NEW COMMENTARY ON THE CODE OF CANON LAW

COMMISSIONED BY
THE CANON LAW SOCIETY OF AMERICA

EDITED BY
JOHN P. BEAL
JAMES A. CORIDEN
THOMAS J. GREEN

PAULIST PRESS
New York, N.Y./Mahwah, N.J.

Acknowledgments

The text of the Code of Canon Law is taken from *Code of Canon Law, Latin-English Edition,* copyright © 1998 by the Canon Law Society of America and is reprinted by permission of the CLSA. Excerpts from the English translation of *Documents on the Liturgy, 1963–1979: Conciliar, Papal and Curial Texts,* © 1982, International Committee on English in the Liturgy, Inc. (ICEL); excerpts from the *Order of Christian Funerals,* © 1985, ICEL; excerpts from the English translation of *Book of Blessings,* © 1988, ICEL; excerpts from the English translation of *Ceremonial of Bishops,* © 1989, ICEL, are used by permission of ICEL. All rights reserved.

Library of Congress Cataloging-in-Publication Data

Beal, John P.
    New Commentary on the Code of Canon Law / edited by John P. Beal,
James A. Coriden, and Thomas J. Green.
       p. ; cm.
    Includes bibliographical references and index.
    ISBN 0–8091–0502–0 (cloth)
    1. Canon law—Sources. I. Coriden, James A. II. Green, Thomas
J. (Thomas Joseph), 1938–   . III. Catholic Church. Codex Juris
Canonici (1983). English. IV. Title.
LAW
262.9'4—dc21

98–49546
CIP

Published by Paulist Press
997 Macarthur Blvd.
Mahwah, N.J. 07430

www.paulistpress.com

Printed and bound in the United States of America

CONTENTS

Knut Walf

PART II
THE HIERARCHICAL CONSTITUTION OF THE CHURCH [cc. 330-572]...................**423**

SECTION I
THE SUPREME AUTHORITY OF THE CHURCH [cc. 330-367] 423

John G. Johnson

Thomas J. Green

Charles D. Balvo

John A. Renken

SECTION II
PARTICULAR CHURCHES AND THEIR GROUPINGS [cc. 368-572]....................501

JOHN G. JOHNSON

BARBARA ANNE CUSACK

JOHN A. RENKEN

Rose M. McDermott, S.S.J.

Sharon L. Holland, I.H.M.

SECTION II
SOCIETIES OF APOSTOLIC LIFE [cc. 731-746]

BOOK III
THE TEACHING FUNCTION OF THE CHURCH [cc. 747-833]

James A. Coriden

Michael A. O'Reilly, O.M.I.

Sharon A. Euart, R.S.M.

JOHN M. HUELS, O.S.M.

FREDERICK R. MCMANUS

ROBERT J. GEISINGER, S.J.

PART III
SACRED PLACES AND TIMES [cc. 1205-1253]

BOOK V
THE TEMPORAL GOODS OF THE CHURCH [cc. 1254-1310]

ROBERT T. KENNEDY

CRAIG A. COX

PART II
THE CONTENTIOUS TRIAL [cc. 1501-1670]

JOHN P. BEAL

SECTION II
THE ORAL CONTENTIOUS PROCESS [cc. 1656-1670]

CRAIG A. COX

PART III
CERTAIN SPECIAL PROCESSES [cc. 1671-1716]

PETER J. JUGIS

THOMAS J. PAPROCKI

Thomas J. Green

Thomas J. Paprocki

Why a new English commentary on the 1983 Code of Canon Law? Because things change.

The earlier work, *The Code of Canon Law: A Text and Commentary,* also commissioned by the Canon Law Society of America, was published in 1985. One could fairly ask why another one is needed, since the code itself remains almost the same as when it was issued in 1983. But much has changed in the nearly twenty years since the authors of the previous commentary did their work.

The Church has changed. The Roman Catholic Church in the United States and worldwide continues to experience remarkable developments in its ministry, in its diocesan and parish life, and in its witness and outreach. Among those experiences, the Church has come to terms with the 1983 Code of Canon Law, a long-awaited revision of the first code, issued in 1917. That revision, eighteen years in the making (1965–1983), took place in the light of the Second Vatican Council (1962–1965), and consciously attempted to translate the council's teachings into rules for the life of the Church. By now the Church has had considerable experience living by those new rules. It is that experience which this new commentary tries to capture and assess.

Canon law has changed. The 1983 code itself has undergone just one formal amendment (the minor additions to canons 750 and 1371 introduced by the May 1998 apostolic letter *Ad tuendam fidem*) since its promulgation. However, many new documents and official interpretations have enlarged and reshaped the canonical scene in the intervening years. The 1988 apostolic constitution on the Roman Curia, the 1990 ritual for the celebration of marriage, the 1993 directory on ecumenism, the 1996 apostolic constitution on papal elections, the 1998 *motu proprio* on episcopal conferences, and especially the 1990 Code of Canons of the Eastern Churches, as well as many other documents, have influenced the meaning and practice of canon law. The Pontifical Council on the Interpretation of Legislative Texts has issued dozens of authentic interpretations of the canons. Scores of decisions made by ecclesiastical tribunals have shed light on the meaning of particular canons. Many other canonical commentaries have appeared in various languages since 1985. Several papal encyclicals and apostolic exhortations as well as the teaching and policy statements of episcopal synods and conferences have given new nuance to the canonical texts and allowed for a new understanding of them. A lot has changed in canon law.

The Canon Law Society of America has done a new English translation of the code. After nearly six years of painstaking effort, consultations, and corrections by a special committee, the society published an entirely new English translation of the 1983 code in 1999. This translation greatly improved upon the 1983 CLSA translation, especially in its accuracy and consistency of language and style. The president of the National Conference of Catholic Bishops granted a *nihil obstat* for the new translation in 1997. This new translation, contained herein, forms the basis for the explanations and reflections that make up this new commentary.

The authors have changed. Of the thirty-six contributors to this commentary, about three-fourths are different from the authors of the 1985 commentary. All are members of the Canon Law Society of America and all hold doctoral degrees in canon law. Seven are women, three are Europeans, and two are Canadians. They pursued their canonical studies at many different schools, North American as well as European. The commentators bring fresh vision and diverse views based on a wide range of pastoral and academic experiences.

The purpose of this commentary is different. The Canon Law Society's board of governors commissioned this new commentary in April 1996. From the outset its purpose was distinct from that of the commentary published in 1985. Both are basically expository and explanatory, that is, they tell the reader what the Church's official rules are and how they are to be understood and applied. Both view the canons as standing under and subject to the teachings of the Second Vatican Council. However, the 1985 commentary focused on the differences between the 1917 and 1983 codes, and how the canons were formed in the long process of revision after the council. This commentary focuses on the lived experience of the canons in use since 1983. It emphasizes the contemporary understanding and applications of the canons based on that experience. The commentators take account of the 1990 Code of Canons of the Eastern Churches, the other relevant documents, and the views expressed by other commentators and authors. The contributors present the state of the question on controverted issues and bring their own views to these ongoing debates.

This commentary is entirely new in purpose and content. It responds to the changes and developments mentioned above. The editors are confident that it will prove to be an indispensable canonical resource for diocesan personnel, parish staffs, seminary and university teachers, indeed for anyone who wishes to understand the rules of the Catholic Church. We judge it to be a worthy complement to the 1985 CLSA *Code of Canon Law: A Text and Commentary*. Our desire is that it serve well the Church, both people and ministers, in their service to God's purpose in the world.

John P. Beal
James A. Coriden
Thomas J. Green

January 17, 2000

ABBREVIATIONS

a.	anno
AA	Vatican II, decr *Apostolicam actuositatem, AAS* 58 (1966) 837–864
AAS	*Acta Apostolicae Sedis*, Rome 1909–
AC	*L'Année Canonique*, Paris 1952–
AcDocVat	*Acta et Documenta Concilio Oecumenico Vaticano II apparando.* Series 1 (Antepraeparatoria), vols. I–IV, Indices: Vatican City, 1960–1961. Series II (Praeparatoria), vols. I–III: Vatican City, 1964–1969
AcSynVat	*Acta Synodalia Sacrosancti Concilii Oecumenici Vaticani II*, vols. I–IV, Indices. Vatican City, 1970–
AER	*American Ecclesiastical Review*, vols. I–XXXII, Philadelphia, 1889–1905; *The Ecclesiastical Review,* Philadelphia, 1905–1943; *The American Ecclesiastical Review*, Washington, D.C., 1944–1974
AG	Vatican II, decr *Ad gentes, AAS* 58 (1966) 947–990
AkK	*Archiv für katholisches Kirchenrecht,* Mainz, 1857–
alloc	allocution
AP	Paul VI, mp *Ad pascendum*, August 15, 1972, *AAS* 64 (1972) 534–540; *CLD* 7, 695–698
apconst	apostolic constitution
apexhort	apostolic exhortation
aplett	apostolic letter
APN	*American Procedural Norms*, July 1, 1970: L. Wrenn, *Annulments*, 3rd ed. (Toledo: CLSA, 1978) 115–119; *Jurist* 30 (1970) 363–368
Apol	*Apollinaris, Commentarium iuris canonici*, Rome, 1928–
ApPen	Apostolic Penitentiary
ApS	John Paul II, aplett *Apostolos suos,* May 21, 1998, *AAS* 90 (1998) 641–658; *Origins* 28:9 (July 30, 1998) 152–158
ApSig	Apostolic Signatura
AS	Paul VI, mp *Apostolica sollicitudo*, September 15, 1965, *AAS* 57 (1965) 775–780; *CLD* 6, 388–393
ASS	*Acta Sanctae Sedis,* Rome, 1865–1908
B.A.C.	Biblioteca de Autores Cristianos
BB	*Book of Blessings*, Approved for Use in the United States of America by the NCCB, prepared by ICEL (Collegeville: Liturgical Press, 1989)

BCL	Bishops' Committee on the Liturgy
BCLN	*Bishops' Committee on the Liturgy Newsletter*
c.	canon
ca.	circa
CanLawStud	Catholic University of America, *Canon Law Studies*
CB	Sacred Congregation for Divine Worship, *Caeremoniale Episcoporum,* September 14, 1984 (Libreria Editrice Vaticana, 1984); *Ceremonial of Bishops* (Collegeville: Liturgical Press, 1989)
cc.	canons
CCC	*Catechism of the Catholic Church* (Washington: USCC, 1994)
CCCB	Canadian Conference of Catholic Bishops
CCE	Congregation for Catholic Education
CCEO	*Code of Canons of the Eastern Churches*
CCS	Congregation for the Causes of Saints
CD	Vatican II, decr *Christus Dominus*, *AAS* 58 (1966) 673–696
CDF	Congregation for the Doctrine of the Faith
CDWDS	Congregation for Divine Worship and the Discipline of the Sacraments
CE	Paul VI, *mp Catholica Ecclesia*, October 23, 1976, *AAS* 68 (1976) 694–696; *CLD* 8, 236–238
CEC	Congregation for the Eastern Churches
CEP	Congregation for the Evangelization of Peoples
CFB	Congregation for Bishops
CFC	Congregation for the Clergy
ch.	chapter
Chiappetta Com	L. Chiappetta, *Il Codice di Diritto Canonico: Commento giuridico-pastorale*, 2 vols. (Naples: Dehoniane, 1988)
Chiappetta Com 1996	L. Chiappetta, *Il Codice di Diritto Canonico: Commento giuridico-pastorale*, 2nd ed., 3 vols. (Rome: Dehoniane, 1996)
CIC	1917 Code of Canon Law (*Codex Iuris Canonici*)
CIC An	*Codex Iuris Canonici Auctoritate Ioannis Pauli II Promulgatus, Fontium Annotatione et Indice Analytico-Alphabetico Auctus* (Libreria Editrice Vaticana, 1989)
CICFontes	*Codicis Iuris Canonici Fontes*, vols. I–IX, ed. P. Gasparri and I. Seredi (Rome, 1923–1939)

CICLSAL	Congregation for Institutes of Consecrated Life and Societies of Apostolic Life
CL	John Paul II, apexhort *Christifideles laici*, December 30, 1988, *AAS* 81 (1989) 393–521; *The Vocation and Mission of the Lay Faithful in the Church and in the World* (Washington: USCC, 1989)
CLA	*Canon Law Abstracts*, 1958–
CLD	*Canon Law Digest*, ed. T. Bouscaren and J. O'Connor. Vols. 1–6, Milwaukee-New York: Bruce, 1934–1969. Vols. 7–10, Chicago: Canon Law Digest, 1975– 1986. Vols. 11–, Washington: CLSA, 1991–
CLSA	Canon Law Society of America
CLSA Com	*The Code of Canon Law: A Text and Commentary*, ed. J. Coriden, T. Green, and D. Heintschel (New York/Mahwah: Paulist, 1985)
CLSANZ	Canon Law Society of Australia and New Zealand
CLSAP	*Canon Law Society of America Proceedings,* 1969–
CLSGBI Com	The Canon Law Society of Great Britain and Ireland, *The Canon Law: Letter and Spirit,* ed. G. Sheehy et al. (Collegeville: Liturgical Press, 1995)
CLS-GBIN	*Canon Law Society of Great Britain and Ireland Newsletter*
CM	Paul VI, *mp Causas matrimoniales*, March 28, 1971, *AAS* 63 (1971) 441–446; L. Wrenn, *Annulments*, 3rd ed. (Toledo: CLSA, 1978) 120–123
CMat	Paul VI, *mp Cum matrimonialium*, September 8, 1973, *AAS* 65 (1973) 577–581; *CLD* 8, 1157–1163
CMIS	World Conference of Secular Institutes
CMSM	Conference of Major Superiors of Men
COD	*Conciliorum Oecumenicorum Decreta*, ed. G. Alberigo et al., 3rd ed. (Bologna: Istituto per le Scienze Religiose, 1973)
CodCom	Pontifical Commission for the Authentic Interpretation of the Canons of the Code of Canon Law
ComCICRec	Pontifical Commission for the Revision of the Code of Canon Law (Pontificia Commissio Codicis Iuris Canonici Recognocendo)
Com Ex	*Comentario Exegetico al Codigo de Derecho Canonico,* ed. A. Marzoa, J. Miras, and R. Rodriguez-Ocaña, 2nd ed., 5 vols. in 8 books (Pamplona: EUNSA, 1997)
Comm	*Communicationes*, Vatican City, 1969–
ComRelMiss	*Commentarium pro Religiosis et Missionariis*, Rome, 1920–
Con	*Concilium, International Journal of Theology,* 1965–
Con Lif	*Consecrated Life*, Chicago: Institute on Religious Life, 1976–

CorpusIC	*Corpus Iuris Canonici*, ed. E. Friedberg, parts I–II (Graz, 1955 and 1959)
CP	Pontifical Commission for the Instruments of Social Communications, *Communio et Progressio,* May 23, 1971, *AAS* 63 (1971) 593–656; *Origins* 1:3 (June 7, 1971) 44–70
CPH	*Clergy Procedural Handbook,* ed. R. Calvo and N. Klinger (Washington: CLSA, 1992)
CR	*Clergy Review*, London, 1931–
CRIS	Congregation for Religious Institutes and Societies of Apostolic Life
CS	*Chicago Studies*, Mundelein, Ill., 1961–
CSIS	Congregation on Seminaries and Institutes of Studies
CT	John Paul II, apexhort *Catechesi tradendae*, October 16, 1979, *AAS* 71 (1979) 1277–1340; *Catechesis in Our Time* (Washington: USCC, 1979)
CTSA	Catholic Theological Society of America
CTSAP	*Catholic Theological Society of America Proceedings,* 1945–
DB	*Rituale Romanum: De Benedictionibus* (Typis Polyglottis Vaticanis, 1984)
DDC	*Dictionnaire de Droit Canonique*, vols. I–VII (Paris: Letouzey et Ané, 1935–1955)
decl	declaration
decr	decree
DH	Vatican II, decr *Dignitatis humanae*, *AAS* 58 (1966) 929–941
"Directives"	Sacred Congregation for the Clergy, "Directive Norms for the Cooperation of the Local Churches among Themselves and Especially for a Better Distribution of Clergy in the World," March 25, 1980, *AAS* 72 (1980) 343f; *CLD* 9, 760–787
Directory	Sacred Congregation for Bishops, *Directorium de Pastorali Ministerio Episcoporum*, February 22, 1973; *Directory on the Pastoral Ministry of Bishops* (Washington: USCC, 1974)
DMC	Sacred Congregation for Divine Worship, *Directory for Masses with Children,* November 1, 1972, AAS 66 (1974) 30–46; *Masses with Children* (Washington: USCC, 1996); *DOL* 276
DOL	*Documents on the Liturgy 1963–1979, Conciliar, Papal and Curial Texts* (Collegeville: Liturgical Press, 1982)
DPM	John Paul II, apconst *Divinus perfectionis magister*, January 25, 1983, *AAS* 75 (1983) 349–355; appendix 1, 661–667, *Code of Canon Law* (Washington: CLSA, 1999)
Droit Canonique	*Droit Canonique*, ed. P. Valdrini, J. Vernay, J-P Durand, and O. Eschappe (Paris: Dalloz, 1989)

DV	Vatican II, dogmatic constitution *Dei Verbum*, *AAS* 58 (1966) 817–830
ECE	John Paul II, apconst *Ex corde Ecclesiae*, August 15, 1990, *AAS* 82 (1990) 1475–1509; *Origins* 20:17 (October 4, 1990) 265–276
Ecum Dir	Pontifical Council for Promoting Christian Unity, *Directoire pour l'application des principes et des normes sur l'oecumenisme*, March 25, 1993, *AAS* 85 (1993) 1039–1119; *Directory for the Application of Principles and Norms on Ecumenism* (Washington: USCC, 1993); *Origins* 23 (1993) 129–160
ED	Secretariat for Promoting Christian Unity, *Ecumenical Directory*, part 1, May 14, 1967, *AAS* 59 (1967) 564–592; *CLD* 6, 716–734
EI	*Enchiridion indulgentiarum*, June 29, 1968, *AAS* 60 (1968) 413–419; *CLD* 7, 675–681
EIC	*Ephemerides Iuris Canonici*, Rome, 1945–1993
EM	Paul VI, *mp De episcoporum muneribus*, June 15, 1966, *AAS* 58 (1966) 467–472; *CLD* 6, 394–400
Emendations	*Emendations in the Liturgical Books Following upon the New Code of Canon Law* (Washington: ICEL, 1984)
EN	Paul VI, *apexhort Evangelii nuntiandi*, December 8, 1975, *AAS* 68 (1976) 5–76; *Evangelization in the Modern World* (Washington: USCC, 1975)
Ench	H. Denzinger and A. Schönmetzer, *Enchiridion symbolorum, definitionum et declarationum de rebus fidei et morum*, 35th ed. (New York, 1974)
EnchVat	*Enchiridion Vaticanum: Documenti ufficiali della Santa Sede* (Bologna: Dehoniane, 1966–1990)
ency	encyclical
EP	Sacred Congregation for the Doctrine of the Faith, decr *De Ecclesiae pastorum vigilantia circa libros*, March 19, 1975, *AAS* 67 (1975) 281–284; *CLD* 8, 991–1004; *Censorship of Books* (Washington: USCC, 1975)
ES	Paul VI, *mp Ecclesiae sanctae*, August 6, 1966, *AAS* 58 (1966) 757–787; *CLD* 6, 264–298; *Norms for Implementation of Four Council Decrees* (Washington: USCC, 1966)
ET	Paul VI, apexhort *Evangelica testificatio*, June 29, 1971, *AAS* 63 (1971) 497–526; *CLD* 7, 425–449; *On the Renewal of Religious Life according to the Teachings of the Second Vatican Council* (Washington: USCC, 1971)
EUNSA	Ediciones Universidad de Navarra, S.A.
"Explanatory Note"	*Nota explicativa praevia* ("Explanatory Note" regarding *Lumen gentium*), *AAS* 57 (1965) 72–75
FC	John Paul II, apexhort *Familiaris consortio*, November 22, 1981, *AAS* 74 (1982) 81–191; *On the Family* (Washington: USCC, 1982)

FL	Congregation for Institutes of Consecrated Life and Societies of Apostolic Life, instr *Congregavit nos in unum Christi amor,* February 2, 1994; *Fraternal Life in Community, Origins* 23/40 (March 24, 1994) 693–712
GCD	Sacred Congregation for the Clergy, *Directorium Catechisticum Generale*, April 11, 1971, *AAS* 64 (1972) 97–176; *General Catechetical Directory* (Washington: USCC, 1971)
GE	Vatican II, decl *Gravissimum educationis, AAS* 58 (1966) 728–739
GIRM	Sacred Congregation for Divine Worship, *Ordo missae editio typica altera* (Typis Polyglottis Vaticanis, 1975); *General Instruction of the Roman Missal*, trans. ICEL (Washington: USCC, 1977)
GS	Vatican II, pastoral constitution *Gaudium et spes, AAS* 58 (1966) 1025–1115
Guidelines	Bishops' Committee on the Permanent Diaconate, *Permanent Deacons in the United States: Guidelines on Their Formation and Ministry* (Washington: USCC, 1971)
Handbuch	*Handbuch des katholischen Kirchenrechts,* ed. J. Listl, H. Muller, and H. Schmitz (Regensburg: Pustet, 1983)
HCWE	*De Sacra Communione et de cultu mysterii Eucharistici extra Missam, editio typica,* June 21, 1973 (Typis Polyglottis Vaticanis, 1973); *Rite of Holy Communion and Worship of the Eucharist outside Mass, DOL* 2091
HPR	*Homiletic Monthly and Catechist,* New York, 1901–1917; *Homiletic and Pastoral Review,* New York, 1917–
HV	Paul VI, ency *Humanae vitae,* July 29, 1968, *AAS* 60 (1968) 489–496; *On the Regulation of Birth* (Washington: USCC, 1968)
IC	*Ius Canonicum,* Pamplona, 1961–
ICEL	International Commission on English in the Liturgy
ID	Paul VI, apconst *Indulgentiarum doctrina,* January 1, 1967, *AAS* 59 (1967) 5–24; *CLD* 6, 570–575; *On Indulgences* (Washington: USCC, 1967)
IDon	Sacred Congregation for Sacraments and Divine Worship, instr *Inaestimabile donum,* April 3, 1980, *AAS* 72 (1980) 331–343; *CLD* 9, 563–574
IE	*Ius Ecclesiae,* Milan, 1988–
IGIC	Sacred Congregation for Divine Worship, *General Introduction to [the Rite of] Christian Initiation* (Washington: USCC, 1977); *DOL* 301
IM	Vatican II, decr *Inter mirifica, AAS* 56 (1964) 145–153
ImCar	Sacred Congregation for the Discipline of the Sacraments, instr *Immensae caritatis,* January 29, 1973, *AAS* 65 (1973) 264–271; *CLD* 8, 477–497
instr	instruction

IO	Sacred Congregation of Rites, instr *Inter oecumenici*, September 26, 1964, *AAS* 56 (1964) 877–900; *CLD* 6, 73–99
IP	*Ius Pontificium*, Rome, 1920–1921, 1941–
J	*The Jurist*, Washington, 1940–
LC	Paul VI, apconst *Laudis canticum*, November 1, 1970, *AAS* 63 (1971) 527–535; *TPS* 16 (1971) 129–131
LCE	J. Martín de Agar, *Legislazione delle Conferenze Episcopali Complementare al C.I.C.* (Milan: Giuffré, 1990)
LCWR	Leadership Conference of Women Religious
LEF	Pontifical Commission for the Revision of the Code of Canon Law, *Lex Ecclesiae Fundamentalis*, April 24, 1980 (Libreria Editrice Vaticana, 1980)
LG	Vatican II, dogmatic constitution *Lumen gentium*, *AAS* 57 (1965) 5–75
littcirc	circular letter
LOTH	*Liturgy of the Hours*
ME	*Il Monitore Ecclesiastico*, Rome, 1876–1948; *Monitor Ecclesiasticus*, Rome, 1948–
MM	Paul VI, *mp Matrimonia mixta*, March 31, 1970, *AAS* 62 (1970) 257–263; *CLD* 7, 711–718
mp	*motu proprio*
MQ	Paul VI, *mp Ministeria quaedam*, August 15, 1972, *AAS* 64 (1972) 529–534; *CLD* 7, 690–698; *Laying Down Certain Norms regarding the Sacred Order of the Diaconate and by Which the Discipline of the First Tonsure, Minor Orders and Subdiaconate in the Latin Church Is Reformed* (Washington: USCC, 1972)
MR	Sacred Congregation for Bishops and Sacred Congregation for Religious and Secular Institutes, decr *Mutuae relationes*, May 14, 1978, *AAS* 70 (1978) 473–506; *CLD* 9, 296–339; *Directives for the Mutual Relations between Bishops and Religious in the Church* (Washington: USCC, 1978)
MS	Congregation for the Doctrine of the Faith, instr *Matrimonii sacramentum,* March 18, 1966, *AAS* 58 (1966) 235–239; *CLD* 6, 592–597
Münster Com	*Münsterischer Kommentar zum Codex Iuris Canonici unter besonderer Berücksichtigung der Rechtslage im Deutschland, Oesterreich und der Schweiz,* ed. K. Ludicke (Essen: Ludgerus Verlag, 1985–)
N	*Notitiae*, Vatican City, 1965–
NCCB	National Conference of Catholic Bishops
NCCB-*CompNm*	National Conference of Catholic Bishops, *Implementation of the 1983 Code of Canon Law Complementary Norms* (Washington: USCC, 1991)

NCDD	National Conference of Diocesan Directors of Religious Education
NCE	*New Catholic Encyclopedia* (New York: McGraw-Hill, 1967)
NFPC	National Federation of Priests' Councils
Norms	National Conference of Catholic Bishops, *Norms for Priestly Formation: A Compendium of Official Documents on Training of Candidates for the Priesthood*, 2 vols. (Washington: USCC, 1993)
NSC	National Conference of Catholic Bishops, *National Statutes for the Catechumenate*, November 11, 1986 (appended to the 1988 adapted version of the *RCIA*)
Nu	*Nuntia*, Vatican City, 1975–
OAKR	*Oesterreichisches Archiv für Kirchenrecht*, Vienna, 1950–
OCF	*Order of Christian Funerals* (Washington: NCCB, 1989)
OE	Vatican II, decr *Orientalium Ecclesiarum*, *AAS* 57 (1965) 76–89
OEx	Sacred Congregation for Divine Worship, *Ordo Exsequiarum*, August 15, 1969 (Typis Polyglottis Vaticanis, 1969); *Rite of Funerals*, BCL-USCC (New York: Catholic Book, 1971)
OrConVir	Sacred Congregation for Divine Worship, *Ordo for the Consecration of Virgins*, May 13, 1970, *DOL* 395
OssRomEng	*L'Osservatore Romano*, English edition
OT	Vatican II, decr *Optatam totius*, *AAS* 58 (1966) 713–727
P	*Periodica de re canonica*, Rome, 1905–
PA	Congregation for the Clergy, directive note *Postquam apostoli*, March 25, 1980, *AAS* 72 (1980) 343–364; *CLD* 9, 760–787
Paen	Paul VI, apconst *Paenitemini*, February 17, 1966, *AAS* 58 (1966) 177–185; *CLD* 6, 675–678
Pamplona Com	*Codigo de derecho canonico*, ed. J. Arrieta et al. (Pamplona: EUNSA, 1983)
Pamplona ComEng	*Code of Canon Law, Annotated* (English), ed. E. Caparros, M. Thériault, and J. Thorn (Montreal: Wilson & LaFleur Limitée, 1993)
Pastoral Care	*Pastoral Care of the Sick: Rites of Anointing and Viaticum* (Collegeville: Liturgical Press, 1983)
PB	John Paul II, apconst *Pastor bonus*, June 28, 1988, *AAS* 80 (1988) 841–912; appendix 2, 679–751, *Code of Canon Law* (Washington: CLSA, 1999)
PC	Vatican II, decr *Perfectae caritatis*, *AAS* 58 (1966) 702–712
PCC	Pontifical Council for Culture
PCCU	Pontifical Council "Cor Unum"

PCDNB	Pontifical Council for Dialogue with Non-Believers
PCF	Pontifical Council for the Family
PCHW	Pontifical Council for Pastoral Assistance to Health Care Workers
PCID	Pontifical Council for Interreligious Dialogue
PCILT	Pontifical Council for the Interpretation of Legislative Texts
PCJP	Pontifical Council for Justice and Peace
PCL	Pontifical Council for the Laity
PCMT	Pontifical Council for the Pastoral Care of Migrants and Itinerant People
PCPCU	Pontifical Council for Promoting Christian Unity
PCSC	Pontifical Council for Social Communications
PDV	John Paul II, apexhort *Pastores dabo vobis*, March 25, 1992, *AAS* 84 (1992) 657–804; *I Will Give You Shepherds* (Washington: USCC, 1992)
PF	Pius XII, *mp Primo feliciter*, March 12, 1948, *AAS* 40 (1948) 283–286
PI	Congregation for Institutes of Consecrated Life and Societies of Apostolic Life, instr *Potissimum institutioni*, March 2, 1990, *AAS* 82 (1990) 472–532
PL	J. P. Migne, *Patrologiae cursus completus*, Series Latina, 221 vols. (Paris, 1844–1855)
Plen	*Congregatio Plenaria diebus 26–29 octobris 1981 habita* (Typis Polyglottis Vaticanis, 1991)
PM	Paul VI, *mp Pastorale munus*, November 30, 1963, *AAS* 56 (1964) 5–12; *CLD* 6, 370–378
PO	Vatican II, decr *Presbyterorum ordinis*, *AAS* 58 (1966) 991–1024
Pospishil Com	V. J. Pospishil, *Eastern Catholic Church Law according to the Code of Canons of the Eastern Churches*, 2nd ed. (Brooklyn: St. Maron, 1996)
PPF	*Program for Priestly Formation*, 4th ed. (Washington: USCC, 1994)
PS	Congregation for the Clergy, littcirc *Presbyteri sacra*, April 11, 1970
QuadStR	*Quaderni di Studio Rotale*, Rome, 1987–
RAnointing	Sacred Congregation for Divine Worship, *Ordo unctionis infirmorum*, December 7, 1972 (Typis Polyglottis Vaticanis, 1972); *Rite of Anointing*, *DOL* 410
Ratio	Sacred Congregation for Catholic Education, *Ratio fundamentalis institutionis sacerdotalis*, January 6, 1970 (Libreria Editrice Vaticana, 1985); *Basic Plan for Priestly Formation* (an English translation can be found in *Norms*)

RBaptC	Sacred Congregation for Divine Worship, *Ordo Baptismi Parvulorum*, May 15, 1969 (Typis Polyglottis Vaticanis, 1969); editio typica, altera, 1973; *Rite for Baptism of Children, DOL* 295
RC	Sacred Congregation for Religious and Secular Institutes, instr *Renovationis causam*, January 6, 1969, *AAS* 61 (1969) 103–120; *On the Renewal of Religious Formation* (Washington: USCC, 1969)
RCIA	Sacred Congregation for Divine Worship, *Ordo initiationis christianae adultorum*, January 6, 1972 (Typis Polyglottis Vaticanis, 1972); *Rite of Christian Initiation of Adults, DOL* 301
RConf	Sacred Congregation for Divine Worship, *Ordo confirmationis*, August 22, 1971 (Typis Polyglottis Vaticanis, 1971); *Rite of Confirmation, DOL* 305
RDC	*Revue de Droit Canonique*, Strasbourg, 1951–
RDCA	Sacred Congregation for Sacraments and Divine Worship, *Rite of Dedication of a Church and an Altar,* May 29, 1977, *DOL* 547
RE	Paul VI, apconst *Regimini Ecclesiae universae*, August 15, 1967, *AAS* 59 (1967) 885–928; *On the Roman Curia* (Washington: USCC, 1967)
REDC	*Revista Española de Derecho Canonico*, Salamanca, 1951–
Rel	Pontifical Commission for the Revision of the Code of Canon Law, *Relatio complectens synthesim animadversionum ab Em. mis. atque Exc. mis. Patribus Commissionis ad ultimum schema Codicis Iuris Canonici Exhibitarum, cum responsionibus a Secretaria et Consultoribus datis* (Typis Polyglottis Vaticanis, 1981)
RfR	*Review for Religious,* Topeka, Kans., 1942–1967; St. Louis, Mo., 1968–
RI	*Regulae Iuris,* Boniface VIII, *Liber Sextus* (1298) in *Corpus Iuris Canonici*
Rites	*The Rites of the Catholic Church,* 2 vols. (New York: Pueblo, 1990–1991)
ROils	Sacred Congregation for Divine Worship, *Ordo benedicendi oleum catechumenorum et infirmorum et conficiendi chrisma,* December 3, 1970 (Typis Polyglottis Vaticanis, 1971); *DOL* 459
RomRot	Tribunal of the Roman Rota
RP	John Paul II, apexhort *Reconciliatio et paenitentia,* December 2 1984, *AAS* 77 (1985) 185–275; *Reconciliation and Penance* (Washington: USCC, 1985)
RPen	Sacred Congregation for Divine Worship, *Ordo Paenitentiae,* December 2, 1973 (Typis Polyglottis Vaticanis, 1974); *Rite of Penance* (Washington: USCC, 1975)
RR	*Roman Replies,* ed. W. Schumacher (Washington: CLSA, 1981–1983)
RRAO	*Roman Replies and CLSA Advisory Opinions, 1984–*
SacM	*Sacramentum Mundi, An Encyclopedia of Theology,* 6 vols. (New York: Herder & Herder, 1968–1970)

Salamanca Com	*Codigo de derecho canonico,* ed. L. de Echeverria et al. (Madrid: Biblioteca de Autores Christianos, 1983)
SapC	John Paul II, apconst *Sapientia christiana*, April 15, 1979, *AAS* 71 (1979) 469–499; *On Ecclesiastical Universities and Faculties* (Washington: USCC, 1979)
SC	Vatican II, constitution *Sacrosanctum Concilium*, *AAS* 66 (1964) 97–134
SCa	John Paul II, apconst *Sacri canones*, October 18, 1990 (promulgation document of *CCEO*)
SCB	Sacred Congregation for Bishops
SCC	Sacred Congregation for the Clergy
SCCE	Sacred Congregation for Catholic Education
SCConc	Sacred Congregation of the Council
SCConsist	Sacred Consistorial Congregation
SCDF	Sacred Congregation for the Doctrine of the Faith
SCDW	Sacred Congregation for Divine Worship
SCOC	Sacred Congregation for the Oriental Churches
SCOf	Sacred Congregation of the Holy Office (former title of the Sacred Congregation for the Doctrine of the Faith)
SCProp	Sacred Congregation for the Evangelization of Nations/Sacred Congregation for the Propagation of the Faith
SCR	Sacred Congregation for Religious
SCRIS	Sacred Congregation for Religious and Secular Institutes
SCRit	Sacred Congregation of Rites
SCSacr	Sacred Congregation for the Discipline of the Sacraments
SCSDW	Sacred Congregation for Sacraments and Divine Worship
SCSU	Sacred Congregation of Seminaries and Universities (former title of the Sacred Congregation for Catholic Education)
SDL	John Paul II, apconst *Sacrae disciplinae leges,* January 25, 1983 (promulgation document of 1983 Code of Canon Law)
SDO	Paul VI, *mp Sacrum diaconatus ordinem*, June 18, 1967, *AAS* 59 (1967) 697–704; *CLD* 6, 577–584
SMC	John Paul II, apconst *Spirituali militum curae*, April 21, 1986, *AAS* 78 (1986) 481–486; *TPS* 31 (1986) 284–288
SoE	Paul VI, *mp Sollicitudo omnium Ecclesiarum*, June 24, 1969, *AAS* 61 (1969) 473–484; *CLD* 7, 277–284

SP	Sacred Penitentiary
SPCU	Secretariat for Promoting Christian Unity
SRRDec	*Sacrae Romanae Rotae Decisiones*, Rome, 1909–
SRS	John Paul II, ency *Sollicitudo rei socialis,* December 30, 1987, *AAS* 80 (1988) 513–586; *On Social Concern* (Washington: USCC, 1988)
SS	Secretariat of State
STh	St. Thomas Aquinas, *Summa Theologiae*
Stud Can	*Studia Canonica*, Ottawa, 1969–
Tanner	*Decrees of the Ecumenical Councils*, ed. Norman P. Tanner, 2 vols. (London/Washington: Sheed & Ward/Georgetown University Press, 1990)
TPS	*The Pope Speaks,* Huntington, Ind., 1954–
TS	*Theological Studies*, Baltimore, 1939–
UR	Vatican II, decr *Unitatis redintegratio*, *AAS* 57 (1965) 90–107
Urbaniana Com	*Commento al Codice di Diritto Canonico,* ed. P. V. Pinto (Rome: Urbaniana Press, 1985)
USCC	United States Catholic Conference
Valencia Com	*Codigo de Derecho Canonico (edición bilingue): Fuentes y Comentarios de Todos los Canones,* ed. A. B. Poveda, 4th ed. (Valencia: EDICEP C.B., 1993)
Variationes	Sacred Congregation for Sacraments and Divine Worship, decr *Promulgato Codice Iuris Canonici*, September 12, 1983; *Notitiae* 19 (1983) 540–555
VC	*Vita Consacrata* (formerly *Vita Religiosa*), Rome, 1964–
Vorgrimler	H. Vorgrimler, ed., *Commentary on the Documents of Vatican II*, 5 vols. (New York: Herder & Herder, 1966–1969)
VR	*Vita Religiosa*, Madrid, 1944–
VS	Congregation for Religious and Secular Institutes, instr *Venite seorsum*, August 15, 1969, *AAS* 61 (1969) 674–690; *CLD* 7, 536–541
VSp	John Paul II, ency *Veritatis splendor*, August 6, 1993, *AAS* 85 (1993) 1133–1228; *The Splendor of Truth* (Washington: USCC, 1994)
W	*Worship*, Collegeville, Minn., 1926–

Theology and Canon Law

Ladislas M. Örsy, S.J.

The issue of the relationship between doctrine and law in the life of the Church has emerged with some force and urgency after Vatican Council II: the theological statements of the Fathers had to be translated into legislative enactments. As faith sought and found new intelligence at the council, the same faith demanded and searched for new norms of action after the council. Thus, while the work of the revision of the Code of Canon Law progressed, theologians and canon lawyers looked for a paradigm that could serve as a guide for the transition from doctrinal insights to juridical norms. In this process two distinct questions emerged:

(1) *What is the place and role of law in the Church?*

(2) *What is the relationship between theology and canon law?*

The first question is an issue of systematic theology; it belongs to ecclesiology. The answer ought to identify, describe, and explain the place and role of law in the living body of the Church. Once such a systematic understanding is reached and articulated, it may fulfill an apologetic scope as well: the origin, purpose, and nature of the law can reveal why and how it ought to be an integral part of the structures and operations of the community.

The second question focuses on a more specific issue: the relationship between theology and canon law; that is, on the mutual interaction between the doctrine of faith (theory) that has all to do with the community's beliefs, and the norms of action (practice) that have all to do with the community's operations.

(1) *What is the place and role of law in the Church?*

The *place* of law is in the Church of Christ where the drama of our redemption is enacted; the *role* of law is to assist the people in the reception of God's saving mysteries.

The Church of Christ, according the teaching of Vatican Council II, "subsists in the Catholic Church, which is governed by the successor of Peter and by the bishops in communion with him. Nevertheless, many elements of sanctification and of truth are found outside its visible confines . . . these are gifts belonging to the Church of Christ" (*LG* 8). It follows that the object of any theological inquiry concerning the Church must be always the whole Christian communion. This rule we should never lose sight of, not even when we are investigating the place and role of law.

At the present, however, the one Church of Christ is broken or wounded since there are divisions among the believers in proclaiming their faith and in ordering the operations of their communities. For this reason, and to avoid a diffuse and complicated inquiry into the varied life of divers denominations, our study about the place and role of law will focus on the Roman Catholic Church. It is our church; moreover, in it the presence and use of canon law can be more easily and securely discerned. Much of what we are going to say, however, with due allowance for differences, is applicable to other churches and ecclesial communities.

Our point of departure is in accepting and professing that the Church is both a truly human community, entrusted to human beings, and a divine mystery (cf. Eph 5:32), the work of the Spirit.

Right from the beginning the Church perceived itself as a human community: the very name of it, *ecclesia,* means "gathering." This fact is of foundational importance because it follows that the internal and natural laws of a human community are relevant for, and operating in, the Church.

Paul the Apostle declared this "gathering" a great *mysterion,* translated into Latin as *sacramentum.* The word was used in a unique sense: the Church was the possessor and dispenser of the word of God and of the grace-filled sacramental rites. The scriptures use various images comprehensible to us to convey some understanding of this mystery: the Church is the coming of God's kingdom, his temple, his sheepfold, the field where he has planted his vineyard, and so forth. Interestingly, all such images point toward some visible and structured reality.

This community, earthly and heavenly at the same time, has not reached its perfection. It is incomplete and unfinished: it must grow and expand in history. It has an absolute need to reach out for authentic values. (Values are good things that can perfect the community, support its life, and sustain its development.) Law is a specific instrument in this process; it prompts and binds the community to strive for its perfection and gives directions for its progress.

As the Church is of a composite nature, so is canon law. In it human elements blend with divine gifts. As the Church is incomplete and unfinished, so is canon law. That the Church is always in need of reform, *ecclesia semper reformanda,* means that canon law, too, is permanently in need of review, *ius canonicum semper revidendum.*

To gain an even fuller understanding of the place and role of law in the Church, let us look at the law's origin, purpose, and nature.

The *origin* of canon law is both in the humanity of the Church and in the divine gifts possessed by the community. Some norms are born from a human need for order and ordered operations; some norms are demanded and generated by divine revelation. In each case reason is the operating agent in bringing order into the life of community, that is, reason enlightened by, and united with, the word of God and energized by divine grace. In this sense, the definition of Aquinas holds: "Law is an ordinance of reason."

The *purpose* of canon law is to assist the Church in fulfilling its task which is to reveal and to communicate God's saving power to the world. Law can help by creating order in the community, an order that leads to tranquillity and peace: a good disposition for the "assembly" to become "light to the nations." The law can be also a

teacher to the people, as the *Torah* once was: guiding them toward the kingdom.

The *nature* of canon law reflects the nature of the Church: *it is truly human* because the Church is a human community; *it has an affinity with the divine* because it is an integral part of the Church as sacrament. In the law itself, human prudence blends with divine wisdom in a close union but without fusion or confusion. This complex nature gives to canon law its incarnational character. Let this character unfold.

As the visible church is *contingent,* so is canon law. Law is meant for this passing world—while charity remains forever. Whenever the law provides for human needs (e.g., when it creates structures and processes not defined by revelation), it is bound to reflect the human qualities of the legislator, such as his horizon, his alertness in gathering information, his capacity for creative insights, his ability to form critical judgments, his prudence in matters practical, his skill in communicating a piece of legislation—and so forth. When the law is implementing divine commands (e.g., concerning the reception of the sacraments), it has a transcendental quality but it does not carry an immunity from human fragility. Even when the law gives effect to an explicit divine precept (e.g., the law that gives effect to the words of Christ to Peter: "Feed my sheep"), it remains conditioned by the historical circumstances of its enactment.

As the Church is *changeable* and reformable, so are its laws; some in their substance, some in their formulation. For this reason, canon law has the potential for development. In the course of history, changes in the rules often prompted and guided the Church in its own growth and expansion. A living social body demands flexible norms. To prevent the onset of rigidity, dying norms ought to be steadily pruned away and new ones created as needed. The decision by the Church to put virtually all its laws into one "code" (imitating a trend among states) has brought many advantages but also contributed significantly to an increase in rigidity. No matter how urgent the need for reform is concerning one subject, it is difficult to introduce major changes in a unified code.

Since the Church is of divine foundation, its laws have an *affinity with the divine*. To a significant extent their scope is to give effect to the *word of God*. Further, the structures that the word creates and the operations that it prompts are part of, or linked to, the *visible sacramental symbol* that is the Church.

The head of the Church is the risen Christ: there is a *personal bond* between him and his people. When the people intelligently and freely give themselves to his Church and observe its laws, they honor him. No such quality can ever exist in civil law.

Every norm in canon law must be *linked to authentic values*, human and/or divine: without such a bond no law can have authority. In other terms, a norm is valid as far as it promotes, supports, and protects a value; otherwise it would not serve the common good. This may happen in a specific way as when a given rule is linked to a defined value, or it can happen in a generic fashion as when a set of rules converge to uphold the value of order and unity in the community. Briefly: norms in themselves have no value; they exist for the sake of values. (The term "value" and the expression "common good" are so close to each other that they are virtually interchangeable.)

We have now come to a position where we are able to gather the elements of our reflections into a unified theory concerning the place and role of law in the Church.

It is part of the external visible sacramental structure of the Church; there it shares the composite nature of the community. In its provisions it can be human; it can display the limitations and weaknesses of our nature. It can also represent divine wisdom and thus testify that God is present among his people. It is contingent and in constant need of reform in order to be in harmony with the rhythm of life of the Church and of the surrounding world; it is constant as far as it gives effect to the word of God.

The best criterion for judging any theory concerning the place and role of law in the Church is in asking how far the theory is able to perceive, understand, affirm, and sustain this delicate balance.

We turn now to the presentation and examination of some of the current theories, but not before a caution is sounded.

The literature seeking to explain the place and role of law in the Church is abundant but it is not easy to handle. The issue itself is new; there is little tradition to guide the inquiries. The thinkers and writers, moreover, do not come from the same background; they start from differing philosophical, theological, and jurisprudential assumptions, often hidden behind their articulated positions. When this happens, the reader is compelled to conjecture the principles that inspired or determined the meaning of their direct statements. Further, as various "schools of thought" developed, they tended to remain isolated within their own boundaries—linguistic, national, or doctrinal. This isolation occasioned more repetitions of positions than mutual exchanges of opinions. In this small field there is a great need for critical dialogue.

We offer hereby a representative selection of various theories with a brief critical assessment. We introduce each one in thesis form, name its author or its supporting school, and then apply the criteria mentioned above for its evaluation.

(a) Theories that fail to perceive the true nature of the Church or the true nature of the law; they are radically deficient.

In the Church of charity there is no place for law: they are mutually exclusive.

This position was articulated and defended (and buttressed with a restricted and fragmented vision of history) by *Rudolf Sohm* (d. 1917). He correctly perceived the primacy of charity in the Church but failed to see the community's need for order. He had, moreover, a limited understanding of law: he saw it as a norm that by its nature demands enforcement through violent actions. For such law, he held, there is no room in the Christian community. His position gained much publicity mainly in Germany; it was frequently used in a modified form to postulate the exclusion of any law in the Christian community. History contradicts the theory: since the first apostolic council in

Jerusalem, Christians have been guided by rules and regulations in their assemblies. A warning from Sohm, however, could be well taken: no law should ever overshadow charity.

The law is autonomous: there is no need to link it to any value.

This is the theory of the school of the *legal positivists*. Their field of vision is restricted to the observable phenomenon of law: anything beyond it they ignore. They do not see the wholesome reality and organic nature of a human community; they sever the law from its natural environment. Their interpretation of the law tends to be literal and rigid, since no "external factors" (hierarchy of values, principles of morality, etc.) must ever be taken into account. The theory of legal positivism has no place in Christian jurisprudence.

Pragmatic positivism, however, is another matter: it is a permanent temptation for religious communities; history shows it. The books of the Old and New Testaments report groups of zealots insisting on the literal observance of the law in disregard of higher values; Jesus himself had to insist that the healing of human persons was more important than the observance of the Sabbath. Pragmatic positivism is no less subversive than the theoretical one but it can camouflage itself as the semblance of the virtue of fidelity or obedience. Every time in a Christian community when the law takes precedence over faith, hope, and charity, we are dealing with a manifestation of pragmatic positivism.

(b) Theories that fail to do justice to the distinctive and intrinsically religious character of canon law.

Canon law is law in the same sense as civil law.

Scholars following this position are often designated as the *Italian School;* in truth they could be of any nationality.

They identify canon law with civil law; for them "law" is not an analogical concept. In consequence, they recognize one kind of jurisprudence only, applicable to all legal systems. The religious origin, scope, and nature of canon law, all that *ap-*

pear to give it a special character, are really irrelevant because they are "meta-legal," that is, outside the orbit of the law. For them, the rules of interpretation are the same in civil law and canon law. In this way, and in this way only, can canon law enter the respected field of legal science.

This approach is severely deficient because the theory detaches canon law from the religious soil that produced it, from the transcendental scope that it serves, and ignores its specific nature shaped by human needs and divine commands. Of course, for this school, it is illegal to give priority to faith, hope, and charity in the interpretation and application of canonical norms.

Canon law is law in the same sense as civil law but its "owner" is the Church.

This theory is often referred to as the position of the *Navarra School* although it can be found worldwide and not all the scholars from Navarra may hold it. Its advocates follow the Italian School in asserting an essential identity between the nature of civil law and canon law, but they affirm the power of the Church over canon law under every aspect: legislation, interpretation, and application. In other terms, for them canon law is not different from civil law but the Church retains jurisdiction over every part of it. This external dependence sets canon law apart from other systems.

The theory is inadequate on several counts. It pays little or no attention to the intrinsic connection between theological realities and canonical commands; it does not promote insightful interpretation on the basis of religious values; it fails to create a climate that favors the participation of the faithful in the preparation and the evaluation of the norms; it reduces the reception of the law into passive acceptance.

(c) Theories that virtually identify canon law with theology.

Canon law is a theological discipline with juridical method.

This "thesis" is usually referred to as the position of the *Munich School* since *Klaus Mörsdorf*

(d. 1989), professor of the university of that city, first proposed it. He created the general category of "theological discipline" and within it the "specific branches" differentiated among themselves by the method they were using. Thus, canon law for him was a theological discipline specified by its juridical method. (Presumably, church history should be differentiated by its historical method.)

The direction of Mörsdorf's intuition was correct: he saw that there must be an organic connection between theology and canon law—notwithstanding their differences. His thesis, however, is hardly more than an "axiom"; it is not an elaborate, cohesive, and critically grounded theory. He does not account with precision for the meaning of "theological discipline"; he gives no satisfactory explanation why method should be the criterion for distinguishing its branches. In fact, the difference between the two disciplines goes much deeper than their respective methods: the one seeks understanding; the other imposes action. The nature of canon law by Mörsdorf's "axiom" should be the same as that of theology; this misrepresents reality to the detriment of both disciplines. When canon law is seen as part of *theo-logia,* it becomes difficult to explain its human limitations.

Canon law is ordinance of faith, ordinatio fidei, *not ordinance of reason,* ordinatio rationis.

This statement sums up, in his own words, the theory of *Eugenio Corecco* (d. 1995), former professor at Fribourg, later bishop of Lugano. He was a disciple of Mörsdorf but went further than his mentor in stressing the divine elements in canon law. He saw faith as the principal agent creating it, and the law so produced as similar to dogma. He gives little attention to the human nature of the pilgrim Church. He does not, therefore, sufficiently account for earthly limitations and failures in the legal system. He perceives, correctly, that the nature of canon law is substantially different from that of civil law, but he brings canon law so close to the doctrine of faith that its humanity and specific practical character virtually disappear. In the interpretation and application of canon law, this theory can lead to an excessive rigidity.

(d) A tentative theory with a sound starting point but as yet incomplete.

The Eucharist is the source of rights and duties in the Church.

Could we conceive of a theory that presents the legal system of the Church as rooted in (or centered on) the Eucharist? The question is legitimate; *Peter Huizing* (d. 1995), former professor at the Gregorian University in Rome, raised it with some insistence. The question is prompted by the belief that the Church (and every particular church) comes into existence when the community celebrates the Eucharist. It should follow that rights and duties are created through the same sacred act and they are sustained and supported by it.

How can we bring further intelligence into this approach?

The expression "the Church comes into existence through the celebration of the Eucharist" means that the risen Christ takes into himself those whom he predestined, called, justified, and glorified (cf. Rom 8:30). He binds them together into one body through the mystery that re-creates his saving deed.

It makes good sense to say that ultimately all rights and duties, all rules and regulations originate in, and remain connected with, this sacred event. An ecclesiastical legislator can be no more than a trustee of the risen Christ.

Canon law, then, can be truly part of the sacramental structure of the Church itself, a sign and symbol of our humanity *that is being redeemed.* Because that humanity is still subject to limitations and failings, so are the legal rules. They, too, are *being redeemed.* The saying that our laws are in need of constant reform (as the Church is) receives a new meaning.

In this unfolding theory, we may find eventually the best explanation of the place and role of law in the Church. Admittedly, it still needs refinement and elaboration. Some practical consequences, however, are discernible. Among the Christian churches, an existing communion in the Eucharist could be seen as far more important than the separation in matters of jurisdiction. Inside the Church, the awareness of the unity of the faithful in the celebration of the Eucharist could become an incentive for the increased participation of the same faithful in decision-making processes. The immense and gratuitous mercy experienced in the Eucharist may eventually help us to see that the structures of the sacrament of penance ought to follow the simplicity of Jesus' forgiving acts and must be free of any legalism. In the long run, sound practical consequences could be the best proofs for the soundness of the theory. "You will know them by their fruits" (Mt 7:16).

This theory still needs the critical challenges of theologians and canon lawyers; it needs even more the response that can come only through the "supernatural sense of faith" that resides in the entire people of God (cf. *LG* 12). It represents a vision that not only is an antidote to legalism but is likely to inspire respect for the law.

In summary, the first group of theories under (a) does not represent adequately the true nature of canon law or of any law; the second group under (b) virtually identifies the nature of canon law with that of civil law and fails to account sufficiently for the religious and ecclesial character of canon law; the third group under (c) sees canon law too much as a theological enterprise and falls short of doing justice to its humanity and juridical nature. All such theories can lead to interpretations that lack internal balance and harmony. The last theory under (d) is well founded and promising but as yet not completed: it should be considered as a report on "faith seeking understanding."

(2) *What is the relationship between theology and canon law?*

To handle the question correctly, an initial explanation of the concepts is warranted.

What is theology?

In a broad sense, *theo-logia*, "God-science," is sacred knowledge received from God through his self-revelation and implanted in the spirit (memory) of the Christian community, then expanded by insightful reflections on its content. The core of it never changes: it is the "Tradition," *id quod traditum est:* all that was given through the mission of Christ and is protected by his Spirit. This gift, however, is like the living seed: in our intelligence it is alive and unfolding. As history progresses, "faith seeks understanding." This search for a deeper knowledge of God's mysteries is sustained by a divine energy, but it is marked also by human limits. No falsehood can corrupt the core, yet our insights are not immune to error. This complex character makes theology unique among all sciences: it is unlike any other.

We are able to express our *theologia* in several ways: in artistic creations, in musical compositions, and in doctrinal propositions. Our attention here focuses on theology in propositions—as we find it, for instance, in our traditional professions of faith and other authoritative doctrinal declarations. All such propositions are affirmations: they respond first to the "essential" question *What is it?* then to the "existential" one *Does it really exist?* For example, in an inquiry about the meaning of the Eucharist, the first response would keep us at an abstract level and give an account of its foundation and its significance in the assembly; the second would move us into the realm of the concrete world of existence and assert that the Eucharist is there. At the end we would know (as we can) what the Eucharist is and that it really exists.

This process of "faith seeking understanding" has been always present in the Church and will never be completed. Nor will it ever be a mere repetition of what is already known because new insights will be emerging until the end of time. The content of the mysteries can never be exhausted: theological knowledge by its very nature keeps expanding.

What is canon law?

The usual definition of modern canon law, which is mostly statutory, contains the following elements: it is a set of norms created by reason enlightened through faith, it intends to bring order into the life of the ecclesial community, it is articulated and promulgated by those who are entrusted with the community's care, and its purpose is to serve the common good. Thus, canon law imposes obligations; that is, it establishes legal bonds from which rights and duties flow.

A better understanding of canon law could be achieved by recalling that in the Christian community an overall obligation *of theological origin* exists prior to any law; it is a bond that binds the faithful to God and to each other; canon law can do no more than to give directions in detail as to how to fulfill this principal obligation in daily life. Canon law, in its essence and existence, depends on a pre-existing theological reality.

As faith moves the community to seek insights into the mysteries, so the same faith prompts the community to organize itself and to create norms of action for the reception of God's gifts. Faith, however, does not articulate the norms: our practical reason does, with the help of some divine wisdom revealed to us and some human ingenuity brought into play.

Every single sentence in canon law is the communication of a decision in view of action; every norm is in an imperative mood. These norms are addressed to persons, they specify obligations, they answer the question *What ought to be done?* The task of every ordinance is to name an action. (Note: for our purposes, a law that prohibits an action falls under the same consideration as the law that prescribes an action; in each case an act of compliance is commanded.)

This process of "faith seeking action" has operated in the Church ever since the communities started to assemble: they had to create ordered structures and converging operations if they wanted to exist at all.

How do theology and canon law relate to each other?

For a response we must turn to the living Church: the Church *generates* theology and canon law; the Church *receives* them.

Whenever a human community, the Church not excepted, operates collectively, it does so in a fashion that follows the pattern of the activity of individual persons. Intelligent persons have a natural longing for knowledge and understanding—so do communities. Free persons have a natural desire for all that can perfect them, they decide to reach out for values that can enrich them—so do communities. The energy that the Spirit infuses into Christians only increases such natural impulses.

The community's search for knowledge revolves principally around God and his saving deeds but it does not end there: the members want to know about values that they—*as a community*—need in order to sustain and nourish their life. The discovery and definition of "values for life" are part and parcel of the theological enterprise. Once the values are identified, they can become objects of desire: the community must decide to reach out for them if it wants to live and grow in the concrete order.

Canon law comes into play when those to whom the care of the social body is entrusted formulate norms, that is, specify and impose actions for the acquisition of values that are indispensable or highly necessary or useful for the life of the group. Of course, not all the values suitable for the community need to be objects of legislation; it will always be a matter of prudence to select the ones that ought to be promoted by legislative acts. Good guidance can come from our long-standing legal experience.

As in the spirit of a human person there is a vital process that begins with the affirmation of values and moves into decision and action for their appropriation, so in the collective spirit of the Church there is a similar process that identifies values and then directs and binds the community to reach out for them.

The connection between theology and canon law is best seen at the depth where they are born: in the spirit of the Church. Both are generated by the operation of one and the same subject, the Church. They come into existence as diverse fruits of an organic process in which there is a sequence of events. First there is a value judgment in the abstract world of theological knowledge, then a decision follows aiming for an action that impacts on the concrete world. There is one organic process moving from the one stage to another, each stage with its specific production.

We find an analogous play of events if we observe the *reception* of theological knowledge and of legal commands. There is one subject receiving, the Church. There are two distinct gifts received: one is knowledge that (when assimilated) leads the people into a deeper understanding of the mysteries; the other consists of commands that (when obeyed) dispose the people to accept God's gifts. This organic process of reception can be successful only if the natural sequence of events is respected: the people should become aware first of the values that sustain and nourish the life of the community, and then they should be given the command of the law for the acquisition of the same values.

The relationship explained.

To our second question we can now give an answer organized in a systematic fashion. Each of the following paragraphs represents a thought unit: they converge toward a full picture.

• The Church is the active agent that generates both theology and canon law. As the Church receives divine mysteries, the faith of the Church seeks understanding, and the resulting knowledge is theology. The faith of the Church seeks also balanced structures and ordered actions in the community for the ongoing reception of God's gifts, and the resulting ordinances form the body of canon law. There is one process of generation with two distinct products.

• The Church is the passive agent in receiving both theology and canon law. When theology is received, the people are nourished with knowledge and understanding. When canon law is received, the people are in possession of authoritative guidance toward actions for the appropriation of values. There is one subject to receive the two distinct products.

• In the spirit of the Church there is an organic and ordered sequence from "doing theology" to "making law." First, values must be known and defined, and then action for their acquisition can be imposed. A similar pattern ought to exist in the reception of the laws: the community should come first to an appreciation of the values, and then move to the observance of the norms.

• The Spirit of God, ever present in Christ's Church, guarantees that the memory of God's saving deeds will never be lost, and that the light that the *Logos* brought into the world will not be overcome by darkness. Hence, at the core of theology there is a participation in God's infallible knowledge. The same Spirit of God protects the Church in its practical decisions so that it can never lose its way toward the fullness of the kingdom, but we have no revelation to tell us that human laws in the Church will always and unfailingly represent the highest degree of prudence. For this reason, canon law has an inner fragility that can be balanced only by its strong attachment to theological values.

• Different dynamics are at work in the interpretation of dogmas and in the interpretation of canonical norms. In our intelligence the meaning of dogmas expands with every new insight into the mysteries—a never-ending process. When we inquire about meaning of a canonical norm, we are searching for a singular action that the norm intends to impose—a process with a precise goal. The two methods are mutually exclusive.

• For a system of laws to be authentic and attractive, it must represent a system of values. In other terms, the structure of the laws must be intimately bonded to a structure of values. Some laws can be directly linked to a specific value; for instance, the prohibition to kill speaks of the value of life. Some other laws must be linked in a general way to the value of good balance and public order in the community; for example, the norms for administrative procedures safeguard justice and protect rights. When a law is not supported by a value, it becomes a destructive force in the community.

• While sound theological and philosophical principles postulate balanced structures and coordinated actions in the Christian community, they do not demand the exclusive use of any particular legal system. The fact that the Roman Catholic Church is using the concepts and institutions of classical Roman law is due to historical circumstances. In an ecumenical age, the catholicity of the Church may eventually require a broader approach to the creation of order in the community.

• The relationship between theology and canon law can be best summarized by saying that in theology the Church contemplative is speaking to the people, and in canon law the Church active is guiding the faithful. There are not, however, two churches; one and the same Church is contemplative and active. There is a season for reflection and there is a season for action. The two operations blend into one but without losing their distinctive characters: they mutually support each other. They together reveal something of the internal life of God's covenanted community.

THE ECCLESIAL VOCATION OF CANON LAWYERS

The ecclesial vocation of canon lawyers is determined by the tasks that they are called to perform in the Church. Such tasks alternate on the level of theory and practice but they are organically connected.

• They have the task to identify the values the community needs in order to prosper: for this they have to enter the field of theology. They must be thoroughly conversant with the theoretical judgments of value, and they must have the capacity to discern the ones that need promotion and support by legislation.

• They must be able to assess the existing capacity of the community to appropriate a given value and to live by it; if this capacity is not there, the legislation will be a failure. This is a prudential judgment concerning a concrete situation. Of course, we are not talking about universal Christian values that the community must accept, but about particular values that allow choices.

• They must have the literary skill for the drafting and interpretation of legal texts.

• They must be observers and prudent judges of the encounter of the *abstract, general,* and *impersonal* legal norms with the *concrete, particular,* and *personal* situations; it is there that the suitability of the law for promoting life in the community reveals itself. They must be able to be of assistance for the application of the correctives of law, such as epiky *(epikeia, epieikeia),* equity, and economy *(oikonomia).*

• Finally, a task of creativity: canon lawyers should be in position to suggest changes in our laws and, as the spirit of the times demands it, propose provisions for new needs in the community.

• To sum up: the ecclesial vocation of canon lawyers is to be trustees for much of the practical operation of the Church; for this they need good theological knowledge of the mysteries, a realistic perception of the practical strength of the people, a creative talent to articulate the needed norms, and a capacity to form prudential judgments to interpret and implement the laws. Thus, and only thus, will canon lawyers implement "the supreme law in the Church" which is "the salvation of souls" (c. 1752).

BIBLIOGRAPHY

Corecco, E. *Théologie et droit canon: Écrits pour une nouvelle théorie générale du droit canon.* Ed. Patrick Le Gal. Fribourg: Éditions Universitaires, 1991.

Erdö, P. *Teologia del diritto canonico. Un approccio storico-istituzionale.* Turin: Giappichelli, 1996.

Granfield, D. *The Inner Experience of Law: A Jurisprudence of Subjectivity.* Washington, D.C.: Catholic University of America, 1988.

Hervada, J. *Coloquios propedeuticos sobre el derecho canonico.* Pamplona: Universidad de Navarra, 1990.

Örsy, L. *Theology and Canon Law: New Horizons for Legislation and Interpretation.* Collegeville, Minn.: Liturgical Press, 1992.

Paul VI. *Allocutiones de iure canonico.* Ed. J. Beyer. 2nd ed. Rome: Università Gregoriana, 1980.

Ramallo, V. *El derecho y el misterio de la Iglesia.* Rome: Università Gregoriana, 1972.

Sohm, R. *Kirchenrecht.* Vol. 1, *Die Geschichtliche Grundlagen.* Vol. 2, *Katholisches Kirchenrecht.* Reprint. Munich, 1923.

Wijlens, M. *Theology and Canon Law: The Theories of Klaus Mörsdorf and Eugenio Corecco.* Lanham, Md.: University Press of America, 1992.

CANONICAL OVERVIEW: 1983–1999

Frederick R. McManus

A canonical commentary must of necessity deal with a succession of individual norms, laws, and statutes. This is especially true of a codified style of law like the Code of Canon Law of the Latin church. Such law is properly considered in text and context, considering that context in the broadest sense possible.

Nonetheless, it is equally sound to survey the universal canon law as a whole, in particular as it develops and changes even in short periods of time, such as during the decade and a half since the 1983 promulgation of the Latin or Western church's code. The survey or overview should be done selectively and broadly, if only not to encroach on the other two introductory essays in this volume or on the commentary regarding the canons themselves.

The broad principles which guided the revision of the 1917 code, as agreed upon in 1967 and as asserted in the papal constitution of 1983, *Sacrae disciplinae leges,* place this body of law, this code, in perspective. It is a perspective that changes in the course of time, a course of time now shortened by the instant, worldwide communication of the churches in the 1990s.

As one prenote, the Christian and Catholic canon law comprises much more than a simple collection of canons common to the Latin church. After all, even the concept of canonical codification is still a novelty, dating only from the beginning of the twentieth century. Codification has its strengths, but is wrongly misconceived as if the code were the only church law. Even more is this problematical because—aside from the liturgical law and the church-state or concordat law outside the code—the Catholic canon law embraces all manner of particular law of the churches at every level: diocesan, provincial, national, regional. In the future, we may, and indeed must, pray that in the providence of God it will embrace as well the law of the churches with which we are not now in full Catholic communion.

Second Vatican Council

This brings us to the critical themes of the Second Vatican Council by which our code and later developments must be judged, whether at the time of promulgation in 1983 or today, almost two decades later. This is a point admirably made and repeated in the mid-eighties by the Latin code's lawmaker, Pope John Paul II, Bishop of Rome.

There was much to be learned from Vatican II, whether as the partial source text of the present Latin code or of subsequent enactments. Certainly the new definition of the Church itself in terms of communion and collegiality, mystery and people, was the chief lesson, coupled with an innovative summons to church dialogue with today's human society. Another insight, in article six of the very significant decree on ecumenism *Unitatis redintegratio,* had been almost alien to modern orthodoxy and orthopraxis, namely, that the Church always stands in need of reform and reformation. Rather pragmatically, this openness to change can be viewed in the canonical developments, good and bad, strong and weak, in the period since 1983.

There are different ways to judge the success or failure of the 1983 code as it stands, always in the light of the most general of the modern general councils. Sometimes the multifold themes of Vatican II were expressed negatively, perhaps most famously when the German Frings denounced a curial dicastery as a scandal to the Church and the Belgian DeSmedt decried the Church's triumphalism, juridicism, and clericalism.

The critique of the Roman Curia was partially answered in the papal reform of 1967, only slightly reflected in the 1983 code, and again partially answered in a second papal reform of 1988. The ongoing problems of juridicism and triumphalism were answered in some measure by the greater canonical concerns, now called pastoral, for charity and service to the people of God, by mitigations or omissions of some more rigid norms, and by attribution of the threefold office of Christ—priest, prophet, shepherd—to all believers. Clericalism, developed over nearly two millennia, has also been happily weakened through the concepts of the basic equality of the baptized, the common priestly ministry of all Christians, and the universal call to holiness.

The council, moreover, was characterized by the absence of condemnations. From the first words uttered by John XXIII on October 11, 1962, it was a positive expression of what the Church is and how its mission of evangelization can be achieved only by the most open and free dialogue with the totality of human culture and society.

The work of reforming and recodifying the 1917 code which governs the Latin church was announced in 1959, along with the council, but had to await action until the council was completed in 1965. The first broad determination of the code's style and content—in a way, how to deal with a changed postconciliar Church—was agreed upon in 1967, with general principles approved by both Paul VI and the Roman synod of bishops assembled that year as "representative of the whole Catholic episcopate."

At that time a series of important principles for the revised code was derived from conciliar teaching: pastoral tone and purpose; charity as well as justice; fundamental equality of believers in their rights (and responsibilities), with power or authority seen as service; and the major principle of subsidiarity, whether in view of the local churches in which the *ecclesia* is present or in their corporate groups, especially the national conferences of bishops acting on behalf of groups of particular or local churches.

Then a series of necessary but somewhat secondary considerations was listed in those principles of 1967: the retention of the code's juridic character but with better protection of rights; better coordination of internal and external forums; the (exceptional) non-territorial personal jurisdictions; fewer and simpler penalties and fewer reservations of canonical faculties and the like;

development of administrative or executive procedures and powers.

In promulgating the 1983 code in the apostolic constitution *Sacrae disciplinae leges*, John Paul added a new stress on key elements of the project: the concept of Church as people of God and as *communio;* collegiality and primacy; participation of all in the threefold office of Christ, with a definition of the rights of all Christians, especially the non-ordained; and commitment to ecumenism—although in fact this last element was barely touched on in the code itself.

Reform of the Roman Curia:
Pastor bonus

Two major reforms in the departments or dicasteries of the Roman Curia took place in this century prior to the 1983 revision of the code. One was accomplished by the apostolic constitution of Pius X *Sapienti consilio* (1908), the second by the apostolic constitution of Paul VI *Regimini Ecclesiae universae* (1967). The latter of course responded to some of the severe criticisms of the Curia by the fathers of Vatican II. Unlike the 1917 code, which took more than twenty canons to define the competence of congregations, tribunals, and offices of the Curia (*CIC* 242–264), the 1983 code has only two canons on the curial institutes (cc. 360–361).

In part the limited number of canons is due to the fact that a further curial reform was under way in 1983; hence the reference to a forthcoming special law. Immediately prior to the 1985 extraordinary session of the Roman synod of bishops, John Paul II consulted with the college of cardinals on the subject. (He did not, however, formally consult on the point with the synod.) Similarly, the conferences of bishops were invited to offer recommendations. The result is the apostolic constitution *Pastor bonus* of June 1988, which is now printed as an appended document in the codes of both East and West.

The pattern of *Pastor bonus* is familiar and traditional: a substantial and valuable introduction followed by almost two hundred articles of norms, general and particular. The introduction is a historical and theoretical exposition, especially important for its treatment of the meaning of service or *diaconia* in the Church, along with the conciliar restoration of the concept of communion; the Church as both collegial and primatial; and the pastoral office of the bishop as shepherd of the particular church with a relation to another bishop, the Bishop of Rome, who fulfills the Petrine or primatial ministry of service. After a summary of the history of the Roman Curia, including the creation of the body or college of cardinals as papal electors, the constitution deals with the present situation of that Curia.

The Second Vatican Council had defined the pope's Curia in positive ways, partially picked up in the canons:

> In exercising the supreme, full, and immediate power over the universal Church, the Roman Pontiff uses the dicasteries of the Roman Curia which then carry out their function—in his name and by his authority —for the good of the churches and in service to the sacred pastors [bishops].

This primary text was from article nine of the conciliar decree on the office of bishops in the Church *Christus Dominus*. There it was immediately followed by a listing of the several reforms desired, new patterns adapted to contemporary needs in names, competence, procedures, and co-ordination, with membership of cardinals and bishops from diverse lands. This was the reform undertaken by Paul VI in 1967 and developed further two decades later in *Pastor bonus*.

The concluding paragraphs of the constitution's introduction are an admirable statement of the curial role and responsibility. They touch on its ministerial and vicarious character; the importance of collegiality, especially with respect to the episcopal college's solicitude for the whole Church; the value of particular usages and practices which by divine law pertain to the pastors of local or particular churches; curial support of the unity of the Church, of faith, and of discipline; and more.

There are, perhaps inevitably, certain contrasts between theory or doctrine and the detailed, concrete norms which constitute the bulk of *Pastor bonus*. These deal with the many departments called dicasteries (congregations, tribunals, councils, with a few secondary institutes). In principle, at least, all the dicasteries enjoy equal juridic status. Only a very few of the general norms need be pointed out here.

For ordinary or regular sessions of the dicasteries, it is enough that members (that is, the cardinals and bishops) resident in Rome be present; for plenary sessions (annual if possible), all the members must be present. Matters of major importance are reserved to general assemblies of this kind.

Aside from judicial sentences, all decisions of major importance must also be submitted for approbation by the Roman Pontiff unless special faculties have already been given to the head of a dicastery. No laws or general decrees with the force of law or derogations from law may be issued without the specific approbation of the Roman Pontiff. Nor is anything "grave and extraordinary" to be undertaken without prior notification of the pope. Regular relationships with particular churches and conferences of bishops should be fostered by seeking their counsel in the preparation of general documents of major importance. Questions proposed to dicasteries should be studied carefully and answered without delay, or at the very least acknowledged.

Practical regulations of this kind are positive and fruitful. They are chosen here, however, because of some indications that they are not observed all the time, in spirit or letter. In general, a measure of tension will inevitably exist between the Roman Curia and the particular churches—and often enough between that Curia and the groups of particular churches, the groups which for the past century and more have gathered in conferences of bishops. The interposition of the new synod of bishops, superior to the college of cardinals in *Christus Dominus* 5 and in the code, and not a part of the Curia at all, has been seen as a possible resolution of such tensions—but this has not developed as yet.

Catholic Higher Education:
Ex corde Ecclesiae

In August 1990 John Paul II issued an apostolic constitution, *Ex corde Ecclesiae,* on Catholic universities and other postsecondary institutions of higher learning; it was complementary to canons 807–814. Published after several years of consultation with conferences of bishops and responsible college and university officials, the constitution had been prepared prior to the death of Paul VI and had been somewhat enlarged by Pope John Paul II. In its final version it spoke more strongly of Catholic higher education as an instrument of evangelization. This fits in well with the council's brief treatment in its declaration on Christian education. There, in *Gravissimum educationis* 10, a goal was expressed:

> Thus [through Catholic colleges and universities] there is accomplished a public, stable, and universal presence of the Christian mind in total commitment to the furtherance of higher culture. The students of these institutions are formed as men and women truly outstanding in learning, ready to undertake weighty responsibilities in society, and witnesses to the faith in the world.

The papal constitution of 1990 was well received in the academic community of the Church for its doctrinal exposition in the introduction and first part, on the identity and mission of service of Catholic higher education. But the second, canonical or dispositive part, the general norms, raised questions that are not yet resolved.

Background

Before the constitution is examined a little more carefully, two prenotes are needed.

First, in the 1917 code all of Catholic higher education (except seminaries) was governed by a single title of canons about "schools" at every level—elementary, middle, and higher (*CIC* 1372–1383). There was only a first step toward clarifying distinctions among these "schools," in particular by reserving to the Apostolic See the establishment of institutions which grant degrees with so-called canonical effects.

By the time of Vatican II, the nomenclature was clearer, helped by an apostolic constitution of Pius XI in 1931, *Deus scientiarum Dominus.* That document raised the standards of faculties and universities in the "sacred" sciences and set such institutions apart. In article ten of the conciliar declaration *Gravissimum educationis,* it was taken for granted that Catholic colleges and universities belonged to a broad, general category corresponding to the same institutions in the general academic world. "Faculties of sacred sciences" or "ecclesiastical faculties" (or even universities) were distinct: they were in the religious field and related areas; they were approved by the Roman See; and, perhaps most important, their degrees were granted by authority of that same Apostolic See. In the 1983 code it became even clearer: distinct chapters of canons were devoted to "Catholic" (and, in a sense, "non-ecclesiastical") higher education (cc. 807–814) and to ecclesiastical universities and faculties, often, but less properly, called pontifical (cc. 815–821).

Second, this excursus on nomenclature was necessary because the constitution *Ex corde Ecclesiae* was preceded by a parallel papal document, *Sapientia christiana* of 1979, released just prior to the promulgation of the code. *Sapientia christiana* was to be complementary to the new canons on ecclesiastical universities and faculties. The constitution had both the usual theoretical and expository sections and then more than ninety normative articles, as well as related articles, more than sixty in number, from the Congregation for Catholic Education.

Again, in the pattern to be followed by the code, the ecclesiastical faculties and universities were distinct from the much more numerous Catholic institutions of higher education. Nevertheless, the traditions of the former were maintained, with Roman control understood to have special meaning in the papal responsibility for degrees with canonical effects.

The New Law for Catholic Colleges and Universities

In turn, *Ex corde Ecclesiae* of 1990 followed a similar pattern, especially in the elaborate consultation that took several years and included a congress in Rome, with representatives from episcopal conferences and representative college and university heads. The latter came, for example, from the International Federation of Catholic Universities and, for the United States, from the Association of Catholic Colleges and Universities. Various proposals affected the final shape of the constitution: a lengthy exposition of the nature and purpose of Catholic higher education—received favorably in the church and academic community, as already mentioned—and a relatively small body of normative articles, only seven in all, with another four transitional norms.

In passing, a few of the expository matters may be mentioned as particularly welcome to the academic community. One is the assertion of both academic freedom and institutional autonomy. Another is the inclusion of the essential characteristics of Catholic postsecondary institutions in terms formulated by the international federation as early as 1972: Christian inspiration of individuals *and* of the educational community as such; reflection and research on human knowledge in the light of Catholic faith; fidelity to the Christian message as it comes through the Church; institutional commitment to service of the people of God and the human family.

The document was welcome because of the expression of priorities—over and above specific missions, such as evangelization, as mentioned above, cultural dialogue, and service to society through teaching and research. The priorities were expressed in terms of the institution being both a college or university *and* Catholic, first the noun, then the adjective, as it has often been put. This was meant to define Catholic higher education as truly satisfying the expectations of academe in human society but always institutionally committed to the Christian and Catholic message.

The positive reception of the bulk of *Ex corde Ecclesiae* did not extend to all of the attached norms by any means. The series of canonical requirements or norms asked, first, for concrete application by the conferences of bishops and, second, for some kind of inclusion of the canon law of *Ex corde Ecclesiae* and its national applications in the foundational documents of individual institutions. The principal questions, still unresolved, relate to the present diversity of the institutions in their foundation, reporting requirements in relation to church authorities, proportions of Catholic teachers, ecclesiastical approbation of regulations of individual institutions, and sharper definitions of ecclesiastical vigilance or control. An issue that has grown in importance, although not enjoined by *Ex corde Ecclesiae* itself, is the procedure for the concession or acknowledgment of the mandate of canon 812 for teachers of theological disciplines—and, more significantly, procedures for revocation of this mandate. (A parallel problem, also not enjoined by the constitution itself, relates to the application of the oath of fidelity upon undertaking an ecclesiastical office to be exercised in the name of the Church in the case of "teachers in any universities whatsoever who teach disciplines which deal with faith or morals"—as described in connection with *Ad tuendam fidem* below.)

Problems are associated with the mandate itself: whether or not it is a novel intrusion into educational autonomy; whether or not it means new authoritarian control by church authorities; whether or not it might lead to loss of academic integrity and repute or of civil recognition and even loss of state aid. This is why an application of the constitution *Ex corde Ecclesiae* in the United States has not been achieved after nearly a decade. In 1996 the National Conference of Catholic Bishops almost unanimously enacted the required national ordinances—eleven juridic norms couched in pastoral language, in three sections each preceded by a rationale. The decree of the conference, however, under the title, "*Ex corde Ecclesiae:* An Application to the United States," did not receive the *recognitio* from the

Apostolic See. Now the conference is left to develop new legislative norms or applications if these can be agreed upon.

Ecumenism:
Directory

The canonical treatment of matters ecumenical in the 1983 code may appear meager, at least in quantity (cc. 755 and 844), given the intrinsic significance of such developments during and after the council. The importance of ecumenism has been recognized at every level of the church community, in liturgical sharing, in dialogues, and in programs. At the level of the Roman See, this was acknowledged by John Paul II in a brief reference in the apostolic constitution *Sacrae disciplinae leges* and eloquently in the encyclical letter *Ut unum sint* of 1995. The latter, while addressing doctrinal and pastoral rather than disciplinary changes, is most notable for seeking dialogue with church leaders and theologians about the forms in which the papal or Petrine primacy can be better exercised. Such dialogue could doubtless lead to profound changes in church institutions and canonical discipline.

The chief concrete development—aside from all the universal and particular ecumenical dialogues—is found in the March 1993 "Directory for the Application of Principles and Norms of Ecumenism." This superseded the earlier directory, which had appeared in two parts (1967 and 1970) and was issued by the Pontifical Council for Promoting Christian Unity, as the former Secretariat has been called since 1988. Although still reflecting the canonical weight and force of directories and general executory decrees (c. 33), the 1993 document has a final note indicating its approbation, confirmation, and promulgation by authority of John Paul II.

So far as canonical discipline is concerned, the revised directory serves as a kind of compendium of regulations applying both the conciliar decrees and the canons without introducing new legislation as such. The discipline includes institutional or structural organization of ecumenical activity of the Catholic Church; Catholic ecumenical formation (formerly the subject of part two of the directory in 1970, but now broadened); liturgical and spiritual activity (including the potentially troubling areas of sacramental sharing); and ecumenical cooperation by way of dialogue and witness.

The disciplinary and institutional elements of the directory are valuable, but more significant is the underlying exposition or rationale. This runs throughout the directory, but is also found in a new first chapter on "The Search for Christian Unity." Paragraphs 9–36 cover such matters as the Church as communion, divisions among Christians and the re-establishment of unity, the complexity and diversity of the ecumenical situation, and sects and new religious movements. This substantive chapter supports and justifies the Catholic ecumenical discipline that is set forth and explained in later chapters.

One final note. This directory may also be judged as reflecting little radical change since the 1983 code, although it was article six of the conciliar decree on ecumenism, *Unitatis redintegratio,* which declared once for all that the pilgrim Church of Christ always stands in need of constant reform. The pontifical council, while juridically equal to other dicasteries of the Roman Curia, must submit the agreed statements of international dialogues and even such regulations as this directory to the scrutiny and judgment of the Congregation for the Doctrine of the Faith. In effect, this congregation is thus a brake upon the ecumenical initiatives of Vatican II.

As a broad example of this potential problem, article eight of the same *Unitatis redintegratio* offers two principles for sharing (once *communicatio in sacris*), especially eucharistic sharing, first, as the sign of the Church's unity, second, as participation in the means of grace. The first principle, not yet achieved, may forbid sharing; the second may commend it. The directory, like canon 844 and the code's norms on mixed marriages, attempts to strike a balance—but of course the positive side to ecumenical progress may dictate further and perhaps radical change in this discipline.

"Collaboration of the Non-Ordained":
Interdicasterial Instruction

This curial document, which was issued in August 1997, is unique in several ways. It bears the signatures of the moderators (prefect, pro-prefect, or president) and secretaries of six congregations and two pontifical councils; it is properly called interdicasterial or interdepartmental. It cites a good number of pertinent canons and liturgical norms as well. And it is approved by John Paul II, not in the usual or common form, but in the now rarer specific form (*in forma specifica*). This surely adds to its juridic weight, although it is still categorized as only an instruction under the precise terms of canon 34.

The breadth of the document—with a foreword and a series of theological principles leading up to thirteen practical articles and a conclusion—is evident from the full title: "Instruction on Certain Questions Regarding the Collaboration of the Non-Ordained Faithful in the Sacred Ministry of Priests." The Roman congregations which joined in preparing the document are, in the order given in the text, those for the clergy, the laity (a pontifical council), the doctrine of the faith, divine worship and the discipline of the sacraments, bishops, the evangelization of peoples, institutes of consecrated life and societies of apostolic life, and the interpretation of legislative texts (a pontifical council).

The title of the interdicasterial instruction is susceptible of a positive and indeed an expansive meaning, namely, one of increasing and enlarging juridical norms for lay participation in the Church's ministries, including the ministries otherwise reserved to bishops and presbyters. For the most part, however, just the opposite is true in both the theological principles and the "practical provisions."

This does not mean that the 1997 instruction omits any positive exposition of the role of the non-ordained. For example, the impetus given by Vatican II and the papal magisterium to lay ecclesial involvement is acknowledged, and "a full recovery of the awareness of the secular nature of the mission of the laity" is therefore sought. The areas of the Church's mission involving the non-ordained are enumerated: culture, arts and theater, scientific research, labor, means of communication, politics, the economy, etc. Other tasks closely associated with the "more restricted area" of the "sacred ministry of the clergy" are called "the great field of complementary activity" of non-ordained persons. These include the teaching of Christian doctrine, certain liturgical actions, and the care of souls.

Undoubtedly the thrust of the instruction, again both in the sections of theoretical elaboration and in the practical norms, moves in a very different and retrogressive direction. This is apparent in the constant definition of limits to lay participation or collaboration and especially in the singling out of aberrations or abuses in almost all the thirteen articles of dispositive "provisions," most of which are divided into subsidiary paragraphs.

The reception of the instruction by the church community in 1997 was largely negative, less because of prescriptions derived from canon law than because of the tone and direction of the document. This negative reaction was expressed by several conferences of bishops, with the assertion that the aberrations alleged had not been experienced in their territories.

The Roman response to this negative reaction or failure in ecclesial reception was twofold. First, it was pointed out that the abuses and aberrations were actually absent in some and possibly in most places, although this fact would hardly explain the general or universal character of the instruction or the specific papal approbation. Second, it was explained that the prescriptions in the practical section were simply gathered from prohibitions in the current church law. This assertion was only partly supported by the abundant citations of canons and other sources in the text of the document. Whether the selectivity or almost uniformly prohibitory nature of the selected norms can be explained in this way is something else, to be taken up below.

Theological Principles

The theological principles of the instruction fall under four headings:

(1) "The Common Priesthood of the Faithful and the Ministerial Priesthood." The emphasis here is on the different *modes* of the faithful's participation in Christ's priesthood, without denying the universality or dignity of the whole community's participation; the ministerial priesthood is rooted in the apostolic priesthood, and the ordained are entrusted with "the authoritative proclamation of the word of God, the administration of the sacraments, and the pastoral direction of the [non-ordained] faithful."

(2) "Unity and Diversity of Ministerial Functions." The functions of the ordained are next affirmed to be "a single indivisible unity in virtue of their singular foundation in Christ." The exercise of the threefold *munera* is therefore "the essence of pastoral ministry," and the exercise of some such functions, in a limited degree, by the non-ordained "does not make pastors of the lay faithful."

(3) "The Indispensability of the Ordained Ministry." Here the opening principle is that "a canonical or juridical determination made by hierarchical authority is necessary for the exercise of the *munus* of teaching or governing." Thus the ministerial priesthood is needed for a community to exist as "Church," else a community would lack the essential "exercise and sacramental action of Christ." Two pastoral demands are a consequence: the promotion of vocations and proper seminary training.

(4) "The Collaboration of the Non-Ordained Faithful in Pastoral Ministry." Finally, the instruction recognizes the collaboration in question as "mutual enrichment of the common Christian vocation." It distinguishes rights and duties of the non-ordained as, first, "those which are theirs in virtue of their secular condition" and, second, those which are "along the lines of collaboration with the sacred ministry of clerics" and to which they therefore have no right. These latter ministries may be entrusted to them, within limits and by deputation, when the ordained ministers are not available—with the hope that the abuse of multiplying such "exceptional" cases will be avoided.

Practical Provisions

As already mentioned, the larger part of the interdicasterial instruction is a recital of abuses or improper practices. This section is often but not always documented from the present law, with frequent comments and interpretations. Nowhere is the role of the Pontifical Council for the Interpretation of Legislative Texts, one of the participating dicasteries, spelled out, and there is no suggestion of authoritative or "authentic" interpretation of the sources for the practical provisions. Yet the council's role lends greater credence to the provisions so long as the law itself—disciplinary, liturgical, or other—rather than some simple recommendation or exhortation is cited.

The practical provisions range from the question of appropriate terminology for ministry, offices, and functions all the way to the possible leadership role at funerals. The latter is a good example of the regular approach to specifics in the instruction: the failure of presbyters and deacons to preside at funerals is explained as related to "growing dechristianization" and "abandonment of religious practice," but the possibility of non-ordained presidency by deputation is recognized "provided that there is a true absence of sacred ministers and that they [the non-ordained] adhere to the prescribed liturgical norms." Article nineteen of the introduction to the *Order of Christian Funerals* is then cited.

Other examples can be selected in which the juridic source of a norm is explicitly mentioned, such as the canons on lay preaching in churches or oratories or canon 517 on the deputed exercise of pastoral care by lay persons, to be viewed as exceptional and never replacing the role of the parish priest. In almost every case, however, cautionary language is added to a norm. This is done regularly to emphasize the exceptional nature of the case of the non-ordained person who is deputed for one or other ministry proper to the ordained.

More problematic, in the series of practical provisions, are cases in which the commentary may go beyond the current law and introduce new restrictions. For example, "Any ceremony associated with the deputation of the non-ordained as collaborators in the ministry of clerics must not have . . . a form analogous to that of the conferral [*sic*] of lector or acolyte." "Homilies in non-eucharistic liturgies may be preached by the non-ordained faithful only when expressly permitted by law." "To avoid any confusion between sacramental liturgical acts presided over by a priest or deacon and other acts which the non-ordained faithful may lead, it is always necessary to use clearly distinct ceremonials, especially for the latter."

It is not that such examples are lacking in logic or reasonableness, but they are fresh injunctions or the like which may exceed the law in force. The same might be said of the proscription of titles employed for the non-ordained even when they are properly deputed: pastor, chaplain, coordinator, moderator. Or: "The non-ordained faithful or a group of them entrusted with a collaboration in the exercise of pastoral care cannot be given the title of 'community leader' or any other expression indicating the same idea."

Without further examples, it should be evident that the instruction is pervasively negative or cautionary or restrictive in direction and purpose. This may be said without asserting that abuses or improper practices do not exist in the Church universal.

A last point may be made: it would probably have been possible to achieve many of the purposes of the 1997 instruction in entirely different and indeed opposite ways. This could have been done through a positive enumeration of all the potential roles and ministries of the non-ordained, with positive encouragement of everything from preaching to presidency at non-eucharistic rites. A further step or stage would have involved more profound exploration of such matters as the exercise of the power of governance (*potestas regiminis*) to see whether the responsibility of the non-ordained might be objectively expanded in the light of historical precedent and the openness of Vatican II. Legal options in many areas, ranging from judicial offices to deliberative votes in councils and conferences, could be assayed in this fashion.

Profession of Faith: Ad tuendam fidem

The decade and a half after the 1983 codification saw radical developments affecting the received profession of faith, in particular as it is obligatory for those listed in canon 833. At the time of the promulgation of the code, the profession of faith in possession was that of 1967. It consisted of the Nicene-Constantinopolitan creed—common to the Catholic Church and most other Christian churches and ecclesial communities and of course celebrated each Sunday by the eucharistic assembly in the Roman and other rites. One brief paragraph was added to this creed in 1967:

> I firmly embrace and accept
> all and everything which has been either defined by the Church's solemn deliberations
> or affirmed and declared by its ordinary magisterium concerning the doctrine of faith and morals,
> according as they are proposed by it,
> especially those things dealing with the Holy Church of Christ,
> its sacraments and the sacrifice of the Mass,
> and the primacy of the Roman Pontiff.

As is evident, this single added paragraph referred to the teachings of the modern ecumenical councils and was formulated in the light of Vatican II. It replaced the lengthier additions made after Trent and Vatican I; it also replaced the antimodernist oath of 1910.

The substantial changes since the code of 1983 took place in two stages over almost a decade.

First Stage

The first development was in 1989 and was itself twofold. The 1967 addition to the creed was replaced by three new paragraphs, to be affirmed by those bound by canon 833. At the same time a new discipline—an oath of fidelity for certain church office-holders—was introduced. All this occurred by decree of the Roman Congregation of the Doctrine of the Faith in the fall of 1989; while the original document was undated and unsigned, without reference to any prior papal approval, this canonical deficiency was later sanated.

The text of the first and third new paragraphs added to the creed itself was closely related to the 1983 code, canons 750 and 752 respectively; the second paragraph, however, was an innovation:

1. With firm faith I believe as well everything contained in God's word, written or handed down in tradition and proposed by the Church—whether by way of solemn judgment or through the ordinary and universal magisterium—as divinely revealed and calling for faith.

2. I also firmly accept and hold each and every thing that is proposed definitively by the Church regarding teaching on faith and morals.

3. Moreover, I adhere with religious *obsequium* of will and intellect to the teachings which either the Roman Pontiff or the college of bishops enunciate when they exercise the authentic magisterium, even if they proclaim those teachings by an act that is not definitive.

The other part of the 1989 decree was a canonical innovation, in this case an oath of fidelity—derived from a variety of sources—for those persons who undertake an ecclesiastical office "to be exercised in the name of the Church." It affected and affects those church officeholders enumerated in canon 833, nn. 5–8, the canon which requires the profession of faith. But the oath was an entirely new obligation and thus a burden on certain persons in the church community. At this point, moreover, the application of the second added paragraph of the creed to members of the Church other than ecclesiastical officeholders was not at issue; such a development would have to await the next stage.

Second Stage

These details have been spelled out so that the 1998 development, the second stage, will be clear. This fresh development was a matter of a change in the code(s)—both the doctrinally based discipline affecting all the members of the Church (both Western and Eastern) and the introduction or expansion of penalties. In this case, the basic action took the form of an apostolic letter, issued *motu proprio* in May 1998 by John Paul II.

The letter *Ad tuendam fidem* offered the traditional exposition of the rationale for the papal action. In particular, it noted that the 1983 code had omitted the matter contained in the second paragraph of the text newly attached to the creed in 1989. This omission was rectified by adding a new second paragraph to canon 750 of the Latin code as well as to canon 598 of the Code of Canons of the Eastern (Catholic) Churches:

Each and every thing which is proposed definitively by the magisterium of the Church concerning the doctrine of faith or morals, that is, each and every thing which is required to safeguard reverently and to expound faithfully the same deposit of faith, is also to be firmly embraced and retained; therefore, one who rejects those propositions which are to be held definitively is opposed to the doctrine of the Catholic Church.

The key words are "proposed definitively" and "to be held definitively." The principal change was to make the new norm—embracing and maintaining certain doctrinal propositions—binding for all the Christian faithful who are obliged to observe the canons of the codes, that is, not merely for those obliged to make the 1989 profession of faith. Determining the extent to which this is a serious enlargement of obligations of assent, distinct from but closely related to divine and Catholic faith (the first paragraph of the profession of faith and the respective c. 750 and *CCEO* 598), will be a task of theologians: perhaps they must develop clearer interpretations of "definitive" teachings. Equally important and difficult is the study of individual teachings to determine which ones belong to each of the three categories of the three appended paragraphs and now in the canons of the codes.

The second new law addressed in *Ad tuendam fidem* is likewise troublesome; it addresses the "just penalty" (*ferendae sententiae*) to be imposed on those persons who violate canon 750, §2, that is, the new canonical text about doctrines "definitively" to be held. With the added reference, the Latin church penal canon 1371 now reads:

The following are to be punished with a just penalty:
    1° in addition to the case mentioned in canon 1364, §1 [apostasy, heresy, schism], a person who teaches a doctrine condemned by the Roman Pontiff or an ecumenical council or who obstinately rejects the doctrine mentioned in [the new] canon 750, §2 or in canon 752 and who does not retract after having been admonished by the Apostolic See or the ordinary.

In effect, the just penalty of canon 1371 (and also the parallel penalty in the Eastern canon 1436, §2) has been extended to include those who obstinately reject definitive teachings. This extension, though logically flowing from the 1989 revision of the profession of faith, has been considered troublesome because the just penalty threatened by the canon can range from the slightest to the ultimate, namely, excommunication from the Christian community.

The apostolic letter *Ad tuendam fidem* of John Paul II thus flowed from the decision to ratify the 1989 revised profession of faith and specifically its inclusion of a different level of church teaching of truths related to Christian and Catholic faith. These teachings are at the next level down from the divine and Catholic faith of canon 750 (and the first paragraph appended to the creed), but at a level superior to teachings which are described in canon 752 (and in the third paragraph)

as proclaimed without a definitive act of the authentic magisterium.

Accompanying the papal document but dated a few weeks later was a commentary from the Congregation for the Doctrine of the Faith. The weight of the curial document, signed by the prefect and secretary of the dicastery but without any mention of papal action or approval, still remains considerable, at least because of its intrinsic argument.

The commentary is a lengthy and helpful discursus on the apostolic letter and its purpose. A single instance may be quoted from the clarifications:

8. With regard to the *nature* of the assent owed [by all the faithful] to the truths set forth by the Church as divinely revealed (those of the first paragraph) and to be held definitively (those of the second paragraph), it is important to emphasize that there is no difference with respect to the full and irrevocable character of the assent which is owed to those teachings. The difference concerns the supernatural virtue of faith: In the case of truths of the first paragraph, the assent is based directly on faith in the authority of the word of God (doctrines *de fide credenda*); in the case of truths of the second paragraph, the assent is based on faith in the Holy Spirit's assistance to the magisterium and on the Catholic doctrine of the infallibility of the magisterium (doctrines *de fide tenenda*).

Having explained the diversity of the relationships between the "definitive" doctrines and revealed truth, the commentary offers a series of examples. Those listed as belonging to the "definitively to be held" category are of greatest interest: understanding of papal infallibility before Vatican I; reservation of priestly ordination to men; illicitness of euthanasia, prostitution, and fornication. These teachings are said to fall into the category of definitive teachings because of their logical relationship to revelation itself. Others in the same category are those related to revelation by historical necessity: legitimacy of the election of the pope; legitimacy of the celebration of an ecumenical council; canonization; the declaration on the invalidity of Anglican ordinations by Leo XIII. The selection of examples, and certainly the last example, was quickly challenged in the theological community as demanding further study. Differences have long existed among theologians on this matter of the binding force of such teachings, generally under the heading of the so-called secondary objects of infallibility.

In summary, in a certain sense the major development involved here was not the 1998 papal action in itself but rather the revision of the canonically required profession of faith in 1989, only a few years after the promulgation of the Latin code—along with the disciplinary norm which introduced a novel oath of fidelity for a large proportion of those already bound by canon 833 to make the profession of faith. However, the recent apostolic letter of 1998 was indeed significant, for it introduced canons binding the whole Church, which require universal acceptance or assent to another category of proclaimed truths under pain of a just penalty for obstinate transgression. This development, however reasonable and logical, has been regarded as an additional and unnecessary burden upon the community of faith.

Conferences of Bishops:
Apostolos suos

In May 1998, after more than a decade of consultation and preparation, John Paul II issued an apostolic letter *motu proprio Apostolos suos,* about conferences of bishops. Its full topic is "the theological and juridical nature of episcopal conferences." With the exception of what are called complementary norms at the end of the papal letter and which constitute new law, the letter is a lengthy, thorough, and doctrinal discourse.

The background is this. In 1985 an extraordinary session of the synod of bishops (that is, one chiefly made up of the elected presidents of the conferences of bishops) was held in Rome to observe the twentieth anniversary of the conclusion of Vatican II. Although not the reason for the gathering by any means, the issue of the nature of conferences of bishops was discussed. It was occasioned in part by the anniversary and in part by a challenge to the teaching office of the conferences of bishops from a minority of synod members, some of whom were members of the Roman Curia. The canonical status of such conferences had of course been revised and determined by the 1965 decree on the pastoral office of bishops *Christus Dominus* 37–38.

The conciliar decree had long since been implemented by means of the interim *motu proprio Ecclesiae sanctae* of 1966 and then with a definitive redaction in the 1983 code. The relationships of episcopacy and primacy were also threshed out in the 1969 extraordinary session of the synod of bishops. And the majority of members of the 1985 synod, "representing the whole Catholic episcopate" and in fact the heads of the conferences, strongly supported the full authority of such bodies and affirmed their pastoral success during the two decades since the council.

Although the synod's final statement was in accord with this majority judgment, it did recommend a study of the nature of such conferences. Pope John Paul entrusted the matter to the Congregation for Bishops, which deals with the conferences on behalf of the Apostolic See in such matters as the *recognitio* or review of their legislative decrees. The congregation's first draft of the requested study was not well received by some conferences, such as the National Conference of Catholic Bishops in the United States. The apostolic letter of 1998 represents the final step in the process begun in 1985. Many had hoped it would be a strong Roman vindication of the nature and role of the modern institute of conferences.

On the contrary, however, this apostolic letter on "the theological and juridical nature of episcopal conferences" insists very strongly upon the power of the individual bishops of particular churches and thus appears to situate the conferences in a somewhat secondary or ancillary role only—apart from their clearly pastoral, nonbinding decisions. It acknowledges but does not enlarge greatly upon the closely analogous nature of conferences and particular councils (cc. 439–446). The latter seem almost intrinsic to the communion of churches since the second century. Yet, despite what some see as a cautionary and even fearsome tone, *Apostolos suos* warmly confirms the pastoral worth of conferences of bishops.

Apostolos suos begins with an introductory chapter on the history and development of the communion of churches and the mission of the apostolic college. It is here that the role of particular or regional councils (both provincial and "plenary") is recognized "from the second century on," that is, considerably antedating the first ecumenical council in 325. After a chapter on "Collegial Union among Bishops," including the kinds of joint pastoral action of the local bishops, conferences of bishops are addressed in their modern (nineteenth- and twentieth-century) character, both theological and juridical. A recital of canonical norms in the third chapter is completed by reflections on the teaching office of the conferences.

On the one hand, the teaching office of conferences is limited and can never be equated with a universal magisterium, even though the members are in full communion with the Roman See. One of many concerns, for example, is that the assembled bishops should be "careful to avoid interfering with the doctrinal work of the bishops of other territories, bearing in mind the wider, even worldwide resonance which the means of social communication give to the events of a particular region." Again, problems are seen in doctrinal statements made "in dealing with new questions and in acting so that the message of Christ enlightens and guides people's consciences in resolving new problems arising from changes in society." On the other hand, canon 753 is cited to affirm the authentic magisterium which the Christian faithful of a given nation or region must see in the common pronouncements of their own bishops:

Although the bishops who are in communion with the head and members of the college [of bishops], whether individually or joined together in conferences of bishops or in particular councils, do not possess infallibility in teaching, they are authentic teachers and instructors of the faith for the Christian faithful entrusted to their care; the Christian faithful are bound to adhere with religious submission of mind [*religioso animi obsequio*] to the authentic magisterium of their bishops.

To understand the new complementary norms which complete *Apostolos suos,* it is necessary to refer to canon 455, §4 of the code. This paragraph introduced a norm not found in the conciliar decree *Christus Dominus;* it constitutes a cautionary and limiting norm. The codal text has just treated general decrees or laws (and general executory decrees) which are disciplinary in nature, and the fourth paragraph adds:

In cases in which neither universal law nor a special mandate of the Apostolic See has granted the power mentioned in §1 [the enactment of general decrees or laws] to a conference of bishops, the competence of each diocesan bishop remains intact, nor is a conference or its president able to act in the name of all the bishops unless each and every bishop has given consent.

Vatican II had limited the juridically obligatory decisions of conferences of bishops to areas attributed to their competence by law or papal mandate. Outside these areas, disciplinary action "in the name of all the bishops" requires unanimity according to the canon just quoted. Of course this was an application or major extension of the old canonical maxim, "What touches all must be treated and approved by all." In turn, the 1998 letter *Apostolos suos* decreed an analogous or parallel restriction on the collegial teaching office of conferences. Article 1 of the complementary norms reads:

In order that the declarations of the conference of bishops referred to in no. 22 of the present letter may constitute authentic magisterium and be published in the name of the conference itself, they must be unanimously approved by the bishops who are members, or receive the *recognitio* of the Apostolic See if approved in plenary session by at least two-thirds of the bishops belonging to the conference and having a deliberative vote.

Most exercises of the teaching office by conferences of bishops are not undertaken with any purpose of obliging the Christian faithful of their territory. Nonetheless *Apostolos suos* does constitute a new restriction upon them in the first article just quoted. The same holds true of the other complementary norms, which, for example, prohibit commissions or other bodies to be deputed to exercise the conference's authentic magisterium.

By way of summary, the analogy between particular councils or synods of ancient Christian times and today's conferences of bishops needs greater exploration. The contemporary institute of conferences differs substantively only in its continuity between assemblies. It also differs, but not intrinsically, in its limited areas of legislative competence. It is surely not impossible, even if unlikely, that conferences of bishops should now have attributed to them the general binding power of particular councils—limited only by requirements of common and universal law and guaranteed by the canonical institute of Roman review or *recognitio* (cc. 445–446).

The application to conferences of the traditional function of councils, which is not now specified in the canons, needs exploration. *Christus Dominus* 36, for example, speaks of particular councils very broadly indeed: "The bishops decreed for various churches [including individual churches] the manner to be observed both in teaching the truths of faith and in the ordering of church discipline." Again, the question deserves further study, even while the new norms of *Apostolos suos* are observed. Whether this expanded conference competency would be considered a concession from the supreme authority of the pope or college of bishops or rather the simple lifting of present reservations is almost immaterial.

A year after *Apostolos suos,* in May 1999, the Roman Congregation for the Clergy addressed a circular letter to the conferences of bishops. Cautionary in tone and further restrictive, it dealt chiefly with doctrinal statements which might constitute authentic or authoritative magisterial pronouncements. These should not undertake, according to the curial letter, to deal with magisterial matters already in force: "Such teachings or parts of them may be quoted in any document of the episcopal conference or commissions without, however, voting upon them." The review or *recognitio* of a conference's doctrinal declaration, if not unanimous, belongs to the Congregation for Bishops or the Congregation for the Evangelization of Peoples, depending on the conference's territory. Should joint or international actions (whether magisterial or legislative) be necessary, the approbation of the Apostolic See is required. Statutes of conferences should be redrawn in accord with the letter and distinguish magisterial declarations from general decrees.

In other matters, for example, the circular letter recommended avoiding bureaucracy in the offices of conferences and asked them "not to replicate at conference level" diocesan curias and other organs. It also asked for a reduction in the number of documents emanating from episcopal commissions. As complementing *Apostolos suos,* the letter will be seen by many canonists and ecclesiologists as further regression from principles of subsidiarity and of regional collegiality of the bishops.

Conclusion

This limited selection of instances of canonical development from the 1983 code to the present calls for a general, objective appraisal of that development. This appraisal should indicate whether progress or regression has taken place in relation to the teaching and discipline of the Second Vatican Council. Few would consider the ecclesial reform of Vatican II minimal, but even it should be only a starting point for the present and the future.

To begin with, neither the few examples described above nor the numerous other lesser instances that might be adduced contain any direct, explicit reversals of conciliar decisions. In fact, this posture may be a problem: even when a different direction is taken, especially in tone or thrust, there is a strong official reluctance to affirm or acknowledge any change. But it is entirely correct to study how both the canonical codification and contemporary developments truly satisfy the implementation of the will of the Church assembled in council. In fact, the venerable concept of ecclesial reception of councils and of canon law needs to be fully reappraised and restored.

In addition, one properly includes in the overall appraisal both words and deeds, especially those of the Bishop of Rome himself. The latter has offered all manner of indispensable exposition and commentary on the life and mission of the Church, often quite distinct from the specific prescriptions of canon law. In fact, these expositions may be more reasonable than the legal "ordinances of reason" themselves. The same holds true, to a lesser degree, of curial pronouncements. The encyclical letters of Paul VI and John Paul II are the principal and invaluable examples, but the expository parts of disciplinary decrees are worthwhile instances as well.

Among the encyclicals, *Ut unum sint* of 1995 has already been mentioned. On the one hand, it does not alter the received discipline in matters ecumenical, but—and this would be true on a somewhat lower level of the revised ecumenical directory—the doctrinal or theoretical treatment is the best support to the present discipline. On the other hand, as noted already, this particular encyclical opens the way to all kinds of disciplinary development and institutional change. The warm invitation to reconsider through Christian dialogue the very forms of exercising the Petrine ministry—if pursued in the direction of change—can have immense effects.

Insights in other papal documents, often without any direct canonical effects at all, may offer striking points not to be overlooked even in a canonical overview. An example is the apostolic letter *Orientale lumen* (also of 1995), which has remarkable affirmations, for example, about Eastern monasticism as a model of baptismal life. In relation to nuns within the Eastern community there is the following striking passage:

> I would also like to mention the splendid witness of nuns in the Christian East. This witness has offered an example of giving full value in the Church to what is specifically feminine, even breaking through the mentality of the time. During recent persecutions, when many male monasteries were forcibly closed, female monasticism kept the torch of the monastic life burning. The nun's charism, with its own specific characteristics, is a visible sign of that motherhood of God to which the Sacred Scripture often refers.

The point is simple: the discipline of canon law may not always demonstrate the positive direction of the Spirit evinced by the Roman Primate. And the canonical developments may sometimes reflect the continued impact of the "prophets of doom" chided by John XXIII and even a serious weakness of confidence in the Spirit-filled community of believers.

Again, genuine progress may be seen sometimes in non-canonical curial developments. Here a noteworthy example is the 1993 document of the Pontifical Biblical Commission entitled "The Interpretation of the Bible in the Church." Praised by John Paul II for its spirit of openness, balance, moderation, and understanding of the word of God as universal, it describes positively the diverse methods and approaches in biblical criticism. Then it analyzes the Catholic interpretation of the Bible within the church community.

The pontifical commission's openness is demonstrated by its favorable analysis of actualization and inculturation in interpretation: first, present-day actualization of biblical interpretation that is done in the light of the "contemporary situation of the people of God" and, second, present-day inculturation according to diversity of place.

Neither concept would have been welcome in the past; they signify true progress. This statement has major implications, not yet realized, for the liturgical hearing of God's word.

Another positive example can be found in a document from the Congregation for the Eastern Churches in 1996, "Instruction for Applying the Liturgical Prescriptions of the Code of Canons of the Eastern Churches." This has a somewhat more canonical tone—and of course pertains directly only to the East—but it is fully in harmony with the concerns of Vatican II, beginning with the constitution on the liturgy, *Sacrosanctum Concilium* (1963): the constitution's sound principles but not its Roman rite usages are maintained. A major feature is the repeated call to the Eastern Catholic churches to observe Eastern traditions faithfully and to correct latinization—including theological latinization. One paragraph makes the point: "In the Eastern tradition, the priest, in addition to assisting, must bless the marriage. To bless means to act as the true minister of the sacrament."

When all this has been said, the canonical developments explained above must still be judged—and some judged harshly. The changes in regard to the profession of faith, the regulations of the ministries of the non-ordained, and the restrictions on the teaching authority of the conferences of bishops do reflect retrogression when compared with the expectations of Vatican II. The splendid reflections of John Paul II about Catholic colleges and universities may be seriously compromised by a style of fresh and authoritarian control of academic institutions.

The Second Vatican Council was, to say the least, open-ended. It was a kind of plateau, in some sense only a beginning. It invited advance and surely not retreat.

Any number of recommendations may be made to curb or reverse change that has moved in the wrong direction. One is the strengthening of the collegiality of the episcopate in practice as well as theory, which many see as now denigrated, especially at the national or regional level. A second is to respect genuine subsidiarity, again in fact as well as principle; such respect recognizes the importance of local churches and, in the same spirit of collegiality and conciliarity, the significance of groups or groupings of churches gathered in the conferences of their bishops. Still another is a fresher development of the concept of communion of the equal baptized members of Christ and of their churches. In quasi-political terms, the retrogressive aberrations of the day call for devolution, whether in an expanded local role in the selection of shepherds of the particular churches or in the fuller participation of all the baptized in the threefold offices of prophet, priest, and shepherd.

In terms of institutional development, respect for authentic conciliarity or synodality may suggest widening the responsibility of the conferences of bishops while making certain that the diocesan shepherd guides his community collegially. It may increase the responsibility of the universal synod of bishops as truly taking the part of the total college of bishops effectively. Some of the "general principles" of codal revision now need to be revisited and embraced more fully, whether in the enhancement of the rights of Christians without needless reservations or in the further, radical reduction of penalties and of legalism itself—rather than the opposite.

To some degree these propositions appear to paint a negative or even pessimistic picture. The fact is that the radical and open developments of the Second Vatican Council—perhaps beginning with John XXIII's celebrated initial words on October 11, 1962—must still contribute to the progression of a church community always in need of reformation. A profound demand is trust in divine Providence and the working of the Spirit of God.

An Overview of the Code of Canons of the Eastern Churches

John D. Faris

A Corpus Iuris Canonici

In promulgating a new common law for all the Eastern Catholic churches, Pope John Paul II drew an anatomical metaphor: "The Church itself, gathered in the one Spirit breathes as though with two lungs—of the East and of the West—and it burns with the love of Christ in one heart having two ventricles."[1] Likewise, during the presentation of that code to the twenty-eighth general congregation of the synod of bishops, the pope accentuated the parity and complementarity of the two codes by stating that the 1983 Latin code and the 1990 Eastern code, along with the 1988 apostolic constitution *Pastor bonus,* constitute a *corpus iuris canonici.* While the elements of the *corpus* are distinct, they are not unrelated. For that reason, Pope John Paul II called for comparative studies of the two codes.[2]

An understanding of both codes is indispensable for Latin and Eastern canonists. It is not possible to retain an inaccurate conception of the Catholic Church as a monolithic, Latin entity, governed by a single body of legislation. To do so is to ignore a significant number of Christian faithful who take pride in their bonds of full communion with the See of Rome.

On a practical level, both codes contain provisions that affect the lives of all Catholics. For example, marriages between Latin and Eastern Catholics are not uncommon. Since each party must observe the requirements of his or her own law, those involved in marriage preparation (or, unfortunately, in annulment processes) must have knowledge of both codes.

In light of Latin canon 17, the parallel passages of the Eastern code can contribute to the interpretation of ambiguous passages in the Latin code.[3] Further, the Eastern code can serve as a supplementary source of law for the Latin church; the arbitration process formulated in the Eastern code (*CCEO* 1168–1174) is an example.[4]

For these reasons, an overview of the Code of Canons of the Eastern Churches is appropriately included in this commentary on the Latin code.

Codex Iuris Canonici Orientalis

During Vatican Council I (1869–1870), the need for a common code for the Eastern churches adapted to the needs of the times was discussed, but no concrete action was taken. Only after the benefits of the 1917 Latin code were appreciated was a serious effort made to create a similar code for the Eastern Catholic churches.

During a plenary session of the Sacred Congregation for the Eastern Church in 1927, the project of a codification of Eastern canon law was formally proposed, unanimously accepted, and referred to Pope Pius XI.

After a few years of preliminary work, Pope Pius XI created the Commission of Cardinals for the Preparatory Studies of the Eastern Codification to formulate the first drafts of the future code.[5] To assist the cardinals in the preparatory work, a College of Delegates, comprised of fourteen priests elected by their respective synods, and a College of Consultors, twelve experts in the sources of Eastern canon law, were created to col-

---

[1] John Paul II, apconst *Sacri canones,* October 18, 1990, *AAS* 82 (1990) 1033–1044.

[2] *AAS* 83 (1991) 490.

[3] See J. Abbass, "Canonical Interpretation by Recourse to 'Parallel Passages,'" in *Two Codes in Comparison* (Rome: Pontificio Istituto Orientale, 1997) 133–149.

[4] See J. Abbass, "The Usefulness of Comparative Studies," in *Two Codes in Comparison,* 278–294.

[5] Commissio Cardinalitia pro Studiis Preparatoriis Codificationis Orientalis. See *AAS* 21 (1929) 669.

lect and publish the canonical sources.[6] From 1930 until 1936 this commission prepared eight drafts of the various sections of the future Eastern code.

In 1935 Pius XI established the Pontifical Commission for the Redaction of Eastern Canon Law[7] and charged it with revising the drafts in light of the comments submitted by the various consultative bodies. By 1945 this commission had formulated a draft of the entire code, the *Codex Iuris Canonici Orientalis*.

In March 1948, Pope Pius XII was given a complete draft of the *Codex Iuris Canonici Orientalis* in a nearly final form. Because some churches immediately needed parts of the new legislation, portions of the canons were promulgated:

Crebrae allatae (CA)—131 canons on marriage promulgated on February 22, 1949; acquired force of law on May 2, 1949.[8]

Sollicitudinem nostram (SN)—576 canons on procedure promulgated on January 6, 1950; acquired force of law on January 6, 1951.[9]

Postquam apostolicis (PA)—325 canons on religious and on temporal goods and the definition of terms promulgated on February 9, 1952; acquired force of law on November 21, 1952.[10]

Cleri sanctitati (CS)—558 canons on rites and persons promulgated on June 2, 1957; acquired legal force on March 25, 1958.[11]

In his 1959 convocation of an ecumenical council Pope John XXIIII indicated that one aspect of the program of *aggiornamento* would be an updating of canonical discipline. He referred specifically to the forthcoming promulgation of the *Codex Iuris Canonici Orientalis*, which was to be a forerunner of the great project.[12] However, it soon became evident that the Eastern Catholic common law would also be affected by the forthcoming conciliar reform, so the entire project was suspended.

Out of 2666 proposed canons, a total of 1574 canons were promulgated in the above-mentioned *motu proprios*. The unpromulgated texts remained in the archives of the preconciliar commission.

Codex Canonum Ecclesiarum Orientalium

Drafting Process

On June 10, 1972, Pope Paul VI established the Pontifical Commission for the Revision of the Code of Eastern Canon Law (hereinafter referred to as the Revision Commission). The Revision Commission was mandated to revise the promulgated canons and the unpromulgated texts of the *Codex Iuris Canonici Orientalis* according to the genuine traditions of the Eastern churches and the principles of the Second Vatican Council.[13] For the benefit of canonists, the Revision Commission inaugurated the publication of *Nuntia*, its official journal that was published in thirty-one issues until 1990.[14]

The first plenary meeting of the Revision Commission took place March 18–23, 1974,[15] during which a set of guidelines was approved that was to provide direction for the codification project.

---

[6] *L'Osservatore Romano*, April 2, 1930. These sources have been published in the *Fonti della Codificazione Orientale*, Series I (13 vols.), Series II (32 vols.), and Series III (14 vols.). See *Nu* 3 (1976) 96–100 and 10 (1980) 119–128.

[7] *AAS* 27 (1935) 306–308.

[8] *AAS* 41 (1949) 89–119.

[9] *AAS* 42 (1950) 5–120.

[10] *AAS* 44 (1952) 65–152.

[11] *AAS* 49 (1957) 433–603.

[12] *AAS* 51 (1959) 65–69.

[13] *AAS* 66 (1974) 647 and *Nu* 1 (1975) 11.

[14] The publication of *Nuntia* began with a mimeographed first edition in 1973 and with a printed edition in 1975. A useful index is found in *Nu* 31 (1990) 44–70. Subsequent to the dissolution of the Revision Commission, *Communicationes* serves as the organ of the PCILT.

[15] *Nu* 30 (1990) 8–88.

Guidelines for Revision of Eastern Canon Law

The *Guidelines for the Revision of the Code of Oriental Canon Law*, approved at the first plenary meeting of the Revision Commission,[16] can be summarized as follows:

1. A *single code* would serve as a common law for all the Eastern Catholic churches; specific matters would be treated in particular law.

2. The code would be inspired by *genuine Eastern sources* and be thoroughly imbued with the Eastern canonical tradition; at the same time, the code would have to accommodate itself to current circumstances and needs, especially regarding Eastern Catholics residing outside the original territory of their churches.

3. In accord with conciliar principles, the *promotion of the unity of churches* would be of primary concern in elaborating the code. The code would need to recognize that the Orthodox churches were called "sister churches" by the council and enjoy the right to govern themselves.

4. The Eastern code would possess a *juridical character* and not be a mere handbook of dogmatic, pastoral, and moral theology.

5. The code would exhibit a *pastoral character* with a concern not only for justice, but also for equity and charity. Bishops and pastors would be given reasonable discretion in order to adapt the canonical provisions to their particular needs.

6. The principle of *subsidiarity* (namely, that what a lower hierarchical institution can accomplish for itself should not be reserved to

a superior authority) was to find expression in the code.

7. The notion of *rite* and the nature and juridical status of *particular churches* would be examined and juridically articulated in the code.

8. Because of the fundamental equality of all the baptized, the laity would be called to cooperate more directly in the Church's apostolate in liturgy, administration, tribunals, and preaching. Sufficient freedom of expression of opinion and initiative of action would be guaranteed.

9. All Catholics were to observe the *same procedural norms*. Each Eastern Catholic church would be permitted to establish its own tribunals to deal with cases in all three instances of a canonical trial up to the final sentence.

10. All automatic (*latae sententiae*) penalties would be eliminated in the Eastern code. Greater emphasis was to be given to the *canonical admonition* prior to the imposition of a penalty. Conforming to Eastern tradition, a canonical penalty would not be considered only as the deprivation of a good; the imposition of positive acts (penance) would also be considered.

Elaboration and Revision of Drafts

The elaboration of the first drafts began in March 1974 with the approval of the *Guidelines* and ended with a May 1980 meeting of the central committee. After the eight drafts were prepared and approved by the superior authority, they were distributed to various consultative bodies for comments. Each draft contained, besides the canons themselves, *praenotanda* (preliminary notes) indicating noteworthy issues and innovations in the text.

---

[16] The *Guidelines* are published in English in *Nu* 3 (1976) 18–24 and *CLD* 8, 29–39.

After each section had been revised in light of the comments, a comprehensive draft of the entire code was prepared. This draft was transmitted in 1986 to the members of the Revision Commission; their responses were then compiled and distributed to the members.[17]

The second plenary meeting of the Revision Commission, held on November 3–14, 1988, marked the final step of the preparation of a text for presentation to the pope.[18] A draft was presented to him on January 28, 1989, after which additional modifications were made.[19]

Promulgation

The *Codex Canonum Ecclesiarum Orientalium* was promulgated by Pope John Paul II with the apostolic constitution *Sacri canones*[20] on October 18, 1990,[21] and acquired the force of law on October 1, 1991. While practical considerations made it impossible for a "co-promulgation" of the code by the Roman Pontiff and the heads of the Eastern Catholic churches,[22] the manner of its promulgation posed certain ecumenical difficulties since Eastern tradition requires that such a body of law be promulgated by a synod.

Proposals were made that the Eastern code be promulgated with the provision that it would serve until full unity is achieved with the Eastern non-Catholic churches.[23] However, the proposal was not accepted since by its very nature the code requires a certain permanence and stability.[24]

Contents and Structure

The Eastern code contains 1546 canons while the Latin code is made up of 1752 canons. The relative brevity of the Eastern code results from several factors. First, and most important, while the Latin code is both the common and particular law of the Latin church, the Eastern code is only the common law for the twenty-one Eastern Catholic churches; many matters are relegated to the particular law of the various churches *sui iuris*. Second, there are certain institutions (e.g., the synod of bishops, Roman Curia, Roman Rota, Apostolic Signatura, cardinals, and papal legates) which, though serving the universal Church, are strictly speaking Latin institutions; hence, the Latin canons 342–367 are briefly referred to in the Eastern code (*CCEO* 46, 48 and 1056). Finally, the drafters of the Eastern code could take advantage of the critiques made of the Latin code and provide a text with greater conciseness.[25]

The Eastern code is occasionally more expansive than the Latin code. The canonical institutions of tradition, rite, and church *sui iuris* are treated only indirectly in Latin canons 111–112, while the Eastern code treats in a detailed manner these institutes, enrollment in a church *sui iuris*, and the preservation of rites (*CCEO* 27–41). The ecclesial groupings of patriarchal, major archiepiscopal, metropolitan, and other churches are extensively treated in the Eastern code (*CCEO* 55–176), while Latin canon 438 describes the patriarchal office as a prerogative of honor only exceptionally endowed with the power of governance.

Although it might be didactically and academically convenient for the Latin and Eastern codes to be similarly organized, it was felt that theological, canonical, and ecumenical difficulties could arise if the Eastern code followed the Latin code too closely.[26] Reminiscent of the ancient Eastern canonical collections, the Eastern code is divided into thirty *titles* (each comprising anywhere from

---

[17] *Nu* 24–25 (1987) 1–268 and 28 (1989) 3–138.
[18] For a report on the meeting, see *Nu* 29 (1989) 3–77.
[19] *Nu* 31 (1990) 37–45.
[20] *AAS* 82 (1990) 1033–1044.
[21] *AAS* 82 (1990) 1061–1353.
[22] *Nu* 28 (1989) 7.
[23] See *OE* 30.
[24] *Sacri Canones, AAS* 82 (1990) 1035–1036. See also *Nu* 28 (1989) 9 and 12; *Nu* 29 (1989) 34–36.

[25] G. Nedungatt, *The Spirit of the Eastern Code* (Rome: Centre for Indian and Inter-religious Studies, 1993) 51.
[26] See *Nu* 9 (1979) 91–92; 11 (1980) 79, 84; 26 (1988) 17–99. See also E. Eid, "The Nature and Structure of the Oriental Code," in *The Code of Canons of the Oriental Churches,* ed. C. Gallagher (Rome: Saint Thomas Christian Fellowship, 1991) 32.

1 to 229 canons), with further subdivisions into chapters, articles, numbers, letters, and the canons themselves.

An Overview of the Eastern Code

The following overview will address only those points of the Eastern code that may interest Latin canonists. Hence, those matters common to both codes are omitted, no matter how canonically important for church discipline, e.g., supreme church authority.

Many canons of the Eastern and Latin codes are substantially the same or even verbatim identical. The canons unique to the Eastern code usually result from the different Eastern traditions or the relative autonomy of Eastern Catholic hierarchical structures.

Title

The preconciliar codification project employed the working title of *Codex Iuris Canonici Orientalis* (Code of Eastern Canon Law), which was retained during the postconciliar revision project: it had been employed in papal documents and was even incorporated in the title of the commission entrusted with the revision.[27] Nevertheless, the aforementioned title posed certain difficulties since it appeared to be only a variation of the title for the Latin code, with the implication that the Eastern code was supplementary to the former. Accordingly, an alternate title was sought.

The title, *Codex Canonum Ecclesiarum Orientalium*, fits because the Latin term *codex* is broadly used to denote a comprehensive systematic arrangement of a body of legislation. The term *canon* accentuates the code's spiritual character and theological foundation and conforms to the long-standing Eastern usage of the term "sacred

canons." The term *Ecclesiarum Orientalium* (Eastern churches) is appropriate since it generically indicates the communities for whom the law is intended.

Preliminary Canons

The six preliminary canons are similar to the preliminary canons of the Latin code in delineating the legal force of the Eastern code. The first canon states that the Eastern code concerns only the twenty-one Eastern *Catholic* churches, an explicit exclusion of the Orthodox churches from the obligations of the code. The canon also states, "...unless, with regard to relations with the Latin church, it is expressly laid down otherwise." The Latin church is included not only in those instances wherein it is *explicitly* mentioned by name (i.e., cc. 37, 41, 207, 322, 432, 696, 860, 916, and 1465); express mention can also be implicit (e.g., cc. 343 and 517, §2). Perhaps the most significant area touching upon Latin-Eastern relations is title II, which addresses enrollment in a church *sui iuris* and the preservation of rites (*CCEO* 29–41).

Based on the ancient Eastern laws (*CCEO* 2), the Eastern code does not generally include liturgical law (*CCEO* 3); nor does it affect agreements entered into or approved[28] by the Holy See (*CCEO* 4) or acquired rights or privileges conceded by the Apostolic See (*CCEO* 5). All common and particular law contrary to the Eastern code or treating matters it re-orders is abrogated; likewise, all customs contrary to the Eastern code but that are neither immemorial nor centenary are revoked (*CCEO* 6).

Rights and Obligations of the Christian Faithful

In treating fundamental rights and obligations, title I (*CCEO* 7–26) is quite similar to the Latin code. However, the Eastern code additionally obliges the Christian faithful to adhere to the word

---

[27] An analysis of the significance of the name of the code and the various possibilities and a proposal for a name are found in G. Nedungatt, "The Title of the New Canonical Legislation," in *Stud Can* 19 (1985) 61–80. See also *Nu* 28 (1989) 13 and 29 (1989) 30–34.

[28] The patriarch may enter into agreements with civil authorities after receiving the assent of the Apostolic See (*CCEO* 98).

of God and the authentic magisterium of the Church, profess it openly, acquire a better understanding of it, put it into practice, and make it fruitful in works of charity (*CCEO* 10).

Churches Sui Iuris *and Rites*

Title II on churches *sui iuris* and rites (*CCEO* 27–41) treats the juridical status of the Eastern and Latin churches and the canonical notions of *tradition* and *rite*. Within the Catholic communion, there are twenty-two ecclesial groupings whose hierarchy enjoys a self-governing power that has either been expressly conceded or recognized by the supreme church authority; these ecclesial groupings are designated as churches *sui iuris* (literally, "of their own right") (*CCEO* 27). Each of the twenty-one Eastern Catholic churches *sui iuris* observes a rite, i.e., a corpus of liturgy, theology, spirituality, and discipline, derived from one of the five Eastern traditions: Alexandrian, Antiochene, Armenian, Chaldean, and Constantinopolitan (*CCEO* 28).

Certain norms treat enrollment in a church *sui iuris*, transfer from one church *sui iuris* to another, or the retention of one's rite upon entrance into the Catholic Church (*CCEO* 29–38), while others articulate the obligation of each of the Christian faithful to foster and preserve the various rites in the Church (*CCEO* 39–41).

Membership in the Catholic Church is never "at large"; instead, a person is enrolled in a specific church *sui iuris*, determined according to law. Whether it is a case of reception of baptism or entrance into full communion, membership is determined by the law as a consequence of the act whether or not the baptism or entrance actually occurs in the church *sui iuris* as stipulated by the law (see c. 111, §2).

Patriarchal Churches

Six of the Eastern Catholic churches are of patriarchal status: Alexandrian, Armenian, Chaldean, Maronite, Melkite, and Syrian. The patriarchal form of ecclesiastical government, recognized by the ancient ecumenical councils, is the most comprehensive expression of the self-governing authority of the Eastern Catholic churches and is structured in title IV, "The Patriarchal Churches" (*CCEO* 51–150). Two conciliar directives shaped the formulation of these canons: (1) the powers of the Eastern Catholic patriarchs were to be restored to the situation which was operative at the time of the union of East and West; and (2) the patriarchs, *along with their synods,* enjoy superior authority in their respective churches.[29] Without determining which authority is superior, the Eastern code casuistically delineates the competence of each of these authorities. In general, the patriarch enjoys executive authority; the patriarchal synod is the highest instance of legislative, judicial, and electoral power in the patriarchal church (*CCEO* 110).

The patriarch is elected by the synod of bishops (*CCEO* 63) and, if he is already an ordained bishop, is enthroned upon acceptance of the election (*CCEO* 75) whereby he acquires his office (*CCEO* 77, §1). However, he cannot validly convoke a synod or ordain a bishop without first receiving a testimonial of ecclesiastical communion from the Roman Pontiff (*CCEO* 77, §2).

The Eastern code envisions, in addition to the patriarchal synod, the institution of a *permanent synod of bishops* (*CCEO* 115–121), i.e., a group comprised of the patriarch and four bishops which functions as an executive committee of the patriarchal synod. It also envisions a *patriarchal convocation* (*CCEO* 140–145), a consultative body comprising all bishops, representatives of clergy, male and female religious, universities, and the laity that is convoked every five years.

Eastern Catholics outside Original Territory

Title IV, chapter 7 (*CCEO* 146–150) regulates the jurisdiction of the patriarch and synods outside the historical territory of the patriarchal churches. For various political, social, and economic reasons, the majorities of several Eastern

[29] *OE* 9.

Catholic churches reside in western countries. At the impetus of Vatican Council II, hierarchies were established to care for those faithful.[30] The population imbalance and the existence of hierarchs outside the territorial boundaries made the issue of the relationship of these communities to the mother church increasingly acute during the codification process.[31]

The relationship between the hierarchs outside the historical territory and the patriarch and synod can be summarized as follows:

The patriarch can validly exercise his power only within the territorial boundaries of the patriarchal church (*CCEO* 78, §2). In the designation of hierarchs outside the patriarchal territory, the patriarchal synod proposes three candidates to the Roman Pontiff, who then makes the appointment (*CCEO* 149). Such hierarchs have the same voting power within the synod of bishops in elections, but their voting rights can be restricted by particular law in other matters (*CCEO* 150, §1).

Legislation enacted by the patriarchal synod of bishops is binding only within the territorial boundaries of the patriarchal church unless: (1) it is liturgical law, in which case it binds all members of the patriarchal church; or (2) it is endowed with the force of law by the eparchial bishop whereby it becomes eparchial law; or (3) it is approved by the Apostolic See in which case it has the force of law everywhere in the world (*CCEO* 150, §§2–3).

Major Archiepiscopal Churches

The governance of the major archiepiscopal churches (at present, the Ukrainian church and the Malabar church) is treated briefly in title V (*CCEO* 151–154). The brevity of this title results from the fact that the major archbishop is canonically equivalent to a patriarch except for the patriarchal title itself (*CCEO* 151) and the requirement that the election of the major archbishop be confirmed by the Roman Pontiff (*CCEO* 153).

[30] *OE* 4, 7 and *AAS* 62 (1970) 179.
[31] See *Nu* 29 (1989) 227.

Metropolitan and Other Churches

A third kind of church *sui iuris,* the metropolitan church, is treated in title VI, chapter 1 (*CCEO* 155–173). The Ethiopian, Malankar, Romanian, and Ruthenian churches have metropolitan structures.

The governance of these churches significantly differs from that of the patriarchal and major archiepiscopal churches. While the patriarchs and major archbishops exercise supra-metropolitan authority (see *CCEO* 56), the metropolitan exercises only supra-episcopal authority (see *CCEO* 157, §1). The metropolitan must request the pallium, a sign of metropolitan authority, from the Roman Pontiff (*CCEO* 156, §1); prior to its imposition, the metropolitan can neither convoke the bishops of his church to the council of hierarchs nor ordain a bishop (*CCEO* 156, §2).

A *council of hierarchs,* comprising all the bishops of the metropolitan church, cooperates with the metropolitan in the governance of the church (*CCEO* 164). The power of this council is more restricted than that of the patriarchal or major-archiepiscopal synod: the council cannot elect the metropolitan or a bishop, but rather proposes three names to the Roman Pontiff who makes the appointment (*CCEO* 168). The legislative authority of the council is also restricted; its laws cannot be promulgated until they have been received by the Apostolic See (*CCEO* 167, §2).

Because of the small number (or, in some cases, the total lack) of hierarchical structures, certain churches *sui iuris* are defined negatively (being neither patriarchal, major archiepiscopal, nor metropolitan) and are placed under the category of "Other Churches" and treated in chapter 2 of title VI (*CCEO* 174–176). The Albanian, Belorussian, Bulgarian, Greek, Hungarian, Italo-Albanian, Križevci, Russian, and Slovak churches fall under this category.

The hierarch governing these churches acts with authority delegated to him by the Apostolic See (*CCEO* 175). Further, when the common law remits a matter to the superior authority of a church *sui iuris,* the hierarch governing this church is the competent authority, but acts only with the consent of the Apostolic See (*CCEO* 176).

Eparchies, Exarchies, and Bishops

Title VII, "Eparchies and Bishops" (*CCEO* 177–310), and title VIII, "Exarchies and Exarchs" (*CCEO* 311–321), treat the fundamental ecclesial groupings of the Church and the episcopacy.

In treating these institutions, the Eastern code employs a terminology appropriate to Eastern usage while the meaning of the terms is substantially identical to that of the Latin code. For example, *eparchial bishop* is the equivalent of a *diocesan bishop* (*CCEO* 177 and c. 369); *hierarch* is the counterpart of *ordinary* (*CCEO* 984 and c. 134). Furthermore, *protosyncellus* is equivalent to the *vicar general* (*CCEO* 245 and c. 475); *syncellus* (*CCEO* 246) is the counterpart of *episcopal vicar* (c. 476). A *protopresbyter* (*CCEO* 276) is comparable to a *vicar forane* (c. 553).

Since they respond to similar pastoral needs and draw upon some of the same canonical precedents, especially the conciliar documents, the canons of this title of the Eastern code are quite similar to their Latin code counterparts.

An interesting addition to the Eastern code definition of eparchial bishops is the reference to the bishops as *vicars and legates of Christ* (*CCEO* 178). Bishops are categorized under two headings: *eparchial bishops* (a bishop to whom an eparchy has been assigned [*CCEO* 178]) and *titular bishops* (a bishop who is without an eparchy [*CCEO* 179], i.e., an auxiliary bishop, a coadjutor bishop, a bishop of the patriarchal curia [cf. *CCEO* 87], and a retired or resigned bishop [*CCEO* 210]).

An *exarchy* is comparable to an *eparchy*, but is not, for some reason, established as such (*CCEO* 311); it is entrusted to the pastoral care of an *exarch*, who functions either in his own name or as the delegate of another (*CCEO* 312). It is generally governed in a manner comparable to that of an eparchy (*CCEO* 313).

Assemblies of Hierarchs

The mobility of people has resulted in a plurality of hierarchies of different churches *sui iuris* established in the same locale. Hierarchs of different churches *sui iuris* are encouraged to meet to discuss common issues (*CCEO* 84; 202). Title IX, "Assemblies of Hierarchs of Several Churches *Sui Iuris*," structures such discussions (*CCEO* 322).[32]

Clerics

Title X, on "Clerics" (*CCEO* 323–398) treats those members of the Christian faithful designated as sacred ministers through ordination. Clerics are either in *major orders* (bishop, priest, and deacon) or in *minor orders* (distinguished by their function, ecclesial service, and liturgical role). Canonical provisions for minor clerics are generally relegated to particular law (*CCEO* 323–327).

The first chapter of the title deals with the promotion of vocations and the formation of clerics (*CCEO* 328–330), seminaries (*CCEO* 331–341), the admission of candidates (*CCEO* 342–343), and formation in the minor seminary (*CCEO* 344 and 346) and the major seminary (*CCEO* 345–356).

Chapter 2 treats the enrollment (*adscriptio*) of a cleric (*CCEO* 357–366) by delineating the various institutes competent to ascribe him (*CCEO* 357) with the eparchy as somewhat normative (*CCEO* 358). While ascription is conceived as a permanent arrangement (*CCEO* 362 and 364), there are circumstances that could necessitate a transfer (*CCEO* 361) and the law delineates the manner in which the transfer is to be executed (*CCEO* 359–360; 365–366).

Chapter 3 (*CCEO* 367–393) delineates clerical rights and obligations while chapter 4 (*CCEO* 394–398) indicates the causes and canonical consequences of the loss of the clerical state.

---

[32] There are seven assemblies under the title of "assembly," "reunion," or "conference." See *Annuario Pontificio 1997* (Vatican City: Libreria Editrice Vaticana, 1997) 1103.

Lay Persons

Title XI on "Lay Persons" (*CCEO* 399–409) opens by defining lay persons negatively, stating that those within this category are Christian faithful who are neither clerics nor religious and whose proper and special state is secular (*CCEO* 399).

Lay persons have the right to participate actively in the liturgical celebrations of any church *sui iuris* according to the norms of the liturgical books (*CCEO* 403, §1). Lay persons are urged to study their own rites in order to foster goodwill and cooperation among the various churches *sui iuris* (*CCEO* 405; 40, §3).

Consecrated Life

Title XII, "Monks and Other Religious as Well as Members of Other Institutes of Consecrated Life," (*CCEO* 410–572) is dedicated to the third "order" or "state" of Christian life and provides in a historical and systematic manner the six institutional and three individual forms of consecrated life as well as societies of apostolic life that are similar but not equivalent to canonical forms of consecrated life.[33]

Chapter 1 on "Monks and Other Religious" (*CCEO* 410–553) deals with monasteries, orders, and congregations, all of which fall under the general classification of *religious institute.*

After general canons operative for religious institutes (*CCEO* 410–432), article 2 is dedicated to *monastic life* (*CCEO* 433–503). Since monastic life is the paradigm for religious life, the third article includes numerous references to article 2 in its treatment of *orders* and *congregations* (*CCEO* 504–553). Unlike the Latin code which recognizes eremetical life as separate from an institute of consecrated life (c. 603), the Eastern code defines *hermits* as members of monasteries *sui iuris*

who have dedicated themselves to contemplation and have separated themselves from the world (*CCEO* 481).

Chapter 2, "Societies of Common Life according to the Manner of Religious" (*CCEO* 553–562) treats a form of consecrated life that does not fall under the category of a religious institute. Members of societies of common life imitate the religious state, but do not make religious vows (*CCEO* 554). The Latin code does not consider these societies within the category of consecrated life (see c. 731, §2).

Chapter 3 (*CCEO* 563–569) provides the essential framework for the fifth institutional form of consecrated life known as the *secular institute,* whose members neither make vows nor lead a common life in the manner of religious; instead, they live in communion with each other as they carry out an apostolic activity in the world (*CCEO* 563).

Chapter 4 (*CCEO* 570–572) treats three forms of individual consecrated life: (1) ascetics who, not belonging to an institute of consecrated life, imitate the eremetical life (see c. 603); (2) consecrated virgins, women who live in the world and dedicate themselves to virginity (see c. 604) are included in the Eastern code as a category of individual consecrated life; and (3) consecrated widows, an ancient institute (*CCEO* 570).

The sixth form of institutional consecrated life is the *society of apostolic life* whose members are without religious vows, but who pursue the particular apostolic life of the society and live in common (*CCEO* 572). Although such institutions do not, strictly speaking, fall in the category of an institute of consecrated life (see c. 731, §1), their inclusion in this title emphasizes their similarities to institutes of consecrated life.

Evangelization

In conformity with the provisions of *Orientalium Ecclesiarum* 3, the Eastern Catholic churches are expressly mandated to participate in the evangelization of the non-baptized.

---

[33] See J. Abbass, "Forms of Consecrated Life Recognized in the Eastern and Latin Codes," in *Two Codes in Comparison*, 23–56.

Emphasizing that the teaching mission to non-believers significantly differs from the ongoing nurturing of the faith of believers, the canons are found in a distinct title (title XIV, "The Evangelization of Peoples" [*CCEO* 584–594]).

Evangelization, to be undertaken under the guidance of the Roman Pontiff, is primarily addressed at the level of the churches *sui iuris* whose competent authorities are to establish a commission to coordinate missionary activity; each eparchy is to have a priest to promote the missions (*CCEO* 585).

Ecclesiastical Magisterium

The preliminary canons of the title "Ecclesiastical Magisterium" (*CCEO* 595–666) include various facets of the magisterial function not enunciated in the Latin code. Responding to the diversity of circumstances of the Eastern churches, the Eastern code asserts that the manner in which the Church teaches must be appropriate to the time and place (*CCEO* 601) and that doctrinal diversity should emphasize the catholicity of the Church (*CCEO* 604). This mission is accomplished through the sciences (*CCEO* 602) and literature and the arts (*CCEO* 603).

Theologians are included as a category of persons entrusted with magisterial obligations and rights (*CCEO* 606). Catechetical commissions at the level of the church *sui iuris* (*CCEO* 622) and the eparchy (*CCEO* 623) are also foreseen.

The various degrees of autonomy of the Eastern Catholic churches are recognized in the approval of liturgical texts (*CCEO* 657). Without prejudice to the protection of civil law, which may or may not be operative in the regions of the Eastern Catholic churches, canonical protection is offered to the intellectual property of authors (*CCEO* 666). Canon 666 also distinguishes between ecclesiastical *permission* and *approval*.

Sacraments

The most extensive title of the Eastern code, title XVI, "Divine Worship and Especially the

Sacraments" (*CCEO* 667–895) comprises preliminary canons on divine worship (*CCEO* 667–674), a separate chapter on each sacrament (chapters 1–7), and a final chapter on sacramentals, sacred times and places, veneration of the saints, vows, and oaths.[34]

The section of preliminary canons opens by describing the sacraments theologically (*CCEO* 667) and regulates the participation of Catholics in non-Catholic liturgical worship (*CCEO* 670, §1), the sharing of Catholic facilities with non-Catholic Christians (*CCEO* 670, §1) and *communicatio in sacris* (*CCEO* 671).

A minister is to celebrate all the sacraments according to the liturgical prescriptions of his own church *sui iuris*, but can also receive permission from the Apostolic See (an indult of bi-ritualism) to celebrate the sacraments according to another rite (*CCEO* 674, §2).

Baptism

The administration of baptism is ordinarily reserved to the pastor (*CCEO* 290, §2), but a priest of the church *sui iuris* in which the person is to be enrolled has priority over a pastor and is not to be denied permission to baptize such a person (*CCEO* 678, §1).

An Eastern non-Catholic can be admitted as a *sponsor* for a baptism if the other sponsor is a Catholic (*CCEO* 685, §3). Likewise, a Western non-Catholic (i.e., a Protestant) can be admitted as a *witness* (c. 874, §2). If the parents are members of different churches *sui iuris,* the ecclesial membership of the child should be ascertained and recorded in the baptismal register (*CCEO* 37 and 689, §1).

Chrismation

In conformity with the ancient discipline of the Church, the presbyter is the ordinary minister of

---

[34] See Congregation for the Eastern Churches, *Instruction for Applying the Liturgical Prescriptions of the Code of Canons of the Eastern Churches* (Vatican City: Libreria Editrice Vaticana, 1996).

chrismation (*CCEO* 694). Eastern presbyters (Catholic and Orthodox) administer chrismation validly to all the Christian faithful, including members of the Latin church (*CCEO* 696, §1). Likewise, the members of Eastern churches validly receive confirmation from Latin presbyters who enjoy the faculty to administer this sacrament (*CCEO* 696, §2). In order for the chrismation to be licit, the Christian faithful should approach their proper minister.

Ordinarily, chrismation is administered in conjunction with baptism; if it must be delayed because of necessity, it is to be administered as soon as possible (*CCEO* 694).

Eucharist

The Eastern code recognizes the tradition of some churches to sanctify Sundays and feast days either through participation in the celebration of the Divine Liturgy or the divine praises as determined by particular law or custom of the churches *sui iuris* (*CCEO* 881, §1).

The Eastern Catholic churches are encouraged to restore the practice of administering the Eucharist in conjunction with baptism and chrismation, i.e., infant communion (*CCEO* 697 and 710).

The concelebration of priests of different Catholic churches is permitted for any suitable reason, especially for manifesting the unity of the churches. Concelebration among bishops and presbyters of different churches *sui iuris* requires the permission of the bishop in whose rite the liturgy is celebrated. In such a concelebration, each presbyter is to wear the vestments and insignia of his rite, but the same eucharistic rite as that of the principal celebrant is to be used (*CCEO* 701). Although Catholics may participate in the liturgical worship of other Christians, Catholic priests are prohibited from concelebrating the Divine Liturgy with non-Catholic priests or ministers (*CCEO* 702).

Penance

Presbyters who have received the faculty of hearing confessions from their proper hierarch

(bishop, major religious superior) can validly and lawfully exercise it everywhere in the world and in the jurisdictions of all Catholic churches *sui iuris* unless forbidden to do so by the local hierarch or ordinary (*CCEO* 722).

Anointing of the Sick

Among the canons treating anointing of the sick (*CCEO* 737–742), the Eastern code encourages the preservation of the custom of anointing of the sick by several priests (*CCEO* 737, §2).

Sacred Ordination

Chapter 6 (*CCEO* 743–775) deals with the administration of sacred orders. Ordination confers the status of cleric upon certain individuals (*CCEO* 323, §2); they are distinguished by degrees as bishops, presbyters, and deacons (*CCEO* 325). While the Latin church abolished minor orders,[35] the institution may be retained in an Eastern church, either for apostolic work or for liturgical functions that are generally regulated by the particular law of the respective church *sui iuris* (*CCEO* 327).

Without the permission of the Apostolic See, an eparchial bishop cannot ordain a candidate subject to him who is enrolled in another church *sui iuris* (*CCEO* 748, §2). Such a permission is also to precede the concession of a dimissorial letter (*CCEO* 752).

Marriage

The sacrament of marriage is treated in chapter 7 (*CCEO* 776–866).

The Latin code exempts Latin Catholics who have abandoned the Catholic Church through a formal act (c. 1117) from the obligation of the canonical marriage form, the impediment of disparity of cult (c. 1086, §1), and the prohibition against mixed marriages (c. 1124). However, the

---

[35] Paul VI, *mp Ministeria quaedam, AAS* 64 (1972) 534–540.

Eastern code makes no exemption for Eastern Catholics. Therefore, anyone baptized in or received into an Eastern Catholic church must observe the canonical form of marriage (*CCEO* 834), is subject to the impediment of disparity of cult (*CCEO* 803), and must obtain permission to marry a baptized non-Catholic (*CCEO* 813).

Out of respect for the legislation binding non-Catholics, especially Eastern non-Catholics, the Eastern code established an innovation in Catholic canon law by providing a legal framework with which to deal with non-Catholics, both the baptized and the non-baptized. While always taking into account the binding, non-dispensable authority of divine law, the Eastern code states that when a Catholic marries a non-Catholic, the law binding either is to be observed (*CCEO* 780).

Since by virtue of divine law Catholic doctrine does not permit divorce and successive remarriage, the prior marriage of the non-Catholic must be adjudicated by a Catholic tribunal. The law on impediments and on form to be considered in adjudicating these marriage cases is the law of the respective churches or ecclesial communities binding the parties at the time of the marriage (*CCEO* 781).

The Latin code refers to the *matrimonial contract* (see cc. 1055, §2 and 1108, §2). While canonical doctrine requires an appraisal of the marriage in the context of contractual law, it is clear that it is a unique kind of contract, i.e., one that communicates the grace of Christ. To emphasize this unique quality of the marriage, the Eastern code employs the term *matrimonial covenant* (*CCEO* 776, §1). Avoiding the use of the phrase *to contract marriage*, the Eastern code refers to the *celebration of marriage* (see *CCEO* 828, §1).

In the Latin church, the ordinary required canonical form is the exchange of consent of the two parties in the presence of a canonically competent local ordinary, priest, or deacon (c. 1108, §1) or, in the absence of a priest or deacon, a lay person (c. 1112) and two witnesses. In the Eastern churches, there is an additional element: the intervention of a priest who blesses the marriage (*CCEO* 828). This sacred rite is required by all Eastern churches because marriage entails a covenant celebrated between three interested parties: the man, the woman, and God. Within the boundaries of his jurisdiction, a local hierarch or pastor can validly bless the marriages of parties whether or not they are his subjects, provided that at least one party is a member of his church *sui iuris;* likewise, within the boundaries of his jurisdiction, a local hierarch or personal pastor can validly bless the marriage of parties when at least one of them is his subject (*CCEO* 829).

While the Latin church affords couples the freedom to choose the parish of either the bride or the groom (c. 1115), the Eastern code reflects the Eastern tradition that the bride follows the groom, and states that the marriage is generally to be celebrated in the parish of the groom unless the particular law of the Eastern church or a just cause excuses (*CCEO* 831, §2). Further, the local hierarch or pastor can licitly bless a marriage in which at least one party is a member of his church *sui iuris* in a place exclusively pertaining to another church *sui iuris,* provided he is within his own territorial boundaries and the hierarch who exercises jurisdiction in that place does not expressly refuse (*CCEO* 831, §1, 3°).

Even for mixed marriages, the required intervention of the priest cannot be dispensed from in the Eastern Catholic churches except for the most grave reasons. Such a dispensation can be granted only by the Apostolic See or the patriarchs (*CCEO* 834). On September 21, 1991, to accommodate the pastoral needs of the faithful, papal legates were delegated the faculty to dispense. Even though Latin diocesan bishops may dispense Latin Catholics from the observance of canonical form (c. 1127, §2), they should be sensitive to the traditions of the Eastern churches when called upon to dispense an Eastern Catholic subject from that observance.

An Eastern Catholic (*CCEO* 834, §2) or a Latin Catholic (c. 1127, §1) can marry an Eastern non-Catholic validly before an Eastern non-Catholic priest. While permission for a mixed marriage and a dispensation from canonical form are required, such requirements are for the sake of lawfulness; their non-observance does not affect the validity of the marriage.

A consequence of the great importance placed by the Eastern churches on the sacramental grace imparted by the celebration of the marriage rite is a difference between the Latin and Eastern codes in recognizing a marriage by proxy. Unlike the Latin code (c. 1105), the Eastern code prohibits marriage by proxy unless the particular law of the pertinent church *sui iuris* determines otherwise (*CCEO* 837).

The impediments to marriage are generally the same in both the Latin and Eastern codes with a few divergencies:

1. The diriment impediment of *abduction* pertains to any abducted person in the Eastern code (*CCEO* 806) whereas it concerns only an abducted woman in the Latin code (c. 1089).

2. The Eastern code alone maintains the impediment of *affinity* in the collateral line, that is, marriage with the brothers or sisters of one's former spouse (*CCEO* 809, §1).

3. The Eastern code alone states that a *null* or *non-existent marriage* (the establishment of common life by those who, being bound to the canonical form, have attempted marriage before a civil official or a non-Catholic minister) can also give rise to the impediment of public propriety (*CCEO* 810, §1, 3°).

4. The impediment of a *spiritual relationship* (between a baptismal sponsor and the person baptized or his or her parents) is maintained in the Eastern code alone (*CCEO* 811, §1).

While the Latin church holds that a marriage based on a future condition is invalid, it admits the possibility that the validity of a marriage could be affected by a present or past condition (c. 1102, §§1–2). A conditional marriage, which does not entail the total giving of one's self, logically requires placing the condition above the marriage. Such a view is not consonant with the Eastern notion of marriage; therefore, a marriage based on any kind of condition cannot validly be celebrated in the Eastern churches (*CCEO* 826).

Baptized Non-Catholics Coming into Full Communion

The Eastern code devotes title XVIII (*CCEO* 896–901) to the reception of baptized persons into the Catholic Church. While the Catholic Church has disavowed all forms of proselytism or pressured conversions (*CCEO* 586),[36] the respect for freedom of conscience requires that persons be allowed to embrace the Catholic faith if they desire to do so. Since an imperfect communion already exists among the baptized, the Eastern code requires only what is absolutely necessary for a baptized non-Catholic to become a Catholic (*CCEO* 896). After receiving suitable doctrinal formation, Eastern non-Catholics are obliged to make only a profession of Catholic faith to be received into the Catholic Church (*CCEO* 897).

The Eastern code determines the competent authority to receive baptized individuals into the Catholic Church (*CCEO* 898), articulates certain caveats regarding the reception of minors (*CCEO* 900), and refers to the required adaptation of these norms when receiving non-Eastern Christians into the Catholic Church (*CCEO* 901).

Ecumenism

While both codes contain many similarities in the area of ecumenism, the extensive reference to ecumenical concerns in *Sacri canones*[37] and the inclusion of a distinct title, XVIII on "Ecumenism"

---

[36] See the statement of the Joint Commission for the Theological Dialogue between the Roman Catholic Church and the Orthodox Church issued subsequent to the Balamand meeting (June 17–24, 1993), "Uniatism, Method of Union of the Past, and the Present Search for Communion." Published in the PCPCU, *Information Service* 83 (1993) 95–99.

[37] See *Code of Canons of the Eastern Churches: Latin-English Edition* (Washington, D.C.: CLSA, 1990) xii–xiii.

(*CCEO* 902–908) indicate that the Eastern code is much more focused in this area. All Christians are obliged to pray and work for unity (*CCEO* 902). Eastern Catholic churches have a special obligation to promote unity through prayer and fidelity to authentic Eastern traditions (*CCEO* 903); each church *sui iuris* is to establish a commission of ecumenical experts and each eparchy, either individually or united with others, is to have a council to promote Christian unity (*CCEO* 904). Directors of Catholic schools, hospitals, and other similar institutions are to be attentive to the spiritual needs of other Christians (*CCEO* 907). In preaching, catechesis, and various forms of social media, special attention is to be given to disseminating accurate information about the tradition of the Catholic and non-Catholic churches (*CCEO* 906). False irenicism, indifferentism, and excessive zeal are not to be confused with the promotion of Christian unity (*CCEO* 905). Finally, besides the approved arrangements for *communicatio in sacris* (see *CCEO* 671), Eastern Catholic churches should cooperate with the non-Catholic churches in works of charity, social justice, and the promotion of peace (*CCEO* 908).

Ecumenical issues are also addressed elsewhere in the Eastern code; these issues include Catholic participation in non-Catholic liturgical worship and the sharing of Catholic buildings, cemeteries, or churches with non-Catholics (*CCEO* 670). Catholic ministers may baptize children of other Christians who lack their own ministers (*CCEO* 681, §5). Finally, the laws governing non-Catholics who marry Eastern Catholics are operative in the celebration of marriage (*CCEO* 780) and the laws governing non-Catholic Christians at the time of their marriage are to be considered when adjudicating the validity of their marriages (*CCEO* 781).

Temporal Goods

Title XXIII, "The Temporal Goods of the Church" (*CCEO* 1007–1054), treats the acquisition and administration of ecclesiastical goods, contracts and alienation, and pious foundations. In general the title follows the pattern of the Latin code.

In applying the principle of subsidiarity, the Eastern code concedes significant autonomy to the various ecclesiastical authorities. For example, the eparchial bishop may set the amounts for taxes and offerings to be made in connection with the celebration of sacraments (*CCEO* 1013); in the Latin church, such amounts are set by the provincial bishops (c. 1264). Another case is the establishment of a maximum amount regarding the alienation of property: while the Latin code determines that the episcopal conference establishes the maximum limit beyond which the permission of the Holy See is required (c. 1292), the Eastern code allows the patriarchal synod of bishops to establish this limit (*CCEO* 1036).

Eastern autonomy in temporal administration is also exemplified by the several references to the particular law of the various churches *sui iuris*. Certain matters in the Eastern code are governed by that law, while the Latin code determines that they depend on the particular law of the conference of bishops which must be reviewed by the Apostolic See.

Procedural Law

Procedural law is treated in title XXII, "Recourse against Administrative Decrees" (*CCEO* 996–1006); title XXIV, "Trials in General" (*CCEO* 1055–1184); title XXV, "The Contentious Trial" (*CCEO* 1185–1356); title XXVI, "Certain Special Procedures" (*CCEO* 1357–1400); and title XXVIII, "The Procedure for Imposing Penalties" (*CCEO* 1468–1487).

At the beginning of the revision process, one guideline adopted by the Revision Commission was that all Catholics should observe the same procedural norms.[38] Hence, the canons of both codes are notably similar. The differences between them generally result from the differences in the hierarchical structures of the Latin and Eastern churches.

[38] *Nu* 3 (1976) 23.

Canons 1062 and 1063 of the Eastern code establish tribunals that are unique to the Eastern patriarchal churches. The patriarchal synod is the superior tribunal of the patriarchal church inside the patriarchal territory (*CCEO* 1062, §1), with due regard for the right of appeal to the Roman Pontiff (*CCEO* 1059) and the reservation of certain cases to him (*CCEO* 1060). This tribunal is comprised of three bishops, elected for a five-year term (*CCEO* 1062, §2) and is competent to judge contentious cases of eparchies or bishops (*CCEO* 1062, §3) and cases reserved to the Roman Rota in the Latin church (*CCEO* 1405, §3, 1°). Among these bishops is a general moderator who exercises vigilance over the tribunals inside the patriarchal territory (*CCEO* 1062, §5); in the Latin church the Apostolic Signatura exercises such vigilance (*CCEO* 1445, §3, 1°). The patriarch is to establish not only the patriarchal synod but also a tribunal of the patriarchal church, distinct from his own eparchial tribunal, to judge certain cases in the first and succeeding instances (*CCEO* 1063).

In addition to first instance tribunals for several eparchies of the same church *sui iuris* (*CCEO* 1067), a common first instance tribunal may be established to adjudicate contentious and penal cases of the faithful of those churches in the territory (*CCEO* 1068).

Another uniquely Eastern canon treats the recruitment of judges and tribunal personnel. An Eastern Catholic bishop can appoint members of other eparchies of his church *sui iuris* or of another church *sui iuris* to serve in his tribunal (*CCEO* 1102).

Sanctions

The Eastern code does not include *latae sententiae* censures, i.e., incurred automatically with the commission of the delict. In the Eastern Catholic churches, penalties must be imposed (*ferendae sententiae*) judicially or administratively (*CCEO* 1402).

Conclusion

This brief exposition of salient points of the Eastern code has attempted to demonstrate that there is a beautiful variety of churches within the Catholic communion of churches. Awareness of disciplinary diversity not only serves the Latin and Eastern Catholic churches, but perhaps can also reassure those Eastern Orthodox churches that are wary of absorption into a Catholic monolith.

BIBLIOGRAPHY

Sources

Congregation for the Eastern Churches. *Instruction for Applying the Liturgical Prescriptions of the Code of Canons of the Eastern Churches.* Vatican City: Libreria Editrice Vaticana, 1996.

John Paul II. Aplet *Orientale lumen*, May 2, 1995. *AAS* 87 (1995) 745–774.

Pontificium Consilium de Legum Textibus Interpretandis. *Codex Canonum Ecclesiarum Orientalium Auctoritate Ioannis Pauli PP. II Promulgatus, Fontium Annotatione Auctus.* Vatican City: Libreria Editrice Vaticana, 1995.

Eastern Churches

Lynch, J. "The Eastern Churches: Historical Background." *J* 51 (1991) 1–17.

Roberson, R. *The Eastern Christian Churches—A Brief Survey,* 6th ed. Rome: Pontifical Oriental Institute, 1999.

Codification Process

Green, T. "Reflections on the Eastern Code Revision Process." *J* 51 (1991) 18–37.

Nedungatt, G. "A New Code for the Oriental Churches." *Vidyajyoti Journal of Theological Reflection* 55 (1991) 265–284.

Pospishil, V. *Ex Occidente Lex.* Carteret, N.J.: St. Mary's Religious Action Fund, 1979.

Žužek, I. "The Ancient Oriental Sources of Canon Law and the Modern Legislation for Oriental Catholics." *Kanon* 1 (1973) 147–159.

Translations

Canon Law Society of America. *Code of Canons of the Eastern Churches: Latin-English Edition.* Washington, D.C.: Canon Law Society of America, 1992.

Nedungatt, G. *A Companion to the Eastern Code.* Kanonika 5. Rome: Edizioni Orientalia Christiana, 1994.

Concordance

Fürst, C.G. *Canones-Synopse zum Codex Iuris Canonici und Codex Canonum Ecclesiarum Orientalium.* Freiburg im Breisgau: Herder, 1992.

Index

Žužek, I. *Index Analyticus Codicis Canonum Ecclesiarum Orientalium.* Kanonika 2. Rome: Pontificium Institutum Orientalium Studiorum, 1992. An addendum to the index was published in *Orientalia Christiana Periodica* 60 (1994) 635–639.

Bibliographies

Soule, W. B. *Eastern Canon Law Bibliography.* Brooklyn, N.Y.: Saint Maron Publications, 1994.

Synek, E. "Bibliographie zum katholischen Ostkirchenrecht." *Kanon* 11 (1993) 79–134.

Commentaries

Faris, J. *The Eastern Catholic Churches: Constitution and Governance according to the Code of Canons of the Eastern Churches.* Brooklyn, N.Y.: Saint Maron Publications, 1993.

Pospishil, V. *Eastern Catholic Church Law.* Brooklyn, N.Y.: Saint Maron Publications, 1996.

Collections of Articles

Abbass, J. *Two Codes in Comparison.* Kanonika 7. Rome: Pontificio Istituto Orientale, 1997.

Chiramel, J., et al., eds. *The Code of Canons of the Eastern Churches—A Study and Interpretation.* Alwaye, India: St. Thomas Academy of Research, 1992.

Gallagher, C., ed. *The Code of Canons of the Eastern Churches.* Rome: Saint Thomas Christian Fellowship, 1991.

Nedungatt, G. *The Spirit of the Eastern Code.* Bangalore, India, 1993.

Pallath, P., ed. *Catholic Eastern Churches—Heritage and Identity.* Rome: Mar Thoma Yogam, 1994.

CCEO *in General*

McManus, F. "The Code of Canons of the Eastern Catholic Churches." *J* 53 (1993) 22–61.

Provost, J. "Some Practical Issues for Latin Canon Lawyers from the Code of Canons of the Eastern Churches." *J* 51 (1991) 38–66.

Žužek, I. "One Code for a Varietas Ecclesiarum." In *Conference Proceedings of Canon Law Society of Australia and New Zealand.* Melbourne, 1993.

Title II – Churches Sui Iuris *and Rites*

Nedungatt, G. "Equal Rights of the Churches in the Catholic Church." *J* 49 (1989) 1–21.

Žužek, I. "The *Ecclesiae Sui Iuris* in the Revision of Canon Law." In *Vatican II Assessment and Perspectives Twenty Five Years After (1962–1987)*, ed. R. Latourelle. Vol. 2. New York/Mahwah: Paulist, 1989.

Title III – Supreme Authority of the Church

Abbass, J. "*Pastor Bonus* and the Eastern Catholic Churches." *Orientalia Christiana Periodica* 60 (1994) 587–610.

Title IV – Patriarchal Churches

Chiramel, J. *The Patriarchal Churches in the Oriental Code.* Alwaye, India: St. Thomas Academy for Research, 1992.

Hajjar, J. "Patriarchal Synods in the New Eastern Code of Canon Law." *Con* 26 (1990) 88–97.

Pallath, P. *The Synod of Bishops of Catholic Oriental Churches.* Rome: Mar Thoma Yogam, 1994.

Žužek, I. "Canons Concerning the Authority of Patriarchs over the Faithful of Their Own Rite Who Live outside the Limits of Patriarchal Territory." *Nu* 6 (1978) 3–33.

Chapter VII – Patriarchal/Synodal Extra-Territorial Power

Abbas, J. "Canonical Dispositions for the Care of Eastern Catholics outside Their Territory." *P* 86 (1997) 321–362.

Thériault, M. "Canonical Questions Brought About by the Presence of Eastern Catholics in Latin Areas in the Light of the *Codex Canonum Ecclesiarum Orientalium.*" *Ius Ecclesiae* 3 (1991) 201–232.

Title IX – Assemblies of Hierarchs

Madathikandam, G. *The Catholic Bishops' Conference of India: An Interecclesial Assembly.* Kerala: Oriental Institute of Religious Studies India Publications, 1995.

Title XI – Laity

Varghese, M. *The Laity and Their Cooperation in Church Governance.* Rome: Pontificium Institutum Orientale, 1996.

Title XII – Monks and Religious

Holland, S. "A Spirit to Animate the Letter: *CCEO* Title XII." *J* 56 (1996) 288–306.

Koluthara, V. *Rightful Autonomy of Religious Institutes.* Rome: Centre for Indian and Interreligious Studies, 1994.

McDermott, R. "Two Approaches to Consecrated Life: The Code of Canons of the Eastern Churches and the Code of Canon Law." *Stud Can* 29 (1995) 193–239.

Pinheiro, A. "Religious Life in the Eastern Code." *Vidyajyoti Journal of Theological Reflection* 60 (September, 1996) 606–617 and (October, 1996) 663–671.

Title XV – Ecclesiastical Magisterium

Nedungatt, G. "The Teaching Function of the Church in Oriental Canon Law." *Stud Can* 23 (1989) 39–60.

Title XVI – Divine Worship and Especially the Sacraments

Gallagher, C. "Marriage in the Revised Canon Law for the Eastern Catholic Churches." *Stud Can* 24 (1990) 69–90.

McManus, F. "Marriage in the Canons of the Eastern Catholic Churches." *J* 54 (1994) 56–80.

Title XVIII – Ecumenism

Fahey, M. "A Note on the 'Code of Canons of the Eastern Churches' and Orthodox/Catholic Reunion." *J* 56 (1996) 456–464.

Green, T. "The Fostering of Ecumenism: Comparative Reflections on the Latin and Eastern Codes." *P* 85 (1996) 397–444.

Title XXIX – Law, Custom, and Administrative Acts

Abbass, J. "Canonical Interpretation by Recourse to 'Parallel Passages': A Comparative Study of the Latin and Eastern Codes." *J* 51 (1991) 293–310.

Bharanikulangara, K. *Particular Law of the Eastern Catholic Churches*. New York: Saint Maron Publications, 1996.

BOOK I
GENERAL NORMS
[cc. 1–203]

INTRODUCTION

John M. Huels, O.S.M.

As the title "General Norms" suggests, the canons of Book I treat fundamental principles and technical rules that have general application to other parts of the code and the science of canon law in general.[1] Knowledge of these rules is essential for canonists and church administrators, especially bishops, other superiors, and curial officials. For pastoral ministry, the more important sections are those treating dispensations (cc. 85–93), physical persons (cc. 96–112), and the power of governance (cc. 129–144), and secondarily those on laws and customs (cc. 7–28).

The 203 canons of Book I are divided into eleven titles. To understand the systematic arrangement of the topics addressed, some fundamental canonical concepts must be understood. The first of these is the power of governance. As in civil governments, the power of governance of the Church is divided into legislative, executive, and judicial powers. The power of governance is the subject of a distinct title in Book I (title VIII), but in fact the entire code and all other universal and particular norms of the Church, including the laws that regulate the offices of teaching (*munus docendi*) and sanctifying (*munus sanctificandi*), pertain to the office of governing (*munus regendi*). Book I is mainly concerned with rules governing legislative and executive powers, while judicial power is the subject of Book VII.

Another fundamental concept is that of "law" itself. Latin and the major European languages have two words to express what in English is conveyed by the single word "law." The Latin word *lex* is specific and means law as legislation, the norms enacted by a legislative authority. The word *ius* is generic, referring to law in a broad sense, and is used for any kind of normative rule: divine law, ecclesiastical law, customs, statutes,

rules of order, norms issued by executive authorities such as the norms contained in documents of the Roman Curia and individual administrative acts. *Ius* also has a subjective sense, in which case it is translated as "right," as in the rights of the faithful, the rights of clergy, etc. Because English translates both *lex* and *ius* (in its objective sense) as "law," the technical precision of the Latin is lost, and mistakes in interpretation can be made. Ordinarily the Latin text of the law must be consulted whenever the word "law" appears in English to determine which meaning is intended.

With these fundamental concepts in mind, it becomes clear that the first five titles of Book I treat different sources of *ius*.[2] The first three titles treat norms that have a general application: title I on laws, which are acts of legislative power; title II on customs, which are norms introduced by the community itself; and title III on general decrees of legislative power and general executory decrees and instructions, which are norms of executive power. Title IV treats acts of executive power that have an individual application, given for individual juridic and physical persons. The subjects of title V are statutes, which are norms governing the internal life of juridic persons, and rules of order that regulate the meetings of groups. Title VI treats physical and juridic persons, those who are capable of acting in law. The remaining titles of Book I provide rules for various fundamental matters of the canonical system: juridic acts, the power of governance, ecclesiastical offices, prescription, and the computation of time.

A further terminological issue must be addressed with particular reference to title III, "General Decrees and Instructions." This title, new to the 1983 code, successfully establishes the principle of "legality," meaning that norms of executive power must always be within the law, and they

---

[1] Cf. ComCICRec, *Schema canonum libri I de normis generalibus* (Typis Polyglottis Vaticanis, 1977), *Praenotanda*, p. 5.

[2] The term *ius vigens* refers to all binding norms currently in force, including customs and administrative norms.

lack all force if contrary to the law. However, from a systematic viewpoint, title III is unsatisfactory. Canons 29–30 deal with legislative decrees, which would fit more logically in title I. Canons 31–34 deal with general executory decrees and instructions, which are specific kinds of general administrative norms, but not the only ones.

The term "general administrative norms" is not found in the code but comes from canonical doctrine (the writings of canonists).[3] General administrative norms are the norms found in documents of the Roman Curia and other executive authorities. They are called "general" because they are directed to a general audience, as opposed to individual administrative acts which affect only individual juridic or physical persons. General administrative norms may be divided into two categories. *Executory norms,* namely, general executory decrees and instructions, depend on the laws they execute, explain, and expound upon. Title III treats only this category of general administrative norms. However, there are many norms in documents of the Roman Curia that have no direct relationship to a specific law. They are aptly called *independent norms,* because they are independent of the law, though not contrary to it.[4] The lack of a systematic

treatment of general administrative norms in title III is not simply a matter of theoretical inelegance but has practical consequences, because it makes the task more difficult for the Church at large to understand the role and assess the weight of the norms contained in the numerous juridical and pastoral documents issued by the Roman Curia.

The Code of Canons of the Eastern Churches includes many of the canons of Book I of the Latin code, but they are arranged much differently, since the Eastern code is not organized into books. A notable difference in the Eastern code is the absence of anything comparable to title III of the Latin code on general decrees and instructions.[5]

Laws and Customs: Canons 1–28

Canons 1–6 show the relationship of the 1983 code to other juridical realities of the Catholic Church. Canons 7–22 establish rules governing ecclesiastical laws in general. Canons 23–28 establish rules governing customs, in particular how they achieve the force of law. In this commentary on canons 1–28, references to *ius* are noted in the Latin while the word "law" is reserved for *lex,* for the act of a legislator, except where "law" is followed by *ius* in parentheses, or when using the standard expressions "canon law" (*ius canonicum*) and "divine law" (*ius divinum*).

---

[3] We rely in particular on the work of E. Labandeira, *Tratado de derecho administrativo canónico,* 2nd ed. (Pamplona: EUNSA, 1993). It is also published in Italian, *Trattato di diritto amministrativo canonico* (Milan: Giuffrè, 1994).

[4] They are given by authorities who have executive power within their competence. See c. 479; *PB* 62, 72, 86, 94,

105, 115. Like executory norms, independent norms lack all force if they are contrary to the law.

[5] On this point, see the report of the *Coetus de normis generalibus* in *Nu,* no. 10 (1980/1) 106–109.

INTRODUCTORY CANONS
[cc. 1–6]

Canons 1–6 treat the relationship of the code to other juridical realities: the law of the Eastern Catholic churches, liturgical norms, agreements with states and political societies, acquired rights and privileges, customs, and the universal and particular norms in existence at the time the code went into force in 1983. These canons are basically the same as they were in the first code of 1917. The first six canons of the Eastern code are comparable, but the material treated in canons 5 and 6 of the Latin code is greatly simplified in canon 6 of the Eastern code; canon 2 of the Eastern code provides a rule parallel to canon 6, §2 of the Latin code, but in different words.[6]

A Code for the Latin Church

Canon 1 — The canons of this Code regard only the Latin Church.

The Roman Catholic Church consists of twenty-two autonomous (*sui iuris*) churches, formerly called "rites," each with its own hierarchy, traditions, and discipline. All of these churches, while remaining juridically distinct, are united under the headship of the bishop of Rome, the pope. This initial canon sets forth the fundamental rule that this code pertains only to the Latin church *sui iuris*. Consequently, it does not bind the members of the Eastern Catholic churches, notwithstanding some canons that allude to them.[7] The twenty-one

---

[6] Canon 2 of the Eastern code states: "The canons of the Code, in which for the most part the ancient law of the Eastern Churches is received or adapted, are to be assessed mainly according to that law." This and subsequent translations of the Eastern code are taken from *Code of Canons of the Eastern Churches: Latin-English Edition* (Washington, D.C.: CLSA, 1992).

[7] See cc. 111–112; 214; 350; 372, §2; 383, §2; 450, §1; 476; 479, §2; 518; 846, §2; 923; 991; 1015, §2; 1021; 1109; 1248, §1.

Eastern churches *sui iuris* have their own particular norms and customs as well as a code of law common to all of them, the Code of Canons of the Eastern Churches.

The 1983 code frequently refers to a church *sui iuris* as a "rite," but since the promulgation of the Eastern code in 1990, the term "rite" is used for the liturgical, theological, spiritual, and disciplinary patrimony of the church. A "church *sui iuris*" is the institutional entity as a whole with its own hierarchy and particular laws (*CCEO* 27–28). The word "rite" also is used to refer strictly to the liturgical tradition observed by a church (cc. 846, §2; 923). The Latin church *sui iuris* observes the Roman rite liturgy or a variation of it, the most notable variation being the Ambrosian rite of Milan. The twenty-one Eastern churches *sui iuris* observe five different liturgical rites, as follows:

1. Alexandrian rite: Coptic church, Ethiopian church.
2. Antiochene rite: Malankar, Maronite, and Syrian churches
3. Byzantine rite: Albanian, Byelorussian, Bulgarian, Greek, Italo-Albanian, Yugoslavian, Melkite, Romanian, Russian, Ruthenian, Slovakian, Ukrainian, and Hungarian churches
4. Chaldean rite: Chaldean and Malabar churches
5. Armenian rite: Armenian church

Liturgical Norms

Canon 2 — For the most part the Code does not define the rites which must be observed in celebrating liturgical actions. Therefore, liturgical laws in force until now retain their force unless one of them is contrary to the canons of the Code.

For the most part (*plerumque*), the code does not contain the norms ordering the liturgy. By saying "for the most part," the legislator implies that there are canons of the code that do regulate the liturgy. These are found in Book IV of the code. The legislator also implies that most laws regulating the liturgy are not found in the code. There is another body of universal ecclesiastical law, even larger than the code, called the liturgical law, consisting of norms too numerous and detailed to be included in the code. These laws are found chiefly in the liturgical books. Another important source of liturgical law since Vatican II is the particular laws on the liturgy enacted by conferences of bishops and diocesan bishops (c. 838). Although canon 2 speaks only of liturgical "laws" (*leges*), the principle stated in this canon also applies to liturgical norms found in documents that are acts of executive rather than legislative power, such as directories or instructions published by a congregation of the Roman Curia on liturgical matters.

All the liturgical books and rites contain an introduction,[8] and some contain additional introductions to the various parts of the rites. These introductions, printed in black, have some theological content, but they are largely juridical in nature. Within the rites themselves are found the rubrics, printed in red, giving the precise directions for the proper execution of the rite. Both the rubrics and the juridical norms of the introductions are true ecclesiastical laws, subject to the same general rules for promulgation, interpretation, revocation, and dispensation as all other ecclesiastical laws (cc. 7–21, 85–93).

Liturgical norms promulgated before the 1983 code are not affected by the code, unless they are contrary to the canons. In fact, after the code was promulgated it was necessary to modify seventy-six norms of the liturgical books to bring them into conformity with the canons.[9] It should be noted in this regard that canon 2 is incomplete, for not only were the liturgical norms *contrary* to the code abrogated, but also abrogated were the liturgical norms that were *completely reordered* by the code in keeping with canon 6, §1, 4°.

From a purely technical viewpoint, canon 2 is unnecessary because the general rules of canon 6, §1, 2° and 4° are applicable also to the liturgical norms. However, the canon has a kind of pastoral and didactic value in that it alerts the canonist and the Christian community at large to the existence of another major and important body of ecclesiastical law apart from the code.

Agreements

Canon 3 — The canons of the Code neither abrogate nor derogate from the agreements entered into by the Apostolic See with nations or other political societies. These agreements therefore continue in force exactly as at present, notwithstanding contrary prescripts of this Code.

A fundamental rule of international relations is that "pacts must be observed" (*pacta sunt servanda*). If one government could unilaterally alter a treaty or other mutual agreement, there could be no order or security among nations. This is the principle at the root of canon 3. The code has no effect on any kind of agreements made between the Apostolic See with nations or other political societies, such as the United Nations, UNESCO, the European Union, etc.[10] Even if a canon is contrary to a provision of such an agreement, the latter prevails.

Agreements (*conventiones*) are of various kinds. A concordat is a general agreement that regulates all the matters of concern to the Church and a particular nation. There are also partial agreements, called protocols, *modi vivendi*, accords, etc., which regulate various kinds of matters. A chief purpose of them is to secure the rights of the Church—in education, ownership

---

[8] These go by several names: general instruction (*institutio generalis*), introductions (*praenotanda*), and general introductions (*praenotanda generalia*), although frequently authors simply call them the *praenotanda*, using the Latin word.

[9] SCSDW, "Variationes in libros liturgicos ad normam Codicis Iuris Canonici nuper promulgati introducendas edidit," *N* 19 (1983) 540–555; ICEL translation, *Emendations in the Liturgical Books Following upon the New Code of Canon Law* (Washington, D.C.: 1984).

[10] Canon 3 of the 1917 code dealt only with agreements with nations.

and free use of property, freedom to practice the faith, etc. Some agreements give rights to the State, for example, the right in some countries that the government be notified of the appointment of a bishop before it is announced, but these rights are conceded only if the rights of the Church are recognized by the State.

Agreements between the Church and the State are not treaties between nations (between a civil government and the Vatican State), but between a nation and the competent authority of the Roman Catholic Church. The Roman Catholic Church is unique among world religions for its highly developed diplomatic relations with civil governments and its participation in world affairs and representation in world organizations. This uniqueness is due not to the fact that the pope is a temporal ruler of the Vatican State, but to the influence of the Church itself with a billion members throughout the world, a unified governance at the universal level, national hierarchies organized into conferences of bishops, and a global corps of papal legates.

The principle that agreements must be observed can be extended to include, not only agreements between Church and State, but all agreements and contracts entered into between any physical or juridic persons in the Church among themselves or with partners outside the Church.[11] Agreements valid at the time the 1983 code came into force are not affected by the code, even if a provision of the agreement be contrary to a canon.

Acquired Rights and Privileges

Canon 4 — Acquired rights and privileges granted to physical or juridic persons up to this time by the Apostolic See remain intact if they are in use and have not been revoked, unless the canons of this Code expressly revoke them.

The purpose of this canon is to protect certain privileges and rights, already lawfully acquired,

from being taken away by the 1983 code. It is an application of canon 9 on the non-retroactivity of law. Privileges granted by the Apostolic See and acquired rights remain effective, even if contrary to the code, unless the law expressly states otherwise.

Acquired Rights

In the context of canon 4, an acquired (or vested) right refers to a right, other than an innate right or a legal right, that a physical or juridic person lawfully acquired before the 1983 code went into effect. There are numerous ways by which a right may be acquired; these include the civil law (c. 22), administrative acts (cc. 48, 59, 76, 85), judicial sentences (e.g., c. 1684), contracts (cc. 192, 1290), prescription (c. 197), a promise to marry (c. 1062), election to office (cc. 147, 178), vows and oaths (cc. 1196, 1203).[12] If an acquired right is contrary to a canon of the code, it is not affected by the code and remains intact unless expressly revoked by the canons of the code. In fact, the code does not explicitly revoke any acquired rights.[13]

An example may help to elucidate the meaning of an acquired right. The 1983 code, unlike the 1917 code, requires that tribunal judges, the defender of the bond, and the promoter of justice have doctorates or licentiates in canon law (cc. 1421, §3; 1435). After the promulgation of the code on January 25, 1983, but before it took effect on November 27, bishops in some dioceses appointed persons to these positions who lacked degrees in canon law. Such appointments, valid under the 1917 code, gave these persons the right

---

[11] *Münster Com,* 3/6.

[12] See also cc. 38; 121; 122; 123; 192; 326, §2; 562; 616, §1; 1222, §2.

[13] However, c. 510, §1, without explicitly mentioning "acquired rights," prohibits parishes from being joined to a chapter of canons, and it makes this prohibition retroactive by requiring the bishop to separate any such parishes from a chapter. This is an express revocation, albeit implicit, of a right. Regarding the difference between express, explicit, and implicit revocation, see the commentary under c. 20.

to the office, even though they did not meet the requirements of the new law. The right was acquired in virtue of the valid appointment, and this right was not affected by requirements of the new law. An appointment is an administrative act—a singular decree—and since the appointments were valid, the persons appointed to be tribunal officials during this period had a right to assume office, even if they did not begin their duties until after the code took effect when the qualifications for the office had changed.

Acquired rights must be distinguished from innate (natural) rights and from legal rights. *Innate rights* come from the divine natural law; they are innate to every human being from birth and include rights such as freedom of religion, the right to a good reputation, the right of parents to see to the education of their children, the right to choose one's vocation and state in life, and many others. Such rights are inviolable and are never lost, even if abused or denied by human authority.

Legal rights, in this context, refer to rights that come to a person in virtue of ecclesiastical law or legal custom, such as rights given by the code to pastors, clergy, religious, and laity (e.g., cc. 533, §2; 278, §1; 670; 229, §2). Such rights are subject to change when the law changes. Otherwise, any right once given in law would be absolute and could never be changed or removed for as long as the person lived, held office, or remained in the clerical or religious state. For example, under the 1917 code, the pastor had a right to two months of vacation each year (*CIC* 464, §2), but the 1983 code reduced this to one month (c. 533, §2). A pastor appointed before November 27, 1983 could not claim that he had an acquired right under the old law to continue taking two months' vacation for as long as he held office. Rights coming from the merely ecclesiastical law, like other ecclesiastical laws, are subject to the general rules of canons 6 and 20, not the exception of canon 4.[14] If a right is granted by the ecclesiastical law, and a subsequent law abrogates the law or dero-

gates from it, the right is thereby lost or is modified in accord with the new law.

Legal rights coming from a custom that has the force of law (cc. 23–26) are also not the acquired rights of canon 4. If a right acquired on the basis of a legal custom is contrary to a canon of the code, it is suppressed unless the code expressly provides otherwise or unless the custom is centenary or immemorial, in which case the ordinary may permit it to continue in keeping with canon 5, §1.

Privileges Granted by the Apostolic See

Privileges are treated in canons 76–84. A privilege is a favor that is an exception to the law granted by the legislator or his delegate to a physical or juridic person. The canon refers to privileges granted by the Apostolic See. If such privileges are still in use, they may continue, even if contrary to the code. For example, a few religious orders have a centuries-old privilege of amending their constitutions without getting the approval of the Holy See. This privilege remains intact, despite the requirement of canon 587, §2. The code revokes contrary privileges in four cases: canons 396, §2; 509, §1; 526, §2; and 1019, §2.

Privileges granted by any legislator lower than the pope (or his delegate) are revoked if they are contrary to the code. This is evident by the inclusion of the words "Apostolic See" in reference to the privileges in question. One opinion holds that a privilege, insofar as it is the source of an acquired right, would not be revoked by the code even if contrary to the code and granted by a legislator lower than the pope.[15] While it is true that a right is acquired by a privilege, nevertheless canon 4 specifically distinguishes acquired rights from privileges. The only practical reason for this distinction in this context is precisely to allow for the continuance of apostolic privileges contrary to the code while revoking contrary privileges granted by lower legislators.

---

[14] It would make more sense systematically (as noted in *Münster Com,* 4/1) if c. 4 were to follow c. 6.

[15] *Com Ex,* 1:273.

Canon 4 will continue to be applicable to juridic persons for as long as the code remains in force since, unlike physical persons, juridic persons are by nature perpetual, unless legally extinguished (c. 120). Consequently, the acquired rights and the apostolic privileges of juridic persons are presumed to endure as long as the juridic persons do, unless the right or privilege be expressly revoked.

Contrary Customs

Canon 5 — §1. Universal or particular customs presently in force which are contrary to the prescripts of these canons and are reprobated by the canons of this Code are absolutely suppressed and are not permitted to revive in the future. Other contrary customs are also considered suppressed unless the Code expressly provides otherwise or unless they are centenary or immemorial customs which can be tolerated if, in the judgment of the ordinary, they cannot be removed due to the circumstances of places and persons.

§2. Universal or particular customs beyond the law (praeter ius) which are in force until now are preserved.

A custom is a normative practice of the community introduced by the community itself, unlike a law, which is a norm introduced by a legislator. Canons 23–28 treat customs in general, including the formation of new customs, but this canon treats only those customs in observance at the time the code went into effect in 1983. The canon is really concerned only with customs contrary to the code, but the second paragraph on customs beyond the law (praeter ius) resolves a question about whether the previous law affected such customs or not. This paragraph makes it clear that customs beyond the law, that is, those which regulate a matter not treated in the law, are unaffected by the code.

The concern of the canon, therefore, is with customs contrary to the code, whether universal or particular. A universal custom is one that exists in a majority of areas of the Latin church, for ex-

ample, the custom of having special decorations in church for Christmas. Most customs are particular, in force in one or more areas or communities but not widespread throughout the Church.

Four categories of contrary custom are distinguished: (1) those that are reprobated by the code; (2) those that the code itself expressly permits to continue; (3) those that are centenary or immemorial; (4) all other contrary customs. The code reprobates contrary customs only in six instances (cc. 396, §2; 423, §1; 526, §2; 1076; 1287, §1; and 1425, §1). These expressly reprobated customs may not be tolerated, even if centenary or immemorial. They are absolutely suppressed by the code and may not revive in the future, that is, they may not become legitimate over the course of time like other contrary customs, unless the law reprobating them itself is abrogated.[16]

In certain instances, the code itself expressly permits the continuance of customs, even those contrary to the norm being expressed in the canon. This may be stated explicitly (cc. 438, 1263, 1279, §1), or contained in a general reference to particular or proper law (ius particulare, ius proprium), which includes customs.[17] The exception may also be expressed without any explicit reference to custom or particular law, for example, in canon 858, §1, which speaks of the right of non-parochial churches to a baptismal font, a right that might be based on a custom.

Centenary customs are those that are at least one hundred years old. Immemorial customs antedate the memory of the oldest persons in the community; they have been observed for as long as anyone can remember. The code has great respect for such long-standing customs. Even if they are contrary to the canons, the ordinary[18] may allow them to continue if he judges, according to the circumstances, that they cannot be removed without causing harm or disturbance in his territory or community. In making this judgment, the ordinary should take into consideration the gravity of

[16] See the commentary below on cc. 23–26.
[17] E.g., cc. 127, §1; 482, §1; 553, §2; 1177, §3; 1672.
[18] See c. 134, §1.

the law and the circumstances of the case (cf. c. 90). He also should take account of minority viewpoints and expert opinions to avoid the danger of a decision made more on the basis of politics than of principle. The ordinary may tolerate the custom either explicitly, by decreeing or declaring that the custom may be observed, or tacitly, by being aware of the custom's continued observance and doing nothing to eradicate it.

Finally, all other customs contrary to the code[19] are also suppressed, that is, they may not be lawfully observed. Unlike customs expressly reprobated, all other contrary customs are capable of reviving in the future and may even obtain the force of law after thirty years of observance in accord with canons 24–26.

Previous Laws

Canon 6 — §1. When this Code takes force, the following are abrogated:
1° **the Code of Canon Law promulgated in 1917;**
2° **other universal or particular laws contrary to the prescripts of this Code unless other provision is expressly made for particular laws;**
3° **any universal or particular penal laws whatsoever issued by the Apostolic See unless they are contained in this Code;**
4° **other universal disciplinary laws regarding matter which this Code completely reorders.**
§2. Insofar as they repeat former law, the canons of this Code must be assessed also in accord with canonical tradition.

The canon intends to provide juridical certainty regarding the relation of the 1983 code to norms previously enacted. It clarifies which of these norms are revoked by the code itself and, conse-quently, which norms remain in force. Although the canon speaks only of *leges,* that is, laws promulgated by legislative authorities, it also encompasses lesser juridical norms of executive authorities, such as those in general documents published by the Roman Curia,[20] certain statutes of juridic persons (c. 94, §3), and the proper law (*ius proprium*) of institutes of consecrated life and societies of apostolic life.[21]

1°. The code of 1917 was abrogated at midnight on November 27, 1983 at the same instant at which the revised code came into effect. This date has great importance in canonical practice, because the validity of juridic acts placed before this date (such as marriages) must be judged in accordance with the law in force at that time, not according to the new law. In addition to the 1917 code itself, all other juridical norms and documents, whether legislative or executive, that were intended to implement the 1917 code are abrogated. With the exceptions mentioned in nn. 2–4 of the canon, all juridical norms contained in documents implementing the decrees of Vatican II are *not* abrogated, since they are not dependent on the 1917 code.

2°. Also abrogated by the 1983 code are other universal or particular laws contrary to the code, unless particular laws are expressly excepted in a canon of the code. A universal law is given for the whole Latin church by the supreme legislator—the pope or the college of bishops. A particular law is given for a particular territory or community within the Church, for example, the law of a diocese or a region of a conference of bishops. All universal laws contrary to a law of the code are abrogated, and all contrary particular laws are abrogated unless the code expressly makes an exception for particular laws (as in cc. 288; 482, §1; 553, §2; 1470, §1; 1561; and 1653, §1).

---

[19] These are, namely, the contrary customs that are not expressly reprobated, not centenary or immemorial, or not expressly excepted by the code.

[20] *Comm* 14 (1982) 131; *Com Ex,* 279–280.
[21] SCRIS, decr, Feb. 2, 1984, *AAS* 76 (1984) 498–499.

3°. Penal laws enacted by the Apostolic See before the 1983 code went into effect, whether particular or universal, are abrogated. An example of penal laws revoked by the code were the penalties established for violations of certain rules governing the election of the pope.[22] Any penal laws enacted by legislators other than the pope or his delegate remain in force, unless they are contrary to the code. This would be the case, for example, if a diocesan law established a different penalty from the code for the same crime; the diocesan law would be abrogated and the law of the code would prevail.

4°. All universal disciplinary laws in effect before the 1983 code are abrogated if they are completely (*ex integro*) reordered by the code. A disciplinary law in this context simply means an ecclesiastical law, as opposed to a divine law.[23] A disciplinary law is completely reordered by the code when its entire subject matter is treated anew by the code. For example, canon 844 completely reordered the discipline on sacramental sharing contained in the 1967 *Ecumenical Directory*.[24] The revocation of law by complete reordering is discussed in the commentary below on canon 20.

The second paragraph of canon 6 provides a principle of interpretation: canons of the code that restate (*referunt*) the former law must *also* be assessed in light of canonical tradition. In saying "also," the law implies that the canonical tradition is not the only source for interpretation; there are other principles, as noted below in the commentary on canons 16–19. The canonical tradition refers here to the expanse of time prior to the 1983 code in which a common understanding of a norm emerged by means of the practice of the Holy See and the writings of canonical scholars. Since many canons of the code are not new but were taken up from previous sources, especially the 1917 code and documents of the Holy See issued after Vatican II, the interpreter of the 1983 code must investigate the canonical tradition in order to achieve a well-grounded interpretation of such canons. Sometimes this investigation will reveal that there is no consensus on the meaning of a norm, in which case the interpreter must decide which arguments are more persuasive.[25]

The Latin word *refero* has several meanings, among them "repeat," "refer to," "reproduce," "represent," "restore," "set forth anew." A canon does not have to repeat exactly the wording of the old law for this principle to apply, so long as the substance of the old law has been legislated anew.

TITLE I
ECCLESIASTICAL LAWS
[cc. 7–22]

The canonical system embraces three bodies of law: divine law, both positive and natural,[26] which

---

[22] Paul VI, apconst *Romano Pontifici eligendo*, October 1, 1975, *AAS* 67 (1975) 609–649. This has been replaced by John Paul II with another apostolic constitution that also contains penal laws. See *Universi Dominici gregis*, February 22, 1996, *AAS* 88 (1996) 305–343; *Origins* 25 (1996) 617, 619–630.

[23] A non-technical meaning of "disciplinary law" is used here. It has the same general sense as seen in a number of other canons referring to "ecclesiastical discipline": 305, §1; 326, §1; 342; 392, §2; 436, §1, 1°; 445; 1317. Thus, procedural laws, penal laws, and merely ecclesiastical constitutive laws are also capable of being integrally reordered, although penal laws have already been treated in subsection three. Cf. cc. 86 and 87, §1.

[24] *ED* 42, 44, 46, 55.

[25] For an illustration of this interpretative principle, see the commentary on c. 18 with respect to exceptions from the law.

[26] The divine law consists of the irreformable truths of the faith, both dogmatic and moral. The divine positive law has its source in revelation, expressed in scripture or tradition; the divine natural law is based on the order of creation and can be known by human reason. Only the supreme authority of the Church can authentically determine what constitutes divine law. See cc. 749–750, 841,

is the law of God binding all people; ecclesiastical law, the law of the Catholic Church that binds only Catholics (c. 11); and civil law (c. 22), certain laws of the respective civil jurisdictions that bind citizens of the State. The rules of this title apply to ecclesiastical law, the human laws of the Church. Divine laws, given by God, are unchangeable by human beings; ecclesiastical laws, human in origin, can be created and abolished by the competent legislative authorities of the Church. Canon law in the broad sense (*ius canonicum*) also includes customs, the subject of the next title (cc. 23–28), and the general norms of executive power, treated in the third title (cc. 29–34).

Although the title of this section indicates that canons 7–22 refer only to legislative acts (*leges*), many of the rules and principles given here are equally applicable to other written sources of the *ius,* especially the norms in juridical documents of the Roman Curia or lesser executive authorities.[27] Canon 17 provides the legal basis for extending these rules to other general norms of executive rather than legislative power. Since comparable rules and principles governing such norms are lacking, other than in canons 31–34, it is necessary to look to parallel places in the law, namely, pertinent canons in this first title of the code. Thus, most of what is said here about laws applies equally to general administrative norms contained in documents issued by executive authorities such as directories, circular letters, notifications, instructions, etc. The only essential difference between laws and general administrative norms is the authority that issues them (legislative or executive), and the only practical difference is that norms of executive authority cannot be contrary to the law of the comparable[28] or higher legislator

(cc. 33, §1; 34). In particular, the following canons of title I of the code may also be applied to general administrative norms: canons 9; 11–14; 15, §2; 17; and 19–21. Canon 31, §2 makes explicit reference to the applicability of canon 8.

The primary source for title I—with the notable exception of canon 22, which was new to the 1983 code—is canons 8–24 of the 1917 code. The comparable section of canons in the Eastern code is found near the end of that code (*CCEO* 1488–1505). It contains three canons with no counterpart in the Latin code, canon 1492 on the extent to which the faithful of the Eastern churches are subject to laws of the supreme authority of the Church, canon 1493 that defines "common law" and "particular law" in the Eastern canon law,[29] and canon 1505 stating the principle that the use of the masculine gender includes the feminine unless the *ius* provides otherwise or it is clear from the nature of the matter.

Title I consists of sixteen canons treating establishment of law (c. 7); promulgation, *vacatio,* and binding force of law (c. 8); non-retroactivity of law (c. 9); invalidating and disqualifying laws (c. 10); subjects of canon law (c. 11); universal and particular laws (cc. 12 and 13); doubts of law and fact (c. 14); ignorance and error (c. 15); official interpretation of law (c. 16); rules for interpretation of law (c. 17); strict interpretation of law (c. 18); cases involving lacunae in the law (c. 19); revocation of law (c. 20); doubtful revocation of law (c. 21); and the canonization of civil laws (c. 22).

Establishment of Law

Canon 7 — A law is established when it is promulgated.

1075, §1. See also cc. 22; 24, §1; 113, §1; 145, §1; 1059; 1163, §2; 1165, §2; 1290; and 1692, §2.

[27] See J. Otaduy's discussion of this point in *Com Ex,* 1:296.

[28] Thus, a dicastery of the Holy See may not validly make a norm contrary to a law of the pope, and the vicar general or episcopal vicar may not validly make a norm contrary to a law of the diocesan bishop.

[29] *CCEO* 1493 states: "§1. Beyond the laws and legitimate customs of the universal Church, this Code also includes by the designation 'common law' (*ius*) the laws and legitimate customs common to all Eastern Churches.

"§2. Included in the designation 'particular law' (*ius*) are all the laws, legitimate customs, statutes and other norms of law (*ius*) which are not common to the universal Church nor to all the Eastern Churches."

A law is a binding norm duly promulgated by a competent legislator for the common good of a community capable of receiving a law.[30] Only a legislator, someone who possesses legislative power, can make a law. The code treats the legislative power of the pope and the college of bishops (cc. 333, 336–337), particular councils and conferences of bishops (cc. 445, 455), and diocesan bishops and their equivalents (cc. 391, §2; 381, §2). The dicasteries of the Roman Curia do not have legislative power; they have executive or judicial power. Only the pope and the college of bishops can delegate legislative power.[31]

A law must be enacted according to the necessary legal formalities. The text of the law must be drafted in writing,[32] approved by the legislator, dated, and signed. Then, the law must be promulgated according to the requirements of canon 8. Finally, the law goes into effect on the established date. Often there are three separate dates marking these various acts: the date of issuance,[33] the date of promulgation, and the date the law has binding force. Likewise, different bodies or officials in addition to the legislator may be involved in these several stages. Decrees of an ecumenical council are approved by the council fathers and confirmed and promulgated by authority of the pope (c. 341, §1). Most of the liturgical rites were promulgated by a decree of the Congregation for Divine Worship on the authority of the pope, who approved them and ordered them to be published.[34] Similarly, a diocesan synod first approves the synodal decrees; the diocesan bishop as sole legislator in the diocese (c. 466) then signs them; and finally the vicar general might see to their promulgation in the manner determined by the bishop.

Laws take various forms in the canonical system: canons of the code, the juridical norms[35] of the introductions and the rubrics of the liturgical books, general decrees (cc. 29–30), the juridical norms contained in certain papal documents such as apostolic constitutions and apostolic letters *motu proprio,*[36] juridical norms in a document of the Roman Curia approved *in forma specifica* by the pope,[37] decrees of a diocesan synod promul-

---

[30] This definition is based on that proposed in earlier drafts of c. 7, which said that a law is "a general norm for the common good of some community given by a competent authority." ComCICRec, *Schema Codicis Iuris Canonici* (1980) and *Codex Iuris Canonici Schema Novissimum* (1982). The reference to the community "capable of receiving law" is not strictly necessary because it is implicit in the notion of the "competent legislator." It is added because it is contained in the definition of general decrees (c. 29), which are laws. It clarifies that not all communities and groups in the Church are capable of receiving a law and, consequently, that the legislator has no power to make laws for these communities as such, even though, as individuals, they are subject to his authority and to the applicable laws of his jurisdiction.

[31] Canons 30, 135, §2; *PB* 18, §2.

[32] The pope sometimes makes a change in law orally, and this change is then reported by the Secretariat of State and published in the *Acta Apostolicae Sedis.*

[33] This is the date listed at the end of a juridical document. Often it is a major feast day or the anniversary of some important event. Rarely does the date of issuance actually coincide with the date the document is first distributed to the public.

[34] All such decrees are found at the beginning of the liturgical rite.

[35] Besides the juridical norms, the liturgical books and many documents of the Holy See also contain statements of a doctrinal, or theological, nature. The latter pertain more to the discipline of theology and the *munus docendi,* the former more to the discipline of canon law and the *munus regendi,* although canonists and theologians alike have an interest in all the norms of church documents.

[36] J. Huels, "A Theory of Juridical Documents Based on Canons 29–34," *Stud Can* 32 (1998) 337–370. The words *motu proprio* mean "on his own initiative," i.e., the document is signed in his own name; it is not a question of the pope delegating legislative power to a Roman dicastery or approving a curial document *in forma specifica.* An apostolic constitution is the most solemn form of papal legislation, followed by the apostolic letter *motu proprio.* See F. Morrisey and M. Thériault, *Papal and Curial Pronouncements: Their Canonical Significance in Light of the Code of Canon Law* (Ottawa: Faculty of Canon Law, St. Paul University, 1995).

[37] Ordinarily, the pope approves a curial document in general fashion (*in forma communi*), which means that the document remains an act of executive power of the curial dicastery that authored it. If he approves it *in forma specifica,* he gives the juridical norms of the document legislative force. For documents published since 1992,

gated by the bishop (c. 466), etc. Moreover, certain acts, such as authentic interpretations of the law (c. 16, §2) and statutes (c. 94, §3), can be given legislative force. The form of the law, or the document in which the law is published, has less juridical significance than the authority who makes the law. All universal laws, for example, have exactly the same juridical value, or weight, regardless of the form in which they are published. However, there is a hierarchy of legislative authorities that makes a real difference in the weight of the laws. The laws of the pope or an ecumenical council (the supreme legislators) are higher than all other ecclesiastical laws; the laws of plenary councils and conferences of bishops are higher than those of provincial councils and diocesan bishops; the laws of provincial councils are higher than those of diocesan bishops. No legislator may validly make a law contrary to a *ius* of a higher legislator.[38]

The legislator may make a law only for a community capable of receiving the law, as discussed below at canon 25. A law is given by the legislator for the community; it has a general character and applies to everyone equally for whom it is made (e.g., all pastors in the Latin church, all religious in the diocese, all the faithful in the episcopal conference region, etc.). The bishop, for example, could not make a law prohibiting an abuse in one parish while allowing it to continue in all others; that would not be a law, but a precept (c. 49), an individual administrative act (cc. 35–93). He could make a law for one parish if the law governed a matter unique to that parish, for example, a law regulating a parish shrine or cemetery.

Law is normative; it is binding. If law were not binding, it could not achieve its end, which is to serve the common good, providing harmony and unity in a society. By establishing rules that all the members of the society are obliged to follow, conflicts in the society are minimized and may readily be resolved by turning to the law itself for the solution, or to the authority who is competent in law to decide the matter. Canon law binds in conscience,[39] unless there are causes that excuse from observance, and in the external forum (the visible life of the Church). Because canon law is binding in conscience, it is not necessary to legislate penalties for the violation of the law, except for serious crimes where penalties are required for the common good. Rather, the faithful are called voluntarily to submit to the demands of the law out of respect for Christ's Church and in the hope of salvation, which is the ultimate goal of canon law (cf. c. 1752).

A characteristic of canon law is its rationality, that is, its reasonableness (cf. c. 24, §2),[40] which means it serves a useful purpose and upholds the common good. This characteristic of reasonableness is not a formal requirement for the creation of law, because a law can be validly made and will externally or formally bind the community even if it is not reasonable. However, the law must be reasonable if it is to achieve its purpose, to foster the

---

the precise words *in forma specifica approbavit* must be contained in the document to verify this special papal approval. See SS, *Regolamento generale della Curia romana*, art. 110, §4, February 4, 1992, *AAS* 84 (1992) 201–267; the provision was repeated in the revised *Regolamento* of 1999, art. 126, §4. See J. Huels, "Interpreting an Instruction Approved *in forma specifica*," *Stud Can* 32 (1998) 5–46. Before 1992, specific papal approval was recognized by other formulas, notably *ex certa scientia*. See V. Gómez-Iglesias, "Naturaleza y origen de la confirmación *ex certa scientia*," *IC* 25 (1985) 91–116.

[38] Canon 135, §2 speaks of a higher *ius,* not a higher *lex;* e.g., a particular law cannot be validly made if it is contrary to a general administrative norm in a document of the Roman Curia, nor can a particular law be made contrary to a universal custom.

[39] Cf. *Comm* 16 (1984) 144. Whether a sin is committed by the violation of a given law is a matter for moral theology and pastoral practice, not the science of canon law. Various factors must be taken into consideration in estimating sinfulness, among which are knowledge of the law, deliberate intent to violate the law, the existence of mitigating factors judged in proportion to the gravity of the law, etc.

[40] Thomas Aquinas defined law in part as an ordinance of reason: *ordinatio rationis ad bonum commune ab eo qui curam habet communitatis promulgata. STh* I-II, q. 90, a. 4.

common good. A reasonable law promotes the welfare of the community, including the individuals who compose it; an unreasonable law is harmful to the common good. Of course, every legislator thinks his law is reasonable when he makes it, but sometimes a well-intentioned law does not live up to the legislator's original expectations. Usually a law is readily received by the community and endures as long as the legislator or his successors consider it useful (cf. c. 20). Sometimes, however, the faithful who are subject to the law, or some of them, find that the law is unreasonable in their circumstances, and an appropriate remedy is sought from the canonical tradition.

The rarest of these "remedies" is the phenomenon of the non-acceptance of law, also known as the non-reception of law, when the majority of the community quietly ignores a law and fails to put it into practice from its very inception, due to the practical impossibility or harm that would come from observing it.[41] Or the law might be accepted in most places, but not in others where a contrary custom develops (cc. 23–27). Likewise, the law initially might be accepted, but could become obsolete or harmful over time and fall into desuetude, the phenomenon known as the intrinsic cessation of law.[42] For good reason, individuals and communities may be dispensed from a law (cc. 85–93); they might be given a privilege exempting them from the law's observance (cc. 76–84); or, in some situations, individuals and small groups may invoke the virtue of *epieikeia* for justifiable reasons.[43] These phenomena, in some respects unique

to the system of canon law, reflect the essential characteristic of the law's rationality. If the law is not serving a reasonable purpose, it is not truly functioning as law should, so an appropriate remedy will be needed, whether this be provided by a competent authority or by the subjects of the law themselves. The subjects of canon law are not passive but are actively involved in determining the law's practical meaning and implementation in the local churches and communities.[44]

Promulgation, Vacatio, *and Binding Force*

Canon 8 — §1. Universal ecclesiastical laws are promulgated by publication in the official commentary, *Acta Apostolicae Sedis,* **unless another manner of promulgation has been prescribed in particular cases. They take force only after three months have elapsed from the date of that issue of the** *Acta* **unless they bind immediately from the very nature of the matter, or the law itself has specifically and expressly established a shorter or longer suspensive period (***vacatio***).**

§2. Particular laws are promulgated in the manner determined by the legislator and begin to oblige a month after the day of promulgation unless the law itself establishes another time period.

Typically, there are several stages of a law's coming into being: (1) the preparation of the text of the law, (2) the approval of the text by the legislator and its issuance on his authority, (3) promulgation, (4) the period when the force of the law is suspended, and (5) the date that the law begins to bind. This canon treats the final three stages. Promulgation is the formal act of publication of a law, which is essential for the law to come into being. If promulgation is omitted or done invalidly, the law has no effect and cannot be enforced. A law does not ordinarily achieve its binding force on the date of its promulgation, but only after a suspensive period called the *vacatio legis,* literally, the "vacation of the law."

[41] G. J. King, "The Acceptance of Law by the Community: A Study of the Writings of Canonists and Theologians," *J* 37 (1977) 233–265; J. Coriden, "The Canonical Doctrine of Reception," *J* 50 (1990) 58–82.

[42] G. Michiels, *Normae generales juris canonici,* 2nd ed. (Paris: Typis Societatis S. Joannis Evangelistae, Desclée, 1949) 1:646–649; J. Huels, "Nonreception of Canon Law by the Community," *New Theology Review* 4 (1991) 47–61.

[43] L. J. Riley, *The History, Nature and Use of Epikia in Moral Theology* (Washington, D.C.: Catholic University of America, 1948). This Greek word is spelled variously by writers in English, most often *epieikeia* or *epikeia*.

[44] L. Örsy, *Theology and Canon Law* (Collegeville: Liturgical Press, 1992) 41–52.

The *vacatio* is the period between the date of promulgation and the date the law goes into effect. Its purpose is to allow the Christian community some time to adjust to the new law, to make necessary arrangements for administration, catechesis of the faithful, and the like. The normal suspensive period is, for universal law, three months from the date of the issue of the *Acta Apostolicae Sedis* (*AAS*) in which the law is published and, for particular laws, one month from the date of promulgation. If the text makes no express mention of the date on which the law is to go into force, then this normal suspensive period is intended, unless by its very nature the law begins to bind immediately.

For a shorter or longer suspensive period, the date the law goes into effect must be expressly stated. Sometimes the suspensive period of a universal law is longer than three months; for example, in the case of a new code that contains many laws, it is necessary to allow more time to get acquainted with and implement them.[45] Some laws bind immediately because of their nature. Among these are laws that are statements of the divine law, authentic interpretations of laws that are merely declarative (c. 16, §2), laws requiring an immediate binding force in order that their purpose be fulfilled, laws that are merely qualifications of or technical points about other laws,[46] laws that are beneficial to the spiritual well-being of the faithful but do not affect the rights of third parties or require any organizational preparation or changes, and laws that revoke an earlier law that has become unnecessary or unjust as a result of a new situation.[47]

Publication in the *Acta Apostolicae Sedis,* the official journal of the Apostolic See, is the ordinary way in which universal laws are promulgated.[48] The first volume of this journal appeared in 1909. Its predecessor was the *Acta Sanctae Sedis,* published from 1865 to 1908. The magisterial and juridical texts of the pope and the more important documents of the Roman Curia are published in the *AAS* in the original language, usually Latin, but occasionally in a modern language like Italian. The language of promulgation is the official version, so any doubts regarding a translation and its interpretation must be resolved by examining the promulgated version. Sometimes the full text of a law is not given in the *AAS,* but only the decree of promulgation. This is the case, for example, with the laws appearing in the liturgical books and rites, which are published separately by the Vatican Press. At other times, an entire book of laws is published in the *AAS,* as in the case of the two codes, the Code of Canon Law and the Code of Canons of the Eastern Churches. The pope can also choose other means of promulgation, for example, by publication of the text in *L'Osservatore Romano.*

Particular laws are promulgated by whatever method the legislator chooses; they begin to bind one month from the date of promulgation, unless something else is expressly stated.[49] A diocesan law, for example, could be promulgated by its publication in the diocesan newspaper or newsletter, by being sent to all the parishes or to all juridic persons, etc. A document containing numerous laws, such as the diocesan synod might draw up, should be promulgated by a general decree of the diocesan bishop (c. 29); it suffices to publish the decree while making the document available only to those concerned. The mode of promulgation for

---

[45] The *vacatio* for the 1983 code was from January 25 to November 27, 1983. For the Eastern code, it was from October 18, 1990 to October 1, 1991.

[46] E.g., SCRIS, decr *Iuris Canonici Codice* and decr *Praescriptis canonum,* February 2, 1984, *AAS* 76 (1984) 499–500; *CLD* 11, 84–85, 91–92.

[47] *Münster Com,* 8/4–8/5.

[48] The 1917 code, c. 9, required publication in the *AAS* only of laws given by the Apostolic See, whereas this code requires all universal laws, including the laws of an ecumenical council, ordinarily to be so promulgated. The former code also made no provision for the promulgation of particular laws.

[49] *CCEO* 1489, §2 specifies no *vacatio* for laws by legislators other than the Apostolic See, but leaves this to the legislators themselves to prescribe.

the law of a particular council or conference of bishops is also determined by the legislators in question (cf. cc. 446, 455, §3), for example, by sending the law to all the diocesan bishops.

Although they are acts of executive rather than legislative power, general executory decrees must likewise be promulgated in accord with the requirements of canon 8 (c. 31, §2). This rule would also apply to other general administrative norms given for the community, whether by the dicasteries of the Roman Curia or other lesser executive authorities. Such norms, given for the community, function in the same way as laws, though of lesser authority, and so must be formally made public to the community. Usually the documents of the Roman Curia containing such norms are published in the *AAS,* but sometimes they appear in other publications of the Apostolic See, such as *L'Osservatore Romano* or *Notitiae,* or as booklets by the Vatican Press, as in the case of lengthy directories. Instructions (c. 34) and related norms and documents intended for the executors of the law are sent directly to the executors in question and begin to bind immediately, unless noted otherwise. Although instructions of the Roman Curia are sometimes published in the *AAS* or other journals of the Apostolic See, this is not required, unless a document is approved *in forma specifica* by the pope, in which case it has the force of law.

Non-retroactivity of Law

Canon 9 — Laws regard the future, not the past, unless they expressly provide for the past.

The principle of the non-retroactivity of law has already been seen in canon 4 with respect to acquired rights, and here it is stated in general fashion. As a rule, law is not retroactive; it affects only future activity, that is, what will take place after the law has gone into force.[50] For example,

the liturgical law states that there should only be one altar in a church, unless an additional altar is located in a separate blessed sacrament chapel.[51] This law is binding only with respect to churches built since 1977, when it went into effect. The side altars in older churches may be removed to conform to the law, but this is not required. Another example is the marriage impediment of spiritual relationship, which existed in the 1917 code (*CIC* 1079, 768), but is not in the 1983 code. Thus, a marriage between a person and his or her godparent would be valid if it took place on or after November 27, 1983, but invalid before. A new law does not change juridical effects brought about under a former law. The legality of an act and its effects must be determined according to the law in force at the time of the act, not a law that went into force after the act took place.

Laws that are expressions of the divine law are always retroactive, as in the case of laws that stipulate the essential elements of capability or will needed to place a juridic act, insofar as they emanate from the divine natural law. For example, certain grounds for the invalidity of marriage in the 1983 code were not in the 1917 code, but they may be applied to marriages celebrated under the former law because they are based on the divine law (e.g., cc. 1095, §3; 1097, §2; 1098).

All authentic interpretations of law that are merely declarative have retroactive force (c. 16, §2).[52] General administrative norms contained in documents of the Roman Curia and other general norms of executive authorities are retroactive, insofar as such norms are merely rephrasing, clarifying, or elaborating on laws that have already been in force. If any such norm enunciates a rule or imposes an obligation not found in the law al-

---

[50] This principle of the non-retroactivity of law is longstanding in canon law, going back to Roman law (C. 1, 14, 7).

[51] *Rite of Dedication of a Church and an Altar,* IV, 7.

[52] It is not always evident which authentic interpretations are merely declarative. This determination is left to the canonical science, as the PCILT does not indicate what kind of interpretation it is making. See L. G. Wrenn, *Authentic Interpretations on the 1983 Code* (Washington, D.C.: CLSA, 1993); hereafter cited as Wrenn, *Authentic Interpretations.*

ready, it is not retroactive but binds only from the moment the document goes into force.

Ecclesiastical laws that have a retroactive effect must expressly (*nominatim*) provide for the past. A law whose retroactive application is doubtful may not be held to be retroactive. Retroactive laws are an exception. They should be made only for pressing reasons or when the benefits are appreciable, especially for the common good, to extend a favor, or to conform obsolete structures and institutes to a new juridical reality, such as that brought about by the reforms of Vatican II. A retroactive law should not be made if it would have an adverse effect on persons or groups, unless there is a substantial and overriding benefit to the common good.[53]

An example of retroactive law is the rule that the penal law more favorable to the offender is to be applied (c. 1313), whether this be the law presently in force or the law in force when the crime was committed. Another example of the law operating retroactively to favor persons is seen in the canonical institute of radical sanation (*sanatio in radice*), whereby an invalid juridic act is made valid and all the effects of the act are recognized retroactively, as if the act had been valid from the beginning (e.g., c. 1161).

Invalidating and Disqualifying Laws

Canon 10 — Only those laws must be considered invalidating or disqualifying which expressly establish that an act is null or that a person is unqualified.

Invalidating laws (*leges irritantes*) establish the necessary requirements of a juridic *act,* such that their non-fulfillment would render the act in-

valid, null and void, not recognized as legally existing. For example, canon 1108, §1 states that the marriage (a juridic act) of a Catholic is valid only if celebrated according to the canonical form. Disqualifying laws (*leges inhabilitantes*) establish the necessary qualifications required of a *person* validly to perform or benefit from a juridic act, such that the act is invalid if the person lacks an essential requirement. For example, canon 658 states that a religious must be at least twenty-one and must have been in temporary vows for at least three years to make perpetual profession validly; and canon 842, §1 states that one who is not baptized cannot validly receive any other sacrament.

Invalidating and disqualifying laws must *expressly* establish, whether explicitly or implicitly, that an act is null or a person is unqualified. The law uses many explicit expressions pertaining to validity and capability, notably *capax esse; dirimere; habere effectum, obtinere effectum* or *sortiri effectum; incapax; inhabilis; invalidus; irritus; nullus; valide; validitas; validus; vi carere; vim habere; vim non habere;* and *vitiare.*[54]

A law is implicitly invalidating or disqualifying when it has no explicit reference to validity or capability. However, an invalidating or disqualifying intent can be demonstrated from the text and context of the law, parallel places in the law, the purpose and circumstances of the law, the mind of the legislator (cf. c. 17), and/or by reference to the canonical tradition (cf. c. 6, §2).[55] If doubt re-

---

[53] E.g., c. 510, §1, based on *ES* 21, §2, establishes the rule that parishes are not to be joined to a chapter of canons, and it requires the diocesan bishop to enforce this rule retroactively. The continuation of a juridic person as pastor would not only be obsolete and anomalous in the new juridic order but, more important, it would adversely affect the common good by depriving the parishioners of the benefits of having an actual person as their pastor.

[54] For canon citations, see X. Ochoa, *Index verborum ac locutionum Codicis iuris canonici,* 2nd ed. (Vatican City: Libreria Editrice Lateranense, 1984).

[55] There is no uniform approach among the commentators on this canon as to the criteria for verifying an implicitly invalidating or disqualifying law. This approach directs the interpreter of the law not to look for certain words in the text but to consider broader factors before concluding whether a law pertains to validity. One must also bear in mind the norm of c. 124, §1.

Some examples of implicitly invalidating and disqualifying laws are cc. 16, §2 (*promulgari debet*); 176; 338, §1; 526, §2; 609, §1; 684, §3; 684, §5; 995, §1; 1012; 1420, §2 (*iudicare nequit*); and c. 1482, §1 (*substituere nequit*). In reference to c. 1012, to say that it per-

mains, the law may not be held to be invalidating or disqualifying.

Canon 10 refers only to the ecclesiastical law, not to requirements for validity that are of the divine law. Sometimes the canons give divine law requirements for validity without any express mention of this,[56] while at other times the canons expressly mention that a requirement of the divine law is for validity or capability.[57]

Subjects of the Law

Canon 11 — Merely ecclesiastical laws bind those who have been baptized in the Catholic Church or received into it, possess the sufficient use of reason, and, unless the law expressly provides otherwise, have completed seven years of age.

The laws intended by the canon are those that impose obligations, laws that command or forbid, those to which subjects of the law are bound (*tenentur*), not laws that confer rights or divine laws that bind everyone. All three conditions of this canon must be met for ecclesiastical laws to bind. The person must: (1) be a Catholic; (2) possess sufficient use of reason; and (3) be at least seven years of age, unless something else is specified in the *ius*.

Catholics

The law recognizes as Catholic anyone baptized in the Catholic Church or received into it. One is baptized in the Catholic Church by a Catholic minister or, in necessity, also by a non-Catholic minister, if the adult recipient or the parents or guardian of an infant intend a baptism into the Catholic Church (cf. c. 97, §2; 99). An infant

of non-Catholic parents or guardian, baptized in danger of death by a Catholic minister,[58] is a member of the church or ecclesial community of the parents or guardian, unless they intended the infant to be baptized and raised as a Catholic, or unless they are not Christians.

Anyone seven or older with the use of reason who was baptized in a non-Catholic church or ecclesial community is received into the full communion of the Catholic Church by means of the *Rite of Reception of Baptized Christians into the Full Communion of the Catholic Church.*[59] Anyone under seven or without the use of reason who was baptized in a non-Catholic church or ecclesial community is received into the Catholic Church simply by a parent or guardian declaring his or her intention orally or in writing to the pastor or local ordinary that the infant is to be received into the Catholic Church and will be raised in the Catholic religion.[60]

Once a Catholic by baptism or reception, one always remains a Catholic (*semel catholicus, semper catholicus*).[61] Even those who have joined another religion, have become atheists or agnostics, or have been excommunicated remain Catholics. Excommunicates lose rights, such as the right to the sacraments, but they are still bound to the obligations of the law; their rights are restored when they are reconciled through the remission of the penalty. In three instances, the code grants an exemption from certain requirements of marriage law for the benefit of Catholics who have left the Church by means of a formal act (cc. 1086, §1; 1117; 1124). Although such Catholics have formally joined another religion or made it known in some formal way that they are not Catholic, they are still Catholic in virtue of baptism or reception

---

tains to validity does not imply a resolution of the theological question as to whether the pope may delegate a presbyter to ordain, but is simply an assertion of the legal reality.

[56] E.g., cc. 845, §1; 880; 924; 960; 965; 987; 998; 1000; 1009, §2; 1057, §1; 1141.

[57] E.g., cc. 842, §1; 849; 864; 889, §1; 900, §1; 1003, §1; 1024; 1084, §1; 1085.

[58] See c. 861; *CCEO* 677.

[59] This rite is contained in the *RCIA*.

[60] See J. Huels, "The Valid Minister of Catholic Baptism and Receiving an Infant into Full Communion," in *Roman Replies and CLSA Advisory Opinions 1999* (Washington, D.C.: CLSA, 1999) 76–79.

[61] The *coetus* revising Book I specifically rejected any notion of the Church as a society that anyone could freely leave at will. *Comm* 14 (1980) 133.

and may be reconciled to the Church whenever they choose to conform to the requirements of the law.

The limitation of canonical obligations to Catholics is one of the most important innovations of the 1983 code. Canon 12 of the 1917 code had bound all the baptized to the ecclesiastical laws of the Catholic Church. The implication of the revised law, based on the doctrine of Vatican II, is that non-Catholic Christians have an ecclesial reality of their own and are bound to the laws of their own church or ecclesial community.[62] In some exceptional instances, non-Catholics are required to observe specific laws of the Church, such as when they wish to become a Catholic,[63] be a party to a case before a church tribunal (c. 1476), marry a Catholic (e.g., cc. 1108, 1118, 1125), or receive a sacrament from a Catholic minister (c. 844, §§ 3–4). It is their own desire to interact in a specific way with the Catholic Church that brings about their subjection to the canonical discipline governing that interaction.

Sufficient Use of Reason

In virtue of the divine natural law, one must have sufficient use of reason to be bound by law. Use of reason refers to the ability to conceptualize, make abstractions, and take responsibility for one's own actions. The minimal use of reason required for the subject of canon law would be that of normal seven-year-old children (cf. c. 97, §2). Persons who lack this minimal reasoning capacity, such as those with severe mental illnesses and de-

velopmental disabilities like mental retardation, cannot morally or legally be bound to the law. They lack adequate mental capacity to understand and remember the law, and to foresee and evaluate the consequences of their own actions. They are legally incompetent (*non sui compos*); they cannot act for themselves in law but must be represented by a guardian or curator.

The canonical notion of "use of reason" cannot be applied without reference to developmental psychology and other pertinent sciences. Intellectual and volitional capacity are acquired gradually as a child develops. The use of reason of the normal seven-year-old child does not make the child capable of all legal or moral acts. It takes considerably more understanding and discretion to commit a mortal sin, profess religious vows, marry, or be ordained than it does to receive Holy Communion or the anointing of the sick. The canon speaks of the *sufficient* use of reason, that which is sufficient for performing the act, exercising the right, or fulfilling the obligation in question.

At Least Seven Years Old

Besides possessing the sufficient use of reason, the subject of the law must also have completed at least seven years of age,[64] unless another age is expressly stated in the *ius* (law or administrative norm).[65] Although some children below the age of seven may have already attained sufficient use of reason (relative to a law in question), still they are not bound to observe the law. The more important canonical obligations binding those who are at least seven and have the use of reason are to attend Mass and refrain from burdensome labor on Sundays and holy days (c. 1247), to confess all

---

[62] *LG* 8; *OE* 5; *UR* 3, 8, 15, 16. *UR* 3 speaks of significant ecclesial elements and endowments that exist in other Christian churches and ecclesial communities, including "visible elements," among which would certainly be their own laws and customs. This is recognized explicitly in *CCEO* 780, §2 in respect to marriage law, which is a fundamental rule equally valid in the Latin canon law.

[63] These would be principally the obligations of the liturgical laws governing the catechumenate and reception into full communion. See J. Huels, *The Catechumenate and the Law* (Chicago: Liturgy Training Publications, 1994), 10–13, 18–20.

[64] In canon law, one completes a year of life at midnight at the end of one's birthday. The seventh birthday is the final day of one's seventh year, so the law begins to bind the next day. See cc. 202–203.

[65] The law sometimes speaks of the "age of discretion." This is to be understood as the age of seven, or a later age at which a person achieves the use of reason if this was not attained by the age of seven.

serious sins at least once a year (c. 989) and, once they have made their first Communion, to receive Communion at least once a year (c. 920). Certain canonical obligations begin to bind at higher ages: fourteen for abstinence (c. 1252), sixteen for subjection to sanctions (c. 1323, 1°), and eighteen for fasting (c. 1252). Likewise, various canonical rights of the faithful are acquired by law at different ages.[66]

Universal and Particular Laws

Canon 12 — §1. Universal laws bind everywhere all those for whom they were issued.

§2. All who are actually present in a certain territory, however, are exempted from universal laws which are not in force in that territory.

§3. Laws established for a particular territory bind those for whom they were issued as well as those who have a domicile or quasi-domicile there and who at the same time are actually residing there, without prejudice to the prescript of can. 13.

Canon 13 — §1. Particular laws are not presumed to be personal but territorial unless it is otherwise evident.

§2. Travelers are not bound:

1° by the particular laws of their own territory as long as they are absent from it unless either the transgression of those laws causes harm in their own territory or the laws are personal;

2° by the laws of the territory in which they are present, with the exception of those laws which provide for public order, which determine the formalities of acts, or which regard immovable goods located in the territory.

§3. Transients are bound by both universal and particular laws which are in force in the place where they are present.

---

[66] See B. F. Griffin, "The Ages of Man," in *Code, Community, Ministry,* 2nd rev. ed., ed. E. G. Pfnausch (Washington, D.C.: CLSA, 1992) 18–20.

Universal laws are made for the Latin church by the supreme legislator—the pope or college of bishops (or their delegate)—and they bind those for whom they were made everywhere they go (e.g., clerics, pastors, all the faithful, etc.). If a particular territory has an exemption from a universal law, anyone present in the territory is exempt from that law, not only those with domicile and quasi-domicile but also travelers.[67] A universal law might not be binding in a specific territory for various reasons: (1) a contrary custom, including desuetude;[68] (2) a contrary particular law, not expressly revoked, that was in force before the universal law went into force (cf. cc. 20, 135, §2), or a contrary particular law that the Holy See made or confirmed; (3) an apostolic privilege (c. 76) or other apostolic indult; or (4) a dispensation for a particular case (c. 85).

Particular laws may be territorial or personal. Personal laws are given for non-territorially defined groups of persons that are capable of receiving a law, such as institutes of consecrated life and societies of apostolic life, personal prelatures, and various associations of the faithful.[69] Personal laws bind the persons for whom they were given wherever they go. The presumption of the law is that particular laws are territorial, unless they are clearly personal.[70] For example, a diocesan bishop makes a law pertaining to the exercise of the apostolate by religious. Although the law is given for members of religious institutes, it is territorial

---

[67] A common example is holy days of obligation. Although there may be an obligation to attend Mass in one's own country on a certain feast, one is exempt when visiting a country that does not observe the feast as a day of obligation.

[68] A contrary custom is a practice of the community contrary to the law; desuetude is the contrary custom of not observing the law for a sustained period.

[69] On the notion of a community capable of receiving a law, see the commentary for c. 25. Statutes of juridic persons, such as the constitutions of religious institutes, are an example of personal law (*ius*) in the broad sense; statutes may also be given legislative force (c. 94, §3).

[70] On the notion of "presumptions" in canon law, see L. Örsy, in *CLSA Com,* 33.

because it applies only to religious who exercise the apostolate in the territory of the diocese. However, a diocesan law governing the spiritual obligations of members of diocesan religious institutes would be a personal law and would apply to the religious even when they are not in the diocese. If there is a doubt as to whether a law is personal, it must be considered territorial.

Canons 12 and 13 are concerned with particular laws that are territorial.[71] Territorial particular laws are given for ecclesiastical territories, especially dioceses, provinces, and the nation or group of nations that makes up a conference of bishops.[72] The diocesan bishop or higher legislator can make laws binding in the diocese. A provincial council or the supreme legislator can make laws for the province. A plenary council, the conference of bishops, or the supreme legislator can make laws for the nation or other territory that makes up the conference. Such territorial particular laws bind those for whom they were issued.[73] As a rule, particular law binds only those who have a domicile or quasi-domicile in the territory (c. 102), and only when they are actually in their territory.

Travelers and Transients

The second and third paragraphs of canon 13 provide special rules governing the observance of particular laws by travelers (*peregrini*) and transients (*vagi*). Travelers are persons who are outside their place of domicile or quasi-domicile; transients have no domicile or quasi-domicile (cc. 100, 107). Along with the rules, several exceptions are given. All these exceptions are subject to strict interpretation, not only because they are exceptions, but also because a broad application of them would restrict the free exercise of personal rights.[74]

Generally, travelers are not bound to the particular laws of their own territory when they are absent from that territory. One exception to this rule has already been noted: personal laws bind everywhere. The other exception is for laws whose transgression would cause harm in one's own territory. Such would include laws that regulate the duties of office, residence, and participation in a diocesan synod or particular council.[75] In all such cases, there must be a real danger of harm in one's own territory or the law does not oblige outside the territory, even if one leaves the territory to avoid observing the law.

As a rule, travelers also are not bound to the laws of the territory in which they are traveling. However, they are bound to laws that provide for public order (*ordo publicus*), determine legal formalities (*sollemnia actuum*), or pertain to immovable goods in that territory.

The concept of *public order* was introduced in the late nineteenth century by canonists who borrowed the idea from civil law, especially from French and Italian jurists. It formally entered canon law in the 1917 code (*CIC* 14, §1, 2°). Laws that protect the public order are those that are so necessary for the good of the community that, when violated, the common good would be harmed.[76] Such laws are indispensable to the society and their violation would be disruptive. Laws that provide for public order include those affecting the exercise of authority (judicial power, administrative offices, parochial functions); governing meetings, public events, and the public celebration of the liturgy; preventing offenses to the faith; and laws given specifically for travelers.[77] The public

---

[71] Universal laws may be seen as either territorial or personal. The effect is the same: they bind everywhere those persons for whom they were issued.

[72] See cc. 368, 391, 431, 439, 445, 447, 455.

[73] Even a pontifical particular law binds only in the territory for which it was made.

[74] On strict interpretation, see the commentary on c. 18.

[75] *Com Ex*, 1:335. For example, a diocesan law says that if a parish priest is going to be away from the parish on a Sunday or holy day and he has no one to replace him, he must notify the local ordinary. The parish priest would not be exempt from this law merely by leaving the diocese, because it would bring harm in his own territory.

[76] Cf. *Comm* 16 (1984) 148.

[77] For example, in a certain diocese, a law requires that visiting priests who stay more than a month in the diocese must receive permission of the local ordinary to exercise public ministry in the diocese. Even though these priests

order should not be confused with uniformity of conduct. While an orderly and well-regulated community is desirable, every community may tolerate reasonable exceptions for travelers.[78]

Formalities of acts are the legal formalities connected with contracts, bequests, administrative and judicial procedures, and other juridic acts (cf. c. 124, §1). *Immovable goods* are land, buildings, and any other structures that are not movable. The observance of laws pertaining to immovable goods and legal formalities follows the legal principle that "the place regulates the act" (*locus regit actum*).

Transients are persons without any domicile or quasi-domicile. They are bound by both universal and particular laws wherever they are at the time. They are fully subjects of the law and enjoy all the rights of the faithful, including the right to pastoral care and liturgical celebrations within the context of parish and diocese (c. 107, §2).

The rules of the Eastern code governing the observance of particular laws are comparable to those of canons 12 and 13 of the Latin code (*CCEO* 1491). The Eastern code does not speak of universal law but of "laws enacted by the supreme authority of the Church," which bind everywhere unless given for a particular territory.[79] It uses the term common law (*ius commune*) for the laws and legitimate customs of the universal Church and for those common to all the Eastern churches *sui iuris*. It uses the term particular law (*ius particulare*) for all laws, legitimate customs, statutes, and other norms of law (*ius*) which are not common to the universal Church or all the Eastern churches.[80]

---

are outside their own territory and do not have quasi-domicile after only a month in the new territory, the particular law in question was made precisely to regulate their situation for the public order of the diocese, for the common good.

[78] See J. H. Hackett, *The Concept of Public Order, Can-LawStud* 399 (1959) 74.

[79] *CCEO* 1491, §1; 1492.

[80] *CCEO* 1493. In the 1917 Latin code, "common law" was used for what is now called "universal law." A vestige of this use can be seen in c. 1362, § 1, 3°.

Doubts of Law and Fact

Canon 14 — Laws, even invalidating and disqualifying ones, do not oblige when there is a doubt about the law. When there is a doubt about a fact, however, ordinaries can dispense from laws provided that, if it concerns a reserved dispensation, the authority to whom it is reserved usually grants it.

Doubt is the state of mind withholding assent between two contradictory propositions. If there exist alternative interpretations of a law or fact, and each is supported by *objective* reasons, this leads to uncertainty. The doubt must be *positive,* founded on reasons pro and con; a negative doubt is ignorance. If someone does not know the meaning of a law or the existence of a fact, this is not objective but subjective doubt, or ignorance. The doubt must also be *probable,* that is, the reasons pro and con are sound.

A doubt of law (*dubium iuris*) occurs when it is impossible to achieve moral certainty concerning the law's meaning, applicability in a particular case, or force. Even experts cannot resolve the doubt. When there is a doubt of law, even if the law is invalidating or incapacitating, the law in question does not oblige. If the doubtful law is beneficial, for example, granting some favor, then one may continue to benefit from the doubtful law. However, if the law imposes an obligation or restricts freedom, the doubtful law does not oblige. The legislator does not want the community to be in confusion about its obligations, but intends the law to give clear directions for ordering ecclesial life.

A doubt of law may pertain to: (1) the meaning of the law; (2) the extent of its application to doubtful cases; (3) its legitimate promulgation and force; or (4) its revocation.[81] Rarely is the meaning of a law objectively doubtful, but it can happen. A doubt about a law's meaning is usually resolved over time by an authentic interpretation

---

[81] On doubtful revocation, see the commentary on cc. 20–21.

(c. 16, §2),[82] by a new law that rephrases the matter with greater clarity, or by developments in canonical doctrine that lead to a consensus among experts that overcomes the doubt.

The doubt might arise not about the meaning of the law but about the extent of its application to doubtful cases. For example, canon 455 requires that general decrees of conferences of bishops be approved by two-thirds of the members and obtain the *recognitio* of the Apostolic See. A doubt arose as to whether general decrees referred only to the general decrees of canons 29–30 or also extended to the general executory decrees of canons 31–33. The response determined that the procedure for the approval of general decrees must also be extended to general executory decrees.[83]

Various doubts may arise concerning the law's legitimate promulgation and force, such as: whether the necessary formalities of promulgation were observed; whether the supreme legislator expressly delegated legislative power or approved a curial decree *in forma specifica;*[84] whether the law is intended to have prescriptive or merely directive force (e.g., calling "guidelines" a diocesan policy intended to be normative); whether the matter was within the legislator's competence (e.g., a diocesan policy requiring reservation of the Blessed Sacrament in the sanctuary of the church rather than in a special chapel as preferred in the universal law).

A doubt of fact (*dubium facti*) refers to a doubt about some concrete fact that pertains to the law's applicability, such as doubts concerning age, relationship, valid baptism, validity of other sacraments and juridic acts, membership in the Catholic Church, etc. When there is a doubt of fact, the ordinary (c. 134) may dispense. The dispensation is necessary in the case of an invalidating or incapacitating law (e.g., a marriage impediment).

The doubt must be objective and positive. In merely subjective doubt, or ignorance, a thorough investigation must be undertaken to the extent possible to ascertain the facts (e.g., as required in canon 869). If the fact is verified, the law applies; if the contrary, it does not. However, if the investigation is inconclusive and the doubt remains, the ordinary may dispense. For example, in a customary society where no birth records are kept, a young man wants to get married. He looks to be about sixteen (cf. c. 1083, §1), but an investigation reveals that no testimonies provide conclusive proof of sufficient age. The ordinary may dispense to permit the marriage. The doubt here is not mere ignorance. A positive reason exists for believing the young man is old enough to marry because he appears to be sixteen, though the contrary possibility cannot be excluded.

In a doubt of fact, the ordinary may also dispense from laws whose dispensation is reserved to higher authority, provided the higher authority usually grants the dispensation.[85] For example, in danger of death, the Apostolic See usually dispenses from the obligations of priestly celibacy, which permits the priest to convalidate an attempted marriage. In a particular case, a priest admits he never wanted to be ordained, so a doubt arises about the validity of his ordination (the *dubium facti*). Since there is no time to resolve the doubt by a canonical process (cc. 1708–1712), the ordinary may dispense from the obligations of

---

[82] The first authentic interpretation of the 1983 code concerned the word *iterum* in canon 917 on receiving Communion more than once a day. The meaning of the canon was doubtful because *iterum* can mean "a second time" or "again." The latter is more open-ended and would have enabled a person to receive Holy Communion as often as he or she attended Mass, not just twice in one day. However, the authentic interpretation determined that the meaning was "a second time." PCILT, August 7, 1984, *AAS* 76 (1984) 746; *Pamplona ComEng,* 1293–1295. *CCC* 1388 must be read in light of this authentic interpretation.

[83] PCILT, August 1, 1985, *AAS* 77 (1985) 771; *Pamplona ComEng,* 1289. This might also be seen as merely declaring that the meaning of "general decree" includes decrees that are both legislative and executory.

[84] Doubt about this can arise only in reference to documents published before June 7, 1992 when a revised *Regolamento generale della Curia romana* went into effect. See commentary on c. 7 above.

[85] See cc. 291; 1047, §§ 1–3; and 1078, §2 for dispensations reserved to the Apostolic See in the code.

celibacy and the subsequent marriage would be presumed valid, even if later the priest survived and the validity of his ordination were upheld.

The ordinary may not dispense in a doubt of fact when the dispensation is reserved to a higher authority who does not usually grant it or when dispensation in doubt is expressly excluded by law. For example, if there is a doubt as to whether a man and woman are related in the direct line or second degree collateral line of consanguinity, marriage is not permitted and a dispensation is not given (cc. 1078, §3; 1091, §4).

The power to dispense in this canon is broader in some respects than the typical rules for dispensation (cc. 85–93). In doubt of fact, any competent ordinary, not just the diocesan bishop (c. 87, §1), may dispense from universal laws; any competent ordinary, not just the local ordinary (c. 88), may dispense from particular laws; and laws reserved to higher authority can be dispensed by the ordinary even if recourse to the higher authority is possible and there is no danger of grave harm in delay (cf. c. 87, §2), provided the higher authority usually dispenses in the circumstances of the case. Under the meaning of reserved laws in canon 14 must also be understood merely ecclesiastical procedural and penal laws (c. 87, §1). Divine laws and constitutive laws may never be dispensed.

Ignorance and Error

Canon 15 — §1. Ignorance or error about invalidating or disqualifying laws does not impede their effect unless it is expressly established otherwise.

§2. Ignorance or error about a law, a penalty, a fact concerning oneself, or a notorious fact concerning another is not presumed; it is presumed about a fact concerning another which is not notorious until the contrary is proven.

Ignorance is lack of knowledge.[86] Error is mistaken judgment. The two are related, since error is based on insufficient knowledge, but it is not a total absence of knowledge; it is an erroneous application of one's knowledge. With respect to invalidating and incapacitating laws, ignorance and error usually have no effect; actions posited in ignorance or error remain valid or invalid, irrespective of what the person thought or judged at the time. Canon 15 upholds stability in the community. Invalidating and incapacitating laws are generally the most important laws in the canonical system. If they were to become ineffectual due to ignorance or error, the legal system would break down; there would never be certainty that juridic acts were valid. Thus, the canon establishes the rule that ignorance or error does not affect invalidating and incapacitating laws, unless it is expressly established otherwise.[87]

For example, a woman marries her second cousin (sixth degree collateral consanguinity), and she erroneously concludes that she has married invalidly because she had heard that a dispensation was necessary to marry a relative. Her mistaken judgment about the application of canon law does not affect the marriage, which is valid, provided she truly consented to marry him (cf. c. 1091, §2). The same principle is true with respect to ignorance. For example, an unbaptized man receives Holy Communion, but is ignorant of the law that baptism is necessary to receive any other sacrament (c. 842, §1). Ignorance does not affect this incapacitating law, and he receives invalidly.

---

[86] The canonical doctrine on ignorance has its roots in Roman law (D. 50, 17, 42; D. 50, 17, 206). This tradition is reflected in rule 13 ("Ignorance of fact excuses, but not of law"), and rule 47 ("Ignorance is presumed where knowledge is not proven") of the *Regulae Juris in Sexto* (hereafter cited as *RI* rule #). Translations of *RI* are from A. Gauthier, *Roman Law and Its Contribution to the Development of Canon Law* (Ottawa: Faculty of Canon Law, St. Paul University, 1996) 108, 112 (hereafter cited as Gauthier).

Inadvertence and forgetfulness, in practical cases, usually may be considered equivalent to ignorance and error.

[87] Some exceptions are the exercise of delegated power in the internal forum in inadvertence (c. 142, §2); common error of fact or law (c. 144); and the effects of ignorance and error on matrimonial consent (cc. 1096–1098).

The second paragraph states a presumption of law (*praesumptio iuris*). A presumption of law refers to a fact that the law presumes. It is a given and need not be proven. Instead, the burden is on the person who wants to prove the opposite. This is the key difference between paragraph one, which admits of no contrary proofs, and paragraph two, which does. The law does not presume ignorance or error about:

1) *A law.* The law always presumes knowledge of the law, even if in fact one is ignorant of it. Ignorance of the law does not excuse, unless the law provides otherwise.

2) *A penalty.* As with a law, knowledge of penalties is presumed. To claim exemption from or mitigation of a penalty, one would have to prove ignorance or error to the extent this is permitted in the law (c. 1323, 2°, 7°; 1324, §1, 8°–9°).

3) *A fact concerning oneself.* The law presumes that all people with the use of reason have knowledge of their own actions and other facts about themselves.

4) *A notorious fact concerning another.* Notorious means well known, something that is public knowledge, that the average person would know about.

Without these presumptions, the legal system would be ineffectual, because anyone who claimed ignorance or error could not be held accountable. In all these cases, the presumption of the law can be overturned, but the burden of proof falls on the person asserting ignorance or error.

The law does presume ignorance or error about a fact concerning another that is not notorious, that is, a fact that is not public knowledge. However, this presumption could be overturned by proofs. For example, a woman married a man who is a homosexual and she now petitions for a declaration of invalidity on the ground of error re-

garding a quality of a person (c. 1097, §2). The court would not initially presume that she knew of the man's sexual orientation at the time she married him, but the evidence of the case might overturn this presumption.

Official Interpretation of Law

Canon 16 — §1. The legislator authentically interprets laws as does the one to whom the same legislator has entrusted the power of authentically interpreting.

§2. An authentic interpretation put forth in the form of law has the same force as the law itself and must be promulgated. If it only declares the words of the law which are certain in themselves, it is retroactive; if it restricts or extends the law, or if it explains a doubtful law, it is not retroactive.

§3. An interpretation in the form of a judicial sentence or of an administrative act in a particular matter, however, does not have the force of law and only binds the persons for whom and affects the matters for which it was given.

Canon law is officially interpreted by the legislator and by judges and administrators. The first two paragraphs treat the authentic interpretation of law by an authority with legislative power; such an interpretation, when given in the form of law, has the force of law and binds everyone for whom it is given. The third paragraph treats the interpretation of laws in concrete cases given in the form of judicial and administrative acts; such a practical interpretation binds only the parties involved in the case.[88]

---

[88] Commentators do not agree whether the term "authentic interpretation" should be limited to an act of the legislator given in the form of law, whether it includes also judicial or administrative interpretations, or whether judicial and administrative interpretations may be either authentic or non-authentic. These views are nicely summarized, with references, in *Münster Com,* 16/10–11. We follow the view that authentic interpretations are only those given in the form of law.

Authentic Interpretation

It has already been noted in the commentary on canon 14 that an authentic interpretation by the legislator can officially resolve a doubt of law. Unlike the Anglo-American common law system where the courts settle the meaning of laws, in canon law the competent legislator determines the law's meaning and resolves doubts about it.[89] The supreme legislator entrusts certain powers of authentically interpreting law to the Pontifical Council for the Interpretation of Legislative Texts (PCILT).[90] Its competence extends to the interpretation of all the universal laws of the Latin church and the common laws of the Eastern churches.[91] Although the PCILT is not empowered to interpret particular laws authentically, it may, when requested, determine whether they are in accord with the universal law.[92]

The power to interpret law as treated in paragraphs one and two is legislative power. There-fore, only the supreme authority may delegate it (c. 135, §2), unless something else is specifically established in the law (*ius*).[93] The authentic interpretation of particular laws pertains to the competent legislator himself or to the supreme authority[94] or delegate of the same. Thus, a law of the conference of bishops is authentically interpreted either by the supreme authority or delegate of the same, or by the conference itself according to the procedure of canon 455. A law of the diocese may be interpreted authentically by the supreme legislator or delegate, or by the diocesan bishop himself.

There are four kinds of authentic interpretation. (1) *Declarative* interpretation merely affirms the meaning of the wording of the law that was already certain. (2) *Restrictive* interpretation narrows the meaning and applicability of the law. (3) *Extensive* interpretation broadens the meaning and applicability of the law beyond what is included in the text of the law. (4) *Explanatory* interpretation explains the meaning of a doubtful law, without extending or restricting its original meaning.

Declarative interpretation does nothing other than affirm the meaning of the law that is clear in itself. With restrictive and extensive interpretation, the applicability of the law is narrowed or broadened so that, effectively, it no longer has the same meaning. Explanatory interpretation makes no change in the literal meaning of the law, but determines the precise meaning of an ambiguous law. Explanatory interpretation is really the only one that resolves a doubt inherent in the wording of the law (cf. c. 14). The other three respond to the question: "Does this law really mean what it says?" A declarative interpretation

---

[89] In its classical period, Roman law was based on case law similar to Anglo-American common law, but with Justinian in the year 529, authentic interpretation was reserved to the emperor (C. 1. 14, 12). In the Middle Ages, canon law received from Roman law the principle that "the one who makes the law is the one who is competent to interpret it" (*Ad quem pertinet iuris constitutio, ad ipsum pertinet interpretatio*). See Gauthier, 20–21.

The legislator refers to the office or organ, not the person; thus it applies to the successors of the legislator or legislative body that made the law.

[90] This is its present name. From 1984 to 1989, before *PB* went into effect, it was called the Pontifical Commission for the Authentic Interpretation of the Code of Canon Law. Before that, Paul VI in 1966 had established the Commission for the Interpretation of the Decrees of the Second Vatican Council. There was also a commission for the interpretation of the 1917 code, and before that a commission for interpreting the decrees of the Council of Trent.

[91] See *PB* 154–158 for the competencies of the PCILT; translation in *Pamplona ComEng,* 1249. For its competency with respect to the common laws of the Eastern churches, see SS, letter, February 27, 1991, *Comm* 23 (1991) 14–15.

[92] *PB* 158.

[93] Only the supreme legislator could make a particular law granting to a lower legislator the faculty to delegate the power of authentically interpreting that legislator's laws.

[94] On this point we accept the view of *Chiappetta Com,* 2nd ed. (1996), 1:59, n. 284, that only the hierarchical superior of the legislator, not any higher legislator, may authentically interpret particular laws.

gives an affirmative answer to the question. A restrictive or extensive interpretation gives a negative answer, affirming that the law does not include this situation (restrictive), or that the law must be seen as also including this situation (extensive).

To have the force of law, authentic interpretations must be put forth in the form of law (*per modum legis*) and promulgated; they go into force after the *vacatio* defined in canon 8 has elapsed. An authentic interpretation given in the form of law has the same force as the law itself. A declarative interpretation has retroactive force, since no change is made to the law whose meaning was not objectively doubtful.[95] Extensive, restrictive, and explanatory interpretations are not retroactive with respect to that part of the law whose meaning is changed or explained.[96] Interpretation of a law that is based on the divine law is always retroactive.[97] In practice, it is often difficult to determine which kind of authentic interpretation of universal law is given, since the PCILT does not indicate this.[98] In cases of doubt as to whether an interpretation is merely declarative, the law may not be applied retroactively.

[95] The 1917 code, c. 17, §2, did not require that a declarative interpretation be issued in the form of law. The value of putting all interpretations in the form of law is that it clarifies the intention of the legislator to interpret the law authentically and consequently it removes doubt about the binding force of the interpretation, although doubt might remain about retroactivity if it is unclear whether the interpretation was declarative.

[96] E.g., the authentic interpretation that general executory decrees are included in the meaning of canon 455, §1 is not retroactive. General executory decrees previously enacted by the conferences of bishops do not need to be submitted to the Holy See for *recognitio,* but only those enacted since the authentic interpretation went into force. See PCILT, response, August 1, 1985, *AAS* 77 (1985) 771; *Pamplona ComEng,* 1289.

[97] See, e.g., the authentic interpretation on c. 1103, August 6, 1987, *AAS* 79 (1987) 1132; *Pamplona ComEng,* 1295.

[98] An attempt at classification is that of Wrenn, *Authentic Interpretations.* This work is a good basis for continuing discussion, but it does not seem necessary to use Wrenn's eight categories when c. 16 speaks of only four.

Interpretations not given in the form of law do not bind juridically.[99] The pope often interprets laws by his comments on them in non-legislative texts, such as his allocutions to the Roman Rota. Although these interpretations have great doctrinal value, they are not authentic interpretations of the law. While an authentic interpretation given in the form of law resolves a doubt and closes the debate, other interpretations (even those of the pope himself) allow insights in jurisprudence and canonical doctrine to continue developing within the general parameters established in the law and church teachings. The legislators of the Church also have teaching authority, but legislative and magisterial acts are distinct and should not be confused.

Judicial and Administrative Interpretation

Laws are also officially interpreted by judicial and executive authorities—by the judges in church tribunals and by church administrators (Vatican congregations, diocesan bishops, major superiors, vicars, etc.). Judicial sentences and individual administrative acts[100] involve interpreting the law and applying it to particular cases. Such interpretation has no impact on the meaning of the law and does not have the force of law, that is, it cannot be enforced generally. Judicial sentences and administrative acts bind only the party or parties for whom they are given. The parties are legally obliged to abide by the decision, notwithstanding their right to appeal or take recourse.

Judicial sentences and administrative decisions do not create binding precedents. Nevertheless, the decisions of the Roman Curia do have a kind of precedential value. The sentences of the Roman Rota have a great impact on other courts around the

[99] Theoretically, a merely declarative interpretation would be binding, even if not given in the form of law, in the sense that the law itself, which the interpretation reiterates, continues to bind. However, there is no juridical certainty that the legislator intends an authentic interpretation unless he gives it in the form of law.

[100] Canons 1607–1618; 35–93.

world. Judges on diocesan and regional tribunals routinely cite decisions of the Rota to strengthen their arguments. The jurisprudence of the Rota has also led to developments in the canon law of marriage, for example, regarding the "psychic grounds" for defective marriage consent (c. 1095) and *dolus* (c. 1098). Likewise, there is a kind of precedent in the administrative arena, since repeated decisions by the Roman Curia contribute to the *praxis curiae* (c. 19) and the canonical tradition (c. 6, §2). Lower level administrators and their advisors look to the practice of the Roman Curia for indications of how to settle similar cases.

Sometimes a Roman dicastery gives a declaration on a law's meaning or execution and it is published in the *Acta Apostolicae Sedis*. Such a decision, if given for a specific physical or juridic person, does not have general application. If the declaration is not directed to anyone in particular, it has general applicability and pertains to the authority of the Roman Curia to issue general administrative norms (cc. 31–34).[101]

Rules for Interpretation

Canon 17 — Ecclesiastical laws must be understood in accord with the proper meaning of the words considered in their text and context. If the meaning remains doubtful and obscure, recourse must be made to parallel places, if there are such, to the purpose and circumstances of the law, and to the mind of the legislator.

The canonical tradition holds in high regard, not only official interpretation by legislators, judges, and administrators, but also the private interpretation of canon law by scholars, which is called doctrinal interpretation. The rules of this canon, as well as those of canons 18 and 19, apply to everyone in-

terpreting canon law—church officials, scholars, and practitioners of the law.

The interpretation of an ecclesiastical law begins with understanding the proper meaning of the key words of the legal text. The "proper meaning" is the way the word or phrase is understood in the canonical tradition—in the practice of the Church and the writings of the "doctors," the canonical scholars. Many canonical words and expressions have a standard, technical meaning that is familiar to canonists but is often not evident to others.[102] Sometimes, this technical meaning cannot be known from the translation, for example, the difference between *lex* and *ius,* which are both translated in English as "law." The Latin text is the official text. If the Latin word is open to various meanings, looking at different translations to see how translators interpret the word is helpful.

The proper meaning of the words is not usually determined solely by examining the text of the law in isolation; the text must be seen in relation to other statements that make up the context of the law.[103] The context refers to related texts in the same book, document, or section in which the law is published, for example, the article, chapter, title, part, or book of the code in which a canon is found, or the introductory section of certain juridical documents that briefly provides the historical context, theoretical underpinnings, and rationale for the norms that follow. The context may often clarify the law's purpose and the way it functions in relationship to other laws surrounding it. By examining this context, the interpreter is better able to grasp the meaning of the key words and phrases of the law, which leads to its correct understanding and application.

If the meaning of the law is not clear from the text and its context, the canon directs the inter-

---

[101] This point is important to keep in mind in assessing the weight of responses of curial dicasteries that are translated in the *Canon Law Digest* and *Roman Replies*. Those that are private in character—given to individuals—are not binding on others, unless they are merely reiterations of the *ius vigens*.

[102] Ordinarily, a text of law does not define its own terms, but it does so now and then, e.g., cc. 29, 34, 48, 49, 59, 76, 85, 100, 102, 134, 145, 435, 573, 607, 710, 731, etc.

[103] See M. R. Torfs, "*Propria verborum significatio:* De l'épistémologie à l'herméneutique," *Stud Can* 29 (1995) 179–192.

preter of the law to make recourse to parallel places if they exist, to the purpose and circumstances of the law, and to the mind of the legislator. Actually, these additional steps are a necessary part of any thorough, scholarly interpretation of a law. While examining the text and context of a law is usually sufficient for applying the law in practical situations, the process delineated in the second sentence of the canon is always necessary for good doctrinal interpretation. This more thorough examination and explanation of the law is illuminating even if the law's meaning is not doubtful and obscure.

The first means given for acquiring a deeper understanding of the law is to look for any parallel places where the matter is treated in juridical texts.[104] These would be norms given elsewhere that treat the same subject or make use of the same rule or principle as that of the law at hand. Consulting the Eastern code to see how it treats a subject in the Latin code is often helpful, because there might be certain differences, as well as similarities, that may shed fuller light on the meaning of the Latin canon. Such parallel passages may also be found in juridical documents other than the two codes. For example, in reference to many canons of Book IV, parallel passages exist in the liturgical books, in the Constitution on the Liturgy of Vatican II, and in postconciliar documents.

Another means of interpreting the law is to seek to uncover the purpose of the law (*ratio legis*). Each law has a specific purpose, besides the overarching purpose of canon law itself, which is the spiritual welfare of the faithful, the *salus animarum* (cf. c. 1752). As noted above, the specific purpose of the law is sometimes discernible from the context, for example, in the introduction to or theological foundations of a juridical text.[105] Often, however, the purpose of the

law is only implicit and requires reflection on the law and its relation to its context, the legal system as a whole, and/or the very mission of the Church. Some authors refer to this purpose of the law as the "value" behind the law, the good that the law seeks to accomplish.[106] If the interpreter can correctly apprehend the values behind the law, understanding of the law is enriched. These values might be theological, moral, philosophical, sociological (for the good of the church society), or strictly legal (such as laws that establish rules or principles of law). For example, the purposes of the law on the impediment of disparity of cult (c. 1086) are to prevent Catholics from marrying someone who could pose dangers to their Christian faith and the Catholic upbringing of the children, and to call attention to the importance of a sacramental marriage. Sometimes, however, the purpose is not at all evident. An old law might be restated just to preserve a long-standing tradition that served the Church well in the past and might still be serviceable in some places and circumstances, for example, the law requiring the faithful to receive Communion at least once a year (c. 920). Discovering the purpose of the law is not a precise science but more of an art, requiring persons with broad knowledge not only of canon law but also of related sciences, especially the theological disciplines.

The circumstances of the law are the relevant historical facts about the matter regulated by the law, factors that led to the immediate creation of the law, and, if the law is being restated or modified later, the circumstances at that time. Investigation of the circumstances takes the interpreter into the field of history, especially church history. The circumstances include the political, social, and ecclesial factors and other influences relevant

---

[104] These are not steps that must be taken successively, but in any order that is most effective with respect to the law in question.

[105] See, e.g., *Ecum Dir* 6 which lists the purposes of the directory. These general purposes of the directory as a whole illuminate the individual purpose of each specific

norm in the directory. The theological values expressed in the directory, especially in part one, provide further insights into the purpose of the juridical norms.

[106] See L. Örsy, *Theology and Canon Law* (Collegeville: Liturgical Press, 1992), *passim;* and M. Wijlens, "The Church Knowing and Acting: Relationship between Theology and Canon Law," *Louvain Studies* 20 (1995) 21–40.

to the making of the law. This might involve study of the law's remote history, discussions about the matter at Vatican II, postconciliar developments, and the various drafts of the law before its most recent promulgation. Knowing such facts and circumstances will often shed light on the law's purpose and meaning.

The mind of the legislator (*mens legislatoris*) does not mean the subjective mind of the legislator or his successor—what he inwardly thinks or wills—because that is largely unknowable and even irrelevant. It is the objective text of the law that must be observed, not what anyone presumes the legislator might have been thinking when he made the law. The mind of the legislator does not refer to a human person's mind at all.[107] Instead, it is a construct, an "institutional figure"[108] signifying the whole institution of the law itself—the canonical system—especially the basic rules, values, and principles that underlie and support it.[109] Knowing this "mind of the legislator" takes considerable study and experience in the field of canon law, and it also requires knowledge of related disciplines, such as ecclesiology and moral theology.

The rules of interpretation in canon 17 are not the only ones observed by canonists. Other commonly used means of enriching the understanding of the law and its function and purpose include consideration of the canonical tradition (c. 6, §2), pertinent customs (cc. 19, 27), general principles of law, the jurisprudence and practice of the Roman Curia, and the constant and common opinion of learned persons, as discussed below under canon 19. Going into such depth in the everyday application of laws is not usually necessary. How-

ever, the use of these additional methods of interpretation leads to a more profound understanding of the law, even of laws whose meaning is not doubtful and obscure, and this benefits both the canonical science and the faithful who are called to observe the law.

Strict Interpretation

Canon 18 — Laws which establish a penalty, restrict the free exercise of rights, or contain an exception from the law are subject to strict interpretation.

To understand this canon, it is necessary to distinguish the categories of strict and broad interpretations from those of restrictive and extensive interpretations. Restrictive and extensive interpretations change the meaning of a law by limiting or broadening its applicability. Only the legislator may offer such an interpretation, in accord with canon 16; it must be promulgated and is not retroactive. Strict and broad interpretations do not change the law's meaning in any way. Strict interpretation limits the law's application to the minimum stated in the law; broad interpretation widens the application of the law to all possible cases that can fall within its meaning. Broad interpretation is normative when a law is favorable; strict interpretation is required when a law is "odious," namely, in the three instances mentioned in this canon.[110]

The definition of membership in a religious institute may be useful in exemplifying these distinctions. A strict interpretation of the law would hold that religious life begins with the profession of temporary vows (c. 654); therefore, odious laws applicable to religious, such as a penal law for violation of an obligation of religious life,[111] may not be applied to novices. A broad interpreta-

---

[107] How, for example, could any one know the mind of the several thousand prelates who are legislators at an ecumenical council?

[108] Otaduy, in *Com Ex*, 1:371.

[109] E.g., the fundamental principle that laws must be interpreted in such a way that they do not result in anything unjust or absurd, which is contrary to the nature of law as an ordinance of reason; the principle that beneficial laws should be broadly interpreted and burdensome laws strictly interpreted; the rule of canonical equity; the role of custom; etc.

[110] This follows from the long-standing canonical principle that odious matters are to be restricted and favors amplified: *Odia restringi, et favores convenit ampliari. RI* 15.

[111] E.g., c. 1392. A novice may be dismissed for not observing religious obligations, but penal laws could not be applied unless the laws were applicable to all the faithful.

tion would hold that religious life begins with the novitiate (c. 646), so novices are in some sense already members of the institute and may participate in many respects as professed members, such as, in accord with proper law, by living and working in the community, by wearing the habit, etc. A restrictive interpretation of religious life would hold that only those in perpetual vows are religious; this would illicitly deny to temporary professed rights that they have in the law (e.g., c. 670). An extensive interpretation would hold that even postulants or associates are members of the institute; this would illicitly extend to them the rights or impose the obligations proper only to professed religious and/or novices.

Penal laws are those for whose violation the law prescribes a penalty.[112] Strict interpretation of penal laws is necessary to protect the rights of persons, including those who have committed or been accused of a crime. A judge or superior cannot penalize someone for an offense that is not a crime in canon law, nor impose a harsher penalty than the law itself establishes. The crime must be gravely imputable by reason of malice or culpability and be committed exactly as stated in the law before the offender is subject to a penalty (c. 1321). For example, the crime of abortion is subject to the penalty of *latae sententiae* (automatic) excommunication (c. 1398), but an attempted abortion, though sinful, is not a crime.[113]

A *law that restricts the free exercise of a right* places one or more limitations on a right recognized in canon law, be it natural, ecclesial, or acquired.[114] The terms of such laws are subject to strict interpretation to enable maximal exercise of personal rights within the letter of the law. For example, all the faithful have a right to receive Holy Communion (cc. 213, 912). To restrict this right, there must be a clear basis in the law,[115] or the right is unlawfully denied. Thus, pastors are not free to extend to parents the requirement of preparation of children for the sacrament (c. 913, §1), and unlawfully deny the sacrament to children whose parents do not participate. Likewise, persons may not be denied the Eucharist whenever the minister considers them unworthy, but there must be positive proof that *all* the terms of the law have been met: (1) they have committed an objectively grave sin that (2) is manifest, and (3) they obstinately (after a warning) continue to commit the sin (c. 915).[116]

There is no consensus among the commentators on either the 1917 or 1983 codes on how to apply the rule that *laws that contain an exception from the law* are subject to strict interpretation.[117] However, it seems evident that this rule should be applied in accord with the axiom on which this canon is based, that "favors are to be broadened and odious things are to be restricted."[118] Therefore, favorable laws, even if they are exceptions to the rule, are subject not to strict but to broad in-

---

[112] E.g., cc. 1364–1399 and John Paul II, apconst *Universi Dominici gregis,* February 22, 1996, *AAS* 88 (1996) 303–343, nn. 58, 80, 81; *Origins* 25 (1996) 617, 619–630.

[113] The authentic interpretation of December 12, 1988 on what constitutes the crime of abortion was extensive and could not have lawfully been made except by the legislator or his delegate. It is not retroactive. *AAS* 80 (1988) 1818; *Pamplona ComEng,* 1297.

[114] In one sense, any law that imposes an obligation or a prohibition limits one's personal freedom, but what is meant here is a right that canon law recognizes as such, including the human rights of the divine natural law.

[115] See cc. 843, §1; 844; 913–919; 1331, §1, 2°; 1332.

[116] Other examples of laws subject to strict interpretation are 13, §2; 171–172; 194, §1, 2°–3°; 643; 656; 694, §1; 823, §1; 874, §1, 3°; 1041–1044; 1078, §2; 1083–1094; 1095; 1117; 1252; 1741.

[117] See F. J. Urrutia, "Adnotationes quaedam ad propositam reformationem Libri Primi Codicis Iuris Canonici," *P* 64 (1975) 649.

[118] *RI* 15. This is listed as one of three sources for c. 19 of the 1917 code (which is c. 18 of the 1983 code). The proximate source for the canon is the comparable provision in the Italian Civil Code of 1865. By adopting it in the canon law, the legislator made more concrete the axiom of rule 15 of the *Regulae Iuris.* The latter, however, comes from the canonical tradition and must be considered in interpreting the meaning of "exceptions" from the law. See c. 6, §2.

terpretation. For example, canon 932, §1 states that the eucharistic celebration is to be carried out in a sacred place unless necessity requires otherwise, in which case it must be in some fitting place. The *rule* is that the Eucharist is to be celebrated in a sacred place; the *exception* is that it may be celebrated in another fitting place in a case of necessity. Since the exception is a favor, the meaning of "case of necessity" calls for a broad interpretation—not only when it is physically impossible to celebrate in a sacred place, but also in cases of pastoral need, such as when it is spiritually beneficial for a group of the faithful occasionally to have a Mass in a school, home, etc. Many laws allow exceptions that grant favors, the terms of which are subject to broad interpretation.[119] Each term or condition of the law must be fulfilled for the exception to apply, but the meaning of each is subject to broad interpretation.

Laws containing an exception from the law must be strictly interpreted, even if the exception grants a favor, whenever broad interpretation would have an "odious" result, in particular, when broad interpretation would infringe upon the exercise of another person's rights or whenever a broad interpretation would be unreasonable. If an exception is favorable to one person or group, but infringes on the rights of another, the exception must be strictly interpreted. For example, if a pontifical religious institute were to claim that its apostolate is exempt from the authority of the diocesan bishop (c. 591), it could not base this claim on some broad understanding of exemption but it would have to prove that a pope had expressly granted this specific exemption that would restrict a fundamental right and obligation of the bishop (cc. 763, 394).[120]

In general, exceptions from the law are odious and require strict interpretation whenever a broad interpretation would be unreasonable, such as when a broad interpretation would weaken the

law's purpose or be harmful to church order. Deeply rooted in the canonical tradition is the conviction that a law must be reasonable,[121] and so it follows that interpretation of law must also be reasonable. If broad interpretation of an exception to the law, though granting a favor, results in an unreasonable application of the law, it is odious and contrary to this canon. Unreasonableness may be demonstrated when a broad interpretation would be contrary to a legal custom or the express policy of the particular territory or community,[122] or when it would be contrary to standard canonical principles and rules.[123]

Cases Involving Lacunae

Canon 19 — If a custom or an express prescript of universal or particular law is lacking in a certain matter, a case, unless it is penal, must be resolved in light of laws issued in similar matters, general principles of law applied with canonical equity, the jurisprudence and practice of the Roman Curia, and the common and constant opinion of learned persons.

This canon provides a remedy for a *lacuna legis*, literally, a "hole in the law." A lacuna occurs, as the canon states, when an express provi-

---

[119] E.g., cc. 230, §3; 844, §§ 2–4; 884, §1; 961, §1; 1116, §1; 1127, §2; 1206; 1352, §1.

[120] For other examples of this kind, see cc. 312, §1, 3°; 377, §4; 523; 1021.

[121] See commentary on cc. 7 and 24.

[122] It is also possible that the particular custom or policy is needlessly strict and needs to be reassessed in light of changing circumstances.

[123] E.g., c. 89 states the basic rule that the pastor and other presbyters and deacons *cannot* grant dispensations from the law, unless this power has been *expressly* granted to them. Since this is a fundamental rule on which the validity of the dispensation is based, one may not broadly interpret the meaning of "expressly granted" to include tacit delegation, despite the fact that the granting of a dispensation is a favor. Thus, when a visiting priest is appointed to substitute for a vacationing pastor, any faculties to dispense must be explicitly granted by law or delegation or implicitly granted by appointing him administrator (c. 540, §1). He cannot simply presume that his appointment as the pastor's replacement tacitly confers all the powers of the pastor.

sion of universal or particular law[124] or a custom[125] is lacking to provide a solution for a concrete case.[126] Laws are meant for the generality of cases, but sometimes no law exactly covers a particular case. Often, customs arise in those areas of the community's life not regulated by law. If there is no law or legal custom, and some matter requires a solution, a lacuna exists.[127] This canon establishes four sources that judges, administrators, scholars, and other interpreters of the law should use to seek a rule, norm, or principle to resolve the case.[128]

1. Laws issued in similar matters.

When there is no precise law or custom for a particular case, the interpreter may find elsewhere in the law a norm issued for a similar matter and, by analogy of law (*anologia legis*), apply it to the case. For example, the law requires a seriously ill person to have attained the use of reason before receiving the sacrament of the anointing of the sick, but it allows children with a serious illness to be anointed before the age of seven provided they have sufficient use of reason to be comforted by the sacrament.[129] However, the universal law says nothing about seriously ill persons who have not attained the use of reason due to a developmental disability such as mental retardation. By analogy of law, they may be anointed if they have sufficient use of reason to be comforted by the sacrament.[130]

2. General principles of law applied with canonical equity.

Pertinent general principles of law (*ius*) may be useful in finding a solution to a case involving a lacuna. Among these are general principles derived from the divine law, both positive and natural; the general principles contained in Book I of the code; the fundamental laws at the beginning of Book II of the code; and other general princi-

---

[124] Although the canon speaks of *lex,* this must be understood in a broad sense to include all written sources of the objective *ius*—laws, general administrative norms, and, when applicable, statutes and ordinances.

[125] This must be a legal custom, one with the force of law (cc. 23–26), if the solution is to be binding, as when given by a judge or administrator who must officially resolve a case. E.g., if a case has been handled the same way for at least thirty years and a legal custom has been established, there is no lacuna. The custom itself has the force of law and must be observed.

[126] The "case" must be understood broadly, not just in terms of administrative and judicial cases, but anytime a lacuna exists and a just solution must be found to resolve the matter. This includes a lacuna caused by an objectively doubtful law (c. 14). Solutions to cases by application of c. 19 pertain only to liceity; an invalidating or incapacitating effect must be expressly stated in the law (c. 10).

[127] According to L. Örsy, a "lacuna in the proper sense occurs when there is a right that must be supported, or an injustice that cries for redress, or a freedom that needs protection, and there is no appropriate provision in the legal system." *CLSA Com*, 37.

[128] *Comm* 17 (1985) 34–35. Administrators who must make a decision for the good of the community and judges who must decide a case *are obliged* to observe c. 19; canonists should use it whenever required by their science or to assist the faithful in finding practical and equitable solutions. The suppletory norm made by an administrator or judge binds only in that case. Solutions derived by canonists and other private persons are not binding but may be adopted more widely to the ex-

tent that the reasoning on which they are based is persuasive.

[129] Canon 1004, §1; *RAnointing,* 12.

[130] Some other examples are: the authority to issue dimissorials, missing in c. 1018, §1 for personal prelatures, is supplied by analogy with c. 295, §1; the requirement for a probationary period before transfer from one religious institute to another (c. 684, §2) can be extended to transfers from one society of apostolic life to another (c. 744, §1); the procedure for the removal and transfer of parish priests (cc. 1740–1747) can be applied to removal and transfer from other offices (c. 193, §1); the norms for the election of the diocesan administrator *in sede vacante* (cc. 423–424) can be applied to the election of the priest in charge of the diocese during an impeded see (c. 414); the rules for the collegial acts of juridic persons (c. 119) can be applied to other groups.

Another notable lacuna in the code is the absence of rules governing general administrative norms and other forms of written *ius* comparable to the rules that exist for *leges* in title I of the code. By analogy of law, pertinent canons from title I can be used to supply for this lacuna.

ples governing canonical institutes and acts.[131] Juridic maxims and principles from Roman law and the canonical tradition are useful, in particular the *Regulae Juris in Sexto*.[132] Principles from contemporary civil law systems might also be helpful, provided they are not contrary to the divine or the canon law and are congenial with the canonical system.

Equity is an ethical principle by which judges and superiors apply the law with mercy. Avoiding mere juridical formalism, they seek an interpretation and enforcement of the law that, while faithful to the law's meaning, take into account the situation of persons and the concrete circumstances of the case, bearing in mind the overall purpose of the law, which is to promote the common good and the *salus animarum* (cf. c. 1752). Equity corrects the rigor of the law and tempers it with mercy. It is a higher form of justice, an expression of Christian love, or charity.[133] Both judges and administrators (bishops, vicars general, religious superiors, parish priests, et al.) must render decisions equitably, applying the law with compassion and keeping in mind the nature of the case and the circumstances of persons. Just as they must always enforce the law with canonical equity, so also must they equitably apply general principles of law (*ius*) in solving a case involving a lacuna.

3. The jurisprudence and practice of the Roman Curia.

Jurisprudence is the science of law that develops from actual judicial cases. The jurisprudence in question is especially that of the Supreme Tribunal of the Apostolic Signatura and the Roman Rota. The Rota is particularly influential in church tribunals around the world as a source of jurisprudence on marriage law. The principal legislation governing the Roman Curia acknowledges this role of the Rota in stating that it "fosters unity of jurisprudence and, by virtue of its own decisions, provides assistance to lower tribunals."[134]

The practice of the Roman Curia refers to the administrative activity of the Roman dicasteries, in particular, the way it resolves specific cases. As for its juridical value, the curial practice is not binding on lower authorities, but is to be taken into account. The curial dicasteries usually develop a common approach to the various kinds of cases that fall within their competence. Knowing the way they handle cases and the decisions they reach may assist local administrators who encounter similar cases. For example, the law says nothing about a person who wishes to receive Communion, but can ingest food and drink only from a stomach tube. May the bishop dispense from the liturgical law[135] to allow Communion to be given through the stomach tube? In reaching

---

[131] Such principles are not usually stated explicitly as principles but are known to be such by reflection upon the entirety of the laws governing a juridic entity. For example, the liturgical laws taken as a whole lead to a number of principles, among them, that the integrity of liturgical celebrations must be protected, that the active participation of the faithful is to be fostered, that preparation for the liturgy is required, that the diocesan bishop has authority over the public exercise of divine worship, that significant adaptations in the liturgy cannot be made except by legislative authorities, that the Catholic liturgy is primarily directed to benefit the Catholic faithful, etc. General principles can likewise be derived for other major juridic institutes, like marriage, diocesan administration, judicial procedures, etc.

[132] The Latin text and an English translation is available in Gauthier, 107–117.

[133] Equity also exists in the civil courts, e.g., when a judge does not apply the maximum penalty in consideration of the circumstances of the convicted person and the crime—a first-time offender, young age, provocation to commit the crime, etc.

Equity should not be confused with *epieikeia*. Equity is applied by interpreters of the law, especially administrators and judges; *epieikeia* is used directly by the subject of the law on his or her own behalf. *Epieikeia* is a virtue by which the subject of the law does not observe the law when, in particular circumstances, a greater good is at stake. See J. Coriden, "Rules for Interpreters," in *The Art of Interpretation* (Washington, D.C., 1982) 5–6.

[134] PB 126; *Pamplona ComEng*, 1239.

[135] HCWE, 21; GIRM, 244–251.

his decision, it might help the bishop to know that the Holy See has granted indults permitting this, but refused an indult for Communion through a nasal tube.[136] The bishop may take this practice of the Roman Curia as a possible solution for his own case.

This rule on consulting the jurisprudence and practice of the Roman Curia is difficult to observe consistently, because the Holy See does not systematically publish its decisions, particularly those in the administrative realm. For the most part, the interpreter must look to private collections, most notably (in English translation) the multi-volume *Canon Law Digest* and *Roman Replies and CLSA Advisory Opinions.*[137]

4. The common and constant opinion of learned persons.

The learned persons (*doctores*) are those who publish scholarly monographs, commentaries, and canonical opinions. When an opinion is both common and constant, it is safe to use as a source for resolving a case where there is no applicable law or custom. A constant opinion is one that endures over an extended period, one that has stood the test of time. The common opinion is the one that becomes dominant by the force of its argumentation and the depth of its reasoning. This is not simply a matter of counting the number of authors who hold one view or another. Sometimes a minority opinion is more persuasive on its merits and should be preferred to the majority opinion. This may happen especially if the minority opinion adds new information not known or considered by earlier authors, and the

common opinion of the past is clearly now incomplete or even obsolete.

A lacuna in penal cases may not be resolved by the means provided in this canon. A judge or superior may not impose a penalty for a case unforeseen in the law, in keeping with the long-standing principle, *nulla poena sine lege.* This exception is intended to protect the right of those accused of a crime not to be punished except according to the law.[138] Analogously, solutions derived from the four sources of this canon may not be applied if they would restrict the free exercise of rights or be unjust or unreasonable (cf. c. 18). Moreover, equity must prevail in solutions derived from all four sources for resolving cases, not just from the application of general principles of law (*ius*).

The four sources of this canon for resolving cases involving a lacuna are equal to each other in value; the order of their presentation does not imply any ranking. The interpreter should use as many of them as may be helpful in reaching a solution for a given case.

Revocation of Law

Canon 20 — A later law abrogates, or derogates from, an earlier law if it states so expressly, is directly contrary to it, or completely reorders the entire matter of the earlier law. A universal law, however, in no way derogates from a particular or special law unless the law expressly provides otherwise.

Divine laws do not change, but ecclesiastical laws, being of human origin, can be revoked partially (derogation) or entirely (abrogation). This canon treats the ways that a law may be revoked by a later law, either expressly or tacitly. The legislator competent to revoke a law is the legislator who promulgated the law, or his successors. The pope may revoke the law of any lower legislator,

---

[136] *CLD* 6, 562–565 records three affirmative replies on the stomach tube, and a negative reply on the nasal tube. These were granted by the Holy Office in the early 1960s before diocesan bishops had the power to dispense from universal disciplinary laws.

[137] Both are published by the CLSA in Washington, D.C. The *CLD* mainly contains public documents, which are a binding source of *ius* and not the subject of c. 19, but it also has numerous private replies. *RR* consists mainly of private replies. These replies are the best source for determining the practice of the Roman Curia with respect to actual cases.

[138] Canon 221, §3 uses the words *ad normam legis,* which means that the faithful may not be punished by canonical penalties on any basis other than legislation.

but it is disputed whether a particular council or conference of bishops may revoke a law of the diocesan bishop.[139]

Express revocation occurs when a later law expressly states that it is revoking an earlier law, either explicitly or implicitly. A law *explicitly* revokes when it unequivocally states that it is derogating from or abrogating one or more previous laws, for example, canon 6, §1, 1°. A law *implicitly* revokes by using a general expression or formula to the effect that previous laws are being abrogated or derogated from, such as "notwithstanding anything to the contrary," "anything presently in force contrary to this law is abrogated," "derogating from other laws in force," etc.

Unlike express revocation, *tacit revocation* makes no mention of the fact that any previous law is being revoked. Tacit revocation occurs when a later law is directly contrary to an earlier law, and when a later law completely reorders the matter of the earlier law.[140]

A later law is directly contrary to an earlier one whenever the two are in opposition to each other, as when the later law permits or commands something that had been prohibited or when it prohibits something that had been permitted or commanded. For example, n. 39 of the 1975 edition of the *General Instruction of the Roman Missal* said that the Alleluia before the gospel at Mass *may* be omitted if not sung, but n. 23 of the 1981 *Lectionary for Mass* says that the Alleluia "must be sung," that is, it *must* be omitted if not sung and may never be recited.

The second way in which a later law tacitly abrogates or derogates from an earlier law is when the later law completely reorders (*de integro ordinet*) the entire subject matter of the earlier law. (1) The revocation affects an entire document when a new document is published treating anew

the entire matter of an earlier one.[141] It is unnecessary for the legislator or executive authority to abrogate expressly the earlier document; the complete reordering of its subject matter in the later document tacitly abrogates it.[142] (2) The revocation may affect all or some of the norms governing a juridic institute (that is, a subject matter or entity regulated by law). For example, canons 873–874 on the qualifications of godparents completely reordered n. 10 of the 1969 *Christian Initiation: General Introduction* by treating anew the whole institute of godparents; and canons 960–963 on general confession and absolution completely reordered the 1973 *Rite of Penance,* nn. 31–34.[143] (3) The abrogation or derogation by a later law may affect only one or several laws or

[141] E.g., the 1993 *Directory for the Application of the Principles and Norms on Ecumenism* completely reordered the previous directory of 1967 and 1970, as well as all other "norms already established for implementing and developing the decisions of the Council given up to the present" (*Ecum Dir* 6). In virtue of this complete reordering of ecumenical law (*ius*), the *ius vigens* on ecumenism consists of the pertinent canons of the Latin and Eastern codes and the 1993 *Ecum Dir,* not any other documents before 1993.

[142] Some authors have suggested that there was no need for the legislator expressly to abrogate the 1917 code in c. 6, §1, 1° of the 1983 code, because this would have been accomplished in virtue of the 1917 code's complete reordering by the 1983 code. However, this may have left uncertainty regarding the status of those parts of the 1917 code that were not treated anew in the 1983 code, so express abrogation probably was necessary.

[143] *Emendations,* 12–13; 17–19 (full citation above at c. 2). The *Emendations* went into effect on the same day as the code (November 27, 1983), so in reality this was express revocation by the legislator. However, those who prepared the changes in the liturgical books did so in light of the principles of cc. 2, 6, and 20. Had the pope not acted expressly, the revocations would have tacitly occurred anyway due to the code's direct contrariety with and complete reordering of those earlier liturgical laws. In this sense, it is perfectly correct to consider the liturgical rites as having been altered by the code, since all the emendations were directly and solely the result of the code's promulgation. The *Emendations* provide numerous examples of the application of the principles of direct contrariety and complete reordering.

[139] *Chiappetta Com,* 2nd ed. (1996), 1:73, n. 337.
[140] Some commentators take a different approach from the one given here. They do not speak of two kinds of express revocation, but treat explicit and implicit as one. They refer to what is here called "tacit" revocation as "implicit" revocation.

norms in an earlier juridical text, leaving the others intact.[144]

The complete reordering of an entire document, and sometimes of an entire institute, is easy to demonstrate. It is more difficult to determine when one or more later laws abrogate or derogate from one or more previous laws by completely reordering their subject matter, because there are so many individual norms in the various documents that might be affected. Often, the code or postcode laws and documents will have completely reordered certain norms in a document, while other norms in the same document will not have been reordered. The following are some indicators of the abrogation of or derogation from a law or general administrative norm due to its complete reordering by a later law:

1. A law (*lex*) restates exactly a general administrative norm or slightly rephrases it without altering its substance; although there is no material difference between the two, the new law has greater juridic value than the administrative norm and must now be considered the *ius vigens*.[145]

2. A new law deals with the same matter as a previous law or norm, but rephrases it such that the new law is incompatible with, even if not directly contrary to, the former law or norm.

3. A new law changes part of an old law or norm but leaves the rest intact; this is a derogation, not abrogation.[146]

4. A new law adds something to an old law or norm such that the old law or norm is now incomplete and cannot stand on its own as the *ius vigens* on the matter; this is "subrogation," a derogation by the addition of new material.[147]

5. The forcefulness of the new law is different from that of a former law or norm, for example, the new law says "must" and the former law or norm said "should." There is no incompatibility in content, but a difference in force.

With respect to the liturgical books published before the 1983 code was promulgated, the Holy See itself made an authoritative judgment concerning what norms needed to be changed in them because of the code. With respect to norms in most documents issued from Vatican II to the 1983 code, there is no authoritative guide on what is still in force, and what is not, in light of the

---

[144] The typical examples of complete reordering given by the authors are usually entire documents and less often whole legal institutes. However, the canon speaks of the complete reordering of a law, using the singular. Thus, even a single law can be totally or partially revoked by being completely reordered by another law.

In the opinion of this author, the category of "complete reordering" includes "direct contrariety." A law that is directly contrary to a new law has been reordered as completely as possible! From this perspective, the category of "direct contrariety" is not necessary.

[145] An earlier general administrative norm, an act of executive power, is formally changed when it is promulgated anew as *lex*. Since law, an act of legislative power, has greater juridic value than an administrative norm, the previous norm with a lower juridic value, though saying the same thing as the new law, cannot be considered the *ius vigens*. To do so would undervalue the new law, and lead to mistakes in interpretation and application, such as if a later general administrative norm were contrary to it. Cf. cc. 33, §1 and 34, §2.

However, a law does not revoke another law (*lex*) by restating it if the former appears in a document that still

has the force of law. Often, for example, a liturgical law is repeated in other liturgical books; this is simply the reiteration of a law that continues to be in force.

[146] For an example, see the commentary on c. 1172 on the qualifications of an exorcist.

[147] This could be considered simply a new law that is not at all incompatible with the previous law but simply adds new elements. In reality, however, the previous law has been changed, because it no longer adequately represents the *ius vigens;* one would incorrectly cite the old law as if it were the law governing the subject matter. The old law is derogated not by changing something in it, but by adding something to it that makes it incomplete on its own.

code and the laws and administrative documents published since the code. Consequently, it falls to canonical doctrine (the writings of scholars) to demonstrate which pre-1983 code norms remain the *ius vigens* and which norms have been completely reordered and therefore abrogated or derogated from by the code and by laws and administrative documents issued after the code.

The revocation of general administrative norms contained in documents issued by executive authorities such as the congregations of the Roman Curia is subject to the rules of canons 33 and 34, §§ 2–3.[148] For example, a new directory abrogates an earlier directory on the same subject; a new law or general administrative norm revokes earlier general administrative norms that are directly contrary to it or that have been completely reordered by the new law or norm.[149] However, a general administrative norm cannot revoke a law or a legal custom.

Particular or Special Norms

The second sentence of canon 20 states a general principle: universal law does not revoke particular or special law unless it expressly says so. *Ius particulare* includes particular laws (*leges*), customs, and general administrative norms (e.g., general executory decrees of a vicar general or an episcopal vicar). Opinions differ on the meaning of the term "special law" (*ius speciale*),[150] but the expression appears to be a way of stressing that the rule of the canon applies not only to the norms

and customs of particular territories, but also to norms and customs of juridic persons. This interpretation is in continuity with canon 22 of the 1917 code, which spoke of "statutes of special places and individual persons"[151] as well as with previous schemas on this canon of the code which referred to "special statutes of persons"[152] or simply "special statutes."[153] In keeping with the principle of canon 6, §2, *ius speciale* may be understood as referring to statutes of juridic persons (c. 94), including the proper law (*ius proprium*) of institutes of consecrated life and societies of apostolic life. However, the change from "statutes" to *ius speciale* indicates that the legislator intended a broader meaning than just statutes. Thus, *ius speciale* means not only the written norms of a juridic person, but also includes their legal customs.

A new universal law revokes neither particular nor special norms, unless the law expressly abrogates or derogates from them as, for example, in canon 5, §1 with respect to contrary customs and in canon 6, §1, 2°–3° with respect to contrary particular laws and particular penal laws. Revocation of particular and special norms by universal law cannot occur tacitly. A particular norm directly contrary to a universal norm remains in force for the subjects of that particular norm, while the universal norm binds everyone else. Nor can a particular or special norm be completely reordered by a universal law. In doubtful cases, the continued viability of the particular and special norms must be upheld (cf. c. 21).

Canon 1502 of the Eastern code expresses the same rules as canon 20. However, it does not mention *ius speciale,* since it is explicit in the Eastern law that the term *ius particulare* includes laws, customs, statutes, and all other particular norms (*CCEO* 1493, §2).[154]

---

[148] The "implicit" revocation mentioned in cc. 33, §2 and 34, §3 also includes tacit revocation.

[149] Instructions and similar norms and documents of the Roman Curia *given for the executors of the law* (c. 34) cannot revoke administrative norms given by the Roman dicasteries *for the community*. E.g., an instruction may be issued to explain and elaborate on the norms of a directory, but it could not revoke any of these norms. That would be contrary to its nature and purpose.

[150] See F. X. Urrutia, "De quibusdam quaestionibus ad librum primum Codicis pertinentibus," *P* 73 (1984) 297–301. See also the standard commentaries on the 1983 code.

[151] *Lex generalis nullatenus derogat locorum specialium et personarum singularium statutis.*

[152] *Comm* 16 (1984) 151, c. 22.

[153] ComCICRec, *Schema Codicis Iuris Canonici,* 1980, c. 20.

[154] In our view, the expression *ius speciale* in c. 20 of the Latin code is not necessary, since the term *ius particulare* encompasses its meaning also in the Latin canon law.

Doubtful Revocation

Canon 21 — In a case of doubt, the revocation of a pre-existing law is not presumed, but later laws must be related to the earlier ones and, insofar as possible, must be harmonized with them.

This canon provides a rule for a doubt about the revocation of a law. A doubt exists when probable reasons exist for and against the revocation of an earlier law by a later one, and even experts are not able to overcome the doubt. The revocation of the earlier law may not be presumed. Instead, one should examine the two together and attempt to harmonize them.

This should not be confused with canon 14, which says that doubtful laws do not oblige. If the revocation of the earlier law is doubtful, it does not bind, but its revocation may not be presumed; one must attempt to harmonize it with the later law. One cannot presume that a law has been revoked, yet, on the other hand, the presumption of non-revocation does not make a doubtful law binding. Although not binding, the earlier law cannot be disregarded, as if it had been certainly revoked. Perhaps the later law did not abrogate the earlier law but merely derogated from it. In this case, it is possible to observe the unaffected part of the earlier law. An authentic interpretation or further changes in the law may also clarify the force of the earlier law.

A law that expressly revokes an earlier law leaves no doubt that the earlier law lacks all force. This is true even of implicit revocation by means of a general formula such as "anything to the contrary notwithstanding."[155] Likewise, a law that is directly contrary to an earlier law leaves no doubt about the revocation of the earlier law; the earlier law is revoked because it is manifestly incompatible and irreconcilable with the later law. How-

ever, a doubt may arise about revocation by the complete reordering of the entire subject matter of the earlier law.

When a new law or series of laws treats the subject matter of a previous law or laws, various questions may arise. Was the reordering by the new law complete (*de integro*)? Was the entire subject matter (*tota materia*) reordered, or only part of it? If the old law contained a provision not mentioned in the new, is the old provision revoked by the complete reordering of the matter in the new law, or does it continue to exist? Is the former law incompatible with the new law, or can both be observed? If such questions are unresolvable, a doubt exists.

This canon prescribes a solution to the problem. In doubt about revocation, an attempt must be made to relate (*trahere*)[156] the new law to the old and see if they can be harmonized. If they can be harmonized, then both should be observed. If only part of the former law can be harmonized with the later law, then only that part should be observed. Such observance cannot be enforced, however, because a doubtful law does not bind (c. 14). This suggests that there may be another purpose for the rule of canon 21. The legislator may be saying that, by making the effort to harmonize the two laws, it could become clear that the two are not wholly incompatible, and thus a true doubt never really existed.

Canonization of Civil Laws

Canon 22 — Civil laws to which the law of the Church yields are to be observed in canon law with the same effects, insofar as they are not contrary to divine law and unless canon law provides otherwise.

In some instances, canon law does not have its own norms on a matter but defers to the civil laws.

---

[155] However, if it is doubtful whether an earlier law is truly *contrary* to the later law, then the presumption favors the continuance of the earlier law, which is to be reconciled with the later.

[156] The Latin words, *trahendae sunt,* mean in this context that the two laws must be examined together and compared with each other.

The rule of this canon says that, whenever the canon law yields (*remittit*) to the civil law, the civil law must be observed and its effects are the same in canon law. This is frequently called the *canonization* of the civil law, because the canonical system adopts as its own and grants complete force to the applicable civil laws. The interpretation and application of such laws must be done according to the rules and standards of the civil law, even by judges, superiors, and others operating within the canonical system. When the civil law conflicts with divine law or canon law, the latter prevails. For example, if a contract to sell church property is valid in the civil law but invalid in the canon law, the ecclesiastical judge or superior must attempt to enforce the canon law.[157]

A better translation of the canon's opening words would be, "*the* civil laws to which the law (*ius*) of the Church yields," because canon law does not yield to civil laws in general, but only in certain matters. The code canonizes the civil laws on guardians of minors, prescription, the merely civil effects of marriage, the document required for a proxy marriage, contracts, possessory actions, and rules for settlements, compromise, and arbitration.[158] By canonizing the civil laws on these matters, the canon law avoids conflicts with the various laws of the many civil jurisdictions throughout the world.

The civil laws (*leges*) in question are all pertinent norms of the State or society—not only legislation but also administrative law, customary law, and other norms. It refers to all levels of the law—international, national, state, county, city (or comparable levels).[159] The term "canon law" (*ius canonicum*) here refers only to ecclesiastical law (*ius*), but generally it has a broader meaning, including both divine law and the various sources of the ecclesiastical law. The explicit mention of the divine law calls attention to the necessity of evaluating the civil laws also in accord with the divine law, for example, as it is expressed in the moral teachings of the Church.

Sometimes the canon law recognizes the applicability and effects of the civil laws on a certain matter without canonizing the laws, that is, without incorporating them into the canonical system itself.[160] In other canons, the code exhorts or requires the observance of the civil laws on a certain matter, which is another way in which the canon law recognizes the applicability of the civil laws without canonizing them.[161] Recognition of the civil laws does not eliminate the possibility that, in individual instances, competent church authorities may determine that a certain civil law should not be observed if it would harm the interests of the Church.

In respect to most legal matters regulated by civil law, canon law says nothing. Morally, citizens are bound to observe legitimate civil laws, but they are obliged to disobey any laws or other directives that "are contrary to the demands of the moral order, to the fundamental rights of persons or the teachings of the Gospel."[162] For the Catholic, two systems of law oblige simultaneously, canon law (including divine law) and legitimate civil laws. While both are binding within separate but parallel systems, the canon law prevails whenever it conflicts with the civil law. Nevertheless, a contrary civil law can still influence the canonical system. For example, canon law does not recognize the validity of civil divorce, yet many ecclesiastical tribunals will not admit petitions for the invalidity of marriage unless civil di-

---

[157] See cc. 638, §3; 1292; 1296.

[158] Canons 98, §2; 197; 1105, §2; 1290; 1500; 1714; and 1716. Since the taking on of civil law obligations frequently involves a restriction on the free exercise of rights by persons operating in the canonical system, this list of canons is limited only to those that certainly canonize the civil law. Cf. c. 18.

[159] The Anglo-American common law system understands "civil law" in different ways. See D. Galles, "The Civil Law," *J* 49 (1989) 241–248.

[160] See cc. 105, §1; 110; 365, §1; 877, §3; 1059, 1672, and 1692, §§ 2, 3; 1071, §1, 2°; 1296; 1540, §2; 1558, §2.

[161] See cc. 231, §2; 362; 668, §§ 1, 4; 1062, §1; 1274, §5; 1284, §2, 2°, 3°; 1286, 1°; 1299, §2.

[162] *CCC* 2238–2242.

vorce proceedings have been finalized, in order to prevent interference from civil authorities in an exclusively ecclesiastical proceeding. Canon law also does not recognize a merely civil marriage by a Catholic, yet such an invalid marriage may have consequences in canon law.[163]

TITLE II
CUSTOM
[cc. 23–28]

In addition to the divine and ecclesiastical law, customs are a major source of the *ius canonicum*. A law is a norm given for the community by a legislative authority; a custom is a norm introduced by the community itself. Customs are often called the "unwritten law," but this is not a definition, because a custom could be written down and it would still be a custom. The key difference between a law and a custom is their respective origins —the legislator for a law, the community for a custom.

In the first millennium, custom was more important than law in ordering the Christian communities. From the twelfth century, legislation grew in importance, but custom continued to enjoy a privileged place. While legislation became the predominant focus of canonists, particularly since the first code of 1917, customs continued to be formed and to shape significant parts of ecclesial life, especially in areas not directly regulated by laws.[164] Today, the convergence of certain demographic, historical, and theological realities has brought about a new awareness of the importance of customs in the inculturation of the Catholic faith within the many thousands of particular communities that make up a world-Church of more than a billion adherents.[165]

Three kinds of practices introduced by the community may be distinguished: an *optional practice,* which the community does not consider to be binding, that is, the majority of the community would not be opposed to the removal of the practice; *factual custom* (custom of fact), which the majority of the community considers binding, but does not have the force of law; and *legal custom,* a custom with the force of law. The canons of title II are concerned with factual and legal customs, in particular, how a factual custom may attain the force of law, which gives the custom legal protection against removal by anyone except the legislator or the community itself.

A custom, like law, is a general norm for the community, a norm that regulates a matter that also could be regulated by law.[166] Custom relates to law in two ways. (1) It is *beyond the law* (*praeter ius*) when the law says nothing about the specific matter regulated by the custom. (2) It is *contrary to law* when it conflicts with what the law prescribes. Traditionally, canonists have recognized a third category of customs *in accord with the law.* However, this tradition needs to be reassessed for three reasons. (1) So-called "custom in accord with law" does not function as true custom, that is, it creates no new norm for the community.[167] It is either simply a way of observing a law in force, or else it may properly be called a custom beyond the law.[168] (2) The code

---

[163] See cc. 194, §1, 3°; 694, §1, 2°; 1041, 3°; 1394.

[164] For a history of canonical custom, see A. Van Hove, *Commentarium Lovaniense in Codicem Iuris Canonici,* vol 1, tome 3: *De consuetudine; De temporis supputatione* (Mechelen, Belgium: H. Dessain, 1933) 18–48.

[165] This point is developed in J. Huels, "Back to the Future: The Role of Custom in a World Church," *CLSAP* 59 (1997) 1–25, especially 1–3.

[166] This need not be a positive norm but could simply be the practice of not observing a law (desuetude). It makes no difference whether the community acts in good or bad faith. Even if the community knowingly disregards a law, this non-observance could become a custom with the force of law. However, as will be seen in c. 24, a custom must be reasonable, at least in the circumstances of the community that observes it, for it to attain the force of law.

[167] On this point, see Otaduy, in *Com Ex,* 1:460–461.

[168] E.g., in a certain diocese it is the "custom" to give the Christmas collection of all the parishes to the priests' re-

does not mention customs in accord with the law. (3) All the canons can be literally and reasonably interpreted without positing a category of custom in accord with the law. Indeed, the law makes more sense without this category.[169]

The law of the Eastern code on custom is substantially the same as that of the Latin code (*CCEO* 1506–1509). A notable difference is that the Eastern code has a brief theological rationale for custom, which states that custom "responds to the action of the Holy Spirit in the ecclesial body" (*CCEO* 1506, §1). Other significant differences will be noted below.

Title II treats the notion of legal custom (c. 23), the requirement that legal customs be reasonable (c. 24), the community capable of inducing a custom (c. 25), the time required to create a custom with the force of law (c. 26), custom as interpreter of law (c. 27), and revocation of custom (c. 28).

Legal Custom

Canon 23 — Only that custom introduced by a community of the faithful and approved by the legislator according to the norm of the following canons has the force of law.

A legal custom is not a law; it remains a custom but has the force of law (*vis legis*).[170] Where the legal custom is in force, the faithful are bound to observe it, unless the community is in the process of forming a custom contrary to it. Whether legal or factual, a custom is a normative practice of a community, that is, the community intends the custom to be binding. However, a legal custom has greater stability than a factual custom and cannot be removed except by a contrary law or custom. This canon establishes the rule that, besides being introduced by an ecclesiastical community (c. 25), a custom must be approved by the legislator to attain the force of law.

The community. Only a community within the Church, as discussed below at canon 25, can introduce an ecclesiastical custom. This does not mean that the community's leader may not introduce it, but the community must want it. If a practice is imposed against the will of the majority of the community, it is not a custom and cannot attain the force of law.

The competent legislator. The supreme legislator may approve any custom, universal or particular. A plenary council or conference of bishops (in accord with canon 455) may approve customs particular to the region. The diocesan bishop may approve diocesan customs. With respect to customs contrary to the law, determination of the competent legislator depends on the extent of the law to which the custom relates. If the custom is contrary to the universal law, only the pope or the college of bishops may approve it. If it is contrary to a particular law, the competent particular legislator, or his hierarchical superior, is the competent legislator. For example, the diocesan bishop or the pope could approve a custom contrary to a diocesan law.

Approval of a custom may be either specific or legal. With *specific* approval, the custom achieves the force of law immediately. Customs may be specifically (*specialiter*) approved (c. 26) either expressly or tacitly. The legislator *expressly* approves a custom by explicitly stating this fact in a public document.[171] He *tacitly* approves a custom

---

tirement fund. This may be seen simply as one way of observing c. 222, §1 or, if the practice is considered normative, as a custom beyond the law, since the law says nothing specifically about Christmas collections.

[169] Canon 28 speaks only of customs contrary to and beyond the law being revoked tacitly by a contrary law or custom. If there were customs in accord with the law, it follows that they could not be tacitly revoked by a contrary law or custom of the community but only expressly by law. This would lead to the absurd conclusion that a community could not change a custom it had introduced!

[170] *CCEO* 1506–1507 speaks of the *vis iuris* instead of the *vis legis,* but no difference in meaning is intended. See *Nu,* n. 10 (1980) 103 and n. 13 (1981) 12.

[171] The privately expressed views of the legislator are juridically irrelevant. Contra *Pamplona ComEng,* 94–95, express approval is not given in the form of law. That would make the custom a law, an act of the legislator, rather than approval precisely as custom, a norm of the community.

when it is certain that he is aware of the custom's existence but does nothing to eliminate it, for example, when he celebrates the Eucharist at which the custom is observed.[172] Specific approval may be given at any time within the thirty years it would have taken the custom to attain the force of law by legal approval.

Legal approval, also called "general" approval,[173] is the usual way that customs are approved and are verified as having obtained the force of law. Legal approval is demonstrated when all the conditions of canons 24–26 are met: the custom must be reasonable and not contrary to the divine law; the community must be capable of receiving a law and must intend to introduce a normative practice; the custom must be observed for thirty continuous and complete years. These rules require no intervention of the legislator. Since it is impossible for the legislator to be aware of every custom, the mechanism of legal approval enables customs to achieve the force of law without his specific approval.

As an aid in understanding the following canons, it may be helpful to summarize the various ways in which customs are distinguished. (1) A custom is *universal* if it is widespread throughout the Latin church or the entire Catholic Church; otherwise, it is *particular*.[174] (2) A custom may be either beyond the law or contrary to it. (3) A custom is legal and has the force of law if the legislator has approved it, in which case only a contrary law or custom can remove it; otherwise it is factual and any competent superior of the community can remove it. Both factual and legal customs are considered normative by the community, unlike optional practices. (4) A custom may be approved specifically by the legislator, whether expressly or tacitly, in which case it attains the force of law immediately, or it may obtain legal approval in accord with canons 24–26, in which case it takes thirty years to attain the force of law. (5) A *centenary* custom is at least one hundred years old; an *immemorial* custom is one that has been observed for as long as anyone can remember.

Reasonableness

Canon 24 — §1. No custom which is contrary to divine law can obtain the force of law.

§2. A custom contrary to or beyond canon law (*praeter ius canonicum*) cannot obtain the force of law unless it is reasonable; a custom which is expressly reprobated in the law, however, is not reasonable.

Ecclesiastical law and custom, although different in origin, have the same purpose—to order the Christian community and promote the spiritual good of the faithful. To be true to this purpose, both law and custom must be rational, or reasonable; both written and customary norms must be "ordinances of reason."[175] If a law or custom is unreasonable, it lacks the essence of a true canonical norm. An unreasonable law must be changed by the legislator, or the community will cease on its own to observe it, the phenomenon called the "intrinsic cessation" of law.[176] If a custom—a norm introduced by a community—is unreasonable, it cannot achieve the force of law, even if it persists for more than thirty years.

Canon 24 states two kinds of customs that are always unreasonable: those contrary to the divine law and those that are expressly reprobated in the

---

[172] *CCEO* 1507, §4 explicitly states that the approval of the legislator may be tacit. The more common opinion of canonical authors is that tacit approval also is possible in the Latin church.

[173] *Comm* 3 (1971) 87; M. Benz, "Die Mitwerkung des Gesetzgebers bei der Entstehung von Gewohnheitsrecht," *AkK* 155 (1986) 466–479, especially 472–474.

[174] Customs, by nature, are particular; by the time they become universal, they are usually taken up into law. An example of a universal custom is the decoration of churches at Christmas.

[175] Thomas Aquinas, *STh* I–II, q. 90, a. 1–4.

[176] In fact, this is a contrary custom. The law mandates or prohibits something, and the community does not do it. Since an obsolete or harmful law is unreasonable, the contrary practice of the community, tolerated by the diocesan bishop or competent superior, restores the rationality of church order.

law (*ius*).[177] Reprobated customs should not be confused with customs that have been abrogated or prohibited in law; the latter may revive and some day become legal; reprobated customs cannot. The juridical text must expressly state that it is reprobating a custom, as with the words *reprobata contraria consuetudine*. The code expressly reprobates contrary customs in six canons.[178] These practices may never attain the force of law as long as the laws that reprobate them remain in force. Unlike customs contrary to divine law that are intrinsically unreasonable, expressly reprobated customs are not necessarily unreasonable by nature, that is, they could be justified in certain circumstances; instead, they must be considered unreasonable simply because of their explicit reprobation in the law.

A custom contrary to or beyond the law (*ius*) may be reasonable or unreasonable. The *ius* to which a *contrary* custom relates could be a law, a general administrative norm, a statute, an ordinance, or a legal custom. A custom *beyond the law* is a practice not regulated by any written norm. All customs contrary to or beyond the *ius* must be reasonable to attain the force of law. Unreasonable customs are those that are against faith or morals, occasion sin, are opposed to the constitution or liberty of the Church, harm the common good, or disrupt the "nerve of ecclesiastical discipline."[179]

The leaders of Christian communities (diocesan bishop, pastor, religious superior, etc.) are responsible for deciding whether a custom is reasonable. By allowing a factual custom to continue, a favorable judgment about the custom's reasonableness is implied; by seeking to eradicate the custom, the superior judges it to be unreasonable. This judgment cannot be based solely on the fact that the custom is contrary to a written norm; otherwise, there would be no role for contrary customs in the canonical system. Rather, it must be based upon a consideration of various criteria depending on the nature of the practice and the circumstances of the case, such as the custom's theological/liturgical propriety, usefulness, meaningfulness to the community, the *gravitas* (cf. c. 90, §1) or importance of the norm to which the custom is contrary, whether it is peacefully observed, whether most of the community wants to keep observing the practice even after learning it is *contra ius,* etc.

The Community

Canon 25 — No custom obtains the force of law unless it has been observed with the intention of introducing a law by a community capable at least of receiving law.

The canon lays down two further requirements for a custom of fact to become a custom with the force of law, both pertaining to the community that introduces the custom. The community must (1) be capable of receiving a law (*lex*), and (2) have the intention of introducing a norm (*ius*).[180]

---

[177] Cf. c. 5, §1. Use of the word *ius* instead of *lex* makes it evident that customs may also be expressly reprobated by other written sources of the objective *ius,* such as the *ius proprium* of institutes of consecrated life and societies of apostolic life. Thus, the reprobation of contrary factual or future customs is not an exclusively legislative power, although legislative power (or a contrary legal custom) is needed to remove a custom that already has the force of law (c. 28). For an opposing view, see H. Socha, in *Münster Com,* 24/3.

[178] Canons 396, §2; 423, §1; 526, §2; 1076; 1287, §1; and 1425, §1.

[179] Such would be customs that impede the exercise of ecclesiastical authority or violate fundamental principles and rules of the canonical system. In 1918, the Holy See ruled that the custom, contrary to the 1917 code, of lay persons serving as judges, auditors, and assessors in tri-

bunals "disrupts the nerve of ecclesiastical discipline and is contrary to the liberty and immunity of the Church." This custom was contrary to a fundamental rule of the 1917 code that only clergy could exercise the power of jurisdiction; it was not just a matter of the disciplinary laws requiring these officials to be priests (*CIC* 118, 1573–1575, 1581). See SCConc, response, December 14, 1918, *AAS* 11 (1919) 128; *CLD* 1, 97–98.

[180] English translations of this canon do not distinguish *lex* from *ius.* No community can introduce a law in the strict sense; that can be done only by a legislative authority.

The community capable of forming a custom that could attain the force of law must be a community for whom a legislator may enact a law. It is not necessary that the community actually have had any legislation enacted for it, so long as it is capable of receiving a law. The community must be an identifiably ecclesiastical community that, while composed of members of the faithful, does not depend for its continuing existence on any particular physical persons. The community must be ecclesiastically recognized, that is, juridically connected to the Catholic Church as a group, not simply as a collectivity of individual Catholics.[181]

Communities that are capable of receiving a law may be divided into three categories: (1) the community that makes up a juridic person;[182] (2) communities and institutions that, although not juridic persons as such, have been canonically established in some way and are subject to ecclesiastical regulation and supervision;[183] and (3) homogeneous groups of persons who belong to entities defined in 1 and 2, for example, the permanent deacons of a diocese, the lay brothers of a clerical religious institute, the faithful who belong to a parish organization, Catholic hospital chaplains in the diocese, etc.

Not capable of receiving a law are individual families and private associations of the faithful whose statutes have not been approved and which are not subject to hierarchical supervision.[184] The key factors in determining whether a community is capable of receiving law are that, as a distinct community and not merely as a collection of individuals, it is juridically tied to the Catholic Church and subject to supervision by someone with legislative power. The legislator competent to supervise the group would also be competent to make a law for it.

For a custom to obtain the force of law, the capable community must have the intention (*animus*) of introducing a norm, namely, a normative practice that the community wishes to observe and maintain. A norm is not a merely optional practice about whose observance and preservation the community is indifferent. The community must consider its custom to be binding. It suffices that the faithful *want* to observe and maintain the custom, even if they are not conscious of this intent. An intention is an act of the will; people can will something without consciously alluding to it in their minds,[185] because the mind and the will are separate though related faculties (cf. cc. 1099–1100). The intention of the community to introduce a norm is usually explicitly manifested only when a superior or minority group within the community attempts to remove the custom. If the community is disturbed by and objects to the attempted removal, the intention to have a binding norm is proven; if the community is unperturbed by the attempt to re-

---

[181] Authors on both the 1917 and 1983 codes apply variously the concept of the "community capable of receiving law." With respect to the 1917 code, see J. P. Cook, *Ecclesiastical Communities and Their Ability to Induce Legal Customs, CanLawStud* 300 (1950).

[182] E.g., all churches *sui iuris,* all particular churches, institutes of consecrated life and societies of apostolic life and their provinces, personal prelatures, parishes, public associations, private associations that have acquired juridic personality after approval of their statutes (c. 322), formally established houses of religious institutes, seminaries, etc.

[183] E.g., private associations that have been approved by ecclesiastical authority and are subject to its regulation; the community that makes up a Catholic institution (such as a university or hospital) which, though not a juridic person, is controlled by a juridic person or Catholic faithful and is subject to canon law; local communities of religious institutes whose members reside in a house that lacks juridic personality but has been established in accord with the proper law of the institute.

[184] Such groups certainly form their own customs, but they are not recognized by canon law as ecclesiastical customs, and they cannot attain the force of law.

[185] E.g., a person wills to avoid physical injury, but this intention need not be conscious to be operative. Many other examples could be given. The canonical doctrine on this issue is surveyed in P. Pellegrino, *L' "animus communitatis" e l' "adprobatio legislatoris" nell' attuale dottrina canonistica della consuetudine antinomica* (Milan: Giuffrè, 1995). S. Gherro offers a different view from that expressed here in "L'*animus communitatis* della consuetudine canonica," *Ephemerides iuris canonici* 38 (1982) 137–139.

move the practice, it is proven that the community does not consider its practice to be binding, and thus the intention to introduce a norm does not exist. The community's indifference shows that the practice is optional and not a real custom.[186]

A custom must be the practice of most members of the community. The majority must intend to introduce a norm, not just tolerate a practice imposed by the community's leadership. A minority practice cannot become a custom with the force of law.

The Eastern code (*CCEO* 1507, §1) mentions nothing about the community's "intention of introducing a law," but says the practice must be "continuous and peaceful" for the period prescribed in law. This suggests an evolution in the mind of the legislator, namely, that the phrase in the Latin code is unnecessary, since it is clear from the very notion of canonical custom that it is a norm introduced by the community. It further suggests that the community's intention to introduce a norm is demonstrated when the custom has been continuously and peacefully observed for thirty years.

The Required Time

Canon 26 — Unless the competent legislator has specifically approved it, a custom contrary to the canon law now in force or one beyond a canonical law (*praeter legem canonicam*) obtains the force of law only if it has been legitimately observed for thirty continuous and complete years. Only a centenary or immemorial custom, however, can prevail against a canonical law which contains a clause prohibiting future customs.

The final rule for the formation of a legal custom is given in this canon, which deals with con-

trary customs and customs beyond the law.[187] Such customs must be observed for thirty continuous and complete years to attain the force of law. If a law prohibits a contrary custom from forming in the future, it could not attain the force of law unless it were legitimately observed for one hundred complete and continuous years (centenary), or unless it were observed as long as anyone in the community could remember (immemorial).[188] A prohibition on future customs does not affect legal customs already existing, which may continue, but it does affect factual customs already in existence that have not yet attained the force of law.

The custom must be *legitimately* observed, meaning "according to the law," especially canons 24–25. The observance must be for thirty *complete* years in accord with canons 202, §2 and 203. It must be *continuous,* that is, without interruption (c. 201, §1).[189] The observance of a custom is in-

---

[186] The purpose of the law on custom may be seen as protecting legal customs from being easily removed, while at the same time allowing the community's leaders the freedom to remove factual customs and optional practices, especially when these are *contra ius.* The only time the law on custom affects the community's practical life is when someone in authority attempts to remove or change a custom.

[187] The canon speaks of custom contrary to the *ius* and beyond the *lex.* Some authors suggest that the use of *praeter legem canonicam* was a mistake, and the law really means *praeter ius,* but we believe an interpretation on the basis of the literal meaning of the text, as required by c. 17, is possible. Thus, the only customs *praeter ius* of concern to the legislator in this canon are those that are beyond the *law (praeter legem),* not customs beyond other kinds of *ius,* such as statutes. This means that there is freedom in particular law (*ius particulare,* but not in the *lex particularis*) to establish a period other than thirty years for the time needed to establish a binding custom that is *praeter ius,* e.g., the constitutions of a religious institute with respect to an internal custom of the community. In the absence of such a particular norm, the rule of c. 26 must be observed (cf. c. 19 on laws passed in similar matters).

[188] The canon speaks of a canonical law (*lex canonica*), not *ius.* This means that if another source of the *ius,* such as a statute, were to prohibit future contrary customs, it would take only thirty years to attain juridical force, or that period determined in the *ius particulare.*

This provision of law has minimal application, as neither the 1917 nor the 1983 code contains a canon prohibiting future customs. A law prohibiting a future contrary custom is not the same as a law revoking or reprobating a contrary custom.

[189] The canonical tradition also holds that the custom must be *free* (not coerced, but desired by the majority), *re-*

terrupted if: (1) the majority of the community ceases to observe it for a time, (2) the custom is continuously observed but for a time the community does not consider it normative (c. 25),[190] or (3) the custom is expressly disapproved by legitimate ecclesiastical authority. The latter refers not only to those with legislative power but also to executive authorities (the Roman Curia, the vicar general, major superiors, etc.) over matters within their competence.[191] The disapproval may be general by means of a public document (cc. 29–34), or directed to a specific community by an individual administrative decree (cc. 48–49). Observance of a contrary custom is also interrupted if a new law or norm is enacted that repeats the law or norm to which the custom was contrary, for example, the repetition of a norm in a new edition of a liturgical book or a revised directory (cf. c. 28). If the custom continues after the interruption, a new period of thirty years would be required for it to attain the force of law, barring no further interruptions.

The rules of this canon apply only to legal, not specific, approbation. The latter is treated above in the commentary on canon 23.

The Best Interpreter

Canon 27 — Custom is the best interpreter of laws.

The interpretation treated in this canon is better understood as interpretation-in-practice rather than the technical interpretation of a law's meaning treated in canons 17–18. Thus, to say that custom is the best interpreter of law means it is the surest and most reliable way of understanding how the law is to be understood and observed within an actual community. The canon is a well-established maxim in the canonical tradition going back to Roman law, whence it came.[192] It is a particularly useful principle for interpreting a universal law in the diverse particular churches. The law given by the universal legislator provides general rules for the entire Latin church, but circumstances within the many particular churches and communities vary considerably. The sound traditions and customs that have endured the test of time in these many settings provide a solid foundation for the practical interpretation of laws that regulate the same matters as do these customs. The canon applies also to particular laws, but to a lesser degree, since particular laws are themselves frequently a way in which matters treated in the universal law are concretized for particular places and communities.

Authors do not agree on exactly which categories of customs are intended by the canon. Some limit its application only to so-called customs in accord with the law. Others say it refers only to factual customs, because legal customs are themselves norms that must be observed, not interpretations of law. We believe that all customs can interpret the law, but in different ways.

Legal customs, in communities where they are in force, do not interpret the law, because they themselves are norms that must be observed, even if contrary to the law. However, for communities struggling to apply the law in practice, the legal customs on the matter observed by other communities could be helpful means of interpretation. Factual customs contrary to the law might be abuses, so they are not a reliable source of interpretation of the law unless their reasonableness in the circumstances is plainly evident and the cus-

---

peated (with a frequency dependent on the nature of the practice and the circumstances), and *public* (not concealed and provable).

[190] This is a theoretical possibility, but rarely possible to prove.

[191] Cf. Michiels, *Normae generales juris canonici,* 2:85. In reality, even lesser superiors, e.g., pastors and local religious superiors, are able to interrupt the observance of a custom pertaining to a matter within their competence. For example, if the pastor eliminates a factual custom contrary to a liturgical law (c. 528, §2), the observance of the custom is effectively interrupted; if it continues under a new pastor, the thirty-year time period must begin again.

[192] D. 1, 3, 27; cf. *RI* 45. The use of *lex* in this canon is traditional, not technical. It should be understood to include all forms of the objective, written *ius*.

tom is tolerated by the ordinary. Customs beyond the law (*praeter ius*) treat matters not regulated in the law, but they are useful in interpreting laws that deal with similar matters. The rule of this canon does not strictly apply to optional practices of the community that popularly are called customs, but lack an essential feature of custom—that it be observed with the intention of introducing a norm (c. 25). However, such practices may be considered in the application of the law, especially given the difficulty of determining whether the community intends its custom to be normative.

Revocation of Custom

Canon 28 — Without prejudice to the prescript of can. 5, a contrary custom or law revokes a custom which is contrary to or beyond the law (*praeter legem*). Unless it makes express mention of them, however, a law does not revoke centenary or immemorial customs, nor does a universal law revoke particular customs.

Canon 5 revokes all customs contrary to the code, with the exceptions noted. Canon 28 provides a general rule for the revocation of all customs, but especially legal customs, since factual customs may be removed by executive authorities as well as by law or custom.

A law may revoke a custom in two ways, expressly or tacitly. A law *expressly* revokes a custom by naming the precise custom or, more commonly, by means of a general formula revoking contrary customs, such as "anything to the contrary notwithstanding." This formula, if it appears in a universal law, revokes only universal customs contrary to the law (which are very rare), but if used in a particular law, it revokes customs contrary to both particular and universal law within that jurisdiction.

A later law *tacitly* revokes a custom simply by being contrary to it, such that the two are incompatible. The custom can no longer be observed at all or in part without conflicting with the new law, thus the abrogation or derogation of the custom by the new law. Likewise, a new legal custom,

contrary to a previous custom, revokes the previous custom. The canon speaks of a contrary custom or law; this is the new law or custom that is contrary to the old custom. The old custom may have been contrary to or beyond the law (*ius*) in force at that time; in either case, it is revoked (abrogated or derogated from) by the later law or legal custom contrary to it.

Two categories of contrary customs may *not* be tacitly revoked by a contrary law but must be expressly revoked. (1) No law tacitly revokes centenary and immemorial customs. A general formula revoking contrary customs must refer specifically to centenary and immemorial customs, or they are not revoked.[193] (2) Universal law does not tacitly revoke contrary particular customs that have the force of law. The universal law must expressly revoke contrary particular customs, either by explicitly stating this,[194] or by means of a general formula that includes particular customs.[195]

The revocation of customs by particular law is a question disputed by authors. Certainly, a particular legislator can revoke, for that particular jurisdiction, any custom within the legislator's competence that is *contrary* to law, whether the custom be contrary to universal or particular law (cf. c. 392). However, some authors maintain that the particular legislator cannot revoke a custom *beyond* the law (*praeter ius*), even within his own jurisdiction, if the custom is also in force in a higher legislator's jurisdiction. For example, a diocesan bishop cannot revoke a national custom

---

[193] E.g., *non obstante quacumque consuetudine etiam centenaria aut immemorabili.*

[194] E.g., *nulla obstante consuetudine contraria etiam particulari.*

[195] E.g., *reprobata quacumque consuetudine,* or *non obstante iure particulari contrario.* The revocation of particular law (*ius*) includes the revocation of particular customs, but the revocation of particular legislation (*lex*) does not affect customs. Universal law could not revoke contrary particular customs with a general formula such as *non obstante consuetudine contraria,* because this formula makes no express mention of particular customs.

beyond the law in his own diocese; that must be done by the conference of bishops, plenary council, or supreme legislator. Since the point is doubtful, this latter opinion must be followed, lest the community's right to observe a legal custom be denied by dubious means or broad interpretation (cf. cc. 14, 18).

A new legal custom tacitly revokes an older custom that is contrary to it, even if the older custom is centenary and immemorial. For example, in a certain parish the people had the custom of praying the rosary after daily Mass, but for the past thirty years it was not observed. The old custom is revoked by desuetude, the contrary practice of not observing it. Nothing prevents the resumption of the custom if the pastor and the community want it, but there is no legal right to resume it as there had been before the thirty years expired.

The canon speaks of customs contrary to or beyond the law (*lex*). Although it speaks only of legislation, the canon may be applied to other forms of the objective *ius*, in keeping with the rule of canon 19 on laws issued in similar matters. For example, a custom of a province of a religious institute is revoked if new constitutions are approved that contain a contrary norm. However, general administrative norms, as in documents of the Roman Curia, cannot revoke legal customs; only the legislator can do this and, with respect to the universal legislator, the revocation of a particular custom must be expressly stated.[196]

Proof of a Custom

A legal custom has the force of law and, if contrary to law, must be observed in place of the law where the custom is in force. In case of a conflict between a superior who wants to remove a custom and a community that wishes to retain it,

the higher superior or judge who is petitioned to decide the case must determine whether a legal custom exists. Unless the legislator has specifically approved the custom, the following are key questions whose answers must be sought by the testimonies of witnesses and/or authentic documents and writings or opinions of experts.

1. Is the community capable of receiving a law, that is, is it a juridically established Catholic community subject to legislative authority, or a homogeneous group within such a community?

2. Is the custom the practice of the majority of the community?[197]

3. Did the community intend to introduce a normative practice, not just an optional one?[198]

4. Has the custom been observed for at least thirty years without interruption? Is the custom centenary or immemorial?

5. Is the custom reasonable?[199]

If a custom has the force of law, the community has the right to maintain it. If the competent legislative authority opposes a legal custom, he may revoke it only by means of a law (c. 8).

---

[196] The only curial documents that could revoke customs are a legislative decree (c. 29) or a document approved *in forma specifica* by the pope; in either case, the legislative power comes from the pope.

[197] This is relative to the nature of the custom. E.g., if the custom occurs only at a particular parish Mass, the majority of people attending that Mass, not all parishioners, constitute the homogeneous community.

[198] Ordinarily, this is indicated when the custom has been continuously and peacefully practiced for thirty years. In a conflict situation, it is also indicated when a significant part of the community opposes removal of the custom.

[199] This is best argued on the basis of principles related to the nature of the custom. E.g., a liturgical custom is reasonable if it conforms to sound principles of liturgical celebration; it is unreasonable if it hinders the ends of the liturgy or obscures its proper nature. Experts must be consulted.

BIBLIOGRAPHY

Books

García Martín, J. *Le Norme Generali del Codex Iuris Canonici*. Rome: Edizioni Istituto Giuridico Claretiano, 1995.

Gauthier, A. *Roman Law and Its Contribution to the Development of Canon Law*. Ottawa: St. Paul University, 1996.

Gherro, S., ed. *Studi sul primo libro del Codex Iuris Canonici*. Padua: CEDAM, 1993.

Giordano, M., et al. *Il diritto della Chiesa: Interpretazione e prassi*. Studi Giuridici 41. Vatican City: Libreria Editrice Vaticana, 1996.

Gruppo Italiano Docenti di Diritto Canonico, eds. *Il diritto nel mistero della Chiesa* 1: *Il diritto nella realtà umana e nella vita della Chiesa; Il Libro 1 del Codice: Le Norme Generali*. 2nd ed. Quaderni di *Appolinaris* 5. Pontificia Università Lateranense, 1988.

Labandeira, E. *Tratado de derecho administrativo canónico*. 2nd ed. Pamplona: EUNSA, 1993.

Michiels, G. *Normae generales juris canonici*. 2nd ed. 3 vols. Paris: Desclée, 1949.

Miñambres, J. *La remisión de la ley canónica al derecho civil*. Rome: Ateneo Romano della Santa Croce, 1992.

Morrisey, F. G. *Papal and Curial Pronouncements: Their Canonical Significance in Light of the Code of Canon Law*. 2nd ed. rev. and updated by M. Thériault. Ottawa: St. Paul University, 1995.

Örsy, L. *Theology and Canon Law: New Horizons for Legislation and Interpretation*. Collegeville: Liturgical Press, 1992.

Van Hove, A. *Commentarium Lovaniense in Codicem Iuris Canonici,* vol. 1, Tome 2: *De legibus ecclesiasticis;* Tome 3: *De consuetudine; De temporis supputatione*. Mechelen, Belgium: H. Dessain, 1930, 1933.

Wrenn, L. G. *Authentic Interpretations on the 1983 Code*. Washington, D.C.: CLSA, 1993.

Articles

Abbass, J. "Canonical Interpretation by Recourse to 'Parallel Passages.'" *J* 51 (1991) 293–310.

Arrieta, J. I. "Il valore giuridico della prassi della Curia romana." *Ius Ecclesiae* 8 (1996) 97–119.

Benz, M. "Die Mitwerkung des Gesetzgebers bei der Entstehung von Gewohnheitsrecht." *AkK* 155 (1986) 466–479.

Castillo Lara, R. J. "De iuris canonici authentica interpretatione in auctoritate pontificae commissionis adimplenda." *Comm* 20 (1988) 265–287.

Coriden, J. A. "The Canonical Doctrine of Reception." *J* 50 (1990) 55–82.

Drössler, B. T. "Bermerkungen zur Interpretationstheorie des CIC/1983." *AkK* 153 (1984) 3–34.

Erdö, P. "Il cattolico, il battezzato e il fedele in piena comunione con la Chiesa cattolica: Osservazioni circa la nozione di 'cattolico' nel CIC (a proposito dei cc. 11 e 96)." *P* 86 (1997) 231–240.

Fernández Arruti, J. Á. "La costumbre en la nueva codificación." In *The New Code of Canon Law: Proceedings of the 5th International Congress of Canon Law,* ed. M. Thériault and J. Thorn, 159–182. Ottawa: St. Paul University, 1986.

Gaudemet, J. "La coutume en droit canonique." *RDC* 38 (1988) 224–251.

Gutiérrez, J. L. "La interpretación literal de la ley." *IC* 35 (1995) 529–560.

Herranz, J. "La interpretación auténtica: El Consejo Pontificio para la Interpretación de los Textos Legislativos." *IC* 35 (1995) 501–527.

Huels, J. M. "Back to the Future: The Role of Custom in a World Church." *CLSAP* 59 (1997) 1–25.

McIntyre, J. P. "The Acquired Right: A New Context." *Stud Can* 26 (1992) 25–38.

Malloy, T. E., and Folmer, J. J. "The Canonization of Civil Law." *CLSAP* 46 (1984) 43–65.

Minelli, C. "La canonizzazione delle leggi civili e la codificazione post conciliare." *P* 85 (1996) 445–487.

Otaduy Guerín, J. "El derecho canónico postconciliar como *ius vetus* (c. 6, §1)." In *The New Code of Canon Law: Proceedings of the 5th International Congress of Canon Law,* ed. M. Thériault and J. Thorn, 115–128. Ottawa: St. Paul University, 1986.

———. "La relación entre el derecho universal y el particular." *IC* 30 (1990) 467–492.

Pree, H. "Traditio canonica: La norma de interpretación del c. 6 §2 del CIC." *Ius Canonicum* 35 (1995) 423–446.

Rubio Rodriguez, J. J. "Los derechos adquiridos en el Codex de 1917 y 1983." *REDC* 39 (1983) 439–450.

Torfs, M. R. *"Propria verborum significatio:* De l'épistémologie à l'herméneutique." *Stud Can* 29 (1995) 179–192.

Urrutia, F. J. "Aequitas canonica." *Apol* 63 (1990) 205–239.

———. "Legis ecclesiasticae definitio." *P* 75 (1986) 303–335.

Valdrini, P. "Unité et pluralité des ensembles législatifs: Droit universel et droit particulier d'après le code de droit canonique latin." *Ius Ecclesiae* 9 (1997) 3–17.

Werneke, M. "Das Gewohnheitsrecht im Gesamtfüge von Universal- und Partikularrecht." *AkK* 156 (1996) 115–131.

TITLE III
GENERAL DECREES AND INSTRUCTIONS
[cc. 29–34]

The first five titles of the code define and regulate different types of normative behavior, moving from the more general and abstract (laws) to the more specific and particularized (statutes and rules of order). Title III serves as a bridge between the generality of law and the particularity of its execution. It moves from the realm of prescribed norms, whether written (laws) or unwritten (customs), to that of the application of those norms, from the legislative to the executive.

The six canons of title III show that terminology and juridic specification do not always coincide with precision. In the canons, the term "general decree" is ambiguous; it may refer to a normative legislative act (a law) or to an executive (or administrative) act of application. The code commission recognized this ambiguity when it stated that "the term decree signifies both laws and the administrative acts which provide for the execution of laws."[1] Canon 29 looks back to the abstract norm of law while canon 30 moves on to new material—the application of law.

General Decrees:
Nature/Identification with Laws

Canon 29 — General decrees, by which a competent legislator issues common prescripts for a community capable of receiving law, are laws properly speaking and are governed by the prescripts of the canons on laws.

Although this canon begins title III, it properly belongs to the category of ecclesiastical law. It is placed here to clarify a distinction between traditional usage and juridic reality. At times, particularly at the level of the episcopal conference or diocese, legislative acts are promulgated under the title of *general decree*. Such general decrees are actually laws. Consequently, only a person (or persons, in the case of a council) who possesses legislative power can issue these decrees. Moreover, as laws, these decrees apply to a "community capable of receiving law." Such a community is one whose ecclesiastical superior possesses legislative authority. Thus, a diocese is such a community, for it is subject to an ecclesiastical superior with legislative authority, that is, to a bishop. A parish, however, would not qualify as a community capable of receiving law, since it is only a part of the community of the diocese and the parish's direct ecclesiastical superior, the pastor, possesses only administrative authority.

Because the decrees are really laws, the prescripts of title I, not the prescripts of title III, apply. Moreover, the presence of this canon underlines the fact that it is only these types of general decrees—that is, decrees promulgated by a legislator—that have the true force of law. As the subsequent canons indicate, general executory decrees do not make law, they apply law.

The confusion caused by this double use of the term "general decree" is illustrated by the question raised concerning the proper interpretation of the term "general decree" in canon 455, §1. Was the reference only to general legislative decrees or also to general executory decrees? An authentic interpretation clarified the issue by indicating that the use of "general decree" included the general executory decrees regulated by canons 31–33.[2]

Limits of the Exercise of Executive Power

Canon 30 — A person who possesses only executive power is not able to issue the general decree

---

[1] *Comm* 3 (1971) 92.

[2] See *AAS* 77 (1985) 771.

mentioned in can. 29 unless, in particular cases, it has been expressly granted to that person by a competent legislator according to the norm of law and the conditions stated in the act of the grant have been observed.

This canon begins the code's normative organization of the executive, or administrative, function of governance, that is, that function of governance which applies laws rather than creates them.[3] It starts out on a negative note—indicating what an executive official cannot do. Those officials entrusted with the application of the law do not have authority to enact new laws, even if such laws are promulgated under the form of general decrees as described in the previous canon.

The canon provides an exception, however. An executive official can validly issue the type of general decree described in canon 29 if that official has received delegation to do so from a competent legislative authority.[4] The limits and conditions for the use of the delegation would be contained in the act of delegation. Since the code itself limits delegation of legislative authority to the supreme authority of the Church, the competent legislative authority mentioned in the canon would be the Roman Pontiff or an ecumenical council.

Purpose/Issuance of General Executory Decrees

Canon 31 — §1. Those who possess executive power are able to issue, within the limits of their competence, general executory decrees, namely, those which more precisely determine the methods to be observed in applying the law or which urge the observance of laws.

§2. With respect to the promulgation and suspensive period (vacatio) of the decrees mentioned in §1, the prescripts of can. 8 are to be observed.

---

[3] For a detailed study of the administrative function of governance in canon law, see E. Labandeira, *Tratado de Derecho Administrativo Canónico* (Pamplona: Ediciones Universidad de Navarra, S.A., 1988).

[4] See c. 135, §2.

Canon 31 introduces the positive regulation of executive (or administrative) activity. In considering this activity, some brief remarks about terminology may be helpful. While canon 135, §1 refers to the division of governance into the legislative, executive, and judicial functions, the code also uses the term "administrative" to refer to the activities of executive authority. For example, title IV of this book concerns singular administrative acts; canon 149, §2 refers to an administrative tribunal; and canon 1400, §2 speaks of an act of administrative power. In these canons, "administrative" refers to the activity of executive authority.

The use of the adjective "administrative" as a reference to the executive function of governance, however, should not be confused with the similar terminology in the code of an "act of administration." The acts of administration mentioned in canons 638, §1 and 1277 are not necessarily acts of executive authority but rather actions involving some use of ecclesiastical goods.

Administrative activity, that activity performed by a person who possesses administrative or executive authority, encompasses the broad and difficult to define area of governance that is neither law-enacting nor formally judicial. It is difficult to define because administrative/executive activity includes applications of laws that are quasi-legislative (for example, the general executory decrees described in this canon) as well as applications that are quasi-judicial (for example, the imposition of a penalty through an administrative process). Administrative activity is that action of governance which carries out the day-to-day application of abstract norms to the concrete circumstances of ecclesial life, apart from those specific activities entrusted to the courts.

Canon 31 regulates that aspect of executive authority that more closely resembles legislative actions. A general executory decree is analogous to a law. Like a law, it is general and abstract. It differs from a law, however, in that it does not create a new norm as such but applies an existing norm more specifically. The general decree depends upon a prior law. General decrees specify the law or urge its observance; they do not create new law.

This distinction is important, particularly in the interpretation of general decrees issued by the Roman congregations. They are executive, not legislative, acts[5] and are thus dependent upon the canons of this section for their proper interpretation.

Although this canon clearly states that general executory decrees are not laws but applications of existing laws, the analogy to law remains. The second paragraph of the canon prescribes that general executory decrees are to be issued in the same way that laws are promulgated.

Subjects of General Executory Decrees

Canon 32 — General executory decrees oblige those who are bound by the laws whose methods of application the same decrees determine or whose observance they urge.

This canon determines those obliged to observe the general executory decrees described in the preceding canon. It does so by stating that those who have to observe a law must also observe the general decrees that further specify that law.

An apparent lack of precision in this canon is that the extent of an administrator's competence does not necessarily coincide with that of the legislator. Canons 12 and 13 determine those who are obliged to observance of a law. A general executory decree, however, obliges only those who are both obliged to the law by virtue of canons 12 and 13 and under the authority of the administrator who issues the general executory decree. While a prescript of the code may well oblige all members of the Latin rite, a general executory decree of an episcopal conference would oblige only those members of the Latin rite under the authority of that particular episcopal conference. The law

may remain uniform, but its application through general executory decrees may vary from one executive authority to another.

The Relation of Decrees to Laws

Canon 33 — §1. General executory decrees, even if they are issued in directories or in documents of another name, do not derogate from laws, and their prescripts which are contrary to laws lack all force.

§2. Such decrees cease to have force by explicit or implicit revocation made by competent authority as well as by cessation of the law for whose execution they were given. They do not, however, cease when the authority of the one who established them expires unless the contrary is expressly provided.

General executory decrees further specify a law or urge its observance.[6] Such decrees, consequently, depend upon the prior existence of the law; they are not equal but subordinate to the law. The first paragraph of canon 33 emphasizes this dependence. An act which fulfills the definition of canon 31, §1, no matter what title it has, can further specify a law but it cannot nullify the provisions of that law. Should it do so, those provisions of the decree which contradict the law have no effect. They are not to be observed nor can they be used as an argument to suggest that the law has been changed or repealed. Only the legislator or a legitimate delegate can change or repeal laws.

Canon 31 indicates how a general executory decree comes into being. The second paragraph of canon 33 describes how a general executory decree ceases. Three possibilities are given. First, the competent authority can repeal the act; if an administrator can issue a general executory decree, the administrator can also repeal that decree.

Second, a general executory decree loses force if the law which it executes ceases to exist. Since a general executory decree depends upon a prior

[5] See *PB,* arts. 18 and 156, *AAS* 80 (1988) 864 and 901, as well as the *Regolamento Generale della Curia Romana,* art. 109, §§1 and 2, *AAS* 84 (1992) 244.

[6] See, for example, the *Ecumenical Directory, AAS* 85 (1993) 1039–1119.

law, its continued existence also depends upon the continued existence of that same law. When the law ceases, so does the decree, since the decree is merely a specific application of the law.

Third, a general executory decree can cease to exist when the administrator who issued it leaves office. This third manner of cessation of a decree, however, is the exception rather than the norm. The general norm is that when an administrator leaves office, the general executory decrees issued by that administrator remain effective. Since general decrees are issued as a necessary or useful specification of the law, they share the law's quality of permanence. Thus, a general executory decree ceases when the issuing administrator leaves office only if the decree expressly provides for that result.

Rules for Instructions

Canon 34 — §1. Instructions clarify the prescripts of laws and elaborate on and determine the methods to be observed in fulfilling them. They are given for the use of those whose duty it is to see that laws are executed and oblige them in the execution of the laws. Those who possess executive power legitimately issue such instructions within the limits of their competence.

§2. The ordinances of instructions do not derogate from laws. If these ordinances cannot be reconciled with the prescripts of laws, they lack all force.

§3. Instructions cease to have force not only by explicit or implicit revocation of the competent authority who issued them or of the superior of that authority but also by the cessation of the law for whose clarification or execution they were given.

The code explicitly includes norms for instructions in order to provide juridic certainty that instructions are *not* laws and that laws cannot be enacted under the title of "Instruction."[7] Rather, like

general executory decrees, instructions are acts of executive authority, that is, administrative acts. Both general executory decrees and instructions are issued by those who possess executive, or administrative, authority. They are both dependent upon a prior law for their existence and effect.

What distinguishes the two are the object and the audience. A general executory decree further specifies a law or urges observance of a law. An instruction, on the other hand, further specifies how the law is to be applied in practice. A general executory decree binds those obliged to observance of the law. An instruction binds subordinate administrators, namely those who are responsible to execute or apply the law.

An instruction, therefore, is a handbook or guideline for those whose responsibilities involve the application of the law in concrete circumstances—people such as pastors, vicars, directors of religious education, etc.[8] The guidelines for the application of the law found in an instruction, however, are not merely suggestions; they oblige those who are responsible for the application of the law. Instructions provide more detailed regulations in an attempt to ensure a more uniform application of the law accommodated to current circumstances. Instructions are based on the presumption that coordination of activity fosters the common good.

Because instructions are a type of executive, or administrative, action, their relationship with the law is similar to that of general executory decrees. The second and third paragraphs of this canon apply the earlier norms of general executory decrees to instructions.

---

[7] *Comm* 14 (1982) 136.

[8] Examples of instructions are those regarding the ecclesial vocation of the theologian, *AAS* 82 (1990) 1550–1570; the study of patristics in seminaries, *AAS* 82 (1990) 607–636; interreligious dialogue, *AAS* 84 (1992) 414–446; social communication, *AAS* 84 (1992) 447–468; the Roman liturgy and inculturation, *AAS* 87 (1995) 288–318; the diocesan synod, *AAS* 89 (1997) 706–721; collaboration of non-ordained faithful in the sacred ministry of priests, *AAS* 89 (1997) 852–877.

TITLE IV
SINGULAR ADMINISTRATIVE ACTS
[cc. 35–93]

CHAPTER I
COMMON NORMS
[cc. 35–47]

The Author of an Administrative Act

Canon 35 — A singular administrative act, whether it is a decree, a precept, or a rescript, can be issued by one who possesses executive power within the limits of that person's competence, without prejudice to the prescript of can. 76, §1.

With title IV, the code begins the normative regulation of the typical activity of an executive authority or administrator—the particularized application of the law to concrete, specific circumstances. It is important to note that not every action of an administrator is an administrative act. An administrator often handles a variety of affairs. Administrators answer correspondence, order office supplies, chair staff meetings, and approve expense accounts. The fact that an action is performed by an administrator does not make that action an administrative act as understood in these canons.

An administrative act is a juridic action. It is an act performed by an administrator as a function of office and intended to have a juridic effect. An administrative act changes the juridic situation of a physical or juridic person. It is consequently a more limited notion than a mere action of an administrator, for it entails a legal consequence.

The current canon categorizes administrative acts as decrees, precepts, or rescripts.[9] A singular administrative act that resolves a controversy or makes a provision is a decree. A precept imposes

an injunction. A rescript answers a request for a favor, that is, a request for some juridic action to which the petitioner does not have a legal right.

Although canons 35–47 provide the general norms for singular administrative acts, inconsistencies of usage do occur in the code. Canons 1400, §2 and 1445, §2 refer to acts of administrative power. Sixteen canons[10] refer to indults, even though an indult is not included here as a type of administrative act. Despite such inconsistencies, however, it is clear that an indult of release from vows issued by the Holy See or a diocesan bishop in accord with canon 691, §2 is an administrative act and must conform to the prescripts of the general norms given here in Book I.

Interpretation of an Administrative Act

Canon 36 — §1. An administrative act must be understood according to the proper meaning of the words and the common manner of speaking. In a case of doubt, those which refer to litigation, pertain to threatening or inflicting penalties, restrict the rights of a person, injure the acquired rights of others, or are contrary to a law which benefits private persons are subject to a strict interpretation; all others are subject to a broad interpretation.

§2. An administrative act must not be extended to other cases besides those expressed.

The rules for the interpretation of an administrative act parallel those given in canons 17 and 18 for the interpretation of laws. As with laws, administrative acts must be understood according to the proper meaning and common usage of the words. The law presumes that an administrator expects to communicate meaning, not confuse the issue, and thus uses a particular language in accord with its own rules of grammar, syntax, and vocabulary. This should not obscure the fact,

---

[9] Canons 48 to 75 provide more specific norms for these three types of singular administrative acts.

[10] Canons 320, §2; 684, §2; 686, §§1, 2; 687; 688, §2; 691, §§1, 2; 692; 693; 726, §2; 727, §1; 728; 743; 745; 1015, §2; 1019, §2; and 1021.

however, that legal systems themselves have particular vocabularies that may attribute a specific meaning to a word even though that word may have other meanings in non-legal contexts.

If there is doubt about the exact meaning or extent of the administrative act, however, additional rules apply. Administrative acts that restrict freedom or the free exercise of rights are to be interpreted strictly, that is, interpreted so as to be limited in their application. This canon lists the cases in which such limitation applies: administrative acts that involve lawsuits, threaten or impose penalties, restrict rights, injure the acquired rights of others, or are to the benefit of private persons and contrary to the law. In other circumstances in which sanctions or the restriction of rights are not at issue, administrative acts are subject to broad interpretation.

Unlike laws, which are general and abstract, singular administrative acts are concrete and individual. They are applications of the law to a particular need. Consequently, the present canon restricts the application of a singular administrative act to the situation for which it was issued. When a *lacuna legis* appears, analogous laws are applied to fill the "gap" in the law. This does not hold true in the sphere of administrative activity. If the need for administrative action arises, the proper response is not to apply another administrative act to the situation by way of analogy, but to request a concrete response from the competent authority.

Written Form of an Administrative Act

Canon 37 — An administrative act which regards the external forum must be put in writing. Furthermore, if it is given in commissorial form, the act of its execution must be put in writing.

In regulating the activity of public officials, the code adopts the practice common to contemporary legal communities—the rule that official acts must be issued in written form. This is not a recommendation for administrators but a requirement. The canon prescribes that an administrative act *must* be issued in writing. The Latin text uses the strongest form of the jussive. Nevertheless, written form is required only for legitimacy, not for validity. According to canon 124, §1, requirements for the validity of juridic acts are to be expressed in the law; in the current canon written form is not expressly required as a condition for validity. Moreover, canon 58, §2 makes explicit provision for acts given orally, which would seem unnecessary if such acts were invalid by law. The canon does not even require that the written document be signed, though some means of authentication seems necessary by virtue of canon 40 below.

The canon does qualify this requirement, however. An administrative act must be issued in writing when it concerns the external forum. The general understanding of governance in the law is that it deals with the external, public order of the community. In fulfilling its mission of sanctification, however, the Church also functions authoritatively in the internal forum, the forum of conscience. In those more unusual circumstances when an authoritative act of executive authority takes place within that forum—some action, for example, by the Apostolic Penitentiary—the requirement of written form does not apply. The canon does not prohibit issuance in writing in such circumstances, but neither does it require it. Singular administrative acts in the internal forum will follow the specific directives which regulate the activities of those executive agencies competent to act in such matters.

The requirement of written documentation in executive activity in the external forum extends not only to the original administrative act but also to the execution of that act when the act is issued in commissorial form. An administrative act is an application of the law to some concrete case. It thus applies to some particular person or persons —whether physical or juridic. It is generally not sufficient that an administrator apply the law. The administrator must also communicate that application to the interested or affected parties. Just as a law that was not promulgated would be an ineffective law, so too an administrative act that was not communicated would remain an ineffectual act of governance.

The communication or execution of an administrative act can take place in two ways. The simplest way would be to notify the affected parties—to hand them the written document, send it to them in the mail, etc. This is a process of simple notification. The written document, or at least its content, is conveyed to the parties in some immediate way.

With new technology, however, new questions arise. May an act be communicated by fax or e-mail? The difficulties with new technologies concern elements of security and authenticity. E-mail can lack appropriate security and cannot be easily authenticated, though further development may resolve these problems. Fax transmittals are more trustworthy than e-mail, since a facsimile can show the actual document, including signatures and seals. The authentic decree, however, remains the written document, at least at present. Canon 40 below, though, seems to take into account developing technology by allowing execution of a decree if "previous notice" of the official act has been received.

At times, simple notification may not be opportune. The administrator and the parties may be at some distance from one another. The content of the act may be of such importance that the administrator wishes to verify that certain conditions are fulfilled or that specific circumstances are verified. In such a case, the administrator may entrust the execution of the act to another person. The law refers to this process as the issuance of an act in commissorial form. The original act is to be executed by means of a secondary instrument.

For example, the supreme moderator of a clerical religious institute of pontifical right may receive a petition for separation from the institute. His decree of dismissal is an administrative act, an act of executive authority, since he is an ordinary in the law. It is an act in the external forum with clear juridic effects. Consequently, he must issue his decree as a written document.

It may happen, however, that the supreme moderator does not merely notify the petitioner of his decision but entrusts the execution of his deci-

sion to the local superior. The local superior must verify that the situation as described in the petition is true. The local superior has a responsibility greater than that of simple notification. The superior, consequently, carries out his executive responsibility in written, verifiable form.

This is a common practice when the executive authority responsible for a decision is removed from the actual situation, as occurs in the activity of the Roman congregations. To help ensure good governance, the execution of an act of governance is entrusted to someone closer to the scene. Because such acts of execution are also decisory, though in a subordinate manner, the law also requires that they be written.

Government by written documentation is the common practice of contemporary societies. It is a practice which canon law accepts and requires in its own regulation of the use of authority. Written documentation has certain advantages. No matter how clear a person may think he or she has been, disputes do arise. A written document provides objective evidence that can be referred to and studied. Even a text can be vague or understood in various ways. If every written act were clear and unambiguous, there would be no reason to provide the norms for interpretation found in canon 36. Yet a written text provides a far better starting point for resolution of a dispute than the parties' recollections of what may have been said or decided. In its option for written documentation, canon law follows the accepted practice of contemporary legal communities.

Limitations on an Administrative Act

Canon 38 — An administrative act, even if it is a rescript given *motu proprio*, lacks effect insofar as it injures the acquired right of another or is contrary to a law or approved custom, unless the competent authority has expressly added a derogating clause.

The use of executive authority, the application of the law to the exigencies of the moment, is not an exact science that follows rigorous and unbending rules of deduction. It is an art, the prudent weighing of myriad factors so that the values professed by the community can be concretely realized at a particular moment and in a particular situation. Such activity requires freedom, flexibility, and good judgment.

Discretionary activity, however, is not unlimited. It is bound by the requirements of justice, the good of the community, and the rights and dignity of individual persons. Administrative activity is discretionary, but it is a structured, regulated discretionary activity.

The current canon places limits upon the discretionary use of executive authority. An administrator may issue an act either because the administrator has received a request for action or because the administrator personally perceives that some action is called for. Nevertheless, the administrative act itself cannot injure another person's acquired right or be contrary to the law or to an approved custom. If the act is issued in violation of one of these three elements, it lacks juridic effect.

The canon notes an exception, however. If an administrative act is issued in violation of one of the elements mentioned above, it lacks effect unless the competent authority has expressly added a derogating clause, that is, a clause explicitly exempting the act from these legal restrictions. Care must be taken in applying this exception. The executive authority who issues an act is not necessarily an authority competent to affix a derogating clause. Who has such competence? The legislator who promulgated the particular law, approved the custom, or regulates the exercise of rights may add such a derogating clause when exercising executive authority. Although the present canons specifically treat the exercise of executive authority in the Church, it must be remembered that there is no division of powers in the Church analogous to that found in contemporary constitutional governments. The Roman Pontiff for the universal Church and the bishops for their particular churches exercise legislative, executive, and judicial functions. Consequently, these authorities, when acting administratively, may derogate from the norms they enacted in their capacity as legislators.

Those who possess legislative authority may also entrust to subsidiary administrators the power to derogate or dispense from laws or approved customs. The universal law in canons 87 and 88 offers an example of such in reference to dispensations. Such derogating authority, however, must be explicitly entrusted in some way. The exercise of executive authority of itself does not include authority to derogate from laws.

Finally, it must be noted that even if a particular administrator does have the authority to derogate in the ways described in this canon, an administrative act issued in violation of a law, an approved custom, or an acquired right still lacks effect unless that administrator specifically adds the derogating clause to the act itself. The administrator must clearly indicate that the action is an exception to the norm.

Conditions Affecting Validity

Canon 39 — Conditions in an administrative act are considered added for validity only when they are expressed by the particles if (*si*), unless (*nisi*), or provided that (*dummodo*).

A community functions more securely and productively if there is stability in its juridic activity. Actions should generally effect what they intend. Consequently, the law generally favors efficacy over inefficacy, validity over invalidity. Canon 39 concretizes this value. An administrative act may include conditions within the text. Nonetheless, these conditions do not affect the validity of the act unless they are expressed in a specific way.

At this point the text becomes somewhat problematic. The official text of the canon seems to give a taxative list. Unlike the norm of canon 10 which prescribes that laws are invalidating or disqualifying only when expressly stated to be such, canon 39 lists specific particles which are to be used in order to indicate a requirement for validity. Conditions in an administrative act affect validity only when they are expressed through the particles *si, nisi,* or *dummodo.* This presents no problem at all if the administrator happens to issue the particular act in Latin. If one of the three particles is used to express a condition, that condition affects the validity of the act. If no particle appears, then there is no condition affecting validity.

Yet what of administrative acts in the vernacular? The only official text of the law is Latin. The three particles in the canon can be expressed in various ways in various languages. Is it sufficient to say in English that "if," "unless," and "provided that" always refer to validity? After all, the English text is not official. If a clause begins "provided that," does that mean that the clause affects the validity of the act whereas a clause that begins "in the event that" does not?

It is worth noting that the Eastern code addresses this issue. Canon 1516 of the Eastern code states, "Conditions attached to administrative acts are considered to affect its [sic] validity only when they are expressed by the particles, *si, nisi, dummodo,* or by similar words in the vernacular."

Application of the law in a language other than Latin presents certain problems when the law determines a specific vocabulary without providing for the use of the vernacular, as occurs here. The Eastern code clearly offers a more effective formulation. The law favors validity. An administrator, consequently, would do well to be very explicit when expressing conditions that affect validity in order to avoid the real possibility of doubt.

Invalid Anticipation of an Administrative Act

Canon 40 — The executor of any administrative act invalidly carries out his or her function before receiving the relevant letter and verifying its authenticity and integrity, unless previous notice of the letter had been communicated to the executor by authority of the one who issued the act.

The preceding canons concern the administrative act itself. Canon 40 begins a series of provisions for the execution of an administrative act. The law now attends to the concrete application of the act, the action through which the exercise of executive authority is put into effect.

As mentioned earlier, an administrator can entrust the application, or execution, of an administrative act to another in two ways. The administrator may ask the executor of the act simply to notify the interested party. In this situation, the executor is merely an intermediary for the purposes of communication. The executor, however, may be entrusted with greater responsibility—the responsibility to issue a decree of execution. In the first method of execution, the administrative act is handed over or made known to the interested party/parties. In the second, an additional administrative act is issued—the act of execution, an act which is also to be issued in writing according to the norm of canon 37.

Before a person fulfills the responsibility of execution, however, he or she must have received and verified the authorization to do so. The executor is not to presume this beforehand. The executor must have received the documentation entrusting execution of the original act and ascertained that it is properly prepared, signed, sealed, etc. and that there are no suspicious or doubtful emendations added to the text. If the executor fails to do this, the execution is invalid.

There is an exception to this requirement for validity. If the administrator who issues the act informs the proposed executor of the commission in a more informal way and the executor acts upon that information, the execution of the act is valid. During the period of revision prior to the promulgation of the code, there was a proposal to eliminate this exception in the new law. The proposal was not accepted, however, on the grounds that the exception reflected a common and often useful practice.[11]

Thus, a member of an institute of consecrated life, because of his future apostolic work or the territory in which he resides, might request a dispensation from canon 1015, §2 so that he can be ordained by a bishop of a different ritual church. As the date of the ordination nears, however, no rescript has been received. His superior telephones the dicastery and determines that the dis-

[11] See *Comm* 14 (1982) 137.

pensation was in fact granted but has been delayed in the mail. Based upon this information, the ceremony takes place even though the official rescript has not been received. The flexibility provided by this exception to the rule is evident and protects the common good and individual welfare from an overly formal approach to governance.

Limitations on the Activity of an Executor

Canon 41 — The executor of an administrative act to whom is entrusted merely the task of execution cannot refuse the execution of this act unless it clearly appears that the act itself is null or cannot be upheld for another grave cause, or the conditions attached to the administrative act itself have not been fulfilled. Nevertheless, if the execution of the administrative act seems inopportune due to the circumstances of person or place, the executor is to suspend the execution. In such cases the executor is to inform immediately the authority who issued the act.

This canon strives to strike a balance between two important values: consistency in government and subsidiarity. In entrusting the execution of an administrative act to another, an administrator must have confidence that the act will be executed as issued, that it will not be changed or modified by the executor. If one cannot rely on a consistent application of decisions, responsible policy and governance become difficult, if not impossible. The law provides for consistency in action. If an administrator entrusts the simple execution of an act to another, the person must execute the act.

On the other hand, an administrator, particularly an administrator at a distance from the actual situation, may be unaware of the local situation or even mistaken in understanding the circumstances of the case. The law attempts to make provision for such situations. The current canon carefully qualifies the requirement of execution when certain circumstances arise.

The general principle requiring execution remains, though with some qualification. A person who receives a mandate of simple execution cannot refuse to execute the act except in three specific situations. An executor is not to execute an administrative act (a) if it is clear that the act is null, in other words, that the administrative act lacks some requirement for its validity; (b) if it cannot be upheld for some serious reason other than nullity, for example, if the administrative act is contrary to an approved custom yet contains no derogating clause; or (c) if the conditions attached to the administrative act have not been fulfilled. It would certainly appear that (c) would be a specific responsibility of any executor—the person on the scene, so to speak. In any event, the executor must immediately inform the issuing authority of what has occurred, since the act is ultimately not the responsibility of the executor but of the issuing administrator.

It could also happen that the executor perceives that if the administrator had understood the local situation, the administrator would not have issued the act. This is, of course, a prudential judgment, a conclusion about the mind of the administrator. The judgment may be correct or not. The law, however, gives weight to the considered judgment of the person on the scene. If the executor judges that the execution of the administrative act is untimely due to some particular circumstance, the executor may delay the execution until he or she clarifies the situation with the issuing authority. Thus, a balance is struck between the authority of the issuer and the prudent judgment of the local person.

Invalid Execution of an Administrative Act

Canon 42 — The executor of an administrative act must proceed according to the norm of the mandate. If, however, the executor did not fulfill the essential conditions attached to the relevant letter and did not observe the substantial form of proceeding, the execution is invalid.

When an administrator entrusts the execution of an administrative act to another person, the administrator may include instructions as to how the execution is to take place. The executor must proceed accordingly. Failure to do so renders the execution either illicit or invalid. Any failure to follow the instructions set forth for the execution of the act would result in an illicit execution. If the document entrusting execution of the act attaches essential conditions for the execution—conditions which must be expressed according to the norm of canon 39 since the document is itself an administrative act—then failure to fulfill those conditions would render the execution invalid. Similarly, if the executor does not substantially observe required procedural formalities, the execution would also be invalid. In other words, the executor must follow at least the general substance of any guidelines indicating how he or she is to carry out the mandated execution.

Although this canon refers to "essential" conditions, it would be more precise and clearer if it had simply repeated the terminology of canon 39, that is, "conditions for validity." Canon 1523 of the Eastern code does so with the result that it is a more precisely formulated norm.

Substitution of an Executor

Canon 43 — The executor of an administrative act can, according to his or her prudent judgment, substitute another as executor unless substitution has been forbidden, the executor has been chosen for personal qualifications, or a substitute has been predetermined. In these cases, however, the executor may entrust the preparatory acts to another.

In general, when a person has been entrusted with the execution of an administrative act, that person can designate a substitute to handle the matter. The freedom to entrust this responsibility to another, however, can be limited by the issuer of the administrative act. The original executive authority may prohibit the use of a substitute or personally designate a particular substitute. The authority may also have chosen the particular executor for some specific reason—because of the person's office (the pastor, the school principal, etc.) or some specific qualification. When such specification is clearly expressed, designating a substitute is also precluded.

Even when substitution is not permitted, the executor is still able to entrust the preparatory acts to another. The person cannot designate someone else to do the actual execution, but can ask another to verify the documents, ensure that the conditions required by the act are fulfilled, take care of any preliminary details, etc. Only the actual execution must be done personally.

Succession in Office of the Executor

Canon 44 — The executor's successor in office can also execute an administrative act unless the executor was chosen for personal qualifications.

The law assumes that when an official is designated to perform an executive function, it is the person as officeholder, not the person as private individual, who is chosen to carry out the responsibility. Thus, when there is a change of office, responsibility follows the office, not the person.[12] The person's successor assumes the responsibility. If the execution of a rescript has been entrusted to the pastor of a parish and the pastor is transferred before executing the rescript, then the new pastor assumes the responsibility of execution.

The law admits an exception to that rule when the person as an individual rather than as an official has been designated to execute an administrative act. In such a case, the responsibility remains with the person apart from the office. Because this is the exception rather than the rule, however, the designating authority must clearly express such a qualification when entrusting an act to an executor.

---

[12] *RI* 46: *Is qui in ius succedit alterius, eo iure, quo ille, uti debebit.* (The one who takes over the responsibilities of another must fulfill the responsibilities which the former had.)

Remedy for Error in the Execution

Canon 45 — If the executor has erred in any way in the execution of an administrative act, the executor is permitted to execute the same act again.

An executor is responsible for implementing the administrative act. The administrative act has priority. It is the original administrative act which intends to apply the law to a concrete need. The important thing, consequently, is to ensure that the act is properly implemented. If the act of implementation is somehow defective, the law is concerned that the defect not overly hinder effective governance. Mistakes in execution can be corrected. If a certain method or specific formalities are required in the execution of an act and the person responsible for the execution makes some mistake, the act of execution can be repeated. In fact, it is the responsibility of the executor to repeat the act of execution if a mistake has been made. After all, it is the original act of governance that is important. The execution of that original act is only a secondary function.

Continuity of Executive Powers

Canon 46 — An administrative act does not cease when the authority of the one who established it expires unless the law expressly provides otherwise.

An administrative act is a public, not a private, act. As an act of executive authority, it is an action done in fulfillment of some office in the Church. When Titius, the bishop of Pamphylia, appoints a pastor, it is the bishop of Pamphylia who makes the appointment, not Titius the private person. When Titius retires and Matthew takes possession of the see, the slate is not wiped clean. The acts of governance of the bishop remain as part of the continuation of the episcopal office.

The importance of this norm is clear. No society could function adequately if every change of office resulted in institutional collapse—the abolition of all previous decisions and provisions. Institutional continuity is an essential component of a stable social group, a safeguard against chaos and uncertainty.

The continued effectiveness of acts of executive authority is provided in the law, but not absolutely. In specific cases, the law may determine that an act is to cease when the authority who issued it leaves office. Because that is the exception, however, and not the rule, the law must make express provision in such cases.

Revocation of an Administrative Act

Canon 47 — The revocation of an administrative act by another administrative act of a competent authority takes effect only from the moment at which the revocation is legitimately made known to the person for whom it has been given.

For the most part, administrative acts take effect when the person affected by the act receives official notification. The same holds true when one administrative act revokes a previous act. When the executive authority issues the new act, the prior act continues in effect until the moment of notification.

CHAPTER II
SINGULAR DECREES AND PRECEPTS
[cc. 48–58]

Singular decrees and precepts are types of administrative acts. The current law distinguishes three forms of administrative activity: the singular decree, the singular precept, and the rescript. The content of the specific administrative act determines its form: singular decrees communicate decisions or provisions; singular precepts impose injunctions; rescripts grant dispensations, privileges, or other types of favors. This chapter sets forth the norms for the first two categories: singular decrees and singular precepts.

The Singular Decree: Concept/Species

Canon 48 — A singular decree is an administrative act issued by a competent executive authority in which a decision is given or a provision is made for a particular case according to the norms of law. Of their nature, these decisions or provisions do not presuppose a petition made by someone.

Canon 48 lists five elements as constitutive of a singular decree:

(1) A singular decree is an administrative act, that is, an action of executive authority which intends some juridic effect.

(2) It must be issued by a competent authority; the official must have a legal basis for action.

(3) It is to be issued according to the norm of law; the exercise of executive authority is discretionary but still confined within legal boundaries.

(4) It communicates a decision or makes some provision; in other words, through the singular administrative decree, the competent executive authority settles some controverted matter or provides for some need of the Church.

(5) It does not presuppose a petition or request for action on the part of another. A singular decree can be in response to some request or it can be the product of the free initiative of the executive authority.

Of these five elements, the fourth concerns the actual content of the act. It is that content which distinguishes the singular decree from other types of administrative acts. The singular decree communicates a decision or makes a provision. In the fulfillment of office, an executive authority may be called upon to settle some dispute or controversy. When confronted with the prosecution of a criminal act, for example, an ordinary may decide to settle the case through an administrative, rather than a judicial, process.[13] The ordinary's decision would consequently be issued in the form of a singular decree.

Executive authorities also issue singular decrees in order to make some provision for the good of the Church. Although the term *provision* refers elsewhere to the process of filling an ecclesiastical office[14] (and, in fact, the decree of appointment to office is one of the most common types of provision), its use here is broader. It has to do with an administrator's responsibility to provide for the specific needs of the community. A particular community may be benefited by the establishment of a new association of the faithful. In response to that perceived benefit, the diocesan bishop may establish the new association by means of a singular decree. A major superior of a clerical religious institute of pontifical right erects a new religious house by means of a singular decree. Through such decrees, executive officials place concrete actions for the common good.

As defined here, a singular decree is a concrete application of the law to a particular situation—whether that be some decision about a disputed issue or a specific response to a perceived need. The singular decree manifests a clearer characteristic of positive action than does the singular precept described in the following canon.

The Singular Precept: Concept

Canon 49 — A singular precept is a decree which directly and legitimately enjoins a specific person or persons to do or omit something, especially in order to urge the observance of law.

Canon 49 offers an example of either the limitations of vocabulary or the difficulties in editing text. The code proposes to distinguish between two concepts: that of a singular decree and that of

[13] See c. 1720.
[14] See cc. 146 and following.

a singular precept. Canon 48 defines the singular decree. In offering its definition of the singular precept, however, this canon refers to it as a decree. If canon 49 had followed the logic of the preceding canon, it would have begun as follows: "A singular precept is an *administrative act*." After all, according to the overall organization of this section of the code, singular decrees and singular precepts are types of administrative acts; the singular precept is not a type of singular decree.

A better formulation in this regard is found in canon 1510, §2, 1° and 2° of the Eastern code. That paragraph begins by stating, "Administrative acts are above all..." and then continues in numbers one and two to distinguish decrees from precepts. The paragraph clearly indicates that both are types of administrative acts and avoids the repetitive and misleading use of the term "decree."

What distinguishes the precept from the decree is the precept's negative character. Although both are actions of an executive authority, a decree has a more positive aspect to it. The decree settles an argument, makes a decision, provides for a concrete need of the community.

The precept, on the other hand, imposes an injunction. Through a precept an administrator orders someone to do something or to refrain from doing something, generally to observe the law or to refrain from behavior in violation of the law. In a real sense, an injunction provides for a need of the community, but it does so through a command or an obligation imposed upon a particular person or group.

An executive authority enjoins such an obligation "directly and legitimately." The precept is imposed directly, not through the mediation of another. It is imposed legitimately, that is, according to the norm of law. The precept must concern something over which the administrator has authority and must be imposed upon a person or persons who fall within the jurisdiction of that same administrator. A diocesan bishop may enjoin one of his own clergy against running for office in a local election, forcefully remind a lax diocesan official to carry out his or her duties, or prohibit an unauthorized liturgical innovation.

Information and Consultation before Decree

Canon 50 — Before issuing a singular decree, an authority is to seek out the necessary information and proofs and, insofar as possible, to hear those whose rights can be injured.

Although this particular chapter concerns singular decrees and precepts, the term "precept" occurs only twice—in the preceding canon and in canon 58, the last canon of the chapter. The intervening canons refer only to singular decrees. Nevertheless, some of the provisions would seem to apply equally to precepts, particularly those which determine such matters as legal effects, notification, and cessation.

After defining singular decrees and precepts, the chapter moves on to their issuance, notification, and interpretation. At first glance, canon 50 may appear so obvious as to make one wonder why it would be included in the law. Yet despite its commonsense reasonableness, it makes an important statement about the use of authority. Acts of governance are not acts of whimsy or caprice but actions intended to realize the common good and the salvation of souls. Thus, the legitimate use of authority requires information and consultation. A penalty cannot be imposed through an administrative process without a prior gathering of evidence.[15] Otherwise it would be an act of injustice rather than of good governance.

The present canon is thus important in this section. An administrative act is to be the result of investigation and considered judgment. Most particularly, those who will be affected by the act are to be informed and consulted insofar as this is possible. Canon 1517, §1 of the Eastern code even more effectively expresses this principle of consultation by stating that those who will be "directly touched" by the decree should be consulted. Some administrative procedures in the Latin code—such as those for the transfer or removal of pastors[16]—more exactly specify the need for in-

---

[15] See cc. 1717 and following.
[16] See cc. 1740 and following.

vestigation and consultation. Nonetheless, the gathering of information is prescribed as a fundamental requirement of administrative action, though not a requirement for the validity of the act.

Written Form of a Decisory Decree

Canon 51 — A decree is to be issued in writing, with the reasons at least summarily expressed if it is a decision.

According to canon 37, singular administrative acts which concern the external forum must be issued in writing. Canon 51 repeats this requirement with a significant addition. A decisory decree must not only be issued in writing but must also give, at least in summary form, the reasons for the decision. It is not enough simply to communicate one's conclusion; the administrator must also give the reasons that led to that conclusion.

As the canon notes, this requirement applies only to decrees which communicate a decision. When an administrative act settles some controversy or decides some disputed issue, the administrator must provide an explanation. If a diocesan bishop chooses to resolve a criminal accusation through an administrative process, his final decree must express the reasons underlying his decision, the logic of the evidence that has led to that decision.

On the other hand, when a diocesan bishop makes provision for an office, the requirements of this canon do not apply. In appointing a pastor, the diocesan bishop does not have to indicate in his decree of appointment why he decided on this particular priest. It is simply presumed that he acts reasonably in making provision for the good of the Church.

The issuance of decisory decrees is more strictly structured because such decrees more frequently affect a person's juridic situation and rights. Decisions resolve disputes. Administrative acts that decide an issue are thus similar to judicial sentences. Like judicial sentences, they are subject to appeal to a higher authority. As a pro-

tection to all parties, the law requires that the logic for the decision be publicly evident.

This requirement has further application in the event of recourse against the decree. Although a person aggrieved by an administrative act can make recourse to the administrator's hierarchical superior for any just reason,[17] recourse to an administrative court can be made only if it is alleged that the act is illegitimate, that is, has violated the law in some way. The norms for the Second Section of the Signatura Apostolica, the administrative court of the Apostolic See, state that recourse to the tribunal against an act of administrative power is possible only when the petitioner contends that the act "violated some law either in the decision-making process or in the procedure used."[18] Although a detailed discussion of the illegitimacy of acts and the competence of the Second Section is beyond the scope of this work, it is sufficient to note that inclusion of the reasons for a decision provides a concrete foundation for determining the legitimacy or illegitimacy of the executive authority's decision-making process.

The canon gives no exceptions or qualifications to its requirement. Although canon 55 deals with situations which exempt the administrator from handing over a written text, no similar provision permits the exclusion of reasons in decisory decrees. This is in contrast to the corresponding provisions of canon 1519, §2 in the Eastern code. This canon also requires a summary of the reasons but adds a qualification: "If there is danger of public or private harm, so that the reasons should not appear in it, they are to be contained in a secret book and revealed, if asked for, to the one who is studying the possibility of interposing recourse against the decree."

This is a limitation to access not found in the Latin code. When an administrator makes use of this exception, only a person contemplating recourse has access—and only if the person requests access, though how the person would know of the secret record is not evident. Since the

---

[17] See c. 1737, §1.
[18] See *PB*, art. 123, §1.

Eastern code also provides for oral notification rather than handing over of the written text in exceptional circumstances, it is not clear what purpose this limitation on a person's right to know actually serves. In this regard, the provision of the Latin Code offers a more concrete protection of rights.

Limited Application of a Singular Decree

Canon 52 — A singular decree has force only in respect to the matters which it decides and for the persons for whom it was given. It obliges these persons everywhere, however, unless it is otherwise evident.

Just as canons 11–13 clarify the scope and application of ecclesiastical laws, so does this canon explain the scope and application of singular decrees and precepts. As noted above, the activity of executive authorities is limited to those actions that fall within the scope of their competence and those persons who are subject to their authority. Canon 52 further specifies the limits of an administrative act.

A singular decree or precept applies only to the matter contained in the decree. It cannot be extended to additional cases or similar situations. If a singular decree decides some issue, that decree does not become a binding precedent for further administrative activity such as a court decision would in the common law tradition. The singular decree applies only to the specific situation concerned.

Likewise, the singular administrative decree applies only to those persons for whom the act was issued. Again, the act cannot be extended to other persons in similar situations. The administrative act is concrete and specific. The law does not acknowledge the legitimacy of application by analogy. If similar situations arise, new acts are required to respond to those situations.

Once an act is legitimately issued and executed, however, it effectively binds the person or persons to whom it was issued until such time as it is withdrawn or otherwise legally abrogated. It binds the person, not the place where the person happens to be, and continues to bind the person or persons even if they move outside the territory of the particular administrator. If a diocesan bishop imposed a censure using an administrative process, the censure continues until revoked even if the person moves to a new diocese. It remains a legitimate and effective act of governance.

Conflicting Decrees

Canon 53 — If decrees are contrary to one another, a particular decree prevails over a general in those matters which are specifically expressed. If they are equally particular or equally general, the decree later in time modifies the earlier to the extent that the later one is contrary to it.

Canon 20 provides rules for determining the applicable norm when a situation of conflict of laws arises. This canon similarly provides for situations of conflict between singular decrees or precepts. The canon considers two possible situations in which singular decrees may deal with the same situation or circumstances: one in which there is a conflict between a general decree and a specific decree; the other in which there is a conflict between two general decrees or two specific decrees. There is an assumption in the canon that the conflicting decrees are products of the same administrative authority, since conflict of authority is a separate issue—the decree of a higher authority supersedes that of a lower authority.

The first case considers the situation in which an executive authority issues a general executory decree, the type of decree which might give guidelines or specifications for some activity. The same authority also issues a singular administrative decree regarding the same activity. This decree provides for the particular situation of a specific parish or group—a parish or group that falls under the administrator's authority and, consequently, under the authority of the general executory decree. However, it conflicts with the general executory decree. In such a circumstance, the provision for the specific situation takes precedence over the more general guidelines. In this, the canon follows the traditional principle given in rule 34 of the *Regulae Iuris: Generi per speciem derogatur,* or "The specific derogates from the general."

The second case concerns a situation in which an executive authority issues two conflicting general decrees or singular decrees without providing for the resolution of the conflict within the texts of the decrees themselves. When such a situation arises, the more recent decree takes precedence. The law presumes that the administrator's intention in providing for the public good is better reflected in the action that is more immediate in time.

Operative Force of a Singular Decree

Canon 54 — §1. A singular decree whose application is entrusted to an executor takes effect from the moment of execution; otherwise, from the moment it is made known to the person by the authority of the one who issued it.

§2. To be enforced, a singular decree must be made known by a legitimate document according to the norm of law.

This norm of law answers the question: When does an administrative act take effect? Acts of governance affect persons and communities. Although their originating source may be the authority of the particular office-holder, they can be concretely effective only if communicated, made public to those subject to the governing authority. Interior intention is not sufficient for an act of governance. The intention must be expressed and communicated in some public way.

The code determines that singular administrative acts become effective at the time of notification, that is, at the time they are made known to the person or persons affected by the act. If the administrative act is one which is to be executed by someone other than the administrator who issued the act, then the act takes effect when the executor fulfills his or her responsibility to communicate the decree. When it is a case of simple

communication of the act, then the act takes effect when the person or persons affected are notified. The basic rule in either case is that administrative acts take effect when the affected parties are informed of them.

Although the basic rule is simple and fairly straightforward, there still remains the question of determining what is meant by notification. Is it enough that the person or persons are told of the administrative act by a third party—for example, by someone in the administrator's office? Is something more official required? The second paragraph responds to this by prescribing that effective notification must be made through a legitimate document according to the norm of law; otherwise, the decree cannot be enforced. In the majority of cases, this means through an official, written document as indicated in canons 37 and 51.

Substitute Form of Communication of a Decree

Canon 55 — Without prejudice to the prescripts of cann. 37 and 51, when a very grave reason prevents the handing over of the written text of a decree, the decree is considered to have been made known if it is read to the person to whom it is destined in the presence of a notary or two witnesses. After a written record of what has occurred has been prepared, all those present must sign it.

A situation may arise when it would be inopportune or inadvisable to hand over a written document. The law permits an exception to the norm only for a very grave reason. A very grave reason would generally be something detrimental to the common good or the good of the persons involved, such as the possibility of scandal or defamation of character. Simple convenience, however, would not appear to be sufficient to justify an exception.

Even if the administrator judges that there is a sufficiently grave reason not to hand over a written document, notification must still occur through some publicly verifiable act. The text of the act is to be read to the person in the presence of either a notary or two witnesses. A testimony of this action—the oral notification before witnesses—is then to be prepared and signed by all the parties and witnesses. This document of attestation then becomes the legal proof of legitimate notification.

Presumptive Communication of a Decree

Canon 56 — A decree is considered to have been made known if the one for whom it is destined has been properly summoned to receive or hear the decree but, without a just cause, did not appear or refused to sign.

The previous canon provides for exceptional circumstances of notification. This canon continues the consideration of such unusual cases. There may well be sufficient reason not to hand over the written document. The administrator may attempt to secure notification according to the norm of the previous canon. Yet the person or persons may simply not cooperate, either by not showing up for the oral notification or by refusing to sign the attestation of notification. If there is a good reason for failure to appear or refusal to sign, then the administrator must take some action to rectify the situation. A new appointment can be scheduled, etc.

On the other hand, the person or persons affected by the administrative act may simply be uncooperative for no good reason, or at least for no apparent good reason. Lack of cooperation cannot be used to obstruct the ongoing governance of a community. In such circumstances, therefore, lack of cooperation does not prevent the legal effectiveness of the administrative act. The law accepts the act as legally notified, even if actual notification has not occurred.

Presumptive Negative Response of Authority

Canon 57 — §1. Whenever the law orders a decree to be issued or an interested party legitimately proposes a petition or recourse to obtain a decree, the competent authority is to provide for the matter within three months from the receipt of the petition or recourse unless the law prescribes some other time period.

§2. When this time period has passed, if the decree has not yet been given, the response is presumed to be negative with respect to the presentation of further recourse.

§3. A presumed negative response does not exempt the competent authority from the obligation of issuing the decree and even of repairing the damage possibly incurred, according to the norm of can. 128.

The previous canon dealt with the situation of an uncooperative subject. This canon considers the situation of the uncooperative or negligent administrator, the situation when no response is forthcoming although some response is indicated. In that event, the law itself provides the response.

An executive authority may be obliged to issue a singular administrative decree either because the law requires it or because a person legitimately requests some action. If an election requires confirmation by a competent executive authority, the competent authority must respond by virtue of canon 179, §§1 and 2. Similarly, if a group of electors legitimately submits a postulation to a competent executive authority by virtue of canon 180, §1, the competent authority has an obligation to respond to the petition. When legal responsibility exists, the administrator must give a response within three months determined according to the norm of canon 202, §2. The only exception to this rule is if a particular norm determines a different time limit.[19]

If an administrator fails to respond despite the obligation to do so, the law itself provides for the administrator's negligence. Once the time limit has passed, a negative response is legally presumed. The canon establishes a general rule: Si-

---

[19] This occurs, for example, in the case of incardination where the competent authorities have four months to respond; see canon 268, §1.

lence means denial. Specific norms, however, can overturn this presumption. Canon 268, §1, for example, provides that in cases of excardination and incardination silence from the competent authorities is to be taken as approval rather than denial. The present canon provides a general rule; the rule, though, can be qualified or even contradicted in specific norms.

The presumption of negative response, however, is with respect to subsequent recourse. The presumed negative response does not resolve the concrete situation requiring some action but offers the possibility of requesting action from the administrative superior. The administrative superior can then either provide for the situation or enjoin the original administrator to take action.

Nor does a response supplied by the law exempt an administrator from the responsibilities and consequences of negligence. The legal obligation to issue a decree remains. Likewise, the administrator is responsible for damages caused by the failure to act.

Cessation of a Singular Decree or Precept

Canon 58 — §1. A singular decree ceases to have force through legitimate revocation by competent authority as well as through cessation of the law for whose execution it was given.

§2. A singular precept not imposed by a legitimate document ceases when the authority of the one who issued it expires.

A singular decree ceases to have effect if competent authority revokes it or the law it applies ceases to have force. In making this provision, the first paragraph follows the norms given for general decrees and instructions in canons 33, §2 and 34, §3. Regarding singular precepts, the second paragraph states that a singular precept that is not imposed by a legitimate document ceases when the official who imposed it leaves office. Otherwise, it remains in effect. A precept given orally, therefore, would have effect only while the particular administrator remained in office.

CHAPTER III
RESCRIPTS
[cc. 59–75]

After having presented the norms concerning the personal precept (*ius*), the code turns next to the favor (*gratia*). A precept is appropriately conveyed in an decree, but a rescript acknowledges a favor granted in response to a request. For perfectly rhetorical reasons, it is important to keep this distinction in mind. Since the precept is principally concerned with observing the law (divine, positive, natural, moral, canon, liturgical), the Church can always oblige. But a favor is just that: a gift, a benefit, a courtesy. By definition, then, we have no claim on favors. So it is well to remember this when requesting an indult of exclaustration or a dispensation from the obligation of celibacy. Also, by reason of the materials, the hierarchical principle prevails in these chapters.

Structurally speaking, chapter 3, which presents the common norms on rescripts (cc. 59–75), follows earlier sections in Book I. Under an organic metaphor, it presents the five essential elements that constitute a rescript: competence, matter, recipient, execution, and cessation. Like the titles on ecclesiastical laws and custom, these three chapters have a beginning, a middle, and an end. They also specify those elements that make singular administrative acts a species of constitutive law.

Canonical Concept of Rescript

Canon 59 — §1. A rescript is an administrative act issued in writing by competent executive authority; of its very nature, a rescript grants a privilege, dispensation, or other favor at someone's request.

§2. The prescripts established for rescripts are valid also for the oral granting of a permission or favors unless it is otherwise evident.

Because the competent authority can always urge following the law, the precept is usually imposed. A favor, on the other hand, requires a petition (*suapte natura*).[1] Addressed to one with ordinary executive power (cc. 136–138), thereby ensuring competence, the petition asks for a favor (*CCEO* 1527, §1). While the canon mentions both privilege and dispensation, which chapters 4 and 5 will explain, it also mentions "or other favor." This may include petitioning for an honorary degree from an ecclesiastical faculty, securing admission in a pontifical society, or requesting a papal blessing to commemorate a particular anniversary or occasion. Or the petition may ask for information, even to resolving a doubt of law. The rescript (from the Latin *rescribere*) acknowledges the petition and grants the request.

The body of the petition, usually a formal letter, should contain the following points: the precise request desired, the worthiness of the recipient, the concrete reasons applicable for this particular case, any supporting testimonials, and an appropriate conclusion. As an administrative act (c. 35), it imports a necessary formality, especially when it goes from one office to another. The rescript itself, as a juridic act (c. 124), will embody all the requisite formalities and solemnities.

The second paragraph, a new provision, pertains largely to permissions which a religious superior or a pastor might grant orally (*CCEO* 1527, §2). While the code surely favors the writing culture, it provides realistically enough for oral acts (e.g., cc. 55, 74). In general, canonists agree that an oral act suffices for validity but not for proof (cc. 74, 131, §3). In addition to competence, the following six canons also condition validity.

---

[1] F. J. Urrutia points to the inadequacy of the translation in modern language editions of the code. See *Les normes générales* (Paris: Tardy, 1994) 135, n. 1.

Canon 60 — Any rescript can be requested by all those who are not expressly prohibited from doing so.

According to the canon, anyone, whether baptized or non-baptized, can effectively (*efficaciter*) request and obtain a rescript.[2] In principle, then, the Church recognizes the capacity and the legitimacy of everyone to petition either the local ordinary or the Apostolic See (e.g., c. 1142). While continental canonists refer to this stance as that of "the passive subject," the nature of the activity itself belies the epithet. Indeed, the law itself grants to catechumens (c. 206) certain favors like receiving blessings (c. 1170) and even Christian burial (c. 1183, §1).[3] The law also indicates those who are expressly excluded from benefiting from favors (cc. 1331, §2, 3°; 1332; 1333, §4). In these cases, however, any penalty has to be declared or proved.

Canon 61 — Unless it is otherwise evident, a rescript can be requested for another even without the person's assent and has force before the person's acceptance, without prejudice to contrary clauses.

The Church has a long history of acknowledging distinguished services and awards various dignities and honors by way of recognition (*RI* 16, 77). Awards ceremonies occur at the local, national, and international levels. These awards, however, presuppose the appropriate requests, of which the recipients are presumably unaware (*CCEO* 1528). So the efficacy of the acknowledgement does not depend on the intention of the recipient but rather on that of the competent authority. In other words, the Church regularly acts on behalf of others, with or without their knowledge (e.g., c. 1164). The validity of the rescript, as a juridic act, derives from the competence of the issuing author-

ity.[4] According to canon 71, the recipient is free to use the favor or not. In the case of a dispensation from the vows of religion, the law provides otherwise (c. 692). A contrary clause, however, relative to the dispensation from celibacy limits that freedom. So the canons allow for both validity and for acceptance.

Canon 62 — A rescript in which no executor is given has effect at the moment the letter is given; other rescripts, at the moment of execution.

The notification of a rescript occurs either directly or indirectly. When the issuing authority mails the favor directly to the petitioner, he acts *in forma gratiosa*. The rescript takes effect according to the date found on the document (*CCEO* 1511). This agrees with the general principle found in *Regulae Iuris* 15, that odious things be restricted and favorable ones extended. If the rescript requires an executor, either necessary or voluntary, this indirect form of notification takes place *in forma commissoria*. This means that he must comply with the norms found in canons 40–45. So the diocesan bishop, as a necessary executor, notifies the petitioner that his rescript of laicization has arrived. In this case the rescript takes effect from the time of notification.

Conditions for Validity

Canon 63 — §1. Subreption, or concealment of the truth, prevents the validity of a rescript if in the request those things were not expressed which according to law, style, and canonical practice must be expressed for validity, unless it is a rescript of favor which is given *motu proprio*.

§2. Obreption, or a statement of falsehood, also prevents the validity of a rescript if not even one proposed motivating reason is true.

---

[2] See *Comm* 17 (1985) 54.
[3] According to the *RCIA*, no. 47, catechumens also have their proper marriage rite.

[4] Does the recipient have to accept the favor? Traditionally, commentators reply in the negative. See F. M. Cappello, *Summa Iuris Canonici*, 4th ed. (Rome: Apud Aedes Universitatis Gregorianae, 1945) 114–15, no. 144.

§3. The motivating reason in rescripts for which there is no executor must be true at the time when the rescript is given; in others, at the time of execution.

Since the rescript concerns a favor, the reasons for granting it must be factually true. In order to uphold this truth-value, the canon forbids both subreption and obreption. Either withholding the truth or lying about the truth constitutes fraud (c. 125, §2) which the canons explicitly prohibit (cc. 67, §2, 69). We are liable to encounter subreption today with somebody applying for admission to a seminary or a religious community.[5] Moreover, the first paragraph adds for validity other criteria: "according to law, style, and canonical practice" (*CCEO* 1529, §1), necessary for the validity of a juridic act (c. 124). By way of exception, a rescript granted *motu proprio* (i.e., spontaneously) derogates from these essential conditions in favor of largesse: "Any favor granted by the prince should remain" (*RI* 16).

The second paragraph indicates the necessary relationship between the motivating reason as cause and the valid rescript as effect.

The third paragraph asserts the existence of the motivating reasons by acknowledging the two modes of notification mentioned in canon 62 (*CCEO* 1529, §1). Although both modes uphold the truth-value intrinsic to any concession, it prevails at different moments. Any executor, either voluntary or necessary, should make sure that the motives are in fact well founded.

Canon 64 — Without prejudice to the authority of the Penitentiary for the internal forum, a favor denied by any dicastery of the Roman Curia cannot be granted validly by any other dicastery of the same Curia or by another competent authority below the Roman Pontiff without the assent of the dicastery before which the matter was initiated.

This canon concerns the use of executive authority at the level of Church universal. Associated

with the Apostolic Penitentiary and the Roman Curia, it represents a principle of good order. Since all the dicasteries are juridically equal (*PB*, art. 2, §2), the petitioner cannot legitimately play one off against another. That is, "What is forbidden directly may not be done indirectly" (*RI* 84). Given multiple competencies of the various congregations, one congregation cannot validly grant what another congregation has denied. Still, another dicastery may review the petition. In that case, validity requires the assent (not the consent) of the prior dicastery; otherwise we are dealing with subreption. Canonical authors say that this assent is tantamount to concession. If circumstances so warrant, the petitioner may have recourse to the Apostolic Penitentiary (*PB*, arts. 117–120) in case of a request denied in the external forum. Needless to say, the Holy Father grants favors freely.

Canon 65 — §1. Without prejudice to the prescripts of §§2 and 3, no one is to petition from another ordinary a favor denied by one's own ordinary unless mention of the denial has been made. When this mention has been made, however, the ordinary is not to grant the favor unless he has obtained the reasons for the denial from the prior ordinary.

§2. A favor denied by a vicar general or by an episcopal vicar cannot be granted validly by another vicar of the same bishop even if the reasons for the denial have been obtained from the vicar who denied it.

§3. A favor denied by a vicar general or by an episcopal vicar and afterwards obtained from the diocesan bishop without any mention made of this denial is invalid. A favor denied by a diocesan bishop, however, even if mention is made of the denial, cannot be obtained validly from his vicar general or episcopal vicar without the consent of the bishop.

This canon essentially applies the same principles at the local level, that of the particular church (*CCEO* 1530). Since one may have several ordinaries, whether proper or cumulative but competent, it is possible to ask each of them at the same

[5] See *RR* (1996) 78–80.

time. This strategy, while not forbidden by the law, seems to violate the spirit of the law (*RI* 88). In short, the canon presents three situations.

The first paragraph, looking to the coherence of the legal system, ensures that a petitioner does not play one office against another, e.g., the ordinary of domicile and the ordinary of quasi-domicile. If the former has denied the request, the latter must be informed of the reasons before granting it. Otherwise the favor will be invalid by reason of fraud.

The second paragraph applies the same principle of inter-communication between the vicars. While their specific competencies may be limited, their executive authority may be very broad. But in the hierarchical order, they are perceived as equals, exercising a share in the bishop's power of governance. Denial here by one vicar precludes recourse to another.

The diocesan bishop surely can grant favors. In the case of a previous denial, the bishop needs to know the reasons for denial, and that for validity. The vicars, after all, act in the name of the bishop. Moreover, according to Urrutia, the bishop can grant a favor *motu proprio,* that is, spontaneously.[6] In this case, he does not need to be informed of previous requests and previous denials, and the favor is valid by reason of the bishop's own authority. However attractive this opinion (especially by way of analogy with the previous canon), it really subverts the norm and encourages duplicity. Nevertheless, the diocesan bishop can reverse a previous refusal. On the other hand, an inferior office cannot reverse the decision of a superior (c. 139). The canon upholds the unity of governance within the diocese.

Canon 66 — A rescript does not become invalid due to an error in the name of the person to whom it is given or by whom it is issued, or of the place where the person resides, or in the matter concerned, provided that, in the judgment of the ordinary, there is no doubt about the person or the matter.

[6] Urrutia, 140, no. 423.

The canon concerns a doubt of fact (c. 14), one that pertains either to the recipient of the favor or to the matter of the rescript itself. The local ordinary or the major religious superior must be personally satisfied that despite any accidental errors relative to the identity, the address, and the contents the rescript is authentic (c. 40). That is, the canon conditions the execution of the rescript on the judgment of the ordinary. Substantial doubt occurs when there is question of the person or the favor intended. The ordinary must resolve any doubt in order to ensure validity.

Contrary Rescripts

Canon 67 — §1. If it happens that two contrary rescripts are obtained for one and the same thing, the particular prevails over the general in those matters which are particularly expressed.

§2. If they are equally particular or equally general, the earlier in time prevails over the later unless there is express mention of the earlier one in the later one or unless the person who obtained the earlier one has not used the rescript out of malice or notable negligence.

§3. In a case of doubt whether a rescript is invalid or not, recourse is to be made to the one who issued it.

The canon concerns contrary rescripts. The first paragraph gives us a principle to resolve any conflict; the second paragraph offers another strategy. In this matter, it is well to recall the legal maxim "It is fitting that odious things be restricted and favorable ones extended" (*RI* 15).

Relative to the object or the matter of the rescript, the first paragraph explains that the more concrete provision prevails over the generic (*RI* 34). This application of the incarnational principle, already established in canon 53, asserts the priority of the specific, the particular, and the concrete over the general. As such, it encourages a certain immediacy in deciding and behaving. In this way, the canonical tradition reverses the philosophical bias which prefers the universal, the general, and the abstract to the concrete and the particular.

The second paragraph offers another strategy should the contrary rescripts be equally particular or equally general. It refers to a priority in time according to the principle "Whoever is prior in time has preference at law" (*RI* 54). Since decrees usually import obligations, they take effect later. But rescripts import favors, which means that they take effect earlier. Moreover, the priority in time involves an acquired right (cc. 36 §1; 38).

This same paragraph notes two exceptions. If the later rescript refers even indirectly (*expresse*) to the previous document, the presumption of priority no longer obtains. In this case, the beneficiary loses the original *ius ad rem* for another. Because the competent authority has either revoked or suspended the earlier rescript, the law respects this intention. The second exception concerns non-use of a rescript through either deceit or notable negligence. For the first, Pope Innocent III established the legal principle at work here in the year 1203: "Fraud and deceit should prove an advantage to no one" (X.1.3.16; F 2:23). "Notable negligence" would indicate that the matter was of little or no importance to the petitioner. In this case, delay harms everyone (*RI* 25). However, canonical authors agree that both fraud and notable negligence would have to be proved.

If the rescripts still remain contrary, the canon provides for recourse (§3). The petitioner can ask the competent authority to clarify the situation. Despite the numerous matters which come to the attention of chancery and curial officials, they are usually quite happy to clarify ambiguous situations.

Notification

Canon 68 — A rescript of the Apostolic See in which no executor is given must be presented to the ordinary of the one who obtained it only when it is prescribed in the same letter, or it concerns public matters, or it is necessary that conditions be verified.

In effect the canon ensures an executor in three specific instances. And this pertains for lawfulness only, not for validity (c. 10). Otherwise the general principle for rescripts given *in forma gratiosa* obtains. Nevertheless, the rescript may require in its wording the recognition by an ordinary (c. 134). Indeed, the text may require such presentation, even for validity. In this case the Apostolic See has clearly conditioned the rescript (c. 39). A second instance of presentation occurs with "public matters." Because persons—both physical and juridic—receive rescripts, their contents often enough bear on the public purposes of the diocese. If a religious community, for example, receives permission to call a school "Catholic" (c. 803, §3), the ordinary should be advised. So public matters pertain to the external forum. Canon 1706 illustrates the principle involved here. "Public" then is opposed to private, and not to occult. Accordingly, because certain faculties granted to religious are considered private, they do not affect the public order directly; the awareness (*visum*) of the ordinary is not required. Finally, a rescript must be presented to an ordinary who will verify that any attached conditions have been fulfilled, viz., that the recipient is a practicing Catholic in good standing. The integrity of the juridic act (c. 124) requires that attention. Since the rescript is valid from the time of its date, commentators discuss when the recipient should present a rescript to the ordinary. As a general rule, the recipient must avoid any suspicion of the deceit and notable negligence of the previous canon.

Canon 69 — A rescript for whose presentation no time is specified can be shown to the executor at any time, provided that there is neither fraud nor malice.

Having qualified the rescript given *in forma gratiosa*, the code proceeds in this and the following canon to consider those given *in forma commissoria*. The first canon turns on the presentation of the rescript to an executor. In general, either the law or the text will determine the time frame. But this canon allows for a situation in which no time has been specified. When does the executor receive the rescript? This canon provides only a negative norm: the avoidance of fraud and malice. To take away deliberately an honor reserved for another presumes imputability (c. 1321, §3).

Canon 70 — If in a rescript the granting of a favor is entrusted to an executor, it is up to the prudent judgment and conscience of the executor to grant or deny the favor.

By definition the rescript confers a favor (*gratia*) which one cannot claim as a right (*ius*). Here, in the case of a rescript granted *in forma commissoria,* the canon concedes a great deal of discretion to the voluntary executor. We find an analogous situation in canon 41. Admittedly, the executor cannot act arbitrarily; the canon stipulates as criteria "the prudent judgment and conscience of the executor." As in the case of decrees, circumstances may very well have changed. The canon leaves the executor free "to grant or deny the favor." Since the favor is perceived as indivisible, the executor must grant or deny the favor as a whole and not by parts. Unlike the necessary executor, who is charged, the voluntary executor takes charge of the whole business.

Supplementary Norms

Canon 71 — No one is bound to use a rescript given only in his or her favor unless bound to do so by a canonical obligation from another source.

The canon envisages two situations. In the case of a perfectly personal (*dumtaxat*) rescript, the code grants complete liberty to the recipient. A priest, for example, may receive a dispensation commuting for him the liturgy of the hours. He is free to avail himself or not of this favor as circumstances warrant. That is, a favor does not become an obligation (*RI* 61). The second instance concerns a rescript given to benefit others. Here, the recipient has an obligation to use it, provided that the obligation derives from a canonical source. Again, a priest may have been granted the faculty to confirm (c. 885, §2). As long as the faithful are well prepared and properly disposed,

he must exercise his faculty (c. 843, §1). The same principles apply to favors given orally. In concrete circumstances, the pastoral context will suggest the appropriate response.

Canon 72 — Rescripts granted by the Apostolic See which have expired can be extended once by the diocesan bishop for a just cause, but not beyond three months.

This new canon indicates the bishop's leadership role in his diocese. The law permits him to extend a favor granted by the Apostolic See under three conditions: "once," "for a just cause," "but not beyond three months." Since a rescript grants a favor which presumably contributes to someone's welfare, the bishop needs only "a just cause" in order to prorogue the favor. By way of respecting the appropriate competencies, he may exercise this faculty once. If necessary, he should be able to renew the favor within the canonical time provided. This means that the bishop does not anticipate the expiration. His decree (c. 62) takes effect after the expiration date, thereby ensuring a duration of three months. The current law uses three months as normative, found, for example, in canons 8, §1; 57, §1; 102, §2; 158, §1; 189, §3; 379; 437, §1; 1623; and 1646.

Canon 73 — Rescripts are not revoked by a contrary law unless the law itself provides otherwise.

This canon illustrates the precise difference between an obligation (*ius*) and a benefit (*gratia*). By definition (c. 59, §1), the rescript represents an exception to the law and therefore requires a strict interpretation (c. 36, §2). So a contrary law does not override the favor conceded, tantamount to an acquired right (c. 36, §1). Indeed, any subsequent law contrary to the rescript looks to the future, not to the past (c. 9). The present norm coheres with the burden of canon 20: a universal law does not derogate from a particular or a special law. How then do rescripts cease? They cease either by another administrative act formally rescinding the favor (c. 47) or by another law with an explicit revocatory clause (c. 20). Just as the legal system favors the stability of the law, it also upholds the permanence of its favors (*CCEO* 1513).

Canon 74 — Although one can use in the internal forum a favor granted orally, the person is bound to prove the favor in the external forum whenever someone legitimately requests it.

Although the code clearly allows for the oral act (c. 59, §2), it prefers the written document (cc. 37, 59, §1). Favors granted orally make sense in the internal forum, either sacramental or extra-sacramental. Because "the forum of conscience" concerns matters at once private and personal, oral favors are used to best advantage there. Moreover, they can be extended lawfully in the external forum provided that some lawful authority does not challenge them. An ordinary, for example, can legitimately ask for some proof according to the principle *Quod non est in actis, non est in mundo* (*CCEO* 1527, §2). The Church ordinarily recognizes three modes of proof: the written document (c. 37), prescription (c. 197), and witnesses (c. 1547). Without adequate proof the beneficiary of an oral act cannot claim the protection of law.

Canon 75 — If a rescript contains a privilege or dispensation, the prescripts of the following canons are also to be observed.

From a rhetorical point of view, the canon sets up a division that accounts for the materials in chapter 4 (privileges) and chapter 5 (dispensations). Canonically speaking, it states that in addition to the common norms for administrative acts (cc. 35–47) and those concerning rescripts (cc. 59–75), both privileges and dispensations also (*insuper*) follow supplemental norms. The general principle of interpretation (c. 36, §1) becomes more precise relative to privileges (c. 77) and dispensations (c. 92). So the special norms will derogate from the common norms according to the principle that the specific takes priority over the generic (*RI* 34).

CHAPTER IV
PRIVILEGES
[cc. 76–84]

Although the revision committee made an effort to clarify the different aspects of church governance—legislative, executive, judicial—they really did not succeed. Admittedly, they added two new titles to Book I, viz., titles III and IV. But the confusion begins early on with canons 30 and 31, which call for excessive refinement. The blurring between legislative and executive authority underlies this chapter as well. Just as the three *munera*—sanctifying, teaching, ruling—are inadequately distinct, so too the power of governance (c. 135, §1) remains imperfectly conceptualized.

Canonical Concept of Privilege

Canon 76 — §1. A privilege is a favor given through a particular act to the benefit of certain physical or juridic persons; it can be granted by the legislator as well as by an executive authority to whom the legislator has granted this power.

§2. Centenary or immemorial possession induces the presumption that a privilege has been granted.

This canon represents a considerable innovation compared with its predecessor, canon 63 in the 1917 code. By simplifying the previous norm, the canon stipulates the specific manner and the singular recipient (*CCEO* 1531). Although the privilege is still seen as a "favorable personal law," it requires the intervention of a legislator. Nevertheless, because it is ordinarily granted by a singular administrative act (*per peculiarem actum*), it may be delegated to one with executive authority (c. 134, §3). The appropriate *relator* indicated that privileges can also be acquired by prescription.[7] As a favor, the privilege acts either against the law (*contra legem*) or apart from the law (*praeter legem*), thereby retaining its legal character. Unlike other favors, however, the privi-

---

[7] See *Comm* 23 (1991) 40.

lege constitutes an objective norm conferred on an individual person, either physical or juridic. So a group or a de facto association of the faithful is not really the proper subject of a privilege. In this somewhat debatable material, the canon indicates four elements: a definition, competence, the beneficiary, and the mode of acquisition.

The second paragraph sets up a presumption of law. Centennial privileges have been in existence for more than a hundred years. Immemorial privileges have existed as long as anyone can remember. The canon is concerned largely with "possession." Presumably the documentation does not exist, but it very well may. Consequently, the presumption may be overturned by contrary proof (c. 1585).

Canon 77 — A privilege must be interpreted according to the norm of can. 36, §1, but that interpretation must always be used by which the beneficiaries of a privilege actually obtain some favor.

The canon stipulates two norms relative to the interpretation of privileges. The first alludes to the common norm found in canon 36, §1, which, for all practical purposes, ensures a strict interpretation, especially in any case of doubt. To the extent that privileges go against (*contra*) or beyond (*praeter*) the law, they become offensive and even detrimental to the common good. Therefore, the narrow reading prevails. On the other hand, the canon recognizes the generosity of the grantor, which requires a liberal interpretation (*CCEO* 1512, §3). That is, as a *lex favorabilis privata*, a privilege should positively concede some benefit (*RI* 61). Nevertheless, following the provision of canon 36, §2, privileges are not to be multiplied.

Types of Privilege

Canon 78 — §1. A privilege is presumed to be perpetual unless the contrary is proved.

§2. A personal privilege, namely one which follows the person, is extinguished with that person's death.

§3. A real privilege ceases through the complete destruction of the thing or place; a local privilege, however, revives if the place is restored within fifty years.

Unless it is clear from the nature of the privilege itself, the law presumes that every privilege is perpetual (*RI* 16). In this respect, it imitates the stability of law (*CCEO* 1532, §1). Still, a privilege can be limited to a specific liturgical season, by the number of cases, or as a temporary expedient (c. 83, §1). The presumption of perpetuity here indicates that a privilege does not cease with the mere passing of time. If somebody has difficulty distinguishing whether certain privileges are personal or real, the following principle should prove helpful: if the privilege is hurtful, consider it personal; if the privilege is favorable, consider it real.[8]

A personal privilege attaches to an individual, whether physical or juridic. According to canonical tradition, the personal privilege so follows the person that it ceases with the death of that person (*CCEO* 1532, §2). According to *Regulae Iuris* 7, "A personal privilege follows the person; it ceases with the individual." This means that it is nontransferrable to family, to friends, or to heirs. The privilege ceases intrinsically when its subject no longer exists. It is equally possible that the competent authority could revoke the privilege so that it would cease extrinsically. In the case of a juridic person, privileges similarly cease either intrinsically (c. 120, §1) or extrinsically (c. 47).

A real privilege attaches to a thing (*res*), usually an office or a place. Generally, a real privilege concerns a dignity or an indulgence. For the privilege to cease, the canon requires the absolute destruction of the thing (e.g., a sacred image) or the place (e.g., a shrine). In principle, then, the nonexistence of the thing or place means the loss of all privileges. Consonant with the spirit of liberality, the canon allows for the principle of revivis-

---

[8] See A. G. Cicognani, *Canon Law*, trans. J. M. O'Hara and F. Brennan, 2nd rev. ed. (Philadelphia: Dolphin Press, 1935) 818.

cence. If, after some disaster, a church, a shrine, or a basilica is rebuilt within fifty years (c. 201, §1), its privileges also revive (*CCEO* 1532, §3). Having treated in this canon the intrinsic cessation of privileges, the code addresses in the next six canons (cc. 79–84) the extrinsic cessation of privileges.

Cessation of Privileges

Canon 79 — A privilege ceases through revocation by the competent authority according to the norm of can. 47, without prejudice to the prescript of can. 81.

The canon illustrates the ordinary practice of the Church: it takes one administrative act to revoke another (c. 47). Administrative acts emanate from ecclesiastical offices. As the office endures, so too does its competence. The legal system calls for the intervention of the appropriate authority to manifest anew his will. This means that privileges do not cease with the passage of time (c. 78, §1), with the expiration of the competence of conceding authority (c. 81), or by any contrary law (c. 73). The legislator or his vicar, in effect, revokes a privilege *per peculiarem actum* (cf. c. 76, §1), by another administrative act, which includes a just and proportionate cause (c. 51) and lawful notification (c. 47). According to the norm, the privilege ceases with the proper notification.

Canon 80 — §1. No privilege ceases through renunciation unless the competent authority has accepted the renunciation.

§2. Any physical person can renounce a privilege granted only in that person's favor.

§3. Individual persons cannot renounce a privilege granted to some juridic person or granted in consideration of the dignity of a place or of a thing, nor is a juridic person free to renounce a privilege granted to it if the renunciation brings disadvantage to the Church or to others.

The canon speaks about the cessation of privileges through renunciation. As Mendonça points

out, "Formal renunciation is not to be confused with non-use or contrary use" (cf. c. 82).[9] Like many other institutes in the Church, this provision requires two moments: a proposal and its acceptance. In other words, the hierarchical principle does not admit of any unilateral decisions (*CCEO* 1533). Until the competent authority has accepted the formal renunciation, the privilege endures. Since any privilege represents an objective, if personal, norm in itself (c. 76, §1), it cannot be renounced by somebody who does not have the competence to establish the norm. This means that a superior with the appropriate legislative or delegated power must by an administrative act derogate from the individual norm.

Without compromising the validity of the general principle just enunciated, the second paragraph allows an individual to renounce a personal favor. The individual in this case is a physical person, not a private juridic person. The canon requires that the privilege to be renounced has been conceded exclusively for one's personal benefit. This makes the individual the exclusive subject of the privilege. Even so, an individual is not free to renounce a privilege assigned to a place, an office, or a community because the physical person is not the proper subject of the privilege and because these privileges are conferred precisely to benefit others.

Accordingly, because the whole is greater than the part (*RI* 35), no individual can renounce on his or her own authority a privilege granted to a juridic person, either public or private (c. 116). Similarly, a physical person cannot renounce a privilege associated with either a place (e.g., a shrine) or a thing (e.g., a sacred image) because the privilege does not belong to his or her proper patrimony. For the most part, privileges assist the faithful in exercising their religious duties (c. 214); in their own way privileges facilitate the pastoral ministry of the Church. So while a juridic person may find a way to renounce a privilege (c. 119, 3°), the interests of the Church, understood broadly, must always be kept in view.

---

[9] See *CLSGBI Com*, 46, no. 164.

Canon 81 — A privilege is not extinguished when the authority of the one who granted it expires unless it has been given with the clause, at our good pleasure (*ad beneplacitum nostrum*), or some other equivalent expression.

This canon represents an exception to the general rule (c. 78, §1). The legislator can condition a privilege (c. 39). Otherwise, privileges derive their permanence from the stability of the offices which grant them. In this sense, the canon recognizes the common norm relative to singular administrative acts (c. 46). The dispositive part of the text will reveal whether or not the legislator has conditioned the privilege. He may very well use an expression like "at our good pleasure" or its equivalent. In this way he signifies his intention to limit the personal privilege to the extent of his own competence, at either the local or the supreme level. As soon as his authority ceases, so too does the privilege.

Canon 82 — A privilege which is not burdensome to others does not cease through non-use or contrary use. If it is to the disadvantage of others, however, it is lost if legitimate prescription takes place.

The canon distinguishes between those privileges that are burdensome to others and those that are not (*CCEO* 1534). This means that some privileges are affirmative and favorable while others are negative and unfavorable to third parties. In the former instance, the canon asserts the general rule that privileges remain permanently (c. 78, §1). A priest, for example, may have received a privilege of celebrating Mass at a portable altar. Still, he prefers saying Mass in a church. Because he acts contrary to his privilege does not mean that he has lost his privilege. The same principle applies to non-use. A priest who has received a commutation for the liturgy of the hours by way of privilege may in fact prefer to recite the breviary. These examples illustrate favorable privileges which do not harm a third party.

The canon goes on to speak of negative privileges. Urrutia cites as examples an exemption from a tax and the faculty of taxing others, clearly onerous to other people.[10] Given the objectivity of the privilege as a singular norm, others in the community must respect it, invoked or not. Nevertheless, this canon recognizes the force of liberative prescription (cc. 197–199). Through non-use of this unfavorable privilege, the beneficiary signifies, at least implicitly, his intention to renounce it (cc. 71, 80, §2); and the affected third parties can take advantage of prescription (*CCEO* 1534). The civil law of prescription must be in place (c. 197); all parties must act in good faith (c. 198); and the matter involved must actually be prescriptible. Privileges that emanate from the Apostolic See are not (c. 199, 2°). Nevertheless, a lesser privilege may very well cease through prescription.

Canon 83 — §1. A privilege ceases through the lapse of the time period or through the completion of the number of cases for which it had been granted, without prejudice to the prescript of can. 142, §2.
§2. It also ceases if, in the judgment of the competent authority, circumstances are so changed in the course of time that it becomes harmful or its use illicit.

The first paragraph refers to temporary privileges, otherwise known as indults. Privileged faculties expire when the time-frame ceases or when the number of cases is complete. Canon 142, §2 makes a provision for the internal forum only; canon 144 supplies in the external forum executive power in the case of common error. The diocesan bishop may prorogue a privilege granted by the Apostolic See once and for only three months (c. 72).

The second paragraph also concerns the intrinsic cessation of privileges. It mentions the disruptive change in circumstances which militates against the final cause of the privilege. Every

---

[10] See F. J. Urrutia, *De normis generalibus* (Rome: Pontificia Universitas Gregoriana (1983) 50.

privilege, after all, is meant to confer a benefit and not to work against a beneficiary (*RI* 61). An appropriate authority makes the determination that a particular privilege is either illicit in its use or detrimental to the Church. With this judgment confirmed, the privilege simply ceases.

Canon 84 — One who abuses the power given by a privilege deserves to be deprived of that privilege. Therefore, when the holder of a privilege has been warned in vain, an ordinary is to deprive the one who gravely abuses it of a privilege which he himself has granted. If the privilege was granted by the Apostolic See, however, an ordinary is bound to notify the Apostolic See.

An abuse of a personal privilege deserves privation. The canon takes notice of three elements: the grave abuse, the inefficacious warning, and the deprivation. A privilege can be abused by exceeding the intended limits, by acting contrary to its original purpose, and by making it an occasion of sin or a source of scandal. The canon speaks of grave abuse which presupposes a habitual intention to disregard the moral order. For this reason the Church lists the deprivation of "privileges previously granted" among the expiatory penalties (cc. 1331, §2, 3°; 1336, §1, 2°). Second, an ordinary, being advised of the abusive situation, must issue a warning lest he seem to give tacit approval to the abuse (*CCEO* 1535). Neither the abuse nor the warning removes the privilege. The privation occurs, finally, when the responsible superior revokes the power (*potestatem*) behind the privilege. Although an ordinary may do this at the local level for a local privilege, in case of an apostolic privilege, he must inform the Holy See.

By way of conclusion, this chapter recognizes six ways of losing a privilege: (1) revocation (c. 79), (2) renunciation (c. 80), (3) expiration (c. 81), (4) prescription (c. 82), (5) cessation (c. 83), and (6) privation (c. 84). However subtle or infrequent these distinctions, the matter bears upon canon 93, which concerns the cessation of dispensations. These supplement the common norm found in canon 47.

CHAPTER V
DISPENSATIONS
[cc. 85–93]

As the commentators like to remind us, this chapter reverses just about one thousand years of church history. So it represents a certain newness, not without its difficulties, that indicates just how successfully the 1983 code reflects the intent of the Second Vatican Council. In effect, it obrogates the materials found in canons 80–86 of the 1917 code.

Although Roman law recognizes the institute that we call dispensation, it applies largely to three areas: the law, penalties, and contracts. During the first millennium of the Church's history, this faculty appears only in the most dramatic instances, e.g., relative to the *lapsi*, the ordinations of heretical or schismatic bishops, the residence of bishops. According to Fournier, the first ecclesiastical tract on dispensations appears with the *Prologus* of Yves of Chartres (d. 1115), a very famous text still discussed by medievalists.[11] De Ghellinck speculates that it may very well have circulated as an independent text in the eleventh century under the title *De consonantia canonum*. Whatever its provenance, it illustrates quite forcefully the broad dispensing power of bishops.

Admittedly, Yves of Chartres was perhaps the best-known canonist of his day. But he was also very pastorally minded, so he thought that bishops should dispense their people whenever they could secure some spiritual good. Influenced largely by Alger of Liège, he taught that justice must be tempered by mercy. Indeed, his letters reveal just how often and liberally the bishop of Chartres dispensed in order to accommodate difficult situations. So Naz, following Brys, gives us a definition of a dispensation which he attributes to Yves of Chartres: "a temporary relaxation of the law's rigor on account of a necessity of circumstances or usefulness to the Church."[12]

---

[11] For this text, see *PL* 161:47–60.

[12] *Mitigatio ad tempus rigoris iuris ob necessitatem temporum vel utilitatem Ecclesiae.* R. Naz, *DDC* 4:1284.

With Gratian, we find another mind-set. Unlike the French canonist, he rallies to the centrist position of Rome. This became for him the surest way of realizing the goals of the Gregorian Reform (1075–1122). According to this model, the *plenitudo potestatis* resides in the Roman pontiff; he delegates jurisdiction as he sees fit. This includes the power of dispensation. For Yves of Chartres, dispensing authority came with episcopal consecration and office. For Gratian, it was delegated by the Holy Father. This situation prevailed in the Church through Vatican I and the 1917 code. With Vatican II, we find the breakthrough, the one that reversed one thousand years of legal history in the Church.

The primary text occurs in *Christus Dominus:*

As successors of the apostles, bishops automatically enjoy in the dioceses entrusted to them all the ordinary, proper, and immediate authority required for the exercise of their pastoral office. But this authority never in any instance infringes upon the power which the Roman Pontiff has, by virtue of his office, of reserving cases to himself or to some other authority. (*CD* 8a; no. 586)

According to this text, diocesan bishops possess by reason of their episcopal order and their canonical mission all the power necessary to supervise that portion of the people of God confided to them. This means that they are no longer to be seen as vicars of the pope or emissaries of the Roman Curia. They have all the necessary authority in their own right. The text continues:

Except when it is a question of matters reserved to the supreme authority of the Church, the general law of the Church gives each diocesan bishop the faculty to grant dispensations in particular cases to the faithful over whom he exercises authority according to the norm of law, provided he judges it helpful for their spiritual welfare. (*CD* 8b; no. 587)

These two paragraphs reflect the new ecclesiology of Vatican II, characterized by the principle of subsidiarity and the union of churches.

To prevent any misunderstanding of the bishop's proper authority, *Lumen gentium* speaks very clearly:

Bishops govern the particular churches entrusted to them as the vicars and ambassadors of Christ.... This power which they personally exercise in Christ's name is proper, ordinary, and immediate, although its exercise is ultimately regulated by the supreme authority of the Church, and can be circumscribed by certain limits, for the advantage of the Church or of the faithful. In virtue of this power, bishops have the sacred right and the duty before the Lord to make laws for their subjects, to pass judgment on them, and to moderate everything pertaining to the ordering of worship and the apostolate. (*LG* 27; no. 351)

This important statement not only completes the work of Vatican I, but in many ways represents the precise achievement of Vatican II. We see its effects in the current code (e.g., c. 381, §1).

The first legislation to respond to this old/new recognition was Pope Paul VI's *motu proprio Pastorale munus,* issued on November 30, 1963.[13] According to Msgr. J. Denis, this document conceded to the bishops a number of faculties which they previously had had to request and renew periodically. He continues: "It consisted...of a concession of the Holy See, not a recognition of what devolved by reason of episcopal consecration as a number of Fathers had called for. The document granted to the bishops all at once forty faculties and eight privileges."[14] Although this *motu proprio* appeared in the midst of Vatican II, it could

---

[13] See *AAS* 56 (1964) 5–12. For the appropriate English translation, see *CLD* 6, 370–378.

[14] Msgr. J. Denis, "L'exercice du pouvoir de dispense des évêques diocésains depuis Vatican II," *AC* 13 (1969) 65–78; here at 67.

not satisfy the bishops, who at that time were working on *Lumen gentium*.

This dogmatic constitution clearly distinguishes the diocesan bishops from the Sovereign Pontiff:

> The pastoral office or the habitual and daily care of the sheep is entrusted to them completely. Nor are they to be regarded as vicars of the Roman Pontiff, for they exercise an authority which is proper to them, and are quite correctly called "prelates," heads of the people whom they govern. Their power, therefore, is not destroyed by the supreme and universal power. On the contrary, it is affirmed, strengthened, and vindicated thereby, since the Holy See unfailingly preserves the form of government established by Christ the Lord in his Church. (*LG* 27; no. 352)

In effect, this means that the papal system of "doling out" faculties to residential bishops had to cease. In his understanding of this development, K. Rahner says that we cannot claim "an absolutely one way real and logical relation of priority or posteriority between the two factors, which are in fact present in each of the two offices (pope and bishop)." So he is satisfied to assert "a *reciprocal* relationship" between them.[15] The apostolic constitution *Pastor bonus* (June 28, 1988) especially alludes to this aspect of hierarchical communion, a clear sign of the *communio* ecclesiology effected by Vatican II.

On June 15, 1966, Pope Paul VI promulgated his *motu proprio De episcoporum muneribus*.[16] Consonant with the teaching of *Christus Dominus* and *Lumen gentium*, the pope offers certain norms relative to the dispensing power of bishops. For Msgr. Denis, the document still looks very much like "pontifical law." For M. Bonnet, however, the text presents a list of those general laws of the Church whose dispensation the Holy Father reserves to himself. So it is not "a concession or a delegation of a papal power made to the bishops, but really a recognition of the bishops' power to dispense."[17] Canonists generally agree that these canons successfully codify the provisions of *De episcoporum muneribus*.

The principal change that occurs in this chapter contradicts canonical tradition. So say the fathers of the code commission.[18] According to the tradition, dispensing power is an expression of legislative power (e.g., *CIC* 80); the present code, however, makes it a species of executive power. Admittedly, this broadens its accessibility, largely because just as legislative authority is to be interpreted narrowly, so executive power is to be interpreted broadly (c. 138). Consequently, those who possess executive (or administrative) power —either by office, by law, or by delegation—exercise real dispensing power.

Does this mean that a lay person can validly dispense? At the present state of the question, there is no easy answer. Unlike J. Vernay in his *Initiation*, who has no difficulty acknowledging all the *Christifideles* as *habiles* for governance,[19] the contributors to the commentary prepared by the Canon Law Society of Great Britain and Ireland, *Letter and Spirit*, seem very reluctant to acknowledge this ecclesial fact.[20] Those canonists who attach the power of jurisdiction exclusively to the power of orders have simply misread the structure of governance in the Church today.[21] Remembering, moreover, what we have already said, that executive power depends on the will of the competent superior, the legislator may very

---

[15] K. Rahner, *Bishops: Their Status and Function* (Montreal: Palm Publishers, 1963) 18–19.

[16] See *AAS* 58 (1966) 467–472. For an appropriate English translation, see *CLD* 6, 394–400.

[17] M. Bonnet, "La 'dispense' dans le Code," *Les cahiers du droit ecclesial* 1 (1984) 51–56, 101–113; here at 103.

[18] See *Comm* 3 (1971) 89–90.

[19] J. Vernay, *Le droit dans l'Église catholique* (Paris: Desclée de Brouwer, 1995) 76–77.

[20] See *CLSGBI Com* 76–77, 129.

[21] On this important but intricate question, which must be understood first historically and then metaphysically (and not vice-versa as the Mörsdorf school proposes), see A. Stickler, "De potestatis sacrae natura et origine," *P* 71 (1982) 65–91.

well intend just that, i.e., "for a particular case." If the competent authority has in fact delegated executive power unconditionally, then that disposition also indicates the mind of the legislator.

Before proceeding to the individual canons, it might be helpful to offer a further reflection. This has to do with the language of dispensation itself. In Roman law, a dispensation referred to any release from the law, from penalties, and from contracts. Although all three institutes involve obligation, the dispensation suspends the obligation and leaves the law intact. To a certain extent, vestiges of this usage remain in the current code. In Christian usage, we find a language of stewardship, i.e., a good steward managing property. So dispensation has to do with both the administration and the distribution of goods. St. Paul echoes this usage in 1 Corinthians 4:1. Canon 992, for example, speaks of the Church dispensing the merits of Christ. Again, we find canons 276, §1; 387; and 1273 reflecting this Christian dimension. Later, a medicinal use entered the language, i.e., the dispensary. The priest, then, was said to be "dispensing" the sacraments. As Urrutia points out, the current code does not refer to this last usage at all.

If we look to dispensation beyond this particular chapter, we find it applied concretely to oaths and vows (cc. 1194, 1196, 1203). In marriage law, the canons speak of a "dispensation" from canonical form (c. 1127). Again, we notice canon 1697 which speaks of a "dispensation from a marriage *ratum et non consummatum*." Each of these instances presupposes a *vinculum* or an obligatory bond, which competent authority relaxes for a just cause. By combining dispensation with *oikonomia*, some contemporary canonists see this institute as a means for constructive innovation. It also provides a way of resolving intolerable marriage situations.

Canonical Concept of Dispensation

Canon 85 — A dispensation, or the relaxation of a merely ecclesiastical law in a particular case, can be granted by those who possess executive power within the limits of their competence, as well as by those who have the power to dispense explicitly or implicitly either by the law itself or by legitimate delegation.

In the literature, canonists refer to dispensation as a *vulnus legis*, that is, a "wounding of the law." If the law is given to ensure the common good, then dispensation looks very much like an exception to the law (*CCEO* 1536, §1). Not surprisingly, then, it requires a strict interpretation according to cc. 18; 36, §1; and 92. Still, the 1983 code uses the concept of dispensation more broadly than this canon would suggest. In addition to the examples mentioned above, canon 527, §2 indicates that a dispensation from certain procedural formalities in effect puts the pastor in possession of his parish.

In addition to the diocesan bishop, who else possesses ordinary executive power? Those equivalent to him in law (cc. 370; 371; 381 §2; 427, §1) and vicars general and episcopal vicars (cc. 134, §1; 479, §1, §2); also religious superiors of clerical institutes of pontifical right (cf. c. 968, §2). The canon also mentions "by the law itself." See, for example, canons 543, §1; 1079; 1086; 1196; 1203; and 1245. Finally, it speaks of "legitimate delegation."

According to canon 129, §1, the clergy are *habiles* of the "power of governance (cf. c. 274, §1). The laity also are *habiles* of being admitted to those ecclesiastical offices which they can assume (c. 228, §1). In short, all the *Christifideles* are capable of receiving executive power. *Regulae Iuris* 68 reminds us: "Someone can delegate another to do what he can do himself." In this instance, the rules of lawful delegation apply: cc. 137–142. This means that the power of dispensation, as an expression of executive power, really participates in the Church's power of governance. Even though the canon speaks of "a particular case," to the extent that competence allows, any dispensation really mitigates, relaxes, or suspends the law.

Exceptions

Canon 86 — Laws are not subject to dispensation to the extent that they define those things which

are essentially constitutive of juridic institutes or acts.

This particular provision originates with *De episcoporum muneribus* iv (*CLD* 6, 396). Constitutive law defines elements that essentially comprise a juridic act (e.g., c. 124, §1) or an institute (e.g., c. 573, §1). According to Michiels, constitutive law refers to "an ecclesiastical law, which positively determines the intrinsic form or the essential elements making up...the determinate nature of the specific act; it takes its origin and complete [juridic] status from canon law."[22] Because both rights and responsibilities emanate from this juridic state, all the essential elements must be present. Otherwise, the missing element(s) invalidate either the act or the institute. Consequently, the diocesan bishop is not free, for example, to dispense any of his subjects thinking of entering consecrated life from taking the three vows of poverty, chastity, and obedience. Similarly, he cannot dispense spouses from giving marital consent. In order to receive any of the sacraments, one must be free. So, for the social sacraments, marriage and orders, freedom is constitutive of the juridic state. As we have seen earlier, administrative acts require proper competence, consultation, and reasons as constitutive elements of their validity. At the present state of theological and canonical reflection, canon 1024 also belongs to constitutive law. Other canonists would also include liturgical law. To the extent that sacred signs constitute the essence of the sacramental system, nobody in the Church is free to alter them, as the Holy Father has recently insisted in his celebrated letter, *Ordinatio sacerdotalis* (May 22, 1994). Still, one can distinguish ceremonies from rites, which means accidents from substances. More liberal canonists, then, allow bishops to dispense from accidental elements.

[22] *Quae scilicet positive determinat* formam intrinsecam, *seu elementa essentialia ipsum actum, qui ex jure canonico initium et totum statum capit, in se esse seu determinata natura constituentia.* See G. Michiels, *Normae generales*, 2nd ed. (Paris and Rome: Desclée, 1949) 1:341.

What emerges from this discussion of constitutive law? We see that any dispensation in the Church must be reasonable, in the sense of "proportionate reason." According to canons 87, §1 and 90, §1, a dispensation can be given only for the "spiritual good" of the faithful and "for a just and reasonable cause." The Church has not confided this faculty to bishops and others in order to damage or destroy those institutions which have served the Church so faithfully and so well over the centuries (*CCEO* 1537). Even though the canons give to the diocesan bishop the faculty to dispense from the constitutions of an institute of diocesan right (c. 595, §2), he is not really free to change the essential purpose or character of the religious group. After all, juridic acts and institutes witness to the Church and her holiness. And for that reason, they need to be protected.

Canon 87 — §1. A diocesan bishop, whenever he judges that it contributes to their spiritual good, is able to dispense the faithful from universal and particular disciplinary laws issued for his territory or his subjects by the supreme authority of the Church. He is not able to dispense, however, from procedural or penal laws nor from those whose dispensation is specially reserved to the Apostolic See or some other authority.

§2. If recourse to the Holy See is difficult and, at the same time, there is danger of grave harm in delay, any ordinary is able to dispense from these same laws even if dispensation is reserved to the Holy See, provided that it concerns a dispensation which the Holy See is accustomed to grant under the same circumstances, without prejudice to the prescript of can. 291.

This important canon obrogates from canon 81 in the 1917 code. That is, it completely reworks and rethinks the previous practice. Grounded in *Christus Dominus* 8 and *De episcoporum muneribus* iv–v, it recognizes the bishop's power of dispensation, not as a concession from the Holy See, but as intrinsic to his power of governance. The reference to "universal and particular disciplinary laws" reminds us that the diocese as a portion of the people of God "constitutes a particular church in which the one, holy, catholic, and apostolic Church of Christ is truly present and operative" (*CD* 11; no. 593). As the diocesan bishop is responsible for upholding the universal laws of the Church (c. 392, §1), so can he dispense from them in a particular instance. As the proper legislator for his people, the diocesan bishop not only makes laws, but he also applies laws (c. 392). Both the nature and the logic of the situation would seem to require broad dispensing power (*CCEO* 1538, §1). In effect, this canon supplies it.

While canonists remark on this advance, we must also note the limitations which the canon(s) impose. Already, we have seen that bishops cannot dispense from constitutive law (c. 86). In the first paragraph of this canon, both procedural and penal laws are excepted. That is, the bishop cannot dispense from procedural law (Book VII and *passim*) precisely because it assists in the protection of rights. By the same token, the bishop cannot dispense from penal law (Book VI) because penalties look to the spiritual conversion of the faithful. This means that the dispensing power of the bishop is restricted to laws that are either (a) universal or (b) particular but also (c) ecclesiastical and (d) disciplinary. The canon also makes it clear that the dispensation by definition pertains not to any general permission but to an individual case.

The canon goes on to speak about those laws "whose dispensation is specially reserved to the Apostolic See or some other authority." According to *De episcoporum muneribus* ix, the sovereign pontiff has reserved about twenty situations to himself. In his commentary, Lefèbvre groups these reserved laws under three headings: those relative to the clergy, to religious, and to the sacraments. Without compiling a taxative list, the current USCC publication *Manual for Bishops* (1992) catalogues the major reservations first for orders and then for matrimony.[23] For a current list, see the appendix at the end of this chapter on dispensations.

As Mendonça points out, some of these reservations the Holy See is wont to dispense; others, not. The practical canonist must have an eye to Roman replies, current jurisprudence, and curial practice. Wrenn's commentary, however critical, seems most timely and useful. O'Reilly notes that in recent years certain authentic interpretations have placed a limit on what would otherwise seem to be the ordinary dispensing power of bishops.

He is referring first to the August 1, 1985 decision which does not allow the bishop to dispense two Catholics from canonical form; second, to the decision on canon 767 which prevents the bishop from dispensing the priest or deacon from giving the homily; third, to the interpretation of canon 705 which denies both active and passive voice to religious bishops. For the same reason, authors have noted that the Holy See has in place very clear guidelines about priests going into politics, so that while the bishops (theoretically) can dispense from c. 287, §2, in practice they seem to defer to the current policy of the Holy See. Finally, we can point to the *Program for Priestly Formation* (4th ed.), no. 263, concerning "the requirements of c. 250."

The second paragraph refers to what canonists call "the urgent case." In effect, it gives not only the diocesan bishop but any ordinary (c. 134, §1) and any other competent authority (c. 137) the power to dispense even from those laws usually reserved to the Holy See. In order to invoke this extraordinary faculty, the canon specifies three conditions—all three of which must be present simultaneously. In order of sequence they are (1) difficult recourse, (2) grave harm in delay, and (3) a dispensation that the Holy See usually does grant (*CCEO* 1538, §2).

The canon really presupposes ordinary mail as the usual means of communicating with either the Holy See or with any other ecclesiastical superior (cf. c. 1079, §4). For one reason or another, the mails will not arrive in time to take care of this "urgent case." The canon reads "difficult"; it does not say "impossible." In order to ensure both privacy and confidentiality, both matters of constitutive justice, the Apostolic See does not readily en-

---

[23] See *A Manual for Bishops*, rev. ed. (Washington, D.C.: NCCB, 1992) 8–11, 12–15.

courage "telecommunications." That is, we must not think ordinarily in terms of Telex, fax, satellite communication, or e-mail. The conservative stance reflects a very basic value, which the Church associates with confidentiality (protected by some twenty-three canons). This means that traditional thinking makes little or no allowance for the Internet. Admittedly, a papal legate may have the necessary dispensing authority as part of his diplomatic faculties, but the canon indicates no necessity of contacting him since he is not mentioned in the definition of "Apostolic See" given in canon 361. Consequently, the interpretation of "difficult recourse" depends very exactly on the prudent judgment of the ordinary involved.

The canon speaks of "grave harm in delay." While the phrase *grave damnum* comes from the moralists, it recalls *Regulae Iuris* 25, that sentence from Paulus to the effect that delay harms everyone. The canonists, however, who comment on this passage do not render the phrase any more specific.[24] It does occur elsewhere in the code: cc. 326, §1; 1328, §2; 1741, §5. It refers to a situation of moral seriousness and not just to an inconvenience. We do know that the first paragraph speaks of "spiritual good" (cf. c. 88) and that canon 90 requires "a just and reasonable cause" for validity. Although the canon itself requires a strict interpretation (c. 36, §1), the reason itself can be broad enough to account for the circumstances of the situation (c. 90). Therefore, the particular case requiring urgency should be able to balance those elements to achieve a practical credibility.

The canon assumes that normally the Holy See would grant the dispensation under the same circumstances. This condition nuances any reasonable application of this canon. The Holy See, for example, does not easily dispense from celibacy, from solemn profession, from apostasy. On the other hand, the ordinary may use this canon to dispense from the law of alienation (c. 1292), from the defect of age (c. 1031, §4), from retroactive validation (c. 1165, §1). The Holy See (ap-

parently) never dispenses from episcopal orders, from the irregularity of abortion, and from the impediment of consanguinity in all degrees of the direct line (cc. 108, 1091, §1). Despite the broad dispensing power of this canon, it presupposes a capacity for better than average discrimination.

Competence

Canon 88 — A local ordinary is able to dispense from diocesan laws and, whenever he judges that it contributes to the good of the faithful, from laws issued by a plenary or provincial council or by the conference of bishops.

The canon reflects the gradual extension of *Pastorale munus* and its faculties to other diocesan officials. What began as a very restrictive concession to the local bishop in a short time applied even to chancellors in the United States. The definition of "local ordinary" here comes from *De episcoporum muneribus* ii, indicating the Church's broader concern to provide canonical answers to pastoral questions.

At this particular point, we may want to emphasize the singularity of the dispensation. That is, it applies by definition to a single case or instance, so this chapter does not envisage any dispensations understood generically (unrestricted) or broadly (unlimited). As we have seen, the individual case, however, may turn on either a physical person or a juridic person. So the local ordinary may dispense an individual or a community from participating, for example, in a diocesan day of penance (c. 1249).

Even though the law gives juridic personality to the ecclesiastical province (c. 432, §2), the competence of the provincial council seems relatively limited in law. In one area, however, the provincial council seems very important indeed: it sets the stipend for Mass offerings (c. 952, §1). If any local ordinary wished to dispense in a particular case, he might well find himself in difficulty with the larger community called diocese or province (cf. c. 1308, §1). In other words, he would have to have a proportionately just reason.

---

[24] For example, see *Chiappetta Com,* 1:104, no. 503.

According to an authentic interpretation issued on August 1, 1985, the decrees issued by an episcopal conference fall under the category of general executory decrees (cc. 31–33). Although these look like laws, they really are not (c. 455, §1). In a number of places, the 1983 code enjoins on the national conference of bishops to establish norms in order to secure a certain uniform practice throughout the conference (cf., for example, c. 1127, §2). Nevertheless, before the norms take any effect, they must be sent to the Holy See for "review" (c. 456). This canon asserts the independence of the diocesan bishop relative to his own particular church (c. 455, §4). Nevertheless, like all of these canons, this one also presupposes hierarchical communion and canonical mission, which import a solicitude for all the churches.

A more delicate question arises with a consideration of liturgical law. Can the local ordinary dispense from liturgical law? Truth to tell, there does not seem to be any general or clear answer to the question today.[25] To the extent that liturgy comprises constitutive law, bishops cannot dispense (c. 86). To the extent that liturgical rubrics and other conditions belong to the Church's disciplinary laws, they can dispense (c. 87, §1).

Nevertheless, the area requires enormous caution. First of all, we are speaking about cult and worship, both of which pertain to the virtue of religion, which, as the highest form of justice, everyone must take very seriously. Second, any dispensation pertains to an individual case and not to any *carte blanche* (cf. c. 838, §4). Third, because the liturgical books require both recognition and approval from the Holy See (cc. 826, §1; 838, §2), they pertain to universal or pontifical law, which would seem to require a proportionately grave reason for any dispensation. While the liturgists may have helped their cause in some respects, they have hindered it in others. As the commentary on canon 2 makes clear, liturgical law is not entirely under their control. This means that they are also obliged to respect and to follow liturgical norms.

[25] See, for example, John Huels's opinion in *RR* (1992) 52–53.

Canon 89 — A pastor and other presbyters or deacons are not able to dispense from universal and particular law unless this power has been expressly granted to them.

In addition to those faculties which the law expressly gives (e.g., cc. 1079, 1080), this canon provides for lawful delegation (c. 137, §1). Indeed, this seems to be the ordinary mode of extending this kind of pastoral care. Often enough, missionary priests and religious are given certain faculties by reason of their situation. So they too fall under the norm of lawful delegation. Where do we find this delegation? The priests customarily find it in the *pagella* which they receive usually at the beginning of their ministry or at the time of a new assignment. It contains explicitly all the ordinary faculties which the bishop is willing to concede to the clergy. In this way, the canon is able to protect two values: the pastoral dimension associated with dispensing power and the clear supervisory role attributed to the diocesan bishop.

Motivating Cause

Canon 90 — §1. One is not to be dispensed from an ecclesiastical law without a just and reasonable cause, after taking into account the circumstances of the case and the gravity of the law from which dispensation is given; otherwise the dispensation is illicit and, unless it is given by the legislator himself or his superior, also invalid.

§2. In a case of doubt concerning the sufficiency of the cause, a dispensation is granted validly and licitly.

This canon, substantially the same as canon 84, §1 in the 1917 code, is based on *De episcoporum muneribus* viii with a reference to *Christus Dominus* 8b. Paul VI writes: "As provided in canon 84, §1, there is required for granting a dispensation a just and reasonable cause, taking into account the gravity of the law from which the dispensation is given (*CCEO* 1536, §2). The spiritual good of the faithful is a legitimate cause for a dispensation."[26] The commentators speak of the proportion required between the law being dispensed and the particular case. A relatively minor law requires a lesser cause. Since the Church attaches validity (c. 10) to the reason given for the dispensation, it must be free from *dolus* (c. 63). In this way, the Church is able to prevent the discipline from being trivialized.

Recognizing that canon law really exists as a subalternated science, we can illustrate its dependence on moral theology in this canon. Moreover, we can cite St. Thomas Aquinas to make this case. Since he explains the institute in his "Treatise on Law," we can expect from him a lucid persuasion (c. 252, §3). The question concerns "whether rulers can dispense from human laws."[27] According to St. Thomas, the good householder must combine prudence with fidelity. Clearly, this article places dispensation within the original Christian context. The argument germane to our present canon turns on the double distinction between faithful and unfaithful, prudent and imprudent. An authentically ecclesial consciousness/ conscience makes it clear where the moral values reside.

The second paragraph resolves any positive doubt (c. 14). As J. Risk points out in his commentary, the doubt must be both positive and objective; otherwise we are not dealing with doubt at all.[28] As in other cases, the law itself resolves any ambiguity (*CCEO* 1536, §3). This means that the dispensation may be illicit but valid. Whether the law actually wishes to accommodate these nominal niceties remains to be seen.

Appropriate Subjects

Canon 91 — Even when outside his territory, one who possesses the power to dispense is able to exercise it with respect to his subjects even though they are absent from the territory, and, unless the contrary is expressly established, also with respect to travelers actually present in the territory, as well as with respect to himself.

This canon actually applies canon 136 on executive power to this particular institute called dispensation. It represents a broader extension than that found in the 1917 code, for it describes a competence at once personal and territorial. As such, it includes three different groups of the faithful: his own people, travelers, and the homeless; the canon also mentions "himself" (*CCEO* 1539). It looks like an application of *Regulae Iuris* 53: who can do "more" can surely do less. While the 1983 code grants to the ordinary this broad dispensing power, it is not entirely clear that Urrutia is correct when he refers to these recipients as "passive subjects." If the validity of any dispensation depends on a just and reasonable cause, we cannot reasonably consider this immanent activity as particularly passive.

Interpretation

Canon 92 — A dispensation is subject to a strict interpretation according to the norm of can. 36, §1, as is the very power to dispense granted for a particular case.

The canon refers to c. 36, §1 which limits administrative acts. To the extent, then, that dispensation represents an exception to the law (c. 18), it requires the restrictive norm (*CCEO* 1512, §4). By narrowing the exceptions to law, the Church is emphasizing the precise value of the law meant to enhance the common good. Once again, we are able to see the coherence of the system at work.

Cessation

Canon 93 — A dispensation which has successive application ceases in the same ways as a privilege as well as by the certain and total cessation of the motivating cause.

---

[26] *CLD* 6, 397.
[27] For St. Thomas's treatment of dispensation, see *STh* 1–2.97.4.
[28] *CLSA Com*, 67.

In general, one administrative act revokes another (cc. 47, 79). But, as we have also seen, the principle of cessation can be written into the rescript. So the canon refers to canon 83 which specifies the causes for cessation of privileges, e.g., the number of cases for which the dispensation was given has expired, or the time-period (e.g., during Advent or Lent) has lapsed, or the circumstances have so changed that the just and reasonable cause no longer applies (*CCEO* 1513, §4). In these ways, the Church implements the strict interpretation associated with dispensation.

The canon mentions privileges explicitly. This recalls a caution which Pope Paul VI made in *De episcoporum muneribus* iv: "The grant of a permission, a faculty, an indult, or an absolution, is not contained in the notion of a dispensation."[29] So by way of concluding this discussion, we offer the following definitions by way of distinguishing dispensation from other juridic acts.

Permission (*licentia*) is the faculty of doing or omitting something which is permitted not in an absolute manner but conditioned by the consent of the lawful authority. Thus, permission is not something done against the law.

A faculty is the extension of a power given by a superior enjoying jurisdiction in the external forum to an inferior so that he/she can do validly, licitly, or without risk something which by its nature or by some positive reservation belongs to a higher superior. For example, the power to confirm can be given to a priest.

The term "indult" designates a special favor given for a determinate period of time; it is distinguished from a privilege which is a special favor granted in perpetuity. Both indult and privilege comprise a positive and objective juridic norm. It is necessary to remark that the term "indult" is applied also to the document granting the concession of the favor, as in the indult of a marriage dispensation.

Outside of sacramental absolution or the acquittal of an accused (a judicial absolution), absolution is the act whereby a superior releases a believer from the medicinal penalties or censures incurred by him (*CIC* 2236). These distinctions make it clear that dispensation is a specific juridic act defined in law and limited in practice.

[29] *CLD* 6, 396.

APPENDIX – DISPENSATIONS AND OTHER MATTERS RESERVED TO THE HOLY SEE

1. Dispensation from the obligation of celibacy as a marriage impediment (cc. 291, 1078, §2, 1°).
2. The grant of a favor of returning to the lay state for deacons and presbyters (c. 290, 3°).
3. Dispensation of the required age in excess of one year for ordination of both deacons and presbyters (cc. 1031, §1, §2, §4).
4. Dispensation from all irregularities to orders if the "fact on which they are based has been brought to the judicial forum" (c. 1047 §1).

5. Dispensation from certain specially reserved irregularities and impediments to receive orders (c. 1047, §2). These include:
   (a) the public delict mentioned in canon 1041, 2° of apostasy, heresy, or schism (c. 1047, §2, 1°);
   (b) the public delict mentioned in canon 1041, 3° of attempted marriage when impeded by a prior bond, orders, or a public perpetual vow of chastity (c. 1047, §2, 1°);

(continued)

(c) the public or occult delict mentioned in canon 1041, 4° of a person who has committed voluntary homicide or procured an abortion and those who positively cooperated in either (c. 1047, §2, 2°);

(d) the impediment of having a wife as mentioned in canon 1042, 1° (n.b., the impediment does not apply to married men destined for the permanent diaconate); see c. 1047, §2, 3°.

6. Dispensation from specially reserved irregularities which preclude the exercise of orders already received (c. 1047, §3). These include:

(a) only public cases mentioned in canon 1041, 3° of attempted marriage when impeded by a prior bond, orders, or a public perpetual vow of chastity (c. 1047, §3);

(b) both public and occult cases mentioned in canon 1041, 4° of a person who has committed voluntary homicide or procured an abortion and those who positively cooperated in either (c. 1047, §3).

7. Dispensation from the minimum number of bishops at an episcopal ordination (c. 1014).

8. Dispensation from the impediment of crime as defined in canon 1090 (c. 1078, §2, 2°).

9. Dispensation from canonical form between two Catholics (c. 1127). See the authentic interpretation of July 5, 1985; *AAS* 77 (1985) 771.

10. Dispensation/dissolution of a non-consummated marriage (cc. 1142, 1698).

11. Dissolution of a marriage "in favor of the faith," where one of the parties was already baptized before or during the marriage to be dissolved.

12. Certain radical sanations (c. 1165). The diocesan bishop is able to grant radical sanations except in two situations (c. 1165, §2):

(a) where an impediment reserved to the Apostolic See by canon 1078, §2 (sacred orders, vow of chastity, coniugicide) is involved; and

(b) where there was an impediment of the natural law or of divine positive law (e.g., prior bond) which has ceased to exist.

13. Suspension, dispensation, or commutation of a promissory oath which would tend to harm others (c. 1203)

14. Excommunication incurred from the desecration of the consecrated eucharistic species (c. 1367).

15. Excommunication incurred from using physical force against the Roman Pontiff (c. 1370).

16. The excommunication of a priest who violated canon 977 by attempting to absolve an accomplice of a sin against the sixth commandment except *in periculo mortis* (c. 1378).

17. The excommunication of a bishop who ordains someone a bishop without a pontifical mandate and the person who was ordained (c. 1382).

18. The excommunication incurred from the *direct* violation of the seal of confession (c. 1388, §1).

19. The reduction of Mass stipends "for a just and necessary cause" (c. 1308, §1).

20. A dispensation exempting the deacon or priest from giving the homily (c. 767). An authentic interpretation was given on June 20, 1987; see *AAS* 79 (1987) 1249.

21. A dispensation from the academic requirements for tribunal personnel relative to canons 1420, §4; 1421, §3; and 1435 "without doubt reserved to the Apostolic See, and more specifically to the Apostolic Signatura" (*PB* 124, no. 2). See *Roman Replies* (1994) 22–24.

22. "Seminaries or study centers sponsoring courses of priestly formation that abbreviate the requirements of canon 250 need the explicit permission of the Congregation for Catholic Education to offer such programs." *Program of Priestly Formation*, 4th ed. (NCCB), 51, no. 263.

BIBLIOGRAPHY

Beal, J. P. "Confining and Structuring Administrative Discretion." *J* 46 (1986) 70–106.

Bonnet, M., and B. David. *Introduction au droit ecclésial et au nouveau Code*. Luçon, France: Les Cahiers du Droit Ecclésial, 1985.

Bouscaren, T. L., A. C. Ellis, and F. N. Korth. *Canon Law: A Text and Commentary*. 4th rev. ed. Milwaukee: Bruce Publishing Co., 1966.

Cicognani, A. G. *Canon Law*. Trans. J. M. O'Hara and F. Brennan. 2nd rev. ed. Philadelphia: Dolphin Press, 1935.

Clergy Procedural Handbook. Ed. R. R. Calvo and N. J. Klinger. Washington, D.C.: CLSA, 1992.

Crowe, F. E. "Law and Insight." *J* 56 (1996) 25–40.

de Koninck, T. *De la dignité humaine*. Paris: Presses Universitaires de France, 1995.

García-Martín, J. *Le Norme Generali del Codex Iuris Canonici*. 2nd ed. Rome: Edizioni Istituto Giuridico Claretiano, 1996.

Gauthier, A. "Juridical Persons in the Code of Canon Law." *Stud Can* 25 (1991) 77–92.

Gy, P.-M. "Traits fondamentaux du droit liturgique." *Maison-Dieu* n.s. 183/184 (1990) 7–22.

Herranz Casado, J. "The Personal Power of Governance of the Diocesan Bishop." *CLSAP* 49 (1987) 16–34.

Krukowski, J. "Notion de l'acte administratif individuel dans le nouveau *Code du Droit Canonique*." In *Dilexit Justitiam: Studia in honorem Aurelii Card. Sabattani*, ed. Z. Grocholewski and V. Carcel Orti, 495–502. Vatican City: Libreria Editrice Vaticana, 1984

Lombardia, P. In *Pamplona ComEng,* 109–122.

McIntyre, J. P. "Rights and Duties Revisited." *J* 56 (1996) 111–127.

Mendonça, A. In *CLSGBI Com,* 37–54.

Michiels, G. *Normae Generales Juris Canonici*. 2nd ed. 2 vols. Paris, Turin, and Rome: Desclée, 1949.

Moodie, M. R. "The Administrator and the Law: Authority and Its Exercise in the Code." *J* 46 (1986) 43–69.

Örsy, L. M. "Moral Theology and Canon Law: The Quest for a Sound Relationship." *TS* 50 (1989) 151–167.

———. *Theology and Canon Law: New Horizons for Legislation and Interpretation*. Collegeville: Liturgical Press, 1992.

Risk, J. H. In *CLSA Com,* 57–69.

Urrutia, F. J. "Administrative Power in the Church according to the Code of Canon Law." *Stud Can* 20 (1986) 253–273.

———. "Le Nouveau Droit Ecclésial." In *Les normes générales*. Paris: Éditions Tardy, 1994.

Wrenn, L. G. *Authentic Interpretations on the 1983 Code*. Washington, D.C.: CLSA, 1993.

TITLE V
STATUTES AND RULES OF ORDER
[cc. 94–95]

This new title indicates the place of statutes and rules of order in the ordinary life of the Church. As such, it marks an advance over the 1917 code which made no such provision. Given the freedom of association, however, which the Church has only recently recognized for both the laity and even (though more reluctantly) for the clergy, the code commission decided to add this new chapter. Admittedly, it pertains to what we might call formal associations and formal meetings. But the 1983 code indicates in many places that statutes are clearly in order. So these norms act as guidelines. Rules of order (as in the Roberts' Rules) govern individual meetings. Indeed, often enough the success of these meetings depends quite exactly on these procedural norms. The Church also recognizes their usefulness. As Bonnet and David observe, statutes describe the nature of an association, whereas the rules govern its internal governance. To the extent that the Church officially recognizes the statutes of a given organization or group, these statutes become a true source of law. We might note by way of an introductory conclusion that both statutes and rules reflect an aspect of church that we may very well associate with the principle of subsidiarity.

Statutes

Canon 94 — §1. Statutes in the proper sense are ordinances which are established according to the norm of law in aggregates of persons (*universitas personarum*) or of things (*universitas rerum*) and which define their purpose, constitution, government, and methods of operation.

§2. The statutes of an aggregate of persons bind only the persons who are its legitimate members; the statutes of an aggregate of things, those who direct it.

§3. Those prescripts of statutes established and promulgated by virtue of legislative power are governed by the prescripts of the canons on laws.

While the first paragraph looks explicitly to juridic persons (Book I, title VI) in the Church, it pertains equally to other associations of the faithful (Book II, part one, title V) as well. "Juridic person" is the name which the Church gives to an ecclesiastical corporation (c. 115). A corporation may be made up of individual persons who constitute the membership (e.g., a religious congregation). This is known in law as *universitas personarum*. On the other hand, a corporation may be made up of things such as property, investments, or monies administered by a board of directors or trustees (e.g., a pious foundation). The code refers to this entity as *universitas rerum*. By definition, an ecclesiastical corporation or juridic person must not only have statutes, but the statutes must also be approved (c. 117).

Other organizations encouraged by the new code may also seek legal personality in the Church. This means that they will have to prepare statutes. The first paragraph presents in outline form the various matters that must be treated. The canon gives us four different titles or chapters that should enable any group to indicate its relevance to the Church (c. 298, §1). The organization's purpose, then, must be compatible with the Church's mission understood in a very broad sense. The constitution would indicate the various ways in which the organization expects to realize its purpose. Governance refers to personnel, what we might recognize as the legal officers of the group. Procedure would include both internal and external operations. The next canon on rules would take care of the internal ordering of business; in all likelihood, a supplementary set of rules would be required to cover outside activities. This outline provides a spine, if you will. Depending on the nature of the organization, the constitutions can be greatly expanded (as, for example, with religious institutes); or they may be kept to a minimum (as, for example, with the college of diocesan consultors). At any rate, the canon indicates the principal points that must be addressed.

In the second paragraph, we see once again how the canon indicates a moral dimension implied by either membership (*universitas personarum*) or responsibility (*universitas rerum*). That is, individuals freely assent to belonging to these different juridic persons. Consequently, any obligations which the canon asserts arise from free choice. No one, for example, can be forced to join a religious community. By the same analogy, an individual should not accept the responsibility for a directorship of a foundation if he/she cannot or will not abide by its statutes. Because juridic persons act *in nomine Ecclesiae,* external behavior must be perceived as compatible with the Church's moral position (c. 209, §1). For this reason, the statutes include a section on members: admission and separation.

The third paragraph indicates that statutes, once established and promulgated, acquire the force of law. If they are approved by competent ecclesiastical authority, they pertain to ecclesiastical law (e.g., c. 587). To this extent, then, statutes can be seen as an authentic source of law. In effect, however, the 1983 code does not indicate just who this "competent authority" might be. If we look to canon 312, §1, however, we find a legal analogue (c. 19) appropriate for this situation: (1) the Holy See for international groups, (2) the conference of bishops for national associations, and (3) the diocesan bishop for local organizations (cf. c. 352, §2).

So far, we have suggested that various associations make up their statutes and present them to competent authority for ecclesiastical approval (c. 322). Indeed, this seems to be the normal procedure, especially for those associations seeking status as private juridic persons (e.g., hospitals). On the other hand, the law recognizes other groupings where the competent ecclesiastical authority in effect imposes statutes on the organizations.

The diocesan bishop, for example, presides over the presbyteral council so that it cannot act apart from the bishop (c. 500, §3). Presumably, this means that he is responsible for its statutes (c. 496) in much the same way that he is responsible for those of the seminary (c. 239, §3). The code also refers to diocesan statutes (cc. 548, §1; 562) and to those for a diocesan pastoral council (c. 513, §1). There are associations of the clergy whose statutes recommend holiness (c. 278, §2). Admittedly, the code does not tell us explicitly who actually writes these statutes; despite this lacuna (c. 19), it seems perfectly clear that the diocesan bishop is responsible for approving them. So too with the different chapters, either cathedral or collegiate (c. 505). In this way, the Church ensures that various groups cannot call themselves "Catholic" until she says that they are (cc. 216, 300).

In the same way, the Apostolic See provides the statutes for a personal prelature (c. 295, §1); it approves those of the episcopal conference (c. 451) and the conference of major superiors (c. 709). Each ecclesiastical university and faculty must have its statutes approved by the Holy See (c. 816, §2). The code also provides statutes for shrines at every level: local, national, and international (c. 1232). All of this, then, emphasizes the obvious: the Church prefers the written over the unwritten.

Rules of Order

Canon 95 — §1. Rules of order (*ordines*) are rules or norms, which must be observed in meetings, whether convened by ecclesiastical authority or freely convoked by the Christian faithful, as well as in other celebrations. They define those things which pertain to the constitution, direction, and ways of proceeding.

§2. These rules of order bind those who participate in these assemblies or celebrations.

Rules of order govern meetings. As such, they facilitate whatever participation the statutes provide for the membership. Moreover, these rules may work at different levels. That is, although they must direct the business at a general meeting, they should be flexible enough to handle a smaller group of directors as well. As we have seen, certain administrative acts require a measure of consultation (c. 50) for their validity (c. 127). Meetings offer an ordinary means of securing this requirement. In order to ensure that these meetings bear fruit, experience (even in the secular sphere) shows that rules of order help.

Once again, the canon points to consensus as a practical norm for ensuring the validity of subsidiarity. Administrators do not really have to listen to every demagogue or dissident as if only the disruptive had access to information or answers. If people wish to participate in a consultative process, they freely accept the rules of order. If the rules of order were not obligatory, then legitimate disruption might seem to be a possible way of proceeding. Such rules, then, would oblige those who participate, for example, in diocesan synods, parish councils, and various chapter meetings. As the more experienced can testify, without such rules all too often these meetings can degenerate into something considerably less than Christian. The canon, therefore, looks very much like a prudential caution.

TITLE VI
PHYSICAL AND JURIDIC PERSONS
[cc. 96–123]

CHAPTER I
THE CANONICAL CONDITION
OF PHYSICAL PERSONS
[cc. 96–112]

The Incarnational Principle

According to the incarnational principle, the concrete fact is more important than the abstract thought, the historical datum more significant than the theoretical explanation. The incarnation lends transcendence to the enfleshed immanence.

In this chapter, we learn that baptism produces two primary effects: (1) it incorporates a person into the Church of Christ and (2) it makes the individual a subject of duties and rights. Concretely, these depend on the person's state in life (cc. 207, 219). For all practical purposes, we find these duties and rights articulated in Book II. There we find the duties and rights proper to all Christians (cc. 208–223), those proper to the laity (cc. 224–231), those proper to the clergy (cc. 273–289), and those proper to religious (cc. 662–672). The responsibilities associated with the state in life render the individual person ever more physical in the Church. The complex and sensitive issue regarding the precise juridic effects of baptism on those who belong to the separated and reformed churches is a matter of dispute among canonists and remains unresolved.

Juridic Effects of Baptism

Canon 96 — By baptism one is incorporated into the Church of Christ and is constituted a person in it with the duties and rights which are proper to Christians in keeping with their condition, insofar as they are in ecclesiastical communion and unless a legitimately issued sanction stands in the way.

As a correlative to canon 204, which describes the spiritual effects of baptism, this canon defines the juridic effects of baptism. The sacrament of baptism grounds the complete incorporation of the individual in the Church and constitutes him/her a person.[1] Given the theological context of canon 204 and the spiritual imperative of canon 210, we are not talking about a naturalistic definition of "person," as found (for example) in Boethius, but a supernatural one, as found in St. Thomas Aquinas (*STh* 1.29.3). That is, the definition moves from *substantia* ("substance") to *subsistens* ("subsistent"). In this way, canon 96 marks an ad-

---

[1] The canon is based on c. 5 of *Lex Ecclesiae Fundamentalis* (1980), understood as the constitutive law of the Church.

vance over canon 87 of the 1917 code. The baptized is not only incorporated into Christ but also invested with rights and obligations. This means that the individual must move from any passive stance to a position of active responsibility.[2] For all practical purposes, this is how the Church understands "person" today.

In order to emphasize the supernatural dimension of the person, the canon mentions three precise points: full communion in the Church (c. 205), a concrete state of life (cc. 207, 219), and the obligations and rights proper to that state of life. By definition, full communion excludes the catechumen (c. 206) and those baptized in the separated and reformed churches (c. 11). As for the state in life, the Church recognizes four: the single, the married, the religious, and the clerical. In effect, every baptized person has a concrete means by which to cooperate in achieving a personal salvation. The current code specifies various responsibilities appropriate to the different states of life. By living out the duties and rights proper to his or her state, the individual cooperates with grace and realizes his or her supernatural destiny. In this way, the canon relativizes the status and condition of the individual Christian. Nevertheless, baptism in the Catholic Church grounds the intelligibility of the Christian vocation.[3]

Baptism constitutes the juridic basis for making one a person in the Catholic Church. Even if the present code principally concerns relations between Catholics and different institutes within the Latin church, it also makes certain provisions for and concessions to non-Catholics. We can cite four separate instances. Relative to non-Catholics, canons 844; 1127, §1; 1142; 1183, §3; 1476; and 1549 surely apply. On the other hand, lack of ecclesial communion imposes certain restrictions, found, for example, in canons 874, §2 and 908.

Moreover, non-Catholics are exempt from observing "merely ecclesiastical law" (cc. 11, 85). In addressing certain ecclesial concerns, the code consistently evinces an awareness of the pluralistic nature of contemporary culture (see, for example, cc. 748, §1; 383, §3; 463, §3; 844; 883, 2°; and 1124).

Finally, the present canon speaks to "a legitimately issued sanction." By definition, penalties are either expiatory or medicinal. Therefore, they may well limit the exercise of certain rights within the Church (c. 1312). Sanctions, in other words, militate against full communion.[4]

Does the Church specify the duties and rights of all of Christ's faithful? According to canons 208–223, it would seem so. That is, by reason of baptism, the faithful participate in the preaching, governing, and sanctifying office of Christ (c. 204, §1). So Book II, by delineating the duties and rights "proper to Christians," emphasizes those spiritual elements that describe the specifically Christian personality. It sets forth fairly systematically the effects of baptism. In addition to ecclesial communion in fact and in behavior (c. 209, §2), we find the call to personal holiness (c. 210). A need for spirituality (c. 214) underlies a concern for Christian education (c. 217) and a specific state of life (c. 219). While these responsibilities inhere in the sacrament of baptism, the Church does condition their exercise according to the norms of full communion and the common good (cc. 209, §1; 223). This provision pertains largely to those members who belong to the separated and reformed churches by reason of an "imperfect communion" (*UR* 3-a).

By referring to baptism as the sacrament which incorporates one "into the Church of Christ," the canon acknowledges the achievement of Vatican II. There, the conciliar fathers distinguished between "the Church of Christ" and the Catholic

---

[2] For this reading, see L. Örsy, "Interpretation in View of Action: A Quest for Clarity and Simplicity (Canon 96)," *J* 52 (1992) 587–597.

[3] The canon presupposes sacramental baptism with water as normative. It envisages neither martyrdom nor baptism by desire.

[4] On the other hand, J. Faris discusses the case of an excommunicate from the Orthodox Church received into full communion with the Catholic Church. See *CLSA Advisory Opinions, 1984–1993*, ed. P. Cogan (Washington, D.C.: CLSA, 1995) 15–17.

Church (*LG* 8-b). They went on to say that the Church of Christ subsists visibly in the Catholic Church (c. 204, §2). In this way they were able to concede to the separated and reformed churches genuine elements of sanctification and truth that promote both religion and devotion. This awareness grounds the seriousness which characterizes the ecumenical movement. In addition, these various gifts impart a dynamism which presses for the unity of the churches, the unity for which Christ himself prayed (Jn 17:21).

Age

Canon 97 — §1. A person who has completed the eighteenth year of age has reached majority; below this age, a person is a minor.

§2. A minor before the completion of the seventh year is called an infant and is considered not responsible for oneself (*non sui compos*). With the completion of the seventh year, however, a minor is presumed to have the use of reason.

Successive canons in this chapter will render our understanding of "physical person" more precise. The code presents five elements which qualify the status of persons in the Church: age, mental condition, residence, legal relationship, and rite. The first paragraph of this canon distinguishes the ages of majority and minority at eighteen; that is, eighteen years completed, putting the adult into his or her nineteenth year (c. 203). The second paragraph defines infants as those who have yet to reach seven years.[5] It also contains two presumptions of law: infants are incapable of acting responsibly, and minors are presumed to have the use of reason. As presumptions of law, they can be overturned by professional evaluations and other evidence. Nevertheless, the intent of the canon is to harmonize the provisions of ecclesiastical law with those of civil law (c. 22).

While Book I contains canons that make certain determinations regarding age, we find other provisions concerning age scattered throughout the code. For the most part, these concern certain responsibilities attached to states in life and various offices. The operative principle seems reasonable: the more difficult the undertaking, the greater the maturity required. The bishop, for example, must be thirty-five years of age (c. 378, §1, 3°), as also the married deacon (c. 1031, §2), and the diocesan administrator (c. 425, §1). According to law, the vicar general, the episcopal vicar (c. 478, §1), and the judicial vicar (c. 1420, §4) must be at least thirty years of age. A priest may be ordained at twenty-five (c. 1031, §1), and religious may make final profession at twenty-one (c. 658, 1°). The age of retirement usually follows local norms, but the code also makes its own recommendations (cc. 354; 401, §1; 538, §3). Most church provisions on age reflect a concern for the experience and maturity that should inform new responsibilities.[6]

Because the current code understands responsibility as essentially developmental, it provides great latitude to the minor. Ordinarily minors live with their parents or guardians (c. 98, §2) and remain subject to their authority. But the code also allows for the emancipated adolescent in the choice of domicile (c. 105, §1). We might think of a college student, for example, or a work situation. A minor can be admitted as a postulant or even as a novice (c. 643, §1, 1°) at seventeen years of age. And while the code avoids the use of "puberty" (except for c. 1096, §2) as a norm, it does permit marriage for a man at sixteen and a woman at fourteen (c. 1083, §1); still, canon 1072 advises customary law as a local norm, and canon 1071, §1, 6° cautions against the marriage of minors. At sixteen, minors can act as sponsors (c. 874, §1, 2°); they are also subject to ecclesiastical penalties (c. 1323, 1°). Again, at fourteen, under certain circumstances, minors can elect baptism in either the Eastern or Western church (c. 111, §2). They are also obliged to observe the law

---

[5] In his commentary on this canon, A. de Fuenmayor (following Michiels) calls this provision a presumption *iuris et de iure*, necessitated "for reasons of juridical certainty." See *Pamplona ComEng*, 123–124.

[6] For this developmental model, see St. Thomas Aquinas, *STh. Supp.* 43.2.

of fasting (c. 1252). Minors under fourteen can act as witnesses, provided that the judge deems it appropriate (c. 1550, §1). In these ways, the Church extends the areas of public accountability, enabling adolescent Christians to take responsibility for their actions within the Church.[7] Ecclesiastical law, therefore, recognizing the flexibility that accords to a developing Christian personality, makes responsibility relative to age.

Majority

Canon 98 — §1. A person who has reached majority has the full exercise of his or her rights.

The first paragraph of this canon seems clear enough: on reaching their majority, adults in the Church are subject to duties and can exercise rights. Even if in the Church duties and rights are limited by one's state in life (e.g., sacred ministers and professed religious have voluntarily renounced certain rights), adult persons are free to exercise their Christian responsibilities by acting in their own name. One's precise status and condition in the Church will render these duties and rights increasingly concrete according to the incarnational principle.

Minority

§2. A minor, in the exercise of his or her rights, remains subject to the authority of parents or guardians except in those matters in which minors are exempted from their authority by divine law or canon law. In what pertains to the appointment of guardians and their authority, the prescripts of civil law are to be observed unless canon law provides otherwise or unless in certain cases the diocesan bishop, for a just cause, has decided to provide for the matter through the appointment of another guardian.

The second paragraph concerns minors, those persons between seven and eighteen years of age. Because they live with their parents, minors obey their parents' wishes. The canon, however, recognizes that both divine and canon law restrict parental authority. That is, minors can exercise provisions of both divine law (e.g., cc. 219; 852, §1; 1101, §2) and of canon law (e.g., cc. 851, 1072, 1550, §1). In effect, this norm encourages parents to form their children in the faith (c. 793, §1). Although the family as an institution seems to be challenged in so many ways today, we recall that the Church celebrates every year the Feast of the Holy Family, which suggests that our understanding of the Christian family belongs to revelation.

This canon also speaks of guardians. This provision originates in Roman law. As Gauthier remarks in his text on Roman law, "In classical law, guardianship of those children without a *paterfamilias* but below the age of puberty was an institution for the protection of such (boys under fourteen years old and girls under twelve)."[8] Even though the canon recognizes the priority of civil law, it assumes that the diocesan bishop can make another determination in specific cases and for a just reason by appointing another guardian. In fact and in law, this assumption seems to be false, despite the assertions of canons 1478 and 1479. Nevertheless, the bishop is to provide for guardianship insofar as he can, as a responsibility in faith, just as canons 1481, §3 and 1646, §3 make special provisions for minors in procedural matters. In other words, minors according to the provisions of law can place juridic acts through others who act on their behalf.

Mental Condition

Canon 99 — Whoever habitually lacks the use of reason is considered not responsible for oneself (*non sui compos*) and is equated with infants.

[7] For a commentary on this perception, see V. D'Souza, *The Juridic Condition and Status of Minors according to the Code of Canon Law*, unpublished dissertation (Ottawa: St. Paul University, 1992).

[8] A. Gauthier, *Roman Law and Its Contribution to the Development of Canon Law* (Ottawa: St. Paul University, 1996) 34.

This canon concerns insanity. It really has to do with natural law. That is, in order to perform a juridic act, the individual person must be rational (c. 11). As a matter of fact, it also pertains to divine law (c. 852, §2). To the extent that one habitually lacks the use of reason, he or she is considered incapable of exercising personal responsibility; this means that he or she cannot place either a moral or a juridic act such as orders (c. 1041, 1°) or marriage (c. 1095). Natural law requires the use of reason in order to assure imputability (cc. 1323, 6°; 1324, §1, 1°).[9]

Except for canon 777, 4°, the code does not usually refer to the physically or mentally handicapped. Nevertheless, those who are mentally handicapped have limited standing at law. Two consequences follow: (1) they cannot place a valid juridic act (c. 124, §1), and (2) they cannot commit a canonical crime (c. 1322). If they have occasion to appear in court, they do so through their curator (c. 1478, §1). It is possible that such individuals do have moments of lucidity. But because the law presumes as norms self-governance (cc. 187, 852, §2), full possession of faculties (cc. 922, 1006), and personal responsibility (c. 97, §2), those who do not meet these provisions are considered legally as infants.

The code recognizes insanity as a legal fact. Like its predecessor, the 1917 code, it refers to *amentia* (cc. 689, §3; 1044, §2, 2°; 1105, §4) as well as senility (c. 1004, §1). Although the law is not principally concerned with pathology, it respects a psychological continuum which moves from the insane to the sane. Modern treatments and more accurate diagnoses considerably improve the state of the mentally handicapped today. Even here, then, the presumption of law yields to contrary proof.

After having considered age and mental capacity, the code addresses residence or domicile in the following canons (cc. 100–107).

[9] For a commentary on this norm, see F. Urrutia, *Les normes générales* (Paris: Editions Tardy, 1994) 254, no. 900, n. 1.

Residence

Canon 100 — A person is said to be: a resident (*incola*) in the place where the person has a domicile; a temporary resident (*advena*) in the place where the person has a quasi-domicile; a traveler (*peregrinus*) if the person is outside the place of a domicile or quasi-domicile which is still retained; a transient (*vagus*) if the person does not have a domicile or quasi-domicile anywhere.

This terminological canon defines persons in the Church in terms of domicile (*ius domicilii*). That is, it specifies the relationship between an individual person and a geographical place, thereby rendering the principle of territoriality (cc. 12, 13) very concrete. Following Roman law, the code recognizes four possibilities: the resident (*incola*), the newcomer (*advena*), the traveler (*peregrinus*), and the homeless (*vagus*). In other words, the kind of residence qualifies the exercise of duties and rights.

Realistically enough, the code accepts the fact of modern mobility, with possibilities ranging from second homes to refugee camps. For canonical purposes, the code is concerned largely with domicile and quasi-domicile. Domicile refers to the place of permanent residence. Classical canonists define this as the place where one spends most of his or her nights. Quasi-domicile refers to a second home, a place for business purposes or for recreation. Since people may very well have a plurality of domiciles, the canon asserts a juridic relationship between the person and a place—any place.

For the most part, domicile and quasi-domicile pertain to matters of both procedural law and substantive law. Relative to procedural law, for example, residence is relevant to such issues as entering a plea (cc. 1408; 1409, §2; 1504, 4°), witnesses in a trial (c. 1552, §1), competence for marriage cases (c. 1673), competence for the separation of spouses (c. 1694), and cases of a marriage *ratum sed non consummatum* (c. 1699, §1).

Residence also plays a part in substantive law. Domicile and quasi-domicile pertain not only to ecclesiastical laws (cc. 12, 13), but also to such matters as membership on the presbyteral council (c. 498, §2), the place of baptism (c. 857, §2), and the sacraments of penance (cc. 967, §2; 971), orders (c. 1016), and marriage (c. 1115).

Residence, therefore, understood either as domicile or quasi-domicile, clearly has juridic effects. As another manifestation of the incarnational principle, it concretizes our understanding of "person" in the Church.

Residence of Children and Neophytes

Canon 101 — §1. The place of origin of a child, even of a neophyte, is that in which the parents had a domicile or, lacking that, a quasi-domicile when the child was born or, if the parents did not have the same domicile or quasi-domicile, that of the mother.

§2. In the case of a child of transients, the place of origin is the actual place of birth; in the case of an abandoned child, it is the place where the child was found.

This canon is concerned with exceptional cases. Like its predecessor, canon 90 of the 1917 code, the first paragraph mentions "the place of origin." The revision committee included this phrase in order to indicate a proper bishop in the case of ordination.[10] But both Urrutia and Mendonça, commenting on canon 1016, find this determination irrelevant. Canonists generally agree that the concept has little juridical significance today.[11] We might say, then, that "the place of origin" does not mean the place of birth; it really refers to the parents' domicile or quasi-domicile.

A neophyte is a convert, a person baptized as an adult, somebody recently baptized. According to canon 1042, §3, a neophyte is simply impeded from orders. That is, the neophyte has to practice

the faith for some years before being admitted to ordination. Three years seems to be a prudential norm.

The second paragraph concerns the children of homeless persons and children who are foundlings. In both instances, the law determines the place of origin. Should the parents or guardians later acquire a domicile or quasi-domicile, the child's place of origin does not change.

Unlike canon 93, §1 of the 1917 code, this canon distinguishes the residences of the two parents and acknowledges the possibility of separate domiciles for estranged spouses. Moreover, the canon favors the mother, thus establishing the basis for distinguishing between the actual place of residence and the legal domicile.

Domicile

Canon 102 — §1. Domicile is acquired by that residence within the territory of a certain parish or at least of a diocese, which either is joined with the intention of remaining there permanently unless called away or has been protracted for five complete years.

After having defined some effects of domicile and quasi-domicile, this canon states their immediate causes. Domicile involves two elements: (1) actual residence for five years or (2) residence with the intention of remaining permanently. While the institute looks backwards to the *fundus,* or an estate of a largely agrarian community, canonists today generally associate it with property and with business interests. These activities have a way of legitimating intent. Nevertheless, the canon states that both elements necessary for permanent residence have been adequately fulfilled after five full years of actual residence, which means that the law itself concedes domicile.[12]

---

[10] *Comm* 6 (1974) 95–96.

[11] See, for example, J. García Martín, *Le Norme Generali del Codex Iuris Canonici* (Rome: Edizioni Istituto Giuridico Claretiano, 1996) 351.

[12] According to the Pio-Benedictine code (c. 92.1), the law granted domicile after a residence of ten years. See F. Cappello, *Summa Iuris Canonici* (Rome: Apud Aedes Universitatis Gregorianae, 1946) 1:156.

The canon allows for a certain flexibility, increasingly necessary in a mobile society. For this reason, the canon mentions "unless called away." Extrinsic circumstances, whether familial or economic, may qualify an original intent. Still, because the territorial principle is involved here (cc. 12, 13), intention is understood as both voluntary and actual. Consequently, an individual may have two permanent residences wherein he or she resides continuously and morally. For example, people may have real domicile in both the city and the country.

The formal intention to reside personally and permanently in a given place is determinative here. In effect, this means that domicile puts the individual in relationship to the local church, both to the parish and the diocese.[13] Accordingly, domicile signifies a communitarian context. That is, it represents the place wherein the individual Catholic is going to work out his or her salvation both historically and personally according to the responsibilities associated with the individual's proper state in life. For this reason, canonists see in these laws the value of stability. In ecclesiastical matters, residence also defines the place of competence (cc. 967, §2; 1115; 1408; 1413; 1673, 2°, 3°). Residence, then, clearly acts as a juridic determinant of "person" in the Church.

§2. Quasi-domicile is acquired by residence within the territory of a certain parish or at least of a diocese, which either is joined with the intention of remaining there for at least three months unless called away or has in fact been protracted for three months.

Quasi-domicile by definition means a temporary residence. Quasi-domicile depends on actual residence in a parish or diocese for three months or on residence with the intention of remaining at least three months. This situation affects (among

others) students, civil servants, consultants, and even business executives. According to their individual situation, they can adapt their intention, which means that people today can also multiply quasi-domiciles. The institute, however, presupposes domicile, thereby setting up a dialectic between the stable and the transitional.

§3. A domicile or quasi-domicile within the territory of a parish is called parochial; within the territory of a diocese, even though not within a parish, diocesan.

Domicile and quasi-domicile place the individual in relationship to the particular church, whether it be the life of the Catholic campus, the local parish, or the diocese. This third paragraph distinguishes between parochial and diocesan domiciles. As a general rule, we say that the specific derogates from the generic (*RI* 34). While in practice the parish affiliation is more effective than the diocesan, the canon actually prefers the diocese. It also envisages those territories, equivalent to dioceses, which have not yet established parishes; these include a territorial prelature, an apostolic vicariate, and an apostolic prefecture (cf. c. 368). According to Cappello, however, in early law the notion of diocesan domicile or quasi-domicile was practically unknown.[14]

Domicile of Religious

Canon 103 — Members of religious institutes and societies of apostolic life acquire a domicile in the place where the house to which they are attached is located; they acquire a quasi-domicile in the house where they are residing, according to the norm of can. 102, §2.

Religious acquire legal domicile by the law itself. That is, according to the law itself as well as their own proper law, those in consecrated life and members of societies of apostolic life are expected to live in properly constituted houses (see

---

[13] In his historical overview of domicile and quasi-domicile, G. Michiels relates these institutes to the sacramental life of the Church. See his *Principia Generalia de Personis in Ecclesia* (Tournai: Desclée, 1955) 107–116.

[14] Cappello, 1:158.

cc. 608; 665, §1; 740). The assignment itself, given by the appropriate superior, determines legal domicile. In fact, the person assigned to a house may be working elsewhere. Nevertheless, the assignment to a house of the institute constitutes domicile for the religious and for the member of a society of apostolic life. It does not require a time frame.

Moreover, the canon provides that religious and members of societies of apostolic life can acquire quasi-domicile according to the provision of canon 102, §2. They may, for example, attend university or require medical attention. Or they may help out in a missionary area. If they reside there for three full months, the law itself gives them quasi-domicile.

This provision can occasion a difficulty for religious priests. If they lack confessional faculties in the place of their assigned house, they must secure faculties for hearing confessions (c. 967, §2) in the diocese of quasi-domicile. That is, new faculties must be obtained from a local ordinary (c. 969, §1).[15] Otherwise, they may exercise the sacrament of reconciliation only within their own houses according to the provision of proper law (cc. 967, §3; 968, §2; 969, §2). Moreover, because members of societies of apostolic life are incardinated into their own society (unless their constitutions provide otherwise), they too are subject to this same procedure (c. 736, §1). This provision, however, does not apply to any clerical members of secular institutes because their priests are already incardinated in a particular church (c. 715, §1). In this way, the Church regulates the relationship between the pontifical institute and the local community, between the universal and the local church.

Domicile of Marriage Partners

Canon 104 — Spouses are to have a common domicile or quasi-domicile; by reason of legiti-

mate separation or some other just cause, both can have their own domicile or quasi-domicile.**

This canon makes a new provision for the current law of the Church. Unlike its predecessor (*CIC* 93, §1), this stipulation allows each of the spouses in marriage to have separate domiciles or quasi-domiciles. Undoubtedly, it derives from the new understanding of marriage as a partnership of life (c. 1055, §1). The partners share equally in establishing this community (c. 1135), which obliges them to a common life (c. 1151). Under normal circumstances, this entails a common domicile, which the canon acknowledges and mandates. What the canon abrogates is the notion of the *necessary* domicile, which previously obliged the wife to the domicile of the husband. Accordingly, for a just reason (including, but not necessarily, separation) either partner can establish his or her own domicile or quasi-domicile. In the case of a partner's abuse, adultery, or divorce (c. 1153, §1), the other partner may lawfully claim another residence. As a matter of fact, it may be practical to do so simply for economic or business reasons. This canon indicates a certain gender equality (e.g., cc. 208, 606) evident today in the universal law of the Church.

Domicile of Minors

Canon 105 — §1. A minor necessarily retains the domicile and quasi-domicile of the one to whose power the minor is subject. A minor who is no longer an infant can also acquire a quasi-domicile of one's own; a minor who is legitimately emancipated according to the norm of civil law can also acquire a domicile of one's own.

This canon speaks to the necessary domicile of minors. Consonant with the provisions of canon 98, §2, this canon provides that minors derive their legal residence from their parents or guardians. Depending on circumstances, however, it allows for a plurality of domiciles and quasi-domiciles. It acknowledges that a minor over seven can acquire quasi-domicile, by going away

---

[15] See W. Woestman, *Sacraments: Initiation, Penance, Anointing of the Sick* (Ottawa: St. Paul University, 1992) 234–235.

to school, for example. Moreover, once he or she has left home, that is, has become emancipated according to the norms of civil law, then the minor acquires domicile according to the provisions of canon 102.

§2. Whoever for some other reason than minority has been placed legitimately under the guardianship or care of another has the domicile and quasi-domicile of the guardian or curator.

Those who habitually lack the use of reason (c. 99) also retain the necessary or involuntary domicile of their curators. As guardians look to the welfare of minors, so curators defend the rights of the mentally impaired. This provision, established by the law itself, represents another form of legal domicile, one which easily accords with both natural and moral law and reflects the *potestas dominativa* associated with the earlier code (cf. *CIC* 501, §1).

Loss of Domicile

Canon 106 — Domicile and quasi-domicile are lost by departure from a place with the intention of not returning, without prejudice to the prescript of can. 105.

This canon simply reverses the provisions of canon 102, §1. That is, it includes two elements: (1) the actual departure from a place and (2) the intention not to return. In other words, mere departure does not mean the loss of domicile. Why not? As an acquired right (*ius domicilii*), domicile requires a strict interpretation according to canon 36, §1. Moreover, since the departure is physically evident, e.g., when one moves the whole household, it points to a permanent arrangement; we are not talking therefore of a tourist or a visitor. The loss of domicile thus includes both actual departure and an actual intention not to return, placed simultaneously.

On the other hand, the law also protects necessary domicile. But this status is also relative, subject to change. That is, the minor attains his majority, the insane gain the use of reason, and the religious transfers to another house.

Pastor and Ordinary

Canon 107 — §1. Through both domicile and quasi-domicile, each person acquires his or her pastor and ordinary.
§2. The proper pastor or ordinary of a transient is the pastor or local ordinary where the transient is actually residing.
§3. The proper pastor of one who has only a diocesan domicile or quasi-domicile is the pastor of the place where the person is actually residing.

This canon explains the juridic effects of domicile. It places the individual person in relationship to the pastor of a specific parish and to a diocesan bishop. As ecclesiastical superiors, they have responsibility for assuring the teaching, sanctifying, and governing offices of the particular church.

Although the canon mentions transients (c. 107, §2), it also mentions quasi-domicile, which includes travelers (c. 107, §1). In effect, every one of the *Christifideles* without exception has both a parish priest and an ordinary. Since this relationship belongs to the constitutive law of the Church, it is not liable to dispensation (c. 86).

After having presented the canons on domicile and its juridical effects, the code turns next to relationships, the fourth determinant of what it means to be a physical person in the Church. It speaks to parentage, whether by kinship or by adoption; to relatives, either by marriage or quasi-affinity; and to rite, either by baptism or by choice. These legal relationships render the person ever more concretely so within the communion that we recognize as Church.

Blood Relationships

Canon 108 — §1. Consanguinity is computed through lines and degrees.
§2. In the direct line there are as many degrees as there are generations or persons, not counting the common ancestor.

§3. In the collateral line there are as many degrees as there are persons in both the lines together, not counting the common ancestor.

Consanguinity, as the etymology suggests, involves a blood relationship between two persons, effected by sexual intercourse or *copula perfecta*. It does not occur by any blood transfusion. In general, when children have the same parents, we have bilateral consanguinity, which establishes a bond between persons descending from the same parents through carnal generation. The canon, therefore, grounds consanguinity not in marriage but in generation, whether the parents are married or not. So the principle of perfect carnal *copula* prescinds from any moral considerations. It recognizes only the act, licit or not, by which the bloodline flows from one person to another.

According to this canon, the current code computes consanguinity by lines and degrees. There are two lines: the direct (e.g., father and son, grandmother and granddaughter) and the collateral (brother and sister, aunt and nephew, cousins). In both, individual persons are related to one another through a common ancestor (*stipes*). Degree measures the closeness or distance of these relationships. In the direct line, the computation of degree is made by counting the acts of generation between the persons or counting the number of persons, then subtracting the common ancestor (e.g., father and son are related in the first degree, grandmother and granddaughter in the second). In the collateral line, degree is computed by counting all the persons on both sides from the common ancestor and subtracting the ancestor (e.g., brother and sister are related in the second degree, aunt and nephew in the third degree, and first cousins in the fourth degree). These mathematics become important in any consideration of the matrimonial impediment (c. 1091).[16]

---

[16] Important considerations are also raised in connection with dispensations from the impediment. See the instruction of the Congregation of Sacraments of August 1, 1931 (*CLD* 1, 514–516) and more recently the rescript of Pope Paul VI to the CDF of January 21, 1977 (*Leges Ecclesiae* 5:7288).

The previous code depended on the Germanic mode of calculation, introduced by Alexander II (1065) and confirmed by Gregory IX (1230). For the sake of clarity, the revision committee reversed this in favor of the Roman method of computation,[17] which accords more easily with the provisions of civil law and those of the Eastern churches (e.g., *CCEO* 918).

As a juridic fact, consanguinity effects certain limitations evident throughout the code: (1) it excludes from specific ecclesiastical offices (cc. 478, §2; 492, §3); (2) it acts as an impediment to marriage (cc. 1091, 1092); (3) it prohibits the sale or lease of ecclesiastical property to certain persons (c. 1298); (4) it prevents the judge, the promoter of justice, the defender of the bond, the assessor, and the auditor from undertaking certain cases (c. 1448); and (5) it exempts one from testifying under certain circumstances (c. 1548, §2, 2°). For most practical purposes, the fourth degree of consanguinity in the collateral line remains normative.

Relationships Resulting from Marriage

Canon 109 — §1. Affinity arises from a valid marriage, even if not consummated, and exists between a man and the blood relatives of the woman and between the woman and the blood relatives of the man.

Affinity describes the relationship that arises from a canonically valid marriage, whether natural or sacramental, whether consummated or not. The relationship is only between the husband and the blood relatives of the wife, and between the wife and the blood relatives of the husband. For example, there is no relationship of affinity between the husband's brother and the wife's sister.

As a juridic bond, with roots in Roman law, affinity is perceived as perpetual. That is, it does not cease with the death of one spouse. Since it

---

[17] *Comm* 6 (1974) 97 and 14 (1982) 141.

pertains only to the blood relations of each of the spouses, it acts as a limited concept in law. In other words, despite the concept of the extended family, relatives do not really become related to relatives. This is the meaning behind the adage *Affinitas non gignit affinitatem.*

§2. It is so computed that those who are blood relatives of the man are related in the same line and degree by affinity to the woman, and vice versa.

Because they do not have lines and degrees of themselves, relationships of affinity are computed like those of consanguinity. The principle, however, remains the same: count the persons. So, in the direct line and first degree, we find a mother-in-law and sons-in-law, a stepfather and a step-daughter. In the collateral line, the second degree includes brothers- and sisters-in-law. Only affinity in the direct line is a matrimonial impediment (c. 1092).

As in the case of consanguinity, so in the case of affinity, the following canons apply: canons 478, §2; 492, §3; 1091; 1092; 1298; 1448; 1548 §2, 2°. The question arises as to whether the impediment of affinity is of divine and natural law, or of merely ecclesiastical law. Current canonical opinion agrees that the impediment of affinity really belongs to ecclesiastical law, which the Church takes very seriously indeed. We see this in the reply of the Holy Office on January 31, 1957, which makes the impediment retroactive (*CLD* 4, 89). On the other hand, we also find an exception in granting a dispensation from canon 1092 by the Sacred Congregation for the Sacraments (*CLD* 11, 265–266). Still, these decisions seem to confirm the opinion that affinity involves a merely legal relationship between people, reflected equally in canon 919 of the Eastern code. Admittedly, a quasi-affinity gives rise to the impediment of public propriety (c. 1093). Yet, on the other hand, the sponsor at baptism (c. 872) accepts de facto and de iure a spiritual relationship (*CIC* 1079) which is no longer an impediment to marriage.

Adoption

Canon 110 — Children who have been adopted according to the norm of civil law are considered the children of the person or persons who have adopted them.

Since the code really has no mechanism or procedure in place to secure the institute of adoption, the Church defers to civil legislation (c. 22). In the previous code, the canons on adoption (*CIC* 1059, 1080) are found among the canons concerned with marriage impediments. In this respect, the code was following the provisions of civil law (cf. *CLD* 8, 634–635). While the code commission wanted to follow civil law procedures in order to secure the fact of adoption, it did not want to canonize the merely civil effects of adoption. Consequently, we find two canons on adoption: canon 110 on the fact of adoption and canon 1094 on its consequence for marriage.

Adoption arises from a legal bond whereby one takes the child (or adult) as one's own with all the rights and duties which would have existed had the child (or adult) been one's own originally. Hence, canon 1094 speaks of "a legal relationship." By mentioning "person or persons," canon 110 allows for single-parent adoptions and same-sex adoptions. It does not specify any age limit. Because the Church acknowledges that adopted children belong to the person or persons who legally adopted them, the juridic effects parallel those of the natural family.

According to canon 877, §3, the episcopal conference is to set norms concerning the baptismal registration of adopted children. How are their baptisms to be recorded (cf. c. 535, §2)? On July 22, 1988 the National Conference of Catholic Bishops promulgated a complementary norm on this.[18] The legislation of other conferences is also available (cf. *CLD* 11, 193–199).

For the most part, the juridic consequences of adoption fall to the adopting parent or parents: (1)

---

[18] *Implementation of the 1983 Code of Canon Law: Complementary Norms* (Washington, D.C.: NCCB, 1991) 10.

relative to status (cc. 98, §2;, 105, §1); (2) to Catholic formation (cc. 774, §2; 793; 796–798; 868, §1, 2°); (3) to the sacramental life of the Church (cc. 851, 2°; 855; 867; 890; 914; 1071, §1, 6°; 1136; 1183, §2); and (4) to church discipline (cc. 1252, 1366).

Rite

Canon 111 — §1. Through the reception of baptism, the child of parents who belong to the Latin Church is enrolled in it, or, if one or the other does not belong to it, both parents have chosen by mutual agreement to have the offspring baptized in the Latin Church. If there is no mutual agreement, however, the child is enrolled in the ritual Church to which the father belongs.

§2. Anyone to be baptized who has completed the fourteenth year of age can freely choose to be baptized in the Latin Church or in another ritual Church *sui iuris*; in that case, the person belongs to the Church which he or she has chosen.

Through the reception of baptism (cc. 96, 204), an individual becomes a member of the Latin church (c. 1), provided that the parents belong to the Western church. The Latin church constitutes a ritual church *sui iuris,* and affiliation with it does not occur by free choice but by means of the norms stipulated in these canons. Although the Latin church acknowledges rites other than the Roman, such as the Ambrosian in Milan (dating from approximately 537) and the Mozarabic in Toledo (dating from approximately 808), neither of these constitutes a ritual church *sui iuris*. So, for all practical purposes, the canon is concerned with the Eastern Catholic churches.

Canon 111 deals with three situations: (1) the child under fourteen years of age who is baptized, (2) the person over fourteen who receives baptism, and (3) transfer from one rite to another after baptism.

In the first situation, if both parents belong to the Latin rite, so too does the child. If only one parent belongs to the Latin rite, so too does the child, provided that both parents agree. If they do

not agree, then the child follows the father's rite, according to long-standing tradition. (Canon 29 of the Eastern code also favors the rite of the father, but permits the child to be enrolled in the mother's ritual church if both parents agree. In the case of an unwed mother, the Eastern code allows the child to follow the mother's rite.)

Hence, ritual enrollment and membership normally conform to the rite of baptism, so that the rite of baptism determines ritual affiliation; baptism acts as a practical norm.[19] However, Eastern rite Catholics have sometimes accepted Latin rite baptism for their children out of necessity (e.g., when no church of their rite is anywhere around) or by mistake (e.g., having lost contact with their ritual heritage) or based on their own preference. In such cases, the child actually belongs to the rite in which it *should have been baptized* in accord with this canon. In other words, neither practical necessities nor natural assimilation effects a transfer from one rite to another. A de facto baptism, when it takes place contrary to the canon, does not create a de iure ritual membership.[20] Consequently, the baptismal rites by themselves do not constitute an absolute norm of ritual membership.

The first paragraph of the canon presents a restrictive norm. Suppose we find a Latin father and an Eastern mother. If both parents agree, can the child be baptized in the Eastern rite? The canon does not permit this. If they both agree, it must be in the Latin church. In no case can parents ascribe their children to a ritual church *sui iuris* other than that to which at least one of them belongs.

The second paragraph allows any candidate for baptism who has completed his or her fourteenth year (c. 203) the freedom to choose his or her own ritual church. We find the same provision in canon 30 of the Eastern code. Admittedly, paragraph two of canon 111 suggests that the baptismal rite also identifies the ritual church *sui*

---

[19] See F. Urrutia, *De normis generalibus: Adnotationes in Codicem: Liber I* (Rome: Pontificia Universitas Gregoriana, 1983) 69.

[20] This position is expressed in *CLD* 1, 85, confirmed in *CLD* 3, 302, and repeated in *RR 1993,* 11–14.

iuris. As a universal norm, this provision admits of no exception. That is, it prevails also in missionary countries. It applies equally to those invalidly or doubtfully baptized. Baptized non-Catholics who wish to convert to Catholicism enjoy the same freedom.

A family may wish to support a variety of rites. For example, in the Ukrainian tradition, the girls follow the mother's rite, and the boys follow that of the father. While this arrangement may prove acceptable theoretically, others dispute its practical wisdom. Since the family, according to Pope Paul VI, acts as "the domestic church," there is much to be said for unity of rite. In other words, multiple rites can act as a source of familial discord.

Change of Rite

Canon 112 — §1. After the reception of baptism, the following are enrolled in another ritual Church *sui iuris*:

    1° a person who has obtained permission from the Apostolic See;

    2° a spouse who, at the time of or during marriage, has declared that he or she is transferring to the ritual Church *sui iuris* of the other spouse; when the marriage has ended, however, the person can freely return to the Latin Church;

    3° before the completion of the fourteenth year of age, the children of those mentioned in nn. 1 and 2 as well as, in a mixed marriage, the children of the Catholic party who has legitimately transferred to another ritual Church; on completion of their fourteenth year, however, they can return to the Latin Church.

This canon concerns the transfer of rite. It can be accomplished in one of three ways. First, the Apostolic See can grant permission (*licentia*) for Latin Catholics to be enrolled in another autonomous ritual church. However, the transfer of an Eastern Catholic to the Latin rite requires for validity consent (*consensus*) of both the eparchial bishop and the diocesan bishop (*CCEO* 32, §2).[21] In such a case, the canon presumes the consent of the Apostolic See.[22] Nevertheless, the burden of this canon falls on the Latin Catholic who wishes to transfer to another autonomous church. This norm derives quite exactly from *Orientalium Ecclesiarum* (no. 460).

Second, a Latin spouse before or during marriage to an Eastern Catholic may declare his or her intention to transfer to the spouse's rite. While this canon treats both spouses as equals, canon 33 of the Eastern code reflects the older discipline, which allows only the woman to transfer. This difference in discipline makes inter-ritual marriage a fairly sensitive issue.[23] The intention to affiliate to one's spouse's rite requires a public declaration. Using canon 1126 by way of analogy, we understand that this declaration must be made before an appropriate pastor and put in writing. Pius XII would insist on two witnesses as well. Moreover, according to canon 526, §2, the baptismal register must be so annotated. Once the marriage is dissolved, however, either by death or annulment, the spouse is free to return to the Latin church. Nevertheless, the perception here is quite clear: because ascription to a ritual church is definitive, it belongs to the status of persons. Consequently, affiliation is understood as belonging to constitutive law and not merely to disciplinary law (cf. *CLD* 9, 51). According to *Pastor bonus* 58 the Congregation for the Eastern Churches is competent to judge the status of persons relative to rite. In practice, it is easier for a Latin Catholic to affiliate with an Eastern church than for an Eastern Catholic to transfer to the Latin rite (cf. *RR* 1995, 28–31).

---

[21] See the commentary of A. Mendonça in *CLSGBI Com*, 63 at no. 226.

[22] See, for example, J. Abbass, *Two Codes in Comparison* (Rome: Pontificio Istituto Orientale, 1997) 287.

[23] For the disparity between the different disciplines, see V. Pospishil, *Eastern Catholic Church Law*, 2nd rev. ed. (New York: St. Maron Publications, 1996) 118–119.

Third, children who are born into an inter-ritual marriage generally follow the rite of their parents (*CLD* 5, 7–8). Children of mixed marriages follow the rite of the Catholic party. When the children have completed their fourteenth birthday, they are free to choose a proper rite. Since the law does not specify any time frame, they can exercise this option at any time (cf. *RR* 1994, 155–157). The provision is compatible with canon 111, §2; we find a correlative in canon 34 of the Eastern code. Any transfer, however, requires an appropriate declaration and annotation (c. 535, §2).

§2. The practice, however prolonged, of receiving the sacraments according to the rite of another ritual Church *sui iuris* does not entail enrollment in that Church.

Ascription to an autonomous ritual church requires a formal recognition and declaration. It does not occur by osmosis, by custom, or by regular attendance at liturgical events. Even prolonged practice does not effect a change in membership (cf. *CCEO* 38). Nevertheless, the code is flexible enough to provide for the spiritual needs of the faithful. So the *Christifideles* are free to receive most of the sacraments fruitfully in any Catholic rite: baptism (c. 861, §2), confirmation (cc. 882, 887), Eucharist (cc. 923, 1248, §1), reconciliation (c. 991), and anointing (cc. 1003, §2; 1004, §1). In effect, the canon distinguishes membership

from liturgical practice.[24] This means that change of ritual church membership occurs in one of the three ways provided for in paragraph one.

Finally, the code provides additional norms relating to the faithful of other rites. The diocesan bishop, in the first place, is directly charged with their pastoral care (c. 383, §2). We also find the possibility of erecting a personal parish based on rite (c. 518). The bishop is free to appoint an episcopal vicar to supervise different rites (cc. 383, §2; 476). The law distinguishes dimissorial letters according to rite (c. 1021). Priests validly assist at local marriages in which one of the parties is of the Latin rite (c. 1109). Canon 846, §2 obliges ministers to celebrate the sacraments according to their own rite. An instruction from the Congregation of Bishops urges diocesan bishops to provide for the spiritual needs of emigrants of different rites (*CLD* 7: 198, 207, 210). These provisions acknowledge that the Church is a vital communion with a rich diversity of traditions, as was taught by the fathers in the Vatican II Decree on Eastern Catholic Churches.

In general, this chapter treats the physical person in terms of substance (i.e., *subsistens*). Later canons in Book II will relate the individual to appropriate activities in the Church. By putting the person in motion, as it were, the code discloses a fairly complete Christian anthropology.[25]

[24] See Pospishil, 116–117.
[25] See, for example, J. McIntyre, "*Lineamenta* for a Christian Anthropology," *P* 85 (1996) 249–276.

CHAPTER II
JURIDIC PERSONS
[cc. 113–123]

Apostolic undertakings often transcend the abilities and life span of individual natural persons and require the combined efforts of many persons continuing over long periods of time. To afford continuity and stability, the legal system of the Church, like other legal systems, creates artificial entities known as juridic persons on which the law confers certain rights, such as the right to own property, the right to enter into contracts, and the right to sue, and imposes certain obligations, such as regard for the common good, accountability to ecclesiastical authority, and liability for debts and for the faithful fulfillment of the intentions of donors. Such entities include dioceses, episcopal conferences, parishes, institutes of consecrated life, societies of apostolic life, seminaries, and some colleges, universities, hospitals, and other educational, charitable, or apostolic endeavors. To aid in adequately understanding the nature and functioning of such entities, the code offers general norms regarding the creation of juridic persons (cc. 114, 117), the major classifications among them (cc. 115, 116), the natural persons who are to represent and act in the name of a juridic person (c. 118), decision-making in juridic persons (c. 119), the termination of juridic persons (c. 120), and the distribution of the assets and liabilities of a juridic person upon its consolidation (c. 121), its division (c. 122), and its extinction (c. 123).

Moral and Juridic Persons

Canon 113 — §1. The Catholic Church and the Apostolic See have the character of a moral person by divine ordinance itself.

§2. In the Church, besides physical persons, there are also juridic persons, that is, subjects in

canon law of obligations and rights which correspond to their nature.

This canon acknowledges the existence of three categories of persons in the Church: natural (physical), moral, and juridic. While the notion of a natural person may be considered self-evident, the notions of moral and juridic persons are not. As so often is the case with technical terminology, however, the code offers no definitions, leaving the matter of definition to canonical jurisprudence.

A moral person is a group or succession of natural persons who are united by a common purpose and, hence, who have a particular relationship to each other and who, because of that relationship, may be conceived of as a single entity. A moral person is what we refer to when we speak of a team, a university class, an association. It is a mental construct, a collectivity thought of as a single entity, but an entity which does not exist, and cannot be conceived of, apart from the people who compose it. One can speak of a moral person having rights and obligations, but they are the cumulative rights and obligations of the members of the group.[1] Since a moral person is a group or collectivity, it may properly be referred to in the plural: "they," "them," "theirs." A moral person precedes, logically and usually chronologically, the establishment of a corresponding juridic person.

Analogously, a moral person may also be understood as an accumulation or mass of material goods or assets which have been set aside for a common purpose and which, therefore, can be conceived of as a single entity, as, for example, a fund, such as a pension, building, or other restricted fund. A fund is a mental construct, a collectivity

---

[1] See A. Gauthier, "Juridical Persons in the Code of Canon Law," *Stud Can* 25 (1991) 81–84; P. Rayanna, "Moral or Juridical Person?" *J* 18 (1958) 460. For an example of the code's recognition of the cumulative rights and obligations of the members of a group, see c. 310.

thought of as a single entity but an entity which does not exist, even in the mind, apart from the assets which compose it. Since such a moral person is a collectivity, it may properly be referred to in the plural: "those." Such a moral person precedes, logically and usually chronologically, the establishment of a corresponding juridic person (known as a foundation).

A juridic person, on the other hand, is an artificial person, distinct from all natural persons or material goods, constituted by competent ecclesiastical authority for an apostolic purpose, with a capacity for continuous existence and with canonical rights and duties like those of a natural person (e.g., to own property, enter into contracts, sue or be sued) conferred upon it by law or by the authority which constitutes it.[2] Like a civil-law corporation, it is a legal construct which can and must be conceived of apart from the natural persons who constitute it, administer it, or for whose benefit it exists.[3] It is not a group or collectivity and may properly be referred to only in the impersonal singular: "it." The establishment of a juridic person follows, logically and usually chronologically, the formation of an underlying moral person, either a group of natural persons or an accumulation of material goods, which serves as the substratum or basis in reality of the juridic person. Of its nature, a juridic person is perpetual and, once established, it can outlast all natural persons or material goods which formed its substratum (see c. 120, §1).

In canon 113, §1, the Catholic Church and the Apostolic See are each said to have the nature of a moral person by divine institution. Affirmation of divine origin makes clear that here the Apostolic See refers only to the papacy, not to the conglomerate of congregations, secretariats, councils, tribunals, and other offices that constitute the Roman Curia (see c. 361). By divine institution the Catholic Church is a group, and the papacy a succession, of natural persons united by a common purpose and conceived of as a single entity. Classification as moral persons distinguishes the Catholic Church and Apostolic See from juridic persons, which are creations of ecclesiastical authority, and affirmation of the divine origin of the Catholic Church and Apostolic See distinguishes them from other moral persons, such as associations of the faithful or funds, which are of human origin.[4]

Canon 113, §2, while affirming the existence of natural (physical) and juridic persons, makes no further mention of moral persons, such as those of human origin of which there are a great number in the Church. This is regrettable, because it leaves Book I of the code without an explicit synthesis of all categories of persons in the Church. The existence of moral persons of human institution is, of course, implied in paragraph one, as it is in other canons of this chapter,[5] in the canons on private associations of the faithful which have not been erected as juridic persons,[6] and in various other canons.[7] There are also numerous *de facto* groups of natural persons which have been formed, without official recognition, to pursue various apostolic works pursuant to the right of the Christian faithful to associate for apostolic purposes;[8] these *de facto* groups or associations also come within the meaning of moral person.

Canonists trained under the 1917 code may find this terminology unfamiliar and perhaps confusing. While in canon 113 the 1983 code acknowledges three categories of persons, the parallel canon in the 1917 code spoke of only two, nat-

---

[2] These essential characteristics of a juridic person are derived from cc. 113, §2; 114, §§1, 2; and 120. For discussion of the nature of a juridic person, see Gauthier, 79–85; Rayanna, 461–462.

[3] See L. Chiappetta, *Il Codice di Diritto Canonico: Commento Giuridico-Pastorale*, 2nd ed. (Rome: Dehoniane, 1996) 1:169.

[4] It would seem that the college of bishops should also be recognized as a moral person of divine origin. *Chiappetta Com 1996*, 1:168.

[5] See cc. 114, §3; 117.

[6] See cc. 310, 321–326.

[7] See, e.g., cc. 495–502 (presbyteral council and college of consultors), cc. 1274–1275 (various diocesan and interdiocesan funds).

[8] See cc. 215, 216; see also R. Pagé, "Associations of the Faithful in the Church," *J* 47 (1987) 169, 172–174; Gauthier, 81–83.

ural (physical) and moral.[9] The 1917 code used the term "moral person" not only of the Catholic Church and Apostolic See, as does the present code, but also to signify what the present code more precisely calls "juridic persons," namely, entities constituted by ecclesiastical authority.[10] The 1917 code did use the term "juridic person," but only three times,[11] and in each instance the context made it clear that "juridic person" was being used synonymously with "moral person."[12] The 1983 code more clearly distinguishes artificial persons (juridic persons constituted by ecclesiastical authority) from groups of persons or accumulations of assets not brought into existence by ecclesiastical authority (moral persons), and among the latter distinguishes moral persons of divine institution (the Catholic Church and Apostolic See) from moral persons of human origin, such as various *de facto* associations or funds.[13]

Creation of Juridic Persons

Canon 114 — §1. Juridic persons are constituted either by the prescript of law or by special grant of competent authority given through a decree. They are aggregates of persons (*universitates personarum*) or of things (*universitates rerum*) ordered for a purpose which is in keeping with the mission of the Church and which transcends the purpose of the individuals.

§2. The purposes mentioned in §1 are understood as those which pertain to works of piety, of the apostolate, or of charity, whether spiritual or temporal.

§3. The competent authority of the Church is not to confer juridic personality except on those aggregates of persons (*universitates personarum*)

or things (*universitates rerum*) which pursue a truly useful purpose and, all things considered, possess the means which are foreseen to be sufficient to achieve their designated purpose.

The primary focus of this canon is on the creation of juridic persons. Paragraph one provides for two alternative modes of creation: by operation of law (*a iure*) and by decree of competent authority (*ab homine*). Paragraph two sets forth the proper purposes for which juridic persons can be created. Paragraph three requires of ecclesiastical authority an informed judgment of the usefulness of the purpose of a proposed juridic person in the light of other endeavors addressing the same or similar needs in the area, and also an informed judgment of the adequacy of resources available to the proposed juridic person for the fulfillment of its purpose.

Although neither this nor any other canon uses the term "creation" in regard to the origin of a juridic person, the term, at least in English, would seem best to describe what is happening, namely, bringing into existence something (an artificial person) that has not existed before and that is not comprised of previously existing components. Some canons, like paragraph one of canon 114, speak of juridic persons being "constituted," while others speak of their being "erected."[14] Each of these terms connotes bringing an entity into existence. Paragraph three of canon 114, however, speaks of juridic personality being "conferred," and other canons speak of it being "given,"[15] "granted,"[16] "obtained,"[17] "acquired,"[18] "possessed,"[19] all of which suggest that juridic personality is not the creation of something new, but simply a juridic enhancement of something already existing. Reconciliation of these apparently

---

[9] *CIC* 99.

[10] Ibid.

[11] *CIC* 687, 1489, 1495, §2.

[12] Compare *CIC* 687 with *CIC* 100; *CIC* 1489 with *CIC* 1491; and *CIC* 1495, §2 with *CIC* 1497. Also see Gauthier, 81, Rayanna, 465.

[13] The Code of Canons of the Eastern Churches has no canon parallel to c. 113, §1 and makes no mention of moral persons. See *CCEO* 920.

[14] Juridic persons are said to be "constituted" in cc. 114, §1; 115, §2; 116, §1; 121; and 313. They are said to be "erected" in cc. 122; 433, §2; and 709.

[15] Canon 116, §2.

[16] Ibid.

[17] Canon 117.

[18] Ibid.

[19] Canons 373; 238, §1; 432, §2; 449, §2; 515, §3.

conflicting notions is afforded by the realization of the relationship that exists between a juridic person, which is an artificial person, and the moral person which precedes it and serves as its substratum or basis in reality.

Prior to (or, rarely, simultaneously with) the creation of a juridic person, it is necessary that there exist a moral person—either a group of natural persons committed to some apostolic purpose, or an accumulation of material goods set aside for an apostolic purpose—to serve as the substratum or basis in reality for the artificial personality of the juridic person. Some authors refer to such a group of persons or assemblage of goods as the material constitutive element of a juridic person (to which must be joined the formal constitutive element of authoritative conferral of juridic personality).[20] Referring to a group of persons or assemblage of goods as a constitutive element of a juridic person, however, ignores the fact that, once established, a juridic person can continue in existence (for as long as one hundred years) without any natural persons or material assets being associated with it (see c. 120, §1). For that reason, it seems less confusing and more accurate to forego the language of constitutive elements when speaking of the group of natural persons or assemblage of material goods which must logically (and usually chronologically) precede the creation of a juridic person, and refer to them instead as the basis in reality or substratum of the newly created juridic person.[21]

Also prior to the creation of a juridic person is the need to draft and obtain approval of the statutes that are to serve as its internal governing document, much like the articles of incorporation and by-laws of a civil-law corporation. In most instances, many of the provisions of such statutes will already have been drafted for the internal governance of the moral person which has preceded and which is to be the substratum of the juridic person; some changes may be necessary, but most provisions should be readily transferable to statutes for the juridic person. No juridic person is to be created without prior approval of its statutes (c. 117). Regrettably, this law of the Church seems not always to be followed by those responsible for the coming into existence of such juridic persons as parishes, which often appear to be lacking statutes altogether.

As noted above, the actual conferral of juridic personality, which always requires the action of competent ecclesiastical authority (see commentary on c. 113), can be either *a iure* or *ab homine*. With only one exception, the 1983 code is consistently explicit in its *a iure* conferral of juridic personality upon such entities as dioceses (c. 373), parishes (c. 515, §3), religious institutes and each of their provinces and individual houses (c. 634, §1), societies of apostolic life and, unless their constitutions provide otherwise, their parts and houses (c. 741, §1), seminaries (c. 238, §1), ecclesiastical provinces (c. 432, §2), episcopal conferences (c. 449, §2), and public associations of the faithful (c. 313). The one exception occurs in regard to secular institutes. No canon explicitly confers juridic personality upon secular institutes. In providing that the administration of the temporal goods of a secular institute is governed by the norms of Book V of the code, however, canon 718 implicitly confers juridic personality upon secular institutes for, while a few canons in Book V govern the goods of natural persons (see, e.g., cc. 1269, 1300), the vast majority of canons in Book V govern the temporal goods only of juridic persons (see c. 1257).

Entities in the Church such as colleges, universities, hospitals, and other apostolically oriented institutions can also serve as the substrata of juridic persons, but juridic personality is not conferred upon such institutions *a iure*. It can be conferred only by decree of competent ecclesiastical authority. While the 1917 code designated local ordinaries as the authorities competent to grant such a decree,[22] the present code contains no ex-

[20] See *Chiappetta Com 1996*, 1:169; P. Pinto, in *Urbaniana Com*, 68; F. D'Ostilio, *Il Diritto Amministrativo della Chiesa* (Vatican City: Libreria Editrice Vaticana, 1995) 23–26.

[21] See E. Molano, in *Pamplona ComEng*, 134–135.

[22] *CIC* 1489, §1.

plicit designation of competent authority in this regard. Recourse may be had, however, to canon 312, the immediate purpose of which is to designate authorities competent to establish public associations of the faithful but which, in conjunction with canons 313 and 322, affords a solid basis for identifying authorities competent to create all juridic persons as well. Canon 313 provides that all public associations of the faithful are *ipso facto* juridic persons; canon 322 states that a private association of the faithful can acquire juridic personality by decree of the same competent authority mentioned in canon 312 for public associations. Thus, juridic persons which have an association of the faithful, public or private, as their underlying substratum can, according to canon 312, be created by decree of the Holy See, or an episcopal conference, or a diocesan bishop, or, with consent of the diocesan bishop, by others acting pursuant to apostolic privilege.

In the absence of any other canon indicating competence for the issuance of a decree conferring juridic personality, it would seem appropriate to look to canon 312, by analogy, for the designation of authorities competent to issue decrees conferring juridic personality upon any entity, including those which do not have officially recognized associations of the faithful as their substrata, such as foundations, the substrata of which are accumulations of material goods, or *de facto* associations of the faithful which, prior to seeking juridic personality, have not sought or received official recognition by ecclesiastical authority.

Confining competence for the creation of juridic persons to the Holy See, episcopal conference, and diocesan bishop is in keeping with canonical tradition which has required episcopal power for the conferral of juridic personality, since such conferral affects the public order of the Church by creating new subjects of canonical rights and obligations.[23] The requirement of a de-

cree, the issuance of which is an act of executive power of governance,[24] is also strongly indicative of episcopal or at least quasi-episcopal power.

While the principal focus of canon 114 is on the creation of juridic persons, a subordinate clause in paragraph one introduces the first of the major distinctions among categories of juridic persons, the distinction between an *universitas personarum* (translated as "aggregate of persons") and an *universitas rerum* (translated as "aggregate of things"). Since this distinction becomes the principal focus of canon 115, commentary on the distinction and on its translation into English is deferred to the commentary on canon 115.

Paragraph one of canon 114 also draws attention to the necessary congruity between the purpose of any ecclesial juridic person and the mission of the Church, which is given added

---

[23] See G. Michiels, *Principia Generalia de Personis in Ecclesia,* 2nd ed. (Tournai: Desclée, 1955) 403–404; R. Kennedy, "McGrath, Maida, Michiels: Introduction to a Study of the Canonical and Civil-Law Status of Church-

Related Institutions in the United States," *J* 50 (1990) 379–384.

Many Catholic colleges, universities, hospitals, and other institutions have been founded by religious institutes, clerical and non-clerical. Without an apostolic privilege, however, no major superior of a religious institute could have created such an institution as a juridic person while the 1917 code was in effect, for erection as a juridic person was reserved to local ordinaries (*CIC* 1489, §1; 686, §2; 687). Though some major superiors were ordinaries (*CIC* 198, §1), none were local ordinaries (*CIC* 198, §2).

Competency for the creation of such institutions as juridic persons under the 1983 code would appear to be even more limited. There is no general grant of competency to local ordinaries as there was in the 1917 code. Rather, as noted in the text above, competency would appear to be limited to the Holy See, episcopal conferences, and diocesan bishops, in the absence of an apostolic privilege conferring competency on others, with the consent of the diocesan bishop required for the valid exercise even of such an apostolic privilege (c. 312, §2). Not even the diocesan administrator is accorded such competency (c. 312, §1, 3°). This would appear to preclude the creation of juridic persons by major superiors of religious institutes in the absence of an apostolic privilege.

For a discussion of the canonical status of church-related institutions in the United States, see the "Note" on that topic following the commentary on c. 123.

[24] Canons 35, 48.

specificity in paragraph two.[25] The practical wisdom of the requirements in paragraph three regarding informed judgments of usefulness and adequacy of resources is self-evident.

Universitas Personarum, Universitas Rerum

Canon 115 — §1. Juridic persons in the Church are either aggregates of persons (*universitates personarum*) or aggregates of things (*universitates rerum*).

§2. An aggregate of persons (*universitas personarum*), which can be constituted only with at least three persons, is collegial if the members determine its action through participation in rendering decisions, whether by equal right or not, according to the norm of law and the statutes; otherwise it is non-collegial.

§3. An aggregate of things (*universitas rerum*), or an autonomous foundation, consists of goods or things, whether spiritual or material, and either one or more physical persons or a college directs it according to the norm of law and the statutes.

The distinction, introduced in canon 114, §1, between juridic persons which in English translation are said to be aggregates of persons and those which are said to be aggregates of things, is the focus of canon 115. The distinction is fundamental and important; it is regrettable that the translation jeopardizes a true understanding both of the distinction and of the nature of a juridic person. It is not that a better translation is available, but simply that the absence of an accurate English word or phrase for the Latin word *universitas* when applied to a juridic person argues strongly for leaving untranslated the terms *universitas personarum* and *universitas rerum* when applied to

juridic persons, as is done with some other technical terminology in the code (see, e.g., cc. 1299, 1445, §1, 1°).

As indicated in the commentary on canon 113, a juridic person is not a group or collectivity, either of natural persons or of material goods. It is not an aggregate. It is an artificial person, an impersonal singular subject of rights and obligations similar to, but totally distinct from, the rights and obligations of natural persons. A juridic person is an "it," not a "they" or "those." The difference is not merely theoretical; it has enormous practical importance.

To speak of a parish, for example, as a community of persons is entirely appropriate from an ecclesiological point of view; canon 515, §1 speaks of a parish in such a sense. From a juridical point of view, however, such a manner of speaking invites canonical misunderstanding and error. Canonically, a parish is a juridic person (c. 515, §3). As such it has a canonical personality of its own distinct from the natural personalities that make up the theological community of the faithful. The temporal goods of a parish are owned by a single legal construct known as the parish; they are not co-owned by an aggregate of persons as are the temporal goods of an association of the faithful which has not been erected as a juridic person (see c. 310). Debts of the parish are not joint liabilities of the parishioners. Actions taken by pastors or others involved in administering the assets of a parish are not subject to challenge in ecclesiastical or civil tribunals on the ground that the actions were contrary to the wishes of the "true owners," the parishioners. A great deal of ill-conceived and unsuccessful but nonetheless expensive litigation, ecclesiastical and civil, has resulted from attempts to vindicate the rights of parishioners to "their" parochial funds or properties, or to compel parishioners, especially wealthy ones, to pay "their" parochial debts. Much of this kind of confusion is traceable to the imprecise speaking of juridic persons, such as parishes, as aggregates of persons.

Paragraph two of canon 115 requires at least three natural persons for the constitution of an *universitas personarum*, thereby seeming to vin-

---

[25] The code contains a variety of expressions for purposes in keeping with the mission of the Church. See, e.g., in addition to c. 114, §2, cc. 215, 298, 1254, §2. In view of the conciliar definition of the apostolate, however, as all activity of the Church dedicated to bringing the world to Christ (*AA* 2), it would be difficult to conceive of any ecclesial purpose not included in "works of the apostolate."

dicate the use of the plural "aggregate of persons" when referring to such a juridic person. In this regard, however, canon 115, §2 is speaking only of the moment in which a juridic person is constituted; canon 120, §2 envisions the possibility of such a juridic person continuing in existence even after the number of natural persons associated with it has diminished to one. Difficult as it is to conceptualize an "aggregate" of one, it seems even more incongruous to use the term "aggregate of persons" to designate an existing juridic person which has been inactive for nearly one hundred years and, hence, in all likelihood would have no natural persons associated with it, as envisioned in canon 120, §1.

For both theoretical and practical reasons, therefore, it is suggested that the terms *universitas personarum* and *universitas rerum,* when used to designate categories of juridic persons, be untranslated, with the understanding that an *universitas personarum* is a juridic person the substratum or basis in reality of which is persons, and an *universitas rerum* is a juridic person the substratum or basis in reality of which is things.

The potential for confusion, and hence the need for care, in the use of terminology in this area is heightened by the fact that the code also employs the same terminology—*universitas personarum* and *universitas rerum*—when referring, not to juridic persons, but to moral persons, groups of natural persons (associations) or accumulations of material goods (funds) which precede the creation of juridic persons and serve as their substrata (see cc. 114, §3 and 117). In these instances, and these alone, it is appropriate to translate *universitas personarum* as an aggregate of persons, and *universitas rerum* as an aggregate of things.

Collegial and Non-collegial Juridic Persons

Canon 115, §2 introduces another major distinction among juridic persons, namely, the distinction between a collegial and non-collegial juridic person. As paragraph two makes clear, this distinction is applicable only to *universitates personarum,* namely, to juridic persons which have as their substrata groups or communities of persons. Such a juridic person is said to be collegial when, according to law or the statutes of the juridic person, all its members (i.e., the members of the underlying moral person which serves as the substratum of the *universitas personarum*) participate in the making of decisions determining the actions of the juridic person. Examples of collegial juridic persons include episcopal conferences and religious institutes. Participation need not be direct; it can be indirect through elected representatives, as in many religious institutes. Moreover, paragraph two makes clear that participation in decision-making need not be by equal right for a juridic person to be classified as collegial; participation by unequal right, as in the case of participation by auxiliary bishops in the decision-making of episcopal conferences (see c. 454), suffices. Examples of non-collegial juridic persons are dioceses and parishes.

Many canonists trained under the 1917 code will find the 1983 code's use of "collegial" and "non-collegial" unfamiliar and perhaps confusing. The terms were used in the 1917 code (*CIC* 99), but without definition. Though not all canonists agreed,[26] the distinction was generally understood in terms similar to the present distinction between an *universitas personarum* and an *universitas rerum;* a collegial (often translated collegiate) juridic person was understood to be one whose basis in reality or substratum was a group of persons, while a non-collegial (non-collegiate) juridic person was understood to have as its substratum a collection of material assets.[27] The present

---

[26] See Gauthier, 85–87.

[27] See Michiels, 377–378; F. Cappello, *Summa Iuris Canonici,* 5th ed. (Rome: Gregorian University, 1951) 1: 187; A. Vermeersch and J. Creusen, *Epitome Iuris Canonici,* 7th ed. (Rome: H. Dessain, 1940) 1:201–202; E. Regatillo, *Institutiones Iuris Canonici,* 6th ed. (Santander: Sal Terrae, 1961) 1:163; S. Sipos, *Enchiridion Iuris Canonici,* 7th ed. (Rome: Herder, 1960) 78; T. Bouscaren, A. Ellis, and F. Korth, *Canon Law: A Text and Commentary,* 4th rev. ed. (Milwaukee: Bruce, 1966) 89.

code confines the distinction between collegial and non-collegial juridic persons to *universitates personarum,* and roots the distinction in differing approaches to decision-making.

Canon 115, §3 addresses the *universitas rerum.* As noted above, the term *universitas rerum,* when used of a juridic person, signifies a juridic person the underlying reality or substratum of which is a collection of goods or things (e.g., real estate, securities, cash) which have been set aside for a particular apostolic purpose (e.g., worship, education, justice, charity) and which, prior to the conferral of juridic personality, are often referred to as funds, such as education, building, or retirement funds.[28] The affairs of an *universitas rerum* are managed in accord with the norms of law and the juridic person's own statutes by one or more natural persons or by a college or group of natural persons. Paragraph three of canon 115 equates such an *universitas rerum* with an autonomous foundation, one of two types of canonical foundations (see c. 1303).

Public and Private Juridic Persons

Canon 116 — §1. Public juridic persons are aggregates of persons (*universitates personarum*) or of things (*universitates rerum*) which are constituted by competent ecclesiastical authority so that, within the purposes set out for them, they fulfill in the name of the Church, according to the norm of the prescripts of the law, the proper function entrusted to them in view of the public good; other juridic persons are private.

§2. Public juridic persons are given this personality either by the law itself or by a special decree of competent authority expressly granting it. Private juridic persons are given this personality only through a special decree of competent authority expressly granting it.

To the distinctions between an *universitas personarum* and an *universitas rerum,* and between a collegial and non-collegial juridic person, this canon adds the distinction between a public and private juridic person. The distinction is new and is an attempt, along with the 1983 code's division of associations of the faithful into public and private, to give effect to the teaching of the Second Vatican Council that all members of the faithful have the right to engage in apostolic action not only by giving assistance to works appropriately founded and governed by the hierarchy but also by founding and governing other apostolically oriented associations and organizations on their own initiative.[29] The codification of this teaching (see cc. 215, 216) required the creation of expanded canonical structures to afford opportunity for the teaching to be put into practice. Thus, private as well as public associations of the faithful (see cc. 298–329), and private as well as public juridic persons, came into being.

The distinction between a public and a private juridic person is essentially the distinction between a juridic person that is closely governed by ecclesiastical authority (public juridic person) and one that, although subject to authority in certain respects,[30] enjoys more autonomy and is governed primarily by its own statutes (private juridic person). The distinction is essentially a difference in relationship to the hierarchy.[31] This is cryptically

---

[28] As noted above, the term *universitas rerum* is also used in the code to designate the fund which precedes the creation of a juridic person and serves as its substratum (see cc. 114, §3; 117).

[29] See *AA* 18, 19, 24, 25; *PO* 8–9.

[30] Within the Church, all persons, natural and juridic, are subject to hierarchical authority in the area of doctrinal and moral integrity (see, e.g., cc. 209; 305; 323; 386, §2; 397); it is also each diocesan bishop's responsibility to urge the observance of all relevant ecclesiastical laws and to guard against abuses (see cc. 392, 305).

[31] The root of the distinction finds expression in the conciliar decree on the apostolate of the laity:

Depending on its various forms and goals, the lay apostolate admits of different types of relationships with the hierarchy. (*AA* 24)

These words are followed by a tracing of different levels of relationship between various apostolic undertakings of the laity and the hierarchy. The 1983 code attempts, with inevitable loss of nuance, to codify complex ecclesiologi-

expressed in canon 116, §1 which speaks of a public juridic person fulfilling entrusted functions "in the name of the Church," a phrase which is generally understood to mean acting pursuant to a mission received from hierarchical authority and under the close supervision and direction of the hierarchy.[32]

A private juridic person, though its statutes require approval by the ecclesiastical authority that creates it (see cc. 117, 114, §1), is understood to act in its own name, not in the name of the Church, that is, not in close relationship to the hierarchy. This general expression of the distinction between public and private juridic persons is given more detailed expression in the specific differences between them indicated in subsequent canons (see, e.g., cc. 118, 120–123, 1257).

A private juridic person is no less Catholic than a public juridic person; it simply enjoys more autonomy, in service to the right of association which belongs to all members of the faithful. Illustrative of that greater autonomy is the provision in Book V of the code according to which the temporal goods of a private juridic person, though clearly dedicated to the work of the Church, are not classified as ecclesiastical goods (*bona ecclesiastica*) or church property and, hence, are not subject to most of the canons in Book V (see cc. 1257, 1258), including the invalidating laws governing acts of extraordinary ad-

ministration, acts of alienation, and some other transactions.[33]

Canon 116, §2 affords alternative ways of conferring public juridic personality: by law or by special decree of competent authority expressly granting such personality. Conferral of private juridic personality can take place only by decree; no private juridic personality is conferred by law. In the several instances, therefore, where juridic personality is conferred by law (see commentary on c. 114) it is always public juridic personality that is conferred; it is unnecessary for the canons dealing with conferral of juridic personality to state that the personality conferred is public.

No law confers juridic personality on Catholic colleges, universities, hospitals, or similar institutions; they can be constituted juridic persons, either public or private, only by decree of competent authority. The decree need not be separate from the decree creating the juridic person; one and the same decree can confer juridic personality and indicate whether it is public or private.

The distinction between public and private juridic persons is not found in the Code of Canons of the Eastern Churches.

Statutes

Canon 117 — No aggregate of persons (*universitas personarum*) or of things (*universitas rerum*), intending to obtain juridic personality, is able to acquire it unless competent authority has approved its statutes.

The statutes of juridic persons are the internal governing documents of such persons in the Church. They are ordinances, analogous to the bylaws of civil-law corporations in many nations including the United States, which set forth the pur-

---

cal notions, involving not just the laity but all members of the faithful, into the succinct juridical categories of private association of the faithful (see cc. 321–326), public association of the faithful (see cc. 312–320), private juridic person, and public juridic person.

[32] See c. 313; Gauthier, 90–91. The phrase is used with the same meaning in cc. 301, §1; 313; 675, §3; 834, §2; 1108, §2; 1192, §1; and 1282. The seeming identification of the Church with the hierarchy, which is implicit in the phrase, unfortunately echoes just such an identification frequently found in the 1917 code, as in *CIC* 684–686 where establishment of associations of the faithful by hierarchical authority was called establishment "by the Church" (*ab Ecclesia*), an identification difficult to reconcile with the people-of-God ecclesiology of Vatican II.

[33] See commentary on cc. 1281, 1291, 1295. Not to be subject to such laws is a factor to consider when selecting a canonical status for a hospital, college, or other church-related institution. See the discussion of the canonical status of church-related institutions in the United States following the commentary on c. 123.

pose, basic organization, structures of authority, governing principles, forms of decision-making, and mode of operation of the juridic person (see cc. 94, 304, 451). It is their function to afford organizational stability.[34] They also serve as instruments for the implementation of the principle of subsidiarity, as many canons remit to statutes the specification of general norms.[35] This is particularly true in regard to private juridic persons (see, e.g., cc. 118; 120, §1; 123). Among many matters remitted to the statutes of public juridic persons are the determination of which types of financial transaction are to be considered acts of extraordinary administration for the particular juridic person[36] and, hence, are to be subject to the invalidating laws which regulate such acts,[37] and the determination of the manner in which the mandated finance council or financial advisors are to assist in the administration of temporal goods.[38] It is the responsibility of the authority competent to approve the statutes to see that they address the matters remitted to them by the law of the Church.[39]

As noted in the commentary on canon 115, the terms *universitas personarum* and *universitas rerum,* inappropriately translated as "aggregates" when referring to juridic persons, are appropriately translated as "aggregates" in canon 117, because in this canon they refer to groups of persons or collections of things prior to the conferral of juridic personality. Canon 117 makes no distinction between juridic personality that is to be con-

ferred by operation of law (*a iure*) and that which is to be conferred by decree of competent authority (*ab homine*); it would seem, therefore, that all juridic persons, public or private, whether their juridic personality is conferred *a iure* or *ab homine,* should have their statutes approved as a prerequisite to the conferral of juridic personality.[40] The implication is clear that all parishes and all dioceses, as juridic persons, should have statutes though, as a matter of fact, many do not. The absence of statutes is no doubt largely due to the absence in the 1917 code, under which most presently existing dioceses and parishes were established, of any general norm requiring statutes.[41] While, strictly speaking, canon 117 can be said to be binding only on juridic persons constituted after the promulgation of the 1983 code (see c. 9) and, hence, only on newly created dioceses and parishes, good governance would seem to call for the enactment and approval of statutes for all existing dioceses and parishes as well.[42] Nor does there seem to be any compelling ecclesiological reason why the statutes of all parishes or all dioceses need to contain identical provisions; diversity, within the parameters of the law, especially in financial matters, would seem to be entirely compatible with Catholic unity (see commentary on c. 1281).[43]

Acts of a Juridic Person

Canon 118 — Representing a public juridic person and acting in its name are those whose competence is acknowledged by universal or particular law or by its own statutes. Representing a private juridic person are those whose competence is granted by statute.

---

[34] See Pagé, 177.

[35] *Chiappetta Com 1996,* 1:175.

[36] See c. 1281, §2.

[37] See c. 1281, §1.

[38] See c. 1280.

[39] While statutes cannot be approved if they contain provisions contrary to the law, it is sometimes required that statutes contain provisions positively conforming to certain canons of the code. See, e.g., c. 1295 which requires statutes (of public juridic persons) to be in conformity with canons 1291–1294. Such a requirement is designed to provide notice, usually to people engaging in financial transactions with a juridic person, that if certain canonical requirements are not fulfilled, the transaction will be canonically invalid. See commentary on c. 1295.

[40] *Chiappetta Com 1996,* 1:175; A. McGrath, in *CLSGBI Com,* 67.

[41] The 1917 code required statutes only of associations of the faithful (*CIC* 689).

[42] See *Chiappetta Com 1996,* 1:175.

[43] The Code of Canons of the Eastern Churches confines the explicit requirement of having approved statutes to juridic persons erected by decree (*CCEO* 922, §1).

Juridic persons have rights to be exercised and obligations to be fulfilled (c. 113, §2); they are capable of acquiring, retaining, administering, and alienating temporal goods (c. 1255); they can sue and be sued in ecclesiastical tribunals (c. 1400, §1, 1°). Being artificial persons,[44] however, juridic persons can act only through natural persons, either as individuals or as groups. Those competent to represent and act on behalf of a public juridic person are often designated by law, especially where public juridic personality has been conferred by law (see, e.g., c. 393 for a diocese, cc. 532, 543, §2, 3° for a parish, c. 238, §2 for a seminary); when not designated by law, they are to be designated in the statutes of the public juridic person. Those who represent and act on behalf of a private juridic person are to be designated in the statutes.

The apparent simplicity of canon 118 masks a source of tension between diocesan bishops and pastors or others who, by law of the Church or by statutes, are said to represent and act in the name of a juridic person in places where the civil-law structure of a diocese does not mirror the canonical structure. Where a diocese is civilly structured as a corporation sole, for example, as in many dioceses in the United States, all, or nearly all, church-related assets are considered to belong to a single corporation whose sole representative is the diocesan bishop. He, and he alone, acts for the corporation. Incompatible with the law of the Church, this method of holding title to church property was long ago disapproved by the Holy See[45] but continues in some places, often giving rise to internal ecclesial disputes and raising other problems for the Church (see commentary on c. 1256). Whatever the civil structure, every effort should be made to see that the laws of the Church regarding the official representation of parishes and other juridic persons in all juridic affairs are faithfully fulfilled.

[44] See commentary on c. 113.
[45] SCConc, July 29, 1911, *CLD* 2 (1956) 443–445.

Canon 119 — With regard to collegial acts, unless the law or statutes provide otherwise:

1° **if it concerns elections, when the majority of those who must be convoked are present, that which is approved by the absolute majority of those present has the force of law; after two indecisive ballots, a vote is to be taken on the two candidates who have obtained the greater number of votes or, if there are several, on the two senior in age; after the third ballot, if a tie remains, the one who is senior in age is considered elected;**

2° **if it concerns other affairs, when an absolute majority of those who must be convoked are present, that which is approved by the absolute majority of those present has the force of law; if after two ballots the votes are equal, the one presiding can break the tie by his or her vote;**

3° **what touches all as individuals, however, must be approved by all.**

Given the location of this canon in a chapter of canons entitled "Juridic Persons," its norms should be understood as applicable only to acts of collegial juridic persons; application to colleges or groups, such as a college of consultors or presbyteral council, which are not themselves juridic persons or do not constitute the total membership of a collegial juridic person, can only be by way of suggested analogy, not direct obligation. Even in regard to collegial juridic persons, the provisions of canon 119 are suppletory; they apply only in the absence of different norms found in law, universal or particular, or in the statutes of a particular juridic person. Viewing the content of canon 119 in the light of contemporary approaches to decision-making, it would seem likely that many collegial juridic persons would incorporate into their statutes provisions governing the conduct of elections and other affairs that differ markedly from the provisions in the canon.

Number one concerns elections and requires, first of all, a quorum composed of a majority of those entitled to be convoked.[46] Given the presence of a quorum, one or, if necessary, two ballots are to be taken in search of an absolute majority (i.e., one more than half) of those present (not merely of valid votes cast[47]) in favor of one candidate. If no candidate has received an absolute majority after the second ballot, a third ballot is to be taken between the two candidates who received the most votes on the second ballot or, if two or more received an equal number of votes, between the two of them who are oldest in age. The canon does not say that an absolute majority is needed on the third ballot, and an official interpretation by the Pontifical Council for the Interpretation of Legislative Texts has stated that on the third ballot a relative majority (i.e., more votes than any other candidate) suffices.[48] If the third ballot results in a tie, the candidate oldest in age is considered elected. The Code of Canons of the Eastern Churches provides that, unless otherwise specified in law, in the event of a tie vote on the third ballot the senior in sacred ordination is to be considered elected in elections between clergy, and the senior in first profession in elections between religious; in other elections, the senior in age is considered elected when the third ballot results in a tie.[49]

Number two deals with matters other than elections, and again provides for decision-making by a quorum composed of a majority of those entitled to be convoked. Given the presence of a quorum, an absolute majority of those present (not merely of valid votes cast) determines the outcome. Unlike elections, the resolution of other matters is not limited to three ballots; discussion and voting can continue until an absolute majority of those present resolves the matter, regardless of how many ballots it may take. The canon provides, however, that if, after two ballots, the voting should result in a tie,[50] the one presiding (over the meeting, not necessarily over the juridic person, although in most cases they would be identical[51]) can break the tie. This is an option, not an obligation, for the one presiding.

As noted above, the provisions of canon 119 are suppletory; they apply only in the absence of other provisions contained in universal or particular law or in the statutes of a particular juridic person. Universal law, for example, requires a two-thirds vote (of members having a deliberative vote) for the passage of general decrees by an episcopal conference (c. 455, §2), and remits to proper law the ordering of elections and other matters handled in chapters of religious institutes (cc. 631, §2; 632). Particular law governing collegial juridic persons in a diocese, or the proper law in institutes of consecrated life, or the statutes of

---

[46] While it is of the essence of a collegial juridic person that all its members participate in decision-making, participation can be direct or indirect through representatives as, for example, through a chapter of a religious institute (see commentary on c. 115, §2). Those who must be convoked to an election or other meeting, therefore, need not comprise the full membership, but only those entitled to vote in a representative capacity.

[47] The parallel canon in the 1917 code required an absolute majority only of valid votes cast (*CIC* 101, §1, 1°); abstentions or votes invalid for any reason were not counted. Under c. 119, 1° of the 1983 code, however, since an absolute majority of those present is required, an abstention or invalid vote is significant and can preclude the reaching of an absolute majority.

[48] *AAS* 82 (1990) 845. The parallel canon in the 1917 code explicitly stated that a relative majority sufficed on the third ballot (*CIC* 101, §1, 1°). Omission of that language in c. 119 of the 1983 code gave rise to a doubt and led to the request for an official interpretation by PCILT. See L. Wrenn, *Authentic Interpretations on the 1983 Code* (Washington, D.C.: CLSA, 1993) 59–61. The Code of Canons of the Eastern Churches restores the explicit mention of the sufficiency of a relative majority on the third ballot. *CCEO* 924, 3°; 956, §1.

[49] *CCEO* 924, 3°; 956, §1. A similar provision distinguishing elections among clergy or religious from other elections was found in the 1917 code (*CIC* 101, §1, 1°).

[50] Since the canon does not so require, the tie need not represent a fifty-fifty split of those present; even when some of those present do not vote or vote invalidly, if a tie results, the one presiding may choose (so long as at least two ballots have been taken) to break the tie. See *Chiappetta Com 1996,* 1:178.

[51] See *Chiappetta Com 1996,* 1:179.

individual collegial juridic persons, public or private, may well and perhaps should contain provisions different from those found in canon 119 to govern elections and other areas of decision-making.

Number three restates an ancient canonical principle, derived from Roman law[52] and included among the *Regulae Iuris* at the end of the Decretals of Boniface VIII.[53] The location of the principle in the code, in a chapter entitled "Juridic Persons" and in a canon dealing with the acts of a collegial juridic person, assists in its proper interpretation. It is a fundamental postulate of decision-making in a collegial juridic person that whatever touches all as individuals, that is, as individual members of a collegial juridic person, must be approved by all. Matters affecting the juridic person as such are to be decided in accord with the norms in numbers one and two (unless otherwise provided in law or statutes), but matters affecting the rights of individual members of the decision-making body itself (namely, the moral person which serves as substratum for the juridic person) must be decided unanimously. Such matters are nearly always procedural, such as a proposal to allow a vacancy in an elected office to be filled by vote of only a committee rather than by the whole body; such a proposal would require unanimous consent of all members, since it touches upon the procedural right of each member of a collegial juridic person to participate in the decision-making (see c. 174, §1). Similarly, where neither universal law nor a special mandate has granted power to an episcopal conference to issue a general decree, neither the episcopal conference nor its president may act in the name of all the bishops unless each and every bishop has given his consent (c. 455, §4).

The suppletory character of canon 119 is stated at its outset ("unless the law or statutes provide otherwise") and is therefore applicable to all three sub-sections, including the last which restates the *regula iuris* requiring unanimity in matters touching all as individuals. Even in regard to this provision of ancient origin, then, particular or proper law or statutes can provide exceptions. Thus, for example, statutes could provide for elections under certain circumstances to be handled by a committee rather than by all members without first obtaining the unanimous consent of all members. This was not the case prior to the 1983 code. Canonical tradition codified in the 1917 code, while allowing exceptions to the provisions regulating elections and the making of other decisions affecting a collegial juridic person as such, did not allow exceptions to the *regula iuris* requiring unanimity in matters affecting all as individuals.[54]

Decision-making in non-collegial juridic persons (e.g., dioceses, parishes), a matter not mentioned in canon 119, is governed by other universal laws, by particular law, and by statutes.[55]

Termination of a Juridic Person

Canon 120 — §1. A juridic person is perpetual by its nature; nevertheless, it is extinguished if it is legitimately suppressed by competent authority or has ceased to act for a hundred years. A private juridic person, furthermore, is extinguished if the association is dissolved according to the norm of its statutes or if, in the judgment of competent authority, the foundation has ceased to exist according to the norm of its statutes.

§2. If even one of the members of a collegial juridic person survives, and the aggregate of persons (*universitas personarum*) has not ceased to exist according to its statutes, that member has the exercise of all the rights of the aggregate (*universitas*).

Essential to an understanding of the nature of a juridic person is an appreciation of its inherent

---

[52] Molano, in *Pamplona ComEng,* 138; *Chiappetta Com 1996,* 1:178.

[53] *RI* 29.

[54] See *CIC* 101, §1, 1°, 2°.

[55] Molano, in *Pamplona ComEng,* 137; Pinto, in *Urbaniana Com,* 71. A general norm to this effect was included in the 1917 code (*CIC* 101, §2) but has been omitted as unnecessary in the 1983 code.

perpetuity, its capacity for continuous existence. As an artificial person (see commentary on c. 113), a juridic person transcends the lives and works of natural persons associated with it at any given time, and continues in existence until terminated in one or another of the ways indicated in this canon.

A public juridic person can be terminated in one of two ways: by legitimate suppression by competent authority or by ceasing to act for a period of one hundred years. The authority competent to suppress a juridic person is usually, but not always, the authority that created it (or established its underlying substratum in instances where juridic personality is conferred *a iure*); some suppressions are reserved to higher authority. The suppression of an institute of consecrated life or a society of apostolic life, even one of diocesan right, for example, is reserved to the Holy See (cc. 584, 732), as is the suppression of the only house of a religious institute (c. 616, §2). At times, even though the authority competent to suppress is the same as the authority to create (or establish the substratum), the law requires consultation of others prior to suppression (see, e.g., cc. 320, §3; 616, §1; 733, §1); failure to consult would negate the legitimacy of the suppression which, in turn, would invalidate the termination.

A public juridic person which has ceased to act for a period of one hundred years would certainly have outlasted the lives of all natural persons ever associated with it, either as members of an *universitas personarum* or as administrators of an *universitas rerum,* and in all likelihood would also have outlasted all the assets which formed any part of the substratum underlying an *universitas rerum.*[56] During the inactive one hundred years the rights and obligations of the juridic person are considered to be dormant; they would revive if someone were to acquire membership in the dormant *universitas personarum* or if material goods were restored to the dormant foundation. If not

revived, the juridic person terminates automatically by operation of law upon the expiration of one hundred years from the day on which the inactivity originated.

A private juridic person can also be terminated by legitimate suppression or by ceasing to act for a period of one hundred years. A private juridic person, however, in accord with its greater autonomy, can also be terminated in other ways provided for in its statutes, such as the reduction below a designated number of members in the association that serves as substratum for an *universitas personarum,* or reduction below a designated value in the assets that serve as substratum for an *universitas rerum* (foundation).

Canon 120, §2 provides that if only one member of a collegial juridic person survives, and the juridic person has not been terminated according to its statutes, all the rights of the juridic person can be exercised (on its behalf) by the surviving member. This provision applies to all public collegial juridic persons because no public juridic person can be terminated according to its statutes; only private juridic persons have the option of providing in their statutes for methods of termination other than the two prescribed in canon 120. So all public, and some private (those whose statutes have not provided for termination prior to or concurrently with the survival of only one member) collegial juridic persons are subject to paragraph two of canon 120.

Consolidation of Juridic Persons

Canon 121 — If aggregates of persons (*universitates personarum*) or of things (*universitates rerum*), which are public juridic persons, are so joined that from them one aggregate (*universitas*) is constituted which also possesses juridic personality, this new juridic person obtains the goods and patrimonial rights proper to the prior ones and assumes the obligations with which they were burdened. With regard to the allocation of goods in particular and to the fulfillment of obligations, however, the intention of the founders and donors as well as acquired rights must be respected.

---

[56] This, alone, would seem to make clear the inappropriateness of speaking of a juridic person as an "aggregate." See commentary on c. 115.

Juridic persons can be combined or united in a variety of ways. There can be federations or confederations of juridic persons (e.g., among religious institutes), each of which retains its juridical identity but seeks limited union with others in sharing talents, experiences, and vision. There can be what, in the United States, are known as mergers of juridic persons, in which one juridic person is absorbed by another (e.g., one parish being absorbed by another) with only one of the previously existing juridic persons retaining its juridical identity.[57]

Canon 121 deals with neither of these kinds of union. Rather, it focuses on what, in the United States, is called a consolidation, in which two or more juridic persons are so joined that each of them loses its own juridical identity and in their stead a new juridic person is constituted.[58] A consolidation involves both the suppression and creation of juridic persons; as such, the intervention of competent authority is necessary, both authority competent to create the new juridic person (see c. 312 and commentary on c. 114) and authority competent to suppress the previously existing juridic persons (see commentary on c. 120). Often, but not always, the same authority is competent both to suppress and to create.[59] The scope of

canon 121 is limited to consolidations of public juridic persons; in accord with the greater autonomy of private juridic persons, norms governing consolidations, mergers, or other forms of union among them are to be found in their statutes.

Temporal goods, property rights, and financial obligations of the two or more consolidating public juridic persons are transferred *a iure* (by the operation of canon 121) to the new juridic person. Although transfer of ownership (known canonically as alienation) of church property (that which belongs to a public juridic person in the Church[60]) is often subject to a number of regulatory norms,[61] such norms do not apply to transfers which are a part of canon 121 consolidations for a number of reasons. As just noted, such transfers occur *a iure,* not pursuant to voluntary decisions made by church administrators (the object of the laws regulating alienation). Moreover, higher ecclesiastical authorities are already involved in the suppression and creation of the juridic persons involved in the consolidation (obviating the need for supervisory involvement of the authorities competent to approve voluntary acts of alienation); and safeguarding the economic viability and stability of public juridic persons whose property is to be alienated, which is the purpose of the laws regulating acts of alienation, is not relevant in a canon 121 consolidation because, by hypothesis, the public juridic persons whose property is being transferred are, simultaneously with the transfer, going out of existence.

Canon 121 does require, however, that in the use of goods and in the fulfillment of obligations transferred to the new juridic person, the intentions of founders and donors be faithfully fulfilled. This is a fundamental principle of canon

[57] References to federations, confederations, and other forms of union may be found in cc. 582; 684, §3; and 1274, §4.

[58] For American usage, see *Black's Law Dictionary,* 6th ed., s.v. "consolidation of corporations"; *Bouvier's Law Dictionary,* 3rd rev. (F. Rawle), 8th ed., s.v. "merger: of corporations." American courts and authors generally distinguish a consolidation from a merger on the ground that in a consolidation all the combining entities are dissolved and lose their identities as a single new entity is created, whereas in a merger one of the combining entities (corporations) continues in existence and absorbs the others. While this is the general usage in the United States, the terms "consolidation" and "merger" have occasionally been used interchangeably. See *Ballentine's Law Dictionary,* 3rd ed., s.v. "merger of corporations."

[59] Although the view has been expressed that in a canon 121 type of union there is no suppression or extinction of the component juridic persons and that they may be said to continue, since their patrimonial rights and liabilities

have been acquired by the new juridic person (McGrath, in *CLSGBI Com,* 70), the wording of the canon would seem to make it clear that the previous juridic persons no longer exist and that the goods, rights, and obligations that were once theirs are no longer so, but belong to the new juridic person. See *Chiappetta Com 1996,* 1:182.

[60] See cc. 1257, §1; 1258.

[61] See cc. 638, §§3, 4; 1291–1294.

law, given expression frequently throughout the code.[62] The Church's concern for justice also finds expression in the requirement that all acquired rights are to be honored notwithstanding the consolidation.

Division of Juridic Persons

Canon 122 — If an aggregate (*universitas*) which possesses public juridic personality is so divided either that a part of it is united with another juridic person or that a distinct public juridic person is erected from the separated part, the ecclesiastical authority competent to make the division, having observed before all else the intention of the founders and donors, the acquired rights, and the approved statutes, must take care personally or through an executor:

1°   that common, divisible, patrimonial goods and rights as well as debts and other obligations are divided among the juridic persons concerned, with due proportion in equity and justice, after all the circumstances and needs of each have been taken into account;

2°   that the use and usufruct of common goods which are not divisible accrue to each juridic person and that the obligations proper to them are imposed upon each, in due proportion determined in equity and justice.

Commentaries on the 1917 code often stated that a juridic person could not be divided; its territory could be divided, but not the person.[63] This was in accord with the wording of the 1917 code which spoke of the division, not of a juridic person, but of the territory of a juridic person (*CIC* 1500), and in accord also with the theoretical view that a person, juridic no less than natural, is indivisible.

The 1983 code adopts a more practical approach. While the division of a diocese or parish usually involves a concomitant change in territorial boundaries, the division of other juridic persons, such as a province of a religious institute or a public association of the faithful or a foundation, need not be based on or involve a division of territory. Accordingly, the present code speaks more broadly (and more abstractly) of the division of the juridic person itself.[64]

In accord with the greater autonomy of private juridic persons, the norms of canon 122 are made applicable only to public juridic persons, leaving to the statutes of private juridic persons the regulation of their division. Several of the principles expressed in canon 122, however, such as equity and justice and faithful observance of the intentions of donors, could well be incorporated into the statutes of private juridic persons.

Canon 122 makes clear that the act of dividing a juridic person and the act of dividing its assets and liabilities are distinct juridic acts. There is no automatic division of assets and liabilities in mathematical proportion, for example, to the number of Catholics or parishes or counties in each diocese in the case of a divided diocese, or in proportion to the size of the territory or number of families in each parish in the case of a divided parish. Rather, divisible assets and liabilities are to be divided in due proportion as dictated by equity and justice in the light of all relevant circumstances, including size of territory and total[65] population, demographic projections, presently available resources, the potential for future re-

---

[62] See cc. 122; 123; 326, §2; 531; 616, §1; 706, 3°; 954; 1267, §3; 1284, §2, 3°, 4°; 1299, §2; 1303, §2; 1304, §1; 1307, §1; 1310, §2.

[63] Cappello, 2:551; Bouscaren-Ellis-Korth, 811. The 1917 code and its commentators rarely used the term "juridic person"; the term "moral person" was used to signify what the present code more precisely calls a "juridic person" (see commentary on c. 113).

[64] The Code of Canons of the Eastern Churches retains the approach of the 1917 code and speaks of the division, not of a juridic person, but of the territory of a juridic person (*CCEO* 929).

[65] The mission of the Church to evangelize and to serve all people precludes any planning that is limited to presently existing Catholic populations.

sources, personnel needs unique to each juridic person, and a host of other factors. Not even canonical ownership of land passes automatically from the present diocese or parish to a newly created one; at times, it is appropriate for the parent diocese or parish to retain ownership of land (e.g., a cemetery) that is situated within the territorial boundaries of the new diocese or parish. Considerations of equity and justice require that there be observed *before all else* the intentions of founders and donors,[66] acquired rights, and the applicable provisions of the statutes of the juridic person being divided.

The use and enjoyment of the benefits of indivisible assets such as a seminary, for example, and the attendant liabilities and obligations, are to be shared according to a plan similarly characterized by due proportion based on equity and justice in the light of all relevant circumstances.

Assets which serve the needs of a diocese or other public juridic person are not always canonically or civilly owned by the diocese or other public juridic person served by them. Independent foundations (see c. 1303, §1, 1°), for example, are often established to provide funds for various educational, health-care, or social service endeavors within a diocese; the assets of such a foundation, since they are not canonically owned by the public juridic person known as the diocese, are not subject to division if the diocese should be divided. The existence of such a foundation, however, is a circumstance relevant to any division of diocesan assets based on equity and justice, for the relative abilities of the parent and newly created dioceses to meet their needs are clearly affected by the existence of the foundation. Equity and justice demand disclosure of such a foundation and its being taken into account when determining the due proportion according to which assets owned by the parent diocese are to be divided between the parent and newly created dioceses. Similar circumstances may be present in the division of a

religious institute or one of its provinces, or in the division of other public juridic persons.

Canon 122 provides that the competent authority to divide assets and liabilities, and to impose the terms of shared use of indivisible assets, is the same authority as that which is competent to divide the juridic person. Ordinarily, this would be the authority competent to create the juridic person (or establish the underlying moral person upon which the law confers juridic personality), such as the Holy See for a diocese (c. 373) or the diocesan bishop for a parish (c. 515, §2). Where not determined by universal law, the designation of competent authority is to be found in proper law (see, e.g., c. 581) or in the statutes of a public juridic person.

The division of assets and liabilities and the imposition of the terms of shared use of indivisible assets is to be carried out by the competent authority personally or through an executor. While the term "executor" is used in a variety of contexts throughout the code, it commonly refers to one who carries out the directives of another, either with or without the exercise of discretion having been committed to the executor.[67] In the context of canon 122 an executor would be given considerable discretion, but always within the parameters set forth in the canon.

When a diocese is divided by the Holy See, it is customary for the Holy See to instruct the diocesan bishops involved to develop a plan for the division and sharing of assets and liabilities. Such an instruction is not tantamount to naming the bishops co-executors to determine by their mutual agreement the final disposition of the assets and liabilities; final decision-making authority rests with the Holy See, or with a third party executor designated by the Holy See to make the final determination in the name of the Holy See. Until any agreement reached by the involved diocesan bishops has been confirmed by the Holy

---

[66] As noted in the commentary on c. 121, this is a cardinal principle of canon law, expressed in many canons (see note 62 above).

[67] For varied contexts in which the term is used see cc. 40–45, 54, §1, 62, 63, §3, 70 (executor of an administrative act); c. 1301 (executor of a pious will); cc. 1654, 1655, §2 (executor of a judicial sentence).

See, or by an executor designated by the Holy See, the canonical division is not completed and, hence, can be reopened for further negotiation at a future time. This is the import of canon 122; it seems not always to be understood by diocesan bishops who sometimes, with their financial advisors and attorneys, think they have definitively settled the division of assets and liabilities by their mutual agreement. Similar misunderstandings can arise in connection with the division of any public juridic person.

Extinction of Juridic Persons

Canon 123 — Upon the extinction of a public juridic person, the allocation of its goods, patrimonial rights, and obligations is governed by law and its statutes; if these give no indication, they go to the juridic person immediately superior, always without prejudice to the intention of the founders and donors and acquired rights. Upon the extinction of a private juridic person, the allocation of its goods and obligations is governed by its own statutes.

Public juridic persons are extinguished only by suppression by competent authority or by being inactive for a period of one hundred years; private juridic persons are extinguished in either of these ways or in any other way specified in their statutes (c. 120, §1). Both public and private juridic persons, however, can provide in their statutes for the allocation of their assets and liabilities upon extinction, unless, in regard to public juridic persons, provision has been made in universal or particular law. Universal law contains such provisions in connection with the suppression of an institute of consecrated life (c. 584), a society of apostolic life (c. 732), and the only house of a religious institute (c. 616, §2), in each case reserving to the Apostolic See the determination of what is to be done with the temporal goods. Universal law directs that provision for the distribution of the goods of a suppressed house (other than the only house) of a religious institute be made in the proper law of each institute (c.

616, §1), and that provision for the distribution of the goods of a suppressed autonomous monastery of nuns be included in the constitutions of the monastery (c. 616, §4).

Canon 123 prescribes that when provision is not made in universal or particular law, and is not made in the statutes of a public juridic person, the assets and liabilities of an extinguished public juridic person go to the immediately superior public juridic person. A relationship of superiority, however, exists only among hierarchically ordered juridic persons, such as a parish, diocese, and the Holy See, or a religious house, province, and institute; other public juridic persons, such as a public association of the faithful, or a university or hospital erected as a public juridic person, or an autonomous foundation, do not have immediately superior juridic persons. Canon 123 is silent as to what happens in such cases.

The 1917 code similarly directed that goods of an extinct juridic person be distributed to the immediately superior juridic person, and was similarly silent as to the goods of juridic persons which were not hierarchically related to other juridic persons (*CIC* 1501). Commentators on the 1917 code concluded that, in such circumstances, the goods should go to the juridic person presided over by the ecclesiastical authority who issued the decree erecting or suppressing the extinct juridic person,[68] or to whom the extinct juridic person was otherwise immediately subject, namely, to either the diocese or the Holy See.[69] Since canon 123 of the present code essentially restates the prior law, and remains silent where the prior law was silent, the norms of canonical interpretation dictate that the jurisprudence developed under the prior law should be followed (see c. 6, §2). This means that, absent relevant provisions in law or in the statutes of a public juridic person, the goods of a public juridic person which has no immediately superior juridic person will, upon extinction, go to the diocese, the episcopal conference, or the Holy See,

[68] Cappello, 2:552.
[69] Regatillo, 2:206; Vermeersch-Creusen, 2:572; Bouscaren-Ellis-Korth, 812.

the juridic persons presided over by the authorities competent to erect a juridic person or to which a juridic person would otherwise be subject (if juridic personality were conferred *a iure*).[70] While in many cases such a disposition would be unobjectionable, in some cases it would be incompatible with the justifiable expectations of the sponsors of a hospital, college, or other institution erected as a public juridic person in its own right by a diocesan bishop but sponsored, staffed, and administered by a religious institute. If the expectation of such a religious institute is that, upon extinction, the assets would revert to the sponsoring religious institute, but such an expectation is not embodied in the statutes of the juridic person, the assets, according to canonical tradition, would go to the diocese. This argues for careful consideration, at the time of drafting the statutes, of what distribution is to be made of assets and liabilities upon the extinction of a public juridic person.

As in canons 121 and 122, and frequently throughout the code,[71] so also in canon 123 the Church's commitment to faithful fulfillment of the intentions of founders and donors finds expression. Acquired rights must also be respected in the allocation of goods and obligations upon the extinction of a public juridic person. Although the wording of canon 123 leaves entirely to the statutes of a private juridic person the allocation of goods and obligations upon extinction, without mention of acquired rights or intentions of donors, such considerations, since they are matters of justice, should not be ignored. In this connection it should be noted that canon 326, §2, in remitting to the statutes of a private association of the faithful (which may or may not have received juridic personality) the allocation of goods upon extinction, explicitly requires the honoring of acquired rights and the intentions of donors.

---

[70] See c. 312 and commentary on c. 114. Chiappetta, without mention of the jurisprudence developed under the 1917 code, appears to be of the same opinion. *Chiappetta Com 1996*, 1:184.

[71] See cc. 326, §2; 531; 616, §1; 706, 3°; 954; 1267, §3; 1284, §2, 3°, 4°; 1299, §2; 1303, §2; 1304, §1; 1307, §1; 1310, §2.

NOTE ON THE CANONICAL STATUS OF CHURCH-RELATED INSTITUTIONS IN THE UNITED STATES

A study of the general norms on juridic persons, coupled with a study of the canons on associations of the Christian faithful (cc. 298–329), leads to the realization that the law of the Church affords a number of options for the canonical status of Catholic colleges, universities, hospitals, and other educational, health-care, and social service institutions. Any endeavor or any person claiming to be Catholic is subject, at least to some degree, to the governance of ecclesiastical authority; it is one of the defining characteristics of being Catholic (see c. 205). Not all Catholic insti-

tutions, however, any more than all Catholic individuals, are subject to ecclesiastical authority in the same way or to the same extent; not all are subject to all of the same laws of the Church. Which laws are applicable to a particular church-related institution depends upon the canonical status of the institution.

Apostolic Work of Sponsor. A Catholic institution may simply be the apostolic work of a sponsoring public juridic person, such as a diocese or religious institute; as such, the institution shares in the canonical status of its sponsor. Canonically, the college, hospital, or other entity is simply the institutionalized apostolate of a public juridic person; those who administer the affairs of the public juridic person are, canonically, ultimately responsible for the affairs of the college, hospital, or other institution, and the assets and liabilities of the institution are, canonically, assets and liabilities of the sponsoring public juridic person. This would seem to have been the original canonical status of many Catholic educational and healthcare institutions in the United States, the vast majority of which were founded by religious institutes, and most likely continues to be the canonical status of many such institutions.

This category of canonical status affords a number of advantages. Since the institution is understood to belong to its sponsor (most often a religious institute or diocese), the level of perceived Catholicity is high, as is the level of sponsor involvement in the work of the institution. Clarity of mission is well served by the close relationship between the institution and its sponsor, and the closeness of relationship yields the sponsor a high degree of control over the Catholic identity of the institution, a control that, in many states of the United States, is civilly protected through the mechanism of reserved powers retained by the sponsor over some of the affairs of a separately incorporated institution.

Notwithstanding the advantages, there are also a number of disadvantages to this canonical status. The close relationship between the institution and its sponsor exposes the sponsor to the risks of liability, canonical and civil, for financial transactions or injury-causing malfeasance or culpable negligence on the part of trustees, employees, or other agents of the institution.[72] Moreover, where

the sponsor is a public juridic person, the assets of an institution that canonically belongs to the sponsor are ecclesiastical goods (see c. 1257, §1) and, as such, are subject to virtually all of the property laws of the Church, including invalidating laws governing acts of extraordinary administration (see cc. 1277, 1281), acts of alienation (see cc. 1291–1294), and some other transactions (see c. 1295). Subjection to these laws often results in Church-State conflicts arising from transactions that are valid at civil law but invalid canonically, or vice versa. A close relationship between an educational institution and its religious sponsor can also endanger the eligibility of the institution for various forms of governmental aid in the United States where state and federal constitutions place limitations on governmental aid to religious endeavors, especially educational ones. These and other disadvantages often argue against the advisability of a Catholic institution seeking or retaining such a canonical status, and in favor of seeking an alternative canonical status.

Public Juridic Person. A church-related institution can be constituted a public juridic person in its own right. While retaining many of the advantages of sharing in the canonical status of a sponsoring public juridic person, this category affords canonical separateness between the institution and its sponsor, thereby reducing the risks of sponsor liability for acts of the institution. Since the institution is a public juridic person, however, its assets are ecclesiastical goods subject to all canon laws governing church property, including the invalidating laws, and resulting Church-State con-

---

[72] The canonical liability of a sponsor could be based upon such canons as c. 128 and would be enforceable in ecclesiastical tribunals, which exist for the vindication of the rights of physical or juridic persons (c. 1400, §1, 1°) and for the resolution of many different kinds of disputes (see, e.g., cc. 1410, 1411, 1413). Civil liability of a spon-

sor could be based upon its extensive control of the affairs of the separately incorporated institution, inducing an American court to "pierce the corporate veil" and impose liability on the sponsor. For discussions of ascending liability in religiously sponsored institutions, see P. Moots and E. Gaffney, Jr., *Church and Campus* (Notre Dame, Ind.: University of Notre Dame, 1979) 10–18; E. Gaffney, Jr., and P. Sorensen, *Ascending Liability in Religious and Other Nonprofit Organizations* (Macon, Ga.: Mercer University, 1984).

flicts mentioned above. As a public juridic person, the institution remains closely governed by ecclesiastical authority (see commentary on c. 116) and, as such, remains vulnerable to characterization by governmental authorities as pervasively sectarian for purposes of determining constitutional eligibility for governmental aid.

Private Juridic Person. A Catholic institution can be constituted a private juridic person in its own right. As such, the institution, although subject to some degree to the ecclesiastical authority that confers juridic personality upon it, enjoys more autonomy than a public juridic person (see commentary on c. 116). Just as the extent of sponsor control, and that of other ecclesiastical authorities, over the institution is less than in the previously mentioned categories of canonical status, so too is the extent of canonical regulation of the financial aspects of the institution. The assets of a private juridic person are not ecclesiastical goods and, therefore, are not subject to most of the laws of the Church governing temporal goods, including the invalidating laws mentioned above (see c. 1257, §2). The lessened extent of ecclesiastical control over the institution also serves to mitigate the institution's vulnerability to characterization as pervasively sectarian for constitutional purposes relating to governmental aid.

Private Association of the Faithful. A church-related institution may be neither the apostolic work of a sponsoring public juridic person, such as a diocese or religious institute, nor a juridic person, public or private, in its own right. It may be the work of a recognized private association of the faithful (see cc. 298–311, 321–326). Though recognized by ecclesiastical authority as truly Catholic, such an association enjoys even more autonomy than a private juridic person. While the assets of a private association of the faithful are not ecclesiastical goods and, hence, are not subject to the canons governing the administration and alienation of church property and certain other financial transactions, the private associa-

tion of the faithful affords no corporate or institutional ownership of assets; the individual members of the association are understood to be co-owners of the assets of the institution and are individually and jointly liable for the debts of the institution (see c. 310).[73]

De Facto Catholic Institution. Options for canonical status of a church-related educational, health-care, or other charitable institution include the *de facto* Catholic institution. This is simply an apostolically oriented institution run by a group of members of the Church who have not sought official recognition by ecclesiastical authority. The institution is Catholic in fact (*reapse*[74]) but juridically the institution as such is only minimally subject to ecclesiastical authority and is bound by only a few laws of the Church,[75] though the individual members of the faithful associated with the institution are, of course, bound by all the laws which govern their relationship as individuals to the hierarchical authority of the Church.[76] Such an institution enjoys a high degree of autonomy but often a lower degree of perceived Catholicity and sponsor involvement, and virtually no degree of sponsor control, if a sponsor is involved at all. This is more likely to be the initial canonical status of a new institutionalized apostolic work than a later status chosen to replace one of the other categories of canonical status.

In the United States, Catholic institutions exist in each of the canonical categories summarized

---

[73] The code also provides for public associations of the faithful, but such associations are, by law, public juridic persons (see c. 313) and, hence, are included in the category of public juridic persons discussed above.

[74] See, e.g., cc. 803, §3; 808.

[75] See, e.g., cc. 216; 300; 803, §3; and 808 which prohibit use of the name or title "Catholic" without the consent of competent ecclesiastical authority.

[76] See Pagé, 169–170, 172–174; Catholic Health Association of the United States, *The Search for Identity: Canonical Sponsorship of Catholic Healthcare* (St. Louis, Mo.: CHA, 1993) 20–21.

above.[77] No one canonical status is always preferable to the others; each has its advantages and disadvantages. The most desirable status for a particular institution will depend on a number of factors. What is important for each presently existing institution (college, university, hospital, nursing home, hospice, and others) is to ascertain, through careful research in the archives both of the institution and of its sponsor, the present canonical status of the institution. Only then should a determination be made as to which of the available options would be the most desirable, in the light of all relevant circumstances.[78] Once that determination is made, the appropriate canonical steps could be taken to effect whatever change in canonical status is desired. These steps may include the creation of a new juridic person and the alienation of assets.[79]

The view has been expressed, criticized, rejected by the Holy See, and yet repeatedly expressed, that civil incorporation has the effect not only of conferring civil-law status upon an institution but also of negating any canonical status whatsoever.[80]

Such a view ignores the fact that Roman Catholic persons and endeavors are subject to two independent legal systems, canonical and civil, and juridic acts under one system have no necessary juridic effects under the other. Just as the creation of a juridic person under canon law is given no automatic recognition under civil laws in the United States, so too, an act of civil incorporation has no necessary effect upon a previously acquired canonical status, nor upon previously acquired canonical ownership of the property of the institution. Just as civil incorporation of a parish or diocese does nothing to alter the canonical status of the parish or diocese, neither does civil incorporation alter the canonical status of an educational or health-care institution that already enjoys canonical status as the institutionalized apostolate of a sponsoring diocese or religious institute.

Nor is any change in canonical status effected by a change in the composition of the governing board of trustees or directors of a Catholic institution. An institution is not owned by its board. Whoever serves on such a board, whether lay, religious, or cleric, member or non-member of a sponsoring religious institute or diocese, is bound to administer the affairs of the institution in accord with the laws, canonical and civil, which govern it and in accord with the institution's internal governing documents, canonical as well as civil. Competent lay persons, no less than competent religious or clerics, are capable of administering church property (see cc. 1282, 1287, §1) and otherwise administering apostolic works sponsored by dioceses or religious institutes. A change in board membership from a majority of clerical or religious members of the sponsor to a majority of lay persons does not necessarily signify a change in the canonical status of a Catholic insti-

---

[77] See *The Search for Identity,* 23; J. Hite and J. Poe, "An Innovative Way to Continue the Ministry," *Health Progress* 73 (1992) 56–58; N. Mulvihill, "Public Juridic Person Ensures Catholic Presence," *Health Progress* 77 (1996) 25–27; B. McMullen, "A Closer Look at Lay Sponsorship," *Health Progress* 77 (1996) 28–30; B. Dunn, "The Evolving Nature of Sponsorship," *Health Progress* 79 (1998) 54–60.

[78] Relevant considerations include the preferences of a sponsor as to how closely involved with the governance and finances of an institution the sponsor wishes to be, the preferences of likely benefactors and constituents as to how much autonomy they would want the institution to have, and civil-law implications of one or another canonical status in various states.

[79] For canonical norms governing the alienation of church property, see cc. 638, §§3, 4; 1291–1294.

[80] This view is often attributed to a monograph authored by John J. McGrath, *Catholic Institutions in the United States: Canonical and Civil Law Status* (Washington, D.C.: Catholic University of America, 1968). For an analysis and evaluation of what became known as "the McGrath thesis," along with evaluative analyses of the views of Adam J. Maida written in response to McGrath

and the position of Gommarus Michiels upon which Maida relied, see R. Kennedy, "McGrath, Maida, Michiels: Introduction to a Study of the Canonical and Civil-Law Status of Church-Related Institutions in the United States," *J* 50 (1990) 351–401. The article includes a detailed account of the rejection of the McGrath view by the Holy See.

tution, nor constitute an alienation of its property; canonically, the property continues to be owned by the sponsor, not by the members of the board.

Nor does the transfer of title to real estate from the sponsor to a newly incorporated institution necessarily effect a change in canonical status or in canonical ownership of the property. Such a transfer could be intended as a true conveyance from the sponsor to the institution, but it need not be so intended. Administrators of church property are obliged to take appropriate steps to safeguard the ownership of ecclesiastical goods "by civilly valid methods" (c. 1284, §2, 2°). Accordingly, placing title to real estate in the name of a civilly incorporated institution is often intended to do no more than gain civil-law separateness to insulate the sponsor from civil-law liability for the actions of the sponsored institution, with no intention to alter the canonical ownership of the property or the canonical status of the institution. For this reason, such transfers of title are frequently not accompanied by efforts to comply with canonical requirements for the valid alienation of church property; no such alienation is intended.[81]

Efforts to ascertain the present canonical status

[81] For a more extensive discussion of the canonical implications of transferring title to real estate, see Kennedy, 371–375.

of a Catholic institution in the United States, therefore, should avoid misleading assumptions about the supposed canonical effects of civil incorporation (or other civil-law structuring) of the institution, or changes in the composition of the institution's board of trustees, or transfers of civil title to real estate. Efforts should concentrate on careful research to determine the original canonical status of the institution and whether or not valid canonical steps were ever taken to alter that original status. Once the present status has been definitively ascertained, a choice of desirable status can be made and steps taken to modify[82] or alter the canonical status accordingly.

[82] Canonical status of an institution can be modified without being replaced by an entirely different category of canonical status. The first status mentioned above, for example—according to which the institution is understood simply to be the apostolic work of a sponsoring public juridic person such as a diocese or religious institute—can be modified (partially altered) by the sponsor relinquishing canonical ownership and control of the finances of the institution (and relinquishing the corresponding civil-law mechanisms employed to protect the sponsor's canonical role in major financial transactions) while retaining control of matters relating to Catholic identity and mission and to the particular charism of the sponsor.

Title VII
Juridic Acts
[cc. 124–128]

For the first time in the history of canon law, the 1983 code contains the norms concerning "juridic acts" under a separate heading. It is only relatively recently that "juridic acts" have been the object of study and systematic treatment in canon law. Although Roman law did not have a technical expression for a juridic act, it did provide the material from which later studies would draw. Jurists in nineteenth century Germany, in particular the Pandectists who studied Roman law, developed a theory of juridic acts which focused on the will of the individual which is necessary for a juridic act. This doctrine had an impact on canon law and is reflected in the 1917 code which regulated different aspects of juridic acts in the beginning of Book II on "Persons" (*CIC* 103–104) and in Book IV on "Processes" (*CIC* 1680, §1 and 1681). In the years that followed, canonists devoted increasing attention to the theory of juridic acts. This led to the decision to treat juridic acts under a separate heading in the 1983 code.

This section in the 1983 code does not contain a definition of a juridic act, but the description by O. Robleda seems to dominate the canonical literature. He writes that it is "an externally manifested act of the will by which a certain juridical effect is intended."[1]

Juridic acts are to be distinguished from *other acts* (c. 128), i.e., acts which have no legal charac-ter because the law does not attach juridic consequences to them or because such consequences are not intended. Examples of other acts would be cooking or walking. Juridic acts are furthermore to be distinguished from juridic *facts* which are facts or actions that have legal consequences by the law itself and for which no will is required. Examples of juridic facts are birth, death, gender, age, mental capacity. In contrast to other acts and juridic facts, a *juridic act* entails two essential aspects: (a) the person acting has a will to do so, i.e., there must be a decision in which all rational faculties are engaged, and (b) the intention of the action is to bring about a certain juridic effect. A juridic act requires a decision to cause a certain consequence which the law attaches to it. Such a consequence can affect oneself or, when the person placing the act has the authority to do so, it can bind others. Examples of juridic acts are the sale of property, contracting marriage, religious profession, conferral of an office, resigning from an office, promulgating a law, and issuing a judicial sentence.

Juridic acts may be unilateral, bilateral, or multilateral. Unilateral acts are those which are issued by one person only and may or may not require notification.[2] A removal from office is an example of a juridic act which becomes effective only when the person who is to be removed has received notification about it. The making of a will, on the other hand, is an example of a juridic act which does not require notification of another party. Bilateral or multilateral acts are those in which two or more persons are involved in the juridic act as is the case in, for example, a contract.

---

[1] O. Robleda, "De Conceptu actus iuridici," *P* 51 (1962) 413–446. Trans. by M. Hughes in "A New Title in the Code: Juridical Acts," *Stud Can* 14 (1980) 391–403. See also W. Onclin: "De requisitis ad actus iuridici exsistentiam et validitatem," in *Studi in onore di Pietro Agostino d'Avack* (Milan: Giuffrè, 1976) III: 399–419. Both Robleda and Onclin personally participated in the commission for the revision of these norms of the 1917 code.

[2] Notification or the reception of notice is not the same as acceptance, because acceptance implies that an action requires someone else's confirmation or approval, thus resulting in a bilateral act. For example: most resignations of office require acceptance (e.g., parish priest, c. 538, §1; bishop, cc. 401 and 411); however, the resignation of the Roman Pontiff needs only to be manifested (c. 332, §2) and thus does not require acceptance.

The five canons in this section begin with an identification of the requirements for a valid juridic act (c. 124, §1). Canon 124, §2 establishes what is required for a juridic act to be presumed valid. The succeeding canons 125–127 list things or causes which might affect the validity of the act. Finally, canon 128 concerns compensation for damage which an external act might have caused. From a systematic point of view, one might question why canon 119 on collegial acts has not been included in this section, since that canon deals with juridic acts and not with physical or juridic persons.

A Valid Juridic Act

Canon 124 — §1. For the validity of a juridic act it is required that the act is placed by a qualified person and includes those things which essentially constitute the act itself as well as the formalities and requirements imposed by law for the validity of the act.

§2. A juridic act placed correctly with respect to its external elements is presumed valid.

Whereas the 1917 code had only a canon determining what would invalidate an act (*CIC* 1680, §1), the 1983 code contains in this canon a positive description of the necessary elements required for a valid juridic act. They concern (1) the person placing the act, (2) the intrinsic nature of the act itself, (3) extrinsic formalities, and (4) other elements which the law requires for validity.

The person placing the act can be a physical person, a juridic person, or a college. The acting subject needs to be qualified—*habilis*—which in canon law means that the person has a right to act in the matter in the broad sense.[3] This means not only that the person is generally able to place acts (see cc. 96–98), but also that the person is qualified for a specific act. Thus, anyone who is *non sui compos* cannot place a juridic act (see cc. 97,

§2 and 99) because such a person cannot place an act of the will. A sentence rendered by a person who lacks the power of judging in the tribunal in which a case is decided is irremediably null (c. 1620, 2°), because that person is not qualified for this specific act.

Not only the acting person, but also the object of the act is relevant. In a juridic act the two go together because the object relates the will to the juridic order. The canon speaks of "things which essentially constitute the act itself." An objection that this phrase was too general was rejected during the revision process with the argument that the phrase could be found in the juridic tradition and would be sufficiently clear.[4] It means that which essentially constitutes an act. When any of the elements that essentially constitute an act are lacking, there is no juridic act and there are no juridic consequences. Thus, a contract implies at least two parties and an exchange of rights, and its object must be possible.[5]

Furthermore, formalities imposed by the law must be fulfilled. Canon law generally allows for freedom regarding the form of an act, but at times requires formalities for legitimacy or validity. Examples of such formalities include that an act be in writing (c. 1524, §3), the signature of the one acting (c. 474), acting in person and not through a representative (c. 833), and the canonical form for marriage (c. 1108). When no formalities are required, the preferred form may be chosen as long as it is somehow communicated and manifest and thus provable.

Other requirements imposed by law need to be fulfilled as well, such as consultations or the obtaining of consent (c. 127).

The second paragraph of the canon establishes a presumption: when the external elements have been placed correctly, the juridic act is presumed to be valid; its invalidity must be proven, i.e., the burden of proof rests with the person alleging in-

---

[3] *Comm* 14 (1982) 145. *CCEO* 931, §1 has kept the words used in the 1977 and 1980 schemas for the Latin code, i.e., *habilis* and *competens*.

[4] *Comm* 14 (1982) 144–145.

[5] E.g., the provision of an office requires its vacancy (c. 153).

validity. In this context it is important to note that canon law differentiates between the intended will and the manifested will: although the manifested will is presumed to be in congruence with the intended will, that presumption may be rescinded. This is what happens in marriage nullity cases which concern the so-called ground of "simulation" (c. 1101, §2).

Canon law, furthermore, recognizes a presumption for a manifestation of the will when the law determines that under certain circumstances the manifested will can be assumed. Thus, a *libellus* is considered as having been accepted when the judge has not accepted or rejected it in the prescribed time (c. 1506). A presumed or interpreted will is allowed only when the law has provided for it, as in the case of the presumed permission from the local ordinary for another diocesan bishop to perform pontifical functions in the former's diocese (c. 390).

Deficient Juridic Acts

Although the external criteria for a valid juridic act might be fulfilled, the act might nevertheless be defective for other reasons. Since juridic acts are human acts, they must be placed knowingly and freely. Canons 125 and 126 consider factors which influence the will or the knowledge of the one placing the act: canon 125 speaks of external reasons, i.e., external force, fear, and malice, and canon 126 speaks of internal reasons, i.e., ignorance and error. These factors do not constitute a taxative list, since other factors derived from the natural law can apply as well.[6]

Force and Fear

Canon 125 — §1. An act placed out of force inflicted on a person from without, which the person was not able to resist in any way, is considered as never to have taken place.

[6] Cf. M. Walser, *Die Rechtshandlung im kanonischen Recht* (Göttingen: Cuvillier, 1994) 172–173.

§2. An act placed out of grave fear, unjustly inflicted, or out of malice is valid unless the law provides otherwise. It can be rescinded, however, through the sentence of a judge, either at the instance of the injured party or of the party's successors in law, or *ex officio*.

When, in placing a juridic act, someone is compelled by force to the extent that the will is totally absent because resistance is not possible, that act is not a human act. Since such an act is externally verifiable, the law itself declares that, as a human act, it is non-existent (*infectus; CCEO* 932, §1 speaks of *nullus*, null); hence, no juridic action in the form of a contestation or complaint of nullity need be taken.

The canon speaks of force inflicted from outside the person. This is also called a direct force and is exercised by a person other than the one acting. Some authors equate external force with physical force (cf. c. 1323, 3°); others include the use of psychic and chemical means as force.

Connected to force is fear. The latter is an indirectly exercised force: the will is influenced by the threat of a severe evil. In contrast with direct force, fear is one of many possible reasons for placing a juridic act; therefore, an act placed under fear is valid, but rescindable. Rescission requires that the fear have been severe, external, unjust, and a cause for the manifestation of the will. What is decisive is that the juridic act was placed in order to avoid the threatened evil.

Malice (*dolus*) is a deliberate concealment of facts or deliberate assertion of what is untrue in order to persuade someone to act in a certain manner. A juridic act is invalid when malice leads to an essential error on the part of the one acting concerning the juridic act; the act must be the result of the malice.

In the case of grave fear or malice, the act placed is valid, but rescindable. There are two reasons for this. First, the person acting is presumed to possess sufficient knowledge and will to place a human act; if that act resulted from grave fear or malice, it can be rescinded through the sentence of a judge. Second, there was an attempt to limit the number of acts which are invalid by the law itself; hence the law itself determines the specific exceptions to this rule.[7]

Since canon law incorporates the civil law of a territory for contracts (c. 1290), rules in civil law might affect the applicability of canon 125 to contracts when it states, "unless the law provides otherwise."

Ignorance and Error

Canon 126 — An act placed out of ignorance or out of error concerning something which constitutes its substance or which amounts to a condition *sine qua non* is invalid. Otherwise it is valid unless the law makes other provision. An act entered into out of ignorance or error, however, can give rise to a rescissory action according to the norm of law.

A person placing a juridic act needs to know what he or she is doing. Ignorance and error with regard to elements that concern the substance of the act or are *sine qua non* conditions cause the act to be invalid. Ignorance is the absence of knowledge, and error is a positive judgment which is objectively false. The juridical effects of ignorance and error are the same because no one can want what is not known. When the ignorance or error concerns a substantive element of the juridic act, that act is invalid. When the ignorance or error concerns an accidental or incidental element, however, the act is valid unless that particular element was the reason for placing the juridic act. Thus, canon 1097, §2 determines that error about a quality of a person does not invalidate a marriage "unless this quality is directly and principally intended."

Less serious acts which were placed based upon ignorance or error may be rescinded. The 1917 code allowed this only for contracts.

Deficiencies in Collegial Juridic Acts

Canons 125–126 apply not only to the acts placed by individuals, but also to those placed by a college. The 1977 and 1980 schemas had a canon addressing in particular what should be done when a member of a college was affected by the deficiencies mentioned in canons 125–126. The canon was omitted, because a collegial act is an act placed by a majority of the members. Hence, with regard to force or fear, as long as the vote is given freely (c. 172, §1, 1°)[8] by a majority of the members, the collegial act is valid.

Obtaining Consent or Counsel

Canon 127 — §1. When it is established by law that in order to place acts a superior needs the consent or counsel of some college or group of persons, the college or group must be convoked according to the norm of can. 166 unless, when it concerns seeking counsel only, particular or proper law provides otherwise. For such acts to be valid, however, it is required that the consent of an absolute majority of those present is obtained or that the counsel of all is sought.

§2. When it is established by law that in order to place acts a superior needs the consent or counsel of certain persons as individuals:

1° if consent is required, the act of a superior who does not seek the consent of those persons or who acts contrary to the opinion of all or any of them is invalid;

2° if counsel is required, the act of a superior who does not hear those persons is invalid; although not obliged to accept their opinion even if unanimous, a superior is nonetheless not to act contrary to that opinion, especially if unanimous, without a reason which is overriding in the superior's judgment.

§3. All whose consent or counsel is required are obliged to offer their opinion sincerely and, if the gravity of the affair requires it, to observe se-

---

[7] The law determines that an act is invalid due to fear or fraud in cc. 172, §1, 1°; 188; 643, §1, 4°; 656, 4°; 735, §2; 1098; 1103; 1191, §3; 1200, §2.

[8] *Comm* 14 (1982) 145.

crecy diligently; moreover, the superior can insist upon this obligation.

In order to place a juridic act validly, a superior at times needs the consent (*consensus*) or counsel (*consilium*) of a third party.[9] Such a third party is, therefore, someone who is hierarchically subordinate[10] to the one who needs the consent or advice. The code does not provide a general norm for obtaining consent or advice from a third party who is hierarchically equal or superior.[11]

Consent or counsel may be obtained from a college or group of persons (§1), or from individuals (§2). All those who give consent or counsel are obliged to offer their opinion sincerely and, when the seriousness of the matter requires it, are asked to observe secrecy (§3). In contrast with the Latin code, the Eastern code has an important additional paragraph indicating that the authority which requires the consent or counsel must provide the necessary information and see to it that the persons answering have freedom to speak their mind (*CCEO* 934, §3). Indeed, giving consent or counsel is not considered a mere formality, but is rather the exercise of a responsibility by the one who is being consulted or asked for counsel; it ought to be based on all the data possible.

The canon addresses the superior who has an obligation to obtain consent or counsel. With this obligation goes the right of others to give consent or counsel. The right or obligation to give or obtain advice (*consilium*) is in the law often expressed through the verb "to hear" (*audire*) and not through the noun *consilium*.[12]

When the law requires the consent or consultation of a college or group of persons, those belonging to it are to be convoked according to canon 166. In the case of a consultation, particular or proper law may provide that a meeting in person is not necessary.

When consent is necessary, an absolute majority of those present is required. A vote ending in a tie may not be interpreted as giving consent. Such a vote implies that consent is not given. Since a superior asks for consent from others, this superior cannot participate in the voting nor break a tie.[13]

The canon states that for consultation the counsel of all ought to be sought. The syntax of this phrase could imply that indeed the opinion of all, whether present or not, is to be obtained. Four arguments, however, militate against this broad interpretation. First, the schemas of 1977, 1980, and 1982 clearly state that all members of the group ought to be *convoked*. Only with the 1982 schema does the possible exception of particular or proper law appear.[14] Second, the exception would make no sense in those cases for which particular or proper law did not foresee that those present would have to be heard. Third, it would seem somewhat illogical to require a consultation of all—including those not present—for *counsel,* whereas *consent,* which is of greater importance, need be obtained only from those present. Fourth, when all persons must be consulted, whether or not they convene, the need to convene in itself di-

---

[9] See, for a detailed analysis of this canon, Elmar Güthoff, *"Consensus" und "consilium" in c. 127 CIC/1983 und c. 934 CCEO* (Würzburg: Echter, 1994).

[10] This is not to be confused with c. 208 according to which all persons are equal in the Church. From an ecclesiological perspective, the word *superior* is therefore not the best. The Eastern code speaks of *auctoritas* (*CCEO* 934).

[11] Two examples: For the alienation of property whose value exceeds the maximum amount, the permission of the Holy See is necessary (c. 1292, §2). A diocesan bishop needs the favorable opinion of the bishop's conference and the permission of the Holy See to delegate a lay person to assist at weddings (c. 1112, §1).

[12] The noun *consilium* usually refers to an advisory body, such as a presbyteral council (*consilium presbyterale*). The use of the verb *audire*, however, does not always imply a right to be heard in the sense of c. 127, as is the case when the subject to be consulted is not clearly identified (e.g., cc. 377, §3 and 1064), when it is left to the discretion of the superior to obtain advice (e.g., cc. 50; 317, §1; 524; 547; 553, §2; 971; 1064) or when those to be heard are not "subordinate" (e.g., cc. 459, §2; 796, §2; 1479).

[13] PCILT, authentic interpretation of May 15, 1985, *AAS* 77 (1985) 771.

[14] It was added because several constitutions of institutes of religious life provided for it. See *Comm* 14 (1982) 146.

minishes tremendously. The purpose of convening is, however, to discuss the matter and exchange thoughts before advice is given. In conclusion, when counsel is asked for, all must be convoked in accord with canon 166, unless particular or proper law provides otherwise. Those who do not respond to the notice of convocation lose the right to be heard. Nevertheless, the superior could ask those not present at the meeting for their counsel, but could not "add" their advice to that given by those who were present.[15] This interpretation implies that superiors have fulfilled their duty when they have heard those present.

Could the superior act validly against the counsel given by a college or group of persons? The canon does not answer this question, but in light of number two of the next paragraph, which considers this situation in relation to counsel given by individuals, it seems that the superior is not bound by the counsel, but would need an overriding reason, at least in the superior's judgment, not to follow it.

The canon speaks of a college (*collegium*) and a group of persons (*coetus*). Since the latter always includes the former, Eastern code canon 934 is correct and less confusing when it speaks solely about a group of persons (*coetus*). For the sake of clarity: the difference between *a collegial act* and giving consent or advice as a group of persons or as a college is that in the latter the superior alone places the act; giving consent is only a prerequisite for the validity of that act. In *a collegial act*, however, the superior is *primus inter pares* and dependent on the majority vote; the superior must act according to the majority decision. Hence, in a collegial act the superior may vote and even break a tie. When simply obtaining consent though, the superior may not vote. In a case where the law determines that the superior is to act together with the council, therefore, canon 127 does not apply, because such a case involves a collegial act.[16]

The second paragraph concerns the obtaining of consent or counsel from individuals. For the validity of the act, all of the individuals need to be asked. Furthermore, when they need to give consent, every single individual must give consent. Even when only one person does not do so, the act placed by the superior is invalid.[17] In the case of counsel, the superior is not to act contrary to the advice given, especially when it is given unanimously, unless the superior has a reason which is overriding, at least subjectively.

The third paragraph contains two obligations for those who are to give consent or counsel. (1) They should give their opinion sincerely. (2) They are to observe secrecy when the gravity of the affair requires it. At times, the superior may even insist on this. The first obligation implies that consent or counsel should be given in virtue of the knowledge, competence, and position that these persons have.[18] Those who are to give consent or counsel must have full information, as Eastern code canon 934, §3 indicates.[19]

Repair of Damage

Canon 128 — Whoever illegitimately inflicts damage upon someone by a juridic act or by any other act placed with malice or negligence is obliged to repair the damage inflicted.

A juridic act or any other act might cause damage to another juridic or physical person.[20] Only

---

[15] See Güthoff, 127–129.

[16] E.g., c. 699 determines that the supreme moderator together with at least four council members is to decide about a dismissal. Because this is a collegial act, the supreme moderator has to execute the decision made by the majority even if the superior him- or herself voted against it. See also c. 119 above.

[17] Not every consent to be given by an individual is to be understood in the sense of c. 127. For example, the consent given by the wife of a candidate for the deaconate is not to be seen in the sense of c. 127. For other examples, see cc. 1177, §2; 764; and 1003, §2.

[18] Cf. c. 212, §3.

[19] Canon 1292, §4 determines that those who are to give advice or consent for alienation are first to be fully informed.

[20] J. Krukowski, "Responsibility for Damage Resulting from Illegal Administrative Acts in the *Code of Canon Law* of 1983," in Consociatio Internationalis Studio Iuris Canonici Promovendo, *Le Nouveau Code de Droit canonique,*

when such a juridic act is placed unlawfully or when an act is placed with malice or culpability is there an obligation for the one who placed the act to compensate for the damage inflicted. This applies to physical and juridic persons. The damage not only concerns property, but might also refer to other "goods" like health, freedom, reputation, or spiritual goods (e.g., sacraments). Furthermore, negligence in performing an act which causes damage might be a reason for reparation, e.g., when a competent authority does not issue an obligatory decree (c. 57, §3). This example shows that canon 128 not only is directed to individuals who might cause damage, but includes damage caused by ecclesiastical officials.[21]

The restoration of damage might require restitution and reparation. Restitution is restoration to the situation which existed before the damage was caused. For example, an object that was illegitimately possessed is returned, or a right or duty that was denied is acknowledged. Reparation is satisfaction. This could be financial or moral. Often restitution and reparation are connected.

Requests for compensation should be made through the legitimate means offered by the Church itself. Canon 221 states that Christian faithful can legitimately vindicate and defend their rights. In fact, procedural law provides a forum in which physical and juridic persons can vindicate their rights (c. 1400, §1). A person who has been damaged through an administrative illegal act can seek hierarchical recourse (c. 1732–1739) and, when necessary, even have recourse to the Apostolic Signatura.[22] Procedural law provides norms concerning actions for repair of damages (cc. 1729–1731), but such norms presume a delict. When no other means are available, an action in virtue of canon 1491 seems possible.

The New Code of Canon Law, ed. M. Thériault and J. Thorn (Ottawa: Université Saint-Paul, 1986) 1:231–242.

[21] See also c. 1389, §2 on abuse of authority through negligence and c. 1281, §3 on damage caused by administrators of ecclesiastical juridical persons.

[22] *PB* 123, §2 determines that in a case of administrative recourse the Apostolic Signatura might decide as well about the restoration of damage.

TITLE VIII
THE POWER OF GOVERNANCE
[cc. 129–144]

One of the major achievements of Vatican II was certainly that of considering ecclesiologically the position of all faithful. The second chapter of the Constitution on the Church, *Lumen gentium*, thus discusses first the "people of God," and subsequently the hierarchy, laity, and religious. The council had recourse to the so-called *munus triplex* theory in considering the different tasks that the faithful have. This theory focuses on the threefold ministry of Christ, namely, that of prophet, priest, and king, and the participation of the faithful therein. Through baptism all share in the priesthood of Christ, but this common priesthood differs in essence from the ministerial or hierarchical priesthood. Crucial for this difference is the sacred power (*potestas sacra*) which the ministerial priest (*sacerdos*) possesses (*LG* 10). It is exactly here that the concepts of *munus* and *potestas* come together.

Traditionally a differentiation has been made between the powers of orders and jurisdiction. It was for Vatican II to answer two questions related to this. The first one concerned the difference between the priesthood and episcopacy: Was the difference only on the level of a superior jurisdiction of the bishop? The second question had arisen after Vatican I, namely: What is the source of the power of jurisdiction of diocesan bishops? Are they mere delegates of the Roman Pontiff?

Vatican II answered these questions by stating that episcopal consecration is the fullness of the sacrament of orders and that the episcopal consecration confers not only the office (*munus*) of sanctifying, but also the offices of teaching and governing (*LG* 21). The diocesan bishop governs his flock as vicar and legate of Christ by authority and, as the council calls it, by sacred power. This power is proper, ordinary, and immediate (*LG* 27). Since the council here made use of both terms, *munera* and *potestas,* and because the Church had traditionally used the language of power for orders and jurisdiction, a "Preliminary Explanatory Note" was added to *Lumen gentium*. It states, in part,

> In *consecration* is given an *ontological* participation in *sacred* functions [*munerum*]. ... The word *functions* is used deliberately, rather than *powers* [*potestatum*], since this latter word could be understood as *ready to go into action*. But for such ready power to be had, it needs *canonical* or *juridical determination* by hierarchical authority.[23]

The council stated that presbyters share with bishops in the priesthood of Christ and thus depend on the bishop for the exercise of their power. The council did not speak about deacons and sacred power or about functions which concern the power of governance. Furthermore, the council never discussed the sacred power of the laity, but affirmed that all the faithful do participate in the threefold ministry of Christ.

As Pope John Paul II mentioned when he promulgated the 1983 code, it is the task of canon law to "translate" these theological insights into concrete canonical norms.[24] The commentary on the following canons will show that the translation of the insights about governance into norms for action was among the most disputed areas in the process of the reform of the 1917 code. Moreover, now that the interpretation and application of these norms have been under way for some time, there is still no unified understanding. It will therefore be important to recall a principle of interpretation mentioned by Pope John Paul II, namely, that the council should remain point of reference when something is not clear: the legislation may not interpret the council, but the council should be the basis for the interpretation of the legislation.

Whereas the code has separate books on the teaching and sanctifying offices (*munera*) of the Church, it lacks a parallel book on the governing office. Book I on general norms contains the title

"The Power of Governance" (*De potestate regiminis*). This title does not correspond to the traditional language of the power of jurisdiction (*iurisdictio*), nor does it speak of the office (*munus*) of governing. It speaks about governing, because that fits better with history and with the teaching of Vatican II concerning the three *munera*.[25] Furthermore, the title is broader than the one in the 1917 code which spoke about "ordinary and delegated power," because the title in the 1983 code does not restrict itself to executive power, but also includes legislative and judicial power.[26]

Who Can Exercise the Power of Governance?

Canon 129 — §1. Those who have received sacred orders are qualified, according to the norm of the prescripts of the law, for the power of governance, which exists in the Church by divine institution and is also called the power of jurisdiction.

§2. Lay members of the Christian faithful can cooperate in the exercise of this same power according to the norm of law.

The first canon of this title attempts to answer the question: who can exercise the power of governance? This question has certainly been one of the most debated issues, not only during the reform of the 1917 code but also in the time after the promulgation of the 1983 code.[27] The debate focuses in particular on the laity and their exercise of the power of governance. The question underlying the debate has to do with the necessity of ordination in order to exercise the power of governance and is closely connected to the question concerning the capacity of the laity to hold office (cf. c. 274, §1).

The discussion has resulted in two (opposing) positions which may be identified as the Roman

---

[23] *LG*, "Explanatory Note," #2 (emphasis in original).
[24] *SDL*, in *AAS* 75 (1983) 11.

[25] *Comm* 9 (1977) 234.
[26] *Comm* 9 (1977) 234.
[27] For an extensive analysis of this canon, see J. P. Beal, "The Exercise of the Power of Governance by Lay People: State of the Question," *J* 55 (1995) 1–92.

school and the Munich school.[28] The positions of the two schools can be understood only in light of the 1917 code which determined that only clerics can obtain the power of jurisdiction (*CIC* 118). Clerics, according to the 1917 code, were all those who had received tonsure. Thus, ordination was not a necessity for obtaining power of jurisdiction.

The Roman school points out that the council did not really speak about the power of jurisdiction, but answered questions about the powers of the bishops and affirmed the oneness of sacred power for the episcopacy. The council neither intended, nor did it in fact speak about, the power of jurisdiction of the laity. This school refers to historical examples which testify to laity having exercised jurisdiction and concludes that, because Vatican II had no intention to break with history, laity can exercise the power of jurisdiction.

The Munich school, however, states that the council clearly decided on the oneness of sacred power which is indivisible. The only source of sacred power is ordination. Hence, laity cannot exercise power of jurisdiction. According to this school, the council restored the unity of the powers of orders and jurisdiction. To state that laity could exercise the power of jurisdiction would therefore be a break with the insight of the council.

In light of these thoughts, both schools proposed changes to the draft texts of the 1983 code.[29] An important result of the discussion concerns the word "cooperate" in the second paragraph of canon 129. It replaced the word "participate" (*partem habere*), which had been in the 1980 and 1982 schemas. The Munich school sees in this change an affirmation that laity cannot exercise jurisdiction and quotes in favor of that interpretation canon 274, §1 which states that only clerics may be given an office which requires either power of

orders or power of jurisdiction. The norm that lay persons may function as judges in collegiate tribunals (c. 1421, §2) is considered to be an aberration which should not be implemented by bishops. To "cooperate" means, therefore, that laity can be involved only in the preparation, accompaniment, and execution of acts of jurisdiction.

The Roman school, while acknowledging the change from "participating" to "cooperating" as a possible weakening of its position, does not give too much weight to this, for the word *cooperatores* is used in other canons as meaning "participation."[30] The determination that only clerics can hold an office which requires the power of orders or of jurisdiction is to be interpreted in light of its text and context, which implies that this norm is to be seen in terms of the rights and duties of clerics. Thus, clerics would have a right to hold an office which requires the power of jurisdiction by reason of the orders received; they would also then have an obligation to exercise that office. The laity, however, have no right to such an office and therefore no obligation to exercise it.

An issue closely related to the question of laity exercising the power of governance is the question of whether laity can be delegated the power of governance. The code does not determine who can be delegated (c. 131). Therefore, some hold that since the laity are not incapable of exercising the power of governance, it is possible for a bishop to delegate a lay person; others deny this possibility.

In conclusion, the question concerning the exercise of the power of governance by the laity is still being debated. Nevertheless, several offices are open to laity which do imply the power of governance, e.g., finance officer of a diocese (c. 494) and of a religious institute (c. 636), member of a diocesan finance council (c. 492), lay person in charge of a parish (c. 517, §2), administrator of ecclesiastical goods (c. 1279), judge (c. 1421, §2), auditor (c. 1428), promoter of justice (c. 1435), and defender of the bond (c. 1435).[31]

---

[28] The literature usually speaks of the German school, but this is incorrect because several German canonists do not hold this position. Considering the scholars who hold this theory, it might be better to speak of the "Munich" school.

[29] See in particular the debate concerning the 1980 schema of the code in *Plen* 33–97 and 177–229.

[30] E.g., in c. 545, §1.

[31] For the power of governance of laity in institutes of consecrated life, see E. McDonough, "The Potestas of Canon

Internal and External Forum

Canon 130 — Of itself, the power of governance is exercised for the external forum; sometimes, however, it is exercised for the internal forum alone, so that the effects which its exercise is meant to have for the external forum are not recognized there, except insofar as the law establishes it in determined cases.

The second of the ten principles governing the revision of the 1917 code concerned a call for a coordination of the external and internal forums. One of the problems had been that the internal forum had also been referred to as the forum of conscience (*CIC* 196). However, the internal and the external forums are together to be seen as distinct from the forum of conscience, because the latter refers to the relationship between God and an individual, but the internal and external forums refer to different "places" (of the effect) of an act of governance. Hence, whether an act is placed in the internal or the external forum, its effect on the forum of conscience is the same.

The major difference between the internal and external forums is the absence of publicity in the internal forum. The external forum is the place in which public and verifiable decisions are made. Hence, names of persons are made public or noted in a register (e.g., the registration of a marriage, c. 1121). In the internal forum, however, there would be no mention of (full) name or nota-

tion in a public register (e.g., a secret marriage, c. 1133). The internal forum itself is divided into the internal sacramental forum and the internal non-sacramental forum. The internal sacramental forum refers to matters decided within the sacrament of penance and therefore additionally protected by the seal of confession. The power of governance may also be exercised in the internal non-sacramental forum.

The decision as to which forum is applicable in a given case should be guided by the following criteria: what is legally or factually known, or possibly going to be known, is to be decided in the external forum; what is secret and likely to remain secret may be decided in the internal forum. The rules for confessional secrecy are always to be respected. The canon clearly prefers the exercise of the power of governance in the external forum.

Persons who have the power of governance for the external forum may use that power in the internal forum also. There are, however, persons who hold offices the power of which are exclusively (penitentiary—cc. 64, 1082, canon penitentiary—c. 508) or partially (confessor—cc. 1079, §3; 1357, §1) for the internal forum.

Decisions made in the internal forum have full effect. Hence, a marriage entered into after a dispensation from an impediment has been granted in the internal forum is valid, even though the legal effects are not recognized in the external forum. Should, however, the impediment become known before the marriage is contracted, that marriage cannot be entered into until a dispensation has been granted in the external forum. It should be noted that the law does provide for some cases in which the act of governance placed in the internal non-sacramental forum is recognized in the external forum (see, for example, c. 1082).

596," *Antonianum* 63 (1988) 551–606 and "Jurisdiction Exercised by Non-ordained Members in Religious Institutes," *CLSAP* 58 (1996) 292–307. In relation to the argument that in a college of judges in which a lay person participates the sacred power is guaranteed because the *majority* of the members do have sacred power, McDonough points out that in a chapter of a clerical pontifical religious institute the number of non-ordained members can far exceed the number of ordained, so that it would be difficult to hold that the college would possess sacred power because of a majority of clerical members. McDonough argues that the factual possibilities according to c. 596 should have an influence on the interpretation of c. 129, §2.

Ordinary and Delegated Power

Canon 131 — §1. The ordinary power of governance is that which is joined to a certain office by the law itself; delegated, that which is granted to a person but not by means of an office.

§2. The ordinary power of governance can be either proper or vicarious.

§3. The burden of proving delegation rests on the one who claims to have been delegated.

Whereas the Roman Pontiff obtains the power of governance upon accepting the election together with the episcopal consecration, and the college of bishops also has full power by divine law, others who have power of governance receive it either by holding an office—in which case it is called ordinary power—or by delegation. The ordinary power attached to an office can be determined by law or in a decree issued by the authority which constitutes and confers the office (c. 145, §2). Delegated power is given to a specific person. The difference between ordinary and delegated power has relevance for the possibility of delegating it to others and for extinguishing it.

The second paragraph of the canon further differentiates between ordinary proper and ordinary vicarious power. Although the code does not give a criterion for the difference between the two, it is generally accepted that the independence of an office is decisive. Thus, some hold offices which are dependent on others and in a sense assist the "main" office. These, then, are offices with ordinary vicarious power. Hence, a diocesan bishop has ordinary proper power, but a vicar general has ordinary vicarious power. The latter's power is ordinary, because it comes with an office, but it is vicarious because it is exercised in the name of another, namely, the bishop.

Although normally the vicar and the "head" (or bishop) are considered to be the same acting person, the 1983 code allows for recourse to the hierarchical superior against an administrative act placed by someone who acted with vicarious power (c. 1737, §1).

Paragraph three of the canon states that the burden of proof of delegation lies with the one who claims to be delegated. Hence, it is highly recommended that the delegation be given in writing (cc. 973 and 1111, §2).

The canon does not determine who may or may not be delegated. In light of canon 129, §2

the question has arisen as to whether lay persons can be given delegated power.[32]

Habitual Faculties

Canon 132 — §1. Habitual faculties are governed by the prescripts for delegated power.

§2. Nevertheless, unless the grant expressly provides otherwise or the ordinary was chosen for personal qualifications, a habitual faculty granted to an ordinary is not withdrawn when the authority of the ordinary to whom it was granted expires, even if he has begun to execute it, but the faculty transfers to any ordinary who succeeds him in governance.

Habitual faculties are one type of delegated faculties. When they are granted to an ordinary in virtue of his office, they do not cease with the cessation of the office holder's authority and may therefore be exercised by the ordinary's successor. This is an exception to the general provision in the law on the cessation of delegated power (see c. 142). Unless otherwise provided in the grant or unless the ordinary was chosen for personal qualifications, habitual faculties do not cease with the cessation of the ordinary's authority.

The vicar general and episcopal vicar also possess the habitual faculties granted to a bishop by the Apostolic See, unless other provisions have been expressly made or the bishop has been chosen because of personal qualifications (cf. c. 479, §3).

Validity of Acts Placed by a Delegate

Canon 133 — §1. A delegate who exceeds the limits of the mandate with respect to either matters or persons does not act at all.

§2. A delegate who carries out those things for which the person was delegated in some manner other than that determined in the mandate is not considered to exceed the limits of the mandate unless the manner was prescribed for validity by the one delegating.

[32] See above, under c. 129.

The first paragraph of the canon concerns the substance of the delegation and the second one the manner of executing it. There are then two reasons which cause an act to be placed invalidly: (1) The person acts beyond the power he or she has been granted. Invalidity could also be due to the limitations of the one who delegates, because what one does not have one cannot give.[33] However, note that delegation given for all cases (*ad universitatem casuum*) is to be broadly interpreted (c. 138). (2) The person does not act in the prescribed way as determined for validity.[34] Canon 39 determines that conditions affecting the validity of administrative acts are expressed with the words "if" (*si*), "unless" (*nisi*), or "provided that" (*dummodo*).

Ordinaries

Canon 134 — §1. In addition to the Roman Pontiff, by the title of ordinary are understood in the law diocesan bishops and others who, even if only temporarily, are placed over some particular church or a community equivalent to it according to the norm of can. 368 as well as those who possess general ordinary executive power in them, namely, vicars general and episcopal vicars; likewise, for their own members, major superiors of clerical religious institutes of pontifical right and of clerical societies of apostolic life of pontifical right who at least possess ordinary executive power.

§2. By the title of local ordinary are understood all those mentioned in §1 except the superiors of religious institutes and of societies of apostolic life.

§3. Within the context of executive power, those things which in the canons are attributed by name to the diocesan bishop are understood to belong only to a diocesan bishop and to the others made equivalent to him in can. 381, §2, excluding the

vicar general and episcopal vicar except by special mandate.

This canon determines who in canon law is considered to be an ordinary and differentiates between personal and local ordinaries. Personal ordinaries are superiors of clerical religious institutes of pontifical right and clerical societies of apostolic life of pontifical right; the others mentioned in paragraph one are local ordinaries. To be added to the list of local ordinaries is the ordinary of a personal prelature (c. 295, §1).

The third paragraph differentiates between a diocesan bishop and those equivalent to him according to canons 381, §2 and 368 on the one hand, and an episcopal vicar and vicar general on the other hand. At times the code prescribes that only the diocesan bishop can act. When a bishop extends this "reserved" power to a vicar general or an episcopal vicar (see c. 479, §§1–2), the latter act not with ordinary vicarious power, but in virtue of delegated power (see c. 131).

Legislative, Executive, and Judicial Power

Canon 135 — §1. The power of governance is distinguished as legislative, executive, and judicial.

§2. Legislative power must be exercised in the manner prescribed by law; that which a legislator below the supreme authority possesses in the Church cannot be validly delegated unless the law explicitly provides otherwise. A lower legislator cannot validly issue a law contrary to higher law.

§3. Judicial power, which judges or judicial colleges possess, must be exercised in the manner prescribed by law and cannot be delegated except to perform acts preparatory to some decree or sentence.

§4. In what pertains to the exercise of executive power, the prescripts of the following canons are to be observed.

The power of governance is subdivided into legislative, executive, and judicial powers. In the Church there has been a long tradition of recogniz-

---

[33] *Nemo potest iuris transferre in alium, quam sibi competere dinoscatur. RI* 79.

[34] A person who exceeds his or her mandate is not *inhabilis*. See c. 124.

ing legislative and judicial power. Since the Council of Trent, decisions have also been made in an administrative way. In the 1983 code this type of governance is called executive power. It is important to note that in the Church those who have legislative power are also the ones who implement the law, that is, who have executive power. The reverse, however, is not true, because the code states that those who have executive power normally have no legislative power (c. 30) and that general executory decrees may not affect the law (cc 30; 33, §1; 34, §1). Nevertheless, a problem may occur when executive power is delegated to exercise legislative power (c. 30), since in principle executive power is subject to legislative power.

An important difference between the so-called *trias politica* of Montesquieu and the three powers in the Church is that in the case of the latter those who have executive power can also become active in the domain of penal law. This occurs, for example, in threatening determinate penalties through a precept (c. 1319, §1) or imposing or declaring a penalty by an extra-judicial decree (c. 1342) in which case the procedure is not judicial but administrative (cf. cc. 1341; 1718, §1, 3°). Furthermore, if circumstances warrant it, an ordinary with executive power can provide for penal remedies even when the accused is acquitted of the charge or when no penalty is imposed (c. 1348).

Due to the absence of administrative tribunals, executive power handles conflicts as well (cc. 1732–1739). Judicial power is normally not exercised personally but through judges (c. 1420), which assures some independence from the executive.

Hence, although the canon distinguishes between legislative, executive, and judicial powers, they are closely connected by reason of the offices and the persons holding them.

The second paragraph of the canon addresses legislative power. The canon does not determine who may legislate, but only states that anybody below the highest authority, that is, the Roman Pontiff (c. 331) and the college of bishops (c. 336), cannot delegate legislative power unless the law provides for it, as is the case, for example, in

canon 30.[35] Furthermore, a law which is contrary to a higher law cannot be enacted by a lower level legislator. Thus, a diocesan bishop is restricted by the law enacted by the Roman Pontiff or Apostolic See; a provincial chapter of a religious institute is restricted by the laws enacted by the general chapter. According to *Pastor bonus*, the Pontifical Council for the Interpretation of Legislative Texts is competent to determine at the request of someone whether particular laws and general decrees issued by lower legislators are in agreement with (*consentanea*) the universal law.[36]

The third paragraph speaks about the judicial power not exercised by the Roman Pontiff or diocesan bishop, but by judges or judicial colleges. This power cannot be delegated by these judges or colleges except to carry out acts which are preparatory to a decree or a decision, as would be the case when an auditor hears parties or witnesses (c. 1428).

The fourth paragraph only refers to the norms contained in the subsequent canons.

The Scope of Executive Power

Canon 136 — Unless the nature of the matter or a prescript of law establishes otherwise, a person is able to exercise executive power over his subjects, even when he or they are outside his territory; he is also able to exercise this power over travelers actually present in the territory if it concerns granting favors or executing universal laws or particular laws which bind them according to the norm of can. 13, §2, n. 2.

The canon describes the scope of executive power in terms of who is subject to that power and where.[37] There are no equivalent canons for the exercise of legislative and judicial power. The

---

[35] For the bishop as legislator, see M. Wijlens, "'For You I Am a Bishop, With You I Am a Christian': The Bishop as Legislator," *J* 56 (1996) 68–91.

[36] *PB* 158.

[37] For the determination of domicile and quasi-domicile, see c. 107.

scope of legislative power is only indirectly determined by way of who is bound by which laws (cc. 11–13). The scope of judicial power is indicated in the determination of competence of the judge (cf. cc. 1404–1416 and c. 1673 for marriage cases).

Delegation of Executive Power

Canon 137 — §1. Ordinary executive power can be delegated both for a single act and for all cases unless the law expressly provides otherwise.

§2. Executive power delegated by the Apostolic See can be subdelegated for a single act or for all cases unless the delegate was chosen for personal qualifications or subdelegation was expressly forbidden.

§3. Executive power delegated by another authority who has ordinary power can be subdelegated only for individual cases if it was delegated for all cases. If it was delegated for a single act or for determined acts, however, it cannot be subdelegated except by express grant of the one delegating.

§4. No subdelegated power can be subdelegated again unless the one delegating has expressly granted this.

Someone holding an office to which is attached ordinary executive power, be it proper or vicarious (see c. 131), may delegate such power. A person who has been delegated may under certain circumstance subdelegate such power. This canon regulates delegation and subdelegation. It should be noted that delegation and subdelegation are not allowed when the law expressly states this (e.g., cc. 508, §1; 969, §1). Of course, a person can subdelegate only what he possesses himself and may exercise legitimately (c. 133).

Interpretation of Ordinary and Delegated Executive Power

Canon 138 — Ordinary executive power as well as power delegated for all cases must be interpreted broadly; any other, however, must be interpreted strictly. Nevertheless, one who has delegated power is understood to have been granted also those things without which the delegate cannot exercise this power.

The canon regulates the interpretation of ordinary executive power and of power that has been delegated. When power is delegated for all cases, it is to be interpreted favorably and therefore broadly. However, when it is not delegated for all cases, a strict interpretation is necessary. This parallels the interpretation of dispensations, for the power to dispense granted for all cases is to be interpreted broadly, but when it is granted for a particular case, the dispensation is to be interpreted strictly (cc. 36, §1; 92) as is the power granted for a particular case (c. 92).

Even though the second part of the canon is not a legal presumption (see c. 1584), it determines that the person who has received delegated power has also been given what is necessary to exercise it.

The Competency of Several Persons to Act

Canon 139 — §1. Unless the law determines otherwise, the fact that a person approaches some competent authority, even a higher one, does not suspend the executive power, whether ordinary or delegated, of another competent authority.

§2. Nevertheless, a lower authority is not to become involved in cases submitted to a higher authority except for a grave and urgent cause; in this case, the lower authority is immediately to notify the higher concerning the matter.

The competence of a person to place an executive act is not suspended when a higher competent authority is approached unless the law prescribes otherwise. The second paragraph, however, states that normally a lower authority should not act when a higher authority has been approached. The norm is a moral exhortation, for even the exception mentioned in the norm touches only the liceity of an act. Any action by the competent lower authority would be valid. Hence, the purpose of the second paragraph is to avoid undermining the higher authority.

The canon provides for a situation where a decision has not been made by anyone. Once, however, a decision has been made, canons 64–65 apply which prescribe what is to be done once a favor has been denied.

Delegation of Several Persons

Canon 140 — §1. When several persons have been delegated *in solidum* to transact the same affair, the one who first begins to deal with it excludes the others from doing so unless that person subsequently was impeded or did not wish to proceed further in carrying it out.

§2. When several persons have been delegated collegially to transact an affair, all must proceed according to the norm of can. 119 unless the mandate has provided otherwise.

§3. Executive power delegated to several persons is presumed to be delegated to them *in solidum*.

The canon provides rules for situations where several people have been delegated jointly (§1) or where a college has been given the delegation (§2). A delegation to individuals jointly is to be distinguished from successive delegation (cf. c. 141).

A delegation granted jointly implies that every single individual is equally fully competent to act, but that the first one who uses the delegated power excludes the others from acting legitimately. They continue to hold the delegated power but may no longer exercise it; hence, if one of these persons should act, it would be valid, but illicit. However, if the first one to take action does not fulfill or terminate his task, the others are equally competent to licitly exercise their delegated power once again. The fact that the first individual is unable or unwilling to proceed in the matter must be established authentically.

When delegated power is given to a college, that power is to be exercised according to canon 119. In distinction to individuals who are jointly delegated, the members of a college do not receive the delegation individually, but only as a college. Hence, they ought to act according to canon 119 unless the delegating person has provided otherwise, e.g., by prescribing that a majority different from the one in canon 119 suffices for approval of an action.

Normally, the act of delegation itself indicates whether it is given to individuals jointly or to a college. Should this not be clear, then it is to be presumed that the delegation has been given to the individuals jointly.

Successive Delegation

Canon 141 — When several persons have been delegated successively, that person is to take care of the affair whose mandate is the earlier and has not been subsequently revoked.

Whereas the previous canon discusses the delegation of several persons jointly, this canon treats the case where persons are delegated successively. However, the canon does not answer a practical problem that may arise, namely, that of determining who has been delegated first. In case of doubt, recourse should be taken to the one who delegated.

If one person has general delegation and another later receives specific delegation, the latter has precedence for this specific case.[38]

The Cessation of Delegated Power

Canon 142 — §1. Delegated power ceases: by fulfillment of the mandate; by expiration of the time or completion of the number of cases for which it was granted; by cessation of the purpose for the delegation; by revocation of the one delegating directly communicated to the delegate as well as by resignation of the delegate made known to and accepted by the one delegating. It does not cease,

---

[38] *RI* 34: *Generi per speciem derogatur.*

however, when the authority of the one delegating expires unless this appears in attached clauses.

§2. Nevertheless, an act of delegated power which is exercised for the internal forum alone and is placed inadvertently after the lapse of the time limit of the grant is valid.

Delegated power ceases:

- by the fulfillment of the mandate;
- by the lapse of time (cf. cc. 202–203) or by the completion of the number of cases for which it was granted;
- by cessation of the final cause of the delegation;
- by the revocation of the one delegating, directly communicated—that is, communicated officially—to the delegate;
- by the resignation of the delegate, made known to and accepted by the one delegating.

However, the delegated power does *not* cease when the authority of the one delegating expires, unless this appears in attached clauses. Thus, a priest who has been delegated to dispense from a matrimonial impediment can still do so even when the bishop who delegated him resigns from his office or is transferred. This would not be the case, however, if the bishop had explicitly determined otherwise.

It should be remembered that subdelegation can never extend beyond what the one subdelegating possesses. Thus, when delegated power was granted for a specific number of cases or a specific time, the subdelegation cannot go beyond those limits.

The second paragraph of canon 142 regulates acts placed in the internal forum after the time allowed has expired and states that such acts are valid. When an act of delegated power is inadvertently exercised after the time for which it was granted, it is valid only when placed in the internal forum, be it sacramental or non-sacramental (cf. c. 130). The delegated power need not have been granted solely for the internal forum.

Cessation of Ordinary Power

Canon 143 — §1. Ordinary power ceases by loss of the office to which it is connected.

§2. Unless the law provides otherwise, ordinary power is suspended if, legitimately, an appeal is made or a recourse is lodged against privation of or removal from office.

Since ordinary power of governance comes with an office (cf. c. 131), it is lost when the office is lost. This is applicable to both proper and vicarious ordinary power. Ecclesiastical office can be lost by way of resignation, transfer, removal, or privation (cc. 184–196). Since the law foresees that a person might appeal or have recourse against a removal or privation (cf. cc. 1353, 1733–1739), it states that in such a case the power held in virtue of that office is suspended. Hence, until the matter is definitely settled, the person continues to hold the office, but may not exercise the power attached to the office. In the meantime the competent authority must make an appropriate provision (c. 1747, §3).

An excommunicated person is prohibited from discharging any ecclesiastical office, ministries, or functions, and is forbidden to place acts of governance (c. 1331, §1). Should a person nevertheless do so, the acts would be valid, but illicit, unless the excommunication had been declared or imposed, in which case the acts would be invalid (c. 1331, §2, 2°). A suspension forbids either all or some acts of the power of governance and the exercise of all or some rights attached to an office (c. 1333, §1, 2°, 3°). Acts nevertheless placed would be illicit but valid, unless a law or precept had determined that the suspended cleric could not validly place acts of governance after a condemnatory or declaratory sentence (c. 1333, §2).

Common Error, Positive and Probable Doubt

Canon 144 — §1. In factual or legal common error and in positive and probable doubt of law or of fact, the Church supplies executive power of governance for both the external and internal forum.

§2. The same norm is applied to the faculties mentioned in cann. 882, 883, 966, and 1111, §1.

It has been a traditional principle that in the interest of the community the Church supplies jurisdiction when a public ecclesiastical office-holder has placed an act for which he or she had no authority. Such jurisdiction concerns, however, only the executive power of governance. The Church supplies this power when the person acting either was not given such power or was given it ineffectively, or when the act was placed after power granted had expired. Supplying the power of governance is a kind of transfer of the power of governance; it is not a sanation.

It should be noted that the Church supplies the power of governance for the common good or the avoidance of general harm. This implies that normally the prescribed formalities of the law are applicable, but that in certain circumstances because of the common good the Church supplies the lacking executive power.[39]

The Church can supply executive power of governance only for cases where the person acting would have been capable (*habiles*) of exercising executive power. Thus, it could never supply a lay person the power to hear a confession, because a lay person is not capable under any circumstance of hearing a confession.

The Church supplies the executive power of governance only when there is a common error which is either factual or legal or when there is a positive and probable doubt. Error is a false judgment. Such an error must be probable, i.e., it must be of such a nature that it is capable of gaining the assent of a prudent person. Hence, it is not simply ignorance. The error is to be *common,* not private;

that is, it is to affect some sort of community. Such a community does not necessarily have to be a canonically established community in the sense of a diocese, parish, or religious community. It could also be a community gathered together for one occasion. That an error is "common" does not mean that a majority of those present hold something to be true, but that there is a public circumstance in which all reasonable persons would naturally conclude that it is true. Thus, to establish common error, it is sufficient that a majority of people, when asked, would reply erroneously to the question. It is also not necessary that in fact a certain number of people actually do make the error, for the Church supplies power when, objectively speaking, reasonable persons would make the error. Common error is also not restricted to situations which occur regularly; it may also be applied to an isolated event, such as a case in which a priest receives the profession of a religious of a pontifical institute of consecrated life without having been delegated by the legitimate superior to do so (c. 656, 5°).

Although the canon presupposes the existence of common error, occasions might arise where common error could be induced, e.g., when a priest has no faculty to hear confession, but enters the confessional because many people want to confess and he is sure that in the given situation people will think he has jurisdiction. In such a situation the Church will supply the faculty.

The second part of the first paragraph concerns positive and probable doubt either about the law or about a fact.[40] Doubt is a state in which the mind is not able to make a decision between contradictory conclusions. Doubt is *positive* when there are probable reasons for one or both decisions, and it is *negative* when there is too little information to support either. The doubt may be probable or improbable, depending on the strength of the foundation. Doubt may have to do with the law, namely, its existence, binding force, meaning, extension, or cessation. Doubt may also

---

[39] Thus, if a priest who is not properly delegated assists at a wedding, the mere fact that he is a priest is not a sufficient reason for the Church to supply the faculty. There must be some degree of common error. In other words, there must be a congregation or at least a few witnesses who assume the priest is duly authorized, otherwise he would not be up there at the altar. Canonical form (cc. 1108–1118) is to be observed, but when the common good calls for it, the Church will supply the faculty.

[40] On the difference between doubt of fact and doubt of law, see c. 14.

have to do with the facts in the sense that there is uncertainty with regard to whether a situation contains all that is necessary for the law to be applicable to it. Examples would be whether the number of cases for which delegated power was granted has been completed (cf. c. 142); or whether danger of death really exists when a dispensation from a marriage impediment is given (cf. c. 1079).

In the case of positive and probable doubt, the Church supplies the power of governance for both the internal and the external forum.

The second paragraph states that the canon applies to the faculties mentioned in canon 883 on the sacrament of confirmation, canon 966 on hearing confession, and canon 1111, §1 on assisting as an official witness at a wedding. Furthermore, the canon applies to the executive power of all superiors and chapters in institutes of consecrated life (c. 596, §3).

The principles mentioned in this canon are applicable to all delegated faculties. It is not clear whether they also apply to someone who has been delegated invalidly for one particular act.

BIBLIOGRAPHY

Juridic Acts

Gauthier, A. "The Juridical Act." In *Roman Law and Its Contribution to the Development of Canon Law*, 75–81. Ottawa: St. Paul University, 1996.

Güthoff, E. *"Consensus" und "consilium" in c. 127 CIC/1983 und c. 934 CCEO.* Würzburg: Echter, 1994.

Hughes, M. "A New Title in the Code: On Juridic Acts." *Stud Can* 14 (1980) 391–403.

Walser, M. *Die Rechtshandlung im kanonischen Recht.* Göttingen: Cuvillier, 1994.

The Power of Governance

Aymans, W., and K. Mörsdorf. *Kanonisches Recht: Lehrbuch aufgrund des Codex iuris canonici.* Vol. 1: *Einleitende Grundfragen, Allgemeine Normen.* Paderborn: Schöningh, 1991.

Beal, J. A. "The Exercise of the Power of Governance by Lay People: State of the Question." *J* 55 (1995) 1–92.

Huysmans, R. *Algemene Normen van het Wetboek van Canoniek Recht.* Leuven: Peeters, 1993.

Socha, H. In *Münster Com*, cc. 124–144.

Torfs, R. "*Auctoritas, potestas, iurisdictio, facultas, officium, munus:* A Conceptual Analysis." *Con* 197 (1988) 63–73.

TITLE IX
ECCLESIASTICAL OFFICES
[cc. 145–196]

The Church has developed various legal structures to carry out its mission of continuing the work of Christ in the world: the listing of common responsibilities arising from Christian initiation for all the Christian faithful (e.g., cc. 208–223), the recognition and promotion of charisms as given by the Spirit, the delegation of individuals for specific tasks (e.g., cc. 137–142), and the institution of ecclesiastical offices. Office provides a key structure in support of the Church's mission, for unlike the other approaches, the creation of an office assures that an important function will be continued in the Church even after the initial officeholder is no longer available. In the Church, an office is a function established in a stable manner by divine or ecclesiastical ordinance, to be carried out for a spiritual purpose by one who has been legitimately named to the office (cc. 145–146).

Historically, ordination and office were tied together. This was the meaning of "relative ordination" as mandated by the early councils of the Church. A person was ordained for service in a particular locality, and was not to move from there. Clergy were identified with the place for which they were ordained. Beginning in the late fourth century, the Roman Empire assured support for clergy through a system parallel to its civil service, but based on this principle of ordination tied to a place. When this form of financial support was lost with the collapse of the empire in the West, a system of "benefice" gradually replaced it; that is, an assured source of income (e.g., from a vineyard, farm, etc.) was tied to the place where the cleric was ordained to serve.

During the Middle Ages, some major shifts took place which affected the Church's discipline on orders and on church offices. With the development of mendicant clergy and due to some other factors, "absolute" ordination was adopted in the West. This meant that ordination was no longer tied to a specific place. At the same time, church offices were recognized as legal entities distinct from their officeholders. But the economic dimension of the office (the benefice system) overshadowed the spiritual function, at least in canon law. Moreover, as a result of the lay investiture controversy, ecclesiastical office became increasingly a clerical concern: only ecclesiastics could confer an office in the Church, and eventually only clergy could be named to church offices.

The 1917 code summed up this clerical monopoly on offices in its canon 145, recognizing a broad sense of office (any function performed for a spiritual purpose), but narrowing the legal use of office to the strict sense of "any function constituted in a stable manner by divine or ecclesiastical ordinance, to be conferred according to the norms of canon law, involving at least some participation in the powers of either orders or jurisdiction." Canon 118 of that code restricted the power of orders and jurisdiction to clergy. Thus, only clergy could be named to church offices. Although offices were divided into benefices and non-beneficiary offices, all of them were restricted to clergy.

The Second Vatican Council affected ecclesiastical offices in several ways. In dealing with financial support for the clergy, the council separated office from benefice, called for a new system of clergy support to replace benefices, and declared that in the future the legal understanding of office was to be any function conferred in a stable manner for a spiritual purpose (*PO* 20). The council also called for a more active involvement of lay persons in the life and mission of the Church, including many functions which are constituted as offices (*AA* 24); indeed, the council encouraged bishops to name lay persons to church offices (*LG* 37).

Keeping these conciliar developments in mind, the drafters of the 1983 code moved the treatment of ecclesiastical offices from the section on clergy, where it appeared in the 1917 code, and located it among the general norms of Book I to make it clear that church offices are no longer restricted to clergy. Similarly, the drafters of the 1990 Code of Canons of the Eastern Churches placed the canons on office in a distinct title by themselves (title XX—*CCEO* 936–978).

In both codes the material is developed in three stages: an introductory canon on office; canons on conferral of office; canons on loss of office.[1]

Concept of Ecclesiastical Office

Canon 145 — §1. An ecclesiastical office is any function constituted in a stable manner by divine or ecclesiastical ordinance to be exercised for a spiritual purpose.

§2. The obligations and rights proper to individual ecclesiastical offices are defined either in the law by which the office is constituted or in the

[1] For commentaries on the present law, see: J. Arrieta, in *Pamplona ComEng*, 155–180; J. Arrieta, in *Com Ex* 1:907–951; W. Aymans, *Kanonisches Recht* (Paderborn: F. Schöningh, 1991) 1:445–502; L. Chiappetta, in *Chiappetta Com*, 2nd ed. (1996) 1:229–288 (nn. 1024–1278); V. De Paolis and A. Montan in *Il diritto nel mistero della Chiesa*, 2nd ed. (Rome: Pontificia Università Lateranense, 1988) 1:402–429; O. Échappé in *Droit Canonique*, 258–263; P. Gefaell, in *Com Ex*, 1:1034–1090; J. García Martín, *Le norme generali del Codex Iuris Canonici* (Rome: Edizioni Istituto Giuridico Claretiano, 1995) 473–583; H. Heimerl and H. Pree, *Kirchenrecht: Allgemeine Normen und Eherecht* (Vienna: Springer, 1983) 121–142; R. Hill, in *CLSA Com*, 98–112; R. Huysmans, *Algemene Normen van het Wetboek van Canoniek Recht* (Leuven: Peeters, 1993) 305–350; J. Manzanares, in *Salamanca Com*, 112–130; G. May, in *Handbuch*, 141–153; A. McGrath, in *CLSGBI Com*, 86–109; J. Miñambres, in *Com Ex*, 1:952–1033; P. Pinto, in *Urbaniana Com*, 86–105; H. Socha, in *Münster Com*; F. Urrutia, *Les normes générales* (Paris: Tardy, 1994) 233–259 (nn. 802–929).

Many of these commentaries compare the 1983 and 1917 codes; see Hill, in *CLSA Com*, for a rather thorough treatment, which will not be repeated here.

decree of the competent authority by which the office is at the same time constituted and conferred.

There are four key concepts in paragraph one.

1. An office is a function (in Latin, munus*).*

Offices are not honorific; they involve doing something. As church offices, they entail doing something on behalf of the Church and of Christ. An office is not for one's own sake, but is to be exercised for the sake of other people.

Munus ("function") is frequently used for the threefold ministry of Christ: to teach, to sanctify, and to govern. Offices in the Church participate in these functions in various ways. Some offices are constitutional, central to the organization and functioning of the Church as the continuation of Christ's mission (e.g., pope, diocesan bishop, pastor). Other offices are auxiliary, assisting in but not central to that mission (offices of the Roman Curia or of a bishops' conference, of a diocesan curia or religious institutes).

The function may be a responsibility the officeholder carries out individually; or it may entail collective or collegial action, such as membership in an ecumenical or particular council, in a conference of bishops or on the council of a religious institute, in the presbyteral council or finance council, and so on.

The function carries with it various obligations and rights. These are to be spelled out in the law or by decree of a competent authority (§2). The power needed to carry out an office is attached to it by the law and is termed ordinary power (c. 131, §1); it can be exercised in the officeholder's own name ("proper" power) or in the name of another ("vicarious" power—see c. 131, §2). Even if the law spells out the obligations and rights of an office, a competent authority can further specify the obligations and rights for some offices; for example, the bishop can further specify for individual episcopal vicars (c. 479, §2), or particular law can modify the role of the diocesan chancellor (c. 482, §1).

An officeholder can be given further powers by delegation, but this is in addition to those responsibilities which belong to the office as such. For example, pastors are often delegated additional powers through "diocesan faculties" to carry out various functions over and above those specified for pastors in the canons (see cc. 528–534).

2. An ecclesiastical office must be constituted by divine or ecclesiastical ordinance.

"Ordinance" (in Latin, *ordinatio*) is a broader term than "law," although laws are an example of ordinances. Ordinances are also contained in some general executive acts (e.g., cc. 29–34) and in statutes (c. 94). Ordinances can have a divine origin (e.g., c. 113, §1); they can also arise from the customs of the community.[2]

Church offices are not created by secular authorities; neither are they created by private individuals or groups. They must have an appropriate canonical origin. This principle calls to mind the tensions of the lay investiture controversy which racked the Church in earlier centuries, and which was settled by emphasizing the Church's control over its own offices.

Commentators commonly list as offices arising from divine ordinance[3] the office of the Petrine ministry (pope), the college of bishops, and the office of diocesan bishop (although the creation of individual dioceses is a matter of ecclesiastical law). Other offices are considered to be constituted by ecclesiastical ordinance.

Some offices come into existence when the juridic structure they serve is created. So, when a diocese is erected, by that very fact the law constitutes the office of diocesan bishop for that diocese (c. 369). When a parish is erected, the law constitutes the office of pastor (c. 515). When the proper authority of a religious institute establishes a province (c. 621) or a house (c. 608), the law itself creates the corresponding office of superior.

Other offices come into existence either when a law creates them (for example, a diocesan law setting up an office of parish religious education

director), or when a competent authority establishes one by decree (e.g., the bishop issues a decree constituting the office of diocesan director of ministry to the handicapped).

3. An office is constituted in a stable manner.

"Stable" here can be understood both in an objective sense (i.e., the office itself continues, even when there is no officeholder) and in a subjective sense (i.e., the person named to the office holds it for a notable period of time).

The canon says an office is "constituted" in a stable manner. This is the objective sense of the term, and is in keeping with canonical tradition. An office is created to assure that a given function will continue in the Church, even after the initial officeholder departs. An office exists for the good of the Church and does not depend on the charisma or gifts of a particular officeholder. This is one of the differences between delegation, which is given to an individual, and an office, which has an existence beyond the individual who carries it out.

Although it is not stated in this canon, offices also entail some subjective stability or "tenure" on the part of the officeholder. Indeed, the Second Vatican Council emphasized this, calling an office a function "conferred" in a stable manner (*PO* 20). It does not make sense to structure a function as an office and then rotate officeholders as through a revolving door. Canon 193 indicates that there are three levels of subjective stability in canon law. Some officeholders are named for an indefinite period of time and in effect have "tenure" for life, e.g., pastors (c. 522). Other officeholders are named for a term, and enjoy stability in office during the length of that term, e.g., a pastor named for a term (c. 522); the diocesan finance officer (c. 494, §2); religious superiors (c. 624, §1); tribunal judges (c. 1422). Finally, there are officeholders who are named at the prudent discretion of the competent authority; but even these enjoy some stability in office, as seen in the discussion of canon 193 below.

Stability does not mean an office is perpetual. Some offices exist only for a time or for certain circumstances, such as those of a diocesan or

---

[2] Socha, in *Münster Com,* 145/2.
[3] *CCEO* 936, §1 terms it more personally, "by the Lord himself."

parish administrator (cc. 430, §1; 540), or that of an official of a synod of bishops (c. 347, §1).

When offices and benefices were so closely related, some offices were considered to be juridic persons.[4] This is no longer true. It is more appropriate to speak of an entity as being established as a juridic person, and an office as serving that entity. For example, a public association of the faithful is a juridic person, but the offices of the association are not juridic persons. Similarly, the office of diocesan bishop is at the service of and represents the juridic person which is the diocese (c. 393), but the office is not itself a juridic person.

4. An office is constituted for a spiritual purpose.

This is in keeping with the purpose of canon law, for the salvation of souls is the supreme law of the Church (c. 1752). Yet a spiritual purpose is not disembodied, as is clear from such mundane realities as temporal goods in the Church which exist for the spiritual purposes of providing for divine worship, the support of clergy and other ministers, and works of the apostolate and charity (c. 1254, §2).

Anyone who performs a function in the Church ultimately does it for a spiritual purpose, but not all such functions are constituted as offices. For example, workers can be employed without their work becoming an ecclesiastical office (see c. 1286). The Church relies on a variety of volunteers in carrying out its mission, but they are not necessarily appointed to an office. Clergy are ordained for a spiritual service in the Church (c. 1008), but do not as such hold an ecclesiastical office; office is distinct from sacred ordination. Lay persons can be admitted on a stable basis to the ministries of lector and acolyte, but in themselves these ministries do not constitute ecclesiastical offices (c. 230, §1). Other lay persons may supply for certain of the duties of ministers in the Church (c. 230, §3), but of itself this does not confer on them an ecclesiastical office.

When a function is constituted as an ecclesiastical office, the effect is that the person who performs that function for a spiritual purpose does so in the name of the Church. The spiritual purpose is provided not on the initiative of the individual, nor as a result of the person's charisma alone, but primarily as an act of the Church, for officeholders act in the name of the Church when they carry out Christ's priestly, prophetic, or royal functions in virtue of their office.[5]

For a function to be constituted as an ecclesiastical office, all four elements must be present: it must be a function, constituted in a stable manner, through divine or ecclesiastical ordinance, and for a spiritual purpose. It is not required, however, that the office involve the exercise of the power of orders or of governance.[6] Some offices are the source of financial support for the officeholder (see c. 195) although generally offices no longer include the element of a benefice (see c. 1274, §1).

Unresolved Issues

Several issues remain unresolved by the provisions of the code. Who is the authority competent to erect an office? To what extent are the obligations and rights of individual offices inviolable? What is the relationship in practice of office and delegation? Are some of the current "positions" in the Church ecclesiastical offices?

(1) Who is the authority competent to erect an office, for example, to constitute the position of parish religious education director as an ecclesiastical office? Certainly the bishop is competent to do this (see c. 381, §1). Can a vicar general, or an episcopal vicar, or even the pastor of a parish? This raises the issue of whether legislative power is needed to erect an office, or if executive power is sufficient.

The question is posed most acutely by canon 145, §2, which permits the obligations and rights

---

[4] See Arrieta, in *Com Ex,* 910–911; *Chiappetta Com 1996,* n. 1036.

[5] *Chiappetta Com 1996,* n. 1025, warns against the danger of bureaucratization which can compromise this spiritual dimension.

[6] This is a major change from the 1917 code, where the legal meaning of office required such participation.

for an office to be specified not only in a law, but also in a decree which both constitutes and confers the office. The word "decree" can be understood in two senses here: a decree which is a law (c. 29) and hence an ordinance of a legislator; and a decree which makes provision of an office (c. 48) and hence an act of someone with executive power.

It is not a question here of activating an office which is already provided for in the law, whether in the code or in particular law, or even in the proper law of an institute of consecrated life or the statutes of a public association. Rather, it is a question of creating a new office. Can an executive decree, such as the appointment to office, result in the creation of an office?

Most commentators on the 1983 code do not address this issue. Socha argues that whatever the kind of decree, it must have sufficient legal force for the office to have objective stability.[7] Hill, on the other hand, argues that it is an administrative, not a legislative, decree and creates a position with subjective stability but without the usual objective stability associated with ecclesiastical office; "it may never have another incumbent" and "is not intended as a permanent position."[8] Huysmans also holds that it is an administrative act, and says it results in either an altogether new type of office, or else an office of a type that happens only rarely in the Church.[9] Arrieta says it results in a true office with objective stability, but may be a temporary office.[10] The Eastern code does not provide much help; it drops the phrase describing the decree as one which both constitutes and confers the office.[11]

As discussed above, "ordinance" can include legislative acts, general executive acts, statutes, and customs. It would seem from this that a vicar general or an episcopal vicar, who enjoy executive power of governance (c. 134), could issue a general executive decree constituting an office and at the same time appointing the first office-holder. However, it is not clear that pastors enjoy that level of executive power.

(2) Can a diocesan bishop change the obligations and rights specified in the law for various offices, such as pastors? This is not a question of dispensing from disciplinary law, but of actually changing by decree the "obligations and rights proper to individual ecclesiastical offices" (c. 145, §2).

The practice has developed in some dioceses to limit the ministry of pastors in certain areas, either as standard policy (e.g., related to marriages), or on an individual basis. A distinction must be made here between regulating the exercise of rights, which ecclesiastical authority is competent to do in view of the common good (c. 223, §2), and the limits placed on lower level legislators against issuing laws contrary to a higher law (c. 135, §2). The bishop is not competent to change the code's listing of obligations and rights for an office, but he is competent to regulate their exercise.

(3) In practice, it can be difficult to distinguish an office from delegation. For example, because of the debate about whether lay persons can be appointed to certain types of offices in the Church (see c. 274, §1), some dioceses have configured their curia not with vicars (who exercise ordinary power in virtue of the office of episcopal vicar), but with "delegates" or "secretaries." These are functions established in a stable manner by the diocesan bishop, which are carried out for the same spiritual purpose for which the office of vicar might have been created.

In effect, these positions are ecclesiastical offices and not just delegation. They fulfill all the requirements of canon 145 for an office, and have been constituted by the competent ecclesiastical authority. Moreover, when the positions become vacant, they are considered "vacant" and not ter-

---

[7] Socha, in *Münster Com,* 145/2–3.

[8] Hill, in *CLSA Com,* 99.

[9] Huysmans, 309.

[10] Arrieta, in *Com Ex,* 918; he mistakenly includes as examples offices which are established by the law rather than by decree, but which are temporary.

[11] *CCEO* 936, §2. The same canon, §3, states that the authority which is competent to establish an office can modify or suppress it, but it does not specify how to determine what authority is competent.

minated, as would be the case with delegation properly so-called.

The officeholders, however, are not "vicars." Canon 478, §1 requires that vicars be priests. These new arrangements make it possible for those who are not priests to hold offices in the service of the diocese.

(4) The revised notion of ecclesiastical office found in the present code raises questions concerning various positions in the Church today. Are they offices? For example, under the previous code, commentators considered parochial vicars not to hold an office as such; under the present law, the position is considered an ecclesiastical office (cc. 545–552).

More difficult to determine is the position of a deacon, religious, or lay person who serves a parish in light of canon 517, §2. The only position mentioned in the canon is that of the priest moderator, which appears to be an office (the canon indicates the rights and duties of this priest). What of the person or persons he supervises? Although they serve "because of a lack of priests," their position is not by that fact unstable. It could be temporary, but as noted earlier, an ecclesiastical office can be temporary (e.g., a diocesan administrator who serves until a new bishop takes office). This may be an example of an office which is constituted and conferred in the letter of appointment.

Principals of Catholic schools and those who teach religion there are given special attention in the canons (see cc. 805–806). Do they hold an ecclesiastical office? The local ordinary has the right to name or approve religion teachers; their position is a stable one and is exercised for a spiritual purpose. It is not yet clear from practice whether these positions have the protections and obligations that come with ecclesiastical office.

Those who teach theology in institutes of higher learning, especially those bound to the profession of faith (c. 833, 7°) who now must also take the oath of fidelity, are considered by the latter document to be assuming an office. In some instances their posts may have been erected as ecclesiastical offices, for example, in countries with concordats regulating such positions. In other countries, colleges and universities which have not been erected as public juridic persons probably do not contain ecclesiastical offices in the strict sense, even for teachers of theology.

Significance of Office

What is the practical import of whether a position is an ecclesiastical office? There are several. First, erecting a position as an ecclesiastical office is a commitment by church officials to the people of God that this function is important enough to be assured on their behalf, even when the initial officeholder is no longer available. Second, as will be discussed below, the law sets various criteria for appointment to an ecclesiastical office. It also provides a procedure for appointment which assures that the criteria will be followed. Thus, the law assures the faithful that they will be served by competent ministers. Third, each office has its own "job description" or list of obligations and rights. An officeholder is assured the right to initiative and is held responsible for fulfilling this job description. That is, the officeholder is presumed to be free to do what is needed to carry out the obligations and rights of the office without need for further authorization, unless this is explicitly required (see c. 138: ordinary power is to be interpreted broadly). On the other hand, there are established expectations to which the officeholder can be held accountable by the proper church authorities. This safeguards both the officeholder and the interests of the community. Finally, the law establishes criteria and procedures for loss of office; it is not done at the whim of a superior. This safeguards the interests of both the officeholder and the community, as well as the concerns of higher authorities.[12]

If a position has not been erected as an office, are there any safeguards for people who perform

---

[12] *CCEO* 937 provides a further practical import, requiring that adequate means be available before erecting an office, both for the office's operations and to remunerate the officeholder.

these important services in the Church today?[13] One safeguard could be contracts, which in canon law generally have the same force as in secular law (c. 1290). Another approach could be a standard diocesan employment policy which incorporates the various safeguards the canons provide for ecclesiastical offices. But it can be questioned why parallel systems need to be developed, when canon law already provides a time-tested system of offices to provide for "human resources" in the Church's mission. If the system of ecclesiastical offices is not being respected in practice, there is little reason to hope that other systems will be effective either.

CHAPTER I
PROVISION OF ECCLESIASTICAL OFFICE
[cc. 146–183]

Chapter 1 of title IX deals with the provision or conferral of ecclesiastical offices. It states some general norms, and then details the various systems for conferring an office. The general norms deal with the need and systems for conferring an office, called "canonical provision" (cc. 146–147), the authority competent to make provision (c. 148), the qualifications needed to receive an office (c. 149), and some limitations in the conferral of office (c. 150–156).

GENERAL NORMS ON PROVISION
[cc. 146–156]

Canonical Provision

Canon 146 — An ecclesiastical office cannot be acquired validly without canonical provision.

This is a basic principle of canon law, formerly contained in the very notion of an ecclesiastical office (CIC 145, §1).[14] The former code even stat-

ed what constitutes provision of an office: "concession of an ecclesiastical office by a competent ecclesiastical authority according to the norms of the sacred canons" (CIC 147, §2).

Because canonical provision is required for validity, any attempt to exercise an office without having received it by canonical provision would be invalid. For example, a priest who tried to take over as pastor of a parish without a proper appointment would not validly assist at a marriage there (see c. 1109).

Canonical provision assures church control over church offices. Since an ecclesiastical office involves acting in the name of the Church, some intervention of church authority is required, whether immediately or remotely (e.g., through legislation approving various ways of making canonical provision).

Canon 147 — The provision of an ecclesiastical office is made: through free conferral by a competent ecclesiastical authority; through installation by the same authority if presentation preceded it; through confirmation or admission granted by the same authority if election or postulation preceded it; finally, through simple election and acceptance by the one elected if the election does not require confirmation.

There are three stages to acquiring an ecclesiastical office: the selection of the candidate, the conferral of the office, and taking possession of the office. This canon describes the various systems for the first two stages.[15]

In free conferral, the same person selects the candidate and confers the office. Presentation means one person selects the candidate(s), another confers the office. Election involves the selection of the candidate according to an electoral process, with conferral by another authority or, in certain cases in which confirmation of the election is not required, free acceptance by the one

---

[13] See P. Erdö, "Ministerium, munus et officium in Codice Iuris Canonici," P 78 (1989) 434–436.
[14] See also CCEO 938.

[15] CCEO 939 is similar but does not mention presentation; other Eastern code canons include presentation in practice (e.g., CCEO 284, §2, religious as pastors).

elected. Postulation is similar to election, but involves the need to dispense an impediment which the electors recognize even as they still desire the candidate. These four systems are discussed in detail below.

Most commentators consider this list to be taxative; i.e., these are the only ways in which canonical provision can take place. The final item in the listing in the canon begins with "finally" (in Latin, *tandem*), which normally indicates this is a closed list. Erdö has demonstrated, however, that the code itself contains other methods, for example, prescription for offices not involving the exercise of sacred orders (c. 199, 6°), or the immediate assumption of the office of administrator by persons so designated in the case of an impeded see (c. 413).[16] As Erdö points out, there appears to be a doubt of law here, and canonical provision by lawful means other than those listed in the canon would be valid in light of canon 14.

The key element in any system of provision is the actual conferral of the office, for at this stage one normally acquires the office (*ius in re*). Church authority is always involved at this stage, whether in actually conferring the office, in legislating a system whereby one acquires the office (for example, through accepting election), or in approving statutes in which an office is created.[17] Various systems of selection, such as presentation or an election which needs confirmation, give the candidate only a right to be named (*ius ad rem*), but not the office itself. The third element of conferral, taking possession, usually does not require any particular formality; this is needed only for certain offices involving more important pastoral responsibili-

ties.[18] In these cases, the office itself (*ius in re*) is acquired only when possession takes place.

Competent Authority

Canon 148 — The provision of offices is also the competence of the authority to whom it belongs to erect, change, and suppress them unless the law establishes otherwise.

"Competent authority" is a phrase used repeatedly in the code, but seldom specified. In this canon, it is specified by referring to the authority who is competent to erect, alter, or suppress an office; but this merely pushes the issue back one degree, without clarifying further the issue of competency.

In some cases competency is clear: the supreme church authority is competent to erect, alter, or suppress an episcopal conference, province, or diocese (cc. 449, §1; 431, §3; 373); the diocesan bishop for parishes (c. 515, §2); the superior specified in the constitutions for erecting various units of a religious institute (cc. 581; 609, §1); and so on. In other cases, as discussed above, there is some question as to the competence of those who do not possess legislative power, although it appears that ordinaries may be included among these competent authorities.

An office can be "erected" either by implementing provisions already existing in law (e.g., when the Holy See erects a diocese, or a diocesan bishop erects a parish) or by the creation of a new office not foreseen in existing law through the promulgation of a new law, the issuing of a decree by a competent authority, the development of a custom, etc.

To "alter" an office can mean to change the configuration of the office (e.g., change the boundaries of a diocese or parish, which changes

---

[16] P. Erdö, "Quaestiones quaedam de provisione officiorum in ecclesia," *P* 77 (1988) 363–379.

[17] For example, in the approval by a competent ecclesiastical authority of the statutes of a public juridic person (c. 117), or specifically of a public association of the faithful (cc. 312, 314) and of the constitutions of a religious institute (c. 587, §2). This would also include the statutes of a parish, which as a public juridic person is to have statutes approved by the competent ecclesiastical authority, but whose statutes could specify various offices within the parish, and who is competent to confer them.

[18] For example, diocesan bishop (c. 382, §2), coadjutor and auxiliary bishops (c. 404, §§1 and 2), pastor (c. 527), and the moderator of a pastoral team *in solidum* (c. 527). The formalities for taking possession of a parish can be dispensed (c. 527, §2).

the extent of the office of the diocese's bishop or parish's pastor—see c. 515, §2); it can also mean to change the obligations and rights which make up the office.[19] The common interpretation of "alter" in this context is to change the configuration or boundaries.

To "suppress" an office is either to suppress the entity which it serves (e.g., to close a parish involves suppression not only of the juridic person of the parish but also of the office of pastor of that parish) or to terminate an office which is not directly tied to such an entity (e.g., to suppress the office of diocesan director for some activity). Some offices are beyond the competence of the diocesan bishop to suppress, for example, the offices of vicar general, judicial vicar, chancellor, and diocesan finance officer (cc. 475, §1; 1420, §1; 482, §1; 494, §1). He is, however, competent to name these officials because this is specifically stated in the canons.

The "law establishes otherwise" in the cases just cited, and also, for example, in canon 509, which gives the diocesan bishop the right to name canons to a chapter of canons even though canon 504 reserves to the Apostolic See the erection, alteration, or suppression of a cathedral chapter. Similarly, a diocesan law could restrict to the diocesan bishop the erection, alteration, or suppression of the office of a parochial assistant (or parish religious education director, or some other parish office), but it could give the pastor the right to name people to these offices.

Those who claim a right to select the candidate, whether through presentation, election, or postulation, have the burden of proof, since theirs is an exception to the general principle stated in this canon.[20]

---

[19] Only the supreme authority can change the body of obligations and rights set by the general law of the Church for an office (e.g., diocesan bishop or parish pastor). Other offices, which are created by particular law, custom, or decree of a competent authority, can be altered by that same authority through combining them, dividing them, or in other ways redesignating the obligations and rights which pertain to those offices.

[20] Hill, in *CLSA Com*, 100.

Qualifications for Office

Canon 149 — §1. To be promoted to an ecclesiastical office, a person must be in the communion of the Church as well as suitable, that is, endowed with those qualities which are required for that office by universal or particular law or by the law of the foundation.

§2. Provision of an ecclesiastical office made to one who lacks the requisite qualities is invalid only if the qualities are expressly required for the validity of the provision by universal or particular law or by the law of the foundation. Otherwise it is valid but can be rescinded by decree of competent authority or by sentence of an administrative tribunal.

§3. Provision of an office made as a result of simony is invalid by the law itself.

The canon sets two general criteria for determining the suitability of a person for ecclesiastical office, leaving to the detailed norms governing individual offices the listing of more specific qualifications. It then discusses what happens when the individual lacks the required qualities. Finally, it addresses the problem of simony.

Communion

The canon requires the person to be "in the communion of the Church." It does not specify what this involves.[21]

Negatively, the candidate must not be under a declared or imposed penalty of excommunication; this renders the exercise of an office invalid (c. 1331, §2, 4°). Similarly, the candidate must not have publicly abandoned the Catholic faith or the Church's communion, for this entails the ipso facto loss of office (c. 194, §1, 2°).

---

[21] See discussion in Arrieta, *Com Ex*, 931; *Chiappetta Com 1996*, nn. 1049–1050. For a contrary opinion, see Socha, in *Münster Com*, 149/2.

CCEO 940, §1 makes no mention of communion as a required quality for provision of office.

Positively, something more than the mere fact of being baptized is needed. An office is exercised on behalf of the Church, so an officeholder must have a positive commitment to the Church. Many commentators take this to mean the person must be a Catholic in "full communion";[22] but the text of the canon does not call for this and a more nuanced view is needed.

First, the canon sets a qualification for candidates which limits the free choice of those who make provision for office; because it is a limitation on their right, the canon is subject to a strict interpretation (see c. 18). Second, the text of the canon itself does not say "full communion" and a strict interpretation must stay with the wording of the text. Third, some canons do require full communion as a qualification for office; e.g., member of a diocesan pastoral council (c. 512, §1), or advocate in a tribunal (c. 1483, which requires the advocate to be a "Catholic" unless the diocesan bishop permits otherwise). If some canons call for full communion as a qualification for office, then the communion required for other offices need not be "full."[23]

Arrieta points out that the degree of communion may vary depending on the office.[24] For example, some offices require the profession of faith (c. 833). Others can be exercised only in hierarchical communion (e.g., cc. 336; 375, §2). Offices which entail the full care of souls can be held only by priests (c. 150).

But could a bishop name a non-Catholic Christian to a diocesan office for which the person is suited (e.g., finance officer or member of the diocesan finance council) if that person is committed to carry out the work in keeping with the bishop's directives and according to the norms of church law? In contrast to the norms on pastoral councils, which require that the lay members be "in full communion with the Catholic Church," members of the diocesan finance council are characterized only as "Christian faithful" without the further requirement of full communion.

Moreover, as disciplinary, non-constitutive law, this qualification can be dispensed in individual cases by the diocesan bishop to permit non-Catholics and even qualified non-Christians to hold an individual ecclesiastical office, provided there is a sufficient reason to do so (see c. 87, §1) and it is not a situation involving procedural law (although, as noted above, procedural law gives the bishop the authority to permit non-Catholics to be named advocates). However, an officeholder acts in the name of the Church and the usual experience is that Catholics are named to offices in the Catholic Church. In the exceptional situation when a non-Catholic is named to an office, it must be clear that the person is informed about the Catholic Church and committed to carry out the office in an appropriate manner.[25]

Suitable

The other qualities required by universal law in general are quite broad. Some offices require priestly orders (c. 150) or sacred orders (c. 199, 6°). There is the question of offices which entail the exercise of the power of governance, which canon 274, §1 says only clergy are capable of receiving, but this restriction is open to question in

---

[22] In addition to Socha, see Aymans, 460; García Martín, 492–493; Huysmans, 314; Manzanares, in *Salamanca Com,* 114; McGrath, in *CLSGBI Com,* 88; and Urrutia, n. 809. Some take it as evident that "full communion" is meant, or cite another commentator in support of their position. Others give reasons; see Socha (cites analogous canons in the code), García Martín (only those in full communion are subject to ecclesiastical law, c. 11), and Manzanares (office serves the communion). Urrutia, however, holds that full communion is only for the liceity, not the validity, of the appointment.

[23] For discussion of "full communion," see c. 205.

[24] Arrieta, in *Com Ex,* 931.

[25] A parallel situation is that of a non-Catholic named to a teaching position on an ecclesiastical faculty. Although a non-Catholic is not given a *missio canonica* but a *venia docendi,* it is likely that faculty positions in these institutions are ecclesiastical offices. On the appointment of non-Catholic teachers, see *SCCE,* "Ordinationes ad Constitutionem Apostolicam 'Sapientia Christiana,'" April 29, 1979, art. 18, *AAS* 71 (1979) 505.

light of exceptions within the law itself (e.g., lay persons can hold the office of judge on an ecclesiastical tribunal; c. 1421, §2). Other qualifications in universal law are set down for individual offices, e.g., bishop (c. 378, §1), pastor (c. 521), parochial vicar (c. 546), religious superior (c. 623), novice director (c. 651, §1), diocesan finance officials (cc. 492, §1 and 494, §1), tribunal officials (cc. 1420, §4; 1421, §3; 1435), etc. But frequently the specifics are left either to the prudential judgment of the superior who is making canonical provision, or to particular or proper law, the law of foundation, or the statutes.

The most common types of qualifications in the code deal with age and experience, academic qualifications or equivalent expertise, character and reputation, and length of time in an organization or in a specific sacred order. There are also restrictions based on blood relationship (e.g., cc. 478, §2 and 492, §3).

The "law of the foundation" is the law established when an office is set up. If it is connected to an ecclesiastical foundation, see canons 1299–1310. Otherwise, the "law of the foundation" is frequently found in the statutes for the office or for the entity it serves (e.g., a public association of the faithful).

Qualifications Missing

Two possibilities are foreseen in canon 149, §2: the qualifications for an office are expressly required for validity, or they are not required for validity. Appointment of a person who lacks the qualifications expressly required for validity is invalid; otherwise, the appointment of a person lacking the qualifications is valid, but it can be rescinded.

Only in a few canons are qualifications for an office expressly and explicitly required for valid appointment.[26] Negatively, a person under a declared or imposed excommunication cannot validly acquire an office (as stated expressly in c. 1331, §2, 4°; see discussion above concerning communion).

In canonical tradition, however, an express requirement can also be stated implicitly (see discussion at c. 10). Here a number of questions arise. How does one determine an implicit but express requirement of a qualification for valid appointment to office? When several qualifications are listed, are all for validity, or are only some, and how can one tell these apart?

Consider the qualifications for judges on a diocesan tribunal (cc. 1420–1421). The judicial vicars and their adjutants "must" (*esse debent*) have certain qualifications (priestly orders, unimpaired reputation, degree in canon law, at least thirty years old). In contrast, other judges "are to be" (*sint*) of unimpaired reputation and degreed in canon law. Are any, some, or all of these qualifications for validity? "Valid" is not explicitly stated in the canons; is validity at least implied by the verb "must"? Can it be found implicitly in the subjunctive "are to be"?[27]

A more difficult problem is posed regarding other offices, such as a bishop's vicars. These exercise the power of governance by office, so theoretically must be priests (c. 274, §1), although, as just noted, this canon admits of exceptions and there may even be a doubt of law as to whether it binds for validity.[28] Although some have held that the bishop's vicars exercise the full care of souls and so must be priests in virtue of canon 150,[29] vicars general and episcopal vicars are limited to the external forum (c. 478, §2) and do not have by office all the authorizations and responsibilities involved in the full care of souls (e.g., Mass for the people, sacrament of anointing). But when the qualifications for a bishop's vicars are given (c. 478, §1), "valid" is not expressly stated explicitly, and the

---

[26] For example, see cc. 150; 425, §1; 521,§1; 546; 623.

[27] This is not only a question of whether the judges have degrees in canon law; but on that topic, see G. Read, "At Least a Licentiate in Canon Law," *CLS-GBIN* n. 61 (June 1984) 34–36, and the criticism of his views by J. Beyer, "Iudex laicus vir vel mulier," *P* 75 (1986) 34–35.

[28] See also c. 129, where clergy are "qualified" and lay persons "can cooperate" in the exercise of the power of governance.

[29] For example, J. Alesandro, in *CLSA Com,* 389, cites c. 150 as a reason why vicars must be priests.

verb form ("are to be"—*sint*) appears weak in terms of an implicit requirement for validity.[30]

These issues should be resolved in each case, keeping in mind the intent of the canon which presumes that an appointment to office is valid unless a missing qualification is expressly required for validity, in accordance with the intent of the revision of the code, which was to reduce the number of invalidating laws.[31]

Effects of Qualifications Missing

If the missing qualification was for validity, the conferral of the office was invalid. Any actions taken in virtue of the office would themselves be invalid. For example, a pastor who lacked a qualification required for valid appointment would not validly assist at marriages in virtue of his office.[32] The actions of a finance officer, religious superior, tribunal judge, etc., taken in virtue of the office, would be invalid if the appointee lacked a qualification required for validity.

If the missing qualification was not required for validity, the appointment is valid and whatever the officeholder did in virtue of the office would itself be valid. However, because of the missing qualification the appointment could be rescinded. The canon lists two ways in which this could happen.

The first is a decree of a competent authority. The competent authority could be the one who conferred the office, or that person's superior, or even the Apostolic See (in virtue of papal primacy). This is not a removal from office but a declaration that the appointment is rescinded due to a missing qualification. It therefore is not subject to the procedures and causes listed in canon 193, but the au-

thority would have to follow the provisions of canons 50–51 and 54 on administrative acts. The lack of qualification could be brought to the competent authority's attention by others (see cc. 57; 212, §§2–3), or may be initiated by the authority.

The second method of rescinding the appointment of someone lacking a qualification for an office is the decision of an administrative tribunal. This provision could be a remnant of the system of administrative tribunals proposed in drafting the code but dropped before its promulgation.[33] On the other hand, it could be the basis of competence for administrative tribunals if they are established by competent authority in dioceses or larger jurisdictions. The only existing administrative tribunal is the Apostolic Signatura.[34]

Simony

Simony is the attempt to buy or sell spiritual things for material benefit. It can be carried out by the one seeking the office, the one conferring the office, or a third party unknown to the recipient. The simony could be active or passive.[35] It is, in effect, an attempt at bribery.

Simony should not be confused with paying a tax or fee for administrative expenses, or with the gift of a donor establishing a new foundation or office. However, care must be taken that the gift is truly for the office, and not an attempt to purchase the position for a given individual.[36]

Limitations in Conferral of Offices

Several limitations or restrictions are placed on those conferring offices. These are based on whether

---

[30] In practice, bishops generally deal with this situation by naming as "secretaries" or "delegates" those who are not priests but carry out responsibilities which might otherwise be done by episcopal vicars.

[31] See Principle 3 for the revision of the code; see also discussion in García Martín, 72.

[32] However, if the diocesan faculties also included delegation from the bishop to assist at any marriages within the diocese, the priest's assistance at a marriage would be valid by that fact.

[33] This might be inferred from the Eastern code, where there is no mention of administrative tribunals in this context; see *CCEO* 940, §2.

[34] See *PB*, art. 123, §3. Prior to *PB* the Second Section of the Signatura was referred to as an administrative tribunal; see *RE*, art. 106–107.

[35] García Martín, 498.

[36] In addition to simony, *CCEO* 946 declares null any provision of office made because of serious fear unjustly inflicted, fraud, or substantial error.

the office entails the care of souls (cc. 150–151); the burden of work involved (c. 152); the availability of the office (cc. 153–154); the effect of supplying for another (c. 155); and the written form for provision (c. 156).

Offices with Care of Souls

The "care of souls" refers to the pastoral activity of the Church to teach, sanctify, and govern the people of God. While the ultimate purpose of church law is the salvation of souls, the "care" of souls is the official activity whereby authorized persons provide ministry to people with a view to their salvation.

The care can be "full" or partial. Offices with the full care of souls encompass the full pastoral work of the Church at the appropriate level, carried out by diocesan bishops for their dioceses, pastors for their parishes, and some chaplains for specialized groups of people (c. 564).[37] This care is addressed to believers and non-believers (c. 771, §2). Other offices share in this pastoral care in part, although they do not entail the "full" care of souls (for example, coadjutor and auxiliary bishops [c. 407 §3], parochial vicars [545, §1], deacons and lay persons involved in the care of souls [c. 517, §2], some chaplains [c. 564]).[38]

The concept of an office with the care of souls is used to set a qualification for appointment to some offices (c. 150), and an expectation concerning the time limit in filling any offices with the care of souls (c. 151).

Canon 150 — An office which entails the full care of souls and for whose fulfillment the exercise of the priestly order is required cannot be conferred validly on one who is not yet a priest.

This is an example of a qualification expressly and explicitly required for valid appointment to an office. It is limited to offices with the full care of souls; it does not limit who can be appointed to offices involved with partial care of souls (e.g., c. 517, §2). It is in addition to whatever other qualifications may be stated in law (e.g., cc. 378, §1; 521, §2), and is repeated expressly for pastors of parishes (c. 521, §1).

The clause "for whose fulfillment the exercise of the priestly order is required" explains and specifies the meaning of an office entailing the full care of souls. Because priestly orders are required to fulfill the office as such, only those who have been ordained priests can be named to such offices. Deacons, including those about to be ordained priests, cannot be named to such an office until they have received priestly ordination.[39]

Canon 151 — The provision of an office which entails the care of souls is not to be deferred without a grave cause.

The implication of this canon is that these are the most important offices in the Church; provision of other offices can be deferred, but not these, unless there is a grave cause.[40]

The canon applies to any system for the provision of these offices, including free conferral, presentation, and election.[41]

No specific standard of time is set by the canon. The office must not be filled precipitously, for it is necessary to attend to what is needed for

---

[37] Socha, in *Münster Com,* 150/3–4, includes as well those who are equivalent in law to a diocesan bishop (see c. 368), the pastor of a quasi-parish (c. 516), and possibly the bishop of a military ordinariate (*SMC,* n. 11, §1, *AAS* 78 [1986] 483) and a parish administrator (in the sense of c. 540, §1).

[38] Socha, in *Münster Com,* 150/4–5, also lists vicars general and episcopal vicars (c. 473, §2), members of the chapter of canons (c. 503), the canon penitentiary or the priest with his function (c. 508), vicars forane (c. 555), chaplains for students (c. 813), rectors of churches (c. 556), superiors in institutes of consecrated life or societies of apostolic life (cc. 618–619, 717, 734), missionaries (c. 784), etc.

[39] *Chiappetta Com 1996,* n. 1056, lists offices for which presbyteral orders are required, whether with full care of souls or not.

[40] *CCEO* 941 uses a different standard: offices conferred without a term are not to be deferred.

[41] Manzanares, in *Salamanca Com,* 115; Socha, in *Münster Com,* 151/1–2.

the care of souls (which is the primary consideration). For example, it takes time to conduct the consultation mandated prior to appointing bishops (c. 377, §3) or pastors (c. 524).

On the other hand, some canons require action within three months at least to propose one or more candidates for any office (by presentation, election, or postulation; see cc. 158, §1; 165). Many commentators argue that the conferral of the office itself must take place within three months after the presentation, election, or postulation; otherwise, recourse can be taken to a higher authority in virtue of canons 57 and 1734–1739.

In the case of a diocesan administrator, "deferral" is limited to a maximum of eight days or the college which is to elect loses its right to do so for that time (c. 421, §1).

The canon includes the possibility of an exception for a "grave cause." Who determines when a cause is grave? If the provision is by a competent authority, that person decides. If a group is to make the provision (e.g., by presentation or election), the authority who is to supply for their inaction is competent to determine if there is a "grave cause."

The gravity of the cause depends on the office to be filled and the care of souls it entails. Examples could include a lack of qualified candidates or a shortage of priests for offices requiring priestly orders.[42]

There is no immediate sanction for not complying with this canon. In the former code, if the time limit was not met, the right to appoint for some offices devolved to a higher authority.[43] This is no longer the case. Failure to comply with this canon does not affect the validity of an appointment, but could constitute negligence of office (see c. 1389, §2).

Incompatible Offices

Canon 152 — Two or more incompatible offices, that is, offices which together cannot be fulfilled

at the same time by the same person, are not to be conferred upon one person.

Generally speaking, incompatibility depends on the officeholder; what is too much for a given person to take on becomes incompatible. The inability to fulfill the several offices could be for various reasons, such as the impossibility of being in two places at the same time,[44] personal conditions of physical or mental health, language requirements, etc.

However, the law does establish some offices as incompatible. For example, the same person cannot be at the same time the diocesan administrator and the diocesan finance officer (c. 423, §2); vicar general or episcopal vicar, and canon penitentiary (c. 478, §2); major superior and provincial finance officer (c. 636, §1); promoter of justice and defender of the bond in the same case (c. 1436, §1); judge or assessor in a subsequent instance if the person acted in any of several capacities in an earlier instance (c. 1447).[45]

Appointment to incompatible offices, however, does not affect the validity of the appointment. The new appointment is valid, but it could be rescinded in light of canon 149, §2.[46] The fact of in-

---

[42] McGrath, in *CLSGBI Com*, 89; Socha, in *Münster Com*, 151/2.

[43] Arrieta, in *Com Ex*, 937.

[44] Diocesan bishops (c. 395, §1) and pastors (c. 533, §1) are to reside in their respective places; this would seem to prohibit being bishop of two dioceses, or pastor of two parishes, at the same time. But the Apostolic See dispenses to permit the first, and the law authorizes the bishop to permit exceptions to residence (c. 533, §1) and thus makes possible the second.

[45] García Martín, 502, and Socha, in *Münster Com*, 151/1–2, also list seminary rector and spiritual director (c. 239, §§1–2), and major superior and novice master (cc. 620, 651 §3) as incompatible. They also consider the ineligibility of relatives of the bishop for certain offices to be a type of incompatibility, although strictly speaking this does not involve two offices for the same person.

[46] Manzanares, in *Salamanca Com*, 155, holds that the earlier office is lost when the incompatible office is assumed; this was true under the 1917 code, but is no longer the case. McGrath, in *CLSGBI Com*, 90, agreeing that incompatibility does not affect validity, notes that it is hard to see how it does not. On the other hand, *CCEO* 942 permits appointment to incompatible offices in a case of "real necessity."

compatibility in the sense of too much for a particular person to take on would be a legitimate impediment leading a cleric to decline an appointment by his bishop (c. 274, §2).

Vacant Offices

An office is vacant when there is no officeholder. The vacancy can be by law (*de iure*), in which case there is no one with a legal claim to the office; and by fact (*de facto*), in which case there is no one who actually is holding the office.

Canon 153 — §1. The provision of an office which by law is not vacant is by that fact invalid and is not validated by subsequent vacancy.

§2. Nevertheless, if it concerns an office which by law is conferred for a determined period of time, provision can be made within six months before the expiration of this time and takes effect from the day of the vacancy of the office.

§3. A promise of some office, no matter by whom it is made, produces no juridic effect.

The first paragraph states the general rule which affects the validity of provision: the office must be vacant by law (*de iure*) in order to make provision of it. An attempt to provide someone with an office before it is legally vacant is not corrected by a subsequent vacancy; a new provision would be needed.

The second paragraph provides for an exception to the general rule. If the office is held for a limited term,[47] a new officeholder can be named six months or less before the end of the current term and takes over when the current term ends. For example, within six months of the end of the term of a pastor, his replacement can be named; similarly, a new religious superior can be named or elected within six months of the current superior's end of term.[48] The office becomes vacant and

the new officeholder takes over when the competent authority communicates the term's end in writing (c. 186).

The Apostolic Signatura has ruled that the transfer of several pastors (serving without a term) which was to take place simultaneously on the same day was invalid because the offices were not vacant at the time the appointments were made.[49] Such a system for appointments is not uncommon. These could be considered promises until the date of effectiveness. Since a promise has no effect (§3), the appointment could be changed without any formalities until the date of effectiveness. Or this may be a situation where competent authority prescribes otherwise in a transfer (see c. 191, §1).

Canon 154 — An office vacant by law, which may still be possessed illegitimately by someone, can be conferred provided that it has been declared properly that the possession is not legitimate and mention of this declaration is made in the letter of conferral.

Two actions are required. The declaration of illegitimate possession would resolve any questions about possession in good faith leading up to prescription for an office not requiring priestly orders (cc. 198, 199, 6°). The mention of *de facto* possession in the letter of conferral prevents the new officeholder from any surprises. Some authors consider this mention to be required for validity of the appointment, but it is only for liceity.[50]

Supplying for Another

Canon 155 — A person who confers an office in the place of another who is negligent or impeded

---

[47] On the concept of limited term, see discussion at c. 186.

[48] Hill, in *CLSA Com,* 101, points out that dispensation by the Apostolic See is possible for provisions prior to the six months.

[49] McGrath, in *CLSGBI Com,* 90, discusses the principles involved.

[50] For example, *Chiappetta Com 1996,* n. 1065; Hill, in *CLSA Com,* 101; and McGrath, in *CLSGBI Com,* 91, say it is for validity. But the "provided that" (*dummodo*) is in the canon, not in an administrative act (where it would have an invalidating effect—c. 39); see Arrieta, in *Com Ex,* 946; García Martín, 505–506; Urrutia, n. 818.

acquires no power thereafter over the person upon whom the office was conferred. The juridic condition of that person, however, is established just as if the provision had been completed according to the ordinary norm of law.

The negligence can be due to an inability to act (ill, exiled, or prohibited from exercising office [e.g., c. 415]), or division within an electoral body, or simple failure to act. The general law permits supplying for negligence when the time limits are not met in presentations (c. 162), elections (c. 165), or postulation (c. 182, §2). It may also happen if a competent authority fails to act in time and recourse is taken to a superior (c. 57).

The purpose of the canon is to clarify that the one who supplies does not by that fact acquire any authority over the officeholder, who remains subject to the usual hierarchical order as if the provision happened properly.

In Writing

Canon 156 — The provision of any office is to be put in writing.

This provides proof of the provision. Most commentators do not consider it necessary for the validity of the provision itself, but there are important arguments that appointment is not effective until the appointee is notified in writing.[51]

ARTICLE 1: FREE CONFERRAL
[c. 157]

Canon 157 — Unless the law explicitly establishes otherwise, it is for the diocesan bishop to provide for ecclesiastical offices in his own particular church by free conferral.

In free conferral, the same authority selects the candidate and confers the office. The canon applies this to diocesan offices, where the diocesan bishop and those equivalent to him in law (but not other local ordinaries unless otherwise specified[52]) is presumed to exercise free conferral within his church.

The general law contains various exceptions. Some pastors are named through presentation or election (c. 523; for example, the pastor of a parish committed to religious); at least about half the members of the presbyteral council are elected (c. 497, 1°). Particular law and the law of foundation can set other exceptions.

Before deciding on a candidate for some offices the bishop is to consult others but he retains free conferral; e.g., diocesan finance officer (c. 494, §1), canons of the cathedral chapter (c. 509, §1), naming of pastors (c. 524); naming a religious to a diocesan office (c. 682, §1).

Free conferral is also exercised by the Roman Pontiff (e.g., c. 377, §1 for naming bishops), and by religious superiors in keeping with their proper law (e.g., c. 625, §3 on naming of other superiors by the supreme moderator).[53]

Once named by free conferral, the person acquires the right to the office (*ius ad rem*) and the office itself (*ius in re*), unless, as for offices such as pastor (c. 527), one must take possession to have the office in full right (*ius in re*).

ARTICLE 2: PRESENTATION
[cc. 158–163]

In free conferral, one person or group has the right to select one or more candidates, but a separate competent authority installs (confers) the office. Examples include a diocesan bishop submit-

---

[51] García Martín, 507, argues that it is required for validity by c. 54, §2; *Chiappetta Com 1996,* n. 1067, points out that curial acts of an ordinary must be signed to be valid (c. 474).

[52] See cc. 565 (chaplains), 805 (religion teachers), and 830 (censors of books) for exceptions where local ordinaries exercise free conferral.

[53] See *Chiappetta Com 1996,* nn. 1070–1080, for lists of who freely confers which offices in a diocese.

ting three names for auxiliary bishop (c. 377, §4), or a religious superior presenting candidates for a diocesan office such as pastor (c. 682, §1).

Canon 158 — §1. Presentation for an ecclesiastical office by a person who has the right of presentation must be made to the authority to whom it belongs to install in that office. Moreover, this must be done within three months from notice of the vacancy of the office unless other provision has been made legitimately.

§2. If some college or group of persons has the right of presentation, the person to be presented is to be designated according to the prescripts of cann. 165–179.

The first rule here is that presentation is made to the person competent to confer the office (see c. 148). Presentation gives the candidate no right to the office (no *ius ad rem*), but does limit the competent authority to considering only the candidate(s) presented.

The second rule is that presentation must be made within three months of notice of vacancy.[54] Exceptions must be "legitimate"; i.e., by law or custom. The law permits an additional month if the candidate refuses (c. 161). There is no time limit set for installing (conferring) the office by competent authority, but failure to act after three months gives rise to the situation of canon 57.

The third rule in the canon applies to groups which have the right to present; they are to select the candidate as if it were an election, although the one thus chosen does not acquire any right to the office, since it is a presentation. No norm is given for how an individual is to select a candidate, but particular law, the law of foundation, or the statutes can require consultations and other processes.

Canon 159 — No one is to be presented unwillingly; therefore, a person who is proposed for

presentation and questioned about his or her intention can be presented unless the person declines within eight useful days.

This is a case when silence is understood as consent. It applies only to whether the name can be submitted; the person can still decline the installation (c. 161, §2). To compute "useful time," see canon 201, §2.

Canon 160 — §1. The person who possesses the right of presentation can present one or even several persons, either at the same time or successively.

§2. No one can present oneself; a college or group of persons, however, can present one of its own members.

Presentation can be of one or several persons. If of several persons, they can be named all at the same time, or in successive times. Proposing other names after the first does not mean the first is withdrawn, or that the first has necessarily been refused; but it does give the competent authority a choice among those presented (see c. 163).[55]

Canon 161 — §1. Unless the law establishes otherwise, a person who has presented one found unsuitable can present another candidate within a month, but once more only.

§2. If the person presented renounces or dies before the installation, the one who has the right of presentation can exercise this right again within a month from the notice of the renunciation or death.

There are three situations in which the three-month time limit is extended. The first is when the candidate has been found unsuitable by the competent authority.[56] The second is when the

---

[54] In light of c. 162, García Martín, 514, and Socha, in *Münster Com,* 158/2, clarify that this is "useful time" (see c. 201, §2).

[55] Although one cannot present one's self for an office, *Chiappetta Com 1996,* n. 1097, describes how exceptions could be worked out.

[56] Recourse is possible against this judgment (see c. 1734) which suspends the time because it suspends the execution of the decree.

candidate declines to be installed. The third is when the candidate dies before installation. In each case, an additional month is given in which to present a new candidate. The following canon characterizes this month as "useful time."

Canon 162 — A person who has not made presentation within the useful time according to the norm of can. 158, §1 and can. 161 as well as one who has twice presented an unsuitable person loses the right of presentation for that case. The authority to whom it belongs to install freely provides for the vacant office, with the assent, however, of the proper ordinary of the person appointed.

This canon enforces the time limits for presentation, but also respects the rights of ordinaries and religious superiors. For example, if a religious superior has failed to meet the time limits, or has twice presented two unsuitable candidates for pastor of a religious parish, the bishop has the right to free conferral for the religious parish this one time. But the bishop has to obtain the assent of the religious superior if he names one of the institute's members as pastor.

Canon 163 — The authority competent to install the person presented according to the norm of law is to install the one legitimately presented whom the authority has found suitable and who has accepted. If several persons legitimately presented have been found suitable, the authority must install one of them.

Installation by the competent authority completes the provision of office by presentation. It involves three steps by the competent authority: determination of the candidate's suitability (see c. 149); determination that the candidate is willing; and the actual installation or conferral of the office, which is to be in writing (c. 156). If several candidates were presented, the competent authority must select which one to install from among those who are suitable and willing. The candidate acquires the right to the office (*ius ad rem*) and

the office itself (*ius in re*), unless, as for offices such as pastor (c. 527), one must take possession to have the office in full right (*ius in re*).[57]

ARTICLE 3: ELECTION
[cc. 164–179]

Through election, an electoral body selects the candidate for an office. The elected person obtains the office either by accepting the election, if no confirmation is needed,[58] or by being confirmed by a competent authority.

Canon 164 — Unless the law has provided otherwise, the prescripts of the following canons are to be observed in canonical elections.

The first place to look for how to conduct an election is in the statutes, proper law, and particular law governing an electoral body. The canons in this article are obligatory for situations not otherwise resolved by the electoral body's own law. This point is repeated in several canons which follow (cc. 165, 167, 174, 176, 179).

Convening the Electors

Canon 165 — Unless the law or the legitimate statutes of a college or group have provided otherwise, if a college or group of persons has the right of election to office, the election is not to be delayed beyond three months of useful time computed from the notice of the vacancy of the office. If this limit has passed without action, the ecclesiastical authority who has the right of confirming the election or the right of providing for the office successively is to make provision freely for the vacant office.

---

[57] *Chiappetta Com 1996,* nn. 1108–1113, lists possible presentations in the code, how the right of presentation can cease definitively, and how it can be suspended.

[58] For example, the Roman Pontiff (c. 332, §1), diocesan administrator (c. 427, §2), supreme moderators of various religious institutes (c. 625, §1).

If a shorter or longer time is not set by the electoral body's own law or other law, it must act within three months ("useful time") of notice of a vacancy to conduct the election or risk losing the right to elect for this time. The competent authority to confirm some elections is given in the code;[59] others are set in proper law. For some offices which do not need confirmation, the law specifies who is to make the provision called for in this canon.[60]

Where the vacancy has not yet occurred, the convocation and election would both be invalid,[61] unless it were a case of an office whose term will run out in six months (c. 153, §2).

Canon 166 — §1. The person presiding over a college or group is to convoke all those belonging to the college or group; the notice of convocation, however, when it must be personal, is valid if it is given in the place of domicile or quasi-domicile or in the place of residence.

§2. If anyone of those to be convoked was overlooked and for that reason was absent, the election is valid. Nevertheless, at the instance of that same person and when the oversight and absence have been proved, the election must be rescinded by the competent authority even if it has been confirmed, provided that it is evident juridically that recourse had been made at least within three days from the notice of the election.

§3. If more than one-third of the electors were overlooked, however, the election is null by the law itself unless all those overlooked were in fact present.

Convocation is by the one who presides according to the group's statutes or the law, or who is otherwise specified in law (e.g., c. 419). The group's rules may specify how convocation is to be made (personally, or by notice, edict, etc.). The convocation is to include the reason why the group is being convened, and the time and place it will meet (c. 167, §1).

All belonging to the college or group are to be convoked, although some commentators argue that it is not necessary to convoke some.[62] If one-third or less are not called, the election is valid but rescindable (§2); if more than one-third are not convoked, the election is invalid by the law itself (§3). In either case, if the persons who were not convoked actually are present, the election is valid and not rescindable.

Individuals who were overlooked and not present for the election have three days from notice of the election to have recourse. It will be necessary to prove that they should have been convoked, were overlooked, were not present, and have made recourse within three days of notice of the election itself. Recourse is to be made to the authority competent to confirm the election; if the election did not need confirmation, recourse is to the authority to whom the group is subject. If the facts are proven, the authority has no choice but to rescind the election.

Canon 167 — §1. When the notice of the convocation has been given legitimately, those present on the day and at the place determined in the same notice have the right to vote. The faculty of voting by letter or proxy is excluded unless the statutes legitimately provide otherwise.

§2. If one of the electors is present in the house where the election occurs but cannot be present at the election due to ill health, his or her written vote is to be sought by the tellers.

Canon 168 — Even if a person has the right to vote in his or her own name under several titles, the person can vote only once.

---

[59] See, for example, cc. 317, §1; 352; 509, §1.

[60] See, e.g., c. 421. In contrast, no competent authority is specified for failure to act in other situations; see cc. 413, §2 and 452, §1.

[61] García Martín, 521.

[62] García Martín, 524: various members who cannot vote need not be called; Urrutia, n. 835: those certainly impeded (c. 167, §2) or who are not capable of voting (c. 171) need not be called. This affects who is to be included among those "to be convoked" in paragraph two or the total number used to determine the number of electors in paragraph three; the group's statutes should clarify the issue.

Elections to an office normally are held in a place designated in the convocation. The statutes could provide for other arrangements (e.g., ballot by mail).

Likewise, unless otherwise specified, the quorum for an election is a majority (over half) of those who must be convoked (c. 119, 1°).

To vote, one must be present in the place at the time of the election. Thus, proxy votes are not usually allowed, although the statutes could provide for them.[63] However, if an elector is ill and not able to come to the room where the election is held but is in the house where the election is held (or in a house attached to that building or at least on the same grounds[64]), the tellers can go to the person for a written ballot.

Only one vote per person is allowed, even if an elector holds several positions which would give the right to vote.[65] On the other hand, if an elector who is present also exercises proxy votes for others, the same person could cast in addition as many ballots as proxies.

Validity of the Election

Canon 169 — For an election to be valid, no one can be admitted to vote who does not belong to the college or group.

Canon 170 — An election whose freedom actually has been impeded in any way is invalid by the law itself.

In these two cases the election itself is invalid. Persons other than the electors can be present for the election, but they cannot vote nor can they impede the freedom of the election itself.

The impairment of freedom is of the electoral group as such; it invalidates if it truly exists and is not just a threat, no matter how the impediment occurs.[66] Anyone who impairs the freedom of an election can be punished in keeping with canon 1375.

Validity of the Vote

Canon 171 — §1. The following are unqualified to vote:
  1° a person incapable of a human act;
  2° a person who lacks active voice;
  3° a person under a penalty of excommunication whether through a judicial sentence or through a decree by which a penalty is imposed or declared;
  4° a person who has defected notoriously from the communion of the Church.
  §2. If one of the above is admitted, the person's vote is null, but the election is valid unless it is evident that, with that vote subtracted, the one elected did not receive the required number of votes.

To vote, one must be eligible. Four sources are given for ineligibility to vote. Incapable of a human act are infants (c. 97, §2), persons who lack the use of reason habitually (c. 99), or who temporarily are deprived of this ability due to illness, drugs, trauma, etc. Active voice is the right to vote; passive voice is the right to be elected.[67] The right to vote can be taken away or restricted as an expiatory penalty (c. 1336 §1, 2°–3°). An excommunication is a medicinal penalty; if it is incurred *latae sententiae* and has not been declared, the person is eligible to vote. Only when it has been properly declared or imposed does it

---

[63] However, statutes for a particular council cannot permit proxy votes (c. 444, §2).

[64] Hill, in *CLSA Com,* 104; Socha, in *Münster Com,* 167/3.

[65] *Chiappetta Com 1996,* n. 1133; Hill, in *CLSA Com,* 104; and Socha, in *Münster Com,* 168/1 hold that the statutes could permit a person several votes if each office is a distinct basis for voting; other commentators do not mention this.

[66] Socha, in *Münster Com,* 170/2–3, lists ten ways in which an election's freedom can be impeded.

[67] For elections to the presbyteral council, c. 498 specifies who has active and passive voice; religious lack active and passive voice who are exclaustrated (c. 687) and who have become bishops (authentic interpretation of April 29, 1986, *AAS* 78 [1986] 1324).

render one ineligible (cf. c. 1331, §2, 2°). To be notorious, defection from the Church's communion must be public by law (e.g., declared by competent authority) or in fact known. Most commentators equate this defection from communion with breaking the bonds of canon 205, but the phrase in canon 171 is more nuanced.[68] Leaving by a formal act is not required, only that the defection be notorious; it is also not required that the person join another church or religion.[69]

The issue of eligibility becomes significant in close votes. To assure stability in office it is important to verify prior to the election the eligibility of electors if any questions arise.

Canon 172 — §1. To be valid, a vote must be:
   1° free; therefore the vote of a person who has been coerced directly or indirectly by grave fear or malice to vote for a certain person or different persons separately is invalid;
   2° secret, certain, absolute, determined.
   §2. Conditions attached to a vote before the election are to be considered as not having been added.

If a vote is to be valid, not only must the elector be eligible to vote, but the elector's action must satisfy five criteria. The vote must be:

Free: this is one of the situations where the "law provides otherwise" regarding a juridic act (c. 125, §2), giving invalidating force to grave fear or *dolus* ("deceit," here translated as "malice"), whether direct or indirect. The "therefore" (*ideoque*) clause specifies the coercion is to vote for a certain person or different persons separately. It would appear the clause is illustrative, not limiting, in the sense that

whatever coercion, fear, or *dolus* is brought to bear regarding the content of a vote would invalidate. If, however, the clause is substantive and not merely illustrative, a strict interpretation (required because it is an exception to c. 125, §2) would seem to limit the invalidating force.[70]

Secret: at least at the time of casting the vote, who votes for whom is not to be made known.[71]

Certain: there is no doubt that the elector intends to vote, and for whom the vote is cast; it would not be certain if it were illegible or blank.

Absolute: the vote itself contains no extrinsic conditions.

Determined: no doubt regarding the person for whom the vote is cast; it would not be determined if, for example, the vote were for "a or b."[72]

Conditions which may have been made prior to the vote are considered worthless in law and do not affect the validity of the vote. But if they were contained in an actual ballot, that individual ballot would be invalid.

Conducting the Voting

Canon 173 — §1. Before an election begins, at least two tellers are to be designated from the membership of the college or group.

---

[68] *CCEO* 953, §1, 3° is more explicit, specifying the Catholic Church.

[69] Does this mean a non-Catholic Christian is ineligible to vote in a canonical election? It would seem so, since electoral bodies in the Church are composed of Catholics. However, experiments with non-Catholic members of various movements directed toward ecumenism raise special issues, which need to be resolved according to the statutes of these movements.

[70] *Chiappetta Com 1996,* n. 1146. However, Miñambres, in *Com Ex,* 999, cautions that the legislator is not giving an exhaustive list of how freedom can be restricted, but does specify that it should relate to the vote and not to something else. Arrieta, in *Pamplona ComEng,* 166, holds that fraud, fear, or coercion unjustly inflicted would invalidate whether it was to vote for or against a specific person. However, Urrutia, n. 849, says the vote would not be invalid if the coercion were to exclude voting for someone; Socha, in *Münster Com,* 142/2, agrees and adds that it would also not invalidate if directed toward voting disjunctively (for A, or B, or C). García Martín, 533, observes that the canon does not address the prohibition against voting for a determined person.

[71] Urrutia, n. 852, observes that secrecy is not affected if the tellers know. *Chiappetta Com 1996,* n. 1148, gives an example of one who is incapable of writing and asks the tellers to complete the ballot.

[72] *CCEO* 954, §1, 2° adds for the last four criteria that any contrary customs are reprobated.

§2. The tellers are to collect the votes, to examine in the presence of the one presiding over the election whether the number of ballots corresponds to the number of electors, to count the votes themselves, and to announce openly how many votes each person has received.

§3. If the number of votes exceeds the number of electors, the voting is without effect.

§4. All the acts of an election are to be transcribed accurately by the secretary and are to be preserved carefully in the archive of the college after they have been signed at least by the same secretary, the one presiding, and the tellers.

Particular law or the statutes of the electoral body may specify a greater number of tellers, and may provide for alternative methods for voting besides ballots (e.g., raising hands, unanimous acclamation, etc.).[73] They may specify how to include proxies in determining the number of votes cast and what disposition is to be made of the ballots.[74]

Canon 174 — §1. Unless the law or the statutes provide otherwise, an election can also be done by compromise, provided that the electors, by unanimous and written consent, transfer the right to elect on that occasion to one or more suitable persons, whether from among the membership or outside it, who are to elect in the name of all by virtue of the faculty received.

§2. If it concerns a college or group composed of clerics alone, those commissioned must be ordained; otherwise the election is invalid.

§3. Those commissioned must observe the prescripts of the law concerning elections and, for the validity of the election, the conditions attached to the compromise agreement which are not contrary to the law; conditions contrary to

the law, however, are to be considered as not having been attached.

Canon 175 — The compromise ceases and the right to vote returns to those authorizing the compromise:

1° by revocation by the college or group before any action was taken;

2° if some condition attached to the compromise agreement was not fulfilled;

3° if the election had been completed but was null.

Compromise is a usual option unless the law or statutes rule it out.[75] Unanimous written consent is required to proceed with this method of electing. It frequently is used to resolve tensions in the electoral body or to negotiate a difficult situation. As an exception, it permits persons who are not members of the electoral body to be commissioned to act on its behalf.

The electoral body can attach conditions to the compromise agreement; provided they are not contrary to law, these conditions are binding on those commissioned to carry it out. The electoral body can also cancel the compromise process, but only before any action has been taken by those commissioned.

The Election

Canon 176 — Unless the law or the statutes provide otherwise, the person who has received the required number of votes according to the norm of can. 119, n. 1 is considered elected and is to be announced as such by the one presiding over the college or group.

Canon 177 — §1. An election must be communicated immediately to the person elected who must inform the one presiding over the college or

---

[73] *Chiappetta Com 1996*, n. 1149, disagrees, because these would violate secrecy. His concern would have to be addressed if such alternatives are allowed by particular law or statutes.

[74] *CCEO* 955, §4 requires the ballots to be destroyed after each ballot or session; see comparable provisions in *CIC* 171, §4.

[75] John Paul II has eliminated compromise as a means for electing the pope; apconst *Universi Dominici gregis,* February 22, 1996, n. 62, *AAS* 88 (1996) 331. Compromise is not included in the Eastern code.

group whether or not he or she accepts the election within eight useful days after receiving the notification; otherwise, the election has no effect.

§2. If the one elected has not accepted, the person loses every right deriving from the election and does not regain any right by subsequent acceptance but can be elected again. A college or group, however, must proceed to a new election within a month from notification of non-acceptance.

Canon 119, 1° is presented as a fall-back provision if nothing is specified in law or the electoral body's statutes. Canon 119, 1° requires an absolute majority (fifty percent plus one) of the votes cast for election on the first and second ballots; if a third ballot is needed, only two candidates are to be voted on (the ones with the most votes; or, if that does not resolve it, the two senior in age with the most votes);[76] if a tie results, then the one senior in age is elected.

The votes are announced by the tellers (c. 173, §2); the formal announcement of who is elected, however, is by the one presiding over the electoral body and brings this stage of the process to a close.

But the winner must first accept the election before the full electoral process is complete. If this step is omitted, the election has no effect.

The communication to the winner, usually by the one presiding over the electoral body, is to be given "immediately." There is no penalty for delay, except that if it goes beyond the three months to conduct the election the right to elect this time is lost.

The person has eight "useful days" (c. 201, §2) to accept or decline. If the person declines or fails to respond within this time, a new election has to be conducted within one month. In the meantime, the person loses any rights acquired from the earlier election but is eligible for election again.

Acquiring Office

Canon 178 — The person elected who has accepted an election which does not need confirmation obtains the office in full right immediately; otherwise, the person acquires only the right to the office.

Canon 179 — §1. If the election requires confirmation, the person elected must personally or through another seek confirmation from the competent authority within eight useful days from the day of acceptance of election; otherwise, the person is deprived of every right unless it has been proved that the person was prevented from seeking confirmation by a just impediment.

§2. The competent authority cannot deny confirmation if the person elected has been found suitable according to the norm of can. 149, §1, and the election was conducted according to the norm of law.

§3. Confirmation must be given in writing.

§4. Before being notified of confirmation, the person elected is not permitted to become involved in the administration of the office, whether in matters spiritual or temporal, and acts possibly placed by the person are null.

§5. Once notified of the confirmation, the one elected obtains the office in full right unless the law provides otherwise.

If the election does not need confirmation (e.g., pope, diocesan administrator, some supreme moderators), by accepting the election the one elected immediately obtains the office in full right (*ius in re*) provided all other requirements of law are met.[77] No further formalities are required.

If the election needs confirmation, acceptance gives the one elected a right to the office (*ius ad rem*), but obtaining the office in full right (*ius in*

---

[76] Here is where particular law or statutes could simplify matters. If one candidate received the highest number, and several candidates received the next highest, is the run-off between the two senior of all the candidates in this pool? Or is it between the one with the highest number, and the senior of those in the second group?

[77] For the pope, episcopal consecration must come first if the one elected is not a bishop (c. 332, §1). If an election is held in the six months before an office becomes vacant (c. 153, §2), taking office is postponed until the vacancy of the office by written notification of the end of the term to the person being replaced (c. 186).

re) occurs only after the process of confirmation has taken place. This process is initiated by the one elected, not the electoral body, and must be done within eight "useful days" of accepting the election under penalty of being deprived of the effects of the election. The competent authority must make a judgment about the suitability of the one elected, and about the lawfulness (not just the validity) of the election itself. If satisfied on both matters, confirmation must be given, and in writing.

Meanwhile, the one elected is to abstain from involvement in the office itself until notified of the confirmation; even then, law can provide further delay.[78]

ARTICLE 4: POSTULATION
[cc. 180–183]

Postulation is a vote by an electoral body for a candidate who is known to be canonically impeded from an office. A competent authority must determine whether to admit the postulation and grant a dispensation from the impediment. The postulated candidate receives the office upon acceptance after dispensation.

Postulation is carried out in the same manner as an election, with the exceptions or specifications which follow.

Canon 180 — §1. If a canonical impediment from which a dispensation can be and customarily is granted prevents the election of a person whom the electors believe to be more suitable and whom they prefer, by their votes they can postulate that person from the competent authority unless the law provides otherwise.

§2. Those commissioned to elect in virtue of a compromise cannot postulate unless this was expressed in the compromise.

---

[78] For example, if installation is required after confirmation; or until the end of the current officeholder's term in an election held early in light of c. 153, §2.

The impediment must be of ecclesiastical law, and one that is usually dispensed. Examples include age, academic degree, ineligibility for re-election, etc.[79]

The person does not have to be objectively the most suited; rather, the electors have to consider this candidate more suitable than others and prefer this choice to others.

An electoral body should always consult its statutes and applicable law to determine whether postulation is ruled out in the case at hand.[80] Moreover, those commissioned to elect by compromise may postulate only if that is included in the compromise agreement.

Canon 181 — §1. At least two-thirds of the votes are required for a postulation to have force.

§2. A vote for postulation must be expressed by the words, *I postulate,* or the equivalent. The formula, *I elect or I postulate,* or the equivalent is valid for election if there is no impediment; otherwise it is valid for postulation.

The members of the electoral body must be aware of the impediment, and of their desire for the candidate despite the impediment. To assure this, the law requires explicit mention of postulation in the ballots cast for the impeded person, and sets a higher standard for election (two-thirds instead of one-half plus one).[81]

---

[79] Urrutia, n. 883, claims it cannot be because the person is not "suitable," although he does not explain why. Socha, in *Münster Com,* 180/1, disputes this. The key is really whether the impediment is one which is usually dispensed. For the Eastern churches, however, this restriction does not apply (*CCEO* 961).

[80] Miñambres, in *Com Ex,* 1023, reports that some authors claim that because there is no provision in the canons on religious for postulation, the restrictions of the previous code apply and for elections at chapters postulation must be authorized in the constitutions. This would not seem applicable in light of c. 6, §1, 1°, but it would be advisable to address the point in constitutions.

[81] *CCEO* 962 does not require specific wording for postulation.

If a third ballot is needed, a candidate without the impediment is elected by an absolute majority (c. 119, 1°); only a candidate with an impediment requires the two-thirds.

Canon 182 — §1. A postulation must be sent within eight useful days by the one presiding to the authority competent to confirm the election, to whom it pertains to grant the dispensation from the impediment, or, if the authority does not have this power, to petition the dispensation from a higher authority. If confirmation is not required, a postulation must be sent to the authority competent to grant the dispensation.

§2. If a postulation has not been sent within the prescribed time, by that fact it is null, and the college or group is deprived of the right of electing or postulating for that occasion unless it is proved that the one presiding had been prevented from sending the postulation by a just impediment or had refrained from sending it at the opportune time by malice or negligence.

§3. The person postulated acquires no right by postulation; the competent authority is not obliged to admit the postulation.

§4. Electors cannot revoke a postulation made to a competent authority unless the authority consents.

Unlike in an election, in a postulation it is not the candidate but the one presiding over the electoral body who must submit the postulation to the competent authority.

If the election requires confirmation, the postulation is sent to that authority. If it does not require confirmation, it is sent to the authority who can dispense.

The time limit of eight "useful days" is important; if it is not observed, the postulation is not only null but the electoral body loses its right to elect for this time. However, in addition to the usual caution that "useful time" does not run when a person is impeded (c. 201, §2), the effect of the delay can also be avoided by proving that the presiding officer failed to act in due time because of "malice" (*dolus*) or negligence. These facts can be brought to the competent authority by any member of the electoral body which would lose its right.[82]

Once it has been sent to a competent authority, a postulation is entirely in that person's hands. Unlike an election where the candidate acquires a right to the office (*ius ad rem*), no such right is acquired with postulation and it is up to the authority's discretion whether to proceed or not. Moreover, if the electors ask to withdraw the postulation, the authority is free to decide whether to grant their request or to proceed with the postulation.[83]

If the authority decides to proceed with the postulation, it must determine whether the postulation was carried out legally and the candidate is otherwise suited for the office; if both are true, it must determine who is authorized to grant the dispensation.

The dispensation itself is to be given by one who is competent to dispense. In a case where the election does not need confirmation, this is done by the authority to whom the postulation was sent. If the election needs confirmation, the dispensation is given by the one competent to confirm if that person has the authority to dispense; otherwise, that authority must seek the dispensation from an authority competent to dispense. This latter is free to dispense or not.

A just cause is required for the dispensation (c. 90). It is for the authority which grants the dispensation to determine the sufficiency of the cause.

Canon 183 — §1. If a postulation has not been admitted by the competent authority, the right of electing reverts to the college or group.

§2. If a postulation has been admitted, however, this is to be made known to the person postulated, who must respond according to the norm of can. 177, §1.

---

[82] Socha, in *Münster Com,* 182/3.

[83] *CCEO* 963, §4 does not permit the electors to seek to revoke a postulation.

§3. A person who accepts a postulation which has been admitted acquires the office in full right immediately.

Unlike an election where the candidate is asked to agree before the results are sent to a competent authority for confirmation, the candidate is not contacted until the authority has determined to admit the postulation. In light of paragraph three, this contact is not made until the dispensation has been granted. Thus, if the person accepts, all that needs to be done has taken place and the person obtains the office in full right (*ius in re*).[84]

CHAPTER II
LOSS OF ECCLESIASTICAL OFFICE
[cc. 184–196]

GENERAL NORMS ON LOSS OF OFFICE
[cc. 184–186]

An office is constituted in a stable manner. It is conferred, however, with varying degrees of stability for the officeholder. In addition to death, which is not listed in the code, there are various other ways by which office can be lost, all involving some intervention of a competent authority. Thus office is never to be lost without at least those who have the responsibility to fill it being notified.

This chapter has three preliminary canons and four articles. It begins with the following statement of general principles.

Canon 184 — §1. An ecclesiastical office is lost by the lapse of a predetermined time, by reaching the age determined by law, by resignation, by transfer, by removal, and by privation.

§2. An ecclesiastical office is not lost by the expiration in any way of the authority of the one

who conferred it unless the law provides otherwise.

§3. Loss of an office which has taken effect is to be made known as soon as possible to all those who have some right over the provision of the office.

In addition to the six ways listed in the canon, there are other ways by which office can be lost. These include death, suppression of the office by competent authority (see c. 148), reasons determined by proper or particular law (see c. 624, §3) or in contracts, and for some offices the expiration of the authority that conferred them (see c. 481, §1).[85]

Unless the law specifies otherwise, office is not lost by the expiration of the authority that conferred it. Unless competent authority intervenes, office is not lost by psychic or physical disability, by incompetence, or by bad behavior. Even when someone is impeded from carrying out official duties, the office is not vacant, only impeded.

Because various people can have rights to provide for an office, all of them are to be notified, for example, the cardinals on the death of the pope, the bishop and the religious superior on the death of a pastor who is a religious.

Canon 185 — The title of emeritus can be conferred upon a person who loses an office by reason of age or of resignation which has been accepted.

Usually this is not automatic but requires the intervention of a competent authority. However, in the case of a bishop, the law itself confers the title.[86] In addition to the situations mentioned in

---

[84] This may not happen immediately, of course, if taking possession is required, or until a vacancy occurs at the end of the current officeholder's term (c. 186) in an election held early in light of c. 153, §2.

[85] *CCEO* 965, §1 covers these by the phrase "besides other cases prescribed by law."

[86] Canon 402, §1 applies this to bishops of dioceses; it has been extended to other bishops (e.g., in the Roman Curia, papal diplomatic corps, etc.); see CFB, "Normae de episcopis ab officio cessantibus," October 31, 1988, *Comm* 20 (1988) 167–168.

the canon, there are other situations in which the title may be conferred when judged appropriate by the competent authority.[87]

Canon 186 — Loss of an office by the lapse of a predetermined time or by the reaching of a certain age takes effect only from the moment when the competent authority communicates it in writing.

Some offices are or can be conferred for a term, or "predetermined time."[88] Once the term is up, the person loses the protection of the term (see c. 193, §2) but remains in office until notified by the competent authority.

If an age limit has been set by law, once the age is reached, the person remains in office until notified. There are no age limits set in the code, but particular law may do so.[89] Cardinals (c. 354), bishops (cc. 401, §1 and 411), and pastors (c. 538, §3) are asked to resign when they reach seventy-five, but this is resignation, not loss of office upon reaching a predetermined age.

In both cases, written notification is required for the cessation from office to take effect, seen by some as an application of canon 54, §2.[90]

---

[87] See Gefaell, in *Com Ex,* 1041; Hill, in *CLSA Com,* 109; Socha, in *Münster Com,* 185/2.

[88] Examples in the code include episcopal vicars who are not auxiliary bishops (c. 477); pastors and priests jointly entrusted with pastoral care of a parish, who are appointed for a term (c. 522); members of the presbyteral council (c. 501, §1) and finance council (c. 492, §2); the college of consultors as such (c. 502, §1) and the diocesan pastoral council as such (513, §1); vicars forane (c. 554, §2); religious superiors (c. 624, §1); moderators of secular institutes (c. 717, §1) and societies of apostolic life (c. 734); judicial vicars, adjutant judicial vicars, and tribunal judges (c. 1422). Other offices can be established with limited terms by particular law, law of foundation, or statutes.

[89] Various officials of the Roman Curia are retired at 65, 70, or 75 years; see *Regolamento generale della Curia Romana,* February 4, 1992, art. 43, *AAS* 84 (1992) 220–221.

[90] As García Martín, 561, argues, this applies to all methods for loss of office which require direct intervention of competent authority.

ARTICLE 1: RESIGNATION
[cc. 187–189]

Resignation is a request initiated by an office-holder to leave the office. If no confirmation was required to obtain the office, resignation consists in notifying those responsible for providing for the office. Otherwise, it must be submitted to a competent authority and does not become effective until that authority gives notice of acceptance in writing.

The article deals with who can resign (cc. 187–188) and the process of resignation (c. 189). Understood but not stated in the canons is that only one who holds an office can resign that office.

Who Can Resign

Canon 187 — Anyone responsible for oneself (*sui compos*) can resign from an ecclesiastical office for a just cause.

Resignation is a juridic act; this canon highlights one of the aspects of what is required for a juridic act (cc. 124–126). To be "responsible for oneself" or *sui compos* requires the person to be of sound mind. Someone suffering from severe mental illness, a mentally disabling stroke, a coma, or otherwise lacking the use of reason (c. 99) is not capable of resigning an office.

The just cause can be the good of the individual as well as the good of the Church, or the good of the office being resigned. It should be proportionate to the importance of the office.

Commentators are divided on whether the canon establishes a right to resign.[91] It at least states a right to submit a resignation.

---

[91] The right to resign is held by Arrieta, in *Pamplona ComEng,* 175; Gefaell, in *Com Ex,* 1047; and Hill, in *CLSA Com,* 109. García Martín, 568, argues that competent authority can refuse a resignation, so the canon does not establish a right of the officeholder vis-à-vis authority. Urrutia, n. 900, claims that particular law can prohibit resignation as under the former code, in which case there would be no "right" to resign.

Canon 188 — A resignation made out of grave fear that is inflicted unjustly or out of malice, substantial error, or simony is invalid by the law itself.

Resignation is not only initiated by the officeholder, and not someone else; it must also be a free act of the officeholder. This canon reinforces the freedom of any juridic act as it applies to resignation.

Not mentioned is an irresistible extrinsic force, whether physical, chemical, or whatever.[92] Canon 125, §1 considers an act placed under such a circumstance as non-existent.

Canon 188 is an example of a case in which "the law provides otherwise," as mentioned in canon 125, §2. Unjustly inflicted grave fear and "malice" or "deceit" (*dolus*) do invalidate the juridic act of resignation; without this provision, these factors would not invalidate but would make the resignation rescindable. The threatened evil which produces the fear must be at least grave in the estimation of the officeholder, and its source must be external to the person.

The process for removing a pastor provides an example of force which is justified (c. 1742, §1). For just cause a bishop can remove a pastor, but first he must give the pastor an opportunity to resign, which is resignation under pressure but the pressure is justified.[93]

Substantial error is a mistaken judgment which affects the essential elements of resignation, in terms of either the cause or motivation for resignation, or the nature of resignation and its consequences.[94] An example could be a diocesan finance officer who mistakenly thinks one must resign when a new bishop is named even though one's term has not expired.

Simony invalidates resignation as it does conferral of office (c. 149, §3). In effect, one cannot "buy off" someone by enticing the person to resign for material considerations, although one could freely resign to accept a "golden parachute"

which does not buy the resignation, but does provide added incentive for it.

Because invalidity in these circumstances is by the law itself, the office does not become vacant even though the resignation may have been accepted. The officeholder or another aggrieved party may take recourse to the competent authority for a declaration of the nullity of resignation.

Process of Resignation

Canon 189 — §1. To be valid, a resignation, whether it requires acceptance or not, must be made to the authority to whom it pertains to make provision of the office in question; this must be done either in writing, or orally in the presence of two witnesses.

§2. The authority is not to accept a resignation which is not based on a just and proportionate cause.

§3. A resignation which requires acceptance lacks all force if it is not accepted within three months; one which does not require acceptance takes effect when it has been communicated by the one resigning according to the norm of law.

§4. A resignation can be revoked by the one resigning as long as it has not taken effect; once it has taken effect it cannot be revoked, but the one who resigned can obtain the office by some other title.

The canon distinguishes resignations which need acceptance from those which do not. Although no general principle is given in the code for determining which category an office belongs to,[95] a practical rule seems to be that no acceptance of resignation is needed if the office did not require direct intervention of competent authority to confer it.[96]

If no acceptance is needed, resignation must be communicated to the authority competent to make

---

[92] Socha, in *Münster Com,* 188/1.
[93] Hill, in *CLSA Com,* 109.
[94] Gefaell, in *Com Ex,* 1052.

[95] *Chiappetta Com 1996,* n. 1230, and Urrutia, n. 905.
[96] For example, Roman Pontiff (c. 332), diocesan administrator (c. 430). Proper law may determine the same for supreme moderators of religious institutes. *Chiappetta Com 1996,* n. 1231, limits it to the first two.

provision (e.g., college of cardinals for the pope, college of consultors for diocesan administrator). This may be done in writing, or orally in the presence of two witnesses, although particular law could require a specific formality. The resignation takes effect immediately upon its legitimate communication to the competent authority, although its effect may be suspended until the one resigning specifies when it is to take effect if this condition was made in the resignation itself (e.g., "I resign effective noon tomorrow").

If acceptance is needed, the effect of the resignation is determined by the competent authority. In addition to receiving proper written or oral communication of the resignation, the authority must also judge whether the person acted freely and responsibly, and whether the cause is just and sufficient to warrant resignation.

If the competent authority does not act within three months, the answer is considered to be negative (§3). Recourse can then be taken if the person seeking to resign so decides.

The competent authority can also refuse the resignation directly, or can accept it. If the resignation is accepted, this must be communicated in writing to the one resigning in order to take effect. There are several reasons for this, even though it is not expressly required in this canon.[97] First, written notification is the general norm for an individual decree to take effect (c. 54, §2). Second, appointment to the office was an administrative act for offices requiring provision, installation, or confirmation; revocation of this act by accepting the resignation takes effect when it is legitimately made known to the officeholder (c. 47). Third, it is required for the provision of paragraph four to make sense; that is, how could one know whether it is still possible to

revoke the resignation, if it took effect without the person being properly notified?

If the authority fails to act within the three months, the resignation lacks all force; therefore, the competent authority cannot subsequently accept the resignation. A new resignation would be required. The Holy See has adopted the practice of accepting a bishop's resignation within the three months but qualifying this as *nunc pro tunc*, i.e., the effect of the resignation is suspended until some future time to be determined by the Apostolic See. But the Apostolic See must then determine that the resignation has taken effect for the office to become vacant, a condition for appointing the successor (c. 153, §1).

The person resigning can also specify when the resignation will take effect if this is done in the letter of resignation. If competent authority accepts the resignation, the resignation will take effect as specified in the letter and the officeholder cannot be removed in the meantime except for cause and following the appropriate procedure for removal.[98] However, if the officeholder submits a "standing resignation" which can be accepted whenever the competent authority decides, the resignation would cease to have any force after three months.[99]

ARTICLE 2: TRANSFER
[cc. 190–191]

Transfer is initiated by the competent authority and results in the vacancy of one office and the provision of another. It need not necessarily carry a negative connotation, but it can be imposed as a penalty (c. 1336, §1, 4°).

---

[97] Because the 1983 code does not include the 1917 code's requirement that acceptance of resignation be communicated in writing to be effective, the commentators are divided. Some hold it is necessary for the acceptance to be effective: *Chiappetta Com 1996*, n. 1234; García Martín, 569; Gefaell, in *Com Ex*, 1057–1058; Heimerl and Pree, 139; Huysmans, 342; Socha, in *Münster Com*, 189/5. Others say it is not: Manzanares, in *Salamanca Com*, 128, and Urrutia, n. 255.

[98] Hill, in *CLSA Com*, 110; but see limitations on this for resignation of pastors when the process of removal has begun (c. 1743).

[99] Hill, in *CLSA Com*, 110, and McGrath, in *CLSGBI Com*, 106. Gefaell, in *Com Ex*, 1056, agrees that such a practice does not appear correct, but claims the code does not exclude it; he does not give a reason, however, or explain why the three-month limit would not apply.

Canon 190 — §1. A transfer can be made only by a person who has the right of providing for the office which is lost as well as for the office which is conferred.

§2. If a transfer is made when the officeholder is unwilling, a grave cause is required and the manner of proceeding prescribed by law is to be observed, always without prejudice to the right of proposing contrary arguments.

§3. To take effect a transfer must be communicated in writing.

The first paragraph clarifies the authority competent to effect a transfer. If that authority does not have the right to provide for both offices, a different process would be required, such as resignation or removal from one office, and provision by another competent authority of the new office.

If the officeholder is willing, a just cause is still required for a transfer. It can be for the common good, the service of the Church, or the good of the officeholder personally.[100] No formalities are stated in the code, other than that the transfer be in writing (§3). Particular law could provide additional procedures.

If the officeholder is unwilling, a grave cause is required. The competent authority is the judge of the gravity of the cause, in light of the offices involved and the circumstances;[101] these should be expressed in writing for the eventuality of a recourse against the transfer. Moreover, the procedure prescribed by law is to be observed. A specific procedure is provided in the code only for the transfer of pastors (cc. 1748–1752) and for transfer as a penalty (penal law must be followed); proper law is to provide for the transfer of superiors (c. 624, §3). Particular law could provide other procedures, but must always provide for the officeholder to propose arguments against the transfer. If the officeholder is under contract, the terms of the contract must be re-

spected.[102] All other transfers are at least subject to the procedures of canons 50–51, since a transfer is expressed in a decree (§3).

If there is no general or particular law governing the transfer, and it is not a penal transfer, a more detailed process could be developed for an individual case by relying on laws passed in similar circumstances (c. 19).[103]

A decree of transfer must be communicated in writing to take effect; it is subject to recourse, which suspends its effect.[104]

Canon 191 — §1. In a transfer, the prior office becomes vacant through the canonical possession of the other office unless the law provides otherwise or competent authority has prescribed otherwise.

§2. The person transferred receives the remuneration assigned to the prior office until the person has taken canonical possession of the other office.

In the transfer of a diocesan bishop the law provides otherwise (c. 418) to the extent that he is no longer diocesan bishop but administrator of the prior diocese until he takes possession of the new one.

Competent authority may make other determinations in the case of various transfers simultaneously.[105]

If recourse has been taken against a decree of transfer, the prior office remains occupied *de iure* while the recourse is resolved. If no recourse has been taken, the prior office becomes vacant

---

[100] García Martín, 570.

[101] The type of the officeholder's subjective stability will affect the gravity of the cause; see c. 193, §§1–3.

[102] See cc. 1290 on contracts, 192 on removal when a contract is involved.

[103] *Chiappetta Com 1996*, n. 1243; Socha, in *Münster Com*, 190/3–4; Urrutia, n. 913. Gefaell, in *Com Ex*, 1063, considers the general prescriptions of law and equity to be sufficient in cases of transfer involving lesser stability.

[104] Gefaell, in *Com Ex*, 1064; see cc. 1734, §1; 1736, §1; 1747, §3; 1752.

[105] Manzanares, in *Salamanca Com*, 129, who notes it is a way to resolve difficulties which could arise from c. 153, §1 in these situations.

through canonical possession of the new office. If the officeholder fails to take possession of the new office, the prior office remains occupied *de iure* and further action (e.g., decree declaring vacancy) would be needed for it to become *de iure* vacant.

Particular law can make other provision for remuneration, provided there is no loss to the officeholders involved. The canon protects against double reimbursement, as well as loss.

ARTICLE 3: REMOVAL
[cc. 192–195]

Removal results in loss of office; it differs from transfer in that, of itself, it does not include provision with another office. It carries the connotation that the officeholder is not conducting the office properly, although not necessarily due to a delict.

Removal can be initiated by competent authority (cc. 192–193), or it can be in virtue of the law itself (c. 194). The law is also sensitive to issues of support.

Removal by Competent Authority

Canon 192 — A person is removed from office either by a decree issued legitimately by competent authority, without prejudice to rights possibly acquired by contract, or by the law itself according to the norm of can. 194.

Canon 193 — §1. A person cannot be removed from an office conferred for an indefinite period of time except for grave causes and according to the manner of proceeding defined by law.

§2. The same is valid for the removal of a person from an office conferred for a definite period of time before this time has elapsed, without prejudice to the prescript of can. 624, § 3.

§3. A person upon whom an office is conferred at the prudent discretion of a competent authority according to the prescripts of the law can,

upon the judgment of the same authority, be removed from that office for a just cause.

§4. To take effect, the decree of removal must be communicated in writing.

The authority competent to remove is the authority competent to provide for the office. If a contract is involved, its provisions must be respected in addition to the causes and procedures specified in canon 193. The terms of the contract are to be interpreted in keeping with the applicable civil law on contracts (see c. 1290). Moreover, third parties (in addition to the officeholder) may have acquired rights through the contract and these must be respected as well.[106]

For the decree of removal to be legitimate, it must be based on sufficient cause and be preceded by the requisite procedure. These vary depending on the type of subjective stability enjoyed by the officeholder being removed.

Three types of subjective stability are listed. Conferral for an indefinite term provides the greatest stability; the officeholder enjoys the presumption of full subjective stability. Conferral for a definite term provides the same kind of subjective stability as conferral for an indefinite term, but only for the duration of the term; once the term has expired, the officeholder remains in office but loses the office with the simple notification that the term has expired; no other cause or procedure is required. Conferral at the prudent discretion of a competent authority has limited protection of subjective stability.

For some offices, the code clearly specifies which type of subjective stability is involved.[107] In

---

[106] *Chiappetta Com 1996,* n. 1258; Gefaell, in *Com Ex,* 1069.

[107] For example, the Roman Pontiff (c. 332), bishops (cc. 401, 411), and pastors not appointed for a term (c. 522) or priests entrusted jointly with pastoral care of a parish without a term (c. 542, 2°), hold office for an indefinite term. See discussion at c. 186 for examples of offices with limited term. Conferral at discretion of competent authority applies to vicars general (c. 477, §1), chancellors and notaries (c. 485), delegates (c. 142, §1),

other situations, the message is mixed: officeholders named for a definite term can be removed as if they were appointed at prudent discretion.[108] Particular law, the law of foundation, or the statutes governing a specific office may clarify which category applies. If there is no specification in law or statutes, is an office to be presumed as conferred for an indeterminate time? Some commentators think so,[109] and the text of *Presbyterorum ordinis* 20 would seem to argue for this.[110]

Offices with Special Stability

For offices conferred for an indefinite time, and during the term for an office conferred in that manner, grave causes are required for removal, and the procedures defined by law must be followed.

Grave causes are to be determined by proper law for religious superiors (c. 624, §3). The code gives some examples of grave causes.[111] Otherwise, grave causes are to be judged in light of equity, the good of souls, the common good, the importance of the office, and so on. The judgment is the responsibility of the one decreeing the removal, but should be substantiated and recorded in view of any eventual recourse.

Procedures are provided for some of these offices,[112] but in general canons 50–51 and particular law will determine how to proceed. If proce-

---

parochial vicars (c. 552), rectors of churches (c. 563), chaplains (c. 572), and any diocesan offices held by religious or members of societies of apostolic life (cc. 682, §2 and 738, §2).

[108] For example, episcopal vicars who are not bishops (c. 477, §1) and vicars forane (c. 554, §§2–3).

[109] For example, Arrieta, in *Pamplona ComEng,* 178, and Socha, in *Münster Com,* 193/1.

[110] Where it defines an office as "conferred" in a stable manner.

[111] For example, for seminary professors (c. 253, §3), pastors (c. 1741).

[112] For example, moderators of public associations (c. 318, §2), diocesan finance officers (c. 494, §2), pastors (cc. 1740–1747).

---

dures are included in an applicable contract, they must be observed. To take effect, the decree of removal must be communicated to the officeholder in writing (§4).

Offices Conferred at Discretion

This is not removal at will or whim, but for a cause. The cause, however, is not so weighty as in the previous types; it must be considered just by the authority who decrees the removal. The cause should be substantiated and recorded in view of any eventual recourse.

No specific procedure is mandated by the canon, but at least the procedures for individual decrees must be followed (cc. 50–51) and, to take effect, the decree of removal must be communicated to the officeholder in writing. Particular law, proper law, the law of foundation, the statutes, or contracts governing the office in question may specify further procedures.

Removal by Law

Canon 194 — §1. The following are removed from an ecclesiastical office by the law itself:

    1° a person who has lost the clerical state;

    2° a person who has publicly defected from the Catholic faith or from the communion of the Church;

    3° a cleric who has attempted marriage even if only civilly.

§2. The removal mentioned in nn. 2 and 3 can be enforced only if it is established by the declaration of a competent authority.

For all three situations competent authority must intervene. The clerical state is lost by declaration of invalidity of orders, imposition of the penalty of dismissal, or dispensation (c. 290); competent authority must act for each of these.

In the other two situations of canon 194, competent authority declares the removal. These both involve delicts by the officeholder, and removal here has the effect of a penalty. The canon is an exception to penal law, for removal from office is a permanent expiatory penalty (c. 1336, §1, 2°) which normally cannot be imposed or declared by decree (c. 1342, §2). Nevertheless, competent authority must determine the facts in the case and provide the officeholder with an opportunity to be heard (c. 50) before issuing the decree containing the reasons for removal and communicating this to the officeholder (c. 51).

Public defection from the *Catholic* faith is similar to but not precisely the same as apostasy (which is total repudiation of *Christian* faith—c. 751); public defection from the communion of the Church is similar to but not precisely the same as schism (which is defection from *Catholic* communion—c. 751).[113] A formal act is not required for the defection in canon 194; the only requirement is that it be public (i.e., known, or likely to become known).[114] Neither is it required that the officeholder join another religion, although this could be an objective indication of defection.

Because clergy are bound by the impediment of orders (c. 1087) and canonical form (c. 1117), they are said to "attempt" marriage. If a dispensation has been given to permit marriage (e.g., for a widowed permanent deacon), canon 194, §1, 3° does not apply. Attempted marriage by lay persons, whether vowed religious or not, is not affected by this canon; neither are other types of sexual misconduct by clergy.[115]

In the case of defection or clergy attempting marriage, the declaration by competent authority is similar to the declaration at the end of a term of office or completion of age. The fact on which loss of office is based does not depend on the authority's declaration, but its effectiveness does. The officeholder remains in office, and actions which require the office are valid, until the declaration of removal is communicated to the officeholder in writing.[116]

Support

Canon 195 — If a person is removed not by the law itself but by a decree of competent authority from an office which provides the person's support, the same authority is to take care that the support is provided for a suitable period, unless other provision is made.

This canon applies directly to those removed by decree of competent authority, not to those removed by law. However, canon 1350 makes a similar provision for clerics when they are penalized, and rights acquired by non-clerical officeholders in virtue of canons 231, §2 and 1286 must also be respected.

Other provision can be made through civil unemployment compensation if available, secular employment or some other church office accepted by the officeholder, conditions of a contract, etc.[117] The competent authority is to determine the length of the "suitable period," but civil law pro-

---

[113] *CCEO* 976, §1, 2° specifies defection from the Catholic Church, which is the same as schism.

Commentators on the Latin code generally do not mark these nuances in the canon, equating communion with full communion in the Catholic Church (c. 205), and the defections the same as those in c. 751.

[114] Socha, in *Münster Com,* 194/2–3; Urrutia, n. 925, confuses this with "notorious."

[115] For example, c. 1395. Socha, in *Münster Com,* 194/4, argues that Hill, in *CLSA Com,* 111, is wrong to say that particular law could remove someone by the law itself for such activities. They may be the basis for removal by competent authority, or even privation (c. 195).

[116] McGrath, in *CLSGBI Com,* 108, claims the office may be vacant *de iure* even without the declaration of competent authority, but as Gefaell, in *Com Ex,* 1083, argues, this is not so. The officeholder continues to act validly, and to receive remuneration, until notified in writing (c. 54, §2).

[117] Socha, in *Münster Com,* 195/2, points out that "other provision" is made for clerics due to incardination, and for members of institutes of consecrated life and societies of apostolic life. For each of these, the diocese or other entity of incardination, and the institute or society, have an obligation to provide for decent support. Gefaell, in *Com Ex,* 1086, cautions that this may not always be true and that each case should be studied carefully.

visions (for example, on unemployment compensation) can provide guidance in this.

ARTICLE 4: PRIVATION
[c. 196]

Canon 196 — §1. Privation from office, namely, a penalty for a delict, can be done only according to the norm of law.

§2. Privation takes effect according to the prescripts of the canons on penal law.

Privation is penal removal from office, one of the expiatory penalties (c. 1336, §1, 2°). It can be imposed only if a delict has been committed and is imputable to the officeholder. The provisions of this canon assure due process protection for the officeholder, as well as a means to safeguard the welfare of the community and the common good.

The procedures for penal law must be followed (cc. 1341–1353, 1717–1728). Thus, as a permanent penalty it cannot be imposed by an administrative decree (c. 1342, §2) but requires a judicial process.[118] Privation cannot be imposed where the law states simply a "just penalty," for it is one of the graver penalties.[119] However, particular law could further specify privation as a penalty where the code lists a "just penalty," although only for very grave necessity (c. 1315, §3). Privation cannot be imposed *latae sententiae* (c. 1336, §2), and can be imposed only if the office is subject to the superior who decrees the penalty (c. 1338, §1).

Penal law is rather complex on when a penalty finally takes effect, so this canon refers the question to penal law. In the interim, officeholders continue to exercise their office unless prohibited by decree (c. 1722).

---

[118] García Martín, 582, and Gefaell, in *Com Ex,* 1089. But Socha, in *Münster Com,* 196/2, seems to rely on the distinction made under the 1917 code between irremovable and movable offices to permit proceeding by decree in the latter type, which does not seem justified under the present code.

[119] See c. 1349; Gefaell, in *Com Ex,* 1089; McGrath, in *CLSGBI Com,* 109; Socha, in *Münster Com,* 196/1. Privation is mentioned directly or indirectly in cc. 1364, §1; 1387; 1389, §1; 1396; 1397; and 1457.

Arrieta, J. In *Pamplona ComEng,* 155–180.

Arrieta, J., J. Miñambres, and P. Gefaell. In *Com Ex,* 1:907–1090.

Aymans, W. *Kanonisches Recht.* Vol. 1: 445–502. Paderborn: F. Schöningh, 1991.

Chiappetta, L. *Chiappetta Com.* 2nd ed. 3 vols. (Rome: Dehoniane, 1996) Vol. 1: 229–288.

De Paolis, V., and A. Montan. *Il diritto nel mistero della Chiesa.* 2nd ed. Vol. 1: 402–429. Rome: Pontificia Università Lateranense, 1988.

D'Ostillio, F. "La provvista degli offici ecclesiastici." *ME* 107 (1982) 51–78.

Échappé O. In *Droit Canonique,* 258–263.

Erdö, P. "Ministerium, munus et officium in Codice Iuris Canonici." *P* 78 (1989) 434–436.

———. "Quaestiones quaedam de provisione officiorum in ecclesia." *P* 77 (1988) 363–379.

García Martín, J. *Le Norme Generali del Codex Iuris Canonici.* Rome: Edizioni Istituto Giuridico Claretiano, 1995.

Hayward, P. "The Apostolic Signatura and Disputes Involving the Transfer of Parish Priests." *CLS-GBIN* 104 (1995) 24–32.

Heimerl, H., and H. Pree. *Kirchenrecht: Allgemeine Normen und Eherecht.* Vienna: Springer, 1983.

Hill, R. In *CLSA Com,* 98–112.

Huysmans, R. *Algemene Normen van het Wetboek van Canoniek Recht.* Leuven: Peeters, 1993.

Manzanares, J. In *Salamanca Com,* 112–130.

May, G. In *Handbuch,* 141–153.

McGrath, A. In *CLSGBI Com,* 86–109.

Pinto, P. In *Urbaniana Com,* 86–105.

Socha, H. In *Münster Com,* vol. 1.

Urrutia, F. *Les normes générales.* Paris: Tardy, 1994.

TITLE X
PRESCRIPTION
[cc. 197–199]

Prescription is a means of acquiring or losing rights, or of freeing oneself from obligations, by the passage of time under conditions prescribed by law. Derived from classical Roman law and further developed under Justinian,[1] prescription is found in virtually all legal systems in the western tradition, including the law of the Church. It is grounded in societal needs for the peace and good order that ensue from bringing closure to disputes, precluding prolonged uncertainty of ownership, curing transactional defects flowing from failure to fulfill formalities, avoiding the bringing of stale claims after witnesses and relevant documentary evidence are no longer available, and encouraging social and economic development and productivity by removing fears of future litigation. While the code uses the sole term "prescription," canonists generally distinguish *acquisitive* prescription (the acquiring of rights, especially ownership of temporal goods) from *liberative* or *extinctive* prescription (the freeing oneself of an obligation).[2] Civil laws employ a variety of terms. In the United States, for example, acquisitive prescription is generally called *adverse possession* when referring to rights to real property, and *prescription* when referring to rights to personal

property; liberative or extinctive prescription is generally referred to in the United States as the operative effect of a *statute of limitations*.

Canon 197 — The Church receives prescription as it is in the civil legislation of the nation in question, without prejudice to the exceptions which are established in the canons of this Code; prescription is a means of acquiring or losing a subjective right as well as of freeing oneself from obligations.

In acknowledging the acceptance by the Church of prescription as found in the applicable civil law, canon 197 effectively "canonizes" the local civil law on the matter except where other canons in the code provide otherwise. Canon 197 is a specification of the general norm found in canon 22 regarding civil laws to which the law of the Church defers.

Exceptions to the canonization of civil laws regarding prescription relate to the requirement of good faith (see c. 198), matters considered by the Church to be totally exempt from prescription (see cc. 199, 1°– 6°; 1492, §1) or partially exempt (see cc. 82; 199, 7°; 1269), and the length of time which must pass before some forms of acquisitive prescription become effective (see c. 1270) or some forms of liberative (extinctive) prescription become effective (see cc. 1362, 1363, 1621).

Canon 198 — No prescription is valid unless it is based in good faith not only at the beginning but through the entire course of time required for prescription, without prejudice to the prescript of can. 1362.

It has never been the purpose of prescription to reward unethical behavior such as theft or the wresting of rights or release from obligations by violent means. Good faith has always been an essential element. The extent of required good faith,

---

[1] W. Buckland, *A Text-Book of Roman Law from Augustus to Justinian*, 3rd rev. ed. (Cambridge, England: Cambridge University, 1966) 241–252; F. Schulz, *Classical Roman Law* (Oxford, England: Oxford University, 1961) 355–361; A. Gauthier, *Roman Law and Its Contribution to the Development of Canon Law*, 2nd ed. (Ottawa: St. Paul University, 1996) 59–61.

[2] L. Chiappetta, *Il Codice di Diritto Canonico: Commento Giuridico-Pastorale*, 2nd ed. (Rome: Dehoniane, 1996) 1:289; P. Pinto, in *Urbaniana Com*, 106; J.- P. Schouppe, *Elementi di Diritto Patrimoniale Canonico* (Milan: Giuffrè, 1997) 74–75.

however, has varied among legal systems. Roman law, both classical and imperial, required good faith only at the beginning of the running of the time for prescription;[3] a good faith purchaser or recipient of a gift, for example, was not deprived of the benefits of prescription upon subsequently learning that the property in question had previously been stolen or otherwise misappropriated. The Church, however, at least since the Fourth Lateran Council,[4] has required good faith throughout the entire running of the prescribed time, both for acquisitive and liberative prescription;[5] it is that stance of the Church that is codified in canon 198 and in the parallel canon of the Code of Canons of the Eastern Churches.[6] Moreover, the Church requires positive good faith, that is, a judgment (even though erroneous) that one possesses property, or exercises a right, or withholds payment of a debt or fulfillment of other obligation, justly, that is, without violating any right of another. One who acts in good conscience acts in good faith.[7]

In the United States, civil law requires good faith throughout the entire running of the prescribed period of adverse possession or statute of limitations but, generally speaking, positive good faith (a judgment of the propriety of one's possession of property, for example, or nonfulfillment of an obligation) is required only at the outset; negative good faith (the absence of fraudulent concealment or other deliberate injustice) suffices thereafter.[8]

The sole exception to the canonical requirement of good faith is in regard to the extinctive prescription of criminal actions according to the norms of canon 1362. The presence or absence of good faith on the part of the offender is irrelevant to the effective running of the prescribed time limits for instituting a criminal action (see commentary on c. 1362).[9]

Canon 199 — The following are not subject to prescription:
1° **rights and obligations which are of the divine natural or positive law;**
2° **rights which can be obtained from apostolic privilege alone;**
3° **rights and obligations which directly regard the spiritual life of the Christian faithful;**
4° **the certain and undoubted boundaries of ecclesiastical territories;**
5° **Mass offerings and obligations;**
6° **provision of an ecclesiastical office which, according to the norm of law, requires the exercise of a sacred order;**
7° **the right of visitation and the obligation of obedience, in such a way that the Christian faithful cannot be visited by any ecclesiastical authority or are no longer subject to any authority.**

This is the principal, but not the only, canon that exempts certain matters from prescription. In addition to the seven exemptions declared in canon 199, judicial actions concerning the status of persons are exempt from prescription (c. 1492, §1), as are certain privileges (see c. 82) and, under some circumstances, sacred objects owned by public juridic persons (see c. 1269).

The first of the canon 199 exemptions are rights and obligations that are of divine law, natural or positive. These would include such rights as the right to be free from any kind of coercion

---

[3] Buckland, 244; Schulz, 358; Gauthier, 61.

[4] Gauthier, 61; S. Woywod and C. Smith, *A Practical Commentary on the Code of Canon Law* (New York: Wagner, 1963) 223.

[5] *Chiappetta Com 1996,* 1:290.

[6] *CCEO* 1541.

[7] Pinto, in *Urbaniana Com,* 106; *Chiappetta Com 1996,* 1:290. See also T. Bouscaren, A. Ellis, and F. Korth, *Canon Law: A Text and Commentary,* 4th rev. ed. (Milwaukee: Bruce, 1966) 819–820.

[8] For a helpful discussion of the element of good faith in civil law approaches to prescription in the United States, see P. Gerstenblith, "The Adverse Possession of Personal Property," *Buffalo Law Review* 37 (1989) 119–163.

[9] The Code of Canons of the Eastern Churches contains a similar exception to the requirement of good faith for prescription (see *CCEO* 1541, 1152).

in choosing a state in life (see c. 219) and the right to a Christian education (see c. 217), and such obligations as that of parents to care for the Christian education of their children (see c. 226, §2). Other obligations and rights of Christian spouses are also considered to be of divine law. It is axiomatic that a right or obligation which flows from divine law cannot be precluded by a law of human origin such as prescription.

Rights which can be obtained only by apostolic privilege, the subject matter of the second of the canon 199 exemptions, include the erection of a public association of the faithful by other than the Holy See, episcopal conference, or diocesan bishop (see c. 312, §1, 3°), and entrusting to others the power to grant indulgences (see c. 995, §2). To declare that a right which can be obtained only by apostolic privilege cannot be obtained by prescription would appear to be a redundant provision of law, but through canon 199, 2° the legislator evidently intends to remove any possible doubt.

Virtually all rights and obligations in the Church relate in some way to the spiritual life of the faithful, for that is the central focus of the Church's mission; some, however, such as rights and obligations in the area of temporal goods, relate only indirectly to the spiritual life. Rights and obligations which relate directly to the spiritual life and, hence, which are exempt by canon 199, 3° from prescription include the rights to worship God according to the prescriptions of one's own approved rite and to follow one's own form of spiritual life so long as it is consonant with the teaching of the Church (see c. 214), and the obligations properly to observe Sundays and other feast days (see c. 1247) and days of penance (see c. 1249).

The certain and undisputed boundaries of ecclesiastical territories compose the fourth category of canon 199 exemptions. The parallel provision in the 1917 code detailed the precise territories included, namely, ecclesiastical provinces, dioceses, parishes, apostolic vicariates and prefectures, and abbacies and prelatures *nullius*.[10] Since the same varieties of ecclesiastical territory continue to be

recognized in the 1983 code (see cc. 368–374, 431),[11] they should be understood as included in canon 199, 4°; the more general language of canon 199, 4°, however, would also include additional categories of ecclesiastical territory provided for in the 1983 code, such as ecclesiastical regions (see c. 433). If a particular boundary is uncertain or disputed, then the boundary is subject to prescription, it being among the purposes of prescription to bring closure to uncertainties and disputes (see commentary introducing title X).

Canon 199, 5° exempts from prescription Mass offerings and obligations. This is in accord with the strictness of the Church's stance in regard to the faithful fulfillment of all Mass obligations (see cc. 947–958, 1308–1309), whether they arise from freely accepted individual stipends or from legitimately established foundations, autonomous or non-autonomous (see c. 1303). No passage of time relieves one from the obligation to celebrate Mass or the designated number of Masses for which one has accepted an offering unless, of course, one has legitimately transferred the offering and obligation to another (see c. 955, §1). The same is true of juridic persons, such as parishes or houses of a religious institute, which have accepted Mass stipends. Nor does passage of time relieve one (e.g., a pastor) from giving to priests who have celebrated stipend Masses the full stipends for Masses celebrated unless the priests have voluntarily relinquished their rights to the stipends.[12]

Canon 199, 6° is a puzzling provision. Earlier canons appear to make clear that no ecclesiastical office can validly be acquired without canonical provision (c. 146), and that canonical provision of an office occurs by free conferral, installation if presentation preceded it, confirmation or admis-

---

[10] *CIC* 1509.

[11] In the 1983 code, abbacies and prelatures *nullius* are called territorial abbacies and prelatures (see c. 370).

[12] Notwithstanding the exemption of Mass offerings and obligations from prescription, the code does provide for the reduction of Mass obligations by certain ecclesiastical authorities in strictly limited circumstances (see commentary on c. 1308).

sion following election or postulation, or "finally" (*tandem*) by simple election and acceptance if confirmation is not required (c. 147). Canon 199, 6° implies, however, that an office which does not require the exercise of a sacred order can also be acquired by prescription, thus adding to the earlier, apparently taxative, list of the ways in which ecclesiastical offices can be acquired. Offices that do not require the exercise of a sacred order include the chancellor (see c. 482), diocesan finance officer (see c. 494), member of a diocesan finance council (see cc. 492–493), and superior in a lay institute of consecrated life.

Even more puzzling is the ambiguity of canon 199, 6° as to whether or not an office which does require the exercise of a sacred order is exempt from prescription only by one who lacks the requisite order. The published history of the drafting of canon 199 is silent on the matter, and the 1917 code did not contain a similar provision. Since one who lacks a sacred order which is expressly required by law for the valid reception of a particular office (see, e.g., cc. 150; 521, §1; 546) cannot validly acquire such an office because of the lack of a required quality (see c. 149, §2), canon 199, 6° would be an unnecessary provision of law if applicable only to those who lack the requisite sacred order for a particular office. It would seem, therefore, that canon 199, 6° is intended to preclude all provision by prescription of an ecclesiastical office which by law requires the exercise of a sacred order, even by those in possession of the requisite sacred order.

One of the defining characteristics and fundamental obligations of a Catholic is the obligation to maintain communion with the universal Church and with one's particular church through obedience to competent ecclesiastical authority (see cc. 205, 209, 212, §1). The hierarchy of the Church, in turn, is obliged to protect the unity of the Church by the promotion of doctrinal and moral integrity and by urging the observance of all ecclesiastical laws (see cc. 392, 747–755). Physical visitation is a means by which ecclesiastical authority can exercise vigilance over Catholic persons, institutions, and activities to verify that, both in commitment and in op-

eration, they are in accord with Catholic teaching and discipline (see cc. 305, 397, §1). Canon 199, 7° exempts from prescription the right of visitation on the part of ecclesiastical authority, and the obligation of obedience on the part of the Christian faithful, in circumstances which would leave one or more members of the faithful without subjection to any ecclesiastical visitation or to any ecclesiastical authority at all. Transfer of the right of visitation from one ecclesiastical authority to another, or transfer of one's obligation of obedience from one authority to another, are not exempt from prescription. Only a loss of the right or obligation that would leave one or more members of the faithful with no obligation to obey any ecclesiastical authority is exempt from prescription. To allow such a loss to occur would permit the dissolution of the bond of ecclesiastical governance which, together with the bonds of the profession of faith and the sacraments, constitute the essential elements of full communion with the Catholic Church (see c. 205).[13]

TITLE XI
COMPUTATION OF TIME
[cc. 200–203]

The manner in which precise moments or periods of time are calculated often has serious consequences for persons subject to the law of the Church. The acquisition, duration, and expiration of many canonical rights and obligations depend upon particular measurements of time, as does eligibility for the reception of sacraments, religious profession, and election or appointment to office, and the validity of numerous juridic acts, especially procedural ones. It was said that over three hundred canons in the 1917 code involved some

---

[13] For a discussion of the application of prescription to the acquisition or loss of rights and obligations relating to temporal goods, see commentary on cc. 1268–1270.

mention of time,[14] and the same has been said of almost two hundred canons in the present code.[15] The final four canons of Book I set forth general norms for the computation of time in matters of canonical significance. The norms, which are intended to minimize ambiguity and afford as much juridical certainty as possible, are greatly simplified from those in the corresponding canons of the 1917 code,[16] and are virtually the same as those in the Code of Canons of the Eastern Churches.[17]

Canon 200 — Unless the law expressly provides otherwise, time is to be computed according to the norm of the following canons.

General norms governing the canonical computation of time begin with an acknowledgment that other norms having the force of law constitute exceptions to the general norms, and are to be followed in the matters to which they apply. Given the large number of canons that involve the reckoning of time, it is not surprising that there are a considerable number of exceptions to the general norms.

Some of the exceptions concern liturgical matters, such as the determination of the beginning of a day on which the faithful are bound to participate in the offering of the Eucharist. The general norm of canon 202 understands a day to begin at midnight; fulfillment of the precept to participate in Mass "on Sundays and other holy days of obligation" (c. 1247), however, may take place on the evening of the preceding day (c. 1248). Some exceptions are a consequence of the canonization of the local civil law regarding contracts (see c. 1290) and prescription (see cc. 197, 1268), as a result of which time is reckoned in such matters in the manner determined by civil law. Procedural

law governing ecclesiastical tribunals, in addition to prescribing a number of time limits of its own, provides for additional time limits to be determined by judges or by the mutual agreement of the parties (see cc. 1465–1466). Particular law of a diocese,[18] the proper law of an institute of consecrated life or a society of apostolic life, the statutes of a public or private juridic person or a college or group,[19] the decree of a diocesan bishop,[20] or custom may, and occasionally do, provide for the computation of certain periods of time in ways different from those set forth in the general norms of this title.

Canon 201 — §1. Continuous time is understood as that which undergoes no interruption.

§2. Useful time is understood as that which a person has to exercise or to pursue a right, so that it does not run for a person who is unaware or unable to act.

This canon introduces a fundamental canonical distinction between continuous time (*tempus continuum*) and useful or available time (*tempus utile*). Continuous time is the ordinary, moment-by-moment passage of time which undergoes no interruption as, for example, aging. Useful time is that which is available for the exercise or pursuit of a right and which does not run in instances of unawareness of the right or of the beginning of the time limit for its exercise, or in instances of inability to act due, for example, to illness. Unawareness, which can be due to ignorance or error, usually interrupts *tempus utile* by delaying its start; inability to act, although in some instances it may delay the beginning of the running of the *tempus utile,* most often intervenes to halt the running of the designated period of time after it has begun.[21]

---

[14] See A. Dubé, *The General Principles for the Reckoning of Time in Canon Law,* CanLawStud 144 (Washington, D.C.: Catholic University of America, 1941) 3.

[15] See A. Mendonça, in *CLSGBI Com,* 111.

[16] *CIC* 31–35.

[17] *CCEO* 1543–1546.

[18] See cc. 8, §2; 1520.

[19] See c. 165.

[20] See, e.g., c. 1751.

[21] Useful time (*tempus utile*) should not be confused with *peremptory time limits.* The latter expression refers to the effect of not acting within a designated time; *tempus*

Very few canons explicitly mention continuous time.[22] Many canons, however, explicitly state that the designated period of time is to be useful time. Though explicit affirmations of useful time are primarily found in canons regulating tribunal procedures,[23] they are also present in canons regarding such matters as presentation for office,[24] election to office,[25] postulation,[26] administrative recourse,[27] and administrative removal of a pastor.[28] Most canons that refer to intervals of time, however, are silent as to whether the time referred to is continuous or available (useful) time. In the absence of explicit or implicit designation, it would seem that continuous time, not *tempus utile,* should be understood as intended by the legislator; *tempus utile* is not to be presumed.[29]

A reasonable view to the contrary could argue that concern for the adequate protection of rights, which is the underlying rationale for *tempus utile* and, indeed, for all procedural law,[30] requires that

a designated period of time be presumed to be *tempus utile* whenever the passage of the interval of time could result in the loss of a procedural right, even if the particular procedural law in question makes no mention of *tempus utile.* Such a view might be said to find support in the wording of canon 162 which speaks of the *tempus utile* provided for in canons 158, §1 and 161 even though neither of those canons refers to the time limits they prescribe as *tempus utile.* The view is appealing and could perhaps find effective expression in an argument drawn from analogy to those procedural canons which do make explicit mention of useful time (see note 23).

On the other hand, a number of considerations lead to the opposite conclusion adopted above. Continuous time is the natural understanding of time, and the legislator's explicit reference to available time in many canons would seem to justify the conclusion that where *tempus utile* is not mentioned, it is not intended. An argument drawn from analogy to canons which mention *tempus utile* would seem to lack cogency in an area where the legislator has explicitly spoken of *tempus utile* in many canons and has not so spoken in others. Moreover, in regard to procedural acts in a tribunal, canon 1467 provides that if the tribunal is closed on the day scheduled for a judicial act, the time limit is extended to the first day that is not a holiday. Such a provision would be unnecessary if all procedural time limits, even those which were not so specified, were understood as *tempus utile;* canon 1467 seems to indicate that procedural time limits not said to be *tempus utile* are to be understood as continuous time, with provision for prorogation of the final day if it should fall on a holiday. Similarly, in canon 1646, which provides for the seeking of *restitutio in integrum* against a sentence in instances of manifest injustice, paragraph three provides that the time limit of three months, mentioned in paragraphs one and two of the canon, does not run as long as the injured person is a minor (and, hence, unable to make the petition). If all procedural time limits that could result in the loss of a procedural right are to be understood as *tempus utile* whether or

utile refers to the manner of computing the passage of a designated period of time. That the two expressions are not synonymous is clear from their occasional appearance together in the same canon (see, e.g., cc. 1630, §1; 1734, §2).

[22] See, e.g., cc. 26; 395, §2; 533, §2; 649, §1.

[23] See, e.g., cc. 1460, §3; 1505, §4; 1592, §2; 1599, §2; 1606; 1630, §1; 1634, §2; 1641, 2°; 1668, §2.

[24] See cc. 159, 162.

[25] See cc. 165; 177, §1; 179, §1.

[26] See c. 182.

[27] See cc. 1734, §2; 1737, §2.

[28] See c. 1744, §1.

[29] See J. Miñambres, in *Com Ex* 1:1109; *Chiappetta Com 1996,* 1:293; Mendonça, in *CLSGBI Com,* 112. The same view seems also to have been the commonly held view among commentators on the 1917 code. See A. Cicognani, *Canon Law,* 2nd rev. ed. (Philadelphia: Dolphin Press, 1935) 692–693; A. Vermeersch and I. Creusen, *Epitome Iuris Canonici,* 7th ed. (Rome: Dessain, 1949) 1:150; F. Cappello, *Summa Iuris Canonici,* 6th ed. (Rome: Gregorian University, 1961) 1:158; M. Conte a Coronata, *Institutiones Iuris Canonici,* 4th ed. (Turin, Italy: Marietti, 1950) 1:68; S. Sipos, *Enchiridion Iuris Canonici* (Rome: Herder, 1960) 46; J. Abbo and J. Hannan, *The Sacred Canons,* 2nd rev. ed. (St. Louis, Mo.: Herder, 1960) 1:67. A contrary view is expressed by Pinto, in *Urbaniana Com,* 108.

[30] See *EM* IV.

not the canon prescribing the time limit so states, paragraph three of canon 1646 would be superfluous; not only minority, but any other cause of inability to place a juridic act would also interrupt the running of the time limit. Canon 1646, like canon 1467, seems to confirm the view that where time limits are not said to refer to available (useful) time, they are to be understood as continuous time, with only such specific prorogations as are mentioned in specific canons.

Since the smallest canonically significant unit of time is a day (see commentary on c. 202), a significant interruption of *tempus utile* results in the addition of a full day to the designated time limit, even though one actually may have been impeded from acting for only a few hours. Not every interruption of *tempus utile,* however, is significant; a *notable* interruption is required in order to have an additional full day added to the period of time allotted for a particular action or condition to have been fulfilled.[31] Some authors would require an interruption to last for the *greater part of a day* in order to be canonically significant.[32] The notions of *notable* and *greater part of a day,* however, are necessarily relative, depending upon the nature and extent of the interruption in relation to the number of hours in the day during which a particular act could be placed. Some acts can be placed only during certain hours of certain days (e.g., a particular tribunal may be open for business only on weekdays from 10 A.M. to 3 P.M.) whereas other acts (e.g., deciding whom to appoint to a particular ecclesiastical office) can take place during a much longer time period on any day. To qualify as *notable,* or as lasting for the *greater part of a day,* an interruption caused by unawareness or inability to act would have to be of longer duration in the latter instances than in the former.[33] It is a matter for the prudent judgment of a judge or superior to de-

termine in a particular case whether or not a sufficiently significant interruption of available (useful) time has occurred to warrant prorogation of the designated time limit.[34]

Canon 202 — §1. In law, a day is understood as a period consisting of 24 continuous hours and begins at midnight unless other provision is expressly made; a week is a period of 7 days; a month is a period of 30 days, and a year is a period of 365 days unless a month and a year are said to be taken as they are in the calendar.

§2. If time is continuous, a month and a year must always be taken as they are in the calendar.

Initial wonder as to why it would be thought necessary to include in a code of canon law statements as to how many hours are in a day, and how many days are in a week, or a month, or a year, eventually yields to the realization that the ambiguities that often characterize everyday speech in such matters are incompatible with the precision demanded by law. When canonical rights, duties, and even the ownership of property are contingent upon the passage of designated intervals of days, weeks, months, or years, it is imperative to know precisely when, for canonical purposes, a day is considered to begin (e.g., at midnight, at dawn, at the opening of office hours), how long it is considered to last (e.g., to the close of office hours, to sunset, to midnight), how many days constitute a week (7 days, or 5 working days, or 6 working days), how many days constitute a month (31 or 30 or 28 or, in a leap year, 29), and how many days constitute a year (360,[35] or 365, or 366).

The primary unit of time for canonical purposes is a day; parts of a day, as a general rule, are not accorded canonical significance.[36] A day is canon-

---

[31] See Dubé, 237–240; Conte a Coronata, 1:68; Vermeersch-Creusen, 1:149; H. Jone, *Commentarium in Codicem Iuris Canonici* (Paderborn, Germany: Schöningh, 1950) 1:56.

[32] See, e.g., *Chiappetta Com 1996,* 1:293; Cappello, 1:158.

[33] See Dubé, 237.

[34] Ibid., 239.

[35] Some computations in the financial world consider a year to be composed of 12 equal months of 30 days each, resulting, for some purposes, in a year of 360 days.

[36] The sole exception in the code is the prescribed one-hour fast prior to the reception of Holy Communion (see c. 919, §1).

ically understood to be a period of 24 continuous hours beginning at midnight, unless otherwise expressly provided (e.g., in particular or proper law). A week is understood to be a period of 7 days, consecutive if computed as continuous time, intermittent (in units of whole days, not parts of a day) if computed as *tempus utile*. A month is understood to be a period of 30 days unless it is to be computed as it is in the calendar (in which case some months will have 30 days while others will have 31 or 28 or, in a leap year, 29 days). A year is a period of 365 days unless it is to be computed as it is in the calendar (in which case leap years will have 366 days).

A month is to be computed as it is in the calendar whenever it is referred to by name or equivalently so (as, e.g., "next month"); similarly, a year is to be computed as it is in the calendar if specifically referred to (e.g., "the year of 2000") or equivalently so (as, e.g., "next year"). Moreover, canon 202, §2 provides that whenever time is to be computed continuously, which is usually the case (see commentary on c. 201), a month and a year are always to be understood as they are in the calendar. Thus, a one-month period of continuous time that begins on January 1 will consist of 31 days; a one-month period of continuous time beginning on February 1 will consist of only 28 (or, in a leap year, 29) days; a one-month period of continuous time beginning on April 1 will consist of 30 days. Similarly, a year of continuous time beginning on January 1, 2000 will consist of 366 days, while a year of continuous time beginning on January 1, 2001 will consist of 365 days.

A month computed as *tempus utile,* however, always consists of 30 unimpeded days which, depending upon the number of canonically significant interruptions (see commentary on c. 201), could last more than 30 calendar days. Similarly, a year computed as *tempus utile* always consists of 365 unimpeded days which could last more than 365 calendar days depending upon the number of canonically significant interruptions.

Canon 203 — §1. The initial day (*a quo*) is not computed in the total unless its beginning coin-cides with the beginning of the day or the law expressly provides otherwise.**

§2. Unless the contrary is established, the final day (*ad quem*) is computed in the total which, if the time consists of one or more months or years, or one or more weeks, is reached at the end of the last day of the same number or, if a month lacks a day of the same number, at the end of the last day of the month.

As is clear from canon 202, the basic unit of time for canonical purposes is a day and, as a general rule subject to exceptions, a day is canonically understood to begin at midnight. Canon 203, §1 declares, also as a general rule subject to exceptions, that canonical intervals of time such as weeks, months, and years begin at the beginning of the day, that is, at midnight, *following* the event that occasions the canonically significant period of time (e.g., birth, temporary religious profession, publication of a sentence, acquiring potentially prescriptive possession of property) unless the event coincides precisely with the beginning of a canonical day (usually midnight). Succinctly stated, the actual day from which a computation is to be made (the *terminus a quo*) is not counted unless the event which occasions the computation coincides with the beginning of the day. This general norm applies both to continuous time and to *tempus utile*.[37]

Conversely, unless expressly provided otherwise, the entire final day (the *terminus ad quem*) *is* counted so that the interval of time is not completed until midnight at the *end* of the final day of the designated interval. This general norm also applies both to continuous time and to *tempus utile*.[38]

One's actual day of birth, therefore, is not counted in the computation of one's age (unless one were born precisely at midnight), and one does not complete a year of age until midnight at the close of one's birthday. Consequently, one cannot licitly be ordained to the priesthood until the day following one's twenty-fifth birthday, since the law requires completion of twenty-five

---

[37] See Miñambres, in *Com Ex,* 1:1115.
[38] Ibid.

years of age (c. 1031, §1), nor can one validly be admitted to perpetual profession in a religious institute until the day following one's twenty-first birthday (see c. 658). Similarly, the three-month period of *de facto* residence required for the acquisition of quasi-domicile, and the five-year period of *de facto* residence required for the acquisition of domicile (see c. 102), do not begin to run until the midnight following one's actual taking up of residence, and are not completed until the midnight following the last day of the three-month or five-year periods.

So, too, in the computation of *tempus utile* as, for example, in computing the ten days within which one may take recourse against rejection of a *libellus* (see c. 1505, §4), the day of rejection (*terminus a quo*) is not counted, and the period of ten unimpeded days begins at midnight at the close of that day; the ten-day period will expire at midnight at the end of the tenth unimpeded[39] day.

Canon 203, §2 also makes explicit what is implicit in canon 202, namely, that weeks, months, and years computed not as *tempus utile* but con-

---

[39] For the meaning of "unimpeded," see commentary on c. 201.

tinuously, which is usually the case (see commentary on c. 201), expire at midnight at the end of the corresponding day of the final week or corresponding date of the final month. A three-week period of continuous time beginning on a Wednesday (i.e., according to c. 203, §1, at midnight at the end of a Wednesday), for example, will expire at midnight at the end of the third ensuing Wednesday. A three-month period of continuous time beginning on November 15 will expire at midnight at the end of February 15. If, however, the final month does not have a corresponding date (as, e.g., when a three-month period begins on November 30), the *terminus ad quem* is considered to have been reached at midnight at the end of the last calendar day in the final month of the designated interval (e.g., in a three-month period beginning on November 30, on February 28 or, in a leap year, on February 29).

Tempus utile, on the other hand, is always computed without regard to the calendar. One month of *tempus utile* beginning on January 31, for example, will not, under any circumstances, expire on February 28; thirty unimpeded days must pass before the one month of *tempus utile* will expire.

BOOK II
THE PEOPLE OF GOD
[cc. 204–746]

Robert J. Kaslyn, S.J.

The title of Book II of the code, "The People of God," not only reflects its content but also indicates a foundational ecclesiological perspective. Both the number of canons which Book II contains (543) as well as this ecclesiological perspective clearly demonstrate the importance of its material. This introduction will address two topics in particular. After presenting an overview of the contents of Book II, the introduction will discuss the ecclesiology presented in the code. Canons 204–207 are of special importance in that they fulfill two important functions: from the specific context, these canons introduce the contents of Book II; from a broader perspective, they present ecclesiological principles foundational to the entire code.[1]

The three major divisions of Book II include: part one, "The Christian Faithful" (the *Christifideles*, cc. 204–329); part two, "The Hierarchical Constitution of the Church" (cc. 330–572); and part three, "Institutes of Consecrated Life and Societies of Apostolic Life" (cc. 573–746).

Part one, "The Christian Faithful," begins with an introduction consisting of four canons generally describing the Christian faithful (cc. 204–207), followed by sixteen canons which constitute title I, "The Obligations and Rights of All the Christian Faithful" (cc. 208–223). The remaining topics in part one include rights and duties specific to lay people (cc. 224–231); the rights and duties of clerics as well as norms on clerical formation, incardination ("enrollment") and excardination, and loss of the clerical state (cc. 232–293). Part one concludes with personal prelatures and associations of the faithful (cc. 294–329). Part two, "The Hierarchical Constitution of the Church," is divided into two primary topics: "The Supreme Authority of the Church" (cc. 330–367) and "Par-

ticular Churches and Their Groupings" (cc. 368–572). The first topic considers the Roman Pontiff and the college of bishops as well as the synod of bishops, cardinals and legates, and the Roman Curia. The second topic, particular churches, includes the function, appointment, and authority of bishops; provinces, metropolitans, and conferences of bishops; and internal diocesan and parochial governance structures. The canons in part three (cc. 573–746) concern religious and secular institutes as well as societies of apostolic life and begin with norms common to all institutes of consecrated life (cc. 573–606). Each of these subjects, however, as well as the other canons in the code, presuppose and build upon the first twenty canons in Book II, namely, canons 204–223. For example, the rights and duties of all the Christian faithful apply not only to lay people but also to clerics and to members of institutes of consecrated life.

Through its arrangement of this material, the Eastern code demonstrates the foundational role of these canons more clearly than does the Latin code. The Eastern code begins with six preliminary canons specifying the scope of the text and then articulates "The Rights and Obligations of All the Christian Faithful" in title I (*CCEO*, cc. 7–26, of which cc. 7–9 correspond to cc. 204–206 of the Latin code).

In Book II itself, the four introductory canons, cc. 204–207, exercise a determinative role for the interpretation not only of the remaining canons in Book II but of the entire code. These canons introduce critical foundational and ecclesiological principles which, as Pope John Paul II states in *Sacrae disciplinae leges*, "characterize the true and genuine image of the Church." Canons 204–207 succinctly describe the Catholic Church and the various relationships (or "degrees of relationship") which all the baptized, through reception of baptism, enjoy with the Catholic Church. This description finds greater elaboration throughout the

---

[1] For other introductions to Book II, see J. Hervada, in *Pamplona ComEng,* 185; and J. Provost, in *CLSA Com,* 117–119.

code, and specifically in Book II, in reference to the mission incumbent upon the baptized, derived from their participation in the threefold functions (*munera*) of Jesus Christ, priest, prophet, and ruler. This mission is variously described: "to promote the growth of the Church and its continual sanctification" (c. 210); to "cooperate in the building up of the Body of Christ" (c. 208); "to promote or sustain apostolic action" (c. 216). This mission, derived from baptism, applies to all the baptized independent of their particular status or condition in the Church.[2]

One approach to the ecclesiology expressed in cc. 204–207 arises from the title of Book II, "The People of God." This title reflects the ecclesiological perspective of *Lumen gentium*, especially chapter 2, itself entitled, "The People of God." According to *Lumen gentium* 9, "It has pleased God, however, to sanctify and save men and women not individually and without regard for what binds them together, but to set them up as a people who would acknowledge him in truth and serve him in holiness." Chapter 2 of *Lumen gentium* provides a more particular description of the people of God: it emphasizes God's initiative, inviting all people to enter into a redemptive relationship with him and the salvific life, death, and resurrection of Jesus Christ, who thereby institutes a new covenant uniting God's people in and through the Holy Spirit. The people of God enjoy

the dignity and freedom of the children of God; their law is Christ's commandment of love; their goal is the kingdom of God; their mission is to be a light for the world.

This description, with its trinitarian emphasis, expands the succinct statement in *Lumen gentium* 4: "the universal church appears as a people made one by the unity of the Father and the Son and the Holy Spirit." Both the concept "the people of God" and its underlying trinitarian foundation find systematic clarification in the ecclesiology of *communio* (*koinonia*). The ecclesiology of *communio* finds expression in various documents issued by Pope John Paul II, the synods of bishops, and the Roman dicasteries.[3] The Congregation for the Doctrine of the Faith issued a document in 1992 entitled, "Letter to the Bishops of the Catholic Church on Some Aspects of the Church

---

[2] See CFC et al., "Some Questions Regarding Collaboration of Nonordained Faithful in Priests' Sacred Ministry" (cited hereafter as "Some Questions"), *Origins* 27 (November 27, 1997) 399, 400–409, followed by "The Instruction: An Explanatory Note," 409–410. This text, approved in *forma specifica* by Pope John Paul II, is an instruction signed by the heads of eight Vatican offices: CFC, PCL, CDF, CDWDS, CFB, CEP, CICLSAL, and PCILT. The instruction explains the meaning of approval in *forma specifica* by the pope: such action "makes it a text bearing his own authority and against which there can be no appeal" (410). The text itself, "Some Questions," aims at clarifying "new forms of 'pastoral activity' of the nonordained on both parochial and diocesan levels" (400) and begins by reiterating the call of all the faithful "to participate actively in the mission and edification of the people of God" (399).

[3] In paragraph 42 of his apostolic exhortation, *VC*, John Paul II situated the mission of members of institutes of consecrated life in the context of the Church as "essentially a mystery of communion" (*Origins* 25 [April 4, 1996] 695). "Some Questions" uses the same context for its discussion of collaboration within the Church (400, #1). CICLSAL continued this theme in its document *FL* which presents religious community as an expression of ecclesial communion (#10). The 1993 *Ecum Dir* uses the ecclesiology of *communio* as a foundation for understanding and promoting the ecumenical movement; see especially paragraphs 13–25 and 92–160 (the latter paragraphs are entitled "IV. Communion in Life and Spiritual Activity Among the Baptized"). Paragraph 24 of the "Final Message for the Synod of Africa" states, "It is the church as family which manifests to the world the Spirit which the Son sent from the Father so that there should be communion among all" (*Origins* 24 [May 19, 1994] 5). See also the *lineamenta* for the special assembly of the synod of bishops for America, "Encounter with the Living Jesus Christ: The Way to Conversion, Communion and Solidarity in America," in *Origins* (26 August 15, 1996) 145, 147–164, especially paragraphs 29–47 "Third Part: Jesus Christ, the Way to Communion," 154–158.

One of the foremost authors on *communio*, J.-M.-R. Tillard, approached the ecclesiology of communion from the perspective of canon law in "Ecclesiology of Communion and Canon Law: The Theological Task of Canon Law: A Theologian's Perspective," in *CLSAP* 58 (1996) 24–34.

Understood as Communion."[4] This letter begins as follows:

> The concept of *communion* (*koinonia*), which appears with a certain prominence in the texts of the Second Vatican Council is very suitable for expressing the core of the mystery of the church and can certainly be a key for the renewal of Catholic ecclesiology. A deeper appreciation of the fact that the church is a communion is indeed a task of special importance which provides ample latitude for theological reflection. (#1)

The canons of the code further elaborate this ecclesiology; general references are provided here with more in-depth commentary found in the analysis of specific canons.

Communio exists first and foremost as a relationship with God, rooted in the presence of the Holy Spirit. Through his Spirit, God invites the individual to participate in the intra-trinitarian communion of Father, Son, and Spirit. Inasmuch as *communio* arises from this participation in the divine life, any discussion of ecclesiology must include this essential dimension. Given the social nature of the human person, salvation, a relationship with God, cannot remain solely between the individual and God but involves a specific community of faith: "For by natural constitution the human person is a social being who cannot live or develop without relations with others" and these relations "bring about the first form of the communion of persons."[5] Thus communion does not remain internal but finds external expression in the reception of baptism.[6] Through this sacramen-

tal initiation, a person is incorporated into Christ, becomes a member of the people of God, and exercises the mission entrusted by Christ to his Church. Through baptism, a person becomes one of the Christian faithful (*Christifideles*, c. 204, §1), who participate in the threefold functions (*munera*) of Christ as priest, prophet, and ruler. All the baptized are therefore placed in communion with God, with all the other baptized, and with the Catholic Church in which the Church of Christ subsists (c. 204, §2).

This ecclesiological perspective provides the necessary background for the first canon in the code: the code applies primarily to Latin Catholics. But Latin Catholics are in communion not only with Eastern Catholics but also with members of separated and reformed churches and ecclesial communities, although in the latter instance the relationship does not express full communion. Further, *communio* forms the theological and canonical basis, for example, of the sacramental sharing of the Eucharist, penance, and anointing of the sick (c. 844) and of the distinction between disparity of cult marriages (which require a dispensation, c. 1086) and so-called mixed marriages (which require only permission, cc. 1124–1129).

Each of the baptized lives in some degree of communion with the Catholic Church; the baptized in full communion are those "joined with Christ in its visible structure by the bonds of the profession of faith, the sacraments, and ecclesiastical governance" (c. 205). The impetus for full communion with the Catholic Church is the Holy Spirit, the origin and continuing inspiration for *communio* itself. In title I of Book II, "The Obligations and Rights of All the Christian Faithful," after the first canon which states the fundamental equality of all the faithful, canon 209 enunciates the obligation incumbent upon the faithful "to maintain communion" (§1) and to fulfill their responsibilities "to the universal Church and the

---

[4] *Origins* 22 (June 15, 1992) 108–112.

[5] *GS* 12.

[6] According to c. 849, baptism is "necessary for salvation by actual reception or at least by desire"; the Church, therefore, does not deny the possibility of salvation to those who have not received this sacrament, who also share to some degree in the divine communion arising from the gift of the Holy Spirit. See, for example, *GS* 10: "It is the church's belief that Christ, who died and

was raised for everyone, offers to the human race through his Spirit the light and strength to respond to its highest calling."

particular church to which they belong." Communion finds its paramount expression in and through the celebration of the Eucharist; this celebration particularizes *communio* as it exists in the Catholic Church, both representing and creating unity among the Christian faithful.[7] According to the *Ecumenical Directory*, "Eucharistic communion is inseparably linked to full ecclesial communion and its visible expression" (#129). Consequently, the Eucharist is celebrated by a community united in faith, sacraments, and governance (cc. 204–205). Canon 844 indicates the conditions under which non-Catholic Christians may exceptionally receive the sacraments of the Eucharist, penance, and anointing of the sick.

The parish, "a certain community of the Christian faithful stably constituted in a particular church" (c. 515), celebrates the Eucharist as a community of faith; this celebration signifies and unites the people of God and builds up the body of Christ (c. 897) and thereby manifests *communio*. In turn, the diocese, "a portion of the people of God . . . entrusted to a bishop for him to shepherd with the cooperation of the presbyterate" (c. 369), expresses *communio* through the celebration of the Eucharist, most particularly as manifested in the Eucharist celebrated by the diocesan bishop in the presence of his presbyters and the people entrusted to his care. The bishops themselves are united by the bond of *communio* among themselves within the episcopal college, "together with its head and never without this head," the Supreme Pontiff (c. 336). This communion finds its clearest expression in an ecumenical council, more specifically, through the Eucharistic celebration presided over by the bishop of Rome. Communion therefore permeates every level of the Church's visible expression in the world and as a result provides the basis for the Christian faithful's lives of prayer and activity.

Communion provides the underlying unity among the different vocations, states of life, and ministries which exist within the Church through the gifts of the Holy Spirit. The Holy Spirit as origin and impetus for *communio* is "the dynamic principle of diversity and unity in the Church" (*CL* 20). Unity does not require uniformity but rather a fundamental recognition of the one mission entrusted to the Church by Jesus Christ himself, a mission which involves the participation of all the faithful in diverse ways.

The ecclesiology of *communio* thus establishes the foundation for synthesizing the various images used to describe the Church—for example, as the people of God, as sacrament, as the Body of Christ. In addition, this ecclesiology provides the ground for understanding and interpreting the code. Thus, as a general principle, the nature and exercise of authority in the Church on all levels must be situated within *communio*: the Church's hierarchical structure exists to serve and foster *communio*, to build up the Church as the Body of Christ, and to ensure the active participation of each of the faithful in the Church's mission. More particularly, *communio* also forms the context for interpreting canons which concern, for example, the mission of lay men and women, of members of institutes of consecrated life, and of clerics in the universal call to holiness; the exercise of the teaching office; the relationship among members of various forms of consecrated life (both among themselves and with others, either Christian faithful or not). All church activity, either in virtue of baptism (participation in the threefold functions [*munera*] of Christ as priest, prophet, and ruler; see c. 204) or in virtue of some type of official authorization by competent ecclesiastical authority (for example, through mandate, delegation, or appointment to ecclesiastical office), must aim at maintaining and fostering *communio* among all the people of God so that the Church continues to proclaim the gospel message. *Communio*, through its origin in the divine life, recognizes the importance of charisms in the Church's life and provides a means and a context for their exercise. Canon law needs to reflect further and to develop specific means to implement the ecclesiology of *communio* in the Church's life, in reference both to those in full communion (c. 205) and to those persons who

---

[7] See, for example, *LG* 3 and 11.

through baptism live in some degree of communion with the Catholic Church.[8]

Finally, the ecclesiology of *communio* indicates the unique nature of law in the Church, distinguishing it from civil law by reason of its trinitarian and sacramental basis. Canon law exists to serve the Church's mission: the salvation of souls (c. 1752).

---

[8] See Tillard, "Ecclesiology of Communion," especially 29–34; and J. Provost, "Structuring the Church as a Communio," in *The Church as Communion,* ed. J. Provost (Washington, D.C.: CLSA, 1984) 191–245.

CANONS AND COMMENTARY

Part I
THE CHRISTIAN FAITHFUL
[cc. 204–329]

INTRODUCTORY CANONS
[cc. 204–207]

The Christian Faithful

Canon 204 — §1. The Christian faithful are those who, inasmuch as they have been incorporated in Christ through baptism, have been constituted as the people of God. For this reason, made sharers in their own way in Christ's priestly, prophetic, and royal function, they are called to exercise the mission which God has entrusted to the Church to fulfill in the world, in accord with the condition proper to each.

§2. This Church, constituted and organized in this world as a society, subsists in the Catholic Church governed by the successor of Peter and the bishops in communion with him.

This canon, in a few but highly nuanced sentences, presents an ecclesiological foundation for the interpretation of the code, a foundation which finds further expansion in the following canons, especially in canons 205–207. These introductory canons contain theological affirmations requiring theological interpretation and analysis prior to canonical explanation and application. The Eastern code presents the same foundation in canon 7.[9]

The first paragraph of canon 204 establishes a fundamental distinction among all people: either they have received the sacrament of baptism or not. All the baptized, therefore, constitute the Christian faithful, the *Christifideles*. Like the other sacraments, baptism has both social and individual effects inasmuch as the sacraments influence not only the relationship between God and a particular individual but necessarily involve a specific community of faith. As the canon describes the ramifications of this sacrament, baptism has a personal, individual effect: incorporation into Christ. This personal relationship with Jesus Christ is presupposed in other consequences of baptism as elaborated by canon 204, §1. But baptism also has a social effect: a person enters into the people of God; more particularly, the person enters into a specific community of faith.

From these relationships—with Christ and with the rest of the people of God—flow two consequences: first, the person, in virtue of baptism, participates in the threefold functions (*mu-*

---

[9] For other analyses of canon 204, see Hervada, in *Pamplona ComEng,* 186; A. McGrath, in *CLSGBI Com,* 115–116; and Provost, in *CLSA Com,* 122–126.

nera) of Christ as priest, prophet, and ruler. Second, the person receives a call (*vocatio*) to exercise the mission of the Church in the world, a mission derived from God and from the person's active response to God's initiative. Both consequences require specific determination: individuals participate in the triple functions (*munera*) each "in their own way," and they exercise this mission in distinct manners, determined in reference to each person's "condition." Before we clarify further these types of determinations, a foundational principle must be understood.

The effects and consequences of baptism expressed in §1 apply to all the baptized, whether Catholic or not. This application to all the baptized forms one of the constitutive principles of a *communio* ecclesiology: by the fact of baptism, each of the baptized enters into a relationship with all other baptized; all the baptized are equal in dignity and all are called to exercise the Church's mission (see c. 208).[10] According to canon 207, "by divine institution" all the Christian faithful are either clerics or laity. Specifically within the code, apart from such theological statements as in this paragraph, the term "Christian faithful" (*Christifideles*) applies to the baptized who live in full communion with the Catholic Church (c. 205). Thus derives a second principle of a *communio* ecclesiology: varying degrees of communion exist, i.e., degrees of relationship with the Catholic Church. Canon 204, following the conciliar texts, does not refer to membership but rather to incorporation; degrees of incorporation exist. "Incorporation" as used in §1 does not necessarily imply "full incorporation"; "communion with the Church" does not necessarily imply "full communion." Incorporation is a more dynamic term than membership, reflecting the ongoing and hopefully deepening relationship between the individual and God and between the individual and the community of faith. Thus, the relationship between a baptized person and the

Catholic Church receives specification along a continuum from "communion" to "full communion" and this specification forms the primary aspect of the "condition" proper to each baptized person.

This *communio* among all of the baptized with the Catholic Church forms the basis for the ecumenical movement.[11] The code refers to ecumenism in canon 755, §1 (the competence of the college of bishops and the Apostolic See in promoting and directing Catholic participation in the ecumenical movement); canon 383, §3 (the bishop's role in fostering ecumenism); and canon 256 (instruction of seminarians in ecumenical concerns). The code also provides more particular actions: canon 463, §3 allows the bishop to invite persons not in full communion to the diocesan synod as observers; canon 825, §2 allows Catholics and "separated brothers and sisters" to cooperate in preparing and publishing translations of scripture with the permission of the conference of bishops; canon 844, §4 establishes conditions for administering the sacraments of penance, Eucharist, and anointing of the sick to Christians who do not enjoy full communion; canon 1183, §3 outlines circumstances in which funeral rites can be granted to baptized non-Catholics; and canons 1124–1129 refer to mixed marriages.

Thus the foundational "condition" of the faithful arises from the reception of baptism; as noted, there are varying degrees of communion with the Catholic Church, and this affects the exercise of rights and duties. A related canon, canon 96, states that the Christian faithful can exercise rights and duties "insofar as they are in ecclesiastical communion"; unlike canon 204, this canon refers to the baptized person primarily from a juridical rather than theological perspective.[12] An individual's condition is also determined by other factors, for example, age (cc. 97–98), mental capacity (c. 99), residence (including but not limited to domicile and quasi-domicile; see cc. 100–107

---

[10] In the context of c. 204, §1, the word "Church" refers to the Church of Christ; §2 clarifies the relationship between the Church of Christ and the Catholic Church.

[11] See, for example, *Ecum Dir*, especially 13–21.

[12] For a further discussion of rights and obligations, see the introduction to title I (cc. 208–223).

and 209, §2). Reception of sacraments also affects one's condition. For example, holy orders establishes further rights and obligations for the one ordained (cc. 207, 1008, 273–289) as does the sacrament of matrimony for the spouses (cc. 226; 774, §2; 1135–1136). An individual's condition also changes when he or she makes a public commitment in an institute of consecrated life (cc. 573 and 662–672). Further, an individual belongs to a particular ritual church (for example, the Latin church or the Ukrainian Catholic Church; see cc. 111–112).[13] Finally, sanctions may affect an individual's standing and thus condition in the Church, provided that these are "legitimately issued" (c. 96).

According to canon 204, the faithful participate through baptism in the threefold functions (*munera*) "in their own way." Two consequences derive from this. First, all the people of God possess a role in exercising the functions of Jesus Christ priest, prophet, and ruler. Through this participation, the Christian faithful continue the mission of Christ entrusted to the Church: to proclaim the gospel and thus continue the work of redemption. The qualifying phrase, "in their own way," refers to the second consequence: each of the faithful receives and accepts a specific vocation from God.[14] The code refers more explicitly to participation in the offices of priest and prophet, less explicitly to the governing office.[15]

Paragraph two, citing *Lumen gentium* 8, expresses a theological principle foundational to a *communio* ecclesiology, namely, the fact that the two terms, "Church of Christ" and "Catholic Church," are not identical with one another;

rather, "this Church [of Christ] ... subsists in the Catholic Church."[16] *Lumen gentium* 8—and this canon which quotes it—thus makes a positive affirmation that the Church founded by Christ continues to exist as a visible society, active in history, guided by the Holy Spirit, and under the leadership of the successor of Peter and the bishops in communion with him (cc. 331 and 336). From the canonical perspective, the most important implications of this teaching—the relationship among all the baptized—refer to the possibility of sacramental sharing (c. 844) and the canons concerned with mixed marriage (cc. 1124–1129). While "many elements of sanctification and of truth are to be found" outside the structure of the Catholic Church,[17] these elements "impel toward Catholic unity."[18] The same texts recognize the unique place held by the Catholic Church: "For it is only through Christ's catholic church, which is the all-embracing means of salvation, that the fullness of the means of salvation can be attained."[19] Any form of religious syncretism, i.e., that all churches are equal, is clearly rejected, a principle also found in the *Ecumenical Directory*, paragraph 17.

By analogy with the Incarnation, the Church exists in the world as a visible reality, a society. But the visible society possesses a distinct purpose: it "serves the Spirit of Christ who vivifies the church towards the growth of the body";[20] this purpose serves as a refutation of attempts to distinguish between, for example, "the Church of law" and "the Church of charity" as though the Church could exist in the world independent of any structure or of any norms.

---

[13] Note the important principle in c. 112, §2: baptism in the Latin church does not necessarily enroll that person into the Latin church.

[14] For specific examples of this participation, see cc. 208–223 (which apply to all the Christian faithful); cc. 224–231 (which pertain to lay Christian faithful); and cc. 273–289 (which apply to clerics).

[15] For further treatment of this topic, see commentary on canons 129 and 228 on clerical and lay eligibility to participate in governing power.

[16] *LG* 8. For a fuller treatment of the phrase, "subsists in," see F. Sullivan, "The Significance of the Vatican II Declaration that the Church of Christ 'Subsists in' the Roman Catholic Church," in *Vatican II: Assessment and Perspectives,* vol. 2, ed. R. Latourelle (New York: Paulist, 1989) 272–287.

[17] *LG* 8. See also, for example, *UR* 3; *UR* 22; and *OE* 25.

[18] *LG* 8.

[19] *UR* 3.

[20] *LG* 8.

Full Communion

Canon 205 — Those baptized are fully in the communion of the Catholic Church on this earth who are joined with Christ in its visible structure by the bonds of the profession of faith, the sacraments, and ecclesiastical governance.

This canon continues the ecclesiological foundation of the code by identifying those persons who live in "full communion" with the Catholic Church (see *CCEO* 8). As discussed in reference to canon 204, all the baptized share some relationship—to a greater or lesser degree—with the Catholic Church. Thus, a distinction exists between "full communion" and "communion," between "full incorporation" and "incorporation"; canon 205 offers basic criteria for determining, in the external forum, which persons live in "full communion" with the Catholic Church.

The canon derives from *Lumen gentium* 14 with two important modifications: it deletes the phrase "possessing the Spirit of Christ" (describing those persons who are "fully incorporated into the society of the Church") and omits one of the bonds, namely, that of communion.[21] While the canon focuses on external criteria for determining full communion, it does not ignore the internal dimension, indicated by the phrase "joined with Christ." *Communio* ecclesiology presupposes the grace of God through this union: the Holy Spirit is constitutive of the Church as *communio*. These three bonds (the profession of faith, the sacraments, and ecclesiastical governance) imply some type of faith relationship with God as a reason for the person to assume freely the obligations inherent in them. The omission of the fourth bond—communion—raises fewer difficulties inasmuch as canon 209 obliges all the Christian faithful to maintain communion with the Church.

The code does not specify the content of the three bonds; inasmuch as breaking full communion restricts rights (c. 96), canon 18, requiring a strict interpretation of such laws, would apply in any attempt to determine that a person is no longer in full communion. Thus, the application of this canon to a particular individual and precise situation requires great caution to avoid violating individual rights, for example, the right to a good reputation (c. 220). In addition, external actions do not always or necessarily correspond to interior dispositions; we must maintain the distinction between the external forum and the internal forum as well as realize that harmony between these two fora does not always exist.

One of the principles for the code revision and approved by the 1967 synod of bishops urged proper coordination between the external and the internal fora so as to avoid conflict between them. The judgment that an individual has in fact broken the bond of full communion pertains primarily to the external forum; it does not necessarily indicate that a person has committed sin. Although an individual's external activities should generally reflect his or her interior dispositions, a conflict could arise between a person's internal faith relationship ("communion") with God and the person's incorporation into the Church. In the external forum, the judgment could be made that a person has broken full communion; this judgment, however, does not necessarily indicate a rupture in the person's interior relationship with God, that the individual has sinned. For example, an apostate from the Catholic faith has clearly broken full communion with the Church (see cc. 751; 1364, §1); God alone judges the effect of such an action on the person's relationship with God.

The conciliar teaching on the hierarchy of truths assists in understanding the first bond, that of the profession of the faith. Not all doctrines taught by the Church carry the same weight: they vary "in their connection with the foundation of the Christian faith"[22] and therefore elicit different responses from the faithful. Canons 750 and 752–754 reflect the hierarchy of truths by distinguishing types of church teaching. The canons begin with the obligation to believe "with divine and Catholic faith all those things contained...in

---

[21] *LG* 14.

[22] *UR* 11.

the one deposit of faith" (c. 750, §1). The following canons apply to teachings that are not contained in the one deposit of faith and therefore elicit different responses: "a religious submission of the intellect and will" to a doctrine of the authentic magisterium concerning faith or morals declared by the pope or college of bishops (c. 752); adherence "with religious submission of mind to the authentic magisterium of their bishops" (c. 753); and observance of constitutions and decrees issued by the legitimate authority of the Church (c. 754). The hierarchy of truths and these differing responses recognize the fact that, although bishops are "authentic teachers, that is teachers endowed with the authority of Christ" (*LG* 25), they do not always engage their teaching authority to its fullest extent.[23] Therefore, each teaching must be analyzed to determine the proper response of the faithful.

As defined in canon 751, heresy applies only to the first category, those teachings which must be believed by divine and catholic faith. As one consequence, the determination that a person has broken the bond of professing the faith must be carefully decided on an individual basis, taking into account the nature of the teaching involved. Further, an apostate, one who totally repudiates the Christian faith (c. 751), has broken this bond and thereby incurs an automatic excommunication (1364, §1). Nonetheless, that individual remains "in communion" with the Catholic Church. Sanctions affect the exercise of rights and obligations (c. 96) and may reflect the breaking of the bond of full communion, but they do not erase the fundamental communion relationship with God and with the Church deriving from baptism. In the practical order, this means that the individual may incur further expiatory penalties (c. 1364, §2) or may request reconciliation with the Church.

The second bond is that of sacraments which "contribute in the greatest way to establish,

strengthen, and manifest ecclesiastical communion" (c. 840). Baptism is the prerequisite for receiving the other sacraments (c. 842, §1); the faithful have a right to receive the sacraments (c. 213) provided that they request the sacraments "at appropriate times, are properly disposed, and are not prohibited by law from receiving them" (c. 843, §1).[24] The sacraments themselves cross the boundaries between "full communion" with the Catholic Church and the lesser degree of communion of baptized non-Catholics with it: for example, canon 1055 states that every marriage between two baptized persons is a sacrament; canon 844 allows for reception of penance, Eucharist, and anointing of the sick by those not in full communion with the Catholic Church in certain circumstances and under specific conditions. Nonetheless, canon 837 articulates the basic principle that liturgical actions in general and the sacraments in particular are celebrations not of private individuals but of the specific community of faith, the Catholic Church, in union with Jesus Christ (see also cc. 834 and 840) and therefore are linked with "full ecclesial communion."[25]

The third bond, that of ecclesiastical governance, requires the same careful interpretation and application as demanded by the bond of profession of the faith; this bond reflects union with the visible or societal structure of the Church, including its hierarchical constitution with the Petrine ministry at the center of the communion. Canon 18, which requires a strict interpretation of canons that restrict rights, again serves to protect individuals: it must be unequivocally demonstrat-

---

[23] CDF, *Instruction on the Ecclesial Vocation of the Theologian* (cited hereafter as *Instruction*), May 24, 1990 (Washington, D.C.: USCC, 1994) 13, #17. For a fuller analysis, see the commentary on these canons.

[24] For examples of such a prohibition, see, for example, c. 1331, §1, 1° which forbids "any ministerial participation in celebrating the sacrifice of the Eucharist" and 2° which forbids the celebration and reception of the sacraments. Canon 915 discusses the reception of the Eucharist by those "obstinately persevering in manifest grave sin."

[25] See *Ecum Dir* 129 and also c. 908 which forbids Catholic priests from concelebrating the Eucharist with priests or ministers of churches or ecclesial communities which do not have full communion with the Catholic Church.

ed that an individual has indeed broken the bond of governance before a judgment is made that full communion has been severed. Canon 751 defines schism as "the refusal of submission to the Supreme Pontiff or of communion with the members of the Church subject to him." One clear example of schism was the behavior of Archbishop Marcel Lefebvre, in particular his unlawful conferral of episcopal ordination on June 30, 1988, in the face of an explicit papal prohibition (see c. 1382). In his apostolic letter, *Ecclesia Dei*, Pope John Paul II described this ordination as constituting a schismatic act insofar as Archbishop Lefebvre's disobedience implied a rejection of the Roman primacy; further, those individuals linked with Archbishop Lefebvre have severed the bonds of full communion with the Catholic Church.[26]

Other cases which might suggest schism, however, are not so apparent. Disagreement with church teaching does not necessarily break the bond of full communion, nor, more specifically, of the bonds of governance or of faith; each case must be carefully analyzed. In the *Instruction on the Ecclesial Vocation of the Theologian*, the Congregation for the Doctrine of the Faith clearly distinguishes between "disagreement with Church teaching" and dissent, recognizing that a theologian can have difficulties with a particular teaching, the arguments used to justify it, or the way in which the teaching is presented and should make these difficulties known to the proper authority.[27] This process can contribute to a greater understanding and appropriation of Church teaching. Such a process does not break the bond of full communion, in contrast with "dissent" as this is presented in the same document. Such dissent "aims at changing the Church following a model of protest" derived from political society and maintains that non-infallible teachings lack any obligatory character.[28] Thus understood, "dissent"

might indicate a severance in full communion, but caution must be used to determine that a particular theologian is exhibiting dissent rather than experiencing "difficulties with Church teaching."

Canon 205 describes those in "full communion" and the criteria for judging its presence. The situation of those who wish to leave the Church is not addressed. On the occasion of Pope John Paul's visit to France in 1996, certain individuals requested that they be "de-baptized." Given the irrevocability of the baptismal character, theology (and the code) does not provide for fulfilling such requests, although specific canons create an exemption from the impediment of disparity of cult and the required form of marriage for those who leave the Church "by a formal act."[29] Aside from this particular situation, these persons are considered bound by church law (c. 11). This position, expressed through the axiom, "Once a Catholic, always a Catholic," reflects the fidelity of God toward an individual—the offer of grace always remains for the individual to accept or reject. From a canonical perspective, the law seeks to preserve clarity in determining who is bound to ecclesiastical laws.

Catechumens

Canon 206 — §1. Catechumens, that is, those who ask by explicit choice under the influence of the Holy Spirit to be incorporated into the Church, are joined to it in a special way. By this same desire, just as by the life of faith, hope, and charity which they lead, they are united with the Church which already cherishes them as its own.

§2. The Church has a special care for catechumens; while it invites them to lead a life of the gospel and introduces them to the celebration of sacred rites, it already grants them various prerogatives which are proper to Christians.

Canon 204 makes a fundamental distinction between persons who have received baptism and

---

[26] John Paul II, aplett *Ecclesia Dei*, July 2, 1988, *Origins* 18 (August 4, 1988) 149, 151–152.

[27] *Instruction*, 18–19, ## 28–31. For additional treatment of this complex topic, see the commentary on c. 218.

[28] *Instruction*, 20–21, #33.

[29] See cc. 1086, §1; 1117; 1124.

those who have not; the baptized live—to a greater or lesser degree—in communion with the Catholic Church. Canon 206 addresses the particular situation of catechumens, that is, unbaptized persons who request incorporation into the Catholic Church (see *CCEO* 9). In the external forum, catechumens do not yet enjoy communion with the Catholic Church inasmuch as they have not fulfilled the essential requirement of baptism.[30] The situation of catechumens thus differs from that of baptized non-Catholics who request full communion with the Catholic Church; the latter already live "in communion" with the Catholic Church and can exercise certain rights (see, e.g., c. 844).

The *Rite of Christian Initiation of Adults* does distinguish among different types of persons requesting full communion: the unbaptized; baptized non-Catholics; uncatechized Catholics who have received only the sacrament of baptism. Their formation is similar, but for the baptized the desire for full communion arises from this sacrament already received.[31] Proper selection and preparation of candidates prior to admission to the catechumenate is important, especially the investigation to determine that nothing impedes the individual's reception of the sacraments. Due pastoral care should address issues connected with the individual's marital history as well as that of his or her spouse.[32]

Book III, "The Teaching Function of the Church," refers to the catechumenate under title II, "The Missionary Action of the Church" (cc. 781–792). The canons envisage a period of pre-catechumenate (c. 788, §1; see c. 787 for preliminary dialogue with non-believers); the catechumenate itself (c. 788, §2); and the post-catechumenate period (the *mystagogia*, c. 789).[33]

Although catechumens do not enjoy communion with the Catholic Church, they are nevertheless "joined to [the Church] in a special way" and "are united with the Church which already cherishes them as its own." This relationship arises from the role of the Holy Spirit in the life of the individual. Neither the code in canon 206 nor its source, *Lumen gentium* 14, provides further specification of this relationship, despite the encouragement in *Ad gentes* 14 that "the juridical status of catechumens should be clearly expressed in the new code." Canon 788, §3 empowers conferences of bishops to determine "what prerogatives are to be recognized as theirs [the catechumens']." The term "prerogatives" is important: inasmuch as they have not yet received baptism, catechumens do not enjoy rights in the Church unless specifically granted to them. For example, canon 1183, §1 considers catechumens as members of the Christian faithful for the purposes of their funeral rites[34] and canon 1170 allows catechumens to receive certain blessings. However, if catechumens wish to enter into marriage with Catholics, they, as unbaptized, must request a dispensation from the impediment of disparity of cult.

The catechumenate can exercise a very important function, not only for the catechumens themselves, but also for the particular church community. The Christian community provides an example of living the virtues of faith, hope, and charity for the catechumens; the catechumens and their desire for full communion encourage the faithful to appreciate and to activate their own faith.[35]

Clergy, Religious, Laity

Canon 207 — §1. By divine institution, there are among the Christian faithful in the Church sacred ministers who in law are also called clerics; the other members of the Christian faithful are called lay persons.

---

[30] See *RCIA* 295–305.

[31] See *RCIA* 295 and c. 869, §2.

[32] See, for example, A. Rehrauer, "Welcome In! Canonical Issues and the RCIA," *CLSAP* 52 (1990) 161–169.

[33] See also cc. 851, 1° and 865 which express the requirements for adult baptism.

[34] See *OEx* 18.

[35] The example and support provided by the community to catechumens is one manifestation of the obligation and right of all the Christian faithful to spread the gospel message (c. 211).

§2. There are members of the Christian faithful from both these groups who, through the profession of the evangelical counsels by means of vows or other sacred bonds recognized and sanctioned by the Church, are consecrated to God in their own special way and contribute to the salvific mission of the Church; although their state does not belong to the hierarchical structure of the Church, it nevertheless belongs to its life and holiness.

This canon is terminological, expressing the distinction between "sacred ministers" and "lay persons" and then specifying those Christian faithful (including both lay persons and sacred ministers) who are "consecrated to God" through professing the evangelical counsels. Canon 323 of the Eastern code describes clerics and thus corresponds to canon 207, §1; there is no equivalent to canon 207, §2.

Canon 207 must be situated within the context of *communio*, that is, the mutually supportive interrelationship of all the Christian faithful in the Church under the guidance of the Holy Spirit. This interrelationship necessarily involves the common mission of all the faithful (c. 204) as well as their "true equality regarding dignity and action" (c. 208) and has as its goal the salvation of all men and women.

The first distinction, between sacred ministers and lay persons, derives from "divine institution."[36] The canon significantly uses the expression "sacred ministers," contrasting it with the juridical term "clerics."[37] This reflects the distinction between the necessity for sacred ministry in the Church and the particular legal condition associated with that ministry, organized under the juridic title "the clerical state." A person becomes a cleric through reception of diaconate (c. 266, §1). Canon 290 presents one clear example of the distinction between sacred ministry and the juridic condition of ministers: ordination, once validly received, never becomes invalid, but an individual may lose "the clerical state." Title III of Book II discusses "Sacred Ministers or Clerics" under the chapter headings "The Formation of Clerics" (cc. 232–264); "The Enrollment, or Incardination, of Clerics" (cc. 265–272); "The Obligations and Rights of Clerics" (cc. 273–289); and "Loss of the Clerical State" (cc. 290–293). Book IV, "The Sanctifying Function of the Church," considers the sacrament of orders in canons 1008–1054; other references to clerics and to the clerical state are found throughout the code, e.g., canon 1333 which describes the penalty of suspension, applicable only to clerics.

The term "sacred ministry" also reflects the conciliar teaching that, in origin, this is a ministry of service so the people of God may attain salvation.[38] Sacred ministers are appointed by God and act in his name, not in the name of the community.[39] *Lumen gentium* 10 emphasizes the interre-

---

[36] See *LG* 32 and c. 1008. The phrase "by divine institution" indicates that sacred ministers are essential to the Church's hierarchical structure; see McGrath, in *CLSGBI Com,* 117 (commentary on c. 207). "Some Questions" emphasizes the necessity of the ministerial priesthood "for a community to exist as 'church'" and quotes *PDV* 16: "The ordained priesthood ought not to be thought of as existing...posterior to the ecclesial community, as if the church could be imagined as already established without this priesthood" (402, #2).

[37] The phrase "sacred ministers" indicates an underlying terminological difficulty, present not only in the code but in the conciliar texts as well. In referring to ordained ministry in the Church, the code uses various expressions: *sacred ministers* (see, for example, cc. 232–293; 1008); *presbyter* (see, for example, cc. 89; 290, 3°; 294), and *sacerdos* (see, for example, cc. 233; 276; 279). For a full listing of such terms, see H. Zapp, *Codex Iuris Canonici Lemmata Stichwortverzeichnis* (Freiburg: Rombach, 1986). On the use of these terms, see, for example, D. Donovan, "Priest," in *The New Encyclopedia of Theology* (Wilmington: Michael Glazier, 1987).

[38] See *LG* 18; see also c. 1025, §2 which requires for licit ordination that a candidate be considered "useful for the ministry of the Church."

[39] See, for example, *PO* 2 and 5. See also Hervada, in *Pamplona ComEng,* 188: "Ministerial priesthood is participation in a divine power and can only be granted by a divine act; its cause is the sacrament of orders that produces the sacramental character at the root of which are the hierarchical *munera* or functions."

lationship between the common priesthood of the faithful and the ministerial priesthood: each in its own way originates from a participation in the one priesthood of Christ. Nonetheless, the two types of priesthood differ in "essence and not simply in degree."[40] This difference forms one basis for distinguishing the participation of all the faithful in the threefold functions (*munera*) of Jesus Christ as priest, prophet, and ruler (see c. 204) and the participation by the ordained in the same *munera* (see c. 1008 and *CL* 22–23). All persons have a distinct role in the Church and all should encourage one another in each one's particular vocation.[41]

The canon does not provide here a description of laity; further articulation of the laity's mission in the Church arises, in part, from their "specific lay vocation" derived from baptism, confirmation, and, for some, marriage; from their participation in the triple *munera* (c. 204); from a consideration of the obligations and rights of all the Christian faithful (see especially cc. 208–223) as well as those particular to the lay Christian faithful (cc. 224–231). According to one of the conciliar sources for this canon, "The laity, however, have the specific vocation to make the church present and active in those places and circumstances

where only through them can it become the salt of the earth."[42]

Whereas the first paragraph is terminological in focus ("sacred ministers," "clerics," "lay persons"), the second paragraph, without using specific terminology, describes some of the Christian faithful who are distinguished by their "profession of the evangelical counsels." The paragraph therefore includes the groups and individuals discussed in part three of Book II: members of institutes of consecrated life; societies of apostolic life; and hermits. These persons profess the evangelical counsels of poverty, chastity, and obedience through vows or other bonds recognized as such by the Church and they thereby further specify their participation in the mission derived from baptism.[43] Further, this specification determines their "state" in the Church: they do not form part of the hierarchical constitution of the Church but rather belong "to its life and holiness" (see c. 210). Finally, as is reiterated in canon 588, §1, this state is neither clerical or lay; the code maintains the qualification found in *Lumen gentium* 43: consecrated life is not "an intermediate condition between the clerical and the lay" states.[44] Nonetheless, by analogy with the distinction between "sacred ministers" and "clerics," the latter indicating a particular legal condition, persons whose profession of the evangelical counsels is recognized and accepted by the Church do have a distinct juridic status. For example, their particular exercise of the obligations and rights of all the faithful is situated within the context of these vows or bonds as well as proper law applicable to them. Further, canons 662–672 present "The Obligations and Rights of Institutes and Their Members"; canons 711–712, 718–719, and 723 do the same for members of secular institutes; and

[40] See *LG* 10. "Some Questions" summarizes the essential difference between the ministerial priesthood and the common priesthood of the faithful in two points: "a) The ministerial priesthood is rooted in the apostolic succession and vested with *potestas sacra*, consisting of the faculty and the responsibility of acting in the person of Christ the head and the shepherd. b) It is a priesthood which renders its sacred ministers servants of Christ and of the church by means of authoritative proclamation of the word of God, the administration of the sacraments and the pastoral direction of the faithful" (401, #1).

[41] See "Some Questions," which states that through the ministerial priesthood "Christ gives to priests, in the Spirit, a particular gift so that they can help the people of God to exercise faithfully and fully the common priesthood which it has received" (400–401, #1, quoting *PDV* 17). See also cc. 394, §2 and 529, §2 for the responsibility of bishops and of pastors in fostering the proper role of laity in the Church's mission. Canon 233, §1 expresses the duty of all the faithful to foster vocations to sacred ministry.

[42] *LG* 33. See also "Some Questions" (Foreword).

[43] See c. 573 for the general description of consecrated life; c. 607, §2 for vows in religious institutes; c. 712 for bonds in secular institutes; c. 731, §2 for bonds in some societies of apostolic life; and c. 603, §2 for the vows or bonds professed by hermits.

[44] *LG* 43.

canons 731, 735, and 737–742 apply to members of societies of apostolic life. One might note that canon 672 applies certain obligations of clerics to members of institutes of consecrated life.

TITLE I
THE OBLIGATIONS AND RIGHTS OF ALL THE CHRISTIAN FAITHFUL
[cc. 208–223]

The code contains several titles which list obligations and rights; of paramount importance are those expressed here. Their importance arises from their placement at the beginning of Book II: these obligations and rights follow directly after the ecclesiological principles expressed in canons 204–207 and serve to develop and particularize these principles in the life of the *communio* that is the Church, the people of God. In other words, canons 208–223 present specific means by which the people of God express their identity and their mission in the world. Book II contains other obligations and rights which pertain to specific groups: "The Obligations and Rights of the Lay Christian Faithful" (cc. 224–231); "The Obligations and Rights of Clerics" (cc. 273–289); "The Obligations and Rights of Institutes and Their Members" (cc. 662–672). In addition to these groups of canons, other duties and rights are found throughout the code. For example, canon 793, §1 expresses the right of parents to educate their children, and canon 1620, 7° nullifies a judicial sentence if the right of defense was denied to either party in the case.

Obligations and rights, analyzed either within the context of the Church or of civil society, comprise a complex topic, involving a number of disparate but related issues: the source of rights and duties; the distinction between civil and ecclesial society; the basis for rights (for example, natural, divine, human positive law, either ecclesiastical or civil); the protection of rights and encouragement of the Christian faithful to use them; the enforce-ment of obligations; recourse against neglect or violation of specific rights.

The approach taken here begins with *communio* ecclesiology as expressive of the Church's nature and mission.[45] In his apostolic constitution promulgating the code, *Sacrae disciplinae leges*, Pope John Paul II explicitly links the participation of the faithful in the threefold functions (*munera*) of Jesus Christ priest, prophet, and ruler with the obligations and rights of the faithful and, in particular, of the laity. This connection indicates that the fundamental basis for understanding and interpreting the rights and duties of the faithful (including those listed in this title as well as others expressed elsewhere) is *communio*, the relationship between the individual and God which finds visible manifestation in the person's incorporation into Christ and the community of faith through the sacrament of baptism.

Rights and duties, therefore, occur within a specifically theological or spiritual context—the Church as the community of faith established by Jesus Christ as the sacrament of salvation until the fulfillment of the kingdom of God through the return of Christ.[46] This community of faith finds its origin and goal in the self-communication of God—*communio* begins and continues with God's initiative. This salvific context also applies to specific rights which are more universal in scope and which thereby pertain to everyone, for example, canon 220, which expresses the right to protect one's privacy. The exercise of this right occurs within the specific context of the Church as *communio*. Certain canons apply to all the baptized under definite conditions. For example, canon 213 expresses the right to receive spiritual help, especially the word of God and the sacraments, from sacred pastors. Although the canon applies primarily to those persons living in full

---

[45] For a fuller elaboration of this ecclesiology, see the introduction to Book II. For other analyses of rights and obligations, see, for example, Provost, in *CLSA Com*, 134–139; Hervada, in *Pamplona ComEng*, 190; McGrath, in *CLSGBI Com*, 118.

[46] See, for example, *LG* 9.

communion with the Catholic Church (c. 205), it also applies to baptized non-Catholics, as governed by canon 844.

From another perspective, the origin of rights also requires this theological context, specifically in reference to God's salvific will. Bishop Walter Kasper suggests two mutually related approaches to understanding the basis of rights. The more traditional approach begins with natural law: rights reflect the fundamental dignity of the human person, a dignity arising from one's human nature as a free being and endowed with the ability to reason. The second approach, more common since Vatican II, begins with the economy of salvation and situates rights within God's plan of salvation for humanity. This plan begins with the creation of men and women in God's image and reaches its culmination in the incarnation of Jesus Christ. Through the incarnation, by which the second person of the Trinity assumed human nature and united it with himself, God imparts a unique dignity to each and every human being.[47] These two approaches are summarized by *Gaudium et spes* 29:

> Since all men and women possessed of a rational soul and created in the image of God have the same nature and the same origin, and since they have been redeemed by Christ and enjoy the same divine calling and destiny, the basic equality which they all share needs to be increasingly recognized.

Each approach provides a balance to the other: the abstract notion of "human nature" as created in God's image and endowed with reason finds its correlative in the reality that each human being—as he or she exists in a particular historical period—has been changed by the incarnation of Jesus Christ. As the Eastern tradition maintains, "God became human so that humans could become divine."[48]

Understanding rights and duties within this theological context—broadly expressed, the economy of salvation—removes certain objections to the idea of "fundamental" rights within the Church—primarily, that the Church cannot be considered the equivalent to civil society; that rights arise from and foster an adversarial relationship between the individual and state authority; that the Church as founded by Christ focuses on a personal faith relationship with God, not on rights. These objections must be taken seriously and not only in the context of obligations and rights. There is still the danger of considering the Church simply as a perfect society, i.e., complete in and of itself, analogous to the civil state. This ecclesiology was prevalent until Vatican II and is operative even today when people might consider the Church as an international business conglomerate which manages itself as such. The Church exists as a visible, organized society only to fulfill the mission entrusted to it by Christ and this mission determines the context for any discussion of obligations and rights.[49] In other words, any ecclesial activity, including the exercise of obligations and rights, must be viewed in terms of its fostering the salvific purpose and mission of the Church.

An emphasis on this salvific mission can also correct the impression that rights arise or exist only in consequence of an adversarial relationship between an individual and civil (or ecclesiastical) authority. The Church was established by the will of Christ and not by a group of individuals acting on their own behalf; rights in the Church, therefore, derive from incorporation into Christ through the sacrament of baptism and not from a social compact among individuals.[50] A relationship with God finds its most specific and visible expression in baptism; this relationship with God necessarily involves the community of faith. The community dimension—incorporation into the Body of Christ, *communio* with God and with other members of the Church—argues

---

[47] W. Kasper, "The Theological Foundations of Human Rights," *J* 50 (1990) 157–161.

[48] See also *LG* 7 and *GS* 22.

[49] See *LG* 8 and, for example, cc. 204 and 1752.

[50] See cc. 96 and 204.

against an excessive individualism in which an overemphasis on individual rights often gives rise to an adversarial relationship not only with authority but also with the other members of the community.

Further, the Church as *communio* provides a basis for understanding the dynamic interrelationship between obligations and rights: each right implies a duty and each duty implies a right. The terminology, "obligations and rights," does not imply a priority of one over the other; they are "essential and inseparable."[51] For example, the Christian faithful have a right to receive spiritual assistance from pastors, especially the word of God and the sacraments (c. 213). The code expresses the same right from a different perspective in canon 843, which requires pastors to provide the sacraments to those properly prepared for them, and canon 767, which requires pastors to preach. The obligation to maintain communion (c. 209) corresponds to the duty of the pastor to have concern for and to promote parochial communion (c. 529, §2).

The emphasis on the community of faith and on the Church's mission finds expression through the arrangement of the canons in this title. Canon 208 begins by stating a general principle, derived from the theology expressed in canons 204–205, namely, that a true equality in dignity and in action exists among all the faithful. This fundamental equality does not remove differences among the Christian faithful; different persons have distinct vocations within the community. Flowing from this principle, canons 209 and 223 act as a framework for specific obligations and rights: both canons refer to the broader context for their exercise. As with the practice of faith, duties and rights in the Church exist within a specific community; they do not emphasize the individual as such but are a means to ensure that the Church as the people of God continues to manifest the reali-

ty of salvation in the world. Canon 209 therefore emphasizes the interrelationship among all the Christian faithful; each one of the faithful has the obligation not only to live within and actively support the *communio* that is the Church but also to foster the interior *communio* with God. Canon 223 provides a more particular context for rights and duties: the common good of the Church, the rights of others, and duties toward other persons. In other words, the common good is not in opposition to obligations and rights but provides the particular context for their proper exercise. Canons 208–223 (and other duties and rights expressed elsewhere in the code) provide a means to ensure that the Church as a visible society not only allows but also actively encourages the mission of all the Christian faithful derived from baptism.

The duties and rights expressed within this framework in canons 210–222 reflect the nature of the Church as *communio*. Certain rights and obligations reflect the fundamental dignity derived from a relationship with God and from baptism and incorporation into the Body of Christ: the right to privacy and a good name and reputation (c. 220); the right to freedom from coercion in choosing a state of life (c. 219); the requirement to lead a holy life (c. 210); the rights to proclaim the divine message of salvation (c. 211) and to promote and sustain apostolic action (c. 216); the right to spiritual assistance, primarily, the sacraments and the word of God (c. 213); the right to worship according to one's rite and to follow one's own spiritual life (c. 214). Other rights and obligations flow from this basic dignity and reflect the organized structure of the Church as well as the variety of functions and vocations within the community: the obligation of Christian obedience (c. 212, §1); the right to express needs and desires and to manifest opinions on ecclesial issues (c. 212, §§2–3); the right to a Christian education (c. 217); the right to legitimate academic freedom of inquiry and expression (c. 218); the right to associate (c. 215); the obligation to provide for the Church's needs and to promote social justice (c. 222); the right to vindicate and defend

---

[51] See, for example, the discussion of this point by Cardinal R. Castillo Lara in "Some General Reflections on the Rights and Duties of the Christian Faithful," *Stud Can* 20 (1986) 21–22.

one's rights, to be judged according to the law applied with equity (c. 221 §§1–2), and not to be punished except in accord with the law (c. 221, §3).[52] These obligations and rights, however categorized, cannot be interpreted in isolation, apart from *communio*—the relationship with God and with the specific community of faith.

This analysis of obligations and rights within the context of the Church as *communio* must also recognize another teaching of Vatican II. While consistently reiterating the teaching of the genuine holiness of the Church found, for example, in the Nicene Creed, the council also recognized the reality that individual men and women do sin. According to *Lumen gentium* 8, "the church, containing sinners in its own bosom, is at one and same time holy and always in need of purification." In other words, the Church is holy inasmuch as it was established by Jesus Christ as the definitive sign of his victory over sin and death. At the same time, however, the Church is on pilgrimage in the world and is ever progressing toward its culmination in Christ.[53] Individuals within the Church can and do sin; at times, the rights of others are violated. Such violations need correction in order for the Church to fulfill its mission. From this perspective, the listing of obligations and rights, such as is found in this title, provide one means for the Church on pilgrimage in this world to strive consistently to fulfill its mission. Thus, canon 221, affirming the right of the Christian faithful to vindicate their rights, is of foremost importance.[54]

Despite the presence of specific obligations and rights in the code, difficulties remain in their practical implementation in the life of the Church. These difficulties arise from a variety of reasons: lack of information about them among both clergy and lay people; deficiencies in procedures for protecting and vindicating rights as well as lack of knowledge about or access to these procedures; lack of support among bishops and clergy; and the complex terminology and careful nuances used in articulating specific obligations and rights.[55] This terminology can create certain difficulties in interpretation and implementation. The canons do not always express a right by using the Latin word *ius*. For example, the right to enjoy a good reputation is expressed passively and negatively: "No one is permitted to harm illegitimately the good reputation which a person possesses" (c. 220).[56] In addition, difficulties emerge as to the precise content, limits, and fulfillment of certain rights, for example, canon 211 and the right to proclaim "the divine message of salvation."[57] At a more foundational level, the implications of *communio* ecclesiology for the life of the Church need further development and articulation, especially in developing Church structures and institutes to reflect the *communio* that is the Church. For example,

> We are still far from having worked out the rights and duties that flow from such a respect; e.g., in matters concerning freedom

---

[52] For a fuller analysis, see commentary on specific canons.

[53] For a further discussion of this topic, see, for example, F. Sullivan, *The Church We Believe In* (New York: Paulist, 1989), especially chapter 4, "Marked with a Genuine though Imperfect Holiness," 66–83.

[54] For a fuller discussion, see the commentary on this canon.

[55] See J. Coriden, "What Became of the Bill of Rights?" *CLSAP* 52 (1990) 47–60.

[56] See also J. Provost, "Protecting and Promoting the Rights of Christians: Some Implications for Church Structure," *J* 46 (1986) 289–342. Provost notes, "At times [a right] may be expressed in terms of an obligation. What I have an obligation to do, I have a right to do. What I have an obligation to provide for you, you have a right to receive" (302).

[57] See "Some General Reflections," 22 where Castillo Lara maintains that the norms in cc. 208–223 are "true duties and rights"; nonetheless, "it is not easy, and perhaps, is not even possible to quantify them and to determine their precise extent or the range of one right's necessity or the concrete exercise of others." For his part, J. McIntyre refers to a "basic ambiguity" present in this title inasmuch as the canons do not adequately answer the question, "Who is obliging the *christifideles* to do or not to do x?" See "Rights and Duties Revisited," *J* 56 (1996) 119.

of conscience within the church, regarding the speedy administration of justice, representations of issues before the hierarchy, and so forth.[58]

Despite such difficulties, this title and other rights and duties found in the code offer a significant contribution to the life of the Church. Further progress is needed in understanding such rights and duties as well as supporting and protecting their use. The obligation of maintaining *communio* (c. 209) requires such progress. All the Christian faithful, whatever their condition, state, or function, must encourage and support one another in their shared mission, both *ad extra* (to the world) and *ad intra* (in the Church itself). The exercise of rights and the fulfillment of duties serve the *communio* that is the Church and guarantee that it fulfills its divine mission.

Fundamental Equality

Canon 208 — From their rebirth in Christ, there exists among all the Christian faithful a true equality regarding dignity and action by which they all cooperate in the building up of the Body of Christ according to each one's own condition and function.

The canon first states a general principle and then clarifies the application of that principle in the Church's life. The general principle states that a "true equality regarding dignity and action" exists among all the Christian faithful. The canon, taken from *Lumen gentium* 32 and found in the Eastern code in canon 11, marks a significant shift in understanding the nature of the Church as an organized society. In the previous code, the Church was perceived as a society of unequals, depending upon whether one had received ordination or not. This fundamental change in perception re-

flects a *communio* ecclesiology and develops theologically the implications arising from the reception of baptism as elaborated in canon 204.[59] Thus, the fundamental equality among all the people of God has a sacramental origin; all the baptized share a personal, individual relationship with Jesus Christ, a relationship which finds visible expression through entrance into a particular faith community by baptism. Through this incorporation into the Body of Christ (c. 204), each of the baptized is a daughter or son of God. In addition, all the baptized share in the priestly, prophetic, and ruling functions (*munera*) of Jesus Christ; they thereby participate in the mission entrusted to the Church by Christ. At its most fundamental level, participation in the Church's mission arises from baptism and not from a mandate or concession of a competent ecclesiastical authority. Nonetheless, difficulties remain in the activation of this participation; adequate structures are not always available to encourage dynamic involvement of the faithful; and some of the faithful remain unaware of their obligations in this regard.

Moving from the principle to its application in the Church's life, the canon then states that this participation is not univocal but rather differs "according to each one's own condition and function." This phrase refers to the diversity concretely existing among the people of God; differences exist in the means by which particular individuals participate in the Church's mission; different levels of responsibility exist. All the faithful share in one baptism, but their participation in the triple functions (*munera*) of Christ differs according to the diversity of vocations and charisms in the Church as well as an individual's specific

---

[58] L. Örsy, "The Theological Task of Canon Law: A Canonist's Perspective," *CLSAP* (1996), 21. See also J. Coriden, "A Challenge: Making the Rights Real," *J* 45 (1985) 1–23.

[59] See McGrath, in *CLSGBI Com,* 118: "The canon is based on the view of the Church as the communion of all the baptized." See also Hervada, in *Pamplona ComEng,* 190: "The *principle of radical equality* means that all those who have received baptism are equal members of the faithful (one is not a member of the faithful to a greater degree having received the sacrament of orders or an ecclesiastical office)."

"condition."[60] All the faithful enjoy the obligations and rights listed in this title; other rights and obligations are listed elsewhere in the code. Together, as one people, the faithful build up the Church and cooperate in its mission. More specific duties come with reception of specific sacraments; the faithful who enter into matrimony assume particular duties. For example, they edify the people of God through their marriage and family (c. 226, §1); each spouse has equal duties and rights within marriage (c. 1135), including that of preserving conjugal life (c. 1151). Parents have added responsibilities: the obligation and right to educate their children, and, more especially, to provide a Christian education (cc. 226, §2; 793; 1136) and they participate in the Church's sanctifying function through their conjugal life (c. 835, §4). Other faithful receive a particular grade of the sacrament of orders (episcopacy, presbyterate, or diaconate—c. 1009), each with its responsibilities.[61] Some of the faithful enter an institute of consecrated life and assume specific obligations.[62] Some people are elected or appointed to an ecclesiastical office and thereby incur specific responsibilities as defined in the code, in particular law, and in the letter of appointment.[63]

In the specific context of obligations and rights, canon 208 declares the requisite foundational principle: obligations and rights as well as their exercise and protection exist within the specific community of faith, the Church as *communio,* which is both a visible, hierarchically structured society and a spiritual community.[64] The interrelationship of all the faithful within the Church and their common dignity, equality, and participation in mission manifest the fundamental unity constitutive of the one body of Christ.[65]

Obligations of Communion

Canon 209 — §1. The Christian faithful, even in their own manner of acting, are always obliged to maintain communion with the Church.

§2. With great diligence they are to fulfill the duties which they owe to the universal Church and the particular church to which they belong according to the prescripts of the law.

Canon 209 expresses a fundamental obligation incumbent upon the baptized. This obligation refers to two aspects or dimensions of an individual's life: the internal, personal response to the divine invitation to enter into a relationship with God and the external expression of that personal response within the community of faith through reception of baptism. The first aspect may be expressed as the obligation of "being communion";[66] the second as a "right and duty obligation." The Eastern code contains the same obligation in canon 12.

As a juridic instrument, the code places emphasis upon the latter dimension of maintaining communion; nonetheless, this obligation and right presuppose the internal faith dimension, "being communion": the person's continuing and hopefully deepening relationship with God; participation in the *communio* which is the intra-Trinitarian life; the free and ongoing response to God and cooperation with the means of salvation. When this internal dimension finds external expression through a relationship with a particular ecclesial community or church by means of baptism, the person enters into some degree of communion with the Catholic Church;[67] the extent of the fulfillment of obligations and the exercise of rights

---

[60] For a fuller elaboration of this term, see the commentary on c. 204.

[61] See, for example, cc. 129, 273–289, 381–402.

[62] See, for example, cc. 207, 662–672.

[63] See cc. 129, 145, 228.

[64] See *LG* 8.

[65] See, for example, *LG* 32.

[66] The phrase "being communion" is found in the *instrumentum laboris* of the 1994 special synod of bishops for Africa: "First and foremost the accent must be placed on 'being' communion, and afterward on 'doing' something. Action cannot precede being." Synod of Bishops, "Final Message of the Synod for Africa," 58, *Origins* 24 (May 19, 1994) 118.

[67] See cc. 204–205.

depends upon whether the individual lives in full communion or not (c. 205). In addition to the degree of ecclesiastical communion, canon 96 further nuances this relationship by adding two other qualifiers to the exercise of duties and rights: "in keeping with their condition" and "unless a legitimately issued sanction stands in the way." Inasmuch as the judgment that an individual is not in full communion with the Catholic Church adversely affects that person's exercise of obligations and rights, canon 18 requires that such a determination be based upon clear and unequivocal grounds.[68]

The interrelationships resulting from *communio* and the consequent obligation to maintain communion affect every aspect of the Church's life and mission. *Communio* finds particular expression through the communion of the faithful (*communio fidelium*), the communion of churches (*communio ecclesiarum*), and hierarchical communion (*communio hierarchica*). The *communio fidelium* recognizes the fundamental unity among all the baptized as the one people of God; all share in a common dignity, equality, and mission (c. 208). The unity of those in full communion with the Catholic Church finds specific manifestation through the bonds of profession of the faith, ecclesiastical governance, and the sacraments (c. 205). The *communio fidelium* is a dynamic reality requiring the active participation of all the faithful in the Church's life and mission. It finds visible expression through public worship, by which the faithful exercise their common priesthood,[69] and through the exercise of obligations and rights.

We may understand the *communio ecclesiarum* from two different viewpoints. According to canon 368, the *communio ecclesiarum* exhibits the bond of unity existing among the particular churches (generally dioceses) with one another; this requires the bond of hierarchical communion within the college of bishops (c. 330). From a second viewpoint, the *communio ecclesiarum*

reflects the bond of unity among the "ritual churches *sui iuris*." These churches are defined as "a group of Christian faithful united by a hierarchy according to the norm of law which the supreme authority of the Church expressly or tacitly recognizes as *sui iuris*" (CCEO 27). The Latin church is one such church *sui iuris*.[70] The unity of the Catholic Church arises from the Spirit-founded *communio* existing among these *sui iuris* churches; consequently, the Church is not simply an aggregate unity as in an association nor is it a federation of independent churches which chose to unite (and thus could choose to separate).[71]

The *communio hierarchica* reflects the bond of unity existing within the Church as hierarchically constituted; the pope "is the perpetual and visible principle and foundation of unity both of the bishops and of the multitude of the faithful"[72] and is obliged to maintain communion (c. 333, §2). In its broadest application, hierarchical communion recognizes that the Church is both a spiritual community and a society with hierarchical structures. In a more specific application, this communion reflects the unity within the Church's hierarchical structure, especially among members of the college of bishops. Thus, for example, *communio hierarchica* is required for a bishop to exercise the functions he received through ordination.[73]

The second paragraph of canon 209 exhorts the faithful to fulfill their duties to the universal and particular church; most often, the exercise of such duties occurs within the particular church and parish to which they belong by reason of domicile

---

[68] See commentary on c. 205.

[69] See, for example, cc. 759, 762–766, and 836.

[70] The code addresses this issue indirectly in cc. 111–112, in reference to baptism and enrollment in a particular church *sui iuris*. On the topic of the relationship among the churches *sui iuris*, see, for example, G. Nedungatt, "Equal Rights of the Churches in the Catholic Church," *J* 49 (1989) 1–22.

[71] See Sullivan, *The Church We Believe In*, especially 34–65 and 84–108; see also, for example, *LG* 23.

[72] *LG* 23.

[73] See c. 375, §2 and the "Preliminary Explanatory Note" to *LG*.

or quasi-domicile.[74] According to canon 107, §1: "Through both domicile and quasi-domicile, each person acquires his or her pastor and ordinary." Inasmuch as laws are presumed to be territorial (c. 13), domicile or quasi-domicile determines the applicability of laws (c. 13, §§2–3) as well as the proper ecclesiastical authority for dispensations and permissions.[75] Canon 529, §2 expresses the pastor's duty to work "so that the faithful have concern for parochial communion, consider themselves members of the diocese and of the universal Church, and participate in and sustain efforts to promote this same communion." Canons 383–394 describe the diocesan bishop's responsibility for promoting communion within his diocese.

From one perspective, the duties owed to the universal and to the particular church depend upon a variety of factors: the person's condition, state in life, and functions within the community.[76] At a more fundamental level, underlying these particular responsibilities is the person's obligation to foster his or her relationship with God, responding to God's invitation to participate in the divine *communio* of Father, Son, and Spirit and to express this participation in the *communio* of the Church. As Pope John Paul states in *Sacrae disciplinae leges*, the law exists to serve faith, grace, and charisms, especially charity, in the Church's life. In other words, the obligation "to maintain communion" is a dynamic one; each of the faithful must apply this obligation to his or her particular situation within the Church. *Communio* requires the active participation of all the faithful in a relationship with God and with other members of the Church; they experience and live this communion through prayer, common worship, service of neighbor, and the fulfillment of their baptismal mission.

---

[74] For the definition of these and related terms, see cc. 100–107.

[75] See c. 87 and, for example, cc. 1077–1082 and 1115 in reference to marriage and c. 975 concerning the faculty to hear confessions.

[76] See the commentary on cc. 204 and 207.

Holiness of Life

Canon 210 — All the Christian faithful must direct their efforts to lead a holy life and to promote the growth of the Church and its continual sanctification, according to their own condition.

This canon reflects both the fundamental equality of the faithful (c. 208) and the twofold dynamism of *communio* which exists on both a personal and communal level (c. 209). The Eastern code contains the same obligation in canon 13. According to *Lumen gentium* 41, "there is one holiness cultivated by all who are led by the Spirit of God"; no one vocation or state in life is "holier" than another. This one call to holiness arises from a personal relationship—*communio*—with God. From an individual's personal relationship with God and consequent acceptance of baptism and full communion with the Catholic Church arises the obligation to lead a holy life and thereby promote not only the individual's own growth in holiness but also that of the Church as a whole. Change and growth are intrinsic to the human person, including his or her spiritual life; the faithful must strive constantly to deepen their communion with God and with the Church.

All of the faithful are called to a life of holiness by which they exercise their participation in the sanctifying function (*munus*) of Jesus Christ the priest. The means by which the individual strives to fulfill this participation depend upon the particular vocation to which one is called by God.[77] This participation can occur either individually or through associations. According to canon 298, §1, one purpose of associations is "to foster a more perfect life." More specifically, canon 387 obliges the diocesan bishop to promote the holiness of the faithful according to each one's proper vocation; further, he is obliged "to show an example of holiness in charity, humility, and simplicity of life"; canons 528–529 specify certain responsibilities of the pastor toward the faithful entrusted to his care. Canon 226, §1 addresses the vocation

---

[77] See cc. 204 and 835.

of the married and canons 774, §2 and 835, §4, the specific vocation of parents. Canon 276 asserts the obligation of clerics to pursue holiness "in a special way" since "they are dispensers of the mysteries of God in the service of His people." Canon 574, §1 states that all institutes of consecrated life pertain "to the life and holiness of the Church." As one consequence, members of institutes should foster their own holiness through means suggested by canons 573, 574, §2, and 662–664 and promote the holiness of the Church as a whole (cc. 673–677). This common pursuit of holiness among all the faithful contributes to the transformation of the world according to God's salvific will.[78]

Proclaim the Gospel

Canon 211 — All the Christian faithful have the duty and right to work so that the divine message of salvation more and more reaches all people in every age and in every land.

Canon 211 expresses a foundational right and obligation arising directly from baptism, which is also found in canon 14 of the Eastern code. Through baptism, each person, whatever his or her condition, participates in the mission of the Church; each person is obliged and possesses the right to proclaim the gospel message.[79] The sacrament of confirmation "strengthens the baptized and obliges them more firmly to be witnesses of Christ by word and deed and to spread and defend the faith" (c. 879). In his apostolic exhortation, *Evangelii nuntiandi*, Pope Paul VI describes this mission of evangelization as "in fact the grace and vocation proper to the Church, her deepest identity."[80] As such, "evangelizing means bringing the Good News into all the strata of humanity, and through its influence transforming humanity from within and making it new."[81]

The nature of the Church as missionary originates in the mission of the Son and of the Holy Spirit, according to the salvific plan of the Father.[82] Further elaboration of this mission occurs within the ecclesiology of *communio*. A relationship with God—participation in the divine communion of Father, Son, and Spirit—cannot remain solely interior but needs visible expression. A relationship with God is also directed outwards, in the proclamation of the good news of salvation and in the cooperation of men and women in the power of the Spirit for the salvation of individuals and of the world.[83]

As one consequence, the right and duty of the Christian faithful to proclaim the gospel arises fundamentally from the sacrament of baptism, not from a mandate of ecclesiastical authority. Such a right and duty reflects the fundamental equality of all the faithful (c. 208) and their participation in the prophetic function (*munus*) of Jesus Christ. "The first means of evangelizing is the witness of an authentically Christian life, given over to God in a communion...and at the same time given to one's neighbor."[84] As with *communio* itself, evangelization has both personal and communal dimensions: the person must be converted first in a free and ongoing response to God's initiative and then work for the transformation of society as a whole through the gospel.

The code presents evangelization both in a broad and in a narrow sense. Canons 211 and 781 express the broader understanding in which all church activity is missionary.[85] From another perspective, canon 786 defines "missionary action" in a more particular sense as the proclamation of the Christian message in areas where it is not yet known; all the faithful can have a role in this proclamation. Both senses of evangelization are

---

[78] See *LG* 40.
[79] See cc. 204–205.
[80] *EN* 8, #14.
[81] Ibid., 11, #18.

[82] See *AG* 2.
[83] For further analysis of *communio* ecclesiology, see the introduction to Book II.
[84] *EN* 23, #41.
[85] See also c. 225, §2, which refers to the special duty of lay people "to imbue and perfect the order of temporal affairs with the spirit of the gospel."

intimately related: specific "missionary action" reflects the Church's fundamental mission in the world.

As noted, the context for all evangelization is the Church as *communio*. The obligations to maintain communion (c. 209) and to foster the common good (c. 223) remind us that the exercise of this mission occurs within the specific community of faith that is the Catholic Church. Ecclesiastical authority has the right to regulate this participation if done in the name of the Church.[86] Further, the different methods used to proclaim the gospel not only reflect the legitimate diversity of the Church manifested through diverse functions and vocations but also manifest an image of the Church as it exists in the world.

The means of evangelization include the entire life of the Church—its spiritual and sacramental life; the variety of vocations in the world (laity, both single and married; parents; clerics; members of institutes of consecrated life and societies of apostolic life); particular groupings (families; parishes; dioceses; associations, both public and private); different roles through participation in the triple functions (*munera*) of Jesus Christ priest, prophet, and ruler. Many of the canons in titles I and II of Book II as well as Book III indicate specific responsibilities for evangelization. Through these and other activities, the faithful fulfill their right and duty to proclaim the gospel.

Obedience—Expression of Needs and Desires— Public Opinion

Canon 212 — §1. Conscious of their own responsibility, the Christian faithful are bound to follow with Christian obedience those things which the sacred pastors, inasmuch as they represent Christ, declare as teachers of the faith or establish as rulers of the Church.

[86] See, for example, limitations on the use of the name "Catholic" in c. 216 in reference to apostolic activity; cc. 300–301, concerning associations; and c. 803, §3, concerning schools.

§2. The Christian faithful are free to make known to the pastors of the Church their needs, especially spiritual ones, and their desires.

§3. According to the knowledge, competence, and prestige which they possess, they have the right and even at times the duty to manifest to the sacred pastors their opinion on matters which pertain to the good of the Church and to make their opinion known to the rest of the Christian faithful, without prejudice to the integrity of faith and morals, with reverence toward their pastors, and attentive to common advantage and the dignity of persons.

The three paragraphs comprising this canon together express the dynamic nature of the Church as *communio*. The Eastern code equivalent is canon 15. Each of the faithful actively participates in the mission of the Church in virtue of baptism (c. 204); each person has a particular vocation to fulfill within the Church (cc. 210–211). But this participation is not primarily an individual endeavor; rather, a mutual interdependence exists by which all work together. This canon therefore expresses various aspects of the dynamic relationship which should exist among all the people of God. This relationship includes obedience to sacred pastors (§1), expressing needs and desires to the same pastors (§2), and manifesting opinions on matters concerning the good of the Church to other Christian faithful (§3). These activities strive for common growth in the faith and its practice and also reflect the legitimate diversity within the Church. As noted in the commentary on canon 209, the duty of maintaining communion requires an active, prayerful, and reflective response on the part of the Christian faithful. As one consequence of this obligation, a particular situation requires careful analysis to determine the appropriate response —obedience or expressing one's needs, desires, or opinions. The faithful may disagree with pastors in a particular situation over a specific issue; provided that the faithful maintain communion with and foster the common good of the Church, they have a right to express their opinions to other faithful. Foundationally, canon 212 reflects "the dignity and the responsibility" of the faithful, their "freedom and space to act"[87] and the Church's nature expressed as *communio:* its organization as a society is directed primarily at fulfilling its mission.[88] The interaction of all the faithful must serve the Church in its mission.

The first paragraph of this canon establishes the specific duty of obedience of the faithful to their sacred pastors as representatives of Christ in two specific areas: in that which pastors declare either as teachers of the faith or as rulers of the Church. A proper understanding of this obligation requires an accurate comprehension of the terms used as well as the context for this obedience, namely, the Church as *communio* in which all the faithful possess a true equality in dignity and activity (c. 208) and all contribute to the sanctification of themselves, of other faithful, and of the Church itself (c. 210). The dynamic nature of *communio* requires mutual cooperation, respect, and interdependence of all the faithful.

"Sacred pastors" are those among the faithful constituted as such through the sacrament of orders (cc. 1008 and 207). Canon 386 describes the diocesan bishop's teaching function and canon 391 his multi-faceted governing function. Within his specific competence, canon 519 discusses the pastor's responsibilities in these areas with the cooperation of other presbyters and deacons and the assistance of lay people. The role of "teachers of the faith" is developed more fully in Book III of the code, with the foundational principle articulated in canon 747. This canon expresses the Church's "duty and innate right...to preach the gospel to all peoples."

Not all Church teaching carries the same weight and authority; an order or hierarchy of truths exists within Christian doctrine, dependent upon the connection between a specific teaching and the foundation of the Christian faith.[89] The code reflects this order or hierarchy of truths in canons 750–754 which indicate the specific responses required of the faithful to Church teaching. The canons begin with the obligation to believe "with divine and Catholic faith all those things contained...in the one deposit of faith" (c. 750, §1). The following canons apply to teachings not contained in the one deposit of faith, which therefore elicit different responses: "a religious submission of the intellect and will" to a doctrine of the authentic magisterium concerning faith or morals declared by the pope or college of bishops (c. 752); adherence "with religious submission of mind to the authentic magisterium of their bishops" (c. 753); and observance of constitutions and decrees issued by the legitimate authority of the Church (c. 754).[90] Canon 749, §3 expresses a necessary principle: "No doctrine is understood as defined infallibly unless this is manifestly evident."

Inasmuch as bishops do not always intend to engage the full extent of their teaching authority when they teach on a specific issue,[91] careful examination of each teaching is required to determine the proper response. Thus, the obedience to which the canon obliges the faithful is not a blind, unquestioning reality but rather an intelligent and reflective response, requiring the Christian education expressed in canons 217 and 793–821. Such an education should provide the means by which the faithful may both appreciate and appropriate their faith and the teaching of the Church. In addition, the source for this canon, *Lumen gentium* 37, suggests that the Christian faithful should model their obedience on that of Christ "who by his obedience unto death opened to all people the blessed way of the freedom of the children of God."

Obedience is also the required response to what sacred pastors prescribe as "rulers of the Church." But the exercise of authority is not an end in and of itself; rather, it must serve the Church as *communio* and aim at fostering the "common good" (c. 223) as well as maintaining communion (c. 209). "Sacred pastors" also must

---

[87] See *LG* 37, and c. 227 in specific reference to the laity.
[88] See *LG* 8.
[89] See *UR* 11.

[90] For a fuller analysis of this complex material, see the commentary on cc. 750–754.
[91] See, for example, *Instruction,* 13, #17.

maintain communion with their fellow believers and this obligation determines the appropriate exercise of authority: to build up the Church as *communio*. In *Sacrae disciplinae leges*, Pope John Paul describes "hierarchical authority as service" as a characteristic of the "true and genuine image of the Church."

The second paragraph of canon 212 expressly recognizes the right of all the faithful to express their needs and their wishes to the sacred pastors, with special emphasis given to spiritual needs. Unfortunately, the canon does not explicitly express the concomitant obligation on the part of sacred pastors to listen attentively to the faithful. As with the first paragraph, the context is the dynamic interrelationship among all the Christian faithful, a relationship founded upon mutual respect and trust, with the goal of helping the Church fulfill its mission as sign of and means to salvation. The basis for this right is the "freedom and confidence which befits children of God and sisters and brothers in Christ."[92] Needs and desires may be expressed either individually or through associations[93] or other corporate structures; they may be expressed orally or in writing. The conciliar context for this right is the Church's mission in the world; such needs and desires should reflect the context of the Church as *communio* in which all the faithful contribute to its mission.[94]

One particular way in which the faithful can express their needs and wishes is through various councils and synods. For example, canon 460 describes the diocesan synod as an assistance to the diocesan bishop for the good of the particular church. Canon 463 allows the bishop great freedom in determining who participates in the synod; he may even include as observers individuals who are not in full communion with the Church. Membership in other assemblies may also include a wide diversity of people; canon 443 discusses membership in particular councils and canon 339, §2 allows the supreme authority of the Church to determine the participation and role of those who are not bishops in an ecumenical council.

The third paragraph unequivocally expresses the right and duty of all the faithful to express their opinion on matters concerning the Church's good to their sacred pastors; the faithful have the right to express their opinion to other Christian faithful as well. Again, the ecclesiology of *communio* provides the context for a proper understanding and exercise of this free exchange, itself a basic human right.[95] Through the expression of opinions on matters affecting the Church, *communio* manifests itself as a dynamic interrelationship among all the Christian faithful. At the same time, however, *communio* also reminds us that no one acts as an individual but rather within a specific community of faith, the Catholic Church, which strives to be faithful to Jesus Christ and to the mission entrusted to it.

In the civil sphere, people have widely divergent experiences of opinions and "opinion polls" as determinative of official policy. These experiences—both negative and positive—have influenced the wording of this paragraph. Each of the faithful has the right and at times the duty to manifest an opinion on matters affecting the Church—including but not limited to the Church's teaching, sanctifying, and ruling functions (*munera*) as well as its conduct in temporal affairs. "Since the Church is a living body, she needs public opinion in order to sustain a giving and taking between her members. Without this, she cannot advance in thought and action."[96]

This paragraph suggests that the opinions of the faithful be directed to sacred pastors, those en-

---

[92] *LG* 37.
[93] See c. 298.
[94] See cc. 210–211.

[95] See J. Coriden, "Freedom of Expression in the Church in Light of Canon 212 (CIC)," *CLSAP* 30 (1995) 147–165, especially 153–155 where he gives examples of the freedom of expression principle in the Church's social teaching and in modern constitutions and declarations.
[96] PCSC, "Pastoral Instruction on the Means of Social Communication" *(CP)* 330, #115. The instruction then cites Pope Pius XII: "Something would be lacking in [the Church's] life if she had no public opinion. Both pastors of souls and lay people would be to blame for this" (ibid.).

trusted with the responsibility of teaching the faith and ruling the Church (§1 and cc. 1008 and 207). Sacred pastors should listen carefully and openly to these opinions; the paragraph also qualifies those expressing an opinion so as to assist pastors in assessing specific opinions: key considerations are the "knowledge, competence, and prestige" of the faithful who express opinions. All the faithful are equal in dignity and action (c. 208) and all participate in the threefold functions (*munera*) of Christ priest, prophet, and ruler in accord with their condition. They therefore have a right to take an active role in the Church. At the same time, however, some of the faithful, availing themselves of the right to a Christian education expressed in canon 217, have obtained the learning necessary to offer an informed and intelligent opinion based upon sound evidence, an opinion which must be taken seriously by sacred pastors.

From the perspective of those exercising the right and at times the duty to express their opinions to pastors and to other Christian faithful, paragraph three adds specific qualifiers of such an expression of opinion: the integrity of faith and morals; reverence toward pastors; common advantage; and the dignity of persons. In other words, expressing opinions occurs within the context of *communio* and should aim at the edification of the Church as a whole, not at its splintering into various groups. The "integrity of faith and morals" requires an understanding of the hierarchy of truths discussed above in reference to paragraph one; fundamentally, freedom to express opinions does not apply to doctrine contained in the deposit of faith as indicated by canons 750 and 751. The other qualifiers of the right—reverence towards pastors, common advantage, human dignity—reflect the obligation to maintain communion (c. 209), the common equality of all the faithful in dignity and activity (c. 208), and the necessity of fostering the common good (c. 223). This right and duty does not exist in the abstract as an absolute right but rather is concretely situated within the particular community of faith.

In 1996, the National Pastoral Life Center prepared a document, released by Cardinal Bernar-

din, entitled "Called to Be Catholic: Church in a Time of Peril." To foster the renewal of the Catholic Church in the United States, the document urges the Church's leadership to reaffirm and promote "authentic unity, acceptable diversity and respectful dialogue."[97] The document has elicited a number of responses, some of which raise concerns that the call for a common ground could conflict with the authentic magisterium of the Church. Cardinal Bevilacqua, for example, fears that some American Catholics wish to change Church teaching to foster greater participation in the Church's life. At times, this desire is directed at "divinely revealed truths" which the faithful treat as "outmoded civil institutions: Discard what is old; endorse what is new!"[98] Archbishop Oscar Lipscomb has addressed a number of criticisms directed at the Common Ground project; first and foremost, he affirms that all dialogue "is accountable to Scripture and to the Catholic tradition, witnessed and conveyed to us by the 'Spirit-filled, living Church' and its magisterium 'exercised by the bishops and the chair of Peter.'"[99] The archbishop also cites *Communio et progressio:* "Those who exercise authority in the church will take care to ensure that there is reasonable exchange of freely held and expressed opinion among the people of God."[100]

A balance needs to be maintained between the right and at times the duty of the faithful to express their opinions on the good of the Church and the concomitant obligation of the Church (as a whole) to remain faithful to the teaching entrusted to it and the more specific function of

---

[97] National Pastoral Life Center, "Called to Be Catholic: Church in a Time of Peril," *Origins* 26 (August 29, 1996) 168.

[98] Cardinal Bevilacqua, "Reaction to the Catholic Common Ground Project," *Origins* 26 (September 12, 1996) 199. This issue also contains reactions (both positive and negative) by Bishop Hubbard, Cardinal Maida, Archbishop Lipscomb, Cardinal Hickey, Archbishop Hurley, and Cardinal Bernardin.

[99] Archbishop Lipscomb, "The Kind of Common Ground Sought," *Origins* 26 (March 27, 1997) 652.

[100] *CP* 331, #116.

bishops, including the bishop of Rome, to be "true and authentic teachers of the faith."[101] This balance reflects the "supernatural sense of the faith" (*sensus fidei*) which does not result from some type of "opinion poll" or "majority vote" but rather "is a gift of grace, given by the Holy Spirit."[102] According to *Lumen gentium* 12, "The universal body of the faithful who have received the anointing of the holy one (see 1 Jn 2, 20 and 27) cannot be mistaken in belief." But the text continues by situating this "supernatural sense of the faith" within the necessary guiding role of the "sacred magisterium." The Holy Spirit sanctifies, guides, and bestows gifts and special graces upon all the faithful for the edification of the Church; all have a mission in the Church; all have a right to contribute to an ever-deepening appreciation of divine truth.[103]

As important as the expression of the right is the means to ensure its usefulness in the life of the Church. If the right exists, then sacred pastors must provide means for its exercise. *Lumen gentium* 37 suggests this right be exercised through "institutions set up for this purpose by the Church." Various institutions have already been established on the diocesan and parochial level. Such institutions can provide means for the exercise of this right, to a greater or lesser degree dependent upon the support given to them by lay people, priests, and bishops. For example, the faithful can participate in diocesan pastoral councils (cc. 511–514) and parish councils (c. 536), presbyteral councils (cc. 495–501), and diocesan synods

(cc. 460–468); diocesan bishops and pastors may develop other options for the exercise of this right.

Spiritual Assistance

Canon 213 — The Christian faithful have the right to receive assistance from the sacred pastors out of the spiritual goods of the Church, especially the word of God and the sacraments.

This right flows from the very origin of *communio* itself, in the self-communication of God directed to the individual and involving the person's free, personal response to this communication. The Eastern code expresses the same right in canon 16. The response to God cannot remain purely internal or individual; it finds external expression within a particular community of faith, primarily through the reception of baptism. The Church's mission continues the salvific presence of Christ in the world and involves a cooperation with the grace of God for the salvation of men and women. As one consequence of God's self-communication, the Church, in order to fulfill its mission, must provide assistance to the faithful from its spiritual goods, especially the word of God and the sacraments. This assistance aims at encouraging the personal transformation of the individual and his or her personal relationship with God as well as facilitating that person's own role in the transformation of the world and in the community's fulfillment of its divinely given mission.

This right to spiritual nurture in word and sacrament finds a corresponding obligation on the part of sacred pastors to fulfill their ministerial duties in and to the Church community: both diocesan bishops and pastors are to foster the vocations of all the Christian faithful entrusted to them and to rely on their assistance in the Church's mission.[104]

Book IV deals with "The Sanctifying Function of the Church." Canon 834 establishes a basic

---

[101] See, for example, *CD* 2.

[102] See F. Sullivan, *Magisterium* (Mahwah, N.J.: Paulist, 1983) 21.

[103] See c. 218 on the right of inquiry and expression and, in reference to the role of theologians, see CDF, *Instruction*. In paragraph 30, the document recognizes the possibility that a theologian's objections to a specific teaching of the magisterium "could contribute to real progress and provide a stimulus to the Magisterium to propose the teaching of the Church in greater depth and with a clearer presentation of the arguments" (18–19). See also L. Örsy, *The Church: Learning and Teaching* (Wilmington: Glazier, 1987).

[104] See cc. 383, 385–387, 394 for the bishop; cc. 528–529 for the pastor.

principle for understanding "spiritual assistance" by describing the "sacred liturgy" through which the Church fulfills the priestly function (*munus*) of Jesus Christ. According to canon 839, the function of sanctifying includes the sacraments, prayer, works of penance and charity, and pious exercises in addition to liturgy and public worship.[105] The sacraments "contribute in the greatest way to establish, strengthen, and manifest ecclesiastical communion" (c. 840); therefore, sacred pastors are obliged to provide adequate preparation for their reception (c. 843, §2) and not to deny the sacraments "to those who seek them at appropriate times, are properly disposed, and are not prohibited by law from receiving them" (c. 843, §1). Although canon 213 applies primarily to the Christian faithful in full communion with the Catholic Church (c. 205), canon 844, §§3–4 extends the reception of the three sacraments of penance, Eucharist, and anointing of the sick to members of the Eastern churches and other Christians who do not have full communion with the Catholic Church under certain restrictions, more stringent for those persons falling into the latter category.

In Book III, "The Teaching Function of the Church," canons 756–780 deal with "The Ministry of the Divine Word." Canon 756, §1 establishes the basic principle that the proclamation of the gospel "has been entrusted principally to the Roman Pontiff and the college of bishops." Canon 756, §2 further specifies this responsibility within the diocese: "An individual bishop...is the moderator of the entire ministry of the word." Canons 757–759 explicate the role of presbyters as "co-workers of the bishops" (c. 757); of deacons "in communion with the bishop and his presbyterate" (c. 757); of members of institutes of consecrated life, who give "witness to the gospel in a special way" (c. 758); and of laity who "co-operate with the bishop and presbyters in the exercise of the ministry of the word" (c. 759). Canons 762–772 regulate preaching, among the forms of which the homily is preeminent (c. 767,

§1); bishops enjoy the right (*ius*) to preach everywhere; presbyters and deacons possess the faculty (*facultas*) to do so (c. 764), and laity "can be permitted to preach in a church or oratory" if necessary or advantageous according to the norms of the conferences of bishops (c. 766).

Given both the responsibility of sacred pastors to provide for the spiritual needs of the faithful as well as the dearth of clergy in some particular churches, sacred pastors may utilize a number of options for providing spiritual care to the Christian faithful. For example, parishes may be entrusted to a deacon or lay person or group of persons under the supervision of a priest (c. 517, §2). In this particular situation, those chosen can, among other responsibilities, administer communion to the sick and dying; be designated to preach and expose the Holy Eucharist; and lead specific rites for the deceased.[106] Further, laity and members of institutes of consecrated life can exercise a catechetical role (c. 776); lay people may receive general delegation to act as official witnesses at marriages (c. 1112); pastors may utilize married couples to ensure adequate preparation for the sacrament of marriage (c. 1063).

Worship and Spirituality

Canon 214 — The Christian faithful have the right to worship God according to the prescripts of their own rite approved by the legitimate pastors of the Church and to follow their own form of spiritual life so long as it is consonant with the doctrine of the Church.

This canon expresses two rights of the faithful: the right to worship according to a particular rite and the right to follow a particular spirituality. Inasmuch as both these rights are exercised within

---

[105] See cc. 836–837.

[106] Bishops' Committee on the Liturgy, *Gathered in Steadfast Faith, Statement on Sunday Worship in the Absence of a Priest* (Washington, D.C.: USCC, 1991) 5, #30. See also "Some Questions" and B. A. Cusack and T. G. Sullivan, *Pastoral Care in Parishes Without a Pastor* (Washington, D.C.: CLSA, 1995).

the Catholic Church, the canon requires approval of a specific rite by "the legitimate pastors of the Church" and the judgment that a particular form of spirituality concurs with Church teaching. The Eastern code expresses these rights in canon 17.

In the Latin church, the word "rite" is used in a variety of contexts: the celebration of a sacrament (for example, the Rite of Marriage) or of a sacramental (for example, the rite of blessing for the site of a new church building) or, more broadly, the way in which liturgy is celebrated (for example, the Roman, Tridentine, or Ambrosian rite). According to canon 28, §1 of the Eastern code, "rite" in the broad sense encompasses "the liturgical, theological, spiritual and disciplinary patrimony, culture and circumstances of history of a distinct people." This patrimony and culture are manifested in a particular church *sui iuris*, "a group of Christian faithful united by a hierarchy according to the norm of law which the supreme authority of the Church expressly or tacitly recognizes as *sui iuris*" (*CCEO* 27). In the latter sense, the Latin church is a church *sui iuris*, one of twenty-two such churches comprising the Catholic Church.[107]

These churches *sui iuris* which comprise the one Catholic Church reflect the principle intrinsic to *communio* that unity does not require uniformity; legitimate diversity should exist within the one Church. As one consequence, the faithful may fulfill certain spiritual obligations in any church *sui iuris* in communion with the Catholic Church. For example, canon 1248, §1 refers to satisfying one's Mass obligation in any Catholic rite; canon 991 expresses the faithful's right to free choice of a confessor, even one of another rite; and canon 923 allows the reception of the Eucharist in any Catholic rite. These options reflect the unity of the Church while simultaneously encouraging and protecting the diversity manifested through the different churches *sui iuris*. Canon 383, §2 requires the diocesan bishop to provide for the spiritual needs of the faithful belonging to a different rite within his diocese, and canon 846, §2 requires ministers to celebrate the sacraments "according to [their] own rite."

Further, although the faithful may receive baptism in any Catholic church, such reception does not necessarily include enrollment in that particular church *sui iuris*.[108] Enrollment in a particular church *sui iuris* affects the reception of certain sacraments in the Latin church. For example, canon 1109 requires for the validity of marriage that at least one of the parties and the assisting minister belong to the Latin rite. If eparchies[109] of another church *sui iuris* have been established for a specific territory, then a Latin bishop cannot grant dispensations from matrimonial impediments to persons legitimately enrolled in that church.[110] Canon 1015, §2 requires an apostolic indult for a Latin rite bishop to ordain lawfully a member of an Eastern rite (see also c. 1021). Finally, the right to worship according to the prescriptions of an approved rite carries the concomitant obligation on the part of ministers to follow faithfully the approved liturgical books.[111]

The second right stated in canon 214, to follow a form of spiritual life consonant with Church teaching, also allows for legitimate diversity and flexibility within the unity of the Catholic Church. This right flows from the personal relationship between God and an individual, the basis of Church *communio*. Various forms of spirituality can contribute to the Church's growth and sanctification as well as to the holiness of the faithful.[112] The qualification "consonant with the doctrine of the Church" is reiterated in canon 839 which obliges

---

[107] See J. Faris, *The Eastern Catholic Churches: Constitution and Governance* (New York: Saint Maron, 1992) 44–66. Various Eastern churches *sui iuris* follow a rite derived from one of the five major Eastern traditions: the Alexandrian, Antiochene, Constantinopolitan, Chaldean, and Armenian (46).

[108] See c. 112, §2; cc. 111–112 state the conditions for enrollment in a particular church *sui iuris* and changes in such enrollment.

[109] See *CCEO* 177, §1; these are the equivalent of dioceses in the Latin church.

[110] See cc. 87 and 136.

[111] See c. 846, §1; see also c. 2.

[112] See c. 210.

local ordinaries to see that "prayers and pious and sacred exercises of the Christian people are fully in keeping with the norms of the Church." Even if certain spiritual practices are congruent with church teaching, tensions may nonetheless arise between an individual's desires and the needs of the community. Compromise is often necessary to foster communion within a particular community; for example, if a group of the faithful wish to pray the rosary together publicly in the church building, the pastor may suggest specific times which do not conflict, for example, with celebrations of the Eucharist.

Association and Assembly

Canon 215 — The Christian faithful are at liberty freely to found and direct associations for purposes of charity or piety or for the promotion of the Christian vocation in the world and to hold meetings for the common pursuit of these purposes.

This canon states two fundamental rights of the faithful: to form associations and to hold meetings.[113] The right to associate finds specific canonical elaboration in canons 298–329 on "Associations of the Christian Faithful." The latter canons reiterate the right articulated here but more clearly situate it within the context of the supervisory role of competent ecclesiastical authority and the varying degrees of recognition, support, or encouragement given to a particular association by the Church. The Eastern code expresses the same fundamental rights in canon 18.

Canon 215 offers examples of the purposes intended by these meetings or associations: charity, piety, or the promotion of the Christian vocation in the world. Canon 298 expands these examples by including the promotion of a more perfect life,

public worship, or Christian teaching, as well as "other works of the apostolate." These broadly apostolic purposes, therefore, demonstrate that the right to meet and to form associations is both a natural right arising from the social nature of the person (AA 18) as well as a right derived from baptism, which situates the person within the community of faith and obliges the person to be involved in the Church's mission (c. 205). The right to associate, therefore, is exercised within the specific community of faith and must serve to build up and unify that community; this is one particular application of the obligation to maintain communion (c. 209). "Associations are not an end in themselves but serve the mission of the Church throughout the world."[114]

Associations contribute to the Church's life and to the fulfillment of its mission. Certain canons encourage the creation of associations. For example, canon 604, §2 suggests that consecrated virgins may form an association "to observe their own resolution more faithfully and to perform by mutual assistance service to the Church." Canon 708 encourages major superiors to associate so that "by common efforts they work to achieve more fully the purpose of the individual institutes." Canon 725 allows a secular institute to "associate to itself...other members of the Christian faithful."[115] Canon 278, §1 asserts the right of secular clerics to associate in order to pursue "purposes in keeping with the clerical state."

Inasmuch as the exercise of the right occurs within the Church as *communio,* church authority has a legitimate role in guiding its use. Canon 305 expresses the general principle that all associations are subject to vigilance by competent church authority. This authority may have more or less involvement, depending on the type of association and its statutes. Canon 300 requires consent by competent authority for an association to use the name "Catholic." Other canons express limitations on the right of association for particular persons; for example, canon 278, §3 forbids clerics

---

[113] Among the conciliar sources for this canon, see *AA* 18–20, which discuss associations in general as well as the role of laity in founding and directing associations; *PO* 8 refers to associations of priests; and *GS* 68, associations of workers.

[114] *AA* 19.
[115] See also cc. 677, §2 and 303.

from establishing or participating in associations if the latter's ends or activities are incompatible with clerical obligations and duties. Canon 287, §2 forbids clerics from having "an active part in political parties and in governing labor unions" unless necessary to protect the common good or the rights of the Church, in the judgment of competent ecclesiastical authority. This prohibition applies to members of institutes of consecrated life in virtue of canon 672; canon 288 exempts permanent deacons from this prohibition unless otherwise determined by particular law. Canon 1374 requires a just penalty to be imposed on a person who "joins an association which plots against the Church."

Canon 215 also states the right of the faithful "to hold meetings for the common pursuit of these purposes." This right flows from the social nature of the person whose growth and development require such interaction.[116] As with the right to form and direct associations, the exercise of the right to hold meetings occurs within the Church as *communio* and must serve to build up the Church and to assist in fulfilling its mission. The canon does not specifically include the right to use parochial or diocesan property to hold meetings; in the absence of an official policy, a careful and prudent judgment will be required in each case.

Apostolic Activity

Canon 216 — Since they participate in the mission of the Church, all the Christian faithful have the right to promote or sustain apostolic action even by their own undertakings, according to their own state and condition. Nevertheless, no undertaking is to claim the name *Catholic* without the consent of competent ecclesiastical authority.

This canon expresses the right of the Christian faithful to exercise the apostolate, a right expressed in the Eastern code in canon 19. This right arises from baptism and the consequent par-

[116] See, for example, *GS* 25.

ticipation of the faithful in the threefold functions (*munera*) of Jesus Christ priest, prophet, and ruler (c. 205). Canon 211 states that the faithful "have the duty and right" to proclaim the gospel; canon 216 further specifies this duty and right by stating explicitly the right to "promote or sustain apostolic action even by their own undertakings." *Apostolicam actuositatem* 6 summarizes the apostolate of the Church and of all its members as "primarily directed to making the message of Christ clear to the world by word and deed and to sharing his grace." *Apostolicam actuositatem* 6–8 further describes the apostolate: it begins with the witness of Christian life from which flows the proclamation of the gospel, the transformation of the temporal sphere, and works of charity.

The apostolate begins with a personal relationship with God which finds visible expression within the community of faith. The faithful must foster their own holiness and that of the Church (c. 210) and this obligation finds energy in the right to participate in the spiritual goods of the Church (c. 213). From this basis, the faithful have the right to proclaim the gospel (c. 211) and they fulfill this right in numerous ways. Canon 761 describes various means used to proclaim Christian doctrine, including preaching and catechesis as well as the press and the instruments of social communication. Lay members of the faithful proclaim the gospel "by word and . . . example" and can "cooperate with the bishop and presbyters in the exercise of the ministry of the word" (c. 759). Canon 225, §2 obliges the laity "to imbue and perfect the order of temporal affairs with the spirit of the gospel." All the faithful are obliged to promote social justice and to assist the poor (c. 222, §2). In his diocese, the bishop is obliged to encourage the faithful in their exercise of the apostolate (c. 394). The pastor requires the aid of the faithful to bring the gospel message to those who do not practice their religion or do not profess the true faith (c. 528, §1); further, the pastor must "recognize and promote" the participation of the lay faithful in the Church's mission (529, §2). The faithful exercise the apostolate by fostering, promoting, and joining associations, both on the national and international levels (cc. 216; 298–329).[117]

Each individual possesses a general vocation—to proclaim the gospel—and a more specific vocation within the community of faith: as a married or single person, cleric, religious, or lay person. These particular vocations help determine the differing modalities in which each individual exercises his or her general vocation. A member of an institute of consecrated life, for example, must remain faithful to the mission and works proper to that institute (c. 677, §1). Canon 774, §2 states the primary responsibility of parents to educate their children in the Christian faith and its practice. Canon 276 obliges clerics "to pursue holiness . . . [as] dispensers of the mysteries of God in the service of His people"; further, "clerics all work for the same purpose, namely, the building up of the Body of Christ" (c. 275, §1). Canon 835 expresses the participation of all the faithful in the sanctifying function (*munus*) of Jesus Christ.

Two of the sources for this canon, *Apostolicam actuositatem* 24 and 25, are found in chapter 5, "Preserving Due Order." This chapter recognizes the need for coordination among all forms of the apostolate, to allow "full scope for the special character of each [apostolate]," to promote the spirit of unity and the charity of fellowship, to pursue common ends and avoid harmful competition.[118] Although the right to promote or sustain apostolic action derives primarily from baptism and not from a mandate of ecclesiastical authority (cc. 204 and 759), the exercise of the right occurs within the context of the Church as a *communio* in which all the faithful exercise their vocation for the good of the Church and its mission.

The canon contains three qualifications of the exercise of the apostolate: the right is exercised by the faithful "according to their own state and condition"[119] and "competent ecclesiastical au-

thority" must consent to the use of the name "Catholic" for a specific work. The use of the name "Catholic" could (at least) suggest that a specific effort represents the Church itself or is officially accepted by the Church. The authority competent to consent to the use of the name "Catholic" would depend on particular circumstances. For example, canons 300 and 312 explain that the authority competent to erect a public association is also competent to allow that association to use the word "Catholic." This competency pertains to the Holy See for international associations; to the conference of bishops for national associations; and to the diocesan bishop for diocesan associations. The same authorities are also competent to allow schools and universities to use the name "Catholic" (cc. 803 and 808).

Two other canons provide a context for the exercise of the apostolate: canon 209 (the duty to maintain communion) and canon 223 (the fostering of the common good). These qualifications of the exercise of the right testify to the diversity present in the Church, in which there is fundamental equality in dignity and in action (c. 208) but also different vocations, roles, and charisms.[120]

Christian Education

Canon 217 — Since they are called by baptism to lead a life in keeping with the teaching of the gospel, the Christian faithful have the right to a Christian education by which they are to be instructed properly to strive for the maturity of the human person and at the same time to know and live the mystery of salvation.

The conciliar declaration *Gravissimum educationis* succinctly states the "inalienable right to an education" for "all people of whatever race, condition, and age"; this right arises from their human dignity.[121] Canon 217 concerns the fulfillment of this natural right within the Christian community, namely, the right to a Christian edu-

[117] See R. DeRoo, "Ecclesial Structures and Social Justice," *CLSAP* 43 (1981) 32–43.

[118] *AA* 23.

[119] For a discussion of both terms, see the commentary on cc. 204 and 207.

[120] See cc. 204 and 207.

[121] *GE* 1.

cation which is also expressed in the Eastern code in canon 20. This specific right is directed toward two interrelated goals: the human maturity of the person and a deepening of the person's relationship with God; the latter is the foundation of *communio*.[122] The individual's cooperation with God's salvific will is expressed through participation in the triple functions (*munera*) of Jesus Christ as priest, prophet, and ruler (c. 205) and in the exercise of the Church's apostolate (c. 216). To achieve these goals, the faithful need an appropriate education.

By using the adjective "Christian" to describe this right, canon 217 broadens its scope to include all the baptized, whether or not they live in full communion with the Catholic Church.[123] The reception of baptism and entrance into a particular ecclesial community or church reflects a continuing maturation process both as a human being and as a person in relationship with God and with a community of faith; all the baptized possess the right to an education that fosters their maturity both as human beings and as children of God. Further, this understanding of Christian education presupposes the conciliar teaching that while "elements of sanctification and of truth" are found outside the Catholic Church, these elements impel towards catholic unity.[124]

In various canons, and especially in Book III, the code refers to a particular specification of this right: the right to a *Catholic* education. For example, canon 226, §2 states that parents "have a most grave obligation and possess the right to educate" their children "according to the doctrine handed on by the Church." The seriousness of this obligation is reinforced in canon 1366 which requires a censure "or other just penalty" for parents or those who take the place of parents if they "hand over their children to be baptized or educated in a non-Catholic religion." In Book III, canon 794, §1 expresses the basic principle: the

Church has a "duty and right" to educate the faithful, and paragraph two states that sacred pastors are obliged to arrange for Catholic education. More specifically, the arrangements for such education are spelled out in canons 773–780 which concern catechetical instruction; canons 793–821 on "Catholic Education"; and canons 807–814 on "Catholic Universities and Other Institutes of Higher Studies." Certain consequences can ensue for the faithful when they acquire a Catholic education. For example, greater weight can be given to their opinions on ecclesial issues offered to sacred pastors and to other Christian faithful (c. 212, §3). In certain cases, a specific educational background can qualify lay people to assume ecclesiastical offices or functions (c. 228, §1), to receive a mandate to teach sacred sciences (c. 229, §3), or to be appointed to teach specific disciplines in a seminary (c. 253, §1).

Freedom in Pursuit of Sacred Sciences

Canon 218 — Those engaged in the sacred disciplines have a just freedom of inquiry and of expressing their opinion prudently on those matters in which they possess expertise, while observing the submission due to the magisterium of the Church.

This canon specifies the particular application of rights expressed elsewhere in the code and in the Vatican II documents, especially the participation in the threefold functions (*munera*) of Jesus Christ priest, prophet, and ruler; the right to Christian education (c. 217); and the right to manifest opinions on issues affecting the good of the Church to sacred pastors and other Christian faithful (c. 212, §3). The Eastern code contains the same application of rights in canon 21. According to *Dignitatis humanae*, "all people are bound to seek for the truth, especially about God and his church," a right based on the dignity of the human person.[125] One significant application

---

[122] See the introduction to Book II and the commentary on c. 209.

[123] See cc. 204–205.

[124] See *LG* 8 and *UR* 3.

[125] *DH* 1; c. 748 includes this same citation.

of these rights occurs in the context of interaction between those persons engaged in the sacred disciplines and the magisterium of the Church. The conciliar source for this canon, *Gaudium et spes* 62, indicates that the term "sacred disciplines" includes all those fields of study which foster a deeper appreciation of the faith and which enable men and women to proclaim the gospel message. Those engaged in these sacred disciplines enjoy a just freedom of inquiry and can prudently express opinions, both of which are necessary to the academic enterprise. The conciliar text also invites theologians "to look for a more appropriate way of communicating doctrine to the people of their time," an invitation based upon the distinction between the deposit of faith and the manner in which this deposit is expressed. Finally, *Gaudium et spes* expresses the desire that the laity will receive appropriate formation in the sacred disciplines in seminaries and universities (c. 229, §2).

The Eastern code recognizes that the contributions of disciplines other than theology, including literature and the arts (*CCEO* 603), assist the faithful in being "led to a more conscious and reflective life of faith" (*CCEO* 602). The Eastern code also explicitly articulates the role of theologians in canon 606. The first paragraph states,

> Theologians with their deeper understanding of the mystery of salvation and with their expertise in the sacred and related sciences as well as in current problems, have the role and duty, faithfully complying with the authentic magisterium of the Church, and of equal importance, utilizing their freedom, to illumine the faith of the Church, to defend it and to contribute to doctrinal progress.

The purpose of such endeavors is to preserve and promote the faith and to manifest the catholicity of the Church through legitimate diversity (*CCEO* 604).

The context for the interaction of theologians and the magisterium is the Church as *communio,* which begins with a person's personal relationship with God and which finds visible expression through baptism into the community of faith (see cc. 204–205; 209). Persons dedicated to the sacred disciplines—as students, teachers, or in researching various topics of academic-pastoral concern—exercise their freedom of inquiry and expression in the church *communio* with the goal of bringing the faithful "to a more refined and more mature life of faith."[126] *Gaudium et spes* 62 also notes the contribution of the secular sciences to the process of deepening Christian formation. This freedom, however, is not without qualifications. While no one can be forced to accept the Catholic faith against his or her conscience (c. 748, §2), once baptized or received into the Church, the person cannot choose to accept or to reject specific articles of the faith. This reflects the bond of the profession of faith, one of the three bonds indicating that a person lives in full communion with the Church (c. 205).[127] The exer-

---

[126] See NCCB, "Doctrinal Responsibilities: Approaches to Promoting Cooperation and Resolving Misunderstandings Between Bishops and Theologians," *Origins* 19 (June 19, 1989) 97, 99–110. The text emphasizes that the ecclesial context of *communio* "is critical for understanding the relationship between bishops and theologians, for encouraging cooperation and for constructing an adequate approach to prevent or to address disputes related to church teaching" (99). The text recognizes the responsibilities both of bishops and of theologians: bishops are "charged to preserve and protect the truth of faith, i.e., to transmit the authentic gospel of Christ" (101) while theologians "discharge their responsibility in fidelity to apostolic faith by meditative appropriation of the faith and by critical inquiry" (102). To fulfill this responsibility, theologians "must expect to exchange constructive criticism with other scholars, other Christians and other interested persons of good will" (102).

[127] A clarification is necessary: the bond of the profession of the faith must include accepting the hierarchy of truths within Christian doctrine; that is, not all teaching carries the same weight, depending upon the connection between a particular doctrine and the foundation of the Christian faith. Canons 750–754 recognize this hierarchy of truths by indicating the different responses to be given to various expressions of church teaching. See the discussion below on the third qualification in the canon; *UR* 11; and commentary on c. 205.

cise of religious liberty, like the exercise of other rights, occurs within the context of the Catholic Church through which "the fullness of the means of salvation can be attained."[128]

This foundational qualification—that the faithful cannot choose which articles of faith to accept or reject—finds expression in the duty to maintain communion (c. 209); scholarship occurs within the particular faith community and aims at increasing the community's appreciation of the faith, both as a whole and as individuals. This forms one aspect of the obligation to foster the common good of the Church (c. 223). Canon 218 further notes that this freedom of inquiry must be "just" (*iusta*; in *CCEO* 21 "lawful"); scholarship is not an end in and of itself but serves the community.[129] Further, opinions are to be expressed prudently, through appropriate journals, meetings of scholars, etc. The aim of such scholarly exchange is to engender discussion and clarification about a specific point, not to sway public opinion to one's side.

A second qualification of academic freedom requires that the individuals must possess expertise in the area under discussion. In other words, these persons have the obligation to secure the appropriate education necessary to investigate various academic-pastoral issues and to disseminate their opinions on such issues; their opinions will hold greater weight in relationship to their academic proficiency and ability to assess the evidence.

A third qualification of this right states that these individuals are to observe the "submission" [*obsequium*] due to the Church's magisterium. All the faithful participate in the teaching function of the Church (see c. 747); however, sacred pastors have a specific responsibility to ensure the probity of that which is taught. As noted in the commentary on canons 205 and 212, differing gradations of official teaching exist, evoking different responses from the faithful. The obligation to "believe with divine and Catholic faith" applies to the one deposit of faith entrusted to the Church (c. 750, §1). The following canons (752–754) apply to teachings not contained in the one deposit of faith and therefore elicit different responses: "a religious submission of the intellect and will" to a doctrine of the authentic magisterium concerning faith or morals declared by the pope or college of bishops (c. 752); adherence "with religious submission of mind to the authentic magisterium of their bishops" (c. 753); and observance of constitutions and decrees issued by the legitimate authority of the Church (c. 754).[130] Further, "no doctrine is understood as defined infallibly unless this is manifestly evident" (c. 749, §3). Appropriate Christian submission therefore requires a well-founded respect for and attempt to understand a particular teaching of the magisterium; all the Christian faithful, both those doing research and the Church's official teachers, should strive for "an ever deeper understanding of the Word of God found in the Scripture and handed on faithfully by the Church's living tradition under the guidance of the Magisterium."[131]

Nonetheless, disagreement with a particular teaching may be the appropriate response in a particular situation (see c. 212, §3) and, in fact, the theologian may have the duty to inform the

---

[128] See *UR* 3.

[129] Hervada, in *Pamplona ComEng,* 194, states that the term *iusta* indicates that this freedom of inquiry is not absolute and is geared to avoiding excessive interpretations of such freedom. He elaborates upon this statement in reference to the submission (*obsequium*) owed to the magisterium: "In the case of the right with which we are concerned, this means that the scope of freedom is limited to the field of the debatable. There is no freedom of opinion regarding the doctrinal propositions duly established by the magisterium" (195). See also McGrath, in *CLSGBI Com,* 123: "It is a 'just,' or lawful, freedom in that it must avoid unfounded or excessive pronouncements." In other words, scholarship aims at a deeper appropriation of the faith by the Christian faithful and should not lead to a disrespect for the magisterium of the Church.

[130] For a fuller analysis of this complex material, see the commentary on cc. 750–754.

[131] *Instruction,* 15, #21. See also *DV* 10 which notes that the "teaching function is not above the word of God but stands at its service."

magisterium of difficulties in a particular non-irreformable teaching, in the way it is presented, or in the argumentation utilized to support it.[132] The Congregation of the Doctrine of the Faith recognizes this duty and also makes a clear distinction between this type of disagreement and "dissent" which it defines in a particular and limited manner as "general opposition to Church teaching which even comes to expression in organized groups."[133] Given this distinction, great caution must be used in applying canon 1371, 1° to particular situations in which an individual ex-

presses such difficulties.[134] Furthermore, *Gaudium et spes* 62 recognizes that "a just freedom of enquiry, of thought and of humble and courageous expression" contributes to the proclamation of the gospel in the contemporary situation.

Choice of State in Life

Canon 219 — All the Christian faithful have the right to be free from any kind of coercion in choosing a state of life.

The conciliar sources for this canon proceed from the exceptional dignity of the human person and the essential equality of all people to the necessity of societies (both civil and ecclesiastical) to provide means and opportunities for people to exercise their "universal and inviolable" rights, including the right to follow their vocation.[135] The Eastern code expresses the same freedom in canon 22. As expressed in canon 219, the Church as *communio* forms the particular context for both understanding and exercising this right. Positively expressed, canon 219 states that the human per-

[132] *Instruction*, 18–19, #30. NCCB, "Doctrinal Responsibilities," includes procedures both for formal and informal dialogue between bishops and theologians when theological disagreements arise. These procedures are cited in NCCB, "'Ex corde Ecclesiae': An Application to the United States," *Origins* 26 (November 28, 1996) 381, 383–384, and adopted "as the appropriate procedure to assure a process acceptable to both bishop and faculty member" (383). Cardinal Laghi, in "Vatican Observations on U.S. Bishops' 'Ex corde Ecclesiae' Application Document," *Origins* 27 (June 12, 1997) 53–55, raises two difficulties with "Doctrinal Responsibilities": the text "does not address the situation of the teacher of theology at the moment of his appointment" and "does not seem to facilitate the exercise of the rights and duties of the local bishop when problems arise" (55).

[133] *Instruction*, 19, #32. In #33, the text describes different aspects of dissent, including "its most radical form" which "aims at changing the Church following a model of protest which takes its inspiration from political society." More often, dissent includes the assertion "that the theologian is not bound to adhere to any Magisterial teaching unless it is infallible." The distinction between "difficulties" and "dissent" in the CDF document demonstrates a basic terminological difficulty; see the discussion by L. Örsy in *The Church*, 90–93. Örsy states, "Thus, 'dissent' is too much of an ambivalent word, with too many existential connotations beyond a purely intellectual significance to be a useful term in theological debates, which by definition are supposed to move on a rational level" (91–92). Nonetheless, he concludes, "All these arguments notwithstanding, it appears that for the time being at least, not only must we live with an unsuitable word, but we have to assert the legitimate right of the faithful to scientific research and to a different opinion through the use of a confusing expression: 'the right to dissent'" (93).

[134] See also c. 18 which states that laws establishing a penalty or restricting the exercise of rights must be strictly interpreted. On August 29, 1997, the CDF issued "Regulations for Doctrinal Examination," with an accompanying "Explanatory Note," *Origins* 27 (September 11, 1997) 221–224. These regulations establish a procedure to be followed by the CDF in its examination of theological writings. Such examinations result from situations "when the influence of a publication exceeds the boundaries of an individual episcopal conference or when the danger to the faith is particularly grave" (art. 2). Experience is needed to determine the strengths and weaknesses in the procedure, particularly in reference to the possible declaration by the CDF that *latae sententiae* penalties have been incurred due to heresy, apostasy, or schism and the inability of recourse against such a declaration (art. 28). The "Explanatory Note" addresses this particular article, stating that it would be "pure and unjustified juridical formalism" to initiate a penal trial or to allow for recourse when the CDF has established "with certainty" that an author is a heretic, an apostate, or schismatic.

[135] See, for example, *GS* 26, 29, and 52.

son needs freedom in order to grow in a relationship with God and to respond to a divine vocation. *Communio* begins with the relationship between the individual and God, a free response to God's invitation to enter into the divine life and the visible expression of this response through baptism into the Church. Freedom from coercion in fundamental life choices is one key aspect of the fundamental dignity of the sons and daughters of God.[136]

Canon 219 does not express a right *to exercise or to fulfill* a specific vocation within the Church. *Gaudium et spes* 29 recognizes that not everyone "is identical in physical capacity and in mental and moral resources." In various places, the code balances the individual's perception of and response to an invitation from God with the pastoral needs and teachings of the community of faith. Canon 214, therefore, states the right of individuals to follow their own form of spiritual life provided it is consonant with church teaching. Canon 1026 requires "due freedom" for the reception of orders and canon 1036 requires from the ordinand a signed and handwritten declaration of his freedom and desire to serve in ecclesiastical ministry. Canon 1025, however, articulates the responsibility of one's proper bishop or competent superior to judge that the individual "is endowed...with the necessary qualities" for ecclesial ministry. Canon 1058 recognizes the basic right of individuals to enter into marriage provided they are not prohibited by law; the consent that brings marriage into existence must be free (c. 1057). A marriage is invalid "if entered into because of force or grave fear from without" (c. 1103). Canon 597 allows any Catholic to be admitted to an institute of consecrated life, provided he or she possesses the right intention and requisite qualities and is not prevented from doing so by an impediment (see also c. 641). Further, canon 643, §1, 4° invalidates admission to the novitiate if one entered the institute as a result of force, grave fear, or fraud. Parents have the obligation of providing for a Christian education

of their children (c. 793, §1) and this includes ensuring their children's freedom in choosing a state in life.[137]

Reputation and Privacy

Canon 220 — No one is permitted to harm illegitimately the good reputation which a person possesses nor to injure the right of any person to protect his or her own privacy.

This canon expresses two rights which proceed from human nature, the right to enjoy a good reputation and the right of the person to protect his or her privacy. The Eastern code expresses the same rights in canon 23. According to *Gaudium et spes* 26, the rights "to one's good name" and "to the protection of one's private life" derive from the "exceptional dignity which belongs to the human person."

The canon protects one's reputation from *illegitimate* harm. In other words, individuals exercise their rights, including the right to a good reputation, within the Church as *communio* (c. 209). To protect both the common good (see c. 223) and the Church itself, individuals may act, even though they might thereby damage someone's reputation. The motivating force of such an action should be a desire to protect another value, for example, the good reputation of the Church or of other individuals and not to ruin one person's reputation; all pertinent circumstances must be taken into account before acting. For example, the code presents various options to safeguard reputations and to ensure that penalties are inflicted only as a last resort. In reference to the preliminary investigation process concerning delicts, canon 1717, §2 requires "care" to ensure protection of a person's good name. Canon 1341 suggests diverse "means of pastoral solicitude" be utilized by an ordinary before beginning a judicial or administrative process which is always a last resort measure in dealing with a problematic situation. Other canons strive to protect a person's reputation. For

---

[136] See, for example, *GS* 29.

[137] See *GS* 52.

example, canon 1335 does not require an individual to reveal the presence of a *latae sententiae* censure when one of the faithful requests a sacrament, sacramental, or act of governance. Canon 1352, §2 provides certain conditions under which an undeclared *latae sententiae* penalty is suspended to preclude "grave scandal or infamy." Canon 1455, §3 gives judges in specific cases the freedom to bind participants to observe secrecy if the danger of damaging the reputation of others is present.

The right to a good reputation is at risk as the Church confronts the issue of sexual misconduct by clerics. The media often accuse ecclesiastical authorities of proceeding too slowly when accusations of sexual abuse, particularly of minors, arise. Church authorities have a responsibility to move expeditiously yet must exercise great caution to protect both the accuser and the cleric involved. At times, a cleric is judged guilty simply due to an accusation; his reputation is damaged and he may experience difficulties in exercising his ministry, even if the accusation is later withdrawn or proven false.[138]

The code contains few explicit references to privacy; indirectly, such a concern for privacy is exemplified in the freedom of seminarians to choose any confessor (c. 240, §1) and the prohibition against securing the opinion of a spiritual director or confessor concerning admission to or dismissal from the seminary.[139] The same freedom of access to a confessor is recognized for members of religious institutes in canon 630, §1 without "prejudice, however, to the discipline of the institute." The latter phrase allows an institute to establish its own norms provided these do not violate an individual's freedom in receiving the

sacrament of penance. Canon 630, §5 specifically forbids a superior from inducing a subject to make a manifestation of conscience.

Questions concerning a proper respect for privacy and reputation can arise during the process of admitting individuals to seminaries and to institutes of consecrated life, most often in reference to psychological and medical testing. Canon 642 allows experts to be consulted concerning a person's suitability for admission to a religious institute but also recognizes the right to privacy and to good reputation by explicitly citing canon 220 in this context. In reference to seminaries, *The Program of Priestly Formation*, paragraph 521, requires throughout the admission process that "the candidate's rights to privacy should be respected and the careful management of confidential materials observed." Officials must carefully balance the right of the institute or seminary to certain information in order to develop an educated judgment as to whether or not they should admit a specific individual and that individual's rights to privacy. Although the individual, by his or her application, agrees to provide certain confidential information, the individual does not thereby forfeit entirely the right to privacy.[140] Finally, seminary and diocesan officials, as well as superiors in institutes of consecrated life, must provide adequate protection of materials placed in the archives, including personnel files, in order to protect the privacy and good reputation of individuals.[141]

Protection of Rights

Canon 221 — §1. The Christian faithful can legitimately vindicate and defend the rights which they possess in the Church in the competent ecclesiastical forum according to the norm of law.

---

[138] See J. Provost, "Some Canonical Considerations Relative to Clerical Sexual Abuse," *J* 52 (1992), 615–641. Provost cautions: "Abuse, which can seriously scar the victim for life, does not need to become the source for public voyeurism. When Church officials are approached with reports of abuse by a cleric, they must be very circumspect in order to respect the rights to which all parties are entitled in this situation" (628).

[139] See cc. 240, §2; 984–985.

[140] See P. Cogan, ed., *CLSA Advisory Opinions 1984–1993* (Washington, D.C.: CLSA, 1995), opinions on c. 241, §1, 44–47; and on cc. 241, §1, 1029, and 1051, 1°, 47–52 which concern the specific issues involved in HIV/AIDS testing.

[141] On the diocesan level, see cc. 486–491 on archives, including secret archives (c. 489).

§2. If they are summoned to a trial by a competent authority, the Christian faithful also have the right to be judged according to the prescripts of the law applied with equity.

§3. The Christian faithful have the right not to be punished with canonical penalties except according to the norm of law.

This canon expresses three principles necessary to ensure that rights are not only recognized but also vindicated with the purpose of guaranteeing that rights do not become meaningless. They apply equally to the Church and to civil society. The Eastern code expresses the same principles in canon 24. The three principles are the right to vindicate and defend rights in a competent church forum (§1); the right of due process according to the prescripts of the law "applied with equity" (§2); and the right (rephrased in positive terms) that sanctions be imposed according to law (§3).

The context for the exercise of these principles is the Church as *communio*, in which all of the faithful enjoy a fundamental equality in dignity and action (c. 208). The source of rights and the basis for their protection is the dignity of the human person as a child of God and a sharer in the divine nature;[142] the Church is empowered by the gospel "to proclaim the rights of humanity" and must promote these rights everywhere.[143] The 1971 synod of bishops acknowledged that for the Church to speak about justice, it must first be just.[144] In 1972, the NCCB approved a resolution stating in part, "The promotion of adequate protection of human rights and freedoms within the Church is central to the bishops' role of service to the people of God."[145] Protecting the rights of the faithful as expressed here in title I, elsewhere in the code, or in any other

law is therefore of fundamental importance for the Church to fulfill its mission in the world.

Vindicate and Defend Rights

Expressing a fundamental principle, the code urges all the Christian faithful "to strive diligently to avoid litigation."[146] Canon 1733, §1, in the section on "Recourse Against Administrative Decrees," urges an "equitable solution" between a person who feels injured by an administrative decree and the author of that decree in order to avoid contention; furthermore, paragraph two of that canon allows the conference of bishops or individual bishops for their own dioceses (if the conference has not done so) to establish norms on procedures, a council or office, as well as means for mediation.

Despite this exhortation to avoid litigation, some attempts at amicable resolution of disputes or at mediation processes fail; the faithful therefore have the right to recourse to the competent ecclesiastical court (§1). Book VII on processes establishes a complex series of norms governing the Church's tribunal system. Canon 1400, §1, 1° defines one object of a trial as "the pursuit or vindication of the rights of physical or juridic persons." In practice, however, the Church's tribunal system primarily deals with cases involving declarations of marriage nullity (see cc. 1060 and 1085, §2). Tribunal personnel often have neither access to jurisprudence concerning the vindication of rights nor the expertise to deal with these issues. Limitations in time, personnel, and resources and the volume of marriage nullity claims lead ordinary tribunals to focus solely on the adjudication of such cases.

---

[142] See *LG* 40.

[143] See *GS* 41.

[144] Synod of Bishops, "The Practice of Justice," in *Justice in the World* (Washington, D.C.: USCC, 1971) 41.

[145] NCCB, *On Due Process* (Washington, D.C.: USCC, 1972). This text includes "The Report of the Canon Law Society of America to the National Conference of

Catholic Bishops on the Subject of Due Process." See also the revised report in *Protection of Rights of Persons in the Church* (Washington, D.C.: CLSA, 1991) and CLSA, *Due Process in Dioceses in the United States 1970–1985* (Washington, D.C.: CLSA, 1987). The introduction to *Due Process in Dioceses* states as its objective "to aid members of the Society in exploring additional steps toward effective procedures for the protection of rights of persons in the Church" (1).

[146] See c. 1446, §1, in reference to tribunals.

Further, canon 1400, §2 requires that controversies arising "from an act of administrative power can be brought only before the superior or an administrative tribunal"; thus, these disputes cannot be brought to the ordinary judicial forum. If, however, administrative tribunals are established for a particular diocese, these tribunals would function judicially while reviewing administrative discretion.

The majority of cases in which people perceive a violation of their rights arises from administrative acts of church authority.[147] According to canon 35, such actions would include decrees, precepts, and rescripts; canon 59, §1 adds privileges, dispensations, or other favors under the term "rescript." If these acts violate the rights of an individual, the latter must proceed administratively through hierarchical recourse and not through the Church's ordinary tribunal system. All of these acts of church authority require executive power of governance (c. 35); however, challenges to acts which do not involve this power of governance might form the basis for adjudication by an ordinary tribunal. For example, many actions taken by various lay officials within the diocesan curia as well as the pastor within his parish would not involve executive power and an individual who felt aggrieved by a specific action could theoretically initiate a case involving an alleged violation of rights in the ordinary tribunal.

Canons 1732–1739 provide the procedure for taking recourse against administrative decrees. The first step is conciliation (1733, §1). If this fails, then the canons outline a specific procedure for individuals to follow, including a request for revocation or emendation of the decree (c. 1734, §1) and recourse to a superior. The superior would be the bishop, if his subordinate issued the decree; or a pertinent dicastery of the Apostolic See if the bishop were involved.[148] The possibility also exists of recourse to the second section of the Apostolic Signatura against a decision by one of the Roman dicasteries; according to c. 1445, §2, the Signatura "deals with conflicts which have arisen from an act of ecclesiastical administrative power."[149]

Other processes for dealing with the perceived or actual violation of rights are currently being developed, actively encouraged by the Canon Law Society of America. *Due Process in Dioceses* made a significant contribution to this process by surveying United States dioceses to determine the existence and experience of due process. Two tables outline both allowable and non-allowable cases; most frequently, cases concern employment issues, followed by school and "pastoral issues."[150]

Canons 1400, §2 and 149, §2 refer to administrative tribunals; the *Protection of Rights* offers models for a proposed diocesan administrative tribunal and regional administrative tribunal. The diocesan administrative tribunal can receive petitions from "any person or group of persons in conflict with a parochial or diocesan administrator or administrative body, other than the diocesan bishop."[151] Two dioceses in the United States—the Archdiocese of Milwaukee and the Archdio-

---

[147] See, for example, R. Kennedy, "Commentary," in *Protection of Rights*, 46: "It is in the area of administrative action that we believe the need for due process is most urgent in the Church." See also J. Beal, "Protecting the Rights of Lay Catholics," *J* 47 (1987) 129–164 and the first issue of *J* 46 (1986) which is devoted to promoting and protecting rights in the Church.

[148] See commentary on c. 360.

[149] See *PB* 123, §§1–3.

[150] *Due Process in Dioceses,* 32–33, Figures 14–15; 70–80, Tables 16 and 17. The text does not specify the topics included under "pastoral issues." See also J. Perry, "Accessibility of Due Process for the Laity," *CLSAP* 51 (1989) 65–82; E. Pfnausch, "Protection of Rights of Persons in the Church: A Hearing," *CLSAP* 54 (1992) 195–207; and D. Barr, J. Bell, J. Perry, P. McGreevy, "CLSA Experiment in Due Process Committee Report," *CLSAP* 56 (1994) 68–79.

[151] *Protection of Rights,* 23: Article I, Section 1. In Barr et al., "CLSA Experiment in Due Process," the administrative process is described as "the crowning piece of the entire due process effort.... The extra-judicial methods have assisted us in some good ways over the years, yet their merely voluntary nature has not always solved the issue of an alleged abridged right or perceived injustice" (76).

cese of Minneapolis-St. Paul—have established administrative tribunals on an interim basis. A regional administrative tribunal has not yet been established. Further analysis and reflection will determine the effectiveness of such tribunals and whether or not other dioceses should be encouraged to establish them.[152]

Due Process Applied with Equity

The second paragraph articulates the right of the faithful to be judged according to the law applied with equity. This right applies both to judicial and to administrative processes and would include specific rights such as the right to a good reputation and the right to protect one's privacy (c. 220). An individual pursuing recourse has the right to canonical advice (c. 1738); time limitations for various procedural steps such as those listed in canon 1734 aim at ensuring a more expeditious response to such a petition. The judicial procedures delineated in Book VII include a number of canons which aim at the protection of the rights of all parties involved. For example, according to canon 1620, 7°, a sentence is vitiated by irremediable nullity if the right of defense is denied; canon 1481 states the right to canonical advice; canon 1598, §1, the right to view the acts of the case (also under pain of nullity); and canon 1628, the right to appeal a sentence.[153]

Canonical equity aims at ensuring that rights are protected or injustices corrected in situations where a strict application of the law might harm these rights or where the law is incapable of correcting an injustice.[154] Equity ensures that the Church's mission of salvation remains paramount (see c. 1752), reflecting the Church as *communio* in which all the faithful, as sons and daughters of God, strive to promote the holiness of the Church itself and of individuals (see c. 210).[155]

Proper Procedure for Penalties

According to canon 1400, §1 a trial has two objects: to vindicate the rights of persons (physical or juridic; 1°) and to impose or declare penalties (2°). Canon 1311 asserts the Church's "innate and proper right to coerce offending members" by sanctions although canon 1341 urges the ordinary to utilize other means of achieving the goals of the penal system, including fraternal correction and rebuke, before beginning a judicial or administrative penal procedure. Further, canon 1321 requires that no one be punished "unless the external violation of a law or precept, committed by the person, is gravely imputable by reason of malice or negligence." An accusation does not necessarily mean the individual is guilty nor that a penalty must be imposed (see c. 1341).

Book VI, "Sanctions in the Church," begins with a general description of offenses and penalties. Penalties are presented as a final option to preserve good order in the church (cc. 1317 and 1341). Canon 1314 expresses a preference for imposed (*ferendae sententiae*) rather than automatic (*latae sententiae*) penalties, thus ensuring the implementation of proper procedure, the protection of individual rights, and the investigation of other, non-penal options in the application of penalties. The Eastern code progresses further by omitting automatic (*latae sententiae*) penalties (*CCEO* 1402). Canons 1321–1330 analyze the subjective elements necessary for a person to be punished;

---

[152] The CLSA Committee on Experiment in Due Process is currently engaged in gathering data to assess the effectiveness of various procedures being utilized in various U.S. dioceses.

[153] For further analysis, see the commentary on Book VII.

[154] Canon 19 addresses such issues in the context of a lacuna in the law; canon 85 provides rules for a dispensation, that is, a "relaxation of a merely ecclesiastical law in a particular case."

[155] For further analysis of canonical equity, see J. Coughlin, "Canonical Equity," *Stud Can* 30 (1996) 403–435. Coughlin concludes that canonical equity "safeguards the natural justice recognized through human reason. It abets the effort of ecclesiastical law always to be open to the possibility of supernatural evangelical love, compassion and mercy. It manifests the hope of the Church for the future by helping to ground the juridical structure of the present in the Tradition" (433).

canons 1322–1324 present factors which remove or diminish imputability and canon 1326 those factors which increase imputability. Canons 1331–1340 state what penalties and other punishments are possible and canons 1341–1353 govern the application of penalties.

To protect the rights of the accused person, canon 1342 indicates a preference for judicial procedure for the application of penalties, especially those with serious consequences. Further protection of the rights of individuals is presented in canons 1717–1731 which govern the penal process. These canons consistently emphasize the protection of an individual's rights. For example, the ordinary must take care to ensure a person's good name is protected (c. 1717, §2); in an administrative process, the accused has the right to information about the accusation and proofs (c. 1720) and the right to an advocate (cc. 1481 and 1723). Further, canon 1728, §1 requires the application of the canons concerned with trials in general to specifically penal trials; canon 1728, §2 states that the accused "is not bound to confess the delict nor can an oath be administered to the accused." The canons on trials include a variety of means to protect the interests of both individuals and the Church community.[156]

While the code recognizes the need for sanctions, it also recognizes that sanctions should be applied only as a last resort, in order to protect the Church and its mission in the world (see c. 1341).

Support of the Church

Canon 222 — §1. The Christian faithful are obliged to assist with the needs of the Church so that the Church has what is necessary for divine worship, for the works of the apostolate and of charity, and for the decent support of ministers.

The first paragraph expresses the duty incumbent upon the Christian faithful "to assist with the

needs of the Church," more specifically, to ensure the Church can continue its divine mission through divine worship, the apostolate, charitable works, and the "decent support" of the Church's ministers. The Eastern code expresses the same duty in canon 25, §1. Canon 1254, §1 states that the Church "by innate right is able to acquire, retain, administer, and alienate temporal goods" for the aforementioned purposes which are explicated in canon 1254, §2.

The conciliar sources for this canon emphasize the necessity of Christians to lead profound Christian lives and to foster the holiness of themselves and of the whole Church (c. 210).[157] This reflects the foundational relationship of *communio* between an individual and God resulting in the duty to maintain communion with the Church (c. 209). According to this basis, the faithful, including laity, religious, and the hierarchy, are actively to support the Church's mission through their time and personal talents as well as through financial support. *Apostolicam actuositatem* 21 specifically calls for the promotion and support of associations among all the faithful "in the ways each finds appropriate." The text also encourages the faithful to hold in high regard international Catholic associations and groups (see c. 298). Through these associations and other means, the Christian faithful actively participate in the Church's mission in the world (c. 211).[158]

Canon 1259 expresses the right of the Church to acquire temporal goods "by every just means," and canon 1260 articulates the Church's right to require the faithful to give financial support. Canon 1261, §2 obliges the bishop to remind the faithful of this obligation and to urge its observance. Canons 1260–1261 manifest a preference

---

[156] See, for example, J. Beal, "To Be or Not To Be: That Is the Question. The Rights of the Accused in the Canonical Penal Process," *CLSAP* 53 (1991) 77–97.

[157] See *AA* 21; *PO* 20–21; and especially *AG* 36.

[158] These themes are echoed in the pastoral letter of the United States bishops, "Stewardship: A Disciple's Response" in *Origins* 22 (December 17, 1992) 457, 459–471. The letter "recognizes the importance of church support, including the sharing of time, talent and treasure" and situates this support "in its broader context —what it means to be a disciple" (Introduction).

for free will offerings and legitimate appeals as sources of income; as one example, canon 1266 allows the local ordinary to require a special collection for "specific parochial, diocesan, national, or universal projects." After appropriate consultation, the diocesan bishop can impose a "moderate tax" for diocesan needs on public juridic persons under his authority; he may also impose an "extraordinary and moderate exaction" on both physical and juridic persons (c. 1263). The faithful also participate in the good administration of finances through their involvement in diocesan (cc. 492–493) and parish finance councils (c. 537), following norms established in Book V, "The Temporal Goods of the Church," and by particular legislation.

All the faithful are obliged to support the Church to the best of their ability. For example, canon 282, §2 urges clerics to use any extra income to provide for the good of the Church and for charitable purposes. Institutes of consecrated life give "collective witness of charity and poverty" and are to contribute from any surpluses for church works and for the poor (c. 640). Individual members of religious institutes, under certain conditions, can make disposition for the use of, and revenue from, their goods before first profession (c. 668, §1). At the same time, the code recognizes other financial demands placed upon the faithful. For example, married people need to provide for their own needs and those of their families (c. 231, §2).

Canon 222, §1 refers to the "decent support of ministers" which includes persons involved in a wide variety of church services. Clerics dedicated to ministry (including deacons, married or not) deserve remuneration consistent with their responsibilities and conditions of time and place (c. 281). Laity have a right "to decent remuneration appropriate to their condition so that they are able to provide decently for their own needs and those of their family" as well as provision for health, pension, and social security benefits (c. 231, §2). The liturgical ministries of lector and acolyte do not, however, confer on the recipient a right to support or remuneration (c. 230, §1). Canon 1286

expresses the responsibility of administrators of goods to pay employees a just and decent wage, and canon 1290 requires them to follow civil law on contracts and payments.[159]

Social Justice and Charity

§2. They are also obliged to promote social justice and, mindful of the precept of the Lord, to assist the poor from their own resources.

This paragraph obliges the faithful to promote social justice and to provide for the poor from their own resources. The Eastern code expresses the same obligation in canon 25, §2. *Apostolicam actuositatem* 8 states that the obligation to promote social justice takes precedence over charity: "The demands of justice should be satisfied at the outset, so as to avoid giving in charitable gifts what is due in the name of justice." Individuals must first work at the eradication of the causes of evil and of social injustice so that works of charity truly reflect the Lord's command to love God and one's neighbor. Jesus Christ has gathered all men and women into "a certain supernatural solidarity"; as one consequence, all people, especially those who enjoy prosperity, must support works of charity and works of social assistance. According to *Gaudium et spes* 26, the social order must favor the good of individuals to allow them to lead "a truly human life." Thus, the dignity of the human person demands social justice; this natural right receives impetus from the teaching of Jesus Christ and the rebirth

---

[159] See NCCB, "Economic Justice for All: Catholic Social Teaching and the U.S. Economy," *Origins* 16 (November 27, 1986) which includes the statement: "We bishops commit ourselves to the principle that those who serve the church—laity, clergy and religious—should receive a sufficient livelihood and the social benefits provided by responsible employers in our nation. These obligations, however, cannot be met without the increased contributions of all the members of the Church" (446, #351). The obligation to support the church "falls on all the members of the community because of their baptism" (ibid.).

of men and women as children of God, reflecting the Church as *communio*.[160]

The paragraph obliges the faithful "to promote social justice"; this forms part of the Church's mission to proclaim the gospel (c. 211). The specific modality and the best means of fulfilling this obligation are to be determined by the individual, depending upon particular circumstances and resources available. Canon 298 suggests as one role of associations the exercise of charitable works and imbuing the temporal order with a Christian spirit. Canon 287, §1 urges clerics "to foster the peace and harmony based on justice" and canon 528, §1 obliges pastors to promote works of social justice. *Vita consecrata* 82 urges members of institutes of consecrated life "to denounce the injustices committed against so many sons and daughters of God and commit themselves to the promotion of justice."

The second obligation, to assist the poor, an obligation rooted in "the precept of the Lord," is "a special form of primacy in the exercise of Christian charity, to which the whole tradition of the Church bears witness."[161] Thus, for example, canon 282, §2 exhorts the clergy to use any excess goods for works of charity. Although the specific precept is not specified, *Apostolicam actuositatem* 8 bases the "law of charity" on the greatest commandment, to "love God with your whole heart and your neighbor as yourself," and on Jesus' identification with all men and women "as the object of charity." *Gaudium et spes* 88 denounces the scandal occurring in societies comprised of a Christian majority in which some have a superfluity of goods while others are "being crucified by hunger, disease, and every kind of wretchedness." This "option for the poor" cannot remain on the abstract level but "must be translated at all levels into concrete actions until it decisively attains a series of reforms."[162] Further, "Christ's example,

no less than his words, is normative for Christians. We know that, at the Last Judgment, we shall all be judged, without distinction, on our practical love of our brothers and sisters."[163]

The obligation to assist the poor is not identified with the evangelical counsel of poverty;[164] not all the faithful are obliged to profess this counsel. Thus, the code recognizes that other just demands are placed on the faithful; for example, canon 231, §2 states the right of the lay persons to have decent remuneration "so that they are able to provide decently for their own needs and those of their family." Nonetheless, *Gaudium et spes* 88 requires that all God's people must give not only from their surplus but from their substance. "At stake is the *dignity of the human person*, whose *defense* and *promotion* have been entrusted to us by the Creator," and therefore all must implement "measures inspired by solidarity and love of preference for the poor."[165]

The Common Good and Limitations of Rights

Canon 223 — §1. In exercising their rights, the Christian faithful, both as individuals and gathered together in associations, must take into account the common good of the Church, the rights of others, and their own duties toward others.

§2. In view of the common good, ecclesiastical authority can direct the exercise of rights which are proper to the Christian faithful.

This canon provides a necessary corrective to an overly individualistic understanding of obligations and rights, a tendency which often prevails in civil society. This corresponds to canon 26 in the Eastern code. As noted in the introduction to this title, canons 209 and 223 form a framework

---

160 See, for example, G. Roche, "The Poor and the *Code of Canon Law:* Some Relevant Issues in Book II," *Stud Can* 30 (1996) 177–219.

161 *SRS* 80, #42.

162 *SRS* 81, #43.

163 John Paul II, message "The Links Between Poverty and Peace," January 1, 1993 (released December 11, 1992), *Origins* 22 (December 24, 1992) 476–479.

164 See c. 600 which states that the evangelical vow of poverty requires a life which "is poor in fact and in spirit."

165 *SRS* 90, #47.

for the listing of obligations and rights of all the Christian faithful; these duties and rights exist within the Church as *communio*.

A *communio* ecclesiology necessarily involves an individual's personal relationship with God but that relationship cannot be seen in isolation, separated from a specific community of faith, the Church. The exercise of rights occurs within the community and must follow "the moral maxim of personal and social responsibility"; that is, both individuals and society as a whole must "have regard to the rights of others, to their own duties towards others, and to the common good of all."[166] Nonetheless, inasmuch as the canon does restrict the exercise of rights, it requires strict interpretation (c. 18).

The canon articulates three factors to be taken into account in the exercise of rights by the faithful: the common good of the Church; the rights of others; and specific duties owed toward other faithful. The second paragraph states the competence of ecclesiastical authority to regulate the exercise of rights "in view of the common good."

Dignitatis humanae 6 describes the common good as "those conditions of social living which enable people to develop their own qualities most fully and easily." In the context of chapter 2, "The Human Community," *Gaudium et spes* 26 describes the common good as "the sum total of the conditions of social life enabling groups and individuals to realize their perfection more fully and readily." The community that is the Church is situated within this human society; the two should exist in harmony inasmuch as the gospel of Jesus Christ serves to safeguard the personal dignity and freedom of men and women.[167] Consequently, "the common good of the Church" refers to the fulfillment of the Church's mission received from Jesus Christ: the "salvation of souls" (see c. 1752). In other words, the exercise of rights occurs within the specific context of the Church as *communio*, i.e., the relationship between an individual and God as well as between the individual and the Church (c. 209). Further, this context also includes the mission entrusted to the Church, to proclaim the gospel (c. 211). Thus, the exercise of rights must serve the Church's mission and, as one consequence, any limitation of the exercise of rights to protect the common good must ensure the fulfillment of this mission and the promotion of communion among all the faithful.

This "common good" context explains the second and third limitations on the exercise of rights: the rights of others and duties owed toward others. Human beings are social by nature; they do not exist in isolation. The Church as *communio* emphasizes the mutual interdependence and cooperation among all the faithful. A responsible exercise of rights presupposes a process of reflection on a number of different factors: the person as an individual with obligations and rights; the person as a member of the community of faith; the person as possessing particular duties toward others arising from a specific office, vocation, or function in the Church; and the exercise of rights by other members of that same community. The exercise of rights must both foster a personal relationship with God as well as facilitate the common vocation of the Church to proclaim the gospel.

The second paragraph allows Church authorities to "direct the exercise" of rights but only to protect and promote the Church's mission in view of the common good. The paragraph does not, therefore, allow or justify the arbitrary exercise of authority; rather, it attempts to ensure that individuals in exercising their rights are mindful of the Church as a communion in which all the faithful are equal in dignity and in action (c. 208) and participate in the proclamation of the gospel (c. 211). Conflicts between individuals and between individuals and the institution can and do arise; canon 221 expresses the necessity of ensuring a proper protection of rights. Individuals who act in some official capacity in the church should strive to avoid contention; for example, canon 50 suggests that, prior to the issuance of a decree, the is-

---

[166] *DH* 7. This moral maxim applies both to civil society and to the Church.

[167] See, for example, *GS* 41.

suing authority should "hear those whose rights can be injured."

According to one conciliar source for this canon, *Gaudium et spes* 75: "But where the exercise of rights is temporarily restricted for the common good, once the circumstances have changed then freedom should be restored as rapidly as possible." Although the context of the conciliar text refers to the political community, this minimal restriction of freedom is also applicable to the Church inasmuch as "no human law is able to safeguard the personal dignity and freedom of humans as fittingly as the gospel which Christ has entrusted to his church."[168] The common good helps ensure that the Church not only proclaims the gospel but also lives the gospel message through the relationships among all the faithful and between the faithful and the world as a whole. God desires the salvation of men and

---

[168] *GS* 41.

women not individually but as the people of God (see *LG* 9); the common good serves to remind the faithful of the necessity of mutual cooperation both with God and with one another within the one community of faith. According to *Gaudium et spes* 41:

> The gospel announces and proclaims the liberty of God's children, rejects every slavery as ultimately resulting from sin, reverently respects the dignity of conscience and its free decision, continually teaches that all human talents should be devoted to God's service and the wellbeing of men and women, and commends all to the love of all.

All the Christian faithful, through their lives of faith, including the appropriate exercise and protection of rights, manifest to the world the Church's fundamental nature as *communio* and thereby proclaim the gospel.

BIBLIOGRAPHY ────────────────────────

Introduction: Ecclesiology (Communio)

Bertrams, W. "Communio, communitas, et societas in Lege Fundamentali Ecclesiae." *P* 61 (1972) 553–604.

─────. "De gradibus 'communionis' in doctrina Concilii Vaticani II." *Gregorianum* 47 (1966) 286–305.

CDF. "Letter to the Bishops of the Catholic Church on Some Aspects of the Church Understood as Communion," May 28, 1992. *Origins* 22 (June 15, 1992) 108–112.

CFC et al. "Some Questions Regarding Collaboration of Nonordained Faithful in Priests' Sacred Ministry." *Origins* 27 (November 27, 1997) 399, 400–409, followed by "The Instruction: An Explanatory Note," 409–410.

Fahey, M. "Ecclesial Community as Communion." In *The Church as Communion*, ed. J. Provost, 4–23. Washington, D.C.: CLSA, 1984.

─────. "Chapter 6: Church. The Contemporary Context of Ecclesiology." In *Systematic Theology*, vol. 2, ed. Francis Schüssler Fiorenza and John Galvin. Minneapolis: Fortress, 1991.

Feiner, J. "Decree on Ecumenism: Commentary on the Decree." In Vorgrimler II, 57–164.

Ghirlanda, G. *Il diritto nella Chiesa mistero di comunione*. Milan: Edizioni Paoline, Rome: Editrice Pontificia Università Gregoriana, 1990.

Granfield, P. "The Church Local and Universal: Realization of Communion." *J* 49 (1989) 449–471.

Hamer, J. *The Church Is a Communion*. London: G. Chapman, 1964.

Hertling, L. *Communio: Church and Papacy in Early Christianity*. Chicago: Loyola University, 1972.

Kaslyn, R. *Communion with the Church and the Code of Canon Law*. Lewiston, N.Y.: Edwin Mellen, 1994.

Kasper, W. *Theology and Church*. New York: Crossroad, 1989.

McDermott, J. "The Biblical Doctrine of Koinonia." *Biblische Zeitschrift* 19 (1975) 64–77, 219–233.

PCPCU. "Directory for the Application of Principles and Norms on Ecumenism." *Origins* 23 (July 29, 1993) 129, 131–160.

Provost, J. "Structuring the Church as a Communio." In *The Church as Communion*, ed. J. Provost, 191–245. Washington, D.C.: CLSA, 1984.

Sullivan, F. *The Church We Believe In: One, Holy, Catholic and Apostolic*. New York: Paulist, 1988.

Synod of Bishops. "Final Message of the Synod for Africa." *Origins* 24 (May 19, 1994) 1, 3–11.

Synod of Bishops, Special Assembly for America. "Encounter with the Living Jesus Christ: The Way to Conversion, Communion and Solidarity in America." *Origins* 26 (August 15, 1996) 145; 147–164.

Tillard, J.-M.-R. *Chair de l'Église, chair du Christ: Aux sources de l'ecclésiologie de communion*. Paris: Les Éditions du Cerf, 1992.

———. "The Church Is a Communion." *One in Christ* 17 (1981) 117–131.

———. "Ecclesiology of Communion and Canon Law. The Theological Task of Canon Law: A Theologian's Perspective." *CLSAP* (1996) 24–34.

———. *Église d'églises: L'ecclésiologie de communion*. Paris, Les Éditions du Cerf, 1987.

———. "Koinônia—Sacrament." *One in Christ* 22 (1986) 104–114.

Urresti, T.D., "The Ontology of Communion and Collegial Structures in the Church." *Concilium* 1.8 (1965) 5–10.

Willebrands, J. "Vatican II's Ecclesiology of Communion." *One in Christ* 23 (1987) 178–191.

Canons 204–207

Bonnet, P. "The *Christifidelis* Restored to His Role as Human Protagonist in the Church." In *Vatican II: Assessment and Perspectives*, vol. 1, ed. R. Latourelle, 540–567. New York: Paulist, 1988.

CDF. *Instruction on the Ecclesial Vocation of the Theologian*, May 24, 1990. Washington, D.C.: USCC, 1994.

CICLSAL. "Fraternal Life in Community," February 2, 1994. *Origins* 23 (March 24, 1994) 693, 695–712.

Hervada, J. In *Pamplona ComEng*, 185–189.

John Paul II. Apexhort *Christifideles laici*. *Origins* 18 (February 9, 1989) 561–595.

———. Apexhort *Vita consecrata*. *Origins* 25 (April 4, 1996) 681, 683–719.

———. Aplett *Ecclesia Dei*, July 2 1988. *Origins* 18 (August 4, 1988) 149, 151–152.

Komonchak, J. "The Local Realization of the Church." In *The Reception of Vatican II*, ed. G. Alberigo, J.-P. Jossua, and J. Komonchak, 77–90. Washington, D.C.: Catholic University of America, 1987.

Laghi, P. "Vatican Observations on U.S. Bishops' 'Ex corde Ecclesiae' Application Document." *Origins* 27 (June 12, 1997) 53–55.

McGrath, A. In *CLSGBI Com*, 115–118.

NCCB. Pastoral Letter "Economic Justice for All: Catholic Social Teaching and the U.S. Economy." *Origins* 16 (November 27, 1986) 408, 410–455.

———. "'Ex corde Ecclesiae': An Application to the United States." *Origins* 26 (November 28, 1996) 381, 383–384.

———. Pastoral Letter "Stewardship: A Disciple's Response." *Origins* 22 (December 17, 1992) 457, 459–471.

National Pastoral Life Center. "Called to Be Catholic: Church in a Time of Peril." *Origins* 26 (August 29, 1996) 165, 167–170.

Provost, J. In *CLSA Com*, 119–134.

Rehrauer, A. "Welcome In! Canonical Issues and the RCIA." *CLSAP* 52 (1990) 161–169.

Sullivan, F. "The Significance of the Vatican II Declaration that the Church of Christ 'Subsists in' the Roman Catholic Church." In *Vatican II: Assessment and Perspectives*, vol. 2, ed. R. Latourelle, 272–287. New York: Paulist, 1989.

———. *Magisterium*. Mahwah, N.J.: Paulist, 1983.

Thomas, R. "Ecumenical Questions in the New Code." *CLSAP* 49 (1987) 45–60.

Tillard, J.-M.-R. *The Bishop of Rome*. Wilmington: Michael Glazier, 1983.

Obligations and Rights of the Christian Faithful (cc. 208–223)

Barr, D., J. Bell, J. Perry, and P. McGreevy. "CLSA Experiment in Due Process Committee Report." *CLSAP* 56 (1994) 68–79.

Bass, R. "Due Process: Conciliation and Arbitration." *CLSAP* 53 (1991) 63–76.

Beal, J. "Administrative Tribunals in the Church: An Idea Whose Time Has Come or an Idea Whose Time Has Gone?" *CLSAP* 55 (1993) 39–71.

———. "Confining and Structuring Administrative Discretion." *J* 46 (1986) 70–106.

———. "Protecting the Rights of Lay Catholics." *J* 47 (1987) 129–164.

———. "To Be or Not To Be: That Is the Question. The Rights of the Accused in the Canonical Penal Process." *CLSAP* 53 (1991) 77–97.

Bevilacqua, A., et al. "Reaction to the Catholic Common Ground Project." *Origins* 26 (September 12, 1996) 197, 199–203.

Beyer, J. "La 'communio' comme critère des droits fondamentaux." In *Les droits fondamentaux du chrétien dans l'Église et dans la société,* 79–96. Fribourg: Éditions Universitaires, 1981.

Bishops' Committee on the Liturgy. *Gathered in Steadfast Faith: Statement on Sunday Worship in the Absence of a Priest*. Washington, D.C.: USCC, 1991.

CLSA. *Due Process in the United States 1970–1985*. Washington, D.C.: CLSA, 1987.

———. *Protection of Rights of Persons in the Church*. Washington, D.C.: CLSA, 1991.

Castillo Lara, R. "Some General Reflections on the Rights and Duties of the Christian Faithful." *Stud Can* 20 (1986) 7–32.

Cogan, P., ed. *CLSA Advisory Opinions 1984–1993*. Washington, D.C.: CLSA, 1995.

CDF. *Instruction on the Ecclesial Vocation of the Theologian*, May 24, 1990. Washington, D.C.: USCC, 1994.

———. "Regulations for Doctrinal Examination" and "Explanatory Note." *Origins* 27 (September 11, 1997) 221–224.

Coriden, J. "Alternate Dispute Resolution in the Church." *CLSAP* 48 (1986) 61–82.

———. "A Challenge: Making the Rights Real." *J* 45 (1985) 1–23.

———. "Freedom of Expression in the Church in Light of Canon 212 (*CIC*)." *CLSAP* 57 (1995) 147–165.

———. "What Became of the Bill of Rights?" *CLSAP* 52 (1990) 47–60.

Coughlin, J. "Canonical Equity." *Stud Can* 30 (1986) 403–435.

Cusack, B. A., and T. G. Sullivan. *Pastoral Care in Parishes Without a Pastor*. Washington, D.C.: CLSA, 1995.

DeRoo, R. "Ecclesial Structures and Social Justice." *CLSAP* 43 (1981) 32–43.

Donovan, D. "Priest." In *The New Encyclopedia of Theology*. Wilmington: Michael Glazier, 1987.

Doyle, J. "The Formal Act of Leaving the Catholic Church." *CLSAP* 54 (1990) 152–160.

Faris, J. *The Eastern Catholic Churches*. New York: Saint Maron, 1992.

Folmer, J. "Promoting and Protecting Rights: An Introduction." *J* 46 (1986) 1–13.

Hervada, J. In *Pamplona ComEng*, 190–197.

Huels, J. "Participation by the Faithful in the Liturgy." *J* 48 (1988) 608–637.

———. "Preparation for the Sacraments: Faith, Rights, Law." *Stud Can* 28 (1994) 33–58.

John Paul II. Message, "The Links Between Poverty and Peace." *Origins* 22 (December 24, 1992) 476–479.

Kasper, W. "The Theological Foundations of Human Rights." *J* 50 (1990) 148–166.

Laghi, P. "Vatican Observations on U.S. Bishops' 'Ex corde Ecclesiae' Application Document." *Origins* 27 (June 12, 1997) 53–55.

Langan, L. "Can There Be a Human Rights Problem in the Church?" *J* 46 (1986) 14–42.

Lipscomb, O. "The Kind of Common Ground Sought." *Origins* 26 (March 27, 1997) 649, 651–655.

McGrath, A. In *CLSGBI Com*, 118–126.

Moodie, M. "Defense of Rights: Developing New Procedural Norms." *J* 47 (1987) 423–449.

Morrisey, F. "What Makes an Institution 'Catholic'?" *J* 47 (1987) 531–544.

NCCB. "Doctrinal Responsibilities: Approaches to Promoting Cooperation and Resolving Misunderstandings Between Bishops and Theologians." *Origins* 19 (June 19,1989) 97, 99–110.

———. "Economic Justice for All: Catholic Social Teaching and the U.S. Economy." *Origins* 16 (November 27, 1986) 408, 410–455.

———. "'Ex corde Ecclesiae': An Application to the United States." *Origins* 26 (November 28, 1996) 381, 383–384.

———. *On Due Process*. Washington, D.C.: USCC, 1972.

———. "Stewardship: A Disciple's Response." *Origins* 22 (December 17, 1992) 457, 459–471.

National Pastoral Life Center. "Called to Be Catholic: Church in a Time of Peril." *Origins* 26 (August 29, 1996) 165, 167–170.

Nedungatt, G. "Equal Rights of the Churches in the Catholic Church." *J* 49 (1989) 1–22.

Örsy, L. *The Church: Learning and Teaching*. Wilmington: Michael Glazier, 1987.

———. "The Theological Task of Canon Law: A Canonist's Perspective." *CLSAP* (1996) 1–23.

Paprocki, T. "Rights of Christians in the Local Church: Canon Law Procedures in Light of Civil Law Principles of Administrative Justice." *Stud Can* 24 (1990) 427–442.

Perry, J. "Accessibility of Due Process for the Laity." *CLSAP* 51 (1989) 65–82.

Pfnausch, E. "Protection of Rights of Persons in the Church: A Hearing." *CLSAP* 54 (1992) 195–207.

Provost, J. In *CLSA Com*, 134–159.

———. "Ecclesial Rights." *CLSAP* 44 (1982) 35–44.

———. "The Nature of Rights in the Church." *CLSAP* 53 (1991) 1–18.

———. "Protecting and Promoting the Rights of Christians: Some Implications for Church Structure." *J* 46 (1986) 289–342.

———. "Some Canonical Considerations Relative to Clerical Sexual Abuse." *J* 52 (1992) 615–641.

Roche, G. "The Poor and the Code of Canon Law: Some Relevant Issues in Book II." *Stud Can* 30 (1996) 177–221.

Sullivan, F. "The Response Due to the Non-Definitive Exercise of the Magisterium (Canon 752)." *Stud Can* 23 (1989) 267–284.

Synod of Bishops. "The Practice of Justice." *Justice in the World*. Washington, D.C.: USCC, 1971.

TITLE II
THE OBLIGATIONS AND RIGHTS OF
THE LAY CHRISTIAN FAITHFUL
[cc. 224–231]

The canons in this title of the code[1] constitute one of the most extensive sections of the law to deal exclusively with the laity.[2] Since the code's promulgation in 1983, many of the issues originally raised by these canons have continued to evolve.[3] The meaning of individual canons remains to be fully discovered, and certain issues, particularly the methods of vindicating lay rights, persist as an important area of canonical development for the future. While many other aspects of

[1] The extensive commentary written by J. Provost in *CLSA Com* provides a substantial historical analysis of these canons that will not be repeated here. Rather, the following commentary will specifically highlight the changes made in this area of the law since the promulgation of the 1983 code and summarize the basic concerns addressed in the individual canons. See Provost, in *CLSA Com*, 159–170.

[2] Canons 208–223 on the rights and duties of all believers also apply to the laity, as well as to clerics. Other canons throughout the code mention the laity. See, for example, cc. 759, 1282, and 1287, §2.

[3] A number of articles concerning the laity were prepared in connection with an April 1987 CLSA symposium on the laity. See *J* 47 (1987) 1–245. The subjects include "Laity in the Renewing Church: Vision and Opportunities," "Laity in Church Law: New Code, New Focus" by F. McManus; "The Church in the World" by N. Provencher; "Who Is a Lay Person?" by A. Prew-Winters; "The Call of the Laity to a Spirituality of Discipleship" by K. Egan; "'In the Manner of a Leaven': The Lay Mission to the Secular World" by M. Place; "Equality, Dignity and Rights of the Laity" by S. Holland; "Protecting the Rights of Lay Catholics" by J. Beal; "Associations of the Faithful in the Church" by R. Pagé; "Conciliar and Canonical Applications of 'Ministry' to the Laity" by E. Rinere; and "Laity and the Inner Working of the Church" by E. McDonough.

the 1983 code have been implemented, the vindication of lay rights has not yet received a great amount of attention, nor have the implications of such rights been clarified to any great extent by any type of canonical process. Many of the faithful do not know of these rights, despite the passage of time. However, as the concept of rights in the Church is further explored and clarified, we will have a clearer idea of the role of the laity.

Unlike the 1917 code, which limited its specific treatment of the laity to two canons affirming the rights of all the Christian faithful to receive the sacraments (*CIC* 682) and prohibiting them from wearing ecclesiastical garments (*CIC* 683), the canons under study here reflect an emphasis on the equality of all the faithful. These canons exhibit a relatively new view of rights for the laity in the Church, but much remains to be explored before their implications are fully realized. Defining the concept of ministry for the laity, in contrast to the ministry of the ordained, continues to be a major topic of discussion in the Church.

The 1987 synod of bishops on the laity[4] together with Pope John Paul II's subsequent apostolic exhortation *Christifideles laici*[5] presented the most extensive treatment of the role of the laity since the promulgation of the 1983 code. Both reaffirm the importance of the laity and highlight the theoretical and practical implications of their baptism in the Church.[6] The *Catechism of the Catholic Church* deals with the subject in a general fashion and refers to this part of

[4] "Message to the People of God," *Origins* 17 (November 12, 1987) 385–387.

[5] *Origins* 18 (February 9, 1989) 561–595.

[6] See *CL* 10–17 for a fuller discussion of the baptism of the laity and their relationship to the Church, their role in the mission of the Church, their secular character with their place in the world, and their own call to holiness in their lives.

the code in several instances.[7] The most recent Roman instruction, entitled "Some Questions Regarding Collaboration of Nonordained Faithful in Priests' Sacred Ministry,"[8] addresses issues of concern regarding the role of the laity in relation to that of the ministerial priesthood. The canons that follow will be reviewed in light of these documents.

Introductory Canon[9]

Canon 224 — In addition to those obligations and rights which are common to all the Christian faithful and those which are established in other canons, the lay Christian faithful are bound by the obligations and possess the rights which are enumerated in the canons of this title.

This introductory canon makes it clear that this section of the code applies directly to the lay faithful. However, it does not limit the application

---

[7] See *CCC* 873–875 (differences between clergy and laity), 897–913 (definition of laity in terms of their vocation together with their relationship to the *munera* of the Church), 940–943 (vocation of laity to a mission in the world and to holiness).

[8] See CFC et al., "Some Questions Regarding Collaboration of Nonordained Faithful in Priests' Sacred Ministry" (cited hereafter as "Some Questions"), *Origins* 27 (November 27, 1997) 399, 400–409, followed by "The Instruction: An Explanatory Note," 409–410. This instruction, approved in *forma specifica* by Pope John Paul II, was signed by the heads of eight Vatican dicasteries: CFC, PCL, CDF, CDWDS, CFB, CEP, CICLSAL, and PCILT. This document proposes to clarify "new forms of 'pastoral activity' of the nonordained on both parochial and diocesan levels" (400). For a canonical evaluation of the document, see J. Huels, "Interpreting an Instruction Approved in *forma specifica*," *Stud Can* 32 (1998) 5–46. Huels views the instruction as a new form of canonical document: a legislative instruction. A short commentary on the document prepared for the Canon Law Society of Great Britain and Ireland looks at the document's relationship to pastoral practices in the United Kingdom. See G. Read, "The Vatican Instruction on Collaborative Ministry," *CLS-GBIN* 113 (March 1998) 15–31.

[9] See also *CCEO* 400.

of the canons only to the laity, as some clerics or religious may be married and be parents, or may have been married in the past.[10]

While this canon does not define the laity, an understanding of the meaning of laity is necessary for an understanding of the canons that follow. A lay person, like a religious or cleric, is a member of the people of God, a baptized member of the Christian faithful with a distinct dignity whose primary function is within the world rather than within the Church's governance structure. Lay persons may have roles in both places, but their primary task is the transformation of the secular world (*AA* 2, 7). All are called to live out their baptismal promises, but the laity do this in their everyday lives, whether they be mothers, doctors, accountants, or street sweepers. Their call to holiness may be through marriage or the single life, as well as through parenthood.

That is not to say that the rights mentioned here are exclusive to the laity. Married deacons exercise the rights of the married and may exercise those of parents. Members of religious institutes with apostolic charisms may serve in the world, rather than in ecclesiastical structures. The most important fact is that no one within the Church stands alone; laity, clergy, and religious are all inexorably linked in the same goal of building up the whole Church.

Mission

Canon 225 — §1. Since, like all the Christian faithful, lay persons are designated by God for the apostolate through baptism and confirmation, they are bound by the general obligation and possess the right as individuals, or joined in associations, to work so that the divine message

---

[10] Permanent deacons may marry prior to their ordination or afterwards with the permission of the Holy See (cc. 1042, 1°; 1087). Diocesan priests or religious may have been married prior to entering into that state, after their children were of age and if their spouse had died or their marriage (to a living spouse) was annulled or dissolved through the proper church process.

of salvation is made known and accepted by all persons everywhere in the world. This obligation is even more compelling in those circumstances in which only through them can people hear the gospel and know Christ.

§2. According to each one's own condition, they are also bound by a particular duty to imbue and perfect the order of temporal affairs with the spirit of the gospel and thus to give witness to Christ, especially in carrying out these same affairs and in exercising secular functions.

The mission of the laity[11] is derived from their incorporation into the Church through the sacraments of initiation. The roles of the laity in society, whether with their families or as individuals, are viewed as instrumental in bringing others to the Church. This canon[12] is divided into two sections; paragraph one notes the obligation of individuals or groups to evangelize the world through the gospel, and paragraph two highlights the special duty of the lay faithful to transform the world through the gospel.

The secular role of the individual lay person is the basis for these actions, although lay persons may associate themselves with others to accomplish the same goals.[13] It is through the exercise of the laity's various roles in the world that others may be brought to faith in Christ. This secular orientation distinguishes the direction of their mission from that of the clergy, in that it emphasizes their complete immersion in their faith through their wide-ranging occupations in the secular world. The one who cleans the streets is under the same obligation to witness to the faith as the one who heals the sick. The implications of this mis-

sion are more specifically enumerated in the canons that follow in this title.

The source for the mission of the laity is their reception of the sacraments of initiation, making God the ultimate beginning of any action. This means that such work does not require the specific formal permission or deputation of church authorities; rather, it is a natural outgrowth of the mission that flows from the grace of the sacraments.[14] That mission may be the evangelization of others through service or the transformation of the secular world into a world permeated with Christ. It can mean inviting a fellow employee to an RCIA session or maintaining moral principles in the workplace. In carrying out their mission, lay persons may work as individuals or as members of teams or organizations. There is no single manner for carrying out the mission of the laity.

Marriage and Family Life[15]

Canon 226 — §1. According to their own vocation, those who live in the marital state are bound

---

[11] See *CCC* 873–875. Also, M. D. Place, "'In the Manner of a Leaven': The Lay Mission to the Secular World," *J* 47 (1989) 86–102.

[12] Canons 401 and 406 of the Eastern code are worded in a similar fashion, although *CCEO* 401 is more specific about the role of the laity in transforming the temporal order.

[13] This transforming action may be carried out with other individuals belonging to official organizations or simply in concert with other persons with similar beliefs.

[14] The laity are "to learn the meaning and value of creation and how to relate it to the glory of God; to assist one another to live holier lives even in their daily occupations; to labor so that human labor, technical skill, civil culture and created goods may be made perfect for the benefit of every last man according to His plan; to work to see that created goods in their own way lead to general progress in human and Christian liberty and so illumine all society with Christ's saving light; to remedy through combined efforts any institutions and conditions of the world which are customarily an inducement to sin and thus imbue culture and human activity with moral values; to seed the world with the Word of God and to open wider the Church's doors so that the message of peace can enter the world" (*LG* 36).

[15] This canon must be studied in the context of the other portions of the code that address marriage (cc. 1055–1165) and various parental issues (cc. 98, §2 [authority over minors]; 111 [determining the Catholic rite of the child]; 529, §1 [relationship with the pastor]; 774, §2, 776, 793, 796–799, 1252 [education/religious education]; 835, §4 [sanctifying office of the Church]; 851, 2°, 855, 857, §2, 867, 868, 872, 874, §1, 1°, 877 [role in baptism of child]; 890, 895 [confirmation]; 914 [Eucharist], 1063 1°, 1136 [duty of parents]; 1071, §1, 6°

by a special duty to work through marriage and the family to build up the people of God.

§2. Since they have given life to their children, parents have a most grave obligation and possess the right to educate them. Therefore, it is for Christian parents particularly to take care of the Christian education of their children according to the doctrine handed on by the Church.

This canon deals with two related issues. The first paragraph[16] deals with the state of marriage and the duties that this vocation entails.[17] The second paragraph[18] relates to the procreation and education of children,[19] a reality which has long been viewed as a central good of marriage.

Marriage

The vocation of marriage has remained an important theme since the promulgation of the 1983 code. *Christifideles laici* mentions the importance of marriage and confirms its central role in the life of the laity.[20] Through marriage, the couple is drawn toward holiness; through married love and the building up of the kingdom of God, they are brought closer to their own salvation. This canon touches on the key theological dimensions of the sacrament.[21] Other canons that deal with marriage[22] must be considered in understanding the present canon properly. Christian marriage is viewed as the domestic Church, and the family is viewed as

a basic unit of the Church as a whole. It is in those tiny churches of the family that the search for salvation is present each day.

Parents

This canon, which mentions the central role of parents in the education of their children, is the first of a veritable bill of parental rights[23] and obligations in the code. While the canon does not state that parents are the first and principal educators of their children, it does make clear that they are the primary educators of their children.[24] Parents are the ones to determine how this education is to be carried out, although their rights regarding religious education are exercised in relation to the corresponding rights and responsibilities of their pastor or the sacramental minister who will administer a specific sacrament.[25] Because of the

---

[opposition to marriage of a minor]; 1478, §§1–3 [judicial procedure involving minors]).

[16] See *CCEO* 407.

[17] See the extensive treatment of various aspects of the sacrament in *CCC* 1601–1666.

[18] There is no corresponding Eastern code canon for this paragraph.

[19] *CCC* 902, 1652, 2249.

[20] Church documents confirming the importance of marriage include *GS* 47–52; *HV* 8–9; and *FC* 11–17.

[21] See also c. 835, §4, which was mentioned earlier; its second sentence highlights the liturgical significance of marriage and parenting.

[22] See footnote 15 for a list of canons pertaining to marriage.

[23] See P. Baillargeon, "The Rights and Duties of Parents in the Sanctification of Their Children," *CLSAP* 54 (1992) 55–71. M. Foster, "The Promotion of the Canonical Rights of Children," *CLSAP* 59 (1997) 163–203. Specific canons that refer to parents are listed in footnote 15. See also *CCC* 2221–2231.

[24] See also c. 774, §2 which instructs parents to form their children in the Christian life. This obligation is repeated in c. 793 §1, which adds that parents are to select the means for the Catholic education of their children.

[25] See cc. 793, §1; 776; and 777. In some places in North America where there has been an increase in the home schooling of children, there has been controversy concerning the exercise of this parental right. Some parents wish to determine the readiness of their child to receive the sacraments (Eucharist, reconciliation, and confirmation) *without* the assistance and oversight of the pastor, even where officially sanctioned church programs for preparation are available. These parents have failed to understand properly their right to teach their child about the Church, in light of their obligation to abide by the teachings of their local bishop and pastor. There may also be difficulties in home schooling situations concerning the appropriate texts and sources of Catholic teaching that are to be used in preparation for sacramental initiation. Some might prefer to choose a text that would not be approved by the local bishop, whether it is a catechism originating prior to Vatican II or one not entirely in accord with current Roman teach-

specific responsibility of the ordained minister to foster a proper reception of the sacraments in accordance with Church teaching, the parents' educational rights are somewhat conditional.[26]

The education of children in the faith is of paramount importance to the future of the Church. Hence, like canon 797, this canon envisions that parents will be free to determine the particular method of Catholic education with the support and recognition of such a right by the State. Parents are theoretically free to select the schools where they will educate their children. However, in practice, it may not always be possible for them to do so.[27]

Civil Liberties[28]

Canon 227 — The lay Christian faithful have the right to have recognized that freedom which all citizens have in the affairs of the earthly city. When using that same freedom, however, they are to take care that their actions are imbued with the spirit of the gospel and are to heed the doctrine set forth by the magisterium of the Church. In matters of opinion, moreover, they are to avoid setting forth their own opinion as the doctrine of the Church.

This canon recognizes the fact that the Christian faithful possess the same civil liberties as other citizens. While the Church spent many cen-

turies supporting limitations of ordinary civil rights,[29] the popes of this era have proclaimed that the basic dignity of human beings must be recognized and protected with appropriate civil liberties to be guaranteed by secular governments.[30] These rights are to be adopted in civil legislation and applied to all members of a given society. A variety of documents of Vatican II[31] provide the foundation for this canon.

Clergy and religious are also recognized as possessing such liberties, but their exercise of some rights is circumscribed in various ways because of their special ministry within the Church.[32]

---

ings. A number of these issues are addressed by M. Foster in "Promotion of the Canonical Rights of Children"; section four is especially helpful in evaluating diocesan policies on religious education with these concerns in mind.

[26] See, for example, c. 843.

[27] A number of countries (including those with concordats with the Holy See) have a governmentally established church, e.g., the Anglican Church in Great Britain. Some of these countries have regulated what religious faith may be taught in any school (state sponsored or not) within their borders, regardless of the faith of the children and their parents, so there is effectively no freedom truly to choose how one's child is educated.

[28] See also *CCEO* 402.

[29] Roman Catholic Church history is marked with institutional actions including the Inquisition or the support of secular governments (monarchical or dictatorial) that did not allow freedom of speech, association, worship, etc., although this has not been the stance of the Holy See during much of the late nineteenth century and during the twentieth century.

[30] See *GS* 26, *AAS* 58 (1966) 1049 which states, "Therefore, there must be made available to all men everything necessary for leading a life truly human, such as food, clothing, and shelter; the right to choose a state of life freely and to found a family, the right to education, to employment, to a good reputation, to respect, to appropriate information, to activity in accord with the upright norm of one's own conscience, to protection of privacy and to rightful freedom in matters religious too." See also John XXIII, ency *Pacem in terris*, April 20, 1963, *AAS* 55 (1963) 257–304. For a fuller discussion of this issue, see D. Hollenbach, *Claims in Conflict: Retrieving and Renewing the Catholic Human Rights Tradition* (New York: Paulist, 1979). See also P. Bolté, *Les droits et la papauté contemporaine: Synthèse et textes* (Montreal: Fides, 1975) 15–83.

[31] *LG* 37 and *GS* 43 are examples of sources of the rights mentioned in the previous note, together with *DH* which addresses such issues in more detail.

[32] For example, c. 285, §3 prevents clerics from holding elective or appointed office in a civil government while c. 287, §2 does not allow them to be active in political parties or to direct labor unions without the permission of the competent authority. Such a decision must be founded on the protection of the rights of the Church or the promotion of the common good. Canon 672 applies these prohibitions to members of religious institutes.

Official Positions

Canon 228 — §1. Lay persons who are found suitable are qualified to be admitted by the sacred pastors to those ecclesiastical offices and functions which they are able to exercise according to the precepts of the law.

§2. Lay persons who excel in necessary knowledge, prudence, and integrity are qualified to assist the pastors of the Church as experts and advisors, even in councils according to the norm of law.

This canon recognizes the ability of the laity to hold ecclesiastical office or cooperate in the exercise of such office. The canon must be examined within the broader context of canons 129, 145, and 274, §1 on lay sharing in ecclesiastical jurisdiction, the elements of an ecclesiastical office, and eligibility for offices requiring orders or jurisdiction. All of these complex issues continue to be debated by canonists and others.[33] The first paragraph of the canon refers to the lay person's suitability and capacity actually to hold an office or exercise a specific function, while the second paragraph is concerned with the lay person's ability to give counsel or offer assistance to the pastors of the Church, especially in various conciliar processes.[34]

The competence to hold an ecclesiastical office hinges on a person's abilities and the nature of the office itself as established by law. Such competence is viewed as relating to the duties that will be undertaken as part of the office. Members of the Christian faithful, whether they be laity or clergy, are to possess the requisite qualifications for that office prior to their appointment. Special attention is to be paid to such qualifications as they relate to a specific position, such as diocesan chancellor (c. 483, §2), a judge in the tribunal (c. 1421) or finance officer (c. 494, §1). The manner in which the particular expertise was obtained is especially important. Married persons may speak expertly on the needs of those exercising their vocation[35] simply on the basis of their own lived experience, while a member of the finance council who must be expert in matters of law and economics would have to have acquired those credentials in a more formal fashion, such as receiving a degree in law or business.[36]

The types of ecclesiastical offices that may be held by lay persons have expanded substantially as the number of clergy has continued to decline. A comprehensive list of offices that might be held by the laity is literally impossible to draw up, since individual bishops have the ability to establish them as necessary; they are not limited to those specifically mentioned in the code. Lay persons currently act as diocesan chancellors and notaries (cc. 482–483, 1437), tribunal judges (c. 1421, §2), tribunal directors, assessors (c. 1424), auditors (c. 1428), promoters of justice or defenders of the bond (cc. 1430, 1432), finance officers (c. 494), members of the diocesan finance (cc. 492–493) and pastoral councils[37] (cc. 511–514),

---

[33] For a thorough examination of the complex canonical dimensions of the issue of lay jurisdiction, see J. Beal, "The Exercise of the Power of Governance by Lay People: State of the Question," *J* 55 (1995) 1–92. This part of the commentary will not deal with these complex issues; however, see the commentary concerning cc. 129 and 145 for a discussion of these issues. See also J. Provost, "The Participation of the Laity in the Governance of the Church," *Stud Can* 19 (1985) 417–448; J. Myers, "Ecclesial Ministries for Lay Persons Within the Diocese: Development and Integration," *CLSAP* (1985) 66–83; B. Cusack, "Power of Governance: Theoretical and Practical Considerations," *CLSAP* (1990) 187–205; F. McManus, "Laity in Church Law: New Code, New Focus," *J* 47 (1987) 11–31.

[34] This section is similar to *CCEO* 408, §1–§3 and 403, §2. *CCEO* 408, §1–§3 emphasizes the admission of laity to ecclesiastical functions by competent authority. *CCEO*

403, §2 strictly requires that there be an ecclesial necessity, or great advantage and a lack of sacred ministers, before certain duties may be entrusted to members of the laity.

[35] For example, in pre-marriage preparation (c. 1063).

[36] Canon 492, §1.

[37] "Some Questions" sets out specific clarifications regarding the roles of various types of councils, including parochial pastoral councils, finance councils, and parish councils in art. 5, nos. 2–5. See *Origins* 27 (November 27, 1997) 405.

as well as pastoral ministers with varying types of authority.[38]

The question of whether lay persons may exercise jurisdiction in the traditional sense of the word is still a difficult one.[39] Lay judges with the requisite credentials (usually a license or doctorate in canon law) do "cooperate" in the exercise of jurisdiction every time they vote as part of a panel of judges (*turnus*) in a church tribunal. Furthermore, the laity have been granted permission to witness marriages when there is a genuine pastoral need.[40] The precise line limiting the exercise of jurisdiction to the ordained appears to be becoming less distinct with time and pastoral practice.

The counsel offered to ordained church officials, referred to in the second paragraph of the canon, is far more common in practice today with the proliferation of parish pastoral and finance councils established by universal[41] and particular church law, together with the same types of bodies at the diocesan level.[42] Diocesan synods,[43] which have become more prevalent in various places around the world, allow for specific input from the laity on a number of controlled subjects.[44] The laity have had difficulties accepting the advisory nature of many of these councils, since they are used to determining their own fate in everyday life. Their understanding of the theology and mission of the Church has evolved as they shape their vision of the future. Many are seeking formal theological education and an opportunity to bring their own gifts for leadership to the challenges of diocesan and parish governance by agreeing to hold ecclesiastical offices.

Theological Formation[45]

Canon 229 — §1. Lay persons are bound by the obligation and possess the right to acquire knowledge of Christian doctrine appropriate to the capacity and condition of each in order for them to be able to live according to this doctrine, announce it themselves, defend it if necessary, and take their part in exercising the apostolate.

§2. They also possess the right to acquire that fuller knowledge of the sacred sciences which are taught in ecclesiastical universities and faculties or in institutes of religious sciences, by attending classes there and pursuing academic degrees.

§3. If the prescripts regarding the requisite suitability have been observed, they are also qualified to receive from legitimate ecclesiastical authority a mandate to teach the sacred sciences.

This canon is divided into three paragraphs, with the first indicating the obligation of the laity to acquire Christian formation and education in keeping with their role in life so they can live a

---

[38] See cc. 516, §2 implicitly, and 517, §2 explicitly on lay leadership in parishes and comparable juridic structures. In part four of the section on theological principles, "Some Questions" also states: "The non-ordained faithful do not enjoy a right to such tasks and functions. Rather, they are 'capable of being admitted by the sacred Pastors...to those functions which, in accordance with the provisions of law, they can discharge'" (*Origins* 27 [November 27, 1997] 402).

[39] See footnote 33.

[40] The code provides for non-clerics to act as official witnesses to marriages in accordance with c. 1112, §1. "Some Questions," in article 10, addresses the issue of the nonordained witnessing marriages by specifying the three criteria necessary to allow this to happen in special circumstances involving a grave shortage of clergy (*Origins* 27 [November 27, 1997] 406). Canon 1116 also allows the contractants themselves to marry without the presence of an official church witness in certain situations, since the parties to the marriage are the ministers of the sacrament.

[41] Canons 536–537.

[42] See "Some Questions," art. 5, nos. 2–5, in *Origins* 27 (November 27, 1997) 402–405.

[43] Canons 460, 463.

[44] Just as the synod of bishops for the whole Church (cc. 342–348) is under the authority of the pope, a diocesan synod is under the authority of the bishop who called it into being (461, §1) and determines the issues that will be addressed. All other members of the synod have only a consultative vote; the legislative power remains with the diocesan bishop (c. 466).

[45] See *CCEO* 404.

fuller Christian life. They are also to be prepared to defend the faith in the world. Each person is granted his or her own special gifts from God, whether it be an intelligence suited for advanced theological study or one that is sufficient to assist in the instruction of children as they prepare for the sacraments of initiation. The canon emphasizes the responsibility of the laity to obtain this knowledge, but does not specify the source from which it is to be obtained. That source could be private study, formal instruction, or life experience within the Christian community.[46]

The second paragraph establishes the right of the laity to acquire a formal education at the Church's institutions of higher learning and to receive academic degrees for their work.[47] In the past, ecclesiastical universities and pontifical faculties approved or established by the Holy See[48] have most often been the exclusive domain of clergy and religious rather than the laity. In North America, this situation has changed drastically over the past twenty years. The lay faithful have actively sought additional education for their own spiritual benefit and to allow them to serve their local communities more fully. With the increasing need to educate the laity as fewer clergy are available, many educational institutions actively recruit lay students or tailor their programs to the laity's needs. The number of lay persons preparing to act as professional ministers after receiving

extensive graduate education has increased dramatically. The presence of lay students with a variety of life experiences has also enriched educational programs that were once reserved solely for young men. Oftentimes, church educational institutions have established specific programs for the preparation of parish ministers, programs that are separate from the seminary curriculum. The trend is likely to continue as these institutions, concerned with defraying the high costs of training clergy, look to the additional funding generated by the instruction of the laity to lighten that financial load.

The third paragraph establishes a qualified right of the laity to teach the sacred sciences.[49] It is the most restricted of the rights mentioned in this canon. Any person seeking such a position must meet the requirements for reception of a canonical mandate.[50] Lay persons currently teach in seminaries and hold mandates to teach in pontifical faculties.

Liturgical Functions[51]

Canon 230 — §1. Lay men who possess the age and qualifications established by decree of the conference of bishops can be admitted on a stable basis through the prescribed liturgical rite to the ministries of lector and acolyte. Nevertheless, the conferral of these ministries does not grant them the right to obtain support or remuneration from the Church.

§2. Lay persons can fulfill the function of lector in liturgical actions by temporary designation. All lay persons can also perform the functions of commentator or cantor, or other functions, according to the norm of law.

[46] For a listing of various lay ministry education programs, see Center for Applied Research in the Apostolate, *Catholic Ministry Formation Directory* (Washington, D.C.: Georgetown University, 1997–1998). This directory is published bi-annually and is compiled through queries to all dioceses in the United States. It includes accredited and unaccredited programs. The same group also publishes *Seminary Formation Directory* and *Diaconate Formation Directory*.

[47] Article 13 of "Some Questions" indicates that proper formation is an important issue and expresses a preference for preparation under proper ecclesiastical authority "in environments other than that of the Seminary, as this is reserved solely for those preparing for the priesthood" (*Origins* 27 [November 27, 1997] 407).

[48] Canon 816, §1.

[49] Canon 253, §2 indicates that the sacred sciences include church history, dogmatic and moral theology, canon law, liturgy, sacred scripture, and philosophy.

[50] Canon 812. The commentary on this canon provides a fuller explanation of the requirement for an ecclesiastical mandate to teach and the relationship between the magisterium and those teaching the sacred sciences.

[51] There is no corresponding canon in the Eastern code.

§3. When the need of the Church warrants it and ministers are lacking, lay persons, even if they are not lectors or acolytes, can also supply certain of their duties, namely, to exercise the ministry of the word, to preside over liturgical prayers, to confer baptism, and to distribute Holy Communion, according to the prescripts of the law.

Interpretations of this canon continue to evolve. Both the laity and the ordained may hold liturgical offices.[52] Much has been written about the differences between the liturgical roles of the laity and the ordained,[53] and there has been some controversy regarding certain official clarifications of the lay-clergy relationship.[54]

Installed Ministries – §1

This paragraph allows only lay men to be installed as lectors and acolytes, without requiring them to be clerics. However, in practice, these ministries continue to be used as steps toward the admission of a candidate to the diaconate or priesthood.[55] One is installed in these ministries by a special ceremony presided over by the appropriate bishop, or the major superior of a clerical religious institute or society of apostolic life. This is the only canon in this title that distinguishes between men and women.

Some priests have refused to apply this law strictly, relying instead on an interpretation of the law that allows for the use of extraordinary ministers.[56] One argument used to justify this practice is

that the canon is unjustly discriminatory toward women, since there is no reason for such a distinction at this time. This is particularly true in light of the Holy See's permission for the use of altar girls. A second justification suggested for using only extraordinary ministers is the level of mobility in modern society in North America, that makes establishing a stable pool of installed lectors and acolytes practically impossible. Many dioceses lack specific norms to govern these ministries.

Installed lectors and acolytes acquire a stability in ministry that goes beyond the exercise of their function during liturgical celebrations. Admission to these ministries must be in keeping with the guidelines of the local episcopal conference and will usually involve a rite of installation.[57] The age for admission to the ministries in the United States is eighteen.[58] These ministries do not entitle the holder to financial remuneration or support. In an October 27, 1977 letter, the Congregation for Divine Worship and the Discipline of the Sacraments permitted conferences of bishops to establish other stable ministries in their own regions.[59]

This canon continues the canonical provisions of *Ministeria quaedam*[60] which eliminated the tonsure, the minor orders, and the subdiaconate

---

[52] Canon 145. The eligibility to hold office with the power of governance poses somewhat different concerns. See the commentary on cc. 129 and 274, §1 regarding these matters.

[53] "Some Questions," passim.

[54] "Some Questions," art. 8, in *Origins* 27 (November 27, 1997) 405–406.

[55] Canon 1035 requires that a man who is to be promoted to the permanent or transitional diaconate have received the ministries of lector and acolyte and exercised these ministries for a suitable time. At least six months must elapse between the conferral of the ministry of acolyte and the diaconate.

[56] See c. 230, §2. In light of the decision to allow the use of female altar servers (*Origins* 23 [April 28, 1994] 777–

779), the restriction of installation in such ministries to men seems unusual. See footnote 61 for additional comments on this topic.

[57] See "Rite of Installation of Readers and Acolytes," in *Rites of the Catholic Church* (New York: Pueblo, 1976) 740–745.

[58] The current NCCB policy on this subject is based on Paul VI, *mp Ministeria quaedam*, August 15, 1972, *AAS* 64 (1972) 529–534; *DOL,* 908–911. The NCCB confirmed the provisions specified in this document during its November 1972 meeting. See *BCLN* 8 (December 1972) 353–354. Under the present NCCB policy, bishops may dispense from the age requirement if the candidate possesses the requisite maturity and judgment to carry out the duties of the ministry. As this commentary is being written, the NCCB is considering establishing norms to govern these ministries.

[59] CDWDS, private reply, *Novit profecto,* October 27, 1977, Prot. N. 1837/77, in *CLD* 9, 602–604; *DOL,* 916–917.

[60] The canon also expresses the liturgical law found in *GIRM,* 66–68.

from the Latin church. The document also provided for what was considered a new recognition of lay ministry in the Church's mission, for it allowed episcopal conferences to request the installation of laity in other ministries if it was deemed helpful in the local situation. The current code does not eliminate this possibility, so other installed ministries could conceivably be created.

It should be noted that a ministry differs from an "office" established in accordance with canon 145. One who acts as a minister in this case may change from one parish or community to the next without needing an additional installation ceremony. However, one who holds an office is much more limited in exercising his or her responsibilities. For example, one who is the pastor of one parish may not exercise the same powers and responsibilities in another parish without a proper appointment.

In the United States, the term "ministry" has been applied to the exercise of all the gifts and talents of the faithful for the benefit of the community. Ministries open to the laity are not limited to those established by law. This has been amply proven over the past two decades as functions of all kinds have proliferated to respond to the various pastoral needs present in society today. Many parishes have established a ministry for "greeting" those who arrive for liturgical functions, who "usher" others to places in the church, or who assist with the education of others in a ministry of education. This is not to suggest that the ordained ministry is not respected or that the laity are acting as clerics, but that the concept of "ministering" to others has become synonymous with church "service" in any capacity. Changing the usage of the term "ministry" so that it would apply only to the ministry of the ordained or those officially installed would be a herculean task, given the evolution which began with the Second Vatican Council. It would also serve little purpose, since it appears that there is no confusion regarding the distinction between the functions of the ordained and those of the laity. If there is no confusion, there is no reason to change. For example, there is no confusion regarding the rights attached to the ministerial priesthood vis-à-vis those of one who exercises a "ministry of hospitality" by serving donuts after Sunday Mass.

Extraordinary Ministries – §2

The other ministries of lector, commentator, and cantor mentioned in the canon are viewed in the same informal way, as distinguished from those requiring a formal installation rite as mentioned in paragraph one of this canon. This paragraph of the canon allows for the establishment of other liturgical functions as necessary, depending on the needs of the local church. Such ministries are open to both women and men, and the canon does not place any age restrictions on those who might seek to fulfill these duties.

The term "temporary designation" seems to mean that those who function according to this paragraph of the canon do so in a way that is not stable, as contrasted with the installed ministries mentioned in paragraph one. The needs of the community at the moment are paramount, so a person deemed suitable by the competent authority may exercise the same responsibilities as an installed minister, but only for a limited period.

In the past, acting as an altar server has been restricted to boys and men, whether installed as acolytes or not (*CIC* 813). However, in 1994 a general permission for the use of female altar servers was granted, subject only to the judgment of the individual bishop in light of the specific circumstances of his own diocese.[61]

---

[61] The CDWDS decision to grant general permission for the use of female altar servers was based on a June 30, 1992 authentic interpretation of the PCILT, which determined that female altar servers could be permitted under c. 230, but called for additional instructions from the CDWDS. The question posed to the PCILT was: "Can service at the altar also be counted among the liturgical functions that lay people, either men or women, can fulfill according to Canon 230, §2 of the Code of Canon Law?" The answer was in the affirmative. This decision was confirmed by Pope John Paul II on July 11, 1992. See *AAS* 86 (1994) 541; *Origins* 23 (April 28, 1994) 777–779. The CDWDS instruction reminds bishops that boys should remain servers at the altar since this has led to vocations in the

Supplying for Ministers – §3

This paragraph of the canon refers to the most extraordinary of circumstances in allowing the laity, whether women or men, to exercise or supply the functions of absent or impeded ministers. In some parts of the Church today, such circumstances are all too common. This canon allows lay persons to act as lectors or ministers of the Eucharist (c. 910, §2), baptism (c. 861, §2), or of the word (c. 759) or to preside over liturgical prayers as established by law. For the laity to act in this way, the Church must need such actions, and clerical ministers must be truly physically or morally unavailable for the exercise of the function.[62] One example of the regulated exercise of such extraordinary ministry is *The Directory for Sunday Celebrations in the Absence of a Priest.*[63]

Formation and Remuneration for Church Service[64]

Canon 231 — §1. Lay persons who permanently or temporarily devote themselves to special service of the Church are obliged to acquire the appropriate formation required to fulfill their function properly and to carry out this function conscientiously, eagerly, and diligently.

§2. Without prejudice to the prescript of can. 230, §1 and with the prescripts of civil law having

been observed, lay persons have the right to decent remuneration appropriate to their condition so that they are able to provide decently for their own needs and those of their family. They also have a right for their social provision, social security, and health benefits to be duly provided.

This canon discusses a pertinent obligation and right of those lay persons who serve the Church either permanently or temporarily. It sets standards for formation and remuneration to be observed by church authorities in light of church teachings on the just wage and benefits to be paid to church workers.

Appropriate Formation – §1

This paragraph obliges the lay person who wishes to serve the Church, either permanently or temporarily, to acquire the proper training and skills to accomplish that work.[65] It is not specified whether that education should be obtained prior to commencing the task.

The type of work covered under this canon may include that of the offices described in canons 145 and 228, §1. These are only examples of the types of activities discharged by those bound by this obligation, since the wording of the canon is broad enough to cover various functions that may not be considered offices in the strict sense. The service involved may be paid, volunteer, temporary, permanent, full-time, or part-time. It may be related to the teaching, governing, or sanctifying ministries of the Church.

All must carry out their functions "conscientiously, eagerly, and diligently." These criteria, which differ from the legally verifiable requirements that are most often included in the canons,

---

past. Furthermore, provision must be made to explain to the faithful the reasons for the change.

[62] See "Some Questions," arts. 8 (Eucharist) and 11 (baptism), *Origins* 27 (November 27, 1997) 405–407. While not specifically mentioning them as extraordinary ministries, this same document also treats the apostolate to the sick (art. 9) and funeral liturgies (art. 12).

[63] This CDWDS document was dated June 2, 1988. See *Origins* 18 (October 20, 1988) 301, 303–307. On July 9, 1991, the NCCB Committee on the Liturgy issued the statement "Gathered in Steadfast Faith: Statement on Sunday Worship in the Absence of a Priest." See also M. Henchal, "A Ministry for Gathering in Steadfast Faith: Lay Presiding," *CLSAP* 54 (1992) 130–146. See "Some Questions," art. 7, *Origins* 27 (November 27, 1997) 405.

[64] *CCEO* 409 is similar to this canon with the exception of the reference to c. 230, §1, since there is no corresponding canon in the Eastern code.

[65] Canons 234–235 refer to clerical formation prior to ordination, and c. 279 obliges clerics to continue their own education throughout their lives. Canons 646–653 and cc. 659–661 specify the general canonical requirements for the formation of novices and professed members of religious institutes; the constitutions of these institutes may also address this subject. The code also requires the formation of members of societies of apostolic life (cc. 735–736) and secular institutes (cc. 722, 724).

are akin to the admonition that a church administrator charged with the oversight of ecclesiastical
goods act with the "diligence of a good householder" (c. 1284, §1) or that a pastor should fulfill
his office "diligently" (c. 529, §1). Such criteria
should be interpreted consistently in light of other
legal provisions.[66]

One must consider the obligation specified in
this canon in light of the basic right of all believers to a Christian education (c. 217). Furthermore,
this canon must also be read in light of canon 229,
§1, which articulates a more general educational
obligation for all laity, regardless of their condition. By contrast, canon 231, §1 addresses the
issue of formation for a specific ecclesial purpose.

In recent years it has been easier for lay persons to receive the appropriate instruction necessary to fulfill this obligation. Various dioceses and
parishes have begun to assist the laity in obtaining
the required education, since their exercise of various offices has become more critical due to a
shortage of both clergy and religious.

The bishops continue to grapple with their
obligation under this canon. On the one hand,
they must contend with an increasingly limited
number of qualified teachers for an ever growing
population. On the other, the funds necessary to
sustain any type of educational program are frequently lacking. The great geographic spread
characterizing the majority of dioceses in North
America presents additional problems, since the
faithful may be unable to avail themselves of any
kind of educational program a bishop can offer.
Practically speaking, while a bishop may establish
mandatory educational requirements for church
workers, if the faithful will not or cannot attend
such training programs, volunteer positions will
go unfilled, or other arrangements will have to be
made. In places where more formal education is
unavailable, alternative programs have begun to
emerge so that the right of the laity to receive ap-

propriate formation may be satisfied and they
may receive the training they need to take on their
responsibilities in the Church.

Just Wages and Benefits – §2

The second paragraph of this canon is grounded
in the Church's social justice teachings on a just
wage and also specifies certain implications of that
teaching regarding employment benefits. Such
benefits would include appropriate wages that respect civil law requirements as well as the right to
social provisions such as health, disability, and retirement insurance that people need to provide decently for themselves and their families. This
"right" under the law has been slow to be realized
in practice in many places, since the Church is
viewed by many—both within and outside it—as
a separate institution immune from the requirements of its own law. In some quarters just compensation and volunteerism are confused. Many
lay persons who serve the Church are not aware of
this teaching or have been reluctant to bring a case
in canonical court for the vindication of this right,
since such an action effectively brands them as
"troublemakers" and in effect makes them unem-
ployable in the Church.

This canon should be viewed in relationship to
canon 1286 in Book V which requires that administrators observe local laws concerning labor in
the employment of church workers[67] and are to
pay employees a just and decent wage so they can
support themselves and their families.[68] Paragraph

---

[66] Additional examples of such criteria include clergy
being called to fulfill their functions "faithfully" (c. 274,
§2) and bishops being admonished to set an example of
charity, humility, and simplicity of life (c. 387).

[67] Canon 1286, 1° states that in the employment of workers
administrators "are to observe meticulously also the civil
laws concerning labor and social policy, according to the
principles handed on by the Church."

[68] Canon 1286, 2° states that administrators "are to pay a
just and decent wage to employees so that they are able
to provide fittingly for their own needs and those of their
dependents." See National Association of Church Personnel Administrators (NACPA), *Just Treatment for
Those Who Work for the Church* (Cincinnati, Ohio:
NACPA, 1986) viii–21; CLSA, "Canonical Standards in
Labor-Management Relations: A Report," *J* 47 (1987)
545–575. Both works discuss the practical applications
of the Church's teaching on justice in this area.

two of canon 231 does not limit these rights only to those who work full time for the Church, but is tailored to make it clear that these rights extend to persons who work without a contract and provide less formal ministerial service. The bishops of the United States have reiterated the importance of this right in their pastoral letter *Economic Justice for All: Catholic Social Teaching and the US Economy*[69] which states, "We bishops commit ourselves to the principle that those who serve the Church—laity, clergy, and religious—should receive a sufficient livelihood and the social benefits provided by responsible employers in our nation."[70] This same document also recognizes the rights of employees to organize and bargain collectively with the institution through whatever association or organization they freely choose.[71] The increase in the number of lay persons working in formal positions within the Church has placed a particularly heavy burden on church institutions to honor this right. Many of the post-1983 code disputes that have arisen in the Church are in the area of employment practices.[72] To deal with these cases, some dioceses have implemented a "due

process" system similar to that approved by the National Conference of Catholic Bishops (NCCB).[73] Most have some type of system on record, even if it differs from the NCCB-approved system.[74]

---

[69] *Origins* 16 (June 5, 1986) 33–76; particularly 65–67, nos. 335–353.

[70] Ibid., 66, no. 348.

[71] Ibid., 66, no. 349.

[72] J. Provost, ed., *Due Process in Dioceses in the United States 1970–1985* (Washington, D.C.: CLSA, 1987) iii–251. This is a report of a CLSA task force whose purpose was to survey the due process experience in the United States.

[73] NCCB, *On Due Process* (Washington, D.C.: USCC, 1972) 1–48. See CLSA, *Protection of Rights of Persons in the Church—Revised Report of the Canon Law Society of America on the Subject of Due Process* (Washington, D.C.: CLSA, 1991) iii–48.

[74] The application of due process procedures differs from diocese to diocese, as do the expertise and commitment of those charged with implementing them. The aforementioned CLSA study on due process documents the history of the application of these procedures. The CLSA is currently conducting an experiment in due process designed to evaluate aspects of conciliation/mediation procedures in smaller dioceses. The same study also surveys the practicality of adding a limited administrative tribunal component to well-established due process (conciliation/mediation/arbitration) systems. For a presentation made to the CLSA membership regarding this project, see "CLSA Experiment in Due Process Committee Report," *CLSAP* 56 (1994) 68–79. Other reports can be found in *CLSAP* 57 (1995) 456–459; *CLSAP* 58 (1996) 427–428; and *CLSAP* 59 (1997) 376–377. The results of the aforementioned experiment were still being compiled as this commentary was being written.

TITLE III
SACRED MINISTERS OR CLERICS
[cc. 232–293]

CHAPTER I
THE FORMATION OF CLERICS
[cc. 232–264]

*The Church's Duty and Right
to Form Sacred Ministers*

Canon 232 — The Church has the duty and the proper and exclusive right to form those who are designated for the sacred ministries.

On the occasion of the commissioning of the apostles, Jesus instructed the eleven as follows:

Full authority has been given to me both in heaven and on earth; go, therefore, and make disciples of all nations. Baptize them in the name "of the Father, and of the Son, and of the Holy Spirit." Teach them to carry out everything I have commanded you. And know that I am with you always, until the end of the world.[1]

The obligations that flow from this command are complemented by the right of the apostles and their successors to carry it out. That fact is expressed absolutely in this canon which introduces the section on the essential work of forming and preparing students in seminaries and religious communities for service to the Church as ordained ministers.[2]

The exercise of the Church's right and the carrying out of this obligation have their roots primarily in the gospel as well as, in more recent

[1] Mt 28:18–20.
[2] Canons 1008 and 1027; *CCEO* 328.

years, the documents of Vatican II that offered a standard teaching on the priesthood. These include *Lumen gentium, Christus Dominus,* and *Presbyterorum ordinis,* together with the documents that provided formation principles and guidelines for the renewal of priestly formation, *Optatam totius* and the Sacred Congregation for Catholic Education's 1970 *Ratio fundamentalis institutionis sacerdotalis.* This latter document was a basic plan to assist bishops in formulating their own particular programs for seminary renewal. An updated 1985 edition of it followed the promulgation of the 1983 Code of Canon Law.[3]

All these works provided direction for the National Conference of Catholic Bishops' publication, the *Program for Priestly Formation.* Its fourth edition reflects the 1990 synod of bishops on "The Formation of Priests in the Circumstances of the Present Day," and Pope John Paul II's post-synodal apostolic exhortation, *Pastores dabo vobis.*[4]

Central to the life and work of the Church is the appropriately formed and well-educated priest who has received as expert as available human, spiritual, and pastoral formation in a seminary. Toward this end, the Church in the United States under its civil laws enjoys the freedom to establish its own seminaries and form its own seminarians for ordination to the priesthood (*DH* 4).

The Task of Nurturing Vocations

Canon 233 — §1. The duty of fostering vocations rests with the entire Christian community so that the needs of the sacred ministry in the universal

[3] The text of the updated *Ratio* may be found in *Norms* I, 15–60.
[4] For the 1990 synod's *Lineamenta,* see *Origins* 19 (June 1, 1989) 33–46; for the synod's *Instrumentum laboris,* see *L'Osservatore Romano* (in English) 30 (1150) (July 23, 1990) 1–6, 11–14; for *PDV* see *Origins* 21 (April 16, 1992) 717–759, esp. n. 4.

Church are provided for sufficiently. This duty especially binds Christian families, educators, and, in a special way, priests, particularly pastors. Diocesan bishops, who most especially are to be concerned for promoting vocations, are to teach the people entrusted to them of the importance of the sacred ministry and of the need for ministers in the Church and are to encourage and support endeavors to foster vocations, especially by means of projects established for that purpose.

§2. Moreover, priests, and especially diocesan bishops, are to have concern that men of a more mature age who consider themselves called to the sacred ministries are prudently assisted in word and deed and duly prepared.

In *Pastores dabo vobis* 34 Pope John Paul II speaks of the "Gospel of vocation" in reference to John 1:35–42 ("Come, and see"). He describes it as the "paradigm, strength and impulse behind [the Church's] mission to care for the birth, discernment and fostering of vocations, particularly those to the priesthood."[5]

Optatam totius has been called the Second Vatican Council's charter of seminary reform and paragraph two is the foundation for this canon. Under the leadership of the diocesan bishop, who has the ultimate responsibility for fostering vocations (c. 385),[6] and with the active cooperation of the diocesan community, responsible and well-planned public relations efforts must be undertaken to promote vocations to the priesthood. The powerful technological tools of modern communication ought to be utilized in order to awaken all Christians to the need for sacred ministers in the Church in the United States and throughout the world (*PDV* 41).

While in some parts of the world there is an increase in the number of priestly vocations, a grave shortage of priests is being felt in other parts (*PDV* 1).[7] "The lack of priests is certainly a sad thing for any Church," said Pope John Paul II (*PDV* 34). An alarm needs to be sounded so that in accord with this canon all the faithful might dutifully attend to the scarcity of priestly vocations.[8]

The *Program for Priestly Formation* 95 points to the necessity for organized programs of assistance in the work of awakening these vocations and building up new feeder systems. The call to priestly ministry should come from the local church, from the parish and all its members. Today many dioceses have responded with varying types of programs aimed at helping an individual begin the process of making an informed decision about a vocation to the priesthood.

Paragraph two of this canon highlights another significant fact in the United States and elsewhere. This is the gradually growing number of men of more mature age responding to the call to the diaconate and priesthood later in life. These callings are generally referred to as "delayed vocations" or "second career vocations."[9] Following up on the call for "colleges for late vocations" in *Optatam totius* 3, this matter was addressed in 1976 by the Sacred Congregation for Catholic Education.[10] The present canon directs that such individuals are to be encouraged and provided for in every way possible, ideally by a specific seminary curriculum of formation and academic programs with suitable adaptations tailored to their special talents and needs.[11]

---

[5] Canons 385 and 791, 1°; CFC, *Directory on the Ministry and Life of Priests* (Vatican City: Libreria Editrice Vaticana, 1994) 32; NCCB, "Statement on Vocations to the Priesthood," *Origins* 19 (November 2, 1989) 358–361.

[6] J. Marshall, "Strengths and Weaknesses of the U.S. Seminaries," *Origins* 17 (January 7, 1988) 527, 1.

[7] For example, the continent of Africa has three times more major seminarians than the continent of North America. For current statistics see the yearly Vatican publication *Annuarium Statisticum Ecclesiae* published by the Secretariat of State.

[8] John Paul II, "Holy Thursday Letter to Priests," *Origins* 18 (April 6, 1989) 732.

[9] "The issue of adult vocations has become more accented in the United States." Letter from SCCE, April 28, 1981, *CLD* 9, 612.

[10] *CLD* 8, 946–955.

[11] *CLD* 9, 615. In a letter of May 27, 1981, Bishop Thomas Kelly, general secretary of the NCCB, ac-

The Eastern code also underscores the shared responsibility of the whole Christian community in becoming involved in the work of fostering vocations. It stresses that the community's outreach must be to boys, young people, and men of "more advanced age."[12]

Minor Seminaries

Canon 234 — §1. Minor seminaries and other similar institutions are to be preserved, where they exist, and fostered; for the sake of fostering vocations, these institutions provide special religious formation together with instruction in the humanities and science. Where the diocesan bishop judges it expedient, he is to erect a minor seminary or similar institution.

§2. Unless in certain cases circumstances indicate otherwise, young men disposed to the priesthood are to be provided with that formation in the humanities and science by which the youth in their own region are prepared to pursue higher studies.

At the other end of the age spectrum are young men studying in minor seminaries or similar institutions (*Ratio* 11–19). These have played a crucial role as the traditional means for fostering priestly vocations among the young.

The Eastern code expresses a wider purpose for a minor seminary. It describes the minor seminary as a place to serve not only those who show signs of a vocation to the sacred ministry but also others who may not seem to be called to the clerical state but, nevertheless, can be pre-

pared to work in certain ministries and apostolic works.[13]

In the United States, Catholic schools and colleges served in the past as reliable feeder systems for providing seminaries with students, but today they are no longer producing many applicants. Enrollments in high school and college seminaries continue to decline as do the number of seminaries for students at these levels.[14]

Even the term "minor seminary" has in some quarters become an unpopular and controversial one and has been replaced for the most part by the term "college seminary." However, while not all are in agreement on their value, some are beginning to take a second look at minor seminaries. The 1990 synod of bishops recognized them as a valid instrument for formation in the early stages of young vocations.[15]

While this canon does not require the establishment of such an institution in each diocese, it does call on the diocesan bishop to maintain and support such institutions where they exist and even to provide for the erection of one, if he judges it expedient. The "mind of the legislator" (c. 17) is rather clear here as it is in the apostolic exhortation *Pastores dabo vobis* 63–64, where the Holy Father stresses the advantages of "minor seminaries" or, if it is not possible to have such an institution, then of other "institutions," e.g., "vocational groups for adolescents and young people."

knowledged that formation for "second career" applicants seems to be best accomplished in a seminary setting which is constructed only for older candidates. He noted that pioneers in this area have been the Pope John XXIII National Seminary in Weston, Massachusetts, and Sacred Heart School of Theology in Hales Corners, Wisconsin.

[12] *CCEO* 329 and 380. See also E. Hemrick and R. Wister, *Readiness for Theological Studies* (Washington, D.C.: NCEA, 1993) 20 on the advantages of having older seminarians.

[13] *CCEO* 331, §1 and 332, §1. See P. Golden, *CLSA Com*, 179 for his description of the use and application of the term "minor seminary"; see also *PO* 3 and *OT* 3. The latter, in endorsing the minor seminary, gives its purpose together with a description of its formational and educational duties. See *PPF* 94–130 for material on high school seminaries and related programs; similar attention is given to college seminaries and related programs in 131–208 with the addition of requirements for philosophical training and undergraduate study of theology.

[14] A dramatic example of this is the fact that in the last quarter of the twentieth century college seminary enrollment dropped by approximately 90 percent. For current statistics see the yearly publication *CARA Seminary Directory*, Washington, D.C.: Georgetown University.

[15] 1990 Synod, "Overview of Synod Proposals," *Origins* 20 (November 8, 1990) 353–355.

As regards preparing and forming these students for priestly ministry, paragraph two of this canon states that their training and education ought to be on a par with that of their peers. This echoes the call of canon 806, §2 for "academically distinguished" formation in Catholic educational institutions. *Gravissimum educationis* 8 is one of the sources for this canon.

The Eastern code urges even more strongly that the minor seminary's curriculum be such that it can lead to a civil diploma so that students can continue to pursue their studies elsewhere if they choose (*CCEO* 344, §3).

Major Seminaries

Canon 235 — §1. Young men who intend to enter the priesthood are to be provided with a suitable spiritual formation and prepared for their proper duties in a major seminary throughout the entire time of formation or, if in the judgment of the diocesan bishop circumstances demand it, for at least four years.

§2. The diocesan bishop is to entrust those who legitimately reside outside a seminary to a devout and suitable priest who is to be watchful that they are carefully formed in the spiritual life and in discipline.

The duties proper to the priesthood that require education and preparation are supported by the qualities listed in the *Program for Priestly Formation* 544 and 545. These include, among others, fidelity to the word of God, commitment to a life of personal prayer, abiding love for the sacramental life of the Church, and acceptance of a lifelong commitment to chaste celibacy. Possession of such qualities, together with manifestations of an apostolic heart, zeal for service, self-awareness, and sound personal identity may provide evidence that a candidate has a sense of ministerial priesthood, that is, a vocation in the Church.

Optatam totius 4 states that major seminaries are necessary for priestly training in the ministries of word, worship, sanctification, and shepherding

(*PDV* 60). Therefore, insofar as it is possible, there is to be adequate formation in these areas in a seminary setting for the whole time of that process. Four years are considered the minimal amount of formation time. Apart from a particular circumstance where the diocesan bishop allows an exception, viz., judging that only four years is sufficient for a candidate,[16] canon 250 calls for two full years to be dedicated to the philosophical disciplines and four to theological disciplines in accord with the local program of priestly formation. A "freestanding seminary" is the ordinary site for this training, but there are also "collaborative seminaries" which have a house of formation where students live while they attend classes at a university.

With due regard for the accepted nature and order of these "collaborative seminaries," a student preparing for the priesthood outside of a seminary would be rare in the United States. Nevertheless, paragraph two of this canon allows the diocesan bishop to grant an exception from paragraph one's requirement that formation and training take place in a major seminary "throughout the entire time of formation" which is six full years. In this case a devout and suitable priest is to be appointed by the diocesan bishop to be the candidate's vigilant formation director.[17]

The Eastern code addresses the same matter except that it speaks neither of a specific number of years nor of those who legitimately reside outside a seminary (*CCEO* 331, §2 and 344, §4).

Permanent Deacons

Canon 236 — According to the prescripts of the conference of bishops, those aspiring to the permanent diaconate are to be formed to nourish a spiritual life and instructed to fulfill correctly the duties proper to that order:

1° young men are to live at least three years in some special house unless the diocesan

---

[16] Explicit permission from the CCE is required to abbreviate a program of formation (*PPF* 263).

[17] *SapC* 72 and 74; *Origins* 9 (June 7, 1979) 33–45.

bishop has established otherwise for grave reasons;

2° men of a more mature age, whether celibate or married, are to spend three years in a program defined by the conference of bishops.

Lumen gentium 29 and *Ad gentes* 16 spoke of restoring the diaconate as a permanent rank of the hierarchy. In June 1967 and August 1972, Pope Paul VI promulgated the *motu proprios Sacrum diaconatus ordinem* and *Ad pascendum* which provided the developing norms for this restoration.[18] In April 1968 the bishops of the United States were among the first to take action by determining that such a restoration was appropriate for the country and desirable for meeting pastoral needs. In August 1968 they received permission from the Holy See to revive the permanent diaconate. Where needed, and with the consent of the local bishop, the permanent diaconate could be restored for married or unmarried men of mature years, the latter at the time being eligible after age twenty-five. A two-year training program was suggested, but the present code extends it to three years, and some dioceses require even more time.

In March 1998, the Congregation for Catholic Education issued *Fundamental Norms for the Formation of Permanent Deacons,* and the Congregation for the Clergy issued the *Directory for the Ministry and Life of Permanent Deacons.* The documents provide universal norms aimed at ensuring consistency in the training and ministry of deacons around the world.[19]

Candidates for the permanent diaconate are bound by the appropriate canons in this chapter on the formation of clerics.[20] The above norm directs the bishops' conference to set up a program for the formation of permanent deacons which is to be governed by norms issued by the same conference. This had been done in 1968 when the U.S. bishops established a Bishops' Committee on the Permanent Diaconate to approve programs established in particular dioceses. In 1971 it published formation guidelines drawing on the experience of a number of existing programs.[21]

Canon 1031, §2 allows an unmarried candidate for the permanent diaconate to be admitted to the diaconate at age twenty-five and a married candidate, with the consent of his wife, at thirty-five. Canon 1031, §3 empowers the conference to set down a norm requiring an older age, and in the United States that has been set for all candidates at thirty-five. When a dispensation from the required age involves more than one year, it is reserved to the Apostolic See.

The conference of bishops decided against requiring a three-year residence for young men in a "special house," but these men are required, along with married candidates, to enter the formation program. At the time of ordination those who are single (both the young and those of more mature years) are bound by the law of celibacy. Celibates and married permanent deacons who later might become widowers are subject to the impediment of sacred orders which would invalidate any attempted marriage, (c. 1087).[22]

The Eastern code calls for adapting the general norms for the formation of clerics to the formation of deacons not destined for the priesthood. It calls for at least three years of formation but "keeping in mind the traditions of their own Church *sui iuris* concerning the service of the liturgy, the word and charity" (*CCEO* 354).

---

[18] *AAS* 59 (1967) 697–704; *CLD* 6, 577–584; *AAS* 64 (1972) 534–540; *CLD* 7, 695–698.

[19] Catholic News Service, March 10, 1998, 10.

[20] See also cc. 281, §3, 288, 1031, §2, 1032, §3, 1037, and 1039.

[21] Bishops' Committee on the Permanent Diaconate, *Permanent Deacons in the United States* (Washington, D.C.: USCC, 1971).

[22] A circular letter of June 6, 1997 from the CDWDS announced new conditions under which permanent deacons widowed after ordination may be dispensed from the impediment of c. 1087. *Origins* 27 (August 28, 1997) 169–171.

Diocesan or Interdiocesan Major Seminaries

Canon 237 — §1. Where it is possible and expedient, there is to be a major seminary in every diocese; otherwise, the students who are preparing for the sacred ministries are to be entrusted to another seminary, or an interdiocesan seminary is to be erected.

§2. An interdiocesan seminary is not to be erected unless the conference of bishops, if the seminary is for its entire territory, or the bishops involved have obtained the prior approval of the Apostolic See for both the erection of the seminary and its statutes.

The spiritual, intellectual, pastoral, and disciplinary training of candidates for the priesthood is to be carried out in a major seminary. In 1997 in the United States there were 77 diocesan and 129 religious seminaries serving 4,645 students.[23] Changes in the last quarter of the twentieth century have radically altered the structure of the seminary. At present there are various types: *freestanding,* a self-contained institution which provides all the components of formation; *university-related,* where parts of the program are provided by a college or university other than the seminary; and *collaborative,* wherein faculty and other resources are shared among several seminaries with each one usually providing its own spiritual formation.

While the legislator prefers, if possible, a major seminary in every diocese, this canon recognizes the fact that many dioceses are not able to establish their own. *Optatam totius* 7 sees interdiocesan seminaries as meeting the needs of either a group of dioceses or of an entire region or nation. An interdiocesan seminary requires the input of all the bishops concerned and the Holy See's approval of both its establishment and its statutes. According to *Pastor bonus* 113, 3 this

approval is granted by the Congregation for Catholic Education.[24]

The related canon in the Eastern code does not mention the approval of the Apostolic See but, depending on the canonical status of the church in question, it does call for the consent of the appropriate eparchial bishop or bishops, a metropolitan authority with the consent of his council of hierarchs, or a synod of bishops of a patriarchal Church (*CCEO* 332, §2 and 334).

Juridic Personality

Canon 238 — §1. Seminaries legitimately erected possess juridic personality in the Church by the law itself.

§2. In the handling of all affairs, the rector of the seminary represents it unless competent authority has established otherwise for certain affairs.

This canon and canon 335 of the Eastern code *ipso iure* constitute all lawfully established seminaries as juridic persons (cc. 113–123), i.e., subjects in church law of appropriate obligations and rights.

Insofar as a seminary is a non-collegial public juridic person (cc. 115, §2 and 116), a physical person, usually the rector, is ordinarily appointed to act as its legal representative. The rector in effect becomes a kind of vicar for the bishop, recommending that the bishop ordain those who have met the requirements of canon 1025 or refuse to do so for those who are "canonically unsuitable" (cf. c. 1026).

The diocesan bishop himself, or the bishops related to an interdiocesan seminary, or even the Holy See could conceivably be the physical person representing a particular seminary.

---

[23] *Official Catholic Directory Anno Domini 1997* (New Providence, N.J.: P. J. Kenedy, 1997), General Summary, 2107; also E. Hemrick and J. Walsh, *Seminarians in the Nineties* (Washington, D.C.: NCEA, 1993).

[24] *Pastor bonus* (June 28, 1988) originally named this dicastery "Congregation of Seminaries and Educational Institutions." On February 26, 1989, the Secretariat of State changed the name to "Congregation for Catholic Education (for Seminaries and Educational Institutions)" (Protocol number 236.026).

Chief Personnel

Canon 239 — §1. Every seminary is to have a rector who presides over it, a vice-rector if one is needed, a finance officer, and, if the students pursue their studies in the seminary itself, teachers who give instruction in various disciplines coordinated in an appropriate manner.

§2. Every seminary is to have at least one spiritual director, though the students remain free to approach other priests who have been designated for this function by the bishop.

§3. The statutes of a seminary are to provide ways through which the other moderators, the teachers, and even the students themselves participate in the responsibility of the rector, especially in maintaining discipline.

The bishop is present in a seminary principally through the ministry of the rector, who is entrusted with the responsibility for its administration (*PDV* 60). So much of a seminary's character and spirit depend on his leadership, his willingness to communicate to the faculty, students, and staff and to delegate management responsibilities at various levels where they can be most suitably carried out. A further description of his work and role may be found in *Optatam totius* 5, the *Program for Priestly Formation* 459–464, and canons 260 and 262. More detailed norms relative to his role are to be drafted into the statutes that are mentioned here in paragraph three, and especially into the particular rule for an individual seminary.[25]

If needed, a vice-rector may be a valuable assistant. The Eastern code makes no mention of a vice-rector (*CCEO* 338, §1), but the *Program for Priestly Formation* 465 mentions a vice-rector "sharing responsibilities for the internal operation of the seminary, especially as the rector attends to external responsibilities."

Our present canon requires a finance officer. The Eastern code qualifies this provision with "if the situation warrants" (*CCEO* 338, §1). In the Latin code, canons 494 and 636 call for a finance officer in dioceses and religious institutes. The *Program for Priestly Formation* 478 views this officer as a business manager or treasurer assisting the rector in the stewardship of the financial and physical resources of the seminary, in budget preparation and implementation, and in supervision of service personnel. The provisions of Book V on "The Temporal Goods of the Church" (see c. 1257, §1) need to be considered in administering the seminary's properties and goods since it is a public juridic person (c. 238, §1).[26]

In addition to the agency of the rector on behalf of the bishop, the latter is present in a seminary in the service of co-responsibility and communion fostered by the rector with the other teachers (*PDV* 60). The bishop is to provide the seminary with its principal administrators and faculty (c. 253) and see to the implementation of *Optatam totius* and the *Program for Priestly Formation* in correspondence with the Code of Canon Law (*PPF* 446; *PDV* 65).

Teachers and instructors are to meet certain academic and canonical qualifications. A description of the seminary's superiors and professors referred to in this canon can be found in *Ratio*.[27]

The *Program for Priestly Formation* 486 indicates that the faculty are appointed by the bishop on the recommendation of the rector in accord with the approved statutes of the seminary. There is a preference for teachers who have advanced degrees in their fields. This preference extends further to those teaching the sacred sciences, including philosophy, who have degrees from an institution recognized by the Holy See. The *Program for Priestly Formation* 485 also requires

---

[25] For a study of the office of rector/president see J. White and R. Wister, *The Study of the Seminary Presidency in Catholic Theological Seminaries* (Pittsburgh, Pa.: Association of Theological Schools, 1995).

[26] For more on finances see K. Schuth, *Reason for the Hope* (Wilmington, Del.: Michael Glazier, 1989) 73–82.

[27] *Norms* I, 27–38; *PPF* 458–478, 484–505. The spiritual formation personnel are addressed in *Norms* I, 44–58 and *PPF* 479–483. For more on faculty see Schuth, 97–110.

that these teachers have a "canonical mission" from the appropriate ecclesiastical authority.[28] The program further states that priests who teach on the seminary faculty should have appropriate experience in pastoral ministry (486).

Under the direction of the rector and in accord with the law, teachers are to work together to draw up a curriculum. Often the rector will appoint an academic dean or dean of the faculty who chairs the cooperative efforts of the teaching staff. Together with the rector, those who teach philosophy and theology and areas that are related to theology, such as scripture, canon law, church history, liturgy, pastoral studies, and the like must make a profession of faith (c. 833) and take an oath of fidelity in accord with the formula published February 27, 1989.[29]

The role and work of the spiritual director are considered by many to be the animating spirit of authentic seminary life.[30] The spiritual director mentioned here in paragraph two is designated by the bishop to assist the rector in coordinating the entire spiritual formation program. The *Program for Priestly Formation* 479–483 details his responsibilities. In accord with this canon, those who provide spiritual direction must be priests appointed by the bishop, and each student may choose one of them as director of his spiritual life.[31]

The statutes mentioned in paragraph three are the governing documents by which a seminary operates; these could include a charter, constitutional norms, bylaws of the board of directors and trustees, the particular seminary's rule, and other administrative regulations.[32] Such documents are to respect the local culture in accordance with the varying circumstances of time and place. The seminary statutes are to provide for faculty and, in a significant change from the past, students also, to share in the concerns of the rector. The discipline and order of seminary life are significant matters,

---

[28]For more on the notion of "canonical mission" see *SapC* 27.1. See also R. Deeley, *The Mandate for Those Who Teach Theology in Institutes of Higher Studies,* JCD dissertation (Rome: Pontificia Universitas Gregoriana, 1986) 2–8.

[29]*AAS* 81 (1989) 104–106; *Origins* 18 (March 16, 1989) 661–663. For an informative study on the strengths and weaknesses of seminarians in academics and formation as seen through the eyes of seminary faculties see E. Hemrick and J. Walsh, *Readiness for Theological Studies* (Washington, D.C.: NCEA, 1993).

[30]"Spiritual direction is regarded by students as the single most important aspect of preparation for priesthood." W. Baumgaertner and K. Schuth, *NCE* 18, 469.

[31]In the 1980s some women faculty members in seminaries were serving as spiritual directors. However, the 1993 *PPF* 323 restricted spiritual direction of seminarians to priests recommended by the rector and approved

by the bishop. See CDWDS, "Scrutinies Regarding the Suitability of Candidates for Orders," Enclosure V, no. 12, November 28, 1998 (Protocol number 589/97). In its guidelines for the preparation of reports concerning the promotion of a candidate to holy orders, it calls for consideration of the regularity of a candidate's spiritual direction and with whom. For a study of those persons responsible for carrying out the spiritual training of students see M. Bartchak, *Responsibility for Providing Spiritual Formation in Diocesan Seminaries according to the 1983 Code of Canon Law with Special Reference to the United States, CanLawStud* 540 (Washington, D.C.: Catholic University of America, 1992). With regard to this canon's recognition of the freedom of students to approach other designated priests and any confessor, whether in the seminary or outside it, which is mentioned in the following canon, see G. McKay, "Spiritual Direction in the Diocesan Seminary: An Interpretation of the Canonical Norms," *Stud Can* 26 (1992) 401–413. The author discusses what he believes to be some confusion in the code's terminology and the present tension between respect for a seminarian's liberty of conscience and the seminary's desire to supervise his spiritual life. He also discusses and interprets the function of the spiritual director mentioned in this canon, the ordinary, and other confessors of c. 240, §1 and the director of one's spiritual life in c. 246, §4. See also *Ratio* 35; *PPF* 111, 145, and 323; *CCEO* 339, §1.

[32]In recent years there has been more diversity in those persons involved in the governance of seminaries. Clergy, religious, and laity more frequently contribute to the makeup of the various seminary boards. While these bodies are not mentioned in the code, they are found in *PPF* 444, 452, and 453. Such boards are expected to assist the bishop, rector, and faculty in developing a basic seminary policy in accord with church law. For more on these kinds of boards, see Schuth, 62–72.

and the canon calls for student participation in these areas according to the provisions of the rule.

Confessors

Canon 240 — §1. In addition to ordinary confessors, other confessors are to come regularly to the seminary. Without prejudice to the discipline of the seminary, students are always free to approach any confessor, whether in the seminary or outside it.

§2. When decisions are made about admitting students to orders or dismissing them from the seminary, the opinion of the spiritual director and confessors can never be sought.

The spiritual director mentioned in the preceding canon and the other priests designated for this function by the bishop can also serve as confessors. This present canon calls for still additional priests to be made available at the seminary on a regular basis to serve as "external" confessors (*PPF* 316).

In keeping with the sacred nature of the sacrament of penance and the anonymity that is its hallmark, this canon guarantees the widest liberty to students in the choice of a confessor, in the seminary or outside of it, within the reasonable limits of the good order of seminary life. Canon 630 provides the same freedom to members of religious institutes.

Out of serious concern for the sacramental seal (c. 983) and for the internal forum, even non-sacramental, those who direct the spiritual life of students and those who hear student confessions are not allowed a voice in the faculty council's determination of students' advancement to orders or continuation in the seminary program. Only external forum material may be used in making such decisions (cc. 984, 985, and 1388).

The Eastern code enjoins similar requirements (*CCEO* 339, §2 and §3).[33]

[33] For a discussion on the relationship of seminary personnel who function primarily in the external forum and

Admission to the Seminary

Canon 241 — §1. A diocesan bishop is to admit to a major seminary only those who are judged qualified to dedicate themselves permanently to the sacred ministries; he is to consider their human, moral, spiritual, and intellectual qualities, their physical and psychic health, and their correct intention.

§2. Before they are accepted, they must submit documents of the reception of baptism and confirmation and any other things required by the prescripts of the program of priestly formation.

§3. If it concerns admitting those who were dismissed from another seminary or religious institute, testimony of the respective superior is also required, especially concerning the cause for their dismissal or departure.

The rector, with the assistance of a vocation director and an admissions board made up of faculty members or other competent persons, ordinarily is charged by the diocesan bishop, whose responsibility it is to carry out the work of admissions. This involves undertaking the interviews and evaluations that are necessary before making a decision to admit or not to admit an applicant.

In addition to the seven qualities listed in paragraph one, *Optatam totius* 6 mentions that careful inquiry is to be made into a candidate's freedom of choice and his capacity for undertaking and carrying out the obligations of pastoral ministry.[34]

In order to meet the requirements of this canon, the admissions board and the rector will need the help of spiritual directors for interviews, medical doctors and other professionals for exam-

those who function primarily in the internal forum see Bartchak, 319–328. See also R. Pelkey, *The Relationship Between the Spiritual Formation Program and the Formation Advisor Relationship at Roman Catholic Seminaries,* doctoral dissertation (San Diego: United States International University, 1995).

[34] For more on the notion of "correct intention" see Paul VI, *Summi Dei Verbum, AAS* 55 (1963) 979–995, esp. 987–988; *TPS* 9 (1964) 239–250, esp. 245; also *Ratio* 39.

ination of an applicant's health, and a psychological assessment to aid in judging his motivation, stability, and capacity (cc. 642 and 1051).[35] The human limitations of each one of these aids needs to be acknowledged so that no single one should serve as a primary basis for a decision. Rather, all of them together should be taken into consideration with due regard for canon 220's concern for respecting a person's right to a good reputation and to privacy.[36]

The Eastern code does not specify the qualities mentioned in this present canon but calls on the appropriate authority to obtain documentary evidence which attests to a candidate's possession of the "required abilities" (*CCEO* 342, §1 and §2).

Serious consideration also needs to be given to canons 1041 and 1042 which list irregularities and impediments that would prevent one from receiving orders. Today members of the Church are faced with a considerable amount of proselytizing by both Christian and non-Christian religious sects. Consequently, there can be a candidate for the seminary who has recently "returned to the Church" from one of these groups but had been baptized and to some degree brought up a Catholic. Perhaps canons 751 and 1041, §2, on committing the delict of heresy, apostasy, or schism, might apply in a specific case; but careful attention is to be given to canons 18 and 1321–1330, on the strict interpretation of penal laws and on penal imputability.

Similarly, in a society where drugs, casual sex, and abortions are easily accessible, a candidate could be irregular for the reception of orders because of an attempted suicide, or cooperation in a successful abortion, or the attempted marriage mentioned in c. 1041, §3, or any of the other irregularities or impediments listed in the code. Canon 1047 explains who can dispense from these.[37]

The *Program for Priestly Formation* 510 calls for caution to be the byword in the admission procedure and states that the benefit of the doubt should be given to the Church. "Notwithstanding the regrettable shortage of priests," *Optatam totius* 6 states, "due strictness should always be brought to bear on the choice and testing of students." Further, it directs that those candidates judged unsuitable for priestly ministry be guided with fatherly kindness to adopt another calling, suggesting that they zealously engage in the lay apostolate.

Besides the documents mentioned in paragraph two of this canon,[38] the *Program for Priestly Formation* 510–528 lists more extensive admission requirements such as evaluations and letters of recommendation from candidates' pastors and teachers, academic records, and standardized test scores (513). Some seminaries also require personally written essays in which the candidate provides a profile of his vision of priestly ministry and why he wishes to choose it.

---

[35] "Evident indeed is the fragile psychological state of a number of candidates to the priesthood in the Western world," 1990 synod, *Lineamenta* 3b, *Origins* 19 (June 1, 1989) 36. See also E. Hemrick and D. Hoge, *Seminary Life and Visions of Priesthood* (Washington, D.C.: NCEA, 1987); E. Hemrick and D. Hoge, *Seminarians in Theology* (Washington, D.C.: NCEA, 1985); *PPF* 517–521. For a discussion on psychological evaluations, privacy, and good reputation, see J. Provost, "Canons 273, 1041 and 1044, Canonical Obedience and Psychological Evaluation," *RRAO 1995,* 43–45.

[36] See S. Euart, "Canon Law and Psychological Testing for Admission to a Seminary," in *Psychology, Counseling and the Seminarian,* ed. R. Wister (Washington, D.C.: NCEA, 1993) 185–193. On the subject of human immunodeficiency virus (HIV) testing as a requirement for seminary admission, see the opinions of J. Anderson, R. Calvo, and R. Gibbons in *CLSA Advisory Opinions, 1984–1993,* ed. P. Cogan (Washington, D.C.: CLSA, 1995) 44–52.

[37] For a further study of the canons related to irregularities and impediments, see C. Cox, "Processes Involving Irregularities and Impediments to the Exercise of Orders," in *Clergy Procedural Handbook,* ed. R. Calvo and N. Klinger (Washington, D.C.: CLSA, 1992) 178–205.

[38] See CDWDS, "Scrutinies Regarding the Suitability of Candidates for Orders," Enclosure I, no. 2, November 28, 1997 (Protocol number 589/97). It states that a candidate's certificates of baptism and confirmation are to be kept in his personal file.

Today the seminary program must call as well for careful screening of an applicant who has obtained a declaration of nullity of his marriage (*PPF* 527).[39] Such a candidate's admission to a seminary does not depend on the previous approval of the Holy See but on the sponsoring ordinary. The *Program for Priestly Formation* 527 states, "While such application should be carefully weighed on a case-by-case basis, the presumption normally is against acceptance."[40]

Similar pastoral concerns are pertinent regarding widowed candidates seeking admission to a major seminary. In judging whether or not to admit a candidate, one needs to keep in mind that the seminary is the place for testing and fostering vocations at their start, so the signs of a vocation need not be in full bloom but only need to have the potential to sprout.[41]

Paragraph three requires further testimony from a superior of another seminary or religious institute relative to an applicant who has been dismissed or who departed from such an institution (see also *CCEO* 342, §3). This requirement is further underscored by the *Program for Priestly Formation*'s statement that the proper authorities have a "serious obligation to consult all previous institutions about the past record of candidates"

(525). This required consultation "must be done in every instance" (526).[42]

In the past, admittance of the above mentioned candidates required the approval of the Holy See. This requirement ceased with the entrance into force of the code, and a private letter from the Secretariat of State on June 6, 1983, indicated it did not seem opportune to reinstate it.[43]

Occasionally some carelessness could occur in this area, especially at a time when applicants for the priesthood are in such short supply, but it would be regrettable to neglect the above required consultation given both the strong language of the *Program of Priestly Formation* and the mandate of canon 242, §2.[44]

National Program of Priestly Formation

Canon 242 — §1. Each nation is to have a program of priestly formation which is to be established by the conference of bishops, attentive to the norms issued by the supreme authority of the Church, and which is to be approved by the Holy See. This program is to be adapted to new circumstances, also with the approval of the Holy See, and is to define the main principles of the instruction to be given in the seminary and general norms adapted to the pastoral needs of each region or province.

§2. All seminaries, both diocesan and interdiocesan, are to observe the norms of the program mentioned in §1.

Optatam totius 1 laid down basic principles for the renewal of priestly formation and mandated each nation and rite to develop its own program to be revised and reviewed by competent authority on a regular basis. In 1970 the Sacred Congregation for Catholic Education's *Ratio* (since revised

---

[39] A. McGrath expresses his concern for the need of a letter from the former spouse stating she has no objection. "Furthermore, it should be determined that the candidate was not the cause of the breakup of the marriage and that there is little or no danger of scandal. Finally, before admitting such a person, the bishop should consider carefully the situation of any children born of the marriage who are still minors." *CLSGBI Com,* 138.

[40] A July 8, 1983 letter from the SCCE to the president of the NCCB stated that a man whose marriage has been declared null by an ecclesiastical tribunal is canonically free and eligible to enter a seminary and be ordained. While cautioning care in the case of a marriage declared null on the ground of the man's "psychological incompetence," the letter stated that the decision to admit such a man to the seminary is within the competence of the ordinary who wishes to sponsor him. *CLD* 10, 204–205; 11, 27–28; *RRAO 1983,* 23–24.

[41] McGrath, in *CLSGBI Com,* 137.

[42] *Ratio* 39. See also CDWDS, "Scrutinies Regarding the Suitability of Candidates for Orders," 8 and Enclosure I, no. 10, November 28, 1997 (Protocol number 589/97).

[43] *CLD* 2, 426; 4, 387; 5, 635; 10, 202–204.

[44] N. Halligan, "Readmission to the Seminary," *J* 20 (1960) 340–342.

in 1985) provided the universal guidelines to assist the national conferences in developing their particular programs.

In the United States *Interim Guidelines for Priestly Formation* were prepared in 1968. These were succeeded by the first edition of the *Program of Priestly Formation* approved by the Holy See and the conference in 1971 (c. 455, §1). This program was revised in subsequent editions in 1976, 1981, and 1992. All the editions reflected the collaboration among the bishops of the United States, together with personnel involved in priestly formation programs and other experts. The 1992 edition was based on the older ecclesiastical documents in addition to 1986 and 1988 documents from the Sacred Congregation for Catholic Education and a joint letter in 1990 from the same congregation and the Congregation for Institutes of Consecrated Life and Societies of Apostolic Life.[45]

This followed an apostolic visitation of seminaries called for by Pope John Paul II and begun in 1983. Additional sources used in preparing the 1992 fourth edition included the 1983 revised Code of Canon Law, the new 1985 edition of the *Ratio,* and various documents from the National Conference of Catholic Bishops, the 1990 synod of bishops, and the subsequent apostolic exhortation of Pope John Paul II, *Pastores dabo vobis.*[46]

---

[45] "Letter to the Bishops of the United States Concerning Free-Standing Seminaries," *Norms* II, 221–240; "Letter to the Bishops of the United States Concerning College-Level Formation of Diocesan Candidates," *Norms* II, 241–250; "Letter to the Bishops of the United States and Religious Provincials on the Formation of Religious Candidates for the Priesthood," *Norms* II, 251–262.

[46] Bishops' Committee on Priestly Formation Secretariat, *Spiritual Formation in the Catholic Seminary* (Washington, D.C.: NCCB, 1984); R. Gariboldi, *Pastoral Formation and Pastoral Field Education in the Catholic Seminary* (Washington, D.C.: NCCB, 1985); the 1990 synod of bishops' *Lineamenta* and *Instrumentum laboris* (see notes under c. 232). See also *PPF,* Preface, 1–8 for a listing of the Vatican II constitutions, decrees, and documents that underlie the *PPF* and various directives from the congregations of the Holy See, many of which may be found in vols. I and II of *Norms.* Today these episco-

The Eastern code calls on the proper authorities within the territorial boundaries of their own church or, by mutual agreement, a whole region, nation, or other churches *sui iuris,* to set forth more precisely the common law for seminaries. The tradition of one's own church *sui iuris* is to be kept in mind and the same authorities can change the program when needed (*CCEO* 330, §1). No mention is made of the Holy See's approval.

Particular Seminary Rule

Canon 243 — In addition, each seminary is to have its own rule, approved by the diocesan bishop, or, if it is an interdiocesan seminary, by the bishops involved, which is to adapt the norms of the program of priestly formation to particular circumstances and especially to determine more precisely the points of discipline which pertain to the daily life of the students and the order of the entire seminary.

In an exercise of the principle of subsidiarity, the diocesan or interdiocesan seminary itself is to draw up its own rule for daily life reflecting local or regional pastoral needs. This rule is to be based on the values found in the particular program mentioned in the previous canon. Only the approval of the diocesan bishop or bishops (in the case of an interdiocesan seminary) is required.

As in any formational institute, discipline and right order are central to the good of the seminary and of its members. Recognizing these needs, the Eastern code states that moderators, officials, teachers, counselors, and students are to "participate in the concerns of the rector especially in the observance of discipline of the seminary" (*CCEO* 337). This broader involvement adds a more inclusive tone to the Eastern code's call for a seminary to have its own statutes as well as its own directory which is to put into effect the norms of the

---

pal norms apply to all seminaries in the United States including those of religious communities preparing candidates for holy orders (c. 659).

program of formation of clerics. Both of these documents are to be approved by the appropriate authority.

Integration of Seminary Programs

Canon 244 — The spiritual formation and doctrinal instruction of the students in a seminary are to be arranged harmoniously and so organized that each student, according to his character, acquires the spirit of the gospel and a close relationship with Christ along with appropriate human maturity.

Inasmuch as through baptism the Christian faithful have been "made sharers in their own way in Christ's priestly, prophetic, and royal function" (c. 204, §1), and more so since "priests are commissioned in a unique way to continue Christ's mission as prophet, priest, and king" (*PPF* 33 and 48), it follows that preparing candidates to teach, to sanctify, and to lead is the object of the seminary formation process.

The importance of this formation and instruction is evident from the fact that before declaring a candidate worthy of the reception of orders, the rector, with the assistance of the faculty, must be able to testify that the candidate manifests evidence of a close relationship with Christ and a personal appropriation of the gospel as seen in his overall manner of living and praying. This presupposes an effort to coordinate the spiritual, intellectual, and pastoral aspects of seminary life, as the *Program of Priestly Formation* does. They are to be integrated so they may serve to lead each individual student to the human maturity required for the exercise of the threefold ministry demanded of a true shepherd of souls, the priest in the likeness of Christ (*OT* 4 and 12). E. Gilbert cites canon 1029 on the requisites for promotion to orders and describes it as "the heart of the law on candidates for orders."[47] That canon is linked very closely to this canon.

[47] *CLSA Com,* 725.

Spiritual Formation Program

Canon 245 — §1. Through their spiritual formation, students are to become equipped to exercise the pastoral ministry fruitfully and are to be formed in a missionary spirit; they are to learn that ministry always carried out in living faith and charity fosters their own sanctification. They also are to learn to cultivate those virtues which are valued highly in human relations so that they are able to achieve an appropriate integration between human and supernatural goods.

§2. Students are so to be formed that, imbued with love of the Church of Christ, they are bound by humble and filial charity to the Roman Pontiff, the successor of Peter, are attached to their own bishop as faithful co-workers, and work together with their brothers. Through common life in the seminary and through relationships of friendship and of association cultivated with others, they are to be prepared for fraternal union with the diocesan presbyterium whose partners they will be in the service of the Church.

Spiritual formation is given pride of place among the various aspects of seminary training, and this canon (together with canons 246 and 247) richly reflects the conciliar teachings and echoes the *Ratio* 44–58, especially 47, 49, and 51. It draws liberally on the council's concern for proper spiritual training and formation of those preparing for priestly service.[48]

Reiterating the universal call to holiness and to mission, the first paragraph emphasizes the importance of guiding candidates to appreciate that the way for them to holiness is by faithfully carrying out the duties that characterize their ministerial calling and define their mission. Canon 276,

[48] See Schuth, 139. In this nationwide study of theologates, the author found that almost every person interviewed stressed the centrality and importance of the personal and spiritual formation of students. See *OT* 8–12 and *PO passim,* especially 3, 8, and 9; C. Merces de Melo, "Priests and Priestly Formation in the 'Code of Canon Law,'" *Stud Can* 27 (1993) 463–464.

§2, 1° lists this fidelity to duty as the first step in the priest's pursuit of perfection.[49]

As for "those virtues which are valued highly in human relations," *Optatam totius* 11 describes them as "sincerity, a constant love of justice, fidelity to one's promises, courtesy in deed, modesty and charity in speech." *Presbyterorum ordinis* 3 provides a similar list, adding Paul's call to the faithful at Philippi to imitate him.[50]

The goals of paragraph two are further stressed in *Presbyterorum ordinis* 7 and 8 on priestly relations with bishops and the bond of priestly brotherhood. *Presbyterorum ordinis* 9 speaks of relations with the laity.[51] Canon 273 on the obligation of clerics to show reverence and obedience to the Supreme Pontiff and their own ordinary supports this canon. The "fraternal union with the diocesan presbyterium," spoken of here, "is also a constitutive factor of [the diocesan priesthood's] identity, mission, and spirituality" (*PPF* 53).

Spiritual Exercises in the Seminary

Canon 246 — §1. The eucharistic celebration is to be the center of the entire life of a seminary in such a way that, sharing in the very love of Christ, the students daily draw strength of spirit for apostolic work and for their spiritual life especially from this richest of sources.

§2. They are to be formed in the celebration of the liturgy of the hours by which the ministers of God pray to God in the name of the Church for all the people entrusted to them, and indeed, for the whole world.

§3. The veneration of the Blessed Virgin Mary, including the marian rosary, mental prayer, and other exercises of piety are to be fostered; through these, students are to acquire a spirit of prayer and gain strength in their vocation.

§4. Students are to become accustomed to approach the sacrament of penance frequently; it is also recommended that each have a director of his spiritual life whom he has freely chosen and to whom he can confidently open his conscience.

§5. Each year students are to make a spiritual retreat.

This canon spells out the initial steps essential to growth in a candidate's vocation and the means to support its exercise throughout life. As in paragraph one here, the *Program of Priestly Formation* also calls for the daily celebration of the Eucharist as part of every seminary and theologate program.[52]

The *Program of Priestly Formation* is more specific than paragraph two of this canon. It calls for the celebration of the liturgy of the hours, especially morning and evening prayer, on a daily basis for all programs.[53] Students are to be formed for the future official ministry of praying "to God in the name of the Church for all the people entrusted to them, and indeed, for the whole world."[54]

The norms in paragraph three on acquiring a spirit of prayer and on strengthening one's vocation are reiterated in the *Program of Priestly Formation* for every level of seminary and theologate life[55] as are those of paragraphs four and five on the sacrament of penance and a yearly retreat.[56]

---

[49] *PPF* 58–59.

[50] "Finally, brothers, whatever is true, whatever is honorable, whatever is just, whatever is pure, whatever is lovely, whatever is gracious, if there is any excellence and if there is anything worthy of praise, think about these things" (Phil 4:8). See also CFC *Directory* 70; *CLD* 9, 871–894; *PDV* 43–44; CDWDS, "Scrutinies Regarding the Suitability of Candidates for Orders," Enclosure V, nos. 2 and 8, March 28, 1997 (Protocol number 589/97).

[51] Bishops' Committee on Priestly Life and Ministry, *As One Who Serves* (Washington, D.C.: USCC, 1977) esp. 33–35.

[52] *PPF* 273 and 312. Other canons in the code call on pastors, religious, and members of secular institutes to see to it that the Eucharist is the center of parish and community life (cc. 528, §2, 608, and 719, §2). It is recommended that priests celebrate the Eucharist daily (c. 276, §2 and 904).

[53] *PPF* 153, 215, 273, 313, and 481.

[54] *PO* 5; *Ratio* 53; cc. 1173–1175.

[55] *PPF* 59, 73–78, 101, 126, 218, 275, 319, 325, and 423.

[56] *PPF* 276, 277, 316, and 317. Appropriate emphasis is given to respect for the conscience and free choice

Later in the code, in the section on the obligations of clerics, canon 276 repeats much of this canon highlighting the means to be used by the cleric in the pursuit of perfection, in addition to the faithful carrying out of the duties of his pastoral ministry.[57]

The Eastern code details the many diverse sources of power for the spiritual life and strength for apostolic labors (*CCEO* 346). This canon is a treasure trove of riches directed much more to the person of the seminarian than to the seminary's canonical structure. While our present canon rightly centers on the celebration of the Eucharist as the core of the entire life of the seminary, the Eastern code begins with a call for formation in the Holy Spirit, "as a familiar companion," that students might "dwell with Christ and . . . seek God in all things." The Divine Liturgy is "the font and culmination of seminary life as it is of the whole Christian life," and assiduous participation in it is exhorted.

Celibacy

Canon 247 — §1. Students are to be prepared through suitable education to observe the state of celibacy and are to learn to honor it as a special gift of God.

§2. They are duly to be informed of the duties and burdens which are proper to sacred ministers of the Church; no difficulty of the priestly life is to be omitted.

This canon speaks of the commitment to and observance of the obligation of priestly celibacy.

It stresses the need for proper preparation of the seminarian during his formation stage and is complemented by canon 277 on the obligation of a cleric to observe celibacy. Seminary education and formation in preparing a candidate to cooperate with this special gift of God must address human, Christian, and priestly maturity, all of which must build on emotional and sexual maturity. After careful seminary training the candidate for holy orders ought to be ready gratefully to "embrace this state, not only as a precept of ecclesiastical law, but as a precious gift of God" (*OT* 10).[58]

In a general way, paragraph two reminds the seminary rector, spiritual director, and faculty of their duty to inform and prepare candidates for all the challenges the priest will confront, no matter how difficult. The Catholic Church is a visible, often provocative, countercultural sign, and the individual who chooses the priestly state is considered to be an anomaly by those whose values and lifestyles are in opposition to what appears to many to be the prevailing culture. Sadly, as a result of a small percentage of priests who have fallen from grace and the wide notoriety given to sexual sins and crimes, priests in some areas may be looked upon suspiciously and so not be as welcome as they may have been in the past. Moreover, the shortage of priests means that the smaller number are expected to do much

---

[58] *OT* 10 does acknowledge the dignity of Christian marriage which the cleric chooses to renounce for the sake of the kingdom of heaven and a "greater measure of the blessedness promised by the Gospel." This same *OT* 10 along with *PO* 16 serve as conciliar bases for the many documents that address the matter of priestly celibacy. Among them are Paul VI, ency *Sacerdotalis caelibatus, AAS* 59 (1967) 657–697 and *TPS* 12 (1967) 291–319; SCCE, *A Guide to Formation in Priestly Celibacy,* April 11, 1974, *Norms* I, 155–205; Bishops' Committee on Priestly Life and Ministry, *A Reflection Guide on Human Sexuality and the Ordained Priesthood* (Washington, D.C.: USCC, 1983); NCCB, *Statement on Celibacy,* November 14, 1969 (Washington, D.C.: USCC, 1969); Third General Synod of Bishops, *The Ministerial Priesthood* (Washington, D.C.: USCC, 1972); CFC, *Directory,* 57–60; *Ratio* 48; *PDV* 50.

---

which each student has in regard to spiritual direction. For an explanation of the role and function of a "director of his spiritual life," see Bartchak, 298–309; also *Ratio* 55 and 56 and related canons 239, §2 above and 276, §2, 5°, 528, §2, 664, 719, §3, and 991.

[57] E. Pfnausch in *The Relationship Between Ministry and Holiness in the Life of the Diocesan Priest, CanLawStud* 543 (Washington, D.C.: Catholic University of America, 1994) reports that in c. 276, §2, 1° the code identified this ministry of the priest as the primary means of fulfilling his obligation to pursue holiness.

more. The resulting stresses on pastoral ministry can lead to physical and emotional problems. Also, the priest in the United States will increasingly find himself alone in his residence. Such loneliness is a very real test that needs to be addressed to prevent it from leading to unhealthy and painful depression.[59]

The Eastern code calls for candidates for ordination "to be properly taught the obligations of clerics and led to undertake and fulfill them magnanimously" (*CCEO* 355). Canons 373 and 374 of the Eastern code address celibacy.

Academic Program

Canon 248 — The doctrinal instruction given is to be directed so that students acquire an extensive and solid learning in the sacred disciplines along with a general culture appropriate to the necessities of place and time, in such way that, grounded in their own faith and nourished thereby, they are able to announce in a suitable way the teaching of the gospel to the people of their own time in a manner adapted to their understanding.

In accord with *Ratio* 59–81, this canon, together with canons 249–254 and the similar canon in the Eastern code (*CCEO* 347), is concerned with doctrinal instruction. The very nature of ordained ministry and "the challenge of the 'new evangelization' to which our Lord is calling the church on the threshold of the third millennium" (*PDV* 51) underscore the importance of intellectual formation. The *Program of Priestly Formation* 335 describes the goal of this formation as "conversion of mind and heart, which is the only sure foundation for a lifetime of teaching and preaching." In educating candidates for the priesthood it is important also that the seminary take into account the nature of the times as well as the pastoral and cultural needs of the region to be served by the priest in teaching and proclaiming the

gospel. On this matter of preaching, canon 769 provides an exhortation similar to what is presented above.[60]

Language Programs

Canon 249 — The program of priestly formation is to provide that students not only are carefully taught their native language but also understand Latin well and have a suitable understanding of those foreign languages which seem necessary or useful for their formation or for the exercise of pastoral ministry.

Several letters and constitutions from the popes and the Holy See have addressed the concerns expressed in this canon.[61] The same demands are made for both high school and college seminary programs in *Optatam totius* 13, which speaks as well of the necessity of studying the liturgical language of one's own rite and encourages knowledge of the languages of holy scripture and tradition. The *Program of Priestly Formation* 119 and 178 further recommends in high school seminaries the study of Greek and at all levels the Spanish language and Hispanic culture, as well as other pastorally appropriate languages and cultures. In recent years many seminaries have made available programs of "English as a Second Language" for the various new immigrants to the United States.[62]

Among the linguistic needs seminary authorities must address is the already serious language gap that results from the fact that seminarians today generally have grown up in communities

---

[59] McGrath, in *CLSGBI Com*, 142.

[60] In relation to this canon see *OT* 13–18; *GS* 58, 62; *AG* 16; *PDV* 51–56; *PPF* 333–396.

[61] Some examples in the last half of the twentieth century are John XXIII, apconst *Veterum sapientia,* Feb. 22, 1962, *AAS* 54 (1962) 129–135; *CLD* 5, 642–649; Paul VI, aplet *Summi Dei Verbum,* Nov. 4, 1963, *AAS* 55 (1963) 993–1003; *TPS* 9 (1963–1964) 239–250; Paul VI, *mp Studia latinitatis,* Feb. 22, 1964, *AAS* 56 (1964) 225–231.

[62] *Ratio* 66–67.

where the vernacular is used extensively and practically exclusively in liturgical celebrations. Latin is no longer heard in the local church and, moreover, is rarely a required course in public or parochial schools. Consequently, the understanding and use of the Latin language have declined dramatically, where they have not disappeared altogether. Candidates come to seminaries today with little or, more often, no background or experience in the Latin language. This is frequently accompanied by lack of a desire to learn it. There are, of course, exceptions and they do take on the challenge.[63]

More to the point, however, this canon once again requires that all candidates for the priesthood understand Latin and that provision be made for such studies in an episcopal conference's program of priestly formation. Articles 119 and 178 of the *Program of Priestly Formation* comply with this canon.

Time Requirements for Education for the Priesthood

Canon 250 — The philosophical and theological studies which are organized in the seminary itself can be pursued either successively or conjointly, in accord with the program of priestly formation. These studies are to encompass at least six full years in such a way that the time dedicated to philosophical disciplines equals two full years and to theological studies four full years.

The time requirement for proper formation is specified here, and the same is found in the Eastern code with the directive that in the philosophical-theological courses the relationship be shown "between all the disciplines and their coherent arrangement" (*CCEO* 348). The requirements of this canon cannot be abbreviated except with the explicit permission of the Congregation for Catholic Education (*PPF* 263 and *PB* 112–113).

[63] Hemrick and Walsh, *Seminarians in the Nineties,* 61.

Besides this canon's time requirements for studies of philosophy and theology,[64] a new pretheology program called for by the Holy Father and the 1990 synod of bishops is in effect in most seminaries. Recognizing the fact that many candidates today enter a seminary later in life with more professional but less church experience, the pretheology program is structured for college graduates with no or insufficient credits in philosophy as well as those judged in need of basic spiritual and human formation before studying theology.[65]

The Study of Philosophy

Canon 251 — Philosophical instruction must be grounded in the perennially valid philosophical heritage and also take into account philosophical investigation over the course of time. It is to be taught in such a way that it perfects the human development of the students, sharpens their minds, and makes them better able to pursue theological studies.

This canon is taken from *Optatam totius* 15 which provides directions on fostering the students' human and intellectual growth and, among other things, stimulating them, "to perceive the connection between philosophical arguments and the mysteries of salvation which theology considers in the higher light of faith."[66] Also taken from *Optatam totius* are the words "the perennially

[64] *Ratio* 42, 60, 70–81; SCCE, *The Study of Philosophy in Seminaries,* 1972; *Norms* I, 97–107; *SapC* 74.1; *Norms* I, 242; c. 1032, §1.

[65] 1990 synod, "Overview of the Synod Proposals," *Origins* 20 (November 8, 1990) 353–354. The synod fathers called for a preparatory period, "the so-called propaedeutic year." *PDV* 62 reiterates the bishops' concern; also *PPF* 13, 14, and 209–248, which are directed toward the formation program at the pre-theology level and 524 relative to flexibility in adapting the program to the needs of the individual student; R. Malone, "What Miracles Should Pre-Theology Programs Accomplish?" *Seminarium* 36 (October-December 1996) 647–665.

[66] *Ratio* 70–75.

valid philosophical heritage," which are found in Pius XII's encyclical *Humani generis*. They refer to the patrimony found in the Church's traditional philosophical cornerstones, the principles of St. Thomas Aquinas who is cited by name in the next canon.[67] Appropriate examination is to be made also of contemporary philosophical investigations as well as those of past eras.

The Eastern code has a similar norm but with the added goal of philosophical formation making students "more suitable for carrying out the ministry by a dialogue with the learned people of this age" (*CCEO* 349).

The Study of Theology

Canon 252 — §1. Theological instruction is to be imparted in the light of faith and under the leadership of the magisterium in such a way that the students understand the entire Catholic doctrine grounded in divine revelation, gain nourishment for their own spiritual life, and are able properly to announce and safeguard it in the exercise of the ministry.

§2. Students are to be instructed in sacred scripture with special diligence in such a way that they acquire a comprehensive view of the whole of sacred scripture.

§3. There are to be classes in dogmatic theology, always grounded in the written word of God together with sacred tradition; through these, students are to learn to penetrate more intimately the mysteries of salvation, especially with St. Thomas as a teacher. There are also to be classes in moral and pastoral theology, canon law, liturgy, ecclesiastical history, and other auxiliary and special disciplines, according to the norm of the prescripts of the program of priestly formation.

This canon is drawn from *Optatam totius* 16, which provides a more detailed ordering of the

wide scope of subjects to be treated in the theological formation of future priests. For the United States, the *Program for Priestly Formation* 364–396 lays down the norms to be followed in establishing a seminary's curriculum for the intellectual formation of its candidates. These adhere closely to the canon's concerns for a proper and adequate theological formation, guided by the magisterium with a special emphasis on sacred scripture and the teachings of St. Thomas and the requirement in paragraph three that provision be made for various other subjects and disciplines.[68]

The Eastern code speaks of teaching the theological disciplines without enumerating them by name and, along with the Latin canon, stresses sacred scripture, calling it "the soul of all theology" influencing all the sacred disciplines. The canon also highlights the teaching of both liturgy and ecumenism (*CCEO* 350).

As St. Thomas finds his way into our present canon, the Eastern code calls on teachers of sacred sciences to follow in the footsteps of the "holy fathers and doctors highly praised by the church, especially of the East," and to draw from the eminent doctrinal treasury handed down by them (*CCEO* 340, §3).

Seminary Professors

Canon 253 — §1. The bishop or bishops concerned are to appoint to the function of teacher in philosophical, theological, and juridic disciplines only those who are outstanding in virtue and have obtained a doctorate or licentiate from a university or faculty recognized by the Holy See.

§2. Care is to be taken that different teachers are appointed to teach sacred scripture, dogmatic theology, moral theology, liturgy, philosophy,

---

[67] *CLD* 6 (1963–1967) 252; *Humani generis,* August 12, 1950, *AAS* 42 (1950) 561–578, and *Catholic Mind* 48 (1950) 688–700.

[68] In connection with the subject matter of this canon see also *DV* 23–24; *Ratio* 76–81; SCCE, instr *The Theological Formation of Future Priests,* February 22, 1976, *Norms* I, 61–95; SCCE, letter *On the Teaching of Canon Law to Those Preparing to Be Priests,* April 2, 1975, *Norms* I, 145–151; SCCE, instr *On Liturgical Formation in Seminaries,* June 3, 1979, *Norms* I, 109–144.

canon law, ecclesiastical history, and other disciplines which must be taught according to their proper methodology.

§3. The authority mentioned in §1 is to remove a teacher who is gravely deficient in his or her function.

The concerns of *Optatam totius* 5 and 18 for competent educators "chosen from among the best" are reflected in this canon. The bishop or bishops are to appoint an able faculty, each member with appropriate academic credentials in his or her own field, together with evident virtue, and evaluate them (*PPF* 497) in their carrying out of their responsibilities. Seven distinct fields are mentioned in paragraph two with reference to other appropriate disciplines that need to be taught "according to their proper methodology." The specific requirement that these individuals hold a canonical degree from a university or faculty recognized by the Holy See (see cc. 815–821) is reiterated in the *Program of Priestly Formation* 486 as a condition of service.[69]

If a teacher proves to be gravely deficient, he or she is to be removed, mindful of the protection of rights provided for in canon 221. Each seminary's faculty manual should be more precise regarding this rather general charge. A teacher who is dismissed and considers himself or herself to be aggrieved may have recourse against such an action.[70]

The Eastern code speaks of teachers' qualifications only in terms of "suitable academic degrees." However, it encourages cooperation among all teachers and moderators to bring about unity of faith and formation among all their various disciplines (*CCEO* 340). Fidelity to doctrine and humble submission to the magisterium and supervision of the Church are required of teachers since they have been given a mandate to teach by ecclesiastical authority (*CCEO* 351).

Sapientia christiana 27.1 and the *Program of Priestly Formation* 485 require as well that a canonical mission be given by the appropriate authority following the professor's profession of faith and oath of fidelity.[71]

Integration of Academic Work and Teaching Methods

Canon 254 — §1. In giving instruction in their disciplines, teachers are to have a constant concern for the intimate unity and harmony of the entire doctrine of the faith so that students find that they learn one science. For this to be realized more suitably, there is to be someone in the seminary who directs the entire curriculum of studies.

§2. Students are to be instructed in such a way that they also become qualified to examine questions by their own appropriate research and with scientific methodology; therefore, there are to be assignments in which the students learn to pursue certain studies through their own efforts under the direction of the teachers.

The integration of academic work is one of the concerns of *Optatam totius* 5 in its call to the seminary faculty to "cultivate the closest harmony of spirit and action." A similar theme is found in this canon.[72]

---

[69] *Ratio* 34 speaks of the equivalent to the degree mentioned above. SCCE, *Norms of Application for the Correct Implementation of the Apostolic Constitution Sapientia Christiana* 17 makes allowance for a teacher with a doctorate that is not a canonical degree as long as he/she has "at least a canonical licentiate." On the canonical degree see *Norms* I, 248, art. 7 and 250, art. 17. See also CCE, *Directives Concerning the Preparation of Seminary Educators* (Rome: Vatican, 1993) 6–16. It acknowledges the scarcity of educators and offers initiatives toward pedagogical renewal to strengthen the life of seminaries.

[70] Canons 1732–1734; *Comm* 14 (1982) 55 at c. 106, §3.

[71] Canon 833; CDF, instr *Donum veritatis* 22, *AAS* 82 (1990) 1550–1570 and *Instruction on the Ecclesial Vocation of the Theologian* (Washington, D.C.: USCC, 1990). For the profession and oath see *Origins* 18 (March 16, 1969) 661–663. On the notion of "canonical mission" see Deeley, *The Mandate for Those Who Teach Theology*, 2–8.

[72] SCCE, *The Theological Formation of Future Priests*, 121–127, *Norms* I, 89–90.

In order to achieve this goal, seminaries ordinarily have an officer who is known as the academic dean or called by some other title. In cooperation with the rector, this dean is to direct the faculty's concerns for unity and harmony of doctrine and the formation of the curriculum into a unified, internally coherent whole as called for in this canon.[73]

Optatam totius 17 further calls for a revision of teaching methods so that doctrinal training is not merely a communicating of ideas. As this canon indicates, students, under the guidance of their teachers, need to be enabled to be more self-reliant in pursuing their studies and research.[74]

There is a related canon in the Eastern code (*CCEO* 340, §2).

Pastoral Program

Canon 255 — Although the entire formation of students in the seminary has a pastoral purpose, strictly pastoral instruction is to be organized through which students learn the principles and skills which, attentive also to the needs of place and time, pertain to the exercise of the ministry of teaching, sanctifying, and governing the people of God.

This canon, together with canons 256–258, addresses the specific principles and skills related to pastoral ministry that are to be learned by seminarians. *Optatam totius* 19 speaks of "the pastoral preoccupation which should characterize every feature of the students' training" and lists papal documents on the life, qualities, and training of priests. To this list today can be added the writings of Pope John Paul II, most especially the much studied *Pastores dabo vobis*.[75]

In the wake of the Second Vatican Council and its emphasis on pastoral formation of seminarians, a significant recent development is the whole new life taken on by this kind of training. An entire in-dustry has grown up in what now is generally referred to as field education. It has become an integral part of the seminary curriculum and is accredited as such.[76]

Field education has been approached in varied ways by different seminaries. Some require a pastoral year apart from the institutional seminary setting, which period of time may be separate from or included in the six-year requirement. Others require parish internship for some months preceding and/or following ordination to the diaconate. Still others require a certain number of pastoral work hours each week in supervised programs throughout the theologate.[77]

The Eastern code adapts the Latin code's canon on pastoral formation to its own students, whether celibate or married (*CCEO* 352, §1).

Instruction in Matters Pertaining to the Sacred Ministry

Canon 256 — §1. Students are to be instructed diligently in those things which in a particular manner pertain to the sacred ministry, especially in catechetical and homiletic skills, in divine worship and particularly the celebration of the sacraments, in relationships with people, even non-Catholics or non-believers, in the administration of a parish, and in the fulfillment of other functions.

---

[73] *Ratio* 27 and 90; *PPF* 351, 466, 467.
[74] *Ratio* 90–91.
[75] *PDV* 58; *OT* 4; *Ratio* 94–99.

[76] For material on pastoral formation through Christian service projects and apostolic programs in high schools, college seminaries, and related programs, as well as for directives on pastoral experiences in pre-theology formation and supervised theological field education in the theologate, see *PPF* 121–124, 180–190, 242–244, 397–440. For more on pastoral theology, see SCCE, *The Theological Formation of Future Priests,* February 22, 1976, *Norms* I, 86; Gariboldi, *Pastoral Formation;* The Center for Human Development, *Formation of Priests: The Challenge of the 1990s* (Washington, D.C.: The Center for Human Development, 1990).

[77] *PPF* 190 encourages seminarians to see the relationship of this apostolic service to prayer, community life, spiritual formation, and the seminary's academic program. See also the norms in *PPF* 180–190, 242–244, 397–440.

§2. Students are to be instructed about the needs of the universal Church in such a way that they have solicitude for the promotion of vocations and for missionary, ecumenical, and other more urgent questions, including social ones.

Optatam totius 19 lists various matters in which seminarians are to be instructed, and this canon draws on it, capturing the vast "job" description of the priest who in an appropriate manner must develop competencies that enable him to be, insofar as possible, "all things to all people in order to save at least some of them" (1 Cor 9:22).[78]

Vatican II's concerns that all should generously foster vocational choices which will assist the whole Church in carrying out her essential missionary labors and that all should cooperate in the ecumenical movement's work of restoring unity among the followers of Christ find mention in this canon and in the following one on instructing students preparing for the priesthood.[79]

Other urgent issues, including the many demands of justice and peace in our country and in our world and the need for a distinctly Christian witness in response, are to be addressed. The social doctrine of the Church is a valuable source for such instruction.[80]

The particular needs of a region where priests are to serve in the name of the Church may well suggest other areas in which specialized training needs to be provided and pastoral skills need to be developed.[81]

The Eastern code also mentions the above areas in addition to instruction in the instruments of social communication, psychology, and pastoral sociology (*CCEO* 352, §2 and §3). The *Program for Priestly Formation* 163 includes these in the section on intellectual formation in a college seminary or related program.

The Missionary and Evangelizing Spirit

Canon 257 — §1. The instruction of students is to provide that they have solicitude not only for the particular church in whose service they are to be incardinated but also for the universal Church, and that they show themselves prepared to devote themselves to particular churches which are in grave need.

§2. The diocesan bishop is to take care that clerics intending to move from their own particular church to a particular church of another region are suitably prepared to exercise the sacred ministry there, that is, that they learn the language of the region and understand its institutions, social conditions, usages, and customs.

Students for the priesthood are to be provided with an awareness, education, and appreciation of both the particular and the universal Church. They must manifest a care and concern for the "universal mission of salvation 'to the ends of the earth'" (Acts 1:8; *PO* 10) and a consequent willingness to serve where the priest is most needed.[82]

Canon 271 also addresses the needs of a particular region laboring under a grave lack of clergy and the obligation of a diocesan bishop in circumstances where one of his priests, "prepared in spirit to preach the Gospel everywhere" (*OT* 20), seeks permission to move to such a region. This is in response to Vatican II's emphasis on the universal dimension of the priesthood and its solicitude for a proper distribution of priests. The council called for the rules about incardination and excardination to be revised in order to answer more effectively the pastoral needs of today (*PO* 10).

---

[78] *Ratio* 94–95.

[79] *Ratio* 96.

[80] See *CCC* 2419–2449 and, among other papal writings, John Paul II, ency *Centesimus annus,* May 1, 1991, *AAS* 83 (1991) 793–867; *Origins* 21 (May 16, 1991) 1–24.

[81] Paragraph one of this canon together with *Ratio* 94 strike a practical note in calling for training in parish administration, an area most seminaries have not been addressing, often due to "course overload."

[82] See *OT* 20; *LG* 17; *Ratio* 96; SCC, *Directive Norms for Cooperation among Local Churches and for a Better Distribution of the Clergy,* March 25, 1980, *AAS* 72 (1980) 343–364, esp. 360–363; *CLD* 9, 760–787, esp. 782–786.

Paragraph two of canon 257 logically follows paragraph one and faithfully reflects various conciliar and postconciliar documents, e.g., *Presbyterorum ordinis* 10; *Christus Dominus* 6; *Ad gentes* 25; *Ecclesiae sanctae* I, 1–3.[83]

Field Education Programs

Canon 258 — In order that students also learn the art of exercising the apostolate in practice, during the course of studies and especially during times of vacation they are to be initiated into pastoral practice by means of appropriate activities, determined by judgment of the ordinary, adapted to the age of the students and the conditions of the places, and always under the direction of a skilled priest.

A major component in the seminary's course of studies is the pastoral implementation of what is being learned by the students. As mentioned above under canon 255, given the conciliar emphasis on pastoral concerns, there has been a significant concentration on pastoral field experiences. The responsibility for directing these activities falls to the post-Vatican II programs of field education, through which seminaries attempt to respond to this canon and canon 255. Candidates at all levels are to experience supervised pastoral practice in sites outside of the seminary.[84]

The reference to vacations as times for initiation into pastoral practice is echoed in *Ratio* 97–99. Summer months often are utilized as opportunities for experiential learning on the part of seminarians, under priestly supervision, as called for by this canon. *Ratio* 99 further allows for other experts to supervise where necessary or appropriate.[85]

In a similar fashion, the Eastern code calls for strengthening pastoral formation with particular emphasis on a pastoral internship during the period of philosophical-theological formation and a diaconal internship before ordination to the priesthood (*CCEO* 353).

Administration of the Seminary

Canon 259 — §1. The diocesan bishop or, for an interdiocesan seminary, the bishops involved are competent to decide those things which pertain to the above-mentioned governance and administration of the seminary.

§2. The diocesan bishop or, for an interdiocesan seminary, the bishops involved are to visit the seminary frequently, to watch over the formation of their own students as well as the philosophical and theological instruction taught in the seminary, and to keep themselves informed about the vocation, character, piety, and progress of the students, especially with a view to the conferral of sacred ordination.

The bishop (or, in the case of a regional or interdiocesan seminary, the group of all the bishops concerned) remains central in the making of decisions for his (or their) seminary. The bishop's primary role in this regard has been a tradition that dates back to the Council of Trent.[86]

Over the past century, however, the Holy See more and more has taken on the direction of the diocesan seminary. In 1983 a study of priestly formation mandated by the Sacred Congregation for Catholic Education began with a visitation of all seminaries in the United States. In 1986 the con-

[83] *CLD* 6, 267.

[84] See Gariboldi, *Pastoral Formation; Ratio* 98; and the many citations under "Pastoral Formation" and "Field Education" in the index of *PPF*.

[85] See also *PPF* 243, which calls for "qualified supervision" on the pre-theology level; 416, which calls for teaching supervisory skills to those who have on-site re-

sponsibility for overseeing pastoral assignments of seminarians; 420 and 436, which speak of the seminary's direction on the theologate level of competent, trained, on-site pastoral supervisors who have respect for the priesthood; and 425, 507, and 534, which address summer placements. For more on field education see Schuth, 191–200.

[86] See J. White's introduction to Schuth's *Reason for the Hope*, 11.

gregation's prefect, Cardinal William Baum, wrote to the American bishops, expressing general satisfaction with their theologates and offering useful commendations and recommendations, especially the need for a clearer concept of the meaning of ordained priesthood.[87]

This canon's second paragraph spells out the responsibilities as well as the rights of those bishops mentioned in paragraph one. While the canon calls for "frequent" visitation, in practice this may be more an ideal than a reality since generally in the order of things it is the rector, or perhaps a vocation director or another delegate appointed by the bishop or bishops who will carry out these specific duties. This delegate must report back to those bishops relative to the students' formation and readiness in the light of the canonical requirements for ordination mandated in canons 1026–1039.

The Eastern code speaks of the same kind of vigilance on the part of the appropriate authority (*CCEO* 356, §2).

The Rector

Canon 260 — In carrying out their proper functions, all must obey the rector, to whom it belongs to care for the daily supervision of the seminary according to the norm of the program of priestly formation and of the rule of the seminary.

The canon is clear: faculty, students, and staff are to obey the rector who is charged with the daily administration of the seminary under the authority of the bishop and in accord with the *Program of Priestly Formation* and the local seminary rules.[88]

The *Program of Priestly Formation* 459–464 (and other places listed in the index under "Rector") provides greater detail about the role of the rector; and each seminary's specific rule is expected to do the same.[89] Ultimately, all are responsible to the bishop, who has the authority to hire or remove members of the teaching and administrative staffs (c. 253, §3).

Duties of the Rector, Director of Studies, and Teachers

Canon 261 — §1. The rector of a seminary and, under his authority, the moderators and teachers for their part are to take care that the students observe exactly the norms prescribed by the program of priestly formation and by the rule of the seminary.

§2. The rector of a seminary and the director of studies are carefully to provide that the teachers properly perform their function according to the prescripts of the program of priestly formation and of the rule of the seminary.

The canon emphasizes the need for faithful observance by all of the norms of the *Program of Priestly Formation* and the rules of the local seminary. The rector, with the cooperation of the faculty and staff, is charged with the responsibility of seeing to this observance on the part of the students.

The rector is further charged, with the help of the dean of studies (c. 254, §1), to supervise the carrying out of duties by the faculty in accord with the prescribed norms and rules. Seminaries ought to have a faculty manual which, among other purposes, provides for evaluation of individual faculty

---

[87] W. Baum, "State of U.S. Free-Standing Seminaries," and Marshall, "Strengths and Weaknesses." With regard to a seminary owned and operated by an exempt religious community, attention is called to *Relationship of the Local Ordinary to the Seminary Owned and Operated by Religious, Norms* I, 315–326. See also *PPF* 6, 12, 38, 87–89, 138, 252, and 255; *PDV* 31 and 74.

[88] P. Golden writes, "This in no way relieves the rector from the responsibility of exercising collegiality and

subsidiarity" (*CLSA Com,* 189). *Ratio* 29 states: "It is the rector's part to keep the staff together, and he should work closely with them in brotherly charity." For more on the particular importance of this office, see C. Peterson, *Spiritual Care in Diocesan Seminaries, CanLawStud* 342 (Washington, D.C.: Catholic University of America, 1966) 74–116.

[89] See commentary on c. 239 above.

performance by the rector, the academic dean, perhaps some other faculty members, and some representative students. All of these evaluations are to be shared with the faculty member for his or her own consideration and benefit.

Exemption from Parochial Jurisdiction

Canon 262 — A seminary is to be exempt from parochial governance. The rector of the seminary or his delegate fulfills the office of pastor for all those who are in the seminary, except for matrimonial matters and without prejudice to the prescript of can. 985.

"All those who are in the seminary" may be served by the rector, who for them holds the office of pastor. P. Golden observes that this exemption is a territorial one, since the seminary property is exempt from the parochial governance of the territorial pastor. The canon applies equally to those who live in the seminary and those who remain in the seminary for only a portion of the day as staff employees usually do.[90]

Canon 985, which is mentioned here, prohibits the rector from hearing a student's confession unless the latter freely asks in a particular case. The present canon also excepts those matrimonial matters addressed in canons 1063–1072 on preparation for marriage and canons 1108–1123 on required formal assistance at marriage. These remain under the jurisdiction of the territorial pastor. Otherwise, by virtue of this canon, the rector has the power to hear the confessions of others, the right and duty to administer the sacrament of the anointing of the sick and Viaticum, to celebrate funerals, and to dispense from the laws of fast and abstinence, the obligation of observing a holy day (c. 1245), and an oath or a vow (cc. 1196 and 1203).[91]

Canon 336, §2 of the Eastern code is largely comparable to Latin canon 262.

Financial Support

Canon 263 — The diocesan bishop or, for an interdiocesan seminary, the bishops involved in a way determined by them through common counsel must take care that provision is made for the establishment and maintenance of the seminary, the support of the students, the remuneration of the teachers, and the other needs of the seminary.

The obligation to provide for the financing and maintenance of the seminary is to be carried out by the diocesan bishop or, for an interdiocesan seminary, by the bishops involved. In the case of an interdiocesan seminary, the contribution of each should not be based simply on the number of students from a specific diocese but rather on the actual financial resources available to each diocese.[92]

Seminary Tax

Canon 264 — §1. In addition to the offering mentioned in can. 1266, a bishop can impose a tax in the diocese to provide for the needs of the seminary.
§2. All ecclesiastical juridic persons, even private ones, which have a seat in the diocese are subject to the tax for the seminary unless they are sustained by alms alone or in fact have a college of students or teachers to promote the common good of the Church. A tax of this type must be general, in proportion to the revenues of those who are subject to it, and determined according to the needs of the seminary.

The bishop, after having consulted with both the finance council and the presbyteral council, can levy a general tax (c. 1263) on juridic persons (cc. 115–116) to raise money for the seminary. Such a tax must be moderate and in proportion to the income of the persons being taxed and the needs of the seminary.

---

[90] Golden, in *CLSA Com,* 189 and footnotes 115–117.

[91] Ibid.; T. Bouscaren, A. Ellis, and F. Korth, *Canon Law,* 4th ed. (Milwaukee: Bruce Publishing Co., 1963) 762; see also c. 530.

[92] *Comm* 14 (1982) 60 at c. 116a. For more on finances see Schuth, 73–82.

Excepted are those supported solely by alms (a contemplative monastery) and those who operate a college for the common good (house of formation or of studies run by a religious community).[93]

---

[93] McGrath, in *CLSGBI Com*, 150.

Canon 1266 allows the bishop to order the taking up of special collections for specific projects, one of which could be the maintenance of the seminary. Usually a special weekend is set aside for this purpose.

The Eastern code addresses in a similar vein the matters found in canons 263–264 (*CCEO* 341).

BIBLIOGRAPHY

Official Sources

CCE. *Directives Concerning the Preparation of Seminary Educators*. Rome: Libreria Editrice Vaticana, 1993.

CFC. *Directory on the Ministry and Life of Priests*. Vatican City: Libreria Editrice Vaticana, 1994.

Some Additional Works

Center for Human Development. *The Challenge of the 1990s: Formation of Priests*. Washington, D.C.: CARA, 1990.

Hemrick, E., and J. Walsh. *Seminarians in the Nineties: A National Study of Seminarians in Theology*. Washington, D.C.: NCEA, 1993.

Schner, G. *Education for Ministry: Reform and Renewal in Theological Education*. Kansas City, Mo.: Sheed & Ward, 1993.

White, J. *The Diocesan Seminary in the United States: A History from the 1870s to the Present*. Notre Dame, Ind.: University of Notre Dame, 1989.

Wister, R., ed. *Psychology, Counseling, and the Seminarian*. Washington, D.C.: NCEA, Seminary Department, 1994.

CHAPTER II
THE ENROLLMENT, OR INCARDINATION,
OF CLERICS
[cc. 265–272]

Incardination is the canonical institution of permanent attachment of bishops, priests, and deacons to a particular church or other ecclesiastical entity for the primary purpose of the service of the people of God. The root of the word "incardination," *cardo,* "hinge," provides a general understanding of the canonical implications. Clerics are linked to the church as a door is attached to a wall; the life of the Church hinges, through incardination, on the service of the ordained ministers who provide the fullness of the sacramental life to the people of God. All clerics are ordained for service; they serve in collaboration with one another, under the direction and authority of ecclesiastical leadership, and always in a bond of service of a particular group of the people of God.[1] Book II, part one, title III, chapter 2 presents the current legislation on incardination: its necessity for all clerics beginning at diaconate, the entities to which clerics are attached, procedures and requirements for moving permanently or temporarily to another place or entity for service, and even an automatic method to change incardination.

The 1983 code uses the two terms *adscriptio,* enrollment, and *incardinatio,* incardination. The 1990 Eastern code only speaks of "enrollment."[2]

The juridic effects are the same. It is first established at diaconate (c. 266) and is changed only with the procedures found in these canons.

Incardination was first articulated in universal church law in canons 111–117 of the 1917 code, but it has been an ancient principle in the history of the Church. Canons 265–272 contain the same basic principles of incardination as the former law, but are innovative in legislating the competent structures for incardinating clerics. This is in response to the teaching of Vatican II.[3] The conciliar sources and principles must be primary in interpreting the current canonical legislation on incardination. The council fathers explicitly insisted that the pastoral ministry of clerics be clearly seen as connected with service, and that this ministry is not only service of the local churches, but also service of the universal Church. Whereas the former law emphasized the disciplinary nature of incardination through the bishop's or superior's vigilance and control, Vatican II returned to the more basic pastoral sense of incardination for the purpose of service. As will be seen, the canons on excardination and temporary service to churches in need are expressions of these conciliar directives.[4] Postconciliar legislation implementing the wishes of the council fathers has been incorporated into the canons on incardination.[5] These canons have indeed provided processes to facilitate the service of

[1] For canonical commentaries on these canons see J. Lynch, in *CLSA Com,* 191–198; L. Chiappetta, in *Chiappetta Com,* 146–161; A. McGrath, in *CLSGBI Com,* 150–155; T. Rincón Pérez, in *Pamplona ComEng,* 223–228. Very helpful and practical is the *Clergy Procedural Handbook* (cited hereafter as *CPH*), ed. R. Calvo and N. Klinger (Washington, D.C.: CLSA, 1992). Most of this book is a commentary on the various implications of the institute of incardination. See esp. 6–49, 67–97.

[2] *CCEO* 357–366. See commentary in *Pospishil Com,* 280–283. Note that different terms are used in the Eastern code: incardination is consistently called enrollment (*adscriptio*) and excardination is called dismissal (*dimissio*).

[3] See *CD* 6, 28–29; *PO* 10.

[4] These canons were discussed during the 1917 code revision process by two study groups, *de clericis* and *de sacra hierarchia;* both groups made explicit efforts to incorporate conciliar teaching in the revised legislation. For reports on discussions see session I (*de clericis*), October 24–28, 1966, *Comm* 16 (1984) 158–167; session 13 (*de sacra hierarchia*), April 9–14, 1973 [not reported]. A synthesis of the work of both groups can be found in *Comm* 33 (1971) 187–191.

[5] These sources will be noted under the appropriate canon.

priests and deacons in other parts of their countries or the world, and bishops and superiors have found that these processes work well. Although no new legislation has been promulgated since the 1983 code,[6] the Holy See remains concerned about the better distribution of priests throughout the world and continues not only to monitor the proportion of priests to people but to provide priests, bishops, and superiors with means of temporary or permanent service.

Necessity[7]

Canon 265 — Every cleric must be incardinated either in a particular church or personal prelature, or in an institute of consecrated life or society endowed with this faculty, in such a way that unattached or transient clerics are not allowed at all.

Canon 265 states the canonical principle that incardination is absolutely necessary for every cleric (bishop, priest, and deacon).[8] Since earliest times the Church has dealt with the problem of unattached clerics, called *vagi,* who roamed from church to church with no accountability to ecclesiastical authority, often causing scandal to the faithful.[9] Incardination combines the traditional understanding of ordination as a commitment to service as well as the Church's obligation to support those who serve it in ordained ministries.[10] No "contract" is required for those ordained to serve the Church. However, incardination fosters and protects the rights and obligations of church communities, priests and deacons, and church leaders. It is in this light that three purposes of incardination can be seen.[11]

First, the faith community has a right to the spiritual riches of the Church to be provided by stable ministers committed to serving a particular community. The law assures the presence of clerics, "public servants," who do not move about but who are bound to the community, live there, and get to know their people. Because only those necessary and useful for service are incardinated, the community is assured of properly equipped ministers who are able to serve them well (see c. 266, §1). The community also assumes responsibility to provide for those things to which the clergy are entitled from the Church, e.g., education, remuneration, benefits, etc.

Second, incardination guarantees the cleric permanent employment as long as he possesses the necessary qualities for service. With his dedication to ministry as an incardinated cleric, he is also assured a permanent source of sustenance (c. 281). Incardination, in theory, guarantees that his rights will be safeguarded (c. 384); these are rights based not only in universal law but also in particular law, e.g., personnel policies, formation, continuing education, etc.

Third, bishops and superiors have a right to depend on the assistance and cooperation of a stable group of priests and deacons who will not be absent for long periods of time and who will not abandon service for ambitious or inappropriate reasons.[12] Through incardination the clergy assume the obligations of ordained ministers (cc. 273–289), monitored by the appropriate vigilance of the competent authority. Incardination is an effective structure for providing accountability for the clergy; when corrective measures are taken, they cannot flee elsewhere.

---

[6] The two directories for priests and deacons have juridically binding force but contain no new legislation. See CFC, *Directory for the Life and Ministry of Priests,* January 31, 1994 (Washington, D.C.: USCC, 1994) n. 26, and CCE and CFC, *Directory for the Ministry and Life of Permanent Deacons,* February 22, 1998 (Washington, D.C.: USCC, 1998) n. 2.

[7] Cf. *CCEO* 357, §1.

[8] *CIC* 111; *PO* 10 *CIC An.*

[9] For a full treatment of the history of incardination see J. T. McBride, *Incardination and Excardination of Seculars: An Historical Synopsis and Commentary, CanLawStud* 145 (Washington, D.C.: Catholic University of America, 1941). Also see J. Lynch, "History of Incardination," in *CPH,* 6–27.

[10] Canon 281.

[11] McBride, 37–39; J. Donlon, "Incardination and Excardination," *CLSAP* (1991) 124–153; J. Provost, in *CPH,* 28–36.

[12] See *LG* 28–29.

Although there is no mention of the perpetual and absolute character of incardination as in canon 112 of the 1917 code, it is permanent and definitive, while allowing for the flexibility called for by the council.

Original Incardination[13]

Canon 266 — §1. Through the reception of the diaconate, a person becomes a cleric and is incardinated in the particular church or personal prelature for whose service he has been advanced.

§2. Through the reception of the diaconate, a perpetually professed religious or a definitively incorporated member of a clerical society of apostolic life is incardinated as a cleric in the same institute or society unless, in the case of societies, the constitutions establish otherwise.

§3. Through the reception of the diaconate, a member of a secular institute is incardinated in the particular church for whose service he has been advanced unless he is incardinated in the institute itself by virtue of a grant of the Apostolic See.

Diaconate is the "door" through which clerics are incardinated. Paul VI determined that a person becomes a cleric at diaconate.[14] Canon 266 states that original or first incardination occurs at diaconate for all clerics and gives examples for each type of cleric.

The law attempts to ensure that only fitting candidates who are necessary and useful for service are ordained; through incardination they are permanently committed to exercise ministry in the particular church. When first admitting candidates to the seminary, church authority must judge them capable of permanent dedication (c. 241). Before incardination, at ordination to the diaconate, there are several canonical requirements (cc. 1024–1039) which include proper formation, fitting age to assume the responsibilities of the

clerical state, possession of necessary qualities, and proof of freedom. If the deacon candidate is married, his wife must give consent. Finally, the candidate must be judged useful for ministry (c. 1025, §2); he is accepted because there is a need for his ministry upon incardination. The candidate himself must be committed "perpetually" to serve the Church (c. 1036). He is free to be incardinated in the diocese of his domicile or to serve in another place of his choice where he intends to "devote himself" (c. 1016).

A secular cleric (diocesan priest or deacon) is incardinated into a particular church, usually a diocese but also its equivalent (i.e., territorial prelature, territorial abbacy, apostolic vicariate, apostolic prefecture, or apostolic administration erected on a stable basis [c. 368]). Although military ordinariates may incardinate clergy, the current practice of the Archdiocese for the Military Services of the United States is not to incardinate. A cleric can also be incardinated in a personal prelature (e.g., Opus Dei, c. 294).

Canon 266, §2 lists the so-called "religious orders" which can also incardinate, such as a clerical institute of consecrated life (cc. 588, §2; 589),[15] or a clerical society of apostolic life (c. 731), unless the constitution states otherwise. The major superior who is competent to incardinate is determined by the constitution and statutes of the institute or society. Although ordination incardinates a religious into the institute or society, this must be seen as an addition to the bond assumed through perpetual vows or definitive incorporation into the institute or society. Through incardination religious become enrolled or attached as clerics to the institute or society.

According to canon 266, §3, secular institutes as a rule do not incardinate unless the Apostolic See has granted an indult; clerics remain incardinated in the diocese and are subject to the diocesan bishop and other ordinaries (c. 715, §1).

---

[13] Cf. *CCEO* 358.

[14] Minor orders are now abrogated and the ministries of lector and acolyte are open to laymen. See Lynch, in *CLSA Com,* 192–193.

[15] A clerical institute of diocesan right remains under the authority of the diocesan bishop, who is the competent authority to issue dimissorial letters (c. 1019, §2).

Formal Process of Incardination[16]

Canon 267 — §1. For a cleric already incardinated to be incardinated validly in another particular church, he must obtain from the diocesan bishop a letter of excardination signed by the same bishop and a letter of incardination from the diocesan bishop of the particular church in which he desires to be incardinated signed by that bishop.

§2. Excardination thus granted does not take effect unless incardination in another particular church has been obtained.

Although incardination binds a cleric to one place, the law provides a means for him to move and to minister permanently elsewhere. The cleric may be incardinated in another particular church (c. 267, §1), or a secular cleric may become incardinated in an institute or society (c. 268, §2).

Canon 267, §1 explains the requirements for the validity of the formal process of incardination and excardination (also called "derived" incardination). The process is the same for priests and deacons[17] and simply consists of two activities: a letter to the cleric from the "sending bishop" (*a quo* bishop) granting excardination, and a letter to the cleric from the "receiving bishop" (*ad quem* bishop) granting incardination. The canon clearly states that these are simultaneous provisions—excardination takes effect only at the moment of incardination. The legislator has thus avoided the possibility that, for however short a time, the cleric is a *vagus* or an unattached, unincardinated ordained minister. The only exception seems to be the dismissed religious who has not found a benevolent bishop (c. 701).

Canon 267, §1 states the elements necessary for the validity of the excardination and incardination.[18] The sending and receiving diocesan bishops (c. 272) respond to the written request of the

cleric. The letters of excardination and incardination are to be in writing.[19] The bishops write to the cleric himself; their letters are not from one bishop to another merely referring to the incardinating/excardinating cleric. The receiving bishop is not to issue a letter of incardination unless he has been assured by the sending bishop that a letter of excardination has been issued. This is usually done as part of the required testimonials from the sending bishop.[20] Both dioceses involved must be specifically mentioned in both letters. The letter is to be signed by the bishop himself for the validity of the juridic act; it must also be notarized by the chancellor or notary.[21] For the good ordering of the Church as well as common courtesy, the receiving bishop should duly notify the sending bishop that the letter of incardination has been issued to the cleric.[22]

Church administrators have been attempting to deal fairly with deacons who have moved from one area of the country to another, usually because of employment or retirement. On March 4, 1995, the Administrative Committee of the NCCB authorized the publication of the "Protocol for the Incardination/Excardination of Deacons."[23] It is meant to assist bishops in applying the canonical norms and does not constitute particular law. Its provisions should be followed insofar as they facilitate the deacon's process of moving from one diocese to another. The protocol envisions the eventual incardination of the deacon, rather than the canonical agreement as stated in canon 271. Briefly, the protocol suggests that the

---

[16] Cf. *CCEO* 359; 364.

[17] See CFC, *Directory for the Ministry and Life of Permanent Deacons*, n. 3.

[18] Sample letters can be found in *CPH*, 77–85.

[19] It is understood that the letter can be typed and printed, as long as the bishop himself signs the document. See. c. 474.

[20] See commentary on c. 269.

[21] The letters of incardination and excardination are juridic acts which are governed by c. 474. See commentary on c. 474.

[22] The Eastern code explicitly states that the incardinating eparchial bishop is to inform the previous eparchial bishop that the cleric has been enrolled (*CCEO* 366, §2).

[23] See memo of March 31, 1995 to U.S. bishops. Also CFC, *Directory for the Ministry and Life of Permanent Deacons*, n. 3.

deacon, when he decides to move, write to both the sending bishop and the receiving bishop, notifying them of the move. He is to state his intention to visit the receiving bishop or his delegate after he arrives. The sending bishop transmits some initial materials to the receiving bishop. After a possible period of supervision and evaluation (a minimum of two years is suggested), the deacon may write to request incardination, thus activating the procedure of canon 267.[24] Although the protocol suggests that the receiving bishop issue a letter of incardination within one month of receiving a copy of the letter of excardination, he is free to accept or reject the petition. Likewise, a bishop who has not implemented the diaconate in his diocese is not bound to incardinate a deacon who has moved there.[25]

Automatic Incardination[26]

Canon 268 — §1. A cleric who has legitimately moved from his own particular church to another is incardinated in the latter particular church by the law itself after five years if he has made such a desire known in writing both to the diocesan bishop of the host church and to his own diocesan bishop and neither of them has expressed opposition in writing to him within four months of receiving the letter.

§2. Through perpetual or definitive admission into an institute of consecrated life or into a society of apostolic life, a cleric who is incardinated in the same institute or society according to the norm of can. 266, §2 is excardinated from his own particular church.

The 1983 code has three forms of automatic incardination; two are found in canon 268.[27] The canon is taken from postconciliar legislation that implemented the council's desire for a better distribution of clergy and more flexible structures for service.[28] The canon also reflects a private reply of the Apostolic Signatura of June 27, 1978, clarifying the conditions for what it called "tacit" or automatic incardination.[29] The provisions of the canon are designed to protect the rights of both the individual cleric and the bishop. The cleric is able to express his desires, receive a clear response within an appropriate period of time, and know with certainty the particular church to which he is bound. The bishop, who is free to respond as he wishes, need not accept the cleric at the time of the request. The bishop needs only to respond in writing within four months. If he follows the norms, he will not find himself suddenly saddled with a cleric he did not want.

Indefinite residence of clerics in dioceses other than their own for a long period of time harms the stable institute of incardination. A cleric should be bound to a particular church and serve there so that no semblance of acephalous or unincardinated clerics cause scandal to the Church.

There are four conditions for automatic incardination:

1. *Five years of legitimate presence in the diocese.*
    The "clock" starts ticking once the cleric has resided legitimately in the diocese for five years. He does not need to be engaged in pastoral ministry or receive any assignment from the bishop, part-time or full-time. The cleric need not have been granted faculties. In fact, the host bishop might not even be aware that the cleric is residing in the diocese. He must merely spend five years

---

[24] There is no mention of *ipso iure* or automatic incardination as in c. 268, although it may apply.

[25] Not explicitly mentioned in the code are incardination and the creation of a new diocese. Incardination is usually determined for priests and deacons in the decree of erection (c. 373). Possible determinants could be their present assignment or the diocese of their domicile, or the issue may be left to the final determination of the bishops, who may even consult with the clergy.

[26] Cf. *CCEO* 360, §2.

[27] The third form deals with the religious cleric who has legitimately left or been dismissed from an institute of consecrated life or a society of apostolic life. See cc. 693; 701; 727, §2; and 743.

[28] *ES* I, 3, §5; *PA* §1.

[29] See *CLD* 9, 52–60.

residing there (*commoratio*) with the consent (or presumed permission) of the two ordinaries. Should either ordinary prohibit residence for any reason, or if the cleric is absent from his diocese or institute against the wishes of his ordinary, the "clock" stops running.

2. *Letter written to both ordinaries.*

The cleric must express in writing his desire to be incardinated in the diocese where he has resided. Although the letter usually is written after the five years of residence, the cleric may have written to one or both bishops at an earlier time. Such a letter suffices to fulfill the second requirement. The letter must clearly indicate the cleric's desire for incardination.

3. *Neither ordinary writes that he opposes the incardination.*

The ordinary's mind must be manifest "clearly, certainly, and to be sure, in writing, and not in vague and, perhaps, ambiguous words." It is best that the bishop should respond immediately to the letter of intent, telling of his "mind": total refusal, or perhaps refusal to accept the request at this time but an openness to doing so later.[30] The response can even be conditional.[31] The law is clear: when either ordinary indicates his opposition in writing, the "clock" stops ticking.

4. *After four months, no response.*

Automatic incardination occurs by the law itself should neither ordinary indicate his opposition in writing after four months of receiving the cleric's letter.

Requirements for Lawful Incardination[32]

Canon 269 — A diocesan bishop is not to allow the incardination of a cleric unless:

---

[30] O. Garcia, "The Assignment of Non-Diocesan Priests," *CLSAP* (1994) 106.

[31] See *RRAO 1994,* 84.

[32] Cf. *CCEO* 366. Note that the text of *CCEO* 366, §2 is not explicitly found in the 1983 code.

1° **the necessity or advantage of his own particular church demands it, and without prejudice to the prescripts of the law concerning the decent support of clerics;**

2° **he is certain from a legitimate document that excardination has been granted and, in addition, has appropriate testimonials from the excardinating diocesan bishop, under secrecy if necessary, concerning the life, behavior, and studies of the cleric;**

3° **the cleric has declared in writing to the same diocesan bishop that he wishes to be dedicated to the service of the new particular church according to the norm of law.**

Canon 269 protects the rights of the faith community and the bishop, who is required to organize the pastoral life of the diocese, especially the administration of the sacraments.

The severe shortage of priests is never a reason to incardinate; the concern of the legislator is clearly "quality" and not "quantity" of clerics. The people of the diocese have a right to ordained ministers who have appropriate preparation, the ability to minister effectively, and the capability to be placed in an assignment which will be useful and necessary to the pastoral life of the diocese. On the other hand, the bishop has the right to rely on stable and competent ordained ministers who are committed to serve him in a spirit of collaboration and mature and responsible obedience. The canon also protects the rights of the cleric. Once incardinated in a perpetual bond of service, he is assured that he will be employed in ministry and receive a just remuneration; he can count on the community and the bishop to support him until he dies.[33]

Because of the difficulties that arise through the misconduct of clergy, bishops are cautious when incardinating a priest or deacon from another diocese or an institute. However, canon 269 provides a thorough checklist—much like the list of requirements necessary before ordination—that

---

[33] For example, see cc. 213, 214, and 281.

assists in ascertaining the suitability of one to be incardinated.[34] The NCCB has developed the "Protocol for the Incardination/Excardination of Deacons" (cited above), which assists in fulfilling the canonical requirements for a deacon's valid and lawful incardination.[35]

The canon lists three matters of concern and investigation, but these are not taxative. There is no chronological order given; it is left to the discretion of the bishop. The following six areas are important to note:

1. *Necessity or usefulness* (c. 269, 1°).

First, the bishop must judge if the cleric's ministry will benefit the diocese. The bishop can insist that the priest or deacon speak the language well and be familiar with the culture and customs of the people he will serve. This requirement is modified in light of a prospective ministry among the faithful of his own home country or language. The canon does not require that the incardinated cleric exercise a "general ministry"; his usefulness to the diocese is very often in a particular ministry among a specific group of the faithful. The judgment of "necessity or advantage" rests with the bishop himself, although he benefits from the advice of appropriate persons and consultative bodies regarding the possible offices or ministries available to the priest or deacon.

2. *Due regard for decent support* (c. 269, 1°).

The bishop cannot incardinate a man whom he cannot support (c. 281), even though the need for the cleric's ministry be very great. In such a case the priest or deacon should go to another diocese where he is needed and can also be supported. The canon again closely connects incardination with the right of the cleric to decent remuneration. Although not a requirement of the canon, the re-

ceiving bishop would do well to discuss with the sending bishop the details of financial concerns, e.g., reimbursement for educational expenses, retirement benefits, pension, etc.[36]

3. *Document concerning excardination* (c. 269, 2°).

The canon does not require that the bishop obtain a copy of the actual letter of excardination written to the cleric, nor does it require that the excardination be granted at a particular time. The letter of excardination, once written, does not have a date of expiration unless specified in the letter itself. However, some statement is necessary attesting to the bishop's grant of excardination. Again, the legislator's concern for *vagi* is evident; at no time should a cleric be without a stable place of service and accountability to legitimate authority for such service.

4. *Documents concerning suitability* (c. 269, 2°).

Of special concern and importance is clear evidence that the cleric is suitable for ministry and is of good character. Should "secrecy" be necessary, the canon ensures that the rights of the community and the bishop are respected while not compromising the cleric's right to privacy (c. 220). It is essential that open communication between the cleric and both bishops be maintained throughout the process. The canon offers three areas that attest to suitability—life, behavior, and studies.[37] Included in the investigation should be documentation concerning an evaluation of the cleric's ministry and testimony as to his good name, character, and clerical lifestyle. Appropriate transcripts and seminary documentation (called *scrutinia*) are to be among the materials sought during the investigation. It is permissible to ask the cleric to undergo a psychological evaluation in order to assist in the assessment of suitability. The cleric must agree to release the confidential information, and the names of those who have access to the in-

---

[34] For commentary on the process in U.S. dioceses, see L. Jarrell, "A Look at Current Practices Surrounding the Transfer of Clerics," *J* 50 (1990) 310–321.

[35] The bishop retains the right to accept or reject the petition of the deacon for incardination.

[36] Provost, in *CPH,* 71.

[37] The canon does not mention the 1917 code's demand (*CIC* 117, 2°) for a background check on the cleric's family.

formation must be clearly stated. For example, a priest or deacon who has been accused of sexual misconduct has a right to be evaluated according to the canonical requirements.[38] The troublesome nature of his past should not immediately prevent another bishop from considering him for incardination. During the investigation the cleric must be cooperative and willing to release confidential materials concerning the accusation, psychological evaluation, and aftercare agreement. The receiving bishop is to make a prudent judgment, surely with consultation,[39] that the cleric's studies, life, and behavior are those of someone necessary and useful to his diocese.[40]

5. *Testimony of dedication to service* (c. 269, 3°).

Finally, the canon requires for the lawfulness of the incardination the declaration, in writing, of the cleric's intention permanently to serve the particular church of incardination.[41] This replaces the oath required by the 1917 code, yet the oath is still a legitimate way to fulfill the requirement of the canon. The canon does not demand that the cleric repeat the promise of obedience made at ordination; however, the receiving bishop becomes his proper ordinary when he is incardinated (c. 273).[42]

---

[38] The mere fact of an accusation is not tantamount to proof of criminal imputability, which usually presupposes a formal process.

[39] An "incardination committee" is very helpful in these cases.

[40] A bishop is free to take what some would call the "risk" of incardinating a cleric who has been accused of misconduct; in making such a decision, the bishop would benefit from the critical advice of others, e.g., a review board of pastoral, canonical, legal, and psychological experts.

[41] The NCCB protocol for deacons does not explicitly require this. It is not contained in any of the sample letters.

[42] The canonical documents that make the incardination effective can be used to "celebrate" the incardination of the cleric and welcome him for service in the diocese. For example, the cleric may be invited to the meeting of a consultative body of priests or deacons (e.g., priests' personnel board, deacons' advisory council) where the bishop signs the letter of incardination and the cleric

6. *Other elements of the process.*

There are other components of the process which are not explicitly included in the canon but which dioceses have found helpful in developing their policy of incardination. For example, many dioceses have instituted a probationary period before a man can begin the formal process for incardination. During that time (three to five years is the usual length)[43] the cleric can experience the atmosphere and life of the local church, and the community can observe in an informal way the ministry and style of the cleric. An initial probationary assignment or assignments can be given.[44] The diocese may screen the individual through the personnel director or the personnel board; this person or persons may handle the entire process and offer a final recommendation to the bishop. An evaluation by the pastor of the cleric's assignment during the probationary period may be helpful. Once the bishop receives the recommendation for incardination, the formal exchange of letters between the two bishops (i.e., excardination and incardination) can take place.

Many dioceses do not have a written incardination policy,[45] even though such a policy need only repeat the requirements of canons 267–269. A written statement is an effective means of expressing the diocese's expectations of those who wish to serve permanently. It outlines the procedure so that the rights and dignity of the priest can be respected during a time of anxiety as to the possible outcome of the process. The canonical requirements can be presented in a clear fashion while being adapted to the needs and experience of the individual diocese and the types of applications for incardination it receives.

---

signs the required statement of his intention to dedicate himself to diocesan service.

[43] Jarrell, 315. For deacons, the NCCB protocol suggests a minimum of two years of probationary service.

[44] The NCCB protocol suggests that, soon after the arrival of the deacon in the new diocese, faculties and an assignment be given.

[45] Jarrell, 314.

Requirements for Lawful Excardination[46]

Canon 270 — Excardination can be licitly granted only for just causes such as the advantage of the Church or the good of the cleric himself. It cannot be denied, however, except for evident, grave causes. A cleric who thinks he has been wronged and has found an accepting bishop, however, is permitted to make recourse against the decision.

Canon 270 complements the previous canon by stating the requisites for lawful excardination. The rights of the cleric to exercise his ministry for the good of another local church or for his own personal needs are protected, while the bishop is granted the right to make a prudential judgment about the request.[47] Canon 270 attempts to balance both sets of rights. However, the canon gives preference to the request of the cleric; the burden of proof to deny the request rests with the bishop. The legislation implements the renewed understanding of the mission of the priest who is, with the bishops, to be solicitous for the welfare of the universal Church *(PO* 10).[48] The sacrament of orders involves the universality of the priestly mission; the canon provides a certain flexibility in order to put into effect the teaching of the council.[49] There is a subtle shift in the attitude of the legislator: the needs of the wider Church and the personal good of the cleric himself normally take preference over the needs of the local church.

Excardination can be granted for "just causes" only. The canon does not give a taxative list of the just causes, but offers two examples.[50] First, the benefit of the Church may call for the excardination. For example, another diocese may have a serious lack of clergy. The canon does not specify which particular church benefits, only the benefit of "the Church." Thus, the excardination may be for the good of the sending diocese in terms of an expression of generosity to the needs of the universal Church. A just cause for the benefit of the particular church would not be merely to be rid of a troublesome priest. However, the receiving bishop may indeed judge such a priest necessary, useful, and suitable for incardination.

The 1983 code adds a new "just cause" to previous legislation on excardination: the personal good of the cleric himself. This includes all aspects of his well-being—spiritual, psychological, physical.[51] His talents may be better used in another place, or his ministry may have become ineffective or lifeless in his diocese of original incardination. Indeed, this is even a way of leaving behind the tension between himself and his own bishop. For deacons, the permanent transfer to another diocese for reasons of employment or retirement suffices as a just cause to petition for excardination.[52] Of course, personal ambition, avarice, selfish reasons, restlessness, or instability are not just causes for excardination.

While a *just reason* is required to grant excardination, the canon states explicitly that a *serious*

---

[46] Cf. *CCEO* 365.

[47] Jarrell suggests that it seems more and more bishops and superiors are refusing excardination while the CFC has frequently responded in favor of the priest in conflict situations. The competent authority "can never let the concern for the local church override the rights of the individual (c. 18)" (Jarrell, 320).

[48] *CCEO* 361 states that this permission is granted to the cleric "mostly for the evangelization of the whole Church."

[49] See also commentary on c. 271.

[50] One diocese's policy states that any one of four reasons will suffice for excardination: serious health problems, desire to be near close family members, desire to enter a religious congregation, desire to work where there is a dearth of clergy (Jarrell, 315–316, n. 6).

[51] See Bishops' Committee on Priestly Life and Ministry, *The Health of American Catholic Priests* (Washington, D.C.: USCC, 1985) and *The Priest and Stress* (Washington, D.C.: USCC, 1982). Although neither document deals explicitly with excardination or temporary service, the issues of health and stress must be taken into account when making a decision about excardination.

[52] The NCCB protocol presumes that the transferring deacon will make his petition to his sending bishop and receiving bishop, yet the deacon retains the right to remain incardinated in his home diocese as well as the right to petition to exercise ministry in the new diocese or not.

reason is necessary to deny it. In practice, the request of the cleric to move should usually be granted unless there are serious reasons in the particular church to reject it. The burden of proof for denial lies with the bishop; however, the canon clearly leaves the decision to him. In other words, the bishop determines the presence of *just cause(s)* for excardination as well as the *serious reason(s)* should it be denied. The bishop's decision can never be arbitrary but always is to be made after careful consideration of all the circumstances of the priest and his own diocese. A serious reason could be the more pressing pastoral needs of the original diocese. This needs to be sensitively balanced with the reasons presented in the request of the priest (c. 384).

Canon 270 recognizes, in practice, the right of the cleric to petition for excardination. The canon emphasizes this by including an explicit reference to his right to take recourse against the decision of the bishop; the canon reminds the priest that he can vindicate his right in appropriate fora. The cleric may bring the matter to the diocesan board of conciliation or arbitration, should it exist in the diocese and be competent in such cases.[53] The cleric is always free to have recourse to the Holy See. In this matter the competent dicastery is the Congregation for the Clergy. The petition for recourse should indicate the reasons why the cleric has asked for excardination and the reasons why it has been denied and include all documentation available; a letter from the receiving bishop should be part of the petition.[54]

Few dioceses have an excardination policy, although, like an incardination policy, such a policy assists in fostering a healthy openness regarding the expectations of the diocese and the individual priest or deacon. The legislation on excardination touches on issues concerning the nature of the priestly vocation, which may begin with a calling to exercise ministry in a particular church and change to a calling to serve the universal Church, e.g., service in the Roman Curia or at the level of the episcopal conference. As a result, bishops should not be hasty in denying clerics' requests and should weigh the impact that such denials have on the morale of the presbyterate.[55]

Temporary Service[56]

Canon 271 — §1. Apart from the case of true necessity of his own particular church, a diocesan bishop is not to deny permission to clerics, whom he knows are prepared and considers suitable and who request it, to move to regions laboring under a grave lack of clergy where they will exercise the sacred ministry. He is also to make provision that the rights and duties of these clerics are determined through a written agreement with the diocesan bishop of the place they request.

§2. A diocesan bishop can grant permission for his clerics to move to another particular church for a predetermined time, which can even be renewed several times. Nevertheless, this is to be done so that these clerics remain incardinated in their own particular church and, when they return to it, possess all the rights which they would have had if they had been dedicated to the sacred ministry there.

§3. For a just cause the diocesan bishop can recall a cleric who has moved legitimately to another particular church while remaining incardinated in his own church provided that the agreements entered into with the other bishop and natural equity are observed; the diocesan bishop of the other particular church, after having observed these same conditions and for a just cause, likewise can deny the same cleric permission for further residence in his territory.

---

[53] See commentary on cc. 1732–1739.

[54] Provost, in *CPH,* 71.

[55] See Bishops' Committee on Priestly Life and Ministry, *Reflections on the Morale of Priests* (Washington, D.C.: USCC, 1989).

[56] The Eastern code parallels to canon 271 are organized differently: c. 271, §1, *CCEO* 360; c. 271, §2, *CCEO* 360, §1 and 362, §2; c. 271 §3, *CCEO* 362, §1.

Vatican II taught that bishops and priests share in solicitude for the good of the whole Church (*LG* 28), and expressed a deep concern for the just distribution of clergy throughout the world (*PO* 10). This preoccupation led to the postconciliar norms of *Ecclesiae sanctae* (I, 3, §2) for temporary service in another part of the world. In 1980 the Congregation for the Clergy issued "Directive Norms for Cooperation Among Local Churches and for a Better Distribution of the Clergy."[57] In 1991, John Paul II established the Interdicasterial Commission for a More Just Distribution of Priests, under the competence of the Congregation for Catholic Education.[58] This commission makes regular reports and sees itself "like an observatory" to detect where a greater presence of clergy is needed. The commission utilizes the services of the Internet in order to facilitate the contact of bishops open to the exchange of priests.[59]

Canon 271 was designed to implement the directives of the council and to meet the needs for the just distribution of clergy, still respecting the stability and permanence of incardination.[60] The canonical institute of temporary transfer, also called aggregation or migration, is found in this canon. The canon is carefully designed to safeguard the rights of the individual cleric who serves outside the diocese of incardination, as well as the rights of the bishops and dioceses involved.

Canon 271, §1 states the basic components of the law on the temporary transfer of a cleric: criteria for the decision, reasons to deny the permission, and the necessity of a written agreement with the receiving bishop. Each of these components needs to be examined separately.

The initiative for the move usually comes from the cleric himself who desires to serve where there is a scarcity of clergy.[61] Note that the canon calls for service in another diocese where the cleric will "exercise the sacred ministry," and not for other reasons, such as secular employment.[62] The cleric may have personal reasons for a request for excardination, such as his health, closeness to family, or even an extended sabbatical or time of renewal. The 1980 norms called for a "special vocation" to serve elsewhere (23), a suitable temperament, and natural gifts, including psychological qualities, constancy of soul, and sincere intent (24). The canon gives the bishop discretion to judge the suitability of the candidate who is "prepared"[63] and fit to serve outside the diocese, and the 1980 norms cautioned ordinaries to exercise great care in finding those who are able and qualified (24). Whereas excardination is granted for "just causes" (c. 270), the permission to transfer hinges on the presence of three factors: dearth of priests, preparedness, and suitability.

The concluding section of the 1980 norms called for the bishop to be solicitous for the good of the universal Church, and even to encourage clerics to serve temporarily elsewhere because of their special gifts and the needs of other churches.[64] As part of his solicitude for the universal Church, the bishop should consider ways in which clerics can serve the Church outside the diocese, e.g., military chaplaincy, service to the Apostolic See, bishops' conference, institutes of

---

[57] March 25, 1980, in *CLD* 9, 760–787. These norms are now substantially contained in c. 271.

[58] See initial report of the commission in *Origins* 20 (1991) 682–685. The report called for a "conveying of forces [of priests] from one pole to another" and pointed to certain priest-rich religious orders which should be open to temporary transfers of their members to dioceses in need.

[59] For example, see Vatican Information Service report on distribution of priests (vis@pressva-vis.va) of July 22, 1997.

[60] For a commentary on c. 271 see Garcia, 97–108. See also J. Beal in *CPH*, 160–168.

[61] This is not just the priest's "subjective attraction" to a particular place but an objective need for priests in the area (Beal, 162).

[62] Garcia, 103.

[63] For such preparation, see *Norms*, n. 25.

[64] The encouragement and support of the bishop are also pertinent to deacons (CFC, *Directory for the Ministry and Life of Permanent Deacons*, n. 3).

study, and interdiocesan seminaries and educational institutions.[65]

However, the reasons to grant the permission are balanced with the concrete needs of the particular church. Again, the bishop has the discretion to make this judgment. The permission may be denied for a case of "true necessity" of the particular church. The reasons for denial of temporary transfer would appear to be less grave than the serious causes needed for a denial of "permanent transfer" through excardination in the previous canon. As in canon 270, the burden of proof is placed on the bishop. However, there has been a shift in mentality in the 1983 code, one that favors the just distribution of clerics and extending help to other particular churches. The bishop, even in the face of the needs of his diocese, should be quite hesitant in denying the permission, for a time, for service outside the diocese where there is a need.[66] Should the cleric request this permission for personal reasons rather than the greater need of another diocese, the bishop has more discretion to deny the permission, since the canon allows him greater latitude to deny in terms of the greater needs of his own diocese. Although not stated in the canon, the receiving bishop presumably also has the right to reject the temporary service of a cleric and has no obligation to accept the services offered, no matter how needy the diocese might be.

As in the 1980 norms, the canon stipulates that an agreement be drawn up between the two bishops.[67] The purpose of the agreement is to safeguard the rights and obligations of all those concerned, while protecting the institute of incardination. The agreement does not presuppose an openness to incardination in the host diocese and

should not be construed to imply such openness. The norms insist that, because it is "absolutely necessary" to define the rights and obligations of the cleric, the agreement is to be drawn up with the involvement of the priest himself and "must, in order that it have legal force, be accepted and signed by the priest" (25). Since the purpose of the agreement is to safeguard the rights and obligations of all parties, especially those of the cleric, it is important that all three parties sign the document, i.e., the cleric and the two bishops.

While the canon stipulates, in general terms, an agreement which makes provisions for "the rights and duties of these clerics," the 1980 norms are more complete and should be followed. The elements of the agreement are as follows (27): length of time of service, duties to be performed, place of ministry and residence, means of support and from whom, social security in case of illness, disability, and old age, and even provision for a time to visit home during the period of service. The agreement cannot be changed unless all parties agree.

The renewal of the agreement (c. 271, §2 states it can be renewed "several times") is based on the same criteria of its creation; the cleric's performance of the ministry should be evaluated as well.[68]

The Office for the Pastoral Care of Migrants and Refugees (PCMR) of the National Conference of Catholic Bishops has drawn up the "Standardized Agreement for Use with Bishops' Conferences of Other Countries for the Exchange of Clergy."[69] Although the bishops requested this agreement to facilitate the temporary service of foreign clergy, few bishops seem to take advantage of the protocol, and most prefer to make their own arrangements.[70] The "Standardized

[65] See Beal, 166–168.
[66] The author agrees with Beal (163), Donlon (141–142), and Lynch (in *CLSA Com,* 197). A dissenting opinion is expressed by Teixeira who states that the "material needs of the particular church of incardination take precedence over such needs elsewhere" ("Clergy Personnel: Policy and Canonical Issues," *J* 45 [1985] 517).
[67] For a sample agreement, see Beal, 176.

[68] Beal, 164.
[69] The current revision is dated December 12, 1990. In September 1995 the PCMR was authorized by the NCCB Committee on Migration to simplify the agreement yet substantially repeat the provisions of the 1990 version. This latest version is being prepared for approval.
[70] The agreement is not particular law and does not bind the bishops.

Agreement" encompasses certain areas of concern for bishops, especially selection of personnel, immigration papers, determining terms of service, and providing necessary orientation both prior to clergy leaving their home countries and upon their arrival in the United States.[71]

Canon 271, §3 addresses the possible recall of the cleric. The sending bishop retains the right to recall the cleric at any time, always respecting the agreement that has been made and "natural equity." Any arbitrary decision is to be avoided by keeping to the terms of the agreement. However, the canon calls for a "just cause" and not a "serious" one. Normally the cleric is recalled when the time period of the agreement has expired. However, should an exception occur, any unfulfilled obligations should be met by the recalling bishop, who is also to be attentive to the particular situation of the cleric. Likewise, the receiving bishop may terminate the agreement and send the cleric home early; the "just cause" stipulated in the canon could be ineffective ministry, problems with adjustment, or personal difficulties.

Canon 271, §2 reviews the canonical status of the cleric temporarily serving outside the diocese and states that he remains incardinated in his home diocese. As in the 1980 norms, he retains all rights and privileges "as if [he] had been engaged in the sacred ministry there without interruption" (30). While the cleric is away, he is the object of the bishop's special solicitude and personal contact (28).[72]

One final note is in order concerning the transfer of deacons.[73] The canon does not pro-

vide for the situation of a deacon who moves to a diocese where there is no diaconate in place. The 1984 NCCB Guidelines on Deacons leave this to the discretion of the receiving bishop,[74] although the deacon's bishop of incardination may try to contact the new bishop and arrange for an assignment. For this reason many deacons choose to work or retire in a diocese where the diaconate is operative so that they can exercise their ministry.

Competent Authority[75]

Canon 272 — A diocesan administrator cannot grant excardination or incardination or even permission to move to another particular church unless the episcopal see has been vacant for a year and he has the consent of the college of consultors.

The canons on incardination are completed with legislation on the competent authority to grant incardination, excardination, and permission to serve outside the diocese. In light of the sacramental bond linking the diocesan bishop, major superior, priests, and deacons and the common care they exercise together for the people of God, it is clear that these three acts are important to the life of the community and the corps of ordained ministers who serve it. Only the diocesan bishop or major superior is competent to grant incardination or excardination or temporary transfer; a vicar general (c. 475) or episcopal vicar (c. 476) is not competent without a special mandate. Should the see be vacant, usually no major changes are permitted (c. 428, §1). The diocesan administrator (generally elected by the college of consultors or appointed by the metropolitan) can grant incardination only under two conditions: the see has been vacant for one year and the college of consultors (c. 502) has given its consent.

[71] The NCCB currently has agreements with other episcopal conferences, i.e., CELAM, Korea, Mexico, Philippines, and Poland. In cases of clergy from these areas, bishops are expected to contact the PCMR. Drafts of agreements have been drawn up with Brazil, Colombia, and Nigeria, while conversations are being held with Haiti and India.
[72] Such contact includes all mailings to clerics and invitations to clerical gatherings and retreats.
[73] See the 1995 NCCB deacon protocol and J. Provost, "Permanent Deacons and the Code," *CLSAP* (1984) 175–191.

[74] "If the new diocese has not implemented the diaconate, the deacon will not exercise his ministry without the permission of the bishop" (n. 120).
[75] Cf. *CCEO* 363.

BIBLIOGRAPHY

Calvo, R., and N. Klinger, eds. *Clergy Procedural Handbook*. Washington, D.C.: CLSA, 1992.

Colagiovanni, E. "Incardinazione ed escardinazione nel Nuovo Codice di Diritto Canonico." *ME* 109 (1984) 49–57.

CCE and CFC. *Basic Norms for the Formation of Permanent Deacons and Directory for the Ministry and Life of Permanent Deacons,* February 22, 1998. Washington, D.C.: USCC, 1998.

CFC. "Directive Norms for Cooperation Among Local Churches and for a Better Distribution of the Clergy," March 25, 1980. *CLD* 9, 760–787.

———. *Directory for the Life and Ministry of Priests,* January 31, 1994. Washington, D.C.: USCC, 1994.

Donlon. J. "Incardination and Excardination." *CLSAP* (1991) 124–153.

Garcia, O. "The Assignment of Non-Diocesan Priests." *CLSAP* (1994) 97–108.

Jarrell, L. "A Look at Current Practices Surrounding the Transfer of Clerics." *J* 50 (1990) 310–321.

McBride, J. T. *Incardination and Excardination of Seculars. CanLawStud* 145. Washington, D.C.: Catholic University of America, 1941.

NCCB. *Permanent Deacons in the United States.* Washington, D.C.: NCCB, 1984.

NCCB, Office for the Pastoral Care of Migrants and Refugees. "Standardized Agreement for Use with Bishops' Conferences of Other Countries for the Exchange of Clergy," December 20, 1990.

NCCB, Secretariat for the Permanent Diaconate. "Protocol for the Incardination/Excardination of Deacons," March 14, 1995.

Teixeira. J. S. "Clergy Personnel: Policy and Canonical Issues." *J* 45 (1985) 502–520.

Vatican Interdicasterial Committee. "For a More Equal Distribution of Priests in the Church." *Origins* 20 (1991) 682–685.

CHAPTER III
THE OBLIGATIONS AND RIGHTS OF CLERICS
[cc. 273–289]

In seventeen canons this chapter treats the obligations and rights of clerics. They are not simple recommendations but binding juridic norms that have validity for the whole Latin church.[1] At the beginning of Book II the code treats the obligations and rights of all the Christian faithful (cc. 208–223). It then takes up the obligations and rights of lay Christians (cc. 224–231) and now turns to the clergy.[2] The clergy and laity enjoy the same fundamental rights and are bound by the same basic obligations. The obligations and rights affirmed here (cc. 273–289) are proper to the clerical state, but must be interpreted in accordance with the obligations and rights of all believers.[3] Certain common rights, such as that of association, are repeated so that there can be no doubt that clerics are entitled to them.[4] Although in the title of the chapter the term "obligations" comes before that of "rights," there was no intention to assign any priority or precedence to one over the other.[5] The rights of the clergy are to be understood as just as important as their obligations.

The study group charged with formulating this section of the code originally considered seven rights, three of which were eventually incorporated in the code: the right of association, the right to a vacation, and the right to fitting and decent remuneration.[6] Of the sixteen obligations proposed, all but one, the obligation to foster vocations, found a place. The rights are interspersed among the obligations. The parallel chapter in the Eastern code is substantially identical, though it is spread over twenty-seven canons (*CCEO* 367–393) and recognizes also the right to a ministry (*CCEO* 371, §1) as well as the responsibilities of a married clergy (*CCEO* 375).

The sources for this chapter are mainly two titles of the 1917 code, "On the Rights and Privileges of Clerics" (*CIC* 118–223) and "On the Obligations of Clerics" (*CIC* 124–144). While the ancient but outmoded privileges no longer find a place in ecclesiastical law,[7] the 1983 code affirms certain rights belonging to clerics that were unknown in the former code. These rights were enunciated in the documents of the Second Vatican Council, especially *Presbyterorum ordinis*

---

[1] Cardinal Willebrands thought that any precepts regarding the life of clerics should be placed in special statutes outside the code. The Secretariat of the Commission replied that the code would be very incomplete without such an important chapter; and, furthermore, these canons are real juridic norms (*Rel,* 62). Thus sanctions may be imposed for the violation of certain obligations such as engaging in trade or business (c. 1392), failure to observe continence and celibacy (cc. 1394, 1395), and serious neglect of the duty of residence (c. 1396).

[2] The obligations and rights of religious are found in cc. 662–672.

[3] *Comm* 14 (1982) 168.

[4] *Comm* 9 (1977) 245.

[5] Cardinal Bernardin sought to have rights placed first in the title as more in conformity with the sacramental constitution of the Church. The Secretariat responded that rights could indeed precede obligations but that was not necessary since both flowed from the sacraments (*Rel,* 62).

[6] Four rights were either eliminated or included elsewhere: the right of cooperating with the bishop in the exercise of ministry, the right to obtain an ecclesiastical ministry, the right to sufficient time for spiritual and intellectual development, the right to have recourse (*Comm* 3 [1971] 195–196 and 16 [1984] 170).

[7] The four were: (1) the privilege of the canon which safeguarded the clergy from real injury; (2) the privilege of the forum which restricted all contentious or criminal cases against the clergy to an ecclesiastical judge; (3) the privilege of immunity which exempted the clergy from military service and public civil offices which are foreign to the clerical state; and (4) the privilege of competence which allowed the clergy burdened with debt to withhold enough resources for their decent support.

(the Decree on the Ministry and Life of Priests). Even when the 1983 code repeats verbatim the 1917 canon, Pope John Paul II has insisted that "the code is a new law and it is to be evaluated primarily in the perspective of the Second Vatican Council, to which it is intended to conform fully."[8] At the same time, according to canon 6, §2, the restatement of the former law must "be assessed also" in light of "canonical tradition." On the whole, it seems that commentaries on this section of the 1983 code have not been sufficiently attuned to the conciliar spirit. "Rarely do authors follow an emphasis on the responsibility of the priest. The council's insistence on the fundamental dignity of the priest, episcopal-presbyteral cooperation in the Church, and the solicitude of the bishop for the priest is not adequately reflected when the canons are explained."[9]

Clerical Reverence and Obedience

Canon 273 — Clerics are bound by a special obligation to show reverence and obedience to the Supreme Pontiff and their own ordinary.

Unlike the two previous drafts of this section of the code which were circulated, in the 1983 code the cleric's obligation of obedience became the lead canon of this chapter.[10] The Holy Father seems to have been responsible for the change,

since he together with a small group of consultors edited the final version. There is no reason to hold, however, that its position implies that obedience takes precedence over the other obligations and rights in this chapter, that it is a primary norm for interpreting the following canons, or that it in any way limits the exercise of a cleric's rights.[11]

The obligation of obedience does not bind only clerics. All the faithful "are bound to follow with Christian obedience those things which the sacred pastors, inasmuch as they represent Christ, declare as teachers of the faith or establish as rulers of the Church" (c. 212, §1). Clerics, however, are bound by "a special obligation." The canon reproduces the 1917 code except for the elimination of the phrase "especially priests" and the addition of the term "the Supreme Pontiff."[12] Yet an identity of formulation must not obscure the freshness of conciliar inspiration. *Presbyterorum ordinis* and *Christus Dominus* (the Decree on the Bishops' Pastoral Office) identified the theological or sacramental basis for the obligation.

According to *Presbyterorum ordinis:*

Priests for their part should keep in mind the fullness of the sacrament of order which bishops enjoy and should reverence in their persons the authority of Christ the supreme pastor.... Priestly obedience, inspired through and through by the spirit of cooperation, is based on that sharing of the episcopal ministry which is conferred on priests by the sacrament of order and the canonical mission.[13]

Similarly, *Christus Dominus* stated:

---

[8] Address to the Roman Rota, January 26, 1984, *Insegnamenti di Giovanni Paolo II* 7/1: 167. Translation in *TPS* 29 (1984) 175.

[9] F. Schneider, *Obedience to the Bishop by the Diocesan Priest in the 1983 Code of Canon Law,* CanLawStud 533 (Washington, D.C.: Catholic University of America, 1990) 314. See canon 384: "With special solicitude, a diocesan bishop is to attend to presbyters and listen to them as assistants and counselors. He is to protect their rights and take care that they correctly fulfill the obligations proper to their state...."

[10] In the 1917 code the canon on obedience (*CIC* 127) was fourth among the obligations. When first discussed by the study group, it was twelfth in a list of sixteen obligations (*Comm* 16 [1984] 184–185). Canon 132 in the 1977 schema was in fifth place; canon 247 in the 1980 schema was in fourth.

[11] Schneider, 226–228.

[12] *CIC* 127: "All clerics, but especially priests, are bound by a special obligation to show reverence and obedience each to his own ordinary." The singling out of priests in the old law was apropos since the term "clerics" also included those who had not received the sacrament of orders but only tonsure and minor orders.

[13] *PO* 7.

All priests, whether diocesan or religious, share and exercise with the bishop the one priesthood of Christ.... The diocesan clergy have, however, a primary role in the care of souls because, being incardinated in or appointed to a particular church, they are wholly dedicated in its service...and accordingly form one priestly body and one family of which the bishop is the father.[14]

The obligation of obedience is based on the relationship between cleric and bishop arising from the reception of the sacrament of orders. The cleric thereby shares in the episcopal ministry. By ordination the cleric becomes incardinated in the diocese and is destined for its service (c. 266, §1).[15] Though the council does refer to the canonical mission, a jurisdictional term, it avoids any connotation of superior and inferior, preferring instead a relationship grounded in ecclesial communion. Nevertheless, the code here seems to have overlooked the spirit of the council in continuing to speak of the "ordinary" with jurisdictional connotations, whereas one finds in canon 384 the more pastoral "diocesan bishop" who "with special solicitude...is to attend to presbyters and listen to them as assistants and counselors."

It may be argued that the code deliberately chose the term "ordinary" because of its greater extension, including, besides the diocesan bishop, vicars general, episcopal vicars, and major superiors of pontifical clerical religious institutes (c. 134, §1). Even so, obedience would be owed primarily to the bishop and to the vicars only as acting in his name. Members of religious institutes and clerical societies of apostolic life at the reception of the diaconate become incardinated as clerics (c. 266, §2) and thereby receive their superior as their own proper ordinary. They do not owe

obedience to the diocesan bishop as their proper ordinary.[16]

The 1983 code states that clerics owe obedience not only to the ordinary but also to the Supreme Pontiff. There was some disagreement about including the pope in a canon that dealt with the cleric's relation to his own bishop.[17] It was further objected that such a reference was bound to the theological opinion that the Roman Pontiff was the universal bishop of the Church.[18] The Secretariat, though, insisted that a cleric is held to render special reverence and obedience not only to his own ordinary but also to the Supreme Pontiff, "who is indeed the ordinary for the whole Church."[19] In fact, canon 331 states clearly that "he possesses supreme, full, immediate, and universal ordinary power in the Church, which he is always able to exercise freely." Not only does the Roman Pontiff possess power over the universal Church, he also has "the primacy of ordinary power over all particular churches and groups of them" (c. 333, §1).[20]

The obedience that a diocesan priest owes his ordinary is called canonical obedience—to distin-

---

[14] CD 28.

[15] Through the reception of the diaconate, religious who are already permanently attached to their communities become affiliated with them as clerics (c. 266, §2). Their obligation of obedience would be in virtue of their religious profession (cc. 601, 654).

[16] For the relation to the bishop of exclaustrated religious see c. 687 and of dismissed religious see c. 693.

[17] Comm 16 (1984) 184.

[18] Cardinal Marty, Rel, 63.

[19] Comm 14 (1982) 168.

[20] Canon 752 requires that "a religious submission of the intellect and will must be given to a doctrine which the Supreme Pontiff or the college of bishops declares concerning faith or morals when they exercise the authentic magisterium," even if not intended as infallible. "The obligation to follow the Magisterium in matters of faith and morals is intrinsically united to all the functions which the priest must perform in the Church. Dissent in this area is to be considered grave, in that it produces scandal and confusion among the faithful" (Directory for the Life and Ministry of Priests, cited hereafter as Directory Priests, n. 62). The observance of liturgical norms "merits special mention in our times." The celebration of the sacraments are acts of Christ and the Church "which the priest administers in the person of Christ and in the name of the Church for the good of the faithful. These have a true right to participate in the liturgical celebrations as the Church wills and not according to the personal likes of a particular minister" (ibid., n. 54).

guish it from the religious obedience owed a religious superior. The obligation of the latter arises from a vow or some other commitment made upon joining a community. Canonical obedience is restricted to those matters that are prescribed by canon law. It is determined by clerical status and office, on the one hand, and by the extent of episcopal jurisdiction, on the other. The bishop is empowered to enforce the universal law that regulates the clerical state, and the clergy are bound to obey in whatever pertains to their state as such.[21] Religious obedience is more extensive in that it embraces all phases of the member's life.

The authority of the bishop to enforce the common law regarding clerical discipline (cc. 273–289) includes the right to interpret the law in accordance with local circumstances. His commands must be in conformity with the spirit of the law. He cannot command anything prohibited by it. A deacon, for example, who is unwilling to be promoted to the priesthood cannot be forced to do so, nor, absent grave cause, can he be forbidden to exercise his diaconal orders (c. 1038). Conversely, the bishop cannot prohibit what the code clearly permits;[22] he cannot, for example, command his priests not to accept Mass offerings (c. 945, §1).

Areas that are not directly connected with the government of the diocese are not inherently within the ambit of episcopal jurisdiction. In civil matters the cleric enjoys all the liberties of every other citizen. Canon 285, §3, however, limits his right to hold public office. He may join any political party, unless it is condemned by the Church; he may vote for any candidate he deems fit. On a debatable political issue, such as a specific constitutional amendment, he may sign petitions and take a position that is at variance with that of the bishop.

Private matters, too, are not subject to episcopal direction. Provided that the priest is not incurring debts, the bishop may not interfere in his personal finances or the disposition of his inheritance, let alone dictate his last will and testament.[23] A bishop is exceeding his power when he legislates that assistant pastors are not to own automobiles.[24] Similarly, a bishop has no right to force a cleric before ordination to take a pledge to abstain from alcoholic beverages for a certain period of time, as was commonly done before the council.

With regard to the personal appearance of clerics, the authority of the bishop is limited to enforcing clerical dress as provided for in canon 284. The 1917 code (CIC 136, §1) required that clerics have a simple hair style. The Second Plenary Council of Baltimore in 1866 had legislated in greater detail, forbidding clerics to grow beards. Since this particular legislation was not opposed to the 1917 code, it remained in effect and could be enforced by the bishop, according to a decision of the Sacred Congregation of the Council.[25] The 1983 code says nothing about hair or beards. In view of widespread acceptance of longer hair and beards, as well as civil court decisions about individual rights in this matter, contemporary custom has evidently prevailed over any restrictions. The former prohibition against clerics wearing rings (CIC 136, §2) no longer applies. Only in extreme cases in which there is danger of genuine scandal may the bishop impose canonical obedience on a cleric to modify his appearance.

---

[21] A particularly difficult question is the right of a bishop to command a cleric to undergo a psychological examination. Canon 220 states that no one may violate the right of another person to protect his privacy, yet canons 1041, 1° and 1044, §2, 2° require the ordinary to consult with experts before judging a cleric who "labors under some form of amentia or other psychic weakness" unfit or fit to fulfill the ministry properly. See J. Provost, *RRAO 1995,* 43–45.

[22] F. Wernz and P. Vidal, *Ius canonicum* (Rome: Pontificiae Universitatis Gregorianae, 1928) II, n. 599, §l, a.

[23] The universal law does not oblige a cleric to make a last will and testament, but particular law may well require it (*Rel,* 68).

[24] J. Sheehan, *The Obligation of Respect and Obedience of Clerics toward Their Ordinary (Canon 127), CanLawStud* 344 (Washington, D.C.: Catholic University of America, 1954) 113.

[25] *Concilii Plenarii Baltimorensis II Acta et Decreta* (Baltimore: John Murphy, 1868) 95, n. 151. SCConc, January 19, 1920, *AAS* 12 (1920) 43.

For clerics who after a warning persistently refuse to obey in a serious matter, the code prescribes the imposition of a just penalty (c. 1371, §2). The penalty would depend upon the gravity of the offense.

It should be noted, in sum, that the special obedience the cleric owes his bishop is based on his sharing in the episcopal ministry through the sacrament of orders and the bond of incardination. The priest or deacon is to cooperate with the bishop in the service of the faithful of a particular church. Canon law does not require unquestioned, let alone joyful obedience. As a recent study has maintained, one "is not bound to conform his mind to the thinking and reasoning of the bishop; he is simply to carry out the order." Canonical obedience, though connected to the virtue of obedience, is quite different from the virtue, which should inform the spiritual life of a cleric just as any one of the faithful. Furthermore, to have recourse against commands which are perceived as unjust is not a sign of "a lack of priestly generosity or spirituality, or of questioning the will of God."[26]

Certain Offices Restricted to Clerics

Canon 274 — §1. Only clerics can obtain offices for whose exercise the power of orders or the power of ecclesiastical governance is required.

By placing this paragraph in the present chapter, the framers of the code indicate that a right is under consideration. The text states that only clerics may receive offices requiring the exercise of orders or the power of government in the Church. Yet it stops short of affirming that clerics have a right to obtain from their bishop "an office, ministry or function [*munus*] to be exercised in the service of the Church" as does canon 371, §1 of the Eastern code. Nevertheless, every cleric when physically and mentally capable does have the right to exercise his orders so long as useful, unless barred by law. Canon 1008 declares that by

the sacrament of orders one is deputed to fulfill the functions (*munera*) of teaching, sanctifying, and ruling; canon 1025, §2 requires that no one be ordained unless his ministry be considered useful for the Church.

An ecclesiastical office is defined in canon 145, §1 as "any function [*munus*] constituted in a stable manner by divine or ecclesiastical ordinance to be exercised for a spiritual purpose." The council itself in reforming the system of benefices proposed this definition (*PO* 20). There is little controversy over the first part of the paragraph limiting offices that require the exercise of orders to clerics. The power of orders of its nature directly promotes the sanctification of the faithful through public worship, especially the Mass, and through the administration of the sacraments. The offices of bishop (c. 375, §1), pastor (c. 521, §1), and parochial vicar (c. 546) are obvious examples of responsibilities requiring the administration of the sacraments. The law itself specifies presbyteral orders for the offices of parochial administrator (c. 539), vicar forane or dean (c. 553, §1), and diocesan administrator (c. 425, §1). To be a member of the presbyteral council (c. 495, §1) or the board of consultors (c. 502, §1) one must also have such orders. Within the diocesan curia the following offices must be filled by priests: moderator of the curia (c. 473, §2), vicar general and episcopal vicar (c. 478, §1), judicial vicar and adjutant judicial vicar (c. 1420, §4).

Offices and Functions Open to the Laity

The last phrase of paragraph one has occasioned great controversy: only clerics can obtain offices for whose exercise "the power of ecclesiastical governance is required." This restriction restates canon 118 of the 1917 code to the effect that "clerics alone are capable of obtaining the power of order or of ecclesiastical jurisdiction." Canon 129, §2 of the 1983 code, however, seems to modify the exclusivity of this clerical prerogative by declaring that lay members of the Christian faithful "can cooperate [*cooperari*]" in the exercise of this same governance or jurisdiction "ac-

[26] Schneider, 320.

cording to the norm of law." The apparently conflicting canons represent a compromise in relation to the as yet unresolved theological dispute about the nature and origin of sacred power in the Church and the accessibility of that power to the laity.[27] One opinion holds to the unity of sacred power which embraces both orders and jurisdiction and is transmitted only through the sacrament of orders so that the participation of the laity in the power of governance is merely extrinsic. The other opinion maintains that the mission of the Church is carried out through three separate powers, the power to sanctify, to teach, and to rule. Through baptism the laity have a capacity to exercise jurisdiction or governance in a subordinate and dependent way.

According to some theologians the council was not wholly successful in defining the precise relationship between the powers of orders and jurisdiction. In *Lumen gentium* it taught that through ordination the offices (*munera*) of teaching and governing were conferred along with that of sanctifying (*LG* 21, 18). The source of governing authority, then, is ordination and not canonical mission (or commission). Canonical mission merely determines the sphere in which jurisdiction may be exercised (*LG* 24). The council further taught that the ministries of the ordained and the laity "differ from one another in essence and not only in degree" (*LG* 10); some functions are reserved exclusively to the ordained. Yet later in the same document one finds that the laity through their baptism and confirmation receive "the capacity to assume from the hierarchy certain ecclesiastical offices [*munera*] that are to be performed for a spiritual purpose" (*LG* 33).[28]

Since the council's position is somewhat of a compromise and, therefore, ambiguous, there is no commonly accepted theological explanation for lay ministry. The Sacred Congregation for the Doctrine of the Faith, in its "Declaration on the Question of the Ordination of Women to the Ministerial Priesthood,"[29] insisted that "it is the Holy Spirit given in ordination who grants participation in the ruling power of the supreme pastor Christ" (n. 6), adding that "the pastoral charge in the Church is normally linked to the sacrament of order." In the official commentary on the document the congregation noted that the participation of some medieval abbesses in ecclesiastical jurisdiction was an abuse. While canonists in the past had admitted the possibility of separating jurisdiction from orders, the council, the document continued, "has tried to determine better the relationship between the two; the council's doctrinal vision will doubtless have effects on discipline."[30] One wonders how this position of the congregation can be reconciled with the fact that the papal *motu proprio Causas matrimoniales* in 1971 permitted a lay man to serve on a panel of three judges in marriage cases. The Pontifical Commission for the Revision of the Code of Canon Law recognized that such lay judges did exercise "jurisdictional power of governing."[31] The commission argued that classical canonists had long held that the pope using his plenary authority could bestow such power and that the lay man's capacity to receive it was affirmed by *Lumen gentium* 33.

The formulation of canons 129 and 274 of the present code was not resolved until the end of the revision process. The participation of the laity in the exercise of governmental power was a special question on the agenda of the last plenary meeting of the commission, October 20–29, 1981. A dossier sent to all the participants beforehand included: (1) the observations of several cardinals on this issue, most notably Cardinal Ratzinger; (2) the opinion of Alfonsus Stickler, Prefect of the Vatican Library and Professor of the History of Canon Law at the Salesianum University, a con-

---

[27] For a thorough exposition of the state of the question see J. Beal, "The Exercise of the Power of Governance by Lay People: State of the Question," *J* 55 (1995) 1–92.

[28] See L. Ligier, "'Lay Ministries' and Their Foundations in the Documents of Vatican II," in *Vatican II Assessment and Perspectives,* ed. R. Latourelle (New York: Paulist, 1989) II: 160–176.

[29] October 15, 1976, *Origins* 6 (1977) 517–524.

[30] *Origins* 6 (1977) 529.

[31] *Comm* 3 (1971) 187.

sultor to the commission; and (3) the opinion of another consultor, Jean Beyer, Dean of the Faculty of Canon Law at the Gregorian University.[32]

Cardinal Ratzinger objected: (a) to the distinction in governmental power between that founded on sacred orders and that not so founded; (b) to the participation of the laity in the exercise of ruling power not based on orders. To say that there was a power not based on sacred orders would be inconsistent with *Lumen gentium* (*LG* 21, 2), which maintained the essential unity of ecclesiastical authority (*sacra potestas*) founded exclusively on the sacrament of orders. He thought it a contradiction to hold, furthermore, that an unordained person is incapable of holding a power but that he may participate in its exercise.

At the final plenary congregation of the commission, the participation of lay persons in the exercise of jurisdiction—in particular as lay associate judges (c. 1421, §2)—was overwhelmingly approved by vote of fifty-two to nine.[33] The definitive formulation of canon 129, though, is a compromise, deliberately ambiguous: "Lay members of the Christian faithful can cooperate in the exercise of this same power [of governance] according to the norm of law." It may be interpreted either that the laity do not have jurisdiction, that all jurisdiction comes only with the sacrament of orders, or that they can indeed be given jurisdiction by the supreme legislator.

As was approved at the plenary congregation, the present code states (c. 1421, §1) that diocesan judges are to be clerics; thus deacons are eligible. The episcopal conference, however, may permit the laity to be appointed judges and, when necessary, one of them can be selected to form a collegiate tribunal (c. 1421, §2). The laity are also eligible to be defenders of the bond and promoters of justice (c. 1435), as well as advocates (c.

1483). They may be assessors (c. 1424) and auditors (c. 1428, §2). They may hold the offices of chancellor, vice chancellor, and notary. The chancellor as defined by law is an archivist, but in many American dioceses the chancellor functions with extensive delegated powers. (See the commentary on c. 482 for a discussion of the difficulties associated with such delegation.)

In financial matters the expertise of the laity is clearly recognized. They may serve on the finance council that must be established in every diocese (c. 492, §1) and fulfill the office of administrator of the temporal goods of a juridic person (c. 1279). A lay person may also be named finance officer, a position that every diocesan bishop must fill (c. 494, §1). The laity similarly serve on the financial council required to be set up in every parish (c. 537). They are to constitute the majority of the diocesan pastoral council (c. 512, §1) and the parish council (c. 536, §1) where these groups are established.

In situations in which there is a scarcity of priests, a bishop may entrust a participation in the exercise of pastoral care to a lay person or group of lay persons (c. 517, §2). The Church's annual statistical report (*Annuarium Statisticum Ecclesiae*) reported that on December 31, 1994, in the United States there were 63 parishes entrusted to permanent deacons, 9 to men religious who were not priests, 188 to women religious, 55 to lay persons, and 58 parishes which were vacant.[34] The laity are authorized to exercise the ministry of the word, to preside over liturgical prayer, to baptize, and to distribute Holy Communion (c. 230, §3). Lay women are not disadvantaged here as they are in receiving the ministries of lector and acolyte (c. 230, §1). The laity may prepare couples for marriage and formally assist at weddings (c. 1112, §1). They are also allowed to bring

---

[32] ComCICRec, *Plen,* 35–97.

[33] Ibid., 211–212. See E. Corecco, "Aspects of the Reception of Vatican II in the Code of Canon Law," in *The Reception of Vatican II,* ed. G. Alberigo, J.-P. Jossua, and J. Komonchak (Washington, D.C.: Catholic University of America, 1987) 288–293.

[34] *Annuarium Statisticum Ecclesiae 1994* (Vatican: Libreria Vaticana, n.d.). The NCCB Secretariat for the Diaconate reported in an internal memorandum that on December 31, 1996 permanent deacons served as administrators of 122 parishes; 67 of these deacons were full-time administrators.

Viaticum to the sick and conduct funeral services (*Rite for the Anointing and Care of the Sick, Praenotanda* n. 29 and *Rite for Funerals, Praenotanda* n. 19).

Even in parishes where there is a priest, the laity can be admitted to preach in church if, in certain circumstances, it is necessary or useful (c. 766). In Masses for children, for example, with the consent of the pastor one of the adults may speak after the gospel, especially if the celebrant finds it difficult to adapt to the mentality of children (*Directory for Masses with Children* n. 24). In other liturgies the homily is reserved to the priest or deacon (c. 767, §1).

In a 1988 apostolic exhortation after the promulgation of the code, John Paul II seems to have offered his own commentary on canon 129, §2, which is also repeated in canon 979, §2 of the Eastern code.

> When necessity and expediency in the Church require it, the pastors, according to established norms from universal law, can entrust to the lay faithful certain offices and roles that are connected to their pastoral ministry but do not require the character of orders. ... The task exercised in virtue of supply takes its legitimacy formally and immediately from the official deputation given by the pastors as well as from its concrete exercise under the guidance of ecclesiastical authority.[35]

Clerical Duty to Accept Assignments

§2. Unless a legitimate impediment excuses them, clerics are bound to undertake and fulfill faithfully a function which their ordinary has entrusted to them.

The obligation to accept and faithfully fulfill an assignment flows from the fact of incardination and the commitment to serve the diocese; sacred orders are conferred that they may be used

[35] *CL* n. 23, *Origins* 18/35 (February 9, 1989) 571.

for the good of the people of God (c. 1025, §2). The obligation of canonical obedience may be imposed only by the bishop or the diocesan administrator. Although the canons on obedience refer to the "ordinary," a term broader than "diocesan bishop," the texts of Vatican II, as noted above, clearly have in mind the special relationship of the diocesan bishop to his priests. The bishop should personally and carefully review decisions of a personnel board. The assignment or duty (*munus*) is to be taken in a wide sense, not necessarily limited to the care of souls. It includes such positions as pastor, assistant pastor, chaplain in a hospital, seminary teacher, or director of a religious institution. For the bishop to impose obedience, according to the interpretation of the Code Commission Secretariat, it is understood that the necessity of the Church truly requires it.[36] The judgment concerning the existence and the duration of the necessity belongs to the ordinary. He could, for example, delay for a time the entrance of a cleric into a religious community.[37]

A cleric with a legitimate impediment cannot be forced to accept an assignment. Poor health, whether physical or psychological, as well as advanced age would be obvious obstacles. The greater the pastoral need to be met, the greater should be the excusing cause. Again, it is up to the ordinary to judge the validity of the reason. A cleric who thinks that he has been aggrieved may have recourse to the Congregation for the Clergy,[38] but meanwhile he should accede to the bishop's command. One who does not comply with the legitimate precepts of the ordinary but persists

[36] *Rel*, 63. The bishop should as far as possible bear in mind the morale of his clergy and appreciate that a "source of stress occurs when a priest is given an assignment that does not fit his interests and abilities or match his expectations" (Bishops' Committee on Priestly Life and Ministry, *The Priest and Stress* [Washington, D.C.: USCC, 1982] 11).

[37] See c. 644 and commentary.

[38] The only other remedy would be mediation or arbitration (c. 1733). The code does provide, however, special procedures for the removal (cc. 1740–1747) and transfer (1748–1752) of pastors.

in disobedience after a warning is to be punished with a just penalty (c. 1371, 2°).

In making assignments, indeed, in exercising authority over his clerics, the bishop is to be guided by the principles of the Second Vatican Council. An intimate relationship is established between them by the sacrament of ordination which confers on priests a share in the episcopal ministry (*PO* 7). The bishop is "to regard his priests, who are his co-workers, as sons and friends, just as Christ called his disciples no longer servants but friends" (*LG* 28). Since priests have a joint responsibility to advance the cause of the Church, obedience to Christ demands that while "they confidently propose their plans and urgently explain the needs of the flock entrusted to them, they should always be prepared to submit to the judgment of those who exercise the chief function in ruling God's church" (*PO* 15).

The bishop for his part has a "sacred duty" to know his priests individually and intimately—"their character and talents, their likes and dislikes, their spiritual life, zeal and plans, their health and economic situation, their family and whatever concerns them...in sincere, friendly dialogue, he converses with them about their work, the offices entrusted to them and also about matters pertaining to the life of the whole diocese" (*Directory for Bishops,* n. 111). With a real appreciation of the principles of co-responsiblity the bishop must enter into a serious consultation before making an assignment that will have a significant impact on the life of a priest.

In the appointment of a permanent deacon the bishop is to ascribe duties "which are congruent with his personal abilities, his celibate or married state, his formation, age, and with his spiritually valid aspirations." The decree of appointment is to clearly specify "the territory in which his ministry is to be exercised or those to whom he is to minister"; it is also to indicate "whether the office conferred is to be discharged on a partial or full-time basis" and to name "the priest who has the *cura animarum*" of the people concerned (*Directory for the Ministry and Life of Permanent Deacons,* n. 8).

Clerical Cooperation

Canon 275 — §1. Since clerics all work for the same purpose, namely, the building up of the Body of Christ, they are to be united among themselves by a bond of brotherhood and prayer and are to strive for cooperation among themselves according to the prescripts of particular law.

This canon, which is new to the 1983 code, is taken from the conciliar document *Presbyterorum ordinis* 8 which stresses the intimate sacramental bond uniting them; though the document does not speak of deacons, they, too, share in the same sacrament. No matter how diverse the apostolates in which they labor, all clerics contribute toward the building up of the Body of Christ. The older should welcome the younger, assisting them to fit into the ministry, and both groups should try to bridge the generation gap through mutual understanding. "They should be particularly concerned about those who are sick, about the afflicted, the overworked, the lonely," in short those experiencing difficulties. The decree notes that apostolic enterprises "must often overstep the boundaries of one parish or diocese": "No priest is sufficiently equipped to carry out his own mission alone and as it were single-handed" (*PO* 7). Parish priests "should therefore collaborate both with other parish priests and with those priests who are exercising a pastoral function in the district (such as vicars forane and deans) or who are engaged in works of an extra-parochial nature" (*CD* 30, 1). The precise nature of the cooperation may be worked out in particular law. Permanent deacons are also held to collaborate with each other and with the bishop to foster the mission of the Church (*Directory for the Ministry and Life of Permanent Deacons,* n. 9).

§2. Clerics are to acknowledge and promote the mission which the laity, each for his or her part, exercise in the Church and in the world.

Again echoing the council, the law calls upon the clergy sincerely to appreciate and promote the place of the laity in the mission of the Church (*PO* 9). The sacred pastors should "confidently assign offices to them in the service of the church, leaving them freedom and scope for activity" (*LG* 37). Whereas an earlier draft of the code was satisfied with clerics "recognizing" the role of the laity, the promulgated version adds the responsibility of positively "promoting" it. This duty is stressed even more forcefully with respect to pastors of parishes (c. 529, §2). The right that the laity have to participate in the Church's mission (c. 225, §1) is paralleled here by the obligation of clerics to see that this right is accorded them and that institutions are available to enable that right to be exercised.

In December 1981 the Pontifical Council on the Laity issued a study document explaining the identity and mission of priests within associations of the laity. It sees the priest as the "architect of unity" both within the association and within the Church at large. He is to guarantee that its goals are essentially religious and not political or social or economic.[39]

Holiness of Life

Canon 276 — §1. In leading their lives, clerics are bound in a special way to pursue holiness since, having been consecrated to God by a new title in the reception of orders, they are dispensers of the mysteries of God in the service of His people.

The formulation of the basic obligation incumbent upon clerics is taken from the conciliar decree *Presbyterorum ordinis*. All Christians through their baptismal consecration are "enabled and obliged even in the midst of human weakness to seek perfection." Clerics, "consecrated to God in a new way by their ordination and made the living instruments of Christ the eternal priest," are bound by a special claim to acquire this perfection (*PO* 12, *LG* 39). "It is through the daily sacred actions, and through the whole of their ministry, which

they carry out in communion with the bishop and their fellow priests that they are set on the right course to perfection of life" (*PO* 12). The 1917 code expressed this duty to acquire holiness in comparative terms: clerics ought to lead a holier life than the laity, both interiorly and exteriorly, and surpass them by example in virtue and good deeds. The council, however, insisted that "all Christians in any state or walk of life are called to the fullness of Christian life and to the perfection of love" (*LG* 40). Though the forms and duties of life are many, "holiness is one" (*LG* 41). The distinctive way for clerics to acquire holiness is through the zealous exercise of their ministry.[40]

§2. In order to be able to pursue this perfection:

1°　they are first of all to fulfill faithfully and tirelessly the duties of the pastoral ministry;

2°　they are to nourish their spiritual life from the two-fold table of sacred scripture and the Eucharist; therefore, priests are earnestly invited to offer the eucharistic sacrifice daily and deacons to participate in its offering daily;

3°　priests and deacons aspiring to the presbyterate are obliged to carry out the liturgy of the hours daily according to the proper and approved liturgical books; permanent deacons, however, are to carry out the same to the extent defined by the conference of bishops;

4°　they are equally bound to make time for spiritual retreats according to the prescripts of particular law;

5°　they are urged to engage in mental prayer regularly, to approach the sacrament of

---

[39] "Identity and Mission of Priests within Associations of the Laity," *Origins* 11 (1982) 533–547.

[40] Canon 368 of the Eastern code states this more succinctly. "Clerics are bound in a special manner to the perfection which Christ proposed to his disciples, since they are consecrated to God in a new way by sacred ordination, so that they may become more suitable instruments of Christ, the eternal priest, in the service of the people of God, and at the same time that they be exemplary models to the flock."

penance frequently, to honor the Virgin Mother of God with particular veneration, and to use other common and particular means of sanctification.

Closely following *Presbyterorum ordinis* (*PO* 13), the canon indicates the means clerics are to use in striving for perfection.[41] After the 1990 synod of bishops on the ministry and life of priests, John Paul II published an apostolic exhortation, *Pastores dabo vobis*.[42] It was followed in 1994 by a *Directory for the Life and Ministry of Priests* issued by the Congregation for the Clergy. Chapter 2 of this instruction, "Priestly Spirituality," elaborates upon the present canon and treats extensively the priestly ideal and the means to achieve it.

Faithful Service of the People

In the pursuit of holiness clerics must first of all strive faithfully and untiringly to fulfill the obligations of their pastoral ministry.[43] What *Lumen gentium* affirmed of bishops can equally be applied to all clerics who share in the episcopal ministry. That ministry zealously fulfilled "will also be for them an outstanding means of sanctification" (*LG* 41). *Presbyterorum ordinis* similarly teaches that priests who dedicate themselves completely to the service of the people "are able, in the holiness with which they have been enriched in Christ, to grow towards the perfection of humanity" (*PO* 12). The 1971 synod of bishops, which is also cited as a source for this part of the canon, summed up the connection of holiness with the fulfillment of the ministry. "The activities of the apostolate for their part furnishing an indispensable nourishment for fostering the spiritual life of the priest: 'By assuming the role of the Good Shepherd, they will find precisely in the pastoral exercise of love the bond of priestly perfection which will unify their lives and activities' (*PO* 14). In the exercise of ministry the presbyter is enlightened and strengthened by the action of the Church and the example of the laity."[44]

Preaching and Eucharist[45]

As preachers of the word they must first make it part of their lives by prayerful meditation upon the scriptures. As dispensers of the mysteries of God it behooves them to seek nourishment at the eucharistic table.[46] "In the mystery of the Eucharistic sacrifice, in which priests fulfill their principal function, the work of our redemption is continually carried out. For this reason the daily celebration of the Eucharist is earnestly recommended. This celebration is an act of Christ and the Church even if it is impossible for the faithful to be present" (*PO* 13). The code adopts this strong recommendation about the daily celebration of the eucharistic sacrifice (c. 904). Note also that deacons are "earnestly" (*enixe*) encouraged to participate in Mass every day.[47]

The conciliar document *Sacrosanctum Concilium* (the Constitution on the Sacred Liturgy) taught that "communal celebration involving the presence and active participation of the faithful" is to be "preferred," as far as possible, to a celebration that is individual and quasi-private. This rule applies with special force to the celebration of the Mass and the administration of the sacraments, even though every Mass has of itself a

---

[41] The means enumerated here are quite similar to those prescribed for the formation of clerics or seminarians (c. 246).

[42] March 25, 1992, *AAS* 84 (1992) 657–804.

[43] See E. Pfnausch, *The Relationship between Ministry and Holiness in the Life of the Diocesan Priest*, CanLawStud 543 (Washington, D.C.: Catholic University of America, 1994).

[44] *The Ministerial Priesthood* (Vatican City: Typis Polyglottis Vaticanis, 1971) 20.

[45] See cc. 762–772.

[46] The reference to the twofold table of nourishment, the scriptures and the Eucharist, appears several times in conciliar documents: *PO* 18, *DV* 21, and *PC* 6.

[47] W. Woestman, "Daily Eucharist in the Postconciliar Church," *Stud Can* 23 (1989) 85–100. See H. Kramer, "The Spiritual Life of the Deacon," in *Foundations for the Renewal of the Diaconate*, trans. D. Bourke et al. (Washington, D.C.: NCCB, 1993) 28–50.

public and social nature (*SC* 27). The code, therefore, provides: "Except for a just and reasonable cause, a priest is not to celebrate the eucharistic sacrifice without the participation of at least some member of the faithful" (c. 906). If such a participant were not readily available, the priest's devotion would be sufficient reason for him to celebrate alone. Whereas an earlier draft of the code "commended" concelebration of the Mass, canon 902 states merely that priests "can" concelebrate unless the good of the faithful urges otherwise.

The Liturgy of the Hours

Among the means for pursuing holiness the council recommended praying the liturgy of the hours. "By praying the Divine Office[48] priests themselves should extend to the different hours of the day the praise and thanksgiving they offer in the celebration of the Eucharist. By the Office they pray to God in the name of the church for the whole people entrusted to them and in fact for the whole world" (*PO* 5).[49] One of the main objectives of *Sacrosanctum Concilium* was to restore the traditional sequence of the hours so that the day would be sanctified. "Lauds as morning prayer and Vespers as evening prayer are the two hinges on which the daily office turns. They must be considered as the chief hours and are to be celebrated as such" (*SC* 89).[50]

In fulfillment of the conciliar mandate, a reformed Divine Office, known as *The Liturgy of the Hours,* was promulgated in 1971. The instruction (printed at the beginning of vol. 1) speaks of the obligation "to recite the whole sequence of Hours each day, preserving as far as possible the genuine relationship of the Hours to the time of day."[51] It introduces distinctions, however, and suggests priorities among the different hours (n. 29). Morning prayer and vespers, as the two hinges on which this liturgy turns, are not to be omitted "unless for a serious reason"; certainly their omission is to be exceptional. Clerics are to "carry out faithfully the Office of Readings, which is above all the liturgical celebration of the word of God" in order to become more perfect as disciples by welcoming that word in themselves. A lesser reason would justify the omission of the Office of Readings. "That the day may be completely sanctified they will desire to recite the middle Hour and Compline, thus commending themselves to God and completing the entire *Opus Dei* before going to bed."[52]

The code, in the spirit of the council and the instruction, imposes on bishops, priests, and deacons the juridic obligation of fulfilling daily the liturgy of the hours (cc. 276, §2, 3° and 1174, §1).[53] The rationale is clear from the council: the sacred ministers are to offer prayer in the name of the Christian community. Far more than a rule of canon law or a specific duty of clerics, the practice of reciting the Office sets up a pattern of prayer in their lives. Canon 1175 requires that "in carrying out the liturgy of the hours, the true time for each hour is to be observed insofar as possible." The canon, like the instruction, leaves to the discretion of the ordained minister the judgment of circumstances permitting any exceptions. "There is of course a danger of self-deception in this kind of decision, but there are certainly reasons or causes which, considered objec-

---

[48] The term "Divine" is used in the sense of "praise of God": "Office" (*officium*) means "a charge, an occupation," a public ritual activity of the community. Sometimes the term "canonical hours" is used.

[49] The code treats the liturgy of the hours in title II of part two of Book IV.

[50] For a history of the development see A. G. Martimort, *The Church at Prayer* (Collegeville, Minn.: Liturgical Press, 1986) IV, 151–275.

[51] ICEL, *The Liturgy of the Hours* (New York: Catholic Book Pub. Co., 1975) I, 38.

[52] Ibid.

[53] "Not all the means are juridically imposed. Clerics are juridically or canonically obliged only to recite the canonical hours daily according to proper and approved liturgical books and to a retreat according to the prescriptions of particular law. The other means of sanctification, of which only the most important are listed, are only recommended" (*Comm* 3 [1971] 193).

tively, do excuse from the Office as from other precepts of Church Law."[54]

The extent to which permanent deacons are required to pray the liturgy of the hours is left to the determination of the episcopal conference.[55] In the United States this obligation to recite the canonical hours extends to morning and evening prayer. The Bishops' Committee on the Liturgy has urged: "In view of the particular style of life and circumstances of most permanent deacons, it is appropriate that this [prayer] be done with their families."[56]

As of November 27, 1977, *The Liturgy of the Hours* became the single official version for use in the United States, approved by the NCCB and confirmed by the Holy See. That translation, as it appears in several authorized editions, or the Latin *Liturgia horarum,* must be used to fulfill the canonical obligation whether prayed in common or by individuals.[57] When non-English texts are used in the United States for the celebration of the liturgy (the Eucharist, the sacraments, and the Divine Office), they must have the approval of the episcopal conference of the country where they are published and have been confirmed by the Holy See.[58] One could use, for example, approved texts in the French, Spanish, Italian, German, or Slovenian languages.

Retreats

Like the requirement of the Divine Office, the requirement of a retreat is juridically imposed rather than merely commended.[59] It is left to particular law to specify the frequency and length of the obligation.[60] In the United States, the Third Plenary Council of Baltimore in 1884 decreed that bishops must schedule retreats for their clergy every year or at least every two years (n. 75). The diocesan bishop was to determine whether it was to be annual or biennial, where it was to take place, its duration, and the method to be followed. This particular law from the nineteenth century remains in effect under the new code just as it did after the 1917 code. In virtue of his legislative power (c. 391, §2) the diocesan bishop can establish particular law regarding retreats for the clergy. "The two most usual modes which may be prescribed by the Bishop in his own Diocese are the day of recollection (possibly monthly) and the annual retreat."[61] In view of the diversity of spiritual needs, it is desirable that some options be made available. Even the former law did not require that the retreat be in common.[62]

Other Recommended Means of Holiness

Unlike the former code (*CIC* 125) which made the diocesan bishop directly responsible for seeing that his clergy carried out such devotional practices as frequent confession, the 1983 code leaves this responsibility to the clerics themselves.

---

[54] *BCLN* 13 (1977) 88. The conciliar *Constitution on the Sacred Liturgy* declared that "in particular cases, and for adequate reasons, ordinaries may dispense their subjects, wholly or in part, from the obligation of reciting the divine office, or they may change it to another obligation" (*SC* 97). Certain religious superiors are considered ordinaries with regard to their own subjects (c. 134, §1).

[55] The NCCB determined as follows: "Although they are not bound by universal church law to say the whole of this prayer every day, permanent deacons should not hold themselves lightly excused from the obligation they have to recite morning and evening prayer" (*Complementary Norms,* 3). The episcopal conferences of Australia, Belgium, England and Wales, France, and Scotland have also made the recitation of morning and evening prayer obligatory (*CLD* 11, 30–31). The Canadian conference has established the same norm (*Code of Canon Law Annotated,* Appendix III, 1314–1315).

[56] *BCLN* 13 (1977) 88.

[57] *BCLN* 13 (1977) 89.

[58] This is the general policy adopted by the NCCB. See *BCLN* 14 (1978) 99.

[59] *Comm* 3 (1971) 193.

[60] Citing c. 533, §2, F. Coccopalmerio maintains that a pastor is to make a retreat every year ("Quaestiones de paroecia in novo Codice," *P* 76 [1987] 72).

[61] *Directory Priests,* no. 85. "In each case, it is necessary that days of recollection and especially annual spiritual retreats be seen as times of prayer and not as courses of theological-pastoral up-dating" (ibid.).

[62] M. Conte A Coronata, *Institutiones Iuris Canonici,* 4th ed. (Turin: Marietti, 1949) I: 217, no. 188.

They are to apply themselves regularly to mental prayer.[63] They are to approach the sacrament of penance frequently (*PO* 18). The code does not offer here or elsewhere any further guidelines on penance. The Sacred Congregation for Religious and Secular Institutes in the *Decree on Confession for Religious* on December 8, 1970, did indicate that "frequently" meant "twice a month."[64] In view of the opinion of commentators on the former law, once a month could be considered frequent. While special devotion to the Blessed Virgin is recommended, the rosary is not singled out. Other more particular norms may be established by the episcopal conference.[65]

Clerical Celibacy

Canon 277 — §1. Clerics are obliged to observe perfect and perpetual continence for the sake of the kingdom of heaven and therefore are bound to celibacy which is a special gift of God by which sacred ministers can adhere more easily to Christ with an undivided heart and are able to dedicate themselves more freely to the service of God and humanity.

The *Directory for the Life and Ministry of Priests* defended this canon as follows: "Convinced of the profound theological and pastoral motives upholding the relationship between celibacy and the priesthood, and enlightened by the testimony which confirms to this day, in spite of painful negative cases, its spiritual and evangelical validity, the Church has reaffirmed in Vatican Council II and repeatedly in teachings of the Pontifical Magisterium the 'firm will to maintain the

law which requires celibacy freely chosen and perpetual for candidates to priestly Ordination in the Latin rite.'"[66] After considerable discussion at the council, the law of celibacy was sustained in *Presbyterorum ordinis*. The decree noted in article 16: "Perfect and perpetual continence for the sake of the kingdom of heaven was recommended by Christ the Lord (Mt 19:12)...and has always been highly esteemed by the Church as a feature of priestly life.[67] For it is at once a sign of pastoral charity and an incentive to it as well as being in a special way a source of spiritual fruitfulness in the world." Still, it must be acknowledged, celibacy is not demanded of the priesthood by its nature, as the practice of married clergy in the primitive church and the tradition of the Eastern churches bear witness.[68] Furthermore, since the 1950s the Latin

---

[63] "Regular time each day for prayer, meditation, and spiritual reading is a *sine qua non* for the unfolding in a priest's life of authentic Christ-centeredness" (Bishops' Committee on Priestly Life and Ministry, *The Priest and Stress*, 18).

[64] *CLD* 7, 532.

[65] *Rel,* 64. The Eastern code (*CCEO* 369) repeats most of the recommendations. While it does not mention mental prayer, it does stress the daily examination of conscience and the importance of spiritual direction.

[66] *Directory Priests,* n. 57.

[67] See J. Lynch, "Marriage and Celibacy of the Clergy: The Discipline of the Western Church: An Historical Synopsis," *J* 32 (1972) 14–38, 189–212; idem, "Critique of the Law of Celibacy in the Catholic Church from the Period of the Reform Councils," in *Celibacy in the Church,* ed. W. Bassett and P. Huizing, *Con* 78 (1972) 57–75.

[68] The Eastern code, while affirming the value of celibacy, asserts the ancient practice of married clergy: "Clerical celibacy chosen for the sake of the kingdom of heaven and suited to the priesthood is to be greatly esteemed everywhere, as supported by the tradition of the whole Church; likewise, the hallowed practice of married clerics in the primitive Church and in the tradition of the Eastern Churches throughout the ages is to be held in honor" (*CCEO* 373). A requirement for the episcopate, however, is that a person "not be bound by a matrimonial bond" (*CCEO* 180, §3).
On December 23, 1929 the Sacred Congregation for the Eastern Church decreed: "Secular priests who have a wife shall not be admitted to exercise the sacred ministry in those countries [the Americas and Australia] but only celibate priests or widowers" (*CLD* 1, 20–21). The Eastern code states in canon 758, §3: "With respect to married men to be admitted to sacred orders, the particular law proper to each autonomous church or the special norms issued by the Apostolic See shall be observed." There is some doubt whether or not the 1929 norms of the Apostolic See are still in effect after the promulgation of the new Eastern code (D. Hamilton, "A Crucial Test for Optional Celibacy," *America* 176 [April 19, 1997] 13–15).

church has cautiously but increasingly permitted the ordination of former Protestant clergymen who are married.[69]

The appropriateness of celibacy to the priesthood rests on theological and spiritual grounds. It very effectively symbolizes the essence of the ministry. The priest is one entrusted with the ministry of Christ; the more complete his dedication, the more credible his work. Through celibacy the priest is consecrated in a new and excellent way to Christ, "for his sake and for the sake of the gospel" (Mk 10:29). "It is a special gift of God through which sacred ministers may more readily cling to Christ with undivided heart and dedicate themselves more freely in him and through him to the service of God and of men."[70]

The last section of article 16 of *Presbyterorum ordinis* attempts to answer the question of how the charism of celibacy that God gives to some (Mt 19:11) can be made obligatory for all priests.

This sacred Council approves and confirms this legislation so far as it concerns those destined for the priesthood, and feels confident in the Spirit that the gift of celibacy, so appropriate to the priesthood of the New Testament, is liberally granted by the Father, provided those who share Christ's

priesthood through the sacrament of Order, and indeed the whole Church, ask for the gift humbly and earnestly.

In the words of one commentator: "Priestly celibacy cannot be fully explained purely theoretically; in the end it is a matter of faith and spiritual experience, otherwise it cannot be fully lived out."[71]

This argumentation makes sense only to the believing Christian; and it becomes all the easier to understand the more one sees the charisma of celibacy as something not extraordinary, but perfectly normal within the framework of God's gracious guidance. Moreover, one may not think of this charisma, that is so deeply embedded in a man's life, as something self-contained, complete, and given all at once, as something a man either has or has not. It should be conceived, rather, as something put by God into a man's concrete historical, anthropological and psychological situation, itself possessing a history and being an adventure—the adventure of faith.[72]

The positive focus of celibacy—"for the sake of the kingdom of heaven"—in the conciliar teaching as well as in the code, is a great improvement over past presentations. "All untenable motives for celibacy—arising from notions of cultic purity or from a subliminal depreciation of the body and of sexuality—are avoided, motives still commonly mentioned until quite recently in official documents."[73]

Under the present discipline, canon 1037 requires that before the reception of the diaconate a candidate who is not married must, in a prescribed rite, assume publicly before God and the Church

---

[69] R. Hill, "Ordination of Married Protestant Ministers," *CLSAP* 51 (1989) 95–100. In the United States a number of married former Episcopal clergymen have been ordained. For the process followed see the then Bishop Bernard Law, the delegate of the SCDF, in *Origins* 11 (1982) 517–519. The Bishops' Conference of England and Wales drew up statutes for admitting married former clergymen of the Church of England to the Roman Catholic priesthood. These statutes were approved by Pope John Paul II June 2, 1995 for a period of four years (*Origins* 25 [1995] 145–148).

[70] This explanation advanced by the council did not appear in the *Schema de Populo Dei* c. 135, §1 or in the 1980 schema but was added in the promulgated canon. Also see R. Garrity, "Spiritual and Canonical Values in Mandatory Priestly Celibacy," *Stud Can* 27 (1993) 217–260.

[71] F. Wulf, in Vorgrimler 4, 283.

[72] Ibid., 287. See G. Versaldi, "Priestly Celibacy from the Canonical and Psychological Points of View," in Latourelle III: 131–157.

[73] Wulf, in Vorgrimler 4, 287.

the obligation of celibacy or have previously made a perpetual vow in a religious institute.

According to canon 1042, 1° "a man who has a wife, unless he is legitimately destined to the permanent diaconate," is impeded from receiving orders. Canon 1031, §2 also envisions married men being ordained to the permanent diaconate. Canon 1087 declares flatly, "Those in sacred orders invalidly attempt marriage." The current discipline of the Latin church is, therefore, that only those married men intended for the permanent diaconate may receive orders and that no one already in orders may subsequently be married.

The 1980 draft of the code would have exempted widowed deacons from the aforementioned impediment sacred orders poses to marriage. Because the arguments for the retention and the suppression of the impediment for the widowed deacons were so difficult to evaluate, the Secretariat referred the decision to the *Plenarium* of the Commission in October 1981. Several reasons were listed for permitting widowed deacons to remarry. Since they had not chosen celibacy but had manifested a vocation to marriage at the time they were ordained, this burdensome obligation ought not be laid upon them. Often, moreover, there were children whose care by a hired servant would pose grave economic difficulty and the danger of incontinence. Other arguments were presented to preclude such remarriage. To permit an ordained minister to marry would be going against a millenarian and even an apostolic tradition;[74] it would thus be

prejudicial to ecumenism insofar as it was at odds with the discipline of the Orthodox churches and contrary to the practice of the Eastern Catholic churches. Such an innovation was also seen as gravely injurious to sacerdotal celibacy. After weighing these considerations, the *Plenarium* by a vote of thirty-eight to thirteen affirmed that a widowed deacon could remarry and continue to exercise his order without special permission or dispensation.[75]

When the 1983 code was promulgated, however, it made no exception for widowed deacons: "Those in sacred orders invalidly attempt marriage" (c. 1087). In order for a deacon who has lost his wife to remarry, a dispensation must be sought from the Apostolic See (c. 1078, §2, 1°).[76] The dispensation has not been granted routinely. In a circular letter of June 6, 1997, the Congregation for Divine Worship and the Discipline of the Sacraments announced that the Holy Father had modified the "current norm which requires three cumulative and simultaneous conditions" to constitute "motivating exceptions for the granting of a dispensation from the prohibition of can. 1087." Henceforth "any one of the three following conditions taken singly" is sufficient "for a favorable consideration of the dispensation from this impediment, namely: (1) the great and proven usefulness of the ministry of the deacon to the dio-

---

[74] The early councils permitted the ordination of married men but did not allow the ordained to marry. At first there was a temporary concession. The Council of Ancyra (314 A.D.) in c. 10 declared: "If deacons at the time of their ordination declare they must marry, and that they cannot be continent, and if accordingly they marry, they may continue in their ministry, because the bishop gave them permission to marry; but if at the time of their ordination they were silent and received the imposition of hands and professed continence, and if later they marry, they ought to cease from their ministry" (*Corpus Iuris Canonici*, c. 8, Dist. 28). Shortly afterwards the Council of Neocaesarea (314–319) affirmed: "If a presbyter takes

a wife, he ought to be deposed from the order" (*Corpus Iuris Canonici*, c. 9, Dist. 28). In 692 A.D. the Council of Trullo which established the basic law for the Eastern churches legislated: "If any ordained person contracts matrimony, let him be deposed; if he wishes to be married, he should become so before his ordination (c. 6, *Apostolic Canons* 26).

[75] *Plen,* 138–149, 292–308.

[76] In danger of death the local ordinary could dispense from the impediment in the case of deacons but not of priests (c. 1079, §1). The NCCB secretariat reported that on December 31, 1996 out of 11,868 permanent deacons in the U.S., 3.7 percent were widowers, and some of these were widowers before their ordination. The secretariat unofficially estimated that about half of the approximately forty petitions for widowed deacons to remarry which are submitted annually receive favorable action.

cese to which he belongs; (2) the fact that he has children of such a tender age as to be in need of motherly care; (3) the fact that he has parents or parents-in-law who are elderly and in need of care."[77]

As noted above, in recent years former Protestant clergymen have been ordained to the priesthood, even though they were married. The Canon Law Society of America has on several occasions addressed the issue of the ordination of married men in the Latin church. A report on the canonical implications of such ordinations was prepared for the society in 1996 by James A. Coriden and James H. Provost.[78] It "presumes the general law of the Church as it applies to all candidates for orders and all ordained ministers in the Church" as it considers the "specific issues raised when married men are being considered for ordination, or have been ordained." The first part of the report treats entrance into sacred ministry: discernment of vocation, formation for ministry, irregularities and impediments, the need of the Church, and assurance of support. The second part studies obligations and rights: the obligation to undertake an assignment; continence and celibacy; community of life; financial support; benefits; stability; and forbidden activities. The report concludes: "Some adjustments for these implications are already possible under the present canon law. The practice of the Roman curia provides guidance for other adjustments to meet these implications."

§2. Clerics are to behave with due prudence towards persons whose company can endanger their obligation to observe continence or give rise to scandal among the faithful.

Since clerics have committed themselves to perfect and perpetual continence, they are warned to be careful about those with whom they associate lest their commitment be endangered and the faithful scandalized.[79] The former code (*CIC* 133) was much more detailed. So as not to give rise to suspicion on the part of others, clerics were not to live under the same roof with or to frequently visit women. Clerics were permitted to dwell only with those whose natural kinship (mother, sister, aunt) or whose irreproachable character and maturity obviated any skepticism about the relationship. The present code does not single out women as the likely cause of scandal; the association with certain males could be just as harmful.

In view of the terrible scandals occasioned by child abuse, clerics must avoid any physical contact with minors that would provoke legitimate comment from reasonable people, such as hugging, tickling, or wrestling. Clerics should not invite children to their rooms or allow them to stay overnight in the rectory. It would also be very imprudent for clerics to go on outings, field trips, or vacations with children unless the parents or other adults were present. The civil law in most jurisdictions defines a minor as one under the age of eighteen.

§3. The diocesan bishop is competent to establish more specific norms concerning this matter and to pass judgment in particular cases concerning the observance of this obligation.

This paragraph affirms the possibility of the direct intervention and judgment of the diocesan bishop in matters concerning the observance of celibacy. The code refrains from establishing more determinate norms for the whole Church be-

---

[77] Protocol number 263/97, *Origins* 27 (1997) 169–171.

[78] *CLSAP* 58 (1996) 438–451. Also see J. McIntyre, "Married Priests: A Research Report," *CLSAP* 56 (1994) 130–152.

[79] "'Chastity' is in the moral order; it is the virtue of correctly ordering one's sexual faculties and drives. 'Continence' is in the order of physical behavior; it describes the non-use of the sexual faculties....'Celibacy' is in the legal order; it describes that state of not being married" (J. Provost, "Offenses against the Sixth Commandment: Toward a Canonical Analysis of Canon 1395," *J* 55 [1995] 650). The parallel canon in the Eastern code is expressed in more positive terms, emphasizing the virtue of chastity: "Clerics, celibate or married, are to excel in the virtue of chastity; it is for the particular law to establish suitable means for pursuing this end" (*CCEO* 374).

cause circumstances vary so much from place to place. It is left to the bishop, therefore, to do so if he considers additional regulations to be necessary or useful. Earlier drafts called upon him to consult the presbyteral council before so acting. Presumably this requirement was seen as an infringement on the bishop's legislative power,[80] yet he is obliged, for example, to consult the council before issuing regulations on the allocation of stole fees (c. 531). In any event the bishop is still free, certainly, to seek advice from any source. The diocesan bishop also has the right to pass judgment on the observance of the obligation of celibacy in particular cases.

It is well within the competence of the bishop to enact norms regarding the association of clerics with minors and to judge inappropriate conduct. If penalties are to be imposed, he must carefully observe the law on sanctions in Book VI, especially canons 1394 and 1395.[81]

Clerical Associations

Canon 278 — §1. Secular clerics have the right to associate with others to pursue purposes in keeping with the clerical state.

The right of secular clerics[82] to form associations is acknowledged for the first time in canon law. Although canon 215 declares that the Christian faithful—which certainly includes clerics—are at liberty to establish organizations, special notice is taken of the clerical right to do so because of its importance and to remove any doubts about it.[83]

Even the right of the faithful to form associations with supernatural objectives was recognized only implicitly in the former code which commended them for joining organizations established by the Church (c. 684). The Sacred Congregation of the Council declared that this was indeed an authentic and natural right.[84] On December 10, 1949, the United Nations in its Universal Declaration of Human Rights asserted: "Everyone has the right to freedom of peaceful assembly and association. No one may be compelled to belong to an association" (art. 21). Pope John XXIII in his 1963 encyclical *Pacem in Terris* 24 offered a fuller explanation of the right.

> From the fact that human beings are by nature social, there arises the right of assembly and association. They have also the right to give the societies of which they are members the form they consider most suitable for the aim they have in view, and to act within such societies on their own initiative and on their own responsibility in order to achieve their desired objectives.... It is most necessary that a wide variety of societies or intermediate bodies be established, equal to the task of accomplishing what the individual cannot by himself efficiently achieve. These societies or intermediate bodies are to be regarded as an indispensable means in safeguarding the dignity and liberty of the human person, without harm to his sense of responsibility.[85]

The right of association is a natural right not dependent upon positive law or human concession. The council, too, insisted that since people are social by nature, they are called upon to exercise an apostolate not only as individuals but in groups. "The group apostolate is in happy harmony therefore with a fundamental need in the faithful, a need that is both human and Christian" (*AA* 18) and "while preserving intact the necessary link with ecclesiastical authority, the laity have the

---

[80] *Rel,* 65.

[81] Provost, "Offenses," 650–663.

[82] The term "secular" rather than "diocesan" clerics was used to distinguish them from clerics belonging to an institute of consecrated life or a society of apostolic life who may be engaged in the parochial ministry of a diocese (*Comm* 14 [1982] 171).

[83] *Comm* 9 (1977) 245: ComCICRec, *Schema de Populo Dei, Praenotanda,* 18.

[84] *Corrienten,* November 13, 1920, *AAS* 13 (1921) 139.

[85] *Pacem in Terris,* English trans. ed. W. Gibbons (Glen Rock, N.J.: Paulist, 1963) 12.

right to establish and direct associations, and to join existing ones" (*AA* 19).

During the debate on *Presbyterorum ordinis,* one of the last conciliar documents to be approved, the commission charged with its drafting noted: "Priests cannot be denied what the council attentive to the dignity of human nature declared as belonging to the laity since it corresponds to natural law."[86] In presenting an intermediate draft of the decree, the commission rejected a proposal that associations of priests be placed under the diocesan bishop or the conference of bishops. These associations pertain to the personal life of priests and the exercise of their legitimate liberty.[87] From a juridical point of view, furthermore, such an exercise of episcopal power would give rise to confusion between the internal and external fora. Practically speaking, also, many priests, out of respect for their ordinary, would be morally forced to join associations directed by him. A polarization would result between diocesan priests who joined associations run by the bishop and those who did not.[88]

§2. Secular clerics are to hold in esteem especially those associations which, having statutes recognized by competent authority, foster their holiness in the exercise of the ministry through a suitable and properly approved rule of life and through fraternal assistance and which promote the unity of clerics among themselves and with their own bishop.

Paragraph two of the canon, without diminishing in any way the unqualified right of clerics to form associations, cites *Presbyterorum ordinis* in singling out certain associations. It especially commends those which by means of statutes rec-

ognized by the competent authority "foster priestly holiness in the exercise of the ministry through a suitable and properly approved rule of life and through brotherly help, and so aim at serving the whole order of priests" (*PO* 8).[89] They thus provide the clergy with fraternal support, encouragement to holiness in the ministry, and a means of promoting unity among themselves and with their bishop. These associations may be diocesan, national, or international in scope. Clerics are not asked to *promote* such approved societies or forbidden to form organizations whose statutes are not submitted to any authority for approval. This paragraph again refers to "secular" clerics and repeats the conciliar text except that it speaks of "competent authority" instead of "competent ecclesiastical authority."

§3. Clerics are to refrain from establishing or participating in associations whose purpose or activity cannot be reconciled with the obligations proper to the clerical state or can prevent the diligent fulfillment of the function entrusted to them by competent ecclesiastical authority.

Here clerics are prohibited from establishing or participating in organizations incompatible with their status or duties. Certainly groups that advocate or practice violence are antithetical to the clerical commitment. On March 8, 1982, the Congregation for the Clergy issued a *Declaration on Associations of Priests, Politics and Labor.* It identified as "irreconcilable with the clerical state, and therefore prohibited to all members of the clergy," those associations of clerics "which directly or indirectly, in a manifest or clandestine manner, pursue aims relating to politics, even if presented under the external aspect of wanting to

---

[86] *AcSynVat* IV, pars 7, 168, *responsum ad Modum* 129.
[87] The Eastern code adds a qualification of the clerical right of association: "Clerics are free . . . to associate with others for the purpose of pursuing ends suitable to the clerical state. However, it belongs to the eparchial bishop to judge authentically concerning this suitability" (*CCEO* 391).
[88] *AcSynVat* IV, pars 6, 395.

[89] The qualification "statutes recognized by competent authority" was added to distinguish them from so-called "patriotic associations" in socialist states. The *responsum ad Modum* 30 noted that the associations the decree was promoting had their own juridic journey: they generally began with the approval of the bishop and finally in most instances ended with the sanction of the Apostolic See.

favor humanitarian ideals, peace and social progress." It saw these groups as sowing division in
the Christian community and blurring the priestly mission. The declaration also stigmatized as
"irreconcilable" with the clerical state those associations

> which intend to unite deacons or presbyters
> in a type of "union" thus reducing their sa-
> cred ministry to a profession or career com-
> parable to functions of a profane character.
> Such associations, in fact, compare the ex-
> ercise of the functions of the ministerial
> priesthood to a relationship of work and
> thus can easily place the clerics in opposi-
> tion to their holy pastors who become con-
> sidered only as givers of work.[90]

At one time it was considered "not expedient"
for clerics to become members or even attend
meetings of the Rotary Clubs (*CLD* 1, 617; 3,
284). Today, however, they may participate fully
in these organizations. In an allocution to the Rotary Clubs of Italy, Paul VI explained that previous "reservations" of the Church were based on a
fear that the clubs might "either be infiltrated by
false ideologies or come to be offered as an all-
sufficient guide to life, to the exclusion of Christian ideals" (*CLD* 6, 511).

In 1973 the Congregation for the Doctrine of
the Faith noted that "episcopal conferences have
from the Apostolic See the faculty of permitting
the inscription of clerics in the Rotary Club" but
not in Masonic organizations (*CLD* 8, 456). The
congregation reaffirmed the same point the next
year: "The prohibition remains in every case
against clerics and religious as well as members
of secular institutes enrolling in any kind of Ma-

sonic association" (*CLD* 8, 1211). Canon 1374,
however, forbids only in a general way membership in those associations which plot against the
Church and does not single out the Masons in this
connection. In an effort to settle the question, the
congregation on November 26, 1983, shortly after
the promulgation of the code, issued a "Declaration on Masonic Associations," which stated that
the Church's position had not changed, that Catholic membership in Masonic lodges was still prohibited.[91]

Permanent deacons also have the right to form
associations to "promote their spiritual life, to
carry out charitable and pious works and pursue
other objectives which are consonant with their
sacramental consecration and mission." They, too,
are forbidden to be involved with any association
or group "even of a civil nature which is incompatible with the clerical state" or which impedes
the fulfillment of their duties. Completely irreconcilable with the clerical state are associations
which, "under the guise of representation, organize deacons into a form of *trade(s) unions or
pressure groups,* thus reducing the sacred ministry
to a secular profession or trade" or "would prejudice the direct and immediate relationship between
every deacon and his bishop" (*Directory for the
Ministry and Life of Permanent Deacons,* n. 11).

Continuing Education

**Canon 279 — §1. Even after ordination to the
priesthood, clerics are to pursue sacred studies
and are to strive after that solid doctrine founded
in sacred scripture, handed on by their predecessors, and commonly accepted by the Church, as
set out especially in the documents of councils
and of the Roman Pontiffs. They are to avoid
profane novelties and pseudo-science.**

**§2. According to the prescripts of particular
law, priests are to attend pastoral lectures held**

---

[90] *Origins* 11 (1982) 647. "Italian newspapers said the directive was aimed specifically at organizations like
Priests for Peace in Hungary, Christian Reality in Yu-
goslavia, and *Pacem in Terris* in Czechoslovakia. These
organizations were said to work in close collaboration
with the Communist government and often to be in open
conflict with the bishops of the nation" (ibid.). The English translation is also found in *CLD* 10, 15–19.

[91] See the commentary on c. 1374 and also R. E. Jenkins,
"The Evolution of the Church's Prohibition against
Catholic Membership in Freemasonry," *J* 56 (1996) 735–
755.

after priestly ordination and, at times established by the same law, are also to attend other lectures, theological meetings, and conferences which offer them the opportunity to acquire a fuller knowledge of the sacred sciences and pastoral methods.

§3. They are also to acquire knowledge of other sciences, especially of those which are connected with the sacred sciences, particularly insofar as such knowledge contributes to the exercise of pastoral ministry.

The Second Vatican Council in several documents stressed the importance of the ongoing training of the clergy. Bishops were urged to encourage institutes and special congresses where priests might come for a renewal of life and "to acquire a deeper understanding of ecclesiastical studies, especially sacred scripture, theology, the more important social problems and new approaches to pastoral work" (*CD* 16). The fullest treatment of the subject is found in *Presbyterorum ordinis*. Priests are exhorted to study the scriptures as the primary source of sacred knowledge. They are to know the tradition of the Church as seen in the teachings of the councils and popes. It is also important for them to keep abreast of developments in secular culture.

Various means are suggested to facilitate study: "courses or congresses, the establishment of centers designed for pastoral studies, the founding of libraries and the proper direction of studies by suitable persons" (*PO* 19). To implement the conciliar directives, Paul VI in his *motu proprio Ecclesiae sanctae* (I, §7) in 1966 required special training for those newly ordained and a program of lectures on pastoral and theological matters for all priests. The Congregation for Catholic Education in January 1970 published a *Ratio fundamentalis* that included a section on post-seminary training (nn. 100–101). The 1973 *Directory for Bishops* stressed the need for a pastoral year immediately following ordination and periodic renewal courses for all priests (n. 114).

The bishops of the United States in *The Program of Continuing Education of Priests* (1972)

affirmed "the right and obligation" of every priest "to continue his spiritual growth and education."[92] The Bishops' Committee on Priestly Life and Ministry in *As One Who Serves* (1977) noted that a priest's "right to strong support" in furthering his education included financial assistance.[93]

The first paragraph of canon 279 stating the obligation of clerics to continue their sacred studies is taken almost verbatim from the previous code (*CIC* 129) except for two concerns emphasized in the council: that the source of doctrine is sacred scripture, and that the tradition of the Church is to be found especially in the documents of the councils and of the popes. *The Directory for the Life and Ministry of Priests* explains the need for ongoing formation:

> Rapid and widespread transformations and a secularized social fabric typical of the contemporary world are what make unavoidable the priest's duty of being adequately prepared, so that he not lose his own identity and so that he might respond to the demands of the new evangelization. To this grave duty corresponds the specific right of the faithful, who feel the effects of priests' solid formation and sanctity in a definite way.[94]

This paragraph places the obligation of continuing education on all clerics, on bishops and permanent deacons as well as on priests. The NCCB Secretariat for the Diaconate conducted a survey in 1995. Almost 70 percent of the dioceses reported having a requirement for the continuing education of permanent deacons. The number of hours

---

[92] (Washington, D.C.: USCC, 1972) n. 3.

[93] *As One Who Serves: Reflections on the Pastoral Ministry of Priests in the United States* (Washington, D.C.: NCCB, 1977) 60.

[94] *Directory Priests,* n. 69. See National Organization for Continuing Education of the Roman Catholic Clergy, *Handbook for Continuing Formation of Priests* (Chicago: NOCERCC, 1994).

of education prescribed per year averaged slightly over twenty.[95] The *Directory for the Ministry and Life of Permanent Deacons* (nn. 63–92) treats extensively the indispensable obligation for both bishops and deacons to pursue an "adequate, integral formation" (n. 63). "With the approval of the bishop, a realistic program of ongoing formation should be drawn up in accordance with the present dispositions, taking due account of factors such as the age and circumstances of deacons, together with the demands made on them by their pastoral ministry" (n. 79).

The second paragraph of the canon requires priests[96] to attend pastoral lectures and theological meetings or conferences in order to develop their knowledge and pastoral techniques. If continuing education is to be effective, structures or programs must be established. It is imperative that they not only be planned but also actually implemented. "A clear work structure is called for: with *objectives, specific topics* and *instruments* to carry them out."[97] Particular law is to determine the specifics of the program. Some dioceses have also made available to the clergy more elaborate options such as the sabbatical.[98] After seven years of service one may be permitted to spend an extended period of time away from normal pastoral duties for purposes of enrichment. On an annual basis clergy may also be entitled to a certain number of days off to attend workshops or other continuing education courses. The priests' *Directory*

insists that the priest himself is "the person primarily responsible for ongoing formation." Based on his capacities and specific talents, he "will strive to furnish himself with books and magazines with sound doctrine and of proven utility, for his spiritual life and the fruitful development of his ministry."[99] The continuing education obligation of the priest carries with it the right to be accorded sufficient time and resources for its fulfillment.

The last paragraph of the canon calls for priests[100] to cultivate other disciplines, especially those that will further their ministerial activity. The priests' *Directory* notes that "a special treatment must be reserved to the questions posed by scientific advances, which are especially influential to the mentality of contemporary men. Priests must be up-to-date and prepared to respond to questions that science may pose in its advancement."[101] The Eastern code succinctly charges clerics to acquire "as much knowledge of profane sciences, especially those sciences connected more intimately with the sacred sciences, such as those which cultured people ought to have" (*CCEO* 372, §3).

Common Life

Canon 280 — Some practice of common life is highly recommended to clerics; where it exists, it must be preserved as far as possible.

Although common life among diocesan clergy had been encouraged by regional councils and popes from the early Middle Ages, the 1917 code for the first time recommended it as a universal norm with specific application to the pastor and his assistants. Commentators agreed that the directive that a parochial assistant live in the rectory was a recommendation rather than a precept except where common life had been customary.

---

[95] *National Study on the Permanent Diaconate of the Catholic Church in the United States: 1994–1995* (Washington, D.C.: USCC, 1996).

[96] Here the canon specifies priests (*sacerdotes*), the only canon among the obligations and rights that does not refer generically to *clerici*. The priests' *Directory* (n. 93) stresses the need for carefully organized formation in the first years of priesthood.

[97] *Directory Priests*, n. 86. See J. S. Duarte, *The Diocesan Bishop's Solicitude for the Intellectual Life of Diocesan Priests,* CanLawStud 547 (Washington, D.C.: Catholic University of America, 1996).

[98] *Directory Priests,* n. 83. See National Association of Church Personnel Administrators, *Priests' Personnel Policies,* rev. ed. (Cincinnati: NACPA, 1990).

[99] *Directory Priests*, n. 87.

[100] The subject of the sentence carries over from the previous sentence.

[101] *Directory Priests,* n. 77.

Some even held that a bishop could not impose it where a contrary custom prevailed.[102]

The common life is generally understood as living under the same roof and sharing the same table. It is not to be confused with the common life of religious that connotes especially a sharing of goods or property. No juridical bond arises as in a society with rules and a superior. The practice of clerics living together is a safeguard of celibacy and a means of fostering other virtues.

The Second Vatican Council, the first ecumenical council to treat the common life of the clergy, took up the subject in *Presbyterorum ordinis*. The bishops were sharply divided over how strongly to recommend community life. One group pointed out how difficult this type of life would be if love and forbearance were lacking. Thus the proposal that it be observed "to the greatest extent possible" was rejected. Another group sought a more emphatic formulation than that in the 1917 code, even if it were not yet feasible to prescribe a *vita communis* for all the clergy. The final text read:

> Moreover, in order to enable priests to find mutual help in cultivating the intellectual and spiritual life, to promote better cooperation amongst them in the ministry, to safeguard them from possible dangers arising from loneliness, it is necessary to develop some kind of common or shared life for them. This can take different forms according to varying personal and pastoral needs: by priests' living together where this is possible, or by their sharing a common table, or at least meeting at frequent intervals. *(PO 8)*

The *Directory for Bishops* also took note of the dangers of a solitary ministry. Bishops were warned to take "special care that priests, especially the young, are not left to work isolated or all alone, as can happen in small or almost deserted places, where for several days a week there is no opportunity to exercise the ministry." It is "very opportune that the bishop suggest ways for them to have community life."[103] Where no form of community life can be maintained, the bishop is urged to arrange "conferences at certain times for the sake of studies, piety and fraternal joy."[104] It is important for priests to experience and foster the sense of communion and solidarity.

The sources listed for canon 280 are the 1917 code (*CIC* 134), *Presbyterorum ordinis* 8, and the bishops' *Directory*, n. 112. The first example of community of life is a common residence. Several new canons in the code offer a means for fostering such a life-style. Although a pastor is ordinarily to live in a parish house close to the church, the local ordinary in particular cases may permit him to live in a house shared by several presbyters (c. 533, §1). Similarly, the parochial vicar, ordinarily obliged to live in the parish, may be permitted to reside in a house common to several priests. Where possible, some manner of common life between the pastor and the parochial vicars is to be encouraged (c. 550). The desire of several priests to live a common life could justify establishing a team ministry (c. 517, §1), "thus making the *communio ministeriorum* of the presbyterium a reality at the parochial level."[105]

When sharing a residence is not feasible, some measures of common life can still be realized. It is especially important for newly ordained priests and deacons to experience some form of common life in their pastoral year (*Directory Priests*, n. 82). Canon 275, §1 requires the clergy "to be united among themselves by a bond of brotherhood and prayer and to strive for cooperation among themselves." Bishops are urged to favor priests' associations that promote holiness "through a suitably regulated life and fraternal charity" (*Directory for Bishops*, no. 109c); the clergy are to hold such societies in high regard (c. 278, §2). Meetings that bishops must arrange for

---

[102] E. Voosen, "De residentia parochorum," *IP* 17 (1937) 52–63, esp. 56, held that the bishop needed the permission of the Holy See to impose common life.

[103] *Directory for Bishops*, n. 112.

[104] Ibid., n. 109.

[105] Corecco, "Aspects of the Reception of Vatican II," 288.

continuing education (c. 279, §2) are opportunities for the clergy to experience fraternal support and brotherhood. Communal participation in liturgical prayer is particularly recommended (*Directory Priests,* no. 29).

At the 1990 synod of bishops devoted to the formation of priests in contemporary circumstances, it was suggested that every diocese have a "kind of mother house for priests in which they could always feel welcome and be supported by their bishop and priest brothers."[106] Accordingly, the priests' *Directory* recommends a "House for Clerics" for holding meetings or gatherings and "also as a reference place for other various circumstances. Such a house should offer all the organizational structure which will make it comfortable and attractive."[107] In summary, one may define *common life* among diocesan priests as *"a number of modes of living a shared life in which the sacramentally-based communion among priests is manifested."*[108] Although the conciliar and later documents refer to priests and the presbyterate, the canon itself is addressed to all clerics. Some provision, therefore, must be made for community life among permanent deacons whether married or not.[109]

---

[106]Laszlo Danko, intervention at the 16th general congregation, October 10, 1990, in G. Caprile, *Il sinodo dei vescovi 1990* (Rome: Edizioni La Civiltà Cattolica, 1991) 286 as quoted by J. Johnston, "Fostering and Preserving the Common Life of Diocesan Priests," JCL thesis, Catholic University of America, 1995, 75.

[107]*Directory Priests,* no. 84.

[108]Johnston, 83.

[109]"The mutual support and fraternity of deacons are not just sociologically or psychologically useful things; they are integral parts of the meaning of their vocation. Deacons are, therefore, encouraged to cultivate a sense of community among themselves. They have a diaconal ministry toward one another, too, which they can exercise in countless ways, both informally and formally, as, for example, by establishing regional or diocesan diaconal communities. In these communities, they can meet regularly to pray and to reflect together about their work, to address common problems, to study together, and to support one another." NCCB, *Permanent Deacons in the United States,* nn. 124–125.

Clerical Remuneration and Support

Canon 281 — §1. Since clerics dedicate themselves to ecclesiastical ministry, they deserve remuneration which is consistent with their condition, taking into account the nature of their function and the conditions of places and times, and by which they can provide for the necessities of their life as well as for the equitable payment of those whose services they need.

Based on their dedication to the ministry, priests, according to the council, are entitled to a just remuneration; "the laborers deserve their wage" (Lk 10:7) and "they who proclaim the Gospel should get their living by the Gospel" (1 Cor 9:14). If, therefore, provision is not forthcoming from another source, "the faithful are duty bound to provide a decent and fitting livelihood for their priests." The obligation "arises from the fact that the priests are working for the benefit of the laity." Bishops should ensure "the decent support of those who hold or have held any office in God's service" (*PO* 20).

The council deliberately chose the term "remuneration" rather than "pay or salary" (*merces*) in order to avoid the usual association of "job and wages."[110] The performance of the ministry establishes a claim to remuneration but not in the same way that a laborer's work creates a right to wages. There could be situations in which the cleric's right would have to give way to the salvation of souls—"which must always be the supreme law in the Church" (c. 1752). The 1917 code, for example, permitted a parish to be erected even if fitting support of the pastor were unavailable, as long as at least the necessities of life could be met (*CIC* 1415, §3). The Pontifical Commission for the Authentic Interpretation of the Code decided in 1945 that a bishop may not leave a parish unfilled because of the financial difficulties of the diocese.[111] The Third Plenary Council of Baltimore urged priests in charge of missions to be

---

[110]*Acta Synodalia* 4, pars 7, p. 226, n. 22.

[111]*CLD* 3, 118

content with their income if it fell below that prescribed by the diocesan statutes. The bishop was not obliged to make up the difference later, if the pastor had received from church income sufficient funds for his shelter and sustenance (n. 273)

The Second Vatican Council went on to elaborate specifics of the support to which priests are entitled. With due regard for differences of time and place as well as the nature of the office held, "the remuneration to be received by each priest should be fundamentally the same for all living in the same circumstances." The amount should be in keeping with their status and "sufficient to ensure that they are able to pay those who work in their service and also are able to give to those in need" as well as to enjoy a vacation for themselves (*PO* 20).

The 1971 synod of bishops insisted that the fitting support of priests was a matter of justice. It declared that their remuneration, which "must be as far as possible, equitable and sufficient, is a duty of justice and must also include social security. Excessive differences in this matter must be removed, especially between priests of the same diocese or jurisdiction."[112]

Canon 281, which seeks to implement the conciliar texts on compensation, is applied to all clerics and not just to priests. It states that "since clerics dedicate themselves to ecclesiastical ministry, they deserve remuneration." It reiterates the conciliar direction that the remuneration be consistent with the nature of the office and in accord with conditions of time and place. The amount, then, would vary for a bishop, pastor, assistant pastor, transitional deacon, and so forth. What would be considered adequate in a Third World country would not be appropriate in the United States. Because of inflation and other economic fluctuations, adjustments should be made from time to time. Increments based on length of service may also be allowed. In general, a cleric's income should be sufficient to enable him to live with fitting dignity in conformity with the general economic conditions of his locality as well as meet

the obligations to which he is subject.[113]

In addition to basic necessities, a suitable livelihood includes sufficient income for continuing education (c. 279), vacation (c. 283, §2), hospitality, charitable giving (c. 282, §2), and provision for the future. The canon further specifies that the cleric should be able to pay a just wage to those who provide him service. John Paul II, referring to clerics employed by the Holy See, noted that they should have the means "to carry out the duties of their state, including responsibilities which they may have in certain cases toward parents or other family members dependent on them."[114]

The context of this canon, in the chapter on rights and obligations of clerics, indicates that the remuneration of the clergy is indeed a matter of right, but it is difficult to determine whether or not it is a right in the strict sense. In fact, nothing is said here about who has the obligation of providing the remuneration. Note that neither the conciliar text (*PO* 20) nor the canon affirms a *right* on the part of the cleric.[115]

Another difficulty presents itself. Is the remuneration due to the fact that the cleric performs ministerial work or due simply to his incardination into the particular church "for whose service he has been advanced" (c. 266, §1)? The answer

---

[112] *Ultimis temporibus, CLD* 7, 364.

[113] P. Hannan, *The Canonical Concept of Congrua Sustentatio for the Secular Clergy, CanLawStud* 302 (Washington, D.C.: Catholic University of America, 1950) 124.

[114] *Origins* 12 (December 9, 1982) 420.

[115] A proposal to use the term *ius* was rejected at the council (*Acta Synodalia* 4, pars 7, p. 226, n. 22). The Revision Commission similarly declined the suggestion of Cardinal Franz König to state in §2 of this canon that clerics enjoyed the right (*iure gaudent*) to social assistance: "The text of the canon seems sufficient for establishing the right itself while avoiding terminology which would place the sacerdotal ministry—broader than 'office' or '*munus*'—in a less appropriate economic context" (*Rel,* 67; *Comm* 14 [1982] 172 ad c. 255, §2). Nevertheless, canon 390, §1 of the Eastern code affirms that "clerics have the right [*jus*] to a suitable sustenance and to receive a just remuneration for carrying out the office or function committed to them." Note, too, that the Eastern code makes a clear distinction between "remuneration" and "sustenance."

has been advanced" (c. 266, §1)? The answer would seem to rest on the meaning of the introductory clause, which begins with the Latin "*cum*" and has the verb in the indicative mood. Is the "*cum*" to be translated "since" (causal sense) or "when" (temporal sense)? The approved translation above has decided in favor of the causal "since." According to the rules of Latin grammar, however, "*cum,*" when followed by a verb in the indicative mood, indicates "when" (temporal); while "*cum*" with a verb in the subjunctive mood indicates "since" (cause). The 1977 draft used the subjunctive mood, which clearly called for the translation, "since they dedicate themselves to the ministry." The final promulgated text uses the indicative mood and the main verb was also changed from the forceful "they *must* receive remuneration" (1977 version) to the present weaker "they *deserve* remuneration." Unless an authentic interpretation of the canon rules otherwise, one could make the argument, at least on the basis of grammar, that a cleric deserves remuneration from the Church when he devotes himself to ecclesiastical ministry. The canon "bases remuneration on the fact that the cleric performs an *ecclesiastical office,* independently of whether or not he is incardinated into the diocese or institute in which he performs this office."[116]

If clerics who are engaged in the ministry deserve remuneration, what may be said of those who are not so engaged? Do all the clergy deserve remuneration or only those who actively engage in the ministry? (Sick and retired clergy are covered in the next paragraph.) The code distinguishes between "remuneration" (as treated in this canon) and "decent support."[117] Canon 269, 1° forbids a diocesan bishop to incardinate a cleric unless "the necessity or advantage of his own particular church demands it, and without prejudice to the prescripts of the law concerning the decent support of clerics." Similarly, canon 384 states that the diocesan bishop "is to take care that provision is made for [the] decent support and social assistance [of his priests], according to the norm of law." Remuneration, on the other hand, is a term that extends beyond what is necessary to meet basic needs. As defined above, it is an amount sufficient to allow, in accordance with the cleric's condition, for continuing education, a vacation, and other reasonable amenities.

Though the Latin code does not assert specifically a cleric's right to ministry, as does the Eastern code (*CCEO* 371, §1), the right to exercise the ministry to which one has been ordained is clearly understood in the law. Rincón Pérez maintains that so long as a cleric is willing to accept an assignment, "the bishop is obliged to provide him not only with basic decent support, but also with remuneration in keeping with his condition."[118]

The "right to exercise orders can be limited only in one of two ways: the imposition of a penalty, or the declaration of an impediment from the exercise of a sacred order which has been received" (cf. c. 1044).[119] Canon 1336, §1, 2° provides that a cleric's right can be restricted by means of an expiatory penalty. Here the right to exercise ministry and the right to remuneration are at issue. Thus, through the infliction of a penalty the remuneration of a cleric could be severely impacted. Canon 1350, §1, however, insists that when penalties are imposed, except that of dismissal from the clerical state, "provision must always be made so that he [the cleric] does not lack those things necessary for his decent support."

The canon on remuneration clearly does not require that the amount be the same for all clerics.

---

[116] V. De Paolis, "The Maintenance of the Clergy," in Latourelle I: 683.

[117] *CCEO* 390, §1 clearly distinguishes the two: "Clerics have the right to a suitable sustenance and to receive a just remuneration for carrying out the office or function committed to them."

[118] T. Rincón Pérez, *Manual de Derecho Canónico*, ed. Instituto Martin de Azpilcueta (Pamplona: EUNSA, 1988) 197–198 cited in J. Provost, "Effects of Incardination," *Clergy Procedural Handbook* (Washington, D.C.: CLSA, 1992) 48. It would seem that a cleric "who stubbornly refuses to accept any and all assignments from his bishop has no claim on remuneration," translator's note, *Pamplona ComEng* 234.

[119] G. Ingels, *RRAO 1997,* 37.

The remuneration is to be "consistent with their condition, taking into account the nature of their function and the conditions of places and times." It is left to particular law to determine the circumstances and conditions that will affect it. "Thus, a diocesan bishop does have the right to establish policies regarding the remuneration of clergy who are unable to exercise the ministry or are impeded from that exercise."[120]

The case of a cleric who has become ineligible for assignment because of culpable criminal activity is particularly complicated. As noted above, complete clerical support may be withdrawn only through the penalty of dismissal from the clerical state (canon 1350, §1). If the cleric is able to support himself in a secular job, the bishop, according to canonists, would fulfill the obligation of support by helping him during the transitional period. "It does not seem that it is the diocese's responsibility to care for the rest of his life for a priest who committed serious crimes, especially if he was informed beforehand of their gravity and the consequences. The priest must assume responsibility for his own actions."[121]

§2. Provision must also be made so that they possess that social assistance which provides for their needs suitably if they suffer from illness, incapacity, or old age.

After considering clerics actively engaged in the ministry, the canon in its second paragraph requires that provision be made for those who are ill, incapacitated, or elderly. The law is merely ap-

plying to the clergy a right which John XXIII affirmed as belonging to every human being: "the right to security in case of sickness, inability to work, widowhood, old age, unemployment, or in any other case in which he is deprived of the means of subsistence through no fault of his own" (*Pacem in terris* 11). "In countries where social security has not yet been adequately organized for the benefit of clergy, episcopal conferences are to make provision...for the setting up of diocesan organizations...for the proper support of priests who suffer from ill health, disability or old age" (*PO* 21).[122] The NCCB on November 18, 1987, adopted "Norms for Priests and Their Third Age," which deal with retirement and health care issues.[123] "The bishop normally should allow any priest to retire when he has reached the age of seventy-five." "Each diocese should guarantee that priests be given adequate support through a long-range, financially independent, and professionally managed pension fund." The dioceses are advised to avail themselves of the resources and expertise "provided by national organizations both within and outside the Church."

§3. Married deacons who devote themselves completely to ecclesiastical ministry deserve remuneration by which they are able to provide for the support of themselves and their families. Those who receive remuneration by reason of a civil profession which they exercise or have exercised, however, are to take care of the needs of themselves and their families from the income derived from it.

This paragraph concerns married deacons.[124] Those who work full time in the ministry are to receive remuneration sufficient to maintain them-

---

[120] Ibid., 38.

[121] F. Morrissey, "Procedures to Be Applied in Cases of Alleged Sexual Misconduct by a Priest," *Stud Can* 26 (1993) 71. According to John Beal, "The diocese may fulfill its obligation to see to the cleric's support by assisting him to find appropriate secular employment," perhaps by "making available vocational counseling and education for a career in an area in which the cleric demonstrates some aptitude and interest" ("Doing What One Can: Canon Law and Clerical Sexual Misconduct," *J* 52 [1992] 681). For other opinions see under c. 281 in *RRAO:* G. Ingels 1989 and J. Provost 1993.

[122] See the commentary on c. 1274 which treats extensively of a fund to meet the need.

[123] NCCB-*CompNm,* 50–52. For a history of and commentary on the development of the norms, see Hesch, 163–180.

[124] All deacons, transitional or permanent, celibate or married, are clerics (c. 266).

selves and their families.[125] This provision specifies one implication of the first paragraph to the effect that clerics deserve remuneration in accord with their condition, which in this case is that of a married person. The paragraph also includes the exception made in the *motu proprio* restoring the permanent diaconate to the effect that those who practice a secular profession should support themselves and their families from its income. However, the important qualification that they support themselves from secular income *"insofar as possible"* which appears in the *motu proprio* is omitted in the canon.[126] Number 119 of the 1984 NCCB diaconate guidelines restates this text of the code.[127] It then continues: "Expenses incurred by deacons in the exercise of their ministry should be recompensed by the agency, institution, or diocese for which the ministry was undertaken." Nothing is said about deacons whose secular income is not enough to provide sufficient remuneration to support their families. Nor is anything said either in the canon or in the *Guidelines* about remuneration for deacons who serve on a part-time basis or about the support that is due those deacons who lose their secular jobs or the support of their families in case of death.[128] If, however, according to canon 231, §2 lay persons who devote themselves

to special service of the Church have the right to remuneration to provide decently for themselves and their family as well as a "right for their social provision, social security, and health benefits," deacons, too, must be so entitled. Canon 1274, §1 requires, furthermore, that a special fund be set up in every diocese "for the support of clerics who offer service for the benefit of the diocese, unless provision is made for them in another way." Paragraph two of the same canon mandates the episcopal conference in an area where no other provision exists to establish a fund "which provides sufficiently for the social security of clerics."

The *Directory for the Ministry and Life of Permanent Deacons* requires deacons who are professionally employed "to provide for their own upkeep from the ensuing emoluments" (n. 15). Both celibate and married deacons who minister full time "have a right to be remunerated according to the general principle of law (c. 281.1) should they have no other source of income" (nn. 17–18). The *Directory* acknowledges the difficulty in attempting to draw up general norms concerning the upkeep of deacons "which are binding in all circumstances, given the great diversity of situations in which deacons work, in various particular churches and countries (n. 15). "It is for particular law to provide opportune norms in the complex matter of reimbursing expenses, including, for example, that those entities and parishes which benefit from the ministry of a deacon have an obligation to reimburse him those expenses incurred in the exercise of his ministry" (n. 20). "Particular law may also determine the obligation devolving on the diocese when a deacon, through no fault of his own, becomes unemployed. Likewise, it will be opportune to define the extent of diocesan liability with regard to the widows and orphans of deceased deacons. Where possible, deacons, before ordination, should subscribe to a mutual assurance (insurance) policy which affords cover for these eventualities" (n. 20).

---

[125] *SDO*, IV, n. 19, *CLD* 6, 581. The employment of permanent deacons in the United States was included in the 1995 survey. About 5 percent of the deacons receive some compensation for diaconal ministry, 5 percent for other ministries. Some 3.4 percent are salaried in full-time ministry, 1.6 percent in part-time ministry; 5.5 percent are salaried in positions such as diocesan director of finance, director of the diocesan diaconate program, and director of religious education (*National Study,* 18).

[126] *SDO*, IV, n. 21, *CLD* 6, 581. The canon also omits the provision in *SDO* n. 20 that "it will be up to the episcopal conference to make specific rules on the decent support of a deacon and of his family if he is married, in accordance with local circumstances." The responsibility is left, therefore, to the diocesan bishop.

[127] Bishops' Committee on the Permanent Diaconate, rev. ed. (Washington, D.C.: NCCB, 1984).

[128] *RRAO 1995,* 45–50. The Eastern code recognizes the right that families of clerics have to support: "[Clerics] also have the right that there be provided for themselves

as well as for their families, if they are married, suitable pension funds, social security as well as health benefits" (*CCEO* 390, §2).

Canon 282 — §1. Clerics are to foster simplicity of life and are to refrain from all things that have a semblance of vanity.

After affirming their right to a decent livelihood, the law considers how the clergy ought to use temporal goods. This canon is based on *Presbyterorum ordinis* 17 which invites priests to "embrace voluntary poverty" in order to "become more clearly conformed to Christ and more ready to devote themselves to the sacred ministry." Priests and bishops alike are "to avoid everything that might in any way antagonize the poor"; "they are to put aside all appearance of vanity in their surroundings" so that "nobody, even the humblest, is ever afraid to visit."

The canon interprets the council's call to voluntary poverty to mean a simple life-style, one that avoids ostentation and luxury. As in the previous canon concerned with clergy support, circumstances of time and place must be taken into account. What would be considered a luxury in one age or locality might be commonplace in another.

§2. They are to wish to use for the good of the Church and works of charity those goods which have come to them on the occasion of the exercise of ecclesiastical office and which are left over after provision has been made for their decent support and for the fulfillment of all the duties of their own state.

Whatever monies bishops and priests receive from the exercise of an ecclesiastical office they are to use primarily for their own decent support and the fulfillment of their duties of state. Any surplus, according to the council, they "should be willing to devote" to the good of the Church or to works of charity. They are not to regard "an ecclesiastical office as a source of profit and are not to spend the income accruing from it for increasing their own fortunes" (*PO* 17).

The canon, therefore, exhorts clerics to use any funds derived from an ecclesiastical office which are not necessary for the maintenance of their status for the good of the Church and for charitable

purposes. The 1977 draft of the canon was more preceptive in character, "they should use" (*destinent*), but was deliberately adjusted to "they are to wish to use" (*velint impendere*).[129] Clerics are thus urged rather than obliged to use superfluous funds in this way. Such monies should not be used for personal enrichment or for investment as capital. The canon is referring to all emoluments received by clerics in the performance of their official duties. Certainly what a cleric inherits or earns by use of his talents in writing or musical composition may be freely accumulated. Clerics, like all the faithful, are bound to assist the poor from their own resources (c. 222, §2). The universal law does not speak of the obligation to make a will in view of varying circumstances throughout the world;[130] however, particular law may well provide suitable norms in this matter.[131]

Clerical Residence and Vacation

Canon 283 — §1. Even if clerics do not have a residential office, they nevertheless are not to be absent from their diocese for a notable period of time, to be determined by particular law, without at least the presumed permission of their proper ordinary.

A cleric must ordinarily reside within his diocese. Since one is ordained for the good of the diocese, he is supposed to have some assignment or at least be at the disposition of the bishop should a need for his services arise. A bishop may permit individual clerics to reside outside the diocese for the good of the Church (c. 271), for personal reasons such as health or continuing education (c. 279, §2), and for any reason he judges justifiable. Particular law will determine the length of time beyond which a cleric needs the permis-

[129] *Comm* 14 (1982) 80–81.

[130] *Rel*, 68.

[131] The Eastern canon 385, §1 is quite similar to this canon in the Latin code but speaks of all the temporal goods a cleric possesses and not just those acquired through the exercise of an ecclesiastical office.

sion of his bishop in order to be legitimately absent. Presumed permission means the prudent judgment of the cleric that under the circumstances the bishop would approve his leaving the diocese. The Commission Secretariat noted that this canon also applies to permanent deacons.[132]

Pastors and parochial vicars responsible for the pastoral care of the faithful are bound by special regulations.[133] Canon 533, §2 requires a pastor who will be away from his parish beyond a week to inform the local ordinary of his absence.[134] According to canon 550, §1 the parochial vicar is obliged to live within the parish or, if appointed for different parishes jointly, in one of them. Nevertheless, for a just cause, the local ordinary can allow him to reside elsewhere, especially in a house shared by several presbyters.

§2. They are entitled, however, to a fitting and sufficient time of vacation each year as determined by universal or particular law.

Presbyterorum ordinis states forcefully: "Priests' remuneration should be such as to allow the priest a proper holiday each year. The bishop should see to it that priests are able to have a holiday" (*PO* 20). In the 1977 draft of the canon the annual vacation was explicitly called a right (*ius*) of clerics.[135] Without explanation the text was later changed to "clerics are entitled to" a vacation.[136] The length of the vacation was to be determined by general or particular law.

The code specifies certain norms for those who hold residential offices. It permits a pastor to take a month's vacation every year, not counting the time spent on retreat (c. 533, §2). The same amount of vacation time is granted the parochial vicar (c. 550, §3). The month may be continuous or spread out in

several periods during the year. This time is in addition to the one or two days off each week that clerics enjoy by custom, at least in the United States. The diocesan bishop may not be absent from his diocese beyond a period of one month, whether that period be a continuous one or an interrupted one; the time spent at the bishops' meetings is not counted (c. 395 §2). As for the coadjutor bishop and the auxiliary bishop, "except for the fulfillment of some other office outside the diocese or for the sake of vacation, which should not extend beyond one month, they should not leave the diocese but for a short period of time (c. 410). Particular law will regulate the vacations of those who do not hold residential offices."[137] The canon says simply that it be annual, fitting, and sufficient (*debito et sufficienti quotannis gaudeant*). To be fitting it should conform to the simple lifestyle called for in the previous canon.

Clerical Dress

Canon 284 — Clerics are to wear suitable ecclesiastical garb according to the norms issued by the conference of bishops and according to legitimate local customs.

On September 8, 1982, Pope John Paul II wrote to the papal vicar of Rome instructing him to promulgate norms regarding the use of clerical and religious garb in the Diocese of Rome. The pope acknowledged that although there are "motivations of an historical, environmental, psychological or social order which can be proposed to the contrary," "motivations of an equal nature exist" in favor of a distinctive attire. He added that the arguments against clerical garb "appear more of a purely human than ecclesiological character." In the pope's view a distinctive sign is valuable "not only because it contributes to the propriety of the priest in his external behavior or in the exercise of his ministry but above all because it gives evidence within the ecclesiastical community of the public witness that each priest is held to give of his own identity and special belonging to God."

---

[132] *Rel*, 63.

[133] "Even if a diocesan bishop has a coadjutor or auxiliary, he is bound by the law of personal residence in the diocese" (c. 395, §1).

[134] The 1981 *Relatio* notes that the consent of the ordinary is implied (p. 127 ad can. 472).

[135] *Comm* 16 (1984) 190.

[136] *Comm* 24 (1992) 277.

[137] *Rel*, 68.

The modern secular city where "the sense of the sacred is so frighteningly weakened" needs "the sign value that religious dress constitutes."[138]

The 1994 *Directory for the Life and Ministry of Priests* treated the obligation of ecclesiastical attire in article 66. It referred to the pope's letter which stressed how important it was in a secularized and materialistic society "that the community be able to recognize the priest, man of God and dispenser of his mysteries, by his attire...which is an unequivocal sign of his dedication and his identity as a public minister." Certainly the priest should be primarily identifiable through his conduct, but his manner of dress also makes known to everyone that he belongs to God and the Church. The priests' *Directory* then clarifies what the canon means by clerical attire: it must be different from lay dress, and conform to the dignity and sacredness of his ministry; its "style and color should be established by the Episcopal Conference" in accord with universal law. "Because of their incoherence with the spirit of this discipline, contrary practices cannot be considered legitimate customs and should be removed by the competent authority. Outside of entirely exceptional cases, a cleric's failure to wear this proper ecclesiastical attire could manifest a weak sense of his identity as one consecrated to God."[139]

Shortly after the appearance of the priests' *Directory,* a Brazilian bishop wrote to the Pontifical Council for the Interpretation of Legislative Texts inquiring whether the section on clerical dress is merely pastoral and exhortative or whether it is also juridically binding. The council responded that though the priests' *Directory* is permeated by a profound pastoral spirit, as a general executory decree it has prescriptive force, obliging those who are bound by the laws with which it deals (c. 32). General executory decrees "more precisely determine the methods to be observed in applying the law" (c. 31, §1). Thus article 66 of the priests' *Directory* contains a general norm which complements canon 284: clerical dress must be distinct from that of the laity; its style and color are to be determined by the episcopal conference. Contrary practices cannot be considered legitimate custom and must be removed by competent ecclesiastical authority. The diocesan bishop is the competent authority to urge obedience to this discipline and to remove contrary practices (c. 392, §2).[140]

In November 1998 the NCCB enacted legislation for the United States which will need final Roman approval. "A black suit and the Roman collar are the appropriate attire for priests, especially in the exercise of their ministry. The use of a cassock in church or at home is at the discretion of the cleric." Rules for wearing the religious habit will be determined by each clerical institute or society.[141]

Inappropriate Clerical Activity

For the last five canons in this chapter on the obligations and rights of clerics, the sources listed in the annotated version of the 1983 code are almost all taken from the 1917 code and pre-Vatican II documents. The canons consider certain negative obligations of clerics, such as avoiding unbecoming and alien pursuits, civil office, trade and business, partisan and political activity, and military service. In the absence of conciliar guidance, when the code repeats the former law, it is to be assessed in accord with the canonical tradition (c. 6). Exceptions from many of the restrictions binding clerics are made in the case of permanent deacons and are noted in a separate canon.[142]

---

[138]*Origins* 12 (November 4, 1982) 344. For the legislation of the bishops' conferences of Australia, England and Wales, Ireland, the Philippines, and Scotland see *CLD* 11, 31–35. Also see *Pamplona ComEng,* Appendix III, 1309–1358.

[139]See C. Mangan and G. Murray, "Why a Priest Should Wear a Roman Collar," *HPR* 95 (November 1995) 62–69.

[140]*Comm* 27 (1995) 192–194.

[141]*America* 179 (December 5, 1998) 4.

[142]Canon 288 "exempts permanent deacons from the obligation of wearing ecclesiastical garb. However, in exceptional circumstances, a diocesan bishop, with due consideration for the practice of neighboring dioceses and with appropriate consultation, may decide that deacons

Canon 285 — §1. Clerics are to refrain completely from all those things which are unbecoming to their state, according to the prescripts of particular law.

Certain activities are forbidden, not because they are evil in themselves but insofar as they are unbecoming to the clerical state. Since the attitude of the people is critical in determining what is unfitting for a cleric, the relativity of time and place must be considered. As "set apart in some way in the midst of the People of God," clerics are "witnesses and dispensers of a life other than that of this earth" (*PO* 3). They must, therefore, maintain a position of dignity in the eyes of the faithful.

The 1917 code (*CIC* 138), after stating the principle that clerics are to abstain absolutely from all things unbecoming their state, proceeded to list a number of examples. They were not to engage in unfitting trades and professions, e.g., such occupations as bartenders, jailers, and taxicab drivers. They were not to gamble *habitually* or play games with considerable money stakes. They were not to carry weapons unless there was just reason for taking such precaution. The former code (*CIC* 140) also forbade the clergy to attend certain entertainments. They were not to be present at spectacles that would be unbecoming the clerical state or give rise to scandal among the people. Among the objectionable spectacles, commentators listed professional prize fights, horse racing, and risqué theatrical productions.

The 1983 code simply states the general rule that clerics should wholly avoid all those things that are unbecoming their state in accordance with the prescripts of particular law. Obviously many of the activities once considered inappropriate for clerics have ceased to be so.[143] People have grown more tolerant, and clerics are no longer looked upon as semi-cloistered individuals on a pedestal.

The Church always expects, nevertheless, that they will conduct themselves in such a way as to maintain the respect of the community at large. In their lives they should witness to the higher values and tastes of society. If necessary, particular law can specify what activity in a given locality would threaten societal esteem of clerics.

Worker Priests

An experiment known as the "Worker Priests," which involved about one hundred individuals, was carried out in France and Belgium from 1944 to 1959. As a means of evangelizing the lower classes, priests took jobs in factories, at docks, and in the construction industry. They supported themselves by their labor without seeking any privileges.

Though such intimate contacts proved beneficial to the cause of religion, they also endangered the spiritual life of the priests. In 1953 the three French cardinals following an interview with the Holy Father declared that the experiment in its present form could not be continued and established several norms for the future. The priests assigned to this apostolate were to spend only a limited time each day in manual labor so as to "safeguard their readiness to meet all the exigencies of their priestly state." They were not to accept any assignments "which might lead to responsibilities in connection with labor unions or other offices which should be left to laymen." Finally, they were not to live by themselves but attached to a parish in which they were to collaborate.[144]

On July 3, 1959, in response to Cardinal Feltin's petition that some priests be allowed to work in factories full time, and not as heretofore only three hours a day, the Holy Office decided that the experiment should be ended. As Cardinal Pizzardo explained, in order to evangelize the workers "it is not absolutely necessary to send priests as workers into the centers of labor, and it is not possible to sacrifice the traditional concept of the

---

should wear some distinctive garb when engaged in formal clerical ministry" (*Permanent Deacons*, no. 130).

[143] It should be noted that one of the sources cited for the canon is a circular letter from the SCConc in 1926 concerning unbecoming recreation (*CLD* 1, 138–140).

[144] *CLD* 4, 97–102.

priesthood to this objective, which is nevertheless one to which the Church clings as one of her most cherished missions." Working in factories or yards is "incompatible with the life and duties of a priest." Besides being unable to fulfill all his duties of prayer, "working in factories or even in less important projects exposes the priest little by little to the dangers of being influenced by his surroundings." The Holy See, the letter continued, asks the bishops of France to consider whether the time has not come to supplement various lay apostolates by creating one or more secular institutes composed of both priests and lay members. The latter could work in factories without limitation of time and the priests could provide the necessary spiritual formation. A gradual phasing out of the current system was allowed "so as to avoid any hasty and too general change or dangerous disturbance in the workers' apostolate."[145]

The council, however, contradicted "the alarming arguments which Cardinal Pizzardo had used in his letter."[146] *Presbyterorum ordinis* observed that although priests are

> assigned different duties, yet they fulfill the one priestly service for the people.... This is true whether the ministry they exercise be parochial or supra-parochial; whether their task be research or teaching, or even if they engage in manual labor and share the lot of the workers, where that appears to be of advantage and has the approval of the competent authority. (*PO* 8).

The reference to worker priests was disputed up to the last draft. The compromise formula states that "competent authority has to approve" such activity, but does not identify that authority.[147]

On October 23, 1965, the bishops of France announced that they were authorizing with the consent of the Holy See "a small number of priests to work full time in factories and yards after a suitable period of preparation." The authorization for manual-wage work was that it was called "an essentially priestly mission" and was to be for an initial period of three years. The Holy See laid down three conditions: (1) the priests must not have responsibility for any labor union activity; (2) they are not to live alone but in pairs or groups and together with other priests so as to avoid a contrast between two categories of priests; and (3) there should be in the same place lay members of the Workers' Catholic Action so that the Church may appear to the workers as it really is, "the laity with their temporal engagements and the priests with their spiritual engagement."[148]

The 1971 synod of bishops affirmed that as a general rule "the priestly ministry ought to be a full-time occupation. Sharing in men's secular activities is by no means to be considered the principal aim nor can such participation suffice to give expression to the specific responsibility of priests. In concrete circumstances it is up to the bishop with his presbyterium and, if necessary, in consultation with the episcopal conference to determine whether secular activity is in accord with the priestly ministry."[149]

Activity Foreign to Clerics

§2. Clerics are to avoid those things which, although not unbecoming, are nevertheless foreign to the clerical state.

Besides activities that are incompatible with the dignity of the clerical state, there are occupations that are foreign to it, but some are not so irreconcilable that they can never be undertaken. The 1917 code (*CIC* 139) enumerated some of the

---

[145] *CLD* 5, 200–205. See O. Arnal, *Priests in Working Class Blue* (New York: Paulist, 1986).

[146] P.-J. Cordes, Vorgrimler 4, 251.

[147] Ibid.

[148] *CLD* 6, 168–169.

[149] *The Ministerial Priesthood,* II, n. 2 (December 9, 1971), *TPS* 16 (1972) 369. A decade later J. Willke could report: "Today there are nearly 10 times as many worker-priests in France as there were in 1954. But no one hears of them anymore. They have not changed greatly in the last 30 years, but the Church has" ("The Worker-Priest: Experiment in France," *America* 150 [April 7, 1984] 257).

professions that, though not considered debasing, were hardly congruent with the spiritual mission of the ministry. Without an apostolic indult, for example, clerics were not to practice medicine or surgery. The new code states only the general principle without any specifics, beyond what is contained in the two following paragraphs of the canon. Again, local sensibilities must be considered in determining what activity is foreign to the clerical state as well as in judging what is wholly unbecoming. At least one commentary holds that the 1961 ban on clerics and religious practicing psychoanalysis is still in force.[150] The Eastern code requires a cleric to obtain the permission of his own proper hierarch in order to exercise any civil profession (*CCEO* 371, §3).[151]

Public Office

§3. Clerics are forbidden to assume public offices which entail a participation in the exercise of civil power.

Lumen gentium 31 carefully distinguished the roles of the laity and the clergy. "To be secular is the special characteristic of the laity. Although those in holy orders may sometimes be engaged in secular activities, or even practice a secular profession, yet by reason of their particular vocation they are principally and expressly ordained to the sacred ministry. . . . It is the special vocation of the laity to seek the kingdom of God by engaging in temporal affairs and directing them according to God's will."

Insofar as the clergy are men of the Church, their engagement in politics could cause confusion regarding the religious mission of the Church. The 1971 synod of bishops explained:

"Since political options are by nature contingent and never in an entirely adequate and perennial way interpret the Gospel, the priest, who is the witness of things to come, must keep a certain distance from any political office or involvement." Whereas the values of the gospel are absolute and independent of culture, politics is rooted in the concrete circumstances of the here and now. "In order to remain a valid sign of unity and be able to preach the Gospel in its entirety," the priest must take care "lest his opinion appear to Christians to be the only legitimate one or become a cause of division among the faithful."[152]

The 1983 code rules definitively without qualification that "clerics are forbidden to hold public offices that call for the exercise of civil power."[153] The 1981 *Relatio* (p. 68) interpreted "civil power" to include legislative, administrative, and judicial authority.[154] The canon is concerned with the exercise of *public authority*. The prohibition extends beyond serving as governor, mayor, judge, senator, and the like, to serving on zoning boards, school boards, transportation commissions, and similar bodies.[155] However, merely advisory positions would not be banned. The law speaks of "assuming" office, which includes both election and appointment to office. Members of religious institutes (c. 672) and of societies of apostolic life (c. 739) are also bound by this canon.

The possibility of exceptions to the prohibition is not raised in the canon. In the 1977 draft (c. 146, §2) there was a provision for the local ordinary to give permission for a cleric to hold such office, but this proviso was ultimately eliminated. Furthermore, the prohibition was strengthened in the final version by the use of the term *vetantur* instead of the subjunctive verb *ne assumant*. Canon 1042, §2 makes the holding of a public office an impediment to ordination until the office is

---

[150] *Pamplona ComEng*, c. 285. See July 15, 1961 *monitum* of the Holy Office, *CLD* 5, 196.

[151] The Eastern code also obliges clerics "to abstain completely from all those things unbecoming to their state, according to the norms determined in detail by particular law, and also to avoid those things which are alien to it" (*CCEO* 382).

[152] "The Ministerial Priesthood," Pt. II, n. 2 (*CLD* 7, 356).

[153] *CCEO* 382, §1 is exactly the same in this regard.

[154] Also see *Comm* 14 (1982) 173 at c. 260.

[155] J. Provost, "Clergy and Religious in Political Office in the U.S.," in *Between God and Caesar*, ed. M. Kolbenschlag (New York: Paulist, 1985) 87.

relinquished and an account rendered according to the civil law.

The question arises, therefore, whether or not the diocesan bishop may dispense from the law forbidding clerics to hold public office. According to canon 87, §1 the bishop may dispense from universal disciplinary laws as often as he judges it helpful for the spiritual good of the faithful and when the matter has not been reserved to the Apostolic See. The *motu proprio De episcoporum muneribus* of Paul VI (1966) specifically reserved to the Holy See any dispensation permitting clerics "to assume public offices which involve the exercise of lay jurisdiction or administration,"[156] but this reservation is not found in the present code.[157] However, John Paul II's adamant opposition to priests and religious serving in public office would urge a bishop to use great caution in evaluating the "just and reasonable cause" required for a dispensation (c. 90).[158]

Canon 288 exempts permanent deacons from the prohibition unless particular law states other-wise. The 1984 *Guidelines on the Diaconate* of the NCCB (n. 131) stipulate: "While the Code of Canon Law permits permanent deacons to hold political office, a deacon should consult with his bishop before seeking or accepting such an office. In particular cases, the bishop may forbid such an undertaking."[159]

Financial Involvement

§4. Without the permission of their ordinary, they are not to take on the management of goods belonging to lay persons or secular offices which entail an obligation of rendering accounts. They are prohibited from giving surety even with their own goods without consultation with their proper ordinary. They also are to refrain from signing promissory notes, namely, those through which they assume an obligation to make payment on demand.

This paragraph repeats the 1917 code (*CIC* 139, §3 and 137) with a slight modification (the substitution of "proper" ordinary for "local" ordinary in the second sentence) and the addition of the reference to promissory notes. The twofold purpose of this regulation, according to the older commentators, was to safeguard clerical decorum and to prevent distractions that would interfere with ministerial duties.[160]

---

[156] IX, 3, b, *CLD* 6, 398.

[157] In a similar case (the right of a bishop to dispense from the canonical form for the marriage of two Catholics) the Pontifical Commission for the Authentic Interpretation of the Code rendered an authentic interpretation that the reservation imposed by *De episcoporum muneribus* (XVII; CLD 6, 399) was still in effect. The commission did not give a reason for its interpretation. According to Wrenn, the likely reason was that "throughout the process of drafting the new Code, it was always *understood* by the drafting commission that such a dispensation was reserved to the Apostolic See" (L. Wrenn, *Authentic Interpretations on the 1983 Code* [Washington, D.C.: CLSA, 1993] 22).

[158] A. McGrath, in *CLSGBI Com,* 163. For some examples of priests in the United States barred from office and for texts of John Paul II on the issue, see J. Lynch, in *CLSA Com,* 224. Theodore McCarrick noted in "The Integration of Catholics and American Political Life": "As you know, the church (especially the present pontiff) has admonished priests and religious against running for public office or serving in political offices because such activity is not consistent with the primary commitment of priestly ministry or religious life, but is more appropriately the realm of the lay person" (*Origins* 17 [June 18, 1987] 80).

[159] The prohibition about holding public office does, however, apply to all religious (c. 672).

[160] "This ruling may seem harsh, but cases brought before the Roman Curia prompted a severer course in order to protect the clerical state from slanders and insinuations which are never so rife as when a clergyman makes mistakes in money matters" (C. Augustine, *A Commentary on the New Code of Canon Law* [St. Louis: B. Herder, 1919] II: 86). "The emphasis of the council and recent church teaching on the dignity of the priest is not well reflected in this norm. Little attempt was made by the consultors to update it taking into account the mature responsibility of the priest. The study group wanted the details of these prohibitions to be assigned to particular law so as better to address modern circumstances; the new canon still presumes a lack of maturity and responsibility in the diocesan priest" (Schneider, 272).

Clerics are not to manage the money or property of lay people without the *permission* of their ordinary. They need permission, therefore, to be guardians of children, executors of wills, or trustees of funds. They would, of course, be permitted to handle the affairs of relatives or close friends who were dependent upon them. They must also have authorization to hold secular offices for which they are legally accountable, such as an official in a savings bank, a cooperative, or a charitable association.

Without *consulting* their ordinary, clerics are not to give surety (e.g., bail), even with their own goods, or to sign promissory notes obliging themselves to pay money on demand. One member of the commission sought to eliminate this clause or at least to substitute an exhortation in place of the necessary permission of the bishop. The secretariat responded that for the sake of prudence the text should remain as it is.[161] Again this paragraph does not apply to permanent deacons (c. 288) but it does apply to religious (c. 672).

The 1977 draft included a fourth paragraph (*CIC* 139, §3) inhibiting clerics from hailing anyone before a lay tribunal or having any part in a lay criminal trial, even to the extent of giving testimony without necessity, unless they had the permission of their ordinary. This paragraph was subsequently dropped.[162]

Business or Trade

Canon 286 — Clerics are prohibited from conducting business or trade personally or through others, for their own advantage or that of others, except with the permission of legitimate ecclesiastical authority.

Clerics are barred from engaging in business. An interpretation of this highly technical and complicated canon must be based on canon 142 of the 1917 code and a 1950 decree of the Sacred Congregation of the Council, the only sources indicated in the annotated edition of the current code. The 1983 code is the same as the former one except for the provision that legitimate ecclesiastical authority may permit such activity. Clerics are forbidden to engage in *negotiatio aut mercatura*. While in practice most canonists treat the terms as synonymous, *negotiatio* refers to all business operations carried on for gain, whereas *mercatura* is restricted to trading, i.e., the buying and selling of merchandise.

Commentators distinguish among several types of commercial enterprises. (1) Trading strictly so-called is buying goods with the intention of selling them unchanged for a profit, whether or not in smaller quantities or newly packaged. Included under this category would be a currency exchange where money itself is bought and sold. Such activity is definitely not lawful for clerics. (2) Industrial business or buying materials with the intention of selling them later at a profit after they have been transformed by one's own labor or that of hired employees is also prohibited. However, publishing or other apostolic enterprises are not forbidden, since they are not undertaken for profit alone.[163] (3) Domestic business is permissible. It consists in the profitable management of more or less permanent investments. A religious community, for example, may sell wine produced from its vineyards. Land, houses, and farms may be purchased with the intention of renting them out later at a profit. (4) Convenience operations which make such items as food, books, and religious articles available to a school or other community are permissible so long as any profit accrues to the organization. (5) With regard to stocks, a distinction must

---

[161] Cardinal Bernardin sought to leave the matter to the discretion of the clergyman, but it was decided to leave the text as it is "for the sake of prudence" (*Rel,* ad c. 260, 68).

[162] The *coetus* dropped the former permission needed for a priest to appear in civil court and be involved in criminal cases (*CIC* 139, §3) precisely because such permission presumed the priest to be a minor in dependence on the bishop. See *Comm* 14 (1982) 82: "Esso risente di una vecchia concezione per cui il sacerdote era considerato quasi un minore alla dipendenza del Vescovo."

[163] J. Dede, "Business Pursuits of Clerics and Religious," *J* 23 (1963) 50–60.

be made between speculation and investment. Investment is the purchase of stocks and bonds with the intention of receiving periodic income. Speculation is carried on, not for the sake of the income accruing, but with the hope that the item purchased will rather quickly increase in value so that it can be resold for a profit. All speculation, which is akin to gambling, is forbidden to clerics, especially such a transaction as short-selling.

The canon forbids clerics to "conduct" (*exercere*) business, that is, on a more or less habitual basis. An isolated act would not violate the law. A cleric may not engage in business either personally or through an agent; he is not allowed to commission an agent to carry on the operation in the cleric's name and at his risk. Clerics are forbidden, furthermore, to carry on such activity either for their own benefit or for that of other persons. Even the intention to devote the proceeds to pious or charitable causes does not justify a cleric's engaging in business.

A March 22, 1950, decree of the Sacred Congregation of the Council declared that any cleric or religious who violated the canon on business activity incurred an excommunication specially reserved to the Holy See. Even the penalty of degradation, which included dismissal from the clerical state, could be invoked.[164] Paul VI in *De episcoporum muneribus* reserved to the Holy See any dispensation for a cleric "to practice business or commerce."[165]

The 1983 code eliminated the automatic excommunication but provides in canon 1392 that "clerics or religious who exercise a trade or business contrary to the prescripts of the canons are to be punished according to the gravity of the delict." The code, nevertheless, makes explicit reference to the possibility of obtaining permission from "legitimate ecclesiastical authority" to engage in such activity. It was recognized under the 1917 code that in cases of necessity, either of the cleric himself or of his family, the ordinary could

allow what would otherwise be forbidden. If a cleric inherited or succeeded to a viable business that could not be relinquished without loss, the permission of the Holy See had to be obtained to continue it. Now a secular cleric is to seek permission from the diocesan bishop and a religious from the major superior.

The Clergy as Signs of Peace

Canon 287 — §1. Most especially, clerics are always to foster the peace and harmony based on justice which are to be observed among people.

The clergy are to be especially zealous promoters of peace. Here the obligation is stated positively in contrast to the negative position of the 1917 code (*CIC* 141) which had forbidden the clergy to participate in any way whatever in civil conflict or public disturbances. The sources for this paragraph stress the need for the clergy to be imbued with an all-embracing concern for concord. "The pastor's task is not limited to individual care of the faithful" but extends to all people; "priests can never be the servants of any human ideology or party" (*PO* 6). "Since God the Father is the beginning and the end of all things, we are all called to be brothers and sisters; we ought to work together without violence and without deceit to build up the world in a spirit of genuine peace" (*GS* 92). It is the Church's mission to preach the gospel message with a consequent demand for justice in the world. "This is the reason why the Church has the right—indeed, even the duty—to proclaim justice on the social, national, and international level, and to denounce instances of injustice when the fundamental rights of people and their very salvation demand it. The Church is not solely responsible for justice in the world; however, she has a proper and specific responsibility that is identified with her mission of giving witness before the world of the need for love and justice contained in the gospel message."[166]

[164] *CLD* 3, 68–69. This decree generated extensive canonical literature. For a bibliography see Dede, 61–62.
[165] IX, 3, d, *CLD* 6, 398.

[166] The 1971 synod of bishops, "Justice in the World," P II, *TPS* 16 (1972) 383.

§2. They are not to have an active part in political parties and in governing labor unions unless, in the judgment of competent ecclesiastical authority, the protection of the rights of the Church or the promotion of the common good requires it.

Though this paragraph has no antecedent in the 1917 code, several Roman decrees barring political activity on the part of the clergy in the decade after World War I are listed as sources.[167] In the post-Vatican II era, the 1971 synod of bishops declared that the "assumption of a role of leadership or a style of active militancy for some political faction must be ruled out by every priest unless in concrete extraordinary circumstances this is really demanded for the good of the community and has indeed the consent of the bishop after consultation with the priests' council and, if the case warrants, with the episcopal conference."[168]

Like canon 285, §3, which prohibits the clergy from holding public office, this restriction on political activity is based on the distinctive role of the clergy vis-à-vis the laity. Political activity ordinarily belongs to lay persons; priests should be "mindful of the maturity of lay persons and must highly value it when there is question of a special sphere in which they are versed."[169]

The present canon, however, is principally focused on the responsibility of the clergy to promote unity in the community. Their ministry is directed to all the faithful, not just to the members of a political party or a trade union. "Since political options are by nature contingent and never in an entirely adequate and perennial way interpret the gospel, the priest, who is the witness of things to come, must keep a certain distance from any political office or involvement."[170] The clergy are not forbidden to *belong* to these organizations; rather, they are not to play an active part in political parties or in the governing of unions. It is important

that the clergy be seen first and foremost as representatives of the Church. It is their responsibility to assist lay persons in forming their own consciences correctly in these complex issues.

There may be circumstances, nonetheless, when it will be necessary for the clergy to become more actively involved in political and union affairs in order to protect the rights of the Church or to promote the common good. It pertains to competent ecclesiastical authority to make this judgment. Note that while the ban on clergy holding office (c. 285, §3) is absolute, though dispensable, the prohibition on political engagement is not absolute. The "competent authority" to authorize such involvement is not specified in the code, as it was in the 1977 draft of the canon (c. 148, §2) and in the 1980 draft (c. 262, §2). Those drafts required permission of the Holy See for bishops or in places where a pontifical ban was in effect; in other places and in the case of priests and deacons, both their own ordinary and the ordinary of the area where the activity was to occur had to approve. It is reasonable to interpret "competent ecclesiastical authority" in terms of these provisions.

Exemptions for Permanent Deacons

Canon 288 — The prescripts of cann. 284, 285, §§3 and 4, 286, and 287, §2 do not bind permanent deacons unless particular law establishes otherwise.

Permanent deacons are bound neither by the norm regarding clerical dress (c. 284) nor by the prohibitions regarding occupations foreign to the clerical state, such as public office, administration of property belonging to the laity, positions requiring accountability (c. 285, §§3 and 4), business and trade (c. 286), and participation in partisan politics or in governing a labor union (c. 287, §2).[171]

---

[167] *CLD* 1, 126–128.
[168] "The Ministerial Priesthood," pt. II, 2, *CLD* 7, 357.
[169] Ibid., 356.
[170] Ibid.

[171] Number 17 of the 1967 *mp Sacrum diaconatus ordinem* restoring the permanent diaconate provided as follows: "Care should be taken that deacons do not carry on a profession or trade which the local ordinary considers

A number of objections were raised about the wording of the canon. It seemed incongruous to some canonists for permanent deacons who are clerics to be exempt from clerical obligations; since they are constituted in the hierarchy of the Church, they represent the Church to the laity. One proposal was to frame the canon positively: deacons are bound by clerical obligations unless legitimate church authority in a concrete case should have determined differently. Another suggestion was to state: "They *are not bound* but the ordinary considering attendant circumstances could prescribe otherwise." A third group thought that permanent deacons should not be held to the norms regarding clerical dress and business affairs but should be obliged not to engage in partisan politics or in running a union. The secretariat of the commission decided to maintain all the exemptions for permanent deacons as listed but to add the clause "unless particular law establishes otherwise."[172]

"Although most deacons will give only part of their time to formal diaconal ministries, they should not neglect the opportunities they have to exercise their ministry in the world or in the marketplace. They do not cease to be deacons when they go to their secular occupations, and there is much that they can do there precisely as deacons. Of course, a deacon should never use his ministry for the purpose of professional or personal gain."[173]

Use of Exemptions Allowed by Civil Law

Canon 289 — §1. Since military service is hardly in keeping with the clerical state, clerics and candidates for sacred orders are not to volunteer for military service except with the permission of their ordinary.

Clerics and candidates for ordination should not volunteer for military service without the permission of the ordinary. This canon applies to deacons as well as priests, since no exclusion of deacons is made as in the previous canon.[174] The l917 code (*CIC* 141) allowed clerics with the permission of the ordinary to volunteer in order to be freed sooner from compulsory service. In the United States, clerics and seminarians have been required to register for selective service but have not been called to serve. Church law in the past and at present does not prevent priests from acting as chaplains in the various branches of the military; permanent deacons also are enrolled in the military. In fact, there is an Archdiocese for the Military Services, U.S.A., originally established on September 8, 1957, as the Military Vicariate.[175] Those who volunteer to be chaplains must have the permission of their ordinary or major religious superior.

§2. Clerics are to use exemptions from exercising functions and public civil offices foreign to the clerical state which laws and agreements or customs grant in their favor unless their proper ordinary has decided otherwise in particular cases.

Clerics are to take advantage of all exemptions from civic duties that the secular law, concordats, or custom may grant them as alien to their state, unless in particular cases their ordinary has judged differently. A cleric, therefore, ought not accept service on a grand or petit jury if federal or state law recognizes the ministry as an excusing cause. A cleric should certainly voice an objection if called to serve on a criminal case.

---

[174] *Comm* 14 (1982) 174 at c. 264.

[175] The apostolic constitution of John Paul II, *Spirituali militum curae* of April 21, 1986 promulgated norms for the military ordinariates throughout the world. For an English translation see *TPS* 31 (1986) 284–291. Furthermore, specific norms would have to be drawn up for each individual ordinariate. See "Statutes of the Military Ordinariate of the United States (Approved August 18, 1987)," in *Occasional Publications Services Review* (Silver Spring, Md.: Archdiocese for the Military Services, USA [*Ordinariatus castrensis*], November 1987) 6–9.

---

unsuitable or which will interfere with the fruitful exercise of their sacred office" (*CLD* 7, 581).

[172] *Rel,* 69.

[173] *Permanent Deacons,* no. 132.

CHAPTER IV
LOSS OF THE CLERICAL STATE
[cc. 290–293]

Through the sacrament of orders one is perpetually marked with an "indelible character" (c. 1008) and definitively incorporated into the clerical state. A diocesan cleric is incardinated perpetually into the diocese; a religious remains incardinated in the institute of consecrated life or society of apostolic life. Both the sacramental and juridical consequences of ordination are meant to last throughout the lifetime of the cleric. Whereas the sacramental character can never be removed, one's juridical status as a member of the clerical state may be lost. This occurs only through death or the procedures stated in law.[1] The cleric may be far from home, not exercise his ministry, or be unfaithful to his duties as a bishop, priest, or deacon, but he remains a cleric. He may leave the Church or totally renounce his faith, yet he remains a cleric. "Severance packages" arranged for a "resigned" priest or deacon have no canonical effect on incardination or ordination.

Therefore, the cleric's status does not change without his knowledge.[2] Whereas the 1917 code spoke of the "reduction" of the cleric to the lay state,[3] the parallel canons of the 1983 code are placed under the rubric "Loss of the Clerical State." The 1983 code consciously implements the insistence of Vatican II on the fundamental equality of Christians flowing from baptism. The disparaging term "reduction" has been dropped from the 1983 code. Similarly, the penalty of degradation (reduction to the lay state, *CIC* 2305) is no longer mentioned in the 1983 code, along with two other penalties reserved to clerics: deposition (suspension from office and deprivations of any benefits accrued from office, *CIC* 2303), and "defrocking" or deprivation of ecclesiastical garb (*CIC* 2304). Only the penalty of dismissal from the clerical state (formerly degradation) remains.

Canons 290–293 contain the current legislation regarding loss of the clerical state and its consequences.[4] They are to be read with the canons on dismissal from the clerical state.[5] Like the previous two chapters of Book II, these canons were the result of the discussions of two study groups.[6] Although the loss of the clerical state is now seen in the more positive light of the fundamental baptismal equality of the Christian faithful, the current legislation is relatively unchanged from the prior law. There are some changes as to the competence of dicasteries as well as a slight modification of procedures. Parallel canons in the 1990 Eastern code are substantially the same.[7]

---

[1] This has been restated for deacons in the 1998 *Directory for the Ministry and Life of Permanent Deacons*, n. 21.

[2] The Holy See continues to make every effort to protect a cleric from the undue interference of his bishop or superior regarding the cleric's status. See commentary below on the previously accepted practice of *ex officio* laicizations.

[3] See Book II, part one, title VI, *De reductione clericorum ad statum laicalem* (*CIC* 211–214).

[4] For other canonical commentaries on these canons see J. Lynch, in *CLSA Com,* 229–238; L. Chiappetta, in *Chiappetta Com,* 406–409; A. McGrath, in *CLSGBI Com,* 166–168; T. Rincón Pérez, in *Pamplona ComEng,* 239–242; D. Hynous, in *Clergy Procedural Handbook* (cited hereafter as *CPH*), ed. R. Calvo and N. Klinger (Washington, D.C.: CLSA, 1992) 238–275.

[5] For example, see commentary on cc. 1317; 1336, §1, 5°; 1425, §1, 2°; and 1717–1731.

[6] These canons were discussed during the 1917 code revision process by the study groups *de clericis* and *de sacra hierarchia: de clericis* session II, April 3–8, 1967, *Comm* 17 (1985) 88–90; session III, December 4–7, 1967, *Comm* 18 (1986) 54–55; session IV, March 4–7, 1968, 18 (1986) 111–112; *de sacra hierarchia,* session 13, April 9–14, 1973 [not reported]; synthesis of the entire process, *Comm* 3 (1971) 196–197.

[7] *CCEO* 394–398. See commentary in *Pospishil Com,* 289–290.

Besides explaining the meaning of the law and the values underlying the canons, this section will investigate the practical implementation of these canonical procedures since the promulgation of the 1983 code.

Three Modes of Loss of Clerical State[8]

Canon 290 — Once validly received, sacred ordination never becomes invalid. A cleric, nevertheless, loses the clerical state:
  1° by a judicial sentence or administrative decree, which declares the invalidity of sacred ordination;
  2° by a penalty of dismissal legitimately imposed;
  3° by rescript of the Apostolic See which grants it to deacons only for grave causes and to presbyters only for most grave causes.

Declaration of Invalidity (1°)

A valid ordination (c. 1024) always remains a valid ordination when conferred by the competent minister through the imposition of hands and the consecratory prayer (c. 1009, §2). Canon 290, 1° states the exception. The ordination can be declared invalid as a result of a judicial procedure resulting in a decision, or by an administrative decree. The current practice of the Holy See has been to discourage petitions of this kind, and therefore it has not admitted this as a practical possibility in recent years.[9] Rather, the Holy See encourages the third mode (c. 290, 3°) for the loss of the clerical state (petition for a return to the lay state and dispensation from celibacy).

The 1917 code was explicit in stating that an ordination coerced by grave fear was an invalid sacrament (*CIC* 214, §1), but this reference is not found in the 1983 code. The candidate must testify, in writing, that he receives orders freely (c.

1036).[10] The other requirements for ordination, including the absence of impediments and irregularities, are for the lawfulness of the sacrament, not validity. In cases of declaring the nullity of ordination, the canonical procedure in canons 1708–1712 must be followed.[11]

In practice, the other two modes of losing the clerical state indicated in canon 290 are the usual means by which the clerical state is lost.

Penalty of Dismissal from the Clerical State (2°)

As noted above, the sole remaining penalty entailing the loss of the clerical state is the perpetual expiatory penalty of dismissal from the clerical state (c. 1336, §1, 5°).[12] The penalty can be inflicted only through a judicial procedure reserved to a collegiate tribunal of three judges (c. 1425, §1, 2°) and then only when the cleric has committed an offense that merits the canonical penalty of dismissal from the clerical state (c. 1317). The canons are careful to preserve the rights of all in the Church, especially in the application of penalties, which must be interpreted strictly.[13] It is essential that bishops and superiors have a proper understanding of the nature of church penalties, especially when they affect the clergy with whom bishops and superiors serve and for whom they are responsible. The penalty of dismissal from the clerical state, though rarely inflicted because of the complexity of the process, safeguards the right of the community to be protected from ordained ministers who are a grave danger to the common good of the Church, and

---

[8] Cf. *CCEO* 394.

[9] Hynous, in *CPH*, 238.

[10] In 1928 the Roman Rota stated that a genuine intention to receive orders is required for validity. See *CLD* 2, 554. For more detailed commentary, see Lynch in *CLSA Com*, 230–231.

[11] The author is not aware of any instances of the use of this procedure since the 1983 code.

[12] See commentary on cc. 1425, §1, 2° and 1717–1731. The remarks here are meant to elucidate the penalty in light of this section of the code.

[13] Canon 18. When all the goals of the penal system cannot otherwise be achieved, penalties are the measure of last resort (c. 1341).

the right of the bishop or superior to protect the community from such a dangerous cleric. At the same time, the rights of the cleric are carefully protected by the strict application of penalties.[14] This penalty remains a legitimate means of last resort when a cleric becomes a serious danger or causes grave scandal, but only in a limited number of situations.

This penalty can never be automatic (c. 1336, §2) nor can it be established by particular law (c. 1317). It can never be used as a penalty outside the seven instances in the 1983 code. The taxative list is as follows: contumacy or serious scandal given in apostasy, heresy, or schism (c. 1364, §2), violation of the sacred species (c. 1367), physical attack on the Holy Father (c. 1370, §1), serious cases of solicitation in confession by a confessor (c. 1387), persistence in attempted marriage after a warning (c. 1394, §1), persistence in concubinage after a warning (c. 1395, §1), persistence in other sexual offenses after a warning, or commission of other sexual offenses through force, threats, or publicly, or with a minor under sixteen (c. 1395, §2).

In recent years, as the Church attempted to deal with the consequences of clerical misconduct, the judicial process demanded for dismissal from the clerical state has been experienced by some as a cumbersome means effectively to separate a cleric from the Church. Most often the third mode of the loss of the clerical state cannot be employed because the cleric refuses to petition spontaneously for a laicization.[15] The NCCB examined various ways by which the penalty of dismissal could be inflicted. This resulted in the approval by the Holy Father of derogations from some of the canonical norms concerning sanctions.[16] However, no new

procedures were added outside of those in canon 290.[17] Throughout the discussion process with the Holy See, it was clear that the protection of the rights of clerics was of great concern. Any possibility that a dismissal procedure might be used by a bishop or superior in an arbitrary way which would infringe on the cleric's rights was to be totally avoided.

The penal process for dismissal could also be legitimately initiated while the cleric has himself submitted a petition for laicization to the Holy See. Should a negative response to the petition be received from Rome, such a penal process could be continued.[18]

Rescript of the Apostolic See (3°)

The usual mode of the loss of the clerical state continues to be the rescript of the Apostolic See (c. 290, 3°).[19] This is so-called "laicization," which not only results in a rescript returning the cleric to the lay state, but also includes a dispensation from the obligation of celibacy.[20] In 1971, after Paul VI's 1967 encyclical on celibacy, the CDF issued norms which revised and simplified

---

[14] See commentary on Book VI for a complete treatment of the penal issues involved.

[15] The CDWDS discussed this matter in its 1991 plenary session. See M. O'Reilly, "Recent Developments in the Laicization of Priests," *J* 52 (1992) 695.

[16] A derogation from the provisions of the canons on clerical sexual abuse of minors was granted by the Holy Father on April 25, 1994: the age in c. 1395, §2 was changed from

below sixteen to below eighteen. Also, the period of prescription regarding the pursuit of criminal actions (cc. 1362 and 1395, §2) was changed. See the commentary on those canons. For a full history of the development of the derogations and an explanation of the derogations themselves, see J. Alesandro, "Canonical Delicts Involving Sexual Misconduct and Dismissal from the Clerical State," *Ius Ecclesiae* 8 (1996) 173–192. (Also found, in substance, in "Dismissal from the Clerical State in Cases of Sexual Misconduct: Recent Derogations," *CLSAP* [1994] 28–67).

[17] See NCCB Canonical Affairs Committee, *Canonical Delicts Involving Sexual Misconduct and Dismissal from the Clerical State* (Washington, D.C.: USCC, 1995).

[18] Alesandro, "Dismissal from the Clerical State," 46. The acts of the laicization request should be introduced into the acts of the case.

[19] *CCEO* 394, 3°. In addition to the Apostolic See, in some cases the patriarch may also grant the laicization, while the dispensation from celibacy is reserved to the Holy Father (*CCEO* 396–397). See commentary in *Pospishil Com,* 289.

[20] See commentary on c. 291.

the process.[21] In 1980 the same congregation published a letter which contained norms governing the procedure.[22] These norms are still in effect.

Since the promulgation of the 1983 code there have been a number of practical changes and improvements in these petitions for both priests and deacons. In 1988, a significant development occurred with the reorganization of the papal curia. *Pastor bonus* assigned competence for "laicizations" of priests and deacons to the Congregation for Divine Worship and Discipline of the Sacraments (art. 68). All cases presented after March 1, 1989, were to be handled by this dicastery. The CDF reviewed all cases that were pending at this time and contacted bishops and superiors who had submitted cases yet had not received a decision. They were asked to update the files with new details about the cases in order to bring them to closure.[23] The CDF retains competence for cases which were submitted to it before the aforementioned date.

The competency of the Congregation for Divine Worship and Discipline of the Sacraments was confirmed in a February 8, 1989, letter of the Secretary of State, indicating that the 1980 norms are still to be employed in processing laicization petitions.[24] This includes all petitions of secular and religious clerics in Latin or other churches *sui*

iuris, in common law or mission territories. A July 25, 1989 letter of the Secretary of State reconfirming this competency replied to an inquiry of the Congregation for Institutes of Consecrated Life and Societies of Apostolic Life regarding competency for processing dispensations from the obligations connected with the diaconate ordinations of religious men.[25]

Since 1989, practical instructions on laicization petitions have been issued by the Congregation for Divine Worship and Discipline of the Sacraments. The "Documents Necessary for the Instruction of a Case for the Dispensation from the Obligations of Priestly Celibacy" contains a checklist of documents necessary for the proper instruction of a case. This was distributed to ordinaries in 1991 through the NCCB.[26] The following year a similar document was distributed concerning the laicization of deacons.[27] Finally, on June 6, 1997, a circular letter was sent to all ordinaries and superiors concerning the laicization of priests and deacons.[28] These documents will be integrated into the following explanations of the laicization processes.

Very helpful in this area are the experiences of church administrators who assist those who have left the active ministry. These experiences cast light on the curial practice (c. 19) regarding the proper interpretation and implementation of the law.[29]

---

[21] The fonts offered by the *CIC An* list the following postconciliar sources for the current law: CDF Norms, January 3, 1971, *CLD* 7, 110–117; CDF Circular Letter, January 13, 1971, *CLD* 7, 119; CDF Declaration, June 26, 1972, *CLD* 7, 121–124; CDF Letter, October 14, 1980, *CLD* 9, 92–96. For an excellent summary of such sources see Rincón Pérez, in *Pamplona ComEng,* 240, and Lynch, in *CLSA Com,* 232–234.

[22] For commentaries on the 1980 norms see the "Procedures for a Dispensation from Priestly Celibacy," published privately by the NCCB Canonical Affairs Committee, and V. Ferrara, "Normae substantivae ac procedurales nunc vigentes in pertractandis causis de dispensatione a coelibatu sacerdotali," *Apol* 62 (1989) 513–540.

[23] After updating the CDF on the outstanding cases, many dioceses reported prompt and favorable responses.

[24] N. 230.139, February 8, 1989, *N* 25 (1989) 485.

[25] Reported in *N* 26 (1991) 53–54.

[26] Msgr. Robert E. Lynch, "Memo to All Bishops," April 19, 1991. The aforementioned set of instructions was presented to the president and vice president of the NCCB during their visit to the Holy See in April 1991. Also in *RRAO 1991,* 2–4.

[27] "Loss of the Clerical State by a Deacon and a Dispensation from all the Obligations of Ordination," attached to the "Memo to All Bishops" of Daniel E. Pilarczyk, May 11, 1992.

[28] Protocol number 263/97: *Origins* 27/11 (August 28, 1997) 169, 170–172.

[29] See M. O'Reilly, "Recent Developments in the Laicization of Priests," *J* 52 (1992) 684–696. For examples of processing petitions see *RR* 1981: 7–8; 1982: 37–38,

The laicization procedures currently followed for deacons and priests will be examined separately, but some common issues can be examined at this point. Canon 290, 3° explicitly includes deacons and priests (*presbyteris*). The congregation still follows the practice that it will not recommend a laicization for a bishop or a superior general or former superior general of a religious institute.[30] The rescript of laicization is a "favor" of the Holy See; it is never to be construed as a right of the cleric. Therefore, a spirit of humility and penance is always the spirit in which the favor is sought; it is never to be seen as a "simple expedient."[31] The bishop or superior of incardination is competent to accept a petition and offers his *votum* on the merits of the case. However, the local ordinary of the place of domicile of the petitioner can be delegated. The Holy See must authorize any other ordinary.

The canon does not make explicit who must petition the Apostolic See—the cleric or the bishop or superior without the consent or knowledge of the cleric (*ex officio* petition). The 1980 norms do not contain the provision for the *ex officio* laicization procedure found in the 1971 norms, according to which the ordinary petitioned the Holy Father without the consent or at times the knowledge of the cleric. Whereas *ex officio* petitions had been accepted in the past, they are only rarely accepted now.[32]

Laicization of Deacons

Canon 290, 3° gives little detail on the procedure for laicization of deacons. It states simply that the Apostolic See grants laicization to deacons "only for grave causes" (*ob graves tantum*

causas*). A frequent "grave cause" accepted by the congregation had been to permit the remarriage of permanent deacons who had been widowed after ordination and who wished to remarry. It was the practice of the Holy See to insist that the deacon be returned to the lay state and dispensed from the obligation of celibacy. However, a statement of June 6, 1997 admitted, "For some time it has become evident that because of this prohibition, grave difficulties have arisen for those who have been widowed after ordination but are desirous of remaining in the diaconal ministry."[33] Under certain conditions, a petition for a dispensation from the impediment of canon 1087 is submitted to the Holy See, not the laicization petition.[34]

The Congregation for Divine Worship and Discipline of the Sacraments[35] has established a simple five-step procedure for the laicization of a transitional or permanent deacon. (1) The deacon makes an explicit request in writing to the Holy Father for the favor of a return to the lay state and the dispensation from celibacy. In the letter he is to state briefly the reasons for the petition, e.g., a transitional deacon wishes to marry. (2) A *curriculum vitae* is prepared, including an explanation of the seriousness of the reasons for the request, the development of events which led to the crisis, and the responsibility for said crisis. (3) The *votum* of the bishop of incardination, which includes his endorsement of the petition, is needed. (4) Various testimonies are submitted, e.g., from superiors, professors, colleagues during the time of formation and during diaconal ministry. It may be appropriate to include the testimony of wife or family members. (5) Finally, the pertinent documentation from the time of formation and the *scrutinia* (c. 1051) for admission to orders are to be collected and included.

The protocol does not call for a table of contents or the numbering of pages, nor does it indi-

---

41–42; 1983: 22–23. Also *RRAO 1985*, 9–10, 20–23; 1987: 26–36; 1988: 8–10; 1989: 10–14, 58–64; 1990: 8–13; 1991: 1–4; 1992: 6–11; 1995: 6–8.

[30] O'Reilly, 691.

[31] Private reply of CDWDS, *RRAO 1995*, 7.

[32] The CDWDS stated that the deacon who will not ask for laicization must be dismissed according to the judicial process, thus implying that it will not accept an *ex officio* petition (1992 Protocol, n. 2).

[33] Circular letter, June 6, 1997, n. 7 (*Origins* 27/11 [August 28, 1997] 171).

[34] See commentary under c. 291.

[35] The habitual faculty to laicize deacons was granted to the cardinal prefect in 1989. See *N* 25 (1989) 486.

cate the number of copies to be sent to the Holy See. However, it is helpful to follow the procedure for priests' laicizations[36] for the good ordering of the case and its being expedited once it reaches Rome. The 1992 protocol has made this process a simple and straightforward one. Deacons who submit their petition usually feel fairly and respectfully treated, and many dioceses report that these dispensations are granted in a timely fashion with few, if any difficulties.

Laicization of Priests

Whereas the procedure for laicizing deacons is rather simple, the case is very different for priests. The reason is obvious: the favor of the rescript for a return to the lay state for a priest is granted only for the most serious reasons (*ob gravissimas causas*). The ordained ministry of the priest is full time, involves the full care of souls, and entails the carrying out of all the rights and obligations of the clerical state with none of the exceptions granted to deacons (c. 288). The "high profile" nature of the priest's life and ministry demands that very serious reasons motivate his petition. These reasons must be firmly documented and supported in the *vota* called for by the current protocol. The purpose of the rescript is to regularize the status of the priest who has left the active ministry, and to allow him to participate fully in the sacramental life of the Church, always attentive to the good of the community and to the avoidance of scandal or confusion regarding a man's status.

The practice continues of speedily processing the petition of a man in danger of death, whatever his age might be. The urgency of the case could even account for a dispensation from the requirement of the signature of the petitioner. The normal informative process is not required, and the entire case can be transmitted by fax to the dicastery.[37]

The most grave reasons for laicization accepted by the dicastery continue to be those in the 1980 norms and those followed by the CDF; i.e., a priest who has long ago left active ministry, has married, and now wishes to reconcile with the Church; one who should not have been ordained because he lacked a due sense of freedom or responsibility, or because, during the time of formation, his competent superiors were not able to judge if he was able to live a celibate life.[38]

A change has occurred in granting the request of a priest under the age of forty. The CDF had the custom of not granting such a petition; the Congregation for Divine Worship and Discipline of the Sacraments was at first open to such a petition should an exceptional motivation be present.[39] By 1995, John Paul II suspended action in these cases in order to give bishops and superiors more time to exhaust every means of persuading the priest to return to the active ministry.[40] However, the 1997 circular letter has reintroduced these motives as a possibility, though they are exceptional in nature. They are to be used when the priest's motives for defection go beyond the ordinary reasons and when grave scandal is present. In other words "there existed in the petitioner, previous to and concomitant with his Sacred Ordination, a psychological or physical condition . . . not taken into serious consideration by those entrusted with formation."[41] Because of the serious nature of the danger of scandal to the Church in these cases, the dicastery has accepted and approved cases which do not include the ordinary process of interviewing witnesses.[42]

---

[36] See commentary below.

[37] Protocol number 263/97, n. 5. The local fax number given is 6988.3499.

[38] There has not been recent evidence that the rescript states that the man "should never have been ordained," although this can be implied from the reasons often given in the petition (sample in Hynous, 272–274).

[39] Among such motives one might note habitual or grave moral or psychological faults present before, during, or after the ordination, cohabitation with women of a scandalous nature, public and habitual disputes with church authorities. See *N* 27 (1991) 43–57 and Hynous, 240.

[40] Private reply of the CDWDS, *RRAO 1995,* 6.

[41] Protocol number 263/97, nn. 3 and 4.

[42] *RRAO 1987,* 26–36. Also *RRAO 1989,* 10–11. CDWDS granted the petition also as a "disciplinary measure" be-

When the aforementioned elements are present, the Congregation for Divine Worship and Discipline of the Sacraments will give "active consideration" to cases of priests under the age of forty and present them to the Holy Father.

The steps of the process will be briefly outlined below.[43] An attentive following of the 1991 "list of documents" provided by the Congregation for Divine Worship and Discipline of the Sacraments has proven to be a straightforward way to instruct the case.[44] The process should not begin unless the bishop or superior has made every attempt to persuade the priest to return to the active ministry. Since the rescript entails a permanent loss of the clerical state, there should be no doubt that the petitioner wishes permanently to return to the lay state. These efforts at clarifying the mind of the petitioner should be documented and placed into the acts of the case.

The petitioner first submits a signed petition to the Holy Father. The letter is written in a spirit of humility and penance and must explicitly include the two requests for a return to the lay state and a dispensation from the obligations of celibacy. The Congregation for Divine Worship and Discipline of the Sacraments calls the *curriculum vitae* the *libellus;* this document presents a "detailed description" of the reasons for leaving the priesthood and why such a decision is irrevocable. It succinctly states significant dates and provides information on the education and assignments of the priest. The ordinary is to summarize the "pastoral attempts" made to dissuade the petitioner from submitting the request (as above) and to include a document of "suspension" of faculties. This is not the penalty of suspension (cc. 1333–1334) but the "withdrawal" of faculties done as a consequence of the decision to petition for a return to the lay state. However, suspension is incurred *latae sententiae* by an attempted civil marriage (c. 1394, §1).

Although the ordinary may decide to instruct the case himself, usually a priest familiar with the process handles most of the work of the case. A canonical degree is helpful but not required. The priest instructor's decree of appointment is included in the acts of the case, with the "explicit statement" that the 1980 norms are to be followed.

Worth noting is the shifting role of the priest instructor in light of curial praxis. In addition to gathering data and documents, the priest instructor must also provide his *votum* (his personal opinion) about the merits of the case. Because he is familiar with many facets of the case and details of the "story" of the petitioner, his *votum* can be very helpful in assisting the Holy See to assess the sometimes convoluted turns in the petitioner's history. He can offer a thorough synthesis of the interview, testimonies, and psychological reports of the case, especially in light of the petitioner's well-being and the good of the Church. Thus, the ordinary's *votum* is simpler. Besides summarizing his recommendation for the granting of the petition, it must contain the explicit statement that the ordinary is certain no scandal will be taken. Should the petitioner live outside his proper ordinary's jurisdiction, a second *votum* of the ordinary of that place is necessary with the same explicit statement.

The Congregation for Divine Worship and Discipline of the Sacraments offers a list of testimonies to be gathered. The list, which is not taxative, includes: interrogations or depositions of witnesses (those indicated by the petitioner or chosen by the instructor), parents and relatives, superiors, companions, priest friends, co-workers, physicians, therapists, psychologists, etc. These testimonies may be submitted in writing, and should be notarized. The petitioner's written consent to release confidential information is required.

The petitioner is interviewed under oath by the instructor in the presence of a notary. Prepared questions are helpful. While the priest instructor will probe areas which the petitioner has given as the reasons for the petition, the former is free to

---

cause the petitioner admitted his guilt and acknowledged the great harm done to the community.

[43] For more detailed presentations see Hynous, 238–276, and O'Reilly, 684–696.

[44] See sample documents in *CPH,* 249–281.

gather narrative details he has deemed crucial in light of the testimony of those in formation, as well as any professionals involved in assisting the petitioner discern his decision to petition the Holy Father. During the interview the petitioner should feel free to add any details not covered by the instructor's questions, and ample room should be given the former to "tell his story."

Other documentation is required: the *scrutinia* (c. 1051), any pertinent documentation from the seminary or house of formation, civil marriage certificate if such a marriage has been attempted, sacramental certificates of spouse and children.

Finally, the case itself should be bound (section dividers are helpful), each page numbered and hand-written pages transcribed, a table of contents prepared, and the entire case authenticated by a notary. Three copies are sent to the Congregation for Divine Worship and Discipline of the Sacraments; the apostolic nunciature is the best way to ensure that the case is sent expeditiously to Rome.[45]

At times, the Congregation for Divine Worship and Discipline of the Sacraments requests additional documentation so that the acts of the case can be completed. The petition could be denied because of inadequate motivation. Should the petition be denied, recourse to the congregation is possible, and more convincing evidence can be offered. The petition can be submitted as many times as the priest desires.

The Church's concern to respect the dignity of all persons is implemented in a unique way through the processes outlined above. The deacon or priest who seeks to be returned to the lay state retains the right to privacy and a good reputation (c. 220). The Congregation for Divine Worship and Discipline of the Sacraments has shown special sensitivity through the protocol and list of required documents circulated for use of ordinaries. Not only do these procedures protect the Church's right to examine carefully each case and reach an appropriate decision as to its disposition, but they also provide a clear and reasonable description of what the cleric can expect during the process. Like the annulment process, these procedures, too, can provide healing and new life for those who have struggled with vocational questions and wish to participate fully in the sacramental life of the Church. Because of the unpredictability of international mail routes as well as the workload of the dicastery, no "time line" can or should be given the cleric regarding the disposition of his petition with the exception of the cleric in danger of death.

Dispensation from Celibacy[46]

Canon 291 — Apart from the case mentioned in can. 290, n. 1, loss of the clerical state does not entail a dispensation from the obligation of celibacy, which only the Roman Pontiff grants.

The Holy Father alone dispenses from the obligation of celibacy (c. 277), unlike some of the other clerical obligations of merely ecclesiastical law. The rescript granting the return to the lay state also contains the dispensation from the obligation of celibacy. It is not possible for a cleric to accept the rescript without also accepting the dispensation from celibacy.[47] The Church continues to uphold the value of celibacy for those in ordained ministries,[48] and canon 291 is an expression of this concern. One exception noted in this canon is the judicial or administrative declaration of the invalidity of orders (c. 290, 1°); in such an instance, no dispensation is necessary.

The Pontiff himself determines occasions when he may wish to grant the favor of the dispensation. A recent example has been the openness of the Holy See to widowed permanent deacons who wish to remarry. In the past, the CDF and the Con-

---

[45] For details on the praxis of the dicastery once it receives the case, see *N* 27 (1991) 53–57 and O'Reilly, 690–695.

[46] Cf. *CCEO* 396.

[47] See the usual rescript issued by the CDWDS, n. 1 (sample in Hynous, 272–274). The 1971 norms stated that the return to the lay state and the dispensation from celibacy were inseparably united (V, 1).

[48] See commentary on c. 277.

gregation for Divine Worship and Discipline of the Sacraments explained the Holy Father's reluctance to grant the dispensation as stemming from the concern that it might weaken the Church's stance on celibacy. However, because of the evidence of the grave difficulties resultant from this practice, "any one of the three following conditions taken singly are sufficient for a favorable consideration of the dispensation from the impediment, namely: the great and proven usefulness of the ministry of the deacon to the diocese to which he belongs; the fact that he has children of such a tender age as to be in need of motherly care; the fact that he has parents or parents-in-law who are elderly and in need of care.[49]

Another example of such a dispensation from celibacy has been the rescripts granted for former non-Catholic priests or ministers who are married and who wish to be ordained to the Catholic priesthood.[50] Most men in this category have been from the Episcopal or Anglican communions. In the United States, Bernard Cardinal Law of Boston has acted as the delegate to the Holy See in these cases. The rescript typically contains these requirements: agreement to the condition that, should his wife die, remarriage is not possible; avoidance of scandal regarding celibacy and undue publicity; and assignment to administrative, social, or educational work rather than the ordinary care of souls. This does not exclude their giving assistance, when pastorally useful, in the full range of priestly duties.

A similar dispensation was given to a former priest of the Polish National Catholic Church through the CDF.[51] Outside the cases of former Episcopal and Anglican married ministers, the apostolic nunciature handles the cases of those married men of other Christian communions and forwards them to the Holy See.

Besides these cases, the dispensation from celibacy is granted very rarely. It is not granted for a laicized transitional deacon who later marries in the Church and then wishes to exercise his diaconal ministry. A response of the CDF in such a case indicated that it has been its "constant practice" in such cases never to admit these men as permanent deacons because of "the implication of the law of ecclesiastical celibacy."[52] Although the scarcity of clergy impelled this dicastery to refer the matter to a "higher authority," the CDF reported that the Holy Father upheld its decision of not granting the dispensation. "This is both to safeguard ecclesiastical celibacy and to avoid the possible consequences that it might have as regards dispensation from priestly celibacy."[53]

Effects of the Loss of the Clerical State[54]

Canon 292 — A cleric who loses the clerical state according to the norm of law loses with it the rights proper to the clerical state and is no longer bound by any obligations of the clerical state, without prejudice to the prescript of can. 291. He is prohibited from exercising the power of orders, without prejudice to the prescript of can. 976. By the loss of the clerical state, he is deprived of all offices, functions, and any delegated power.

The loss of the clerical state has a number of consequences, which pertain, for the most part, to all three modes of loss, i.e., invalidity, dismissal, and laicization.[55] Because he is no longer a member of the clerical state, he is no longer bound by its obligations nor does he enjoy any of its rights (cc. 273–289).[56] For example, he is not to wear ecclesiastical garb or be addressed by titles used

---

[49] CDWDS, Protocol number 263/97, n. 8: *Origins* 27/11 (August 28, 1997) 171.

[50] For samples of such rescripts, see *RRAO 1989,* 7–10.

[51] *RRAO 1986,* 20–22.

[52] Ibid., 18–19.

[53] Ibid., 19.

[54] Cf. *CCEO* 395.

[55] The contents of c. 292 are reiterated and elaborated on in the usual rescript of laicization.

[56] However, like any lay person, he too is encouraged to pray the liturgy of the hours (c. 1174, §2) and employ all the pertinent means he chooses to foster his spiritual life. These may indeed be very similar to the means he used as a priest or deacon, e.g., daily Mass, scripture meditation, rosary, etc. (see c. 276).

by ordained ministers. He has no right to remuneration, with due regard for the obligation of the bishop or superior when a cleric is punished by dismissal.[57]

While the juridical consequences of ordination can be lost, the power of orders can never be. However, the cleric in question is forbidden the exercise of sacred orders, with the exception stated in canon 976.[58] Obviously this exception does not apply when the invalidity of ordination is declared. Finally, canon 292 states that by the very fact of the loss of the clerical state an individual is deprived[59] of clerical offices, functions, and any delegated power granted to him as a cleric.

Canon 292 implies the obvious and more positive consequence of the loss of the clerical state, i.e., a return to the lay state with all its rights and obligations. These are enjoyed and to be fulfilled according to the norm of law just as they are applied for any other lay person. These are limited only when specifically restricted in the law itself, the rescript of laicization, or the decree of dismissal. Because a strict interpretation is necessary when limiting the free exercise of rights (c. 18), it is important to examine carefully the typical rescript now issued by the Congregation for Divine Worship and Discipline of the Sacraments.[60]

The rescript is crafted to protect two important values. First, the good ordering of the community in its worship and celebration of the sacraments is paramount; the community has the right to receive the spiritual riches of the Church from its ordained ministers who fulfill the obligations incumbent on them. The stability of the clergy is closely connected to the stability of local communities. Second, the rescript makes every effort to avoid confusion of the faithful and, more importantly, scandal.[61]

Besides the consequences contained in canon 292, the rescript can contain other explicit prohibitions. The rescript ordinarily granted for a laicized deacon contains no special prohibitions.[62] The case is quite different for the laicized priest. He can never deliver a homily,[63] be a special minister of the Eucharist, or have a directive office in the pastoral field.[64] He can have no function (*munus*) whatsoever in a seminary or an equivalent institution, e.g., a house of formation [4 (c)]. In a secondary institute of study dependent on church authority (e.g., Catholic graduate school, college, or university), he can have no directive function (*munus*, e.g., president or administrator) or teaching office (*officium*) [4 (c)]. In similar institutions not dependent on church authority (e.g., secular college or university), he cannot teach theology or subjects closely connected to theology. In Catholic elementary or high schools, he may not have a directive function (e.g., principal or other school administrative office) or teach theology. In this case, however, the rescript authorizes the ordinary to dispense should there be no scandal present [4 (d)]. This applies only to teaching theology, not to holding a directive office. Finally, the laicized priest cannot teach religion in non-Catholic high schools or elementary schools without the dispensation of the ordinary.

The rescript also contains a caution regarding the celebration of marriage; it is to be done in a prudent way without undue display (*sine pompa vel exteriore apparatu*) (3). Finally, the laicized

---

[57] When the dismissed cleric is "truly in need" because of the penalty, the ordinary must see to his proper care (c. 1350, §2).

[58] A dismissed or laicized priest can hear the confession of a person in danger of death validly and licitly, even if a priest with the proper faculty is present. The CDWDS rescript, n. 4 (b) also refers to c. 986, §2, which obliges any priest, when a person is in danger of death, to hear the confession.

[59] This should not be taken as the penalty of deposition in the 1917 code (*CIC* 2303) or the "deprivation" in the 1983 code (c. 1336, §1, 2°).

[60] This is almost identical to the rescript issued by the CDF. Each individual rescript now issued by the CDWDS must be carefully scrutinized to see what restrictions are included.

[61] It is important to point out that not only can one give scandal, but the community must *take* scandal. It would be good to monitor the reaction of the community in this area.

[62] This rescript contains an explicit reference to c. 1350, §2.

[63] See commentary on c. 767, §1.

[64] N. 4 (b). See Lynch, in *CLSA Comm,* 237.

priest who has been civilly married ought not to live in a place where his condition is known. This provision, too, can be dispensed from by the ordinary of the place where the petitioner lives should the ordinary judge there is no danger of scandal (5).[65]

It must be remembered that these restrictions are to be interpreted strictly; in all other areas the cleric returned to the lay state enjoys the same rights and is bound by the same duties as all lay persons. The rescript reminds the ordinary who communicates the rescript to encourage the man to live in harmony with the Church and participate fully in its life. Full and appropriate liturgical participation includes, for example, proclaiming the word, leading song and participation in the choir, offering reflections during services of the word, or giving a "witness talk," etc.

Although deprived of clerical offices and functions, the laicized priest is able to exercise roles or hold offices outside those prohibited in the rescript, e.g., he may serve on the diocesan pastoral council or the parish finance council; he may be named a delegate to the diocesan synod; he may be a lay judge on the tribunal.[66]

The rescript also directs the ordinary who notifies the priest to impose some work of piety or charity. The bishop or superior may leave the nature of this work to the man himself. Finally, a brief report should be sent to the Congregation for Divine Worship and Discipline of the Sacraments at a later date to notify it that the rescript has been executed and explain if there has been any "wonderment" of the faithful at its being granted.

Return to the Clerical State[67]

Canon 293 — A cleric who loses the clerical state cannot be enrolled among clerics again except through a rescript of the Apostolic See.

Chapter 4 of title III of part one of Book II concludes with a canon which addresses the case of a cleric who has lost the clerical state and who wishes to return to the diaconal or priestly ministry. The canon states the necessary requirement simply and directly: a rescript of the Holy See is necessary;[68] no further procedure is specified.[69] This theoretically applies to the case of a man whose ordination was declared invalid[70] and to one who was dismissed from the clerical state. In the practical order, it usually applies to one who was granted the rescript of laicization (and dispensation from celibacy) and who wishes to exercise ordained ministry once again.[71]

The practical steps to be followed are rather simple, and M. Souckar outlines them briefly: beginning the process, formal process, formation, and permission to readmit.[72] He stresses three pastoral considerations, i.e., observance by the petitioner and ordinary of civil, canonical, and moral responsibilities during the investigation; readiness of the ordinary to support the cleric financially during the period of formation; and a presentation of the readmitted priest or deacon to the other clerics and the community.[73]

The process begins when the laicized cleric approaches a bishop or superior who designates an instructor for the case. This begins the "formal process" wherein the instructor investigates the precise canonical status of the deacon or priest, as

---

[65] For a discussion of the possible dispensations see "The Dispensing Power of the Diocesan Bishop and Conditions in the Rescript of Laicization," issued by the NCCB Canonical Affairs Committee, July 2, 1987.

[66] RRAO 1984–1993, 78–81. For a slightly dissenting opinion, see 81–82.

[67] Cf. CCEO 398.

[68] When the patriarch has granted the laicization, he is competent to readmit the cleric (CCEO 398). See commentary in Pospishil Com, 290.

[69] A 1987 private reply of the CFC stated that a procedure would be issued "in the near future," but to date no such protocol has been given. See RRAO 1988, 10.

[70] Although the term "readmission" to a state that one never possessed is not accurate, the canon indicates that a rescript is needed should such a person seek to be ordained.

[71] In light of the 1997 circular letter of the CDWDS, it will prove interesting if laicized deacons who remarried after laicization ask to be reinstated in the diaconal ministry.

[72] For a thorough commentary on this issue, see M. Souckar, "Return to Ministry of Dispensed Priests," J 54 (1994) 605–616.

[73] Ibid., 615.

well as any natural obligations that he may have (e.g., a spouse whom he may have divorced or who has died, children). The petitioner writes a personal letter to the Holy Father making the request and explaining his style of life since the favor of laicization was granted; the letter should state, of course, that a bishop or superior is willing to accept him. References to witnesses to his behavior and lifestyle are helpful. An interview is conducted which addresses the concerns of the Apostolic See[74] and the diocese or institute, e.g., financial or moral obligations, a proposed course of study, the preclusion of scandal.[75] The bishop or superior should express his *votum* recommending that the request be granted and indicating that he is willing to incardinate the priest once the *nihil obstat* of the Holy See is granted. The peti-

tion is forwarded to the same congregation which granted the rescript of laicization. The next stage starts when the congregation receives the petition and lets the bishop or superior know its favorable opinion so that an intense time of formation (usually at least six months) can begin. Usually the man lives in a monastery or religious house, although a seminary would seem to be acceptable. A supervisor should be assigned who can offer instructions and make evaluations in the pastoral setting; spiritual direction on a regular basis is important.[76] The final step is the permission to readmit into the clerical state; it can be granted once the period of formation has been successfully completed. The congregation is informed and the *nihil obstat* is requested. When the rescript is received, it should be immediately executed by the bishop, and the cleric should be immediately incardinated into the diocese or institute.

[74] See *RRAO 1990,* 73–74. The congregation which processed the laicization petition handles the petition for a return to ministry (Souckar, 612, n. 16).

[75] See *RRAO 1990,* 70–74.

[76] Souckar, 613.

BIBLIOGRAPHY

Alesandro, J. "Canonical Delicts Involving Sexual Misconduct and Dismissal from the Clerical State." *Ius Ecclesiae* 8 (1996) 173–192.

———. "Dismissal from the Clerical State in Cases of Sexual Misconduct: Recent Derogations." *CLSAP* (1994) 28–67.

Calvo, R., and N. Klinger, eds. *Clergy Procedural Handbook.* Washington, D.C.: CLSA, 1992.

Ferrara, V. "Normae substantivae ac procedurales nunc vigentes in pertractandis causis de dispensatione a coelibatu sacerdotali." *Apol* 62 (1989) 513–540.

Morrisey, F. "The Pastoral and Juridical Dimensions of Dismissal from the Clerical State." *CLSAP* (1991) 221–239.

NCCB, Canonical Affairs Committee. "Procedures for a Dispensation from Priestly Celibacy." Privately circulated.

———. *Canonical Delicts Involving Sexual Misconduct and Dismissal from the Clerical State.* Washington, D.C.: USCC, 1995.

O'Reilly, M. "Recent Developments in the Laicization of Priests." *J* 52 (1992) 684–696.

Provost, J. "The Involvement of Dispensed Priests in the Official Ministry of the Church." *J* 34 (1974) 143–152.

Souckar, M. "Return to Ministry of Dispensed Priests." *J* 54 (1994) 605–616.

Title IV
Personal Prelatures
[cc. 294–297]

The only prelatures which were known at the time of Vatican II were prelatures *nullius* which, with the advent of the 1983 code, became known as territorial prelatures. Unlike a personal prelature, a territorial prelature is assimilated in law to a diocese (c. 368); its prelate governs it as its proper pastor, in a manner similar to that of a diocesan bishop (c. 370) to whom he is the equivalent in law (c. 381, § 2). Since they are located in the code between clerics and associations of the Christian faithful, rather than in the part that deals with the Church's hierarchical constitution, it is clear that personal prelatures are neither associations of the Christian faithful nor particular churches. This ended the debate between the holders of two differing opinions on whether personal prelatures were particular churches; both opinions were prevalent after the council and during the code revision process, indeed, right up to its final phase.[1]

In any event, in light of the context in which the idea of personal prelatures took shape during Vatican II, it is also clear that they do not belong to the Church's hierarchical constitution.[2] In fact, not only is the topic never considered in *Lumen gentium* or in *Christus Dominus,* but the decree *Presbyterorum ordinis* 10 treats it only in the context of the distribution of priests and priestly vocations. Personal prelatures must therefore be considered as administrative entities with the power to incardinate secular priests who are given an adapted formation to provide for various pastoral needs.[3] The institution of personal prelatures is not directed to "the proper distribution of priests" as an end in itself, but more toward the goal of facilitating various forms of pastoral activities for different social strata in a given region, nation, or continent.

Paul VI fleshed out this new conciliar institution[4] in his *motu proprio Ecclesiae sanctae.* He did it in the same context as *Presbyterorum ordinis* 10: for a better distribution of the clergy.[5] *Ecclesiae sanctae* I, 4 determined that the Apostolic See was the competent authority to erect personal prelatures, that they were to be founded to facilitate particular pastoral activities, and that they were to be constituted by secular priests incardinated in the prelature. Each prelature was to have its own statutes. Beyond that, nothing was to prevent lay persons, whether single or married, from dedicating themselves with their professional skill to the service of these works and projects after making an agreement with the prelature.[6] Finally, episcopal conferences were to be consulted before

---

[1] For an exhaustive historical analysis of cc. 294–297, see W. J. Stetson and J. Hervada, "Personal Prelatures from Vatican II to the New Code: An Hermeneutical Study of Canons 294–297," *J* 45 (1985) 379–418. The authors conclude that "in any case, the systematic arrangement of a body of laws is always something secondary" (416). See also J. Hervada, in *Com Ex* II/1, 401. This may be right, but if the place of an institution in the code is not always an affirmation of its nature, it nevertheless remains significant in clarifying what the institution is not. And that is never a secondary consideration. This is indeed the opinion of G. Ghirlanda. He contends that we must never forget that the legislator changed the systematic organization of the canons on personal prelatures in the preparatory schemata. This change meant that these prelatures could not be viewed as equivalent to a particular church or considered as belonging to the Church's hierarchical structure. See G. Ghirlanda, "De differentia Praelaturam personalem inter et Ordinariatum militarem

seu castrensem" *P* 76 (1987) 228. The author extensively studies the evolution of the pertinent texts in the code (227–236).

[2] See Ghirlanda, 221.

[3] Ibid., 223.

[4] *AAS* 58 (1966) 1007.

[5] Ibid., 760–761.

[6] Ibid.

a personal prelature was erected, and the rights of local ordinaries were to be respected in the exercise of its activities (*PO* 10).

Some may have thought that the elements expressed in *Ecclesiae sanctae* were sufficiently clear and in keeping with the conciliar approach to constitute the juridical framework within which a personal prelature could evolve. But such does not appear to be the case if we consider the extensive discussions leading up to the formulation of the current law and the doubts of the code commission itself regarding where such prelatures were to be situated in the code. Evidently amid all the discussions there was a serious search for a canonical definition or a theological understanding of personal prelatures. However, the legislator offers no such definition or understanding in the four canons of the code describing the new institution. And the Eastern code does not shed further light on this point, since it does not deal at all with personal prelatures. Personal prelatures have been described as "jurisdictional entities established by the Holy See within the hierarchical pastoral activity of the Church as an instrument for the performance of particular pastoral and missionary endeavors."[7] But this approach does not satisfy everyone. In fact, there is no doubt about the place where such prelatures are situated in the code: they cannot and should not be considered as jurisdictional entities belonging to the Church's hierarchical constitution; rather, they are societal institutions or administrative entities established to promote a more equitable distribution of the clergy.[8]

Be that as it may, an ecclesial structure may be of a hierarchical type while not belonging to the

Church's hierarchical constitution.[9] The content of the canons on personal prelatures does not permit us to say more. Neither their establishment by the Apostolic See (c. 294), their government (c. 295), the potential presence of lay people (c. 296), nor their relations with local ordinaries (c. 297) permit us, in fact, to believe that they were some forgotten element of the Church's hierarchical constitution which was discovered at the last moment by Vatican II. They are what they were in the mind of the council fathers: a means to provide for "not only the proper distribution of priests . . . but also the carrying out of special pastoral projects" (*PO* 10). Developed later by Paul VI in *Ecclesiae sanctae,* the institution of such prelatures has been set out in the present canons and becomes operational with statutes approved by the Holy See, giving each personal prelature its proper configuration.

Purpose and Competent Authority

Canon 294 — After the conferences of bishops involved have been heard, the Apostolic See can erect personal prelatures, which consist of presbyters and deacons of the secular clergy, to promote a suitable distribution of presbyters or to accomplish particular pastoral or missionary works for various regions or for different social groups.

The first words of the Latin text speak of the two possible objectives of personal prelatures,

---

[7] J. L. Gutiérrez, "Personal Prelatures," in *Pamplona ComEng,* 242.

[8] Ghirlanda, 234. This goes against the conclusions of Stetson and Hervada, for whom "they are prelatic, hierarchical, jurisdictional structures of the People of God. The proper place for personal prelatures in the Code is among the institutions belonging to the hierarchical constitution of the Church" ("Personal Prelatures," 416).

[9] For Hervada (*Com Ex* II/1, 399–400) personal prelatures are new forms of the organization of the Church's constitutional structure in addition to already existing structures such as the pope, bishops, episcopal conferences, territorial prelatures, apostolic vicariates, etc. Moreover, for J. I. Arrieta (*Com Ex* II/1, 680) there are three main types of ecclesiastical circumscriptions: ordinary territorial circumscriptions, missionary territorial circumscriptions, and personal circumscriptions. Personal prelatures belong to the last type of category along with personal dioceses, military ordinariates, and ordinariates for Eastern rite faithful. This would mean that the prelate of a personal prelature would be equivalent to a diocesan bishop in law. However, this is simply not the case.

i.e., the promotion of a better distribution of priests and the accomplishment of particular pastoral and missionary tasks. Since the canon also states that a personal prelature consists of secular priests and deacons, we might conclude that its main purpose is the better distribution of clerics and not only of priests, even though *Ecclesiae sanctae* did not mention deacons. Priests and deacons are therefore the natural members of a personal prelature. However, this does not exclude lay persons, who may also dedicate themselves to the particular tasks of the prelature (c. 296).

The second important element of this canon concerns the authority competent to erect personal prelatures: the Apostolic See through the Congregation for Bishops.[10] It is important to note here that the text speaks of "erection" by the Holy See and not of "recognition" or "approval." This is not the only place in the code where the Holy See alone "erects," that is, gives a legal existence and a juridical status to an organization, an institution, or a structure. It erects public international associations (c. 312, §1, 1°), particular churches (c. 373), conferences of bishops (c. 449, §1), etc.

In some of these cases—for example, an international association—there could be a preexisting entity which at this point in its existence has its statutes. And as for a personal prelature, what is it before it is erected? A society of apostolic life? A clerical association? A secular institute? The question is not without importance, as it refers to the origins—and therefore to the founders—of the prelature. Canonical erection should not be confused with the foundation of such an entity. And it must matter that the founders, perhaps, had intended first of all a society of apostolic life or an association of the faithful or a secular institute. The intention to found a personal prelature may not have been present at first. In any case, the founding intention cannot be disassociated from the history of an organization.

Finally, the canon states that the Holy See will not establish personal prelatures without having first consulted with the episcopal conferences involved. It remains to be seen which episcopal conferences are involved, and why they are to be consulted. At least the episcopal conference of the place where the prelature is to be established must be consulted, along with those of the territories where the preexisting institution was present and where it will accomplish its mission, once it is erected as a prelature. As for other bishops and local ordinaries, the statutes of each personal prelature will determine the nature of their mutual relationships.

Statutes and Government

Canon 295 — §1. The statutes established by the Apostolic See govern a personal prelature, and a prelate presides over it as the proper ordinary; he has the right to erect a national or international seminary and even to incardinate students and promote them to orders under title of service to the prelature.

§2. The prelate must see to both the spiritual formation and decent support of those whom he has promoted under the above-mentioned title.

Like the last two canons of this title, this one deals with statutes, which provide each prelature with its distinctive configuration. The statutes are established by the Apostolic See (*ab Apostolica Sede conditis*) and become particular law for the prelature. Unlike statutes, constitutions, and other norms concerning associations and institutes of consecrated life—which are either recognized or approved by the competent authority and remain private laws—the statutes of a personal prelature are laws enacted by the Holy See.[11] The same expression—*ab Apostolica Sede conditis*—is found in the apostolic constitution *Spirituali militum curae,* which deals with the proper statutes of each military ordinariate.[12]

[10] See *PB* 80.

[11] See E. Caparros, "A New Hierarchical Structure for New Pastoral Needs: Personal Prelatures," *Philippiniana Sacra* 24 (1989) 392, note 41.
[12] Ibid., note 42.

If the statutes constitute a particular set of laws for each prelature, they must take into account the existing framework of universal law, which determines those elements which personal prelatures may have in common. Evidently, since the statutes are the written expression of the specific nature of the prelature, they will vary according to its uniqueness and goals. This is why the code does not go into too much detail. This is also why canon 295, §1 states simply that "a prelate presides over [each prelature] as the proper ordinary." Even though canon 134, §1 does not mention the prelate in its list of ordinaries, which seems exhaustive, the present canon calls the head of a personal prelature an ordinary. Therefore, as any ordinary, he can, for example, dispense from universal disciplinary laws in certain extraordinary circumstances (c. 87, §2). The statutes of each prelature are to determine the scope and limitations of the powers of the prelate, along with the other structures of government and internal organization.[13] Whatever the ultimate goals or nature of the personal prelature, universal law takes into account the fact that its prelate, being an ordinary, will eventually have to deal with local ordinaries (c. 297).

According to the nature of the prelature, its prelate has the right to establish proper structures for the recruitment and formation of its members by setting up seminaries. Here we are evidently dealing with major seminaries within the context of the canons on the formation of the clergy (cc. 232–264). However, the prelate can also establish minor seminaries (c. 234). To ascertain whether the prelature's major seminary must follow the episcopal conference program for priestly formation (c. 242), the goals of the prelature should no doubt be considered, although its seminarians are future secular priests and deacons. All the clergy of the prelature are incardinated into it. The prelate calls them to orders and is able to ordain them, if he has received episcopal ordination.

Although the code no longer refers to titles of ordination, canon 295, §1 still mentions that the prelature's candidates for orders will be called "under title of service to the prelature."[14] Finally the canon logically points to the prelate's responsibility for the spiritual formation and the decent support of the clergy of the prelature.

Lay Involvement in a Personal Prelature

Canon 296 — Lay persons can dedicate themselves to the apostolic works of a personal prelature by agreements entered into with the prelature. The statutes, however, are to determine suitably the manner of this organic cooperation and the principal duties and rights connected to it.

As is clear from the two preceding canons, a personal prelature is in fact a clerical institution, particularly when we consider its members. But the lay faithful may also (*possunt*) consecrate themselves to the pastoral works of the prelature. The level and nature of their collaboration will be determined by the statutes. For example, a simple contract might determine the rights and obligations of both parties. This contract would also have to consider certain civil law dispositions in these matters.

The text speaks of an "organic cooperation," referring no doubt to a form of integration into the prelature, so that, as lay faithful, individuals may carry out their role in its apostolic tasks. Even if the role of the lay faithful may be of great importance in a given prelature, they do not belong to its nature in the sense that personal prelatures could exist without the presence of lay associates.

This organic presence of lay associates in the prelature does not change its particular nature, nor does it change the status of these lay people. Their presence does not technically make of the prelature a portion of the people of God, like a diocese,[15] nor do these members become detached from the jurisdiction of the local ordinary where they have a domicile or quasi-domicile. The local ordinary remains the competent author-

---

[13] See Hervada, in *Com Ex* II/1, 409.

[14] See T. Green, in *CLSA Com,* 242.
[15] Ibid.

ity regarding certain acts of the Christian life which require faculties. We speak here of those acts which concern the juridical status of persons, as in the case of marriage, especially as regards the dispensation of certain impediments (c. 1078, §1). The competence of the prelate regarding the lay faithful usually extends to the pastoral activities of the prelate within the framework of the statutes. These lay faithful continue to belong to their local parish; this implies a respect for certain prerogatives specifically entrusted to the pastor (c. 530).

Normally, if the powers of the prelate and of the local ordinary are to be applied to the same persons, such powers do not deal with the same matters. Unlike the jurisdiction of military ordinaries, which is cumulative with that of the local ordinary since both jurisdictions may apply to the same matters, the prelate's jurisdiction is rather mixed in nature[16] and is determined by the statutes of the prelate. However, this does not prevent lay members who cooperate organically in the pastoral tasks of the prelate from benefiting also from the pastoral ministry of its clergy.

Prelature-Local Ordinary Relationships

Canon 297 — The statutes likewise are to define the relations of the personal prelature with the local ordinaries in whose particular churches the prelature itself exercises or desires to exercise its pastoral or missionary works, with the previous consent of the diocesan bishop.

Normally all personal prelatures exercise their pastoral activities within the territorial limits of a particular church or a community of the faithful assimilated to a particular church (c. 368). The pastoral tasks of the prelature must therefore be integrated within the larger pastoral objectives of the diocese in order to avoid potential conflicts. While the preceding canon considers the exercise of authority by the prelate over the lay faithful of

the prelature, distinct from that of the local ordinary over these same lay persons, canon 297 deals explicitly with the relations between the personal prelature and the ordinaries of the places where it is to exercise its mission. Like *Presbyterorum ordinis* 10 and *Ecclesiae sanctae* I, 4, this canon gives particular attention to the nature of these relationships. Evidently harmonious relations will lead to an effective accomplishment of the prelature's mission.

Here again, the statutes are to determine the essentials of this relationship, i.e., the framework within which they will be established while keeping in mind the specific nature and purpose of the prelature. If this involves education, for instance, these relations will not be the same as in the case of hospital care or ministry to refugees or prisoners. Whatever the elements found in the particular laws of the prelature, universal law requires the consent of the diocesan bishop or his equivalent in law (c. 381, §2) if a personal prelature is to exercise its pastoral or missionary activities within a particular church.

The legislator has been entirely coherent in establishing the provisions on the pastoral office of a bishop and clarifying the nature of the powers needed for the accomplishment of that office. Canon 394, §1 invites him to favor various forms of the apostolate within his diocese, but he is also responsible for coordinating these activities, with "due regard for the proper character of each." What is determined in canon 305, §2 for associations of Christian faithful and in canons 678, 681, and 682 regarding the apostolic works of religious in a diocese, canon 297 determines *mutatis mutandis* for personal prelatures.

TITLE V

ASSOCIATIONS OF THE CHRISTIAN FAITHFUL
[cc. 298–329]

Among the rights of the faithful recognized by the Code of Canon Law, there is at least one that the Church has already recognized in civil soci-

---

[16] Gutiérrez, in *Pamplona ComEng,* 244.

ety: the right to associate.[17] In itself, there is not much which is very new in the statement that the faithful "are at liberty freely to found and direct associations" (c. 215). What is new in this legal provision does not lie in the fact that the faithful can gather in associations, but rather that this capacity is recognized as a fundamental right of all the faithful, whatever their state in the Church: lay person, priest, religious, or bishop.

By the very fact of its presence in the "bill of rights and duties" of believers in the Church (cc. 208–223), the right of association becomes something to be protected, to be claimed, and also to be promoted.

The faithful thus find formally proclaimed the right to associate in the Church, a right which the Church has already recognized for the members of civil society. But this is the proclamation of an existing right, not the concession or creation of a new right. Indeed, from the first centuries of the Church the faithful have organized in order to care for the needs of the sick and other necessities. During the middle ages, spiritual fraternities appeared, then groupings which formed around convents to participate in their spiritual merits. Other associations for prayer multiplied, composed only of lay persons and having the following purposes: development of devotion to God and the saints; the practice of charity towards one's neighbor; and the exercise of a spirit of penance.[18] How many institutes of consecrated life started by being associations of the faithful?

The 1917 code treated of associations of the faithful (*CIC* 684–725). It witnessed to what was in practice the right of association at that stage in the Church's history. The 1983 code, while conserving several basic elements of the older legislation on associations of the faithful, elaborates these elements by adding some precision to them, some distinctions, and greater possibilities for new associations. In its turn, the new code wit-

nesses to this facet of contemporary church life. But the treatment of associations of the faithful this time is more than a description of what already exists. It is like a legal framework designed to govern in practice the exercise of the right of association recognized by canon 215:

> The Christian faithful are at liberty freely to found and direct associations for purposes of charity or piety or for the promotion of the Christian vocation in the world and to hold meetings for the common pursuit of these purposes.

Three brief comments must be made on this canon.[19]

First, the text affirms the principle of the capacity of each of the faithful to found and to govern associations freely. The association which a believer founds can remain a de facto association, without official juridic status, or it can be recognized as a private association, or even be erected into a public association.

If each of the faithful has the right to found an association, the responsible authority in the community reserves the right to intervene when the members of an association or its leaders seek to acquire an official status in the community. No one, however, is required to seek such a status.

Second, canon 215 does not exhaustively list the purposes to be pursued by associations. They are for "purposes of charity or piety or for the promotion of the Christian vocation in the world." These are general objectives which serve as a framework for the more detailed statement of canon 298, §1.

Finally, canon 215 must also be read in light of the following canon, which in effect bears on the right of initiative of the faithful: "All the Christian faithful have the right to promote or sustain apostolic action even by their own undertakings" (c. 216).

---

[17] See ency *Pacem in terris, AAS* 55 (1963) 262–263.

[18] See R. Naz, *Traité de droit canonique,* 2nd ed. (Paris: Letouzey et Ané, 1954) I:749.

[19] For a lengthy commentary on the right to associate, see L. Navarro, *Diritto di associazione e associazioni di fedeli* (Milan: Giuffrè, 1991) 3–33.

The fundamental right of the faithful to associate for purposes in conformity with the Christian life can be exercised without their being subject to the canons on associations of the faithful (cc. 298–329); that is, unless an association wishes to acquire the status of a private or public association, or wishes to adopt a name, such as "Catholic" for example, which signifies a formal status.

That an association does not wish to acquire a recognized status or take a name signifying such does not mean that it is beyond any intervention by the competent ecclesiastical authority. Other rights and obligations are in question when the common good is touched: "In exercising their rights, the Christian faithful, both as individuals and gathered together in associations, must take into account the common good of the Church, the rights of others, and their own duties toward others" (c. 223, §1).

If the common good is affected in one way or another by an association of the faithful, the competent authority can and at times must intervene: "In view of the common good, ecclesiastical authority can direct the exercise of rights which are proper to the Christian faithful" (c. 223, §2). The text does not say how, but presumably those responsible for the community can always exercise their right to intervene whenever the public order is concerned. When an association has a formal canonical status, it can be suppressed (cc. 320 and 326). When it does not, it remains, as "all associations of the Christian faithful . . . subject to the vigilance of competent ecclesiastical authority which is to take care that the integrity of faith and morals is preserved in them and is to watch so that abuse does not creep into ecclesiastical discipline" (c. 305, §1). Certainly the competent authority always can and sometimes must warn the faithful against a de facto association. It can even go so far as to condemn it.

During the past few years there has been a significant increase in the Church of associations of the Christian faithful, particularly lay associations. A certain number of these have asked for official recognition from the competent authorities. At times these authorities will be called upon, for various reasons, to judge whether an association of Christian faithful conforms to the requirements of the Church.

It will be insufficient merely to examine the goals of an association before giving one's judgment. There is a need for objective, verifiable criteria in order to avoid an arbitrary decision. In 1987, the members of the synod of bishops on the laity focused their attention on the phenomenon of the growing number of lay associations and the lack of objective criteria to permit a recognition of their legitimacy. This is why, in his apostolic exhortation *Christifideles laici,* John Paul II enumerated a list of five "criteria of ecclesiality" which must be found in any association of the Christian faithful. The purpose of these criteria is to verify the fundamental mark of the legitimacy of such associations: their ecclesial character. Here then are the criteria: the primacy given to the call of every Christian to holiness, the responsibility of professing the Catholic faith, the witness to a strong and authentic communion with the pope and local bishop, conformity to and participation in the Church's apostolic goals, and a commitment to a presence in human society.[20]

Besides these criteria, the pope also listed eight actual fruits of legitimate associations, for example: "the renewed appreciation for prayer, contemplation, liturgical, and sacramental life; a readiness to participate in programs and church activities at the local, national, and international levels; a desire to be present as Christians in various settings of social life; and the creation and awakening of charitable, cultural, and spiritual works, the spirit of detachment, and evangelical poverty leading to a greater generosity in charity toward all."[21] When found in an association, those fruits enable one to ascertain whether the necessary criteria of ecclesiality are present.[22]

---

[20] See *CL* 30; also J. Provost, "Approaches to Catholic Identity in Church Law," *Con* 255 (1994) 21–23.

[21] Ibid.

[22] See R. Pagé, "Note sur les 'critères d'ecclésialité pour les associations de laïcs,'" *Stud Can* 24 (1990) 460–462.

The part of the code dealing with associations of the faithful can also be considered as the legal framework establishing the juridic status of associations of the faithful in the Church. Thirty-two canons (ten less than in the 1917 code) are contained in four chapters. The first chapter presents the basic norms common to all associations of the faithful having a status in the Church. Among other things, we learn here that de facto associations can exist in the Church. Chapter 2 deals with public associations, and chapter 3 with private associations. The final chapter dedicates three canons to associations of lay persons in particular.

Apart from the fundamental right to associate (*CCEO* 18, which is the same as c. 215), the Eastern code deals with associations of the faithful in eleven canons (*CCEO* 573–583) within one title (XIII), compared to the thirty-two canons of the Latin code. The canons are all similar to the corresponding ones in the Latin code but highlight the essentials only. The basic distinctions between public and private associations are found in the Eastern code; however, it provides no specific or detailed norms for each of these types or for lay associations. Evidently, particular law will have a major role to play. The Eastern canons list the competent authorities and mention their right and responsibility of vigilance; the canons also set forth the principles which form the basis for respecting the rights and obligations of the members of the associations. Each norm is clear, although there will inevitably be difficulties in their application. Undoubtedly the more detailed norms of the Latin code will be helpful as parallel norms.

CHAPTER I
COMMON NORMS
[cc. 298–311]

For the most part, these norms deal directly with associations of the faithful having a juridic status in the Church, whether these be public or private associations. But de facto associations are also affected by several of these norms.

NATURE OF ASSOCIATIONS OF THE FAITHFUL
[cc. 298–311]

Only by describing the purposes of associations of the faithful, their diverse categories and organization, and the situation of their members, is it possible to develop a precise idea of their nature. But these are only common denominators. Each association then adopts its own configuration, which establishes its specificity.

Description and Ends

Canon 298 — §1. In the Church there are associations distinct from institutes of consecrated life and societies of apostolic life; in these associations the Christian faithful, whether clerics, lay persons, or clerics and lay persons together, strive in a common endeavor to foster a more perfect life, to promote public worship or Christian doctrine, or to exercise other works of the apostolate such as initiatives of evangelization, works of piety or charity, and those which animate the temporal order with a Christian spirit.

§2. The Christian faithful are to join especially those associations which competent ecclesiastical authority has erected, praised, or commended.

The first paragraph of this canon contains the elements essential not only for grasping the nature of associations of the faithful, but also for clarifying and guiding the choice of the juridic status to be granted or denied to an association.

"In the Church there are associations distinct from institutes of consecrated life and societies of apostolic life...." The image of the typical association in the Church—experienced in institutes of consecrated life and societies of apostolic life—is profiled in these words. In proceeding by way of comparison, the text is reduced to explaining associations of the faithful negatively: they are not groups of the faithful organized as in institutes of consecrated life and societies of apostolic life, and their members are not bound by vows or other sacred bonds by which the evangelical counsels are assumed.

"...in these associations the Christian faithful, whether clerics, lay persons, or clerics and lay persons together...." Not only can associations of the faithful group together exclusively lay people, religious, or clergy, but these can also be together in the same association. The fact of being a member of an association of the faithful does not change the status of a person in the Church, as does the fact of religious profession or priestly ordination.

"...strive in a common endeavor to foster a more perfect life, to promote public worship or Christian doctrine, or to exercise other works of the apostolate such as initiatives of evangelization, works of piety or charity, and those which animate the temporal order with a Christian spirit." Canon 215 indicates three generic purposes justifying the exercise of the right of association: charity, piety, and the promotion of the Christian vocation in the world. Canon 298, §1 seeks in effect to explicate these three purposes, but without thereby precisely listing them in an exclusive fashion. Indeed, the precise objectives of associations of the faithful can be as numerous and varied as there are facets to Christian life. However, the purposes expressed in canon 298 must serve as criteria in examining an association's request for recognition presented to the competent authority. These purposes can be sketched as follows:

(a) fostering a more perfect life;
(b) promoting public worship;
(c) promoting Christian doctrine;
(d) exercising other works of the apostolate such as initiatives of
     i.   evangelization
     ii. works of piety
     iii. works of charity
     iv. animation of the temporal order with the Christian spirit.

To judge from this list, there is room for an infinite number of associations of the faithful. The phrase "other works of the apostolate such as..." leaves room for a very broad interpretation. For instance, certain institutes of consecrated life have recently transferred to lay people some of their apostolic works whether in health care or in education. Some of these lay associations now want to be considered as sharing in the Church's mission and are requesting appropriate recognition. In certain places, an association of Christian faithful is formed whose apostolate consists in directing a health care facility, a school, or another endeavor within the framework of the Church's mission.[23] The foundation of a college or a university as a private association of the faithful recognized in the Church may even be one way of obtaining an initial formal recognition of the Catholic identity of the college or university.[24]

Paragraph two of canon 298, in inviting the faithful to enroll "especially [in] those associations which competent ecclesiastical authority has erected" (c. 312, §1), implies that besides public and private associations, with their corresponding juridic status, there are some associations, born quite naturally from the right of association, which remain without official status and which can be called simply de facto associations. But those associations, while remaining de facto, may receive a "pastoral" recognition from competent authority by being praised or commended.

CATEGORIES
[cc. 299–303]

The 1917 code spoke of various kinds of associations of the faithful, such as pious unions or sodalities, confraternities, etc. The new code no longer uses this terminology. Without making sharp or systematic distinctions, the code does refer to various types of associations, for example, "Catholic associations," or "clerical associations," or "third orders." In speaking of "private associations" and "public associations," it refers to the juridic status of associations of the faithful.

---

[23] See F. Morrisey, "What Makes an Institution 'Catholic,'" *J* 47 (1987) 538–539.

[24] See J. Provost, "The Canonical Aspects of Catholic Identity in the Light of *Ex corde Ecclesiae*," *Stud Can* 25 (1991) 170–171.

Private Associations[25]

Canon 299 — §1. By means of a private agreement made among themselves, the Christian faithful are free to establish associations to pursue the purposes mentioned in can. 298, §1, without prejudice to the prescript of can. 301, §1.

§2. Even if ecclesiastical authority praises or commends them, associations of this type are called private associations.

§3. No private association of the Christian faithful is recognized in the Church unless competent authority reviews its statutes.

The first paragraph of this canon basically repeats canon 215 on the right to associate. But it contains two noteworthy elements. First, the expression "by means of a private agreement made among themselves" corresponds to the above term, "de facto associations." It must not be confused with the more technical term, "private associations," which appears in paragraph two. Second, besides restating canon 215, canon 299, §1 excludes some purposes which associations formed by private agreement might take up, namely what pertains directly to the competence of ecclesiastical authority such as teaching doctrine in the name of the Church.

If an association formed by private agreement is praised or commended by ecclesiastical authority, this does not in itself make the association either public or private. Praise or commendation is equivalent to a "pastoral" recognition, and does not grant any juridical status.[26]

That no private association of the faithful is formally recognized "in the Church unless competent authority reviews its statutes" does not mean that an association of the faithful formed by a private agreement is not recognized at all in the Church if its statutes have not been reviewed by

the competent authority.[27] It means simply that any de facto association, or one formed by a private agreement, which wishes to obtain the status of a "private association" in the Church (cc. 321–326), must have its statutes reviewed by the competent authority. Thus a de facto association is neither irregular nor illegal. Rather, it would be illegal if it pretended to have the status of a "private association" without its statutes having been recognized.

Catholic Associations

Canon 300 — No association is to assume the name *Catholic* without the consent of competent ecclesiastical authority according to the norm of can. 312.

It is not only associations which are forbidden to take the name "Catholic" without the consent of the competent ecclesiastical authority. Canon 216, in affirming the existence of the right of apostolic initiative, forbids any undertaking born from this right to assume the name "Catholic" without the consent of that authority. More precisely yet, "even if it is in fact Catholic, no school is to bear the name *Catholic school* without the consent of competent ecclesiastical authority" (c. 803, §3).

Evidently the name "Catholic" constitutes a special recommendation, since it carries one of the marks of the Church itself. Hence, it is precisely the competent ecclesiastical authority which has a strict right to supervise the use of this term which qualifies the Church itself. "Catholic" is something which is universal, in the sense of "without borders." In this Catholic Church there subsists the Church of Christ, into which each baptized person is incorporated (c. 204, §2).[28]

[25] Cf. *CCEO* 573, §2.

[26] See Canadian Conference of Catholic Bishops, *Recognition of National Catholic Associations—Guidelines for the CCCB and Associations of the Faithful* (CCCB Guidelines) (Ottawa: CCCB, 1993) 44.

[27] See R. Pagé, "La reconnaissance des associations de fidèles," *Stud Can* 19 (1985) 332–333.

[28] For further reflections on Catholic identity, see Provost, "Canonical Aspects of Catholic Identity," 159–168.

Public Associations[29]

Canon 301 — §1. It is for the competent ecclesiastical authority alone to erect associations of the Christian faithful which propose to hand on Christian doctrine in the name of the Church or to promote public worship, or which intend other purposes whose pursuit is of its nature reserved to the same ecclesiastical authority.

§2. Competent ecclesiastical authority, if it has judged it expedient, can also erect associations of the Christian faithful to pursue directly or indirectly other spiritual purposes whose accomplishment has not been sufficiently provided for through the initiatives of private persons.

§3. Associations of the Christian faithful which are erected by competent ecclesiastical authority are called public associations.

The first paragraph of canon 301 affirms the exclusive right of the competent ecclesiastical authority to erect certain types of associations of the faithful: those which set out to promote public worship, or those which aim at other ends whose pursuit is reserved by their nature to ecclesiastical authority.

Canon 298, §1 already mentioned the promotion of public worship or Christian doctrine as purposes for associations of the faithful. Canon 301, §l does not, however, limit the participation of the faithful to associations which devote themselves to such purposes. It only reserves the right to the competent ecclesiastical authority to erect such associations. Obviously, the reason is that they intend to teach Christian doctrine in the name of the Church and to promote public worship, activities within the competence of ecclesiastical authority.

Beyond this exclusive right, the competent authority can see to the assuring of the pursuit of certain other spiritual ends "whose accomplishment has not been sufficiently provided for through the initiatives of private persons." It can then itself erect some associations of the faithful "if it has judged it expedient" (§2).

[29] Cf. *CCEO* 573, §1 and 574.

When the competent ecclesiastical authority does erect an association of the faithful, this is called a "public association." It is, then, the fact of being "erected" by church authority that makes an association of the faithful "public" while it is a private association if it is "recognized." The conditions for obtaining these types of juridic status will be developed below.

Clerical Associations

Canon 302 — Those associations of the Christian faithful are called clerical which are under the direction of clerics, assume the exercise of sacred orders, and are recognized as such by competent authority.

Three conditions are needed for an association to be called "clerical": (1) it must be under the direction of clergy; (2) it must presume the exercise of sacred orders; (3) it must be recognized as such by competent authority.

These three conditions have to be fulfilled at the same time. That an association of the faithful be under the direction of clergy is not sufficient to make it a "clerical" association. That it assumes the exercise of sacred orders is not sufficient either. Moreover, this second condition does not mean that a clerical association must necessarily be formed exclusively of clergy.

An association could be formed uniquely of deacons, or exclusively of priests. Could the conference of bishops be called a clerical association in the terms of canon 302? It is quite difficult to give a positive answer, since the conference of bishops is not a free association (cf. c. 450). In fact, it is an expression of the *affectus collegialis* that belongs to the nature of the episcopate. However, the bishops may organize a clerical association open only to their colleagues; for example, for their spiritual needs.

Third Orders

Canon 303 — Associations whose members share in the spirit of some religious institute while in secular life, lead an apostolic life, and strive for

Christian perfection under the higher direction of the same institute are called third orders or some other appropriate name.

The old code distinguished three types of associations of the faithful: secular third orders, confraternities, and pious unions. Canon 303 retains only the name of the first type, third orders. But it considerably expands its meaning.

In the old code, a secular third order designated lay persons living in the world the spiritual and apostolic values of a religious order composed of men (the first order) or women (the second order) (*CIC* 702–706). The new code permits associations of the faithful to be called "third orders" if their members participate in the spirit of any religious institute while living in the world. The name "third order" is thus no longer only descriptive, and by that fact it is no longer exclusive. Another characteristic of these third orders or associations which have "some other appropriate name" is their being "under the higher direction" of the institute which inspires them.

ORGANIZATION
[cc. 304–305]

Since an association of the faithful is a society, it is a place where rights are exercised, where obligations are acquired, and where a common end or common good is pursued. As with any society, an association therefore needs a modicum of organization in order to be for its members the most effective means possible for promoting the purposes which they are pursuing.

Statutes[30]

Canon 304 — §1. All public or private associations of the Christian faithful, by whatever title or name they are called, are to have their own statutes which define the purpose or social objective of the association, its seat, government, and conditions required for membership and which determine the

manner of its acting, attentive, however, to the necessity or advantage of time and place.

§2. They are to choose a title or name for themselves adapted to the usage of time and place, selected above all with regard to their intended purpose.

An association's statutes are a significant element of its juridic condition. As was previously stated in canon 299, §3, it is the review of its statutes which brings about the recognition of a private association in the Church. Other canons frequently refer to the content of the statutes.

The statutes have such importance because they represent the stable element of an organization, somewhat like a constitution does for a state. They are a key point of reference for both the rights and obligations of the members. The statutes are the stable reminder of the group's nature and objectives. This is why canon 304, §1 makes no exceptions: whether they are public or private, "by whatever title or name they are called," associations of the faithful "are to have their own statutes."

The canon prescribes the essential elements which must be inserted in the statutes. They must define the end or social objective of the association, its headquarters, its mode of government, and the conditions required for membership. They must determine the association's modes of action.

On the whole, the statutes of an association must contain sufficient elements to permit a member of the faithful who is interested in becoming a part of it to have the clearest understanding possible before joining it. Many other canons of the code deal with statutes and can potentially provide an inspiration for developing the statutes of an association of the faithful, e.g., canons 94, 451, 506, 587, and 1232.

Vigilance by Competent Authority[31]

Canon 305 — §1. All associations of the Christian faithful are subject to the vigilance of competent ecclesiastical authority which is to take care that

---

[30] Cf. *CCEO* 576, §1.

[31] Cf. *CCEO* 577.

the integrity of faith and morals is preserved in them and is to watch so that abuse does not creep into ecclesiastical discipline. This authority therefore has the duty and right to inspect them according to the norm of law and the statutes. These associations are also subject to the governance of this same authority according to the prescripts of the canons which follow.

§2. Associations of any kind are subject to the vigilance of the Holy See; diocesan associations and other associations to the extent that they work in the diocese are subject to the vigilance of the local ordinary.

The Church's mission is to lead all human persons to unity, to build up the Body of Christ. While awaiting the definitive attainment of this end, the Church is the sacrament of that unity to which humanity is called. Church leaders are particularly sensitive to anything that expresses the communion of the faithful. They are therefore directly concerned with associations, as they are whenever public order is affected. This is why the present canon might theoretically apply equally to any association of the faithful, whether it has a juridic status in the Church or not. However, even if the text speaks without greater precision of "all associations of the Christian faithful" (§1) and of "associations of any kind" (§2) it seems evident from the context that it envisions here only those associations that are "public" and "private" as distinct from de facto associations.

The competent authority has the right and duty in virtue of its mission to exercise vigilance in the Christian community. In granting a juridic status to an association of the faithful, the Church becomes particularly involved in its life and activities. It follows, therefore, that even if the scope of the Church's right and duty of vigilance is not expanded, it at least acquires a particular significance by being defined by universal law and by proper law as expressed in the statutes. The right and duty of vigilance are exercised then "according to the norm of law and the statutes."

The object of the competent authority's vigilance is to preserve the integrity of faith and

morals, and to "watch so that abuse does not creep into ecclesiastical discipline" (§1). But it includes many other aspects determined in the following canons.

Concretely, the Holy See constitutes the authority competent to exercise vigilance over any association of the faithful, whether it be public, private, diocesan, national, or international. The local ordinary exercises vigilance over diocesan associations, "and other associations to the extent that they work in the diocese" (§2). The local ordinary can thus intervene, if this is needed, not only when a diocesan association of the faithful has its headquarters in his own diocese, but also when an association—which may or may not be diocesan—carries on its work in his diocese even though it has its headquarters elsewhere. The manner of intervention as well as the situation calling for such intervention can vary according to the case and the nature of the association.

MEMBERS
[cc. 306–308]

Members constitute the most important element of an association of the faithful. They are its principal agents. Since associations of the faithful are voluntary by nature, the faithful must know that their rights will be protected or promoted, but also that they assume obligations by joining an association. It is against this background that several prescriptions of law are written about the statutes, the most fundamental of which deal with how members of the faithful are admitted to and dismissed from an association.

Conditions of Belonging

Canon 306 — In order for a person to possess the rights and privileges of an association and the indulgences and other spiritual favors granted to the same association, it is necessary and sufficient that the person has been validly received into it and has not been legitimately dismissed from it according to the prescripts of law and the proper statutes of the association.

This canon mentions the two fundamental conditions for someone to enjoy the rights and advantages furnished by an association: that the person "has been validly received into it and has not been legitimately dismissed from it." These conditions are presented here as principles. The following canons will return to them. But the present canon refers to the "proper statutes of the association," those which contain the conditions for a valid reception into the association as well as those governing a legitimate dismissal.

Admission[32]

Canon 307 — §1. The reception of members is to be done according to the norm of law and the statutes of each association.

§2. The same person can be enrolled in several associations.

§3. Members of religious institutes can join associations according to the norm of their proper law with the consent of their superior.

As already prescribed in canon 304, §1, the association's statutes must contain the "conditions required for membership." Since associations of the faithful envision the fulfillment of some aspect of the mission of the Church, each in its own way, then "the same person can be enrolled in several associations" (c. 307, §2). However, the former code (*CIC* 705) prohibited members of a third order from being members of another third order.

Even while recognizing the fundamental right of association for members of religious institutes, paragraph three is careful to refer to the constitutions of each institute as well as to require the superior's consent. Not every association of the faithful, in effect, can be consonant with every type of religious institute. One has only to think of an institute of contemplative life. How could a member be involved in the activities of an association dedicated to the apostolate toward migrants or students? Furthermore, such a person could not

"be summoned to furnish assistance in the various pastoral ministries" (c. 674).

Dismissal[33]

Canon 308 — No one legitimately enrolled is to be dismissed from an association except for a just cause according to the norm of law and the statutes.

Even if canon 304, §1 does not require that the conditions for dismissal from an association of the faithful be written into the statutes, this goes without saying, since in any case they are included in the conditions for admission. In effect, if people wish to be admitted into an association, they must make a commitment to espouse its purposes, modes of action, government, etc. If some members no longer respect this commitment, they could be considered to have excluded themselves from the association. However, that is not sufficient. The statutes protect the rights and duties of the members as well as of the association itself; they must specify what causes will justify a dismissal, and even the procedures which will lead to it.

FUNCTIONING
[cc. 309–311]

Whether or not they are erected as juridic persons, associations of the faithful must be able to function in a way which will enable them to attain their end and which permits their members to attain their individual ends.

Internal Functioning

Canon 309 — According to the norm of law and the statutes, legitimately established associations have the right to issue particular norms respecting the association itself, to hold meetings, and to designate moderators, officials, other officers, and administrators of goods.

---

[32] Cf. *CCEO* 578.

[33] Cf. *CCEO* 581.

The term "legitimately established" applies to private as well as public associations. However, the working out of this right "to issue particular norms" will vary according to the association's juridic status. More precise qualifications of this right will be discussed below.

Rights and Obligations of a Private Association

Canon 310 — A private association which has not been established as a juridic person cannot, as such, be a subject of obligations and rights. Nevertheless, the members of the Christian faithful associated together in it can jointly contract obligations and can acquire and possess rights and goods as co-owners and co-possessors; they are able to exercise these rights and obligations through an agent or a proxy.

As expressed in the previous canon, every association of the faithful has the right to issue rules concerning its own internal workings. But for an association to have an external function—or better, for it to be the subject of rights and obligations besides those which it has in regard to its own members—it must have a juridic personality. However, as will be discussed below, only public associations acquire a juridic personality by the very decree which erects them as public associations. For a private association to have a juridic personality, it must expressly request it and fulfill the conditions set forth in the law.

What happens if a private association does not request juridic personality? Although it cannot as such be the subject of rights and obligations, its members "can jointly contract obligations and can acquire and possess rights and goods as co-owners and co-possessors." Individual members are therefore responsible for their respective obligations and rights contracted jointly.

It should be noted that goods held jointly are not ecclesiastical goods and thus are not subject to canonical norms regulating these, e.g., those in Book V. They remain private goods. Since the association cannot act as a body or a juridic person, the members cannot exercise the rights and obligations they have contracted except by an agent or proxy. Obviously, all of these issues must be dealt with in the statutes.

Cooperation among Associations

Canon 311 — Members of institutes of consecrated life who preside over or assist associations in some way united to their institute are to take care that these associations give assistance to the works of the apostolate which already exist in a diocese, especially cooperating, under the direction of the local ordinary, with associations which are ordered to the exercise of the apostolate in the diocese.

This canon deals especially with associations that are governed by canon 303, those which "are called third orders or some other appropriate name."[34] Canon 311 basically reminds the directors or associate directors of these associations that, while they are dedicated to the works and mission of the institute which inspires them, they are primarily a means of serving the mission of the faithful. Therefore, they cannot distance themselves from "the works of the apostolate which already exist in a diocese."

The preferred way to assist diocesan works is by cooperation, "under the direction of the local ordinary, with associations which are ordered to the exercise of the apostolate in the diocese." *Mutatis mutandis* a similar provision applies to institutes of consecrated life (see c. 778). This is, moreover, the meaning of canon 305, §2, which speaks of the vigilance role of the local ordinary.

---

[34] Christian faithful (laity, clerics, or religious) may be associated with an institute of consecrated life to participate in its spiritual life and its apostolate. Most of the time they will remain individually associated. However, sometimes they will be gathered in an association. Canon 311 does not pertain to the former; it does pertain to the latter. Actually, the code does not deal with individuals associated with institutes of consecrated life.

CHAPTER II
PUBLIC ASSOCIATIONS
OF THE CHRISTIAN FAITHFUL
[cc. 312–320]

This chapter of the code presents the characteristic traits of public associations of the faithful. The canons cover their nature, the admission of members, their moderator and chaplain, the administration of their goods, and finally their suppression.

NATURE
[cc. 312–315]

The most distinctive feature of public associations is the fact that they are erected by competent authority and by this very fact receive a juridic personality.

Authority Competent to Erect
Public Associations[35]

Canon 312 — §1. The authority competent to erect public associations is:

1° the Holy See for universal and international associations;

2° the conference of bishops in its own territory for national associations, that is, those which from their founding are directed toward activity throughout the whole nation;

3° the diocesan bishop in his own territory, but not a diocesan administrator, for diocesan associations, except, however, for those associations whose right of erection has been reserved to others by apostolic privilege.

§2. Written consent of the diocesan bishop is required for the valid erection of an association or section of an association in a diocese even if it is done by virtue of apostolic privilege. Nevertheless, the consent given by a diocesan bishop for

the erection of a house of a religious institute is also valid for the erection in the same house or church attached to it of an association which is proper to that institute.

The expression "the authority competent" has been used several times in this section of the code. Each time it has been used in the sense of canon 312.

According to paragraph one, the authority competent to erect public associations varies depending on their territorial scope. If the association is universal and international, then it belongs to the Holy See to erect it.[36] If the association is to be national, then the conference of bishops erects it. The diocesan bishop erects diocesan associations, unless the association is one "whose right of erection has been reserved to others by apostolic privilege." For example, establishing sodalities of the rosary is reserved to the Dominican Order.[37] The second paragraph of this canon, however, conditions the valid exercise of this privilege on the written consent of the diocesan bishop. One should recall that the competent authority is the same for the approval of private associations (cf. c. 299, §3).

Unless it was founded by the Holy See itself or by the conference of bishops according to the terms of canon 301, an association of the faithful begins by being erected as a diocesan association,

---

[35] Cf. *CCEO* 575.

[36] According to an internal document of the PCL, in 1996 forty-eight associations of Christian lay faithful had received recognition as international private associations or had been erected as international public associations; and thirteen others had requested an international (§1) status that was being examined. It is interesting to note that among the forty-eight associations that have received international status, forty-four were recognized as private associations. Some private ones received their status for three years, some for five years, some indefinitely. Since a public association is granted juridic personality which is perpetual by its nature (c. 120), it is strange to note that one of the four public associations received its status for three years.

[37] See E. Kneal, in *CLSA Com*, 250.

usually after having been a de facto association and perhaps praised or recommended by the competent authority. Once erected in one diocese, an association does not have to be erected again by the bishop of another diocese in order to work there, since it has already been erected. But it obviously must obtain the agreement of the local bishop before beginning to work or to establish itself there, somewhat like religious institutes (cc. 678–683) and personal prelatures (c. 297).

A diocesan association which spreads to many or even all the dioceses of a bishops' conference does not thereby become a "national" association.[38] Moreover, if such an association were to become established in several countries, it would not become "international" or "universal" in a legal sense. To become "national" or "international," it must be erected as such by the competent authority, either the bishops' conference or the Holy See respectively.

It should be noted that the bishops of an ecclesiastical province (c. 431) or region (c. 433) of a bishops' conference are not considered to be the competent authority for erecting an association of the faithful. Of course, each of the bishops of a district could praise or authorize the activities of such an association or establish it in their respective dioceses. All the bishops of the area could obviously issue a joint communiqué praising an association. But this does not give it a different juridic status.

Canon 312, §2 prescribes that a diocesan association cannot validly be erected unless the diocesan bishop consents in writing. No exception is made, even for an association or the section of an association which can be erected only by someone else in virtue of an apostolic privilege; even here, the written consent of the diocesan bishop is needed. On the other hand, the consent of the bishop to erect the house of a religious institute in his diocese "is also valid for the erection in the same house or church attached to it of an association which is proper to that institute."

[38] See CCCB Guidelines, 26.

Juridic Personality

Canon 313 — Through the same decree by which the competent ecclesiastical authority according to the norm of can. 312 erects it, a public association and even a confederation of public associations is constituted a juridic person and, to the extent it is required, receives a mission for the purposes which it proposes to pursue in the name of the Church.

An association of the faithful is constituted as a juridic person by the very decree which erects it as a public association. This is one of the characteristics which distinguishes it from a private association, which has to make an explicit request if it wishes to acquire a juridic personality (c. 322, §1).

A public association can receive "a mission for the purposes which it proposes to pursue in the name of the Church," to the extent that such mission is required. An association of the faithful which receives such a canonical mission acquires a public juridic personality in the terms of canon 116, §1.

The fact that an association of the faithful acquires a public juridic personality in being erected as a public association has a special impact on the laws which affect it. This is because, up to a certain point, the Church endorses its objectives, its manner of acting, etc., since it gives the association a mission to act in its name.

What canon 313 says about public associations also applies to confederations of public associations. Such confederations are treated nowhere else in the code. Since canon 313 places them on the same level as public associations in regard to their erection, one may conclude that there can be groupings of public associations which are de facto confederations and which need not be erected by competent authority. If they are so erected, they obtain public or private juridic personality, depending on whether they receive a mission to act in the name of the Church.

Approval of Statutes[39]

Canon 314 — The statutes of each public association and their revision or change need the approval of the ecclesiastical authority competent to erect the association according to the norm of can. 312, §1.

Since a public association acquires a juridic personality in being erected, its statutes must be approved by the competent authority. In effect, according to canon 117, "no aggregate of persons (*universitas personarum*) or of things (*universitas rerum*), intending to obtain juridic personality, is able to acquire it unless competent authority has approved its statutes." Obviously, the same is true for any change in the statutes.

Here an approval is required, not just a recognition as in the case of private associations (c. 299, §3). As will be seen below (c. 322, §2), if a private association wishes to obtain a juridic personality, its statutes must be approved and not merely recognized. Evidently, the effects of recognition are not the same as those of approval; through approval the Church commits itself to a greater degree, to the same extent that it commits itself when it grants juridic personality. Such personality implies a set of rights and duties which are limited, as are those of physical persons (c. 223).

Right of Initiative

Canon 315 — Public associations are able on their own initiative to undertake endeavors in keeping with their own character. These endeavors are governed according to the norm of the statutes, though under the higher direction of the ecclesiastical authority mentioned in can. 312, §1.

Canon 315 merely recognizes for public associations, which are juridic persons, what canon 216 has already recognized for physical persons.

[39] Cf. *CCEO* 576.

The right of initiative which is recognized for the former, however, must be exercised in conformity with their proper character, "according to the norm of the statutes," and "under the higher direction of the ecclesiastical authority."

Admission of Members

Canon 316 — §1. A person who has publicly rejected the Catholic faith, has defected from ecclesiastical communion, or has been punished by an imposed or declared excommunication cannot be received validly into public associations.

§2. Those enrolled legitimately who fall into the situation mentioned in §1, after being warned, are to be dismissed from the association, with due regard for its statutes and without prejudice to the right of recourse to the ecclesiastical authority mentioned in can. 312, §1.

The statutes of any association, public or private, must define the conditions of membership. To impose some conditions is the most legitimate right of an association. No one can ever be obliged to join an association, but one must know the conditions in advance. The criteria for admitting members will be determined greatly by the ends and means of the association in question.

However, there are some important limits in regard to the exercise of this right to define the conditions of membership by public associations. Canon 316 establishes that they cannot validly admit to their membership someone who has publicly rejected the Catholic faith, been separated from the communion of the Church, or been subject to an imposed or declared excommunication.

Understandably, a person in one of these situations cannot be part of a public association, given the purpose of associations of the faithful in general and the particular nature of public associations, which act in the name of the Church. The minimal condition of membership in such associations is fulfilling the first duty of any of the Christian faithful, i.e., maintaining communion with the Church (c. 209, §1).

It is not always easy to apply the provision of canon 316. The difficulty is not located at the level of the logical consistency on which this prescription is based. It consists rather in the criteria used to identify "a person who has publicly rejected the Catholic faith, or has defected from ecclesiastical communion." There is no difficulty in regard to "an imposed or declared excommunication," since there would be documents to prove this.

The question, then, is to know at what moment a person has publicly rejected the Catholic faith or abandoned communion with the Church. On one hand, there must be a rejection of the Catholic faith, and this must be public; on the other hand, a person must distance himself or herself from the communion of the Church.

The first case can occur when someone crosses over publicly from the Catholic faith to, for example, the Lutheran faith. The second case could happen when someone abandons communion with the (Catholic) Church but without joining any other ecclesial community. Undoubtedly the mere fact of no longer going to Mass would not be enough to indicate abandonment of the Catholic communion. Moreover, each case would have to be examined separately.[40]

The provisions of paragraph one apply equally to the dismissal of persons legitimately inscribed in a public association. Canon 308 has already foreseen that a member legitimately admitted in an association can be dismissed. However, this can be done only with due regard for its statutes and without prejudice to the right of recourse to the competent authority.

MODERATOR AND CHAPLAIN
[cc. 317–318]

Among the positions required for the effective working of an association of the faithful, cer-

---

[40] See Kneal, in *CLSA Com,* 251–252. The author discusses various possible criteria for judging each case.

tainly the most important are those of moderator and of chaplain or ecclesiastical assistant. Since a public association acts in the name of the Church, the competent authority always plays an important role in the process not only of designating but also of removing those who hold these positions.

Designation

Canon 317 — §1. Unless the statutes provide otherwise, it is for the ecclesiastical authority mentioned in can. 312, §1 to confirm the moderator of a public association elected by the public association itself, install the one presented, or appoint the moderator in his own right. The same ecclesiastical authority also appoints the chaplain or ecclesiastical assistant, after having heard the major officials of the association, when it is expedient.

§2. The norm stated in §1 is also valid for associations which members of religious institutes erect outside their own churches or houses in virtue of apostolic privilege. In associations which members of religious institutes erect in their own church or house, however, the nomination or confirmation of the moderator and chaplain pertains to the superior of the institute, according to the norm of the statutes.

§3. In associations which are not clerical, lay persons are able to exercise the function of moderator. A chaplain or ecclesiastical assistant is not to assume that function unless the statutes provide otherwise.

§4. Those who exercise leadership in political parties are not to be moderators in public associations of the Christian faithful which are ordered directly to the exercise of the apostolate.

The dispositions vary depending on whether the moderator or the chaplain is being named.

(a) *Moderator.* The code often uses the term "moderator," but without ever defining it. Despite several variations depending on the context, the moderator is always someone responsible, a sponsor, a coordinator. In the law for religious it is used in the sense of a superior. It is used in the same sense in the canons on associations of the faithful. For example, canon 320, §3 speaks of the "moderator and other major officials."

The language of canon 317, §1 echoes that of the canons on ecclesiastical offices, summed up in canon 147: "The provision of an ecclesiastical office is made: through free conferral by a competent ecclesiastical authority; through installation by the same authority if presentation preceded it; through confirmation or admission granted by the same authority if election or postulation preceded it."

It is up to the statutes to determine if the public association will elect its moderator, who must then be confirmed by the competent authority, or will present the moderator to be installed by that same authority, or will even have the moderator directly named by the competent authority. The statutes could provide something else. But whether it is through election, presentation, or nomination by the competent authority, the procedure to be followed is that which is provided for each of these approaches in the canons on ecclesiastical offices (cc. 157–179).

The same is true for associations which "members of religious institutes erect outside their own churches or houses in virtue of apostolic privilege." But if religious erect associations in their own church or house, the superior of the institute names or confirms the moderator.

Lay persons, religious men and women, and clergy can be moderators in associations of the faithful. However, the code also specifies certain restrictions. Lay persons cannot be moderators in clerical associations. Normally, the chaplain cannot exercise the job of moderator at the same time because of a conflict of fora. Those who exercise leadership in political parties cannot be moderators in public associations "which are ordered directly to the exercise of the apostolate." Obviously, the reason is that public associations act in the name of the Church (c. 313) while political parties, by their very nature, are exclusive of

those who are not members of them. The provision here seeks to avoid any danger of confusion or conflict on both sides.

(b) *Chaplain.* The function of chaplain is clearly defined in canon 564. He is "a priest to whom is entrusted in a stable manner the pastoral care, at least in part, of some community or particular group of the Christian faithful." It is then necessarily a priest, whom canon 317, §1 also calls by the name of "ecclesiastical assistant."

He is named by the competent ecclesiastical authority, who may decide to consult the major officials of the association before proceeding to name the chaplain. Likewise the authority which is competent to erect the association is also the one who names the chaplain in an association erected by members of religious institutes outside their churches or houses. If the association is erected by members of a religious institute in their own church or house, then the superior of the institute names the chaplain.

Removal

Canon 318 — §1. In special circumstances and where grave reasons require it, the ecclesiastical authority mentioned in can. 312, §1 can designate a trustee who is to direct the association for a time in its name.

§2. The person who appointed or confirmed the moderator of a public association can remove the moderator for a just cause, after the person has heard, however, the moderator and the major officials of the association according to the norm of the statutes. The person who appointed a chaplain can remove him according to the norm of cann. 192–195.

Habitually in the code the power to remove an official corresponds to the power to appoint such an official. Similarly, those who accept a mandate because they fulfill certain legal requirements ought not to be surprised that the mandating authority may revoke such a mandate if those requirements are no longer fulfilled.

But removal is not the only option in a problematic situation. In fact, it could be an extreme solution, or perhaps not the best one. In special circumstances and where grave reasons require it, the competent authority might judge that a trustee is to be named to direct the association temporarily. The canon mentions neither what circumstances nor what reasons may justify such action. This is similar to placing someone under a tutor or guardian. The naming of such a trustee, obviously, is exceptional and can only be temporary. It is not always a step necessarily tied to the dismissal of the moderator. It is easy to imagine that in certain circumstances it would not be good to name a new moderator; a key task of the trustee would often be that of assessing the situation in this regard.

If the moderator was elected or presented, the competent authority who confirmed or instituted such a one could remove the person, but not without first having heard the moderator as well as the major officials of the association as indicated in the statutes. There must, evidently, be a just cause to remove a moderator.

The removal of the chaplain is subject to the prescriptions of canons 192–195 on ecclesiastical offices.

Administration of Goods[41]

Canon 319 — §1. Unless other provision has been made, a legitimately erected public association administers the goods which it possesses according to the norm of the statutes under the higher direction of the ecclesiastical authority mentioned in can. 312, §1, to which it must render an account of administration each year.

§2. It must also render to the same authority a faithful account of the expenditure of the offerings and alms which it has collected.

Since public associations become juridic persons by the decree which erects them as public associations, one consequence is that their goods have become "ecclesiastical goods." They are regulated by the canons of Book V on temporal goods, as well as by their own statutes (c. 1257, §1).

The fact that these goods are ecclesiastical goods does not remove them from the possession or ownership of the public associations of the faithful. In effect, under the supreme authority of the Roman Pontiff, the ownership of goods belongs to that juridic person which has acquired them legitimately (c. 1256). But their administration is subject to considerable restrictions.

Besides conforming to the provisions of its statutes approved by the competent authority, a public association "must render an account of administration each year" to that same authority. The use of offerings and alms is also subject to such reporting. The form according to which such reports are to be made will usually be determined in the statutes or by local custom in accord with canon 1287.

Suppression[42]

Canon 320 — §1. Only the Holy See can suppress associations it has erected.

§2. For grave causes, a conference of bishops can suppress associations it has erected. A diocesan bishop can suppress associations he has erected and also associations which members of religious institutes have erected through apostolic indult with the consent of the diocesan bishop.

§3. The competent authority is not to suppress a public association unless the authority has heard its moderator and other major officials.

A public association can be suppressed by the same authority which erected it, whether it be the Holy See, the conference of bishops, or the diocesan bishop. The diocesan bishop, in addition to being able to suppress associations which he himself has erected, can also suppress those erected by members of religious institutes in virtue of an apostolic indult, but which required his consent. Nevertheless, a competent authority cannot sup-

---

[41] Cf. *CCEO* 582.

[42] Cf. *CCEO* 583.

press a public association without having heard the moderator and other major officers.

The provisions for the suppression of a private association are slightly different (c. 326, §1). Therefore, it will be important to determine if an association that received its canonical status before 1983 is a private or a public association according to the new code.[43] Those two categories of associations did not exist in the former code.

In the case of suppression, an association can always take hierarchical recourse against the decree of the competent authority (cc. 1732–1739). The competent authority to deal with such recourse depends on the type of association. It could be the Pontifical Council for the Laity,[44] the Congregation for the Clergy,[45] or the Congregation for Institutes of Consecrated Life and Societies of Apostolic Life[46] if a lay association has been founded to become eventually an institute of consecrated life or a society of apostolic life.

After a public association has been suppressed, its goods must be distributed according to the provisions of the statutes. Of course, the practical application of those provisions may depend on an existing civil charter of incorporation. On the other hand, this charter is supposed to be in conformity with canonical statutes. If the statutes give no indication of how the goods are to be distributed, they go to the juridic person immediately superior, always without prejudice to the intention of the founders and donors and acquired rights (c. 123). In principle, the determination of the juridic person immediately superior depends on the character of the association (international, national, or diocesan). It will be the Holy See, the conference of bishops, or the diocese, unless the suppressed association is part of a confederation of public associations (c. 313). Such a confederation is a ju-

ridic person and may be considered as the juridic person immediately superior.

CHAPTER III
PRIVATE ASSOCIATIONS OF THE CHRISTIAN FAITHFUL
[cc. 321–326]

Private associations of the faithful constitute perhaps the most striking fruit of the renewal of the law concerning associations in the Church. None of the prescriptions of the current chapter was found in the 1917 code.

A simple reading of these prescriptions leaves the impression that private associations of the faithful enjoy considerable freedom on several very important points such as the choice of juridic personality, the designation of officers and spiritual counselor, and the administration of goods. However, this does not eliminate the responsibility of the competent authority already treated in the chapter on the norms common to all associations of the faithful: this is made explicit on certain points in the present chapter.

NATURE
[cc. 321–322]

If associations of the faithful become public associations by being erected as such by the competent authority, who must approve their statutes, they become private associations when they are praised or recommended and their statutes are recognized by this same authority (c. 299).

Autonomy

Canon 321 — The Christian faithful guide and direct private associations according to the prescripts of the statutes.

The minimum required of an association of the faithful which wishes to obtain the status of a private association is the drawing up of statutes with a view to their being recognized. The fact that

---

[43] See R. Pagé, "La Signature apostolique et la suppression du statut canonique de l'Armée de Marie," *Stud Can* 25 (1991) 407–408.
[44] *PB* 134.
[45] *PB* 95.
[46] *PB* 111.

these statutes may be recognized by the competent authority as respecting the rights of persons and the minimal norms common to all associations of the faithful underlie canon 321, which acknowledges the competency of the faithful to guide and direct their private associations.

In fact, the statutes will be recognized if they contain the elements defining the framework in which the private association's autonomy will evolve. Such a "framework" implies limits, since a private association is subject to the vigilance of the competent authority. Its autonomy, therefore, is not absolute, any more than is the freedom of de facto associations or that of the individual faithful.

Acquiring a Juridic Personality

Canon 322 — §1. A private association of the Christian faithful can acquire juridic personality through a formal decree of the competent ecclesiastical authority mentioned in can. 312.

§2. No private association of the Christian faithful can acquire juridic personality unless the ecclesiastical authority mentioned in can. 312, §1 has approved its statutes. Approval of the statutes, however, does not change the private nature of the association.

A public association acquires public juridic personality by being erected as such by the competent authority. A private association, however, must expressly request such personality if it wishes to be the subject of corporate rights and duties. In this situation, the authority which can give it juridic personality is the same as the authority which is competent to recognize its status as a private association.

A formal decree of the competent authority is always required for a private association to acquire juridic personality. Although a simple recognition of its statutes is enough to give it the status of a private association, these statutes must now be approved in order for the private association to receive juridic personality (c. 117). This approval, even if it is more demanding than a simple recog-

nition, "does not change the private nature of the association."

Will such an association which asks for juridic personality receive a private juridic personality? Since a public juridic person fulfills its specific tasks in the name of the Church (see c. 116, §1) and since this is a characteristic of a public association of the faithful, undoubtedly there would seem to be a certain discrepancy if a private association were to be granted public juridic personality.[47]

FUNCTIONING
[cc. 323–325]

In comparison with public associations, private associations enjoy a rather notable freedom of activity. Such freedom, of course, is not absolute, just as there is no absolute freedom for the persons who are members of a private association.

Vigilance by Competent Authority

Canon 323 — §1. Although private associations of the Christian faithful possess autonomy according to the norm of can. 321, they are subject to the vigilance of ecclesiastical authority according to the norm of can. 305 and even to the governance of the same authority.

§2. It also pertains to ecclesiastical authority, while respecting the autonomy proper to private associations, to be watchful and careful that dissipation of their energies is avoided and that their exercise of the apostolate is ordered to the common good.

Even as it reaffirms the autonomy of private associations, canon 323 defines the limits of its exercise. This reflects canon 223 that gives the competent authority the right to regulate the exercise of the rights of Christ's faithful, such as the right to associate (c. 215) in view of fostering the

---

[47] For further discussion of this question, see Navarro, *Diritto di associazione,* 92–103.

common good. Canon 323 first recalls that, like any association, private associations are subject to the governance and vigilance of the competent authority regarding the integrity of faith and morals, and are to observe ecclesiastical discipline (c. 305). It then reminds private associations of the right and duty of competent authority to intervene if their action does not correspond to the expectations raised in seeking recognition, and if their apostolate is not ordered toward the common good.

Designation of Officers and Spiritual Advisors

Canon 324 — §1. A private association of the Christian faithful freely designates its moderator and officials according to the norm of the statutes.

§2. A private association of the Christian faithful can freely choose a spiritual advisor, if it desires one, from among the priests exercising ministry legitimately in the diocese; nevertheless, he needs the confirmation of the local ordinary.

Canon 309 establishes that "legitimately established associations" have the right to designate their moderators, etc., "according to the norm of law and the statutes." In contrast with what applies to public associations, which "according to the norm of law" must have their moderator confirmed, instituted, or named by competent church authority, private associations freely designate theirs, as well as their officers. This must, however, be done according to the approved statutes.

While in public associations the chaplain or ecclesiastical assistant is named by the competent authority, in private associations this person, called a "spiritual advisor," is freely chosen by the association itself. Despite differences between the names designating these functions, the person must always be a priest. The spiritual counselor of a private association must be exercising ministry legitimately in the diocese. No matter what authority was competent to approve the private as-

sociation, the choice of a spiritual counselor requires the confirmation of the local ordinary.

It is conceivable that not every association of the faithful will be able to find a priest to take on this role. If no priest is available, could a deacon, a lay religious, or another lay person do this? Yes, as long as distinctly priestly acts are performed by a priest, for example, confession and Eucharist. Therefore, deacons or lay people can supply certain functions usually performed by the spiritual advisor who is normally a priest. To avoid confusion with a properly priestly role, the term "spiritual advisor" should not be used for such a deacon or lay person.[48] In the event, each association is to find an appropriate term.

Administration of Goods

Canon 325 — §1. A private association of the Christian faithful freely administers those goods it possesses according to the prescripts of the statutes, without prejudice to the right of competent ecclesiastical authority to exercise vigilance so that the goods are used for the purposes of the association.

§2. A private association is subject to the authority of the local ordinary according to the norm of can. 1301 in what pertains to the administration and distribution of goods which have been donated or left to it for pious causes.

Canon 325 presupposes that the private association has not sought to become a juridic person, and that, consequently, the members of the private association can acquire and possess goods as co-owners and co-possessors (c. 310). The statutes must mention the right of the members to acquire goods, which would make more understandable the provisions of canon 325, §1 that "a private association of the Christian faithful freely adminis-

---

[48] See CFC et al., instr "Some Questions Regarding Collaboration of Nonordained Faithful in Priests' Sacred Ministry," art. 1, *Origins* 27/24 (November 27, 1997) 402–403.

ters those goods it possesses according to the prescripts of the statutes." But it is also understandable that the competent authority has the right "to exercise vigilance so that the goods are used for the purposes of the association." This gives it the right to intervene should an abuse arise in this regard. Such a provision is unnecessary for public associations since, having public juridic personality, the provisions of Book V are relevant to them. For example, canon 1276, §1 gives ordinaries the right to exercise vigilance over the administration of all the goods which belong to public juridic persons subject to them.

Since the competent authority is to be watchful over the proper use of the association's goods, the association is subject to the local ordinary regarding the administration and distribution of goods destined for pious causes. The text does not distinguish between diocesan, national, or international associations. This is because "the ordinary is the executor of all pious wills" in his diocese (c. 1301, §1).

Extinction

Canon 326 — §1. A private association of the Christian faithful ceases to exist according to the norm of its statutes. The competent authority can also suppress it if its activity causes grave harm to ecclesiastical doctrine or discipline or is a scandal to the faithful.

§2. The allocation of the goods of an association which has ceased to exist must be determined according to the norm of its statutes, without prejudice to acquired rights and the intention of the donors.

The statutes must provide for the fact that an association which began in time can also disappear in time, whether this be because it no longer has enough members, or no longer meets a need, or for any other reason. It could always merge with another association.

There is, however, yet another means of extinction provided for by the general law, and that is suppression. This means of extinction should not be surprising, if the preceding observations are taken into account. Even if a private association enjoys significant autonomy in its action, this autonomy cannot be more extensive than what pertains to the individual faithful who make it up.

In the preceding canons of this title, the vigilance of the competent authority has been mentioned frequently. This vigilance is relevant to three major areas of ecclesial life: faith, morals, and discipline. Depending on the gravity of the abuse, the nature of the intervention by authority can vary. At an extreme point, it could go so far as the suppression of the association by the authority which recognized it.

Evidently, this is an extreme step which must be proportionate to the gravity of the cause, and which presupposes that other means of addressing the problem have been tried. Above all, a concern for the common good or public order must guide such a decision.

The statutes are to provide for the distribution of the goods of an association extinguished by suppression or otherwise. If it is not a juridic person, then the statutes should have provided that the members are co-owners and co-possessors of the private association's goods (c. 310). Yet rights acquired by others must also be respected, such as rights acquired by contracts with other physical or juridic persons. Also, the will of donors must be respected if, for example, the association received any legacies or accepted any foundations. In any event, it must always be remembered that certain civil law provisions may need to be observed to avoid any possible civil suits.

CHAPTER IV
SPECIAL NORMS FOR ASSOCIATIONS OF THE LAITY
[cc. 327–329]

The norms studied so far apply without distinction to any association of the faithful, whether lay or not. It is the chosen juridic status which determines which norms are to apply, regardless of the clerical, lay, or religious character of the association. The only exception, perhaps, is canon 302 on "clerical" associations.

The three "special" norms of this chapter bring nothing specific to the nature of associations of lay persons. None of them even gives an exact notion of lay associations. At least canon 42 of the 1977 schema on the people of God said that, for all practical purposes, associations which do not correspond to the description of clerical associations are called "lay." It is probably a good thing that the commission did not keep this formulation, since members of religious institutes or priests may be members of non-clerical associations. Therefore, any possible confusion is avoided.

Hence the recognized or approved statutes will have to determine whether an association is a lay association. Will it always be appropriate to do this? Determining the ends, means of action, and at times the leadership of the association will most often be enough to clarify that it is a lay association.

Even if some clergy or religious could be members, as in third orders, these associations "under the higher direction" of a religious institute (c. 303) are indeed lay associations. Canon 328 speaks, moreover, of those who direct lay associations, without further precision.

Importance

Canon 327 — Lay members of the Christian faithful are to hold in esteem associations established for the spiritual purposes mentioned in can. 298, especially those which propose to animate the temporal order with the Christian spirit and in this way greatly foster an intimate union between faith and life.

Lay persons are invited to prefer those associations of the faithful whose ends correspond directly to their distinctive role in fulfilling the Church's mission, and which can be held by no one else.

This canon faithfully reflects canon 225, the first one in the list of rights and obligations proper to lay faithful who are "bound by the general obligation and possess the right as individuals, or joined in associations, to work so that the divine message of salvation is made known and accepted by all persons everywhere in the world." This in no way diminishes the importance of associations whose purpose is personal perfection or piety. The Church knows well that there is no true apostolate which is not rooted in an authentic spirituality.[49] This is why, moreover, lay persons are invited to esteem those associations "which propose to animate the temporal order with the Christian spirit and in this way greatly foster an intimate union between faith and life."

Mutual Cooperation

Canon 328 — Those who preside over associations of the laity, even those which have been erected by virtue of apostolic privilege, are to take care that their associations cooperate with other associations of the Christian faithful where it is expedient and willingly assist various Christian works, especially those in the same territory.

When the legislation on associations of the faithful is reviewed in its entirety, it is clear that no association can close in on itself, or focus solely on the proper and exclusive good of its members. Several canons call for—at the very least—openness to cooperation with other associations.

The present canon reflects canons 311, 323, and other canons on the right and duty of competent ecclesiastical authority to exercise vigilance. The diocesan bishop is directly concerned for any association working in his diocese. He is to foster various forms of the apostolate in the diocese and take care that in the entire diocese or in its particular districts, all the works of the apostolate are coordinated under his direction, with due regard for their distinctive character (c. 394, §1).

[49] See *AA* 3.

Formation of Members

Canon 329 — Moderators of associations of the laity are to take care that the members of the association are duly formed to exercise the apostolate proper to the laity.

This prescription is self-explanatory. The organization itself must provide that everything is done so that the members of a lay association are formed adequately to accomplish their proper work.

But more must be said. Lay persons have the right to expect this formation. In effect, according to canon 229, §1, "lay persons are bound by the obligation and possess the right to acquire knowledge of Christian doctrine appropriate to the capacity and condition of each in order for them to be able to live according to this doctrine, announce it themselves, defend it if necessary, and take their part in exercising the apostolate." A lay association could be a privileged place not only for fulfilling this obligation, but for demanding the exercise of this fundamental right.

Conclusion

The activities proper to lay associations of the faithful depend on various factors which to a great extent constitute their limits as defined in law. These limits relate for the most part to the question of juridic status, but also to the reservation by competent authority of certain foundations whose ends relate directly to its own ends.

An examination of the legal dispositions on associations of the faithful makes it clear that their freedom of action diminishes as they are more formally recognized by those in charge of the community. So long as they remain de facto associations, they have the same freedom as the members who make them up, aside from that of adopting the name "Catholic" (c. 300). This is the fundamental exercise of the right of association. The ecclesial and secular activities of these associations are as varied and diversified as the mission of the Church or the nature of Christian life.

However, the faithful are invited to join "especially those associations which competent ecclesiastical authority has erected, praised, or commended" (c. 298, §2). Here is where the juridic status of associations of the faithful becomes a question.

Besides reminding us that every association of the faithful is not necessarily erected, praised, or commended and that de facto associations can exist, canon 298, §2 clarifies the meaning of the recognition of associations of the faithful by the competent authority. For their potential members, this recognition provides, at least in principle, a guarantee of their doctrinal authenticity, their communion with the leaders of the ecclesial community, and the conformity of their activities with the Church's mission.

In the very act of recognizing an association, the episcopate exercises its role of vigilance by a means which is proper to it. From the viewpoint of the association, recognition brings a confirmation of its validity, and sometimes this is an important element reassuring the faithful desiring to join it. Of course, recognition also provides a voice for the association. For example, to the question: "Whether a group of faithful, lacking juridical personality and even recognition as envisaged in canon 299, §3, can legitimately make hierarchical recourse against a decree of its own diocesan bishop," the Pontifical Commission for the Authentic Interpretation of the Code of Canon Law (the former name of the Pontifical Council for the Interpretation of Legislative Texts) responded: "*Negative* as a group."[50] The commission added that they can make a recourse as individual members of the group, singly or together, but not as an association.

It should be recalled that associations are not obliged to seek recognition. But likewise the competent authority is not bound to recognize

---

[50] *AAS* 80 (1988) 1818.

every association which asks for such recognition. The conditions set forth in the law must be observed. However, there is one condition the law does not contain, and that is the test of time which the authority could always require prior to acceding to a request for recognition.[51]

Recognition imposes certain constraints on the freedom of an association. However, it also offers certain advantages. For example, such recognition assures people that the association conforms to the Church's mission.

The norms to be observed in erecting a public association are much more demanding than those which deal with the recognition of a private association. This is because the Church

feels itself more committed when it erects an association of the faithful as a public association. But the same is true on the part of the association, which must respond to various exigencies even while leaving greater room for interventions by competent authority.

Does all this mean that the range of ecclesial and secular activities varies according to an association's juridic status? It would seem so. For example, in receiving a public juridic personality, a public association receives a mission to act in the name of the Church, and its goods become ecclesiastical goods. Any change in orientation or mission is subject to approval by the competent authority, even as the administration of its goods is subject to the general law concerning the temporal goods of the Church.

---

[51] See CCCB Guidelines, 43–45.

BIBLIOGRAPHY

Personal Prelatures

Caparros, E. "A New Hierarchical Structure for New Pastoral Needs: Personal Prelatures." *Philippiniana Sacra* 24 (1989) 379–417.

Ghirlanda, G. "De differentia Praelaturam personalem inter et Ordinariatum militarem seu castrensem." *P* 86 (1987) 219–251.

Hervada, J. In *Com Ex* II/1, 398–417.

O'Reilly, M. "Personal Prelatures and Ecclesial Communion." *Stud Can* 18 (1984) 439–456.

Stetson, W. J., and J. Hervada. "Personal Prelatures from Vatican II to the New Code: An Hermeneutical Study of Canons 294–297." *J* 45 (1985) 379–418.

Associations of the Christian Faithful

Amos, J. R. "A Legal History of Associations of the Faithful." *Stud Can* 21 (1987) 271–297.

Canadian Catholic Conference of Bishops. *Recognition of National Catholic Associations—Guidelines for the CCCB and Associations of the Faithful.* Ottawa: CCCB, 1993.

Galante, J. "Consecrated Life: New Forms and New Institutes." *CLSAP* (1986) 118–125.

Huot, D. M. "Associations of the Faithful and their Dependence with Regard to the Sacred Congregation for Religious and for Secular Institutes and the Pontifical Council for the Laity." *Con Lif* 10 (1986) 101–116, 205–224.

Modde, M. "Lay Governance in Catholic Institutions." *CLSAP* (1992) 185–194.

Morrisey, F. G. "What Makes an Institution 'Catholic'?" *J* 47 (1987) 531–544.

Navarro, L. *Diritto di associazione e associazioni di fedeli.* Milan: Giuffrè, 1991.

Pagé, R. "Les associations de fidèles: reconnaissance et érection." *Stud Can* 19 (1985) 327–338.

———. "Associations of the Faithful in the Church." *J* 47 (1987) 165–203.

———. "Note sur les 'critères d'écclésialité pour les associations de laïcs.'" *Stud Can* 24 (1990) 455–463.

———. "La Signature apostolique et la suppression du statut canonique de l'Armée de Marie." *Stud Can* 25 (1991) 403–415.

Provost, J., "Approaches to Catholic Identity in Church Law." *Con* 255 (1994) 15–25.

———. "The Canonical Aspects of Catholic Identity in the Light of *Ex corde Ecclesiae*." *Stud Can* 25 (1991) 155–191.

Knut Walf

Translated by Ronny Jenkins

Part II
THE HIERARCHICAL CONSTITUTION OF THE CHURCH
[cc. 330–572]

SECTION I
THE SUPREME AUTHORITY OF THE CHURCH
[cc. 330–367]

Scarcely any concept at the last council was so frequently mentioned as that of collegiality between the pope and bishops. The First Vatican Council (1869/1870), which was concerned in a particular way with the position of the pope (primacy, infallibility), was an interrupted, incomplete council. It did not clarify the status of the bishops, particularly their juridical relationship to the pope. The central document of the Second Vatican Council, the dogmatic constitution *Lumen gentium*, dealt with this fundamental question of Catholic ecclesiology.

That the constitution was dealing with a sensitive point of ecclesiology is clear from the fact that it was accompanied by a preliminary "Explanatory Note" through the initiative of Paul VI, a unique event in conciliar history. The "Explanatory Note" refers essentially to the central, third chapter of the constitution, which treats the "hierarchical structure of the Church, in particular the office of bishop."

Right from the beginning, the "Explanatory Note" addresses the delicate notion of collegiality, more precisely the word *collegium* (college). A significant assertion in the "Explanatory Note," as will be seen, is that *collegium* (college) was "not to be understood in a juridical sense." Consequently, interpretation of the corresponding conciliar expression was apparently to be restricted to a non-juridical, purely pastoral meaning. It is im-

portant to mention this in a commentary on canons 330–341 since these canons, with practically no exceptions, build on the aforementioned ecclesiological document.

But even the statements of the constitution itself were (and are) not unambiguous and clear (see *LG* 22, 1). *On the one hand,* the constitution speaks of the pope and bishops as being united together as Peter and the other apostles who "form a unique apostolic college." As proof of the practice of collegiality, the council mentions the principle of communion in the early Church, the practice of gathering in councils, and the ancient tradition of several bishops attending the consecration of a newly elected bishop. *On the other hand,* in the same paragraph, the document speaks of the "collegial design and nature of the episcopal *office.*"[1] As it continues to treat the subject, the council returns again to the description of the "college or body of bishops" (*LG* 22, 2). This last combination of terms was and is of great significance for an understanding of the conciliar notion of collegiality. Namely, *collegium* (college) is quite certainly a juridical notion whose meaning does not correspond to the ecclesiological notion of the council. Concerned Roman theologians frequently pointed this out even during the council itself. They feared the revival of the idea of a collegial constitution of the Church, since in legal terminology *collegium* (college) signifies a *societas aequalium,* a society of equals or of those of equal rank. The idea of a collegial constitution was developed on wholly different grounds by Protestant Church-State lawyers of the early modern era (Christoph Matthäus Pfaff and others). However, such ideas had already been discussed at the First Vatican Council, viewed as not without danger to

[1] This conceptual diversity suffuses the documents of the Second Vatican Council on the relationship between the primacy and the episcopacy. Consequently, it also permeates the corresponding provisions of the code.

the Catholic Church, and almost completely rejected. The "Explanatory Note" is also directed against these ideas. The Note clarifies that *collegium* (college) is not to be understood in the conciliar texts as "a group of equals."

Despite this assertion of the "Explanatory Note" and the use of other terms in the conciliar texts and the Constitution on the Church to describe the college of bishops,[2] the ambiguous term *collegium* (college) remained. The 1983 code recognizes the same term and uses it in constitutional law (cc. 336–341).

There is another difficulty besides that of the juridical limitation of the term *collegium:* the parallel drawn between Peter and the other apostles on the one hand, and the pope and bishops on the other. The "Explanatory Note" speaks of the parallel in this way: This "parallelism...does not include the transfer of the extraordinary power of the apostles to their successors or, as is obvious, an *equality* between the head and members of the college, but only a proportionality between the first term of the analogy (Peter–apostles) and the second (Pope–bishops)."

This scholastic distinction must have been difficult to understand. Thus, the "Explanatory Note" had to return to this problematic issue in its third point. The clarification expressed by this point is of the highest significance for constitutional law; namely, that the college of bishops, according to the teaching of the council, is also a "bearer of supreme and full power over the universal Church." However, the college possesses this power only with its head, the pope, who necessarily belongs to the college of bishops. Therefore the Note states: "In other words, the distinction does not hold between the bishop of Rome on the one hand, and all the bishops together on the other, but between the bishop of Rome as separate from, and the bishop of Rome united with the

---

[2] Among such terms were *corpus Episcoporum* (body of bishops), *corpus episcopale* (episcopal body), *ordo Episcoporum* (order of bishops), *ordo episcopalis* (episcopal order), etc.

other bishops." It is interesting to note the guarded use of "bishop of Rome" (rather than Petrine office or pope) to emphasize the pope's obvious membership in the college of bishops through his position as bishop of Rome.

Finally, a further problem was to differentiate the power of the pope or primacy from that of the college of bishops. The "Explanatory Note" was clear on this point as well: although the college has "always existed," it is not always "fully functional." Significantly, the phrase "fully functional" was enclosed in quotation marks in the "Explanatory Note." At the same time, the phrase addressing the power of the pope was underlined, stressing the fact that he could exercise his power or authority "at any time according to his discretion."

If the college of bishops were to be active "from time to time in a strictly collegial act," it would require the "consent of the head," that is, of the pope. Indeed, the "Explanatory Note" emphasized that the college of bishops *cannot* act in any way without the pope. This follows from the notion of *collegium* (college). Furthermore, this hierarchical communion is "strongly rooted in tradition."

Such remarks are historically contestable. There have been situations, for instance, in which bishops assembled in a council have acted without or even against the pope (or popes); indeed, they had to act for the good of the Church. Hierarchical communion between pope and bishops has been striven after as an ideal of communion from ancient times. However, for a large period of church history this ideal has been a distant one. In fact, large parts of the one Church are no longer in hierarchical communion with the pope.

The problem is aggravated and intensified by the comment with which the "Explanatory Note" concludes: "Without hierarchical communion the sacramental-ontological office, which is to be distinguished from the canonical-juridical point of view, *cannot* be exercised. However, the commission was of the opinion that it should not delve into questions of *liceity* and *validity,* but that they should be left to theological research. This is especially true of the power that is actually exercised by the separated Oriental churches and about which there are various doctrinal opinions."

On the one hand, this position maintains that without hierarchical communion the office cannot be exercised. On the other hand, it leaves open the question of liceity as well as validity.[3]

The Principle of Collegiality and the Current Legal Form of the Church

Without any doubt, the incorporation of the principle of collegiality was the greatest difficulty in drafting the 1983 code.

The pope is the head of the college of bishops, an assertion naturally not found in the 1917 code. However, this notion was added to the 1983 code, which emphasizes the primacy of the pope more so than did the corresponding provisions of the earlier code. He is the "vicar of Christ," and "shepherd of the universal Church on earth." These descriptions of the papal office are also found in the Constitution on the Church, even if in different formulations (*LG* 22, 2).

The constitution of the Catholic Church is based on two fundamental offices, that of the pope (primacy) and that of the bishop (episcopacy). For long periods church history has been marked by a tension between primacy and episcopacy. And there have always been times in which extreme positions developed in favor of one side or the other. For instance, there have been inclinations to strengthen the position of the bishops against the pope (episcopalism), or movements that sought to rewrite the function of the council to subordinate the pope to it (conciliarism). Conversely, the popes have continuously tried to safeguard their primacy and, whenever possible, expand it (papalism). Even the last two ecumenical councils, the First and Second Vatican Councils, were marked by struggles over this fundamental eccle-

siological question. Thus the dogmatic proclamation of papal primacy at the First Vatican Council brought primacy to its high point, while it was at least the intention of the Second Vatican Council to restore the balance between primacy and episcopacy disrupted by Vatican I. This balance had already been upset in the Counter Reformation measures of the Council of Trent (1545–1563), which reduced bishops to the level of papal delegates. Subsequently a bitter opposition to this tendency arose in numerous particular churches, especially in France (Gallicanism), in German regions (Febronianism) and in Austria (Josephinism). All these movements had mixed origins. Legitimate claims of the bishops and the particular churches to cultivate and further develop their own traditions often (in fact, almost always) fused with the initiatives of princes and rulers to create national and state churches. But both vehement critics and supporters of these three movements, which—with certain qualifications—one could unite under the notion of a *Catholic Enlightenment,* stood firm in maintaining that the papacy be the *centrum unitatis* (center of unity) of the Church. It was a difficult issue then, as it is today, for theologians and "ordained shepherds" to agree on a convincing boundary between an acceptable centralized function of the primacy and an oppressive papal centralism.

The best solution to the problem was found by the Second Vatican Council, even if postconciliar developments in ecclesial politics and law have demonstrated the weaknesses, loopholes, and ambivalence in the council's ecclesiology. The council fathers wanted especially to outline the significance and function of the office of bishop. Characteristic of this attempt is the fact that the central, third chapter of *Lumen gentium* bears the title "The hierarchical structure of the Church, and in particular the office of bishop." Right at the beginning of this chapter the unifying function of the Petrine office is emphasized. The description of this office as "an everlasting and visible principle and foundation of the unity of faith and communion" (*LG* 18, 2) sounds like the formulations of the thought-

---

[3] In 1966 Joseph Ratzinger referred to the special difficulties of the "Explanatory Note" in his commentary on it. See Vorgrimler, 1:348–359.

ful and critical theologians of the ecclesial Enlightenment. Similarly, *Lumen gentium* 23 speaks of the principle of unity, but not of the previously mentioned theological principle of communion which was emphasized so strongly after the council, and was often used as an unsuitable means of covering up the structural tension between particular churches and the center.

The college of bishops, "in which the apostolic body continues...is also the subject of supreme and full power over the universal Church" (c. 336). However, the college of bishops can use this power only together with the pope, that is, with his consent. Therefore, the universal ecclesial power of the episcopal college, which can be expressed in a special way in an ecumenical council, is thoroughly restricted.

The pope possesses not only power over the universal Church, but also "primacy" (*principatus* —c. 333, §1) over all particular churches and their groupings. Despite an ever increasing defense of this ecclesiological position, clearly the danger of competition for jurisdiction between the pope and bishops must be addressed. Moreover, the code emphasizes that by the primacy of ordinary papal power the proper, ordinary, and immediate power which the bishops possess over the particular churches entrusted to them is at the same time strengthened and protected (c. 333, §1). It is difficult to interpret this statement of the code. At the same time, it seems to demonstrate correctly that the pope is always bound by communion with the other (!) bishops and the universal Church (c. 333, §2). In short, papal decisions and actions that do not agree with the conviction of the bishops and the ecclesial community are unthinkable and impossible, at least from a moral point of view.

Finally, in this legal system there is *no* legal remedy against official abuse of the supreme office. Canon 333, §3 states succinctly: "No appeal or recourse is permitted against a sentence or decree of the Roman Pontiff." Only the confidence that the pope exercises his office in the Spirit of Christ gives this spiritual law a modicum of reliability. In the history of the Church, popes who have not possessed the fullness of power that the current law assigns the pope have abused their power. In those times, ideas arose that only the college of bishops, united in an ecumenical council, could govern the Church in such difficult times and exceptional situations. The current church law does not consider, much less regulate, such emergency situations that are at least fundamentally possible.

Primacy and Episcopacy

The supreme and most distinguished expression of collegiality between primacy and episcopacy, between pope and bishops, was and is the ecumenical council.

It is all the more conspicuous, therefore, how badly the council is treated in the new legal documents of the Catholic Church. The 1976 draft of the Fundamental Law of the Church (*Lex Ecclesiae Fundamentalis,* or *LEF*) dealt with the council only after dealing with the various institutes in which the pope and bishops work together, but which nonetheless depend on the pope's primacy (see c. 334). The final 1980 draft of the Fundamental Law[4] corrected this mistaken assessment of the council (*LEF*/1980, c. 35). The content and formulation of canons 330–341 of the 1983 code essentially agree with canons 29–39 of that 1980 draft.

In the 1983 code, the provisions on the council are found in the chapter on the pope and college of bishops. They are located in the second part (art. 2) which deals with the college of bishops.

The first canon of this part does not concern itself with the council, but with the college of bishops. The formulation of this canon is a synthesis of key ideas in *Lumen gentium* 22, 2. However, the positive function of the college of bishops is not mentioned here, as it was in *Lumen gentium*. The subordination of the college of bishops to the pope is too strongly emphasized.

What is currently described in the 1983 code as the "power" of the episcopal college over the universal Church was applied to the ecumenical

---

[4] The draft is dated April 24, 1980.

council in the former code; namely, the ecumenical council was said to exercise supreme power (*suprema potestas*) over the universal Church. The term *plena* (full) has now been added to *suprema* (supreme) in reference to the power of the college of bishops in light of *Lumen gentium* 22, 2. But what that term adds or expresses is not apparent.

If the episcopal college, like the pope, is a subject of supreme and full power over the universal Church, the question naturally arises: in what way does or can the college exercise its power? Again, like *Lumen gentium* 22, 2 and 23, 1, canon 337 of the 1983 code mentions three possibilities for the exercise of this power:

— in an ecumenical (general) council;
— in another form of collegial cooperation of all bishops; such a form of action (for instance, a so-called epistolary council [*Briefkonzil*]) must be convened and freely accepted by the pope;
— in other forms of collegial cooperation chosen and promoted by the pope.[5]

The 1983 code uses the word "power" in reference to the first two ways of collegial action in the same sense as that expressed in canon 336: "supreme and full power" (*suprema et plena potestas*). It is notable that *no direct* reference is made to this. Hence, in contradistinction to the earlier code, the current code no longer states that the ecumenical council exercises supreme power (*suprema potestas*) over the universal Church (see *CIC* 228, §1). This is all the more notable since the current descriptions of or terms regarding the primacy have been combined in a cruder way. Moreover, the ecumenical council is included as one of the three possibilities for collegial action, all of which can be carried out in different ways. The former law had two institutions that exercised or could exercise supreme power, namely, the pope and the ecumenical council (together with the pope!). But this is no longer so clear in the

new legal situation. The former juridical position of the ecumenical council has been extensively neutralized by the integration of the ecumenical council under the superior notion of "college of bishops," and by its inclusion in a *series* of possible means of collegial action. Thus, in light of this legal position, one can ask whether or not it is even necessary for an ecumenical council ever to take place again.

In light of the above, canon 749, §2 must be emphasized. It establishes that the college of bishops possesses the infallibility of the magisterium when the bishops are united in an ecumenical council. But the college of bishops can also make an infallible pronouncement when "dispersed throughout the world." Here too, in extraordinarily important questions, the new law sees the possibility of a so-called epistolary council (*Briefkonzil*).

The new provisions concerning the council, partly changed from those of the former law, and the legal or systematic arrangement of these provisions in the 1983 code reveal that the independence and significance of the council as a legal institute have been reduced. The new legal provisions seem to be governed by the concern that the primacy of the pope never be infringed upon by the principle of collegiality in any manner. The formulations use theologically sound concepts to describe the real situation of papal primacy in such a way that the true intention is concealed rather than plainly presented. The constant interchange in the use of the two terms *munus* (office, task, *service*) and *potestas* (authority, *power*) makes this especially clear.

Although the continuing implementation of the Second Vatican Council demonstrates how necessary and indispensable a council is in times of ecclesial crisis, the new code further undermines the legal significance of the council in comparison to the former code. While the 1917 code treated the legal position of the council (*CIC* 222–229) immediately after the provisions on the pope (*CIC* 218–221), the provisions on the ecumenical council in the 1983 code were appropriated into one chapter that deals with the pope and the college of

[5] *Promovere* can also mean "produce."

bishops. It is noteworthy that while other forms of collegial actions of the pope and bishops are given their own chapters (for example, the synod of bishops, the college of cardinals), the council is not.

The central statement about the power of the college of bishops was taken from the definitions regarding the council and appropriated by canon 336, which begins with these definitions and comprehensively outlines the dominant juridical position of the pope in the college of bishops.

The terms formerly used to describe the power of the pope and the council over the Church were notably modified and, in the case of the council, restricted. According to the 1983 code, the pope now enjoys supreme, full, immediate, and universal ordinary power in the Church (*gaudet suprema, plena, immediata et universali in Ecclesia ordinaria potestate*). The college of bishops, on the other hand, exercises power over the entire Church in an ecumenical council (*potestatem in universam Ecclesiam exercet in Concilio Oecumenico*). As was already mentioned, the term "supreme" qualifying "power" (*suprema potestas*) that the former code recognized and mentioned was deleted.

The relevant literature on the council continuously emphasizes that Vatican II reordered the relationship between the pope and bishops or placed it on a new or completely rethought foundation. Such assertions certainly go too far. Supported by the postconciliar praxis, one can more legitimately maintain merely that certain theological, that is, ecclesiological emphases were articulated in a different way. "Despite a difficult struggle [i.e., at Vatican II], the relationship between papal and episcopal power remained fundamentally that of the regulation of 1870."[6] The notions of *collegiality* and the *synodal element* are constantly mentioned in literature that evaluates the council positively. But what they mean must be established. As it became clear after the council, these notions need to be clarified concretely, and they mean little in and of themselves for the structural building up of the Church. Even worse, such notions and

their unclear content can be misused in order to conceal persistently the true and effective relationships of power.

Perhaps the single significant change that Vatican II brought about in the relationship between the pope and bishops exists in *one* word, the adjective *plena* (full) that was added to the *potestas* (power) of the ecumenical council (*LG* 22). The 1917 code retained the fine distinction in which the pope possessed supreme and full power of jurisdiction (*suprema et plena potestas iurisdictionis*) over the entire Church (*CIC* 218), while the council possessed merely supreme power (*suprema potestas*) (*CIC* 228). However, *Lumen gentium* 22 recognized that the order of bishops (*ordo Episcoporum*) also possessed supreme and full power (*suprema ac plena potestas*). But this statement was anxiously qualified in various ways. To avoid any misunderstandings, the power of the pope in this context was stressed by attaching the term "universal" (*universalis*) to "full" (*plena*) and "supreme" (*suprema*). Canon 29, §2 of the 1980 draft of the Fundamental Law went even further by describing the power of the pope as supreme, full, immediate, and universal (*suprema, plena, immediata, et universalis*), a formulation contained in canon 331 of the 1983 code.

In this connection, an ambiguity of Vatican II should be mentioned. The term "immediate" (*immediata*) was not used in *Lumen gentium* when referring to the power of the pope. This first occurred in the decree *Christus Dominus,* which was given less attention, as a rule, especially by ecclesiologists. Furthermore, *Lumen gentium* did speak of an immediate power (*potestas immediata*) of the diocesan bishop over his see. This "transference" of a phrase or part of a phrase is certainly not accidental. The power of the pope has an immediate effect even in the particular churches. Thus, it must be said that in the sphere of the local churches the competing powers of the pope and bishops *can* indirectly put bishops back on the level of papal delegates (*delegati papae*) in the sense of the Council of Trent.

The foregoing examples demonstrate that from a juridical standpoint the texts of Vatican II are

---

[6] T. Eschenburg, *Über Autorität* (Frankfurt am Main: Suhrkamp, 1976) 35.

full of problems and inconsistencies. At least Vatican I used clear language, something Vatican II did not achieve, and probably did not strive for. This was particularly true concerning a central issue for Vatican II: the demarcation of papal and episcopal power, and thus the jurisdictional primacy of the pope.

It is thus noteworthy that Vatican II does not speak of primacy of jurisdiction (*primatus iurisdictionis*). Instead, it uses the phrase "sacred primacy" (*sacer primatus*). The well-known German canonist Klaus Mörsdorf writes concerning this: "The failure to use the word *iurisdictio* is cause for thought since changes in terminology often bring with them changes in the thing itself."[7] What is unfortunate about this fact is that behind the juridically vague notion of sacred primacy (*sacer primatus*) lies concealed the old, juridically precise notion of the primacy of jurisdiction. For the sake of comparison, a glance at the 1980 draft of the Fundamental Law is worthwhile. Canon 29, §2 spoke in terms of the ordinary power (*potestas ordinaria*) of the pope *in* the (universal) Church (see c. 331).

[7] K. Mörsdorf, "Das oberste Hirtenamt des Papstes im Lichte des Zuordnungsverhältnisses von Gesamtkirche und Teilkirchen," *Études de Droit et d'Histoire* (1976) 321.

CANONS AND COMMENTARY

CHAPTER I
THE ROMAN PONTIFF AND THE COLLEGE OF BISHOPS
[cc. 330–341][8]

Introductory Canon

Canon 330 — Just as by the Lord's decision Saint Peter and the other Apostles constitute one college, so in a like manner the Roman Pontiff, the successor of Peter, and the bishops, the successors of the Apostles, are united among themselves.

The introductory canon (c. 330) of the chapter of the code that discusses the juridical status of the pope and college of bishops (cc. 330–341) declares in extensive agreement with the Dogmatic Constitution on the Church, *Lumen gentium* 22, 1, and the "Explanatory Note" (n. 1): "Just as by the Lord's decision Saint Peter and the other Apostles constitute one [apostolic] college, so in a like manner the Roman Pontiff, the successor of Peter, and the bishops, the successors of the Apostles, are united among themselves." The bracketed word "apostolic" was not appropriated by the code from the conciliar text. It was found in the earlier drafts of the Fundamental Law (*LEF*/1969: c. 31, §3; 1971: c. 21, §3) but was later excised. A definition comparable to that of the current canon 330 did not appear in the revised text of 1976–1977. In the final 1980 draft of the Fundamental Law (c. 29, §1), the word *collegium* (college) was even replaced with *coetus* (grouping).[9] The for-

[8] For helpful reflections on these canons see J. Provost, in *CLSA Com,* 258–281; O. Stoffel, in *Münster Com,* on such canons.

[9] See below for more on this issue. *LEF*/1980 c. 29, §1 reads: "Dominus Iesus Christus, Ipse quidem Ecclesiae suae Caput invisibile summusque angularis lapis ac aeternus Pastor manens, Ecclesiae suae pastores esse voluit Apostolos, eisque praeposuit Petrum, ut universo caritatis coetui praesideret atque perpetuum ac visibile unitatis fidei et communionis esset principium et fundamentum."

mulation "in a like manner" stresses that this comparison deals merely with a proportional equality. The selection of the adjective "apostolic" should apparently contribute to clarifying the difference between Peter and the (other) apostles, between the pope and bishops.

Collegium (College)

In this introductory canon, the code mentions the principle of unity: "Just as by the Lord's decision Saint Peter and the other Apostles constitute one college [*collegium*], so in a like manner the Roman Pontiff, the successor of Peter, and the bishops, the successors of the Apostles, are united among themselves." The concept of college (*collegium*) has been juridically loaded down by Roman law, and burdened by certain interpretations during the history of the Church. In Roman law the members of a college were given equal rights (*societas aequalium*). The college reached its decisions in the presence of the members called together in accordance with the regulations. Thus, the unity of time and place was required if a college wished to reach binding decisions. Historically, the term is especially burdened by eighteenth-century Protestant collegial theory appropriated by Catholic episcopalists (Josephinists, Febronians) and adapted to the Catholic ecclesial structure. According to this view, the bishops form the college as rectors of the Church (*Rectores Ecclesiae*). From this it followed, according to the episcopalists, that the Christian or Catholic Church possessed a collegial structure.[10]

Because the term "college" (*collegium*) was open to many possible interpretations, conservative members of Vatican II opposed the use of the concept early on. The conservative side also presented alternative terms which made their way into the conciliar texts and partly into the code and the drafts of the Fundamental Law: *ordo*

[10] K. Walf, *Das bischöfliche Amt in der Sicht josephinischer Kirchenrechtler,* Forschungen zur kirchlichen Rechtsgeschichte und zum Kirchenrecht, vol. 13 (Cologne-Vienna: Böhlau, 1975).

(order), *corpus* (body), *fraternitas* (fraternity), *coetus* (grouping).

In order to preclude any misunderstanding, Pope Paul VI expressly stated in the "Explanatory Note" to *Lumen gentium* that *collegium* (college) was not to be understood in a "*strictly juridical sense*" ("Explanatory Note," 1).

Canon 330 is one of the most important provisions of the code. Based on the foundational insights and decisions of the Second Vatican Council, the canon defines the relationship between the pope and the college of bishops. The introductory formula *statuente Domino* ("the Lord's decision") makes it clear that the canon is treating a matter of divine law. Even though the formulation is recent, the content has been established by Christ according to Catholic doctrinal teaching. This means that the content of this definition cannot be changed. The fathers of Vatican II used an analogical form of expression in formulating the content: the first part of the analogy speaks of a historical fact which the second part, with its statement on the prevailing ecclesial structure, is set against. This applies as well to the proportional arrangement of the individual parts: Saint Peter: the pope, successor of Peter; the other apostles: the bishops, the successors of the apostles. The word *ceteri* (the others) was added to the conciliar text by those authors[11] who wished to clarify that Peter too was one of the apostles and so a member of the *one* college. Thus, Peter is not to be seen as separate from the college.

A proportional identity arises out of the two parts of the canon. One could also call it a proportional relationship. At the transition point between both parts is the formula *pari ratione* ("in a like manner"). There was a conscious choice not to use "in the same way" (*eadem ratione*). As spelled out in the "Explanatory Note," there is no "transmission of the extraordinary authority of the apostles to their successors" ("Explanatory Note," 1). Although the impression can arise that the apostles and college of bishops are equal, when

[11] This happened especially due to the initiative of the exegete Cardinal Alfrink, Archbishop of Utrecht (Holland).

such an impression is examined in light of the "Explanatory Note," it becomes clear that there are considerable differences between the two colleges. While the Catholic tradition assigns responsibility for the entire Church to all the apostles, bishops are given responsibility only for their particular churches. The bishops are not successors of a definite apostle, but are "by reason of divine appointment placed on the level of the apostles" (*LG* 20c)." The bishops, united as they are in the college of bishops, bear responsibility not only for their own particular church, but also for the universal Church.

A comparison between canon 330 and canon 329 of the 1917 code clarifies the ecclesiological advance brought about by the Second Vatican Council and the 1983 code. The latter canon described the bishops as successors of the apostles who govern their particular churches under the authority of the pope.

Canon 330 and canon 42 of the Eastern code stand in literal agreement. In the 1980 draft of the Fundamental Law, the content of canon 330 was contained in canon 29, §2.

ARTICLE 1: THE ROMAN PONTIFF
[cc. 331–335]

Bishop of the Roman Church

Canon 331 — The bishop of the Roman Church, in whom continues the office given by the Lord uniquely to Peter, the first of the Apostles, and to be transmitted to his successors, is the head of the college of bishops, the Vicar of Christ, and the pastor of the universal Church on earth. By virtue of his office he possesses supreme, full, immediate, and universal ordinary power in the Church, which he is always able to exercise freely.

This canon emphasizes the singular position of Peter. The office (*munus*) which the Lord gave uniquely (*singulariter*) to Peter continues (*permanet*) in the person of the current bishop of Rome. As in canon 330, the appointment or disposal of the office by the Lord Jesus Christ is stressed.

The following definition of papal power brings together terms from numerous historical, i.e., earlier, definitions, resulting in an accumulation of such adjectives. According to canon 331, the pope enjoys, by reason of his office [*munus*], "supreme, full, immediate, and universal ordinary power [*potestas*] in the Church." Canon 218, §1 of the 1917 code contained the phrase "supreme and full [power]," and canon 218, §2 used the phrase "ordinary and immediate [power]." The 1917 code did not use the adjective "universal" (*universalis*). This adjective, together with the phrase "full and supreme [power]," was taken from *Lumen gentium* 22, 2. Thus, the individual elements of this definition are not at all new. What is new is the combination of these terms. In the context of a juridical description of collegiality, the combination suggests a definition of the primacy unlike any other known in the history of canon law.

Canon law derives the extensive fullness of power of the Petrine office from the will and mission of Jesus and the function of that Petrine office, namely, to guarantee the unity of the faith and the Church. The pope "possesses supreme, full, immediate, and universal ordinary power in the Church, which he is always able to exercise freely" (c. 331).

The canon mentions the functions or characteristics of the pope in somewhat of an odd order: bishop of the Roman church, bearer of the Petrine office, head of the college of bishops, vicar of Christ, pastor of the universal Church. Undoubtedly the function of "Vicar of Christ" is inappropriately ranked. Actually, none of the functions or characteristics are ranked according to their theological, ecclesiological, or canonical relevance.

Canon 331 begins by referring to the function of the pope as bishop. According to the canon's formulation, he is the bishop of the "Roman Church," not (as sometimes translated) "Bishop of the church of Rome." This description is found only in canon 331. Otherwise, the description "Roman Pontiff" (*Romanus Pontifex*) is used. The "function" of the pope is stressed through the use of *munus*, a concept of the Second Vatican Council that means service or task, and not mainly or primarily office. Concrete assertions follow from this rather moderate formulation.

Papal Titles

The pope is the head of the college of bishops, vicar of Christ, and shepherd of the universal Church.

Head of the College of Bishops: The use of this title, which has a long prior history,[12] is closely connected to the Second Vatican Council (*LG* 22b). In the conciliar texts, as well as in the code, the function of the pope as head of the college of bishops is often and effectively stressed. In the code this is especially so in canon 336. Without the head, the college of bishops does not bear supreme and full power over the entire Church.

Vicar of Christ (Vicarius Christi): Traditionally this title was used by the Roman emperors of the East, while the pope was called the vicar of Peter or *Vicarius Petri*. Popes since Innocent III (1198–1216) have used the designation "Vicar of Christ" as a stable—i.e., solemn—title, although one which has no legal definition or juridical relevance. While *Lumen gentium* applies the title to bishops as well, the code somewhat surprisingly reserves it to the pope alone. With the promulgation of the 1983 code, the inclusion of this title occasioned unnecessary irritation in other Christian churches.

Pastor of the Universal Church: This title is also laden with ambivalence. It can give the impression that the pope is the bishop of the universal Church. Canon 333 points in this direction when it speaks of the pope's power "over the universal Church." Therefore, it must be stressed here that *Lumen gentium* speaks clearly of the bishops and not the pope as vicars and envoys of Christ (*LG* 27a). The Second Vatican Council deliberately chose this unambiguous expression since the Council of Trent had wrongly placed bishops in the position of being papal delegates.[13] Thus, one should appreciate that the choice of the title "pastor of the universal Church" now emphasizes the pastoral function of the papal office, while previous councils (Florence, Vatican I) stressed the function of the pope as head of the universal Church. Since this canon, in which the pope is called the "pastor of the universal Church," is found in the 1983 code, whose provisions "affect only the Latin Church" (c. 1), there should have been a provision in the same canon clarifying the difference between the universal Church and the Latin church.

Besides these titles, the pope possesses further functions with regard to particular churches, and so, further titles that are not mentioned in canon 331: he is the metropolitan of the Roman ecclesial province, primate of Italy, and patriarch of the West. Only the title of metropolitan still carries concrete rights, essentially the right of supervision of the suffragan bishops of the (Roman) ecclesial province as provided for in canons 435–437. According to canon 438 the other titles are now simply honorific titles in the Latin church.

Definition of the Power of Jurisdiction

The second part of canon 331 describes the papal power of jurisdiction. The pope possesses supreme, full, immediate, and universal ordinary power in the Church. There is one conspicuous difference in terminology within the canon: the first sentence speaks of the "universal Church," and the second simply of "the Church." According to canon 1 the description of the papal power of jurisdiction in the Latin code is valid only for the Latin church. Canon 43 of the Eastern code contains a nearly identical definition of papal jurisdiction for the Eastern churches in union with Rome.

The relevant text in *Lumen gentium* (22b) does not mention the terms "immediate" and "ordi-

---

[12] Y. Congar, *La collégialité épiscopale: Histoire et théologie* (Paris: Cerf, 1965).

[13] Conc. Trid., sess. VI, *de ref.*, c. 2.

nary." Canon 218, §1 of the 1917 code used the terms "supreme" and "full," and canon 218, §2 spoke of "ordinary" and "immediate," but the term "universal" was not mentioned in the 1917 code in connection with papal power.[14] On the other hand, that code contained the term "episcopal," and the current code does not. The term "immediate," which was inserted into the code from the conciliar text, has a wide-ranging significance, which canon 333, §1 makes especially clear. The meanings of the terms overlap and partially intersect so that it is difficult to comment on them separately. It should also be mentioned that the pope's position in the universal Church is ultimately defined with the word *potestas,* which means power, dominion, office, but especially power or authority. The Second Vatican Council had previously avoided the use of this word or concept in reference to all offices in the Church. Instead, it preferred the word or concept *munus,* since it expressed the ministerial character of any ecclesial office or function.

Supreme Power: This superlative gives the impression that the pope's power is unique. This impression is not correct, however, since according to the current law the college of bishops possesses "supreme . . . power over the universal Church" (c. 336) even if only together with the pope. (The difficulties of interpretation that arise out of this will be addressed further in connection with canon 336.) Nevertheless, further legal provisions support or strengthen the phrase "supreme power": There is no appeal against a papal judgment or decree (c. 333, §3). By reason of the pope's primacy, every member of the faithful can always bring his or her contentious or penal case before the Holy See for judgment in all instances and at any procedural stage (c. 1417, §1). The pope is head of the college of bishops (c. 336), supreme shepherd and teacher (c. 749, §1), and he can be judged by no one (c. 1404). Until Vatican I, popes sought recognition of supreme papal

power in the Church from civil governments.[15] At that time, the idea supporting this position was that the State and the Catholic Church were both perfect societies (*societates perfectae*).[16] A remnant of this position is found in canon 204, §2.

Full Power: This phrase is also found in the description of the power of the college of bishops (c. 336). Thus there are two official institutional authorities with full, or more precisely, with "supreme and full" power in the Church, the pope and the college of bishops. The decisive difference lies in the fact that the pope exercises his power "always freely" (c. 331), while the college of bishops exercises it only together with the pope. This legal construction is not without risks in light of conflicts that have occasionally arisen in church history. For instance, at the time of the Council of Constance (1414–18) three popes fought for power. In that particular case, the college of bishops, united in the council, clarified the situation both theoretically and practically.

The term "full" was used by Vatican I in defining the primacy of jurisdiction.[17] According to Vatican II, it would have been a mistake to restrict "full" to the power of jurisdiction. Consequently, *Lumen gentium* 21b and canon 375, §2 both state that all bishops by consecration receive the offices of sanctifying, teaching, and governing. This broadening of the concept "full" leads to new difficulties in interpretation concerning the general origin of the power of jurisdiction. However, in reference to the papal office, the question is clearly answered. The pope receives full (and supreme) power by acceptance of a legitimate election together with episcopal ordination (c. 332, §1).

Immediate Power: This phrase was found in the central text of the First Vatican Council on the jurisdictional primacy of the pope.[18] It was also

---

[14] Canon 218, §1, however, spoke of the papal power of jurisdiction over the universal Church (*universa Ecclesia*).

[15] Conc. Vat. I, sess. IV, c. 3.

[16] K. Walf, "Die katholische Kirche—eine 'societas perfecta'?" *Theologische Quartalschrift* 157 (1977) 107–118.

[17] Conc. Vat. I, sess. IV, c. 3.

[18] Ibid.

found in canon 218, §2 of the 1917 code. The 1983 code clearly defines the matter in canon 333, §1, about which further comments will be made. "Immediate" means that the pope can intervene directly on all levels of ecclesial jurisdiction. Such papal power should be conceived of and employed to strengthen and protect the power of the bishops in their particular churches as well as the rights of the faithful.[19] Until the First Vatican Council, this statement of immediate papal jurisdiction explicitly contained the pope's claim to have contact with the faithful without interference from civil power. The current law implicitly renews this claim in this canon.

Universal Power: This phrase is also laden with history, and so in a certain way burdened by it. Pope Boniface VIII (1294–1303), in his bull *Unam sanctam* (1302), gave an exaggerated form to his notion of papal power as a universal power over all crowns and peoples and a spiritual preeminence over states. Although popes Leo XIII (1885) and Pius XII (1955) officially distanced themselves from such ideas, this historically and currently unrealistic notion is still extant. The term "universal power" is found in the texts of both the First and Second Vatican Councils, but not in the 1917 code. If one were to interpret it in light of canon 218, §1 of the 1917 code, one would have to conclude that papal power means power over the universal (Catholic) Church and not simply the Latin church. Interpreted in this way, the phrase says essentially the same thing as other terms used in this canon, thus bringing essentially nothing new to them.

Ordinary Power: This canon is to be evaluated in light of the meaning of canon 131, §1. By accepting the papal office according to the regulation of canon 332, §1, the pope obtains ordinary, proper power of governance. The Catholic Church recognizes two offices with preeminent ordinary, proper power of governance: the office of the pope and the office of the diocesan bishop (and those equiv-

alent to him according to c. 381, §2). Other ordinaries such as vicars general possess vicarious power of governance.[20] The bishop of Rome is, so to speak, ordinary of the universal Church.

The pope can always freely exercise this power. For centuries this point has been expressed in this or a similar way. Today the formulation possesses primarily intra-ecclesial significance in light of the strict separation of ecclesial (religious) and civil spheres of interest. However, because of its history it still contains an unmistakable, final purpose directed against civil power. In the current world order, the matter is significant inasmuch as the pope or Apostolic See is recognized as a subject of international law. This is explored further in the commentary on canons 3, 113, and 362–367. The intra-ecclesial significance of the phrase is seen in connection with canon 333, §3, according to which neither appeal nor recourse is possible against a papal decree, and in relation to canon 1375, which penalizes those who impede ecclesiastical power generally, and so those who impede the exercise of papal power as well.

The Second Vatican Council introduced the notion of *munus* into Catholic ecclesiology. The notion, which had its origin in Protestant theology, means ministry, task, office.[21] However, the drafting of the 1983 code again relied on the use of the traditional notion of *potestas* (power, authority). The meaning of the concept *munus* is to be emphasized in light of canon 331, which speaks of the power of the pope in a very particular way. The term *munus* is used in canon 375, §2, which describes the competencies of the bishop. It should be recalled clearly that the very strictly

---

[19] See the already mentioned provision of c. 1417.

[20] See c. 134, §1, which lists those who are "ordinaries" in canon law. It should be noted that certain religious superiors exercise power somewhat comparable to bishops, but only for their own members.

[21] The term has a long history. The appropriation of the Protestant teaching on the threefold office into the Catholic sphere is due largely to the work of the Vienna canonist George Phillips (d. 1872), who converted to the Catholic Church in 1828.

held formulation of the papal power of jurisdiction undergoes not only a certain qualification, but also a clear correction in canon 331. The Catholic Church holds in an unbroken tradition that the power of orders (*potestas ordinis*) has precedence over the power of jurisdiction. The 1983 code also makes it clear that the pope's power of jurisdiction has its foundation in the fact that he is a bishop; namely, the bishop of Rome. It is not entirely clear whether or not these two statements of the code are to be separated one from the other. Canon 332, §1 says that the pope first obtains power "in the Church" when he has received episcopal ordination, while canon 331 connects his being a bishop clearly with "the Roman Church." From time immemorial bishops have been elected pope, that is, as bishop of Rome. This obvious point obscures a difficulty, since bishops are always bishops of a particular diocese, even the so-called titular bishops who are ordained with the title of a defunct diocese.

In any case, canons 331 and 332 must be interpreted with the help of canon 375 since the latter's content, theologically speaking, prevails over the power of jurisdiction contained in canons 331 and 332 due to the precedence of the power of orders. Vatican II, with its doctrine of the threefold ministry or office, was not the first to see the relevance of this and bring it out clearly into the open. The 1917 code also spoke of it in canon 218, §2, which stated that the power of the pope is "truly episcopal" (*vere episcopalis*).

One can also interpret the power of the pope in accordance with canon 375, §2 and the teaching on the threefold ministry or office. In the first place, the pope as bishop exercises the ministry of sanctification (*munus sanctificandi*). Book IV of the code is dedicated to this ministry. The bishop of Rome is included along with all other bishops when canon 835, §1 describes them as the "principal dispensers of the mysteries of God." Even if the pope is not specifically mentioned in this central canon, it corresponds to Catholic ecclesiology, which (as has been mentioned) affirms the priority of the power of orders over the power of jurisdiction. While the bishop possesses the highest

office in the more important hierarchy of orders, the pope has the highest position in the hierarchy of jurisdiction. Only later canons (e.g., c. 838) will define the competencies of the Apostolic See (the term "pope" will not be used there!).

Additionally, the pope exercises the ministry of teaching (*munus docendi*). Clear statements on this matter are found in Book III of the code (*De Ecclesiae munere docendi*). The pope possesses infallibility in the teaching office "by virtue of his office [*munus*]" when he "as the supreme pastor...proclaims by definitive act that a doctrine of faith or morals is to be held" (c. 749, §1). The college of bishops possesses infallibility in the teaching office only in union with the pope (c. 749, §2; see the corresponding commentary). The teaching authority of the pope and the other members of the college of bishops is grounded in their episcopal character. The bishops are "authentic teachers endowed with the authority of Christ. ...[Therefore, the faithful must follow] with religious obedience a teaching of their bishop concerning matters of faith or morals which he pronounces in the name of Christ" (*LG* 25a). With reference to the entire Church, the task of preaching the gospel has been entrusted primarily to the pope and college of bishops (c. 756, §1).

Finally, the pope exercises the office of governing (*munus regendi*) the universal Church. The word *munus* (ministry or office) appears in canon 331. However, as already mentioned, it is strongly governed by the traditional notion of *potestas* (power, authority). As far as the governing office is concerned, the Catholic Church follows the differentiation of powers in the sense of Montesquieu (legislative, judicial, administrative). But it must be expressly emphasized here that this does not imply a division of powers or even reciprocal controls of the powers. The Catholic Church holds the unity of powers (the pope over the universal Church, the bishops over the particular churches) and recognizes merely a distinction, and not a difference in the three powers.

With regard to legislative power, the pope is the legislator for the universal Church. As a rule, he himself exercises this power except for very limited competencies of the congregations of the Roman Curia in this area. Papal laws appear under various and manifold forms, a fact that can lead to certain confusion. They can be promulgated as constitutions or as *motu proprios*. The laws of the papal congregations, which generally carry the same binding character, are generally published as decrees, although they can also be in the form of instructions or ordinances. General (papal) laws are promulgated through publication in the official publication *Acta Apostolicae Sedis* (c. 8, §1).

The pope is also the supreme judge "for the entire Catholic world." This noteworthy expression is found in canon 1442. Although this canon speaks of the fact that the pope can exercise his judicial power either personally or through the ordinary tribunals of the Apostolic See or judges delegated by him, it has been quite a while since the pope has judged cases himself. While he does not normally delegate his legislative power, the pope regularly delegates his judicial power. The Catholic opinion, however, is that the pope "himself" judges by means of the tribunals of the Apostolic See or delegated judges; that is, the delegated judges on the papal judgment seat decide cases in his name. In other words, since there is no division of powers, these tribunals or judges do not decide cases independently of the pope. Yet, since time immemorial, there has never been a case in which the pope has had a direct or indirect influence on the administration of justice in his courts. At the most, he has admonished the judges. He has done so especially in recent years in addresses to the Roman Rota on questions concerning marriage nullity.

As has already been said, the pope can be judged by no one (c. 1404). He has competence in canonical matters regarding heads of state, cardinals, papal envoys, and bishops (only in penal matters). These and other rights or prerogatives are mentioned in canon 1405. As already mentioned, "by reason of the primacy" every member of the faithful may appeal to the Apostolic See in every contentious and penal canonical procedure and in every phase of a procedure (c. 1417). The papal tribunals are mentioned only briefly in the code (c. 360). Further regulations are found in the

June 28, 1988, apostolic constitution *Pastor bonus* (art. 117–130). There are three papal tribunals: the Apostolic Signatura, the Roman Rota, and the Apostolic Penitentiary. The last one is not a tribunal in the proper sense. Rather, it is an administrative body that grants absolutions and especially dispensations in the internal forum.

Finally, the pope exercises a supreme and extensive (as well as difficult to grasp) executive power over the universal Church. This power is expressed primarily and best in the multitude of administrative competencies of the congregations of the Roman Curia (cc. 360–361; *PB*). Furthermore, the pope is supported by his legates in exercising this power (cc. 362–367). In this context it should also be mentioned that the extent of his exercise of executive power appears in his supervision of particular churches and institutes of consecrated life (orders, congregations, etc.). This supervision occurs by means of quinquennial reports and *ad limina* visits of the local ordinaries to Rome (c. 400), his dominant influence on the naming of bishops and equivalent ordinaries, on the division of ecclesial territories, in ordination and marriage law (in those dispensations reserved to the pope), and in many other areas. Through decrees of the Second Vatican Council, papal executive power was reduced in some areas from what it had become through the centuries, especially in the decrees of the Council of Trent and Vatican I which developed the centralized structure of the Catholic Church. Still, the enormous potential of papal executive power is still overly prevalent and dominating.

Canon 331 and canon 43 of the Eastern code extensively coincide. There is only a slight change of wording. At the end of its canon, the Eastern code uses *potest* instead of *valet*. This makes little difference in the meaning. There is agreement, but also a great difference between canon 331 and canon 29, §2 of the 1980 draft of the Fundamental Law.[22]

---

[22] "Ecclesiae Romae Episcopus, in quo permanet munus a Domino singulariter Petro, primo Apostolorum, concessum et successoribus eius transmittendum, Collegii Episcoporum est Caput, Vicarius Christi atque universae Ec-

Papal Election and Resignation

Canon 332 — §1. The Roman Pontiff obtains full and supreme power in the Church by his acceptance of legitimate election together with episcopal consecration. Therefore, a person elected to the supreme pontificate who is marked with episcopal character obtains this power from the moment of acceptance. If the person elected lacks episcopal character, however, he is to be ordained a bishop immediately.

§2. If it happens that the Roman Pontiff resigns his office, it is required for validity that the resignation is made freely and properly manifested but not that it is accepted by anyone.

As already expressed in the commentary on canon 331, the law is concerned with the question of how the bearers of papal, as well as episcopal, office receive their power. Hence, the difference between the power of orders and the power of governance takes on special importance. As far as the papal office is concerned, along with the extensive powers, competencies, and rights connected to it, the law states that the pope receives "full and supreme power in the Church by his acceptance of legitimate election together with episcopal consecration" (c. 332, §1). Thus, if a bishop is elected pope, which has been the normal case for a long time, he receives all the rights of the papal office by accepting the election.

The details of the papal election are not regulated by the code although it mentions essential elements of that election, such as the fact that active voice in a papal election belongs exclusively to cardinals (c. 349). Throughout this century, provisions concerning papal elections have been issued more and more through special papal legislation.[23] The most recent example is the apostolic constitu-

tion *Universi Dominici gregis* of February 22, 1996, which provided new regulations for the "vacancy of the Apostolic See and the election of the pope of Rome." Since the Third Lateran Council (1179), and thus for more than eight hundred years, the pope had to be elected by a two-thirds majority of the cardinals.[24] Currently, an absolute majority is de facto required since, according to the new provisions, unsuccessful balloting that takes place by traditional means can be passed over in favor of another method of election. The 1975 election rules provided for this as well, but the change in election method had to be approved by all legitimate electors while the new and now valid rules require only an absolute majority.

In the postconciliar period, several changes in the method of papal elections took place. The number of cardinal electors was limited to 120. Cardinals possessed active voice in an election only until the completion of their eightieth birthday (*Universi* 33). There was no discussion of the variously expressed desires in the postconciliar period to change papal elections completely, for instance, to allow election by all bishops or at least all diocesan bishops, etc. Nor at present are there any such proposals to consider.

In principle, according to canon 1024,[25] every rational Catholic man is eligible. Actually, however, since 1378 only cardinals have been elected pope.

Canon 332, §1 uses only the terms "full" and "supreme" to describe the power that the pope possesses "in" the Church. This is similar to the description of the college of bishops in c. 336![26] The canon says only how he receives the power, not from whom. According to the traditional position, he receives it from God. The "how" is further clarified by three elements: legitimate elec-

---

clesiae his in terris Pastor; qui ideo vi muneris sui suprema, plena, immediata et universali in Ecclesia gaudet ordinaria potestate, quam semper libere exercere valet."

[23] After the 1917 code one may note the 1945 apconst *Vacantis Apostolicae Sedis,* the 1962 *mp Summi Pontificis Electio,* and the 1975 apconst *Romano Pontifici Eligendo.*

[24] The 1975 apconst *Romano Pontifici Eligendo* stated in n. 65 that for the election of a new pope a two-thirds plus one majority was required. See T. Reese, "Revolution in Papal Elections," *America* (April 13, 1996) 4.

[25] Canon 1024: "A baptized male alone receives sacred ordination validly."

[26] However, the order of the terms is changed.

tion, free acceptance of the election, episcopal consecration. It is noteworthy that the second part of canon 332, §1 states positively what should actually read as follows: If a non-bishop is elected pope, this legitimately elected person does not receive power in the Church through acceptance of the election. This canon again expresses the pre-eminence of the power of orders over the power of jurisdiction. On the other hand, canon 219 of the 1917 code stated that the legitimately elected person received full power of supreme jurisdiction by divine right by accepting the election. That code did not recognize the essential connection between jurisdiction and the power of orders.

The new law correctly provides for the resignation of a pope even if in a limited measure (c. 332, §2). Such a resignation must be freely submitted and duly manifested. However, its acceptance is not a requirement. The general provisions on resignation of an office are contained in canons 187–189. These legal regulations are only guidelines since, due to his supreme power, the pope can always pass new laws, and stands above already valid laws (*Papa supra omnes canones*). Until now only one pope has relatively "freely" resigned his office, i.e., Celestine V (1294, d. 1296).

The resignation from office of the pope must be sufficiently manifested and requires no acceptance "by anyone." The recipient of the "manifestation" is not specified. Some commentators are of the opinion that the college of cardinals or its dean as the competent electoral body must be informed of the resignation.

Quite clearly there is a *lacuna* in canon law, since it makes no legal provisions for a case in which the pope is temporarily or permanently incapacitated, e.g., due to political obstruction, physical or mental illness, etc. Canon 335 states merely that if the "Roman See" is fully impeded no innovations are to take place in the governance of the universal Church.

In addition to a few insignificant rearrangements or modifications of individual words as well as stylistic improvements, there is an interesting difference between canon 332 and canon 44 of the Eastern code. In paragraph one, instead of the words *consecratio episcopalis* (episcopal consecration), the Eastern code contains the more juridical phrase *ordinatio episcopalis* (episcopal ordination). There is no substantial difference between canon 332 and canon 30 of the 1980 draft of the Fundamental Law although there are a few formal differences.

Exercise of Primacy

Canon 333 — §1. By virtue of his office, the Roman Pontiff not only possesses power over the universal Church but also obtains the primacy of ordinary power over all particular churches and groups of them. Moreover, this primacy strengthens and protects the proper, ordinary, and immediate power which bishops possess in the particular churches entrusted to their care.

§2. In fulfilling the office of supreme pastor of the Church, the Roman Pontiff is always joined in communion with the other bishops and with the universal Church. He nevertheless has the right, according to the needs of the Church, to determine the manner, whether personal or collegial, of exercising this office.

§3. No appeal or recourse is permitted against a sentence or decree of the Roman Pontiff.

Canon 333, whose content is connected to that of canon 331, describes the papal primacy of power, and an especially significant aspect of this power, the primacy (*principatus*) of ordinary power that the pope possesses over all particular churches. The issue here is the extremely delicate problem of the so-called concurring power of jurisdiction of the pope and bishop in the particular churches. The notion of *principatus ordinariae potestatis* (primacy of ordinary power) was not introduced by the 1983 code. The author of the code was supported by the 1965 papal decree *Christus Dominus* (n. 2). In this context, generally speaking, one can wonder what influence a reference to paragraphs 22 and 27 of *Lumen gentium* would have had on *Christus Dominus* or the drafts of the Fundamental Law since the constitution emphasized the independence of the bishops over against the pope.[27] The *principatus ordinariae potestatis* (primacy of ordinary power) is a concept of the *First,* not of the Second Vatican Council. The expression arises out of the third chapter (*De primatu Romani Pontificis*) of the dogmatic constitution *Pastor aeternus* of Vatican I. Even the addition in canon 333, §1 according to which "this primacy strengthens and protects the proper, ordinary, and immediate power which bishops possess in the particular churches entrusted to their care" is based on the same First Vatican Council text.

This canon is based on older legal documents.[28] However, it is new to ecclesial law if one disregards the non-promulgated canon 31 of the 1980 draft of the Fundamental Law.

As was mentioned, paragraph one regulates one of the most difficult issues of Catholic ecclesial structure, that of the so-called concurring power of jurisdiction of the pope and bishops over their particular churches and their groupings. The Latin terminology and the content of the words used are hardly suitable for translation into modern languages, as the translations of the code in various languages make clear. The central notion of paragraph one is *principatus,* inadequately translated into English as "primacy." *Principatus* is related to *princeps.* In the Roman Empire this word described the emperor. This association is consciously aroused here, suggesting that the pope also has an imperial preeminence in the Catholic Church.

It is very much a question of whether or not this canon agrees with the spirit of the Second Vatican Council. In *Lumen gentium* the council had to overcome the ever present danger in church history of an extreme papalism on the one hand, and a just as extreme episcopalism on the other hand.

Therefore it refrained from viewing bishops as papal delegates as the Council of Trent had seen them. It also gave up the earlier concession system (concessions of the pope to the bishops, especially in the form of the so-called quinquennial faculties)[29] in favor of a system of reservations (the pope reserves certain rights to himself). The council expressly stated in *Lumen gentium* that bishops are "not to be understood as vicars of the bishop of Rome, for they have their own proper power, and are truly heads of the people they govern.... [Therefore,] their power is not eliminated by the supreme and universal power, but is affirmed, strengthened, and safeguarded by it" (*LG* 27b). A part of this text is found in the current canon 333, §1, but clearly it was appropriated into that canon in a very particular way.

Canon 333, §1 must also be understood together with canons 375 and 381, §1, in which the power of the bishop (i.e., the diocesan bishop) is described. Paul VI had attempted to demarcate the competencies of the pope and bishops in his 1963 *motu proprio Pastorale munus* as well as in his 1966 *motu proprio De episcoporum muneribus;* these attempts were not entirely successful. Later work on the 1983 code also proved unsuccessful in establishing objective limits to papal power over against that of the bishops.[30] On the one hand, canon 381, §1 speaks of "all ordinary, proper, and immediate power" of the diocesan bishop over his particular church. On the other hand, it contains an even clearer exception in favor of papal power, that is, when there is a legal provision or a decree of the pope. Canon 591 should also be mentioned in this context: the pope can "exempt institutes of consecrated life from the governance of local ordinaries and sub-

---

[27] One need think only of *LG* 22, 2, which concerns the bishops in their relation to the pope: "They are not to be understood as vicars of the bishop of Rome, for they have their own proper power, and are rightly called heads of the people they govern."

[28] See, for instance, *CIC* 218, §2 and various texts in *LG* and *CD*.

[29] The faculties (*facultates*) were given the diocesan bishops every five years (*quinque anni*) by the pope, especially in the areas of marriage and penal law. Opposed to this system, which was introduced in the seventeenth century, were the German Febronians. According to them the bishops possessed these faculties in their own right.

[30] *Comm* 8 (1976) 89.

ject them to himself alone or to another ecclesiastical authority."

In canon 333, §1, the play with the terms *munus* (ministry, office) and *potestas* (power, authority) is also noteworthy. First of all, the position of the pope is described with the softer term *munus,* which is used in canon 375, §2 to describe the competence of the bishops. It is also stated there that the bishops stand in *hierarchical* communion (*communio*) with the head of the college, that is, the pope. This early church concept of communion has been viewed by some canonists as a guarantee against the head of the college abusing his power of jurisdiction (*potestas*). On the occasion of the promulgation of the code, Pope John Paul II in the apostolic constitution *Sacrae disciplinae leges* expressly referred to the "doctrine in which the Church is seen as a *communion* and which therefore determines the relations which are to exist between the particular churches and the universal Church, and between collegiality and the primacy." The code still does not recognize legal provisions against possible abuses of the primacy although the "Explanatory Note" to *Lumen gentium* clearly stated that *communio* is "not some vague *feeling,* but an *organic reality* that requires a legal form" ("Explanatory Note" 2).[31] This is precisely what the code did not accomplish, and this is one of its central weaknesses.

How *communio* is to be understood in contemporary Catholic ecclesiology is found in canons 204, §2 and 205. According to those canons, the Church is governed by the successor of Peter and the bishops in communion with him (*in eius communione*). "Full communion" with the Catholic Church is explained by the triad: confession of faith, acceptance of the (seven) sacraments, and ecclesial governance (the pope and the bishops united with him). When one of these three criteria is lacking, in traditional terms it becomes a matter of heresy (with reference to confession of faith and sacraments), schism (with regard to ecclesial

governance), or apostasy, provided that there is a complete abandonment of the faith and separation from the Church.

Canon 333, §2 of the code also explains how one is to understand the concurring jurisdiction of the pope and bishop in a particular church. This definition is completely new, and is not found either in the former code or in the declarations of the Second Vatican Council. It first appeared in the process of drafting the 1976 version of the Fundamental Law. From there it was appropriated by the 1983 code. This provision states: "In fulfilling the office of supreme pastor of the Church, the Roman Pontiff is always joined in communion with the other bishops and with the universal Church. He nevertheless has the right, according to the needs of the Church, to determine the manner, whether personal or collegial, of exercising this office."

According to this provision, the pope can intervene in the affairs of particular churches according to his own discretion. The word "communion" is even mentioned in this canon. From the early days of the Church, this word described the communion of the particular churches, but primarily the communion of faith of the particular churches with Rome. In particular, then, when the pope sees that the "communion" between Rome and a particular church is endangered, he can intervene in a personal or "collegial" manner. "Collegial" is to be interpreted in this context in which it appears. The pope *can,* as is his duty, govern the affairs of the universal Church as well as the particular churches with the help of the college of bishops. He may do so with the college as a whole (for instance, in an ecumenical council or through a so-called epistolary council [*Briefkonzil*]) or through the selection of representatives of the college of bishops (e.g., through a synod of bishops over whose composition the pope has extensive influence).

The terms *munus* and *communio* are both found in canon 333, §2. It is noteworthy that the term "hierarchical" is not used here in connection with communion, but it is still to be understood in the sense in which canon 375, §2 uses it. The ter-

---

[31] O. Saier, *"Communio" in der Lehre des Zweiten Vatikanischen Konzils* (Munich: Max Hueber, 1973).

minology of canon 330 is also applicable to canon 333, §2. The former canon uses "Peter and the other Apostles," while the latter uses "the Roman Pontiff... with the other bishops." But canon 333, §2 then refers again to the objective reality. The pope decides whether to exercise his office (*munus*) personally or collegially. Further qualifications of what the possible collegial exercise of the office implies are found in canon 334.

Canon 333, §3 contains the very old provision that there is no legal recourse against a judgment or decree of the pope. Canon 1404 of the procedural law corresponds to it by stating that the pope (here *Prima Sedes* or First [episcopal] See) can be brought to trial by no one. According to the decrees of the Council of Constance (1414–1418; the decrees *Sacrosancta* and *Frequens*), which were reaffirmed by the Council of Basel (1431–1439), an ecumenical council stands above the pope. However, popes later provided penalties for an appeal to a council (see *CIC* 2332). Current law threatens a penalty for those who seek recourse to an ecumenical council or the college of bishops against a measure of the pope (c. 1372).

The primacy of the pope is safeguarded through numerous individual provisions of the code. According to canon 361, the terms "Apostolic See" and "Holy See" also describe the pope. The pope possesses exclusive rights regarding an ecumenical council and other activities of the college of bishops (cc. 337–338; 341). Currently the nomination of bishops rests exclusively in his hands. On the one hand, diocesan bishops are obliged to make a report to the pope (c. 399). On the other hand, the pope controls the particular churches through his envoys (cc. 362–367). Clerics are bound in a particular way to obey the pope (c. 273). This is also true for members of institutes of consecrated life (religious—c. 590, §2). Authority to dispense from the obligation of celibacy is reserved to the pope alone (c. 291), as is the dissolution of a non-consummated marriage between the baptized (cc. 1142; 1698, §2). The pope possesses the faculty to hear confessions in the entire Church (c. 967, §1), and he can dispense from private vows at any time

and in any case (c. 1196). Furthermore, he has authority over the ownership of ecclesiastical goods (c. 1256), and he possesses the power of supreme administration and disposal of ecclesiastical goods (c. 1273). The pope alone has competence in certain processes (judging heads of state, cardinals, etc.—c. 1405, §1). Without papal permission, a judge cannot rule on a legal act or document expressly confirmed by the pope (c. 1405, §2). Recourse against a papal decree is not possible (cc. 1732; 333, §3). Reservations and provisions in favor of papal power are found in all parts of the code, for example, the right to review decrees of particular councils (c. 446) or of bishops' conferences (c. 455, §2) or the right to grant dispensations from impediments in ordination and marriage law.

There are merely terminological rather than substantial differences between canon 333 and canon 45 of the Eastern code. The assertion of canon 333 is found in canon 31 of the 1980 draft of the Fundamental Law, although in a different formulation.[32]

Assistance in Exercising Primacy

Canon 334 — Bishops assist the Roman Pontiff in exercising his office. They are able to render him cooperative assistance in various ways, among

---

[32] *LEF*/1980, c. 31: "§1. Romanus Pontifex, quippe qui tamquam omnium fidelium pastor ad bonum Ecclesiae universae et ad bonum singularum Ecclesiarum missus sit, vi huius sui muneris, non modo in universam Ecclesiam potestate gaudet, sed et super omnes Ecclesias particulares earumque coetus ordinariae potestatis obtinet principatum, quo quidem insimul roboratur atque vindicatur potestas propria, ordinaria et immediata qua in Ecclesias particulares suae curae commissas Episcopi pollent.

"§2. Romanus Pontifex in munere supremi Ecclesiae Pastoris explendo, communione cum ceteris Episcopis immo et universa Ecclesia semper est coniunctus; ipsi ius tamen est, iuxta Ecclesiae necessitates, determinare modum, sive personalem sive collegialem, huius muneris exercendi.

"§3. A sententia Romani Pontificis non datur appellatio."

which is the synod of bishops. The cardinals also assist him, as do other persons and various institutes according to the needs of the times. In his name and by his authority, all these persons and institutes fulfill the function entrusted to them for the good of all the churches, according to the norms defined by law.

Canon 334 mentions some possibilities for cooperation between bishops and the pope in the exercise of the papal office: the synod of bishops (cc. 342–348), cardinals (cc. 349–359), and "other persons and various institutes according to the needs of the times." The "institutes" refer first of all to the Roman Curia (cc. 360–361) as well as the papal diplomatic corps (cc. 362–367).[33]

Thus canon 334 provides further clarifications of the final phrase of canon 333, §2, which states that the pope can exercise his office in a collegial manner. The former law limited the collegial exercise of the papal office both actually and legally to cooperation between the pope and the college of cardinals (*CIC* 230). However, various documents of Vatican II, such as *Christus Dominus* 9 and 10, as well as a series of postconciliar documents, broadened the circle of those able to participate in this collegiality. Of current significance is the apostolic constitution *Pastor bonus*.

Canon 334 corresponds to the ecclesiology of Vatican II when it lists the bishops first among the co-workers (*cooperatores,* derived from the word *cooperatrix* used in the Latin text). *Cooperator* can also mean "assistant." More likely this is the sense given to the word in the other formulations according to which bishops, cardinals, and other persons carry out this task "in his [the pope's] name and by his authority." The canon makes special mention of the synod of bishops (cc. 342–

348), an institute first suggested by the Second Vatican Council. The fact that ecumenical councils are not mentioned in this canon is appropriate from an ecclesiological standpoint since they do not act in the name and under the authority of the pope. Rather, they are an institute of a unique nature. In this context, one should recall that in a council the college of bishops exercises power over the universal Church together with its head, the pope (c. 337, §1).

In canon 32 of the 1980 draft of the Fundamental Law, the content of the current canon 334 was clearly subdivided into two paragraphs.[34] The first paragraph mentioned the bishops as well as the synod of bishops, and the second paragraph mentioned the cardinals and the Roman Curia, in order to stress their distinct foundations, namely, either *ordo* (orders) or the power of jurisdiction derived from the pope. Controversial discussions concerning the function of the college of cardinals occasionally took place at Vatican II, especially concerning the extent to which this college truly represented the world-wide episcopate. The compromise solution to these critiques resulted in the creation of the new institute of the synod of bishops as well as the internationalization of the college of cardinals.

Apart from a few stylistic differences, there are two textual differences between canon 334 and canon 46 of the Eastern code. The Eastern code expressly mentions not only the cardinals, but also the Roman Curia as well as the papal legates as institutions or persons assisting the pope (as some commentators on c. 334 do). Moreover, the

---

[33] K. Walf, *Die Entwicklung des päpstlichen Gesandtschaftswesens in dem Zeitabschnitt zwischen Dekretalenrecht und Wiener Kongreß (1159–1815),* Münchener Theologische Studien, Kanonistische Abteilung, vol. 24 (Munich: Max Hueber, 1966); idem, "Das Motuproprio Pauls VI über das Amt der päpstlichen Gesandten," *AkK* 138 (1969) 113–125.

[34] *LEF*/1980, c. 32: "§1. In eius munere supremi Ecclesiae pastoris exercendo, Romano Pontifici praesto sunt Episcopi, qui auxilio ei esse valent variis rationibus, inter quas est Synodus Episcoporum, coetus scilicet in quem Episcopi ex diversis orbis regionibus selecti statis temporibus conveniunt.

"§2. In eodem munere exercendo, Romano Pontifici praeterea auxilio sunt Patres Cardinales, necnon aliae personae itemque varia secundum temporum necessitates instituta; quae personae omnes et instituta, nomine et auctoritate Ipsius, munus sibi commissum explent, in bonum omnium Ecclesiarum, iuxta normas iure definitas."

phrase at the end of canon 334, "according to the norms defined by law," is enlarged to read: "according to the norm of law established by the Roman Pontiff himself."

Interim Governance of Apostolic See

Canon 335 — When the Roman See is vacant or entirely impeded, nothing is to be altered in the governance of the universal Church; the special laws issued for these circumstances, however, are to be observed.

During the time between the death of a pope and the election of his successor, the Roman See in considered vacant. According to canon 335, during such times, as well as during those in which the pope is impeded from exercising his office, there can be no innovations in the governance of the universal Church (*Sede vacante nihil innovetur*). When the see is vacant, the college of cardinals assumes the immediate care of the daily business of the Holy See. Essentially, during this time the activity of the college of cardinals is directed to the swift and orderly completion of the papal election. The tasks and rights of the cardinals and the Roman Curia during a vacant see are regulated by the apostolic constitution *Universi Dominici gregis*. The parts of the constitution regarding daily operations while the see is vacant can *possibly* be used also in times when the pope is fully impeded from exercising his office. A clear legal provision or even a separate law does not exist. In the realm of possibilities, the provisions of the code for an impeded episcopal see (cc. 412–415) could be used in the case of an impeded Apostolic See. Moreover, the provisions of the code for a vacant episcopal see, especially canon 428, §1, could be applied analogously since it would be a case of the vacancy of the episcopal see of Rome.

As has been mentioned, while the Roman See is vacant, the college of cardinals assumes the governance of the universal Church. But the college obviously cannot issue any acts involving the power of jurisdiction that have been reserved to the pope. It can merely regulate daily and urgent affairs, and only within the limits of the boundaries set out by *Universi Dominici gregis* (see c. 359). The offices of the cardinals, those who are heads of the congregations of the Roman Curia, as well as that of the cardinal secretary of state, expire with the vacant see. Actually, the function of the college of cardinals remains during the vacant see even if limited to preparing for and completing the papal election. Before the papal election conclave begins, those cardinals present in Rome gather daily for a meeting of the college. A vacant see has further legal consequences. An ecumenical council is immediately interrupted (c. 340) as is a synod of bishops (c. 347, §2). However, the office of a papal legate does not expire with the vacant see unless the papal letter of appointment establishes otherwise (c. 367).

There are merely stylistic differences between canon 335 and canon 47 of the Eastern code. Canon 33 of the 1980 draft of the Fundamental Law contained the additional provision that the exercise of the ministry of the pope is suspended while the see is vacant or impeded. Thus, during these times it ceases functioning.[35]

ARTICLE 2: THE COLLEGE OF BISHOPS
[cc. 336–341]

Description

Canon 336 — The college of bishops, whose head is the Supreme Pontiff and whose members are bishops by virtue of sacramental consecration and hierarchical communion with the head and members of the college and in which the apostolic body continues, together with its head and never without this head, is also the subject of supreme and full power over the universal Church.

---

[35] *LEF*/1980, c. 33: "Sede romana vacante aut prorsus impedita, *supremi Pastoris muneris exercitium suspenditur* et nihil innovetur in Ecclesiae universae regimine: serventur autem leges speciales pro iisdem adiunctis iam latae."

Canon 336 must be the one canon of the code that gives rise to the largest number of difficulties in interpretation. It bears a fundamental significance for Catholic ecclesiology, and it is a product of the Second Vatican Council. Accordingly, the composition of the text, as opposed to its actual content, has no prior model in the history of canon law. It is based on *Lumen gentium* 20, 22, 23 and the "Explanatory Note" as well as on *Christus Dominus* and *Ad gentes*. It simplifies canon 29, §3 of the 1980 version of the Fundamental Law.[36] As mentioned above, an entirely new composition arose out of these texts. It is noteworthy that the tenor of the source texts emphasizes in a special way the exceptional significance of the college of bishops while canon 336 serves to stress the supremacy of the pope over the college of bishops. As far as the organization of the legal text is concerned, a remarkable change should be noted. The 1917 code spoke of the ecumenical council (*CIC* 222–229) in the chapter following the chapter on the pope (*CIC* 218–221). That chapter on the council is no longer formally recognized by the 1983 code. Rather, its provisions were appropriated, in a transformed fashion, into an "article" entitled "The College of Bishops." That is how canon 336 was shaped. There is a connection between canon 336 and canon 228, §1 of the 1917 code as far as content is concerned. Both canons speak of supreme power in the Church: in the 1917 code in reference to the ecumenical council, and in the 1983 code in reference to the college of bishops.

---

[36] *LEF*/1980, c. 29, §3: "Una cum Romano Pontifice ceteri Episcopi, in quibus nempe omnibus perseverat munus pascendi Ecclesiam omnibus Apostolis concessum et successoribus eorum transmittendum, Corpus constituunt seu Collegium Episcoporum, cuius Caput est Summus Pontifex, Petri successor, et cuius membra sunt Episcopi vi sacramentalis consecrationis et hierarchica communione cum Collegii Capite et membris; quod Collegium Episcoporum, in quo Corpus apostolicum continuo perseverat, una cum Capite suo, et numquam sine hoc Capite, subiectum quoque supremae et plenae potestatis in universam Ecclesiam exsistit, quae quidem potestas nonnisi consentiente Romano Pontifice exerceri potest."

The use of the term "power" or "authority" (*potestas*) is of great importance in this canon, just as it was in the provisions on the power of the pope in canon 331. The 1917 code used such terms far less frequently than the 1983 code does, and then only in reference to both the pope and the ecumenical council. At least the use of the terms in the former law was thoroughly adequate for describing clearly the power of jurisdiction of the pope and the council. As regards the council, the 1917 code spoke of a "supreme power" over the universal Church. The 1983 code is more reserved with regard to the power of the council. Canon 337 speaks merely of a "power" of the ecumenical council over the universal Church. Nevertheless, canon 336 now contains two terms in its description of the power of the college of bishops. It exercises "supreme and full" power with regard to the universal Church.

Canon 336 is the only self-contained statement in the code concerning the college of bishops. As opposed to the rather detailed section on the pope, there are no more statements on the function and tasks of the college in the code besides the provisions of canon 337, §2 and §3. Instead, one finds merely the traditional statements concerning the ecumenical council (with modifications). Canon 336 speaks of membership in the college of bishops, its origin in the apostolic college, the function of the pope as head of the college, and the power of the college of bishops.

Membership in the College of Bishops

Bishops are members of the college of bishops based on their consecration *and* hierarchical communion with the head of the college, that is, the pope, as well as with the other members of the college. The unbreakable connection between both requirements is continuously emphasized in Catholic ecclesiology (*LG* 22a; c. 375, §2). The word order used in this statement is important, since the element of consecration is of greater importance than that of jurisdiction (i.e., the power of jurisdiction and hierarchical jurisdiction). Bishops receive the three *munera* with consecration: the office of sanctifying, of teaching, and of governing (*LG* 21b; c. 375, §2). This ontological participation is determined by hierarchical communion. According to number two of the "Explanatory Note," the determination of power occurs through hierarchical authority according to rules approved by the supreme authority. "Supreme authority" (*suprema auctoritas*) in the texts of Vatican II is an expression synonymous with the pope. It is clear that the appropriate rules for the determination of power (*potestas*) must be made by the pope. The statement of the "Explanatory Note" that the determination itself must come "through hierarchical authority" is rather vague. According to Catholic tradition, the hierarchical authority for or over the universal Church is the pope, and for or over the particular church is the bishop or ordinaries equivalent to him (c. 381, §2; see c. 368).

According to Catholic doctrine, hierarchical communion includes acceptance of the (jurisdictional) primacy of the pope. Concerning this, the "Explanatory Note" (n. 3) says that the head of the college of bishops must be "the bearer of the supreme and full power over the entire Church," and "his office as Vicar of Christ and Shepherd of the Universal Church must be protected from being diminished."

The "Explanatory Note," and with it the Second Vatican Council, found brief but not thoroughly clear words for dealing with the question of validly ordained bishops who are not in hierarchical communion with the pope and the bishops united with him. On the one hand, the council maintained that the *munus* (office) *cannot* be exercised without hierarchical communion. On the other hand, it did not want to go into the questions of liceity and validity. These questions were expressly left to further theological research.

Apostolic Origin

The provisions of canon 336 on the apostolic origin of the college of bishops bring to mind the provisions of canon 330, although there is an essential difference between them. The word "col-

lege" and its legal notion have a central place in canon 330. Canon 336, on the other hand, uses the word "body" (*corpus*), which was given priority by the conservative faction at the Second Vatican Council (*LG* 22b). In another place, the council used an alternative and more functional phrase for the apostolic college: "stable group" (*coetus stabilis*—*LG* 19). However, "college" remained the dominant term in the council as well as in canon 336. This correctly corresponds to the word's more juridical meaning as compared to the terms *corpus* and *coetus*. At the same time, mention can be made of the change in the order of *collegium* and *corpus* from canon 29, §3 of the 1980 version of the Fundamental Law to canon 336. The term "apostolic" has a traditional place in the phrase "apostolic succession" (*successio apostolica*) in which *all* bishops stand. The phrase seeks to express the fact that current bishops by the reception of ordination (*ordo*) are united in an unbroken tradition and historical continuity with an apostle chosen by Jesus. This also (indirectly) highlights the greater significance of the power of ordination over the power of jurisdiction.

The Function of the Pope as Head of the College

The emphasis on the function of the pope as head of the college in canon 336 is noteworthy, especially since it occurs in the one canon of the code dedicated exclusively to the college of bishops. The word or the concept "head" (*caput*) appears four times in this brief text. In terms of content, canon 336 is based on numbers 3 and 4 of the "Explanatory Note," which are dedicated solely to the function of the pope as head of the college. Accordingly, without its head the college of bishops does *not* possess supreme and full power over the universal Church. This does not agree with historical facts, with the very notion of a college, or with the teachings of the legitimate ecumenical councils of Constance and Basel. Thus it can—indeed, must—be said that the ecclesiological doctrine on the primacy and its relationship to the episcopacy has changed. And yet, given historical experiences, a situation similar to that which occurred in the fifteenth century cannot be ruled out in the future of the Church; namely, the question of how the Church must deal on a structural level with a schismatic or heretical pope. This question is not addressed by current church law. The problem is heightened by the fact that, according to currently operative church law, the college of bishops cannot act without its head. In contrast, the head (the pope) can act or exercise power over the universal Church without the college of bishops. Collegial acts of the bishops always require the *consent* of the pope (*LG* 22b; cc. 341, 343). This was treated expressly by the "Explanatory Note" (n. 4). The term "consent" is used "so that no one thinks of *dependence* on someone who stands *outside*." The expression calls to mind the communion between the head and the members. The question naturally arises, therefore, whether the college of bishops even possesses a "proper" power or whether its power is derived from the head since without the head it cannot even exercise its power. It should be noted as well that papal power is in no way derived from the college of bishops. Rather, it is exercised by the mandate of Christ. Furthermore, it should be clearly seen that diverse types and origins of the power of jurisdiction are spoken of in this context. As far as the essentially greater power of orders is concerned, there is but the one *ordo* (orders), which the pope and bishops possess equally.

The Authority of the College of Bishops

The college of bishops possesses supreme and full power over the universal Church and is thus also responsible for it. It is noteworthy that the ecclesial legislator, in both the wording of canons as well as in the divisions of material, speaks always first concerning the pope and then concerning the college of bishops, something that is contrary to the unambiguous teaching of the Second Vatican Council and canon 330 of the code. The ecclesiologically correct order is found only in canons 330, 336, and 755, §1. In contrast, canon 782 refers first to the pope and then to the college of bishops. A reference to the comparable power of

the pope and college of bishops represented in an ecumenical council is found in canon 1732, according to which the decrees published by them have a special value.

Finally, the formulations of canon 336 express a general ambiguity in postconciliar Catholic ecclesiology. Certainly the conciliar teaching has hopefully put a final end to the earlier extreme positions of papalism and conciliarism (conciliar theory). Still, Paul VI's insight into the necessity of the "Explanatory Note" has shown that there are ambiguities and difficulties of interpretation in the Dogmatic Constitution on the Church.[37] The "Explanatory Note" itself is ultimately not clear in every regard. It leaves room for further theological research. This has led to at least two consequences following the council. The first is that theologians and canonists have taken two different positions. The first sees the college of bishops with the pope as its head as the bearer of supreme power in the Church. This view is held primarily, although not exclusively, by theologians (e.g., Congar, Rahner, Schillebeeckx). Others, primarily canonists (e.g., Corecco, Mörsdorf), maintain that the pope and college of bishops are two inadequately distinct subjects of supreme power. The second consequence, which cannot be overlooked, is that as a result especially of the 1983 code, but also of the numerous legally relevant postconciliar acts of the pope, a de facto strengthening of the emphasis on papal power in the universal Church has occurred. The 1992 letter of the Congregation for the Doctrine of the Faith *Communionis notio* should be mentioned in this regard.[38]

There are only two terminological differences between canon 336 and canon 49 of the Eastern code, possibly out of consideration for the Eastern churches in union with Rome: instead of *Summus*

---

[37] K. Walf, "Lakunen und Zweideutigkeiten in der Ekklesiologie des II. Vatikanums," in *Kirche im Wandel—eine kritische Zwischenbilanz nach dem zweiten Vatikanum*, ed. G. Alberigo, Y. Congar, and H. J. Pottmeyer (Düsseldorf: Patmos, 1982) 195–207.

[38] CDF, letter to the bishops of the Catholic Church *Communionis notio*, May 28, 1992, *AAS* 85 (1993) 838–850.

Pontifex ("Supreme Pontiff") one finds *Romanus Pontifex* ("Roman Pontiff") and in the place of "sacramental consecration" one finds "sacramental ordination."

Exercise of Power

Canon 337 — §1. The college of bishops exercises power over the universal Church in a solemn manner in an ecumenical council.

§2. It exercises the same power through the united action of the bishops dispersed in the world, which the Roman Pontiff has publicly declared or freely accepted as such so that it becomes a true collegial act.

§3. It is for the Roman Pontiff, according to the needs of the Church, to select and promote the ways by which the college of bishops is to exercise its function collegially regarding the universal Church.

Canon 337 speaks of the diverse forms of the exercise of the supreme power of the college of bishops over the universal Church. The ecumenical council, based on the decrees of Vatican II (*LG* 22b; "Explanatory Note," 3; *CD* 4), is now but one possibility, even if it is the first or most preeminent. There are two other forms, with the form and structure of the third involving the power of the pope expressly exercised on his own initiative. Hence one must speak of a relativization of the traditional significance of the ecumenical council. To be perfectly clear, it must be said that even the ecumenical council and the so-called epistolary council mentioned in paragraph two occur only at the initiative of the pope. The college of bishops is seen as a reality having a purely abstract importance, whose realization in the forms mentioned in this canon depends on the initiative of the pope. Only through him can the college become an acting subject of supreme and full power over the universal Church. The threat of sanctions in canon 1372 applies to recourse taken to the college of bishops, since the canon provides a penalty for recourse against an act of the pope "to an ecumenical council or the college of bish-

ops" (one should note the word order!). The first two paragraphs of canon 337 are based on *Lumen gentium* 22 and *Christus Dominus* 4. Paragraph three has been taken from the "Explanatory Note" (n. 3).

The Ecumenical Council (§1)

According to the provisions of the 1917 code (*CIC* 228, §1), the ecumenical council possessed supreme power over the universal Church. This phrase has been dropped. According to the currently operative formulation, the college of bishops exercises this power "in an ecumenical council." Since the college of bishops is thus an active subject, the definition of its power in canon 336 ("supreme and full power") applies. The essential structural elements of an ecumenical council are mentioned in or regulated by canons 338–341. However, the code says nothing about the term "ecumenical." According to the Catholic Church's own understanding, the term "ecumenical" applies to a council whose participants are bishops and other persons (c. 339) who accept the function of the pope as head.

According to Catholic calculations, the Second Vatican Council was the twenty-first ecumenical council. Other Christian churches, foremost among them the Orthodox, agree with the Catholic Church only in recognizing the first four councils as ecumenical (Nicea, Constantinople I, Ephesus, Chalcedon). The emperors had a great influence at the early councils. They convened the councils and also made their dominant authority felt during the course of the council. The medieval emperors of the Holy Roman Empire attempted to carry on this tradition, but their influence remained relatively limited. On the other hand, the influence of popes on the council grew. Since the Council of Florence (1431–1445) the pope's influence has been dominant at all councils with the exception of the Councils of Constance and Basel. Councils have served in a special way in times of ecclesial crisis by deciding disputed questions of ecclesial doctrine and discipline. The last three councils (Trent, Vatican I and II) were and are of outstanding significance for the current law of the Church. In former times, due to the insufficient means of communication, councils were representative ecclesial gatherings only in a very limited sense. Only the two Vatican councils can be referred to as ecumenical. Still, despite their designation as ecumenical councils, they were actually councils of only the Catholic Church (the Latin church and the Eastern churches united with Rome). Incidentally and surprisingly, Catholic Church law, structurally speaking, recognizes no council (or synod) that is exclusively and solely for the Latin church.

United Exercise of Office (§2)

One of the most problematic provisions of the 1983 code is found in paragraph two. It states that "through the united action of the bishops dispersed in the world...it becomes a true collegial act." According to references to the source of this text, it is based on *Lumen gentium* 22. But, as far as this question is concerned, that source text contains a much more general formulation ("The same collegial power can be exercised together with the pope by the bishops living throughout the world..., such that a truly collegial act results"). If one takes seriously as a juridical concept the term "collegial act" found in both formulations, the idea that bishops dispersed throughout the world could posit such an act is highly questionable. The prerequisites for a collegial act are that it be placed at the same time, in the same place, by the members of the college convoked according to the regulations of the statutes. That these prerequisites do not exist or are not guaranteed in the situation mentioned in canon 337, §2 was also sensed by the legislator since he formulated the end of the canon to read: "so that it becomes a truly collegial act." In canon 341, §2 the code again speaks of this possibility. Interestingly, that canon speaks of the college taking "truly collegial action in another way."

So far there have been no provisions or regulations governing the exercise of this juridical possibility, nor has there yet been a need for such a possibility. Usually this regulation is understood as referring to an epistolary council [*Briefkonzil*].

In the past, bishops were consulted by Pius XII before the proclamation of the dogma of the bodily assumption of Mary into heaven (1950), and other popes made similar inquiries during the last 150 years. It has also been occasionally asserted that the synod of bishops issues collegial acts vicariously (!), which is an expression of episcopal collegiality. These examples are troubling. The synod of bishops itself in its most comprehensive form, namely, as an ordinary general gathering, is merely a representation of the college of bishops, and was conceived as such from the beginning. Besides, an epistolary council does not possess the already mentioned criteria for a collegial act. Canon 337, §2 is based on *Lumen gentium* 22b where, in fact, these same provisions are made. Even those statements of the council were interpreted in various ways.

Canon 337 makes provisions similar to those of canon 333, §2. It is up to the pope to determine whether and how the college of bishops should collegially exercise its mission regarding the universal Church. Even here problems can arise if the pope, for whatever reason, is not prepared to allow the college to exercise its task. One of the most important legal actions in the Church occurs without the pope, that is, the papal election. This is also a collegial act, even if it involves only the college of cardinals and not the entire college of bishops. Still, according to current opinion, the college of cardinals is representative of the college of bishops. However, one senses a certain ambivalence in the code when paragraph two speaks of the pope being able to accept freely a united action of the bishops. Apparently, this refers to a subsequent acceptance of the action. There is an unmistakable parallel with canon 341 (confirmation of conciliar decrees or free acceptance of conciliar decrees by the pope). This invites further reflection on the differences between the two processes.

The Role of the Pope (§3)

It is the pope's right to confirm the collegial form of action of the college of bishops. As has already been mentioned, this text originates from part three of the "Explanatory Note." It contains the formulation according to which the pope directs, promotes, and approves collegial actions in light of the good of the Church "according to his own judgment." This wording was not appropriated by the code; instead, the provision of the code was strengthened through a not-so-subtle wording which maintains that this is a prerogative or right of the pope.

There is no difference in content between canon 337 and canon 50 of the Eastern code. The former canon corresponds to canon 35 of the 1980 version of the Fundamental Law.

Ecumenical Council: Role of the Pope

Canon 338 — §1. It is for the Roman Pontiff alone to convoke an ecumenical council, preside over it personally or through others, transfer, suspend, or dissolve a council, and to approve its decrees.

§2. It is for the Roman Pontiff to determine the matters to be treated in a council and establish the order to be observed in a council. To the questions proposed by the Roman Pontiff, the council fathers can add others which are to be approved by the Roman Pontiff.

This canon presents special provisions regarding the ecumenical council. While appropriating extensively the provisions of the 1917 code (*CIC* 222–229), the 1983 code also made changes that arise only partly out of the decrees of the Second Vatican Council.

Canon 338 reflects the content of canons 222 and 226 of the 1917 code as well as *Lumen gentium* 22b and the "Explanatory Note" (n. 3).

It is the pope's right to convoke an ecumenical council. *Lumen gentium* 22b addressed this point a bit more extensively. An ecumenical council occurs only when it is determined to be such by the pope or at least recognized by him. Only in that context did the council speak of a "prerogative" of the bishop of Rome to convene councils. If canon 338 has redefined the content of canon 222,

§1 of the 1917 code by another wording of it, this must be viewed as an ecclesiological step backwards. Certainly the formulation of the council took into consideration historical experiences. The first councils were convened by Roman emperors, even if on the advice of bishops. Medieval councils too occurred at the initiative of emperors and others, rather than absolutely or solely at the popes' initiative. The wording of the code, according to which it belongs to the pope *alone* to convene an ecumenical council, permits the sole interpretation that this is a prerequisite for the validity of the council.

It also belongs to the pope to preside at the council. He can permit others to represent him, something that happened, for instance, at the Second Vatican Council. Furthermore, the pope (alone) can transfer the place where the council is held, interrupt its work for a certain period of time, or dissolve it. This form of dissolving a council is to be distinguished from the interruption of a council regulated by canon 340 at the death of a pope. Conceivably a majority of the council fathers might oppose a dissolution of the council by the pope. However, the decrees of such a council would acquire validity only if the pope or his successor freely accepted them (see c. 337, §2).

This canon further mentions the (sole) right of the pope to approve the decrees of the council. Canon 341, §1 also speaks of this. We find here evidence of an inconsistent redaction of the canons, and discrepancies on this point between both canons are proof of different ecclesiologies. Canon 338, §1 follows the teaching of Vatican I (*CIC* 222, §2) by granting the pope alone the right to approve decrees. Canon 341, §1, on the other hand, follows the view of Vatican II by maintaining that the pope approves the decrees "together with the council fathers."[39]

Canon 338, §2 regulates the rather technical or formal aspects of a council. Every responsibility and initiative lies legitimately with the pope. He

---

[39] This was the formula for approving council documents used in Vatican II.

determines the matters the council will address, although the "council fathers" can add to them with the approval of the pope. Council fathers include all bishops as well as those who are nominated by the pope according to canon 339, §2 to be participants in the council. Finally, the pope alone confirms the topics of a council. One might question whether this filtration process in the preparation of a council corresponds to the idea of collegiality, since a council, according to canon 337, §1, is an occasion during which the college of bishops exercises power over the universal Church. In preparation for the Second Vatican Council, commissions, conferences of bishops, orders, universities, scientific organizations, etc., all made recommendations to the Roman Curia or reacted to suggestions that came from institutions of the Curia. This often very time-consuming process can give rise to the impression that the topics of the council were also determined by these persons and institutions. In fact, however, the topics on the daily agenda of the council were those to which the pope had consented. In this way, Paul VI expressly excluded discussion of the important topics of birth control and clerical celibacy from the Second Vatican Council.

The order to be followed in a council is determined by the pope.[40]

Apart from rather small terminological differences, canon 338 corresponds to canon 51 of the Eastern code. It corresponds literally to canon 36 of the 1980 version of the Fundamental Law.

Participants at a Council

Canon 339 — §1. All the bishops and only the bishops who are members of the college of bishops have the right and duty to take part in an ecumenical council with a deliberative vote.

§2. Moreover, some others who are not bishops can be called to an ecumenical council by the supreme authority of the Church, to whom it belongs to determine their roles in the council.

[40] See *Ordo Concilii Oecumenici Vaticani II celebrandi,* AAS 54 (1962) 609–631.

Canon 339 possesses great ecclesiological significance. It contains changes in traditional canon law that in themselves bear welcome consequences in the evaluation of episcopal consecration, but which are also partly alarming. This is clearly demonstrated by a comparison between canon 339 and canon 223 of the 1917 code.

Canon 339, §1 is based on *Christus Dominus* 4.[41] It gives all bishops (diocesan as well as titular and emeritus bishops) the right to take part in the council with a deliberative vote. The former law granted this right to titular bishops as well, but included the possibility of reserving it.[42] Participants in the council also have the right to vote. They must be members of the college of bishops, that is, they must fulfill the requirements of canons 336 and 375, §2: episcopal consecration as well as hierarchical communion with the pope and the other members of the college of bishops. Participation in a council is described as a right and duty (*officium*) of bishops. The translation of *officium* as "duty" is certainly correct, even though the notion of *officium* has a more extensive connotation, namely, that of an office. The former law's provision for the appointment of a proxy (without the right to vote) in cases where a member was legitimately prevented from attending a council has been dropped.

The now clear provision of paragraph one is welcome. The group of participants has been limited to bishops alone in accord with the ecclesiology of the Second Vatican Council. The 1917 code mentioned a series of other legitimate participants: cardinals (even if they had not been consecrated bishops), diocesan bishops not yet consecrated, abbots and prelates *nullius,* abbot primates, and superiors general of exempt religious orders of clerics. Earlier councils also included secular representatives among their participants, although these individuals were not

[41] It is noteworthy that this source was not reported in the sources for the code.
[42] *CIC* 223, §2: "unless it was expressly precluded in the convocation" ("nisi aliud in convocatione expresse caveatur").

granted the right to vote. The decisive difference is that until Vatican II the right to participate in an ecumenical council and the right to vote in one were considered to be exercises of the power of jurisdiction, which in the case of titular bishops was seen as something conferred by the pope. Since the Second Vatican Council both rights have been based on episcopal consecration, an indication of the high esteem given it in the council's ecclesiology.

It is quite regrettable that the clear description of the right to participate and vote has been seriously attenuated in paragraph two. Some "others" who are not bishops can be called to participate in a council. Apparently the canon envisions only a small number of such persons. It was once assumed, with regard to the *synod of bishops,* that the pope could appoint up to an additional fifteen percent of its members beyond the number that the law provided for. Although this limit has been dropped from the code, if the need arose, one could apply this method of determining the number of participants in an ecumenical council. Although theoretically this provision could be applied to the pope and/or the college of bishops, some maintain that the ecclesial legislator intended it to apply exclusively to the pope. In the texts of the Second Vatican Council it was reserved to the pope. The whole context of the canons on the ecumenical council also supports the view that at least in this canon the pope alone is intended to have this right. The "supreme authority" determines the roles of those appointed by him to a council.

A structural change for the Catholic Church that does not correspond to the ecclesiology of the Second Vatican Council lies concealed in the subordinate clause of canon 339, §2, which does not state what type of vote these appointees have. The supreme authority is to determine whether they will have a deliberative vote or merely a consultative vote. The 1917 code gave detailed provisions concerning who would have a deliberative vote. Following the ecclesiological view current at the time, a deliberative vote was granted to persons who were not bishops only if they were ecclesiastical dignitaries with a higher power of jurisdiction. At the same time, a deliberative vote was expressly denied to theologians and canonists who had been invited to the council as experts (*periti; CIC* 223, §3). According to the new provision, it is left to the (not clearly defined) "supreme authority" to determine the type of vote the appointed members will have.

Apart from a few small terminological changes (*obligatio,* "obligation," instead of *officium,* "duty," in §1), canon 339 corresponds to canon 52 of the Eastern code. The former text also corresponds to canon 37 of the 1980 version of the Fundamental Law.

Automatic Interruption

Canon 340 — If the Apostolic See becomes vacant during the celebration of a council, the council is interrupted by the law itself until the new Supreme Pontiff orders it to be continued or dissolves it.

Canon 340 is comparable to canon 229 of the 1917 code although it is worded more generally. The earlier provision regulated the dissolution of a council only in the case of the death of a pope. The new regulation includes the possibility of the resignation of a pope as a cause of a vacant Roman See. Moreover, up until recently it was envisioned that a new pope would reconvene the council and bring it to completion. Now it is clearly stated that a new pope can also dissolve a council.

According to the "Explanatory Note" (n. 4), every collegial act of the college of bishops requires the consent of its head. This statement is the reason for this canon. The canon also demonstrates the consequences of the traditional provision "Sede vacante nihil innovetur" ("When a see is vacant nothing is to be altered"—cc. 335; 428, §1) as well as of canon 336, according to which the pope is head of the college of bishops. The council cannot dissolve itself during a vacant see, since the right of dissolving a council is reserved to the pope (c. 338, §1).

As with canon 332, §2, there are important and clearly possible situations that are not regulated by canon 340. As opposed to canon 335, there is no mention in this canon of the possibility of the pope being "entirely impeded." Furthermore, regulations are lacking in this canon, as they are in the canons on the pope himself, for the possibility of incapacity resulting from physical or psychic causes, for cases in which the pope is prevented from exercising his office (e.g., due to political causes), or for the possibility of a pope or competing popes committing heretical or schismatic acts. All of the foregoing incidents are attested to in church history (cf. Council of Constance, 1414–1418). This canon, as well as the canons on the pope, demonstrate a certain reluctance for regulating by means of the law a breakdown in papal power.

With regard to content, there is no difference between canon 340 and canon 53 of the Eastern code. Canon 340 corresponds literally to canon 38 of the 1980 version of the Fundamental Law.

Binding Force of Decrees

Canon 341 — §1. The decrees of an ecumenical council do not have obligatory force unless they have been approved by the Roman Pontiff together with the council fathers, confirmed by him, and promulgated at his order.

§2. To have obligatory force, decrees which the college of bishops issues when it places a truly collegial action in another way initiated or freely accepted by the Roman Pontiff need the same confirmation and promulgation.

Paragraph one broadens the formulation of canon 227 of the 1917 code on the basis of conciliar ecclesiology (*LG* 22b) and corrects an unfortunate inconsistency in the final redaction of canon 338, §1 of the 1983 code. Paragraph two similarly takes into consideration expressions of the Second Vatican Council and corresponding other provisions of the 1983 code whereby collegial acts of the college of bishops could take place in ways other than in an ecumenical council.

Paragraph one describes the three stages leading to a legally binding conciliar decree. The first involves the pope "together with the council fathers," and the last two involve the pope alone. The first step, referred to as approval (*approbatio*), is the foundation of the entire process. As far as this stage is concerned, the canon makes it clear that the head and members of the college work together. Without the head, the pope, this step cannot be completed. With regard to the indispensable cooperation of the council fathers, there is no mention here of the required majority. The regulation of this matter is left to the procedural rules of an ecumenical council. However, it would certainly have been wise to include a fundamental reference to it in the code. As to the meaning of the phrase "together with the council fathers," commentaries on the code generally speak only of a "majority," which could also mean a simple majority of those present at the council with a right to vote, and not the usual qualified majority.

After the collegial act of approval (*approbatio*) come the primatial acts of confirmation (*confirmatio*) and promulgation (*promulgatio*). These correspond to canon 227 of the 1917 code. The subsequent free approval of conciliar decrees, as foreseen by *Lumen gentium* 22b and still found in the drafts of the Fundamental Law,[43] was eliminated.

The fact that two primatial acts must follow a collegial act in order for conciliar decrees to become legally binding is ecclesiologically dubious and, from a legal standpoint, not without logical problems. On the one hand, the collegial act of approval by the pope and the other council fathers is necessary for the legally binding character of a decree since it is a decree of the college of bishops represented in a council. On the other hand, according to canon 341, the primatial acts of confirmation and promulgation are necessarily involved. They follow the constitutive act of ap-

---

[43] In c. 46, §1 of the 1971 draft of the *LEF*, the phrase is "or at least freely accepted by him." *Herder-Korrespondenz* 25 (1971) 244.

proval. However, they apparently possess the same legal quality as approval.

Pope Paul VI used the following formula of promulgation for the acts of the Second Vatican Council: "What is expressed in this constitution (decree, declaration) in whole and in part, has been approved by the fathers. And we, by virtue of the apostolic authority granted us by Christ, approve, decide, and decree it, together with the venerable fathers in the Holy Spirit, and inasmuch as it has been so ordered by the council, we command that it be promulgated for the glory of God." The same pope signed the documents with the significant title "Bishop of the Catholic Church" (*Catholicae Ecclesiae Episcopus*).

Paragraph two regulates the possibility of the college of bishops, not gathered in a council, taking collegial action in another manner. (see c. 337, §2). The legal difficulty that such a (not yet realized) act conceals has been discussed in the commentary on canon 337. The formal steps necessary for such an act to achieve a legally binding character are the same as those necessary in a council: confirmation and promulgation by the pope. Since this act must be "initiated or freely accepted by the Roman Pontiff," his cooperation is required for the act to come into being. However, it is noteworthy that in this case the term *approbatio* (approval) is not used as it is in the case of a council (§1). As has already been mentioned, the notion was expressly rejected that the pope can accept collegial acts of the college of bishops subsequent to their having taken place.

It is highly questionable that a concept as important as *approbare* (approve) would be used in different senses in canons 338, §1 and 341.

Canon 341 and canon 54 of the Eastern code diverge only in some details of wording, but not in regard to content. Canon 341 corresponds to canon 39 of the 1980 version of the Fundamental Law. There is merely a small stylistic difference in paragraph one.

BIBLIOGRAPHY

The Roman Pontiff and the College of Bishops

Aymans, W. *Kirchenrechtliche Beiträge zur Ekklesiologie*. Berlin: Duncker & Humblot, 1995.

Aymans, W., and K. Mörsdorf. *Kanonisches Recht: Lehrbuch aufgrund des Codex Iuris Canonici. Band II: Verfassungs- und Vereinigungsrecht*. Paderborn: Schöningh, 1997.

Bertrams, W. "De subiecto supremae potestatis Ecclesiae." *P* 54 (1965) 173–232.

D'Onorio, J. B. *Le pape et le gouvernment de l'Église*. Paris: Fleurus-Tardy, 1992.

Komonchak, J. "The Ecumenical Council in the New Code of Canon Law." *Con* 167 (1983) 100–105.

Krämer, P. *Kirchenrecht II: Ortskirche—Gesamtkirche*. Stuttgart: Kohlhammer, 1993.

Longhitano, A. "Il libro II: Il Popolo di Dio." In *Il nuovo codice di diritto canonico*, ed. J. Beyer, 60–79. Turin: Leumann, 1985.

Mörsdorf, K. *Schriften zum kanonischen Recht*. Ed. W. Aymans et al. Paderborn: Schöningh, 1989.

Stoffel, O. In *Münster Com* at cc. 330–341.

CHAPTER II
THE SYNOD OF BISHOPS
[cc. 342–348]

During the preparation for the Second Vatican Council, several bishops suggested the establishment of some kind of permanent council whereby the bishops could exercise their authority over the universal Church, but this idea had little influence on the two schemas on bishops which were drafted for the first session of the council. In written comments on these drafts, several bishops repeated the proposal that some kind of episcopal council be created. By the time the schema on bishops and diocesan governance came up for discussion, the council had endorsed the proposition that, under the headship of the pope, the episcopal college was the subject of supreme power in the universal Church. The discussion could thus focus on appropriate ways to exercise this power.

In the light of this discussion, and in the light of papal comments indicating that Paul VI would welcome suggestions of ways in which bishops could more effectively assist him in carrying out his responsibilities, the drafting committee prepared a revised draft of the schema which included the following paragraph:

5. [The Central Coetus or Council]. Since the universal mission of the Supreme Pontiff demands greater resources of help and assistance each day, the Fathers of this Holy Council vehemently wish that some bishops from the different regions of the world may offer to the Supreme Pastor of the Church more effective aid, in a manner to be determined at the proper time, even, if it should please the Supreme Pontiff, coming together in a certain *coetus* or council, which could at the same time be a sign of the participation of all the bishops in solicitude for the universal Church.[1]

The drafting committee did not intend this gingerly worded paragraph to mean that the proposed council of bishops involved an exercise of *episcopal* ministry; the institute would exist "only to assist the Supreme Pontiff in the government of the universal Church."[2] This intention did not satisfy all the bishops, but the Fathers never resolved the issue. On September 14, 1965 Pope Paul VI anticipated (or forestalled) the achievement of a conciliar consensus by announcing his impending creation of the synod of bishops.[3] He formally established the institute the following day.[4]

Even so cursory an account of the conception of the synod of bishops demonstrates that the institute can be understood in at least two not entirely complementary ways. On the one hand, one can view its creation as a papal response to some bishops' expectations that a structure should exist through which the college of bishops might exercise their supreme power over the universal Church.[5] On the other hand, one can view the synod as an instru-

---

[1] *AcSynVat,* III, 2:23–24.

[2] *AcSynVat,* III, 4:127.

[3] Pope Paul VI, alloc "In hoc laetamur," September 14, 1965, *AAS* 57 (1965) 794–804.

[4] Pope Paul VI, *mp Apostolica sollicitudo,* September 15, 1965, *AAS* 57 (1965) 775–780. The commentary will cite the *mp* as *AS* with the articles in Roman numerals and paragraphs in Arabic.

[5] This view found official representation in the treatment of the synod in the *Directory on the Pastoral Ministry of Bishops.* The SCB situated its brief comments on the synod, not in part two, chapter 2, The Bishops' Collaboration with the Roman Pontiff (§§44–49), but in part two, chapter 3, Collaboration of the Bishops with the Episcopal College (§§50–53). Cf. SCB, *Directory on the Pastoral Ministry of Bishops,* trans. Benedictine Monks of the Seminary of Christ the King (Ottawa: Canadian Catholic Conference, 1974) §29, 52.

ment by means of which the pope allows bishops to assist him in the exercise of his ministry.[6] It seems evident that the conciliar drafting commission strongly advocated the second view,[7] and Pope Paul VI never disavowed it. The phrasing of some of the following canons (the synod meets "to assist the Roman Pontiff"—c. 342; the pope may *give* the synod deliberative power—c. 343) reflects the same view.[8] However, if the synod was not conceived and does not function as an instrument for the exercise of the power of the college of bishops, then the Church's government structure suffers from a handicap: the Church has recognized herself as endowed with a power but has not created an ordinary means for exercising it.

The seven canons of this chapter comprise only one source of law governing the synod. The 1965 *motu proprio Apostolica sollicitudo* contains more detailed prescriptions concerning the nature, purpose, and procedures of the institute; and it constitutes an authentic expression of the canonical tradition in the light of which the canons must be interpreted (cf. c. 6, §2). Moreover, the *Ordo Synodi Episcoporum Celebrandae*[9] contains norms about the structures and procedures of the synod. It is

therefore necessary to refer to these documents in interpreting the canons.

The first two canons in this chapter define the synod and specify its function. Canon 344 lists some papal prerogatives vis à vis the synod. Canon 345 indicates the three forms of celebration of a synod (ordinary, extraordinary, and special), and canon 346 discusses the membership of each form. Canon 347 discusses an ordinary and an extraordinary way in which the celebration of a synod might cease. Canon 348 describes the officials necessary for the operation of the synod.

All of these canons are new, because the synod did not exist at the time the 1917 code was formulated, and the materials from which they are crafted come from *Apostolica sollicitudo,* from the *Ordo,* and from *Christus Dominus* 5.

Definition

Canon 342 — The synod of bishops is a group of bishops who have been chosen from different regions of the world and meet together at fixed times to foster closer unity between the Roman Pontiff and bishops, to assist the Roman Pontiff with their counsel in the preservation and growth of faith and morals and in the observance and strengthening of ecclesiastical discipline, and to consider questions pertaining to the activity of the Church in the world.

This canon is one of three officially promulgated definitions of the synod. The first and most detailed is contained in the first two norms of *Apostolica sollicitudo:*

I. . . . The Synod of Bishops, whereby bishops chosen from various parts of the world lend their valuable assistance to the Supreme Pastor of the Church, is so constituted as to be: a) a central ecclesiastical institution, b) representing the complete Catholic episcopate, c) by its nature perpetual, d) as for its structure, performing its duties for a time and when called upon.

---

[6] See, for example, J. L. Gutiérrez, "Chapter II: The Synod of Bishops," in *Pamplona ComEng,* 271: "The Synod of Bishops is not a form of exercising collegiality in the governance of the Church, but it *is* a way of collaborating with the Roman Pontiff in his primatial function."

[7] For a detailed and persuasive argument in favor of this conclusion, cf. J. Arrieta, "El sinodo de los obispos: criterios que enmarcan su evolución normativa," *Ius Canonicum* 24 (1984) 51–85.

[8] The positioning of the canons in the code is ambiguous. The chapter on the synod could be seen either as the completion of the code's treatment of the college of bishops or as the beginning of its discussion of the instruments of papal government.

[9] This document was originally issued by the SS prior to the celebration of the 1967 synod (*AAS* 59 [1967] 775–780). It was revised in the light of experience prior to the 1969 synod (*AAS* 61 [1969] 525–539; *CLD* 7, 322–338). At the recommendation of the 1969 synod, some additions were made prior to the 1971 synod (*AAS* 63 [1971] 702–704; *CLD* 7, 338–341). The commentary will cite the *Ordo* by reference to its articles.

II. By its very nature it is the task of the Synod of Bishops to inform and give advice. It may also have deliberative power, when such power is conferred upon it by the Sovereign Pontiff, who will in such cases confirm the decisions of the Synod.

1. The general aims of the Synod of Bishops are: a) To encourage close union and valued assistance between the Sovereign Pontiff and the bishops of the entire world; b) To insure that direct and real information is provided on questions and situations touching upon the internal action of the Church and its necessary activity in the world of today; c) To facilitate agreement on essential points of doctrine and on methods of procedure in the life of the Church.

2. The special and proximate ends of the Synod of Bishops are: a) To communicate useful information; b) To proffer advice on the topics proposed for discussion in the individual meetings of the Synod.[10]

The text from *Christus Dominus* 5 is vaguer and shorter:

Bishops from various parts of the world, chosen through ways and procedures established or to be established by the Roman Pontiff, will render especially helpful assistance to the supreme pastor of the Church in a council to be known by the proper name of Synod of Bishops. Since it will be acting in the name of the entire Catholic episcopate, it will at the same time demonstrate that all the bishops in hierarchical communion share in the responsibility for the universal Church.[11]

Like its progenitors, the definition in canon 342 specifies what the synod of bishops is (a gathering of bishops from around the world) and the purposes for which it exists: (a) the fostering of com-

munion, especially between the pope and his brother bishops; (b) assisting the pope in discharging his responsibilities; and (c) formulating possible answers to questions arising from the changing situation of the Church in the world.[12] Unlike the conciliar decree, the canon says nothing about the representative function of the synod[13] nor about its manifestation of the episcopal college's responsibility for the universal Church. Unlike the *motu proprio,* the canon pays little attention to the information-gathering and information-sharing possibilities of the synod. The canon's more matter-of-fact approach to the institute need not imply a repudiation of the council's or Pope Paul VI's views. It may reflect only the humble realization that the law is not the best forum for resolving theological questions.

Authority of the Synod

Canon 343 — It is for the synod of bishops to discuss the questions for consideration and express its wishes but not to resolve them or issue decrees about them unless in certain cases the Roman

[12] McGrath prefers a fourfold division of synod functions: (1) fostering communion; (2) assisting the pope "in the defense and development of faith and morals"; (3) assisting the pope "in the preservation and strengthening of ecclesiastical discipline"; and (4) considering the mission of the Church in the world. A. McGrath, "Chapter II: The Synod of Bishops," in *CLSGBI Com,* 197. Because the canon itself uses three parallel purpose clauses to specify the synod's functions, this author prefers the threefold division.

[13] From available documentation it would appear that the committee responsible for drafting this section of the code deliberately excluded from the text language parallel to the phrase "acting on behalf of the whole Catholic episcopate." Three reasons for this exclusion emerged during the discussion: (1) if the phrase were true, the synod ought to have deliberative power, and it does not; (2) the synod has functioned as an institute of the Latin church rather than of the whole Church; (3) the special assembly of the synod certainly does not represent the *whole* episcopate. *Comm* 14 (1982) 92–93. See also J. Tomko, "Il sinodo dei vescovi e Giovanni Paolo II," in *Il Sinodo dei Vescovi,* ed. J. Tomko (Rome: Libreria Editrice Vaticana, 1985) 27.

[10] *AAS* 57 (1965) 776–777.
[11] *AAS* 58 (1966) 675.

Pontiff has endowed it with deliberative power, in which case he ratifies the decisions of the synod.

"To issue decrees" is technical language: the synod of bishops is not a legislature. It is *by nature* a consultative body.[14] Rather than resolving the issues on its agenda, the synod offers the pope a wealth of information and makes suggestions, from among which the pope is free to choose or not, as he deems best.[15]

The canon envisages the possibility—not realized as of this writing—that the pope might endow the synod with decision-making power, but only for specific cases. In such an event the synod would be exercising delegated papal power (cf. c. 131, §1).[16]

Relationship with the Pope

Canon 344 — The synod of bishops is directly subject to the authority of the Roman Pontiff who:
  1° **convokes a synod as often as it seems opportune to him and designates the place where its sessions are to be held;**
  2° **ratifies the election of members who must be elected according to the norm of special law and designates and appoints other members;**
  3° **determines at an appropriate time before the celebration of a synod the contents of the questions to be treated, according to the norm of special law;**
  4° **defines the agenda;**
  5° **presides at the synod personally or through others;**

6° **concludes, transfers, suspends, and dissolves the synod.**

This list of papal prerogatives is derived almost verbatim from *Apostolica sollicitudo* III. Number two of the canon supplements the reference to the pope's right to certify the election of some of the members with an accurate reference to his right to appoint others. The "norm(s) of special law" to which the canon refers are *Apostolica sollicitudo* VII and article 6 of the *Ordo*.[17] *Apostolica sollicitudo* III, 3 had expressed the preference that the assembly's topic be determined "at least six months, if possible, before the date for the convening of the Synod."[18] The canon more generously refers to "an appropriate time." It defers to particular law further specification of the method of determining the topic.[19] *Apostolica sollicitudo* contained a norm on "dispatching of material to those who are to take part in the discussion." The code omits this, too, apparently because it is a matter more properly dealt with in particular law.

These papal rights and duties are similar to those the pope exercises vis à vis the ecumenical council (cf. c. 338). Clearly, the laws governing the celebration of ecumenical councils served as a model for the laws governing the synod—with two significant differences. Possibly because participation in an ecumenical council is the right and duty of all and only bishops (c. 339, §1), the pope has no right (indeed, no *need*) to confirm the election of any members, although he does have the right (as does the college itself, acting under his headship) to call others who are not bishops to an ecumenical council and determine their partici-

---

[14] Cf. *AS* II: "By its very nature it is the task of the Synod of Bishops to inform and give advice." *AAS* 57 (1965) 776–777.

[15] It has become customary for ordinary sessions of the synod of bishops to prepare for the pope lists of "propositions" which, with the assistance of the *consilium,* he uses to prepare an apostolic exhortation.

[16] For a synopsis of the positions various authors take on the source of the power exercised by the synod, cf. J. Johnson, "The Synod of Bishops: An Exploration of Its Nature and Function," *Stud Can* 20 (1986) 298–305.

[17] The election must be by secret ballot. Each representative must be elected in turn—i.e., the first must be elected before the conference begins to vote on the second, etc. The *Ordo* even contains advice on the qualifications of candidates (6, §2, 5°).

[18] *AAS* 57 (1965) 777.

[19] In accordance with article 13, §5, 1° of the *Ordo,* the council of the general secretariat generally polls the synods of Eastern churches and the episcopal conferences about suitable topics, collates the responses, and presents a list of potential topics to the pope.

pation in it (c. 339, §2). The participants in an ecumenical council, unlike the participants in a synod, can add other questions for the council to discuss, subject to papal approval (c. 338, §2).

Forms of Assembly and Membership

Canon 345 — The synod of bishops can be assembled in a general session, that is, one which treats matters that directly pertain to the good of the universal Church; such a session is either ordinary or extraordinary. It can also be assembled in a special session, namely, one which considers affairs that directly pertain to a determinate region or regions.

Apostolica sollicitudo IV treated each form of celebration (general, extraordinary, and special) as a distinct species. The canon, following article 4 of the *Ordo,* is more systematic: there are two species (general and special), depending on whether the synod in question is convoked to discuss matters of concern to the entire Church or matters of concern primarily to a given territory.[20] The first species contains two sub-species (ordinary and extraordinary) depending on the urgency of the questions to be discussed.

Canon 346 — §1. A synod of bishops assembled in an ordinary general session consists of members of whom the greater part are bishops elected for each session by the conferences of bishops according to the method determined by the special law of the synod; others are designated by virtue of the same law; others are appointed directly by

the Roman Pontiff; to these are added some members of clerical religious institutes elected according to the norm of the same special law.

Ordinary general sessions of the synod are celebrated with some regularity (1967, 1971, 1974, 1977, 1980, 1983, 1987, 1990, 1994). They have dealt with such issues as evangelization, the role of the laity, family life, justice, the formation of priests, and reconciliation and penance. The distinguishing characteristic of the ordinary session is that the majority of its episcopal participants are elected by the episcopal conferences: a conference with twenty-five or fewer members elects one representative; a conference with fifty or fewer elects two; a conference with one hundred or fewer elects three; and a conference with more than one hundred elects four.[21] In addition, the assembly includes: (1) the patriarchs, major archbishops, and metropolitans of Eastern *sui iuris* churches; (2) representatives of religious elected by the Union of Superiors General; (3) the cardinal prefects of Roman dicasteries; (4) and any papal appointees.[22] Generally more than two hundred ecclesiastics participate in an ordinary general assembly of the synod of bishops.

§2. A synod of bishops gathered in an extraordinary general session to treat affairs which require a speedy solution consists of members of whom the greater part are bishops designated by the special law of the synod by reason of the office which they hold; others are appointed directly by the Roman Pontiff; to these are added some members of clerical religious institutes elected according to the norm of the same law.

As of this writing there have been two extraordinary synods—one called in 1969 to discuss collegiality, and one convoked in 1985 to celebrate the twentieth anniversary of Vatican II. In neither case were there "affairs which require[d] a speedy

---

[20] According to c. 433, §1, an ecclesiastical *region* is a grouping of some (but not all) of the ecclesiastical provinces within the territory of a single episcopal conference. The first draft of c. 433, by contrast, proposed the gathering into an ecclesiastical region of all of the provinces in a given nation. See *Comm* 17 (1985) 97–98 for background discussion and p. 105 for the original text of c. 12. It seems likely that c. 345 retains this earlier meaning. In other words, a special synod would be convoked, not for New England, but for an entire country (the Netherlands) or several countries (Africa).

[21] Cf. *Ordo,* 6, §1, 3°.

[22] Cf. *AS* V; *Ordo,* 5. According to *AS* X, papal appointees ought not to exceed 15 percent of the other members.

solution." Why Pope Paul VI decided to convoke an extraordinary synod for 1969 is still a mystery.[23] Pope John Paul II regarded the celebration of a synod as a fitting commemoration of a significant episode in the life of the Church.[24] No crisis precipitated either assembly.

A more distinguishing characteristic of the extraordinary assembly is that the majority of its participants serve *ex officio*. The categories of membership are identical with those of the ordinary assembly: hierarchs from the Eastern *sui iuris* churches, prefects of Roman dicasteries, representatives of religious, papal appointees, and representatives of episcopal conferences. Instead of electing representatives, however, the episcopal conferences send their presidents.[25] Because these officials are already known, assembling the participants in such a synod (as opposed to other elements of preparation) can be fairly rapid. Because each episcopal conference sends a single representative, the assembly is also smaller than an ordinary session. The synod of 1969, for example, had 146 participants.

§3. A synod of bishops gathered in a special session consists of members especially selected from those regions for which it was called, according to the norm of the special law which governs the synod.

The first special session of the synod of bishops was the 1980 synod for the Netherlands.[26]

[23] Cf. J. Johnson, *The Synod of Bishops: An Analysis of Its Legal Development* (Washington, D.C.: Catholic University of America, 1986) 46–50, for a discussion of the preparation for this synod. If a sense of urgency marks the celebration of an extraordinary session, it is puzzling that more time elapsed between the convocation and assembly of the 1969 *extraordinary* session of the synod than between the convocation and assembly of the 1967 *ordinary* session.

[24] Cf. the remarks of J. Tomko, then the general secretary of the Synod of Bishops, "Why an Extraordinary Synod?" *Origins* 14 (1984–1985) 622–623.

[25] *AS* VI; *Ordo*, 5, §2, 1°, b and c.

[26] This classification follows T. Reese, *Inside the Vatican: The Politics and Organization of the Catholic Church*

There have been special synods for Europe (1991), Africa (1994), and Lebanon (1995).[27] Synods for the Americas, Asia, and possibly Oceania[28] are in the planning stages.[29]

The members of a special synod come from the same general categories as those for the participants in general synods. All participants, however, including the prefects of Roman dicasteries, must have some connection with the territory for which the synod is being celebrated.[30]

This particular form of synod can raise serious questions. How can one understand a special

(Cambridge, Mass.: Harvard University, 1996) 45. J. Schotte ("The Synod of Bishops: A Permanent yet Adaptable Church Institution," *Stud Can* 26 [1992] 299–300) calls the Dutch synod "particular" rather than "special" because it occurred before the promulgation of the 1983 code and because it involved all rather than representatives of the bishops from the Netherlands. For a more detailed exposition of arguments in favor of Schotte's position, cf. Johnson, *The Synod of Bishops: An Analysis*, 185–193.

[27] Reese, 45. Schotte offers an overview of the European synod (300–304) and brief comments on the synods for Lebanon (304) and Africa (304–305). G. Caprile, *Il Sinodo dei Vescovi 1991: Assemblea Speciale per L'Europa* (Rome: La Civiltà Cattolica, 1992) is a detailed discussion of the European synod.

[28] In his aplett, "Tertio millennio adveniente," *AAS* 87 (1995) 30–31, Pope John Paul II announced his intention to convoke these synods. See Reese, 45, 47 for brief comments on the preparations for the synods for the Americas and Asia. The preliminary outline (*lineamenta*) for the American synod ("Encounter with the Living Jesus Christ: Way to Conversion, Communion and Solidarity") was published in *Origins* 26 (1996) 145–164. The *lineamenta* for the Asian synod ("Jesus Christ the Savior: Mission of Love and Service in Asia") appeared in *Origins* 26 (1997) 501–520.

[29] Most commentaries (J. Provost, in *CLSA Com*, 285; McGrath, in *CLSGBI Com*, 198; Gutiérrez, in *Pamplona ComEng*, 274) classify the Ukrainian synod of 1980 as a special synod. Johnson (*The Synod of Bishops: An Analysis*, 210–214) argues that it does not fit that category. There have recently been other synods of Eastern hierarchs: another synod of Ukrainian bishops in February 1991 and a synod of the Armenian Catholic Church in November, 1992.

[30] Cf. *AS* VII; *Ordo*, 5, §3.

synod as a *consilium* (advisory council) for the entire Church?[31] The synod exists to offer advice to the pope; how effective can such an institute be in addressing issues of concern to only some particular churches?[32] For example, if the bishops of the Netherlands had gathered in plenary council rather than in a special synod, they would have been capable of making decisions and issuing decrees, provided their acts received a papal *recognitio* (cf. cc. 445 and 446). Gathered in special synod, however, the bishops could in theory do no more than propose suggestions to the pope.[33]

Conclusion or Suspension of an Assembly

Canon 347 — §1. When the Roman Pontiff concludes a session of the synod of bishops, the function entrusted in it to the bishops and other members ceases.

§2. If the Apostolic See becomes vacant after a synod is convoked or during its celebration, the session of the synod and the function entrusted to its members are suspended by the law itself until the new Pontiff has decided to dissolve or continue the session.[34]

This canon deals with two ways in which a synod might come to an end. Canon 344, 6° and

particular law add a third. (1) When the pope convokes a session of the synod of bishops, he specifies the date on which the participants will convene and the date on which he anticipates the session will conclude.[35] When the synod completes its work on the assigned date, its participants with the exception of the members of the *consilium* (cf. c. 348, §1) cease to have any official status (*AS* XI). Although the synod itself is a permanent institute, membership in a synod is always *ad hoc*.

(2) When any diocese falls vacant, "nothing is to be altered" (c. 428, §1). When the Roman See falls vacant, the prohibition against innovations extends to the governance of the universal Church (c. 335). Even an ecumenical council, in which the college of bishops exercises its own supreme power over the universal Church (c. 337, §1), is suspended in the event of the pope's death (c. 340). It is therefore only logical that a session of the synod of bishops, one of whose principal functions is "to assist the Roman Pontiff," would come to a halt during the vacancy of the chair of Peter. Like the parallel canon concerning the ecumenical council (c. 340), paragraph two does not decree the *dissolution* of the synod. The new pontiff is free to decree its continuance; but he is also free to dissolve it or change the focus of its discussion. During the interval, those whose membership in the synod had received papal approval would continue to be members; and officers who had been appointed for the session would continue to be officers; but they would not function.

(3) Article 1, §7 of the *Ordo* notes that the pope has the authority "to transfer, suspend, and dissolve the synod."[36] The pope's authority over the synod is complete: if its activities no longer seem useful to him, he can simply decree that its session is at end. Were he to do so, the members and officers of the particular session would cease to be so.

---

[31] Cf. J. Beyer, "De synodi episcoporum natura melius determinanda," *P* 84 (1995) 615–616.

[32] Cf. J. Arrieta, "Circa la natura giuridica delle conferenze generali dell' episcopato latinoamericano," *Ius Ecclesiae* 5 (1993) 866.

[33] The synod actually issued, with formal papal approval, a substantial document—something of a joint pastoral letter: *AAS* 72 (1980) 215–232 (French text) and 232–250 (Dutch text). The European (cf. *Origins* 21 [1991] 457–465) and African (cf. *Origins* 24 [1994] 1–11) synods likewise issued final documents which do not appear to have been published in *AAS*.

[34] Article 17, §4 of the *Ordo* is slightly different: "If it should happen that the Supreme Pontiff departs this life after the convocation of a meeting of the Synod or during its celebration, the meeting is by that fact suspended until the new Pontiff has decreed that it is to be resumed or has convoked a new meeting." *AAS* 61 (1969) 533; *CLD* 7, 331.

[35] Cf., for example, Pope Paul VI, alloc "Il Cardinale," December 23, 1966, *AAS* 59 (1967) 54; the first synod was summoned for September 29, 1967, and its work was to be completed on October 24, 1967.

[36] *AAS* 661 (1969) 526; *CLD* 7, 323.

Secretariat of the Synod

Canon 348 — §1. The synod of bishops has a permanent general secretariat presided over by a general secretary who is appointed by the Roman Pontiff and assisted by the council of the secretariat. This council consists of bishops, some of whom are elected by the synod of bishops itself according to the norm of special law while others are appointed by the Roman Pontiff. The function of all these ceases when a new general session begins.

Apostolica sollicitudo XII had decreed that the institute would have "a permanent or general secretary, who will be provided with an appropriate number of assistants,"[37] but said nothing about his duties. The most recent version of the *Ordo* amply fills that *lacuna*.[38] The general secretary is appointed by the pope and serves at the pope's good pleasure (article 12, §1). He accordingly performs any tasks given him by the pope (§2). He participates in the sessions of the synod, directs the activities of the secretariat (§3), and chairs the council of the general secretariat (§4). With papal approval, he prepares the agenda for meetings of the council and reports to the pope about those meetings. He is responsible for communications from the pope to episcopal conferences and to other interested parties. He keeps curial officials, Eastern hierarchs, and presidents of episcopal conferences abreast of the activities of the synod. He fulfills any responsibilities assigned to him by the synod itself. He "collects, arranges, and preserves" the acts and documents of the synod. In fulfilling these responsibilities, he enjoys the services of assistants whom he can appoint with papal approval (§6).

One of the major conclusions of the 1969 first extraordinary synod of bishops was that the general secretariat needed reorganization in order to make both it and the synod more effective. The 1971 additions to the *Ordo* were intended to accomplish this end. Article 13 created a "council of the general secretariat" of the synod of bishops. It consists of fifteen members, twelve of whom are to be elected by the participants at the end of each general assembly.[39] The three remaining members are papal appointees. Because a large majority of the members of the council would be participants in the concluding session of the synod, they would be well positioned to assist in presenting to the pope the synod's recommendations and in implementing whatever he returned to them for execution. They would also be able to assist the general secretary in gathering suggestions from episcopal conferences and Eastern synods concerning possible topics for future synods and in preparing for the celebration of the next synod. The members of the council of the secretariat are not *ex officio* members of the succeeding assembly of the synod.[40]

§2. Furthermore, for each session of the synod of bishops one or more special secretaries are constituted who are appointed by the Roman Pontiff and remain in the office entrusted to them only until the session of the synod has been completed.

The special secretary is an expert in the matter to be discussed by a given assembly of the synod of bishops (*Ordo* 14, §1). The *Ordo* provides that one special secretary is to be appointed for each topic treated in a given session. The special secretary is heavily involved in the development of the synodal process. He assists the *relator*[41] in prepar-

---

[37] *AAS* 57 (1965) 779.

[38] The following comments on the role of the general secretary derive from article 12 of the "revised and augmented" *Ordo, AAS* 63 (1971) 702–704; *CLD* 7, 338–341.

[39] Article 13, §2 of the *Ordo* prescribes that the election of the council should take into account the geographical distribution of bishops. In practice this has meant electing three representatives from Europe, Africa, the Americas, and Asia/Oceania/Australia respectively.

[40] Cf. *AAS* 72 (1980) 767.

[41] The *relator* is a bishop appointed by the pope to prepare and read a preliminary report on the question(s) to be addressed by the synod. He assists the synod in coming to conclusions about its topic. Cf. *Ordo, 30.*

ing and presenting the preliminary report that commences the genuine work of each synod. If the delegated presidents decide that a special study commission is necessary to assist the synod in completing its work, the special secretary attends all meetings of that commission. After the participants have discussed the agenda, both in general assembly and in small, language-based discussion groups, they express their opinions in writing. It is the task of the special secretary to collect these observations and reduce them to some kind of order. A printed copy of his summary serves as the basis for the final voting of the assembly. After the work of the synod is concluded, the special secretary assists the general secretary in preparing a report on its labors and conclusions.

BIBLIOGRAPHY

Official Documents

Paul VI. *Mp Apostolica sollicitudo,* September 15, 1965. *AAS* 57 (1965) 775–780; *CLD* 6, 388–393.

Council for the Public Affairs of the Church. *Ordo Synodi Episcoporum Celebrandae Recognitus et Auctus,* June 24, 1969. *AAS* 61 (1969) 525–539; *CLD* 7, 323–337.

———. *Ordo Synodi Episcoporum Celebrandae Recognitus et Auctus nonnullis additamentis perficitur,* August 20, 1971. *AAS* 63 (1971) 702–704; *CLD* 7, 338–341.

Studies

Antón, A. "Episcoporum Synodus: Partes agens totius catholici episcopatus." *P* 57 (1968) 495–527.

———. *Primado y Colegialidad: Sus relaciones a la luz del primer Sinodo extraordinario.* Madrid: B.A.C., 1970.

Arrieta, J. "Lo sviluppo istituzionale del sinodo dei vescovi." *Ius Ecclesiae* 4 (1992) 342–348.

———. "Verso una collegialità piu effettiva nel sinodo dei vescovi." *La revista del clero italiano* 64 (1983) 290–302, 482–498, 562–576.

Aymans, W. "Kritische Erwägungen zum formalen Beschlussfassungsrecht der Bischofssynode." *AkK* 137 (1968) 125–138.

Bertrams, W. "Commentarium in Litteras Apostolicas 'Apostolica Sollicitudo' Papae Pauli VI." *P* 55 (1966) 115–132.

———. "De Synodi Episcoporum potestate cooperandi in exercitio potestatis primatialis." *P* 57 (1968) 528–540.

Beyer, J. "De Synodi Episcoporum natura melius determinanda." *P* 84 (1995) 609–626.

Fagiolo, V. "Il Synodus Episcoporum." *EIC* 25 (1969) 9–64.

Foley, D. *The Synod of Bishops: Its Canonical Structure and Proceedings.* Washington, D.C.: Catholic University of America, 1973.

Gutiérrez, J. L. "Chapter II: The Synod of Bishops." In *Pamplona ComEng,* 270–275.

Johnson, J. *The Synod of Bishops: An Analysis of Its Legal Development.* Washington, D.C.: Catholic University of America, 1986.

McGrath, A. "Chapter II: The Synod of Bishops." In *CLSGBI Com,* 196–200.

Provost, J. "Part II: The Hierarchical Constitution of the Church [cc. 330–572]." In *CLSA Com,* 258–310.

Rausch, T. "The Synod of Bishops: Improving the Synod Process." *J* 49 (1989) 248–257.

Reese, T. *Inside the Vatican: The Politics and Organization of the Catholic Church.* Cambridge, Mass.: Harvard University, 1996, 42–65.

Schotte, J. "The Synod of Bishops: A Permanent yet Adaptable Institution." *Stud Can* 26 (1992) 289–306.

Tomko, J., ed. *Il Sinodo dei Vescovi: Natura—Metodo—Perspettive.* Rome: Libreria Editrice Vaticana, 1985.

Trisco, R. "The Synod of Bishops and the Second Vatican Council." *AER* 157 (1967) 145–160.

Urru, A. "Istituti per l'esercizio della collegialità e del primato: Il concilio ecumenico e il sinodo dei vescovi." *ME* 115 (1990) 569–589.

Zurowski, M. "Synodus episcoporum in quantum 'partes agens totius catholici episcopatus.'" *P* 62 (1973) 375–391.

CHAPTER III
THE CARDINALS OF THE HOLY ROMAN
CHURCH
[cc. 349–359][1]

Unlike the recent institution of the synod of bishops, the college of cardinals is an ecclesiastical law institution with a long history of papal service. Although certain Eastern patriarchs may occasionally be members of this college, the cardinals are a distinctly Latin church phenomenon which is not treated in the Eastern code. While the synod of bishops has addressed various noteworthy postconciliar ecclesial concerns, the cardinals have continued to exercise significant ecclesial influence due to several factors.

First of all, the cardinals elect the pope, and most popes have come from their ranks. Second, contemporary popes, especially John Paul II, have increasingly sought their corporate counsel in addressing significant issues such as curial reform and Vatican finances. Third, as individuals, they occupy major curial positions and increasingly govern major sees around the world.

Before examining the canons on cardinals, this commentary will place them briefly in their proper historical context.[2]

Name

The term "cardinal" comes from the Latin word for hinge (*cardo*). In the early church a cleric was ordained to a particular post for life. This position was his "title" and he was called a "titular" there. If he changed his attachment from the title to which he was ordained to some other position, he was said to have been "incardinated" in the new position. This reflected the meaning of *cardo,* or hinge, that attaches a door to the wall. Such clergy were called "cardinals," not "titulars." The former term was used throughout the Western church and was accepted as a technical canonical term by the time of Pope Gregory the Great (590–604).

Some clerics were transferred (becoming "cardinals" instead of "titulars") because of their outstanding ability. Bishops, such as the bishop of Rome, wanted to utilize that ability; and gradually such clerics became pivotal episcopal aides (another meaning of *cardo*).

Roman liturgical practice influenced a unique use of "cardinal." Priests assigned to the various ancient house churches ("titles") were asked to provide liturgical services at the major shrines of the martyrs, e.g., the basilicas of Saints Peter, Paul, Mary Major, and the Lateran. When providing such services, these priests were known as "cardinals," for they were inserted there temporarily, acting outside their proper church or "title." This was the origin of today's "cardinal presbyters."

The bishops of the suburban towns around Rome performed episcopal services at the Lateran, the cathedral church of Rome. They were "titulars" in their own dioceses but "cardinals" when functioning liturgically at the Lateran. In addition to having a liturgical role, cardinals were increas-

[1] For some helpful canonical reflections on these canons see A. Abate, in *Urbaniana Com,* 207–212; J. Arrieta, "Il collegio cardinalizio," in *Diritto dell'Organizzazione Ecclesiastica* (Milan: Giuffré, 1997) 281–298; C. Fürst, in *Com Ex,* 626–641; J. Gutiérrez, in *Pamplona ComEng,* 275–283; P. Leisching, in *Handbuch,* 277–281; A. McGrath, in *CLSGBI Com,* 200–205; J. Provost, in *CLSA Com,* 286–292; J. Sanchez y Sanchez, in *Salamanca Com,* 202–208; R. Sobanski, "Il concilio ecumenico, il sinodo dei vescovi, il collegio cardinalizio," in *Collegialità e primato* (Bologna: Dehoniane, 1993) 112–120; O. Stoffel, in *Münster Com.* For some informative reflections of a political scientist, see also T. Reese, "The College of Cardinals," in *Inside the Vatican* (Cambridge: Harvard University, 1996) 66–105.

[2] See C. G. Fürst, *Cardinalis: Prolegomena zu einer Rechtsgeschichte des römischen Kardinalskollegiums* (Munich: W. Fink, 1967); S. Kuttner, *"Cardinalis:* The History of a Canonical Concept," *Traditio* 3 (1945) 129–214; P. van Lierde and A. Giraud, *What Is a Cardinal?* (New York: Hawthorn, 1964).

ingly consulted by the pope on various ecclesial issues. This was the origin of today's "cardinal bishops," who are attached to the seven suburbicarian sees around Rome.

Especially after the popes took over the civil governance of Rome, various social services were provided by deacons, who initially were direct papal aides attached to the Lateran palace. Later, however, they were also sent to *diaconiae* or social service centers throughout Rome, each with a chapel attached. Their significant role in administering church goods for the poor eventually gave rise to today's "cardinal deacons."

The aforementioned "cardinals" increasingly became the pope's pivotal aides in discharging his responsibilities as bishop of Rome and head of the college of bishops. They served as envoys in carrying out special papal commissions, including representing the pope at ecumenical councils.

Rise of the Cardinalate

The reform aspirations of the eleventh century popes led them to call various like-minded spirits to Rome where various churches were attributed to them without any burden of daily service. Such "cardinals" became the cornerstone of ecclesial reform. Presumably such a cadre of committed clergy would improve the pastoral life of Rome and carry the renewal of Christian life to other places in the Church.

A key development enhancing the status of this "college of cardinals" was a 1059 decree of Nicholas II on papal elections, attributing a key electoral role first to the cardinal bishops and then to the cardinal presbyters and deacons. The rest of the clergy and faithful were subsequently to ratify the election. In 1179 the Third Lateran Council determined the exclusive electoral competency of the cardinals without the other clergy and faithful.

Besides having this competency, the cardinals were increasingly involved in universal church governance to the point where some authors viewed them as sharing in the fullness of papal power and succeeding the apostolic college. However, canonists generally insisted that most of

their rights were derived from the pope even when the Roman See was vacant.[3]

Increasingly, from the late eleventh century, one notes the development of consistories, or meetings of the cardinals, during which the pope consulted them on various spiritual and temporal issues, e.g., choice of bishops, sending of papal legates, etc.

The cardinals' prestige was further enhanced because of their missions as papal legates, their receiving broad powers, and their participating in papal ceremonies. A significant development was the naming of abbots and residential bishops from outside Rome as cardinals. They enjoyed a certain precedence over other hierarchs including patriarchs.

Reforms of the College of Cardinals

Sixtus V (1585–1590) significantly reformed the college of cardinals. He fixed its number at seventy (see *CIC* 231, §1), specified various requirements to improve the quality of its members, and strove to internationalize it. Sixtus also reformed the Roman Curia, placing cardinals at the head of its fifteen congregations. Their importance was increasingly linked to this role, and the aforementioned consistories accordingly were much less influential than they had been from the twelfth to the sixteenth centuries.

The next significant change in the college of cardinals occurred only in the 1960s and 1970s although it was not discussed at Vatican II. Besides increasing the number of cardinals, John XXIII decreed that they all should be ordained bishops.[4] Paul VI reorganized the college's internal structure and imposed certain age restrictions.

---

[3] G. Alberigo, *Cardinalato e collegialità: Studi sull'ecclesiologia tra l'XI e il XIV secolo* (Florence: Vallecchi, 1969); Y. Congar, "Notes sur le destin de l'idée de collégialité épiscopale en occident au moyen âge (XIIe-XVIe siècles)," in *La collégialité épiscopale: Histoire et théologie,* 99–129 (Paris: Cerf, 1965).

[4] John XXIII, *mp Cum gravissima,* April 15, 1962, *CLD* 5, 273–274.

For example, cardinals at seventy-five years of age were obliged to resign from the various Roman curial dicasteries and other institutions which they headed. Furthermore, at eighty years of age they lost their offices in the Curia and in Vatican City and could no longer elect the pope.[5]

The 1983 code reflects many of these reforms, although it does not explicitly restate the age limit on papal electors, which is still operative. The code situates the cardinals between the synod of bishops (cc. 342–348) and the Roman Curia (cc. 360–361); all of these institutes can be understood properly only in light of special law governing them.

The code clarifies certain basic issues regarding membership in and the functioning of the college of cardinals. However, it generally leaves the details of its inner operations to its statutes or special law, contained particularly in contemporary papal documents mentioned in this commentary. This law retains its force unless it specifically contradicts the code. Frankly, it is not always clear why certain issues are treated in the code and not in special law, e.g., movement within cardinalatial ranks (c. 350, §§5–6).

The canons describe the notion and basic role of the college of cardinals, its triple ranks, certain movements from one rank to another, the creation of cardinals, the organization of the college (e.g., dean), resignation from curial leadership positions, and the cooperative relationship of cardinals with the pope.

The aforementioned changes in the status of cardinals are basically reaffirmed in post-1983 code documents of John Paul II such as the 1988 apostolic constitution *Pastor bonus* (Roman Curia reform) and the 1996 apostolic constitution *Universi Dominici gregis* (papal election).

College of Cardinals: Notion and Purpose

Canon 349 — The cardinals of the Holy Roman Church constitute a special college which pro-vides for the election of the Roman Pontiff according to the norm of special law. The cardinals assist the Roman Pontiff either collegially when they are convoked to deal with questions of major importance, or individually when they help the Roman Pontiff through the various offices they perform, especially in the daily care of the universal Church.**

This introductory constitutional canon describes the notion and three major functions of the college of cardinals. First of all (although Paul VI had considered possibly including certain members of the council of the synod in the papal electoral college),[6] the cardinals are exclusively competent to elect the pope according to special law.[7] Furthermore, they fulfill an interim governance role for the universal Church and Vatican City when the Apostolic See is vacant (see cc. 359, 335). In its own way the college of cardinals is both *Roman* and *universal* in character because of its ties (at least titular) to the various Roman churches and the fact that cardinals are chosen from around the world.

The cardinals also constitute a special advisory body that the pope consults regularly on significant ecclesial issues. Finally, they individually assist the pope in various ways, especially by heading special curial offices for universal church governance. This chapter explicates certain implications of the earlier cryptic reference to the cardinals' assisting the pope in various ways (c. 334).

Canon 349 modifies the 1917 code (*CIC* 230) in light of various contemporary *motu proprios*.

---

[5] Paul VI, *mp Sacro Cardinalis consilio*, February 26, 1965, *CLD* 6, 312–313; idem, *mp Ingravescentem aetatem*, November 21, 1970, *CLD* 7, 143–145.

[6] Sanchez y Sanchez, in *Salamanca Com*, 202–203.

[7] John Paul II, apconst *Universi Dominici gregis*, February 22, 1996, *AAS* 88 (1996) 305–343; Eng. trans.: *Origins* 25/37 (March 7, 1996) 617; 619–630. See J. Foster, "The Election of the Roman Pontiff: An Examination of Canon 332, §1 and Recent Special Legislation," *J* 56 (1996) 691–705; E. Williamson, "The Apostolic Constitution *Universi Dominici gregis*," *CLSGBIN* no. 109 (March 1997) 95–104; Reese, 74–105. The code does not include all the significant provisions of such special law, e.g., the limitation of the electoral college to 120 members (*Universi*, introduction).

The former code spoke only generically of the cardinals as papal counselors and assistants. The present code describes their functions more precisely. It refers to them as a "special college" rather than as the "senate of the Roman Pontiff," and especially mentions their responsibility to elect the pope.

The use of the term "college" rather than "senate" is noteworthy. In the Middle Ages some viewed the college of cardinals as succeeding not only the apostolic college, precisely as a college, but also the ancient Roman Senate in governing Rome, the Papal States, and the universal Church.[8] However, the revised code replaces this secular analogue with language which is more ecclesial than civil.

The phrase "college of cardinals" means a specific juridic collegial body, which functions under the leadership of the dean (c. 352, §1) according to the law on public collegiate juridic persons (cc. 115, §2; 116, §1). The cardinals assist the Roman Pontiff *collegially* by advising him on major ecclesial issues and *individually* by sharing in the daily care of the universal Church, e.g., service as papal legates (c. 358).

Cardinals advise the pope collegially especially in consistories (c. 353) and other general meetings, which John Paul II has convoked more frequently to revitalize the institution. Unlike the synod of bishops, which performs its generally consultative function on a temporary and occasional basis, the college of cardinals is available for such a role on a somewhat more permanent and ongoing basis.[9] The cardinals also head various curial offices or serve as members of various curial congregations for five-year terms (*PB* 5, 1) even if they primarily govern a particular church elsewhere in the world.

---

[8] C. Lefebvre, "Les origines et le rôle du cardinalat au moyen âge," *Apol* 41 (1968) 59–70.

[9] Interestingly enough, it is not only the whole college of cardinals that performs such a collegial consultative function. A papally appointed board of fifteen cardinals advises the pope on economic and organic matters pertaining to the administration of the Holy See (*PB* 24–25).

Ranks

Canon 350 — §1. The college of cardinals is divided into three orders: the episcopal order, to which belong cardinals to whom the Roman Pontiff assigns title of a suburbicarian church and Eastern patriarchs who have been brought into the college of cardinals; the presbyteral order; and the diaconal order.

§2. The Roman Pontiff assigns each of the cardinals of the presbyteral or diaconal orders his own title or *diaconia* in Rome.

§3. Eastern patriarchs who have been made members of the college of cardinals have their own patriarchal see as a title.

§4. The cardinal dean holds as his title the Diocese of Ostia together with the other church he already has as a title.

§5. Through a choice made in consistory and approved by the Supreme Pontiff and with priority of order and promotion observed, cardinals from the presbyteral order can transfer to another title, and cardinals from the diaconal order to another *diaconia* and if they have been in the diaconal order for ten full years, even to the presbyteral order.

§6. A cardinal transferring through choice from the diaconal order to the presbyteral order takes precedence over all those cardinal presbyters who were brought into the cardinalate after him.

Canon 351 on eligibility to be a cardinal, the exclusive papal choice of cardinals, and the mode of announcing such a choice presumably should have preceded this canon on the organization of the college of cardinals. However, such is not the case.

Although all cardinals are to be bishops (unless dispensed) and hence are basically equal (c. 351, §1), they are ranked within the college of cardinals in terms of the three clerical ranks of bishop, presbyter, and deacon. This division reflects the college's historical roots in the Roman presbyterate,[10] a purely formal relationship with-

---

[10] See introductory historical material at the beginning of this chapter. During the code revision process John Paul

out juridical implications. Rather than reflecting a true communion of ministerial orders, which was true when the college contained bishops, priests, and deacons, the present organization more notably expresses episcopal collegiality.

Cardinal presbyters or deacons may opt to change the church or *diaconia* to which they are assigned, and the latter may move from the rank of deacon to that of presbyter. They are to do so in consistory (c. 353) and such a change requires papal approval. Considerations of seniority in terms of ordination and promotion to the college are especially relevant here. This is probably the only instance in the code of one's acquiring a right by declaration with papal approval.

This canon reflects former provisions on the organization of the college and possible options within it (*CIC* 231, 236), as modified by John XXIII[11] and Paul VI.[12]

There are two types of cardinal *bishops:* those appointed by the pope to one of the seven suburbicarian dioceses surrounding Rome and Eastern patriarchs named to the college. Some have questioned whether patriarchs ought to belong to such a quintessentially Roman institution. However, they keep the title of their patriarchal church, giving some indication of their special status within the college and embodying a concern to respond to such criticism. Furthermore, they do not vote for the cardinal dean (c. 352, §2).

Seven suburbicarian sees surround Rome: Albano, Ostia, Porto and Santa Rufina, Palestrina, Sabina and Mentana, Frascati, and Velletri. Cardinal bishops are appointed to six of these; in addition to his titular see, the cardinal dean holds title to the see of Ostia (c. 350, §4). Interestingly enough, the honorary title gives the cardinal no legal-pastoral authority over the suburbicarian see

(c. 357, §1); rather, another bishop provides pastoral care for its people.[13]

Since the 1961 *motu proprio Ad suburbicarias dioceses* of John XXIII, cardinal presbyters may not opt to become cardinal bishops, who are named solely by the pope.

Cardinal *presbyters* are assigned one of the *tituli* (titular churches) in Rome; this is perhaps the clearest symbol of the college's historic tie to the Roman church. In consistory cardinal presbyters can later opt to change to a vacant title with papal approval. Like cardinal bishops, cardinal presbyters have no legal-pastoral authority in their titular church (c. 357, §1), but they are expected to support it financially.[14] The largest number of cardinals are cardinal presbyters, and this number has varied most significantly throughout history.

Cardinal *deacons* are assigned one of the *diaconiae* or aid stations that used to be staffed by deacons in early medieval Rome. Their relationship to the church is the same as that of the other cardinals (c. 357, §1). Cardinal deacons are curial officials and prior to 1965 were often not bishops. In consistory and with papal approval they can change the *diaconia* to which they are assigned; and, after ten years as a cardinal deacon, they may become cardinal presbyters. If they do so, they outrank cardinal presbyters who were named after the former were named cardinal deacons.

While the number of cardinals has varied historically, the former code, like Sixtus V (1586), fixed their number at seventy: six bishops, fifty presbyters, and fourteen deacons (*CIC* 231, §1). However, since John XXIII there has been no maximum number, although since Paul VI only 120 may vote in the papal election. Presumably this figure sufficiently represents the Church's universality in such a central decisional process.[15]

II rejected a proposal to drop this traditional threefold distinction because of its contemporary inappropriateness despite its historic origins. See *Comm* 14 (1982) 182.

[11] John XXIII, *mp Ad suburbicarias dioceses,* March 10, 1961, *CLD* 5, 275–276.

[12] Paul VI, *mp Ad purpuratorum patrum,* February 11, 1965, *CLD* 6, 310–311.

[13] John XXIII, *mp Suburbicariis sedibus,* April 11, 1962, *CLD* 5, 270–272.

[14] Paul VI, *mp Ad hoc usque tempus,* April 15, 1969, *CLD* 7, 146–147.

[15] Paul VI, *mp Romano Pontifici eligendo,* October 1, 1975, *CLD* 8, 146. For the current law, see introduction

Creation of Cardinals

Canon 351 — §1. The Roman Pontiff freely selects men to be promoted as cardinals, who have been ordained at least into the order of the presbyterate and are especially outstanding in doctrine, morals, piety, and prudence in action; those who are not yet bishops must receive episcopal consecration.

§2. Cardinals are created by a decree of the Roman Pontiff which is made public in the presence of the college of cardinals. From the moment of the announcement they are bound by the duties and possess the rights defined by law.

§3. When the Roman Pontiff has announced the selection of a person to the dignity of cardinal but reserves the name of the person *in pectore*, the one promoted is not bound in the meantime by any of the duties of cardinals nor does he possess any of their rights. After the Roman Pontiff has made his name public, however, he is bound by the same duties and possesses the same rights; he possesses the right of precedence, though, from the day of reservation *in pectore*.

Cardinals are freely chosen by the pope without any juridic claims by states or particular episcopal sees. Prescinding from whatever consultation actually occurs, the pope is not required to consult any group or individual. Nor, as noted above, is there any fixed number of cardinals.

The canon simplifies the former code (*CIC* 232–233) and reflects John XXIII's *motu proprio Cum gravissima*.[16]

The qualifications of cardinals are stated broadly (§1). The 1917 code contained more detailed requirements, such as the exclusion of those

not of legitimate birth or subject to various irregularities (*CIC* 232, §2). These requirements reflected efforts to address difficulties prompted by the unwarranted influence of members of the college or secular authorities.

To be eligible one must be at least a priest and characterized by outstanding doctrinal gifts, moral character, and practical administrative and pastoral experience. This latter point is particularly significant given the college's important consultative role. Furthermore, since the time of John XXIII, cardinals are generally to be bishops; hence the qualifications for bishops also seem pertinent. For example, one must be at least thirty-five years old, five years ordained, and expert in the sacred sciences even if lacking a doctorate or a licentiate (c. 378, §1). Occasionally the pope dispenses from such qualifications; for example, certain cardinals have been dispensed from becoming bishops, e.g., theologians Hans Urs von Balthasar, Yves Congar, Henri de Lubac. Interestingly enough, today such cardinal presbyters would not automatically have a deliberative vote at an ecumenical council as was the case in the 1917 code (c. 339, §1; *CIC* 223, §1, 1°).

The choice of cardinals seems to reflect a concern for a body representative of both older established churches and younger churches. Among those named cardinals one notes especially heads of prominent sees such as New York or Paris, significant curial officials, and those who have served in the Vatican diplomatic corps. Certain Eastern patriarchs may also be named cardinals.

The pope formally announces the new cardinals in a consistory with the existing members of the college of cardinals (§2). Occasionally he may withhold the name of one selected for the college, keeping it in his heart (*in pectore*), perhaps because of Church-State conflicts rendering such an announcement inappropriate at a given time (§3).

Such an announcement of new cardinals takes place in a secret consistory. This reflects the time when the college served as the papal court and appointments to the cardinalatial dignity were subject to debate and required the consent of the col-

to *Universi*. According to the 1997 *Annuario Pontificio* there were 6 cardinal bishops, 128 cardinal priests, and 17 cardinal deacons, making a total of 151 cardinals. However, on January 18, 1998 John Paul II named 22 new cardinals, temporarily waiving the papal elector limit of 120 since there were then 123 potential electors. See *Origins* 27/32 (January 29, 1998) 530.

[16] John XXIII, *mp Cum gravissima,* April 15, 1962, *CLD* 5, 273–274.

lege. Today this is more of a formality. The subsequent formal public consistory involves conferring the ring and the biretta and assigning a titular church or *diaconia.*

From the moment of the aforementioned announcement, the new cardinals enjoy the full rights of cardinals, including that of electing the pope. They also assume various obligations specified in the code (e.g., cc. 354; 356) and in special law. Those whose names are not published, however, neither possess cardinalatial rights nor are bound by their duties. If the pope dies without revealing their names, the appointment ceases. If, however, he later reveals their names, those cardinals enjoy the rights of precedence as if their names had been published on the date the appointment *in pectore* was announced.

The code no longer lists in detail here various obligations and privileges of cardinals (*CIC* 234–235, 239).[17] However, certain prerogatives of cardinals in the code might be mentioned. They are personally exempt from the jurisdiction of local bishops (c. 357, §2). They have the unrestricted faculty to hear confessions everywhere in the world (c. 967, §1). They may be buried in their church (c. 1242). The pope alone may judge them in formal processes (c. 1405, §1, 2°), and they may choose the place where they testify in such processes (c. 1558, §2).

Dean of the College

Canon 352 — §1. The dean presides over the college of cardinals; if he is impeded, the assistant dean takes his place. Neither the dean nor the assistant dean possesses any power of governance over the other cardinals but is considered as first among equals.

§2. When the office of dean is vacant, the cardinals who possess title to a suburbicarian church and they alone are to elect one from their own group who is to act as dean of the college; the assistant dean, if he is present, or else the oldest among them, presides at this election. They are to submit the name of the person elected to the Roman Pontiff who is competent to approve him.

§3. The assistant dean is elected in the same manner as that described in §2, with the dean himself presiding. The Roman Pontiff is also competent to approve the election of the assistant dean.

§4. If the dean and assistant dean do not have a domicile in Rome, they are to acquire one there.

As a collegial juridic person (c. 115, §2) the college of cardinals has its own officials. Chief among these are the dean and assistant dean, whose election is provided for in this canon, which revises the former law (*CIC* 237).

Paul VI[18] changed the former provision whereby the dean was automatically the cardinal who had been cardinal bishop the longest. Now the selection is by vote, but the vote and the candidates are restricted to the cardinals who have a title to a suburbicarian diocese without any other restrictions. Hence the cardinals who are patriarchs may not vote in such an election or be elected dean. The election must be approved by the pope. The same provisions govern the election of the assistant dean.

Thereafter the dean and assistant dean must reside in Rome, the seat of the college as a juridic person. Such residence should facilitate their discharging various functions in the college of cardinals—with the dean serving as first among equals without any juridic power over his peers. The dean ex officio holds title to the see of Ostia as well as his other titular see (c. 350, §4).

Besides carrying out the various internal functions within the college that are governed by its own norms, the dean has several key responsibili-

---

[17] H. Hynes, *The Privileges of Cardinals—Commentary with Historical Notes* (Washington, D.C.: Catholic University of America, 1945). Many of these privileges are irrelevant today given the significant postconciliar enhancement of the episcopal office.

[18] Paul VI, *mp Sacro Cardinalium consilio,* February 26, 1965, *CLD* 6, 312–313.

ties when the Apostolic See is vacant.[19] For example, he convenes the general congregations, or regular meetings of the cardinals, prior to the conclave that elects the new pope (*Universi* 9) and sends the official notice to all the cardinals to come to the conclave (*Universi* 19). If he is not over eighty years old himself, he also chairs the conclave (e.g., *Universi* 53, 87). Otherwise the assistant dean takes his place in the conclave. If he, too, is over eighty, then the cardinal elector who is first in rank and age takes their place. If the dean is in the conclave, he has the right to consecrate the newly elected pope if the one elected is not already a bishop (c. 355, §1).

Consistories[20]

Canon 353 — §1. The cardinals especially assist the supreme pastor of the Church through collegial action in consistories in which they are gathered by order of the Roman Pontiff who presides. Consistories are either ordinary or extraordinary.

§2. For an ordinary consistory, all the cardinals, at least those present in Rome, are called together to be consulted concerning certain grave matters which occur rather frequently or to carry out certain very solemn acts.

§3. For an extraordinary consistory, which is celebrated when particular needs of the Church or the treatment of more grave affairs suggests it, all the cardinals are called together.

§4. Only the ordinary consistory in which some solemnities are celebrated can be public, that is, when prelates, representatives of civil societies, and others who have been invited to it are admitted in addition to the cardinals.

---

[19] For a somewhat more detailed treatment of the role of the dean and other officials such as the cardinal camerlengo (chamberlain) of the Roman church and the cardinal camerlengo (chamberlain) of the college of cardinals, see Arrieta, 290–293.

[20] For some informative comments on consistories, see Arrieta, 293–295, and Reese, 69–74. The latter offers some helpful information regarding the format of consistories, which the code does not mention.

This canon deals with a significant way in which the cardinals assist the pope collegially in governing the universal Church, i.e., through various consistories. A consistory is a formal gathering of the college of cardinals, chaired by the pope, which has a couple of forms, i.e., ordinary (generally secret but sometimes public) and extraordinary. The topics addressed by such consistories have been determined by tradition, changing pastoral practice, and the college's internal regulations.

Originally the papal consistory was a meeting characterized by open discussion between the pope and the cardinals. However, such consistories gradually became highly formalized events like European royal court ceremonies and served more of a ceremonial than a genuinely consultative purpose.

The 1917 code did not describe consistories. This new canon may reflect an effort to revitalize a consultative institution whose functioning had become somewhat *pro forma* over the years. Although the synods of bishops frequently address noteworthy ecclesial issues, John Paul II has increasingly consulted the college of cardinals on diverse matters of universal church governance. Actually, the precise rationale for the pope's consulting the synod on certain issues and consistories of cardinals on others is not entirely clear.

The new organization of consistories envisions both ordinary and extraordinary sessions, although there is not always an appreciable difference between the two.

Ordinary consistories deal with serious but regularly recurring issues or carry out certain more solemn acts, e.g., creation of new cardinals or canonization of saints. At least all the cardinals resident in Rome must be invited to be present for such a consistory.

Extraordinary consistories are held when the special pastoral, organizational, and governmental needs of the Church suggest it, e.g., Roman Curia reform or Vatican finances. Or, on occasion, it may be necessary to deal with more serious and pressing affairs. John Paul II has held such consistories more frequently than his immediate predecessors.[21] All the cardinals are to be called to an extraordinary consistory, even those living outside Rome (*PB* 23).

Normally a consistory is held in secret although the press, various civil and ecclesiastical dignitaries, and the public at large can be invited to certain ordinary consistories, e.g., those involving canonizations, the conferral of the pallium,[22] or the public celebration of the creation of new cardinals.

Resignation from Curial Offices

Canon 354 — The cardinals who preside over dicasteries and other permanent institutes of the Roman Curia and Vatican City and who have completed the seventy-fifth year of age are asked to submit their resignation from office to the Roman Pontiff who will see to the matter after considering the circumstances.

This canon does not concern resignation from the college of cardinals.[23] Rather it states that cardinals presiding over curial dicasteries and other permanent institutions are subject to the regulations that apply to other curial officers concerning resignation at age seventy-five (*PB* 5, 2).

The code treats this issue in a manner comparable to that of the resignation of bishops (cc. 401, 411) and pastors (c. 538, §3) at age seventy-five. Such officials are requested to submit their resignation; however, they do not automatically lose their office because an age limit has been reached

(c. 184, §1). Furthermore, they actually lose their office only after the competent authority (i.e., the pope vis-à-vis cardinals) communicates it in writing (c. 186, §1). The competent authority is also to see to the provision of appropriate support for the retiree (c. 281).

This innovation was introduced by Paul VI in the *motu proprio Ingravescentem aetatem*.[24] That document also prescribed that when cardinals reach the age of eighty, they automatically cease being members of curial congregations (*PB* 5, 2) and can no longer be electors for a new pope (*Universi* 33). Aging cardinals would presumably be unduly burdened by such weighty deliberations although they may participate in pre-conclave discussions (*Universi*, Introduction). The code commission debated this matter at some length during the 1981 plenary session and finally decided not to include this latter provision in the code but to leave it to the special law on cardinals.[25] Again one wonders why certain provisions on cardinals are placed in the code and others in special law.

Functions of Cardinal Dean/ Senior Cardinal Deacon

Canon 355 — §1. The cardinal dean is competent to ordain as a bishop the one elected as Roman Pontiff if he needs to be ordained; if the dean is impeded, the assistant dean has the same right, and if he is impeded, the oldest cardinal from the episcopal order.

§2. The senior cardinal deacon announces the name of the newly elected Supreme Pontiff to the people; likewise, in the place of the Roman Pontiff, he places the pallium upon metropolitans or hands it over to their proxies.

The college of cardinals has a special relationship with the pope. The next five canons (cc. 355–359) spell out certain aspects of this relationship regarding the election of the pope, personal

---

[21] Reese identifies six such extraordinary consistories, the first being held in November 1979 and the most recent in June 1994. They have considered such issues as Roman Curia reform, Vatican finances, the reform of the code, threats to human life, the emergence of sects, and preparation for the millennium (Reese, 71).

[22] See the commentary on c. 437.

[23] The code does not address the issue of one's ceasing to be a cardinal, but *Universi* 36 on papal electors mentions the exclusion of cardinals who have been canonically deposed (presumably dismissed from the clerical state) or whose resignation as cardinals has been accepted by the pope.

[24] Paul VI, *mp Ingravescentem aetatem*, November 21, 1970, *CLD* 7, 143-145.

[25] *Plen*, 374–376.

contact with him, special missions the cardinals perform on his behalf, and their role when the Apostolic See is vacant. In light of this relationship, cardinals also enjoy a special personal exemption from the jurisdiction of local bishops.

These canons simplify the 1917 code (*CIC* 239, §§2 and 3; 240; and 241) in light of *motu proprios* of John XXIII[26] and Paul VI.[27]

Canon 355 restates the ancient privilege of the dean of the college to consecrate the one elected pope if he is not already a bishop; it also provides for the situation where the dean may be impeded from doing so (§1; *Universi* 88–90). The canon also affirms that the senior cardinal deacon has the privilege of announcing the election of a pope (§2; *Universi* 89). Furthermore, in the pope's absence the senior cardinal deacon bestows the pallium on metropolitans, or archbishops who head an ecclesiastical province (cc. 435–438), or gives it to their proxies. This ritual symbolizes the communion between the Roman See and ecclesiastical provinces around the world (see c. 437).

Cooperation of Cardinals with Pope

Canon 356 — Cardinals are obliged to cooperate assiduously with the Roman Pontiff; therefore, cardinals who exercise any office in the curia and who are not diocesan bishops are obliged to reside in Rome. Cardinals who have the care of some diocese as the diocesan bishop are to go to Rome whenever the Roman Pontiff calls them.

Cardinals are to share the pope's solicitude for the universal Church in various ways, collegial and individual. While canon 353 on consistories focuses on collegial assistance, this canon seems to emphasize individual cooperation with the pope. To assure that cardinals may "cooperate assiduously" with him, they have been traditionally required to reside in Rome unless they are diocesan bishops

[26] John XXIII, *mp Suburbicariis sedibus,* April 11, 1962, *CLD* 5, 270–272.
[27] Paul VI, *mp Ad hoc usque tempus,* April 15, 1969, *CLD* 7, 146–147.

elsewhere. However, even such bishops formerly had to obtain the pope's permission to leave Rome when they came to the city (*CIC* 238).

That provision is now somewhat revised, and the present canon expresses a concern to revitalize the college and ensure cardinals' availability to assist the pope. Cardinals exercising a curial office who are not diocesan bishops must reside in Rome; however, retired curial cardinals are not so obliged. Furthermore, cardinals who are diocesan bishops do not have the same obligation, given their primary duty to reside in their dioceses (c. 395). However, they must come to Rome whenever the pope calls them, be it for a consistory or for curial service. Indeed, the assignment of titular churches symbolizes their ongoing tie to the church of Rome, although the former legal fiction that they are part of the Roman clergy is no longer operative.

Relationship to Titular Church/ Personal Exemption

Canon 357 — §1. The cardinals who have been assigned title to a suburbicarian church or a church in Rome are to promote the good of these dioceses or churches by counsel and patronage after they have taken possession of them. Nevertheless, they possess no power of governance over them nor are they to intervene in any way in those matters which pertain to the administration of their goods, their discipline, or the service of the churches.

§2. In those matters which pertain to their own person, cardinals living outside of Rome and outside their own diocese are exempt from the power of governance of the bishop of the diocese in which they are residing.

Unlike the former code (*CIC* 240), the current code stipulates that cardinals have no pastoral jurisdiction, spiritual or temporal, in their titular churches in Rome or in the suburbicarian dioceses. In fact, despite certain honorary prerogatives, they are explicitly prohibited from interfering in the governance of such churches, which is the prerogative of the competent authority, e.g., the cardinal vicar of Rome. However, their titular relationship requires that they foster the well-being of such churches after formally taking possession of them (§1).

Given the significant ecclesial role of cardinals, when they are outside Rome and outside their own dioceses if they are diocesan bishops, they are personally exempt from the local episcopal authority (§2). This exemption is not as broad as the liturgical privileges that cardinals formerly enjoyed (*CIC* 239, §1), although some of those privileges are now part of the expanded competency of diocesan bishops. The exemption corresponds more to the general norm that pastoral activities in a diocese are always subject to the diocesan bishop although some persons may be exempt from his authority in their personal lives. For example, members of religious institutes enjoy an appropriate autonomy of life (c. 586, §1) while still being subject to the diocesan bishop in certain pastoral, liturgical, and educational matters (c. 678, §1).

Special Missions for the Pope

Canon 358 — A cardinal to whom the Roman Pontiff entrusts the function of representing him in some solemn celebration or among some group of persons as a *legatus a latere,* that is, as his alter ego, as well as one to whom the Roman Pontiff entrusts the fulfillment of a certain pastoral function as his special envoy (*missus specialis*) has competence only over those things which the Roman Pontiff commits to him.

In addition to relying on the regular and stable service of pontifical legates, who are treated in canons 362–367, the pope often entrusts special temporary missions to individual cardinals. The former code addressed this matter, perhaps more logically, in the chapter on such legates (*CIC* 266).

Canon 358 specifies two types of missions, only the first of which was in the former code. One is more ceremonial in nature (*legatus a latere,* literally, a legate from the side [of the pope], or his alter ego), e.g., a cardinal representing the pope at a eucharistic congress. The other is more pastoral in nature (*missus specialis,* or one especially sent), e.g., a cardinal representing the pope in a situation such as that in Bosnia, where political conflict jeopardizes the Church's task of evangelization. Both types of envoys enjoy only the authority granted them by the pope for the given task.

Vacancy of Apostolic See

Canon 359 — When the Apostolic See is vacant, the college of cardinals possesses only that power in the Church which is attributed to it in special law.

During the vacancy of the Apostolic See, the college of cardinals has a special role in ensuring a certain continuity in universal church governance (see c. 335). It exercises this temporary governance role in accord with special law, e.g., especially the 1996 apostolic constitution *Universi Dominici gregis.*

Given the general prohibition of any innovations during a vacant see (cc. 335; 428, §1), the role of the college is a limited one, and it must strictly comply with the special law governing that situation.[28] Neither the college of bishops nor the college of cardinals possesses primatial power at this time.

The cardinals have no power regarding matters within the exclusive competence of the pope dur-

---

[28] See *Universi* 1–32 on the vacancy of the Holy See. Norms 1–6 govern the competence of the college of cardinals. Norms 7–13 regulate the composition and specific functions of pre-conclave congregations, or meetings, of cardinals. Norms 14–26 provide for the functioning of certain necessary curial offices, e.g., that of the cardinal chamberlain of the holy Roman church, who handles various practical details related to the death and funeral of the pope and safeguards and administers the goods and temporal rights of the Holy See. These norms also provide for the exercise of certain faculties by the curial dicasteries (e.g., congregations, councils, tribunals, offices, etc.—*PB* 2) during the vacancy. Norms 27–32 deal with the deceased pope.

ing his lifetime. Rather, they are limited to dealing with ordinary ecclesiastical business, treating non-deferrable matters, and preparing for the conclave.

They may not change the papal election norms or any other papal norms. They may not make decisions binding a future pope. They are not to prejudice the rights of the Apostolic See or the diocese of Rome. They are competent, however, to resolve questions about the meaning of *Universi Dominici gregis* by majority vote. They may also decide by majority vote matters viewed as urgent by the majority (c. 119, 2°). They also possess all the civil power of the pope concerning the government of Vatican City State, yet they can issue pertinent decrees only in emergency situations.

CHAPTER IV
THE ROMAN CURIA
[cc. 360–361]

Canon 360 — The Supreme Pontiff usually conducts the affairs of the universal Church through the Roman Curia which performs its function in his name and by his authority for the good and service of the churches. The Roman Curia consists of the Secretariat of State or the Papal Secretariat, the Council for the Public Affairs of the Church, congregations, tribunals, and other institutes; the constitution and competence of all these are defined in special law.

Canon 361 — In this Code, the term Apostolic See or Holy See refers not only to the Roman Pontiff but also to the Secretariat of State, the Council for the Public Affairs of the Church, and other institutes of the Roman Curia, unless it is otherwise apparent from the nature of the matter or the context of the words.

Introduction

Significant officeholders often need the assistance of others in discharging their responsibilities. There is and has been great diversity in the ways of rendering such assistance. The matter

may be left to the officeholder's discretion, but more often the law specifies detailed supportive structures in order to foster the common good.

Despite the Church's primarily supernatural dimension, its distinctly human character makes it subject to human variables in carrying out its mission in space and time. The bishops as successors of the apostles continue Christ's threefold mission in collaboration with others, e.g., the diocesan curia (cc. 469–494).

This is also true for the pope who, as bishop of Rome and successor of Peter, has distinctive spiritual and temporal responsibilities. In discharging their expanding responsibilities, popes have increasingly required the collaboration of others, which has been gradually systematized historically on a permanent and stable basis in the Roman Curia (henceforth Curia).

The 1917 code treated the Curia's structure and competency in some detail while not mentioning its purpose (*CIC* 242–264). However, canons 360–361 sketch only its basic nature, purpose, and structure while most details are left to special law. According to canon 360, which has no Eastern code counterpart, the Curia is an instrument enabling the pope to deal with various issues affecting the universal Church.

The Curia is expected to serve the good of the particular churches (c. 368);[29] it acts in the pope's name and by his authority. When the code was promulgated in 1983, the Curia essentially encompassed the Secretariat of State, the Council for the Public Affairs of the Church, the congregations, tribunals, and other institutes (c. 360). However, the code's terminology here needs to be updated slightly in light of post-1983 code curial developments, especially the 1988 apostolic constitution of John Paul II, *Pastor bonus.*[30] The Curia's rich

---

[29] *Christus Dominus* 9 spoke explicitly also of curial service of the bishops, who head and represent their particular churches in the communion of churches. This motif is crucial in properly evaluating contemporary curial reform.

[30] For the original text of *Pastor bonus,* see *AAS* 80 (1988) 841–934; for an unofficial English translation see *Pamplona ComEng,* 1166–1279. For some helpful canonical

and varied history, its successes and failures reflect various reform efforts with successive curial forms embryonically contained in their predecessors.

It is important to have some understanding of the Curia's history and operations. Hence this introduction briefly discusses that history, especially during the twentieth century. The bulk of this commentary will briefly describe the various curial dicasteries in light of the 1983 code, but especially in terms of *Pastor bonus*. Occasional reference will be made to the 1992 *Regolamento* governing the operation of the curial dicasteries.[31]

reflections on canons 360–361 but especially on *Pastor bonus,* see W. Aymans and K. Mörsdorf, *Kanonisches Recht: Lehrbuch aufgrund des Codex Iuris Canonici, Band II: Verfassungs- und Vereinigungsrecht* (Paderborn: Schöningh, 1997) 242–264. In preparing these reflections the author found especially helpful V. De Paolis, "La Curia Romana secondo la costituzione *Pastor Bonus,*" in *Collegialità e primato* (Bologna: Dehoniane, 1993) 125–187. See also G. Ghirlanda, *Il diritto nella Chiesa mistero di comunione* (Rome: Edizioni Paoline, 1990) 519–526; D. Gutiérrez, in *Valencia Com,* 189–190; J. Gutiérrez, in *Pamplona ComEng,* 283–287; McGrath, in *CLSGBI Com,* 206; Stoffel, in *Münster Com* at cc. 360–361; A. Viana, in *Com Ex* II/1, 646–655. For the most extensive reflections on *Pastor bonus,* see P. Bonnet and C. Gullo, ed., *La Curia Romana nella Cost. Ap. Pastor Bonus (La Curia Romana)* (Vatican City: Libreria Editrice Vaticana, 1990). For helpful reflections on canons 360–361 written in light of the 1967 apostolic constitution *Regimini Ecclesiae Universae,* see Gutiérrez, in *Pamplona ComEng,* 267–269; I. Perez de Heredia y Valle, in *Handbuch,* 281–295; Provost, in *CLSA Com,* 292–300; Sanchez y Sanchez, in *Salamanca Com,* 208–210; A. Sousa Costa, in *Urbaniana Com,* 213–214. For some informative reflections on the Curia by a political scientist, see T. Reese, *Inside the Vatican* (Cambridge: Harvard University, 1996) 106–139 (especially); 140–172; 202–229. For a helpful overview of the competencies of the various Roman dicasteries, see "The Roman Curia," in *Official Catholic Directory 1998* (New Providence, N.J.: Kenedy, 1997) A-29/A-31.

[31] Secretariat of State, *Regolamento Generale della Curia Romana,* February 4, 1992, *AAS* 84 (1992) 201–267. This document is divided into two general parts: personnel and structure of curial dicasteries (arts. 1–81) and general procedural norms (arts. 82–127). Regrettably, no English translation is yet available.

History of the Curia[32]

The basic curial structure today can be traced to the following popes:

(a) Sixtus V: January 22, 1588 constitution *Immensa aeterni Dei.*

(b) Pius X: June 29, 1908 constitution *Sapienti consilio.*

(c) Paul VI: August 15, 1967 constitution *Regimini.*

(d) John Paul II: June 28, 1988 constitution *Pastor bonus.*

After a few words about the first three constitutions, we will briefly note the significant theological-juridical principles underlying *Pastor bonus,* some of its key organizational norms, and certain details about the individual curial dicasteries and comparable institutions.

a. *Sixtus V:* Immensa aeterni Dei *(1588)*

Sixtus did not create the Curia, since there was a pre-existing complex of papal collaborators in liturgical, administrative, and judicial matters somewhat comparable to the imperial court. Such collaborators (particularly cardinals) aided the pope in governing the diocese of Rome and the universal Church, especially as church governance became increasingly centralized during the second millennium.

Sixtus V systematized the work of the various congregations of cardinals which operated permanently or temporarily in a fragmentary or partial fashion. Besides setting up a "college of cardinals," he created smaller "colleges" to deal with specific issues. To cope with the burdens of his office, he sought the assistance of others and carefully delineated their responsibilities.

[32] For a slightly more detailed curial history see J. Provost, in *CLSA Com,* 292–294. For a rather extensive history, see N. del Re, *La Curia Romana: Lineamenti storico-giuridici,* 3rd rev. ed. (Rome: Ed. di Storia e Letteratura, 1970). See also J. Sanchez y Sanchez, "La Curia Romana hasta Pablo VI," *REDC* 32 (1976) 439–458; A. Stickler, "Le riforme della Curia nella storia della Chiesa," in *La Curia Romana,* 1–15.

b. Pius X: Sapienti consilio *(1908)*

Despite certain curial developments after Sixtus, the next significant curial reform did not occur for three centuries. The curial reorganization of Pius X was largely incorporated in the 1917 code. Despite the historical organizational variables, there was one constant factor: the Curia was a complex of dicasteries aiding the pope in governing the universal Church. Furthermore, the Curia encompassed congregations (*CIC* 246–257), tribunals (*CIC* 258–259), and offices (*CIC* 260–264).

c. Paul VI: Regimini *(1967)*

Ecclesial changes influenced especially by two world wars and the experience of Vatican II prompted further curial reform. For example, there had been a significant conciliar critique of the Curia, especially in light of the emerging themes of collegiality, the enhanced role of the laity, and the Curia's mission to serve the bishops, the particular churches, and the universal Church. Papal and collegial power needed to be integrated better in an era of more decentralized governance structures (*CD* 9).

In *Regimini* Paul VI basically maintained the traditional curial structure of congregations, tribunals, and offices but also dropped certain older entities and added secretariats. He defined more clearly curial competencies and procedures and facilitated the coordination of the various dicasteries. He appointed certain diocesan bishops to curial positions to internationalize the Curia and specified five-year terms and age limits for key curialists. The Secretariat of State and the Council for the Public Affairs of the Church assumed especially significant roles.

Regimini was the basis for John Paul II's distinctive curial reorganization initiatives, which ultimately led to the promulgation of *Pastor bonus* in 1988. A key feature of *Pastor bonus* was its effort to offer a theological-juridical rationale for the Curia within the context of the communion of churches and episcopal collegiality.[33]

---

[33] For a thoughtful critique of *Pastor bonus* given its own stated goals and the curial reform expectations of the

Such a rationale preceded the detailed organizational norms.

d. Theological and Juridical Principles in Pastor bonus

Whatever may be the historic and continuing tensions between the particular churches and the Curia, *Pastor bonus* highlights its pastoral character rooted in the ecclesial service calling of Peter and his successors.

The pope's primatial office entails service of the universal Church, the particular churches, and the individual faithful. His task is especially to foster the unity of the diverse ministerial functions in the Church.

The Curia is not a divine law reality like the papacy but rather an ecclesiastical law response to the varying requirements of the Petrine ministry. The Curia is ideally both pastoral and ministerial in character; it is not of the essence of the Church but it has a profoundly ecclesial character.

The Petrine ministry is to serve the college of bishops and individual bishops in building up the Church as a communion of the faithful with God and among themselves. The reciprocal communion of and communication between pope and bishops is extremely important in fostering unity of faith, sacramental life, and discipline (c. 205).

While the Curia is evidently closely linked to the pope, it should also be viewed ideally as linked to all bishops. Its being composed significantly of cardinals and bishops bespeaks a certain "collegial" character although not in the proper sense of the term.

---

conciliar fathers, canonists, and the 1969 synod, see J. Provost, "*Pastor bonus:* Reflections on the Reorganization of the Roman Curia," *J* 48 (1988) 499–535. Space does not permit a proper examination of contemporary concerns about the exercise of papal primacy and functioning of the Curia. However, several non-canonical sources seem worth citing in this connection. See Reese, 270–283; M. Buckley, *Papal Primacy and the Episcopate* (New York: Crossroad, 1998); P. Zagano and T. Tilley, eds., *The Exercise of the Primacy: Continuing the Dialogue* (New York: Crossroad, 1998).

The Curia also expresses the solicitude of bishops vis-à-vis the universal Church; this solicitude is shared with the pope and depends on him. While fostering ecclesial unity in service of the pope, the Curia is also to protect legitimate diversity in the various particular churches.

Pastor bonus highlights the significance of the quinquennial *ad limina* visits of bishops to the pope (c. 400), which enable them mutually to address various pressing pastoral problems. These visits may help greatly to foster church unity and serve the values of catholicity and collegiality. Proper preparation for such visits includes the timely forwarding to the Curia of the corresponding quinquennial reports (c. 399).

The Curia exercises vicarious papal power in virtue of its essential and foundational relationship with the pope (cf. c. 334 implicitly). It is called to express his will in fostering the good of the particular churches and serving their bishops. Such a subsidiary and subordinate relationship to the pope gives the Curia its distinctive authority but also limits its prerogatives.

The Petrine primacy and the Roman episcopate pertain to the office of the pope and are institutionally differentiated in the complex reality of the Apostolic See. The diocese of Rome is governed by the pope not precisely in virtue of canonical mission but in virtue of the fullness of his power as successor of Peter and head of the episcopal college (cf. c. 332 on papal election).

Canon 361 does not strictly identify the Apostolic See and the Curia. The Apostolic See as identified with the office of the primacy is indeed a moral person in virtue of divine law and independent from the State (c. 113, §1). However, the Curia is an historically-conditioned institute of ecclesiastical law. It is to be clearly distinguished from the papal office from which it derives and from which it differs in terms of the nature and extent of its authority.

Although canon 361 must be updated slightly in light of the terminology of *Pastor bonus*,[34] the

canon provides a useful rule of canonical interpretation. Hence it might be situated more appropriately in Book I on general norms as it was formerly (*CIC* 7). The canon clarifies the meaning of the frequently used terms "Apostolic See"[35] or "Holy See"[36] in the code. Unless they clearly mean the pope (e.g., c. 340 on the vacancy of the Apostolic See), then they include the various curial dicasteries and other institutes.

Certain practical principles highlighted in *Pastor bonus* may help one evaluate the adequacy of contemporary curial reforms:

- The Curia is to be reformed in light of contemporary pastoral exigencies in continuity with Vatican II and *Regimini*.
- The legal renewal exemplified in the 1983 code[37] is to be duly implemented. However, curial activities are also regulated by special law (e.g., *PB*) and the special rules governing the individual dicasteries.
- Curial organisms are to be better adapted to their various governmental and pastoral purposes.
- Collaboration (e.g., communication in preparing documents) among the dicasteries is imperative.

---

[34] In identifying the Curia, c. 361 speaks of the "Secretariat of State, the Council for the Public Affairs of the Church, and other institutes of the Roman Curia." However, *PB* 1 speaks simply of the Curia as a "complex of dicasteries and institutes." Furthermore, *PB* 2, §1 indicates that the term "dicasteries" means the "Secretariat of State, Congregations, Tribunals, Councils and Offices, namely the Apostolic Camera, the Administration of the Patrimony of the Apostolic See, and the Prefecture for the Economic Affairs of the Holy See." The Council for the Public Affairs of the Church no longer exists as such; its functions are fulfilled by the second section of the Secretariat of State. See also *CCEO* 48.

[35] For a list of over 130 code references to "Apostolic See," see X. Ochoa, *Index verborum ac locutionum Codicis Iuris Canonici,* 2nd ed. (Vatican City: Libreria Editrice Lateranense, 1984) 436–437.

[36] For a list of over forty code references to "Holy See," see Ochoa, 428.

[37] While *PB* was promulgated prior to the 1990 Eastern code, curial activities must also be assessed in terms of their fidelity to that significant text which, along with *PB* and the 1983 code, constitutes the basic legal corpus of the Catholic Church.

— Curial structure and activity are to correspond closely to conciliar ecclesiology.

General Norms in Pastor bonus

1. Notion of Curia (PB 1)

The Curia is a complex of dicasteries serving the pope (*PB* 1). Such dicasteries include the Secretariat of State, nine congregations, three tribunals, twelve councils, and three offices. The Curia facilitates the pope's service of the universal Church and the particular churches. It is to reinforce the unity of faith and communion of the people of God and promote the Church's proper mission in the world.

2. Structure of Dicasteries (PB 2–10)

(a) Equal Dignity of Dicasteries

While the dicasteries are technically juridically equal, they are not equal in importance or power. Normally no dicastery has any power over another; each responds directly to the pope regarding its activity. However, in the case of alleged legal violations, each dicastery is subject to the judgment of the Signatura or supreme court (*PB* 123) regarding the former's compliance with the law. De facto the dicasteries occasionally need to respond to the secretary of state, given his immediate relationship with the pope.

(b) Ordinary Structure of Dicasteries

A cardinal prefect or archbishop president heads the dicasteries (*PB* 3, §1). Only selected cardinals or bishops are normally dicastery members with five-year terms; yet occasionally additional clerics or other faithful may be members of certain councils with due regard for the general restriction of governance functions to clerics (cc. 129, 274).

The dicastery secretary supervises its personnel and expedites its business.

The consultors are clerics or laity chosen stably or on an *ad hoc* basis for their competence and prudence, generally in light of the criterion of universality. Normally they study issues individually and prepare written opinions, but there may be an occasional collegial consultation.

Major curial officials and other collaborators are chosen in light of the above criteria. The particular churches and religious institutes and societies are invited to supply personnel.

3. Procedures

(a) Competencies of Dicasteries (cf. PB 13)

This is usually determined by the nature of the material, e.g., sacraments and divine worship, unless it is explicitly determined otherwise, e.g., a personal criterion such as the Eastern Catholic faithful.

The congregations, or at least dicasteries with executive power, generally handle issues exceeding the competence of individual bishops and their groupings and therefore reserved to the Holy See or committed to the dicasteries by the pope.

Given their preeminently pastoral nature, pontifical councils study serious ecclesial problems transcending the scope and resources of the particular churches and foster pastoral initiatives for the good of the universal Church.

The tribunals and other dicasteries with judicial power judge disputed issues referred to the Holy See or reserved to it in law (e.g., c. 1405).

Unless the pope provides otherwise, the Signatura resolves conflicts of interdicasterial competence when a complex issue potentially pertains to more than one dicastery (*PB* 20).

Issues of mixed competency clearly involve more than one dicastery. For example, the CDF is necessarily involved whenever a question addressed to another dicastery has doctrinal-moral implications, e.g., ecumenical policy. In such circumstances there are two possibilities: an interdicasterial consultation with an independent decision by each dicastery or a single solution by a joint commission (*PB* 21; *Regolamento* 85–95).

(b) Treatment of Various Questions (PB 15)

All issues are treated by the curial executive or judicial dicasteries according to law. The three key legal sources of curial activity in descending importance are the codes, *Pastor bonus* (constitutive law), and the *Regolamento* (cf. c. 95). The individual dicasteries also have their own special law, which must normally be obtained when consulting them (cf. *PB* 37–38).[38] All such curial activity is ideally to foster justice, the good of the Church, and the salvation of persons (c. 1752).

(c) Plenary Assemblies (PB 23)

Ordinary daily decisions are made by the dicastery head, the secretary, and other minor officials. However, some significant questions (e.g., policy decisions) are reserved to plenary assemblies (*plenaria*) potentially involving all dicastery members. Extraordinary *plenaria* occur once a year and involve all the members; ordinary *plenaria,* however, occur more frequently and involve the members living in Rome.

(d) Papal Approval (PB 18; cf. also PB 15)

The various dicasteries are to execute the pope's wishes willingly, since they function vicariously in his name and with his authority. He alone acts with properly papal authority.

The dicasteries (e.g., congregations) do not have *legislative* power unless they have a special papal mandate expressly delegating such power (cf. cc. 29–30; *Regolamento* 110). They neither can derogate from universal law nor authentically interpret it, which is the task of the Pontifical Council for the Interpretation of Legislative Texts (*PB* 154–158).

Judicial power is generally exercised only by tribunals such as the Rota and the Signatura.

Executive power is generally exercised only by the congregations and not the councils barring certain exceptions, e.g., Council for the Laity vis-à-vis lay associations (*PB* 134). Within the areas of their competency, dicasteries with executive power may issue general executory decrees (cc. 31–33) or instructions (c. 34).

---

[38] By way of exception one may find the latest (April 16, 1994) norms of the Rota in *AAS* 86 (1994) 508–540. For the still operative March 1968 norms of the Signatura see X. Ochoa, ed., *Lex Ecclesiae* (Rome: Commentarium pro Religiosis, 1972) 3, 5321–5332; *CLD* 7, 246–272.

With due regard for the specific procedures of the papal tribunals in issuing sentences, there are various ways in which the pope intervenes in other curial activities. In three instances they remain *distinctly curial acts* against which one may possibly take recourse although they are posited in the pope's name and so have a distinctive authority. First of all, he must approve all major curial decisions, e.g., publication of a congregation document (common papal approval—*Regolamento* 115–116). Second, he may grant a dicastery special faculties to exceed its ordinary competency. Third, he may sanate a curial act that exceeds a dicastery's ordinary competence or violates ordinary procedures.

Fourth, however, the pope may make a dicastery act his own by giving it a special type of approval (*in forma specifica*) according to specific conditions articulated in *Regolamento* 110. This papal intervention changes the nature of such an act; it becomes a properly papal act, and neither recourse nor appeal is possible against it (cc. 1404; 1406, §1).

(e) Hierarchic Recourse (PB 19; Regolamento 118–122)

One may make hierarchic recourse (cc. 1732–1739) against lower level administrative acts to the various dicasteries in light of the nature of the matter. For example, the Congregation for the Clergy normally reviews recourse against episcopal disciplinary or penal action against clerics.

There is a limited possibility of such recourse to the Signatura against alleged legal violations in the administrative acts of the dicasteries (c. 1445, §2; *PB* 123).

4. Meetings of Cardinals

As presidents, prefects, or members of the dicasteries the cardinals (cc. 349–359) play a central curial role. For example, several times a year, by papal mandate, the cardinal dicastery heads meet to examine key issues, coordinate curial efforts, and exchange information (*PB* 22).

A separate council of fifteen cardinals aided by experts is to advise the pope on Holy See organizational and economic problems (*PB* 24–25). Its establishment reflects a concern about safeguarding and administering the capital destined for charitable and religious works. Various heads of particular churches are named for five-year terms. The council normally meets twice a year after being convened by the secretary of state.

Specific Curial Structures in **Pastor bonus**[39]

We now briefly describe the various curial dicasteries, especially their areas of competency.[40]

[39] After discussing the Secretariat of State (*PB* 39–47) we will briefly discuss the following nine *congregations:* Doctrine of the Faith (*PB* 48–55), Eastern Churches (*PB* 56–61), Divine Worship-Sacraments (*PB* 62–70), Causes of Saints (*PB* 71–74), Bishops (*PB* 75–84), Evangelization of Peoples (*PB* 85–92), Clergy (*PB* 93–104), Institutes of Consecrated Life and Societies of Apostolic Life (*PB* 105–111), and Catholic Education (*PB* 112–116).

Then we will consider the three *tribunals:* Apostolic Penitentiary (*PB* 117–120), Signatura (*PB* 121–125), and Rota (*PB* 126–130).

Subsequently we will comment on the twelve *councils:* Laity (*PB* 131–134), Christian Unity (*PB* 135–138), Family (*PB* 139–141), Justice and Peace (*PB* 142–144), "Cor Unum" (*PB* 145–148), Migrants and Itinerant People (*PB* 149–151), Health Care Workers (*PB* 152–153), Interpretation of Legislative Texts (*PB* 154–158), Interreligious Dialogue (*PB* 159–162), Dialogue with Non-Believers (*PB* 163–165), Culture (*PB* 166–168), and Social Communications (*PB* 169–170).

After briefly discussing certain *commissions,* we deal with three *offices:* Apostolic Camera (*PB* 171), Patrimony of the Apostolic See (*PB* 172–175), and Prefecture for the Economic Affairs of the Holy See (*PB* 176–179).

Finally we will briefly consider two other *institutes:* the Prefecture of the Papal Household (*PB* 180–181) and the Office for the Liturgical Celebrations of the Supreme Pontiff (*PB* 182).

[40] For a more detailed examination of the dicasteries, see the pertinent bibliographical references mentioned in connection with each dicastery. For specific details on the personnel, addresses, and phone numbers of the various dicasteries, see the annual *Annuario Pontificio* published by the Vatican Press. While the various dicasteries issue numerous documents in discharging their responsi-

Secretariat of State (*PB* 39–47)[41]

The Secretariat occupies a central curial position. Headed by the cardinal secretary of state, it enjoys a particularly close relationship to the pope in the daily exercise of his supreme mission. It has a comprehensive competence, be it vis-à-vis other dicasteries or in terms of its own distinctive responsibilities.

The Secretariat's first section for general ecclesial business (*PB* 41–44) is directed by the cardinal secretary's deputy. It examines extraordinary issues transcending the competency of individual dicasteries, coordinates curial activities, monitors the work of papal legates (cc. 362–367), draws up apostolic letters, and oversees publications such as *Acta Apostolicae Sedis* and *L'Osservatore Romano.*

The Secretariat's second section for governmental affairs (*PB* 45–47) is directed by its own secretary, aided by an undersecretary and a body of cardinals and bishops. This section handles such matters as accrediting diplomatic representatives, supervising the activity of papal legates, assuring Holy See representation in international institutes and meetings, drawing up concordats (c. 3), and expediting episcopal nominations and seeing to the establishment and modification of particular churches requiring negotiations with civil governments (cf. *PB* 78).

Congregations[42]

The congregations, which have surrendered some of their former preeminence to the Secretariat of State, have a distinctive organization.

bilities, limitations of space preclude listing such documents in the following brief comments on those responsibilities. For observations on such documents, see the individual commentaries on the pertinent canons.

[41] See R. Bertagna, "La Segreteria di Stato," in *La Curia Romana,* 163–176; V. Buonomo, "La Segreteria di Stato: Competenze nella funzione diplomatica," in ibid., 177–188.

[42] See P. Palazzini, "Le Congregazioni," in *La Curia Romana,* 189–206.

Technically, a "congregation" is a group of cardinals and bishops who collegially address particular ecclesial concerns such as education on behalf of supreme church authority and in service to the particular churches. Each congregation is normally chaired by a "prefect," who is assisted by a secretary (usually a titular archbishop) and a staff whose size varies from congregation to congregation.

The congregation's membership includes both cardinals resident in Rome and cardinals and bishops who head dioceses around the world and reflect distinctive ecclesial experiences.[43] The congregation gathers annually for a plenary meeting (*plenarium*) to discuss major pastoral matters and make policy decisions on matters within its competence.

Ordinary meetings of all the members who are in Rome are held regularly throughout the year. Theoretically, all major decisions implementing policy are made or affirmed at these meetings. The agenda for them and accompanying documentation are developed by the congregation's staff.

The cardinal prefect, secretary, and major staff personnel meet frequently to carry on the ordinary business of the congregation in light of the policy set by the plenary session and decisions reached in the ordinary meetings. This group (the *congressus*) also decides how to handle issues brought to the congregation's attention: whether to submit them directly to the pope, place them on the agenda for a plenary session, or address them in an ordinary meeting.

The congregations draw on experts in their respective fields, usually those living in Rome but also others from around the world. Consultors can be asked their advice by mail. They can also be called to meetings of the council of consultors where their advice is sought as a body (*consulta*).

Certain congregations are responsible comprehensively for various ecclesial concerns affecting only a certain group of people, e.g., Eastern Churches or Evangelization of Peoples. However,

other congregations are responsible for only a given ecclesial concern that affects all the faithful, e.g., CDF in doctrinal matters.

For a long time, the congregations were called "sacred," probably because they dealt with various sacred or religious issues. However, this is no longer true, perhaps because such nomenclature seems inappropriate in characterizing such bureaucratic entities even given their religious concerns.

1. *Congregation for the Doctrine of the Faith* (CDF) (*PB* 48–55).[44] While all congregations are technically juridically equal (*PB* 2, §2), the CDF enjoys a certain preeminence given its comprehensive competence to promote (*PB* 49–50) and safeguard (*PB* 51) the integrity of faith and morals throughout the Church. Accordingly, other dicasteries must submit proposed documents to the CDF for prior review in light of such doctrinal concerns (*PB* 54).[45] The CDF is also expected to assist the bishops in exercising their individual and corporate teaching roles.

In promoting the faith, the CDF is to foster studies of the faith in light of new questions posed by science and culture. The Pontifical Biblical Commission and the International Theological Commission assist in that enterprise (*PB* 55).

In safeguarding the faith against errors, the CDF examines new teachings and opinions, books, and other writings, utilizing its own norms for doctrinal examination. It also occasionally punishes crimes against faith or morals, e.g., in celebrating the sacraments, especially penance (*PB* 52).[46]

The CDF also handles privilege of the faith cases (*PB* 53). Furthermore, it reviews requests for dispensations from celibacy arising before 1989

---

[43] Paul VI, *mp Pro comperto sane*, August 6, 1967, *CLD* 6, 322–324.

[44] See A. Silvistrelli, "La Congregazione per la Dottrina della Fede," in *La Curia Romana*, 225–237.

[45] See, for example, *PB* 137, §1 on the Council for Promoting Christian Unity's consultation with the CDF before publishing ecumenical documents. See also *PB* 161 regarding the Pontifical Council for Interreligious Dialogue.

[46] See commentary on cc. 1364, 1387–1388.

(cc. 290, 3°–292). It proceeds administratively or judicially depending on the nature of the issue.

2. *Congregation for the Eastern Churches* (*PB* 56–61).[47] The name of this congregation reflects conciliar teaching on the equality of the diverse ritual churches *sui iuris* that form the worldwide Catholic communion.[48] In addition to the assigned cardinals, the various Eastern patriarchs and major metropolitans are automatically congregation members as is the president of the Council for Promoting Christian Unity. The congregation officials and consultors should reflect the aforementioned ritual diversity (*PB* 57).

This congregation exercises for members of the Eastern Catholic churches a comprehensive competency in various teaching, sanctifying, or governing areas which would be handled by different Latin church congregations, e.g., Bishops, Catholic Education, etc. This is the case even in mixed matters involving Latin as well as Eastern Catholics where consultation with the corresponding other dicasteries may be necessary (*PB* 58). Furthermore, this congregation has exclusive responsibility for ecclesial activities in specific geographic areas (e.g., Middle East) traditionally ministered to by Eastern Catholic churches (*PB* 60). There are, however, exceptions to this broad competency, e.g., doctrinal matters (CDF) or judicial matters (Signatura or Rota) (*PB* 58, §2).

The congregation has a special relationship to the Pontifical Councils for Promoting Christian Unity and Interreligious Dialogue given their common ecumenical concerns (*PB* 57, §1; 61).

[47] See M. Brogi, "La Congregazione per le Chiese Orientali," in *La Curia Romana,* 239–267.

[48] Besides the Latin church there are twenty-one Eastern Catholic churches corresponding to five Eastern liturgical traditions: Alexandrian, Antiochian, Byzantine (Constantinopolitan), Chaldean, and Armenian. See V. Pospishil, *Eastern Catholic Church Law,* 2nd ed. (Staten Island: St. Maron, 1996) 15–28. For a thoughtful overview of all the Eastern churches including those not in full communion, see R. Roberson, *The Eastern Catholic Churches,* 5th ed. (Rome: Edizioni Orientalia Christiana, 1995).

3. *Congregation for Divine Worship and the Discipline of the Sacraments* (*PB* 62–70).[49] This congregation underwent some noteworthy postconciliar organizational changes both before and after the 1983 code was promulgated.[50] In 1984 the Congregation for Divine Worship and the Congregation for Sacraments were separated into two distinct congregations headed by the same prefect. *Pastor bonus,* however, again unified the two congregations in one dicastery, appropriately viewing liturgy and the sacraments in an integrated fashion.

The congregation's *worship* section moderates and promotes the liturgy, monitors the development and revision of liturgical texts, reviews episcopal conference translations and adaptations of such texts (c. 838, §3), communicates with various liturgical commissions, fosters international liturgical meetings, and oversees the observance of liturgical norms (c. 838, §2) (*PB* 64–66).

The congregation's *discipline of the sacraments* section fosters the integrity of their celebration and deals with such issues as granting dispensations from non-consummated marriages (cc. 1142, 1697–1706), processing the laicization of clerics (c. 290, 3°), and adjudicating allegations of the invalidity of ordination (cc. 290, 1°; 1708–1712) (*PB* 63, 67–68).

This congregation is competent for the whole Latin church, including those areas under the Congregation for the Evangelization of Peoples.

4. *Congregation for the Causes of Saints* (*PB* 71–74).[51] This congregation deals with the beatification and canonization of saints in the Latin and Eastern Catholic churches and monitors the authentication and preservation of relics.

The congregation works through three offices. The first one (the "judicial office") establishes and implements the procedures for beatification

[49] See R. Melli, "La Congregazione del Culto Divino e della Disciplina dei Sacramenti," in *La Curia Romana,* 269–280.

[50] See Provost, in *CLSA Com,* 298.

[51] See A. Eszer, "La Congregazione delle Cause dei Santi: Il nuovo ordinamento," in *La Curia Romana,* 309–329.

and canonization cases (c. 1403), which are initially processed in local dioceses. The second office, that of the promoter general of the faith (the so-called "devil's advocate"), examines any objections to the sanctity of a proposed saint and assures the integrity of the procedure. A third office, the historico-hagiographical office, investigates cases for which there are no living witnesses and through careful historical research is to determine the heroic virtue of persons whose causes have been presented long after their death.

5. *Congregation for Bishops* (*PB* 75–84).[52] This congregation is principally responsible for overseeing the constitution and provision of particular churches and the exercise of the episcopal ministry along with the Congregations for the Eastern Churches and the Evangelization of Peoples and the Secretariat of State.

The Congregation for Bishops provides for the erection, division, suppression, or other changes in dioceses (c. 373), ecclesiastical provinces (c. 431, §3), regions (c. 433), military ordinariates, and personal prelatures (c. 294). Likewise, it oversees the selection of bishops, apostolic administrators, military ordinaries, and various vicars or prelates with personal jurisdiction. When civil governments are involved in such decision-making, the congregation proceeds in close consultation with the second section of the Secretariat of State (c. 377).

The congregation receives the five-year report on the diocese (c. 399) submitted by diocesan bishops and arranges for the corresponding *ad limina* visits of bishops (c. 400—*Regolamento* 123–127). Occasionally it orders an apostolic visitation of a diocese,[53] and it deals with whatever else touches bishops personally in their ministry or retirement.

---

[52] See M. Costalunga, "La Congregazione per i Vescovi," in *La Curia Romana,* 281–307.

[53] See *J* 49 (1989) 341–567 for detailed theological-canonical reflections on apostolic visitation prompted especially by a publicized 1986 visitation of the Archdiocese of Seattle, Washington.

The congregation also handles matters concerning particular councils (cc. 439–446) and episcopal conferences (cc. 447–459). In the latter instance it sees to their establishment and reviews their statutes; and in both instances it reviews their legislative enactments after appropriate consultation with the pertinent other dicasteries.

6. *Congregation for the Evangelization of Peoples* (*PB* 85–92).[54] For centuries this ancient congregation has exercised extensive jurisdiction in territories considered still to be "missionary," i.e., where the ordinary diocesan organization has not been fully established for various reasons. However, that somewhat broad competency has been somewhat restricted during the twentieth century. For example, tribunals such as the Rota and Signatura exercise exclusive judicial competency even in missionary territories.

The congregation is primarily responsible for directing and coordinating the world-wide work of evangelization and missionary cooperation except in areas subject to the Congregation for the Eastern Churches. Among other things, this entails fostering theological research, assisting the pastoral work of missionaries and developing appropriate norms for such work, fostering missionary vocations, and promoting missionary works such as the Society for the Propagation of the Faith.

Like the Congregation for Bishops, this congregation establishes and modifies ecclesiastical circumscriptions and provides for church leaders in missionary areas. It monitors the activities of missionary societies of apostolic life as well as the distinctly missionary work of members of institutes of consecrated life, individually and corporately.

The congregation administers its own funds and other goods destined for the missions, but must report on this administration to the Prefecture for Economic Affairs of the Holy See (*PB* 176–179).

---

[54] See V. De Paolis, "La Congregazione per l'Evangelizzazione dei Popoli," in *La Curia Romana,* 359–378.

7. *Congregation for the Clergy* (*PB* 93–104).[55] This congregation was formerly the Sacred Congregation of the Council, established to implement and interpret the decrees of the Council of Trent. Hence, the congregation has extensive responsibilities transcending the realm of clerical life and ministry.

Three offices exist within this congregation. The first deals with the life and ministry primarily of the secular clergy, ranging from their holiness of life to continuing education, pastoral ministry, and their appropriate distribution throughout the Church. This office exercises vigilance over priests in pastoral ministry regarding their fidelity to clerical discipline and also oversees the activity of presbyteral councils (cc. 495–501). This congregation also oversees the functioning of diocesan (cc. 511–514) and parish pastoral councils (c. 536), although such entities involve laity and religious as well as clergy.

The second office addresses questions of preaching and catechetics (cc. 762–780). It is to promote and approve pastoral and catechetical directories prepared by episcopal conferences (c. 775, §2) and may itself indicate opportune norms for the religious instruction of children, youth, and adults after consultation with the CDF.

The third office is competent for matters of temporal administration, e.g., expediting Holy See permission to alienate ecclesiastical goods (c. 1292, §2). Similarly it oversees the proper administration of Mass obligations, pious foundations, pious wills, and legacies (cc. 1308, §1; 1310, §3). It is also concerned about the proper support and social security of clergy (c. 281).

8. *Congregation for Institutes of Consecrated Life and for Societies of Apostolic Life* (*PB* 105–111).[56] The name of this congregation (CICLSAL) reflects the twofold structure of the pertinent canons of the 1983 code. After general norms (cc. 573–606), it deals with institutes of consecrated life (cc. 607–730) and societies of apostolic life (cc. 731–746).

With due regard for the competency of other congregations (e.g., Evangelization of Peoples for missionary institutes), CICLSAL is primarily responsible for promoting and supervising the living of the evangelical counsels of poverty, chastity, and obedience. It does this for formally recognized institutes or societies, individuals such as hermits (c. 603) or consecrated virgins (c. 604), and other forms of consecrated life (c. 605).

While assisting institutes and societies to flourish with fidelity to the spirit of their founders in serving the Church's mission, CICLSAL exercises certain pastoral governance functions. For example, it establishes new institutes or societies or advises bishops on their comparable initiatives (c. 579); it approves constitutions (c. 587, §2); it authorizes the alienation of property where necessary (c. 638, §3); it grants indults of departure in various institutes or societies (c. 691, §2) and confirms dismissals from pontifical institutes or societies (c. 700). CICLSAL also establishes conferences of major superiors of men and women, approves their statutes, and monitors their activities to assist them in achieving their purpose (cc. 708–709).

9. *Congregation for Catholic Education* (*PB* 112–116).[57] This congregation deals with the varied dimensions of the Church's educational mission, except for catechetics (Congregation for the Clergy).

The Congregation for Catholic Education oversees the varied dimensions of the formation of sacred ministers: spiritual, doctrinal, and pastoral. For example, it approves episcopal confer-

---

[55] See A. Lauro, "La Congregazione per il Clero," in *La Curia Romana,* 331–342.

[56] See M. Linscott, "La Congregazione per gli Istituti di Vita Consecrata e per le Società di Vita Apostolica," in *La Curia Romana,* 343–358.

[57] See T. Bertone, "La Congregazione per l'Educazione Cattolica," in *La Curia Romana,* 379–394. While *PB* called this dicastery "The Congregation of Seminaries and Educational Institutions," its current more representative name was indicated in a February 26, 1989 letter of the Secretariat of State (prot. no. 236.026).

ence programs of priestly formation (c. 242). It also exercises a certain vigilance over the direction, discipline, and temporal administration of seminaries.

The congregation's responsibility to promote and organize Catholic education in light of basic magisterial principles technically encompasses elementary, secondary, college, and university level education. However, in the post-1983 code period, the most noteworthy congregation attention has been focused on the post-secondary level of Catholic colleges and universities.

The authority the congregation exercises over educational institutions varies depending on the degree to which the Holy See is juridically involved in their governance. For example, such jurisdiction is much more extensive in ecclesiastical universities and faculties (cc. 815–821) than in other Catholic universities and institutions of higher studies (cc. 807–814).

Tribunals[58]

The Roman Curia contains three tribunals, each of which has a unique organization and specialized competence[59] (unchanged in *PB*) in exercising the pope's judicial power. The Apostolic Penitentiary deals with internal forum matters, sacramental or non-sacramental (*PB* 117–120), while the Roman Rota and the Apostolic Signatura address external forum concerns. The Rota is the preeminent appellate tribunal in second and higher instances, e.g., fostering the protection of rights and assuring a unified jurisprudence. Occasionally it handles first instance cases, e.g., those involving heads of state (*PB* 126–130). The Signatura functions both judicially and administratively in ensuring the correct administration of justice in the Church (*PB* 121–125). It reviews

various procedural challenges to Rotal sentences, resolves conflicts of competency among Roman dicasteries, and hears recourses against administrative acts of such dicasteries.

Since the code does not mention the Apostolic Penitentiary, a few words are warranted regarding its functioning.[60] From the early Middle Ages a cardinal has customarily been named to absolve from censures reserved to the pope. His competence was gradually restricted to the internal forum, and today he functions at the universal church level in many ways similar to the canon penitentiary at the diocesan level (c. 508). The Penitentiary grants various internal forum indulgences, favors, absolutions, dispensations, commutations, sanations, and condonations. In deciding such issues, the cardinal penitentiary is assisted by a regent, a theologian, a canonist, and other officials.

Pontifical Councils (PB 131–170)[61]

In *Regimini* Paul VI added a new dicastery called a "secretariat" to the traditional triad of congregations, tribunals, and offices. Later additional secretariats, councils, and commissions were added; however, it was frequently difficult to clarify their precise juridic status. For example, the same term "council" designated the juridically significant Council for the Public Affairs of the Church and the less juridically significant, however pastorally important, Council for the Pastoral Care of Migrants and the Apostolate of the Sea and Air.

Pastor bonus reorganized the juridic profile and activity of such councils, whose focus differs from older curial entities such as congregations. The latter exercise various governance tasks while

---

[58] See Z. Grocholewski. "I Tribunali," in *La Curia Romana,* 395–418.

[59] The competence of the Rota (cc. 1443–1444; 1405, §3) and the Signatura (c. 1445), unlike the competence of other curial dicasteries, is also mentioned in Book VII of the code. See the commentary on the pertinent canons.

[60] See L. DeMagistris and U. M. Todeschini, "La Penitenzieria Apostolica," in *La Curia Romana,* 419–429. For a somewhat detailed treatment including questions about whether the Penitentiary should technically be considered a tribunal, see Aymans and Mörsdorf, 254–257.

[61] See T. Mauro, "I Consigli: Finalità, organizzazione e natura," in *La Curia Romana,* 431–442.

the former are primarily engaged in activities of promotion, study, providing information, and consultation in service of the particular churches. Furthermore, some councils such as those for the laity and the family have lay members.

Pastor bonus mentions twelve councils, some of which have a certain autonomy while others depend on other dicasteries. For example, the Council for Social Communications closely collaborates with the Secretariat of State (*PB* 169, §2).

The term "council" indicates the stability and relative independence of such organisms. The term "commission" was dropped because it seemed to indicate an undue dependency. Despite their various tasks, the councils have a similar purpose: promotional service of the ecclesial community.

It is sometimes difficult to clarify how the councils differ from the traditional dicasteries. However, while the latter generally address inner church issues, the councils frequently focus on extra-ecclesial pastoral and human concerns, e.g., various dialogue-oriented councils such as Christian Unity (*PB* 135–138) or Interreligious Dialogue (*PB* 159–162).

While most councils primarily focus on the study and promotion of pastoral life, some exercise certain governmental functions. For example, in implementing the conciliar ecumenical decrees and the two codes, the Pontifical Council for Promoting Christian Unity issued the 1993 Ecumenical Directory, a general executory decree addressing various ecumenical policy issues (*PB* 136; cc. 31–33).

We will now briefly indicate the competency of the various councils.

1. *Pontifical Council for the Laity* (*PB* 131–134).[62] This council promotes and coordinates the apostolate of the laity, discusses issues affecting their Christian life, and handles whatever concerns distinctly lay associations.

2. *Pontifical Council for Promoting Christian Unity* (*PB* 135–138). This council fosters ecumenical activity at all levels in fidelity to Vatican II (c. 755). It monitors the activity of various ecumenical groups and oversees the conducting of various bilateral and multilateral dialogues with various Christians not in full communion. It collaborates especially with the CDF and the Congregation for the Eastern Churches. Furthermore, a special commission handles religious relationships with the Jews.

3. *Pontifical Council for the Family* (*PB* 139–141). This council promotes the pastoral care of families and fosters their dignity in the Church and in civil society. It strives to understand better the Church's official teaching on marriage and the family in light of contemporary challenges.

4. *Pontifical Council for Justice and Peace* (*PB* 142–144). This council fosters justice and peace in the world in light of the gospel and the Church's social teaching. It deals with issues of the development of peoples and human rights, especially in collaboration with the Secretariat of State.

5. *Pontifical Council "Cor Unum"* (*PB* 145–148). This council, closely linked to the preceding one, expresses the Church's concern for the needy, fosters pertinent research on human development, and coordinates relief efforts.

6. *Pontifical Council for the Pastoral Care of Migrants and Itinerant People* (*PB* 149–151).[63] This council expresses the Church's pastoral care for those forced to leave their native land or lacking one. It also seeks to motivate the particular churches to care for migrants, refugees, nomads, seafarers, airport and airline employees, etc.

7. *Pontifical Council for Pastoral Assistance to Health Care Workers* (*PB* 152–153). This council reflects the Church's solicitude for the sick, espe-

[62] See S. Berlingò, "Il Pontificio Consiglio per i Laici," in *La Curia Romana,* 443–453.

[63] See J. Beyer, "Il Pontificio Consiglio della Pastorale per i Migranti e gli Itineranti," in *La Curia Romana,* 455–466.

cially by aiding health care workers in ministering in light of church teaching.

8. *Pontifical Council for the Interpretation of Legislative Texts* (*PB* 154–158).[64] This canonically significant council authentically interprets universal laws for both the Latin and Eastern churches (c. 16, §1; *CCEO* 1498, §1) and publishes such interpretations with papal confirmation. It assists the other dicasteries in ensuring that their general executory decrees and instructions conform to universal law and are expressed in the proper juridic form. The council also examines the juridical aspects of the general decrees of episcopal conferences during the necessary review (*recognitio*) process (cc. 455, §2; 456). Finally, at the request of interested parties, the council may review the conformity to universal law of particular laws and general decrees issued by other lower level legislators such as diocesan bishops.

9. *Pontifical Council for Interreligious Dialogue* (*PB* 159–162). This council fosters relations with non-Christian believers and promotes greater mutual esteem and sharing of information between them and Christians. The council especially is to collaborate with the CDF, the Congregation for the Eastern Churches, and the Congregation for the Evangelization of Peoples. A special office handles religious relations with Moslems.

10. *Pontifical Council for Dialogue with Non-Believers* (*PB* 163–165). This council studies the contemporary phenomenon of atheism as well as the lack of faith and religion. It also fosters relations with cooperative atheists and non-believers.[65]

---

[64] See J. Herranz, "Il Pontificio Consiglio per l'Interpretazione dei Testi Legislativi," in *La Curia Romana,* 467–481.

[65] On March 25, 1993 this council was integrated with the Pontifical Council for Culture. See John Paul II, *mp Inde a pontificatus, AAS* 85 (1993) 549–552. Also related to the latter council, though independent from it, is the Pontifical Commission on the Preservation of the Church's Artistic and Historical Patrimony (*PB* 99–104).

11. *Pontifical Council for Culture* (*PB* 166–168). This council embodies the Church's concern about the faith-culture relationship by fostering appropriate dialogues with those involved in science, literature, and the arts. It collaborates with the Secretariat of State in dealing with cultural activities involving states and international agencies.

12. *Pontifical Council for Social Communications* (*PB* 169–170). In strict collaboration with the Secretariat of State, this council treats of questions involving the communications media so that they may be imbued with a human and Christian spirit (c. 822) and so better communicate the gospel and duly foster civil culture and *mores*.

Commissions[66]

The Curia contains numerous commissions, such as the Pontifical Commission for Latin America, which is attached to the Congregation for Bishops (*PB* 83–84). The commissions vary in different ways, e.g., in terms of their newness, their permanent or temporary character, their relationship to an existing dicastery, their necessary or discretionary nature, their authority, and their possible interdicasterial dimension, e.g., regarding a more equitable distribution of priests (cf. *PB* 95, §2).

However diverse they may be, such commissions respond to curial exigencies of adaptability, flexibility, and therefore efficiency—characteristics which occasionally are lacking in the older established dicasteries given their somewhat more fixed structure, competency, and procedure.

Generally the commissions are purely consultative or promotional without governmental power, yet they also function vicariously in the pope's name. They usually operate according to *Regolamento* 93–95, the special norms of a given dicastery, and their own proper statutes.

---

[66] See G. Dalla Torre, "Le Commissioni," in *La Curia Romana,* 207–224.

Offices (PB 171–179)[67]

From the outset, in addition to the congregations and tribunals, there have been other curial organizations with different structures depending on their competencies, leadership personnel, and the immediacy of their relationship to the pope, in whose name they function. A personal rather than collegial style of functioning characterizes their exercise of various technical executive functions, generally but not exclusively economic in character.

The term "offices" used in *Pastor bonus* seems to be a convenient nomenclature for heterogeneous departments which support the Curia but whose competence and powers have not always been clearly delineated.

Three offices are mentioned: the Apostolic Camera, which manages the Holy See when the see is vacant (*PB* 171), the Administration of the Patrimony of the Apostolic See, which administers its temporal goods (*PB* 172–175), and the Prefecture for the Economic Affairs of the Holy See, which establishes the annual Holy See budget, prepares the annual financial report, and supervises the economic activities of the dicasteries (*PB* 176–179).

Other Institutes of the Roman Curia
(PB 180–182)

Finally, there are two other bodies which, while not technically "dicasteries" like the preceding entities (*PB* 2, §§1 and 3), are called "other institutes of the Roman Curia": the Prefecture of the Papal Household, which monitors its internal order (*PB* 180–181), and the Office for the Liturgical Celebrations of the Supreme Pontiff (*PB* 182).

Institutions Linked to Holy See (PB 186–193)

These are varied entities which respond to certain Holy See exigencies although they do not directly serve the Petrine ministry, e.g., archives, Vatican Library, Academy of Sciences, The Fabric (maintenance) of St. Peter's Basilica.[68]

---

[67] See F. Salerno, "Gli Uffici," in *La Curia Romana,* 483–503.

[68] Various other agencies or persons are mentioned in *Pastor bonus* despite not being situated under any of the aforementioned categories, e.g., the central labor office (*PB* 136) and the translation center (*PB* 16). See Gutiérrez, in *Pamplona ComEng,* 286.

CHAPTER V
LEGATES OF THE ROMAN PONTIFF
[cc. 362–367]

Since the earliest times of the Church's history, the Roman Pontiffs have sent legates to represent them, such as, for example, at the major ecumenical councils.[1] As the practice developed over the centuries, legates were sent also to civil authorities, with permanent papal representation beginning to appear by the end of the fifteenth century. The period following the Council of Trent brought about reforms regarding the preparation, designation, and functions of pontifical legates. These reforms were consolidated in the subsequent centuries, leading to the current practice by which the Roman Pontiff sends legates to particular churches and to civil authorities in order to act as his representatives in a permanent and stable fashion.

The principal source for the canons that follow is the 1969 *motu proprio Sollicitudo omnium ecclesiarum,* which responded to the desire expressed during the Second Vatican Council regarding a clarification of the role of the pontifical legates in relation to the proper pastoral ministry of the bishops.[2]

The reorganization of the Roman Curia brought about by the 1988 apostolic constitution *Pastor bonus* did not directly affect the pontifical legates[3] nor does the 1990 Code of Canons of the Eastern Churches contain legislation on this matter.

---

[1] See the commentary by J. Provost in *CLSA Com,* 300–301.

[2] *CD* 9. See the introduction to *SoE* and A. Talamanca, "I rappresentanti pontifici nella nuova normativa canonica," in *Vitam impendere vero: Scritti in onore di Pio Ciprotti,* ed. W. Schulz and G. Feliciani (Vatican City: Libreria Editrice Vaticana, 1986) 276–288.

[3] The competencies attributed to the two Sections of the Secretariat of State are virtually the same as those of the earlier configuration. See *PB* 39–47, *AAS* 80 (1988) 870–872.

Right of Legation

Canon 362 — The Roman Pontiff has the innate and independent right to appoint, send, transfer, and recall his own legates either to particular churches in various nations or regions or to states and public authorities. The norms of international law are to be observed in what pertains to the mission and recall of legates appointed to states.

The Roman Pontiff, in exercising his responsibilities as the visible head and the principal spiritual leader of the Catholic Church, makes use of representatives or legates to act as liaisons both to the particular churches and to the states and public authorities throughout the world.

The right of the Roman Pontiff to appoint, send, transfer, and recall his legates is innate, that is, proper to his office, since he can freely exercise supreme, full, immediate, and universal ordinary power in the Church (c. 331).

The canon, based substantially on *Sollicitudo* III, 1, reflects the theological reality that, as the successor of Peter, the Roman Pontiff is "a permanent and visible source and foundation of unity of faith and fellowship"[4] and has the mission to confirm his brother bishops and the people of God in the faith, in that *communio* which is the Church. The bishops, as pastors of the particular churches spread throughout the world, exercise their office collegially, in communion with and under the authority of the Roman Pontiff. In this context, with due regard for the external, social, and juridical dimensions of the Church, the pontifical legates are recognized as an effective, though certainly not exclusive, means of maintaining the bonds which link the Roman Pontiff with the bishops of the world, as well as with all the members of the Christian faithful.

Following the internal logic of the canon, the pontifical legates are sent, first of all, to the par-

---

[4] *LG* 18.

ticular churches, as an expression and extension of the aforesaid mission of the Roman Pontiff. Therefore, they have a primarily ecclesial role.

The pontifical legates are sent also to states and public authorities. The Church addresses itself to every aspect of human life in exercising its mission to proclaim the gospel to all, to communicate to society Christian values, and to safeguard the rights of the Christian faithful as well as the transcendent quality and the fundamental rights of all human persons. Therefore the Church attempts to engage in constructive dialogue with political authorities and with the international community of nations and supranational organizations.[5] In this secular aspect of their mission, the pontifical legates exercise a role which is rooted in a fundamentally ecclesial reality.

For their part, states and public authorities, recognizing the particular mission of the Church, send representatives, or ambassadors, to the Roman Pontiff. Hence, the Holy See exercises a right of active (sending) and passive (receiving) legation.

The Roman Pontiff sends his legates in virtue of his spiritual and moral authority, rather than as the supreme temporal ruler of the State of Vatican City. To illustrate this point, during the nearly sixty-year period when the Roman Pontiff did not possess a territory, the international community, in accord with a long accepted practice,[6] continued to recognize his right to send legates and receive ambassadors. In fact, during that period, the number of diplomatic missions accredited to the Holy See increased.

The Roman Pontiff exercises his rights concerning the pontifical legates independently, since he is not subject to any other authority, either civil or ecclesiastical.

History is replete with attempts on the part of civil authorities to circumscribe, either totally or partially, the rights of the Roman Pontiff regarding his legates. These have included attempts to limit them to merely diplomatic or political functions, in order to control the Church and to hinder contacts, whether on the part of the hierarchy or of the lay faithful, between the particular churches and the Apostolic See.

The usefulness of sending pontifical legates has, at times, been questioned within the Church. During the Second Vatican Council, while the bishops as a whole requested greater clarity regarding the role of the pontifical legates, some went so far as to suggest that the practice was an anachronism and should be totally suppressed. The idea was not entirely new since, prior to the twentieth century, some bishops opposed the sending of pontifical legates, considering them to be usurpers of their rights, and therefore tried to restrict their activities, ironically, to merely ceremonial or diplomatic functions.

Lastly, with regard to the sending and recalling of legates appointed to states, the canon refers to the norms of international law, which are contained in the Vienna Convention on Diplomatic Relations.[7]

Types of Legates

Canon 363 — §1. To the legates of the Roman Pontiff is entrusted the office of representing the Roman Pontiff in a stable manner to particular churches or also to the states and public authorities to which they are sent.

§2. Those who are designated as delegates or observers in a pontifical mission at international councils or at conferences and meetings also represent the Apostolic See.

---

[5] The annual address of the Holy Father to the diplomatic corps accredited to the Holy See, published in *AAS,* can be a useful resource regarding the concerns of the Church vis-à-vis the current world situation.

[6] For a thorough exposition of this topic, see R. J. Graham, *Vatican Diplomacy: A Study of Church and State on the International Plane* (Princeton, N.J.: Princeton University, 1959).

[7] The Vienna Convention was organized by the United Nations, and the final document was signed on April 18, 1961 by representatives of the nations of the world and of the Holy See. For the full text, see United Nations, *Treaty Series* (1964) 96–126.

The canon, which synthesizes the contents of *Sollicitudo* I and II, distinguishes between those pontifical legates who represent the Roman Pontiff on a stable basis and those who are appointed as observers or delegates for a particular occasion.

The majority of the pontifical legates referred to in the first paragraph of the canon exercise the dual function of representatives to particular churches and to states and public authorities.

Heretofore a distinction was made between the nuncio, who enjoys the prerogative of the deanship of the diplomatic corps from the moment that he presents his credential letters, in conformity with the multi-century tradition codified in article 16 of the Vienna Convention,[8] and the pro-nuncio, whose place in the order of precedence is determined by seniority, that is, by the date of his accreditation. However, there has been a recent change, according to which the latter type of pontifical legate is to be given the designation of nuncio, whether or not he is the dean, and the title pro-nuncio is no longer to be used.[9]

At present, the Holy See maintains diplomatic relations with more than 165 countries, while the total number of nuncios and pro-nuncios is just over one hundred, since several have concurrent accreditation to more than one country.[10] The prerogative of the deanship is enjoyed in most countries of Central and South America, in many countries in Europe, and in some countries in Asia and Africa.

The pontifical legates who represent the Roman Pontiff only to the particular churches are given the title apostolic delegate.[11] Since more and more countries have established diplomatic relations with the Holy See, the number of delegations has decreased in recent years, such that there are now fewer than a dozen.[12]

The pontifical legates who represent the Roman Pontiff in a stable manner as nuncio, pro-nuncio, or apostolic delegate have the rank of titular archbishop, and are usually, but not exclusively, selected from among those ecclesiastics who already serve in pontifical representations.

The second paragraph of the canon refers to those persons who represent the Apostolic See in a sphere of increasing importance in today's world, the growing number of regional, continental, and world-wide international organizations, both governmental and non-governmental.

A number of these institutions, such as the United Nations Organization, are of such importance that permanent missions have been established;[13] for others, representatives are designated *ad hoc*.

---

[8] The article reads as follows:

"1. Heads of mission shall take precedence in their respective classes in the order of the date and time of taking up their functions in accordance with Article 13.

"2. Alterations in the credentials of a head of mission not involving any change of class shall not affect his precedence.

"3. This article is without prejudice to any practice accepted by the receiving State regarding the precedence of the representative of the Holy See."

[9] There remain very few pontifical legates with the title of pro-nuncio.

[10] A concrete example, taken from the author's experience, is the apostolic nunciature in Accra, accredited concurrently to Ghana, Togo, and Benin.

[11] From 1893 until 1984, the pontifical legate resident in Washington was an apostolic delegate.

[12] Other titles mentioned in *SoE* are either no longer used (*internuncio*), or are exceedingly rare (*apostolic visitor, regent, chargé d'affaires with instructions*). The title *chargé d'affaires ad interim* is used commonly in the temporary absence of the head of any diplomatic mission.

[13] At present the Roman Pontiff sends permanent representatives, either as members with the right to vote, or as observers without said right (See *SoE* II, §1), to the following international governmental organizations: the U.N. (New York); the Office of the U.N. and its Specialized Agencies (Geneva); the International Atomic Energy Commission, the Office of the U.N. and the U.N. Organization for Industrial Development, the Organization for Security and Co-operation in Europe (Vienna); the U.N. Organizations and Organisms for Food and Agriculture, and the World Tourist Organization (Rome); UNESCO (Paris); the European Union (Brussels); the Council of Europe (Strasbourg); the Organization of the American States (Washington); and the International Committee of Military Medicine. Furthermore, the Holy See is a member of other international governmental organizations, such as INTELSAT, under the title of the

Concrete examples of recent major international meetings that have drawn world-wide attention particularly to the role played by the Holy See delegations were the United Nations Conferences on Population, in Cairo (1994), and on Women, in Beijing (1995). The aforesaid delegations included not only permanent pontifical legates but also members chosen from among the clergy, religious, and the laity, both men and women.[14]

These institutions and conferences have become a key forum for the Holy See. Through pontifical legates, the Holy See gives voice to the Church's concern for the principal moral and social issues of the day which affect the lives not only of the Christian faithful but also of all the people of the world. In recent years, the Roman Pontiffs have increasingly addressed themselves to these organizations and to events organized by them, in order to draw the world's attention to many serious problems affecting the dignity of the human person.[15]

Ecclesial Responsibilities

Canon 364 — The principal function of a pontifical legate is daily to make stronger and more effective the bonds of unity which exist between the Apostolic See and particular churches. Therefore, it pertains to the pontifical legate for his own jurisdiction:

1° to send information to the Apostolic See concerning the conditions of particular churches and everything that touches the life of the Church and the good of souls;

Vatican City State. The Holy See sends representatives as well to about ten non-governmental organizations.

[14] The delegation sent to Beijing was headed by Dr. Mary Ann Glendon, Professor of Law at Harvard University.

[15] The degree of the Holy See's involvement in the international arena can be seen in the annual publication *Le Saint-Siège et les Organisations internationales*. A quick survey reveals that the Roman Pontiff is represented by personnel from the Secretariat of State, by permanent observers and/or members of their staffs, and by persons appointed specifically for a particular meeting.

2° to assist bishops by action and counsel while leaving intact the exercise of their legitimate power;

3° to foster close relations with the conference of bishops by offering it assistance in every way;

4° regarding the nomination of bishops, to transmit or propose to the Apostolic See the names of candidates and to instruct the informational process concerning those to be promoted, according to the norms given by the Apostolic See;

5° to strive to promote matters which pertain to the peace, progress, and cooperative effort of peoples;

6° to collaborate with bishops so that suitable relations are fostered between the Catholic Church and other Churches or ecclesial communities, and even non-Christian religions;

7° in associated action with bishops, to protect those things which pertain to the mission of the Church and the Apostolic See before the leaders of the state;

8° in addition, to exercise the faculties and to fulfill other mandates which the Apostolic See entrusts to him.

The principal obligations of the pontifical legate are directly related to and draw their *raison d'être* from the pope's ministry as a visible sign of unity for the whole Church, such that the legate acts as a liaison between the Apostolic See and the particular churches.

The canon, drawn from *Sollicitudo* IV–VIII, lists various functions of the legate, the first of which is to keep the Apostolic See informed regarding the conditions of the Church and of the Christian faithful in the territory to which the legate is sent (1°). Assisted by an understanding of the local language, culture, history, and traditions, the legate carries out his mission most effectively by means of personal visits to dioceses, seminaries, religious houses, parishes, and other institutions and communities.

This enables him to acquire first-hand knowledge regarding the life and activity of the Church, including customs, pastoral initiatives, and developments, at all levels, as well as the material and civil circumstances which affect the life of the people.[16]

The informational role of the pontifical legate in this regard is certainly not exclusive, since the Apostolic See is also informed about the conditions of the particular churches in other ways, e.g., papal visits around the world.

The pontifical legate plays an important role also regarding the local bishops. He neither replaces the local bishops nor exercises a supervisory function over them (2°). The bishops retain their right to deal directly with the Apostolic See, even if at times, in specific matters, the opinion of the pontifical legate is also sought. The relationship between the pontifical legate and the local bishops is intended to be mutually cooperative since the particular church may, at times, face difficult problems and can benefit from the legate's expertise and fraternal counsel. The pontifical legate makes present to the local bishops the unifying and strengthening presence of the Roman Pontiff, especially in political situations in which the particular church may be isolated, and communicates to them documents, directives, and initiatives which emanate from the Apostolic See. The pontifical legates also transmit to the Apostolic See publications, initiatives, and concerns which originate in the particular churches.

Similarly, the pontifical legate is to maintain a good relationship with the episcopal conference, respecting and safeguarding its rightful role (3°). While not a member (c. 450, §2), the pontifical legate is to take part in at least a part of its plenary meeting, and he can participate in other sessions at the invitation of the bishops or in virtue of a particular mandate. In conjunction with the episcopal conference, the pontifical legate can assist in coordinating the promotion of the mission of the Church and in dealing with specific problems, to whose resolution he can contribute his own point of view, as well as papal and curial insights. He also cooperates with the episcopal conference regarding the creation, division, and suppression of ecclesiastical circumscriptions. By his counsel and activity, he can provide valuable assistance, when needed, in helping to maintain the inner unity and cohesion of the episcopal conference. In conformity with the law (c. 456), the proceedings of the conference assemblies and decrees are sent to the Apostolic See, normally by the pontifical legate, who may add observations or an evaluation.

Furthermore, given the renewed emphasis on the importance of the *ad limina* visit, the pontifical legate is requested to assist in setting up and organizing the visit.[17]

A primary function of the pontifical legate is transmitting and proposing the names of those to be considered as candidates for the episcopacy, and the instruction of the informative process concerning the individual candidates (4°). The process is governed by universal law (c. 377) and by particular law.[18] The pontifical legate submits the *ternus* with a personal evaluation and informs the Holy See concerning the local conditions and the needs of the particular church, the actual state of the diocese or territory, and the qualities of the person to be considered. In this matter, the pontifical legate is to respect the discipline of the Eastern churches and the praxis regarding the designation of candidates for ecclesiastical circumscriptions entrusted to religious communities and under the

---

[16] As indicated in *PB* 41, §1, the First Section of the Secretariat of State, for General Affairs, is responsible for the ordering of the functions and activities of the representatives of the Holy See, especially regarding the particular churches. *AAS* 80 (1988) 870. For other specific details on such representatives see also the "Regolamento per le Rappresentanze Pontificie," published by the Secretariat of State, Vatican City, February 22, 1994.

[17] See Appendix I of *PB*, n. 7, regarding the pastoral significance of the *ad limina* visit (*PB* 28–32). *AAS* 80 (1988) 917.

[18] Council for the Public Affairs of the Church, *Normae de promovendis ad Episcopale Ministerium in Ecclesia Latina, AAS* 64 (1972) 386–391.

jurisdiction of the Congregation for the Evangelization of Peoples. In addition, several circumscriptions in Europe have acquired rights regarding the selection of bishops.[19] The process of selecting bishops has experienced continual developments throughout the history of the Church and, despite occasional criticism,[20] the pontifical legates carry out fairly wide consultation in order to avoid partial views and to have as complete information as possible to send to the Apostolic See.

The pontifical legate has responsibilities as well in other areas of the Church's life.

In recent decades the popes have taken a much more active role regarding the sphere of human development, the moral dimensions of economic and social problems faced especially by developing nations, the peaceful resolution of conflicts, and international relations in general. The pontifical legate therefore has an increasingly visible role in promoting the teaching of the Catholic Church and the moral leadership of the Roman Pontiff, often involving active participation in public forums dealing with such issues (5°).

Similarly, recent decades have seen an increase in initiatives and documents on the part of the Apostolic See regarding ecumenism and the relationship of the Catholic Church to non-Christian religious communities and to the different cultures existing in the world (6°). In cooperation with the bishops of the particular churches, the pontifical legate has a role in fostering such relations. Concrete examples include personal participation in ecumenical dialogue and in ceremonial and liturgical occasions, as well as contacts of a more private and personal nature, afforded often by the presentation of pontifical messages and the publication of Holy See documents.

The pontifical legate, in concerted action with the local bishops, seeks to protect that which pertains to the mission of the Church and the Apostolic See, especially regarding the preaching of the gospel and the exercise of the apostolate, in relations with the political and social leaders of the State (7°).

Lastly, the pontifical legate may be given other mandates and faculties, some of which relate to the liturgy, such as the imparting of the apostolic blessing, the administration of the sacraments, and various dispensations.[21] Under certain circumstances, the pontifical legate can also be entrusted with the care of a particular church.[22]

The canon does not mention the role of the pontifical legate regarding institutes of consecrated life and societies of apostolic life. The norms contained in *Sollicitudo* IX, which remain valid, indicate that the pontifical legate has the responsibility to help promote and consolidate the conferences of major superiors and to assist in coordinating their apostolic activity. He should be invited to take part in the opening sessions of the plenary assemblies of the conferences of major superiors of men and women religious, and he is to receive a copy of the acts, in order to transmit them to the competent dicastery. In addition, his counsel is to be sought regarding the granting of pontifical status to an institute of consecrated life which has its principal house in his territory.

The pontifical legate can also assist in fostering good relations between the episcopal conference and the conferences of major superiors.[23]

---

[19] R. Metz, "Papal Legates and the Appointment of Bishops," *J* 52 (1992) 272–275.

[20] Ibid., 259–284. See also C. Corral, "Response to Rene Metz," *J* 52 (1992) 285–293.

[21] See the *Index facultatum legatis pontificiis tributarum* (1986) and the *Facultates Legatis Romani Pontificis concessae* (1992) published, respectively, by the Congregation for Bishops and the Congregation for Eastern Churches, as well as the earlier *Facultates nuntiorum, internuntiorum et delegatorum apostolicorum* (1968) and *Index facultatum nuntiis, pro-nuntiis et delegatis apostolicis in territoriis missionum tributarum* (1971), published, respectively, by the Sacred Congregation for Bishops and the Sacred Congregation for the Evangelization of Peoples.

[22] The appointment of pontifical legates as apostolic administrators of Estonia, Southern Albania, and Transcarpathia for the Latin rite were recent examples.

[23] An example would be to encourage the establishment of the mixed commission, consisting of bishops and major superiors, men and women, as indicated in *MR* 63.

Diplomatic Responsibilities

Canon 365 — §1. It is also the special function of a pontifical legate who at the same time acts as a legate to states according to the norms of international law:

    1° to promote and foster relations between the Apostolic See and the authorities of the state;

    2° to deal with questions which pertain to relations between Church and state and in a special way to deal with the drafting and implementation of concordats and other agreements of this type.

    §2. In conducting the affairs mentioned in §1, a pontifical legate, as circumstances suggest, is not to neglect to seek the opinion and counsel of the bishops of the ecclesiastical jurisdiction and is to inform them of the course of affairs.

This canon, in rephrasing somewhat *Sollicitudo* X, indicates that, as the representative of the Roman Pontiff to the State and to public authorities, the pontifical legate has a particular responsibility to promote and foster relations between them and the Apostolic See.[24] The exercise of this function reflects as well the specific character of the Church and the Holy See, which, far from trying to gain any political advantage, seek rather to promote the common good and the resolution of conflicts in a peaceful manner, by negotiation and dialogue. This particular philosophy is reflected in the fact that pontifical legates are sent to nations with a great diversity of cultures and political systems, and exercise their functions even when the states to which they are sent are engaged in armed conflict.

In those countries where the pontifical legate is also the dean of the diplomatic corps, there are additional duties regarding the relations between the members of the diplomatic corps and the receiving state. As dean, the pontifical legate has the duty of representing the whole diplomatic corps to the government and receives the ambassadors and other heads of diplomatic missions at the beginning and the end of their term of service.

The responsibilities of the pontifical legate in maintaining good relations between the state and the particular churches often involve such fields as education, health care, and other social programs in which both the particular churches and the public authorities are involved. Such responsibilities may be exercised in concert with or supervised by government departments or ministries. These relations may also involve issues concerning the temporal goods of the Church, such as incorporation, registration and taxation, and, in some areas, restitution of goods and properties confiscated by past governments. The activity and the personal commitment of the pontifical legate aim to guarantee the rights of the Church, and to propose and promote the values it upholds for the common good of all.

The rights of the Church concerning the free exercise of its mission are sometimes guaranteed by a written agreement, such as a concordat or a *modus vivendi,* between the Holy See and the state, whether in whole or in part (e.g., the states of the Federal Republic of Germany). Agreements of this kind usually deal with issues such as access to places of worship, the establishment of religious schools and the teaching of religion in state or public schools, and the provision of religious services to prisoners and military personnel. The pontifical legate has particular responsibilities in the negotiations with the state and in drafting and signing the document on behalf of the Holy See.

The pontifical legate exercises these functions in concrete situations and profits from the advice and counsel of the bishops of the particular church, who have first-hand knowledge of local conditions and are directly affected by government policies. Moreover, in virtue of their status as members of the diplomatic corps, the pontifical legates must be attentive regarding their involvement in the political or internal affairs of the state to which they are accredited. Hence, close coop-

---

[24] In conformity with *PB* 46, 3°, the Second Section of the Secretariat of State, for Relations with States, is responsible for dealing with the pontifical representatives in the specific area of its activities. *AAS* 80 (1988) 872.

eration between the pontifical legate and the local bishops is essential, since the latter, as citizens, have the right to be involved in the affairs of their own country, in conformity with the prescriptions of canon 287, §2. In addition, some concordats stipulate that further details or accords regarding their implementation are to be worked out with the local episcopal conferences.

Privileges of Legates

Canon 366 — In view of the particular character of the function of a legate:
   1° **the seat of a pontifical legation is exempt from the power of governance of the local ordinary unless it is a question of celebrating marriages;**
   2° **after he has notified in advance the local ordinaries insofar as possible, a pontifical legate is permitted to perform liturgical celebrations in all churches of his legation, even in pontificals.**

In order to safeguard the legitimate autonomy of the pontifical legate, this canon, which is based on *Sollicitudo* XII, indicates that he is exempted from the governing power of the local ordinary, except for the celebration of marriage, for which delegation is needed, in conformity with the law.

The pontifical representation has a chapel in which the pontifical legate celebrates the sacred liturgy and administers other sacraments, often for members of the diplomatic corps, for the families of the personnel of the mission, and for others who have some relationship with the pontifical legation.[25]

Frequently, the pontifical legate is invited to celebrate public liturgical functions during visits to the particular churches of the territory in which he exercises his mission and, more commonly, in the place of his residence. The law points out what

would appear to be common courtesy, that the pontifical legate inform the local ordinaries with regard to such liturgical activities. Such apostolic activity, in fact, serves to demonstrate the unity that exists between the universal Church and the particular church, which is keenly felt by the participants, and to sustain the particular churches in times of difficulty.

The pontifical legates enjoy the privilege, in procedural law, of being judged by the Roman Pontiff alone (c. 1405, §1, 3°).

Duration in Office

Canon 367 — The function of a pontifical legate does not cease when the Apostolic See becomes vacant unless the pontifical letter establishes otherwise; it does cease, however, when the mandate has been fulfilled, when the legate has been notified of recall, or when the Roman Pontiff accepts the legate's resignation.

The last canon of this chapter, similar to *Sollicitudo* III, 2 and 3, is rather straightforward. Unlike the norms regarding the dicasteries of the Roman Curia, which stipulate that, during the vacancy of the Apostolic See, the mandate of those who preside over them expires, the same rule does not normally apply to the pontifical legate, ostensibly to safeguard the important principles of permanence and stability.[26]

Normally, during the course of the years of papal service, a pontifical legate will be assigned to more than one representation. In conformity with the norms of international law, when a pontifical legate who is also accredited to a state ceases from office, letters of recall are drawn up. These are usually presented to the government when the legate's successor presents the new letters of credence. Apostolic delegates would simply take leave of the particular church.

---

[25] In some circumstances, e.g., where the mission may be located in a diplomatic enclave or there is little access to a local parish, the chapel of the pontifical legation functions as an oratory.

[26] John Paul II, *Universi Dominici gregis, AAS* 88 (1996) 305–343. Article 21 reiterates what is contained in the code, namely, that the *munus* and *potestas* of the pontifical legates do not cease with the vacancy of the Apostolic See.

Cessation from office also occurs as a result of transfer to a different mission, such as the appointment as a residential bishop in the pontifical legate's country of origin or as head of a dicastery of the Roman Curia.

The retirement of the pontifical legate is governed according to principles contained in particular law, which are similar to those which govern superior prelates of the Roman Curia. Namely, the pontifical legate, upon reaching the completion of his seventy-fifth year, ceases from his functions.

Provision is also made for resignation or retirement prior to the aforesaid age limit in circumstances similar to those for bishops (c. 401, §2); such a resignation must be accepted by the Roman Pontiff to be effective.

BIBLIOGRAPHY

Studies Prior to Vatican II

Graham, R. J. *Vatican Diplomacy: A Study of Church and State on the International Plane.* Princeton, N.J.: Princeton University, 1959.

Paro, G. *The Right of Papal Legation.* Washington, D.C.: Catholic University of America, 1947.

Staffa, D. *Le Delegazioni Apostoliche.* Rome/New York: Desclée, 1959.

Commentaries on the 1983 Code of Canon Law

Chiappetta, L. *Il Codice di Diritto Canonico: Commento Giuridico Pastorale.* Naples: Dehoniane, 1988.

"De Romani Pontificis Legatis." In *Pamplona ComEng,* 239–244.

"Les Légats du Pontife Romain." In *Code de Droit Canonique Annoté,* ed. A. Soria-Vasco, H. Laplane, and M.-A. Chueca, 252–256. Paris: Cerf, 1989.

McGrath, A. "Papal Legates." In *CLSGBI Com,* 206–209.

Petroncelli-Hübler, F. "De Romani Pontificis Legatis." In *Com Ex,* 656–674.

Provost, J. "The Legates of the Roman Pontiff." In *CLSA Com,* 300–305.

Official Documents

CFB. *Index facultatum legatis pontificiis tributarum.* Typis Polyglottis Vaticanis, 1986.

CEC. *Facultates Legatis Romani Pontificis concessae.* Typis Polyglottis Vaticanis, 1992.

Ciprotti, P., and Talamanca, A., eds. *I concordati di Pio XII (1939–1958).* Milan: Giuffré, 1976.

———. *I concordati di Giovanni XXIII e dei primi anni di Paolo VI (1958–1974).* Milan: Giuffré, 1976.

Mercati, A. *Raccolta di Concordati su materie ecclesiastiche tra la Santa Sede e le Autorità Civili.* Vol. 1 (1908–1914); vol. 2 (1915–1954). Rome: Tipografia Polyglotta Vaticana, 1919 and 1954.

Paul VI. *Mp Sollicitudo omnium Ecclesiarum,* June 24, 1969. *AAS* 61 (1969) 473–484; *CLD* 7, 277–284.

SCB. "Facultates nuntiorum, internuntiorum et delegatorum apostolicorum." *EnchVat,* 13th ed. Vol. 3, 26–45. Bologna: Dehoniane, 1985. *CLD* 5, 293–306.

Schoppe, L. *Konkordate seit 1800: Originaltext und deutsche Übersetzung der geltenden Konkordate.* Frankfurt: Metzner, 1964.

————. *Neue Konkordate und konkordatare Verein-barung: Abschlüsse in den Jahren 1964 bis 1969.* Hamburg, 1970.

SCProp. "Index facultatum nuntiis, pro-nuntiis et delegatis apostolicis in territoriis missionum tributarum." *EnchVat,* 13th ed. Vol. 4, 34–43. Bologna: Dehoniane, 1985. *CLD* 7, 285–289.

Studies

Arrieta, J. *Diritto dell'Organizzazione Ecclesiastica.* Milan: Giuffré, 1997.

Bassett, W., ed. *The Choosing of Bishops.* Hartford, Conn.: CLSA, 1971.

Bertagna, B. "Santa Sede ed Organizzazioni Internazionali." *ME* 107 (1982) 102–159, 284–306, 383–428.

Blet, P. *Histoire de la représentation diplomatique du Saint-Siège: Des origines à l'aube du XIXe siècle.* Vatican City: Archivio Vaticano, 1982.

Braida, P. V. A. "L'ufficio dei rappresentanti del Romano Pontefice." *Apol* 52 (1979) 175–199.

Cardinale, H. *The Holy See and the International Order.* Gerrards Cross, England: Colin Smythe, 1976.

Castro, R. *La Misión del Representante Pontifico, Modelos Históricos y Orientaciones del Magisterio.* Rome: Typis Pontificae Universitatis Gregorianae, 1989.

Cavalli, F. "Il Motu proprio Sollicitudo omnium Ecclesiarum sull'ufficio dei rappresentanti pontifici." *La Civiltà Cattolica* 120 (1969) 34–43.

Ciprotti, P. "Note sparse sulla precedenza dei rappresentanti diplomatici della Santa Sede." *Il Diritto Ecclesiastico* (1987) 1:240–249.

Coriden, J. "Diplomatic Recognition of the Holy See." *J* 48 (1988) 483–498.

Corral, C. "Response to René Metz." *J* 52 (1992) 285–293.

deEcheverria, L. "Funciones de los legados del Romano Pontífice." *REDC* 25 (1969) 581–636.

————. "The Pope's Representatives." In *The Roman Curia and the Communion of Churches,* ed. P. Huizing and K Walf, 56–63. *Con* 127. New York: Seabury, 1979.

D'Onorio, J.-B. *La Nomination des Evêques: Procédures Canoniques et Conventions Diplomatiques.* Paris: Tardy, 1986.

Dupuy, A. *La Diplomatie du Saint-Siège après le IIe Concile du Vatican.* Paris: Téqui, 1980.

Granfield, P. "The Church Local and Universal: Realization of Communion." *J* 49 (1989) 449–471.

Hennesey, J. "Papal Diplomacy and the Contemporary Church." In *The Once and Future Church,* ed. J. Coriden, 179–204. New York: Alba House, 1971.

Huizing, P., and K. Walf, eds. *Electing Our Own Bishops.* New York: Seabury, 1980.

Jiménez-Urresti, T., ed. *Structures of the Church.* *Con* 58. New York: Herder & Herder, 1970.

Köck, H. F. "Die multilaterale Diplomatie des Heiligen Stuhls." *OAKR* 32 (1981) 204–226.

Krämer, P. "Episcopal Conferences and the Apostolic See." *J* 48 (1988) 134–145.

Laghi, P. "The Role of the Apostolic Pro-Nuncio." *Origins* 14 (1984) 390–391.

Lallou, W. *The Fifty Years of the Apostolic Delegation: Washington. D.C. 1893–1943.* Jersey City, N.J.: St. Anthony Guild, 1943.

Le Tourneau, D. "Les légats pontificaux dans le Code de 1983, vingt ans après la constitution apostolique 'Sollicitudo omnium Ecclesiarum.'" *AC* 32 (1989) 229–260.

Marini, L. "The Apostolic Delegate: His Role in Ecclesiastical Law." JCL dissertation. Catholic University of America, 1983.

Metz, R. "Le désignation des évêques dans le droit actuel: Étude comparative entre le Code latin de 1983 et le Code oriental de 1990." *Stud Can* 27 (1993) 321–334.

———. "L'indépendence de l'Église dans le choix des évêques à Vatican II et dans le Code de 1983, aboutissement d'un demi-siècle d'effort diplomatique." *RDC* 37 (1987) 143–170.

———. "Papal Legates and the Appointment of Bishops." *J* 52 (1992) 259–284.

Minnerath, R. *L'Église et les états concordataires (1846–1981): La souveraineté spirituelle.* Paris: Cerf, 1983.

Oliveri, M. *The Representatives: The Real Nature and Function of Papal Legates.* Gerrards Cross, England: Van Duren, 1981.

Petroncelli Hübler, F. "De Romani pontificis legatis: Note in margine alla nuova normativa codiciale." In *Raccolta di Scritti in onore di Pio Fedele,* ed. G. Barberini, 555–590. Perugia: Università degli Studi di Perugia, 1984.

Reese, T. J. *Inside the Vatican: The Politics and the Organization of the Catholic Church.* Cambridge, Mass.: Harvard University, 1996.

Robinson, G. J. "Papal Representatives in the Context of Collegiality." In *Le Nouveau Code de Droit Canonique—The New Code of Canon Law: Actes du Ve Congrès International du Droit Canonique. Ottawa. 19–24 Août 1984,* ed. M. Theriault and J. Thorn, 481–495. Ottawa: St. Paul's University, 1986.

Talamanca, A. "I rappresentanti pontifici nella nuova normativa canonica." In *Vitam impendere vero: Scritti in onore di Pio Ciprotti,* ed. W. Schulz and G. Feliciani, 277–296. Vatican City: Libreria Editrice Vaticana, 1986.

Walf, K. "Der Apostolische Pronuntius: Neue Sinngebung für einen alten Terminus technicus." *AkK* 134 (1965) 376–381.

Wister, R. *The Establishment of the Apostolic Delegation in the United States of America: The Satolli Mission. 1892–1896.* Rome: Pontificia Universitas Gregoriana, 1981.

SECTION II
PARTICULAR CHURCHES
AND THEIR GROUPINGS
[cc. 368–572]

TITLE I
PARTICULAR CHURCHES
AND THE AUTHORITY ESTABLISHED IN THEM
[cc. 368–430]

In *Sacrae disciplinae leges,* the apostolic constitution whereby he promulgated the 1983 Code of Canon Law, Pope John Paul II says:

Among the elements which characterize the true and genuine image of the Church we should emphasize especially the following: . . . the doctrine in which the Church is seen as a *communio* and which therefore determines the relations which are to exist between the particular churches and the universal Church, and between collegiality and the primacy.

An appropriate understanding of the particular church is essential for a right understanding of the Church established by Christ, which by its own profession is catholic. Canons 368–430 contain the Latin church's legislation about the particular churches (the most common form of which is the diocese), their bishops (or equivalent leadership figures), and their pastoral governance in extraordinary circumstances when the particular church temporarily is impeded or vacant.

The Church of Christ is a *communio* of believers. The 1993 *Directory for the Application of Principles and Norms on Ecumenism* says that the communion in which all Christians believe and for which we hope "is realized concretely in the particular churches, each of which is gathered together around its bishop. In each of these 'the one, holy, catholic and apostolic church of Christ is truly present and alive.' This communion is, by its very nature, universal."[1] The directory continues:

Thus the bishops guarantee that the churches of which they are the ministers continue the one church of Christ founded on the faith and ministry of the apostles. They coordinate the spiritual energies and the gifts of the faithful and their associates toward the building up of the church and of the full exercise of its mission.

Each particular church, united within itself and in the communion of the one, holy, catholic and apostolic church, is sent forth in the name of Christ and in the power of the Spirit to bring the Gospel of the kingdom to more and more people, offering them this communion with God. . . .

Communion within the particular churches and between them is a gift of God.[2]

This same theme of ecclesial communion is found in the first chapter of the 1984 *Ceremonial of Bishops,* promulgated soon after the 1983 code had become operative in the Latin church. The ceremonial says:

Hence the dignity of the Church of Christ is embodied in the particular Churches. Each such Church is not simply a group of people who on their own choose to band together for some common endeavor; rather each Church is a gift that comes down from the Father of lights. Nor are the particular Churches to be regarded merely as administrative divisions of the people of God. In

---

[1] *Ecum Dir* 13.
[2] Ibid., 14–16.

their own way they contain and manifest the nature of the universal Church, which issued from the side of Christ crucified, which lives and grows through the Eucharist, which is espoused to Christ, and which, as their mother, cares for all the faithful.... Just as the universal Church is present and manifested in the particular Churches, so too each particular Church contributes its own distinctive gifts to the other Churches and to the Church as a whole....

As Christ's vicar and representative, marked with the fullness of the sacrament of orders, the bishop leads the particular Church in communion with the pope and under his authority.[3]

In this commentary, special consideration is given to the Church's living understanding of these canons since the promulgation of the 1983 code. Particular focus is placed on any post-codal legislation which touches upon the material covered in canons 368–430.

Structure

Book II of the Code of Canon Law, entitled "The People of God," is divided into three parts: the Christian faithful (part one, cc. 208–329), the hierarchical constitution of the Church (part two, cc. 330–572), and institutes of consecrated life and societies of apostolic life (part three, cc. 573–746).

Part two is divided into two sections: the supreme authority of the Church (section one, cc. 330–367) and particular churches and their groupings (section two, cc. 368–572).

Section two has three titles: particular churches and the authority established in them (title I, cc. 368–430), groupings of particular churches (title II, cc. 431–459), and the internal organization of particular churches (title III, cc. 460–572).[4]

---

[3] *CB* 2, 4–5.

[4] For a discussion of the dialogue in the *coetus de sacra hierarchia* leading to this sequence of the material in sec-

Title I, considered here, is divided into three chapters (two of which are subdivided into articles):

Chapter I – Particular churches (cc. 368–374)
Chapter II – Bishops (cc. 375–411)
   Art. 1 – Bishops in general (cc. 375–380)
   Art. 2 – Diocesan bishops (cc. 381–402)
   Art. 3 – Coadjutor and auxiliary bishops (cc. 403–411)
Chapter III – The impeded see and the vacant see (cc. 412–430)
   Art. 1 – The impeded see (cc. 412–415)
   Art. 2 – The vacant see (cc. 416–430)

Historical Context

Most of the content of canons 368–430 reflects similar canons in Book II (*De personis*) of the 1917 code, which often presents the material differently. The 1917 code contained no canons precisely describing the diocese and other kinds of particular churches, nor were these groupings called *particular churches;* any understanding of them must be gleaned from the 1917 code's treatment of their leaders. Canons 293–311 treated apostolic vicars and apostolic prefects, and canons 319–328 treated prelates *nullius* and abbots *nullius,* called collectively *inferior prelates;* these canons came at the end of title VII, "The supreme power of the Church and those who participate in it by ecclesiastical law." These church authorities were considered to be exercising vicarious papal power, and so norms about them were contained among the canons on supreme ecclesiastical power.

tion two, see T. Green, "Persons and Structures in the Church," *J* 45 (1985) 44–47. The deliberate choice was made to place title I before title II. The pope (treated in section one) and the bishops (treated in section two, title I) are divine law realities, and should be treated together. Groupings of particular churches (provinces, regions, metropolitans, particular councils, and conferences of bishops—treated in section two, title II) are ecclesiastical law realities, and rightly placed after the treatment of the divine law institutes. This is the result of a 47–2 vote of the October 1981 *Plenarium.*

Title VIII of Book II treated episcopal power and those who share in it. It contained two chapters on bishops: chapter 1 on "bishops" (*CIC* 329–333 dealing with the appointment of all bishops and *CIC* 334–349 on the ministry of residential [diocesan] bishops), and chapter 2 on "coadjutor and auxiliary bishops" (*CIC* 350–355).

The treatment of the impeded and vacant see was combined into chapter 7 of title VIII (*CIC* 429–444).

The 1967 synod of bishops approved ten principles to guide the revision of the 1917 code,[5] three of which have particular significance in considering canons 368–430. *Principle four* directed that the office of bishop was to be presented positively in the revised code; in accord with conciliar teaching, especially that of *Christus Dominus* 8, bishops should be given all the faculties needed to exercise their pastoral ministry—except in cases explicitly reserved to the supreme authority or to some other authority. *Principle five* called for an application of the principle of subsidiarity in the Church. Like principle four, principle five recognizes the fact that diocesan bishops, as successors to the apostles, possess all the ordinary, proper, and immediate power to perform their pastoral function—unless the Supreme Pontiff has reserved some case to himself or to another authority. Although canon law must remain uniform for the entire Church, there is also place for particular legislation, especially in the matter of administration of temporal goods (which must regard local civil laws and diverse economic variables); while general procedural laws must be uniform throughout the Church, local authorities will enact norms to be observed in local tribunals. Finally, *principle eight* said that territory should remain the usual determinant of jurisdiction, although serious reasons (e.g., the rite or nationality of the faithful) may require other determinants, at least together with territory.

The history of the revision of the 1917 code and the creation of the 1983 code is beyond the scope of this commentary, and is readily available elsewhere.[6] Suffice it to note that the key sources for canons 368–430 are the following: the 1917 code, three conciliar documents (especially *Lumen gentium* 19–28, *Christus Dominus* 11–26, and *Sacrosanctum Concilium* 41), and two post-conciliar documents (especially *Ecclesiae sanctae* I, 10–13, and the *Directory on the Pastoral Ministry of Bishops*).

Eastern Code

The Eastern code does not treat particular churches in the same manner as does the Latin law, since the term *particular church* is understood differently among the Eastern churches than in the Latin church.[7] Material similar to that of canons 368–430 is found in the Eastern code title VII, *eparchies and bishops,* chapter 1, *bishops* (*CCEO* 177–234). After three preliminary canons (*CCEO* 177–179) the chapter contains the following four articles:

Art. 1 – The election of bishops (*CCEO* 180–189)
Art. 2 – The rights and obligations of eparchial bishops (*CCEO* 190–211)
Art. 3 – Coadjutor bishops and auxiliary bishops (*CCEO* 212–218)
Art. 4 – The vacant or impeded eparchial see (*CCEO* 219–233)

The chapter concludes with a single canon (*CCEO* 234) which treats *apostolic administrators,* specific norms about which are not found in the 1983 code although such an authority figure does exist in practice in the Latin church.

---

[5] *Comm* 1 (1969) 77–85. For more discussion about these principles, see J. Alesandro, "The Revision of the *Code of Canon Law:* A Background Study," *Stud Can* 24 (1990) 106–110.

[6] For a commentary placing more emphasis on the development of the canons of the 1983 code, especially as compared with the 1917 code, see T. Green, "Particular Churches and the Authority Established in Them," in *CLSA Com,* 311–349. See also appendix I of this commentary, which traces the revision process reported in *Comm.*

[7] See fn. 10, below.

CHAPTER I
PARTICULAR CHURCHES
[cc. 368–374][8]

Chapter 1 identifies the canonical meaning of the *particular church* (c. 368) and then explains in more detail the six kinds of particular churches: diocese (c. 369), territorial prelature (c. 370), territorial abbacy (c. 370), apostolic vicariate (c. 371, §1), apostolic prefecture (c. 371, §1), and apostolic administration erected in a stable manner (c. 372, §2). As a rule a particular church is defined by territory, though some other criterion of determination may exist (e.g., the rite of the faithful) (c. 372). Only the supreme authority of the Church erects a particular church which, when erected, possesses juridic personality by law (c. 373). Each particular church is to be divided into distinct parts or parishes, neighboring ones of which can be joined into groups such as vicariates forane (c. 374).

These canons expand significantly canons 215–217 of the 1917 code which simply explained that the supreme authority of the Church could erect or modify an ecclesiastical province, diocese, abbey *nullius,* or vicariate *nullius* (*CIC* 215, §1), that the abbey *nullius* and the vicariate *nullius* were likened to a diocese (*CIC* 215, §2), that the territory of a diocese was to be divided into parishes (*CIC* 216), that several nearby parishes were to be united into regions called vicariates forane, deaneries (*decanatus*), or archpresbyteries (*CIC* 217, §1), and that, if such regional grouping seemed impossible or inopportune, the bishop was to consult the Holy See (*CIC* 217, §2). The canons of the 1917 code did not describe a *particular church* or the kinds of particular churches. Apostolic vicars and apostolic prefects (*CIC*

293–311) and prelates *nullius* and abbots *nullius* (*CIC* 319–328), all figures likened to residential bishops, were treated in the section on the supreme authority of the Church since they participated in papal power.

Canon 177, §1 of the Eastern code on the eparchy is similar to canon 369 on the diocese, and canon 177, §2 of the Eastern code is similar to canon 373 on the power competent to modify dioceses. Canon 311 of the Eastern code on the exarchy is similar to the apostolic vicariate in canon 371, §1. Other similar canons about particular churches are not in the Eastern code, and the eparchy and exarchy are not called *particular churches,* a term avoided in the Eastern code.[9]

Types of Particular Churches

Canon 368 — Particular churches, in which and from which the one and only Catholic Church exists, are first of all dioceses, to which, unless it is otherwise evident, are likened a territorial prelature and territorial abbacy, an apostolic vicariate and an apostolic prefecture, and an apostolic administration erected in a stable manner.

This preliminary canon explains *particular church* as the term is understood in the code.[10] In

---

[8] For the history of the development of these canons, see *Comm* 3 (1971) 188; 4 (1972) 39–43; 12 (1980) 275–285; 14 (1982) 201–204; 18 (1986) 54–57, 99–102, 112–114; 24 (1992) 56–57, 309–310. Other commentaries: *CLSGBI Com,* 209–213; *Pamplona ComEng,* 292–297.

[9] *Nu* 9 (1979) 5–6; J. Faris, *The Eastern Catholic Churches* (New York: St. Maron, 1992) 403–404, 409–410, n. 3.
[10] *Particular church* is a term applied in a variety of ways in Vatican Council II. In *LG* it refers to dioceses or their groupings. In *AG* it refers to all the churches in a given region or social context. In *CD* it refers to dioceses. In *OE* it refers to the ritual churches or *faithful sui iuris* who are identified in *CCEO* 27 as a *church sui iuris.* The council also uses the term *local church* a number of times. The term *particular church* was abandoned by those drafting the Eastern code since the Latin code uses the term in c. 368 to designate dioceses and structures like dioceses. See *Nu* 9 (1979) 5–6; also G. Routhier, "'Église locale' ou 'église particulière,'" *Stud Can* 25 (1991) 277–334. Routhier discusses the terms *local church* and *particular church;* he argues in favor of using the former term, even though the Latin code has

words reflecting Vatican II, the canon describes particular churches as those in which and from which the one and only Catholic Church exists. *Lumen gentium* 23 says that in and from the particular churches there comes into being the one and only Catholic Church.[11] Each particular church is constituted after the model of the universal Church. Within each particular church the bishop is the visible source and foundation of unity, and the Roman Pontiff is the perpetual and visible source and foundation of unity both of the bishops and of all the faithful. Each bishop represents his own particular church; all bishops, together with the pope, represent the whole Church in a bond of peace, love, and unity.

In this code, *particular church* refers first of all to dioceses (described in c. 369).[12] Further, unless the contrary is evident, the term is also understood to describe five other kinds of gatherings of the faithful which are likened to (*assimilantur*) dioceses: territorial prelatures, territorial abbacies, apostolic vicariates, apostolic prefectures, and apostolic administrations erected in a stable manner.[13]

The persons who head these communities are equivalent in law to a diocesan bishop even if they have not received episcopal ordination, unless the contrary is evident either from the nature of the matter[14] or the prescript of law (c. 381, §2). They are also *local ordinaries* (c. 134, §2).

Particular churches are commonly limited to a definite territory such that all the faithful living therein form the particular church, though some other criterion of identification can exist (see c. 372). Territoriality is not, however, considered a constitutive element of a particular church; it is a specifying or determining element whereby a particular church is identified.

Pastor bonus explains the competency of the various dicasteries of the Roman Curia in the establishment of particular churches and in the appointment of bishops or other heads of these churches. In the Latin church, the Congregation for Bishops examines what pertains to the establishment and provision of particular churches and to the exercise of the episcopal function therein, without prejudice to the competence of the Congregation for the Evangelization of Peoples for mission territories of the Latin church. The Congregation for Bishops also deals with everything concerning the constitution, division, union, suppression, and other modifications of particular churches and groups of them (*PB* 75–76). It proceeds only in consultation with the "Section for Relations with States" of the Secretariat of State when dealing with civil governments in establishing or modifying particular churches or their groups (*PB* 78; see *PB* 47, §1). In mission territories, the Congregation for the Evangelization of Peoples deals with everything pertaining to the establishment and modification of ecclesiastical territories, and carries out the other functions that the Congregation for Bishops fulfills elsewhere (*PB* 89).

---

selected the latter. See also P. Granfield, "The Church Local and Universal," *J* 49 (1989) 453–455.

[11] See also *LG* 13, 26; *CD* 11; *AG* 19–20.

[12] During the process of revising the 1917 code, personal prelatures were initially included among the particular churches. It was decided in time, however, that these are not particular churches, and so treatment of them should be elsewhere in the law. Personal prelatures are discussed in cc. 294–298 in the first part of Book II, located between the treatment of clergy and associations of the Christian faithful. Nonetheless, the Congregation for Bishops is the competent Roman dicastery for everything involving personal prelatures: *PB* 80. See P. Rodríguez, *Particular Churches and Personal Prelatures* (Dublin: Four Courts, 1986).

[13] A. Longhitano explains that the first two of these five kinds of particular churches have a definitive form and differ from dioceses only for historical reasons or because of the size of the territory; the last three have an initial form and are on the way to being erected into dioceses when circumstances permit. "Le chiese particolari," in A. Longhitano et al., *Chiesa particolare e strutture di communione* (Bologna: Dehoniane, 1985) 31.

[14] According to the nature of the matter, presbyteral leadership figures cannot place those acts which require episcopal ordination (e.g., the power to ordain). Presbyters who govern particular churches can perform other acts otherwise reserved in law to the diocesan bishop, unless a given law forbids this.

On April 21, 1986, Pope John Paul II issued *Spirituali militum curae*,[15] the apostolic constitution on the military ordinariate. Military ordinariates are juridically likened to a diocese (*dioecesibus iuridice assimilantur*); they are special ecclesiastical districts governed by proper statutes issued by the Apostolic See.[16] Their ordinary, normally a bishop, has the rights and duties of a diocesan bishop unless the nature of things or particular statutes determine otherwise.[17] He is freely appointed (or confirmed, if legitimately designated) by the Supreme Pontiff.[18] He is subject to the Congregation for Bishops or the Congregation for the Evangelization of Peoples,[19] and belongs to the conference of bishops.[20]

---

[15] This apconst replaces the instruction *Sollemne semper* of April 23, 1951, *AAS* 45 (1951) 562–565; *CLD* 3, 113–117. *SMC* asked each military ordinariate to present its proposed statutes to the Apostolic See for examination within a year of July 21, 1986, the effective date of this law. The only reference to the military ordinariate in the 1983 code is c. 569, which says that military chaplains are governed by special laws.

[16] *SMC* I, §1. *SMC* II, §4 compares the military ordinariate to "*other* particular churches" (*alias ecclesias particulares*) which reveals that in the mind of the legislator the military ordinariate is a form of the *particular church*. J. Beyer agrees, and writes: "Hence the ordinariate to the forces is correctly termed a particular church" ("Commentary on the Apostolic Constitution *Spirituali militum curae,*" *CLS-GBIN* 76 [December, 1988] 59). D. LeTourneau, however, concludes that the military ordinariate is not a particular church (although it is very much like one) but instead is a personal prelature, in "La nouvelle organisation de l'Ordinariat aux Armées," *SC* 21 (1987) 37–66. There appears to be no basis for LeTourneau's position.

[17] *SMC* II, §1.

[18] *SMC* II, §2.

[19] *SMC* XI.

[20] *SMC* III. *SMC* adds other particulars about the governance of the military ordinariate, among which are the following. The military ordinary is to make a quinquennial report on the affairs of the ordinariate, and is to make the *ad limina* visit to Rome (XII). The ordinary is normally to be free from other duties involving the care of souls (II, §3). He has jurisdiction which is personal (concerning all who are part of the ordinariate), ordinary (in both the internal and external fora), and proper but

The six kinds of particular churches identified in the code (but not the military ordinariate, whose norms were promulgated after the code) are described in detail in the immediately following canons.

Notion of Diocese

Canon 369 — A diocese is a portion of the people of God which is entrusted to a bishop for him to shepherd with the cooperation of the presbyterate, so that, adhering to its pastor and gathered by him in the Holy Spirit through the gospel and the Eucharist, it constitutes a particular church in which the one, holy, catholic, and apostolic Church of Christ is truly present and operative.

The most common form of particular church is the diocese, described in this canon with words taken verbatim from *Christus Dominus* 11.[21] The diocese is a portion of the people of God; its pastoral care is entrusted to a bishop for him to shepherd with the cooperation of the presbyterate.[22]

---

cumulative (i.e., simultaneous with that of the diocesan bishop, since those belonging to the ordinariate do not cease to be faithful of the particular church where they have domicile or quasi-domicile) (IV; see also V, VII, X). Clerics may incardinate in the military ordinariate, which may operate its own seminary (VI, §§3–4). There is to be a presbyteral council (VI, §5). Special statutes for each military ordinariate will address various issues: the place of the military ordinary's church and curia; whether he will have a vicar (or vicars) general and other curial officials; details about the clerics of the ordinariate during and after their time of service; provisions for the impeded or vacant see; the existence of a pastoral council for the entire ordinariate or part of it; the maintenance of sacramental records; the status of a tribunal for the ordinariate (XII–XIV).

[21] *CCEO* 177, §1.

[22] The presbyterate includes all the priests resident in and/or ministering in the diocese: i.e., priests incardinated in the diocese, priests incardinated in another particular church, priests of a personal prelature, and priests who are members of institutes of consecrated life or societies of apostolic life. The diocesan bishop also has a special relationship of collaboration and cooperation with other bishops assigned to serve under his leadership in the diocese: the

The canon reveals the constitutive elements of a diocese: the bishop, his presbyterate, the people of God. The bishop gathers this portion of the people of God in the Holy Spirit through the gospel and the Eucharist. The diocese is a particular church in which the one, holy, catholic, and apostolic Church of Christ is truly present and operative. The diocese is not a mere administrative division of the universal Church. The role of the bishop is presented not in terms of his power but of his shepherding or pastoral ministry.

One observes that the description of a diocese does not mention territoriality. The canon focuses upon the people of God who form the particular church. Nonetheless, according to canon 372 every particular church is generally limited to a definite territory, although some other criterion of determination may exist, such as the rite of the faithful.

The diocese is the particular church to which are likened other forms of particular churches (c. 368). The diocesan bishop is the central figure in the particular church to which the heads of other particular churches are juridically equivalent, unless the nature of the matter or a prescript of law determines otherwise (c. 381, §2).

Notions of Territorial Prelature/ Territorial Abbacy

Canon 370 — A territorial prelature or territorial abbacy is a certain portion of the people of God which is defined territorially and whose care, due to special circumstances, is entrusted to some prelate or abbot who governs it as its proper pastor just like a diocesan bishop.

This canon identifies two other kinds of particular churches: the territorial prelature and the territorial abbacy.[23] These are portions of the people

of God with specific territorial boundaries; due to special circumstances their care is entrusted to a prelate or abbot[24] as proper pastor. These authority figures govern their particular churches just like a diocesan bishop unless the nature of the matter or the law specifies otherwise (see c. 381, §2).[25]

The territorial prelature, formerly called a prelature *nullius dioeceseos* (i.e., attached to no diocese), has its own territory, faithful, and clergy and a prelate (who generally has received episcopal ordination). It is separated from any diocese. The prelate governs the prelature in the manner of a diocesan bishop, and is named by the Supreme Pontiff.[26]

The territorial abbacy, formerly called an abbacy *nullius dioeceseos* (i.e., attached to no diocese), also has its own territory, faithful, and clergy; the abbot of the nearby monastery governs it in the manner of a diocesan bishop. It is separated from any diocese. The abbot (who generally has not received episcopal ordination) is named by the Supreme Pontiff.[27]

---

coadjutor bishop, the auxiliary with special faculties, and the auxiliary without special faculties (c. 407).

[23] *CIC* 319–327. In these nine canons, the 1917 code treated the prelate and abbot *nullius* as "inferior prelates" and in the section dealing with the supreme (papal) power of the church, not in the section dealing with bishops.

[24] On October 23, 1970, Pope Paul VI issued his *mp Catholica Ecclesia* which decreed that in the future no abbacies *nullius* were to be erected except under very special circumstances; those currently existing for the most part should be turned over to other ecclesiastical circumscriptions (in accord with the mind of Vatican II in *CD* 23); those whose territory is turned over totally to another circumscription will be governed by common law, unless special law has been decreed in individual instances by the Apostolic See; and normally the abbot should not possess episcopal orders unless such is demanded by the spiritual authority or special historical status of the abbacy, which embraces a portion of the people of God. *AAS* 68 (1976) 694–695; *CLD* 8, 236–238.

[25] *CIC* 319, §2 had legislated that a prelature or abbacy *nullius* with fewer than three parishes is governed by particular law and not the code. However, similar legislation does not exist in the 1983 code.

[26] The *Annuario Pontificio per l'Anno 1998* identifies 52 territorial prelatures (1029–1042).

[27] The *Annuario Pontificio per l'Anno 1998* identifies 15 territorial abbacies (1043–1046).

Notions of Apostolic Vicariate/
Apostolic Prefecture

Canon 371 — §1. An apostolic vicariate or apostolic prefecture is a certain portion of the people of God which has not yet been established as a diocese due to special circumstances and which, to be shepherded, is entrusted to an apostolic vicar or apostolic prefect who governs it in the name of the Supreme Pontiff.

This canon describes two types of particular churches found in missionary lands and not yet established as dioceses: the apostolic prefecture and the apostolic vicariate.[28] Commonly, a mission *sui iuris*[29] first becomes an apostolic prefec-

---

[28] *CIC* 293–311. In these nineteen canons, the 1917 code treated the apostolic vicar and the apostolic prefect in the section dealing with the supreme (papal) power of the Church, not in the section dealing with bishops.

The *Annuario Pontificio per l'Anno 1998* identifies 75 apostolic vicariates (1060–1076) and 44 apostolic prefectures (1077–1083). It identifies 7 missions *sui iuris* (1086–1087). In the Eastern churches, the equivalent of an apostolic vicariate is the *exarchy,* described as a portion of the people of God not erected as an eparchy (diocese) within territorial or other kinds of limits (*CCEO* 311). See *Annuario Pontificio per l'Anno 1998,* p. 1820.

The revision commission (during very early meetings occurring on December 4–5, 1967) acknowledged that the apostolic vicariate and apostolic prefecture had merely political origins: they arose to avoid conflict between the Holy See and Spain-Portugal during the days of colonial expansion. Some of these apostolic vicariates and apostolic prefectures became even more developed than dioceses in areas such as organization of the apostolate, numbers of vocations, intensity of the Christian life, etc. The revision commission was also aware that, in today's world, there exist jurisdictional structures (e.g., military ordinariates, ordinariates for migrants, sailors, etc.) which did not exist at the time when the 1917 code was promulgated. It was felt that the revised code should provide structures accommodated to concrete social circumstances and pastoral needs. See *Comm* 18 (1986) 59–60.

[29] The term *mission sui iuris* is the name given to a mission territory not yet part of an apostolic vicariate or an apostolic prefecture. It is governed by an ecclesiastical superior who provides the personnel and other resources for

---

ture; this then becomes an apostolic vicariate; finally, it becomes a diocese. The pastoral care of these two kinds of particular churches is entrusted to an apostolic prefect or an apostolic vicar. Normally, the prefect is not a bishop, but the vicar is a bishop.[30] The prefect and the vicar are equivalent to a diocesan bishop, unless the nature of the matter or the law specifies otherwise (see c. 381, §2). They govern their particular churches in the name of the Supreme Pontiff, so their power is called *ordinary* (attached to their office) and *vicarious* (not proper) power (see c. 131, §2).

Pastor bonus 89 says that in mission territories the Congregation for the Evangelization of Peoples deals with the establishment and modification of "ecclesiastical territories" and the appointment of bishops or others to head them. In fact, the congregation carries out in mission territories all the functions that the Congregation for Bishops fulfills elsewhere.

Notion of Apostolic Administration
Erected on a Stable Basis

§2. An apostolic administration is a certain portion of the people of God which is not erected as a diocese by the Supreme Pontiff due to special and particularly grave reasons and whose pastoral care is entrusted to an apostolic administrator who governs it in the name of the Supreme Pontiff.

This canon identifies a sixth kind of particular church: the apostolic administration erected in a stable manner.[31] This kind of particular church was not identified in the 1917 code.[32] It is a por-

---

it. This kind of ecclesiastical jurisdiction came into being with the decree *Excelsum* of September 12, 1896. See *Annuario Pontificio per l'Anno 1998,* p. 1823.

[30] If they are bishops, they are *titular* bishops, not diocesan ones (see c. 376).

[31] The *Annuario Pontificio per l'Anno 1998* identifies 10 apostolic administrations stably erected (1084–1085).

[32] The 1917 code did, however, make reference to the figure of an *apostolic administrator,* a prelate whom the Supreme Pontiff, for grave and special reasons, appointed

tion of the people of God which for special and particularly grave reasons is not established as a diocese by the Supreme Pontiff. Its pastoral care is entrusted to an apostolic administrator who governs in the name of the Supreme Pontiff, and who is the legal equivalent of a diocesan bishop unless the nature of the matter or the law specifies otherwise (see c. 381, §2). Like the apostolic vicar or apostolic prefect, the apostolic administrator also governs with *ordinary* (attached to his office) and *vicarious* (not proper) power.

Pastor bonus 47, §1 explains that the provision of particular churches in special situations and by mandate of the Supreme Pontiff, in consultation with the competent dicasteries of the Roman Curia, is handled by the second section of the Secretariat of State, the "Section for Relations with States," which governs relations with states and deals with heads of government. The creation of an apostolic administration permanently established is handled by this second section.[33]

either to a vacant or filled see, whether for a time or perpetually (*CIC* 312). He could be appointed *sede plena* if the residential bishop was incapacitated by illness, advanced age, etc.; in this instance the jurisdiction of the diocesan bishop and his vicar general was suspended. The apostolic administrator's rights, duties, and privileges were identified in his letter of appointment and in *CIC* 313–318. The apostolic administrator's role ceased when the new bishop took canonical possession of the diocese (but not if the pope or current bishop should die). Even though the kind of apostolic administrator mentioned in the 1917 code is not referenced in the 1983 law, nothing prevents the Supreme Pontiff from appointing an apostolic administrator as characterized in the 1917 code, and indeed in some places such an apostolic administrator has been appointed in recent years.

The *apostolic administrator* in *CCEO* 234 is similar to the figure identified in the 1917 code. The Eastern code says that, for serious and special reasons, the Roman Pontiff sometimes entrusts the government of an eparchy (diocese), whether vacant or not, to an apostolic administrator; his rights, obligations, and privileges are identified in his letter of appointment.

[33] Pope John Paul II established a permanent interdicasterial commission on March 18, 1989 to establish and modify particular churches and to identify their leaders. The commission is headed by the secretary of state and com-

Territoriality of a Particular Church

Canon 372 — §1. As a rule, a portion of the people of God which constitutes a diocese or other particular church is limited to a definite territory so that it includes all the faithful living in the territory.

§2. Nevertheless, where in the judgment of the supreme authority of the Church it seems advantageous after the conferences of bishops concerned have been heard, particular churches distinguished by the rite of the faithful or some other similar reason can be erected in the same territory.

The first paragraph explains that normally a particular church is identified by a specific geographical territory, such that all the faithful who live in the territory belong to it. Territoriality is not a constitutive element of a particular church, but a determining element of the portion of the people of God who are defined as a particular church.[34] Territorial dwelling place (i.e., domicile or quasi-domicile) determines a person's pastor and ordinary (see c. 107).[35]

The second paragraph says that, nonetheless, within the same territory particular churches can be erected which distinguish the faithful by rite or some other factor. These can be established if judged opportune by the supreme authority of the Church after it has heard the concerned episcopal conference. Such a particular church is called

posed also of the prefect of the Congregation for Bishops and the secretaries and under-secretaries of both the Secretariat and the Congregation. *AAS* 81 (1989) 580–581.

[34] "Guiding Principles," principle eight: Territoriality should be the usual criterion for church governance. There is no reference to territory as determining an eparchy in the Eastern code. See Faris, 403–404.

[35] In a similar fashion, c. 518 lays down the general rule that a parish is territorial, but also states that *personal parishes* can be erected; these are determined by reason of the rite, language, nationality, or some other factor distinguishing the Christian faithful of some territory (e.g., c. 813 on campus parishes).

"personal" or "ritual."[36] *Christus Dominus* had called for a review of diocesan boundaries as soon as possible after Vatican II; this paragraph reflects that conciliar vision.[37] Even if a particular church is established on the basis of some criterion other than territoriality, however, territory is still a determining criterion—such that, for example, all the faithful of a given rite within a given territory form a particular church.[38]

The territoriality (or other criterion) is determined by the supreme authority of the Church when it erects the particular church (c. 373).

Competent Authority to Establish/ Juridic Personality

Canon 373 — It is only for the supreme authority to erect particular churches; those legitimately erected possess juridic personality by the law itself.

Only the supreme authority of the Church is competent to erect a particular church of any kind,[39] which necessarily will maintain a certain stability and which will be modified only after serious consideration. The Congregation for Bishops oversees everything concerning the constitution, division, union, suppression, and other modification of particular churches and their groupings for non-missionary territories of the Latin church.[40] In mission territories, the Congregation for the

Evangelization of Peoples deals with these same matters.[41]

When a particular church is legitimately established, it *ipso iure* acquires juridic personality (see cc. 113–123). The diocesan bishop represents the diocese in all juridic affairs (c. 393), as do those who preside over the other particular churches (see c. 381, §2).

Parishes and Vicariates Forane

Canon 374 — §1. Every diocese or other particular church is to be divided into distinct parts or parishes.

§2. To foster pastoral care through common action, several neighboring parishes can be joined into special groups, such as vicariates forane.

Every particular church is to be divided into distinct parts, known as parishes.[42] The erection of parishes is obligatory, not optional. The code describes the parish in canon 515, §1 as a "certain community of the Christian faithful stably constituted in a particular church, whose pastoral care is entrusted to a pastor (*parochus*) as its proper pastor (*pastor*) under the authority of the diocesan bishop."[43] Only the diocesan bishop can erect, suppress, or alter the parish, but first he must hear the presbyteral council (c. 515, §2). Once it is legitimately erected, a parish acquires

---

[36] *Directory* 172.

[37] *CD* 22–24. *CD* had specifically decreed that if pastoral care cannot be provided adequately for the faithful of a different rite through the ministry of the diocesan bishop, an episcopal vicar, or priests and parishes, then a proper hierarchy for the different rites may be established for them.

[38] See "Guiding Principles," principle eight: *Comm* 1 (1969) 84.

[39] *CIC* 215, §1; *CCEO* 177, §2. *SMC* I, §2 states that new military ordinariates are erected by the Apostolic See, after it has consulted the conference of bishops.

[40] *PB* 76; see also *PB* 78 which says that the Congregation for Bishops must proceed only in consultation with the

Section for Relations with States of the Secretariat of State when dealing with civil governments in the matter of establishing or modifying particular churches (and see 47, §1).

[41] *PB* 89.

[42] *CIC* 216, §3; *Directory* 174–177. The 1917 code equivalent of a parish in an apostolic vicariate or apostolic prefecture was called a *quasi-parish*. The 1983 code says a quasi-parish is the equivalent of a parish but is not yet erected as one because of particular circumstances (c. 516, §1).

[43] If the particular church in which the parish exists is not a diocese, the authority competent to erect, suppress, or otherwise alter it is the head of the community who is the equivalent of the diocesan bishop (see c. 381, §2).

juridic personality (c. 515, §3; see also cc. 516–552 on parishes).

Paragraph two of this canon says that to foster pastoral care through common action, several neighboring parishes can be joined together into specific groups such as vicariates forane, also called deaneries (see cc. 553–555). Their establishment is optional, depending only on the decision of the one who heads the particular church.[44]

The code also provides the possibility of appointing an episcopal vicar to serve as local ordinary in a specific part of the diocese, rather than a vicar forane who is not a local ordinary (see c. 476).

CHAPTER II
BISHOPS
[cc. 375–411][45]

Chapter 2 is divided into three articles. Article 1 (cc. 375–380) is about bishops in general; article 2 (cc. 381–402), the longest one, is about diocesan bishops; and article 3 (cc. 403–411) is about coadjutor and auxiliary bishops.

These canons are similar to canons 329–355 of the 1917 code, two chapters of a title dealing with episcopal power and those who participate in it: chapter 1 (*CIC* 329–349) concerning "bishops" though diocesan (residential) bishops were the principal focus, and chapter 2 (*CIC* 350–355) concerning coadjutor and auxiliary bishops. The 1983

code divides all this material into three parts: bishops in general, diocesan bishops, and coadjutor and auxiliary bishops.

The Eastern code treats eparchies (dioceses) and bishops in canons 177–218: two preliminary canons about bishops (*CCEO* 178–179) are followed by three articles which treat the election of bishops (*CCEO* 180–189), the rights and obligations of eparchial bishops (*CCEO* 190–211), and coadjutor and auxiliary bishops (*CCEO* 212–218).

ARTICLE 1: BISHOPS IN GENERAL
[cc. 375–380][46]

The canons of this article treat bishops in general.[47] The office of bishop originates from divine institution, and confers the powers to sanctify, teach, and govern—powers to be exercised in hierarchical communion with the head and other members of the college of bishops (c. 375). A bishop is either a diocesan or titular one (c. 376). Norms about the process of appointment (c. 377) and qualifications for office (c. 378) are identified, as is the requirement that episcopal consecration normally be received within three months from receiving the apostolic letter of appointment and before taking canonical possession of the specific office (c. 379). Before taking canonical pos-

---

[44] Canon 217 of the 1917 code required the bishop to divide his territory into regions or districts composed of several parishes; these regions or districts were called vicariates forane, deaneries, archpresbyteries, etc. If this arrangement seemed impossible or inopportune, the bishop was required to consult the Holy See. From very early in the revision process, it was concluded that such consultation with the Holy See was unnecessary and that the diocesan bishop alone should determine whether or not to arrange parishes into such groups. See *Comm* 17 (1985) 97. Also *Directory* 184–188.

[45] Other commentaries: *CLSGBI Com,* 213–234; *Pamplona ComEng,* 297–319.

[46] For the history of the development of these canons, see *Comm* 3 (1971) 188; 5 (1973) 217–219; 12 (1980) 285–293; 14 (1982) 204–206; 18 (1986) 94–97, 116–128, 131–133, 157–160; 19 (1987) 106, 107–109, 131–134; 24 (1992) 33–36, 315–316, 340–343.

[47] The 1983 code contains, literally, hundreds of references to bishops, ordinaries, and local ordinaries. X. Ochoa, *Index verborum ac locutionum codicis iuris canonici,* 2nd ed. (Rome: Libreria Editrice Lateranense, 1984) 166–172, 322–324 identifies the following references: *ordinarius* (86), *ordinarius competens* (4), *ordinarius loci* (128), *ordinarius proprius* (18), *episcopatus* (8), *episcopi* (231), *episcopus auxiliaris* (33), *episcopus coadiutor* (26), *episcopus dioecesanus* (303), *episcopus dioecesis* (8), *episcopus ordinans* (3), *episcopus proprius* (16), *episcopus suffraganeus* (8), *episcopus titularis* (5).

session of his office, the one promoted is to make the profession of faith and take the oath of fidelity to the Apostolic See according to the approved formula (c. 380).[48]

Institution and Functions of Bishops

Canon 375 — §1. Bishops, who by divine institution succeed to the place of the Apostles through the Holy Spirit who has been given to them, are constituted pastors in the Church, so that they are teachers of doctrine, priests of sacred worship, and ministers of governance.

§2. Through episcopal consecration itself, bishops receive with the function of sanctifying also the functions of teaching and governing; by their nature, however, these can only be exercised in hierarchical communion with the head and members of the college.

This canon expresses a theological teaching about the institution and functions of the office of bishop.[49] Through the Holy Spirit and by divine institution, bishops are successors to the apostles. Bishops are pastors in the Church so that they are teachers of doctrine, priests of sacred worship, and ministers of governance. They receive through episcopal consecration itself these three *munera* (sanctifying, teaching, governing) which, by their nature, can be exercised only in hierarchical communion with the head and other members of the episcopal college (see c. 336).

This doctrine reflects *Lumen gentium* 19–21 and *Christus Dominus* 2.

A priest becomes a member of the episcopal college through episcopal ordination and hierarchical communion with the head of the college and its other members (see c. 336). Two moments must be distinguished: episcopal ordination and canonical mission. By reason of *ordination,* the bishop receives an ontological share in the sacred functions of Christ (teaching, sanctifying, governing). By *canonical mission,* given through hierarchical authority and required for such functions to become active, he is appointed to a particular office or assigned to certain persons for whom he performs these functions. Such sacred functions are discharged by different bishops who cooperate hierarchically with each other according to the will of Christ.[50] Thus, transcending the particular canonical mission of individual bishops and considering their episcopal consecration and membership within the college of bishops, there exists a true and basic equality among the bishops, under the primacy of the Supreme Pontiff (see cc. 330, 336). The power of bishops "cannot be exercised in an entirely autonomous or independent manner. Rather they must act in accord with the *communio* structures given by Christ to the Church: that is, in communion with the whole of the episcopal body, and in submission to the one who is its head."[51]

Diocesan/Titular Bishops

Canon 376 — Bishops to whom the care of some diocese is entrusted are called *diocesan;* others are called *titular.*

The code says all bishops belong to one of two categories: *diocesan*[52] or *titular*. A *diocesan* bishop is one to whom is entrusted the care of a

---

[48] Canons 375–380 concern individual bishops; see cc. 336–341 for the code's treatment of the college of bishops, and cc. 431–459 for the code's consideration of the collaboration of bishops in groupings of particular churches (i.e., ecclesiastical provinces, ecclesiastical regions, particular councils, conferences of bishops). See also cc. 705–707 on norms about religious raised to the episcopate. A response from the PCILT promulgated December 4, 1986 indicates that a religious bishop lacks active and passive voice in his own institute: *AAS* 78 (1986) 1324. L. Wrenn, *Authentic Interpretations on the 1983 Code* (Washington, D.C.: CLSA, 1993) 27–28.

[49] *CIC* 329, §1; *Directory* 32–38.

[50] *LG,* Preliminary Explanatory Note 2; *CD* 11; *Directory* 39–43.

[51] J. Herranz, "The Personal Power of Governance of the Diocesan Bishop," *CLSAP* (1987) 20.

[52] Canon 334 of the 1917 code termed them *residential* bishops.

diocese.[53] Any other bishop is called a *titular* bishop.[54]

Titular bishops hold a title other than that of diocesan bishop. They comprise the following categories:

(1) coadjutor bishops, with the title of "Coadjutor Bishop of N."[55]
(2) retired diocesan bishops, with the title of "Former Bishop of N."[56]

(3) all other bishops to whom is assigned title of a "titular see," with the title of "Titular Bishop of N."—that is, auxiliary bishops; legates of the Holy See; territorial abbots; apostolic vicars; apostolic administrators; those assigned specialized service in the Church (e.g., in the Roman Curia); and any others who are not coadjutor, diocesan, or retired diocesan bishops.

A *titular see* is a diocese which no longer has a diocesan bishop. In earlier days the head of these sees was called a "bishop *in partibus infidelium* (i.e., among the infidels)"; Pope Leo XIII changed the designation to "titular bishop."[57] Titular bishops have no jurisdiction in the titular church but enjoy the privileges and honors of the episcopal order.[58]

Canon 450 provides that the members of the conference of bishops by law are all the diocesan bishops in the territory, their legal equivalents, coadjutor bishops, auxiliary bishops, and other titular bishops who perform in that territory a special function entrusted to them by the Apostolic See or the conference of bishops itself. Ordinaries of another rite may be invited; they have a consultative vote, unless the statutes of the conference decree otherwise. The papal legate and other titular bishops are not by law members of the conference. Canon 454 determines that diocesan bishops, their equivalents in law, and coadjutor bishops have a deliberative vote in plenary meetings of the episcopal conference. The statutes of the conference may give a deliberative or consultative vote to auxiliary bishops and other titular bishops.

The canons of this chapter mention many rights and duties of diocesan and titular bishops;

---

[53] The head of a territorial prelature, who is the canonical equivalent of a diocesan bishop (cf. c. 381, §2), holds the title of "Bishop-Prelate" of his prelature. On October 17, 1977, the SCB forwarded a letter to the Code Revision Commission indicating that Pope Paul VI had provided that prelates *nullius* who are bishops will no longer be assigned the title of an extinct episcopal see but will be designated with the title "Bishop-Prelate of N." The letter states: "This provision, which strengthens the real bond which is established between the said prelate and the particular church entrusted to his pastoral care, is intended to bring into reality the wish expressed on various occasions by the episcopate on the equalization of prelates for the dioceses." *Comm* 9 (1977) 224; *CLD* 8, 238–239.

[54] Canon 179 of the Eastern code says titular bishops are those to whom an eparchy has not been entrusted for governing in their own name, whatever other function in the Church they exercise or have exercised.

[55] On August 31, 1976, the SCB informed the Sacred Council for the Public Affairs of the Church that Pope Paul VI had provided that henceforth a coadjutor with the right of succession in the Latin church would hold title *nunc pro tunc* (i.e., "now for then") to the particular church for which he is destined, and no longer to an extinct episcopal see. The congregation also said that further study would be conducted concerning the status of prelates *nullius. Comm* 9 (1977) 233; *CLD* 8, 252–253. For the conclusion about prelates *nullius,* see fn. 53, above.

[56] On November 7, 1970, the prefect of the SCB informed all papal representatives that Pope Paul VI, in an audience of October 31, 1970, decided that henceforth retired diocesan bishops would no longer be transferred to a titular church but would continue to be addressed with the name of the see they had served preceded by the term "former" or its equivalent. Currently resigned bishops were given the option of retaining the name of the titular church to which they had been assigned or being designated as "Former Bishop of N." *Comm* 10 (1978) 18; *CLD* 9, 204–205.

[57] Pope Leo XIII made this change in his aplett *In Suprema,* of June 10, 1882. See *Annuario Pontificio per l'Anno 1998,* pp. 1818–1819.

[58] The 1917 code said that a titular bishop could not exercise any power in his titular see and did not take possession of it; in charity he could occasionally apply a Mass for the people of the see, though there was no obligation to do so (*CIC* 348). A parallel canon does not exist in the 1983 code.

other rights and obligations are found elsewhere throughout the code. In addition, all bishops retain their basic rights and obligations as members of the Christian faithful (cc. 208–223) and as clerics (cc. 273–289), as appropriate.

Appointment of Bishops

Canon 377 — §1. The Supreme Pontiff freely appoints bishops or confirms those legitimately elected.

§2. At least every three years, bishops of an ecclesiastical province or, where circumstances suggest it, of a conference of bishops, are in common counsel and in secret to compose a list of presbyters, even including members of institutes of consecrated life, who are more suitable for the episcopate. They are to send it to the Apostolic See, without prejudice to the right of each bishop individually to make known to the Apostolic See the names of presbyters whom he considers worthy of and suited to the episcopal function.

§3. Unless it is legitimately established otherwise, whenever a diocesan or coadjutor bishop must be appointed, as regards what is called the *terna* to be proposed to the Apostolic See, the pontifical legate is to seek individually and to communicate to the Apostolic See together with his own opinion the suggestions of the metropolitan and suffragans of the province to which the diocese to be provided for belongs or with which it is joined in some grouping, and the suggestions of the president of the conference of bishops. The pontifical legate, moreover, is to hear some members of the college of consultors and cathedral chapter and, if he judges it expedient, is also to seek individually and in secret the opinion of others from both the secular and non-secular clergy and from laity outstanding in wisdom.

§4. Unless other provision has been legitimately made, a diocesan bishop who judges that an auxiliary should be given to his diocese is to propose to the Apostolic See a list of at least three presbyters more suitable for this office.

§5. In the future, no rights and privileges of election, nomination, presentation, or designation of bishops are granted to civil authorities.

The process of the appointment of a bishop involves several distinct steps.[59] First, an individual presbyter is judged to be a potential candidate for the episcopacy; this judgment can take place in various ways. Next, the Supreme Pontiff appoints him to the episcopacy (or confirms a candidate who has been legitimately elected) and confers a canonical mission. Then, the presbyter receives episcopal consecration. Finally, the bishop takes canonical possession of his office as diocesan, coadjutor, or auxiliary bishop. The code contains canons about each of these steps.

Paragraph one of canon 377 underscores the right of the Church to nominate and appoint bishops.[60] Specifically, it identifies the central role of the Supreme Pontiff in their appointment: he freely either (1) appoints bishops or (2) confirms those who have been legitimately elected.[61] Papal

---

[59] F. Sarrazin, "La nomination des évêques dans l'Église latine," *Stud Can* 20 (1986) 367–407. The author overviews the methods of appointing bishops employed by the Church throughout history, with special emphasis on the procedures listed in the 1917 and 1983 codes. See also T. Reese, *Archbishop* (New York: Harper and Row, 1989) 1–52. One finds interesting discussions among the bishops on the issue of episcopal selection in Archbishop John Quinn's Oxford lecture, "Concerning the Papacy," *Origins* 26 (July 18, 1996) 119–128, and responses from Bishop James McHugh, "What Is the 'New Situation'?" *Origins* 26 (August 29, 1996) 119–128; John Cardinal O'Connor, "Reflections on Church Governance," ibid., 171–175; and Archbishop Rembert Weakland, "The Local Churches and the Church of Rome," ibid., 176–177.

[60] *CD* 20.

[61] *CIC* 329, §§2–3; 332, §1; *CCEO* 181. The 1983 code adds that the pope also confirms those who have been legitimately elected, as takes place in such places as Germany (most dioceses), Austria (Salzburg), and Switzerland (Chur, St. Gall, and Basel) where the chapters of canons (cc. 503–510) elect episcopal candidates; their election is confirmed by the pope. Also, the President of the French Republic has the right to designate the bishops

appointment or confirmation safeguards the *communio* which must exist between the universal Church and the particular church which the new bishop will shepherd. The law clearly states that the Apostolic See[62] makes the definitive judgment on a candidate's suitability for the office of bishop (c. 378, §2), and before his consecration the bishop-elect must take an oath of fidelity to the Apostolic See (c. 380). The Congregation for Bishops handles everything concerning the appointment of diocesan, coadjutor, and auxiliary bishops for non-mission territories of the Latin church;[63] the Congregation for the Evangelization of Peoples handles their appointment for mission territories.[64]

Paragraph two requires bishops to identify presbyters who are suitable candidates for the episcopacy;[65] this identification is to be renewed (revised) on a regular basis. At least every three years, the bishops of a province (or of an episcopal conference, if circumstances suggest it) are to compose in common and in secret[66] a list of presbyters, including members of institutes of consecrated life, who are suitable to become bishops (without reference to a specific vacancy). This list is to be sent to the Apostolic See. It is useful in the further process for the appointment of bishops outlined in paragraphs three and four of this canon. Moreover, the law expresses the right of each bishop individually to propose to the Apostolic See the names of presbyters whom he judges worthy and suitable to become bishops.

Paragraph three explains the process for the appointment of a *diocesan* bishop or a *coadjutor* bishop.[67] The focus is upon the needs of the particular church, and the Holy See guides the process. Unless another provision has been made, the pontifical legate[68] plays a central role. He is to

---

of Strasbourg and Metz. See R. Metz, "Papal Legates and the Appointment of Bishops," *J* 52 (1992) 272–275.

[62] Canon 361 explains that the term *Apostolic See* or *Holy See* refers to the Roman Pontiff and others: the Secretariat of State, the Council for the Public Affairs of the Church, and other institutes of the Roman Curia, unless it is otherwise apparent from the nature of the matter or the context of the words.

[63] *PB* 77; see also 47, §1.

[64] *PB* 89.

[65] See also Sacred Council for the Public Affairs of the Church, *Episcoporum delectum,* March 25, 1972, *AAS* 64 (1972) 386–391. English translation: "Norms for the Promotion of Candidates to the Episcopal Ministry in the Latin Church," *CLD* 8, 366–372. These norms explain the process of consultation prior to the appointment of bishops in the Latin church, and are reflected in canon 377. They continue to be applicable unless contradicted by the code, since their subject matter has not been completely revised by the 1983 code (see c. 6, §1, 4°). Note also that *ES* I, 10 asked episcopal conferences to propose each year the names of suitable candidates for the episcopacy; see *CD* 20. See *CCEO* 182, §§2–4: generally the Eastern code tends to provide for somewhat greater input from the particular churches in the selection of bishops. The Roman Pontiff must give assent to each candidate proposed by the synod of bishops. See Faris, 421–422; *Pospishil Com,* 210.

[66] Even the voting of the bishops gathered is to be done in a secret fashion. See *Episcoporum delectum,* VII, 2. The secrecy has many values: it permits a candid expression of opinions about the candidate, it respects his good name and reputation, it avoids the hurt which can come when expectations of appointment are not fulfilled, it bypasses publicity and lobbying for or against candidates, etc. See also the instruction on papal secrecy from the Secretariat of State, *Secreta continere,* February 4, 1974, *AAS* 66 (1974) 89–92. English translation: *CLD* 8, 205–210.

[67] Since the code envisions that the coadjutor bishop is to become the diocesan bishop when the see is vacant (c. 403, §3), the process for his appointment is effectively the same as that for the appointment of one who will be the diocesan bishop immediately.

[68] Canon 363, §1 explains that the pontifical legate has the duty to represent the Roman Pontiff in a stable manner to the particular churches, or to the states and public authorities to which the legates are sent. Canon 364 says that the principal function of a legate is daily to make more strong and more effective the bonds of unity existing between the Apostolic See and the particular churches, and then outlines some of the ways in which this principal function is achieved. Canon 364, 4° says that, regarding the nomination of bishops, the pontifical legate is to transmit or propose to the Apostolic See the names of candidates and to instruct the informational process con-

send to the Apostolic See the list or *terna* of candidates for the office in question, composed after he has sought out individually the suggestions of the metropolitan and suffragans of the province (see cc. 435–436) in which the diocese which will receive the diocesan or coadjutor bishop is located, and the suggestions of the president of the episcopal conference. The legate is to communicate these suggestions to the Apostolic See along with his own opinion. He is also to hear some members of the college of consultors (c. 502) and of the cathedral chapter (cc. 503–510).[69] If he judges it opportune, he may also obtain individually and secretly the opinion of others: secular clergy, religious clergy, and laity outstanding in wisdom.[70]

Paragraph four explains the process for the appointment of an *auxiliary* bishop—a process simpler than that for the appointment of a diocesan or coadjutor bishop.[71] Unless some other provision has been made legitimately, when a diocesan bishop judges that his diocese needs an auxiliary (see c. 403, §1), he is to propose to the Apostolic See a list of *at least* three suitable presbyters. This canon does not identify precisely the role of the pontifical legate in the discernment and appointment process, nor does the law require consultation with other bishops (e.g., those of the province) on either the need of the diocese for an auxiliary or on the suitability of a candidate for the office.

The last paragraph of this canon insists that hereafter civil authorities are to be given no rights and privileges of election, nomination, presentation, or designation of bishops. This provides the Church greater freedom in the selection of its bishops without any intervention of civil government. This norm reiterates *Christus Dominus* 20, which also invited dialogue between the Holy See and those governments which were able to propose episcopal candidates, with the object of the governments' freely waiving their rights and privileges of election, nomination, or presentation of sees.

Qualifications to Be a Bishop

Canon 378 — §1. In regard to the suitability of a candidate for the episcopacy, it is required that he is:

1° **outstanding in solid faith, good morals, piety, zeal for souls, wisdom, prudence, and human virtues, and endowed with other qualities which make him suitable to fulfill the office in question;**

2° **of good reputation;**

3° **at least thirty-five years old;**

4° **ordained to the presbyterate for at least five years;**

5° **in possession of a doctorate or at least a licentiate in sacred scripture, theology, or canon law from an institute of higher studies approved by the Apostolic See, or at least truly expert in the same disciplines.**

§2. The definitive judgment concerning the suitability of the one to be promoted pertains to the Apostolic See.

The code identifies in this canon those qualities which are required for a presbyter to become a bishop.[72] A presbyter must have certain positive human gifts, including talents needed to fulfill the given episcopal office: consideration is given both to the qualifications of the candidate and the

---

cerning presbyters to be promoted, according to the norms issued by the Apostolic See. For more on the role of the pontifical legate, see cc. 362–367.

[69] The law does not state that members of the presbyteral council (cc. 495–501) are to be involved in the consultation process since the council does not exist *sede vacante* (c. 501, §2).

[70] Canon 377, §3 requires that the papal legate consult certain persons who have clear leadership roles in the diocese (e.g., the college of consultors or the cathedral chapter) and gives him free discretion to consult others. See c. 524 on a similar process of consultation before a diocesan bishop appoints a pastor. The bishop is to listen to the vicar forane and may consult some other presbyters and lay persons.

[71] CD 26.

[72] CIC 331, §§1–2; CCEO 180; *Directory* 21–31.

requirements of the office for which he is being considered.[73] The candidate must have a good reputation. He must be at least thirty-five years old and ordained a presbyter for at least five years. He must also have a doctorate or licentiate in scripture, theology, or canon law from an institute of higher studies approved by the Apostolic See, or at least be truly expert in these areas.[74]

Paragraph two explains that the definitive (but not only) judgment on the suitability of a presbyter for the episcopacy rests with the Apostolic See.[75] Others, however, also make a judgment about a candidate's suitability (e.g., the bishops of the ecclesiastical province), though their judgment would not be considered definitive.

Requirement of Episcopal Consecration

Canon 379 — Unless he is prevented by a legitimate impediment, whoever has been promoted to the episcopacy must receive episcopal consecration within three months from the receipt of the apostolic letter and before he takes possession of his office.

A presbyter promoted to the episcopacy must receive episcopal consecration within three months of receiving the apostolic letter and before

he takes canonical possession of his office, unless he is held back by a legitimate impediment.[76]

Canon 1014 says that, unless the Apostolic See grants a dispensation, the principal consecrating bishop is to be joined by at least two other consecrating bishops; it is especially appropriate that together with these three all the bishops present also co-consecrate the bishop-elect. This symbolizes clearly the episcopal *communio*.

Canon 1013 says that no bishop is to consecrate another bishop unless it is first evident that the pontifical mandate exists. Canon 1382 explains that if a bishop consecrates another as bishop without a pontifical mandate, both receive a *latae sententiae* excommunication whose remission is reserved to the Apostolic See.

Unless he is prevented from doing so by some legitimate impediment (e.g., an illness), a presbyter becoming a diocesan bishop must take canonical possession of the diocese within four months of receipt of the apostolic letter of appointment; if he is already a bishop, within two months of receiving the letter (c. 382, §2).

Profession of Faith/Oath of Fidelity

Canon 380 — Before he takes canonical possession of his office, the one promoted is to make the profession of faith and take the oath of fidelity to the Apostolic See according to the formula approved by the Apostolic See.

In addition to receiving episcopal consecration before taking canonical possession of his office,

---

[73] Presumably, the needs of a diocese will surface during the consultation process led by the pontifical legate (see c. 377, §3) and from the quinquennial report on the state of the diocese (c. 399).

[74] The 1917 code had required that a candidate for the episcopacy be legitimate by birth (not even legitimated by the subsequent marriage of his parents) and be at least thirty years of age (*CIC* 331, §1, 1°–2°). The 1983 code makes absolutely no reference to legitimacy as a requirement, and raises the minimum age to thirty-five, perhaps because of a clearer sense of the significance and burdens of the office.

[75] *CIC* 331, §3. *PB* identifies the dicasteries competent to judge on the suitability of candidates in the Latin church: the Section for Relations with States of the SS (in special circumstances and by mandate of the Supreme Pontiff, and in consultation with the other competent dicasteries, art. 47, §1), the CEP for mission territories (*PB* 89), the CFB for other particular churches (*PB* 77; see 78).

[76] *CIC* 333 had required that a candidate receive episcopal consecration within three months of receiving the apostolic letters, and go to his diocese within four months. See *CCEO* 188, §1, which gives the eparchial bishop-elect three months to receive episcopal consecration from the day of proclamation or receipt of the apostolic letter of appointment, and four months to take canonical possession of the eparchy from the same day. See *CB* 1129–1132 on the election of the bishop, 1133–1137 on the ordination of the bishop, 1138–1140 on taking possession of the diocese, and 1141–1148 on reception of the bishop in his cathedral church.

the presbyter promoted is to make a profession of faith (see c. 833, 3°) and take an oath of fidelity to the Apostolic See, in accord with the formula approved by the same Apostolic See.[77]

ARTICLE 2: DIOCESAN BISHOPS
[cc. 381–402][78]

Article 2 is devoted to the office of diocesan bishop. It explains that the diocesan bishop has the ordinary, proper, and immediate power needed to exercise his office, and that some of this power can be reserved only by the Supreme Pontiff (c. 381, §1). Those who lead other particular churches are legally equivalent to him, unless otherwise apparent by the law or the nature of the matter (c. 381, §2). The diocesan bishop may exercise his role only after taking canonical possession of his office (c. 382).

The diocesan bishop is to have special pastoral concern for Catholics, other Christians, and the unbaptized (c. 383), and is to attend to presbyters with special solicitude (c. 384). He is to foster vocations to ministry and consecrated life, with special care for priestly and missionary vocations (c. 385).

He is to preach frequently and to oversee all aspects of the ministry of the word in the diocese (c. 386). He is to be a good example and to promote the holiness of all the faithful, especially through the celebration of the sacraments (c. 387). He must offer the *Missa pro populo* on the prescribed days (c. 388) and should frequently preside at Masses in the cathedral and other churches, especially on holy days and solemnities (c. 389). He performs pontifical functions throughout the diocese (c. 390).

The diocesan bishop governs the diocese with legislative power (always to be exercised personally), executive power (shared especially with his vicars general and episcopal vicars; it is simply *delegated* to others, such as chancellors and vice-chancellors), and judicial power (shared with his judicial vicar and judges) (c. 391). He is to promote universal church discipline and to guard against abuses (c. 392). He represents the diocese in all juridic affairs (c. 393).

The diocesan bishop is to foster and coordinate the works of the apostolate, and to urge the faithful to assume their proper roles in it (c. 394).

He is to reside in the diocese and not be absent for lengthy periods of time (c. 395) and to make pastoral visitations throughout the diocese (cc. 396–398). He presents the quinquennial report to the Holy See (c. 399) on the occasion of his *ad limina* visit (c. 400).

The diocesan bishop is to offer his resignation at age seventy-five, or earlier if he is burdened by ill health or another limiting factor (c. 401). He then becomes bishop emeritus of the diocese and may maintain residence therein; the diocese is responsible to provide for his retirement, under the caring oversight of the episcopal conference (c. 402).

Scope of Power of a Diocesan Bishop

Canon 381 — §1. A diocesan bishop in the diocese entrusted to him has all ordinary, proper, and immediate power which is required for the exercise of his pastoral function except for cases which the law or a decree of the Supreme Pontiff reserves to the supreme authority or to another ecclesiastical authority.

§2. Those who preside over the other communities of the faithful mentioned in can. 368 are

---

[77] *CIC* 332, §2; *CCEO* 187, §2. The CDF issued the text of the profession of faith (replacing the profession issued in 1967, *AAS* 59 [1967] 1058) and the oath of fidelity, both of which became effective on March 1, 1989 (see *AAS* 81 (1989) 104–106). That oath of fidelity is intended for the persons mentioned in c. 833, 5°–8°, not for bishops. The "oath of fidelity to the Apostolic See" required of bishops seemingly has not been officially published. See H. Schmitz, "'Professio fidei' and 'Iusiurandum fidelitatis,'" *AkK* 157 (1988) 353–429.

[78] For the history of the development of these canons, see *Comm* 3 (1971) 188; 5 (1973) 219–224; 12 (1980) 293–308; 14 (1982) 206–208; 18 (1986) 128–130, 134–157, 161–170; 19 (1987) 109–116, 135–142; 24 (1992) 37–39, 316–320, 343–350.

equivalent in law to a diocesan bishop unless it is otherwise apparent from the nature of the matter or from a prescript of law.

A diocesan bishop possesses in his diocese all the ordinary, proper, and immediate power needed to perform his pastoral ministry.[79] This teaching reflects the doctrine in *Lumen gentium* 27,[80] which explains that bishops are not to be considered vicars of the Roman Pontiff, but that they exercise the power they possess in their own right and are true prelates of the people they govern. They are vicars and legates of Christ, and their power comes from him.[81] This power of governance is a sacred and personal power which is radically conferred by episcopal ordination; it becomes a juridical power by means of canonical mission from supreme authority.[82]

This canon incorporates guiding principles four and five for the revision of the code.[83] *Principle four* calls for a positive presentation of the powers of the episcopal office and for fewer cases being reserved to the supreme authority or another authority in the church. Bishops should have the legal authority to exercise their pastoral leadership, notwithstanding the power of the Roman Pontiff, given him by office, to reserve cases to himself or to assign them to another authority.

Principle five proposes the application of the principle of subsidiarity by which bishops and other infra-universal leaders will be given more discretionary authority. Reserved cases must be clearly delineated, and there should be a greater latitude for particular legislation.

The diocesan bishop's power of governance is distinguished as legislative, executive, and judicial (c. 391, §1). He uses these pastoral powers, which come to him from Christ, to lead the people of his particular church; he also leads and shepherds continually by the model of his own life (see c. 387).

The power of a diocesan bishop is *ordinary* (related to his office as diocesan bishop), *proper* (exercised in his own name, not vicariously in the name of another), and *immediate* (directed toward all in the diocese without the mediation of another).[84] *Lumen gentium* 27 and *Christus Dominus* 8 explain that he exercises this power personally in the name of Christ, even though the supreme authority of the Church can control and limit its exercise, whether by the law or by a decree of the Supreme Pontiff.[85] This can be done when it

---

[79] *CIC* 334, §1; *CCEO* 178; *Directory* 42. See Herranz, 16–34; T. Green, "The Pastoral Governance Role of the Diocesan Bishop: Foundations, Scope and Limitations," *J* 49 (1989) 472–506.

[80] See also *CD* 8, 11.

[81] The 1983 code does not explicitly state that bishops are vicars of Christ, though the Roman Pontiff is so described (c. 331). The Eastern code, however, says that the eparchial (diocesan) bishop governs in his own name the eparchy (diocese) entrusted to him as a vicar and legate of Christ (*CCEO* 178).

[82] Herranz states: "That is to say consecration and canonical mission form a power of governance of a personal nature, whose complete entitlement and juridical and moral responsibility affects only the conscience of the diocesan pastor in an immediate and non-transferable way" (18).

[83] *Comm* 1 (1969) 80–81.

[84] *SMC* IV says that military ordinaries, who normally are bishops, have all the rights and duties of diocesan bishops. Their jurisdiction is personal (it can be exercised over those who belong to the ordinariate even if they are beyond national boundaries), ordinary, and proper *but cumulative*—that is, the jurisdiction of the military ordinary is in addition to that of the diocesan bishop since the faithful of the ordinariate do not cease being part of the particular church of the diocesan bishop where they have a domicile or a quasi-domicile (c. 102).

[85] See Green, "The Pastoral Governance Role of the Diocesan Bishop," 492–503. Green comments that there needs to be a continuing effort to define the episcopal office positively and that each "bishop is situated in a hierarchial framework in relationship to his brother bishops, particularly the pope. The episcopal office necessarily implies an openness to collegial activity in its fullest sense or otherwise, and a solidarity with and a solicitude for the universal Church.... The bishop needs to be sensitive to the transdiocesan implications of his governance of the diocese given its links to the other churches in the *communio,* especially Rome the *prima sedes.*... Papal

would be useful for the Church and when the faithful require it. In these cases the exercise of power is reserved either to the supreme authority or to some other authority in the Church (e.g., episcopal conferences, bishops of the province, an auxiliary bishop with special faculties). Certainly fewer powers of the diocesan bishop are reserved to another ecclesiastical authority in the 1983 code than in former legislation.[86]

Equivalent in law to a diocesan bishop are the heads of those other particular churches mentioned in canon 368, unless the contrary is evident either from the nature of the matter (e.g., an act requiring episcopal orders as regards a presbyter head of such a church) or a prescript of the law, even if they exercise power vicariously in the name of the Supreme Pontiff rather than properly.[87] All of these must make the profession of faith and take the oath of fidelity, even if they are not ordained as bishops (see c. 833, 3°).

Taking Possession of a Diocese

Canon 382 — §1. One promoted as bishop cannot assume the exercise of the office entrusted to him before he has taken canonical possession of the

authority is supreme, full and universal, and thereby differentiated from that of the diocesan bishop; it extends to faith, morals and church governance, and entails a primacy not simply of honor but of real legislative, administrative, and judicial jurisdiction. Accordingly he may reserve certain issues to himself in view of the unity and advantage of the people of God" (492–493).

[86] M. Wijlens comments that "the 1983 code no longer uses the concept of concession, but that of reservation. Accordingly, the pope is not said to 'concede' to the bishops the power to dispense, but a bishop has every power he needs, with the exception of what the Roman Pontiff reserves to himself or to some other authority (c. 87, §1). This not only provides a greater autonomy for the bishop; it implies an increased responsibility as well." "'For You I Am a Bishop, With You I Am a Christian': The Bishop as Legislator," *J* 56 (1996) 74, n. 22.

[87] *CIC* 215, §2. *SMC* II says that military ordinaries, who normally are bishops, enjoy the rights and are bound by the duties of diocesan bishops, unless the nature of the matter or particular statutes say otherwise.

diocese. Nevertheless, he is able to exercise offices which he already had in the same diocese at the time of promotion, without prejudice to the prescript of can. 409, §2.

§2. Unless he is prevented by a legitimate impediment, one promoted to the office of diocesan bishop must take canonical possession of his diocese within four months of receipt of the apostolic letter if he has not already been consecrated a bishop; if he has already been consecrated, within two months from receipt of this letter.

§3. A bishop takes canonical possession of a diocese when he personally or through a proxy has shown the apostolic letter in the same diocese to the college of consultors in the presence of the chancellor of the curia, who records the event. In newly erected dioceses, he takes canonical possession when he has seen to the communication of the same letter to the clergy and people present in the cathedral church, with the senior presbyter among those present recording the event.

§4. It is strongly recommended that the taking of canonical possession be done within a liturgical act in the cathedral church with the clergy and people gathered together.

This canon deals with a bishop taking possession of the diocese to which he is appointed.[88] He exercises full governance in his diocese as soon as the canonical possession occurs. Unless he is held back by a legitimate impediment, if he is already a bishop, he must take canonical possession within two months of receiving the apostolic letter of appointment; if he is not yet a bishop, within four months. Canon 379 requires a presbyter named a bishop to receive episcopal consecration within three months from receipt of the apostolic letter of appointment, unless he is prevented by a legitimate impediment; certainly, the consecration must precede taking canonical possession of the diocese.

[88] *CIC* 333; 334, §§2–3; *CCEO* 188, §2; 189. The Eastern code says the eparchial bishop must take canonical possession of the eparchy within four months from the day of episcopal election or appointment.

Canon 418 says that when a diocesan bishop receives certain notice of his transfer to another diocese and until he takes canonical possession of it, in the diocese from which he is being transferred he obtains the power of a diocesan administrator and continues to receive his full remuneration from that see. The former diocese becomes vacant on the day he takes canonical possession of the new diocese.

The one promoted cannot exercise the office entrusted to him before he has taken canonical possession. He can, however, exercise an office which he already has in the diocese at the time of his promotion, without prejudice to canon 409, §2.

Canonical possession of a diocese takes place when the bishop, personally or through a proxy, shows the apostolic letter to the college of consultors (c. 502); the chancellor (cc. 482–485) is to be present to record the event.[89] If he is being appointed to a newly erected diocese, the bishop shows the apostolic letter to the clergy and people in the cathedral church, and the senior presbyter present records the event.[90]

The canon strongly recommends that taking canonical possession be done in a liturgical act in the cathedral, in the presence of clergy and others.[91]

The Bishop as Pastor

Canon 383 — §1. In exercising the function of a pastor, a diocesan bishop is to show himself concerned for all the Christian faithful entrusted to his care, of whatever age, condition, or nationality they are, whether living in the territory or staying there temporarily; he is also to extend an apostolic spirit to those who are not able to make

sufficient use of ordinary pastoral care because of the condition of their life and to those who no longer practice their religion.

§2. If he has faithful of a different rite in his diocese, he is to provide for their spiritual needs either through priests or parishes of the same rite or through an episcopal vicar.

§3. He is to act with humanity and charity toward the brothers and sisters who are not in full communion with the Catholic Church and is to foster ecumenism as it is understood by the Church.

§4. He is to consider the non-baptized as committed to him in the Lord, so that there shines on them the charity of Christ whose witness a bishop must be before all people.

Every bishop is constituted a pastor in the Church (c. 375, §1). The diocesan bishop is pastor of his particular church. This canon identifies some of the specific groups who are subjects of his pastoral care: Catholics (even those of another *sui iuris* church), baptized non-Catholic Christians, and the non-baptized.

The first paragraph says the diocesan bishop is to be concerned for all the Christian faithful present in the diocese, even if they are there only temporarily. He is to offer special pastoral care to those who cannot make use of ordinary means of such care and those who have ceased religious practice.[92] The exact practical application of this canon will depend upon the unique character of the particular church. The canon reflects *Christus Dominus* 11, 16, and 18.

The second paragraph says that the diocesan bishop is to provide spiritual care to Catholics of other *sui iuris* churches.[93] This may be done through priests, parishes, or even an episcopal vicar (c. 476). This corresponds to the right of the Christian faithful "to worship God according to the prescripts of their own rite approved by the legitimate pastors of the Church" (c. 214). It reflects the teaching of *Christus Dominus* 23 (3).

---

[89] The chancellor, present to record the event of the bishop taking canonical possession of the diocese, is exercising his or her role as notary of the curia (c. 482, §3; see c. 484).

[90] See c. 404 on the manner in which a coadjutor and an auxiliary bishop take canonical possession of their offices.

[91] *SC* 41; *CB* 1138–1148.

[92] *CCEO* 192, §1; *Directory* 153–157.

[93] *CCEO* 193.

The third paragraph tells the diocesan bishop to be humble and charitable toward Christians who are not in full communion with the Catholic Church, and to foster ecumenism according to the mind of the Church. *Lumen gentium* 27 and *Christus Dominus* 11 and 16 teach the same.[94]

Finally, the fourth paragraph says the diocesan bishop is to regard the unbaptized also as committed to his care in the Lord, and is to evidence Christ-like charity toward them.[95] *Christus Dominus* 11 and 16 is reflected in this provision.

Bishop's Relation to Presbyters

Canon 384 — With special solicitude, a diocesan bishop is to attend to presbyters and listen to them as assistants and counselors. He is to protect their rights and take care that they correctly fulfill the obligations proper to their state and that the means and institutions which they need to foster spiritual and intellectual life are available to them. He also is to take care that provision is made for their decent support and social assistance, according to the norm of law.

The diocesan bishop is to attend to his presbyters with special solicitude; he is to regard them as assistants and counselors.[96] He is to protect

their rights. He is to see that they fulfill their obligations, and that they have the necessary resources to foster their spiritual and intellectual life. He is to care for their decent support and social assistance. Canon 384 identifies the diocesan bishop as the source of care, challenge, and support of priests in exercising their rights and fulfilling their obligations.[97] This canon reflects the conciliar doctrine of *Lumen gentium* 28, *Christus Dominus* 16, and *Presbyterorum ordinis* 20–21.

The diocesan bishop receives assistance and advice from his presbyters not only as individuals but also in groups, such as the presbyteral council (cc. 495–501) and the college of consultors (c. 502). The diocesan bishop is to hear the presbyteral council, which exists to promote the pastoral good of the diocese (c. 495, §1) in affairs of greater importance (c. 500, §2). The college of consultors assists the diocesan bishop in the several specific areas identified in the law, most of which concern diocesan temporalities.[98] Furthermore, if it exists, the diocesan bishop also receives assistance from the episcopal council (composed of vicars general and episcopal vicars, who must be priests), which serves to foster pastoral action more suitably (c. 473, §4). In addi-

---

[94] See c. 755 on the duty of bishops to foster ecumenism, in accord with prescripts issued by the supreme authority of the Church; see also cc. 844 (*communicatio in sacris*), 933 (permission for a priest to celebrate the Eucharist in a non-Catholic place of worship), 1124–1129 (mixed marriages), and 1183, §3 (funeral rites of baptized non-Catholics). See also *Directory* 48, 158. *Ecum Dir* 4 says: "The bishops individually for their own dioceses and collegially for the whole church are, under the authority of the Holy See, responsible for ecumenical policy and practice." The *Ecum Dir* in its comprehensiveness will help clarify the bishop's ecumenical role much more fully than the code. See also B. Griffin, "The Challenge of Ecumenism for Canonists," *CLSAP* (1993) 17–38.

[95] *CCEO* 192, §3; *Directory* 159.

[96] See John Paul II, "Pastores dabo vobis," *Origins* 21 (April 16, 1992) 717, 719–759; CFC, *Directory for the Life and Ministry of Priests* (Vatican City: Libreria Editrice Vaticana, 1994).

[97] The obligations and rights common to all clerics are identified in cc. 273–289, as well as elsewhere throughout the code. Specific rights and duties are also assigned to clergy with particular offices in the church (e.g., vicars general, episcopal vicars, vicars forane, pastors, rectors, etc.). See *CCEO* 192, §4. Note that *CCEO* 192, §5 says the eparchial bishop is to see that the families of married clerics are provided with adequate support, appropriate protection, social assistance, and health insurance. See also *Directory* 107–117. *CCEO* 194 says the eparchial bishop can confer certain honorific dignities on clerics; such a canon is not found in the Latin code.

[98] The diocesan bishop needs the *consent* of the college of consultors to perform acts of extraordinary administration, as defined by the episcopal conference (c. 1277), and to alienate diocesan property whose proposed value is between the minimum and maximum amounts defined by the episcopal conference (c. 1292, §1). He needs the college's *advice* to appoint and remove the diocesan finance officer (c. 494, §§1–2).

tion, the diocesan bishop receives the assistance of that group of pastors commonly identified as pastor consultors[99] in the processes to remove (cc. 1742, §1; 1745) or transfer (c. 1750) a pastor unwilling to be removed or transferred.

Although canon 384 does not mention deacons, it is reasonable to expect that the diocesan bishop will also care for and nurture them in their ministry.[100] He will also have special concern for their families, if the permanent deacons are married.[101]

Fostering of Vocations

Canon 385 — As much as possible, a diocesan bishop is to foster vocations to different ministries and to consecrated life, with special care shown for priestly and missionary vocations.

The diocesan bishop is to foster vocations to the various ministries and to consecrated life.[102] He is to have special care for priestly and missionary vocations. This canon reflects *Christus Dominus* 15, which says the bishop should foster vocations to priesthood, religious life, and missionary works; the canon is more broad, since it tells the bishop to foster vocations to various *ministries* as well.[103] Although the promotion of ecclesial vocations is a concern of the whole Church, canon 233 says that diocesan bishops most especially are to be concerned with promoting voca-

tions to the clerical state, including vocations of men of more mature age. They are also to promote vocations to the missions (c. 791, 1°).

The Bishop as Teacher

Canon 386 — §1. A diocesan bishop, frequently preaching in person, is bound to propose and explain to the faithful the truths of the faith which are to be believed and applied to morals. He is also to take care that the prescripts of the canons on the ministry of the word, especially those on the homily and catechetical instruction, are carefully observed so that the whole Christian doctrine is handed on to all.

§2. Through more suitable means, he is firmly to protect the integrity and unity of the faith to be believed, while nonetheless acknowledging a just freedom in further investigating its truths.

Every bishop is a teacher of doctrine (c. 375, §1).[104] This canon identifies the aspects of the role of the diocesan bishop as a teacher of the faith[105] and reflects the doctrine of *Christus Dominus* 12–14.

The first paragraph of the canon says that the diocesan bishop teaches in a variety of ways. He is to preach in person frequently. He is bound to propose and explain truths of the faith and morals. He is to make sure that the canons dealing with the ministry of the word are observed carefully—with a special eye on the homily and catechetical formation. Canon 756, §2 says the diocesan bishop is the moderator of the entire ministry of the word within the diocese; he exercises the function of proclaiming the gospel there.[106]

---

[99] No specific name is given to this group in the code.

[100] The code distinguishes transitional deacons from permanent deacons, who may be married. Canon 288 explains that permanent deacons are not bound by some of the canons which bind other clerics, unless particular law establishes otherwise.

[101] See Bishops' Committee on the Permanent Diaconate, *Foundations for the Renewal of the Diaconate* (Washington, D.C.: NCCB/USCC, 1993); NCCB, *Permanent Deacons,* 3rd ed. (Washington, D.C.: USCC, 1995).

[102] See *CCEO* 195, which mentions the eparchial bishop fostering vocations to priestly, diaconal, and monastic life; to institutes of consecrated life; and to the missions. See also *Directory* 118–119.

[103] See also *OT* 2; *AG* 20.

[104] The teaching role of the diocesan bishop is understood properly only by a thorough study of Book III of the code. See also NCCB, *The Teaching Ministry of the Diocesan Bishop: A Pastoral Reflection* (Washington, D.C.: NCCB, 1992); J. Tobin, "The Diocesan Bishop as Moderator of the Entire Ministry of the Word," *CLSANZ Proceedings* (1988) 51–84.

[105] *CIC* 336, §2; *CCEO* 196, 623, §1; *Directory* 55–65, 75.

[106] Canons 757–759 explain that the ministry of the word and proclamation of the gospel is also shared by pres-

All sacred ministers are to hold the function of preaching in great esteem (c. 762), and bishops have the right to preach the word of God everywhere, including churches and oratories of religious institutes of pontifical right, unless the local bishop has expressly forbidden it in particular cases (c. 763). Bishops and all pastors of souls are to take care that the word of God is preached to the faithful who have special pastoral needs, and are even to proclaim the gospel to non-believers since they too are subjects of pastoral care (c. 771). All are to observe the norms on preaching issued by the diocesan bishop (c. 772, §1).

The diocesan bishop is to issue norms for catechetics: to make sure that suitable instruments of catechesis are available (perhaps even by preparing a catechism) and to foster and coordinate catechetical endeavors (c. 775, §1). Pastors are to see that all catechetical formation is accomplished in accord with norms established by the diocesan bishop (c. 777).

Canon 823, §2 gives every bishop specific rights and duties regarding social communications: (1) to be watchful that writings and the means of social communication do no harm to the faith and morals of the Christian faithful, (2) to demand that writings about faith and morals be submitted to their judgment before publication, and (3) to condemn writings harmful to correct faith and good morals.[107] These rights and duties rest with a diocesan bishop in a special way within his particular church.

The Christian faithful have the right to instruction in the Catholic faith in order "to know and live the mystery of salvation" (c. 217). As the principal teacher of doctrine in his particular church, the diocesan bishop will also take care that the truths of faith and morals are communicated by those who share his prophetic mission.

Canon 253 tells bishops to appoint qualified seminary professors and to remove those gravely deficient. Canon 805 gives the diocesan bishop (and other local ordinaries) the right to appoint or approve religion teachers, and to remove them if necessary. Canon 810, §2 gives diocesan bishops the right and duty to be vigilant that Catholic doctrine is taught faithfully in Catholic universities.

The second paragraph of canon 386 teaches that the diocesan bishop is also to be firm in protecting the integrity and unity of the faith, while at the same time admitting a just freedom in further investigating the truths of the faith. Canon 212, §3 says that knowledgeable and qualified members of the Christian faithful have the right and occasionally even the duty to manifest to the sacred pastors their opinion on what pertains to the good of the Church, but without prejudice to the integrity of faith and morals. Canon 218 gives those engaged in the sacred disciplines "a just freedom of inquiry and of expressing their opinion prudently on those matters in which they possess expertise, while observing the submission due to the magisterium of the Church."[108]

The Bishop as Sanctifier

Canon 387 — Since the diocesan bishop is mindful of his obligation to show an example of holiness in charity, humility, and simplicity of life, he is to strive to promote in every way the holiness of the Christian faithful according to the proper vocation of each. Since he is the principal dispenser of the mysteries of God, he is to endeavor constantly that the Christian faithful entrusted to his care grow in grace through the celebration of the sacraments and that they understand and live the paschal mystery.

byters, deacons, members of institutes of consecrated life, and baptized and confirmed lay persons.

[107] For more specifics about the role of the diocesan bishop in overseeing the instruments of social communication and books, see also cc. 824–827.

[108] See CDF, "Instruction on the Ecclesial Vocation of the Theologian," *Origins* 20 (July 5, 1990) 117, 119–126; NCCB, "Doctrinal Responsibilities: Approaches to Promoting Cooperation and Resolving Misunderstandings between Bishops and Theologians," *Origins* 19 (June 29, 1989) 97, 99–110.

Every bishop is a priest of sacred worship (c. 375, §1).[109] This canon considers the sanctifying role of the diocesan bishop.[110] He has a special obligation to promote the holiness of the Christian faithful of his particular church. He is to be a personal model of holiness in charity, humility, and simplicity of life. He is to help every person grow in holiness according to each one's proper vocation.[111]

The diocesan bishop is the principal dispenser of the mysteries of God within his diocese. He is to endeavor constantly that the people in his care grow in grace through the sacraments, and that they understand and live the paschal mystery. These words reflect the teaching of *Lumen gentium* 26–27 and *Christus Dominus* 15.

Canon 213 insists that the "Christian faithful have the right to receive assistance from the sacred pastors out of the spiritual goods of the Church, especially the word of God and the sacraments." Canon 387 identifies the bishop's role in assuring this assistance.

Canon 835, §1 says that the sanctifying function of the Church is exercised in the first place by the bishops; it calls bishops "the high priests, the principal dispensers of the mysteries of God,

and the directors, promoters, and guardians of the entire liturgical life in the church entrusted to them." Canon 837, §1 says that liturgical actions are "celebrations of the Church itself which is *the sacrament of unity,* that is, a holy people gathered and ordered under the bishops." The diocesan bishop is to issue liturgical norms, within the scope of his competence, which bind throughout his particular church (c. 838, §4); with other local ordinaries, the diocesan bishop is "to take care that the prayers and pious and sacred exercises of the Christian people are fully in keeping with the norms of the Church" (c. 839, §2).

Mass for the People

Canon 388 — §1. After the diocesan bishop has taken possession of the diocese, he must apply a Mass for the people entrusted to him each Sunday and on the other holy days of obligation in his region.

§2. The bishop himself must personally celebrate and apply a Mass for the people on the days mentioned in §1. If he is legitimately impeded from this celebration, however, he is to apply the Masses either on the same days through another or on other days himself.

§3. A bishop to whom other dioceses besides his own have been entrusted, even under title of administration, satisfies the obligation by applying one Mass for all the people entrusted to him.

§4. A bishop who has not satisfied the obligation mentioned in §§1–3 is to apply as soon as possible as many Masses for the people as he has omitted.

After he has taken canonical possession of the diocese, the diocesan bishop is obliged to offer a Mass for the people of the particular church on each Sunday and holy day of obligation in the region.[112] This is a personal obligation. If he is

---

[109] The sanctifying role of the diocesan bishop is understood properly only by a thorough study of Book IV of the code. See also T. Green, "The Church's Sanctifying Mission: Some Aspects of the Normative Role of the Diocesan Bishop," *Stud Can* 25 (1991) 245–276. The author discusses the sanctifying mission of the diocesan bishop as the moderator, promoter, and guardian of diocesan liturgical life, especially as this role is presented in Book IV and with particular attention to his liturgical governance function (i.e., his policy-setting or normative role). See also T. Green, "The Church's Sanctifying Mission: Some Aspects of the Role of Episcopal Conferences," in *Ius Sequitur Vitam: Law Follows Life, Studies in Canon Law Presented to P. J. M. Huizing* (Louvain: University Press, 1991) 57–88.

[110] *CCEO* 197; *Directory* 21–23, 28.

[111] Canon 210 says that all the Christian faithful must direct their efforts to lead a holy life and to promote the growth and sanctification of the Church, according to their own condition. The special obligation of clerics to pursue holiness is explained in detail in c. 276.

[112] *CIC* 339, §§1, 4–6. *CCEO* 198 says the eparchial bishop is to celebrate the Divine Liturgy frequently for his people, and must celebrate on the days prescribed by the particular law of his church *sui iuris.* The Eastern code

legitimately impeded, however, the diocesan bishop is to apply these Masses on these days through another, or on other days himself. If other dioceses have been entrusted to him (even as administrator only), he may offer one *Missa pro populo* for all the faithful given to his care. If he has failed in any of this, he is to apply as soon as possible as many Masses that he has omitted.[113]

The Bishop as Eucharistic Presider

Canon 389 — He is frequently to preside at the celebration of the Most Holy Eucharist in the cathedral church or another church of his diocese, especially on holy days of obligation and other solemnities.

Every bishop is a priest of sacred worship (c. 375, §1). The diocesan bishop is to preside frequently at the Eucharist in the cathedral and other churches in the diocese, especially on holy days of obligation and other solemnities.[114] The *Ceremonial of Bishops* says:

> The cathedral church is the church that is the site of the bishop's cathedra or chair, the sign of his teaching office and pastoral power in the particular Church, and a sign also of the unity of believers in the faith that the bishop proclaims as shepherd of the Lord's flock.
>
> In this church, on the more solemn liturgical days, the bishop presides at the liturgy. There also, unless pastoral considerations suggest otherwise, he consecrates the sacred chrism and confers the sacrament of holy orders....

With good reason, then, the cathedral church should be regarded as the center of the liturgical life of the diocese.[115]

Sacrosanctum Concilium 41 says that the bishop is the high priest of his flock; therefore, all should hold in the greatest esteem liturgical life in the diocese centered around him, especially in the cathedral. It teaches that "the principal manifestation of the Church consists in the full, active participation of all God's holy people in the same liturgical celebrations, especially in the same Eucharist, in one prayer, at one altar, at which the bishop presides, surrounded by his college of priests and by his ministers."

Canon 899, §2 says that in the eucharistic gathering the people of God are called together with the bishop (or, under his authority, a presbyter) presiding and acting in the name of Christ; according to a diversity of orders and functions, all the faithful who are present unite in the one celebration. Canon 837, §1 recalls that all liturgical actions are celebrations of the Church, that is, a holy people gathered and ordered under the bishops; liturgical actions belong to the whole Church, a sacrament of unity, but touch individuals according to the diversity of orders, functions, and actual participation.

Churches are sacred buildings designated for divine worship to which the faithful have the right of entry for divine worship (c. 1214). The law envisions that the diocesan bishop regularly celebrates the Eucharist in them, and presumes that the faithful are present. The law does not state (nor does it exclude) that the diocesan bishop should celebrate the Eucharist regularly in oratories, which are places designated for divine worship for the benefit of some group and to which others may have access with the consent of the competent superior (c. 1223).[116]

---

makes no mention of his celebrating on different days if he is legitimately impeded, or of his designating others to celebrate in his place on the designated days.

[113] Canon 534 explains that the pastor has a similar obligation to offer the *Missa pro populo* for the people of his parish.

[114] *CCEO* 199, §3; *Directory* 81.

[115] *CB* 42, 44; see also 43–54.

[116] Canon 1227 says bishops (diocesan and titular) can establish a private chapel for themselves with the same rights as an oratory. By definition a "private chapel" is a

Exercise of Pontificals

Canon 390 — A diocesan bishop can perform pontifical functions in his entire diocese but not outside his own diocese without the express, or at least reasonably presumed, consent of the local ordinary.

The diocesan bishop can perform pontifical functions everywhere in his diocese.[117] Outside his diocese, however, the diocesan bishop may perform them only with the express (or at least reasonably presumed) consent of the local ordinary.[118] "The pontifical insignia belonging to a bishop are: the ring, the pastoral staff, and the miter, as well as the pallium, if he is entitled to its use."[119]

Aspects of Bishop's Governmental Role

Canon 391 — §1. It is for the diocesan bishop to govern the particular church entrusted to him with legislative, executive, and judicial power according to the norm of law.
§2. The bishop exercises legislative power himself. He exercises executive power either personally or through vicars general or episcopal vicars according to the norm of law. He exercises judicial power either personally or through the judicial vicar and judges according to the norm of law.

Every bishop is a minister of governance (c. 375, §1).[120] He has all the ordinary, proper, and immediate power he needs for the exercise of his pastoral office, unless some matter is reserved by the Supreme Pontiff to the supreme authority of the Church or to some other authority, such as the episcopal conference (c. 381, §1). He also leads by his own personal example of holiness in charity, humility, and simplicity of life (c. 387).

The first paragraph[121] of canon 391 says the diocesan bishop governs his particular church with legislative, executive, and judicial power.[122] His power of governance, however, is not absolute or arbitrary: he must act "according to the norm of law." He must respect laws stemming from higher authority (c. 135, §2) and can dispense from them only in accord with the laws of the code (see cc. 85–93). This power of governance is given to the diocesan bishop to enable him to serve the faithful in the particular church who are in communion with the universal Church.

The second paragraph explains how the diocesan bishop exercises his governing powers.[123] He is the sole legislator of the diocese; he exercises legislative power alone.[124] His legislative authority cannot be delegated validly to another, and he cannot issue a law contrary to a higher law (c. 135, §2).[125] He may legislate through a diocesan

place of divine worship for the benefit of one or more physical persons (c. 1226). Since all sacred functions can be performed by law in an oratory (c. 1225), and since the bishop's chapel has the same rights as an oratory, Mass and other sacred functions can be celebrated within it.

[117] *CIC* 337; *CCEO* 200; *Directory* 81.

[118] For specifics on pontifical functions, see *CB, passim.*

[119] *CB* 57, which continues: "The *ring* is the symbol of the bishop's fidelity to and nuptial bond with the Church, his spouse, and he is to wear it always" (58). The other pontificals are worn during liturgies: 59–62. See *CIC* 337, §2, which indicates that the pontifical insignia are the staff and miter.

[120] See Herranz, 22–27; Green, "The Pastoral Governance Role of the Diocesan Bishop," 483–490.

[121] See *CIC* 335, §1, which identifies three kinds of power: legislative, judicial, and coercive. The 1983 code speaks of executive power rather than coercive. See *CCEO* 191, §1; *Directory* 32–38.

[122] Canon 135, §1 teaches that the power of governance in the Church is distinguished as legislative, executive, and judicial.

[123] *CIC* 362; 366, §1; 368; 369; 1572; 1573; *CCEO* 191, §2.

[124] Wijlens suggests that a coadjutor or auxiliary bishop would be able to exercise legislative power if he had been granted such special faculties, as mentioned in c. 403, §§2–3 (71, n. 11).

[125] Wijlens comments that many canonical institutions exist to assist the bishop not only in his pastoral ministry but also in his legislative task (e.g., the presbyteral council,

synod (c. 466)[126] or, outside the diocesan synod, by general decrees (c. 29).[127] As diocesan legislator, he is competent to interpret his diocesan laws (c. 16, §1) which he promulgates in the manner he determines and which bind within one month of promulgation, unless the law specifies another period of time (c. 8, §2). He can abrogate, or derogate from, diocesan laws (see c. 20). He can also issue penal laws and, for serious necessity, can add other penalties in his diocese to the penal laws established in universal law; further, if universal law provides for an indeterminate or facultative penalty, he can establish within his diocese a determinate or obligatory penalty for the delict (c. 1315; see also c. 1316).

The diocesan bishop exercises his executive power either alone or through his vicar(s) general (c. 475) and episcopal vicars (c. 476), according to the norms of law (see also cc. 477–481). By office the vicar(s) general and episcopal vicars

are local ordinaries in the diocese along with the diocesan bishop (c. 134, §3).[128] They exercise their executive power according to canons 136–144. However, the bishop occasionally delegates some of his executive power to the chancellor.[129] The code identifies many administrative responsibilities which are to be exercised only by the diocesan bishop (not by the local ordinary); if the diocesan bishop wishes to delegate these to the vicars general and episcopal vicars, he must do so through a specific mandate (c. 134, §3).[130]

The diocesan bishop exercises his judicial power either alone as the judge of first instance in his diocese (c. 1419) or most commonly through others (his judicial vicar, adjutant judicial vicar[s],

the diocesan pastoral council, the diocesan synod); though he is the sole legislator of the diocese the bishop may rely on the recommendations of these groups so he does not legislate in a vacuum. Always the bishop is bound to promote the common discipline of the church and to urge the observance of all ecclesiastical laws (c. 392, §1). Moreover, according to c. 135, §2, no laws promulgated by the diocesan bishop are to be contrary to a higher law: "The bishop has responsibility not only for his own local church, but also for the universal Church. This implies that the bishop as legislator must keep in mind the unity of the local church with the universal Church whenever he decides to create a new law. He should never promulgate a law that is harmful to the unity of the Church even if it appears to serve the needs of the local church" (86–87).

[126] Canon 466 teaches that the diocesan bishop is the only legislator in the diocesan synod, and that other members of the synod possess only a consultative vote. This collaboration, though only consultative, can have a very significant impact in shaping diocesan policy and life. Only the diocesan bishop signs the synodal declarations and decrees, and only he can authorize their publication.

[127] Canon 29 says that by general decrees a competent legislator issues common prescripts for a community capable of receiving law; general decrees are laws properly speaking.

[128] The law gives local ordinaries power to dispense from certain merely ecclesiastical laws: e.g., c. 88 (diocesan laws, laws from a plenary or provincial council, laws from the episcopal conference), cc. 1078–1080, 1127, §2 (marriage impediments and canonical form for marriage), cc. 1196, 1°, 1203 (private vows and oaths), etc.

[129] Herranz comments that "delegated power...is a delicate juridic instrument decentralizing power." He notes that in some countries the diocesan chancellor has been delegated broad powers of governance and says, "It would be less appropriate to make use of the diocesan chancellor, as used to be done in some countries in the past, when the figure of the episcopal vicar 'for a certain type of business' did not exist in law. In fact the chancellor, whether or not a cleric, does not share in the power of governance 'vi officii': his functions are fundamentally those of a notary or secretary of the curia (cfr. can. 482). And particular law could not change the nature of such an ecclesiastical office." He says that the legislator has introduced the episcopal vicar into the code and that "this figure reduces the need for the bishop to delegate his executive power.... There is nothing unusual about the pastoral organization of a diocese, especially the larger and more complex ones, which would include several episcopal vicars" (31–33). See also G. Mesure, *The Diocesan Chancellor in Canon Law and Practice in United States' Archdioceses* (Washington, D.C.: Catholic University of America, 1997). He explains that diocesan chancellors in the United States commonly have acted in capacities and with powers as if they were vicars general.

[130] See H. Müller, "De speciali episcopi mandato iuxta CIC/1983," *P* 79 (1990) 229–235.

and diocesan judges—cc. 1420–1421),[131] according to the norms of law. With the approval of the Apostolic See, several diocesan bishops may establish a single tribunal of first instance for their dioceses in place of individual diocesan tribunals, whether for all cases or certain types of cases; in such a situation, the several diocesan bishops exercise their judicial power together (c. 1423), though one bishop generally functions as moderator of the tribunal.

Fostering Common Discipline

Canon 392 — §1. Since he must protect the unity of the universal Church, a bishop is bound to promote the common discipline of the whole Church and therefore to urge the observance of all ecclesiastical laws.

§2. He is to exercise vigilance so that abuses do not creep into ecclesiastical discipline, especially regarding the ministry of the word, the celebration of the sacraments and sacramentals, the worship of God and the veneration of the saints, and the administration of goods.

Paragraph one expresses the general norm that the diocesan bishop is to protect the unity of the universal Church.[132] Therefore, he is to promote the common discipline of the Church and to urge the observance of all ecclesiastical laws, whatever their origin may be.[133]

Paragraph two specifies the general norm.[134] The diocesan bishop is to have special vigilance

---

[131] Canon 135, §3 says that the judicial power possessed by judges or judicial colleges must be exercised in the manner prescribed in the law; it can be delegated only to perform acts preparatory to some decree or sentence.

[132] *CIC* 336, §1; *CCEO* 201, §1.

[133] Ecclesiastical laws may originate from the supreme authority of the church but also from particular councils (cc. 445–446), the episcopal conference (c. 455), or the diocesan bishop himself (see c. 391, §2).

[134] *CIC* 336, §2 added to this listing matters of faith and morals, catechetical instruction, and Catholic schools. The 1983 code treats these matters in c. 386. See *CCEO* 201, §2; *Directory* 65, 83, 87, 133–138.

---

that abuses do not enter the ecclesiastical discipline, especially regarding the ministry of the word (cc. 756–780), the celebration of sacraments and sacramentals (cc. 840–1172), divine worship and veneration of the saints (cc. 834–839, 1186–1190), and the administration of goods (cc. 1254–1310). Even this more specific listing, however, cannot be considered an exhaustive litany of the areas of the pastoral oversight of the diocesan bishop.

Problems may arise in the correct exercise of the pastoral function of bishops. In such an instance, the Congregation for Bishops is competent to offer assistance of every kind. If necessary, the congregation may initiate a general apostolic visitation, perhaps in agreement with other concerned dicasteries of the Roman Curia. After the visitation, the congregation evaluates its results and proposes to the Supreme Pontiff any appropriate actions to be taken.[135]

Juridic Representative of the Diocese

Canon 393 — The diocesan bishop represents his diocese in all its juridic affairs.

Once it has been legitimately erected, the diocese possesses juridic personality *ipso iure* (c. 373). The diocesan bishop is the agent who represents the diocese in all its juridic affairs.[136]

This canon is new: it is not found in the 1917 code which had only indicated that the local ordinary can stand in trials concerning the cathedral church or the episcopal temporal goods (*CIC* 1653, §1). Canon 393 makes it clear that the diocesan bishop represents his diocese in *all*

---

[135] *PB* 79. In mission territories, such an apostolic visitation would be initiated, overseen, and concluded by the CEP: *PB* 89. See the CLSA Committee for the Study of Apostolic Visitation and the Limitation of Powers of a Diocesan Bishop, "Apostolic Visitation, Accountability, and the Rights of the Local Church," *J* 49 (1989) 341–346.

[136] *CCEO* 201.

juridic affairs, not only in a trial involving the cathedral or episcopal temporalities.[137]

Fostering of Apostolate

Canon 394 — §1. A bishop is to foster various forms of the apostolate in the diocese and is to take care that in the entire diocese or in its particular districts, all the works of the apostolate are coordinated under his direction, with due regard for the proper character of each.

§2. He is to insist upon the duty which binds the faithful to exercise the apostolate according to each one's condition and ability and is to exhort them to participate in and assist the various works of the apostolate according to the needs of place and time.

This canon reflects the teaching of *Christus Dominus* 17.[138] The diocesan bishop is to foster the various forms of the apostolate in the diocese. He is to take care that all apostolic works are coordinated under his direction throughout the whole diocese and its various parts, and with due regard for the proper character of each.

Apostolicam actuositatem 2 teaches that every activity of the Church which is intended to spread the kingdom of God is to be called the "apostolate." The Church exercises the apostolate through all its members, though in different ways. The conciliar decree says in clear terms that "the Christian vocation is, of its nature, a vocation to the apostolate as well." All are called to play an active role in the work of the Church. Canon 394, §2 says that the diocesan bishop is to insist on the

duty of the faithful[139] to exercise the apostolate, and is to exhort them to participate in and assist the various works of the apostolate, with due regard for the needs of place and time.

The role of the faithful in the apostolate is identified several times among the rights and duties of all the Christian faithful. Canon 210 says that, according to the proper condition of each, they are to promote the growth and continual sanctification of the Church. Canon 211 reminds them of the obligation and right to work so the divine message of salvation reaches people of every age and place. Canon 215 mentions their right to found and direct associations for purposes of charity, piety, or the promotion of the Christian vocation; the faithful may hold meetings to pursue these purposes. Canon 216 gives all the Christian faithful the right to promote or sustain apostolic action by their own undertakings, according to their state and condition. To be called *Catholic,* however, the undertaking must have the consent of the competent ecclesiastical authority.

Canon 298, §1 says that associations of the faithful exist to exercise works of the apostolate such as evangelization, works of piety or of charity, and works which animate the temporal order with a Christian spirit.

Furthermore, the law also indicates that the diocesan bishop has a special rapport with the religious who exercise the apostolate in his diocese (see especially cc. 678–683).

Obligation of Residence

Canon 395 — §1. Even if a diocesan bishop has a coadjutor or auxiliary, he is bound by the law of personal residence in the diocese.

§2. Apart from *ad limina* visits, councils, synods of bishops, conferences of bishops which he

---

[137]The 1983 code also says that in juridic affairs the rector represents the seminary (unless the competent authority determines otherwise for certain matters, c. 238, §2), and the pastor represents the parish (c. 532).

[138]See *CCEO* 203; *Directory* 139–161. Canon 275, §2 says all clerics are to acknowledge and promote the mission of the laity in the Church and the world, and c. 529, §2 says pastors are to do the same, even by fostering lay associations for religious purposes.

[139]The Christian faithful include clerics and lay persons; individuals from each group may live the consecrated life (c. 207). Hence, c. 394, §2 says the bishop is to insist on the duty of clergy and lay persons, consecrated or not, to exercise the apostolate according to each one's condition and ability, with an awareness of the needs of place and time.

must attend, or some other duty legitimately entrusted to him, he can be absent from his diocese for a reasonable cause but not beyond a month, whether continuous or interrupted, and provided that he makes provision so that the diocese will suffer no detriment from his absence.

§3. He is not to be absent from the diocese on Christmas, during Holy Week, and on Easter, Pentecost, and the Feast of the Body and Blood of Christ, except for a grave and urgent cause.

§4. If a bishop has been illegitimately absent from the diocese for more than six months, the metropolitan is to inform the Apostolic See of his absence; if it concerns the metropolitan, the senior suffragan is to do so.

Canon 283 says that all clerics, even those without a residential office, are not to leave their diocese for a notable period without at least the presumed permission of their proper ordinary, and that universal and particular law are to determine the time for a due and sufficient annual vacation. This rather general norm is made more specific for diocesan bishops in canon 395.

The diocesan bishop has a personal obligation to reside in the diocese, even if he has a coadjutor or auxiliary.[140] The pastoral work of the diocesan bishop requires a physical presence so that he can

personally and actively perform his many responsibilities in his particular church.[141] When he is away from his diocese, he remains its diocesan bishop and must provide for the continued pastoral care of the particular church through others. Even if the diocese has coadjutor or auxiliary bishops, their function is fundamentally different from that of the diocesan bishop, whom they are called to assist and whose role they do not replace.

The diocesan bishop can be absent from his diocese for a reasonable cause but not beyond a month, continuous or interrupted. This includes his vacation time. He must take care that the diocese suffers no detriment from his absence.[142] In addition he may be absent from the diocese for the *ad limina* visit, councils, synods of bishops, conferences of bishops, or some other duty legitimately entrusted to him.[143] He may also be away when he makes his retreat (see c. 276, §2, 4°). The revised *Form for the Quinquennial Report,* issued in 1997 by the Congregation for Bishops, asks the diocesan bishop to report about his absence from the diocese: "motives, frequency, effects on the pastoral governance of the diocese."[144]

Except for a grave and urgent cause, the diocesan bishop is not to be absent from the diocese on

---

[140] See PCILT, "Obbligo del vescovo di risiedere in diocesi (circa il canone 395 CIC)," September 12, 1996, *Comm* 28 (1996) 182–186. The presence of a bishop at gatherings of the conference of bishops is justified when the conference's statutes state a given bishop *must* be present. A superior authority may also confer another office on a bishop occasioning his absence from the diocese. Finally, a bishop should count his vacation time within the month-long period of his absence from the diocese; further, also within this month he would include such things as: giving retreats outside the diocese to persons not from his diocese, attending lectures or conferences, meetings of various regional or national groups (associations, movements, etc.), visiting foreign missions, leading religious and cultural pilgrimages not organized by the diocese, etc. The document insists that bishops exhibit their solicitude for all the Church best when they minister well to the people of their own particular churches.

[141] *CIC* 338; *CCEO* 204.

[142] Canon 533, §§2–3 deals with the absence of a pastor from his parish. The pastor is given an annual vacation of one month, taken in whole or parts, in addition to his time for annual spiritual retreat. If he is absent from the parish for more than a week, he is to inform the local ordinary. The diocesan bishop is to issue norms which provide for the care of the parish by a priest with necessary faculties while the pastor is absent.

[143] *CIC* 338, §2 had forbidden the bishop to add vacation days to the *ad limina* visit or to add them to days which take him away from the diocese for other reasons, or to combine vacations of two years into one period. It had permitted, however, that each bishop take a vacation not to exceed a maximum of three months per year, continuous or interrupted.

[144] Congregatio pro Episcopis, *Formulae Relationis Quinquennialis* (Vatican City: Libreria Editrice Vaticana, 1997). English translation from the same congregation: *Form for the Quinquennial Report,* III, 10, hereafter cited as *FRQ.*

Christmas, during Holy Week, on Easter, Pentecost, and Corpus Christi.[145]

If a diocesan bishop is illegitimately absent from his diocese for more than six months, the metropolitan[146] is to inform the Apostolic See. If it is the metropolitan himself who is absent, the senior suffragan bishop is to do so. One recalls the norm of canon 1396 that a person who violates the obligation of residence which binds by reason of ecclesiastical office is to be punished with a just penalty—including the possibility, after a warning, even of privation from office.[147]

Obligation of Visitation

Canon 396 — §1. A bishop is obliged to visit the diocese annually either in whole or in part, so that he visits the entire diocese at least every five years either personally or, if he has been legitimately impeded, through the coadjutor bishop, an auxiliary, vicar general, episcopal vicar, or another presbyter.

§2. A bishop is permitted to choose the clerics he prefers as companions and assistants on a visitation; any contrary privilege or custom is reprobated.

Since he is pastor of his particular church, the diocesan bishop has the obligation to visit the diocese on a regular basis.[148] The visitation is an occasion for the diocesan bishop to know the faithful entrusted to his care and to see the various institutions, places, and things present in the diocese.[149] The *Ceremonial of Bishops* says: "The bishop in fulfilling the obligation to visit the parishes or local communities of his diocese should not appear to be satisfying a purely administrative duty. Rather the faithful should see in him the herald of the Gospel, the teacher, shepherd, and high priest of his flock."[150] The information the diocesan bishop gathers through the pastoral visitation process may assist his preparation of the *ad limina* report (c. 399) made every fifth year to the Apostolic See. Canons 396–398 concern his obligation to visit his diocese, the scope of this obligation, and the style of his visitation.

Canon 396, §1 says that the diocesan bishop is obliged to visit the diocese annually, either in whole or part, such that at least every five years he visits the entire diocese. He is to make this visitation either personally or, if he is legitimately impeded, through another—specifically, through the coadjutor bishop, an auxiliary bishop, a vicar general, an episcopal vicar, or another presbyter.[151] The canon does not provide for the visitation to be accomplished through deacons or lay persons.

Canon 396, §2 says that when the diocesan bishop makes the episcopal visitation, he is allowed to choose the clerics (i.e., bishops, presbyters, or deacons)[152] who will accompany him as

---

[145] *CIC* 338, §3 had also forbidden the bishop to be absent during the entire time of Advent and Lent.

[146] Canon 435 says that the metropolitan is the archbishop of his diocese and presides over an ecclesiastical province. The office of metropolitan is joined with an episcopal see determined or approved by the Roman Pontiff. The metropolitan's very limited competencies within the suffragan dioceses of his province are outlined in canon 436.

[147] The Eastern code does not contain the threat of a sanction for unlawful absence.

[148] *CIC* 343. Paragraph one of this canon had identified the following several reasons for the visitation: the preservation of sound and orthodox doctrine, the defense of morality, the correction of abuses, the promotion of peace, simplicity, piety, and docility in the people and

the clergy, and the establishment of anything which seems profitable for religion in light of the circumstances. Such a listing had been included in earlier drafts of canon 396, but was suppressed since it was judged evident and unnecessary: *Comm* 12 (1980) 305. See *CCEO* 205, §1; *Directory* 166–170.

[149] *CD* 23 (2) said that a factor in the revision of diocesan boundaries should be facilitating the exercise of the duty of the bishop to carry out his pastoral visitations, perhaps assisted by others.

[150] *CB* 1177; see also 1178–1184.

[151] Canon 555, §4 says that the vicar forane (dean) is to visit the parishes of his district in accord with the regulations made by the diocesan bishop.

[152] Canon 207, §1 says that clerics are the sacred ministers in the Church. Canon 1008 teaches that the sacrament of

companions and assistants. Any contrary privilege or custom is reprobated.[153]

If the diocesan bishop fails to conduct the visitation, the Holy See may approve the metropolitan's conducting it in a suffragan diocese (c. 436, §1, 2°).

Scope of Visitation

Canon 397 — §1. Persons, Catholic institutions, and sacred things and places, which are located within the area of the diocese, are subject to ordinary episcopal visitation.

§2. A bishop can visit members of religious institutes of pontifical right and their houses only in the cases expressed in law.

This canon identifies the scope of the visitation of a bishop within his diocese.[154] Subject to the ordinary visitation of the diocesan bishop are the persons, Catholic institutions, sacred things, and sacred places located within the diocese.

The diocesan bishop can visit members and houses of religious institutes[155] of pontifical right only in cases expressed by law.[156] Canon 683, §1 says that at the time of his pastoral visitation and

also in cases of necessity, the diocesan bishop (personally or through another) can visit these specific works entrusted to religious: churches and oratories which the faithful habitually attend, schools, and other works of religion or charity; he cannot visit those schools which are open exclusively to an institute's own members. Canon 683, §2 adds that, should the diocesan bishop discover abuses during the visitation process, if he warns the religious superior in vain, he can take steps to correct the abuses even on his own authority. Canon 806, §1 gives the diocesan bishop the right to watch over and visit the Catholic schools of his territory, even those founded or directed by religious; he can also issue prescripts regulating Catholic schools of the diocese, even those directed by religious.[157]

Canon 1224, §1 says the ordinary (personally or through another) is to visit a place destined to become an oratory to make sure it is properly prepared; only thereafter is he to grant permission to establish the oratory.[158]

Canon 366, 1° says that the seat of a pontifical legation is exempt from the power of governance of the local ordinary, except in marriage matters. The seat is also exempt from the diocesan bishop's visitation.

Style of Visitation

Canon 398 — A bishop is to strive to complete the pastoral visitation with due diligence. He is to take care that he does not burden or impose a hardship on anyone through unnecessary expenses.

---

orders marks them with an indelible character and consecrates them to nourish the people of God, fulfilling in the person of Christ the Head the functions of teaching, sanctifying, and governing. Canon 1009, §1 identifies the three orders: the episcopate, the presbyterate, and the diaconate.

[153] Canon 24, §2 teaches that any custom expressly reprobated by the law is not reasonable, and therefore cannot obtain the force of law.

[154] CIC 344, §1; CCEO 204, §§2–3; Directory 118–119, 168.

[155] This canon does not prevent a diocesan bishop from visiting a secular institute (cc. 710–730).

[156] CD 35; ES I, 38–40. Canon 397, §2 concerns the diocesan bishop's visitation of members and houses of religious institutes of *pontifical* right. Canon 628, §2 says the diocesan bishop has the right and duty to visit, even with respect to religious discipline, the *autonomous monasteries* mentioned in c. 615 and individual houses of an institute of *diocesan* right located within his own territory.

[157] Canon 806, §1 adds, however, that the diocesan bishop is not to interfere with the autonomy of religious regarding the internal direction of their schools.

[158] Interestingly, the code does not require any episcopal visitation before the erection of a church, though more extensive consultation is envisioned. The diocesan bishop is to hear the presbyteral council and the rectors of neighboring churches (c. 1215, §2). The law mentions, however, that even if the diocesan bishop has given religious his consent to establish a new house in his diocese, they must also obtain his permission before erecting a church (c. 1215, §3).

The diocesan bishop is to perform the pastoral visitation with due diligence.[159] He is to be careful that he does not burden or impose a hardship on anyone by unnecessary expenses.

Quinquennial Report

Canon 399 — §1. Every five years a diocesan bishop is bound to make a report to the Supreme Pontiff on the state of the diocese entrusted to him, according to the form and time determined by the Apostolic See.

§2. If the year determined for submitting a report falls entirely or in part within the first two years of his governance of a diocese, a bishop can refrain from making and submitting his report on this one occasion.

This canon concerns the so-called *Quinquennial Report*.[160] Every five years every diocesan bishop[161] is to present a report to the Supreme Pontiff on the state of his diocese. The format of the report is determined by the Apostolic See, as is the time it is to be submitted. It is to be sent to the Congregation for Bishops six months before the time set for the visit. In addition to this report, each diocesan bishop submits an annual statistical report to the Central Statistical Office of the Secretariat of State.[162]

Pastor bonus says that the *Quinquennial Report* "is to be examined with all diligence by the competent dicasteries, and their remarks are to be shared with a special committee convened for this purpose so that a brief synthesis of these may be drawn up and readily at hand in the meetings."[163] The Congregation for Bishops is competent to study the quinquennial reports presented by the bishops on the occasion of the *ad limina* visit, for the particular churches assigned to its care.[164]

The diocesan bishop can refrain from making this report on one occasion only: if the year for submitting it falls entirely or partly within the first two years of his pastoral governance of the diocese (§2).

In 1997 the Congregation for Bishops issued a revised *Form for the Quinquennial Report*. Its introductory remarks indicate that the Holy Father is given a synthesis of each quinquennial report before his private audience with each diocesan bishop, and that the preparation of the quinquennial on the local level "affords a privileged occasion for reflection on the situation of the diocese and pastoral planning for its future."[165] The diocesan bishop is to adapt the extensive schema to the circumstances of his particular church, and is urged to be objective, precise, and succinct in providing the requested information. It is important for him to include pastoral difficulties, their causes, and the means used to resolve them; he is also to enumerate pastoral issues yet to be resolved. Reports on confidential matters may be sent directly to the various dicasteries of the Roman Curia.[166] The document invites the diocesan bishop to involve his closest collaborators in drawing up

---

[159] *CIC* 346. This canon had added that the bishop is not to seek or accept any gift of any kind, and any contrary custom is to be considered unreasonable; local custom is to be observed, however, regarding travel costs, food, and lodging for him and his companions. There is no parallel canon in the Eastern code. See also *Directory* 170.

[160] *CIC* 340. Paragraph two of this canon had listed the specific years that bishops from the various nations were to make the quinquennial report; this is omitted in the present law. Remaining in effect is the decree issued on June 29, 1975, by the SCB, in consultation with other interested dicasteries of the Roman Curia, entitled *Ad Romanam Ecclesiam,* which fixes the years in which the diocesan bishops will make the *ad limina* visit and prepare the quinquennial report: *AAS* 67 (1975) 674–676; *CLD* 8, 246–250. See *CCEO* 206, §2. The CEC handles everything concerning the quinquennial reports for the Eastern churches (*PB* 58, §1).

[161] *SMC* XII says that the military ordinary is to present a report to the Holy See on the affairs of the ordinariate every five years, according to the prescribed formula, in accord with the norm of c. 399.

[162] *PB* 44.
[163] *PB* 32.
[164] *PB* 81.
[165] *FRQ,* Intro., n. 2.
[166] *FRQ,* Intro., nn. 3, 5.

the quinquennial report, but adds that the bishop's own contribution is essential. This is true especially when evaluating his own ministry, giving a general assessment of the situation of the diocese, and discussing the diocesan pastoral plan with its future goals and the means to achieve them).[167]

The *Form for the Quinquennial Report* contains twenty-two sections, most of which begin with a comparison of statistics regarding January 1 of the first year of the quinquennium and December 31 of the last year of the quinquennium.[168] The sections, and their major divisions, are the following:

    I. Pastoral and Administrative Organization of the Diocese
       A. Diocesan Ordinary
       B. Other Bishops Working or Residing in the Diocese
       C. Vicars General and Episcopal Vicars
       D. Diocesan Synod
       E. Pastoral-Administrative Offices and Consultative Diocesan Agencies
       F. Cathedral of the Diocese
       G. Division of the Diocese into Deaneries
       H. The Bishop's Evaluation and Personal Judgment on the Effectiveness and Efficiency of the Above Listed Offices, Agencies and Tribunals
    II. Identification and General Religious Situation of the Diocese
    III. The Ministry of the Diocesan Bishop
    IV. Liturgical and Sacramental Life, The Cult of Saints
    V. Catholic Education
    VI. Catechesis
    VII. Life and Ministry of the Clergy
    VIII. Institutes of Consecrated Life and Societies of Apostolic Life
    IX. Missionary Cooperation

    X. The Laity
    XI. Ecumenism
    XII. Other Religions
    XIII. Pastoral Care of the Family
    XIV. Evangelization of Culture
    XV. Social Communications
    XVI. Social Justice and the Social Teaching of the Church
    XVII. Christian Charity and Human Development
    XVIII. Health Care
    XIX. Pastoral Care of Migrants and Pilgrims
    XX. Artistic and Historical Patrimony of the Church
    XXI. Financial State of the Diocese
    XXII. General Assessment and Outlook for the Future

An overview of these sections and a careful reading of the entire *Form for the Quinquennial Report* show that the diocesan bishop is asked to render an account of the many pastoral obligations he has in his particular church. These are listed here in these canons on the role of the diocesan bishop and elsewhere throughout the code and in other legislation as well.

Ad Limina Visit

Canon 400 — §1. Unless the Apostolic See has established otherwise, during the year in which he is bound to submit a report to the Supreme Pontiff, a diocesan bishop is to go to Rome to venerate the tombs of the Blessed Apostles Peter and Paul and to present himself to the Roman Pontiff.

§2. A bishop is to satisfy the above-mentioned obligation personally unless he is legitimately impeded. In that case, he is to satisfy it through his coadjutor, if he has one, or auxiliary, or a suitable priest of his presbyterate who resides in his diocese.

§3. An apostolic vicar can satisfy this obligation through a proxy, even one living in Rome. This obligation does not bind an apostolic prefect.

---

[167] *FRQ*, Intro., n. 6.
[168] Section II is largely statistics. Sections III–XXI are divided into two parts: "A. Statistics" and "B. Description."

Unless the Apostolic See determines otherwise, during the year when the diocesan bishop[169] is to submit his *Quinquennial Report,* he is to go to Rome to venerate the tombs of the apostles Peter and Paul and to present himself to the Roman Pontiff.[170] This visit is known as the *ad limina* (literally, *to the threshold*) visit; it has three principal stages: the pilgrimage to the tombs of Peter and Paul and their veneration, the meeting with the Supreme Pontiff, and the meetings with the officials of the dicasteries of the Roman Curia.[171] Titular bishops do not have this obligation.

Pope John Paul II explains that the *ad limina* visit is an occasion when every bishop exercises his inviolable right and duty to approach the successor of Peter.[172] He states in the introduction to his apostolic constitution, *Pastor bonus:*

These visits have a special meaning all of their own, in keeping with ecclesiological and pastoral principles explained above. Indeed, they are first of all an opportunity of the greatest importance, and they constitute, as it were, the center of the highest ministry committed to the Supreme Pontiff. For then the pastor of the universal Church talks and communicates with the pastors of the particular churches, who have come to him in order to see Cephas (cf. Gal. 1:18), to deal with him concerning the problems of their dioceses, face to face and in private, and so to share with him the solicitude for all the Churches (cf. 2 Cor. 11:28). For these reasons, communion and unity in the innermost life of the Church are fostered to

the highest degree through the *ad limina* visits.[173]

He adds that in these meetings the pope confirms and supports his brother bishops in faith and charity; the bonds of hierarchical communion are strengthened; and the catholicity of the Church and the unity of the episcopal college are manifested openly.[174]

Pastor bonus teaches that the *ad limina* visits also engage bishops in dialogue with officials of the dicasteries of the Roman Curia: information is shared and deepened, and advice and suggestions are offered for the good and progress of the Church and for the observance of common ecclesiastical discipline.[175]

The Congregation for Bishops is competent to handle all matters related to the *ad limina* visits for the particular churches assigned to its care. The congregation studies the quinquennial reports and is available to the bishops when they arrive in Rome, especially to see to arrangements for visits with the Supreme Pontiff and for other meetings and pilgrimages. After the *ad limina* visit, the congregation also communicates in writing to the bishops the conclusions concerning their dioceses.[176] *Pastor bonus* announces that the Congregation for Bishops, in consultation with other interested congregations, is preparing a directory to assist bishops in preparation for the *ad limina* reports.[177]

In 1988, the Congregation for Bishops issued the *Directory for the Ad Limina Visit*[178] which contains two principal parts. The first part discusses three phases of the *ad limina* visit: remote preparation (involving a time of reflection and prayer, writing the quinquennial report, dialogue with the

---

[169] *SMC* XII also says that the military ordinary is to make the *ad limina* visit prescribed by c. 400, §§1–2.

[170] *CIC* 341, §1; *CCEO* 208, §1.

[171] *PB* 31. See also Appendix I of *PB,* which offers a lengthy and inspiring reflection on the pastoral significance of the *ad limina* visit. The CEC handles everything concerning the *ad limina* visits for the Eastern churches (*PB* 58, §1).

[172] *PB,* Intro., 10.

[173] Ibid.

[174] *PB* 29.

[175] *PB* 30.

[176] *PB* 81.

[177] *PB,* App. I, 6.

[178] CFB, *Directory for the Ad Limina Visit* (Vatican City: Libreria Editrice Vaticana, 1988). *Comm* 20 (1988) 156–165.

papal representative), intermediate preparation (involving dialogue with the Coordinating Office of the Congregation for Bishops), and the execution of the *ad limina* visit (involving pilgrimage to and veneration of the apostles' tombs, the meeting with the Holy Father, and contacts with officials of the dicasteries of the Roman Curia). The second part of the *Directory* contains three texts to help bishops better understand the richness of the *ad limina* visits: Joseph Cardinal Ratzinger addresses theological issues, Lucas Cardinal Moreira Neves addresses spiritual-pastoral issues, and Monsignor Vincente Cárcel Ortí addresses historico-juridical issues.

The second paragraph of canon 400 says that the diocesan bishop is to make this visit personally.[179] If he is legitimately impeded from doing so, he satisfies this obligation through his coadjutor or auxiliary, or through a suitable priest who resides in his diocese.

An apostolic vicar can choose to satisfy this obligation through a proxy, even one living in Rome.[180] An apostolic prefect, however, does not have this obligation. No reference is made to an *ad limina* visit made by the apostolic administrator mentioned in canon 371, §2. The heads of these three kinds of particular churches govern with vicarious power, in the name of the Supreme Pontiff.

Retirement from Office

Canon 401 — §1. A diocesan bishop who has completed the seventy-fifth year of age is requested to present his resignation from office to the Supreme Pontiff, who will make provision after he has examined all the circumstances.

§2. A diocesan bishop who has become less able to fulfill his office because of ill health or some other grave cause is earnestly requested to present his resignation from office.

The 1983 code is the first codified legislation asking for the retirement of bishops, both diocesan

[179] *CIC* 342.
[180] *CIC* 299.

(c. 401) and coadjutor and auxiliary (c. 411). A diocesan bishop who has completed his seventy-fifth year is asked (*rogatur*) to submit his resignation to the Supreme Pontiff.[181] Strictly speaking, the law does not *require* resignation, but seeks voluntary resignation. The resignation must be accepted by the Supreme Pontiff,[182] who will make a provision after he has studied all the circumstances. *Christus Dominus* 21 had urged diocesan bishops (and their equivalents) who had become less capable of performing their roles because of age or other serious reason to resign voluntarily or at the request of competent authority; no specific age was mentioned. Without explanation, *Ecclesiae sanctae* I, 11 set seventy-five as the age for voluntary resignation, but did not mention retirement for reasons other than age. Canon 401, §1 reflects the voluntary request for retirement of all bishops at age seventy-five.[183]

A diocesan bishop is earnestly asked (*enixe rogatur*) to submit his resignation if he has become less able to fulfill his office due to ill health or some other grave cause (c. 401, §2). The "grave cause" is not further specified, but entails something other than ill health or advanced age, which are already mentioned in the canon. The code here makes a stronger request (*enixe*) for voluntary retirement than when the diocesan bishop reaches

[181] *CCEO* 210.
[182] Canon 416. The resignation does not take place *ipso facto,* but must be accepted by the pope. See cc. 187–189 on resignation from ecclesiastical offices.
[183] Resignation to be offered at age seventy-five is also requested of cardinals who preside over dicasteries and other permanent institutes of the Roman Curia and Vatican City (c. 354; see *PB* 5, §2), coadjutor and auxiliary bishops (c. 411), and pastors (c. 538, §3). Non-cardinal moderators and secretaries of Roman dicasteries cease holding office at age seventy-five, and other members of congregations lose their office at age eighty (*PB* 5, §2). Judges (auditors) of the Roman Rota retire at age seventy-four, and undersecretaries of dicasteries resign at age seventy; major and minor officials of dicasteries resign at age seventy (if they are clergy or religious) or sixty-five (if they are lay): *Regolamento Generale della Curia Romana* 43, §§4–6, February 4, 1992; *AAS* 84 (1992) 220–221.

the age of seventy-five, but once again the resignation is not, strictly speaking, *required.*

A diocese does not become vacant at the moment the diocesan bishop submits his resignation for whatever reason; it becomes vacant only when the Roman Pontiff accepts the resignation (c. 416).

Status of Diocesan Bishop Emeritus

Canon 402 — §1. A bishop whose resignation from office has been accepted retains the title of emeritus of his diocese and can retain a place of residence in that diocese if he so desires, unless in certain cases the Apostolic See provides otherwise because of special circumstances.

§2. The conference of bishops must take care that suitable and decent support is provided for a retired bishop, with attention given to the primary obligation which binds the diocese he has served.

Once his resignation has been accepted by the Supreme Pontiff, the diocesan bishop immediately becomes a titular bishop and holds the title of bishop *emeritus* of his diocese.[184] Unlike the custom in the past, he does not receive title to a titular church *in partibus infidelium* (in the territory of unbelievers) but instead holds the title of "Former Bishop of N." This symbolizes an ongoing relationship to the people whom he had previously served as diocesan bishop.

The retired diocesan bishop can retain a place of residence in the diocese if he so chooses, unless in certain cases the Apostolic See makes another provision because of special circumstances. A retired *religious* bishop may choose to live outside the house of his institute, unless the Apostolic See has determined otherwise (c. 707, §1).

The conference of bishops must make sure that suitable and decent support is provided to a retired diocesan bishop, although the primary obligation rests with the diocese he served. This canon reflects the discipline of *Christus Dominus*

---

[184] *CCEO* 211.

21 and *Ecclesiae sanctae* I, 11. If a retired religious bishop has served a diocese, that diocese is to provide his sustenance unless his own institute wishes to do so; otherwise the Apostolic See is to provide (c. 707, §2).[185]

Retired bishops continue to be members of the college of bishops (c. 336) and to be pastors in the Church who are teachers of doctrine, priests of sacred worship, and ministers of governance (c. 375, §1). They still have the right and duty to take part in an ecumenical council with a deliberative vote (c. 339, §1). They also can be called to particular councils and have a deliberative vote within them if they are so called (c. 443, §1, 3°).[186]

On October 31, 1988, the Congregation for Bishops issued norms for retired bishops.[187] The

---

[185] At its November 13, 1995, meeting, the NCCB approved a plan proposed by the ad hoc Committee on Bishops' Life and Ministry, which gives retired bishops a monthly stipend of $1,300. Also provided are other "basic benefits" which include: appropriate housing and board, health and welfare benefits (including major medical and the full cost of all medical and hospital care), an office with secretarial assistance as needed, and suitable funeral and burial. In addition, retired bishops are to receive a car for personal use, and transportation, food, and lodging expenses for NCCB meetings, *ad limina* visits, and provincial and regional meetings, workshops, and retreats. These norms were last considered in 1990, and will be reviewed again in 2000. See Mark Pattison, "Bishops Revise, OK Retirement Plan for Retired Colleagues," Catholic News Service, November 14, 1995.

[186] See T. Green, "Deliberative Vote for Retired Bishops in Teaching Matters," *J* 54 (1994) 15–21. Green discusses the possibility and advisability of retired bishops having a deliberative vote in decisions of the conference of bishops. He notes: "Relatively few conference statutes provide for a deliberative vote by retired bishops in conference deliberations. A fair number of conference statutes envision a consultative vote for such bishops. However, the great majority of conference statutes in Europe and the Americas do not explicitly refer to the involvement of retired bishops, whatever may be the de facto practice of involving them in conference activities" (19).

[187] Congregatio pro Episcopis, "Normae de episcopis ab officio cessante," *Comm* 20 (1988) 167–168. Unofficial translation: *CLS-GBIN* 79 (September 1989) 17–19.

norms acknowledge that retired bishops have the right and duty to take part in an ecumenical council (c. 339, §1). They are to be consulted about questions of a general nature just like other bishops, so that their proven pastoral experience may be shared. Like other bishops, they are to be sent documents from the Holy See, especially from the Holy Father. They may be consultants to and adjunct members of dicasteries of the Roman Curia. They may be selected by episcopal conferences to participate in synods of bishops.[188] They may have a role in the work of episcopal conferences, even if they have no vote; they should receive documents from the conference. They should also receive documents from their diocese and be informed of the various activities of the diocesan community; special care should be taken to provide financial support for them within the limits of diocesan resources. The entire Church is encouraged to make retired bishops feel they are part of its life.[189]

On December 3, 1991, the Pontifical Council for the Interpretation of Legislative Texts promulgated an authentic interpretation of canon 346, §1 stating that retired diocesan bishops (c. 402, §1) can be elected by the conference of bishops as members of the synod of bishops. This clarifies the meaning of canon 346, §1.[190]

ARTICLE 3: COADJUTOR AND AUXILIARY BISHOPS [cc. 403–411][191]

Diocesan bishops are entrusted with the pastoral care of a diocese (c. 376). Article 3 treats three categories of bishops who may serve in a diocese with the diocesan bishop and under his leadership: the coadjutor (who has the right of succession to the office of diocesan bishop), the auxiliary with special faculties, and the auxiliary without special faculties. The article contains the norms on their appointment (c. 403) and explains how they take canonical possession of their office (c. 404). The scope of their ministry is identified (c. 405). The diocesan bishop is to appoint them as vicars general or, in the case of the auxiliaries without special faculties, at least as episcopal vicars (c. 406). Under the leadership of the diocesan bishop, these bishops are to collaborate together and consult each other so they work in harmony (c. 407). They should perform pontificals and other episcopal functions when so directed by the diocesan bishop (c. 408). They are obliged to reside in the diocese and are given a month-long vacation (c. 410). The norms on the resignation of a diocesan bishop also apply to coadjutor and auxiliary bishops (c. 411).

When the see is vacant, the coadjutor immediately becomes the diocesan bishop; the auxiliaries retain their current powers and faculties until a

---

[188] Bishop Anthony Pilla reported in a letter to the U.S. bishops, dated May 16, 1997, that the Vatican document "Criteria for Participation at the Special Assembly for America" states specifically "that the election of delegates to any synod is to be conducted by and from the members of the episcopal conference who have active and passive vote according to the statutes in force at the moment." He noted that the NCCB had erred in permitting retired bishops to vote on synod delegates, but that Pope John Paul II had granted a sanation of the votes. The retired delegate elected, Archbishop John Quinn, however, was not qualified to be a synod delegate, so a replacement for him would need to be elected at the bishops' June 19–21, 1997 meeting. *Origins* 27 (1997) 34.

[189] G. Read, "Norms of Bishops Leaving Office," *CLS-GBIN* 79 (September 1989) 20–22.

[190] *AAS* 83 (1991) 1093. Some may suggest this interpretation is expansive, since by universal legislation retired

bishops are not *de iure* members of the conference (c. 450, §2) and therefore not eligible for synod membership which is limited to conference members (c. 346, §1). Others, however, will suggest that the interpretation is simply declarative, since no legislation restricts the conference of bishops from electing a retired bishop to synod membership; see Wrenn, 62–63. In any event, the interpretation is helpful, since the October 31, 1988 norms from the Congregation for Bishops do not appear to be legislative in nature. One notes, further, that the interpretation refers only to retired *diocesan* bishops. See Green, "Deliberative Vote for Retired Bishops," 11–12, n. 23.

[191] For the history of the development of these canons, see *Comm* 3 (1971) 188; 5 (1973) 223–224; 7 (1975) 161–172; 12 (1980) 309–314; 19 (1987) 117–130, 143–145; 24 (1992) 40–41.

new diocesan bishop takes possession of the see (c. 409).

These canons reflect the teaching of *Christus Dominus* 25–26 and *Ecclesiae sanctae* I, 13.

Appointment of Coadjutor/Auxiliary

Canon 403 — §1. When the pastoral needs of a diocese suggest it, one or more auxiliary bishops are to be appointed at the request of the diocesan bishop. An auxiliary bishop does not possess the right of succession.

§2. In more serious circumstances, even of a personal nature, an auxiliary bishop provided with special faculties can be given to a diocesan bishop.

§3. If it appears more opportune to the Holy See, it can appoint *ex officio* a coadjutor bishop who also has special faculties. A coadjutor bishop possesses the right of succession.

This preliminary canon identifies three kinds of bishops who may serve in a diocese together with the diocesan bishop: the auxiliary bishop, the auxiliary bishop with special faculties, and the coadjutor bishop.[192] All are appointed to service of

the diocese, not the person of the diocesan bishop, even though some personal characteristic of the diocesan bishop (e.g., poor health) may occasion the appointment of the latter two types of auxiliaries.[193] All are titular bishops (c. 376); however, the coadjutor holds the title of "Coadjutor Bishop of N." while the auxiliaries hold the title to a titular church.[194]

The auxiliary bishop[195] with or without special faculties does not have the right of succession. One or more are appointed at the request of the diocesan bishop when the pastoral needs of the diocese suggest it. *Christus Dominus* 25 suggests that an auxiliary may be appointed when the diocesan bishop on his own cannot provide sufficiently well for the good of the faithful of his diocese because of the great size of the diocese, the number of inhabitants, some special pastoral problem, or some other reasons.

The auxiliary bishop with special faculties[196] can be given to a diocesan bishop in more serious

---

[192] *CIC* 350. The 1917 code had identified a coadjutor given to the person of the bishop with the right of succession; the coadjutor given to the see without the right of succession; and the coadjutor (called the *auxiliary*) given to the bishop without the right of succession. When the see became vacant, the coadjutor with the right of succession immediately became the ordinary of the diocese if he had taken canonical possession; the coadjutor given to the see continued his office during the vacancy; and the auxiliary lost his office unless the apostolic letters of appointment had provided otherwise (see *CIC* 355).

See also *CCEO* 212. The Eastern code identifies two kinds of bishops who serve together with the eparchial bishop: *coadjutor bishops* who can be appointed ex officio, who have special powers, and who have the right of succession; and *auxiliary bishops*. No reference is made to auxiliary bishops with special faculties. *CCEO* 234, however, provides norms for apostolic administrators appointed by the Roman Pontiff for serious and special reasons, whether *sede plena* or *sede vacante*. See also *Directory* 199.

[193] See c. 377, §3 on the procedure for the appointment of a coadjutor bishop, and c. 377, §4 on the procedure for the appointment of an auxiliary.

[194] For more on this issue, see the commentary on c. 376.

[195] See M. Foster, "The Role of Auxiliary Bishops," *J* 51 (1991) 423–430. Foster concludes his study as follows: "The conciliar principles derived from *Christus Dominus, Ecclesiae Sanctae* I, and the *Directory on the Pastoral Ministry of Bishops* influenced the formulation of the canons on auxiliary bishops. These four principles of pastoral need, unity in diocesan governance, episcopal status, and a close working relationship between the diocesan bishop and his auxiliaries are the basic frame of reference within which one can view the role of auxiliary bishops in the life of the local church" (430). See also CLSA Committee for Research and Education on Rights and Pastoral Responsibilities of Bishops, "Report of a CLSA Survey on Auxiliary Bishops," *J* 53 (1993) 354–361.

[196] The Eastern code does not make provision for this kind of auxiliary bishop; it does, however, identify an *apostolic administrator* who may, for grave and special reasons, be appointed by the Roman Pontiff even to a see which is not vacant (*CCEO* 234). A similar figure was found in *CIC* 312–318, but is not mentioned in the 1983 code though in fact apostolic administrators are still appointed in Latin dioceses. This apostolic administra-

circumstances, even of a personal nature. Interestingly, the code does not say this kind of auxiliary is appointed necessarily at the request of the diocesan bishop.

The coadjutor bishop has the right of succession. This means that the diocese does not become vacant when the current diocesan bishop ceases to hold office in one of the ways identified in canon 416, provided that the coadjutor has taken canonical possession of his office; instead, diocesan governance passes immediately to the coadjutor, who then is the new diocesan bishop. If the see is impeded, the coadjutor assumes immediate interim governance of the diocese unless the Holy See determines otherwise (c. 413, §1). He is appointed ex officio by the Holy See (not specifically at the request of the diocesan bishop) when this arrangement seems more opportune, and is endowed with special faculties to be determined in the letter of appointment. It is not envisioned that any diocese have more than one coadjutor bishop.

The law gives special consideration to the coadjutor and the auxiliary with special faculties. They are to aid the diocesan bishop in the entire governance of the diocese and to take his place if he is absent or impeded (c. 405, §2). They are to be appointed vicars general, and the diocesan bishop is to entrust to them before others those things which by law require a special mandate (c. 406, §1). They and the diocesan bishop are to consult one another on matters of major importance (c. 407, §1). Since their special faculties restrict the rights of the diocesan bishop, those faculties must be strictly interpreted (see c. 18).[197]

Other canons specify further the rights and duties of coadjutor and all auxiliary bishops. They have the right and duty to take part in an ecumenical council with a deliberative vote (c. 339, §1). They must be called to particular councils and have the right to a deliberative vote in them (c. 443, §1, 2°). They belong to the conference of bishops by the law itself (c. 450, §1); coadjutor bishops have a deliberative vote in plenary meetings of the conference (c. 454, §1) and auxiliary bishops have a consultative or deliberative vote according to the statutes of the conference (c. 454, §2). They are to be called to and participate in a diocesan synod (c. 463, §1, 1°). They are to serve as vicars general or episcopal vicars, with corresponding rights and duties (cc. 475–481) and, as such, may belong to the episcopal council of the curia where that council exists (c. 473, §4). Auxiliary bishops, however, may not serve as presidents or pro-presidents of the conference of bishops or a gathering of bishops of an ecclesiastical region.[198]

Taking Possession of Office

Canon 404 — §1. A coadjutor bishop takes possession of his office when he, either personally or through a proxy, has shown the apostolic letter of appointment to the diocesan bishop and college of consultors in the presence of the chancellor of the curia, who records the event.

§2. An auxiliary bishop takes possession of his office when he has shown the apostolic letter of appointment to the diocesan bishop in the presence of the chancellor of the curia, who records the event.

---

tor may function very much like the auxiliary bishop with special faculties in c. 403, §2 of the Latin code; certainly the faculties of an apostolic administrator will need to be clearly delineated since no listing of them is found in the current Latin code. See J. Huels, "The Correction and Punishment of a Diocesan Bishop," *J* 49 (1989) 529–530.

[197] Huels, 527–528. He adds: "It is possible that the special faculties may be contrary to the general law by limiting

the diocesan bishop's authority in certain areas. Even if the apostolic letter of appointment contains provisions against the common law, the letter must be acknowledged as holding precedence, and the diocesan bishop may not act contrary to it" (528). The faculties are examples of delegated power.

[198] This incapacity of the auxiliary bishop is found in a response of the PCILT promulgated March 15, 1989: *AAS* 81 (1989) 388. See Wrenn, 52–54.

§3. If the diocesan bishop is completely impeded, however, it suffices that both the coadjutor bishop and the auxiliary bishop show the apostolic letter of appointment to the college of consultors in the presence of the chancellor of the curia.

Canon 382, §1 forbids one appointed as diocesan bishop to exercise his office before taking canonical possession of it. In a related fashion, the coadjutor and auxiliary also are expected to take canonical possession of their offices before they begin their pastoral ministry.[199]

The coadjutor takes possession of his office when, personally or through a proxy, he has shown his apostolic letter of appointment to the diocesan bishop (unless he is completely impeded) and the college of consultors; the chancellor is to be present to record the event. This arrangement is quite similar to the manner in which a diocesan bishop takes possession of his diocese: the diocesan bishop presents his apostolic letter to the college of consultors in the presence of the chancellor (c. 382, §3). This reflects the fact that the coadjutor has the right of succession: he will become the diocesan bishop immediately upon the death of the current diocesan bishop, his resignation accepted by the Roman Pontiff, his transfer, or his deprivation of office (see cc. 409, §1; 416).

An auxiliary bishop (even one with special faculties) takes possession of his office when he has shown his apostolic letter of appointment only to the diocesan bishop (not also to the college of consultors); the chancellor is to be present to record the event. The law does not mention the auxiliary doing this through a proxy as it does in the case of a coadjutor bishop.

If the diocesan bishop is completely impeded (see c. 412), the coadjutor and the auxiliary may show the apostolic letter of appointment to the college of consultors, instead of to the diocesan bishop. The chancellor is to be present presumably to record the event, though the code does not specify exactly so in this instance; the chancellor

presumably would also record the fact that the diocesan bishop was completely impeded. The code does not mention taking possession of office being done through a proxy.

When the diocesan bishop takes canonical possession of his office, the code strongly recommends that this be done in a liturgical act at the cathedral with clergy and others gathered together (c. 382, §4). The code does not say the same for the coadjutor or auxiliary bishops, though it certainly does not oppose a public liturgical celebration in which canonical possession takes place. The former is envisioned more as a public celebration, and the latter more as a simple administrative act.

Rights and Obligations in General

Canon 405 — §1. A coadjutor bishop and an auxiliary bishop have the obligations and rights which are determined in the prescripts of the following canons and are defined in the letter of their appointment.

§2. A coadjutor bishop and the auxiliary bishop mentioned in can. 403, §2 assist the diocesan bishop in the entire governance of the diocese and take his place if he is absent or impeded.

The first paragraph of this canon says that the rights and obligations of coadjutor bishops and auxiliary bishops (with or without special faculties) are explained both in their letter of appointment and in the following canons.[200]

Paragraph two says that the coadjutor and the auxiliary with special faculties assist the diocesan bishop in the governance of the entire diocese, and they take his place if he is absent or impeded (see c. 413, §1). They are to be appointed vicars general, and the diocesan bishop is to entrust to them before others whatever by law requires a special mandate (c. 406, §1). Further, they are to consult each other on matters of major importance in order to foster the present and future good of the diocese (c. 407, §1).

---

[199] CIC 353; CCEO 214.

[200] CIC 351, §§1–2; CCEO 213.

Appointment as Vicar General/Episcopal Vicar

Canon 406 — §1. The diocesan bishop is to appoint a coadjutor bishop and the auxiliary bishop mentioned in can. 403, §2 as vicar general. Moreover, the diocesan bishop is to entrust to him before others those things which by law require a special mandate.

§2. Unless the apostolic letter has provided otherwise and without prejudice to the provision of §1, a diocesan bishop is to appoint his auxiliary or auxiliaries as vicars general or at least as episcopal vicars, dependent only on his authority or that of the coadjutor bishop or auxiliary bishop mentioned in can. 403, §2.

Appointment by the Holy See to be a coadjutor or an auxiliary bishop (even though special faculties may be granted in their letter of appointment) does not confer the office of *local ordinary* in the diocese. Canon 406 expects the diocesan bishop to appoint his coadjutor and auxiliary as local ordinaries of the diocese with him, whether as vicars general or episcopal vicars.[201] *Christus Dominus* 26, which is reflected in this canon, adds that the coadjutor and auxiliary are dependent on the authority of the diocesan bishop.[202]

Because of the preeminent diocesan status of the coadjutor and the auxiliary with special faculties, they are to be appointed by the diocesan bishop as vicars general (§1). *Christus Dominus* 27 says that the vicar general holds a preeminent position in the diocesan curia; it also says that episcopal vicars may be appointed to promote the good government of the diocese with the same powers of the vicar general but over a specific part of the diocese, a specific kind of affair (e.g., education, evangelization, liturgy, etc.), or a specific group of the faithful (such as those of a particular rite). The vicar general and episcopal vicar exercise *vicariously* (not properly, or in their own name) the ordinary power of executive governance as defined by the law; by special mandate,

they may be delegated even executive powers otherwise belonging to the diocesan bishop alone (e.g., the power to appoint a parochial administrator).[203] The law asks the diocesan bishop to entrust to the coadjutor and the auxiliary with special faculties before others those things which by law require this special mandate (see c. 134, §3). All this illustrates that they, before others, share with the diocesan bishop in a special way the general pastoral governance of the diocese.

Unless the apostolic letter says otherwise, the diocesan bishop is to appoint his auxiliaries without special faculties as vicars general or episcopal vicars (§2). These auxiliaries are to be dependent solely on the authority of the diocesan bishop, the coadjutor bishop, or the auxiliary bishop with special faculties.

Episcopal Consultation and Collaboration

Canon 407 — §1. In order to foster the present and future good of the diocese as much as possible, a diocesan bishop, a coadjutor, and the auxiliary mentioned in can. 403, §2 are to consult one another on matters of major importance.

§2. In considering cases of major importance, especially of a pastoral character, a diocesan bishop is to wish to consult the auxiliary bishops before others.

§3. Since a coadjutor bishop and an auxiliary bishop are called to share in the solicitude of the diocesan bishop, they are to exercise their duties in such a way that they proceed in harmony with him in effort and intention.

The diocesan bishop, the coadjutor, and the auxiliary with special faculties are to consult each other on matters of major importance in order to

---

[201] *CIC* 351, §3; *CCEO* 215, §§1–2; *Directory* 199, 201.
[202] See also *ES* I, 13.

[203] Appendix II of this commentary identifies rights and responsibilities which belong by law to the *diocesan bishop;* for another local ordinary to perform any of these functions requires that he receive a special mandate from the diocesan bishop. Even a mandate is useless, however, if the action requires episcopal ordination and the local ordinary is a presbyter, not a bishop.

foster the present and future good of the diocese (§1).[204] A very close bond of collaboration exists between the diocesan bishop and these others, closer than that existing between the diocesan bishop and an auxiliary bishop without special faculties.

When considering cases of major importance, especially pastoral ones, the diocesan bishop is to consult his auxiliaries before others (§2).[205]

The coadjutor and auxiliaries share in the solicitude of the diocesan bishop; therefore they are to perform their duties in harmony with him in effort and intention (§3).[206] The law places strong emphasis on the importance of diocesan unity; this unity is evident in collaboration and harmony among the bishops serving the diocese.

Assistance Rendered the Diocesan Bishop

Canon 408 — §1. A coadjutor bishop and an auxiliary bishop who are not prevented by a just impediment are obliged to perform pontificals and other functions to which the diocesan bishop is bound whenever the diocesan bishop requires it.

§2. A diocesan bishop is not to entrust habitually to another the episcopal rights and functions which a coadjutor or auxiliary bishop can exercise.

Whenever the diocesan bishop requires it, the coadjutor and the auxiliary bishops are to perform pontificals and other functions to which the diocesan bishop is bound, unless they are prevented by a just impediment (§1).[207] They are not bound to substitute for the diocesan bishop in fulfilling strictly personal responsibilities which he has assumed on his own.

The diocesan bishop is not to entrust habitually to another any of the episcopal rights and roles which a coadjutor or auxiliary can exercise (§2).[208] This reflects the close collaboration which should exist between the diocesan bishop and his coadjutor or auxiliary, and the importance of the episcopal office.

Vacancy of See

Canon 409 — §1. When the episcopal see is vacant, the coadjutor bishop immediately becomes the bishop of the diocese for which he had been appointed provided that he has legitimately taken possession of it.

§2. When the episcopal see is vacant and unless competent authority has established otherwise, an auxiliary bishop preserves all and only those powers and faculties which he possessed as vicar general or episcopal vicar while the see was filled until a new bishop has taken possession of the see. If he has not been designated to the function of diocesan administrator, he is to exercise this same power, conferred by law, under the authority of the diocesan administrator who presides over the governance of the diocese.

The see becomes vacant in one of four ways: death of the diocesan bishop, his resignation accepted by the pope, his transfer, or privation of office made known to him (see c. 416). This canon concerns the destiny of the coadjutor and the auxiliary bishops when the vacancy occurs.[209]

Chistus Dominus 25 determined that the auxiliary bishop is not to lose his powers and faculties when the see becomes vacant, unless competent authority determines otherwise. It also recommended that the auxiliary (or, if there were several, one of them) should be assigned the governance of the diocese during the vacancy. *Ecclesiae*

---

[204] *Directory* 199.

[205] Canon 500, §2 says that the diocesan bishop is to listen also to the presbyteral council in matters of greater importance (*in negotiis maioris momenti*), above and beyond the specific instances in which he must consult it to act validly.

[206] *CCEO* 215, §4.

[207] *CIC* 351, §4; *CCEO* 215, §3.

[208] *CIC* 351, §3; *CCEO* 216.

[209] *CIC* 355. *CIC* 355, §2 said that the auxiliary lost his office when the see became vacant, unless his apostolic letter provided otherwise. See also *CCEO* 224.

sanctae I, 13 reiterated the fact that the auxiliary does not lose his powers as vicar general or episcopal vicar during the vacancy, but acknowledged the fact that the auxiliary might not be elected as diocesan administrator. If he is not elected the diocesan administrator, during the vacancy the auxiliary retains the powers he had as vicar general or episcopal vicar, until the new diocesan bishop takes possession of the see. During the vacancy, the auxiliary is to serve in full accord with the diocesan administrator, who is primarily responsible for diocesan governance. The code commission refused to legislate that an auxiliary must be designated diocesan administrator; this would unnecessarily have restricted the electoral prerogatives of the college of consultors.[210]

When the see becomes vacant, if there is a coadjutor, he immediately becomes the diocesan bishop, provided he has legitimately taken possession of his office in the manner explained in c. 404, §1 (§1).[211]

If there is no coadjutor and therefore the see is truly vacant, the means of providing governance in the diocese is explained in canons 416–430. In such a case, unless competent authority has decided otherwise, an auxiliary (both one with special faculties and one without them) loses his office (c. 481, §1) yet retains all the powers he had as vicar general or episcopal vicar while the see was filled until the new diocesan bishop takes possession of the see.[212] The new diocesan bishop, after he takes canonical possession, needs to reappoint the auxiliaries as his vicars general or episcopal vicars (§2; c. 406).

If the auxiliary is not designated as diocesan administrator, he is to exercise his powers (which he retains during the vacancy) under the authority of the diocesan administrator who governs the diocese until its new bishop takes possession of it.

Obligation of Residence

Canon 410 — Like the diocesan bishop, a coadjutor bishop and an auxiliary bishop are obliged to reside in the diocese. Except for a brief time, they are not to be absent from it other than to fulfill some duty outside the diocese or for vacation, which is not to exceed one month.

Like the diocesan bishop (c. 395), the coadjutor and auxiliary bishops have the duty of personal residence in the diocese.[213] Even though they are not heads of the particular church, they may be absent from it only for a brief time to fulfill some duty (e.g., episcopal conference committee work), and may enjoy a vacation not to exceed a month.

Canon 395, which concerns the absence of the diocesan bishop from the diocese for other work and vacation, specifies certain events (the *ad limina* visits, councils, the synod of bishops, or the episcopal conference) that legitimate such absence; it mentions certain days (Christmas, Holy Week, Easter, Pentecost, Corpus Christi) when the diocesan bishop is not to be absent from the diocese except for an urgent or grave reason. The canon also indicates that the metropolitan is to report an illegitimate absence beyond six months to the Apostolic See. Canon 410 does not contain similar provisions for a coadjutor or auxiliary, but simply says they are not to be outside the diocese except for a brief time for their annual vacation, which is not to exceed a month, or for fulfilling a duty outside the diocese.

Resignation from Office

Canon 411 — The prescripts of cann. 401 and 402, §2 on resignation from office apply to a coadjutor and auxiliary bishop.

The coadjutor and auxiliary bishops, like the diocesan bishop, are asked to submit their resignation at age seventy-five to the Supreme Pontiff

---

[210] *Comm* 14 (1982) 209.

[211] *CCEO* 222.

[212] This is an example of executive power delegated by the law.

[213] *CIC* 354; *CCEO* 217.

who will decide on accepting it after he has examined all the circumstances (see c. 401 §1).[214] They are earnestly asked to resign at an earlier age if they become less able to perform their office due to illness or some other grave cause (see c. 401, §2).[215]

The episcopal conference must take care that the retired coadjutor and auxiliary have suitable and decent support, the primary obligation for which binds the diocese which they served before retirement (see c. 402, §2).

This canon does not specify the title of these retired bishops,[216] nor is reference made to the bishops' residence in the diocese; both of these matters are considered in the code's treatment of retired diocesan bishops (c. 402, §1). It is reasonable to presume that appropriate adaptations are to be made in the norms on retired diocesan bishops.

CHAPTER III
THE IMPEDED SEE AND THE VACANT SEE
[cc. 412–430][217]

These canons make special provisions when the pastoral governance of a diocese is interrupted, either because the diocesan bishop is impeded (cc. 412–415) or because he no longer

holds his office as diocesan bishop and the see has become vacant (cc. 416–430).

ARTICLE 1: THE IMPEDED SEE
[cc. 412–415]

This article begins with a definition of the code's understanding of the *impeded see* (c. 412). It then provides norms for the interim governance of the diocese. This is to be exercised either by the coadjutor; or, if there is no coadjutor, by the priest identified on a secret list created by the diocesan bishop and preserved by the chancellor; or, if there is no list, by a priest selected by the college of consultors (c. 413). The rights and obligations of the interim diocesan leader, who has no specific title in the law, are outlined (c. 414). Finally, a canon explains that special provision is to be made by the Holy See if a diocesan bishop is subject to an ecclesiastical penalty which prevents his exercising his governance role (c. 415).[218]

Notion of Impeded See

Canon 412 — An episcopal see is understood to be impeded if by reason of captivity, banishment, exile, or incapacity a diocesan bishop is clearly prevented from fulfilling his pastoral function in the diocese, so that he is not able to communicate with those in his diocese even by letter.

A diocese is considered *impeded* when its bishop is clearly prevented from performing his pastoral role, such that he cannot communicate with the faithful of the diocese even by letter.[219]

---

[214] *CCEO* 218.

[215] *CD* 21 and *ES* I, 11 considered only the resignation of diocesan bishops. Canon 411 applies the conciliar doctrine also to the coadjutor and auxiliary. The coadjutor has the right of succession to become diocesan bishop, so the same age limits and other requirements for continued pastoral ministry of a diocesan bishop would logically apply also to him.

[216] *CCEO* 218 says that the retired coadjutor and auxiliary bishops are given the title *emeritus* of the office previously held.

[217] For the history of the development of these canons, see *Comm* 3 (1971) 188; 5 (1973) 233–235; 13 (1981) 140–146; 14 (1982) 220; 24 (1992) 32, 103–108, 130–137, 163–167, 204–205, 227–229. Other commentaries: *CLSGBI Com,* 234–241; *Pamplona ComEng,* 320– 328.

[218] *CIC* 429. The 1917 code devoted only this one canon to the impeded see. The same is true of the Eastern code: *CCEO* 233.

[219] The code does not speak precisely of an *impeded* parish, but c. 539 foresees that a parochial administrator (that is, a priest who substitutes for a pastor in accord with c. 540) may be appointed by the diocesan bishop for a number of reasons: (1) captivity, (2) exile, (3) banishment, (4) incapacity, (5) ill health, or (6) some other cause.

This situation can result from the four reasons identified in this canon: (1) captivity, (2) banishment, (3) exile, or (4) personal incapacity. The first three factors are extrinsic to the diocesan bishop, but the last concerns his human capacity itself.

The canon does not indicate who makes the determination that the diocese is, in fact, impeded. Dialogue with the metropolitan (or senior suffragan, if the metropolitan see is impeded) and the papal representative is prudent and appropriate to determine whether the diocese is, in fact, impeded.

If the bishop is able to communicate by letter with the diocese, the see is not considered impeded from a canonical point of view. He is able to govern the diocese, and can delegate others to govern in his absence, perhaps even with special mandates (see c. 134, §3).

The diocese ceases to be impeded when the circumstances creating the impeded situation cease (e.g., when a diocesan bishop is no longer in captivity, banishment, or exile; when he becomes able to communicate with the diocese at least by letter even under these circumstances; when his personal capacity to govern is restored, etc.). If there is doubt, recourse should be made to the Apostolic See which is to have been informed immediately about the impeded see (c. 413, §3).

Determination of Interim Diocesan Leader

Canon 413 — §1. When a see is impeded, the coadjutor bishop, if there is one, has governance of the diocese unless the Holy See has provided otherwise. If there is none or he is impeded, governance passes to an auxiliary bishop, the vicar general, an episcopal vicar, or another priest, following the order of persons established in the list which the diocesan bishop is to draw up as soon as possible after taking possession of the diocese. The list, which must be communicated to the metropolitan, is to be renewed at least every three years and preserved in secret by the chancellor.

§2. If there is no coadjutor bishop or he is impeded and the list mentioned in §1 is not available, it is for the college of consultors to select a priest to govern the diocese.

§3. The one who has assumed the governance of a diocese according to the norm of §§1 or 2 is to advise the Holy See as soon as possible of the impeded see and the function he has assumed.

When the diocese is impeded, the Holy See may make special arrangements for its governance. Otherwise, the governance rests with the coadjutor bishop, if there is one and if he has taken canonical possession of his office. If there is no coadjutor or if he too is impeded,[220] diocesan governance rests with the first available person identified on a list[221] of priests created for this purpose by the diocesan bishop soon after taking

[220] Mention must be made of the auxiliary bishop with special faculties (c. 403, §2) who, like a coadjutor bishop, is to assist the diocesan bishop in the entire governance of the diocese and is to take his place when he is absent or impeded (*impeditus*). Does this not indicate that when the diocese is impeded, if there is no coadjutor, the auxiliary with special faculties is to assume interim governance, and that recourse is to be made to the secret list of priests only if there is also no such auxiliary with special faculties? There is a certain parity between the coadjutor and the auxiliary with special faculties—e.g., cc. 405, §1 and 406, §1.

[221] *CIC* 429, the single canon treating the impeded see, did not make mention of this secret list composed by the diocesan bishop. It said the vicar general or another cleric assumed governance when the bishop was impeded, and that the bishop could delegate several to succeed each other in office; if these were not available, the cathedral chapter elected a vicar who took on governance with the power of a vicar capitular (diocesan administrator).

CCEO 233, §1 says that when the see is impeded its governance passes to the coadjutor or, if there is no coadjutor, to the protosyncellus (vicar general), syncellus (episcopal vicar), or another suitable priest designated by the eparchial bishop, who at a suitable time can designate several to succeed one another in office. No mention is made of a secret list as in the 1983 code. *CCEO* 233, §2 says that if no such priest is available, the college of eparchial consultors elects a priest to govern the eparchy.

canonical possession of the diocese and to be renewed (i.e., confirmed or changed) at least every three years. Those listed must be priests. The canon mentions as likely possibilities the auxiliary bishop, vicar general, or episcopal vicar, but these are only *possibilities:* the diocesan bishop is entirely free to name them or others. A number of priests may be named on this list, which is to be communicated to the metropolitan and preserved in secret by the chancellor of the diocesan bishop. If it concerns the metropolitan see, it would be reasonable for the metropolitan's secret list to be maintained by his chancellor and the senior suffragan bishop, even though the canon does not make this specific provision.[222]

If the diocese is impeded and there is neither a coadjutor nor the list of priests drawn up by the diocesan bishop, the college of consultors (see c. 502)[223] selects a priest to govern the diocese. This priest assumes governance immediately upon his acceptance of the selection made by the college.

The code does not provide any title for the bishop or presbyter who governs the diocese temporarily while it is impeded, whether he is the coadjutor, the priest named on the secret list by the diocesan bishop, or the priest chosen by the college of consultors. He is not properly called the *diocesan administrator,* since this is a technical term in law for "the one who is to govern the [vacant] diocese temporarily" (see c. 421, §1).

The code requires the person who governs the impeded see temporarily to inform the Holy See as soon as possible both that the see is impeded

and that he has assumed its temporary governance. The Holy See may decide to make other determinations after it has been informed of the status of the diocesan bishop.

The function of this interim diocesan leader ceases when the diocese is no longer impeded or when the Holy See makes other provision. Although the law does not specifically mention it, if the interim diocesan leader ceases his function while the see remains impeded (whether by his death, resignation, etc.), another interim diocesan leader must be determined in accord with canon 413, §§1–2, unless the Holy See then makes another provision.

Status of Interim Diocesan Leader

Canon 414 — Whoever has been called according to the norm of can. 413 to exercise the pastoral care of a diocese temporarily and only for the period in which the see is impeded is bound by the obligations and possesses the power in the exercise of the pastoral care of the diocese which a diocesan administrator has by law.

The temporary leader of the impeded see exercises pastoral care for the diocese only while it remains impeded. During this time he is bound by the obligations and possesses the powers given in law to a diocesan administrator, i.e., the priest who temporarily governs a vacant see (c. 421).[224] These obligations and rights are identified especially in canons 427–429.[225] His role ceases when the see is no longer impeded, or when the Apostolic See makes other provision.

---

[222] Such a presumption is in keeping with the role of the senior suffragan in relation to the metropolitan, identified for example in cc. 395, §4; 415; 421, §2; 425, §3. This is a good example of a *lacuna iuris* situation (c. 19).

[223] Canon 502, §2 says that when the see is impeded or vacant, the priest member oldest in ordination presides over the college until the one who temporarily replaces the diocesan bishop takes office. Canon 502, §3 says that the conference of bishops can establish that the functions of the college of consultors be entrusted to the cathedral chapter.

[224] Canon 525, 2° specifies that this interim diocesan leader may appoint pastors when the see has been impeded for one year. *CCEO* 233, §1 says that the priest who governs the impeded eparchy has the powers and rights of a protosyncellus (vicar general).

[225] See the commentary on c. 427, which identifies other rights and obligations of a diocesan administrator listed in the code. The diocesan administrator can perform some acts only with the consent of the college of consultors, and/or only after the see has been vacant for a year.

Penalized Diocesan Bishop

Canon 415 — If an ecclesiastical penalty prevents a diocesan bishop from exercising his function, the metropolitan or, if there is none or it concerns him, the suffragan senior in promotion, is to have recourse immediately to the Holy See so that it will make provision.

If a diocesan bishop is unable to function due to an ecclesiastical penalty, the see is not "impeded" in the senses identified in canon 412. Still, special provision must be made for the governance of the diocese while the penalty remains. In such a situation, the metropolitan is to have immediate recourse to the Holy See so that it will make provision for the pastoral governance of the diocese. If there is no metropolitan, or if it is the metropolitan himself who is bound by the ecclesiastical penalty, the suffragan bishop senior in promotion has the duty to inform the Holy See.[226]

Most penalties bind a guilty party only after they have been imposed; these are called *ferendae sententiae* penalties (c. 1314). Only the Roman Pontiff is competent to impose penalties on bishops (see c. 1405, §1, 3°). In such an instance, the Holy See would already know if a penalty is being imposed upon a diocesan bishop, and provision would have been made for diocesan governance without the intervention of the metropolitan. It is reasonable to conclude, therefore, that canon 415 concerns penalties which are incurred *ipso facto* when the delict is committed. These are called *latae sententiae* penalties (c. 1314), and the involvement of the metropolitan identified in this canon appears to be limited to such instances.[227]

---

[226] *CIC* 429, §5. There is no parallel canon in the Eastern code.

[227] Huels, 530–540. Two delicts which only bishops may commit are identified in c. 1382 (consecration of a bishop without a pontifical mandate, which may result in a *latae sententiae* excommunication reserved to the Apostolic See) and c. 1383 (ordination of a non-subject as a deacon or presbyter without legitimate dimissorial letters, which may result in a prohibition from conferring the order for one year).

When the function of the diocesan bishop is suspended, the power of his vicars general and episcopal vicars is also suspended unless they are bishops, given their close dependence on him for the exercise of their office (c. 481, §2; see also cc. 406, 409).

ARTICLE 2: THE VACANT SEE
[cc. 416–430]

This article provides norms for diocesan governance when the see is vacant. It begins with a definition of the code's understanding of the *vacant see* (c. 416). It explains that the diocesan bishop and his vicars retain their power until they are certain of the vacancy (c. 417), and provides norms to govern the diocese when the diocesan bishop is transferred to another see (c. 418). Special norms apply in an apostolic vicariate or prefecture (c. 420).

As soon as a diocese becomes vacant, its immediate governance devolves either upon the senior auxiliary bishop or, if there is none, upon the college of consultors (c. 419). This interim leader is to inform the Apostolic See of the death of the diocesan bishop (c. 422) and has the powers of a vicar general (c. 426). Thereafter, the college of consultors is to elect a diocesan administrator (c. 421) according to the norms of canons 165–178 (c. 424). Only one diocesan administrator is to be elected, and he cannot be the diocesan finance officer (c. 423). His qualifications are identified (c. 425) as are his obligations and powers (cc. 427, 429). The function of the diocesan administrator ceases when the new diocesan bishop takes possession of the diocese, or by the diocesan administrator's resignation, removal by the Holy See, or death (c. 430).

Nothing is to be modified during the vacancy, and nothing is to be done that is prejudicial to the see (c. 428).

Notion of Vacant See

Canon 416 — An episcopal see is vacant upon the death of a diocesan bishop, resignation accepted

by the Roman Pontiff, transfer, or privation made known to the bishop.

A diocese is considered *vacant* when it no longer has a diocesan bishop.[228] Such a vacancy can result from four causes: (1) the death of the diocesan bishop, (2) the resignation of the diocesan bishop which has been accepted by the Roman Pontiff, (3) the transfer of the diocesan bishop, or (4) the privation of office of the diocesan bishop which has been communicated to him.[229]

If the diocesan bishop wishes to resign, his resignation (by letter, or orally in the presence of two witnesses) must be made to the Roman Pontiff (see c. 189, §1). Canon 189, §3 indicates that a resignation which requires acceptance lacks force if it is not accepted within three months.

If the diocesan bishop is being transferred, his former diocese is considered vacant only from the day he takes canonical possession of the new diocese (c. 418, §1).

If the diocese has a coadjutor bishop who has taken canonical possession of his office (see c. 404, §1), he immediately becomes the diocesan bishop when the current one ceases to hold office (c. 409, §1). The diocese never actually becomes vacant.

Validity of Vicars' Acts

Canon 417 — Everything that a vicar general or episcopal vicar does has force until they have received certain notice of the death of the diocesan bishop. Likewise, everything that a diocesan bishop, a vicar general, or an episcopal vicar does has force until they have received certain notice of the above-mentioned pontifical acts.

When the diocesan bishop dies, the acts of his vicar general or episcopal vicar have force until they have certain notice of the death, even though the diocese is actually vacant from the moment of the bishop's death. When the see is vacant for one of the reasons other than death identified in canon 416, the acts of the diocesan bishop, his vicar general, or episcopal vicar have force until they have certain notice that the see has become vacant.[230] The obvious reason for the provisions of this canon is to provide efficacious pastoral care (valid acts of governance) for the faithful of the diocese, and to give a certain legal security to such vicars regarding the exercise of their office.

If the vicar general or episcopal vicar is an auxiliary bishop, however, when the see is vacant, the auxiliary retains the powers he had while the see was filled and until a new diocesan bishop takes possession of the see (c. 409, §2). This provision reflects earlier legal enactments on this point. *Christus Dominus* 26 stated that the powers and faculties of an auxiliary were not terminated when the diocesan bishop departed from his office.[231] *Ecclesiae sanctae* I, 13 (3) specified further that, unless other provisions were made by the competent authority in a particular case, an auxiliary retained the powers he had as vicar general or episcopal vicar before the see was vacant; he retained these powers during the vacancy even

---

[228] A parish is vacant when it no longer has a pastor (c. 539). Such a vacancy can result from: (1) removal or transfer of the pastor by the diocesan bishop done according to the norm of law (cc. 682, §2; 1740–1752); (2) resignation of the pastor accepted by the diocesan bishop; (3) lapse of time if the pastor was appointed for a definite period of time in accord with particular law (c. 522); (4) death of the pastor (c. 538, §1).

[229] *CIC* 430, §1; *CCEO* 219. *CB* contains directives on the occasion of the transferral or resignation of the diocesan bishop (n. 1156) and on the occasion of his death (nn. 1157–1165). It also says that "when the see becomes vacant, the diocesan administrator should ask the clergy and people to offer their prayers that the pastor chosen will be one who can meet the needs of the local Church" (n. 1166).

[230] *CIC* 430, §2; *CCEO* 224.

[231] *CD* 26 also urged that, unless there existed grave reasons to the contrary, the duty of governing the diocese *sede vacante* was to be entrusted to the auxiliary bishop or, if there were several, to one of them. This recommendation, however, never became law.

if he were not appointed the diocesan administrator and until the new diocesan bishop took canonical possession of his office.[232]

Vacancy Because of Transfer of Diocesan Bishop

Canon 418 — §1. Upon certain notice of transfer, a bishop must claim the diocese to which he has been transferred (*ad quam*) and take canonical possession of it within two months. On the day that he takes possession of the new diocese, however, the diocese from which he has been transferred (*a qua*) is vacant.

§2. Upon certain notice of transfer until the canonical possession of the new diocese, a transferred bishop in the diocese from which he has been transferred:

1° obtains the power of a diocesan administrator and is bound by the obligations of the same; all power of the vicar general and episcopal vicar ceases, without prejudice to can. 409, §2;

2° receives the entire remuneration proper to this office.

When a diocesan bishop is transferred to another see, he must take canonical possession of it within two months (§1; see also c. 382, §2). The former diocese is vacant on the day he takes canonical possession of the new one (see c. 191, §1).[233] If the diocese has a coadjutor bishop who has taken possession of his office, he assumes the role of diocesan bishop as soon as the current bishop takes canonical possession of his new diocese (c. 409, §1).

When the diocesan bishop receives certain notice that he is transferred, his present diocese is not technically vacant, but he loses the power of a diocesan bishop.[234] He immediately obtains instead the power of a diocesan administrator, and continues to receive his full remuneration from this diocese (see also c. 191, §2). The obligations and rights of a diocesan administrator are identified in canons 427–429. When he takes canonical possession of the new diocese, his rights and obligations in the former diocese cease (§2).

All the power of the vicars general and episcopal vicars ceases when the diocesan bishop receives certain notice of his transfer to another diocese, without prejudice to the prescript of canon 409, §2, which says that an auxiliary bishop in a vacant see retains the powers he had as vicar general or episcopal vicar until a new diocesan bishop takes canonical possession of the see. If the former vicars general and episcopal vicars are to continue a ministry similar to that which they had been performing as vicars, they will need delegated power to do so (see c. 131, §1).

Interim Government Before Administrator

Canon 419 — When a see is vacant and until the designation of a diocesan administrator, the governance of a diocese devolves upon the auxiliary bishop or, if there are several, upon the one who is senior in promotion. If there is no auxiliary bishop, however, it devolves upon the college of consultors unless the Holy See has provided otherwise. The one who so assumes governance of the diocese is to convoke without delay the college competent to designate a diocesan administrator.

This canon identifies who assumes the interim responsibility of diocesan governance immediately upon the vacancy of the see before the designation of a diocesan administrator.[235] When the dio-

---

[232] See also *ES* I, 14, (5), which repeats that an auxiliary bishop who is an episcopal vicar does not lose that power during the vacancy of the diocese.

[233] *CIC* 430, §3. The 1917 code had given the bishop four months to take possession. Two months are given in *CCEO* 223.

[234] *CIC* 194, §2; 430, §3, 1° and 3°.

[235] See *CIC* 427; 431, §1. The latter had said the governance of the vacant diocese devolved immediately upon the cathedral chapter (college of consultors) unless an apostolic administrator (*CIC* 312–318) had been appointed or the Holy See made other provisions. See *CCEO* 221, 2°.

cese becomes vacant but before a diocesan administrator is designated, the auxiliary bishop immediately assumes the interim governance; if there are several auxiliary bishops, the one senior in promotion governs. This norm, new to the 1983 code, further enhances the role of the auxiliary bishop.[236]

If there is no auxiliary bishop, the interim diocesan responsibility immediately devolves upon the college of consultors (see c. 502)[237] as a body, unless the Holy See has made some other provision.[238] The priest oldest in ordination presides over the college of consultors when the see is impeded or vacant, before the one who temporarily replaces the diocesan bishop assumes his office (c. 502, §2).

Whoever assumes interim diocesan governance has the power of a vicar general, not of a diocesan bishop (c. 426; see c. 134, §3). Such an interim leadership figure is to convoke without delay the college competent to designate the diocesan administrator, and is immediately also to inform the Apostolic See of the death of the diocesan bishop (c. 422).

Interim Government in Missions

Canon 420 — When the see is vacant in an apostolic vicariate or prefecture, the governance is assumed by the pro-vicar or pro-prefect, appointed only for this purpose by the vicar or prefect immediately after the vicar or prefect has taken possession of the vicariate or prefecture, unless the Holy See has established otherwise.

When the vacancy occurs in an apostolic vicariate or an apostolic prefecture (whose leader governs vicariously in the name of the Supreme Pontiff, c. 371, §1), the governance is immediately assumed by the pro-vicar or the pro-prefect.[239] This is a priest appointed for this purpose by the apostolic vicar or apostolic prefect immediately upon taking possession of the particular church, unless the Holy See has made some other provision.[240] The vicar or prefect must nominate the pro-vicar or pro-prefect immediately upon taking possession, just as, immediately upon taking possession of a diocese, the diocesan bishop must identify those who would govern the diocese if it becomes impeded (c. 413, §1).

Election of Diocesan Administrator

Canon 421 — §1. The college of consultors must elect a diocesan administrator, namely the one who is to govern the diocese temporarily, within eight days from receiving notice of the vacancy of an episcopal see and without prejudice to the prescript of can. 502, §3.

§2. If a diocesan administrator has not been elected legitimately within the prescribed time for whatever cause, his designation devolves upon the metropolitan, and if the metropolitan church itself is vacant or both the metropolitan and the suffragan churches are vacant, it devolves upon the suffragan bishop senior in promotion.

---

[236] Again, if the diocese has a coadjutor bishop, it never becomes vacant with the departure of the diocesan bishop; pastoral governance passes to the coadjutor who immediately becomes the new diocesan bishop provided he has taken canonical possession of his office.

[237] Canon 502, §3 says that the conference of bishops can determine that the functions of the college of consultors are to be entrusted to the cathedral chapter.

[238] The Holy See may, for example, appoint an *apostolic administrator* to govern the diocese until a new diocesan bishop takes his canonical possession of it.

[239] *CIC* 309, §§1–2. There is no parallel canon in the Eastern code.

[240] There is no presbyteral council (and consequently no college of consultors, c. 502) in the apostolic vicariate or apostolic prefecture. Instead, the vicar or prefect establishes a council of at least three missionary presbyters whose opinion, even by letter, he is to hear in more serious matters (c. 495, §2). These particular churches are not yet dioceses, and their leader governs in the name of the Supreme Pontiff with vicarious (not proper) power. Special provisions apply, among which is the determination of the person to govern during vacancy.

When the see is vacant, a diocesan administrator must be constituted.[241] The college of consultors must elect a diocesan administrator within eight days of receiving notice of the vacancy of the diocese (§1). The episcopal conference can determine that the functions of the college of consultors be entrusted to the cathedral chapter (c. 502, §3; see cc. 503–510).

The diocesan administrator is the priest who governs the diocese during its vacancy. In the 1917 code he was called the vicar capitular (*CIC* 432–444).

If the administrator has not been legitimately elected within the first eight days of the vacancy of the diocese, the metropolitan is to designate the diocesan administrator (§2). The college of consultors loses its right of election, and the metropolitan has no legal responsibility to consult the college when he designates the diocesan administrator.

The diocesan administrator may not be legitimately elected for a number of reasons: (1) because the eight available days have passed without the college of consultors taking any action (c. 421, §1); (2) because more than one diocesan administrator was elected (c. 423, §1); (3) because the election was invalid inasmuch as it was not conducted according to the norms of canons 165–178, which are required for validity (c. 424); or (4) because the one elected lacks the necessary qualifications for office (c. 425, §1).

If the metropolitan see is vacant, or if both the metropolitan see and the suffragan see are vacant, and the diocesan administrator has not been elected, the suffragan bishop senior in promotion is to designate the diocesan administrator (see also c. 425, §3).

Notification of Holy See

Canon 422 — An auxiliary bishop or, if there is none, the college of consultors is to inform the Apostolic See of the death of a bishop as soon as possible. The one elected as diocesan administrator is to do the same concerning his own election.

[241] *CIC* 427; 432 §§1–2; *CCEO* 221.

The one who assumes diocesan governance immediately upon the death of the diocesan bishop (i.e., the auxiliary bishop or the college of consultors, c. 419) is to inform the Apostolic See as soon as possible (*quantocius*) about the bishop's death. This notification, commonly done through the papal representative, is to take place before the election of the diocesan administrator.[242]

Once he has been elected, the diocesan administrator is to inform the Apostolic See about his own election. This is similar to the obligation of the one who governs the impeded see (c. 413, §3).

Only One Administrator/ Distinct from Finance Officer

Canon 423 — §1. One diocesan administrator is to be designated; any contrary custom is reprobated. Otherwise, the election is invalid.

§2. A diocesan administrator is not to be the finance officer at the same time. Therefore, if the finance officer of the diocese has been elected as administrator, the finance council is to elect a temporary finance officer.

A vacant see can have only one diocesan administrator; this assures unified diocesan governance. Otherwise, the election is invalid.[243] Any contrary custom is expressly reprobated by the law and, therefore, is unreasonable and cannot obtain the force of law (c. 24, §2).

One person cannot be diocesan administrator and finance officer at the same time. If the finance officer is elected diocesan administrator, the finance council is to elect a temporary finance officer who performs the tasks of the finance officer while he serves as diocesan administrator.[244]

[242] *CIC* 432, §4; *CCEO* 221.

[243] *CIC* 433, §1; *CCEO* 225, §1.

[244] Here is a rare instance of appointment to a diocesan office by a corporate body; the only other example of such an appointment is the "pastor consultors" chosen by the presbyteral council from a list presented to it by the diocesan bishop (c. 1742, §1). By contrast, the 1917 code had envisioned the election of both a *vicar capitular* (diocesan administrator) and an *oeconomus* by the

The separation of the roles of diocesan administrator and finance officer limits even the perception of any financial misconduct during the vacancy. When the vacancy ends, the original finance officer resumes his role, and the function of the temporary finance officer ceases.

Election of Diocesan Administrator

Canon 424 — A diocesan administrator is to be elected according to the norm of cann. 165–178.

The diocesan administrator, whether chosen by the college of consultors or by the cathedral chapter, is to be *elected* according to the norms of canons 165–178 on elections.[245] The particular statutes of the college of consultors may specify some of the options mentioned in those canons.[246] The one who assumes diocesan governance immediately upon the vacancy (c. 419) is competent to convoke the college of consultors.

Qualifications of Diocesan Administrator

Canon 425 — §1. Only a priest who has completed thirty-five years of age and has not already been elected, appointed, or presented for the same vacant see can be designated validly to the function of diocesan administrator.

§2. A priest who is outstanding in doctrine and prudence is to be elected as diocesan administrator.

§3. If the conditions previously mentioned in §1 have been neglected, the metropolitan or, if the metropolitan church itself is vacant, the suffragan bishop senior in promotion, after he has ascertained the truth of the matter, is to designate an administrator in his place. The acts of the one who was elected contrary to the prescripts of §1, however, are null by the law itself.

This canon considers the qualifications to be found in the priest elected as diocesan administrator.[247] Paragraph one legislates that, for the validity of his appointment, the diocesan administrator must be a priest (*sacerdos:* i.e., a bishop or a presbyter) who has completed thirty-five years of age. He cannot have been already elected, appointed, or presented for the same vacant see.[248]

The second paragraph says that, for liceity, the one elected must be outstanding in doctrine and prudence.

The third paragraph provides for the case in which no diocesan administrator has been validly elected. If the conditions of the first paragraph have been neglected, the metropolitan is to ascertain the truth of the matter and then to designate a diocesan administrator in virtue of his pastoral oversight role in the province. The college of consultors is no longer competent to elect him; it has lost that right. If the metropolitan see is vacant, this task is performed by the suffragan bishop senior in appointment.

Since there is no valid designation of a diocesan administrator, all acts performed by the one invalidly elected are invalid.[249] Likewise, the acts

---

cathedral chapter; these two roles could be fulfilled by the same person (*CIC* 433, §3). The *oeconomus* (or several of them) was to be a trustworthy and competent person appointed if the chapter had the function of collecting revenues (*CIC* 432–433). In the United States the diocesan consultors did not have the responsibility of collecting revenues or maintaining the *mensa episcopalis,* so the appointment of an *oeconomus* would have been superfluous. See *CCEO* 225, §2.

[245] *CIC* 432, §2; 433, §2; *CCEO* 221.

[246] See cc. 167, §1 (permitting votes by letter or proxy); 174, §1 (forbidding an election by compromise); and 176 (identifying the majority of votes necessary to be elected as different from the norm of c. 119, 1°).

[247] *CIC* 434. *CIC* 434, §1 had said that the vicar capitular could be thirty years old. The higher age here parallels a similar provision for bishops in c. 378, §1, 3°. (Note the other parallels in qualifications for a candidate for episcopacy—e.g., c. 378, §1, 3° and 5°.) See *CCEO* 227.

[248] These specific issues pertain only in places where the cathedral chapter elects the bishop or where civil authorities propose a candidate for the episcopacy (see c. 377, §§1, 5).

[249] Canon 421, §2 requires the intervention of the metropolitan (or, for the metropolitan see, the suffragan

of those appointed to office by him or delegated by him are also invalid, since he has no power to appoint or delegate.

Status of One Governing a Diocese Before Administrator

Canon 426 — When a see is vacant, the person who is to govern the diocese before the designation of a diocesan administrator possesses the power which the law grants to a vicar general.

In the very brief period when the see is vacant and before the diocesan administrator is elected, the one who assumes the immediate governance of the diocese (i.e., the auxiliary bishop or the college of consultors, c. 419) has the power given by law to a vicar general.[250]

Canon 479, §1 says that by office the vicar general has the executive power over the entire diocese which the law gives to the diocesan bishop —that is, the power to place all administrative acts except those which the bishop has reserved to himself or which the law says require a special mandate from the bishop (c. 134, §3).[251] He is a local ordinary (c. 134, §2).

Obligations and Powers of Diocesan Administrator

Canon 427 — §1. A diocesan administrator is bound by the obligations and possesses the power of a diocesan bishop, excluding those matters which are excepted by their nature or by the law itself.

§2. When he has accepted election, the diocesan administrator obtains power and no other confirmation is required, without prejudice to the obligation mentioned in can. 833, n. 4.

The first paragraph of this canon says that the diocesan administrator has the obligations and powers of a diocesan bishop—except for those which are excluded (1) by the nature of the matter or (2) by the law itself.[252]

Several acts are excluded from the powers of a diocesan administrator by the law itself: A diocesan administrator can *never* perform the following acts:

- to approve diocesan associations of the faithful (c. 312, §1, 3°)
- to confer a canonry in places where canons exist in cathedral or collegial churches (c. 509, §1)[253]
- to entrust a parish to a clerical religious institute or clerical society of apostolic life (c. 520, §1)
- to remove the judicial vicar and adjutant judicial vicars (c. 1420, §5).

A diocesan administrator can perform the following acts *only with the consent of the college of consultors:*

- to remove the chancellor and other notaries (c. 485)
- to issue dimissorial letters for ordination, but never to those who have been denied orders by the diocesan bishop (c. 1018).

A diocesan administrator can grant excardination, incardination, or even permission to move to another particular church, *only after the see is vacant for one year* and with the *consent of the college of consultors* (c. 272). Finally, a diocesan administrator can name pastors *only after the see has been vacant for one year* (c. 525, 2°).

---

senior by appointment) when the college of consultors has failed to elect a diocesan administrator within eight days of being notified of the vacancy of the episcopal see.

[250] *CIC* 435. Actually, no vicar general exists in a vacant diocese (see cc. 417; 481, §1). See *CCEO* 221, 2°. Some may suggest that this canon would be placed more appropriately after canon 419, which also governs the situation before the designation of the administrator.

[251] See also cc. 475–481.

[252] *CIC* 435, §§1–2; *CCEO* 229.

[253] Canons do not exist in the United States.

The second paragraph says that when the diocesan administrator has been elected, he assumes the power of his office and he needs no other confirmation (see c. 178). Nonetheless, he must make the profession of faith in the presence of the college of consultors according to the formula approved by the Apostolic See (c. 833, 4°).[254]

No Innovations During Vacancy

Canon 428 — §1. When a see is vacant, nothing is to be altered.

§2. Those who temporarily care for the governance of the diocese are forbidden to do anything which can be prejudicial in some way to the diocese or episcopal rights. They, and consequently all others, are specifically prohibited, whether personally or through another, from removing or destroying any documents of the diocesan curia or from changing anything in them.

The first paragraph expresses succinctly the general norm that when the diocese is vacant, nothing is to be innovated.[255] The provisional nature of the diocesan administrator's function is eminently clear here. Care must be taken to maintain the status quo of the diocese until the new diocesan bishop takes canonical possession of it. Nonetheless, the life of the particular church continues and certain determinations must be made. The commentary on canon 427 above identifies certain actions which the diocesan administrator may never take, may take only with the consent of the college of consultors, or may take after the see has been vacant for a full year (perhaps with the consent of the consultors). Nonetheless, the general principle enunciated in paragraph one of canon 428 maintains its significance.

The second paragraph highlights certain actions always forbidden during the vacancy, and

thereby further specifies the more general norm of the first paragraph.[256] All who govern the diocese temporarily (this includes the one who assumes diocesan governance immediately upon the vacancy [c. 419] and the diocesan administrator [c. 421, §1]) are specifically forbidden to do anything which could be prejudicial to the diocese or episcopal rights. These diocesan leaders, and all other persons as well, are forbidden to remove, destroy, or modify any documents of the diocesan curia, whether personally or through another. Access to the secret archive or safe of the diocese is forbidden except in case of true necessity, in which case only the diocesan administrator personally is permitted to open it (c. 490, §2). Those who violate this canon may be punished with a just penalty, according to the gravity of the delict (see c. 1391, 1°).

Residence/Mass for the People

Canon 429 — A diocesan administrator is obliged to reside in the diocese and to apply Mass for the people according to the norm of can. 388.

Canon 427, §1 says the diocesan administrator has the obligations of a diocesan bishop unless such are excepted by their nature or by the law. This canon specifies two certain obligations of the diocesan administrator: he is to reside in the diocese and to apply the *Missa pro populo*. These are obligations of a diocesan bishop identified in cc. 395, §1 and 388, respectively.[257]

Cessation of Ministry of Diocesan Administrator

Canon 430 — §1. The function of a diocesan administrator ceases when the new bishop has taken possession of the diocese.

§2. The removal of a diocesan administrator is reserved to the Holy See. If an administrator resigns, the resignation must be presented in au-

---

[254] *CIC* 438.

[255] *CIC* 436; *CCEO* 228, §1. Similar norms proscribe innovations during the vacancy of the Roman See (c. 335) and of a parish (c. 540, §2).

[256] *CIC* 435, §3; *CCEO* 228, §2.

[257] *CIC* 440. There is no parallel canon in the Eastern code.

thentic form to the college competent to elect, but it does not need acceptance. If a diocesan administrator has been removed, resigns, or dies, another diocesan administrator is to be elected according to the norm of can. 421.

The function of the diocesan administrator ceases in the four ways identified in this canon: (1) the new diocesan bishop's taking canonical possession of the diocese, (2) the diocesan administrator's removal by the Holy See, (3) his resignation, or (4) his death.[258]

The function of the diocesan administrator ceases when the new bishop takes possession of the diocese in accord with the prescript of c. 382, §3. The administrator retains his power as administrator after the new diocesan bishop has been identified and until the latter takes canonical possession of the diocese, since the new bishop is not permitted to exercise governance in the diocese before he has taken canonical possession of it (c. 382, §1). Even if the diocesan administrator is appointed the diocesan bishop, he retains only the powers of a diocesan administrator until he takes canonical possession of the diocese (c. 382).[259]

The function of the diocesan administrator may also cease before the new diocesan bishop takes canonical possession of the diocese for two reasons other than the administrator's own death: his removal by the Holy See, or his resignation. Only the Holy See is competent to remove a validly elected diocesan administrator (see c. 192); the college of consultors that elected him cannot remove him.[260]

If the diocesan administrator wishes to resign, he must present his resignation in authentic form to the college of consultors. The resignation is valid even without acceptance by the group competent to elect (see c. 189, §3) but must be communicated according to the proper legal form (that is, either in writing, or orally in the presence of two witnesses, c. 189, §1).

If the diocesan administrator is removed, resigns, or dies, a new diocesan administrator is to be elected in the usual way by the college of consultors (§2; c. 421).

---

[258] *CIC* 443; *CCEO* 231.

[259] *CIC* 444 had required the new bishop to seek a report on their offices, jurisdiction, and administration during the vacancy from the cathedral chapter, vicar capitular, *oeconomus,* and other officials. This requirement is omitted from the revised code, though some may still wisely do what *CIC* 444 had required. Canon 540, §3, however, expects the parochial administrator to render an account to the pastor after the administrator has completed his function.

 CCEO 232 says that when the eparchial see is vacant the eparchial finance officer administers ecclesiastical goods under the authority of the eparchial administrator; the eparchial finance officer must give an account of his administration to the new eparchial bishop and, thereafter, ceases to hold office unless confirmed in it by the new bishop.

[260] Of course, the norm of c. 194 on the removal from an ecclesiastical office by the law itself also pertains to the diocesan administrator.

APPENDIX I – REVISION OF THE 1917 CODE

Dates of Meetings	*Comm*	Pages
December 4–7, 1967	18 (1986)	54–74; 94–97; 99–102
March 4–7, 1968	18 (1986)	111–170
December 16–21, 1968	19 (1987)	106–123, 131–145
April 14–19, 1969	24 (1992)	32–41
February 2–9, 1970	24 (1992)	56–57
October 5–10, 1970	24 (1992)	103–115
February 15–20, 1971	24 (1992)	103–137; 163–167
December 13–18, 1971	24 (1992)	204–205; 227–228
May 15–20, 1971	3 (1971)	186–189
	4 (1972)	39–43
November 20–23, 1972	5 (1973)	216–224; 233–235
April 9–14, 1973	24 (1992)	309–310; 315–320; 340–350
February 18–22, 1974	7 (1975)	161–163
December 2–6, 1974	7 (1975)	163–172
March 10–15, 1980	12 (1980)	275–314
April 18, 1980	13 (1981)	140–146
May 13, 1980	13 (1981)	298–302
July 16, 1981 – *Relatio*	14 (1982)	201–220

The code identifies the *diocesan bishop* as the agent responsible in the following matters; other *local ordinaries* cannot perform these actions or exercise these powers without a special mandate and perhaps not even then if the episcopacy is required. Some are rights, others are obligations.[261]

- to extend an expired rescript granted by the Apostolic See once, but not beyond three months (c. 72)
- to dispense from certain disciplinary laws (c. 87, §1)[262]
- to designate a guardian for a minor (c. 98, §2)
- to confer ecclesiastical offices in the particular church entrusted to them (c. 157)
  - curial officials (c. 470)
  - moderator of the curia (c. 473, §§2–3)
  - vicar general (c. 475)
  - episcopal vicars (c. 476)
  - chancellor, vice-chancellors, and notaries (cc. 482–483 – implicit)
  - diocesan finance officer (c. 494, §1)
  - priest with faculties equivalent to a canon penitentiary (c. 508, §2)
  - canons (c. 509)
  - priest members of a "team ministry" and their moderator (cc. 517, §1 – implicit; 544)
  - deacons, lay persons, and communities of persons who are not priests, to whom is entrusted a participation in the exercise of pastoral care of a parish (c. 517, §2)
  - pastor (cc. 523–524)
  - parochial administrator (c. 539)

[261] This list identifies some of the principal matters for which the *diocesan bishop* is the responsible agent. See also NCCB, *A Manual for Bishops: Rights and Responsibilities of Diocesan Bishops in the Revised Code of Canon Law,* rev. ed. (Washington, D.C.: NCCB, 1992).

[262] A response from the PCILT promulgated August 1, 1985 decreed that the diocesan bishop may not dispense from canonical form for the marriage of two Catholics: *AAS* 77 (1985) 771. Wrenn, 21–22. A response from the same council promulgated September 3, 1987 also explains that the diocesan bishop cannot dispense from the prescription of c. 767, §1 by which a homily is reserved to priests and deacons: *AAS* 79 (1987) 1249. Wrenn, 41–43.

- parochial vicars (c. 547)
- vicars forane (c. 553, §2)
- rectors of churches (c. 557)
- judicial vicar (c. 1420, §1)
- adjutant judicial vicars (c. 1420, §3 – implicit)
- diocesan judges (c. 1421, §1)
- tribunal auditors (c. 1428)
- promoter of justice (c. 1435)
- defender of the bond (c. 1435)
- to determine whether seminarians are to be formed outside a seminary, and to entrust them to a devout and suitable priest (c. 235, §2)
- to admit candidates to the major seminary (c. 241, §1)
- to make decisions about seminary governance and administration (c. 259, §1)
- to visit the seminary and oversee formation (c. 259, §2)
- to impose a seminary tax (c. 264, §1)
- to issue letters of incardination and excardination (c. 267, §1)
- to oppose in writing *ipso iure* incardination/excardination (c. 268, §1)
- to decide about incardination (c. 269)
- to grant clerics permission to move to another particular church, and to recall them (c. 271)
- to establish diocesan public associations (c. 312, §1, 3°)
- to convoke, preside over, choose members of (when the law makes no specific determinations), suspend, and dissolve the diocesan synod (cc. 462–463; 468, §1)
- to determine promises of faithful discharge of office to be made by curial officials, and to define terms of their secrecy (c. 471)
- to establish an episcopal council (c. 473, §4)
- to remove from ecclesiastical offices
  - vicars general and episcopal vicars (c. 477, §1)
  - chancellors (vice-chancellors), and notaries (c. 485)
  - diocesan finance officer (c. 494, §2 – implicit)
  - pastors (c. 538, §1; 1740–1747)

(continued)

- parochial vicar (c. 552)
- vicar forane (c. 554, §3)
- judges (c. 1422 – implicit)
- promoter of justice (c. 1436, §2)
- defender of the bond (c. 1436, §2)
- to preside over the diocesan finance council (c. 492, §1)
- to establish a diocesan budget and oversee diocesan expenditures (c. 494, §3)
- to approve presbyteral council statutes (c. 496)
- to name freely some presbyteral council members (c. 497, 3°)
- to convoke, preside over, set the agenda for, and dissolve the presbyteral council (cc. 500–501)
- to choose members of and preside over the college of consultors (c. 502, §§1–2)
- to approve cathedral/collegial chapter statutes (c. 505)
- to separate parishes from chapters of canons (c. 510, §1)
- to establish norms for a pastor and a chapter of the same church (c. 510, §3)
- to establish, convoke, preside over, choose members of, and make public the work of the diocesan pastoral council (cc. 511–514)
- to erect, suppress, or alter parishes (c. 515, §2) or quasi-parishes (c. 516 §1 – implicit)
- to provide pastoral care where a (quasi-)parish cannot be erected (c. 516, §2)
- to determine conditions for entrusting a participation in the exercise of pastoral care in a parish to a deacon, to a lay person, or to a community of persons who are not priests (c. 517, §2)
- to entrust a parish to a clerical religious institute or society of apostolic life (c. 520, §1)
- to require establishment of parish pastoral councils (c. 536, §1)
- to accept the resignation of a pastor, and to provide for his retirement (c. 538, §3)
- to determine rights and duties of parochial vicars (c. 548, §1)
- to erect diocesan institutes of consecrated life (c. 579) which remain under his special care (c. 594)

- to approve and modify constitutions of diocesan institutes of consecrated life, to grant dispensations from the constitutions, and to oversee the more significant business matters of these institutes (c. 595)
- to receive the vows or bonds of hermits, and to guide their lives (c. 603, §2)
- to consecrate virgins (c. 604, §1)
- to discern new gifts of consecrated life in the Church and to aid their promoters (c. 605)
- to give written consent to erect houses of religious institutes (c. 609, §1)
- to consent for a religious house to perform apostolic works different from those for which it was founded (c. 612)
- to give special vigilance to an autonomous monastery (c. 615); to preside at elections of its superiors (c. 625, §2); to visit it even with respect to religious discipline (c. 628, §2, 1°); to grant dismissal of members (c. 699, §2)
- to visit even with respect to internal discipline individual houses of diocesan religious institutes (c. 628, §2, 2°)
- to enter cloisters of monasteries of nuns, to allow others to enter, and to permit the nuns to leave if truly necessary (c. 667, §4)
- to consult mutually with religious superiors in organizing apostolic works (c. 678, §3)
- to prohibit a religious from living in his diocese (c. 679)
- to entrust works to religious, to direct them, and to enter into written agreements about them (c. 681)
- to confer ecclesiastical offices on religious, and remove them (c. 682)
- to visit the churches, oratories, schools, and works of religious, and to address any abuses discovered (c. 683)
- to extend an indult of exclaustration beyond three years for religious of diocesan institutes, or to impose exclaustration upon the same (c. 686, §§1, 3)
- to confirm an indult of departure of temporarily professed religious belonging to diocesan institutes and autonomous monasteries (c. 688, §2)

- to grant an indult of departure of perpetually professed religious belonging to diocesan institutes (c. 691, §2) and of perpetually incorporated members of diocesan secular institutes (c. 727, §1)
- to receive a religious cleric for incardination, at least experimentally, and to refuse incardination of the same (c. 693)
- to confirm the decree of dismissal of religious of institutes of diocesan right (c. 700)
- to give prior written permission to erect a house and to establish a local community of a society of apostolic life, and to be consulted for its suppression (c. 733, §1)
- to call members of institutes of consecrated life to assist in proclaiming the gospel (c. 758)
- to prohibit a bishop from preaching in the diocese (c. 763)
- to issue norms on preaching (c. 772, §1)
- to issue norms on catechesis, to make catechetical instruments available, and to coordinate catechetical endeavors (c. 775, §1; see c. 777)
- to oversee missionary activity in missionary dioceses, and to enter into contracts with missionary institutes (c. 790, §1)
- to consent to religious establishing schools (c. 801)
- to regulate and oversee Catholic religious education in schools and the media (c. 804, §1)
- to exercise vigilance over and to visit Catholic schools (c. 806, §1)
- to exercise vigilance over Catholic universities (c. 810, §2)
- to provide pastoral care for students at Catholic universities, other institutes of higher education, and ecclesiastical universities and faculties by erecting a parish or providing priests, and to provide Catholic centers at universities, even non-Catholic ones (cc. 813, 818)
- to send outstanding young people and clerics to ecclesiastical universities and faculties (c. 819)
- to establish higher institutes of religious sciences, whenever possible (c. 821)

- to guard against harmful publications/media, to require writings on faith and morals be submitted to his judgment, and to repudiate works contrary to faith and morals (c. 823)
- to determine when "in grave necessity" the sacraments of penance, Eucharist, and anointing may be administered to non-Catholic Christians (c. 844, §4), after appropriate consultation with the competent non-Catholic authority (c. 844, §5)
- to permit baptism in hospitals, outside cases of necessity (c. 860, §2)
- to baptize persons fourteen years of age and older (c. 863)
- to delegate the faculty to confirm to one or more specific presbyters (c. 884, §1)
- to associate priests with him in confirming on an ad hoc basis (c. 884, §2)
- to make a judgment about eucharistic processions through public streets, and to issue norms about them (c. 944)
- to determine whether the conditions for general absolution exist (c. 961, §2)
- to forbid a bishop to hear confessions (c. 967, §1)
- to issue norms on the communal anointing of the sick (c. 1002)
- to ordain his own subjects, or to grant dimissorials to another bishop (cc. 1015, §1; 1018, §1, 1°; 1020–1021)
- to give permission in his diocese for a bishop to confer orders (c. 1017)
- to place restrictions in dimissorial letters, or to revoke them (c. 1023)
- to judge the suitability and usefulness of candidates for orders (cc. 1025, §§1–2; 1029; 1052, §1)
- to see that candidates are instructed about the order to be received (c. 1028)
- to forbid, for a canonical reason, the advance of a transitional deacon to the presbyterate (c. 1030)
- to determine the length of the pastoral internship of a transitional deacon (c. 1032, §2)
- to admit one to candidacy for orders (c. 1034, §1)

(continued)

- to receive signed hand-written declarations of freedom and intention from candidates for diaconate and presbyterate (c. 1036)
- to determine if a serious cause prevents a transitional deacon, refusing advance to presbyterate, from exercising the diaconate (c. 1038)
- to make certain candidates have made the preordination retreat of at least five days (c. 1039)
- to issue an authentic certificate of ordination (c. 1053, §2)
- to delegate qualified lay persons to assist at marriages after favorable vote of the conference of bishops and approval of the Holy See (c. 1112, §1)
- to issue norms on the marriage register (c. 1121, §1)
- to grant radical sanations of individual marriages unless an impediment of divine or natural law has ceased or dispensation is reserved to the Apostolic See (c. 1165, §2)
- to dedicate a sacred place, and to commission another bishop or presbyter to do so (c. 1206)
- to bless churches, or to delegate another priest to do so (c. 1207)
- to give written consent to erect a church, even for religious (c. 1215)
- to relegate a church to profane but not sordid use (c. 1222)
- to determine special feast and penitential days (c. 1244, §2)
- to issue prescriptions on pastors' dispensing or commuting days of obligation or penance (c. 1245)
- to impose taxes in accord with the norm of law (c. 1263)[263]
- to involve the diocesan finance council in significant economic activity, and even to obtain their consent for acts of "extraordinary administration" (c. 1277)
- to assign special functions to the diocesan finance officer (c. 1278)
- to determine acts exceeding ordinary administration (c. 1281, §2)
- to alienate ecclesiastical goods of the diocese according to the norms of law, which often requires the consent of the finance council, the college of consultors, and the concerned parties (c. 1292, §1)
- to reduce Mass obligations in cases defined by law (c. 1308, §§3–4)
- to transfer Mass obligations (c. 1309)
- to see that penal laws are uniform in the same city or region (c. 1316)
- to remit a non-declared *latae sententiae* penalty in confession (c. 1355, §2)
- to make determinations in certain procedural matters
  - to entrust more difficult or more significant cases to three or five judges (c. 1425, §2)
  - to involve the promoter of justice in contentious cases (c. 1431, §1)
  - to permit extern judges to acquire judicial proofs (c. 1469, §2)
  - to execute sentences issued in first instance in the diocese (c. 1653, §1)
  - to decree separation of spouses or to permit them to approach civil court (c. 1692, §§1–2)
  - to receive a petition for dissolution of a non-consummated marriage (c. 1699, §1), to permit either party to have a legal expert (c. 1701, §2), to prepare his own opinion (c. 1704, §1), to send the acts to the Apostolic See (c. 1705, §1), and to receive the rescript of dispensation from the Apostolic See (c. 1706)
  - to make a declaration of presumed death (c. 1707)
  - to establish an office or council of mediation (c. 1733, §2)

[263] The PCILT issued a decree promulgated August 10, 1989 indicating that the diocesan bishop cannot tax the external schools of religious institutes of pontifical right: *AAS* 81 (1989) 991. Wrenn, 57–58.

BIBLIOGRAPHY

Primary Sources

Bishops' Committee on the Permanent Diaconate. *Foundations for the Renewal of the Diaconate.* Washington, D.C.: NCCB/USCC, 1993.

CDF. "Instruction on the Ecclesial Vocation of the Theologian." *Origins* 20 (July 5, 1990) 117, 119–126.

CDWDS. *Caeremoniale Episcoporum,* September 14, 1984. Vatican City: Libreria Editrice Vaticana, 1984. ICEL translation: *Ceremonial of Bishops.* Collegeville: Liturgical Press, 1989.

CFB. *Directory for the Ad Limina Visit.* Vatican City: Libreria Editrice Vaticana, 1988.

———. *Form for the Quinquennial Report.* Vatican City: Libreria Editrice Vaticana, 1997.

———. "Normae de episcopis ab officio cessante," October 31, 1988. *Comm* 20 (1988) 167–168. Unofficial translation *CLSG-BIN* 79 (September 1989) 17–19.

CFC. *Directory for the Life and Ministry of Priests,* January 31, 1994. Vatican City: Libreria Editrice Vaticana, 1994.

John Paul II. Apconst *Pastor bonus,* June 28, 1988. *AAS* 80 (1988) 841–924, 1867. Unofficial translation: *Code of Canon Law, Annotated,* ed. E. Caparros, et al. Montreal: Wilson and Lafleur, 1993. Pp. 1167–1279 (alternating).

———. Apexhort *Pastores dabo vobis,* March 25, 1992. *Origins* 21 (April 16, 1992) 717, 719–759.

———. Apconst *Spirituali militum curae,* April 21, 1986. *AAS* 78 (1986) 481–486. Unofficial translation: *TPS* 31 (1986) 284–288.

NCCB. "Doctrinal Responsibilities: Approaches to Promoting Cooperation and Resolving Misunderstandings between Bishops and Theologians." *Origins* 19 (June 29, 1989) 97, 99–110.

———. *A Manual for Bishops: Rights and Responsibilities of Diocesan Bishops in the Revised Code of Canon Law.* Rev. ed. Washington, D.C.: NCCB, 1992.

———. *Permanent Deacons.* 3rd ed. Washington, D.C.: USCC, 1995.

———. *The Teaching Ministry of the Diocesan Bishop: A Pastoral Reflection.* Washington, D.C.: NCCB, 1992.

PCPCU. *Directory for the Application of Principles and Norms on Ecumenism,* March 25, 1993. *Origins* 23 (July 29, 1993) 129, 131–160.

Secretariat of State. "Regolamento Generale della Curia Romana," February 4, 1992. *AAS* 84 (1992) 201–267.

Secondary Sources

Austin, R. "The Particular Church and the Universal Church in the 1983 *Code of Canon Law.*" *Stud Can* 22 (1988) 339–357.

BCL. *Ceremonial of Bishops: A Reader.* Washington, D.C.: USCC, 1994.

Beal, J. "The Apostolic Visitation of a Diocese: A Canonico-Historical Investigation." *J* 49 (1989) 347–398.

Caparros, E., M. Theriault, and J. Thorn, eds. *Code of Canon Law Annotated.* Montreal: Wilson and LeFleur, 1993.

Cappellini, E. "La tutela dei diritti delle communità territoriali: diocesi e parrocchia." *ME* 113 (1988) 85–104.

Cárcel Ortí, V. "Legislazione e magistero di Giovanni Paolo II sulla visita 'ad limina apostolorum.'" *ME* 118 (1993) 451–500.

CLSA Committee for Research and Education on Rights and Pastoral Responsibilities of Bishops. "Report of a CLSA Survey on Auxiliary Bishops." *J* 53 (1993) 354–361.

CLSA Committee for the Study of Apostolic Visitation and the Limitation of Powers of a Diocesan Bishop. "Apostolic Visitation, Accountability, and the Rights of the Local Church." *J* 49 (1989) 341–346.

Faris, J. D. *The Eastern Catholic Churches: Constitution and Governance.* New York: St. Maron Publications, 1992.

Foster, M. "The Role of Auxiliary Bishops." *J* 51 (1991) 423–430.

Ghirlanda, G. "Adnotatio ad responsum authenticum circa can. 346, §1." *P* 81 (1992) 347–350.

———. "La chiesa particolare: Natura e tipologia." *ME* 115 (1990) 551–568.

Granfield, P. "The Church Local and Universal: Realization of Communion." *J* 49 (1989) 449–471.

Green, T. "The Church's Sanctifying Mission: Some Aspects of the Normative Role of the Diocesan Bishop." *Stud Can* 35 (1991) 245–276.

———. "The Church's Sanctifying Mission: Some Aspects of the Role of Episcopal Conferences." In *Ius Sequitur Vitam: Law Follows Life, Studies in Canon Law Presented to P. J. M. Huizing,* 57–88. Louvain: University Press, 1991.

———. "Deliberative Vote for Retired Bishops in Teaching Matters." *J* 54 (1994) 1–21.

———. "The Diocesan Bishop in the Revised Code: Some Introductory Reflections." *J* 42 (1982) 320–347.

———. "The Pastoral Governance Role of the Diocesan Bishop: Foundations, Scope and Limitations." *J* 49 (1989) 472–506.

———. "Persons and Structures in the Church: Reflections on Selected Issues in Book II." *J* 45 (1985) 24–94.

———. "Rights and Duties of Diocesan Bishops." *CLSAP* (1983) 18–36.

———. "Shepherding the Patrimony of the Poor: Diocesan and Parish Structures of Financial Administration." *J* 56 (1997) 706–734.

Griffin, B. "The Challenge of Ecumenism for Canonists." *CLSAP* (1993) 17–38.

Herranz, J. "The Personal Power of Governance of the Diocesan Bishop." *CLSAP* (1987) 16–34; reprinted in *Comm* 20 (1988) 288–310.

Huels, J. M. "The Correction and Punishment of a Diocesan Bishop." *J* 49 (1989) 507–542.

Legrand, H. "Reflections on Conferences and Diocesan Bishops." *J* 48 (1988) 130–133.

Longhitano, A., et al. *Chiesa particolare e strutture di communione.* Bologna: Dehoniane, 1985.

Mallett, J., ed. *The Ministry of Governance.* Washington, D.C.: CLSA, 1986.

McHugh, J. "What Is the 'New Situation'?" *Origins* 26 (August 29, 1996) 175–176.

Metz, R. "La désignation des évêques dans le droit actuel: Étude comparative entre le Code latin de 1983 et le Code oriental de 1990." *Stud Can* 27 (1993) 321–334.

———. "Papal Legates and the Appointment of Bishops." *J* 52 (1992) 259–284.

Montini, G. P. "Ecclesia universalis an ecclesia universa?" *P* 74 (1985) 43–62.

Müller, H. "De speciali episcopi mandato iuxta CIC/1983." *P* 79 (1990) 219–241.

———. "How the Local Church Lives and Affirms Its Catholicity." *J* 52 (1992) 340–364.

———. "The Relationship Between the Episcopal Conference and the Diocesan Bishop." *J* 48 (1988) 111–129.

O'Connor, J. "Reflections on Church Governance." *Origins* 26 (August 29, 1996) 171–175.

PCILT, ed. *Ius in Vita et in Missione Ecclesiae.* Vatican City: Libreria Editrice Vaticana, 1994.

Pospishil, V. J. *Eastern Catholic Church Law.* 2nd rev. ed. Staten Island: Saint Maron Publications, 1996.

Provost, J. "Appointment of a Diocesan Administrator or a Coadjutor." *CLSA Advisory Opinions 1984–1993,* ed. P. Cogan, 90–91. Washington, D.C.: CLSA, 1995.

Quinn, J. "Considering the Papacy." *Origins* 26 (July 18, 1996) 119–128.

Read, G. "Norms on Bishops Leaving Office." *CLS-GBIN* 79 (September 1989) 20–22.

———. "Retired Bishops as Members of the Synod of Bishops: A Comment on the Interpretation of Can. 346, §1 dated 2nd July 1991." *CLS-GBIN* 89 (March 1992) 6–8.

Reese, T. *Archbishop.* New York: Harper and Row, 1989.

———. *A Flock of Shepherds: The National Conference of Catholic Bishops.* Kansas City: Sheed and Ward, 1992.

———, ed. *Episcopal Conferences: Historical, Canonical, and Theological Studies.* Washington, D.C.: Georgetown University, 1989.

Rodríguez, P. *Particular Churches and Personal Prelatures.* Dublin: Four Courts, 1986.

Routhier, G. "'Église locale' ou 'église particulière': Querelle sémantique ou opinion théologique?" *Stud Can* 25 (1991) 277–334.

Ruini, C. "Il vescovo e la communione nella chiesa particolare." *ME* 116 (1991) 227–241.

Sarrazin, F. "La nomination des évêques dans l'église latine." *Stud Can* 20 (1986) 367–407.

Sheehy, G., et al., eds. *The Canon Law: Letter and Spirit.* Collegeville: Liturgical Press, 1995.

Thomas, F. "The Bishop in His Teaching Office and Those Who Assist Him." *Stud Can* 21 (1987) 229–238.

Tobin, J. "The Diocesan Bishop as Moderator of the Entire Ministry of the Word." *CLSANZ* (1988) 51–84.

Weakland, R. "The Local Churches and the Church of Rome." *Origins* 26 (August 29, 1996) 176–177.

Wijlens, M. "'For You I Am a Bishop, With You I Am a Christian': The Bishop as Legislator." *J* 56 (1996) 68–91.

Wrenn, L. *Authentic Interpretations on the 1983 Code.* Washington, D.C.: CLSA, 1993.

TITLE II
GROUPINGS OF PARTICULAR CHURCHES
[cc. 431–459]

The 1917 code's canons on "Patriarchs, Primates, and Metropolitans" (*CIC* 270–280) and on "Plenary and Provincial Councils" (*CIC* 281–292) were sandwiched between chapters on "Legates of the Roman Pontiff" (*CIC* 265–270) and "Apostolic Vicariates and Prefectures" (*CIC* 293–211), under the rubric, "The Supreme Power and Those Who by Church Law Share in It." Provinces merited only passing notice as the territories over which metropolitans and provincial councils exercised authority. This organization of material could easily give the impression that the authority exercised by metropolitans and by particular councils, like the power exercised by legates and apostolic vicars, was delegated papal power, and that provinces were only administrative units of the universal church.

The 1983 code's treatment of provinces, metropolitans, particular councils, and episcopal conferences is differently situated. The code does not approach these institutes under the rubric of the supreme church authority but in a section devoted to particular churches and their groupings (cc. 368–572). After a title concerning particular churches and their shepherds (cc. 368–430) comes the present title dealing with groupings of particular churches (cc. 431–459). This organization of material does not suggest that metropolitans, particular councils, and episcopal conferences are vehicles for the exercise of papal power.

One should probably resist the temptation to exaggerate the significance of the change. Common sense could argue that the governance of groupings of particular churches need not involve a sharing in the supreme power.[1] When an archbishop cele-

brates a pontifical Mass in a parish church located within the territory of one of his suffragans, is he really exercising the supreme power? On the other hand, it is difficult not to see in the structure of this section of the 1983 code something of the new mindset (*novus mentis habitus*) about which Pope Paul VI spoke. Ideas recovered or more forcefully emphasized by the Second Vatican Council clearly constitute the background against which the reader will understand these canons.

(1) If a diocese is a particular church in and from which the one and only Catholic Church comes into being (*LG* 23; cf. *CD* 11), it is more than an administrative unit of the universal Church. In and through it the Church of Christ manifests itself in a particular place at a particular time. When such particular churches come together to promote their common dedication to the mission of the Church (cc. 431, §1; 434; 445; 447), their assemblies ought also to reflect something more than administrative efficiency. It may be too early to say how these gatherings exhibit the structure of the Church, but the 1983 code's organization seems open and flexible enough to accommodate doctrinal development.

(2) If the authority to shepherd a particular church is conveyed by episcopal ordination,[2] then, when ministering routinely to the particular churches entrusted to their care, bishops are exercising their own episcopal rather than delegated papal power (*LG* 27). Overarching papal power and the power of the college of bishops coordinate (and sometimes limit) the exercise of this episcopal power so as to allow the whole Church to grow harmoniously toward its goal. Intermediate structures such as provincial councils and

---

[1] See, for example, the remarks of one consultor during the February 13, 1980 session of the *coetus* responsible for

the revision of this section of the code (*Comm* 12 [1980] 244–245).

[2] The essential proviso is that such authority can be exercised only in hierarchical communion with the head and members of the college of bishops (*LG* 21).

episcopal conferences can be seen as vehicles provided or sanctioned by supreme authority for the more effective exercise of episcopal authority.

(3) As members of the college entrusted with responsibility for the well-being of the universal Church, each individual bishop has a right and duty to be "solicitous" for the whole Church (*LG* 23). Gatherings of bishops to provide for the better shepherding of the particular churches over which they individually preside are a forum within which this solicitude comes to practical expression. The 1983 code's emphasis on the fostering of relationships among neighboring bishops (c. 431, §1) and on the joint exercise of pastoral *munera* (c. 447) seems to acknowledge that effective shepherding is always a collaborative[3] endeavor.

This title of the code consists of four chapters that are not logically parallel. Chapter 1 comprises four canons, two each on ecclesiastical provinces and ecclesiastical regions (cc. 431–434). In the 1977 schema on the People of God (hereafter "schema") the latter were coterminous with nations. It would therefore have been quite logical for the next chapters to address the institutes that exercise authority within the province (the metropolitan and the provincial council) and then those which exercise it within the region (the regional— now *plenary*—council and the episcopal conference).[4] However, the neatness of this pattern has

been somewhat disordered by the change in meaning of *region*. *Regions* are now optional gatherings of provinces within the territory over which a single episcopal conference exercises authority. A gathering of the bishops of an ecclesiastical region has no proper name in the code: canon 434 calls it a *conventus*, a meeting, assembly, or "coming together" of the involved bishops.

The chapter on provinces and regions is followed by chapters on metropolitans (who exercise authority within the provinces—cc. 435–438) and particular councils (one type of which, the provincial council, also exercises authority within a province—cc. 439–446). The chapter on particular councils also discusses plenary councils because the norms on membership, procedure, and authority of both institutes are virtually identical. The final chapter in the title addresses episcopal conferences (cc. 447–459). Strictly speaking, an episcopal conference is not, as the rubric might lead one to suspect, a *coetus* of particular churches; it is a gathering of the chief shepherds of particular churches. In the practical order, however, this distinction may be academic: at least in the United States of America, particular councils as envisaged by the canons almost never occur.

The principal sources of the following canons are the 1917 code, the conciliar decree *Christus Dominus,* and the 1966 *motu proprio Ecclesiae sanctae.* With one exception[5] there are no exact parallels in the Code of Canons of the Eastern Churches.

---

[3] One hesitates to use the term *collegial* here. Strictly collegial acts involve the entire episcopal college. On the other hand, "the episcopal function is by its very nature 'collegial.' This essential connection of each bishop with the college brings it about that the acts of only one bishop, even if they are personal, also imply a collegial dimension so long as he remains in hierarchical communion" (A. Antón, "The Theological 'Status' of Episcopal Conferences," *J* 48 [1988] 205). If this be true of the solitary activity of the individual bishop, how much more should it be true of the activity of bishops working together in provinces, in particular councils, or in episcopal conferences!

[4] The schema in fact used the opposite order: because article I (concerning particular councils) began with canons on regional (i.e., national) councils, article II dealt with the other national institute, the episcopal conference; and article III dealt with the other provincial institute, the

CHAPTER I
ECCLESIASTICAL PROVINCES
AND ECCLESIASTICAL REGIONS
[cc. 431–434]

The four canons in this chapter comprise two loosely parallel pairs dealing respectively with ec-

---

metropolitan. The canons in chapter 1 of the present code were called "preliminary canons."

[5] Canon 437 concerning the pallium corresponds with c. 156, §1 of the Eastern code.

clesiastical provinces (cc. 431 and 432) and ecclesiastical regions (cc. 433 and 434). Canons 431, §1 and 434 specify the purposes for which these institutes exist. Canons 431, §3 and 433, §1 indicate how they come into being. Canons 432, §2 and 433, §2 discuss their juridic personality. Canons 432, §1 and 434 note who exercises authority within them.

Ecclesiastical Provinces

Canon 431 — §1. To promote the common pastoral action of different neighboring dioceses according to the circumstances of persons and places and to foster more suitably the relations of the diocesan bishops among themselves, neighboring particular churches are to be brought together into ecclesiastical provinces limited to a certain territory.

This canon, without antecedent in the 1917 code, consists of (a) two parallel purpose clauses specifying the values the law seeks to promote and (b) an impersonally expressed norm of action.

The norm of action is clear: the particular churches within specified territories must be gathered into provinces. Canon 368 defines *particular churches* as (1) dioceses; (2) territorial prelatures; (3) territorial abbacies; (4) apostolic vicariates; (5) apostolic prefectures; and (6) apostolic administrations "erected in a stable manner." Canon 431, §3 indicates upon whom falls the obligation of grouping these particular churches into provinces: the supreme authority of the Church.

The canon's two parallel purpose clauses provide reasons for the establishment of provinces: (1) it will make it easier for neighboring particular churches to collaborate; (2) it will foster communion among the shepherds of their constitutive particular churches. The qualification, *iuxta personarum et locorum adiuncta,* demonstrates the legislator's realization that "common pastoral action" is not an absolute value: local circumstances may indicate that within a given province the well-being of the people of God as a whole or the people of God within one or another particular

church will be best served by independent action on the part of one or several dioceses. The law does not see the fostering of *communio* among the shepherds, and therefore among the flocks, as subject to any similar qualification.

§2. As a rule, exempt dioceses are no longer to exist. Therefore, individual dioceses and other particular churches within the territory of some ecclesiastical province must be joined to this ecclesiastical province.

The source of this canon, also without a 1917 code parallel, is *Christus Dominus* 40, 2: "As a general rule all dioceses and other territorial divisions which are by law equivalent to dioceses should be attached to an ecclesiastical province. Therefore dioceses which are now directly subject to the Apostolic See and not united to any other are either to be brought together to form a new ecclesiastical province, if that be possible, or else attached to that province which is nearer or more convenient. They are to be made subject to the metropolitan jurisdiction of the archbishop, in keeping with the norms of common law."[6] The canon consists of two norms of action derived from the principles expressed in §1. Given the importance of the values identified therein, the existence of particular churches that respond directly to the Holy See and are not associated with any province does not make much sense. A freedom not to collaborate with neighboring particular churches is not a privilege; it is a failure to appreciate the universal Church as a *communion of particular churches.* Henceforth, no particular church ought to be considered (*ne habeatur*) exempt from the provincial structure. The canon, following the council, does qualify this dictate: *pro regula,* as a rule.[7] The legislator does not ex-

---

[6] *AAS* 58 (1966) 694.

[7] The expression appears in three other canons. Canon 372, §1 declares that dioceses should *pro regula* include all and only the faithful who live within a given territory. Nevertheless, paragraph two recognizes that special circumstances might require the erection of personal dio-

clude *a priori* the possibility that particular circumstances might require that some particular church not be joined to some province.[8]

The second clause of the paragraph strongly prescribes (*ascribi debent*) the assimilation of hitherto exempt particular churches into the provinces within whose territorial limits they lie. Paragraph three specifies the subject of this impersonally expressed obligation: the supreme power in the Church.

§3. It is only for the supreme authority of the Church to establish, suppress, or alter ecclesiastical provinces after having heard the bishops involved.

The source of this canon is canon 215, §1 of the 1917 code which claimed for the supreme *power* (changed to *authority* in the present code) of the Church the sole prerogative to "erect or otherwise circumscribe, divide, combine, or suppress" provinces and particular churches. The former code made no mention of any requirement for prior consultation with the bishops, territorial prelates, etc., who might be affected by the exercise of this prerogative.

---

ceses, e.g., for members of a different rite. Canon 475, §2 prescribes that *pro regula* there should be only one vicar general, but allows for exceptions due to "pastoral reasons." Canon 857, §2 indicates that adults should be baptized in their own parish church and infants in the parish church of their parents, "unless a just cause suggests otherwise." Only in c. 431, §2 is the expression *pro regula* not immediately followed by an explicit recognition that circumstances might make observing the general rule unduly difficult. The *coetus* responsible for drafting this section of the code added the expression lest the canon impose an inflexible norm out of harmony with some situations. *Comm* 12 (1980) 253.

[8] *CLD* 7, 124 reports a private SCB rescript, dated June 28, 1972, withdrawing the Diocese of Berlin from the jurisdiction of the Archdiocese of Wroclaw, Poland, and making it immediately subject to the Holy See. G. Read points to "the dioceses in Switzerland in which there are no provinces" as other examples of still-existing particular churches that have not been joined to an ecclesiastical province. G. Read, "Section II: Particular Churches and their Groupings," in *CLSGBI Com,* 242.

Lumen gentium 21 teaches that bishops can exercise their sacred power only in hierarchical communion with the head and members of the college of bishops. Assigning each bishop a specific office as well as delineating the sphere of its exercise is a function of the supreme authority within the Church.

According to canon 331, by virtue of his office the pope "possesses supreme, full, immediate, and universal ordinary power in the Church." He usually conducts the business of the universal Church "through the Roman Curia" (c. 360). According to article 76 of *Pastor bonus,* everything concerning the "constitution, division, union, suppression, or other changes of particular churches and their groupings" belongs to the Congregation for Bishops. According to article 89, the same responsibility in mission lands belongs to the Congregation for Evangelization of Peoples. It is therefore through these dicasteries that the pope would fulfill his right and duty "to establish, suppress, or alter ecclesiastical provinces."

According to canon 336, the episcopal college, "together with its head and never without this head, is also the subject of supreme and full power over the universal Church." Nothing in the text of canon 431, §3 would prevent the college of bishops from establishing, suppressing, or changing ecclesiastical provinces. Indeed, the Second Vatican Council can be thought of as having exercised just this power when it mandated the suppression of the institute of "exempt" particular churches.

Although nothing in law precludes the collegial creation or suppression of an ecclesiastical province, such an activity would be very difficult in practice. The entire episcopal college is the subject of the power in question; but, apart from the convocation of an ecumenical council, the entire college lacks a vehicle for the exercise of this power. For all practical purposes, therefore, only the Holy See can erect, suppress, or change the makeup of an ecclesiastical province.

The canon prescribes that the bishops likely to be affected by the decision should be heard beforehand. This prescription appears to be a particular application of canon 50: "Before issuing a singular decree, an authority is to seek out the necessary information and proofs and, insofar as possible, to hear those whose rights can be injured." One of the functions of the provincial structure is the fostering of common pastoral activity in the light of local circumstances (c. 431, §1). If only in order to prepare the quinquennial report (c. 399, §1), a bishop must be sensitive to these circumstances. Hence, the Holy See would want to consult with the bishops of the affected local churches, not so much to prevent injury to the personal interests of the bishops themselves, but more to avail itself of the information and insights only these shepherds could provide.[9]

Authority in Province

Canon 432 — §1. The provincial council and the metropolitan possess authority in an ecclesiastical province according to the norm of law.

A province, like a particular church or even the universal Church, needs a physical person or a group of physical persons to represent it and to coordinate the activities of its members. This paragraph, part of whose material derives from canon 272 of the 1917 code, identifies two institutes that fulfill this function: the provincial council and the metropolitan. The norms of law defining the metropolitan's exercise of this authority[10] are found primarily in chapter 2 (cc. 435–437) of the current title; those dealing with the provincial council are found primarily in chapter 3 (cc. 439, §2; 440; 442–446).

§2. An ecclesiastical province possesses juridic personality by the law itself.

This paragraph indicates the juridic nature of the ecclesiastical provinces whose existence is mandated in canon 431: they are juridic persons, "subjects in canon law of obligations and rights which correspond to their nature" (c. 113, §2), "aggregates of persons or of things ordered for a purpose which is in keeping with the mission of the Church and which transcends the purpose of the individuals" (c. 114, §1).[11] A province enjoys this legal status *ipso iure:* it cannot exist as a province without therefore being a juridic person. As such it can own property, make contracts, receive bequests, stand in court—in short, engage in whatever business is necessary for the accomplishment of its mission.

It would appear that a province is a *public* juridic person as defined in canon 116, §1: it is constituted by competent ecclesiastical authority (the Holy See) to fulfill "the proper function entrusted to [it] in view of the public good." Canon 118 states that the person or persons entitled to represent a public juridic person must be specified in universal law, in particular law, or in the statutes of the juridic person. Canon 432, §1 functions as the necessary acknowledgment in universal law of the rights and duties of the metropolitan[12] and of the provincial council in this regard.

Ecclesiastical Regions

Canon 433 — §1. If it seems advantageous, especially in nations where particular churches are more numerous, the Holy See can unite neighboring ecclesiastical provinces into ecclesiastical regions at the request of the conference of bishops.

---

[9] *ES* I, 42 had "established the competence of the conference of bishops to provide information" about the erection, suppression, or alteration of ecclesiastical provinces. Canon 431, §3 appears to eliminate from the process the involvement of the conference. Cf. J. Arrieta, "Title II—Groupings of Particular Churches," in *Pamplona ComEng,* 329.

[10] Read, in *CLSGBI Com,* 242, correctly observes that the metropolitan has no legislative power over the province and very limited executive power. His judicial authority is limited to particular cases.

[11] A juridic person in canon law is roughly analogous to a corporation in civil law. It appears that, at least in the United States of America, provinces are not civilly incorporated.

[12] "Based on an analogy of law (see cc. 19, 118, 435), the Metropolitan represents the province in juridical matters in the same way as the Bishop represents the diocese (see Can. 393)." Read, in *CLSGBI Com,* 242.

The material in this canon parallels the material in canon 431, §§1 and 3, and is without antecedent in the 1917 code. *Christus Dominus* 40, 3 had urged that, when it seemed useful, provinces should be gathered into ecclesiastical regions, for which regulations should be formulated.[13] The 1977 schema proposed that all of the provinces of a single nation constitute an ecclesiastical region (c. 187, §2), which could be subdivided into "regional districts" (c. 187, §5).[14] The optional institute envisaged by the 1983 code, by contrast, is an intermediate structure between the province and the nation—i.e., it is roughly what the schema had termed a "regional district."[15]

Canon 433, §1 is a complex conditional sentence. The main clause in the indicative recognizes that the Holy See has the power to gather provinces into ecclesiastical regions. The canon presupposes that the Holy See will do this, not on its own initiative, but in response to a request from the episcopal conference of the territory in question. The same considerations that necessitate the grouping of particular churches into provinces (cf. c. 431, §1) can suggest the usefulness of grouping provinces into regions: the fostering of common pastoral action and the enhancing of effective collegiality among neighboring bishops. In relatively small countries (e.g., Belgium) these values may be adequately realized through regular meetings of the episcopal conferences. Where there are many provinces, however (e.g., Italy), there might be some point in having an intermediate level of organization.[16] The initiative for proposing the establishment of such a structure belongs to the affected bishops, acting through the episcopal conference.

The phrasing of this canon is entirely concessive: it acknowledges a power to act, but imposes no obligation to do so. It should be noted that *Ecclesiae sanctae* I, 42 directed episcopal conferences to determine whether "the good of souls" urged the erection of such regions. If so, the conferences were to make proposals to the Holy See concerning their correct ordering.[17]

§2. An ecclesiastical region can be erected as a juridic person.

The purely optional character of the ecclesiastical region is underscored by this canon. The establishment of a region, unlike that of a province, does not automatically endow it with juridic personality. Because canon 433, §1 views the Holy See as the authority competent to erect a region, one can infer that the Holy See is likewise the authority competent to endow it with juridic personality.[18]

Canon 434 — It belongs to a meeting of the bishops of an ecclesiastical region to foster cooperation and common pastoral action in the region.

---

[13] *AAS* 58 (1966) 694.

[14] For a clear presentation of the evolution of the meaning of the term, see J. Provost, "Title II— Groupings of Particular Churches," in *CLSA Com,* 353. See also the original *coetus* discussion of the formulation of the canons on ecclesiastical regions in *Comm* 17 (1985) 97–98.

[15] J. Listl notes that this and the following canons are products of the final redaction of the 1983 code: they were not to be found even in the March 25, 1982 *Schema novissimum* of the code. The lateness of the appearance of these canons demonstrates how controversial were questions about the nature and function of ecclesiastical regions. J. Listl, "§33 Plenarkonzil und Bischofskonferenz," in *Handbuch,* 305. The unsettled state of these questions, in turn, might explain the code's restrained treatment of this optional institute.

[16] J. Gutiérrez reports that since 1919 Italy has been divided into 17 pastoral regions called conciliar regions. J. Gutiérrez, "Capítulo VI Organización Jerarquica de la Iglesia," in *Manual de Derecho Canonico* (Pamplona: Universidad de Navarra, 1988) 352.

[17] *AAS* 58 (1966) 774–775.

[18] Chapter VII of the Bylaws of the NCCB (= Article XIV of the Bylaws of the USCC) states, "For the purposes of the National Conference of Catholic Bishops, the archdioceses and dioceses of the United States will be grouped into regions as designated by the Administrative Committee." These regions are not examples of the canonically erected regions with which cc. 433 and 434 are concerned. According to Sister Sharon Euart, RSM, Associate General Secretary of the NCCB, "there is no uniform manner of operation among the regions. Each has a regional chairman elected by the members of the regions and regional representation on the Administrative Committee and Board" (private communication).

Nevertheless, such a meeting does not have the powers attributed to a conference of bishops in the canons of this Code unless the Holy See has specifically granted it certain powers.

Without antecedent in the 1917 code, this canon parallels canon 432, §1 concerning the province. There are two foci of authority in the province, but only one in a region; and its authority is rather weakly defined. The two clauses of this canon specify what the *conventus* ("meeting" or "assembly") of the bishops of a region can and cannot do. In the absence of a special grant of power from the Holy See, such an assembly lacks the powers which the code attributes to the episcopal conference. On the other hand, because it is not a particular council, it lacks the powers proper to a provincial or plenary council (cf. c. 445). Although such an assembly is responsible for fostering "cooperation and common pastoral action in the region," the canon gives no indication that individual bishops are legally bound to observe decisions reached by the assembly.[19]

Despite its obvious lack of juridic authority, such a *conventus* cannot be chaired by an auxiliary bishop.[20]

---

[19] Arrieta observes, "This assembly does not usually exercise a governing power that is binding on the member bishops." However, if granted peculiar faculties by the Holy See, "it will exercise some kind of the power of governance" when it uses those faculties (*Pamplona ComEng,* 330). In other words, the power exercised by such an assembly of bishops would always be delegated power. Because the legislative power of an authority lower than the supreme authority cannot be delegated (cf. c. 135, §2), Read dryly concludes, "It is clear that the Bishops at a regional meeting cannot do more than reach joint decisions to be implemented on the basis of their individual episcopal authority within their own dioceses" (*CLSGBI Com,* 243).

[20] *AAS* 81 (1989) 388. The code likewise reserves the presidency of a plenary council (c. 441, 3°) and (if the metropolitan is impeded from acting) of a provincial council (c. 442, §2) to *diocesan* bishops. For the arguments in favor of reserving the presidential role to diocesan bishops see R. Castillo Lara, "De episcoporum conferentiarum praesidentia," *Comm* 21 (1989) 95–97. See the commentary on c. 452 for a précis of his arguments.

CHAPTER II
METROPOLITANS
[cc. 435–438]

The world into which Christianity first spread was, long before the Roman conquest, a world of city states. Some urban centers exercised considerable political, economic, and cultural influence over their less important neighbors; and their becoming the seats of Roman provincial government heightened their prestige. Christian communities sprang up first in these centers, and the evangelization of other cities and towns began there. These "mother" churches (metropolitan sees) accordingly acquired certain prerogatives over their "daughter" churches, a development that reached its climax in the growth of the great patriarchal sees.

This process was attenuated in the West, partly because it was less thoroughly urbanized, partly because of the preeminence of Rome. Although history has known doughty metropolitans like Hincmar of Rheims, current law accords the metropolitan very limited authority.

The four canons of this chapter are based on canons 272 through 281 of the 1917 code. A preliminary canon (c. 435) defines the office of metropolitan. Canon 436 specifies the rights and duties of the office. Canon 437 deals with the pallium, a vestment symbolizing the communion between the metropolitan and the pope. Canon 438 is a kind of appendix, noting that the titles of patriarch and primate are purely honorific in the West.

Definition

Canon 435 — A metropolitan, who is the archbishop of his diocese, presides over an ecclesiastical province. The office of metropolitan is joined with an episcopal see determined or approved by the Roman Pontiff.

This canon, a reworking of canon 272 of the 1917 code, combines elements of constitutional law and definition. Canon 432, §1 states that within the norms of law the competent authority in the province is the metropolitan and the provincial council. This raises the questions, "Who is the metropolitan? What norms of law govern his activity?" Canon 435 answers the first question, and canon 436 answers the second.

The former code appeared to identify the titles *metropolitan* and *archbishop*. The current canon is more exact: the title of *archbishop* can be given to a non-residential bishop—for example, the pronuncio to the United States of America. A metropolitan is a residential archbishop, the chief shepherd of a particular church to which the office of presiding over the province has been attached either by papal determination or with papal approbation. The chief shepherds of the other particular churches belonging to the province are called *suffragans*. The former code categorized the task of presiding over the province as a *dignity*. Canon 435 more appropriately calls it an *officium*. Canon 145, §1 defines *officium* as "any function constituted in a stable manner by divine or ecclesiastical ordinance to be exercised for a spiritual purpose." To facilitate achieving the purposes of provinces (cf. c. 431, §1), in each province church law entrusts in a stable manner certain functions to the chief shepherd of a determinate particular church.

Authority

Canon 436 — §1. In the suffragan dioceses, a metropolitan is competent:
   1° to exercise vigilance so that the faith and ecclesiastical discipline are observed carefully and to inform the Roman Pontiff of abuses, if there are any;
   2° to conduct a canonical visitation for a cause previously approved by the Apostolic See if a suffragan has neglected it;
   3° to designate a diocesan administrator according to the norm of cann. 421, §2, and 425, §3.

This simplification[21] of canon 274 of the 1917 code is a taxative (cf. c. 436, §3) specification of

the duties (and corresponding rights or prerogatives) of the metropolitan vis à vis the dioceses of his suffragans.[22] Within his own particular church

of the 1917 code concerned the presentation of a candidate for a benefice. The institution of presentation has been suppressed (cf. *Comm* 12 [1980] 273). (2) Canon 274, 2° concerned indulgences, an institute that has been greatly simplified: cf. Paul VI, apconst *Indulgentiarum doctrina,* January 1, 1967, *AAS* 59 (1967) 5–24; *CLD* 6, 570–575). See the commentary on cc. 992–997. (3) Canon 274, 6° was reworked into c. 436, §3 of the current code. (4) Canon 274, 7°–8° dealt with tribunal issues now relegated to procedural law (cf. *Comm* 12 [1980] 273; also *Comm* 14 [1982] 190).

[22] Canon 442, §1 lists other obligations of the metropolitan vis-à-vis a provincial council; and c. 442, §2 notes his right and duty to preside over such a council unless he is legitimately impeded. The metropolitan presumably would preside over the triennial meeting of the bishops of the province during which they compose a list of presbyters "who are more suitable for the episcopate" (c. 377, §2). One likewise presumes that the metropolitan would preside at the non-conciliar "meeting of the bishops of the province to determine by decree for the entire province the offering to be given for the celebration and application of a Mass" (c. 952, §1). According to c. 413, §1, "as soon as possible after taking possession of the diocese," each bishop is to prepare a list of persons who are (in their listed order) to assume the governance of the impeded see. A copy of this list, which must reviewed at least every three years, is to be provided to the metropolitan (cf. the commentary on this canon). The metropolitan is likewise entitled to receive copies of any declarations or decrees emanating from diocesan synods celebrated within his province (c. 467), but the canons do not imply that he has any power to disallow or revise either the aforementioned list or the declarations and decrees. Canon 501, §3 requires a suffragan bishop to consult his metropolitan before dissolving a "presbyteral council [which] does not fulfill the function entrusted to it for the good of the diocese or gravely abuses it." However, the phrasing of the canon makes it obvious that the metropolitan has no authority to overrule the suffragan's decision, for the canon speaks of consultation (*facta consultatione*), not of consent. Furthermore, it requires the metropolitan to consult "the suffragan bishop senior in promotion" before dissolving the archdiocesan presbyteral council; and no suffragan, not even the most senior, has a supervisory function vis à vis his metropolitan. In none of these instances does the law grant the metropolitan any power of governance within the suffragan dioceses.

[21] The items from the 1917 code omitted from the present code are not particularly significant. (1) Canon 274, 1°

the archbishop possesses all of the rights and duties of a diocesan bishop: these are not in question in this section of the code.[23]

Canon 392, §1 situates a diocesan bishop's disciplinary role within the context of his concern for the unity of the universal Church. His guarding against abuses (c. 392, §2) is a particular expression of this concern: false or inaccurate teaching, irreverent or otherwise improper worship, and maladministration are disruptive of the harmony and good order without which the people of God cannot fulfill their mission and grow in charity. The metropolitan exercises a similar but more circumscribed oversight over the entire province. Unlike the diocesan bishop, who has "all ordinary, proper, and immediate power" necessary for shepherding the particular church entrusted to his care (cf. c. 381, §1), the metropolitan has no authority to intervene on his own initiative in the affairs of the dioceses of his suffragans. He has instead the right and duty to inform the pope (who does have "ordinary power over all particular churches"—c. 333, §1) of any abuses in the area of faith or discipline.

Canons 395 and 415 offer two examples of the metropolitan's exercise of this kind of vigilance.[24] According to canon 395, §4, if a suffragan absents himself from his diocese for longer than six months, the metropolitan is obliged to inform the Holy See of his absence. Canon 415, in turn, prescribes that the metropolitan is to take immediate recourse to the Holy See if one of his suffragans should be prevented by an ecclesiastical penalty from fulfilling his episcopal duties.[25]

Canon 396, §1 specifies the diocesan bishop's obligation to visit his diocese at least once every five years. If a bishop neglects this duty, the met-

ropolitan can fulfill the obligation, but only with the prior approval of the Holy See.

If a suffragan see falls vacant, the college of consultors is to elect a diocesan administrator within eight days. If it fails to do so (c. 421, §1), or if the administrator elected (a) is not a priest, or (b) is not at least thirty-five, or (c) was previously elected, nominated, or presented for the same vacant see[26] (c. 425, §1), the metropolitan has the right and the duty to appoint a diocesan administrator.

The phrasing of canon 436, §1, 1°, 2°, and 3° indicates how rarely a metropolitan can involve himself in the governance of the particular churches of his brother bishops. Potentially the most important of his prerogatives—the right and duty to appoint a diocesan administrator—is assumed by the senior suffragan when the metropolitan see itself is vacant (cc. 421, §2; 425, §3). It is obvious that the canons do not see the metropolitan as a kind of "super bishop."

§2. Where circumstances demand it, the Apostolic See can endow a metropolitan with special functions and power to be determined in particular law.

There are large cities—e.g., São Paulo[27] and Paris[28]—which have been divided into several particular churches, one of which is the archdiocese. The need for fostering common pastoral action, evident in any province (c. 431, §1), is critical in such situations.[29] This new canon recognizes that the Holy See may provide for the special needs of such

---

[23] See the relevant commentary on cc. 381–402.

[24] The obligations specified by these canons belong to the senior suffragan if the metropolitan is the delinquent.

[25] According to c. 1405, §1, 3°, only the pope can serve as judge in penal cases involving bishops. See the relevant commentary on this canon. Presumably c. 415 would be of particular importance only when the suffragan had incurred an automatic penalty.

[26] The Holy See is the final arbiter of a person's suitability to be a bishop (c. 378, §2). A candidate who was nominated, presented, or elected to the office of bishop of a specific see but not confirmed by Rome has already been judged by Rome unsuitable to serve as shepherd of that particular flock. This implicit judgment of unsuitability prevents a group of diocesan priests from later selecting him for the same post.

[27] *Comm* 12 (1980) 273.

[28] Read, in *CLSGBI Com*, 244.

[29] For a more technical discussion of this issue, see Arrieta, in *Pamplona ComEng*, 332.

a province by endowing the metropolitan with additional responsibilities and authority. The canon expresses the preference that these peculiar rights and duties be regulated by particular law.

§3. The metropolitan has no other power of governance in the suffragan dioceses. He can perform sacred functions, however, as if he were a bishop in his own diocese in all churches, but he is first to inform the diocesan bishop if the church is the cathedral.

The list of rights and duties of metropolitans in canon 436, §1 is intended to be taxative: with the exception of the circumstances detailed in canon 436, §2, common law does not recognize the metropolitan as having any other governmental power[30] within the dioceses of his suffragans. This canon concedes that the metropolitan does enjoy a liturgical prerogative (not really a power) not shared by non-metropolitans. Canon 390 prescribes that a bishop "can perform pontifical functions in his entire diocese" but not *outside* his diocese "without the express, or at least reasonably presumed, consent of the local ordinary."[31] The

metropolitan, by contrast, can pontificate throughout the province without anyone's consent. If he intends to preside in the cathedral of one of his suffragans, the canon obliges him to notify the latter beforehand; but the suffragan has no legal right to prevent the celebration.

The Pallium

Canon 437 — §1. Within three months from the reception of episcopal consecration or if he has already been consecrated, from the canonical provision, a metropolitan is obliged to request the pallium from the Roman Pontiff either personally or through a proxy. The pallium signifies the power which the metropolitan, in communion with the Roman Church, has by law in his own province.

This canon is virtually identical with canon 275 of the 1917 code.[32] The pallium is a kind of white woolen collar, roughly two and a half inches wide, with pendants in front and back. Decorated with six black silk crosses, it is secured with gold pins on top of the chasuble. It is woven from the wool of two lambs that are blessed at Saint John Lateran on the feast of Saint Agnes. On the vigil of the feast of Saints Peter and Paul the new pallia are taken to the crypt of Saint Peter where they are blessed by the pope at vespers. They are kept there overnight and are given to the new archbishops in a special ceremony on the feast.[33] The pallium used to be more widely given.[34] In response to Vatican II's call for a reform of the

---

[30] The metropolitan's tribunal may or may not have appellate jurisdiction over the cases originating in his suffragans' tribunals (cf. c. 1438, 1°). In some areas (for example, Canada) regional appellate tribunals have been established instead; and in other areas the tribunals within a single province appeal to each other in "round robin" fashion (Tribunal A to Tribunal B; Tribunal B to Tribunal C; Tribunal C to Tribunal D; Tribunal D to Tribunal A). If the metropolitan's tribunal does have appellate jurisdiction over the tribunals of his suffragans, it also enjoys first instance jurisdiction in actions concerning "the rights or temporal goods of a juridic person represented by [any suffragan] bishop" (cf. c. 1419, §2). In any event, the appellate jurisdiction his tribunal might enjoy over the cases heard in first instance before his suffragans' tribunals does not imply that the metropolitan is the moderator of any tribunal other than his own.

[31] In the light of *SC* 41, this is a highly sensible norm: the Church becomes most clearly visible when the bishop, assisted by his fellow ministers, presides over the Eucharist with his flock. The symbolism is less clear when the bishop is presiding over a brother bishop's flock.

[32] The *ius vigens* more precisely describes the pallium as symbolizing, not *archepiscopal* power (cf. the commentary on c. 435), but the power which a *metropolitan* exercises as such within his own province.

[33] For a sprightly discussion of the history of the pallium, the ceremonies involved in blessing it, and the correct way to wear it, see J.-C. Noonan, Jr., *The Church Visible: The Ceremonial Life and Protocol of the Roman Catholic Church* (New York: Viking, 1996) 359–363.

[34] For example, *Cleri sanctitati* 321, §1 required all Eastern rite metropolitans outside patriarchates to obtain a pallium. *AAS* 49 (1957) 529.

laws governing the rights and privileges of metropolitans (*CD* 40, 2), Pope Paul VI decreed that the pallium would henceforth be conferred only on metropolitans and on the Latin patriarch of Jerusalem.[35]

The canon establishes a duty for the newly created archbishop. It is not the responsibility of the Holy See to endow him with the pallium; it is his responsibility to seek one from the pope. His seeking the pallium vividly represents the communion with the church of Rome it will be his special responsibility to foster throughout his province. According to canon 379, someone who is not a bishop is obliged to seek episcopal consecration within three months of his receiving his letter of appointment. A non-bishop appointed to a metropolitan see might therefore have a maximum of six months within which to petition the pope for his pallium. A bishop transferred to the metropolitan see, on the other hand, must ask for the pallium within three months of his appointment. The former code (*CIC* 276) and *Cleri sanctitati* (c. 321, §2) forbade new metropolitans from exercising certain of their powers until they had obtained the pallium. This restriction was eliminated from the 1983 code to avoid giving the impression that the pallium itself conferred power and to avoid the inconvenience of limiting a metropolitan's exercise of his authority until the next consistory.[36]

This canon has an exact parallel in the Eastern code canon 156, §1. Certain Eastern churches have a metropolitan rather than patriarchal structure. According to canon 151, §1 of the Eastern code, such a church "is presided over by a metropolitan of a determined see who is appointed by the Roman Pontiff and assisted by a council of hierarchs according to the norm of law." It is autonomous in the sense that it is not subject to the authority of a patriarch or a major archbishop. It is directly subject to the authority of the pope,

who can be thought of as exercising patriarchal authority over it.[37] Faris lists five Eastern Catholic churches (Ethiopian, Malabar, Malankar, Romanian, and Ruthenian) with a metropolitan structure.[38] The metropolitans of these churches, like the Latin rite metropolitans, are obliged to obtain from the pope a pallium as "a sign of [their] metropolitan power and full communion" with the Roman church. Like the 1917 code, but unlike the 1983 code, the Eastern code prohibits a metropolitan from exercising certain functions prior to the reception of the pallium: he "cannot convoke the council of hierarchs or ordain bishops" (*CCEO* 156, §2).

§2. A metropolitan can use the pallium according to the norm of liturgical laws within any church of the ecclesiastical province over which he presides, but not outside it, even if the diocesan bishop gives his assent.

This canon simplifies canon 277 of the 1917 code. It recognizes two limitations on the metropolitan's right to wear the pallium. The first is liturgical. Because the pallium is a vestment, its use is naturally regulated by liturgical law. The *Ceremonial of Bishops* 62 prescribes that, after a residential archbishop has received the pallium, he wear it to celebrate the stational Mass,[39] other Masses celebrated with great solemnity,[40] ordinations, blessings of abbots and abbesses, consecrations of virgins, and dedications of churches and altars. The second limitation on the wearing of the

---

[35] Paul VI, *mp Inter eximia,* May 11, 1978, *AAS* 70 (1978) 442.

[36] *Comm* 12 (1980) 274.

[37] J. D. Faris, *The Eastern Catholic Churches: Constitution and Governance According to the Code of Canons of the Eastern Churches* (New York: Saint Maron, 1992) 375; *Pospishil Com,* 196–198.

[38] Faris, 375.

[39] According to *CB* 119, a stational Mass is celebrated "when the bishop, as high priest of his flock, celebrates the eucharist . . . in the cathedral, surrounded by his college of presbyters and by his ministers, and with the full, active participation of all God's holy people."

[40] H. Mauritz, "§34 Die Kirchenprovinz," in *Handbuch,* 328, n. 8, lists some two dozen principal feasts on which the pallium might be worn.

pallium is territorial: the metropolitan may wear it in every church located within the province over which he presides but in no other church. Because it is a symbol of the authority he exercises precisely as a metropolitan, it would make little sense for him to wear it in places where he lacks that authority.[41]

§3. A metropolitan needs a new pallium if he is transferred to another metropolitan see.

This canon reproduces the provisions of canon 278 of the 1917 code, omitting the reference to a metropolitan's "losing" his pallium.[42] Because the pallium represents a metropolitan's authority over a specific province, it might be unseemly for him to use the same pallium in another province. Moreover, the act of requesting the pallium could be seen as a distinctive act of harmony between the province and the church of Rome.

Patriarchs and Primates

Canon 438 — The titles of patriarch and primate entail no power of governance in the Latin Church apart from a prerogative of honor unless in some matters the contrary is clear from apostolic privilege or approved custom.

In the Western church there exists only one genuine patriarch, the pope.[43] Nevertheless, although they lack the authority patriarchs exercise in the Eastern churches, several prelates enjoy the title *patriarch:* the Latin Patriarch of Jerusalem,

the Patriarch of Venice, the Patriarch of Lisbon, the Patriarch of the East Indies, and the Patriarch of the West Indies.[44] The title of *primate* likewise is purely honorific in current Latin rite law. This canon, a slight reworking of canon 271 of the former code, concedes that the Holy See might grant a given patriarch or primate special powers,[45] or that a given patriarch or primate might acquire such powers by custom;[46] but it notes that the titles in themselves do not imply any power of governance.

**CHAPTER III
PARTICULAR COUNCILS
[cc. 439–446]**

When the Second Vatican Council expressed its earnest desire "that the venerable institute of synods and [particular] councils flourish with new vigor" (*CD* 36),[47] the Fathers were recommending the more frequent and widespread use of one of the most ancient elements of the Church's governmental structure. Luke writes that, when controversies erupted at Antioch concerning the necessity of circumcision for salvation, the leaders of that community sent representatives to meet with the leadership of the Jerusalem community to formulate a common response to the question (Acts 15). Whatever the historical accuracy of Luke's account, the leaders of Christian communities early developed the habit of meeting with their neighbors to discuss such issues as the date of Easter, controverted doctrinal matters, and the proper treatment of members who lapsed during persecutions. Particular councils such as those held at Carthage in North Africa and Elvira and Toledo in Spain were influential in the development of canon law. The celebration of particular councils was a critical factor in the success of the Carolingian reform. More recently, the Councils of Baltimore had a lasting impact on the

---

[41] There are at least two exceptions to this rule: the Latin Patriarch of Jerusalem and the Patriarch of Lisbon enjoy the privilege of wearing their pallia even outside their provinces. Cf. *Comm* 14 (1982) 190.

[42] Wearing the pallium is a privilege rather than an obligation. A metropolitan who "lost" his pallium would not therefore be obliged to seek a new one. On the other hand, the law does not appear to prohibit him from seeking a replacement for a lost, stolen, or damaged pallium.

[43] *Comm* 12 (1980) 271.

[44] Gutiérrez, 352–353.

[45] See the commentary on cc. 76–84 on privileges.

[46] See the commentary on cc. 23–28 on custom.

[47] *AAS* 58 (1966) 692.

development of church life in the United States of America.[48]

From Vatican II's expression of the wish that this institute "flourish with new vigor" one can easily conclude that particular councils were not then flourishing at all. Indeed, the 1917 code's requirement that a provincial council be convoked at least once every twenty years (*CIC* 283) was largely a dead letter. Although at least two countries (Poland[49] and the Philippines[50]) have recently convoked plenary councils, the decades following Vatican II do not appear to have witnessed a proliferation of particular councils.[51] It is possible that the institute is falling into desuetude.

---

[48] Two easily accessible overviews of the history of particular councils are: F. J. Murphy, *Legislative Powers of the Provincial Council* (Washington, D.C.: Catholic University of America, 1947) 1–28; and E. O. Poblete, *The Plenary Council* (Washington, D.C.: Catholic University of America, 1958) 1–19. For an excellent analysis of the vicissitudes of particular councils, cf. J. Provost, "Particular Councils," in *The New Code of Canon Law,* ed. M. Theriault and J. Thorn (Ottawa: St. Paul University, 1986) 1:538–542.

[49] "Regolamento del II Sinodo Plenario," in *Ius Ecclesiae* 5 (1993) 403–407, with a commentary: T. Pieronek, "Nota al Regolamento del II Sinodo Plenario Polacco," *Ius Ecclesiae* 5 (1993) 407–411.

[50] "Second Plenary Council of the Philippines Directory," *Ius Ecclesiae* 6 (1994) 813–825, with an appended commentary: A. Opalalic, "The Second Plenary Council of the Philippines," *Ius Ecclesiae* 6 (1994) 825–832. This council was celebrated from January 20, 1991 to February 17, 1991.

[51] For example, in preparation for drafting this commentary, the author informally polled the thirty-one provinces of the United States of America. Since 1983, none of the twenty responding provinces has held a council of the sort the code envisions. The bishops of these provinces meet regularly, with varying degrees of formality; and several provinces have Catholic conferences involving non-episcopal participation. Two provinces have institutes called *provincial councils* which meet once or twice each year. One of them welcomes the participation of representative priests, but neither of these councils seems to be what the code envisions. If the promulgation of a new code, some of whose norms require adaptations of particular legislation, does not spur intense conciliar activity, nothing is likely to do so.

Not everyone views that prospect with alarm. J. Gutiérrez, for example, argues that the purposes served by particular councils can be more efficiently achieved in other ways: plenary sessions of the episcopal conference can substitute for the celebration of plenary councils, and informal meetings of the bishops of a province can take the place of provincial councils.[52] Certainly these alternatives require less preparation and prior consultation,[53] and they almost certainly would be less cumbersome and easier to manage.[54]

Against the commendable pragmatism of this position at least two counter arguments can be mounted, one of which is admittedly purely technical. Respecting the traditional value of particular councils, the code recognizes their legislative competence (c. 445). The more or less informal gatherings of the bishops of a province are not really as such subjects of governmental power, and the legislative authority of the episcopal conference is strictly defined (c. 455, §1). Hence, a particular council, whether provincial or plenary, has greater legislative competence than either of the alternatives of which Gutiérrez speaks. The more important defense of the continuing relevance of particular councils, however, is ecclesiological. The informal gathering of the bishops of a province is precisely a gathering *of bishops*. An episcopal conference is likewise (by definition!) an assembly *of bishops* (c. 447). A particular council, by contrast, is a gathering of the faithful, both clergy and lay, both religious and secular. Although only bishops may actually cast ballots in such gatherings (c. 443, §§1–2), all the participants may speak; and during the celebration of such a council the Church as a hierarchically ordered community of believers is graphically displayed. Surely there is some value in a vehicle for

---

[52] Gutiérrez, 354. The above-cited survey indicates that bishops do tend to meet in provincial gatherings, sometimes as frequently as four or six times a year.

[53] Pieronek, 408, reports that preparatory work for the Polish Plenary Synod began in 1987.

[54] Opalalic, 826, reports that the plenary council recently celebrated in the Philippines involved 489 participants.

decision making that so well expresses the nature of the Church.

The eight canons in this chapter are all norms of action, and most of them involve reworking the material found in canons 281 through 291 of the 1917 code. Two introductory canons distinguish between plenary councils and provincial councils. There follow two canons indicating who is responsible for convoking, determining the agenda of, and presiding over these councils. Two canons deal with the participants in particular councils. One canon specifies the scope of the authority of particular councils, and a final canon addresses the aftermath of the celebration of a council.

Plenary Councils

Canon 439 — §1. A plenary council, that is, one for all the particular churches of the same conference of bishops, is to be celebrated whenever it seems necessary or useful to the conference of bishops, with the approval of the Apostolic See.

This canon, modeled (with some significant differences) on canon 281 of the 1917 code, (a) defines *plenary* councils, (b) contains a norm governing the frequency of their celebration, and (c) notes the need for papal approval before their convocation.

(a) A *plenary* council is a gathering of representatives from all the particular churches within the territory of a single episcopal conference. Most episcopal conferences are responsible for all the local churches within a nation (cf. c. 448, §1); but some exercise jurisdiction over only a portion of the territory of a nation (e.g., Puerto Rico, England and Wales) or over the territories of several countries (Gambia, Sierra Leone, and Liberia) (cf. c. 448, §2). According to this canon, a council involving the leadership of all the particular churches of Puerto Rico would be a plenary council. A gathering of representatives from all the particular churches in the state of California would not. Under the discipline of the 1917 code, by contrast, any council involving the leadership of particular churches from more than one

ecclesiastical province was a plenary council (*CIC* 281).

(b) At least as far back as the Council of Nicea,[55] universal law has urged the frequent celebration of particular councils. This canon realistically entrusts the decision about the necessity or the usefulness of celebrating a plenary council to the discretion of the episcopal conference.[56] Conferences must hold plenary sessions at least annually (cf. c. 453), and these regular sessions involve the participation of the chief shepherds of all the particular churches that would be involved in the celebration of a plenary council. The conference can adequately discuss and decide many issues whose resolution, under the 1917 code, would have required the convocation of a plenary council.[57] The canon does not indicate how the

[55] See Murphy, 3–6, for an overview of early attempts to foster the frequent celebration of councils.

[56] The initial draft of this canon prescribed the celebration of regional (= *plenary* in the 1983 code) councils "at least every twenty years and whenever the episcopal conference of the region, with the approval of the Apostolic See, judged it necessary or useful" (*Comm* 17 [1985] 106). Hence, Arrieta, in *Pamplona ComEng*, 334–335, contends that a norm requiring the celebration of plenary councils at fixed intervals "would have implicitly entailed the approval of the Holy See." The text of c. 439, §1, by contrast, ensures Roman participation in every decision to convoke a plenary council and also allows the episcopal conference more freedom to decide when such a council might be useful. Cf. *Comm* 12 (1980) 256.

[57] An episcopal conference, however, is by definition an assembly of bishops (cf. c. 447). A plenary council involves the participation of many non-bishops, even non-clerics. An observation from the *Praenotanda* to the 1977 schema *De Populo Dei* seems apposite here: "But it seems necessary that at certain times a broader discussion be had concerning the necessities of the region or province, in which not only the bishops who are members of the episcopal conference, but also several others whom it appears impossible to invite to each and every meeting of the conference." *Comm* 4 (1972) 47–48. The document adverts to two distinct and important advantages of holding councils: (1) they allow a more comprehensive discussion of some issues than would be possible in the regular sessions of the conference; and (2) they provide for the participation of non-bishops whose in-

conference is to decide on the need for celebrating a plenary council. The matter apparently can be addressed in the statutes of each conference.[58]

(c) The approval of the Holy See is necessary before a plenary council can be convoked.[59] The phrasing of the canon[60] implies that the approval of the Holy See must be concurrent with the judgment of the conference: just as the conference's authority over the council does not cease with convoking it, so the Holy See's authority is not exhausted by approving of the convocation. The 1917 code provided for continued Roman involvement in the conciliar process by requiring that a papal legate convoke and preside over the plenary council (cf. *CIC* 281). Although requiring the *recognitio* of the Holy See before enactments of a plenary council can be promulgated (cf. c. 446 and the commentary, below), the 1983 code does not make explicit provision for such continuing Roman involvement.[61]

§2. The norm established in §1 is valid also for the celebration of a provincial council in an ecclesiastical province whose boundaries coincide with the territory of a nation.

There are episcopal conferences whose individual territories comprise single provinces. Every provincial council in such a setting would, by the definition given in canon 439, §1, be a plenary council.[62] The convocation of such a particular council is governed by the rules for plenary councils rather than by the rules for provincial councils. Thus, the conference (in which auxiliary bishops and other titular bishops may have a vote—cf. c. 454, §2) rather than a majority of the diocesan bishops (cf. c. 440, §1) determines whether the council should be convoked; and the approval of the Holy See must be sought before its convocation.

Provincial Councils

Canon 440 — §1. A provincial council for the different particular churches of the same ecclesiasti-

---

sights could not practically be made available during regular sessions of the conference. Neither of these values has lost its validity.

[58] This was the view of the *coetus* (*Comm* 14 [1982] 193). Without offering supporting arguments, Arrieta, in *Pamplona ComEng,* 335, implies instead that the provisions of c. 455, §2 would apply: the motion to call a plenary council would need the approval of a two-thirds majority of the voting members of the conference.

[59] The *coetus* expressed the matter forcefully: "The final decision about the necessity or usefulness of celebrating [plenary] councils...belongs to the Holy See." *Comm* 14 (1982) 192. The reason for this reservation is that the celebration of such a council "involves the exercise of supradiocesan power—especially legislative—which goes beyond the ambit of the power of the individual bishops or even the episcopal conference." Ibid.

[60] The requirement of Holy See approval is expressed as an ablative absolute using a present active participle indicating simultaneity between the activity of the Holy See (giving approval) and that of the conference (deeming the celebration of a council useful).

[61] Nor does the code make explicit provision for the participation in the council of the papal representative to the country for which the plenary council is being celebrated. When discussing the first draft of the canon on participants in particular councils, the *coetus* was unable to achieve consensus about the presence or the voting status of the papal legate.

Cf. *Comm* 17 (1985) 100. The *coetus* apparently decided not to mention the legate's potential participation (cf. c. 193 of the 1977 schema). Because a papal representative would ordinarily be one of the "titular bishops who perform in the territory a special function" (cf. c. 443, §1, 3°), one might conclude that he should be invited and would enjoy a deliberative vote. On the other hand, unlike other titular bishops with special functions in the territory (cf. c. 450, §1), the papal legate is not by law a member of the episcopal conference (c. 450, §2). Thus, the other bishops who must be invited to the plenary council are *de iure* members of the conference. If the legislator had intended the legate, who was not a *de iure* member of the conference convoking the plenary council, to be the only *de iure* participant in that council, would he not have expressed his intention more clearly? Other commentators take no position on this question.

[62] Provost, "Particular Councils," 547, observes, "For provinces in approximately forty-eight nations, provincial councils are equivalent to plenary councils because the province and nation are coterminous." He also notes that "in forty-three nations it would be possible to have a national synod even though no provincial or plenary council could be held there, since there is only one diocese and it is coterminous with the national boundaries." The law makes no special provisions for this situation.

cal province is to be celebrated whenever it seems opportune in the judgment of the majority of the diocesan bishops of the province, without prejudice to can. 439, §2.

Canon 283 of the 1917 code, the source of this canon, required the celebration of a provincial council at least once every twenty years. It came from a long line of unfortunately futile laws mandating the frequent celebration of particular councils. This new canon leaves the decision about the celebration of a provincial council to the wisdom of a majority of the diocesan bishops of the province.[63] The canon implies a definition of a *provincial* council: an official gathering of representatives of all the particular churches within a single ecclesiastical province.

§2. When a metropolitan see is vacant, a provincial council is not to be convoked.

Canon 284 of the 1917 code envisaged the celebration of a provincial council when the metropolitan see was vacant or impeded. In that event, the suffragan who was most senior by reason of his appointment to a suffragan see assumed the responsibilities of the non-existent or incapacitated metropolitan. This new canon simply forbids the celebration of a provincial council when there is no metropolitan.

Authority over Particular Councils

Canon 441 — It is for the conference of bishops:
  1° to convoke a plenary council;
  2° to select the place to celebrate the council within the territory of the conference of bishops;
  3° to select from among the diocesan bishops a president of the plenary council whom the Apostolic See must approve;
  4° to determine the agenda and questions to be treated, set the opening and duration of a plenary council, transfer, extend, and dissolve it.

This canon, a conflation and reworking of material found in canons 281 and 288 of the 1917 code, details some[64] of the rights and the duties of the episcopal conference vis à vis a plenary council celebrated for its territory. According to the former code, the ordinaries of several provinces could petition the pope for permission to celebrate a plenary council. The pope would then appoint a legate to convoke and preside over the council. In the current law, it is the prerogative of the conference, after obtaining approval from the Holy See (c. 439, §1), to convoke the plenary council and to select its president (who must be a diocesan bishop and requires Roman approval).[65] The Pio-Benedictine Code authorized the president —i.e., the papal legate—to set the agenda and to open, transfer, prorogue, or end the council. These rights and duties now belong to the conference. While the decision to convoke the council, the selection of its site, the specification of its opening and (anticipated) closing sessions, and the election of the president might all take place before

---

[63] By virtue of c. 381, §2, territorial prelates, territorial abbots, apostolic vicars, apostolic prefects, and apostolic administrators appointed on a stable basis (c. 368) are included in the term *diocesan bishops,* as are diocesan administrators by virtue of c. 427, §1. Note, however, the different terminology in c. 442, §1: "with the consent of the majority of the *suffragan* bishops...."

[64] V., 2. of the "Regulations for the II Plenary Synod" issued (with Roman approval) by the Polish Episcopal Conference lists other prerogatives of the conference— e.g., determining the composition of synodal commissions, supervising the work of those commissions, and the like (*Ius Ecclesiae* 5 [1993] 404–405). Hence, the list in c. 441 must represent a minimal description of the conference's authority, not the maximum extent of its scope.

[65] While commendably reflecting the English language's aversion to the passive voice, the translation of c. 441, 3° might give the impression that the canon imposes on the Holy See an obligation to approve the candidate. The Latin uses the gerundive: "*praesidem...approbandum.*" The sense is that the candidate needs papal approval before he can function as president. The Holy See is quite free to reject the candidate.

the council begins, decisions about transferring it, prolonging its celebration, or ending it early could be made only during or between its sessions. It would therefore seem prudent for the conference to make provisions for going into plenary session should the situation of the plenary council so require.[66]

Canon 442 — §1. It is for the metropolitan with the consent of the majority of the suffragan bishops:
1° to convoke a provincial council;
2° to select the place to celebrate the provincial council within the territory of the province;
3° to determine the agenda and questions to be treated, set the opening and duration of the provincial council, transfer, extend, and dissolve it.
§2. It is for the metropolitan or, if he is legitimately impeded, a suffragan bishop elected by the other suffragan bishops to preside over a provincial council.

This canon, which reworks material found in canons 284 and 288 of the 1917 code, specifies the rights and duties of the metropolitan vis-à-vis a particular council for his province. There are a few significant differences between the codes.

(1) The 1917 code provided for the holding of a provincial council during the vacancy of the metropolitan see. In that event, the suffragan most senior in terms of appointment to a suffragan see had the right and duty to convoke the council, to determine where it would be celebrated, and to preside over the council (*CIC* 284). The 1983 code prohibits the celebration of a provincial council when the metropolitan see is vacant (c. 440, §2).

(2) The 1983 code allows the suffragans to elect the council president if the metropolitan is legitimately prevented from acting.[67] As has just been noted, the 1917 code prescribed that the senior suffragan would act in the absence or incapacity of the metropolitan (*CIC* 284).

(3) The 1917 code authorized the *president,* who might be the metropolitan or might be the senior suffragan, to set the agenda and open, transfer, prorogue, or end the council (*CIC* 288). The 1983 code attributes these rights and duties, not to the *president,* but to the metropolitan (c. 442, §1, 2° and 3°). If councils were celebrated more frequently, this change might occasion some difficulty: a metropolitan might convoke a provincial council, determine its venue, and set its agenda, but then fall sick. The suffragans could elect a president; but would he be able to extend the council for another session, transfer it to a more convenient locale, or conclude it earlier than anticipated? The senior suffragan unquestionably had this authority under the 1917 code. The 1983 code has achieved a stylistically more elegant formulation at the cost of leaving this question unanswered.

(4) The 1917 code did not require the *consent* of the suffragans before the metropolitan (or senior suffragan) convoked a council. Presumably, the requirement that a council be celebrated at

---

[66] Cf. Section 1, 1, of the "Second Plenary Council of the Philippines Directory": "The Conference may exercise its pertinent prerogatives at any time even during the very celebration of the council. Hence, duly convoked, the Conference can legitimately meet emergency situations and respond to contingencies." *Ius Ecclesiae* 6 (1994) 814.

[67] Provost, in *CLSA Com,* 359, notes that "'legitimate' reasons are not necessarily physical; given the pastoral emphasis in the code, pastoral reasons may be sufficient for a metropolitan to consider himself legitimately impeded." One of the suffragans, for example, might be more able to cope with the demands of presiding or might be more skilled at doing so. Read, in *CLSGBI Com,* 242, points to the definition of an *impeded* see found in c. 412: the bishop is *completely* prevented from exercising his pastoral ministry because of imprisonment, banishment, exile, or incapacity. The canon adds a particular measure of the incapacity: the poor man is unable to communicate even by letter. Read does allow that ill-health might also prove an impediment. His conclusion, "if he is both willing and able to preside, then the suffragans cannot prevent him," is well-taken; but Provost's point —that a lesser incapacity might induce him to see himself as incapable—also deserves consideration.

least every twenty years (c. 283) was sufficient warrant for his acting. Before he determined its meeting place, however, the convoker needed to *hear* (not *obtain the consent of*) all who were obliged to participate with a deliberative vote (c. 284, 1°). Moreover, before the president determined the order of discussion, etc., he needed "the consent of the Fathers." In the new discipline the metropolitan requires the *consent* of the majority of the suffragans (who are not the only participants obliged to participate with deliberative vote) before doing any of this.[68]

(5) The 1917 code expressed some preference for the celebration of a provincial council in the metropolitan's see (*metropolitana ecclesia ne negligatur*). However, this preference has disappeared from the new code.

The current canon enhances the suffragans' responsibility for the preparation for and development of a provincial council. The metropolitan, except as the presiding officer during sessions,

[68] While lucidly phrased, the canon leaves some room for puzzlement here. (1) The metropolitan is a *diocesan* bishop but not a *suffragan* bishop. Canon 440, §1 requires the celebration of a provincial council whenever a majority of the *diocesan* bishops of the province deems it opportune, but c. 442, §1 allows the metropolitan to convoke a provincial council only with the consent of a majority of the *suffragan* bishops. In a province containing an odd number of dioceses, the anomalous situation could arise in which c. 440, §1 would require the celebration of a council (because the metropolitan and half of the suffragans thought it prudent) but c. 442, §1 would not authorize the metropolitan to convoke it (because only half of the suffragans would consent). (2) A related question arises about those who are not diocesan bishops but who preside over particular churches. They are equivalent to diocesan bishops in law. One presumes that, although they are not "suffragan bishops," they should be included in the tally required by c. 442, §1. Read, in *CLSGBI Com,* 247, argues to the contrary: "The term suffragan Bishop must be understood as a corollary of the 'suffragan dioceses' of Can. 436. Territorial prelatures, vicariates and prefectures are not suffragan dioceses, even though they are linked to a province; thus, it would appear that the prelate, even if in fact a Bishop, does not have a voting right at this preliminary stage." Other commentators do not address this issue.

acts only in concert with his brother bishops. The provincial council is clearly not an instrument whereby the metropolitan accomplishes his own objectives, however praiseworthy. It is instead a vehicle whereby the leaders of all the particular churches in the province, with due regard for appropriate input from a representative cross-section of the members of their dioceses, exercise collectively their responsibility for the faithful.

Participants in Particular Councils

Canon 443 — §1. The following must be called to particular councils and have the right of a deliberative vote in them:
    1° diocesan bishops;
    2° coadjutor and auxiliary bishops;
    3° other titular bishops who perform in the territory a special function committed to them by the Apostolic See or the conference of bishops.
  §2. Other titular bishops, even retired ones, living in the territory can be called to particular councils; they also have the right of a deliberative vote.
  §3. The following must be called to particular councils but with only a consultative vote:
    1° the vicars general and episcopal vicars of all the particular churches in the territory;
    2° major superiors of religious institutes and societies of apostolic life in a number for both men and women which the conference of bishops or the bishops of the province are to determine; these superiors are to be elected respectively by all the major superiors of the institutes and societies which have a seat in the territory;
    3° rectors of ecclesiastical and Catholic universities and deans of faculties of theology and of canon law, which have a seat in the territory;
    4° some rectors of major seminaries elected by the rectors of the seminaries which are located in the territory, in a number to be determined as in n. 2.
  §4. Presbyters and other members of the Christian faithful can also be called to particular

councils, but with only a consultative vote and in such a way that their number does not exceed half the number of those mentioned in §§1–3.

§5. Moreover, cathedral chapters and the presbyteral council and pastoral council of each particular church are to be invited to provincial councils in such a way that each of them sends two of their members designated collegially by them; however, they have only a consultative vote.

§6. Others can also be invited as guests to particular councils, if it is expedient in the judgment of the conference of bishops for a plenary council, or of the metropolitan together with the suffragan bishops for a provincial council.

The 1917 code dealt separately with participants in plenary (*CIC* 282) and provincial (*CIC* 286) councils. This canon lists those who must or may be invited to particular councils, allowing for adaptations to fit the circumstances.

The canon distinguishes participants (§§1–5) from guests (§6), participants who must be invited (§§1, 3, and 5) from participants who may be invited (§§2, 4), and participants who can both speak and vote (§§1–2) from participants who can speak but cannot vote (§§3–5).

The possibility of inviting *guests* was not considered in the 1917 code. Paragraph six may be a happy result of the experience of having observers at Vatican II and sessions of the synod of bishops. The text clearly distinguishes these guests (*etiam alii*) from the bishops, clerics, and lay persons who can be invited but have no legal right to be summoned. The conclusion seems inescapable that these guests are not to be regarded as participants in conciliar discussions.[69]

The only participants who can vote on questions the council seeks to answer are the bishops (§§1–2) and those—including administrators of

vacant dioceses—who are legally equivalent to diocesan bishops. Voting is seen as so bound up with the bishop's leadership role that any bishop who is invited to participate must be allowed to vote. All other participants in a council have the right to speak, but not to vote.

The participants who must be invited to the council include at least representatives of all those who exercise a supervisory role over the pastoral activities of the Church within the territory for which the council is being celebrated. Thus, the list of those who must be invited includes all bishops who are officially ministering within the territory, all vicars general and other episcopal vicars, elected representatives of the major superiors of religious congregations "which have a seat in the territory," all rectors of Catholic and ecclesiastical universities and deans of faculties of theology and canon law, elected representatives of rectors of major seminaries in the territory, and two representatives from each cathedral chapter (where these exist), presbyteral council, and diocesan pastoral council within the territory. Even if only those who must be invited were invited to a particular council, it seems inevitable that there would be lay participation: among the members should be at least some representatives from religious congregations of women as well as some lay members of diocesan pastoral councils.

In addition, the council could invite the participation of retired bishops, bishops who, although actually within the territory, are not engaged in pastoral work there, and a restricted number[70] of priests[71] and lay persons.

---

[69] Provost, in *CLSA Com,* 361; also Read, in *CLSGBI Com,* 249. The latter prudently adds, "This does not, however, mean that they might not be invited to speak to the assembly if they would wish to do so; on the contrary, at least courtesy would require that they ought to be so invited and, if they accept, that their expressions of opinion or advice be given careful attention."

[70] The method of calculating their number is somewhat cumbersome. One adds the number of bishops, vicars, religious superiors, and academics (but not the number of representatives from cathedral chapters, presbyteral councils, and pastoral councils) and divides the sum by two. Fewer than that number may be invited. Although the commentaries do not analyze the reasons for limiting the number of additional participants, Provost, "Particular Councils," 549, does allude to "the danger of pressure groups attempting to take over a gathering."

[71] Canon 282, §3 of the 1917 code envisaged the invitation of religious or secular *clerics*—a broader term than

This canon suggests that a particular council will be a sizable gathering. If only those who must be invited are summoned, each diocese would send at least one bishop, one vicar general, two members of the priests' council, and two members of the pastoral council; and there would be religious and some academics as well. Moreover, the heterogeneous makeup of the council makes it evident that the council is a gathering of particular *churches,* not merely a gathering of the clergy who minister to those particular churches. Such widespread participation ought to ensure that the bishops who actually vote within the council will have a breadth and depth of information that otherwise might not be available to them.

Duties of Participants

Canon 444 — §1. All who are called to particular councils must attend them unless they are prevented by a just impediment, about which they are bound to inform the president of the council.

This canon, for which no exact parallel existed in the 1917 code, specifies two obligations incumbent on all who are invited to a particular council: (1) they must participate; and (2) if unable to participate because of a *just* impediment, they must inform the president of their reason for being absent.[72] Canon 286, §4 of the former code

stated that invited major superiors of exempt religious or monastic congregations were obliged either to participate or to notify the council of their reason for non-attendance. Canon 289 forbade anyone who was obliged to participate in a council from leaving after it had begun unless he had proven either to the legate (in the case of a plenary council) or to the "Fathers" (in the case of a provincial council) his just reason for leaving. With respect to the right and duty to participate, the new code does not discriminate among participants. It thereby implies that the anticipated contributions of all the participants will be of great value. Invitations to a council are not arbitrary. Either the law itself (in the case of those who must be invited) or the bishops who are convoking the council (in the case of those who may be invited) consider the involvement of all the invited participants to be essential to the proper development of the conciliar process.[73]

Although the code's treatment of particular councils says nothing about the style of any member's participation, it may not be amiss to advert to canon 465 on the diocesan synod: "All proposed questions are subject to the free discussion of the members during sessions of the synod." This canon implies that all members of a diocesan synod have the right and the duty to contribute

---

priests, especially within that discipline. According to c. 108, §1 of the former code, anyone who had received at least first tonsure was a cleric. On the assumption that the code does not want to exclude the participation of permanent deacons, one might urge that they, too, could be invited as participants.

[72] The canon provides that one might be excused from the obligation of participation in a council if prevented "by a just impediment." Read, in *CLSGBI Com,* 249, offers as examples of a "just impediment": "illness, a serious commitment which cannot without harm be abandoned or postponed, [or] an urgent personal or familial situation." The canon says nothing about joining the deliberations after the council has begun (i.e., after the impediment has ceased). Unlike the 1917 code (*CIC* 298), it has no stipulations with regard to leaving early.

[73] For Arrieta (in *Pamplona ComEng,* 337), non-voting participants in a council "do not properly exercise a function of governance as such; their votes are merely consultative." Two contrary observations come to mind. (1) Canon 129, §2, states that "lay members of the Christian faithful can cooperate in the exercise of [the] power" of governance. According to c. 445, the particular council (not just certain members of it) enjoys the power of governance. Does not this imply that all of the members of such a council at least "cooperate in the exercise" of this same power? (2) Much more is involved in reaching a decision than simply making the choice. Cf. R. Kennedy, "Shared Responsibility in Ecclesial Decision Making," *Stud Can* 14 (1980) 5–23. To speak of the participation of non-voting members as "merely consultative" surely undermines the influence of background research, the formulation of proposals, the expression of arguments, and the like. See the balanced exposition in Provost, "Particular Councils," 549–550.

freely and intelligently to the discussion of all issues on the agenda. If the Christian faithful generally enjoy the right "to make known to the pastors of the Church their needs, especially spiritual ones, and their desires" (c. 212, §2), this right becomes particularly urgent within a council whose very purpose is to make "provision . . . for the pastoral needs of the people of God" (c. 445). Canon 212, §3 goes further: "According to the knowledge, competence, and prestige which they possess, they have the right and even at times the duty to manifest to the sacred pastors their opinion on matters which pertain to the good of the Church." From the fact that they have been invited to a particular council, one must infer that all the participants have the requisite "knowledge, competence, and prestige" and that they therefore have both the right and the duty to contribute freely to the conciliar discussions.[74]

§2. Those who are called to particular councils and have a deliberative vote in them can send a proxy if they are prevented by a just impediment; the proxy has only a consultative vote.

Although the cooperation of all the members of a particular council is important, the role of those whose vote determines the outcome is decisive. As noted above, the only voting members of a council are bishops or those legally equivalent to diocesan bishops. Not only are they presumably exceptionally gifted with faith, zeal, wisdom, and the like (cf. c. 378, §1, 1°), and not only are they endowed by episcopal ordination with a peculiar charism for guiding the flock, but they also, as chief shepherds of particular churches or titular bishops charged with other pastoral responsibilities within the territory, will be responsible for implementing the decisions of the council. This canon accordingly recognizes the special importance of the input from bishops. It allows the

bishop who is invited to a council but unable to attend to send a proxy.[75] The proxy may speak and may therefore convey to the council the insights of the absent bishop, but he or she may not vote.[76]

Authority of Particular Councils

Canon 445 — A particular council, for its own territory, takes care that provision is made for the pastoral needs of the people of God and possesses the power of governance, especially legislative power, so that, always without prejudice to the universal law of the Church, it is able to decide what seems opportune for the increase of the faith, the organization of common pastoral action, and the regulation of morals and of the common ecclesiastical discipline which is to be observed, promoted, and protected.

This canon expresses more forcefully than canon 290 of the 1917 code the primary responsibility of a particular council and the authority it enjoys to fulfill that responsibility. The responsibility is stated in general terms: the council "takes care that provision is made for the pastoral needs of the people of God." One might broadly categorize such necessities as the Word, the sacraments, and good order; or one might look at the goods to which the faithful have a legally recognized right (see, for example, cc. 213, 214, 217, etc.). The

---

[74] Canon 127, §3 appears to be a parallel canon: "All those whose consent or counsel is required [before a superior places a juridic act] are obliged to offer their opinion sincerely."

[75] The canon prescribes no necessary qualifications for serving as a proxy. It does not, in other words, exclude non-bishops or even non-clerics from assuming this function.

[76] In denying a deliberative vote to the proxy, the canon echoes c. 287, §2 of the 1917 code. The *coetus* apparently agreed with its secretary's fear that it might be somehow dangerous to give proxies a deliberative vote (*Comm* 12 [1980] 261). The commentaries do not analyze the reason for not allowing proxies to vote. The canon does not distinguish between proxies who are bishops (e.g., a retired auxiliary representing a diocesan bishop) and proxies who are not. Presumably it would make such a distinction if the lack of episcopal character were the reason for not allowing the proxies to vote.

point is that the purposes of a particular council are conceived in the broadest possible terms. The canon indicates two limitations: (a) the direct concern of the council is the territory for which the council was convoked; and (b) the universal laws of the Church may limit the options the council considers.

To meet these broad obligations the council has equally broad powers. It enjoys "the power of governance, especially legislative power."[77] *Regimen,* literally, "governmental power," is that species of the sacred power with which the Church is endowed which functions primarily in the external forum (c. 130) and supports the Church's ministry of ruling/serving.[78] Canon 135, §1 divides governmental power into legislative, executive, and judicial power. Councils have historically fulfilled a variety of governmental functions, including judicial; but they have been especially effective as legislative bodies. According to this canon, a particular council enjoys the sacred power necessary to do whatever seems appropriate: (a) to foster the growth of faith; (b) to coordinate common pastoral action; and (c) to preserve the good order and moral health of the community.[79] This phrasing of the council's aims is considerably more positive than the one found in canon 290 of the 1917 code: "to moderate morals, to correct abuses, to resolve controversies, and to preserve or bring about one and the same discipline." Councils have effectively corrected abuses and resolved controversies; but they might also be summoned, not to fix what is broken, but to foster conditions in which an already healthy community might become still more vital.

Conciliar Decrees

Canon 446 — When a particular council has ended, the president is to take care that all the acts of the council are sent to the Apostolic See. Decrees issued by a council are not to be promulgated until the Apostolic See has reviewed them. It is for the council itself to define the manner of promulgation of the decrees and the time when the promulgated decrees begin to oblige.

This slight revision of canon 291, §1 of the 1917 code[80] contains three somewhat related clauses.

(1) It imposes on the president an obligation to forward to the Holy See all of the acts of the council. This requirement can be viewed as an attempt on the part of the Holy See to oversee the activities of bishops. It can also be seen as a recognition of communion: what happens in every particular

---

[77] It is interesting that c. 447, concerning the nature and purpose of the episcopal conference, speaks of "pastoral functions" (*munera . . . pastoralia*) rather than governmental power. By the same token, c. 455 tightly circumscribes the legislative capacity of the conference.

[78] Particular councils have also issued authoritative teachings, as c. 753 recognizes (cf. the commentary), but one may question whether authentic *teaching* is an exercise of *governmental* power: "In the church there is *an authority to teach, a doctrinal authority;* it is the authority to proclaim the Word. In the Church there is also an *authority to impose an action,* which is mostly known under the name of *juridical authority.* The task of the former is to communicate knowledge that saves; the task of the latter is to establish well-measured balances in the community . . . so that all can live, pray, and work in peace. . . . There is a radical difference between affirming the truth and imposing an action." L. Örsy, "Teaching Authority of Episcopal Conferences," in *Episcopal Conferences: Historical, Canonical and Theological Studies,* ed. T. Reese (Washington, D.C.: Georgetown University, 1989) 241.

[79] The canons dealing with an ecumenical council (cc. 337–341) contain no description of the scope of that institute's authority. A parallel canon concerning the diocesan synod (c. 460) provides a similarly vague description of its purposes: to "offer assistance to the diocesan bishop for the good of the whole diocesan community."

[80] Canon 290, §2 of the 1917 code was suppressed. Its first clause stated the obvious: that the laws made by a particular council bind everywhere within the territory (cf. c. 12, §3). Its second clause denied to local ordinaries the power to dispense from them "except in particular cases and for a just cause." Canon 87, §1 of the current code already provides that the diocesan bishop, "whenever he judges that it contributes to their spiritual good," *can* dispense the faithful from such laws."

church is of interest to other particular churches, and particular churches most easily reinforce their communion with each other by tending to their communion with the church of Rome.

(2) The canon requires a *recognitio* from the Holy See before any laws issued by the particular council can be promulgated.[81] If universal law limits the legislative competence of a particular council, then someone needs to review the proposed legislation of a particular council to ensure that it does not conflict with universal law.[82] Because a particular council does not enjoy the power to legislate against the universal law of the Church, any attempted enactments of this sort would be invalid. Thus, the request for *recognitio* can eliminate the danger of invalid legislation.

(3) The canon recognizes the right and duty of the particular council to determine how its laws should be promulgated and when (after their promulgation) they should become effective. The act of promulgation gives birth to a law as law (c. 7). Because the council rather than the Holy See promulgates the law, the *recognitio* does not translate a conciliar decree into papal legislation. A particular council does not propose that the pope legislate on certain questions affecting the pertinent particular churches but prepares such legislation on its own initiative. Once the proper dicastery has given its *recognitio,* the council promulgates its own decrees. They remain, from first to last, conciliar rather than papal acts.[83]

CHAPTER IV
CONFERENCES OF BISHOPS
[cc. 447–459]

Nearly one hundred fifty years ago Belgium's bishops began meeting regularly at the archbishop's residence in Mechlin.[84] Thus, without further

---

[81] For a balanced and thorough analysis of the *recognitio,* cf. J. Manzanares, "Papal Reservation and *Recognitio:* Considerations and Proposals," *J* 52 (1992) 228–254, especially 234–239. The author argues that the institute ensures that the decrees of a particular council will be free from error and not imprudent or harmful to the universal Church (235).

[82] Provost (in *CLSA Com,* 362, and "Particular Councils," 554–555) sketches some serious difficulties that have emerged from the *recognitio* process. "It has also been used," he reports, "for other purposes, including that of imposing on local churches a discipline which they themselves had not voted to assume" (*CLSA Com,* 362). This would appear to constitute a perversion of the institute. *Recognitio* can safeguard the communion of the universal Church by preventing one group of particular churches from adopting practices that would be disruptive of the harmony of the whole; such is the value the law seems designed to serve. However, using the process to impose on the faithful practices they did not dream of assuming is likely to provoke disharmony between the universal Church and the pertinent group of particular churches.

[83] The laws would not begin to bind until the *vacatio legis* has elapsed (i.e., one month from the date of promulgation, unless the law itself determines otherwise). See the commentary on c. 8, §2. Unless the law in question was a personal law or its violation would cause harm in their own territory (cf. c. 13, §2, 1°), travelers are not bound by the council's legislation when they are away from the territory under the council's jurisdiction (cf. c. 12, §3). See the pertinent commentary on the canons on ecclesiastical laws.

[84] Easily accessible histories of episcopal conferences include: Provost, in *CLSA Com,* 363–364; P. Huizing, "The Structure of Episcopal Conferences," *J* 28 (1968) 163–176; R. Kutner, *The Development, Structure, and Competence of the Episcopal Conference* (Washington, D.C.: Catholic University of America, 1972) 1–64. Good accounts of the particular councils which performed similar functions earlier are: H.-J. Sieben, "Episcopal Conferences in Light of Particular Councils during the First Millennium," *J* 48 (1988) 30–56; A. García y García, "Episcopal Conferences in Light of Particular Councils during the Second Millennium," *J* 48 (1988) 57–67; B. Daley, "Structures of Charity: Bishops' Gatherings and the See of Rome in the Early Church," in Reese, *Episcopal Conferences,* 25–58. Good accounts of the history of the NCCB include E. McKeon, "The National Bishops' Conference: an Analysis of Its Origins," *Catholic Historical Review* 66 (1980) 565–583; G. Fogarty, "The Authority of the National Catholic Welfare Conference," in Reese, *Episcopal Conferences,* 85–103; E. McKeon, "The 'National Idea' in the History of the American Episcopal Conference," in Reese, *Episcopal Conferences,* 59–84.

ado, began what evolved into the episcopal conference. Within a few years the bishops of Germany, of Bavaria, of Austria, of Italy, and of Ireland were following suit. Often with explicit papal encouragement, such national assemblies of bishops became widespread in the late nineteenth century. Changing circumstances—revolutions, economic dislocations, the dominance of secular liberalism, etc.—posed problems for which bishops sought common solutions; and these gatherings provided a convenient forum for exchanging information and opinions on such problems. Given their fortunate experience of this institute which had developed without specific legal warrant, it is not surprising that the Fathers of Vatican II chose to give formal status to the conference:

> Nowadays especially, bishops are frequently unable to fulfill their office suitably and fruitfully unless they work more harmoniously and closely every day with other bishops. Episcopal conferences, already established in many nations, have furnished outstanding proofs of more fruitful apostolate. Therefore, this most sacred Synod considers it supremely opportune everywhere that bishops belonging to the same nation or region form an association and meet together at fixed times. Thus, when the insights of prudence and experience have been shared and views exchanged, there will emerge a holy union of energies in the service of the common good of the churches.[85]

Although there was widespread agreement about the good conferences could do, there was no unanimity about other issues such as their theological status.[86] Good laws should reflect sound

theological reflection, but a canonical commentary is not the place to discuss controversies concerning the theological status of the institute[87] or the limits of its teaching authority[88] or other more technical questions.[89] Suffice it to say that two sources of suspicion of the conference have left their fingerprints on the canons of this chapter. On the one hand, there is fear that conferences might become seedbeds of nationalism or other attempts to undermine papal authority over the universal Church. On the other hand, there is

sensus . . . in affirming the 'pastoral usefulness' or even more the 'necessity' of episcopal conferences for the Church in the present circumstances and on the other hand there is a great disparity of opinions when it is a question of clarifying their theological status more precisely."

[87] See John Paul II, *aplett Apostolos suos,* May 21, 1998, *Origins* 28 (1998) 152. See also R. Lettmann, "Episcopal Conferences in the New Canon Law," *Stud Can* 14 (1980) 349–355; J. Komonchak, "Episcopal Conferences," *CS* 27 (1988) 311–328; A. Antón, 185–212, with a comprehensive bibliography on 213–219.

[88] Thoughtful essays on this issue include J. Manzanares, "The Teaching Authority of Episcopal Conferences," *J* 48 (1988) 234–263; A. Dulles, "Doctrinal Authority of Episcopal Conferences," in Reese, *Episcopal Conferences,* 207–232; L. Örsy, "Teaching Authority of Episcopal Conferences," in Reese, *Episcopal Conferences,* 233–252; J. Green, *Conferences of Bishops and the Exercise of the Munus Docendi of the Church* (Rome: Gregorian University, 1987); T. Green, "The Church's Teaching Mission: Some Aspects of the Normative Role of Episcopal Conferences," *Stud Can* 27 (1993) 23–57.

[89] The Final Report of the 1985 Second Extraordinary Assembly of the Synod of Bishops called for further study of the nature and authority of episcopal conferences (cf. *Origins* 15 [1985] 449: "It is hoped that the study of their theological 'status' and above all the problem of their doctrinal authority might be made explicit in a deeper and more extensive way"). In response, the CFB prepared a "working paper" (*instrumentum laboris*) which was circulated in 1988 (cf. *Origins* 17 [1988] 731–737). Some sense of the complexity of the questions involved emerges from reviewing this document in conjunction with the excellent collection in Reese, *Episcopal Conferences* and the papers from the Salamanca colloquium on the nature of episcopal conferences (*J* 48 [1988] 1–407).

[85] *CD* 37; *AAS* 58 (1966) 693. *ES* I, 41, §1 required that conferences be quickly (*quam cito*) established where they were not in existence.

[86] Cf. A. Antón, "The Theological 'Status' of Episcopal Conferences," *J* 48 (1988) 185–186: "It can appear paradoxical that on the one hand there is a general con-

concern that the conferences might unduly limit the divine law authority each bishop enjoys within in his own diocese.

The thirteen canons in this chapter are not easy to outline. Canon 447 provides a descriptive definition of the conference. Canon 449 indicates how the conference comes into being. Canons 448 and 450 discuss the makeup of the conference, territorially and personally. Canon 451 requires each conference to prepare its own statutes and provides some guidelines about their contents. Canons 452, 457, and 458 deal with officers each conference must have. Canons 453 through 456 treat the plenary session of the conference, prescribing its minimum frequency, the voting rights of some members, the limits of its legislative authority, and the aftermath of its deliberations. Canon 459 discusses the implications of interactions among conferences.

Christus Dominus 38 is the source from which most of these canons were quarried. Some few modifications were inspired by general legal principles and by attempts to quiet fears of the conference's potential influence. Although the law envisages the participation in the conference by Eastern hierarchs, the institute has evolved as a creature of the Latin church;[90] and although there are certain similarities between conferences and Eastern patriarchal synods, there are no exact parallels for these canons in the Eastern code.

Definition

Canon 447 — A conference of bishops, a permanent institution, is a group of bishops of some nation or certain territory who jointly exercise certain pastoral functions for the Christian faithful of their territory in order to promote the greater good which the Church offers to humanity, especially through forms and programs of the apostolate fittingly adapted to the circumstances of time and place, according to the norm of law.

This canon is derived almost verbatim from *Christus Dominus* 38, 1: "An episcopal conference is a kind of council in which the bishops of a given nation or territory jointly exercise their pastoral office by way of promoting that greater good which the Church offers mankind, especially through forms and programs of the apostolate which are fittingly adapted to the circumstances of the age."[91] The canon slightly modifies the conciliar text.

(1) Unlike *Christus Dominus* it classifies the conference as a *permanent institution.* Canon 449, §2 states that a legitimately erected conference enjoys juridic personality *ipso iure,* and every juridic person is perpetual by nature (c. 120, §1). During the revision process, there arose a question regarding how an institute that exists only when its members are meeting could be called *permanent.* The secretary of the drafting committee replied that a conference is permanent because it has a permanent secretariat and standing commissions.[92]

(2) Unlike *Christus Dominus,* the canon mentions "the Christian faithful of their territory" as the beneficiaries of the bishops' pastoral ministry. Canon 383, §3, however, directs the diocesan bishop to conduct himself with *humanitas* and love toward his sisters and brothers who are not in full communion with the Catholic Church. Canon 383, §4 commends to his loving attention the unbaptized who live within his territory. At least indirectly, non-Catholics are subjects of an individual bishop's pastoral concern; and canon 447 surely does not intend to deny episcopal conferences the right and duty to minister to them.

(3) The canon qualifies the purpose of the conference with the phrase *ad normam iuris*— "according to the norm of law." The qualification

---

[90] *ApS,* n. 1, explicitly differentiates between Eastern synods and episcopal conferences: "The Oriental Churches headed by Patriarchs and Major Archbishops are governed by their respective Synods of Bishops, endowed with legislative, judicial and, in certain cases, administrative power... the present document does not deal with these. Hence, no analogy may be drawn between such Synods and episcopal Conferences."

[91] *AAS* 70 (1968) 693.
[92] *Comm* 12 (1980) 263. See Arrieta, in *Pamplona ComEng,* 339.

might have no particular meaning: every legal institute acts according to the law. It might also reflect a concern to prevent the conference from enjoying too broad a governmental competency, especially in legislative areas.[93]

The canon is a lengthy, densely packed definition. It states what a conference is: a permanent assembly of the bishops from a defined territory. It indicates what the bishops do: they collaborate in meeting the needs of their flocks.[94] It gives the reason for their doing so: they wish to promote, not just the "common good" which earthly governments seek, but the greater good—the salvation of souls (cf. c. 1752)—which the Church offers to all. It prescribes the method they adopt in pursuing their goals: they accommodate their pastoral activities to changing circumstances of time and place. The canon does not describe the nature or the limits of the legislative power of this institute. These matters are dealt with in canon 455.

Territorial Limits

Canon 448 — §1. As a general rule, a conference of bishops includes those who preside over all the particular churches of the same nation, according to the norm of can. 450.

---

[93] The *coetus* was unanimous in not wanting the conference to develop into an intrusive bureaucracy—a curia between the diocesan curia and the Roman Curia. Cf. *Comm* 12 (1980) 263. Even as late as the 1980 schema bishops were worrying that the powers of the conference might unduly limit the legitimate authority of the individual bishops. Cf. *Comm* 14 (1982) 195–196.

[94] Arrieta, in *Pamplona ComEng,* 339, writes that "conferences of bishops should not only be conceived as bodies of legislative centralization and collective power of governance..., but as organs enabling bishops to cooperate in their ministry...so that their individual responsibility may be better fulfilled through the counsel and experiences of others." He rightly warns against a preoccupation with issues of power to the exclusion of issues of service. Similarly, Gutiérrez, 356, stresses that the purpose of the conference is to express *communio.* It facilitates an exchange of views and experiences among bishops so that each might better exercise his own authority in his own diocese.

§2. If, however, in the judgment of the Apostolic See, having heard the diocesan bishops concerned, the circumstances of persons or things suggest it, a conference of bishops can be erected for a territory of lesser or greater area, so that it only includes either bishops of some particular churches constituted in a certain territory or those who preside over particular churches in different nations. It is for the Apostolic See to establish special norms for each of them.

The preceding canon left unanswered two important questions about the make-up of the conference: who are included in the term *bishops* (*coetus episcoporum*), and what are the limits of the territory from which they come? This canon, inspired by *Christus Dominus* 38, 2, answers the second question. Canon 450 answers the first.

Paragraph one prescribes a rule to which paragraph two allows an exception. A conference usually consists of the chief shepherds of all and only the particular churches of a single nation. Canon 450, §1 indicates the persons to be included in the category "those who preside over... particular churches."

There are two possible deviations from the general rule: (a) a conference might include some rather than all the diocesan bishops in a given nation; or (b) a conference might include the diocesan bishops of more than one nation. Paragraph two allows the erection of an episcopal conference for only some of the bishops of a nation (e.g., Puerto Rico, England and Wales) and for the bishops of more than one nation (e.g., Gambia, Liberia, and Sierra Leone).[95] *Christus Dominus* 38, 5 allowed *the bishops* of more than one nation to establish a single conference *with papal approval.* The code, by contrast, reserves to the Holy See the authority to establish, suppress, or alter episcopal conferences (cf. c. 449, §1). Hence, this canon attributes to the Holy See rather than to the concerned bishops the prerogative of deciding that the circumstances of the particular churches in ques-

---

[95] See Provost, "Particular Councils," 546, n. 33, for a list of conferences transcending national boundaries.

tion suggest not following national boundaries in determining the membership of the episcopal conference. The canon allows the Holy See wide latitude in making this determination: "*si adiuncta id suadeant*"—"if the circumstances so suggest"—not a particularly strong condition. The canon does prescribe that the affected bishops be consulted beforehand. This requirement recognizes that these men should be extremely well-informed about the "circumstances of persons or things" which justify the exceptional structuring of the conference in question.

Establishment and Legal Nature

Canon 449 — §1. It is only for the supreme authority of the Church to erect, suppress, or alter conferences of bishops, after having heard the bishops concerned.

The probable inspiration for this canon was canon 251, §1 of the 1917 code: "It is the sole prerogative of the supreme ecclesiastical power to erect, otherwise circumscribe, divide, unite, and/or suppress ecclesiastical provinces, dioceses, abbacies, and prelatures *nullius,* apostolic vicariates, and apostolic prefectures." The code has described the episcopal conference as a vehicle for the exercise of episcopal *munera.* Establishing, suppressing, or changing conferences is one way in which the supreme power coordinates the exercise of episcopal power for the good of the universal Church.[96]

§2. A legitimately erected conference of bishops possesses juridic personality by the law itself.

[96] Cf. Read, in *CLSGBI Com,* 251: "Although the origins of the Bishops' Conference lie in the spontaneous collaboration and communication between neighboring Bishops, the authority to establish, suppress, or alter the composition of these Conferences is reserved exclusively to the Holy See." Of course, the law did not recognize the "spontaneous gatherings" as subjects of *regimen.* Now that the conferences are seen as exercising sacred power, however, the Holy See is understandably concerned with coordinating their activity.

Without a forerunner in the 1917 code, this canon has parallels in canons 432, §2 (concerning ecclesiastical provinces) and 373 (concerning the diocese). The episcopal conference quite clearly fits the definition of a public juridic person: it is established by competent ecclesiastical authority (the Holy See) to fulfill in the name of the Church specific tasks entrusted to it for the public good (cf. c. 116, §1). Unlike such public juridic persons as a diocese or a religious congregation, however, the conference is not always "there"—i.e., it is not permanently in session. Between its assemblies one should think of the conference's legal personality as carried by its president, its general secretariat, its *permanent council* of bishops, and its various commissions.

Membership

Canon 450 — §1. To a conference of bishops belong by the law itself all diocesan bishops in the territory, those equivalent to them in law, coadjutor bishops, auxiliary bishops, and other titular bishops who perform in the same territory a special function entrusted to them by the Apostolic See or conference of bishops. Ordinaries of another rite can also be invited though in such a way that they have only a consultative vote unless the statutes of the conference of bishops decree otherwise.

§2. Other titular bishops and the legate of the Roman Pontiff are not by law members of a conference of bishops.

Derived from *Christus Dominus* 38, 2, this canon answers the question, who are included in the term *bishops* in the definition of the conference (*coetus episcoporum*)? By law the conference includes all those who preside over particular churches[97] *of the Latin church,* all coadjutor bishops (auxiliary bishops with the right of succession —c. 403, §3), all auxiliary bishops (titular bishops

[97] Arrieta, in *Pamplona ComEng,* 341, following c. 427, §1, notes that the diocesan administrator would be an *ipso iure* member of the conference.

appointed to assist a diocesan bishop in meeting the pastoral needs of the diocese—c. 403, §1), and all other titular bishops who have been entrusted either by the Holy See or by the conference itself with specific ministries within the territory.[98] *Christus Dominus* 38, 2 included within the *de iure* membership the local ordinaries of other rites. The code allows the conference to invite the participation of Eastern hierarchs and to determine their voting status.[99] The code's more circumspect approach[100] seems prudent, especially inasmuch as the conference has certain liturgical responsibilities (cf. cc. 838, §3; 851, 1°; 891; etc.) in the fulfillment of which Eastern pastors[101] might not wish to participate.

With the exception of non-bishops who preside over particular churches and are therefore on the same legal footing as bishops (cf. c. 381, §2), the

canon says nothing about participation in the conference by non-bishops. If the conference is a *coetus episcoporum,* it is logical not to expect non-bishops to be members; but if the conference is, as suggested by the rubric of this title of the code, a *coetus ecclesiarum particularium,* its membership should include more than just the chief shepherds.[102] According to an authentic interpretation of *Christus Dominus* 38, §2, priests, religious, and lay persons *can* be invited to participate in the conference, if the statutes so provide, "but only in individual matters and cases and with only a consultative vote."[103] This interpretation parallels the provisions of canon 443, §§3–5, concerning the kind of participation in particular councils allowed to non-bishops.

Paragraph two does not forbid a conference from inviting the participation of papal legates[104]

---

[98] Read, in *CLSGBI Com,* 252 helpfully suggests that two factors determine *ipso iure* membership in the conference: episcopal ordination and an office involving governing. "Of the two, the more significant is that of pastoral office; some titular Bishops, although obviously in episcopal orders, need not be invited... whereas a non-episcopal, territorial prelate or abbot has a right to attend with a deliberative vote."

[99] According to Article II, a), 1) of the Statutes of the NCCB, all diocesan bishops, coadjutors, and auxiliaries *of any rite* are *de iure* members of the conference. Eastern bishops can speak but cannot vote and are not counted as part of the quorum when questions affecting only the Latin church are being decided (Article IV, b). The Statutes of the Bishops' Conference of England and Wales invite the Apostolic Exarch for Ukrainians to accept membership (Article 3), but apparently without vote (cf. Articles 6 and 7). Article 2, 2) of the Statutes of the German Bishops' Conference offers consultative membership to those who preside over particular churches of the various Eastern churches *sui iuris.*

[100] This canon differs both from the conciliar decree and from the norm concerning episcopal participation in particular councils. According to c. 443, §2, any bishop invited to participate in a council has the right to a deliberative vote.

[101] Read, in *CLSGBI Com,* 252, sees "no reason why [Eastern] auxiliaries or titular Bishops" should not be invited. He cautions, however, that the conference "is essentially an institution for cooperation among Bishops belonging to the Latin Rite."

[102] J. Zizioulas, an Orthodox metropolitan, would argue to the contrary that the conference would function more clearly as a gathering of particular churches if its voting membership were restricted to diocesan bishops. He points to modern Orthodox synods in which only diocesan bishops take part but which are understood as gatherings of churches through their bishops. Cf. J. Zizioulas, "The Institution of Episcopal Conferences: An Orthodox Reflection," *J* 48 (1988) 377–378. His argument has many points of contact with the justification R. Castillo Lara offers for not allowing an auxiliary bishop to serve as president of an episcopal conference. Cf. R. Castillo Lara, 95–97.

[103] *AAS* 62 (1970) 793; *CLD* 7, 292. Arrieta, in *Pamplona ComEng,* 341 regards these non-bishops as *guests.* However, c. 443, §§4 and 6, a parallel canon concerning particular councils (cf. cc. 17 and 19), clearly distinguishes between non-episcopal, non-voting *participants,* on the one hand, and *guests,* on the other. Unlike such guests at particular councils, non-episcopal participants in a conference could have a consultative vote.

[104] Arrieta, in *Pamplona ComEng,* 341 points out that the papal legate "will attend the first meeting of each plenary session... and will be entitled to attend others if he is invited... or is sent by the Apostolic See (cf. *Comm* 17 [1985] 100)"; but his citation from *Comm* documents a *coetus* discussion of the participation of the papal legate in *particular councils.* Actual practice is diverse. According to Article VII of the NCCB Statutes, the pro-nuncio is welcome to attend all plenary sessions and should be invited to speak. The Statutes of the German Bishops' Con-

or other titular bishops: the statutes may extend such an invitation and may even endow these prelates with a deliberative vote. The paragraph merely denies that prelates not mentioned in §1 have a legal right to participate in the conference.

Statutes

Canon 451 — Each conference of bishops is to prepare its own statutes which must be reviewed by the Apostolic See and which are to organize, among other things, the plenary meetings of the conference which are to be held and to provide for a permanent council of bishops, a general secretariat of the conference, and also other offices and commissions which, in the judgment of the conference, more effectively help it to achieve its purpose.

Canon 449, §2 provides that every legitimately erected episcopal conference enjoys legal personality. In the light of canon 116, §1, the conference must be a *public* juridic person: having been erected by competent authority, it has a specific mission concerning the public good which it fulfills in the name of the Church. Hence, in accordance with canon 117, it must have statutes that are approved by the proper ecclesiastical authority. Canon 451 applies to episcopal conferences the general norm of action applicable to all similar legal institutes: each conference is responsible for preparing its own statutes. Canon 454, §§1–2 prescribes that only diocesan bishops, those equivalent to them in law, and coadjutors can vote on proposed statutes or amendments to them.

According to canon 94, §1, statutes define the "purpose, constitution, government, and methods of operation" of an organization. They bind all

and only the members of the organization in question (c. 94, §2). Canon 451 specifies more exactly the necessary contents of the statutes of an episcopal conference.[105] The *purpose* of the conference is already described in canon 447, the provisions of which tend to be echoed in various statutes. The *establishment* of the conference belongs to the supreme authority in the Church (c. 449, §1). The decree of erection would indicate territorial limits on *membership*—whether the conference in question included all or only some of the chief shepherds of particular churches within a given country, or whether it included all or only some of the chief shepherds of several neighboring countries (c. 448). The statutes themselves would have to determine whether ordinaries of Eastern *sui iuris* churches, titular bishops who are not coadjutors or auxiliaries, and papal legates are also members. The statutes would also determine whether auxiliary bishops and other titular bishops should enjoy a consultative or a deliberative vote (c. 454, §2) and whether ordinaries of Eastern *sui iuris* churches should have a deliberative vote (c. 450, §1). With respect to the *government* of the conference, canon 451 requires every conference to have a permanent council of bishops and a general secretary.[106] Canon 452, §1 requires the conference to have an elected president and a properly designated person to act in his stead when he is lawfully impeded. The conference may have additional officers and commissions, in which case the statutes must describe them. The statutes would need to determine how these officers are selected, what their terms of office are, what their duties are, and so on. With respect to *procedures,* canons 451 and 453 insist that the statutes contain provisions governing plenary sessions of the conference.

---

ference (Article 2, §2) require inviting the papal nuncio to the opening session. The Statutes of the Bishops' Conference of England and Wales provide for the pro-nuncio's attendance at "at least one session" of each plenary assembly (Article 4). Article 7, §2 of the statutes of the CCCB prescribes that "the conference invites the Pro Nuncio to meet the Members and address the meeting."

[105] Article 4 of *ApS* requires the statutes to take cognizance of that *aplett*'s norms governing the issuing of doctrinal statements.

[106] *CD* 38, 3 had listed a general secretary, a permanent council of bishops, and episcopal commissions as examples of offices that might aid a conference in fulfilling its mission.

The drafting of these statutes obviously requires considerable care. Canon 451 indicates that the statutes must be reviewed by the Holy See. According to article 82 of *Pastor bonus,* the Congregation for Bishops is the dicastery responsible for giving the necessary *recognitio* for conferences in non-missionary territories. *Pastor bonus* 89 indicates that the Congregation for the Evangelization of Peoples fulfills this function for conferences in mission territories.[107] The Pontifical Council for the Interpretation of Legislative Texts provides these congregations beforehand with a juridic evaluation of the proposed statutes (*PB* 157).[108] J. Gutiérrez reports that most conferences receive only a five-year approval for their statutes. The consequent periodic review of the statutes can facilitate a conference's more adequate adaptation to its particular situation.[109]

Officers

Canon 452 — §1. Each conference of bishops is to elect a president for itself, is to determine who is to perform the function of pro-president when the president is legitimately impeded, and is to designate a general secretary, according to the norm of the statutes.

§2. The president of a conference, and, when he is legitimately impeded, the pro-president, preside not only over the general meetings of the conference of bishops but also over the permanent council.

Although universal law allows the conference wide latitude in determining its own structures and procedures, this new canon establishes certain requirements with respect to its officers.

(1) The code requires each conference to have a president. In addition to the prerogatives and responsibilities with which the statutes endow him, he has the right and duty of: (a) presiding at plenary sessions; (b) presiding at sessions of the permanent council of bishops; (c) transmitting to the Holy See, after each plenary session, the minutes of the session and any general decrees issued by that session (c. 456). The canon requires that the president be elected. Unless the statutes provide otherwise, the provisions of canons 164–179 would govern the election. According to a May 23, 1988 authentic interpretation issued by the Pontifical Council for the Interpretation of Legislative Texts, an auxiliary bishop cannot be elected president of an episcopal conference.[110] The statutes would also indicate how the president would legally represent the conference as a juridic person (c. 118).

(2) Lest the work of the conference cease during the president's sickness or other incapacity, the statutes must make provision for someone to exercise his functions when he is legitimately impeded. The canon does not require that the conference have an office of vice-president, much less that its incumbent be elected. A conference could conceivably choose to allow the immediate past president or the senior diocesan (arch)bishop or the general secretary (if otherwise qualified) or the primate to fulfill these tasks.[111] The May 23, 1988 authentic interpretation cited immediately

---

[107] Gutiérrez, 358 mentions the CEC as well; but is not the episcopal conference an institute of the Latin church?

[108] For a discussion of the procedure, cf. I. Žužek, "Authentic Interpretation," *CLSAP* 57 (1995) 71.

[109] Cf. Gutiérrez, 358. As of this writing, the process of revising the statutes and by-laws of the NCCB has begun, but no changes will be effective for several years (private communication from Sister Sharon Euart, RSM, Associate General Secretary of the NCCB).

[110] *AAS* 81 (1989) 388; *CLD* 7, 292. Cf. also R. Castillo Lara, 94–98. The argument adopted by the council runs roughly as follows. The episcopal conference is by nature concerned with the coordination of the pastoral functions of the bishops of its territory. But an auxiliary bishop as such does not enjoy any personal pastoral responsibility in the diocese. Therefore he is not a "*pleno iure*" member of the conference (96). Because the president of the conference is the personal representative of the conference, and because he exercises such important responsibilities on its behalf (96), it is inappropriate (97) to allow an auxiliary to occupy that office. For a respectful critique of these arguments, cf. G. McKay, "Episcopal Conferences and Auxiliary Bishops," *CLS-GBIN* 80 (1989) 8–16.

[111] Read, in *CLSGBI Com,* 253, mentions the possibility of a permanent vice-president.

above prevents an auxiliary bishop from being designated to do so.

(3) The canon does require that there be an official with the title and duties of *general secretary*. Certain of those duties are prescribed by canon 458. The statutes should specify other responsibilities, his/her qualifications, the method of his/her selection, the term of office, and so on. The canon does not require that the general secretary be a bishop or even a cleric.[112] If a bishop, he would appear to enjoy *ipso iure* membership in the conference: he would be a titular bishop to whom the conference had entrusted a special function within its territory (c. 450, §1).

Meetings

Canon 453 — Plenary meetings of a conference of bishops are to be held at least once each year and, in addition, whenever particular circumstances require it, according to the prescripts of the statutes.

The canons do not define a *plenary* session. *Pastor bonus* 11 distinguishes between *plenary* sessions of a Roman dicastery (to which all members, wherever they live, must be invited) and *ordinary* sessions (to which only the members who happen to be in Rome need be invited). Because a conference necessarily involves bishops who are scattered over a country, such a distinction probably does not apply to sessions of an episcopal conference. Thus, the term *plenary* probably denotes a session of the conference to which all members have the right to be invited, in which voting takes place (cf. c. 454) and general decrees may be issued (cf. c. 455, §2). Such a session must be held at least annually. It may be held more frequently if the statutes so provide or if special circumstances require such a session. The statutes might provide a procedure for convoking a plenary session in the latter case.[113]

Voting Rights

Canon 454 — §1. By the law itself, diocesan bishops, those who are equivalent to them in law, and coadjutor bishops have a deliberative vote in plenary meetings of a conference of bishops.

§2. Auxiliary bishops and other titular bishops who belong to a conference of bishops have a deliberative or consultative vote according to the prescripts of the statutes of the conference. Nonetheless, only those mentioned in §1 have a deliberative vote in drawing up or changing the statutes.

This canon reworks material found in *Christus Dominus* 38, 2. It makes several important distinctions. In the first place, there is the distinction between a *deliberative* and a *consultative* vote.[114] A consultative vote is not the power to vote at all; it is the right to speak about an issue under discussion.[115] A deliberative vote is the power to cast a ballot to determine the outcome of a discussion. The canon therefore distinguishes between those who can address the assembly and those who can vote when the assembly is reaching a decision. All bishops who are members of a conference have the right to speak, but not all of them have the right to vote.

A second distinction is between the right to vote granted (or recognized) by universal law, on the one hand, and the right to vote granted by the statutes of the conference, on the other. All prelates who actually preside over particular churches and all coadjutor bishops have the first, and the statutes cannot deprive them of this right. All other bishops belonging to the conference have the voting status accorded them by the

proval of the Administrative Committee." The Statutes of the Bishops' Conference of England and Wales allow "the President or, in his absence, the Vice President, after consultation with the Standing Committee,... to convene further meetings."

[114] Cf. the commentary on c. 127 for a more detailed discussion of this issue.

[115] Cf. Provost, "Particular Councils," 549–550, on the importance of a consultative vote.

[112] Read, in *CLSGBI Com,* 256.

[113] Article V of the NCCB Statutes, for example, authorizes the president to convoke a plenary assembly "with ap-

statutes.[116] The statutes may deny them the power to vote or may limit their exercise of the right.[117]

Finally, the canon distinguishes the enacting or amending of the statutes from the resolution of all other issues. This is somewhat analogous to the distinction in the United States of America between drawing up or amending the Constitution and enacting legislation. Only the chief shepherds of particular churches and coadjutor bishops can vote on proposed statutes or amendments.[118]

Authority

Canon 455 — §1. A conference of bishops can only issue general decrees in cases where universal law has prescribed it or a special mandate of the Apostolic See has established it either *motu proprio* or at the request of the conference itself.[119]

Christus Dominus 38, 4 is the source of this canon: "Decisions of the episcopal conference... are to have juridically binding force in those cases and in those only which are prescribed by common law or determined by special mandate of the Apostolic See, given spontaneously or in response to a petition from the conference itself."[120]

According to canon 29, "General decrees... are laws properly speaking." Canon 455, §1 is accordingly a rule of recognition specifying the extent of the legislative power of the episcopal conference. It is also an invalidating law (cf. c. 10): if a conference has power only in certain cases (*tantummodo potest in causis*), it invalidly attempts to legislate outside those cases.

Although some (perhaps many) canonists and ecclesiologists would prefer otherwise, neither the council nor the code envisages the conference as a *primarily* legislative institute.[121] A particular council, by contrast, "possesses the power of governance, especially legislative power" (c. 445). Its legislative authority is a given unless it attempts to act in contravention of universal law or unless the Holy See refuses to grant the requisite *recognitio* (c. 446). The conference, on the other hand, cannot propose legislation unless some prescription of universal law so requires[122] or so allows, or

---

[116] *ApS* 17 cautions that in granting a deliberative vote to these bishops the statutes should take account of "the proportion between diocesan bishops and auxiliary and other titular bishops... in order that a possible majority of the latter may not condition the pastoral government of the diocesan bishops."

[117] For example, the Statutes of the Bishops' Conference of England and Wales, Article 7, allow "only diocesan bishops, those equivalent to them in law and coadjutor bishops" to vote on financial questions. Article XIV of the Statutes of the NCCB has a similar provision (excluding coadjutors): "In the determination of diocesan quotas or of special assessments in individual dioceses, or special collections not prescribed by the Holy See..." The exclusion of coadjutors is curious inasmuch as they are mentioned in canon 454, §1 as having an *ipso iure* right to vote.

[118] For discussions of reasons for not allowing auxiliaries to vote on these issues see Arrieta, in *Pamplona ComEng*, 342, and Lettmann, 359, n.19.

[119] *ApS*, article 1, parallels this canon: "In order that the doctrinal declarations of the conference of bishops referred to in No. 22 of the present letter may constitute authentic magisterium and be published in the name of the conference itself, they must be unanimously approved by the bishops who are members or receive the *recognitio* of the Apostolic See if approved in plenary assembly by at least two-thirds of the bishops belonging to the conference and having a deliberative vote." Unlike the canon, the *aplett* does not require the conference to receive authorization either from the law or from the

Holy See before considering a doctrinal declaration. In this respect, the teaching authority of the conference is somewhat less circumscribed than its legislative authority. On the other hand, no act of legislation requires the unanimous approval of all members (*ApS* does not distinguish here between those with and those without *ipso iure* right to vote). In this respect the conference's teaching authority is more limited than its legislative authority. On this point see c. 753 and its commentary.

[120] *AAS* 58 (1966) 693.

[121] In the mind of the drafting committee, for example, "the episcopal conference is not understood primarily as a legislative assembly... but is especially an organ of union and intercommunication among bishops." *Comm* 14 (1982) 199.

[122] Listl, in *Handbuch*, 313, following Bertrams and Manzanares, distinguishes the conference's proper, ordinary power (i.e., the power to act with which the law endows the conference) from the delegated power it would enjoy if the Holy See empowered it to act in a given case.

unless the Holy See has given prior approval.[123] Thus, the legislative competence of the conference is more tightly circumscribed than that of the particular council.[124]

However limited, the legislative competence of the conference is nonetheless genuine. According to canon 131, §1, governmental power which is attached by law to an office is *ordinary.* Whenever the conference legislates in the light of provisions of universal law, it is therefore exercising the ordinary power proper to itself. Whenever the Holy See authorizes the conference to legislate, however, the conference would be exercising delegated papal power.[125]

Book I of the code distinguishes between *general decrees* (c. 29) and *general executory decrees,* which "more precisely determine the methods to be observed in applying the law or which urge the observance of laws" (c. 31, §1). Relying on this distinction, some authors have argued that canon

455 does not limit the conference's power to issue general executory decrees.[126] However, on July 5, 1985 the Pontifical Commission for the Authentic Interpretation of the Code of Canon Law ruled that "the term *general decrees* employed in canon 455, §1 includes also the general executory decrees treated in canons 31–33."[127] Hence, an episcopal conference's power to issue general executory decrees is subject to the same limitations as its power to legislate.

Several lists of the cases in which universal law either prescribes or allows the conference to legislate have been published.[128] The differences among them result from some imprecision in the formulation of the universal laws: it is not always clear whether the activity they require or permit is *legislative.*[129]

---

[123] The verbs in the canon's subordinate clause (*praescripserit* and *statuerit*) are perfect subjunctives. The use of the perfect tense underscores the priority of the action of universal authority: the universal legislator must enact an enabling law or the Holy See must grant the requisite mandate before the conference begins to establish its law. The drafting committee was most emphatic on this point: "An indiscriminate concession of legislative power to the episcopal conference would be detrimental, not only to the authority of the Holy See, but also to the authority which each bishop enjoys in his own diocese, and would also be contrary to the mind and the words of the Second Vatican Council" (*Comm* 15 [1982] 199).

[124] H. Schwendenwein suggests that the conference also has (limited) *judicial* power: it can authorize the establishment of regional appellate courts and the use of lay judges. H. Schwendenwein, *Das neue Kirchenrecht* (Graz: Styria, 1983) 229. This authorization is actually an exercise of administrative rather than judicial power.

[125] So T. Green, "The Authority of Episcopal Conferences: Some Normative and Doctrinal Considerations," *CLSAP* 51 (1989) 125: "The conferences as such (as distinct from their committees) are permanent collegial subjects of ordinary proper power.... Yet such conferences may occasionally exercise delegated authority if a Holy See mandate is required for their issuing a general decree."

[126] Provost, in *CLSA Com,* 369 makes a particularly strong case in favor of this conclusion.

[127] *AAS* 77 (1985) 771.

[128] Most authoritatively, on November 8, 1983 the cardinal secretary of state sent to all presidents of episcopal conferences (1) a list of 22 cases for which conferences *could* enact particular laws complementing the code and (2) a list of 21 cases for which the conference *should* enact complementary particular legislation. *Comm* 15 (1983) 135–139. Listl, in *Handbuch,* 314–320 lists 80 instances of potential legislative activity by conferences. Provost, in *CLSA Com,* 370–372 distinguishes 29 clear instances of potential lawmaking ("cases in which the code authorizes [and at times requires] conferences to adopt" particular laws) and 53 cases in which conference activity is less certainly legislative. T. Green ("The Normative Role of Episcopal Conferences in the 1983 Code," in Reese, *Episcopal Conferences,* 168–175) provides a list of 43 areas of "normative competence for Episcopal Conferences." See the appendix to this section of the commentary for a table documenting the legislative activity of the NCCB and the CCCB.

[129] Cf. Provost, in *CLSA Com,* 370: "Does canon 1126 authorize the conference to determine how the general law for the declaration and promises in a mixed marriage is to be applied in its territory, or does it make a new particular law for the subject matter?" Cf. also T. Green, "The Church's Teaching Mission," 24, n. 2: "The Code uses diverse legal formulations to specify conference normative competencies. Furthermore, there does not always seem to be a clear consensus among the commentators on the issue if they even address it at all."

§2. The decrees mentioned in §1, in order to be enacted validly in a plenary meeting, must be passed by at least a two thirds vote of the prelates who belong to the conference and possess a deliberative vote. They do not obtain binding force unless they have been legitimately promulgated after having been reviewed by the Apostolic See.

This canon, too, is derived from *Christus Dominus* 38, 4: "Decisions of the episcopal conference, provided they have been made lawfully and by the choice of at least two-thirds of the prelates who have a deliberative vote in the conference, and have been reviewed by the Apostolic See, are to have juridically binding force."[130] The canon is a rule of recognition: it prescribes the procedures which must be followed, under pain of invalidity, before a general decree enacted by an episcopal conference can be recognized as a law.[131]

In reaching its decisions a particular council would presumably follow, *mutatis mutandis,* canon 119, 2°: "When an absolute majority of those who must be convoked are present, that which is approved by the absolute majority of those present has the force of law." The decision of a majority of those who (a) are present and (b) have the right to vote would be decisive. However, the conference follows different rules in legislating. As in a particular council, only those who have a deliberative vote can cast votes; but the votes are tallied differently, and a different majority is required. In a council, only an absolute majority is required: 50 percent plus one vote. In a conference, the approval of at least $66\,^2\!/_3$ percent is required. In a council, the majority is determined on the basis of those who are present. If fifty shepherds should attend, but only forty actually do so, the requisite majority is twenty-one, not twenty-six. In the conference,

the majority is determined on the basis of all members who have a deliberative vote *whether or not they are present*. If fifty should attend, but only forty actually do so, the necessary majority remains thirty-four, not twenty-seven. Absentee ballots can be critically important.

After the conference has followed the procedure for enacting a general decree, three additional elements (only two of which are explicitly mentioned in the canon) are necessary before it becomes effective.

(1) The decree must receive the *recognitio* from the Apostolic See. In accordance with *Pastor bonus,* the proposed legislation would be sent either to the Congregation for Bishops (*PB* 82) or, if the conference were located in missionary territory, to the Congregation for the Evangelization of Peoples (*PB* 89). Before authorizing the *recognitio,* the appropriate congregation consults with the Pontifical Council for the Interpretation of Legislative Texts to ensure that the proposed law is consistent with universal laws and uses correct legal language.[132] The *recognitio* does not convert episcopal legislation into papal legislation,[133] but it does guarantee that the proposed particular laws do not conflict with universal legislation and do not threaten the well-being of the universal Church.[134]

(2) In accordance with canon 7, the approved decree must next be promulgated. Until promul-

---

[130] *AAS* 58 (1966) 693.

[131] Canon 135, §2 prohibits the valid delegation of legislative power by anyone except the supreme authority of the Church, unless the law provides otherwise. Hence, the conference cannot delegate its law-making power to its committees. See an authentic interpretation on this point dated June 10, 1966, *AAS* 60 (1968) 361; *CLD* 7, 131.

[132] Žužek, "Authentic," 71, notes that the conference's use of language is sometimes problematic.

[133] Listl, in *Handbuch,* 313; also P. Krämer, "Episcopal Conferences and the Apostolic See," *J* 48 (1988) 137–138. See Provost, "Particular Councils," 552, on the *recognitio* of laws enacted by particular councils.

[134] D. Murray has a sanguine view of the *recognitio* process. "The Holy See not merely confirm the decree but enters actively into its formulation.... This can be seen as heightening the degree of collegiality involved. The unity with the Head of the College which must be at least implicitly present in every truly collegial act is here rendered quite explicit." D. Murray, "The Legislative Authority of the Episcopal Conference," *Stud Can* 20 (1986) 45. However, the pope's rewriting the text of a decree formulated by several dozen of his brother bishops might seem an odd exercise of collegiality.

gation, the proposed decree is not "established" or "given birth" as a law.

(3) Finally, after the promulgation of the decree a specified time (the *vacatio legis*) must elapse before the decree begins to bind (c. 8, §2).

§3. The conference of bishops itself determines the manner of promulgation and the time when the decrees take effect.

This canon is in some respects a deduction from and in other respects an adaptation of canon 8, §2: "Particular laws are promulgated in the manner determined by the legislator and begin to oblige a month after the day of [their] promulgation unless the law itself establishes another time period." The conference has the authority to decide how it will promulgate its general decrees. The conference might establish, within its statutes, a routine form of promulgation (just as c. 8, §1 prescribes publication in *Acta Apostolicae Sedis* as the routine form of promulgation for universal laws);[135] or the proposed decree might contain provisions about its eventual promulgation; or the conference might even defer to another plenary session the decision about promulgation.[136] Similarly, provisions for the *vacatio legis* could be made in the conference's statutes, in the decree itself, or in the instrument of promulgation. In the absence of any such provisions, canon 8, §2 would presumably come into play, and particular laws would begin to bind one month after the day of their promulgation.

§4. In cases in which neither universal law nor a special mandate of the Apostolic See has granted the power mentioned in §1 to a conference of bish-

ops, the competence of each diocesan bishop remains intact, nor is a conference or its president able to act in the name of all the bishops unless each and every bishop has given consent.

Each bishop enjoys proper, ordinary, and immediate power over the flock entrusted to him (*LG* 27). He is engraced by ordination with all the authority necessary for him to serve the people whose proper shepherd he is. Some bishops have long expressed the fear that episcopal conferences might usurp this legitimate episcopal power. This canon seeks to allay their fears. The code commission appears to view the legislative authority of the conference as a kind of limit which the supreme authority of the Church has imposed on the exercise of the individual bishop's authority.[137] Apart from the cases specified in canon 455, §1, the individual bishop's power remains intact. The canon emphasizes this by making explicit with reference to the conference and its president the general principle, "What touches all as individuals, however, must be approved by all" (cf. c. 119, 3°). When neither the canons nor the pope has authorized the conference to legislate, the majority of the conference cannot enforce its will upon even a single reluctant bishop.

This is not to say, however, that the "sense" of the conference has no weight at all. Quite the contrary, as the *Directory on the Pastoral Ministry of Bishops* declares,

> There are other decisions and regulations of the conference which do not have a juridical binding force, and as a rule the bishop makes them his own with a view to unity and charity with his brother bishops unless serious reasons he has carefully considered in the Lord prevent it. He promulgates these decisions and norms in his diocese in his own name and proper authority whenever the conference cannot definitively circumscribe

---

[135] Cf. article 16, 1 of the Statutes of the German Bishops' Conference; also Schwendenwein, 228 concerning similar provisions for the Austrian episcopal conference.

[136] J. Provost questions the lack of any consistent approach to promulgating conference norms: "The Promulgation of Universal and Particular Law in the Ten Years Since the Code," in *Ius in Vita et in Missione Ecclesiae* (Rome: Libreria Editrice Vaticana, 1994) 631–634.

[137] Hence, in the light of c. 18, the conditions c. 455 places on the exercise of the conference's power would require strict interpretation.

the power which each bishop personally discharges in the name of Christ (*LG* 27).[138]

The *Directory* states that the fostering of communion among the bishops ("unity and charity") generally requires the individual bishop to act in harmony with the common understanding of the conference, even when that common understanding is not juridically binding, and even when he previously disputed it.[139] Such an interpretation of conference initiatives sees cooperation as enhancing rather than undermining the authority of the individual bishop (cf. *CD* 37).

Communication with the Holy See

Canon 456 — When a plenary meeting of a conference of bishops has ended, the president is to send a report of the acts of the conference and its decrees to the Apostolic See so that the acts are brought to its notice and it can review the decrees if there are any.

This new canon parallels canon 446 concerning the conclusion of a particular council. Proposed decrees cannot be promulgated and cannot become effective without the *recognitio* (cf. c. 455, §2); hence, someone needs to forward them to Rome for appropriate review. The fostering of communion

likewise requires that other particular churches—especially the Roman church—be kept informed of even non-legislative initiatives. The president as the legal representative of the conference is the appropriate person to further these goals.

The Permanent Council

Canon 457 — It is for the permanent council of bishops to take care that the agenda for a plenary session of a conference is prepared and that decisions made in plenary session are properly executed. It is also for the council to take care of other affairs which are entrusted to it according to the norm of the statutes.

Though a permanent institute, the episcopal conference is not permanently in session. Between sessions its work is supervised by a permanent council of bishops. The statutes of each conference are to specify the composition and responsibilities of this body.[140] This canon prescribes the minimum competency of such a council. The council (not the general secretary) is responsible for preparing for plenary meetings and for overseeing the implementations of decisions of prior meetings. Through the permanent council the conference continues functioning even when not in session.

The General Secretariat

Canon 458 — It is for the general secretariat:
   1° to prepare a report of the acts and decrees of a plenary meeting of a conference and

---

[138] SCB, *Directory on the Pastoral Ministry of Bishops,* Benedictine Monks of the Seminary of Christ the King, trans. (Ottawa: Canadian Catholic Conference, 1974) 113, n. 212 b.

[139] Article 16 of the Statutes of the Bishops' Conference of England and Wales takes an interesting approach: "Proposals approved by an absolute majority of those present with a deliberative vote at the Plenary Assembly become *Official Conference Resolutions.* Although lacking juridical binding force, those resolutions will normally be observed by all members in the spirit of collegial unity. Such observance will be presumed unless, on occasion, individual bishops indicate otherwise, either during the Plenary Assembly or later by informing the President." Article XII of the NCCB statutes recommends the observance of similar measures "as an expression of collegial responsibility and in a spirit of unity and charity with their brother bishops."

[140] The Statutes of the CCCB provide for a 14-member board (Articles 10–12) and an Executive [*sic*] consisting of the president, the vice president, and two councilors. The Statutes of the Bishops' Conference of England and Wales establish a Standing Committee consisting of the president, the vice-president, the metropolitan archbishops, and the chairs of the departments of the conference (Articles 19–21). The NCCB has an Administrative Committee (Article IX) and a smaller Executive Committee "to deal with urgent conference matters when the Administrative Committee is not in session" (Article X).

the acts of the permanent council of bishops, to communicate the same to all the members of the conference, and to draw up other acts whose preparation the president of the conference or the permanent council entrusts to the general secretary;

2° to communicate to neighboring conferences of bishops the acts and documents which the conference in plenary meeting or the permanent council of bishops decides to send to them.

The tasks of the general secretary of the conference are similar to those of the chancellor of a diocese (cf. cc. 482, 484). He/she is responsible for preparing various official documents, taking proper care of them, and communicating them to members of the conference or to the proper officials of neighboring conferences (at the direction of the conference itself or the permanent council). Communicating with the Holy See about legitimate conference business is the responsibility, not of the general secretary, but of the president (cf. c. 456).

Relations Among Conferences

Canon 459 — §1. Relations between conferences of bishops, especially neighboring ones, are to be fostered in order to promote and protect the greater good.

§2. Whenever conferences enter into actions or programs having an international character, however, the Apostolic See must be heard.

Christus Dominus 38, 5 encouraged contacts among episcopal conferences; and *Ecclesiae sanctae* I, 41, 5 suggested areas in which such contacts would be particularly important:

(a) communicating the principal decisions, especially in pastoral life and action;

(b) sending texts or reports of the decisions of the conference or the acts and documents by the bishops collectively;

(c) reporting the various apostolic enterprises proposed or recommended by the episcopal conference which could be of use in similar circumstances;

(d) proposing those questions of grave import which in our times and in particular circumstances seem of the greatest importance;

(e) indicating the dangers or errors making ground in their own country which might also creep into other nations, so that suitable means should be taken in good time to prevent them or remove or confine them.[141]

Intercommunication between conferences will, at a minimum, foster better understanding among bishops and may lead to common solutions to otherwise intractable problems. Universal legislation therefore strongly encourages it.[142]

Because the Holy See is responsible for the well-being of the entire communion of churches, however, it has a legitimate interest in ecclesiastical undertakings with international implications. *Ecclesiae sanctae* I, 41, 4 had required that conferences *advise* the Holy See about such initiatives beforehand (*praemoneatur*). The canon requires that the Holy See be *heard* (*audiatur*). Neither text demands papal approval of the initiative, but both implicitly enable the Holy See to forbid anything that seems particularly unwise[143] and to encourage especially prudent initiatives.

---

[141] *AAS* 58 (1966) 774; *CLD* 6, 283–284.

[142] Because of the complexity of the issue and limitations of space, the reader must look elsewhere for a discussion of the various structures that have developed to foster communications among conferences especially in Europe, Latin America, and Africa. Detailed discussions are available in I. Fürer, "Episcopal Conferences in Their Mutual Relations," *J* 48 (1988) 153–174; and J. Hortal, "Relationships Among Episcopates," *J* 48 (1988) 175–180.

[143] Unless the power to impose such restrictions is used cautiously, however, the legitimate initiatives of the bishops might be unduly curtailed.

PARTICULAR LEGISLATION[144] ENACTED BY THE NCCB AND THE CCCB

Reference to the 1983 Code[145]	NCCB Norms[146]	CCCB Norms[147]
c. 8, §2: method of promulgation		SC (21) 210–211: publication in the series "Official Document—Document officiel"; generally, one month *vacatio legis*
c. 230, §1: ministries of lector and acolyte		SC (22) 222–223: candidates must be 21
c. 236: formation of permanent deacons		SC (22) 462–465
c. 242: program of priestly formation	J 398: 4th edition of *Program of Priestly Formation*	SC (22) 216–217
c. 276, §2, 3°: permanent deacons and Liturgy of the Hours	J 399: "permanent deacons should not hold themselves lightly excused" from morning and evening prayer	SC (22) 204–205: permanent deacons must pray Lauds and Vespers
c. 284: clerical dress		SC (22) 458–459: clerics must dress in such a way as to be identifiable as clerics
c. 451: statutes		SC (20) 220–229
c. 455, §3: method of promulgation		SC (21) 210–211: publication in the series "Official Document—Document officiel"; generally, one month *vacatio legis*
c. 496: norms on presbyteral councils		SC (22) 458–461

(continued)

[144] The reader is encouraged to consult the code itself and the relevant commentary for discussion of the norms in question. The table can provide only an overview of the kind and extent of legislative activity on the part of two conferences.

[145] NCCB documentation (cf. the following footnote) recognizes 84 canons authorizing legislative activity by the conference. Neither the NCCB nor the CCCB has issued that many decrees. The table will not take cognizance of canons on which neither conference has yet acted.

[146] The NCCB has promulgated its decrees in various ways. The most recent documentation can be found in S. Euart, "Complementary Norms Implementing the 1983 Code of Canon Law by the National Conference of Catholic Bishops," *J* 53 (1993) 396–434. In this table, the decree will be cited as *J* and page number.

[147] As of this writing documentation of 37 decrees is available in various issues of *Stud Can*. In the table, the decree will be cited as SC (volume number), and page number.

Reference to the 1983 Code	NCCB Norms	CCCB Norms
c. 502, §3: cathedral chapters and diocesan consultors		SC (19) 170–171: where chapters of canons exist, they may be given the responsibilities the code gives to diocesan consultors
c. 522: term of office for pastors	J 399–400: six-year terms, renewable at discretion of diocesan bishop	SC (19) 172–173: after consultation with presbyteral council, bishop can appoint pastors to renewable six-year terms
c. 538, §3: the support of retired pastors	J 400: diocesan bishops may develop policies in accordance with *Norms for Priests and Their Third Age*	SC (22) 478–481: bishops must establish retirement funds
c. 766: norms on lay preaching		SC (19) 174–177: diocesan bishop can allow lay preaching when there are no clergy, when liturgy of word is celebrated without clergy, when seminarians are learning, in other special circumstances
c. 772, §2: norms on radio or television talks on doctrine	J 401: diocesan bishops can *provisionally* establish their own guidelines	SC (22) 206–207: only explicitly recognized "Catholic" programs are Catholic; media workers need special training
c. 788, §3: statutes on the catechumenate	J 401: cf. *National Statutes for the Catechumenate*	SC (22) 218–221
c. 792: programs welcoming people from mission lands		SC (24) 466–467: priests coming to study in Canada need a letter from their ordinary attesting to their good standing; priests from mission countries seeking to work in Canada need letters from the ordinary *a quo* and the ordinary of the place where they wish to work

Reference to the 1983 Code	NCCB Norms	CCCB Norms
c. 804: Catholic education in schools		SC (22) 472–473: reaffirmed norms already in force
c. 830: a list of censors		SC (22) 476–477: the conference will compile and regularly revise such a list
c. 831: norms governing participation of priests or religious in media	J 402: diocesan bishops can *provisionally* establish their own guidelines	SC (22) 468–471: regular participants need authorization from their proper superiors and the ordinary of the place; conference should be informed of regular media commitments by clerics or religious; regular participants need proper training
c. 851: norms on adult baptisms		SC (25) 486–489
c. 877, §3: recording baptisms of adopted children	J 402: diocesan bishops can *provisionally* establish their own guidelines	SC (22) 208–211: generally infants are not baptized before adoption; civil law prescriptions to be followed for registration and issuing of certificates
c. 891: age for confirmation	*Origins* 24 (1994) 2: "between the age of discretion . . . and 18 years of age, within the limits determined by the diocesan bishop"	SC (21) 200–201: candidates are confirmed "at the age determined in the approved catechetical programs"
c. 961, 2°: criteria for using general absolution	J 404: "a long while" in the canon means "one month"	
c. 964, §2: norms concerning confessionals		SC (20) 212–213
c. 1031: age for ordination	J 404–405: minimum age for ordination to permanent diaconate is thirty-five; diocesan bishop can dispense up to one year	

(*continued*)

Reference to the 1983 Code	NCCB Norms	CCCB Norms
c. 1067: norms governing prenuptial investigations	J 405: diocesan bishops can *provisionally* establish their own norms	SC (25) 492–495
c. 1067: the banns		SC (25) 498–501: banns no longer obligatory, but parties may request them or diocesan regulations may so recommend
c. 1083, §2: age for marriage		SC (21) 202–203: minimum age for liceity is eighteen, but ordinary may dispense
c. 1112: lay witnesses of marriage	J 406: the conference will entertain requests for the faculty to delegate lay witnesses	SC (19) 168–169
c. 1126: promises for mixed marriages	J 406: 1970 norms were reaffirmed	SC (24) 474–477: promises made orally in presence of parish priest or his delegate
c. 1127, §2: dispensations from canonical form	J 407: 1970 norms were reaffirmed	SC (21) 204–207
c. 1236, §1: materials used for fixed altars		SC (22) 214–215: "natural stone, or any solid, worthy material approved by the diocesan bishop"
c. 1246: days of obligation	J 408: six holy days; January 1st, August 15th, and November 1st are *not* days of obligation if they fall on Saturday or Monday	SC (19) 178–179: Sundays plus Christmas and January 1st
c. 1253: norms for fast and abstinence	J 409: 1966 norms were reaffirmed; J 409–410: the minimum age at which fasting becomes obligatory is eighteen	SC (19) 180–181: Ash Wednesday and Good Friday are days of fast and abstinence; Fridays are days of abstinence, but faithful can substitute other practices
c. 1262: norms governing contributions of the faithful	J 410: diocesan bishops can establish their own norms	SC (24) 470–471

Reference to the 1983 Code	NCCB Norms	CCCB Norms
c. 1277: the meaning of "extraordinary" administration	J 410–411	SC (19) 184–185
c. 1292: alienation of church property	J 411–414: maximum amount of $3,000,000	SC (19) 188–189; SC (22) 454–455: the "minimum" amount is 10% of the "maximum"
c. 1297: norms concerning leasing church property	J 414; cf. J 410–411	SC (22) 200–203
c. 1421, §2: lay persons as ecclesiastical judges	J 414	SC (19) 164–165
c. 1425, §1: collegiate tribunals	J 415: diocesan bishops can entrust first instance trials to single clerical judges	SC (19) 166–167
c. 1439, §2: tribunals of second instance	J 416: conference will act when petition for such action has been made	

Acerbi, A. "The Development of the Canons on Conferences and the Apostolic See." *J* 48 (1988) 146–152.

Antón, A. "The Theological 'Status' of Episcopal Conferences." *J* 48 (1988) 185–219.

Arrieta, J. "Title II—Groupings of Particular Churches." In *Pamplona ComEng,* 328–345.

Canadian Conference of Catholic Bishops. *Complementary Norms to the 1983 Code of Canon Law.* Ottawa: CCCB, 1996.

Dulles, A. "Doctrinal Authority of Episcopal Conferences." In *Episcopal Conferences: Historical, Canonical and Theological Studies,* ed. T. Reese, 207–232. Washington, D.C.: Georgetown University, 1989.

Feliciani, G. "Episcopal Conferences from Vatican II to the 1983 Code." *J* 48 (1988) 11–25.

———. *Le Conferenze Episcopali.* Bologna: Il Mulino, 1974.

Fogarty, G. "The Authority of the National Catholic Welfare Conference." In *Episcopal Conferences: Historical, Canonical and Theological Studies,* ed. T. Reese, 85–103. Washington, D.C.: Georgetown University, 1989.

Fürer, I. "Episcopal Conferences in their Mutual Relations." *J* 48 (1988) 153–174.

García y García, A. "Episcopal Conferences in Light of Particular Councils during the Second Millennium." *J* 48 (1988) 57–67.

Ghirlanda, G. "De episcoporum conferentia deque exercitio potestatis magisterii." *P* 87 (1987) 573–604.

Green, J. *Conferences of Bishops and the Exercise of the 'Munus Docendi' of the Church.* Rome: Gregorian University, 1987.

Green, T. "The Authority of Episcopal Conferences: Some Normative and Doctrinal Considerations." *CLSAP* 51 (1989) 123–136.

———. "The Church's Teaching Mission: Some Aspects of the Normative Role of Episcopal Conferences." *Stud Can* 27 (1993) 23–57.

———. "The Normative Role of Episcopal Conferences in the 1983 Code." In *Episcopal Conferences: Historical, Canonical and Theological Studies,* ed. T. Reese, 137–175. Washington, D.C.: Georgetown University, 1989.

Gutiérrez, J. "Capitulo VI Organización Jerarquica de la Iglesia." In *Manual de Derecho Canonico,* 291–371. Pamplona: Universidad de Navarra, S.A., 1988.

Hortal, J. "Relationships among Episcopates." *J* 48 (1988) 175–180.

John Paul II. *Mp The Theological and Juridical Nature of Episcopal Conferences. Origins* 28 (July 30, 1998) 152–158.

Huizing, P. "The Structure of Episcopal Conferences." *J* 28 (1968) 163–176.

Iban. I., ed. *Gli statuti delle conferenze episcopali II America.* Padua: CEDAM, 1989.

Komonchak, J. "Episcopal Conferences." *CS* 27 (1988) 311–328.

Krämer, P. "Episcopal Conferences and the Apostolic See." *J* 48 (1988) 134–145.

Kutner, R. *The Development, Structure, and Competence of the Episcopal Conference.* Washington, D.C.: Catholic University of America, 1972.

Lettmann, R. "Episcopal Conferences in the New Canon Law." *Stud Can* 14 (1980) 347–367.

Listl, J. "Plenarkonzil und Bischofskonferenz." In *Handbuch,* ed. J. Listl et al., 304–324. Regensburg: Pustet, 1983.

Manzanares, J. "The Teaching Authority of Episcopal Conferences." *J* 48 (1988) 234–263.

Maritz, H. "Die Kirchenprovinz: Provinzialkonzil und Metropolit." In *Handbuch,* ed. J. Listl et al., 325–329. Regensburg: Pustet, 1983.

McKeown, E. "The National Bishops' Conference: An Analysis of Its Origin." *The Catholic Historical Review* 66 (1980) 565–583.

———. "The 'National Idea' in the History of the American Episcopal Conference." In *Episcopal Conferences: Historical, Canonical and Theological Studies,* ed. T. Reese, 59–84. Washington, D.C.: Georgetown University, 1989.

Müller, H. "The Relationship between the Episcopal Conference and the Diocesan Bishop." *J* 48 (1988) 111–129.

Murray, D. "The Legislative Authority of the Episcopal Conference." *Stud Can* 20 (1986) 33–47.

NCCB. *Implementation of the 1983 Code Complementary Norms.* Washington, D.C.: USCC, 1991.

Örsy, L. "Reflections on the Teaching Authority of the Episcopal Conferences." In *Episcopal Conferences: Historical, Canonical and Theological Studies,* ed. T. Reese, 233–252. Washington, D.C.: Georgetown University, 1989.

Poblete, E. *The Plenary Council: A Historical Synopsis and a Commentary.* Washington, D.C.: Catholic University of America, 1958.

Popek, A. *The Rights and Obligations of Metropolitans: A Historical Synopsis and Commentary.* Washington, D.C.: Catholic University of America, 1957.

Provost, J. "Particular Councils." In *The New Code of Canon Law: Proceedings of the 5th International Congress of Canon Law,* ed. M. Theriault and J. Thorn, 1:537–561. Ottawa: Faculty of Canon Law, 1984.

———. "Title II—Groupings of Particular Churches." In *CLSA Com,* 350–377.

Ratzinger, J., and V. Messori. *The Ratzinger Report.* San Francisco: Ignatius Press, 1985.

Read, G. "Section II: Particular Churches and Their Groupings." In *CLSGBI Com,* 209–313.

Reese, T. *A Flock of Shepherds: The National Conference of Catholic Bishops.* Kansas City, Mo.: Sheed and Ward, 1992.

Schwendenwein, H. *Das neue Kirchenrecht.* Graz: Verlag Styria, 1983.

Sieben, H.-J. "Episcopal Conferences in the Light of Particular Councils during the First Millennium." *J* 48 (1988) 68–106.

Sobanski, R. "The Theology and Juridic Status of Episcopal Conferences at the Second Vatican Council." *J* 48 (1988) 68–106.

Tillard, J. "The Theological Significance of Local Churches for Episcopal Conferences." *J* 48 (1988) 220–226.

Urrutia, F. "De exercitio muneris docendi a conferentiis episcoporum." *P* 66 (1987) 605–636.

TITLE III
THE INTERNAL ORDERING OF PARTICULAR CHURCHES
[cc. 460–572]

CHAPTER I
THE DIOCESAN SYNOD
[cc. 460–468]

While varying according to the needs of the age in both purpose and constitution, diocesan synods have been utilized by the Church since the fourth century as vehicles for pastoral governance. In earlier centuries, synods were structured for wide-ranging purposes, from electing bishops to planning strategies for combating threats to the Church's stability from such matters as heresies and clerical misconduct.[1] Previous universal legislation required annual celebrations of diocesan synods for the purpose of local promulgation of provincial council legislation[2] and later for the purpose of ensuring consistent reform and correction of abuses.[3] The 1917 code devoted seven canons to the diocesan synod (*CIC* 356–362) including one that called for the convocation of a diocesan synod every ten years, a norm that was rarely observed. The current code on this topic (cc. 460–468) provides more episcopal discretion both in the frequency of convening a diocesan synod and in its design and execution. The canons in this chapter address the concept and constitu-

tion of a synod as well as its convening and cessation. The most recent document on diocesan synods was a joint instruction[4] by the Congregation for Bishops and the Congregation for the Evangelization of Peoples.[5] This document provides many details related to preparing for and conducting a synod.[6] In some instances, 1917 code requirements not included in the present law are set forth as required or necessary elements of a synod in this document.[7] In other cases, new "requirements" not mentioned in the code are contained in the document.[8] A careful review of this document would seem to be an important preliminary step in any consideration of convening a synod.

---

[1] For a fuller study of the history of synods, see L. Jennings, "A Renewed Understanding of the Diocesan Synod," *Stud Can* 20 (1986) 320–329.

[2] Fourth Lateran Council (1215). See J. D. Mansi, *Sacrorum conciliorum nova et amplissima collectio,* vol. XXII, col. 991.

[3] Council of Trent (1563), sess. XXIV, *de ref.,* c. 2; sess. XXV, *de ref.,* cc. 4, 10.

[4] Canon 34 defines the purpose of an instruction: to "clarify the prescripts of laws and elaborate on and determine the methods to be observed in fulfilling them."

[5] CFB and CEP, *Instruction on Diocesan Synods* (July 8, 1997). See *Origins* 27 (October 23, 1997) 324–331.

[6] For example, it discusses the practicalities of observing the liturgical norms of the *Caeremoniale Episcoporum* for the opening and closing liturgies as well as any other liturgies celebrated during the synod.

[7] For example, under the 1917 code, the bishop was to establish one or more preparatory commissions of clerics to prepare the drafts of synodal texts if opportune (*CIC* 360, §1). Earlier drafts of the law retained these bodies but the code commission specifically deleted them later (cf. *Rel,* 111). The 1983 code makes no reference to such commissions, clerical or not, even though the practicality of such would seem unquestioned for the ordering of the material to be discussed and deliberated upon at the synod.

[8] For example, the 1997 instruction refers to the constitution of a preparatory commission as an "obligation" of the bishop and provides extensive detail on its structure, composition, and purpose (*Origins* 27 [October 23, 1997] 326–327). Likewise the instruction states that the commission is to assist in the preparation of a required synodal directory, again a practical tool but one not mentioned in the code and hence not strictly obligatory. Since an instruction is to "clarify," "elaborate on," and "determine the methods" for observance of law, but not to issue new law, it is difficult to see how this document could add new obligations binding in law.

In the Eastern churches, a parallel institute to the diocesan synod is the eparchial assembly.[9] It, too, is a representative body composed of members of the Christian faithful who are periodically convened at the discretion of the eparch to advise him on matters of import for the eparchy.[10] The eparchial bishop convenes and presides over the assembly, personally or through a representative, and transfers, postpones, suspends, or dissolves it.[11] Like the diocesan synod (c. 463), the eparchial assembly is composed of members who must be convened by reason of office, members who are elected on a representational basis, and members who may be invited by the eparchial bishop.[12] Unlike the norms on diocesan synod members, the eparchial assembly norms make explicit provision for the election of deacon representatives.[13] With due regard for the right of the eparchial bishop to determine the agenda and the right of the faithful to propose questions for consideration at the assembly, he is to establish one or more preparatory commissions to organize matters to be discussed.[14] Like the diocesan bishop in the synod, the eparchial bishop is the sole legislator in the assembly.[15] He communicates the synod results according to particular law.[16]

The Nature and Purpose of a Diocesan Synod

Canon 460 — A diocesan synod is a group of selected priests and other members of the Christian faithful of a particular church who offer assistance to the diocesan bishop for the good of the whole diocesan community according to the norm of the following canons.

This introductory canon describes a diocesan synod, stating in general terms its nature as well as those who comprise it and its basic purpose. The synod is described from the outset in terms of its essential characteristic, namely, that it is a group or assembly (*coetus*) of the people of God.[17] This primary description of the synod is consistent with our contemporary understanding of the Church as the people of God and the diocese as a portion of the people of God. The synod's functional and organizational elements flow from its basic constitution.

Those who comprise this synodal group are generally designated as "selected priests and other members of the Christian faithful." The following canons provide more specific determinations regarding who must be convened and others who could be called to form the synod, but this initial determination of membership establishes a broad base of representation. Contrary to previous practice and legislation, the synod is no longer an exclusively clerical or presbyteral gathering. The phrase "other members of the Christian faithful" would obviously embrace any and all of those not included in the designation "selected priests." Therefore, the synod composition presumably would include deacons, laity, and members of institutes of consecrated life and/or societies of apostolic life, to the extent that these are present in the diocese.

While this chapter of the code is entitled "*Diocesan* Synod," canon 460 refers to the ambit of the synod as the "particular church," thus making it and the following norms applicable to other forms of particular churches.[18] These comments, however, will emphasize the diocese rather than other types of particular churches.

The purpose of the diocesan synod is clearly stated: to "offer assistance to the diocesan bishop for the good of the whole diocesan community."

---

[9] *CCEO* 235–242.
[10] *CCEO* 235–236.
[11] *CCEO* 237.
[12] *CCEO* 238.
[13] *CCEO* 238, §1, 8°.
[14] *CCEO* 240.
[15] *CCEO* 241.
[16] *CCEO* 242.

[17] The code commission specifically opted to use the word *coetus* here, indicating that it is the assembly that is significant, rather than the alternate word, "meeting" (*conventus*), which would have placed more emphasis on the vehicle used to achieve the purpose of the gathering. See *Comm* 12 [1980] 315.
[18] Cf. cc. 368–371.

This primary function of the synod reflects a concrete means by which the faithful exercise some of their rights and fulfill some of their obligations as recognized by the code. Among these rights and duties are building up the Body of Christ (canon 208), promoting the growth of the Church (canon 210), making known their spiritual needs (canon 212, §2), and expressing to their sacred pastors their opinion on matters which pertain to the good of the Church (canon 212, §3).

It has been traditional to designate the primary focus of the synod as assisting the bishop in the fulfillment of his legislative function. In discussing this portion of the code, the commission indicated its presumption that legislative activity was a primary synodal function,[19] but the final text does not make explicit this underlying expectation. Therefore, in the years since the promulgation of the code, a wide variety of formats and structures have been utilized for diocesan synods. In some cases, and often shortly after the promulgation of the 1983 code, the synod was the vehicle by which the diocesan bishop prepared a whole range of particular legislation called for in the code. In other cases, the synod process was utilized as a forum for planning, setting strategies, and establishing a unified diocesan vision, with little or no specific legislative activity. In some instances, the synodal activity was largely centralized, with diocesan personnel and agencies preparing texts and agenda items to lead to particular legislation. In other instances, a more decentralized, "grass roots" approach called for the faithful of the diocese to surface key issues for examination by the synod with little or no emphasis on legislation as an end product.[20]

This divergence in approach frequently reflected the episcopal leadership style in the given diocese as well as the needs of the local church. The "offering of assistance for the good of the diocese" was seen to have pastoral implications beyond the issuing of legislation. However, this same divergence may have motivated the July 1997 *Instruction on Diocesan Synods* issued by the Congregation for Bishops and the Congregation for the Evangelization of Peoples. Its prologue indicates some concerns about various forms of "diocesan assemblies" which "often include elements of diocesan [s]ynods [but]...lack a precise canonical character."[21] It is clear from the instruction and its appendix that these Roman dicasteries are calling for a shift back to the legislative function as the primary synodal focus. The appendix provides a lengthy listing of the various areas in which the code calls for diocesan norms or particular legislation.

The synod's attention is to be directed toward the "good of the whole diocesan community," and it is to this end that those who comprise the synod offer their assistance to the diocesan bishop.[22] The instruction more precisely describes what constitutes this "good of the whole." Within the larger context of the Church's pastoral activity which involves both communion and mission, the following are seen as works of the synod: promoting "acceptance of the Church's salvific doctrine" and encouraging the following of Christ; furthering "apostolic zeal" as a foundation for the Church's pastoral activities; attending to "the continued betterment of clerical life, the formation of clergy and the promotion of [priestly and religious life] vocations"; building up and fostering ecclesial unity through synodal documents that "accurately reflect the universal Magisterium of the Church"; "shaping pastoral activities" within the liturgical, spiritual, and canonical tradition; studying existing diocesan norms and reforming or expanding them as needed; evaluating the adequacy of existing pastoral programs; and proposing "new pastoral plans" as needed.[23]

After defining the diocesan synod, canon 460 indicates that the synod is to be governed by the

---

[19] *Comm* 12 (1980) 315.

[20] For other examples of the varying ways synod issues have been raised, see A. Rehrauer, "The Diocesan Synod," *CLSAP* 49 (1987) 12.

[21] *Origins* 27 (October 23, 1997) 324.

[22] For possible areas of synodal activity to "offer assistance to the diocesan bishop," see Jennings, 342.

[23] *Origins* 27 (October 23, 1997) 325.

canonical norms that follow, which will be reviewed in the following comments.

Convocation of a Synod

Canon 461 — §1. A diocesan synod is to be celebrated in individual particular churches when circumstances suggest it in the judgment of the diocesan bishop after he has heard the presbyteral council.

§2. If a bishop has the care of several dioceses or has the care of one as the proper bishop but of another as administrator, he can convoke one diocesan synod for all the dioceses entrusted to him.

As noted above, the 1917 norm (*CIC* 356, §1) requiring the convening of a synod every ten years was rarely observed. In many dioceses, prior to the 1983 code, there were few who could recall a previous synod having occurred. At various stages in the drafting of canon 461, §1 different norms were proposed on the frequency of a synod. These proposals ranged from the previous ten-year interval with a possible extension of an additional ten years,[24] to deleting any time reference at all and making the convocation of a synod an option for the diocesan bishop to consider.[25]

In the final text, it is expected that a diocesan synod will be a usual part of diocesan life, but the discretion of the diocesan bishop is respected in determining its frequency. The diocesan bishop is to exercise his prudent judgment regarding when "circumstances suggest" the convening of a synod. As part of his judgment process, he must seek the counsel of his presbyteral council. This consultation is consistent with the primary function of that advisory body to "assist as much as possible the bishop in the governance of the diocese . . . to promote the pastoral good of the [diocese]."[26] Depending on local circumstances and episcopal leadership preferences, the diocesan bishop may

choose to widen the circle of consultation regarding the appropriateness of convening a synod. Nothing in this canon precludes his consulting also with the diocesan pastoral council. Since this latter consultative body is designated to "investigate, consider, and propose practical conclusions about those things which pertain to pastoral works in the diocese,"[27] the diocesan bishop might have the pastoral council consider the advantages of a diocesan synod and propose their conclusions in that regard to him. Likewise, the bishop could choose to consult with other advisory groups who assist him. While these various consultations could help the bishop in his determinations regarding a synod, the only canonically required consultation is that of the presbyteral council.

The second paragraph of this canon also provides for some discretion on the part of the diocesan bishop. If two or more dioceses have been entrusted to his care, he may choose to convene a single synod for all of them. Such a situation could occur even if he is appointed as administrator in the additional diocese[s]. He would have to have been named administrator of that diocese in a more or less permanent manner[28] rather than in the situation of a vacant see since in this latter situation a synod ceases (c. 468, §2). Likewise, canon 462, §1 specifically excludes the convening of a synod by one who temporarily governs a diocese.

Prior to convening the joint synod, however, the diocesan bishop would need to make the same determination as for a synod in a single diocese, namely, that circumstances warrant it. Given the variations among dioceses, one may not assume that what is timely in one diocese is necessarily so in another. These same variations may make synodal recommendations which are appropriate in one diocese ineffectual in the next. Perhaps for these reasons the canon does not encourage this type of "corporate synod" but simply allows it.

In determining the timeliness of this alternate form of synod, the diocesan bishop must consult

---

[24] *Comm* 12 (1980) 315.
[25] *Comm* 14 (1982) 210.
[26] Canon 495, §1.

[27] Canon 511.
[28] See, for example, c. 371.

with the presbyteral council of each diocese affected. He will also need to convene members from each diocese in accord with the norms that follow. This latter consideration in itself may advise against this type of synod since the number of members convened could preclude effective interchange.

Canon 462 — §1. The diocesan bishop alone convokes a diocesan synod, but not one who temporarily presides over a diocese.

§2. The diocesan bishop presides over a diocesan synod. He can, however, delegate a vicar general or episcopal vicar to fulfill this responsibility for individual sessions of the synod.

The diocesan bishop is the one to whom the governance of the diocese has been principally committed and it is he who exercises the pastoral function within the diocese with ordinary, proper, and immediate power appropriate to his office.[29] Thus he alone has the authority to convoke a diocesan synod.

A diocesan administrator who presides over the diocese in a temporary fashion, as on the occasion of a vacant or impeded see, does not have the full scope of authority of a diocesan bishop.[30] In various diocesan matters his authority is circumscribed.[31] His ability to act in more significant diocesan administrative issues is even more restricted.[32] Because a diocesan synod is an exceptional event, it is logical that a diocesan adminis-

trator lacks the authority to convene a synod. This restriction is consistent with the age-old principle, "*Sede vacante, nihil innovetur.*"[33]

Just as the diocesan bishop convokes the synod, usually by means of a formal decree,[34] so also he normally presides over it. The second paragraph of this canon states this norm and then provides for an exception to it, namely, that for individual sessions of the synod, a vicar general or episcopal vicar can fulfill this function in his stead. The one who substitutes for the diocesan bishop is to do so only for individual sessions; a diocesan bishop would presumably not delegate another to act for him throughout the entirety of the synod. Prior to invoking this exception, it would be advisable to review the synod's primary purpose, that is, to offer assistance to the diocesan bishop. Having another person preside over the synod would seem to run counter to this primary function. This canon specifically designates a vicar general or episcopal vicar as those to whom delegation may be given.

The actual issuing of synodal documents is part of the legislative governance function of the diocesan bishop and cannot, therefore, be delegated.[35] Presiding over the synod, however, is part of the executive governance function of the diocesan bishop and can, therefore, be delegated. As with other forms of delegation, the diocesan bishop should designate in writing the specific person who is to act in his place.[36] In those dioceses with more than one vicar general and/or episcopal vicar, priority should be given to "one already invested with the episcopal dignity (Coadjutor or Auxiliary Bishop)."[37]

This canon presumes that the synod is not a solitary event but rather will consist of a series of

---

[29] Canons 381, 391.

[30] See c. 427, §1.

[31] The administrator cannot issue dimissorial letters under ordinary circumstances without the consent of the college of consultors (c. 1018, §1), nor can he issue dimissorial letters previously denied by the bishop (c. 1018, §2). He can allow access to the secret archives only in necessity (c. 490, §2). His removal of the chancellor or other notaries from office requires the consent of the college of consultors (c. 485).

[32] For example, during a vacant see the administrator can neither establish public associations of the Christian faithful (c. 312, §1, 3°) nor entrust a parish to a religious institute (c. 520, §1).

[33] Canon 428, §1: "When a see is vacant, nothing is to be altered."

[34] See cc. 48, 50–51. The CFB *Instruction* indicates that the issuance of this decree is required, usually on the occasion of a significant liturgical feast. *Origins* 27 (October 23, 1997) 326.

[35] Canon 135, §2.

[36] See c. 131, §3.

[37] *Origins* 27 (October 23, 1997) 325.

sessions. "The synodal sessions should be arranged over a period of time to study the questions raised during the sessions, as well as to make interventions during the discussions."[38]

Membership of the Diocesan Synod

Canon 463 — §1. The following must be called to a diocesan synod as members of the synod and are obliged to participate in it:

1° **a coadjutor bishop and auxiliary bishops;**

2° **vicars general, episcopal vicars, and the judicial vicar;**

3° **canons of the cathedral church;**

4° **members of the presbyteral council;**

5° **lay members of the Christian faithful, even members of institutes of consecrated life, chosen by the pastoral council in a manner and number to be determined by the diocesan bishop or, where this council does not exist, in a manner determined by the diocesan bishop;**

6° **the rector of the diocesan major seminary;**

7° **vicars forane;**

8° **at least one presbyter from each vicariate forane, chosen by all those who have the care of souls there; also another presbyter must be chosen who, if the first is impeded, is to take his place;**

9° **some superiors of religious institutes and of societies of apostolic life which have a house in the diocese, chosen in a number and manner determined by the diocesan bishop.**

§2. The diocesan bishop can also call others to a diocesan synod as members of the synod; they can be clerics, members of institutes of consecrated life, or lay members of the Christian faithful.

§3. If the diocesan bishop has judged it opportune, he can invite as observers to the diocesan synod other ministers or members of Churches or ecclesial communities which are not in full communion with the Catholic Church.

[38] Ibid., 328.

This canon provides a lengthy list of those who either must or can be called to comprise the synod. The bishop's obligation to convene certain persons is balanced by their obligation to participate in it, and the fact that the diocesan bishop must convene certain persons gives them a right to attend. However, he enjoys a degree of discretion in relation to those he may choose to call to the synod either as members or observers.

The list of synod participants designated in canon 463 can be divided into several categories: members who are called by reason of the office they hold; members who are to be selected by various groups or individuals; members who are designated by the diocesan bishop; those who can be invited to participate as observers.[39]

The first paragraph of this canon indicates those whom the diocesan bishop is obliged to call as members of the synod. First among this group (c. 463, §1, 1°) are the coadjutor bishop and any auxiliary bishops. Their presence at a synod is consistent both with their general diocesan leadership role and the purpose of the synod. Since these bishops are to "assist the diocesan bishop in the entire governance of the diocese,"[40] and the synod is convened to "offer assistance to the diocesan bishop for the good of the whole [diocese],"[41] their presence and participation in the synod are logical. If the provisions of canon 406 were observed, however, namely that coadjutor and auxiliary bishops are to be named vicars general or episcopal vicars, they would be included among those who must be convened by reason of those offices as designated in the following category.

[39] G. Read in *CLSGBI Com,* 259 observes that the synod is not an open assembly or pastoral congress to which all who wish may be admitted. Such an opinion is consistent with the caution in the CFB *Instruction* that diocesan assemblies be distinguished from synods. It would not be contrary to the law, however, for the diocesan bishop to invite the entire population of a very small diocese as synod participants; he would have to consider the practicality of such a plan.

[40] Canon 405, §2.

[41] Canon 460.

Because they assist the diocesan bishop in the executive governance of the diocese, either in its entirety or in designated regions or activities, vicars general and episcopal vicars are logically among those who must be called as members of the synod (c. 463, §1, 2°). The judicial vicar exercises a similar role in relation to the bishop's judicial function and, therefore, also is included among those whom the diocesan bishop must convene.[42]

The third group who must participate in the synod (c. 463, §1, 3°) are the canons of the cathedral church. In many dioceses there is no such group and thus this portion of the canon would be inapplicable. Some mention should be made, however, of a change in legislation in this area which does appear to be significant. Under the 1917 code, if there were no cathedral chapter, the diocesan consultors were to be called in their place (*CIC* 358, §1, 2°). This provision is not found in the current law. Some would say that, because of the fact that the subsequent group mentioned among those who must be called is the presbyteral council (c. 463, §1, 4°), the consultors would necessarily be included.[43] However, the term of office of an individual consultor may exceed his term on the presbyteral council. Thus, he would be a member of the college of consultors without being a member of the council. Under such circumstances, certain members of the college of consultors might not be obliged to participate in the synod or have a right to do so. Obviously, because he may appoint additional members (c. 462, §2), the diocesan bishop could supply for this apparent *lacuna* in the law by his personal appointment of any such individuals.

As just mentioned, the members of the presbyteral council are among those whom the diocesan bishop must convene. Their presence is also consistent with their role as the preeminent diocesan consultative body. The presbyteral council exists to "assist the bishop in the governance of the diocese . . . to promote as much as possible the pastoral good of [the diocese],"[44] and the purpose of the synod is offering assistance for the good of the diocese. The presbyteral council is the one group which must be consulted by the diocesan bishop prior to his decision to convoke a synod; their presence at the synod is, therefore, logical as well.

All of the aforementioned synod members are necessarily presbyters by reason of the requirements of the offices they hold or the roles they play. Subsequently, the membership of the synod is expanded to include more representation from the whole of the people of God.

Certain lay members of the Christian faithful must be called as members of the synod (c. 463, §1, 5°); the manner in which they are designated for synodal membership may vary from diocese to diocese. If there is a pastoral council[45] in the diocese, it is to be involved in the designation of the lay membership of the synod. While laity are among the members of the pastoral council, this canon does not seem to require that those who serve on it be named to the synod, rather they are simply to be involved in the selection process. It is the bishop's prerogative to determine the manner in which the selection takes place as well as the number of persons selected. If there is no pastoral council, the diocesan bishop is to designate some other means by which these lay members are chosen for membership in the synod.

While the members of the synod need not be the same as those of the pastoral council, the 1997 instruction suggests that the same principles governing the representative membership of the council and the qualities expected of council members be utilized in selecting the members of the synod.[46] Thus they are to be "selected in such a way that they truly reflect the entire portion of the people of God which constitutes the diocese, with consideration given to the different areas of the diocese, so-

---

[42] Judicial vicars were not included in an earlier version of this canon but were added, without comment or explanation, in the 1980 schema (*Comm* 12 [1980] 317).

[43] D. Ross, "Participation in the Synod," *ME* 116 (1991) 464.

[44] Canon 495, §1.

[45] Canons 511–514.

[46] *Origins* 27 (October 23, 1997) 325–326.

cial conditions and professions, and the role which they have in the apostolate whether individually or joined with others."[47] They are also to be chosen because they are "outstanding in firm faith, good morals, and prudence."[48]

Among the lay participants can be included members of religious and secular institutes. It would appear to be within the authority of the diocesan bishop to indicate a certain number or proportion of the lay members who are to come from such institutes when he designates the manner of selection. Alternately, since he retains the right to name additional members, he could determine that the synod membership does not adequately represent the full scope of that portion of the people of God entrusted to him, and name members of such institutes as well as members of societies of apostolic life who are not specifically included among those listed for potential membership.

Clerical members of institutes of consecrated life or societies of apostolic life are not included under this title of membership. However, they may be members under other titles of mandatory membership or by reason of personal designation by the diocesan bishop to ensure proper representation of the diocese at large.

Given the prescriptions of paragraph three of canon 463, those to be included among these lay members would be Catholics in full communion. The 1997 instruction specifies that these lay members of the faithful are to be "in a canonically regular situation in order to take part in the [s]ynod."[49]

While clerics are also members of the pastoral council, their membership in the synod is based on other reasons. Deacons may also serve on the pastoral council. However, neither in this provision for synod membership nor in the other categories of obligatory synod members does it ap-

pear to be required that any deacons be called to membership in the synod. However, the diocesan bishop could designate such clerics as members of the synod.

Also to be named to the synod is the rector of the diocesan major seminary if such exists in the diocese (c. 463, §1, 6°). Rectors of other seminaries, either those of religious institutes or minor seminaries or interdiocesan seminaries, are not mandatory participants in the synod. The presence of the seminary rector is appropriate because of his significance in the formation of those who will assume positions of leadership in the diocese.

Given their role in the coordination of pastoral activity in a region of the diocese,[50] the presence of the vicars forane as members of the synod (c. 463, §1, 7°) contributes to the fulfillment of its purpose. While each vicar exercises his coordinating function only within a portion of the diocese, the cumulative presence of all of these vicars provides a representation of the needs and conditions of the diocese as a whole before the synod.

The next category of persons to be selected for membership in the synod are the priests of the diocese (c. 463, §1, 8°). In order to ensure a presbyteral representation from the whole of the diocese similar to that of the lay representation, at least one priest from each vicariate forane is to be selected for membership. This provision states the minimum number of priests from each vicariate, but the diocesan bishop could designate a larger number or, in fact, in dioceses with fewer priests he could designate the whole of the presbyterate as synod members.[51]

If there is to be a selection process, the canon does not specify the manner of selection, merely those who are to be selected and those who do the selecting. Obviously, from the very wording of the canon, those to be selected under this provision are priests, but the canon does not designate them as diocesan, secular,[52] or members of insti-

---

[47] Canon 512, §2.

[48] Canon 512, §3.

[49] *Origins* 27 (October 23, 1997) 326. As an instruction this document is not making new law. It may be clarifying the meaning of "full communion" in this context.

[50] Canon 555, §1, 1°.

[51] *Origins* 27 (October 23, 1997) 326.

[52] The category "secular" includes members of personal prelatures (c. 294).

tutes of consecrated life or societies of apostolic life. Therefore, a priest from any of these categories would appear to be eligible for synod membership.

Those who do the selecting are "those who have the care of souls" in each vicariate forane. Priests, deacons, and laity can have the "care of souls." There is a distinction, however, between those who hold offices entailing "full care of souls," which offices are restricted to priests, and those who hold other offices entailing partial care of souls and are not required to be priests.[53] The context of this canon would seem to indicate that "those who have the care of souls" and are involved in the selection process for priest representatives from each vicariate forane to the synod are themselves priests of that territory. Again, the selectors are not restricted to diocesan priests but to all priests of the vicariate.

The selection process is to be designated by the diocesan bishop. It could include an election which follows the norms for canonical elections[54] or some other process for choosing synodal representatives. Since the presbyteral council of a diocese is also to be a representative body[55] whose selection process and criteria are designated in its statutes, that already established selection process could be reviewed as a possible model for the manner of synod selections.

While elsewhere in the synod legislation[56] synod members are prohibited from sending a substitute if they are impeded from attending, there is a contrary provision for these presbyteral synodal representatives. In the vicariate forane selection process, a second priest is also to be designated should the originally selected one be impeded from participation. The canon addresses the situation in which the original representative, impeded from participation in one session of the synod, becomes capable of participation in subsequent sessions.

[53] See Ross, 473.
[54] Canons 164–179.
[55] Canon 499.
[56] Canon 464.

The final category of members who must be called to the synod are superiors of religious institutes and societies of apostolic life (c. 463, §1, 9°). The manner of selection for these synod members is not determined in the law but rather by the diocesan bishop who also specifies the number of individuals.

There are two prerequisites for those who are eligible for selection under this title: they must be superiors and their institute or society must have a house in the diocese. The canon neither designates the individual as a major superior[57] nor requires that the superior be domiciled within the diocese. An institute could have a house within the diocese, and the major superior of that institute, residing elsewhere, could be selected for synod membership. The diocesan bishop should take such considerations into account as he designates the manner in which the selection process is to proceed.

The superiors mentioned in the canon are those of religious institutes and societies of apostolic life; there is no distinction here between those which are clerical and those which are lay. Nor are secular institutes included in this canon even though they may be present within the diocese. The diocesan bishop could include a representative from this category under the provisions of paragraph two.

Regardless of the title under which these synodal representative are called, their designation as members should be communicated in writing by the diocesan bishop. Likewise, their acceptance of membership should be communicated to him in writing. The canon does not address a situation in which an individual is designated for membership either by reason of office or representative selection yet later loses the foundation upon which the membership was based, either prior to or during the course of the synod. For example, a priest could have been selected as a vicariate representative during the preparatory stages, and at some point prior to the actual gathering of the synod he has been transferred to an assignment which takes

[57] Canon 620.

him out of the vicariate he is chosen to represent. He would not appear to be impeded as such, but the basis for his selection no longer exists. Such could also be the case of a vicar general or episcopal vicar who ceases from such office during the course of the synod.

Having completed in paragraph one the designation of those who must be called to synod membership, the canon leaves to the discretion of the diocesan bishop the designation of additional members. While these additional members are not mandated, once named to the synod, they are full members with the right to full participation. In naming additional members, the diocesan bishop will want to take into account "those ecclesial vocations or the various apostolic works not sufficiently represented among elected members, to give adequate expression to the true make-up of the diocese."[58] It is under the auspices of this free selection process that the diocesan bishop will want to consider those categories of persons noted already as not being included under a mandatory title, such as deacons, superiors of secular institutes, or members of societies of apostolic life. Again, both selection and acceptance should be communicated in writing.

The final paragraph of this canon provides for an additional category of persons to attend the synod. They are distinct from those already mentioned since they are not formally members of the synod but are rather observers. These observers can be designated at the discretion of the diocesan bishop from among the ministers and members of other Christian churches or ecclesial communities not in full communion with the Catholic Church. As observers they lack the right to participate in consultative votes, but they could be given the right to a voice in the discussions. Their presence would add an ecumenical dimension to the matters under consideration by the synod, thus reflecting the experience of Vatican II itself.[59] A practical recommendation in the 1997 instruction is that these observers be selected in consultation

with the leadership of the churches or ecclesial communities involved.[60]

The canon does not seem to provide for the selection of non-Christians as synod observers. However, such a selection would appear to be within the discretion of the diocesan bishop.[61] An interfaith component could be a significant factor, especially in those regions where there is a large number of non-Christians or significant interaction with members and leaders of non-Christian religions such as Judaism or Islam.

Canon 464 — If a member of the synod is prevented by a legitimate impediment, the member cannot send a proxy to attend it in his or her name. The member, however, is to inform the diocesan bishop of this impediment.

With the exception noted above regarding the substitute for the presbyteral representative from a vicariate forane, other members of the synod may not send a substitute or proxy in their place if they are impeded from attending. This restriction applies to all members of the synod, both those who must be convened and those whom the diocesan bishop chooses to convene. While individual members who are impeded are not permitted on their own authority to send a substitute or proxy, the diocesan bishop could establish a manner of designating a substitute, and he himself could admit that person to the synod. Since certain individuals, such as lay persons chosen by the pastoral council (c. 463, §1, 5°) or superiors (c. 463, §1, 9°), are to be selected in a "manner determined by the diocesan bishop," this manner could include a means of designating an alternate whom the diocesan bishop could admit to the synod.[62]

The individual who is impeded from participation is to inform the diocesan bishop of this fact.

[58] *Origins* 27 (October 23, 1997) 326.
[59] Ibid.

[60] Ibid.
[61] J. Alesandro, in *CLSA Com*, 381.
[62] Since this canon applies only to those who are "members," unless the diocesan bishop has determined otherwise, observers (c. 463, §3) may send substitutes if unable to attend personally. See Alesandro, in *CLSA Com*, 381.

Such a communication would ordinarily be in writing but the canon does not require this. Informing the bishop in a timely fashion would be important if he intends to name a substitute. The canon does not distinguish between absence from the synod as a whole or from an individual session.

Finally, it should be noted that all synod members must make a profession of faith before the synod discussions commence (c. 833, 1°). Ordinarily the profession takes place after the first solemn session. The bishop makes his profession in the presence of the gathered synod. The other members are to do so in the presence of the diocesan bishop as president of the synod or his delegate. Obviously this same requirement cannot be imposed on those who are merely observers. The formula for the profession of faith is that issued in 1989.[63]

Synod Participation and Outcomes

Canon 465 — All proposed questions are subject to the free discussion of the members during sessions of the synod.

The matters to be studied at the synod arise from and are shaped by the experience of the local church. Even in those situations in which the synod is engaged in a process of drafting particular legislation in compliance with universal law, there will be variations among the churches in adapting the directives of that law. In order that the fullest experience of the synodal process might be possible, this canon assures that the members of the synod have the right to discuss freely the matters before the synod. Such free discussion would preclude the devolution of the synod into merely a perfunctory gathering to rubber stamp decisions already made.

Once called to the synod, the members have a concrete opportunity to exercise several of their rights as members of the Christian faithful. They can make known their needs and desires,[64] and express their opinions[65] based on their individual knowledge and competence. For example, parents who have experienced a need for more coordinated sacramental preparation for their children could raise that concern during discussions of diocesan educational directions. Those who have special expertise in religious education could, likewise, help frame issues surrounding age-appropriate catechetics. The synod participants can also further their education into Christian maturity[66] or engage freely in theological discussions according to their expertise.[67]

Free discussion and the exercise of one's rights in the context of a synod should not result, however, in any sense of disorder or disharmony. Careful preparation of general rules of order or procedural norms can produce sessions which are well ordered and yet allow for interaction and discussion.[68] While, as noted above, the diocesan bishop or his delegate presides over the synodal sessions, the presider need not be the one who coordinates or facilitates the discussion. In his presiding role, however, the diocesan bishop has the ultimate responsibility to see to the good order of the synod. Such good order would obviously include managing the manner in which interventions are made, questions are raised, and issues are discussed. The presider's responsibility would include seeing to it that mechanisms are in place to achieve these ends while not necessarily having to manage them personally. Additionally, the good order of the synod would include the responsibility of seeing to it that the synod deliberations contribute to or at least do not detract from the good of the diocese.[69]

---

[63] *AAS* 81 (1989) 104–105.
[64] Canon 212, §2.
[65] Canon 212, §3.
[66] Canon 217.
[67] Canon 218.
[68] *Origins* 27 (October 23, 1997) 328.
[69] The CFB *Instruction* states that, in light of the diocesan bishop's concern for the bonds which unite the particular and the universal Church, he is to exclude from the discussion any matters "discordant with the perennial doctrine of the Church or the Magisterium or concerning material reserved to Supreme ecclesiastical authority or to other ecclesiastical authorities." Like-

Canon 466 — The only legislator in a diocesan synod is the diocesan bishop; the other members of the synod possess only a consultative vote. Only he signs the synodal declarations and decrees, which can be published by his authority alone.

Within the diocese entrusted to his care, the diocesan bishop exercises his pastoral governance role with legislative, executive, and judicial power.[70] Unlike the latter two powers, legislative power cannot be delegated but must be exercised personally.[71] Canon 466 is consistent with this principle and highlights the bishop's central role within the synod as the only legislator.

As with other areas of diocesan governance, the bishop exercises his episcopal office not in isolation but in consultation with other members of the Christian faithful. The other members of the synod, in assisting the diocesan bishop, play a consultative role. This role, however, is a significant one. While the final decision on matters before the synod rests with the diocesan bishop, the entire decision-making process is a consultative one involving all the members of the synod.[72]

The opinions of the members of the synod may be sought by the bishop even by means of consultative votes on various issues before them. "Since the [s]ynod is not a college with decisional capacity, such votes are not intended as a binding majority decision.... [R]ather... their purpose is to indicate the degree of concurrence among the synodal members with regard to a given proposal."[73] Remaining free in his ultimate decision, the diocesan bishop "may wish to accept the view ex-

pressed by the members of the [s]ynod, unless there should exist [in his prudential judgment] some grave obstacle."[74]

The issuance and publication of the synod decrees are legislative acts of the diocesan bishop. Since he is the sole legislator, it is appropriate that he alone sign the decrees and authorize their publication. With this promulgation of synodal legislation, the diocesan bishop may either establish a specific suspensive period (*vacatio legis*) before it takes effect or allow the general norm of one month from the promulgation date to be the effective date.[75]

Canon 467 — The diocesan bishop is to communicate the texts of the synodal declarations and decrees to the metropolitan and the conference of bishops.

Synodal legislation applies only within the diocese. Nonetheless, the sharing of the results of the synod with the metropolitan and the conference of bishops promotes ecclesial communion at the provincial and conference level. However, the legislation need not be confirmed at these other levels.[76] Nor is there a need for Roman review (*recognitio*) as is true for episcopal conference (c. 455, §2) or particular council (c. 446) norms.

Earlier drafts of this canon had also required that the synodal legislation be communicated to the Apostolic See. This requirement was eventually omitted because the consultors judged that it evoked an ecclesiology that was too centralized.[77] However, the 1997 instruction reintroduces a call for the communication of the synodal documents to the Apostolic See, either to the Congregation for Bishops or to the Congregation for the Evangelization of Peoples, through the appropriate pontifical representative in the region.[78] The rationale for the inclusion of this "requirement," particularly in

---

wise the bishop is cautioned not to allow the use of the synod as a vehicle to transmit similarly contrary opinions or polls to higher authority. *Origins* 27 (October 23, 1997) 328.

[70] Canon 391, §1.

[71] Canons 391, §2; 135, §2.

[72] For more on consultative decision-making, see R. Kennedy, "Shared Responsibility in Ecclesial Decision-Making," *Stud Can* 14 (1980) 5–23.

[73] *Origins* 27 (October 23, 1997) 328.

[74] Ibid.

[75] Canon 8, §2.

[76] Alesandro, in *CLSA Com,* 382.

[77] *Rel,* 111.

[78] *Origins* 27 (October 23, 1997) 328–329.

light of the reasons for its previous omission, is not mentioned in the document and may indicate renewed efforts toward centralization. Again, the instruction mentions communication and does not imply the need for confirmation or approval of the synodal documents.

Cessation of a Synod

Canon 468 — §1. The diocesan bishop is competent to suspend or dissolve a diocesan synod according to his prudent judgment.

§2. When an episcopal see is vacant or impeded, a diocesan synod is interrupted by the law itself until the succeeding diocesan bishop has decided that it is to be continued or has declared it terminated.

Just as the diocesan bishop is the competent authority to convene a synod, so also is he capable of suspending or dissolving the synod. He is to do so based on his own prudent judgment, that is, based on some reasons that are at least as serious as the fact of ending the synod. Because of the presbyteral council's consultative role in more important matters of diocesan governance, such as holding a synod,[79] the council would be an appropriate source of advice before the bishop decides to suspend or dissolve a synod.[80] The decision to suspend or dissolve the synod should be communicated in writing unless such a step is impossible. If the decision is for suspension of the synod, rather than its dissolution, and the suspension is not indefinite, a resumption date should also be communicated.

In addition to the bishop's suspension or dissolution of the synod, the law itself decrees its interruption during the time a see is vacant or impeded. A see becomes vacant with the diocesan bishop's death, his resignation accepted by the pope, his transfer, or his removal from office once notice has been communicated to him.[81] The

inability of the diocesan bishop to communicate with and therefore care for the people entrusted to him, either by reason of his captivity, banishment, exile, or incapacity, results in an impeded see.[82]

Only the succeeding diocesan bishop is able to continue or terminate the synod; a diocesan administrator of a vacant see or the individual who assumes governance of an impeded see may not do so. The new diocesan bishop remains free to reconstitute the synod or to dissolve it. In his reconvening of the synod he is also free to alter its membership, procedures, or agenda.

CHAPTER II
THE DIOCESAN CURIA
[cc. 469–494]

A diocese is entrusted to the diocesan bishop for his pastoral care.[83] He is not alone, however, in fulfilling the responsibilities entrusted to him. One of the vehicles available to assist him in his administration of the diocese is his curia. The five canons that introduce this chapter provide general norms on the operation and coordination of the curia. The subsequent articles in this chapter address specific institutes and persons who comprise the curia.

The corresponding article in the Code of Canons of the Eastern Churches consists of only two canons. The first provides a lengthier, but still not comprehensive, list of curial members than does the corresponding canon under our consideration.[84] Like his counterpart, the diocesan bishop, the eparchial bishop is free both to appoint those who will serve in the eparchial curia and to remove them from office.[85] Members of the eparchial curia are bound to take an oath of office and

---

[79] Canon 500, §2.
[80] *Origins* 27 (October 23, 1997) 328.
[81] Canon 416.

[82] Canon 412.
[83] Canons 369, 381.
[84] Compare *CCEO* 243, §2, which lists ten specific curial offices or institutes, with the more generic statement of c. 469.
[85] *CCEO* 244, §1.

make a promise of secrecy similar to that of their Latin colleagues.[86]

Meaning, Purpose, and Composition of the Curia

Canon 469 — The diocesan curia consists of those institutions and persons which assist the bishop in the governance of the whole diocese, especially in guiding pastoral action, in caring for the administration of the diocese, and in exercising judicial power.

This initial canon defines the diocesan curia as consisting of both persons and institutions. The curia consists of those individuals as well as those structures which exist to assist the diocesan bishop in his governance responsibilities. The canon highlights a threefold focus for the function of the diocesan curia: guiding pastoral action, conducting general administration, and exercising judicial power.

Beyond these general designations, however, the diocesan bishop has broad discretion in determining the structure and composition of the diocesan curia. Subsequent articles in this chapter will provide more specific norms on certain required officers of diocesan administration such as vicars, chancellors, and finance officers. Even within these required areas the diocesan bishop has a great degree of latitude in specific applications of the law. He is free to make his own determinations in such matters as: the areas of concern assigned to vicars, if and how many vice chancellors shall be appointed, how the finance officer should relate to others involved in financial matters such as development directors or fund raisers. The size and complexity of the diocesan curia will vary with the needs of different dioceses.

Common components of the diocesan curia will include "pastoral, social-charitable, and liturgical departments."[87] Among the usual divisions of that portion of the diocesan curia responsible

for pastoral matters are such areas as schools and religious education.

The overall purpose of the curia is to assist the diocesan bishop in discharging his pastoral governance responsibilities. The curial offices exist "to be the means for studying, planning and carrying through the pastoral program which the bishop weighs and ponders together with his [presbyteral and pastoral] councils."[88]

Canon 470 — The appointment of those who exercise offices in the diocesan curia pertains to the diocesan bishop.

Consistent with the purpose of the diocesan curia, namely, to assist the diocesan bishop in discharging his governance role, this canon designates him as the one authorized to make appointments to curial offices. While every diocese, using tools and processes developed within the human resources field,[89] will have established its own practical means of surfacing, interviewing, and presenting candidates for various offices, the final appointment to office rests with the diocesan bishop.[90] There are some specific provisions in law for appointment to certain offices; for example, the bishop must consult the finance council and college of consultors prior to appointing the finance officer.[91]

Some curial positions clearly exist as ecclesiastical offices, that is, "function[s] constituted in a stable manner by divine or ecclesiastical ordinance to be exercised for a spiritual purpose."[92] They are established as such by universal law. Universal

---

[86] *CCEO* 244, §2.
[87] *Directory* 200.

[88] Ibid.
[89] The National Association of Church Personnel Administrators (NACPA), headquartered in Cincinnati, Ohio, can serve dioceses in their development and evaluation of personnel systems. NACPA attempts to integrate good management and human resources principles with pastoral values.
[90] See c. 157 on free conferral of offices in the diocese.
[91] Canon 494, §1. See also Read, in *CLSGBI Com,* 262.
[92] Canon 145, §1. A complete review of the general norms on ecclesiastical office would be useful prior to establishing or realigning any curial offices.

law, however, is not the only source of ecclesiastical office; the diocesan bishop can establish ecclesiastical offices by means of particular law.

With the establishment of an office its rights and obligations are defined.[93] Certain criteria, such as one's being in the communion of the Church and capable of discharging the office[94] must be met before an individual can be provided with an office. In some cases being an ordained presbyter is a prerequisite for an office, for example when it entails the full care of souls[95] as in the case of a pastor,[96] or when the law establishes such a prerequisite as in the case of a vicar general or episcopal vicar.[97]

The appointment to office can be for a designated or an indefinite period of time. Once the office is conferred on a person, there is a presumption of stability. However, the degree of stability will vary. A vicar general can be removed freely at the bishop's discretion; a pastor, however, can be removed only after a formal process. Because of this stability in office, an individual can be removed from the office only for cause, and in some instances according to established procedures.[98] Furthermore, even removal from office does not necessarily terminate a financial responsibility toward the individual.[99] Civil contract provisions[100] as well as the demands of social justice[101] will dictate financial arrangements to be made upon termination.

Although not required for validity, appointments to curial offices should be made in writ-

---

[93] Canon 145, §2.
[94] Canon 149, §1.
[95] Canon 150.
[96] Canon 521, §1.
[97] Canon 478, §1.
[98] Canons 192–195.
[99] Canon 195.
[100] Canon 1290.
[101] See NACPA, *Just Treatment for Those Who Work for the Church* (Cincinnati: NACPA, 1986). See also CLSA, "Canonical Standards in Labor-Management Relations: A Report," *CLSAP* (1987) 311–335, for a correlation between the Church's social teaching and its institutional responsibility toward church workers.

ing[102] and notarized by the chancellor or another ecclesiastical notary.[103]

While it is important to apply the norms on ecclesiastical offices to some curial members, it is not always easy when viewing diocesan organizational charts or management systems, to determine which, if any, curial positions have been constituted as ecclesiastical offices by particular law. Not every position within the diocesan curia needs to be established as an office in order to contribute to the ministry and work of the diocese.

Canon 471 — All those who are admitted to offices in the curia must:
   1° promise to fulfill their function faithfully according to the manner determined by law or by the bishop;
   2° observe secrecy within the limits and according to the manner determined by law or by the bishop.

Once it has been determined which curial positions are truly constituted as ecclesiastical offices, the norms of this canon are applied to them. It imposes two obligations on the officeholder: one, to promise faithful fulfillment of the obligations of the office and two, to preserve the confidentiality required by the office. The means by which the promise is communicated and the person to whom it is communicated are not specified in the canon. The promise of fidelity to the obligations of the office would presumably be made to the diocesan bishop or his delegate. Since it is the diocesan bishop who appoints to office and, in the case of offices established under particular law, defines the office, this conclusion seems appropriate.[104] The promise should be made in writing and a written record of it kept on file.

---

[102] Canon 156.
[103] Canon 474.
[104] This conclusion is also consistent with c. 833, 5° which determines that the vicar general, episcopal vicar, and judicial vicar, all curial officers, make their profession of faith in the presence of the diocesan bishop or his delegate.

The obligation of observing the necessary level of secrecy could be seen as an expectation of faithful fulfillment of the office, and, therefore, it could be included as an element of the promise noted above. The level of secrecy to be maintained is that which is defined in the law[105] or by the bishop himself. Obviously, if an office holder is to be held accountable, the confidentiality expected of the person must be clearly communicated, preferably in the written position description or in a general policy manual or personnel handbook.

Canon 472 — The prescripts of Book VII, *Processes,* are to be observed regarding cases and persons which belong to the exercise of judicial power in the curia. The prescripts of the following canons, however, are to be observed regarding those things which pertain to the administration of the diocese.

As noted in the canon which introduced this chapter, the work of the diocesan curia is pastoral, administrative, and judicial. For judicial matters the norms of Book VII, devoted to procedures, are to be applied. For all other curial activity, the norms in the remainder of this chapter are to be observed. The fact that there are different canonical norms to govern the judicial function as opposed to the pastoral or administrative does not mean that the tribunal is completely separated or isolated from the rest of the curia; tribunal personnel are truly part of the curia as stated in canon 469. When personnel or other matters distinct from the internal working of the judicial processes are being considered within the curia, input from and communication with tribunal personnel or their representative would be important.

---

[105]In some cases the law determines the degree of confidentiality to be observed. For example, members of the presbyteral council are not to divulge the contents of their meetings (c. 500, §2), and judges and other tribunal personnel are bound to varying degrees of secrecy based on the nature of the case before them (c. 1455).

Coordination of Curial Activity

Canon 473 — §1. A diocesan bishop must take care that all the affairs which belong to the administration of the whole diocese are duly coordinated and are ordered to attain more suitably the good of the portion of the people of God entrusted to him.

§2. It is for the diocesan bishop himself to coordinate the pastoral action of the vicars general or episcopal vicars. Where it is expedient, a moderator of the curia can be appointed who must be a priest and who, under the authority of the bishop, is to coordinate those things which pertain to the treatment of administrative affairs and to take care that the other members of the curia properly fulfill the office entrusted to them.

§3. Unless in the judgment of the bishop local circumstances suggest otherwise, the vicar general or if there are several, one of the vicars general, is to be appointed moderator of the curia.

§4. Where the bishop has judged it expedient, he can establish an episcopal council, consisting of the vicars general and episcopal vicars, to foster pastoral action more suitably.

Regardless of the simplicity or complexity of the curial structure, whenever two or more persons or offices are functioning to serve a common end, as they are intended to do within the curia as a whole, coordination of their activities is essential. Likewise, the diocesan bishop is obliged to see that all the works of the apostolate are coordinated (c. 394, §1). This canon provides a variety of ways in which that coordination can occur. It is to be noted that, while none of the means of coordination proposed in the canon is mandatory, the practice of coordination is an expectation.

As the one ultimately responsible for the ministry of the diocesan curia, the diocesan bishop is also ultimately responsible for the coordination of the activities of the curia. While different management styles and structural configurations will result in more or less direct episcopal involvement in the daily activity of the various curial offices, the diocesan bishop remains the chief pastor and leader of the diocese. Hence, his coordination of the activities of those whom he appoints to curial offices is truly an integral component of his episcopal office.

One model of curial organization includes the appointment of various vicars to assume ordinary, executive authority over the whole diocese or over various parts of the diocese or apostolic functions within the diocese.[106] As vicars, they act in the name and stead of the diocesan bishop. Hence, it is proper that the diocesan bishop himself be designated as responsible for the coordination of their pastoral activities.

In those circumstances in which the diocesan bishop deems it appropriate, rather than coordinating all of the curial activities himself, he can designate someone, provided it is a priest, to coordinate the work of other members of the curia. This individual, aptly named a moderator of the curia, functions under the authority of the diocesan bishop to assist him in his coordination of the administrative activities of the curia.

This section of the canon seems to distinguish between the curial activity of the vicars, designating it as "pastoral," and the curial activity of others, indicating that it is "administrative." Should the diocesan bishop determine that it is in the best interests of the diocese to name a moderator of the curia, therefore, it would seem that the coordination function of this individual would be in relation to administrative activities rather than pastoral ones. There will be situations, however, in which the two realms of activity are so interrelated as to be virtually indistinguishable. Furthermore, the moderator of the curia would not direct the work of the vicars but that of others in the curia.[107] It needs to be kept in mind, however, that, in many dioceses, the heads of the various curial departments are designated as episcopal vicars. In such a case, the coordination of the departmental activities within the curia would be appropriate to a moderator of the curia. Clear

lines of authority, accountability, and responsibility would be essential whatever design of coordination is enacted.

Having designated very generically the function of the moderator of the curia and set one prerequisite, presbyteral orders, the canon sets an additional, though not mandatory, standard, namely that the moderator of the curia be a vicar general (§3). The fact that the moderator also holds the office of vicar general does not mean that he automatically, as moderator, assumes a directive role over all other vicars, either general or episcopal. As noted above, the coordination of the pastoral activity of these vicars is primarily an episcopal function. As also noted above, however, there may be situations in which the administrative functions of the vicars would come under the direction of the moderator of the curia.

One final, optional vehicle for curial coordination is found in the last paragraph of the canon. Paragraph two established the principle that the diocesan bishop is responsible for the coordination of the pastoral activity of the vicars; paragraph four presents him with a means to exercise that responsibility. If he judges it to be useful in the context of his own curia, the diocesan bishop could establish a council composed of his vicars general and episcopal vicars. The purpose of this episcopal council seems clear. It exists as a means to examine and promote the coordination of the pastoral activities entrusted to the vicars.

The coordination of the work of the curia is essential if it is to provide true pastoral and administrative service to the diocese and not devolve into simply a series of bureaucratic structures with a life of their own divorced from the mission of the diocese. The means of coordination, however, can be many and varied based on a diocese's structural complexity, size, location, geographic spread, and praxis. Those vehicles for coordination that are suggested but not mandated in this canon can serve as a starting point for the diocesan bishop to determine the most appropriate means for curial coordination in his own diocese. He is also free to determine some of his own.

[106] For more on the roles of vicars, see the comments on cc. 475–481.

[107] Alesandro, in *CLSA Com,* 385.

For example, some bishops have found it helpful to meet regularly, monthly or weekly depending on the size and complexity of the curial structure, with those individuals, whether they be vicars or others,[108] charged with the management of various aspects of the curia. This group often forms a kind of "cabinet" for the diocesan bishop, ensuring that he is kept informed of the programs and projects being developed as well as the issues of concern being raised from or about various groups in the diocese. These meetings also provide the bishop with the opportunity to chart the course of the work of the curia, seeing that it is consistent with his own vision of the mission of the diocese.

Other forms of coordination can include annual or more frequent meetings of the entire staff of the curia with the diocesan bishop. Such meetings can provide the opportunity for an annual "state of the diocese" report from the diocesan bishop and can be a source of spiritual support and pastoral encouragement for those who serve the bishop and the diocese in various capacities, including administrative and support staff. These types of meetings will often include announcements of specific goals toward which all will strive in a concerted effort for the good of the diocese.

Canon 474 — For validity, acts of the curia which are to have juridic effect must be signed by the ordinary from whom they emanate; they must also be signed by the chancellor of the curia or a notary. The chancellor, moreover, is bound to inform the moderator of the curia concerning such acts.

For the diocesan bishop and his curia, written records of actions serve not only as proofs that something occurred but also as historical signposts of the diocese's evolution. This canon is deceptively simple; documents are to be signed, notarized, and communicated appropriately. However, beneath the surface of this simplicity, some technical canonical points need to be addressed.

The phrase "acts of the curia" (*acta curiae*) has a specific meaning. It does not refer to all of the daily, physical actions taken by the members of the curia. Nor does it refer to those actions called "juridic acts."[109] Rather, it refers to the formal, written documents which emanate from some members of the curia. While we are usually more accustomed to referring to judicial documentation as acts ("acts of the case" or "publication of the acts"), the administrative arena also generates "acts."

The acts, or documents, referenced in this canon are, even more specifically, those which are to have a juridic effect, that is, those which make something legally effective. These kinds of documents must be signed by the ordinary who issued them and countersigned or notarized by the chancellor or another ecclesiastical notary. The signature of the ordinary is for the validity of the curial act. Because the canon does not expressly state that the signature of the chancellor or notary is also required for the validity of the act, failure to obtain this countersignature would not invalidate it.[110] Examples of such curial acts would be incardination or excardination documents,[111] letters of appointment to office,[112] decrees establishing parish churches or chapels,[113] or other types of decrees,[114] dispensations,[115] or rescripts.[116]

This canon specifically refers to those curial acts issued by ordinaries. While they are not the

---

[108] Various organizational structures exist in dioceses. In some cases the works of the curia are divided into departments or secretariats. Heads of these divisions are called, variously, delegates, directors, secretaries. Such persons do not necessarily have to be priests. See J. Provost, "Canonical Reflection on Selected Issues in Diocesan Governance," in *The Ministry of Governance,* ed. J. Mallet (Washington, D.C.: CLSA, 1986) 230.

[109] See cc. 124–128.
[110] See c. 10 for an expression of this principle.
[111] Canon 267, §1.
[112] Canon 156.
[113] Canon 1215, §1.
[114] Canon 51.
[115] Canon 85.
[116] Canon 59.

only persons who could issue such acts,[117] this canon governs only their acts. Therefore, if a curial act emanates from someone other than an ordinary, it would appear to be valid even if not properly signed or notarized. However, prescinding from issues of validity, good practice would dictate that such important acts be signed and notarized. Obviously, if the chancellor is the agent of the act, it should be notarized by another notary.

The signature of the chancellor would seem to serve two purposes. First, the chancellor attests by signature to the authenticity of the document. Second, as the one charged with the responsibility of gathering, arranging, and safeguarding curial acts,[118] the chancellor would need to be made aware of the issuance of such acts and serving as notary provides the opportunity for such an awareness.

While the chancellor is responsible for the coordination of curial acts, the moderator of the curia is responsible for the coordination of activity affected by such acts. Therefore, the final clause in this canon is appropriate. The chancellor is to inform the moderator of the curia of the issuance of any such acts so that the latter may assess their impact on the administrative activities of the curia as a whole. In those dioceses where there is no moderator of the curia, the chancellor would need to be aware of who would hold a parallel position, such as a vicar general, and provide the same information to that individual.

ARTICLE 1: VICARS GENERAL AND EPISCOPAL VICARS
[cc. 475–481]

This article begins a description of a series of curial offices, some of which are mandatory. While the office of vicar general had existed under the previous code (*CIC* 366–371), it was not a required office as it is now. A new office, that of

episcopal vicar, introduced through the teaching of Vatican II[119] and postconciliar norms,[120] is also incorporated into the law through the canons of this article. The offices of both vicar general and episcopal vicar are addressed also in canon 134 which includes them among those designated as ordinaries and local ordinaries who possess ordinary general executive power of governance. The scope of their power is circumscribed in the same canon whereby those administrative actions which are attributed directly to the diocesan bishop in the law are understood to pertain to him alone; vicars general and episcopal vicars require a special mandate for such actions.

Two similar offices are designated in the Code of Canons of the Eastern Churches.[121] The titles are different, "protosyncellus" for vicar general and "syncellus" for episcopal vicar, but the roles are parallel. With minor variations,[122] the norms between the two codes are almost identical. Provisions specific to the Eastern churches[123] can be found, but the type and scope of power, the manner of appointment to office, and the means of ceasing from office are the same.

Vicar General: Definition

Canon 475 — §1. In each diocese the diocesan bishop must appoint a vicar general who is provided with ordinary power according to the norm of the following canons and who is to assist him in the governance of the whole diocese.

§2. As a general rule, one vicar general is to be appointed unless the size of the diocese, the number of inhabitants, or other pastoral reasons suggest otherwise.

---

[117] Certain members of the curia, such as a chancellor, may be delegated to issue acts which have a juridic effect.

[118] Canon 482, §1.

[119] *CD* 27.

[120] *ES* I.14.

[121] See, for example, *CCEO* 245–251.

[122] For example, among the qualifications for the office, celibacy is indicated as an expectation, admitting of particular law exceptions (*CCEO* 247, §2). Because celibacy is the norm for priests in the Latin church, such a requirement is not stated here.

[123] For example, the issue of the insignia of such offices is addressed in *CCEO* 250.

This canon introduces the first of the mandatory curial offices, that of the vicar general, whom every diocesan bishop must appoint. By reason of his office, a vicar acts in the name of another authority, exercising the executive authority of the diocesan bishop. The vicar general has ordinary power, attached to his office,[124] but it is vicarious, not proper,[125] because he exercises it not in his own name but in the name of the diocesan bishop. The power of the vicar general is executive in nature[126] and its scope is designated as the whole diocese. The main function of the vicar general is broadly described as being of assistance to the diocesan bishop in his executive governance role.

The second paragraph of this canon expresses a general principle but also allows for an exception. Ordinarily there is to be a single vicar general in the diocese. The reason for this general rule would flow logically from the nature of the office itself. The possibility of confusion of roles and overlapping functions increases when more persons exercise the same authority with the same scope of action, in this case ordinary executive power for the entire diocese. The potential for conflict and confusion can be reduced by an effectively functioning episcopal council[127] and well established expectations for and lines of communication among those who exercise the same authority.

While presumably only one vicar general will be appointed in the diocese, the diocesan bishop may name more than one, prompted by the size, population, or the pastoral needs of the diocese. In deciding to name more than one vicar general, the diocesan bishop will want to weigh these needs over and against the disadvantages of overlapping positions of authority.

It was not uncommon in the past to utilize the office of vicar general as an honorific title for priests or bishops, frequently retired bishops.

There was often a tacit understanding, if not an explicit agreement, that the individual would not function in that capacity. Under the norms of the code such a designation would seem inappropriate. To vest someone with such broad executive power with the expectation that it not be exercised seems to be an empty gesture. Likewise, it seems inappropriate to appoint an individual as an additional vicar general with the understanding that he will act only in the absence of the diocesan bishop and the vicar general who regularly exercises that office.

In addition to those matters attributed in law to an ordinary or local ordinary, a vicar general may also be designated by mandate of the diocesan bishop to exercise authority which the law accords exclusively to the diocesan bishop. Examples of functions that are, at times, delegated to a vicar general include appointing individuals to pastoral offices,[128] issuing incardination or excardination documents,[129] issuing dimissorial letters,[130] permitting the establishment of a church or relegating it to secular use.[131]

Episcopal Vicar: Definition

Canon 476 — Whenever the correct governance of a diocese requires it, the diocesan bishop can also appoint one or more episcopal vicars, namely, those who in a specific part of the diocese or in a certain type of affairs or over the faithful of a specific rite or over certain groups of persons possess the same ordinary power which a vicar general has by universal law, according to the norm of the following canons.

Among the curial offices which can be established at the discretion of the diocesan bishop is that of episcopal vicar. In deciding whether or not to operate with a curial system which includes episcopal vicars, the diocesan bishop will take

[124] Canon 131, §1.
[125] Canon 131, §2.
[126] Canon 135, §1.
[127] Canon 473, §4.

[128] Canons 524 and 539.
[129] Canon 267, §1.
[130] Canon 1018, §1, 1°.
[131] Canons 1215, §1 and 1222.

into account what is required for effective governance in his particular diocese.

The role of the episcopal vicar is described as parallel to that of the vicar general. However, whereas the vicar general's executive authority is exercised in relation to the entire diocese, an episcopal vicar's similar authority is more circumscribed. He exercises his authority within a more restricted range in relation to a specific territory of the diocese, a specific type of activity, such as education, clergy, or health care, or a specific category of persons designated by rite or by some other characteristic such as language or culture.

In establishing the office of episcopal vicar, the diocesan bishop will need to "define accurately the area of [the episcopal vicar's] authority lest the jurisdiction of several persons should overlap or become doubtful."[132] Once the scope of authority is specified, an episcopal vicar exercises ordinary, vicarious, executive power in that distinct arena. In assigning areas of responsibility to the episcopal vicar, the diocesan bishop could also specify those actions, ordinarily reserved to himself, which are to be delegated by mandate to the episcopal vicar. Again, if a system of episcopal vicars is established in a diocese, the management of their activities is essential and should be handled within an episcopal council or a similar vehicle of coordination.

Appointment to Office

Canon 477 — §1. The diocesan bishop freely appoints a vicar general and an episcopal vicar and can freely remove them, without prejudice to the prescript of can. 406. An episcopal vicar who is not an auxiliary bishop is to be appointed only for a time to be determined in the act of appointment.

§2. When a vicar general is absent or legitimately impeded, a diocesan bishop can appoint another to take his place; the same norm applies to an episcopal vicar.

The diocesan bishop freely appoints both vicars general and episcopal vicars without necessarily having to consult anyone.[133] Likewise, he has the authority to remove them from the same offices[134] but within some limits. A coadjutor bishop and an auxiliary bishop endowed with special faculties must be appointed vicar general.[135] Other auxiliary bishops are to be named vicars general or at least episcopal vicars.[136]

The office of vicar general or episcopal vicar is not reserved to bishops, however. A priest may, and in those dioceses without a coadjutor or auxiliary bishop must, likewise be appointed as vicar general. In the case of appointment of a priest as vicar general, it is for an indefinite period of time. In the appointment of a priest to the office of episcopal vicar, there must be a designated term of office, not specified in the universal law. The priest could be renewed in office repeatedly. The term of office in either case should be designated when the office is established by the diocesan bishop or at least when the office is conferred. Because the offices of both the vicar general and the episcopal vicar are ecclesiastical offices, the general norms on office must be observed, such as making the appointment in writing, for liceity.[137]

Circumstances such as illness or required presence outside the diocese could cause a vicar general or episcopal vicar to be absent or impeded. In such a situation the diocesan bishop may appoint a substitute, just as he is free under any circumstances to name additional vicars. The canon does not state that such absence from the diocese or other impediment results in a loss of office for the original designee; an additional vicar is simply named. The "substitute" vicar must meet the requirements for a vicar and exercises his full authority. Likewise, his appointment should be made in writing, and his scope of authority, additional

---

[132] *Directory* 202.

[133] Canon 157.
[134] Canons 192–195.
[135] Canon 406, §1.
[136] Canon 406, §2.
[137] Canon 156.

mandates, or restrictions as well as the period for which the appointment is effective should be specifically stated.

Qualifications of Vicars

Canon 478 — §1. A vicar general and an episcopal vicar are to be priests not less than thirty years old, doctors or licensed in canon law or theology or at least truly expert in these disciplines, and recommended by sound doctrine, integrity, prudence, and experience in handling matters.

§2. The function of vicar general and episcopal vicar can neither be coupled with the function of canon penitentiary nor be entrusted to blood relatives of the bishop up to the fourth degree.

The previous canons having set forth some basic premises regarding vicars, this canon designates the positive qualifications of the office holders as well as restrictions regarding who can be appointed to the office. The qualifications listed include canonical status, personal qualities, and professional credentials and are the same for both vicars general and episcopal vicars.

Questions have been raised regarding the validity of the appointment of someone who lacks any or all of the listed qualifications.[138] This issue involves the application of canon 10 which states: "Only those laws must be considered invalidating or disqualifying which expressly establish that an act is null or that a person is unqualified." Also to be considered is the statement of canon 149, §2 that the conferral of an ecclesiastical office on someone who lacks the required qualities for the office "is invalid only if the qualities are expressly required for the validity of the provision." One could argue that there is no expressly stated, invalidating condition attached to canon 478. On the other hand, while not containing an explicit reference to validity, the canon's use of the subjunctive form of the verb "to be" (*sint*) could be an example of an implicit requirement for

validity.[139] Both the role of the vicar, namely acting in the person of the bishop, and the expressly stated requirement of orders in this canon would seem to give more weight to the opinion that priesthood is required for the validity of the appointment. Without definitively resolving these issues of validity or invalidity, however, we can proceed with an analysis of these expected qualifications for office as expressed in the canon.

Both a vicar general and an episcopal vicar are to be priests. Obviously, a bishop is also qualified for such an appointment (see c. 406). The requirement of priestly orders for vicars is usually related to their significant representative role in relation to the diocesan bishop as his executive "alter ego." Also given as a reason for this qualification is their exercise, by office, of executive power of governance and the restrictive provision that only clerics can be named to offices which require the exercise of the power of governance.[140]

In addition to their priestly status, vicars general and episcopal vicars are also to possess certain personal qualities. These include the minimum age of thirty and personal characteristics deemed appropriate to the fulfillment of the office. Given the broad range of authority exercised by vicars general and episcopal vicars, there is an expectation that they be held to and have demonstrated a high standard of behavior described in terms of their doctrinal soundness, personal integrity, and prudence.

The nature of their role also requires certain professional qualifications, e.g., an advanced degree, either a licentiate or doctorate in canon law or theology. If this degree is lacking, there should be some demonstrated expertise in these areas of study.

---

[138] For a detailed discussion of this matter see J. Provost, "Canonical Reflection," 224–230.

[139] Ibid., 225–226.

[140] Canon 274, §1. Although all "clerics" including deacons are theoretically eligible for such offices, c. 478 speaks specifically of priests (bishops) as vicars, unlike c. 1421, §1 which speaks generically of clerics as judges. One should also note the need to reconcile the restrictive provision of c. 274, §1 with c. 1421, §2 which allows lay persons to be appointed judges in collegiate tribunals, an office requiring the exercise of governance.

While the first paragraph states expectations of the office holder in a positive way, the second paragraph restricts those who can be appointed to these offices. In line with the prohibition on appointing persons to incompatible offices,[141] the same person cannot fulfill the role of canon penitentiary (c. 508, §1) and vicar general or episcopal vicar. The vicar general is to function in the external forum whereas the canon penitentiary's role is in internal forum matters. Conflicts between the fora could arise if one person were to serve in both roles.[142]

Lest there be any appearances of favoritism or conflict of interest, the diocesan bishop is not to name any of his close relatives to these offices. The degree of blood relationship is computed canonically; there are as many degrees as there are blood relatives on each side excluding the common ancestor. By this computation, brothers, nephews, or uncles of the diocesan bishop, his second and third degree relatives, are excluded from the office of vicar general or episcopal vicar. The prohibition arises from a blood relationship "up to" the fourth degree; it does not say "up to and including."[143] Therefore, a fourth degree relative of the diocesan bishop, a first cousin, would be eligible to be a vicar.[144]

The Power of Vicars

Canon 479 — §1. By virtue of office, the vicar general has the executive power over the whole diocese which belongs to the diocesan bishop by law, namely, the power to place all administrative acts except those, however, which the bishop has reserved to himself or which require a special mandate of the bishop by law.

§2. By the law itself an episcopal vicar has the same power mentioned in §1 but only over the specific part of the territory or the type of affairs or the faithful of a specific rite or group for which he was appointed, except those cases which the bishop has reserved to himself or to a vicar general or which require a special mandate of the bishop by law.

§3. Within the limit of their competence, the habitual faculties granted by the Apostolic See to the bishop and the execution of rescripts also pertain to a vicar general and an episcopal vicar, unless it has been expressly provided otherwise or the personal qualifications of the diocesan bishop were chosen.

Both the type and scope of the authority of the vicars are detailed in this canon, beginning in paragraph one with a vicar general's power and moving in paragraph two to that of the episcopal vicar. After addressing the vicars' ordinary power, the canon, in paragraph three, covers an area of delegated power.

The type of power exercised by a vicar general is ordinary because it is attached to the office itself[145] and vicarious because it is exercised in the name of the diocesan bishop.[146] It is further specified as being executive power as distinct from legislative or judicial power.[147] His executive power allows a vicar general to place administrative acts such as issuing decrees, precepts, or rescripts.[148]

The scope of a vicar general's power is quite extensive, encompassing the entire diocese and being almost equivalent to that of the diocesan bishop. There are limits on this power, however. In addition to its being restricted to the executive arena, there are two further limitations. As noted above, when the law specifically mentions the diocesan bishop in the executive arena, a vicar general is constrained from acting without an episcopal mandate.[149] Likewise, the diocesan bishop

[141] Canon 152.

[142] Alesandro, in *CLSA Com,* 389.

[143] For comparison see c. 1091, §2.

[144] For a variant opinion, namely, that first cousins of the bishop are also excluded from this office, see Alesandro, in *CLSA Com,* 389.

[145] Canon 131, §1.

[146] Canon 131, §2.

[147] Canon 135.

[148] Canon 35.

[149] Canon 134, §3.

may reserve additional matters to himself. In those cases, even though the law does not use the words "diocesan bishop," the vicar general still cannot act.

Obviously, any matters which are entrusted to a vicar general by mandate should be clearly specified. In the mandate the diocesan bishop should either list all areas being delegated to a vicar general or make a general statement delegating him to act in all administrative matters and then listing, if any, those matters he reserves to himself.

Consistent with the scope of an episcopal vicar's office is the scope of his power. While it is parallel in type to that of a vicar general, its range of exercise is more restricted. An episcopal vicar exercises his power only in relation to the territory, activity, or persons entrusted to him by office. The same additional limitations noted above in relation to a vicar general's power also apply to an episcopal vicar; he cannot act where the law specifies "diocesan bishop" or where the diocesan bishop has reserved certain matters to himself. In addition to reserving certain functions to himself, a diocesan bishop may also restrict them to a vicar general, another possible limit on the scope of an episcopal vicar's power.

The final paragraph of this canon addresses certain delegated power that may be applicable to vicars general or episcopal vicars. If, by some special concession, habitual faculties are granted to a diocesan bishop by the Apostolic See, vicars general and episcopal vicars are understood to enjoy them as well. Again, the scope of the exercise of these faculties is consistent with the differing roles of the vicars; a vicar general exercises them anywhere in the diocese and an episcopal vicar within the parameters of his office.

Finally, unless the diocesan bishop has been specifically empowered to execute a rescript because of his personal qualifications, a vicar general or episcopal vicar can also execute them. This canon appears to be parallel to canon 43 which describes the execution of administrative acts in general: "unless ... the executor has been chosen for personal qualifications," another per-

son can be substituted for the named executor. The exclusion of a vicar, however, must be clearly stated in the document naming the diocesan bishop as executor. Such an exclusion is not presumed.

Canon 480 — A vicar general and an episcopal vicar must report to the diocesan bishop concerning the more important affairs which are to be handled or have been handled, and they are never to act contrary to the intention and mind of the diocesan bishop.

Because of their close connection with the diocesan bishop, acting in his person and stead, vicars general and episcopal vicars must maintain a close relationship with him. This relationship encompasses both regular communications and ongoing harmony of action. Despite the extensive executive power of vicars general and episcopal vicars, the diocesan bishop remains ultimately responsible for all diocesan affairs. Therefore, an appropriate reporting relationship between him and his vicars is essential.[150]

In determining both the means and frequency of communication, the size and complexity of the diocese will need to be considered. There will also need to be a balance between so little communication that the diocesan bishop becomes removed from important dimensions of diocesan governance and so much communication that he becomes encumbered with nonessential details. Use of the option of an episcopal council may be an effective means of ensuring sustained communication regarding the more important matters already undertaken or anticipated by vicars.

Again, because of their close connection with the diocesan bishop, vicars will have to ensure that their actions are not in conflict with his intentions. The regular communication noted in this canon, effected either by means of an epis-

---

[150] A similar collaborative relationship is expected between the diocesan bishop and his auxiliary or coadjutor bishops (c. 407) as well as between a pastor and parochial vicar (c. 548, §3).

copal council or some other vehicle, will serve also to keep vicars informed about the mind and will of the diocesan bishop. It will likewise present an opportunity to report on favors which may have been refused by the diocesan bishop and which, therefore, cannot validly be granted by vicars.[151]

Cessation from Office

Canon 481 — §1. The power of a vicar general and an episcopal vicar ceases at the expiration of the time of the mandate, by resignation, by removal made known to them by the diocesan bishop, without prejudice to cann. 406 and 409, and at the vacancy of the episcopal see.

§2. When the function of the diocesan bishop is suspended, the power of a vicar general and an episcopal vicar is suspended also unless they are bishops.

A number of the general norms on loss of office are applied here to the offices of vicar general and episcopal vicar. Therefore, the applicable provisions of canons 184 to 196 need to be considered. Also to be kept in mind is the special stability of these offices when they are held by coadjutor or auxiliary bishops.[152]

Both the power attached to the office of vicar general or episcopal vicar as well as any of their delegated power expires when either the term for which they were appointed or the time period for the exercise of the mandate expires. Such an expiration takes effect when it is communicated in writing to the episcopal vicar by the diocesan bishop (c. 186).

A second means by which the office of vicar is lost is resignation. The resignation is to be submitted to the one who has the authority to appoint to the office, in this case the diocesan bishop. The resignation is to be in writing or, if given orally, before two witnesses (c. 189, §1). There is no pro-

vision in this canon that the resignation must be accepted by the diocesan bishop as is true for pastors (c. 538, §1). Therefore, upon its communication, the resignation becomes effective.

Finally, priest vicars can be removed from the office of vicar. A simple auxiliary bishop can be removed as a vicar general but must then be named an episcopal vicar. The general provisions for removal from office are to be observed here. The competent authority to issue the decree of removal[153] is the diocesan bishop. Since they serve at his discretion, vicars can be removed for a just cause by the diocesan bishop without any prescribed procedure.[154] Consistent with the general norm on removal from office,[155] the removal is valid only after the proper issuance and communication of the decree.

In addition, vicars also cease from office when a see is vacant through the death, resignation, transfer, or removal of the diocesan bishop (c. 416). This fact applies to coadjutor and auxiliary bishops as well as priests who hold these offices. With a vacant see, a coadjutor automatically assumes the office of diocesan bishop and, therefore, ceases from the office of vicar general. With a vacant see, an auxiliary bishop ceases from his office as vicar but retains the powers and faculties attached to the office and exercises them, delegated by law, under the authority of the diocesan administrator.[156] With the filling of the office of diocesan bishop, new appointments of vicars general and episcopal vicars must be made.

If the diocesan bishop is suspended from office, priest vicars also have their power suspended, consistent with their significant dependence upon him. However, bishops who hold these offices retain them and all power attached to them even during the suspension of the diocesan bishop.

---

[151] Canon 65, §3.
[152] Canon 406.

[153] Canon 192.
[154] Canon 193, §3.
[155] Canon 193, §4.
[156] Canon 409, §2.

ARTICLE 2: THE CHANCELLOR,
OTHER NOTARIES, AND THE ARCHIVES
[cc. 482–491]

The canons in this second article on the diocesan curia provide general descriptions of how records of administrative activity within the diocese are to be authenticated and maintained and under whose responsibility. They also indicate the levels of security to be exercised in relation to record storage and treat issues of access to such records.

The three topics of chancellor, notaries, and archives are also addressed in the Code of Canons of the Eastern Churches (*CCEO* 252–261). The subject matter is almost identical to that of the Latin code. There are two significant differences however: the office of chancellor is restricted to a presbyter or deacon (*CCEO* 252, §1); the protosyncellus rather than the moderator of the curia joins the chancellor in granting access to the archives (*CCEO* 257, §1).[157]

The Chancellor, Vice-Chancellor, and Notaries

Canon 482 — §1. In every curia a chancellor is to be appointed whose principal function, unless particular law establishes otherwise, is to take care that acts of the curia are gathered, arranged, and safeguarded in the archive of the curia.

§2. If it seems necessary, the chancellor can be given an assistant whose title is to be vice-chancellor.

§3. By reason of being chancellor and vice-chancellor they are notaries and secretaries of the curia.

The office of chancellor is a mandatory office within the diocesan curia (§1). According to this introductory canon, the primary function of the chancellor is to maintain the curial records. However, the history and practice indicate otherwise,

especially in the United States.[158] The chancellor's records management function entails gathering, arranging, and safeguarding such materials. The size and complexity of a given diocese and its activities will dictate the procedures to be used in fulfilling these tasks. The canon itself allows for local adaptation of the role of the chancellor. In larger dioceses with many curial offices, the chancellor may play a supervisory role in relation to the records generated in the various offices. Such supervision would include the establishment of records management as well as retention and access guidelines. The volume of records generated by a multi-faceted office, for example Catholic Charities, could make it unreasonable for the chancellor personally to manage the records. A records policy, however, would designate what records are of such significance that they should be maintained indefinitely and transferred to the diocesan archives in accord with a determined schedule.

While the chancellor has the responsibility to see that the curial records are properly maintained, the actual task of systematic arrangement and preservation will often be assumed by a professional archivist if the chancellor is not trained

---

[157] There is no provision for a moderator of the curia in the Eastern code.

[158] It has been the practice in the United States, for many years, to assign to the chancellor additional functions beyond those designated in the canons on this office. Not infrequently, the chancellor is also named a vicar general with ordinary power of governance or is delegated broad governance responsibilities through the issuance of faculties from the diocesan bishop. By reason of the office of vicar or as a result of these faculties, chancellors frequently grant dispensations from marriage impediments. In other cases, while not being appointed to an additional office or given delegated faculties, the chancellor, if appropriately qualified, functions as a canonical advisor to the bishop and/or within the curia. For purposes of this commentary, however, the chancellor's role and function will be addressed as stated in the canons. For more on the diverse functions of chancellors in the United States, see G. Mesure, *The Diocesan Chancellor in Law and Praxis in Archdioceses in the United States, CanLawStud* 551 (Washington, D.C.: Catholic University of America, 1997).

or skilled in these areas. In fact, the drafters of this canon assumed that such a professional would be available especially for maintenance of historical records.[159]

While this canon does not delineate which "acts of the curia" are to be gathered and maintained by the chancellor, other canons give guidance in this regard. For example, canon 1053, §1 states that documents relating to ordination are to be carefully preserved and records maintained in the curial archives. Canon 1208 makes a similar reference to the document which attests to the blessing or dedication of a church or the blessing of a cemetery. Additional considerations regarding the contents of the curial archives will be addressed below.[160]

The size and nature of a given diocese may necessitate the appointment of an assistant to the chancellor who is designated as a vice-chancellor (§2). The role of the vice-chancellor in a specific diocese will be determined by the tasks given to its chancellor. Likewise, the vice-chancellor assists in fulfilling the responsibilities designated in paragraph one of this canon. In some dioceses more than one vice-chancellor is appointed and there is no canonical prohibition against this practice. However, practically speaking, the tasks of the various persons assigned to the chancery should be clearly delineated and properly coordinated.

Besides the offices of chancellor and vice-chancellor, the canon also treats of the offices of notary and secretary of the curia. The function of a notary is addressed in the following canon. Certain events require the action of the chancellor as notary. The presentation of apostolic letters by a newly appointed diocesan bishop, as well as a coadjutor or auxiliary bishop, is to be recorded by the chancellor.[161] The chancellor is to notify the moderator of the curia, if one is appointed in a given diocese, of the issuance of curial acts which have a juridic effect and, in some instances, will also notarize those acts.[162]

The stable functions mentioned in this canon are clearly ecclesiastical offices. Therefore, the general norms on office should be reviewed for their application to these offices.[163] Canon 482 does not specify who makes the appointment to the offices of chancellor or vice-chancellor. However, canon 470, which states that the diocesan bishop appoints those who exercise offices within the diocesan curia, would apply in this case.

Canon 483 — §1. Besides the chancellor, other notaries can be appointed whose writing or signature establishes authenticity for any acts, for judicial acts only, or for acts of a certain case or affair only.

§2. The chancellor and notaries must be of unimpaired reputation and above all suspicion. In cases in which the reputation of a priest can be called into question, the notary must be a priest.

While the appointment of a chancellor is mandated, the appointment of additional notaries is an option that can be exercised by the diocesan bishop. In contrast to the chancellor and vice chancellor who, by the law itself, are notaries authorized to authenticate by signature all acts of the curia, these additional notaries may have more circumscribed roles. They may be appointed as notaries for judicial acts[164] alone or for certain other specified acts or types of cases or even for an individual event. The areas of competence for these notaries should be indicated in their letters of appointment.

The general function of an ecclesiastical notary is similar to that of a civil notary or notary public.

159 *Comm* 14 (1982) 214. See also NCCB, "A Document on Ecclesiastical Archives," November 22, 1974, in *Pastoral Letters of the United States Catholic Bishops, III,* ed. H. Nolan (Washington, D.C.: USCC, 1983) 470–471, and D. Morrow, "The Chancellor as Archivist," *CLSAP* (1988) 225–227.

160 For a sample listing of materials for archival preservation, see S. Holland, "Archives: In Service of Culture and Learning," *J* 46 (1986) 630–631.

161 Canons 382, §3 and 404, §§1, 2.

162 Canon 474.

163 Canons 145–196.

164 See c. 1437 for the role of a notary in judicial processes.

By the act of signing a document the notary attests to its authenticity. The range and variety of acts and documents that a notary will encounter and authenticate will depend on the nature of the diocese and the position description for the individual.

Since the notary's signature authenticates documents, there must be no hint of dishonesty or taint of suspicion regarding his or her character. Therefore, the chancellor and other notaries are to be people of unimpaired reputation. Other qualifications for ecclesiastical office in general are applicable to these offices. Hence, the chancellor and other notaries must be in communion with the Church and capable of fulfilling the requirements of the office.[165] Upon their appointment, which should be committed to writing,[166] the chancellor and other notaries are obliged to promise to discharge the obligations of the office faithfully.[167] The qualifications for appointment to office within the curia would also be applicable. Hence, the person must be able to maintain the levels of confidentiality required of the position.[168]

Other than the personal qualities noted above and the qualifications for all office-holders, the canons state no additional requirements for the office of chancellor or notary. The chancellor need not be a priest as in the 1917 code (*CIC* 372, §1). However, in those cases which involve the reputation of a priest, the notary must be a priest, although the law does not specify the reasons for such a requirement.[169] The canon itself speaks of the "reputation of a priest" and there may be the presumption that only another priest would be prepared to deal with the facts of such cases and maintain the required level of confidentiality. Examples of such cases in the administrative sphere would be the declaration of an impediment to the exercise of orders,[170] the instruction or notarizing of documents for a laicization case[171] or the removal of a pastor.[172] In the judicial sphere, an example would be a penal process involving a priest.[173] If there is no priest notary, an *ad hoc* appointment is possible. Also, since this requirement of priestly orders is not expressly stated as being for validity, a lay person could serve in this role. The required confidentiality binding all notaries (c. 471, 2°) should be sufficient to guarantee that the priest's reputation would remain unharmed.[174]

Functions of Notaries

Canon 484 — It is the duty of notaries:
  1° **to draw up the acts and instruments regarding decrees, dispositions, obligations, or other things which require their action;**
  2° **to record faithfully in writing what has taken place and to sign it with a notation of the place, day, month, and year;**
  3° **having observed what is required, to furnish acts or instruments to one who legitimately requests them from the records and to declare copies of them to be in conformity with the original.**

In addition to their role in authenticating documents, notaries also have the responsibility of drawing up documents, such as decrees, in their correct form. Therefore, they must be sufficiently familiar with the norms affecting such documents.

Notaries are also to provide written records of transactions, records that include the pertinent date and place. The notary's signature on such a document authenticates it. Examples of such records would be minutes of required episcopal consulta-

---

[165] Canon 149.

[166] Canon 156.

[167] Canon 471, 1°.

[168] Canon 471, 2°.

[169] Commentaries on the previous and current law do not address the reasons for this restriction; it is simply stated as a fact.

[170] Canon 1044, §2, 2°.

[171] Canon 290, 3°. See also CDF, "Procedural Norms Regarding a Dispensation from Priestly Celibacy," October 14, 1980, *AAS* 72 (1980) 1132–1137; *CLD* 9, 92–99.

[172] Canons 1740–1747.

[173] Canons 1717–1731.

[174] Alesandro, in *CLSA Com*, 394.

tions such as those with the presbyteral council regarding parish modifications[175] or with the college of consultors or finance council to obtain their consent for the alienation of property.[176]

In addition to creating documents, notaries also have certain responsibilities regarding documents contained in the archives. Notaries are authorized to show to those who legitimately request them documents or other records from the archives. The canon does not indicate who determines that the request for documents is legitimate. The legitimacy of such a request could be based on the person's right to documents which pertain to his or her personal status or which are public in nature.[177] This canon does not give notaries who are not the chancellor the right to have full access to the archives or to permit others such access. Not only do notaries authenticate original documents, they also verify the fact that copies conform to the original. One reason for the chancellor to be both archivist and notary seems to be that the one who cares for the storage of documents can also retrieve and authenticate them.[178] This authentication can be by means of a signature with the notation "conforms with the original." Some authenticated documents or verified copies may be necessary during ecclesiastical processes since such documents can have probative value before an ecclesiastical court.[179]

Failure to fulfill the obligations attached to the office of notary can have serious consequences. For example, the falsification of documents could make the notary liable to a just penalty.[180]

Removal from Office

Canon 485 — The chancellor and other notaries can be freely removed from office by the diocesan bishop, but not by a diocesan administrator except with the consent of the college of consultors.

Chancellors or notaries can be appointed for a definite or an undetermined period of time. Chancellors and notaries are freely appointed to office and removed from it by the diocesan bishop. This canon, however, is deceptively simple. While they hold office at the will of the bishop, they cannot lose office merely at his whim. Canon 193, §3 requires that there be a just cause for their removal from office. Dioceses should have established procedures for such removals to ensure that justice and equity are served.

A decree of removal is to be issued in writing for validity.[181] Since it is a document which has juridic effect, it should also be notarized. Removal from the office of chancellor or notary does not necessarily sever the diocese's financial obligations to the individual.[182] Minimal support may still be due the individual if it is not provided in some other form, e.g., unemployment compensation or a severance package. When chancellors or notaries are employed under a contract, care will need to be taken that those contractual arrangements are consistent with the canonical provisions for removal or other type of loss of office. In addition to being lost through removal from office by episcopal decree, these offices can also be lost by the law itself.[183]

The diocesan bishop himself may remove these individuals from office. When the see is vacant, a diocesan administrator can remove them only with the consent of the college of consultors. Such a provision is consistent with the principle of keeping changes to a minimum when the see is vacant. The diocesan administrator is not prohibited from appointing a new chancellor if that of-

---

[175] Canon 515, §2.
[176] Canon 1292, §1.
[177] Canons 487, §2; 1540, §§1–2. See also Holland, 626–628.
[178] J. Price, *The Diocesan Chancellor, CanLawStud* 167 (Washington, D.C.: Catholic University of America, 1942).
[179] See cc. 1539–1546 on the use of documents as proofs in a trial. Canon 1544 in particular states that "documents do not have probative force in a trial unless they are originals or authentic copies."
[180] Canon 1391.

[181] Canon 193, §4.
[182] Canon 195.
[183] See c. 194.

fice becomes vacant during the time of his administration. It would be prudent, however, that such an appointment be made in consultation with the college of consultors and only for the time that the see is vacant.[184]

The Archives

The remaining canons in this article (cc. 486–491) focus on the structure and maintenance of the diocesan archives which are divided into three categories: general, secret, and historic. Three norms apply to the general archive, two to the secret, and one to the historical.

General Archive

Canon 486 — §1. All documents which regard the diocese or parishes must be protected with the greatest care.

§2. In every curia there is to be erected in a safe place a diocesan archive, or record storage area, in which instruments and written documents which pertain to the spiritual and temporal affairs of the diocese are to be safeguarded after being properly filed and diligently secured.

§3. An inventory, or catalog, of the documents which are contained in the archive is to be kept with a brief synopsis of each written document.

The first paragraph of this canon states the general principle that the preservation of documents is a serious diocesan and parish responsibility. While these canons emphasize the diocesan archive,[185] there can be a connection with the parish if the diocesan archive also contains copies of some relevant parish documents. To safeguard valuable documents and provide insurance against the possibility of destruction of important parochial records, many dioceses maintain back-up copies of parish registers or other important documents such as titles to parish property. These diocesan

records are often maintained in microfilm or microfiche form. Computer or digital files are also being employed for such back-up purposes.

The establishment of a diocesan archive or records storage area in the curia is mandatory. The canon requires that it be in a safe place but does not provide more detail on the provisions used for such safety. Professional archivists will be of assistance in assessing the appropriateness of the selected site, taking into consideration such conditions as temperature stability, humidity levels, lighting, and storage containers. Unless the chancellor is a trained archivist, such consultation would be important in fulfilling his or her role. As the volume of records increases in a diocese, some dioceses maintain more than one physical location for the contents of the archive. Provided each site in the curia is safe and able to be secured according to canonical standards, this practice would not violate the norms.

The canon describes the contents of the archive very generically as "instruments and written documents which pertain to the spiritual and temporal affairs of the diocese" (§2). Other canons specify certain documents and records which must be maintained.

For example, canon 1053, §1 states that documents relating to ordination are to be carefully preserved and records maintained in the curial archive. Canon 1208 makes a similar reference to the document which attests to the blessing or dedication of church or the blessing of a cemetery. Canon 1283, 3° requires administrators of ecclesiastical goods to maintain an inventory of property, updating it as needed, a copy of which they are to preserve in the diocesan archive. These same administrators are to maintain copies of property deeds and titles in the diocesan archive provided it can be done conveniently (c. 1284, §2, 9°). Canon 1306, §2 requires that copies of charter documents for pious foundations are also to be preserved in the diocesan archive.

The acts and records of judicial processes are also to be retained, but the canons are not clear on whether they are maintained in the general diocesan archive or in a separate tribunal archive.

---

[184] R. Pagé, *Les Églises particulières* (Montreal: Les Éditions Paulines, 1985) 101.

[185] For the required parish archive, see c. 535, §4.

Arguments can be made for either opinion. Canon 469 includes the tribunal within the institutes and persons of the diocesan curia. However, canon 472 applies the norms of Book VII, "Processes," to the cases and persons involved in judicial processes. The site for the final depository of tribunal records is not specified in Book VII. Canon 1475, §1 simply states that copies of documents belonging to private persons are to be retained without indicating the site; and canon 1475, §2 addresses access to these records but does not state where they are found. Interestingly enough, the latter canon mentions the chancellor in describing the process of according such access. The chancellor cannot provide copies without a mandate from the judge but, provided this requirement is met, access to these records by the chancellor seems legitimate. Therefore, one could conclude that the records of the tribunal archive are assimilated into the diocesan archive. The chancellor would preserve them with the special security their nature would demand and be bound by special norms on access. However, other commentators would maintain that tribunals are expected to preserve their judicial acts and records separately from the diocesan archive.[186]

Records affecting the temporal affairs of the diocese would include deeds and titles to property as well as civil, corporate documents. Finance offices will generate volumes of records, many of which are maintained in accord with accounting standards and civil law requirements. For such records, retention schedules and maintenance policies should be established respecting distinctly financial and archival concerns. The roles and responsibilities of the finance officials and the archivist should be clear. The same considerations are also pertinent to personnel records. Records retention and access policies should comply with standards within the human resource field as well as with civil law requirements.

In properly filing and storing the contents of the archive, one will need to address such issues

[186] L. Wrenn, in *CLSA Com,* 965.

as the transfer of active files from various departments and offices to the archive for permanent storage. This type of transfer will involve the purging of unnecessary or duplicate records as well as assessing the value of records either to serve historical purposes or to produce proof of certain acts in the future. The archivist determines the value of records based on their administrative, legal, fiscal, historic, or sacramental uses.

The securing of records is an important dimension of their safeguarding. Securing includes the physical placement of the records in a site that can be closed off from general access, an issue addressed in the following canon, as well as providing for their long-term security by proper storage techniques.

The secure storage of records and documents is not an end in itself. They are stored in order to serve as documentary proofs of facts. These records can also provide historical evidence regarding decisions made and actions taken. Storage of records and documents without a means of retrieval would be meaningless. Therefore, the third paragraph of canon 486 addresses this concern. A well ordered inventory of archival holdings is essential if records are to be retrievable and usable. Chancellors should consider the standards within the archival profession for such catalogs and inventories. Computer programs have been developed in the field and can be invaluable in maintaining these types of catalogs and inventories, but manual systems based on standard archival descriptive practices can provide adequate access to records. Consideration should be given to providing electronic access to catalogs of records of archival holdings which have historical significance and could serve researchers. Access to the catalog of such holdings would not appear to violate the expectation that the records themselves be secured.

Security and Access

Canon 487 — §1. The archive must be locked and only the bishop and chancellor are to have its key. No one is permitted to enter except with the per-

mission either of the bishop or of both the moderator of the curia and the chancellor.

§2. Interested parties have the right to obtain personally or through a proxy an authentic written copy or photocopy of documents which by their nature are public and which pertain to their personal status.

This canon addresses both security and access issues. Because of the significance of the documents and records contained therein, the archive is to be secured and access to the documents limited. The canon refers to the archives as "locked," but there are various means by which security can be maintained in addition to the traditional lock and key approach. Security can be maintained by means of a vault whose combination is confidential. Other highly technological means of security have been developed, such as card-key access, computer identification, etc., and their viability for potential diocesan use will need to be assessed at the local level. When the canon refers to possession of the "key" to the archive, it should be understood to apply to these other means of access as well.

Only two persons are mentioned as being authorized to hold the key to the archive: the bishop (presumably the diocesan bishop) and the chancellor. With due regard for their essential obligations regarding the security of diocesan records, it may be necessary to provide a means of access when neither person is available. The bishop could, for example, allow the moderator of the curia, if one exists in the diocese, or the vicar general to be entrusted with a key for use when the bishop and chancellor are absent, especially if their absence is foreseen to extend for some length of time.

Access to the archive is limited. However, the statement in this canon regarding such access must be carefully interpreted. The responsibilities of the chancellor obviously demand ongoing access to the archive. Therefore, the phrase "no one" cannot be taken literally. Likewise, if a professional archivist is to assist the chancellor in organizing and maintaining the archive, reasonable

access must be permitted that person. Policies and procedures can be developed at the local level to govern this type of access. Such policies would include provisions for obtaining access as well as restrictions on such access for the archivist.

While access to the archive is to be controlled, it is not absolutely forbidden. The diocesan bishop can allow access on his own authority. Likewise, he can delegate someone else to grant such permission. Because the canon does not refer to "ordinary" or "local ordinary" but rather to "bishop," a vicar general or episcopal vicar cannot permit access without a special mandate.[187] The moderator of the curia cannot grant access on his own authority; he can do so only jointly with the chancellor. Again, the diocesan bishop could delegate either of them to grant access in his name, and then each could act independently of the other.

The permission for access to the archive can be granted for one occasion only, for a limited amount of time, or for general, ongoing access. Chancery secretaries, for example, may be granted ongoing access to assist in the general clerical work involved in maintaining the archive. Each diocesan bishop will need to assess his curial needs to determine those persons who should be granted permission for temporary or ongoing access to the archive. Issues related to access to the historical archive for legitimate purposes such as research will be addressed below.

Separate from the issue of access to the archive itself is the issue of access to documents or records contained therein. This matter is handled in the second paragraph of the canon. Those persons whose personal status is addressed in the document have a right to access to it provided its nature is public. Public ecclesiastical documents are those which have been drawn up by an ecclesiastical official according to legal formalities.[188] Individuals can exercise their right to access such documents by requesting an authenticated copy, either written or electronically produced. Examples of such documents would include sacramen-

---

[187] Canon 134, §3.
[188] Canon 1540, §1.

tal records which may be retained in the diocesan archive, decrees which affect individuals' personal status such as a decree establishing an ecclesiastical office which they hold, and rescripts such as laicization documents. Individuals may exercise this right personally or through a proxy.

Lest there be any inference of preferential treatment or an infringement of a right to access, a bishop should establish a diocesan policy describing which records shall be considered under the canon's category of "documents which by their nature are public and which pertain to.... personal status." In the absence of such a policy, individual decisions would be in the hands of the chancellor. It can be argued that all sacramental records are public in nature, since those sacraments for which records are kept are all public in nature and affect one's ecclesiastical status. However, questions can be raised regarding which of these records pertain to the individual's personal status. Given an increased interest in genealogical studies, more requests for sacramental records of ancestors have been forwarded to chanceries. Some researchers maintain that one's ancestors' records do, by extension, affect one's own personal status. Others hold that general access to sacramental records could result in violations of the right to privacy and personal reputation[189] given the forthrightness with which some annotations in records, such as illegitimacy, have been made. To avoid conflicts, it would be helpful for dioceses to establish policies on access which address potentially conflictual matters.[190]

Removal of Documents

Canon 488 — It is not permitted to remove documents from the archive except for a brief time only and with the consent either of the bishop or of both the moderator of the curia and the chancellor.

[189] Canon 220.
[190] For issues to be addressed, see M. Breitenbeck, "Practical Addendum on Policy-Making," in *Confidentiality in the United States* (Washington, D.C.: CLSA, 1988), 163–165.

The holdings of the archive are to be maintained in their integrity. Therefore, documents generally are not to be removed. However, this canon does provide standards by which documents can temporarily be removed from their usual place of storage. The time constraints on such removal are not specified beyond the reference to a "brief time." Local policy and custom should determine the length of time. The chancellor should establish a system of tracking documents temporarily out of their usual place of storage; requiring an "out-card" specifying the document removed, the date of removal, and the person into whose custody it was transferred is a simple system to utilize.

Authorization for removal of documents parallels authorization for access to the archive. The same principles noted above regarding permissions can be applied here.

The Secret Archive

Canon 489 — §1. In the diocesan curia there is also to be a secret archive, or at least in the common archive there is to be a safe or cabinet, completely closed and locked, which cannot be removed; in it documents to be kept secret are to be protected most securely.

§2. Each year documents of criminal cases in matters of morals, in which the accused parties have died or ten years have elapsed from the condemnatory sentence, are to be destroyed. A brief summary of what occurred along with the text of the definitive sentence is to be retained.

In addition to the general archive, each diocese must maintain a secret archive. The documents contained in the secret archive are held under even greater security than those in the general archive. This security is ensured through special means used to store the material and special norms authorizing access to the secret archives.

The secret archive can be a distinct site or a specially secured portion of the general archive. A permanent safe or other type of self-contained and securely locked depository is to be used if there is no separate site.

The first paragraph of this canon provides a general description of the contents of the secret archives, "documents to be kept secret," but does not list such documents. One example of its contents, "documents of criminal cases in matters of morals," is found in the second paragraph of this canon. An illustrative list could be constructed by reference to other parts of the code. For example, a book or registry for recording dispensations from occult marriage impediments in the non-sacramental internal forum is to be maintained in the secret archive (c. 1082). Likewise, the secret archive is to contain a register for noting of secret marriages (c. 1133). Proofs of rebukes or warnings issued in the form of a penal remedy are to be kept in the secret archive (c. 1339, §3) as are pre-investigative and investigative materials or documents relating to any penal process (c. 1719). In addition to those items delineated in the code, the diocesan bishop may determine that other materials or documents[191] be stored there because of their sensitive or secret nature or because dissemination or revelation of them could seriously damage an individual's reputation or cause scandal within the community.[192] While it is the responsibility of the chancellor to maintain the secret archive, it is the diocesan bishop who in part determines the contents. He may delegate the chancellor to share this task.

Certain documents maintained in the secret archive have a distinct retention schedule (§2). Any documents relating to criminal cases involving matters of morals are to be destroyed under two circumstances: the death of the accused or the lapse of ten years from the condemnatory sentence. However, even though the full documentation is destroyed, a summary of the acts and a copy of the sentence are to be retained.[193]

Access to the Secret Archive

Canon 490 — §1. Only the bishop is to have the key to the secret archive.

§2. When a see is vacant, the secret archive or safe is not to be opened except in a case of true necessity by the diocesan administrator himself.

§3. Documents are not to be removed from the secret archive or safe.

Because the secret archive contains documents which are of their nature confidential or highly sensitive, access to it is extremely guarded. The bishop alone holds the key or, in the case of a separate vault or safe, the combination or electronic access (§1). The canon does not specify who may use this key but, in keeping with the chancellor's responsibilities, the bishop could logically allow him or her access to the secret archive as necessary to store documents, make notations in the registers retained there, and destroy documents (c. 489). The diocesan bishop would not seem to be personally responsible for discharging these functions but would need to make such access possible.

---

[191] Examples of documents not required by law to be stored in the secret archive include records of dispensation from impediments or irregularities for orders (cc. 1047–1048) or decrees of dismissal from religious institutes (c. 700). See J. Alesandro, in *CLSA Com,* 397 and E. Rinere, "The Confidentiality of Written Documents in Canon Law," in *Confidentiality in the United States,* 131.

[192] Pagé, 104–105.

[193] Relying on a 1941 reply from the code commission (*CLD* 2, 132), Read concludes that the retention of a summary of the acts and a copy of the sentence applies only to the ten-year provision, not the death of the accused (*CLSGBI Com,* 273). The ten-year peremptory time limit for a complaint of nullity against a sentence (c. 1621) appears to be the basis for the retention of the full acts during that time period. If that were the only basis for the retention, then complete destruction would seem to be appropriate at that time. The fact that they are retained, even in summary form, beyond the ten-year period would seem to indicate that their retention also has a value for historical purposes, even though access to such records is tightly controlled. Therefore, an argument can be made for keeping a summary of the acts even upon the death of the accused.

The diocesan bishop could allow a second copy of the key or other means of access to be held by the moderator of the curia or vicar general and to be used in their presence by the chancellor. Such a provision would maintain the higher level of security appropriate to the secret archive but still allow for reasonable and necessary access.[194] This latter provision would neither violate the secret nature of the archive nor provide unlimited perusal of its contents even by the chancellor.

During a vacant see, given the limited authority of the diocesan administrator, he is permitted to open the secret archive only when it is truly necessary. Since there are to be no innovations during a vacant see and the destruction of documents according to canon 489, §2 could be interpreted as such an innovation, access by others to the secret archives would seem unnecessary and not permissible.

Because of the sensitive nature of the documents contained in the secret archive, the removal of materials, either in their original form or copied, is prohibited (§3). This prohibition, however, is not absolute. Some documentation may licitly be removed from the secret archive. For example, if materials from a preliminary penal investigation are to be used in the process itself, they will need to be accessed.[195] In the case of a secret marriage, if the secret should cease because maintaining it would cause scandal or harm to the sanctity of marriage (c. 1132), any records relating to the marriage could be transferred from the secret archive to a public register in the diocesan curia or parish.[196]

The Historical Archives

Canon 491 — §1. A diocesan bishop is to take care that the acts and documents of the archives

of cathedral, collegiate, parochial, and other churches in his territory are also diligently preserved and that inventories or catalogs are made in duplicate, one of which is to be preserved in the archive of the church and the other in the diocesan archive.

§2. A diocesan bishop is also to take care that there is an historical archive in the diocese and that documents having historical value are diligently protected and systematically ordered in it.

§3. In order to inspect or remove the acts and documents mentioned in §§1 and 2, the norms established by the diocesan bishop are to be observed.

This final canon in the article addresses parish and other church records, the diocesan historical archive, and the issue of access to these various records. Canon 535, §4 requires that each parish maintain an archive; canon 491, §1 extends this requirement to other churches as well. The diocesan bishop is to see that such archives are maintained. He could also designate the types of records and documents to be retained there. Furthermore, he could require that, in addition to the copies of inventories and catalogs that are to be stored in the diocesan archive, copies of more important documents also be kept in the curial archive for safekeeping against destruction. Canon 535, §5 requires that older parish documents be guarded with special care. The diocesan bishop could require that they also be copied or stored in the diocesan archive.

Archival science has developed as a specialized field. Experts in this area are invaluable to a diocese in fulfilling its responsibility for the preservation of important historical records. It is not feasible that every parish retain the services of a professional archivist. Therefore, if one is employed by the diocese, or if the chancellor is such a professional, that person's position description should include consultative services to parishes and other diocesan institutions. Since the bishop is obliged to inspect such records personally or through a delegate (c. 535, §4), he could delegate such a professional archivist to assist him in the inspection

---

[194] See Read, in *CLSGBI Com,* 272 and Alesandro, in *CLSA Com,* 397 for similar opinions. The 1977 schema on the people of God also enabled the chancellor to hold a second copy of the key.

[195] Canon 1719.

[196] For a similar interpretation, see D. Kelly, in *CLSGBI Com,* 639.

and assessment of the quality of parochial archives. Diocesan archivists may also provide regional in-service programs for those charged with maintaining parochial or other ecclesial records. If a diocese employs a professional archivist, such an individual should have professional contact with other ecclesiastical archivists.[197]

The preservation of parochial and other church records is also a significant issue when parishes are merged or suppressed or churches are closed. Clearly established norms and procedures should ensure that such records are not destroyed or lost and that access to them is provided for.

This issue is even more critical regarding sacramental records. In some cases, dioceses have determined that the records of merged parishes will be maintained at the new parish that results from the merger. In cases of suppression, records of the former parish are often maintained by the parish which assumes responsibility for the suppressed parish's previous territory, or, if there is more than one, a designated parish. In other cases, dioceses have determined that all documents and registers from merged or suppressed parishes will be maintained in the diocesan archive. Regardless of the option chosen, there should be consistency in practice and carefully maintained indications of where documents and registers can be located.[198]

Besides parochial documents that may have historical value, other material significant to the history of the diocese is to be maintained in an historical archive. Such material will often require special treatment for preservation.[199] Again, specialists in archival science should be employed either to as-

sume such tasks or advise other diocese personnel who will perform them. Smaller dioceses where human or financial resources are more lacking may be able to obtain the services of professional archivists or at least individuals with some training in historical preservation through local historical societies. Such individuals may find it beneficial to aid dioceses, since many early records of events in a region may exist only within the diocesan curia. It might be possible to provide a catalog of the diocesan historical holdings to local historical societies as well.

The material held in the historical archive should be readily available for purposes of research. The diocesan bishop is to issue norms regarding access to and removal of material from church and historical archives (§3). In establishing such norms, the bishop will need to balance issues of security with those of scholarly research. He can use standards established for access to government archives as well as those for access to ecclesiastical ones, such as the Vatican archives.[200] Professional diocesan archivists have discussed this issue and developed sample access policies.[201]

ARTICLE 3: THE FINANCE COUNCIL AND THE FINANCE OFFICER
[cc. 492–494]

This article, with two canons devoted to the finance council and one to the finance officer, is de-

---

[197] For example, such professional contact takes place through the Association of Catholic Diocesan Archivists, which holds regular national meetings for the purpose of exchange and continuing education in this specialty.

[198] It is especially helpful to make a notation in the *Official Catholic Directory,* where one can locate records for parishes that no longer exist.

[199] Professional archivists regularly consider such issues as the use of acid-free containers for storage of documents and the removal of metal fasteners, as well as provision for handling particularly fragile documents.

[200] John Paul II, allocution to the College of Cardinals, December 22, 1978, in *CLD* 9, 169–171.

[201] For further reflections on the issue of access from the perspective of professional diocesan archivists, see M. Hussey, "Access to Diocesan Archives: Some Historical Reflections," T. Slavin, "Diocesan Archives and the Question of Access," R. Patkus, "ACDA and the Question of Access," and D. Ward, "Confidentiality in Archival Files in the Code of Canon Law," in *Preparing for the 90's: Strategies for Diocesan Archivists and Records Managers* (Chicago: Association of Catholic Diocesan Archivists, 1993) 38–69. See also the ACDA project "Guidelines for Access to Diocesan Archives" (1991).

ceptively simple. It must be read in conjunction with the correlative canons in other books of the code, especially those in Book V, "The Temporal Goods of the Church," and Book I, "General Norms." While the Church has an essential spiritual dimension, it is not removed from the material world, including the world of property and finances. "It is, therefore, totally impossible to make a sharp division between the theology of the nature of the Church and the Church's behavior in economic and financial affairs."[202] The canons in this article need to be read and understood in light of larger issues, such as the credibility of the Church's proclamation of stewardship, honesty, justice, and integrity reflected in its internal management as well as its spoken message. The roles of the finance council and finance officer include not only their administrative and financial expertise, but also their participation in the mission of the Church itself.

Eastern Churches: The Eparchial Finance Officer and Finance Council

The Code of Canons of the Eastern Churches in only two canons (*CCEO* 262 and 263) provides more detail than the Latin code on these topics. The two topics are also addressed in opposite order from the Latin code. The term of office of the finance officer is not defined in common law but is to be determined by particular law (*CCEO* 262, §2); canon 263 establishes no term of office for finance council members.

The eparchial bishop must consult the same two bodies as his Latin church counterpart, the consultors (*CCEO* 271) and finance council, prior to the appointment or removal of the finance officer (*CCEO* 262, §1); and his or her removal prior to the expiration of the term of office requires a serious cause. Instead of submitting the annual report to the finance council, the eparchial finance officer submits it to the eparchial bishop but

through that council (*CCEO* 262, §4). A cross-reference to canon 232 provides more detail on the role of the finance officer during a vacant see. Like his counterpart in the Latin church, the eparchial bishop presides over the eparchial finance council and appoints its members. Unlike a Latin diocesan bishop, however, the eparchial bishop must first consult the college of eparchial consultors or another group designated by particular law before appointing finance council members (*CCEO* 263, §1). Their function, i.e., fulfilling the duties assigned by common law as well as preparing a budget and reviewing the annual report, is the same as in the Latin code (*CCEO* 263, §5). Unlike the Latin code, canon 262, §2 designates the eparchial finance officer as a member of the finance council.

Constitution and Membership of the Finance Council

Canon 492 — §1. In every diocese a finance council is to be established, over which the diocesan bishop himself or his delegate presides and which consists of at least three members of the Christian faithful truly expert in financial affairs and civil law, outstanding in integrity, and appointed by the bishop.

§2. Members of the finance council are to be appointed for five years, but at the end of this period they can be appointed for other five year terms.

§3. Persons who are related to the bishop up to the fourth degree of consanguinity or affinity are excluded from the finance council.

The finance council is an obligatory consultative body in the diocese and is established by the diocesan bishop. The diocesan bishop need not preside over the financial council personally; he may delegate another to preside in his place. Given his ultimate responsibility for the financial administration of the diocese, however, it would be advisable for the bishop to preside himself. Whenever the diocesan bishop is required to hear or receive consent from the finance council, his

---

[202] W. Bayerlein, "The Role of the Laity," in *The Finances of the Church,* ed. W. Bassett and P. Huizing, *Con* 117 (New York: Seabury, 1979) 89.

personal attendance at the meetings would be even more appropriate.

The finance council is to have at least three members. Its size is determined by the diocesan bishop himself. Given the importance of some of its actions, such as considering issues of extraordinary administration or alienation of property, it would seem advisable to consider a larger body for more diverse expertise among the members.[203] However, too large a body could become unwieldy for discussion and deliberation. Since in some instances its consent is required, if more members are to be appointed, an uneven number will make the outcome of a decisive vote clearer.

The members of the finance council are taken from among the "members of the Christian faithful."[204] Since this term comprises all categories of persons, the finance council could consist of all bishops, priests, deacons, or laity including religious in each category. Or it could include a variety of such persons. While the finance council is not required to be representational,[205] it would seem advisable that it include both clergy and laity.

Regardless of the categories of persons who constitute the finance council, what is essential is that they be experts in the matters that come before them. Their financial and civil law expertise rather than their ecclesiastical status is what recommends their place on the council. While not excluding the possibility that priests may be experts in these fields, in many dioceses the finance council will be an excellent arena to utilize the gifts of the laity, or even of deacons whose secular professions include these fields. Canon 228, §2 states that "lay persons who excel in necessary knowledge, prudence, and integrity are qualified to assist the pastors of the Church as experts and advisors, even in councils." Accordingly, the diocesan bishop will be well served to draw on their talents for his finance council.

In addition to having technical expertise, the members of the finance council are also to possess certain personal characteristics that recommend them for such an important ecclesial responsibility. They are to be noted for their integrity, which will assist the Church in its dedication to principles of administrative honesty and forestall any implications of scandal in relation to the Church's patrimony.

In light of canon 228, they should possess the prudence necessary to deliberate properly and make wise decisions in light of the larger ecclesial context. Their prudential judgment will be required for decisions that take into account not only the best financial or legal results but also fundamental ecclesial principles.

Since they may be involved in investment matters, they will need to be aware of certain ethical standards by which investment decisions are made.[206] If they are consulted about major build-

---

[203] Expertise in such matters as civil law, investing, and real estate would be valuable to the bishop.

[204] Opinions vary as to whether or not the members of the finance council, as well as the diocesan finance officer, must be Catholic. The basis for these varying positions is the interpretation of c. 149, §1 which states the requirements for holding an ecclesiastical office. That canon states that office holders must be "in the communion of the Church." Canon 205 describes those who are Catholic or in *full* communion. Full communion is stated as a requirement for some but not all offices; members of the diocesan pastoral council, for example, must be in full communion (c. 512, §1). Some commentators hold that full communion is intended in c. 149, §1 and, therefore, the members of the finance council must be Catholic. Others maintain that only baptism is required for members of the finance council. For more on this issue, see J. Provost, "Canonical Reflections," 224–227; N. Cafardi, "Religious Affiliation of the Diocesan Finance Officer," in *CLSA Advisory Opinions: 1984–1993*, ed. P. Cogan (Washington, D.C.: CLSA, 1995) 99–102; T. Green, "Shepherding the Patrimony of the Poor," *J* 56 (1996) 714.

[205] Both the presbyteral council (c. 495, §1) and the pastoral council (c. 512, §2) do have such a requirement.

[206] In their pastoral letter, "Economic Justice for All: Catholic Social Teaching and the U.S. Economy" (*Origins* 27 [November 27, 1986] 409–455) the U.S. bishops stated: "Although it is a moral and legal fiduciary responsibility...to ensure an adequate return on investment for the support of the work of the church,...stewardship embraces broader moral concerns....We...praise efforts to develop alternative investment policies, especially those which support enterprises that promote eco-

ing or construction projects, they will need to be cognizant of the Church's social teaching on just wages and the right of laborers to organize. These principles are as important as financial or legal expertise.

Therefore, the diocesan bishop, or a member of his diocesan curia who has studied the Church's social teaching, should provide some type of orientation for members of the finance council. Ethical standards of financial administration should also be delineated. The diocesan pastoral council could also draw up guidelines for the diocesan bishop to apply to diocesan and parochial finances.

The members of the finance council are appointed by the diocesan bishop. As with all ecclesiastical appointments, this should be done in writing[207] and notarized,[208] although the appointments would be valid nonetheless. The requirement of a promise of service and confidentiality[209] would apply to the members of the finance council.

Paragraph two of this canon provides that the members of the finance council are to be appointed for a five-year term. There is no limit to the number of terms that a member can serve on the finance council. In determining whether or not to renew terms, which he can do indefinitely, the diocesan bishop should weigh the advantages of stability over and against the value of new ideas and insights brought by new members. There is some value in retaining existing members and adding new ones periodically. Members of the council may resign from their positions,[210] but they can be removed before the expiration of their term only for a grave reason.[211]

Lest there be any hint of scandal or perceptions of personal financial gain on the part of the dioce-

san bishop, the members of the finance council are not to be his close relatives. Excluded are blood or legal relatives up to the fourth degree, i.e., brothers/ sisters, nieces/nephews, uncles/aunts, as well as their spouses. The canon states that the exclusion arises from a relationship "up to" the fourth degree; it does not say "up to and including" that degree.[212] Therefore, a fourth degree relative of the diocesan bishop, such as a first cousin or that individual's spouse, could serve on the finance council.

Although it is not stated in this canon, the finance council remains in place even during a vacant see,[213] unlike other consultative bodies such as the presbyteral council[214] and the diocesan pastoral council.[215] Such a conclusion is clear from the fact that if the finance officer is chosen as the diocesan administrator, the finance council is to select an interim finance officer since he cannot fulfill both roles simultaneously (c. 423, §2). If the finance council ceased to exist with the vacant see, it could not fulfill such a function.

Function of the Finance Council

Canon 493 — In addition to the functions entrusted to it in Book V, *The Temporal Goods of the Church,* the finance council prepares each year, according to the directions of the diocesan bishop, a budget of the income and expenditures which are foreseen for the entire governance of the diocese in the coming year and at the end of the year examines an account of the revenues and expenses.

This canon specifies the function of the finance council.[216] While always operating under the direction of the diocesan bishop, the finance council bears a great deal of responsibility for

---

nomic development in depressed communities and which help the church respond to local and regional needs" (446).

[207] Canon 156.

[208] Canon 484, 2°.

[209] Canon 471.

[210] See cc. 187–189 for the prescriptions on resignation.

[211] Canon 193, §2.

[212] For purposes of comparison, see c. 1091, §2.

[213] Pagé, 109.

[214] Canon 501, §2.

[215] Canon 513, §2.

[216] For a more detailed description of the functions of the finance council in light of Book V, see A. Farrelly, "The Diocesan Finance Council," *Stud Can* 23 (1989) 149–166.

proper management of the finances and administration of the diocese itself as well as other ecclesial entities within the diocese.

In addition to the reference to the relevant norms of Book V, this canon designates specific tasks for the finance council. It is responsible for the annual preparation of the diocesan budget and an annual review of the diocesan financial report prepared by the finance officer. The manner in which the budget is prepared and the financial review conducted is left to the bishop's discretion. In many cases, the available resources for the upcoming fiscal year are calculated so as to set forth from the outset a benchmark for achieving a balance between income and expenses.

The size and complexity of the diocesan curia and other agencies or institutions which are financially supported by the diocese will dictate more or less sophisticated procedures for budget preparation. Consistent with the principle of subsidiarity, it would be appropriate that the various offices, departments, institutions, and agencies which are supported by diocesan funds be involved at least in the initial stages of budget preparation.

In many dioceses, office or department budgets are submitted to an individual, frequently the finance officer or the moderator of the curia, who makes adjustments to arrive at a preliminary balanced budget for presentation to the finance council for its final adjustments.

In other dioceses, a team approach is taken in preparing a preliminary budget from the individual ones submitted by various constituents. Those who comprise an administrative cabinet or other type of "senior management" group within the diocesan curia work together to coordinate the financial needs of the various offices and agencies into a coherent whole from which a preliminary budget is prepared for submission to the finance council. An advantage of this second approach is the degree of ownership for the work of the diocese as a whole which emerges. Also, when the end-product is a corporate effort, there is less possibility of resentment among curial offices or departments based on necessarily uneven financial

allocations. A spirit of cooperation in maintaining a solid financial base for the mission of the diocese can replace a more competitive atmosphere, especially as resources are limited.

Regardless of the approach taken in preparing an initial draft of a budget for the finance council, the diocesan budget should be based on the priorities of the diocese as a whole. The diocesan bishop should undertake a regular, if not annual, review of diocesan needs and priorities and share his vision with all of those involved in budget preparations.

The final responsibility for preparing the budget to be submitted to the diocesan bishop rests with the finance council. In reviewing the annual budget, it may be involved not only in allocating funds but also in making recommendations regarding fund-raising.[217] In some dioceses a development or stewardship committee may exist to coordinate the raising of funds, but the finance council could offer a valuable service to this group from its perspective of budget preparation and annual review.

A second annual function of the finance council is examining the finance report for the year's income and expense activities. The finance officer is responsible for the preparation of the annual finance report[218] and usually utilizes the services of a professional auditing agency in doing so. However, the finance council is to examine the report carefully in light of both the finances and the mission of the diocese. As the chief financial advisors of the diocesan bishop, they should call to his attention any matters that seem to need more immediate attention, such as consistent over-spending in a particular area of the budget. They should also raise concerns for the long-term financial welfare of the diocese if deficit spending occurs or if other fund balances appear to be in question.

The annual review will also be the occasion for the finance council to ensure that funds designated for restricted purposes have been allocated

[217] Farrelly, 154.
[218] Canon 494, §4.

only to those purposes.[219] It may also use that opportunity to review the status of various endowments or foundations.[220]

Upon completion of its review of the annual finance report, the finance council may also assist the diocesan bishop in preparing his required public financial accounting report to the faithful of the diocese.[221] It may also use that opportunity to review and possibly alter the various diocesan procedures and standards, both financial and ethical.

Besides the annual budget and financial review obligations of the finance council, it has additional responsibilities that may arise at various times during the year, e.g., pursuant to the prescriptions of Book V.

At times the diocesan bishop must seek the advice of the finance council and at other times its consent. The obligation to consult is not easily dismissed. Canon 127 makes it clear that the validity of certain of the diocesan bishop's actions depends on his observance of the aforementioned requirements. When counsel is to be sought, he must listen to the opinions of those convened regarding the matter under consideration; even though he is not bound to observe their recommendations, he should not lightly dismiss them, especially when there is a consensus. When consent is required, the diocesan bishop cannot act validly without the vote of an absolute majority of those present.

The following decisions of the bishop require his consulting the finance council:[222]

(1) the imposition of a moderate tax on public juridic persons subject to his authority (c. 1263);

(2) the imposition of an extraordinary tax on other juridic and physical persons (c. 1263);

(3) the performance of more important acts of administration (c. 1277);

(4) the determination of limits of ordinary administration of those subject to him (c. 1281, §2);

(5) the designation of appropriate investment strategies for goods assigned to an endowment (c. 1305);

(6) the diminishment of obligations arising from a foundation when their fulfillment becomes impossible (c. 1310, §2).

The following decisions of the bishop require the consent of the finance council:[223]

(1) the performance of acts of extraordinary administration (c. 1277);

(2) the alienation of property beyond a stipulated amount determined by the conference of bishops (c. 1292, §1);

(3) the completion of any transaction, in addition to alienation, which could worsen the financial condition of the diocese (c. 1295).

In addition, the diocesan bishop must consult the finance council before selecting or removing the diocesan finance officer (c. 494, §§1–2). Finally, as noted above, the finance council itself selects a new finance officer if he is chosen as diocesan administrator at the time of a vacant see.

The diocesan finance council, through its wide range of responsibilities and activities, is an important advisory group to the diocesan bishop and to the diocese as a whole as it assists him in his pastoral office. "Material goods are a necessary part of the Church's mission. Diocesan management of such goods is to be in harmony with that mission. The diocesan finance council plays a vital role in this work."[224]

---

[219] Canon 1267, §3.
[220] Canon 1305.
[221] Canon 1287, §2. See also Farrelly, 158.
[222] For a more detailed examination of these norms from Book V, see the pertinent commentary.

[223] Ibid.
[224] Farrelly, 166.

The Diocesan Finance Officer

Canon 494 — §1. In every diocese, after having heard the college of consultors and the finance council, the bishop is to appoint a finance officer who is truly expert in financial affairs and absolutely distinguished for honesty.

§2. The finance officer is to be appointed for a five year term but can be appointed for other five year terms at the end of this period. The finance officer is not to be removed while in this function except for a grave cause to be assessed by the bishop after he has heard the college of consultors and the finance council.

§3. It is for the finance officer to administer the goods of the diocese under the authority of the bishop in accord with the budget determined by the finance council and, from the income of the diocese, to meet expenses which the bishop or others designated by him have legitimately authorized.

§4. At the end of the year, the finance officer must render an account of receipts and expenditures to the finance council.

Among the more stable offices in the diocesan curia is that of the finance officer. Unlike other curial officials, such as episcopal vicars, whose appointments are optional, the finance officer holds a mandated office. Unlike other curial officials, such as vicars, who cease from office during a vacant see, the finance officer remains in office. Unlike other curial officials, such as chancellors or vicars, who can be freely removed from office for just cause, the finance officer can be removed only for grave cause.

Under normal circumstances, the finance officer is appointed by the diocesan bishop. However, when a see is vacant, if the finance officer is chosen as diocesan administrator, he is to be replaced by someone appointed by the finance council, a rare example of a significant diocesan appointment by someone other than the bishop. If during a vacant see the finance officer resigns or dies, the diocesan administrator may appoint a finance officer, because he generally has the rights and obligations of a diocesan bishop.[225] Therefore, except for very brief intervals, a diocese would never be without a finance officer.

Prior to appointing the finance officer, the diocesan bishop must consult both the college of consultors and the finance council. However, he does not need their consent for the appointment. This consultative process is understandable, especially because of the close working relationship the finance officer will need to have with the finance council. The finance officer will frequently be required to prepare reports for consideration of the consultors and the finance council members on matters of extraordinary administration or alienation.

Since the canons on ecclesiastical office apply in this case, the individual appointed needs to meet the general requirements for office, namely communion with the Church[226] and suitability for the position, i.e., possession of the qualities required for the office.[227] The qualifications of the finance officer are twofold: professional and personal. Not only must the lay person or cleric have expertise in the area of finances, usually as a certified public accountant or a member of a similar profession, but he or she must also be noted for personal honesty and integrity.

A further indicator of stability in office for the finance officer is the requirement of a term of office. The diocesan bishop appoints the finance officer for a five-year term which is renewable without limit. As with all ecclesiastical appointments, this should be done in writing[228] and notarized,[229] although the appointments would be valid nonetheless. The requirement of a promise of service and confidentiality[230] applies to the finance officer as well as to other curial officials.

---

[225] Canon 427, §1.

[226] See above at note 204 for discussion of the appointment of a non-Catholic.

[227] Canon 149, §1.

[228] Canon 156.

[229] Canon 484, 2°.

[230] Canon 471.

The diocesan bishop can remove the finance officer prior to the fulfillment of his or her term only for grave cause. Even with such a cause, such as misappropriation of funds, the bishop must seek the advice of both the college of consultors and the finance council for validity. The diocesan bishop himself judges the seriousness of the cause and actually executes the decree of removal in writing. However, such a removal from office might not sever all diocesan responsibility for the finance officer. Any civil contractual obligations must be met[231] as well as requirements of financial support unless there are other provisions for such support.[232]

The function of the finance officer is stated in broad terms in paragraph three of this canon. Serving under the authority of the diocesan bishop, and operating within the scope of the budget prepared by the finance council, the finance officer administers the goods of the diocese. The diocesan bishop himself remains the administrator of such goods, but the finance officer provides the administrative services. The finance officer serves as a comptroller and disburses or authorizes the disbursement of funds to cover expenses according to diocesan policies.

Besides carrying out the functions stated in this canon, the finance officer may also serve the diocesan bishop by providing administrative services, such as assisting in budget preparation or the annual financial review, in relation to other juridic persons subject to the diocesan bishop or those which do not have their own administrator.[233] In such cases, the role and responsibility of the finance officer should be clearly understood by those entities.

The final responsibility assigned to the finance officer is the preparation of an annual report to the finance council. This report will usually be prepared under the direction of the finance officer but actually rendered by outside auditors. While the finance officer is not a member of the finance council, he or she may attend its meetings as staff to the council. The finance officer should at least attend the meeting at which the annual report is examined.

CHAPTER III
THE PRESBYTERAL COUNCIL
AND THE COLLEGE OF CONSULTORS
[cc. 495–502]

Among the consultative bodies required by the code are the presbyteral council and the college of consultors. Both are advisory groups composed of priests[234] who are to assist the diocesan bishop in his pastoral governance of the portion of the people of God entrusted to him. While the two groups have a connection with one another, they also have separate and distinct functions.[235] As with other consultative groups in the code, these two bodies serve an important role in the process of decision making within the diocese.[236]

Under the 1917 code diocesan consultors were to be appointed provided the diocese had no cathedral chapter (*CIC* 423–428).[237] The present code requires the establishment of a college of consultors in every diocese. The presbyteral council had no parallel in the 1917 code but finds its roots in the Vatican II mandate to reorganize the existing diocesan consultative groups according to contemporary needs.[238] Because of the close connection between the diocesan bishop and his

---

[231] Canon 192.
[232] Canon 195.
[233] Canons 1278; 1276, §1; 1279, §1.

[234] It appears that presbyteral orders is a constitutive element of membership in either body. Therefore, the diocesan bishop could not dispense from this provision to allow deacons or lay persons to be members of either body.
[235] For the relationship between the two bodies and their distinctive functions, see J. Provost, "Presbyteral Councils and Colleges of Consultors: Current Law and Some Diocesan Statutes," *CLSAP* (1987) 194–211.
[236] For a summary of the importance of consultation in decision making, see J. Provost, "Canonical Reflections," 232–235.
[237] See below on chapters of canons (cc. 503–510).
[238] *CD* 27.

presbyterate, Vatican II called for them to constitute "one priesthood" composed of different functions.[239] Based on this close communion, Vatican II counseled bishops to "listen to [the priests], indeed, consult them, and have discussions with them about those matters which concern the necessities of pastoral work and the welfare of the diocese."[240] The vehicle for such consultation was described as "a group or senate of priests to represent the presbytery" and its purpose set forth as giving "assistance to the bishop in his governance of the diocese."[241] This conciliar directive was further refined in the implementing legislation of *Ecclesiae sanctae*,[242] in which the establishment of such an assembly of priests was made a requirement for dioceses.

The current canonical legislation on presbyteral councils is consistent with these conciliar and postconciliar foundations. It develops in more detail some of the previous legislation but still allows for considerable diversity based on local ecclesial circumstances. While the canons set forth general principles on the council's form, membership, and manner of functioning, it is the local diocesan bishop who shapes the council according to the needs of the particular church. This chapter consists of seven canons on the presbyteral council and one canon on the college of consultors.

Eastern Churches: Presbyteral Council and College of Eparchial Consultors

The Code of Canons of the Eastern Churches addresses these two canonical institutes in canons 264 to 271. In both the sequence of topics and content, these canons basically parallel those of the Latin code.

Establishment and Purpose of the Presbyteral Council

Canon 495 — §1. In each diocese a presbyteral council is to be established, that is, a group of priests which, representing the presbyterate, is to be like a senate of the bishop and which assists the bishop in the governance of the diocese according to the norm of law to promote as much as possible the pastoral good of the portion of the people of God entrusted to him.

§2. In apostolic vicariates and prefectures, the vicar or prefect is to establish a council of at least three missionary presbyters whose opinion, even by letter, he is to hear in more serious matters.

The establishment of a presbyteral council is required in every diocese.[243] Whereas the 1917 code referred to the chapter of canons and, by analogy, the diocesan consultors as the "senate" of the bishop, this canon reserves that description to the presbyteral council. This title, "senate," accurately describes the role of the council and its style of interaction with the diocesan bishop. While there are certain matters that the law requires the diocesan bishop to take to the presbyteral council, there is also a wide range of pastoral concerns about which the diocesan bishop will want to seek the counsel of this group of priests who are to act as his collaborators in the pastoral care of the diocese.[244] The presbyterate as a body always acts in relation to the bishop.[245] Thus, as a "senate" this group serves a representational as well as an advisory role. The entire presbyterate functions as collaborators with the diocesan bishop in his pastoral care of the diocese;[246] this council symbolizes, represents, and concretizes that collaboration by its direct interaction with the diocesan bishop in a manner that

[239] *LG* 28.

[240] *PO* 7.

[241] Ibid.

[242] *ES* I, 15, 1. The SCC circular letter, *De consiliis presbyteralibus*, April 11, 1970 (*AAS* 62 [1970] 459–465; *CLD* 7, 383–390) provided additional clarification and detail regarding these councils.

[243] It is also required in every eparchy (*CCEO* 264).

[244] See comments below on c. 500, §2.

[245] For a summary of the theological relationship between the presbyterate and the episcopal office, see Pagé, 116–119.

[246] Canon 384.

ordinarily would not be feasible with the entire presbyterate of a diocese. The council members do not supplant the role of the entire presbyterate as "assistants and counselors"[247] to the diocesan bishop but rather facilitate the process by which he attends and listens to them.

Some councils employ a committee structure within their organization with each committee charged with a specific area of concern, such as spirituality or social concerns. These committees meet to address certain issues, undertake background research for council discussion, and study various proposals that have come to the council. Even broader representation from among the presbyterate is possible when committee membership extends to priests not sitting on the council.

Paragraph two of this canon takes into account the special situation found in apostolic vicariates and prefectures. The law's accommodation to their circumstances allows for a smaller council. However, it must be composed of at least three members. The canon also provides an alternate means of obtaining their advice, namely by letter rather than by formal meetings. Nonetheless, the purpose of the council, providing counsel in matters of importance to the particular church, remains the same.

Statutes of the Presbyteral Council

Canon 496 — The presbyteral council is to have its own statutes approved by the diocesan bishop, attentive to the norms issued by the conference of bishops.

Each presbyteral council is to have its own governing documents, referred to in this canon as "statutes."[248] While these documents are not technically statutes in the sense of canon 94,[249] the ele-

ments found in formal statutes could be used to shape these presbyteral council documents; formal statutes define the purpose, constitution, government, and methods of operation of a body such as the council.

The canon does not designate who has the responsibility to draft the statutes of the council. Since a council does not exist until its statutes are established, the council itself does not write the statutes. In reality, in many dioceses, initial statutes have been drawn up by a task force or committee charged with that mission. Regardless of the source of the text of the statutes, it is the diocesan bishop who must approve them for them to have juridic effect. As with any document having legal effect, the statutes must be signed by him and notarized by the chancellor or another notary.[250]

While the content of presbyteral council statutes may vary greatly from diocese to diocese, taking into account local circumstances, subsequent canons determine certain elements that they must contain. These elements include: the manner of election of members,[251] the designation of ex officio members,[252] election rights of certain priests,[253] election procedures,[254] and terms of office of members.[255]

The canon indicates that the presbyteral council statutes are to be attentive to the norms issued by the conference of bishops. Earlier provisions for presbyteral council statutes appeared to expect more uniformity among the councils within the territory of a conference. They went so far as to refer to "common regulations" for these councils.[256] Were a conference of bishops to issue such norms and were they to receive a Vatican *recogni-*

---

tion of this canon and see c. 94 as applicable. See, for example, Alesandro, in *CLSA Com,* 402; J. Arrieta, in *Pamplona ComEng,* 365.

[250] Canon 474.
[251] Canon 497, 1°.
[252] Canon 497, 2°.
[253] Canon 498, §2.
[254] Canon 499.
[255] Canon 501, §1.
[256] *ES,* I, n. 17.

---

[247] Ibid.
[248] See also *CCEO* 265.
[249] Canon 94 uses the term *statutes* to refer to the governing documents of juridic persons, and the presbyteral council is not a juridic person. See Pagé, 124–125. However, other commentaries differ in their interpreta-

tio, the individual bishops would be bound to observe them.[257]

Presbyteral Council Membership and Election of Members

The following three canons address various issues relating to membership on the presbyteral council.[258] While deferring to local statutes in some cases, the canons set forth some universal expectations. These universal norms are consistent with the expectations of the role of the council: to be a representative body of the presbyterate and to assist the diocesan bishop in his governance function. Thus, there is provision for electing members from among the presbyterate at large, seating those who have specific functions within the diocese, and naming members by episcopal discretion. A manner of election must be part of the statutes and must be formulated in such a way as to guarantee the representational nature of the council. The rights of certain members of the presbyterate in relation to council elections are also designated by universal law.

Canon 497 — In what pertains to the designation of members of the presbyteral council:
   1° **the priests themselves are freely to elect about half, according to the norm of the following canons and of the statutes;**
   2° **according to the norm of the statutes, some priests must be *ex officio* members, that is, members who are to belong to the council by reason of the office entrusted to them;**
   3° **the diocesan bishop is freely entitled to appoint others.**

This canon provides three means of attaining membership on the presbyteral council: by election, by office, or by episcopal appointment. Approximately half of the members are to be chosen by the presbyterate in a manner prescribed in the council statutes. The following canon will designate specifics regarding electoral rights. Regardless of the means of designation, once priests are on the council, there does not appear to be any distinction among the members; they share an equality of place on the council even though some, by statute, may be designated for certain organizational functions, such as moderator or secretary.

Free election is the means for designating approximately half of the members on the council. The phrase "about half" appears to be a compromise and lacks the legal precision one would expect. Previous documents on presbyteral councils had specified that the majority of the membership should result from election.[259] It will be for the statutes to make more precise the specific meaning of "about half" the membership.

The second category of membership is *ex officio*. By reason of the office they hold, certain members of the presbyterate are appropriate members of the council. Again, the statutes should specify which offices constitute the basis for council membership in light of the role the council plays. Since the council is to serve the diocesan bishop in his governance function, those who hold significant governance offices in the diocese would be suitable for council membership. The vicar general and episcopal vicars, especially if there is one designated in relation to the priests of the diocese, would be among those individuals to be considered for *ex officio* membership. Likewise, to facilitate the interaction between the council and the diocesan curia in aiding the bishop in diocesan governance, the moderator of the curia, especially if he is not a vicar general, would be an appropriate *ex officio* member of the council.

The presbyteral council is to serve as a key advisory body to the diocesan bishop. Thus, if, after considering the membership of the council achieved

---

[257] At the time of this writing, the NCCB has not issued any norms on this matter. It did, however, issue theological, canonical, and pastoral reflections on such councils. See "United in Service: Reflections on the Presbyteral Council," *Origins* 21 (December 5, 1991) 409, 411–421.

[258] See also *CCEO* 266–268.

[259] *De consiliis presbyteralibus* 7.

by these two previous means of designation, the diocesan bishop should determine that additional members would enhance the function of the council, he remains free to name them. He is not required to do so, nor do the statutes necessarily have to make such a provision since this right of appointment is contained in the universal law. In making any such appointments, the diocesan bishop would not be permitted, however, to override the provision that "about half" the membership be elected.

Canon 498 — §1. The following have the right of election, both active and passive, in constituting a presbyteral council:

    1° all secular priests incardinated in the diocese;

    2° secular priests not incardinated in the diocese and priests who are members of some religious institute or society of apostolic life, who reside in the diocese and exercise some office for the good of the diocese.

    §2. To the extent that the statutes provide for it, the same right of election can be conferred on other priests who have a domicile or quasi-domicile in the diocese.

This canon provides more specific determinations regarding election rights. It addresses both the right to elect council members and the right to be elected as a council member. The first paragraph provides a universal norm for the right to active and passive voice and the second allows the statutes of the particular council to extend the right to others.

The first category of priests possessing active and passive voice in council elections are those who are incardinated in the diocese. While incardination occurs with diaconal ordination,[260] incardination alone is an insufficient basis for these election rights since only priests, not deacons, are eligible to vote and be elected members of the council. It is incardination which is the foundation upon which this right rests, not office, domi-

cile, or residence. Thus, as long as a priest remains incardinated in the diocese, active or retired, resident or not, he retains his rights regarding council elections. Since ecclesiastical authority can regulate the exercise of rights in light of the common good,[261] there may be some cases in which a priest, though still technically incardinated in a diocese, may not be permitted to exercise his electoral rights. For example, a priest who, though not laicized, has left the active ministry or one who is absent from the diocese without authorization for a considerable period of time may be so restricted.[262] The exercise of rights should never be regulated arbitrarily. Therefore, to help avoid any abuse of discretionary authority, it would be appropriate for the council statutes to delineate carefully those ineligible to participate in the election process.

The second category of priests who have the right to active and passive voice in council elections is found in part two of paragraph one. It actually consists of several different categories of priests. What they have in common is that, unlike the priests noted above, they are not incardinated in the diocese; likewise, they reside in the diocese. Neither domicile nor quasi-domicile is a prerequisite for council membership in this case. Residence alone, however, is not sufficient. It is required that they exercise some "office for the good of the diocese." This requirement is consistent with the purpose of the council, to assist the bishop in promoting the pastoral welfare of the people of the diocese. Because the canon does not clarify what constitutes an "office for the good of the diocese," the statutes should more clearly define the meaning of this phrase as it is applied in the individual diocese.

The first group under this heading is made up of secular priests. This category would include diocesan priests incardinated in another diocese and members of personal prelatures.[263] The second

---

[260] Canon 266, §1.

[261] Canon 223.

[262] Alesandro, in *CLSA Com,* 403.

[263] In its *Declaration Regarding the Prelature of the Holy Cross and Opus Dei* (August 23, 1982) the SCB specifi-

category of those resident in the diocese and possessing electoral rights consists of members of institutes of consecrated life, both members of religious institutes and members of secular institutes. This latter group would include those incardinated either into another diocese or the institute itself.[264] The final category of priests mentioned in this section is made up of members of societies of apostolic life who may be incardinated in another diocese or the society itself.[265]

The second paragraph of the canon proposes the possibility of extending electoral rights to other priests who are not in any of the categories already noted. The council statutes would need to make provision for such an extension of rights and clearly delineate to whom such rights are to be accorded. Unlike those priests who exercise an office for the good of the diocese, who need merely reside in the diocese, the members of this latter group must have a domicile or quasi-domicile there. However, they need not be providing any ministry for the benefit of the diocese. This category could include priests who remain incardinated in their own dioceses but have a retirement home in the diocese where they now maintain domicile. Likewise, it could include priests who have established a quasi-domicile by reason of a program of extended studies within the diocese.

Canon 499 — The manner of electing members of the presbyteral council must be determined in the statutes in such a way that, insofar as possible, the priests of the presbyterate are represented, taking into account especially the different ministries and various regions of the diocese.

The preceding canon established the criteria for electoral rights; this canon addresses the exercise of those rights by determining how elections are to be conducted. The canon allows broad discretion in the manner in which elections are held, requiring, however, that election procedures be established in the council's statutes. The council is, of its nature, to be representative of the presbyterate. Within the latitude allowed for diverse electoral procedures, the code encourages that the election results contribute to the representative nature of the council. This canon points out two bases of representation in particular, ministry and geography. In establishing electoral procedures, the statutes could specify other criteria for a representative council, such as age or membership in institutes of consecrated life or societies of apostolic life.

In some dioceses, elections are conducted primarily along territorial lines with the priests of each deanery, vicariate, or district having the right to elect a representative. In other dioceses, consideration is given to electing age-group representatives or representatives from various ministerial groupings, such as parochial ministry, educational ministry, or health-care ministry. A combination of both methods is employed in yet other dioceses. The canon, however, while encouraging that the elections result in a representative council, does not require elections by regional or ministerial groupings. Consideration could be given to general elections among the presbyterate for their determination of membership from among all eligible priests. The diocesan bishop could then assure appropriate representation by means of his own appointments to the council. More broadly based elections help avoid a sense of members' representing a distinctive constituency.[266] Their counsel to the bishop is to take into account the good of the entire diocese, not merely a given territory or segment of the population they "represent." A council that is reflective of the presbyterate of the whole diocese can assure that legitimate interests of various groups or areas, such as urban, rural, or ethnic

cally referred to the clergy of the prelature as belonging to the secular clergy. With regard to presbyteral councils, in the same document the SCB stated: "As regards the constitution of presbyteral councils, they [priests of the prelature] enjoy active and passive voice" (*AAS* 75 [1982] 464; *CLD* 10, 129). This canon would, however, place the additional requirement of exercising an office for the good of the diocese as noted above.

[264] Canon 266, §3.
[265] Canon 266, §2.

[266] Alesandro, in *CLSA Com,* 403–404.

concerns, are brought before the council in its deliberations.

Manner of Operation of the Presbyteral Council

Canon 500 — §1. It is for the diocesan bishop to convoke the presbyteral council, preside over it, and determine the questions to be treated by it or receive proposals from the members.

§2. The presbyteral council possesses only a consultative vote; the diocesan bishop is to hear it in affairs of greater importance but needs its consent only in cases expressly defined by law.

§3. The presbyteral council is not able to act without the diocesan bishop who alone has charge of making public those things which have been established according to the norm of §2.

In addressing how the presbyteral council is to function, this canon[267] necessarily concentrates to a great degree on the relationship between the council and the diocesan bishop. Since the council is "to be like a senate of the bishop,"[268] its function cannot be seen apart from the bishop. He convenes the council, presides over it, and sets its agenda.[269] The council's proper role is that of an advisory body to the bishop. As such, it is more than an association of priests with its own agenda. The council's very existence is dependent on the diocesan bishop.[270]

The manner in which the aforementioned three roles of the diocesan bishop are exercised is not delineated in the canon. The frequency with which he is to convoke the council is not stated. Commentators differ on whether or not council statutes could legitimately state the frequency of meetings.[271] However, the statutes could set a

standard for the frequency of meetings and, since the bishop approves the statutes, his freedom is duly protected. Obviously such a schedule could be modified at the discretion of the diocesan bishop. He could cancel meetings which are not seen as necessary or convene the council for additional meetings if there is a pressing need for the council's input on a matter requiring more immediate attention. The canon does not specify the manner in which the diocesan bishop convenes the council. To assure a legitimate convocation, the statutes should specify the procedure for convening the council. This provision takes on added importance when the counsel of the group is required for the validity of the bishop's actions.[272]

There are, likewise, no provisions for the manner in which the diocesan bishop presides over the council. He may do so personally or through another.[273] Should he elect to preside through another, the statutes should designate who (such as the vicar general) is eligible and the bishop should issue an episcopal mandate designating the individual as the council presider.[274] Given the role of the council and its relationship with him, the diocesan bishop should normally preside with

---

[267] See also *CCEO* 269.

[268] Canon 495, §1.

[269] This role of the bishop is comparable to that of the pope vis-à-vis the synod (cc. 342–348), presiding, setting agenda, etc.

[270] For more on this relationship see comments below under c. 501.

[271] Pagé maintains that the statutes could determine the frequency or regularity of the meetings but cautions against

meetings for the mere sake of meeting without sufficient cause or agenda (141). Arrieta, in *Pamplona ComEng,* holds that such statutory regulation of the frequency of meetings would violate the bishop's right to convoke the council (367).

[272] Canon 127, §1 states that, for the validity of an action that requires counsel, the one required to seek such counsel must convoke the group either in the same manner as convening a group for elections (c. 166) or in accord with particular law. The council statutes could state the manner of convoking the group. The diocesan bishop would be bound to follow such a procedure if his consultation of the council were to be valid. Some matters require such counsel, e.g., establishing or suppressing parishes (c. 515, §2). Failure to convene the council legitimately could result in an invalid consultation and hence an invalid action in relation to the parish.

[273] For a more extended discussion of the various meanings of "presiding" and arguments favoring the conclusion that the bishop need not preside personally, see Pagé, 142–144.

[274] Canon 134, §3.

other provisions available for exceptional cases. The fact that the bishop is to preside does not preclude others fulfilling tasks such as chairing or facilitating meetings.

An additional role of the bishop is determining the questions to be treated by the council or receiving proposals from members. This action would usually be referred to as "setting the agenda." Again, the diocesan bishop may do so personally or utilize the services of an individual or committee to assist in this process. Certain matters must be brought to the council[275] for their consultation. When circumstances warrant, these issues would be part of the agenda for a council meeting. However, the council will almost certainly meet far more often than such matters would dictate. These other meetings will involve a broad range of matters in which the input from the council will assist the bishop in his governance of the diocese. Agenda items in this category can arise either from the bishop or from the council members. Many councils have developed processes by which issues or proposals generated from the presbyterate at large or from other members of the faithful can be directed to the council for their consideration. Likewise, the diocesan bishop may find it helpful at times to utilize the services of his diocesan pastoral council to surface issues for the consideration of the presbyteral council.

The second paragraph of canon 501 specifies the role and authority of the council in relation to the diocesan bishop. While the diocesan bishop must take certain matters to the council for its consideration, ultimately the bishop himself must decide about taking action on these matters. He makes his decision in light of the advice given by the council, but it does not make the decision for him given its role as advisory to the bishop. Thus council members are said to have a consultative vote only. However, their consultation helps shape the decision since the bishop is to come to them prior to making a decision, and their input must be considered by him. As his council, the members assist him in the decision-making process and thus are an essential part of the decision even though they do not actually make it.

Some of the "affairs of greater importance" about which the diocesan bishop is to consult with the council are defined by law; other such matters will be at his own discretion. This paragraph indicates that the bishop needs the consent of the council "only in cases expressly defined by law." Commentators differ regarding whether or not any such cases exist in the universal law.[276]

The final paragraph of the canon is also consistent with the advisory nature of the council. Since the council members do not have an existence apart from the one whom they advise and since they do not convene themselves or establish their own agenda, they can never act without or apart from the bishop. Likewise, since the decisions are ultimately the diocesan bishop's, so also is the right to make public those deliberations and decisions. The manner in which he publicizes them is also at his discretion. He need not do so personally;

---

[275] The diocesan bishop must bring the following matters to the presbyteral council for their consultation: the decision to convene a diocesan synod (c. 461, §1); the establishment, suppression, or notable alteration of parishes (c. 515, §2); the allocation of offerings made by the faithful for parochial services and the remuneration of clerics for the same (c. 531); the determination that there should be a pastoral council in each parish (c. 536, §1); the decision to build a new church (c. 1215, §2); the decision that a church, no longer able to be used for worship, be relegated to profane use (c. 1222, §2); the exercise of his right to impose a moderate tax on juridic persons subject to him (c. 1263). He must also propose names to the council for its establishment of a standing group of pastors from whom he will choose two to assist him in removing or involuntarily transferring a pastor (cc. 1742, §1; 1745, 2°; 1750).

[276] See Read, in *CLSGBI Com* for the opinion that no such cases exist in universal law but that the diocesan bishop could issue particular law which would establish certain matters requiring consent (277). See Arrieta, in *Pamplona ComEng* for the opinion that selection of the pastor consultors (c. 1742, §1) is a matter in which the consent of the presbyteral council is required rather than merely counsel (367). *CCEO* 269, §2 refers to the bishop's needing consent only in cases expressly determined in common law.

he may use the services of others to prepare and disseminate the information. The statutes may define the manner in which minutes and other council materials are published and distributed. Such communication assists the diocesan bishop in his general relationship with the presbyterate at large. It also serves to keep the larger group informed of the issues being addressed by the council and aids in ensuring a smoother transition of new members onto the council.

Term and Cessation of the Presbyteral Council

Canon 501 — §1. Members of the presbyteral council are to be designated for a time determined in the statutes, in such a way, however, that the entire council or some part of it is renewed within five years.

§2. When a see is vacant, the presbyteral council ceases and the college of consultors fulfills its functions. Within a year of taking possession, a bishop must establish the presbyteral council anew.

§3. If the presbyteral council does not fulfill the function entrusted to it for the good of the diocese or gravely abuses it, the diocesan bishop, after having consulted with the metropolitan, or, if it concerns the metropolitan see itself, with the suffragan bishop senior in promotion, can dissolve it but must establish it anew within a year.

The presbyteral council has stability but not permanence.[277] Its members are not designated for life, and it does not continue in existence under any and all circumstances. This canon addresses both issues, stability and transience. Stability on the council is achieved through the terms of members, to be determined by the council statutes. These terms, however, should not be of such a duration that there is little or no turnover of membership. The council is to be renewed, entirely or in part, within five years. The diocesan bishop through the statutes could determine that the en-

tire council will remain stable for five years, at which time an entirely new council will be seated.[278] Alternately, he could decide that a gradual turnover during the five-year period would be more appropriate to the needs of the diocese. Either method would contribute to the stability that makes a presbyteral council effective.

Since the council cannot act without the diocesan bishop, the council ceases to exist at the time of a vacant see. At that time any matters which the council would ordinarily handle are directed to the college of consultors. Because the presbyteral council is a required body (c. 495, §1), however, once the see is no longer vacant, a new council must be convened within the year. The new diocesan bishop certainly would be free to reconvene the same members who had served under the previous bishop, but they would still be a new council.

Only under the most serious circumstances can the diocesan bishop suppress the presbyteral council. There must be evidence that the council members are not fulfilling their proper function or are abusing their role. The canon gives no examples of what would constitute this serious a dereliction of duty. Presumably obstinate refusal to assemble when convened by the bishop or a failure to address issues of major importance he presents to them would be grounds for the council's dissolution. In order to monitor such a serious act of discretionary authority, the canon makes provision for prior consultation. Suffragan bishops must consult with the metropolitan and the metropolitan with the senior suffragan bishop. While the diocesan bishop is not bound to accede to the advice given, his failure to consult could result in the invalidity of the dissolution.[279]

The dissolution of a presbyteral council would be a rare event. If it were to be done, however, a properly notarized, written decree should be issued with the reasons for the decision given, at

---

[277] See also *CCEO* 270.

[278] The statutes would need to make provision for situations in which members cease from office who are on the council because of the office they hold.

[279] Canon 127, §2, 2°.

least in summary form.[280] If a council is suppressed, it cannot remain so indefinitely; the bishop must establish a new council within a year. The canon does not make any provision regarding actions requiring consultation of the presbyteral council during the time of its suppression. Since the college of consultors exists as a separate entity, it does not cease with the dissolution of the council. The legislator may have intended that the provision of the preceding paragraph also be applicable here. Hence, as in the case of a vacant see, the consultors act in lieu of the council.

College of Consultors

Canon 502 — §1. From among the members of the presbyteral council and in a number not less than six nor more than twelve, the diocesan bishop freely appoints some priests who are to constitute for five years a college of consultors, to which belongs the functions determined by law. When the five years elapse, however, it continues to exercise its proper functions until a new college is established.

§2. The diocesan bishop presides over the college of consultors. When a see is impeded or vacant, however, the one who temporarily takes the place of the bishop or, if he has not yet been appointed, the priest who is senior in ordination in the college of consultors presides.

§3. The conference of bishops can establish that the functions of the college of consultors are to be entrusted to the cathedral chapter.

§4. In an apostolic vicariate and prefecture, the council of the mission mentioned in can. 495, §2 has the functions of the college of consultors unless the law establishes otherwise.

The college of consultors is a required body in the diocese.[281] Its constitution, membership, functions, and duration are all dictated by universal law. This canon does not describe the role of the

college of consultors, unlike canon 495 which called the presbyteral council a kind of senate. The nature of that role emerges, however, from the various canons which assign responsibilities to the college.

The diocesan bishop freely appoints members to the college of consultors, but he is limited in the pool of candidates from which he may draw; he must select members of the college from among the members of the presbyteral council. Therefore, the consultors must be priests or bishops. Once one becomes a member of the college of consultors, however, that membership is independent of presbyteral council membership. Thus, one could cease to serve on the presbyteral council and still retain membership on the college of consultors.[282]

Members are appointed for five-year terms.[283] Again, this term is independent of any term a college member may have as a member of the presbyteral council. However, when a new college is constituted, it must be constituted from presbyteral council members. One's membership on the college does not cease merely by expiration of time. Notification of the cessation from office must be communicated in writing (c. 186). The college may continue in existence beyond its five-year term; by the law itself it continues until replaced by a new college.

The size of the college of consultors is at the discretion of the diocesan bishop within the bounds set by this canon. There must be at least six members but no more than twelve. Consultors who cease from office need to be replaced only if

---

[280] Canon 51.
[281] See also *CCEO* 271.

[282] This issue was addressed in a response from the PCILT. See *AAS* 76 (1984) 747; *RRAO 1990,* 112. An analysis of this interpretation can be found in L. Wrenn, *Authentic Interpretations on the 1983 Code* (Washington, D.C.: CLSA, 1993) 15–16.
[283] For an opinion that the individual members do not have terms but that the college as a whole is constituted for five years, that the members "are named as a group and remain in office as a group for the five year period, or even longer if a new group has not been named," see Provost, "Presbyteral Councils and Colleges of Consultors," 198.

the total number would fall below the required six.[284]

The following functions of the college of consultors are determined by law:

(1) when a see has been vacant for a year, a diocesan administrator can grant excardination or incardination only with the consent of the college of consultors (c. 272);

(2) some of the members are to be consulted by the pontifical legate prior to selection of a diocesan or coadjutor bishop (c. 377, §3);

(3) a coadjutor bishop takes possession of his office by showing his letter of appointment to the diocesan bishop and the college of consultors (c. 404, §1);

(4) if the see is impeded, a coadjutor and auxiliary bishop take office by showing their letters of appointment to the college of consultors (c. 404, §3);

(5) when a see is impeded and there is no coadjutor, or he also is impeded, the college of consultors is to select a priest to govern the diocese if the diocesan order of succession is not available (c. 413, §2);

(6) if there is no auxiliary bishop, the college assumes the governance of a vacant see in the interim before the selection of a diocesan administrator (c. 419);

(7) the college is to elect a diocesan administrator within eight days of receiving notice that the see is vacant (c. 421, §1);

(8) in the absence of an auxiliary bishop, the college is to notify the Apostolic See of the death of the diocesan bishop (c. 422);

(9) chancellors and other notaries cannot be removed from office by a diocesan administrator without the consent of the college (c. 485);

(10) prior to naming a finance officer, the diocesan bishop is to consult with the college (c. 494, §1);

(11) the finance officer cannot be removed from office during his term without the diocesan bishop's having also consulted the college (c. 494, §2);

(12) the diocesan administrator is to make his profession of faith in the presence of the college (c. 833, 4°);

(13) the college must give its consent before the diocesan administrator can issue dimissorial letters (c. 1018, §1, 2°);

(14) the diocesan bishop must consult with the college prior to placing more important acts of administration (c. 1277);

(15) the diocesan bishop, likewise, needs the college's consent for acts of extraordinary administration (c. 1277);

(16) the diocesan bishop also needs its consent for alienation of property beyond the amount specified by the conference of bishops (c. 1292, §1).

The diocesan bishop is certainly free to take up additional matters with the college of consultors, seeking its advice on issues of import for the diocese. Its consultative role, however, is not to supplant that of the presbyteral council.

Under ordinary circumstances the diocesan bishop presides over the college of consultors. However, when a see is vacant or impeded, that role is assumed by the one who takes his place. Since the consultors themselves are to select the diocesan administrator when a see is vacant, there will obviously be an interim time when there is no one in the place of the diocesan bishop to preside. In that case, the consultor who is senior by ordination presides over the college.

Two final paragraphs of this canon deal with somewhat exceptional cases. In some situations, a conference of bishops may determine that those functions listed above which the law assigns to

[284] Ibid. See also *CCEO* 271, §3 which explicates this point.

the college of consultors can be exercised by the cathedral chapter. The missionary council, which takes the place of a presbyteral council in apostolic vicariates and prefectures, also fulfills the functions of the college of consultors unless there is another provision in law.[285]

CHAPTER IV
CHAPTERS OF CANONS
[cc. 503–510]

This chapter of the code contains only eight canons, considerably reduced from the thirty-two found in the 1917 code (*CIC* 391–422). Chapters of canons evolved over history[286] and now exist only in a few places. The presbyteral council and college of consultors fulfill many of the functions previously assigned to the chapter.[287] The main role of the chapter is now liturgical, although in some places the chapter enjoys certain prerogatives such as a significant role in the selection of bishops.[288] The code mainly addresses organizational issues such as statutes, membership, and remuneration of the chapter of canons. Only one paragraph in this section applies to dioceses which do not have a chapter of canons; the bishop must appoint a priest to fulfill the role ordinarily assumed by the canon penitentiary (c. 508, §2). There is no corresponding section in the Eastern code.

---

[285] One such special provision occurs during the vacant or impeded see; whereas in a diocese the college of consultors assumes governance, in an apostolic vicariate or prefecture the pro-vicar or pro-prefect assumes that role (c. 420).

[286] For a historical summary, see J. Abbo and J. Hannan, *The Sacred Canons,* vol. 1 (St. Louis: Herder Book Co., 1960) 400–401.

[287] The only exception to this norm would occur if a conference of bishops determined that the role of the college of consultors were to be entrusted to the cathedral chapter (c. 502, §3).

[288] See, for example, R. Metz, "Papal Legates and the Appointment of Bishops," *J* 52 (1992) 259–294.

Role of the Chapter of Canons

Canon 503 — A chapter of canons, whether cathedral or collegial, is a college of priests which performs more solemn liturgical functions in a cathedral or collegial church. In addition, it is for the cathedral chapter to fulfill the functions which the law or the diocesan bishop entrusts to it.

The canon describes the chapter of canons as a group of priests who fulfill a liturgical function. There are two types of chapters of canons, cathedral and collegiate. The former group is connected with the cathedral church of a diocese and the latter with any other church. The cathedral chapter no longer serves as the bishop's "senate and counsel" (*CIC* 391, §1); nor does it assume authority during a vacant see (*CIC* 431–435, 443); these functions are now performed by the presbyteral council and the college of consultors.

Establishment, Modification, and Suppression

Canon 504 — The erection, alteration, or suppression of a cathedral chapter is reserved to the Apostolic See.

This canon applies to cathedral chapters only.[289] Their establishment and suppression as well as any alteration are reserved to the Apostolic See. Although earlier drafts of this canon had applied the same reservation to collegial chapters,[290] the diocesan bishop has this authority over collegial chapters.

Statutes

Canon 505 — Each and every chapter, whether cathedral or collegial, is to have its own statutes, drawn up through a legitimate capitular act and

---

[289] Arrieta, in *Pamplona ComEng,* applies this reservation to both types of chapters (371).

[290] *Comm* 13 (1981) 135.

approved by the diocesan bishop. These statutes are neither to be changed nor abrogated except with the approval of the same diocesan bishop.

The chapter itself draws up its statutes; but they are approved, abrogated, or changed by the diocesan bishop alone. The statutes themselves will determine the requirements for the legitimacy of the capitular act. The diocesan bishop should put his approval, abrogation, or alteration of the statutes in writing (c. 474). These documents are not technically statutes in the sense of canon 94.[291] Many of the elements found in formal statutes, however, are listed as required elements of chapter statutes in the following canon.

Canon 506 — §1. The statutes of a chapter are to determine the constitution of the chapter and the number of canons, always without prejudice to the laws of its foundation. They are to define those things which the chapter and individual canons are to do in the performance of divine worship and ministry. They are to determine the meetings in which the affairs of the chapter are handled and establish the conditions required for the validity and liceity of those affairs, without prejudice to the prescripts of universal law.

§2. The statutes are also to define the compensation, whether stable or to be given on the occasion of the performance of some function, and, attentive to the norms issued by the Holy See, the insignia of the canons.

The statutes define the type of chapter, the number of members, corporate and individual responsibilities for worship and other ministry, the scheduling and conduct of meetings, and the requirements for the chapter's valid and licit acts. The statutes are also to designate the amount and

manner of compensation of the canons, whether ongoing or related to the performance of a specific function, as well as the insignia to be worn by members in accord with universal norms.[292]

Organization of Chapters

Canon 507 — §1. One of the canons is to preside over the chapter; other offices are also to be constituted according to the norm of the statutes, after the practice prevailing in the region has been taken into consideration.

§2. Other offices can be entrusted to clerics who do not belong to the chapter; through these offices they assist the canons according to the norm of the statutes.

This canon declares that one of the members is to preside over the chapter but does not establish the manner of determining this presidency. The statutes should include this provision. The president could be elected by the members or appointed by the diocesan bishop.[293] The statutes can also establish other offices in keeping with local custom. In addition to naming offices held by chapter members, the statutes may determine other auxiliary offices which can be held by clerics who are not members.

The Canon Penitentiary

Canon 508 — §1. By virtue of office, the canon penitentiary of a cathedral church and of a collegial church has the ordinary faculty, which he cannot delegate to others, of absolving in the sacramental forum outsiders within the diocese and members of the diocese even outside the territory of the diocese from undeclared *latae sententiae* censures not reserved to the Apostolic See.

---

[291] Canon 94 uses the term *statutes* to refer to the governing documents of juridic persons and the chapter is not a juridic person. However, one commentator differs in this interpretation of the status of the chapter and describes it as a public juridic person. See Read, in *CLSGBI Com*, 280.

[292] The most recent norms on insignia were issued in the form of a March 18, 1987 CFC circular letter to presidents of conferences of bishops. See *AAS* 79 (1987) 603–604.

[293] See comments under c. 509.

§2. Where there is no chapter, the diocesan bishop is to appoint a priest to fulfill the same function.

This canon addresses the ecclesiastical office of canon penitentiary. The canon penitentiary possesses the ordinary faculty to remit, in the internal sacramental forum, all undeclared *latae sententiae* censures[294] which are not reserved to the Apostolic See.[295] However, he cannot delegate this faculty to others. He exercises this faculty on behalf of any penitents who approach him within his own diocesan territory; if he is outside his territory he can absolve only members of his diocese.

In those dioceses without a chapter of canons, the diocesan bishop is to appoint a priest with the same faculties as a canon penitentiary. In place of such an appointment, the bishop could delegate all priests to remit undeclared, unreserved, *latae sententiae* censures.[296]

Appointment of Canons

Canon 509 — §1. After having heard the chapter, it is for the diocesan bishop, but not a diocesan administrator, to confer each and every canonry, both in a cathedral church and in a collegial church; every contrary privilege is revoked. It is for the same bishop to confirm the person elected by the chapter to preside over it.

§2. A diocesan bishop is to confer canonries only upon priests outstanding in doctrine and integrity of life, who have laudably exercised the ministry.

The diocesan bishop enjoys the right of free conferral of the office of canon, both cathedral and collegial (cf. c. 157). However, this same right does not transfer to the diocesan administrator when the see is vacant. Prior to making any such appointments, the bishop is to consult the appropriate chapter. He is not required to accede to its opinion, but the appointment would be invalid if he did not consult it at all.[297]

The latter part of paragraph one addresses the bishop's right to confirm in office a priest elected as president of the chapter. The meaning of this stipulation was clarified by an authoritative code commission interpretation issued on January 24, 1989.[298] The question was raised whether canon 509, §1 requires that the chapter elect its president. From the negative response given in the interpretation, we can conclude that the diocesan bishop is free to appoint the president but that, if the statutes call for an election, the diocesan bishop has the right to confirm the election.[299] The general norms on confirmation of an election require that the elected individual, unless legitimately impeded, request confirmation, personally or through another, within eight useful days (c. 179, §1). The bishop cannot refuse confirmation if the election was valid and the person is suitable (c. 179, §2). He is to communicate his confirmation in writing (c. 179, §3) at which time the one elected obtains all the rights associated with the office (c. 179, §5).

The second paragraph of canon 509 states the qualifications of chapter members. They are to be priests noted for their sound doctrine and integrity of life who have a proven record of ministry. These same qualities are among those required for other significant diocesan offices, such as vicar general or episcopal vicar.[300] In contrast with the qualifications for these offices, however, there is neither an age requirement for chapter members nor restrictions on the appointment of the bishop's close relatives.[301]

Relationship with Parishes

Canon 510 — §1. Parishes are no longer to be joined to a chapter of canons; the diocesan bishop

[294] Canons 1331–1335.
[295] For censures reserved to the Apostolic See, see cc. 1367; 1370, §1; 1378, §1; 1382; 1388, §1.
[296] See Alesandro, in *CLSA Com,* 409.

[297] Canon 127, §1.
[298] See *AAS* 81 (1989) 99; *RRAO 1989,* 105.
[299] L. Wrenn, *Authentic Interpretations,* 55–56.
[300] Canon 478, §1.
[301] Canon 478, §2.

is to separate from a chapter those parishes which are united to it.

§2. In a church which is at the same time parochial and capitular, a pastor is to be designated, whether chosen from among the members of the chapter or not. This pastor is bound by all the duties and possesses the rights and faculties which are proper to a pastor according to the norm of law.

§3. It is for the diocesan bishop to establish definite norms which fittingly integrate the pastoral duties of the pastor and the functions proper to the chapter, taking care that the pastor is not a hindrance to capitular functions nor the chapter to parochial functions. The diocesan bishop, who above all is to take care that the pastoral needs of the faithful are aptly provided for, is to resolve conflicts if they occur.

§4. Alms given to a church which is at the same time parochial and capitular are presumed given to the parish unless it is otherwise evident.

The 1917 code provided for three possible scenarios when the cathedral or collegiate church was also the parish church: the parish could be joined fully (*pleno iure*) to the chapter which would technically be the pastor although one member of the chapter would function as a parochial vicar and provide ordinary pastoral care (*CIC* 402; 471, §1); the office of pastor was one of the benefices (*CIC* 1409) given to a particular chapter member (*CIC* 415); the chapter and parish were separate entities, sharing a common church. Canon 510 prohibits all but the third option; parishes may no longer be united with a chapter.[302] Likewise, the diocesan bishop is to sever the connection of parishes previously united to a chapter.

The canon does allow a church to be both parochial and capitular, but in such cases a pastor is to be appointed with all of the rights and obligation of other pastors.[303] The pastor may be a

member of the chapter or another priest as the bishop determines. The pastoral care of the parishioners takes precedence over any chapter function (c. 1752). In order to avoid conflicts, the bishop is to set norms governing the relationship between the duties of the pastor and the role of the chapter. If conflicts do arise, the bishop is likewise the final arbiter.

The final paragraph clarifies financial issues. Offerings given to the church are presumed to be given to the parish, not the chapter (cf. c. 1267, §1). This presumption would be overturned only by proof that the chapter was the intended recipient, e.g., a will specifically naming the chapter as the beneficiary.

CHAPTER V
THE PASTORAL COUNCIL
[cc. 511–514]

The roots of the diocesan pastoral council are evident in conciliar documents and postconciliar literature.[304] The clearest conciliar foundation for its existence and composition was the statement in *Christus Dominus* 27: "It is highly desirable that in every diocese a pastoral council be established, presided over by the diocesan bishop himself, in which clergy, religious and laity specially chosen for the purpose will participate." This same source stated the general purpose of this council as being "to investigate matters relating to pastoral activities, to consider them, and to formulate practical conclusions concerning them." In a similar vein, *Ad gentes* 30 promoted the coordination of the diocesan apostolate and missionary activity by means of "a pastoral council in which clergy, religious and lay people would have a part through elected delegates" and stated that the diocesan bishop "should, as far as possible, establish" such a council.

---

[302] See c. 520, §1 for a similar prohibition against naming a juridic person as pastor of a parish.

[303] See, for example, cc. 528–538.

[304] For an overview and analysis of the development of pastoral councils, see J. Renken, "Pastoral Councils: Pastoral Planning and Dialogue Among the People of God," *J* 53 (1993) 132–154.

Besides these conciliar texts,[305] postconciliar documents promoted the establishment of a diocesan pastoral council and provided more specificity regarding its function and means of operation. The *motu proprio Ecclesiae sanctae* I, 16 reiterated that the pastoral council was strongly commended and set forth six additional points:

(1) in fulfilling its function of examining and considering pastoral work and proposing practical conclusions, the council assists in promoting the life of the gospel among the people of God;

(2) the establishment of a pastoral council can be accomplished in different ways, is convened as the diocesan bishop finds it helpful, is consultative in nature, and is ordinarily permanent although there may be a temporary character to its membership and various activities;

(3) the council includes clergy, religious, and laity;

(4) the accomplishment of its work will require study and cooperation with other groups and institutions involved in the same fields of study;

(5) pastoral councils can be interritual in composition;

(6) the diocesan bishop has broad discretion in deciding other matters relating to the pastoral council.

Ecclesiae sanctae I, 17 suggests that, in implementing the norms on councils, the bishops of a conference should consult together and issue common regulatory norms for their dioceses.[306] It

also advises that diocesan bishops coordinate the various councils within their dioceses by defining their different competencies, promoting their mutual cooperation, and providing common or continuing sessions among them.

The 1971 synod of bishops also briefly referred to the diocesan pastoral council. Its function is to provide, after study and consideration, conclusions for the systematic arrangement and effective implementation of the diocesan pastoral program.

The most extensive postconciliar document relating solely to diocesan pastoral councils was the 1973 circular letter issued by the Congregation for the Clergy.[307] The document once again pointed out that such councils are important and helpful and quoted directly from *Christus Dominus* 27 on their purpose. Having restated the areas of competence from the conciliar source, the document proceeded to point out areas which are beyond the pastoral council's competence, such as doctrinal questions or moral issues. The document stated that pastoral questions which involve matters of jurisdiction are more rightly directed to the senate of priests, but the diocesan bishop may bring such matters to the pastoral council for its consideration provided he also undertakes the required canonical consultation. The circular letter highlighted the council's representative nature, though not in a strictly juridical sense, and pointed out that since most believers in any diocese are lay, the majority of the pastoral council should also be lay. This document reiterated the council's consultative nature but also pointed out that the diocesan bishop is to consider its judgments seriously. The relationship between the diocesan bishop and the pastoral council is clear; the diocesan bishop is to preside over it, and it ceases when the see is vacant.

The 1973 *Directory on the Pastoral Ministry of Bishops* reiterated the conciliar and early postconciliar statements on pastoral councils and their function (n. 204). The *Directory* noted that such councils were highly recommended, even though

---

[305] The only additional conciliar reference is in a footnote to *Presbyterorum ordinis,* n. 7, indicating that the priests' senate is distinguished from the diocesan pastoral council because this latter group includes laity and its function is confined to the investigation of pastoral matters, not the management of the diocese.

[306] This suggestion of common norms within a conference territory was abandoned during the revision process, and it was determined that no reference be made to such common norms (*Comm* 13 [1981] 149).

[307] SCC, "Pastoral Council" (January 25, 1973), in *CLD* 8, 280–288.

not mandatory, and that the diocesan bishop should have great respect for council recommendations since the pastoral council offers him "the serious and settled cooperation of the ecclesiastical community." This same document also encouraged parish pastoral councils and highlighted the possible linkage between them and the diocesan pastoral council.

In scope, content, and sequence the canons on the pastoral council (*CCEO* 272–275) in the Code of Canons of the Eastern Churches parallel the legislation in the Latin code except that in the Eastern code the annual convening of the pastoral council is not required (c. 514, §2).

Establishment and Purpose of a Pastoral Council

Canon 511 — In every diocese and to the extent that pastoral circumstances suggest it, a pastoral council is to be constituted which under the authority of the bishop investigates, considers, and proposes practical conclusions about those things which pertain to pastoral works in the diocese.

Consistent with its conciliar sources, the canon proposes that a diocesan pastoral council be established by the diocesan bishop in every diocese. While such councils are not mandatory, conciliar and postconciliar endorsement of such councils would suggest that, unless pastoral circumstances warrant otherwise, the bishop should establish such a council. In the drafting stages there were efforts to strengthen the encouragement of councils, more in line with the conciliar texts. However, it was ultimately determined that circumstances among dioceses were quite diverse so the canon should not mandate councils.[308]

The threefold and interrelated purposes of the pastoral council (*CD* 27) are cited in the canon. The council is to investigate, consider, and propose practical conclusions in relation to the pastoral works of the diocese. In the coordination of the pastoral activity of a diocese, these three func-

tions are usually components of what is referred to as "pastoral planning."[309]

The fact that the diocesan pastoral council is specifically charged with such a planning function does not mean that it necessarily proceeds with the task in isolation. In many dioceses, among the various curial offices there is one devoted to planning, or the task itself, if not the title, is assigned to a curial office that has other responsibilities as well, e.g., educational policy making. In those dioceses where such a planning office exists, there needs to be a careful delineation of the relationship between the planning function of the pastoral council and that of the diocesan office. In some cases, personnel from the diocesan curial planning office serve as staff to the pastoral council. The work of one body should not be seen as in competition with or opposed to the work of the other. The function of the diocesan office is to assist the diocesan bishop in directing pastoral activity and administering the diocese (c. 469). However, the pastoral council's function is not a directive or administrative one.

The canon does not delineate specific issues for the council to investigate, to ponder, and about which to probe conclusions. However, the 1973 circular letter can provide some pertinent suggestions:

> The pastoral council, therefore, can give the bishop great help by presenting him with proposals and suggestions: regarding missionary, catechetical and apostolic undertakings within the diocese; concerning the promotion of doctrinal formation and the sacramental life of the faithful; concerning pastoral activities to help the priests in the various social and territorial areas of the diocese; concerning public opinion on matters pertaining to the Church as it is more likely to be fostered in the present time, etc. The pastoral council can also be extremely useful for mutual communication of experiences and for proposed undertak-

[308] *Rel*, 120.

[309] Renken, 146–147.

ings of various types by which the concrete needs of the people of the diocese may become clearer to the bishop and a more opportune means of pastoral action may be suggested to him. (n. 9)

The special circumstances of each diocese as well as its needs at a given moment in history will help shape the agenda of the pastoral council.

The council functions under the authority of the diocesan bishop. Issues to be addressed flow from him to the council or are addressed from the council to him. The council can serve the diocesan bishop well by assisting him in setting the direction of the diocese in various pastoral matters as well as by surfacing for him areas of pastoral concern among the faithful entrusted to his care.

The scope of the council's activity is the diocese. Despite some early indications that interdiocesan or supradiocesan councils might be explored, these suggestions were not developed. Concerns that pastoral councils might involve themselves in matters beyond the diocese were raised during the revision process; the canon clearly limits the role of the pastoral council to the diocese.[310]

Pastoral Council Membership

Canon 512 — §1. A pastoral council consists of members of the Christian faithful who are in full communion with the Catholic Church—clerics, members of institutes of consecrated life, and especially laity—who are designated in a manner determined by the diocesan bishop.

§2. The Christian faithful who are designated to a pastoral council are to be selected in such a way that they truly reflect the entire portion of the people of God which constitutes the diocese, with consideration given to the different areas of the diocese, social conditions and professions, and the role which they have in the apostolate whether individually or joined with others.

§3. No one except members of the Christian faithful outstanding in firm faith, good morals, and prudence is to be designated to a pastoral council.

In three paragraphs, this canon provides various details on the membership of the diocesan pastoral council. Members are to be drawn from the whole range of Christian faithful, namely clergy, members of institutes of consecrated life, and especially laity. They are to be in full communion with the Catholic Church (c. 205). Beyond these general descriptions, paragraph one establishes the broad discretionary authority of the diocesan bishop to clarify how membership is determined, from election or appointment or ex officio designation. The priority to be given to lay membership on the council is consistent with the 1973 circular letter principle that, since laity constitute the largest portion of the population of the diocese, they should be the majority of the council as well.

Paragraph two expresses other ways in which the council is to reflect the make-up of the diocese. Regardless of the membership selection process utilized by the diocesan bishop, the council should be a microcosm of the diocese as a whole. The council is not representative in the sense that its membership is based on the size of the population of a given area or component of the diocese, or in the sense that members represent constituents and their vested interests. The council is to reflect the membership of the diocese as a whole rather than being representative of its various parts. The council should be a microcosm of the diocese, whose welfare is to be considered in council deliberations.[311] Therefore, the diocesan bishop is to consider geographic, social and professional, as well as apostolic bases for council membership. In those dioceses with distinctive ethnic or language components, the overall membership of the council may also include those factors. In some cases, after an initial selection process has been completed, the diocesan bishop may make additional appointments to

---

[310] *Rel*, 120.

[311] Renken, 152.

round out the membership so it is truly reflective of the diocese.

Just as establishing the manner of selection is left to the discretion of the diocesan bishop, so also is the determination of the size of the council, which will be affected by the size and complexity of the diocese. The council should be large enough to be reflective of the diocese and yet not so large that it defeats the council's purpose to investigate, consider, and propose pastoral conclusions. Too large a group can make interaction among members in discharging these tasks difficult or impossible. Too small a group cannot be reflective of the diocese in presenting diverse views and concerns to the bishop; too large a group can make it impossible for him to take effective counsel.

Besides the prerequisite of full communion with the Catholic Church, council members are also to be noted for their firm faith, good morals, and prudence (§3). These same characteristics are noted elsewhere when the code regulates membership in certain groups or eligibility for certain offices.[312]

Since those who constitute the pastoral council can be considered canonical office holders (c. 145), regardless of the selection process utilized by the diocesan bishop, the norms on appointment to office should be observed once the determination of membership has been made. A letter of appointment signed by the bishop and notarized should be sent to each member, even one who may serve in an ex officio capacity.

Canon 513 — §1. A pastoral council is constituted for a period of time according to the prescripts of the statutes which are issued by the bishop.

§2. When the see is vacant, a pastoral council ceases.

This brief canon presents two norms which highlight the council's fundamental consultative relationship with the diocesan bishop, who has the authority to determine the manner of that relationship. Although the council is not technically a juridic person, the bishop issues "statutes" to govern its workings. Such provisions are comparable to laws and are formally promulgated by the diocesan bishop and interpreted by him.[313]

Among the elements the statutes address is the term of office of the council members. Once established as an institution of the diocese, and not dissolved, the council has a permanent quality to it. In some cases it will be disbanded and reconstituted in its entirety according to a designated schedule, such as every three years. In other cases, members serve a set term, and there is a gradual turnover of the entire membership over a period of years. The statutes establish the term of office of the council members.

Also, because the council serves in a close relationship with the diocesan bishop, when the see is vacant, the council ceases to exist. This norm is consistent with the cessation or suspension of other bodies during a vacant see.[314] Unlike the canonical norms for the resumption of other bodies, however, there are no norms for the resumption of the pastoral council; the new diocesan bishop has full discretion in seeing to its reestablishment, determining its membership, and issuing its statutes, with any appropriate modifications.

Authority of the Pastoral Council

Canon 514 — §1. A pastoral council possesses only a consultative vote. It belongs to the diocesan bishop alone to convoke it according to the needs of the apostolate and to preside over it; it

---

[312] See, for example, the general requirement for lay persons to serve as experts or advisors individually or in councils (c. 228, §2); the personal characteristics to be found in candidates for the college of cardinals (c. 351, §1), bishops (c. 378, §1, 1°), diocesan administrators (c. 425, §2), vicars general or episcopal vicars (c. 478, §1).

[313] Canon 94, §3 establishes the general norm that statutes issued by one with legislative power, as is the case with the diocesan bishop, are governed by the canons on laws. See also n. 249 in this connection.

[314] The diocesan synod is suspended during a vacant see (c. 468, §2) and the presbyteral council ceases (c. 501, §2).

also belongs to him alone to make public what has been done in the council.

§2. The pastoral council is to be convoked at least once a year.

The pastoral council has been consistently viewed as a consultative rather than a deliberative body. It is not like the diocesan finance council, whose role is at times consultative and at other times deliberative, with certain matters referred by law for its consent; there are no canonical requirements that any matters be taken to the pastoral council for consultative or deliberative action. Its consultative nature, however, does not detract from its potential to serve as a valuable tool for consultation in setting pastoral directions for the diocese.[315]

Again, in line with the diocesan bishop's relationship with the council, he has the authority to convene it and preside over it. The pastoral needs of the diocese will determine the frequency with which the council gathers. However, once he establishes it, the diocesan bishop must convene the council at least once a year.

In presiding over the council, the diocesan bishop need not chair its meetings. Ordinarily he will preside at the meetings personally. However, he may delegate another to preside in his place. If this option is selected, avenues of communication between the delegate and the bishop will have to be carefully established to ensure that the council is an effective vehicle for consultation.

The statutes of the council should determine levels of and expectations regarding confidentiality. The diocesan bishop alone has the authority to make council matters public. The vehicles for doing so can include the publication of minutes, the issuance of annual reports, media conferences, etc. Again, the bishop can make matters public personally or through a delegate, e.g., a diocesan communications officer.

Conclusion

The impact and use of diocesan pastoral councils in the United States have been the subject of three major studies since their inception. The first study was conducted in 1972 at the same time that a feasibility study for a national pastoral council was undertaken by the NCCB. A second study took place in 1984 as a project of the NCCB Committee on the Laity. The results of this latter study resulted in a publication of findings complete with reporting on specific dioceses where diocesan pastoral councils had been successfully established.[316] In 1997 a new study of diocesan pastoral councils was proposed as a joint project of the NCCB Committee on Pastoral Practices and the Secretariat for Family, Laity, Women and Youth. The Canon Law Society of America joined as a partner in the project as a result of a membership resolution at the 1996 annual convention.[317] The current study will include survey data from all dioceses and eparchies in the United States as well as an analysis of the implications of the data.[318]

[315] Renken, 153.

[316] NCCB Committee on the Laity, *Building the Local Church: Shared Responsibility in Diocesan Pastoral Councils* (Washington, D.C.: USCC, 1984).

[317] *CLSAP* (1996) 504–506.

[318] *Diocesan and Eparchial Pastoral Councils: A National Profile* (Washington, D.C.: Center for Applied Research in the Apostolate, 1998).

Association of Catholic Diocesan Archivists. *Preparing for the 90's: Strategies for Diocesan Archivists and Records Managers.* Chicago: Association of Catholic Diocesan Archivists, 1993.

Bassett, W., and P. Huizing, eds. *The Finances of the Church.* New York: Seabury, 1979.

Breitenbeck, M. "Practical Addendum on Policy-Making." In *Confidentiality in the United States,* 163–165. Washington, D.C.: CLSA, 1988

Cafardi, N. "Religious Affiliation of the Diocesan Finance Officer." In *CLSA Advisory Opinions: 1984–1993,* ed. P. Cogan, 99–102. Washington, D.C.: CLSA, 1995.

CFB and CEP. *Instruction on Diocesan Synods,* July 8, 1997. *Origins* 27 (October 23, 1997) 324–331.

CLSA, "Canonical Standards in Labor-Management Relations: A Report." *CLSAP* (1987) 311–335.

Diocesan and Eparchial Councils: A National Profile. Washington, D.C.: Center for Applied Research in the Apostolate, 1998.

Farrelly, A. "The Diocesan Finance Council." *Stud Can* 23 (1989) 149–166.

Green, T. "Shepherding the Patrimony of the Poor." *J* 56 (1996) 706–734.

Holland, S. "Archives: In Service of Culture and Learning." *J* 46 (1986) 630–631.

Jennings, L. "A Renewed Understanding of the Diocesan Synod." *Stud Can* 20 (1986) 320–329.

Kennedy, R. "Shared Responsibility in Ecclesial Decision-Making." *Stud Can* 14 (1980) 5–23.

Metz, R. "Papal Legates and the Appointment of Bishops." *J* 52 (1992) 259–294.

Morrow, D. "The Chancellor as Archivist." *CLSAP* (1988) 225–227.

National Association of Church Personnel Administrators. *Just Treatment for Those Who Work for the Church.* Cincinnati: National Association of Church Personnel Administrators, 1986.

NCCB. "A Document on Ecclesiastical Archives," November 22, 1974. In *Pastoral Letters of the United States Catholic Bishops, III,* ed. H. Nolan, 470–471. Washington, D.C.: USCC, 1983.

———. "Economic Justice for All: Catholic Social Teaching and the U.S. Economy." *Origins* 27 (November 27, 1986) 409–455.

———. "United in Service: Reflections on the Presbyteral Council." *Origins* 21 (December 5, 1991) 409, 411–421.

NCCB Committee on the Laity. *Building the Local Church: Shared Responsibility in Diocesan Pastoral Councils.* Washington, D.C.: USCC, 1984.

Pagé, R. *Les Églises particulières.* Montreal: Les Éditions Paulines, 1985.

Provost, J. "Canonical Reflection on Selected Issues in Diocesan Governance." In *The Ministry of Governance,* ed. J. Mallett, 209–251. Washington, D.C.: CLSA, 1986.

———. "Presbyteral Councils and Colleges of Consultors: Current Law and Some Diocesan Statutes." *CLSAP* (1987) 194–211.

Rehrauer, A. "The Diocesan Synod." *CLSAP* 49 (1987) 1–15.

Renken, J. "Pastoral Councils: Pastoral Planning and Dialogue Among the People of God." *J* 53 (1993) 132–154.

Rinere, E. "The Confidentiality of Written Documents in Canon Law." In *Confidentiality in the United States,* 125–144. Washington, D.C.: CLSA, 1988.

Ross, D. "Participation in the Synod." *ME* 116 (1991) 462–482.

Wrenn, L. *Authentic Interpretations on the 1983 Code,* 15–16, 55–56. Washington, D.C.: CLSA, 1993.

CHAPTER VI
PARISHES, PASTORS,
AND PAROCHIAL VICARS
[cc. 515–552][1]

PARISHES AND PASTORS
[cc. 515–544]

In speaking to a group of French bishops during their *ad limina* visit on January 25, 1997, Pope John Paul II reflected on the importance of the parish in the life of each diocese. He said:

> [In] close collaboration with the other pastoral groups, it is essentially the parish which gives the Church concrete life, so that she may be open to all. Whatever its size, it is not merely an association. It must be a home where the members of the Body of Christ gather together, open to meeting God the Father, full of love and Savior in his Son, incorporated into the Church by the Holy Spirit at the time of their Baptism, and ready to accept their brothers and sisters with fraternal love, whatever their condition or origins.
>
> The parish institution is meant to provide the church's great services: prayer in common and the reading of God's Word, celebrations, especially that of the Eucharist, catechesis for children and the adult catechumenate, the ongoing formation of the faithful, communications designed to make the Christian message known, services of charity and solidarity and the local work of movements. In brief, the image of the sanctuary which is its visible sign, it is a building to be erected together, a body to bring to life and develop

together, a community where God's gifts are received and where the baptized generously make their response of faith, hope and love to the call of the Gospel. At this time when pastoral structures are being renewed, it will be appropriate to resume the in-depth study of the ecclesiological teaching of the Second Vatican Council, in the Constitution on the Church *Lumen gentium* and in the various documents providing directives, especially those concerning priests and the laity.[2]

The Holy Father continued his reflections by discussing parish pastoral planning (consolidation of parishes or the creation of new parishes), collaboration between priests and lay persons in parishes (in pastoral councils and leadership teams), and various other elements of parish life.

Over a year later, on May 21, 1998, Pope John Paul II commented on the parish in the midst of reflections on the life and ministry of priests. The occasion was the *ad limina* visit of bishops from Michigan and Ohio in the United States. Underscoring the central, vital, and irreplaceable role of prayer in the life of every priest, the pope said:

> Indeed prayer for the needs of the church and the individual faithful is so important that serious thought should be given to reorganizing priestly and parish life to ensure that priests have time to devote to this essential task individually and in common. Liturgical and personal prayer, not the tasks of management, must define the rhythms of a priest's life, even in the busiest of parishes.[3]

[1] For other commentaries on these canons, see G. Read, "Chapter IV: Parishes, Parish Priests and Assistant Priests," in *CLSGBI Com*, 285–302; J. Calvo, "Parishes, Parish Priests and Assistant Priests," in *Pamplona ComEng*, 377–398.

[2] John Paul II, "The Vocation of the Parish," January 25, 1997 talk to the third group of French bishops on the *ad limina* visit. *OssRomEng* 1477 (February 5, 1997) 5. Reprinted in *Church* 13/2 (Summer, 1997) 43–46.

[3] John Paul II, "Priests, Their Life and Ministry," May 21, 1998 talk to the bishops of Michigan and Ohio on their *ad limina* visit, *Origins* 28 (June 18, 1998) 74.

To implement the vision of Pope John Paul II about the parish in ecclesial life requires, among many other important things, a clear and accurate understanding of the ecclesiastical legislation on the parish, its pastor, and other persons who serve the parochial community.

This commentary analyzes the universal law on pastors and parishes for the Latin church, contained in the Code of Canon Law, canons 515–544. The analysis considers each canon in relation to other legislation, including the 1917 code and conciliar and postconciliar texts. Consideration is given occasionally to the deliberations of those responsible for the creation of the canons during the revision of the 1917 code. The commentary gives special consideration to the Church's living understanding of the canons since the promulgation of the 1983 code, especially as that understanding has been expressed in further legislation and official teachings.

A history of the parish in the life of the Catholic Church is beyond the limited scope of this commentary.[4] Likewise, a detailed account of the revision of the 1917 code is beyond the scope of this commentary.[5]

Relation to the 1917 Code

Canons 515–544 of the 1983 code reflect canons 451–470 of the 1917 code. The 1917 code treated the parish within the context of the legislation on its pastor. The parish was bestowed upon the priest as a title (*in titulum*—meaning he rightfully possessed it), and it was his benefice[6] (*CIC*

1409–1488). Canon 216, §§1, 3–4 of the 1917 code briefly described the parish; this canon is reflected in canons 374 (in the chapter on particular churches), and 515, §§1–2 and 518 (in the chapter on parishes).

The current legislation considers the parish as a community of the faithful stably constituted within a particular church, whose pastoral care is entrusted to a pastor under the authority of the diocesan bishop. Norms about the pastor are considered within the context of norms on the parish, which is no longer considered his benefice.

The 1983 code contains a number of other notable changes from the 1917 code. The diocesan bishop has the power to erect, suppress, or alter all parishes, after having heard his presbyteral council (c. 515, §2). The parish is a juridic person by law (c. 515, §3). Quasi-parishes may exist in every particular church; they are understood as definite communities which are *not yet* erected as parishes (c. 516). The diocesan bishop may entrust the pastoral care of a parish (or parishes) to several priests *in solidum* (that is, jointly) with the requirement that one be the moderator of the group (c. 517, §1). When there is a lack of priests, two options are possible: (1) the diocesan bishop may arrange for a share in the exercise of parochial pastoral care to be entrusted to a deacon, lay person, or group of non-priests, in which case a priest with the powers and faculties of a pastor directs the pastoral care (c. 517, §2), or (2) the diocesan bishop may entrust the pastoral care of several neighboring parishes to the same pastor (c. 526, §1). Personal parishes may be erected without the approval of the Apostolic See (c. 518). Only a physical person can be a pastor (c. 520, §1). The distinction between irremovable and removable pastors is eliminated, and the con-

---

[4] See J. Coriden, *The Parish in Catholic Tradition: History, Theology and Canon Law* (New York: Paulist, 1997).

[5] In this connection, see T. Green, "Persons and Structures in the Church: Reflections on Selected Issues in Book II," *J* 45 (1985) 57–62; J. Janicki, "Parishes, Pastors, and Parochial Vicars (cc. 515–552)," in *CLSA Com*, 413–443; J. Lynch, "The Parochial Ministry in the New Code of Canon Law," *J* 42 (1982) 383–421.

[6] *CIC* 1409 described an ecclesiastical benefice as a juridic entity perpetually established or erected by competent authority, and consisting of a sacred office and a right to revenue from the endowment connected to that office.

PO 20 called for the system of benefices to be abandoned or else so reformed that the principal emphasis was placed on the office with a secondary emphasis on the endowment itself. Canon 1272 of the 1983 code urges the gradual elimination of benefices and the placing of their income and endowment (*corpus*) into the diocesan institute for priests' support mentioned in c. 1274, §1.

ference of bishops can permit the diocesan bishop to appoint pastors for a specific term (c. 522). Each pastor is requested to submit his resignation at age seventy-five (c. 538, §3). After he has heard the presbyteral council, the diocesan bishop may require the establishment of a pastoral council in every parish (c. 536). A finance council, however, must be established in every parish; its role is to assist the pastor in administering parochial temporal goods (c. 537). The pastor represents the parish in all juridic affairs, and is to take care that its goods are administered appropriately and legally (c. 532).

Parish legislation in the current code is built upon the law of the 1917 code and the Church's subsequent lived experience, especially legal changes called for by the Second Vatican Council[7] and selected postconciliar documents.[8]

Following Vatican Council II, the Pontifical Commission for the Revision of the Code of Canon Law began to create revised law for the Latin church. The initial revision of the law on parishes and pastors was the work of the *coetus De sacra hierarchia*.[9] In 1977 the commission sent to the world's bishops and pontifical faculties the *Schema Canonum Libri II De populo Dei*,[10] which included proposed canons (cc. 349–376) on parishes and pastors. Responses were due by the end of 1978, and were later studied by the commission[11] which produced the 1980 *Schema Codicis Iuris Canonici*.[12] On August 22, 1981, Pericles Cardinal Felici, president of the commission, sent to commission members a *Relatio*[13] in

which the secretariat and consultors reported and responded to various suggestions of the commission, and made some changes in the schema. The plenary session of the commission, enlarged by fifteen members, took place in Rome on October 20–29, 1981;[14] further changes were introduced; and the 1982 *Codex Iuris Canonici, Schema novissimum*[15] was sent to the Holy Father. Pope John Paul II studied the text with a small group of consultors, and episcopal conferences were informed that he would accept any further suggestions about the code. The revised Latin code was promulgated on January 25, 1983, and became effective on November 27, 1983.

Eastern Code

The universal legislation on parishes for the Eastern churches is contained in title VII (Eparchies and Bishops), chapter 3 (Parishes, Pastors, and Parochial Vicars), canons 279–303 of the Eastern code. The canons are generally similar to those in the 1983 code, with some notable exceptions.[16]

The Eastern code allows the eparchial bishop to erect personal parishes only after he has heard the presbyteral council (*CCEO* 280, §1). The eparchial bishop needs a grave cause to remove from the pastoral care of the pastor any non-exempt groups, buildings, and places in the pastor's territory (*CCEO* 283). A pastor is not to be named for a determined period unless: (1) it concerns a member of a religious institute or society of common life in the manner of religious; (2) a candidate agrees to this in writing; (3) it concerns a special case, in which instance the consent of the college of eparchial consultors is required; or (4) the particular law of his church *sui iuris* permits it (*CCEO* 284, §3). If a pastor is married,

---

[7] Especially *Christus Dominus* 18, 23, 28, 30–32 and *Presbyterorum ordinis* 6–9. These and other *fontes* for each specific canon are identified in *CIC An.*

[8] Especially *Ecclesiae sanctae* I, 8, 18–21 and the *Directory.*

[9] *Comm* 4 (1972) 39–50; 5 (1973) 216–235; 6 (1974) 44–46; 8 (1976) 23–31; 24 (1992) 109–114, 137–159, 167–176; 25 (1993) 179–209.

[10] ComCICRec, *Schema canonum Libri II De populo Dei* (Vatican City: Libreria Editrice Vaticana, 1977).

[11] *Comm* 13 (1981) 146–151, 271–294, 304–308.

[12] ComCICRec, *Schema Codicis Iuris Canonici* (Vatican City: Libreria Editrice Vaticana, 1980).

[13] *Comm* 14 (1982) 123, 221–230.

[14] *Comm* 13 (1981) 256–270.

[15] ComCICRec, *Codex Iuris Canonici, Schema novissimum* (Vatican City: Libreria Editrice Vaticana, 1982).

[16] The Eastern code canons which are parallel to those of the 1983 code are indicated in the footnotes to each Latin canon throughout this commentary.

good morals are required of his wife and his children who live with him (*CCEO* 285, §2). If the particular law of a church *sui iuris* permits a parish to be entrusted to several presbyters, the same law is to define more accurately the role of the moderator and other members of the group (*CCEO* 287, §2). Only three sacred functions (sacraments of Christian initiation, blessing of marriages, and ecclesiastical funeral rites) belong to the pastor; the parochial vicar needs at least the presumed permission of the pastor to perform them (*CCEO* 290, §2). The particular law of each church *sui iuris* is to prescribe when the pastor is to celebrate the Divine Liturgy for the people (*CCEO* 294) and to determine the nature and necessity of parish councils for pastoral affairs and for financial matters (*CCEO* 295).

The Eastern code makes no mention of quasi-parishes, special pastoral care for communities which cannot be erected as parishes or quasi-parishes (c. 516), or the entrusting of a participation in the exercise of pastoral care to an individual (or community) who is not a priest (c. 517, §2).

Notion of Parish[17]

Canon 515 — §1. A parish is a certain community of the Christian faithful stably constituted in a particular church, whose pastoral care is entrusted to a pastor (*parochus*) as its proper pastor (*pastor*) under the authority of the diocesan bishop.

This preliminary canon describes the elements[18] of the parish: it is (1) a certain community of the

Christian faithful stably constituted in a particular church (2) whose pastoral care is entrusted to a pastor (*parochus*) as its proper pastor (*pastor*) under the authority of the diocesan bishop.[19] The parish is a part of the particular church, not an autonomous entity; the diocesan bishop who leads that church has authority over the pastor of each parish therein.[20]

whose pastoral care is entrusted to a priest. "L'affidamento della parrocchia ad un gruppo di sacerdoti in solidum o a fedeli non sacerdoti nonché ad un istituto religioso," in *La parrocchia,* 51.

F. Coccopalmerio identifies seven elements of a parish: (1) community of the faithful; (2) generally determined only by a territory; (3) in a particular church; (4) stably constituted; (5) having a pastor as its proper pastor; (6) under the authority of the diocesan bishop; (7) with the cooperation of presbyters, deacons, and laity. *De paroecia* (Rome: Pontificia Università Gregoriana, 1991) 3–12.

J.-C. Périsset says the constitutive elements of the parish are (1) the community of the faithful and (2) pastoral care from its proper pastor; territoriality is extrinsic to the determination of the community. *La Paroisse: Commentaire des canons 515–572* (Paris: Tardy, 1989) 13.

S. Euart says the parish has four *fundamental* elements: (1) community, (2) stable basis, (3) pastor, (4) diocesan bishop. "Parishes without a Resident Pastor: Reflections on the Provisions and Conditions of Canon 517, §2 and Its Implications," *J* 54 (1994) 374.

A. Sánchez-Gil identifies four elements which configure a parish: (1) a certain community of the Christian faithful, (2) stably constituted in a particular church, (3) whose pastoral care under the authority of the diocesan bishop (4) is entrusted to a pastor (*parochus*) as its proper pastor (*pastor*). "Circa la portata della qualifica del parroco quale pastore proprio della comunità parrocchiale," *Ius Ecclesiae* 8 (1996) 217–230.

---

[17] Cf. *CCEO* 279. The Eastern code does not say that the pastor (*parochus*) is the parish's "proper pastor (*pastor*) under the authority of the diocesan [eparchial] bishop."

[18] J. Arrieta identifies two essential elements of a parish: (1) a group of the faithful and (2) the proper pastor (*parochus*). These must be united to a bishop in his pastoral care for a portion of the people of God. "La parrocchia come comunità di fedeli e soggetto canonicamente unitario," in *La parrochia,* Studi giuridici, 24 (Vatican City: Libreria Editrice Vaticana, 1997) 28.

A. Gauthier also sees two elements as comprising a parish: (1) a community of the Christian faithful (2)

[19] In American usage, *pastor* and *parochus* are rendered by the same term, *pastor*. Canons 515, §1 and 519 explain that the *parochus* is the proper *pastor* of a parish; these are the only two canons where the two terms appear together. Elsewhere, it is often helpful or even necessary to distinguish which term is being used. Every *parochus* is *pastor* for his parish; but not every *pastor* is a *parochus* since, for example, the diocesan bishop is also a *pastor* (see c. 369).

[20] Canon 555, §1, 1° recognizes the fact that not all possible pastoral activity in a diocese is contained in the parish when it identifies the first role of the vicar forane

Canon 374 requires that every diocese or other particular church be divided into distinct parts or parishes. The parish, then, is a distinct part (*distincta pars*) of a particular church. This reflects the 1917 code which said that the territory of every diocese was to be divided into distinct territorial parts (*distinctas partes territoriales*) called parishes; to each part was to be assigned its own church with a definite part of the population and its own rector as the proper pastor who was responsible for the necessary care of souls (*CIC* 216, §§1, 3).

Not included in the current description of a parish (see cc. 374 and 515, §1) is the *parish church.* One may not conclude, however, that a parish no longer should have its own church. Several canons elsewhere in the code refer to the parish church.[21] The church building is simply no longer included in the description of the parish.

Also not explicitly included in the description of the parish (see cc. 374 and 515, §1) is the element of *territory,* although it is the principal determining factor in establishing a parish (c. 518).

Canon 515, §1 follows the teachings of Vatican Council II. *Sacrosanctum Concilium* 42 explains that the parish represents the visible Church, and that efforts must be made to foster a parish's liturgical life and relation to the bishop, and to encourage a sense of community:

> But as it is impossible for the bishop always and everywhere to preside over the whole

flock of his church, he must of necessity establish groupings of the faithful; and, among these, parishes, set up locally under a pastor who takes the place of the bishop, are the most important, for in some way they represent the visible Church constituted throughout the world.

Therefore the liturgical life of the parish and its relation to the bishop must be fostered in the spirit and practice of the laity and clergy. Efforts must also be made to encourage a sense of community within the parish, above all in the common celebration of the Sunday Mass.

Lumen gentium 26 teaches that the true Church of Christ is present in all local assemblies of the faithful. United with their bishops, the people are nurtured by word and Eucharist. In each parish (and other altar communities) charity and unity are to be evident :

> This Church of Christ is really present in all legitimately organized local groups of the faithful, which, in so far as they are united to their pastors, are also quite appropriately called Churches in the New Testament. For these are in fact, in their own localities, the new people called by God, in the power of the Holy Spirit and as the result of full conviction (cf. 1 Thess. 1:15). In them the faithful are gathered together through the preaching of the Gospel of Christ, and the mystery of the Lord's Supper is celebrated. ... In each altar community, under the sacred ministry of the bishop, a manifest symbol is to be seen of that charity and "unity of the mystical body without which there can be no salvation" [St. Thomas, *Summa Theol.* III, q. 73, a. 3]. [22]

---

as promoting and coordinating common pastoral activity within the vicariate.

[21] See cc. 510, §§2, 4 (on churches which are both parochial and capitular); 857, §2 (on the place for baptism); 858, §1 (on the baptismal font); 859 (on baptism outside a parish church); 934, §1, 1° (on reservation of the Eucharist); 1118, §1 (on the place for marriage between two Catholics, or between a Catholic and a baptized non-Catholic); 1177, §§1, 3 (on the place for funerals); 1217, §2 (on the dedication of parish churches by a solemn rite); 1248, §2 (on the liturgy of the word in a parish church when Mass is not possible on a Sunday or other holy day of obligation).

[22] Those drafting this text during Vatican II deliberately understood such "churches" to be infra-diocesan structures, especially parishes and other groups, all of whom remain dependent on the bishop. *ActSynVat* III, 1, 253.

Ad gentes 37 teaches that the communities of the parish and the diocese must bear witness to Christ before the nations; in these communities, the people of God live and, in a certain sense, become manifest. *Christus Dominus* 30 says that pastors "are in a special sense collaborators with the bishop. They are given, in a specific section of the diocese, and under the authority of the bishop, the care of souls as their particular shepherd," and *Christus Dominus* 31 explains that "basically,... parochial responsibility has to do with the good of souls." *Apostolicam actuositatem* 10 teaches that the action of lay persons in church communities is so necessary that, without it, the apostolate of the Church's pastors will often be unable to obtain its full effect; in specific reflection about the parish, the decree says:

> The parish offers an outstanding example of community apostolate, for it gathers into a unity all the human diversities that are found there and inserts them into the universality of the Church. The laity should develop the habit of working in the parish in close union with their priests, of bringing before the ecclesial community their own problems, world problems, and questions regarding man's salvation, to examine them together and solve them by general discussion. According to their abilities the laity ought to cooperate in all the apostolic and missionary enterprises of their ecclesial family.
>
> The laity will continuously cultivate the "feeling for the diocese," of which the parish is a kind of cell; they will be always ready on the invitation of their bishop to make their own contribution to diocesan undertakings. Indeed they will not confine their cooperation within the limits of the parish or diocese, but will endeavor, in response to the needs of towns and rural districts, to extend it to interparochial, interdiocesan, national and international spheres.

The parish is not to be taken so much as an administrative division (territorial or personal) of the diocese entrusted to a pastor, but rather as a community established to provide pastoral care of a group of persons within the particular church. It is an individual, non-autonomous portion of the diocesan community.[23]

Competent Authority to Erect, Suppress, or Alter Parishes[24]

§2. It is only for the diocesan bishop to erect, suppress, or alter parishes. He is neither to erect, suppress, nor alter notably parishes, unless he has heard the presbyteral council.

The code identifies the diocesan bishop as the competent authority in the particular church to erect, suppress, or alter parishes.[25] To *erect* a parish is to bring it into existence. To *suppress* a parish is to end its existence. To *alter* a parish admits a number of possibilities: e.g., to join two or more parishes; to divide a parish into more than one; to change a parish from territorial to personal, or vice versa; to modify parish boundaries, etc.[26]

---

[23] Arrieta, 28–29. See also G. Montini, "Stabilità del parroco e permanenza nell'ufficio parrocchiale," in *La parrocchia,* 126–129.

[24] Cf. *CCEO* 280, §2.

[25] A distinction must be made between suppressing or otherwise modifying a *parish* (c. 515, §2) and relegating a *church building* (parochial or other) to "profane but not sordid use" (c. 1222). The discussion here is only about the former.

[26] For some helpful canonical and practical reflections on modifying parishes, see J. Provost, "Some Canonical Considerations on Closing Parishes," *J* 53 (1993) 362–370. In discussing the involvement of the presbyteral council, Provost says: "It would be a mistake for the planning process to complete a total package, and then inform the presbyteral council on the results. Even though in some sense this is indeed consultation (that is, the presbyteral council could recommend against the package, or recommend major modifications in it), the impression can be given that the council is being brought in too late for its advice to be significant. That impression would seem to be in violation of the council's role in canon 515, §2" (364–365). The canonical issues involved in closing several parishes in the Archdiocese of Chicago are reported in T. Paprocki, "Parish Closings

The diocesan bishop erects, suppresses, or alters parishes only after having heard the presbyteral council; otherwise, his action is invalid (see c. 127, §1); he is not obliged, however, to follow the council's recommendations (see c. 500, §2). The diocesan bishop also remains entirely free to listen to the advice and wisdom of other groups (e.g., diocesan and parish pastoral councils, religious institutes, episcopal council, etc.) and individuals (e.g., vicars general, episcopal vicars, vicars forane, pastors, parishioners, etc.)

Since a parish is a juridic person (a public, non-collegiate *universitas personarum*),[27] the norms on joining juridic persons (c. 121), on dividing them (c. 122), and on extinguishing them (c. 123) apply also in the cases of joining, dividing, or suppressing parishes. These canons also require respect for acquired rights and the intentions of founders and donors.

Christus Dominus 32 explained that concern for the salvation of souls is to be the motive for determining or reconsidering the erection, suppression, or other modifications of parishes, and that the diocesan bishop may act in these matters on his own authority. Following the council, *Ecclesiae sanctae* I, 21 (1) discussed parish modifications:

Every possible effort should be made that parishes where, because of too great a popu-

lation or too large a territory or for any cause whatsoever, apostolic activity can be exercised only with difficulty or less effectively, should be suitably divided or dismembered, as the circumstances require. And likewise parishes which are too small should be united as conditions and circumstances demand.

Ecclesiae sanctae I, 21 (3) reiterated the diocesan bishop's power to erect, suppress, or change parishes, but added that he is first to hear the presbyteral council. Special arrangements must be made when agreements between the Apostolic See and civil governments, or the acquired rights of physical or moral (juridic) persons, affect the modification of parishes.[28]

The *Directory on the Pastoral Ministry of Bishops* suggested the establishment of a diocesan commission for new parishes which, in collaboration with the presbyteral council and other concerned commissions, would handle matters concerning the erection of new parishes and the construction of new church buildings.[29] The *Directory* also mentioned the organization and timely erection of new parishes, modification of parochial boundaries, and non-parochial apostolic centers and worship places.[30]

The 1917 code treated the modification of parishes under the more general legislation on the modification of benefices (*CIC* 1419–1430); furthermore, it required a special apostolic indult to establish personal parishes; and any personal parishes already existing were not to be changed without consulting the Apostolic See (*CIC* 216, §4). The 1983 code, however, does not consider parishes as benefices; canon 515, §2 is the principal legal text concerning modifications of parishes. No further Holy See involvement is required to modify any parishes, e.g., personal parishes.

and Administrative Recourse to the Apostolic See: Recent Experiences of the Archdiocese of Chicago," *J* 55 (1995) 875–896. Paprocki explains that the Apostolic Signatura will grant "active legitimation (standing to sue) in the case of a closed parish...to former parishioners even if the pastor or parochial administrator does not participate in the recourse or moreover if he is actively opposed to it.... In a sense, the Signatura has taken a very progressive step by recognizing the voice of lay parishioners in the life of a parish" (893). He concludes his report by explaining that, in the end, the Apostolic See will not substitute its own judgment on the *substantive* issue of closing a parish (since that decision rests with the diocesan bishop alone, c. 515, §2) but may require a correction of a defective canonical *process*. See also J. Coriden, "The Vindication of Parish Rights," *J* 54 (1994) 32–34, nn. 13, 15.

[27] See cc. 115, §2; 116.

[28] Agreements between the Apostolic See and civil governments fall within the competence of the Second Section of the SS (*PB* 45–47); other parish matters are within the competence of the CFC (*PB* 97, 1°).

[29] *Directory* 178.

[30] *Directory* 176–177, 179–180.

A just cause is needed for the modification of parishes; the exercise of pastoral leadership should not be arbitrary.[31] The diocesan bishop must hear his presbyteral council *before* he erects, suppresses, or otherwise modifies a parish; he is not to approach the council after he has already made his decision. In order to make an informed recommendation, the council must first have received detailed and necessary information regarding the parish. If the bishop intends to modify a parish, before issuing the decree he must seek out the necessary information and proofs and must hear those whose rights can be injured (c. 50).[32] The decree is to be issued in writing, with the reasons at least summarily expressed (c. 51).

Franz Daneels, an official of the Supreme Tribunal of the Apostolic Signatura, explains that the attempt to prove that suppression of a parish violates a whole series of fundamental rights and duties of the Christian faithful "attempts to prove too much, and so in fact proves nothing," and that the claim that suppression violates the right of immigrants to preserve their proper spiritual patrimony is not persuasive since "a personal parish is not the only way to preserve" the patrimony of immigrant people.[33] He comments that the Supreme Tribunal may identify errors in the process of suppressing a parish, but not in the decision itself:

While the Apostolic Signatura, in two cases, has decreed a violation of the law *in procedendo* for a parish, it has never decreed a violation of the law *in decernendo* in any of the cases it has treated. In fact, to suppress a parish, it suffices that there be a just cause, and it is very difficult to prove the lack of a just cause. One should therefore reflect seriously before presenting to the Apostolic Signatura a recourse against the suppression of a parish.

It appears also from the cases studied at the Apostolic Signatura that bishops do not take lightly the painful decision of suppressing a parish.[34]

The diocesan bishop will be careful not only to observe all the canon laws when a parish is modified, but will also be attentive to the civil law provisions as these pertain to the erection, suppression, or notable alteration of a parish.[35]

Juridic Personality of the Parish[36]

§3. A legitimately erected parish possesses juridic personality by the law itself.

---

[31] F. Daneels, "The Suppression of Parishes and the Reduction of a Church to Profane Use in the Light of the Jurisprudence of the Apostolic Signatura," *Forum* 8 (1997) 287.

[32] Ibid., 288. He adds: "Personally, I do not think that the parish and the parishioners have such a 'right' in the strict sense of the term since, according to canon 120 §1 a juridic person can be legitimately suppressed by the competent authority and canon 515 §2 does not require in this case the prior consultation of the parish or of the parishioners. However, I maintain that for the sake of prudence it is of the utmost importance to involve the parish in some way or another in the process for deciding about its suppression, which does not seem to be the common practice."

[33] Daneels, 289.

[34] Ibid.

[35] See J. Myers, "Suppression and Merger of Parishes: Brief Overview of Canonical Issues," in *CLSA Advisory Opinions, 1984–1993,* ed. P. Cogan (Washington, D.C.: CLSA, 1995) 110–113. The Sacred Congregation for the Council issued a *private letter* to the ordinaries of the United States on July 29, 1911 on the proper way to incorporate parochial property. It said that *parish corporation* is preferable, with five trustees (the bishop, vicar general, pastor, and two lay parishioners appointed by the others) for every parish. They may never act validly without the "sanction" of the bishop. Even if such a corporation is impossible in certain instances, dioceses should work toward such an arrangement. In the interim they may retain the *corporation sole* with the understanding that the bishop must hear and, in more important matters, receive consent from the college of consultors and the interested parties. The method called *in fee simple* is to be entirely abandoned. *CLD* 2, 443–445.

[36] Cf. *CCEO* 280, §3.

Once a parish has been legitimately erected, it possesses juridic personality by the law.[37] The juridic personality is not granted by the diocesan bishop, though he alone has competence to erect (suppress or notably alter) a parish.[38] A juridic person is a subject in canon law of obligations and rights which correspond to its nature (c. 113, §2); by its nature every juridic person is perpetual (c. 120, §1). The parish is a public juridic person (c. 116). It is a non-collegial *universitas personarum,* that is, a *universitas* whose members do *not* determine its actions through common decision making (c. 115, §2).[39] The pastor alone represents it in all juridic affairs according to the norm of law; he is to take care that parochial goods are administered according to the norm of canons 1281–1288 (c. 532; see c. 118).

Like any other juridic person, the parish is capable of acquiring, retaining, administering, and alienating temporal goods according to the norm of law (c. 1255). Under the supreme authority of the Roman Pontiff, ownership of its goods belongs to the parish which has acquired them legitimately (c. 1256). Its temporal goods are considered *ecclesiastical goods* which are governed by the canons on temporal goods (c. 1257, §1).

The 1917 code did not contain a canon stating so directly that the parish has juridic personality, but instead taught that benefices were non-collegiate moral persons (*CIC* 99) and identified parishes as benefices (e.g., *CIC* 1423, 1425–1427).

Quasi-Parishes/Other Communities[40]

Canon 516 — §1. Unless the law provides otherwise, a quasi-parish is equivalent to a parish; a quasi-parish is a definite community of the Christian faithful in a particular church, entrusted to a priest as its proper pastor but not yet erected as a parish because of particular circumstances.

This canon describes a quasi-parish. It is (1) a definite community of the Christian faithful in a particular church (2) entrusted to a priest as its proper pastor (*pastor*) (3) but not yet erected as a parish because of particular circumstances. Unless the law provides otherwise, a quasi-parish is equivalent to a parish (e.g., it has juridic personality by the law itself, it is "territorial" or "personal," etc.).[41]

Unlike a parish, a quasi-parish is not seen as permanent: it is a temporary structure on its way, eventually, to becoming a parish. It is "not yet" (*nondum*) established as a parish.[42] The law does

---

[37] The parish, considered as a *juridic person,* is the entity created by the juridic act of the bishop erecting it as a parish (c. 515, §2). Theoretically, the community may disperse, but the parish, as a juridic person, will continue to exist until it is extinguished according to the norms of law: i.e., either by decree of legitimate authority, or by cessation of all activity for a period of one hundred years (c. 120, §1).

[38] Canon 114, §1 says that juridic personality is given either by the law itself or by decree of competent authority. Parishes obtain juridic personality by law.

[39] An authentic interpretation by the PCILT indicated that a group of lay persons without juridic personality (or even the recognition mentioned in c. 299, §3) cannot, precisely as a group, legitimately make recourse against a decree of the diocesan bishop. They can, however, "as individual members of the Christian faithful, whether singly or together, provided that their grievance is real" [author's translation]; the judge must have suitable discretion in estimating the gravity of the grievance. This interpretation was issued on April 29, 1987 and approved by Pope John Paul II on June 20, 1987. *AAS* 80 (1988) 1818. Further, a November 12, 1987 decision of the Apostolic Signatura explains that the capacity to have recourse is not recognized for a group of the Christian faithful which does not have juridic personality, but it is recognized for persons acting as individuals, singly or together. (Prot. No. 17447/85 C.A.) *Comm* 20 (1988) 88–94 at 91. See also L. Wrenn, *Authentic Interpretations on the 1983 Code* (Washington, D.C.: CLSA, 1993) 46–47.

[40] A parallel canon does not exist in the Eastern code.

[41] Coccopalmerio, 57–58.

[42] Coccopalmerio suggests that the reasons why a quasi-parish is "not yet" a parish may be *extrinsic* (e.g., problems with civil authorities) or *intrinsic* (e.g., little or no financial means) (55).

not lay down any specifications for when a quasi-parish becomes a parish.[43]

Many dioceses contain so-called "mission churches" whose canonical status may be uncertain. Such a church may simply be another worship site within a parish, in which case it would be a non-parochial church. It may, however, belong to what the 1983 code calls a quasi-parish, which has the characteristics identified in canon 516, §1 and would be a community "not yet" erected as a parish.[44] When the time comes, however, the diocesan bishop must first hear the presbyteral council before he erects the parish (c. 515, §2).

In the 1917 code *quasi-parishes* were divisions of apostolic vicariates or apostolic prefectures; they existed in only these mission areas (*CIC* 216, §3). Their location in missionary lands was what primarily distinguished them from parishes.[45] Their pastors were called *quasi-pastors* (*CIC* 451, §2, 1°). Now, quasi-parishes may exist in any particular church (in the missions and elsewhere), and what primarily distinguishes them from parishes is the fact that they are not yet established as parishes. Each quasi-parish has its own *pastor*.[46]

Other Communities[47]

§2. When certain communities cannot be erected as parishes or quasi-parishes, the dioce-

san bishop is to provide for their pastoral care in another way.

This paragraph envisions that some communities of the faithful may exist which cannot be erected as parishes or even as quasi-parishes. Their pastoral care is to be provided by the diocesan bishop in some other way. The code envisions that within a particular church may be found non-parochial churches and their rectors (cc. 556–563), and chaplaincies and chaplains (cc. 564–572).[48] These may serve particular communities of the faithful. Beyond this, canon 516, §2 does not identify precisely who the non-parochial communities may be; the diocesan bishop must make the prudent determination,[49] and in so doing may freely seek the advice of the presbyteral council.

Parish(es) Entrusted to Several Priests "In Solidum"[50]

Canon 517 — §1. When circumstances require it, the pastoral care of a parish or of different par-

---

[43] T. Green suggests that changing a quasi-parish to a parish seems to reflect a judgment that the "definitive community" now enjoys a certain *stability*—the "key characteristic" which differentiates a parish (c. 515, §1) from a quasi-parish (c. 516, §1) and from a community which is neither a parish nor a quasi-parish (c. 516, §2). "Mission Parishes (Quasi-Parishes) Changed to Status of Parish," in *CLSA Advisory Opinions, 1984–1993*, ed. P. Cogan (Washington, D.C.: CLSA, 1995) 113–114.

[44] See T. Green, in T. Green, J. Provost, and R. Wiatrowski, "Establishment of a Parish That is both Territorial and Personal," in *RRAO 1994*, 106.

[45] The 1977 schema made no reference to quasi-parishes, which reappeared only in c. 455 of the 1980 schema.

[46] Coccopalmerio suggests the *pastor* should be called the "quasi-pastor" (*quasi-parochus*) (57–58). The code is silent on the name of the figure. He has the power of governance in the quasi-parish (see c. 519).

[47] A parallel canon does not exist in the Eastern code.

[48] See also c. 510 on capitular churches and chapters of canons.

[49] Canon 813 says the diocesan bishop is to provide pastoral care for university students by erecting for them a parish or by at least designating a priest stably for them; it also says that even at non-Catholic universities spiritual assistance should be offered to the youth through university centers. Seemingly, these "university centers" fulfill the norm of c. 516, §2. The *Directory* (174) also envisions the possibility of non-parochial "centers of the apostolate" being established with a more or less organic and stable structure to meet the pastoral needs of particular places and groups. The *Directory* (183) mentions "missions with the charge of souls" and the "pastoral house" or "pastoral center" (all existing within the territory of a parish) to provide for the pastoral care of certain special groups (such as migrants). The 1983 code does not refer specifically to such structures by name, but c. 516, §2 is the basis for particular law creating them and comparable structures within the diocese.

[50] *CCEO* 287, §2 says that the particular law of the proper autonomous church may allow a parish to be entrusted to several presbyters, and is to determine accurately the rights and obligations both of the moderator (who directs

ishes together can be entrusted to several priests *in solidum*, with the requirement, however, that in exercising pastoral care one of them must be the moderator, namely, the one who is to direct the joint action and to answer for it to the bishop.

This canon is new to the 1983 code.[51] It permits the diocesan bishop, when circumstances require it, to entrust the pastoral care of one or more parishes to several priests *in solidum* (that is, jointly), one of whom is the moderator of the group in the exercise of the pastoral care. This moderator directs the joint action of the several priests and answers for it to the bishop, although all the priests together are responsible for their pastoral activity. Only one priest may be the moderator (c. 526, §2; see c. 520, §1), and he alone takes possession of the parish (canon 527, §2). For the other priests, the profession of faith replaces taking possession (c. 542, 3°). The moderator alone represents the parish in juridic affairs (c. 543, §2, 3°).

In everything else, however, all the priests to whom the parish is entrusted *in solidum* have the same rights and duties.[52] Each must be endowed with the qualities required to become a pastor (c. 542, 1°; see c. 521). Each must possess stability in office and be appointed for a definite period of time, or for a specific period, as is the case for every pastor (c. 542, 2°; see c. 522). Each must be considered suited to exercise pastoral care in the parish, according to the judgment of the diocesan bishop who is to make his determination as he does for ordinary pastors (c. 542, 2°; see c. 524). Each obtains pastoral care from the moment of taking possession (c. 542, 3°). Each is bound by the obligation of residence (c. 543, §2, 1°). Each is obliged to perform the functions of a pastor mentioned in canons 528–530, according to an arrangement the priests *in solidum* establish (c. 543, §1). Only one of them, however, offers the Mass for the people, according to the arrangement they establish by common counsel (c. 543, §2, 2°; see c. 534). Further, each has the faculty to assist at marriages and all the dispensing powers of a pastor; these powers, however, are to be exercised under the direction of the moderator (c. 543, §1).

If one of the priests, even the moderator, ceases from office[53] or becomes incapable of exercising his pastoral function, the parish(es) entrusted to the priests *in solidum* does not become vacant. If the priest involved is the moderator, the diocesan bishop must appoint another moderator. Until that appointment is made, the priest in the group who is senior in appointment fulfills the moderator's function (c. 544).

Canon 526, §1 states the general principle that a pastor is to have the parochial care of only one parish, but admits that exceptionally (e.g., because of a lack of priests or other circumstances) several neighboring parishes can be entrusted to the same pastor. Canon 517, §1 readily accepts the possibility that the priests *in solidum* may have pastoral care of more than one parish, a unique characteristic of this unique arrangement.

The earliest recorded comments by the *coetus De sacra hierarchia* about the intention of those drafting this canon explain that the group of priests is not a "juridic person" to whom the pastoral care of the parish or parishes is entrusted. Rather, they are individual priests who together or jointly assume pastoral care. Monsignor William Onclin, relator of the *coetus,* reports:

---

the common action and reports on it to the eparchial bishop) and of the other presbyters. The Eastern code, however, neither employs the technical term *in solidum* when referring to this arrangement nor contains canons parallel to cc. 542–544 on such an arrangement.

[51] In the 1917 code each parish could have only one pastor who had the actual care of souls; any contrary custom was reprobated and any contrary privilege whatsoever was revoked (*CIC* 460, §2). A similar norm is found in c. 526, §2, which explains, however, that a parish may have only one pastor *or one moderator according to the norm of c. 517, §1.* At several times and places in the past, a parish had been entrusted to several pastors with clear endorsement of church authorities: see Gauthier, 38–42.

[52] Coccopalmerio says that the pastor is the group itself, but the group is not a juridic person (102).

[53] The priest, even the moderator, may cease from office in the same ways as a pastor (c. 538, §§1–2).

It is a general rule that all the priests constituting the *coetus* have *in solidum* the duties proper to a pastor. *In solidum* they are bound to the duties of teaching, sanctifying, and governing the individual parishes.... *In solidum* they also are obliged to fulfill the functions which are to be performed by a pastor and which can be performed by others only with the pastor's permission. Moreover, the group of priests itself must determine which duties and which functions are to be performed by the individual priests of the group. Therefore, the concrete pastoral duties of a pastor to which each individual is bound must be defined in the arrangement they establish under the leadership of the moderator.[54]

The pastoral care rests with all of them simultaneously, but one of them directs the common or joint action and is the person responsible for it.[55]

The 1981 *Relatio* admits that the novel concept in canon 517, §1 is not sanctioned in Vatican II, but seems useful for some circumstances. The arrangement is "truly exceptional" and is to be implemented only "when circumstances require it." The moderator cannot be placed on the same level as an ordinary pastor.[56] The fact that the moderator "is to direct the joint action" signifies that this action is to be collegial; all the priests *in solidum* have the juridic faculties proper to a pastor. The moderator cannot be understood as the only one "endowed with the power of a pastor."[57]

Diaconal and Lay Participation in Parochial Pastoral Care[58]

§2. If, because of a lack of priests, the diocesan bishop has decided that participation in the exercise of the pastoral care of a parish is to be entrusted to a deacon, to another person who is not a priest, or to a community of persons, he is to appoint some priest who, provided with the powers and faculties of a pastor, is to direct the pastoral care.

This canon is new to the 1983 code. It permits the diocesan bishop, because of a lack of priests, to entrust participation in the pastoral care of a parish to a deacon, another person who is not a priest, or a community of persons who are not priests. In this situation, the bishop is to appoint a priest, provided with the powers and faculties of a pastor, to direct the pastoral care.[59]

The implications and novelty of this canon occasion special study of its development and application. The earliest discussions about it were reported by Monsignor William Onclin, relator of the *coetus De sacra hierarchia:*

In modern circumstances, it can be impossible to name a pastor for individual parishes since in many regions there is a shortage of priests. In these instances the care of souls must be provided for in another way. Two or three parishes can be united *aeque principaliter,* such that one and the same pastor is appointed for them. Also, a group of priests can be appointed for different parishes at the same time to have care for them jointly. Further, if there is such a shortage of priests that even this cannot be done, it may be necessary to grant some participation in the exercise of pastoral care to some persons not marked with the priestly character

---

[54] *Comm* 8 (1976) 30. [Author's translation.]
[55] *Comm* 8 (1976) 29–30.
[56] *Comm* 14 (1982) 221.
[57] *Comm* 14 (1982) 222.
[58] A parallel canon does not exist in the Eastern code.

[59] Canon 519 legislates that a pastor carries out his functions with the cooperation of other presbyters and deacons and the assistance of the laity. A variety of such cooperating/assisting roles in fact exists throughout the Church. However, c. 517, §2 is not about those arrangements; rather, it concerns the situation where there is no pastor and the diocesan bishop decides that, due to the lack of available priests, participation in the exercise of pastoral care is entrusted to person(s) who are not priests, under the direction of a priest with a pastor's powers and faculties. See Coccopalmerio, 109–110.

or to some community of persons. In this case, however, it is necessary to appoint a priest who directs that pastoral care as the proper pastor and who possesses the proper power of a pastor.[60]

Canon 349, §2 of the 1977 schema said:

If, because of a lack of priests, the diocesan bishop has decided that participation in the exercise of the pastoral care of a parish is to be entrusted to some person not marked with the priestly character or to a community of persons, he is to appoint some priest who, possessing the power of a pastor, directs the pastoral care as the proper pastor of the parish.[61]

Following consultation with the world's hierarchy and other consultative groups on the 1977 *Schema Canonum Libri II, De Populo Dei,* the *coetus* on the people of God met on April 19, 1980. Some of its members did not welcome the notion that a parish be entrusted even in part to anyone other than a priest. The secretary of the code commission, Archbishop Rosalio José Castillo Lara, however, related his experience in Venezuela where the pastoral care of some communities of the faithful (called *vicariates*) was fruitfully entrusted to a community of women religious in those things which do not require priestly orders.[62] As a result of his intervention, all accepted the proposed canon in which two changes were made:

(1) the priest was said to be "endowed with" (*instructus*), rather than "possessing" (*gaudens*), the powers of a pastor, and (2) the words "as the proper pastor of the parish" (*uti proprius paroeciae pastor*) were suppressed in order neither to restrict excessively the role of this non-priest leadership figure nor to compress too much the scope of the competence of such a person.[63]

The *coetus* again discussed this canon on May 14, 1980. The proposed canon was modified to indicate that a certain participation in the pastoral care of a parish could be entrusted "to some deacon or even a lay member of the Christian faithful or to a community of them." Furthermore, some priest was to be appointed who, endowed with the power of a pastor, directs the pastoral care and administration, which office the priest can fulfill simultaneously for many such parishes.[64] Neither of these changes, however, appeared in the 1980 schema.[65]

In the 1981 *Relatio* the code commission explained that it is not necessary to state that this arrangement is "extraordinary and temporary" since the beginning of the canon speaks about a shortage of priests (*ob penuriam sacerdotum*). Furthermore, saying the priest "directs the pastoral care" is a broader expression than saying that he "exercises offices which require the power of orders and the power of ecclesiastical governance connected to holy orders." Finally, it was not necessary explicitly to mention "deacons" who always have a certain ordinary and permanent participation in the exercise of the pastoral care of a parish, since the canon concerns only granting some participation to those who have no share in the ministerial priesthood.[66]

Following the code commission *plenarium* in October, 1981, the commission presented to Pope John Paul II a version of canon 517, §2 similar to

---

[60] *Comm* 8 (1976) 24. [Author's translation.]

[61] Canon 349, §2. *Comm* 13 (1981) 147. [Author's translation.]

[62] Interestingly, in *CIC An* the only source for c. 517, §2 is a November 19, 1976 instruction of the SCProp, *La fonction évangélisatrice,* about the parish evangelization role of religious women in missionary countries where these women perform various administrative, pastoral, and liturgical functions in the absence of a priest. See X. Ochoa, ed., *Leges Ecclesiae (1973–1978)* (Rome: Commentarium pro Religiosis, 1980) 5, n. 4476, pp. 7260–7267. See further comments on the instruction in Périsset, 200.

[63] *Comm* 13 (1981) 149.

[64] Canon 349-ter, §3. *Comm* 13 (1981) 306.

[65] Canon 456, §2 of the 1980 schema. ComCICRec, *Schema Codicis Iuris Canonici* (Vatican City: Typis Polyglottis Vaticanis, 1980).

[66] *Comm* 14 (1982) 222.

the current text. However, it described the priest as having the "power of a pastor."[67] In the period before promulgation, two changes were made: the text now speaks of "the powers *and faculties* of a pastor" and the term "deacon" was inserted into the canon.

Several conclusions become evident from this overview of the development of canon 517, §2. First, the intervention of Archbishop Castillo Lara about his experience of women religious serving vicariates in Venezuela favorably influenced the members of the *coetus De Populo Dei* in 1980. Second, from the beginning this arrangement was envisioned as a response to the shortage of priests. The canon cannot be implemented otherwise. Third, from the beginning the canon consistently indicated that a priest was to direct the pastoral care exercised by the person(s) not ordained to the presbyterate. Initially, the priest was said to be the proper pastor of the parish who possessed the power of a pastor. Later versions of the canon, however, deliberately avoided saying the priest is the proper pastor but instead explained that he possesses the powers (and, finally, also the faculties) of a pastor. Properly speaking, however, he is not the pastor (*parochus*) of the parish(es).[68] Fourth, also from the beginning, the decision to implement the canon has rested with the diocesan bishop. Finally, no *title* is given to the priest who directs the pastoral care with the powers and faculties of a pastor, or to the deacon or lay person(s) who participate in the exercise of parochial pastoral care.

This canon is being implemented in many parts of the world, including in the United States. To assure its proper implementation, the Holy See in November 1997 issued the *Instruction on Certain Questions Regarding the Collaboration of the Non-Ordained Faithful in the Sacred Ministry of Priests.*[69] It offers a number of helpful directives

to clarify the meaning of the canon, guide its further implementation, and correct any inappropriate applications.

Discussing lay collaboration in priestly ministry in general, the *Instruction* says that appropriate titles are to be given to lay persons who serve in the Church: "It is unlawful for the non-ordained faithful to assume titles such as 'pastor,' 'coordinator,' 'moderator' or other such similar titles which can confuse their role and that of the pastor, who is always a bishop or priest [presbyter]."[70] The *Instruction* gives no specific titles concerning the application of canon 517, §2. The deacon or lay person(s), however, should be called neither the "moderator" of the parish nor its "coordinator," a term which has become common in the United States.[71] Nor should the person be called the "community leader."[72]

The *Instruction* explains that canon 517, §2 provides an "extraordinary form of collaboration" and says:

> The right understanding and application of this canon...requires that this exceptional

Sacred Ministry of Priests (Washington, D.C.: USCC, 1997). See also *AAS* 89 (1997) 852–877. The USCC version will be cited subsequently.

[70] *Instruction*, p. 14, art. 1, §3. The Latin term used twice for "pastor" is *pastor* (not *parochus*). The document explains that pastoral care is properly the task of bishops and presbyters. The footnote to art. 1, §3 adds: "Such examples [of terms which can confuse the role of the laity with that of the pastor, who is always a priest or bishop] should include all those linguistic expressions which in languages of the various countries are similar or equal and indicate a directive role of leadership or such vicarious activity."

[71] Seemingly the term "coordinator" was commonly chosen, with all good intentions, in an attempt to identify the person(s) who serves in a parish under the leadership of the priest directing the pastoral care. The canon, however, states that the deacon, lay person, or community has only a "participation" in the exercise of parochial pastoral care, while the priest possessing the powers and faculties of a pastor "directs" the pastoral care.

[72] *Instruction*, p. 20, art. 4, §1, note 76. Would an acceptable title for the deacon or lay person(s) perhaps be "parish life *collaborator*," terminology which reflects the theme of the *Instruction*?

[67] ComCICRec, *Codex Iuris Canonici, Schema novissimum iuxta placita Patrum Commissionis emendatum atque Summo Pontifici praesentatum* (Vatican City: Typis Polyglottis Vaticanis, 1982) c. 517, §2.

[68] Coccopalmerio, 109.

[69] CFC et al., *Instruction on Certain Questions Regarding the Collaboration of the Non-Ordained Faithful in the*

provision be used only with strict adherence to conditions contained in it. These are:

a) *ob sacerdotum penuriam* [because of a lack of priests] and not for reasons of convenience or ambiguous "advancement of the laity," etc.

b) this is *participatio in exercitio curae pastoralis* [participation in the exercise of pastoral care] and not directing, coordinating, moderating, or governing the parish; these competencies, according to the canon, are the competencies of a priest alone.

Because these are exceptional cases, before employing them, other possibilities should be availed of, such as using the services of retired priests still capable of such service, or entrusting several parishes to one priest or to a *coetus sacerdotum* [group of priests] [cf. *CIC*, can. 517, §1].

In any event, the preference which this canon gives to deacons can not be overlooked.

The same canon, however, reaffirms that these forms of participation in the pastoral care of parishes cannot, in any way, replace the office of parish priest [*parochus*]. The same canon decrees that "Episcopus dioecesanus ... sacerdotem constituat aliquem qui potestatibus et facultatibus parochi instructus, curam pastoralem moderetur [the diocesan bishop ... is to appoint some priest who, provided with the powers and faculties of a pastor, is to direct the pastoral care]." Indeed, the office of parish priest [*parochus*] can be assigned validly only to a priest (cf. c. 521, §1) even in cases where there is a shortage of clergy.[73]

The *Instruction* will occasion a review of every aspect of the application of the extraordinary form of collaboration envisioned by canon 517, §2, throughout the Church.

A careful study of the history and teaching of the canon leads to the following conclusions about the pastoral leadership arrangement it authorizes:

(1) *Establishment*. The arrangement is established by the diocesan bishop, most likely after appropriate investigation and consultation.[74]

(2) *Requirement: Shortage of Priests to Be Pastor*. The arrangement is possible only when there is a true shortage of priests to fill all parochial and other positions (e.g., curial, seminary, university, etc.) in the particular church. The diocesan bishop must make the prudent judgment about such a shortage. When it ceases, so does the possibility of implementing this canon.[75] The arrangement is clearly exceptional.[76]

---

[73] *Instruction*, pp. 19–20, art. 4, §1. The footnote ending this quotation adds: "The non-ordained faithful or a group of them entrusted with a collaboration in the exercise of pastoral care cannot be given the title of 'community leader' or any other expression indicating the same idea." Clearly, the community leader is the priest possessing the powers and faculties of a pastor and directing the pastoral care. The lay person(s) participate in the exercise of the parochial pastoral care; they do not lead the community.

[74] Canon 526, §1 allows a pastor to be entrusted with the care of several neighboring parishes when there is a lack of priests (*ob penuriam sacerdotum*—the same terminology as c. 517, §2) or in other circumstances. If the diocesan bishop implements the arrangement envisioned in c. 517, §2, he should probably indicate why that arrangement was chosen rather than the possibility permitted by c. 526, §1. Perhaps the existing burdens on the clergy would be a key reason for such a decision.

[75] Pope John Paul II spoke on July 2, 1993 to a group of American bishops during their *ad limina* visit: "It is not a wise pastoral strategy to adopt plans which would assume as normal, let alone desirable, that a parish community be without a priest pastor. To interpret the decreased number of active priests—a situation which we pray will soon pass—as a providential sign that lay persons are to replace priests is irreconcilable with the mind of Christ and of the church. The royal priesthood of the laity is never furthered by obscuring the ministerial priesthood of the ordained, which makes priests not only celebrants of the eucharist, but also spiritual fathers, guides and teachers of the faithful entrusted to them." "On Parishes, Lay Ministry and Women" *Origins* 23 (July 15, 1993) 125.

[76] One recalls c. 151 which legislates that the provision of an office entailing the care of souls is not to be deferred

(3) *Priest-Director.* The arrangement requires the appointment of a priest with the powers and faculties of a pastor who is to direct the pastoral care of the parish.[77] He is the community leader but he is not technically the pastor *(parochus)* of the parish. There is no pastor. The parish is vacant.[78]

(4) *Deacons and Lay Persons Participating in Pastoral Care.* The arrangement also involves the entrusting of a participation in the exercise of parochial pastoral care to a deacon, a lay person, or a community of persons who are not priests.[79] These persons *participate* in pastoral care, but do not exercise the *full* care of souls, for such an office can be validly conferred only on a priest (c. 150).

The code does not give this person(s) any title, and the *Instruction* excludes a number of designations. Any title should reflect appropriately the

mind of the Church and the canonical role of such figure(s). If a community of persons is given a share in the exercise of parochial pastoral care, one of them should be designated as the leader of the group, or at least its contact person or liaison with the priest-director and others in the diocese.

(5) *Role Descriptions.* Dioceses will find it extremely helpful, indeed necessary, to develop role descriptions for the priest-director and the parish life collaborator(s). These role descriptions will reflect the universal legislation (identified in the code, the *Instruction,* and elsewhere) as well as local particulars such as the precise ways in which the deacon, lay person, or community members will participate in the exercise of pastoral care in a *specific* parish.[80]

Territoriality or Other Determining Factor[81]

Canon 518 — As a general rule a parish is to be territorial, that is, one which includes all the Christian faithful of a certain territory. When it is expedient, however, personal parishes are to be established determined by reason of the rite, language, or nationality of the Christian faithful of some territory, or even for some other reason.

This canon teaches that parishes are either *territorial* or *personal.* A parish is generally territorial— that is, it includes all the Christian faithful of a given territory.[82] When it is expedient, however, a

---

without a grave cause. When the shortage of priests mentioned in c. 517, §2 ceases, the diocesan bishop would provide for the parish(es) in the ordinary way. There no longer exists a grave reason (the priest shortage) to occasion deferring the appointment of a pastor who has the full care of souls (see cc. 150; 515, §1; 519).

[77] Seemingly c. 517, §2 gives to the priest-director the powers and faculties of a pastor so no further grant of them is needed from the diocesan bishop, and this law itself establishes the role of priest-director as an ecclesiastical office (c. 145).

[78] This conclusion follows the detailed study of the history of the development of this canon. Some may suggest, however, based on merely a surface reading of c. 517, §2, that it provides legislation for a parish with a pastor *(parochus)* with whom others participate in pastoral care as "pastoral associates," "parish assistants," etc., exercising functions otherwise performed by a priest. Nothing in the canon's development supports this application as the intent of those who drafted it.

[79] The canon refers to the person or community that participates in the exercise of parish pastoral care, but in such an indirect fashion that it appears that the canon does not certainly establish the office held by the person or community (c. 145, §1). Particular law should establish the office (c. 145, §2) and define the obligations and rights of the office holder(s).

[80] In some situations there exists, in addition to the priest-director, another priest who regularly celebrates priestly functions in the parish(es). Care must be taken to assure that the latter priest has the necessary faculties to perform his tasks. Canon 517, §2 envisions, however, that the priest-director is the one with the powers and faculties of a pastor. One may rightly question the advisability of routinely involving yet another priest in an arrangement which is certainly exceptional, temporary, and canonically somewhat vague.

[81] Cf. *CCEO* 280, §1. The eparchial bishop may judge it expedient to establish personal parishes after he has consulted the presbyteral council.

[82] The 1967 synod of bishops approved ten principles to guide the revision of the 1917 code. Principle eight says

personal parish may be established; such a parish is determined by reason of the rite, language, nationality, or some other factor affecting the persons living in some territory.[83] Personal parishes have some social base, and are created to facilitate pastoral care.[84] Canon 813 suggests that the diocesan bishop consider establishing a parish for university students (or providing for their pastoral care at least by designating priests stably for them); seemingly, the university parish is an example of a personal parish. The apostolic constitution *Spirituali militum curae* says that priests who are appointed as military chaplains have the rights and duties of a pastor (*parochus*), unless the nature of things or particular statutes dictate otherwise; their jurisdiction is *cumulative* with that of the local pastor, just like the jurisdiction of the military ordinary is *cumulative* with that of the diocesan bishop.[85]

The mere attendance, even regular attendance, at liturgical celebrations in the church of a territorial or personal parish does not necessarily make one a member of that parish. If the parish is territorial, membership comes from having a domicile or quasi-domicile in its boundaries (cc. 102, §3; 107, §1).[86] If the parish is personal, membership comes from belonging to the group for which the parish was established. To belong to the personal parish, one must belong to the group for which it was established.[87]

In a sense, each parish is both territorial and personal, but its designation as one or the other indicates which of these two characteristics is dominant. If a parish is considered *territorial,* all the persons in the territory belong to it (whether they have "enrolled" or "registered" in the parish, or not). If a parish is considered *personal,* it still has some territorial limits (at the utmost, the territorial limits of the particular church). Further, some suggest that a single parish may be both territorial *and* personal.[88]

The 1917 code had also legislated the general rule that a parish is territorial: a distinct territorial part of the diocese (*distincta pars territorialis*) with its proper church, people, and rector as its proper pastor (*CIC* 216, §§1, 3). To establish personal parishes (whether for persons speaking a specific language in the same region as a territorial parish, for a specific family, etc.) required a special apostolic indult. If personal parishes already existed, they could be changed only after consultation with the Apostolic See (*CIC* 216, §4).

Following Vatican Council II, the Sacred Congregation for Bishops issued an instruction *On the Pastoral Care of Immigrants* which recommended the establishment of personal parishes for immigrants who use the same language whether

---

that territory should remain the usual criterion of jurisdiction, although serious reasons (e.g., the rite or nationality of the faithful) may require other criteria, at least together with territory. *Comm* 1 (1969) 77–85.

[83] *CD* 23 suggests that creating special parishes may be an appropriate way to provide pastoral care for people of a different language group. Other ways include appointing priests who speak the language or appointing an episcopal vicar well versed in it. See c. 476 on the episcopal vicar appointed for certain groups of the faithful.

[84] Périsset, 47.

[85] John Paul II, apconst *Spirituali militum curae,* April 21, 1986, VII, *AAS* 78 (1986) 481–486 at 484. English translation: *TPS* 31 (1986) 284–288 at 286–287.

[86] Further, the proper pastor (and parish) of a transient is the pastor (and parish) where the transient is actually residing (c. 107, §2). The proper pastor (and parish) of one with only a diocesan domicile or quasi-domicile is the pastor (and parish) of the place where the person is actually residing (c. 107, §3).

[87] This is especially important for marriages. The pastor of a personal parish may assist validly only at marriages where at least one of the parties is his parishioner (c. 1110). Otherwise, the marriage is invalid by reason of lack of canonical form, because the pastor had no jurisdiction to assist at it. The pastor of a territorial parish, however, assists validly at the marriages of subjects and non-subjects (provided that one of them is of the Latin rite), so long as he is within the territory of his parish and not under a declared or imposed censure.

[88] For example, they suggest that a territorial parish may simultaneously be erected as the personal parish for all the Hispanics of a broader territory (or even of the entire diocese), or the territorial parish in a university city may simultaneously be erected as the personal parish for all students, faculty, and staff of the university wherever they may reside. See Green, Provost, and Wiatrowski, 102–110.

they take up permanent residence or constantly change. Or the local ordinary could establish a "mission with the care of souls" with its own territory within the boundaries of one (or more) territorial parishes; this mission would exist for particular groups of persons who lived there for any reason over a period of time. If neither a personal parish nor a mission were appropriate, the local ordinary could designate a chaplain or missionary who spoke the migrants' language and served in a defined territory; if the number of migrants was very large, the chaplain or missionary could be appointed as a *vicar cooperator* of one or several parishes. The chaplain or missionary was to conduct sacred services in some church, chapel, or seminary oratory—if necessary, even in a parish church.[89]

Notion of Pastor[90]

Canon 519 — The pastor (*parochus*) is the proper pastor (*pastor*) of the parish entrusted to him, exercising the pastoral care of the community committed to him under the authority of the diocesan bishop in whose ministry of Christ he has been called to share, so that for that same community he carries out the functions of teaching, sanctifying, and governing, also with the cooperation of other presbyters or deacons and with the assistance of lay members of the Christian faithful, according to the norm of law.

This canon describes the pastor. The pastor (*parochus*) is the proper pastor (*pastor*)[91] of the parish entrusted to him. He exercises pastoral care in the parish community under the authority of the diocesan bishop in whose ministry of Christ

he has been called to share. He extends pastoral care to the parishioners by fulfilling the functions of teaching, sanctifying, and governing,[92] with the cooperation of other presbyters[93] or deacons[94] and with the assistance of lay members of the Christian faithful (e.g., as lectors and extraordinary ministers of the Eucharist [c. 230, §3], catechists [c. 785, §1], those involved with marriage preparation and family enrichment [c. 1063], etc.), according to the norms of the law.

The pastor is not simply the delegate of the diocesan bishop. Within his parish, he functions with ordinary power, given him in law by reason of the office he holds.[95] His power is proper, exercised in his own name. He exercises pastoral care in the parish *ex officio* but under the authority of the diocesan bishop (c. 515, §1).

For the validity of his appointment, the pastor must be a presbyter (c. 521, §1). For its liceity, he must also be outstanding in sound doctrine and integrity of morals, endowed with zeal for souls and other virtues, and possessing other qualities required by universal or particular law for the parish in question (c. 521, §2).

---

[89] SCB, instr *De pastoralis migratorum cura,* August 22, 1969, n. 31, *AAS* 61 (1969) 614–643 at 630–633. English translation: *CLD* 6, 192–220 at 207–209.

[90] Cf. *CCEO* 281, §1. The Eastern code says here that a pastor must be a presbyter (see c. 521, §1).

[91] He is the "proper pastor" for such celebrations as baptisms (cc. 851, 2°; 855; 858, §2; etc.), marriages (c. 1108, §1), funerals (c. 1177, §1), etc.

[92] The "pastoral care" of the pastor is described in greater detail in cc. 528–530, 534, and elsewhere throughout the code. See *CD* 30.

[93] A *parochial vicar* is a presbyter who is a co-worker of the pastor; he shares in the pastor's solicitude, either for the entire parish, for a determined part of the parish, or even in specific ministry in more than one parish (c. 545). No title is given in the universal law for any other presbyter who may cooperate with the pastor (e.g., a priest in residence, a pastor emeritus, etc.). That the pastor collaborates with other priests is a practical application of the teaching of *PO* 7: "No priest is sufficiently equipped to carry out his mission alone and as it were single-handed. He can do so only by joining forces with other priests, under the leadership of those who are rulers of the Church."

[94] No specific title is given to the deacon in the parish. The code mentions the deacon only twice in the canons on parishes, i.e., cc. 517, §2 and 519.

[95] Canon 131 teaches that the ordinary power of governance is that which is joined to a certain office by the law itself (§1) and can be either proper or vicarious (§2). The power of a pastor is proper ordinary power.

The 1917 code had defined the pastor either as a priest (*sacerdos*) or a moral person to whom a parish is entrusted *in titulum* (that is, with rightful possession) with the care of souls to be exercised under the authority of the local ordinary (*CIC* 451, §1).[96] A moral (juridic) person, however, can no longer be appointed pastor of a parish (see c. 520, §1).

Entrusting a Parish to Clerical Religious Institutes and Clerical Societies of Apostolic Life[97]

Canon 520 — §1. A juridic person is not to be a pastor. With the consent of the competent superior, however, a diocesan bishop, but not a diocesan administrator, can entrust a parish to a clerical religious institute or clerical society of apostolic life, even by erecting it in a church of the institute or society, with the requirement, however, that one presbyter is to be the pastor of the parish or, if the pastoral care is entrusted to several *in solidum*, the moderator as mentioned in can. 517, §1.

§2. The entrusting of a parish mentioned in §1 can be made either perpetually or for a specific, predetermined time. In either case it is to be made by means of a written agreement between the diocesan bishop and the competent superior of the institute or society, which expressly and accurately defines, among other things, the work to be accomplished, the persons to be assigned to the parish, and the financial arrangements.

---

[96] *CIC* 451, §2 said that quasi-pastors and parochial vicars who were endowed with full parochial powers were equivalent to pastors; the powers of military chaplains were determined by the particular prescripts of the Holy See.

[97] Cf. *CCEO* 281, §2; 282; see also *CCEO* 284, §2. In this general context the Eastern code inserts a canon on the non-exemption of persons and places within a parish: "The eparchial bishop is not to remove from the pastor the partial or total care of certain groups of persons, buildings, and places which are in the territory of the parish and are not exempt by law, except for a grave cause" (*CCEO* 283). No parallel canon exists in the 1983 code.

A physical person is to be the pastor of a parish: a juridic person is not to be a pastor.

The 1917 code had permitted, with an indult of the Apostolic See, a parish to be united *pleno iure* to a moral person (e.g., a religious house, a capitular church, etc.), in such a fashion that the moral person was its pastor (*CIC* 452, §1). In this scenario the superior of the moral person nominated a priest, called a *parochial vicar,* who would exercise the actual care for souls, and presented him to the bishop for installation. To the vicar belonged exclusively the entire care of souls with all the rights and duties of a pastor (*CIC* 471). Canon 520, §1 makes it clear that the aforementioned arrangement is no longer permitted. Indeed, canon 510, §1 says precisely that a parish can no longer be joined to a chapter of canons, and the diocesan bishop is to separate from a chapter those parishes which are united to it.[98]

Christus Dominus 35 (1) urged superiors of non-contemplative religious institutes to cooperate with the bishop, especially in light of the shortage of diocesan clergy and urgent pastoral needs, even by taking responsibility for parishes on a temporary basis.[99]

With the consent of the competent superior, however, a diocesan bishop (but not a diocesan administrator)[100] can entrust a parish to a clerical

---

[98] Canon 510, §§2–4 envisions the possibility, however, of one church being both parochial and capitular. In this situation a priest, whether belonging to the chapter or not, is to be appointed its proper pastor (*parochus*). The diocesan bishop is to establish definite norms to integrate fittingly the functions of the pastor and those of the chapter. Neither should hinder the other. If any conflict arises, the diocesan bishop is to resolve it, primarily in view of the pastoral needs of the parishioners. Further, alms given to the church are presumed given to the parish (not the chapter), unless the contrary is evident. A canon parallel to c. 510 is not found in the Eastern code.

[99] *ES* I, 33 (1) implemented *CD* 35 (1) and was quite similar to c. 520, except that the canon says the *diocesan bishop* entrusts the parish whereas *ES* said the *local ordinary* can do it. Gauthier recounts a serious reluctance to entrust a parish to religious in past centuries (57).

[100] That the diocesan administrator is forbidden to establish this arrangement is a practical application of the norm:

religious institute or to a clerical society of apostolic life.[101] The bishop can even erect the parish in a church of the institute or society. In this situation, one presbyter is to be the pastor or, if the parish is entrusted to several priests *in solidum* (c. 517, §1), the moderator of the group. This arrangement can be made either perpetually or for a time. A written bilateral agreement between the diocesan bishop and the competent superior of the institute or society is called for; the agreement is expressly and accurately to define, among other things, (1) the work to be accomplished, (2) the persons to be assigned to the parish, and (3) the financial arrangements. In addition, it should mention the length of the agreement, especially if it is for a specific time.

When a parish is entrusted to such an institute or society, the care of souls remains subject to the diocesan bishop (see c. 678, §1) and all laws about a parish, both universal and particular, must be observed. The diocesan bishop and the other local ordinaries, however, are not to become involved in the internal discipline of the religious serving the parish; rather, they are to preserve and safeguard the autonomy of the religious as regards their internal governance (see cc. 586, 732).

Canon 520 concerns entrusting a *parish* to an institute or society. This is not the same as what occurs when a diocesan bishop enters into an agreement with a competent superior on the assignment of an *individual priest member* to a parish (e.g., as its pastor).[102]

Qualifications of Pastors[103]

Canon 521 — §1. To become a pastor validly, one must be in the sacred order of the presbyterate.

§2. Moreover, he is to be outstanding in sound doctrine and integrity of morals and endowed with zeal for souls and other virtues; he is also to possess those qualities which are required by universal or particular law to care for the parish in question.

§3. For the office of pastor to be conferred on someone, his suitability must be clearly evident by some means determined by the diocesan bishop, even by means of an examination.

For validity, a pastor must be a presbyter (of course, a bishop may also be appointed a pastor by the diocesan bishop).[104] A deacon or lay person cannot be appointed validly to the office of pastor. For liceity, the presbyter is to be outstanding in doctrine and integrity of morals, endowed with zeal for souls and other virtues; he is also to have those other qualities required by law (universal or particular) to care for the particular parish.[105] His suitability for the office of pastor must be clearly evident by some means determined by the diocesan bishop—perhaps even by means of an examination. In many dioceses in the United States, mechanisms are in place for the regular evaluation of a pastor's ministry performed by qualified diocesan personnel, perhaps especially before renewing a six-year term of office.[106]

"When a see is vacant, nothing is to be altered" (c. 428, §1).

[101] The 1981 *Relatio* says a parish is not to be entrusted to a secular institute, but to a specific priest who belongs to it. Further, the arrangement permitted in c. 520 is better left to the discretion of the diocesan bishop than the conference of bishops. *Comm* 14 (1982) 222.

[102] Canon 682 pertains to this arrangement; see also c. 538, §2. *ES* I, 33 (2) says: "The local ordinary may also, with the approval of his superior, appoint a religious as parish priest [pastor] of a parish which is not entrusted to a religious institute. This is to be done by special and appropriate agreement with the competent superior of the same institute."

[103] Cf. *CCEO* 281, §1; 285, §1. The Eastern code does not refer to the suitability of a candidate being determined by the eparchial bishop using some method, perhaps even an exam. *CCEO* 285, §2, discussing a pastor's qualifications, says: "If a presbyter is married, good morals are required in his wife and his children who live with him."

[104] This is an application of c. 150: "An office which entails the full care of souls and for whose fulfillment the exercise of the priestly order is required cannot be conferred validly on one who is not yet a priest."

[105] See *CD* 31.

[106] B. Dunn, "The Evaluation of Pastors," in *RRAO 1997*, 45–46; and "Transition Evaluation Processes in Parishes," ibid., 46–47. K. McDonough, "'I Never Knew What You

Paragraphs one and two repeat substantially canon 454, §§1–2 of the 1917 code. Ascertaining a candidate's suitability for the office of pastor was a grave obligation of the local ordinary (not precisely the diocesan bishop). Among other things, the candidate was to be examined on doctrinal matters before the local ordinary and two synodal examiners: this exam could be dispensed if the priest were well known for his theological doctrine (*CIC* 459).[107]

Stability of Office of Pastor[108]

Canon 522 — A pastor must possess stability and therefore is to be appointed for an indefinite period of time. The diocesan bishop can appoint him only for a specific period if the conference of bishops has permitted this by a decree.

A pastor must possess stability in office[109] for the good of souls (*CD* 31). As a rule, therefore, a pastor is to be appointed for an *indefinite* period of time. The rule admits an exception: if the conference of bishops has permitted it by a decree,[110] the diocesan bishop may appoint a pastor for a *specific* period of time.

The 1917 code had legislated that pastors should have stability, but they could be removed according to the norm of law. Not all pastors enjoyed the same stability. Some were designated as *irremovable* (enjoying greater stability) and others as *removable* (with less stability). Since pastors of either category could be removed, there was technically no such thing as a true "irremovable pastor," but the process to remove an unwilling irremovable pastor (*CIC* 2147–2156) was more involved than that to remove an unwilling removable pastor (*CIC* 2157–2161). *Christus Dominus* 31 called for the elimination of the distinction between irremovable and removable pastors, and a simplification of the procedure to remove or transfer pastors for the good of souls. The conciliar decree, however, did not envision appointment of pastors for specific periods,[111] which is new legislation for the Church in the current code.

The 1983 code does not distinguish between irremovable and removable pastors. Now all pastors enjoy the same kind of stability in office and are subject to the same removal process (cc. 1740–1747).

At its November 1983 meeting, the NCCB approved a decree that diocesan bishops may appoint pastors for a limited period of time, with the specific length of the tenure and renewability being left to the former's determination. This decree was reviewed by the Congregation for Bishops on May 16, 1984 (prot. no. 1887/84/6). A letter from Archbishop Pio Laghi, apostolic pro-nuncio, on September 4, 1984 (prot. no. 3517/84/6) gave as the approved final decree the following:

> In accord with canon 522, the National Conference of Catholic Bishops decrees that diocesan bishops may appoint pastors

Really Thought of Me': Evaluation of Pastors and the Issue of Unassignability," *Stud Can* 32 (1998) 145–156.

[107] *CIC* 459, §4 mentioned the *concursus,* a kind of competitive examination, which was to continue to be used where the practice was common until the Apostolic See decreed otherwise. *CD* 31, however, stated clearly that the *concursus* is to be rescinded wherever it exists.

[108] *CCEO* 284, §3 says a pastor possesses stability in office, but may be appointed for a determined period in four instances: (1) if the pastor is a member of a religious institute or a society of common life in the manner of religious; (2) if the candidate agrees to this in writing; (3) if it concerns a special case, in which instance the consent of the college of eparchial consultors is required; and (4) if the particular law of the proper autonomous church permits it.

[109] This canon also applies to the priests to whom a parish(es) is entrusted *in solidum* in accord with the norm of c. 517, §1 (see c. 542, 2°).

[110] See c. 455 about conference legislative decrees. Decrees approved at a plenary meeting must be passed by at least two-thirds of the prelates who belong to the conference and possess a deliberative vote. The decrees obtain binding force when they are legitimately promulgated following review by the Apostolic See (§2).

[111] See also *ES* I, 20 (1)–(2), which implements the teaching of *CD;* it, too, makes no mention of specific terms for pastors.

to a six-year term of office. The possibility of renewing this term is left to the discretion of the diocesan bishop.[112]

This decree was promulgated by the president of the NCCB/USCC on September 24, 1984. Therefore, in the United States, a diocesan bishop may choose to appoint pastors for a six-year period, repeatedly renewable, but he is not bound to do so.[113] He may continue to appoint pastors for an indefinite period.[114]

If a pastor is appointed for a definite term, his office ends not precisely when the six years have passed but when the competent authority communicates to him in writing that the years have passed and the term has ended (see c. 186). If the pastor is not so informed, he retains the office of pastor even though the six years have passed but can be legitimately removed by the competent authority anytime thereafter.

Furthermore, the pastor appointed for a definite term is free to seek a transfer before the term is completed. The diocesan bishop is also free to invite him to accept a transfer to another parish. If the pastor refuses, the diocesan bishop may use the process for the transfer of an unwilling pastor (cc. 1748–1752).

Provision of the Office of Pastor[115]

Canon 523 — Without prejudice to the prescript of can. 682, §1, the provision of the office of pastor belongs to the diocesan bishop, and indeed by free conferral, unless someone has the right of presentation or election.

The provision of the office of pastor belongs to the diocesan bishop usually by free conferral (see c. 157).[116] Someone, however, may have the right of presentation or election of the priest,[117] in which case the diocesan bishop (or even the diocesan administrator, c. 525, 1°) installs or confirms him as pastor.[118] Further, if a religious priest is to be appointed as pastor by the diocesan bishop, the priest's competent superior must present him or at least consent to his appointment (c. 682, §1); in this situation, too, the appointment is made by the diocesan bishop.

The 1917 code stated that the local ordinary had the right to nominate and install pastors, and added that the appointment of some pastors was reserved to the Holy See (*CIC* 455, §1). These norms are no longer operative. The *diocesan bishop* (not other local ordinaries)[119] appoints pastors; the code does not reserve to the Holy See the appointment of some pastors.

---

[112] NCCB-*Comp Nm*, 5.

[113] Lynch identifies a number of arguments for and against a definite term of office for pastors: "The limited rather than lifelong tenure is seen by some as a valuable way to assure pastoral evaluation and accountability. Their arguments in favor of rotation of pastors generally hold: (1) it promotes the introduction of new and creative ideas in a parish; (2) it spreads different pastoral experiences and charisms over a larger area; (3) it permits priests to become pastors at an earlier age. Opponents to a limited term point to the difficulties a pastor experiences in becoming acquainted with an entirely different scene and his frustration at leaving programs uncompleted. They also think it prevents a pastor from knowing his people well and forces parishioners to adjust themselves to different pastoral orientations. An effective pastoral council, however, could ensure a large measure of continuity in parish projects" (397).

[114] Indeed, the diocesan bishop may choose to appoint certain pastors for the six-year renewable term but others indefinitely. Some may, however, question the advisability of such a non-uniform practice in the same particular church.

[115] Cf. *CCEO* 284, §1.

[116] All the norms on the provision of an ecclesiastical office (cc. 146–156) apply in the free conferral of the office of pastor.

[117] No law forbids the continued granting of the right of presentation or election; *CD* 31, however, called for their abrogation so the diocesan bishop could more easily and efficiently make provision for parishes. Thus, the future granting of these rights opposes the conciliar position.

[118] If the diocesan bishop should refuse to install or confirm one legitimately presented or elected, the candidate would have the right to recourse to the competent ecclesiastical authority (i.e., the CFC).

[119] Vicars general and episcopal vicars (i.e., the other local ordinaries in a diocese) may appoint pastors only if they have received the special mandate to do so from their diocesan bishop (see c. 134, §3).

The 1917 code also envisioned the possibility of some persons having been granted the privilege of electing or presenting a pastor (*CIC* 455, §1). *Christus Dominus* 28 states that bishops must have the requisite liberty in making appointments, and that all rights and privileges which in any way restrict that right should accordingly be eliminated. Referring specifically to parish appointments, *Christus Dominus* 31 says:

> Basically... parochial responsibility has to do with the good of souls. It follows that, if a bishop is more easily and efficiently to make provision for the parishes, all rights whatsoever of presentation, nomination and reservation should be abrogated, without prejudice, however, to the rights of religious.

Canon 523 admits the possibility that the right of presentation and election of pastors may still be operative in some situations, notwithstanding the conciliar call for the abrogation of these privileges. Further, canon 525, 1° gives to the diocesan administrator of a vacant see (see c. 421, §1) and to the bishop or presbyter who temporarily governs an impeded see (see c. 413, §§1–2) the power to install or confirm presbyters who have been legitimately presented or elected for a parish. Canon 525, 2° determines that they may appoint other pastors if the see has been vacant or impeded for a year.

Suitability of Pastor[120]

Canon 524 — A diocesan bishop is to entrust a vacant parish to the one whom he considers suited to fulfill its parochial care, after weighing all the circumstances and without any favoritism. To make a judgment about suitability, he is to hear the vicar forane and conduct appropriate investigations, having heard certain presbyters and lay members of the Christian faithful, if it is warranted.

This canon requires the diocesan bishop to entrust a vacant parish to a priest whom he judges

[120] Cf. *CCEO* 285, §3.

suitable to fulfill its pastoral care, after he has weighed all the circumstances and without any favoritism.[121] Canon 521, §§2–3 identifies characteristics which a candidate for pastor must possess, and says that his suitability must be clearly evident by some means determined by the bishop, even by means of an examination. Canon 524 adds that the diocesan bishop will judge the priest's suitability also by hearing the vicar forane (see cc. 553–555)[122] and conducting appropriate investigations, hearing certain presbyters and lay persons, if war-

[121] See *CIC* 459, §1. The *Directory* (98) identifies as a fundamental principle of a bishop's pastoral rule that he must place the right people in the right places for the good of souls, "employing talents in as fitting and useful a way as possible for the service of the community."

[122] *ES* 19 (2) says that the diocesan bishop should consult the vicars forane when nominating, transferring, or removing pastors in the deanery. Canon 547 suggests that the diocesan bishop also hear the vicar forane before appointing parochial vicars. If the pastor or parochial vicar is being moved from one vicariate forane to another, the diocesan bishop might appropriately consult both vicars forane.

Some (e.g., Coccopalmerio, Read) question if the diocesan bishop's appointment of a pastor without hearing the vicar forane is valid (see c. 127, §2, 2°), since the Latin term (*audiat*) is the same as found elsewhere when the diocesan bishop's action is invalid without such consultation (see, e.g., cc. 494, §2; 1277). For example, Coccopalmerio says emphatically that the diocesan bishop's appointment of a pastor is invalid if he has not heard the vicar forane; the diocesan bishop may hear the vicar forane through another (e.g., the vicar general or episcopal vicar, who must have a *special mandate*) (123). Read says that the bishop is required to consult the vicar forane in whose vicariate the vacant parish is located; "such a consultation is necessary if the appointment is to be valid (see Can. 127 §2, 2°)" (290).

Others (e.g., Brewer), however, say that the diocesan bishop probably validly appoints a pastor even if he fails to hear the vicar forane, since the office of vicar forane is not required by law. (Those consulted in cc. 494, §2 and 1277, however, hold required offices.) D. Brewer, "Canon 524 and the Systematic Participation of the Laity in the Selection of Pastors," *Stud Can* 29 (1995) 485, n. 13.

Whether the bishop's action is valid or not without such consultation, the canon expects him to hear the vicar forane before appointing a pastor. Such consultation is prudent and can prove helpful in clarifying the qualifications of the candidate.

ranted.[123] The presbyters involved may be members of the priests' personnel board, and the laity may be members of the parish pastoral council who, in their planning role, prepare a parish profile to assist the diocesan bishop in his discernment.

The appointment of a pastor to a vacant parish is not to be deferred without a grave cause (see c. 151).[124] Indeed, the 1917 code had insisted that the local ordinary not delay the appointment of a pastor to a vacant parish beyond six months, unless special circumstances called for a greater delay (*CIC* 458). The current code does not set a time within which the diocesan bishop must appoint a pastor.

The parish being conferred freely by the diocesan bishop must be a *vacant* parish: otherwise, the provision is invalid (see c. 153, §1). However, if the current pastor has been appointed for a six-year term which will expire in six months, the diocesan bishop may validly appoint the successor pastor whose term takes effect when his predecessor's term ends (see c. 153, §2). The mere promise of a pastorate by the diocesan bishop has no juridic effect (see c. 153, §3).

Parochial Appointments During Impeded/Vacant See[125]

Canon 525 — When a see is vacant or impeded, it belongs to the diocesan administrator or another who governs the diocese temporarily:

1° to install or confirm presbyters who have been legitimately presented or elected for a parish;

2° to appoint pastors if the see has been vacant or impeded for a year.

The diocesan administrator of a vacant see (see c. 421, §1) or the bishop or presbyter who governs the diocese temporarily when it is impeded (see c. 413, §§1–2) is able: (1) to install or confirm presbyters who have been legitimately presented or elected for a parish, and (2) to appoint pastors if the see has been vacant or impeded for a year.[126] That the interim leader of the diocese may appoint pastors after the see has been vacant or impeded for a year is an application of the norm that the provision of an office entailing the care of souls (such as a pastorate) is not to be deferred without a grave cause (c. 151).

One Parish Per Pastor[127]

Canon 526 — §1. A pastor is to have the parochial care of only one parish; nevertheless, because of a lack of priests or other circumstances, the care of several neighboring parishes can be entrusted to the same pastor.

As a general rule, a pastor is to have the pastoral care of only one parish.[128] Nevertheless, be-

---

[123] See J. Myers, "Consultation for the Appointment of Pastors," in *CLSA Advisory Opinions, 1984–1993*, ed. P. Cogan (Washington, D.C.: CLSA, 1995), 137–138.

[124] One will rightly question the appropriateness of assigning a *parochial administrator* (cc. 539–541), rather than a pastor, to a parish for a lengthy period. The parochial administrator is envisioned as a temporary substitute either for a pastor who is impeded or for a pastor in a vacant parish. The parochial administrator should not become, for all practical purposes, stably appointed to the parish: the pastor, not the parochial administrator, possesses stability (c. 522).

[125] Cf. *CCEO* 286.

[126] See *CIC* 455, §2, which had given the vicar capitular (called the diocesan administrator in the 1983 code) the ability to appoint parochial vicars, a right not specifically mentioned in c. 525. Nonetheless, the diocesan administrator has this right in light of c. 427, which gives him the powers of a diocesan bishop, except those excluded by their nature or by the law. Canon 547 on the appointment of a parochial vicar does not preclude his appointment by the diocesan administrator. Also, c. 552 states that the diocesan administrator can *remove* a parochial vicar for a just cause.

[127] Cf. *CCEO* 287, §1.

[128] Canon 152 says that two or more incompatible offices (i.e., offices which cannot be fulfilled together at the same time by the same person) are not to be conferred upon one person. The "Observations Concerning Cases in Which the Pastoral Care of More than One Parish Is Entrusted to a Single Pastor," issued by the PCILT on November 13, 1997, says that nothing in c. 526, §1 indicates that the same priest cannot be *parochus* (pastor)

cause of a lack of priests or other circumstances, the pastoral care of several neighboring parishes can be entrusted to the same pastor.[129]

The Latin phrase "because of a lack of priests" (*ob penuriam sacerdotum*) is the same phrase used in canon 517, §2. Thus, when there is a priest shortage the code demonstrates two options for a diocesan bishop: (1) the appointment of a pastor to more than one parish, or (2) the arrangement envisioned in c. 517, §2. The 1997 multi-dicastery *Instruction* makes it clear that the former arrangement is preferred, and says that before implementing c. 517, §2 "other possibilities should be availed of, such as using the services of retired priests still capable of such services, of entrusting several parishes to one priest or to a *coetus sacerdotum*."[130]

The pastoral care of several neighboring parishes can be entrusted to one pastor in a number of ways. He can be pastor of all the parishes (c. 519). He can be pastor of one (or some) and parochial administrator of the other(s) (c. 539). He can be the pastor of one (or some) and the priest endowed with the powers or faculties of a pastor (i.e., the so-called "priest-director") in the arrangement of canon 517, §2 in the other(s).[131]

If, in fact, more than one neighboring parish is conferred upon the same pastor, he will need to take possession of *each* according to the norm of canon 527. However, if the priest is pastor of one parish but not pastor of the others (e.g., if he is their parochial administrator or priest-director), he takes possession only of the parish for which he is the pastor. The other parishes would be vacant (without a pastor) but would be receiving pastoral care through the other arrangements.

Canon 460, §1 of the 1917 code had allowed a pastor to have title to multiple parishes if they were united *aeque principaliter,* i.e., if each retained its own legal personality and none was subject to the others. Canon 1423, §1 of that code had permitted such a union of parishes on account of the need of the Church or great and evident usefulness.[132] The pastor was the pastor of the *united* parishes. The 1983 code, however, permits a pastor to be assigned to more than one parish without requiring their union. Each parish to which the same priest is assigned remains an independent juridic person.

---

of neighboring parishes: "There is nothing in either the Code or in the *Acta* documenting the process of the revision of the Code which would determine or suggest that the priest mentioned in c. 526 could not be nominated pastor in each parish entrusted to his care." Furthermore, the incompatibility mentioned in c. 152 is a question "of fact, rather than of law." The PCILT also adds: "Although one can imagine particular cases in which two pastorates would be incompatible (by reason of the needs or size of the parishes or the distance that separates them), present experience in many dioceses confirms that there could be situations in which a single priest would be able to provide adequate pastoral care in more than one parish." The *parochus* (pastor) of multiple parishes may offer one Mass for the people (c. 534, §2). The observations add that if a *parochus* of more than one parish is to be removed (cc. 1740–1747), a single investigation may occur but the decision for the pastor's removal must be made for each individual parish, with causes of removal shown for each particular parish. *Comm* 30 (1998) 28–30. See also P. Erdö, "De incompatibilitate officiorum, specialiter paroeciarum: Adnotationes ad cann. 152 et 526," *P* 80 (1991) 521–522.

[129] Since a parish is no longer a benefice, the remuneration of the pastor of more than one parish will be determined by the diocesan bishop rather than the former's receiving income from the multiple (incompatible) benefices.

[130] *Instruction,* art. 4, §1. The instruction does not forbid implementing the arrangement of c. 517, §2 when there

are not enough priests to assign a pastor to each individual parish; it says, however, that other arrangements should be used instead, and identifies three: (1) the utilization of the services of retired priests able to serve a parish, (2) the entrusting of several parishes to one priest, and (3) the group arrangement envisioned in c. 517, §1. There is no indication that these options are listed in order of preference.

[131] See J. Provost, "Priests Serving as Pastors in More than One Parish," in *CLSA Advisory Opinions,* 124–126.

[132] *CIC* 1423, §3 required that the union of the parishes *aeque principaliter* be a perpetual arrangement (*in perpetuum*). Still, the local ordinary retained the right to divide or dismember parishes (*CIC* 1427).

One Pastor Per Parish[133]

§2. In the same parish there is to be only one pastor or moderator in accord with the norm of can. 517, §1; any contrary custom is reprobated and any contrary privilege whatsoever is revoked.

In each parish there is to be only one pastor or, if it has been entrusted to several priests *in solidum* (c. 517, §1), one moderator. Any contrary custom is reprobated and any contrary privilege is revoked.[134] This canon repeats almost literally canon 460, §2 of the 1917 code, and adds the reference to the arrangement of canon 517, §1.

Taking Possession of the Parish[135]

Canon 527 — §1. The person who has been promoted to carry out the pastoral care of a parish obtains this care and is bound to exercise it from the moment of taking possession.

§2. The local ordinary or a priest delegated by him places the pastor in possession; he is to observe the method accepted by particular law or legitimate custom. The same ordinary, however, can dispense from that method for a just cause; in this case, the notification of the dispensation to the parish replaces the taking of possession.

§3. The local ordinary is to prescribe the time within which possession of a parish must be taken.

When this has elapsed without action, he can declare the parish vacant unless there was a just impediment.

Becoming a pastor involves three elements: (1) the diocesan bishop making provision of the office, (2) the candidate making the profession of faith (see c. 833, 6°), and (3) the candidate taking possession of the office. Canon 527 concerns the last element.

The priest appointed pastor obtains the pastoral care of the parish and is bound to exercise it from the moment he takes possession of the parish. Before that time he has no powers whatsoever in the parish. The local ordinary prescribes the time within which the priest must take possession of the parish. If this period elapses without action and unless he judges that there is a just impediment, the local ordinary can declare the parish vacant.

A pastor is placed in possession of the parish by the local ordinary or by a priest delegated by him; he is to observe the method of placing in possession which is accepted by particular law or legitimate custom.[136] For a just cause, the same local ordinary can dispense from that method; in this case, the notification of the dispensation to the parish replaces the taking of possession.[137] This canon provides significant room for adaptation to local circumstances on the manner in which the pastor takes possession of the parish.

---

[133] *CCEO* 287, §2 incorporates the discipline of canon 517, §1, and says that the issues addressed in cc. 542–544 are to be determined by the particular law of the proper autonomous church.

[134] See cc. 28 (on revoking customs) and 79 (on revoking privileges).

[135] Cf. *CCEO* 288. The manner of taking canonical possession of a parish is determined by particular law. The Eastern code does not make reference to canonical possession being taken by the moderator or other members of the group of priests to whom is entrusted a parish; seemingly, this must be determined by the particular law of the proper autonomous church which allows the arrangement (*CCEO* 287, §1). In the 1983 code, c. 542, 3° says the moderator alone is placed in possession of a parish, and the profession of faith replaces such a taking possession for the other presbyters.

[136] For rituals of the installation of a pastor, see *CB*, "Part VIII: Liturgical Celebrations in Connection with Official Acts Pertaining to the Government of a Diocese," "Chapter 3: Introduction of a New Parish Priest (Pastor) into His Parish," 1185–1198. No. 1185 says the pastor is to make the profession of faith either before the installation or during it. See also *BB*, "Appendix I: Order for the Installation of a Pastor," 2012–2045. No. 2012 recommends that the installation take place at a Mass on the first Sunday after the appointment is effective, with the bishop or his delegate presiding.

[137] Canon 833, 6° says the profession of faith must be made by the pastor "at the beginning of [his] function," without further specification. If the pastor is dispensed from taking possession in the way required by particular law or legitimate custom, he must still make the profession of faith at the beginning of his pastoral function.

The 1917 code also legislated that a pastor obtained the care of souls from the moment he took possession of his parish, and that before or while taking possession he was to make the required profession of faith (*CIC* 461); the means of taking possession, the time to do so, and the consequences of failing to do so were treated in canon 1444 of the 1917 code, on taking possession of benefices.[138]

Pastor as Minister of the Word[139]

Canon 528 — §1. A pastor is obliged to make provision so that the word of God is proclaimed in its entirety to those living in the parish; for this reason, he is to take care that the lay members of the Christian faithful are instructed in the truths of the faith, especially by giving a homily on Sundays and holy days of obligation and by offering catechetical instruction. He is to foster works through which the spirit of the gospel is promoted, even in what pertains to social justice. He is to have particular care for the Catholic education of children and youth. He is to make every effort, even with the collaboration of the Christian faithful, so that the message of the gospel comes also to those who have ceased the practice of their religion or do not profess the true faith.

Canon 519 teaches that, under the authority of the diocesan bishop, the pastor carries out for his parishioners the functions of teaching, sanctifying, and governing. According to the norms of law, he does this in cooperation with other presbyters or deacons, and with the assistance of the laity. Together with many other canons throughout the code and elsewhere, canons 528–530 illustrate how the pastor fulfills these functions.

Canon 528, §1 discusses the pastor's role as minister of the word. He is to make provision that the word is proclaimed entirely in the parish (see cc. 213, 757). He is to see that the laity are instructed in the truths of the faith, especially by homilies on Sundays and holy days of obligation (see c. 767, §2) and by catechetical instruction (see cc. 776–777). He is to foster works which promote the spirit of the gospel, even in matters of social justice (see c. 222, §2). He is to have particular care for the Catholic education of children and youth (see cc. 217, 229, 793–806). In collaboration with others, he is to see that the gospel message comes to those who have ceased the practice of their religion and who do not profess the true faith.

Other canons also identify the pastor's role in the ministry of the word. According to the prescripts of the diocesan bishop, he is to arrange for spiritual exercises, sacred missions, or other forms of preaching adapted to the pastoral needs of the parish (c. 770). He is to see that the word is proclaimed to those who, because of their condition of life, do not have sufficient common and ordinary pastoral care or lack it completely (c. 771, §1), and to non-believers (c. 771, §2).

Pastor as Minister of Sanctification[140]

§2. The pastor is to see to it that the Most Holy Eucharist is the center of the parish assembly of the faithful. He is to work so that the Christian faithful are nourished through the devout celebration of the sacraments and, in a special way, that they frequently approach the sacraments of the Most Holy Eucharist and penance. He is also to endeavor that they are led to practice prayer even as families and take part consciously and actively in the sacred liturgy which, under the authority of the diocesan bishop, the pastor must direct in his own parish and is bound to watch over so that no abuses creep in.

This canon discusses the sanctifying role of the pastor. He is to see that the Most Holy Eucharist

---

[138] *CIC* 1445 permitted a pastor to take possession of a parish through a proxy, but *CIC* 1407 said that, in any case, the pastor had to make the profession of faith personally.

[139] Cf. *CCEO* 289, §1. See also *CIC* 467, 469; *SC* 35, 52; *UR* 11; *CD* 30; *PO* 6, 9.

[140] Cf. *CCEO* 289, §2. See also *CIC* 467–468; *SC* 42, 59; *CD* 30.

is at the center of parochial life (see cc. 897–898). He is to work for the sanctification of the parishioners (see cc. 210; 212, §2; 213–214), especially through the Eucharist and penance. He is to encourage family prayer (see cc. 851, 2°; 1248, §2), and to lead the faithful to conscious and active participation in the sacred liturgy (see cc. 835, §4; 837; 898). Under the authority of the diocesan bishop (see c. 839, §2), he is to direct the liturgy in the parish and to prevent liturgical abuses. In addition, the canons on the parish identify a number of sanctifying functions especially entrusted to a pastor (c. 530) and require that he offer the Mass for the people of his parish on every Sunday and holy day of obligation (c. 534).

Several other canons make explicit reference to the pastor's role in sanctifying his parishioners. The canons concern his role in baptism (cc. 851, 2°; 855; 858, §2; 861, §2; 867, §1; 874, §1, 1°–2°; 877, §§1–2; 878; 1706); confirmation (cc. 883, 3°; 890; 895–896); the Eucharist (cc. 911; 914; 958, §1); penance (c. 968, §1); orders (cc. 1043, 1054); marriage (cc. 1067; 1069–1070; 1079, §2; 1081; 1105, §2; 1106; 1108, §1; 1109–1110; 1111, §1; 1114–1115; 1118, §1; 1121; 1122, §2; 1123; 1706); and funerals (c. 1177, §2).

For a just cause, the pastor can dispense his parishioners everywhere and travelers in his parish from private vows, provided the dispensation does not injure another's acquired right (c. 1196, 1°). He may dispense from promissory oaths, provided this does not jeopardize others who refuse to remit the obligation of the oath (c. 1203). In individual cases, he can dispense from the obligation of observing a Sunday or holy day of obligation, or a day of penance; likewise, he can commute these obligations into other pious works (c. 1245).

Pastor as Minister of Pastoral Governance[141]

Canon 529 — §1. In order to fulfill his office diligently, a pastor is to strive to know the faithful entrusted to his care. Therefore he is to visit families,

---

[141]Cf. *CCEO* 289, §3; *CIC* 468; *CD* 18, 30; *PO* 6.

sharing especially in the cares, anxieties, and griefs of the faithful, strengthening them in the Lord, and prudently correcting them if they are failing in certain areas. With generous love he is to help the sick, particularly those close to death, by refreshing them solicitously with the sacraments and commending their souls to God; with particular diligence he is to seek out the poor, the afflicted, the lonely, those exiled from their country, and similarly those weighed down by special difficulties. He is to work so that spouses and parents are supported in fulfilling their proper duties and is to foster growth of Christian life in the family.

This canon identifies several aspects of the pastor's ministry of pastoral governance. He is to strive to know his parishioners, and so he visits families, shares parishioners' cares, anxieties, and griefs, strengthens them, and prudently corrects them as necessary. He is to have a generous love for the sick, refreshing them with the sacraments and commending their souls to God. He seeks out the poor, the afflicted, the lonely, the exiled, and all those weighed down by special difficulties. He supports spouses and parents in fulfilling their proper duties, and fosters the growth of Christian family life.

In order to perform these pastoral functions effectively, the pastor must not have repeated and extended absences from his parish. Therefore, he is to live in a rectory near the parish church; however, the local ordinary can permit him to live elsewhere, especially in a house shared by several presbyters, provided that his parochial functions are properly and suitably provided for (c. 533, §1). He is provided an annual spiritual retreat, and a maximum of one continuous or interrupted month for vacation, unless there is a grave reason to the contrary (c. 533, §2). The grave reason could be parochial needs, especially in places suffering a grave lack of priests. The diocesan bishop is to establish norms to assure that a priest, endowed with the necessary faculties, is available to provide pastoral care in the parish whenever the pastor is absent for any reason (c. 533, §3).

Pastor, Role of the Laity, Ecclesial Communion[142]

§2. A pastor is to recognize and promote the proper part which the lay members of the Christian faithful have in the mission of the Church, by fostering their associations for the purposes of religion. He is to cooperate with his own bishop and the presbyterate of the diocese, also working so that the faithful have concern for parochial communion, consider themselves members of the diocese and of the universal Church, and participate in and sustain efforts to promote this same communion.

This canon identifies the duty of the pastor in promoting the role of the laity and in working for ecclesial communion.[143] He is to recognize and promote the role of the laity in the mission of the Church (see cc. 208, 211, 224–231) by fostering associations for the purposes of religion (see cc. 215; 223, §1; 225, §1; 327–329). He furthers ecclesial communion as he cooperates with his own bishop and fellow presbyters in the diocese and as he works so that the faithful have concern for parochial *communio,* realize they are members of the diocese and of the universal Church, and participate in and sustain efforts to promote this ecclesial *communio* (see cc. 209, 223).

Functions Especially Entrusted to the Pastor[144]

Canon 530 — The following functions are especially entrusted to a pastor:

1° the administration of baptism;
2° the administration of the sacrament of confirmation to those who are in danger of death, according to the norm of can. 883, n. 3;
3° the administration of Viaticum and of the anointing of the sick, without prejudice to the prescript of can. 1003, §§2 and 3, and the imparting of the apostolic blessing;
4° the assistance at marriages and the nuptial blessing;
5° the performance of funeral rites;
6° the blessing of the baptismal font at Easter time, the leading of processions outside the church, and solemn blessings outside the church;
7° the more solemn eucharistic celebration on Sundays and holy days of obligation.

Inasmuch as he is the proper pastor of the parish, it is appropriate that the pastor personally perform certain important functions within the community, especially in liturgical celebrations.[145] This canon identifies certain functions which by law are especially entrusted to a pastor: (1) the administration of baptism; (2) the administration of confirmation to those who are in danger of death; (3) the administration of Viaticum and of the anointing of the sick, and the imparting of the apostolic blessing; (4) the assistance at marriages and the nuptial blessing; (5) the performance of funeral rites; (6) the blessing of the baptismal font at Easter time, the leading of processions outside the church building, and solemn blessings outside the church building; and (7) the more solemn eucharistic celebration on Sundays and holy days of obligation.[146]

Canon 462 of the 1917 code contained a similar listing of functions which were said to be "re-

---

[142] See *CD* 30; *PO* 7–9.
[143] Those drafting the 1983 code deliberately limited the term *communio* to references to the Church (ecclesial communion) and to the Eucharist (eucharistic communion). *Comm* 15 (1983) 222.
[144] Cf. *CCEO* 290, §2. The Eastern code simply says that sacred functions of greater importance belong to (*spectant ad*) the pastor, e.g., the celebration of the sacraments of Christian initiation, the blessing of marriages, and ecclesiastical funeral rites. The parochial vicar is not permitted to perform these functions except with the permission, at least presumed, of the pastor.

[145] Périsset, 133.
[146] Canon 534 obliges the pastor to apply a Mass for the people on each Sunday and holy day of obligation. If necessary he may offer the Mass on same day through another, or on other days himself.

served to" the pastor. No one else was to perform these functions without his permission. The 1983 code says the functions in canon 530 are "especially entrusted to" (*not* exclusively reserved to) the pastor.[147] He does not have the same right to discharge these functions as he had in the earlier legislation.[148] He has the responsibility to exercise vigilance over these very important functions. Accordingly, the rector of a church is not permitted to perform the functions listed in canon 530, 1°–6° in the church entrusted to him unless the pastor consents or, as the matter warrants, delegates him (c. 558).[149] Moreover, canon 566, §1 gives to chaplains, for those entrusted to their care, ordinary power to perform two functions similar to those especially entrusted to a pastor: to administer Viaticum and anointing of the sick, and to confirm those who are in danger of death.

Other canons also empower the pastor to perform certain functions: to hear confessions (c. 968, §1), to dispense from some marriage impediments in danger of death (c. 1079, §2) or when everything is prepared for the wedding (c. 1080, §1), to dispense from private vows (c. 1196, 1°) or to commute them (c. 1197), to suspend, dispense, or commute a promissory oath (c. 1203), and to dispense or commute the obligation of holy days and days of penance (c. 1245).

"Stole Fees"[150]

Canon 531 — Although another person has performed a certain parochial function, that person is to put the offerings received from the Christian faithful on that occasion in the parochial account, unless in the case of voluntary offerings the contrary intention of the donor is certain. The diocesan bishop, after having heard the presbyteral council, is competent to establish prescripts which provide for the allocation of these offerings

and the remuneration of clerics fulfilling the same function.

Canon 1264, 2° expects the bishops of each province to specify the amount of the offerings on the occasion of the administration of the sacraments and sacramentals. Canon 1267, §1 says that offerings given to any superior or administrator of a juridic person are presumed to be given to the juridic person itself, unless the contrary is established.[151] Thus, when a pastor performs certain parochial functions (including those which are said to be especially entrusted to him), any "stole fees" given on the occasion are presumably given to the parish, unless it is clear that the voluntary offering is given him personally.

Canon 531 concerns the occasion when a cleric other than the pastor performs a certain parochial function. It requires that offerings received by him are to be put into the parochial account, unless in the case of voluntary offerings the donor's contrary intention is clear. The diocesan bishop, after he has heard the presbyteral council, is competent to establish prescripts for the allocation of these offerings and for the remuneration of the clerics who fulfill these functions.

Canon 551 legislates that the prescripts of canon 531 are to be observed regarding offerings which the faithful give to a parochial vicar when he performs a pastoral ministry.

These norms evidently apply whether or not the parochial functions are performed in the parish church.

Inasmuch as the pastor, parochial vicar, and the other clerics performing parochial functions are to place the aforementioned offerings into the parish account, they evidently are not expected to find a source of livelihood in these "stole fees." Canon 281 treats the remuneration of all clerics, which certainly includes pastors and parochial vicars. Since they devote themselves to sacred ministry, clerics deserve remuneration consistent with their

---

[147] *Comm* 13 (1981) 281; 14 (1982) 225.
[148] J. Provost and R. Hill, "Stole Fees," in *CLSA Advisory Opinions, 1984–1993*, 139–142.
[149] See also c. 1219.
[150] Cf. *CCEO* 291.

[151] Canon 1267, §2 adds that these offerings cannot be refused except for a just cause and, in matters of greater importance, without the permission of the ordinary.

condition, taking into account their roles and circumstances of places and times. The remuneration should provide for their own necessities and for the equitable payment of those whose services they need. Provisions must also be made for social assistance which provides for their needs if such clerics suffer illness, incapacity, or old age.

Presbyterorum ordinis 20 had called for the provision of just remuneration for all priests, an obligation which binds all the faithful and about which the bishop is to remind them. The remuneration of the priests should be fundamentally the same for all living in the same circumstances. It should reflect their status and enable them to give a salary to those who work for them and to assist the needy. It should also allow the priest an annual holiday. The decree says further:

> It is, however, to the office that sacred ministers fulfill that the greatest importance must be attached. For this reason the so-called system of benefices is to be abandoned or else reformed in such a way that the part that has to do with the benefice—that is, the right to the revenues attached to the endowment of the office—shall be regarded as secondary and the principal emphasis in law given to the ecclesiastical office itself. This should in the future be understood as any office conferred in a permanent fashion and to be exercised for a spiritual purpose.[152]

Presbyterorum ordinis 21 calls for the establishment of common funds to provide for the social security of priests and the health care of priests.[153]

Canon 531 deals with offerings given on the occasion of the administration of parochial functions. It does *not* deal with Mass offerings. Any priest celebrating or concelebrating a Mass is permitted to receive an offering to apply the Mass for a specific intention (c. 945, §1); he has the right to keep one such offering per day, except on Christmas when he may retain three Mass offerings (c. 951, §1).[154]

Canon 463, §3 of the 1917 code entitled the pastor to receive and retain stole fees. If another performed any parochial functions, the offerings still belonged to the pastor, unless it was clear that the donor wished the other priest to retain the sum exceeding the ordinary tax. The pastor, however, was exhorted not to refuse gratuitous ministry to needy persons.[155] Canon 531 shows a significant shift from the former law inasmuch as stole fees given to pastors (and all other clerics) belong to the parish, not the pastor.

Juridic Representation of the Parish and Administration of Parochial Goods[156]

Canon 532 — In all juridic affairs the pastor represents the parish according to the norm of law. He is to take care that the goods of the parish are administered according to the norm of cann. 1281–1288.

The pastor represents the parish in all juridic affairs, according to the norm of the law. He is to take care that parochial goods are administered according to the norm of canons 1281–1288. If the

---

[152] *ES* I, 8 says that the ComCICRec is to reform the system of benefices. "In the meantime bishops, having heard the views of the councils of priests, are to see that revenues are equitably distributed, even those revenues deriving from benefices." In areas where revenues for the clergy derive entirely or in great part from the offerings of the faithful, a special agency should be established in each diocese to collect these offerings. See also *PO* 21 and c. 1274.

[153] See c. 1274.

[154] Mass offerings are treated in cc. 945–958; see *CIC* 824–844, where the offerings are also called "stipends."

[155] Canon 848 states: "The minister is to seek nothing for the administration of the sacraments beyond the offerings defined by competent authority, always taking care that the needy are not deprived of the assistance of the sacraments because of poverty."

[156] Cf. *CCEO* 290, §1. While the Eastern code omits saying that the pastor must take care that the goods of the parish are administered according to canons parallel to cc. 1281–1288 (*CCEO* 1024–1026, 1028–1032), this is clearly expected of him.

pastoral care of a parish or parishes is entrusted to several priests *in solidum,* only the moderator represents the parish(es) in juridic affairs (c. 543, §2, 3°) and is responsible for the administration of parochial goods.[157]

Canon 537 requires the establishment of a finance council in every parish. Its role is to assist the pastor in the administration of parochial goods.[158] Diocesan norms may further specify its role. The very existence of the parish finance council makes it clear that the pastor is not expected to administer the goods of the parish in isolation.[159]

Canon 118 says that those representing a public juridic person and acting in its name are those whose competence is acknowledged by universal or particular law or by its own statutes. The parish is a juridic person by law (c. 515, §3). Canon 532 is universal law identifying the pastor as the legal representative of the parish. It applies canon 1279, §1, which states that the person who directs a juridic person is the administrator of its ecclesiastical goods. The pastor is the administrator of the goods of the parish, as administration is understood in canons 1281–1288. The role of the finance council is to assist the pastor in his role as administrator of parochial goods; the finance council cannot be conceived of as an administrative body, since administration is the pastor's competence.[160] Any particular legislation on the parish finance council must be careful not to compromise the canonical function of the pastor as administrator of parochial goods.

Any civil determinations about the parish and its goods must reflect these canons. The pastor alone is to represent the parish. He alone is to see to it that parochial goods are appropriately administered, according to the norms of canon law (es-

pecially cc. 1281–1288) and civil law. In addition, diocesan particular law may address the civil involvement of a pastor on behalf of the parish.

Residence of the Pastor[161]

Canon 533 — §1. A pastor is obliged to reside in a rectory near the church. Nevertheless, in particular cases and if there is a just cause, the local ordinary can permit him to reside elsewhere, especially in a house shared by several presbyters, provided that the performance of parochial functions is properly and suitably provided for.

As a general rule, a pastor is obliged to reside in the rectory[162] near the church.[163] In particular cases and for a just cause, the local ordinary can permit the pastor to reside somewhere else, especially in a house shared by several presbyters; in this situation, provision is to be made that parochial functions are performed properly and suitably. In related legislation, canon 550, §1 says the parochial vicar is obliged to reside in the parish (the canon does not call specifically for residence in the rectory) or, if he is assigned to several parishes, in one of them. For a just cause the local ordinary can permit the parochial vicar to reside elsewhere, especially in a house shared by several presbyters, provided this is not detrimental to his pastoral functions. Furthermore, canon 550, §2 requires the local ordinary to take care that some manner of common life in the rectory is fostered between the pastor and parochial vicars where this can be done.[164]

---

[157] Canon 555, §1, 3° says the vicar forane has the duty and right to see that ecclesiastical goods are administered carefully.

[158] Canon 1276 says the ordinary is to oversee the administration of ecclesiastical goods. Canon 1280 requires every juridic person to have a finance council or at least two counselors to assist its administrator.

[159] Périsset, 146.

[160] Coccopalmerio, 205–206.

[161] Cf. *CCEO* 292, §1.

[162] The canon presumes that the rectory (literally, the "parish house," *domus parochialis*) is near the parish church. The vicar forane has the duty and right to see that the rectory is cared for with proper diligence (c. 555, §1, 3°).

[163] See A. Longhitano, "L'obbligo della residenza del parroco e la reggenza della parrocchia durante la sua assenza," in *La parrocchia,* 155–174.

[164] *CIC* 476, §5 said the vicar cooperator was obliged to reside in the parish according to diocesan statutes, laudable customs, or episcopal prescripts, and therefore the ordinary was to take care prudently that he lived in the parochial house.

Christus Dominus 30 (1) said that for the better ordering of the care of souls, priests are strongly recommended to live in common, especially when they are attached to the same parish: "This on the one hand is helpful to their apostolate work, and on the other gives to the faithful an example of charity and unity."[165]

Canon 533, §1 applies to pastors the general norm for clerics contained in canon 280, which highly recommends some practice of common life to clerics, and asks that common living be preserved as far as possible in places where it already exists.[166]

Canon 465, §1 of the 1917 code had required the pastor to live in a rectory near the parochial church, but the local ordinary could permit him to live elsewhere, provided the house was not so distant from the church that his parochial functions would suffer any detriment. This legislation is basically repeated in the current law.

Vacation and Absence of the Pastor[167]

§2. Unless there is a grave reason to the contrary, a pastor is permitted to be absent from the parish each year for vacation for at most one continuous or interrupted month; those days which the pastor spends once a year in spiritual retreat are not computed in the time of vacation. In order to be absent from the parish for more than a week, however, a pastor is bound to inform the local ordinary.

§3. It is for the diocesan bishop to establish norms which see to it that during the absence of the pastor, a priest endowed with the necessary faculties provides for the care of the parish.

Unless there is a grave contrary reason, a pastor is permitted to be absent from the parish for vacation each year for a period of one month, continuous or interrupted. His time for annual spiritual retreat is not computed as part of his vacation period. Canon 550, §3 gives the parochial vicar the same right as a pastor concerning vacation—i.e., the period of one month, continuous or interrupted, unless there is a grave reason to the contrary.

Canon 283, §2 entitles all clerics to a fitting and sufficient time of annual vacation, to be determined by universal or particular law. *Presbyterorum ordinis* 20 had said that priests' remuneration should be sufficient to provide an annual vacation. Canons 533, §2 and 550, §3 are universal law applications for pastors and parochial vicars of the more general norm of canon 283, §2 for all clerics.

The pastor is to have time for an annual retreat; the days at retreat are not to be counted among the days available for vacation. Canon 276, §2, 4° obliges all clergy to make time for spiritual retreats, according to the norms of particular law. Canon 533, §2 applies the more general norm to the pastor: it expects that his spiritual retreat will be *annual,* and its days do not detract from his vacation time. The code provides no similar norm on an annual retreat or its relation to vacation days for parochial vicars.

If the pastor is to be absent from the parish for more than a week, he is to inform the local ordinary. The diocesan bishop is to establish norms which see to it that a priest endowed with the necessary faculties provides for the pastoral care of the parish while the pastor is absent.[168] The same norms may consider who substitutes for an absent moderator of a group of priests entrusted *in solidum* with the pastoral care of a parish or parishes.[169] The absence may be expected (e.g., a vacation) or unexpected.

---

[165] See also *PO* 8, which recommends that priests foster community life or social relations with each other.

[166] See *CIC* 134.

[167] Cf. *CCEO* 292, §§2–3.

[168] The 1917 code had not required such norms. If the pastor's absence will be more lengthy, cc. 539; 541, §1; and 549 would apply. Among the faculties to be given to the priest who substitutes for the pastor is that of assisting at marriages (c. 1111).

[169] The norms may identify the substitute as the priest of the group who is senior by appointment (see c. 544) or, if they were appointed together, senior by ordination.

Canon 465, §§2–6 of the 1917 code was legislation about the pastor's vacation. It gave him *two* months of vacation each year, continuous or interrupted, not including the days for annual retreat. When the pastor was absent for more than a week, he required a legitimate cause (which could include vacation), the written permission of the ordinary, and a substitute approved by the same ordinary. If the pastor were a religious, he would also need the consent of his superior and a substitute approved by both the ordinary and the superior. If the pastor had to leave the parish suddenly for a grave reason and had to be gone for longer than a week, the pastor had to inform the ordinary in writing as soon as possible, explain the reason for his absence, and obey the bishop's mandates. Finally, if any pastor were gone for less than a week, he must also provide for the needs of the faithful, especially in particular circumstances. The 1917 code did not regulate the vacation of the parochial vicar.

Mass for the People[170]

Canon 534 — §1. After a pastor has taken possession of his parish, he is obliged to apply a Mass for the people entrusted to him on each Sunday and holy day of obligation in his diocese. If he is legitimately impeded from this celebration, however, he is to apply it on the same days through another or on other days himself.

§2. A pastor who has the care of several parishes is bound to apply only one Mass for the entire people entrusted to him on the days mentioned in §1.

§3. A pastor who has not satisfied the obligation mentioned in §§1 and 2 is to apply as soon as possible as many Masses for the people as he has omitted.

Once he has taken possession of the parish (see canon 527), the pastor is obliged to apply a Mass

---

[170] Cf. *CCEO* 294. The Eastern code simply says the pastor is frequently to celebrate the Divine Liturgy for the people, and is bound to do so on the days prescribed by the particular law of his autonomous church.

for the people entrusted to him on each Sunday and holy day of obligation observed in his diocese.[171] If he has care of several parishes, he is bound to apply one Mass for the entire people entrusted to his care.

If the pastor is legitimately impeded from this celebration, he is to apply the Mass either on the same day through another priest, or on another day himself. If he has not satisfied these obligations, he is to apply as soon as possible as many Masses for the people as he has omitted.

Canon 540, §1 says the parochial administrator is bound by the same duties and possesses the same rights as a pastor, unless the diocesan bishop states otherwise. This means that the parochial administrator has the obligation of the Mass for the people. If for some reason a parish has both a pastor and a parochial administrator (see c. 539), either the diocesan bishop or the pastor and parochial administrator among themselves must determine which of the two will fulfill this obligation. Presumably, in such a situation the obligation remains with the pastor, unless other provision is made.

When a parish or parishes are entrusted to priests *in solidum* (c. 517, §1), the priests together are obliged to see to the offering of a Mass for the people according to an agreement established by common counsel (c. 543, §2, 2°). If more than one parish is entrusted to them, one Mass for the people suffices for all the parishes.

When a parish becomes vacant or the pastor becomes impeded and before a parochial administrator is appointed, the parochial vicar (or, if there

---

[171] J. Provost considers the opinion of several canonists regarding the Mass for the people, and concludes that: (1) one may not accept a stipend for the Mass for the people; (2) while celebrating the Mass for the people, one may not apply it for another intention for which a stipend was received; and (3) one may accept a stipend for a second Mass on the day when one offered a Mass for the people, since the latter arises from pastoral responsibility rather than from an obligation in justice (*ex titulo iustitiae*) due to the income of a benefice. "Retention of Stipend for a Second Mass and Mass for the People," in *RRAO 1994*, 110–111.

are several, the parochial vicar senior in appointment) assumes governance of the parish (c. 541, §1). Furthermore, unless the diocesan bishop has provided otherwise (c. 533, §3) and unless a parochial administrator is appointed, whenever a pastor is absent, the norms of canon 541, §1 apply: the parochial vicar has all the obligations of the pastor except that of applying the Mass for the people (c. 549).[172]

Canon 534 is similar to canon 388 which requires the diocesan bishop to offer a Mass for the people entrusted to his care. It also reflects closely the former code in canons 466 (for the pastor) and 339 (for the bishop of the diocese). That code, however, required the diocesan bishop or pastor to offer the Mass for the people on several more days each year, even if the days had been suppressed in the locale. Further, the pastor was expected to celebrate the Mass in the parish church, unless there existed circumstances warranting its celebration elsewhere, and he needed the permission of the local ordinary to celebrate on a day other than the appropriate one. The current legislation makes no reference to the place where the Mass for the people must be celebrated, and the pastor needs no special permission to offer it on some other day (a legitimate cause, as determined by the pastor himself, suffices).

Parochial Registers, Seal, and Archive[173]

Canon 535 — §1. Each parish is to have parochial registers, that is, those of baptisms, marriages, deaths, and others as prescribed by the conference of bishops or the diocesan bishop. The pastor is to see to it that these registers are accurately inscribed and carefully preserved.

§2. In the baptismal register are also to be noted confirmation and those things which pertain to the canonical status of the Christian faithful by reason of marriage, without prejudice to the prescript of can. 1133, of adoption, of the re-ception of sacred orders, of perpetual profession made in a religious institute, and of change of rite. These notations are always to be noted on a baptismal certificate.

§3. Each parish is to have its own seal. Documents regarding the canonical status of the Christian faithful and all acts which can have juridic importance are to be signed by the pastor or his delegate and sealed with the parochial seal.

§4. In each parish there is to be a storage area, or archive, in which the parochial registers are protected along with letters of bishops and other documents which are to be preserved for reason of necessity or advantage. The pastor is to take care that all of these things, which are to be inspected by the diocesan bishop or his delegate at the time of visitation or at some other opportune time, do not come into the hands of outsiders.

§5. Older parochial registers are also to be carefully protected according to the prescripts of particular law.

Each parish is to have parochial registers,[174] and the pastor is to see that they are accurately inscribed and carefully preserved. The specific registers envisioned are for baptisms (cc. 877–878), marriages (c. 1121), deaths (c. 1182), and other events as prescribed either by the conference of bishops or the diocesan bishop. Examples of registers which may be required by particular law are the confirmation register (c. 895), the first communion register, and the register for the reception of baptized non-Catholics into full communion.[175] The pastor has the obligation to see that the parochial registers are accurately inscribed and carefully preserved. The vicar forane is to see that they are inscribed correctly and protected appropriately (c. 555, §1, 3°); when a pastor is ill or

---

[172] Canon 548, §2 says clearly that the parochial vicar is normally not obliged to offer the Mass for the people.

[173] Cf. CCEO 296.

[174] See C. Cox and J. Koury, "Regulations Concerning the Format of Sacramental Registers," in CLSA Advisory Opinions, 1984–1993, 144–147.

[175] Particular law may mandate a register of parish history. Coccopalmerio (211) says particular law may require the confirmation register and the parish census book, each of which was called for by CIC 470, §1.

dies, the vicar forane must make provision that the parochial registers and documents (as well as sacred furnishings and everything else belonging to the parish) are not lost or removed (c. 555, §3).

Special consideration is given to the baptismal register. It is to contain not only data concerning a person's baptism but also data about confirmation (c. 895), marriage (cc. 1122–1123, 1685, 1706), adoption (c. 877, §3), reception of sacred orders (c. 1054), perpetual religious profession, and change of rite. All these annotations are always to be noted on a baptismal certificate.

Other canons mention other books to be maintained by each parish. Canon 788, §1 mentions the book inscribing the names of catechumens. Canon 958 calls for a parochial book recording Mass offerings and obligations; canon 1307, §2 calls for an additional book to record the offerings and obligations of pious foundations. The pastor, as administrator of the juridic person which is the parish, must also keep well organized books of parochial receipts and expenditures (c. 1284, §2, 7°).

Every parish is also to have its own seal which, with the signature of the pastor or his delegate, is to be placed on documents regarding the canonical status of the Christian faithful and on all acts which have juridic importance.

Each parish is to have its own archive (or storage area) which protects letters of bishops and other documents to be preserved that are necessary or useful. The pastor is to make sure that the contents of the archives do not come into the hands of outsiders. The diocesan bishop or his delegate is to inspect the archive at the time of the visitation (see cc. 396–398).[176] The archive would certainly contain the aforementioned parish books and the prenuptial investigation files (see c. 1067).

---

[176] Canon 555, §4 requires the vicar forane to visit the parishes of his vicariate according to the determination of the diocesan bishop. He may be the person appropriately designated by the diocesan bishop to inspect the parish registers and the other contents of each parish archive.

Particular law is to establish prescripts concerning the careful protection of older parochial records. These reflect the lived faith of past generations in the locale.

Canon 470 of the 1917 code had mentioned a parish census book among the parochial registers, but made no reference to other books being required by the conference of bishops or the diocesan bishop. It had also required an authentic copy of all parish records (except the census book) to be sent annually to the diocesan curia, a requirement absent from the current law. Finally, it made no reference to the careful protection of older parochial registers.

Parish Pastoral Council[177]

Canon 536 — §1. If the diocesan bishop judges it opportune after he has heard the presbyteral council, a pastoral council is to be established in each parish, over which the pastor presides and in which the Christian faithful, together with those who share in pastoral care by virtue of their office in the parish, assist in fostering pastoral activity.

§2. A pastoral council possesses a consultative vote only and is governed by the norms established by the diocesan bishop.

The 1917 code did not mention a parish pastoral council. The current universal law does not require its establishment, but allows the diocesan bishop to require it in all the parishes of his diocese after he has heard the presbyteral council. The universal law does, however, identify some of the characteristics to be found in pastoral councils, if they are established in parishes (whether by mandate of the diocesan bishop or not). The pastor presides over the pastoral council, which is composed of the Christian faithful and those who share pastoral care by virtue of their office in the

---

[177] CCEO 295 says that particular law of each autonomous church is to establish norms for parish councils dealing with pastoral matters. See cc. 511–514 for legislation on the *diocesan* pastoral council (CCEO 272–275).

parish.[178] The council assists the pastor in fostering pastoral activity, possesses a consultative vote only, and is governed by norms established by the diocesan bishop.[179]

The origin of legislation on parish pastoral councils is the same as that on diocesan pastoral councils.[180] *Christus Dominus* 27 said that it is highly desirable to establish a diocesan pastoral council composed of clergy, religious, and laity; its function is to investigate and consider matters relating to pastoral activity and to formulate practical conclusions."[181] A number of postconciliar documents further elaborated the role of the diocesan pastoral council.[182] The Sacred Congregation for the Clergy issued a circular letter on pastoral councils on January 25, 1973, which stated that nothing prevents "the institution within the diocese of councils of the same nature and function [as diocesan pastoral councils], whether parochial or regional."[183] On May 31, 1973, the Sacred Congregation for Bishops issued its *Directory* for bishops which invited the establishment of parish pastoral councils to be aligned with the diocesan pastoral council.[184]

The vision developed in these conciliar and postconciliar sources is reflected in canons 511–514 on the diocesan pastoral council and in canon 536 on the parish pastoral council. The vision leads to the insight that *pastoral councils exist to do pastoral planning.* They investigate pastoral works, consider (study) them, and propose practical conclusions about them: this is pastoral planning. Pastoral councils perform their planning function in an advisory or consultative way.

The 1997 *Instruction on Certain Questions Regarding the Collaboration of the Non-Ordained Faithful in the Sacred Ministry of Priests* lists the parish pastoral council and the parish finance council among the structures for collaboration in the particular church "so necessary to that ecclesial renewal called for by the Second Vatican Council [which] have produced many positive results and have been codified in canonical legislation. They represent a form of active participation in the life and mission of the Church as communion."[185] The *Instruction* underscores that the parish pastoral and finance councils "enjoy a consultative vote only and cannot in any way become deliberative structures."[186] The *Instruction* clarifies the central role of the pastor who receives advice from the pastoral council:

> It is for the parish priest to preside at parochial councils. They are to be considered invalid, and hence null and void, any deliberations entered into (or decisions taken) by a parochial council which has not been presided over by the parish priest or which has assembled contrary to his wishes.[187]

---

[178] Paul VI, *SDO,* June 18, 1967, n. 24, *AAS* 59 (1967) 697–704 at 702, says: "If it can be done, deacons are to have a role in pastoral councils." [Author's translation.] No. 24 is missing from the document as it appears in *CLD* 6, 582.

[179] See P. Marcuzzi, "Il consiglio pastorale parrocchiale," in PCILT, *Ius in Vita et in Missione Ecclesiae* (Vatican City: Libreria Editrice Vaticana, 1994) 437–463.

[180] A detailed history of the development of pastoral councils in ecclesial life (and in the 1983 code) is found in J. Renken, "Pastoral Councils: Pastoral Planning and Dialogue Among the People of God," *J* 53 (1993) 132–154.

[181] Later, *AG* 30 and *PO* 7, n. 41, also refer to the diocesan pastoral council, citing *CD* 27.

[182] *ES* 1, 16, 17; Second Synod of Bishops, *Ultimis temporibus,* November 30, 1971, II, 3, *CLD* 7, 364; SCC, littcirc *Omnes Christifideles,* January 25, 1973, *CLD* 8, 283; *Directory* 204.

[183] *CLD* 8, 287–288.

[184] *AA* 26 mentions diocesan and parish councils with another purpose: "to assist in apostolic work,... [to] take care of the mutual coordinating of the various lay associations and undertakings, the autonomy and particular nature of each remaining untouched." These may be un-

derstood as "coordinating councils of apostolic works" (or a similar term). They are not pastoral councils which advise on pastoral planning, a conclusion reached by a careful study of postconciliar documents and the history of the development of canons 511–514 and 536 in *Comm.* See Renken, "Pastoral Councils," 147–149; Marcuzzi, 438–441.

[185] *Instruction,* p. 21, article 5.

[186] *Instruction,* p. 21, article 5, §2.

[187] *Instruction,* p. 21, article 5, §3.

The *Instruction* also mentions that ordinaries may avail themselves of special study groups of experts to examine particular questions, but that these may not be constituted as structures parallel to the parish pastoral council or the parish finance council. "Neither may such a group deprive these structures of their lawful authority. Where structures of this kind have arisen in the past because of local custom or through special circumstances, those measures deemed necessary to conform such structures to the current universal law of the Church must be taken."[188]

Canon 536 says that, after he has heard the presbyteral council, the diocesan bishop may mandate the establishment of a pastoral council in every parish. If he does not issue such a mandate, the council is not required. Nonetheless, it still may be established in individual parishes at the discretion of the pastor.[189]

Parish Finance Council[190]

Canon 537 — In each parish there is to be a finance council which is governed, in addition to universal law, by norms issued by the diocesan bishop and in which the Christian faithful, selected according to these same norms, are to assist the pastor in the administration of the goods of the parish, without prejudice to the prescript of can. 532.

The universal law requires the establishment of a finance council in every parish. The parish finance council is governed by universal law (which contains very few norms about it) and also by norms which the diocesan bishop issues. It is composed of members of the Christian faithful who are selected according to these diocesan norms. Its purpose is to assist the pastor in the administration of parochial goods.[191] Nonetheless, in all juridic affairs the pastor represents the parish and is to take care that parochial goods are administered according to the norm of canons 1281–1288 (see c. 532). Canon 537 applies to the parish the more general norm of canon 1280 which legislates that each juridic person is to have its own finance council or at least two counselors who assist the administrator of the juridic person.

In 1997 the Holy See issued the *Instruction on Certain Questions Regarding the Collaboration of the Non-Ordained Faithful in the Sacred Ministry of Priests* which identifies the parish finance council as a collaborative structure necessary for conciliar renewal, consultative in nature, requiring the presence of the pastor for the validity of its proceedings, and not to be confused with parallel structures with a different origin or purpose.[192]

The 1917 code did not specifically mention a parish finance council.[193] *Presbyterorum ordinis* 17 said that priests are to manage ecclesiastical property according to ecclesiastical laws and with the help, as far as possible, of skilled lay persons.

Canons 536 and 537 illustrate that each parish *may* have two parish councils: a parish *pastoral*

---

[188] *Instruction,* p. 22, article 5, §5.

[189] Diocesan norms requiring the establishment of *parish pastoral councils* may include provisions for the dissolution of a council which does not perform its function appropriately. Canon 501, §3 permits the dissolution of a presbyteral council which does not fulfill its function or abuses it. The diocesan bishop may dissolve it after he has consulted the metropolitan, and must reestablish it within a year. Similarly diocesan norms on the *parish finance council* may provide for the possibility of dissolving it, with the requirement of reestablishing it within a very short time (c. 537). See J. Cuneo, "Pastor's Right to Dissolve the Parish Council," in *CLSA Advisory Opinions, 1984–1993,* 150–152.

[190] *CCEO* 295 says that the particular law of each autonomous church is to establish norms for parish councils dealing with financial matters. See cc. 492–493 for legislation on the *diocesan* finance council (*CCEO* 263).

[191] *Mutatis mutandis,* diocesan norms on the parish finance council may reflect norms on the diocesan finance council, found in universal law (cc. 492–493) and particular law.

[192] *Instruction,* pp. 21–22, article 5, §§2–3, 5. For a more extensive treatment of the *Instruction*'s teachings, see the commentary on c. 536.

[193] But see *CIC* 1183–1184; 1520, §§1–2; 1521, §1; 1525, §1.

council (obligatory only if the diocesan bishop so judges) and a parish *finance* council (obligatory in all parishes by the universal law). The former assists in pastoral planning, and the latter in the administration of parochial goods. Their roles are distinct, and each must be careful to retain its proper focus should they collaborate with one another.

Cessation of Office of Pastor[194]

Canon 538 — §1. A pastor ceases from office by removal or transfer carried out by the diocesan bishop according to the norm of law, by resignation made by the pastor himself for a just cause and accepted by the same bishop for validity, and by lapse of time if he had been appointed for a definite period according to the prescripts of particular law mentioned in can. 522.

§2. A pastor who is a member of a religious institute or is incardinated in a society of apostolic life is removed according to the norm of can. 682, §2.

§3. When a pastor has completed seventy-five years of age, he is requested to submit his resignation from office to the diocesan bishop who is to decide to accept or defer it after he has considered all the circumstances of the person and place. Attentive to the norms established by the conference of bishops, the diocesan bishop must provide suitable support and housing for a retired pastor.

If a pastor is a religious or is incardinated in a society of apostolic life, he is removed from office at the discretion either of the diocesan bishop or his competent superior (c. 682, §2). While the diocesan bishop provides the office of pastor (c. 523), both he and the competent superior may terminate the appointment of a pastor who is a member of a religious institute or a society of apostolic life.[195]

---

[194] Cf. *CCEO* 297.

[195] See *CIC* 455, §5. This canon added that if one or the other opposed the removal of the religious pastor, recourse could be made *in devolutivo,* i.e., without suspensive effect.

In other cases, pastors end their function in the four ways identified in canon 538, §1: (1) removal, (2) transfer, (3) resignation, and (4) lapse of time, if they were appointed for a definite period.

1. Removal[196]

A pastor, whether appointed for an indefinite or specific period, may be removed from office by the diocesan bishop (cc. 192; 193, §§1–2), who is bound to observe the norms on removal contained in canons 1740–1747.[197] Removal requires a grave cause (c. 193, §1), among which canon 1741 identifies especially the following:[198]

(1) a manner of acting by the pastor which brings grave detriment or disturbance to ecclesiastical communion;

(2) ineptitude or a permanent infirmity of mind or body which renders the pastor unable to fulfill his functions usefully;

(3) loss of a good reputation among upright and responsible parishioners or an aversion to the pastor which it appears will not cease in a brief time;

(4) grave neglect or violation of parochial duties which persists after a warning;

(5) poor administration of temporal affairs with grave damage to the Church whenever another remedy to this harm cannot be found.

In addition, the pastor (like any holder of an ecclesiastical office) is removed from office by the law itself if he (1) loses the clerical state, (2) publicly defects from the Catholic faith or from the communion of the Church, or (3) attempts

---

[196] A detailed analysis of the process of removing or transferring a pastor is beyond the immediate scope of this commentary, and is given elsewhere. See the detailed and scholarly article by Z. Grocholewski, "Trasferimento e rimozione del parroco," in *La parrocchia,* 199–247.

[197] See *CIC* 2147–2156 on removing irremovable pastors, and 2157–2161 on removing removable pastors.

[198] This listing is illustrative only; the diocesan bishop may identify other reasons for removal.

marriage, even if only civilly (c. 194, §1). Deprivation of the office can also be an expiatory penalty (c. 1336, §1, 2°).

One notes that age is not listed as a reason to remove a pastor from office, notwithstanding the norm of canon 538, §3 encouraging him to retire at seventy five.

The removal must be communicated in writing to take effect (c. 193, §4), and the diocesan bishop must provide suitable support for the removed pastor (cc. 195; 1746; 1747, §2).

2. Transfer

A pastor may be transferred by the diocesan bishop (c. 190, §1). If the pastor is unwilling, a grave cause is required and the diocesan bishop must observe the norms on transfer (cc. 1748–1752).[199] The transfer must be communicated in writing to take effect (c. 190, §3).

3. Resignation

Canons 187–189 on resignation in general from ecclesiastical offices apply to the resignation of a pastor. Resignation requires a just cause (c. 187; see c. 189, §2). It is invalid if made out of grave fear unjustly inflicted, malice, substantial error, or simony (c. 188). The resignation must be presented to the diocesan bishop (i.e., the authority who provides the office) in writing or orally before two witnesses (c. 189, §1). Since the resignation requires the diocesan bishop's acceptance, if it is not accepted within three months of its presentation, it lacks all force (c. 189, §3). Until the resignation has been accepted by the diocesan bishop, the pastor is able to revoke it (c. 189, §4).

A pastor may offer his resignation to the diocesan bishop for a just cause; the resignation must be accepted by the diocesan bishop for its validity. A pastor is requested to submit his resignation when he has reached the age of seventy-five; after he has considered all the circumstances of the person and the place, the diocesan bishop is to decide to accept the resignation or to defer it. If he

accepts the resignation, the diocesan bishop is to provide suitable support and housing for the retired pastor in light of norms established by the conference of bishops.

The 1917 code had not contained a norm inviting the resignation of pastors. *Christus Dominus* 31, however, had stated:

> Parish priests who on account of advanced years or for some other grave reason are unable to perform their duties adequately and fruitfully are earnestly requested to tender their resignation spontaneously, or when the bishop invites them to do so. The bishop will make suitable provision for the support of those who retire.

The conciliar decree did not mention a specific age for retirement, but *Ecclesiae sanctae* 20 (3) called for retirement at age seventy-five:

> In the execution of prescription number 31 of the Decree *Christus Dominus* all parish priests are requested voluntarily to submit their resignation to their own bishop not later than the completion of their seventy-fifth year. The bishop having considered all the circumstances of place and person shall decide whether to accept, or defer acceptance of, the resignation. The bishop shall make appropriate provision for the living and residence of those who resign.[200]

At its November, 1987 meeting, the NCCB decreed that diocesan bishops are to establish a diocesan policy for the retirement of priests:

> In accord with the prescriptions of canon 538, §3, the National Conference of Catholic Bishops authorizes diocesan bishops to

---

[199] See c. 191; *CIC* 2162–2167.

[200] Pope Paul VI restated this invitation to pastors (and bishops) to resign voluntarily no later than their seventy-fifth birthday in his *mp* on the retirement of cardinals, *Ingravescentem aetatem,* November 21, 1970, *AAS* 62 (1970) 810–813; *CLD* 7, 143–145.

develop diocesan policy for the requirement of priests in accord with the provisions of *Norms for Priests and Their Third Age.*[201]

This decree was reviewed by the Congregation for the Clergy, whose approval was communicated through a letter from the apostolic pro-nuncio on January 19, 1988 (Prot. No. 5465/87/4). The *Norms for Priests and Their Third Age*[202] was promulgated on February 23, 1988. These norms reiterate the universal norm that "pastors are asked to submit their letters of resignation by the age of seventy-five" but adds that the diocesan bishop, "in consultation with the presbyteral council, can adopt a diocesan policy which allows priests, for pastoral or personal reasons, to retire from diocesan assignment at an earlier age."[203]

In the 1997 *Instruction on Certain Questions Regarding the Collaboration of the Non-Ordained Faithful in the Sacred Ministry of Priests,* the Holy See discusses the cessation of the office of pastor and, specifically, the resignation of a pastor at age seventy-five:

> It must be noted that the parish priest [*parochus*] is the proper pastor [*pastor*] of the parish entrusted to him and remains such until his pastoral office shall have ceased.
>
> The presentation of resignation at the age of 75 by a parish priest does not of itself [*ipso iure*] terminate his pastoral office. Such takes effect only when the diocesan bishop, following the prudent consideration of all the circumstances, shall have definitively accepted his resignation in accordance with Canon 538, §3 and communicated such to him in writing. In the light of those situations where scarcity of priests exists, the use of special prudence in this matter would be judicious.

In view of the right of every cleric to exercise the ministry proper to him, and in the absence of any grave health or disciplinary reasons, it should be noted that having reached the age of 75 does not constitute a binding reason for the diocesan bishop to accept a parish priest's resignation. This also serves to avoid a functional concept of the Sacred Ministry.[204]

4. Lapse of Time

A pastor ceases exercising his office by the lapse of time if he has been appointed for a definite period according to particular law (see c. 522). In the United States the diocesan bishop may appoint a pastor for a specific term of six years, continually renewable. In such a situation the pastor loses his office only from the moment when, after the specific period has passed, the competent authority communicates this in writing to him (c. 186).

Before his term is completed, a grave cause is required to transfer an unwilling pastor (c. 190, §2) or to remove him (c. 193, §2), and the norms on transfer and removal become operative.

Parochial Administrator: Appointment and Notion[205]

Canon 539 — When a parish becomes vacant or when a pastor is prevented from exercising his pastoral function in the parish by reason of captivity, exile or banishment, incapacity or ill health, or some other cause, the diocesan bishop is to designate as soon as possible a parochial administrator, that is, a priest who takes the place of the pastor according to the norm of can. 540.

A parish is *vacant* when its pastor has died or ceased functioning for one of the reasons identified in canon 538. A pastor is *impeded* who,

---

[201] NCCB-*CompNm,* 6. For a more in-depth commentary, see J. Hesch, "The 1987 NCCB Norms for Priests and Their Third Age," *J* 54 (1994) 387–408.

[202] See NCCB-*CompNm,* 50–52.

[203] Ibid., 50. See also cc. 281, §2; 1274.

[204] *Instruction,* 20, art. 4, §2. See CFC, *Directory for the Life and Ministry of Priests* (Vatican City: Libreria Editrice Vaticana, 1994) n. 44.

[205] Cf. *CCEO* 298.

though he remains in office, is prevented from exercising his pastoral function by reason of captivity, exile or banishment, incapacity or ill health, or some other cause. When a parish is vacant or impeded, the diocesan bishop must designate as soon as possible a parochial administrator (that is, a priest who takes the place of a pastor according to the norm of c. 540).

Canon 472, 1° of the 1917 code said that when the parish was vacant, the local ordinary was to appoint as soon as possible an economic or administrative vicar (*vicarius oeconomus*); if a religious priest were to be appointed, his religious superior had to consent. Canon 475, §1 of the 1917 code said that when the pastor was incapable of discharging his duties properly due to old age, mental debility, incompetence, blindness, or other permanent cause, the local ordinary was to give a helping vicar (*vicarius adiutor*) to the pastor; if the parish had been entrusted to religious, the superior was to present this helping vicar to the bishop for appointment.

Parochial Administrator: Duties and Rights[206]

Canon 540 — §1. A parochial administrator is bound by the same duties and possesses the same rights as a pastor unless the diocesan bishop establishes otherwise.

§2. A parochial administrator is not permitted to do anything which prejudices the rights of the pastor or can harm parochial goods.

§3. After he has completed his function, a parochial administrator is to render an account to the pastor.

A parochial administrator is a *priest* who takes the place of a pastor in a parish which is vacant or whose pastor is impeded[207] (c. 539). The law

does not further identify his qualifications for office, but certainly he must have the capacities to perform this temporary role. By definition a parochial administrator does not have stability in office (see c. 522); by nature his appointment is temporary. The law avoids giving any period of time within which the diocesan bishop must appoint a pastor to a parish served by a parochial administrator.[208]

A parochial administrator has all the duties and possesses the same rights as a pastor unless the diocesan bishop establishes otherwise;[209] among other things, this means the parochial administrator is obliged to offer the Mass for the people (c. 534). He is not permitted to do anything which prejudices the rights of a pastor or which can harm parochial goods.[210] When he has completed his function, he is to render an account to the pastor.

The 1917 code mentioned two kinds of parochial vicars[211] who assisted in parishes in these situations: the *vicarius oeconomus* (who served when the parish is vacant) and the *vicarius adiutor* (who served when the pastor is impeded).

---

[206] Cf. *CCEO* 299.

[207] The canon identifies some possible reasons for the pastor's being prevented from exercising his role: captivity, exile or banishment, incapacity or illness, or some other cause. The reasons listed are merely illustrative, not exhaustive. See P. Marcuzzi, "La vacanza della parrocchia

e l'amministratore parrocchiale," in *La parrocchia,* 61–83.

[208] *CIC* 458 expected a pastor to be appointed within six months of a parochial vacancy, unless particular circumstances called for a longer vacancy. The 1983 code does not contain this specification. See J. Provost, "Parochial Administrator's Length of Office and the Bishop's Obligation to Name a Pastor," in *CLSA Advisory Opinions, 1984–1993,* 152–154.

[209] The canon allows the diocesan bishop to focus more precisely the role of the diocesan administrator, especially if the parish is not vacant (for example, the diocesan bishop may determine whether the pastor or the parochial administrator offers the Mass for the people).

[210] Similarly, the diocesan administrator is not to alter anything and is forbidden to do anything prejudicial to the diocese or episcopal rights (c. 428; see also c. 414).

[211] The other parochial vicars mentioned in the 1917 code were the *vicarius* of the moral person to whom a parish is entrusted (*CIC* 471), the *vicarius substitutus* (*CIC* 474), and the *vicarius cooperator* (*CIC* 476).

Interim Parochial Governance[212]

Canon 541 — §1. When a parish becomes vacant or a pastor has been impeded from exercising his pastoral function and before the appointment of a parochial administrator, the parochial vicar is to assume the governance of the parish temporarily. If there are several vicars, the one who is senior in appointment or, if there are no vicars, a pastor determined by particular law assumes this governance.

§2. The one who has assumed the governance of a parish according to the norm of §1 is immediately to inform the local ordinary about the vacancy of the parish.

When a parish is vacant or a pastor is impeded from performing his function, the diocesan bishop is to designate a parochial administrator as soon as possible (see c. 539). Before the parochial administrator is appointed, a priest must assume temporarily the governance of the parish. If there is one parochial vicar, he assumes temporary governance. If there are several parochial vicars, the one senior by appointment assumes it. If there are no parochial vicars, the code expects particular law to identify a pastor to assume interim parochial governance.[213] The code gives no particular title to this presbyter who assumes temporary parochial governance.

The first responsibility of whoever has assumed the temporary governance of the parish is to inform the local ordinary immediately of the vacancy of the parish or, presumably, of the impeded status of the pastor.

This canon basically repeats the norm of canon 472, 2°–3° of the former code, which had also stated that, if there are no parochial vicars,

---

[212] Cf. *CCEO* 300. The Eastern code says that, if there are no parochial vicars, the nearest pastor assumes temporary governance; the eparchial bishop is to determine at an early date (*tempestive*) which parish is considered closer to which parish.

[213] Particular law may select the nearest pastor, the vicar forane, or some other presbyter. No recommendation is given in the code.

interim parochial governance was to be assumed by the *nearest* pastor as designated by the local ordinary in or outside of a diocesan synod. Further, if the parish had been assigned to religious, the superior of the house would assume interim parochial governance.

Parish(es) Entrusted to Several Priests "In Solidum": Qualifications, Appointment, and Canonical Possession

Canon 542 — Priests to whom the pastoral care of some parish or of different parishes together is entrusted *in solidum* according to the norm of can. 517, §1:

1° must be endowed with the qualities mentioned in can. 521;

2° are to be appointed or installed according to the norm of the prescripts of cann. 522 and 524;

3° obtain pastoral care only from the moment of taking possession; their moderator is placed in possession according to the norm of the prescripts of can. 527, §2; for the other priests, however, a legitimately made profession of faith replaces taking possession.

Canons 542–544 concern the governance of parish(es) entrusted to several priests *in solidum* in accord with the norm of canon 517, §1.[214] Canon 542 concerns the qualifications, appointment, and taking canonical possession of the parish(es) by such priests. Canon 543 concerns their tasks, functions, and obligations. Canon 544 concerns the cessation of office of one of them, or his incapacity to perform his function.

When the pastoral care of a parish or of different parishes together is entrusted to several priests *in solidum*, each priest must be endowed with the qualities mentioned in canon 521 including, for validity, presbyteral ordination. Each is to be ap-

---

[214] The issues in cc. 542–544 are to be determined by the particular law of each proper autonomous Eastern church (*CCEO* 287, §2).

pointed for an indefinite or specific period of time (c. 522) and the diocesan bishop is to judge the priests' suitability (c. 524). Further, each obtains pastoral care from the moment of taking possession of the parish: the moderator is placed in possession according to the prescripts of canon 527, §2, but the profession of faith (c. 833, 6°) replaces taking possession for the other priests.

Parish(es) Entrusted to Several Priests "In Solidum": Tasks, Functions, and Obligations

Canon 543 — §1. If the pastoral care of some parish or of different parishes together is entrusted to priests *in solidum,* each of them is obliged to perform the tasks and functions of pastor mentioned in cann. 528, 529, and 530 according to the arrangement they establish. All of them have the faculty of assisting at marriages and all the powers to dispense granted to a pastor by law; these are to be exercised, however, under the direction of the moderator.

§2. All the priests who belong to the group:
1° are bound by the obligation of residence;
2° are to establish through common counsel an arrangement by which one of them is to celebrate a Mass for the people according to the norm of can. 534;
3° the moderator alone represents in juridic affairs the parish or parishes entrusted to the group.

When the pastoral care of a parish or of different parishes together is entrusted to several priests *in solidum,* each is obliged to perform all the tasks and functions of a pastor enumerated in canons 528–530, according to the arrangement the priests establish. Each has the faculty to assist at marriages (cc. 1108–1111) and all the powers to grant dispensations which are granted to a pastor by law (see cc. 89; 1079, §2; 1080; 1196, 1°; 1203; 1245); this faculty and these powers are to be exercised under the direction of the moderator.

All the priests are bound by the obligation of residence (see c. 533, §1). They are to establish

through common counsel an arrangement whereby one of them is to celebrate the Mass for the people (see c. 534). In juridic affairs, only the moderator represents the parish(es) (see c. 532); therefore, only he has the obligation to take care that the goods of the parish are administered according to the norm of canons 1281–1288, and he is to be assisted by the parish finance council in that administration (c. 537). Certainly, the other priests may also be involved with these administrative functions, even though only the moderator represents the parish(es) in a proper canonical sense.

Parish(es) Entrusted to Several Priests "In Solidum": Cessation of Office of a Priest or Incapacity to Exercise His Pastoral Function

Canon 544 — When a priest from the group mentioned in can. 517, §1 or its moderator ceases from office as well as when one of them becomes incapable of exercising his pastoral function, the parish or parishes whose care is entrusted to the group do not become vacant. It is for the diocesan bishop, however, to appoint another moderator; before someone is appointed by the bishop, the priest in the group who is senior in appointment is to fulfill this function.

When the pastoral care of a parish or of different parishes together is entrusted to several priests *in solidum* (c. 517, §1), the parish or parishes do not become vacant when one of the priests or its moderator ceases from office or becomes incapable of exercising his function. If this situation concerns the moderator, the diocesan bishop is to appoint another moderator and, in the meantime, the priest of the group senior by appointment fulfills the moderator's function. If all the remaining priests were appointed at the same time, the seniority may be determined by ordination or age.[215]

The parish or parishes entrusted to several priests *in solidum* become vacant only when all the priests cease from office.

---

[215]This could be determined by particular law.

APPENDIX I – PARTICULAR LEGISLATION ON PARISHES

The 1983 code calls for particular legislation on parishes in a number of areas in order to apply the more general universal law to the unique circumstances of the particular churches:

Particular Law of the Conference of Bishops

– on permitting a diocesan bishop to appoint a pastor for a specific period of time (c. 522; see c. 538, §1)

– on required parochial registers in addition to those for baptisms, marriages, and deaths (c. 535, §1)

– on suitable support and housing to be provided to a retired pastor (c. 538, §3)

Particular Law of the Diocese

– on the requirements for the pastor of a given parish (c. 521, §2)

– on the method whereby the pastor takes possession of his parish (c. 527, §2)

– on the allocation of offerings received on the occasion of performing parochial functions, and on the remuneration of the clerics performing them (c. 531)

– on providing pastoral care in a parish when the pastor is absent through a priest endowed with the necessary faculties (c. 533, §3; see c. 549)

– on required parochial registers in addition to those for baptisms, marriages, and deaths (c. 535, §1)

– on protecting older parochial registers (c. 535, §5)

– on requiring the establishment of a pastoral council in each parish, and on its operation (c. 536)

– on the specific operation of the parish finance council (c. 537)

– on which pastor is to assume immediate governance of a parish when the parish is vacant or the pastor is impeded, if the parish has no parochial vicars (c. 541, §1)

– on the obligations and rights of a parochial vicar (c. 548, §1)

The 1983 code mentions the roles of the diocesan bishop, the local ordinary, and the diocesan administrator in the life of parishes:

Role of the Diocesan Bishop

- to oversee the pastoral care of the parish (cc. 515, §1; 519)
- to erect, suppress, or notably alter parishes, after hearing the presbyteral council (c. 515, §2)
- to establish quasi-parishes (c. 516, §1—implicit)
- to provide pastoral care in some other way for certain communities which cannot be erected as parishes or quasi-parishes (c. 516, §2)
- to entrust the pastoral care of a parish or parishes to a group of priests *in solidum* with one of them functioning as moderator (c. 517, §1)
- to decide that a participation in the exercise of the pastoral care of a parish is to be entrusted to a deacon, lay person, or community of non-priests, under the direction of a priest endowed with the powers and faculties of a pastor (c. 517, §2)
- to entrust a parish to a clerical religious institute or a clerical society of apostolic life, and to enter into the appropriate written agreement (c. 520)
- to determine the suitability of a presbyter to be a pastor, even by means of an examination (c. 521, §3; see c. 542, 1°)
- to appoint a pastor for an indefinite or specific period of time (c. 522; see c. 542, 2°)
- to provide the office of pastor by free conferral, unless someone has the right of presentation or election, and without prejudice to canon 682, §1 (c. 523)
- to entrust a vacant parish to one whom he considers suited, after he has heard the vicar forane and, if warranted, certain presbyters and lay persons (c. 524; see c. 542, 2°)
- to oversee the pastor's direction of the sacred liturgy (c. 528, §2)

- to receive cooperation from the pastor in promoting and sustaining ecclesial communion (c. 529, §2)
- to issue prescripts on the allocation of offerings received on the occasion of certain parochial functions, and on the remuneration of clerics fulfilling them (c. 531)
- to establish norms on providing pastoral care in a parish through a priest endowed with the necessary faculties when the pastor is absent (c. 533, §3; see c. 549)
- to prescribe parochial registers in addition to those for baptisms, marriages, and deaths (c. 535, §1)
- to inspect the parochial archive at the time of visitation or another time (c. 535, §4)
- to require the establishment in each parish of a pastoral council, and to establish norms on its operation (c. 536)
- to issue specific norms on the operation of the parish finance council (c. 537)
- to remove or transfer a pastor, and to accept a pastor's resignation (c. 538, §1)
- to receive a pastor's resignation at age seventy-five, to accept or defer it, and to provide suitable support and housing for him (c. 538, §3)
- to designate a parochial administrator (c. 539) who has the same rights and duties as a pastor unless the diocesan bishop determines otherwise (c. 540, §1)
- to issue particular law on which pastor is to assume immediate governance of a parish when the parish is vacant or the pastor is impeded, if the parish has no parochial vicars (c. 541, §1—implicit; see c. 549)
- to appoint another moderator of the group of priests *in solidum* to whom is entrusted together the pastoral care of a parish or parishes, when the moderator ceases from office or becomes incapable of performing his office (c. 544)
- to appoint a parochial vicar (c. 547) and to define his obligations and rights (c. 548, §§1–2)
- to remove the parochial vicar (c. 552)

Role of the Local Ordinary

- to place a pastor in possession of his parish, observing the method accepted by particular law or legitimate custom, or to dispense from that method for a just cause (c. 527, §2; see c. 542, 3°)
- to prescribe the time within which a pastor must take possession, and to be able to declare the parish vacant if the time has elapsed and he has not taken possession without a just impediment (c. 527, §3)
- to permit the pastor to reside in a place other than the rectory near the church, especially in a house shared by several presbyters (c. 533, §1)
- to be informed when the pastor will be absent for more than a week (c. 533, §2)
- to permit the parochial vicar to reside outside the parish, especially in a house shared by several presbyters (c. 550, §1)
- to take care that some manner of common life in the rectory is fostered between the pastor and parochial vicars, where this can be done (c. 550, §2)

Role of the Diocesan Administrator[216]

Permitted

- to install or confirm as pastor those presbyters who have been legitimately presented or elected for a parish (c. 525, 1°)*
- to appoint pastors if the see has been vacant or impeded for a year (c. 525, 2°)*
- to remove the parochial vicar (c. 552)

Not Permitted

- to entrust a parish to a clerical religious institute or a clerical society of apostolic life, and to enter into the appropriate written agreement (c. 520)
- to appoint pastors unless the see has been vacant or impeded for a year (c. 525, 2°)*

---

[216] Those roles marked with an asterisk (*) also belong to the person who temporarily governs an impeded see (c. 413, §§1–2)

BIBLIOGRAPHY

Primary Sources

Book of Blessings, prep. ICEL. Collegeville: Liturgical Press, 1989.

CDW. *Caeremoniale Episcoporum,* September 14, 1984. Vatican City: Libreria Editrice Vaticana, 1984. ICEL translation: *Ceremonial of Bishops.* Collegeville: Liturgical Press, 1989.

CFC. *Directory for the Ministry and Life of Priests,* January 31, 1994. Vatican City: Libreria Editrice Vaticana, 1994.

CFC et al. *Instruction on Certain Questions Regarding the Collaboration of the Non-Ordained Faithful in the Sacred Ministry of Priests,* August 15, 1997. Washington, D.C.: USCC, 1997. *AAS* 89 (1997) 852–877.

John Paul II. "On Parishes, Lay Ministry and Women" (*ad limina* address to bishops from Baltimore, Washington, Atlanta, and Miami, July 2, 1993). *Origins* 23 (July 15, 1993) 124–126.

——. "Priests, Their Life and Ministry" (*ad limina* address to bishops from Michigan and Ohio, May 21, 1998). *Origins* 28 (June 18, 1998) 73–75.

——. Apconst *Spirituali militum curae,* April 21, 1986. *AAS* 78 (1986) 481–486. Unofficial translation: *TPS* 31 (1986) 284–288.

——. "The Vocation of the Parish" (*ad limina* address to the third group of French bishops, January 25, 1997). *OssRomEng* (February 5, 1997) 5, 8.

NCCB. *Implementation of the 1983 Code of Canon Law: Complementary Norms,* April 26, 1991. Washington, D.C.: USCC, 1991.

Ochoa, X., ed. *Leges Ecclesiae (1973–1978).* Rome: Commentarium pro Religiosis, 1980.

Paul VI. *Mp Pastoralis migratorum cura,* August 15, 1969. *AAS* 61 (1969) 601–602. English translation: *CLD* 6, 190–192.

——. *Mp Sacrum diaconatus ordinem,* June 18, 1967. *AAS* 59 (1967) 697–704. See *CLD* 6, 577–584.

PCILT. "Observations Concerning Cases in Which the Pastoral Care of More than One Parish Is Entrusted to a Single Pastor," November 13, 1997. *Comm* 30 (1998) 28–32.

SCB. *Directory for the Pastoral Ministry of Bishops,* May 31, 1973. Ottawa: CCCB, 1974.

——. *Inst De pastorali migratorum cura,* August 22, 1969. *AAS* 61 (1969) 614–643. English translation: *CLD* 6, 192–220.

Secondary Sources

Books/Dissertations

Applegate, G. "Selected Canonical Issues in the Closing of Parishes." JCL dissertation. Catholic University of America, 1996.

Chester, T. "Select Canonical Issues in Diocesan Plans for Parish Restructuring." JCL dissertation. Catholic University of America, 1997.

Coady, J. *The Appointment of Pastors. CanLawStud* 52. Washington, D.C.: Catholic University of America, 1929.

Coccopalmerio, F. *De paroecia.* Rome: Editrice Pontificia Università Gregoriana, 1991.

Coriden, J. *The Parish in Catholic Tradition: History, Theology and Canon Law.* New York: Paulist, 1997.

Cote, M. "Cura Animarum According to Vatican II." JCL dissertation. Catholic University of America, 1981.

Cusack, B., and T. Sullivan. *Pastoral Care in Parishes Without a Pastor: Applications of Canon 517, §2.* Washington, D.C.: CLSA, 1995.

Downey, D. "The Retirement of Diocesan Priests." JCL dissertation. Catholic University of America, 1994.

Faris, J. *Eastern Catholic Churches: Constitution and Governance.* Brooklyn: St. Maron, 1992.

Hesch, J. *A Canonical Commentary on Selected Personnel Policies in the United States of America Regarding Decent Support of Diocesan Priests in Active Ministry. CanLawStud* 544. Washington, D.C.: Catholic University of America, 1994.

Koudelka, C. *Pastors: Their Rights and Duties According to the New Code of Canon Law. CanLawStud* 11. Washington, D.C.: Catholic University of America, 1921.

McCann, R. "Remuneration and Honest Sustenance for Clerics in Twentieth-Century Canon Law." JCL dissertation. Catholic University of America, 1994.

Mundy, T. *The Union of Parishes: An Historical Synopsis and Commentary. CanLawStud* 204. Washington, D.C.: Catholic University of America, 1945.

Myers, J. "The Qualifications of Clergy for the Office of Pastor." JCL dissertation. Catholic University of America, 1976.

O'Connell, P. *The Concept of the Parish in the Light of the Second Vatican Council. CanLawStud* 470. Washington, D.C.: Catholic University of America, 1969.

Périsset, J.-C. *La Paroisse: Commentaire des canons 515–572.* Paris: Tardy, 1989.

Pospishil, V. *Eastern Catholic Church Law.* Brooklyn: St. Maron, 1993.

Prendeville, E. "Lay Parish Coordinators: Some Canonical Considerations on the Implementation of Canon 517, §2 of the Revised Code of Canon Law." JCL dissertation. Catholic University of America, 1996.

Quant, R. "Non-Territorial Parishes in the 1983 Code of Canon Law: An Examination of Canon 518." JCL dissertation. Catholic University of America, 1996.

Articles

Arrieta, J. "La parrocchia come comunità di fedeli e soggetto canonicamente unitario." In *La parrocchia* (Studi giuridici, 24) 21– 36. Vatican City: Libreria Editrice Vaticana, 1997.

Berlingò, S. "Il consiglio pastorale della parrocchia." In *La parrocchia* (Studi giuridici, 24) 249–266. Vatican City: Libreria Editrice Vaticana, 1997.

Brewer, D. "Canon 524 and the Systematic Participation of the Laity in the Selection of Pastors." *Stud Can* 29 (1995) 481–492.

Calvo, J. "Parishes, Parish Priests and Assistant Priests." In *Pamplona ComEng,* 377–398.

Carlson, R. "The Parish According to the Revised Law." *Stud Can* 19 (1985) 5–16.

Coriden, J. "The Foundations of the Rights of Parishes: The Bases for the Canonical Right of Parishes and Other Local Catholic Communities." In PCILT, *Ius in Vita et in Missione Ecclesiae,* 505–525. Vatican City: Libreria Editrice Vaticana, 1994.

———. "The Rights of Parishes." *Stud Can* 28 (1994) 293–309.

———. "The Vindication of Parish Rights." *J* 54 (1994) 22–39.

Cox, C., and J. Koury. "Regulations Concerning the Format of Sacramental Registers." In *CLSA Advisory Opinions, 1984–1993,* ed. P. Cogan, 144–147. Washington, D.C.: CLSA, 1995.

Cuneo, J. "Pastor's Right to Dissolve the Parish Council." In *CLSA Advisory Opinions, 1984–1993,* ed. P. Cogan, 150–152. Washington, D.C.: CLSA, 1995.

Dalton, W. "Parish Councils or Parish Pastoral Councils?" *Stud Can* 22 (1988) 169–185.

Daneels, F. "Soppressione, unione di parrocchie e riduzione ad uso profano della chiesa parrocchiale." In *La parrocchia* (Studi giuridici, 24) 85–112. Vatican City: Libreria Editrice Vaticana, 1997.

———. "The Suppression of Parishes and the Reduction of a Church to Profane Use in the Light of the Jurisprudence of the Apostolic Signatura." *Forum* 8 (1997) 287–293.

De Paolis, V. "Il consiglio per gli affari economici ed i beni patrimoniali della parrocchia." In *La parrocchia* (Studi giuridici, 24) 267–288. Vatican City: Libreria Editrice Vaticana, 1997.

Doran, T. "Rights and Duties of Pastors." *CLSAP* (1993) 182–192.

Dugan, P. "Changes in Baptismal Records." In *RRAO 1997,* 51–52.

Dunn, B. "The Evaluation of Pastors." In *RRAO 1997,* 45–46.

———. "Transition Evaluation Processes in Parishes." In *RRAO 1997,* 46–47.

Erdö, P. "De incompatibilitate officiorum, specialiter paroeciarum: Adnotationes ad cann. 152 et 526." *P* 80 (1991) 499–522.

Euart, S. "Parishes without a Resident Pastor: Reflections on the Provisions and Conditions of Canon 517, §2 and Its Implications." *J* 54 (1994) 369–386.

Fürst, C. "La parrocchia nel Codice di Diritto Canonico delle Chiese Orientali (CCEO)." In *La parrocchia* (Studi giuridici, 24) 289–307. Vatican City: Libreria Editrice Vaticana, 1997.

Gauthier, A. "L'affidamento della parrocchia ad un gruppo di sacerdoti in solidum o a fedeli non sacerdoti nonché ad un istituto religioso." In *La parrocchia* (Studi giuridici, 24) 61–83. Vatican City: Libreria Editrice Vaticana, 1997.

Green, T. "Mission Parishes (Quasi-Parishes) Changed to Status of Parish." In *CLSA Advisory Opinions, 1984–1993,* ed. P. Cogan, 113– 114. Washington, D.C.: CLSA, 1995.

———. "Persons and Structures in the Church: Reflections on Selected Issues in Book II." *J* 45 (1985) 24–94.

Green, T., J. Provost, and R. Wiatroski. "Establishment of a Parish That Is Both Territorial and Personal." In *RRAO 1994,* 102–110.

Griffin, B. "Canon 517: Jurisdiction for Laity." In *CLSA Advisory Opinions, 1984–1993,* ed. P. Cogan, 115–123. Washington, D.C.: CLSA, 1995.

Grocholewski, Z. "Trasferimento e rimozione del parroco." In *La parrocchia* (Studi giuridici, 24) 199–147. Vatican City: Libreria Editrice Vaticana, 1997.

Hesch, J. "The 1987 NCCB Norms for Priests and Their Third Age." *J* 54 (1994) 387–408.

Hill, R. "The Mass *Pro Populo* and Acceptance of Other Intentions." In *CLSA Advisory Opinions, 1984–1993,* ed. P. Cogan, 144. Washington, D.C.: CLSA, 1995.

———. "Parish Membership on Other Than Territorial Basis." In *CLSA Advisory Opinions, 1984–1993,* ed. P. Cogan, 126–128. Washington, D.C.: CLSA, 1995.

Huels, J. "Confirmation of Baptized Catholics in a Schismatic Church." In *CLSA Advisory Opinions, 1984–1993,* ed. P. Cogan, 147–150. Washington, D.C.: CLSA, 1995.

Longhitano, A. "L'amministratore ed i vicari parrocchiali." In *La parrocchia* (Studi giuridici, 24) 175–197. Vatican City: Libreria Editrice Vaticana, 1997.

———. "L'obbligo della residenza del parroco e la reggenza della parrocchia durante la sua assenza. In *La parrocchia* (Studi giuridici, 24) 155–174. Vatican City: Libreria Editrice Vaticana, 1997.

Lynch, J. "The Parochial Ministry in the New Code of Canon Law." *J* 42 (1982) 383–421.

Mariconti, G. "Il parroco promotore di comunione nella communità parrocchiale." *ME* 116 (1991) 243–259.

Marcuzzi, P. "Il consiglio pastorale parrocchiale." In PCILT, *Ius in Vita et in Missione Ecclesiae*, 437–463. Vatican City: Libreria Editrice Vaticana, 1994.

———. "La vacanza della parrocchia e l'amministratore parrocchiale." In *La parrocchia* (Studi giuridici, 24) 61–83. Vatican City: Libreria Editrice Vaticana, 1997.

McDonough, K. "'I Never Knew What You Thought of Me': Evaluation of Pastors and the Issue of Unassignability." *Stud Can* 32 (1998) 145–156.

Montini, G. "Stabilità del parroco e permanenza nell'ufficio parrocchiale." In *La parrocchia* (Studi giuridici, 24) 125–153. Vatican City: Libreria Editrice Vaticana, 1997.

Myers, J. "Consultation for the Appointment of Pastors." In *CLSA Advisory Opinions, 1984–1993*, ed. P. Cogan, 137–138. Washington, D.C.: CLSA, 1995.

———. "Suppression and Merger of Parishes: Brief Overview of Canonical Issues." In *CLSA Advisory Opinions, 1984–1993*, ed. P. Cogan, 110–113. Washington, D.C.: CLSA, 1995.

Paprocki, T. "Parish Closings and Administrative Recourse to the Apostolic See: Recent Experiences of the Archdiocese of Chicago." *J* 55 (1995) 875–896.

Provost, J. "Diocesan Policies Toward Pastors with Limited Terms of Office." In *CLSA Advisory Opinions, 1984–1993*, ed. P. Cogan, 135–137. Washington, D.C.: CLSA, 1995.

———. "Disposition of Stole Fees." In *CLSA Advisory Opinions, 1984–1993*, ed. P. Cogan, 142–143. Washington, D.C.: CLSA, 1995.

———. "Lay Co-Pastors—Improper Terminology." In *CLSA Advisory Opinions, 1984–1993*, ed. P. Cogan, 115. Washington, D.C.: CLSA, 1995.

———. "Limited Tenure of Office for Pastors." In *CLSA Advisory Opinions, 1984–1993*, ed. P. Cogan, 132–135. Washington, D.C.: CLSA, 1995.

———. "Limited Tenure of Office for Pastors and Others." In *CLSA Advisory Opinions, 1984–1993*, ed. P. Cogan, 129–132. Washington, D.C.: CLSA, 1995.

———. "Non-Retroactivity of Term Appointments for Pastors." In *CLSA Advisory Opinions, 1984–1993*, ed. P. Cogan, 128. Washington, D.C.: CLSA, 1995.

———. "Parochial Administrator's Length of Office and the Bishop's Obligation to Name a Pastor." In *CLSA Advisory Opinions, 1984–1993*, ed. P. Cogan, 152–154. Washington, D.C.: CLSA, 1995.

———. "Pastor of More Than One Parish." In *RRAO 1997*, 48–51.

———. "Priests Serving as Pastors in More Than One Parish." In *CLSA Advisory Opinions, 1984–1993*, ed. P. Cogan, 124–126. Washington, D.C.: CLSA, 1995.

———. "Reappointment of Pastor." In *RRAO 1997*, 47–48.

———. "Retention of Stipend for a Second Mass and Mass for the People." In *RRAO 1994*, 110–111.

———. "Rights of Pastors Being Transferred Concerning Appointment." In *CLSA Advisory Opinions, 1984–1993*, ed. P. Cogan, 138–139. Washington, D.C.: CLSA, 1995.

———. "Some Canonical Considerations on Closing Parishes." *J* 53 (1993) 362–370.

Provost, J., and R. Hill. "Stole Fees." In *CLSA Advisory Opinions, 1984–1993*, ed. P. Cogan, 139–142. Washington, D.C.: CLSA, 1995.

Read, G. "Pastors, Parish Priests and Assistant Priests." In *CLSGBI Com*, 285–302.

Renken, J. "Parishes Without a Resident Pastor: Comments on Canon 517, §2." *CLSAP* 50 (1988) 249–263.

———. "Pastoral Councils: Pastoral Planning and Dialogue Among the People of God." *J* 53 (1993) 132–154.

———. "The Parish: Community of the Christian Faithful within the Particular Church: Reflections on Some Aspects of Parochial Communio." *CLSAP* (1998).

Sánchez-Gil, A. "Circa la portata della qualifica del parroco quale pastore proprio della comunità parrocchiale." *IE* 8 (1996) 217–230.

Viana, A. "El parroco, pastor proprio de la parroquia." *IC* 29 (1989) 467–481.

PAROCHIAL VICARS[1]
[cc. 545–552]

The 1917 code contained the law on parochial vicars in a special chapter (*CIC* 471–478). Different kinds of vicars were defined: vicar *oeconomus* (*CIC* 472–473), who was equivalent to the present parochial administrator assigned when a parish is impeded or vacant; vicar *substitutus* (*CIC* 474), a supply priest during the pastor's vacation or other absence; vicar *adjutor* (*CIC* 475), who was given to a pastor who was impeded from fulfilling his duties because of old age, mental problems, inadequate skills, blindness, or other permanent reason; and the vicar *cooperator* (*CIC* 474), who was substantially equivalent to the present law's parochial vicar. "Associate pastor," "assistant pastor," and "curate" are equivalent terms used in English speaking countries. The law for the Eastern churches is substantially the same as that in the Latin code (*CCEO* 301–303).

The Office of Parochial Vicar

Canon 545 — §1. Whenever it is necessary or opportune in order to carry out the pastoral care of a parish fittingly, one or more parochial vicars can be associated with the pastor. As co-workers with the pastor and sharers in his solicitude, they are to offer service in the pastoral ministry by common counsel and effort with the pastor and under his authority.

§2. A parochial vicar can be assigned either to assist in exercising the entire pastoral ministry for the whole parish, a determined part of the parish, or a certain group of the Christian faithful of the parish, or even to assist in fulfilling a specific ministry in different parishes together.

[1] For some other reflections on these canons see J. Calvo, in *Pamplona ComEng,* 398–402; J. Janicki, in *CLSA Com,* 437–440; G. Read, in *CLSGBI Com,* 302–305.

The Second Vatican Council provides the basic principles for the harmonious relationship and ministry of the pastor and parochial vicar or vicars:

> Curates, as co-workers with the parish priest, should be eager and fervent in their daily exercise of their pastoral ministry under the authority of the parish priest. There should therefore be a fraternal relationship between the parish priest and his curates, mutual charity and respect, and they should assist each other by advice, practical help and examples, providing with harmonious will and a common zeal for the needs of a parish. (*CD* 30)

The parochial vicar shares with the pastor the threefold ministry of teaching, sanctifying, and governing, but there are certain distinctions between them. Certain sacramental and liturgical functions are reserved to the pastor (c. 530). The parochial vicar needs the pastor's agreement to celebrate baptisms, confirmation, and anointing of the sick in danger of death, and to conduct funerals. The parochial vicar does not have delegation to assist at marriages by reason of office but requires either general or special delegation from the local ordinary or the pastor. Even if he has general delegation, he also requires the pastor's agreement to witness a specific marriage in the parish (c. 1114). Only the pastor represents the parish in juridic affairs (c. 532). The parochial vicar does not have the obligation of the Mass for the people (c. 534). The parochial vicar is accountable to the pastor and shares in pastoral ministry under his authority; in this way the vicar differs from the members of the pastoral team (c. 517, §1) who share pastoral authority *in solidum*. In other words, all team members are bound by all the obligations of the pastor.

Ordinarily a parochial vicar is assigned for full pastoral service in the parish. However, the bishop (or even the pastor) may assign him to a specific geographic area in a parish such as a mission or station, or for a specific ministry such as youth ministry, campus ministry, or ministry to an ethnic or language group in the parish. A new element in the law permits the bishop to assign him to fulfill a certain type of ministry in several parishes. In such a case, the letter of appointment should specify the ministry, the manner of remuneration by the several parishes, and his accountability.

Certain parallels can be noted between the pastor (*parochus*) and his parochial vicars and the bishop and his diocesan vicars such as the vicar general with executive power for the entire diocese, and the episcopal vicar who may be appointed to exercise such power for a territory within the diocese, for a specific ministry or business, or for the faithful of a determined rite or group (c. 479).

Requirement of Priestly Ordination

Canon 546 — To be appointed a parochial vicar validly, one must be in the sacred order of the presbyterate.

Only presbyters may validly be appointed as parochial vicars. This canon applies the more general norm in canon 150: "An office which entails the full care of souls and for whose fulfillment the exercise of the priestly order is required cannot be conferred validly on one who is not yet a priest." However, we can distinguish between specifically presbyterial functions and the broad range of pastoral services to be rendered at the parish level and provided by parish deacons, lay pastoral ministers or associates, and catechists. Such pastoral associates are usually church professionals and employees rather than office holders (c. 145), with rights and obligations specified in diocesan personnel manuals and parish job descriptions. However, if parish deacons are assigned by the bishop with stable obligations determined by him, they hold ecclesiastical offices.

Appointment of Parochial Vicar

Canon 547 — The diocesan bishop freely appoints a parochial vicar, after he has heard, if he has judged it opportune, the pastor or pastors of the parishes for which the parochial vicar is appointed and the vicar forane, without prejudice to the prescript of can. 682, §1.

The 1917 code required the local ordinary to consult with the pastor before assigning a vicar cooperator (*CIC* 476, §3). In the present law the bishop ordinarily provides for the office of pastor by free conferral after consulting the vicar forane (cc. 523–524). Likewise the bishop provides for the office of parochial vicar by free conferral; if he judges it opportune, he consults the pastor or pastors of the parishes for which the vicar is appointed as well as the vicar forane. In this country, by particular law or diocesan practice, the bishop ordinarily consults the priest personnel board rather than the vicar forane. It is rare to appoint a parochial vicar without at least some consultation with the pastor. However, the law does not technically require such consultation.

The Eastern code recommends consultation with the pastor before the appointment of a parochial vicar, but omits references to the protopresbyter, who is equivalent to a vicar forane (*CCEO* 301, §3).

The appointment of a parochial vicar who is a member of an institute of consecrated life or a clerical society of apostolic life follows the usual permission of canon 682, §1. The appointment is made by the bishop upon presentation of the candidate by the superior of the institute or society or at least with his consent.

The diocesan bishop may delegate a vicar general or episcopal vicar to assign parochial vicars provided he issues a special mandate to do so (c. 479, §§1–2).

Rights and Obligations of the Parochial Vicar

Canon 548 — §1. The obligations and rights of a parochial vicar, besides being defined in the canons of this chapter, diocesan statutes, and the

letter of the diocesan bishop, are more specifically determined in the mandate of the pastor.

§2. Unless the letter of the diocesan bishop expressly provides otherwise, a parochial vicar is obliged to assist the pastor in the entire parochial ministry by reason of office, except for the application of the Mass for the people, and to substitute for the pastor if the situation arises according to the norm of law.

§3. A parochial vicar is to report to the pastor regularly concerning proposed and existing pastoral endeavors in such a way that the pastor and the vicar or vicars, through common efforts, are able to provide for the pastoral care of the parish for which they are together responsible.

As a cleric the parochial vicar has the rights and obligations accorded all clerics by universal law (cc. 273–289). His rights and obligations by reason of office are determined by the pertinent canons of this chapter of the code (cc. 545–552). Such obligations include the obligations to provide general pastoral care (c. 545, §1), to cooperate with the pastor (c. 545, §1 and c. 548, §3), to substitute for the pastor in his absence (c. 549), and to reside within the parish (c. 550, §1). The parochial vicar has the right to a vacation (c. 550, §3). He is not required to apply Mass for the people even when acting as a substitute in the pastor's absence (c. 549). Other rights and obligations may be added by diocesan statutes or other particular law such as a personnel manual. The letter of appointment from the diocesan bishop may also specify certain rights and obligations. The pastor may further specify the obligations of the parochial vicar in a more detailed job description or other mandate.

Ordinarily the parochial vicar exercises his office by fulfilling pastoral obligations for the entire parish. The fundamental pastoral obligations are contained in canon 528 (the pastor as teacher and sanctifier) and canon 529 (the pastor as shepherd and community leader). The bishop's letter of appointment, however, can limit the parochial vicar's ministry to a particular part of the parish or to a certain group of the Christian faithful (c. 545, §2).

The parochial vicar and the pastor are advised to consult and plan together. Such consultation may be informal; in larger parishes it ordinarily occurs in regular staff meetings with the pastor, his parochial vicars, and pastoral ministers.

Parochial Vicar as Substitute for the Pastor

Canon 549 — Unless the diocesan bishop has provided otherwise according to the norm of can. 533, §3 and unless a parochial administrator has been appointed, the prescripts of can. 541, §1 are to be observed when the pastor is absent. In this case, the vicar is also bound by all the obligations of the pastor, except the obligation of applying Mass for the people.

The 1917 code provided for a special vicar *substitutus* when the pastor was absent (*CIC* 474). The present law makes the following provisions:

The diocesan bishop should enact particular law providing for the pastoral care of a parish by a priest with the necessary faculties during the absence of the pastor (c. 533, §3). Such an absence could be due to a sabbatical, a vacation, a retreat, an illness, or an emergency. Diocesan norms may require the pastor to obtain his own substitute and inform the bishop or may assign a neighboring pastor to supply in case of emergencies. In the absence of such norms the parochial vicar is empowered to act as substitute. If there is more than one parochial vicar, the senior vicar in terms of appointment assumes the governance of the parish (c. 541, §1). If the pastor's absence is long term because of his captivity, exile, banishment, incapacity, ill health, or some other cause, a parochial administrator is to be appointed who substitutes for the pastor and replaces the parochial vicar acting as temporary substitute (cc. 539–540).

Ordinarily the parochial vicar substitutes when the pastor is on sabbatical, vacation, or retreat. The pastor may be absent from the parish for one month each year, not including his retreat (c. 533, §2); particular law may grant additional time for continuing education. If any absence is more than a week, the bishop is to be informed. The present canon transfers the needed faculties of the pastor to the parochial vicar during such absences.

Residency of the Parochial Vicar

Canon 550 — §1. A parochial vicar is obliged to reside in the parish or, if he has been appointed for different parishes jointly, in one of them. Nevertheless, for a just cause the local ordinary can allow him to reside elsewhere, especially in a house shared by several presbyters, provided that this is not detrimental to the performance of his pastoral functions.

§2. The local ordinary is to take care that some manner of common life in the rectory is fostered between the pastor and the vicars where this can be done.

§3. A parochial vicar possesses the same right as a pastor concerning the time of vacation.

The pastor is obliged to reside in a parish house close to the church. However, the local ordinary can permit him to live elsewhere, especially in a house shared by other presbyters (c. 533, §1). Similarly, the parochial vicar is obliged to reside within the parish or one of the parishes to which he is assigned. The local ordinary may also permit him to reside elsewhere, especially in a house shared by other presbyters.

In the United States, particularly in the missions, pastors often lived in apartments attached to the church. Later, rectories were built, and the pastor and his parochial vicars lived in rooms or apartments in the same building where offices and meeting rooms were located. More and more dioceses are pursuing alternatives to the rectory system. The present canon does not require the pastor and parochial vicar to share the same house, or for either to live in the parish office building. The canon leaves other alternatives up to the bishop but encourages both the pastor and the parochial vicar to live in a residence shared by other priests. Some community of life between the pastor and parochial vicar is also encouraged (c. 280).

The pastor and parochial vicar possess the same right to vacation time, namely one continu-

ous or uninterrupted month (c. 533, §2). Just as the pastor's retreat is not counted in his vacation days, the parochial vicar also has the right to a month's vacation in addition to his annual retreat.

Voluntary Offerings

Canon 551 — The prescripts of can. 531 are to be observed in regards to offerings which the Christian faithful give to a vicar on the occasion of the performance of pastoral ministry.

Mass stipends belong to the priest who celebrates or concelebrates the Eucharist. The amount is set by a provincial council, by the bishops of the province, or by local custom (c. 952). However, the present canon refers to voluntary offerings (previously called stole fees) given on the occasion of celebrating certain sacraments or sacramentals. The amount of the offering is set by the bishops of the province or by local custom. Such offerings are usually given on the occasion of baptisms, marriages, and funerals, and sometimes even when communion is brought to the sick. The offering belongs to the parish, not to the parochial vicar, unless it is obvious that the donor wanted the offering to be a personal gift. The parochial vicar is remunerated for his ministry by a salary, living expenses, and benefits which are paid from the parish account (c. 281).

Removal of the Parochial Vicar

Canon 552 — The diocesan bishop or diocesan administrator can remove a parochial vicar for a just cause, without prejudice to the prescript of can. 682, §2.

The pastor is normally named for an indefinite period of time (c. 522); hence a grave cause is required for his removal (c. 193, §1). Canon 1741 lists five causes which the law considers serious enough for removal of a pastor. They include bringing grave harm to the ecclesiastical community, permanent illness of mind or body rendering his ministry ineffective, hatred of the people, grave neglect of office, and poor administration.

Other grave reasons may also be cause for removal. The parochial vicar, however, is appointed at the prudent discretion of the bishop and can be removed for a just cause; an unjust cause or arbitrary removal is of course excluded. A grave cause, however, is not required. The pastor has far more stability in office than the parochial vicar.

The procedure for removing pastors is contained in canons 1740–1747. There is no similar procedure for the removal of parochial vicars. General norms on removal from office (cc. 192–195) and on individual administrative decrees (cc. 48–58) are applicable. The decision should be in writing and the reasons given (c. 193, §4). The diocesan administrator as well as the diocesan bishop may remove the parochial vicar. Finally, a parochial vicar who is a religious may be removed at the discretion of the diocesan bishop after notifying the religious superior or by the religious superior after notifying the bishop. Neither requires the consent of the other (c. 682, §2).

CHAPTER VII
VICARS FORANE[2]
[cc. 553–555]

The institute of vicar forane is basically unchanged from the 1917 code (*CIC* 445–450). The 1917 code made it mandatory to divide the diocese into vicariates forane, deaneries, or archpresbyterates, although the bishop could seek permission from the Holy See not to do so (*CIC* 217). The office of archpriest can be traced to the fourth century. The deanery was originally a grouping of ten parishes. The modern concept of the vicar forane dates back to the sixteenth century under the inspiration of St. Charles Borromeo. The term "forane" originally meant the outlying or rural parts of the diocese where the bishop's presence and pastoral concern could be made visible by a vicar. More recently, bishops have appointed pas-

toral vicars with the title of urban vicars for urban and metropolitan districts.

Canon 374, §1 requires that a diocese be divided into parishes. Supra-parochial divisions are not required. Canon 374, §2 permits several neighboring parishes to be joined together in order to foster pastoral care through common action. Vicariates forane are named as an example of such groupings. The bishop can also create a region or district in the diocese and place an episcopal vicar in charge (c. 476). The episcopal vicar is a local ordinary and as such possesses ordinary general executive power (c. 134). The vicar forane does not possess the power of governance in the strict sense but exercises vicarious ordinary pastoral authority as a representative of the bishop. Episcopal vicars may be in charge of several vicariates forane or may substitute for the vicar forane in dioceses where only one supra-parochial structure is instituted: that of the district governed by an episcopal vicar. Finally, pastoral zones may be created within a vicariate composed of two or more parishes served by a common pastor or pastoral team.

The *Directory on the Pastoral Ministry of Bishops* (189) recommends that in large dioceses urban or rural vicariates be joined into pastoral regions with episcopal vicars as their heads. Episcopal vicars could also be appointed for particular groups of the faithful whose special care is entrusted to them (e.g., women religious, the laity of various social or religious categories, etc.) (*CD* 27; *ES* I, 14: 1–5).

Similarly, the *Directory* (184) suggests that in addition to territorially defined vicariates forane there can be personal, ritual, or functional deaneries, such as a deanery consisting of hospital chaplains or an ethnic vicariate for a particular language or ethnic group in a region.

The Eastern code requires the eparchial bishop to consult the presbyteral council before establishing, changing, or suppressing a district consisting of several parishes (*CCEO* 276, §2). While this is not required in the Latin code, the *Directory* (186) recommends that the bishop consult the priests' council before drawing up general constitutions for the deaneries or vicariates forane of the diocese. The

---

[2] For other reflections on these canons see Calvo, in *Pamplona ComEng*, 402–404; Janicki, in *CLSA Com*, 440–443; Read, in *CLSGBI Com*, 306–307.

constitution should define the composition of each deanery, the title of the leader, his faculties, and regulations for expediting the work of the vicariate. Otherwise, the Eastern code (*CCEO* 276–278) is substantially the same as the Latin code.

Finally, too much weight should not be placed on the location of the canons on the vicar forane. In the 1917 code the canons on vicars forane (*CIC* 445–450) immediately preceded the canons on pastors (*CIC* 451–470). In the Eastern code as well the canons on protopresbyters (*CCEO* 276–278) immediately precede the canons on parishes, pastors, and parochial vicars. In the present Latin code, vicars forane are treated in the canons following parishes and parish personnel (cc. 515–552), perhaps because the division of the diocese into parishes is required and vicariates forane are now optional.

Title and Appointment of the Vicar Forane

Canon 553 — §1. A vicar forane, who is also called a dean, an archpriest, or some other name, is a priest who is placed over a vicariate forane.

§2. Unless particular law establishes otherwise, the diocesan bishop appoints the vicar forane, after he has heard the priests who exercise ministry in the vicariate in question according to his own prudent judgment.

Title

The vicar forane is known in some countries or dioceses as the dean, archpriest, urban vicar, area vicar, etc. In the Eastern churches he is known as a protopresbyter. These offices in both the Eastern and Western church were described by Vatican II (*CD* 30) and subsequent legislation (*ES* I, 19).

Appointment

A vicar forane is appointed by the diocesan bishop. Since the term "local ordinary" is not used, a vicar general or episcopal vicar could not appoint a vicar forane without a special mandate.

The law recommends that before appointing a vicar forane, the bishop consult with the priests who exercise ministry in the vicariate.

The canon also permits particular law to determine another way of naming the vicar forane. In some places, for example, the priests of the area select a candidate for appointment by the bishop. A broader selection process including members of the Christian faithful is also possible, provided the candidate is a priest; deacons and lay persons are excluded from the office of vicar forane.

Since a vicar forane is defined in law as a priest who is placed over a vicariate forane, the bishop may not dispense from the requirement of priesthood in order to appoint someone who is not a priest (c. 86).

Qualifications, Term of Office, Removal of the Vicar Forane

Canon 554 — §1. For the office of vicar forane, which is not tied to the office of pastor of a certain parish, the bishop is to select a priest whom he has judged suitable, after he has considered the circumstances of place and time.

§2. A vicar forane is to be appointed for a certain period of time determined by particular law.

§3. The diocesan bishop can freely remove a vicar forane from office for a just cause in accord with his own prudent judgment.

Qualifications

Both the 1917 code (*CIC* 446, §1) and the Eastern code (*CCEO* 277, §1) encourage the appointment of a pastor as vicar forane. The Latin code requires only that a suitable priest be appointed; he may be a pastor, a parochial vicar, a retired priest, or a chaplain; he may come from the diocesan priesthood, a religious institute, or society of apostolic life (c. 554, §1).

The office of vicar forane is not attached to a particular parish. Although attachment to a parish was not required by the 1917 code, it was customary in some places to designate a parish in the deanery as the central parish whose pastor was automatically the dean.

Suitability for the office ought to be judged in terms of the job description outlined in canon 555.

The *Directory on the Pastoral Ministry of Bishops* (187) recommends criteria for judging the suitability of a candidate for the office of vicar forane. He must be a priest who:

1. personally exercises the care of souls.
2. resides in the district.
3. is respected by the clergy and people for his learning, prudence, piety, and apostolic work.
4. is a person to whom the bishop may suitably grant faculties for the vicariate.
5. is able to promote and coordinate the joint pastoral program in the territory.

Term of Office

Like the episcopal vicar who is not an auxiliary bishop (c. 477, §1), the judicial vicar, his adjutant, and the diocesan judges (c. 1422), and members of the college of consultors (c. 502, §1), the vicar forane is to be appointed for a term of office. The length of the term and the question of re-appointment are to be determined by particular law either at the diocesan level (episcopal decree or diocesan synod) or perhaps by the conference of bishops (*Directory* 187). The appointment should be in writing (c. 156). Any faculties or additional powers or responsibilities not stated in common or particular law should be included in the letter of appointment.

Removal from Office

Because the vicar forane acts on behalf of the diocesan bishop in certain pastoral affairs, the bishop must have the freedom to appoint and remove the vicar. The law requires that there be a just cause for removal; an arbitrary or unjust reason is excluded. However, a serious cause is not required. Grave reasons ordinarily are required for the removal from office conferred for a speci-

fied period of time before the term has expired (c. 193, §2). The vicar forane is an exception. In order to be effective, the decree of removal must be communicated in writing (c. 193, §4). A just cause for removal might include failure to fulfill the job requirements or the urgent need to assign the vicar forane other duties incompatible with the office.

Faculties, Duties, and Rights of the Vicar Forane

Canon 555 — §1. In addition to the faculties legitimately given to him by particular law, the vicar forane has the duty and right:

1° of promoting and coordinating common pastoral activity in the vicariate;

2° of seeing to it that the clerics of his district lead a life in keeping with their state and perform their duties diligently;

3° of seeing to it that religious functions are celebrated according to the prescripts of the sacred liturgy, that the beauty and elegance of churches and sacred furnishings are maintained carefully, especially in the eucharistic celebration and custody of the Most Blessed Sacrament, that the parochial registers are inscribed correctly and protected appropriately, that ecclesiastical goods are administered carefully, and finally that the rectory is cared for with proper diligence.

§2. In the vicariate entrusted to him, the vicar forane:

1° is to see to it that, according to the prescripts of particular law and at the times stated, the clerics attend lectures, theological meetings, or conferences according to the norm of can. 279, §2;

2° is to take care that spiritual supports are available to the presbyters of his district, and likewise to be concerned especially for those who find themselves in more difficult circumstances or are beset by problems.

§3. The vicar forane is to take care that the pastors of his district whom he knows to be gravely ill do not lack spiritual and material aids and that the funeral rites of those who have died are celebrated worthily. He is also to make provision so that, on the occasion of illness or death, the registers, documents, sacred furnishings, and other things which belong to the Church are not lost or removed.

§4. A vicar forane is obliged to visit the parishes of his district according to the determination made by the diocesan bishop.

Particular law may legitimately grant certain faculties to the vicar forane. Among these faculties, pastoral needs might suggest the granting of certain matrimonial dispensations and permissions, granting of faculties for confession to visiting priests, or the faculty to administer confirmation (c. 884, §1).

The duties and rights attached to the office of vicar forane are ultimately the responsibility of the diocesan bishop. The vicar forane acts as the bishop's vicar in carrying out these responsibilities. This vicarious authority is pastoral, not governmental in the strict sense. The vicar forane is not a local ordinary. The responsibilities of the vicar forane listed in this canon could be further defined by particular law. A set of statutes or regulations for directing the work of the vicariate would also be helpful (*Directory* 186).

The code defines four general areas of rights and duties of the vicar forane to be further specified by particular law.

Promotion and Coordination
of Common Pastoral Activity

The diocesan bishop is to promote and coordinate the various aspects of the apostolate within the diocese and its individual districts (c. 394, §1). The activity of the diocesan pastoral council may be coordinated with that of parish pastoral councils; parish councils grouped together in areas such as vicariates could choose representatives to serve on the diocesan council (*Directory*

204). The vicar forane assists the diocesan bishop as his vicar for apostolic and pastoral coordination. In doing so he is to respect the autonomy of the parishes and other institutions in his district. In accordance with diocesan policies and episcopal directives, he convenes the association of the vicariate's clergy, the representatives of parish pastoral councils, staffs of parishes and institutions involved in the apostolate and pastoral care, and members of laity involved in apostolic movements and associations.

Supervision of Clergy

The diocesan bishop is expected to demonstrate a special concern for his presbyters, protecting their rights, seeing that they fulfill the obligations proper to their state, making available means and institutions to foster their intellectual and spiritual life, providing for their decent support and social assistance (c. 384). The vicar forane acts as the bishop's vicar in exercising this broad pastoral responsibility toward the presbyters of the district and other clerics. He is concerned with the life-style and ministerial duties of the clergy (priests and deacons) in the district. Paragraphs two and three of the canon specify certain implications of such pastoral concern:

1. *Continuing education of the clergy.* Canon 279, §2 requires priests to attend pastoral and theological lectures, meetings, and conferences in accordance with prescriptions of particular law. The vicar forane reminds the clerics in the district to attend such functions or may even organize study days as directed by the diocesan bishop.

2. *Spiritual needs of the presbyterate.* The vicar forane assists the presbyters of his district to deepen their spiritual lives by encouraging days of recollection, attendance at retreats, and other means.

3. *Social assistance for the clergy.* Finally, the vicar forane is to embody a special concern

for the pastors in his district who are seriously ill or need social assistance. He is charged with seeing to the details of their funerals, and ensuring the protection of the books, documents, sacred furnishings, and other things which belong to the Church.

Supervision of Liturgical and Temporal Administration

The diocesan bishop is to exercise vigilance throughout the diocese in the areas of ministry of the word, celebration of the sacraments and sacramentals, divine worship and veneration of the saints, and the administration of goods (c. 392, §2). The vicar forane assists him in fulfilling his duty of oversight by supervising liturgical functions in his district, the care of churches, the celebration of sacramentals, custody of the Blessed Sacrament, the maintenance of ecclesiastical records, especially of the sacraments, and the administration of parish goods, as well as general maintenance of the parish house and office.

Visitation of the Parishes in the Vicariate

The diocesan bishop is to complete a pastoral visitation of his diocese every five years, either personally or through another priest (e.g., his auxiliary bishop, vicar general, or episcopal vicar). He may enlist the vicar forane to assist in this visitation (c. 396). The vicar forane is also obliged to visit the vicariate by reason of his own office. The diocesan bishop is to regulate the frequency of the visitation, the pastoral issues to be discussed, and the manner of reporting to the bishop. At the very least the visitation should include the three general areas of common pastoral activities, life-style and ministerial duties of the clergy, and liturgical and temporal administration. When the bishop is legitimately hindered from personally visiting his diocese, visitation by the vicar forane might be an adequate substitute.

In addition to the responsibilities listed in this canon, the vicar forane is treated in other places in the code and in the *Directory on the Pastoral Ministry of Bishops:*

– Vicars forane are to be called to the diocesan synod as its members and are obliged to participate in it (c. 463, §1, 7°).

– The diocesan bishop is to hear the vicar forane when making a judgment as to the suitability of appointing a pastor to a vacant parish (c. 524). The *Directory* recommends that the vicar also be consulted when a pastor is transferred or removed (*Directory* 187 citing *CD* 29–30 and *ES* I, 19).

– If he judges it opportune, the diocesan bishop hears the vicar forane as well as the pastor or pastors before appointing a parochial vicar (c. 547).

Finally some deans may be chosen as *ex officio* members of the presbyteral council and the diocesan pastoral council unless the bishop makes other arrangements (*Directory* 188).

CHAPTER VIII
RECTORS OF CHURCHES AND CHAPLAINS
[cc. 556–572]

ARTICLE 1: RECTORS OF CHURCHES[3]
[cc. 556–563]

The Office of Rector

Canon 556 — Rectors of churches are understood here as priests to whom is committed the care of some church which is neither parochial nor capitular nor connected to a house of a religious community or society of apostolic life which celebrates services in it.

Rectors are given the care of a church building, i.e., a sacred building designed for divine worship to which the faithful have the right of

---

[3] For other reflections on these canons see Calvo, in *Pamplona ComEng,* 404–406; Janicki, in *CLSA Com,* 443–445; Read, in *CLSGBI Com,* 308–310.

entry for divine worship, especially its public exercise (c. 1214). The rector has at least minimal pastoral responsibilities and must be a priest. The rector, like the chaplain, treated subsequently, exercises some spiritual care of persons and is generally subordinate to the ministry of the local pastor. Because priesthood is constitutive of the office of rector, it cannot be dispensed from as a qualification for the office (c. 86).

The church entrusted to a rector may not be a parish church (or mission of a parish), a capitular church, or a church connected with the house of a religious community or of a society of apostolic life actually used by these communities. However, other churches which may belong to such groups but are not used by them have rectors appointed or installed by the diocesan bishop.

In the United States, the pastor of the cathedral is sometimes referred to as the rector, but this is not a canonical term. In many countries the cathedral is not a parish and is entrusted to a rector in the sense of this canon. However, in the United States cathedrals are usually parish churches as well as churches for the diocese.

Appointment of Rectors

Canon 557 — §1. The diocesan bishop freely appoints the rector of a church, without prejudice to the right of election or presentation if someone legitimately has it; in that case, it is for the diocesan bishop to confirm or install the rector.

§2. Even if a church belongs to some clerical religious institute of pontifical right, the diocesan bishop is competent to install the rector presented by the superior.

§3. The rector of a church which is connected with a seminary or other college which is governed by clerics is the rector of the seminary or college unless the diocesan bishop has determined otherwise.

Ordinarily it is the diocesan bishop who appoints the rector of a church. The vicar general and episcopal vicar require a special mandate to do so,

although canon 563 permits all these authority figures to remove the rector for a just cause.

In addition to free episcopal appointment, two other methods of provision of the office of rector are possible. If some other person or community has the right to elect or present a candidate, the diocesan bishop confirms the person elected (cc. 164–183) or installs the person presented (cc. 158–163). Finally, even if the church belongs to a clerical religious institute of pontifical right, the diocesan bishop installs the rector presented by the superior (c. 557, §2).

On the other hand, the rector of a seminary or college run by clerics is also the rector of the church connected with the institution. However, the bishop can make an exception.

Rights of Rectors

Canon 558 — Without prejudice to the prescript of can. 262, a rector is not permitted to perform the parochial functions mentioned in can. 530, nn. 1–6 in the church entrusted to him unless the pastor consents or, if the matter warrants it, delegates.

The rector is not allowed to perform the parochial functions especially entrusted to the pastor of the local parish unless he has the pastor's consent or has been directed to do so by the local ordinary (c. 560). In accordance with canon 530:

1. The rector may not administer solemn baptism. Ordinarily the rector would not conduct a catechumenate unless directed to do so by the local ordinary or with the permission of the pastor.

2. The rector may not administer confirmation even in danger of death without at least the presumed permission of the local pastor.

3. The rector may not administer Viaticum and anointing of the sick without at least the pastor's presumed permission.

4. The rector may not assist at marriages without delegation from the pastor and his permission to celebrate the marriage at the rector's church.

5. The rector may not conduct funerals unless he first informs the departed person's pastor.

6. Ordinarily the rector's church does not have a baptismal font. The rector may not lead competing processions in the territory of the parish. The celebration of Mass on Sundays and holy days of obligation should not conflict with the parish Masses.

The local ordinary, however, may direct the rector to celebrate some or all of these services for people who attend the church (c. 560).

Offerings received from the Christian faithful for parochial functions belong to the parish account unless the donor states otherwise (c. 531). The diocesan bishop, however, after consulting the presbyteral council, may decide to allocate all or a portion of these donations to the rector or his church.

The seminary is exempt from parochial governance (c. 262). Hence its rector is an exception to the general prohibition on the activities of rectors expressed in this canon. The seminary rector fulfills the office of pastor for all who are in the seminary with two exceptions: (1) He may not assist at marriage without proper delegation from the pastor or local ordinary nor may he delegate official ministers to assist at marriage (c. 1111); (2) he may not normally hear the confessions of the students (c. 985).

Liturgical Celebrations by the Rector

Canon 559 — A rector can perform liturgical celebrations, even solemn ones, in the church entrusted to him, without prejudice to the legitimate laws of the foundation, and provided that, in the judgment of the local ordinary, they do not harm parochial ministry in any way.

The rector of a church is ordinarily limited to non-parochial liturgical celebrations, e.g., the celebration of the Eucharist and the sacrament of reconciliation, the liturgy of the hours, exposition of the Blessed Sacrament, benediction, etc. The parochial functions listed in canon 530, 1°–6° are excluded from the rector's competency without permission of the pastor.

Other Parochial Services
Which May Be Assigned to the Rector

Canon 560 — When the local ordinary considers it opportune, he can order a rector to celebrate in his church particular functions, even parochial ones, for the people and to make the church available for certain groups of the Christian faithful to conduct liturgical celebrations there.

The local ordinary may direct the rector to celebrate certain liturgical functions, even the parochial functions in canon 530, 1°–6° for the people who attend the church. He may also direct the rector to make the church available to other groups in the diocese who may not have their own church.

Required Permission of the Rector

Canon 561 — No one is permitted to celebrate the Eucharist, administer the sacraments, or perform other sacred functions in the church without the permission of the rector or another legitimate superior; this permission must be granted or denied according to the norm of law.

Since the rector is responsible for the proper celebration of liturgical functions in his church, his permission is required to use the church. Another legitimate superior such as the local ordinary or religious superior to whom the church belongs may also grant such a permission.

Canon 903 gives the norms for permitting a priest to celebrate Mass (the "celebret"). Canon 764 requires the presumed permission of the rector before a presbyter or deacon may preach.

Duties of Rectors

Canon 562 — The rector of a church, under the authority of the local ordinary and observing the legitimate statutes and acquired rights, is obliged to see to it that sacred functions are celebrated worthily in the church according to the liturgical norms and prescripts of the canons, that obligations are fulfilled faithfully, that goods are administered diligently, that the maintenance and beauty of sacred furnishings and buildings are provided for, and that nothing whatever occurs which is in any way unfitting to the holiness of the place and the reverence due to a house of God.

The principal responsibilities of a rector are listed in this canon:

1. To see that liturgical and canonical norms are followed in the celebration of sacred functions.

2. To see that special obligations associated with the church are fulfilled, e.g., prayers for donors or benefactors, Mass obligations and foundation Masses, etc.

3. To administer the goods of the church and maintain its furnishings and building.

4. To prevent use of the building in any way out of harmony with a sacred place.

In exercising these responsibilities, the rector is accountable to the local ordinary, not the pastor. He is bound to respect particular law and acquired rights which affect the church.

Removal of the Rector

Canon 563 — Without prejudice to the prescript of can. 682, §2, the local ordinary, for a just cause and according to his own prudent judgment, can remove the rector of a church from office, even if he had been elected or presented by others.

The diocesan bishop freely names the rector of a church, confirms the person elected, or installs the priest presented by a superior. However, the local ordinary, i.e., the diocesan bishop, the vicar general, or the episcopal vicar can remove the rector for a just cause. An unjust or arbitrary cause is excluded; however, a grave cause is not required. Notification of removal must be in writing (c. 193, §4). If the rector is appointed for a term, the letter of appointment should clarify whether removal may be effected for a just cause at the discretion of the local ordinary, or whether a grave cause is required. As always, a religious rector may be removed by the diocesan bishop who appointed him without the consent of the superior but with prior notice (c. 682, §2). The superior may also remove the rector with prior notice to the bishop.

The bishop does not have to obtain anyone's permission before he removes a rector who has been confirmed after election or installed upon presentation.

ARTICLE 2: CHAPLAINS
[cc. 564–572]

The Office of Chaplain[4]

Canon 564 — A chaplain is a priest to whom is entrusted in a stable manner the pastoral care, at least in part, of some community or particular group of the Christian faithful, which is to be exercised according to the norm of universal and particular law.

Canonically, a chaplain is a priest who serves in a stable manner "some community" or "particular group of the Christian faithful" (c. 516, §2). Although the office is pastoral, the chaplain is not a pastor; he does not serve a parish (c. 515) or quasi-parish (c. 516, §1). He may serve an institution

---

[4] For other reflections on the canons see Calvo, in *Pamplona ComEng*, 406–408; Janicki, in *CLSA Com*, 445–447; Read, in *CLSGBI Com*, 310–313.

such as a school, hospital, or prison, or he may serve a group such as immigrants, sailors and their passengers, or the military. He is not the rector of a church unless a non-parochial church is attached to the house of a community or group. The stability attaches to the office and not to the group, which may be itinerant or transient in nature.

A deacon or lay minister cannot be a chaplain in the canonical sense. The current usage of the word "chaplain" to refer to anyone engaged in pastoral activity in hospitals, prisons, schools, etc., whether lay or religious, is a broad and analogous use of the term. The August 15, 1997 multi-congregation instruction on collaboration of the non-ordained faithful in the ministry of the priest forbids such usage (art. 1, §3).[5]

The canons in this article regulate the exercise of the canonical office of chaplain, yet there are other references to chaplains in the code. For example, canons 317–318 deal with chaplains of associations of the Christian faithful, and canon 813 refers to university chaplains. Other canons treat the right and duty of chaplains to bring Viaticum to the sick (c. 911), and to celebrate funeral rites in the church or oratory of a non-clerical institute of consecrated life or society of apostolic life (c. 1179).

Particular law should make more specific the basic framework on chaplains established by the code. Particular law should also determine the rights and obligations and norms regarding the appointment and removal of pastoral workers who assist chaplains as well as their relationship to him.

In summary, the code mentions several types of chaplains:

- The chaplain in hospitals, in prisons, and on board ship (c. 566, §2)
- The chaplain to a house of a lay religious institute (c. 567, §1)
- The chaplain to migrants, exiles, refugees, nomads, sailors (cc. 568; 383, §1)

[5] *AAS* 89 (1997) 863; *Origins* 27/24 (November 27, 1997) 403.

- Military chaplains (c. 569; apconst *Spirituali militum curae,* April 21, 1986)
- The chaplain of a community or group with a non-parochial church (c. 570)
- The chaplain of an association of the Christian faithful (c. 317)
- The university chaplain for campus ministry (c. 813)

Particular law may establish other chaplaincies, e.g., to orphanages, boarding schools, airports, lay movements even without non-parochial churches, etc.

Appointment of Chaplains

Canon 565 — Unless the law provides otherwise or someone legitimately has special rights, a chaplain is appointed by the local ordinary to whom it also belongs to install the one presented or to confirm the one elected.

A chaplain is appointed in four ways:

1. He may be freely appointed and removed by the local ordinary, namely the diocesan bishop, vicar general, or episcopal vicar. By contrast pastors, parochial vicars, and vicars forane are appointed by the diocesan bishop and may be removed by him. Rectors of churches are also appointed by the diocesan bishop but may be removed by the local ordinary.

2. A chaplain may be presented by another authority, e.g., the administrator of a hospital, the principal of a school, a religious superior if this is specified in law. The person presented is installed by the local ordinary.

3. The chaplain may be elected by the group, e.g., a confraternity or other association of the faithful (c. 317). The local ordinary confirms the one elected.

4. The law may provide another manner for provision of this office or special rights of appointment may legitimately belong to someone

other than the local ordinary. Military chaplains are governed by special laws (c. 569). Special agreements with the Holy See (concordats) may specify the right to appoint certain chaplains. The authority competent to erect a public association of the Christian faithful has the right by law to name the chaplain (c. 317, §1). Likewise the superior of an institute names or confirms the chaplain for an association erected by members of a religious institute in their own church or house (c. 317, §2).

Faculties of Chaplains

Canon 566 — §1. A chaplain must be provided with all the faculties which proper pastoral care requires. In addition to those which are granted by particular law or special delegation, a chaplain possesses by virtue of office the faculty of hearing the confessions of the faithful entrusted to his care, of preaching the word of God to them, of administering Viaticum and the anointing of the sick, and of conferring the sacrament of confirmation on those who are in danger of death.

§2. In hospitals, prisons, and on sea journeys, a chaplain, moreover, has the faculty, to be exercised only in those places, of absolving from *latae sententiae* censures which are neither reserved nor declared, without prejudice, however, to the prescript of can. 976.

Since the chaplain is entrusted with some pastoral care of a community or group of the faithful which has not been or cannot be erected as a parish or even established as a quasi-parish (c. 516, §2), this canon lists the basic faculties needed for him to exercise pastoral care in a responsible fashion. The following faculties granted by universal law are attached to this office:

- to hear confessions of the faithful entrusted to his care
- to preach the word of God to them
- to administer Viaticum
- to anoint the sick
- to confirm those who are in danger of death.

Particular law or special delegation may grant additional faculties when needed, as, for example, in campus ministry, refugee camps, etc. Among such faculties are the authorization to perform solemn baptism, assist at marriages, and conduct funerals. Such faculties should be granted in writing. Particular law or the letter of appointment should also include norms on keeping sacramental records, informing the parish priest when sacraments are administered to his subjects, cumulative rights of the faithful to receive the sacraments from the chaplain as well as from their own pastor, etc.

Because of the difficulty of having recourse to the competent authority, chaplains to hospitals and prisons and on board ship have faculties to absolve from *latae sententiae* censures which are not reserved or declared. This faculty may be exercised in ordinary circumstances and is not limited to danger-of-death situations in which case every priest can absolve from all censures and sins (c. 976). This faculty is also more extensive than the faculty granted to the canon penitentiary which is limited to the sacramental forum (c. 508, §1).

Chaplains of Lay Religious

Canon 567 — §1. The local ordinary is not to proceed to the appointment of a chaplain to a house of a lay religious institute without consulting the superior, who has the right to propose a specific priest after the superior has heard the community.

§2. It is for the chaplain to celebrate or direct liturgical functions; nevertheless, he is not permitted to involve himself in the internal governance of the institute.

The local ordinary must consult with the superior before appointing a chaplain for the house of a lay religious institute. The superior has the right to propose a priest for the office after consulting the community. After this consultation, the superior is free to provide the more suitable candidate; and the local ordinary is equally free to appoint the more suitable candidate.

The chaplain may be the confessor for the house. The superior is nevertheless obliged to arrange for suitable confessors to be available for the members (c. 630, §2).

As in the 1917 code (*CIC* 524, §3), the present canon prohibits the chaplain from interfering in the internal government of the institute. His responsibility is limited to the celebration or supervision of liturgical functions.

Chaplains of Migrants and Others Deprived of Ordinary Pastoral Care

Canon 568 — As far as possible, chaplains are to be appointed for those who are not able to avail themselves of the ordinary care of pastors because of the condition of their lives, such as migrants, exiles, refugees, nomads, sailors.

Ordinary pastoral care is exercised by pastors (c. 519) and pastoral teams (c. 517). According to this canon the local ordinary is responsible for providing pastoral care for groups that cannot avail themselves of the services provided in parishes or quasi-parishes (c. 383, §1). The canon lists as examples of such groups migrants, exiles, refugees, nomads, and sailors. To this list could be added travelers, airport personnel, students (c. 813), and those confined to institutions such as hospitals and prisons.

Campus Ministers or University Chaplains

Canon 813 instructs the diocesan bishop to provide pastoral care for students by creating parishes for them, or establishing university centers at both Catholic and non-Catholic universities and appointing chaplains to serve these.

Chaplains to Public Associations of the Christian Faithful

The Holy See in the case of international associations, the conference of bishops for national associations, and the diocesan bishop (not the vicar general or episcopal vicar) for diocesan associations names the chaplain for public associations of the Christian faithful after hearing the major officials, unless of course the statutes provide otherwise (c. 317, §1). The chaplain may not act as moderator or chairman of non-clerical associations unless the statutes provide otherwise (c. 317, §3).

Military Chaplains

Canon 569 — Military chaplains are governed by special laws.

The special laws referred to in this canon are contained in the apostolic constitution of John Paul II *Spirituali militum curae*[6] and in statutes approved by the Holy See for each country.

Apostolic vicariates and military ordinariates are established by the Holy See in many parts of the world to provide for the pastoral needs of military personnel. Military chaplains are the equivalent of pastors of personal parishes. Besides the faculties mentioned in canon 566 they are usually granted pastoral faculties for solemn baptism, assisting at marriages, and conducting funerals. In the United States the military ordinariate (archdiocese) has its own chancery and tribunal. Its sacramental records are kept in central archives at that chancery office.

The jurisdiction of the military ordinary and of the chaplains is cumulative with that of the diocesan bishop and the local pastors. If there is no military chaplain to minister to their needs, the proper pastor of the territory where the military base is located has pastoral responsibility for military personnel in his parish.

Chaplains of a Non-Parochial Church

Canon 570 — If a non-parochial church is connected to the seat of a community or group, the chaplain is to be the rector of that church, unless the care of the community or of the church requires otherwise.

[6] April 21, 1986, *AAS* 78 (1986) 481–486.

This canon should be read in conjunction with canon 560 on the pastoral services of the rector of a church. Rectors of churches are ordinarily limited to liturgical celebrations such as Mass and the liturgy of the word and may not celebrate services specially entrusted to the pastor (c. 530) such as solemn baptism, assistance at marriage, conducting funerals, confirmation in danger of death, and even Viaticum and anointing of the sick without at least the presumed consent of the pastor (c. 558). However, the local ordinary may instruct the rector to provide even these parochial functions for the faithful who attend the church and to make the church available for groups of the Christian faithful (c. 560).

Canon 570 states that when the headquarters of a religious community, secular institute, society of apostolic life, or association of the Christian faithful is attached to a non-parochial church, the chaplain of the group should usually be appointed the rector of the church. As rector he performs liturgical functions in the church for the public. He also has those faculties granted him by law for the pastoral care of his community (c. 566). Finally, he may be granted certain parochial faculties either as rector of the church or as chaplain of his community or both.

The canon ends by admitting that even if the headquarters of a community or group is attached to a non-parochial church, the office of chaplain and rector may be separated.

Chaplain's Relation to the Local Pastor

Canon 571 — In the exercise of his pastoral function, a chaplain is to preserve a fitting relationship with the pastor.

The chaplain's role is complementary or supplementary to that of the local pastor. It is the duty of the chaplain to coordinate his ministry with the parish and to maintain good communications with the pastor. If the chaplain is given special faculties to celebrate solemn baptism, to witness marriages, and to conduct funerals, special agreements need to be arranged between the parish and chaplaincy and the directives of the local ordinary communicated to the pastor. For example, when the chaplain serves a hospital within the parish boundaries, arrangements should be made to cover emergencies when the chaplain is away. Conflicts between the chaplain and local pastor should preferably be settled by them; but if this proves impossible, they should be referred to the local ordinary for resolution.

Removal of Chaplains

Canon 572 — In what pertains to the removal of a chaplain, the prescript of can. 563 is to be observed.

The law for the removal of a rector (c. 563) is applicable to the removal of a chaplain. The chaplain as well as the rector can be removed for a just cause by the local ordinary in accord with his own judgment. While an unjust or arbitrary cause is excluded, a grave cause is not required.

The law does not discuss the situation where a chaplain is appointed for a term of office. Ordinarily a grave cause is required for removal from office of someone appointed for a term before the term has expired (c. 193, §2). However, although the vicar forane is appointed for a term, he may be removed for a just cause as an exception to the general norm (c. 554, §3). The same exception seems relevant to the ordinary in removing a chaplain whom he has freely appointed to a term. To avoid confusion, the letter of appointment should clarify whether appointment to a term of office implies the possibility of removal for a grave cause only or whether the chaplain continues to serve at the discretion of the local ordinary and may be removed for a just cause.

Religious chaplains can be removed from office by the local ordinary or superior after notifying the other but without necessarily receiving the other's consent (c. 682, §2).

Rose M. McDermott, S.S.J.

Part III
INSTITUTES OF CONSECRATED LIFE AND SOCIETIES OF APOSTOLIC LIFE
[cc. 573–746]

Part three of Book II describes the Christian faithful from both the clerical and lay states who assume the three evangelical counsels by public vow or other sacred bond or who live in the spirit of the counsels in common life and a shared apostolic or missionary work. While they are gifts of the Spirit and an integral part of the life and holiness of the Church, these institutes and societies do not belong to its hierarchical structure addressed in Book II, part two, canons 330–572 of the code.

Part three of Book II is divided into two sections. Section one provides both general norms (cc. 573–606) and particular norms for religious institutes (cc. 607–709) and secular institutes (cc. 710–730). Members of these institutes of consecrated life assume the evangelical counsels of chastity, poverty, and obedience through a public vow or other sacred bond. Section two legislates for societies of apostolic life (cc. 731–746) in which members share common life and engage in apostolic or missionary work. These persons live in the spirit of the evangelical counsels which in some societies are embraced by a bond defined in the constitutions (c. 731, §2).

Although there are distinctions made between religious and secular institutes and between them as institutes of consecrated life and societies of apostolic life, twenty-one of the general norms for institutes of consecrated life apply to societies of apostolic life. Likewise, canons 598–602 apply to societies of apostolic life in which the members embrace the evangelical counsels by some bond defined in the constitutions (c. 732). Fourteen norms for religious institutes explicitly or implicitly apply to secular institutes;[1] forty-six canons for religious institutes explicitly or implicitly apply to societies of apostolic life.[2] This juridical overlapping shows the unity and complementarity of the Spirit's gifts and the difficulty of describing spiritual realities in legal terms. Besides these institutes and societies, there are individual Christian faithful who live an eremitical life (c. 603) or a life of consecrated virginity (c. 604) under the direction of the diocesan bishop. These two ancient forms of consecrated life have been renewed since the Second Vatican Council. Finally, the Church remains ever open to the gifts of the Spirit and the possibility of new forms of consecrated life (c. 605).[3]

Part three of Book II reflects the development of consecrated life in the history of the Church. From the New Testament to the present, there have been men and women under the inspiration of the Holy Spirit who have sought to live the example and teachings of Christ. Church authority studies and approves this vocation in a variety of forms: consecrated widowhood and virginity rooted in the New Testament; the eremitical life of the silence of solitude; monasticism and its daily horarium of liturgy, labor, contemplation, and meals in common; mendicancy characterized by poverty, preaching, charitable works, and mobility; the apostolic life offering the fruits of contemplation through dedicated apostolic service; and secular institutes with their hidden leaven-like presence in the world. Some faithful seek to follow Christ, poor, chaste, and obedient through assuming the counsels by public vow[4] or some other sacred bond in institutes[5] or individually.[6] Still others live

---

[1] See cc. 715, §2; 727, §2; 729; 730.

[2] See cc. 733; 734; 735, §2; 738, §§1–2; 741, §1; 743; 744; 746.

[3] A. Neri, "Nuove forme di vita consacrata (can. 605–CIC): Profili giuridici," *ComRelMiss* 75/3–4 (1994) 253–308.

[4] Canon 607, §2.

[5] Canon 712.

[6] Canon 603, §2.

the spirit of the counsels with or without vows or other bonds, either living in common in a society[7] or alone[8] in service to the Church.[9] The norms in this part of Book II are rooted in the rich legal tradition of the Church and in conciliar documents[10] and postconciliar texts.[11] Much criticism was directed at the 1977 draft on institutes of life consecrated by the evangelical counsels for its "levelling" of all institutes and attempting to categorize a variety of religious institutes. However, the code commission *coetus* on religious law contributed much in introducing principles that directed the laborious task of revising the 1917 code. The legislation was to respect: (1) the spiritual nature of this vocation, (2) the nature, spirit, and end of each institute, (3) subsidiarity with references to the proper law, (4) the cooperative nature of governance in institutes, and (5) the equality between institutes of men and women. These principles guided the *coetus* in its unenviable task of ordering the gifts of the Spirit within a legal framework.[12]

Title XII of the Code of Canons of the Eastern Churches approaches consecrated life from an historical perspective in contrast to the more theoretical ordering of the Latin code. In the Eastern code, monastic religious life provides the pattern for religious orders and congregations as well as all other forms of consecrated life. The Eastern code legislates in detail for institutes of consecrated life, whereas the Latin text leaves significant latitude to the proper law of these institutes. There are other noteworthy distinctions between these two codes of law for consecrated life which order the gifts of the Spirit in accord with differing cultures and ecclesiastical structures.[13]

The 174 canons in part three of Book II of the Latin code show the evolution of this vocation in the Church. Some of the canons contain content which requires special examination: (1) exemption,[14] (2) governance in lay institutes,[15] (3) extraordinary administration,[16] (4) public vow,[17] and (5) juridical effects of eremitic life and consecrated virginity.[18]

Pope John Paul II's apostolic exhortation *Vita Consecrata,* issued after the 1994 synod of bishops, addresses the canonical issues raised by the synod members on the following topics: (1) new institutes, new forms, and new evangelical lifestyles,[19] (2) mixed institutes and equal rights of members,[20] (3) cloister for nuns,[21] (4) the nature and structure of associates joined to institutes,[22] (5) the order of virgins,[23] and (6) mutual relations between bishops and religious.[24] Furthermore, the pope exhorted institutes and their members to serve the special needs of today: the ecumenical movement and interreligious dialogue,[25] the new evangelization and inculturation,[26] evangelical poverty at the service of the

---

[7] Canon 731.

[8] Canon 604.

[9] L. Cada et al., "The Evolution of Religious Life: A Historical Model," in *Shaping the Coming Age of Religious Life,* 2nd ed. (Massachusetts: Affirmation Books, 1985) 11–50; J. Padberg, "Memory, Vision and Structure: Historical Perspectives on the Experience of Religious Life in the Church," in *Religious in the U.S. Church* (Mahwah, N.J.: Paulist, 1985) 64–78.

[10] *LG* VI; *PC; CD* 33–35; *AG* 18, 40.

[11] *ES* I: 22–40; II; III: 15–21; *RC, VS, ET,* and *MR.*

[12] ComCICRec, *Schema of Canons on Institutes of Life Consecrated by Profession of the Evangelical Counsels,* Eng. trans. by USCC (Washington, D.C.: 1977) 9–25.

[13] J. Abbass, "Forms of Consecrated Life Recognized in the Eastern and Latin Codes," *ComRelMiss* 76/1–2 (1995) 5–38; S. Holland, "A Spirit to Animate the Letter: CCEO Title XII," *J* 56/1 (1996) 288–306; R. McDermott, "Two Approaches to Consecrated Life: *The Code of Canons of the Eastern Churches* and the *Code of Canon Law*," *Stud Can* 29 (1995) 193–239.

[14] Canon 591.

[15] Canon 596, §1, §3.

[16] Canon 638, §1.

[17] Canons 607; 1192, §1.

[18] Canons 603, 604.

[19] *VC* 12, 62.

[20] *VC* 61.

[21] *VC* 59.

[22] *VC* 54–56.

[23] *VC* 57.

[24] *VC* 48–50.

[25] *VC* 101–102.

[26] *VC* 79–81.

poor,[27] and the field of social communications.[28] At the threshold of a new millennium, Pope John Paul II observed that consecrated life has "not

only a glorious history to remember and recount, but also a great history still to be accomplished!"[29]

[29] VC 110; R. McDermott, "The Ninth Ordinary Session of the Synod of Bishops: Four Moments and Six Canonical Issues," *ComRelMiss* 77/3–4 (1996) 261–294.

[27] VC 90.
[28] VC 99.

CANONS AND COMMENTARY

SECTION I
INSTITUTES OF CONSECRATED LIFE
[cc. 573–730]

TITLE I
NORMS COMMON TO ALL INSTITUTES OF CONSECRATED LIFE
[cc. 573–606]

Nature of Consecrated Life[30]

Canon 573 — §1. The life consecrated through the profession of the evangelical counsels is a stable form of living by which faithful, following Christ more closely under the action of the Holy Spirit, are totally dedicated to God who is loved most of all, so that, having been dedicated by a new and special title to His honor, to the building up of the Church, and to the salvation of the world, they strive for the perfection of charity in the service of the kingdom of God and, having been made an outstanding sign in the Church, foretell the heavenly glory.

This foundational canon employs both spiritual and juridical norms in describing the vocation to

consecrated life. Inspired by the Spirit, some of the faithful deepen their baptismal consecration through a free and total self-donation to God, who is loved above all through a new and special title or commitment.[31] This vocation is rooted in and more fully expresses the radical consecration of baptism.[32] Through profession of the evangelical counsels, both clerics and laity[33] seek a closer imitation of the chaste, poor, and obedient Christ[34] and strive for the perfection of charity in a permanent form of life.[35] The Church has long recognized the profession of the evangelical counsels as a kind of second baptism, a profound insertion into the Paschal Mystery of Christ.[36] Competent ecclesiastical authority constitutes consecrated life as a stable way of life with moral, social, and juridical effects.[37]

Trinitarian and Christological dimensions characterize life consecrated by the profession of the evangelical counsels lived in accord with the ap-

[30] *CCEO* 410 describes the religious state within the same theological context and seems to be a combination of cc. 573, §1 and 607, §2.

[31] Note that chapter 5 of *LG* deals with all those incorporated into Christ through baptism, whereas chapter 6 treats those called to consecrated life. In the 1983 code, the Christian faithful are provided for in the first section of Book II, and those consecrated through the profession of the evangelical counsels are addressed in this third part of Book II.

[32] *LG* 44, *PC* 5.
[33] Canon 207, §1.
[34] Mt 19:11–12, 21–29; Lk 9:23; Phil 2:7–8; *LG* 46.
[35] *LG* 39.
[36] *LG* 45.
[37] *CIC* 487; cc. 116; 120, §1; 607, §2; 712.

proved proper law of a particular institute.[38] Prompted by grace and motivated by charity, some of the faithful respond to this vocation and witness Christ's own life in love of the Father, openness to the Spirit, and service to people. The vocation manifests prophetic, apostolic, and eschatological elements. It witnesses to the very nature of the Church, contributes to its salvific mission, and anticipates eternal life.[39]

§2. The Christian faithful freely assume this form of living in institutes of consecrated life canonically erected by competent authority of the Church. Through vows or other sacred bonds according to the proper laws of the institutes, they profess the evangelical counsels of chastity, poverty, and obedience and, through the charity to which the counsels lead, are joined in a special way to the Church and its mystery.

Throughout the centuries, holy men and women guided by the Spirit have brought before the Church diverse expressions or ways of living the evangelical counsels. From these gifts of the Spirit, a wonderful variety of forms of consecrated life have been approved and canonically established by competent ecclesiastical authority.[40] This is an important concept, since consecrated life is a gift of the Spirit which the Church receives with gratitude and constitutes as a permanent way of life. Canons 603 and 604 describe hermits and consecrated virgins, individual persons totally dedicated to Christ.[41] Other canons in this section of the code provide for aggregates of persons or institutes of consecrated life.

Some members of the Christian faithful experience a call from God and an attraction to one of these canonically approved institutes of consecrated life. They respond of their own free will[42] and assume the obligations of the evangelical counsels of chastity, poverty, and obedience through vows or other sacred bonds in accord with the proper law of the institute.[43] While some institutes stipulate more or less than the three traditional evangelical counsels in the prescribed profession formula of the institute, all include the essential elements of Christ's total self-offering.[44]

Ecclesistical authority has great reverence for the proper law of each institute of consecrated life. Composed of constitutive or foundational norms approved by ecclesiastical authority and statutory or practical directives approved by the general chapter, the proper law articulates the nature, spirit, and purpose of the institute. It serves as a pedagogic and exhortatory document introducing candidates to the particular gift of God to be lived for the Church and encouraging members to persevere in their call. Imitating Christ's life in accord with a gift of the Spirit, the person lives a life of charity, witnesses gospel values, and is inextricably bound to the Church and its mystery in a special way.[45]

---

[38] Canons 578, 587.

[39] LG 43; VC 14–22; cc. 673, 713.

[40] LG 45, VC 5–11; see also cc. 116; 120, §1. Only competent ecclesiastical authority can change the nature of or suppress such institutes.

[41] Hermits undertake the three evangelical counsels by vows or other sacred bonds (c. 603, §2). Consecrated virgins assume a life of perpetual virginity and follow a way of life prescribed by the diocesan bishop (c. 604).

[42] Canons 219; 643, §1, 4°; 656, §4; 658; 721, §3.

[43] LG 43–44; cc. 607, §2; 712. The constitutions of each institute determine the kind of commitment and the proper object of the sacred bonds (cc. 587, §1; 598, §1). The bond is defined in the constitutions of societies of apostolic life in which the members assume the evangelical counsels (cc. 731, §2; 732).

[44] The Sermon on the Mount called all Christians to the living of the evangelical counsels. Members of religious and secular institutes profess to live chastity, poverty, and obedience in a more radical way in accord with the proper law of a specific institute. Formulas of profession differ. Members of one institute may profess obedience to the proper law which provides the way in which the evangelical counsels are lived. The formulas of other institutes contain a fourth vow or sacred promise of some particular virtue proper to the institute. A profession of stability and conversion of life, a vow to practice mercy or service to the destitute, and a vow of obedience to the Holy Father would be some examples included in the act of profession.

[45] LG 44; VC 29, 33.

Ecclesial Dimension of Consecrated Life[46]

Canon 574 — §1. The state of those who profess the evangelical counsels in institutes of this type belongs to the life and holiness of the Church and must be fostered and promoted by all in the Church.

This canon emphasizes the ecclesial nature of life consecrated by the evangelical counsels. The state neither belongs to the hierarchical ordering of the Church, nor is it an intermediate level between the clerical and lay state. Rather, consecrated life reflects the prophetic nature of the Church and enjoys a certain freedom and autonomy.[47] Each institute contributes to the life and holiness of the Church through its own gift.[48] Diocesan bishops, as well as all of the faithful, have a pastoral duty to promote and foster consecrated life.[49]

§2. Certain Christian faithful are specially called by God to this state so that they possess a special gift in the life of the Church and contribute to its salvific mission, according to the purpose and spirit of the institute.

Both clerics and laity can be called by God to respond through grace to live this state of consecrated life (c. 207, §2).[50] Guided by the Spirit, they enjoy a special gift in the Church and contribute to its salvific mission in accord with the spirit and purpose of their institute.[51]

Counsels Modeled on Christ

Canon 575 — The evangelical counsels, based on the teaching and examples of Christ the Teacher, are a divine gift which the Church has received

from the Lord and preserves always through His grace.

Christ lived and taught the evangelical counsels of chastity, poverty, and obedience.[52] Of the many gospel counsels, these three best express his own consecration in the Paschal Mystery,[53] his love and obedience to the Father even to death on the cross.[54] Prominent in the life of the Mother of God,[55] chastity, poverty, and obedience have significant relevance in the Church. Throughout the centuries countless men and women as hermits, monastics, mendicants, apostolic religious, and secular persons have dedicated themselves through a total self-offering to live these evangelical counsels in imitation of Christ.[56] Through this total self-offering, the person manifests the Trinitarian and Christological characteristics which should mark every Christian life.[57] The counsels are a radical living of gospel spirituality and a continuance of Christ's life and mission.[58] The Church makes every effort to preserve and promote this divine gift. In studying and approving constitutions submitted by institutes of consecrated life, ecclesiastical authority ensures that the evangelical counsels are preserved and lived in accord with the nature and spirit of the institute.[59]

Church Interprets, Orders the Counsels

Canon 576 — It is for the competent authority of the Church to interpret the evangelical counsels, to direct their practice by laws, and by canonical approbation to establish the stable forms of living deriving from them, and also, for its part, to take care that the institutes grow and flourish according to the spirit of the founders and sound traditions.

---

[46] Cf. *CCEO* 411.
[47] Canon 586.
[48] *LG* 43, *PC* 1.
[49] *LG* 44; *PC* 24; *MR* 28; *VC* 49; cc. 385, 387; see also *FC* 53, *AAS* 74 (1982) 81–91, esp. 81.
[50] *LG* 43.
[51] *LG* 43–44, *PC* 2, *VC* 36.

[52] *LG* 43, *PC* 1.
[53] Jn 17:18–19.
[54] Phil 2:8.
[55] *LG* 46, *VC* 112.
[56] *PC* 12–14, 16–17; *VC* 6–11.
[57] *VC* 21.
[58] Mt 9:9, 19:16–22, 20:20–27; Lk 18:18–23.
[59] *LG* 42–43, 46; *PC* 1; *VC* 18, 20–21, 30; c. 587, §1.

This juridic canon reflects conciliar teaching and recognizes the fourfold responsibility of church authority regarding the evangelical counsels: (1) to interpret the evangelical counsels, (2) to legislate for their practice, (3) to constitute stable forms of living them, and (4) to monitor the growth and development of the institutes in accord with their particular charism.[60]

In some instances the Apostolic See acts; in others the diocesan bishop has this responsibility. Only the Apostolic See can approve new forms of consecrated life[61] and erect or approve institutes of pontifical right.[62] Diocesan bishops erect institutes of diocesan right in the particular churches they govern.[63]

An institute of consecrated life ordinarily begins with a small gathering or association of the faithful.[64] Even before formal approval, such an association would fall under the vigilance of the diocesan bishop. He or his delegate would monitor the life and activity of the *de facto* association.[65] The practice of Christian virtue and expressions of the evangelical counsels can be misguided or carried to excess. Competent church authority judges the genuineness of a founding charism and the manner in which the counsels are lived so as to build up the life and holiness of the Church.[66]

Ecclesiastical approval gives assurance and stability to those drawn to the institute and to the ecclesial community that this form of life is in accord with gospel spirituality and church doctrine. Church authority exerts a vigilance in pointing out any departures from the spirit of the founder or the sound traditions of the institute. The members have primary responsibility in nurturing and fostering their gift for the whole Church. Gospel spirituality, the spirit of the founder, church teaching, and the needs of today's world are the criteria that the Church places before canonically approved institutes to enable them to grow and flourish.[67]

Variety of Gifts, Institutes

Canon 577 — In the Church there are a great many institutes of consecrated life which have different gifts according to the grace which has been given them: they more closely follow Christ who prays, or announces the kingdom of God, or does good to people, or lives with people in the world, yet who always does the will of the Father.

The Spirit has blessed the Church throughout its history with a wonderful variety of institutes of consecrated life. Each reflects a particular way of living Christ's life in obedience to the Father's will. All manifest the commandment of love and are as branches of the one vine integrated into the life of the Church. Through the gifts given to the holy founders and foundresses of institutes, the members of those institutes continue Christ's witness through fidelity to their proper charism.[68]

Some live lives of prayer, sacrifice, and penance in a more contemplative lifestyle;[69] others announce the kingdom of God in apostolic institutes dedicated to preaching, missionary activity, or some form of spiritual or corporal work of mercy.[70] Still others live a consecrated secularity as spiritual leaven in the world.[71] The institutes reflect a rich complementarity of gifts. Contemplative institutes share in the mission of the Church through their contributions of prayer and sacrifice. Apostolic and secular institutes find the source for the vitality of their activity in contemplation. Each institute presents Christ in a particular way and at a particular time of salvation history. All share Christ's mission of carrying out the Father's will for the salvation of the world.[72]

---

[60] *LG* 12, 45.
[61] Canon 605.
[62] Canon 593.
[63] Canon 579.
[64] Canon 215.
[65] Canons 305; 397, §1.
[66] *LG* 45.

[67] *PC* 2.
[68] *PC* 8, *VC* 5–12.
[69] Canon 674, *PC* 7, *AG* 40, *VC* 8.
[70] Canon 675, *PC* 8, *VC* 9.
[71] Canon 710, *PC* 11, *VC* 10.
[72] *LG* 36, 46; *PC* 8; *VC* 5, 6–12.

Fidelity to Patrimony[73]

Canon 578 — All must observe faithfully the mind and designs of the founders regarding the nature, purpose, spirit, and character of an institute, which have been sanctioned by competent ecclesiastical authority, and its sound traditions, all of which constitute the patrimony of the same institute.

Fidelity to the spiritual patrimony of the institute becomes a sacred obligation for all institutes and their members. All that the founder or foundress intended regarding the nature (religious or secular), purpose (contemplation or apostolic service), spirit (particular spirituality), and character (monastic, conventual, apostolic) of the institute approved by competent ecclesiastical authority, as well as its wholesome traditions constitute the institute's patrimony.[74] Approved as a public juridic person in the Church, the institute and each of its members have a grave obligation to safeguard and promote this patrimony.

It can happen that accretions unrelated to the original inspiration and purpose of the founder or foundress become attached to and even approved constituent elements of the proper law of a particular institute of consecrated life. Such accretions prompt a reexamination of the original nature, spirit, and purpose of the institute. At times, the Church calls institutes to examine their proper law, particularly the fundamental code or constitutions, in order to ensure that the rich spiritual patrimony perdures.[75]

Erection and Suppression

The next seven canons (cc. 579–585) address the erection, suppression, and structural organization of institutes of consecrated life. The principles of autonomy, or respect for the institute's ability for internal governance, and subsidiarity, or allowing decisions to be made at the appropriate level with accountability to the higher authority, underlie these canons.

Ecclesiastical authority regulates the critical moments of erection and suppression of institutes of consecrated life, as well as any other structural change which would affect the identity and autonomy of an institute. The competent authority in the institute makes decisions for internal structural changes. The norms show how the Church protects gifts given her by the Spirit, guards the rights of both institutes and members, and regulates the temporal goods of suppressed institutes.

Erection of Diocesan Right Institute[76]

Canon 579 — Diocesan bishops, each in his own territory, can erect institutes of consecrated life by formal decree, provided that the Apostolic See has been consulted.

In erecting institutes of consecrated life, the Apostolic See is concerned that they not duplicate existing ones, prove useless, or lack sufficient resources to achieve their purposes.[77] Since 1900, diocesan bishops have been able to erect religious congregations of diocesan right[78] but the bishops

---

[73] *CCEO* 426 prescribes the same fidelity to the patrimony of the institute for each and every religious.

[74] *PC* 2b, *ES* II: 14. The latter text instructed that whatever was out of date, changed with the passage of time, or only of local application was to be excluded from the basic texts of institutes.

[75] *VC* 37, 96–103. Pope John Paul II encourages institutes of consecrated life to creative fidelity in adapting the purposes of their institutes to the present needs of the people of God.

[76] The eparchial bishop can erect monasteries *sui iuris* (*CCEO* 435, §1), congregations (*CCEO* 506, §1), societies of apostolic life (*CCEO* 556), and secular institutes (*CCEO* 566). He cannot erect orders (*CCEO* 505, §1).

[77] *PC* 19. There has been a caution with regard to multiplying religious institutes since the Fourth Lateran Council in 1215 up to and including the Second Vatican Council. In promoting institutes, consideration should also be given to the needs of the people of the particular church, their culture, way of life, and local customs.

[78] See *AAS* 14 (1992) 644; *CLD* 1, 267–269, 272. The former code distinguished between religious institutes as

are required to consult the Apostolic See before erecting these congregations.[79] The present norm provides that the bishop can erect an institute of consecrated life after such consultation. Ordinarily, institutes of consecrated life have humble beginnings. The diocesan bishop can initiate the process, but usually it begins with a small group of persons coming together as a *de facto* association.[80] The bishop or his delegate studies the association with regard to its nature and usefulness to the particular church, careful to ensure that it does not duplicate already existing institutes.[81] The association may possess unique features that differ significantly from already approved forms of consecrated life and require further scrutiny and approval by the Apostolic See.[82]

If the group meets the requirements for one of the existing forms of consecrated life, shows originality, attracts members, and proves resourceful, the diocesan bishop through a formal decree can erect it as a public association of the faithful and approve its statutes.[83] These statutes are the foundation for what will later be the proper law of the institute of consecrated life. At this point, the members of the association may want to make private vows with the consent of the bishop.[84] If the association is clerical,[85] the clerics belonging to it remain incardinated in their respective dioceses, religious institutes, or societies of apostolic life until the association is formally erected as an institute of consecrated life.

If the association continues to thrive, a brief is sent to the appropriate Roman congregation to ob-

tain the *nihil obstat* before either the diocesan bishop or one equivalent to him in law[86] erects it as an institute of consecrated life of diocesan right.[87] The Congregation for Institutes of Consecrated Life has a thorough procedure for examining the materials to ensure correct doctrine. Consultation with the Apostolic See would seem to be required for the validity of the erection. When the *nihil obstat* is obtained, the diocesan bishop or his equivalent in law erects the institute of consecrated life by a formal decree. If the association is erected as a clerical institute of diocesan right,[88] the clerics become incardinated into it at the time of their perpetual profession or definitive incorporation, unless the constitutions prescribe otherwise.[89]

Formal erection as an institute of consecrated life of diocesan right presents the institute as an authentic expression of the gospel empowered to carry on its apostolate in the name of the Church. It remains the responsibility of the diocesan bishop to guide and encourage the growth of the institute in accordance with its proper nature, spirit, and end.[90]

Aggregation of Institute[91]

Canon 580 — The aggregation of one institute of consecrated life to another is reserved to the competent authority of the aggregating institute; the canonical autonomy of the aggregated institute is always to be preserved.

This canon addresses a relationship between institutes of consecrated life that does not interfere

orders, or those with solemn vows, and congregations, or those with simple vows (*CIC* 488, §2).
[79] *CLD* 1, 268–269.
[80] *LG* 45; cc. 215, 299.
[81] Canon 305, §1. The proliferation of institutes has been a constant concern of the Church. See *PC* 19, *VC* 12.
[82] Canon 605. In his apostolic exhortation, *Vita consecrata* 62, John Paul II deemed it appropriate to set up a commission to deal with questions relating to new forms of consecrated life.
[83] Canons 312–314.
[84] Canon 1192, §1.
[85] Canon 302.

[86] Canons 381, §2; 368.
[87] These guidelines are found in *CLD* 7, 458–459. The Congregation for Institutes of Consecrated Life and Societies of Apostolic Life, the Congregation for the Evangelization of Peoples, or the Congregation for the Eastern Churches would be the appropriate congregation.
[88] Canon 588, §2.
[89] Canon 268, §2.
[90] Canon 576; M. Joyce and R. McDermott, "Canon 579: Erection of a Diocesan Institute," *RRAO 1984–1993*, 159–163.
[91] Cf. *CCEO* 440, §1.

with the autonomy of the individual institutes. Aggregation refers to the spiritual bond or affiliation between first, second, and third orders of mendicants (Dominicans, Franciscans, Carmelites, Augustinians, etc.). Another example is the affiliation of Benedictine monasteries of women religious with Benedictine monasteries of men. The institutes share a common spirituality and support one another in their consecrated life. Some secular institutes are aggregated to religious institutes.[92]

The institute desiring aggregation would petition for it, and the act of aggregation would be reserved to the competent authority (superior general or general chapter) of the aggregating institute according to its proper law. The norm states that the aggregating authority has no jurisdiction over the aggregated institute. This bonding of institutes of consecrated life enables them to collaborate and share personnel and resources in preserving and promoting their spirituality and works, while each institute maintains its distinct nature and autonomy.[93]

Structural Divisions of Institute[94]

Canon 581 — To divide an institute into parts, by whatever name they are called, to erect new parts, to join those erected, or to redefine their boundaries belongs to the competent authority of the institute, according to the norm of the constitutions.

This canon employs the principle of subsidiarity in recognizing the competence of the proper authority of an institute to order its internal structures. The authority (supreme moderator or general chapter) and the parts to which the institute can be divided are defined in the constitutions.[95] Some institutes name the general chapter as the competent authority; others prefer to leave such structural adjustments to the supreme moderator and council. The general council meets more regularly than the chapter and may be better informed regarding particular geographic areas and availability of personnel.

The competent authority can divide the institute into parts (provinces,[96] vice-provinces, regions),[97] erect new parts, and join or realign those already existing according to the norms of the constitutions. The nature, size, and purpose of an institute often determine its particular structure. Such structures are effective channels in distributing personnel and resources to carry on the work of the institute.

There may be no provision in the constitutions to erect a needed structure, e.g., a province. Or the competent authority may need to suppress all of the provinces due to the small number of members. Such acts require a constitutional change which would be authorized by the competent ecclesiastical authority after a two-thirds vote of the general chapter.[98] Lack of personnel and resources often necessitates the union of existing parts, as well as the suppression of parts of the institute.[99] While the norm does not require consultation with the diocesan bishops of the places where such changes are made, courtesy and concern for the mission of the particular churches certainly warrant informing bishops of the structural changes of the institute in their dioceses.[100]

---

[92] *CLD* 3, 156.

[93] At times in accord with the will of the founder and the institutes concerned, the Apostolic See has permitted institutes of women religious to be directed by an institute of men religious who share the same founder. For examples, the Daughters of Charity of St. Vincent dePaul are directed by the superior general of the Congregation of the Mission (Vincentians); the Daughters of Mary, Help of Christians, by the superior general of the Salesians; and the Daughters of Wisdom by the superior general of the Montfort Fathers. See E. Gambari, *Religious Life* (Boston: Daughters of St. Paul, 1986) 461.

[94] Cf. *CCEO* 508, §§2–3; 556.

[95] Canon 587, §1.

[96] Canon 621.

[97] The constitution and erection of houses are provided for in cc. 608 and 609.

[98] Canons 587, §2; 593; 595, §1.

[99] Canon 585.

[100] The diocesan bishop's consent is required for the erection of a house (c. 609, §1) and he is to be consulted at the suppression of a house (c. 616, §1).

Mergers/Unions/Confederations/Federations[101]

Canon 582 — Mergers and unions of institutes of consecrated life are reserved to the Apostolic See only; confederations and federations are also reserved to it.

The structures described in this canon extend beyond the internal life and governance of the institutes involved. In addition, merger (fusion) and union affect the juridical nature, governance, and autonomy of the institutes involved.[102] The Apostolic See approves all mergers and unions of institutes of consecrated life. Neither of these two terms is defined; they are often used interchangeably and imply the extinction of one or more juridical persons.

The term "merger" (fusion) is most often employed to describe the extinction of one institute through union with another. This often occurs when a smaller institute begins to lose its vitality due to a lack of personnel or resources and seeks to unite with another institute that is similar to it in nature, spirit, and goals. Conciliar and postconciliar documents encourage such mergers or fusions, particularly when there seems to be no reasonable hope for growth and development in an institute.[103] The smaller or less prosperous institute loses its identity while being absorbed into the larger one.[104]

Another type of union is the coming together of two or more institutes, all of which lose their identity to form a new institute. The institute is erected from the uniting ones with a new name and personality. This union would necessitate the structuring of governance, the drafting of proper law, and all other requisites for the formation of a new institute.[105]

In all such mergers or unions, the good of the Church, each institute, and the individual members should be the foremost concerns.[106] Such restructuring needs to address all civil and canonical issues regarding personnel, temporal goods, and apostolic works involved in the union. There should be careful remote and proximate spiritual, psychological, and juridical preparation of the members of the institutes involved, particularly when the identity of the institute is lost.[107] Individual members have the freedom to choose to belong to the new entity, to transfer to another institute, or to petition for an indult of departure from the institute with a dispensation from their sacred bonds.[108]

A federation occurs when certain institutes sharing the same nature and spirit join together for common purposes, while each institute retains its autonomy. Some examples of federations would be the congregations of Benedictine and Cistercian monasteries[109] and canons regular such as the Premonstratensians. Each of the abbeys, monasteries, or canonries retains its autonomy, while all are under a superior of the congregation who does not possess the full authority of major superiors.[110] Federations of monasteries of nuns provide mutual assistance in areas such as formation, finances, personnel transfers for reasons of health or education, and the opening of new foundations with volunteers from the respective monasteries. Several apostolic institutes of like charism, such as the Sisters of St. Joseph, have federations to foster their spirit and mutually support one another. The statutes of each federation or congregation of monasteries provide details regarding these issues.

Confederations are groupings of federations into a still larger structure. Examples of this phenomenon are the Confederation of Benedictine Monasteries and the Confederation of Canonries of St. Augustine. The confederation is composed of monastic or canonical congregations presided over

---

[101] *CCEO* 439, §§1–3 provides for the erection of a federation; *CCEO* 440, §§2–3 provides for its suppression.
[102] *PC* 21–22, *ES* II: 39–41.
[103] *PC* 21, *ES* II: 41.
[104] *CLD* 6, 445–446; 7, 459–461; 8, 324–325; 9, 292–294.
[105] *CLD* 9, 294–295; C. Darcy, *The Institute of the Sisters of Mercy of the Americas: The Canonical Development of the Proposed Governance Model* (New York: University Press, 1993).

[106] *ES* II: 40.
[107] *CLD* 8, 324.
[108] Darcy, 167–170.
[109] Canon 613.
[110] Canon 620.

by a major superior with limited powers determined in the statutes of the confederation.[111] Again, there is no loss of the autonomy of the individual monastery or abbey. The formation of federations and confederations, composed of monasteries, abbeys, or canonries that share the same nature, spirit, and end, as well as the approval of their statutes are reserved to the Apostolic See. These unions enable the institutes to support one another morally through research and study of their common patrimony and spirituality, while retaining their identity and autonomy. Certain limited powers are given to the president of the federation or confederation in the statutes approved by the Apostolic See in order to give stability to the structure.

Unlike aggregation, which is described in canon 580 and its commentary, the effects of structures such as mergers, unions, federations, and confederations extend beyond the internal governance of the individual institutes. In mergers and unions, some institutes lose their original identity. In federations and confederations, there is a yielding of a limited but certain power over the institute to an authority beyond the institute. Hence, the erections of such structures are reserved to the Apostolic See.[112] The Congregation for Institutes of Consecrated Life and Societies of Apostolic Life recognizes the grave importance of protecting the rights of institutes and/or individual members in all such ventures. In mergers and unions, the dicastery provides certain options for members unwilling to join the new structure. Prescribed procedures must be carried out carefully to ensure justice and equity for all concerned.[113]

Matters Approved by Apostolic See

Canon 583 — Changes in institutes of consecrated life affecting those things which had been approved by the Apostolic See cannot be made without its permission.

This norm reflects a basic principle of law. The competent authority that erects or approves elements of an institute of consecrated life is the same authority to authorize a change in these elements or a dispensation for the institute. No inferior authority can change without permission what is reserved to the Apostolic See.[114] The inferior authority would seek the change from the higher authority. Only the Apostolic See can approve changes in the constitutions of institutes of pontifical right.[115] If the Apostolic See has intervened in any matters pertaining to the constitutions of institutes of diocesan right, the bishop of the principal seat of the institute is not competent to permit changes in those matters without the approval of the Apostolic See.[116]

In subsequent norms, there are references to various competent authorities: the Apostolic See, diocesan bishop, general chapter, supreme moderator, or other major superior. In terms of authority, diocesan bishops, general chapters, and major superiors of institutes of consecrated life are inferior to the Apostolic See. If the Apostolic See intervenes or approves certain measures for an institute of consecrated life, neither the diocesan bishop nor the internal authorities of the institute can approve or effect changes in the same without authorization from the Apostolic See.

Suppression of Institute[117]

Canon 584 — The suppression of an institute pertains only to the Apostolic See; a decision regarding the temporal goods of the institute is also reserved to the Apostolic See.

The norm shows the legislator's reverence for a gift of the Spirit given for the life and holiness of the Church as well as for the perpetual and universal nature of a public juridical person.[118] An in-

---

[111] Canon 620.

[112] PB 106, par. 2.

[113] See, for example, CLD 7, 543–545; 8, 320–323; Darcy, 167–171.

[114] No bishop, for example, could make changes in mergers, unions, federations, or confederations (c. 582).

[115] Canon 587, §2.

[116] Canon 595, §1.

[117] Cf. CCEO 438, 507, 556, 566.

[118] Canons 120; 574, §1; 590, §1.

stitute of consecrated life is a gift to the universal Church with a potential for witness and service to many particular churches. Only the Apostolic See can suppress such an institute. The norm constitutes an exception to the general principle that the authority competent to erect can suppress, since a diocesan bishop cannot suppress an institute of diocesan right which he erected. Because of the extreme consequences of such an act, grave reasons are required for this course of action, e.g., few surviving members with little hope of development.[119] The suppression of an institute of consecrated life implies the cessation of its spiritual patrimony (c. 578) as well as its temporal goods.

It is rare that an institute of consecrated life gives grave scandal, deviating from its original spirit and end. In such an instance, suppression would be a penal measure. However, in most instances, an institute is no longer able to sustain itself because of a lack of vocations over a prolonged period of time. Conciliar and postconciliar documents encourage such institutes to merge or unite.[120] Besides through a formal act of suppression, an institute can cease to exist if it has remained inactive for a hundred years and there are no surviving members.[121] In all such sad and grave situations, it is important to remember the wise counsel of Pope John Paul II:

> While individual Institutes have no claim to permanence, the consecrated life itself will continue to sustain among the faithful the response of love towards God and neighbor. (Thus) it is necessary to distinguish the historical destiny of a specific Institute or form of consecrated life from the ecclesial mission of the consecrated life as such. The former is affected by changing circumstances, the latter is destined to perdure.[122]

The Apostolic See disposes of the temporal goods of the suppressed institute, even if these consist of but one house.[123] In such an instance one must attend to the proper law of the institute, its liabilities, the will of founders or donors, acquired rights, and provision for any surviving members.[124] All is to be accomplished in equity and charity with due regard for the rights of those concerned.

Suppression of Parts of Institute

Canon 585 — It belongs to the competent authority of an institute to suppress its parts.

The suppression of parts of an institute complements the provisions of canon 581 on its division, and should be included in its constitutions or fundamental law along with norms on its erection and realignment. Such internal structures of an institute would include: provinces, vice provinces, regions, and/or districts. Canon 616 provides for the suppression of houses of a religious institute. The competent authority of an institute can suppress its parts. Ordinarily, there must be a grave or very serious reason for such an action, since it has implications for the life and mission of the Church as well as for the institute. As with a suppressed house of religious,[125] concern for the pastoral needs of the people of the particular church and courtesy would prompt the major superior to be in consultation with the diocesan bishop in whose diocese the structure or part of the institute is located. The temporal goods of the suppressed part belong to the institute and are to be disposed of in accord with canon and civil law as well as the institute's proper law, the will of the founder, and any acquired rights.[126]

Autonomy of Life/Governance

Canon 586 — §1. A just autonomy of life, especially of governance, is acknowledged for individual institutes, by which they possess their own discipline

---

[119] *PC* 21, *ES* II: 41.
[120] *PC* 21, *ES* II: 41, c. 583.
[121] Canon 120.
[122] *VC* 63.

[123] Canon 616, §2.
[124] Canons 123; 1257, §1; 1258; 1300.
[125] Canon 616, §1.
[126] Canons 123, 1300.

in the Church and are able to preserve their own patrimony intact, as mentioned in can. 578.

Ecclesiastical authority reverences the gift of each approved institute of consecrated life and gives it the necessary authority to preserve and foster its patrimony as described in canon 578. This norm employs the principle of subsidiarity rooted in conciliar and postconciliar documents. Each approved institute is a public juridical person[127] witnessing gospel spirituality and contributing to the Church's mission. It enjoys a rightful autonomy of life, particularly in governance through which it orders its life and ensures proper discipline of the members. This autonomy is not absolute, since all institutes of consecrated life are subject to ecclesiastical authorities in accord with the universal law. Several norms in the universal law ensure autonomy to all institutes in accord with their particular nature, character, and purpose.[128] Autonomy applies to the internal life and governance of the institute; however, members of institutes of consecrated life are subject to diocesan bishops in matters pertaining to the care of souls, public exercise of divine worship, and other apostolic works.[129]

Superiors and chapters of institutes of consecrated life possess authority according to universal and proper law in areas of internal governance: formation, profession/incorporation, missioning members, administering temporal goods, visitation, and separation from the institute. Moreover, the universal law emphasizes the obligation of all members of each institute to preserve and foster the institute's special gift by a life of fidelity to their vocation.[130]

§2. It is for local ordinaries to preserve and safeguard this autonomy.

As pastor of the particular church, the diocesan bishop is responsible to know, respect, promote, and coordinate the vocation and mission of institutes for the good of the faithful.[131] The law obliges him and other clergy to support and assist consecrated persons, enabling them to offer their witness and service in the many spiritual and pastoral initiatives of the diocese, always remaining faithful to their proper nature and end.[132] For their part, institutes of consecrated life and their members cannot invoke autonomy in external apostolic initiatives which should always be carried out in dialogue between bishops and the competent authorities of the various institutes.[133]

Proper Law of Institute

Canon 587 — §1. To protect more faithfully the proper vocation and identity of each institute, the fundamental code or constitutions of every institute must contain, besides those things which are to be observed as stated in can. 578, fundamental norms regarding governance of the institute, the discipline of members, incorporation and formation of members, and the proper object of the sacred bonds.

This canon addresses the practical instrument through which the patrimony of an institute of consecrated life is preserved and lived. Each institute has its own proper law (*ius proprium*), as distinguished from the universal law and the particular law of dioceses and episcopal conferences. This proper law by which the institute is ordered consists of two parts: a fundamental code, or constitutions, and a supplementary text, or statutes.[134] Both terms are used in the canons addressing in-

---

[127] Canon 634, §1.

[128] Canons 580; 591; 593; 594; 596, §2; 614; 615; 732.

[129] Canon 678, §1. However, even in the external works of the institute, the bishop is obliged to respect their autonomy (cc. 674; 678, §2; 680; 681, §1; 683, §1).

[130] Canons 661, 662, 673.

[131] Canon 385.

[132] Canon 680.

[133] Canon 678, *VC* 49–50.

[134] Some institutes have provincial statutes or directories which determine specific applications of the constitutions and/or general statutes for the particular situation or culture. The provincial statutes are approved by the supreme moderator of the institute.

stitutes of consecrated life. The proper law serves the institute in ways that are both pedagogic and exhortatory. It teaches candidates and other externs the nature, character, and purpose of the institute; it calls members to persevere and mature in accord with the obligations they assumed at the time of incorporation into the institute.

The fundamental code (constitutions) contains the essential elements describing the patrimony of the institute[135] and the basic norms pertaining to governance, temporal goods, formation, incorporation, the proper object of the sacred bonds, and the discipline of members. Several canons in this section of the code contain elements that are to be included in this fundamental law.

Regarding governance, constitutions should describe the basic structures of governance, the convocation and membership of the general chapter, how major moderators are constituted, their terms of office, councils and how decision-making is effected, and all essential elements of local governance.

In areas of formation and incorporation, the constitutions or fundamental code should contain a description of the various stages of formation, their requirements, purpose, and length; the competent authority to admit or refuse admission to different stages; the juridical effects of temporary and perpetual or definitive profession; the nature of the sacred bonds and the rights and obligations assumed at temporary and perpetual or definitive profession.

The constitutions should contain the essential elements of the religious or secular life, key elements in living the spiritual life, and the juridical process for separation from the institute.

Regarding the administration of temporal goods, the fundamental code should include the key elements for ordinary and extraordinary administration, as well as for acts of alienation of the temporal goods of the institute.

If the canons indicate that certain elements be in accord with the constitutions, they must be placed in that fundamental code. If the canons

state that the elements be in the proper law of the institute, they can be placed either in the constitutions or in the statutory section of the proper law.[136]

Institutes and their members have the obligation of obeying the canons of the code applicable to them, and there is no need to repeat these norms in the proper law of the institute. They can be implicitly included with a phrase such as "in accord with universal law," or "in accord with the norms of canon law." However, it is advisable that some canons of major importance be known by the members and added as an appendix to the constitutions of an institute of consecrated life for ready reference.[137]

§2. A code of this type is approved by competent authority of the Church and can be changed only with its consent.

The fundamental code describes the gift of the Holy Spirit to the Church and contains the essential elements through which it is preserved and developed. Therefore, its approval and any changes in it are reserved to the competent ecclesiastical authority. The initial approval of the fundamental code or constitutions takes place at the time of the erection of the institute of consecrated life. The Congregation for Institutes of Consecrated Life and Societies of Apostolic Life approves the constitutions of an institute of pontifical right (an institute erected or approved by the Apostolic See)

---

[135] Canon 578.

[136] For an outline of canons that belong in the constitutions or in either the constitutions or statutes of an institute of consecrated life, see J. Hite, "Canons That Refer to the Constitutions and Proper Law of Institutes of Consecrated Life and Societies of Apostolic Life," in *A Handbook on Canons 573–746* (hereafter Hite, *Handbk*), ed. J. Hite, S. Holland, and D. Ward (Collegeville: Liturgical Press, 1985) 371–381.

[137] For example, major superiors and vocation directors involved in interviewing or admitting candidates to the institute should be aware of the invalidating impediments to admission to the novitiate (c. 643, §1). Major superiors should know when the consent or advice of the council is required in the universal law. A good summation of the latter can be found in Hite, *Handbk,* 392–398.

and confirms any changes legitimately introduced into them.[138] The diocesan bishop of the principal seat of the institute has this same competence for an institute of diocesan right (an institute erected by a diocesan bishop) except in matters in which the Apostolic See has intervened.[139] If the members of the institute want to modify the constitutions, a two-thirds vote of the general chapter[140] is needed, and the petition for the change together with the recommended revised text is presented to the competent ecclesiastical authority.

Dispensations from the proper law depend on the nature of the law and the authority with the right to dispense. If the dispensation is from a norm of the universal law, it would be petitioned of the Apostolic See;[141] in the case of institutes of diocesan right, the diocesan bishop can grant the dispensation from the constitutions in a particular case.[142]

Major superiors of clerical religious institutes and societies of apostolic life of pontifical right are ordinaries for their members;[143] they can dispense from disciplinary laws, both universal and proper for their members, if it is difficult to make recourse to the Holy See and there is danger of grave harm in delay. This also applies to those dispensations reserved to the Holy See, provided the dispensation is one which the Holy See customarily grants in similar circumstances without prejudice to canon 291.[144] It is always good to study the text of the approved constitutions; many permit superiors to grant dispensations in routine matters.[145]

§3. In this code spiritual and juridic elements are to be joined together suitably; nevertheless, norms are not to be multiplied without necessity.

[138] Canon 593.
[139] Canon 595, §1.
[140] Canon 631, §1.
[141] Canons 593; 595, §1.
[142] Canon 595, §2.
[143] Canon 134.
[144] Canon 87, §2.
[145] B. Gangoiti, "The Power of Major Superiors to Dispense from Common Laws and from the Laws of Their Own Institute," *Con Lif* 15/1 (1990) 85–99.

This paragraph reflects the first of the basic principles that guided the *coetus* in revising the universal law on consecrated life.[146] It is difficult to discuss a divine vocation in purely juridical terms without introducing spiritual elements that express a life totally dedicated to God. Recognizing this, the legislator requires that, in the formulation of the fundamental code or constitutions of an institute of consecrated life, the spiritual nature of the vocation be respected. Juridical norms fall short of describing the inspiration and spirit of the founder. However, the fundamental code is a juridical text that contains the essential elements of the vocation. Clarity, precision, and economy should be the hallmarks of the fundamental code; unnecessary norms should not be part of this document. Some institutes include pertinent canons in the appendix of the fundamental law or constitutions for easy referral.

§4. Other norms established by competent authority of an institute are to be collected suitably in other codes and, moreover, can be reviewed appropriately and adapted according to the needs of places and times.

There are norms in proper law that, while not as essential as constitutive elements, are nevertheless necessary for the harmonious ordering of the institute. Institutes have general statutes or directories with norms that follow from and determine more specific applications of the fundamental code. Often provinces of institutes have provincial statutes providing for particular provinces of the institute in a variety of cultures and geographic locations. The general chapter approves and enacts general statutes for the entire institute; provincial chapters approve and promulgate provincial statutes for the province. These same bodies can interpret, modify, or abrogate the norms they enact. Provincial statutes formulated or modified by the provincial chapter must be approved by the su-

[146] ComCICRec, *Schema of Canons on Institutes of Life Consecrated by Profession of the Evangelical Counsels (Draft)* (Washington, D.C.: USCC, 1977) xiii.

preme moderator of the institute in accord with its proper law.

In addition to having juridical texts, many institutes of consecrated life have formularies or books of prayer, spiritual exercises, traditions, and customs indigenous to the institute. While not legal texts, these books are revered in the institute and reflect its sound traditions.

Clerical/Lay Institutes

Canon 588 — §1. By its very nature, the state of consecrated life is neither clerical nor lay.

Although they are described as "clerical" or "lay," institutes of consecrated life are neither clerical nor lay in essence. Rather, Christian faithful from both the clerical and lay states inspired by the Holy Spirit are drawn to a particular charism, consecrated to God through the profession of the evangelical counsels, and serve the mission of the Church.[147]

The Clerical Institute[148]

§2. That institute is called clerical which, by reason of the purpose or design intended by the founder or by virtue of legitimate tradition, is under the direction of clerics, assumes the exercise of sacred orders, and is recognized as such by the authority of the Church.

An institute is said to be clerical if, in accord with the design of the founder and/or legitimate tradition, it meets the following criteria: (1) it is under the supervision of clerics, (2) it assumes the exercise of sacred orders, and (3) it is recognized as such by ecclesiastical authority.[149] The Society of Jesus (Jesuits) and the Congregation of the Most Holy Redeemer (Redemptorists) are exam-

ples of clerical institutes. Many clerical institutes have lay brothers who had not been permitted to hold office in the institute. Conciliar and postconciliar documents provided that brothers take a more active part in the life and governance of the clerical institute and be eligible for certain offices.[150] However, the offices of superior and vicar were reserved to clerics.[151]

Deacons as well as priests are clerics.[152] If a member of a clerical institute wishes to remain a permanent deacon and there is no provision in the proper law, the general chapter would petition for such a provision to be included in the constitutions of the institute.[153]

The Lay Institute

§3. That institute is called lay which, recognized as such by the authority of the Church, has by virtue of its nature, character, and purpose a proper function defined by the founder or by legitimate tradition, which does not include the exercise of sacred orders.

An institute is called lay if, in accord with the purpose of the founder and/or legitimate tradition, it meets the following conditions: (1) the end or function of the institute does not include the exercise of sacred orders and (2) it is recognized as lay by ecclesiastical authority. All institutes of women and brothers are lay institutes. Conciliar

---

[147] *LG* 43; c. 207, §2.

[148] *CCEO* 505, §3; 554, §2.

[149] This is more descriptive than *CIC* 488,4° where the distinction seemed to be based on the number of clerics in the institute.

[150] *PC* 15, *ES* II: 27.

[151] Gradually, brothers were permitted to be local superiors by rescript. See *CLD* 7, 467–471; 8, 342–343; 9, 341, 346. In one reported case, an OFM Cap. brother was permitted to be vice-provincial. The rescript required that a priest be designated by name to carry out acts of jurisdiction requiring orders (*CLD* 10, 106–107). See W. Woestman, "De Institutis Clericalibus Vitae Consecratae et Superioribus Non Clericis," *ME* 110 (1985) 411–420.

Subsequent to the 1994 synod of bishops on consecrated life, Pope John Paul II established a special commission to study the issues surrounding the concept of "mixed institutes" (*VC* 61).

[152] Canon 207, §1.

[153] Paul VI, *mp Sacrum diaconatus ordinem* 32, June 18, 1967, *AAS* 59 (1967) 697. See *CLD* 6, 583–584.

teaching permitted general chapters of institutes of brothers to decide if some members could be admitted to orders, while the lay character of the institute remained intact.[154] In such institutes, admission to orders would be regulated by the code[155] and the proper law of the institute. While some institutes of brothers have availed themselves of this provision, others have not, e.g., the Brothers of the Christian Schools.

Competent ecclesiastical authority decides the clerical or lay status of the institute after a study of its nature, spirit, and purpose when the institute is approved and erected as a public juridical person in the Church.

At present, there is an interesting discussion regarding this norm as institutes review their founders' original inspiration and design. St. Francis desired that the members of his institute, both clerical and lay, would be brothers with equal rights and obligations. Some members describe the Franciscan Order as a "mixed institute." The issue is being studied by a special commission in Rome and by individual Franciscan institutes to determine how best to describe and live the original inspiration.[156]

Institute of Pontifical/Diocesan Right[157]

Canon 589 — An institute of consecrated life is said to be of pontifical right if the Apostolic See has erected it or approved it through a formal decree. It is said to be of diocesan right, however, if it has been erected by a diocesan bishop but has not obtained a decree of approval from the Apostolic See.

Institutes of consecrated life have their own proper autonomy,[158] but it is not absolute. They are subject to ecclesiastical authority in accord with their pontifical or diocesan right status in those internal matters of governance and discipline which exceed the competence of legitimate authority within the institute.[159]

An institute erected or approved through a formal decree by the Apostolic See is an institute of pontifical right. Some diocesan right institutes petition for pontifical right status after significant growth in personnel and expansion into several dioceses. Institutes of pontifical right are immediately subject to the Apostolic See in internal matters exceeding the competence of the authority within the institute. The Congregation for Institutes of Consecrated Life and Societies of Apostolic Life and the Congregation for the Evangelization of Peoples have authority over institutes of pontifical right.[160]

A diocesan right institute is erected by a diocesan bishop[161] and has not sought and obtained a decree of approval as a pontifical institute from the Apostolic See. The diocesan bishop of the principal see of the institute would be competent in those concerns of internal governance and discipline exceeding the competence of the legitimate superiors within the institute. Institutes of diocesan right remain under the special vigilance of the diocesan bishop in several matters.[162]

The authority of ecclesiastical superiors should not be confused with that of the competent internal superiors of the institute. An institute of consecrated life enjoys a rightful autonomy of life, particularly of governance.[163] Ecclesiastical authorities respect and safeguard this autonomy given to institutes to protect and develop their proper gifts and would address only those matters which extend beyond the competence of internal authority, i.e., the approval of changes in the fundamental code[164] and serious matters such as sub-

---

[154] PC 10, CLD 7, 135–136.
[155] Canon 1019.
[156] See note 151; PC 15; prop. 10, VC 61.
[157] Cf. CCEO 413; 434; 505; 554, §2; 563, §2.
[158] Canon 586.

[159] Canons 593, 594. See also c. 732.
[160] PB 90, 108. Religious institutes of the Eastern churches *sui iuris* are subject to the CEC.
[161] Canon 579.
[162] Canons 625, §2; 628, §2, 2°; 637; 638, §4; 688, §2; 700.
[163] Canon 586; V. Koluthara, *Rightful Autonomy of Religious Institutes* (Rome: CHS, 1994).
[164] Canon 587, §2.

stantial alienations of temporal goods[165] or definitive departures from the institute.[166]

Subjection to Supreme Authority

**Canon 590 — §1. Inasmuch as institutes of conse-
crated life are dedicated in a special way to the
service of God and of the whole Church, they are
subject to the supreme authority of the Church in
a special way.**

This norm attests to the ecclesial and universal
character of each institute in that it is a special
gift of the Spirit for the life and holiness of the
Church.[167] As public juridic persons, institutes of
consecrated life belong at the very heart of the
Church and have a special relationship with the
Roman Pontiff and the college of bishops. A
diocesan bishop seeks the *nihil obstat* of the
Apostolic See before he erects an institute of
consecrated life.[168] The authority possessed by
competent authority within these institutes (superiors and chapters) comes from God through the
ministry of the Church.[169] Only the Apostolic See
can suppress an institute of consecrated life,
whether it be of pontifical or diocesan right.[170]

**§2. Individual members are also bound to obey
the Supreme Pontiff as their highest superior by
reason of the sacred bond of obedience.[171]**

The pope possesses supreme, full, immediate,
and universal ordinary power in the Church which
he can always freely exercise.[172] While all of the
Christian faithful are subject to him, members of institutes of consecrated life are subject to him as
their ecclesiastical superior in a special way through

their bond of obedience. While it would be rare, the
pope can command members of institutes of consecrated life to do something within the context of
their proper law. Likewise, he can delegate his authority to one of the congregations of the Roman
curia.[173] In the constitutions of the Society of Jesus,
provision is made for some members to profess a
fourth vow of obedience to the pope regarding their
mission.[174] Religious consecrated bishops remain
religious, but they are subject to the pope alone by
reason of their vow of obedience.[175]

Exemption of Institutes[176]

**Canon 591 — In order to provide better for the
good of institutes and the needs of the apostolate,
the Supreme Pontiff, by reason of his primacy in
the universal Church and with a view to common
advantage, can exempt institutes of consecrated
life from the governance of local ordinaries and
subject them to himself alone or to another ecclesiastical authority.**

While institutes of consecrated life enjoy autonomy in life and governance, they do not act independent of church authority. From earliest times,
popes secured the autonomy of monasteries in
granting them exemption or protection in their internal life from interference by bishops. Gradually,
religious orders and even some congregations were
exempt or attached to the Apostolic See, particularly regarding their apostolic activity.[177] Popes were
careful to note that this exemption, while providing
for the general good of the Church, did not preclude the obedience of religious to bishops in their
exercise of episcopal authority.

---

[165] Canon 638, §§3–4.
[166] Canon 691, §2.
[167] *LG* 44, *VC* 29.
[168] Canon 579.
[169] Canons 618, 631.
[170] Canon 584.
[171] Cf. *CCEO* 412, §1; 555; 564.
[172] Canon 331.

[173] These congregations act in the pope's name and by his
authority (c. 360). CICLSAL has competence for institutes of consecrated life (*PB* 105–111); CEP enjoys
competence over missionary societies of apostolic life
(*PB* 90, par. 2).
[174] Gambari, 117, fn. 13.
[175] Canon 705.
[176] Cf. *CCEO* 412, §2.
[177] See *CIC* 488, §2; 615; 618, §1.

Conciliar teaching on the Church as *communio,* the greater authority given diocesan bishops in the particular churches, and the jurisdiction given to all major superiors of clerical religious institutes and societies of apostolic life of pontifical right have greatly mitigated the importance of exemption.[178] In his concern for the universal Church and by reason of his supreme authority, the pope can remove an institute of consecrated life and its members from the authority of diocesan bishops and subject them to himself alone.[179] However, many provisions once reserved to exempt institutes are now applicable to all clerical institutes of pontifical right.[180] Therefore, it is difficult to explain the nature of exempt institutes. There seems little distinction between exempt clerical institutes and clerical institutes of pontifical right. Exemption refers primarily to the internal ordering of institutes of consecrated life, since all institutes are subject to the governance of diocesan bishops in the care of souls, the public exercise of divine worship, and other works of the apostolate.[181]

Pope John Paul II encourages religious to a fruitful and ordered ecclesial communion:

> It is helpful to recall that, in coordinating their service to the universal Church with their service to the particular Churches, Institutes may not invoke rightful autonomy, or even the exemption which a number of them enjoy, in order to justify choices which actually conflict with the demands of organic communion called for by a healthy ecclesial life. Instead, the pastoral initiatives of consecrated persons should be determined and carried out in cordial and open dialogue

between Bishops and Superiors of the different Institutes. Special attention by Bishops to the vocation and mission of Institutes and respect by the latter for the ministry of Bishops, with ready acceptance of their concrete pastoral directives for the life of the Diocese, these are two intimately linked expressions of that one ecclesial charity by which all work to build up the organic communion—charismatic and at the same time hierarchically structured—of the whole People of God.[182]

Communion with Apostolic See[183]

Canon 592 — §1. In order better to foster the communion of institutes with the Apostolic See, each supreme moderator is to send a brief report of the state and life of the institute to the Apostolic See, in a manner and at a time established by the latter.

This canon obliges the supreme moderator of an institute of consecrated life to make brief periodic reports on the state of the institute in order that communion with the Apostolic See be preserved and strengthened. The norm implicitly shows the responsibility of the Apostolic See to remain informed of the institutes through these reports.

Until 1967, the institute's report was extremely detailed and had to be sent to Rome every five years.[184] In a circular letter in 1988, the Congregation for Religious and Secular Institutes advised the supreme moderators of institutes of consecrated life and societies of apostolic life that the report presented to the general chapter by the general council could be sent to that dicastery in a more

---

[178]*LG* 45; *CD* 35, par. 3; and *AG* 30. For an explanation of the principle of exemption, see J. Huels, "The Demise of Religious Exemption," *J* 54 (1994) 40–55; and idem, "What Became of Exemption?" *Conference of Major Superiors of Men Forum* 66 (Spring, 1994) 8–16.

[179]*CD* 35, 3–4; *ES* I: 22–40; *AG* 30; and *MR* 22.

[180]Canons 134; 397, §2; 596, §2; etc.

[181]Canon 678, §1.

[182]*VC* 49.

[183]Cf. *CCEO* 419. In the Eastern churches the report is sent every five years to the authority to which the institute is immediately subject. Superiors of institutes of eparchial or patriarchal right send a copy of the report to the Apostolic See.

[184]*CLD* 7, 479–480.

concise form. If the general chapter did not take place every five or six years, the report was still to be sent to the congregation every six years.[185] Both the canon and the letter address the supreme moderator; there is no mention of this obligation for the superior of an autonomous monastery or house. The periodic report should contain information on: statistics regarding members, houses, and provinces; the government, discipline, and life of the institute; programs for vocations and formation; experience of common life and the apostolate; financial condition and voluntary or involuntary separations from the institute.[186]

§2. The moderators of every institute are to promote knowledge of documents of the Holy See which regard the members entrusted to them and are to take care about their observance.

Moderators of institutes have the obligation to promote knowledge of the documents of the Holy See which affect the members entrusted to them and to be concerned about their observance. In some institutes, these documents were read aloud along with the constitutions during certain seasons.[187] The provision assists moderators in fostering the vocations of those entrusted to them. Today, many members have easier access to ecclesial documents in their institute's libraries or in places of apostolic service. After the Second Vatican Council, moderators of institutes of consecrated life initiated programs of renewal and adaptation in keeping with conciliar teachings. John Paul II's apostolic exhortation *Vita consecrata*[188] is an example of a document on consecrated life that moderators and other members should read and implement.[189]

Apostolic See/Pontifical Right Institutes[190]

Canon 593 — Without prejudice to the prescript of can. 586, institutes of pontifical right are immediately and exclusively subject to the power of the Apostolic See in regards to internal governance and discipline.

The autonomy[191] accorded each institute through which it orders its life and protects its patrimony pertains to the internal life of the institute but is not absolute.[192] Institutes of pontifical right are subject to the Apostolic See regarding internal matters that extend beyond the competence of moderators governing the institute.[193] This norm applies also to societies of apostolic life,[194] and there are several examples of such accountability in the law.[195]

Diocesan Bishop/Diocesan Right Institutes[196]

Canon 594 — Without prejudice to can. 586, an institute of diocesan right remains under the special care of the diocesan bishop.

Institutes of diocesan right likewise have a rightful autonomy of life in internal matters, but they remain subject to the diocesan bishop in those matters which exceed the competence of internal authorities. Bishops are ecclesiastical authorities, not internal moderators of institutes. They should not interfere in those affairs clearly prescribed for the moderators of the institute in

---

[185] *AAS* 80 (1980) 104–107.

[186] Ibid.; c. 704.

[187] *CIC* 509, §2, 1°.

[188] The apostolic exhortation can be found in *Origins* 25/41 (April 4, 1996) 681, 683–719.

[189] This norm applies also to societies of apostolic life. See c. 732.

[190] Cf. *CCEO* 413.

[191] Canon 586, §1.

[192] All institutes are subject to the diocesan bishop in matters concerning divine worship, care of souls, and apostolic works (c. 678, §1). See *CD* 35, 4; *AG* 30; *ES* I: 22–40; *MR* 52–53; *VC* 49. See also V. Koluthara, *Rightful Autonomy of Religious Institutes.*

[193] *PB* 108.

[194] Canon 732.

[195] Canons 583; 584; 587, §2; 638, §3; 684, §5; 686, §1; 686, §3; 691, §2; 700; 727, §1; 729; 730; 732; 741; 743; 744, §2; 746.

[196] Cf. *CCEO* 413.

universal or proper law. The code offers several examples of the authority of bishops regarding diocesan institutes.[197]

Bishop/Principal Seat of Institute[198]

Canon 595 — §1. It is for the bishop of the principal seat to approve the constitutions and confirm changes legitimately introduced into them, without prejudice to those things which the Apostolic See has taken in hand, and also to treat affairs of greater importance affecting the whole institute which exceed the power of internal authority, after he has consulted the other diocesan bishops, however, if the institute has spread to several dioceses.

An institute of diocesan right enjoys a relationship with the diocesan bishop of its principal seat (generalate) which is parallel to that of the relationship of an institute of pontifical right with the Apostolic See. The diocesan bishop approves the constitutions of the institute of diocesan right once he receives the *nihil obstat*[199] for its erection from the Apostolic See. He also approves any modifications in this fundamental code recommended by a two-thirds vote of the general chapter of the institute.[200] The exception here would be in any matter in which the Apostolic See has intervened.

The diocesan bishop of the principal seat of the institute addresses issues of greater importance affecting the entire institute which exceed the power of its competent authority, after consulting with the other diocesan bishops where the institute has spread.[201] This latter provision respects both the universal character of the institute and the importance of consultation with the bishops in dioceses where the religious give witness and serve.[202]

§2. A diocesan bishop can grant dispensations from the constitutions in particular cases.

A dispensation is the relaxation of an ecclesiastical law in a particular case.[203] It would seem that the norm does not refer to ordinary matters of discipline which the proper law leaves to the judgment of the competent moderator. Likewise, it does not apply to the universal law for consecrated life, but to the norms of the constitutions. A dispensation is given in a particular case;[204] if it affects the entire institute, then it would seem that the diocesan bishop of the principal seat of the institute would dispense from it.

Internal Authority of Institutes[205]

Canon 596 — §1. Superiors and chapters of institutes possess that power over members which is defined in universal law and the constitutions.

An approved institute of consecrated life enjoys internal autonomy to govern itself and protect its patrimony. The universal law and the proper law of the institute describe the nature and the limits of this power. Superiors and chapters of institutes of consecrated life and societies of apostolic life possess ecclesiastical power of governance within the limits of universal and proper law. This ecclesiastical power is public authority given by the Church and carried out in its name.[206]

---

[197] Canons 628, §2, 2°; 637; 638, §4; 686, §3; 688, §2; 691, §2; 700; 727, §1; 729; and cc. 732, 741, 746 regarding societies of apostolic life.

[198] Cf. *CCEO* 414; 554, §2; 566.

[199] *PB* 106, 1; c. 579.

[200] The bishop of the principal seat of the institute also presides at the election of the supreme moderator of the institute (c. 625, §2).

[201] The bishops of the dioceses where the houses of an institute are located have certain responsibilities toward the houses and members. See cc. 628, §2, 1°–2°; 637; 638, §4; 686, §3; 688, §2; 691, §2; 700; 727, §1; 729; 732; 741, §1; 746.

[202] This norm applies also to societies of apostolic life of diocesan right (cc. 732, 734).

[203] Canon 85.

[204] Canon 87.

[205] Cf. *CCEO* 441, §1; 511, §1; 557.

[206] *CLD* 3, 119; *CLD* 6, 425–433; cc. 617–640, 717, 732, 734.

Superiors and chapters of institutes can bind members with general or particular norms, insist on their implementation, and admonish offending members (c. 618). The competent superiors of institutes admit to the novitiate and profession, provide for formation, appoint to offices and apostolates, monitor the life and discipline of the institute, administer temporal goods, and process voluntary and involuntary separation from the institute. This norm recognizes and supports the autonomy of institutes in their internal life and governance. Canons 617–640 address the internal governance of religious institutes; canon 717, of secular institutes; canons 732 and 734, of societies of apostolic life. The constitutions of an institute should clearly define the nature and extent of the power of the superiors and chapters at each level of government.

§2. In clerical religious institutes of pontifical right, however, they also possess ecclesiastical power of governance for both the external and internal forum.[207]

The second section of this norm follows from canon 129, §1. Superiors and chapters of clerical religious institutes of pontifical right also possess ordinary executive power or jurisdiction for both the internal and external forum for their members.[208] The same is true for superiors of clerical societies of apostolic life of pontifical right.[209]

Superiors and chapters of clerical secular institutes of pontifical right are not included in this norm, since the members of these institutes are incardinated into the dioceses they serve. Only in very few cases are members incardinated into the secular institute by apostolic indult.[210]

§3. The prescripts of cann. 131, 133, and 137–144 apply to the power mentioned in §1.

This section of the canon applies the norms governing the exercise of the executive power of governance or jurisdiction to superiors and chapters mentioned in canon 596, §1. The canons describe ordinary (proper or vicarious) and delegated power of governance (c. 131), the use of delegated power (c. 133), the delegation and subdelegation of ordinary executive power and its interpretation (cc. 137–138), the effects of approaching higher authority (c. 139), the provisions for several persons delegated in the same manner (cc. 140–141), and the cessation or suspension of the power (cc. 142–143). Canon 144 addresses jurisdiction supplied by the Church (*Ecclesia supplet*) in cases of common error and positive and probable doubt. There are many unresolved questions and continuing discussion on the nature of the exercise of the ecclesiastical power of governance by lay persons. Developments in this area of law will surely affect the role of authority in lay institutes of consecrated life.[211]

---

[207] Cf. *CCEO* 441, §2; 511, §2; 557.

[208] In the former code (*CIC* 198, §1; 501), only superiors and chapters of clerical exempt religious institutes had ecclesiastical jurisdiction in accord with the code and their constitutions. Paul VI in *Cum admotae,* November 6, 1964, extended ecclesiastical jurisdiction to superiors general of clerical religious institutes, clerical societies of apostolic life, and clerical secular institutes of pontifical right with regard to their ordained subjects incardinated in the institute. See *CLD* 6, 147–153.

In the present code, the major superiors (c. 620) of clerical religious institutes of pontifical right and major superiors of clerical societies of apostolic life of pontifical right are ordinaries for their own subjects (c. 134, §1).

[209] Canon 732.

[210] Canon 266, §3; see also c. 715.

[211] There is much discussion about the exercise of jurisdiction by lay persons in the Church based on c. 129, §2, which provides that lay persons can cooperate in the exercise of ecclesiastical governing power. See, for example, J. Beal, "The Exercise of Jurisdiction by Lay Religious," *Bulletin on Issues of Religious Law* 13 (Winter, 1997) 1–6; also idem, "The Exercise of the Power of Governance by Lay People: State of the Question," *J* 55/1 (1995) 1–92; J. Pfab, "The Right and Duty of the Superior General to Intervene in Certain Matters," *Con Lif* 11/1 (1986) 84–97; J. Provost, "The Participation of the Laity in the Governance of the Church," *Stud Can* (1983) 417–449.

Qualifications for Admission[212]

Canon 597 — §1. Any Catholic endowed with a right intention who has the qualities required by universal and proper law and who is not prevented by any impediment can be admitted into an institute of consecrated life.

This canon provides the essential elements for admission to all institutes of consecrated life and societies of apostolic life.[213] Each institute and society is unique and often prescribes other more specific requisites or qualities for admission in its proper law. Admission presupposes a response to a divine call, the grace to make a total dedication of self in praise of God and service in the Church.[214] It is left to the competent authorities in keeping with the provisions of universal and proper law to judge the person's suitability for consecrated life. Subsequent canons[215] and the proper laws of the respective institutes and societies have more detailed provisions to assist those making this determination.

The person must be a Catholic, one who has been baptized in or received into the Catholic Church, sharing the same faith, sacraments, and ecclesiastical governance.[216] Proofs of Catholicity will be certificates of baptism and confirmation.[217] If a person from another Catholic church *sui iuris* requests admission to a religious institute of the Latin church, the person can licitly be admitted with permission of the Apostolic See.[218] If the person leaves the institute, he or she returns to the rite of the church of baptism.

The person must have the right intention. Right intention or motivation refers to the reason that brought the person to request admission to the institute. The ideal intent is to offer a total gift of oneself in service to God and others in accord with the spirit and mission of the institute. The person may not yet have reached this level of spiritual maturity, but the qualities of faith, generosity, and selflessness should certainly be present in response to the question, "What prompted you to enter this institute?" Often, the best incentive for a person is the witness of a member of the institute; the candidate desires to emulate such a life of dedication.

The person being admitted must have the requisite qualities in universal and proper law. Subsequent canons on admission to institutes and societies as well as the pertinent proper laws will address the qualities of health, suitable disposition, and sufficient maturity.[219] These qualities can, if necessary, be established by the use of experts in the medical field and behavioral sciences with due regard for privacy and the reputation of the candidate.[220] Such qualities should be considered in view of the particular nature of the institute.[221]

The person can be prevented from admission by impediments set down in the universal or proper law. Canons 643, §1; 721, §1; and 735, §2 address invalidating impediments for admission to institutes and societies in the universal law. Proper law can set down other invalidating impediments.[222] Requirements for licit admission to an institute of consecrated life that are set forth in universal law are addressed subsequently in this commentary.[223]

§2. No one can be admitted without suitable preparation.

---

[212] Cf. *CCEO* 448–449; 517, §1; 518.

[213] Canon 732.

[214] *LG* 42; *PC* 1; *ET* 1, 4.

[215] Canons 641–645, 720–721, 735.

[216] Canon 205.

[217] Canon 645, §1.

[218] This procedure, called "accommodation," is not addressed in the Latin code, but is provided for in *CCEO* 451; 517, §2. Permission can be obtained from the apostolic nuncio.

[219] Canons 642; 721, §3; 735, §§1–2

[220] Canons 642, 220.

[221] Canons 642; 735, §2.

[222] Canons 643, §2; 721, §2.

[223] Canons 644–645; 721, §2; 735, §2. See also Congregation for Catholic Education/Seminaries, "Instruction on Admitting Candidates Coming from Other Seminaries or Religious Communities," *Origins* 26/22 (November 14, 1996) 358–360.

The norm leaves to the proper law of individual institutes the norms for the preparatory period before a person begins the canonical formation period in the life of the institute or society. The format and duration of this initial preparation should be ordered in keeping with the nature and end of the institute or society, as well as the needs of the candidate. Christian principles, a deeper knowledge of Christ, liturgical prayer, and the spiritual tradition of the institute should be included in this important time of preparation.[224]

Observance of Proper Law

Canon 598 — §1. Each institute, attentive to its own character and purposes, is to define in its constitutions the manner in which the evangelical counsels of chastity, poverty, and obedience must be observed for its way of living.

The evangelical counsels of chastity, poverty and obedience are of the very essence of consecrated life.[225] Canon 587, §1 and this norm oblige each institute and society in which the members embrace the counsels to prescribe in its fundamental code or constitutions the proper object and manner of living the public vows or other sacred bonds in accord with the nature and spirit of the institute. The next three canons will provide the essential elements or what is applicable to all institutes and societies in which the members embrace the three counsels by vow or other sacred bond. The content of these norms should be incorporated into the constitutions. However, in accord with the nature, spirit, and purpose of the institute, there are other specifics with regard to the way poverty or obedience may be lived in particular institutes.

The canon shows the importance of the constitutions in protecting the patrimony of the institute and in guiding the members in the following of Christ, chaste, poor, and obedient, in accord with the particular nature of the institute.

§2. Moreover, all members must not only observe the evangelical counsels faithfully and fully but also arrange their life according to the proper law of the institute and thereby strive for the perfection of their state.[226]

Members assume the evangelical counsels and accept the obligations of their call as described in the proper law of the institute. That is why from the very beginnings of the formative process they are introduced to the law of the institute. Profession is made in a particular institute and according to its constitutions.[227] This clearly shows their obligations and protects them from arbitrary commands of superiors contrary to proper law. They are obliged to live in accord with the proper law of the institute. The constitutions approved by competent ecclesiastical authority contain essential elements regarding the evangelical counsels and other responsibilities assumed with membership in the institute. Through these fundamental norms, the members order their lives in striving for the perfection of charity according to the patrimony and traditions of the institute.[228]

The Evangelical Counsels

Canons 599–601 contain norms regarding the three evangelical counsels of chastity, poverty, and obedience. Societies of apostolic life in which the members embrace the counsels by a sacred bond defined in the constitutions are also bound by these canons.[229] Each institute and society provides more specific norms in its constitutive law

---

[224] *PI* 42–44. While these directives are for formation in religious institutes, they are also helpful to those involved in formation work in secular institutes and societies of apostolic life. *VC* 65–68.

[225] *LG* 41–47, *PC* 12–14, c. 573. In religious institutes, the members make profession of the counsels by public vows (cc. 607, §2; 654). In secular institutes and societies of apostolic life the constitutions determine the kind of bond (cc. 712; 731, §2).

[226] Cf. *CCEO* 426.

[227] Canon 654.

[228] Canons 578; 587, §1.

[229] Canons 731, §2; 732.

for the living of the evangelical counsels in accord with the nature, spirit, and purpose of the institute or society.

Chastity

Canon 599 — The evangelical counsel of chastity assumed for the sake of the kingdom of heaven, which is a sign of the world to come and a source of more abundant fruitfulness in an undivided heart, entails the obligation of perfect continence in celibacy.

All Christians are obliged to live chaste lives in accord with their vocations. Through the profession of evangelical chastity, a person in imitation of Christ sacrifices marriage and those acts pertaining to the marriage state for the sake of the kingdom. The evangelical counsel of chastity obliges a person to live a celibate life in perfect continence.[230] This counsel assumed for the sake of the kingdom frees the heart for greater love of God and people, enables a wholehearted dedication to the apostolate of the institute, and challenges a hedonistic culture.[231]

Unlike poverty and obedience, evangelical chastity admits of no degrees or gradations. General instructions on admission to institutes and policies of institutes of consecrated life help in determining candidates who can live a chaste, celibate lifestyle. Proper laws encourage members in the values of prayer, self-discipline, health care, and supportive friendships as means of persevering in their commitment.[232]

---

[230]This is true likewise for clerics (c. 277, §1) with the exclusion of permanent married deacons.

[231]PC 12, VC 88.

[232]PC 12; PI 13. Persons bound by a public perpetual vow of chastity in a religious institute invalidly attempt marriage (c. 1088). Such an action would lead to the incurring of certain penalties, e.g., cc. 694, §1, 2°; 194, §1, 3°, 1394, §§1–2. Members of secular institutes and societies of apostolic life would be dismissed from their respective institutes (cc. 729, 746). There are penalties for other offenses against the counsel of chastity, e.g., cc. 695; 696, §1; 1395.

Poverty

Canon 600 — The evangelical counsel of poverty in imitation of Christ who, although he was rich, was made poor for us, entails, besides a life which is poor in fact and in spirit and is to be led productively in moderation and foreign to earthly riches, a dependence and limitation in the use and disposition of goods according to the norm of the proper law of each institute.

All Christians are called to poverty of spirit inspiring them to share their goods and resources with the less fortunate of the world.[233] Those who assume the evangelical counsel of poverty imitate Christ and commit to a life that is poor in fact as well as in spirit.[234] They are obliged to labor in accord with the nature and ends of the institute and in dependence on the institute.[235] Both the universal law and the proper law of the institute regulate the limits, use, and disposition of their temporal goods.[236]

Besides the individual witness given by members through their personal lives, collective witness to evangelical poverty is given by institutes of consecrated life.[237] It should be noted that this is evangelical poverty rooted in the nature of the institute and willed by the members in imitation of Christ and for the mission of the Church. It is not the poverty of destitution experienced by so many persons deprived of the basic necessities of life and a poverty which Christ and his Church strive to eliminate.

Unlike the counsel of chastity, poverty admits of a wide variety of expressions in accord with the nature, spirit, and purpose of each institute. The effects and obligations of a vow of poverty made in a religious institute with common life can differ significantly from those assumed in a secular institute with a more individualized lifestyle.

---

[233]Acts 2:44–45; 4:32–35.

[234]2 Cor 8:9; PC 13.

[235]Canon 670.

[236]PC 13; cc. 668; 712; 722, §2; 732; 741, §2.

[237]Canons 634, §2; 635, §2; 640; 718.

Likewise, the juridical effects of the vow of poverty made in a contemplative institute may differ from those of the vow of poverty made in an apostolic institute.

The various apostolates of institutes of consecrated life witness to the dignity of human labor and the life of service to which the members are called. While education, health care, and social services are traditional apostolates, frequently members of institutes work in other areas to alleviate hunger, ignorance, sickness, unemployment, and the deprivation of basic liberties. Often, too, from their own resources they help provide for those in such circumstances. By their example and teachings, some institutes and their members encourage respect for natural resources and challenge others to reduce consumption through greater simplicity of life and the curbing of wants.[238]

Obedience

Canon 601 — The evangelical counsel of obedience, undertaken in a spirit of faith and love in the following of Christ obedient unto death, requires the submission of the will to legitimate superiors, who stand in the place of God, when they command according to the proper constitutions.

Christ's obedience to the Father's will even to his death on the cross is a central mystery of the Christian life and the motivating force for the sacred bond of obedience.[239] Imitating Christ's love of God's will, members of institutes of consecrated life are to submit their wills in a spirit of faith and love to legitimate superiors who receive their authority from God through the ministry of the Church.[240] In a spirit of service and concern for the members, superiors give commands in accord with the universal law and the proper constitutions of the institute.[241] Thus, authority and obedience practiced in institutes of consecrated life reflect the Fa-

ther's love of Christ and Christ's obedience to the Father.

Sharing a charism or gift of the Spirit, those in authority and other members of the institute are to seek God's will in a spirit of peace, love, unity, and concern for the good of the Church, the institute, and each member. However, this searching ceases with the decision of the superior, who is indispensable in every community. Even small or satellite communities should have a superior vested with personal authority to whom the members are accountable. There is no provision in law for communities without superiors or for "team governance."[242]

The authority entrusted to the superior by the Church is not absolute. The superior must always respect the human dignity of the member, conform to universal and proper law, and exercise authority in a spirit of charity. The member should know when he or she is commanded by virtue of the vow or bond in a grave matter.[243] In obeying the commands of superiors, members live in a spirit of faith and in imitation of Christ who always did the Father's will. Their way of life testifies to the truth that there is no contradiction between obedience and freedom.[244]

Communion of Life

Canon 602 — The life of brothers or sisters proper to each institute, by which all the members are united together as a special family in Christ, is to

---

[238] PC 13, PI 14, VC 89–90, c. 640.

[239] PC 14.

[240] PC 14, c. 618.

[241] PC 14, ES II: 18. Canon 590, §2 recognizes the Supreme Pontiff as the highest superior of members of institutes of consecrated life whom they are bound to obey by reason of their sacred bond of obedience.

[242] ET 25; VC 43, 92; c. 618. See also CICLSAL, instr Fraternal Life in Community, *Congregavit nos in unum Christi amor (FL)*, February 2, 1994, *Origins* 23/40 (March 24, 1994) 693, 695–712, esp. 47–53, 58–64.

[243] It should be made very clear to the member that he or she is being commanded by virtue of the vow of obedience. Also, all formalities have to be fulfilled by the superior in order to command by virtue of the vow, e.g., the issuance of a canonical warning commanding in the name of obedience. The constitutions should indicate clearly which superiors can give such commands. A formal canonical warning is given in writing or before two witnesses to a member for a grave offense. See cc. 697, §2; 729; 746.

[244] PC 14, PI 13, VC 91.

be defined in such a way that it becomes a mutual support for all in fulfilling the vocation of each. Moreover, by their communion as brothers or sisters rooted and founded in charity, members are to be an example of universal reconciliation in Christ.

The norm addresses fraternal life (*vita fraterna*) as distinguished from life in community or the canonical common life prescribed for religious institutes.[245] Members of institutes share their baptismal life and a gift of the Holy Spirit which unites them as a family in Christ. Their love and concern for one another witness to the mystery of the ecclesial communion in which the Trinity dwells. Through mutual support they carry out the purpose of their institute and manifest the "reconciling power of grace which overcomes the divisive tendencies present in the human heart and in society."[246]

This communion in love is evident not only in religious and secular institutes, but also in societies of apostolic life where members live common life. Hermits, consecrated virgins, widows and widowers in their generous response to the gifts of the Spirit witness Christ's love for His Father and all humanity.[247]

Eremitical Life[248]

Canon 603 — §1. In addition to institutes of consecrated life, the Church recognizes the eremitic

or anchoritic life by which the Christian faithful devote their life to the praise of God and the salvation of the world through a stricter withdrawal from the world, the silence of solitude, and assiduous prayer and penance.

Paragraph one describes the eremitical or anchoritic[249] life which traces its roots to the third century and the desert fathers such as Paul and Anthony. This ancient form of consecrated life marked the beginnings of monasticism in the Church. Men and women experienced the call to live in the solitude of silence, prayer, fasting, and penance in love of God and intercession for the world. They witness the sublime vocation of being always with the Lord.[250]

The norm does not address the eremitical lifestyle provided for in the proper law of some religious institutes such as the Carthusians, Camaldolese, and Carmelites. Professed members of these institutes live as hermits under obedience to their legitimate superiors in accord with their proper law.[251] Rather, it addresses solitary men or women living under the authority of a diocesan bishop.

§2. A hermit is recognized by law as one dedicated to God in consecrated life if he or she pub-

---

[245] Members of religious institutes ordinarily live together in a house of the institute, share its resources, receive support from the institute, and are missioned to an apostolate in the name of the institute. See cc. 607, §2; 665; 668, §3; 670; 678, §2. Members of societies of apostolic life are also obliged to live common life in accord with their proper law (c. 740).

[246] *VC* 41.

[247] *PC* 15, *VC* 42. While *VC* 42 includes widows and widowers, there is no norm for consecrated widows and widowers in the Latin code. However, canon 570 of the Eastern code permits particular law of *sui iuris* churches to provide for consecrated widows.

[248] Cf. *CCEO* 481–485. The five canons in the Eastern code describe the hermit as a perpetually professed

member of a monastery *sui iuris* who, with the permission of and subject to the superior, gives himself/herself over totally to contemplation and lives the eremetical life in accord with the typicon or proper law of the monastery.

[249] While the terms are used interchangeably, the term "anchorite" applies to a solitary living near and provided for by a community of the faithful, or a religious living the eremitical lifestyle in accord with the norms of the proper law under the authority of the competent superior.

[250] *LG* 43, *PC* 1, *VC* 7.

[251] The 1977 draft of this canon (c. 92, §2) recognized a hermit as one who professed the three evangelical counsels stabilized by vow and observed his/her proper rule of life under the guidance of the local ordinary or a competent religious moderator. The Eastern code provides for religious as hermits in cc. 481–485. Solitaries who are not religious and live such lives in accord with the particular law of a *sui iuris* church are called ascetics in the Eastern code (*CCEO* 570).

licly professes in the hands of the diocesan bishop the three evangelical counsels, confirmed by vow or other sacred bond, and observes a proper program of living under his direction.[252]

Paragraph two of the norm provides the juridical norms for this form of consecrated life. A person publicly professes chastity, poverty, and obedience by means of a vow or other sacred bond in the hands of the diocesan bishop.[253] Likewise, he or she lives a plan of life approved by the bishop and under his direction. The diocesan bishop may delegate another, e.g., the vicar for religious, to monitor the hermit.

One contemplating an eremitical lifestyle should follow the counsel of a wise and experienced spiritual director. The qualities required for admission to an institute of consecrated life can be applied to this vocation.[254] It would seem within the competence of the diocesan bishop to dispense from the vow or other sacred bond of the hermit,[255] or to dismiss the hermit from this form of consecrated life for a grave reason.[256]

Order of Virgins[257]

Canon 604 — §1. Similar to these forms of consecrated life is the order of virgins who, expressing the holy resolution of following Christ more closely, are consecrated to God by the diocesan bishop according to the approved liturgical rite, are mys-

tically betrothed to Christ, the Son of God, and are dedicated to the service of the Church.

Both men and women lived consecrated virginity in the early Church. The practice led to the formulation of a solemn rite in the *Roman Pontifical* which constituted the candidate a sacred person, a sign of the Church as Bride of Christ, and an eschatological witness of the world to come.[258] Gradually, only certain orders of contemplative nuns used the ancient solemn rite within the context of their profession ceremonies.[259] The Constitution on the Liturgy ordered the revision of the rite which was published on May 31, 1970.[260] The diocesan bishop may consecrate nuns and women living in the world under the following conditions:

> *nuns:* a) that they have never married nor lived in public or flagrant violation of chastity; b) that they have made their final profession, either in the same rite or on an earlier occasion; c) that their religious family uses this rite because of long-established custom or by new permission of the competent authority.

> *women living in the world:* a) that they have never been married nor lived in public or flagrant violation of chastity; b) that by their age, prudence, and universally attested good

---

[252] Cf. *CCEO* 484.

[253] While the term "public vows" is used only in c. 607, §2, describing a religious institute, it would seem that vows made by a hermit in the hands of the diocesan bishop meet the description of c. 1192, §1. However, the hermit's perpetual vow of chastity is not a diriment impediment to marriage (c. 1088).

[254] Canon 597.

[255] The diocesan bishop is competent to grant an indult of departure to members of institutes of consecrated life. See cc. 691, §2 and 727, §1.

[256] H. MacDonald, "Hermits: The Juridical Implications of Canon 603," *Stud Can* 26 (1992) 163–189; R. McDermott, "Recent Developments in Consecrated Life," *Bulletin on Issues of Religious Law* 9 (Fall, 1993) 1–9.

[257] Cf. *CCEO* 570.

[258] *OrConVir* 1.

[259] Despite the ancient beginnings of consecrated virginity, in 1927 the Sacred Congregation for Religious refused the request of bishops for the faculty to consecrate women living in the world as virgins (*CLD* 1, 266). However, by 1950, diocesan bishops and Benedictine abbots in the U.S. could confer the consecration of virgins on Benedictine sisters of simple perpetual vows (*CLD* 4, 166–168). This faculty extended the provision in art. III.3 of the apconst *Sponsa Christi* of Pope Pius XII (November 21, 1950) which reserved the ancient solemn rite of the consecration of virgins for nuns (*CLD* 3, 234).

[260] *SC* 80; SCDW (May 31, 1970), *AAS* 62 (1970) 650; *CLD* 7, 421–425. The revised rite provides only for women, but par. 34 of the *instrumentum laboris* for the 1994 synod of bishops raised the possibility of this form of life for men.

character they give assurance of perseverance in a life of chastity dedicated to the service of the Church and of their neighbor; c)
that they be admitted to this consecration by
the bishop who is the local ordinary.[261]

The rite further indicates that it is for the bishop
to decide on the conditions under which women
living in the world are to undertake a life of perpetual virginity.[262] While they make no profession
of the evangelical counsels, a life lived in the spirit
of the evangelical counsels is implied. Through
their *sanctum propositum* or sacred resolution they
consecrate their chastity for love of Christ and in
service to the Church. Their consecration is received through the ministry of the diocesan bishop.[263] These women resolve to live celibate, chaste
lives in perfect continence and are dedicated to the
service of the Church in their respective dioceses.
The ritual provides for the giving of the veil and
ring in accord with local custom.

**§2. In order to observe their own resolution
more faithfully and to perform by mutual assistance service to the Church in harmony with their
proper state, virgins can be associated together.**

Virgins can offer mutual support to one another
in their sacred resolution and service to the Church
through associations. This is not obligatory for a
consecrated virgin, and the norm is not referring to
community life[264] of institutes of consecrated life
nor the common life lived by members of religious institutes and societies of apostolic life.[265]

New Forms of Consecrated Life[266]

**Canon 605 — The approval of new forms of con-
secrated life is reserved only to the Apostolic See.
Diocesan bishops, however, are to strive to discern new gifts of consecrated life granted to the
Church by the Holy Spirit and are to assist promoters so that these can express their proposals
as well as possible and protect them by appropriate statutes; the general norms contained in this
section are especially to be utilized.**

The norm shows the openness of the Church to
recognize the gifts of the Spirit that contribute to
its life and holiness. New forms of consecrated
life would be forms distinct from those already
approved by the Apostolic See and described in
this section of the code.[267] Only the Apostolic See
can approve new forms and give them juridical
status.[268] For example, secular institutes as a form
of consecrated life were approved in 1947.[269]
Diocesan bishops assist the Apostolic See in discerning the vitality and authenticity of such gifts
in their respective churches. The general norms in
this section of the code (cc. 573–606) serve as
guides to the bishops in this process. Also, the
pope has set up a commission to deal with questions relating to new forms of consecrated life and

---

[261] *OrConVir* 3–5.

[262] Ibid., 5.

[263] The code does not provide for the consecration of widows as does *CCEO* 570. Nothing would prohibit a widow
from making a private vow of perpetual chastity as a sign
of the kingdom of God, devoting herself to prayer and the
service of the Church. Decisions such as this should always be made after serious prayer, reflection, and the
counsel of an experienced spiritual director.

[264] Canon 602.

[265] German Bishops' Pastoral, "Consecrated Virgins in the
World," trans. R. Barringer, *Canadian Catholic Review*

(January 1988) 17–19; A. Jiminez, "El Ordo 'Virgenes
Consagradas' a la luz del Codigo vigente," *ComRelMiss*
75 (1994) 221–242; D. Pichard, "The Renewal of the
Consecration of Virgins," *RfR* (January/February 1986)
17–24; A. Selvaggi, "An Ancient Rite Restored—Consecrated Virgins Living in the World," *Canadian Catholic Review* (January 1987) 6–11.

[266] Cf. *CCEO* 571.

[267] The forms of consecrated life approved by the Church
are hermits (c. 603), religious institutes (c. 607, §2), and
secular institutes (c. 710). The order of virgins (c. 604,
§1) and societies of apostolic life (c. 731, §1) are described in law as "approaching" (*accedunt*) consecrated
life. This distinction seems to be made because a profession of the three evangelical counsels is not required for
these vocations.

[268] *VC* 12.

[269] Pius XII, apconst *Provida Mater Ecclesia*, February 2,
1947, *AAS* 39 (1947) 114–124.

to determine criteria to assist diocesan bishops in discerning them.[270]

History teaches that new forms do not supplant the former ones, but often evolve from them. They are yet another way of following the chaste, poor, and obedient Christ in striving for perfect charity.[271] It is important that such new forms possess the essential theological and canonical elements proper to consecrated life as described in this section of the law.[272]

Canon 606 — Those things which are established for institutes of consecrated life and their members are equally valid in law for either sex, unless it is otherwise evident from the context of the wording or the nature of the matter.

This norm reflects one of the principles directing the labors of the committee in revising the 1917 code. The code treats institutes of men and women equally, unless the nature of the matter or some particular situation warrants otherwise. While the former code contained the same norm,[273] there is greater equality achieved in the present law. For example, the diocesan bishop or his delegate no longer presides at the elections of women's institutes of pontifical right, nor does he interview women candidates before their admission to religious profession.[274]

The norms do make distinctions between clerical and lay institutes and diocesan and pontifical right institutes. The provisions for the cloister of contemplative nuns in canon 667, §§3–4 seem somewhat discriminatory, since the nuns cannot

provide for cloister in accord with the nature and end of their institute. Also, the diocesan bishop permits entrance and egress from these *sui iuris* monasteries of nuns.[275] The bishops at the 1994 synod addressed cloister for nuns[276] and proposed to the Supreme Pontiff that more authority be given major superiors of nuns in granting dispensations from enclosure for just and sufficient reasons.[277] In response, the pope assured a study of cloister which would consider the many forms and degrees of monastic and contemplative life.[278]

TITLE II
RELIGIOUS INSTITUTES
[cc. 607–709]

In title II, 103 canons address religious institutes, one form of consecrated life. The title begins with an introductory canon describing the nature and purpose of the religious vocation and religious institutes. The title then is divided into six chapters on religious institutes: (1) the organizational structure of a religious institute in a particular church, (2) the institute's internal governance and the administration of temporal goods, (3) the admission of candidates and formation of members, (4) the obligations and rights of institutes and members, (5) the apostolates of institutes, and (6) the separation of members. Two final chapters consider a religious named bishop and the conferences of major superiors.

Nature/End of Religious Life[279]

Canon 607 — §1. As a consecration of the whole person, religious life manifests in the Church a wonderful marriage brought about by God, a

---

[270] Prop. 13, *VC* 62. See also J. Galante, "Consecrated Life: New Forms and New Institutes," *CLSAP* (1986) 118–125; R. McDermott, "Recent Developments in Consecrated Life"; A. Neri, "Nuove forme di vita consacrata (can. 605–CIC): Profili giuridici," *ComRelMiss* 75/3–4 (1994) 253–308.

[271] *VC* 12.

[272] Ibid.

[273] *CIC* 490.

[274] R. McDermott, *The Legal Condition of Women in the Church: Shifting Policies and Norms* (Washington, D.C.: Catholic University of America, 1979).

[275] Canon 667, §§3–4.

[276] *ES* II, 30–31; *PC* 7, 16; *VS* VI.

[277] Canon 667, §4; prop. 22, *VC* 59.

[278] *VC* 59, par. 5.

[279] *CCEO* 410 gives a theological description of the religious state which is similar to the description of religious life in c. 607.

sign of the future age. Thus the religious brings to perfection a total self-giving as a sacrifice offered to God, through which his or her whole existence becomes a continuous worship of God in charity.

Paragraph one contains a theological description of religious life, one form of consecrated life. In making profession of the evangelical counsels, the religious offers a total self-donation to God in order to derive even more fruit from the grace of baptism. The entire life of the religious becomes a continuous worship of God and service to his people in love. Religious life witnesses to Christ's love for his Church and foreshadows the future kingdom.[280] Besides giving canonical status to religious life, the Church sets it forth liturgically as a state of consecration to God. It receives the vows of religious,[281] intercedes for them in its public prayer, bestows on them a spiritual blessing, and associates their self-offering with the sacrifice of the Eucharist.[282] Living the fullness of the gospel through the profession of the evangelical counsels, religious offer a witness to the Church far exceeding any apostolic service.[283] While there are essential elements in this consecration, each institute further expresses it in accord with its own nature, spirit, and end.[284]

Religious Institute: Juridical Elements[285]

§2. A religious institute is a society in which members, according to proper law, pronounce public vows, either perpetual or temporary which are to be renewed, however, when the period of time has elapsed, and lead a life of brothers or sisters in common.

Paragraph two provides the juridical elements of a religious institute. It is a society, an organized group of persons with a special nature, spirit, and end. When canonically erected, a religious institute becomes a public juridical person.[286] The members of a religious institute (1) profess public vows and (2) live community life in common as brothers or sisters.

1. Public Vows

A vow is a deliberate and free promise made to God concerning a possible and better good which must be fulfilled by reason of the virtue of religion.[287] A public vow is a vow accepted in the name of the Church by a legitimate superior.[288] There are requirements in the code for the validity and liceity of religious profession which will be discussed in subsequent canons.[289] The law no longer distinguishes between solemn and simple vows in religious institutes. Canons 599–601 contain the essential elements of the evangelical counsels; the effects of profession are described in the constitutions of each institute.

Members of religious institutes are required to make temporary vows for the time defined in the proper law.[290] Temporary profession pre-

---

[280] *LG* 44; *PC* 12; *ET* 13; *VC* 26, 84.

[281] Canons 656, 5°; 658.

[282] *LG* 45; *VC* 8–9.

[283] *LG* 44; c. 673.

[284] CDW, "Rite of Religious Profession" (February 2, 1970) in *The Rites of the Catholic Church*, vol. 2 (Collegeville: Liturgical Press, 1991) 199–297. See esp. 204, par. 4.

[285] Cf. *CCEO* 410.

[286] Canons 116; 634, §1. See cc. 579, 589 for the beginnings and approval of religious institutes.

[287] Canon 1191, §1. Public vows constitute both temporary and perpetual religious profession. *RC* permitted institutes to substitute promises or another form of bond in place of temporary profession. See SCRIS, instr. *Renovationis causam,* January 6, 1969, *AAS* 61 (1969) 103; *CLD* 7, 487–508. However, John Paul II ruled against this proposed provision and it was excluded from the 1980 schema. (Sec. of State, August 12, 1980, Prot. no. 41829). Secular institutes and some societies of apostolic life assume the counsels by vows or other sacred bonds defined in the constitutions (cc. 712; 731, §2).

[288] Canon 1192, §1.

[289] Canons 656, 658, 668. The proper law of the institute can posit other requirements.

[290] Canon 655. The time in temporary vows may not be less than three years nor more than six years. In a particular case, the competent superior in accord with the proper law can extend the period of temporary profession, but

sumes the right intention on the part of the religious of moving toward perpetual or definitive profession.

Final profession in a religious institute may be in the form of perpetual vows or perpetually renewed vows. No matter which form, the profession is perpetual or definitive, i.e., for life. In institutes where the members perpetually renew temporary vows, the constitutions should state clearly the time at which the member is definitively incorporated into the institute.[291]

2. Common Life

Besides the fraternal/sisterly life described in canon 602, members of religious institutes are obliged to common life. It is left to the proper law of the institute to describe the way common life is lived in accord with the nature of the institute. Some elements of the common life can be found in canon 665, §1 (residence in a house of institute), canons 668, §3 and 670 (sharing resources), and canon 669 (common habit or style of dress). Members of institutes dedicated to contemplation share this hidden apostolate (c. 674). Institutes dedicated to works of the apostolate have works proper to the institute, i.e., works which derive from the very nature and purpose of the institute (c. 675, §1). Members are missioned in the name of the institute (cc. 671, 682). The Eucharist is the central focus of the local community of all religious institutes (cc. 608, 934, §1, 1°) and the members share communal prayer (c. 663, §2).

Public Witness[292]

§3. The public witness to be rendered by religious to Christ and the Church entails a separation from the world proper to the character and purpose of each institute.

Consecrated and sent forth to carry on Christ's mission, religious are intimately concerned for and involved in the world, yet separated from it by their public witness of the chaste, poor, and obedient Christ.[293] It is precisely this witness that sets religious apart from worldly values and achievements which are often antithetical to Christian life and the nature and purpose of their institutes.[294] Religious live a common life of prayer and mutual support in chaste celibacy, labor, and dependence on the institute. They sacrifice personal goals for the goals of the institute in service to the Church. These values challenge the promiscuity, hedonism, and individualism often prevalent in society.[295]

CHAPTER I
RELIGIOUS HOUSES AND THEIR ERECTION AND SUPPRESSION
[cc. 608–616]

Religious institutes enjoy a universal character; their members witness and serve wherever the mission of the Church extends. In reality, however, houses are situated and members serve within a particular church. This chapter addresses the constitution and erection of houses of a variety of religious institutes, the rights and responsibilities accorded the houses and their members, the apostolic works within the particular church, the suppression of erected houses, and the disposition of their temporal goods.

---

the entire time spent in temporary vows may not exceed nine years (c. 657, §2).

[291] The code does not explicitly describe perpetually renewed temporary vows. But the two forms of final profession can be implicitly recognized in cc. 623; 1019, §1; and 1052, §2. The time for definitive profession is left to the proper law of the institute and should be stated in the constitutions.

[292] Cf. *CCEO* 410.

[293] The traditional *fuga mundi* or flight from the world has taken on a more nuanced meaning since the teachings of the Second Vatican Council, particularly *Gaudium et spes*. Apostolic religious labor among the people of God and witness the values of their vowed lives. Cloistered religious embrace the world in hiddenness through prayer and penance (*LG* 46; *PC* 7; *AG* 40; *VC* 8; cc. 673–675).

[294] *PC* 24; c. 673.

[295] *VC* 45.

Constituted House[296]

Canon 608 — A religious community must live in a legitimately established house under the authority of a superior designated according to the norm of law. Each house is to have at least an oratory in which the Eucharist is to be celebrated and reserved so that it is truly the center of the community.

This norm addresses a constituted house as distinct from a canonically erected house as described in canon 609.[297] Many houses of religious such as faculty houses, parish convents, rectories, residences for religious in hospital or social service ministries are constituted houses. More than one house or community of religious can be constituted within a larger building; often satellite houses are constituted within the generalate or provincialate. At times, large faculty houses accommodate the religious of two or more religious institutes. The elements necessary for a constituted house are the following:

1. The house must be legitimately constituted by the competent authority in accord with the proper law of the institute. Often such houses are established in response to the needs of a particular apostolate or to those of members engaged in addressing diversified apostolates in a given area. Courtesy, good mutual relations, and a possible future need for sacred ministers would prompt the superior to advise the diocesan bishop and the pastor of the parish in which the house is located.

2. The religious community lives under the authority of a superior designated according to the norm of law. In the case of small or satellite communities,[298] the members may be accountable to a provincial or regional superior. In larger communities, a local superior resides in the house possessing personal authority in accord with canon 618 and the proper law of the institute.

3. The house is to have an oratory in which the Eucharist is celebrated and reserved as the center of the community. This right is congruent with the obligations of religious institutes and their members.[299] The Eucharist is the center of the community. The local ordinary has the responsibility of examining the suitability of the place and the arrangement provided for the oratory in houses of lay religious institutes; the competent major superior in accord with the proper law designates the place for clerical religious institutes of pontifical right.[300] While this right should not be denied religious, reverence for the Eucharist warrants serious consideration both on the part of the local ordinary and the major superior in situations where care and safety may present difficulty.

Erected House[301]

Canon 609 — §1. Houses of a religious institute are erected by the authority competent according to the constitutions, with the previous written consent of the diocesan bishop.

Once a house is canonically erected, the law gives it juridical personality[302] with all of the rights and obligations pertaining to public juridical persons unless limited by the proper law of the institute. Often, it is the generalate or provincialate of an institute which is canonically

---

[296] There does not seem to be an equivalent norm in the Eastern code.
[297] See S. Holland, "'Religious House' according to Canon 608," *J* 50 (1990) 524–552.
[298] *ET* 40–41. At times, two or three religious live in common and serve one or more apostolates.
[299] Canons 662; 663, §2.
[300] Canons 134, §1; 1223; 1224. A religious should be designated to care for the oratory, and the Eucharist should be celebrated there at least twice a month (c. 934, §2).
[301] *CCEO* 436, §2 and 509, §1, providing for the erection of dependent or filial monasteries and houses of orders and congregations, are similar to c. 609, §1.
[302] Canons 634, §1; 116, §2.

erected.[303] The bishop gives previous consent through a written decree which would seem to be a condition for validity. The competent authority to erect the house should be named in the constitutions or fundamental code. An erected house of the institute has greater stability than the residences or faculty houses constituted for an apostolic need. Here, too, good mutual relations and the need for sacred ministers on the part of lay religious would prompt the superior to advise the pastor of the parish in which the house is located.

Erection of Monastery of Nuns[304]

§2. In addition, the permission of the Apostolic See is required to erect a monastery of nuns.

In the case of a monastery of nuns, the permission of the Apostolic See is also required before its erection. These monasteries are *sui iuris* in character or autonomous. Therefore, it would seem that there is concern regarding the ability of the monastery to fulfill the requirements to be addressed in the next canon. The permission of the Apostolic See would precede the consent of the diocesan bishop. However, the bishop or his delegate should thoroughly investigate the potential of the monastery to sustain itself before presenting the petition to the Congregation for Institutes of Consecrated Life and Societies of Apostolic Life.

Usefulness to Particular Church

Canon 610 — §1. The erection of houses takes place with consideration for their advantage to the Church and the institute and with suitable

safeguards for those things which are required to carry out properly the religious life of the members according to the proper purposes and spirit of the institute.**

A public juridic person is by its nature perpetual.[305] Concerns for its usefulness to the particular church and the institute should be seriously considered by the diocesan bishop and the major superior before the canonical erection of a house takes place. The norm shows the essential requisites to erect a house. The religious institute does not need to own the building in which the religious house is canonically erected. Besides the usefulness of the house, the community and each member must have those things necessary for the living out of their lives in accord with the nature and end of the institute. Practical measures of sufficient members, financial resources, and the availability of appropriate apostolate(s) ensure the stability of the house, the care of the members, and the ability to carry on the life and works of the institute. The perpetuity of a canonically erected house distinguishes it from the house that is constituted in order to accommodate a specific pastoral need, e.g., a parochial school.

Provision for Members

§2. No house is to be erected unless it can be judged prudently that the needs of the members will be provided for suitably.

Both the diocesan bishop who gives his written consent and the major superior who erects the house in accord with the constitutions of the institute must study thoroughly its viability. Sufficient members, an apostolate that addresses the needs of the people, the presence and work of other religious in the area, support of the members, and availability of sacred ministers are some considerations to be taken into account in determining this viability. Since the house will become a public juridic person with rights and obligations, prudence

---

[303] At times major superiors request the consent of the bishop required for a canonically erected house, since the juridical status of the house has implications for chapter delegates and temporal goods in the constitutions of the institute.

[304] *CCEO* 434 provides for the erection of monasteries *sui iuris* by the Apostolic See (pontifical right), the patriarch (patriarchal right), and the eparch (eparchial right).

[305] Canon 120, §1.

and justice to both the particular church and the institute would require that the members have the essentials necessary to live in accord with the nature, spirit, and end of the institute.

Rights Flowing from Consent of Diocesan Bishop

Canon 611 — The consent of the diocesan bishop to erect a religious house of any institute entails the right:

1° to lead a life according to the character and proper purposes of the institute;

The diocesan bishop's consent to erect a house assures the following rights:

Members have the right to live their life in accord with the character and purpose of their institute.[306] This provision in law assures the autonomy of the institute.[307] The norm is in keeping with canon 610, §1 regarding the establishment of religious houses.

2° to exercise the works proper to the institute according to the norm of law and without prejudice to the conditions attached to the consent;[308]

Members have the right to engage in works proper to their institute in accord with canon law and the law of the institute. Works proper to the institute would be those that derive from its very nature, spirit, and end.[309] It may be that, in giving his consent, the diocesan bishop indicates specific works in keeping with the pastoral needs of the diocese. The religious would then be limited to performing those works. They would need to seek the consent of the bishop to perform other apostolates even though proper to the institute.[310]

3° for clerical institutes to have a church, without prejudice to the prescript of can. 1215, §3 and to perform sacred ministries, after the requirements of the law have been observed.[311]

Members of a clerical institute[312] have the right to a church, but the diocesan bishop must agree to the site.[313] This is a practical provision, inasmuch as the church of the religious may interfere with a parish church or may not be necessary. Often clerical religious are entrusted with a parish church, and waive this right. Clerics of these institutes have the right to carry out sacred ministries in accord with the law. They would need faculties for hearing confessions[314] and for assisting at marriages.[315] Any requirements of particular law with regard to preaching[316] and liturgical laws[317] should be observed, as well as respect for parochial functions.[318] It is important that the consent of the bishop be most clear regarding any conditions or limitations placed on the works proper to a religious institute.

Change(s) in Apostolic Works[319]

Canon 612 — For a religious house to be converted to apostolic works different from those for which it was established, the consent of the diocesan bishop is required, but not if it concerns a change which refers only to internal governance

---

[306] This right would include the right to have the reservation of the Blessed Sacrament (cc. 608; 934, §1, 1°). In lay religious institutes, the local ordinary would examine the construction and arrangement (cc. 1223–1224).

[307] Canon 586, §1.

[308] Cf. *CCEO* 437, §1; 509, §2. Written permission of the eparchial bishop is required in the case of any monastery for the construction and opening of schools, guest-houses, or similar buildings distinct from the monastery (c. 437, §2).

[309] Canons 675, §1; 677, §1; *CCEO* 437, §1; 509, §2.

[310] Canons 381, §1; 383; 678, §1.

[311] Cf. *CCEO* 437, §1; 509, §2.

[312] Canon 588, §2. The norm includes clerical institutes of diocesan right.

[313] Canon 1215, §3.

[314] Canons 966, §1; 969, §1.

[315] Canon 1108, §1.

[316] Canon 764; 772, §1.

[317] Canon 678, §1.

[318] Canon 530.

[319] Cf. *CCEO* 437, §3; 509, §2.

and discipline, without prejudice to the laws of the foundation.

This norm follows from canon 611, 2° and protects two values already established in the code. It respects the authority of the diocesan bishop in his pastoral care of the people of the diocese.[320] It also assures the rightful autonomy of religious in their internal life and governance.[321] It is important to know the conditions attached to the consent of the diocesan bishop to erect a religious house.[322] If the bishop gives his consent to erect a house without any conditions attached, the religious have the right to exercise all works proper to the institute. An attitude of courtesy and a concern for good mutual relations would prompt advising the bishop of the apostolic activity of the institute and of any changes subsequent to his initial consent. Such decisions have implications for the pastoral care of the diocese for which the bishop is responsible. If the bishop gave his consent to erect the house only for the apostolate of teaching, then his consent would have to be obtained to change this work or to initiate another work proper to the institute. For example, if the religious decided to initiate a soup kitchen in this house for the poor of the area, they would need the bishop's consent.

It is different if the change involves the internal life or discipline of the institute. For example, if the religious institute decides to move its novitiate house or villa for senior members to the house under discussion, there is no need to procure the consent of the diocesan bishop. This alteration pertains to the internal life and discipline of the institute. Again, an attitude of courtesy and concern for good relations would prompt notifying the bishop of this change in the internal life of the religious house. Such internal changes often necessitate the services of a confessor or chaplain, and the major superior petitions the diocesan bishop for a sacred minister.

[320] Canons 383; 678, §1.
[321] Canon 586, §1.
[322] Canon 611, 2°.

Houses of Canons Regular and Monks[323]

Canon 613 — §1. A religious house of canons regular or of monks under the governance and care of its own moderator is autonomous unless the constitutions state otherwise.

Houses of canons regular and monks enjoy a tradition of autonomy with their own moderator as major superior, unless the fundamental code determines otherwise.[324] These autonomous houses of male religious often unite in congregations or confederations[325] with limited authority given to an abbot primate or moderator in accord with the statutes.[326]

Moderator of Autonomous House[327]

§2. The moderator of an autonomous house is a major superior by law.

The moderator of an autonomous house is a major superior by law.[328] In autonomous clerical houses of pontifical right, the moderator is an ordinary.[329] While the abbot primate or superior of a monastic congregation or confederation is comparable to a major superior, he would not have all the power which universal law grants to major superiors. It would be necessary to study the statutes of the respective congregation or confederation in order to determine his limited authority as first among equals.

Aggregation of Monastery of Nuns[330]

Canon 614 — Monasteries of nuns associated to an institute of men maintain their own way of life

[323] Cf. *CCEO* 433, §2.
[324] Canons 613, §2; 620.
[325] Canon 582.
[326] Canon 620.
[327] Cf. *CCEO* 418, §1.
[328] Canon 620; the canon provides that the vicars of these moderators are also major superiors.
[329] Canon 134, §1.
[330] There does not seem to be a canon similar to this norm in the Eastern code.

and governance according to the constitutions. Mutual rights and obligations are to be defined in such a way that spiritual good can come from the association.

This norm applies to monasteries of nuns, women religious with solemn vows.[331] Many of these monasteries are autonomous; others are joined together as a monastic congregation under a major superior. Many monasteries of nuns associate or aggregate with monasteries of men of the same institute, e.g., Passionists, Carmelites, Poor Clares, Benedictines, Cistercians, Norbertines, Dominicans, Carthusians. At times, as explained in the commentary on canon 580, these bonds involve more than spiritual affiliation.

It is clear from the present norm that the monasteries of nuns enjoy the autonomy of life and governance assured to all religious in canon 586, §1. The constitutions or documents in each case provide norms that describe the association and enable it to be mutually enriching. At times, monasteries of men provide confessors, chaplains, spiritual guides, and professors who assist the nuns in initial and ongoing formation as well as in other areas of religious life. Through mutual efforts these men and women religious enhance the patrimony and wholesome traditions they share.

Sui Iuris *Monastery*[332]

Canon 615 — An autonomous monastery which does not have another major superior besides its own moderator and is not associated to another institute of religious in such a way that the superior of the latter possesses true power over such a monastery as determined by the constitutions is entrusted to the special vigilance of the diocesan bishop according to the norm of law.

This canon applies for the most part to monasteries of nuns, although there could be isolated monasteries of men. The monasteries do not belong to a monastic or canonical congregation of monasteries with centralized authority and a superior with limited power. This provision in the universal law for such a *sui iuris* monastery, i.e., the vigilance of the diocesan bishop, protects the rights of the members and renders the superior of the monastery accountable for his/her actions.

Such monasteries enjoy a just autonomy of life and governance.[333] Canon 609, §2 requires the permission of the Apostolic See for the erection of these monasteries. Most are of pontifical right, immediately and exclusively subject to the authority of the Apostolic See in internal discipline and governance,[334] as well as for approval of, changes in, and dispensations from their constitutions.[335] The moderator of a *sui iuris* monastery is a major superior;[336] there is no accountability to a higher superior. The vigilance of the diocesan bishop in no way interferes with the true authority of the moderator, but affords a certain monitoring of the more important government activities such as elections, religious discipline, finances, egress, departure, and dismissal.[337]

Suppression of House[338]

Canon 616 — §1. The supreme moderator can suppress a legitimately erected religious house according to the norm of the constitutions, after the diocesan bishop has been consulted. The proper law of the institute is to make provision for the goods of the suppressed house, without prejudice

---

[331] *CIC* 488, 7°. The 1983 code does not distinguish between solemn and simple profession. The constitutions of religious institutes provide for the effects of the vow of poverty; the public perpetual vow of chastity in a religious institute is a diriment impediment to marriage (c. 1088).

[332] Cf. *CCEO* 433, §2.

[333] Canon 586.

[334] Canon 593.

[335] Canon 587.

[336] Canon 620.

[337] The following canons show the vigilance of the diocesan bishop: cc. 625, §2; 628, §2, 1°; 637; 638, §4; 667, §4; 688, §2; 699, §2.

[338] *CCEO* 510 requires prior consultation with the eparchial bishop for the validity of the suppression of a house of an order or congregation.

to the intentions of the founders or donors or to legitimately acquired rights.

The norm addresses the suppression of a canonically erected religious house.[339] This act is reserved to the supreme moderator in accord with the provisions of the constitutions. The constitutions may require the consent of the council in such an important matter. It would be important that the law distinguish clearly between the suppression of a canonically erected house[340] which this norm addresses and the withdrawal of members from a constituted house of the institute.[341] The latter is not an act of suppression, since a constituted house is not a juridic person. Withdrawal of the members could be effected by another major superior, e.g., a provincial superior, in accord with the proper law.

In most instances, suppression and/or withdrawal are not enviable tasks, inasmuch as such decisions necessarily weaken the vitality of the institute and limit its contribution to the mission of the particular church. A shortage of members and financial difficulties often prompt such action. The diocesan bishop is to be consulted before the decision is made, but his displeasure or opposition to the suppression does not impede the action of the supreme moderator who is obliged to act for the good of the institute. In such instances a concern for the people of God and mutual relations with the bishop would prompt the supreme moderator in case of suppression or competent major superior in case of withdrawal to give ample advance notice. The diocesan bishop bears the responsibility for the care of souls of the diocese and he would need to assess the situation. Since this norm addresses a public juridical person, all provisions in Book V regarding ecclesiastical goods,[342] as well as civil law, the will of the founders, the donors, and all vested rights are to be observed. The proper law of the institute should

make provisions for the allocation of the temporal goods of a suppressed house.[343]

Suppression of Only House[344]

§2. The suppression of the only house of an institute belongs to the Holy See, to which the decision regarding the goods in that case is also reserved.

A house of the institute is normally distinguished from the institute.[345] The suppression of its only house would seem to terminate the life and activity of the institute. For this reason, the suppression pertains to the Congregation for Institutes of Consecrated Life and Societies of Apostolic Life, since it is equivalent to suppressing the institute. The congregation reserves the right to determine what is to be done with the temporal goods in such a case. The care of the surviving members of the institute is of primary concern. Likewise, attention must be given to all of the issues mentioned in the first paragraph of this norm in accord with Book V on temporal goods[346] and the pertinent civil law.

Suppression of Autonomous House[347]

§3. To suppress the autonomous house mentioned in can. 613 belongs to the general chapter, unless the constitutions state otherwise.

---

[339] Canon 609.
[340] Ibid.
[341] Canon 608.
[342] Canon 1257.

[343] Canon 123.
[344] *CCEO* 510, 507. The Apostolic See suppresses the only house of an order and disposes the property. The Apostolic See or the patriarch within the territorial boundaries of the matriarchal church can suppress the only house of a congregation of patriarchal or eparchial right after consultation with interested parties and with the consent of the permanent synod and of the Apostolic See.
[345] Canon 584, §1.
[346] Canon 1257, §1.
[347] *CCEO* 438 provides for the suppression of *sui iuris* or filial pontifical, patriarchial, and eparchial right monasteries as well as subsidiary monasteries and for the disposition of property.

The suppression of a self-governing house described in canon 613 should be provided for in the constitutions. If there is no such provision, the general chapter[348] decides. Since there is no mention of the disposition of the temporal goods, it would seem the constitutions should provide for such. If not, the general chapter would do so in keeping with all that is required with regard to the disposition of the goods of a public juridical person.

Suppression of Sui Iuris *Monastery of Nuns*[349]

§4. To suppress an autonomous monastery of nuns belongs to the Apostolic See, with due regard to the prescripts of the constitutions concerning its goods.

---

[348] Canon 631, §1.
[349] *CCEO* 438, §2.

An autonomous monastery of nuns cannot be erected without the permission of the Apostolic See.[350] Although the monastery remains under the vigilance of the diocesan bishop,[351] the Congregation for Institutes of Consecrated Life and Societies of Apostolic Life reserves the right to suppress such a *sui iuris* monastery. The constitutions should provide for its temporal goods. In the absence of such, the Apostolic See would provide. The welfare of the surviving nuns is to be safeguarded. Furthermore, the norms in Book V on ecclesiastical goods, provisions of civil law, as well as the will of founders and donors and invested rights are to be observed.

---

[350] Canon 609, §2.
[351] Canon 615.

BIBLIOGRAPHY

Bibliographical material for canons 573–616 can be found after the commentary on canon 746.

CHAPTER II
THE GOVERNANCE OF INSTITUTES
[cc. 617–640]

Governance in a religious institute occurs through three coalescing instrumentalities: persons, bodies, and laws. Individuals with personal authority govern the institute in accord with the norm of law. Bodies may be collegial or noncollegial, e.g., chapters, councils, and other lawfully designated groups. Laws may be universal, particular for a region or diocese, or proper to the institute. Governance in every religious institute incorporates these three elements with variations reflecting its spirit and character. The canons of this chapter on governance, and in fact the entire part three of Book II of the code, emphasize the importance of the institute's own law. The proper law applies the Church's general law to a particular institute, expressing its charism, its spirit, and the intent of the founder.

ARTICLE 1: SUPERIORS AND COUNCILS
[cc. 617–630]

Authority of Superiors

Canon 617 — Superiors are to fulfill their function and exercise their power according to the norm of universal and proper law.

Canon 617 introduces the fourteen canons on superiors and councils. It identifies the legal source of power exercised by religious superiors as the universal law of the Church and the proper law of the institute;[1] these provide parameters and

some of the processes for superiors' exercise of their office.[2] Universal law includes law promulgated for the entire Latin church or for all Latin church religious institutes; proper law includes the institute's constitution and secondary document, often called a directory or statutes, as well as chapter enactments and other legislation of the institute. Canon 617 and the two following canons apply to superiors at all levels within religious institutes. The broad wording of these canons provides for the differing traditions found within the various institutes.

Superiors need to be cognizant both of universal law pertaining specifically to religious and of other universal law affecting the members, the institute, or its apostolate. Examples of universal law which could limit or augment the exercise of a superior's function or power would be the canons on juridic persons and juridic acts, those dealing with fundamental Christian obligations and rights, and many of the norms in Book V having to do with temporal goods.[3] In addition, universal law identifies the diocesan bishop as having the pastoral care of the apostolates within his diocese and superiors in apostolic institutes need to be mindful of his responsibilities in overseeing the institute's apostolate.[4]

Exercise of Authority

Canon 618 — Superiors are to exercise their power, received from God through the ministry of the Church, in a spirit of service. Therefore, docile to the will of God in fulfilling their function, they are to govern their subjects as sons or daughters of God and, promoting the voluntary

---

[1] The Eastern code distinguishes between monks and other religious, i.e., those in orders and congregations. *CCEO* 441 identifies the legal source of power for the superior of a monastery and *CCEO* 511 does the same for the superior of an order or congregation.

[2] T. Rincón Pérez adds that this canon serves as a reminder that superiors themselves are subject to both universal law and the institute's proper law. See *Pamplona ComEng*, 430.

[3] See cc. 113–128, 208–223, and 1254–1310.

[4] See cc. 394 and 673–683 and *MR* 52–59.

obedience of their subjects with reverence for the human person, they are to listen to them willingly and foster their common endeavor for the good of the institute and the Church, but without prejudice to the authority of superiors to decide and prescribe what must be done.

This canon, largely based on *Perfectae caritatis* 14, combines theological, spiritual, and legal understandings of the power exercised by superiors in a religious institute. It also describes the pastoral manner in which the superior is to exercise his or her authority.[5]

The canon asserts that superiors receive their power from God through the ministry of the Church, and, like all power in the Church, it is to be exercised in a spirit of service. Religious institutes receive their ecclesial identity through recognition by the Church, and superiors exercise lawful authority within their institutes because of this intermediary ministry of the Church and their legitimate selection in accord with the proper law. Canon 618 then indicates the close connection between the source and purpose of this power and the manner of its exercise. The canon incorporates the conciliar teaching on promoting greater participation of members in the internal governance of the institute.[6] Superiors themselves are to seek the will of God and relate to their subjects as the children of God whom they are; superiors are to be open to the insights and opinions of the members, and are to foster the good of the institute and the Church.

The canon concludes by unequivocally affirming the superior's authority and responsibility to decide and to take action, a right in no way diminished by participative pre-decisional consultative processes. The superior acts, of course, according to the norm of universal and particular law. Superiors should also cultivate an ecclesial awareness because many of their decisions have ramifications external to the religious institute.

[5] No equivalent theological and pastoral description of the superior's role is found in the Eastern code.
[6] *PC* 4 and 14.

Although the superior has a personal responsibility to each member under his or her care, the superior need not always exercise this responsibility personally. At times personal intervention may be neither possible nor advisable; for instance, the general superior of a large international institute cannot possibly hear each member personally before acting. Superiors themselves, or the institute's proper law, may designate other persons or structures at various levels of the institute to assist the superior in serving the members.

The words "power" (*potestas*) and "authority" (*auctoritas*) are both used in this canon; they are related to each other but are not identical. Power is the ability or capacity to act. All power, whether natural, physical, intellectual, or spiritual, has its source in God. Authority, on the other hand, connotes the possession or use of a power whose exercise is grounded in some moral or legal right. Superiors possess power by virtue of their office, and they are to exercise their authority in accord with its purposes.

The authority of superiors in religious institutes has as its correlative the obedience of the members. Neither exists without the other; each actualizes the other. In exercising their function, superiors serve the members and, consequently, the Church. This canon speaks of superiors promoting the voluntary obedience of the members. In fact, there is no other kind. Ecclesiastical superiors in general and religious superiors in particular possess only moral and legal authority, not physical power, with respect to the members. Superiors may, however, exercise this authority by restricting, penalizing, or dismissing members for appropriate cause.

Threefold Office

Canon 619 — Superiors are to devote themselves diligently to their office and together with the members entrusted to them are to strive to build a community of brothers or sisters in Christ, in which God is sought and loved before all things. Therefore, they are to nourish the members regularly with the food of the word of God and are to

draw them to the celebration of the sacred liturgy. They are to be an example to them in cultivating virtues and in the observance of the laws and traditions of their own institute; they are to meet the personal needs of the members appropriately, solicitously to care for and visit the sick, to correct the restless, to console the faint of heart, and to be patient toward all.

This canon describes the superior's threefold office of teaching, sanctifying, and governing, an organization of functions found throughout the code.[7] The pastoral manner in which superiors are to exercise their office is emphasized by the canon's exhortative rather than prescriptive tone, unlike many of the more juridic norms for superiors found elsewhere.[8] The wording of this canon derives partly from *Perfectae caritatis* 6 which was directed to all members of religious institutes; here it guides the superior in fulfilling his or her pastoral responsibility toward the members.

Although the threefold functions of teaching, sanctifying, and governing are distinct, they often overlap in their exercise. The superior exercises the teaching function by breaking open the word of God and by the personal example of a religious life. The superior exercises the sanctifying function by centering the life of the community in God and drawing it to liturgical celebration, by example of personal virtue and religious discipline, and by solicitude for all. The superior exercises the governing function by animating the community, by coordinating and responding appropriately to the personal needs of members, and by correcting, consoling, and encouraging members as needed.[9] While all in the institute share many of these responsibilities by virtue of membership, the superior has a particular respon-

sibility by virtue of office. Centuries of experience of religious life, as well as recent documents from the Holy See, confirm the pivotal and personal role of the superior in the animation of the community.[10]

The canon concludes by naming certain especially needy members for whom the superior should have particular solicitude—the sick, the restless, the faint of heart. This canon echoes the call of the prior canon for the superior to exercise power in a spirit of service; it challenges superiors not only to see to it that these members have the care they need, but even to minister personally to them when possible.

The superior's role as described here may seem daunting, but it reflects the demanding spiritual, personal, interpersonal, and legal responsibilities assumed with this office.

Major Superiors

Canon 620 — Those who govern an entire institute, a province of an institute or part equivalent to a province, or an autonomous house, as well as their vicars, are major superiors. Comparable to these are an abbot primate and a superior of a monastic congregation, who nonetheless do not have all the power which universal law grants to major superiors.

This canon defines major superiors and those comparable to them.[11] The level and scope of responsibility exercised, rather than the number of persons for whom one is responsible, identify a superior as a major superior. Major superiors are individual physical persons who exercise authority by reason of their office over a whole institute, a province of an institute, a part of the institute equivalent to a province, or an autonomous or *sui iuris* house. Also identified as major superiors are the vicars of these persons, that is, those persons designated by the institute's proper law to take the

---

[7] See c. 375 re bishops, cc. 528–529 re pastors, and the organization of the code itself, especially Books III and IV. *CCEO* 421 similarly describes the superior in both monasteries and in orders and congregations.

[8] For example, cc. 625, 639, 647, and 686.

[9] For a more extensive development of this threefold responsibility, see *MR* 13.

[10] *FL* 47–53 and *VC* 43.

[11] *CCEO* 418 gives a comparable definition of major superiors.

place of an absent or impeded major superior. However, those substituting for a major superior in an *ad hoc* manner, exercising delegated power, are not major superiors.[12]

The canon also identifies as comparable to major superiors the abbot primate and the superior of a monastic congregation comprised of several or many independent foundations (e.g., Benedictines and Trappists); however, such persons do not possess all the authority of a major superior over the constituent monasteries of the institute. The particular scope of responsibilities of such an abbot or superior will vary from institute to institute according to its proper law.

In clerical religious institutes of pontifical right, major superiors are also ordinaries who, in virtue of this ecclesiastical power of governance, exercise certain additional powers regarding their own members, e.g., granting dimissorial letters, faculties, and dispensations, giving blessings, and imposing or remitting penalties.[13] The proper law of each institute should identify clearly the respective roles of the supreme moderator and other major superiors in the institute.

Provinces

Canon 621 — A grouping of several houses which constitutes an immediate part of the same institute under the same superior and has been canonically erected by legitimate authority is called a province.

This canon defines a province as a grouping of several houses of an institute under one superior, a grouping canonically erected by legitimate authority in such a way that the resulting entity is an immediate part of the institute.[14] In other words,

the resulting unit relates directly to the highest superior of the institute with no intervening levels of government. Each separate province, upon establishment, is usually comprised of at least three separate houses.[15]

The proper law of the institute, specifically the constitutions, should indicate the authority competent to establish or suppress provinces or other equivalent units. This authority may reside with the highest superior after receiving the advice or consent of the council or with the general chapter of the institute. The 1917 code reserved to the Holy See the right to erect and suppress provinces, but in accord with the 1983 code the revised constitutions of most religious institutes now identify an internal authority.[16]

As a result of apostolic realignments, diminishing numbers of members, and new missionary endeavors, religious institutes sometimes find it necessary or helpful to reorganize their internal governance structures. In doing so it is important to identify the status of each governmental unit of the resulting structure, i.e., whether it is a province or its equivalent which, by the law, has its own juridic personality and whose superior is, consequently, a major superior exercising authority by reason of office. Other organizational units, such as regions or sectors, do not enjoy separate juridic personality and the nature of the unit superior's authority would be different.

Extent of Superior's Authority

Canon 622 — The supreme moderator holds power over all the provinces, houses, and members of an institute; this power is to be exercised according to proper law. Other superiors possess power within the limits of their function.

The code frequently uses generic terms descriptive of an office, a role, or an entity rather than appropriating a particular title from one or another tradition or culture. The term "supreme

---

[12] Neither chapters nor authorities external to the institute can be called superiors in the strict sense of the word, according to Rincón Pérez. See *Pamplona ComEng,* 431.

[13] See c. 596, §2 for the general statement of this power and cc. 967, §3; 968, §2; 969, §2; and 1019, §1 for some specific articulations.

[14] *CCEO* 508, §1 recognizes provinces within orders and congregations and defines them similarly.

[15] Canon 115, §2.

[16] Canon 581.

moderator" is an example of this.[17] The supreme moderator is the highest superior, having authority over the entire institute, all provinces and equivalent subdivisions, all houses and all members of the institute.[18] In many institutes the highest superior is called "president" or "superior general," but different traditions identify the person who holds this office with a title incorporating the institute's spirit or tradition such as "minister general" in the Franciscan tradition, "father abbot" in the Benedictine tradition, or "prioress general" and "master general" in the Dominican tradition.

The authority of the supreme moderator is exercised in accord with the proper law of the institute; the scope and expression of this authority can vary greatly. Institutes with a more centralized government may give considerable authority to the supreme moderator. In other institutes, whose organizational structure provides for provinces or regions, more authority may reside at a lower level with provincial superiors or, occasionally, with local superiors. The proper law of each institute should establish clearly the limits of authority to be exercised by superiors at each level and provide for the coordination of those responsibilities which are shared.

Prerequisite for Office

Canon 623 — In order for members to be appointed or elected validly to the function of superior, a suitable time is required after perpetual or definitive profession, to be determined by proper law, or if it concerns major superiors, by the constitutions.

The role of superiors, whether major or local, is integral to the internal life of the religious institute. Hence the common law of the Church seeks to ensure that only persons experienced in the way of life of the institute and committed to it are named as superiors.[19] This canon specifies that eligibility for appointment or election as superior at any level, whether major or local, requires that the member be perpetually or definitively professed. The election or appointment of a novice, a member in temporary vows, or a transfer member still in the probationary period would be invalid, unless a postulation has been admitted.[20]

In addition to the threshold requirement of perpetual or definitive incorporation, the proper law of the institute identifies any additional requirements for the office of superior. For instance, each institute designates what additional period of time after final profession is suitable before a member becomes eligible for the office of superior; in a clerical religious institute, superiors may be required to be ordained. When these additional requirements concern the office of major superior, they are to be in the constitution; for other superiors, inclusion in the statutes or other secondary document of the institute suffices.

Other requirements of the 1917 code, such as age and legitimacy of birth, intended to protect the office of superior from unworthy officeholders and ensure it appropriate respect, no longer obtain. Institutes may establish in their proper law other requirements for the office of superior which accord with the institute's charism, spirit, and tradition and which respect the cultures within which it

---

[17] The Eastern code uses the term "superior" for one who governs a monastery and "superior general" for one who governs an order or congregation.

[18] In recent years some religious institutes of men which traditionally have been composed of both ordained and non-ordained members have sought a dispensation from the prohibition against a non-ordained superior exercising authority over the ordained members, thus allowing the institute to choose those persons best qualified to lead it regardless of their status. In each case, however, the dispensation has required that a priest be delegated to carry out all acts of jurisdiction. See *CLD* 9, 346; *CLD* 10, 106–107.

[19] The requirements for superior in the Eastern code are more restrictive than those in the Latin code. *CCEO* 442 requires that the superior of a monastery be at least ten years professed and forty years of age, and *CCEO* 513 requires that major superiors in orders and congregations be at least ten years professed and, in addition, that general superiors be at least thirty-five years old.

[20] Canons 180–183.

serves. However, an institute should not define eligibility for the office of superior too narrowly; the gifts of the Spirit, present in many guises, are to be welcomed in its service. On a practical level, for the good of the institute, efforts should be made to increase the pool of those available for this ministry through mentoring, personal encouragement, and ongoing educational opportunities.

Term of Office

Canon 624 — §1. Superiors are to be constituted for a certain and appropriate period of time according to the nature and need of the institute, unless the constitutions determine otherwise for the supreme moderator and for superiors of an autonomous house.

§2. Proper law is to provide suitable norms so that superiors, constituted for a definite time, do not remain too long in offices of governance without interruption.

§3. Nevertheless, they can be removed from office during their function or be transferred to another for reasons established in proper law.

Canon 624 circumscribes the exercise of authority by superiors in two ways: (1) by limiting the time any one person may serve in the office of superior, and (2) by providing methods by which a superior may be relieved of office.[21] The general directives of the canon are applicable to all superiors. The proper law of each institute is to explicitate these directives for the particular institute.

All superiors, both major and local, are to have specific and limited terms of office, except for the two situations discussed below. Indefinite terms are proscribed. The length of the term of office may vary from institute to institute and even from one level of superior to another within the same

institute, according to its nature and needs. For instance, an international missionary institute would have very different needs from those of a small semi-cloistered institute engaged in retreat work or a large apostolic institute whose members are concentrated in a few neighboring dioceses.

The two exceptions to the general requirement of a definite and limited term of office are the supreme moderator of an institute and the superior of an autonomous house. If an institute, according to its tradition, elects the highest superior for life, it may continue to do so, incorporating this provision into its constitutions, e.g., the Society of Jesus and some Benedictine monasteries.

The canon also suggests a rationale for term limitations and a general approach to their implementation. Fixed and limited terms in office are intended to ensure regular change in leadership at every level of the institute, and its proper law is to make suitable provision that this happens. In the constitutions and secondary documents of religious institutes, revised in accord with Vatican Council II,[22] the terms of superiors frequently vary greatly from one institute to another. Some institutes allow for several short successive terms for local superiors while other institutes designate a single longer term without the possibility of an immediate second term. Some institutes require an interval before the same person would again be eligible for the office of superior. Each institute must balance the need for continuity, stability, and the time necessary for the superior to know the members and plan responsibly with the need to develop leadership and benefit from new blood and new energy.

The canon also affirms the possibility of removal or transfer of a superior during his or her term in office (§3). Removal from office may be necessitated by illness, incapacity, incompetence, conflicting responsibilities, or other serious reasons. Transfer to another office may be prompted by a greater need elsewhere or personal needs or desires made known by the superior during his or her term of office. The reasons for removal or transfer of superiors and an appropriate process

---

[21] In *CCEO* 444 the term of the superior of a *sui iuris* monastery is indeterminate, and resignation is required upon completion of seventy-five years of age. Canon 514 of the Eastern code is similar to the Latin code in prescribing certain and limited terms for superiors in orders and congregations.

[22] *PC* 3.

should be prescribed, at least generically, in the institute's proper law, i.e., in the constitution for the major superior and in other legislation for other superiors. Also relevant are the general norms regarding transfer and removal from ecclesiastical office.[23]

Besides removal or transfer, resignation is another means through which a superior may lose his or her office. A superior should resign only for serious reason, and the resignation must be submitted in writing to the authority competent to make provision for the office, e.g., the one who appointed the superior, or the next immediate superior if the superior was elected by an electoral body. Unless the proper law provides otherwise, the resignation of the supreme moderator is tendered to the general chapter if it is in session or, if the chapter is not in session, to the Congregation for Institutes of Consecrated Life and Societies of Apostolic Life for pontifical institutes and the diocesan bishop for diocesan institutes.

Manner of Designating Superiors

Canon 625 — §1. The supreme moderator of an institute is to be designated by canonical election according to the norm of the constitutions.

§2. The bishop of the principal seat presides at the elections of a superior of the autonomous monastery mentioned in can. 615 and of the supreme moderator of an institute of diocesan right.

§3. Other superiors are to be constituted according to the norm of the constitutions, but in such a way that, if they are elected, they need the confirmation of a competent major superior; if they are appointed by a superior, however, a suitable consultation is to precede.

This canon regulates the manner in which superiors are designated.[24] The supreme moderator

is designated by canonical election, which is regulated by canons 164–179 and any complementary norms in the proper law of the institute.[25] For most institutes the general chapter elects the supreme moderator; however, certain institutes, small in number and limited geographically, have received approval for direct election of the supreme moderator by all of the perpetually or definitively professed members. Requests from larger institutes to allow direct election of the supreme moderator have been consistently denied by the Congregation for Institutes of Consecrated Life and Societies of Apostolic Life. Because election is both a religious act and a juridic act, certain conditions should be present: an atmosphere of prayerful discernment, knowledge of potential candidates, objectivity, freedom of voters, allowance for the convergence of insight in the assembly, and the avoidance of politicking or campaigning.[26]

The election of the supreme moderator of the institute is a significant ecclesial event, hence institutes sometimes invite the diocesan bishop to be present for the election. However, his role in the election of major superiors has changed substantially with the 1983 code, and the constitutions of many institutes have been modified accordingly. He now presides only at the election of superiors of autonomous monasteries, i.e., those with no other major superior and no jurisdictional link with another institute, and at elections in diocesan institutes both of men and women. The responsibility to preside falls to the bishop of the diocese where the generalate is located. Since the responsibility of presiding at elections no longer entails the right to confirm or rescind the election, this responsibility may be and often is delegated. The bishop or his delegate does not preside at

---

[23] Canons 190–195.

[24] Canons 443 and 515 of the Eastern code treat similar material regarding the designation of superiors in monasteries and in orders and congregations, respectively.

[25] Rincón Pérez is of the opinion that the institute's proper law regarding elections must conform to the universal law for canonical elections (see *Pamplona ComEng*, 434), but E. Williamson implies that legitimate exceptions exist (see *CLSGBI Com*, 343).

[26] *CLD* 7, 480; *CLD* 8, 354–357; *CLD* 9, 356–358; and *CLD* 10, 102–106.

other elections (e.g., election of members of the council) or at the chapter of affairs.

Most institutes have, in addition to a supreme moderator, provincial, regional, and/or local superiors. This canon also provides for their designation, either by appointment or by election, emphasizing the importance of the institute's proper law. For those elected, confirmation by the competent major superior is required before the office is actually acquired. The institute's proper law may require the prior consent or advice of the council, but the confirmation itself is an act of the individual person with whom the authority rests. The capacity to confirm entails the capacity to deny the confirmation.[27] If an election is not confirmed, the electing body proceeds to another election. For those offices of superior designated by appointment, a suitable consultation is to precede the appointment. This requirement reflects the strong tradition of some religious institutes and the code's emphasis that those who are affected have some part in selecting superiors.

Besides the two ways of designating superiors mentioned in this canon there is also the possibility of postulation, unless this method is specifically proscribed by the constitution. Postulation, no longer reserved by law to extraordinary cases, allows the members of an electoral body, e.g., a general chapter, to request designation of a person barred by a canonical impediment, e.g., a limitation on number of terms, but who is otherwise deemed qualified for the office. The results of the postulation are forwarded to the authority competent to dispense from the impediment. For example, the postulation of the supreme moderator of a pontifical institute is forwarded to the Congregation for Institutes of Consecrated Life and Societies of Apostolic Life; that of the supreme moderator of a diocesan institute to the diocesan bishop; and that of a provincial superior to the supreme moderator of the institute for referral to the proper ecclesiastical authority. If the dispensation is not

granted, the electing body, upon being informed, elects another person. The requirements for postulation differ from those of election and canons 180–183 need to be followed carefully.

Abuses to Be Avoided

Canon 626 — Superiors in the conferral of offices and members in elections are to observe the norms of universal and proper law, are to abstain from any abuse or partiality, and are to appoint or elect those whom they know in the Lord to be truly worthy and suitable, having nothing before their eyes but God and the good of the institute. Moreover, in elections they are to avoid any procurement of votes, either directly or indirectly, whether for themselves or for others.

This canon looks to the dispositions of those responsible for appointing or electing superiors and other office holders, and it proscribes certain actions detrimental to an open and free selection.[28] Those responsible for designating officeholders must first know the requirements of their own proper law and the norms of the code pertaining to elections, rights and obligations, and related matters. In addition, those responsible, whether superiors or other members, are called to act with the same impartiality expected of those elected or appointed in the exercise of their office, that is, they are to place the good of the institute above personal preference.

Actions specifically proscribed in this canon are abuse and partiality, and, in the case of elections, the procuring of votes either directly or indirectly, for oneself or for others. Abuse would include deliberate deception, impeding or manipulating the election process in any way, voting by those not eligible, etc. In the past, religious institutes often conducted elections in secret and in silence; at times this hindered capitulars from voting knowledgeably. Appropriate discernment, both personal and communal, is now understood to require knowledge about persons who are being consid-

[27] Canon 179 details procedures and time constraints for confirming elections. However, any provisions of proper law would supersede the universal law

[28] There is no comparable norm in the Eastern code.

ered for office. Such information is often not immediately accessible to all the members of a group involved in designating a person for office, e.g., council members giving advice or consent before the superior appoints or chapter members electing a supreme moderator and council members. The need to seek information about candidates is especially important in large institutes and in those with diverse and/or international apostolates.

The supplementary documents of some institutes identify appropriate means of promoting respectful discussion and obtaining consultation prior to the selection of superiors. Other institutes leave the design and conduct of these procedures to the competent authority. Discussion and consultation may include pre-chapter gatherings of the entire institute for reflection on qualities and roles, circulation of *curricula vitae* of prospective candidates, preference balloting by the membership, and open forums for the presentation of views by candidates. In addition, individuals may seek information through personal consultation.

A delicate balance needs to be maintained in the conduct of these various participative processes. While those responsible for designating officeholders need adequate knowledge, the persons being considered maintain their right to privacy and their good reputation.[29] Any discussion of persons should be respectful, sensitive, and confidential. If an institute or province conducts a discussion forum, a candidate need not participate. Similarly, if an institute conducts a preference ballot among the membership, the appointing superior or the electoral body is not bound to these results, unless the institute's own law specifically states otherwise. The freedom of the superior or of the electing body is presumed; any restriction on it must be explicit.[30]

This canon does not indicate the consequences of its violation. However, an election whose freedom is impaired in any way whatever is invalid.[31] For the sake of peace in the community, any sus-

picion or allegation either of abuse or of procurement of votes should be taken seriously and investigated by the authority competent to do so. Should an election be deemed invalid, the competent superior would have to declare it so and call a new election.

Role of Council

Canon 627 — §1. According to the norm of the constitutions, superiors are to have their own council, whose assistance they must use in carrying out their function.

§2. In addition to the cases prescribed in universal law, proper law is to determine the cases which require consent or counsel to act validly; such consent or counsel must be obtained according to the norm of can. 127.

Although every superior exercises personal authority, this canon requires that superiors be assisted by a council in fulfilling their responsibilities.[32] The council is normally not a decision-making body but is an integral part of the decision-making process regarding serious matters. Council members give advice or consent as required by the institute's proper law, but they also assist the superior by sharing insights, evaluating initiatives, raising issues, extending support, and generally participating in council discussions with candor, courage, and creativity.

It is important to note the distinct roles of superior and council, i.e., that the superior *has* a council and is not part of it. One practical consequence of this distinction is manifested when the council votes: the superior is attentive to but does not vote with the council.[33] The only exception in

---

[29] Canon 220.
[30] Canon 18.
[31] Canon 170.

[32] Canon 422 of the Eastern code specifies a permanent council for all superiors.
[33] In 1985 the Holy See issued an authentic interpretation on this matter; see *CLD* 11, 16. For further discussion see L. Wrenn, *Authentic Interpretations on the 1983 Code* (Washington, D.C.: Canon Law Society of America, 1993) 19–20 and Rincón Pérez in *Pamplona ComEng,* 435. Nevertheless, the proper law of some institutes, usually older institutes whose traditions predate

universal law concerns the dismissal of a member; such a vote is taken as a collegial body with the supreme moderator's vote carrying the same weight as that of each council member.[34]

Canon 627 leaves to the constitutions of each institute decisions regarding the composition of the council at each level of the institute, the manner of operating, and the qualifications for the role of councilor.[35] If the general council is composed of fewer than four persons, provision should be made in the proper law for augmenting the council in the event of a dismissal because the dismissal process requires for validity at least four members of the council.[36] Other matters for which the institute's proper law should make provision are the manner of selecting councilors, qualifications for eligibility, frequency of meetings, and circumstances in which the entire local community could serve as the local council.

In many religious institutes councilors also carry out administrative responsibilities in the service of their institutes. Council members are chosen because of their wisdom, experience, and ability to assist the superior with good advice and appropriate consent. The distribution of administrative responsibilities usually occurs following the selection of the council members. Position descriptions for any administrative responsibilities, with clear lines of communication and accountability and with opportunity for evaluation of these administrative responsibilities, enable council members serving in these positions to separate council roles from other administrative roles.

Certain offices or functions within the institute present some difficulties and conflicts of interest, making them incompatible with council membership, e.g., members responsible for formation and spiritual directors of other members of the insti-

tute. Such members should not participate in council decisions affecting persons whom they direct. Other offices within the institute, such as that of treasurer or secretary, do not raise the moral dilemmas presented by the positions of novice director or spiritual director, but if such officers serve as council members, this could limit the range of insight, wisdom, or diversity of experience brought to the council discussions. Each institute may determine the composition of the council, having only the good of the institute in mind, and such provisions should be incorporated into its proper law.

The superior is required to use the assistance of the council in two ways, namely in seeking its advice or its consent when expressly determined in universal and proper law. The council's consent or advice is required by the universal law in more than a dozen instances, most of them concerning the status of members or the temporal goods of the institute.[37] An institute's proper law may include additional instances when the council's advice or consent is required in accord with canon 127. These instances often flow out of an institute's tradition and spirit, but they should not be so numerous as to hamper the superior unnecessarily or prevent appropriate flexibility and timeliness in responding to situations. Even if the code requires only the *advice* of the council, the institute's proper law may require *consent*.

When the universal law or the proper law of the institute requires the advice or consent of the council, an act placed without such advice or consent is invalid. Canon 127 gives details regarding how this advice or consent is to be sought and rendered. The council must be convened as a group, not informed and polled individually. In the case of consent, the consent of an absolute majority of council members present must be obtained. In the case of advice, the advice of all council members present is to be sought. Those whose advice or consent is sought must be adequately informed of relevant matters, and their

---

the codification of law, provide for situations in which the superior votes collegially with the council.

[34] Canon 699, §1.

[35] Religious institutes belonging to the Eastern churches may determine in their proper law whether local houses with six or fewer members are to have a council. See *CCEO* 422, §2.

[36] Canon 699, §1.

[37] See, e.g., cc. 638, §3; 647, §§1–2; 656, 3°; 684, §1; 688, §2; 690, §1; and 694, §2.

advice or consent is to be given forthrightly. Finally, when advice or consent is required, the superior may bind the council to secrecy, if the nature of the matter requires it.

In accord with canon 127, when consent is required and the council vote results in a tie, the required consent has not been received, and the superior may neither act nor break the tie by voting himself or herself.[38] When consent is required and has been given by the council, the superior is free to act but is not bound to do so. For a serious reason, perhaps based on confidential information known only to the superior, he or she may refrain from acting. Should the superior act without having obtained the required advice or consent, the act is invalid.

With due regard for the limitations placed on the superior's authority by the occasional requirements of advice and consent, it should be noted that the actions taken after receiving the necessary advice or consent are actions of the superior and not of the council. The requirements of advice and consent are intended to serve the good of the community by bringing to the decision-making process a wider range of knowledge and experience, thereby preventing ill-advised or arbitrary actions regarding the members and the goods of the institute.

Visitation

Canon 628 — §1. The superiors whom the proper law of the institute designates for this function are to visit the houses and members entrusted to them at stated times according to the norms of this same proper law.

§2. It is the right and duty of a diocesan bishop to visit even with respect to religious discipline:

1° the autonomous monasteries mentioned in can. 615;

2° individual houses of an institute of diocesan right located in his own territory.

§3. Members are to act with trust toward a visitator, to whose legitimate questioning they are bound to respond according to the truth in charity. Moreover, it is not permitted for anyone in any way to divert members from this obligation or otherwise to impede the scope of the visitation.

Visitation of religious houses is an ancient and respected institution within religious life; it symbolizes communion within the institute and with the larger Church and, at the same time, provides a vehicle for support, communication, and correction. This canon discusses the various ways in which visitation occurs.[39]

The most common form of visitation is carried out by a superior of the institute designated in accord with the institute's own law. Which superior or superiors hold this responsibility and the frequency and manner of visitation are left to that proper law. Major superiors are ordinarily charged with this duty at least once during their term in office. In large institutes or in special circumstances, e.g., the protracted illness of the superior, responsibility for visitation may be delegated. Besides making the ordinary visitations identified in the proper law, supreme moderators may visit a house of the institute at any time in virtue of the authority vested in them according to canon 622.

During the visitation the superior or delegate usually meets privately with each member and with the local community as a group, depending on the purpose of the visitation. The superior may also meet with the diocesan bishop, the pastor of the parish in which the house is located, or the administrator of the apostolic work.

Visitation is a privileged opportunity for the superior to come to know the members of the institute, to hear first-hand their hopes and burdens, and to offer encouragement and support. It also enables the superior to learn about the apostolates of members of apostolic institutes, to meet some of those with whom and to whom they min-

---

[38] See note 33, above, and the commentary on c. 127 for a fuller discussion of the requirements of advice and consent.

[39] Canons 414, §§1, 3° and 2, and *CCEO* 420, §§1–2 regulate internal and hierarchical visitation.

ister, and to give some direction when appropriate. Visitation likewise provides members time and opportunity to share important aspects of their lives, to seek direction or advice, to request a change of assignment, and to discuss community issues and apostolic initiatives. Furthermore, visitation enables the superior to address in a timely and knowledgeable manner any problems with religious discipline. In religious institutes whose structure includes an intermediate level of provinces or their equivalent, coordination of visitations and careful attention to the principles of subsidiarity and co-responsibility are necessary for good order.

The diocesan bishop also has a limited responsibility regarding visitation of religious institutes (§2). He has the right and the duty to visit the autonomous monasteries and all individual houses of diocesan right institutes located within his diocese. This would include both the principal house (general house) of the latter and any of its houses located within the diocese (c. 615). By such visitation the bishop affords these religious access to ecclesiastical authority. He may investigate any laxity in religious discipline, or he may simply support the religious in their way of life. The code is silent regarding the frequency of the diocesan bishop's visitation; therefore he may go as often as he judges desirable. However, since diocesan institutes have superiors designated in their proper law for visitation, these superiors and the diocesan bishop should coordinate the focus and timing of their visitations to preclude duplicating work or unduly burdening the members.

The members have certain responsibilities in relation to a visitator. The fabric of religious life is woven from trust, and this canon exhorts members to extend that trust to those who conduct an official visitation. Regardless of the purpose of a visitation, religious are obliged to respond truthfully and charitably to any legitimate question asked by the visitator. One limitation on such legitimate questioning would be the prohibition of superiors from inducing from any member a manifestation of conscience (c. 630, §5). How-

ever, all religious in the house and any other persons, lay or clerical, must respect the visitator and in no way impede the purpose of the visitation.

Obligation of Residence

Canon 629 — Superiors are to reside in their respective houses, and are not to absent themselves from their house except according to the norm of proper law.

The superior's obligation to reside in his or her own house is intended to ensure the fulfillment of his or her responsibilities by reason of office.[40] Previous canons have identified in a general way some of the superior's responsibilities: to build community, to give personal example of the religious life, to listen willingly to members, to foster cooperation, to assist members in need. Such personal availability and service is difficult to achieve at a distance. Bishops and pastors are obliged to a similar residency for similar reasons.[41]

The obligation of residence binds all superiors, major and local. Major superiors are to reside in their principal house (general or provincial house) even when another member has been designated as the local superior. By "house" is meant a lawfully constituted house designated according to law; it need not be identified with one particular building. A religious "house" may be constituted as one part of a large community, or it may be constituted from several small residences grouped together and designated as a unit under one superior.[42]

The obligation of residence is not absolute; superiors may be absent from their respective houses according to the institute's own law. Lawful absences may be occasioned by apostolic service, temporary responsibilities related to the institute, vacation and retreat, and other just causes in ac-

---

[40] Canon 446 of the Eastern code also requires that the superior of a monastery reside in the monastery.
[41] Canons 395 and 533.
[42] Canon 608.

cord with the proper law. Some religious institutes find it impractical, if not impossible, to have a local superior residing in every house where religious reside. This is particularly true for some apostolic institutes whose members live in small communities or alone. The norm obliges superiors to residence in their respective houses in accord with the institute's proper law. This allows the institute, in keeping with its own tradition and needs, to identify as area or regional superiors members who reside in one place and serve as superior for several small communities.

Confessors and Freedom of Members

Canon 630 — §1. Superiors are to recognize the due freedom of their members regarding the sacrament of penance and direction of conscience, without prejudice, however, to the discipline of the institute.

§2. According to the norm of proper law, superiors are to be concerned that suitable confessors are available to the members, to whom the members can confess frequently.

§3. In monasteries of nuns, in houses of formation, and in more numerous lay communities, there are to be ordinary confessors approved by the local ordinary after consultation with the community; nevertheless, there is no obligation to approach them.

§4. Superiors are not to hear the confessions of subjects unless the members request it on their own initiative.

§5. Members are to approach superiors with trust, to whom they can freely and on their own initiative open their minds. Superiors, however, are forbidden to induce the members in any way to make a manifestation of conscience to them.

This canon balances the individual's freedom of conscience with the common good of the institute manifested through religious discipline. The canon is located in the section on governance, placing the burden primarily on superiors to respect appropriate boundaries and ensure the avail-

ability of confessors and spiritual directors,[43] while at the same time maintaining religious discipline. This canon is an abbreviated and more pastoral treatment of the 1917 code's regulations regarding confessors for religious (*CIC* 518–530 and 874–876). None of the former restrictions remain; all religious, including women, may choose those from whom they will seek the sacrament of reconciliation and spiritual direction. This canon reflects the emphasis on freedom of conscience found in the conciliar documents and elsewhere in this code.[44] The canon calls for a careful but generous balancing of individual needs with the common good and for mature discretion by both superiors and members.

The first paragraph of the canon resembles the teaching of *Perfectae caritatis* 14, establishing the freedom of each member regarding the frequency, content, and choice of minister in matters of sacramental confession and direction of conscience. All superiors are to recognize and facilitate this freedom as long as it does not undermine the religious discipline of the institute. In cloistered or semi-cloistered institutes the exercise of this right must be balanced with the obligation of enclosure and the disruption to individual and community life which frequent absences might entail. For all religious institutes the freedom to choose a spiritual director may have financial implications, because full-time spiritual guides or directors are entitled to just compensation.

Superiors have the responsibility to ensure the availability of suitable confessors in keeping with the proper law of the institute, but particular circumstances (e.g., remote location of religious house, special needs, dearth of priests) may limit what is reasonably possible. The diocesan bishop

---

[43] *CCEO* 475 and 539 require the appointment of confessors (and spiritual fathers for the monastery), and *CCEO* 473, §2, 2° speaks of free and frequent approach to them, but none of these canons makes as strong a statement about the freedom of the members in these and related matters.

[44] For instance, see *DH* 1–3, 10–11 and cc. 214–215, 219, 240, 748, and 985, *inter alia.*

and superiors of clerical institutes can be helpful in identifying suitable and available confessors. The appointment of regular or ordinary confessors assures availability and provides continuity to those who avail themselves of such confessors. Other practical measures to be considered might include planning community reconciliation services during certain liturgical seasons when several confessors could be available, budgeting realistically for these spiritual services, assuring transportation for members, and the like.

The third paragraph specifies for particular situations the more general admonitions of the prior two paragraphs. The superior is to see that ordinary confessors, approved by the local ordinary, are appointed for certain communities. These communities—monasteries of nuns,[45] houses of formation and larger communities of lay religious—are to be consulted regarding these confessors. More than one ordinary confessor may be appointed to address various community needs. Although the superior has the obligation to provide ordinary confessors, no member of the community need avail himself or herself of them.

The next paragraph applies only to presbyteral superiors in clerical religious institutes. Although such superiors usually possess the faculty to hear confessions of their subjects,[46] they are enjoined from doing so by this canon unless the subject spontaneously requests it. This canon parallels other canons which discourage rectors of seminaries and formation houses, novice directors, and others from hearing the confessions of those under their charge.[47]

The final paragraph of the canon deals with manifestation of conscience, an activity differing from both sacramental confession and spiritual direction although sometimes only by a fine line. Such a manifestation of conscience includes disclosure of all matters of the interior life, both graced and sinful. Some early traditions of religious life considered the superior to be the spiritual father or mother of the community and expected members to manifest their consciences to the superior. The advantages and the dangers of this practice are evident, but the 1917 code (*CIC* 530) and this canon make it clear that any manifestation of conscience is to be the member's free choice.

This final paragraph reiterates the context of trust and freedom that should characterize superior-member relationships; this relationship parallels that between religious and a visitator (c. 628, §3) and complements the willing listening expected of superiors in canon 618. However, all superiors and formation personnel, such as novice directors, are forbidden to induce a manifestation of conscience from those under their charge. Such inducement can be direct, e.g., through questioning, threats, promises, etc., or indirect, e.g., through praise of the practice, disapproval of those who fail to use it, and other forms of manipulation.[48]

Problems regarding manifestation of conscience have arisen recently in situations of alleged sexual misconduct. A superior may not require or pressure the member to admit wrongdoing; in fact, by so doing, he or she may even jeopardize the case before civil law should it go to trial. On the other hand, if a trusting relationship exists with the superior, the member might wish to unburden himself or herself by acknowledging the misconduct or the harm done and seeking help.

The last two paragraphs of this canon provide a double safeguard. They discourage undue pressure on an individual religious in the internal forum and, at the same time, free the superior from any perception by community members that information received in the internal forum has been used in the external forum. Accordingly a superior should not lightly disregard this protective wall, weighing carefully the potential for a conflict in roles if a member requests sacramental

---

[45] See cc. 614–615.
[46] Canon 968, §2.
[47] See cc. 985 and 239, §2–240.

[48] G. McKay, "Spiritual Direction in the Diocesan Seminary," *Stud Can* 26 (1992) 401–413.

confession, spiritual direction, or manifestation of conscience.

ARTICLE 2: CHAPTERS
[cc. 631–633]

Chapters, whether general, provincial, or local, have a long and respected history within religious life.[49] They are based on the theological conviction that the Spirit gifts all members for the good of the community and that unity and reconciliation in Christ are possible. Chapters are the legal manifestations of the principles of representation, participation, and subsidiarity, principles deeply grounded in both Eastern and Western Christianity since the time of the early Church. These principles were reemphasized by Vatican Council II and influenced the revision of the Church's legal codes. Much of what is contained in the following three canons is general in nature, leaving to the proper law of each institute the determination of particulars appropriate to it.

General Chapter

Canon 631 — §1. The general chapter, which holds supreme authority in the institute according to the norm of the constitutions, is to be composed in such a way that, representing the entire institute, it becomes a true sign of its unity in charity. It is for the general chapter principally: to protect the patrimony of the institute mentioned in can. 578, promote suitable renewal according to that patrimony, elect the supreme moderator, treat affairs of greater importance, and issue norms which all are bound to obey.

§2. The constitutions are to define the composition and extent of the power of a chapter; proper

law is to determine further the order to be observed in the celebration of the chapter, especially in what pertains to elections and the manner of handling affairs.

§3. According to the norms determined in proper law, not only provinces and local communities, but also any member can freely send wishes and suggestions to a general chapter.

This canon describes the purpose and functioning of a general chapter.[50] The general chapter is a collegial body at the highest level of the institute, representative of the entire institute, in which each participant has equal voice and vote. While in session it holds supreme authority in the institute, in accord with the constitution.

The extent of the general chapter's authority may vary somewhat from institute to institute; for instance, one institute's constitution may reserve to the general chapter what another gives to the general superior and council. However, this canon delineates five areas of responsibility pertaining to every general chapter, responsibilities which may neither be ignored nor delegated to some other authority.

Foremost among the responsibilities of a general chapter is the duty to protect the patrimony, or sacred legacy, of the institute (c. 578). This foundational duty to protect the institute's precious heritage is an all-embracing yet elusive mandate. Sometimes it calls for specific and, perhaps, bold or radical actions; however, this responsibility generally serves as a touchstone, lens, or common vision by which the chapter reviews reports, discusses issues, and weighs proposed actions. In all these situations the general chapter is enjoined to take those actions necessary to strengthen and hand on the institute's patrimony.

Other chapter responsibilities mentioned in this canon specify how this primary duty is to be carried out. First, it is to promote suitable renewal in accord with the institute's patrimony. Inherent in this call for renewal is the recognition of ongo-

---

[49] The term *chapter* originated with the early monks who gathered daily as a community to listen to a reading from the *Rule of St. Benedict*. Gradually this gathering included discussion and decisions related to the application of the rule. By the thirteenth century general chapters were required of all religious institutes.

[50] *CCEO* 441, §1; 511; and 512 provide for synaxes (chapters) but leave most regulations to the proper law.

ing change within the institute, the Church, the culture, and the world. Concomitant with this is the recognition that renewal is not achieved once for all time. Basic criteria for ongoing renewal can be found in *Perfectae caritatis* 2 and subsequent documents.[51]

The second specific responsibility of the general chapter is to elect the supreme moderator of the institute. The person elected has the responsibility, with the assistance of the council, to carry forward chapter decisions and directions[52] in conjunction with the ordinary governance of the institute. The third specific responsibility of the general chapter is to treat major business matters, which will vary among institutes depending on their nature, size, and tradition. The proper law of the institute may indicate certain decisions to be chapter matter, but certainly included would be a change in the legal status of the institute, a major shift in apostolic thrust, and any proposal regarding merger, union, or dissolution. The fourth specific responsibility of the general chapter is to publish somewhat general norms binding all members of the institute while still allowing for interpretation and application by the competent authority.

Whatever its size, authority, and composition, the general chapter is to be representative of the whole institute and to be a sign of its unity. Capitulars should be drawn from a broad range of members with different ages, apostolates, and geographic regions represented. In order to ensure broad representation, a balance between *ex officio* members, i.e., those who are capitulars by reason of the office they hold, and delegates or elected members needs to be achieved. Many constitutions provide that *ex officio* members are not to exceed one-third of the total body; other institutes achieve the balance by naming and limiting those offices entailing an *ex officio* seat at chapter.

In keeping with the proper law of the institute, delegates may be elected either at large, i.e., by the entire membership of the institute, or by a sub-

group of the institute, such as a province, a region, a local house, or an age group. Each capitular brings his or her own gifts, experience, education, and expertise, offering these for the good of the institute through service in the chapter. Regardless of whether a capitular is *ex officio* or elected, he or she does not represent a "constituency" or carry a particular agenda, theological perspective, or mandate for action. The common good of the institute and its precious heritage are to be served by each participant in the general chapter.

At times it may be necessary to convoke an extraordinary general chapter. This entails the election of delegates according to the norms of proper law. The constitutions should specify the competent authority to convoke such a chapter and any special regulations regarding it.

The second paragraph of canon 631 also highlights the importance of the institute's proper law. The constitution defines the make-up of the chapter and the extent of its authority. Usually the secondary document or other legislation elaborates further directives for the conduct of the business of the general chapter, e.g., the timing of elections vis-à-vis the other matters of business, the number of sessions, the role of committees, if such exist, the manner of proceeding, and expectations regarding participation by the capitulars and others. International institutes or multi-cultural institutes must be sensitive but clear about expectations of participation to ensure the peaceful and orderly conduct of business.

Because of the nature of the institute or apostolic demands, some institutes prefer to hold a chapter of elections some months prior to the chapter of affairs, giving those elected to office time to prepare for the transition. Other institutes prefer to hold the chapter of affairs first, identifying particular directions for the institute and observing potential leaders during chapter discussions, and conclude the chapter with elections. The nature and tradition of the institute will determine how each institute views these pivotal events and incorporates them into its proper law.

The actual agenda and the manner of conducting business are determined by the members of

---

[51] See *ES* II: 15–19; *ET* 5–7 and 11, *inter alia*.

[52] See commentary on c. 625.

the chapter after it has convened. A steering committee or a facilitator may propose certain approaches or topics for discussion, but the chapter itself decides both the agenda and the manner of proceeding, in keeping with its proper law. A chapter, however, may not alter for its own sessions any matter contained in the constitution, e.g., the composition of the chapter body. If some change in these constitutionally determined matters seems advisable, the chapter by a two-thirds vote may seek approval for the change from the competent ecclesiastical authority. For institutes of pontifical right the competent authority is the Congregation for Institutes of Consecrated Life and Societies of Apostolic Life; for institutes of diocesan right it is the diocesan bishop of the diocese in which the general house is located. The changes, if approved, would become effective for subsequent chapters.

The final paragraph of the canon further illustrates the principles of participation and representation by providing every member of the institute the opportunity to voice his or her wishes and suggestions to the general chapter. Methods and vehicles for making known these concerns may vary from institute to institute and even from one chapter to another within the same institute. The nature of the issues under consideration, exigencies of time and context, and the institute's customary mode of operating will all influence this consultative process. Regional preparatory meetings, open hearings, written survey instruments, and other forums may be utilized to test proposals or elicit suggestions, but every individual member and any group of members has this legally protected right to send wishes or suggestions in writing to the chapter as a whole or to any individual delegate. Concomitant with the right to make such representation is the right to be heard. However, the chapter itself determines the manner of hearing, the disposition of these wishes and suggestions, and the shape of its own agenda.

Chapters of the whole, in which every perpetually or definitively professed member is a capitular, are the customary practice in some monasteries and smaller institutes, a practice which is in-

corporated into their constitutions. For a serious reason and for a particular general chapter, other institutes may seek a dispensation from their constitutions to permit the universal suffrage of all members with active and passive voice. However, a self-selected general chapter, i.e., one whose members comprise all perpetually or definitively professed members who so choose, violates the general principle and the right of all members of the institute to have a real and effective part in choosing the chapter members.[53]

Many institutes seek to encourage greater participation of all members in the work of the chapter. In addition to the above-mentioned vehicles for participation preparatory to the convening of the chapter, the institute's proper law may designate ways in which others may participate with the capitulars in the chapter deliberations, e.g., by active listening and prayerful support, by research and committee work, by discussion on the chapter floor. These others might include the general membership of the institute, associates and co-ministers in its apostolic works, experts on topics under discussion, and invited guests. However, only the capitulars, in whom the responsibility of protecting the institute's precious heritage is invested, vote on chapter matters.

Other Chapters and Assemblies

Canon 632 — Proper law is to determine accurately what is to pertain to other chapters of the institute and to other similar assemblies, namely, what pertains to their nature, authority, composition, way of proceeding and time of celebration.

Besides the general chapter, provincial, regional, or local chapters and other assemblies or gatherings enable members to participate in the life and direction of the institute.[54] If an institute is constituted with a provincial level of government or its equivalent, the constitution provides for provincial chap-

---

[53] *ES* II: 4 and 18.

[54] The Eastern code does not mention other synaxes or assemblies, leaving their provision to the typicon or statutes.

ters. The manner of conducting provincial chapters and details related to other regular community gatherings are usually found in the institute's secondary document or in supplementary legislation such as provincial statutes or chapter enactments. The changeable nature of some other assemblies and institute-wide gatherings suggests a more flexible approach for such matters as their frequency, composition, and procedures.

This brief and quite general canon allows each institute great latitude in determining the nature, authority, frequency, and composition of these other chapters. Because they often deal with more regional matters and are often celebrated closer to local communities, they can energize a region or province, generating an enthusiasm and commitment which general chapters, because they are often at a distance, do not. Each institute must seek ways of gathering the membership in keeping with its own nature, spirit, and tradition.

Other Means of Participation

Canon 633 — §1. Organs of participation or consultation are to fulfill faithfully the function entrusted to them according to the norm of universal and proper law and to express in their own way the concern and participation of all the members for the good of the entire institute or community.

§2. In establishing and using these means of participation and consultation, wise discretion is to be observed and their procedures are to conform to the character and purpose of the institute.

The last canon in this section dealing with representation and participation offers both encouragement and caution regarding other organs of participation and consultation.[55] Such vehicles have a long and respected history in many institutes, often originating in their early days and incorporated into their customs and documents. Such participatory organs may be *ad hoc* or standing bodies, elected or appointed, local, re-

gional, or institute-wide. Examples of such include boards of formation, dispute resolution groups, preference ballots, local community meetings, extended councils, planning committees, commissions entrusted with promoting justice issues, transition teams, finance councils, task forces, speak-outs, and opinionnaires. Their common purpose is to enable members to participate in promoting the good of the institute. These organs of participation should be congruent with the character of the institute and operate in accord with the universal law and the institute's proper law. They operate under the authority of the competent superior, in whom resides the responsibility to decide and take action after having considered all input.[56]

ARTICLE 3: TEMPORAL GOODS AND THEIR ADMINISTRATION [cc. 634–640]

The seven canons in this article specify and apply to religious institutes the general law of the Church on temporal goods found in Book V of the code. The norms in Book V generally apply to religious institutes but there are some exceptions. These two sections of the law must be read carefully. Wherever they differ, the norms for religious supersede those in the general law and, as in other situations, the constitutions of a religious institute approved by competent ecclesiastical authority take precedence over the common law.

The Church owns temporal goods, referred to as "ecclesiastical goods," in order to further its mission.[57] The code does not define temporal goods, but in keeping with the canonical legal tradition they are understood to include both material resources such as real property, whether moveable or immovable, and intangible or incorporeal things such as legal rights and obligations, titles, offices, annuities, as well as the more common cash, stocks, and bonds. The oversight or ad-

---

[55] There is no comparable norm in the Eastern code.

[56] Canon 618.

[57] Canon 1257.

ministration of these temporal goods is one dimension of governance in a religious institute. In carrying out their responsibilities, superiors and others sharing in the governance of religious institutes (e.g., councils, chapters, financial administrators) need to be knowledgeable of the universal law of the Church regarding temporal goods, the proper law of their institute, and any applicable civil law. The proper law of the institute plays an important role in determining how each particular institute witnesses to evangelical poverty, uses temporal goods, and administers its assets.

The following canons deal only with those temporal goods belonging to the religious institute or another public juridic person, such as a province; they do not apply to goods or property belonging to an individual religious, which is dealt with in canon 668.

Capacity Regarding Temporal Goods

Canon 634 — §1. As juridic persons by the law itself, institutes, provinces, and houses are capable of acquiring, possessing, administering, and alienating temporal goods unless this capacity is excluded or restricted in the constitutions.

§2. Nevertheless, they are to avoid any appearance of excess, immoderate wealth, and accumulation of goods.

This canon recognizes the capacity and asserts the right of religious institutes, provinces, or local houses as juridic persons to acquire, possess, administer, and alienate temporal goods.[58] Local houses which have been formally erected in accord with canons 609–610 possess juridic personality and thus may own property. The formal erection of a religious house differs from the lawful constitution of a local community, as described in canon 608. Many apostolic religious institutes of

men and women in the United States have chosen over the years to establish local communities but not to erect religious houses with the requisite formalities. The mobility of members, the centrality of the apostolic commitment of these institutes, difficulties with communication, and the like have been factors in such decisions. Consequently, many local communities or residences of apostolic religious are not religious houses with separate juridic personality and thus may not acquire, possess, administer, and alienate temporal goods in their own right.

An institute's constitutions can restrict or completely exclude its capacity to own property under canon law. Such a restriction may apply to the entire institute or to a part of the institute, e.g., provinces or local houses. In circumstances where a restriction or limitation on the ownership of property exists, the superior at that level administers the temporal goods in accord with the proper law, but ownership may belong at another level. In such situations the canonical obligations and corresponding restrictions pertaining to the property should be incorporated into any pertinent civil law documents.

Superiors and others responsible under canon law for administering temporal goods must ensure that their ownership is safeguarded through civilly valid methods.[59] In the United States this usually entails incorporation as a not-for-profit corporation, thus giving the institute, province, or house legal personality under civil law. In establishing the civil entity, care should be taken that the structure and distribution of powers in the civil corporation enable those responsible under canon law (i.e., usually the superior aided by the council) to act under civil law.

In the United States, religious institutes, provinces, and those local houses with the capacity for canonical ownership often choose to incorporate apostolic works separately from the religious institute itself. This can be done to protect the religious institute and its assets from potential liability, in recognition that an apostolate has matured suffi-

---

[58] *CCEO* 423 asserts a similar capacity, while acknowledging the existence of exclusions and limitations on this capacity for some monasteries, orders, and the like. *CCEO* 424 urges the use and administration of property in keeping with the poverty of the institute.

[59] Canon 1284, §2, 2°.

ciently to assume additional responsibility and independence, as a step toward initiating a collaborative endeavor with another entity, or simply as a matter of policy. The separate civil incorporation of the apostolate does not affect the status of the property as ecclesiastical goods unless they are directly or indirectly alienated.[60]

The second paragraph of the canon provides the context for the capacity and right spoken of in the first paragraph. The exhortation to avoid all appearance of luxury and wealth is taken directly from *Perfectae caritatis* 13, which, in turn, echoes *Lumen gentium* 13 and *Gaudium et spes* 68–72 on stewardship and the use of the goods of this world. This second paragraph is directly tied to the exhortation against inappropriate use of material goods and finds its positive counterpart in canon 640, which urges religious institutes to give collective witness to poverty and charity. While individual members of an institute take the vow of poverty, those who administer its goods must do so in accord with its general purposes. Furthermore, the corporate body of the religious institute, province, or house shares responsibility for creating the conditions which support the living out of the individual member's vow of poverty.

Regulation of Temporal Goods

Canon 635 — §1. Since the temporal goods of religious institutes are ecclesiastical, they are governed by the prescripts of Book V, *The Temporal Goods of the Church*, unless other provision is expressly made.

§2. Nevertheless, each institute is to establish suitable norms concerning the use and administration of goods, by which the poverty proper to it is to be fostered, protected, and expressed.

Temporal goods are ecclesiastical goods or not depending on the canonical standing of the owner.[61] If the owner of the goods is a public juridic person in the Church, such as a religious institute or province, its temporal goods are, by that fact, ecclesiastical goods. Thus, all goods owned by a religious institute or province, whether religious in nature such as a shrine or a chalice or secular in nature such as real estate or an oil well, are considered ecclesiastical goods and are governed by the norms of Book V.[62] Conversely, temporal goods owned by an individual religious are not ecclesiastical goods because the owner is not a public juridic person.

The principles of stewardship, subsidiarity, and accountability permeate Book V and should be evident also in administering the goods of a religious institute. One example of the principle of subsidiarity, found in the second paragraph of this canon, is its emphasis on the institute's taking responsibility for expressing its particular charism. This paragraph links concern about the appropriate handling of ecclesiastical goods with concern for the special character of a religious institute. Each institute is to apply the general law of the Church, found in the following canons and in Book V, in such a way that the poverty characteristic of that particular institute is fostered, protected, and expressed. Community practices, the manner of acquiring temporal goods (e.g., begging), modes of sharing within the institute and with those in need, the balance of dependence and interdependence, and the like are to be integrated into the particular law of each institute.

Finance Officer

Canon 636 — §1. In each institute and likewise in each province which is governed by a major superior, there is to be a finance officer, distinct from the major superior and constituted according to the norm of proper law, who is to manage the administration of goods under the direction of the respective superior. Insofar as possible, a finance officer distinct from the local superior is to be designated even in local communities.

---

[60] See cc. 638, §1 and 1291–1296.
[61] Canon 1257, §1.
[62] *CCEO* 425 similarly subjects the temporal goods of religious institutes to the common norms for temporal goods.

§2. At the time and in the manner established by proper law, finance officers and other administrators are to render an account of their administration to the competent authority.

Another expression of subsidiarity in governance is the requirement of this canon that each religious institute and province divide the responsibilities entailed in financial administration.[63] Implicitly acknowledging that local communities may not have the capacity for distinct offices of superior and finance officer, canon 636 nevertheless urges that these offices be separate even on the local level to the extent possible. Similar requirements are made of other juridic persons in the Church.[64] Distinguishing financial responsibility from the general responsibilities of major superiors highlights the importance of specialized expertise in this work and, at the same time, checks the power of the superior. This is a specialized set of responsibilities, and the person who carries them out is to be a distinct person from the major superior, although the superior ultimately bears responsibility for them. In addition, this function is an *office* which presumes a certain stability; it is not a task assigned temporarily to one person and then another. The proper law of the institute often provides for terms for the financial officer, in a manner similar to but not necessarily concurrent with the provision for other offices such as secretary. Finally, the general admonitions regarding those named to office in a religious institute are applicable. In other words, they are to be truly worthy and suitable, and those responsible for naming them should have nothing in mind but God and the good of the institute (c. 626).

The canon does not indicate how the financial administrator is to be selected, but only that it be done according to the norm of proper law. The major superior may appoint after consultation with the council, but free conferral, appointment with the consent of the council, or election by a chapter or by universal suffrage are possible modes of selection. The manner of selection should maximize the probability of identifying a competent finance officer.

The qualifications for this office are implicit rather than explicit. The underlying dynamic is that the finance officer shares with the major superior the responsibility for the institute's temporal goods, with the finance officer acting under the direction of the major superior.[65] The finance officer should understand the requirements of both canon law and civil law regarding temporal goods, be skilled in financial administration, and be known for his or her personal integrity.

The canon does not state that the finance officer must be a member of the institute, and this silence, together with other factors, has given rise to a question on this point. Some commentators, believing that the office is internal to the institute, hold that the finance officer should be a member of the institute; others hold that any such restriction must be explicit.[66] Each institute should follow its own proper law in this matter pending further study.

At times, due to a dearth of qualified persons within the institute itself and the complexity of services required, the institute may look beyond its own membership to supplement the services provided by the finance officer. This assistance may take the form of contracted services from, for example, an investment management firm, a payroll company, or consultants. The institute may also hire salaried personnel, such as a comp-

---

[63] *CCEO* 447 and 516 make provision for a finance officer in monasteries and other religious institutes, respectively.

[64] See cc. 423 and 492–494 regarding diocesan financial administration and c. 537 regarding parish financial administration.

[65] See c. 1279.

[66] See, for instance, D. O'Connor and R. Smith, "Qualifications of a Treasurer in an Institute of Consecrated Life," in *CLSA Advisory Opinions 1984–1993*, ed. Patrick Cogan (Washington, D.C.: CLSA, 1995) 178–179 and 180–181 respectively and Rincón Pérez in *Pamplona ComEng*, 440, who addresses the question for the local level only. For an opinion open to a non-member serving as finance officer see R. McDermott, "The Finance Administrator of a Religious Institute," in *RRAO 1997*, 58–59.

troller, an internal auditor, or even a director of financial services. In addition, some institutes establish financial advisory councils, comprised of both members and non-members skilled in various related fields, who assist the superior and the finance officer with their expertise and experience. Financial advisory councils are required for dioceses (c. 492), parishes (c. 537), and other juridic persons (c. 1280) and are common in religious institutes, but in religious institutes the council may serve this function, with specialized advice sought as needed.[67] However the finances of the institute are organized, the major superior ultimately bears responsibility for its financial administration.

The second paragraph of the canon articulates the principles of subsidiarity and accountability by requiring that the finance officer and other administrators render an account of their actions. The time and manner of doing so will vary depending on the size and nature of the institute and the level of responsibility of the administrators, but the institute should provide for this important function in its proper law. If the supreme moderator is expected to present a financial report to the general chapter, this should be articulated in the constitution or secondary document. Other reporting expectations may be more appropriately placed in provincial statutes, chapter enactments, administrative manuals, position descriptions, and other directives. An annual independent audit, or one done at regular intervals, provides a starting point for financial reporting. The finance officer of an institute, province, or local house which is incorporated under civil law may also have reporting responsibilities to various civil authorities, the fulfillment of which is understood to be a canonical requirement through the "canonization" of civil law (c. 1284, §2, 2°–3°). Other expectations enumerated in this same canon reflect good management practice and bind finance officers in religious institutes.

Accountability of Certain Institutes

Canon 637 — The autonomous monasteries mentioned in can. 615 must render an account of their administration to the local ordinary once a year. Moreover, the local ordinary has the right to be informed about the financial reports of a religious house of diocesan right.

The legal relationship between the diocesan bishop and a religious institute varies depending on the type of institute. He is to be especially vigilant regarding autonomous monasteries with no other external superiors and no jurisdictional link to other monasteries.[68] An institute of diocesan right is committed to his special care.[69] Canon 637 speaks generically about the financial aspects of this "special vigilance" and "special care."[70]

Each year autonomous monasteries, both of men and of women, are to submit a written financial report to the diocesan bishop; its content and format should be mutually determined by the bishop and the superior.

Diocesan institutes, both of men and of women, have a slightly different financial tie to the diocesan bishop. He has the right to be informed about the financial affairs of each religious house of diocesan right within his diocese. However, this does not necessarily entail the right to be informed about the entire institute, but rather the right to be informed about each house formally erected as a religious house within the diocese. This would include the general house if it is located within the diocese. The manner and content of this exchange of information are left to the determination of those involved, but it should be done in such a manner as to accomplish the intent of the norm, i.e., the exercise of vigilance or special care while still honoring the institute's internal autonomy.

The law itself does not indicate how controverted matters are to be handled. As a general

[67] See *Comm* 27 (1995) 102.

[68] See c. 615.
[69] See c. 594.
[70] The Eastern code has no comparable norm.

principle the code recommends peaceful means of arriving at mutual agreement, such as seeking common counsel, mediation by wise persons, and further study.[71] However, if differences persist, the institute always may take administrative recourse. While the bishop may curtail the apostolic activities of the institute within the diocese, he may not suppress it.

Extraordinary Administration and Alienation

Canon 638 — §1. Within the scope of universal law, it belongs to proper law to determine acts which exceed the limit and manner of ordinary administration and to establish what is necessary to place an act of extraordinary administration validly.

§2. In addition to superiors, the officials who are designated for this in proper law also validly incur expenses and perform juridic acts of ordinary administration within the limits of their function.

§3. For the validity of alienation and of any other affair in which the patrimonial condition of a juridic person can worsen, the written permission of the competent superior with the consent of the council is required. Nevertheless, if it concerns an affair which exceeds the amount defined by the Holy See for each region, or things given to the Church by vow, or things precious for artistic or historical reasons, the permission of the Holy See itself is also required.

§4. For the autonomous monasteries mentioned in can. 615 and for institutes of diocesan right, it is also necessary to have the written consent of the local ordinary.

This canon and the following one regulate the kinds of financial and business matters which superiors and finance officers might deal with in the course of their work.[72] These canons specify for religious institutes some differences from the common law on temporal goods found in Book V, highlighting the importance of the institute's proper law in defining roles and establishing limits in matters related to temporal goods.

Canon 638 indicates that each institute, in accord with its own character, nature, and condition is to distinguish in its proper law what is ordinary administration from what is extraordinary administration. Ordinary administration entails the conservation and expenditure of resources and the oversight of financial matters needed for the day-to-day management of the goods of the institute. Examples of ordinary administration might include such actions as meeting a payroll, depositing money in various accounts, overseeing an investment portfolio, and maintaining and repairing a building, even a general house. Extraordinary administration entails those actions, short of alienation, which the finance officer or other administrator may not carry out by reason of office or delegated authority and which require some additional form of authorization. Examples of extraordinary administration would be the expenditure of money above a certain set limit, the transfer of goods from one province to another or from one house to another within the same institute, the refusal of a gift or the acceptance of a gift with significant conditions, the replacement of furniture and equipment, or the renegotiation of a loan.

In a manner which is in keeping with the universal law, each institute must determine what is ordinary and what is extraordinary administration and clarify the further authorizations necessary before placing acts of extraordinary administration. Because of the great differences between institutes, what is extraordinary administration in one institute could be ordinary administration in another (e.g., limitations on expenditures). Similarly, some institutes reserve authorization for acts of extraordinary administration to the superior alone, while other institutes require the permission of the superior with the consent of the council. Still other institutes reserve to the chapter authorization for certain acts of extraordinary administration, such as the purchase or sale of certain types of property

---

[71] See c. 1733.

[72] The Eastern code has no comparable norm directed specifically toward religious institutes.

or a major renovation of the general house. Any act of extraordinary administration placed without first fulfilling the requirements for validity of the proper law is considered invalid in canon law.

The second paragraph of the canon identifies who may place acts of ordinary administration. Such acts include incurring debt up to a specified limit and performing juridic acts in the name of the institute, such as entering into contracts, passing title to property, or managing investments. Superiors and finance officers by virtue of their office and other "officials" named for this purpose in accord with the proper law may act within the limits of their authority. Others who could be authorized to place certain such acts might include an investment oversight committee, a comptroller or bursar, a pension board, the director of the physical plant, and others. Each person or entity so authorized should be given, in writing, definite parameters and clear processes for additional authorization, when such is necessary.

The third and fourth paragraphs treat alienation of property, an act distinct from either ordinary or extraordinary administration. Alienation, as described in the third paragraph, includes both the conveyance or transfer of ownership and any other transaction by which the patrimonial condition of the juridic person is adversely affected. This broad understanding of what is subject to the norms on alienation of property specifies for religious institutes the common law for all juridic persons found in canon 1295. Among actions generally agreed to constitute an alienation would be the sale of significant property; the spending of assets for one purpose from an account/fund reserved or immobilized for another purpose, such as an endowment fund; entering into a long-term lease; effectively handing over the control or ownership of an institution to another group/board; borrowing a substantial amount of money; and taking out a mortgage.[73]

Certain norms are to be observed in order validly to alienate ecclesiastical property belonging to a religious institute, province, or house or to carry out any transaction which would adversely affect it. The first requirement for validity is that permission of the competent superior with the consent of the council be obtained in writing. This requirement differs from the general norm of canon 1292, which requires the consent of a finance council. For religious institutes the consent of the council suffices unless the proper law of the institute indicates otherwise. In addition to the written permission required by this canon, other requirements of the canons in Book V must be fulfilled, e.g., a just cause and at least two written estimates or expert appraisals.[74] If the intended transaction exceeds the current ceiling defined for religious institutes in the United States by the Holy See,[75] *or* if the items to be alienated are precious art, have historical value, or were given to the institute as a result of a vow, the Holy See's permission is also required for the validity of the act. For religious institutes the request for permission to alienate property above the limit established is transmitted to the Congregation for Institutes of Consecrated Life and Societies of Apostolic Life together with the supporting documentation.[76]

Besides the information mentioned above and supporting financial documentation, a statement in writing is needed from the diocesan bishop. For diocesan religious institutes and for autonomous monasteries, this supporting letter should approve

---

[73] F. Morrisey, "Ordinary and Extraordinary Administration: Canon 1277," *J* 48 (1988) 709–726; and "The Alienation of Temporal Goods in Contemporary Practice," *Stud Can* 29 (1995) 293–316.

[74] See c. 1293. The canon does not specify how many expert opinions are required, but the common opinion is that there must be at least two.

[75] Currently the amount approved by the Holy See for the dioceses of the United States and the amount approved by CICLSAL for religious institutes and societies of apostolic life in the United States are the same—three million dollars.

[76] A few religious institutes are subject to a different dicastery of the Holy See: institutes which are primarily missionary in nature and institutes belonging to an Eastern *sui iuris* church. These institutes request permissions for alienation of property from the CEP and the CEC respectively.

the anticipated alienation. Although the canon is silent about a similar requirement for pontifical institutes seeking permission to alienate property, the current practice of the Holy See is to request the opinion (*votum*) of the diocesan bishop before granting permission. The opinion sought is that of the diocesan bishop of the place of the property, given his responsibility for the pastoral care of the diocese.

If an autonomous monastery or a diocesan institute wishes to alienate property as described above and if the value of the goods to be alienated is below the maximum set by the Holy See, the autonomous monastery or diocesan institute must obtain the written consent of the local ordinary in order to alienate the property. For a diocesan institute seeking to alienate property located in a diocese other than that of the principal house (general house), the involvement of two local ordinaries is required. The *consent* of the local ordinary of the general house and the *opinion* (*votum*) of the local ordinary of the place where the property is located must be transmitted to the Congregation for Institutes of Consecrated Life and Societies of Apostolic Life with the request to alienate and the other supporting documentation.[77]

Responsibility for Debts and Obligations

Canon 639 — §1. If a juridic person has contracted debts and obligations even with the permission of the superiors, it is bound to answer for them.

§2. If a member has entered into a contract concerning his or her own goods with the permission of the superior, the member must answer for it, but if the business of the institute was conducted by mandate of the superior, the institute must answer.

§3. If a religious has entered into a contract without any permission of superiors, he or she must answer, but not the juridic person.

§4. It is a fixed rule, however, that an action can always be brought against one who has profited from the contract entered into.

[77] See c. 595, §1.

§5. Religious superiors are to take care that they do not permit debts to be contracted unless it is certain that the interest on the debt can be paid off from ordinary income and that the capital sum can be paid off through legitimate amortization within a period that is not too long.

This canon provides clear principles for assigning responsibility and possible liability which might result from the various business transactions undertaken by a religious institute, its officers, and its members.[78] The juridic person itself—the religious institute, province, or local house—is responsible for its debts and other obligations; responsibility does not lie with the superior whose permission was given to enter into those obligations. In other words, under canon law these are corporate, not personal obligations.

The second principle distinguishes actions taken on behalf of the institute from personal actions. If a member, even with the permission of the superior, incurs an obligation or loss as a result of a contract regarding some matter related to his or her personal property, the member, not the institute, remains responsible to meet the obligation.[79] In fulfilling these personal obligations a member may be required to use his or her personal property, if such exists. However, if a member incurs an obligation while conducting the business of the institute in accord with the directives of the superior, the institute, not the individual member, is responsible to meet this obligation.

This canonical principle is deceptively simple as stated but may have serious civil ramifications. For instance, if a member of the institute is assigned or missioned to a particular apostolate by the superior, it is sometimes difficult to distinguish between actions and liability for which the institute is responsible and those for which the individ-

[78] *CCEO* 468, §§2–3 articulate some of the principles of this canon.

[79] The personal property of an individual member is governed by c. 668.

ual member is responsible. Civil actions seeking restitution and/or damages have varied considerably in assigning responsibility. The proper law of the institute should distinguish clearly between personal and institutional responsibility.

The third principle for determining responsibility is the simplest and the easiest to apply. Any contract or obligation entered into by an individual religious without the permission of the competent superior remains the responsibility of the member and not of the institute. Examples might include personal credit card or gambling debts, contracts or promissory notes related to one's personal property, or obligations for a child. The institute, province, or local house has no legal responsibility to assist in these matters, but the competent superior may choose to do so out of charity, to avoid public scandal or civil action, or to preserve the institute's name.

The legal principle contained in the fourth paragraph derives from the Roman law tradition and is applicable under both canon and civil law. Regardless of who is ultimately responsible for an obligation, legal action or redress can be brought against an agent, whether administrator, finance officer, or individual member, who has profited inappropriately from a contract. The competent superior or other official with standing in the institute is empowered to bring such an action. In situations which cannot be resolved internally and for which civil action is contemplated, prior written permission of the proper ordinary is required.[80]

The final principle of canon 639 is applicable to any administrator considering the assumption of a debt, but is directed as a general exhortation to superiors whose permission is required before the juridic person may encumber itself with a debt. Before granting the necessary permission, superiors should be apprised of the financial implications of the debt, ascertaining that the interest can be paid from ordinary income and the principal repaid within a reasonable time. Because religious institutes and their financial status vary greatly, so too will their ordinary income

and what is considered a reasonable repayment time.

Evangelical Witness

Canon 640 — Taking into account local conditions, institutes are to strive to give, as it were, a collective witness of charity and poverty and are to contribute according to their ability something from their own goods to provide for the needs of the Church and the support of the poor.

This canon acknowledges differences in culture, social location, and economic standing between institutes while at the same time calling all institutes to give corporate witness to charity and poverty (*PC* 13).[81] One concrete way in which institutes can give this witness is by contributing to the needs of the Church and the care of the poor. In so doing, institutes also witness to and build communion among the churches and within the Church.

This canon's exhortation to give a collective witness of charity and poverty can provide impetus for communal reflection on the institute's tradition regarding evangelical poverty and be an occasion for developing a communal consciousness regarding simplicity and moderation.[82] A spirit of generosity is to be encouraged among all members, but responsibility for sharing the goods of the institute with others belongs primarily to those charged with the care of these goods, i.e., superiors, finance officers, and other administrators. Any distribution of goods is to be carried out within the context of the norms on temporal goods and in conjunction with the obligations in justice which religious institutes have to their own members, to employees, and to others who depend on them.[83]

---

[80] Canon 1288.

[81] The Eastern code has no comparable norm.
[82] All religious are called to evangelical poverty, moderation, and simplicity in accord with the charism of the institute (c. 600).
[83] Canon 1286, 2°.

CHAPTER III
THE ADMISSION OF CANDIDATES
AND THE FORMATION OF MEMBERS
[cc. 641–661]

The renewal in religious life called for by Vatican II has focused attention on the importance of formation in the life of a religious institute. Several documents, beginning with the council decree *Perfectae caritatis,* including the interim legislation contained in the instruction *Renovationis causam* (1969), and culminating with the instruction *Potissimum instituti* (1990) which is devoted entirely to formation, have broadened, updated, and integrated the understanding of formation. Formation, understood as growth in the following of Christ, is a life-long process with physical, moral, intellectual, and spiritual dimensions. It begins even before a candidate applies for admission; in fact, the deepening faith and growing maturity of the candidate enables him or her to consider a vocation to the religious life.

Formation is no longer viewed as a series of detailed regulations to be observed minutely, but rather as a set of underlying principles to be adapted to the charism and nature of each institute and to the culture and conditions in which it is situated. Significant shifts evident in the revised norms on formation include insights from the behavioral sciences, recognition of the need for active collaboration of the individuals in formation, an extension of the period of initial formation, greater freedom for each religious institute to design its own formation program, and, for apostolic institutes, the inclusion of apostolic experiences as integral to the formation process.

New members are both the recipients and the agents of formation; the new members and the receiving community participate in a mutually enriching and growth-producing process. The future fidelity and vitality of a religious institute depends, under the action of the Spirit, on the quality and commitment of its newer members. Hence those entrusted with screening, admitting, and forming new members hold a sacred trust. Certain minimal requirements for admission, novitiate,

profession, and initial formation are specified in the following canons, but considerable flexibility is left to individual institutes to apply, adapt, and augment these norms.

ARTICLE 1: ADMISSION TO THE NOVITIATE
[cc. 641–645]

Admission to Novitiate

Canon 641 — The right to admit candidates to the novitiate belongs to major superiors according to the norm of proper law.

Life in the religious institute begins with the novitiate. Admission to the novitiate is a significant event for the institute, for the candidate, and for the Church, and decisions regarding admission appropriately pertain to the major superior.[84] In institutes with an intermediate level of governance (e.g., provinces) the proper law determines which major superior validly admits to the novitiate. Similarly, the proper law of each institute indicates whether a vote of the council, deliberative or consultative, is necessary prior to the major superior's admission of a candidate. The major superior entrusted with admitting candidates should endeavor to have personal contact with the candidate, if possible, so that the superior's judgment confirms the recommendations of those who have been working with the candidate.

This canon, which empowers the major superior to decide regarding admission to the novitiate, complements and specifies canon 597 which speaks of the general or foundational qualifications for admission to an institute of consecrated life. Canon 597, §2 states that no one may be ad-

---

[84] Within the Eastern churches, monasticism is the prototype and model of the other forms of religious life. Hence the Eastern code treats the phenomenon of religious life under three subdivisions: (1) general canons, (2) monasteries, and (3) orders and congregations. *CCEO* 453, §1 and 519 identify who admits to a monastery and an order or congregation, respectively.

mitted without suitable preparation. In contrast to the 1917 code (*CIC* 539–541), which required a period of postulancy for all religious except those preparing for orders, this code is silent regarding what suitable preparation entails, thus permitting each institute to determine and incorporate into its proper law the manner in which candidates are to be assessed and prepared for admission to religious life. Recent Holy See documents have urged that candidates have some type of probationary period prior to admission.[85] Such a pre-novitiate preparatory period enables the institute to ascertain whether candidates have had basic catechesis in the faith and possess sufficient knowledge and maturity, the proper disposition, and the capacity to grow in assuming the obligations of religious life.[86]

Suitability of Candidates

Canon 642 — With vigilant care, superiors are only to admit those who, besides the required age, have the health, suitable character, and sufficient qualities of maturity to embrace the proper life of the institute. This health, character, and maturity are to be verified even by using experts, if necessary, without prejudice to the prescript of can. 220.

This canon, derived in part from *Renovationis causam* 14, reminds the admitting superior of his or her serious responsibility to ensure a candidate's suitability before admission to the novitiate.[87] In addition to the candidate's standing in the Church[88] and requisite age,[89] other issues to be considered are the candidate's health, character, and maturity. Each of these three criteria offers a continuum of possibilities, the assessment of

which is to be made in relation to the nature of the particular institute.

The applicant's physical and mental health is best attested to by professionals credentialed in the respective disciplines.[90] Signed release forms allow the results of such tests to be shared with the responsible superior in the institute. Many institutes require applicants to present various medical evaluations including dental, ocular, and general physical, often using a reporting format supplied by the institute. Medical advances which now enable the detection of HIV infection, chronic or debilitating diseases, and certain genetic predispositions present difficult moral issues to those charged with drawing up admissions policies and recommending applicants. Issues of confidentiality, ongoing responsibility to the applicant to whom such information may be new, and concern for the good of the institute and its ability to assume long-term financial risk pose serious dilemmas to institutes which require this specialized testing.

Psychological assessments, commonly combining in-depth interviews and standardized tests, are widely used and generally found beneficial. However, institutes must choose carefully experts who understand and respect the religious life; these are the best suited to evaluate potential members. Protecting the confidentiality of test results and destroying such results when they have outlived their validity pose serious concerns when evaluating potential candidates. Results of medical and psychological testing should be used in a manner which fosters understanding and growth, whether or not the applicant is admitted.

Suitability of character and sufficient maturity can usually be established through less formal but equally effective means, including long-term contact with the institute or one of its representatives, visits to the applicant's home and ordinary milieu, and the candidate's frequent or extended participation in the life of the institute prior to admis-

---

[85] *RC* 11 and *PI* 43–44.

[86] *RC* 11–12, *PI* 42, and *VC* 65.

[87] *CCEO* 448; 453, §2; and 517 require that a candidate's suitability, intention, and freedom be ascertained before admission to a monastery or an order or congregation.

[88] Canons 597 and 645.

[89] Canon 643.

[90] Both Rincón Pérez and Williamson express some reservation about requiring psychological assessments on a regular basis. See *Pamplona ComEng,* 444 and *CLSGBI Com,* 355.

sion. The maturity required at this stage has both human and Christian elements, should be age- and culture-appropriate, and should evidence the capacity for growth in relation to the demands of life in that particular institute, e.g., the demands of community life.[91]

The responsibility of judging suitability for admission lies with the superior, who often relies on the recommendations of those religious delegated to screen and/or accompany applicants, the assessments of professionals, and other pertinent information. In seeking the information needed to arrive at a determination, superiors are admonished to consider canon 220, avoiding damage to the good reputation of both the applicant and the institute and respecting the candidate's right to privacy. At the very least, this requires superiors to make discreet inquiries and proscribes them and others delegated to assess candidates from requiring a manifestation of conscience.[92] What is sought in this gathering of information is a reasonable assessment of the candidate's capacity to live the life to which he or she is requesting admission and his or her commitment to that endeavor. Such an assessment is neither certain nor final; a candidate who is not admitted may reapply later, and one who is admitted will continue to be evaluated during the subsequent years of formation.

Impediments to Valid Admission

Canon 643 — §1. The following are admitted to the novitiate invalidly:

1° one who has not yet completed seventeen years of age;

2° a spouse, while the marriage continues to exist;

3° one who is currently bound by a sacred bond to some institute of consecrated life or is incorporated in some society of apos-

tolic life, without prejudice to the prescript of can. 684;

4° one who enters the institute induced by force, grave fear, or malice, or the one whom a superior, induced in the same way, has received;

5° one who has concealed his or her incorporation in some institute of consecrated life or in some society of apostolic life.

§2. Proper law can establish other impediments even for validity of admission or can attach conditions.

This canon enumerates the five impediments of universal law which render admission to the novitiate invalid; the institute's proper law may add other invalidating impediments or conditions.[93] The five impediments of universal law are applicable equally to male and female applicants and to pontifical and diocesan right institutes. The existence of any one of these impediments, whether known or occult, invalidates the novitiate.

To be validly admitted to the novitiate, a candidate must be seventeen years of age (1°). However, prior to the 1983 code, the universal law permitted a candidate to be validly admitted to the novitiate at the age of fifteen. In the culture and context of the United States, both fifteen and seventeen seem young for the maturity presumed by such a decision; however, this minimum age for admission applies to all Latin church religious institutes in diverse cultures around the world. Individual institutes, however, may set a higher age for admission, in keeping with their own formation program and cultural milieu.[94]

An applicant may not be admitted to the novitiate who is bound by an existing marriage bond

---

[91] *PI* 42–43.

[92] Canon 630 protects the freedom of members of the institute from any pressure to make a manifestation of conscience to superiors. A comparable freedom is extended to those not yet members.

[93] *CCEO* 450 enumerates the requirements for valid admission to the novitiate of a monastery, and *CCEO* 517 lists similar requirements for orders and congregations.

[94] *CCEO* 450 and 517 establish eighteen as the minimum age for admission to the novitiate of an Eastern church monastery and seventeen as the minimum age for admission to the novitiate of an Eastern church order or congregation.

(2°). If the bond no longer exists, due to the death of the spouse or a declaration of nullity, the person is free to enter the novitiate. If the marriage has broken down but has not been declared null, or if a couple mutually agrees to renounce marital rights and relationships in order to seek admission to religious institutes, a dispensation from the Holy See must be sought.[95] However, before admitting an applicant from the annulled marriage or before seeking a dispensation from the Holy See, superiors should ascertain that the applicant has fulfilled all natural obligations resulting from the marriage, such as care of children, support of the former spouse, and fulfillment of debts. Furthermore, if the failed marriage was annulled on psychological grounds, the candidate may be asked for a written release in order to obtain further information from the competent tribunal regarding the annulment.

A person currently bound by vow or other sacred bond in an institute of consecrated life or society of apostolic life may not be admitted to another religious institute (3°). Freedom from such an impediment is achieved either by the expiration of the bond if it is temporary, or, if the bond is definitive, by an indult of departure from the current institute, which entails a dispensation from the obligations of the existing sacred bond.[96] A person bound by vows or other sacred bonds might also seek to transfer from one institute to another (c. 684).

The fourth universal law impediment to valid admission to the novitiate is the presence of force, grave fear, or fraud, either on the part of the candidate or on the part of the admitting superior (4°). Force means physical coercion, an uncommon circumstance in present-day North America; grave fear is a disturbance of the mind or the in-

timidation resulting from a perceived impending danger; and fraud means intentional deception in a serious matter.

This fourth impediment specifies for the juridic act of admitting to the novitiate what canon 125 requires for the validity of any juridic act. Since every juridic act is an act of the will, it must be a free act, which means that both the candidate and the superior must be substantially free from constraint. Force, grave fear, or fraud which diminishes or vitiates the freedom or knowledge of either the candidate or the admitting superior or both invalidates the admission.[97] This impediment requires that the candidate disclose honestly the facts about his or her life situation so that the admitting superior has sufficient knowledge on which to act.

The final code impediment to a valid admission concerns the concealment of one's incorporation in another institute of consecrated life or society of apostolic life (5°). By incorporation is meant profession of vows or commitment through other sacred bonds, even temporary.[98] The 1917 code (*CIC* 542, §1, 5°) established the *fact* of incorporation as an impediment. While this canon recognizes the seriousness of a prior commitment, it ties the invalidity to the *dishonesty* evidenced in failing to disclose such important information.

Paragraph two of canon 643 permits a religious institute to establish in its proper law other invalidating impediments to admission or other conditions for admission. Such impediments, as in the prior code, may be illegitimate birth, ongoing financial responsibilities, or the support of family members or other dependents. Institutes may also determine a higher age or an age beyond which a candidate will not be admitted, a requisite level of education or work experience, or other culturally related criteria. The proper law should clearly indicate whether such additional requirements are intended for validity or liceity. A dis-

---

[95] Circumstances giving rise to a decree of separation can be found in cc. 1151–1153 and 1692. See also *CLD* 9, 371–372; *CLD* 10, 112–113; and *CLD* 11, 86–90 for some individual cases. For a fuller discussion of the admission of a married candidate see R. McDermott, "Admission to the Novitiate: Canon 643. 1. 2°," *Bulletin on Issues of Religious Law* 7 (Spring, 1991) 7–8.

[96] Canon 692.

[97] Consent to marriage is similarly invalidated by the presence in either party of force, grave fear, or fraud. See cc. 1098 and 1103.

[98] Canon 654.

pensation may be sought from any of these additional requirements unless the proper law indicates otherwise.[99]

The canon does not address the implications either for the admitting superior or for the candidate should the candidate be admitted in the face of invalidating impediments. The 1983 code does not penalize a superior who acts contrary to the five invalidating impediments of universal law, as the prior code did (*CIC* 2352 and 2411). However, an invalid admission remains invalid and all subsequent acts dependent on a valid novitiate (i.e., profession, certain appointments, and elections) would also be invalid. To address such a situation, a retroactive validation, called a *sanatio in radice,* i.e., a making whole from the beginning, may be sought from the Holy See.[100]

Particular Cases

Canon 644 — Superiors are not to admit to the novitiate secular clerics without consulting their proper ordinary nor those who, burdened by debts, cannot repay them.

This canon gives supplementary regulations regarding admission to the novitiate for particular cases.[101] Superiors are to consult with the proper ordinary of a secular deacon or presbyter before admitting him to the novitiate.[102] The proper ordi-

nary is the diocesan bishop of the cleric's diocese of incardination or, in cases in which the see is vacant or impeded, the requirement is satisfied by consultation with the vicar general, administrator, or other person legitimately acting in the place of the proper ordinary. The fact that the cleric has informed his proper ordinary of his intention to seek admission does not satisfy the requirement of this canon. The superior himself is to consult, either orally or in writing; written documentation of the consultation should be retained as part of the candidate's personal file. Such consultation provides an opportunity to become informed about the cleric's background and suitability for religious life.

A superior is not to admit persons with debts which they are unable to repay. If an applicant were habitually insolvent, a natural concern should arise about the applicant's responsibility, character and/or maturity, as well as possible scandal and/or liability involving the institute. However, if a set of unusual and untoward circumstances results in the candidate's filing for personal bankruptcy, the institute should delay consideration of admission, even for some years, until the candidate's financial affairs are in order.[103]

Admission of a person in either of the above situations is illicit, i.e., contrary to the law, but it does not invalidate the admission.

Documentation and Other Information

Canon 645 — §1. Before candidates are admitted to the novitiate, they must show proof of baptism, confirmation, and free status.

§2. If it concerns the admission of clerics or those who had been admitted in another institute of consecrated life, in a society of apostolic life, or in a seminary, there is additionally required the testimony of, respectively, the local ordinary, the

---

[99] See c. 85.

[100] The request for a *sanatio* is more common with regard to marriage. See cc. 1161–1165. With regard to sanating an invalid profession, Rincón Pérez opines that the absence of the prior code's explicit provision argues for the unavailability of such recourse. See *Pamplona ComEng,* 450. No opinion is given regarding the sanation of an invalid novitiate.

[101] *CCEO* 452, 454, and 517 indicate additional requirements for licit admission to a monastery, an order, or a congregation. *CCEO* 452, §2 names specific family obligations (e.g., children, parents, grandparents in need) which could prevent admission. Unlike the Latin code, *CCEO* 454 mentions the furnishing of a dowry where required by the proper law of the monastery.

[102] Since the sacrament of orders is not conferred on members of religious institutes or societies of apostolic life

until after perpetual or definitive profession (c. 1019), these clerics are prevented from entrance into another institute by the invalidating impediment of c. 643, §1, 3°.

[103] Under United States civil law, filing for bankruptcy protection does not eliminate all obligations and liabilities.

major superior of the institute or society, or the rector of the seminary.

§3. Proper law can require other proof about the requisite suitability of candidates and freedom from impediments.

§4. Superiors can also seek other information, even under secrecy, if it seems necessary to them.

As part of the process of ascertaining suitability for admission to the novitiate, certain documentary evidence is gathered. This canon identifies the basic documentation to be assembled, allowing the institute to require other evidence either as a general practice or for a particular situation.[104] The burden of gathering this documentation is usually placed on the applicant, unless it concerns an unusual or confidential matter.

Before admission, candidates are required to show proof of baptism, confirmation, and free status.[105] Proof of the first two is usually established by a recent (within the past six months) and authenticated (with seal) certificate issued by the parish of baptism containing information drawn from the parish sacramental register. Official notations on the baptismal certificate attest to the fact, date, and place of confirmation, marriage, orders, and/or religious profession. If the annotations on the baptismal certificate are incomplete (e.g., the sacrament of confirmation was conferred elsewhere and not recorded at the place of baptism,

the candidate was married outside the church, and the like) additional authenticated certificates will have to be sought from other parishes, dioceses, religious institutes, and civil jurisdictions.

Proof of free status is established by either the absence of any official notation on the baptismal certificate regarding marriage, orders, or religious profession or the presence of notations regarding the annulment of the marriage, an indult of laicization, or an indult of departure from a religious institute. In the case of a prior marriage, copies of the marriage license and civil divorce decree are also necessary to assure that civil affairs are in order. If some or all of the records cannot be obtained due to fire, war, or other upheaval affecting church and/or civil records, the testimony of one witness or even other proofs and testimony suffice.[106]

Besides the basic sacramental documentation and evidence of free status required of all applicants, a cleric or another person who was previously admitted to (1) another institute of consecrated life, (2) a society of apostolic life, or (3) a seminary must also present testimony from the respective superiors of those institutions. A cleric obtains such from the local ordinary, and others from either the major superior of the institute or society or the rector of the seminary. This official statement testifies to the fact of the applicant's prior admission to the institute, society, or seminary; it is helpful if this statement also gives a brief history of the person's life during that time and the circumstances of his or her departure.

In addition to the documentation required by the universal law, other documents, such as additional proofs of suitability and freedom of all applicants or only in certain circumstances, may be required by an institute's own law. This documentation might include official college transcripts, professional certificates or licenses, employment records, proof of military service or immigration status, letters of recommendation from the applicant's pastor or spiritual director,

---

[104] *CCEO* 453, §3 and 519 address in a general manner the documentation and testimonials to be gathered prior to admission to a monastery or to an order or congregation respectively, leaving specific application to the proper law.

[105] Besides attesting to a foundational level of formation in the faith, certificates of baptism and confirmation may alert admissions personnel that an applicant is actually a member of a *sui iuris* Eastern church. The licit admission of such a candidate requires an indult of accommodation either from the head of the *sui iuris* Eastern church (i.e., the patriarch, major archbishop, or metropolitan) or, in the United States, from the apostolic pro-nuncio who may grant such an indult. For a brief discussion of this matter see J. Abbass, "Canonical Dispositions for the Care of Eastern Catholics outside Their Territory," *P* 86 (1997) 336–338.

[106] See cc. 876, 894, and 1547–1573 and c. 1707 for cases of presumed death of the spouse.

etc. Since applications from older, more experienced candidates are increasingly common in the United States, additional supporting information about the candidate's prior life and work is increasingly important.

The final paragraph of the canon gives superiors broad discretion in seeking whatever other information they may need to make an informed decision regarding the admission of a candidate. This does not entitle the superior to secret information, but rather allows the superior to seek other information under secrecy, i.e., without making known the fact or the circumstances of the inquiry. This inquiry may, of course, entail sensitive matters, and the superior must carefully observe the candidate's right to a good reputation and to privacy (c. 220).

ARTICLE 2: THE NOVITIATE AND FORMATION OF NOVICES
[cc. 646–653]

Purpose of Novitiate

Canon 646 — The novitiate, through which life in an institute is begun, is arranged so that the novices better understand their divine vocation, and indeed one which is proper to the institute, experience the manner of living of the institute, and form their mind and heart in its spirit, and so that their intention and suitability are tested.

Life in a religious institute begins with admission to the novitiate.[107] The novitiate, a preparation for life in the institute, is an intense period of formation characterized by initiation into its life, mission, spirituality, and history; personal configuration to the paschal mystery; and discernment regarding the novice's vocation to religious life in this particular institute.[108] The novitiate and, in a

less intense manner, the subsequent periods of formation allow the candidates to discover, assimilate and deepen their identity as religious.[109] During the novitiate the responsibility for growing into the institute's particular way of following Christ through an integral initiation rests both with the novices themselves and with those charged with their direction.

The initiation which characterizes the novitiate goes far beyond simple instruction. The location of the novitiate, its programs, instructions, experiences, and activities are all directed toward deepening this initiation and testing the authenticity of the call to a life commitment in this particular institute.[110] Each institute should have its own program of formation reflecting its own nature, charism, and spirituality.[111] This program should be grounded in the institute's way of life and should incorporate the fundamental principles of Christian and religious formation, but it should be flexible enough to be adapted over time to changing circumstances.

The Novitiate House

Canon 647 — §1. The erection, transfer, and suppression of a novitiate house are to be done through written decree of the supreme moderator of the institute with the consent of the council.

§2. To be valid, a novitiate must be made in a house properly designated for this purpose. In particular cases and as an exception, by grant of the supreme moderator with the consent of the council, a candidate can make the novitiate in another house of the institute under the direction of some approved religious who acts in the place of the director of novices.

§3. A major superior can permit a group of novices to reside for a certain period of time in another house of the institute designated by the superior.

---

[107] *CCEO* 455 and 520 indicate how the novitiate begins in a monastery or in an order or congregation, but the Eastern code has no norm comparable to c. 646.

[108] *PI* 47.

[109] *PI* 6.

[110] *PI* 47.

[111] See c. 659, §§2–3 and *PI* 4.

Besides being a program, the novitiate is also a place. Its location and circumstances, both critical issues throughout the history of religious life, testify to the importance of the novitiate experience for the life of the individual and of the institute. The three paragraphs of this canon govern the fundamental decisions regarding the location of the novitiate and the exceptions which may be made regarding it.[112]

The supreme moderator of the institute, with the consent of the council, has the authority to establish, transfer, or suppress a novitiate house (§1).[113] Even in large international institutes with numerous provinces, only the supreme moderator may take such an action, which is executed by means of a written decree.[114] If the novitiate is to be established as a new foundation, i.e., in a location where there is no other formally established house of the institute, the diocesan bishop must also give his written consent.[115] One novitiate or several novitiates may be established for the entire institute. For good reason, there may be more than one novitiate within a given province. The novitiate program should be conducted in a culture and language familiar to the novices to avoid cultural disorientation or language barriers which could obstruct the intensive spiritual journey which begins in the novitiate. This also enables appropriate vocational discernment by formators familiar with the culture. In establishing a novitiate, care should be taken that the house and environs be appropriate to the institute's collective witness to poverty[116] while still being accessible to courses and other means of formation. On the other hand, the novitiate community should not be located within an apostolic community totally inserted within a poor milieu because, at this stage, the demands of formation must take precedence over the apostolic advantages of insertion among the poor.[117]

The novitiate is generally made in a house designated by formal decree as the novitiate (§2). Several exceptions to this rule are possible which, with conditions carefully observed, provide both for appropriate accommodation to particular circumstances and for the conditions conducive to this period of intense formation. The first truly exceptional case involves a novice whom the supreme moderator, with the consent of the council, determines may make his or her novitiate in another house of the institute and under the direction of a religious who assumes the role of director of novices. Reasons prompting this decision might include age, language, culture, physical disability, or other circumstances, together with the conviction that the particular novice could not benefit fully from the program in the established novitiate. The religious selected to serve as director of this novice is not required to be perpetually or definitively professed as is the director of novices,[118] but the supreme moderator would hardly choose a temporarily professed member or a member in the process of transfer to direct a novice.[119]

The second exception to the general rule of conducting the novitiate in the designated novitiate house permits the novices as a group to be assigned to another house of the institute for a definite period of time (§3). A temporary relocation

---

[112] CCEO 456, 521, and 522 provide norms for determining where the novitiate will take place for candidates for a monastery or for an order or congregation respectively. The superior of a monastery must consult with the council before locating the novitiate in another monastery; its consent is not required as it is for superiors of orders and congregations and for superiors in Latin institutes.

[113] The present legislation first appeared in 1969 in the special norms of RC 16–19, which gave to the highest superior the authority to determine the place of the novitiate, with the consent of the council. Prior to these norms, permission from either the Holy See or the diocesan bishop was required.

[114] See cc. 35–58.

[115] See cc. 609–612 regarding the erection of houses of the institute.

[116] Canons 634, §2 and 640.

[117] PI 28 and 50.

[118] Canon 651, §1.

[119] Williamson implies that the director assigned to an individual novice making novitiate in another house represents the director of novices but is not himself/herself the director. See CLSGBI Com, 358.

might be occasioned by the accessibility to a particular workshop or ministerial experience, a vacation at another house of the institute, some potential danger (e.g., environmental, political, criminal, etc.) at the novitiate house, or the opportunity to study the charism with other novices from the same religious tradition. The competent major superior makes this determination of venue and also designates the house; because this relocation is understood to be of short duration and not a change in location of the novitiate, the canon does not require the permission of the supreme moderator although the proper law may do so.

The third exception to the general rule pertains to apostolic religious institutes which may permit novices to have apostolic experiences outside of the novitiate house (c. 648).[120]

This canon presumes that a group makes up the novitiate community, a condition sometimes difficult to provide given the current dearth of candidates in some religious institutes. In order to provide a formative community, enrich the formation experience, and make the best use of human and material resources, many religious institutes participate in collaborative formation efforts. These efforts, some in effect for many years, take place both through permanent centers and through periodic services. In several regions of the United States where there are clusters of formation houses, novices often participate in weekly inter-congregational programs on theological, biblical, ascetical, and developmental topics pertinent to initial formation.

In addition, in a few instances, institutes stemming from the same foundation and/or sharing similar charisms have established common novitiates in which novices from several institutes are formed. These collaborative efforts, which provide the one or two novices belonging to a single institute the benefit of the community, vitality, and stimulus of a larger group of novices being formed in a similar charism, tradition, and spirituality, are formally established and carefully supervised by the respective major superiors. Together

the major superiors have sought dispensation from the Congregation for Institutes of Consecrated Life and Societies of Apostolic Life from canon 651, which requires that the director of novices be a member of the novice's own institute, before establishing such a novitiate.[121]

Length of Novitiate

Canon 648 — §1. To be valid, a novitiate must include twelve months spent in the community itself of the novitiate, without prejudice to the prescript of can. 647, §3.

§2. To complete the formation of novices, in addition to the period mentioned in §1, the constitutions can establish one or more periods of apostolic exercises to be spent outside the community of the novitiate.

§3. The novitiate is not to last longer than two years.

Canon 648 indicates the minimum and the maximum time of the novitiate.[122] The experience of novitiate is not tied to a particular location, but rather to the group which forms the novitiate community, wherever it may be located. This shift from *place* to *community* is consistent with the prior canon which allows the novitiate community, at the discretion of the major superior, to be located for a time at a house of the institute other

---

[120] See commentary on c. 648, §2.

[121] Inter-institutional novitiates which have existed in the United States include the Dominican Common Novitiate near St. Louis, Missouri, the Sisters of Charity Collaborative Novitiate in New Jersey, and, prior to their foundation in 1991 as a single institute as the Sisters of Mercy of the Americas, a Sister of Mercy novitiate which had several locations.

[122] *CCEO* 457 and 523 stipulate the length of the novitiate for monasteries and for orders and congregations respectively and take cognizance of absences. Two significant differences from the common law for Latin institutes are noted: 1) there is a requirement for a full and continuous three-year novitiate for monasteries in which there is no period of temporary profession; and 2) specific mention of apostolic experience as part of the novitiate is made only for orders and congregations, not monasteries.

than the novitiate house. Also, the designation of *twelve months,* instead of the *complete and unbroken year* as previously required, may shorten by a few days the minimum required (with the possibility of 360 days instead of 365 in some instances). It allows for some flexibility in accommodating changed circumstances in religious institutes and in facilitating the integration of the unique calling to apostolic religious life.

The second paragraph of the canon allows for periods of apostolic activity as part of the novitiate, a provision first introduced in *Renovationis causam* 23–25. Apostolic periods enable the novice to learn about and participate in the works of the institute; to experience community life as lived by its active, professed members; to come to know other members besides those in the novitiate community; to continue the process of integration of prayer and ministry; and to assess better his or her suitability to the life and ministry of the institute. If an institute wishes apostolic experience to be an integral part of the formation of its members, the constitutions should incorporate at least a general reference to this. The timing, location, content, and duration of these experiences are determined by the director of novices, within the parameters of proper law. The novice director also determines whether all or some of the novices are to be assigned to apostolic experiences, unless proper law determines otherwise. These apostolic experiences are to be selected because of their contribution to the formation of the novice and not primarily because of the needs of the apostolate.

Some candidates for the novitiate who are older and/or well established in their careers request a leave of absence from their positions to enter the novitiate. This arrangement assures the candidate of employment and some financial security should a decision be made to terminate the novitiate. A novice with a leave from the former place of employment may return there for his or her apostolic experience if the following conditions are fulfilled: 1) the work is related to the apostolic end of the institute, 2) the required twelve months of the novitiate have been completed, and 3) this experi-

ence truly contributes toward the formation of the novice for life in the institute, and the work is truly an apostolic activity.[123]

The maximum length of the novitiate is two years (§3), a time frame consistent throughout the change and experimentation of the last three decades. Acknowledging a two-year novitiate as normative, the code empowers the major superior, if the institute's proper law allows, to prolong the novitiate for up to an additional six months. This additional time may be granted if there is some uncertainty, either on the part of the novice or of the institute, concerning suitability for profession.[124] The norm of a two-year novitiate provides a reasonable time frame for discernment and decision-making, enabling the candidate to move forward with his or her life if the decision is against remaining with the institute or, alternatively, providing a solid foundation for the ongoing formation which will follow during the time of temporary profession and throughout the religious life.

Absence from the Novitiate

Canon 649 — §1. Without prejudice to the prescripts of can. 647, §3 and can. 648, §2, an absence from the novitiate house which lasts more than three months, either continuous or interrupted, renders the novitiate invalid. An absence which lasts more than fifteen days must be made up.

§2. With the permission of the competent major superior, first profession can be anticipated, but not by more than fifteen days.

Time spent in the novitiate is both gift and necessity. For those seeking to share its life, the religious institute provides the instruction, experiences, structure, support, and encouragement that will enable them to enter fully into the institute's life. This canon seeks to protect this period of intense formation, ensuring sufficient free-

[123] *PI* 48.
[124] See c. 653, §2.

dom, accountability, and continuity to accomplish its ends.[125] Any absence from the novitiate house exceeding three months (i.e., 90 days), whether continuous or intermittent, invalidates the entire novitiate, thus requiring an entirely new novitiate. Time spent within the novitiate community at another house of the institute designated by the major superior (c. 647, §3) and time spent on apostolic experiences (c. 648, §2) are not included when counting the invalidating three months. Examples of what might be included in those three months would be incidents of serious illness requiring hospitalization or recuperation elsewhere, family circumstances such as a parent's illness or death which would require the novice to go home, periods of military service, and periods of vacation or retreat which are not a part of the novitiate formation program. Any absence of fifteen days or more is to be made up, i.e., the number of days over fifteen is to be added to the length of the novitiate. However, common law does not require making up an absence of fifteen days or fewer.

There is another way in which the time of the novitiate may be shortened without any concern for making up the time (§2). The competent major superior may permit first profession to be anticipated by up to fifteen days. The major superior whose permission is required is the major superior competent to admit the novice to profession.[126]

Although this canon seems to emphasize numbers and the counting of days, its underlying concern is to protect the time set aside for novitiate from undue shortening or misuse. Perhaps even more so now than in the past, present-day circumstances require stability and a certain degree of distancing from former activities and relationships to enable the novices to enter fully and

peacefully into the intense journey they have undertaken. In all these considerations the element of time plays an important role.

Director of Novices

Canon 650 — §1. The scope of the novitiate demands that novices be formed under the guidance of a director according to the program of formation defined in proper law.

§2. Governance of the novices is reserved to one director under the authority of the major superiors.

This canon indicates the twofold obligation of the novice director: (1) to carry out the program of formation, and (2) to govern the novices.[127] It is a single responsibility with two distinct aspects. Each person enters the novitiate at a different level of human and Christian development, but brings a commitment to enter fully into the formation process and an expectation that the institute will provide instruction and direction and require certain things. The novice director serves as companion and guide in this mutual process in accord with the formation program determined in the proper law of the institute. Flexibility within the formation program and sensitivity and skill on the part of the director will enable the director to adapt the program to the needs of each novice, thus facilitating the spiritual journey.

The care and guidance of the novices are reserved solely to the director. Past practice, now modified, of physically separating the novices from professed members and of prohibiting communication between them, served to establish, *inter alia,* that the novices were under the exclusive direction of the novice director. With the greater interaction between professed religious and novices characteristic of current formation programs and with two or more persons often working together on formation teams, the well-

---

[125] *CCEO* 457, §2 and 523, §1 regulate absence during the novitiate. The Eastern code makes no provision for anticipating first profession.

[126] The superior competent to admit to the novitiate may not be the superior competent to admit to profession. The institute's proper law should clearly indicate both. See cc. 641 and 656, 3°.

[127] *CCEO* 458 and 524, §3 indicate the duties and responsibilities of the novice director in monasteries and in orders and congregations, respectively.

being of the novices requires the clarity of a single, clearly identified person as director.

The novice remains under the authority of the novice director as long as he or she remains a novice, even if temporarily residing elsewhere, e.g., during an apostolic experience, a vacation, or a home visit. Another member of the institute may be the superior of the house of assignment or the administrator of the apostolic work, but the novice director determines the parameters of the apostolic experience, the duration of the time away from the novitiate, and other elements of the novice's life.

The director of novices alone directs and governs the novices, but he or she in turn is subject to the authority of the major superior(s) of the institute, both as an office holder and personally, as a member of the institute. As director of novices, he or she is accountable for the formation program to the major superior who appointed him or her to the position. However, if the institute has a single novitiate in which novices from various provinces participate, the major superiors of the several provinces share with the supreme moderator responsibility for oversight of the novitiate.

The major superiors ultimately are responsible to see that the institute's program of formation is being carried out and that the novices are being appropriately directed. Major superiors need adequate information to be confident of the formation program and supportive of the director without interfering. For instance, a provincial superior from whose province novices are making their novitiate in a single congregational novitiate should be apprised regularly of their progress, and they remain free to contact the provincial superior. However, the provincial superior must be careful neither to undermine the authority of the director nor to interfere with the director's shaping of the formation process.

Formation Personnel

Canon 651 — §1. The director of novices is to be a member of the institute who has professed perpetual vows and has been legitimately designated.

§2. If necessary, the director can be given assistants who are subject to the director in regard to the supervision of the novices and the program of formation.

§3. Members who are carefully prepared and who, not impeded by other duties, can carry out this function fruitfully and in a stable manner are to be placed in charge of the formation of novices.

The director must be a perpetually or definitively professed member of the institute and be designated in accord with the law.[128] The first qualification seems self-evident, even minimalist; persons entrusted with forming new members in the life and spirit of the institute should themselves be steeped in its spirit and experienced in the many dimensions of its life. If an institute requires other qualifications for novice director, these should be found in its proper law. Additional qualifications might include a minimum age, a certain number of years in perpetual or definitive profession, or specific academic, apostolic, or spiritual experience.[129] Personal attributes should include an inner serenity, availability, maturity, patience, understanding, and a true affection for those entrusted to his or her care.[130]

The manner in which the director is designated is determined by the institute's proper law. Because this office is critical to the institute's life, the proper law often requires that the competent major superior appoint the director only after receiving either the advice or the consent of the council. The proper law of the institute may also indicate a term of office and/or a maximum time during which a person may serve in this office.

---

[128] *CCEO* 458, §1 and 524, §1 stipulate the qualifications of novice director for monasteries and for orders and congregations, respectively.

[129] Several qualifications from the 1917 code (*CIC* 559) no longer obtain, including the requirement that the novice director in a clerical institute be a presbyter. However, for Eastern church religious institutes, *CCEO* 458, §1 and 524, §1 require that the novice director be professed ten years. Furthermore, in a clerical order or congregation, he must be a presbyter.

[130] *PI* 31.

Depending on the number of novices, the circumstances of the novitiate, and the director's particular gifts, the director may be given assistants to help in implementing the program of formation. No qualifications are specified for these assistants, leaving the competent superior wide discretion in choosing them. They may work with the director on a full-time basis, or they may assist by giving certain instructions, by living in the formation community, by acting as consultants, or by any combination of responsibilities. However, an assistant to the director of novices holds an office and should be designated on a stable basis. The presence of assistants increases the gifts and skills available for the instruction and direction of the novices, expands the religious life models with whom they relate, and provides the possibility of a team approach to formation. Although the novice director remains responsible both for the governance of the novices and for the formation program, assistants can greatly enrich the quality of the formation experience. Besides those members of the institute who are named as assistants to the novice director, other persons—lay, clergy, or members of other religious institutes—may assist in forming the novices through educational presentations, reflection experiences, apostolic supervision, spiritual direction, or the like.

Because the novice director should be well prepared for this important work, some institutes have begun the practice of identifying the next director a year or two before the position will be vacant. This enables the novice director-elect to prepare himself or herself by study in theology, spirituality, or the history of the institute, by supervision in direction or counseling, or by whatever may be needed for the responsibilities ahead. Preparation for the ministry of formation is an arduous, time-consuming, and sometimes expensive endeavor. For this reason, larger and better established institutes are encouraged to assist newer foundations in this ministry by sharing members who are well prepared.[131]

[131] VC 66.

Upon taking office, the novice director should be freed of any other obligations which could impede the fulfillment of this primary responsibility. The novitiate is the place of the novice director's ministry, and any other responsibilities assumed would have to be flexible enough to allow the director to be consistently available to the novices. This does not preclude all other ministry, but cautions against obligations which could prove to be too time-consuming, emotionally draining, or geographically distant. In fact, limited apostolic ministry compatible with this primary responsibility may offer a beneficial counterpoint to the intense work of a director.

The Formation Process

Canon 652 — §1. It is for the director and assistants to discern and test the vocation of the novices and to form them gradually to lead correctly the life of perfection proper to the institute.

§2. Novices are to be led to cultivate human and Christian virtues; through prayer and self-denial they are to be introduced to a fuller way of perfection; they are to be taught to contemplate the mystery of salvation and to read and meditate on the sacred scriptures; they are to be prepared to cultivate the worship of God in the sacred liturgy; they are to learn a manner of leading a life consecrated to God and humanity in Christ through the evangelical counsels; they are to be instructed regarding the character and spirit, the purpose and discipline, the history and life of the institute; and they are to be imbued with love for the Church and its sacred pastors.

§3. Conscious of their own responsibility, the novices are to collaborate actively with their director in such a way that they faithfully respond to the grace of a divine vocation.

§4. Members of the institute are to take care that they cooperate for their part in the work of formation of the novices through example of life and prayer.

§5. The time of the novitiate mentioned in can. 648, §1 is to be devoted solely to the task of formation and consequently novices are not to be oc-

cupied with studies and functions which do not directly serve this formation.

Canon 652 describes in some detail the content and dynamic specific to formation during the novitiate.[132] Its fundamental purpose is to discern the vocation of the novices and to prepare them for life in the institute. The novice director has, in effect, been entrusted with the future of the institute. The director together with any assistants gradually forms the novices in its rich tradition and the perennial wisdom of the following of Christ while, at the same time, incorporating the unique gifts and future promise of each new member. While engaged in this task, the director must also arrive at a judgment about the existence of a religious vocation to this particular institute. Formation personnel must progressively evaluate whether each novice has the capacities required by the Church and the institute at this time and make appropriate recommendations to the responsible major superior.

The integral formation of the novice has physical, moral, intellectual, affective, and especially spiritual dimensions.[133] The second paragraph of this canon summarizes the areas to be included in the formation program of the novitiate. These include prayer and asceticism, study of scripture, practice and study of liturgy, understanding of consecrated life, the history and spirit of the institute, and an ecclesial awareness. The teaching function of the novice director will be fully engaged adapting this content to the different levels of human and Christian development of the novices. Any studies undertaken during the novitiate, whether for academic credit or within the novitiate house, should have for their primary purpose formation in religious life.

Formation is a collaborative enterprise engaging both the formation personnel and the novices.[134] Individual novices are primarily responsible for their own formation and are encouraged to participate actively in the formation process through spirited study and application, ongoing self-evaluation, and honest communication with the director. Ultimately, the novice must decide whether to request admission to first profession and bring the fruit of this formation to whatever way of life he or she lives out.

Although the novice director alone governs the novices and is responsible for the formation program, the other members of the institute bear a corporate responsibility for growing together and contributing to the development of new members. They do this by the witness of their lives, by their prayer, and by the general climate of community life to which they contribute and which in turn forms new members in the particular character and spirit of the institute.

The basic twelve months of the novitiate, i.e., the minimum period required by canon 648, §1, is to be devoted entirely to the formation of the novices for life in the institute. This will include study, prayer, manual or intellectual labor, and community experience, but all these activities should be directed toward the work of formation. Preparation for a profession, courses for matriculation, and purely secular study do not contribute directly to the formation which should mark this period and therefore should not be undertaken at this time. Even pastoral activity during this time should be assigned with the formation of the novice in mind rather than the needs of the apostolate or of the institute.

Departure and Termination

Canon 653 — §1. A novice can freely leave an institute; moreover, the competent authority of the institute can dismiss a novice.

§2. At the end of the novitiate, if judged suitable, a novice is to be admitted to temporary pro-

---

[132]*CCEO* 459 describes the content of the novitiate of a monastery and urges that novices be free of responsibilities which are incompatible with the novitiate. *CCEO* 525, §1 treats orders and congregations similarly. However, there is neither mention of the role of other members in forming novices nor explicit mention of the novice's responsibility to cooperate in this process.
[133]*PI* 33–35.

[134]*RC* 32 and *PI* 32.

fession; otherwise the novice is to be dismissed. If there is doubt about the suitability of a novice, the major superior can extend the time of probation according to the norm of proper law, but not beyond six months.

This canon discusses the several ways of terminating the novitiate.[135] In each situation the novice or the superior acts freely because the novice has no legal bond with the institute.

At any time during the novitiate up until first profession the novice may freely leave the institute, and the competent authority within the institute may dismiss the novice. The decision to terminate the novitiate usually entails mutual discernment on the part of both the novice and the director, reflecting the nature of the growing relationship between the novice and the institute. However, there is no obligation that such discernment take place or that the decision be mutual. Both parties are bound by the natural obligations of justice and charity which require kindness, truth-telling, and confidentiality at the very least. The superior competent to dismiss the novice and any internal procedures to be observed are to be found in the proper law. The superior competent to dismiss a novice is usually the superior competent to admit to the novitiate; some institutes require the advice or consent of the council before the superior acts. A record of the novice's admission to the novitiate and some indication of the circumstances surrounding its termination should be retained for future reference, should the candidate reapply to the same or to another institute or to a seminary.

When the time for the novitiate prescribed by the institute's proper law has been completed, the novice is either to be admitted to temporary profession or dismissed. If a novice's suitability for profession is still in question, the major superior may extend the novitiate for up to an additional six months. The question of suitability may arise from the candidate, the novice director, or the major superior; however, the recommendations of the formation personnel who have worked directly with the novice should weigh heavily in arriving at such a decision. The major superior competent according to the institute's proper law makes the decision to extend the novitiate, observing any requirements of proper law.

ARTICLE 3: RELIGIOUS PROFESSION
[cc. 654–658]

In the Church's tradition, religious profession is considered to be a special and fruitful deepening of one's baptismal consecration.[136] By religious profession a person, responding to God's call, freely hands over his or her life to the following of Christ according to the way of life of a particular institute. Profession brings together the action of God and the response of the person, and the religious institute provides the context and support for living the call faithfully.[137]

Religious profession takes place during a liturgical celebration described in the *Rite of Religious Profession*; this rite, approved for use in 1970[138] and contained in the *Roman Ritual,* supplants all former ceremonials or rituals. The rite provides flexibility, however, to incorporate particular traditions and customs of each institute. In this rite the competent religious superior (whether lay or cleric), acting in the name of the Church and the institute, receives the vows of those making profession. The rite of profession ordinarily takes place in the context of the eucharistic liturgy, thus uniting the self-offering of those making profession with the eucharistic sacrifice.

[135] *CCEO* 461, providing for the termination of the novitiate of a monastery and alternatives at its completion, is almost identical to c. 653. *CCEO* 525, §1 applies these same regulations to an order or congregation.

[136] *LG* 44 and *VC* 30–33.
[137] See c. 607 and *PI* 10.
[138] The revised *Rite of Religious Profession* is dated February 2, 1970. See *AAS* 62 (1970) 553. The rite was translated by ICEL and was emended twice, in 1975 and 1984. The most recent edition in English was published by the USCC in Washington, D.C. in 1989.

Religious Profession

Canon 654 — By religious profession, members assume the observance of the three evangelical counsels by public vow, are consecrated to God through the ministry of the Church, and are incorporated into the institute with the rights and duties defined by law.

Religious profession has three distinct but inseparable effects: (1) members assume by public vow the observance of the three evangelical counsels of chastity, poverty, and obedience; (2) members are consecrated to God through the action of the Church; and (3) members become incorporated into a particular religious institute with all concomitant rights and duties.[139] In addition, a cleric being admitted to a religious institute is simultaneously incardinated into it and excardinated from his own proper diocese at the time of perpetual or definitive profession.[140]

Vows are considered to be public when they are accepted in the name of the Church by a legitimate superior; otherwise they are considered to be private.[141] In religious profession the vows are accepted by the religious superior competent according to the institute's proper law who acts in its name and in the name of the Church.

The common law does not identify or regulate which institutes will have their members profess solemn vows and which profess simple vows.[142] Instead, each institute identifies in its own proper law the obligations and rights resulting from pro-

fession. In some institutes the obligations and rights are equivalent to those formerly legislated for solemn vows, e.g., renouncing the capacity to own property. In the proper law of other institutes the obligations and rights of profession are equivalent to those formerly identified with simple vows, e.g., retaining the capacity to own property but renouncing its independent use.

The evangelical counsels of chastity, poverty, and obedience may be explicitly enunciated in the profession, or, in accord with the institute's tradition, they may be included by reference to the institute's constitution or its way of life. Some religious institutes also include in the act of profession an additional vow particular to their spirit and charism, e.g., a vow of stability or service of the poor. Each religious institute develops its own formula for profession which is included in its constitution; if the proper law permits, institutes may allow members to personalize the vow formula by affixing some additional expression of intention or devotion at the beginning or at the end of the common vow formula.

The obligations and rights assumed with profession may vary for those making temporary profession and those making perpetual profession. For example, in many institutes voting rights may be restricted for those under temporary profession. The obligations and rights acquired with profession include, but are not limited to, those obligations and rights enunciated in canons 662–672 which are further specified and elaborated in the proper law of the institute.

Temporary Profession

Canon 655 — Temporary profession is to be made for a period defined in proper law; it is not to be less than three years nor longer than six.

Temporary profession is a relatively new phenomenon in the history of religious life. It was first introduced as a common practice for Latin rite religious in 1857 during a period when new apostolic institutes of both men and women were proliferating, and the provision appears to have

---

[139] *CCEO* 462; 469; 526, §1; 531; 533; and 534 regulate the effects of profession, whether temporary or perpetual, in a monastery, order, or congregation. Perpetual profession in a monastery or an order involves renunciation of goods and the capacity for subsequent ownership. Besides those effects specified for religious belonging to Latin church institutes, upon perpetual profession in an Eastern church monastery a member loses by the law itself any office he or she may have held.

[140] Canon 268, §2.

[141] Canon 1192, §1.

[142] Both *solemn* and *simple* vows are acknowledged but not defined in c. 1192, §2.

been directed toward giving institutes more latitude in screening out members.[143] With the 1917 code a three-year period of temporary profession became normative, but this period could be extended if, upon the completion of the three years, the member was not yet of age to make perpetual profession.[144] In 1969 *Renovationis causam* retained the requirement of temporary commitment prior to perpetual profession, extended the period of temporary profession up to nine years, and added the option of another type of commitment or bond at the completion of the novitiate, i.e., the making of a promise to the institute.[145] This alternative form of commitment was eliminated with the promulgation of the 1983 code.[146] Presently each institute in its proper law is to establish the particulars of temporary profession, i.e., length of profession, evaluation procedures, requirements for renewal, and the like, while remaining within the parameters of a three-year minimum and a six-year maximum.[147] However, canon 657, §2 gives to the competent superior the ability to extend the period of temporary profession for up to nine years in particular cases.

---

[143] S.C. super Statu Regularium, ency *Neminem latet,* March 19, 1857, in *Collectanea in Usum Secretariae S. Congregationis Episcoporum et Regularium,* ed. G. Bizzarri (Rome: Propaganda Fide, 1885) 853–855. See L. Iriarte, "Giving Support to One's Vocational Journey," *Consecrated Life* 21:1 (1997) 79.

[144] *CIC* 574.

[145] *RC* 7 and 34.

[146] On February 2, 1984 CRIS issued the decree *Praescriptis canonum,* which reiterated the provisions of c. 653, §2 and made provision for those religious currently bound by promises, some of which had been indeterminate in length, rather than temporary profession. *AAS* 76 (1984) 500; *CLD* 11, 91–92.

[147] *CCEO* 463, 465, and 526 provide for temporary profession in monasteries, orders, and congregations. However, in accord with their proper law many monasteries have only perpetual profession preceded by a three-year novitiate. In orders and congregations temporary profession is made for a minimum of three and a maximum of six years.

Validity of Temporary Profession

Canon 656 — For the validity of temporary profession it is required that:
    1° the person who is to make it has completed at least eighteen years of age;
    2° the novitiate has been validly completed;
    3° admission has been given freely by the competent superior with the vote of the council according to the norm of law;
    4° the profession is expressed and made without force, grave fear, or malice;
    5° the profession is received by a legitimate superior personally or through another.

This canon identifies five requirements necessary for the validity of temporary profession.[148] The absence of any one of these requirements, whether known or occult, invalidates the profession. The first requirement, a minimum age of eighteen, is consonant with the minimum age of seventeen required for admission to the novitiate.[149] The proper law of the institute may require a higher age. The second requirement, the completion of a valid novitiate, presupposes that all the conditions for admission to the novitiate have been fulfilled. Furthermore it requires that the duration and location of the novitiate have complied with canons 647–649 and that any other conditions for validity required by the proper law of the institute have been satisfied.[150]

Temporary profession is a juridic act which alters a person's ecclesial status and brings into existence legal obligations on the part of both the person and the institute. For the candidate validly to make religious profession, he or she must be admitted by the superior competent to do so after

---

[148] *CCEO* 463 and 527 provide norms for the validity of temporary profession.

[149] Canon 643, §1, 1°.

[150] A novice in danger of death who so requests may make profession although he or she has not completed the novitiate. Should the novice recover, he or she resumes the prior status as novice. *AAS* 15 (1923) 156–158 and *Comm* 15 (1983) 72–73.

obtaining either the advice or the consent of the council according to the institute's proper law.

To be valid, this juridic act of the superior must be free from coercion of any kind. The superior competent to admit to profession may differ from the one competent to admit to the novitiate; each should be clearly designated in the proper law of the institute. Any other provisions of universal or proper law, e.g., consultation with the monastic chapter, must also be followed. The formal act of admitting to profession follows upon the written or explicit request on the part of the candidate.

Further, for the validity of temporary profession it is necessary that the profession be made freely, clearly, and unambiguously. Usually this is accomplished by pronouncing the profession aloud in the presence of witnesses, but other modes of profession are possible, e.g., written profession for someone unable to speak. Because profession is an act of the will requiring the consent of the candidate, any force, grave fear, or deceit on the part of the candidate invalidates the act.[151]

Finally, the profession must be received by the superior competent according to the proper law either personally or through one delegated to receive the profession. Contrary to prior practice in some religious institutes, especially diocesan religious institutes, it is not the bishop or the priest presiding at the liturgy who receives the profession, but the superior competent according to the proper law of the institute.

Renewal of Profession and Perpetual Profession

Canon 657 — §1. When the period for which profession was made has elapsed, a religious who freely petitions and is judged suitable is to be admitted to renewal of profession or to perpetual profession; otherwise, the religious is to depart.

§2. If it seems opportune, however, the competent superior can extend the period of temporary profession according to proper law, but in such a way that the total period in which the member is bound by temporary vows does not exceed nine years.

§3. Perpetual profession can be anticipated for a just cause, but not by more than three months.

Canon 657 regulates the renewal, extension, and termination of temporary profession and provides for the anticipation of perpetual or definitive profession.[152] This canon should be read in conjunction with the proper law of the institute which specifies these matters for the particular institute.

At the completion of the period of temporary profession the common law provides three options: (1) renewal of temporary profession, (2) commitment by perpetual or definitive profession, or (3) departure from the institute. Each action has juridic consequences. The possibility or requirement of renewal of temporary profession,[153] its duration, and procedures for admission to renewal of vows are governed by the institute's proper law. Since the period of temporary profession is intended to be a time of continuing formation, an assessment of suitability is important at each juncture. Expectations and goals are reviewed with the candidate, ministerial growth is

---

[151] See commentary on c. 643, §1, 4°. Under the 1917 code the bishop or his delegate usually visited institutes of women religious and privately interviewed each candidate for profession to ensure that she was requesting profession freely and with an adequate understanding of the obligations entailed.

[152] *CCEO* 526, §2 governs admission to renewal of temporary profession in an order or congregation, c. 546, §1 protects the freedom to leave the order or congregation at the expiration of temporary profession, and c. 547, §1 regulates the exclusion of a member in temporary vows from subsequent profession. *CCEO* 463 and 465 apply these same regulations to monasteries in which temporary profession is customary in accord with their proper law. No provision is made for anticipation of perpetual profession.

[153] In some institutes members make annual vows during the period of temporary profession, thus requiring at least three successive professions before the religious is eligible to make perpetual profession.

assessed for members of active apostolic institutes, and the local community in which the temporarily professed member has lived frequently participates in the evaluative process in some manner. Following the candidate's request for renewal of profession, the competent superior, acting in accord with the proper law, may admit the member to renewal.

The second option at the completion of the period of temporary profession is perpetual or definitive profession. If the requisite minimum of three years in temporary profession has elapsed and if the proper law of the institute permits, the candidate may request perpetual or definitive profession. Ongoing direction and evaluation are expected components of the formation process during the entire period of temporary profession, but most institutes provide for a special evaluation and discernment prior to the recommendation of the formation personnel and the decision of the competent superior. Once the decision to admit has been conveyed to the member, a time of immediate preparation usually precedes the actual profession, in accord with the institute's proper law and program of formation.

The decision to exclude a member from subsequent profession, whether temporary or perpetual, requires a just cause and consultation with the council.[154] The proper law may specify requirements or guidelines in addition to those required by the common law. The decision not to admit to subsequent profession is not a dismissal *per se* which is considered to be punitive in nature,[155] but it has many legal effects similar to dismissal. Although the final decision belongs to the competent superior in accord with the proper law, a decision not to admit a candidate to subsequent profession, either temporary or perpetual (definitive), should not, in justice, come as a surprise to the candidate. Written documentation in the candidate's file, copies of which have been made available to the candidate, should presage and support the decision.

A member's decision not to request either renewal of temporary profession or perpetual or definitive profession *or* the superior's decision not to admit the member results necessarily in the third alternative, i.e., departure from the institute. This development at the expiration of temporary profession terminates the legal bond between the institute and the member, now no longer a religious.

The second paragraph of the canon gives to the competent superior the freedom to extend, in particular cases, the time designated in the proper law for temporary profession.[156] Unless the proper law states otherwise, the superior determines whether an extension is to be granted, as well as its duration. The extension may be for a few months, a year, or longer provided that the total time in temporary profession does not exceed nine years. Reasons for extension might include uncertainty on the part of either the member or the institute regarding a permanent commitment, the desire for more apostolic experience, the member's young age, the necessity of completing certain components of the formation program, etc.

The final paragraph of the canon affords the religious institute some flexibility in determining the actual date of profession. The perpetual or definitive profession may be anticipated by up to three months if there is just cause. This canon provides an exception to canon 655, allowing the minimum period of three years in temporary profession to be shortened by up to three months. Examples of a just cause which might occasion the anticipation of a perpetual or definitive profession might include the demands of an apostolate or of an institute of higher learning at which the mem-

---

[154] Canon 689 deals with the causes and procedures related to exclusion of members under temporary profession from subsequent profession.

[155] For the dismissal of a member, even one in temporary profession, c. 689 requires a cause which is sufficiently serious, external, imputable, and juridically proven.

[156] In contrast to *RC* 37, which permitted nine years in temporary profession for all members if the religious institute so chose, the current law allows nine years only by way of exception.

ber is a student, the advantage of celebrating profession on a particular community feast or during a particular liturgical season, the constraints of immigration law, or the like.

This canon speaks only of anticipating perpetual or definitive profession; it does not address the question of anticipating the renewal of temporary profession. However, since some flexibility is accorded to the competent superior in a more serious matter (i.e., anticipating perpetual or definitive profession), presumably renewal of temporary profession, a lesser matter, could also be anticipated up to the same amount of time (three months) and for a similar just cause.[157]

Two other expectations related to perpetual or definitive profession are found in other sections of the code. Canon 668, §1 requires that religious execute a will valid in civil law at least before perpetual or definitive profession.[158] Such a will provides for any property which the religious possesses at the time or might later inherit. Many religious institutes require that this will be executed prior to first profession or as soon thereafter as the religious is of age to do so.

A second concern is the obligation of the religious institute to notify the parish of baptism of the perpetual or definitive profession of any of its members (c. 535, §2).[159] The institute should also notify the parish of baptism of any subsequent indult of departure, as the parish records should accurately reflect the person's canonical status.

Validity of Perpetual Profession

Canon 658 — In addition to the conditions mentioned in can. 656, nn. 3, 4, and 5 and others imposed by proper law, the following are required for the validity of perpetual profession:

1° the completion of at least twenty-one years of age;

2° previous temporary profession of at least three years, without prejudice to the prescript of can. 657, §3.

To the requirements for a valid temporary profession already enumerated in canon 656, 3°–5°, this canon adds two additional requirements for a valid perpetual or definitive profession.[160] For this kind of permanent commitment the member must be at least twenty-one years old and must have completed at least three years in temporary profession, allowing for the anticipation of perpetual or definitive profession (c. 657, §3). If any of these five requirements is lacking, the profession is invalid.

With the minimum age of eighteen required for admission to temporary profession and the minimum requirement of three years in temporary profession, the only circumstance in which the minimum age of twenty-one for perpetual or definitive profession might be an issue would occur if the perpetual or definitive profession were anticipated (c. 657, §3). Such a convergence of circumstances would be unusual and, if deemed appropriate, a dispensation from the minimum age of twenty-one could be sought from the Congregation for Institutes of Consecrated Life and Societies of Apostolic Life for pontifical institutes or from the diocesan bishop for diocesan institutes.

To these basic requirements for validity of perpetual or definitive profession found in canons 656 and 658, the proper law of a religious institute may add other requirements for validity.

---

[157] *RI* 35. The 1917 code explicitly allowed the anticipation of temporary profession by up to one month, but did not permit anticipation of perpetual or definitive profession (*CIC* 577, §2).

[158] *CCEO* 530 similarly requires that members of orders and congregations execute a will valid in civil law at least prior to perpetual profession. Before perpetual monastic profession members must renounce ownership of all goods while any subsequent goods acquired by the member accrue to the monastery (*CCEO* 467–468).

[159] *CCEO* 470 and 535, §2 require notifying as soon as possible the pastor of the parish in which the baptism is recorded.

[160] *CCEO* 464 gives norms for the validity of perpetual monastic profession and *CCEO* 532 regulates perpetual profession in orders and congregations.

ARTICLE 4: THE FORMATION OF RELIGIOUS
[cc. 659–661]

The three canons in this article deal with the post-novitiate formation of religious. The purpose of all formation is to enable persons to discover and then to assimilate and deepen their identity as religious.[161] While initial formation is directed toward assisting the person to discern his or her vocation and to acquire sufficient understanding and autonomy for living the religious commitment, ongoing formation assists the religious to become increasingly open to the Spirit through attentiveness to the "signs of the times," to deepen fidelity to the charism, and to integrate and develop these movements through dynamic growth in the concrete circumstances of life.[162]

This article on formation for all religious is an innovation with this code; previously only the formation of those religious destined for ordination was addressed. Formation is now understood as a right and an obligation for all religious and a life-long and co-responsible process.

Continuing Formation

Canon 659 — §1. In individual institutes the formation of all the members is to be continued after first profession so that they lead the proper life of the institute more fully and carry out its mission more suitably.

§2. Therefore, proper law must define the program of this formation and its duration, attentive to the needs of the Church and the conditions of people and times, insofar as the purpose and character of the institute require it.

§3. Universal law and the program of studies proper to the institute govern the formation of members who are preparing to receive holy orders.

The first paragraph of this canon identifies the dual focus of formation in a religious institute:

living fully the life of the particular institute and participating suitably in its mission. First profession inaugurates a new phase of formation in which the fruits of the novitiate are reaped and human and spiritual growth continues.[163] This period benefits from both the dynamism and the stability of the recent commitment.[164] Members in temporary profession continue in formation following a definite program outlined in the proper law of the institute. Its format, scope, and duration will vary from institute to institute inspired by the institute's charism and in keeping with its purpose and character.[165] Formation at this stage will include establishing a basic theological and philosophical foundation if that has not already been done, preparation for and integration of apostolic ministry, and spiritual guidance directed toward the discernment of God's action in the person and in the world. The institute also has the responsibility of providing favorable conditions for growth in consecrated life, a formative community life, and competent directors.[166]

The third paragraph of the canon addresses the formation of those religious preparing for ordination. Besides being formed as religious they are also formed in accord with the universal law and the institute's own law regarding preparation for ordained ministry.[167] The conciliar teachings regarding the preparation of priests are concretized in canons 242–264, and the NCCB has developed

---

[161] *PI* 6.

[162] *PI* 67 and *VC* 69–70.

[163] *CCEO* 471 and 536 address continuing formation in monasteries and in orders and congregations, respectively. Neither canon specifically addresses the period following first profession. Those members preparing for ordained ministry are governed by the canons on the formation of clerics, especially *CCEO* 330 and 340.

[164] *PI* 59 and *VC* 68.

[165] For instance, *PI* 75 states that formation in contemplative religious institutes will be less intensive and more informal than that in apostolic religious institutes because of the stability of the members and the absence of outside activities in contemplative religious institutes.

[166] *PI* 60.

[167] CCE, *Ratio fundamentalis institutionis sacerdotalis ad normam Novi Codicis Iuris Canonici Recognita* (Vatican City: Libreria Editrice Vaticana, 1985), *AAS* 62 (1970) 321–365.

in its *Program of Priestly Formation* norms adapted to the pastoral situation in the United States.[168] Although the entire formation of priests and deacons is imbued with a pastoral dimension, the pastoral formation of those in religious institutes should be adapted to the end of their institute, thereby fostering in them the gift which their respective institute is to the Church.[169]

Components of Continuing Formation

Canon 660 — §1. Formation is to be systematic, adapted to the capacity of the members, spiritual and apostolic, doctrinal and at the same time practical. Suitable degrees, both ecclesiastical and civil, are also to be obtained when appropriate.

§2. During the time of this formation, offices and tasks which may impede it are not to be entrusted to the members.

This canon offers guidance for the formation of those in temporary profession and those preparing for ministry, both ordained and non-ordained.[170] It places the burden of organization, content, duration, and cultural and pedagogical adaptation of formation on the institute.[171] In accord with canon 659, §2, each institute is to have its own program of formation which is to be systematic, accessible to those being formed, and holistic. It should include spiritual, apostolic, doctrinal, and practical elements and should ordinarily lead to accreditation in the form of professional degrees and certification in the proposed areas of ministry.

This extended period of formation can be both rich and rigorous; those immersed in it need time for reflection and integration to benefit fully. Those in formation should be left free from other responsibilities which are not compatible with the expectations of the formation program. Even members who entered the institute with their professional preparation completed are still in formation during this time and they need to participate fully in the formation program, i.e., theological and scriptural study, apostolic experience, pastoral reflection and integration, and spiritual development. Apostolic commitments, ecclesial and social experiences, and academic study all need to be harmonized with the rest of the program for this stage of formation.[172]

Responsibility for Continuing Formation

Canon 661 — Through their entire life, religious are to continue diligently their spiritual, doctrinal, and practical formation. Superiors, moreover, are to provide them with the resources and time for this.

This brief norm captures one of the signal conciliar contributions to the renewal of religious life, calling for life-long formation for all religious.[173] Continuing formation, whether in apostolic or contemplative institutes, is an intrinsic requirement of religious life; no religious can claim to be completely conformed to Christ, and therefore none is exempt from the obligation of striving for human and spiritual maturity.[174] Each institute is to have as an integrated part of its formation program a plan which addresses the whole of life, is grounded in the institute's charism[175] and respon-

---

[168] Bishops' Committee on Priestly Formation, *Program of Priestly Formation*, November 1992, 4th ed. (Washington, D.C.: USCC, 1993). Both the canons and the *PPF* address the spiritual, pastoral, theological, philosophical, doctrinal, scriptural, and ecumenical formation of those preparing for ordained ministry.

[169] *VC* 105.

[170] *CCEO,* 471, §1 briefly specifies the purposes of continuing formation for monasteries.

[171] *PI* 60 identifies this burden as a grave responsibility of the institute.

[172] *PC* 18 cautioned against assigning a religious to an apostolic ministry immediately after the novitiate. See also *PI* 62–65.

[173] *PC* 18 and *ES* II: 15–19. The Eastern code has no comparable norm.

[174] *VC* 69.

[175] *VC* 68; *MR* 11 speaks of the charism as a gift of the Spirit to the founder/foundress, which is to be transmitted to the followers to be lived, deepened, and developed.

sive to the signs of the Spirit, and leads toward conversion of heart.

Formation is a dynamic process with intellectual, spiritual, apostolic, and physical dimensions. Religious superiors must provide encouragement, leadership,[176] resources, and time for this process to continue, but the individual religious have the primary responsibility to take advantage of formation opportunities and dispose themselves to the action of the Spirit.

CHAPTER IV
THE OBLIGATIONS AND RIGHTS
OF INSTITUTES AND THEIR MEMBERS
[cc. 662–672]

This chapter contains some, but not all, of the obligations and rights of religious institutes and their members. Besides those obligations and rights articulated here, other obligations and rights pertinent to religious institutes and their members can be found in the canons on the obligations and rights of all the Christian faithful (cc. 208–223); those of the ordained (cc. 273–289); the fundamental rights and obligations assumed with profession of the evangelical counsels (cc. 598–601); the basic autonomy of life pertaining to each institute (c. 586); the expectation that each member participate in the life of the institute (cc. 631–633), and certain procedural protections for both the institute and the members. In addition, other obligations and rights arising from particular responsibilities *as religious* can be found in the canons on juridic persons, temporal goods, the teaching office of the church, and the like.

The institute's proper law is important in the norms of this chapter as it has been elsewhere. Many canons in this chapter enunciate a general principle and leave its application or specification to the particular institute. The contemporary diversity among religious institutes reflects the shift from the uniformity characteristic of preconciliar

legislation to the more charism-specific expressions evident in the life and ministry of religious institutes today.

The phrases "rights and obligations" and "obligations and rights" are used interchangeably in various parts of the code.[177] In several of the following canons, as elsewhere in the code, the positing of an obligation gives rise implicitly to a right to the means of fulfilling it, e.g., time, information, opportunity, etc. All rights and obligations in the Church are grounded in the fundamental equality of the people of God and are understood in the context of the Church as a *communio*. Rights and obligations of religious institutes and of individual religious likewise are derived from the fundamental equality of all members before God and within the institute. The exercise of rights and obligations is moderated by the communal nature of a religious institute and its place within the larger ecclesial communion.[178] Rights and obligations, therefore, are claims *in* community and claims *of* community.

Following of Christ

Canon 662 — Religious are to have as the supreme rule of life the following of Christ proposed in the gospel and expressed in the constitutions of their own institute.

This canon expresses succinctly the Church's fundamental understanding of religious life as the following of Christ in a particular way.[179] The wording is taken from *Perfectae caritatis* 2,

---

[176] *PI* 71 states that superiors should designate a member of the institute to be responsible for continuing formation.

[177] See, for instance, cc. 212, §3; 223; 226, §2; 231; 278; 793; and 794.

[178] See c. 223.

[179] The Eastern code does not contain a separate section delineating the rights and obligations of members and of religious institutes. Instead, the articulation of obligations and rights is interspersed throughout title XII, chapter 1: *Monks and Other Religious* (CCEO 410–572). *CCEO* 410 refers to the religious state as a closer following of Christ, and *CCEO* 433, §1 identifies the monastery as the place where members strive toward evangelical perfection by observing the rules and tradi-

which states that the following of Christ as set forth in the gospel is the purpose of religious life and its supreme law, i.e., both its means and its goal. Each institute expresses in its constitutions the particular way in which it expresses and witnesses to that following of Christ, in accord with the gift it has been given.[180] The following of Christ, however, includes not only the obvious external obligations assumed with the evangelical counsels and the specific expectations of a particular rule, but moves beyond them to interior conversion of heart and mind, a gradual and life-long process.

Spiritual Exercises

Canon 663 — §1. The first and foremost duty of all religious is to be the contemplation of divine things and assiduous union with God in prayer.

§2. Members are to make every effort to participate in the eucharistic sacrifice daily, to receive the most sacred Body of Christ, and to adore the Lord himself present in the sacrament.

§3. They are to devote themselves to the reading of sacred scripture and mental prayer, to celebrate worthily the liturgy of the hours according to the prescripts of proper law, without prejudice to the obligation for clerics mentioned in can. 276, §2, n. 3, and to perform other exercises of piety.

§4. With special veneration, they are to honor the Virgin Mother of God, the example and protector of all consecrated life, also through the marian rosary.

§5. They are to observe faithfully an annual period of sacred retreat.

The way of life articulated in the previous canon needs to be nourished by an intentional and affective relationship with God. This canon reflects the importance of prayer in the religious life and presents a series of recommendations (with

one exception) encouraging religious to avail themselves of authentic sources of Christian spirituality which, with time and grace, lead toward greater union with God.[181] The canon is framed as a series of duties, but it could as easily be framed as a series of rights, for the end result of all the recommended exercises is dependent upon the interior disposition of the individual religious.[182] The individual religious is primarily responsible for fulfilling the exhortations enunciated in this canon since religious, like other adults in the Church, are presumed capable, knowledgeable, and responsible for their own actions. Comparable exhortations regarding the spiritual exercises of clerics and seminarians are found elsewhere in the code.[183]

Vatican Council II taught that the Eucharist is both the summit and source of the Christian life;[184] religious, who belong to the life and holiness of the Church, are encouraged to make every effort to participate as fully as possible in this central salvific event. This second paragraph of the canon also reflects the Church's current teaching regarding receiving communion as often as one participates in the liturgy, and it suggests a balanced approach to the reservation and adoration of the sacrament. While enunciating an ideal toward which the religious is to strive, the canon implicitly acknowledges that certain circumstances may preclude its fulfillment, e.g., the demands of the apostolate, geographic distance, ill health, personal dispositions, lack of ministers, etc.

The third and fourth paragraphs of the canon urge that religious regularly use the various means available for expressing devotion and growing in union with God. The reading of sacred scripture, a practice not generally encouraged in the past, is here recommended for religious. Mental prayer or

---

tions of the monastic life. No comparable statement is given regarding other religious.

[180] See c. 577.

[181] *CCEO* 473 and 538 identify the religious exercises expected of monks and other religious respectively. Both norms oblige the superior to see that these obligations are fulfilled.

[182] *PC* 2 (e).

[183] See cc. 276 and 246.

[184] *SC* 10.

meditation, celebration of the liturgy of the hours, veneration of Mary as Mother of God, recitation of the rosary, and other exercises of piety are also recommended; certain of these may be specified in the proper law of the institute while others may be a matter of personal preference.[185] Other pious exercises might include devotional renewal of vows, community feast days or fast days, ascetical practices during the penitential season, customary prayers for benefactors or on the occasion of a jubilee or upon the death of a member, the stations of the cross, and the like. For ordained religious, the celebration of the liturgy of the hours is an obligation arising from ordination.[186]

The final paragraph of the canon recommends an annual retreat, whose duration and manner may be specified in the institute's proper law with some flexibility usually left to the individual religious. The retreat is usually a time of quiet reflection, enabling the religious to set aside the usual order of life in order to enter into more intense prayer, to review his or her life direction, to receive spiritual guidance, and to be especially open to the action of the Spirit.

Interior Conversion

Canon 664 — Religious are to strive after conversion of the soul toward God, to examine their conscience, even daily, and to approach the sacrament of penance frequently.

The Christian life is a journey toward God, and the religious life, a particular form of the Christian life, witnesses to the single-minded focus of that journey. Religious are to strive toward God and the things of God,[187] always alert to those things which hold them back from God. To assist

in this continuing journey to God, two practices are recommended: (1) regular, even daily, examination of conscience, and (2) frequent approach to the sacrament of penance.[188] At the beginning of each Eucharist the penitential rite provides a regular opportunity to call to mind sins and failings, but the daily examination of conscience recommended here provides a more extended structure for this assessment before God. Furthermore, some religious institutes customarily gather as community at regular intervals or at certain seasons of the year for a communal examination of conscience and ritual of reconciliation.

The second means of conversion recommended by the canon is frequent approach to the sacrament of penance. This canon does not impose a strict obligation because every Christian, including religious, has great freedom in this regard.[189] No one is obliged to approach the sacrament of penance unless he or she is conscious of serious sin.[190] However, frequent recourse to the sacrament can be a source of grace to the religious, providing an opportunity to acknowledge sinfulness and weakness and offering the assistance of a spiritual guide.

Absence

Canon 665 — §1. Observing common life, religious are to live in their own religious house and are not to be absent from it except with the permission of their superior. If it concerns a lengthy absence from the house, however, the major superior, with the consent of the council and for a just cause, can permit a member to live outside a house of the institute, but not for more than a year, except for the purpose of caring for ill

---

[185] *PC* 6 and *ES* II: 21 urged religious institutes to cultivate a spirit of prayer, giving priority to meditation over multiple recited prayers.

[186] Canons 276, §2, 3° and 1174, §1.

[187] Canon 573, §1 speaks of religious as striving toward the perfection of charity, suggesting thereby the essence of God.

[188] *CCEO* 474 and 538, §3 address the frequency of confession for monks and for other religious respectively.

[189] See commentary on c. 630, §§2–3 for discussion of the choice of confessor. This norm notably modifies *CIC* 521, which obliged women religious to confess to the assigned confessor at certain times of the year or at least to approach him for his blessing.

[190] Canon 989.

health, of studies, or of exercising an apostolate in the name of the institute.

§2. A member who is absent from a religious house illegitimately with the intention of withdrawing from the power of the superiors is to be sought out solicitously by them and is to be helped to return to and persevere in his or her vocation.

This canon focuses on absence from the religious house; it is not primarily concerned with community life or common life. After articulating the expectation that religious ordinarily live in a house legitimately constituted by the superior (cc. 607–608), this canon specifies basic norms for absence from it.[191] The basic obligation itself and the norms of this canon are subject to some variation in accord with the proper law of the institute. Similarly, the manner in which the superior handles an unauthorized absence may also vary depending on circumstances. These norms apply equally to temporarily and perpetually or definitively professed members.

First, absence from a religious house necessitates permission from a superior. Second, if the absence is to be lengthy, the *major* superior's permission is required; hence, permission for shorter absences may be granted by a local superior unless the proper law indicates otherwise.[192] The institute's proper law may clarify what constitutes a lengthy absence, but more frequently it is left to the prudent judgment of the local superior, who must take into account the ordinary practice of the institute and the particular circumstances.

Third, when an absence is of such duration that the major superior is involved, permission for no more than one year may be granted for a just cause with the consent of the council. Fourth, if the ab-

sence exceeds one year, the major superior, with the consent of the council, may grant the permission only for the following reasons: (1) caring for the member's ill health, physical or mental, (2) pursuit of studies, or (3) exercising an apostolate in the name of the institute. Study has long been recognized as a reason for absence from the institute, but caring for ill health and exercising the apostolate in the name of the institute are more recent. If absence from the religious house is sought for some other reason, e.g., vocational discernment, exclaustration may be more appropriate.[193]

Frequently religious request permission for an extended absence to care for an aging parent. These requests arise largely as a result of such demographic changes as smaller families, greater mobility with many siblings living at great distances from the family home, and greater longevity of parents. Such an absence often results in a long-term commitment which is difficult to discontinue once begun and should be weighed carefully for its impact both on the religious and on the institute.[194] When there truly is a need, the institute should do what it can to support the religious in fulfilling this familial obligation. It may be possible to arrange for an apostolic assignment in keeping with the nature of the institute which will allow the religious to share in caring for the aging parent.[195]

The fifth and final norm of this canon provides for a member who is absent without permission and with the intention of withdrawing from the authority of the superior. The pastoral tone of the

---

[191] *CCEO* 478 gives norms for absence from a monastery and *CCEO* 495 and 550 provide for unlawfully absent members of monasteries and of orders and congregations respectively.

[192] For example, for monasteries of contemplative nuns which observe papal cloister, the reasons for which permission to be absent may be granted are limited, and such nuns also require at least the habitual permission of the local ordinary. *VS*, norm 7.

[193] See commentary on cc. 686–687.

[194] *FL* 65(b) urges that other arrangements be attempted to avoid excessively long absences, but accords the final decision to the superior.

[195] J. Torres, "Absence from the Religious House," *Con Lif* 19 (1995) 80–81 is of the opinion that, depending on the institute and its proper law, such an absence may be granted provided that the care of the parents is an apostolate undertaken in the name of the institute. However, Williamson states that care of aging parents does not qualify for granting an absence exceeding one year. See *CLSGBI Com*, 369. See also Rincón Pérez, in *Pamplona ComEng*, 455.

canon leaves much discretion to the prudential judgment of the superior, who is to seek out the absent member, offer assistance in returning, and encourage perseverance in the religious life. The canon stipulates no automatic consequences for the absent member, distinguishing the fact of absence from the complexity of human motivation.

Every effort is to be made to restore the member's relationship with the institute. However, if the member persists in the illegitimate absence, the superior may and probably should eventually take action against the member. An appropriate penalty may be imposed if the member has persisted in ignoring the warning of the superior,[196] or dismissal from the institute may result after an appropriate process if the member has been absent for six months or longer.[197]

Use of the Media

Canon 666 — In the use of means of social communication, necessary discretion is to be observed and those things are to be avoided which are harmful to one's vocation and dangerous to the chastity of a consecrated person.

This canon reflects an increasing awareness of the extraordinary influence of the communication media, for good and for ill.[198] The considerable benefits and potential dangers inherent in mass communications were addressed at Vatican Council II and in subsequent documents.[199] Religious, together with others, are encouraged to become skilled and discerning users of the various media of communication to further their own growth and

to ensure that the various media be effective vehicles of evangelization.[200] Among the means of communication would be the traditional print media of newspapers, books, and magazines, the imaging media of television, film, and video, and the burgeoning new electronic media of the Internet, teleconferencing, e-mail, and the like. Recent documents directed to religious caution them about the content, pervasiveness, and potential for manipulation by overly controlled media.[201]

Strictly speaking, this canon articulates neither a right nor an obligation; rather, it exhorts religious and religious institutes to exercise discretion regarding the means of communication. Misuse, abuse, or overuse of the media of communication can be detrimental to the individual religious and to community life. Individual religious may effectively isolate themselves from the community by absorption in TV, videos, films, or the Internet. Radios, stereos, and TV programs may intrude on the privacy of others, disrupt the spirit of recollection, and interfere with communal sharing. Media saturated with violence and sex may inure religious, and others, to suffering or inappropriate behavior, and indiscriminate exposure to certain themes and images may jeopardize chastity. On the other hand, mass communications make accessible information and experiences that can enrich individual religious and the community. Many institutes use these media to further continuing formation, enable consultation, facilitate the apostolate of the institute, promote vocations, share pertinent congregational information in a timely manner, and pursue many other initiatives. International institutes find the electronic media indispensable for regular communication, even, at times, conducting meetings by teleconference.

Contemplative institutes use the various means of social communication with great profit, but, in

---

[196] Canon 1371, 2°.

[197] Canon 696, §1.

[198] The Eastern code has no comparable norm for monks or other religious.

[199] *Inter mirifica,* December 4, 1964, *AAS* 56 (1964) 145–153; Pontifical Commission for Social Communications, *Communio et progressio,* January 29, 1971, *AAS* 63 (1971) 593–656; *FL* 34; *VC* 99; General Secretariat of the Synod of Bishops and the Pre-Synod Council, *Working Paper for the Synod of America, Origins* 27/13 (September 11, 1997) 208–209.

[200] See *CP* 110–111; *FL* 34; and *VC* 99, in which John Paul II says that religious "have a duty to learn the language of the media in order to speak effectively of Christ to our contemporaries."

[201] *FL* 4(d) and 34; *VC* 99.

keeping with their choice of a greater separation from the world, they must preserve carefully an atmosphere of recollection according to their proper law.[202]

Enclosure

Canon 667 — §1. In all houses, cloister adapted to the character and mission of the institute is to be observed according to the determinations of proper law, with some part of a religious house always reserved to the members alone.

§2. A stricter discipline of cloister must be observed in monasteries ordered to contemplative life.

§3. Monasteries of nuns which are ordered entirely to contemplative life must observe *papal* cloister, that is, cloister according to the norms given by the Apostolic See. Other monasteries of nuns are to observe a cloister adapted to their proper character and defined in the constitutions.

§4. For a just cause, a diocesan bishop has the faculty of entering the cloister of monasteries of nuns which are in his diocese and, for a grave cause and with the consent of the superior, of permitting others to be admitted to the cloister and the nuns to leave it for a truly necessary period of time.

This canon regulates the *fact* of cloister in every religious house and makes some general distinctions in the *type* of cloister among contemplative monasteries.[203] Religious institutes are to provide in their proper law for appropriate cloister given their character and spirit, and are to provide whatever safeguards are necessary to protect that cloister. The canon implicitly obliges individual religious to observe the cloister specific to that institute both for their own benefit and to assure all members of privacy, an atmosphere conducive to prayer and recollection, and an opportunity for community life.

Cloister[204] refers both to the law which regulates the separation of religious from those outside the religious house and also to the actual space (rooms, buildings, gardens, walkways, etc.) set aside for the exclusive use of the religious. The first paragraph of the canon incorporates both meanings, the second and third paragraphs refer primarily to the law of cloister, and the last paragraph refers primarily to the reserved space itself.

Cloister has a long and checkered ecclesial history which reaches back into the early Christian era. At times cloister was embraced voluntarily and at other times it was imposed by ecclesiastical authorities.[205] For most of its history the cloister required of women religious was more stringent than that required of men religious. This same pattern continues with the current legislation.[206]

For members of active apostolic religious institutes, the word *cloister* is largely synonymous with that part of the religious house reserved to the members alone. Each apostolic institute may determine what part of the house is to be so reserved, balancing the ministry of hospitality with the needs of the community. With the increase of smaller communities and of communities inserted among the very poor, the ability to reserve some part of the house to the members alone may be difficult; to achieve the purposes of this norm some institutes have determined that some parts of the house are reserved to the members alone during certain times of the day.

The last three paragraphs of the canon deal with the stricter discipline of cloister observed in contemplative monasteries. Several distinctions are made among these monasteries with different degrees of cloister expected accordingly. Monasteries of monks entirely ordered to the contempla-

---

[202] *FL* 34.

[203] *CCEO* 477 and 541 give norms for enclosure for monasteries and other religious respectively.

[204] Both *cloister* and *exclaustration* are derived from the same Latin root, *clausura,* meaning walls or enclosure.

[205] In 1298, through the apostolic constitution *Periculoso,* Boniface VIII imposed strict cloister on all women religious, even on institutes founded for active apostolates.

[206] For example, see cc. 609, §2 and 616, §4 which require Holy See involvement before a monastery of nuns may be erected or suppressed; similar requirements do not pertain to monasteries of monks.

tive life are bound to a stricter discipline of clois-ter, but they are not required to observe *papal* cloister.[207] *Papal* cloister, i.e., cloister regulated by the Apostolic See, is required of monasteries of nuns which are entirely ordered to the contempla-tive life, e.g., many Discalced Carmelite, Domini-can, Passionist, and Trappistine nuns. The current norms for *papal* cloister are contained in the in-struction *Venite seorsum,* published in 1969.[208] These norms, *inter alia,* require a material separa-tion, bind all in the monastery (postulants, nov-ices, and professed nuns alike), delineate who may enter the enclosure, and discourage egress from the monastery, effectively giving the local ordi-nary supervision of the enclosure.[209]

Other monasteries of nuns, i.e., those not en-tirely ordered to contemplation but which instead combine it with some apostolic work like teach-ing or retreat work, are not bound by *papal* clois-ter but observe a cloister adapted to their charac-ter. This cloister, considered to be constitutive of their way of life, is to be defined in the constitu-tion. Among such monasteries would be some Poor Clare monasteries, most monasteries of the Order of the Visitation, and certain monasteries in the Good Shepherd tradition.

The final paragraph of the canon, which deals exclusively with monasteries of nuns, places on the diocesan bishop the primary responsibility for interpreting the law of cloister, whether *papal* or constitutional, for all monasteries of nuns located

within his diocese. For a just cause he may enter the cloister; this would include a formal visitation (c. 628, §2), a pastoral visit, a business matter, a chapter of elections, and the like. For a grave cause the diocesan bishop with the consent of the superior of the monastery may permit others to enter the cloister and the nuns to leave. The canon contains an added caution that the nuns be permit-ted out of the cloister only for the length of time which is truly necessary. A grave cause might in-clude a physical danger, a serious illness, neces-sary construction or renovation of the monastery, some internal difficulty requiring outside interven-tion, and the like. The bishop may permit entrance to the cloister to such persons as workers, medical personnel, security personnel, specialized instruc-tors, confessors, and spiritual directors. His per-mission may be habitual; hence specific permis-sion may not be necessary for each instance. This paragraph of the canon reiterates in general terms *Venite seorsum* 7 and 8, which list the circum-stances and the categories of persons for which permission for entrance and egress may be given.

Regulation of Personal Property

Canon 668 — §1. Before first profession, mem-bers are to cede the administration of their goods to whomever they prefer and, unless the constitu-tions state otherwise, are to make disposition freely for their use and revenue. Moreover, at least before perpetual profession, they are to make a will which is to be valid also in civil law.

§2. To change these dispositions for a just cause and to place any act regarding temporal goods, they need the permission of the superior competent according to the norm of proper law.

§3. Whatever a religious acquires through per-sonal effort or by reason of the institute, the reli-gious acquires for the institute. Whatever accrues to a religious in any way by reason of pension, subsidy, or insurance is acquired for the institute unless proper law states otherwise.

§4. A person who must renounce fully his or her goods due to the nature of the institute is to make that renunciation before perpetual profes-

---

[207] For a discussion of some of the questions arising from the distinctions among contemplative monasteries see V. Dammertz, "The Juridical Structure of Contemplative Life," *Con Lif* 6/1 (1982) 33–39.

[208] SCRIS, *Venite seorsum,* August 15, 1969, *AAS* 61 (1969) 674–690.

[209] In addition to requiring the habitual consent of the local ordinary, egress from a monastery of nuns observing papal cloister also requires the consent (at least habitual) of the regular superior, if there is one. The regular supe-rior would be the major superior of the male religious order with which the monastery of nuns is associated; e.g., the superior general of the Order of Discalced Car-melites (men) would have oversight for those monaster-ies of Discalced Carmelite nuns under his care.

sion in a form valid, as far as possible, even in civil law; it is to take effect from the day of profession. A perpetually professed religious who wishes to renounce his or her goods either partially or totally according to the norm of proper law and with the permission of the supreme moderator is to do the same.

§5. A professed religious who has renounced his or her goods fully due to the nature of the institute loses the capacity of acquiring and possessing and therefore invalidly places acts contrary to the vow of poverty. Moreover, whatever accrues to the professed after renunciation belongs to the institute according to the norm of proper law.

Canon 600 describes the effects of the evangelical counsel of poverty assumed at the time of profession. Canon 668 regulates the practical expression of the obligations assumed with that evangelical counsel, distinguishing between the personal property of the individual religious and income generated by the individual but belonging to the institute. This canon encourages simplicity, communal sharing, and detachment from all that is not God. Each institute, in keeping with its nature, character, and spirit, will express these values and specify these practicalities in its own distinct manner.

The first paragraph of the canon provides for religious who, by reason of the constitution of the institute, may own personal property.[210] Three different acts are envisioned: (1) cession of administration of property; (2) disposition of use of property and revenue received from it; and (3) execution of a will.[211] The first two actions provide for the property of the religious while he or she is living, and the will provides for the disposition of the

property after death. These three actions are necessary because the religious retains the capacity for ownership of property but, in keeping with the obligations assumed with profession, is no longer canonically free to act independently regarding this personal property.

This norm requires that a religious who owns any property cede the administration and make provision for its use and revenue (sometimes called usufruct) before first profession. If the religious does not own any property at the time of first profession but subsequently becomes the owner of property, e.g., through inheritance, the religious must at the time of acquisition provide for the property by ceding administration and making provision for its use and revenue. Although the canon does not require that these two actions be done through civilly valid instruments, it is usually advisable that they be done so, particularly if the value of the property is significant; the requirements of the particular civil jurisdiction should be followed carefully. Once these instruments are in place, the religious should have no further involvement with the property or its revenue.

The religious may designate a family member, a law firm, a bank, the religious institute, or any other party to administer the property. The willingness of such a party to assume the responsibility and any pertinent fees should be ascertained before the designation. Should the religious institute be named, the treasurer of the institute or province and his or her successors in office, as the administrator of the goods of the institute, would assume this responsibility under the authority of the major superior. However, some religious institutes have constitutional restrictions against designating the institute as the beneficiary of the use and revenue of the property.[212] Absent such a restriction, the religious may cede administration and make provision for the use and revenue of the property as he or she chooses.

---

[210] Property is the generic term used to include real estate (e.g., land, buildings); incorporeal goods (e.g., rights, obligations, titles from which benefits accrue); works of art or other goods which have religious or historical value; shares, investments, funds, or arrangements of any kind which entitle the holder to some benefit.

[211] *CCEO* 467; 525, §2; and 530 regulate similar acts on the part of monks and other religious.

[212] Such regulations arose out of concern that novices/members be entirely free in disposing of their property and that there be no question regarding the motivation for admission to profession.

A will is to be executed at least before perpetual profession, whether or not the member owns any personal property. The proper law of many institutes requires that the will be executed prior to temporary profession if the religious is of legal age to do so. The will is to be executed in a manner and form which are valid under the civil law of the place of execution. Most institutes have a model will available which members may use or adapt to their particular needs. However, members are entirely free to use other forms and wordings if they are civilly valid. With the increased age of admission, institutes often find that a member has already executed a will prior to admission to the institute; there is no need to execute another will prior to profession unless the religious wishes to do so.

Once the determinations required in the first paragraph of the canon have been made, a religious may not alter them without permission. The second paragraph provides for changing the documents already in place and placing other acts regarding temporal goods.[213] The authority to permit a change in these documents or the placing of another type of business or financial act now resides with the superior competent according to the institute's proper law,[214] and any just cause may be sufficient reason to grant the permission. A just cause may be broadly interpreted to include any reasonable request, e.g., a substantial alteration in the value of the property, the death of the administrator or of an appointee, a family need, or even a need of the institute to which the religious wishes

to contribute. It is important to note that this norm requires the permission of the competent superior before the religious places any act regarding temporal goods; this would include goods belonging to the religious or to another person. Therefore, if a religious wishes to assume power of attorney for an ailing parent, act as executor of a will, or enter into a contract for employment, royalties, or the like, the competent superior's permission is required.[215]

Following the two paragraphs dealing with the disposition of personal property, the third paragraph delineates what is *not* the personal property of the member. After profession anything which a member acquires as a result of his or her work— e.g., stipends, salaries, bonuses, fees, royalties, and the like—belongs to the institute. Anything a member receives by way of pension, subsidy, or insurance likewise belongs to the institute, unless the proper law states otherwise. One exception would be pensions or other benefits accruing to an individual religious from employment prior to admission to the institute; many institutes determine such benefits to be personal property, whether they are received in a lump sum or paid out regularly over a number of years.[216] All other income, including pensions, insurance settlements, lottery winnings, death benefits, social security or Medicare payments, and salaries, even though issued in the name of the individual religious, belongs to the institute. To avoid any misunderstandings at a later time, a religious institute might wish to establish through a civilly valid document the financial relationship between the member and the institute.

Inheritances received from family members remain personal property, but other legacies, bequests, or gifts are usually the property of the institute, unless the proper law of the institute deter-

---

[213] *CCEO* 529, §4 provides for a change in the disposition of goods for those religious who, after perpetual profession, retain the capacity of ownership.

[214] Canon 583 of the 1917 code required that all those under simple vows, both men and women, have permission of the Holy See to change a will; those under solemn vows had already renounced any personal property as well as the capacity to own property. For a change in a document regarding cession of administration or the disposition of use and usufruct, nuns (i.e., members of monasteries), in addition to other conditions, had to receive the permission of the local ordinary and the regular superior, if the monastery was subject to regulars (*CIC* 580).

[215] See also cc. 639, §§2–3 and 672.

[216] For a discussion of pensions and subsidies received as a result of military service prior to religious profession see SCR, decr, March 16, 1922, *AAS* 14 (1922) 196. See also F. Morrisey, "The Vow of Poverty and Personal Patrimony," *CLS-GBIN* 72 (December 1987) 28–30.

mines otherwise. Inheritances become part of a person's personal property and must be handled as in paragraphs one and two above. In situations where there is doubt regarding the facts of the situation or the intention of the benefactor, the gifts are considered to belong to the institute.[217] The proper law of the institute should provide for the handling of personal gifts, e.g., a Christmas gift from a family member, while at the same time preserving simplicity of life, the bond of unity, and the common life of the institute; distinctions, opportunities, or access to material goods, e.g., cars, based on family wealth have no place in a religious institute.

The fourth and fifth paragraphs of this canon govern the renunciation of property by religious. Some institutes, by their nature, require members to renounce ownership of property, both that which is presently owned and any which might be acquired in the future. This obligation is specified in the constitutions of the institute. Religious belonging to such an institute become, by perpetual profession, canonically incapable of acquiring or owning property of any kind; and, as a result, any contrary act is considered invalid. Members of such institutes make this renunciation just before perpetual profession, to be effective at the time of the profession, and in a civilly valid form as far as possible.[218] Any property which comes to an individual religious after a profession with these effects, if accepted, accrues to the institute. A gift or a legacy may always be refused, but if the recipient who has renounced the capacity of ownership accepts the gift or legacy, the title to the property would revert to the institute, province, or house in accord with the proper law.

Other institutes which do not by their nature require a member to renounce personal property and the capacity of ownership may permit perpetually or definitively professed members to renounce property either in whole or in part. Typically, in such institutes, the proper law requires that in order to renounce property the member must have a certain number of years (e.g., ten or fifteen) in perpetual or definitive profession and obtain the permission of the supreme moderator. Any other provisions of proper law must also be carefully observed. If a religious in this type of institute renounces all or part of his or her presently owned property, he or she still retains the capacity to own property and may, in fact, acquire some additional property in the future. This additional property would be provided for at the time of acquisition either through a cession of administration, another renunciation, or a combination of both. The individual religious freely chooses the beneficiary of the renounced property. The beneficiary may be the institute, a family member or friend in need, a charitable endeavor, or some combination thereof. Some religious institutes limit what an individual religious may renounce in favor of the institute to protect both the individual and the institute.

Still other religious institutes do not permit renunciation, seeking rather to ensure that the member is provided for should he or she leave the institute in the future. In situations where renunciation is permitted, the supreme moderator should weigh carefully the facts of each case before acceding to a member's request to renounce his or her property.

Dress

Canon 669 — §1. Religious are to wear the habit of the institute, made according to the norm of proper law, as a sign of their consecration and as a witness to poverty.

§2. Clerical religious of an institute which does not have a proper habit are to wear clerical dress according to the norm of can. 284.

This canon articulates a general obligation of religious, namely, wearing the habit or dress of the institute, without specifying particulars.[219]

---

[217] See c. 1267, §1.

[218] Civil law in the United States does not recognize the renunciation of the capacity for ownership; therefore an additional civilly valid act of renunciation is required upon any subsequent acquisition.

[219] *CCEO* 476 and 540 regulate the habit or dress of monks and of other religious respectively.

What the habit or garb of the institute is and when it is to be worn are matters left to the proper law of the institute.[220] The obligation of wearing the habit of the institute is explained as a sign of consecration and a witness to poverty.[221]

The discretion left to each institute in this matter reflects the principle of subsidiarity operative throughout the norms for religious, providing for the widely diverse traditions, circumstances, and apostolates of religious institutes throughout the world. For most institutes deriving from a monastic tradition, the habit identifies the tradition and signifies certain dimensions of the monastic life, e.g., separation from the world, simplicity of life, manual labor. For some apostolic institutes of more recent origin, a distinctive habit is an anomaly and an accretion because apostolic institutes of both men and women often adopted as their attire the dress of the ordinary people of their age and locale.[222] Some institutes of women religious have traditionally worn a veil while others have never worn a veil.[223]

The continuing discussion surrounding the attire of religious, focused primarily on the dress of women religious, suggests that something else is at issue, something perhaps not integral to canonical principles and values. The dress of religious priests and brothers is rarely discussed by the media, the general public, or internal church documents.[224] On the other hand, the dress of religious women seems to function for some today in much the same way as enclosure functioned in an earlier era; in addition to being a sign of consecration, it is also seen as a source of protection against physical harm and a touchstone of authentic religious life. Each religious institute, in keeping with its nature, charism, and legitimate customs, has the responsibility to identify in its proper law how the members of the institute are to dress, and each member has the obligation to dress in accord with this.

The second paragraph of the canon deals with those clerical religious whose institutes do not have their own proper habit or dress. Such clerics are to wear clerical dress in accord with canon 284.[225] This norm directs clerics to wear suitable ecclesiastical garb in accord with the episcopal conference norms and legitimate local custom; however, it is silent regarding times, circumstances, or the particulars of dress. Religious clerics are bound by the norms of the place where they reside; episcopal conference norms and local customs may vary from region to region, requir-

---

[220] Williamson interprets this canon as requiring all religious to wear a distinctive habit. See *CLSGBI Com*, 374.

[221] *PC* 17 emphasizes the aspect of consecration, and *ET* 22 discusses the habit in the context of poverty.

[222] In the seventeenth century Vincent de Paul forbade the Daughters of Charity to wear a habit to avoid their being identified as religious and cloistered. Members of the several branches of the Congregation of Saint Joseph of Medaille which trace their origin to P. Medaille originally dressed as ordinary women of the French countryside. Elizabeth Seton and her American Sisters of Charity wore the simple black "widow's weeds" common in the United States during the early nineteenth century.

[223] The Religious Teachers Filippini (MFP), founded in Italy in 1694, the Missionary Servants of the Blessed Trinity (MSBT), founded in the United States in 1912, and the Sisters of Social Service (SSS), founded in Hungary in 1923, are examples of institutes whose members have never worn a veil.

[224] E. McDonough comments: "For members of non-monastic institutes of men, the habit—if they had one—was traditionally a significant form of clothing occasionally donned for community or liturgical exercises or for professional or pastoral services. In contrast, for all institutes of women—with rare exceptions—the habit was traditionally their primary identification symbol and was also often the only clothes they had to wear. Additionally, the habit issue highlights a significant difference in response to legal norms on the part of men and of women. That is, the 1917 code required that habits be worn by all members of all institutes at all times, both inside and outside the religious house. Women consistently did what the law said, while men rather consistently did not." From "Beyond the Liberal Model," in *Studies in Canon Law Presented to P. J. M. Huizing*, ed. J. H. Provost and K. Walf (Louvain: Louvain University, 1991) 105–106.

[225] In c. 669 the word *habitus* is translated as "habit" while it is translated as "garb" in c. 284 on the clothing of clerics.

ing adjustments on the part of these religious clerics when they minister in a different territory.

Obligation of the Institute to Support the Members

Canon 670 — An institute must supply the members with all those things which are necessary to achieve the purpose of their vocation, according to the norm of the constitutions.

The obligations of religious toward the institute are articulated in this chapter and elsewhere throughout the code.[226] This canon cryptically enunciates the overarching correlative obligation of the religious institute toward the members, highlighting the interdependence of rights and duties within the Church's legal system.[227]

The religious institute is charged with the welfare—spiritual, intellectual, physical, and material—of its members, to the degree that anyone can be responsible for another. The common law does not determine either what is "necessary" or what "achieving the purpose of their vocation" means, but gives some direction by indicating fundamental components of life in a religious institute. Two general categories of necessities for achieving the purpose of one's vocation suggest themselves: (1) those structures and processes required to participate in the life of the institute; and (2) material goods and support.[228] Included in the structures and processes would be such items as approved constitutions, formation—both initial and ongoing—some form of consultative and/or deliberative structures or procedures, community life, and an opportunity to participate in the mission of the institute. In the second category, material goods and support would be such things as food, clothing, housing, medical care, academic preparation for apostolic work (for active institutes), and other goods, equipment, and opportunities in keeping with the nature and spirit of the institute.

The appropriate provision and effective use of these necessities requires planning, allocation of resources, both human and material, and a comprehensive understanding of the charism and spirit of the institute. The constitutions of the institute indicate the required structures and processes. Other structures and procedures deemed necessary or useful may supplement those which are required according to the institute's proper law. That law and legitimate customs of the institute will give some guidance about what is appropriate with regard to material necessities. Superiors and councils are responsible to provide material goods (e.g., clothing, vehicles, computers, counseling, vacation, and the like) in keeping with the nature and spirit of the institute, while still allowing for mature choices by the members. The material needs of members of missionary, contemplative, and apostolic institutes may vary considerably.

Superiors in institutes with limited financial resources may need to make some difficult decisions regarding their allocation. For instance, the extraordinary expense entailed in providing one or two needy members with the best available medical or long-term psychological care may compromise the institute's ability to meet other needs such as preparing members for the apostolate or caring adequately for a large number of elderly members. In those institutes which are financially secure, the demands of evangelical poverty[229] and the collective witness to charity and poverty in the use of goods of the institute[230] may call for decisions to do without even what could be afforded.[231]

---

[226] For some of these obligations, see the introduction to this chapter.

[227] The Eastern code has no comparable norm.

[228] Other commentators organize these necessary elements differently. See D. Andres, *El derecho de los religiosos* (Madrid/Rome: Publicationes Claretianas y Commentarium pro Religiosis, 1983) 475; S. Euart, "Religious Institutes and the Juridical Relationship of the Members to the Institute," *J* 51 (1991) 103–118; and E. McDonough, "The Protection of Rights in Religious Institutes," *J* 46 (1986) 164–204.

[229] Canon 600.

[230] Canon 640.

[231] A reflection paper published in 1995 by a Joint CMSM/ LCWR Task Force on Health Care for Religious, *A Vi-*

In making and implementing decisions, superiors must remember the uniqueness of each member and that what is necessary will vary from member to member and from time to time. Professional preparation or updating, health-care needs, opportunity for family visits, time for leisure or sabbatical will differ greatly depending upon the person and upon circumstances. Usually the religious, being an adult, is capable of assessing and requesting what he or she needs. At other times, due to severe depression, addiction, total absorption in the apostolate, or the like, a member may need the special care and intervention of the superior so that he or she receives the assistance needed.

External Duties and Offices

Canon 671 — A religious is not to accept functions and offices outside the institute without the permission of a legitimate superior.

This canon specifies certain practical implications arising from the obligation of obedience which religious assume at profession.[232] In addition to governing their members within the ambit of the religious institute, superiors have a responsibility for members who minister elsewhere. Religious are obliged to obtain the permission of their legitimate superiors before accepting functions and offices outside the institute.[233] The purpose of this regulation is to ensure the availability

of the members for the life and mission of the institute and to foster congruence between the activities of members and the charism of the institute.

The canon is broadly written and encompasses a wide array of functions and offices. It affects religious employed full-time by a diocesan or supra-diocesan organization (e.g., Catholic Charities, a state Catholic conference, the NCCB, or a Vatican dicastery)[234] and those employed by one or several other religious institutes (e.g., director at a retreat center owned and operated by another religious institute, faculty member employed by a consortium of theologates, religious hired to oversee the corporate responsibility activities of another institute). Similarly, the canon covers religious employed by an institution, an agency, or an initiative with no formal church affiliation (e.g., a public university, a non-denominational hospice, a humanitarian organization such as Bread for the World and the like). Whatever form it may take, the work of a religious entails being sent in mission and in communion with the ecclesial purposes of the institute, thus requiring action on the part of the superior competent according to its proper law.[235]

This canon also applies to part-time and/or volunteer work in which a religious may be involved, e.g., serving as a trustee of an institution, significant involvement (not simply membership) in a professional society or other organization, regular ministry at a prison, hospital, or other institution, major writing commitments, regular engagement as a consultant, or any other obligation which entails considerable time and responsibility. Of particular concern would be situations involving the signing of contracts[236] or responsibility for the financial or legal affairs of another.

---

sion of Life, Health, Sickness, and Death for Religious, invites religious to face the ambiguities inherent in life, sickness, and death and to assess what is appropriate care for sick and/or aging religious.

[232] Canon 601 requires submission to legitimate superiors in accord with the proper law of the institute, and c. 598, §2 calls members to organize their lives in accord with this same proper law.

[233] CCEO 431, §1 requires that monks have the written permission of the major superior before accepting either dignities or offices outside the monastery. In addition, CCEO 469 stipulates that upon perpetual monastic profession a religious loses any office which he or she previously held.

[234] Canons 678; 681, §2; and 682 call for consultation, written agreements, and coordination when a religious is working under the aegis of a diocese. As general guides for good management and just procedure, these norms could reasonably apply to situations involving religious employed by other church institutions and agencies.

[235] ET 25.

[236] Canon 639, §§2–3 regulates the signing of contracts by individual members.

This canon is not intended to curtail the initiative of the religious or to limit apostolic outreach. It is intended to assure that the time and energies of the religious are expended on endeavors in keeping with the charism and nature of the institute and that the individual religious is not overextended. The manner of obtaining the required permission would be determined by the proper law and customary practices of the institute.

Before assuming any full-time function or office outside the institute, the religious should obtain permission from the appropriate superior in accord with the institute's proper law. The religious should also have the agreement and support of the superior (major or local depending on the proper law) for part-time and/or volunteer responsibilities which are supplementary to one's primary ministry but which may be time-consuming (e.g., presidency of a professional society, commitment to do a weekly radio spot), controversial (e.g., chaplain to a local chapter of Dignity, serving on the state parole board), or unusual for a member of that particular institute (e.g., social outreach activity in a cloistered monastery). For other functions and offices the local superior usually has the necessary authority. In circumstances in which permission is customarily given, it may be tacit or implicit. However, religious should be candid about their activities, keeping superiors informed of their involvements and being open to their advice and direction. Most religious enjoy a variety of interests, and religious institutes generally support those activities and avocations which are in keeping with the nature of the institute and its mission.

Other Obligations

Canon 672 — Religious are bound by the prescripts of cann. 277, 285, 286, 287, and 289, and religious clerics additionally by the prescripts of can. 279, §2; in lay institutes of pontifical right, the proper major superior can grant the permission mentioned in can. 285, §4.

Besides the general obligations assumed with religious profession, their specification in proper law, and the obligations enumerated in this chapter, this final canon obliges religious to observe certain additional clerical prohibitions and rules of conduct found in the canons on the obligations of clerics.[237] With one exception these regulations apply to all religious, both lay and clerical, but the manner in which they apply to religious may differ from the manner in which they apply to diocesan clerics.

The canons referenced in canon 672 apply to religious because, like the ordained, religious are by profession public ministers in the Church, and certain activities have been judged generally inappropriate or unbecoming for public ecclesial ministers. The canons referenced here express caution with regard to some activities and proscribe others, allowing for exceptions with the permission of the appropriate authority.

The regulations referenced in this canon which apply to religious are summarized here.[238] Canon 277 obliges them to prudence in associating with persons who might endanger consecrated chastity or scandalize the faithful, and it further obliges religious to comply with the pertinent directives of the diocesan bishop. Canon 285 prohibits certain occupations or activities because they are considered unbecoming or alien to public ecclesial ministers, and it prohibits the unauthorized exercise of certain secular offices and activities which entail the exercise of civil power or involve financial administration/transactions. Canon 286 prohibits the conducting of business or trade without the permission of the legitimate ecclesiastical authority. Canon 287 prohibits religious from taking an active role in political parties or labor unions unless certain conditions are met. Canon 289 discourages them from volunteering for military service and encourages them to avail themselves of applicable civil law exemptions from civil duties

---

[237] CCEO 427 binds monks and other religious to all clerical obligations found in the common law unless the law or the nature of the matter indicates otherwise.

[238] For fuller discussion of the content of these canons, see the commentary on the canons regarding the obligations and rights of clerics (cc. 273–289).

and offices. Canon 279, §2 obliges clerical religious to the same continuing education requirements that affect secular clerics. The competent superiors of the institute are to oversee compliance with these regulations, reproving and correcting religious who violate them.[239] In accord with the seriousness of the offense the superior may warn the religious, issue a precept, or even initiate a dismissal process if the religious is recalcitrant.[240]

The final clause in canon 672 indicates that the major superior may permit members of lay institutes of pontifical right to engage in certain activities and secular offices which entail financial responsibility (c. 285, §4).[241] The major superior may also grant such a permission to members of clerical institutes of pontifical right because the canon requires permission of the cleric's ordinary who, in clerical pontifical institutes, is the major superior.

Canon 672 is silent about who may grant the permissions and/or dispensations for the other activities, occupations, and functions proscribed in this rather comprehensive canon. The canons themselves variously state "according to the prescripts of particular law" (cc. 279, §2 and 285, §1); "with the permission of legitimate ecclesiastical authority" (c. 286); "in the judgment of competent ecclesiastical authority" (c. 287, §2); and "of their [proper] ordinary" (c. 289, §§1–2). The major superior of a clerical pontifical institute is the proper ordinary for its members, and, consequently, he may grant the permission required by canon 289. For members of other institutes (i.e., clerical diocesan institutes and lay pontifical institutes of both men and women) the permission required by canon 289 and the judgment called for by canon 287, §2 are twofold. A religious may not engage in these activities without the permission of his or her own superior in virtue of canon 671, and when these activities affect a particular church the further permission of the diocesan bishop, as coordinator of the apostolate of the diocese, appears to be required.[242] He may dispense religious from any of the prohibitions contained in these canons which impact the apostolate of his diocese.[243]

---

[239] Only after all other options are exhausted may the diocesan bishop involve himself in the disciplining of a religious. See cc. 679 and 683, §2.

[240] Canon 1392 refers specifically to religious who practice trade or business in violation of the canons, and urges punishment in accord with the seriousness of the offense; canon 696 addresses in a general manner the reasons for which a religious may be dismissed.

[241] Serving as power of attorney for an elderly parent, as legal guardian or conservator for a minor, or as executor of an estate would be examples of activities requiring permission of the major superior.

[242] The overlapping jurisdictions of the major superior and the diocesan bishop in this regard can be problematic; e.g., the charism of the religious institute may not be understood by the bishop; or the responsibilities of the activity or office may cross the boundaries of several dioceses.

[243] See c. 87, §1. However, recent practice suggests that the Holy See generally opposes granting dispensations from c. 285, §3, which prohibits assuming public offices entailing the exercise of civil power. However, developments in recent years, e.g., in South Africa and Vietnam, suggest that some dispensations have been granted.

BIBLIOGRAPHY

Bibliographical material for canons 617–672 can be found after the commentary on canon 746.

CHAPTER V
THE APOSTOLATE OF INSTITUTES[1]
[cc. 673–683]

Consecration cannot be considered apart from mission. Religious institutes are aggregates of consecrated persons ordered toward the mission of the Church in accord with the nature, spirit, and end of each institute. This is true whether religious institutes are dedicated to contemplation or apostolic action. It is likewise true whether the members serve in a corporate apostolate of the institute or perform an individual service in the name of the institute. Through prayer, penance, and charity, religious conform themselves ever more fully to Christ as they address human needs in various cultures and particular churches. In cooperation and collaboration with bishops and other Christian faithful, religious manifest ecclesial communion and build up the life and holiness of the Church.[2]

Primary Apostolate of Religious[3]

Canon 673 — The apostolate of all religious consists first of all in the witness of their consecrated life, which they are bound to foster by prayer and penance.

Religious witness to Christ by living a life of total dedication through the profession of the counsels. Prayer and penance sustain and nurture their consecration which testifies to the yearning of the Bride for union with her Spouse. The Church esteems this witness and recognizes it as the primary apostolate of religious in the mission of the Church. Following the example and teachings of Christ, religious testify that the world cannot be transformed without the spirit of the beatitudes.[4]

Institutes Dedicated to Contemplation

Canon 674 — Institutes which are entirely ordered to contemplation always hold a distinguished place in the mystical Body of Christ: for they offer an extraordinary sacrifice of praise to God, illumine the people of God with the richest fruits of holiness, move it by their example, and extend it with hidden apostolic fruitfulness. For this reason, members of these institutes cannot be summoned to furnish assistance in the various pastoral ministries however much the need of the active apostolate urges it.

This norm protects the patrimony of institutes dedicated entirely to contemplation by their very nature. Members of these institutes imitate Christ in his prayer on the mountain and offer their entire lives to God in service to others through divine worship, asceticism, contemplation, and charity. They hold a preeminent place in the Church, and the Christian faithful recognize their houses as sources of blessings and graces.

These religious contribute immeasurably to the apostolic fruitfulness of the Church. Since the contemplative life is of the very essence of these institutes, their members cannot be called to participate in apostolic works however great the need. Many offer hospitality and pastoral care through retreats, spiritual directors, and confessors in accord with the nature and end of the institute. The synod on consecrated life praised the witness of contemplative institutes and encouraged their contribution to interreligious dialogue

---

[1] There is no chapter on the apostolate of religious institutes in the Eastern code.

[2] *LG* 42, 44–46; *PC* 5–10, 14, 20; *ES* I: 23–40; *MR* 14, 28, 33–37, 46, 52; *VC* 48–53, 72, 96–99. See also G. Ghirlanda, "Relations between Religious Institutes and Diocesan Bishops," *Con Lif* 14/1 (1989) 37–71.

[3] The Eastern code has no canons comparable to canons 673–677.

[4] *LG* 31b, 44; *PC* 1, 2, 6, 24; *ET* 53; *VC* 33–35, 72.

in younger churches where other religions predominate.[5]

Institutes Dedicated to Apostolic Activity

Canon 675 — §1. Apostolic action belongs to the very nature of institutes dedicated to works of the apostolate. Accordingly, the whole life of the members is to be imbued with an apostolic spirit; indeed the whole apostolic action is to be informed by a religious spirit.

A wonderful variety of apostolic religious institutes exists in the Church. Their apostolates flow from the very nature and spirit of these institutes. Members of apostolic institutes experience and live the dynamic unity between contemplation and apostolic activity.[6]

§2. Apostolic action is to proceed always from an intimate union with God and is to confirm and foster this union.

Contemplation and communion with God sustain and nourish apostolic service. A solid spiritual life enables religious to see all things in God and God in all things. Christ exemplifies for these religious a profound communion with the Father joined to an intense life of service. They bring God to the people in their apostolates and the people to God in prayer.[7]

§3. Apostolic action, to be exercised in the name and by the mandate of the Church, is to be carried out in the communion of the Church.

As public juridical persons, religious institutes perform their apostolic activities in the name of the Church. At times a diocesan bishop invites a

religious institute to his diocese or consents to its request to erect a house and carry on works proper to it.[8] At other times the diocesan bishop may entrust certain works to a particular institute.[9] Both the religious serving in the apostolates proper or entrusted to the institute and an individual religious assigned by the competent superior to an apostolate perform their work in obedience to their superiors and the diocesan bishops.[10] Mindful of the distinct charism of religious institutes, the diocesan bishop encourages and coordinates their apostolates within the diocese.[11] He meets with major superiors in cordial and open dialogue to assure the organic communion of the diocese, to implement its pastoral directives, and to promote the nature and end of each institute.[12]

Apostolate of Lay Institutes

Canon 676 — Lay institutes, whether of men or of women, participate in the pastoral function of the Church through spiritual and corporal works of mercy and offer the most diverse services to people. Therefore, they are to persevere faithfully in the grace of their vocation.

The canon shows the regard of the Church for lay institutes of men and women and encourages fidelity to this special vocation. By its nature, life consecrated by the profession of the evangelical counsels is neither lay nor clerical.[13] The consecration of lay men and women constitutes a state of life complete in itself and of inestimable value to the Church and the individual apart from sacred ministry.[14] Lay religious require the formation and professional training needed for the witness and service they offer the ecclesial community. These

---

[5] *PC* 7, 9; *AG* 40; *ES* I: 36; *VC* 8, 101. See also SCRIS, "The Contemplative Dimension of Religious Life," March 1980, *CLD* 9, 410–431.
[6] *PC* 8, 20; *VC* 9.
[7] *PC* 8; *VC* 9, 74, 93.

[8] Canon 611, §2.
[9] Canon 681.
[10] Canon 678, §§1–2.
[11] Canon 394.
[12] *VC* 49.
[13] Canon 588, §1.
[14] *PC* 10.

religious are distinct from the laity by reason of their consecration which expresses a total self-donation to Christ and all people through a specific gift approved by the Church.[15]

Fidelity/Accommodation of Proper Works

Canon 677 — §1. Superiors and members are to retain faithfully the mission and works proper to the institute. Nevertheless, attentive to the necessities of times and places, they are to accommodate them prudently, even employing new and opportune means.

This norm exhorts superiors and other members to remain faithful to those works proper to the institute, that is, those flowing from the spirit of the founder and traditionally carried on by the members of the institute. Works such as education, health care, and social services need to be accommodated to contemporary time, and advancements in the various sciences. The synod on consecrated life encouraged religious in the apostolate of education and pointed to new apostolic endeavors.[16]

Associations Joined to Religious Institutes

§2. Moreover, if they have associations of the Christian faithful joined to them, institutes are to assist them with special care so that they are imbued with the genuine spirit of their family.

From earliest times lay persons have sought to learn and live the spirituality of certain religious institutes while following their own vocation in the world. At one time, only religious orders with apostolic indults could join lay persons to their institutes. Now many new forms of associations as well as oblates[17] and third orders secular[18] live the spirituality and participate in the works of particular religious institutes.[19] The law is concerned that institutes form these associates in the true spirit of the religious family without sacrificing the identity of the institute.

Associates extend the spirituality of religious institutes into the marketplace of the world. A great love of the Church and fidelity to the spirituality of the institute should characterize their endeavors.[20] Some associates hold positions of responsibility in the apostolic works of the institute. In such instances, they are accountable to the competent religious superiors in accord with the directives for associates and volunteers.[21] Like religious, they are subject to the diocesan bishop in these works and should cooperate and collaborate with others in promoting ecclesial communion.[22]

Obedience to Diocesan Bishop[23]

Canon 678 — §1. Religious are subject to the power of bishops whom they are bound to follow with devoted submission and reverence in those matters which regard the care of souls, the public exercise of divine worship, and other works of the apostolate.

As pastors of the particular churches, diocesan bishops promote, coordinate, and exercise due

---

[15] Canon 207, §2; VC 60.

[16] VC 96–99. New apostolates include evangelizing culture, participating in social communications, serving Christian unity, and advancing ecumenical and interreligious dialogues.

[17] Oblates are men and women joined to a monastery or an abbey while living out the spirituality of the institute in their lay vocation. The Benedictines and Premonstratensians have oblates.

[18] Third orders are associations of lay persons initiated by St. Francis. They are joined to mendicant orders (Franciscans, Carmelites, Dominicans, Augustinians). They have a rather complex structure of governance and enjoy a certain autonomy for their own lay vocation.

[19] ES I: 35; cc. 303; 311; 320, §2.

[20] ES I: 35; c. 311; VC 56.

[21] VC 56.

[22] Canons 311, 328–329.

[23] Cf. CCEO 415, §1. In this norm, religious are also subject to the authority of the local hierarch in matters which pertain to "what becomes the clerical state."

vigilance over all pastoral activity in their dioceses.[24] In works proper to the institute and in works entrusted to them, religious are subject to the authority of bishops in all that pertains to the care of souls,[25] the public exercise of divine worship,[26] and all other apostolic works.[27] Bishops should welcome and support the services of religious, while religious should work in full communion with the bishops. Through cordial dialogue, major superiors and bishops direct the pastoral initiatives of religious in accord with the needs of the people. Mutual trust, collaboration, and cooperation between bishops and religious will benefit the entire Church.[28]

Obedience to Superiors[29]

§2. In exercising an external apostolate, religious are also subject to their proper superiors and must remain faithful to the discipline of the institute. The bishops themselves are not to fail to urge this obligation if the case warrants it.

This paragraph shows the dual authority to which religious are subject in performing apostolic works. Superiors hold primary responsibility for the life and mission of their institutes. They serve as guides for their brothers or sisters in their spiritual and apostolic life.[30] Bishops, while not interfering in the internal life and governance, have the responsibility to promote and foster the life and works of the religious institutes present in the particular churches.[31]

Mutual Relations of Bishops/Major Superiors[32]

§3. In organizing the works of the apostolate of religious, diocesan bishops and religious superiors must proceed through mutual consultation.

All apostolic activity is directed to providing care for persons and responding to human need. Diocesan bishops who direct the pastoral life of the diocese and religious superiors who mission members of their respective institutes should meet periodically to discern how best to carry out the pastoral plan of the particular church. Bishops should recognize, esteem, and welcome the gifts of religious institutes, while superiors should offer their spiritual and pastoral resources in building up the life and holiness of the diocese. This mutual trust and cooperation witness to ecclesial communion and bring quality service to all in need.[33]

Religious Prohibited from Residing in Diocese[34]

Canon 679 — When a most grave cause demands it, a diocesan bishop can prohibit a member of a religious institute from residing in the diocese if his or her major superior, after having been informed, has neglected to make provision; moreover, the matter is to be referred immediately to the Holy See.

This norm seems to introduce an exception to the autonomy of life and governance the law grants to institutes of consecrated life and which diocesan bishops are obliged to preserve and safeguard.[35] Three conditions must be present before

---

[24] *CD* 35.4; *ES* I: 25–26; *MR* 53; cc. 375, 392, 394.
[25] Canon 150.
[26] Canon 834. This includes the public celebration of divine worship within the religious community.
[27] Canon 394.
[28] *VC* 49.
[29] Cf. *CCEO* 543. The canon addresses specifically a religious who is a pastor.
[30] Canon 596; *VC* 43.
[31] Canon 586, §2; *VC* 48–49.

[32] Cf. *CCEO* 416.
[33] *VC* 48–50.
[34] *CCEO* 415, §4 provides that religious who have committed a delict outside their house and have not been punished by their proper superior, having been warned by the local hierarch, can be punished by that hierarch even if they have lawfully left and have returned to the house.
[35] Canon 586, §2.

the diocesan bishop can prohibit a religious from living in the diocese: (1) there must be a most grave reason, (2) the proper major superior, having been informed, neglects to act, and (3) the matter is to be referred immediately to the Holy See.

It would seem that the very grave reason would be some action related to matters in which religious are subject to the authority of the bishops[36] or a violation of ecclesial or civil law causing public scandal. The case would be highly unlikely, since major superiors recognize their responsibility to address such complaints against a member.[37] The diocesan bishop should take great care to secure correct information lest the reputation of the religious and the good name of the institute be harmed.[38] The religious and/or the major superior would have the right to recourse to the Congregation for Bishops against an action of the diocesan bishop perceived to be unjust. The norm presents a serious problem in the case of a religious belonging to a *sui iuris* monastery or a small institute of diocesan right in which the only house or houses of the institute are situated in the one diocese or particular church.

Mutual Relations: Institutes and Secular Clergy

Canon 680 — Among the various institutes and also between them and the secular clergy, there is to be fostered an ordered cooperation and a coordination under the direction of the diocesan bishop of all the works and apostolic activities, without prejudice to the character and purpose of individual institutes and the laws of the foundation.

In carrying out the diocesan pastoral plan under the direction of the diocesan bishop, mutual trust, cooperation, and collaboration should exist among institutes and between them and the secular clergy.[39] All share the one Spirit and follow the one Christ in carrying out the mission of the Church. Faithful to the nature and purpose of their own institutes,[40] religious should recognize the authority of the diocesan bishop and esteem the vocations and pastoral service of clerics, other religious, and all persons in the diocese.[41] On his part, the diocesan bishop should understand and promote among the faithful of the diocese, particularly the secular clerics, the right and obligation of religious to observe the spirit and character of their institute ratified by ecclesiastical authority.[42]

The diocesan bishop can further promote this cooperation between consecrated persons and the secular clergy by providing courses in diocesan seminaries on the history and spirituality of consecrated life. Major superiors can include courses in the curriculum of their formation programs on ecclesiology and the spirituality of the secular clergy.[43]

Works Entrusted to Religious[44]

Canon 681 — §1. Works which a diocesan bishop entrusts to religious are subject to the authority and direction of the same bishop, without prejudice to the right of religious superiors according to the norm of can. 678, §§2 and 3.

At times the diocesan bishop recognizes that members of a certain religious institute could best accomplish certain works because of the nature and end of the institute and the professional training of the members. Parishes, parochial and diocesan schools, hospitals, health care facilities, and social services are a few examples of such works entrusted to religious. The bishop should know and appreciate the gifts of the religious in-

---

[36] Canons 678, §1; 1320.
[37] Canon 678, §2.
[38] Canon 220.
[39] *CD* 35.5.
[40] Canon 586, §1.
[41] Structures such as the diocesan synod (c. 463, §1, 1°, 5°, 9°) and the diocesan pastoral council (c. 512, §1) can facilitate the apostolic involvement of religious; see also *VC* 52.
[42] Canons 578; 586, §2.
[43] *ES* I: 28; *VC* 50.
[44] Cf. *CCEO* 415, §3.

stitutes in the diocese, while religious should respond generously to his request in sharing their gifts with the ecclesial community.

Works entrusted to religious by the diocesan bishop, even though they are proper to or derived from the very nature of the institute, remain under his authority.[45] This does not preclude the vigilance of the competent superiors responsible for the life and discipline of their members to see to their faithful execution of the works. Besides failing to serve the needs of the diocese, the religious institute could be liable for poor or inappropriate administration of church properties if its members were negligent.[46]

Written Agreement for Entrusted Works[47]

§2. In these cases, the diocesan bishop and the competent superior of the institute are to draw up a written agreement which, among other things, is to define expressly and accurately those things which pertain to the work to be accomplished, the members to be devoted to it, and economic matters.

When the diocesan bishop entrusts a work to religious, there are many issues to be addressed so as to ensure the harmonious carrying out of the work. Among such considerations are the following: personnel, responsibilities, compensation, health benefits, insurance, transportation, housing, provision for retreats, vacations, sick leave, etc. If such agreements are not drawn up, inequities and misunderstandings can occur for either or both the diocese and the religious institute. Such agreements assure justice and clarity for both the bishop entrusting the work and the competent superior who missions the religious.[48]

Agreements made for a specified period of time with provision for renewal of contract, revision after renegotiation, and the termination by either party within a designated period of time preclude problematic situations. In such agreements the bishop represents the diocese, while the superior represents the institute.[49] Religious serving as individuals in a diocesan or parochial apostolate should also have these agreements. This issue should be on the agenda in meetings between the diocesan bishop and religious superiors.

Ecclesiastical Office – Conferral[50]

Canon 682 — §1. If it concerns conferring an ecclesiastical office in a diocese upon some religious, the diocesan bishop appoints the religious, with the competent superior making the presentation, or at least assenting to the appointment.

The diocesan bishop provides for the discharge of ecclesiastical offices in the diocese,[51] while the competent superior missions the members of a religious institute. If the bishop requests a certain religious or the major superior presents a member to serve in a particular office,[52] the work should be compatible with the character and purpose of the religious institute.[53] The diocesan bishop appoints the religious to the office with the assent or consent of the competent superior.[54] It is well to have a

---

[45] ES I: 29(2); MR 57.

[46] ES I: 29(2); cc. 678, §2; 1289.

[47] The Eastern code has no canon comparable to this norm.

[48] For a comprehensive study of this issue, see S. Kain, *Written Agreements between Bishops and Religious for Entrusted Diocesan Works, CanLawStud* 550 (Washington, D.C.: Catholic University, 1996).

[49] ES I: 30.2; MR 57b; c. 520; V. De Paolis, "Schema of an Agreement for the Assignment of a Parish to Religious," *Con Lif* 12/1–2 (1987–88) 1: 129–146, 2: 218–242.

[50] Cf. CCEO 284, §2; 431, §1.

[51] Canon 157.

[52] See cc. 158–163. Major superiors have the right to present a religious to the diocesan bishop for an ecclesiastical office in the diocese in accord with the provisions of the law.

[53] Canon 680.

[54] For such offices, see cc. 473, §2; 475; 476; 482; 494; 521, §1; 546; 556; 564; 1420; 1421, §2; 1424; 1435; 1437; 1477. Some offices, such as vicar general, episcopal vicar, judicial vicar, pastor, parochial vicar, rector of a church, and chaplain, require that the religious be a priest.

written agreement between the diocese and the religious institute to afford stability for the diocese and the religious in carrying out the office.[55]

Ecclesiastical Office – Removal[56]

§2. A religious can be removed from the office entrusted to him or her at the discretion either of the entrusting authority after having informed the religious superior or of the superior after having informed the one entrusting; neither requires the consent of the other.

The norm addresses removal from office,[57] not deprivation of office[58] which involves a penal process. Either the bishop who appointed the religious or the superior who presented or consented to the member's accepting the office can remove him or her from an ecclesiastical office. The provisions of the written agreement should be honored. The norm provides that prior notification should be given to the other competent authority, so as to provide for the office or the assignment of the religious. It would seem that a just cause would prompt such an action.[59] It could be that the gifts of the individual religious are needed in a particular work of the institute outside the diocese. It is important to remember that the primary responsibility of the religious is to the institute, not to a particular diocese.

Arbitrary administrative changes by competent superiors or diocesan bishops without appropriate consultation with the parties involved offer poor witness of ecclesial communion, cause instability in service to the diocese, and contribute to lack of trust and poor relations between the bishop and religious. The pastoral care and spiritual needs of people must always be the ultimate concern of those responsible for missioning or appointing others to sacred ministry or apostolic service. Notification of removal should be given to the religious in writing by the bishop or religious superior.[60] It would seem, too, that if injustice is perceived, the grieved party can take administrative recourse to the appropriate congregation.[61]

Visitation of Diocesan Bishop[62]

Canon 683 — §1. At the time of pastoral visitation and also in the case of necessity, the diocesan bishop, either personally or through another, can visit churches and oratories which the Christian faithful habitually attend, schools, and other works of religion or charity, whether spiritual or temporal, entrusted to religious, but not schools which are open exclusively to the institute's own students.

Religious are subject to the diocesan bishop in all that pertains to the care of souls, public worship, and other apostolic works.[63] The diocesan bishop or his delegate visits the places where these works are carried out by religious during the ordinary pastoral visitation[64] or in case of necessity. Places to which the Christian faithful have access such as churches or schools could be works proper to the religious or works entrusted to the institute by the diocesan bishop.

While the canon employs the term "entrusted" regarding works of charity or religion, the phrase

---

[55] MR 58.

[56] The Eastern code has no norm comparable to this section of the canon.

[57] Canons 192–195.

[58] Canon 196.

[59] ES I: 32; MR 58; c. 193, §3.

[60] Canon 193, §4.

[61] The diocesan bishop would have recourse to CICLSAL, while the major superior and/or the religious would have recourse to the CFB. The procedure for recourse, including that for a religious removed from the office of pastor, would be in accord with cc. 1732–1739.

[62] Cf. CCEO §415, §2; 420, §3. Canon 420, §3 provides that the local hierarch must visit all religious houses if the major superior who has the right of visitation has not made a visitation after five years and, after being warned by the local hierarch, still has neglected to visit them.

[63] Canon 678, §1.

[64] Canons 392; 394; 396–397; 806, §1. See R. Hill, "The Apostolate of Institutes," in J. Hite et al., eds., A Handbook on Canons 573–746 (Collegeville: Liturgical Press, 1985) 219–220, note 34.

would seem to be used in the generic sense, since works proper to religious institutes are entrusted to them by the Church at the time of their approval as public juridical persons.[65] Also, the norm excludes from the episcopal visitation only those schools operated exclusively for the institute's own members. Such schools would be aspirancies, novitiates, minor or major seminaries, juniorates, and scholasticates which only candidates and members of the institute attend.

Correction of Abuses[66]

§2. If by chance he has discovered abuses and the religious superior has been warned in vain, he himself can make provision on his own authority.

Superiors have the primary responsibility for monitoring the activities of their members in living the life and performing the works of the institute. If the bishop discovers abuses while on his visitation of the apostolic works undertaken by religious, he should notify the competent superior. If the superior does not resolve the problem, the bishop can address and correct the abuse. Such abuses may be in reference to the ministry of the word, the celebration of the sacraments and sacramentals, the teaching of doctrine, the administration of temporal goods,[67] and conformity with the provisions of civil law. In case of serious violations, he can even impose penalties.[68] This right of the diocesan bishop follows from his pastoral responsibility for the care of souls in the diocese and his obligation to ensure compliance with the law.[69]

[65] *ES* I: 38–39.

[66] Cf. *CCEO* 415, §2; 417. Canon 417 provides that if abuses have crept into houses of institutes of patriarchal or of pontifical right or into their churches, and the superior, warned by the local hierarch, has failed to take care of these abuses, the hierarch is obliged to defer the matter without delay to the attention of the authority to whom the institute is immediately subject.

[67] Canon 392, §2.

[68] Canon 1320.

[69] Canons 381, §1; 392.

BIBLIOGRAPHY

Bibliographical material for canons 673–683 can be found after the commentary on canon 746.

CHAPTER VI
SEPARATION OF MEMBERS
FROM THE INSTITUTE
[cc. 684–704]

The canons dealing with separation are extensive and detailed in an effort to recognize and protect the rights of both individuals and institutes. Some of the norms which are fully developed here for religious institutes are subsequently referred to in the canons on secular institutes and societies of apostolic life.

The forms of separation from an institute are diverse: transfer from one institute to another; exclaustration, whether requested or imposed, as a form of temporary separation; and definitive departure through a requested indult or a process of dismissal.

Not all of these options are open to members not yet perpetually professed or definitively incorporated. In some cases the process differs, not only according to the status of the member, but also according to whether the institute is of pontifical or diocesan right.

As will be indicated in the following sections, the canons regarding separation of members from an institute are among those in the Eastern code's title XII which differ significantly from the Latin code.

ARTICLE 1: TRANSFER TO ANOTHER INSTITUTE
[cc. 684–685]

A religious seeking permission to transfer is contemplating a change of juridic incorporation while maintaining his or her religious consecration. Shortly after the Second Vatican Council, transfers were sometimes motivated by a desire for a more or less rapid pace of renewal. As changes in rules of life took place and certain aspects of discipline were relaxed, it also became more feasible for religious to pursue the contemplative life or a missionary vocation, which their physical stamina had not permitted before.

Years of experience have shown, however, that not all attractions to a more contemplative religious life are, indeed, true vocations to the cloister. Likewise, experience has shown the real hardship of leaving behind the shared charism and history of an institute in order to join another where one has no roots. One of the more important elements in successful transfers has been a common spirituality and/or orientation in mission between the two institutes.

Process of Transfer

Canon 684 — §1. A member in perpetual vows cannot transfer from one religious institute to another except by a grant of the supreme moderator of each institute and with the consent of their respective councils.

§2. After completing a probation which is to last at least three years, the member can be admitted to perpetual profession in the new institute. If the member refuses to make this profession or is not admitted to make it by competent superiors, however, the member is to return to the original institute unless an indult of secularization has been obtained.

§3. For a religious to transfer from an autonomous monastery to another of the same institute or federation or confederation, the consent of the major superior of each monastery and of the chapter of the receiving monastery is required and is sufficient, without prejudice to other requirements established by proper law; a new profession is not required.

§4. Proper law is to determine the time and manner of the probation which must precede the profession of a member in the new institute.

§5. For a transfer to be made to a secular institute or a society of apostolic life or from them to a

religious institute, permission of the Holy See is required, whose mandates must be observed.

Only a religious in perpetual vows may apply for a transfer to another institute; and in centralized institutes, only the superiors general can grant the permission with the consent of their councils. Although the canon does not clearly indicate this, it is the major superior of an autonomous monastery (c. 615) who can permit a transfer into or out of the monastery, observing other norms of proper and universal law.

A religious wishing to transfer should put his or her desire and the motivation for it in writing, requesting the consent from each institute. Such an individual may already have gone through a period of absence (c. 665) or a time of exclaustration, in order to begin to discern the potential move. He or she may have actually spent time with the intended institute.

The receiving institute has a right to request a reasonable amount of information about the prospective member, such as might be provided by a curriculum vitae. This would include apostolic experience and indicate if there have been periods of exclaustration or incapacitating illness. While normal rules of confidentiality must be observed, it would be irresponsible for a superior general simply to give consent for transfer of a religious who has a history of chronic physical or psychological illness or of substance abuse or who is facing accusations before a civil tribunal.

If a religious's own superior apparently refuses permission without sincere motivation, one may have recourse to higher ecclesiastical authority, according to the status of one's institute. However, this can usually be avoided by personal and confidential contact between the superiors general involved. While transfer is not a right, strictly speaking, a rightly motivated religious in perpetual vows should not be forced to request an indult of departure to change institutes.

In their arrangements, the superiors should clarify certain points such as whether, and for how long, the individual will be carried on the original institute's health insurance and the dates on which the probationary period will begin and end. Provision should also be made for suitable notification of the original institute of a decision for or against permanent incorporation in the new institute.

By the law itself, the probationary period for those transferring is a minimum of three years. The code leaves to proper law the specific determination of the length and manner of probation. Some institutes may permit or require more than three years. However, it should be remembered that the individuals involved are perpetually professed religious, not novices; they are learning the charism, spirituality, way of life, and mission of a new institute. They are not new to the practice of the evangelical counsels, but must integrate the way in which they are observed in the new institute.

The permission to enter into a probationary period does not oblige either the individual or the institute to complete the process with perpetual profession. The decision to admit the individual seeking transfer to perpetual profession in the new institute is a distinct decision left in the hands of the competent superior and council according to the proper law of the receiving institute. If the individual decides not to seek perpetual profession, or is not accepted, he or she must return to the original institute unless an indult of departure has been received. (The use of the term "secularization" in the canon seems to be inadvertent.) If the individual wishes an indult of departure, normally it should be requested through the original institute of which the religious is still a professed member.

The third paragraph of the canon provides for transfers within a particular monastic family. Here it is clearly stated that the competent superiors are major superiors. In this case, only the consent of the chapter of the receiving monastery is required at the level of the universal law. Any other norms of proper law must be observed. Since both monasteries are of the same family and share the same rule, a new profession is not required.

Because of the particular circumstances and traditions of monasteries of the same institute, federation, or confederation, this paragraph of the canon became the object of an authentic interpretation. It clarified that for such monasteries, religious in temporary profession were also included under paragraph three.[1]

When a proposed transfer involves institutes of a different type, the consent of the supreme moderators and their councils is no longer sufficient. For a religious to transfer to a secular institute or a society of apostolic life, or for a religious institute to accept a member of a secular institute or a society, the permission must come from the Holy See. The same Holy See permission is relevant to members of secular institutes (c. 730) and societies of apostolic life (c. 744, §2) who wish to transfer to institutes of a different type.

Because religious and secular institutes have diverse life-styles and approaches to mission, and because institutes of consecrated life and societies have quite different practices regarding the assumption and observance of the evangelical counsels, the members will have experienced different approaches to formation. All of these factors help explain why such transfers are reserved to the Holy See and why, at times, specific provisions or conditions may be included as part of the permission. The same norms apply regardless of whether the institute or society is of pontifical or diocesan right.

As interest grows in the life of hermits (c. 603) and of consecrated virgins (c. 604), it has been asked whether a transfer is possible in these cases. Technically it is not, since no institute or society with its superiors and councils is involved. Hermits and consecrated virgins are recognized canonically as individual, not collective, forms of consecrated life.

One who wishes to pass from a religious institute to one of these individual forms of consecration must request an indult of departure in the usual way. To enter into the new state, the individual must follow the necessary procedures for

[1] CodCom, April 29, 1987, *AAS* 79 (1987) 1249. See also L. Wrenn, *Authentic Interpretations on the 1983 Code* (Washington, D.C.: CLSA, 1993) 36–38.

being accepted by the diocesan bishop. If all of the necessary arrangements have actually been made, the indult may be requested to take effect at the time of receiving the consecration of virgins from the bishop or of pronouncing eremitical vows in his hands. Because of the great diversity between these life-styles, however, and because many bishops wisely require probationary periods before accepting individuals into these forms of consecration, it is often best, following serious discernment, to receive an indult of departure and then begin or continue preparations for definitive acceptance into the new state. Private vows or promises could be made if desired or if required by the bishop as a part of the preparation.

The question also arises about passing between approved institutes of consecrated life or societies of apostolic life and various forms of associations of the faithful. Once again, the canons on transfer cannot be applied. One wishing to make such a move must legitimately leave his or her institute or society and join the new association according to its internal procedures for accepting new members. Likewise, a member of an association cannot simply transfer to an institute of consecrated life or a society of apostolic life, even if the association is in the process of becoming such an institute or society. The individual must proceed through the normal steps for entering the institute or society.

Status of the Transferring Member

Canon 685 — §1. Until a person makes profession in the new institute, the rights and obligations which the member had in the former institute are suspended although the vows remain. Nevertheless, from the beginning of probation, the member is bound to the observance of the proper law of the new institute.

§2. Through profession in the new institute, the member is incorporated into it while the preceding vows, rights, and obligations cease.

The status of a religious during the probationary period is truly a provisional one. While still technically a member of the original institute, with the right to return there, the rights and obligations flowing from that membership are suspended in favor of observance of the proper law of the new institute. In particular, the observance of the evangelical counsels and the relationship to authority are those of the new institute. Active and passive voice in the original institute are suspended and are not acquired in the new institute until the religious actually becomes a member of it through profession.

When, in fact, the transferring religious makes perpetual profession in the new institute, there is not a new consecration to God, but a new locus of incorporation, with the resulting rights and obligations according to the new proper law.

A transfer between an institute with simple vows and one with solemn vows requires additional attention to the vow of poverty. One who originally professed solemn vows does not reacquire renounced personal patrimony; however he or she does reacquire the capacity to inherit which, canonically, had been lost. In the case of a future inheritance, attention will have to be given to the cession of administration and possibly to the adjustment of one's will.

If, however, the transfer is to an institute with solemn vows, a transferring religious will have to make the total renunciation called for in canon 668, §§4–5 at the time of the new profession. The previous act of cession will be terminated and the will adjusted as necessary.

In all cases, prior to the new profession any documents regarding personal patrimony must be appropriately reexamined and revised as necessary. The will and other legal documents pertaining to the individual would be returned at this point. With the new profession, the incardination of a religious deacon or priest passes to the new institute. In a word, the profession in the new institute effects full incorporation into it as a perpetually professed member.

Experience with such transfers has raised certain practical questions which an institute should consider. Since transferring religious have not interrupted their religious life, they should logically be inserted into the "ranks" of the new institute according to their original profession dates and celebrate jubilees according to the practice of the new institute, dating these accordingly from entrance into the novitiate, first vows, or perpetual profession in their original institute.

Institutes might profitably interpret how they will apply their constitution's requirements for certain offices. Where the role of superior or some other office requires a certain number of years of perpetual profession, it should be made clear, in the case of those who have transferred, if this will be calculated from their profession in the new institute or in the original one. This matter, unlike the matter of "rank" or celebrating jubilees, involves the issue of how much knowledge of and experience in the institute is necessary for fulfilling the office in question.

The transfer process in the Eastern code[2] is not limited to religious in perpetual vows. It almost always requires some intervention of external ecclesiastical authority and normally calls for the observance of the entire time of novitiate. Unlike the Latin code, the Eastern code has detailed provisions regarding monasteries.

ARTICLE 2: DEPARTURE FROM AN INSTITUTE [cc. 686–693]

Under the title of departure, the canons deal with the diverse categories of exclaustration and indults of departure, and with the specific questions of exclusion from further profession and of readmission to the same institute of one who has left it. Particular provisions are included for clerics.

Exclaustration

Canon 686 — §1. With the consent of the council, the supreme moderator for a grave cause can grant an indult of exclaustration to a member professed by perpetual vows, but not for more than three years, and if it concerns a cleric, with

[2] *CCEO* 487–488 and 544–545.

the prior consent of the ordinary of the place in which he must reside. To extend an indult or to grant it for more than three years is reserved to the Holy See, or to the diocesan bishop if it concerns institutes of diocesan right.

§2. It is only for the Apostolic See to grant an indult of exclaustration for nuns.

§3. At the petition of the supreme moderator with the consent of the council, exclaustration can be imposed by the Holy See on a member of an institute of pontifical right, or by a diocesan bishop on a member of an institute of diocesan right, for grave causes, with equity and charity observed.

It is useful to note from the outset that exclaustration is not the same as the permission to be absent from a house of the institute (c. 665). The "grave cause" warranting exclaustration is something beyond the care of health, the pursuit of studies, and the exercise of an apostolate in the name of the institute. The juridic status of an individual on exclaustration (c. 687) also demonstrates a conscious distancing of the individual from the institute, which is not the case in a simple permission of absence.[3]

The same expression of a grave cause (*gravi de causa*) is used here and in canon 688, §2 regarding the voluntary departure of a religious in temporary vows. By way of distinction, the case of a perpetually professed seeking an indult of departure requires the gravest of causes (*ob gravissimas causas,* c. 691, §1). These terms are not easily quantified or explained. Nevertheless, certain examples can suggest criteria for the judgment of superiors.

The discernment of one's vocation has frequently been cited as a motive for granting a period of exclaustration. Likewise, exclaustration is often

recommended as a transitional time for one who intends to leave definitively. However, it is doubtful if exclaustration is necessarily the best solution for resolving a vocational crisis and for receiving the help necessary in such circumstances.[4]

In many congregations, when a religious has a filial duty to care for an aged or dying parent, the matter is handled through a permission of absence. Such a religious is not seeking to separate, even temporarily, from the institute, but is impelled to accept a physical separation to fulfill this act of filial charity.

On the other hand, some religious, without permission, have undertaken apostolic projects which are not recognized by superiors as works in the name of the institute. After dialogue, a new apostolic assignment may be given but not accepted. Such a religious, hoping to maintain his or her project without leaving the institute, may seek exclaustration. While the religious has the right to ask, the superiors are not obliged to grant the request. The desire to avoid the demands of legitimate authority does not seem to constitute a grave cause for exclaustration.

By contrast, there may be cases of serious psychological needs which are better served by the distancing of exclaustration. Counseling undertaken to deal with trauma, such as abuse suffered in childhood, may also involve vocational discernment. Sometimes not all issues can be handled at the same time, but reasonable parameters should be set with the assistance of professional counselors who understand religious life.

Requests to the Holy See, or to the diocesan bishop, for an extension of exclaustration after three years must be judged in light of the motives indicated by the religious and the accompanying opinion of the superior and the council. The latter may also wish to recommend the duration of an extension. In some cases the Holy See, rather than determining the extension of exclaustration, may grant to the superior general the faculty necessary

---

[3] Some commentators consider a period of less than one year as absence (see c. 665) rather than exclaustration. See T. Rincón Pérez, in *Pamplona ComEng,* 467. However, the motives for a request and the implications of the resulting juridic status would apparently have to be taken into consideration in each case.

[4] J. Torres, "La procedura di esclaustrazione del consacrato," in *I procedimenti speciali nel diritto canonico* (Vatican City: Libreria Editrice Vaticana, 1992) 321.

to do so according to his or her discretion, and with the consent of the council.

A cleric requires the added prior consent of the ordinary of the place where he intends to reside. In some cases exclaustration may be requested precisely in view of seeking diocesan incardination. This desire is more appropriately handled under canon 693. However, in each case, it is essential that there be clarity on the part of both religious and bishop regarding the exercise of orders and any intent regarding incardination.

If a religious priest is not seeking incardination or even the exercise of sacred orders, the matter is more complex. Historically, the concept of "qualified exclaustration" was developed, with the hope of preventing laicization in cases of vocational doubt. It essentially permitted and required the priest to live as a lay person in using the sacraments, and dispensed him from all clerical obligations except celibacy for a specified amount of time. This form of exclaustration is used only where there is hope for the individual's return to priestly life.[5]

The code reserves the exclaustration of nuns to the Apostolic See. Most cloistered nuns are of the type described in canon 615, having no supreme moderator of their own. The request of a nun for exclaustration would be processed internally according to the constitutions and forwarded to the Holy See, often either through the diocesan bishop or through appointed personnel of an order of men with a special supervisory relationship to the nuns in question.

Imposed Exclaustration

The imposition of exclaustration on a religious is also reserved to the ecclesiastical authority competent according to the pontifical or diocesan status of the institute. In the latter case, the canon does not specify which bishop is competent. It would seem most plausible, however, to make the request of the bishop within whose jurisdiction the religious is living at the time of the petition.

[5] Ibid., 329–331.

The initiative in these cases comes from the institute, not the individual religious. The superior general with the consent of his or her council may request the exclaustration for grave causes. The qualification of the cause is the same as in cases of voluntary exclaustration, but the process is obviously more complex since the individual in question has not requested it. The canon calls for equity and charity in an effort to avoid overly harsh treatment of one who, in the judgment of the superior, must be removed from the community for the well-being of the other members.

In today's less structured community life, individuals with problems arising from personality disorders, childhood abuse, or substance abuse may experience some difficulty living in community. Often unwittingly, they become disruptive of it. Treatment for substance abuse or counseling for healing from childhood trauma are the preferred solutions. To be successful, these solutions need to be accompanied by the support of an informed community. However, the willingness of the individual and the capacity of the community to respond are not always present.

Where, for the good of the community, it becomes necessary to insist that an individual live out of community, the major superior, having heard the council, may initiate a process toward imposed exclaustration. The process is somewhat parallel to that for dismissal, but is necessarily different because the causal behavior often is not fully culpable. The individual must be warned that this process is under consideration, told the reasons why, encouraged to change, and informed of the right of self-defense directly to the major superior or to the supreme moderator. Unlike the process for dismissal, the process for imposed exclaustration does not require two warnings, but the efforts to assist and to warn the religious, as well as the responses, should be put in writing, even if first given verbally in the presence of two witnesses. These acts will be forwarded to the superior general.

If the individual, objectively speaking, seems to need treatment for substance abuse or a psychological evaluation and/or counseling, this should be offered and even urged, prior to initiating the process of imposing exclaustration. However, such treatment cannot be forced on an individual under obedience, with a threat of imposed exclaustration or dismissal for failure to comply.

A petition to the competent ecclesiastical authority for imposed exclaustration should include: the request of the superior general with an extract from the council meeting at which consent was given, a summary of the efforts made to assist the individual over a period of time, the concrete cause for requesting the exclaustration, the individual's response to the warning, and an indication of how the institute intends to observe equity and charity toward the individual. Since the very causes for imposed exclaustration may also be ones which limit the individual's ability to support himself or herself, specific attention must be given to this matter.

While perhaps necessary at times for the well-being of a larger number of religious, this remedy, developed after the formulation of the 1917 code largely for the sake of cloistered monasteries,[6] poses serious problems as well. In many cases it must be asked if living alone is a desired solution for certain personalities. Nevertheless, all pertinent factors must be taken into consideration and presented in the petition.

The specific case of clerics is not treated separately here, but would be conditioned by the provisions of canons 686, §1 and 687.

Exclaustration may be imposed for a specific period of time, thus building in a review, or it may be imposed without a time limit. In the latter case, it ends only by being lifted by the same authority which imposed it. Although it is not stated in the document imposing the exclaustration, such cases may give rise to administrative recourse to the Apostolic See.

Status of the Exclaustrated

Canon 687 — An exclaustrated member is considered freed from the obligations which cannot

[6] Ibid., 327.

be reconciled with the new condition of his or her life, yet remains dependent upon and under the care of superiors and also of the local ordinary, especially if the member is a cleric. The member can wear the habit of the institute unless the indult determines otherwise. Nevertheless, the member lacks active and passive voice.

The canonical status of all exclaustrated individuals is essentially the same. The individual, while living out of community, is in fact still a member of the institute under vow. Celibate chastity remains unaltered; usually an individual is expected to be self-supporting, having discretion in the use of earnings, and consequently is also subject to civil norms for taxation; obedience is largely suspended in daily living, but dependence on and care from the religious superior remain. The exclaustrated religious is also under the local ordinary, presumably with particular reference to apostolic activities. This is particularly the case of religious clerics, who will have already received the consent of the same ordinary. In the case of other religious, the local ordinary should be informed of the exclaustrated religious's presence in the diocese by the competent superior, who in turn should be informed if the religious moves. The reasons for which exclaustration was requested or imposed will help suggest how much contact between the superior and the religious is desirable.

While still a member, the exclaustrated religious clearly is not living the usual life of a religious. In helping the religious get settled, the institute should not provide a community-owned car or allow the continued use of congregational credit cards. In certain circumstances, an institute may have to take civil means to clarify the distancing between the institute and the individual to distinguish the locus of liability for financial transactions or criminal behavior.

The indult, according to the situation, may prohibit the use of the institute's habit. A decision on this will also be influenced by the motivations for the exclaustration, and the living and work situations of the religious. Another clear indication of the individual's unusual status is the loss of active and passive voice. There is an internal logic in this, since the individual is neither living within the institute nor subject to its usual patterns of governance.

Voluntary exclaustration in the Eastern code[7] is granted only by the competent ecclesiastical authority to which the monastery, order, or congregation is subject. The effects of the indult are similar except for the obligation to remove the habit and the fact that the individual is subject to the eparchial bishop of the place where he or she lives, rather than to the religious superior. Exclaustration may also be imposed by the aforementioned ecclesiastical authority at the request of the competent superior with the consent of his or her council.[8]

Separation of Members in Temporary Vows

Canon 688 — §1. A person who wishes to leave an institute can depart from it when the time of profession has been completed.

§2. During the time of temporary profession, a person who asks to leave the institute for a grave cause can obtain an indult of departure from the supreme moderator with the consent of the council in an institute of pontifical right. In institutes of diocesan right and in the monasteries mentioned in can. 615, however, the bishop of the house of assignment must confirm the indult for it to be valid.

Those who have made vows for a specific period of time may freely leave at their expiration, or may request an indult to leave if the vows have not yet expired. One who wishes to leave at the expiration of vows will make this known to the superior, most probably at the time when there would otherwise be a request for admission to renewal. On the other hand, one who, in ongoing dialogue with superiors, has been advised that admission to renewal or to perpetual vows probably

will not be granted may decide not to make the request.

In congregations where temporary vows are made for a number of years at a time, a religious in temporary vows may for grave reasons[9] request an indult to leave without waiting for the expiration of vows. The gravity of the cause will be discerned together with the formation director and with the competent major superior. Those who are convinced of having erred regarding a religious vocation or who find insupportable the observance of the vows or of common life may find it better for themselves and for the community to face this honestly and to move on to another form of Christian life. Formators and superiors must seek the delicate balance between emphasizing the seriousness of a vow and recognizing the necessity of some to be released from their obligations.

The supreme moderator with the consent of the council may issue the indult of departure in pontifical or diocesan institutes.[10] However, in the latter case, for validity, the indult must be confirmed by the diocesan bishop of the house to which the religious is assigned. This confirmation is also required for religious of canon 615 monasteries. In this case, unless proper law provides otherwise, the major superior would act with the council's consent.

Since perpetual profession is required for admission to the diaconate,[11] there are no particular difficulties for temporarily professed members of clerical institutes.

Canon 692, on the time when the indult takes effect, applies equally to those in temporary or perpetual vows.

---

[7] *CCEO* 489, 491, and 548.

[8] *CCEO* 490 and 548.

[9] For a discussion of such a grave cause see J. Torres, "La dispensa dai voti e dal giuramento," in *I procedimenti,* 359– 360.

[10] The granting of this faculty to supreme moderators of lay religious institutes raised the question of whether they had the power to dispense from vows. See Rincón Pérez, in *Pamplona ComEng,* 468–469. However, since canon 692 clarifies that the dispensation comes from the law itself, the clerical or lay condition of the moderator is a moot question.

[11] See cc. 266, §2; 1019, §1.

The Eastern canons provide in a similar way for granting an indult of departure for religious in temporary vows.[12]

Exclusion from Further Profession

Canon 689 — §1. If there are just causes, the competent major superior, after having heard the council, can exclude a member from making a subsequent profession when the period of temporary profession has been completed.

§2. Physical or psychic illness, even contracted after profession, which in the judgment of experts renders the member mentioned in §1 unsuited to lead the life of the institute constitutes a cause for not admitting the member to renew profession or to make perpetual profession, unless the illness had been contracted through the negligence of the institute or through work performed in the institute.

§3. If, however, a religious becomes insane during the period of temporary vows, even though unable to make a new profession, the religious cannot be dismissed from the institute.

The language of the code shifts when speaking of excluding a religious from the renewing of vows or from perpetual profession. Here the canon speaks of just causes (*iustae causae*) and gives explicit norms in some of the cases which could be the most controversial.

The competent major superior is the one who, according to proper law, has the authority to admit to profession at the point of renewal or at the point of perpetual vows. In many institutes, the renewal may be provided for at the provincial level, while perpetual vows may be reserved to the superior general. In any case, unless approved proper law explicitly states otherwise, the major superior is required only to hear the council.

The major superior may seek the consent or advice of the council in the sense of canon 656, 3° and receive a negative vote. However, in applying the present canon, the major superior who has se-

rious doubts about admitting a religious to further profession must present the perceived just causes to the council. Only after hearing the council may he or she exclude the religious.

The usual just causes for non-renewal of vows will be serious failures in observing the vows and a common life in charity. In charity and justice, these concerns will have been pointed out to the individual by those responsible for his or her formation. At times it is more charitable and just to assist an individual in returning to lay life than to continue to give a candidate the benefit of the doubt where serious questions about the person's suitability for religious life persist.

A decree resulting from the 1970 *Plenaria* of the Sacred Congregation for Religious and Secular Institutes[13] significantly redefined "just cause" for exclusion from further profession. Its provisions underlie canon 689, §2, with the addition of the final exceptive clause.

If the religious themselves do not see that they are physically or psychologically unsuited for the particular institute, or for religious life in general, the competent superior must have recourse to appropriate experts to apply the canon. While the canons do not grant a right to renewal of vows or to perpetual profession, but rather require for validity of vows that the individual be admitted by the competent superior (c. 656, 3°), the present canon does require a just cause for exclusion. To assure this in the case of illness, medical experts are to be used, with due respect for confidentiality and personal privacy (c. 220). Presumably a religious whose case is doubtful and who wishes to be admitted to further profession will cooperate in releasing necessary information to the competent superior.

The expert opinion is to address the individual's suitability for the life of the institute. Clearly, what is necessary for missions beyond one's own culture, or what is necessary for the cloistered life, will differ from what is required for other forms of apostolic religious life. A particular institute's way

---

[12] *CCEO* 496 and 546, §2.

[13] SCRIS, *Dum canonicarum,* December 8, 1970, *AAS* 63 (1971) 318–319; *CLD* 7, 531–533.

of living poverty or its community life-style may be pertinent factors. In an era when many potential candidates have suffered some form of childhood trauma and/or have been involved in substance abuse, problems may surface during the early years of profession which were not evident at the time of entrance, even to the candidate. Such persons must be treated with charity, yet justice toward the individual and the institute is also a central concern. One who is dealing with too many personal issues often cannot also make the necessary adjustment to religious life.

The final clause of paragraph two further protects the individual. A young religious who, in the course of apostolic experience, has contracted an illness or suffered an injury cannot be refused profession for that reason. Likewise, if an institute has been negligent toward an individual and this has resulted in serious illness, the illness itself cannot be a cause to refuse further profession. The subjectivity possible in judging such cases is a cause of concern. At the same time, these provisions remind institutes to provide reasonable health care for all of their members.

The case of one who becomes insane (*amens*) is different. Since such an individual is unable freely to request renewal or to depart, he or she is, as it were, suspended in the state of temporary profession, although the temporary vows expire. The individual cannot be dismissed but rather must receive appropriate treatment and care. The institute should consult with parents or close relatives regarding their wishes in the matter. If treatment enables the individual to act responsibly, in due time a decision will be made by both the religious and the institute regarding further profession.

The Eastern canon 547 makes the same provision for excluding members in temporary vows from renewing vows or from perpetual profession.

Readmission to the Same Institute

Canon 690 — §1. The supreme moderator with the consent of the council can readmit without the burden of repeating the novitiate one who **had legitimately left the institute after completing the novitiate or after profession. Moreover, it will be for the same moderator to determine an appropriate probation prior to temporary profession and the time of vows to precede perpetual profession, according to the norm of cann. 655 and 657.**

§2. The superior of an autonomous monastery with the consent of the council possesses the same faculty.

This canon applies only to readmission to the same institute which one has left, and not to a generic readmission to religious life. Competency to readmit is reserved to the supreme moderator with the consent of the council. In institutes where a provincial superior usually admits to the institute, his or her role in readmission is consultative.

Readmission to an institute without the necessity of repeating the novitiate applies to one who has completed the novitiate, or left following profession, whether temporary or perpetual. While not explicitly stated, most authors judge that the canon does not apply to those who were dismissed.[14]

The canon does not explicitly state if it intends completion of the novitiate according to the minimum required by the code for validity (c. 648, §1) or if it intends the full time required according to proper law, which frequently is longer. If the minimum is taken as the norm, the superior readmitting the individual would take this factor into consideration in determining the length of probation before profession.

The supreme moderator will determine the amount of time necessary for an individual as a period of probation or preparation prior to tempo-

---

[14] See V. De Paolis, *La vita consacrata nella Chiesa* (Bologna: Dehoniane, 1991) 380; E. Gambari, *I Religiosi nel Codice* (Milan: Ancora, 1986) 354–355; G. Girotti, in *Urbaniana Com,* 432; and E. Williamson, in *CLSGBI Com,* 387. The authors do not consider those who have been legitimately dismissed as being included among those who have "legitimately left" the institute. Canon 702's explicit reference to both those who have departed and those who have been dismissed supports this interpretation.

rary profession. In all cases there will be a period of reintegration, which may vary depending on when an individual left and for how long a time he or she was away from the institute. Likewise, in all cases there will be temporary profession.

Some have questioned whether or not the final phrase of the canon regarding the time of vows to precede perpetual profession is to be interpreted according to *Renovationis causam* 38, which took into consideration the years of temporary vows completed by an individual prior to leaving the institute.[15] However, the canon does not justify such an interpretation, but rather refers to the canons which state the minimum canonical requirements for valid admission to temporary and to perpetual vows (cc. 655, 657). What the present canon does allow is a relaxation of proper law which, for example, may require six years in temporary vows before admission to perpetual profession. In accordance with canon 690, the superior general could permit a readmitted member to make perpetual profession after only three years in temporary vows, regardless of the time previously spent under vows.

All that the canon allows to superiors general is equally applicable to the superiors of autonomous monasteries, which are defined in canons 613, §1 and 615. Canon 613, §2 defines the superiors of autonomous houses as major superiors. Since candidates in these cases normally enter the monastery, as such, rather than a centralized institute, this is a logical adaptation of the canon provided by the law itself.

Under the Eastern code, the possibility of reentry into an institute is mentioned only in the canons on monasteries. Those returning must repeat the novitiate and profession "as if they have never entered religious life."[16]

---

[15] SCRIS, instr *Renovationis causam,* January 6, l969, *AAS* 61 (1969) 103–120. Article 38–II required a minimum of one year before perpetual profession, "or no less than the period of temporary probation which he would have had to complete before perpetual profession at the time he left the institute."

[16] *CCEO* 493, §2.

Departure of the Perpetually Professed

Canon 691 — §1. A perpetually professed religious is not to request an indult of departure from an institute except for the gravest of causes considered before the Lord. The religious is to present a petition to the supreme moderator of the institute who is to transmit it along with a personal opinion and the opinion of the council to the competent authority.

§2. In institutes of pontifical right, an indult of this type is reserved to the Apostolic See. In institutes of diocesan right, however, the bishop of the diocese in which the house of assignment is situated can also grant it.

The act of perpetual profession is truly intended to be for all of one's life in all its aspects. Only the gravest of causes (*ob gravissimas causas*) justifies requesting an indult of departure; this petition will have been tested in serious spiritual discernment. If the religious superior has been directly involved in this discernment process, there is a better possibility of distinguishing temporary crises occasioned by some particular event or circumstance from those very grave causes which indicate a real inability to persevere in observing the evangelical counsels or community life. In some cases the admission to perpetual vows may have been poorly discerned.[17]

The granting of the indult for the perpetually professed is reserved to the competent ecclesiastical authority, but the petition must first be reviewed by the authority of the institute. Proper law may provide that the petition be presented first at the provincial level if such exists. The canon,

---

[17] The 1995 *Statistical Yearbook of the Church* published by the Secretariat of State lists the departure of 398 religious priests of pontifical institutes and 46 priest members of pontifical societies of apostolic life during l995 (378). In pontifical institutes of women, there were 198 departures from autonomous houses and 2666 from centralized institutes in 1995 (384–385). Among non-priest members of pontifical institutes of men, 1169 religious departed in 1995, as did 74 members of societies of apostolic life (531).

however, requires that the supreme moderator receive the petition and forward it to the appropriate ecclesiastical authority. It is not essential that the petition be addressed to the Holy Father or to the bishop; it may also be addressed to the general superior. What is essential is that the request stating the motives for the petition be written and signed by the petitioner.

The code does not require the consent of the general council, and it should not be required by proper law because the congregation is not competent to grant the indult. What is necessary is that the superior general express his or her own opinion in the matter, and that of the council. Nevertheless, the petition must be forwarded to the competent authority, whatever be the opinion of the superior and the council. That opinion is important since the individual requesting an indult does not always give a full account of his or her difficulties.

In forwarding the petition, the superior should also include a brief curriculum vitae of the religious, indicating dates of birth, entry, and profession as well as major apostolic activities and periods of formal education. If there have been periods of absence or of exclaustration, they should also be noted.

The granting of the indult of departure in pontifical institutes is reserved to the Apostolic See. Diocesan institutes presumably could also send their request to the Apostolic See, but the diocesan bishop of the house of assignment can also grant it. The "also" could refer to this bishop, in addition to the bishop of the principal seat of the institute. In any event, the common practice would be to turn to the diocesan bishop of the house of assignment, who possibly knows the religious better.

The major superior of a canon 615 monastery would forward the request for departure to the Holy See. The particular provisions for clerics are treated in canon 693.

The indult of departure for the perpetually professed is provided for similarly in the Eastern code: canon 492 for monasteries and canon 549 for orders and congregations. The particular pro-

visions for clerics are found in Eastern code canons 494 and 549, §3.

Juridic Effect of the Indult

Canon 692 — Unless it has been rejected by the member in the act of notification, an indult of departure granted legitimately and made known to the member entails by the law itself dispensation from the vows and from all the obligations arising from profession.

During a discussion of the procedure for an indult of departure with any religious, whether of temporary or of perpetual vows, it could be very beneficial to point out the content of this canon in advance. The basic principles involved are those found in canons 59–71 on rescripts. The indult of departure is entrusted to the general superior who forwards it to ecclesiastical authority, and it takes effect when it is made known to the member (see c. 62). The petitioner presumably desires the rescript; thus it takes effect once it has been granted and communicated.

Nevertheless, since one is not bound to use a rescript "given only in his or her favor" unless bound by another canonical obligation (c. 71), an individual may reject the rescript in the act of notification. If in the interval between the petition and the receipt of the rescript the motivating cause has changed, the individual may, in fact, reject the indult. If the individual has had a change of heart, he or she should reject the rescript when it is communicated; otherwise the indult is effective immediately. If, in fact, it is rejected, then the individual is expected to remain in or return to full observance of religious life.

Superiors should not confuse the validity of the indult of departure from the institute with the member's signing of documents acknowledging receipt of the rescript, of financial assistance (c. 702), and of personal documents, e.g., baptismal certificate, diplomas, will. A refusal of the rescript because of disagreement over such assistance means that the individual must fully return to the institute, or petition anew. A personal acceptance of the indult or its retention when communicated through the mail, accompanied by a refusal to sign other documents, does not affect the validity of the rescript. The indult, legitimately granted and communicated to the petitioner, results *ipso iure* in dispensation from one's vows and from all obligations arising from profession.

The code does not specify a method of communication. The superior general is often at a distance from the petitioner and, in large institutes, the channels followed in making the request will be followed in communicating the rescript. Even a provincial may be at some distance, but presumably will know the individual; this will dictate the wisdom of communicating the rescript in person, through another, or through the mail.

The Eastern canon 493 on monasteries is essentially the same as the above, adding explicitly that obligations arising from sacred orders are not dispensed. This provision is applied to orders and congregations by canon 549, §3.

Departure of Clerics

Canon 693 — If a member is a cleric, an indult is not granted before he finds a bishop who incardinates him in the diocese or at least receives him experimentally. If he is received experimentally, he is incardinated into the diocese by the law itself after five years have passed, unless the bishop has refused him.

In the case of a religious cleric, whether deacon or priest, the canon presumes a desire to leave religious life, but not the clerical state. Hence in these cases, an indult of departure is not granted (*non conceditur*)[18] before a bishop has agreed to receive the cleric directly for incardination or to receive him experimentally.

If the cleric is received experimentally into the diocese, a special indult of secularization *ad ex-*

perimentum[19] is provided. This allows the religious cleric to remain outside his institute, in the diocese, up to the limit of the five-year experimental period. If he is subsequently incardinated in the diocese by the bishop during that period, or incardinated by the law *ipso iure* at the end of the five-year period, his departure from the institute is effected. Should he be refused incardination, he must return to his institute.

Because a superior general can grant exclaustration only for three years (c. 686, §1), and incardination by the law requires five years' experimentation, exclaustration is not usually the best solution for a religious cleric seeking diocesan incardination. However, a period of exclaustration for three years may possibly result in the bishop's readiness to incardinate the cleric immediately. In that case, the bishop's letter is added to the usual documents required by canon 691 for a simple indult of departure.

The cases not envisioned by the canon, but which continue to occur, are those of religious clerics who wish to terminate their membership in the religious institute, but who either have not found or do not seek a bishop who will incardinate them. These individuals most frequently state that they intend neither to exercise sacred orders nor to marry; however, they do not choose to seek laicization. It is preferable that they be assisted in seeking laicization. However, in those cases where an indult of departure has been granted, it states that the individual may not exercise sacred orders. Furthermore, while the vows and other obligations arising from religious profession are dispensed, the obligation of priestly celibacy remains.[20]

If a religious cleric seeks laicization through the Congregation for Divine Worship and the Discipline of the Sacraments, that dicastery is competent to dispense from religious vows at the same time.[21]

---

[18] It has been questioned whether this phrase of the canon prohibits the granting of an indult or expresses what is customary. Current practice, while cautious, favors the latter interpretation.

[19] Torres, "La dispensa," 370, and "La procedura," 330–331.

[20] On this point see *CLD* 11, 97–98.

[21] See CDWDS, littcirc, June 6, 1997, *Origins* 27 (August 28, 1997) 169–172.

Canon 494 of the Eastern code clearly indicates the status of a monk in sacred orders who receives an indult of departure and the ways in which he may be incardinated in a diocese. Canon 549, §3 applies to other religious in sacred orders what the above canon states for monks.

ARTICLE 3: DISMISSAL OF MEMBERS
[cc. 694–704]

Three distinct canonical procedures are provided for the dismissal of a religious in temporary or perpetual vows.[22]

The first form is *ipso facto* dismissal (c. 694). Second, canon 695 presents the circumstances under which dismissal is required by law. Third, canon 696 introduces those other circumstances under which a member may be dismissed. These rather precise and detailed administrative procedures have been clarified through authentic interpretations; furthermore, they all admit of administrative recourse. However, as will be seen, certain concepts are borrowed from penal law. This fact, together with the grave effects of dismissal (i.e., cessation of all vows, rights, and obligations derived from profession—c. 701), make it clear that the canons are to be strictly interpreted (c. 18).

Ipso facto Dismissal

Canon 694 — §1. A member must be held as *ipso facto* dismissed from an institute who:

    1° has defected notoriously from the Catholic faith;

    2° has contracted marriage or attempted it, even only civilly.

§2. In these cases, after the proofs have been collected, the major superior with the council is to issue without any delay a declaration of fact so that the dismissal is established juridically.

---

[22] For a summary of the changes here from the 1917 code see Rincón Pérez, in *Pamplona ComEng,* 471–472.

In the cases described here, the performance of the act itself (*ipso facto*) effects the member's dismissal from the institute. While the major superior must collect proofs to establish the fact juridically, it is not the superior's declaration which effects the dismissal.

The determination of notorious defection from the Catholic faith is not a simple matter in every case. It surely is not present in every statement critical of the Church's teaching or practice. Canon 750 clarifies somewhat precisely yet generically the content of Catholic faith. However, this canon on dismissal does not mention any of the delicts defined in canon 751: heresy, apostasy, or schism, each of which entails a *latae sententiae* excommunication (c. 1364, §1).

The notorious nature of one's defection is not simply a matter of popular opinion regarding the individual. Rather, there must be clear proof in the external forum. A case of notorious defection would be that of a religious who, without seeking an indult of departure, has, in fact, joined another Christian or non-Christian faith community, consistently substituting that community's public worship for that of the Catholic Church. In some cases, individuals may have begun studies for official ministry in such a community. If, after having acted publicly in this way, the religious seeks an indult of departure, the major superior, having reviewed the proofs with the council, should simply declare the fact of dismissal (c. 694, §1, 1°).

If, in the above case, the defection is doubtful, but there is a petition for an indult of departure, it should be handled according to canon 688, §2 or canon 691. If there is doubt about the notoriety of the defection, and there is no request for an indult, it may be more prudent to follow the procedure for facultative dismissal (c. 696).

Cases of marriage or attempted marriage are more easily proven through written documents. In all such cases, including that of one in temporary vows, there follows *ipso facto* dismissal, with the effects expressed in canon 701. Furthermore, a public perpetual vow of chastity in a religious institute renders marriage invalid (c. 1088). Likewise, a perpetually professed religious cleric who attempts marriage incurs a *latae sententiae* suspension; a non-clerical religious incurs a *latae sententiae* interdict (c. 1394).

Since the superior's declaration does not effect the dismissal, this process is not reserved to the highest superior. It is a major superior (c. 620) who acts with the council; the canon does not specify a vote in this case, but a common reflection on the proofs. The declaration, which must not be delayed once proof is obtained, should state the objective facts: the name of the person, the factual cause of dismissal, and the declaration of the fact of dismissal in virtue of this canon. The declaration, duly signed by the major superior and a notary, should be communicated to the individual concerned, placed in the individual's file, and, if handled at the provincial level, communicated to the generalate. It should be noted that canon 702 applies also to dismissed members.

Norms regulating *ipso facto* dismissal in the Eastern code[23] are essentially the same as those above, with the added useful provision that the ecclesiastical authority to which the monastery, order, or congregation is subject should be informed.

Mandatory Dismissal

Canon 695 — §1. A member must be dismissed for the delicts mentioned in cann. 1397, 1398, and 1395, unless in the delicts mentioned in can. 1395, §2, the superior decides that dismissal is not completely necessary and that correction of the member, restitution of justice, and reparation of scandal can be resolved sufficiently in another way.

§2. In these cases, after the proofs regarding the facts and imputability have been collected, the major superior is to make known the accusation and proofs to the member to be dismissed, giving the member the opportunity for self-defense. All the acts, signed by the major superior and a notary, together with the responses of the member, **put in writing and signed by that member, are to be transmitted to the supreme moderator.**

Cases of mandatory dismissal are indicated through references to delicts found in Book VI of the code.[24] In brief, canon 1397 involves homicide, fraudulent or forcible kidnapping or detention, mutilation or grave wounding of another. Canon 1398 deals with one who procures a completed abortion. Canon 1395, §1 deals with living in concubinage, or persisting in a scandalous situation involving an external sin against the sixth commandment. Canon 1395, §2 then speaks of other offenses against the same commandment, committed by force or threats or publicly or with a minor below the age of sixteen. Private acts with a consenting adult would not be considered under this particular paragraph.

Two preliminary observations are warranted. First, the present canon on mandatory dismissal applies each of these delicts to all religious. Thus, the procuring of an abortion pertains not only to women religious but also to a religious priest or brother actively involved in such an abortion. Similarly, although canon 1395 defines a delict for clerics, canon 695 makes the same acts the cause for dismissal of any religious.[25]

Second, the canon makes a clear distinction in the case of canon 1395, §2. Not every case of such a delict entails obligatory dismissal. Consideration must be given to the possible reform of the offender, the restitution of justice, and the reparation of scandal. In addition, the delicts in paragraph one are continuing offenses, whereas those in paragraph two seem to be single acts. In this context, the offender might be reformed, justice might possibly be restored, and scandal could

---

[24] See commentary regarding cc. 1397, 1398, and 1395.

[25] De Paolis observes that, on this point, the canon is poorly written. Canon 695 speaks of dismissal for delicts, yet in the case of canon 1395 only clerics are the subject of the delict. Nevertheless, De Paolis states that the sense of the canon seems obvious: even non-clerical religious are to be dismissed for committing the acts listed in canon 1395 (387).

---

[23] *CCEO* 497 and 551.

be repaired through other penalties or non-penal measures on the part of the institute.

In today's climate of litigation against priests and religious men and women on charges of child sexual abuse, the superior's decision in such cases requires great prudence, with due regard for the input of experienced legal counsel.

The procedure in cases of mandatory dismissal begins at the level of a major superior, if there is one other than the superior general. He or she must collect the proofs regarding the fact and imputability of the alleged delict, observing certain principles from penal law. Canon 1321, §3 expresses the principle that imputability is presumed where an external legal violation has occurred, unless it is otherwise apparent. Thus, it is particularly important first to have proof of the fact, and then consider canons 1322–1327 on exempting, mitigating, or aggravating circumstances.[26]

In such cases of mandatory dismissal, the council need not be consulted before beginning the process, as in the case of facultative dismissal (c. 696). Once the proofs are gathered, the accusations and the proofs are made known to the religious and the individual is given an opportunity for self-defense. While presumably the member's self-defense will be written and signed as part of the acts transmitted to the superior general, canon 698 also provides the option of offering one's defense directly to the highest superior.

The religious in this situation should be treated with sincere pastoral concern. At the same time, however, such cases should be handled expeditiously. At some point in the process, depending on the circumstances, the religious should also be informed of the possible penal implications of his or her acts. If simultaneously civil law action is taken against the individual, another prudent judgment may have to be made regarding the timeliness of the dismissal process.

It is important to note that since the intermediate major superior makes no decision in the matter, the council has no formal role. All of the acts, whatever their probative force regarding the facts

or the imputability, are signed by that superior and a notary (usually the provincial secretary) and forwarded to the superior general.[27]

In these cases, the procedure then continues with the collegial act of the general council (c. 699). Since the law requires dismissal for the delicts listed, the decision to be made by the superior general with the council is whether the acts constitute proof of the fact and the imputability of the legal violation. If the answer to this question is yes, then the decree is to be issued (c. 700). If the case involves a violation of canon 1395, §2, a decision must be made as to how to proceed in reforming the offender, restoring justice, and repairing scandal, if it seems that dismissal is not necessary.[28]

There is no parallel to canon 695 in the Eastern code.

Facultative Dismissal

Canon 696 — §1. A member can also be dismissed for other causes provided that they are grave, external, imputable, and juridically proven such as: habitual neglect of the obligations of consecrated life; repeated violations of the sacred bonds; stubborn disobedience to the legitimate prescripts of superiors in a grave matter; grave scandal arising from the culpable behavior of the member; stubborn upholding or diffusion of doctrines condemned by the magisterium of the Church; public adherence to ideologies infected by materialism or atheism; the illegitimate absence mentioned in can. 665, §2, lasting six months; other causes of

---

[26] De Paolis, 389.

[27] In cases of alleged abortion, medical proofs of the fact cannot always be procured. Likewise, even if there is strong evidence that the act probably occurred, there may be equally clear evidence of circumstances which mitigate imputability and call for a solution other than dismissal. The same mitigating circumstances also exempt from the *latae sententiae* penalty for abortion (c. 1324, §3).

[28] De Paolis notes that possibly there are cases other than those of canon 1395, §2, when measures other than dismissal might be taken, in consultation with the Holy See (390).

similar gravity which the proper law of the institute may determine.

§2. For the dismissal of a member in temporary vows, even causes of lesser gravity established in proper law are sufficient.

The motives justifying facultative dismissal are extensive but not taxative. They touch upon essential areas of religious life, its public witness and ecclesial communion. In every case, such causes must be grave, external, imputable, and juridically proven. The seriousness of the process is further manifested in the qualifying words such as "habitual," "repeated," "stubborn," "grave," "culpable," "public." Isolated acts, acts involving less serious matters, acts entailing mitigated imputability, or acts not provable in the external forum cannot become the cause of dismissal. At each stage of the process these aspects of the case are to be examined, and warnings are to be repeated enabling the individual to terminate the behavior for which dismissal is threatened. It should be noted that in the case of illegitimate absence, the process cannot be initiated prior to a six-month absence.

If proper law adds other causes of dismissal for perpetually professed members, these causes must be of similar gravity. However, religious in temporary vows can be dismissed for less grave causes, such as a lack of religious spirit which causes scandal. These causes are to be established in proper law.

Unless temporary profession has been made for several years, or the situation, while not covered by canons 694 or 695, is nevertheless extremely serious, it is advisable to await the expiration of the vows. Normally the individual will have been made aware of the problems and advised that he or she will probably not be accepted for further profession, in accord with canon 689, §1. If, however, the dismissal is to be pursued, the following canons are to be observed.

Canonical Warnings

Canon 697 — In the cases mentioned in can. 696, if the major superior, after having heard the council, has decided that a process of dismissal must be begun:

1° the major superior is to collect or complete the proofs;

2° the major superior is to warn the member in writing or before two witnesses with an explicit threat of subsequent dismissal unless the member reforms, with the cause for dismissal clearly indicated and full opportunity for self-defense given to the member; if the warning occurs in vain, however, the superior is to proceed to another warning after an intervening space of at least fifteen days;

3° if this warning also occurs in vain and the major superior with the council decides that incorrigibility is sufficiently evident and that the defenses of the member are insufficient, after fifteen days have elapsed from the last warning without effect, the major superior is to transmit to the supreme moderator all the acts, signed personally and by a notary, along with the signed responses of the member.

In cases of facultative dismissal, unless there is no major superior other than the superior general, the process of dismissal is initiated by an intermediate major superior such as a provincial.[29] The first formal step, to be documented in the acts of the case, is the meeting of the major superior with the council. After hearing the council, a major superior who decides to proceed collects or completes the proofs. Depending on the cause, these may include documents, writings, letters, formal obediences issued by the same superior, etc.

The next step, the formal canonical warnings, should always be put in writing, even if they are first communicated verbally in the presence of two witnesses. These warnings must be clear, complete, and precise in justice to the individual and as a basis for an eventual decree. The cause indi-

---

[29] In the spirit of canon 1341, the superior will have made various pastoral efforts to correct the behavior of the religious before initiating a dismissal process.

cated in the warnings will be the same as that eventually written in the decree and cannot change as the case proceeds. Although a member may be guilty of various violations of his or her religious obligations, it is better to proceed with one juridically proven cause which is clearly grave, external, and imputable rather than trying to include everything in the canonical warnings.

Each warning must clearly indicate the cause warranting dismissal and explicitly threaten subsequent dismissal if the member does not reform. What is expected on the part of the individual must be clear and measurable: compliance with an explicit obedience, return to a designated house by a specific date, written retraction of condemned teachings, etc. It is not acceptable, however, to require the religious to request an indult of departure to avoid dismissal, nor may one be forced by this threat into psychological counseling or substance abuse treatment. These require a free act on the part of the individual. The warnings must also provide the individual with full opportunity for self-defense. This may be through personal meetings, by letter to the major superior, or through direct communication with the superior general (c. 698).

A religious threatened with dismissal may request the assistance of a canonist, a vicar or delegate for religious, or some other qualified person.

The code requires two such warnings, with an interval of at least fifteen days between them. When the warning has been given in person, the days count from that date. When it is communicated in writing, the days would count from the day on which the individual receives the warning. Thus, it is preferable, whenever possible, to send such letters through some form of registered mail which will result in proof of delivery. In some circumstances, the letter should be delivered in person, and this can then be attested to in the acts. In extreme cases, when the whereabouts of the religious cannot be determined, the canonical warnings may be expedited by posting them in the most recent house of assignment.

Although the canon does not state fifteen days of "useful time," it is more prudent to follow the principle of canon 201, §2, discounting Sundays and holidays. Beyond this formality, there must be a reasonable consideration of location, postal service, and circumstances permitting compliance with the warning or receipt of a response.

The second warning should be essentially the same in content as the first, with due regard for any possible defense received. If the first warning is in vain, the superior is to proceed to the second. Obviously, if the individual complies with what was required, the process is terminated. If there is a defense, but one which the superior considers inadequate, the process continues to the second warning, without any required consultation with the council. If the individual at this point spontaneously requests an indult of departure, it may be processed in the usual way, rather than proceeding with dismissal.

After a second warning and a second period of at least fifteen days, the superior's council must be involved in the process again. However, the canon does not state its explicit role: "the major superior with the council decides." From this it is at least evident that the formality of consent is not required.[30] The minutes of the council meeting will record the decision taken by the superior after having heard the council. The superior with the council examines two points: whether the incorrigibility of the member is evident and whether the defenses are insufficient. Perhaps the individual has sufficiently convinced the superior and council of his or her intent and capacity to reform. Likewise, the defenses may be sufficient to convince the superior and council that the accusations against the religious were exaggerated and not actually a cause for dismissal. If so, the process ends; if not, the case is referred to the superior general, who proceeds in accord with canon 699.[31]

---

[30] See canon 127, §1 for the distinction between consent and counsel. Williamson, without explanation, refers to consent of the council in this context (*CLSGBI Com*, 392). De Paolis, on the other hand, interprets the canon as calling for the hearing of the council (393).

[31] If there is no intermediate major superior, the general superior will have handled all of the preceding steps.

The acts which must be transmitted to the superior general will include: the minutes of the first meeting prior to beginning the process; the significant proofs upon which the case is based; the two warning letters with some proof of receipt; the defenses of the member received in writing or signed by the member if given orally and later put into writing; the minutes of the council meeting to consider incorrigibility and the sufficiency of defense. The acts are to be signed by the major superior and a notary, normally the provincial secretary.

At this point in the process, the acts of dismissal involving a religious of those monasteries mentioned in canon 615 would be forwarded to the diocesan bishop for his decision (c. 699, §2).

Access to the Supreme Moderator

Canon 698 — In all the cases mentioned in cann. 695 and 696, the right of the member to communicate with and to offer defenses directly to the supreme moderator always remains intact.

In all mandatory or facultative dismissal cases, where the institute's structures include intermediate major superiors, this canon recognizes the right of the religious to offer his or her self-defense directly to the highest superior. However, this does not interrupt the process begun at the lower level. The major superior must complete the acts to be transmitted to the general superior according to the procedure indicated in canons 695 and 697. Obviously, matters will be greatly facilitated if the intermediate major superior has been informed of the fact that the defense of the religious has been sent and/or received by the general superior, thus completing the acts.

Decision on Dismissal

Canon 699 — §1. The supreme moderator with the council, which must consist of at least four members for validity, is to proceed collegially to the accurate consideration of the proofs, arguments, and defenses; if it has been decided through secret ballot, the supreme moderator is **to issue a decree of dismissal with the reasons in law and in fact expressed at least summarily for validity.**

§2. In the autonomous monasteries mentioned in can. 615, it belongs to the diocesan bishop, to whom the superior is to submit the acts examined by the council, to decide on dismissal.

The formal decision regarding dismissal is made collegially by the general superior with the council. Two points condition the validity of the act; these deal with the composition of the council and the content of the decree.

The council must, for validity, consist of at least four members in addition to the superior general. In institutes without four general councilors, proper law should indicate who is to be called, or specify how the decision is made. In the absence of these provisions in proper law, the superior general should, with the consent of the council, choose a perpetually professed member who is prudent and experienced to complete the required number.

The council is to study all of the acts submitted to determine whether the religious in question is to be dismissed. In this secret collegial vote, the superior general and councilors all have equal voice in deciding the matter. This is not a question of the council giving consent, subject to canon 127. If an absolute majority votes in favor of dismissal, the superior general is to issue the decree. While the canon does not require more than this, a seriously divided vote inevitably raises doubts about the dismissal being justified. The letter accompanying the decree to be confirmed by ecclesiastical authority should indicate the vote, unanimous or otherwise. The decision is made by a collegial vote, but the decree is to be issued by the superior general.[32]

The second point of the canon touching the validity of the decree concerns its content. It must, for validity, contain the reason for dismissal, in

---

[32] See c. 48 on individual decrees issued by one having executive authority. On the decree being an act of the superior general, see also De Paolis, 394.

law and in fact, at least in summary form. As noted earlier, these will be the points already set forth in the canonical warnings. The decree will express that a specific matter is cause for dismissal in universal (c. 696, §1) and proper law and then indicate factually the individual's violation in this matter as the reason for dismissal.

The above procedure is the same whether the institute is of pontifical or diocesan right. However, for canon 615 monasteries, the diocesan bishop makes the decision, there being no general superior. Because these monasteries are of pontifical right, he then forwards the decree to the Holy See for confirmation (c. 700).

Confirmation of the Decree

Canon 700 — A decree of dismissal does not have effect unless it has been confirmed by the Holy See, to which the decree and all the acts must be transmitted; if it concerns an institute of diocesan right, confirmation belongs to the bishop of the diocese where the house to which the religious has been attached is situated. To be valid, however, the decree must indicate the right which the dismissed possesses to make recourse to the competent authority within ten days from receiving notification. The recourse has suspensive effect.

The necessity of having the decree of dismissal confirmed by the Holy See or by the bishop of the house to which the religious has been attached, before it takes effect, gave rise to certain questions. Was the religious in question to be informed of the decree before or after its confirmation? Did the religious have a right to know that the process was at this stage, or would such notification place the superior in an untenable position if the confirmation were delayed or refused? The March 21, 1986 authentic interpretation stated that the confirmation was to be sought first.[33]

This canon adds a further point regarding the validity of the decree to those factors listed in canon 699, §1. The decree must include the right

of the dismissed to make recourse to the competent authority within ten days from receiving notification of dismissal. Given the above authentic interpretation, this clearly refers to notification of the confirmed decree. If made within the ten days, the recourse has suspensive effect by the law itself; in short, the decree of dismissal has no effect as yet. Presumably the canon intends the ten "useful" days as provided for in canon 1734, §2 regarding recourse against administrative decrees.

There remained, however, the question as to who was the competent authority. This also occasioned an authentic interpretation, given together with that regarding notification of the decree. The question posed asked if the authority competent to receive the suspensive recourse was the Congregation for Religious and Secular Institutes which confirmed the decree, or the Supreme Tribunal of the Apostolic Signatura. The response: affirmative to the first; negative to the second.[34] The interpretation has not ended discussion over the appropriateness of the congregation which confirms the decree also being the body which rules on recourse against such a confirmation. However, the interpretation has made clear to institutes and their members what avenues to follow.

Despite such authoritative confirmation, the decree actually remains an act of the superior general, to whom the religious has had access as author of the decree throughout the process (c. 698). The canons on administrative recourse cannot be applied literally since this is a distinct procedure provided for in religious law. Nevertheless, there is a certain logic in directing the recourse to the Congregation for Institutes of Consecrated Life and Societies of Apostolic Life as hierarchical superior of the author of the decree (c. 1737, §1).

The fact remains that, following an unsuccessful recourse to the confirming dicastery, a dismissed religious may have recourse to the Apostolic Signatura following the norms for hierarchical re-

---

[33] *AAS* 78 (1986) 1323.

[34] Ibid. For comments on these two interpretations, see also A. Stankiewicz, *P* 77 (1988) 149–158 and L. Wrenn, *Authentic Interpretations*, 24–26.

course (cc. 1734–1739). The continued suspensive effect of the recourse must be decided according to these canons. Such recourse should have some firm foundation, above all in procedural law. A canonist asked to assist a religious in such a recourse should have access to the full acts of the case to avoid useless procedures and delays occasioned by partial information. The institute must pay the expenses of a recourse to the Signatura.

The authentic interpretation on recourse does not deal with diocesan institutes, but its logical application to them would make the diocesan bishop the first avenue of recourse, followed by the Congregation for Institutes of Consecrated Life and Societies of Apostolic Life.

Juridic Effect of the Decree

Canon 701 — By legitimate dismissal, vows as well as the rights and obligations deriving from profession cease *ipso facto*. Nevertheless, if the member is a cleric, he cannot exercise sacred orders until he finds a bishop who receives him into the diocese after an appropriate probation according to the norm of can. 693 or at least permits him to exercise sacred orders.

The effects of legitimate dismissal follow *ipso facto,* in all types of dismissal. All that derives from religious profession ceases: vows, rights, and obligations. This phrase, "deriving from profession," is of juridic significance, since other obligations may remain. This is particularly true for the dismissed cleric who remains bound by clerical celibacy. Such a clerical dismissal clearly results in the anomaly of a cleric without incardination. Unlike a cleric with an indult granted to cover a period *ad experimentum*[35] with a view to diocesan incardination, the dismissed cleric is no longer a member of his institute.[36]

The canon itself prohibits the exercise of sacred orders until a bishop permits this. The obligation of celibacy remains unless laicization has been obtained. Sometimes such a cleric has been living away from his institute for some time and has not been exercising orders. When it is clear that he intends neither to return nor to regularize his status, the institute sometimes chooses to proceed to dismissal. When a bishop allows a priest dismissed from a religious institute or a society with the faculty of incardination to exercise sacred ministry in the diocese, he should establish clearly in writing whether a period of experimentation toward incardination is being initiated (c. 268, §1).

In treating facultative dismissal of a professed religious, the Eastern code provides differently for those in temporary vows.[37] In these cases, for which "a lack of religious spirit which can be a cause of scandal to others" (*CCEO* 552, §1, 2°) is sufficient cause, the superior general may act with the consent of the council, unless the statutes reserve this to another authority. The code itself reserves the confirmation of dismissal of those in temporary profession to hierarchical authority in the case of *sui iuris* monasteries.[38]

In the case of the perpetually professed, orders and congregations follow canons 500–503 provided for monks and nuns, with the added clarification that the competent authority is the superior general.[39] The full canonical process is spelled out, without, however, a listing of causes of dismissal. The most significant procedural difference is the provision at the point of recourse for a petition that the case be handled judicially rather than through administrative recourse. This is not an option, however, if the Apostolic See has confirmed the decree.[40] The competent tribunal is that of the authority immediately superior to the one which has confirmed the decree.[41]

---

[35] See c. 693.

[36] For two opinions on the status of a dismissed cleric see T. Green and R. Wiatrowski, *CLSA Advisory Opinions: 1984–1993,* ed. P. Cogan (Washington D.C.: CLSA, 1995) 205–210.

[37] *CCEO* 499 and 552.

[38] *CCEO* 499.

[39] *CCEO* 553.

[40] *CCEO* 501, §2. See also R. Metz, *Le Nouveau Droit des Eglises Orientales Catholiques* (Paris: Cerf, 1997) 175, 167–169.

[41] *CCEO* 501, §4.

The effects of dismissal are similar to those of the Latin code, except that those dismissed *ipso iure* are not considered released from the bonds and obligations stemming from profession.[42] Thus, in order to regularize his or her status, the religious dismissed *ipso iure* must pursue the normal canonical procedures for seeking the dispensation from vows and, according to the particular case, the lifting of sanctions and irregularities for the exercise of orders.[43]

Concluding Canons

The three final canons of chapter 6 are not specifically related to those immediately preceding on dismissal. Rather, they deal with certain other points touching various areas of separation.

Assisting Those Who Leave

Canon 702 — §1. Those who depart from a religious institute legitimately or have been dismissed from it legitimately can request nothing from the institute for any work done in it.

§2. Nevertheless, the institute is to observe equity and the charity of the gospel toward a member who is separated from it.

The two parts of canon 702 strike a balance. The religious who departs from the institute has no right to ask recompense for years of work in the institute. One must remember the interrelatedness of canon 668, §3 on a community of goods created through observance of the vow of poverty, and canon 670 on the obligations of the institute to support the members through that community of goods. The religious has not owned his or her earnings and has accumulated nothing. On the other hand, he or she has received formation, education, food, shelter, and all that was reasonably necessary to fulfill his or her vocation. Thus, one who leaves the institute has received much, but aside from possible personal patrimony, he or she has nothing. Thus, the canon's second paragraph speaks of treating the departing member with equity and gospel charity. The same logic explains the canon's inclusion even of those who have been legitimately dismissed.

The use of the term "equity," rather than "justice," indicates that cases vary and not every departing member will receive the same assistance. Factors entering into the discernment of how to observe equity and gospel charity include age, health, education, employable skills, personal patrimony, investment in work-related and/or government pension programs, the financial status of the institute, and its capacity to support all of its members into the future. A prior period of exclaustration may have included funds for helping a departing religious get established. At any point in such processes, it is best that financial arrangements be in writing. As canon 692 is better understood, there should be fewer cases of confusion over a departing member's refusing to sign a financial statement while not really wishing to refuse the indult of departure.

Various legal instruments may be used to assist departing members in an ongoing way, rather than by giving a lump sum. With proper care, these can be used without harm to the institute.[44]

Expulsion from a House

Canon 703 — In the case of grave external scandal or of most grave imminent harm to the institute, a member can be expelled immediately from

---

[42] *CCEO* 502. On this point see C. Pujol, *La Vita Religiosa Orientale* (Rome: Pontificio Istituto Orientale, 1994) 390. There is an interesting similarity between this provision and canon 669 of the 1917 code.

[43] The code commission did not wish to permit a situation in which, by way of a delict, one would be freed from all bonds flowing from monastic profession or appear to be in a state to seek diocesan incardination. *Nu* 16 (1983) 70–71 and 28 (1989) 70.

[44] For a detailed canonical and civil discussion of this canon, see M. Welch and P. Campbell, "Provisions for Departing Members," *Bulletin on Issues of Religious Law* 12 (Fall, 1996).

a religious house by the major superior or, if there is danger in delay, by the local superior with the consent of the council. If it is necessary, the major superior is to take care to begin a process of dismissal according to the norm of law or is to refer the matter to the Apostolic See.

The application of this canon is and should be very rare. Although it follows the canons on dismissal, this provision is clearly not a form of dismissal from the institute. However, under certain circumstances it may be necessary to begin a formal dismissal process.

Immediate expulsion from a religious house is justified only by grave external scandal and most grave imminent harm to the institute. The scandal here must be external, not internal to the community; the danger must be imminent, that is, already present and threatening.[45]

Expulsion as such is a provisional measure. If dismissal is called for, the applicable procedure is to be initiated according to the canons. In other cases, the matter is to be referred to the Apostolic See for further indications on how to proceed. In such cases a member may, of course, spontaneously request an indult of departure.

A major superior may expel the member on his or her own authority; however, if it is urgent that a local superior act, the council must have given consent. Obviously, the major superior who will take the next step must be informed immediately.[46]

Periodic Report of Separations

Canon 704 — In the report referred to in can. 592, §1, which is to be sent to the Apostolic See, mention is to be made of members who have been separated from the institute in any way.

In a circular letter dated January 2, 1988,[47] the Congregation for Religious and Secular Institutes provided guidelines for the reports referred to in this canon. When providing membership statistics, the institute will include information regarding those who have separated from it.

---

[45] De Paolis, 397. In commenting on the parallel material in *CCEO* 498 and 551, Pujol observes that such scandal or harm may be increased if civil legal action has been taken or if there is publicity through the media (381).

[46] For other comments on this canon, see J. Beyer, *Le Droit de la Vie Consacrée* (Paris: Tardy, 1988) 2:201, and Williamson, in *CLSGBI Com,* 395.

[47] *AAS* 80 (1988) 104–106; *Con Lif* 14 (1988) 266–267. A commentary by E. Sastre Santos follows the text of the documents for religious and for secular institutes, 270–287.

BIBLIOGRAPHY

Bibliographical material for canons 684–704 can be found after the commentary on canon 746.

CHAPTER VII
RELIGIOUS RAISED TO THE EPISCOPATE[1]
[cc. 705–707]

Religious life belongs to the life and holiness of the Church; however, it is not part of the hierarchical structure of the Church.[2] At times the Roman Pontiff calls an individual religious to serve as a diocesan or titular bishop (c. 376) or in an office equivalent to that of a diocesan bishop (cc. 368, 381, §2).[3] To serve as pastor of the Christian faithful would not be incompatible with the vocation of one who has offered a total gift of self to God in service to his people through the profession of the evangelical counsels. However, certain adjustments need to be made, particularly in the areas of obedience and poverty, in order to free the religious for this more extensive service to the Church.

Juridical Status of the Religious[4]

Canon 705 — A religious raised to the episcopate remains a member of his institute but is subject only to the Roman Pontiff by virtue of the vow of obedience and is not bound by obligations which he himself prudently judges cannot be reconciled with his condition.

The religious remains a member of his institute and is bound by the obligations of religious life that are not incompatible with his office as bishop.

Appointment to the episcopal office removes him from the authority of the superiors at all levels in his institute and renders him immediately subject to the Roman Pontiff by reason of his vow of obedience.[5] Any office the religious held within or beyond the religious institute would cease with his appointment as bishop.

Appointment to the episcopal office implies serious obligations toward a community of the Christian faithful. The norm permits the religious appointed a bishop to make prudential judgments in dispensing himself from obligations of religious life that are incompatible with the demands of his office. The obligations of common life,[6] traditional or devotional practices of the religious institute,[7] and restrictions on the use of personal goods resultant from the vow of poverty[8] addressed in the next canon are some examples of such possibly incompatible obligations.

Effects on Vow of Poverty[9]

Canon 706 — The religious mentioned above:
1° if he has lost the right of ownership of goods through profession, has the use, revenue, and administration of goods which accrue to him; a diocesan bishop and the others mentioned in can. 381, §2, however, acquire property on behalf of the particular church; others, on behalf of the institute or the Holy See insofar as the institute is capable or not of possession;

This canon provides for adjustments in the vow of poverty for the religious appointed a bishop. Number one applies to a religious who has re-

---

[1] Beyer observes that the content of these canons could be more appropriately placed in the section on bishops or in general norms on consecrated life, since they can apply to clerics belonging to secular institutes or societies of apostolic life. The principle of c. 19 provides that the provisions of cc. 705–707 would apply in such similar cases. See Beyer, *Le Droit de la Vie Consacrée* (Paris: Editions Tardy, 1988) 2: 206.

[2] *LG* 44.

[3] Canons 705–707 apply to cardinals, inasmuch as they are consecrated bishops when promoted to the cardinalate (c. 351, §1).

[4] Cf. *CCEO* 431, §2.

[5] Canon 590, §2. For example, the religious consecrated a bishop would no longer be subject to religious superiors in accord with c. 671.

[6] Canon 607, §2.

[7] Canons 662; 663, §3.

[8] Canon 668.

[9] Cf. *CCEO* 431, §3, 1°.

nounced the ownership of goods by religious profession.[10] The religious does not regain the ownership he renounced, but he does enjoy the administration, use, and revenues of goods that come to him during the time he holds episcopal office. If he is a diocesan bishop or equivalent to a diocesan bishop,[11] he acquires the ownership of the goods for the particular church he serves. Titular bishops acquire the ownership of such goods for their own institute, if it is capable of ownership;[12] otherwise, ownership is acquired by the Apostolic See.

> 2°   if he has not lost the right of ownership of goods through profession, recovers the use, revenue, and administration of the goods which he had; those things which accrue to him afterwards he fully acquires for himself;[13]

If the religious bishop did not renounce the ownership of his goods by religious profession,[14] he regains the administration, use, and revenues of the temporal goods that already belong to him, as well as those goods coming to him through the episcopal office. He acquires the ownership of those temporal goods which come to him personally as remuneration or gift while he serves as bishop. However, it would seem that the bishop remains bound by the spirit of his vow of poverty in the administration and use of all temporal goods.

> 3°   in either case, however, must dispose of goods according to the intention of the donors when they do not accrue to him personally.[15]

The legislation of Book V, "The Temporal Goods of the Church," binds the religious as a bishop.

Goods that do not come to the bishop personally (*intuitu personae*) must be disposed of in accord with the intention of the donors or testators.[16]

Retired Bishop Religious

Canon 707 — §1. A retired religious bishop can choose a place of residence even outside the houses of his institute, unless the Apostolic See has provided otherwise.[17]

A retired bishop has the right to choose a place of residence in or outside his institute, unless the Apostolic See has provided otherwise.[18]

§2. If he has served some diocese, can. 402, §2 is to be observed with respect to his appropriate and worthy support, unless his own institute wishes to provide such support; otherwise the Apostolic See is to provide in another manner.

While a religious institute may offer to provide for a retired bishop who is one of its members, the primary obligation for the bishop's suitable and decent support belongs to the particular church he served given his ongoing pastoral relationship to that people of God.[19] Episcopal conferences must ensure that suitable and worthy provision be made for a bishop who retires.[20]

The retired religious bishop continues to be a member of the episcopal college.[21] He can participate in an ecumenical council with a deliberative vote[22] and exercise collegial activity.[23] A retired diocesan bishop retains the title of emeritus of his diocese and has the right to be buried in its cathedral.[24]

---

[10] Canon 668, §§4–5.
[11] Canon 381, §2.
[12] Canon 634, §1.
[13] Cf. *CCEO* 431, §3, 2°.
[14] Canon 668, §1.
[15] Cf. *CCEO* 431, §3, 3°.
[16] Canons 1267, §3; 1300–1306; 1310.
[17] Cf. *CCEO* 431, §2, 2°.
[18] Canons 401; 402, §1.
[19] Canons 368; 381, §2.
[20] Canons 402, §2; 411.
[21] Canon 336.
[22] Canon 339.
[23] Canon 377, §2.
[24] Canons 402, §1; 1242; CFB, October 31, 1988, *Comm* 20 (1988) 167–168.

The canons do not address the issue of active and passive voice in the religious institute for an active or retired bishop.[25] However, on May 17, 1986, John Paul II approved a response of the Pontifical Council for the Interpretation of Legislative Texts. The response was in the negative as to whether a religious consecrated bishop enjoyed active or passive voice in his religious institute. Neither the question nor the response distinguished between an active and retired bishop.[26]

CHAPTER VIII
CONFERENCES OF MAJOR SUPERIORS
[cc. 708–709]

Conferences and councils of major superiors of religious institutes bear witness to ecclesial communion. While they date back to 1898, Pope Pius XII promoted these structures by convoking the International Congress of the States of Perfection in 1950, enabling religious institutes to offer mutual assistance to one another through common efforts. By the 1950s, six international and over one hundred fifty national conferences existed with at least thirty of the latter composed of both men and women religious. These structures have been helpful in promoting collaboration among the religious institutes and between them and the bishops in the dioceses and episcopal conferences.[27]

---

[25] *CCEO* 431, §2, 1°–2° provides that the religious elevated to the episcopacy lacks active and passive voice in his own monastery, order, or congregation. Having fulfilled his office and returned to his religious institute, he can regain active and passive voice if the typicon (law proper to monasteries) or statutes (law proper to orders and congregations) permit.

[26] *AAS* 78 (1986) 1324. For discussions of this issue, see D. J. Andres, "De religioso episcopo carente voce activa et passiva in proprio instituto," *ComRelMiss* 68 (1987) 294–308; J. Beyer's commentary in *P* 77 (1988) 158–162. Wrenn recognizes the response as seemingly new law and an ultra-restrictive interpretation. See L. Wrenn, *Authentic Interpretations on the 1983 Code* (Washington, D.C.: CLSA, 1993) 27–28.

[27] G. Ghirlanda, "Nature and Institutional Ends of the Conferences of Men and Women Religious Superiors," *Con Lif*

Nature/End of Conferences[28]

Canon 708 — Major superiors can be associated usefully in conferences or councils so that by common efforts they work to achieve more fully the purpose of the individual institutes, always without prejudice to their autonomy, character, and proper spirit, or to transact common affairs, or to establish appropriate coordination and cooperation with the conferences of bishops and also with individual bishops.

The norm describes the optional nature of the conferences and councils composed of major superiors[29] of religious institutes.[30] The structures have three basic tasks: (1) to achieve more fully the purpose of individual institutes, (2) to transact common affairs, and (3) to establish coordination and cooperation with the conferences of bishops and individual bishops.[31] Unlike episcopal conferences, conferences and councils of religious do not possess the power of governance.[32] Rather, they enjoy persuasive power to promote consecrated life within the life and mission of the Church.[33] The structures must always respect the patrimony and autonomy of each institute.[34] They address issues of

---

19/2 (1993) 85–106. For an understanding of these structures, see *CD* 35, 5–6; *PC* 22–23; *AG* 33; *ES* II: 42–43; *MR* 21, 61–66; *PA* 21; *VC* 50, 52; G. Nardin, "De accommodata renovatione statuum perfectionis...motus unionis inter status perfectionis," *ComRelMiss* 39 (1960) 165–195.

[28] The Eastern code has no canons comparable to cc. 708–709.

[29] Canon 620. See *CLD* 7, 462–467 for the statutes of the Union of Superiors General (USG), which was formally erected as the Roman Union of Superiors General in 1957; see *CLD* 6, 448–455, 472–478 for the erection and statutes of the International Union of Superioresses General (UISG).

[30] The World Conference of Secular Institutes (WCSI) was established and its statutes approved on May 23, 1974; see *CLD* 8, 313–315; 11, 113.

[31] *PC* 23 also lists as a purpose of such conferences and councils a more equitable distribution of apostolic efforts of religious in missionary territories, which is not included in the canon.

[32] *MR* 21.

[33] *VC* 53.

[34] Canon 586, §1.

common concern to all religious institutes and stimulate coordination and cooperation between them and the episcopal conferences as well as with individual bishops in their respective dioceses.

Pope John Paul II recommends that mixed commissions of bishops and major superiors be formed at the national level. He suggests structures whereby delegates from conferences of major superiors be invited to conferences of bishops, and delegates from episcopal conferences be invited to conferences and councils of major superiors.[35] Finally, he encourages seminaries to offer courses in the theology and spirituality of consecrated life, and religious formation programs to provide courses on the theology and structure of the particular church. Such education at the formative stages of vocations would greatly contribute to the effectiveness of mutual relations between bishops and religious.[36]

Erection/Approval of Statutes

Canon 709 — Conferences of major superiors are to have their own statutes approved by the Holy See, by which alone they can be erected even as a juridic person and under whose supreme direction they remain.

The Congregation for Institutes of Consecrated Life and Societies of Apostolic Life establishes conferences and councils as juridical persons[37] and approves their statutes. Likewise, the same congregation exercises a vigilance over these structures in order that their activities may be directed to achieving their purposes.[38] It is impor-

tant that the members of conferences and councils maintain contact with the Holy See.[39]

In the United States, the Conference of Major Superiors of Men (CMSM) was erected on September 12, 1957, and the Conference of Major Superiors of Women (CMSW) was erected on December 12, 1959. Subsequently, the Conference of Major Superiors of Women changed its name to Leadership Conference of Women Religious (LCWR).[40] On June 13, 1992, CICLSAL established the Council of Major Superiors of Women Religious (CMSWR) in the United States. This structure parallels but does not supplant the already existing LCWR. Major superiors must meet certain additional criteria for membership in the CMSWR. The council has pledged to cooperate with the NCCB and the two already existing conferences of major superiors in the United States.[41]

---

[35] *VC* 50. This issue was addressed in *MR* 61–65.

[36] *VC* 50.

[37] Canons 113, §2; 114, §1; 117.

[38] *PB* 109.

[39] *ES* II: 42; *MR* 67; *VC* 53. This is accomplished by a council formed from the USG and UISG that meets with CICLSAL; major superiors of religious institutes dedicated to missionary activity meet with CEP. Major superiors of national conferences of men and women religious hold annual meetings and send reports of them to CICLSAL.

[40] The secretariats of the two conferences are located at 8808 Cameron St., Silver Spring, Maryland 20910. In cooperation with the National Conference of Vicars for Religious and the CLSA the two conferences publish the *Bulletin on Issues of Religious Law.* On November 25, 1954, the Canadian Religious Conference (CRC), an association of major superiors of men and women religious of Canada, was established. The address of the CRC is 324 Laurier E., Ottawa, Ontario K1N 6P6. See *CLD* 11, 104–109 for the establishment of the Conference of Major Superiors of France and the Union of European Conferences of Major Superiors.

[41] For further information on this council, see CICLSAL, "New Council of Major Superiors of Women Religious." *Origins* 22/9 (July 23, 1992) 157, 159–163.

BIBLIOGRAPHY _____

Bibliographical material for canons 705–709 can be found after the commentary on canon 746.

TITLE III
SECULAR INSTITUTES
[cc. 710–730]

The fiftieth anniversary of the February 2, 1947 apostolic constitution *Provida Mater Ecclesia*[1] occasioned new reflections on the unique identity of secular institutes in ecclesial life today.[2] Addressing an international colloquium celebrating the occasion in Rome, Pope John Paul II recognized in *Provida Mater* a prophetic inspiration in which Pope Pius XII anticipated certain great themes of Vatican Council II.[3] The document, in recognizing what today would be called a new form of consecrated life, is indeed the *magna carta* of secular institutes,[4] providing also their particular law prior to the 1983 code. Two complementary documents followed: Pius XII's *motu proprio Primo feliciter* (March 12, 1948)[5] and the instruction from the Sacred Congregation for Religious, *Cum sanctissimus* (March 19, 1948).[6]

The eloquent language of Pius XII, calling upon members to be salt which does not lose its savor, light in darkness, and the leaven of Christ permeating every strata of society,[7] paved the way for later synthetic expressions such as consecrated secularity and secular consecration.[8]

As the conciliar theology of the laity and the role of the Church in the contemporary world have evolved, so also has the role of secular institutes as the "experimental laboratory" in which the Church can test concretely her relations with the world.[9] The ever deepening understanding of the vocation of consecrated secularity is reflected anew in the 1996 apostolic exhortation *Vita consecrata*. Members live their consecration to God in the world as "a leaven of wisdom and a witness of grace within cultural, economic and political life."[10]

The organization of the Latin code provides norms common to all institutes of consecrated life[11] that complement these twenty-one canons explicitly dedicated to secular institutes. In contrast, the Eastern code is structured around religious life as such, with an accent on monasticism. Consequently, its brief treatment of secular institutes[12] requires certain additional repetitions or references to religious law.[13] However, the main

---

[1] *AAS* 39 (1947) 114–124; *CLD* 3, 135–146.

[2] Statistics on secular institutes as of 1996 show a total of 191 recognized institutes. Of these, 187 depend on CICLSAL and four on CEC. Of the former, 61 are of pontifical right and 126 are diocesan. The vast majority of these are institutes of women (156). Ten institutes are of laymen, seventeen are clerical, and four have various branches. "Istituti secolari secondo l'archivio della CIVCSVA," *ComRelMiss* 78 (1997) 311.

[3] John Paul II, "Bearing Witness to Christ in Secular Life," *OssRomEng* (February 12, 1997) 5, nn. 1–2.

[4] J. Dorronsoro, "Cinquantesimo della *Provida Mater*," *Informationes* 23 (1997) 53. This article contains a brief history of the document. For a brief history of institutes, see also S. Holland in *CLSA Com,* 521 and E. Williamson in *CLSGBI Com,* 398–399.

[5] *AAS* 40 (1948) 283–286; *CLD* 3, 147–151.

[6] *AAS* 40 (1948) 293–297; *CLD* 3, 151–157.

[7] *Provida Mater Ecclesia,* Intro.

[8] The addresses of Pope Paul VI to secular institutes were characterized by such expressions. See *Secular Institutes, Documents* (Rome: CMIS, 1998) 77–100.

[9] Paul VI. "A Living Presence in the Service of the World and the Church," in *Secular Institutes, Documents,* 97. The theme of the 1996 CMIS Congress in Brazil was "How to Be an Experimental Laboratory in the Third Millennium." See *Dialogue* 24 (1996) 65–140.

[10] *VC* 10. *AAS* 88 (1996) 377–486; *Origins* 25 (April 4, 1996) 681; 683–720.

[11] Canons 573–606. For background on the significance of this structure, see Holland, in *CLSA Com,* 543.

[12] *CCEO* 653–659.

[13] For example, *CCEO* 563, §2 refers to *CCEO* 505, §2 for the status of institutes as pontifical, patriarchal, and eparchial; *CCEO* 564 reiterates the obligation of obedience to the Roman Pontiff; *CCEO* 566 refers back to a series of canons dealing with the erection and suppression of institutes and their dependence on ecclesiastical authority.

reason there are only seven canons is found in canon 569 of the Eastern code. The particular law of each *sui iuris* church is to make further provisions for such institutes.

Identity

Canon 710 — A secular institute is an institute of consecrated life in which the Christian faithful, living in the world, strive for the perfection of charity and seek to contribute to the sanctification of the world, especially from within.

The canon's point of departure may be said to be canon 573 where the conciliar doctrine on consecrated life is summarized. To that fundamental teaching taken from *Lumen gentium* VI and *Perfectae caritatis* is added the peculiar note of secular institutes: consecration lived in the world, contributing to its sanctification from within. This phrase touches the essence of such institutes. Italian Franciscan Agostino Gemelli (1875–1959) in his *Pro memoria* (1939) setting forth the possibility of such a life, insisted that members, rather than seeking to affect the world from outside, would work, "as it were, within the world."[14]

The phrase was subsequently echoed in *Primo feliciter* II and in *Perfectae caritatis* 11, before being adopted here and in canon 713, §2. Likewise *Vita consecrata* recognizes a "specific blending of presence in the world and consecration," making present in society *the newness and power of Christ's Kingdom.*"[15] J. Dorronsoro, undersecretary for secular institutes at the Congregation for Institutes of Consecrated Life and Societies of Apostolic Life, calls this blending a real symbiosis, in which consecration and secularity do not weaken each other but rather give meaning to all of the daily activities and the entire life of the members. In this way they are open and available to the will of God who called them in the world and for the world.[16]

State of Members

Canon 711 — The consecration of a member of a secular institute does not change the member's proper canonical condition among the people of God, whether lay or clerical, with due regard for the prescripts of the law which refer to institutes of consecrated life.

Canon 588 states that consecrated life, of its nature, is neither clerical nor lay. Its paragraphs two and three then clarify how institutes are recognized as either clerical or lay. This is a common norm applying to all institutes of consecrated life. From another angle, canon 207 identifies all of the Christian faithful as either clerics or laity. The canon's second paragraph then helps clarify the point that through profession of the evangelical counsels the lives of those called are consecrated to God "in their own special way." Thus, one who professes vows in a religious institute is known as a religious. Those who assume the evangelical counsels through sacred bonds in a secular institute are consecrated precisely in their condition as secular priests or lay persons.[17] Canons regulating religious life do not apply unless explicitly invoked by the code; the norms common to all institutes of consecrated life (cc. 573–606) are noted here as applicable.

The teaching of *Vita consecrata* develops more clearly the relationship of baptismal consecration, in which every new and special consecration is

---

[14] "Le associazioni di laici consacrati a Dio nel mondo," in *Secolarità e Vita Consacrata* (Milan: Ancora, 1966) 424.

[15] *VC* 10. As regards the earlier phrase *quoad substantiam vere religiosa,* used to identify secular institutes as religious in substance, see T. Rincón Pérez, in *Pamplona ComEng,* 479. While intended by Gemelli and Pius XII to defend the full consecration of life in secular institutes, the use of the phrase tended to perpetuate confusion regarding the particular identity of the newly recognized institutes. Thus it was not employed in *PC* 11.

[16] "Con il cuore di Cristo aperto sul mondo," *OssRom* (February 2, 1997) 7.

[17] Based on c. 207, §2, Rincón Pérez refers to these persons as belonging to the *"status consecratorum."* *Pamplona ComEng,* 480.

rooted,[18] and that undertaken through profession of the evangelical counsels. All are called to holiness of life, to chastity according to their state, to obedience to God and the Church, and to a reasonable detachment from temporal possessions. Not all, however, are called to celibate chastity or to a particular form of poverty and obedience according to the charism of an institute.[19] A new consecration has been added to the members' secular state; they have not been removed from it, but in a sense, more deeply rooted in it.

The Eastern code's description of secular institutes also includes this concept, noting that members, whether clerical or lay, remain in their own state, "in respect to all canonical effects" (*CCEO* 563, §1, 4°).

Both codes have now clearly affirmed the reality of a lay secular consecration which in earlier decades had been placed in doubt.

Evangelical Counsels

Canon 712 — Without prejudice to the prescripts of cann. 598–601, the constitutions are to establish the sacred bonds by which the evangelical counsels are assumed in the institute and are to define the obligations which these same bonds bring about; the proper secularity of the institute, however, is always to be preserved in its way of life.

The constitutions of every institute of consecrated life must describe its particular way of observing the evangelical counsels (c. 598). According to the founding charism's orientation for the spirituality, way of life, and mission of the institute, there will be different accents on the manner of living chastity, poverty, and obedience (cc. 599–601), always within the context of the Church's magisterium and legislation. The constitutions of secular institutes must also define what sacred bonds will be used to assume the aforementioned counsels.

The bonds are called sacred; they effect the consecration of the members of the institute. A vow is a promise made to God which must be fulfilled by reason of the virtue of religion.[20] For the assumption of chastity, the secular institutes were, from the beginning, required to use a vow, an oath, or a consecration binding in conscience.[21]

A further specific point is that the secularity of the institute is not to be lost in defining the obligation of the evangelical counsels. Celibate chastity will be lived in the midst of one's lay colleagues or brother priests. The evangelical poverty of members of secular institutes will most frequently be observed individually. Members earn their living, take appropriate measures for their health care and future retirement, and contribute to the support of their institute according to their means and internal norms. Their accountability is basically to the moderators of the institute. Likewise, secular obedience is oriented to the more individual situation of the member, living and working as the leaven of the gospel. Important decisions or changes in one's life are discerned with moderators. Institutes that have one or more common works will have to provide for involvement in such works in terms of both the obedience of members and the support of such members engaged in these works.

While institutes that use vows do not necessarily receive them "in the name of the Church" as public vows, the regulation of these vows by the code and proper law, and the manner of dispensing from their obligations, argue against calling them purely private vows.[22]

Apostolate

Canon 713 — §1. Members of these institutes express and exercise their own consecration in apostolic activity, and like leaven they strive to imbue all things with the spirit of the gospel for the strengthening and growth of the Body of Christ.

---

[18] See *LG* 44 and *PC* 5.
[19] *VC* 30.

[20] Canon 1191, §1.
[21] *Provida Mater Ecclesia*, III-2. The same text provides for the use of a vow or a promise for poverty and obedience, according to the constitutions.
[22] See cc. 726–728 regarding dispensation from sacred bonds; canon 1196 explains dispensation from private vows.

§2. In the world and from the world, lay members participate in the evangelizing function of the Church whether through the witness of a Christian life and of fidelity toward their own consecration, or through the assistance they offer to order temporal things according to God and to inform the world by the power of the gospel. They also cooperate in the service of the ecclesial community according to their own secular way of life.

§3. Through the witness of consecrated life especially in the presbyterate, clerical members help their brothers by a particular apostolic charity, and by their sacred ministry among the people of God they bring about the sanctification of the world.

Although secular institutes are sometimes said to be characterized by three elements, consecration, secularity, and apostolate, it is more in harmony with the image of leaven to understand the integration of consecration and secularity as becoming apostolate.[23] The image of leaven used by Pius XII[24] was repeated in *Perfectae caritatis* 11 with specific reference to secular institutes. A year earlier, *Lumen gentium* had used the term "secular" to characterize the laity as a whole, recognizing their special apostolate as one of leaven, sanctifying the world from within and seeking to order temporal affairs according to the spirit of the gospel.[25]

Paragraph one speaks of all members of secular institutes. The sphere of their apostolic activities may be as diverse as the discreet presence of a consecrated secular in parliament and the public priestly ministry of a member of a clerical secular institute. The terminology of the paragraph is largely based on texts addressed to the laity, but it is applicable also to the clerics mentioned in paragraph three.

Paragraph two reiterates the theme of working in and from within the world, whatever may be the specific context of a lay member's life. Those who are fully engaged in a secular profession or field of labor bring to it the witness of their lives. This is their way of participating in the Church's evangelizing mission. Wherever one is, gospel values are to be brought to bear on the situation—be it office, factory, field, commerce, or politics. These truly secular spheres of labor are most specifically seen as being affected by a leavening presence which is consecrated and consecrating.

Members of lay secular institutes more directly engaged in ecclesial service, whether full-time or as volunteers, are to function in that capacity in accord with their secular way of life.[26]

Pope John Paul II, while accenting the particular value of this witness, makes it clear that values such as honesty, competence, and fidelity to duty are not enough. Presuming these, he insists it is a matter of "putting on the mind of Jesus Christ in order to be signs of his love in the world." This, he states, is "the meaning and the goal of authentic Christian secularity, and thus the purpose and value of the Christian consecration lived in secular institutes."[27]

Speaking of the Church's mission of initial evangelization, John Paul II notes how secular institute members, in fields "more suited to their lay vocation," are able to evangelize society in all of its aspects, including the laws and structures which regulate it.[28] Two other fields of mission are specifically recommended to secular institute members: the educational structures of the state[29] and the field of social communications. In this latter area they are asked to assist in the religious

---

[23] Canon 722, §2 calls for a formation in which candidates learn "to transform their whole life into the apostolate."

[24] *Provida Mater Ecclesia,* Intro., and *PF,* Intro.

[25] See *LG* 31.

[26] Appropriate to lay secular institutes, therefore, is the teaching of John Paul II's apostolic exhortation *Christifideles laici,* December 30, 1988, *AAS* 81 (1989) 393–521; *Origins* 18 (1989) 561, 563–595. Likewise of interest is the August 15, 1997 instruction which was jointly promulgated by the heads of eight Roman dicasteries, on "Some Questions Regarding Collaboration of Non-Ordained Faithful in Priests' Sacred Ministry," *Origins* 27 (1997) 397, 399–409.

[27] John Paul II, "Bearing Witness," n. 6

[28] *VC* 78.

[29] *VC* 97.

formation of media personnel to offset the inappropriate use of the media and to improve the quality of programming, especially with respect to moral law and human and Christian values.[30]

Although questions are occasionally raised about the meaning of secular institutes of priests,[31] they existed long before *Provida Mater.*[32] The recognition of institutes as both clerical and lay came in *Provida Mater,* art. I and was reiterated in *Perfectae caritatis* 11.

The canon recognizes clerical members as having two broad spheres for their leavening apostolic presence and activity: in the midst of their brother priests, and among the people of God. Canon 711 makes it clear that the assumption of the evangelical counsels does not change a member's status as a diocesan or secular priest. Canon 266, §3 favors diocesan incardination, as referred to in canon 715. *Vita consecrata* sees in the clerical secular institutes a source of spiritual riches for the member and for his ministry. He is helped in "living more deeply the spirituality proper to priesthood" and is thereby further enabled "to be a leaven of communion and apostolic generosity" among the clergy.[33]

In this context, it is helpful to return to *Presbyterorum ordinis* 3 which, discussing the place of priests in the world, presents them as chosen and appointed for the things of God but as remaining with all as brothers. Here, Jesus the Incarnate One, who became like us in all things but sin, is the model. Priests are set apart "in the midst of the people of God, but this is not in order to be separated from that people." Through assumption of the evangelical counsels in a secular institute, a priest is more deeply rooted in this specific priestly vocation.

The priest's ministry is indeed directed more toward the people to be evangelized than toward temporal realities as such. However, in the end, the persons evangelized and sanctified are enabled to guide such realities to God and to animate them with the spirit of the gospel.[34]

Life Style

Canon 714 — Members are to lead their lives in the ordinary conditions of the world according to the norm of the constitutions, whether alone, or in their own families, or in a group living as brothers or sisters.

The possibility of different living situations for members of secular institutes is simply another reflection of their identity as lay persons remaining in their secular context, or as clergy living as do other priests of their diocese. While obviously the members are not prohibited from living together—indeed some community of life among clerics is recommended in canon 280—secular institutes are distinctly different from religious institutes in this matter. Members share the bond of a common vocation as described in canon 602. When living together, their life style will be informed by those values but not regulated by canon 607, §2 on the common life of religious.[35]

---

[30] *VC* 99. For further development of this theme of lay secular institute members living their consecration at the heart of the world, see E. Tresalti, "The Past and Future of Secular Institutes," *Dialogue* 24 (1996) 82–86.

[31] For a discussion of this question, see S. Holland, "Secular Institutes: Can They Be Both Clerical and Lay?" *CLSAP* 49 (1987) 135–144.

[32] The French Jesuit Pierre de Clorivière founded such a group at the time of the suppression of the Jesuits in France. It continued from 1791 to 1835 and was reorganized in 1918, receiving recognition in 1952 as the secular institute, Society of the Heart of Christ. J. Beyer, *Les Instituts Séculiers* (Paris: D.D.B., 1954) 35–50.

[33] *VC* 10. On this point see also V. De Paolis, *La vita consacrata nella Chiesa* (Bologna: Centro Editoriale Dehoniano, 1991) 415.

[34] C. Rocchetta, "La vita basata sui consigli evangelici è segno della libertà per Dio," *OssRom* (February 2, 1997) 7.

[35] De Paolis, 413. Beyer, in view of the distinctive secularity of the institutes, sees a preference expressed in the canon's ordering of the options. Most desirable is the first, i.e., living alone; then, living with family members. The third option of group living, although it may be necessary in certain circumstances, is deemed less desirable for lay members. J. Beyer, *Le Droit de la Vié Consacrée* (Paris: Tardy, 1988) 2:232.

An earlier draft of the canon prohibited wearing any external sign of consecration.[36] However, the matter is better left to the principle of canon 711 which recognizes the secular status of members as clerical or lay. Both this discussion of an external sign, and that of the living situation of members, accentuate the difference between the nature of this state and the public and communal nature of the religious state. The Eastern code explicitly states that secular institute members do not imitate the life style of religious (*CCEO* 563, §1, 3°).

Provida Mater called for one or more houses according to practical needs; these houses could include residences of major moderators; a location for certain steps of formation, retreats, and gatherings; and a place for members who cannot or should not remain on their own.[37] When the instruction *Cum sanctissimus* clarified certain criteria for approving secular institutes, it mentioned such houses. This was immediately followed by a stress on the importance of "steering clear of things incompatible with a true Secular Institute life, e.g., clothing and common life of a Religious type."[38]

Clerics

Canon 715 — §1. Clerical members incardinated in a diocese are subject to the diocesan bishop, without prejudice to those things which regard consecrated life in their own institute.

§2. Those who are incardinated in an institute according to the norm of can. 266, §3, however, are subject to the bishop like religious if they are appointed to the proper works of the institute or to the governance of the institute.

The canons generally presume diocesan incardination for clerics in secular institutes. Other aspects of their lives which pertain to their membership in a particular institute are respected by the canon. Matters such as a particular spirituality, a way of observing evangelical poverty, institute meetings, assemblies, and retreats would be regulated by approved proper law and subject to moderators of the institute. As clerics incardinated in the diocese, clerical members of secular institutes are subject to the diocesan bishop in the usual way and enjoy the same essential rights and obligations.[39]

If a clerical secular institute has the faculty to incardinate by concession of the Holy See (c. 266, §3), this renders the relationship of such clerics to the bishop closer to that of religious in certain circumstances. The canon mentions dedication to the proper works or involvement in the governance of the institute. This latter must also be worked out in cases of diocesan incardination, especially if the institute is large and the role time consuming.[40]

The other matter which must be considered here is the fact that the major moderators of clerical secular institutes of pontifical right are not ordinaries (c. 134, §1), nor are they authorized to grant dimissorial letters (c. 1019, §1) for their members. Thus, unless special provision has been made in approving the institute and its proper law, the members' ordination is governed by the law for seculars.[41]

The Eastern code makes essentially the same provision, with the added possibility of patriarchal concession of incardination in a patriarchal institute (*CCEO* 565).

Spirit of Communion

Canon 716 — §1. All members are to participate actively in the life of the institute according to proper law.

§2. Members of the same institute are to preserve communion among themselves, caring solicitously for a spirit of unity and a genuine relationship as brothers or sisters.

---

[36] On this point see Beyer, *Le Droit,* 2:231–232, and Rincón Pérez, in *Pamplona ComEng,* 481.

[37] *Provida Mater Ecclesia,* III-4.

[38] *Cum sanctissimus* 7 c-d.

[39] On the advisability of a cleric informing his bishop of his incorporation in a secular institute, see Beyer, *Le Droit,* 2:232–233, and Williamson, in *CLSGBI Com,* 401.

[40] DePaolis warns against excessive emphasis on diocesan incardination as the criterion of an institute's secularity (*La vita consacrata,* 416).

[41] See c. 1019, §2.

Because secular institute members frequently neither live nor work together, greater efforts may be required to maintain that unity required by their common charism. Responsibility for the institute's spirit, the attraction of vocations, the formation of members, and the building of communion cannot be left to moderators alone. This canon further expresses for secular institutes the principles enunciated in canon 602 of the common norms. Deliberately avoiding explicitly religious language, it calls for union in Christ of those who share the same vocation and charism.

According to their capacity, all members need to be available to assist in forming candidates, to assume roles in government, and to assist in providing internal services. Likewise, all are urged to make permanent formation sessions a priority, and to be responsive to consultations from moderators.

Governance

Canon 717 — §1. The constitutions are to prescribe the proper manner of governance; they are to define the time during which the moderators hold their office and the manner by which they are designated.

§2. No one is to be designated as supreme moderator who is not incorporated definitively.

§3. Those who have been placed in charge of the governance of an institute are to take care that its unity of spirit is preserved and that the active participation of the members is promoted.

In contrast to the governance of religious institutes, the governance of secular institutes appears to be minimally regulated. What is said primarily touches upon moderators and what must be provided for in the constitutions. One may draw from the common norms the recognition of an institute's rightful autonomy of life, especially of governance[42] and of the authority of its superiors and chapters.[43]

---

[42] Canon 586.
[43] Canon 596.

The constitutions must provide for the way of choosing moderators at each level and the length of their terms (§1). The supreme moderator must be definitively incorporated (§2). The third paragraph of the canon outlines broadly the moderator's role in promoting the unity and participation urged upon all (c. 716).

The subsequent canons directly or indirectly address further governance issues. Moderators will have a role in administering any goods belonging to the institute (c. 718); they will be available to members for spiritual direction and advice (c. 719, §4); major moderators and their councils are competent to admit to probation and to the assumption of bonds (c. 720); moderators must be attentive to the permanent spiritual formation of members (c. 724, §2); moderators and councils will act in cases of separation from the institute (cc. 726–727; 729–730).

The constitutions must complete the description of roles and structures. There may be major moderators at more than one level and councils must exist and be consulted in certain matters. Except for canon 596 from the common norms, there is no mention of chapters or similar representative gatherings. These must be appropriately included in the constitutions.

The canons are also silent on conferences of secular institutes, although their existence was already foreseen in *Perfectae caritatis* 23. Today, these are seen as important instruments of communion with the Holy See and of coordination and promotion of mutual relations with episcopal conferences.[44] The World Conference of Secular Institutes (CMIS) was formally approved by the Holy See in 1974.[45] The 1997 *Annuario Pontificio* also lists an international conference for Latin America.[46]

---

[44] *VC* 53.
[45] E. Tresalti, "Past and Future," 82.
[46] Page 1689. For a history of the U.S. Conference (USCSI) see B. M. Ottinger, "History of Secular Institutes in the United States," in *Secular Institutes in the 1983 Code* (Westminster, Md.: Christian Classics, 1988) 13–19.

Administration of Goods

Canon 718 — The administration of the goods of an institute, which must express and foster evangelical poverty, is governed by the norms of Book V, *The Temporal Goods of the Church*, and by the proper law of the institute. Likewise, proper law is to define the obligations of the institute, especially financial ones, towards members who carry on work for it.

As public juridic persons in the Church, secular institutes must administer any goods pertaining to them in accordance with Book V of the code. The canon requires consonance with evangelical poverty, which is not to be equated with the collective witness expected of religious institutes.[47] Because of the whole manner of life and ministry of secular institutes, they are less likely to own many houses, institutions, or designated funds than religious institutes which require these to support their members.

Practical questions raised by the canon must be addressed in proper law according to the institute's specific nature. If some members are engaged full-time in internal services or works of the institute, provision must be made for matters such as their support, insurance, and retirement.

The Eastern code attributes juridic personality not only to institutes but also to their lawfully erected provinces and houses (*CCEO* 567). References to religious law require proper law to regulate the use and administration of goods with reference to poverty and to ensure the observance of the Eastern norms parallel to those in Book V of the Latin code (*CCEO* 1007–1054).

Spiritual Duties

Canon 719 — §1. For members to respond faithfully to their vocation and for their apostolic action to proceed from their union with Christ, they are to devote themselves diligently to prayer, to

give themselves in a fitting way to the reading of sacred scripture, to observe an annual period of spiritual retreat, and to perform other spiritual exercises according to proper law.

§2. The celebration of the Eucharist, daily if possible, is to be the source and strength of their whole consecrated life.

§3. They are to approach freely the sacrament of penance which they are to receive frequently.

§4. They are to obtain freely necessary direction of conscience and to seek counsel of this kind even from the moderators, if they wish.

Secular institute members must have a profound spiritual life of sacramental and personal prayer, which will enable them to live their vocation faithfully and which ensures that their apostolic activity proceeds from union with Christ. The great fonts of the spiritual life are outlined, with explicit reference to spiritual direction, a subject not addressed in the parallel canons on religious life.[48] On the other hand, the recitation of the liturgy of the hours, recommended to all consecrated persons in *Vita consecrata*,[49] is left to proper law.[50] In the case of clerical institutes, these spiritual obligations are clearly mentioned as part of the member's clerical obligations.[51]

Admission

Canon 720 — The right of admission into the institute, either for probation or for the assumption of sacred bonds, whether temporary or perpetual or definitive, belongs to the major moderators with their council, according to the norm of the constitutions.

The canon on admission is supplemented by canon 597, which requires that the prospective member be Catholic, of right intention, and pos-

---

[47] Canon 640.

[48] Canons 663–664.

[49] *VC* 95.

[50] Williamson also notes that the canon makes no reference to Marian devotion (*CLSBGI Com*, 403).

[51] Canon 276, §2, 3°, 5°.

sess the qualities and be free of the impediments mentioned in universal and proper law. Several specific points must be added in each institute's constitutions: which major superior admits new members and what vote of the council is required in the case of probation and at each stage of assuming sacred bonds.

Invalidating Impediments

Canon 721 — §1. A person is admitted to initial probation invalidly:

   1° who has not yet attained the age of majority;

   2° who is bound currently by a sacred bond in some institute of consecrated life or is incorporated in a society of apostolic life;

   3° a spouse, while the marriage continues to exist.

§2. The constitutions can establish other impediments to admission even for validity or can attach conditions.

§3. Moreover, to be received, the person must have the maturity necessary to lead rightly the proper life of the institute.

The code maintains for secular institutes three of the five impediments listed for the religious novitiate.[52] For the validity of admission to initial probation, individuals must have reached their canonical majority, that is, have completed their eighteenth year.[53] They may not be bound by another life commitment: sacred bonds in an institute of consecrated life, incorporation in a society of apostolic life, or marriage bonds (§1). Although the canon does not refer to transfers when listing sacred bonds and incorporation, there is no impediment in those cases (c. 730).

When it is a question of a marriage bond, the impediment ceases with the death of the spouse or the issuance of a decree of nullity. Cases involving civil divorce are considered cautiously when there is a request for a dispensation from the im-

pediment. Besides taking into account the usual requirements for membership, the institute will also consider any hope of marital reconciliation, the status and attitude of the former spouse, and provisions for children. Canonically, a decree of separation issued by the diocesan bishop will also be required (c. 1692, §1).

The elements of the religious law impediment regarding force, grave fear, or fraud (c. 643, 4°) must be interpreted according to canon 125 on the effect of those factors on any juridic act. The life style of consecrated seculars, however, is less likely to make these institutes appear as a place of refuge or security from the world. The religious law impediment of having concealed previous incorporation in another institute of consecrated life or society of apostolic life (c. 643, 5°) could be added in constitutions (§2). Adding impediments which affect validity should be weighed carefully, and such impediments should refer to facts which can be objectively verified.

The third paragraph here is a good example of a very significant criterion which cannot be readily measured and proven. Individuals and moderators must make prudential judgments; then the progressive stages of probation and formation allow for periodic evaluations. If an institute uses experts in evaluating prospective members, it must observe canon 220 on the individual's right to his or her good reputation and to privacy.

The Eastern code applies to secular institutes the list of invalidating impediments pertinent to monastic novitiates, orders, and congregations (*CCEO* 568, §1).[54]

Initial Probation

Canon 722 — §1. Initial probation is to be ordered in a way that the candidates understand more fittingly their own divine vocation, and indeed, the one proper to the institute, and that they are trained in the spirit and way of life of the institute.

---

[52] See c. 643, §1.

[53] See c. 97, §1.

[54] See *CCEO* 450.

§2. Candidates are properly to be formed to lead a life according to the evangelical counsels and are to be taught to transform their whole life into the apostolate, employing those forms of evangelization which better respond to the purpose, spirit, and character of the institute.

§3. The constitutions are to define the manner and length of this probation before first taking on sacred bonds in the institute; the length is not to be less than two years.

The canon provides broad areas of content for initial probation, calling attention again to the specific nature of the vocation to secular consecration. The constitutions must provide most of the specifics, but, in every institute, the length of this period before sacred bonds must be no less than two years. The fact that secular institutes do not necessarily have a full-time residential formation program like a religious novitiate explains the longer required minimum probationary period.

The code basically outlines the key concerns of the probationary period: an understanding of a vocation to consecrated life and formation in the particular spirit and way of life of the institute; formation in living the evangelical counsels with the distinctive secularity of the institute; formation for a life fully translated into apostolate which, like leaven, strives to imbue all things with the spirit of the gospel; formation as laity to share in the Church's evangelizing tasks, using the means which most clearly respond to the purpose, spirit, and character of the institute; formation for ordering and informing the temporal order according to the values of the gospel; formation as ecclesial men and women, thinking with the Church; formation in a life of prayer, both personal and liturgical, enabling the institute's members to fulfill fruitfully those obligations mentioned in canon 719.

A 1980 document on formation in secular institutes resulted from a study carried out by the Sacred Congregation for Religious and Secular Institutes.[55] The document recognized the specific problems of formation in institutes: the synthesis of faith, consecration, and secular life; finding appropriate times and places for professionally employed persons to engage in formation activities, whether as candidates or formators; an ecclesial milieu in which the vocation is often misunderstood.[56] The document indicates various particular aspects of formation: the spiritual, doctrinal-biblical, and theological; the psychological, moral, and ascetical; formation for the secular apostolate; and professional formation.[57]

The second paragraph of the canon reiterates the fact that one's whole life is transformed into apostolate. In harmony with this, the formation text insists that work, professional activity, and every type of presence in society must become both a means of personal sanctification and a way of inserting Christian values, above all charity, into a world to be sanctified from within.

While not explicitly stated, it is understood that clerical institutes must observe the universal norms of law in preparation for the reception of orders.

Incorporation

Canon 723 — §1. When the period of initial probation has elapsed, a candidate who is judged suitable is to assume the three evangelical counsels strengthened by a sacred bond or is to depart from the institute.

§2. This first incorporation is to be temporary according to the norm of the constitutions; it is not to be less than five years.

§3. When the period of this incorporation has elapsed, the member who is judged suitable is to be admitted to perpetual incorporation or to definitive incorporation, that is, with temporary bonds that are always to be renewed.

§4. Definitive incorporation is equivalent to perpetual incorporation with regard to the specific juridic effects established in the constitutions.

[55] SCRIS, "Formation in Secular Institutes," in *Secular Institutes, Documents,* 113–126.

[56] Ibid. II-B, 115.
[57] Ibid. III-D, 118–121.

The constitutions of each institute will state who is competent to judge suitability to assume the evangelical counsels initially, perpetually, or definitively (c. 720). They will also specify what sacred bonds are used (c. 712). With the first assumption of the evangelical counsels, strengthened by sacred bonds, the individual leaves the probationary stage and becomes incorporated in the institute for a specific time. The first period of incorporation must last a minimum of five years, whether the bonds are taken immediately for the full time or with renewals during the five years. No maximum time in temporary bonds is specified, but the constitutions should distinguish temporary from definitive incorporation.

An institute's proper law must also clarify its practice of perpetual and/or definitive incorporation. The canon gives a basic explanation of definitive incorporation: the bonds are made for a specific period of time—as distinct from making them for life—but they are always to be renewed. That is, there is no longer the sense of the initial, temporary incorporation at the end of which it is clear that the individual and the moderators must again discern its continuation. According to paragraph four, the juridic effects of definitive and perpetual incorporation will be equivalent for those matters established in the constitutions. As noted, the code establishes definitive incorporation as a requirement for a supreme moderator (c. 717, §2).[58]

Ongoing Formation

Canon 724 — §1. Formation after the first assumption of sacred bonds is to be continued without interruption according to the constitutions.

§2. Members are to be formed in divine and human things at the same time; moreover, moderators of the institute are to have a serious concern for the continued spiritual formation of the members.

It is commonly understood today that formation in consecrated life must continue for the whole of one's life. This was already explicitly stated for secular institutes in *Perfectae caritatis* 11, which called for this integration of the human and divine.

Addressing the 1996 World Congress in Brazil, E. Tresalti urged the necessity of support and training for living out the "secularity-consecration synthesis." This training must enable members to "stand on their own two feet as Christians in a world which refuses the values of the Gospel."[59]

Likewise, *Vita consecrata* accentuates the fact that formation, integrating every aspect of the consecrated person's life, never ends precisely because it aims at transformation of the whole person in identification with Christ.[60]

Associates

Canon 725 — An institute can associate to itself by some bond determined in the constitutions other members of the Christian faithful who are to strive for evangelical perfection according to the spirit of the institute and are to participate in its mission.

In distinguishing which existing associations could be canonically established as secular institutes, *Provida Mater* specified that members "in the strict sense" assume the three evangelical counsels.[61] More specifically, *Cum sanctissimus* added that there could be "members attached and incorporated in various degrees who aspire to the perfect life of the gospel, and try to live it in their own situation but do not, or cannot, rise to a commitment to all three counsels at a higher level."[62] A 1976 study on married people and secular institutes concluded that they "necessarily belong to S.I. as members in the wider sense."[63]

---

[58] Rincón Pérez refers to definitive incorporation as "potentially perpetual" (*Pamplona ComEng,* 485).

[59] Tresalti, "Past and Future," 85.
[60] *VC* 65. Numbers 69–71 explicitly discuss continuing formation.
[61] *Provida Mater Ecclesia,* III, §2.
[62] *Cum sanctissimus* 7 a.
[63] SCRIS, "Married People and the Secular Institutes," in *Secular Institutes, Documents,* 111. See also De Paolis

Vita consecrata further clarifies the distinction between baptismal consecration, with its evangelical demands on all, and that further consecration which is rooted in baptism but is not a necessary consequence of it. In particular, the call to and gift of celibacy are characteristic of the consecrated life.[64]

Discussing this point at the 1996 World Congress, Martine Carrez-Maratray noted that many institutes are experimenting with associates, especially couples. In doing so, they seek communion through a shared spirit in mission, without confusion of their respective states of life.[65] Besides referring to an association formalized in accordance with constitutions as provided for in the canon, *Vita consecrata,* in discussing cooperation with the laity also notes that secular institute members "relate to other members of the faithful at the level of everyday life."[66]

Departure of the Temporarily Incorporated

Canon 726 — §1. When the period of temporary incorporation has elapsed, a member is able to leave the institute freely or the major moderator, after having heard the council, can exclude a member for a just cause from the renewal of the sacred bonds.

§2. For a grave cause, a temporarily incorporated member who freely petitions it is able to obtain an indult of departure from the supreme moderator with the consent of the council.

Either the individual or the major moderator may take the initiative to terminate the relationship when the period of temporary incorporation has concluded. One is free to depart when the sacred bonds expire, or a major moderator may exclude

the individual from renewal for a just cause. The present canon does not specify any such causes, unlike canon 689 on religious institutes, nor are such causes generally applicable, since they presuppose the more corporate life-style and mission of religious. Rather, a failure or inability to live the life of the evangelical counsels in a secular context, to fulfill the obligations of the spiritual and apostolic life, or to participate in the life of the institute according to proper law would constitute just causes of exclusion from renewal.

A grave cause is necessary to request an indult of departure during temporary incorporation. The competent authority is the supreme moderator with the consent of the council, without distinction between pontifical and diocesan institutes. The effects of the indult are given in canon 728.

Departure of the Perpetually Incorporated

Canon 727 — §1. After having considered the matter seriously before the Lord, a perpetually incorporated member who wishes to leave the institute is to seek an indult of departure from the Apostolic See through the supreme moderator if the institute is of pontifical right; otherwise the member may also seek it from the diocesan bishop, as it is defined in the constitutions.

§2. If it concerns a cleric incardinated in the institute, the prescript of can. 693 is to be observed.

A request for an indult of departure by a perpetually incorporated member is transmitted to ecclesiastical authority: the Apostolic See or the diocesan bishop.[67] Further particulars are to be found in the constitutions. The request is pro-

---

who states that the faithful associated with an institute, sharing in some way in its spirituality and apostolate, are not, by that fact, incorporated in it (*La vita consacrata,* 423).

[64] *VC* 30.

[65] M. Carrez-Maratray, "Speech," *Dialogue* 24 (1996) 77.

[66] *VC* 54.

[67] Beyer notes that the term *etiam* in the Latin text is of considerable importance. Because of the practice of discretion in some institutes, that is, of not making one's membership commonly known, those of diocesan right may prefer to petition the indult through the Apostolic See (*Le Droit,* 2:268). On this point De Paolis concludes that the bishop does not enjoy the competency to grant the indult unless this competency is provided for in the constitutions (*La vita consacrata,* 424).

cessed through the supreme moderator. The canon is silent regarding the council; thus, unless the constitutions state otherwise, the council is not involved.

A question may be raised as to the procedure to be followed in the case of those who are definitively incorporated, "with temporary bonds that are always to be renewed" (c. 723, §3). Unless it is so stated in the constitutions (cf. c. 723, §4), these bonds should not simply be equated with perpetual incorporation, requiring recourse to ecclesiastical authority.[68] J. Beyer believes that allowing the supreme moderator to permit these departures favors respect of the freedom of the individual, secularity, and discretion.[69] Clearly, an institute which uses this option must make appropriate provisions in its proper law.

The above applies equally to clerics with diocesan incardination. However, if the cleric has been incardinated in the institute, canon 693 from religious law must be observed.

Juridic Effect of an Indult of Departure

Canon 728 — When an indult of departure has been granted legitimately, all the bonds as well as the rights and obligations deriving from incorporation cease.

The canon is a simple, straightforward statement. With a legitimately granted indult of departure, the bonds and all that arose from the resulting incorporation cease, whether on the part of the individual or of the institute. By contrast, all that arises from baptismal consecration and priestly ordination remains unchanged.

Dismissal

Canon 729 — A member is dismissed from an institute according to the norm of cann. 694 and 695; moreover, the constitutions are to determine other causes for dismissal provided that they are **proportionately grave, external, imputable, and juridically proven, and the method of proceeding established in cann. 697–700 is to be observed. The prescript of can. 701 applies to one dismissed.**

By way of exception, this canon borrows large portions of religious law. The norms for *ipso facto* dismissal (c. 694) and for obligatory dismissal (c. 695) are simply incorporated. In the case of facultative dismissal, the pertinent canonical principles are repeated, but the list of causes is omitted (see c. 696, §1). In their own constitutions, institutes may list causes for dismissal which are appropriate to the secular nature of these institutes. Since the canon refers explicitly to constitutions and not to proper law in general, these causes will have been approved by ecclesiastical authority.

The procedure for dismissal is according to canons 697–700, with the inclusion of canon 701 on the effects of the pertinent decree.

The Eastern code leaves the decree of dismissal of a perpetually incorporated member to the institute's statutes, but requires its approval by the eparchial bishop or a higher ecclesiastical authority before it is executed.[70] This quite general treatment of such a sensitive matter must be understood in light of the reservation of more detailed norms for secular institutes to the particular law of each *sui iuris* church (*CCEO* 569).

Transfer

Canon 730 — In order for a member of a secular institute to transfer to another secular institute, the prescripts of cann. 684, §§1, 2, 4, and 685 are to be observed; moreover, for transfer to be made to a religious institute or to a society of apostolic life or from them to a secular institute, the permission of the Apostolic See is required, whose mandates must be observed.

In the case of transfers, religious law is again borrowed, although the section on monasteries is omitted (c. 684, §3) and the provisions for trans-

---

[68] See also Williamson, in *CLSGBI Com,* 406.
[69] Beyer, *Le Droit,* 2:267–268.

[70] *CCEO* 568, §2.

fer between different types of institutes and societies are adapted (c. 684, §5). Thus the competency for allowing transfers between secular institutes remains with the internal authority, while those involving religious or members of societies of apostolic life require the permission of the Apostolic See. This latter provision is true regardless of whether the institutes involved are pontifical or diocesan. The diverse bonds employed and the diverse forms of incorporation provided for in religious institutes, secular institutes, and societies of apostolic life may occasion certain provisions or "mandates" from the Apostolic See when granting the permission for transfer, in order to supply details not contained in universal law.

BIBLIOGRAPHY

Bibliographical material for canons 710–730 can be found after the commentary on canon 746.

Sharon L. Holland, I.H.M.

SECTION II
SOCIETIES OF APOSTOLIC LIFE
[cc. 731–746]

A glance at history helps explain the charismatic and juridic identity of societies of apostolic life and why the code dedicates a distinct section to them. Two broad periods are identifiable: the first includes the sixteenth and seventeenth centuries and the second takes in the nineteenth century and the beginning of the twentieth.[1]

Many of the best known societies from the first period were founded in France where widespread poverty and misery were compounded by the attitude of a society little disposed to assist its poor. These were the circumstances that gave rise to the Oratory of Jesus and Mary Immaculate under the guidance of Pierre de Bérulle in 1611, the Company of Priests of S. Sulpice founded by Jean-Jacques Olier in 1642, and the Congregation of Jesus and Mary (Eudists), founded by St. John Eudes in 1643.

These three founders were fathers of a school of French spirituality which contributed greatly to the formation of society in France in those difficult times. Even today, both the Sulpicians and the Eudists continue to be engaged in seminary formation, a work of critical importance following the Council of Trent.

Two other great societies of the first period are the Congregation of the Mission founded by St. Vincent de Paul in 1625 and the Daughters of Charity founded by St. Vincent and St. Louise de Marillac in 1633. St. Vincent de Paul sought to revitalize the faith through popular missions, reinforcing the work of the parishes. What was new in

his society was the accent on mission. His priests would be secular priests, living in community and working for the salvation of rural people. This mission, not consecration of life through profession of the evangelical counsels, would be their principal identity.

The founders also sought a greater flexibility of life for the Daughters of Charity than would have been possible in the religious life of that time. The words of St. Vincent are well known: the Daughters would have as their monastery the houses of the poor; as their cell, a rented room; as their chapel, the parish church; and as their cloister, the streets of the city.

While the societies of the first period focused their attention primarily on the local population, those of the second period took impetus from the movement of world exploration. With the fleets of the world powers went the first evangelizers: religious priests, especially Dominicans, Franciscans, and Jesuits. These orders produced great missionaries, but for many it was difficult to reconcile the demands of religious observance with those of missionary life.

In 1622 Pope Gregory XV founded the Congregation for the Propagation of the Faith to separate church authority from colonial governments and to provide a centralized authority for the missions in the newly discovered territories. The first society of a new type followed in 1660 with the creation of the Paris Foreign Mission Society. This was a society of secular priests exclusively dedicated to the missions. It served as a model for groups which developed later, largely in the nineteenth century.

In this second period there were diverse foundations but, most frequently, new societies were founded for the missions abroad. These included: the Society of African Missions (1856), the Missionary Society of St. Joseph of Mill Hill (1866), the Missionaries of Africa ("White Fathers," 1868), the Maryknoll Foreign Mission Society (1911), and

---

[1] The 1998 *Annuario Pontificio* lists thirty pontifical societies of men and nine of women. Of the former, fifteen relate to CEP and one to CEC. The others and all of the women's societies relate to CICLSAL (1494–1503 and 1704–1705).

892

the Missionary Society of St. Columban (1917). Also founded during this period, but with a scope broader than the foreign missions, was the Society of the Catholic Apostolate (Pallottines, 1835).[2]

Prior to the 1917 code, these clerical societies were often referred to as secular congregations. In that code they appeared in Book II, *De personis* (On Persons), part two, *De religiosis* (On Religious), under the specific title XVII, *De societatibus sive virorum sive mulierum in communi viventium sine votis* (On Societies of Men or Women Leading a Common Life without Vows). Many canons were borrowed from religious law, but the members clearly were not bound by religious vows. Nevertheless, they were said to live in a way that "imitated" religious life (*CIC* 673, §1).

During the code revision process, the 1977 draft of canons on consecrated life treated societies together with religious institutes and secular institutes as a third category of institutes of consecrated life, entitled *De institutis vitae apostolicae consociatae* (On Institutes of Associated Apostolic Life). This positioning and identity were sharply debated during the 1980 code commission meetings because of the great diversity among societies and the diversity of views regarding the meaning of consecrated life and the means of undertaking it.[3]

Following the publication of the 1983 code, an interesting exchange of correspondence between representatives of missionary societies, the Pontifical Commission for the Interpretation of the Code, and the Sacred Congregation for the Evangelization of Peoples resulted in the determination that those missionary societies recognized under title XVII of the 1917 code now fell under the 1983 code's canons on societies of apostolic life. The option of being considered clerical associations according to the canons on associations of the faithful (cc. 298–329) was not seen as appropriate, since those canons envision neither incardination in a clerical association nor the exercise of the power of governance (*potestas regiminis*), both of which are very important for these missionary societies.[4]

The difficulty of giving the societies a single juridic identity is reflected also in the Code of Canons of the Eastern Churches. There, within title XII, "Monks and Other Religious as well as Members of Other Institutes of Consecrated Life" (*CCEO* 410–572), two separate sections speak of societies: chapter 2, "Societies of Common Life according to the Manner of Religious" (*CCEO* 554–562), and chapter 4, "Other Forms of Consecrated Life and Societies of Apostolic Life" (*CCEO* 570–572). Within the latter, only Eastern code canon 572 is dedicated to societies.

---

[2] For additional historical background on such societies, see C. Duster, *The Canonical Status of Members of Missionary Societies of Apostolic Life of Pontifical Right* (Rome: Columban Fathers, 1994).

[3] *Comm* 13 (1981) 377–387.

[4] J. Beyer. *Le Droit de la Vie Consacrée* (Paris: Tardy, 1988) 1: 196–198.

CANONS AND COMMENTARY

Identity

Canon 731 — §1. Societies of apostolic life resemble institutes of consecrated life; their members, without religious vows, pursue the apostolic purpose proper to the society and, leading a life in common as brothers or sisters according to their proper manner of life, strive for the perfection of charity through the observance of the constitutions.

§2. Among these are societies in which members assume the evangelical counsels by some bond defined in the constitutions.

This canon presents the key identifying characteristic of societies: the pursuit of their proper apostolic purpose. In common with all Christians, members seek the perfection of charity; as members of their particular society, they do so through observance of their constitutions.

The juridic identity of societies is presented by way of comparison. The former phrase regarding "imitation" of religious life has been replaced by the statement that societies "resemble" institutes of consecrated life. The canon further clarifies the fact that societies do not have religious vows. Not surprisingly, the proper translation and interpretation of *accedunt* is still controverted.[5] Historically, the primary point of comparison with religious seems to have been with reference to common life. Nevertheless, the distinctive way of living common life in societies must be spelled out in proper law.

In the end, it is most helpful to glean the positive elements of the identity of such societies from universal law, remembering that their constitutions will provide further detail.

As a rule, where religious law has not been invoked, it should not be considered applicable to societies. The post-synodal apostolic exhortation, *Vita consecrata,* recognizes that each society pursues its particular apostolic or missionary end and that the "specific identity of this form of life is to be preserved and promoted."[6] Indeed the specific nature of societies of apostolic life demonstrates that the apostolate, rightly understood as a mission received from the Lord Jesus, may in itself constitute a way to holiness, to the perfection of charity.[7]

It is common to all societies to be active in the apostolate, living a common life and pursuing charity through observance of their constitutions. According to the second paragraph of the canon, some societies assume the evangelical counsels. The bond by which they do so, according to their constitutions, may be a vow (though not a religious vow), a promise, an oath, or a written contract. It is essential that, in addition to identifying the kind of bond by which the counsels are assumed, the constitutions state the more specific manner of observing them.

On the one hand, this second paragraph of the canon recognizes the real diversity among societies. On the other, it continues to fuel the debate over whether such societies really belong in the category of institutes of consecrated life.[8] Some consider it an anomaly to have members assume the evangelical counsels in a society which is not considered to be an institute of consecrated life.[9]

The Eastern code canon 572 is essentially the same as canon 731, §1, with the added provision that these societies are regulated by the particular law of their own church *sui iuris* or that issued by

---

[5] J. Bonfils, "De societatibus vitae apostolicae," in *Com Ex,* 1882–1883. See also T. Rincón Pérez, in *Pamplona ComEng,* 488–489. While clearly noting that societies are not institutes of consecrated life, the latter author returns to the earlier language, stating that many of the norms regulating societies are in "imitation" (*ad instar*) of religious or consecrated life.

[6] *AAS* 88 (1996) 377–486, n. 11; *Origins* 25 (1996) 681, 683–719.

[7] Bonfils, "De societatibus," 1918.

[8] Strongly opposed to such a categorization is Bonfils, "De societatibus," 1918; in favor of such recognition for at least some societies is J. Beyer, "De novo iure circa vitae consecratae instituta et eorum sodales quaesita et dubia solvenda," *P* 73 (1984) 413–417.

[9] See E. Williamson, in *CLSGBI Com,* 408.

the Apostolic See. In contrast, Eastern code canon 554, §1 speaks of societies of common life in the manner of religious (*ad instar religiosorum*) in which the members assume the evangelical counsels. Unlike canon 731, §2, it provides for this assumption of the counsels by sacred bonds.

Applicable Canons from Religious Law

Canon 732 — Those things which are established in cann. 578–597 and 606 apply to societies of apostolic life, without prejudice, however, to the nature of each society; moreover, cann. 598–602 apply to the societies mentioned in can. 731, §2.

Canon 732 necessarily has two parts to accommodate the diversity provided for in the preceding canon. The canons applicable to societies of apostolic life are borrowed from the norms common to all institutes of consecrated life,[10] excluding the initial canons which more specifically deal with consecration through profession of the evangelical counsels.[11] However, the use of the canons invoked is conditioned by the phrase "without prejudice...to the nature of each society."

The first such reference, canon 578, speaks of fidelity to the intent of the founder or foundress. This is followed by general norms which regulate: erection, aggregation, divisions, mergers, changes subject to the Holy See, suppression, autonomy, proper law, types of institutes (clerical or lay; diocesan or pontifical), exemption, communication with the Holy See, chapters, and general norms for admission.[12] Canon 606 affirms the equal applicability of the law to societies of men and of women.

In addition to the above, another set of canons is invoked to provide further for those societies mentioned in canon 731, §2. These canons broadly regulate the evangelical counsels[13] and communitarian life (*vita fraterna*) for both religious and secular institutes. Canon 602 speaks of that spiritual communion which binds members of the same institute or society; it is not, however, the common life of religious or of societies. Thus, it is not clear why this canon is applied only to those societies referred to in canon 731, §2.

Eastern code canon 554, §2 similarly applies a number of canons from religious law to the societies treated in chapter 2. Further, canon 554, §3 equates the members of such societies with religious in what pertains to canonical effects unless the law provides otherwise or it is apparent from the nature of the matter.

Houses and Communities

Canon 733 — §1. The competent authority of the society erects a house and establishes a local community with the previous written consent of the diocesan bishop, who must also be consulted concerning its suppression.

§2. Consent to erect a house entails the right to have at least an oratory in which the Most Holy Eucharist is to be celebrated and reserved.

The constitutions of each society must establish which internal authority—normally a major superior with advice or consent of the council—is competent to erect a house or establish a local community. In either case, the role of the diocesan bishop is constant; his prior written consent is necessary for the erection or establishment of a house, and he is to be consulted prior to its suppression. Given his essential role in the coordination of apostolates in the particular church,[14] these contacts with the diocesan bishop must be carried out in a timely fashion, especially when the withdrawal of members is involved. Thus, the canon needs to be read in conjunction with canon 738, §2 regarding apostolic activities and canon 740 on the common life of members.

The canons do not explicitly present the differences between an erected house and an established community. However, one example is present in paragraph two of the canon, which attaches

---

[10] Canons 573–606.
[11] Canons 573–577.
[12] Canons 579–597.
[13] Canons 598–601.

[14] Cf. c. 394.

to the consent to erect a house the right to have at least an oratory. This paragraph was added out of deference to women's societies.[15]

It is noteworthy that here the canons on religious houses have not been invoked[16] and the concepts of house and community are separable in a way religious law does not permit.

As regards erecting and suppressing societies, their provinces, and their houses, Eastern code canon 556 invokes the canons provided for religious congregations.

Governance

Canon 734 — The constitutions determine the governance of a society, with cann. 617–633 observed according to the nature of each society.

In the matter of the governance of societies, there is once again a broad recourse to the canons regulating religious institutes. However, it is important to note the recurring phrase "according to the nature of each society."[17] Particulars for the application of the canons must be sought in the approved constitutions.

The canons involved make up two of three articles on religious governance. The third article on the administration of temporal goods is mentioned in canon 741. Canons 617–630 deal with superiors at all levels and their councils, while canons 631–633 discuss chapters and other organs of participation and consultation. Canon 596 on the power of superiors and chapters was already applied to all societies by canon 732. In applying those canons which deal more explicitly with the relationship of authority and obedience

---

[15] *Comm* 13 (1981) 391.

[16] Canons 608–616.

[17] By way of example, Bonfils points out the unique structure of the Oratory of St. Philip Neri, which does not have a superior general but rather a general congress and a delegate of the Apostolic See. He also notes that the Daughters of Charity elect a superior general in their own chapter, but are also subject to the superior general of the Congregation of the Mission who names a director general for them ("De societatibus," 1894).

in the life of members[18] it must be remembered that not all societies formally assume the evangelical counsels. A society member's relationship to its moderators is broadly stated in canon 738, §1.

While recognizing that the statutes of each society must determine its government, Eastern code canon 557 lists as applicable a number of canons from the law regulating congregations (*CCEO* 422; 511–515).

Becoming a Member

Canon 735 — §1. The proper law of each society determines the admission, probation, incorporation, and formation of members.

§2. In what pertains to admission into a society, the conditions established in cann. 642–645 are to be observed.

§3. Proper law must determine the manner of probation and formation, especially doctrinal, spiritual, and apostolic, adapted to the purpose and character of the society, in such a way that the members, recognizing their divine vocation, are suitably prepared for the mission and life of the society.

The canon highlights the primacy of proper law in determining the way in which each society must adequately provide for the admission, probation, incorporation, and formation of the members. Only canons 642–645 are borrowed from religious law. These provide for the criteria, requirements, impediments, and necessary documents for admission. Omitted is canon 641, which states that major superiors have the right to admit to the religious novitiate. Canon 732 invokes canon 597 from the general norms on requirements for admission and the necessity of suitable preparation.

The final paragraph of the canon provides a sort of checklist for the elaboration of proper law. The goal of formation is helping members recognize their vocation and providing for well integrated doctrinal, spiritual, and apostolic training which will prepare the candidate to fulfill the mis-

---

[18] See, for example, cc. 618–619 and 622.

sion and live the life of the particular society. Thus, missionary societies may require aspects of formation not required for members of societies working in their own country and culture. Canon 736, §2 further specifies the formation required in clerical societies. Since universal law provides extensively for priestly formation, particular attention may have to be given to formative programs in societies of women or of laymen.

Because of the vast diversity among societies, proper law must state clearly the modality and meaning of incorporation. Canon 737 views incorporation as the basis for rights and obligations in the society. The fact that the assumption of the evangelical counsels is not normative for all societies helps clarify the fact that such an act is not necessarily the means of incorporation. Some societies use an oath and others a promise to effect incorporation, even if other bonds are used for the assumption of the evangelical counsels. Proper law must indicate whether there is temporary incorporation prior to that which is definitive. The specific terms used must also be clear, since some societies speak of "aggregation" rather than "incorporation" in the case of clerics who are incardinated in a diocese rather than in the society.[19]

Eastern code canon 559, §1 obliges societies to observe the norms regarding invalidating impediments to the novitiate in religious institutes (*CCEO* 450), and the norm indicating when the Apostolic See needs to grant permission to admit a candidate from another church *sui iuris* (*CCEO* 451).

Incardination

Canon 736 — §1. In clerical societies, clerics are incardinated in the society itself unless the constitutions establish otherwise.

§2. In those things which belong to the program of studies and to the reception of orders, **the norms for secular clerics are to be observed, without prejudice to §1.**

The actual legislation making incardination in the society normative results from considerable historical evolution. The early "secular congregations" were made up of diocesan priests, incardinated in their dioceses, who came together for a particular mission either in foreign territories or in their own particular church. Before the 1917 code, the Sacred Congregation for the Propagation of the Faith permitted the use of the title of mission (*titulus missionis*) for ordination. That code did not speak directly of incardination in the society,[20] but the dicastery customarily granted indults of excardination from the diocese for incardination in a society.[21]

Without prejudice to the right of incardination, paragraph two states that the norms for studies and reception of orders in societies are those for secular clerics. It should be noted, however, that canon 1019, §1 recognizes the competency of major moderators of pontifical clerical societies of apostolic life to grant dimissorial letters on behalf of their members. Those moderators are identified as ordinaries in canon 134, §1.[22]

Eastern code canon 560 provides for incardination in societies, without reference to an option of diocesan incardination. It is the major superior who may present dimissorial letters, according to the statutes of the society. No distinction is made between pontifical, patriarchal, and diocesan societies.

Obligations and Rights

Canon 737 — Incorporation entails on the part of the members the obligations and rights de-

---

[19] Bonfils, "De societatibus," 1897–1899. Here the author also points out the need to distinguish associates and affiliates who may be attached in some way to a society without full incorporation.

[20] *CIC* 678.

[21] Duster, 154–157.

[22] On the question of incardination in societies of diocesan right, see Williamson, in *CLSBGI Com,* 410, n. 1. While this incardination is provided for in c. 266, §2, major superiors of diocesan societies are still not ordinaries according to c. 134, §1.

fined in the constitutions and on the part of the society concern for leading the members to the purpose of their proper vocation according to the constitutions.

Incorporation involves a mutuality of obligations and rights between members and the society. These must be clearly defined in the constitutions. Canon 732's inclusion of canon 587 provides a broad outline of the content to be included in various parts of proper law. The diversity among societies, however, entails considerable latitude in that law, especially with reference to the evangelical counsels. Subsequently, canons 738–740 further specify the content of the rights and obligations.

This canon does not distinguish between those temporarily and those definitively incorporated. However, any implications of this difference for obligations and rights should be clarified where necessary in proper law.

Eastern code canon 561 refers to rights and obligations as determined in statutes, with an accent on clerical obligations where applicable.

Relationship to Authority

Canon 738 — §1. All members are subject to their proper moderators according to the norm of the constitutions in those matters which regard the internal life and discipline of the society.

§2. They are also subject to the diocesan bishop in those matters which regard public worship, the care of souls, and other works of the apostolate, with attention to cann. 679–683.

§3. The constitutions or particular agreements define the relations of a member incardinated in a diocese with his own bishop.

The canon sets forth in broad strokes the relationship of members to the authority of their moderators and to that of the diocesan bishop. In light of the just autonomy of a society (c. 586, §1), its moderators govern its internal life according to its spiritual patrimony, its manner of living common life, the observance of the evangelical counsels in societies mentioned in canon 731, §2, and the

workings and decisions of various governance structures.

The provisions of paragraph two flow from the very nature of the episcopal office in the diocese.[23] The exercise of public worship, the care of souls, and other works of the apostolate are necessarily subject to the diocesan bishop's authority. Other canons from religious law are introduced with the expression, "with attention to cann. 679–683."

The Eastern code similarly expresses the diocesan bishop's authority. The equivalent norm (*CCEO* 415, §1) is applied to societies in Eastern canon 554, §2. The role of moderators is treated broadly in Eastern canon 557 on governance, without specific reference to the apostolate.

The subject of incardination in the diocese implicitly alluded to in canon 736, §1 is the subject of particular attention here in paragraph three. Particular agreements must be entered into between bishops and societies if this issue is not already regulated by the constitutions. If a society member is incardinated in his diocese of origin, but goes to work in another diocese, the need for clarity is all the more evident.[24]

Obligations of Clerics

Canon 739 — In addition to the obligations to which members as members are subject according to the constitutions, they are bound by the common obligations of clerics unless it is otherwise evident from the nature of the thing or the context.

Continuing the discussion of the obligations and rights of members of societies, this canon

---

[23] For example, see cc. 392 and 394.

[24] Models of various types of agreements between societies and bishops regarding the incardination, mission, and support of clerical members are given in J. Bonfils, *Les Sociétés de Vie Apostolique* (Paris: Cerf, 1990) 177–182. Duster, 248–254, discusses the advantages and disadvantages of the option of diocesan incardination according to the experience of missionary societies.

states that the common obligations of clerics are normally binding (cc. 273–289). The present canon, however, does not indicate specific canons or distinguish between lay and clerical societies as does canon 672 on religious institutes. Rather, the key to the application of the various common obligations of clerics is found in the final clause, "unless it is otherwise evident from the nature of the thing or the context." According to these principles, certain obligations obviously do not bind societies of women or the lay members of clerical societies. Further, certain rights and obligations which flow directly from incardination in a diocese will be appropriately adjusted and expressed in proper law for members incardinated in the society.

Eastern code canon 561 is equivalent to canon 739. The parallel listing of obligations and rights of clerics is found in the Eastern canons 367–393. For societies with sacred bonds, the Eastern code adds a separate canon on obedience to the Roman Pontiff, in virtue of the bond of obedience (*CCEO* 555).

Common Life

Canon 740 — Members must live in a house or in a legitimately established community and must observe common life according to the norm of proper law, which also governs absences from the house or community.

This canon obliges society members to live in a house or community (cf. c. 733) and observe common life according to proper law. However, society members are not bound to the same kind of common life as religious, and canon 665 on absences is not applicable. Hence, proper law must provide norms for absences. This provision is dictated by the historical development of these societies and their thoroughly apostolic orientation. While community life is an obligation, it is always in service of the mission.

A 1994 document on community life specifically addresses religious institutes; however, as number 1 of the text notes, it also applies "to communities in societies of apostolic life, bearing in mind their specific character and proper legislation."[25] On this point, Pinto attributes to the legislator a tendency to create in these communities stable centers for the apostolate rather than residences (*sedes*) of religious life.[26] Thus, the accent remains on going out in mission more than on the corporate witness expected of a local religious community.

The diversity of societies may dictate varying practices regarding common life and absences from a house or community. For example, societies dedicated to priestly formation may have houses erected in seminaries. Societies dedicated to work in mission territories may have centers to which the members belong, and from which they go out for extended periods of ministry alone. Thus Bonfils notes that a member must belong to a community but might not habitually live there, though remaining a member of it.[27] Proper law must provide for various living situations, above all in terms of the apostolic orientation of the society. For example, although what is expressed in the canon remains normative, proper law may provide for one or more members to live with secular priests or members of another institute or society, while remaining dependent on their own superior.[28]

Proper law must also provide for absences for reasons other than the apostolate.[29]

There is no parallel canon for the societies presented in the Eastern code which live in imitation of religious common life (*CCEO* 554–562). The particular law which must regulate the societies mentioned in Eastern canon 572 could make provisions similar to those of the Latin code.

---

[25] CICLSAL, *Fraternal Life in Community,* February 2, 1994, *Origins* 23 (1994) 695.
[26] P. V. Pinto, in *Urbaniana Com,* 465.
[27] Bonfils, "De societatibus," 1909.
[28] Ibid., 1910.
[29] Ibid. On this point, Bonfils speaks of other possible causes: the health of the member or of his or her parents; family necessities; study or formation.

Temporal Goods

Canon 741 — §1. Societies and, unless the constitutions determine otherwise, their parts and houses are juridic persons and, as such, capable of acquiring, possessing, administering, and alienating temporal goods according to the norm of the prescripts of Book V, *The Temporal Goods of the Church,* of cann. 636, 638, and 639, and of proper law.

§2. According to the norm of proper law, members are also capable of acquiring, possessing, administering, and disposing of temporal goods, but whatever comes to them on behalf of the society is acquired by the society.

In essence, the canon applies to societies of apostolic life the canonical norms regulating the temporal goods of public juridic persons in the Church. The constitutions must provide for appropriate regulations on temporalities if provinces and houses do not have juridic personality. In addition to observing Book V of the code, societies are to observe canons 636, 638, and 639 on religious institutes, together with their proper law. The canons mentioned deal respectively with finance officers and reports, ordinary and extraordinary administration and alienation, and the liability of the juridic person or the individual member in contracting debts. However, those canons which stress the collective witness of religious institutes to charity and poverty are not cited here.[30]

Canon 741, §2 specifies a particular characteristic of societies. According to proper law, their members enjoy a wider sphere of autonomy regarding personal financial matters than do religious. This capacity is a logical consequence of the fact that society members do not take a religious vow of poverty. Thus, proper law will also clarify the essential distinction between personal patrimony and that which comes to a member "on behalf of the society." There is a wide diversity among societies, from those observing a poverty

similar to that of religious, to those allowing a quite broad autonomy even including such matters as Mass stipends.[31]

Eastern code canon 558 similarly reflects the basic principles for the administration of goods of juridic persons. At the same time, it allows society members a greater autonomy in acquiring and administering goods personally (*CCEO* 558, §3) than might be expected in societies identified as living a common life in the manner of religious.

Departure and Dismissal before Definitive Incorporation

Canon 742 — The constitutions of each society govern the departure and dismissal of a member not yet definitively incorporated.

Until a member is definitively incorporated in the society, his or her departure or dismissal is to be regulated by the constitutions. This follows logically from the diverse modes of incorporation available to societies which are regulated entirely by proper law. The fact that this material must be in approved constitutions further provides for that clarity and justice which are especially important in cases of dismissal. A member should have information on who has the right to dismiss him or her and, at least in general, on the reasons permitting such action.

Eastern code canon 562, §4 states that the statutes of each society must determine who has the authority to dispense from the sacred bonds. Paragraph three of the same canon provides for the dismissal of the temporarily incorporated, observing Eastern canon 552 which regulates the matter in orders and congregations.

Departure of Definitively Incorporated Members

Canon 743 — Without prejudice to the prescript of can. 693, a definitively incorporated member

[30] See cc. 634, §2; 635, §2; and 640.

[31] Bonfils, "De societatibus," 1912.

can obtain an indult of departure from the society from the supreme moderator with the consent of the council, unless it is reserved to the Holy See according to the constitutions; with the indult, the rights and obligations deriving from incorporation cease.

An indult of departure requested by a definitively incorporated member can be granted by the supreme moderator with the consent of the council, unless the constitutions reserve this authority to the Holy See.[32] Canon 693 must be observed in the case of a cleric incardinated in the society. The rights and obligations deriving from incorporation cease with the indult.

In Eastern code canon 562, §4, this matter is left entirely to the statutes of each society.

Transfer

Canon 744 — §1. It is equally reserved to the supreme moderator with the consent of the council to grant permission for a definitively incorporated member to transfer to another society of apostolic life; the rights and obligations proper to the society are suspended in the meantime, without prejudice to the right of returning before definitive incorporation in the new society.

§2. Transfer to an institute of consecrated life or from one to a society of apostolic life requires the permission of the Holy See, whose mandates must be observed.

The transfer of a definitively incorporated member to another society may be authorized by the supreme moderators with the consent of their councils. Transfer to a religious institute or a secular institute, however, requires the permission of the Holy See. This latter norm, reflecting an awareness of the diversity of types of institutes and voca-

tions, is parallel to canon 684, §5 on religious institutes and canon 730 on secular institutes.

While the individual's rights and obligations in the original society are suspended during the transfer process, the code itself does not speak of rights and obligations in the new society. In view of varying forms of incorporation, proper law needs to be clear regarding the length of the probationary period and the rights and obligations of one transferring. When the request for transfer must be submitted to the Holy See, its mandates can provide for what may be lacking in proper law or any other particulars which need clarification. For example, the indult permitting a religious to transfer to a society without vows may expressly provide for when and how the vows are dispensed. Requests to transfer should include not only the petition signed by the individual, but also the letters of both supreme moderators following consent of their respective councils. In all instances, the right to return to one's original society or institute before definitive incorporation in the new is protected.

Transfers between the societies mentioned in Eastern code canon 554 and those between societies and religious institutes are treated in canon 562, §1 and 2. Among the differences from the Latin code are the intervention of the Apostolic See when different churches *sui iuris* are involved and the necessity of making a full novitiate when transferring from a society to a religious institute. No reference is made to secular institutes in this context.

Permission to Live outside the Society

Canon 745 — The supreme moderator with the consent of the council can grant an indult to live outside the society to a definitively incorporated member, but not for more than three years; the rights and obligations which cannot be reconciled with the new condition of the member are suspended, but the member remains under the care of the moderators. If it concerns a cleric, moreover, the consent of the ordinary of the place in

[32] The reservation of this decision to the Holy See is more common in societies of women with vows. *Comm* 13 (1981) 397.

which he must reside is required, under whose care and dependence he also remains.

This canon must be clearly distinguished from canon 740, which leaves to proper law provision for absences from a house or community of the society. This permission to live "outside the society" for a maximum of three years is reserved to the supreme moderator with the consent of the council and is similar to the concept of exclaustration in religious institutes (cc. 686–687). However, the parallel canons are not invoked. A cleric must have the consent of the ordinary of the place where he will reside and, presumably, if he is incardinated in a diocese different from the one where he will reside, will have made the required consultation mentioned in canon 271. While a member lives outside the society, those rights and obligations which are not reconcilable with this new condition are suspended. Clerics remain under the double care of the moderator and the bishop. Proper law may need to specify further the obligations and rights to be adjusted.

This matter is not addressed in the Eastern code canons on societies.

Dismissal of the Definitively Incorporated

Canon 746 — For the dismissal of a definitively incorporated member, cann. 694–704 are to be observed with appropriate adaptations.

In the case of the dismissal of definitively incorporated members, reference is made to the entire article on the dismissal of religious (cc. 694–704). These canons are to be observed with adaptations appropriate to the nature of a society (*congrua congruis referendo*). For example, references to sacred bonds and the obligations of consecrated life, which are found in the list of causes for dismissal (c. 696, §1) will need to be adapted in a society's proper law. Likewise, while the same procedures apply to the dismissal of religious in temporary vows (c. 696, §2), these formalities are required by the code only for definitively incorporated members of societies. The dismissal of those not yet definitively incorporated is left to the constitutions of each society (c. 742).

The Eastern code likewise refers to the law for religious in handling dismissals of society members (c. 562, §3).

(The material listed below serves as a comprehensive bibliography for part three of Book II—canons 573–746.)

Documents

CCE. "Directives Concerning the Preparation of Seminary Educators." *Origins* 23 (1994) 557, 559–571.

———. "Instruction on Admitting Candidates Coming from Other Seminaries or Religious Communities." *Origins* 26/22 (November 14, 1996) 358–360.

———. *Ordo Professionis,* Rite of Religious Profession, February 2, 1970. In *The Rites of the Catholic Church* 2: 199–297. Collegeville: Liturgical Press, 1991.

CICLSAL. *Congregavit nos in unum Christi amor,* "Fraternal Life in Community," February 2, 1994. *Origins* 23/40 (March 24, 1994) 693, 695–712.

———. Directive *Potissimum institutionis,* February 2, 1990. *AAS* 82 (1990) 470–532; *Origins* 19 (1990) 677, 679–699.

ComCICRec. *Schema Canonum de Institutis Vitae Consecratae per Professionem Consiliorum Evangelicorum.* Rome, 1977; Trans. USCC, Washington, D.C., 1977.

CRIS. *Praescriptis canonum,* February 2, 1984. *AAS* 76 (1984) 500; *CLD* 11, 91–92.

Paul VI. Alloc *Magno gaudio,* May 23, 1964. *CLD* 6, 429–431.

SCCE. *Ratio fundamentalis institutionis sacerdotalis ad normam novi codicis iuris canonici recognita.* Vatican Press, March 19, 1985.

SCDW. *Mos virgines consecrandi,* Introduction to the Rite of Consecration to a Life of Virginity, May 31, 1970.

———. *Sacris religionis vinculis,* Introduction to the Rite of Initiation to the Religious Life, February 1, 1970.

SCR. Decree on pensions and subsidies for military service prior to religious profession, March 16, 1922. *AAS* 14 (1922) 196.

SCRIS. *La plenaria,* The Contemplative Dimension of Religious Life, January, 1981. *Origins* 10 (1981) 550–555.

———. *Le scelte evangeliche,* Religious and Human Advancement, January, 1981.

———. *Par une lettre,* Acts of special general chapters, July 10, 1972.

———. *Processus judicialis,* Decree on the expulsion of religious who have taken perpetual vows in an exempt clerical religious institute, March 2, 1974.

———. *Sacra congregatio,* On help to be given to those who leave a religious institute, January 25, 1974.

Commentaries on Consecrated Life

Andres, D. J. *Il Diritto dei Religiosi: Commento al Codice Versione della Seconda Edizione Spagnola.* Rome: Editrice Commentarium pro Religiosis, 1984.

Beyer, J. *Il Diritto della Vita Consacrata.* Milan: Editrice Ancora Milano, 1989.

———. *Le Droit de la Vie Consacrée.* 2 vols. Paris: Editions Tardy, 1988.

De Paolis, V. *La vita consacrata nella Chiesa.* Bologna: Centro Editoriale Dehoniano, 1991.

Gambari, E. *I Religiosi nel Codice Commento ai Singoli Canoni.* Milan: Editrice Ancora Milano, 1986.

————. *Religious Life according to Vatican II and the New Code of Canon Law*. Boston: Daughters of St. Paul, 1986.

Hite, J., S. Holland, and D. Ward. *Religious Institutes, Secular Institutes, Societies of Apostolic Life: A Handbook on Canons 573–746*. Collegeville: Liturgical Press, 1985.

General Works

Azevedo, M. *The Consecrated Life: Crossroads and Directions*. Trans. G. Cook. New York: Orbis, 1995.

————. *Vocation for Mission: The Challenge of Religious Life Today*. Mahwah, N.J.: Paulist, 1988.

Cada, L., R. Fitz, et al. *Shaping the Coming Age of Religious Life*. 2nd ed. New York: Seabury, 1985.

Cogan, P. J., ed. *Selected Issues in Religious Law—Bulletin on Issues of Religious Law 1985–1995*. Washington, D.C.: CLSA, 1997.

Cole, B., and P. Conner. *Christian Totality: Theology of the Consecrated Life*. Bombay: St. Paul Pub., 1992.

Fleming, D., and E. McDonough, eds. *The Church & Consecrated Life—the Best of the Review*. St. Louis: *RfR,* 1996.

Khoury, J. *Vie Consacrée*. Rome: n.p., 1983.

Knowles, D. *From Pachomius to Ignatius*. Oxford: Clarendon, 1966.

Lozano, J. M. *Discipleship: Towards an Understanding of Religious Life*. Trans. B. Wilczynski. Chicago/Los Angeles/Manila: Claret Center for Resources in Spirituality, 1980.

————. *Life as Parable: Reinterpreting the Religious Life*. New York/Mahwah, N.J.: Paulist, 1986.

Moloney, F. J. *Disciples and Prophets: A Biblical Model for the Religious Life*. New York: Crossroad, 1981.

The 1983 Code

General Norms

Abbass, J. "Forms of Consecrated Life Recognized in the Eastern and Latin Codes." *ComRelMiss* 76/1–2 (1995) 5–38.

Beyer, J. "L'ordine delle virgini." *VC* 22 (1986) 591–602.

Cabra, G. "A Reflection for the Synod on the Consecrated Life." *Con Lif* 19/1 (1995) 45–59.

Darcy, C. *The Institute of the Sisters of Mercy of the Americas: The Canonical Development of the Proposed Governance Model*. New York: University Press, 1993.

De Paolis, V. "The New Forms of Consecrated Life." *Con Lif* 19/2 (1996) 62–85.

Desautels, D. C. "An Early Christian Rite Revised: Consecrated Virgins Living in the World." *RfR* 49 (1990) 567–580.

Gangoiti, B. "The Power of Major Superiors to Dispense from Common Laws and from the Laws of Their Own Institute." *Con Lif* 15 (1990) 85–99.

German Bishops' Pastoral. "Consecrated Virgins in the World." Trans. R. Barringer. *Canadian Catholic Review* (January 1988) 17–19.

Holland, S. "A Spirit to Animate the Letter: CCEO Title XII." *J* 56/1 (1996) 288–306.

Huels, J. "The Demise of Religious Exemption." *J* 54/1 (1994) 40–55.

————. "What Became of Exemption?" *Conference of Major Superiors of Men Forum* 66 (Spring 1994) 8–16.

Jimenez, A. "El Ordo 'Virgenes Consagradas' a la luz del Codigo vigente." *ComRelMiss* 75 (1994) 221–242.

MacDonald, H. "Hermits: The Juridical Implications of Canon 603." *Stud Can* 26 (1992) 163–189.

McDermott, R. "The Ninth Ordinary Session of the Synod of Bishops: Four Moments and Six Canonical Issues." *ComRelMiss* 77/3–4 (1996) 261–294.

———. "Two Approaches to Consecrated Life: *The Code of Canons of the Eastern Churches* and the *Code of Canon Law.*" *Stud Can* 29 (1995) 193–239.

Neri, A. "Nuove forme di vita consacrata (can. 605-CIC): Profili giuridici." *ComRelMiss* 75/3–4 (1994) 253–308.

O'Hara, E. "Religious Issues of Dissolution, Mergers, Aggregations." *CLSAP* 49 (1987) 155–168.

Pfab, J. "The Episcopal Vicar for Religious." *Con Lif* 14/1 (1989) 81–93.

Pichard, D. "The Renewal of the Consecration of Virgins." *RfR* (January/February 1986) 17–24.

Selvaggi, A. "An Ancient Rite Restored—Consecrated Virgins Living in the World." *Canadian Catholic Review* (January 1987) 6–11.

Torres, J. "Ecclesiastical Approval of Constitutions—Meaning and Scope." *Con Lif* 9:1 (1984) 120–130.

Religious Institutes

Holland, S. "'Religious House' according to Canon 608." *J* 50 (1990) 524–552.

McDonough, E. "Religious Houses—Acquisition of Rights." *CLSAP* 46 (October 1984) 149–160.

Governance in Religious Institutes

Beal, J. "The Exercise of Jurisdiction by Lay Religious." *Bulletin on Issues of Religious Law* 13 (Winter, 1997) 1–6.

———. "The Exercise of the Power of Governance by Lay People: State of the Question." *J* 55/1 (1995) 1–92.

Dammertz, V. "The Juridical Structure of Contemplative Life." *Con Lif* 6/1 (1982) 33–39.

Darcy, C. "Models of Participation in Religious Community Chapters." *CLSAP* (1995) 181–200.

De Paolis, V. "Administrative Recourses and Recourses within Religious Institutes." *Con Lif* 18/1–2 (1993) 1: 90–114; 2: 58–81.

———. "An possit superior religiosus suffragium ferre cum suo consilio vel suo voto dirimere paritatem sui consilii." *P* 76 (1987) 413–446.

Koluthara, V. *Rightful Autonomy of Religious Institutes.* Rome: Dharmaram Pub., 1994.

McDonough, E. "Beyond the Liberal Model." *Studies in Canon Law Presented to P. Huizing.* Ed. J. Provost and K. Walf. Louvain: Louvain University, 1991.

———. "General Chapters: Current Legislation." *RfR* 55/4 (1996) 431–435.

———. "General Chapters: Historic Background." *RfR* 55/3 (1996) 320–325.

———. "The *Potestas* of Religious Superiors according to Canon 596." *RfR* 55/1 (January/February 1996) 87–91.

Nygren, D., and M. Ukeritis. "Religious-Leadership Competencies." *RfR* 52/3 (May/June 1993) 390–417.

Pfab, J. "The Right and Duty of the Superior General to Intervene in Certain Matters." *Con Lif* 11/1 (1986) 84–97.

Provost, J. "The Participation of the Laity in the Governance of the Church." *Stud Can* (1983) 417–449.

Radcliffe, T. "Towards a Spirituality of Government." *Religious Life Review* 36 (July/August 1997) 199–213.

Woestman, W. "De institutis clericalibus vitae consecratae et superioribus non clericis." *ME* 110 (1985) 411–420.

Temporal Goods

Connolly, M. "Creative Stewardship among Religious Communities, the Challenge of the 1990's." *CLSAP* 50 (1988) 233–248.

De Paolis, V. "Temporal Goods of the Church in the New Code, with Particular Reference to Institutes of Consecrated Life." *J* 43 (1983) 2: 343–360.

Kennedy, R. "McGrath, Maida, Michiels: Introduction to a Study of the Canonical and Civil-Law Status of Church-Related Institutions in the United States." *J* 50 (1990) 351–401.

Morrisey, F. "Ordinary and Extraordinary Administration." *J* 48 (1988) 709–726.

———. "The Alienation of Temporal Goods in Contemporary Practice." *Stud Can* 29/2 (1995) 293–316.

———. "The Conveyance of Ecclesiastical Goods." *CLSAP* 38 (1976) 123–137.

Admission of Candidates and Formation of Members

Con Lif 16 (1991). The entire volume contains articles on the document *Potissimum institutionis,* the directives on formation in religious institutes published by CICLSAL on February 2, 1990, *AAS* 82 (1990) 470–532; *Origins* 19 (1990) 677, 679–699.

Hill, R. "Admitting Former Members." *RfR* 45 (1986) 621–624.

———. "Denial of Profession." *RfR* 47 (1988) 934–939.

Loftus, J. "Victims of Abuse as Candidates." *RfR* 45 (1986) 725–738.

Obligations and Rights of Institutes and Their Members

Arnold, F. "Religious Obedience in a World in Search of Freedom and Maturity." *UISG Bulletin* n. 101 (1996) 34–41.

CMSM/LCWR Task Force on Health Care for Religious. *A Vision of Life, Health, Sickness and Death for Religious.* Silver Spring: CMSM/LCWR, 1995.

Euart, S. "Religious Institutes and the Juridical Relationship of the Members of the Institute." *J* 51 (1991) 103–118.

Koonamparampil, J. "Clerical Obligations Applied to the Religious: An Exegesis of Canon 672." *ComRelMiss* 69 (1988) 111–144, 271–284, 365–383.

McDermott, R. "Evangelical Poverty and the Vow in Religious Life." *Religious Life Review* 36 (November/December 1997) 357–367.

McDonough, E. "Cloister of Nuns: From the 1917 Code to the 1994 Synod." *RfR* 54 (1995) 772–778.

———. "The Protection of Rights in Religious Institutes." *J* 46 (1986) 164–204.

———."Understanding 'Obligations and Rights' in Church Law." *RfR* 49 (1990) 779–784.

McKay, G. "Spiritual Direction in the Diocesan Seminary." *Stud Can* 26 (1992) 401–413.

Morrisey, F. "The Vow of Poverty and Personal Patrimony." *CLS-GBIN* 72 (December 1987) 26–34.

Torres, J. "Absence from a Religious House." *Con Lif* 19/1 (1995) 69–103.

The Apostolate of Institutes

Bonfils, J. "'*Mutuae Relationes*' Ten Years Later." *Con Lif* 17/2 (1992) 122–134.

De Paolis, V. "Schema of an Agreement for the Assignment of a Parish to Religious." *Con Lif* 12/1–2 (1987–88) 1: 129–146; 2: 218–242.

Fullenbach, J. "Reflections on the Theological Foundation for Lay Association into Religious Institutes." *UISG Bulletin* n. 97 (1995) 22–31.

Gambari, E. "Affiliation of the Laity to Religious Institutes: A Canonist's Analysis." *CMSM Forum* 55 (Winter, 1990) 17–27.

Ghirlanda, G. "Relations between Religious Institutes and Diocesan Bishops." *Con Lif* 14:1 (1989) 37–71.

Hubbard, H. "The Collaboration Needed by Bishops and Religious." *Origins* 19 (Oct. 19, 1989) 332–336.

Jarrell, L. "Associate and the Relationship to the Religious Institute." *Legal Bulletin* 66 (June 1993) 32–38.

Kain, S. *Written Agreements between Bishops and Religious for Entrusted Diocesan Works.* Washington, D.C.: Catholic University, 1996.

Kolhensblag, M., ed. *Between God and Caesar.* Ramsey, N.J.: Paulist, 1985.

NCCB. "Proposed Guidelines on the Assessment of Clergy and Religious for Assignment." *Canon Law Newsletter* (March 1994) 3, 6–7.

O'Connor, D. "Lay Associate Programs: Some Canonical and Practical Considerations." *RfR* 44 (1985) 256–267.

Pagé, R. "Associations of the Faithful in the Church." *J* 47 (1987) 165–203.

Pfab, J. "The Particular Church and the Consecrated Life." *Con Lif* 19/1 (1995) 59–68.

Provost, J. "Clergy and Religious in Political Office." *J* 44 (1984) 276–303.

Separation of Members

Gomez-Iglesias, V. "El decreto de expulsión del canon 700 y las garantias iuridicas del afectado." *IC* 28 (1987) 643–670.

Hill, R. "Clarification of Dismissal: Canon 700." *RfR* 46 (1987) 782–786.

———."Departure of a Religious Priest or Deacon." *RfR* 46/6 (November/December 1987) 935–938.

McDermott, R. "Canon 702, 2: Equity and Charity to Separated Members." *CLSAP* (October 15–18, 1990) 120–133.

McDonough, E. "Communicating and Indult of Departure." *RfR* 51/5 (September/October 1992) 782–788.

———. "Exclaustration: Canonical Categories and Current Practice." *J* 49/2 (1989) 568–606.

"Procedure for the Separation of Members from Their Institute." *Con Lif* 10/1 (1986) 87–92; *CLD* 11, 92–98.

Ruessmann, M. "Aspects of Exclaustration." *P* 84 (1995) 237–266.

Torres, J. "Dispensation from Vows." *Con Lif* 18/2 (1995) 82–102.

———. "Procedure for the Exclaustration of a Religious." *Con Lif* 18/1 (1993) 47–73.

Welch, M., and P. Campbell. "Provisions for Departing Members." *Bulletin on Issues of Religious Law* 12 (Fall, 1996) 1–16.

Religious Raised to Episcopate

Andres, D. J. "De religioso episcopo carente voce activa et passiva in proprio Instituto." *ComRelMiss* 68 (1987) 294–308.

Goyeneche, S. "Various Queries and Replies." *ComRelMiss* 33 (1954) 54–59; 36 (1957) 225–226; 39 (1960) 72–75; 43 (1964) 174–175.

Conferences of Major Superiors

CICLSAL. "New Council of Major Superiors of Women Religious." *Origins* 22/9 (July 23, 1992) 157, 159–163.

Ghirlanda, G. "Nature and Institutional Ends of the Conferences of Men and Women Religious Superiors." *Con Lif* 19/2 (1993) 85–106.

Nardin, G. "De accommodata renovatione statuum perfectionis . . . motus unionis inter status perfectionis." *ComRelMiss* 39 (1960) 165–195.

Secular Institutes

ComRelMiss 18 (1997). Issue dedicated to secular institutes on 30th anniversary of *Provida Mater Ecclesia,* with extensive bibliography.

CRIS. "Secular Institutes—Informative Document." *CLD* 11, 109–131.

Holland, S. "Instituta saecularia et Codex 1983." *P* 74 (1985) 511–533.

O'Connor, D. "Two Forms of Consecrated Life: Religious and Secular Institutes." *RfR* 45 (1986) 205–219.

Secular Institutes, Documents. Rome: CMIS, 1998.

Walsh, D. A. *The New Law on Secular Institutes. An Historical Synopsis and a Commentary.* Washington, D.C.: Catholic University of America, 1953.

"World Congress of Secular Institutes." *Con Lif* 14/2 (1989) 305–347.

Societies of Apostolic Life

Bonfils, J. *Les Sociétés de Vie Apostolique.* Paris: Cerf, 1990.

Duster, C. *The Canonical Status of Members of Missionary Societies of Apostolic Life of Pontifical Right.* Rome: Columban Fathers, 1994.

Finn, T. J. "An Old Entity—a New Name: Societies of Apostolic Life." *Stud Can* 20 (1986) 439–456.

BOOK III
THE TEACHING FUNCTION OF THE CHURCH
[cc. 747–833]

James A. Coriden

Teaching is central to the purpose and mission of the Church:

> Go, therefore, and make disciples of all nations, baptizing them in the name of the Father, and of the Son, and of the Holy Spirit, teaching them to observe all that I have commanded you. (Mt 28:19–20)

Everyone in the Church participates in this "prophetic function" of announcing the good news of Jesus Christ (cc. 204, 211) and helping one another to become his disciples. Hence the canons of this book relate to all of the Christian faithful because all have a part to play.

The five titles within the book deal with: (1) the ministry of the divine word, including preaching and catechesis, (2) missionary activity, (3) Catholic education, including schools, colleges, and ecclesiastical universities and faculties, (4) media of communications, and (5) the profession of faith. A major theme of the book is the assignment of responsibility for the various aspects of the entire teaching mission.

Because these proclamatory, formational, and educational ministries are gathered here in one location and given a highlighted place in the revised code does not imply that the teaching functions are separate from the sanctifying and pastoring functions. They are not. These activities are most often closely associated, like preaching within liturgical celebrations, and they are profoundly interdependent. They are separated here for disciplinary clarity, but in the life of the Church they must work together in harmony, like voices in a choir.

The Code of Canons of the Eastern Churches regulates these same ministries under four distinct titles: number 14 on evangelization (*CCEO* 584–594), 15 on the magisterium, including preaching, catechesis, catholic education, and media of communications (*CCEO* 595–666), 17 on bringing baptized non-Catholics into full communion (*CCEO* 896–901), and 18 on ecumenism (*CCEO* 902–908).

CANONS AND COMMENTARY

INTRODUCTORY CANONS
[cc. 747–755]

**The Church's Duty and Right
to Preach the Gospel**

Canon 747 — §1. The Church, to which Christ the Lord has entrusted the deposit of faith so that with the assistance of the Holy Spirit it might protect the revealed truth reverently, examine it more closely, and proclaim and expound it faithfully, has the duty and innate right, independent of any human power whatsoever, to preach the gospel to all peoples, also using the means of social communication proper to it.

§2. It belongs to the Church always and everywhere to announce moral principles, even about the social order, and to render judgment concerning any human affairs insofar as the fundamental rights of the human person or the salvation of souls requires it.

The Church exists in order to proclaim the gospel message. Jesus said, "Go into the whole world and proclaim the gospel to every creature" (Mk 16:15). This doctrinal canon reminds everyone of that solemn duty and right. It echoes the language of both the First and Second Vatican Councils; *Lumen gentium* 12, *Dei verbum* 7–10, and *Dignitatis humanae* 13 provide the most helpful conciliar background for the canon's first paragraph.

The Church as a whole, the holy people of God, is the active subject of this teaching function. It is not only the function of the ordained or of professional theologians; everyone in the Church has a role to play. They do so with the constant help of the Holy Spirit. The Spirit of truth arouses and sustains a "sense of the faith" in the universal body of the faithful, and the same Spirit distributes gifts to the faithful of every rank.

The entire Church, under the Spirit's guidance, dynamically engages God's revealed truth, safeguarding it, searching for a more profound grasp of it, faithfully announcing and explaining it.

The Church, as a result of the Lord's command, claims that its right to proclaim the gospel is "natively its own," and not dependent on any civil or state authority's concession, permission, or toleration.

The second paragraph further specifies the Church's teaching function in the moral and social orders. It is to be understood in the sense of *Dignitatis humanae* 14 and *Gaudium et spes* 76. The Church's mission is in the religious order, not in the political, economic, or social orders. Yet its properly religious role can contribute to the building up and strengthening of the human community (*GS* 42). To this end the Church announces moral principles, even on social issues.[1] The Church can also make judgments when basic human rights or the salvation of souls seem to require it; in making such discernments the Church uses "all and only those means appropriate to the

---

[1] Two major pastoral letters of the NCCB are fine examples of this social teaching: *The Challenge of Peace: God's Promise and Our Response* (Washington, D.C.: USCC, 1983) and *Economic Justice for All: Catholic Social Teaching and the U.S. Economy* (Washington, D.C.: USCC, 1986).

gospel and the good of all"; its contribution is "to increase the spread of justice and charity within nations and between nations" (*GS* 76).

The Obligation and Right to Search for Truth and to Embrace It

Canon 748 — §1. All persons are bound to seek the truth in those things which regard God and his Church and by virtue of divine law are bound by the obligation and possess the right of embracing and observing the truth which they have come to know.

§2. No one is ever permitted to coerce persons to embrace the Catholic faith against their conscience.

Human dignity demands that persons should enjoy the use of their own judgment and freedom in making decisions. They should be free to base their own actions on their consciences, and not be coerced by internal (psychological) or external pressures.

However, all persons also have a moral obligation to seek the truth, especially religious truth, about God and about his Church. Once that quest is complete, once the truth is known, then they are obliged to hold on to the truth and regulate their lives in accord with it.

It is an obvious consequence of these teachings that no one can be forced to accept the Catholic faith, or any other faith for that matter, against his or her conscience.

This is the position articulated in the Declaration on Religious Freedom of the Second Vatican Council (specifically *DH* 1–3). That document is the basis for this canon and the context in which it should be read.

The first paragraph states two different responsibilities: (1) to seek the truth about God and his Church, and then, (2) having recognized that truth, to cling to it and live by it. Both are rights which belong to everyone.

The principle of the duty and freedom to search for religious truth is one which should pervade the life of the Church, for it is grounded not only on the dignity of the human person, but on the essential freedom of the act of faith. "The act of faith is by its very nature voluntary" (*DH* 10). A healthy atmosphere of freedom should characterize the community of faith.

The second paragraph traces the outer boundary of this zone of religious freedom: no coercion. The Code of Canons of the Eastern Churches (*CCEO* 586 in title XV on evangelization) is much more thoroughgoing; not only are force and untoward influences to be avoided, but the Church should show itself as an attractive community within which religious freedom is honored:

> It is strictly forbidden to compel someone, to persuade him or her in an inappropriate way, or to allure him or her to join the church; all the Christian faithful are to be concerned that the right to religious freedom is vindicated so that no one is driven away from the church by adverse harassment.

Infallibility of the Pope and of the College of Bishops

Canon 749 — §1. By virtue of his office, the Supreme Pontiff possesses infallibility in teaching when as the supreme pastor and teacher of all the Christian faithful, who strengthens his brothers and sisters in the faith, he proclaims by definitive act that a doctrine of faith or morals is to be held.

§2. The college of bishops also possesses infallibility in teaching when the bishops gathered together in an ecumenical council exercise the magisterium as teachers and judges of faith and morals who declare for the universal Church that a doctrine of faith or morals is to be held definitively; or when dispersed throughout the world but preserving the bond of communion among themselves and with the successor of Peter and teaching authentically together with the Roman Pontiff matters of faith or morals, they agree that a particular proposition is to be held definitively.

§3. No doctrine is understood as defined infallibly unless this is manifestly evident.

The narrowly circumscribed and almost-never-exercised prerogative of teaching infallibly, here attributed to the papal and episcopal offices, should be seen within the larger and more basic indefectibility and inerrancy of the Church itself. "The universal body of the faithful who have received the anointing of the holy one (see 1 Jn 2:20, 27) cannot be mistaken in belief" (*LG* 12).

Nearly all of the vast amount of papal teaching, i.e., encyclicals, exhortations, letters, addresses, homilies, etc., is non-infallible. That is, most of the time the pope makes no pretense of teaching definitively, of defining doctrines. The charism of infallibility is not only most rarely employed (twice in the last century and a half), but it is restricted by all of the conditions stated in the first paragraph of the canon.

Similarly, even when the college of bishops teaches solemnly, as it did at the Second Vatican Council, it does not exercise its infallible authority. If it wished to teach infallibly within or outside of an ecumenical council, the college would have to do so quite explicitly, that is, with the expressed intention to act infallibly and the agreement that an opinion is to be definitively held (*tamquam definitive tenendam*).[2]

The doctrine of infallibility has long roots in the history of the Church, but its solemn articula-

[2] The statement by the CDF of October 28, 1995 (*Origins* 25 [November 30, 1995] 401, 403), that the teaching to the effect that the Church has no authority to confer priestly ordination on women requires the definitive assent of the faithful since "it has been set forth infallibly by the ordinary and universal Magisterium" is an exaggeration. The teaching (restated in the aplett *Ordinatio sacerdotalis*, May 22, 1994, *Origins* 24 [June 9, 1994] 50–52) does not meet the test of explicitness; neither the pope nor the college of bishops declared that they were making an infallible definition, nor has it been demonstrated that the whole body of Catholic bishops has taught the doctrine in such a way as to oblige the faithful to give it definitive assent. Consequently its infallibility can hardly be considered "manifestly evident." For a careful discussion of this point, see "Tradition and the Ordination of Women," a document of the Catholic Theological Society of America of June, 1997 (*Origins* 27:5 [June 19, 1997] 75–79).

tion took place in the final session of the First Vatican Council (a. 1870). This canon should be viewed from that perspective and in the context of the more recent restatement of the teaching in *Lumen gentium* 25.

The third paragraph of the canon is perhaps the most important canonically. Unless a teaching is clearly established as infallibly defined, it is not infallible. *Manifeste* means manifestly, plainly, evidently. Doctrines which are assumed or deduced or inferred to be infallible do not so qualify. The action of teaching infallibly must be clear and unambiguous, so that it does not engender confusion.

Matters of Faith and Matters Connected to Faith

Canon 750 — §1. A person must believe with divine and Catholic faith all those things contained in the word of God, written or handed on, that is, in the one deposit of faith entrusted to the Church, and at the same time proposed as divinely revealed either by the solemn magisterium of the Church or by its ordinary and universal magisterium which is manifested by the common adherence of the Christian faithful under the leadership of the sacred magisterium; therefore all are bound to avoid any doctrines whatsoever contrary to them.

§2. Each and every thing which is proposed definitively by the magisterium of the Church concerning the doctrine of faith and morals, that is, each and every thing which is required to safeguard reverently and to expound faithfully the same deposit of faith, is also to be firmly embraced and retained; therefore, one who refuses those propositions which are to be held definitively is opposed to the doctrine of the Catholic Church.

Among all the things taught by the Church, what *must* be believed? The first paragraph of this canon answers that question by describing God's revelation, that single confluence made up of the written word of holy scripture and the spoken word of tradition, to which the believer gives the assent of faith. The faith is called "divine" because it responds to God's self-revelation, and cause it responds to God's self-revelation, and "catholic" because it is proposed by the Church as divinely revealed.

The doctrine contained in the first paragraph was taught at the First Vatican Council (in the dogmatic constitution *Dei Filius,* chapter 3, and then modified in light of *Lumen gentium* 25 and *Dei verbum* 10 of the Second Vatican Council.

One important addition to the paragraph is the notion of "reception." The "common adherence of the Christian faithful" (*communi adhaesione Christifidelium*) is what makes manifest a teaching which emanates from the ordinary and universal magisterium. The people's "sense of faith" (*sensus fidei*), aroused and sustained by the Spirit of truth, receives the word of God and adheres unfailingly to the faith (*LG* 12). The Spirit facilitates the interaction between God's holy word and the belief of God's holy people.

> Thus it is clear that, by God's wise design, tradition, scripture and the church's teaching function are so connected and associated that one does not stand without the others, but all together, and each in its own way, subject to the action of the one Holy Spirit, contribute effectively to the salvation of souls. (*DV* 10)

The paragraph reminds every believer to avoid any teaching that is contrary to these core doctrines.

The second paragraph of this canon was added to the code (and to the Code of Canons of the Eastern Churches) by Pope John Paul II on May 18, 1998.[3] It refers to truths which, although not divinely revealed, are necessarily connected, either historically or logically, with revealed truths, providing that those connected truths have been proposed definitively by the Church's teaching authority.

---

[3] Apostolic letter issued *motu proprio, Ad tuendam fidem* (*Origins* 28:8 [July 16, 1998] 113–116). In keeping with c. 8, the paragraph became effective three months after the date of the issue of *AAS* in which it was published, July 1, 1998 (*AAS* 90 [1998] 457–461).

The Congregation of the Doctrine of the Faith in 1989 published a new formula for the profession of faith which is to be taken by those listed in canon 833.[4] The formula includes a reference to this category of "definitively proposed" doctrines and states that they are to be "accepted and held" (not "believed," since they are not themselves divinely revealed). This present paragraph was added to the codes in 1998 to make the canons correspond to the formula for the profession of faith.

"Definitively proposed" doctrines are those solemnly defined by the pope or by an ecumenical council or taught infallibly by the ordinary and universal magisterium as teachings to be definitively held (*LG* 25).[5]

A person who obstinately rejects such teachings and fails to retract after being warned by the Apostolic See or an ordinary may be punished in accord with canon 1371, 1°.

Heresy, Apostasy, Schism

Canon 751 — Heresy is the obstinate denial or obstinate doubt after the reception of baptism of some truth which is to be believed by divine and Catholic faith; apostasy is the total repudiation of the Christian faith; schism is the refusal of submission to the Supreme Pontiff or of communion with the members of the Church subject to him.

Previous to the Second Vatican Council the canonical context for these offenses was the Protestant Reformation, that is, the perceived errors and divisions associated with those sixteenth-century events. Now the context is ecumenical.

---

[4] *L'Osservatore Romano,* February 25, 1989, p. 6; *AAS* 81 (1989) 104–106. See the *Report of the Catholic Theological Society of America Committee on the Profession of Faith and the Oath of Fidelity,* April 15, 1990.

[5] A letter of June 29, 1998, signed by Cardinal Ratzinger (*Origins* 28:8 [July 16, 1998] 116–119), offered an explanation of the three categories of teachings contained in the 1989 formula of profession of faith and in this canon and c. 752. Paragraph 11 of that letter suggests several examples of truths which the congregation considers "definitively proposed."

The concepts of heresy, apostasy, and schism must be viewed within the framework of communion, the several elements of which are detailed in *Lumen gentium* 14 and 15 and in *Unitatis redintegratio* 3. Christians are joined together by much more than the profession of common doctrine, not the least of which unifying factors is charity.

Indeed, the terms heresy, apostasy, and schism are no longer used of those born and baptized outside the visible communion of the Catholic Church. The offenses can be ascribed only to Catholics, those baptized into the Catholic Church or later received into it (*UR* 3; *ED* 19–20).

Heresy, apostasy, and schism are considered to be grave offenses against revealed truth and ecclesial communion, especially in a Church which takes both its doctrine and its communion very seriously. Because the possible consequences of these actions are so drastic, the notions must be correctly understood and narrowly construed.

If the elements of these offenses are ever verified, they can lead to loss of ecclesiastical office (c. 194, §1, 2°), to dismissal from one's religious community (c. 694, §1, 1°), to irregularity for receiving holy orders (c. 1041, §2) or for exercising them (c. 1044, §1, 2°), to dismissal from the clerical state (c. 1364, §2), to excommunication (c. 1364, §1), and even to denial of ecclesiastical funeral rites (c. 1184, §1, 1°).

The anomaly about these severe consequences is that some of the most serious of them are "automatic or self-imposed" (*ipso iure, ipso facto, latae sententiae*), while the alleged offenses are often quite complex, nuanced, and vigorously disputed, except in the extremely rare event that the persons themselves admit to being in heresy, apostasy, or schism. In other words, this system of sanctions for serious doctrinal deviations does not work. When a person denies the offense, the sanctions can be justly imposed or declared only by means of a canonical process (cc. 1717–1728), which is almost never employed.[6]

---

[6] The canonical process was not used, for example, when the Congregation for the Doctrine of the Faith declared on January 2, 1997, that Tissa Balasuriya, a Sri Lankan

Heresy is a denial or doubt of "a truth which is to be believed with divine and Catholic faith" (cf. c. 750, §1; but the crime of heresy applies only to this narrow category of truths; it does not extend to the "secondary object of infallibility," i.e., those truths necessary to preserve and expound the deposit of faith, c. 750, §2); these are central truths like the Incarnation and Resurrection of the Lord, and not at all like the morality of artificial contraception or the discipline of not ordaining women to the priesthood.

The denial or doubt must be born of "bad faith" (*mala fide*, see *Comm* 7:2 [1975] 150, and the *praenotanda* to the 1977 schema on the Church's teaching office, no. 3), that is, positions taken with full knowledge, deliberate intent, and the understanding that they are contrary to divine and catholic faith. The denial or doubt must be pertinacious, that is, obstinate, defiant, and enduring, even after a process of reflection, reconsideration, dialogue, and attempted reconciliation.

Apostasy is the complete rejection and repudiation of the Christian (not only Catholic) faith. It implies much more than a withdrawal, distancing, separation, or abandonment of the faith. Like heresy, it requires full knowledge, deliberation, and persistence; it is neither sudden nor momentary.

Schism is more than mere refusal of communion. The canon uses the term *detrectatio* (in place of *recusat* in the 1917 code), implying an adamant refusal and persistent rejection of communion.[7] The solemn duty to maintain communion is stated in canon 209, but the elements of communion are

many more than those summarized in canon 205, for example, possession of the Spirit and the life of grace (see *LG* 14 and 15, *UR* 3).

This canon on grave offenses against belief and communion is oddly placed among the canons on the teaching function of the Church. The Eastern code placed its treatment of these same issues within the "penal sanctions" section (*CCEO* 1436 and 1437). It wisely avoided "automatic" penalties and called for warnings before any punishment is imposed.

Teachings of the Pope and College of Bishops

Canon 752 — Although not an assent of faith, a religious submission of the intellect and will must be given to a doctrine which the Supreme Pontiff or the college of bishops declares concerning faith or morals when they exercise the authentic magisterium, even if they do not intend to proclaim it by definitive act; therefore, the Christian faithful are to take care to avoid those things which do not agree with it.

Nearly all of the teaching of the pope and the college of bishops is non-definitive. This includes papal encyclicals, letters, and constitutions, as well as the documents of ecumenical councils. This canon attempts to describe the response which the faithful ought to give to this solemn but non-infallible teaching. It clearly distinguishes this response from "the assent of faith," which is due only to what is contained in divine revelation.

The canon uses the technical expression *"religiosum obsequium intellectus et voluntatis,"* here rendered as "a religious submission of the intellect and will." An exact translation of *obsequium* is difficult, but "submission" is not the best one because it exaggerates the force of the Latin. Such English terms as "respect," "deference," "concurrence," "adherence," "compliance," or "allegiance" would be better translations of *obsequium*.[8]

---

theologian, had incurred excommunication *latae sententiae* (*Origins* 26:32 [January 30, 1997] 528–530). The congregation *subsequently* issued a new set of internal "Regulations for Doctrinal Examination" (August 29, 1997; *Origins* 27:13 [September 11, 1997] 221–224) which included an assertion (in art. 28) of its authority to declare such penalties without "a penal trial according to canon law," an exception to universal law.

[7] For example, Archbishop Marcel Lefebvre led his followers into effective schism in the early 1970s, shortly after the Second Vatican Council, but he was excommunicated only in 1988 after illegally ordaining four bishops.

[8] For a discussion of this point, see the writings by Boyle, Sullivan, and Blyskal in the bibliography at the end of Book III.

The point is not precision of language so much as the appropriate response to truth. The pope and the college of bishops exercise their authentic teaching authority even when they teach in a non-definitive manner. The proper reception of that teaching is usually acceptance, because the teaching enjoys a strong presumption of correctness. However, that same teaching authority has been mistaken in the past, for example in regard to the teachings of Galileo Galilei, and almost surely will be mistaken sometimes in the future. Hence, it would be wrong to expect the faithful to give absolute or unconditional obedience to it. That is what the canon points out: what is due to this authentic but non-infallible teaching is not the assent of faith but a respectful religious deference of intellect and will, and an avoidance of teachings which do not concur with it. The canon leaves room for dissent when such honest disagreement is based on preponderant evidence.[9]

The principal source for the canon is *Lumen gentium* 25. Among other things, the conciliar text recalls that these teachings are not all of the same import or weight; the level of the doctrine is indicated by the nature of the document, the repetition of the teaching, and the tenor of the language used to express it. (See also *UR* 11 on the intrinsic hierarchy of truths.)

This canon should also be viewed alongside canon 212, §1 on the Christian obedience due to bishops as teachers of the faith, and canon 218 on theological freedom of inquiry and expression, both in the section on the obligations and rights of all the Christian faithful.

A penal provision related to this canon was added to the 1983 code at the last minute; i.e., it did not appear in its present form in the draft approved by the Commission for Revision in 1981. Canon 1371, 1° provides for the possible punishment, after official admonition, of one who pertinaciously rejects the kind of non-definitive teach-

ing described in canon 752. This intemperate provision ill accords with the duty and freedom to search for truth affirmed above in canons 748 and 218. It gives the impression that the Church is intolerant of legitimate debate or opposed to the development of doctrine. This punitive provision was not included in the 1990 Code of Canons of the Eastern Churches (cf. *CCEO* 1436, §2).

Teaching Authority of Bishops

Canon 753 — Although the bishops who are in communion with the head and members of the college, whether individually or joined together in conferences of bishops or in particular councils, do not possess infallibility in teaching, they are authentic teachers and instructors of the faith for the Christian faithful entrusted to their care; the Christian faithful are bound to adhere with religious submission of mind to the authentic magisterium of their bishops.

Bishops teach with authority when gathered in episcopal conferences or in local councils (i.e., plenary or provincial councils), and even when acting individually, for instance, when issuing a pastoral letter. Since bishops have been given an official teaching function in the Church, the faithful entrusted to them should give their teachings sincere and religious deference.[10] It is even more important here, when considering the teaching authority of individual bishops and of groups of bishops (as over against the authority of the entire college of bishops), to distinguish the response of religious respect from the assent of faith, and to discern the various levels of the doctrines being taught. To put it simply, there is greater danger of error here.

Bishops are not only not infallible, they are sometimes mistaken. What then is the nature of their authentic magisterium or teaching authority? Bishops stand in the shoes of James, Paul, Timo-

---

[9] The book of readings edited by Charles Curran and Richard McCormick, listed in the bibliography, provides a thorough discussion of the issue of dissent in the Church.

[10] Again "submission" is too strong an English translation of *"obsequium"* in this canon; see the comments on the preceding canon for more suitable expressions.

thy, and Titus; they are overseers of churches who are charged to proclaim the word and to teach sound doctrine (e.g., 2 Tim 4:1–4). They are heralds of the faith, teachers endowed with the authority of Christ, witnesses to divine and catholic faith, yet they are also fallible (*LG* 25).

The authoritative teaching of bishops must be seen within the context of the primary subject of inerrancy within the Church, namely, the holy people of God, "the universal body of the faithful who have received the anointing of the holy one" (*LG* 12). Hence, the condition, expressed in the canon, that the bishops are "in communion with the head and members of the college." Their teaching is authoritative when in harmony with that of the whole Church.

The bishops' teaching authority must also be viewed in the context of the churches which they head. The canon says they are authoritative teachers of those "Christian faithful entrusted to their care." The bishop's witness to the faith is not separate from or over against the community's faith (though there are times when a prophetic challenge to the community is called for). The bishop is a believer among believers. He has no special source of revelation or inspiration. The bishop and all the other teachers and learners who assist him are all together reliant on the Holy Spirit. They seek and find the truth, under the Spirit's tutelage, in prayer, in study, and in conversation with one another. It is in this context that "the faithful ought to concur with their bishop's judgment concerning faith and morals which he delivers in the name of Christ" (*LG* 25).

This canon should be read along with canons 212, §1, 386, and 756, §2 on the teaching ministry of bishops.

After the council there was some controversy about the teaching authority of episcopal conferences. In light of this canon, the authentic and collegiate teaching role of the conferences in the Church's magisterium seems obvious.[11]

The Eastern code, in canons 600–606, provides an expanded treatment of these issues with rich detail and helpful nuance in its section on the teaching function of bishops.

Teaching by Decree

Canon 754 — All the Christian faithful are obliged to observe the constitutions and decrees which the legitimate authority of the Church issues in order to propose doctrine and to proscribe erroneous opinions, particularly those which the Roman Pontiff or the college of bishops puts forth.

This canon is an illustration of the juridicization of the teaching office. It is not derived from the Second Vatican Council, but it is a refurbished relic from the 1917 code (*CIC* 1324).

The canon, like its predecessor of 1917, speaks of constitutions and decrees. It refers to enactments like the dogmatic constitutions of the First Vatican Council (1870, *Dei Filius* on the Catholic faith and *Pastor aeternus* on the Church of Christ) and the decree of the Congregation of the Holy Office (1907, *Lamentabili* on the errors of the Modernists). But it also refers to the constitutions from the Second Vatican Council (1963, *Sacrosanctum Concilium* on the sacred liturgy; 1964, *Lumen gentium* on the Church; and 1965, *Dei verbum* on divine revelation and *Gaudium et spes* on the Church in the modern world), and its several decrees (e.g., on ecumenism, on the pastoral office of bishops, on the renewal of religious life, on the apostolate of the laity, etc.).

There is no language here of "the assent of faith" or of "religious respect of intellect and will" as in the foregoing canons. Here it is the

---

[11] As obvious as it might seem, an apostolic letter issued *motu proprio* by John Paul II on May 21, 1998, *Apostolos suos* (*AAS* 90 [1998] 641–658; *Origins* 28:9 [July 30,

1998] 152–158), circumscribed the teaching authority of episcopal conferences very narrowly. Bishops gathered in conferences are authentic teachers and instructors of the faith, but conferences may issue doctrinal declarations only when the bishops approve them *unanimously* or when the declarations have received the *recognitio* of the Apostolic See (par. 22 and art. 1).

language of law: the faithful are "obliged to observe constitutions and decrees" issued by legitimate church authority. The authorities in question are especially the pope and the college of bishops, but the canon has been expanded to include bishops acting individually or in conference, synod, or particular council (see preceding canon).

The canon comes from an age when it was thought that truth could be imposed and error proscribed by edict. However, in 1965 the council taught that "truth imposes itself solely by the force of its own truth, as it enters the mind at once gently and with power" (*DH* 1).

The canon has no parallel in the 1990 Code of Canons of the Eastern Churches.

The Ecumenical Movement

Canon 755 — §1. It is above all for the entire college of bishops and the Apostolic See to foster and direct among Catholics the ecumenical movement whose purpose is the restoration among all Christians of the unity which the Church is bound to promote by the will of Christ.

§2. It is likewise for the bishops and, according to the norm of law, the conferences of bishops to promote this same unity and to impart practical norms according to the various needs and opportunities of the circumstances; they are to be attentive to the prescripts issued by the supreme authority of the Church.

The Catholic Church joined the ecumenical movement late, but did so with commitment and enthusiasm. The Decree on Ecumenism of the Second Vatican Council was a dramatic breakthrough; it signaled the Church's serious engagement in the movement toward Christian unity. This canon, derived from that decree (*UR* 4), is a canonical capsule of the Church's commitment. Its operative words are "foster...the ecumenical movement" and "promote...the restoration of unity among all Christians" because that is Christ's will.

By stark contrast, canon 1325, §3 of the 1917 code forbade Catholics to engage in debates or conferences with non-Catholics without the permission of the Holy See.

The canon indicates three levels of official responsibility for this positive promotion of Christian unity: (1) the college of bishops and the Apostolic See are to foster and direct it, (2) the bishops' conferences are to promote and issue practical norms for it, and (3) individual bishops are to do the same in their own churches.

The Pontifical Council for Promoting Christian Unity in 1993 issued a "Directory for the Application of Principles and Norms on Ecumenism,"[12] which summed up and superseded previous guidelines. The document was compiled to help both pastors and people; it is an instrument at the service of the whole Church, intended to motivate, enlighten, and guide ecumenical activity.

The ecumenical movement sometimes appears to move with glacial speed, but great progress has been made since the Second Vatican Council. Local initiatives are responsible for some of the most encouraging forward motion, for example, the bilateral dialogues at the national level and innumerable joint projects, both symbolic and substantial, at the diocesan and parish levels. The work must press on for it is the Lord's will "that all may be one" (Jn 17:21).

The 1990 Eastern code devotes an entire title to "Ecumenism or Fostering the Unity of Christians" (*CCEO* 902–908), which encourages the movement in many ways, and specifically recommends that Christians cooperate in common projects whenever possible: works of social justice, charity, human rights, and peace should not be done separately but together (*CCEO* 908).

See also canons 11, 204–205, 256, §1, 364, 6°, 383, §3, 463, §3, 844, 874, §2, 933, 1124–1129, 1183, §3 of the 1983 code on matters related to ecumenism. A few bishops' conferences have issued norms on ecumenism for their territories (see *LCE* at c. 755 or *Pamplona ComEng,* Appendix III); the NCCB has not done so as yet, except in the area of mixed marriages.

---

[12] March 23, 1993, *AAS* 85 (1993) 1039–1119; *Origins* 23:9 (July 29, 1993) 129–160.

TITLE I
THE MINISTRY OF THE DIVINE WORD
[cc. 756–780]

The entire people of God share in the prophetic role of Christ (*munus propheticum Christi*), hence all participate in the ministry of proclaiming God's holy word. This fundamental teaching of the Second Vatican Council (cf. *LG* 12, 35, *GS* 41–42, *DV* 1, 7–10) rules the entire book on the Church's teaching office and, in particular, this section on the ministry of the divine word. In other words, the one absolutely compelling mandate is that the word of God be proclaimed. Who does it and how they carry it out are secondary considerations. All are responsible to see that it is done.

The "divine word" of the title must be understood in a large sense. It includes not only the written words of the Old and New Testaments, but also tradition, both the originating apostolic message and its subsequent ecclesial transmission and interpretation. Indeed, it means the very Word of God made flesh in the person of Jesus Christ. The divine word, then, is God revealing himself to humankind in ongoing ways through the power of the Holy Spirit.

The "ministry of the divine word" encompasses all the ways that the mystery of God's self-revelation is communicated to humanity, especially in and through the mission of the Church. In this title preaching and catechesis occupy center stage.

The six introductory canons (cc. 756–761), in general and sweeping terms, attempt to do two things: the first four assign responsibilities for the ministry and the last two describe the scope of the ministry.

The first four canons give an impression of completeness and symmetry. They describe the roles of pope, bishops, presbyters, pastors and other pastoral care-givers, deacons, religious, and laity. Everyone has a place in the ministry of the word.

The canons convey a further impression of theological symmetry: pope and bishops are entrusted with the *munus* (function) of announcing the gospel; it is *proprium* (proper) to presbyters, pastors, and others have the *officium* (office); deacons serve (*inservire*) in the ministry of the word; religious, because of their consecration to God, render testimony to the gospel in a special way and are appropriately (*convenienter*) called upon to help; and lay persons, in virtue of their baptism and confirmation, are witnesses (*testes*) to the gospel message and may be called upon (*vocari*) to cooperate in the exercise of the ministry with the bishop and presbyters. However, these various descriptive terms were not employed consistently in the council documents or in the code. They are simply attempts to describe the different roles, and the underlying theological rationale strains under the effort of trying to distinguish them. Some are distinctions without real differences.

The reality is that everyone in the Church has the radical duty and right to participate in the ministry of the divine word by virtue of their initiation (baptism, confirmation, Eucharist), communion, and possession of the Spirit of Christ (*LG* 11–14). Some have further rights and responsibilities in regard to this ministry by virtue of their share in the sacrament of orders and their ecclesiastical office. All must be able and qualified in order to exercise the ministry in the name of the Church. To put it negatively, the Church needs to have ways of indicating who is *not* able or qualified to minister in its name, whether it is a bishop, presbyter, deacon, or lay person. That is the purpose of this elaborate system of canonical distinctions.

These canons (756–761) stand alongside those at the outset of Book II, The People of God, specifically canons 204, §1, 211, 213, 225, §1, and 230, §3, as the first principles of this ministry. They are doctrinal and foundational, which gives them a certain juridic priority. They resemble constitutional provisions which take precedence over statutes.

Roles of the Pope and the Bishops

Canon 756 — §1. With respect to the universal Church, the function of proclaiming the gospel

THE MINISTRY OF THE DIVINE WORD

has been entrusted principally to the Roman Pontiff and the college of bishops.

§2. With respect to the particular church entrusted to him, an individual bishop, who is the moderator of the entire ministry of the word within it, exercises that function; sometimes several bishops fulfill this function jointly with respect to different churches at once, according to the norm of law.

The first paragraph is drawn both from the 1917 code (*CIC* 1327, §1) and from the Second Vatican Council (*LG* 23 and 25, *CD* 3 and 12). "The charge of announcing the gospel throughout the world belongs to the body of shepherds, to all of whom in common Christ gave the command and imposed a common office" (*LG* 23). It specifies the supervisory role of the pope and bishops within the ministry of the word which pertains to the whole Church, and it points to the direct teaching which is associated with the modern exercise of the Petrine office and with the college of bishops when gathered in council.

The second paragraph, from the same sources (*CIC* 1327, §2; *LG* 23 and 25, *CD* 3 and 12), speaks of the bishop's role as "moderator of the ministry of the word" in the diocesan church entrusted to him. Canon 386 further details the bishop's teaching duties, and canons 212, §1 and 753 ask the faithful to respect and obey his teachings. This paragraph, like canon 753, alludes to the legitimate and valuable proclamatory function of bishops teaching together, jointly in groupings, in state conferences, provinces, regions, nations, or ritual churches (*sui iuris*). For example, the bishops' conferences in the U.S., Canada, and other places have distinguished themselves by announcing the gospel in pastoral messages on many urgent issues.

This canon finds no parallel in the 1990 Eastern code.

Roles of Presbyters and Deacons

Canon 757 — It is proper for presbyters, who are co-workers of the bishops, to proclaim the gospel of God; this duty binds especially pastors and others to whom the care of souls is entrusted with respect to the people committed to them. It is also for deacons to serve the people of God in the ministry of the word in communion with the bishop and his presbyterate.

The canon firmly asserts the privileged responsibilities of presbyters and deacons "to proclaim the gospel of God" and "to serve the people of God in the ministry of the word." But in doing so, the canon attempts to build theologically artificial levels within the ministry of the word for bishops, presbyters, and deacons. Granted the supervisory or "moderating" role of the bishop, all three grades of holy orders have an innate duty toward the proclamation of the word. That is to say, it is "proper" (*proprium*) for all three to announce the gospel of God and serve the people in the ministry of the word.

To explain, all three orders, episcopate, presbyterate, and diaconate, fulfill the function of teaching in the person of Christ the Head (*in persona Christi capitis munera docendi...adimplentes;* cc. 1008 and 1009). In their ordination rites, all three are given explicit charges related to the ministry of the word. Surely all three are bound to serve the people of God in that ministry "in communion" with one another, bishops and presbyters no less than deacons. Deacons are co-workers (*cooperatores*) with bishops just as presbyters are. All three are sacred ministers, in proper and permanent grades of the "hierarchy," and all are strengthened by sacramental grace.

There may be disciplinary reasons to assert greater control over the public ministry of the word for deacons and for presbyters (cf. c. 764), but there is little theological justification for doing so. Indeed, it would seem, based on the foregoing, that all three grades of holy orders participate in the Church's magisterium, that is, in its official teaching office.

The canon calls attention to the special obligation of pastors and "others to whom the care of souls is entrusted," like chaplains, rectors of churches, and missionaries. It does not refer explicitly to those deacons, religious, and laity who are given the pastoral care of parishes in virtue of canon 517, §2 (because here the context indicates that the subject is presbyters), but those persons too share in this office (*officium*) and are bound by the duty to proclaim the gospel of God.

The canon is based on *Lumen gentium* 28 and 29, *Christus Dominus* 30, *Presbyterorum ordinis* 4, and canon 1327, §2 of the 1917 code. Canons 528, §1, 771, 773, and 794, §2 also speak of duties related to the ministry of the word.

The comparable canon (*CCEO* 608) in the Code of Canons of the Eastern Churches makes it clear that for all three orders, bishops, presbyters and deacons, the ministry of the word of God is their first and foremost duty (*primum munus*).

Roles of Religious Women and Men

Canon 758 — By virtue of their consecration to God, members of institutes of consecrated life give witness to the gospel in a special way and the bishop appropriately calls upon them as a help in proclaiming the gospel.

Members of religious communities, individually and through the institutions they have sponsored, have made incalculable contributions to the ministry of God's holy word throughout history. Their dedication to teaching, missionary activity, catechetical formation, preaching, higher education, seminary instruction, research, and publication is a precious legacy and a continuing blessing for the people of God. The mention of community "family names" evokes the dimensions of their gifts: the ancient monastic groups (like the Benedictines), the medieval mendicant orders (Franciscan, Dominican, Carmelite, Augustinian), and more modern congregations and societies of apostolic life (Jesuits, Sisters of Mercy, Sisters of Charity, Redemptorists, Paulists).

This canon recognizes and promotes two distinct contributions which religious women and men make: (1) their lives witness to the gospel in a special way, and (2) they are enlisted to assist in the public proclamation of the gospel. Religious

carry out both categories of activity in virtue of their consecration to God through their religious vows. This is in addition to their right and duty to share in the ministry of the word as lay persons or as sacred ministers.

The canon has both ancient and modern roots. The language used to describe the assistance which religious offer in proclaiming the gospel is drawn from the Fourth Lateran Council (a. 1215), and was echoed in the Council of Trent (a. 1563) as well as in the 1917 code (*CIC* 1327, §2). (However, those sources spoke only of men, *viri idonei*.) The teaching about the gospel witness of religious life comes directly from *Lumen gentium* 44.

Canons 591, 678, 680, as well as *Perfectae caritatis* 8–11 and *Mutuae relationes* 4 should be read in conjunction with this canon.

Roles of Lay Women and Men

Canon 759 — By virtue of baptism and confirmation, lay members of the Christian faithful are witnesses of the gospel message by word and the example of a Christian life; they can also be called upon to cooperate with the bishop and presbyters in the exercise of the ministry of the word.

Lay people have their office and right to the apostolate from their union with Christ their head. They are brought into the mystical body of Christ by baptism, strengthened by the power of the Spirit in confirmation, and assigned (*deputantur*) to apostolic work by the Lord himself. (*AA* 3)

This canon is another expression of the full participation of the laity in the life and mission of the Church. Here it is in the area of the Church's continuation of Christ's prophetic role, the proclamation of the gospel. The canon expresses two quite distinct modes of lay activity: (1) the witness which lay persons give to the gospel message by their words and the example of their lives, and (2) their exercise of the ministry of the word.

The first of these has the larger scope: how Christian men and women embody their faith, hope, and love as they go about their family lives, their work, and their social and political involvements. They are empowered to do this effectively by their baptism and confirmation, by their ongoing nourishment at the tables of the word and Eucharist, and by the enlivening action of the Spirit.

Lay persons are radically enabled for the ministry of the word by the same forces. But now the element of being "called upon (*vocari*) to cooperate with the bishop and presbyters in the exercise of the ministry of the word" is introduced as an indication of the need for regulation and control of the Church's public ministry. In other words, someone needs to make judgments about the suitability of those who minister in the name of the Church.

The 1990 Eastern code expresses the lay role more clearly, but also more restrictively: the faithful are to take part willingly in this ministry, according to each one's aptitude, state of life, and received mandate (*CCEO* 608).

The conciliar sources for this canon (*LG* 33, 35, *AA* 3, 6, 10, 25, and *AG* 41) shed great light on it, and these canons should be read along with it: 204, 211, 225–231, and 766.

Purpose and Sources of the Ministry of the Word

Canon 760 — The mystery of Christ is to be set forth completely and faithfully in the ministry of the word, which must be based upon sacred scripture, tradition, liturgy, the magisterium, and the life of the Church.

This terse canon asserts the central goal and chief resources of the Church's ministry of the divine word. It gives a sense of focus, but it is so generic as to be unhelpful. It was omitted from the 1990 Eastern code.

The canon is based on two passages from the Decree on the Pastoral Office of Bishops (nos. 12 and 14) which describe the teaching responsibilities of bishops.

The "mystery of Christ" is a summary expression for the whole of salvation history of which Jesus Christ is the center. It does not imply a Christocentrism which downplays the roles of Father or Holy Spirit, or the responses of redeemed humankind.

To propound the Christian mystery "completely and faithfully" means to do so in a balanced and full manner, with regard for the "hierarchy of truths" (*UR* 11), and without distortion, exaggeration, or diminution. (For example, no minister of the word should fixate on a single moral or social teaching or one particular devotion to the neglect of the entire gospel message.)

The list of five sources or grounds upon which the ministry should be based is borrowed from the guidelines on catechetical instruction: the scriptures, tradition, liturgy, official teaching authority, and the life of the Church (which presumably includes the Code of Canon Law). The list is neither restrictive nor exhaustive; the canon simply suggests broad categories of reliable resources for the ministry.

Means for Carrying Out the Ministry

Canon 761 — The various means available are to be used to proclaim Christian doctrine: first of all preaching and catechetical instruction, which always hold the principal place, but also the presentation of doctrine in schools, academies, conferences, and meetings of every type and its diffusion through public declarations in the press or in other instruments of social communication by legitimate authority on the occasion of certain events.

The canon basically encourages the use of whatever means are available to proclaim the good news of Jesus Christ, but adds: never overlook preaching and catechesis.

The canon is an almost verbatim transposition from the Decree on the Pastoral Office of Bishops (*CD* 13). Transposed in this way, it does not provide useful guidance for the ministry. A clear list of recommended means of evangelization and catechesis, as provided in canons 777 and 1063, would have been more effective.

This canon was not included in the Eastern code.

The expression "Christian doctrine" is here suddenly substituted for "divine word," "gospel of God," and "gospel message," which were used in the other canons of this section. But the switch in terms has no significance; it is simply the language of *Christus Dominus* 13.

The insertion of the words "by legitimate authority" in reference to public declarations in the media (the words did not appear in *CD* 13) calls to mind the possible misunderstandings which can result from privately held media outlets which present themselves as authentically Catholic.

The canon emphasizes the importance of the two forms of the ministry of the word which are the subjects of the two chapters which follow, the preaching of the word and catechetical formation.

CHAPTER I
THE PREACHING OF THE WORD OF GOD
[cc. 762–772]

Preaching is the proclamation of the good news of salvation. It is the spoken announcement of the saving message of God carried on in the Holy Spirit. For Christians, Jesus Christ himself, the Word incarnate, epitomizes that message. The whole Christian community is engaged in retelling the story of Jesus. The purpose of preaching is to arouse the response of faith and conversion of life.

The Church's primary concern is that the word of God be preached and preached effectively. Important but secondary concerns revolve around questions regarding who does the preaching, in what contexts and circumstances, and with whose authorization.

Preaching as a Ministerial Priority

Canon 762 — Sacred ministers, among whose principal duties is the proclamation of the gospel of God to all, are to hold the function of preaching in esteem since the people of God are first brought together by the word of the living God, which it is certainly right to require from the mouth of priests.

The Church, which is made up of local communities of believers, is called together, formed, and built up by the preaching of the word of the living God. Because preaching is so vital to the health and growth of the people of God, it is preeminent among the forms of the ministry of the word. The unmistakable point of this canon is to emphasize the priority of preaching.

This claim about the effect of the preaching of the word of God on the Church is neither an empty platitude nor a mere abstraction. It is a verifiable reality. Local churches thrive on good, authentic preaching, and where the ministry of the word amounts to thin gruel, the local congregation becomes anemic and emaciated.

> There is such force and power in the word of God that it stands as the church's support and strength, affording her children sturdiness in faith, food for the soul, and an unfailing fount of spiritual life. (*DV* 21)

The subject of the canon is sacred ministers, that is, bishops, presbyters, and deacons. Proclaiming the gospel is their number-one priority and privilege. This does not mean that it is their exclusive prerogative. All the baptized who are in communion and possess the Spirit participate in the ministry of the word (cf. cc. 211, 225, §1, and 759), and now they have an explicitly acknowledged share in the preaching ministry (cc. 230, 766).

Even more important than the laity's rightful role in preaching is the right of everyone in the Church to hear God's holy word. This very basic right is clearly stated in canon 213. It is the correlative claim to this statement of ministerial priority.

The rhetorical insertion into the canon of words from the prophet Malachi about requiring "the word from the mouth of priests" (*ex ore sacerdotum*) should not mislead. The canon refers to the ministry of all the ordained, not only presbyters. Malachi spoke, of course, about the levitical priesthood of the Old Testament, and, in fact, found fault with their performance of the ministry of God's word (see Mal 2:1–9).

The sources for this canon are the rich teachings of the Second Vatican Council, namely *Lumen gentium* 25 and *Presbyterorum ordinis* 4. Canons 386, §1, 528, §1, 836, and 1008 should also be consulted.

The canon does not have a counterpart in the Code of Canons of the Eastern Churches.

Bishops Can Preach Everywhere

Canon 763 — Bishops have the right to preach the word of God everywhere, including in churches and oratories of religious institutes of pontifical right, unless the local bishop has expressly forbidden it in particular cases.

All bishops, whether diocesan ordinaries, auxiliaries, or even retired, have the right to preach the word of God anywhere in the world. The canon thus recognizes that a bishop's right and duty to preach is based on sacramental ordination and communion (rather than on his jurisdiction or *missio canonica*), and that every bishop, as a member of the college of bishops, shares a responsibility for proclaiming the gospel in the Church universal (see *LG* 21, 24–25, *CD* 3–4, and c. 756, §1).

The bishop's prerogative extends to preaching in the churches and chapels of religious institutes, which is normally subject to authorization by the superior of the community (c. 765).

A bishop can be forbidden by the local diocesan bishop to exercise this right to preach within his diocese, but only in particular instances and for a serious reason, for example, that the bishop is known to be preaching error or folly. This provision recognizes that the diocesan bishop is the moderator of the ministry of the word in the church entrusted to him (c. 756, §2).

Diocesan bishops have the personal duty to preach frequently to their own people (c. 386, §1).

Presbyters and Deacons Can Preach Everywhere

Canon 764 — Without prejudice to the prescript of can. 765, presbyters and deacons possess the faculty of preaching everywhere; this faculty is to be exercised with at least the presumed consent of the rector of the church, unless the competent ordinary has restricted or taken away the faculty or particular law requires express permission.

With this canon the Church grants the faculty to all those ordained to the presbyterate or diaconate to preach anywhere in the world. The faculty is given on the basis of their sacramental ordination and their ongoing communion, not because of an office they possess or of a canonical mission they have been given. It applies to diocesan and religious clergy.

The Second Vatican Council taught that all sacred ministers, bishops, presbyters, and deacons share in the teaching mission of the Church and preach the gospel by virtue of their sacramental ordination (*LG* 28–29, *CD* 28, *PO* 4). This is in addition to their rightful role in the prophetic office of Christ that stems from their full incorporation into the Church, a role which they share with lay persons.

Presbyters and deacons do not share the same responsibility that the bishops have for the proclamation of the gospel to the whole Church (c. 756, §1), but they are co-workers (*cooperatores*) with their bishop in the diocese, and they are required to maintain communion with their bishop as well as with the presbyterate and diaconate in that diocese (as is implied in c. 757). The faculty to preach is not a personal privilege to be exercised in isolation from the ecclesial community.

Practical questions sometimes arise about the aptitude and actual ability to preach on the part of some of the ordained. Have they been adequately prepared for this esteemed ministry? Have they studied the scriptures and the tradition of the

Church? Have they been trained in public speaking? Even if once able, are they still capable of preaching effectively?

Because the Church must be able to regulate the exercise of its ministry of preaching, the canon provides for four sources of limitations or restrictions on the faculty of presbyters and deacons to preach:

(1) A competent ordinary can restrict or remove the faculty. The "competent ordinary" includes the ordinary of the place where the presbyter or deacon is incardinated, the major religious superior of the institute to which he belongs, or the ordinary of the place where the presbyter or deacon resides or intends to preach. The restriction or withdrawal of the faculty can be temporary or permanent, partial or total. The action should be expressed in writing and should include the precise terms and conditions of the limitation as well as the reasons for it. Such action should not be taken without hearing the person whose faculty is being restricted (cf. c. 50). Any restriction of an ordained minister's faculty to preach is a serious matter, and as such requires serious reasons.

(2) Particular legislation may require a permission (*licentia*) to preach in addition to the faculty related to ordination. A bishops' conference, religious chapter, provincial council, or diocesan bishop (cf. c. 772, §1) could make rules requiring certain levels of preparation or qualification for this permission to preach.

(3) The person in charge (*rector*) of the local church, whose consent is required for a person to preach there, may refuse that consent. Pastors, chaplains, moderators of team ministry, and those entrusted with the pastoral care of parishes (c. 517, §2) all have a responsibility to see that the word of God is proclaimed to the people with integrity (c. 528, §1). Consequently, they have some authority over whoever preaches to their communities. The consent of those in charge, which presbyters or deacons may presume, may also be refused for a serious reason. (See also c. 561.)

(4) Religious superiors may refuse permission (*licentia*) for a presbyter or deacon to preach to their community in their own churches or chapels (c. 765). Again, this is a serious matter, and should be done only for serious reasons.

The central thrust of this canon is to enable and facilitate the preaching of God's holy word. Its limiting provisions are means to assure the quality of that preaching, not to impede or suppress it.

The canons use several different terms to express authorization to preach: a right (*ius*) of bishops, faculty (*facultas*) of presbyters and deacons, permission (*licentia*) given by rule-making authorities or religious superiors, consent (*consensus*) given by those in charge of local churches, permission (*admitti possunt*) for lay persons called upon to preach. Not too much should be made of these distinctions. They are simply positive canonical terms used in an effort to promote the effective preaching of the gospel while safeguarding its integrity. They might be compared to differently shaped handles which can be grasped in order to remove pots and pans from the stove.

The 1990 Eastern code makes similar provisions for the preaching ministry in canons 610–613. It notes that recourse against decrees forbidding someone to preach are made *in devolutivo* (as *CIC* 1340, §3 also provided), meaning that the ban remains in effect while the matter is under recourse.

Preaching to Religious

Canon 765 — Preaching to religious in their churches or oratories requires the permission of the superior competent according to the norm of the constitutions.

The canon respects the legitimate autonomy of religious institutes (c. 586), and requires presbyters and deacons to have the permission of the religious superior to preach to the members of his or her community. It refers to all religious, clerical or lay, female or male, of diocesan or pontifical right. A bishop (c. 763) and the community's own chaplain (c. 566, §1) do not require this permission.

Lay Preaching

Canon 766 — Lay persons can be permitted to preach in a church or oratory, if necessity requires it in certain circumstances or it seems advantageous in particular cases, according to the prescripts of the conference of bishops and without prejudice to can. 767, §1.

This canon provides a broad warrant for lay preaching. Its positive stance recognizes the fundamental capacity and radical responsibility for preaching shared by all who are fully incorporated in the Church.

The Second Vatican Council repeatedly asserted the participation of all the Christian faithful in the prophetic office (*munus propheticum*) of Christ and of the Church by virtue of their Christian initiation, maintenance of communion, and possession of the Holy Spirit (see *LG* 12, 17, 31, 33, 35, *DV* 10, *GS* 41, *AA* 2, 3, 6, 10, 25). This active participation in proclaiming God's message emerged in the code in several places, namely, canons 204, 211, 225, 228–230, 759. This canon's empowerment of lay preaching is one more instance of the impact of this rich vein of conciliar teaching on church discipline.

The canon does not view lay preaching as a substitute for clerical ministry, nor does it require that other ministers be lacking. There is no reason to describe this lay ministerial role as exceptional, abnormal, or extraordinary (as at least one commentator and a recent document have done[13]). It is a fully legitimate lay function which has now become commonplace in the Catholic Church. The same language could have been used for the preaching ministry as was used in the canons on other forms of the teaching office, e.g., canon 774, §1, "solicitude for catechesis belongs to all members of the Church according to each one's role," or canon 784 for lay missionaries.

The term "lay persons" includes religious women and men, in other words, all those who are not ordained. No distinction is made between men and women. There is no specification regarding age or training, but the ability and preparation to preach must naturally be considered.

Preaching takes many forms (e.g., instructions, exhortations, devotional or doctrinal sermons, explanations of biblical texts, mission talks, sacramental preparations, etc.), both within and outside of liturgical settings. This canon states the general principle of admissibility of lay persons to preach, while drawing attention to the single limitation regarding the homily stated in the following canon.[14]

The phrase "in a church or oratory" draws attention to the public and official nature of the preaching. In other words, qualified lay persons may be called upon to preach wherever preaching takes place.

The expression "can be permitted" (*admitti possunt*) implies that someone's permission is required. However, it does not imply the need for a canonical mission or mandate (see *AA* 24; *CCEO* 610, §4, by contrast, does call for a mandate for laity to preach). The permission or consent to preach could be presumed or implicit in an appointment to pastoral office, or it can be explicitly granted, for a given event, for a period of time, or permanently.

The diocesan bishop can give permission for lay persons to preach; he is the moderator of the

---

[13] E.g., E. Tejero, *Pamplona ComEng,* 504. The instruction, "Some Questions Regarding Collaboration of Nonordained Faithful in Priests' Sacred Ministry," issued by the CFC (and signed by seven other curial offices) on August 15, 1997 (*AAS* 89 [1997] 852–877; *Origins* 27:24 [November 27, 1997] 397–409), also uses the unfortunate language of the "exceptional nature of such cases" (art. 2, n. 3).

[14] See the "Directory for Sunday Celebrations in the Absence of a Priest," CDWDS, June 2, 1988, *Origins* 18:19 (October 20, 1988) 301–307, and see art. 3 of the August 15, 1997, instruction mentioned in note 13, above.

ministry of the word in the diocese (c. 756, §2). However, pastors and others who are in charge of "churches or oratories" can also do so; they consent to the preaching of presbyters and deacons (c. 764), they are obliged to see that homilies are preached (c. 767, §4), and they have the responsibility to see that the word of God is proclaimed to the people (c. 528, §1). The religious superior named in canon 765 could permit a qualified lay person to preach to the members of the community. (Pastors, others in charge of churches or oratories, and religious superiors could have their ability to authorize lay preachers limited by diocesan or conference-wide regulations.)

The phrase "if necessity requires" implies circumstances when, for example, a parish or other local congregation has been entrusted to the pastoral care of a lay person or when no presbyters or deacons are available[15] or able to preach, e.g., because of language deficiency, inability to communicate with children, physical disability, or weariness at the end of a long weekend of ministry.

"If . . . it seems advantageous in particular cases" means simply that it seems useful or helpful for the people on this occasion to have a qualified lay person preach, e.g., a mother on Mother's Day, a visiting missionary, a representative of a social or educational apostolate.[16]

Diocesan bishops may issue norms or guidelines for preaching by lay persons and ordained persons for their diocesan churches (c. 756, §2, 772, §1), and many have done so. However, this canon assumes that each bishops' conference will draw up its own "prescripts." Many conferences have done so.[17] The bishops of the United States approved a set of "Guidelines for Lay Preaching"

in November, 1988,[18] but they were not approved by the Holy See because they were not enacted as obligatory. Another set was formulated, but it failed to get the two-thirds vote required for passage in the conference. This delay may actually have been helpful. The agreed-upon guidelines were made publicly available to assist those seeking guidance, and moreover some of the "prescripts" passed by other conferences appear unduly restrictive, e.g., requiring annual deputation of lay preachers by the diocesan bishop. The extensive and positive experience of lay preaching in North America is creating a favorable climate which should make the eventual "prescripts" more realistic.

The quality and effectiveness of preaching is a central issue, whether performed by ordained or lay persons. The ministry is demanding and difficult. It requires thorough learning, especially in scripture and theology, Christian maturity and experience, communication and language skills, familiarity with the community, imagination, and time to prepare well. The word of God is living and powerful, and the Holy Spirit will stir the hearts of its hearers, but the preacher must work hard, using every talent and resource, to make the experience of the "preaching moment" effective.

The Homily

Canon 767 — §1. Among the forms of preaching, the homily, which is part of the liturgy itself and is reserved to a priest or deacon, is preeminent; in the homily the mysteries of faith and the norms of Christian life are to be explained from the sacred text during the course of the liturgical year.

§2. A homily must be given at all Masses on Sundays and holy days of obligation which are celebrated with a congregation, and it cannot be omitted except for a grave cause.

§3. It is strongly recommended that if there is a sufficient congregation, a homily is to be given

---

[15] "In some areas, circumstances can arise in which a shortage of sacred ministers and permanent, objectively verifiable situations of need or advantage exist that would recommend the admission of the nonordained faithful to preaching." August 15, 1997, instruction from the CFC et al., art. 2, n. 4.

[16] The first and obvious meaning of *utilitas* in the canon is "useful"; there is no reason to render it in English as "advantageous."

[17] See *LCE* at c. 766 or *Pamplona ComEng*, Appendix III.

[18] *Origins* 18:25 (December 1, 1988) 402–404.

even at Masses celebrated during the week, especially during the time of Advent and Lent or on
the occasion of some feast day or a sorrowful
event.

**§4. It is for the pastor or rector of a church to
take care that these prescripts are observed conscientiously.**

The canon strongly asserts the eminent position of the homily among all other forms of
preaching of God's word, and provides for its inclusion within virtually all public celebrations of
Mass.

A homily is here described as the exposition of
"the mysteries of faith and the norms of Christian
life" from the sacred scriptures throughout the
Church's liturgical cycle. This description is from
the Vatican Council's Constitution on the Sacred
Liturgy (*SC* 52). A more complete description,
given in a document implementing the constitution, includes the context of the celebration and
needs of the congregation which hears the homily
(*IO* 54). The excellent instruction issued by the
U.S. bishops' conference, *Fulfilled in Your Hearing: The Homily in the Sunday Assembly* (1982),
offers a fuller vision of the homiletic experience
as a mutually interpretative event. The homilist is
a mediator of meaning who enables the community to recognize God's active presence and to respond with more gospel-like lives.

The canon refers to homilies presented within
eucharistic liturgies. This is clear from the text
and its sources (see *CLSA Com* 553). This means
that homilies in other liturgical contexts are not
reserved to presbyters and deacons, at least not in
virtue of this canon.

The reservation of the homily at Mass to priests
and deacons has occasioned considerable discussion in the years since the code.[19] Because the
homily is an integral part of the liturgical action, it
is more than fitting that it should be preached by
the one leading that celebration. The unity between word and sacrament is more clearly seen

that way. The identity of chief celebrant and
homilist is a liturgical norm and preference. Still,
liturgical regulations permit exceptions, e.g., another priest or deacon (*GIRM* 42), or a lay person
at Masses for children (*DMC* 24).

This reservation was further emphasized by a
one-word negative response, given without explanation in 1987 by the Pontifical Commission for
the Authentic Interpretation of the Code, to the
question, "Whether the diocesan bishop can dispense from the norm of canon 767, §1, which reserves the homily to a priest or deacon?"[20] Normally a diocesan bishop can dispense from a disciplinary law for the spiritual good of his people,
and this is a disciplinary law. Hence, the interpretation is enigmatic as well as laconic.

Some canonists (e.g., Provost, Huels, Fox,
Fuentes[21]) argue that the canon is a constitutive
law (one which contains the essential components
of an institute), and thus is beyond the bishop's
dispensing power for that reason (c. 86). They say
that is what is implied in the commission's response. They allege, in other words, that the
reservation to a priest or deacon is of the essence
of a homily; if anyone else delivers it, it simply is
not a homily, no matter the context or content.
Call it an exhortation, a reflection, an explanation
of the biblical text, and lay persons can be admitted to deliver it.

This opinion is unpersuasive and unlikely. It
descends into sheer nominalism (i.e., the nature of
a thing depends on what it is called). It would
mean that lay persons could be invited to give
homilies at the Eucharist at any time, as long as
they were not *called* homilies. This kind of "se-
mantic legerdemain" is probably not what the
commission had in mind. Other indications that
this is a purely disciplinary reservation and not a
declaration of a constitutive law are the following:
none of the source documents (e.g., *SC, IO,
GIRM*, etc.) define the homily in terms of who
preaches it; the canons of the code are not nor-

---

[19] See, for example, art. 3 of the August 15, 1997, instruction of the CFC referred to in note 13, above.

[20] *AAS* 79 (1987) 1249.

[21] The works in which their opinions are expressed are
cited in the bibliography at the end of Book III.

mally where liturgical rites are defined (c. 2); and in the 1990 Code of Canons of the Eastern Churches the reservation of the homily to priests or deacons is clearly separated from the description of the homily (*CCEO* 614, §1 and §4).[22]

The commission's restrictive response, denying the bishop's ability to dispense, was simply its way of reserving the dispensation to the Apostolic See (c. 87, §1; Urrutia and Wrenn share this opinion[23]), without giving any reason for it.

The reservation of the homily at the Eucharist to priests and deacons is a general rule which admits of exceptions. The bishop is one; surely bishops can give homilies! (Actually, the Latin word used in this canon for priests, *sacerdotes,* includes bishops.) Another exception, at Masses for children, was mentioned above. When the presider cannot speak, or speak adequately, the language of the assembled people, it is an obvious case of necessity. Infirmity, exhaustion, and old age on the part of the presiding priest can be other excusing causes for inviting some other qualified and prepared person to deliver the homily.

The rule that the liturgical president preaches the homily at Mass is a good one and is to be observed when reasonably possible (*PO* 4). However, as with other disciplinary norms, there is room for the application of pastoral discretion. Two criteria are suggested by the previous canon: "if necessity requires it in certain circumstances

or it seems advantageous in particular cases." An occasional exception for good reasons does not constitute a violation for one who usually observes the rule conscientiously, i.e., the principle of substantial observance can be applied.

One must not lose sight of the primary value in all of this: the word of God must be preached to the people of God. It is the right of the people and the first duty of those ordained to serve them (cc. 213, 757, 762).

The second paragraph of the canon, taken from *Sacrosanctum Concilium* 52, is a strong reminder that a homily is to be preached at all Sunday and holy day Masses. It would be preferable to have a qualified preacher other than the presiding presbyter give the homily rather than to omit it.

The third paragraph (based on *SC* 42) urges that homilies be preached at all Masses celebrated with people present, and singles out some especially appropriate occasions.

The final paragraph assigns responsibility for seeing to it that homilies are presented. It rests with the one in charge of the local church, that is, the pastor, rector, chaplain, or one entrusted with pastoral care of a parish (c. 517, §2; see c. 528, §1 for the pastoral priority).

The Content of Preaching

Canon 768 — §1. Those who proclaim the divine word are to propose first of all to the Christian faithful those things which one must believe and do for the glory of God and the salvation of humanity.

§2. They are also to impart to the faithful the doctrine which the magisterium of the Church sets forth concerning the dignity and freedom of the human person, the unity and stability of the family and its duties, the obligations which people have from being joined together in society, and the ordering of temporal affairs according to the plan established by God.

Canon 760 outlined the chief sources for the ministry of the word. Canon 768 presents, in two

---

[22] The (now named) Council on Interpretation of Legal Texts was a signatory to the August 15, 1997, instruction of the CFC (cited above in note 9). This was an obvious opportunity to clarify the reason for their 1987 decision. The instruction states that "the diocesan bishop cannot dispense from the canonical norm since this is not merely a disciplinary law but one which touches upon the closely connected functions of teaching and sanctifying" (art. 3, n. 1). This reasoning either rewrites or dismisses canon 87; it invents a new category of non-dispensable laws, i.e., more than disciplinary but less than constitutive.

[23] Their works can be found in the bibliography at the end of Book III.

paragraphs, a very brief synopsis of the content of Christian preaching.

The first paragraph, which is a revision of canon 1347, §1 of the 1917 code, is stated in sweeping generality with classic terseness and symmetry: proclaim what must be believed and done for the glory of God and the salvation of humankind. Preaching is to be salvific, not merely instructional.

The second paragraph, more prolix, focuses on the presentation of the Church's social teaching. It is derived from *Christus Dominus* 12 and *Gaudium et spes* 40–42, and those key sources should be consulted for a fuller context and more detailed description of this vital task.

Canon 616 of the Eastern code contains an improved summary of this same content.

Adapting Preaching to the Assembly

Canon 769 — Christian doctrine is to be set forth in a way accommodated to the condition of the listeners and in a manner adapted to the needs of the times.

The ministry of preaching must be attuned to its audiences. Abstract and generic "religionspeak" simply does not communicate. The language and idiom of the people, their culture and economic condition, their social and political setting, the present situation in this neighborhood—these factors must be among the preacher's first concerns.

This canon's admonition to accommodate the message to the hearers and the times may be self-evident. (Indeed it was not included in the Eastern code.) However, the sources, *Christus Dominus* 13, *Presbyterorum ordinis* 4, and *Gaudium et spes* 4, are eloquent in their concern for the concrete human condition and the need to speak to the actual needs, anxieties, and problems of the community. To this end the preacher must seek and promote dialogue with those among whom he or she lives (*CD* 13; the canon's use of the expression "Christian doctrine" is drawn from this same source). Canon 248 also speaks of the need for

ministers to be able to announce the gospel to the people of their own time and in a manner suited to their understanding.

Special Forms of Preaching

Canon 770 — At certain times according to the prescripts of the diocesan bishop, pastors are to arrange for those types of preaching which are called spiritual exercises and sacred missions or for other forms of preaching adapted to needs.

The routines of human life need occasional variation. The "Sunday after Sunday" pattern of homilies needs to be supplemented sometimes by "special events" related to the ministry of the word. This canon suggests a pair of "old favorites," parish retreats and missions, but it really is a reminder to provide special types of preaching or parish renewal in response to local needs. Scripture discussion groups may be a more effective means than formal preaching events, but the two are not mutually exclusive.

Pastors of parishes and others in charge of local congregations are to see that it happens in their churches; the diocesan bishop is to issue directives about it, if that seems advisable.

Outreach

Canon 771 — §1. Pastors of souls, especially bishops and pastors, are to be concerned that the word of God is also proclaimed to those of the faithful who because of the condition of their life do not have sufficient common and ordinary pastoral care or lack it completely.

§2. They are also to make provision that the message of the gospel reaches non-believers living in the territory since the care of souls must also extend to them no less than to the faithful.

Here and elsewhere in the code (e.g., cc. 383, 528–529) pastoral care-givers and bishops are reminded of their responsibility for "the others," those Catholics who are not in church on Sun-

day, and those in their areas who are not believers. Reaching out to these diverse groups with
God's word of life is not easy, but it is a high-
priority duty for local congregations as well as
their leaders.

The first paragraph envisions groups like migrants, exiles, refugees, travelers, vacationers,
handicapped, disabled, military personnel, prisoners, nursing home patients, and those confined to
their own homes. Bringing the good news of salvation to persons in such diverse circumstances is a
challenge for local churches. Modern media of
communications, e.g., telephone, radio, television,
film, cassettes, Internet connections, compact
disks, and the wide range of print media, all need
to be used. But the organized ministry of one-on-
one personal visitors may be even more effective
and rewarding. The sources for this section are
Christus Dominus 18 and *Evangelii nuntiandi* 52
and 56.

The second paragraph of the canon is a reminder that outreach to non-believers and the
unchurched is also a serious pastoral concern.
Evangelization is not just for "the young churches" in what are regarded as "mission lands." It is a
mandate for all churches. A rich theological and
pastoral context for this task can be found in the
documents on which it is based: *Sacrosanctum
Concilium* 9, *Lumen gentium* 16, *Christus Dominus* 13, *Ad gentes* 10 and 20, *Evangelii nuntiandi*
55 and 58.

The Apostle Paul's piercing questions still
challenge our churches:

> How can they believe in him of whom they
> have not heard? And how can they hear with-
> out someone to preach? And how can people
> preach unless they are sent? As it is written,
> "How beautiful are the feet of those who
> bring the good news!" (Rom 10:14–15)

Norms for the Ministry of Preaching

**Canon 772 — §1. In the exercise of preaching,
moreover, all are to observe the norms issued by
the diocesan bishop.**

**§2. In giving a radio or television talk on Chris-
tian doctrine, the prescripts established by the
conference of bishops are to be observed.**

Paragraph one reminds everyone that if the
diocesan bishop issues norms for preaching within
the diocesan church, they oblige everyone: presbyters, deacons, religious, and laity. The bishop as
moderator of the ministry of the word has the authority to do so (cc. 756, §2, 386, §1, 392, §2).
Since the preaching agenda is largely determined
by the *Lectionary* and the lives of the people, one
might think no other norms are needed. However,
the preparations and qualifications for preachers,
their continuing education, and their systematic
evaluation are important matters, and some bishops have articulated such standards for their
churches.

The second paragraph recognizes that radio
and television broadcast across diocesan boundaries, that they have an immense influence, and
that special talent and training are needed for effective ministry in these media. Hence, the canon
suggests that the national bishops' conference can
issue obligatory norms on such media presentations on "Christian doctrine." Several bishops'
conferences have done so;[24] in 1984 the U.S. bishops said, "Until a study is completed, the NCCB
authorizes diocesan bishops to establish guidelines for expounding Christian doctrine on radio
and TV programs for their own dioceses."[25]

Two important instructions on mass media
have been issued since the Second Vatican Council by what is now called the Pontifical Commission for Social Communications, *Communio et
progressio*[26] and *Aetatis novae*.[27] Both provide
valuable guidance.

---

[24] See *Pamplona ComEng,* Appendix III, or *LCE* at c. 772.
[25] NCCB *Complimentary Norms* (Washington, D.C.:
NCCB, 1991) 7.
[26] May 23, 1971, *AAS* 63 (1971) 593–656; *Catholic Mind*
69 (Oct., 1971) 22–61.
[27] February 20, 1992, *AAS* 84 (1992) 447–468; *Origins* 21
(1992) 659–677.

CHAPTER II
CATECHETICAL INSTRUCTION
[cc. 773–780]

Catechetics, the other paramount form of the ministry of the divine word along with preaching, is the subject of this chapter.

Catechesis is that form of the ministry of the word which is directed to those who have heard the gospel message and responded in faith. It looks to making that faith living, explicit, and operative. Catechesis includes both the teaching of Christian doctrine in an organic and systematic way and the experience of Christian living; the desired result is an initiation into the fullness of Christian life. It is aimed at the faithful of all ages, from very young children to adults well on in years.

This ministry, like that of preaching, is one in which the teaching and sanctifying functions of the Church are joined.

> Catechetical formation... illuminates and strengthens faith, nourishes a life in harmony with the spirit of Christ, leads to a conscious and active participation in the liturgical mystery, and prompts to apostolic action. (*GE* 4)

The Church has issued several major documents since the Second Vatican Council which have helped to promote and shape this ministry, e.g., the *General Catechetical Directory* (1971), the apostolic exhortations *Evangelization in the Modern World* (1975) and *Catechesis in Our Time* (1979), the *Catechism of the Catholic Church* (1992), and the *General Directory for Catechesis* (1997). The NCCB published a national catechetical directory in 1979, *Sharing the Light of Faith*. These documents should be consulted, in conjunction with the following canons, for a more complete and accurate vision of the ministry.

The *Catechism of the Catholic Church* came, not as a result of any call from the council, but from a recommendation of the 1985 synod of bishops. It is intended as a "reference text" which bishops and publishers can use when writing local and regional catechisms. Pope John Paul II de-

scribed it as "a statement of the Church's faith and of Catholic doctrine" and "a sure norm for teaching the faith."[28] It has no special canonical or doctrinal significance, that is, its use is not obligatory and it does not change the hierarchy of truths or level of certainty of Catholic teachings.

The *General Catechetical Directory* of 1971 was revised and updated, and it was issued by the Congregation of the Clergy on September 18, 1997, as the *General Directory for Catechesis*. This *Directory* is intended as a normative orientation, guide, and support for the evangelization efforts of the particular churches.

The 1990 Eastern code (*CCEO* 617–630) treats catechetical formation more fully and with some interestingly different provisions than these present canons.

Pastoral Responsibility

Canon 773 — It is a proper and grave duty especially of pastors of souls to take care of the catechesis of the Christian people so that the living faith of the faithful becomes manifest and active through doctrinal instruction and the experience of Christian life.

This initial canon makes it crystal clear that pastoral leaders, the bishop in the diocese and the pastor (or others to whom the care of local churches is entrusted) in the parish, have a grave duty to provide catechetical formation for their people. Everyone in the community has a role to play, but the "pastors of souls" must see that the job gets done. It is one of their most serious responsibilities. Canons 386, §1, 528, §1, and 843, §2 reiterate this obligation of bishops and pastors.

The canon is drawn from canon 1329 of the 1917 code, *Christus Dominus* 14, *Gravissimum educationis* 4, and *Catechesi tradendae* 1, 14–16, 24, 62–64; they provide powerful motivation and background for its provisions.

---

[28] Apconst *Fidei depositum* 3, October 11, 1992, *AAS* 86 (1992) 113–118; *Origins* 22:31 (January 14, 1993) 525–529.

The wording of the canon itself adds a valuable dimension to its conciliar sources. The goal of catechesis is that the living faith of the Christian faithful become "manifest and active," a real guiding force in their lives. The catechetical process accomplishes this end by means of "the experience of Christian life" as well as by doctrinal formation. This experiential learning comes from living and interacting with other committed Christians in family, neighborhood, school, and local church; it is powerfully formative, a paramount catechetical influence. Liturgical catechesis is an integral part of this ongoing formation in Christ.

Canon 617 of the Code of Canons of the Eastern Churches focuses the catechetical task on the formation of the Christian disciple and a deepening of the commitment to the person of Christ.

A Concern of All Members of the Church, Especially Parents

Canon 774 — §1. Under the direction of legitimate ecclesiastical authority, solicitude for catechesis belongs to all members of the Church according to each one's role.

§2. Parents above others are obliged to form their children by word and example in faith and in the practice of Christian life; sponsors and those who take the place of parents are bound by an equal obligation.

Every member of the Christian community shares responsibility for the catechetical endeavor; it is vital to the health and vigor of the local church as well as the diocesan and universal churches. All the faithful participate in the prophetic function of Christ and his Church, of which catechesis is a major element (*LG* 12, 35, *AA* 10, *CT* 16, 63–70; cc. 211, 225, §1, 759).

Parents have the primary responsibility for the growth in faith and Christian life of those to whom they have given the gift of life. The canon emphasizes the priority of the parental role (*prae ceteris*), but it also adds that those who take the place of parents, like guardians, foster parents, or godparents, also share in this solemn duty.[29] Regarding the parental role, see also canons 226, §2, 776, 793, 851, §2, 872, 890, 914, 1136, 1366.

Facilitation of Catechetics and Catechisms

Canon 775 — §1. Having observed the prescripts issued by the Apostolic See, it is for the diocesan bishop to issue norms for catechetics, to make provision that suitable instruments of catechesis are available, even by preparing a catechism if it seems opportune, and to foster and coordinate catechetical endeavors.

§2. If it seems useful, it is for the conference of bishops to take care that catechisms are issued for its territory, with the previous approval of the Apostolic See.

§3. The conference of bishops can establish a catechetical office whose primary function is to assist individual dioceses in catechetical matters.

This canon details some of the responsibilities of diocesan bishops and bishops' conferences for the ministry of catechesis. It also asserts the controls over the ministry exercised by the Apostolic See.

The first paragraph lists three categories of duties or prerogatives of the diocesan bishop: (1) to manage or guide the ministry in the diocese by issuing regulations or guidelines, (2) to make catechetical materials and resources available for those performing the ministry, even to the extent of commissioning or writing a catechism, and (3) to promote and coordinate the catechetical enterprise in the diocese. These diverse activities are usually carried out by a diocesan office of religious education; they give vitally important assistance to Christian formation in the churches of the diocese. In all of this, the bishop is to observe the rules given by the Holy See.[30]

Diocesan bishops can approve for publication catechisms and other catechetical materials writ-

---

[29] Sources: *LG* 11, 35, *GE* 3, 6–8, *AA* 11, 30, *GS* 48, *CT* 16, 68.

[30] The Congregations of the Clergy and of the Doctrine of the Faith have competence (*PB* 94).

ten or published within their dioceses (c. 827, §1).

This first paragraph is based on the teachings of the Second Vatican Council and subsequent documents which provide very valuable background.[31]

The second paragraph grants to the national bishops' conferences the authority to issue catechisms for their entire territory (or territories, if several conferences were to do so jointly), if they think it would be useful. But if they do publish them, they must first obtain approval from the Holy See. This part of the canon comes from *Catechesi tradendae* 50 and the *General Catechetical Directory* 46, 119, 134.

The final paragraph simply suggests that episcopal conferences may set up catechetical offices to assist dioceses in the ministry of religious education (*GCD* 128).

The United States Catholic Conference has never published a national catechism nor has it established a national catechetical office, except for an office to promote the *Catechism of the Catholic Church.*

The counterpart canons in the Eastern code are 621 and 622.

Parish Catechetical Ministry

Canon 776 — By virtue of his function, a pastor is bound to take care of the catechetical formation of adults, youth, and children, to which purpose he is to use the help of the clerics attached to the parish, of members of institutes of consecrated life and of societies of apostolic life, taking into account the character of each institute, and of lay members of the Christian faithful, especially of catechists. None of these are to refuse to offer their help willingly unless they are legitimately impeded. The pastor is to promote and foster the function of parents in the family catechesis mentioned in can. 774, §2.

The canon specifies the responsibilities of pastors to lead the catechetical formation of the local church. This duty is one of the highest priorities of the pastoral office (cc. 528, §1, 761, 773). It pertains to pastors and others similarly situated, i.e., those entrusted with the pastoral leadership of local congregations (e.g., c. 517, §2). The canon challenges pastors to organize and coordinate the central ministry of religious education in their local church, or to assure its accomplishment by others, e.g., directors of religious education. (Such persons must be well prepared and justly remunerated; cf. c. 231.)

The canon names four categories of recipients of catechesis and three categories of persons to assist with the task.

The pastor is to provide for the religious formation of four groups: adults, young people, children, and parents who are responsible for their own "family catechesis." Each group has its special needs and requires a distinct catechetical approach (c. 777).

Three categories of "willing helpers" are suggested by the canon: (1) any and all bishops, presbyters, and deacons attached to the parish, (2) men and women religious, with due regard for the nature and mission of their communities, and (3) lay persons, especially trained catechists. So vital is this apostolate to the welfare of the local church that these persons should generously respond to the pastor's invitation to assist.[32]

Special Catechetical Needs

Canon 777 — Attentive to the norms established by the diocesan bishop, a pastor is to take care in a special way:

1° that suitable catechesis is imparted for the celebration of the sacraments;

2° that through catechetical instruction imparted for an appropriate period of time

---

[31] *LG* 25, 27, *CD* 2, 13–14, *GE* 2, *GCD* 106–109, 116–126, *CT* 63.

[32] The canon had precedents in the 1917 *CIC*, 1330–1334, but it is more proximately drawn from *LG* 28–29, *CD* 30, 35, *PC* 8, *AA* 3, 10, *PO* 4–9, *EN* 68–71, and *CT* 64–67. The corresponding canon in the Eastern code is 624.

children are prepared properly for the first reception of the sacraments of penance and the Most Holy Eucharist and for the sacrament of confirmation;

3° that having received first communion, these children are enriched more fully and deeply through catechetical formation;

4° that catechetical instruction is given also to those who are physically or mentally impeded, insofar as their condition permits;

5° that the faith of youth and adults is strengthened, enlightened, and developed through various means and endeavors.

The canon raises up several "catechetical moments" or groups with special formational needs, and states the pastor's duty to attend to them. The wording of the canon (*"parochus curet"* followed by a series of verbs in the passive voice) indicates that the pastor is to see that these things are done, not that he is required to do them all himself. The canon illustrates the close interrelation between the teaching and sanctifying offices in the Church; sacramental catechesis is one point at which the two coincide.

Five situations or categories of persons are mentioned.

(1) Catechesis for the celebration of the sacraments. The general principle of preparation for the sacraments is stated again in c. 843, §2. It encompasses all sorts of formative assistance, from a few words before Mass and again before Holy Communion each day to several months of preparation for the sacrament of matrimony (*SC* 14, *GE* 4, *GCD* 25, 56–59, *CT* 23).

(2) Preparation of children for first penance, first Communion, and confirmation. A suitable length of time should be devoted to catechetical formation before the first reception of these sacraments, surely a matter of weeks at least. Canons 913–914 and 890 reiterate the importance of this sacramental preparation (*CD* 30, *GCD* 79–81, 91, *CT* 37).

(3) Catechesis after the reception of first Communion. The formation of children in their faith must be fostered by all appropriate means after they have come to the eucharistic table of the Lord. Their religious development must continue alongside their growth and development as persons (see c. 795 as well as *CT* 38–40, 42, 45).

(4) Catechetical formation of the disabled or handicapped. Whether their disability, illness, or injury is mental or physical, and even though their numbers within the local church are few, the religious education of these members of the faithful must not be neglected. Obviously it will be adapted to their special situations (*GCD* 91, *CT* 41).

(5) Faith development of young people and adults. Adult religious education is of special importance because of the influence that mature Christians have on the entire local church. This category of pastoral action also includes matrimonial catechesis (cc. 1063–1064), which is a concern of the whole community (*GCD* 92–97, *RCIA* 19–20, 98–132, *CT* 39–45).

The Code of Canons of the Eastern Churches counterpart (*CCEO* 619) places the responsibility for catechetical formation on "the parish itself and every ecclesial community."

Catechesis in Institutions of Religious Women and Men

Canon 778 — Religious superiors and superiors of societies of apostolic life are to take care that catechetical instruction is imparted diligently in their churches, schools, and other works entrusted to them in any way.

Religious orders and congregations of men and women have distinguished themselves for the faith formation they have provided in their myriad institutions, e.g., grade and high schools, colleges, hospitals, parishes, missions, chapels, shrines, and information centers. This canon urges the superiors of those religious communities to see to it that such catechetical efforts are continued and fostered in every possible way. The focus here is on the institutional endeavors conducted by religious, rather than the personal assistance which their members often give to local churches (c. 776). The canon is based on *Christus Dominus* 35, *Evangelii nuntiandi* 69, and *Catechesi tradendae* 65.

Means of Catechetical Formation

Canon 779 — Catechetical instruction is to be given by using all helps, teaching aids, and instruments of social communication which seem more effective so that the faithful, in a manner adapted to their character, capabilities and age, and conditions of life, are able to learn Catholic doctrine more fully and put it into practice more suitably.

This canon echoes canon 761 by saying "use whatever means that are available to get the job done." There it was the more sweeping challenge of proclaiming the word of God; here it is the narrower yet huge task of the catechetical formation of the Christian faithful.

The stated goal is that the faithful learn Christian teaching and put it into practice. Whatever pedagogical methods or means of communication which are appropriate and effective should be utilized to accomplish that end, from good example

to television programs, from catechisms to compact disks. The principle of adaptation must always be respected: the means are to be suited to the conditions of the readers, hearers, or viewers: their age, background, abilities, and social situation must always be factored in.[33]

Formation of Catechists

Canon 780 — Local ordinaries are to take care that catechists are duly prepared to fulfill their function properly, namely, that continuing formation is made available to them, that they understand the doctrine of the Church appropriately, and that they learn in theory and in practice the methods proper to the teaching disciplines.

This final canon draws attention to the need for initial and ongoing education for those who actually carry out the catechetical ministry. Local ordinaries (meaning vicars general and episcopal vicars in addition to diocesan bishops, c. 134) have the responsibility of seeing that this crucial level of formation is provided for their catechists. Both content and methods are included: knowledge of the Church's teaching as well as educational theory and practice.[34]

---

[33] Sources of the canon include *IM* 3, 6, 13–14, 17, *CD* 13–14, *AG* 26, *GCD* 116–124, *EN* 40, 45, *CT* 17, 22, 31, 46, 51, 55.

[34] The canon is drawn from *CD* 14, *DV* 25, *AG* 15, 17, *GCD* 108–115, *EN* 73, *CT* 15, 63, 66, 71.

BIBLIOGRAPHY

Bibliographical material for canons 747–780 can be found after the commentary on canon 833.

Michael A. O'Reilly, O.M.I.

Title II
The Missionary Action of the Church
[cc. 781–792]

In the 1917 code, the norms regarding the missionary action of the Church were rather sparse and actually spread throughout that code, but a body of missionary law had been formed apart, especially through the so-called decennial missionary faculties and other sources. Many suggestions had been presented to the preparatory commission for Vatican Council II and eventually a tentative schema or draft on the missionary apostolate was drawn up. After many vicissitudes, eventually the decree *Ad gentes*, on the missionary activity of the Church, was duly promulgated on December 5, 1965, and brought into operation by Paul VI with the *motu proprio Ecclesiae sanctae* on August 6, 1966. In the aftermath of the council and the development of the missionary churches the present code in this section has happily brought together a number of important canonical principles governing the missionary action of the Church.

The canons in this title of the code are based not only on the long canonical tradition of the Church with regard to the missions but also on the conciliar documents, especially *Lumen gentium* and *Ad gentes*, as well as relevant papal and curial postconciliar documents.

A number of important documents have been issued since the promulgation of the code. They throw light, theological as well as ecclesial, on the missionary apostolate of the Church—especially the encyclical letter *Redemptoris missio*,[1] on the mission of Christ the redeemer and the permanent validity of the Church's missionary mandate, and the apostolic exhortation *Ecclesia in Africa*, on the Church in Africa and its evangelizing mission toward the year 2000,[2] both from John Paul II. The *Catechism of the Catholic Church*, published by order of John Paul II on October 11, 1992, has a section entitled "Mission—a requirement of the Church's catholicity" (nn. 849–856).

Canons 584–594 in the 1990 Code of Canons of the Eastern Churches, which correspond to canons 781–792 in the 1983 Code of Canon Law, are also of interest. In the first place, there is a special title XIV on "The Evangelization of Peoples," separate from the following title which deals with the magisterium. The canons themselves cover many of the matters dealt with in the 1983 code, but there are significant differences and even omissions, to some of which reference will be made in the appropriate place. The synod of bishops of the patriarchal churches or the council of hierarchs of the other *sui iuris* churches seem more involved than the conferences of bishops in the Latin church (*CCEO* 585, §2). However, it must be remembered that the Eastern code contains common norms for all the Eastern churches but each *sui iuris* church has also its own particular law.

All Share in Mission Activity

Canon 781 — Since the whole Church is by its nature missionary and the work of evangelization must be held as a fundamental duty of the people of God, all the Christian faithful, conscious of their responsibility, are to assume their part in missionary work.

Before leaving his eleven disciples, Christ gave them their mission: "Full authority has been given to me both in heaven and on earth; go, therefore, and make disciples of all the nations;

---

[1] December 7, 1990, *AAS* 83 (1991) 249–340; Vatican English translation.

[2] September 9, 1995, *AAS* 88 (1996) 5–82; Vatican English translation.

baptize them 'in the name of the Father and of the Son and of the Holy Spirit.' Teach them to carry out everything I have commanded you. And know that I am with you always until the end of the world" (Mt 28:18–20). This is the mandate which Christ left his Church; though it was given directly to the apostles, nevertheless it applies to the whole Church, which by its nature is missionary (*AG* 2), so that the work of evangelization is a basic duty of the people of God (*AG* 35). Not only is the universal Church missionary, but every particular church is also sent forth to the nations. The missionary mandate of the Church is not only as it were institutional or a matter for the Church's hierarchy and for those sent forth specifically "on the missions," but is personal "to all the Christian faithful who, conscious of their responsibility, are to assume their part in missionary work" (*AG* 35). What that part will be depends much on individual possibilities but certainly all are called upon to witness to the gospel and its values. In *Redemptoris missio* John Paul II notes that "the witness of a Christian life is the first and irreplaceable form of mission; Christ whose mission we continue is the 'witness' *par excellence* and the model of all Christian witness." The pope then goes on to detail means of witnessing in the Christian family, in the ecclesial community, and especially in concern for people, in charity towards the poor, the weak, and those who suffer (*Redemptoris missio* 42). The faithful may, indeed, also be called on to participate directly in missionary works of one kind or another or at least to help the work of the missions not only by their prayers but also by providing the necessary resources for the fulfilling of the missionary apostolate (cc. 791 and 1266).

Roles of Pope and Bishops in Mission Work

Canon 782 — §1. The Roman Pontiff and the college of bishops have the supreme direction and coordination of endeavors and actions which belong to missionary work and missionary cooperation.

§2. As sponsors of the universal Church and of all the churches, individual bishops are to have special solicitude for missionary work, especially by initiating, fostering, and sustaining missionary endeavors in their own particular Churches.

The Roman Pontiff, both personally and as the head of the college of bishops, has a very important role in proclaiming the gospel to the whole world, not only in teaching but also in his pastoral and missionary activities. The popes over the centuries have been very much aware of this and those especially of the present century have done much for the spread of the gospel message throughout the world.

Canon 1350 of the 1917 code, having said that local ordinaries and parish priests should regard non-Catholics residing in their territories as commended to their care in the Lord, then goes on in the second paragraph to assert that in other territories the entire care of the mission to non-Catholics is exclusively reserved to the Apostolic See. Vatican II in its constitution *Lumen gentium* determined that "the task of announcing the Gospel in the whole world belongs to the body of pastors (bishops) to whom, as a group, Christ gave a general injunction and imposed a general obligation, as Pope Celestine called to the attention of the Fathers of the Council of Ephesus. Consequently, the bishops, each for his own part, in as far as the due performance of their own duty permits, are obliged to enter into collaboration with one another and with Peter's successor, to whom in a special way the noble task of propagating the Christian name was entrusted" (*LG* 23). The decree *Ad gentes* likewise asserts that "all bishops, as members of the body of bishops which succeeds to the college of the Apostles, are consecrated not for one diocese alone, but for the salvation of the whole world" (*AG* 38). "Since the responsibility of preaching the Gospel throughout the whole world falls primarily on the body of bishops, then the synod of bishops...among matters of general importance, should pay special attention to missionary activity which is the greatest and holiest duty of the Church" (*AG* 29). In the different general assemblies of the synod of bishops the needs of the evangelization of peoples were many times expressed. The third general assembly in 1974 was devoted to the theme of evangelization in the modern world and resulted in the apostolic exhortation of Paul VI *Evangelii nuntiandi*. More recently the Holy Father has set about organizing special assemblies of the synod for different geographical areas of the Church. The Special Assembly for Africa was held in 1994 and the following year John Paul II published the previously mentioned apostolic exhortation *Ecclesia in Africa*, which is a rich mine of both mission theology and practice, attuned to the special needs of the particular churches in Africa. Special assemblies for the Americas (1997), Asia (1998), and Oceania (1998) have also taken place.

The pope exercises his function of direction and coordination of the missionary efforts of the Church with the aid especially of the Congregation for the Evangelization of Peoples, formerly known as the Congregation "De Propaganda Fide." Vatican II asked that "in a manner and according to norms which should be laid down by the pope, selected representatives of all those who are engaged in missionary work should have an active part in the direction of this congregation and also a deliberative vote: that is, bishops of the whole world, after consultation with episcopal conferences, and also the heads of institutes and pontifical agencies. These should all be called together at set times and, subject to the authority of the pope, should exercise supreme control over all missionary work."[3] The council also asked that the congregation "have a permanent body of consultors and experts" and that "institutes of religious women, regional missionary undertakings and lay organizations, especially those which are international, should be suitably represented."[4] Paul VI immediately implemented this decree of the council in his *motu proprio Ecclesiae sanctae*, laying down that "twelve Prelates from the missions; four from other regions; four Superiors of Institutes; four from the Pontifical Mission Societies be assigned to this Congregation to take part

in the Plenary Sessions, with a deliberative vote." It also made provision for some others to be called with a consultative vote.[5] With the reorganization of the Roman Curia by John Paul II, the role of the Congregation for the Evangelization of Peoples remains paramount in the direction and coordination of the missionary apostolate but its function in other respects in missionary territories is somewhat diminished.[6]

The bishops individually are to have a special solicitude for missionary work, especially by initiating, sponsoring, and sustaining missionary endeavors in their own particular churches. As in the 1917 code, they must consider as commended to their apostolic zeal not only the brothers and sisters who are not in full communion with the Catholic Church, but also the non-baptized in their territories (c. 383, §§3–4). "Each Bishop too, as the Pastor of a particular Church, has a wide-ranging missionary duty. It falls to him as the ruler and center of unity in the diocesan apostolate, to promote missionary activity, to direct and coordinate it . . ."[7] These initiatives may indeed be diocesan, such as allowing some of his diocesan priests to undertake a *Fidei donum*[8] apostolate in a mission-field, or undertaking some work in favor of a missionary territory, "twinning" or other projects.[9] On the other hand, the initiatives or activities may be organized by other groups or individuals, in which case it pertains to the diocesan bishop, "not indeed to extinguish the Spirit,

---

[3] *AG* 29.
[4] Ibid.

[5] *ES* III, 15–16. An instruction was drawn up by the Congregation for the Propagation of the Faith determining more fully the role of these newly associated members in the congregation and also of the consultors. This document, 2/26/1968, was not published in the *AAS* but can be found in X. Ochoa, *Leges Ecclesiae*, vol. 3 (Rome: Commentarium pro religiosis, 1995), n. 3633 and in *CLD* 7, 225–229.
[6] *PB* 85–92.
[7] *Redemptoris missio* 63.
[8] Pius XII, ency *Fidei donum*, April 21, 1957, *AAS* 49 (1957) 225; *The Pope Speaks* 4 (1957) 295.
[9] SCProp, instr *Quo aptius*, 2/24/1969, on the regulation of missionary cooperation of bishops relative to *Pontifical Missionary Works* as well as regarding particular diocesan endeavors for the benefit of the missions. *AAS* 61 (1969) 276–280; *CLD* 7, 839–845.

but to test all things and to hold fast to that which is good."[10]

The code does not assign a specific role to the conferences of bishops in regard to the missionary apostolate except in relation to the catechumenate (c. 788, §3) and hospitality for those coming from mission territories (c. 792). John Paul II, however, has exhorted bishops and conferences of bishops to act generously in implementing the norms regarding cooperation between particular churches and especially regarding the better distribution of clergy in the world.[11] Vatican II in the decree *Ad gentes* had assigned other functions or at least had made several other recommendations to conferences of bishops, but evidently it was decided not to enact laws on these points so as to respect the authority and discretion of the diocesan bishop.

Religious to Engage in Mission Action

Canon 783 — Since by virtue of their consecration members of institutes of consecrated life dedicate themselves to the service of the Church, they are obliged to engage in missionary action in a special way and in a manner proper to their institute.

From the early centuries, monks blazed the missionary trail: St. Augustine of Canterbury and his Benedictine companions to England in 597, St. Columbanus and other Celtic monks to various parts of the continent of Europe in the sixth century, St. Boniface to Germany in 719. With the rise of the various religious orders and congregations, right down to the present time, their members have provided a solid phalanx of missionary personnel.

Members of institutes of consecrated life are totally dedicated, by a new and special title, to God and his honor, to the building up of the Church, and to the salvation of the world.[12] How religious will engage in missionary activity depends on the nature of their institute. All religious will contribute to the missionary apostolate by the witness of their consecrated life of prayer and penance (c. 673). Contemplative religious, by the witness of their hidden lives of prayer, call down on the missionary activity of the Church the richest fruits of holiness and hidden apostolic fruitfulness (cf. c. 674). St. Thérèse of the Child Jesus, a contemplative Carmelite nun of Lisieux, was proclaimed patroness of the missions by Pius XI.[13] All religious, whether they belong to institutes dedicated to the direct missionary apostolate or not, do aid the missions by their prayers and other endeavors.

The popes and Vatican II have expressed the desire that institutes of contemplative life establish communities in mission territory, with the religious living their lives in a manner adapted to the genuine religious traditions of the people and bearing an outstanding witness among non-Christians to the majesty and love of God and to union in Christ.[14] Moreover, different forms of consecrated life should be promoted in the new churches, without, however, needless multiplication of institutes, so that the Church's religious tradition can be handed on in a manner in keeping with the character and outlook of each nation; account should be taken also of the traditions of asceticism and contemplation present in certain ancient cultures.[15]

On account of the missionary apostolate of institutes of consecrated life and its close connection with the consecrated life itself, the Holy Father has set up an inter-dicasterial commission of the Congregation for the Evangelization of Peoples and the Congregation for Institutes of Consecrated Life and Societies of Apostolic Life.[16]

Missionaries

Canon 784 — Missionaries, that is, those whom competent ecclesiastical authority sends to carry

[10] *LG* 12.

[11] *Redemptoris missio* 64. SCC, Directive Norms, *Postquam apostoli*, March 25, 1980, *AAS* 72 (1980) 343–364; *CLD* 9, 760–787.

[12] *LG* 44; cf. c. 573, §1.

[13] SCRit, 12/14/1927, *AAS* 20 (1928) 147–148, and 3/13/1929, *AAS* 21 (1929) 195.

[14] *AG* 40.

[15] Cf. *AG* 18.

[16] Cf. *PB* 21, §2.

out missionary work, can be chosen from among natives or non-natives, whether secular clerics, members of institutes of consecrated life or of societies of apostolic life, or other lay members of the Christian faithful.

Although the obligation of spreading the faith falls individually on every disciple of Christ, still the Lord Christ has always called from the number of his disciples those he has chosen that they might be with him so that he might send them to preach to the nations. So the Holy Spirit, who shares his gifts as he wills for the common good, implants in the hearts of individuals a missionary vocation and at the same time raises up institutes in the Church who take on the duty of evangelization, which pertains to the whole Church, and make it as it were their own special task.

Those people who are endowed with the proper natural temperament, have the necessary qualities and outlook, and are ready to undertake missionary work have a special vocation, whether they are natives of the place or foreigners, priests, religious or lay people. Having been sent by legitimate authority they go forth in faith and obedience to those who are far from Christ, as ministers of the Gospel, set aside for the work to which they have been called.[17]

The council documents and the 1983 code have broadened the notion of missionary. While hitherto there was no specific canonical definition of the term *missionary,* nevertheless it was usually considered applicable in the strict sense only to priests working among unbelievers for the propagation of the faith, whereas the others—sisters, brothers, lay associates, etc.—were regarded as auxiliary missionaries.[18] The present canon indi-

cates that to be a missionary one must be sent by competent ecclesiastical authority. In a generic sense, persons may be assigned to the missions by the Apostolic See or even by a diocese or by a missionary institute or organization, according to its approved norms, but juridically that person is assigned to missionary work by the competent ecclesiastical authority of the territory. To be a missionary means that the person is a herald of the gospel and laboring for the implantation of the Church (c. 786).

Missionaries may be diocesan clergy, bishops, priests, or deacons; not only may seminarians be recruited to join the clergy of a missionary circumscription but priests or deacons already incardinated in their home dioceses may be allowed to transfer by excardination/incardination to a missionary circumscription, or they may be permitted to spend even a prolonged period on loan to the missions, sometimes in association with a missionary institute. Indeed there have been some notable examples of bishops who on retirement from the pastoral care of a diocese have volunteered to work for a time as simple missionaries in a mission area.

The Code of Canons of the Eastern Churches has a norm regarding priests which has no counterpart in the Latin code, though the spirit is certainly there:

> *CCEO* 593 — §1. All the presbyters of whatever condition working in missionary territories and forming one presbyterate are to cooperate zealously in the work of evangelization.
>
> §2. They are to freely cooperate according to can. 908 with all other Christian missionaries so that together witness is given to Christ the Lord.

Missionaries may be members of religious or secular institutes or of societies of apostolic life. In the past the religious orders and congregations have been in the forefront of the missionary endeavor and have recruited members also from the area which they were sent to evangelize. Since the

---

[17] *AG* 23.

[18] See *Dictionnaire de Théologie Catholique,* "Missions, personnel étranger" (J.-B. Piolet); *Dictionnaire de Droit Canonique,* "Missionnaire" (R. Naz).

founding of the Paris Foreign Missionary Society in 1660, about twenty other such missionary societies of secular priests have been founded in different countries. These missionary societies include Maryknoll, Mill Hill, Quebec, Scarboro, St. Columban and St. Patrick Societies, and others recently established in mission territories and sending their members as missionaries even to other areas.

A phenomenon of the twentieth century has been the participation of members of the laity in the direct missionary apostolate, sometimes as individuals, more often as belonging to some particular missionary group or as associates of a missionary institute. In recruiting lay persons for the missions, "stress should be laid on the sincere intention of serving the missions, on suitable preparation, professional specialization, as it is called, and on the need for spending a suitable period of time on the missions. . . . The social security of such lay persons should be assured"[19] (cf. c. 231).

In the past, only those who came from abroad to a mission territory were regarded as missionaries, but since the council and according to the code, missionaries may very well be persons from the mission territory itself who are committed to evangelizing their own people or, eventually, to going elsewhere to spread the gospel.

Catechists

Canon 785 — §1. Catechists are to be used in carrying out missionary work; catechists are lay members of the Christian faithful, duly instructed and outstanding in Christian life, who devote themselves to setting forth the teaching of the gospel and to organizing liturgies and works of charity under the direction of a missionary.

§2. Catechists are to be formed in schools designated for this purpose or, where such schools are lacking, under the direction of missionaries.

Catechists have had and still have a very important role to play in the missionary apostolate.

Here we are dealing with lay members of the faithful who assist the missionaries in the important work of expounding the gospel message and organizing liturgical functions and works of charity. Especially in places where the missionary is a foreigner, the catechist who is one of the people, speaking their language and cognizant of their culture, can be a very important aid. Those selected for this office should be outstanding in their Christian life and must be properly instructed for the office which they are to fulfill. Vatican II suggested that "it would be desirable too, wherever it seems opportune, to confer the canonical mission on properly trained catechists in the course of a public liturgical celebration, so that in the eyes of the people they might serve the cause of the faith with greater authority."[20] It had, indeed, been suggested by some that an "instituted ministry of catechist" might be established; Paul VI decided to grant to conferences of bishops which request the faculty from the Holy See the power to institute new ministries which they shall judge to be truly necessary or very useful in their region, ministries which would be open to men and women.[21] However, nothing seems to have come of this suggestion.

Besides expounding the gospel message to the catechumens and to those already baptized, the catechist has an important role in organizing liturgical functions, especially in the absence of the missionary priest. Thus the catechist is indicated as minister of baptism (c. 861, §2) and may be designated as an extraordinary minister of the Eucharist (c. 910, §2) or to assist at marriages in the name of the Church (c. 1112) or, according to the *Roman Ritual,* to impart certain sacramentals or to preside at the funeral service. In particular, the catechist ought to organize prayer services or, in the absence of a sacred minister, a liturgy of the word on Sundays and holy days (c. 1248, §2).[22]

---

[19] *ES* III, 24.

[20] *AG* 17.
[21] CDWDS, October 27, 1977, *CLD* 9, 602–604.
[22] CDWDS, June 2, 1988, *Directorium de Celebrationibus Dominicalibus Absente Presbytero* (Typis Poliglottis Vaticanis, 1988).

The catechist, too, has a responsibility regarding charitable activity. Everything, however, is to be done under the direction of the missionary.

Catechists are to be well instructed so that they may be able to discharge their office properly. "Their training must be in accordance with cultural progress and such that as true co-workers of the priestly order, they will be able to perform their task as well as possible."[23] Normally, catechists should be formed in schools specially designated for the purpose, where "while studying Catholic doctrine with special reference to the Bible and the liturgy, as also catechetical method and pastoral practice, they would also model themselves on the lives of truly Christian people and tirelessly strive for piety and holiness of life."[24] By a decree of May 25, 1980, the Congregation for Catholic Education erected the Institute for Missionary Catechesis at the Pontifical University Urbaniana, Rome. In many mission regions there are schools for the preparation of catechists. Where it is not possible to found such schools, the catechists should be properly formed under the direction of the missionaries.

The council determined that "those who give themselves fully to this work [full-time catechists] should be assured by being paid a just wage, of a decent standard of living and social security"[25] (cc. 231 and 1286).

Missionary Action

Canon 786 — The Church accomplishes the specifically missionary action which implants the Church among peoples or groups where it has not yet taken root especially by sending heralds of the gospel until the young churches are established fully, that is, when they are provided with the proper resources and sufficient means to be able to carry out the work of evangelization themselves.

There has long been discussion with regard to the final aim of missionary action. Certainly the apostles were told, "Go into the whole world and proclaim the good news to all creation" (Mk 16:15), but, as we see especially in the Acts of the Apostles and Pauline epistles, they established local churches to carry on their mission. In this canon, the specifically missionary activity by the heralds of the gospel is seen as arriving at its completion by the implantation of the Church among peoples or groups where it has not yet taken root, and this activity is to continue until the young churches are established fully.

Normally, a mission is initiated when the Holy See, under the juridical form of *commissio*,[26] entrusts to the care of a religious institute or society of apostolic life or, recently, a local church,[27] a

---

[23] *AG* 17.
[24] Ibid.
[25] Ibid.

[26] This system of *commissio* has long existed and an instruction of the Congregation of Propaganda, December 8, 1929 (*AAS* 22 [1930] 111–115 and *CLD* 1, 637–643), regulated the interrelationship between the missionary circumscription and the institute or society and the respective superiors. Vatican II envisaged the development of such missions and the termination of the commission (*AG* 32). Paul VI presupposed the continuance of the *commissio* in his *mp ES* I, n. 24. The instruction *Relationes in territoriis* of the CEP, February 24, 1969 (*AAS* 61 [1969] 281–287 and *CLD* 7, 845–851), determined that the juridical system of *commissio* or entrustment is abrogated as regards dioceses of mission territories but continues to obtain in missionary circumscriptions which have not yet been established as dioceses. *PB* explicitly refers to the congregation committing or entrusting mission territories to institutes (art. 89). More recently, questions were raised as to whether the norms of the 1929 instruction were still in force in vicariates and prefectures apostolic. A private reply of the CEP published in *Omnis Terra* (March 1992, 126–128), said that the system of *commissio* continues to be regulated fundamentally by the 1929 instruction, but a subsequent private reply of the PCILT affirmed that only those norms that are not contrary to the Code of Canon Law remain in force (January 19, 1994, in *Roman Replies and CLSA Advisory Opinions*, 1994, 6–10). In a matter of such importance in many missionary areas, a more authoritative declaration or a new instruction, taking account of the new code, would seem called for.

[27] *PB* 89; the prefecture *Leticia*, Amazonas in Colombia, was committed to the care of the diocese of *Santa Rosa de Osos*, March 4, 1989 (*AAS* 81 [1989] 711).

territory, erecting it into a *missio sui iuris*,[28] an apostolic prefecture, or vicariate and designates one of the members of the institute or society as superior of the mission or prefect apostolic or eventually a bishop as vicar apostolic, all of whom "govern it in the name of the Supreme Pontiff" (c. 371, §1).[29] At this stage the aim of all

[28] This missionary circumscription is not mentioned specifically in the code but there are a number, mostly of quite recent erection, mentioned in the *Annuario Pontificio*, 1997, 1079–1080. The jurisprudence of the CEP applies basically the same norms as are applicable to prefects apostolic, *servatis servandis*, but excluding the prelatial insignia (cf. relevant particular decrees, *CLD* 3, 73–75); J. García Martín, "Origen de Las Misiones Independientes o 'Sui Iuris' y de sus Superiores Eclesiasticos," *ComRelMiss* 74 (1993) 265–324.

[29] When a mission territory is entrusted to the care of a particular institute or society, the practice of the CEP is to ask the superior general to submit a terna of names of suitable candidates for the office of ecclesiastical superior of the mission, whether as superior or prefect apostolic or vicar apostolic. Even after the erection of regular dioceses, if practically all the clergy are members of the institute or society, it may well continue the same practice. There is no reference to this practice in the code (cc. 364, 4° and 377, §3) nor in *PB* 89. However, Paul VI, in his *mp Sollicitudo omnium ecclesiarum*, of June 24, 1969, regulating the functions of the representatives of the Holy See, in VI regarding the appointment of bishops and other ordinaries, states that "the practice [retains its force] for proposing candidates for those ecclesiastical jurisdictions which have been entrusted to religious communities and are subject to the authority of the Congregation for the Evangelization of Nations" (*AAS* 61 [1960] 473 and *CLD* 7, 277–284); see also Council for Public Affairs of the Church, March 25, 1972, Norms for the Selection of Candidates for the Episcopacy in the Latin Church, art. 1, 2 (*AAS* 64 [1972] 386 and *CLD* 7, 366–373); V. Bartocetti, *Ius Constitutionale Missionum* (Rome, 1947); J. García Martin, "Las Relaciones entre Ordinarios del Lugar e Institutos Religiosos en las Misiones segun el Codigo de Derecho Canonico 1983," *ComRelMiss* 65 (1984) 121–166; M. Gerin, *Le Gouvernement des Missions* (Quebec, 1944); G. J. Lafontaine, *Relations Canoniques entre le Missionnaire et Ses Supérieurs*, Catholic University of America Canon Law dissertation #252 (Sherbrooke, Que., 1947); S. Masarei, *De Missionum Institutione et de Relationibus inter Superiores Missionum et Superiores Religiosos*

should be "that the new Christian community might grow into a local church which will, in due course, be ruled by its own pastor and have its own clergy, with a genuine laity existing and working alongside the hierarchy."[30]

When the Church has sufficiently developed in a given country or area, the Holy See erects the regular hierarchy of dioceses and provinces and the system of *commissio* ceases. Even then, however, the particular churches may not be autosufficient; they may not yet have fully developed nor reached their full maturity, with their own clergy and the necessary resources to carry on their mission; they may still depend heavily on the institute or society to which the territory was hitherto entrusted or other outside help for personnel and resources. With the cessation of the *commissio*, the religious working in the missions will do so according to suitable contracts or agreements according to canons 681, §2 and 790, §1, 2°.[31] Moreover, such "young" churches may well remain under the direction of the Congregation for the Evangelization of Peoples.

Vatican II expressed the desire that "in order that the missionary zeal might flourish among their fellow countrymen it would help greatly if the young churches took part in the universal mission of the Church as soon as possible and sent missionaries to preach the Gospel throughout the

(Rome, 1940); I. Ting Pong Lee, "Relationes inter Ordinarios Locorum et Instituta Missionalia," *ComRelMiss* 51 (1970) 34–54; idem, "De Iuridico Mandati Systemate in Missionibus," *ComRelMiss* 51 (1970) 151–167, 238–258; 52 (1971) 43–59, 167–187.

[30] *AG* 21, 32.

[31] *AG* 32. The instruction, *Relationes*, provided general norms regarding contracts or agreements between ordinaries of mission territories and missionary institutes, that is, orders, congregations, institutes, and associations of men or women which are working in the missions. It provides for the possibility of two types of contract or agreement, one where, at the request of the mission ordinary, the Holy See gives a mandate to the missionary institute for its particular work, or the other a simple contract or agreement between the diocesan bishop and the competent superiors. In fact, the CEP issued sample copies of both types (*CLD* 7, 852–861).

whole world, even though they are themselves still short of clergy."[32]

Missionary Dialogue

Canon 787 — §1. By the witness of their life and word, missionaries are to establish a sincere dialogue with those who do not believe in Christ so that, in a manner adapted to their own temperament and culture, avenues are opened enabling them to understand the message of the gospel.

§2. Missionaries are to take care that they teach the truths of faith to those whom they consider prepared to receive the gospel message so that they can be admitted to receive baptism when they freely request it.

Mission fundamentally concerns proclaiming the gospel message to those who "know not Christ." However, the missionaries, by witness of their life and their words, must endeavor to establish sincere dialogue with those whom they hope to evangelize. If this dialogue is to be fruitful, it must be done in great sensitivity and respect for the culture and temperament of those to whom they are sent, mindful that in many cases there is already a very ancient and rich culture. There must also be respect for the great religions of the world and also for the values of the traditional religions, which have remained in their original socio-cultural environment.[33]

The establishment of the local churches should be accompanied by suitable inculturation of the expression of the faith and its practice. Vatican II and various subsequent documents have called for this process.[34] "Through inculturation the Church makes the Gospel incarnate in different cultures and at the same time introduces peoples, together with their cultures, into her own community."[35] It

will need knowledge of the culture and discernment as to how to integrate the gospel message within it. The possibilities of such inculturation will vary from culture to culture but certain areas are specifically referred to in conciliar or subsequent documents: theology or at least expounding the faith,[36] church life and structures,[37] the liturgy,[38] consecrated life,[39] marriage and the family.[40] The Code of Canons of the Eastern Churches emphasizes this point: "The evangelization of the nations should be so done that, preserving the integrity of faith and morals, the Gospel can be expressed in the culture of individual peoples, namely, in catechetics, in their own liturgical rites, in sacred art, in particular law, and, in short, in the whole ecclesial life" (*CCEO* 584, §2).

---

[32] *AG* 20.

[33] PCID, Letter to Presidents of Episcopal Conferences in Africa, Asia, the Americas, and Oceania, Nov. 21, 1993, *L'Osservatore Romano* (Engl.), 1/26/1994.

[34] *GS* 58; *EN* 62–63.

[35] *Redemptoris missio* 52–54; *Ecclesia in Africa* 59–64; *Catechesi tradendae* (October 16, 1979), 53.

[36] Paul VI, addressing bishops from all Africa gathered at Kampala, Uganda, for a symposium, July 31, 1969, dealt with this question and enunciated two principles: First, your church must be Catholic. "That is, it must be entirely founded upon the identical, essential, constitutional patrimony of the self-same teaching of Christ, as professed by the authentic and authoritative tradition of the one true Church.... To make sure the message of revealed doctrine cannot be altered, the Church has even set down her treasure of truth in certain conceptual and verbal formulas. Even when these formulas are at times difficult, she obliges us to preserve them textually. ...Granted this first reply, however, we now come to the second. The expression, that is the language and mode of manifesting this one Faith, may be manifold; hence it may be original, suited to the tongue, the style, the character, the genius and the culture, of the one who professes the one Faith. From this point of view, a certain pluralism is not only legitimate, but desirable. An adaptation of the Christian life in the fields of pastoral, ritual, didactic and spiritual activities is not only possible but even favoured by the Church" (*AAS* 61 [1969] 576–577).

[37] *Ecclesia in Africa* 62.

[38] *SC* 37–40; CDWDS, Instruction on the Roman Liturgy and Inculturation, January 25, 1994, *AAS* 87 (1995) 288–314; *Origins* 23 (1993–1994) 745–756.

[39] *AG* 18, 40; Joint Letter of SCRIS and SCProp on Religious Life in Africa, June 3, 1978, *CLD* 9, 273–280.

[40] In *FC* 10, two principles are enunciated: compatibility of the various cultures with the gospel and communion with the universal Church.

Those who are ready to receive the gospel message are to be instructed in the truths of the faith so that, if they freely request it, they may receive baptism (c. 865, §1). Freedom in embracing the Catholic faith has been a sacred principle from earliest times and was explicitly stated in canon 1351 of the 1917 code: *Ad amplexandam fidem catholicam nemo invitus cogatur.* Pius XII, in reaction to an accusation of "forced conversions," cited this canon and then went back to Lactantius (ca. 305–310): "There is no need of force or injury, for religion cannot be forced; to move the will words rather than blows are to be used.... And so we keep no one against his will—for one who lacks devotion and faith is useless to God.... There is nothing so voluntary as religion; for if the heart of the one who offers sacrifice is turned away, religion is gone, it is nothing..."[41] The Eastern code is even more severe as it asserts, "It is strictly forbidden to compel someone, to persuade him in an inappropriate way or to allure him to join the Church" (*CCEO* 586). Probably mindful of errors of history, that code also insists on the freedom of catechumens to join any *sui iuris* church (*CCEO* 588).

The Catechumenate

Canon 788 — §1. When the period of the pre-catechumenate has been completed, those who have made known their intention to embrace faith in Christ are to be admitted to the catechumenate in liturgical ceremonies and their names are to be inscribed in the book designated for this purpose.

§2. Through instruction and the first experience of Christian life, catechumens are to be initiated suitably into the mystery of salvation and introduced into the life of the faith, the liturgy, the charity of the people of God, and the apostolate.

§3. It is for the conference of bishops to issue statutes which regulate the catechumenate by de-

termining what things must be expected of the catechumens and by defining what prerogatives are to be recognized as theirs.

The catechumenate, as a period of several months or sometimes even years of formation for entering into the Christian community, dates from the pre-Nicene period of the Church's history. In 1614, after the Council of Trent, Paul V issued the *Rituale Romanum*, which contained the rite of adult baptism. This rite did contain the various liturgical elements of different stages of Christian formation but all combined into the one liturgical service. Consequently, the catechumenate as such fell into desuetude. At the request of various local ordinaries especially from mission territories, John XXIII, by a decree of the Congregation of Rites on April 16, 1962, approved an Order of Baptism of Adults according to seven stages of the catechumenate. Vatican II in its Constitution on the Liturgy decreed, "The catechumenate for adults, comprising several distinct steps, is to be restored and brought into use at the discretion of the local Ordinary. By this means the time of the catechumenate, which is intended as a period of suitable instruction, may be sanctified by sacred rites to be celebrated at successive intervals of time" and also "both rites for the baptism of adults are to be revised, not only the simpler rite but also, taking into account the restored catechumenate, the more solemn rite."[42] The new *Rite of Christian Initiation of Adults* was promulgated by a decree of the Congregation for Divine Worship on January 6, 1972.[43]

The present canon considers two distinct periods, the precatechumenate and the catechumenate proper. The precatechumenate is regarded as having great importance and ordinarily is not to be omitted. It is a time of evangelization: in faith and constancy the living God is proclaimed, as is Jesus Christ whom he sent for the salvation of all mankind. Thus those who are not yet Christians,

---

[41] Allocution to the Rota, October 6, 1946, *AAS* 38 (1946) 391–397; *CLD* 3, 650–657; W. H. Woestman, ed., *Papal Allocutions to the Roman Rota 1939–1994* (Ottawa: St. Paul University, 1994) 39–45.

[42] *SC* 64, 66.

[43] CDW, *Ordo Initiationis Christianae Adultorum,* January 6, 1972, reimpressio emendata, 1974, *AAS* 64 (1972) 252; *CLD* 7, 596.

their hearts opened by the Holy Spirit, may believe and be freely converted to the Lord.[44]

Admission to the catechumenate takes place when the period of the precatechumenate has been completed and the candidates have been grounded in the basic fundamentals of the Christian life and teaching. The rite, as given in the *Rite of Christian Initiation of Adults*, takes place in an assembly of the faithful. After the celebration of the rite, the names of those who have been admitted are entered in the register of catechumens, along with the names of the minister and sponsors and the date and place of admission.[45] The catechumens set out on a spiritual journey of deepening evangelization and of Christian living; it is a real apprenticeship through prayer and especially the liturgy, through the witness of their lives as an apostolate, and through the charity of the people of God.[46] The period of the catechumenate is divided into different stages, each with its own liturgical initiation and with a given specific purpose. The rite itself provides for suitable adaptation by the bishops' conference, the bishop, or the minister (*RCIA* 64–67). Vatican II declared, "In mission countries, in addition to what is furnished by the Christian tradition, those elements of initiation rites may be admitted which are already in use among some peoples insofar as they can be adapted to the Christian ritual."[47]

The council had said that "the juridical status of catechumens should be clearly defined in the new Code of Canon Law. Since they are already joined to the Church, they are already of the household of Christ, and are quite frequently already living a life of faith, hope and charity."[48] The code, however, did not go into this question at length but rather left it to the conference of bishops to lay down norms regarding the catechumenate, deciding what the catechumens are to do and what prerogatives they should enjoy. According to the code, catechumens may receive blessings (c. 1170) and also sacramentals publicly administered, as canon 1149 of the 1917 code was officially interpreted.[49] Catechumens are unbaptized and in the marriage law are treated as such; however, the postconciliar revised Marriage Rite contains a special rite for celebrating a marriage between a Catholic and a catechumen or a non-Christian.[50] In case of death, catechumens are counted as among the faithful in regard to funeral rites (c. 1183, §1).

There are various other areas where the canonical situation of catechumens might be regulated, such as the obligations of the catechumens, participation in parish life, membership in associations of the faithful, etc.

Those Newly Initiated

Canon 789 — Neophytes are to be formed through suitable instruction to understand the gospel truth more deeply and to fulfill the duties assumed through baptism; they are to be imbued with a sincere love for Christ and his Church.

After they have received the sacraments of Christian initiation, the neophytes are to be nurtured in the faith by being brought to a fuller understanding of the paschal mystery. Accompanied not only by their sponsors but also by the Christian community, they continue their meditation on the gospel and share in the Eucharist, in church life, and in the performance of works of charity.[51] A neophyte is impeded from receiving orders, unless, in the judgment of the ordinary, he has been sufficiently tested (c. 1042, 3°).

Vatican II insisted: "The ecumenical spirit should be nourished among neophytes; they must appreciate that their brothers who believe in

---

[44] *RCIA*, Introduction, 9–11.
[45] *RCIA*, Introduction, 14–17.
[46] *RCIA*, Introduction, 18–26.
[47] *SC* 65, 37–40.
[48] *AG* 14.

[49] SCRit, March 8, 1919, *AAS* 11 (1919) 144; *CLD* 1, 557.
[50] *Ordo Celebrandi Matrimonium*, editio typica altera, March 19, 1990. Chapter 4, "Ordo celebrandi matrimonium inter partem catholicam et partem catechumenam vel non christianam."
[51] *RCIA*, Introduction, 37–40.

Christ are disciples of Christ, and having being reborn in baptism share in many of the blessings of the people of God."[52]

Diocesan Bishops in Mission Territories

Canon 790 — §1. It is for the diocesan bishop in the territories of a mission:

   1° to promote, direct, and coordinate endeavors and works which pertain to missionary action;

   2° to take care that appropriate agreements are entered into with moderators of institutes which dedicate themselves to missionary work and that relations with them result in the good of the mission.

§2. All missionaries, even religious and their assistants living in his jurisdiction, are subject to the prescripts issued by the diocesan bishop mentioned in §1, n. 1.

This canon indicates the rights and responsibilities of the diocesan bishop in mission territories. Its context is the establishment of regular dioceses in missionary territories.[53]

While vicars and prefects apostolic or even superiors of *missiones sui iuris*, according to the norms of canons 368 and 381, §2, are equivalent in law to diocesan bishops, nevertheless their relationship with the superiors of the religious institutes to which the given mission circumscription is entrusted is fundamentally regulated by the norms of the *commissio* or the proper *Statuta*[54] approved by the Holy See or whatever mutual agreements may have been entered into. In all cases, however, the principles of canon 790 are valid.

"It is the responsibility of the diocesan bishop, as head of the diocesan apostolate and its center of unity, to promote, guide, and coordinate missionary activity, so that the spontaneous zeal of

those who engage in this work may be safeguarded and fostered."[55] The canon speaks of both new initiatives and already established works concerning missionary activity. On the missions as elsewhere, the diocesan bishop and those equivalent to the diocesan bishop ought to promote mission activity in close consultation with their missionaries and with the religious superiors (c. 678, §3), especially with the superiors of the institute or society to which the care of the mission may have been entrusted.

The council and canon 790, §1, 2° both speak of the necessity of proper agreements being drawn up between the head of the mission and the moderators of institutes engaged in missionary activity. The canon speaks of agreements, not necessarily of contracts, which might well require civil formalities and entail civil consequences (c. 1290). The Holy See has laid down some general principles regarding these agreements, whether with the so-called mandate or not,[56] and consultations between the bishops' conferences and the major superiors on the matter may be desirable. In any case, within the necessary parameters, agreements should be freely worked out between the bishop or other head of the mission and the competent major superior; neither the bishops' conference nor the bishops may impose one form of agreement. The aim of the agreements is to ensure clarity regarding the mutual rights and obligations of the ecclesiastical authorities and of institutes and their members and to contribute to the good of the mission. In an analogous case, canon 681, §2 asks specifically for a written agreement; certainly the agreement of canon 790, §2 should likewise be written. The content of the agreements is not specified in the code but the specimen agreements supplied by the Congregation for the Evangelization of Peoples gave good indications of what is required: clauses regarding the work un-

---

[52] *AG* 15.

[53] *AG* 30.

[54] Cf. *CIC* 296–297; W. Van der Marck, *Statuta pro Missionibus Recentiora* (Munster: Aschendorff, 1958).

[55] *AG* 30.

[56] SCProp, instr *Relationes*, Feb. 24, 1969, *AAS* 61 (1969) 281–287; *CLD* 7, 845–861; there are non-obligatory samples of agreements, one with the "mandate" and the other without.

dertaken, the personnel and their preparation, the respective roles of the diocesan bishop and of the religious superior, the matter of temporal goods, their ownership and administration, revenues, by whom expenditures are covered, etc. Especially if an institute has been a long time in the missionary territory, certain matters regarding the ownership of some properties may be very complex and must be regulated in a just and equitable manner.[57]

The question of the subjection of religious to the local ordinary in missionary activity has had a long history. In the last century, Leo XIII issued an apostolic constitution, *Romanos Pontifices*, on May 8, 1881, directly for England and Wales but later extended elsewhere; many of its norms were incorporated into the 1917 code. Vatican II in its decree *Ad gentes* (32) speaks of the submission of institutes and ecclesiastical associations of every kind to the local ordinary in all that concerns missionary activity. The canon speaks not only of the religious but also of their helpers residing in the territory; nowadays institutes or societies often recruit lay associates as missionaries to help in the apostolate.

Support for Missionary Activity

Canon 791 — To foster missionary cooperation in individual dioceses:

  1° **missionary vocations are to be promoted;**
  2° **a priest is to be designated to promote effectively endeavors for the missions, especially the *Pontifical Missionary Works;***
  3° **an annual day for the missions is to be celebrated;**
  4° **a suitable offering for the missions is to be contributed each year and sent to the Holy See.**

While the preceding canon deals with the diocesan bishops in missionary territories, the present canon deals with fostering missionary cooperation throughout the universal Church.

1° – Vocations

As much as possible, a diocesan bishop is to foster vocations to different ministries and to consecrated life, with special care shown for priestly and missionary vocations (c. 385). The promotion of missionary vocations is a very important obligation of the diocesan bishop. In addition to encouraging such vocations, he might afford suitable help for educating and preparing people for these ministries. Vatican II even suggested "that bishops, being conscious of the grave shortage of priests which impedes the evangelization of many regions, would after proper training send to those dioceses which lack clergy some of their best priests who offer themselves for mission work, where at least for a time they would exercise the missionary ministry in a spirit of service."[58]

2° – A Priest to Promote the Missions

Paul VI, in implementing the conciliar decree *Ad gentes*, laid down that "a priest shall be appointed in each diocese to effectively promote the work of the missions. He will also take part in the pastoral council."[59] The code indicates that this priest should especially promote the *Pontifical Missionary Works*.

The *Pontifical Missionary Works* are: *The Pontifical Work for the Propagation of the Faith*, founded by Pauline Jaricot in 1819 to obtain prayers and modest alms for the missions; *The Pontifical Work of the Holy Childhood*, founded by Bishop Forbin Janson at the suggestion of Pauline Jaricot in 1843 to get children involved in the missionary apostolate; *The Pontifical Work of St. Peter the Apostle for Native Clergy*, founded also in France in 1889 by Stéphanie Cottin-Bigard and her daughter Jeanne. To these we may add *The Pious Missionary Union of the Clergy*, founded in

---

[57] I. Ting Pong Lee, "De Bonis in Missionibus: Quaedam de bonorum assignatione in missionibus criteria crisi subiciuntur," *ComRelMiss* 57 (1976) 335–348; 58 (1977) 35–46, 137–148, 210–223, 346–355; 59 (1978) 38–49: G. Vromant, *Ius Missionariorum, 6, De Bonis Temporalibus*, 1953.

[58] *AG* 38.
[59] *ES* III, 4.

Italy in 1916 by Fr. Paolo Manna, encouraged by Bishop Guido Maria Conforti, who in 1898 had founded the Congregation of St. Francis Xavier for the Missions; originally intended for the clergy, this organization later opened membership to seminarians and to religious men and women and it is now simply known as the *Pontifical Missionary Union*. These four associations, which originated in private initiatives, flourished and were encouraged by successive popes.[60] Since the time of Pius XI, the "Pope of the Missions," they have been coordinated:[61] "The four Pontifical Societies would henceforth be set up as one Institution, depending on the Sacred Congregation for the Evangelization of Peoples. However, each work, while keeping its identity and pursuing its own ends, should have its particular regulations, as well as its general secretariat and national secretariat.... In view of the great diversity of pastoral situations, structures and mentalities in the different Churches, the Pontifical Mission-Aid Societies will have to show flexibility in their organization and methods, so as to adapt to local conditions."[62] Vatican II desired that these works should be given first place because they are a means by which Catholics are imbued from infancy with a truly universal outlook, and also a means for instigating an effective collecting of funds for all the missions, each according to its needs.[63] Dioceses or missionary institutes may have other organizations for aiding the missions,

but priority is to be given to the pontifical works and confusion among the faithful is to be avoided. The organization may vary from diocese to diocese and some dioceses may have a special office dedicated to this purpose. Preferably in each diocese one director will be appointed for all four Pontifical Works. Should the bishop designate a different priest as delegate for the missions, this person should give fullest support to the diocesan director of the Pontifical Works.[64]

3 ° – Day for the Missions

Pius XI established the Annual Mission Day for the second last Sunday of October.[65] While Mission Day is still generally celebrated on that day, nevertheless the conference of bishops or the bishop could fix another day. The Holy Father publishes a special message every year for Mission Day. The collection of funds for the Propagation of the Faith usually takes place on that day.

4 ° – Financial Aid for the Missions

The missions are to be supported not only by promoting the National Collection for the Missions (cc. 1266, 1267, §3) but also by subscribing over and above that collection of donations from the faithful, from diocesan and parochial funds (cc. 1271, 640).

Vatican II noted that "in their conferences the bishops should consider...the particular contribution, in proportion to its income, which each diocese will be obliged to make every year for the work of the missions."[66] Paul VI in *Ecclesiae sanctae*, III, 8, is more precise: "Since the voluntary offerings of the faithful for the missions are by no means adequate, it is recommended that as soon as possible a certain sum be fixed to be paid each year out of their own resources by the diocese itself and by the parishes and the other diocesan communities to be distributed by the Holy

---

[60] S. De Angelis, *De Fidelium Associationibus*, 1959, II, nn. 688–695, 759–768. G. Vromant, *Ius Missionariorum, 3, De Fidelium Associationibus,* 1955, 135–151; new statutes for the *Pontifical Works* were approved by a decree of the CEP, June 26, 1980, cf. *Bibliographia Missionaria* 44 (1980) Quaderno 23, Text, 361–374, Commentary by J. López-Gay, 380–392.

[61] Pius XI, *mp Romanorum pontificum*, May 3, 1922, *AAS* 14 (1922) 321–330; *mp Decessor noster*, June 24, 1929, *AAS* 21 (1929) 342–349; Instruction of the Congregation of Propaganda, March 14, 1937, *AAS* 29 (1937) 476–477.

[62] *Statutes of the Pontifical Missionary Societies*, June 26, 1980, nn. 31, 29.

[63] *AG* 38.

[64] *Statutes of the Pontifical Missionary Societies*, chapter 2, art. 1, n. 6.

[65] SCRit, April 14, 1926, *AAS* 19 (1927) 23; *P* 16 (1927) 31.

[66] *AG* 38.

See, without diminution of the other offerings of the faithful."[67]

Welcome and Care for Those from Mission Lands

Canon 792 — Conferences of bishops are to establish and promote works by which those who come to their territory from mission lands for the sake of work or study are received as brothers and sisters and assisted with adequate pastoral care.

Vatican II expressed concern for immigrants from mission lands: "In order that immigrants from mission lands may be properly received and given appropriate pastoral care by the bishops of older Christian lands, cooperation with missionary bishops is necessary."[68]

In most countries, especially in some urban centers, there may be numbers of immigrants, clerics, religious, or lay people, from mission countries. Some may come for a temporary stay for university studies, for health reasons, etc., while others may intend remaining indefinitely in the guest country for work or to build a new life; still others may be refugees, fleeing from persecution of one kind or another. For all, the local church must provide a fraternal welcome and adequate pastoral care. The pastoral needs can be very varied. The canon asks the conference of bishops to establish or promote works to assist these immigrants and help provide pastoral care. Cooperation with the missionary bishops of the places from which the immigrants come may be necessary in order to find priests who know the language and the culture of these immigrants to minister to them until they have become completely integrated into the guest country. The presence of immigrants from the mission countries may be a mutually enriching experience for the host church and for the immigrants.

[67] T. Scalzotto, "Contributo 'Ecclesiae sanctae,' origine del termine e presuppositi conciliari," *Bibliographia Missionaria* 41 (1977) Quaderno 20, 207–209.
[68] *AG* 23.

BIBLIOGRAPHY

Bibliographical material for canons 781–792 can be found after the commentary on canon 833.

TITLE III
CATHOLIC EDUCATION
[cc. 793–821]

The first three canons in the revised code's treatment of Catholic education clearly reflect the conciliar teaching of the Declaration on Christian Education, *Gravissimum educationis,* in asserting the rights and responsibilities of parents regarding the education of their children in general and their Catholic education in particular. Likewise, the canons reflect an openness to the situation in the modern world. The introductory canons of title III contain basic principles of church teaching which inform the subsequent three chapters: "Schools" (cc. 796–806), "Catholic Universities and Other Institutes of Higher Studies" (cc. 807–814), and "Ecclesiastical Universities and Faculties" (cc. 815–821).

Parental Rights and Obligations

Canon 793 — §1. Parents and those who take their place are bound by the obligation and possess the right of educating their offspring. Catholic parents also have the duty and right of choosing those means and institutions through which they can provide more suitably for the Catholic education of their children, according to local circumstances.

§2. Parents also have the right to that assistance, to be furnished by civil society, which they need to secure the Catholic education of their children.

The first paragraph, based on *Gravissimum educationis* 3, 6, focuses on the rights and obligations of parents and those who legitimately take their place (e.g., guardians, foster parents, adoptive parents) to (1) educate their children and (2) select the most suitable means and schools for the Catholic education of their children. These two

assertions of parental rights and responsibilities are fundamental, that is, primary and inalienable, in regard to the education of their children. Parallel provisions on the rights and duties of parents for the Christian education of their children are contained in canon 226, §2. Often identified as a foundational canonical provision in support for home schooling, canon 793, §1 recognizes the primary educational role of parents within the broad framework of Catholic education and suggests, as does the title of this section, that not all education that is Catholic need take place within the school setting.

Paragraph two asserts the right of parents to receive needed assistance from the State in order to ensure a Catholic education for their children. This assertion, while lacking specificity as to the responsibilities of the State or the nature of the assistance, encompasses religious education as an integral and essential component of Catholic education.[1]

Right and Duty of the Church

Canon 794 — §1. The duty and right of educating belongs in a special way to the Church, to which has been divinely entrusted the mission of assisting persons so that they are able to reach the fullness of the Christian life.

§2. Pastors of souls have the duty of arranging everything so that all the faithful have a Catholic education.

Paragraph one, based on *Gravissimum educationis,* Introduction, 3, grounds the Church's role

[1] Cf. *Dignitatis humanae* 5; Congregation for Catholic Education, decl *The Catholic School,* March 19, 1977 (Washington, D.C.: USCC, 1977) nn. 81, 82; Congregation for Catholic Education, instr "The Religious Dimension of Education in a Catholic School," April 7, 1988, *Origins* 18/14 (September 15, 1988) 213, 215–228.

in education in its divine mission to assist all men and women in their efforts to achieve the fullness of the Christian life. By means of education, the Church, working for the realization of God's plan, carries out its mission of evangelization to proclaim the mystery of salvation to all people and to renew all things in Christ.

Paragraph two assigns primary responsibility to pastors of souls (bishops and parish priests) for making arrangements so that everyone has the opportunity for a Catholic education. Although all members of the Christian faithful share in this responsibility, bishops and pastors are given the additional responsibility to serve as promoters and coordinators of the educational efforts. For the diocesan bishop, in particular, this duty includes the responsibility of coordinating educational undertakings throughout the diocese and ensuring that as many young people as possible have access to the Church's educational apostolate (c. 394, §1).

Goals of Education

Canon 795 — Since true education must strive for complete formation of the human person that looks to his or her final end as well as to the common good of societies, children and youth are to be nurtured in such a way that they are able to develop their physical, moral, and intellectual talents harmoniously, acquire a more perfect sense of responsibility and right use of freedom, and are formed to participate actively in social life.

Taken directly from the first paragraph of *Gravissimum educationis,* this canon reiterates the goals of education in the process of human formation and the individual's right to an education. It describes the educational process as a holistic undertaking, focusing on the formation of the whole person: developmental, promoting the growth and harmonious development in the various stages of the individual's physical, moral, intellectual, and spiritual life; and social, acknowledging the importance of the common good of society and the rights and duties that derive from re-

sponsible participation in society and the Church. Similar provisions are contained in canon 629 of the Code of Canons of the Eastern Churches.

CHAPTER I
SCHOOLS
[cc. 796–806]

Role of Schools

Canon 796 — §1. Among the means to foster education, the Christian faithful are to hold schools in esteem; schools are the principal assistance to parents in fulfilling the function of education.

§2. Parents must cooperate closely with the teachers of the schools to which they entrust their children to be educated; moreover, teachers in fulfilling their duty are to collaborate very closely with parents, who are to be heard willingly and for whom associations or meetings are to be established and highly esteemed.

The first paragraph singles out schools as the primary means of assisting parents in carrying out their duty to educate their children. In recognizing the role of schools, the canon exhorts all the Christian faithful to acknowledge their importance. Paragraph one is based on *Gravissimum educationis* 5, which describes in some detail the goals of a Catholic school. Catholic school educators and parents alike could benefit from assessing Catholic school education in the light of the source document.

The importance of Catholic schools is reaffirmed in the 1997 circular letter from the Congregation for Catholic Education, "The Catholic School on the Threshold of the Third Millennium,"[2] which situates the Catholic school, first and foremost, within the Church's evangelizing mission in the world and describes the Catholic school

---

[2] Congregation for Catholic Education, littcirc "The Catholic School on the Threshold of the Third Millennium," December 28, 1997, *L'Osservatore Romano* 16 (April 22, 1998) 8–10.

as "the privileged environment in which Christian education is carried out" (n. 11).

Paragraph two is a call to mutual collaboration exhorting both parents and teachers to work together in the educational enterprise. Parents are admonished to cooperate with teachers, and teachers are urged to work closely with parents. This collaboration should be identified by a willingness on the part of teachers to listen to parents and the establishment of teacher associations.[3]

Freedom of Parents

Canon 797 — Parents must possess a true freedom in choosing schools; therefore, the Christian faithful must be concerned that civil society recognizes this freedom for parents and even supports it with subsidies; distributive justice is to be observed.

This canon is a strong affirmation of the true freedom of parents in the selection of schools for their children. It also contains an admonition to all the Christian faithful to ensure that civil governments recognize, promote, and safeguard this freedom. Civil authority must recognize the right of parents to choose with genuine freedom suitable schools for their children. Moreover, the principle of distributive justice should guide the State in the allocation of public subsidies so that parents are not penalized in exercising their right to select schools for their children in accord with their conscience.

The principal source of this canon is *Gravissimum educationis* 6. It also reflects the teaching of *Dignitatis humanae* 5.

Parental Responsibility for Catholic Education

Canon 798 — Parents are to entrust their children to those schools which provide a Catholic educa-

tion. If they are unable to do this, they are obliged to take care that suitable Catholic education is provided for their children outside the schools.

This canon articulates the obligation of parents to ensure the Catholic education of their children. The Catholic school is one means through which a Catholic education may be provided.

The law presupposes a distinction between the officially sponsored Catholic school of canon 803 and other educational institutions that provide a Catholic education. Other educational alternatives that the law might envision are public, private, or state-funded schools where the Catholic faith is taught.

The canon contains no prohibition against the use of non-Catholic schools. Rather, it provides direction for parents who are unable to send their children to schools that provide a Catholic education. In such cases, parents are to see to it that the children receive an appropriate Catholic education outside of the school setting. The law does not identify reasons or conditions that might prevent parents from sending their children to Catholic schools. Some reasons might include availability, distance, cost, cultural or political conditions. Regardless of the reasons that prevent parents from sending their children to Catholic schools, they are obliged to see to it that the children receive a Catholic education outside of school. The Catholic school is viewed in the law as a means, not an end.

The canon does not suggest how this Catholic education might be attained. Nonetheless, the obligation that rests with parents is a serious one.

Parents, Society, and Religious Education

Canon 799 — The Christian faithful are to strive so that in civil society the laws which regulate the formation of youth also provide for their religious and moral education in the schools themselves, according to the conscience of the parents.

This canon recognizes the inalienable right of parents over the religious and moral education of

---

[3] See *The Catholic School,* nn. 60–61, which extends the call for cooperation and collaboration to the entire school community. See also "The Catholic School on the Threshold of the Third Millennium," n. 20.

their children. It also urges the Christian faithful to ensure that civil society acknowledges and safeguards this right, particularly by promoting just legislation on educational matters for schools regulated by civil authority. While the canon does not suggest that all schools become Catholic schools, it does support the provision of religious and moral education in public schools or schools regulated by the State. *Gravissimum educationis* 7, the source of this canon, acknowledges the role and contribution of civil authority, with due regard for the pluralistic character of modern society, in ensuring "that the education of their children in all schools is given in accordance with the moral and religious principles of the family" (*GE* 7).

Establishment and Promotion of Catholic Schools

Canon 800 — §1. The Church has the right to establish and direct schools of any discipline, type, and level.

§2. The Christian faithful are to foster Catholic schools, assisting in their establishment and maintenance according to their means.

The first paragraph contains a strong assertion of the Church's right to establish and conduct any type of school at any grade level. Based on this claim the Church, i.e., the people of God, has the freedom to initiate and control educational ventures across a broad range that includes, for example, elementary and secondary schools, colleges and postgraduate schools, with academic, professional, or vocational curricula. The importance of the exercise of this right on the part of the Church, as expressed in *Gravissimum educationis* 8, the source for this canon along with canon 1375 of the 1917 code, is threefold: to preserve freedom of conscience, to protect the rights of parents, and to provide for the advancement of culture (*GE* 8).

Paragraph two identifies an important role for the Christian faithful in relation to the promotion of Catholic schools. The faithful are admonished

to encourage Catholic schools and support them in accord with their resources. Based on *Gravissimum educationis* 8 and 9, the exhortation extends to all the faithful, not only to parents whose children attend Catholic schools. The assistance called for is not limited to financial aid; it can include moral support, volunteer work, assistance in promotion, recruitment, administration and development, continuing education for faculty, etc. The importance of the exhortation is more strongly stated in the conciliar source document which urges "pastors of the Church and all the faithful to spare no sacrifice" in their efforts to make Catholic schools more effective, especially in their concern for the poor, those without the benefit of family, and those who lack the gift of faith (*GE* 9).

In his 1987 address to Catholic educators in New Orleans, Louisiana, Pope John Paul II reaffirmed his support of Catholic schools. He stated:

> The presence of the Church in the field of education is wonderfully manifested in the vast and dynamic network of schools and educational programs extending from preschool through the adult years. The entire ecclesial community—bishops, priests, religious, the laity—the Church in all her parts, is called to value ever more deeply the importance of this task and mission, and to give it full and enthusiastic support.[4]

The bishops of the United States also reaffirmed the importance of Catholic elementary and secondary schools in their 1990 statement *In Support of Catholic Elementary and Secondary Schools* and called for an expansion of this "vitally important ministry of the Church."[5]

---

[4] John Paul II, "Catholic Education: Gift to the Church, Gift to the Nation," *Origins* 17/17 (October 8, 1987) 279.

[5] USCC, *In Support of Catholic Elementary and Secondary Schools* (Washington, D.C.: USCC, 1990) 9. See also "The Religious Dimension of Education in a Catholic School" for its "enthusiastic encouragement" to dioceses and religious institutes wishing to establish new schools (41).

Religious Institutes and the Apostolate of Education

Canon 801 — Religious institutes whose proper mission is education, retaining their mission faithfully, are also to strive to devote themselves to Catholic education through their schools, established with the consent of the diocesan bishop.

Canon 801 is a new canon directed to religious institutes whose mission includes the apostolate of education. The canon commends religious institutes for retaining their commitment to education and, recognizing the long-standing contribution of countless women and men religious to the apostolate of Catholic education, encourages religious to continue this commitment. In response to the call for renewal by the Second Vatican Council, religious institutes initiated efforts to adapt their lives and works to the spirit of their founders and the needs of the time. In this process, some religious institutes moved into new apostolates and decreased their involvement in the Catholic school apostolate.[6] The canon urges religious to continue this valuable work in their own schools. The concluding admonition of the canon should be considered in the context of canons 673–683 on the apostolate of religious. Sources for the canon include *Christus Dominus* 35, *Ecclesiae sanctae* I, 29–30, 39, and the Declaration of the Congregation for Catholic Education, *The Catholic School,* 74–76, 89.

Schools with a Christian Spirit

Canon 802 — §1. If schools which offer an education imbued with a Christian spirit are not available, it is for the diocesan bishop to take care that they are established.

§2. Where it is expedient, the diocesan bishop is to make provision for the establishment of pro-fessional schools, technical schools, and other schools required by special needs.**

The first paragraph states the direct responsibility of the diocesan bishop to establish schools imbued with a Christian spirit if they are lacking in his diocese. Based on canon 1379, §1 of the 1917 code, canon 802, §1 differs from the former law in two ways. Whereas canon 1379, §1 of the 1917 code refers to "Catholic elementary and secondary schools," this canon refers more generally to "schools which offer an education imbued with a Christian spirit." The more general description of schools in canon 802, §1 may allow the diocesan bishop to satisfy his responsibility in educational settings other than the Catholic school (e.g., cooperative ventures with ecumenical partners, released time arrangements, etc.). The second change in the law designates the diocesan bishop, rather than the more inclusive "ordinary of place," as the responsible agent.

Paragraph two exhorts the diocesan bishop to take into consideration the needs of the local situation before determining what kinds of schools should be established. The canon offers the examples of professional and technical schools, but leaves open the possibility that local and contemporary needs may require other schools as well. The source of both paragraphs of the canon is *Gravissimum educationis* 9.

What Makes a School "Catholic"?

Canon 803 — §1. A Catholic school is understood as one which a competent ecclesiastical authority or a public ecclesiastical juridic person directs or which ecclesiastical authority recognizes as such through a written document.

§2. The instruction and education in a Catholic school must be grounded in the principles of Catholic doctrine; teachers are to be outstanding in correct doctrine and integrity of life.

§3. Even if it is in fact Catholic, no school is to bear the name *Catholic school* without the consent of competent ecclesiastical authority.

---

[6] For a discussion of the involvement of religious in the school apostolate, see *The Catholic School,* 74–76, and "The Catholic School on the Threshold of the Third Millennium," 13.

Canon 803 addresses the specific character of the Catholic school, namely, what makes a school Catholic. The canon offers both extrinsic and intrinsic criteria. Paragraph one considers the school's juridic relationship to competent ecclesiastical authority. Under this extrinsic criterion, to be Catholic the school must be under the direction of church authority or a public juridic person (cf. cc. 113–123), or it must be recognized by church authority, through a written document, as a Catholic school.

Diocesan schools are supervised by the diocesan bishop or his delegate. Parish schools are under the supervision of the pastor who carries out his responsibilities "under the authority of the diocesan bishop" (c. 519). Schools established and operated by religious institutes are supervised by the sponsoring religious institutes which are by law themselves public ecclesiastical juridic persons (c. 634, §1). Yet such schools can be established only with the consent of the diocesan bishop (c. 801) and are subject to oversight by the diocesan bishop (c. 806, §1). Schools established by and operated under the sponsorship of the laity can be considered "Catholic" only after they have received a written document from competent ecclesiastical authority. The canon offers no criteria for a bishop's decision to grant or deny this designation to a school in the latter category.

Paragraph three provides further that no school, even if it is truly Catholic, can use the name "Catholic" without the consent of competent church authority. Authorization by competent ecclesiastical authority to use the name "Catholic" is a legal criterion, similar to the requirement of canon 216 concerning apostolic undertakings of the Christian faithful and canon 808 with regard to colleges and universities wishing to use the name "Catholic." Derived from *Apostolicam actuositatem* 24 on relations with the hierarchy, canon 803, §3 reflects the Church's concern that forms of the apostolate that assist the Church in fulfilling its mission be explicitly recognized by competent church authority (*AA* 24).

The juridic bond that exists between the diocesan bishop and the Catholic school, though essential to the Catholic identity of the school, is not in itself sufficient to guarantee the school's Catholic character. Paragraph two speaks of two intrinsic criteria, namely, the commitment to root the formational and educational experience in the principles of Catholic teaching and the expectation that teachers in Catholic schools be outstanding in their teaching of doctrine and their moral integrity.

Like the Latin code, the Eastern code requires both extrinsic and intrinsic criteria for determining a school's catholicity. The Eastern code, however, provides a fuller, more comprehensive description of the Catholic school. Canon 634, §1 of the Eastern code adopts the seminal definition of the Catholic school expressed in *Gravissimum educationis* 8, not incorporated into the Latin code. The canon highlights the importance of the "spirit of freedom and love" in the Catholic school community and an atmosphere conducive to the development of the Christian personality of each young person. It stresses the importance of integrating appropriate cultural development with knowledge illumined by a greater understanding of faith. The canon also, unlike the Latin code, calls for appropriate educational adaptations in situations in which non-Catholic students are present.

Vigilance for Catholic Religious Formation and Education

Canon 804 — §1. The Catholic religious instruction and education which are imparted in any schools whatsoever or are provided through the various instruments of social communication are subject to the authority of the Church. It is for the conference of bishops to issue general norms about this field of action and for the diocesan bishop to regulate and watch over it.

§2. The local ordinary is to be concerned that those who are designated teachers of religious instruction in schools, even in non-Catholic ones, are outstanding in correct doctrine, the witness of a Christian life, and teaching skill.

Paragraph one provides a framework for ensuring the distinctive Catholic character of the Catholic school. It clearly states that Catholic religious formation and education are subject to the authority of the Church, whether they are provided in Catholic schools or in any other type of school (*quibuslibet*) or by means of any form of social communication (e.g., films, recordings, telecommunications, print media, etc.). Responsibility is assigned to church authority at two levels: the episcopal conference for issuance of general regulations governing religious formation and education, and the diocesan bishop for vigilance and supervision of such educational efforts. The extension of this norm to any school whatsoever raises the issue of control and oversight of institutions and situations not subject to the governance of the diocesan bishop. Catholic religious education, however, is subject to church authority, in virtue of its teaching mission, and to those entrusted with responsibility for carrying out this mission. Religious education carried out in Catholic schools or in other educational settings, including a home-schooling setting, falls within the scope of this canon. The precise way in which the vigilance role is structured in non-Catholic situations should take into account local political and cultural circumstances.

Paragraph two focuses on one aspect of the religious education programs in Catholic and non-Catholic schools, namely, the quality of the teachers of religion. The responsibility of the diocesan bishop for vigilance and supervision of the religious education effort is shared in paragraph two with the local ordinary (cf. c. 134). The canon cites three areas in which teachers of religion are to be distinguished: the teaching of Catholic doctrine, the witness of their lives, and their skills as teachers. The expression of pastoral concern called for in the canon is not described. It is left to the judgment of the local ordinary to determine the appropriate form of expression in each local situation in accord with any national norms issued by the episcopal conference.

Approval and Removal of Religion Teachers

Canon 805 — For his own diocese, the local ordinary has the right to appoint or approve teachers of religion and even to remove them or demand that they be removed if a reason of religion or morals requires it.

This canon specifies the authority of the local ordinary and extends it to the right of appointing and removing teachers of religion. This authority can be delegated to others such as an episcopal vicar for education, superintendent, school administrator, etc. (cf. c. 134). The canon points to such a possibility in the use of "or approve" and "or demand that they be removed," suggesting that an intermediate level of authority might be involved in the appointment process in certain situations. Moreover, the 1981 *Relatio* confirms this suggestion and states that local practice should be respected: "It is to be noted that the canon looks to either nomination *or approval* as an appropriate equivalent where it is not the custom to nominate" (p. 180). The Eastern code in canon 636, §1 authorizes the eparchial bishop to name or approve teachers of Catholic religion as well as remove them or demand their removal for reasons of faith or morals.

Canon 805 roots the removal of religion teachers in the general reasons "of religion or morals." Practically speaking, offenses or deficiencies of faith and morals would have to be of a serious nature to warrant removal. In such cases, the need for appropriate protection of substantive and procedural rights of all parties involved should be respected and observed.

Vigilance and Visitation of Catholic Schools

Canon 806 — §1. The diocesan bishop has the right to watch over and visit the Catholic schools in his territory, even those which members of religious institutes have founded or direct. He also issues prescripts which pertain to the general regulation of Catholic schools; these prescripts are

valid also for schools which these religious direct, without prejudice, however, to their autonomy regarding the internal direction of their schools.

§2. Directors of Catholic schools are to take care under the watchfulness of the local ordinary that the instruction which is given in them is at least as academically distinguished as that in the other schools of the area.

Paragraph one is a strong assertion of the diocesan bishop's right of vigilance over and visitation of Catholic schools in his territory including schools sponsored by religious institutes (cf. c. 803). By extending the right of visitation to schools operated by religious institutes, canon 806, §1 abrogates the privilege granted prior to the 1917 code which exempted the schools of some religious (regulars) from visitation by the diocesan bishop (*CD* 35, 4).[7]

In determining what schools fall under the bishop's right of visitation, the text of the canon, "Catholic schools," and the context of the norm, its placement in the chapter on elementary and secondary schools, provide some direction. Since the code distinguishes among schools, universities and institutes of higher studies, and ecclesiastical universities and faculties, and regulates the latter two groups elsewhere in the code, the application of the bishop's right of visitation as enunciated in canon 806, §1 is focused on elementary and secondary Catholic schools. This line of reasoning is consistent with that of the code commission as stated in the *Relatio:* "Universities and institutes of higher studies do not come under the chapter on schools" (p. 179). Internal schools of religious institutes which are open only to students belonging to the respective institute are excluded from the bishop's right of visitation by canon 683, §1 (cf. *ES* I, 39).

The canon does not provide guidance for the scope of the bishop's visitation, particularly as it concerns schools operated by religious. However,

since this canon has to do with the bishop's responsibility and oversight for the quality of Catholic education provided in his diocese, his visitation should focus on those aspects of the program that affect the faith development of the students most directly.

Canon 806, §1 also authorizes the diocesan bishop to issue regulations governing the educational policies of Catholic schools described in canon 803, §1 as well as schools operated by religious institutes. These general regulations should not prejudice the legitimate autonomy religious have in directing their own schools (e.g., hiring of teachers and staff). Both sections of paragraph one are based on *Christus Dominus* 35, 4.

Paragraph two is directed to school administrators and focuses on the quality of the educational program in the school. It exhorts those responsible for the instructional program to see to it that the curriculum is as academically excellent as that of nearby schools. Though not explicitly stated, paragraph two reflects the ideals of Catholic education expressed in *Gravissimum educationis* 8–9.

CHAPTER II
CATHOLIC UNIVERSITIES AND OTHER INSTITUTES OF HIGHER STUDIES
[cc. 807–814]

The canons contained in this brief chapter are new. No parallel chapter existed in the 1917 code. Since the promulgation of the code, few, if any, sections of the revised law have received such attention, discussion, and scrutiny as have the canons on Catholic higher education. Canons 807–814 concern specifically Catholic universities and other institutes of higher education and are distinct from those dealing with Catholic schools (cc. 796–806) and ecclesiastical universities and faculties (cc. 815–821). Drawn principally from *Gravissimum educationis* 10, the canons in this chapter generally reflect the conciliar understanding of the university as a place of convergence between faith and reason, identify ways in which a university can be Catholic,

---

[7] Cf. T. Bouscaren and A. Ellis, *Canon Law: A Text and Commentary* (Milwaukee: Bruce Publishing Co., 1946) 700–701.

acknowledge the importance of research and freedom of scientific inquiry, and specify the role of ecclesiastical authority in the preservation of doctrinal integrity.

At the time the code was promulgated it was well known among members of the hierarchy and the leadership of Catholic colleges and universities that a pontifical document on Catholic universities was being prepared by the Holy See. In the years immediately following the promulgation of the revised code, numerous drafts of the proposed document were prepared and reviewed by means of a highly consultative process involving the hierarchy and representatives of Catholic higher education throughout the world. The long-awaited apostolic constitution *Ex corde Ecclesiae* was issued by Pope John Paul II on August 15, 1990.[8] Thus, it is a *lex peculiaris* or special law governing Catholic institutions of higher learning. *Ex corde Ecclesiae* contains a strong affirmation of the value and importance of Catholic colleges and universities and a call to renewal and re-examination of Catholic higher education in light of the gospel and culture.

Essentially a teaching document, *Ex corde Ecclesiae* is intended to serve as "a sort of 'magna carta'" for Catholic universities (*ECE* 8). In addition to providing doctrinal and theological perspectives on Catholic universities, the apostolic constitution is also a legal document containing a series of "general norms" based on the Code of Canon Law and complementary church legislation governing Catholic universities (*ECE*, General Norms, article 1, §1).[9]

Since the appearance of *Ex corde Ecclesiae,* U.S. bishops and presidents of Catholic colleges and universities in the United States have worked together in a common effort to implement article 1, §2 of the general norms which requires episcopal conferences (and other assemblies of Catholic hierarchy in the Eastern Catholic churches) to apply the norms concretely at the local and regional levels. This effort has been marked by a level of cooperation and collaboration never before experienced between bishops and Catholic college and university presidents.

Following the promulgation of *Ex corde Ecclesiae,* Archbishop Daniel E. Pilarczyk, president of the National Conference of Catholic Bishops, appointed Bishop John J. Leibrecht, Bishop of Springfield-Cape Giradeau, to serve as chairman of the NCCB Ad Hoc Committee on the Implementation of *Ex corde Ecclesiae*.[10] He also appointed presidential consultants and resource persons to assist the committee.[11] The committee worked from February 1991 through November 1996 preparing *ordinationes* for the application of *Ex corde Ecclesiae* in the United States for submission to the U.S. bishops for approval and subsequent submission to the Holy See for the required *recognitio* in accord with canon 455, §2.

The first major draft of the proposed document was the focus of extensive consultation with members of the hierarchy, sponsoring religious

---

[8] John Paul II, apconst *Ex corde Ecclesiae,* August 15, 1990, *AAS* 82 (1990) 1475–1509; English translation published in *Origins* 20/17 (October 4, 1990) 265, 267–276.

[9] A few commentaries have been written on *Ex corde Ecclesiae.* See, for example, J. Provost, "A Canonical Commentary on *Ex corde Ecclesiae*," in J. Langan, ed., *Catholic Universities in Church and Society: A Dialogue on 'Ex corde Ecclesiae'* (Washington, D.C.: Georgetown University, 1993) 105–136; P. de Pooter, "L'Université catholique: Au service de l'Eglise et de la société," *Ius Ecclesiae* 4 (1992) 45–78.

[10] Other members of the committee include: Cardinals Adam Maida and James Hickey; Archbishops Oscar H. Lipscomb and Francis B. Schulte; Bishops James A. Griffin and James W. Malone.

[11] Appointed as presidential consultants were: Reverend William J. Byron, SJ (The Catholic University of America), Dr. Dorothy McKenna Brown (Rosemont College), Brother Raymond Fitz, SM (The University of Dayton), Dr. Norman C. Francis (Xavier University of Louisiana), Sister Karen M. Kennelly, CSJ (Mount St. Mary's College-Los Angeles), Reverend Edward A. Malloy, CSC (University of Notre Dame), Reverend J. Donald Monan, SJ (Boston College), and Dr. Matthew Quinn (Carroll College). Resource persons: Sister Alice Gallin, OSU (Association of Catholic Colleges and Universities), Monsignor Frederick McManus (The Catholic University of America).

bodies, learned societies, presidents, faculty members, and trustees of Catholic colleges and universities throughout the country. The various consultations helped identify key issues that called for continued dialogue between bishops and university officials. Among the more challenging issues facing the committee were the relationship between church authority and institutional authority, the scope and limitations of academic freedom, elements and visible expressions of Catholic identity in Catholic colleges and universities, and the meaning of the mandate of canon 812 for Catholic professors of theological disciplines in Catholic colleges and universities and its implications for Catholic postsecondary institutions in the United States.

Because the draft appeared to be unsatisfactory as too juridical, a final draft, more pastoral in character (containing three parts, each one with separate expository and normative sections) was submitted by the committee to the members of the episcopal conference in 1996.

In November 1996 the proposed document, "*Ex corde Ecclesiae:* An Application to the United States," a general decree requiring the affirmative vote of a two-thirds majority of the *de iure* members of the episcopal conference, was overwhelmingly approved by the bishops by a vote of 224 affirmative and 6 negative.

Immediately following the action of the bishops, the approved text was transmitted to the Prefect of the Congregation for Catholic Education for review and *recognitio*. In April 1997, Pio Cardinal Laghi, prefect of the Congregation for Catholic Education, wrote to Bishop Anthony M. Pilla, president of the NCCB, requesting that a further draft of the "ordinances" be drawn up in light of observations on the text from the Congregation for Catholic Education. In its general observations, the congregation indicated that the text lacked the "necessary juridical elements" for the effective functioning of the Catholic university as "Catholic"; that the ordinances were to have a true juridic character; and that the structure of the ordinances reflect more explicitly the essential elements required by the general norms. Cardinal

Laghi also informed Bishop Pilla that the revised text, following approval by the Congregation for Catholic Education, would be forwarded to the Congregation for Bishops which is competent to grant the *recognitio*.[12]

The process for the development of the new draft was initiated with the appointment of a subcommittee of canonists, under the chairmanship of Anthony Cardinal Bevilacqua, to review the observations of the Holy See and to provide the text with appropriate canonical language and, specifically, to offer recommendations regarding the implementation of canon 812. The subcommittee's work will be presented to the Implementation Committee for its consideration and possible adoption. The Implementation Committee will present its text for approbation by the bishops and submission to the Holy See.

Right to Establish and Govern Universities

Canon 807 — The Church has the right to erect and direct universities, which contribute to a more profound human culture, the fuller development of the human person, and the fulfillment of the teaching function of the Church.

The first canon of this chapter provides a strong assertion of the Church's right to establish and operate institutions of higher education and offers a description of the purpose of such institutions. Catholic colleges and universities contribute to: (1) the advancement of human culture; (2) the development of the human person; and (3) fulfillment of the Church's teaching mission. The canon is drawn from *Gravissimum educationis* 10 which guarantees to the various disciplines in a Catholic university treatment that is consonant with their own principles and methods and carried out with freedom of scientific inquiry (c. 218).

---

[12] For the texts of "*Ex corde Ecclesiae:* An Application to the United States," Cardinal Laghi's letter of April 23, 1997, and the Observations of the Congregation for Catholic Education, see *Origins* 27:4 (June 12, 1997) 53–55.

The object of this impartial inquiry is to ensure that the Catholic university becomes, through a deeper understanding of the disciplines and attentiveness to changing circumstances and research, the place where faith and reason converge (*GE* 10). John Paul II speaks to this rationale for a Catholic university in *Ex corde Ecclesiae*:

> ...a Catholic university is distinguished by its free search for the whole truth about nature, man and God. The present age is in urgent need of this kind of disinterested service, namely of proclaiming the meaning of truth, that fundamental value without which freedom, justice and human dignity are extinguished. By means of a kind of universal humanism a Catholic university is completely dedicated to the research of all aspects of the truth in their essential connection with the supreme Truth, who is God. ...It is in the context of the impartial search for truth that the relationship between faith and reason is brought to light and meaning. (*ECE* 4, 5)

Use of the Title "Catholic"

Canon 808 — Even if it is in fact Catholic, no university is to bear the title or name of *Catholic university* without the consent of competent ecclesiastical authority.

This canon provides a legal distinction between colleges and universities that are in fact (*reapse*) Catholic and those that are authorized to use the title or name "Catholic."[13] The permission of competent ecclesiastical authority is required for a college or university to call itself "Catholic." Derived from *Apostolicam actuositatem* 24, the canon reflects the conciliar teaching on apostolic endeavors initiated by the laity and the relationship of the hierarchy to such enterprises, namely that no apostolic enterprise may claim the name

"Catholic" without authorization from competent church authority. Although similar to canon 803, §3 on elementary and secondary schools, canon 808 does not describe precisely what a Catholic university is in the same way that canon 803, §3 describes a Catholic school. *Ex corde Ecclesiae* presents a classification of existing Catholic universities (*ECE,* art. 1, §3) as well as categories for the future establishment of Catholic universities (*ECE,* art. 3).

The application of this norm in practice, that is, the criteria used to grant or deny authorization, is not provided in the code. Interestingly, *Ex corde Ecclesiae* makes no explicit reference to this requirement. It does, however, provide guidance for its application in its enunciation of "essential characteristics" of a Catholic university as "Catholic":

> 1. A Christian inspiration not only of individuals but of the university community as such; 2. a continuing reflection in the light of the Catholic faith upon the growing treasury of human knowledge, to which it seeks to contribute by its own research; 3. fidelity to the Christian message as it comes to us through the Church; 4. an institutional commitment to the service of the people of God and of the human family in their pilgrimage to the transcendent goal which gives meaning to life. (*ECE* 13)[14]

The apostolic constitution summarizes Catholic identity in stating that "being both a University and Catholic, it must be both a community of scholars representing various branches of human knowledge, and an academic institution in which

---

[13] See also canon 216 on apostolic endeavors and canon 300 on associations of the Christian faithful.

[14] For the source document of these characteristics, *ECE* cites "The Catholic University in the Modern World," the final document of the Second International Congress of Delegates of Catholic Universities, Rome, November 20–29, 1972, Section 1. For text, see A. Gallin, *American Catholic Higher Education: Essential Documents 1967–1990* (Notre Dame, Ind.: University of Notre Dame, 1992) 37–57.

Catholicism is vitally present and operative" (*ECE* 14).

The Eastern code provides a more detailed explanation of the nature, purpose, and characteristics of Catholic universities. Several of the canons on Catholic universities in the Eastern code differ from the Latin code's canons in regard to the definition of the goals of Catholic universities (*CCEO* 640, §1), the pursuit of academic disciplines (*CCEO* 641), and the authority competent to establish or approve Catholic universities (*CCEO* 642). Eastern code canons 640, §1 and 641, based on *Gravissimum educationis* 10, are taken almost verbatim from the conciliar source. Eastern code canon 642 authorizes the higher administrative authority of a church *sui iuris* (e.g., patriarch with synod) to establish or approve a Catholic university following consultation with the Holy See. No explicit provision parallel to canon 808 is found in the Eastern code.

Right of Episcopal Conferences to Establish Universities

Canon 809 — If it is possible and expedient, conferences of bishops are to take care that there are universities or at least faculties suitably spread through their territory, in which the various disciplines are studied and taught, with their academic autonomy preserved and in light of Catholic doctrine.

Echoing the teaching of *Gravissimum educationis* 10, this canon is directed to the episcopal conference and obliges the bishops to see to the establishment of Catholic universities or Catholic faculties throughout the territory of their conference. The obligation takes into account local circumstances and applies only if it is possible and expedient. The purpose of these universities and faculties, though described briefly in the canon, is significant for the standard it sets for Catholic universities, namely, the preservation of academic autonomy with due regard for Catholic teaching.

Ex corde Ecclesiae speaks eloquently to the importance of this standard:

> Every Catholic university…possesses that institutional autonomy necessary to perform its functions effectively and guarantees its members academic freedom, so long as the rights of the individual person and of the community are preserved within the confines of truth and the common good. (*ECE* 12)[15]

Drawn from *Gaudium et spes* 59, the apostolic constitution expresses three elements which constitute the boundaries of academic freedom: respect for the rights of others (individuals and community); respect for the confines of truth; respect for the common good. While not enunciated in canon 809, they continue to serve as limitations on the exercise of academic freedom.[16]

As a goal to be achieved or a standard against which a Catholic university may be measured, the educational function described in canon 809 is difficult to particularize in practice. Practical judgments on the part of the appropriate authorities will have to be made, with due caution.

Responsibility for the Appointment of Teachers and Observance of Catholic Doctrine

Canon 810 — §1. The authority competent according to the statutes has the duty to make provision so that teachers are appointed in Catholic universities who besides their scientific and pedagogical qualifications are outstanding in integrity of doctrine and probity of life and that they are removed from their function when they lack these requirements; the manner of proceeding defined in the statutes is to be observed.

---

[15] See also *ECE,* General Norms, art. 2, §5. Paragraph 5 uses the terms "autonomy" and "freedom" in describing the nature of a Catholic university: autonomy to develop its identity and pursue its mission and freedom in research and teaching within the limits noted in n. 12 of the apostolic constitution. The phrase "academic autonomy" (*scientifica autonomia*) is not used in *ECE.*

[16] See also *Gaudium et spes* 62 which concludes the constitution's treatment of the development of culture and speaks as well about integrity and freedom of inquiry and expression by both lay and clerical theologians.

§2. The conferences of bishops and diocesan bishops concerned have the duty and right of being watchful so that the principles of Catholic doctrine are observed faithfully in these same universities.

Canon 810 defines the authorities competent to determine the quality of teachers appointed to Catholic universities and to watch over the observance of Catholic doctrine. It is intended to respect the legitimate autonomy of the academic institution, the Catholic character of the university, and the responsibility of competent ecclesiastical authority for the correct faithful observance of Catholic teaching in these same universities.

Regarding the appointment and removal of teachers in Catholic colleges and universities, the procedures specified in the statutes of the institution are to be carefully observed. The internal authorities of a Catholic university, in determining the suitability of candidates, are to take into consideration their "scientific and pedagogical qualifications" and their "integrity of doctrine and probity of life." Procedures for the removal of teachers lacking the same qualities should also be delineated in the statutes of the institution.

While paragraph one provides general guidance concerning acceptable norms for the appointment and removal of teachers in Catholic colleges and universities, specific criteria and procedures should be developed by the individual institutions to assist in the application of the norms. It is incumbent upon the administrative leadership of Catholic universities to ensure that the statutes of the institution embody standards of fairness and acceptable practice so as to avoid arbitrariness of judgment about the scholarship and personal witness of individual members of the faculty.[17]

Paragraph two places responsibility for vigilance over the observance of Catholic doctrine with episcopal conferences and diocesan bishops. Bishops, as successors of the apostles (c. 753), are authoritative teachers of the faith (c. 386, §1) and competent to make judgments concerning the observance of Catholic teaching. For Catholic colleges and universities, *Ex corde Ecclesiae* describes the role of the diocesan bishop if, in his vigilance, he determines that Catholic teaching is not being faithfully observed:

> Each Bishop has the responsibility to promote the welfare of the Catholic universities in his diocese and has the right and duty to watch over the preservation and strengthening of their Catholic character. If problems should arise concerning this Catholic character, the local Bishop is to take the initiatives necessary to resolve the matter, working with the competent university authorities in accordance with established procedures and, if necessary, with the help of the Holy See. (*ECE*, art. 5, §2)

Ex corde Ecclesiae describes the *ius vigilandi* of the diocesan bishop as a kind of pastoral oversight for the preservation and strengthening of the Catholic character of the institution. The diocesan bishop is not authorized to intervene directly into the internal matters of the Catholic university. In his role of vigilance, he is to work closely with the internal authorities, according to established procedures, to correct the situation. This process implies a relationship characterized by trust, mutual respect, and communication between the diocesan bishop and university officials. It suggests a spirit of cooperation and collaboration in the realization of the goals of the Catholic university.

Canon 810, §2 attributes to episcopal conferences the right and duty to exercise vigilance over the observance of Catholic teaching in colleges and universities. Ecclesiastical competence belongs to the individual diocesan bishop and to the episcopal conference. The canon provides neither procedures for intervention by the episcopal conference nor procedures for the resolution of possible conflicts that could arise between the bishop and the episcopal conference. Presumably, such procedures would have to be developed at the

---

[17] It is clear that the framers of §1 intended it to apply to university administrators as well as to teachers. See 1981 *Relatio* 182–183.

level of the episcopal conference and approved by the bishops of the territory.

Provision for Theological Studies

Canon 811 — §1. The competent ecclesiastical authority is to take care that in Catholic universities a faculty or institute or at least a chair of theology is erected in which classes are also given for lay students.

§2. In individual Catholic universities, there are to be classes which especially treat those theological questions which are connected to the disciplines of their faculties.

Paragraph one urges ecclesiastical authority to see that educational opportunities for the study of theology are provided at Catholic colleges and universities, especially for lay students. Based on *Gravissimum educationis* 10, this canon offers three options for structuring a program of theology in Catholic universities: a faculty (i.e., a college, department, or the like), an institute, or a chair of theology. University officials, considering the particular local situation, are to determine the most appropriate form of theological presence. Here, as in other canons of title III, the competent ecclesiastical authority is left unspecified. It could be the Holy See, episcopal conferences, diocesan bishops, or certain religious superiors of sponsoring religious bodies.

The second paragraph of this canon reflects the concern that theological studies not be isolated from other academic disciplines in the educational enterprise. Drawn from *Gravissimum educationis* 10 and *Gaudium et spes* 62, paragraph two promotes efforts to harmonize faith and culture. *Ex corde Ecclesiae,* building on the conciliar teaching, describes the unique role of theology in the dialogue between faith and reason as serving all other disciplines in their search for meaning (*ECE* 19). At the same time, the interaction between theology and the other disciplines "enriches theology, offering it a better understanding of the world today, and making theological research more relevant to current needs" (*ECE* 19). The interaction

inherent in such efforts to harmonize faith and culture challenges Catholic colleges and universities to seek new and more suitable means of communicating theological reflection and Catholic doctrine to the men and women of this age.

Ecclesiastical Authorization for Professors of Theological Disciplines in Catholic Colleges and Universities

Canon 812 — Those who teach theological disciplines in any institutes of higher studies whatsoever must have a mandate from the competent ecclesiastical authority.

Mandate

This canon requires ecclesiastical authorization for teachers of theological disciplines in Catholic institutions of higher learning. The canon and the notion of the mandate are innovations in the law of the Church on Catholic colleges and universities.[18] The intent of the canon is to preserve the orthodoxy of Catholic doctrine. The requirement of the mandate represents a juridical response to a potential danger to the faith and an effort to protect the rights of the faithful and the good of the Church.

Following promulgation of the revised code in 1983 there was considerable apprehension and concern in U.S. academe about the innovation of the mandate. This was due primarily to the perception that implementation of the mandate of canon 812 would mean new intervention on the part of church authority in Catholic higher education.

The precise meaning of the mandate (*mandatum*) is not clear. Early drafts of canon 812 required a canonical mission (*missio canonica*) for those who taught theological or related disciplines in any kind of institution of higher learning (1977 schema, c. 64). In the 1980 schema, the wording of this canon was the same as in the 1977 text. The 1981 *Relatio,* in response to concerns about the new requirement, contained two significant changes in the text of the canon: *aut cum theolo-*

---

[18] See also canon 229, §3 for reference to the mandate.

gia conexas was dropped and *mandatum* was substituted for *missio canonica,* the reasoning being that the ecclesiastical authorization under consideration was not fully equivalent to a true canonical mission.[19] No explanation was offered as to why "canonical mission" in this context would not be a "true canonical mission."

The notion of canonical mission (*missio canonica*) as applied to teaching in the Church is rooted in conciliar legislation of the Middle Ages concerning requirements for preaching. Condemnations against those who held positions that denied the necessity of ecclesiastical authorization for preaching were issued, for example, by the Council of Verona in 1184, the Fourth Lateran Council, the Council of Constance, and the Council of Trent.[20] Later, in the nineteenth century, canonical mission was applied more broadly to all public instruction with the federalization of schools and universities in Germany. The Church required all teachers of theology to have an ecclesiastical (canonical) mission from the bishop to ensure freedom from intervention by the state in the teaching of theology at all levels of education.[21]

In the 1917 code the term *missio canonica* was used to describe the principal means of acquiring the power of jurisdiction, a power that could be exercised only by clergy. Yet commentators on the 1917 code applied the term to liturgical preaching and to the entire ministry of teaching, including catechetical teaching. The basis of this usage was canon 1328 which used the term *missio* to describe the authorization needed for the ministry of preaching. The placement of canon 1328 in the 1917 code and the organization of the section in which the canon appeared supported the opinion that the *missio* required in the canons applied to the broader ministry of teaching, including catechetical teaching as well as preaching.

At the same time, the application of canon 1328 to the entire ministry of ecclesiastical teaching raised questions regarding the practical application of the *missio* to lay persons. While the *missio* of canon 1328 of the 1917 code was understood as ecclesiastical authorization to perform a special function, it was considered to be a form of authorization distinct from the *missio canonica* of the same code.

The requirement of a canonical mission for some form of public ecclesiastical teaching became an explicit part of universal law in the norms of the 1931 apostolic constitution *Deus scientiarum Dominus* governing ecclesiastical faculties and universities.[22] Among the requirements for faculty selection was the provision that each professor receive a "canonical mission" for teaching from the chancellor after having received the *nihil obstat* from the Holy See.

In 1979, the apostolic constitution *Sapientia christiana* was promulgated by Pope John Paul II. This document, replacing the previous norms regulating ecclesiastical faculties and universities, retains the requirement of a canonical mission for teachers of disciplines related to faith and morals; other teachers require permission to teach (*venia docendi*).[23]

The deletion of *missio canonica* and the insertion of *mandatum* in the final version of canon 812 of the revised code does not suggest that the

---

[19] *Communicationes* 15 (1983) 105.

[20] See Concilium Veronense, C. 9, X *de haereticis,* V. 7; Concilium Lateranense IV, C. 3, X *de haereticis,* V. 7; Martinus V, bull *Inter cunctas,* February 22, 1418, art. 14; Concilium Tridentinum, sessio XXIII, *de ecclesiastica hierarchia et ordinatione,* c. 7. For references to Lateran Council IV and Council of Trent, see Tanner I: 234–235 and II: 744, respectively. For texts of the Council of Verona and the bull *Inter cunctas,* see Denzinger, *Enchiridion Symbolorum: Definitionum et Declarationum de Rebus Fidei et Morum* (Freiburg: Herder, 1963) 761/402 and 1164/594, respectively.

[21] See, for example, H. Flatten, "Missio Canonica," in *Verkundigung und Glaube: Festschrift für Franz X. Arnold,* ed. T. Filthaut and J. Jungmann (Freiburg-Br.: Herder, 1958) 123–141; J. Haring, *Das Lehramt des katholischen Theologie: Festschrift des Grazer Universität für 1926* (Graz: Meyerhoff, 1926).

[22] Pius XI, apconst *Deus scientiarum Dominus,* May 24, 1931, *AAS* 23 (1931) 252, art. 21, n. 5.

[23] John Paul II, apconst *Sapientia christiana,* April 15, 1979, *AAS* 71 (1979) 469–499, art. 27, §1.

drafters considered ecclesiastical authorization unnecessary. Rather, it would seem that the deletion of *missio canonica* simply reflected concern about the nature of the ecclesiastical authorization required for public ecclesiastical teaching. Since the *missio canonica* was not considered to be "fully equated with a true canonical mission," its deletion and its replacement with *mandatum* seems related to the association of *missio canonica* with jurisdiction and the conferral of ecclesiastical office.

The use of *mandatum* rather than *missio canonica* in the promulgated version of canon 812 indicates that the "mandate" is neither a delegation nor a granting of jurisdiction. It does not give the one mandated disciplinary authority over others in the Church. Nor does it confer an ecclesiastical office.

The distinction between *missio canonica* and *mandatum* has also been sought in the Second Vatican Council's Decree on the Apostolate of the Laity.[24] In article 24 of the decree the council fathers set forth differing degrees of relationship between the lay apostolate and the hierarchy, beginning with the more remote relationships and moving to closer relationships in which the laity are fully subject to the hierarchy. In so doing, the council taught that there are certain forms of the apostolate of the laity which the hierarchy joins more closely to its own apostolic endeavors without depriving the apostolate of the laity of its own nature, individuality, and initiative. This act of joining some forms of the apostolate of the laity to that of the hierarchy is called a *mandatum*.

The same article 24 refers to another form of relationship between the laity and hierarchy in which the hierarchy "entrusts" to the laity some functions that are more closely connected with the pastoral duties of the hierarchy. Such functions include the teaching of Christian doctrine, certain liturgical actions, and the care of souls. The decree uses the term *missio* to describe those "entrusted" functions that are fully subject to the direction of the hierarchy.

Although this distinction may provide some insight into the meaning of the *mandatum* of canon 812, it is not all that clear. From the earliest discussion of the Preparatory Commission on the Apostolate of the Laity it was obvious that no real clarity existed on the meaning of "mandate." The concept was confused with the notion of canonical mission and with other juridical meanings of "mandate." The Conciliar Commission for the Apostolate of the Laity made further attempts to clarify the distinction between mandate and canonical mission by appending lengthy explanatory notes to the 1963 schema.[25] One of the explanatory notes listed the areas of apostolic activity requiring a *missio canonica,* which included teaching Christian doctrine in a public manner.[26]

The final text of the decree was presented in 1965; it contained no changes in the distinction between *mandatum* and *missio canonica.* Further clarity in the application of the two notions was lost as a result of the Conciliar Commission's decision to delete the accompanying explanatory notes.

What does seem clear from the promulgated decree is that the council considered *missio* and *mandatum* to be two distinct concepts. Mission connotes entrusting to the laity certain tasks and certain offices which are considered to be proper to the hierarchy but which require neither the power of orders nor the power of jurisdiction for their lawful exercise. Mandate refers to those apostolic activities which remain activities proper to the laity in virtue of baptism, but which, at times, are joined more closely to the apostolic responsibility of the bishop. When acting pursuant to a mandate, a lay person acts, it would seem, on his or her own and in communion with the bishop, but not in the name of the bishop or the church hierarchy.

Based on the canonical history of the notions of *missio canonica* and *mandatum,* it seems that the two concepts are distinct and that the change from "canonical mission" to "mandate" in canon 812 is not without significance. It would also seem that

---

[24] *Apostolicam actuositatem,* November 18, 1965, *AAS* 58 (1966) 837–864, art. 24.

[25] *ActSynVat* III, 4:677–678.
[26] Ibid., 681.

the meaning of the term *mandatum* set forth in the Decree on the Apostolate of the Laity signifies a relationship between bishops and theologians in which theology is carried out in communion with church hierarchy and in a manner respectful of the proper roles of bishops and theologians.

Ex corde Ecclesiae refers to the relationship between bishops and theologians as "interrelated" whereby bishops are to encourage the "creative work" of theologians and theologians are to respect the authority of bishops and "assent to Catholic doctrine according to the degree of authority with which it is taught" (*ECE* 29). The apostolic constitution characterizes the relationship between bishops and theologians as one of "dialogue" (*ECE* 29), a notion which is indispensable in acknowledging the unique role of each participant.

In terms of the purpose of canon 812, namely, to uphold the orthodoxy of Catholic teaching, it would seem that the mandate signifies that the theologian is within the full communion of the Catholic Church and possesses the qualities set forth in canon 810 for teachers in Catholic colleges and universities, namely, "integrity of doctrine and probity of life" (c. 810, §1).

Who Is Bound?

As a legal norm, canon 812 involves a "right-and-duty" situation, that is, the granting, withdrawal, or denial of a mandate for teachers of theological disciplines. The requirement is in the nature of a restriction upon the rights of those engaged in sacred disciplines to freedom of expression and prudent expression (c. 218).[27] As a restriction on the free exercise of rights, canon 812 should be interpreted strictly, that is, as narrowly as is consistent with the ordinary meaning of the words (c. 18). Therefore, wherever the text of

canon 812 is subject to differing interpretations, the stricter or narrower meaning should be given because of the context of the canon as a restriction upon the free exercise of rights.

The opening words of canon 812 identify the subject of the ecclesiastical requirement. The canon imposes the direct legal requirement to obtain a mandate on individual persons who teach or intend to teach theological disciplines in Catholic institutions of higher education. This includes lay men and women as well as clergy and religious. Canon 229, §3 recognizes the capacity of lay persons who have the necessary credentials and competence to receive this mandate to teach the sacred sciences.

This canon applies to Roman Catholics of the Latin church in virtue of canon 11 and would not apply to non-Catholics who teach theology in Catholic colleges and universities. *Ex corde Ecclesiae* supports this understanding when it refers to "Catholic theologians" as those who fulfill a mandate from the Church (*ECE,* art. 4, §3).

Theological Disciplines

Precisely what "theological disciplines" means in canon 812 is not clear. As noted above, the insertion of this term was the result of a textual change during the revision process. Canons 64 and 767 of the 1977 and 1980 schemata, respectively, described the endeavors for which authorization was required as "*lectiones theologicas aut cum theologia conexas.*" This wording was changed in the *Relatio* to "*disciplinas theologicas.*"[28] The effect of the textual change was to narrow the scope of the required authorization to "theological disciplines," omitting reference to those disciplines "connected with theology."

The meaning of "theological disciplines" might be understood in light of article 51 of the norms for the correct implementation of the apostolic constitution *Sapientia christiana* issued by the Congregation for Catholic Education in 1979. Under the heading of "theological disciplines,"

---

[27] Related canons that affirm basic ecclesial rights of the Christian faithful are canon 211 on the duty and right of the faithful to spread the gospel and canon 216 which acknowledges the right of the faithful, in accord with each one's condition and state, to promote and support apostolic undertakings of their own initiative.

[28] *Communicationes* 15 (1983) 57–109.

article 51 lists the following topics: scripture, fundamental, dogmatic, moral, spiritual, and pastoral theology, liturgy, church history, patrology, archeology, and canon law.[29] In looking to parallel places for the meaning of "theological disciplines," care should be taken not to broaden the notion beyond the academic disciplines of Catholic theology or beyond the disciplines that are formally theological. Programs of study focusing on pastoral ministry, methodology of religious education, comparative religion, and history and sociology of religion, for example, would seem not to be considered "theological disciplines" in the strict sense and, therefore, would be beyond the scope of canon 812.

Competent Ecclesiastical Authority

Those who teach theological disciplines in Catholic colleges and universities are to receive a mandate from "competent ecclesiastical authority." Early drafts of the canon did not designate any source for the required authorization.[30] The words "competent ecclesiastical authority" were inserted in the 1981 *Relatio*. The canon does not indicate precisely what authority is competent to grant the mandate.[31]

Since the authority is not specifically identified, it would seem that the canon intends there to be more than one authority in the Church competent to grant the mandate. The Holy See is surely capable of granting the mandate (c. 331). Canon 810 assigns the duty and right of vigilance over Catholic doctrine in Catholic institutions of higher learning to conferences of bishops and diocesan bishops (c. 810, §2). It would follow that such authorities would also be competent to grant the

required mandate to those who teach such doctrine. Additionally, it might be argued that religious ordinaries could also grant the mandate to members of their own institutes teaching in their own institutions.

The law does not restrict the granting of the mandate to bishops or religious ordinaries personally. Therefore, as an act of ordinary executive power, it would seem that the granting of the mandate may be delegated to others according to the norms of law, arguably to lay persons as well as clerics (c. 137, §1). The extent to which others besides the diocesan bishop and the conference of bishops may be competent to grant the mandate of canon 812 will depend on the extent to which the diocesan bishop or the conference of bishops chooses to delegate such responsibility.

Procedures for Granting or Withdrawing

The code does not specify any procedures for the granting or withdrawing of the required mandate of canon 812. It does, however, provide some guidance regarding which principles should be considered in the development of such procedures to ensure fairness in their application. As noted above, canon 812 is a legal norm in the nature of a restriction of the rights of those engaged in the sacred disciplines to freedom of inquiry and prudent expression (c. 218) and, as such, should be interpreted strictly. The concluding sentence of *Gaudium et spes* 62 also provides guidance by assuring a lawful freedom of inquiry, thought, and expression to those who dedicate themselves to theological studies.

Procedures for the application of the canon, that is, the granting or withdrawal of the mandate, should take into account the basic human right to one's good reputation (c. 220) and the foreseeable effects upon the reputations of those involved. Such procedures should also consider the juridical protection offered in the code for the individual to vindicate or defend his or her rights before a competent forum in the Church (c. 221).

Any procedure for the application of the mandate must respect the rights of both theologians

---

[29] Congregation for Catholic Education, *Ordinationes ad Constitutionem Apostolicam 'Sapientia christiana' (Normae speciales)*, art. 51, *AAS* 71 (1979) 513. English translation in USCC, *On Ecclesiastical Universities and Faculties* (1979) 69–70.

[30] See canons 64 and 767 in the 1977 and 1980 schemata, respectively.

[31] See canon 312, §1 for an example of a listing of competent church authorities.

and bishops. As teachers of the faith, bishops are to provide episcopal supervision over the transmission of the faith and to safeguard the integrity of Catholic teaching (c. 753). When the right of the bishop to protect the rights of the Church and its members to receive the faith integrally and faithfully is in tension with the theologian's rights enumerated above, mutual trust, cooperation, and dialogue are placed in jeopardy unless a just and equitable resolution is sought. Concrete application of the norms of *Ex corde Ecclesiae* at the local and regional levels (*ECE*, art. 1, §2) should take into account the rights and responsibilities of all involved in order to "forestall disputes and if such disputes arise to promote their resolution for the good of the faithful."[32]

Pastoral Care of Catholic Students

Canon 813 — The diocesan bishop is to have earnest pastoral care for students, even by erecting a parish or at least by designating priests stably for this, and is to make provision that at universities, even non-Catholic ones, there are Catholic university centers which give assistance, especially spiritual assistance, to youth.

This canon explicitly assigns to the diocesan bishop pastoral responsibility for the pastoral care of Catholic students. Based on *Gravissimum educationis* 10, the pastoral concern extends to students attending both Catholic and non-Catholic colleges and universities. The canon

specifies what it is that the diocesan bishop is to do. He is to establish a university parish for the students or at least assign priest chaplains on a stable basis for this ministry. "Catholic university centers" are also to be provided to assist students studying at Catholic and non-Catholic institutions. The Eastern code also expresses the pastoral responsibility of the hierarchs to care for the spiritual well being of students (*CCEO* 645). The Eastern canon speaks of "carefully chosen and prepared Christian faithful" as exercising the pastoral ministry.

Ex corde Ecclesiae refers to "pastoral ministry" as a "constitutive element of a Catholic university" (*ECE* 38), a part of the mission of the Church within the university, and an opportunity for all members of the university community to "integrate faith with life" (*ECE* 38). The apostolic constitution views this ministry as indispensable for Catholic students as they prepare themselves for "active participation in the life of the Church" (*ECE* 41). It urges close cooperation between the university and the local church in providing pastoral care for the university community and invites all members of the university community "to assist in the work of pastoral ministry and to collaborate in its activities" (*ECE*, art. 6, §2).

Application of Canons 807–813

Canon 814 — The prescripts established for universities apply equally to other institutes of higher learning.

This canon is a terminological canon. It simply clarifies that the application of the preceding canons extends not only to universities but to all institutions of higher studies.

---

[32] NCCB, *Doctrinal Responsibilities: Approaches to Promoting Cooperation and Resolving Misunderstandings Between Bishops and Theologians* (Washington, D.C.: USCC, 1989) 2.

BIBLIOGRAPHY

Bibliographical material for canons 793–814 can be found after the commentary on canon 833.

CHAPTER III
ECCLESIASTICAL UNIVERSITIES
AND FACULTIES
[cc. 815–821]

These seven canons—the last of which properly belongs in the preceding chapter—can best be understood as a very brief summary of the special or "peculiar" law governing postsecondary educational institutions which are ecclesiastical in status. Perhaps "papal" or even "canonical" would be more logical than "ecclesiastical." Popularly but not correctly, ecclesiastical faculties, programs, and degrees are often called "pontifical," but this is an honorific term only. It indicates the origin and dignity of an academic institution, but not its canonical status.

Ecclesiastical universities and faculties have their own Catholic ethos and are a species of Catholic academic institutions. (This is true also of seminaries, to the extent that they too have academic programs. Seminaries, however, are governed by canons 232–264 of Book II on "The Formation of Clerics" rather than by the canons of Book III; in addition, seminaries themselves may be or may possess ecclesiastical faculties.) Nevertheless, ecclesiastical faculties are carefully distinguished from the Catholic universities, colleges, and other institutions of the preceding chapter, canons 807–814. This nomenclature and distinction have only gradually become clear in the period since the 1917 code. That code embraced institutions at every level in the single title *De scholis* (*CIC* 1372–1383) and, in dealing with institutions of higher education, treated them as directly subject to the Apostolic See and as issuing academic degrees with effects at canon law (especially *CIC* 1376–1378). Today the meaning of "ecclesiastical" in this connection is carefully distinguished from "Catholic."

In the United States there are no ecclesiastical universities, and the very few ecclesiastical faculties are chiefly seminaries or theologates. The single exception is The Catholic University of America in Washington: this is a Catholic rather than an ecclesiastical institution, but it has three ecclesiastical faculties, i.e., the departments of theology and canon law and a school of philosophy.

The special law is found now in the apostolic constitution *Sapientia christiana* of 1979 prepared under Paul VI and promulgated early in the period of John Paul II, together with ordinances or norms of application issued by the competent dicastery of the Roman Curia.[1] This constitution remains in effect in virtue of canon 6, §1, 4° of the 1983 code. The background of the special law is an apostolic constitution of Pius XI, *Deus scientiarum Dominus*.[2] In 1931 this lengthy document radically raised academic standards, requirements, and expectations of higher educational institutions within the Church.

In its brief declaration on Christian education, Vatican II devoted an expository paragraph to the subject, followed by a mandate to ecclesiastical faculties:

> The Church has high expectations from the work of the faculties of the sacred sciences. For to them the Church confides the very serious task of preparing its own students not only for the priestly ministry but especially for teaching in seats of higher ecclesiastical studies, for advancing branches of knowledge by their own efforts, and for undertaking the more arduous challenges of the intellectual apostolate. It is also the responsibility of these faculties to explore the various areas of the

[1] April 15, 1979, *AAS* 71 (1979) 469–499; the *Ordinationes* issued by the Congregation for Catholic Education, dated April 29 of the same year, follow directly, 500–521.

[2] May 24, 1931, *AAS* 23 (1931) 241–262; norms of application, SCSU, *Sacra Congregatio,* June 6, 1931, *AAS* 23 (1931) 263–284.

sacred disciplines so that day by day a deeper understanding of divine revelation will be developed, the treasure of Christian wisdom handed down by our ancestors will be more fully opened up, dialogue will be fostered with our separated brothers and sisters and with non-Christians, and responses will be found to questions raised by the development of doctrine.[3]

The council then mandated that ecclesiastical faculties revise their own statutes,[4] thus in effect asking for an updating of *Deus scientiarum Dominus*. Instead, the Congregation for Catholic Education (formerly the Congregations for Seminaries and Universities) took the initiative and, after interim steps[5] and extensive worldwide consultation, prepared the special law of the 1979 papal constitution and the accompanying ordinances.[6]

So far as the canon law of the Eastern Catholic churches is concerned, a brief article (*CCEO* 646–650) is substantially similar to the corresponding canons of the Latin code, but developed in different language. No application of any canons in the chapter on "Catholic Universities" (*CCEO* 640–645) is made to ecclesiastical universities and faculties, as is done in the Latin church's code.

Nature and Purpose

Canon 815 — Ecclesiastical universities or faculties, which are to investigate the sacred disciplines or those connected to the sacred and to instruct students scientifically in the same disciplines, are proper to the Church by virtue of its function to announce the revealed truth.

The assertion in canon 815 is abbreviated from *Gravissimum educationis* 11 (quoted above) so as to refer directly to the twin research and instructional roles of institutions which cover the so-called sacred sciences, themselves supportive of the Church's mission of proclaiming revealed truth. These "ecclesiastical" universities and faculties, as already mentioned, are formally distinguished from universities, colleges, schools, and other academic institutions called "Catholic," which themselves may (and indeed should) also include sacred or religious studies as well as more general disciplines such as arts and sciences or letters, physical sciences, and professional studies.

In these ecclesiastical academic institutions the sacred sciences and subjects or disciplines related to them are, in the first place, theology, canon law, and philosophy; related areas of study embrace biblical and catechetical studies, liturgical studies, church history, and the like. Certain social studies may be included among these disciplines, such as sociology and education. As of 1979 there were some twenty-seven kinds of ecclesiastical faculties, institutes *ad instar,* or specialized sectors within faculties or the like.[7] Faculties—ordinarily called schools, departments, or colleges in American usage—are the principal academic entities; several of them may constitute an ecclesiastical university.

The significant point is that the many "Catholic" universities which embrace non-ecclesiastical or non-sacred disciplines already mentioned, such as arts and sciences or letters, physical sciences, and professional studies, are not included in the category covered here. Understandably, this limits greatly the number of ecclesiastical universities.

Approbation and Statutes

Canon 816 — §1. Ecclesiastical universities and faculties can be established only through erection by the Apostolic See or with its approval; their higher direction also pertains to it.

---

[3] *GE* 11.
[4] Ibid.
[5] In particular, *Normae quaedam,* March 24, 1974 (n. 113/66/F).
[6] For texts, see A. Gallin, ed., *American Catholic Higher Education: Essential Documents, 1967–1990* (Notre Dame, Ind.: University of Notre Dame, 1992) 63–69, 87–127.

[7] Ordinances, appendix II.

§2. Individual ecclesiastical universities and faculties must have their own statutes and plan of studies approved by the Apostolic See.

The first paragraph of canon 816 makes clear that the original constitution, erection, or establishment of ecclesiastical academic entities belongs to the Apostolic See in some cases, while in others their subsequent approbation by that Roman See is enough—whether this is by way of probationary approval or definitive inclusion among such bodies. In either case canonical governance belongs formally to the Apostolic See.

At the same time, paragraph two requires that every institution have its own internal statutes of governance as well as plans or programs of studies. Statutes and programs, drawn up in accord with the canons and the special law of *Sapientia christiana,* in turn require Roman approval.

In the Eastern churches, besides this kind of academic institution erected by the Apostolic Roman See itself, universities and faculties erected by the "higher administrative authority of a Church *sui iuris"* after prior consultation with the Roman See are also considered ecclesiastical by Eastern code canons 649 and 642, §1. In particular, "within the territorial boundaries of a patriarchal Church this higher authority is the patriarch with the consent of the synod of bishops of the patriarchal Church" (*CCEO* 642, §2).

Academic Degrees

Canon 817 — No university or faculty which has not been erected or approved by the Apostolic See is able to confer academic degrees which have canonical effects in the Church.

The preceding canons have determined the first two characteristics of ecclesiastical universities and faculties: first and most important, the defined areas of study, namely, sacred and related disciplines; second, papal or curial constitution or approbation. Canon 817 adds a third element, the conferral of appropriate academic degrees by authority of or in the name of the Apostolic See. This reservation or limitation of degree-granting power is confined strictly to institutions that are erected or approved by the Roman See. The degrees in question are the baccalaureate, the licentiate or license, and the doctorate or *laurea.*

The significance of this canon, in its reference to degrees which have canonical effects in the Church—as distinct from degrees which have effects or recognition in society at large—is demonstrated in the several canons that exemplify these canonical effects: 253, §1 (doctorate or licentiate for teachers of philosophical, theological, and juridical disciplines in seminaries); 378, §1, 5° (degrees or expertise in scripture, theology, or canon law for candidates for the episcopacy); 478, §1 (degrees or expertise in canon law or theology for vicars general and episcopal vicars); 1420, §4 (doctorates or at least licentiates in canon law for judicial vicars or adjutant judicial vicars); 1421, §3 (same requirement for judges); 1435 (same requirement for promoters of justice and defenders of the bond). In the cases where an equivalent expertise is mentioned in a canon, the requirement of a canonical degree may be readily satisfied, for example, by suitable experience.

The special law may make additional requirements: for permanent teachers in ecclesiastical faculties, for example, "a suitable doctorate or equivalent title or exceptional and singular scientific accomplishment."[8] The 1979 norms of application are in turn more specific: "If the discipline is sacred or connected with the sacred, the doctorate must be canonical. In the event that the doctorate is not canonical, the teacher will usually be required to have at least a canonical licentiate."[9]

Such canonical requirements for appointments are of course over and above the recognition that such degrees with canonical effects have in the church community. It is, moreover, usual and de-

---

[8] *SapC* 25, §1, 2.
[9] Art. 17.

sirable for ecclesiastical institutions to seek and obtain civil recognition of the respective ecclesiastical degrees. This may be achieved through a civil charter or certificate of incorporation (usual in the United States) or by concordat; alternatively, again by way of a civil charter or the like, an institution may confer two degrees, one canonical, one civil, for completion of a single academic program of studies.

Application of Canons on Catholic Universities

Canon 818 — The prescripts established for Catholic universities in cann. 810, 812, and 813 are also valid for ecclesiastical universities and faculties.

Despite the distinctive status already mentioned, canon 818 applies three canons from the chapter on "Catholic Universities and Other Institutes of Higher Studies" to the ecclesiastical institutions of this chapter. At the very least this suggests the comparable nature of the different enterprises within church life.

Canon 810 is especially important because, in virtue of canon 818, it determines that the (ordinarily internal) "authority competent according to the statutes" will have, even in ecclesiastical faculties and universities, responsibility for appointment and removal of teachers (§1). Similarly, the immediate responsibility for vigilance "that the principles of Catholic doctrine are observed faithfully" pertains first to the respective conference of bishops and next to the diocesan bishop (§2). In neither case is the ultimate power of the Apostolic See mitigated, but the principle of subsidiarity is respected.

Next, the application of *canon 812* to ecclesiastical universities and faculties creates a seeming contradiction in the law. On the one hand, the special law of *Sapientia christiana* demands that teachers of "disciplines concerning faith or morals must receive ... a canonical mission from the chancellor or his delegate, for they do not teach on their own authority but by virtue of the

mission they have received from the Church."[10] The original language of "canonical mission" in the draft of canon 812 was deliberately changed to "mandate" (without further qualification or elaboration) as a kind of mitigation or amelioration, since "canonical mission" was felt to be less appropriate. Whatever the difference between mandate and mission, it may thus appear that the stronger expression found in *Sapientia christiana* remains in effect, given the further demands of that special law for teachers in ecclesiastical universities and faculties (profession of faith, grant of mission by the chancellor or delegate, declaration of *nihil obstat* by the Apostolic See). It is nevertheless arguable and more logical that the present canon's incorporation of canon 812 by reference suppresses the institute or usage of canonical mission in *Sapientia christiana,* leaving only the mandate of canon 812 in force.

The inclusion of *canon 813* is a less complex requirement, namely, that the diocesan bishop is to satisfy pastoral concerns in ecclesiastical universities and faculties as well as in other academic institutions by establishing a parish or assigning priests on a stable basis, as well as by providing centers for spiritual assistance.

The Eastern code omits entirely this kind of application to ecclesiastical universities and faculties and makes no cross-reference to its canons on Catholic universities (found in *CCEO* 640– 645).

Students

Canon 819 — To the extent that the good of a diocese, a religious institute, or even the universal Church itself requires it, diocesan bishops or the competent superiors of the institutes must send to ecclesiastical universities or faculties youth, clerics, and members, who are outstanding in character, virtue, and talent.

The canon needs little commentary. It places the duty upon diocesan bishops and superiors of

---

[10] Art. 27, §1.

religious institutes to send qualified students to the institutions of learning that undertake the mission of the sacred sciences or disciplines. The conciliar documents on Christian education and on priestly formation use similar language but without specific reference to ecclesiastical universities and faculties.[11]

Cooperation

Canon 820 — The moderators and professors of ecclesiastical universities and faculties are to take care that the various faculties of the university offer mutual assistance as their subject matter allows and that there is mutual cooperation between their own university or faculty and other universities and faculties, even non-ecclesiastical ones, by which they work together for the greater advance of knowledge through common effort, meetings, coordinated scientific research, and other means.

Again, the canon and its desirable goals—mutual assistance of faculties, cooperation with other institutions, including non-ecclesiastical ones, and coordinated scientific research—are clear in themselves. These kinds of relationships are urged both in *Sapientia christiana* and, for non-ecclesiastical Catholic academic institutions, in the 1990 apostolic constitution *Ex corde Ecclesiae*. More important, various kinds of cooperation were strongly urged by the fathers of Vatican II.[12]

[11] See *GE* 10; *OT* 18.
[12] See *GE* 12; *GS* 62.

Establishment of Other Institutes

Canon 821 — The conference of bishops and the diocesan bishop are to make provision so that where possible, higher institutes of the religious sciences are established, namely, those which teach the theological disciplines and other disciplines which pertain to Christian culture.

This canon was originally intended for the previous chapter about Catholic institutes of higher studies (canons 807–814), as is evident from its language, since the responsibility is stated as that of the respective conference of bishops and diocesan bishop. The institutes resulting from their efforts are not thought of as having ecclesiastical status. In particular, they do not enjoy constitution or approval by the Roman See as do the universities and faculties or the like which are addressed in the present chapter of canons. Moreover, they are not governed by canons 815–820 or *Sapientia christiana* but by canons 807–814.

The present relocation of the canon by the commission on revision on the grounds that institutes of this kind "ought to depend entirely on ecclesiastical authority, otherwise they inevitably produce serious disagreements"[13] may thus be misleading. Nevertheless, the anomalous placement of the canon, originally designed to follow canon 814, does not detract from the hope that such institutes will be set up for religious studies, namely, theological disciplines and other areas of study important for Christian culture in general.

[13] *Rel* 184.

BIBLIOGRAPHY ───────────────────────

Bibliographical material for canons 815–821 can be found after the commentary on canon 833.

TITLE IV
INSTRUMENTS OF SOCIAL COMMUNICATION AND BOOKS IN PARTICULAR
[cc. 822 – 832]

The canons of this title represent the latest chapter in the Church's long relationship with the media. Almost since the invention of the printing press, the Church has tried to use the means of communications for its own evangelizing and teaching purposes, while at the same time trying to protect its members from harmful exposure to media which it judged to be dangerous. The printing press was invented about the year 1455; the first general legislation in the Church on the prior censorship of books was in 1487. A set of rules on the prohibition of books was issued just after the Council of Trent in 1564; the Congregation of the Index of forbidden books was established in 1571.

The prohibition of books and the Index were finally abandoned in 1966, just after the Second Vatican Council. In 1975 the rules on the pre-publication censorship of books were radically revised, and these canons reflect that revision. After an initial canon on the promotion and use of all media in pursuit of the Church's mission, most of the canons are concerned with the prior censorship of a very narrow range of official or semi-official publications, i.e., biblical and liturgical texts, prayer books, catechisms, religious textbooks, and literature distributed in churches. The *imprimatur* is now limited in practice to these categories of books.

These regulations on the use of the media must be viewed against the background of the fundamental rights and duties of the Christian faithful: to help with the communication of God's message of salvation (c. 211), to make their needs and opinions known (c. 212), and to be informed (*Communio et progressio* 119; see commentary on c. 822).

The Eastern code treats this material in canons 651 through 666.

The Church and the Media

Canon 822 — §1. The pastors of the Church, using a right proper to the Church in fulfilling their function, are to endeavor to make use of the instruments of social communication.

§2. These same pastors are to take care to teach the faithful that they are bound by the duty of cooperating so that a human and Christian spirit enlivens the use of instruments of social communication.

§3. All the Christian faithful, especially those who in any way have a role in the regulation or use of the same instruments, are to be concerned to offer assistance in pastoral action so that the Church exercises its function effectively through these instruments.

This first canon calls for the Church to use all of the modern means of mass communication for its own central tasks of announcing the gospel message and assisting humankind. It echoes the clarion call of the council's Decree on Mass Media:

> The Catholic church has been founded by Christ our Lord to bring salvation to all and is under an obligation to proclaim the gospel. It considers it part of its mission to spread the message of salvation through the media, and to instruct people on their proper use. (*IM* 3)

The three paragraphs of the canon ask for three different things: (1) for the bishops to be diligent in making use of the media for the Church's purposes, (2) for those same bishops to be sure the people know their duty to try to imbue the media with an ethos that is truly human and Christian, and (3) for the faithful, especially those persons who are themselves in the media, to lend a hand with those two media-related tasks.

The canon is the single most positive and clear encouragement in the code for the Church's engagement with the communications media (which includes film, radio, television, all forms of print, and newly developing electronic forms), but several other canons repeat the theme, e.g., 747, 761, 772, §2, 779, 804, §1, 823, §1, 831, §2, 1063, 1°.

Since the media pervade and shape contemporary cultures, for better or worse, it would be difficult to overstate the importance of this challenge for the Church. The real leadership and lion's share of this huge twofold apostolic effort has been and will be borne by lay women and men as well as men's and women's religious communities.

The canon is drawn from *Inter mirifica* 1–3, 13, and 16, but it should be read in conjunction with two subsequent instructions from what is now called the Pontifical Council for Social Communications, *Communio et progressio,*[1] and *Aetatis novae.*[2] The corresponding canon of the Eastern code is 651; it has a slightly different tenor.

Pastoral Vigilance over Writings

Canon 823 — §1. In order to preserve the integrity of the truths of faith and morals, the pastors of the Church have the duty and right to be watchful so that no harm is done to the faith or morals of the Christian faithful through writings or the use of instruments of social communication. They also have the duty and right to demand that writings to be published by the Christian faithful which touch upon faith or morals be submitted to their judgment and have the duty and right to condemn writings which harm correct faith or good morals.

§2. Bishops, individually or gathered in particular councils or conferences of bishops, have the duty and right mentioned in §1 with regard to the Christian faithful entrusted to their care; the supreme authority of the Church, however, has this duty and right with regard to the entire people of God.

The contrast between this canon and the one preceding it is dramatic. Here "the pastors of the Church," meaning the bishops and the pope, are called upon to safeguard their people from harm. There they were urged to use the media to proclaim the gospel and to motivate the laity to suffuse the media with a human and Christian spirit. Both are functions of the Church's teaching office, one defensive, the other positive.

This entire canon was taken nearly verbatim from the introduction to the Holy Office Instruction on Vigilance over Books, *Ecclesiae pastorum.*[3] The subject in the instruction was "writings," but the words "or the use of instruments of social communication" were inserted in the first paragraph of the canon.

The first paragraph specifies three sets of duties and rights assigned to the bishops: (1) to be vigilant lest harm come to the faithful through writings or the use of mass media,[4] (2) to demand that writings by the faithful on faith or morals be submitted to them for judgment before publication, and (3) to reprove writings which harm faith or morals. (The English word "condemn" is an unfortunate and exaggerated translation of *reprobare;* it should be "reprove" or at most "denounce.") All three rights and duties are bestowed in the interest of preserving the integrity of truth.

The second paragraph makes clear who the "pastors of the Church" are: bishops, individually or gathered in conferences or local councils, for those faithful entrusted to them, and the college of bishops together with the pope for the universal Church. The Congregation for the Doctrine of the

---

[1] May 23, 1971, *AAS* 63 (1971) 593–656; *TPS* 16 (1971) 245–283.

[2] February 2, 1992, *AAS* 84 (1992) 447–468; *Origins* 21 (1991–1992) 669–677.

[3] March 19, 1975, *AAS* 67 (1975) 281–284; *CLD* 8, 991–996.

[4] Note that the "media" are included only here; the rest of the paragraph refers exclusively to "writings."

Faith, which exercises this responsibility on behalf of the pope (see *PB* 51), has issued a document related to this vigilance, Instruction on Some Aspects of the Use of the Instruments of Social Communications in Promoting the Doctrine of the Faith.[5] It restates, interprets, and supplements the discipline contained in these canons.

The assignment of these daunting responsibilities and corresponding prerogatives call to mind similar broad strokes of canons 749 and 756 on infallible teaching authority and the supervision of the ministry of the word.

The duties of the bishops do not excuse or exonerate the laity, religious, and other ministers from their rightful role in this part of the teaching office; they not only read the books, and see and hear the media, but they do most of the writing and producing of them as well. Many are well qualified and duty-bound to make judgments about them and their potential for good or ill.

The second set of duties and rights, that of demanding that writings on faith or morals be submitted for pre-publication review and judgment, would seem to imply that authors or publishers have a corresponding obligation to proffer their books for that purpose. But such is not the case. Only the narrow categories of publications given in the following canons (specifically cc. 825–828) are required to be submitted. The vast majority of writings, even those on theology and morality, are not subject to prior censorship in virtue of this canon. Canon 827, §3 *recommends* that some writings be voluntarily submitted to the judgment of the local ordinary, but hardly any diocesan bishops or bishops' conferences have *required* them to be submitted.

The submission of writings for scrutiny and the process of their denunciation are restrictions on the author's and publisher's free exercise of the right of expression (cc. 212, §2 and §3, 218), and therefore these rules must be strictly interpreted (c. 18).

Canon 652 in the Eastern code covers the same ground, but somewhat more positively.

[5] March 30, 1992, *Comm* 24 (1992) 18–27; *Origins* 22:6 (June 6, 1992) 92–96.

Competent Local Ordinaries; Meaning of Books

Canon 824 — §1. Unless it is established otherwise, the local ordinary whose permission or approval to publish books must be sought according to the canons of this title is the proper local ordinary of the author or the ordinary of the place where the books are published.

§2. Those things established regarding books in the canons of this title must be applied to any writings whatsoever which are destined for public distribution, unless it is otherwise evident.

This canon, which introduces the canonical scheme for the pre-publication censorship of certain writings, speaks of three distinct matters: (1) which local ordinaries are competent to make the necessary evaluation, (2) what constitutes a "book" in these canons, and (3) the distinction between permission and approval.

(1) Location determines competence, that is, the canonical residence of the author and the publisher specify the local ordinaries who may be asked to examine the book in question, and either grant or deny the required approval or permission. The rules on domicile are canons 102–107. The term "local ordinaries" includes vicars general and episcopal vicars as well as diocesan bishops (c. 134).

If a book has multiple authors and they have diverse domiciles, any of their local ordinaries are competent. If an author has more than one domicile or both a domicile and a quasi-domicile, then any one of the author's local ordinaries can be asked. Similarly, if a publishing house has more than one official location, e.g., New York and London, the ordinaries of all those places are competent.

Authors and publishers have a right to an answer to their requests for permission or approval to publish. If one ordinary denies permission to publish, another competent ordinary may be requested to grant it; however, the author or publisher is obliged to inform the second ordinary of the prior refusal, and the second ordinary should ascertain the reasons from the first (c. 65).

(2) The canon states that "books" means "any writings whatsoever which are destined for public distribution." The criteria are "writings" intended for general availability, whether by sale or free gift. The size of the publication does not matter, nor does the mode of print production, i.e., linotype, multilith, photocopy, facsimile, etc. Books include pamphlets, tracts, and booklets as well as books. Electronic "publication" was not envisioned by the canon, e.g., e-mail, servers, websites, CD-ROMs, other Internet or World Wide Web communications; they do not require submission for approval. Journals, magazines, periodicals, and newspapers are not required to have an *imprimatur;* for the most part they are not among the categories of publications which need prior approval, or the frequency of their issuance prevents effective prior review.

Publications which are private, with a restricted circulation, are not considered "destined for public distribution," e.g., a professor's class notes, internal documents, reports or drafts circulated within companies, organizations, or professional societies.

Other media, sound or visual, are also not included in this category of "books"; hence recordings, audio or video, cassettes, disks, or records are not subject to prior censorship.

(3) The canon mentions two terms for indicating a favorable judgment on a book submitted for pre-publication review, "permission" (*licentia*) and "approval" (*approbatio*). Unlike the corresponding Eastern code canon 661, this canon offers no definition or description of the terms. They are virtually indistinguishable. The canons use them interchangeably, e.g., in canon 827, §4. The Congregation for the Doctrine of the Faith instruction of 1992 indicates that the two have exactly the same effects (n. 7.2). It is a distinction without a difference. Both terms express an essentially negative judgment: there is nothing objectionable, nothing contrary to the Church's authentic teaching authority on faith or morals.

Only those publications specifically mentioned in the canons which follow are required to be submitted for pre-publication censorship.

Books of the Sacred Scriptures

Canon 825 — §1. Books of the sacred scriptures cannot be published unless the Apostolic See or the conference of bishops has approved them. For the publication of their translations into the vernacular, it is also required that they be approved by the same authority and provided with necessary and sufficient annotations.

§2. With the permission of the conference of bishops, Catholic members of the Christian faithful in collaboration with separated brothers and sisters can prepare and publish translations of the sacred scriptures provided with appropriate annotations.

The scriptures are a most precious heritage of the Church and the churches. As such they must be made "available to all the Christian faithful" by means of "appropriate and correct translations made into different languages" (*DV* 22). The purpose of this canon is to safeguard that process.

Publication of the books of the scriptures, in their original languages or in translation, must be approved in advance either by the Apostolic See or by a conference of bishops. In practice, the Congregation for the Doctrine of the Faith has reserved to itself the approval of vernacular translations of the scriptures if they are to be used in the liturgy, e.g., as part of the *Lectionary,* in virtue of canon 838, §2. The congregation's 1975 instruction, *Ecclesiae pastorum* 2, permitted the local ordinary to authorize publication of versions or translations of the scriptures. With the code that authority was limited to the bishops' conferences, and, in effect, to the Holy See alone. Such is the process of centralization of authority and the erosion of subsidiarity.

A set of guidelines for the ecumenical preparation of biblical translations was published by the Secretariat for Christian Unity and the United Bible Societies in 1968 and revised in 1987.[6]

---

[6] November 16, 1987, *Enchiridion Vaticanum,* v. 10 (Bologna: Dehoniane, 1989) 2266–2319.

This canon is based on *Dei verbum* 22 and 25, as well as on *Ecclesiae pastorum* 2. The corresponding canon in the Eastern code is 655.

Liturgical Books and Prayer Books

Canon 826 — §1. The prescripts of can. 838 are to be observed concerning liturgical books.

§2. To reprint liturgical books, their translations into the vernacular, or their parts, an attestation of the ordinary of the place where they are published must establish their agreement with the approved edition.

§3. Books of prayers for the public or private use of the faithful are not to be published without the permission of the local ordinary.

These rules reflect the Church's concerns for the authenticity of the liturgical and devotional life of its members. The entire canon is derived immediately from the Congregation for the Doctrine of the Faith instruction *Ecclesiae pastorum* 3, but similar regulations were included in the 1917 code, canons 1257, 1390, and 1385, §1, 2°. The conciliar sources for the first paragraph demonstrate a concern for the adaptation and inculturation of the liturgy and other prayerful practices, as well as for their approval by competent authority.[7]

The first paragraph simply refers to canon 838 which designates the roles of the Apostolic See, episcopal conferences, and diocesan bishops in the supervision of the liturgy and the issuance of liturgical books.

The second paragraph specifies the duty of the local ordinary of the place of publication to attest that newly issued liturgical books or their vernacular translations accurately conform to the official texts. The judgment is expressed as *concordat cum originali*. The additional burdens of authorizations, permissions, copyrights, and royalty payments for liturgical publications are nicely summarized by J. M. Gonzalez del Valle in his commentary on canon 826.[8]

[7] *SC* 22.2, 36, 39, 40, *OE* 5, *UR* 15, *AG* 22, *GS* 58.
[8] *Pamplona ComEng,* 536.

The International Commission for English in the Liturgy (ICEL) prepares translations of liturgical texts for the Catholic churches of the English-speaking world.

The third paragraph illustrates the vital role of genuine Christian piety or popular religious practices and the Church's concern for their doctrinal and spiritual authenticity within the wide boundaries of the Church's many spiritual traditions (see cc. 214 and 839, and *SC* 12 and 13). The local ordinary is to give permission for the publication of prayer books, whether for public or private use. These include books or pamphlets of prayers or devotions, but not books on spirituality, meditation books, or aids in spiritual development.

Canons 656 and 657 of the Eastern code roughly correspond to this canon.

Catechisms, Textbooks, and Books Available in Churches

Canon 827 — §1. To be published, catechisms and other writings pertaining to catechetical instruction or their translations require the approval of the local ordinary, without prejudice to the prescript of can. 775, §2.

§2. Books which regard questions pertaining to sacred scripture, theology, canon law, ecclesiastical history, and religious or moral disciplines cannot be used as texts on which instruction is based in elementary, middle, or higher schools unless they have been published with the approval of competent ecclesiastical authority or have been approved by it subsequently.

§3. It is recommended that books dealing with the matters mentioned in §2, although not used as texts in instruction, as well as writings which especially concern religion or good morals are submitted to the judgment of the local ordinary.

§4. Books or other writings dealing with questions of religion or morals cannot be exhibited, sold, or distributed in churches or oratories unless they have been published with the permission of competent ecclesiastical authority or approved by it subsequently.

This canon requires an *imprimatur* for three distinct categories of books: (1) catechisms and other catechetical instructional writings, (2) textbooks in areas related to scripture, theology, and other sacred disciplines, and (3) writings on religion or morality which are displayed, sold, or given away in church. All three, like the liturgical books (c. 826) and collections of ecclesiastical decrees (c. 828), are the kinds of publications which people often consider or assume to be "official and reliable."

The categories must be narrowly construed because the requirement of submitting such books for censorship is a restriction of the right of expression (c. 18).

All four paragraphs of this canon are drawn from the 1975 Congregation for the Doctrine of the Faith instruction *Ecclesiae pastorum* 4; the first three were more remotely derived from the similar but more sweeping categories required by canon 1385, §1, 2° of the 1917 code.

The ecclesiastical authority competent to grant the required approvals or permissions are the local ordinaries identified in canon 824, §1.

(1) Catechisms and other writings related to catechetical formation include things like workbooks, teachers' manuals, and similar materials, but not writings about catechetics or the teaching of religion. Translations of these writings require approval even though the originals were approved in order to assure that the translated texts are appropriately expressed for their new linguistic and cultural setting.

(2) Textbooks are those written and used for classroom instruction; they outline the course and provide the written material upon which it is based. Books of supplemental readings for reference or background purposes, even when used as required readings for courses, are not included under the canon. The textbooks requiring approval before or after publication are those on sacred scripture, theology, canon law, church history, and religious or moral disciplines. The great bulk of religious and theological publications are neither written nor used as textbooks. The canon refers to schools at all levels, from primary school through college, at least those which are officially Catholic (c. 803).

The third paragraph of the canon recommends that the foregoing categories of books and all those writings related to religion or morality, even though not textbooks, be voluntarily submitted to the judgment of the local ordinary. This sometimes occurs, since such approval might enhance the value of some kinds of books and provide assurance to concerned readers, but the practice is not widespread.

(3) Books and pamphlets dealing with matters of religion or morals which are displayed, sold, or distributed in church are to receive the approval of a local ordinary prior to or after publication. The prior permission (*licentia*) or subsequent approval (*approbatio*) mean no more here than elsewhere; that is, they are essentially negative judgments that the works are not harmful to faith or morals.

The 1990 Code of Canons of the Eastern Churches treats these same matters somewhat differently in canons 658, 659, and 665.

Collections of Acts or Decrees

Canon 828 — It is not permitted to reprint collections of decrees or acts published by some ecclesiastical authority unless the prior permission of the same authority has been obtained and the conditions prescribed by it have been observed.

The canon's prohibition is limited to *republication* of *collections* of *decrees* (official legislative or administrative enactments) or *acts* (official proceedings). But it is broader than canon 1389 of the 1917 code on which it is based; that canon referred only to collections of decrees of the congregations of the Roman Curia. This one includes other ecclesiastical authorities, e.g., individual bishops, conferences of bishops, or chapters of religious congregations. It does not extend to purely historical documents.

The obvious concern is for the accuracy and completeness of such official rules and records.

However, there can also be issues of copyright and royalty payments.

The canon is a rather curious remnant of Pope Leo XIII's 1897 constitution[9] on the prohibition and censure of books on which the 1917 code's treatment of this whole area was based. This provision was not included in the 1990 Eastern code.

Permissions Limited to Original Texts

Canon 829 — The approval or permission to publish some work is valid for the original text but not for new editions or translations of the same.

When ecclesiastical approval for a publication is obtained, it applies only to the original text submitted for judgment, not to subsequent editions or translations of it. Those later texts could vary substantially from the original. However, a simple reprinting of the original work is not considered a new edition.[10]

Censors of Books

Canon 830 — §1. The conference of bishops can compile a list of censors outstanding in knowledge, correct doctrine, and prudence to be available to diocesan curias or can also establish a commission of censors which local ordinaries can consult; the right of each local ordinary to entrust judgment regarding books to persons he approves, however, remains intact.

§2. In fulfilling this office, laying aside any favoritism, the censor is to consider only the doctrine of the Church concerning faith and morals as it is proposed by the ecclesiastical magisterium.

§3. A censor must give his or her opinion in writing; if it is favorable, the ordinary, according to his own prudent judgment, is to grant permission for publication to take place, with his name and the time and place of the permission granted

expressed. **If he does not grant permission, the ordinary is to communicate the reasons for the denial to the author of the work.**

This canon awkwardly describes the way that the process of prior censorship is supposed to work. It is derived almost verbatim from *Ecclesiae pastorum* 6, but there were similar provisions in canons 1393 and 1394 of the 1917 code. The scope of books subject to prior review is quite narrow (see cc. 824–828); hence the process is now relatively rare.

The canon speaks of four phases of the procedure: (1) how the censors are designated, (2) the criteria by which they are to make their judgments, (3) how they are to forward their opinion to the ordinary, and (4) what is involved in the ordinary's subsequent granting or denial of the requested permission.

(1) The first paragraph suggests three possible sources for those who are to review books before publication: (a) each local ordinary can do the work himself or entrust it to someone he approves, (b) the conference of bishops can compile and make available a list of censors it considers able to assist dioceses with this function, and (c) the conference can establish a board of censors which the local ordinaries could consult. A few conferences of bishops have taken action to assemble lists of censors; apparently none have established commissions of censors. The NCCB has done neither; there does not seem to be any need.

Censors, whether lay persons or ordained ministers, are to be "outstanding in knowledge, correct doctrine, and prudence." Obviously they should possess competence in the area in which they are asked to evaluate writings, and have a fair and balanced outlook.

(2) The second paragraph gives two criteria for censors to follow when judging a book. One is negative: not to be prejudiced by a predisposition toward the author, favorable or unfavorable. The judgment is to be made on the work submitted, not on the person of the author. All extraneous issues must be sedulously screened out.

---

[9] *Officiorum ac munerum,* Jan. 25, 1897, *CIC Fontes* III, 502–512.

[10] CDF 1992 "Instruction," 9; see c. 823 above.

The second criterion is positive: the Church's teaching on faith and morals as presented by its own teaching authority. The single category of "doctrine of the Church" does not imply that books must simply conform to everything taught by anyone in authority, regardless of its truth claim. It means that theological levels of teaching must be respected, e.g., distinguishing those things which are divinely revealed from those which are commonly accepted, freely disputed, etc. In other words, the "hierarchy of truths" (*UR* 11) must always be considered as well as the need for authors to be in dialogue with the cultures and voices of their age (*GS* 44, 54, 62, *AG* 22).

The judgment which the censor is called upon to make is whether this writing is or is not likely to be harmful to the faith or morals of the people (c. 823, §1). That is to say, the purpose of pre-publication review of these "official" or seemingly official documents is a pastoral one. Can the faithful rely on them and not be endangered by them? The censor is *not* asked to answer other questions about the publication: Will it sell? Is it opportune? Will it make an effective textbook or catechism?

"The examination preceding the granting of permission calls for the greatest of care and seriousness, with consideration given both to the rights of the authors (c. 218) and of all the faithful (cc. 213, 217)."[11]

It is hyperbole to suggest that "ecclesiastical permission constitutes both a juridical and moral guarantee for the authors, publishers, and the readers" ("Instruction," 10.1), but that exaggerated evaluation of the permission does not diminish the high levels of seriousness and fairness required of the censor's examination.

(3) The censor gives his judgment of the work to the ordinary in writing, dated and signed. Obviously it should contain the reasons on which it is based, especially if it is a negative judgment. An affirmative evaluation by the censor is traditionally

[11] CDF 1992 "Instruction," 10.2.

termed a "*nihil obstat,*" there is nothing standing in the way of publication.

(4) The ordinary, if the censor's decision was favorable, then makes his own prudent judgment to grant the permission to publish ("*imprimatur,*" it may be published). This implies that the ordinary's decision is an independent one, and may take in wider pastoral issues, e.g., opportuneness, but a negative judgment after a positive recommendation from the censor demands serious justification. If the censor's judgment was negative, the ordinary still has an independent decision to make; he can concur with the censor, but he must give the author the reasons for his denial of permission; or he can give the book to another censor or review it himself and then take favorable action.

Relations with authors should always be conducted in a constructive spirit of respectful dialogue and ecclesial communion.[12]

The permission to publish is to be given with the name of the ordinary and the date and place in which it was given. Permission to publish is not a blessing or praise of a book, nor does it imply agreement with the contents.

If the requested permission is denied, the author may ask it of another competent ordinary (cc. 65, §1, 824, §1) or have administrative recourse to the Congregation for the Doctrine of the Faith (cc. 1732–1739, "Instruction," 10.3).

The permission to publish can be conditioned, e.g., in a scholarly rather than popular journal, or for use only in colleges ("Instruction," 8.4), but this conditioned permission would appear to be both unusual and problematic.

The canon does not require that the permission (together with the name, date, and place of issuance) be printed in the published book, but the Commission for the Authentic Interpretation of the Code, in a response which extended the canon's provision, said that it should be.[13] The diocesan

[12] "Instruction," 12.3; cf. also *Cooperation Between Theologians and the Ecclesiastical Magisterium,* ed. L. O'-Donovan (Washington, D.C.: CLSA, 1982).
[13] April 29, 1987, *AAS* 79 (1987) 1249. L. Wrenn, *Authen-*

bishop could dispense from this requirement if there were a good reason.

Canon 664 of the Eastern code parallels this canon.

Writing in Unfriendly Journals; Radio and Television Programs

Canon 831 — §1. Except for a just and reasonable cause, the Christian faithful are not to write anything for newspapers, magazines, or periodicals which are accustomed to attack openly the Catholic religion or good morals; clerics and members of religious institutes, however, are to do so only with the permission of the local ordinary.

§2. It is for the conference of bishops to establish norms concerning the requirements for clerics and members of religious institutes to take part on radio or television in dealing with questions of Catholic doctrine or morals.

The canon treats of two very different things: (1) writing in newspapers or magazines which openly attack the Catholic religion or good morals, and (2) clerics and religious taking part in radio or television programs about Catholic teaching or morals.

The first paragraph comes directly from *Ecclesiae pastorum* 5.2, and is a modification of canon 1386, §2 of the 1917 code. It is a prohibition against cooperation with those who are manifestly inimical to the Church or to moral life; it is not about the content of one's writings. It speaks of publications which regularly, openly, and actively attack the Catholic religion or moral values, not those which might be perceived by some subtly to undermine those institutions. Of lay persons the canon asks that they not lend their name or presence to such publications, unless, in their own judgment, there is just and reasonable cause for

doing so, e.g., refuting error or defending truth. Of ordained ministers or members of religious communities, because of their public identification with the Church, the canon asks that they obtain the permission of the local ordinary (c. 824, §1) to make such written appearances. The 1992 Congregation for the Doctrine of the Faith "Instruction," 13, suggests that the local ordinary give careful consideration to such requests and the circumstances in which such permissions might be granted.

The second paragraph is a specification of canon 772, §2 on bishops' conferences' regulation of radio and television presentations of Christian teaching. Both canons recognize that radio and television transcend diocesan boundaries, have great influence, and therefore require more than local attention. This canon asks only for some norms regarding the media appearances of ordained ministers and religious women and men,[14] because these persons are perceived to be public representatives of the Church. The programmatic areas covered by the canon are "Catholic doctrine or morals," not, for example, history, culture, or politics.

Many conferences of bishops have enacted norms for such participation in radio and television programs, e.g., setting forth requisite qualifications and procedures for granting permissions.[15] The U.S. Conference of Bishops in 1984 issued a provisional decision authorizing individual diocesan bishops to issue guidelines for such participation.

The Code of Canons of the Eastern Churches covers the same ground in canons 660 and 653.

Publications of Religious Women and Men

Canon 832 — Members of religious institutes also need permission of their major superior accord-

---

tic Interpretations on the 1983 Code (Washington, D.C.: CLSA, 1993) 39–40, is of the opinion that the interpretation is simply declarative rather than extensive.

[14] Members of secular institutes and societies of apostolic life are not bound. Canon 18 requires a strict interpretation of "religious institutes."

[15] See *LCE* or *Pamplona ComEng* at c. 831.

ing to the norm of the constitutions in order to publish writings dealing with questions of religion or morals.

The canon is much narrower in scope than its predecessor, canon 1385, §3 of the 1917 code, but more demanding than *Ecclesiae pastorum* 5, which made it only a recommendation rather than a requirement. It is quite similar to canon 662, §2 of the Eastern code.

Women and men who are members of religious institutes[16] are included, and they are to follow their own constitutions regarding the appropriate major superior and the procedures for gaining the permission to publish. (The clerical members of personal prelatures and their affiliated lay persons are governed in this matter by their statutes.)

The canon simply states that the member of the religious institute needs the permission of his or her major superior, but the 1992 Congregation for the Doctrine of the Faith "Instruction," 16 and 17, goes well beyond the canon. The instruction says that the religious superiors have the responsibility of granting permission for their members to publish writings dealing with questions of religion or morals. They should not do so, the instruction states, without obtaining the prior judgment of at least one reliable censor, and satisfying themselves that the work does not contain anything harmful to faith or morals. Since the congregation lacks legislative authority, the provisions of its instruction (see c. 34) which add duties not included in the canon are to be considered prudent counsel rather than canonical obligations.

It is clear that, by virtue of this canon, religious require permission to publish writings only in the areas of religion and morals, not in any other areas of learning, opinion, or culture.

---

[16] As in the previous canon, this does not extend to members of secular institutes or societies of apostolic life (c. 18).

TITLE V
THE PROFESSION OF FAITH
[c. 833]

Profession of Faith and Oath of Fidelity

Canon 833 — The following are obliged personally to make a profession of faith according to the formula approved by the Apostolic See:

1° **in the presence of the president or his delegate, all those who attend with either a deliberative or consultative vote an ecumenical or particular council, a synod of bishops, and a diocesan synod; the president, however, makes it in the presence of the council or synod;**

2° **those promoted to the cardinalatial dignity, according to the statutes of the sacred college;**

3° **in the presence of the one delegated by the Apostolic See, all those promoted to the episcopate as well as those who are equivalent to a diocesan bishop;**

4° **in the presence of the college of consultors, the diocesan administrator;**

5° **in the presence of the diocesan bishop or his delegate, vicars general, episcopal vicars, and judicial vicars;**

6° **in the presence of the local ordinary or his delegate and at the beginning of their function, pastors, the rector of a seminary, and teachers of theology and philosophy in seminaries; those to be promoted to the order of the diaconate;**

7° **in the presence of the grand chancellor or, in his absence, in the presence of the local ordinary or their delegates, the rector of an ecclesiastical or Catholic university, when the rector's function begins; in the presence of the rector if he is a priest or in the presence of the local ordinary or their delegates, teachers in any universities whatsoever who teach disciplines pertaining to faith or morals, when they begin their function;**

8° **Superiors in clerical religious institutes and societies of apostolic life, according to the norm of the constitutions.**

A profession of faith is a virtuous act, and here it is made a canonical obligation on the occasion of the assumption of certain duties or offices, most of which are related to the teaching function of the Church. The public manifestation of belief bears witness to the community that the person entrusted with a teaching role shares their authentic and apostolic faith. Such public recitals are an ancient part of the Church's life, e.g., at baptisms, eucharistic celebrations, ordinations, and the inception of some ministerial offices. This canon replaces canons 1406–1408 of the 1917 code.

The obligation to make a personal profession of faith falls directly on the person who has agreed to assume the office, dignity, or duty. The list of those obliged should be considered taxative; that is to say, the canonical obligation does not extend to any others, even though the list of persons includes only a tiny fraction of those in the Church who actually do the teaching of the faith.

The canon requires that the profession of faith be made "according to the formula approved by the Apostolic See." When the code was promulgated in 1983, that formula was a modified form of the ancient Nicene-Constantinopolitan creed which was issued in 1967 after the Second Vatican Council and well accepted throughout the Catholic world. However, in a hasty action on February 25, 1989,[17] the Congregation for the Doctrine of the Faith published in *L'Osservatore Romano* a new, theologically ambiguous, and controversial formula. The ensuing confusion over the meaning of the three final paragraphs of this new formula together with a delay in providing its approved vernacular translations has

clouded the understanding and observance of this canon.

In the same action the Congregation for the Doctrine of the Faith added an entirely new canonical obligation: an extension of the duty to take an oath of fidelity upon the assumption of office to the categories of persons listed in subparagraphs five through eight of this canon. Since the Congregation lacks legislative authority, it obtained the requisite sanction of the pope to promulgate this new rule.[18]

An oath of fidelity, like a profession of faith, is a very serious religious act. In a promissory oath of this kind one calls upon God to witness the sincerity and reliability of one's promise to fulfill the duties of the office which is being assumed. It is similar to a bishop's oath of fidelity when assuming his office (c. 380), and there are other examples of such oaths in the code, e.g., in tribunals (c. 1454), by administrators of church property (c. 1283, 1°; cf. also cc. 1199–1204). But the new Congregation for the Doctrine of the Faith formula for the oath takes it well beyond a promise faithfully to fulfill the duties of office and remain in communion with the Church; its sweeping final paragraphs make one *swear* to observe all ecclesiastical laws and to obey whatever bishops declare as authentic teachers or prescribe as leaders of the Church.

Unlike the provision of the 1917 code (*CIC* 2403) there is no canonical penalty for failing to make the profession of faith or the oath of fidelity. Nor does such a failure to make them prevent one from accepting an office or exercising one which has been assumed. In other words, the profession and oath are not qualifications for office which affect the validity of appointments.

When a diocesan bishop is convinced that it would be for the spiritual good of the faithful, he can, in particular cases, dispense from the obser-

---

[17] The new rules for the Roman Curia, which would have required review by the PCILT, were to go into effect four days later. *PB* 156, 158.

[18] Rescript from an audience, published by CDF on Sept. 19, 1989, *AAS* 81 (1989) 1169; the original texts of the profession of faith and oath of fidelity were published in *AAS* 81 (1989) 104–106; their English translation appears on pp. 1853–1854 of this volume.

vance of this canon (cc. 85, 87); for example, if the bishop were already fully assured of the faith and fidelity of the person and there was a truly serious difficulty in making the acts of professing and swearing in this instance, he could issue a dispensation.

The profession and oath-taking can either be witnessed in private or incorporated into a liturgical ceremony of installation.

This canon has no counterpart in the 1990 Code of Canons of the Eastern Churches.

BIBLIOGRAPHY

(The material listed below serves as a comprehensive bibliography for Book III.)

Teaching Function

Arrieta, J. "The Active Subject of the Church's Teaching Office (Canons 747–748)." *Stud Can* 23 (1989) 243–256.

Blyskal, L. "*Obsequium:* A Case Study." *J* 48 (1988) 559–589.

Boyle, J. *Church Teaching Authority: Historical and Theological Studies.* Notre Dame: University of Notre Dame, 1995.

Burkhard, J. "*Sensus fidei:* Meaning, Role, and Future of a Teaching of Vatican II." *Louvain Studies* 17 (1992) 18–34.

———. "*Sensus fidei:* Theological Reflection Since Vatican II: I. 1956–1984 and II. 1985–1989." *Heythrop Journal* 34 (1993) 41–59 and 123–136.

Castillo Lara, R. "Le Livre III du CIC de 1983: histoire et principes." *AC* 31 (1988) 17–54.

CDF. "Instruction on the Ecclesial Vocation of the Theologian (*Donum veritatis;* May 24, 1990)." *AAS* 82 (1990) 1550–1570; *Origins* 20 (1990) 117–126.

Curran, C., and R. McCormick. *Dissent in the Church.* Readings in Moral Theology, No. 6. New York: Paulist, 1988.

Di Mattia, G. "Annuncio del messagio: Inadimpienze e tutela." *Apol* (1993) 251–272.

Eno, R. *Teaching Authority in the Early Church.* Wilmington: Glazier, 1984.

Errazuriz, C. "La Dimensione Giuridica del *Munus Docendi* nella Chiesa." *IE* 1 (1989) 177–193.

———. *Il "Munus Docendi Ecclesiae": Diritti e doveri dei fideli.* Milan: Giuffre, 1991.

Fagiolo, V. "Il Munus Docendi: I canoni introduttivi del Codex e la dottrina conciliare del Magistero autoritativo della Chiesa." *ME* 112 (1987) 19–42.

Fuchs, J. "Origines d'une trilogie ecclésiologique à l'époque rationaliste de la théologie." *Revue des sciences philosophiques et théologiques* 53 (1969) 185–211.

Gaillardetz, R. *Witnesses to the Faith: Community, Infallibility, and the Ordinary Magisterium of Bishops.* New York: Paulist, 1992.

———. *Teaching with Authority: A Theology of the Magisterium in the Church.* Collegeville, Minn.: Liturgical Press, 1997.

Gangoiti, B. "La Dottrina Sociale della Chiesa nel Codice di diritto Canonico del 1983." *Angelicum* 70 (1993) 255–278.

Ghirlanda, G., and F. Urrutia. "De Episcoporum Conferentia deque exercitio potestatis magisterii" (article, critique, and exchange). *P* 76 (1987) 573–667

Grant, T. "Social Justice in the 1983 Code of Canon Law: An Examination of Selected Canons." *J* 49 (1989) 112–145.

Green, T. "The Teaching Function of the Church: A Comparison of Selected Canons in the Latin and Eastern Codes." *J* 55 (1995) 93–140.

———. "The Church's Teaching Mission: Some Aspects of the Normative Role of Episcopal Conferences." *Stud Can* 27 (1993) 23–57.

Grisez, G., and F. Sullivan. "The Ordinary Magisterium's Infallibility." *TS* 55 (1994) 720–738.

Gruppo Italiano Docenti di Diritto Canonico. *La Funzione di Insegnare della Chiesa*. Milan: Glossa, 1994.

Henn, W. "The Hierarchy of Truths Twenty Years Later." *TS* 48 (1987) 439–471.

Metz, J.-B., and E. Schillebeeckx. *The Teaching Authority of the Believers*. Concilium 180. Edinburgh: Clark, 1985.

Nedungatt, G. "Magisterio ecclesiastico nei due Codici." *Apol* (1992) 313–328.

Örsy, L. *The Church: Learning and Teaching*. Wilmington: Glazier, 1987.

Sobanski, R. "Les canons 753 et 754: Problemes choisis." *Stud Can* 23 (1989) 285–298.

Sullivan, F. *Magisterium: Teaching Authority in the Catholic Church*. New York: Paulist, 1983.

———. "The Response Due to the Non-Definitive Exercise of the *Magisterium* (Canon 752)." *Stud Can* 23 (1989) 267–283.

———. *Creative Fidelity: Weighing and Interpreting Documents of the Magisterium*. New York: Paulist, 1996.

Urrutia, F. "Bibliographia de libro III C.I.C." *P* 76 (1987) 525–572.

———. "La réponse aux textes du magistère pontifical non infaillible." *AC* 31 (1988) 95–115.

Walf, K. "L'infaillibilité comme la voit le *Code de droit canonique* (canons 749–750)." *Stud Can* 23 (1989) 257–266.

Ecumenism

Green, T. "The Fostering of Ecumenism: Comparative Reflections on the Latin and Eastern Codes." *P* 85 (1996) 397–444.

———. "Changing Ecumenical Horizons: Their Impact on the 1983 Code." *J* 56:1 (1996) 427–455.

Griffin, B. "The Challenge of Ecumenism for Canonists." *CLSAP* 55 (1993) 17–38.

Manna, S. "Delimitations et elements de la formation oecumenique (canon 755)." *Stud Can* 23 (1989) 299–323.

PCPCU. "Directory for the Application of Principles and Norms on Ecumenism," March 25, 1993. *Origins* 23:9 (July 29, 1993) 129–160; also Washington, D.C.: USCC, 1993.

Preaching

CDW. "Directory for Sunday Celebrations in the Absence of a Priest," June 2, 1988. *Origins* 18:19 (Oct. 20, 1988) 301–307.

Feliciani, G. "La predication des laics dans le code." *AC* 31 (1988) 117–130.

Fox, J. "The Homily and the Authentic Interpretation of Canon 767.1." *Apol* 62 (1989) 123–169.

Fuentes, J. "Del Ministerio de la Palabra Divina." In *Com Ex* III/1, 74–158.

Hilkert, M. *Naming Grace: Preaching and the Sacramental Imagination.* New York: Continuum, 1997.

Huels, J. "The Ministry of the Divine Word (Canons 756–761)." *Stud Can* 23 (1989) 325–344.

———. "The Law of Lay Preaching: Interpretation and Implementation." *CLSAP* 52 (1990) 61–79.

———. *More Disputed Questions in the Liturgy.* Chicago: Liturgy Training Pub., 1996.

Martin de Agar, J. "Note sul Diritto particolare delle Conferenze Episcopali." *IE* 2 (1990) 593–632.

Norris, P. "Lay Preaching and Canon Law: Who May give a Homily?" *Stud Can* 24 (1990) 443–454.

Provost, J. "Brought Together by the Word of the Living God (Canons 762–772)." *Stud Can* 23 (1989) 345–371.

Robitaille, L. "An Examination of the Various Forms of Preaching: Toward an Understanding of the Homily and Canons 766–767." *CLSAP* 58 (1996) 308–325.

Schulz, W. "Problemi canonistici circa la Predicazione dei Laici nella normativa della Conferenza Tedesca." *Apol* 62 (1989) 171–180.

Urrutia, F. "Responsa Pontificiae Commissionis Codicis Iuris Canonici authentice interpretando." *P* 77 (1988) 613–628.

Wallace, J. "Reconsidering the Parish Mission." *Worship* 67:4 (July, 1993) 340–351.

Wrenn, L. *Authentic Interpretations on the 1983 Code.* Washington, D.C.: CLSA, 1993.

Catechetics

Barrett, R. "The Normative Status of the Catechism." *P* 85 (1996) 9–34.

———. "The Right to Integral Catechesis as a Fundamental Right of the Christian Faithful." *Apol* 67 (1994) 179–206.

Bertone, T. "La catechesi nel Codice di Diritto canonico." *ME* 112 (1987) 43–52.

The Catechetical Documents: A Parish Resource. Chicago: Liturgical Training Pub., 1997.

Fuentes, J. "The Active Participants in Catechesis and Their Dependence on the Magisterium (Canons 773–780)." *Stud Can* 23 (1989) 373–386.

Marthaler, B., ed. *Introducing the Catechism of the Catholic Church: Traditional Themes and Contemporary Issues.* New York: Paulist, 1994.

Passicos, J. "Le statut des instruments de catechese dans le Code." *AC* 31 (1988) 147–156.

Missionary Action

García Martin, J. *L'Azione Missionaria della Chiesa nella Legislazione Canonica.* Rome: Ediurcla, 1993.

———. "Las relaciones entre Ordinarios del Lugar e Institutos en las Misiones segun el Codigo de Derecho Canonico 1983." *ComRelMiss* 65 (1984) 121–166.

———. "De Religiosorum Regimine in Missionibus." *ComRelMiss* 65 (1984) 283–304; 355–378.

Greco, J. "De ordinatione activitatis missionalis." *P* 55 (1966) 289–314.

Henkel, W. "I destinatari della *Missio ad gentes*." *Euntes Docete* 44 (1991) 225–239.

Huels, J. M. *The Catechumenate and the Law.* Chicago: Liturgy Training Pub., 1994.

Jacqueline, B. L'Organisation de la coopération missionnaire après le Concile Oecuménique Vatican II. *AC* (1974) 125–142.

Lopez-Gay, J. "Ecclesiology in the Missiological Thinking of the Post Conciliar Years." *Bibliografia Missionaria* 46 (1982) 371–381.

Lombardia, P. "El estatuto juridico del catecumeno segun los textos del Vaticano II." *IC* (1966) 529–562.

Martimort, G. A. "Catéchuménat et initiation chrétienne des adultes." *Notitiae* 21 (1985) 382–393.

Nebreda, A. "The Mission of the Church and Missionary Activity." *Teaching All Nations* (1972) 163–177.

Quitugua, D. C. *The Vicar Apostolic in the 1983 Code of Canon Law.* Rome: St. Thomas University, 1995.

Reuter, A. "De novis rationibus iuris missionalis a Concilio Vaticano II inductis vel indictis." *Euntes Docete* (1975) 293–315.

———. "The Missions in the New Code of Canon Law." *Bibliografia Missionaria* 46 (1982) 361–370.

———. "Religious and Missions according to the New Code of Canon Law." *Bibliographia Missionaria* 47 (1983) 367–376.

———. "The Missionary Activity of the Church (Canons 781–792)." *Stud Can* 23 (1989) 387–407.

Rossignol, R. "Vatican II and the Missionary Responsibility of the Particular Church." *Indian Theological Studies* (1980) 34–46.

Ting Pong Lee, I. "De Actione Ecclesae Missionali in Novo Codex Iuris Canonici." *ComRelMiss* 64 (1983) 97–106.

Urrutia, F. J. "Catechumenatus iuxta Concilium Oecumenicum Vaticanum Secundum." *P* 63 (1974) 121–144.

———. *De Ecclesiae Munere Docendi.* Rome: PUG, 1983.

Catholic Education

Beal, J. "Where's the Body? Where's the Blood? The Teaching Authority of the Diocesan Bishop and the Rights of Catholic School Teachers." *CLSA Proceedings* 30 (1995) 91–128.

CCE. *The Catholic School,* March 19, 1977. Washington, D.C.: USCC, 1977.

———. "The Religious Dimension of Education in a Catholic School." *Origins* 18 (September 15, 1988) 213, 215–228.

———. "The Catholic School on the Threshold of the Third Millennium," December 28, 1997. *L'Osservatore Romano* 16 (April 22, 1998) 8–10.

Conn, J. *Catholic Universities in the United States and Ecclesiastical Authority.* Analecta Gregoriana 259. Rome: Editrice Pontificia Università Gregoriana, 1991.

Cusack, B. *A Study of the Relationship Between the Diocesan Bishop and Catholic Schools Below the Level of Higher Education in the U.S.: Canons 801–806 of the Code of Canon Law.* Canon Law Studies #525. Ann Arbor, Mich.: University Microfilms, 1988.

Deeley, R. *The Mandate for Those Who Teach Theology in Institutes of Higher Studies.* JCD dissertation at the Gregorian University. Rome: Tipografia di Patrizio Graziani, 1986.

Euart, S. *Church-State Implications in the United States of Canon 812 of the 1983 Code of Canon Law.* Canon Law Studies #526. Washington, D.C.: Catholic University of America, 1988.

———. "Theologians and the Mandate to Teach." *Origins* 23/27 (December 16, 1993) 465, 467–472.

Gallin, A., ed. *American Catholic Higher Education: Essential Documents 1967–1990.* Notre Dame, Ind.: University of Notre Dame, 1992.

Langan, J., ed. *Catholic Universities in Church and Society: A Dialogue on 'Ex corde Ecclesiae.'* Washington, D.C.: Georgetown University, 1993.

NCCB. "Bishops and Theologians: Promoting Cooperation, Resolving Misunderstandings." *Origins* 19 (June 29, 1989) 97–110.

Örsy, L. *The Church: Learning and Teaching.* Wilmington, Del.: Michael Glazier, 1987.

Morrisey, F. "The Rights of Parents in the Education of Their Children (Canons 796–806)." *Stud Can* 23/2 (1989) 429–444.

O'Brien, D. *From the Heart of the American Church: Catholic Higher Education and American Culture.* Maryknoll, N.Y.: Orbis, 1994.

Peters, E. *Home-Schooling and the Code of Canon Law.* Mt. Royal, Va.: Christendom College, 1988.

Provost, J. "Approaches to Catholic Identity in the Law." *Concilium* 5 (1994) 15–25.

———. "A Canonical Commentary on *Ex corde Ecclesiae.*" In *Catholic Universities in Church and Society: A Dialogue on 'Ex corde Ecclesiae,'* ed. J. Langan, 105–136. Washington, D.C.: Georgetown University, 1993.

———. "The Canonical Aspects of Catholic Identity in *Ex corde Ecclesiae.*" *Stud Can* 25/2 (1991) 155–192.

Urrutia, F. "Ecclesiastical Universities and Faculties." *Stud Can* 23/2 (1989) 459–469.

Valdrini, P. "Les universités catholiques: exercise d'un droit et contrôle de son exercice (canons 807–814)." *Stud Can* 23 (1989) 445–458.

Media and Books

Baura, E. "Il Permisso per la Publicazione di Scritti." *IE* 1 (1989) 249–256.

CDF. "Instruction on Some Aspects of the Use of Instruments of Social Communication in Promoting the Doctrine of the Faith," March 30, 1992. *Comm* 24 (1992) 18–27; *Origins* 22:6 (June 6, 1992) 92–96.

"Congregazione della Dottrina della Fede. Istruzione circa alcuni aspetti degli strumenti de communicazione sociale nella promozione della dottrina della fede, 30 Marzo 1992. Con *nota* di C. J. Errazuriz." *IE* 5 (1993) 365–380.

Coriden, J. "The End of the *Imprimatur.*" *J* 44 (1984) 339–356.

Profession of Faith

Betti, U. "Professione di fede e giuramento di fedeltà: Considerazioni dottrinali." *Notitiae* 25 (1989) 321–325.

CDF. "Professio fidei, Iusiurandum fidelitatis," March 1, 1989. *AAS* 81 (1989) 104–106; "Rescript Approving the Formula of the Profession of Faith and the Oath of Fidelity." *AAS* 81 (1989) 1169; *Comm* 21 (1989) 22–34, 112–118.

CTSA. *Report of the CTSA Committee on the Profession of Faith and the Oath of Fidelity,* April 15, 1990. Washington, D.C.: CTSA, 1990.

De Fleurquin, L. "The Profession of Faith and the Oath of Fidelity: A Manifestation of Seriousness and Loyalty in the Life of the Church (Canon 833)." *Stud Can* 23 (1989) 485–499.

Jukes, J. "Profession of Faith and the Oath of Fidelity: Some Questions of Canonical and Practical Interest." *CLS-GBIN* 81 (1990) 12–17.

Keenan, J. "Compelling Assent: Magisterium, Conscience, and Oaths." *Irish Theological Quarterly* 57 (1991) 209–227.

McManus, F. "The Profession of Faith and the Oath of Fidelity." *CLSAP* 53 (1991) 190–220.

Örsy, L. *The Profession of Faith and the Oath of Fidelity: A Theological and Canonical Analysis.* Wilmington, Del.: Glazier, 1990.

Page, R. "Le document sur la profession de foi et le serment de fidélité." *SC* 24 (1990) 51–69.

Schmitz, H. "'Professio Fidei' und 'Iusiurandum fidelitatis'—Glaudensbekennis und Trueid: Wiederbelebung des Antimodernisteneides?" *AkK* 157 (1988) 353–429.

Thils, G. "La nouvelle 'Profession de foi' et *Lumen Gentium,* 25." *Revue Théologique de Louvain* 20 (1989) 336–343.

Urrutia, F. "Iusiurandum fidelitatis." *P* 80 (1991) 559–578.

BOOK IV
THE SANCTIFYING FUNCTION OF THE CHURCH
[cc. 834–1253]

Frederick R. McManus

The canons of the fourth book of the code govern the liturgical life and celebrations of the Latin church. These include above all the celebration of baptism and Eucharist and the other sacraments, together with sacramentals and the ecclesial prayer. A small number of canons refer to other religious and devotional practices of the Christian community; these practices are understood to be closely related to the liturgy, but they are not a formal part of the Church's public and official corporate worship.

Although Book IV itself may be seen as a very selective collection of liturgical laws, that term is generally reserved, somewhat more narrowly, for the juridic norms that govern the actual celebration of the sacraments and other services of Catholic worship. This is the sense of canon 2: for the most part the code does not define or determine the rites themselves, and all the liturgical laws falling outside the code retain their full canonical force—unless they are contradicted, and thus abrogated, by the code.

The liturgical laws common to the universal Latin church are to be found chiefly in the official Roman liturgical books, both in their introductions or prenotes (*praenotanda*) and in the rubrical directives which describe the rites and accompany the appointed texts. They are also in related juridic documents, e.g., apostolic constitutions and letters.[1] Particular liturgical laws are found in the corresponding official liturgical books of various nations and regions, as well as in decrees and statutes of dioceses and of groups of particular churches which follow the Roman rite.

In addition, although the code does not advert to this distinction, there are non-Roman rites of the Latin church, the most notable now being the Ambrosian rite of Milan.[2] Such non-Roman Western rites, whether of particular churches or of religious orders,[3] were preserved in the post-Tridentine reform of the Roman liturgical books, provided they had at least two hundred years' standing. Today, although diminished in number and in influence, these rites too may have their own liturgical books and laws. Together the Roman rite and the non-Roman rites of the Latin church are called the Latin rites, and all these are equally governed by the code.

The norms of Book IV, unlike the much larger body of uncodified liturgical legislation, are more often concerned with the liturgy from the viewpoint of its extrinsic discipline, e.g., canonical requirements for ministers or recipients of sacraments or for proper times or places of celebration. In other words, the canons are generally not ritual regulations and are distinct from them. As is evident, however, such a distinction can be made only imperfectly, and many canons of Book IV do affect liturgical celebrations directly (as did corresponding parts of *CIC*).[4] Such canons are usually somewhat basic norms or foundational doctrine rather than rubrical directions. When an individual chapter within the title on a given sacrament is called "The Celebration" of the respective sacrament, the canons are relatively few and general; most of the liturgical discipline itself is found outside the code, as canon 2 determines once for all.

---

[1] The source material for existing, postconciliar liturgical legislation of the universal Latin church is collected and translated into English in ICEL, *Documents on the Liturgy, 1963–1979: Conciliar, Papal, and Curial Texts* (Collegeville: Liturgical Press, 1982), from which translations below are taken. Cited as *DOL,* with the number of the corresponding sections into which each of the 554 documents are divided.

[2] See A. A. King, *Liturgies of the Primatial Sees* (Milwaukee: Bruce, 1957).

[3] See A. A. King, *Liturgies of the Religious Orders* (Milwaukee: Bruce, 1955).

[4] *CIC* is used in this commentary to refer to the 1917 *Codex Iuris Canonici.* Canons which are referred to without *CIC* are those of the present, revised code of 1983.

To put the distinction differently, matters that are proximately liturgical or sacramental are considered to be subjects of the liturgical law, while matters affecting the celebrations remotely or less directly are dealt with in the code's discipline. In the twentieth century the respective competencies of certain dicasteries or departments of the Roman Curia have reflected such a distinction. Since March 1989 it may be recognized in the two sections of the Congregation for Divine Worship and the Discipline of the Sacraments, a division based on this distinction.

The distinction also explains why Book IV does not deal with all parts of the liturgy. Such significant elements as the church year, music, and art are not directly touched, nor is there any effort to give a balanced or proportionate treatment of each sacrament or other rite. Because the canons do not include the body of liturgical laws, the commentary that follows offers some guidance to such norms, so that the canons themselves may be understood in their broader context. It must always be understood that the liturgical law is an integral part of the canon law, with the same weight and force as the rest of the law, but with its own special characteristics.

The New Eastern Code of Canon Law

In the Code of Canons of the Eastern (Catholic) Churches promulgated by John Paul II in 1990, title XVI ("Divine Worship and Especially the Sacraments") corresponds to Book IV of the Latin church's code, but has only about half the number of canons. In the Eastern code, canons 667–895 are divided into chapters on the seven sacraments—with chapter 6 on sacred ordinations divided into four articles and chapter 7 on marriage divided into eight articles. In a pattern similar to that of the Latin code (below), these chapters are followed by chapter 8: "Sacramentals, Sacred Times and Places, Veneration of the Saints, Vow and Oath," again in five articles.

As would be expected, there are many differences in discipline, given the different historical, theological, cultural, and canonical traditions of the Eastern churches as a whole and the particular, autonomous (*sui iuris*) churches of the East. This is evident in instances of liturgical laws that reflect the several liturgical rites that are a part of the patrimony of the several churches. In many places there is a close dependence of the Eastern code upon the earlier code of the Latin church, but a major effort was always made to respect the disciplinary traditions of the East and to strengthen further diversity in particular law.

The Eastern canons were supplemented by a significant document in 1996: "Instruction for Applying the Liturgical Prescriptions of the Code of Canons of the Eastern Churches."[5] This is an expository expansion based upon the canons, with constant emphasis upon the preservation of Eastern liturgical traditions and a return to those usages whenever possible—certainly in preference to the usages of the Latin church, however much some principles and norms of the conciliar constitution on the Roman rite, "in the very nature of things, affect other rites as well."[6] At times the instruction emphasizes the differences strongly; a major example is in number 82:

> It should be noted that the obligation of the sacred rite, and thus of the priestly blessing, for the validity of the Marriage is specific to Eastern law. In the Latin Church, simply the presence of the local Ordinary, or the parish priest, or a priest or deacon delegated by either of them is required. In the Eastern tradition, the priest, in addition to assisting, must bless the Marriage. To bless means to act as the true minister of the sacrament, in virtue of his priestly power to sanctify, so that the spouses may be united by God in the image of the flawless nuptial union of Christ with the Church and be consecrated to each other by sacramental grace.

[5] CEC, January 6, 1996 (Rome: Libreria Editrice Vaticana, 1996).
[6] *SC* 3.

Comparison with the 1917 Code of Canon Law

Book IV is a radical departure from the corresponding Book III of the 1917 code, not so much in the content of the canons themselves as in their selection and especially their arrangement. This difference is essential to an understanding of the present law.

Following the medieval categories of canon law, which treated persons and things separately, Book III of the 1917 code (*CIC* 726–1551) dealt with such diverse "things" as simony, sacraments, sacred places (including funeral rites) and sacred times, divine worship, the Church's teaching office, benefices, and church property. The revised codification employs instead the categories accepted by Vatican II, namely, the *munera* or functions of (1) teaching (now Book III), (2) sanctifying (Book IV), and (3) ruling (Book II, principally in part two); the canons on church property now constitute Book V.

This pattern confines Book IV to the church order that affects the full liturgical and sacramental life of the Christian people.

Book IV also reflects a major simplification in the quantity as well as in the substance of the canons; it reduces about six hundred canons of the 1917 code to little more than four hundred.

Much of this simplification has been achieved by the elimination of minute prescriptions and by leaving to the liturgical laws outside the code (and/or to particular law) matters not necessary in the codification. Sometimes the reduction in the number of canons suggests the lesser significance of the matter treated or the changed circumstances of Christian life. For example, canons on indulgences have been reduced from twenty-six (*CIC* 911–936) to six (cc. 992–997); the eight canons on the reservation of the absolution from sins in the sacrament of penance (*CIC* 893–900) have been suppressed.

In general, the revision of the canons has been influenced by the decrees of Vatican II, by the revised liturgical books or *Ordines* of the 1960s and 1970s and other implementing documents of the postconciliar period, and by the pastoral and other principles which governed the whole reform of the Roman liturgy.[7] The most significant departure from the 1917 code, however, is the rearrangement or reordering of canons.

Sequence of the Canons of Book IV

The sequence of canons in the 1917 code treated the seven sacraments of the Church not as the mysteries celebrated by the Christian community in the liturgical assembly but almost exclusively as the means of sanctification given by God through the ministry of the ordained ministers or clergy. Thus it was only after the canons on the sacraments (and sacred places and times) that divine worship itself was taken up (beginning with *CIC* 1255).

A similar sequence was originally planned for the revised code. In the first schema circulated for comment by the episcopate (1975), the seven sacraments were again treated as in the 1917 code.[8] An initial canon identified them as "the principal means of sanctification and salvation" but made no reference to their being liturgical acts of cult or worship of God. Another schema, for sacred places, sacred times, and divine cult (1977), again retained the sequence (and orientation) of the former code.[9]

In the light of comments regarding these schemata and, even more significant, the explicit teaching of Vatican II, the sequence was reversed. The liturgy is first treated as a whole, then (1) "The Sacraments" (cc. 840–1165), (2) "Other Acts of Divine Worship" (cc. 1166–1204), and (3) "Sacred Places and Times" (cc. 1205–1253). These three headings constitute the three parts of Book IV.

[7] "Principia Quae Codicem Iuris Canonici Recognitionem Dirigant," *Comm* 1 (1969) 77–85.

[8] ComCICRec, *Schema documenti pontificii quo disciplina canonica de sacramentis recognoscitur* (Vatican City: Typis Polyglottis Vaticanis, 1975).

[9] ComCICRec, *Schema canonum libri IV de Ecclesiae munere sanctificandi* (Vatican City: Typis Polyglottis Vaticanis, 1977).

This order flows from Vatican II's critical correction and amplification of the earlier teaching of Pius XII on the liturgy. In the 1947 encyclical *Mediator Dei,* the liturgy was defined principally in terms of the public worship offered to the Father by the Church, that is, by Christ and his members.[10] The 1963 conciliar constitution on the liturgy, *Sacrosanctum Concilium*—which along with the 1964 dogmatic constitution *Lumen gentium* and the 1965 pastoral constitution *Gaudium et spes* (for the canons on marriage) mainly influenced Book IV—enlarged this definition. The liturgy embraces both the sanctification of humankind by God and the ecclesial acts of cult offered by Christ the Head and his members, all within an understanding of the basic nature of liturgical acts as "signs perceptible to the senses."[11]

In addition, the council formally redefined the seven sacraments not only as signifying the divine grace which they impart by the action of Christ (*ex opere Christi*) but as sacraments of faith, which "make people holy, build up the Body of Christ, and give worship to God." They were described as celebrations (as well as ministrations) which "most effectively dispose the faithful to receive this [divine] grace in a fruitful manner, to worship God rightly, and to practice charity."[12]

This development is reflected in the fundamental doctrinal canons of Book IV, 834, §1 and 840, which are derived from *Sacrosanctum Concilium* 7 and 59 respectively. It is reflected to a lesser degree in the title of Book IV, "The Sanctifying Function of the Church." While this phrasing may at first glance appear to restrict the canons to the action of God through the Church and the Church's ordained ministers upon the rest of the faithful, the canons themselves include both sanctification and worship or cult—that is, the totality of public liturgy. The Latin expression in the title (*munus sanctificandi*) is intended to include the entirety of the Church's "exercise of the priestly office of Jesus Christ." This ecclesial function or office of sanctifying, which is regularly mentioned in conciliar documents along with the function of teaching and the function of ruling, has itself a twofold meaning: *sanctificare* means both "to make holy" and "to glorify the Holy One [God]" and was thus considered a suitable term for the divine liturgy as defined by Vatican II. In the title of Book IV, as well as in the arrangement and content of the canons, sanctification is thus understood to include worship or cult.

Nature of Liturgical Law

In recent years there has been considerable discussion, especially among English-speaking commentators, about the nature (or style) and weight of the liturgical law. In part this is a response to the greater flexibility and openness to adaptation and variation that have been written into the liturgical norms themselves; in part it reflects the pastoral situation canonized in the conciliar texts and especially the style of the 1963 constitution on the liturgy—and the twentieth-century liturgical renewal or movement which the constitution embodies.

First of all, it is clear and certain that the canons (including the seminal c. 2, which indicates that liturgical laws, though outside the codification, continue in full canonical force) and the liturgical books themselves consider such norms to be an integral and preceptive part of the ecclesiastical or canon law. The ordinary canonical principles of promulgation and interpretation, for example, and the canonical institutes such as custom and dispensation are equally applicable to the liturgical laws. At the same time, many of the liturgical laws may be categorized in traditional terms as non-preceptive or directive only (or even as simply descriptive of rites) or as facultative, that is, as offering choices and options. Their great number and diversity—one reason why they are not easily subject to codification or inclusion in the code of the Latin church—require, even more

---

[10] November 30, 1947, *AAS* 39 (1947) 528–529.
[11] *SC* 7.
[12] *SC* 59.

than other parts of canon law, an appreciation of the comparative weight of the form they take: all the way from a conciliar constitution to minor instructions and even simple declarations of an authoritative kind.[13] These forms seem to go far beyond the relatively simple forms determined in the general norms in the titles of the code on laws (cc. 7–22), custom (cc. 23–28), and general decrees and instructions (cc. 29–34). This is especially true because of the characteristic form of the liturgical books, their introductions (*praenotanda*) and rubrics.

Thus the liturgical law may sometimes be considered almost radically different from other parts of canon law, both in the matters affected and in style. This is suggested by the titles of important postconciliar studies: *New Liturgy, New Laws* by R. K. Seasoltz[14] and *Liturgical Law: New Style, New Spirit* by T. Richstatter.[15]

The liturgical celebrations of sacraments and other services are public and communal actions implicating the whole person of each member of the Christian assembly. They are matters of the most intimate faith and piety, which are articulated communally. The norms that govern them are as often aesthetic and artistic as they are juridic or canonical. Since the celebrations are to be the authentic worship of the Church as it is gathered in a particular place at a particular time, accomplished in forms and words that are both personal and impersonal, individual and common, the liturgical norms easily come into conflict with actual situations. The constitution on the liturgy followed the traditional pattern of expository and doctrinal introductions which precede the dispositive norms, and the norms mandating the reform were sometimes hortatory and broadly stated.

This pattern has been followed in the new liturgical books which the constitution decreed should be revised and promulgated. Thus, along with the historical, ecclesiological, and theological reappraisal of the Church's liturgy, it was inevitable that a different spirit would inform the liturgical laws themselves.

Whether the axiom *lex orandi, lex credendi* is taken in its traditional sense to mean that the liturgy is a norm of faith—as it is surely a principal theological source—or is taken to mean, according to Pius XII, that the law of belief should determine the liturgical text and rite,[16] it is evident that the liturgy is a fit subject for authoritative legislation: at every point it involves the Christian faith which it proclaims; it is a touchstone of the communion of churches and of the congregations of the particular or local church; it is the preeminent social and public action of the Christian community; it has the nature of rite or ritual, with recurring forms and patterns that are evidently subject to canonical discipline and normative custom.

In summary, while the liturgical celebration is not easily governed or moderated because it is ultimately the celebration of the mysteries in the Spirit, the laws affecting this celebration are urged with all the force of the rest of canon law. The rationale is sometimes the same as that of the rest of canon law, sometimes different. The rationale for liturgical law involves the public order and common good sought in the services and celebrations, the communion of the churches and Christian communities which celebrate the liturgy, and the manifestation of the common Christian faith, as just mentioned. It involves as well the important relationship of liturgical presidency to the pastoral office of those who govern the liturgy and, finally, the special matter of the quality and style of actual celebration.

The renewed tone and spirit that infuse the laws and the relative weight of their demands in the face of conflicting pastoral expectations have

---

[13] F. R. McManus, "Liturgical Law and Difficult Cases," *W* 48 (1974) 347–366.

[14] Collegeville: Liturgical Press, 1980.

[15] Chicago: Franciscan Herald Press, 1977. See also W. Kelley, "The Authority of Liturgical Laws," *J* 28 (1968) 397–424; J. M. Huels, "The Interpretation of Liturgical Law," *W* 55 (1981) 218–237.

[16] *Mediator Dei, AAS* 39 (1947) 540–541.

led to a legitimate openness. This recognizes the religious value of diversity and is an invitation to cultural adaptation or liturgical inculturation. All these factors must be kept in mind in the interpretation of the canons themselves and all other kinds of liturgical law, with a special concern not only for the immediate text and context but also for the larger context of celebration.

Liturgical Books

The recurrent sources listed for the canons on sacraments and divine worship in the 1917 code were the Roman liturgical books "restored by decree of the holy council of Trent and issued by command of" several popes after that council. The norms of those modern liturgical books became in some instances the canons of the 1917 code. After the promulgation of the code, it became necessary to revise the prenotes of the *Roman Ritual* in instances where canon law had been changed; this was done in an edition of the ritual in 1925. The process for the 1983 codification now in force was similar. The Roman liturgical books, this time as "restored by decree of the holy ecumenical council of Vatican II and promulgated by authority of Pope Paul VI" (or, later, of John Paul II) are a major source for the canons of Book IV. Papal and curial documents issued during the period beginning in 1964 were also used as sources.

The post-Tridentine liturgical books, exclusive of the books of chant such as the *Roman Gradual* and the *Roman Antiphonal,* were formally enumerated in 1946 as the *Roman Breviary, Roman Missal, Roman Ritual, Roman Pontifical, Roman Martyrology, Ceremonial of Bishops, Memoriale Rituum* (for smaller churches), *Octavarium* (for the offices of local octaves), and the collection of decrees, *Decreta Authentica,* of the Congregation of Sacred Rites.[17] Of these, the *Roman Missal* for the Eucharist (1570), the *Roman Pontifical* (1596) and *Roman Ritual* (1614) for the other sacraments and rites, and the *Roman Breviary* for the daily

prayer of the Church (1568) were the most important and basic.

These major Roman liturgical books, with the exception of the ritual, were imposed as binding upon the whole Latin church. An exception, to preserve the other venerable rites of the West such as Ambrosian, Mozarabic, and Gallican, as well as the "uses" of many particular churches and religious orders, was made in cases in which a different rite had been followed for at least two hundred years.

Aside from the considerable increase in the number of saints' feasts, the four principal Roman liturgical books of the post-Tridentine period were not greatly altered until the beginning of the twentieth century. Even then, in the reform initiated by Pope Pius X, the revisions were principally by way of the simplification of regulations and the strengthening of the temporal cycle of the church year. No significant ritual changes were made in the celebrations which the liturgical books govern by their texts and rubrics.

The reform was taken up again by authority of Pius XII with the establishment of a commission for this purpose in 1948, and a series of revisions resulted in the publication of several sections of liturgical books, including the reformed rites of Holy Week in 1951 and 1955. After John XXIII announced the convening of Vatican II, he placed the unfinished work of the reform commission on the conciliar agenda when he authorized a new code of rubrics in 1962. Finally, in the 1963 conciliar constitution a reform of all the Roman liturgical books was formally decreed. It mandated specific norms and principles for that reform and included laws governing further adaptation of the liturgy, especially in the light of cultural and other diversity in the different nations and regions, once the Roman revision could be completed.[18]

The several parts of the Roman liturgical books were prepared by the Consilium for the Implementation of the Constitution on the Liturgy (1964) and promulgated by authority of Paul VI,

---

[17] SCRit, decr, August 10, 1946, *AAS* 38 (1946) 371–372.

[18] *SC* 21–40.

in decrees of the Congregation of Sacred Rites (until 1969), later by the Sacred Congregation for Divine Worship (1969–1975), and still later by the Congregation for Sacraments and Divine Worship. In the latest curial reform promulgated in 1988, effective the following year, competence over the Roman books belongs to the Congregation for Divine Worship and the Discipline of the Sacraments.

The revised *Roman Missal* appeared in three parts: the *Order of Mass* (promulgated April 6, 1969), the *Lectionary for Mass* (order of readings, May 25, 1969; second edition, January 21, 1980), and *Missal* (presidential prayers or sacramentary, April 3, 1969; second edition, March 27, 1975). The *Roman Calendar,* for both the Eucharist and the liturgy of the hours, was promulgated March 21, 1969.

The *Roman Ritual* includes several parts (formerly called "titles" in the one-volume ritual of 1614): *Rite of Marriage* (March 19, 1969; second edition, March 19, 1990), *Rite of Baptism for Children* (May 15, 1969), *Rite of Funerals* (August 15, 1969), *Rite of Religious Profession* (February 2, 1970), *Rite of Christian Initiation of Adults* (January 6, 1972), *Rite of Anointing and Pastoral Care of the Sick* (December 7, 1972), *Holy Communion and Worship of the Eucharist outside Mass* (June 21, 1973), *Rite of Penance* (December 2, 1973), and the *Book of Blessings* (May 31, 1984).

The *Roman Pontifical* includes the *Ordination of Deacons, Priests, and Bishops* (August 15, 1968; second edition, called *Ordination of Bishops, Presbyters, and Deacons,* June 29, 1989), *Rite of Consecration to a Life of Virginity* (May 31, 1970), *Rite of Blessing an Abbot or Abbess* (November 9, 1970), *Rite of the Blessing of Oils, Rite of Consecrating the Chrism* (December 3, 1970), *Rite of Confirmation* (August 22, 1971), *Rite of Institution of Readers and Acolytes, etc.* (December 3, 1972), and *Dedication of a Church and an Altar* (May 29, 1977). A related volume, the *Ceremonial of Bishops* (September 14, 1984), is no longer counted among the liturgical books, since it does not contain liturgical texts used by the ministers.

The *Liturgy of the Hours according to the Roman Rite (The Divine Office)* was promulgated April 11, 1971 and replaced the *Roman Breviary.*

Corresponding liturgical books in English and in the other languages have been published. Those in English are ordinarily prepared by the International Commission on English in the Liturgy, established in 1963 by a joint commission of Catholic bishops' conferences.[19] The "typical" edition of each vernacular liturgical book has the approbation of the conference of bishops for its territory and the confirmation (review or *recognitio*) of the Apostolic See.

Liturgical Laws and the Code

The contents of the liturgical books have their own canonical significance because of their inclusion of liturgical laws. They provide, moreover, interpretative background for the pertinent canons of the code which have been revised in the light of the new liturgical books or which are derived from them. Since their contents do not ordinarily follow the style of canons, they are able to provide, sometimes at length, the *ratio* or rationale for the laws. This includes doctrinal, catechetical, pastoral, historical, and other information and, according to circumstances, may be important in understanding the canons of Book IV.

There is a theoretical question about the possible conflict between the liturgical laws outside the code, particularly those in the liturgical books recently revised by decree of Vatican II, and the canons of Book IV. Such a question of conflict must be resolved in the individual case, but the principles are relatively simple.

First, the liturgical laws (in the liturgical books and other sources, including the documents of Vatican II and postconciliar legislation) retain

---

[19] See F. R. McManus, "ICEL: The First Years," in *Shaping English Liturgy,* ed. P. C. Finn and J. M. Schellman (Washington, D.C.: Pastoral Press, 1990) 433–459.

their force, in accord with canon 2, unless clearly abrogated by a contrary prescription of the code.

Second, a later law (in this hypothetical instance, a prescription of a canon) abrogates or derogates from an earlier law, in accord with canon 20, in three instances: if it expressly so states (which does not occur in the canons of Book IV), if it is directly contrary to the earlier law (which must be established in the individual case), or if it entirely rearranges the subject matter of the earlier law (which does not occur in Book IV in relation to uncodified liturgical laws).

Third, in the examination of an instance of apparent conflict or contradiction, the presumption is in favor of the continuance of the existing liturgical law. In accord with canon 21, in a case of doubt the revocation of an existing (liturgical or other) law by a subsequent canon or other law is not presumed: the later law is to be related to the former and, to the extent possible, harmonized with it. Thus the resolution of conflicts between the norms of the liturgical books will be made, in case of doubt, in favor of the liturgical law. So far as the liturgical books themselves are concerned, a list of variations made necessary by the promulgation of the code was issued in a decree of September 12, 1983, a few weeks before the new code became effective.[20] Some of the emendations were substantive; most merely brought the language, numbering, and references of the *praenotanda* into formal conformity with the code.

[20] SCSDW, decr *Promulgato Codice Iuris Canonici, N* 19 (1983) 540–555. English translation, "Emendations in the Liturgical Books Following upon the New Code of Canon Law" (Washington, D.C.: ICEL, 1984).

Canons and Commentary

Introductory Canons
[cc. 834–839]

Six introductory canons govern Book IV as a whole, which includes sacraments, other acts of divine worship, and sacred places and times. The six canons are both explanatory or doctrinal and normative: they include (1) a definition of the liturgy (c. 834); (2) liturgical offices and ministries (c. 835); (3) the responsibility of the ordained to arouse the faith that is necessary for the exercise of the common priesthood (c. 836); (4) a norm of preference about communal celebration of the liturgy (c. 837); (5) a determination of the ecclesiastical authorities who have power to moderate or regulate the liturgy (c. 838); and (6) the responsibility for non-liturgical practices (c. 839).

These canons replace the basic norms of canons 1255–1264 of the 1917 code, which were the introductory canons of the title on divine worship.

Certain of those canons, those which do not appear here or elsewhere in the codification, are simply abrogated. In particular this is true of the old canons on the desirability of the separation of women and men in church or at sacred rites[21] (women with heads covered, men bareheaded),[22] and the rule that women religious permitted to sing in church not be visible to the congregation.[23] On the other hand, canons 1261, §1 (concerning abuses in divine worship) and 1264, §1 (concerning improper music in church) of the 1917 code, while formally and canonically abrogated, continue to oblige morally, quite apart from positive ecclesiastical law.

There is a considerable lacuna at this point in the Code of Canons of the Eastern Churches. The

[21] *CIC* 1262, §1.
[22] *CIC* 1262, §2.
[23] *CIC* 1264, §2.

heading of title XVI of that code (*CCEO* 667–895) and in particular its introductory canons (*CCEO* 667–674) embrace the entirety of divine worship and especially the seven sacraments. Yet there is nothing in the preliminary canons like the Latin code's definition of the liturgy, the role of ordained ministers and the liturgical assembly as a whole, the location of regulatory power over the liturgy, non-liturgical exercises, and the like— even though such matters are a concern of the Church universal, both East and West, as clearly intended by *Sacrosanctum Concilium* 3–4. Some of these matters are partially addressed in other contexts of the Eastern code.

Definition of the Liturgy

Canon 834 — §1. The Church fulfills its sanctifying function in a particular way through the sacred liturgy, which is an exercise of the priestly function of Jesus Christ. In the sacred liturgy the sanctification of humanity is signified through sensible signs and effected in a manner proper to each sign. In the sacred liturgy, the whole public worship of God is carried out by the Head and members of the mystical Body of Jesus Christ.

§2. Such worship takes place when it is carried out in the name of the Church by persons legitimately designated and through acts approved by the authority of the Church.

The text of paragraph one, which has no precedent in the 1917 code, is derived from *Sacrosanctum Concilium* 7. It is slightly rephrased from the conciliar constitution on the liturgy to make it serve as an explanation of the way in which the ecclesial function or office of sanctifying is accomplished, namely, in the liturgy. Since the latter does not exhaust the entire life of the Church[24] nor is it the entirety of ecclesial sanctification (which includes other prayers and devotional exercises not strictly assimilated to the official liturgy),[25] the liturgy is said to fulfill

this office of the Church in a special way, indeed in an entirely special way that "far surpasses any other."[26] This concept is explained by Vatican II: the liturgy is "the summit toward which the activity of the Church is directed; at the same time it is the fount from which all the Church's power flows."[27]

The definition of the liturgy from *Sacrosanctum Concilium* 7 is partially derived from Pius XII (*Mediator Dei*), as already noted, but it has been considerably modified and amplified, especially to include the sacramental concept of signs and the action of divine sanctification as well as worship offered to God by and in Christ. Although the explanation of signs perceptible to the senses, as signifying and bringing about sanctification, is primarily applicable to the seven sacraments, the statement is made of the liturgy as a whole, which has innumerable signs over and above those central to the seven sacraments.

The language of paragraph two occurs in canon 1256 of the 1917 code, but in a rather different context. There it was a definition of public cult (other than sacraments) offered to God and the saints, as opposed to private cult. Here, however, paragraph two provides instead a canonical distinction between liturgical services and other cultic activity of the church community or of individual Christians. There are two elements to the distinction.

First and of less practical significance, in order to be considered liturgy the activity must be "carried out in the name of the Church by persons legitimately designated." This designation comes primarily from baptism and is enjoyed by all the faithful; it is the sharing in the common priesthood mentioned in canon 836 and described by Vatican II: "The faithful are deputed by the baptismal character to the worship of the Christian religion."[28] In this primary sense, the canon means that the liturgy is carried out by the baptized members of the Christian community.

---

[24] *SC* 9.
[25] See c. 839.

[26] *SC* 13.
[27] *SC* 10.
[28] *LG* 11; *SC* 14.

At times this element has been understood as referring only to the presidency of an ordained minister that is requisite for certain but not all liturgical celebrations. In other instances, it has been understood as referring to the liturgical presidency of the non-ordained, who may be designated, in a manner not determined by the canon, for this purpose.[29] Examples of the latter include the non-ordained who lead services of the word of God, assist at marriages, preside at funeral services, etc.

A particular question has arisen in the past about the liturgical nature of the private praying of the liturgy of the hours by a person who does not possess the explicit deputation or mandate given to the ordained, to religious, etc. This question has been effectively resolved by the conciliar decision that all lay persons should be encouraged to celebrate the liturgical office of prayer, preferably "with the priests, or among themselves, or even individually."[30] This decision has been formally incorporated in the revised liturgy of the hours[31] and is a specific application of the deputation to (public) cult of all the baptized (above). See also canon 1174, §2.

The second element of the distinction in canon 834, §2 is more useful as a canonical means to identify and determine liturgical actions, namely, that these be "approved by the authority of the Church." The usual but not exclusive means of approbation is by way of inclusion of rites in official liturgical books, as determined in canon 838, §§2 and 3. Thus it is possible to define as liturgical, in the sense of this canon, any rite which appears in an approved liturgical book and to define as non-liturgical or extra-liturgical all other prayers and devotional practices.

Nonetheless, since such other practices may themselves have various degrees of ecclesiastical approbation, it may be expected that the competent authority will indicate whether a rite, approved but not included in an official book, is formally recognized as part of the public, corporate liturgy of the Church. As indicated in canon 839, the non-liturgical devotional life of the Church may include both private and communal practices, the latter being considered either pious or sacred services.

It is important to add that the revised liturgical books of the Roman rite themselves incorporate by reference various services the specific elements of which (texts, order of parts) may not be formally prescribed or described. This inclusion, as a means of approbation, makes such services properly liturgical. Examples are certain penitential services, for which the *Rite of Penance* gives examples, and the services of the word of God on the occasion of the visitation of the sick or exposition of the Blessed Sacrament. Another instance of inclusion in the liturgy by reference is found in *Sacrosanctum Concilium* 98: the approved short offices of religious and other institutes, which are obligatory for the members, satisfy the requirements of being "the public prayer of the Church."[32]

Liturgical Offices and Ministries

Canon 835 — §1. The bishops in the first place exercise the sanctifying function; they are the high priests, the principal dispensers of the mysteries of God, and the directors, promoters, and guardians of the entire liturgical life in the church entrusted to them.

§2. Presbyters also exercise this function; sharing in the priesthood of Christ and as his ministers under the authority of the bishop, they are consecrated to celebrate divine worship and to sanctify the people.

§3. Deacons have a part in the celebration of divine worship according to the norm of the prescripts of the law.

§4. The other members of the Christian faithful also have their own part in the function of sanctifying by participating actively in their own way in liturgical celebrations, especially the Eu-

---

[29] *SC* 35, §4.

[30] *SC* 100.

[31] *General Instruction of the Liturgy of the Hours,* February 2, 1971, nn. 20–32, *DOL* 3450–3462.

[32] *DOL* 98.

charist. Parents share in a particular way in this function by leading a conjugal life in a Christian spirit and by seeing to the Christian education of their children.

This canon, with the exception of the final clause of paragraph four, was inserted from the proposed but never promulgated *Fundamental Law of the Church* (1980).[33] It is doctrinal rather than preceptive or prescriptive. The explanation of the role of the ordained ministers in paragraphs one through three reflects a more tentative statement in the conciliar constitution on the Church, *Lumen gentium:* "The divinely instituted ecclesiastical ministry is exercised in different orders by those who, already in antiquity, are called bishops, presbyters, and deacons."[34] The canon itself might have been placed more logically after canons 836–837 (the latter derived from *SC* 26–27), in which the total Church is understood as celebrating the liturgy. It should be clear that, in accord with canon 834's definition, radically and fundamentally it is the whole community of the faithful, the Church itself, which celebrates the liturgy in union with its Head, the Lord Jesus, and that the common priesthood of all the baptized, to be mentioned in canon 836, is logically prior to the ordained, ministerial priesthood.

In paragraph one of canon 835 the sanctifying role of the bishop, most evident when he presides at the liturgy and especially at the eucharistic liturgy, is seen to extend to his authoritative governance of the liturgy as director, promoter, and guardian. This responsibility is rooted in his sacramental ordination. On the one hand, Vatican II formally taught that "episcopal consecration bestows the fullness of the sacrament of orders... the high priesthood, the summit of the sacred ministry."[35] Thus it put an end to theories which challenged the sacramentality of episcopal ordination and saw the episcopate only as the highest degree of the ordinary or simple priesthood of

presbyters.[36] On the other hand, the conciliar fathers saw the sacramental ordination or consecration (the terms are interchangeable) of a bishop as the source or root of the "offices of teaching and governing" as well as of sanctifying, while insisting that these other functions, "of their very nature, can be exercised only in hierarchic communion with the head of the college and its members."[37]

The (diocesan) bishop is described as the director of the entire liturgical life of the particular church, an expression used in the liturgical books as well,[38] because the direction or regulation of the liturgy belongs to him. He is described as the promoter of the liturgy,[39] whether directly or through commissions and other means. He is described as guardian, or custodian, of the liturgy in that he safeguards its integrity and authenticity within the particular church. This canonical responsibility in turn is founded on the liturgical presidency of the diocesan bishop.

Again following the Dogmatic Constitution on the Church, paragraph two sees the members of the presbyterate as participants in the (special, ordained, or ministerial) priesthood but dependent upon the bishop: the members of the order of presbyters are seen as having "a limited share of the full priesthood [of the bishops]: episcopal consecration is the primary and comprehensive instance of sacramental ordination to office."[40] (The Latin texts are generally careful to use *presbyter* for presbyters or priests of the second order, *sacerdos* in reference to both bishops and presbyters. In English the context often permits the word "priests" to be used and understood as referring either to members of both orders or to presbyters alone; the canonical usage in English is now to follow the Latin distinctions with precision.)

The bishops, as "sharers in [Christ's] consecration and mission... in turn have lawfully handed

---

[33] *LEF* 67.
[34] *LG* 28.
[35] *LG* 21.

[36] See Vorgrimler 1:193.
[37] *LG* 21.
[38] E.g., *RPenance,* n. 9, *DOL* 3074.
[39] In the sense of *SC* 14–19, 41–46.
[40] Vorgrimler 1:193.

on to different individuals in the Church [namely, presbyters and deacons] in varying degrees a participation in this ministry."[41] In direct reference to the principal liturgical role of presiding at the Eucharist, the *Roman Missal* explains: "Every authentic celebration of the eucharist is directed by the bishop, either in person or through the presbyters, who are his helpers."[42]

In the liturgical constitution, the content of paragraphs one and two is expressed in more expansive terms that are critical to an understanding of the liturgy as the principal manifestation of the Church and also of the relation of the two offices of liturgical presidency, episcopate and presbyterate:

The bishop is to be looked on as the high priest of his flock, the faithful's life in Christ in some way deriving from him and depending on him.

Therefore all should hold in great esteem the liturgical life of the diocese centered around the bishop, especially in his cathedral church; they must be convinced that the preeminent manifestation of the Church is present in the full, active participation of all God's holy people in these liturgical celebrations, especially in the same eucharist, in a single prayer, at one altar at which the bishop presides, surrounded by his college of presbyters and by his ministers.

But because it is impossible for the bishop always and everywhere to preside over the whole flock in his Church, he cannot do otherwise than establish lesser groupings of the faithful. Among these the parishes, set up locally under a pastor taking the place of the bishop, are the most important: in some manner they represent the visible Church established throughout the world.[43]

With regard to the order of deacons, paragraph three uses only the most general language, quite different from the preceding paragraphs which extol the orders of bishops and presbyters. It leaves to the liturgical books the determination of specific parts to be taken by the deacons of the Church. The functions proper to deacons had already been defined (and enlarged) by Vatican II, not only in connection with the restoration of the permanent diaconate but also in reference to all deacons,[44] who share in

the *diaconia* of liturgy, word, and charity. Insofar as competent authority assigns them [i.e., either in the law generally or in the case of the individual deacon], the [liturgical] duties of the deacon are to administer baptism solemnly; care for the eucharist and give holy communion; assist at and bless marriages in the name of the Church; carry viaticum to the dying; read the Scriptures to the people and exhort and instruct them; preside over worship and prayer; administer sacramentals; officiate at funeral and burial rites.[45]

See canon 1169, §3 for a formal limitation upon the liturgical office of deacons that was introduced after Vatican II.[46] It is understood, moreover, that deacons preside at the liturgy only in the absence of the bishop and presbyter.

The rest of the Christian faithful, by active participation in celebrations of the liturgy, have their own part in the office of sanctification. The concept *participatio actuosa* is ultimately derived from a statement of Pius X in 1903 about the primary and indispensable source of the Christian spirit, namely, "active participation [*la participazione attiva* in the original and authentic text] in the sacred mysteries and in the public and

---

[41] *LG* 28.
[42] *GIRM* 59, *DOL* 1449.
[43] *SC* 41–42. The language is revised in part from Saint Ignatius of Antioch.

[44] Commission for Interpretation of Decrees of Vatican II, March 26, 1968, *AAS* 60 (1968) 363, *DOL* 2547.
[45] *LG* 29.
[46] Commission for Interpretation of Decrees of Vatican II, November 13, 1974, *AAS* 66 (1974) 667, *DOL* 2592.

solemn prayer of the Church."[47] This concept is the recurring theme of the constitution on the liturgy and all the liturgical books. In the context of canon 835, §4, the other members of the Church are contrasted with the ordained ministers in the preceding paragraphs and their role is said to be carried out in their own manner or mode (*suo modo*).

In the first place, the role of the faithful is that of the members of the praying people assembled in a congregation; their common or congregational parts are defined in the liturgical books, both in principle and in particular instances. Canon 836 gives the fundamental principle in virtue of which all the faithful (including the ordained) share, namely, the common priesthood; canon 837 enlarges somewhat upon communal participation. The phrase "in their own way" in canon 835, §4 thus refers to the hierarchic and communal nature of the liturgy in the full assembly of the Church.

In addition, there is indirect reference (as there is direct reference in c. 837, §1) to special liturgical roles or ministries which some of the faithful, other than the ordained, may and should carry out. These include those for which liturgical institution is required (at present only the lay ministries of reader and acolyte in the Latin church, mentioned in c. 230, §1; other lay ministries with formal liturgical institution were originally contemplated); those for which some deputation or commission is expected (such as the ministry of reader on a less stable basis, as in c. 230, §2); and the many specific ministries referred to in the introductions to the liturgical books, both during the liturgical rites themselves and in preparation for them.[48]

A new document was issued on August 15, 1997, by the Roman Curia: "Instruction on Certain Questions Regarding the Collaboration of the Non-ordained Faithful in the Sacred Ministry of Priests." It is unique in bearing the signatures of the responsible officials of eight distinct dicasteries of the Apostolic See; as an instruction it is also most exceptional in its approval "in specific form" by John Paul II rather than with the common approval and authorization to publish that are ordinarily granted by the Roman Pontiff. Nevertheless, in accord with canon 34, §2, the new instruction does not alter or in any way derogate from the canons and other laws to which it refers. Several articles among the "practical provisions" of the instruction deal with the lay exercise of ministries related to canon 835, §4 (and c. 837, §1): the homily (art. 3), liturgical celebrations (6), presidency at Sunday celebrations (7), eucharistic ministers (8), other sacraments (9–11), and funerals (12). The thrust of the instruction is to restrict narrowly the occasions and pastoral circumstances in which lay persons exercise ministries ordinarily performed by priests, but this is always done without instituting any change in the existing laws about lay ministries.

The final clause of paragraph four, which did not appear in the drafts of the *Fundamental Law of the Church* from which the canon is derived, deals with a very different if related matter: the sanctifying function of parents in relation to their children, both through the Christian style of their married life and through the Christian upbringing of the children that they undertake. (See also c. 774, §2.) In this context the clause may appear to be out of place; it can best be understood as a single and significant illustration of the breadth of the sanctifying function which every Christian believer enjoys in relation to others (children to parents and to their sisters and brothers, spouse to spouse and to other family members, neighbor to neighbor, worker to worker, etc.), not only in the liturgical celebrations of the Church but in every dimension of Christian living.

Responsibility of Ordained Ministers

Canon 836 — Since Christian worship, in which the common priesthood of the Christian faithful is carried out, is a work which proceeds from faith and is based on it, sacred ministers are to

---

[47] *Mp Tra le sollecitudini,* November 22, 1903, *AAS* 36 (1903–1904) 329–339.

[48] E.g., for the Eucharist, *GIRM,* nn. 67–70, *DOL* 1457–1460; for initiation, *RCIA,* nn. 41–48, *DOL* 2368–2375.

take care to arouse and enlighten this faith diligently, especially through the ministry of the word, which gives birth to and nourishes the faith.

The canon, without direct precedent in the 1917 code, first expounds the need for faith for the exercise of the common (general, universal, primary) priesthood of the Christian faithful, then enjoins the ordained to support the faith of others, especially through the ministry of the word.

The expository part of the canon flows from the conciliar definition employed in canon 834 (the "exercise of the priestly function of Jesus Christ") and is an assertion of the relation of faith to liturgical celebration: "Before people can come to the liturgy they must be called to faith and to conversion."[49] Not only must the church community proclaim the gospel to non-believers; it must "ever preach faith and penance to believers, prepare them for the sacraments, teach them to observe all that Christ has commanded, and invite them to all the works of charity, worship, and the apostolate."[50] In particular, the chief liturgical celebrations are called "sacraments of faith" because they "not only presuppose faith, but by words and objects they also nourish, strengthen, and express it."[51] In turn, the common priesthood is defined:

> By rebirth and the anointing of the Holy Spirit the baptized are consecrated as a spiritual house and a holy priesthood.... Though they differ from one another in essence and not only in degree, the universal priesthood of believers and the ministerial or hierarchic priesthood are nonetheless interrelated: each of them in its own special way is a sharing in the one priesthood of Christ.[52]

The second element of the canon, and the first explicit norm for conduct in Book IV, is directed to the members of the hierarchic priesthood, the ordained ministers. They are bound to arouse and illumine the faith of the other sharers in the common priesthood, specifically in relation to the liturgical celebrations. A similar conciliar injunction is:

> Pastors must therefore realize that when the liturgy is celebrated something more is required than the mere observance of the laws governing valid and lawful celebration; it is also their duty to ensure that the faithful take part fully aware of what they are doing, actively engaged in the rite, and enriched by its effects.[53]

The reference to the ministry of the word as the special means to stimulate and nourish faith is a specific application, here in the context of the faith needed to exercise the common priesthood, of the many canons of Book III, title I, which speak of the responsibility of the ordained in relation to the word of God.[54] It has particular significance for the liturgy, in which the celebration of the word is intimately and inextricably related to the celebration of the Eucharist and the other sacraments. The liturgical reform itself is based in part on norms derived from the formative (or didactic) nature of the liturgy, in which the ministry of the word of God is to be better integrated, enlarged, and enriched. While the ministry of the word is very evident in the homily, it is exercised in other ways liturgically, both in preparation for the celebration (liturgical catechesis) and in the rites themselves, all in support of the faith that is celebrated. A governing principle of the liturgical reform mandated by the council is this: "In sacred celebrations there is to be more reading from holy Scripture and it is to be more varied and apposite."[55] This norm is the basis for the introduction

---

[49] *SC* 9.
[50] Ibid.
[51] *SC* 59; see c. 840.
[52] *LG* 10.

[53] *SC* 11.
[54] See cc. 756–757, 762–764, 767–773, 776–777.
[55] *SC* 35.

of biblical readings in major rites (confirmation, anointing, penance) and in minor rites (such as blessings and other sacramentals).

A conciliar injunction is related to the present canon:

> Because the spoken word is part of the liturgical service, the best place for it, consistent with the nature of the rite, is to be indicated even in the rubrics; the ministry of preaching is to be fulfilled with exactitude and fidelity. Preaching should draw its content mainly from scriptural and liturgical sources, being a proclamation of God's wonderful works in the history of salvation, the mystery of Christ, ever present and active within us, especially in the celebration of the liturgy.[56]

Common Celebration and Participation

Canon 837 — §1. Liturgical actions are not private actions but celebrations of the Church itself which is _the sacrament of unity,_ that is, a holy people gathered and ordered under the bishops. Liturgical actions therefore belong to the whole body of the Church and manifest and affect it; they touch its individual members in different ways, however, according to the diversity of orders, functions, and actual participation.

§2. Inasmuch as liturgical actions by their nature entail a common celebration, they are to be celebrated with the presence and active participation of the Christian faithful where possible.

The first paragraph is, like canon 834, a description or definition of liturgical celebrations; it is directly quoted from _Sacrosanctum Concilium_ 26, where it introduces the norms for liturgical change which are drawn from the hierarchic and communal nature of the liturgy. In the present context it is the reason for the norm of participation given in paragraph two; in _Sacrosanctum Concilium_ it precedes a series of liturgical principles and/or laws which it was not necessary to include in the canons, although they remain in force: each person should perform his or her own role in the liturgy; those with special liturgical ministries (servers, readers, choir members, etc.) should perform their offices with piety and decorum, be imbued with the spirit of the liturgy, and be properly prepared; the people should take part by acclamations, responses, psalmody, antiphons, and songs, as well as by actions, gestures, postures, and, at proper times, reverent silence, with the various roles of the people spelled out in the liturgical books; only distinctions based upon liturgical function, holy orders, and honor to civil authorities may be attended to in the liturgy.[57]

Unlike paragraph one, which is descriptive and defining, the next paragraph is an explicit norm for conduct; it too is derived from the conciliar decree:

> Whenever rites, according to their specific nature, make provision for communal celebration involving the presence and active participation of the faithful, it is to be stressed that this way of celebrating them is to be preferred, as far as possible, to a celebration that is individual and, so to speak, private. This applies with especial force to the celebration of Mass and the administration of the sacraments, even though every Mass has of itself a public and social character.[58]

The canon expresses the conciliar injunction even more forcefully, but without altering it; the present canonical context does not demand that the public and social character of the so-called _Missa privata,_ auricular confession, or individual praying of the liturgy of the hours be formally defended. The circumstances, whether of sacramental penance or the celebration of a minor sacramental blessing, which may give a quasi-private appearance to an ecclesial rite are acknowledged, but the preference in all cases possible is for com-

[56] SC 35, 2.

[57] SC 26–32.
[58] SC 27.

munal celebration, with the presence and active participation of the faithful.

Moderation of the Liturgy

Direction of the Liturgy

Canon 838 — §1. The direction of the sacred liturgy depends solely on the authority of the Church which resides in the Apostolic See and, according to the norm of law, the diocesan bishop.

As a whole, this fundamental canon is intended to determine the place within the church community where the power to govern, regulate, or moderate the liturgy resides.

With the clarifying addition of the word "diocesan," the first paragraph is taken verbatim from *Sacrosanctum Concilium* 22, §1. The first clause, vindicating the right of the Church to regulate the liturgy, is a matter of public ecclesiastical law and appeared in canon 1260 of the 1917 code in a different form but with a similar purpose: "In the exercise of worship the ministers of the Church must depend exclusively on ecclesiastical superiors." This language was directed against attempts at civil intervention in the governance of the liturgy, especially during the nineteenth century. Thus it denies any regulatory competence in matters of liturgy to those outside the church community.

Other than in countries where church freedom of worship is suppressed or diminished, the final, relative clause of this paragraph is now more important. The language serves to name the specific places within the Church where canonical power over the liturgy is found, namely, in the Bishop of Rome and in the other bishops who preside over local churches or dioceses—as well as in the respective conferences of bishops in which the diocesan and other bishops of a region act together, as *Sacrosanctum Concilium* 22, §2 added immediately.

The determination is based upon, but radically derogates from, canon 1257 of the 1917 code, which attributed the regulation or ordering of the liturgy exclusively to the Apostolic See. Although the parallel might have been more precise had "Roman Pontiff" and "diocesan bishop" (or even "Apostolic See" and "episcopal see") been used, the conciliar intent is clear: to remove the ultimate reservation of the regulation of the liturgy to the Apostolic See as a "major cause" and to acknowledge that the regulation of the liturgy pertains also to the diocesan bishop "in accord with the [liturgical] law," which may be the written law or, as so important in the evolution of the liturgy and its norms, custom.

That some elements in the governance of the liturgy are removed from the authority of the diocesan church is indicated by the expression *ad normam iuris* (according to the norm of law), in relation to the individual bishop. The liturgical law will therefore determine whether the bishop may act or is limited, for example, by the common liturgical law of the Latin church or the particular law of the conference of bishops or even of a provincial or plenary council.

The principle of *Christus Dominus* 8a (and of c. 381, §1) is applicable: there is a presumption that the bishop has all the power over the governance of the liturgy that is required for the exercise of his pastoral office, always excepting cases reserved to the supreme authority or to another ecclesiastical authority. (The responsibility of the diocesan bishop is further described in paragraph four of the canon.)

Apostolic See

§2. It is for the Apostolic See to order the sacred liturgy of the universal Church, publish liturgical books and review their translations in vernacular languages, and exercise vigilance that liturgical regulations are observed faithfully everywhere.

While this paragraph recognizes the basic modification in the law required by *Sacrosanctum Concilium* 22, §1 (namely, by suppressing the adverb "exclusively" in the description of the Apostolic See's authority), it reserves to the Apostolic

Roman See the right to publish the liturgical books of the universal (Latin) Church. These are the liturgical books in Latin, now revised by decree of Vatican II and promulgated by papal authority. It is in harmony with these that the particular liturgical books, now in the vernacular languages, are prepared and issued by the respective territorial authorities, the conferences of bishops.[59]

As explained at the beginning of this commentary on Book IV, the principal liturgical books of the Roman rite were issued in official form during the decades following the Council of Trent, which in 1563 had entrusted their revision to the Roman See. The *Roman Breviary, Roman Missal, Roman Pontifical,* and *Roman Ritual,* along with ancillary volumes such as the *Roman Martyrology* and *Ceremonial of Bishops,* were re-edited and somewhat augmented but remained substantially unchanged until the present century. Increasingly they displaced the liturgical usages of particular churches within the Latin church.

The canon refers directly to the new Roman liturgical books issued in sections beginning in 1968 with the ordination rites (a part of the *Roman Pontifical*) and completed for the most part in the 1970s. These official books, issued in Latin, are published in a basic and exemplary edition, called the *editio typica,* by the Apostolic See itself (that is, by decree of the appropriate dicastery, now the Congregation for Divine Worship and the Discipline of the Sacraments). The republication of such Latin editions in whole or part requires an attestation of the ordinary of the place of publication (the language used is *concordat cum originali*), in accord with canon 826, §2; the same norm is applicable to republication of vernacular liturgical books.

The canon next speaks of the power of the Apostolic See with respect to such parallel vernacular versions of official liturgical books, which are primarily the responsibility of the respective conferences of bishops. This is explained below under the next paragraph of the canon. The Apostolic See reviews such editions and accords them

confirmation or *recognitio* (review or recognition).[60] Finally, paragraph two speaks of the broad power and responsibility of the Roman See to see to the observance of the liturgical law throughout the Church.

Conferences of Bishops

§3. It pertains to the conferences of bishops to prepare and publish, after the prior review of the Holy See, translations of liturgical books in vernacular languages, adapted appropriately within the limits defined in the liturgical books themselves.

The third paragraph of the canon represents a succinct conflation of several norms of *Sacrosanctum Concilium,* which all retain their force. To begin with, the power of the conferences is stated in general terms in article 22, §2, not repeated in the canons: "In virtue of power conceded by law, the regulation of the liturgy within certain defined limits belongs also" to the conferences.

More specifically, it is the responsibility of the conferences of bishops (or other territorial bodies such as plenary councils) to determine the use and extent of the introduction of the vernacular into liturgical celebrations, the decisions being subject to approval, that is, confirmation, by the Apostolic See.[61] It is also the responsibility of the conferences to approve the translations (nothing being said in the constitution about confirmation by the Apostolic See);[62] potential adaptations of the revised Roman liturgy are to be indicated in the rubrics of the (Latin) liturgical books themselves,[63] and the conferences are to determine such potential or anticipated adaptations (again, nothing being said in the constitution about confirmation by the Apostolic See).[64] Finally, the con-

---

[59] *SC* 63, b.

[60] *SC* 36, §3 speaks only of the confirmation of the *acta* of the episcopal conferences concerning the vernacular; *SC* 63, b speaks of confirmation (*recognitio*) of the rituals.
[61] *SC* 36, §3.
[62] *SC* 36, §4.
[63] *SC* 38.
[64] *SC* 39.

ferences are to prepare particular rituals adapted to the needs of their territories and to introduce them after prior review (*recognitio* or confirmation) by the Apostolic See.[65]

The summary of these norms of the conciliar constitution in paragraph three of the canon leaves intact the several elements. In any event, these retain their force as part of the liturgical law and are to be understood in the same sense as before.[66] In particular, the canon preserves the relationship of the canonical action of the conferences of bishops in the publication of vernacular liturgical books to the canonical action of the Apostolic See. The former is described as the preparation and publication of the books; *Sacrosanctum Concilium* speaks to the same effect but, in clearer harmony with the decree on the pastoral office of bishops in the Church, *Christus Dominus* 37, §4, the liturgical constitution allocates to the conferences of bishops the canonical approbation of texts and the preparation and introduction of the ritual books themselves. The canonical action of the Apostolic See, on the other hand, is described alternatively as approving (in the sense of confirming)[67] and as reviewing or recognizing (*recognitio*) prior to promulgation.[68] The language of the canon is an application of what is stated in canon 455, §2, itself based upon *Christus Dominus* 38, §4: the approval of particular liturgical books is an instance of the cases, referred to in canon 455, §1, where the conference of bishops has primary competence.

In explaining this relationship more precisely, the conciliar commission on the liturgy stated that a law enacted by the conference of bishops is subsequently acknowledged and completed by the Apostolic See; while this subsequent action, called *recognitio* in the canon, adds juridic and moral weight, it does not change the nature of the law.[69] The latter proceeds from the legislative power of the conference rather than from that of the Apostolic See. During the recodification process an ef-

fort was made to reserve, in effect, the approbation of particular liturgical books to the Roman See; after protest the conciliar language was introduced.

This third paragraph of canon 838 appears to limit, but does not limit, the power of the conferences of bishops to the approval of vernacular liturgical books and to adaptations foreseen in the Latin books. Despite its omission at this point, *Sacrosanctum Concilium* 22, §2 remains in effect, as already noted. Canon 841 also refers to the responsibility of conferences of bishops and may be seen as an oblique inclusion of the intent of the conciliar decision about the power called *moderatio*. Primarily the acknowledgment of the location of (legislative) power in the present paragraph pertains to the conferences, in accord with canons 447–459; a fortiori it is applicable to other bodies of particular churches such as councils, in accord with canons 439–446. The conciliar constitution deliberately avoided deciding whether this right belongs to the conferences of bishops by divine or human law,[70] but it is an expression of the collegiality (*affectus collegialis*) of the bishops of a given territory or region, a relationship traditionally described as conciliarity.[71]

The revised liturgical books list in their introductions (*praenotanda*) the liturgical adaptations that are foreseen as falling within the competence of the respective conferences of bishops, depending upon the culture and traditions of various peoples (as well as other variations or accommodations which lie within the competence of the diocesan bishop or even of the presiding minister); both *Sacrosanctum Concilium* and postconciliar liturgical legislation not found in the liturgical books indicate further areas of competence of the conferences. It is to adaptations of this sort or at this level alone that paragraph three refers.

Over and above such matters, the possibility of the conferences initiating "more profound liturgical adaptations" (i.e., those not anticipated in the Latin liturgical books) is also within their competence, in accord with the conciliar constitution:

---

[65] *SC* 63, b.
[66] See c. 6, §2.
[67] *SC* 36, §3.
[68] *SC* 63, b.
[69] *AcSynVat* I, 4:288.

[70] Ibid.
[71] *LG* 23.

1. The competent, territorial ecclesiastical authority mentioned in art. 22 §2 [of *SC*] must, in this matter, carefully and prudently weigh what elements from the traditions and culture of individual peoples may be appropriately admitted into divine worship. They are to propose to the Apostolic See adaptations which are considered useful or necessary that will be introduced with its consent.

2. To ensure that adaptations are made with all the circumspection they demand, the Apostolic See will grant power to this same territorial ecclesiastical authority to permit and to direct, as the case requires, the necessary preliminary experiments within certain groups suited for the purpose and for a fixed time.

3. Because liturgical laws often involve special difficulties with respect to adaptation, particularly in mission lands, experts in these matters must be employed to formulate them.[72]

The two levels of such developments, lesser or ordinary adaptations (*SC* 38–39) and more profound adaptations (*SC* 40), demand respectively the recognition of the Roman See or its consent. The distinction was considered to involve a "very diverse process" by the conciliar liturgical commission when it submitted the matter to the conciliar fathers for vote.

In 1994 the competent Roman congregation issued a lengthy instruction on the Roman liturgy and inculturation, enlarging upon these norms and offering a somewhat more discursive treatment of the reasoning behind such continuing liturgical progress and development.[73]

The canon (like the 1994 instruction) does not refer to a final possibility, namely, the role of the conferences of bishops or other bodies in the development of a new rite, i.e., a new non-Roman rite of the Latin church, which may be acknowledged in the future as being of equal right and dignity with the Roman liturgy. This possibility of a new non-Roman rite and the other conciliar decisions mentioned in *Sacrosanctum Concilium* 40 retain their force despite the fact that they have not been incorporated into the revised code.[74]

Diocesan Bishop

§4. Within the limits of his competence, it pertains to the diocesan bishop in the church entrusted to him to issue liturgical norms which bind everyone.

This final paragraph enlarges the simple reference to the diocesan bishop in paragraph one of this canon and is a specification of the legislative and other power of the diocesan bishop as this is described doctrinally in canon 835, §1.

It belongs to the bishop to enact liturgical norms within the limits of his competence, that is, unless it is circumscribed or restricted in some way.[75] A similar norm was found in canon 1261, §2, of the 1917 code; there, however, the enactment of diocesan laws was in terms of enforcing the observance of the existing (and common) prescriptions of the canons on worship, the avoidance of superstitious practice in the daily life of the faithful, and the exclusion of anything alien to the faith, out of harmony with ecclesiastical tradition, or commercialization.[76] The acknowledgment in *Sacrosanctum Concilium* 22, §1, repeated in this paragraph of canon 838, radically changes the norm of canon 1257 of the 1917 code: the regulation of the liturgy pertains to the bishop and is no longer exclusively or uniquely the responsibility of the Apostolic See.

---

[72] *SC* 40.

[73] CDWDS, instr *Varietates legitimae,* January 25, 1994, *AAS* 87 (1994) 288–314. This was the fourth instruction on implementation of *Sacrosanctum Concilium.*

[74] *SC* 4; see *AcSynVat* I, 3:121.

[75] See "ad normam iuris" of §1 of this canon; also *CD* 8 a and c. 381, §1.

[76] *CIC* 1261, §1.

The final clause of paragraph four, stating that all are bound by diocesan liturgical law, is an inclusive statement. It avoids the possibility of exceptions to or exemptions from the binding force of such laws. This is in harmony with the conciliar decree that religious exemption from diocesan authority is not applicable to "the public exercise of divine worship," unless the religious are of a different liturgical rite.[77] Since the code applies only to the Latin church, however, the diocesan bishop of a particular church cannot issue norms for the celebration of liturgical rites of the Eastern Catholic churches, even if, in the absence of an Eastern eparchy or exarchy in the territory, Eastern members of the faithful may be otherwise subject to his authority.

The canons of the Eastern churches differ greatly from canon 838 and its four paragraphs. Canon 668, §2 of the Eastern code refers the question of the locus of regulatory power over the liturgy to that code's canon 657 on official liturgical books. In that canon the approbation of liturgical texts is reserved to the patriarch with the consent of the synod of bishops or, in metropolitan churches *sui iuris,* to the metropolitan with the consent of the council of hierarchs; in both cases prior review (*recognitio*) by the Apostolic Roman See is required. In other Eastern churches the approbation itself is reserved to the Apostolic See, which may establish limits within which bishops and their assemblies may grant that approbation (§1).

Next, canon 657, §2 of the Eastern code again differs from the law of the Latin church, permitting the enumerated authorities to issue the requisite canonical approbation of translations of liturgical books into vernacular languages, but with only an obligation to report to the Apostolic See, that is, without requesting any Roman *recognitio;* this norm of a simple report or notification, however, is applicable only in the patriarchal churches and the metropolitan churches *sui iuris.*

In the different context of "eparchies and bishops," the liturgical responsibility of the eparchial or local bishop is determined in language corresponding somewhat to Latin canons 835, §1 and 838, §4. The bishop is described as "moderator, promoter, and guardian of the entire liturgical life of the eparchy" with the duty to be "vigilant that it [the liturgical life] be fostered as much as possible and ordered according to the prescriptions and legitimate customs of his own Church *sui iuris.*" The basic conciliar norm found in *Sacrosanctum Concilium* 22, §1 and now in Latin canon 838, §1 on the liturgical regulatory power of the Bishop of Rome and of the diocesan (eparchial) bishop does not appear in the Eastern code.

With regard to liturgical reforms or development, all Eastern hierarchs are constrained by canon 40, §1 of the Eastern code, not only to see to the preservation of their own rite, but also "not [to] admit changes in it except by reasons of its organic progress, keeping in mind, however, mutual goodwill and the unity of Christians." This shows direct concern for the liturgical rite possessed in common with other Christian churches of the East and clearly flows from *Orientalium Ecclesiarum* 6.

Other Prayers and Devotional Services

Canon 839 — §1. The Church carries out the function of sanctifying also by other means, both by prayers in which it asks God to sanctify the Christian faithful in truth, and by works of penance and charity which greatly help to root and strengthen the kingdom of Christ in souls and contribute to the salvation of the world.

§2. Local ordinaries are to take care that the prayers and pious and sacred exercises of the Christian people are fully in keeping with the norms of the Church.

The first paragraph of this canon, which is doctrinal rather than normative, was added in the final stages of the revision process. It describes the breadth of the (non- or extra-liturgical) sanctifying function of the Church and is an application of the meaning of canon 834, §1. The Church exercises that function or office "in a particular way" in the liturgy, which is the source and sum-

[77] CD 35.

mit of church life, but the sanctifying function also embraces all the dimensions listed in canon 839, §1. So far as regulation or governance is concerned, these actions of the church community are likewise subject to the canonical power of church authorities, as already determined in canon 838.

In turn paragraph one introduces paragraph two, which is directly derived from the liturgical constitution of Vatican II and governs the Church's diverse acts and services of prayer and piety that are not considered liturgical in the strict sense. Thus paragraph two replaces canons 1259 (prohibiting prayers and exercises of piety in churches or oratories without the express permission of the local ordinary) and 1261 (requiring local ordinaries to exclude abuses from public and private divine cult and from the daily life of the faithful) of the 1917 code, and does so with more positive language. It is concerned with prayers and devotional exercises or services which are not strictly liturgical in the sense of canon 834.

"Pious" exercises, mentioned first, are communal celebrations (or even individual practices) which lack authoritative recognition as liturgical— but which may be highly endorsed and even ordered by the Apostolic See. "Sacred" exercises are proper to particular churches and have "special dignity if they are undertaken by mandate of the bishops according to customs or books lawfully approved."[78] These latter, while not formally admitted into the liturgy of the Roman or non-Roman rites of the Latin church, are officially recognized by particular (diocesan) churches or groups of churches; thus they are closely analogous to the liturgy as it is understood in the strict and usual sense but differ from pious devotions in general, which receive a more general, sometimes universal, approval or encouragement. The theoretical question of whether so-called sacred services at some point become a kind of diocesan liturgy is not resolved either by *Sacrosanctum Concilium* 13 or by paragraph two of the canon.[79]

For the publication of prayer books that contain pious and sacred exercises, see canon 826, §3.

The norms of the Church, with which the prayers and practices in question must be in harmony, are basically the following: "These devotions should be so fashioned that they harmonize with the liturgical seasons, accord with the sacred liturgy, are in some way derived from it, and lead the people to it, since, in fact, the liturgy by its very nature far surpasses any of them."[80] The conformity of contemporary services of the word of God commanded by these norms is evident;[81] it is the responsibility of local ordinaries to see that all other services be reappraised in the light of the conciliar norm.

It is no longer necessary, however, that prayers and exercises of piety be reviewed and expressly approved by the local ordinary for use in churches or oratories,[82] and local ordinaries are no longer prohibited from approving new litanies for public recitation.[83]

Part I
THE SACRAMENTS
[cc. 840–1165]

The canons on the seven sacraments of the Church constitute well over three-quarters of Book IV. The number of canons is large, partly because the sacraments are the principal elements of the liturgy, partly because the discipline of the sacraments, in varying degrees, has given rise to special needs for order and regulation in the Church. After nine preliminary canons of an introductory or general character, this first part of Book IV is divided straightforwardly into seven titles corresponding to the seven sacraments. In this it differs from the

[78] *SC* 13.
[79] See Vorgrimler 1:16–17.

[80] *SC* 13.
[81] *SC* 35, 4.
[82] *CIC* 1259, §1.
[83] *CIC* 1259, §2.

arrangement of the constitution on the liturgy, which has one chapter devoted to the Eucharist alone and another chapter on the other sacraments and the sacramentals. (The latter are treated in *Sacrosanctum Concilium,* chapter 3, as lesser signs or sacraments; in the canons they are treated among other actions of divine worship, in part two of Book IV—cc. 1166–1204.) The arrangement of the titles in the codification gives primary emphasis to the sequence of the initiatory sacraments: baptism, confirmation, and Eucharist, in accord with the basic statement in canon 842, §2.

Aside from the very first canon of part one and single introductory canons for each title, no formal doctrinal or theological statements about the sacraments are given. There is no need from a disciplinary viewpoint to enter into theological questions about the greater or lesser significance of individual sacraments, e.g., the primacy of baptism and Eucharist or the complementary and subordinate nature of confirmation in relation to baptism and total Christian initiation.

Matter and Form

The canons of Book IV assume the Scholastic doctrine of matter and form, especially in relation to the seven sacraments, even though these distinctions are not readily accommodated to penance and matrimony. At times they are concerned, at least for canonical purposes, with what is minimally necessary for validity in the Latin church, without touching on such questions directly for the other churches. This minimal demand, however, is never to be taken to be what is usual or desirable, and such an understanding of the canons (and of the liturgical books in cases like celebrations in circumstances of emergency) must be avoided. On the contrary, the liturgical books are at great pains to support the fullness of celebration, insisting upon the offices and ministries of the entire community and seeking always the authenticity of signs—not only the signs that are central and considered operative and essential but all signs and elements.

Neither do the canons enter into theological discussions of the divine determination or institution of those elements without which these would not be Christian sacraments in the understanding and acceptance of the Church. They take for granted that the central form of words must indeed be the words (in whatever language) prescribed in the liturgical books of the Latin church but that these are not only different in other churches, including those in full communion with the Catholic Church, but are subject to change and determination by ecclesiastical authority. This has been amply demonstrated by the postconciliar reform of Paul VI, who introduced a new consecratory prayer for episcopal ordination, new forms for confirmation and anointing of the sick, etc. Moreover, he authorized new eucharistic prayers with a variety of epicleses, albeit a single (but revised) form of institutional narrative or consecration.

In this area the teaching of Pius XII in 1947 has been followed,[84] namely, that the (verbal) *form* of a sacrament is not the minimal formula that is essential; as reiterated by Paul VI in the reform of the rites of ordination: "The form consists in the words of the consecratory prayer, of which the following belong to the essence and are consequently required for validity: [there follow the short formulas for the respective orders of deacons, presbyters, and bishops]."[85] The same principle is observed in the rite of penance, when again a distinction is made between the integral form of sacramental absolution ("God the Father of mercies...") and the essential words, traditional in the Latin church since the sixteenth century ("I absolve you...").[86] This question is not unrelated to ecumenical considerations, because of long-standing disputes be-

---

[84] Apconst *Sacramentum ordinis,* November 30, 1947, *AAS* 40 (1948) 6; *DOL* 2608.

[85] Apconst *Pontificalis Romani,* July 18, 1968, *AAS* 60 (1968) 372–373, *DOL* 2609–2611.

[86] *RPenance* 19, *DOL* 3084; 40, *DOL* 3105. Declarative or indicative formulas of absolution were gradually introduced in the Middle Ages under the influence of the Scholastics.

tween East and West about the central and minimal form required in the anaphora or eucharistic prayer. An initial attempt to speak of this in a joint statement of delegates of the Orthodox and Catholic Churches reads:

> The eucharistic mystery is accomplished in the prayer which joins together the words by which the Word made flesh instituted the sacrament and the epiclesis in which the Church, moved by faith, entreats the Father, through the Son, to send the Spirit so that in the unique offering of the incarnate Son, everything may be consummated in unity.[87]

A similar recognition of a changed ecclesiastical discipline underlies the canons in respect to the central and essential *matter* or action of the sacraments. The minimal requirement for validity is specified by the canons, but without entering into past disputes. This position too derives from Pius XII who, in relation to the matter of the sacrament of orders, declared that, regardless of what had been required or had been taught to be required in the past (at least within the Latin church) as essential for validity, henceforward the ritual laying on of hands would suffice.[88] The possibility of change is likewise illustrated in the ritual of Paul VI, for example, in the case of confirmation, where the essential matter is described, for the Latin church, as "anointing with chrism on the forehead, which is done by the laying on of the hand"—but not to the denigration of the full laying on of hands which takes place before the anointing, "even if it is not of the essence of the sacramental rite."[89]

---

[87] Joint Roman Catholic-Orthodox Commission for Theological Dialogue, "The Mystery of the Church and of the Eucharist in the Light of the Mystery of the Holy Trinity," July 6, 1982, *Origins* 12 (1982) 157–160.

[88] See above, notes 84 and 85.

[89] Apconst *Divinae consortium naturae*, August 15, 1971, *AAS* 63 (1971) 663–664, *DOL* 2507.

In summary, the canons are careful to determine, generally in the language already used in papal documents or the liturgical books, the matter and form minimally essential but do not (1) enter into theological or other questions more deeply, (2) overstate the laws, which may affect the Latin church only, or (3) propose that the celebration is in any way integral or complete merely by the satisfaction of the minimal requirement.

For the responsible authority in the determination of what is necessary for valid sacraments, see canon 841.

INTRODUCTORY CANONS
[cc. 840–848]

The preliminary canons on the sacraments (cc. 840–848) are general in character, affecting all the titles and canons of part one of Book IV. The more notable changes introduced in the revision of the preliminary canons are the following: (1) the definition of sacraments in general (c. 840); (2) an explicit norm on the initiatory sacraments of baptism, confirmation, and Eucharist (c. 842, §2); and (3) the new discipline on certain sharing in sacraments (*communicatio in sacris*) with other Christians (c. 844).

Definition of the Sacraments

Canon 840 — The sacraments of the New Testament were instituted by Christ the Lord and entrusted to the Church. As actions of Christ and the Church, they are signs and means which express and strengthen the faith, render worship to God, and effect the sanctification of humanity and thus contribute in the greatest way to establish, strengthen, and manifest ecclesiastical communion. Accordingly, in the celebration of the sacraments the sacred ministers and the other members of the Christian faithful must use the greatest veneration and necessary diligence.

Although the giving or administering of a sacrament by a Christian minister and the receiving of a sacrament by another Christian remain correct expressions, preference is given here and elsewhere in the canons (as in the revised liturgical books) to "celebration" of sacraments by the whole Christian community. For the same reason, the formulation of the canon is explicit in speaking of both the ordained ministers and the rest of the faithful as engaged in common celebration.

The most significant part of the canon is its explanation of the nature of sacraments (which were described merely as "the principal means of sanctification and salvation" in *CIC* 731, §1). This is in accord with *Sacrosanctum Concilium* 59:

> The purpose of the sacraments is to make people holy, to build up the Body of Christ, and, finally, to give worship to God; but being signs they also have a teaching function. They not only presuppose faith, but by words and objects they also nourish, strengthen, and express it; that is why they are called "sacraments of faith." They do indeed impart grace, but, in addition, the very act of celebrating them disposes the faithful most effectively to receive this grace in a fruitful manner, to worship God rightly, and to practice charity.[90]

The influence of the conciliar statement on the canon is seen in the understanding of sacraments (1) as signs and means of expressing and strengthening faith, (2) as actions (of Christ and the Church) of worship as well as of sanctification,[91] and (3) as constitutive of the Church. The first two of these elements were entirely missing from early drafts of the new canon. As explained at the beginning of the commentary on Book IV, the inclusion of references to faith and to worship reflects a major development in the canonical (and doctrinal) understanding of the sacramental signs of faith, which are both ecclesial celebrations of worship and means of grace.

Requisites for the Validity of Sacraments

Canon 841 — Since the sacraments are the same for the whole Church and belong to the divine deposit, it is only for the supreme authority of the Church to approve or define the requirements for their validity; it is for the same or another competent authority according to the norm of can. 838 §§3 and 4 to decide what pertains to their licit celebration, administration, and reception and to the order to be observed in their celebration.

This canon was derived from the draft of the proposed *Fundamental Law of the Church*[92] (1980) and was added at this point only in the final stages of the recodification. It locates the ecclesial authority responsible for (1) the determination of what is requisite for the validity of sacraments and (2) the determination of all other matters relating to the celebration of sacraments.

With regard to the first element, see the commentary above on matter and form as determined by the Church. One point needs repetition: the concern lest, because the minimal requisites need to be determined, these should be thought to suffice doctrinally, liturgically, or pastorally. The present canon reserves the approval or definition of what is necessary for validity, genuineness, or reality of sacraments to "the supreme authority of the Church." This terminology is used in the code to refer to the body or order of bishops as "the subject of supreme and full power over the universal Church, together with the Roman Pontiff and never without this head, a power which it cannot exercise without the consent of the Roman Pontiff."[93]

The expression is likewise used of the Bishop of Rome himself acting as head of the college or order of bishops; he is said to have "a full, supreme, and universal power, which he is always able to exercise freely."[94] The exercise of this power by Pius XII and Paul VI in altering the requisites for validity of matter and form has already

---

[90] *DOL* 59.
[91] *SC* 7.

[92] *LEF* 68, §2.
[93] *LG* 22.
[94] Ibid.

been mentioned above at the beginning of the commentary on part one of Book IV. The supreme authority of the college of bishops, that is, of the Bishop of Rome and the other bishops in hierarchic communion, is stated in canonical terms in canons 330, 331, and 336. Canon 669 of the Eastern code includes the first part of Latin canon 841, but not the second part (treated below).

The second part of the canon treats all else which may be decreed for the lawful celebration, ministration, and reception of sacraments as well as the order of their celebration. This may be decreed by either the supreme authority already mentioned or by the other authorities named in canon 838, §§3 and 4, namely, the conferences of bishops and the individual diocesan bishop, as the canon law of the liturgy may determine.

Canon 841 thus has the effect, with regard to the seven sacraments, of clarifying and reinforcing canon 838. What remains in the final clause, however, is a very general and possibly ambiguous norm: it determines neither the borders or limits of the respective powers nor their interaction and potential.

Sacraments of Initiation

Canon 842 — §1. A person who has not received baptism cannot be admitted validly to the other sacraments.

§2. The sacraments of baptism, confirmation, and the Most Holy Eucharist are interrelated in such a way that they are required for full Christian initiation.

No exception is made to the norm of paragraph one. The sacraments may be received only by Christian believers, those who have and profess the Christian faith. But the believer, before he or she may be admitted to any other sacrament, must first be baptized. As canon 1170 indicates, this norm does not hold true of other rites of the Church, such as sacramentals, which may be given to catechumens and also to those who are not Catholics.

In early drafts of paragraph one, the canon was explicitly related to the prescriptions on sacra-

ments to be received by Christian believers who are not Catholics (see c. 844); here it stands as a basic norm. On the question of valid baptism, see canon 849.

Without any direct precedent in the 1917 code, paragraph two summarizes the doctrine that the three sacraments of baptism, confirmation, and Eucharist are so closely related as to be necessary for full Christian initiation. As is evident, the completion of initiation through full participation in the eucharistic celebration continues throughout the Christian life, unlike baptism and confirmation, which may be celebrated by and for an individual only once.[95]

The sequence of the initiatory sacraments had to be stated at this point, in accord with tradition and the conciliar efforts at restoration of that tradition, because pastoral circumstances and other causes in very many places disrupt the order in which the initiatory sacraments are celebrated for Catholics of the Latin church. In the Latin church the interrelation of the initiatory sacraments is most clearly seen only when the sacraments are celebrated as the climax of the catechumenal formation of new believers, i.e., persons who become Christians after reaching the use of reason, in accord with canon 852, §1. Then complete Christian initiation—baptism with confirmation followed by first eucharistic communion—is celebrated on a single occasion.

The widespread practice of postponing the sacrament of confirmation beyond the age of reason, despite canon 891, coupled with the practice (since the beginning of the twentieth century) of first receiving the Eucharist at about the age of reason, has given rise to an entirely different sequence in the case of those baptized in infancy: baptism, Eucharist, confirmation. If, in addition, the baptized child receives the sacrament of penance before the Eucharist, a still further alteration in the theological, liturgical, and canonical sequence occurs: baptism, penance, Eucharist, confirmation.

In those parts of the Latin church where baptized children are confirmed either as infants or at

[95] See c. 845, §1.

least before their first admission to eucharistic communion, the question does not arise in the same way, although the relation of the three sacraments to which the canon refers may not be so evident because of the great interval between baptism/confirmation and Eucharist. Nor does the question arise at all in the practice of the Eastern churches where, according to a more venerable tradition, the children of Christian families are fully initiated in infancy, receiving the initiatory sacraments in a single rite just as does an adult neophyte in the Latin church (c. 866)—"adult" in this instance referring to anyone who has reached the use of reason, as just mentioned.

Both the 1917 code and the present codification respect the traditional sequence of the initiatory sacraments by the order of the titles on these sacraments. The same is true of the conciliar documents and the revised liturgical books, in which the following explanation is given:

> Through baptism men and women are incorporated into Christ. They are formed into God's people and they obtain forgiveness of all their sins. They are rescued from the power of darkness and brought to the dignity of adopted children.... Signed with the gift of the Spirit in confirmation, Christians more perfectly become the image of their Lord and are filled with the Holy Spirit. ...Finally, they come to the table of the eucharist to eat the flesh and drink the blood of the Son of Man so that they may have eternal life and show forth the unity of God's people.... Thus the three sacraments of initiation closely combine to bring the faithful to the full stature of Christ and to enable them to carry out the mission of the entire people of God in the Church and in the world.[96]

The documents of Vatican II and the revised liturgical books are realistic about achieving a complete or immediate restoration of the tradition

[96] *IGIC,* n. 2, *DOL* 2251.

of the initiatory sacraments celebrated together or at least in sequence. Even if the sequence is upset in practice, *Sacrosanctum Concilium* 71 provides that at least during the celebration of confirmation the relationship and sequence of the sacraments should be clearly manifested:

> The rite of confirmation is also to be revised so that the intimate connection of this sacrament with the whole of Christian initiation may stand out more clearly; for this reason it is fitting for candidates to renew their baptismal promises just before they are confirmed.
>
> Confirmation may be conferred within Mass when convenient...

The revised rites make the point even more effectively than the constitution, and canon 842, §2 states the norm which has application to the first three titles of part one. Nevertheless the norm may appear to be only an ideal wherever the sequence of sacraments indicated by the canons is not observed, as is permitted by canon 891.

Although in complete harmony with the Eastern liturgical and canonical tradition, as already noted, the text of canon 842, §2 does not appear in the Eastern code. On the one hand, the norms of interrelatedness of the three sacraments of initiation and their sequence are held by both East and West, and thus paragraph two can almost be taken for granted in the Eastern code. On the other hand, the Eastern tradition of full Christian initiation of infants in a single celebration (baptism, chrismation with holy myron, and eucharistic communion) is not observed in the Latin church. (See *CCEO* 695, §1 and 710.)

Duties of Ministers and Others

Canon 843 — §1. Sacred ministers cannot deny the sacraments to those who seek them at appropriate times, are properly disposed, and are not prohibited by law from receiving them.

§2. Pastors of souls and other members of the Christian faithful, according to their respective

ecclesiastical function, have the duty to take care that those who seek the sacraments are prepared to receive them by proper evangelization and catechetical instruction, attentive to the norms issued by competent authority.

Canon 213 asserts the right of the faithful to receive spiritual goods, especially the word of God and the sacraments. These are elements of the full liturgical participation by the Christian people that is "their right and duty by reason of their baptism."[97] From this right flows the norm of paragraph one of the present canon, which prohibits any denial of the sacraments by the ordained ministers of the Church without cause.

The disqualifications for which people may be denied the sacraments are clear enough when specified in the law, e.g., irregularities for orders in canon 1041 and possible denial of the Eucharist in canon 915. It is less clear when a request for sacramental ministrations is to be judged opportune or inopportune, reasonable or unreasonable, appropriate or inappropriate; a question might arise, for example, in connection with auricular confession in canon 986, §1. Ordinarily the minister may make a judgment about the timing of a request for sacramental ministries, but the nature of his ministry suggests that he should err on the side of willingness to serve.

Similarly, almost always the proper disposition of faith and devotion can be judged adequately only by the person who seeks the sacrament. Although a judgment of this kind can and sometimes must be made by the minister, the canon establishes a presumption in favor of the Christian person.

There is a parallel to paragraph two of this canon in canon 836, which speaks of the obligation of ordained ministers to arouse and strengthen the faith of others for their exercise of the common priesthood in liturgical celebrations. Here, however, the evangelizing and catechizing responsibility is, first, that of those who exercise a pastoral office and, second, that of all members of

the Church, lay and ordained, depending upon their ecclesial office or function of whatever kind. The duty, moreover, is specifically in relation to preparation for the sacraments.

The intent of paragraph two of canon 843 is best illustrated in the repeated admonitions of the liturgical books. They describe the appropriate preparation for those who are to receive sacraments and the means to provide it. Such explanations are generally contained in sections entitled "Offices and Ministries" in the *praenotanda* of the respective books. These sections speak in detail of pastors, other ordained ministers, catechists, parents, families, and indeed the Christian community at large as having a role in the preparation of others for the sacraments. Such *praenotanda* are examples of norms issued by competent authority; other examples include diocesan, regional, or national norms (i.e., laws) and guidelines, pastoral directories, and the like.

While the canon as a whole applies directly, because of its placement at the head of the canons on the sacraments (part one), to the seven sacraments alone, it can be applied analogously to other elements of the liturgy such as the ecclesial prayer or liturgy of the hours and the sacramentals. In the case of such celebrations or ministrations, similar responsibilities—ministerial response to requests and the appropriate preparation of recipients—may be indicated in the liturgical books.

Sharing in Sacraments

The next canon treats sacramental or liturgical sharing (*communicatio*) in the reception of three of the seven sacraments—penance, Eucharist, and anointing of the sick—in distinct and carefully defined circumstances: (1) in the case of Catholics who may receive the sacraments from ministers not in full communion with the Catholic Church and (2) in the case of Christians who are not themselves in full communion with the Catholic Church but who may seek the sacraments from its ministers. It does not treat other kinds of sharing in worship or spiritual things, i.e., those not involving the

[97] *SC* 14.

reception of sacraments. Neither does it treat the other sacraments, including the sacrament of marriage, which has its own discipline (see cc. 1124–1129). For Catholic responsibility in the promotion of ecumenical dialogue and activity with other Christian believers, see canon 755 (and cc. 902–908 of the Eastern code).

As a whole, the canon is the fruit of Vatican II's deliberations on ecumenism and replaces canon 731, §2 of the former code. The latter contained an absolute prohibition of sacramental ministrations to "heretics or schismatics, even those erring in good faith and asking for the sacraments," without prior reconciliation. (Even under that canon, which admitted no exceptions in the text, it was understood that in danger of death, penance and anointing might be given conditionally in certain circumstances.) In addition, canon 1258 of the 1917 code is abrogated by omission: it prohibited all active participation by Catholics in non-Catholic sacred rites; it tolerated passive or merely material presence under specified and limited conditions.

Although the canon provides rather specific norms, the underlying principles remain those of Vatican II's decree on ecumenism, *Unitatis redintegratio*. Sharing in sacred things (*communicatio in sacris*)

> may not be regarded as a means to be used indiscriminately toward restoring Christian unity. Such sharing is dependent mainly on two principles: the unity of the Church, of which it is a sign, and the sharing in the means of grace. Its function as a sign often rules out *communicatio in sacris*. Its being a source of grace sometimes favors it. Unless the conference of bishops, following the norm of its own statutes, or the Holy See has ruled otherwise, the local bishop is the authority competent to decide with prudence what the right course of action should be in view of all the circumstances of time, place, and people.[98]

[98] *UR* 8.

Canon 844 — §1. Catholic ministers administer the sacraments licitly to Catholic members of the Christian faithful alone, who likewise receive them licitly from Catholic ministers alone, without prejudice to the prescripts of §§2, 3, and 4 of this canon, and can. 861, §2.

§2. Whenever necessity requires it or true spiritual advantage suggests it, and provided that danger of error or of indifferentism is avoided, the Christian faithful for whom it is physically or morally impossible to approach a Catholic minister are permitted to receive the sacraments of penance, Eucharist, and anointing of the sick from non-Catholic ministers in whose Churches these sacraments are valid.

§3. Catholic ministers administer the sacraments of penance, Eucharist, and anointing of the sick licitly to members of Eastern Churches which do not have full communion with the Catholic Church if they seek such on their own accord and are properly disposed. This is also valid for members of other Churches which in the judgment of the Apostolic See are in the same condition in regard to the sacraments as these Eastern Churches.

§4. If the danger of death is present or if, in the judgment of the diocesan bishop or conference of bishops, some other grave necessity urges it, Catholic ministers administer these same sacraments licitly also to other Christians not having full communion with the Catholic Church, who cannot approach a minister of their own community and who seek such on their own accord, provided that they manifest Catholic faith in respect to these sacraments and are properly disposed.

§5. For the cases mentioned in §§2, 3, and 4, the diocesan bishop or conference of bishops is not to issue general norms except after consultation at least with the local competent authority of the interested non-Catholic Church or community.

In paragraph one of the canon, the intent is clear, namely, to define the outer limits of permissible sharing in sacraments, aside from any questions of validity or invalidity. (Canon 861, §2 is treated as an exception because it contemplates the giving of baptism in case of necessity by "any person with the right intention.") It is concerned only with licit or lawful giving and receiving of sacraments, the basic question of validity having been determined in principle by canon 842, §1, namely, that only a baptized Christian may receive any other sacrament validly. The exceptions to the first paragraph's general norm are in the three succeeding paragraphs.

These three succeeding paragraphs are concerned, moreover, with exceptions in the cases of penance, Eucharist, and anointing of the sick only. The sacraments received but once, as determined in canon 845, §1 (baptism, confirmation, orders), are not at issue since these may be received only within one's own communion—aside from the case of baptism just mentioned. In an earlier and more severe redaction of the canon the introduction of an explicit prohibition with regard to the other sacraments was proposed.

As noted already, the sacrament of marriage is treated elsewhere in the canons in chapter 4 of title VII on mixed marriages. This is done in part because of the common teaching in the Latin church (but not in the Eastern churches) that the spouses are the ministers of this sacrament. Thus there are distinct considerations of giving and receiving the sacrament of marriage when one of the persons is a baptized non-Catholic.

The second paragraph makes an initial concession, for the three sacraments only, so that Catholics may request and receive one or other of these sacraments from a minister of a non-Catholic church. The conditions are explicit and clear: (1) either necessity or genuine spiritual advantage; (2) physical or moral impossibility (such as serious inconvenience) of receiving the sacrament from a Catholic minister; (3) the absence of the danger of error or indifferentism; and (4) provided the sacrament is validly celebrated in the other church.

Thus paragraph two stands as an exception to paragraph one, applying only to Catholics as recipients of sacraments. The presence or absence of the requisite conditions must be determined in individual cases by the Catholic subject to the canon law. The law does not mention, but the Catholic should take into account, the discipline of the other church or ecclesial community in which he or she seeks to receive one or more of these sacraments.

Next, paragraph three of canon 844 gives a norm for the Catholic minister and his ministration of one of the three sacraments to persons not in the full communion of the Catholic Church. Again the conditions for the exception permitting the ministration are explicit: (1) in favor of members of the Eastern churches with which the Catholic Church is not in full communion, provided (2) such individuals act voluntarily (when asking for the sacraments), and (3) are properly disposed.

The same exception or concession is then extended in careful language by paragraph three to members of other (non-Catholic) churches, but with an additional requirement: the Apostolic Roman See must have judged that such churches are "in the same condition" as the Eastern churches "in regard to the sacraments." A comparison of paragraph three with paragraphs two and four of the canon helps to interpret the expression, "in the same condition": the Eastern churches do indeed possess valid sacraments of penance, Eucharist, and anointing of the sick and their members share "Catholic faith" in these sacraments.

No determination is made by the canon concerning what churches are meant, that is, what churches may be considered by the Apostolic See to be "in the same condition" as the Eastern churches with regard to the sacraments in question. Postconciliar directives from the Secretariat, now Pontifical Council, for Promoting Christian Unity explain that the problem or hesitation arises because of the failure of some Western churches and ecclesial communities to share "the same ecclesiological and sacramental bases that particularly unite us to the Churches of the East."[99] More specifically, the expectation, spelled out in greater detail in the ecumenical dialogue, is that a church

[99] SPCU, decl, January 7, 1970, n. 6, *AAS* 62 (1970) 184–188, *DOL* 1029.

is to "have kept the substance of eucharistic teaching, the sacrament of orders, and apostolic succession"[100] in order to be judged as having valid sacraments of penance, Eucharist, and anointing of the sick.

Some guidance in this matter is provided by Vatican II's Decree on Ecumenism, which singles out the Anglican communion among Western churches and ecclesial communities as one occupying "a special place among those communions in which Catholic traditions and institutions in part continue to exist."[101] There has been, however, no formal judgment published by the Apostolic See concerning the Anglican or other Reformation communions as churches in the same condition or situation as the Eastern churches.

One affirmative Roman judgment has been reached with regard to the Polish National Catholic Church in the United States and Canada, namely, that this church is in the same condition as the Eastern churches, as just described, in regard to these three sacraments.[102]

The source of the developments in paragraphs two and three, as described above, to be found in the conciliar decree, *Orientalium Ecclesiarum,* affecting the Catholic Eastern churches and here made applicable to the Latin church as well. The text reads:

> When Eastern Christians separated in good faith from the Catholic Church request it of their own accord and are rightly disposed, they may be admitted to the sacraments of penance, eucharist, and anointing. Moreover, Catholics may request these same sacraments of ministers of other Eastern Churches having valid sacraments on any occasion of need or genuine spiritual bene-

fit when access to a Catholic priest is physically or morally impossible.[103]

In effect the canon, besides applying the Eastern norms to Catholics of the Latin church and to Catholic ministers, extends the concession to other non-Eastern churches, but only after the Apostolic See has made the favorable judgment referred to above.

Next, canon 844 makes a clear distinction between those covered by paragraph three and those covered by paragraph four. In that paragraph, a more limited exception is applied to other Christians not within full Catholic communion. With regard to the latter, who are neither Eastern Christians nor in the same situation as the East, the requirements are several: (1) a serious need (whether danger of death or, in the judgment of the diocesan bishop or of the conference of bishops, other grave necessity); (2) inability to approach their own minister; (3) a voluntary request by the recipient; (4) manifestation of Catholic faith concerning the sacrament in question; and (5) a proper disposition to receive the sacrament.

With regard to the serious need, the Secretariat for Promoting Christian Unity has given as examples the situation of persons in prison or under persecution or, aside from such cases of suffering and danger, the situation of persons who live at some distance from their own communion. This is of course not an exhaustive list of such cases, and the judgment belongs to the diocesan bishop or, if it should have issued norms or guidelines for such cases, the conference of bishops.[104]

Since, if possible, the principle of reciprocity should be respected in ecumenical relationships, paragraph five has been added to canon 844 so that no general norms will be issued on the matters in the three preceding paragraphs without consultation with at least a local authority of the respective church or community and preferably

---

[100] SPCU, communication, Oct. 17, 1973, n. 9, *AAS* 65 (1973) 616–619, *DOL* 1061.

[101] *UR* 13.

[102] Guidelines issued by the NCCB Committee on Ecumenical and Interreligious Affairs, March 13, 1996, after receiving a favorable decision from the Pontifical Council for Promoting Christian Unity.

[103] *OE* 27.

[104] SPCU, instr, June 1, 1972, n. 6, *AAS* 64 (1972) 518–525, *DOL* 1050.

with some superior authority. It is easy to see the underlying purpose: not to act unilaterally in possible opposition to the discipline of another church or ecclesial community.

Nevertheless, the language of paragraph five is carefully constructed to leave the diocesan bishop (and the conference of bishops, which has preemptive power in accord with Vatican II's Decree on Ecumenism)[105] free to act in individual cases or in issuing general norms even if the consultation with the competent authority of the other communion is not favorable.

Neither the canon as a whole nor the extensive elaborations of the problem address such particular questions as the seriousness of the need, all other conditions being verified, in cases of proposed sacramental sharing on occasions of legitimate and desirable presence and other participation in the eucharistic celebration of other communions, e.g., in connection with a marriage or an ecumenical dialogue. The language of the conciliar decree itself remains somewhat negative: such sharing "may not be regarded as a means to be used indiscriminately toward restoring Christian unity."[106]

In resolving individual cases and in the issuance of norms of a more general nature, both diocesan bishops and conferences of bishops should take into account the successive statements of the Secretariat, now Pontifical Council, for Promoting Christian Unity. The *Ecumenical Directory*[107] in particular is to be considered "not as a collection of advisory principles which one can freely accept or ignore but as an authentic instruction, an exposition of the discipline to which all who wish to serve ecumenism truly should submit themselves."[108]

Canon 671 of the Eastern code corresponds closely and almost verbatim to Latin canon 844,

which itself is in effect a development of *Orientalium Ecclesiarum* 27, as mentioned above. An additional Eastern code canon, 670, is much more expansive with regard to other kinds of liturgical sharing with other Christians: paragraph one affirms positively the legitimacy of Catholic presence and participation in worship for a just cause, while observing particular norms of the eparchial bishop or superior authority "by reason of the degree of communion [of the other church] with the Catholic Church"; paragraph two affirms the right of the eparchial bishop to permit other Christians to use a Catholic building or cemetery or church when needed. While treated positively in the *Ecumenical Directory,* these provisions of canon 670 of the Eastern code are omitted in the code of the Latin church.

More important, instead of Latin canon 745 and its limited if general requirements for the promotion of Christian unity, the Code of Canons of the Eastern Churches has two titles on ecumenical matters, thirteen canons in all. Title XVII (*CCEO* 896–901) deals with "Baptized Non-Catholics Coming into Full Communion with the Catholic Church." Title XVIII (*CCEO* 902–908) strongly insists upon the specifics of ecumenical activity and promotion: "Ecumenism or Fostering the Union of Christians."

For the special question of concelebration by priests under the presidency of a bishop or presbyter of another church, see canon 908 (and corresponding *CCEO* 702).

Repetition of Sacraments

Canon 845 — §1. Since the sacraments of baptism, confirmation, and orders imprint a character, they cannot be repeated.

§2. If after completing a diligent inquiry a prudent doubt still exists whether the sacraments mentioned in §1 were actually or validly conferred, they are to be conferred conditionally.

The canon does not enter into a doctrinal or theological exposition of the "character" of the

---

[105] *UR* 8.

[106] Quoted above from *UR* 8.

[107] Issued by SPCU in two parts in 1967 and 1970, and in a second, revised edition on March 25, 1993, "Directory for the Application of the Principles and Norms of Ecumenism." See especially nn. 116–136.

[108] SPCU, decl, January 7, 1970, n. 8, *DOL* 1031.

three sacraments,[109] which explains their permanent effect (membership in the Church in the case of baptism and confirmation, the pastoral office in the case of orders), but paragraph one states both the tradition and the discipline that these sacraments cannot be repeated.

The language of paragraph two has been carefully phrased to avoid even suggesting a "repetition" of these sacraments, which would be null and sacrilegious. It avoids saying "again" for the sake of precision, since a conditional celebration or ministration of one of these sacraments ("if you were not baptized..." etc.) by definition is not a second conferral of the sacrament. More important, the introduction of a requirement for a diligent investigation stresses that conditional conferral of these sacraments must not be indiscriminate.

Perhaps the principal instance of this possibility is in the reception of Christians into full communion with the Catholic Church. In reference to this, the *Roman Ritual* is explicit:

> The sacrament of baptism may not be repeated and conditional baptism is not permitted unless there is a prudent doubt about the fact or validity of the baptism already received. If after serious investigation it seems necessary—because of such prudent doubt—to confer baptism again conditionally, the minister should explain beforehand the reasons why baptism is conferred conditionally in this instance and he should administer it in the private form.[110]

This norm is in harmony with the careful exposition in the *Ecumenical Directory* on the subject.[111] The matter is also taken up in canon 869.

Observance of the Liturgical Laws

Canon 846 — §1. In celebrating the sacraments the liturgical books approved by competent authority are to be observed faithfully; accordingly, no one is to add, omit, or alter anything in them on one's own authority.

§2. The minister is to celebrate the sacraments according to the minister's own rite.

This canon has a complex history, at least for paragraph one. On the one hand, paragraph one appears to be unequivocal in requiring that the approved liturgical books be followed in the celebration of the seven sacraments; on the other hand, the reprobation of contrary customs in the 1917 code[112] has been suppressed. The substance of this norm remains unchanged from the old law, and it thus leaves open the traditional possibility of distinguishing the binding (preceptive) norms of the liturgical books affecting sacraments from those which are merely directive or even descriptive.

The second clause of paragraph one is derived literally from *Sacrosanctum Concilium* 22, §3 and, remotely, from the teaching of Pius XII. In 1947 the latter denied the right to moderate the liturgy to anyone other than the Roman Pontiff or to introduce change "at the decision of private persons, even if they belong to the orders of the clergy [including bishops]."[113] Having recognized that the regulation of the liturgy pertains to the Apostolic See *and* the diocesan bishop, and indeed also to the conferences of bishops of particular churches, *Sacrosanctum Concilium* 22, §3 reads: "No other person, not even if he is a priest, may on his own add, remove, or change anything in the liturgy."

The prohibition, which refers to the liturgy as a whole, is here applied to the seven sacraments only. This apparent mislocation of the canon is partially compensated for by canons which require the observance of the liturgical laws in the

---

[109] Trent, sess. VII, *de sac. in genere,* can. 9; sess. XXIII, *de ordine,* c. 4, can. 4.

[110] *RCIA,* appendix, "Rite of Receiving Baptized Christians into the Full Communion of the Catholic Church," n. 7, *DOL* 2482.

[111] See the lengthy treatment of baptism in nn. 92–101, especially 99–101.

[112] *CIC* 818, with reference to the eucharistic celebration.

[113] *Mediator Dei, AAS* 39 (1947) 544.

case of sacramentals (c. 1167, §2) and funerals (c. 1176, §2).

The prohibition of additions, omissions, and changes in the celebrations of the sacraments is made without qualification, but it must be qualified by the fact that the revised liturgical books themselves incorporate very numerous instances of accommodation (regularly at the discretion of the minister), i.e., permitted substitutions and choices, alternative texts, etc. The norm, moreover, does not speak to the possibility of contrary liturgical customs or pastoral situations in which the liturgical laws may not bind.[114]

The other paragraph of canon 846 is directed to the ministers of sacraments. The practical determination of the rite to be followed (Roman, Ambrosian, Byzantine, etc.) is made in accord with the proper rite of the (presiding) minister. In this case the text speaks of sacraments only, not of other liturgical services, to which it may logically be applied. The authentic ritual traditions of the different churches are to be respected;[115] if a minister has or may have the care of a community which is of a rite different from his own, he may be permitted by indult to preside according to that rite—the so-called bi-ritual faculty. In concelebration, the rite to be followed is that of the presiding celebrant.

One important difference from canon 733, §2 of the 1917 code is that the former law applied the norm to everyone (*unusquisque*), not merely to the minister. In the 1983 code it is an unrestricted matter for persons other than the minister of a sacrament; all Latin church Catholics may participate in other Catholic rites. But conciliar injunctions about the preservation of the rites of the several churches, especially those of the Eastern churches, which are in every way equal to the Roman and other rites of the Latin church, remain in full force.[116]

Holy Oils

Canon 847 — §1. In administering the sacraments in which holy oils must be used, the minister must use oils pressed from olives or other plants and, without prejudice to the prescript of can. 999, n. 2, consecrated or blessed recently by a bishop; he is not to use old oils unless it is necessary.

§2. The pastor is to obtain the holy oils from his own bishop and is to preserve them diligently with proper care.

This canon introduces the possibility of using plant oils other than olive oil in the celebration of the sacraments. The former requirement, to use olive oil or, in the case of chrism, olive oil and balsam, was altered in the revision of the pertinent part of the *Roman Pontifical:* "The matter suitable for a sacrament is olive oil or, according to local conditions, another oil extracted from plants.... Chrism is made of [olive or other plant] oil and some aromatic substance,"[117] that is, perfume or other sweet-smelling matter.

The same change was affirmed formally by Paul VI, in reference to the sacrament of anointing of the sick:

> Since olive oil, which has been prescribed until now for the valid celebration of the sacrament, is unobtainable or difficult to obtain in some parts of the world, we have decreed, at the request of a number of bishops, that from now on, according to circumstances, another kind of oil can also be used, provided it is derived from plants and is thus similar to olive oil.[118]

Although the actual use of the oil of catechumens is much diminished in the revised Roman rite, its significance is described traditionally along with the more important chrism and oil of the sick:

---

[114] See the treatment of the nature of liturgical law at the beginning of the commentary on Book IV.

[115] *SC* 3–4; *OE* 6. See also the instruction of January 6, 1996 for the Eastern liturgies, cited above.

[116] Ibid.; also *OE* 3.

[117] *ROils* 3–4, *DOL* 3863–3864.

[118] Apconst *Sacram Unctionem infirmorum,* November 30, 1972, *AAS* 65 (1973) 5–9, *DOL* 3317.

The Christian liturgy has adopted the Old Testament usage of anointing kings, priests, and prophets with consecratory oil because they prefigured Christ, whose name means "the anointed of the Lord."

Similarly, chrism is a sign that Christians, incorporated by baptism into the paschal mystery of Christ, dying, buried, and rising with him [see *SC* 6], are sharers in his kingly and prophetic priesthood and that by confirmation they receive the spiritual anointing of the Spirit who is given to them.

The oil of catechumens extends the effect of the baptismal exorcisms: it strengthens the candidates with the power to renounce the devil and sin before they go to the font of life for rebirth.

The oil of the sick, for the use of which James [see 5:14] is the witness, provides the sick with a remedy for both spiritual and bodily illness, so that they may have strength to bear up under evil and obtain pardon for their sins.[119]

The former requirement that the oil of the sick be blessed by the bishop is mitigated in canon 999. According to that canon, those who in law are equivalent to a diocesan bishop and, in case of necessity, any presbyter may bless this oil; the latter may do so only in the actual celebration of the sacrament (that is, not as a part of the Holy Thursday rite or on other occasions). A further exception, not mentioned in the present canon, is that "in the case of the baptism of adults, presbyters have the faculty to bless [the oil of catechumens] before the anointing at the designated stage of the catechumenate."[120] Moreover, the very use of the oil of catechumens in the baptism of children and in the Christian initiation of adults is dependent upon its continuance by decision of the conference of bishops; in the United States the pastoral need for and desirability of using the oil of cate-

chumens is left to the judgment of the minister. It is no longer used in the ordination of priests, whose hands are now ritually anointed with chrism instead.

Canon 734, §1 of the 1917 code was somewhat more specific about the use of oils recently blessed, speaking of those blessed by the bishop on the preceding Holy Thursday, but the substance of this prescription remains unchanged: for the worthy signification of the oils, they should be fresh and free flowing. The recodification suppresses, by omission, the practice of adding unblessed oil to the blessed oils when the supply runs low.[121]

Canon 735 of the former law may be quoted to indicate how the worthy custody of the blessed oils has now been expressed only in general terms:

> The parish priest must seek the holy oils from his ordinary and keep them carefully in the church in a safe and becoming place under lock; nor should he keep them at home, unless with the ordinary's permission, because of necessity or other reasonable cause.

The requirement of obtaining the oils from one's own bishop is retained: it is a sign of communion of the local parishes and congregations with the bishop and with one another. The keeping of the oils in church in the traditional ambry remains appropriate but is no longer specified, the canon asking only for a diligent and becoming custody. For the carrying of the oil of the sick on one's person and the like, see canon 1003, §3.

In this connection the *Roman Pontifical,* after giving the rite for the blessing and consecration of the oils in the chrism Mass, concludes: "In the sacristy the bishop may instruct the priests about the reverent use and safe custody of the holy oils."[122]

---

[119] *ROils* 2, *DOL* 3862.
[120] *ROils* 7, *DOL* 3867.

[121] *CIC* 734, §2.
[122] *ROils* 28.

Offerings for Sacraments

Canon 848 — The minister is to seek nothing for the administration of the sacraments beyond the offerings defined by competent authority, always taking care that the needy are not deprived of the assistance of the sacraments because of poverty.

Although the canons on simony in the 1917 code[123] no longer precede the canons on the sacraments, the present canon indicates a concern for the reverence due to sacred things, and especially the reverence due to sacraments, and the need to avoid even the appearance of profit-seeking from sacramental ministrations. Any request (or, a fortiori, exaction) of payment for the giving of a sacrament over and above the established offerings is prohibited.

[123] *CIC* 727–730.

According to canon 1264, 2°, the offering should be determined by the meeting of bishops of each ecclesiastical province; this is understood to be a limit imposed by decision of the provincial meeting, not a tax which must be exacted on the occasion of the celebration of sacraments (and sacramentals). Canon 952, §§1 and 2 makes a similar rule for the determination of the offering for Mass, which is the responsibility of the provincial council or the meeting of bishops of the province; in the absence of such a decree, the offering is left to diocesan custom. The canon does not prohibit offerings or gifts that are entirely voluntary, but there may be particular law on this matter.

The clause proscribing abuses by which the poor may be deprived of the sacraments because of their lack of offerings is new. Although the canon does not apply the principle to sacramentals and other acts of worship, the obligation exists apart from positive ecclesiastical law.

For the application of this norm to funeral rites, see canon 1181.

BIBLIOGRAPHY

Abbo, J., and J. Hannan. *The Sacred Canons.* 2nd ed. 2 vols. St. Louis: B. Herder, 1960.

BCL. *Environment and Art in Catholic Worship.* Washington, D.C.: NCCB, 1978.

Bugnini, A., ed. *Documenta Pontificia ad Instaurationem Liturgicam Spectantia (1903–1953).* Rome: Edizioni Liturgiche, 1953. II *(1953–1959).* Rome, 1959.

———. *La Riforma Liturgica (1948–1975).* Rome: CLV–Edizioni Liturgiche, 1983. In English: *The Reform of the Liturgy 1948–1975.* Collegeville: Liturgical Press, 1990.

Callewaert, C. *Liturgicae Institutiones.* 2 vols. Bruges, 1925–1929.

Chupungco, A. *Cultural Adaptation of the Liturgy.* New York: Paulist, 1982.

———. *Liturgies of the Future: The Process and Methods of Inculturation.* New York: Paulist, 1985.

Gordon, I. "Constitutio de S. Liturgia et canones 1256–1257." *P* 54 (1964) 89–140.

Green, T. "The Revision of Sacramental Law: Perspectives on the Sacraments Other Than Marriage." *Stud Can* 11 (1977) 261–327.

Huels, J. "The Interpretation of Liturgical Law." *W* 55 (1981) 218–327.

———. *The Interpretation of the Law on Communion under Both Kinds. CanLawStud* 505. Washington, D.C.: Catholic University of America, 1982.

———. *Liturgical Law: An Introduction.* American Essays in Liturgy, 4. Washington, D.C.: Pastoral Press, 1987.

ICEL. *Documents on the Liturgy, 1963–1979: Conciliar, Papal, and Curial Texts.* Collegeville: Liturgical Press, 1982.

———. *The Rites of the Catholic Church.* New York: Pueblo, 1976–.

Jones, C., G. Wainwright, and E. Yarnold, eds. *The Study of Liturgy.* New York: Oxford University, 1978.

Kaczynski, R., ed. *Enchiridion Documentorum Instaurationis Liturgicae.* I, Turin: Marietti, 1975; II, Rome, 1988.

Kelley, W. "The Authority of Liturgical Laws." *J* 28 (1968) 397–424.

The Liturgy Documents: A Parish Resource. 3rd ed. Chicago: Liturgy Training Pub., 1991.

McManus, F. "Liturgical Law." In *Handbook for Liturgical Studies,* ed. A. Chupungco, 1:399–420. Collegeville, Liturgical Press, 1997.

———. "Liturgical Law and Difficult Cases." *W* 48 (1974) 347–366.

———. *Sacramental Liturgy.* New York: Herder & Herder, 1967.

———. "The Juridical Power of the Bishop in the Constitution on the Sacred Liturgy." In *The Church and the Liturgy (Con),* 33–39. New York: Paulist, 1965.

———, ed. *Thirty Years of Liturgical Renewal: Statements of the Bishops' Committee on the Liturgy.* Washington, D.C.: NCCB, 1987.

Manzanares Marijuan, J. *Liturgia y Decentralización en Concilio Vaticano II.* Rome, 1970.

Martimort, A. "Structures and Laws of Liturgical Celebration." In *The Church at Prayer,* 1: 85–225. Collegeville: Liturgical Press, 1987.

Oppenheim, P. *Institutiones Systematico-historicae in Sacram Liturgiam.* Tom. II–IV, *Tractatus de Iure Liturgico.* Turin: Marietti, 1939–1940.

Regatillo, E. *Ius Sacramentarium.* 3rd ed. Santander: Sal Terrae, 1960.

Richstatter, T. *Liturgical Law: New Style, New Spirit.* Chicago: Franciscan Herald, 1977.

———. "Changing Style of Liturgical Law." *J* 38 (1978) 415–425.

Ryan, G. T. *The Sacristy Manual.* Chicago: Liturgy Training Pub., 1993.

Seasoltz, R. K. *The New Liturgy: A Documentation, 1903–1965.* New York: Herder & Herder, 1966.

———. *New Liturgy, New Laws.* Collegeville: Liturgical Press, 1980.

TITLE I
BAPTISM
[cc. 849–878]

By treating baptism before all the other sacraments in part one of Book IV, the code affirms this sacrament as the precondition for a valid reception of all the others[1] and as the first of the three sacraments necessary for full Christian initiation.[2] The thirty canons that comprise this title reflect the distinction between adult and infant baptism and the corresponding disciplines presented in the current rituals.[3]

An introductory canon summarizes the Church's faith in the sacrament and the fundamental canonical requirements for its validity. The remaining canons fall under the following five chapter headings: the celebration of the sacrament (cc. 850–860); the minister (cc. 861–863); those to be baptized (cc. 864–871); sponsors (cc. 872–874); and registration and proof of baptism (cc. 875–878). With necessary adaptations, the code's treatment of all the other sacraments, except marriage, follows this same structure.

The chief difference between the present legislation and that of the 1917 code is the current law's insistence on the importance of preparation for baptism, particularly for adult candidates, and, to a lesser extent, for parents of infants. This insistence on preparation is a corollary to canon 836 which sees all Christian worship as an action "which proceeds from faith and is based on it," and charges sacred ministers to "arouse and enlighten this faith diligently, especially through the ministry of the word, which gives birth to and nourishes the faith." So strong is the code's insistence on preparation for baptism that it calls for

[1] Canons 842, §1 and 849.
[2] Canon 842, §2.
[3] *RCIA, RBaptC.*

the deferral of the sacrament when the faith which preparation is meant to foster is totally lacking.

Since the promulgation of the revised code in 1983 there have been no substantial authoritative developments in the law governing or the rites for celebrating baptism or the other sacraments of initiation. However, the widespread use of the *Rite of Christian Initiation of Adults* has led to a variety of pastoral applications of the canons and increased implementation of options and adaptations permitted in the *Roman Ritual.*

The Code of Canons of the Eastern Churches has fewer canons on baptism (17 canons) than does the revised Latin code (30 canons). One reason for this difference is that the Latin code makes a more pronounced distinction between the remote preparation, the required catechesis, and the rite to be used for the baptism of adults and those for the baptism of infants than does the Eastern code. Other factors which account for fewer canons in the Eastern code are the absence in it of any explicit treatment of the blessing of the baptismal water (c. 853), the distinction between baptism by pouring and baptism by immersion (c. 854), the name taken or given at baptism (c. 855), the days on which baptism may be celebrated (c. 856), the baptismal font (c. 858), the referral of adults fourteen years of age or older to the bishop for baptism (c. 863), the conferral of confirmation on adults who are baptized and the celebration of baptism during the celebration of the Eucharist (c. 866), the cases of doubts about the reception of baptism and conditional baptism (c. 869), and the specification of the number of sponsors and their sex (c. 873). The ordering of the canons in the Eastern code is also markedly different from that in the Latin code.

There are also three rather substantive differences between the two codes. First, the Latin code prohibits the celebration of baptism in a private home except in cases of necessity (c. 860, §1) whereas the law for the Eastern churches allows it in less extreme situations (*CCEO* 687, §2). Second, the Eastern code does not restrict the celebration of baptism in hospitals as the Latin code does (c. 860, §2). Third, while the Latin code calls for the celebration of infant baptism within the first weeks after birth (c. 867, §1), the Eastern code calls for the baptism of infants as soon as possible after birth (*CCEO* 686, §1).

Essential Theological and Canonical Elements

Canon 849 — Baptism, the gateway to the sacraments and necessary for salvation by actual reception or at least by desire, is validly conferred only by a washing of true water with the proper form of words. Through baptism men and women are freed from sin, are reborn as children of God, and, configured to Christ by an indelible character, are incorporated into the Church.

This introductory canon summarizes the most important dogmatic and theological elements of baptism, together with some of its juridical elements. The first of the dogmatic elements mentioned is the affirmation, drawn from a number of sources including the parallel canon of the 1917 code,[4] *Lumen gentium* 11,[5] and *Introduction to the Rite of Christian Initiation* 3,[6] that baptism is the gateway to the other sacraments. This notion of baptism as the gateway to all the other sacraments is also presented in more juridical terms in several canons already treated: canon 96, which deals with baptism as the means by which one is incorporated into the Church and constituted as a person in it; canon 204, §1, which treats baptism as the means by which one is incorporated into Christ and thereby participates in the threefold office of priest, prophet, and king; and canon 842,

§1, which explicitly treats baptism as the first of the sacraments to be received. This primacy of baptism will also be repeated in numerous places in the code, particularly in the introductory canons to the other sacraments.[7]

A second dogmatic assertion of the canon is the necessity of baptism for salvation.[8] The fundamental necessity of baptism is the rationale underlying subsequent canons dealing with baptism in cases of necessity.[9] The doctrine of the necessity of baptism is also the key to interpreting correctly the whole discipline of baptism, in particular the canonical and liturgical regulations for the proper minister of the sacrament.[10]

The necessity of baptism explains the canon's reference to baptism of desire, even though such baptism carries with it no juridical consequences,[11] to qualify properly the principle that outside the Church there is no salvation, which is the dogmatic foundation of this canon. Without specific mention of baptism of desire, the canon would appear to state incorrectly that baptism with water is necessary for salvation.[12]

Lumen gentium reaffirmed the teaching of the Church regarding baptism of desire in a passage cited by the annotated *Codex Iuris Canonici* as a source for the present canon:

> Those who, through no fault of their own, do not know the Gospel of Christ or his Church,

---

[4] *CIC* 737, §1.
[5] *LG* 11: "The faithful are appointed by their baptismal character to Christian religious worship."
[6] *IGIC* 3: "Baptism, the door to life and to the kingdom of God, is the first sacrament of the new Law."
[7] Canons 879; 889, §1; 912; 959; 996; 998; 1004; 1024; 1055; 1061, §1.
[8] Trent, sess. VI, *de iustificatione*, c. 4; sess. VII, *Decr. de sacramentis, de sacramento baptismi*, c. 5. *CCC* 1129, 1157.
[9] See cc. 853, 857, 860–862, 871.
[10] E. Tejero, in *Pamplona ComEng*, 561.
[11] *CCEO* 675, §1, the parallel to the Latin code, does not refer explicitly to baptism of desire in connection with the necessity of baptism for salvation. Rather, it states in §2: "Only by the actual reception of baptism is a person made capable for the other sacraments."
[12] *Ench* 3866–3873. For a clarification of the relationship between baptism by water and by desire in interpreting the doctrine that "outside the Church there is no salvation," see CDF, *Letter to the Archbishop of Boston*, August 8, 1949, *Ench* 3866–3873; *CLD* 3, 525–530.

but who nevertheless seek God with a sincere heart, and, moved by grace, try in their actions to do his will as they know it through the dictates of their conscience—those too may achieve eternal salvation. Nor shall divine providence deny the assistance necessary for salvation to those who, without any fault of theirs, have not yet arrived at an explicit knowledge of God, and who, not without grace, strive to lead a good life.[13]

During the final redaction of the 1980 schema of the code, it was suggested that the distinction between baptism with water and baptism of desire should be dropped since the latter produced no juridic effects. The suggestion was rejected because of the doctrinal importance of the distinction.[14] The canon makes no explicit reference to baptism of blood, which occurs when a catechumen suffers martyrdom, since it is a specific form of baptism of desire.[15]

The canon delineates four other theological consequences of baptism.[16] It frees one from sin, both original and personal,[17] a truth recapitulated in the Creed's formula: "one baptism for the forgiveness of sins." Baptism gives one a new birth as a child of God.[18] *Lumen gentium* 40 affirmed that the followers of Christ have been made "children of God in the baptism of faith and partakers of the divine nature." This baptismal regeneration in Christ also recalls that the baptized possess the "spirit of adoption" (Rom 8:15) and have become "sharers of the divine nature" (2 Pet 1:4).[19]

---

[13] *LG* 16.

[14] *Comm* 15 (1983) 177.

[15] *CCC* 1258.

[16] *CCEO* 675, §1 mentions the same four theological consequences.

[17] Trent, sess. VI, *de iustificatione,* c. 4; *CCC* 1213, 1226 and, with regard to infants who die without baptism, *CCC* 1261.

[18] *CCC* 1214.

[19] See also *Roman Catechism* II, 5 which describes baptism as a "sacrament of regeneration" by means of water and the word; Council of Florence, *Bulla reunionis Armenorum, Ench* 1314.

Baptism configures one to Christ[20] because through it one becomes a participant in the salvific mystery of Christ's death and resurrection. The indelible character of baptism mentioned in canon 849 stresses the permanence of this configuration. Configuration to Christ also has ecclesial effects: the baptized are made sharers in the priestly, prophetic, and royal functions of Christ and his mission (c. 204). Incorporation into the Church is an effect of configuration to Christ. Canon 849 does not explicitly mention the properly juridical effects of incorporation into Christ and the Church since they have already been articulated in canon 96 (constitution of juridical personality in the Church with the duties and rights proper to Christians in keeping with their status and condition).

Lumen gentium 11 is the source from which canon 849 draws these primarily theological elements of baptism:

> Incorporated into the Church by Baptism, the faithful are appointed by their baptismal character to Christian religious worship; reborn as children of God, they must profess before all the faith they have received from God through the Church.

The *Rite of Baptism* expands considerably on these theological elements.[21]

When all of these theological effects are considered together, it can be said that baptism confers three distinct kinds of "personality" on the baptized: a spiritual or mystical personality through their relationship to God begun in baptism; an ecclesial personality as members of the Christian faithful by their incorporation into the Church; and a juridical personality with canonical rights and obligations by their being placed in a relationship to the hierarchy and the rest of the Christian faithful. The weight or importance to be attributed to these three types of personality depends on the perspective from which they are viewed. From the perspective of the ultimate mission of the Church,

---

[20] 1 Cor 12:12–13; 27.

[21] *IGIC* 3–6.

the salvation of humankind, the mystical personality is clearly the most important. From the perspective of the Church as the people of God, united and distinguished by a network of mutual rights and duties, the juridical personality takes precedence over the others. Ecclesial personality functions as the bridge between the other two personalities since, on the one hand, it signifies a bond of love which exists among all the Christian faithful, and, on the other, it is clearly oriented toward the final end of the Church as the universal sacrament of salvation.[22]

The explicitly juridical elements of the canon are the requirements for a valid baptism: a washing with water accompanied by the proper verbal formula. "Washing" underscores the root meaning of the Greek *baptizein,* to "plunge" or "immerse,"[23] and anticipates the preference in canon 854 for immersion over pouring, a preference made more forcefully in the *Rite.*[24] Baptism by sprinkling, which was explicitly permitted by the 1917 code,[25] is not mentioned in the present code.[26]

The canon specifies only that the water used for baptism must be "true" water. The parallel canon of the 1917 code[27] had added the qualifier "natural," which has not been retained in the present canon. Concerning the words or form to be used in the sacrament, the canon stipulates only that they be the "proper" (*debita*) form, and that they accompany the immersion or pouring. The proper words in the Latin church are: "N., I baptize you in the name of the Father, and of the Son, and of the Holy Spirit." The *Rite* adds that in the case of immersion, the person or the person's head is to be immersed three times, and, in the case of pouring, the water is to be poured three times over the head while the words of the form are being invoked.[28]

Earlier commentators noted other conditions that must be met for the words used in baptism to be "proper." The words must clearly indicate the one baptizing as well as the one being baptized and the fact that the baptism is indeed taking place at that moment. Thus, if one person pronounces the baptismal formula and another person immerses or pours the water, the baptism is invalid, since the separation of the two actions renders the words inaccurate. The one who pronounces the words, "*I baptize* you," is not the same person who actually baptizes by pouring the water. The words must also refer to the Trinity of persons both individually and in their unity.[29] Were one to refer to the Trinity by such terms as "creator, sustainer, and sanctifier," the baptism would also be invalid since these words do not refer to a Trinity of *persons,* even if it were the intention of the minister to do so. Some commentators also hold invalid the baptism in which the formula used is, "You are baptized . . . ," since it does not express the fact that the baptism is being conferred at the present moment. However, this formula is and has long been customary in the Eastern churches. Therefore, it would be difficult to argue that the use of this formula by a minister in the Western church results in the invalidity of the baptism. If the minister omits the person's name and says simply, "I baptize you . . . ," this omission would not invalidate the baptism. The word "you" clearly indicates the person being baptized, just as the pronoun "I" clearly indicates the one baptizing.[30]

Two requirements for validity not mentioned in the canon are the proper intention of the baptizing minister and, in the baptism of an adult, the proper intention of the one being baptized. It appears that the canon simply takes the presence of both of these intentions for granted.[31] However,

---

[22] D. Composta, in *Urbaniana Com,* 526–527.
[23] *CCC* 1214.
[24] *IGIC* 22.
[25] *CIC* 758.
[26] Canon 854.
[27] *CIC* 737, §1.
[28] *RCIA* 226 (USA). All references to the *RCIA* are given for the Latin *editio typica,* unless "USA" follows the ref-

erence, in which case the approved American translation is to be understood.
[29] E. Regatillo, *Ius Sacramentarium,* 3rd ed. (Santander: Sal Terrae, 1960) 33, n. 38.
[30] See J. Huels, "Canon 849: Defect of Form in Baptism," in *CLSA Advisory Opinions 1984–1993* (Washington, D.C.: CLSA, 1995) 252–253.
[31] F. McManus, in *CLSA Com,* 615.

the necessity of the proper intention of both the minister and the adult recipient of baptism is alluded to in canon 869, §2, where an insoluble doubt about the sufficiency of either intention allows baptism to be celebrated conditionally.

CHAPTER I
THE CELEBRATION OF BAPTISM
[cc. 850–860]

All of the chapters in Book IV which treat the celebration of the various sacraments highlight only particular and rather diverse aspects of their celebration, and, in accord with canon 2, leave a much fuller presentation of the laws and rubrics governing the celebration of the sacraments to the various ritual books. The chapter on the celebration of baptism is no exception. Consequently, the following eleven canons present an organized, but also uneven, overview of the celebration: a summary treatment of the proper rite for the celebration (c. 850); preparation requirements for adult and infant baptism (c. 851); the use of reason as the criterion for determining whether the adult or infant rite is to be used (c. 852); two additional norms on the use of water (cc. 853–854); the name given at baptism (c. 855); and five canons—almost half the canons in the chapter—on the time and place of baptism (cc. 856–860).

Two features of this chapter should also be noted. First, the canons are consistently attentive to the distinctions between adult and infant baptism. They reflect the normative nature of the initiation of adults much more than do the canons on confirmation. Second, the canons exhibit an awareness, explicit or implicit, that, when baptism is celebrated in cases of urgency, the requirements of all of these canons may be omitted.

The Rites of Baptism

Canon 850 — Baptism is administered according to the order prescribed in the approved liturgical books, except in case of urgent necessity when
only those things required for the validity of the sacrament must be observed.

The first of these canons deals with the question of the liturgical rite to be followed and directs the minister to "approved liturgical books" of the *Roman Ritual,* the *Rite of Christian Initiation of Adults* (1972),[32] and the *Rite of Baptism for Children* (rev. 1973),[33] together with the adaptations of these rites approved by the episcopal conference[34] and the diocesan bishop,[35] as well as the wide range of options and adaptations available to the minister.[36] Each of these rites is really a collection of different rites for baptism in varying circumstances.

The principal liturgical rite for the celebration of adult baptism is called "Rite of Christian Initiation of Adults," which envisions a rather lengthy process during which the candidate is led through successive periods of preparation which are punctuated by liturgical celebrations of the different stages that mark the adult's progress toward baptism. The *Rite* makes clear the normative quality of this first rite by presenting it as the first option to be used and by grouping all the other rites in part two as "Rites for Particular Circumstances." It is this first rite to which the following canon (c. 851) will explicitly refer when it describes the kind of baptismal preparation required for adults.

Part two of the *Rite of Christian Initiation of Adults* contains five other rites for adult baptism, which are secondary to the normative rite referred to above. The first of these derivative rites presented in the English translation of the *editio typica*[37] is "Christian Initiation of Children Who Have

---

[32] *DOL* 2328–2488.

[33] *DOL* 2285–2315.

[34] *RCIA* 64–66, *DOL* 2391–2392. *National Statutes for the Catechumenate* (Washington, D.C.: NCCB, 1986); *RBaptC* 30–33, *DOL* 2279–2282.

[35] *RCIA* 63, *DOL* 2393.

[36] *RCIA* 64, *DOL* 2394. *RBaptC* 34–35, *DOL* 2283–2284.

[37] It should be noted that the English translation of the Latin *editio typica* rearranges the order of the "Rites for Particular Circumstances." The rationale for the reordering of the rites is presented in the foreword to the English edition, viii–xi.

Reached Catechetical Age."[38] Although children of catechetical age are not usually considered to be adults, canon 852, §1 stipulates that the adult rite is to be used when the candidate for baptism has reached the use of reason. This rite, then, responds to the need for adaptations of the normative rite in the case of unbaptized children.

"Christian Initiation of Adults in Exceptional Circumstances"[39] is the second derivative rite. Exceptional circumstances include sickness, old age, change of residence, or a long absence for travel which may prevent a candidate from celebrating all the rites of the catechumenal process.[40] The extraordinary circumstances permitting the use of the abbreviated rite also are present when the candidate has already attained "a depth of Christian conversion and a degree of religious maturity that lead the local bishop to decide that the candidate may receive baptism without delay."[41] In both cases the permission of the bishop is needed to dispense with the use of the normative rite.

The *Rite of Christian Initiation of Adults* provides for an even more abbreviated celebration of baptism in the rite entitled "Christian Initiation of a Person in Danger of Death,"[42] which is designed particularly for use by catechists and other lay persons when priests or deacons are unavailable.[43] The present canon authorizes the minister to omit any merely liturgical rite in danger of death situations "when only those things required for the validity of the sacrament must be observed."[44] But, when there is still some time for a celebration slightly expanded beyond what is required for validity, the *Rite* directs the priest or deacon minister to use the rite for exceptional circumstances with appropriate adaptations for the case of a dying person.[45]

The two final rites of Christian initiation are not rites of baptism at all. "Preparation of Uncatechized Adults for Confirmation and Eucharist"[46] is designed for those who have already been baptized as Catholics, but who never completed the catechesis which would have led them to confirmation and Eucharist at the usual ages.

The final rite in the English edition, "Reception of Baptized Christians into the Full Communion of the Catholic Church,"[47] is, in the Latin edition, an appendix to the previously treated collection of rites. It is designed for those who were previously baptized in a non-Catholic church or ecclesial community and who now seek full communion with the Catholic Church. If there is an insoluble doubt about the validity of the previous baptism, conditional baptism can be celebrated "in the private form" (c. 869, §2).[48] Here, "private form" is to be understood in its usual sense: not public, or not in public view.[49]

All of these separate rites of the *Rite of Christian Initiation of Adults* call for the reception of confirmation and Eucharist in keeping with canon 842, §2 which requires the celebration of all three sacraments for full Christian initiation.

While adult baptism is recognized as normative because it most clearly demonstrates baptism as a sacrament of conversion and highlights the interrelationship among the three sacraments of initiation, the most frequently used form of celebration is the baptism of infants or of children who have not reached the age of reason.[50] The *Rite of Baptism for Children* is also a collection of rites for different circumstances. The "Rite of Baptism for Several Children"[51] is presented first since it demonstrates more clearly the communal nature of the celebration of the sacraments (c. 837, §2).[52] The "Rite of Baptism for

---

[38] *RCIA* 306–346, *DOL* 2458–2475.
[39] *RCIA* 331–369 (USA), *DOL* 2433–2441.
[40] *RCIA* 274, *DOL* 2438.
[41] *RCIA* 240, *DOL* 2433.
[42] *RCIA* 370–399 (USA), *DOL* 2442–2446.
[43] *RCIA* 280, *DOL* 2444.
[44] *RCIA* 281, *DOL* 2445.
[45] *RCIA* 280, *DOL* 2444.

[46] *RCIA* 400–474 (USA), *DOL* 2447–2457.
[47] *RCIA* 473–504 (USA), *DOL* 2476–2488.
[48] *RCIA*, Appendix, 7.
[49] McManus, in *CSLA Com*, 615.
[50] See c. 852.
[51] *RBaptC* 32–71.
[52] See McManus, in *CLSA Com*, 616.

One Child"[53] is identical with the communal rite, except for grammatical changes from the plural to the singular. The "Rite of Baptism for a Large Number of Children"[54] makes allowances for multiple ministers and for communal responses so as not to unduly prolong the celebration.

A shorter version of the rite, the "Rite of Baptism Administered by a Catechist When No Priest or Deacon is Available,"[55] is to be used when a priest or deacon is absent (c. 861, §2). It alters the formulas for the blessings and allows for multiple ministers and other adaptations in the case of a large number of children to be baptized. Shortest of all is the "Rite of Baptism for Children in Danger of Death When No Priest or Deacon Is Available."[56] If, however, a priest or deacon is readily available, the *Rite* allows him to use this shorter form; if a priest is present and has chrism, it also directs him to confer confirmation in place of the postbaptismal anointing.[57] The "Rite of Bringing a Baptized Child to the Church"[58] is designed to complete the baptisms of children who were previously baptized, usually in case of emergency or danger-of-death situations, by celebrating the other rites, blessings, and anointings which were omitted.

Thus, when canon 850 states that baptism is administered "according to the order prescribed in the approved liturgical books," it is referring to all these rites, with the understanding that the rite appropriate for the age of the candidate and circumstances attending the baptism will be used. As already noted, the rites themselves make provision for conferring baptism in cases of necessity or danger-of-death situations, but they permit the reduction of the celebration to what is required for validity alone only when there is absolutely no time for any additional ceremonies.[59]

---

[53] *RBaptC* 72–106.

[54] *RBaptC* 107–131.

[55] *RBaptC* 132–164.

[56] *RBaptC* 157–164.

[57] *RBaptC* 22.

[58] *RBaptC* 165–185.

[59] Canon 683 of the Eastern code determines the rite to be followed; the exception for danger of death is treated in *CCEO* 676.

Formation for Baptism

Canon 851 — The celebration of baptism must be prepared properly; consequently:

1° an adult who intends to receive baptism is to be admitted to the catechumenate and is to be led insofar as possible through the various stages to sacramental initiation, according to the order of initiation adapted by the conference of bishops and the special norms issued by it;

2° the parents of an infant to be baptized and those who are to undertake the function of sponsor are to be instructed properly on the meaning of this sacrament and the obligations attached to it. The pastor personally or through others is to take care that the parents are properly instructed through both pastoral advice and common prayer, bringing several families together and, where possible, visiting them.

The canon is an application to baptism of the norms of canon 836, which enjoins ordained ministers to nurture the faith and progressively enlighten it particularly through the ministry of the word, and of canon 843, §2, which charges all the Christian faithful to be diligent that "those who seek the sacraments are prepared to receive them by proper evangelization and catechetical instruction." First, the canon stipulates the preparation necessary for adults seeking baptism, and presents the restored catechumenate as the preferred context for this preparation. The Eastern code makes no reference to the preparation of adults for baptism through the various periods and stages of the catechumenate. Second, the canon treats the preparation of parents who have presented their children for baptism as the responsibility primarily of the pastor.[60]

The normative *ordo* for the Christian initiation of adults is the celebration of the rites of the cate-

---

[60] Canon 686, §2 of the Eastern code has a less specific treatment of the pastor's responsibilities regarding infant baptism.

chumenate in successive stages. The use of this *ordo* became mandatory in the United States on September 1, 1988. The canon identifies this rite as the preferred form of preparation for adults seeking baptism.[61]

The preparation called for is not limited to the "various stages" (*varios gradus*) which the canon mentions. The *Rite* uses the term "stages" to denote the principal liturgical celebrations[62] which mark the adult's transition from one period of formation to the next. The significance of these principal rites can be appreciated only when they are viewed in connection with the respective purposes of the four periods of formation.

The first period of formation is termed "precatechumenate," a time set aside for evangelization which leads the adult to an initial conversion "away from sin and into the mystery of God's love."[63] There is no fixed duration or structure for this period of inquiry and introduction to gospel values. During this period the *Rite* calls the adults inquirers. The initial conversion which this period strives for is celebrated by the first stage, the "Rite of Acceptance into the Order of Catechumens."[64]

Acceptance into the catechumenate has a double effect. First, the person receives a new title. The adult is no longer termed an "inquirer," but a "catechumen." Second, the adult acquires the first rudimentary elements of juridic status in the Church. According to conciliar teaching, catechumens who seek incorporation into the Church are by that very intention joined to it. "With love and solicitude Mother Church already embraces them as her own."[65] *Ad gentes* states that catechumens

"are already joined to the Church, already part of Christ's household."[66]

The council's recognition of the status of catechumens in the Church is incorporated into the code in canon 206 which describes them as "joined to [the Church] in a special way" and entitles them to "various prerogatives which are proper to Christians," and which include blessings and sacramentals,[67] repeated anointings with the oil of catechumens,[68] marriage with a baptized Catholic[69] or with another catechumen,[70] and Christian burial.[71] Since their incorporation into the Church comes only with baptism,[72] catechumens are not yet *persons* in the Church and subjects of rights and duties.[73] However, in light of conciliar teaching and the revised canons, they cannot simply be equated with the rest of the unbaptized. One can say that, by their acceptance into the catechumenate, their baptism has already begun. While not yet unqualified members of the faithful, they can already be recognized as Catholic Christians by their initial conversion to Christ.

Acceptance into the catechumenate marks the transition to the second period of formation, the catechumenate properly speaking.[74] It is an extended period of formation in Christian living through catechesis, prayer, and witness to living the gospel. The Church sustains catechumens throughout this period by a variety of liturgical rites.[75] The period of the catechumenate is brought

---

[61] For an overview of the development of the catechumenate in Vatican Council II and the genesis of its inclusion in this canon, see McManus, in *CLSA Com,* 616–617.

[62] The *Rite* calls for many kinds of liturgical celebrations in addition to the principal rites. Blessings, anointings, scrutinies, presentation of the Creed and of the Lord's Prayer, and exorcisms are celebrated primarily during the period of the catechumenate proper and the period of enlightenment.

[63] *RCIA* 9–13, *DOL* 2336–2340.

[64] *RCIA* 14–20, *DOL* 2341–2347.

[65] *LG* 14.

[66] *AG* 14.

[67] Canon 1170.

[68] *RCIA* 98–101 (USA).

[69] *Rite of Marriage* 55.

[70] *RCIA* 18, *DOL* 2345.

[71] Canon 1183.

[72] Canon 96.

[73] Ibid.

[74] In common parlance, "catechumenate" is often used to refer to the entire formation period for adult initiation. The *Rite* uses it in the strict sense as referring only to the second period of formation.

[75] *RCIA* 19–20, *DOL* 2346–2347. These rites include celebrations of the word, blessings, anointings, presentations of the Creed and the Lord's Prayer, the rite of *ephphetha* and the rite of sending the catechumens to the Rite of

to a close with the celebration of the second principal rite: election or enrollment of names.[76]

After the rite of election, the adults are called the "elect" and begin the third period of formation, that of enlightenment,[77] which is to coincide with the season of Lent. More than a continuation of catechetical instruction, the period of enlightenment is a time for spiritual reflection in order to "enlighten the minds and hearts of the elect with a deeper knowledge of Christ."[78] As was the case during the period of the catechumenate, the period of enlightenment is punctuated by numerous liturgical rites.[79] This period is brought to completion at the Easter Vigil with the celebration of baptism, confirmation, and Eucharist, after which the elect are called "neophytes."

Christian initiation does not end with the reception of these three sacraments. The fourth and final period of initiation is that of postbaptismal catechesis or mystagogy.[80] Its purpose is to afford the neophytes the opportunity to deepen their grasp of the paschal mystery by sharing in the Eucharist, meditating on the gospel, and doing works of charity.[81] Although this period ends in a formal sense on Pentecost,[82] ongoing postbaptismal catechesis and continuing conversion are the responsibility of all the baptized. In fact, this kind of ongoing formation is what the second half

of the canon requires for parents who present their children for baptism.

It is apparent that the preparation of adults envisioned by the *Rite* is far more than the mere "instruction" called for in the 1917 code.[83] It is a process of immersion into the Christian life through catechesis, prayer, spiritual growth and direction, apostolic service, and commitment to Christ, all of which are sustained and deepened through liturgical celebration. It is this kind of formation that the canon sees as the norm of adult preparation for baptism. However, it does not require that all the elements of this normative process be celebrated in every case, but only "insofar as possible." This qualification is in harmony with the *Rite* which itself provides for abbreviated formation processes in various circumstances, as was noted above. The *Rite*'s insistence on the normative character of the catechumenal process is stronger than the canon's, since it notes that any abbreviated form of adult initiation, except in danger-of-death situations, is allowed only in individual cases, and even then only with permission of the bishop.[84]

When Vatican Council II called for the restoration of the catechumenate,[85] it intended to leave this restoration to the discretion of each local ordinary, who would "set up the program of the catechumenate and lay down norms according to local needs."[86] However, the present code grants conferences of bishops authority in regulating the liturgy, an authority which preempts that of the local diocesan bishop.[87] The canon reflects this postconciliar development when it says that adult formation for baptism is to be carried out "according to the order of initiation adapted by the conference of bishops and the special norms issued by it."[88]

Election when it is celebrated by the bishop. See *RCIA* 81–117 (USA).

[76] "The step is called election because the acceptance made by the Church is founded on the election by God, in whose name the Church acts. The step is also called the enrollment of names because as a pledge of fidelity the candidates inscribe their names in the book that lists those who have been chosen for initiation." *RCIA* 22, *DOL* 2349.

[77] *RCIA* 138–205 (USA).

[78] *RCIA* 25, *DOL* 2352.

[79] These rites include the scrutinies, the presentations of the Creed and the Lord's Prayer if these were not celebrated during the catechumenal period, the recitation of the Creed, and the choosing of a baptismal name. See *RCIA* 140–205 (USA).

[80] *RCIA* 37–40, *DOL* 2364–2367. *RCIA* 235–239, *DOL* 2428–2432.

[81] *RCIA* 37, *DOL* 2364.

[82] *RCIA* 237, *DOL* 2430.

[83] *CIC* 752, §2.

[84] *RCIA* 240, *DOL* 2433. See also "National Statutes for the Catechumenate," in *RCIA* (USA), Appendix III, nn. 19–20.

[85] *SC* 64.

[86] Ibid.

[87] Canon 838, §§3–4.

[88] The special norms for the United States are the *National Statutes for the Catechumenate*.

The second half of canon 851 also treats the preparation of adults, not as candidates for baptism but as parents or sponsors presenting infants for the sacrament. The canon mentions summarily only two aspects of this preparation: instruction and formation. The parents and godparents are to be instructed about the meaning of the sacrament and the responsibilities proper to parents and godparents which arise from it. The *Rite of Baptism for Children* adds only that parents "should be provided with suitable means such as books, letters addressed to them, and catechisms designed for families."[89]

The canon also calls for the formation of parents and godparents through pastoral direction and common prayer. The text is taken almost verbatim from the *Rite*.[90] The true importance of preparation for parents presenting their children for baptism will be highlighted again in canon 868, §1, 2° which provides that, when the parents or those who care for a child in their place have received no preparation and there is no hope that they will participate in postbaptismal catechesis, the child's baptism may be postponed indefinitely.

The canon recognizes the role of the pastor in the preparation of parents, and notes that his responsibilities may be shared with other members of the community. The *Rite* also notes the role of the bishop in the preparation process by recalling his duty "to coordinate such pastoral efforts in the diocese, with the help also of deacons and lay people."[91]

Clarification of the Terms "Adult" and "Infant"

Canon 852 — §1. The prescripts of the canons on adult baptism are to be applied to all those who, no longer infants, have attained the use of reason.

§2. A person who is not responsible for oneself (*non sui compos*) is also regarded as an infant with respect to baptism.

Since the previous canon distinguished between the baptisms of adults and those of infants, the present canon defines the terms "adult" and "infant" for purposes of determining those subject to the prescriptions of the canons on adult baptism.[92] According to canon 97, §2, those who have not completed their seventh year are, for canonical purposes, "infants" and, therefore, not responsible for themselves (*non sui compos*). After the completion of their seventh year, they are presumed to have the use of reason (to be *sui compos*). The present canon does not make any explicit reference to chronological age, but applies these principles of age *and* use of reason to determine those subject to the prescriptions for adult baptism. For purposes of baptism, anyone who is not an infant is an adult, is presumed to have the use of reason, and is, therefore, subject to the requirements and rites for adult baptism.

Children over the age of seven are subject to the prescriptions of the canons regulating adult baptism because they "are capable of receiving and nurturing a personal faith and of recognizing an obligation in conscience"[93] and can undertake the personal preparation for baptism characteristic of an adult. From this perspective, the second paragraph of the canon is not an exception to the first, but rather an application of it. Should one not have the use of reason, then one is not an adult, and is, therefore, a subject for infant baptism, regardless of chronological age.

The *Rite of Christian Initiation of Adults* provides a rite for children and adolescents considered to be adults in virtue of canon 852, "Christian Initiation of Children Who Have Reached Catechetical Age."[94] Christian initiation of children and adolescents is to be extended over time and re-

---

[89] *RBaptC* 5, 1, *DOL* 2289.
[90] Ibid.
[91] *RBaptC* 7, 1, *DOL* 2291.

[92] Canon 682 of the Eastern code distinguishes between adult and infant candidates for baptism, but only in terms of the preparation required for the sacrament. No distinction between adults and infants is made in terms of the rite of baptism to be used in its celebration.
[93] *RCIA* 306, *DOL* 2458.
[94] *RCIA* 306–346, *DOL* 2458–2475.

quires their personal conversion, in proportion to their age, as well as catechesis and education.[95]

The extent to which pastoral practice follows these prescriptions for Christian initiation of children is difficult to assess. The *National Statutes for the Catechumenate* state that the formation of children considered to be adults by canon 851, §1 "should follow the general pattern of the ordinary catechumenate as far as possible" and that they are to receive all the sacraments of initiation at the Easter Vigil, together with the older catechumens.[96] Nevertheless, it appears that pastoral practice varies. Not infrequently, parishes have no process other than the religious education program or Catholic school by which unbaptized children of catechetical age can be prepared for Christian initiation. Younger children of catechetical age are often baptized in the infant rite in a ceremony that does not allow them to receive the Eucharist immediately following their baptisms. Often confirmation is delayed until the newly baptized children can receive this sacrament along with their classmates in the religious education program or Catholic school who were baptized as infants. By qualifying the mandatory character of the catechumenate for children with the phrase "as far as possible," the *National Statutes* provide room for exceptions. Nevertheless, exceptions should be made only when no program exists for catechumenal formation of children of catechetical age. The intention of the law is clearly that some structure for the catechumenal formation for children ought to exist. In order to comply with the law, parishes able to establish such a structure should not delay in doing so.

A further distinction regarding age will be introduced in canon 863: the baptisms of adults who are fourteen or older are to be referred to the bishop. The present canon does not deal with this distinction, since its primary concern is the determination of the rite to be used, not the proper minister of the sacrament.

---

[95] *RCIA* 307, *DOL* 2459.
[96] *NSC* 18.

Baptismal Water

Canon 853 — Apart from a case of necessity, the water to be used in conferring baptism must be blessed according to the prescripts of the liturgical books.

Water used for baptism should be blessed, normally during the celebration of the baptism itself.[97] Using unblessed water does not affect the validity of the sacrament since canon 849, which treats the requirements for validity, does not mention blessing the water. The rites for both adult and infant baptism provide for blessing the water during the course of the celebration.[98] In adult baptism, the water is normally blessed during the Easter Vigil. If water blessed during the Easter Vigil is available, it is to be used but not to be blessed again for any subsequent infant baptism during the Easter season.[99] When the minister of baptism is not a priest or deacon but a catechist or other person designated to baptize, the water cannot be blessed during the ceremony, but, if possible, water already blessed should be used.

The *Rite* notes some additional concerns about the water used at baptism. It should be clean, so that the baptism can express more fully its sacramental symbolism as a washing. Clean water is also required for hygienic reasons. In cold climates, the water should be heated prior to the celebration. The ritual also recognizes that the baptismal font may be equipped with running water. In this case, the water is blessed while flowing. Outside the Easter season, the water should be blessed at every celebration of the sacrament.[100]

Immersion and Pouring

Canon 854 — Baptism is to be conferred either by immersion or by pouring; the prescripts of the conference of bishops are to be observed.

[97] The Eastern code makes no reference to the blessing of baptismal water.
[98] *RCIA* 311 (USA); *RBaptC* 54.
[99] *SC* 70; *IGIC* 21, *DOL* 2270.
[100] *IGIC* 18, 20–21, *DOL* 2267, 2269–2270.

The canon mentions only two licit manners in which the water is to be used in the celebration of baptism: immersion of the person into the water, or pouring the water over the person.[101] The order in which these two manners of baptizing appear in the canon indicates a preference for immersion. Immersion was the common manner of baptizing from the earliest days of the Church until the end of the twelfth century when pouring became more common.[102] The *Roman Ritual* of Paul V (1614) allowed baptism by immersion to continue in those areas where this custom had been retained.[103] Immersion is still the ordinary practice of the Eastern churches. Immersion is a particularly appropriate symbol of the rebirth that comes with baptism by dying with Christ and rising with him to new life.[104] The preference for immersion over pouring (infusion) is also affirmed in the *Rite*.[105]

The 1917 code allowed baptism by immersion and pouring, and by a combination of both in which the candidates stood in a pool and water was poured over their heads. Neither the present canon nor the *Rite* explicitly allows for this combination. The *Rite* does allow partial immersion, in which only the head of the person is immersed.[106] While the ritual expresses a clear preference for baptism by immersion, it also cautions that local custom should be taken into account "so that in different traditions and circumstances there will be a clear understanding that this washing is not just a purification rite but the sacrament of being joined to Christ."[107]

Although the 1917 code permitted sprinkling as a licit manner of baptizing, the revised code does not retain this option. During the revision of the code it was proposed that sprinkling be retained. However, it was suppressed on the ground that the use of water is meant symbolize a real washing, something that sprinkling fails to do.[108] The *Rite* notes that "either immersion or infusion *should* be chosen."[109] This use of "should" implies that while sprinkling would be illicit, it would nonetheless be valid.

Finally, the canon notes that, when baptizing either by immersion or by pouring, the prescriptions of the bishops' conference are to be followed. In the United States, such prescriptions are found in the *National Statutes for the Catechumenate,* which state a clear preference for immersion, even if only partial immersion.[110] The provision for more frequent use of immersion may require remodeling the baptistries in churches and should be a factor considered carefully when new churches are being planned.[111]

Baptismal Name

Canon 855 — Parents, sponsors, and the pastor are to take care that a name foreign to Christian sensibility is not given.

The 1917 code imposed restrictions on the choice of names given at baptism.[112] They had to be "Christian names," that is, names of saints or names derived from Christian virtues (Faith, Constance, Joy, etc.). At infant baptisms, the minister had to add Christian names if the parents themselves had not chosen them.

The first relaxation of these restrictions, intended particularly for areas where non-Christian

---

[101] The Eastern code makes no distinction between pouring and immersion in the canons on baptism.

[102] *Chiappetta Com,* 3133.

[103] *Rituale Romanum,* tit. II, cap. II, 20: "Where there exists the custom of baptizing by immersion ... "

[104] Rom 6:3–11; Col 2:12.

[105] *IGIC* 22, *DOL* 2271: "Either the rite of immersion, which is more suitable as a symbol of participation in the death and resurrection of Christ, or the rite of infusion may lawfully be used in the celebration of baptism."

[106] *RCIA* 220 (USA).

[107] *RCIA* 32, *DOL* 2359.

[108] *Comm* 13 (1981) 216–217.

[109] *RCIA* 32, *DOL* 2359. Emphasis added.

[110] *NSC* 17.

[111] BCL, *Environment and Art in Catholic Worship* (Washington, D.C.: NCCB, 1978) 39, n. 76.

[112] *CIC* 761.

religions predominated, came with the restoration of the catechumenate in 1972. Although a Christian name was still preferred, a name more reflective of the culture could be chosen, provided that it had a Christian meaning.[113]

The canon allows even greater flexibility.[114] While the preference for a Christian name continues, any name can be given, as long as it is not offensive to Christian belief. Since what is offensive varies from culture to culture, the canon provides ample latitude to accommodate these cultural differences.[115] Moreover, the canon entrusts the responsibility of naming the child primarily to the parents, and only secondarily to the sponsor and pastor. Canon 761 of the 1917 code had entrusted this responsibility primarily to the pastor.

In the *Rite of Infant Baptism,* the conferral of the baptismal name takes place through a question posed to the parents by the minister at the very beginning of the celebration ("What name do you give your child?"). The *Rite of Christian Initiation of Adults* has a distinct rite for the conferral of a name and allows for the possibility that catechumens may change their names as a result of their conversion to Christ.[116] The *Rite* grants conferences of bishops the authority to issue norms regarding the candidates' choosing new names "in regions where it is the practice of non-Christian religions to give a new name to initiates."[117] The National Conference of Catholic Bishops has determined that, in the United States, a new name is normally not to be given at the baptism of adults. However, it has given diocesan bishops the discretion to permit the giving of new names to persons from those cultures in which it is the practice of non-Christian religions to take or give a new name.

---

[113]*RCIA* 88. Note that the text now reflects the greater freedom in choosing a name as does c. 855.

[114]The Eastern code makes no reference at all to the name given at baptism.

[115]D. Kelly, in *CLSGBI Com,* 471.

[116]*RCIA* 73, 200, 202 (USA).

[117]*RCIA* 33, *DOL* 2392, n. 4.

Time of Celebration

Canon 856 — Although baptism can be celebrated on any day, it is nevertheless recommended that it be celebrated ordinarily on Sunday or, if possible, at the Easter Vigil.

Baptism can be celebrated on any day. However, the canon singles out Sundays and the Easter Vigil as particularly appropriate times for the celebration of the sacrament.[118] The reasons for this preference are explained in the ritual:

> To bring out the paschal character of baptism, it is recommended that the sacrament be celebrated during the Easter Vigil or on Sunday, when the Church commemorates the Lord's resurrection.[119]

By citing the Easter Vigil first, the ritual implies that it takes precedence over Sundays, even in the case of children.

The canon, however, states an explicit preference for celebrating baptism on Sundays and adds that the Easter Vigil is appropriate "if possible." During the code revision process, it was suggested that, since adult baptism is the normative rite, the canon should indicate a marked preference for the Easter Vigil, rather than for "any Sunday."[120] The suggestion was rejected on the ground, that, while the Easter Vigil is the "privileged" time for baptism, it is not the time at which baptism is "usually" celebrated. Moreover, to delay baptism for several months, perhaps for as much as a year, until the Easter Vigil, would be contrary to the prescription of canon 867 which obliges parents to present their children for baptism within the first weeks after birth. Thus, the canon reflects the *normal* as opposed to the *normative* time for baptism, at least in the case of infant baptism. In the

---

[118]The Eastern code mentions no preferences for or restrictions on the time of celebration of baptism.

[119]*RBaptC* 9, *DOL* 2293.

[120]*Comm* 15 (1983) 179.

case of adults, the *Rite* continues to see the Easter Vigil as both the normal and normative time for celebrating baptism.[121] Only for serious pastoral reasons can the sacraments of initiation for adults be celebrated outside the Easter Vigil, and then preferably during the Easter season. In addition, the program of immediate preparation of adults for initiation during Lent must be retained.[122]

The canon says nothing about celebrating infant baptism during a Sunday Mass. The ritual highlights the benefit of celebrating baptism during Sunday Mass, but cautions that "this should not be done too often."[123]

Place of Baptism

Canon 857 — §1. Apart from a case of necessity, the proper place of baptism is a church or oratory.

§2. As a rule an adult is to be baptized in his or her parish church and an infant in the parish church of the parents unless a just cause suggests otherwise.

Canons 857–860 deal with different aspects of the place where baptism can be celebrated. Canon 857 deals with the sacred building where the baptism is to take place. Canon 858 treats the baptismal font. Canons 859 and 860 give exceptions to the general rule stated in canon 857 that baptism should be celebrated in a church or oratory.

Canon 837, §2 asserts the general principle that sacraments should be celebrated in the assembly of the faithful. Since a parish church is the place *par excellence* where the faithful assemble, the canon states a strong preference for the celebration of baptism in a church or oratory[124] (§1), especially a parish church (§2). Although baptism can be permitted in an oratory, not all the faithful may have

general access to an oratory. Consequently, the canon treats oratories as secondary places for baptism. However, private chapels[125] are not mentioned as ordinary places for baptism. Thus, the selection of the place for baptism is not dictated by parochial rights as it was in canon 773 of the 1917 code, but rather by theological and liturgical concerns. Since baptism incorporates a person into the universal community of the faithful, this incorporation is best signified through incorporation into a concrete local community in and through which "there comes into being the one and only Catholic Church" (*LG* 23).[126] So important is this principle that the canon allows the celebration of baptism in a place other than a church or oratory only in cases of necessity. Examples of cases of necessity are treated in canons 859 and 860.

The *Rite of Infant Baptism* explains the reason for the preference for celebrating baptism in a parish church: "so that baptism may clearly appear as the sacrament of the Church's faith and of incorporation into the people of God."[127] That these celebrations in the parish should be communal is seen clearly in the *Rite*'s stipulation that, in the case of infant baptism, all the babies to be baptized on a given day are to be baptized in a common celebration and not in separate celebrations at different times on the same day.[128]

Canon 857, §2 determines the specific parish church in which a person's baptism is to take place. "As a rule," the baptism is to be celebrated in the parish church of the adult candidates, or the parish church of the parents of infants. The canon does not require that the parish church of baptism be the one proper to a person by reason of his or her domicile.[129] It has become increasingly common for people to belong to parishes which are theirs not by reason of their domicile, but by reason of their personal choice. The law presumes that adult candidates for baptism have completed

---

[121] *RCIA* 49, *DOL* 2376.
[122] *RCIA* 58, *DOL* 2385.
[123] *RBaptC* 9.
[124] For "church," see c. 1214; for "oratory," see c. 1223. Note that c. 687, §1 of the Eastern code also stipulates a "parish church" for the celebration of baptism, with the same exception regarding the case of necessity. It also makes an exception for "legitimate customs."

[125] See c. 1226.
[126] See *Chiappetta Com,* 3137.
[127] *RBaptC* 10, *DOL* 2294.
[128] *IGIC* 27, *DOL* 2276.
[129] See c. 107.

the catechumenal stages of baptismal preparation. As a result, they have acquired a proper parish through their acceptance into the catechumenate. The proper parish church of infants is that of their parents. Canon 857, §2 allows the celebration of baptism in a church or oratory other than the parish church proper to an adult candidate or an infant's parents for a just cause. Only in cases of necessity may baptism be lawfully celebrated outside a church or oratory; only a "just cause," a much less demanding standard, is required to celebrate baptism in a church or oratory other than the parish church proper to the adult candidates or the infants' parents.

The Baptismal Font

Canon 858 — §1. Every parish church is to have a baptismal font, without prejudice to the cumulative right already acquired by other churches.

§2. After having heard the local pastor, the local ordinary can permit or order for the convenience of the faithful that there also be a baptismal font in another church or oratory within the boundaries of the parish.

The requirement that every parish church have a baptismal font is simply a corollary of the previous canon which designates the parish church as the normal and preferred place for the celebration of baptism.[130] Nevertheless, like canon 774, §1 of the 1917 code, canon 858 recognizes that churches or oratories other than parish churches may have acquired the right to have a baptismal font and allows them the right to retain them. To prevent abuses that had detracted from the role of the parish church as the primary place for celebrating baptism, canon 774, §1 of the 1917 code revoked and reprobated privileges and customs that granted non-parochial churches and oratories rights to baptismal fonts and that excluded the rights of parish churches to possess baptismal fonts.[131] Thus, any

right to a baptismal font possessed by a non-parochial church or oratory is cumulative with that of the parish church. Other churches *may* have a baptismal font, but a parish church *must* have one.[132]

Like canon 774, §2 of the 1917 code, the present canon allows the local ordinary to grant other churches or oratories the right to a baptismal font, if there is a pastoral need for additional places for baptism within the territory of a parish. Distance from the parish church (as suggested by the following canon 859) and ethnic, cultural, or other sub-groupings within the parish are examples of situations in which appropriate pastoral convenience may call for a baptismal font in a non-parochial church or oratory. The requirement that, before permitting a non-parochial church or oratory to have a baptismal font, the local ordinary at least consult with the pastor is meant to ensure that the addition of a baptismal font in another part of the parish will not undermine the unity of the parish or lessen the importance of the parish church as the normal place of assembly of the faithful.

The canon's primary concern is that every parish church have a baptismal font, even though, if the pastoral good of the faithful so requires, other churches or oratories may have already acquired or may yet acquire fonts. The ritual treats such matters as the construction of the font[133] and its location within the church,[134] and notes that it "should be spotlessly clean."[135]

Other Churches or Fitting Places

Canon 859 — If because of distance or other circumstances the one to be baptized cannot go or be brought to the parish church or to the other church or oratory mentioned in can. 858, §2 without grave inconvenience, baptism can and must be conferred in another nearer church or oratory, or even in another fitting place.

---

[130] The Eastern code makes no reference to the baptismal font.

[131] See the commentary on c. 24, §2 on reprobated customs.

[132] See McManus, in *CLSA Com,* 621.

[133] *IGIC* 19, *DOL* 2268.

[134] *IGIC* 25, *DOL* 2274.

[135] *IGIC* 19.

If it is gravely inconvenient for an adult candidate to come to or for parents to bring their infants to their parish church, there is a "just cause" for allowing baptism to be celebrated elsewhere (c. 857, §2).[136] When going to one of the churches or oratories that have acquired the right to a baptismal font (c. 858, §2) would also result in grave inconvenience, baptism may be celebrated in a "fitting place" other than a church or oratory. The canon does not specify any criteria for judging a place to be "fitting," nor does it require any permissions for celebrating the baptism in a fitting place other than a church or oratory. However, the following canon will make it clear that, apart from cases of necessity, private homes and hospitals are not considered to be fitting places for baptism, since to celebrate baptism in these places requires the permission, respectively, of the local ordinary or diocesan bishop.

If the conditions for celebrating baptism in another church or oratory or in another fitting place are met, then the minister "can" and "must" celebrate baptism. The "can" indicates that it is not illicit to celebrate baptism in this other location; the "must" emphasizes that the fact baptism takes place is more important than where it is celebrated.

Private Homes and Hospitals

Canon 860 — §1. Apart from a case of necessity, baptism is not to be conferred in private houses, unless the local ordinary has permitted it for a grave cause.

§2. Except in a case of necessity or for some other compelling pastoral reason, baptism is not to be celebrated in hospitals unless the diocesan bishop has established otherwise.

Although baptism in a parish church is the norm, the code recognizes exceptions to this norm to allow the lawful celebration of baptism elsewhere. Canon 860 represents an "exception" to the other exceptions, since additional permissions are required to celebrate baptisms in private homes and hospitals. This restriction flows from the principle which allows all the other exceptional places of baptism to be permissible: they allow for a representative assembly of the faithful that is called for in every celebration of the sacraments.[137]

Private homes and hospitals are treated in successive paragraphs because the circumstances and the authorities competent to grant the permission required for the liceity of baptisms in these places are different. The canon allows the celebration of baptism in a private home without the prior permission of the local ordinary only in cases of necessity.[138] This norm is consistent with the *Rite*.[139] However, the *Rite* limits the cases of necessity when no permission is required for baptisms in private homes to the situation of danger of death and does not foresee that baptisms might be permitted in private homes in other circumstances. The canon is more permissive than the *Rite*, however, since it allows for celebration of baptism in a private home not only in danger-of-death situations, but also for some other "grave cause" and with the permission of the local ordinary.

The second paragraph deals with the more pastorally frequent situation of baptizing in hospitals. The canon respects the tension between two basic principles: sacraments are to be celebrated in a communal setting, and baptism is necessary for salvation.[140] In deference to the communal nature of sacramental celebration, the canon restricts baptism in hospitals more than it does baptism in pri-

---

[136] The Eastern code does not make explicit reference to "another" church for celebrating baptism. Canon 687, §1 of the Eastern code states that baptism is to be celebrated "in a parish church" and does not specify, as does c. 857, §2 of the Latin code, either the parish church of an adult or the parish church of the parents in the case of infant baptism. Thus, there is no need for the Eastern code to make any provision for "another" church.

[137] See c. 837, §2.

[138] Canon 687, §2 of the Eastern code is less restrictive. It allows for the celebration of baptism in a private home "according to the prescriptions of particular law or with the permission of the local hierarch." It does not require a "grave cause" as does the Latin code.

[139] *RBaptC* 12, *DOL* 2296.

[140] See commentary on c. 849.

vate homes by requiring the permission of the diocesan bishop, not merely that of the local ordinary.[141] In deference to the necessity of baptism for salvation, it allows baptism in hospitals not only in danger-of-death situations but for "some *other* compelling pastoral reason." This second paragraph draws heavily from the *Rite*.[142]

CHAPTER II
THE MINISTER OF BAPTISM
[cc. 861–863]

Three canons treat the minister of baptism. Canon 861 defines the ordinary and extraordinary ministers and the circumstances in which the latter may lawfully baptize; canon 862 imposes territorial restrictions on the exercise of this ministry by ordinary ministers; and canon 863 notes the circumstances in which the diocesan bishop is the proper minister of baptism.

Ordinary and Extraordinary Ministers

Canon 861 — §1. The ordinary minister of baptism is a bishop, a presbyter, or a deacon, without prejudice to the prescript of can. 530, n. 1.

§2. When an ordinary minister is absent or impeded, a catechist or another person designated for this function by the local ordinary, or in a case of necessity any person with the right intention, confers baptism licitly. Pastors of souls, especially the pastor of a parish, are to be concerned that the Christian faithful are taught the correct way to baptize.

The ritual uses the term "ministry" to include a wide variety of functions during both the preparation for and celebration of baptism. Parents, sponsors, godparents, catechists, indeed the whole community of the faithful are mentioned explicitly as those charged with ministries and offices in

baptism.[143] The code uses "minister" in the more restricted sense of "celebrant" as is clear in the three canons of this chapter. The ordinary minister of baptism is one who has received the sacrament of orders: a bishop, a presbyter, or a deacon.[144]

Canon 741 of the 1917 code did not include deacons among the ordinary ministers of baptism. It spoke of deacons only as extraordinary ministers of baptism who needed a justifying reason to baptize as well as the permission of the local ordinary or pastor. However, this discipline was abrogated long before the promulgation of the present code. Vatican Council II "restored the diaconate as a distinct and permanent rank of the hierarchy" and conferred upon deacons "the duty to administer baptism solemnly."[145]

A slight restriction on the ability of ordinary ministers to baptize lawfully is suggested by the reference in canon 861 to canon 530, 1° which lists those functions that, while no longer reserved to the pastor, are considered as "especially entrusted" to him. Among these is the right to administer baptism in his parish.

All persons (including non-Catholics and even non-Christians) are considered potential extraordinary ministers of baptism. The second paragraph of canon 861 delineates two situations in which extraordinary ministers may baptize lawfully. The first is when an ordinary minister of baptism is not present or is impeded from administering the sacrament. The term "absent" means that a cleric is not physically present. The term "impeded" suggests that a minister may be present or could easily be present, but is physically or

---

[141] The Eastern code places no restrictions on celebrating baptism in a hospital.

[142] *RBaptC* 13, *DOL* 2297.

[143] *RCIA* 41–48, *DOL* 2368–2375. *RBaptC* 4–7, *DOL* 2288–2291.

[144] Canon 677, §§1–2 of the Eastern code speaks only of a priest as the ordinary minister of baptism, since chrismation, which only a priest can confer, immediately follows baptism in ordinary situations. The deacon may serve only as an extraordinary minister of baptism in cases of necessity.

[145] *LG* 29. See also *IGIC* 11, *DOL* 2260. The conciliar directive that deacons confer solemn baptism entered canon law with Paul VI, *mp Sacrum diaconatus ordinem*, v, 22, 2, June 18, 1967, *AAS* 59 (1967) 702.

morally prevented from exercising his function. For example, a laicized priest or a priest under suspension or some other censure is impeded from administering baptism. In these cases, a lay person previously deputed by the local ordinary is the extraordinary minister. In keeping with *Sacrosanctum Concilium* 68, the canon specifically mentions catechists as lay people who can appropriately be deputed as extraordinary ministers of baptism.[146] The canon does not, however, reserve this ministry to catechists, as is obvious from the words "or another person."[147] The ritual provides the "Rite of Baptism for Children Administered by a Catechist When No Priest or Deacon Is Available," an abbreviated rite for baptism by an extraordinary minister when ordained ministers are absent or impeded.[148] These situations are common in mission territories as well as in areas of this country which suffer from a scarcity of priests and deacons.

Paragraph two also provides for an extraordinary minister in cases of necessity. The *Rite* is clearer than the canon that these cases of necessity are danger-of-death situations. In these situations, the extraordinary minister is any person, baptized or not, as long as he or she has the right intention, that is, the intention of the Church. For danger-of-death situations, the ritual provides a "Rite of Baptism for Children in Danger of Death When No

Priest or Deacon Is Available." Even an ordinary minister may use this rite if he is present.[149] This rite reflects the concern of the Church that, even in situations of danger of death, the celebration of baptism should have an ecclesial dimension. If death is imminent, however, then all ceremonies are omitted except those required for the validity of baptism: the washing with water and the proper verbal formula.

Because any member of the faithful is a potential minister of baptism, the final sentence in the canon is an exhortation to parish priests, and to pastors in particular, to ensure that the faithful are properly educated in the correct way to baptize. The *Rite* explains:

> All lay persons, since they belong to the priestly people, and especially parents and, by reason of their work, catechists, midwives, family or social workers or nurses of the sick, as well as physicians and surgeons, should be thoroughly aware, according to their capacities, of the proper method of baptizing in case of emergency. They should be taught by parish priests, deacons, and catechists. Bishops should provide appropriate means within their diocese for such instruction.[150]

Territorial Restrictions on Ordinary Ministers

Canon 862 — Except in a case of necessity, no one is permitted to confer baptism in the territory of another without the required permission, not even upon his own subjects.

Although this canon makes no explicit reference to canon 530, its prohibition of any ordinary minister, including a bishop, from administering baptism outside his own territory is an application of the same principle. The restriction can also be seen as an application of canon 857, §2 which identifies the subject's own parish church as the

---

[146] Canon 677, §2 of the Eastern code presents, in descending order of priority, a more specific listing of who can function as the minister of baptism in cases of necessity: deacons, another cleric, a member of an institute of consecrated life, or any member of the Christian faithful. Parents can baptize their child only if none of these other people is available.

[147] During the final revision of the 1980 schema of the code, it was proposed that if the canon was going to mention a specific office, such as catechist, the canon should also explicitly mention lectors and acolytes as instituted ministries prior to mentioning catechists. Otherwise, no specific office should be singled out. The suggestion was rejected on the grounds that the catechist's role as minister of baptism was already foreseen by the council. See *Comm* 15 (1983) 180. See *SC* 68. See also *RBaptC* 20, *DOL* 2304.

[148] *RBaptC* 132–134, *DOL* 2304–2306.

[149] *RBaptC* 21, *DOL* 2305.

[150] *IGIC* 17, *DOL* 2266.

preferred place for baptism. Since by baptism one enters the Christian community, the local parish church where the faith of the baptized will be nourished and grow is normally the appropriate place for a person to enter the community of the faithful. The principle underlying the present canon is evident in canons 877–878 which deal with proving and recording baptisms. When proof of baptism is needed, the baptismal register of the person's home parish is the usual place to seek it.

The canon admits of only two circumstances when one ordinary minister of baptism can lawfully celebrate baptism in the territory of another: (1) when there a case of necessity, and (2) when the minister has received the required, and not merely tacit, permission of the one in whose territory he is baptizing. The seriousness of this norm is underscored by the phrase "not even upon his own subjects."

A Restriction on Presbyter and Deacon Ministers

Canon 863 — The baptism of adults, at least of those who have completed their fourteenth year, is to be deferred to the diocesan bishop so that he himself administers it if he has judged it expedient.

The final canon dealing with the proper minister of baptism presents the special case of the baptisms of adults fourteen and older; the celebration of baptism in this case is reserved to the bishop in conformity with the *Rite of Christian Initiation of Adults*.[151] The *Rite* affirms that the bishop is the preferred minister of all the sacraments of initiation, as well as of the rite of election, for all adults,[152] since the whole catechumenal process is placed under his care as the chief liturgist of the diocese.[153] The *Rite* specifies only "the bishop," although it obviously intends the diocesan bishop.

The canon is more explicit on this point than is the ritual.

Nevertheless, the canon calls for the referral to the bishop not of the baptisms of all those considered "adults" for purposes of the rite,[154] but only the baptisms of those fourteen years of age and older.[155] The reason for choosing fourteen years of age is not clear. It does not correspond with the age of majority in the new code (eighteen),[156] nor does it correspond with the age of discretion when young people become adults for purposes of baptism (c. 852, §1). Canon 817 of the 1980 schema had proposed sixteen as the age at which adult baptisms should be referred to the bishop. One member of the committee noted that the choice of the age of sixteen was rather arbitrary.[157] Although the age was later reduced to fourteen, it still appears just as arbitrary.

The canon does not require the diocesan bishop to be the minister of baptism for all adults over fourteen years of age, but obliges the pastor to refer these candidates to him in the event the bishop wants to reserve their baptism to himself. The canon does not prevent the bishop from reserving to himself the baptism of adults younger than fourteen, nor from setting a higher age for those adults whose baptisms he reserves to himself, nor even from reserving all adult baptisms to himself. Should the bishop decide not to reserve any adult baptisms to himself, he can grant the faculty to his priests to be the minister of baptism for all adults over the age of fourteen.

CHAPTER III
THOSE TO BE BAPTIZED
[cc. 864–871]

The title of this chapter, "Those to Be Baptized," is a significant departure from that of the

---

[151] The Eastern code makes no mention of referring candidates for baptism to an ecclesiastical authority higher than the priest.

[152] *RCIA* 44, *DOL* 2371. See also *IGIC* 12, *DOL* 2261.

[153] See c. 835, §1.

[154] See c. 852, §1.

[155] The parallel in the *CIC* 744 also refers adults to the bishop but with no specification of age.

[156] See c. 97, §1.

[157] *Comm* 15 (1983) 180.

former code which used the term "recipients" or "subjects" of baptism. These terms are not appropriate for adults "who consciously and freely seek the living God and enter the way of faith and conversion as the Holy Spirit opens their hearts."[158]

The topics of these eight canons are logically, although unevenly, divided into four areas: the universal capacity for baptism (c. 864); the requisites for adult baptism (cc. 865–866); the requisites for infant baptism (cc. 867–868); and the special situations of conditional baptism, baptism of abandoned children, and baptism of aborted fetuses (cc. 869–871). The canons carefully distinguish between adult baptism and infant baptism. By presenting the canons on adult baptism first, the code implicitly recognizes the normative character of adult baptism.

Universal Capacity for Baptism

Canon 864 — Every person not yet baptized and only such a person is capable of baptism.

This primarily theological canon, reflecting Jesus' command that the gospel be preached to all nations and to every creature,[159] is a concise statement of the absolute universality of the juridic capacity for baptism from which no human being can ever be excluded. To be a "person" is to be capable of baptism. Since the contemporary understanding of the human person necessarily entails that a person is a living being, the canon does not repeat the stipulation of the former code that the person be alive.[160] Neither baptism nor any other sacrament can ever be conferred on a person who is clearly dead.

That the person be "not yet baptized" recognizes that the ontological change which baptism produces is by its very nature unrepeatable as already noted in canon 845, §1. Once one has been claimed by Christ through baptism, the relationship is absolutely irrevocable.

Because the gift of salvation is offered to all human beings without exception, nothing whatsoever can ever eradicate this capacity. Although the juridic capacity for baptism is unconditional, the following canons deal with various conditions of age, Christian education, and preparation that affect the lawfulness of the exercise of a person's fundamental capacity for baptism.[161] These conditions must be fulfilled for the full effect of the sacrament to take root in those to be baptized.

Prerequisites for Adult Candidates

Canon 865 — §1. For an adult to be baptized, the person must have manifested the intention to receive baptism, have been instructed sufficiently about the truths of the faith and Christian obligations, and have been tested in the Christian life through the catechumenate. The adult is also to be urged to have sorrow for personal sins.

§2. An adult in danger of death can be baptized if, having some knowledge of the principal truths of the faith, the person has manifested in any way at all the intention to receive baptism and promises to observe the commandments of the Christian religion.

The canon distinguishes between the prerequisites for adult baptism in normal situations and in danger-of-death situations.[162] Paragraph one lists four requirements which differ in their importance for the validity of the baptism.[163] These requirements touch the faculties constitutive of the human person: the will, the intellect, the capacity to act, and the human heart.

First, an adult's intention to be baptized must be externally manifested, since the will to be baptized is necessary for the validity of the sacrament. No one who has attained the use of reason can be validly baptized against his or her will.[164] The

---

[158] *RCIA* 1, *DOL* 2328.
[159] See Mt 28:19; Mk 16:15–16; Jn 3:5.
[160] *CIC* 745.

[161] See Composta, in *Urbaniana Com,* 331.
[162] Canon 682 of the Eastern code calls for similar prerequisites.
[163] See Tejero, in *Pamplona ComEng,* 566.
[164] SCOf, *In foliis,* August 3, 1860, *Collectanea S. Congregationis de propaganda fide; seu Decreta, instructiones,*

manifest will called for by the canon can be a positive act of the will (the opposite of an express will not to be baptized), a habitual act of the will (an act of the will made previously and never withdrawn), or even an implicit act of the will (the adult or, more commonly, a child of catechetical age intends to do what Christ or the Church wills). Because even a habitual or implicit intention suffices for the validity of baptism, an unconscious person can also be baptized validly, even though the canon does not explicitly state this.[165] Without some intention of the will, an adult cannot be validly baptized. The concern of the canon is not directly with the actual will of the adult candidate, which is required for the validity of baptism, but rather with the external manifestation of that will, which is required for the liceity of baptism.

The second prerequisite touches on the faculty of the intellect: the adult must be sufficiently instructed in the truths of the faith and in the obligations which that faith entails. The canon does not make explicit what those truths of the faith are. They would certainly include the existence of God, the final judgment, the incarnation, the resurrection, and the Trinity.[166] The canon presumes the preparation supplied through the catechumenal process called for in canon 851, 1°. When candidates for adult baptism are children of catechetical age, the requirement of knowledge of the faith must be adapted to their age, as well as to their culture, background, and environment.[167] Although knowledge of the faith is obviously important for one called to live the Christian life, only a person's lack of faith itself and not deficiencies in knowledge of the faith would invalidate his or her baptism.

The third requirement touches on the adult's capacity to put his or her faith into practice by living the Christian life and considers the catechu-

menate as the locus *par excellence* for testing that faith. The catechumenate also furnishes the pastor and community the opportunity to evaluate the candidate's readiness for baptism.

The final requirement touches on the heart: the adult is urged to express sorrow for personal sins which will be forgiven through reception of the sacrament. The term "urged" indicates that such sorrow for personal sins is not required for the validity of baptism.

Paragraph two treats the prerequisites for adult baptism in danger-of-death situations. With the exception of sorrow for sin, which is not mentioned in this paragraph, the prerequisites are relaxations of the requirements listed in paragraph one. The will to be baptized may be manifested "in any way at all," even only implicitly. The adult is required to have only "some" knowledge of the "principal truths" of the faith, not the "sufficient" knowledge called for in normal situations. Nor does the canon mention the obligations flowing from that faith as did paragraph one; rather, the adult is to promise "to observe the commandments of the Christian religion" if he or she recovers.

These mitigated prerequisites are to be presumed to have been met when the adult is a catechumen. When the adult in danger of death is not a catechumen, he or she

> must give serious indications of being converted to Christ and of renouncing pagan worship and must not be seen to be attached to anything that conflicts with the moral life. The person must also make a promise to go through the complete cycle of initiation upon recovering.[168]

Completion of the Sacraments of Initiation

Canon 866 — Unless there is a grave reason to the contrary, an adult who is baptized is to be confirmed immediately after baptism and is to participate in the eucharistic celebration also by receiving communion.

rescripta pro apostolicis missionibus, I, Ann. 1622–1866, nn. 1–1299 (Rome: SCProp, 1907) n. 1198, pp. 655–656.

[165] The 1917 code recognized this explicitly in c. 752, §3.

[166] Tejero, in *Pamplona ComEng,* 566.

[167] W. Woestman, *Sacraments* (Ottawa: Saint Paul University, 1996) 59.

[168] *RCIA* 279, *DOL* 2422.

The seriousness of the requirement that the other sacraments of initiation follow immediately upon an adult's reception of baptism, even in danger-of-death situations, is indicated by the fact that the code requires "a grave reason" to defer these other sacraments.[169] The language of the 1917 code was a little stronger. It required that the newly baptized assist at Mass and receive communion immediately (*statim*) after baptism unless a "grave and urgent reason" prevented it.[170] During the formulation of the present code both lighter and stricter reasons were proposed for departure from the norm that adults receive all three sacraments of initiation in a continuous ceremony. An early schema called only for a "just" reason to defer confirmation.[171] The 1980 schema called for a "grave" reason as does the present code, although it was proposed that the canon call for a "most grave" (*gravissima*) reason for not completing baptism immediately with confirmation and Eucharist.[172]

The *Rite* uses less preceptive terminology: "A priest who baptizes should confer confirmation after the baptism . . . , and whenever possible . . . should give the Eucharist."[173] The present canon uses stronger terms. The adult who is baptized "is to be confirmed . . . and is to participate in the eucharistic celebration," an obligation further intensified by the opening phrase "unless there is a grave reason to the contrary." Examples of such a grave

reason are given in the rite for adult initiation in danger-of-death situations: when a priest baptizes and does not have chrism or lacks the time and materials needed for celebration of the Eucharist.[174]

The canon is a corollary to canon 842, §2 which speaks of the interrelationship of all three of the sacraments of initiation.

The Time for Celebrating Infant Baptism

Canon 867 — §1. Parents are obliged to take care that infants are baptized in the first few weeks; as soon as possible after the birth or even before it, they are to go to the pastor to request the sacrament for their child and to be prepared properly for it.

§2. An infant in danger of death is to be baptized without delay.

Canons 867–868 present the prerequisites for lawful infant baptism. Canon 867 treats the appropriate length of time between an infant's birth and his or her baptism; canon 868 states what is required of parents for the licit celebration of their children's baptism. The canons require nothing of the infants themselves. Like canons 865–866, these canons distinguish between baptism in ordinary and in extraordinary circumstances.

The time for celebrating infant baptism has varied throughout history. In the ancient Church infant baptism was celebrated in conjunction with adult initiation, primarily on Easter and Pentecost. During the Dark and Middle Ages, the precariousness of life led to the increasing practice of baptizing infants as soon as possible after birth. This practice was mandated by the Council of Florence[175] which decreed that infants are to be baptized as soon as possible (*quamprimum*), either immediately after birth or in the first month of life. This was the practice reflected in the 1917

---

[169] The absence of a parallel canon in the Eastern code reflects the long practice of the Eastern churches of celebrating in one ceremony all three sacraments of initiation for infants, not just for adults as is the case in the Western churches.

[170] *CIC* 753, §1. This canon did not, however, allow the priest who baptized an adult to confirm him or her. Since few Latin rite priests had the faculty to confirm, the reception of confirmation and Eucharist by adults who were baptized took place at different ceremonies, often separated by a considerable period of time, and not in the context of the same liturgical celebration as called for by the present ritual and canon.

[171] *Comm* 13 (1981) 222.

[172] *Comm* 15 (1983) 181.

[173] *RCIA* 280, *DOL* 2444.

[174] Ibid. Although a priest may bless the oil of the sick during the celebration of the sacrament of anointing (c. 999, 2°) he may never consecrate chrism (c. 880, §2).

[175] Council of Florence, sess. XI, *Bulla unionis Coptorum, DOL* 576.

code,[176] which left the determination of the exact meaning of *quamprimum* to particular law. In the United States, the Plenary Council of Baltimore interpreted *quamprimum* to mean "at once."[177] Thus, it was not uncommon for mothers not to be present for the baptism of their own children.

The present law reflects a middle ground between these two traditions. Canon 867 does not use the word *quamprimum* to determine the appropriate time for infant baptism but calls for baptism during "the first few weeks" of an infant's life. The following canon will call for a greater interval between birth and baptism if the parents' lack of faith leaves no hope that the infant will be brought up in the practice of the faith. Canon 856 sees the Easter Vigil as the privileged time for baptism of both adults and infants and recalls that this was the time for infant baptism in the ancient tradition of the Church.

The change in discipline reflects the postconciliar theology of baptism summarized in canon 849. Since popular piety may still think of the baptism of infants only in terms of the removal of original sin and insurance against limbo, the sense of urgency is shifted from the baptism itself to the catechesis of the infant's parents about baptism and their formation for raising their child in the faith. It is this catechesis and formation that are to occur *quamprimum* after the infant's birth or even before it. The necessity of this preparation is the reason for the code's greater flexibility regarding the time when an infant is to be baptized.[178] Besides the need for time to provide proper preparation to the parents, the *Rite* mentions other reasons for an interval between an infant's birth and his or her baptism: the welfare of the child, the health of the mother, and the time needed to plan the ceremony.[179] The *Rite* also authorizes episco-

pal conferences "to determine a longer interval between birth and baptism."[180]

Parental Prerequisites for Infant Baptism

Canon 868 — §1. For an infant to be baptized licitly:
  1° the parents or at least one of them or the person who legitimately takes their place must consent;
  2° there must be a founded hope that the infant will be brought up in the Catholic religion; if such hope is altogether lacking, the baptism is to be delayed according to the prescripts of particular law after the parents have been advised about the reason.

§2. An infant of Catholic parents or even of non-Catholic parents is baptized licitly in danger of death even against the will of the parents.

The canon distinguishes between prerequisites for parents in ordinary situations and in danger-of-death situations. The opening line of the canon makes it clear that these prerequisites are only for the liceity of the baptism and not for its validity.

The canon stipulates two prerequisites in ordinary situations. The first is that it be the will of the parents to have the infant baptized. By presenting a child for baptism, the parents accept the responsibility to see that the fruits of the sacrament come to realization as the child matures. This responsibility cannot be accepted if the parents are unwilling to have their child baptized. While, in ideal situations, both parents would share this willingness, the willingness of one of them or of a guardian or a person who takes the place of the parent is sufficient to render the baptism lawful.

The parents' desire for their child's baptism must be sincere. Normally, this sincerity is evidenced by their own practice of the faith and by the fact that they do not view baptism as a mere social convention.[181] This sincerity is the basis for

---

[176] *CIC* 770.
[177] For a historical development of the time for celebrating infant baptism, see McManus, in *CLSA Com,* 626.
[178] Canon 686, §1 of the Eastern code calls for baptism to be celebrated as soon as possible "according to legitimate custom."
[179] *RBaptC* 8, *DOL* 2292.

[180] *RBaptC* 25, *DOL* 2309.
[181] See CDF, *Reply to Bishop B. Henrion of Dapango,* July 13, 1970, *DOL* 2318, n. 2.

the well-founded hope that the child will be raised in the practice of the faith which the canon requires for the lawfulness of the baptism. If this well-founded hope is lacking, the celebration of the sacrament is to be delayed. The canon draws from an earlier instruction issued by the Congregation for the Doctrine of the Faith:

> Pastoral action regarding the baptism of infants must, in the concrete order, be governed by two principles, the second of which is subordinate to the first. (1) Baptism, which is necessary for salvation, is a sign and instrument of God's prevenient love which frees us from original sin and gives us a share in the divine life: considered on its own merits, the gift of these blessings for infants must not be put off. (2) Assurances must be given that this gift will be able to grow through a genuine education in faith and in Christian living, that the sacrament may attain its full "truth." As a rule, these assurances are given within the Christian community. If, on the other hand, these assurances are not in reality serious, that fact can be reason for postponing the sacrament. Finally, if it is certain that there are no assurances, the sacrament must be denied.[182]

The consequence of a clear lack of any well-founded hope of the child being raised in the faith is somewhat softened in the canon. If assurances are altogether lacking, the baptism is not to be denied outright, as was stipulated in the instruction from the Congregation, but rather "delayed."[183] Since the

canon calls for a postponement rather than a denial of baptism, the pastor should maintain contact with the parents and offer whatever help they may need so that, in time, they will be able to supply the assurance the canon calls for, and proceed to the celebration of their child's baptism.

The canon imposes two additional requirements on those who make the decision to postpone an infant's baptism because of the absence of founded hope that the child will be raised in the faith. First, the postponement must follow the prescripts of particular law, either of a diocesan bishop or of the episcopal conference. Second, the baptism is to be postponed only after the parents have been informed of the reasons for this action. The canon is concerned that the postponement of the baptism not further alienate them from the Church, and, by making their reconciliation more difficult, cause additional delays in the celebration of the infant's baptism.

The formulation of canon 868, §2 followed a tortuous path during the code revision process due to differing opinions among the consultors regarding the liceity of baptizing infants in danger-of-death situations against the explicit wishes of their parents or those who take the parents' place. In the first schema of the canons on baptism, the norm on infant baptism in danger-of-death situations was the exact opposite of that in the present canon: the baptism of an infant against the wishes of the parents was judged *illicit*.[184] In the course of discussion among consultors, the canon was rephrased several times between 1978 and 1983. The first revised version continued to assert the unlawfulness of baptizing infants in danger of death against the will of their parents. It stated, however, that, in danger-of-death situations, the baptism of an infant of Catholic or non-Catholic parents was licit, provided that this was not con-

---

[182] CDF, instr *Pastoralis actio,* n. 28, October 20, 1980, *AAS* 72 (1980) 1137–1156.

[183] In a private response ten years previous to *Pastoralis actio,* the Congregation for the Doctrine of the Faith called not for postponing or denying the sacrament when the assurances were insufficient, but for "the enrollment of the child with a view to its being baptized later [and] further pastoral meetings as a way of preparing them [the parents] for the rite of reception of the child for baptism." This enrollment was seen as analogous to the enrollment of adults in the catechumenate. See CDF, *Reply,*

June 13, 1970, in *N* 7 (1971) 69–70, *DOL* 2317–2318. The later instruction by the same congregation rejected this alternative so that there would be no confusion between such a rite of enrollment of children and baptism. See McManus, in *CLSA Com,* 627.

[184] *Comm* 3 (1971) 200.

trary to the will of the parents.[185] A slightly more restrictive formulation was proposed by the addition of the phrase "and provided that no danger of hatred of religion result."[186] Further discussion led to a substantial change in the proposed formulation of the canon: the baptism was to be considered *licit* even if both the parents were expressly opposed to the baptism, provided that no danger of hatred of religion would result.[187] This was the version proposed in the 1980 schema. The final revision eliminated the phrase regarding "hatred of religion" on the ground that the fact that such hatred may result was not as important as the salvation of the infant through baptism. The result of these discussions was the canon in its present form.

In situations of danger of death, it is lawful to baptize an infant against the express will of the infant's parents. However, it is clear that the canon in no way advocates that a child, even in danger of death, be baptized against the express will of the parents. It simply presents a juridical clarification of the liceity of a baptism administered under those conditions.

Conditional Baptism

Canon 869 — §1. If there is a doubt whether a person has been baptized or whether baptism was conferred validly and the doubt remains after a serious investigation, baptism is to be conferred conditionally.

§2. Those baptized in a non-Catholic ecclesial community must not be baptized conditionally unless, after an examination of the matter and the form of the words used in the conferral of baptism and a consideration of the intention of the baptized adult and the minister of the baptism, a serious reason exists to doubt the validity of the baptism.

§3. If in the cases mentioned in §§1 and 2 the conferral or validity of the baptism remains doubtful, baptism is not to be conferred until after the doctrine of the sacrament of baptism is explained to the person to be baptized, if an adult, and the reasons of the doubtful validity of the baptism are explained to the person or, in the case of an infant, to the parents.

The canon is an application to baptism of the principle stated in canon 845, §1 regarding (1) the non-repeatability of baptism, confirmation, and sacred orders, the sacraments which impose a character, and (2) the conditions under which these sacraments may be conferred conditionally when there is serious doubt as to whether they were conferred at all or whether they were conferred validly.

The general norm for conditional baptism is based on two underlying principles: the unrepeatability of baptism, and the necessity of baptism for the valid reception of any other sacrament. It is little more than a restatement of canon 845. Two types of doubt may arise: a doubt about the fact of the baptism (whether it was ever received at all) and a doubt about the validity of the baptism previously conferred. The fact of a baptism may be doubtful if no record of it can be produced and there are no witnesses to the baptism. Doubt about the validity of a baptism may arise if there is reason to question whether the washing with water was omitted, whether the required verbal form was used, or whether the minister or the one baptized as an adult had the proper intentions. The canon calls for a serious investigation to attempt to resolve such doubts (see c. 845, §2). If a doubt still persists after this investigation, conditional baptism is to be conferred.[188]

When a person was baptized in a non-Catholic church or ecclesial community, there is usually no doubt whatsoever about the fact that the baptism occurred; the only area of doubt is whether or not the baptism was conferred validly. Since the person was baptized a Christian, the law presumes that the baptism was valid. The reasons for doubting the validity of the baptism conferred in the non-Catholic church or ecclesial community must be supported by sufficient evidence to call the reliabil-

---

[185] *Comm* 13 (1981) 223.
[186] *Comm* 13 (1981) 224.
[187] Ibid.

[188] The Eastern code has no parallel canon on conditional baptism.

ity of this presumption into question. Therefore, those baptized in non-Catholic Christian churches and ecclesial communities are not to be baptized conditionally unless a serious doubt or a positive and probable doubt remains even after a thorough investigation of the matter. This caution reflects the 1967 *Ecumenical Directory* which prohibits the indiscriminate conditional baptism of those already baptized in a non-Catholic Christian community: "The practice of conditional baptism of all without distinction who desire to enter full communion with the Catholic Church cannot be approved."[189]

To safeguard the integrity of baptism and to respect the ecclesial nature of non-Catholic churches and ecclesial communities,[190] the areas which must be investigated before conferring conditional baptism include: the matter and the verbal formula used, the intention of the one baptized, and the intention of the minister of baptism. The investigation should consider first the norms, rituals, and customs of the non-Catholic ecclesial community to determine whether or not what the community generally does when baptizing results in valid baptism. If this investigation reveals no doubt about the validity of baptism conferred in that community, doubt can persist only if there is evidence that the minister did not follow the approved rites of his or her own community.

Non-Catholic ecclesial communities whose baptisms are recognized as valid by the Catholic Church include, besides all Eastern non-Catholics: African Methodist Episcopal, Amish, Anglican, Assembly of God, Baptists, Evangelical United Brethren, Church of the Brethren, Church of God, Congregational Church, Disciples of Christ, Episcopalians, Evangelical Churches, Lutherans, Methodists, Liberal Catholic Church, Old Catholics, Old Roman Catholics, Church of the Nazarene, Polish National Church, Presbyterian Church, Reformed Churches, Seventh Day Adventists, and the United Church of Christ.[191]

The question of conditional baptism usually arises when an adult, previously baptized in a non-Catholic Christian community, seeks full communion with the Catholic Church. The *Rite* calls for the prudent investigation as explained in paragraph two of the canon:

> The sacrament of baptism may not be repeated and conditional baptism is not permitted unless there is a prudent doubt about the fact or validity of the baptism already received. If after serious investigation it seems necessary—because of such prudent doubt—to confer baptism again conditionally, the minister should explain beforehand the reasons why baptism is conferred conditionally in this instance and he should administer it in the private form. The local Ordinary shall determine, in individual cases, what rites are to be included or excluded in conditional baptism.[192]

The third paragraph of canon 869 is a pastoral norm which is drawn primarily from the *Rite*. It presumes that the conditions for a conditional baptism outlined in the two previous paragraphs have been met. Before the conditional baptism takes place, and in order to avoid any misunderstanding, the canon calls for an explanation of the doctrine of baptism and the reasons for the conditional baptism. These explanations are to be given to the adult candidate directly and to the parents in the case of infant baptism.

The canon does not include the statement in the *Rite* that the conditional baptism is to be celebrated privately. The 1917 code distinguished between solemn and private baptism. Baptism was solemn when all the ceremonies were celebrated, private when they were not.[193] This distinction has not been retained in the revised code. The "private"

---

[189] *Ecum Dir* I, 14.
[190] *Ecum Dir* I, 13.
[191] J. Huels, *The Pastoral Companion* (Chicago: Franciscan Herald Press, 1986) 51.

[192] *RCIA*, Appendix, "Rite of Receiving Baptized Christians into the Full Communion of the Catholic Church," 7, *DOL* 2482.
[193] *CIC* 755, §1 and 759.

baptism called for in the *Rite* is one that is not celebrated publicly. The reasons for this preference are the same as those that prompt the *Rite* to recommend restraint when receiving into full communion one baptized in a non-Catholic community:

Any appearance of triumphalism should be carefully avoided and the manner of celebrating this Mass should be decided beforehand and with a view to the particular circumstances. Both the ecumenical implications and the bond between the candidate and the parish community should be considered. Often it will be preferable to celebrate the Mass with only a few relatives and friends.[194]

Not all the rites and ceremonies need be celebrated in a conditional baptism. Sometimes, it is sufficient simply to supply those ceremonies whose omission or defect gave rise to doubts about the validity of the original baptism. The *Rite* notes that this determination is to be left to the local ordinary.

Baptism of an Abandoned Child

Canon 870 — An abandoned infant or a foundling is to be baptized unless after diligent investigation the baptism of the infant is established.

The last two canons of this chapter deal with special cases of baptism. Canon 870 treats the baptism of an abandoned child; canon 871 that of an aborted but viable fetus.[195]

In canon 869, the presumption was that baptism conferred in a non-Catholic church or ecclesial community is valid until the contrary is proven. In canon 870, the presumption is reversed. Abandoned children are presumed not to have been baptized until the contrary is proven. Whereas

canon 869 called for a diligent investigation to overturn the presumption that the original baptism was valid, the present canon calls for a similar investigation to rebut the presumption that an abandoned child was not baptized.

The canon is also an exception to canon 868, §1, 2° which stipulates that in order to baptize an infant, there must be a founded hope that the child will be raised in the practice of the faith, and that this assurance is the responsibility of the parents or guardian. No such guarantees can be given in the case of an abandoned child. Therefore, the assurance of Catholic upbringing will have to come from those who will care for the child. Until it is determined that a Catholic will be entrusted with the care of the abandoned child, there should be no rush to baptize the child, outside a danger-of-death situation.

Baptism of an Aborted Fetus

Canon 871 — If aborted fetuses are alive, they are to be baptized insofar as possible.

The 1917 code contained several canons on baptizing fetuses.[196] These detailed norms stipulated when to baptize absolutely and conditionally depending on the manner in which the child was aborted. The present canon reduces all these norms to one. Regardless of how the abortion occurred, baptism is to be conferred as long as the fetus is alive. If the fetus is clearly dead, baptism cannot be conferred.[197] Although the canon does not explicitly address the case of doubt, a doubtfully living fetus should be baptized conditionally, as provided for in the 1917 code.[198]

It is highly unlikely that a priest, deacon, catechist, or another person designated to baptize will

---

[194] *RCIA,* Appendix, "Rite of Receiving Baptized Christians into the Full Communion of the Catholic Church," 3, *DOL* 2478.

[195] Canon 680 of the Eastern code treats the case of a fetus and c. 681, §2 that of a foundling.

[196] *CIC* 746–748.

[197] See *Pastoral Care* 224: "It may be necessary to explain to the family of the person who is dead that sacraments are celebrated for the living, not for the dead, and that the dead are effectively helped by the prayers of the living."

[198] *CIC* 745.

be present for the baptism of a fetus. The *Rite* presumes this situation, and, referring to canon 861, §2, it reminds pastors of their obligation to instruct lay people, especially "midwives, family or social workers or nurses of the sick, as well as physicians and surgeons" on how to baptize.[199]

CHAPTER IV
SPONSORS
[cc. 872–874]

The three canons of this chapter give a summary treatment of the office of sponsor.[200] Canon 872 speaks in very general terms of the responsibility of sponsors. Canon 873 specifies the number of sponsors. Canon 874 lists the qualifications for this office.

Responsibilities of Sponsors

Canon 872 — Insofar as possible, a person to be baptized is to be given a sponsor who assists an adult in Christian initiation or together with the parents presents an infant for baptism. A sponsor also helps the baptized person to lead a Christian life in keeping with baptism and to fulfill faithfully the obligations inherent in it.

The canon defines the sponsor as one who assists an adult in Christian initiation, or who, together with the parents, presents an infant at baptism. While the Canon Law Society of America (CLSA) translation of the code uses the word "sponsor" for this office, the official Latin text uses the terms *patrinus* and *matrina,* which are more accurately translated as "godfather" and "godmother." The role and function of godparents, properly speaking, are treated more extensively in the *Rite.* The *General Introduction to Christian Initiation* delineates the role of the godparent:

It is a very ancient custom of the Church that adults are not admitted to baptism without a godparent, a member of the Christian community who will assist them at least in the final preparation for baptism and after baptism will help them persevere in the faith and in their lives as Christians.

In the baptism of children, as well, a godparent is to be present in order to represent the expansion of the spiritual family of the one to be baptized and the role of the Church as a mother. As occasion offers, the godparent helps the parents to lead the child to profess the faith and to show this by living it.

At least in the final rites of the catechumenate and in the actual celebration of baptism, the godparent's part is to testify to the faith of the adult candidate or, together with the parents, to profess the Church's faith, in which the child is being baptized.[201]

The *General Introduction* then proceeds to list the qualifications of "godparents." These correspond word for word with the qualifications listed in canon 874 for "sponsors." Thus, one should be aware that the English translation of the code consistently uses the term "sponsor" for what the Latin text of the code terms "godparents" (*patrinus, matrina*). It should also be noted that the *Rite of Christian Initiation of Adults* uses the term "godparents" for those who perform the functions mentioned in canon 872.

This confusion in translation would cause no problem, except that the *Rite* uses the term "sponsor" for an office which is quite distinct from that of godparent:

Any candidate seeking admission as a catechumen is accompanied by a sponsor, that is, a man or woman who has known and assisted the candidate and stands as a witness to the candidate's moral character, faith, and intention. It may happen that this sponsor is

---

[199] *IGIC* 17, *DOL* 2266.

[200] A similar treatment of sponsors is found in cc. 684–686 of the Eastern code.

[201] *IGIC* 8–9, *DOL* 2257–2258.

not the one who will serve as godparent (*patrinus, matrina*) for the periods of purification, enlightenment, and mystagogy; in that case, another person takes the sponsor's place in the role of godparent.

But on the day of election, at the celebration of the sacraments, and during the period of mystagogy the candidate is accompanied by a godparent (*patrinus, matrina*). This is a person chosen by the candidate on the basis of example, good qualities, and friendship, delegated by the local Christian community, and approved by the priest.[202]

According to the *Rite,* the offices of sponsor and godparent are distinct. The sponsor is one who assists the catechumen during the initial stages of the journey, while the godparent accompanies the candidate at the celebration of the rite of election, at the baptism, and during the period of post-baptismal catechesis.

In presenting the responsibilities of sponsors (godparents), canon 872 mentions first the responsibility unique to adult baptism, then the responsibility unique to infant baptism, and finally two additional responsibilities common to both.

The responsibility unique to adult baptism is "to assist an adult in Christian initiation." This "assistance" is explained more fully in the *Rite:* to assist an adult "for the periods of purification, enlightenment, and mystagogy,"[203] that is, for the *final* stages of initiation. The responsibility of the sponsor at the baptism of an infant is shared conjointly with the parents: "to present an infant for baptism." Responsibilities common to both adult and infant baptism are: to assist the one baptized in living the Christian life and in fulfilling faithfully the obligations flowing from it. The *Rite* expands on these roles:

It is the responsibility of the godparent to show the candidate how to practice the Gospel in personal and social life and to be for

the candidate a bearer of Christian witness and a guardian over growth in the baptismal life. Chosen before the candidate's election, the godparent fulfills this office publicly from the day of the election, testifying to the community about the candidate. The godparents continue to be important during the time after reception of the sacraments when the neophyte needs to be assisted to remain true to the baptismal promises.[204]

The *Rite* says little about godparents in infant baptism: "Because of the natural relationship, parents have a more important ministry and role in the baptism of infants than the godparents."[205] The *Rite* then develops five areas of responsibility for parents, but never mentions godparents again, except to note that each child may have a godfather and a godmother.[206]

A sponsor (godparent) is not necessary for a valid and licit baptism, although it is clear that his or her presence is desired and preferred. The presence of a sponsor at adult baptism "is a very ancient custom of the Church."[207] The presence of a sponsor at infant baptism is also desirable "in order to represent the expansion of the spiritual family of the one to be baptized and the role of the Church as a mother."[208]

Canon 762 of the 1917 code spoke of a spiritual relationship that arose from serving as a sponsor in a solemn baptism. This relationship had a juridical consequence. It gave rise to an impediment to marriage between the sponsor and the one baptized. In the present code this diriment impediment has been abrogated.

Although the canon says nothing about a sponsor's presence through a proxy, this silence is not to be understood as barring the use of a proxy to stand in for an absent sponsor.

---

[202] *RCIA* 42–43, *DOL* 2369–2370.
[203] Ibid.

[204] *RCIA* 43, *DOL* 2370.
[205] *RBaptC* 5, *DOL* 2289.
[206] *RBaptC* 6, *DOL* 2290.
[207] *IGIC* 8, *DOL* 2257.
[208] Ibid.

Number of Sponsors

Canon 873 — There is to be only one male sponsor or one female sponsor or one of each.

The canon designates the number of sponsors permitted at the celebration of both adult and infant baptism. It allows for either one sponsor, male or female, or two, one male and one female.[209] The rite of adult baptism always speaks of the sponsor in the singular, indicating perhaps a preference for only one sponsor. The *Rite of Baptism for Children* states more clearly, "Each child may have a godfather and a godmother; the word 'godparents' is used in the *Rite* to describe both."[210] This indicates that the *Rite* seems to prefer that two sponsors be present at the baptism. In any case, the canon allows for both of these preferences. The use of the term "godparents" rather than "sponsors" makes obvious the stipulation that if two are present, they should not be of the same sex.

The canon does not permit more than two sponsors. This may call for some pastoral sensitivity in those cultures in which it is traditional for more than two people to be designated as godparents or sponsors. In such a case it is advisable for the minister to consult with the parents prior to the baptism and determine which two names (one male, one female) will be inscribed in the baptismal register.

Prerequisites for Sponsors

Canon 874 — §1. To be permitted to take on the function of sponsor a person must:
1° be designated by the one to be baptized, by the parents or the person who takes their place, or in their absence by the pastor or minister and have the aptitude and intention of fulfilling this function;
2° have completed the sixteenth year of age, unless the diocesan bishop has established

another age, or the pastor or minister has granted an exception for a just cause;
3° be a Catholic who has been confirmed and has already received the most holy sacrament of the Eucharist and who leads a life of faith in keeping with the function to be taken on;
4° not be bound by any canonical penalty legitimately imposed or declared;
5° not be the father or mother of the one to be baptized.
§2. A baptized person who belongs to a non-Catholic ecclesial community is not to participate except together with a Catholic sponsor and then only as a witness of the baptism.

The first paragraph lists five prerequisites for exercising the office of sponsor. First, the sponsor must be properly designated. In infant baptism, the choice of sponsors belongs first to the parents, then to those who take the parents' place, and finally to the parish priest. For adult baptism, the adult himself or herself designates the sponsor.

Second, the sponsor must be at least sixteen years old. However, the diocesan bishop may determine a different age. In individual cases, the pastor or the minister of the sacrament can, for a just reason, make an exception either to the canonical age or to the age established by the diocesan bishop.

Third, because of the theological interrelatedness of the sacraments of initiation, the sponsor must be a fully initiated Catholic. Since the sponsor's role extends beyond the ceremony of baptism and includes the responsibility "to help the baptized person to lead a Christian life in keeping with baptism and to fulfill faithfully the obligations inherent in it" (c. 872), it is only fitting that the sponsor be a Catholic who has already received the sacraments of confirmation and the Eucharist. But even a fully initiated Catholic may be restricted from exercising the office of sponsor if he or she does not live the faith in a manner that is in keeping with the responsibilities of this office. Thus, people who do not participate regularly in the Eucharist or who are liv-

---

[209] Canon 684, §1 of the Eastern code places no limitation on the number of sponsors.
[210] *RBaptC* 7, *DOL* 2290.

ing in marriages not recognized by the Church may not be qualified to function as sponsors. Fourth, those who labor under a declared or imposed canonical penalty are barred from serving as sponsors.

Fifth, parents are prohibited from being sponsors of their own children. The parents are primarily responsible for raising the child in the faith.[211] The godparents' role is simply to assist them. However, the role of the sponsor becomes more critical when the parents fail in their responsibility. Thus, the canon clearly distinguishes between the role of parent and that of godparent. The canon does not, however, repeat the 1917 code's disqualification of religious, priests, and deacons and spouses of adult candidates from undertaking the office of sponsor.[212]

The second paragraph permits a non-Catholic Christian to exercise the role of a Christian witness in the celebration of baptism. The witness does not replace the sponsor. The canon responds to the pastoral situation in which, often for merely social reasons, the parents want to choose as a sponsor a relative or close friend who is Christian but not Catholic. The canon tries to balance the tension between the canonical and sacramental role of the sponsor and a merely social understanding of this office:

> For reasons of kinship or friendship, a Christian of another Communion, having a convinced faith in Christ, can be admitted along with the Catholic godparent as a Christian witness to a baptism. In similar circumstances, a Catholic can fulfill this role for a member of a Community separated from us. In these cases the responsibility for the Christian upbringing of the candidate falls *per se* on the godparent who is a member of the Church or Ecclesial Community in which the infant is baptized.[213]

The canon repeats the stipulation of the *Ecumenical Directory* that the Christian witness may function only with a Catholic sponsor, that is, with a sponsor who meets the canonical prerequisites for the office.

The second paragraph does not make explicit allowance for a member of a separated Eastern church to serve as a sponsor, and not merely as a Christian witness, at the baptism of a Roman Catholic, even though this explicit recognition was proposed during the drafting of the present code.[214] Canon 685, §3 of the Eastern code does, however, explicitly permit non-Catholic members of Eastern churches to be sponsors at Catholic baptisms. The 1967 *Ecumenical Directory,* whose provisions are still in force, also allows a separated Eastern Christian to undertake the role of sponsor:

> It is permissible for a just reason to accept one of the faithful of an Eastern Church as godparent along with a Catholic godparent at the baptism of a Catholic infant or adult, as long as the Catholic upbringing of the one being baptized is provided for and there is assurance that the person is fit to be a godparent. A Catholic invited to stand as a godparent at a baptism in an Eastern Church is not forbidden to do so. In such cases the duty of looking out for the Christian upbringing of the baptized falls first upon the godparent belonging to the Church in which the child is baptized.[215]

It is not permissible, however, for a member of a separated Eastern church to function as a sponsor in a Catholic baptism unless there is also a Catholic sponsor.[216] The Eastern code makes this point clear in canon 685, §3.

---

[211] *SC* 67. See also *RBaptC* 5, *DOL* 2289.
[212] See *CIC* 765, 3° and 766, 4°, 5°.
[213] *Ecum Dir* 57.

[214] See *Comm* 15 (1983) 230–231.
[215] *Ecum Dir* 48.
[216] See J. Cuneo, "Canon 874: Members of Greek Orthodox Church as Sponsors at Catholic Baptism," in *CLSA Advisory Opinions* (Washington, D.C.: CLSA, 1995), 261–264.

CHAPTER V
THE PROOF AND REGISTRATION
OF THE CONFERRAL OF BAPTISM
[cc. 875–878]

The final four canons treat first the means of establishing the fact of baptism, or, in other words, the proof of baptism (cc. 875–876), and second the registration or recording of that fact (cc. 877–878).

Establishing Proof of Baptism

Canon 875 — A person who administers baptism is to take care that, unless a sponsor is present, there is at least a witness who can attest to the conferral of the baptism.

Canon 876 — To prove the conferral of baptism, if prejudicial to no one, the declaration of one witness beyond all exception is sufficient or the oath of the one baptized if the person received baptism as an adult.

Canons 875 and 876 are concerned that there be living witnesses of the baptism who can verify that it took place. In contemporary society, witnesses are particularly important forms of proof in civil and criminal trials. Otherwise, documents or certificates which attest to the occurrence of an event are more common and even preferred. The first two canons on proofs reflect a cultural milieu where proof by documents is not the rule but the exception, and where witnesses are the usual means for providing proof. Nevertheless, the canons have practical relevance for those situations in which a baptismal record cannot be produced.

Canon 875 concerns a baptism at which there was no sponsor, who is ordinarily the principal witness to the baptism. This situation is most likely to occur in the case of baptism in danger-of-death situations. The canon places a responsibility on the minister to see that some other witness is present who will be able to verify that the baptism did indeed take place.

Canon 876 establishes the probative value of the testimony of a witness to a baptism. The testimony of a single witness is sufficient to establish the fact of a baptism. If the person was baptized as an adult, the word of the baptized person is sufficient to establish proof of baptism. This canon is an exception to the general rule that the testimony of a single witness cannot normally provide full proof (c. 1573).

The canon notes that for the testimony of a single witness to provide full proof of baptism, the witness must be above suspicion, i.e., the witness's honesty must be above reproach. The canon states that the testimony of a single witness, even an honest one, or the testimony of the baptized adult alone may not be sufficient proof in "prejudicial" cases. A prejudicial case is one in which the rights of another person may be adversely affected, such as a contested marriage case if the declaration of nullity rests on the proof or disproof of a person's baptism. In cases such as this, the testimony of a single witness may be judged insufficient and more convincing proof may be required.[217]

Recording the Baptism

Canon 877 — §1. The pastor of the place where the baptism is celebrated must carefully and without any delay record in the baptismal register the names of the baptized, with mention made of the minister, parents, sponsors, witnesses, if any, the place and date of the conferral of the baptism, and the date and place of birth.

§2. If it concerns a child born to an unmarried mother, the name of the mother must be inserted, if her maternity is established publicly or if she seeks it willingly in writing or before two witnesses. Moreover, the name of the father must be inscribed if a public document or his own declaration before the pastor and two witnesses proves his paternity; in other cases, the name of the baptized is inscribed with no mention of the name of the father or the parents.

---

[217] See commentary on c. 1573.

§3. If it concerns an adopted child, the names of those adopting are to be inscribed and, at least if it is done in the civil records of the region, also the names of the natural parents according to the norm of §§1 and 2, with due regard for the prescripts of the conference of bishops.

Canon 878 — If the baptism was not administered by the pastor or in his presence, the minister of baptism, whoever it is, must inform the pastor of the parish in which it was administered of the conferral of the baptism, so that he records the baptism according to the norm of can. 877, §1.

The last two canons deal with the person charged with recording the fact of the celebration of baptism and the kind of information to be recorded.

Canon 877 deals with the recording of baptism when the pastor, and by extension, an associate pastor, is the minister of the sacrament. The first paragraph simply mentions the kind of information normally to be recorded in the baptismal register whether the person baptized was an adult or an infant: the names of the person baptized, of the minister, of the parents, and of the sponsors and witnesses; the place and date of birth of the baptized person; and the date and place of baptism.

The remaining two paragraphs treat special situations which pertain only to the baptism of children. The second paragraph explains the kind of information to be recorded or not recorded when the parents of the baptized child are not married. The intent of this paragraph is to protect the reputations of the parents of an illegitimate child. The third paragraph deals with information to be recorded or not recorded when the baptized child has been adopted. Paragraph three tries to find a balance between the desirability of a complete record of baptism, which includes the names of the natural parents, and respect for the civil requirements which may demand the concealment of the names of the natural parents.

Canon 878 treats the case when someone other than the parish priest was the minister of baptism. The baptism may have been conferred licitly in an emergency situation or in a non-parochial church or oratory within the parish territory. It may also have been conferred illicitly, perhaps by a relative of the family at home without permission of the pastor. The point of the canon is simply to ensure that, even in these situations, the fact of the baptism is recorded in the register of the parish in which the baptism took place.

Although it is not explicitly stated in these canons, the baptismal register is primary, since other sacraments for whose celebration proof may be needed (confirmation, marriage, orders) and other events affecting a person's ecclesial status (religious profession, declaration of nullity of marriage) are also to be noted in the person's baptismal record. This explains the canon's emphasis that the record of the baptism be kept in the parish where it was celebrated, since this is the first place contacted when proof of baptism, the reception of other sacraments, or other events determining a person's ecclesial status is needed.

TITLE II
THE SACRAMENT OF CONFIRMATION
[cc. 879–896]

The eighteen canons which constitute the code's treatment of the sacrament of confirmation give little hint of the differing theological emphases, changes in discipline, and controversies which have marked the historical development of this sacrament. Some of these controversies continue to the present day, most notably those surrounding the age of confirmation, the sequence of reception of the sacraments of initiation in pastoral practice, and, to a lesser extent, the minister of the sacrament. In order to understand the code's treatment of confirmation, and to perceive more accurately the continuing questions regarding the current discipline of this sacrament, a limited historical overview is necessary. This historical overview will concentrate on the three areas of current discussion mentioned above.

Most historical treatises on confirmation recognize the *Apostolic Tradition* of Hippolytus (c. 215–220) as the earliest documentary evidence that we have of this sacrament:

> After this pouring the consecrated oil and laying his hand on his head he says, "I anoint you with holy oil in God the Father Almighty and Christ Jesus and the Holy Spirit." And sealing him on the forehead, he shall give him the kiss and say, "The Lord be with you." And he who has been sealed shall say: "And with your spirit."[218]

In recent years, however, attempts have been made to trace the origins of confirmation back beyond the third century to a structural component of ancient liturgies termed the "dismissal rite" (*missa*) which closed or sealed a particular liturgical rite and was accompanied by an imposition of hands and a blessing, but without, necessarily, the use of oil.[219] Nevertheless, as the citation from Hippolytus indicates, the rudiments of confirmation as we know it are already in place by the third century: the bishop as minister, prayer over the neophytes, anointing with oil on the forehead, verbal (Trinitarian) formula, and kiss of peace.

Until the early part of the fourth century, the bishop remained the sole minister of the sacrament in both the Eastern and the Western churches. Confirmation was administered immediately following the baptismal washing and then the Eucharist was celebrated. The interrelationship between the three sacraments of initiation was clearly evident in both theology and practice, an interrelationship which has again become prominent in the West, but only to a limited degree.

Beginning with the Edict of Constantine in 313, however, a series of developments gave rise to widely divergent disciplines with consequently different theologies and emphases. As Christianity emerged from the catacombs, its popularity increased dramatically, not always due to religious conversion or spiritual motives. The lengthy period of catechumenal formation and conversion became truncated, and, most significant of all in terms of confirmation, it became increasingly difficult for the bishop to retain his earlier distinction as the sole minister not only of confirmation but of all the sacraments of initiation.

In both East and West, by necessity, presbyters (and, in their absence, deacons) became the usual ministers of baptism.[220] But in the East they also became the usual ministers of confirmation with the result that the reception of the sacraments of initiation continued to manifest their essential interrelationship. To this day, the Eastern discipline and theology of confirmation give greater emphasis to the unity of the sacraments of initiation.[221] In the West, however, the retention of the bishop's role as the principal or even exclusive minister of confirmation resulted in a temporal separation between this sacrament and baptism. The theological consequence was that confirmation now stressed the union of the newly confirmed with the pastor of the whole particular church and not just with their local community or parish, and made more clear the connection of the confirmed with the apostolic origins and mission of the Church.[222]

With the fall of the Roman Empire in the West in the sixth century, communities became widely scattered and remote, conditions making it even more difficult for the bishop to remain the sole minister of confirmation. While presbyters baptized, the bishop came later, sometimes much later, to complete or "confirm" the baptism by anointing with chrism. Liturgical norms distinguished the anointing with chrism by a presbyter immediately following the baptismal washing from a second anointing with chrism by the bishop.[223]

---

[218] Hippolytus, *The Apostolic Tradition*, 22. Trans. in P. F. Palmer, *Sacraments and Worship* (Westminster: Newman, 1955) 8.

[219] See A. Kavanagh, *Confirmation: Origins and Reform* (New York: Pueblo, 1988) 31.

[220] Council of Elvira, c. 77.

[221] See *CCEO* 694, 695, 697.

[222] See *CCC* 1292.

[223] Council of Toledo, c. 20.

In time, the discipline of the bishop as sole minister of confirmation was no longer universal in the West. The Council of Toledo drafted prohibitions on the consecration of chrism by presbyters and imposed limits on presbyters acting as ministers of confirmation, but did not forbid their confirming in the absence of a bishop.[224]

A letter of Innocent I to the bishop of Gubbio in 416 attests to the practice of presbyter-ministers of confirmation, but calls for an end to this practice.[225] No doubt, the practice of presbyteral confirming continued and in some areas became the custom, as is confirmed by the letter of Gregory I to the bishop of Cagliari a hundred and fifty years later.[226] The letter reveals that the faithful of Cagliari "were scandalized by the introduction of a new discipline regarding the conferral of the sacrament of confirmation."[227] The "new discipline" was the papal prohibition of confirmation by presbyters. A compromise was reached: it was the bishop's place to confirm, but presbyters could confirm in his absence.[228]

The practice of presbyters confirming continued as a general custom until the eleventh century in Spain and Portugal, but in Germany and what is now France presbyteral confirming was allowed by synodal legislation only in danger of death. Not until the Council of Trent was the practice of allowing presbyters to confirm formally condemned, primarily because the reformers had allowed presbyters this role.[229] Thus, the practice finally came to an end in the West.

Due to the temporal separation of baptism and confirmation in the West, differing theologies of confirmation developed in an attempt to supply confirmation with a uniqueness that its ritual distinction from baptism alone failed to do. Since confirmation was celebrated later in life, there gradually developed an understanding that the effects of the sacrament paralleled the age at which the sacrament was received, an understanding which has continued to recent times. The *Baltimore Catechism* defined the sacrament as that which makes one a "strong and perfect Christian and a soldier of Jesus Christ." The effect of confirmation as making one a "soldier of Christ" (*miles Christi*) developed as a result of the Crusades, but it is also mentioned in much more recent authoritative documents.[230] At present it is often understood primarily as a sacrament of Christian maturity and a sacrament of service to the Church and community. These emphases are certainly elements of a theology of confirmation, but they tend to eclipse the relationship of confirmation to baptism and the Eucharist.

While the Eastern churches have preserved confirmation as the completion of baptism for both adults and infants, the general reservation of confirmation in the West to the bishop has resulted in a wide variety of ages at which the sacrament is received. Since confirmation was inevitably delayed beyond infancy, it was rarely conferred prior to use of reason. This practice has long since become normative, particularly after the definitive suppression of presbyter-ministers of confirmation of infants and children by the Council of Trent. Both the 1917 code and the revised code stipulate the age of reason, generally accepted as seven years, as the appropriate time for confirmation. However, the sacrament is generally delayed well beyond that age.

The primary factor governing the determination of the appropriate age for confirmation is the theological understanding of its nature, effects, and relationship to baptism. Those who see confirmation primarily as a sacrament of maturity consider the age of seven far too young. Those who see confirmation primarily as the comple-

[224] R. J. Barrett, "Confirmation: A Discipline Revisited," *J* 52 (1992) 698.

[225] See *Ench* 215.

[226] Gregory I, Ep. 26, *ad Januarium,* in *PL* 77:696.

[227] Barrett, 699.

[228] Ibid.

[229] Barrett, 700–702.

[230] See SCSacr, *Spiritus Sancti munera,* in *AAS* 38 (1946) 349–350: "...suffused with the fullness of grace and marked with the character of soldiers of Christ, they may be equipped in fact and by profession for every good work." *CLD* 3, 303–311.

tion of baptism and stress the ancient ordering of the reception of the sacraments of initiation consider seven years of age the latest time for its reception. In the United States, the bishops' conference determined in 1993 that the "uniform" age for confirmation in this country is anywhere between seven and eighteen years of age, a decision which confirms the wide variety of current pastoral practice.[231]

Although the discipline on the minister of confirmation and the age for its reception have varied widely, the order in which the sacraments of initiation are celebrated has been much more constant. Until the latter part of the nineteenth century confirmation was celebrated after baptism and prior to the Eucharist. As confirmation came to be delayed in the West, so did first reception of the Eucharist. Thus, the traditional ordering of the sacraments of initiation was maintained even though they were celebrated in separate ceremonies.

The first change in this ordering occurred in France in the latter part of the nineteenth century when several dioceses developed the practice of not confirming until after reception of first Eucharist. While Rome complained about this practice, it was not suppressed.[232] Such a reordering of the sacraments, however, became more universal following the promulgation in 1910 of *Quam singulari* by Pius X, which introduced the discipline of admitting children to first Eucharist at the age of reason, or the age of seven. The encyclical said nothing about the ordering of other sacraments, particularly confirmation and penance. However, as a result of the practical problems connected with catechizing children simultaneously for the reception of confirmation, Eucharist, and penance, the reception of first Eucharist came to precede the celebration of confirmation. The connection of confirmation to baptism which the prior ordering of the sacraments had maintained was broken and the sacrament became even more distant from baptism.

In 1963 Vatican Council II called for a reform of confirmation with a view to restoring its original connection with the other sacraments of initiation:

> The rite of confirmation is also to be revised in order that the intimate connection of this sacrament with the whole of Christian initiation may stand out more clearly; for this reason it is fitting for candidates to renew their baptismal promises just before they are confirmed.[233]

The text still presumes a celebration of confirmation apart from baptism, but nevertheless reveals its clear intent to relate these two sacraments more closely to one another.

The actual revision was accomplished and promulgated eight years later.[234] In the apostolic constitution promulgating the revised *Rite of Confirmation* Paul VI stated:

> The aim of this work has been that the intimate connection of this sacrament with the whole of Christian initiation may stand out more clearly. But the link between confirmation and the other sacraments of initiation is more easily perceived not simply from the fact that their rites have been more closely conjoined; the rite and the words by which confirmation is conferred also make this link clear.[235]

> Confirmation is so closely linked with the holy Eucharist that the faithful, after being signed by baptism and confirmation, are incorporated fully into the Body of Christ by participation in the Eucharist.[236]

[231] W. Levada, "Reflections on the Age of Confirmation," *TS* 57 (1996) 302.

[232] Barrett, 703.

[233] *SC* 71.

[234] Congregation for Divine Worship, *Ordo confirmationis,* August 22, 1971 (Vatican City: Typis Polyglottis Vaticanis, 1971); *Rite of Confirmation, DOL* 305, 2510–2528.

[235] Paul VI, apconst *Divinae consortium naturae,* August 15, 1971, *AAS* 63 (1971) 658, *DOL* 2500.

[236] *Divinae consortium naturae, AAS* 63 (1971) 660, *DOL* 2502.

It is true that, in the 1971 *Rite of Confirmation*, the other sacraments of initiation were "more closely conjoined," but not to the extent that they would be a year later with the promulgation of the adult rite of Christian initiation. The 1971 revised rite presumed that baptism had been celebrated some time prior to confirmation, as is clear from the opening line of the rite: "Those who have been baptized continue on the path of Christian initiation through the sacrament of confirmation."[237]

The rite does note that "adult catechumens . . . are to be confirmed immediately after baptism,"[238] but does not supply a liturgical rite for this celebration.

The rite designates the bishop as the "primary" and "normal" minister of the sacrament and offers a scriptural and theological justification for this tradition in the West:

The primary minister of confirmation is the bishop. Normally a bishop administers the sacrament so that there will be a clearer reference to the first pouring forth of the Holy Spirit on Pentecost: after the apostles were filled with the Holy Spirit, they themselves gave the Spirit to the faithful through the laying on of hands. Thus the reception of the Spirit through the ministry of the bishop shows the close bond that joins the confirmed to the Church and the mandate received from Christ to bear witness to him before all.[239]

However, in a major shift from that tradition, the rite gives to presbyters the faculty to confirm adults whom they baptize or receive into full communion,[240] a faculty which will be recognized in canon 883, 2°. With regard to the age of confirmation, the rite retains the age of seven, although for the first time it recognizes the pastoral practice which often delays confirmation to a later age:

With regard to children, in the Latin Church the administration of confirmation is generally delayed until about the seventh year. For pastoral reasons, however, especially to implant deeply in the lives of the faithful complete obedience to Christ the Lord and a firm witnessing to him, the conferences of bishops may set an age that seems more suitable. This means that the sacrament is given, after the formation proper to it, when the recipients are more mature."[241]

Those parts of the 1971 *Rite of Confirmation* dealing with adult confirmation are now treated much more expansively in the 1972 *Rite of Christian Initiation of Adults*.[242] Much more than the 1971 *Rite of Confirmation*, the *Rite of Christian Initiation of Adults* restores the ancient tradition of the Church regarding the liturgical and theological significance of confirmation and calls for its celebration immediately after the baptismal washing in the context of the celebration of the Eucharist at the Easter Vigil:

According to the ancient practice preserved in the Roman liturgy, adults are not to be baptized without receiving confirmation immediately afterward unless serious reasons prevent this. This combination signifies the unity of the paschal mystery, the link between the mission of the Son and the outpouring of the Holy Spirit, and the connection between the two sacraments through which the Son and the Spirit come with the Father to those baptized.[243]

---

[237] *RConf* 1, *DOL* 2510.
[238] *RConf* 3, *DOL* 2512.
[239] *RConf* 7, *DOL* 2516.
[240] Ibid.
[241] Ibid.
[242] Congregation for Divine Worship, *Ordo initiationis christianae adultorum*, January 6, 1972 (Vatican City: Typis Polyglottis Vaticanis, 1972); *RCIA* 305, *DOL* 2328–2488.
[243] *RCIA* 34, *DOL* 2361.

Since the *Rite of Christian Initiation of Adults* is the normative rite for adult confirmation, the use of the 1971 *Rite of Confirmation* in adult confirmation is restricted to those exceptional cases[244] in which the adult has not experienced the catechumenal formation periods and celebrations called for by the code and the adult rite.

The principal concerns and tensions that have surfaced in the course of the historical development of confirmation underlie the code's treatment of the sacrament: the nature and effects of confirmation, the minister, the appropriate age for its reception, and the order of its reception in relation to baptism and Eucharist.

The structure of title II repeats that of title I: an introductory theological canon (c. 879), two canons on the celebration of confirmation (cc. 880–881), seven canons on the minister of confirmation (cc. 882–888), three canons on those to be confirmed (cc. 889–891), two canons on sponsors (cc. 892–893), and finally two canons on proof and records (cc. 894–896).

There are far fewer canons on confirmation than there are on baptism, primarily because of the restored unity between this sacrament and baptism for adults. Such requirements as the preparation for the celebration of and sponsors in adult confirmation have already been treated in the canons on baptism. Despite the restoration of the catechumenate, the canons themselves presume a celebration of confirmation apart from baptism. Although the unified rite of celebrating confirmation together with baptism and Eucharist is normative, the canons reflect the more common or frequent situation in which confirmation is celebrated as a separate and distinct rite.[245]

The canons also presume that confirmation is celebrated before the reception of first Eucharist, even when baptism was celebrated several years before confirmation. Consequently, the canons do not reflect the ordering of the sacraments most common in the United States: baptism, penance, Eucharist, and confirmation. Canon 891 allows

confirmation to be deferred until a later age after the reception of first Eucharist. Nevertheless, the code treats this as an exception to the order retained in all the liturgical books according to which confirmation is followed by first reception of the Eucharist.

The treatment of confirmation in the Eastern code shows some marked differences from that in the Latin code. There are far fewer canons on confirmation in the Eastern code (only six), compared with eighteen canons in the Latin code. One major difference lies in the way the two codes legislate on the minister of the sacrament, to which the Latin code devotes seven canons but the Eastern code only two.[246] The reason for this difference is that in the Eastern churches, the presbyter is the ordinary minister of the sacrament, while in the West the presbyter can function as the minister only within the parameters spelled out in canons 883–887. A second other major difference is the significantly greater emphasis in the Eastern code on the unity of the sacraments of initiation.[247] For the Eastern churches, the celebration of confirmation apart from baptism[248] and the Eucharist is clearly exceptional, while, except in the case of adults, it is generally the rule in the West. The third major difference is the age at which this sacrament is administered. The Eastern code reaffirms the ancient Eastern tradition of confirming infants[249] while the Latin code specifies that confirmation is conferred "at about the age of discretion."[250] Finally, the Eastern code does not refer to this sacrament as "confirmation," but as "chrismation with holy myron" or simply "chrismation."

---

[244] See *RCIA* 240, *DOL* 2433.
[245] See McManus, in *CLSA Com,* 632.
[246] See *CCEO* 694, 696.
[247] See especially *CCEO* 697.
[248] *CCEO* 697 speaks of the Eucharist as the perfection of sacramental initiation. However, it does not state that the Eucharist is to be celebrated in conjunction with baptism and confirmation, but "as soon as possible" afterward. *CCEO* 710, dealing with recipients of the Eucharist, confirms that infants receive the Eucharist some time after baptism and chrismation, according to prescriptions of each church *sui iuris* "with suitable due precautions."
[249] See *CCEO* 695.
[250] Canon 891.

Nature and Effects of Confirmation

Canon 879 — The sacrament of confirmation strengthens the baptized and obliges them more firmly to be witnesses of Christ by word and deed and to spread and defend the faith. It imprints a character, enriches by the gift of the Holy Spirit the baptized continuing on the path of Christian initiation, and binds them more perfectly to the Church.

The initial canon on confirmation is a theological summary of the nature and effects of the sacrament and is drawn from the revised rite of 1971:

> Those who have been baptized continue on the path of Christian initiation through the sacrament of confirmation. In this sacrament they receive the Holy Spirit whom the Lord sent upon the apostles on Pentecost.
>
> This giving of the Holy Spirit conforms believers more fully to Christ and strengthens them so that they may bear witness to Christ for the building up of his Body in faith and love. They are so marked with the character or seal of the Lord that the sacrament of confirmation cannot be repeated.[251]

This citation from the 1971 *Rite of Confirmation* in turn draws heavily from conciliar teaching:

> By the sacrament of confirmation they are more perfectly bound to the Church and are endowed with the special strength of the Holy Spirit. Hence they are, as true witnesses of Christ, more strictly obliged to spread and defend the faith by word and deed.[252]
>
> As members of the living Christ, incorporated into him and made like him by baptism, confirmation and the Eucharist, all the faithful have an obligation to collaborate in

the expansion and spread of his Body, so that they might bring it to fullness as soon as possible.[253]

Confirmation is an unrepeatable gift which is the Holy Spirit. The canon avoids any speculation on the nature of the sacramental character which was treated in canon 845, §1. The text of the canon is more nuanced than the rite in its description of the action of the Holy Spirit. The canon sees the Holy Spirit as "enriching" what was already begun in baptism, whereas the rite states that in confirmation one "receives" the Holy Spirit. The canon, then, presents a more balanced view in which the Holy Spirit is seen as acting in both baptism and confirmation.

One effect of the gift of the Spirit is that it strengthens those who are confirmed, and in addition obliges them more firmly to be witnesses to Christ, a theme drawn almost verbatim from the rite. Finally, the confirmed person is enabled by the Holy Spirit "to spread and defend the faith." The notion of spreading the faith is drawn from the rite, which uses the terminology "building up his Body," but even more explicitly from the teaching of *Lumen gentium* and *Ad gentes* cited above.

The canon departs from the 1971 rite when it speaks of confirmation as binding one "more perfectly to the Church." The rite's focus is more christocentric: the sacrament "conforms believers more fully to Christ." The canon's stress on the ecclesial effect of confirmation flows from *Lumen gentium* and *Ad gentes*.

That confirmation enables one to "defend the faith" is drawn from *Lumen gentium* 11 and echoes a more martial understanding of confirmation as a sacrament by which the person becomes a "soldier of Christ."[254]

The canon's reference to the candidates for confirmation as "the baptized continuing on the path of Christian initiation" presumes a prior celebration of

---

[251] *RConf* 1–2, *DOL* 2510–2511.
[252] *LG* 11.
[253] *AG* 36.
[254] *CCEO* 692 refrains from using martial terminology; instead, it describes those confirmed as "more proper witnesses and co-builders in the Kingdom of God."

baptism. Confirmation is seen as a continuation of Christian initiation begun earlier with baptism.[255]

In light of the history of this sacrament, one might wonder whether the canon presents a theological synthesis of confirmation or merely a listing of different theologies of confirmation which have been emphasized at one time or another in the course of its development. One such theology which sees confirmation as intimately related to baptism is apparent in the phrase "continuing on the path of Christian initiation" and finds its expression in the rite: "They [the apostles] received the power of giving the Holy Spirit to others and so completing the work of baptism."[256] This theology is also evident in the apostolic constitution of Paul VI which promulgated the revised rite:

> Then those who believed the apostles' preaching were baptized and they too received "the gift of the Holy Spirit." From that time on, the apostles, in fulfillment of Christ's wish, imparted to the newly baptized by the laying on of hands the gift of the Spirit that completes the grace of baptism. This is why the Letter to the Hebrews listed among the first elements of Christian instruction the teaching about baptism and the laying on of hands.[257]

A second theology, which considers confirmation principally as the reception of the Holy Spirit, is in evidence in the canon's phrase, "enriches by the gift of the Holy Spirit"; and in the rite's, "Bishops...have the power of giving the Holy Spirit to the baptized."[258] This theology is also found in Paul VI's apostolic constitution:

> From ancient times the conferring of the gift of the Holy Spirit has been carried out in the

Church through various rites. These rites have undergone many changes in the East and the West, but always keeping as their meaning the conferring of the Holy Spirit.[259]

A third theology, which sees confirmation as the fulfillment of the events of Pentecost and emphasizes not so much the gift of the Holy Spirit as the plurality of gifts for the unity of the Church, is not as pronounced in the canon as it is in the rite:

> On the day of Pentecost the apostles received the Holy Spirit as the Lord had promised. ...In our day the coming of the Holy Spirit in confirmation is no longer marked by the gift of tongues, but we know his coming by faith. He fills our hearts with the love of God, brings us together in one faith but in different vocations and works within us to make the Church one and holy. Christ gives varied gifts to his Church, and the Spirit distributes them among the members of Christ's body to build up the holy people of God in unity and love.[260]

A fourth theology, which considers confirmation primarily as the source of spiritual power, is reflected in the canon's phrase, "confirmation strengthens the baptized," but this theology is even more clearly expressed in the rite:

> The gift of the Holy Spirit which you are to receive will be a spiritual sign and seal to make you more like Christ and more perfect members of the Church.... You have already been baptized into Christ and now you will receive the power of his Spirit.[261]

The theology of confirmation most clearly reflected in the canon is one that sees confirmation as a sacrament of spiritual maturity in witnessing

---

[255] Such a reference to the baptized is, of course, absent from *CCEO* 692.

[256] *RConf* 22, *Rites*, 487.

[257] *Divinae consortium naturae, AAS* 63 (1971) 659, *DOL* 2501.

[258] *RConf* 22, *Rites*, 487.

[259] *Divinae consortium naturae, AAS* 63 (1971) 660, *DOL* 2503.

[260] *RConf* 22, *Rites*, 488.

[261] Ibid.

to the faith, spreading it, and defending it. This is also clear in the rite, which adds the responsibility of service:

You must be witnesses before all the world to his suffering, death and resurrection; your way of life should at all times reflect the goodness of Christ.... Be active members of the Church, alive in Jesus Christ. Under the guidance of the Holy Spirit give your lives completely in the service of all, as did Christ, who came not to be served but to serve.[262]

Some of these theologies are complementary. Confirmation as the sacrament of the Holy Spirit, the sacrament of the plurality of gifts of the Holy Spirit for the unity of the Church, and the sacrament of the spiritual power of the Holy Spirit can easily be understood as complementary aspects of one sacrament. But the two remaining theologies are often seen as competing. Confirmation as a sacrament intimately linked with baptism from which it cannot be separated, and confirmation as a sacrament of maturity are not easily harmonized. Those who see confirmation primarily as the completion of baptism tend to call for reception of the sacrament at a much earlier age, preferably prior to or in conjunction with first reception of the Eucharist. Those who see confirmation as a sacrament of maturity, which is the predominant theme in many current catechetical texts, call for more extensive preparation for confirmation after a person's first reception of the Eucharist and the deferral of the reception of the sacrament well beyond the age of seven.

CHAPTER I
THE CELEBRATION OF CONFIRMATION
[cc. 880–881]

The code devotes only two canons to the celebration of confirmation. The first treats the essential

matter and form necessary for the validity of the sacrament; the second deals with the place and liturgical context for its celebration. The brevity of this treatment is an implicit recognition that, in the normative rite of adult initiation, confirmation is celebrated together with baptism. Therefore, much of what was specified earlier for the celebration of baptism applies also to the celebration of confirmation.

Essential Elements of the Sacrament

Canon 880 — §1. The sacrament of confirmation is conferred by the anointing of chrism on the forehead, which is done by the imposition of the hand and through the words prescribed in the approved liturgical books.

§2. The chrism to be used in the sacrament of confirmation must be consecrated by a bishop even if a presbyter administers the sacrament.

Although the discipline of confirmation has varied widely throughout its history, the essential elements of the imposition of the hand and anointing with oil have remained constant. Nevertheless, the relationship between these two actions has received different emphases in the course of this development. Canon 780 of the 1917 code described the anointing and the imposition of hands as two distinct actions which accompany one another: "The sacrament of confirmation shall be conferred by the imposition of the hand accompanied by the anointing of the forehead with chrism."[263] Greater stress was placed on the anointing, since the imposition of hands accompanied it. The present canon restores a more ancient understanding of these essential elements by not treating them as two distinct actions. Rather, the anointing is performed *by* the imposition of the hand. The source of this shift in emphasis is Paul VI's apostolic constitution *Divinae consortium naturae* which promulgated the 1971 revised *Rite of Confirmation*. In that document the Holy Father sketched the development of the relationship

---

[262] *RConf* 22, *Rites*, 488.

[263] *CIC* 780.

between the anointing and the imposition of the hand. In the descriptions of the essential rite given by Innocent III and Innocent IV, the anointing and imposition of the hand were not two distinct actions, but rather one: the anointing which signifies the laying on of the hand:

> Our predecessor Innocent III wrote: "The anointing of the forehead with chrism signifies the laying on of the hand, the other name for which is confirmation, since through it the Holy Spirit is given for growth and strength." Another of our predecessors, Innocent IV, mentions that the apostles conferred the Holy Spirit "through the laying on of the hand, which confirmation or the anointing of the forehead with chrism represents."[264]

It is evident that these descriptions of the anointing and laying on of the hand are clearly reflected in the text of the current canon, as well as in the words of Paul VI:

> From what we have recalled, it is clear that in the administration of confirmation in the East and the West, though in different ways, the most important place was occupied by the anointing, which in a certain way represents the apostolic laying on of hands.[265]

The first part of paragraph one of the canon is taken verbatim from this apostolic constitution:

> The sacrament of confirmation is conferred through the anointing with Chrism on the forehead which is done by the laying on of the hand, and through the words: Be sealed with the gift of the Holy Spirit.[266]

Thus, both the code and the *Rite* state that the anointing is done by the laying on of the hand. This connection is made more visible when the minister lays the palm of his hand on the head of the one to be confirmed while anointing the forehead with the thumb. However, laying the palm on the head is not the imposition of the hand *per se,* for the code and the rite are quite explicit that it is the anointing itself which constitutes the laying on of the hand. This is confirmed in an authoritative interpretation:

> Query: According to the Apostolic Constitution *Divinae consortium naturae,* must the minister in carrying out the act of anointing with chrism lay his outstretched hand on the head of the one being confirmed or is an anointing with the thumb sufficient?

> Reply: To the first, no; to the second, yes, according to the document. The intent is: anointing with chrism done as described sufficiently expresses the laying on of hands.[267]

There is often confusion of the imposition of the hand, which is done by anointing and which is of the essence of the sacrament, with an immediately preceding rite, what the ritual terms "the laying on of hands."[268] In this rite, the minister faces the people, and invites them to pray silently. Then the minister and any concelebrants "lay hands upon all the candidates (by extending their hands over them)" and the minister alone begins the deprecative prayer, "All powerful God..." The apostolic constitution notes the distinction between the two and terms the essential rite the "laying on of *the hand*" and the preceding, nonessential, rite the "laying on of *hands:*"

In the rites of the Latin Church a laying of hands on those to be confirmed prior to

[264] *Divinae consortium naturae, AAS* 63 (1971) 661, *DOL* 2504.

[265] *Divinae consortium naturae, AAS* 63 (1971) 663, *DOL* 2506.

[266] *Divinae consortium naturae, AAS* 63 (1971) 663, *DOL* 2507.

[267] Pontifical Commission for the Interpretation of the Decrees of Vatican Council II, reply, June 9, 1972, *AAS* 64 (1972) 526, *DOL* 2529.

[268] *RConf* 24, *Rites,* 489–490.

anointing them with chrism was always pre-scribed.... But the laying of hands on the elect, carried out with the prescribed prayer before the anointing, is still to be regarded as very important, even if it is not of the essence of the sacramental rite: it contributes to the complete perfection of the rite and to a more thorough understanding of the sacra-ment. It is evident that this prior laying on of *hands* differs from the later laying on of *the hand* in the anointing of the forehead.[269]

Although the distinction is clear in the apostolic constitution, on the pastoral level it is not. The rit-ual itself contributes to this confusion by entitling the non-essential rite "The Laying On of Hands," which is followed immediately by "The Anoint-ing with Chrism" in which neither the text nor the rubrics give any indication that this anointing is also the essential laying on of the hand.

The apostolic constitution also changed the verbal formula to which the last phrase of para-graph one refers. The Holy Father noted that the Byzantine expression "the seal of the Holy Spirit" can be traced back to the fourth century. The tra-ditional Latin form had been: "I sign you with the sign of the cross and confirm you with the chrism of salvation. In the name of the Father and of the Son and of the Holy Spirit." However, this form was not stabilized until the thirteenth century. Paul VI preferred the Byzantine expression, not because of its antiquity, but because of the promi-nence it attributes to the role of the Holy Spirit.[270] It is this ancient Byzantine expression which, modified slightly, has become the formula in the liturgical books to which the canon refers: "N., be sealed with the gift of the Holy Spirit."

In the now abrogated formula of the Latin church, it was clear that the anointing on the fore-head was done with the sign of the cross. The new formulary does not mention the sign of the cross,

nor does the apostolic constitution state that the anointing is to be done in the form of a cross. The *praenotanda* of the *Rite of Confirmation* also make no reference to the sign of the cross.[271] How-ever, the rubrics make explicit that the anointing is to be done by the sign of the cross.[272]

The second paragraph of canon 880 is an applica-tion to confirmation of the norm of canon 847 and states that the chrism used in the anointing of the forehead must always be consecrated by a bishop.[273] This holds true even when a presbyter is the minis-ter of confirmation. Although a presbyter may con-firm in certain circumstances, he cannot consecrate the chrism. The canon makes no provision for ex-ceptions in danger-of-death situations. If the priest does not have chrism consecrated by a bishop, he cannot consecrate it himself, even though he may bless the oil of the sick and the oil of catechu-mens[274] in cases of necessity.[275] Although the canon states that the chrism must be consecrated by a [i.e., any] bishop, canon 847, §2 states that the priest should secure the oil from his own diocesan bishop as a way of stressing the link between a priest using the oil and the bishop as the principal liturgical cel-ebrant of the particular church.[276]

The canon makes no reference to the oil itself other than calling it chrism. Canon 847, §1 notes that while olive oil is preferred, oil pressed from other plants may also be used, to which "some aromatic substance is added."[277] The rite explains the significance of chrism:

The chrism is a sign that Christians, incor-porated by baptism into the paschal mystery of Christ, dying, buried and rising with him, are sharers in his kingly and prophetic priesthood and that by confirmation they re-

---

[269] *Divinae consortium naturae, AAS* 63 (1971) 664, *DOL* 2505, 2507.

[270] *Divinae consortium naturae, AAS* 63 (1971) 663, *DOL* 2505.

[271] See *RConf* 9, *DOL* 2518.

[272] *RConf* 27, *Rites,* 490.

[273] *ROils* 6, *DOL* 3866. *CCEO* 693, while making refer-ence to particular law, also reserves the confection of the myron to a bishop or the patriarch.

[274] *ROils* 7, *DOL* 3837.

[275] Canon 999, 2°.

[276] See c. 835, §1.

[277] *ROils* 4, *DOL* 3864.

ceive the spiritual anointing of the Spirit who is given to them.[278]

Place of Celebration

Canon 881 — It is desirable to celebrate the sacrament of confirmation in a church and during Mass; for a just and reasonable cause, however, it can be celebrated outside Mass and in any worthy place.

In the normative rite of adult initiation, the place for celebrating confirmation is the place where the baptism is celebrated. Thus, the canon implicitly refers to the norms governing the proper place of celebrating baptism given in canons 857–860.

The canon states a double preference: the celebration should take place in a church, and in conjunction with a celebration of the Eucharist.[279] Both preferences of the canon receive a more expansive and stronger treatment in the rite, which also provides the rationale for these preferences:

> Adult catechumens and children who are baptized at an age when they are old enough for catechesis should ordinarily be admitted to confirmation and the Eucharist at the same time as they receive baptism. If this is impossible they should receive confirmation at another community celebration. Similarly, adults who were baptized in infancy should, after suitable preparation, receive confirmation and the Eucharist at a community celebration.[280]

Confirmation takes place as a rule within Mass in order that the fundamental connection of this sacrament with all of Christian initiation may stand out in a clearer light. Christian initiation reaches its culmination in the communion of the body and blood of Christ. The newly confirmed therefore participate in the Eucharist, which completes their Christian initiation.[281]

The canon also reflects the conciliar teaching which called for the revision of the rite:

> Confirmation may be conferred within Mass when convenient; as for the rite outside Mass, a formulary is to be composed for use as an introduction.[282]

The code has a much stronger preference for the celebration of confirmation during a Mass than did the council, which called for celebration within Mass only "if convenient." The reason for this change is clear. Between the council and the revision of the code, the rites of the sacraments, and especially the rite for adult initiation, were revised. With the restoration of the integral unity of the sacraments of initiation, the celebration of the Eucharist became necessary, since the neophytes are called to participate in it.

However, the canon does allow for confirmation to be celebrated in a place other than a church and outside of Mass "for a just and reasonable cause." The *Rite* itself suggests what would be such a just and reasonable cause for celebrating confirmation outside Mass: when those confirmed will not receive first Eucharist, something which may occur when the candidates are children.[283]

The revised *Rite of Confirmation* contains a "Rite of Confirmation outside Mass," which includes the celebration of the word. The inclusion of the liturgy of the word more than satisfies the call made at the council for a formulary to be composed and used when the rite is celebrated outside Mass.

The rite does not give any explicit indication of when the celebration of confirmation may take place "in any worthy place" as allowed for in the canon. The "Rite of Confirmation of a Person in Danger of Death" would most likely be celebrated outside a church, but not necessarily in "a worthy place."

---

[278] *ROils* 2, *DOL* 3862.
[279] The Eastern code makes no reference to the place of confirmation.
[280] *RConf* 11, *DOL* 2520.

[281] *RConf* 13, *DOL* 2522.
[282] *SC* 71.
[283] *RConf* 13, *DOL* 2522.

CHAPTER II
THE MINISTER OF CONFIRMATION
[cc. 882–888]

Because of the substantial disciplinary change allowing presbyters to confirm in a number of circumstances, the treatment of the minister of confirmation in chapter 2 contains the largest number of canons of any chapter in the code's treatment of confirmation, The historical development of confirmation attests to the fact that the minister of confirmation in the Latin church has not always been a bishop. In some localities, confirmation by a presbyter was a custom which Rome grudgingly tolerated and finally suppressed in the sixteenth century. This suppression created problems during the age of discovery and its attendant rapid missionary expansion, which coincided with the Counter Reformation. The paucity of bishops in missionary territories prompted repeated requests to Rome for a wider concession to non-bishops of the faculty to confirm. Most of these requests were denied, since the reformers allowed this practice. When the heat of the Counter Reformation began to cool, the faculty to confirm was granted to vicars apostolic.[284] By the nineteenth century the faculty to confirm was regularly granted to individual presbyters in mission territories, but it could only be used in the absence of a bishop.[285]

Canon 782 of the 1917 code recognized the faculty by law of those equivalent in law to a bishop (abbots, prelates *nullius,* apostolic prefects, and vicars) to confirm within the confines of their territory. Presbyters had no general faculty from the law to confirm, although it could be conceded to them by the Holy See.[286] However, such concessions were rare. Pius XII was the first to break the long tradition that presbyters had no faculty by law to confirm when he granted this faculty to pastors and some other presbyters with the full care of souls in cases of danger of death.[287] However, in these cases, the faculty could be exercised only in the absence of a bishop. In subsequent years, this faculty was gradually extended to more and more priests in pastoral ministry, but its concession was reserved to the Holy See.[288] In 1963 Pope Paul VI allowed diocesan bishops to grant this faculty to presbyters.[289] The revised *Rite of Confirmation* (1971) significantly expanded the faculty by law for presbyters to confirm by extending it to: those presbyters equivalent in law to diocesan bishops within the limit of their territory, presbyters who have the mandate to baptize adults or children of catechetical age or who admit already baptized adults or children of catechetical age to full communion with the Catholic Church, and, in danger-of-death situations, presbyters who hold some office in the Church or who are parochial vicars.[290] The *Rite's* expansion of this faculty for presbyters to confirm is the source of the code's legislation, particularly in canon 883.

The canons follow a logical order in presenting the discipline governing the minister of confirmation: a general norm on the ordinary minister and special[291] ministers of the sacrament (c. 882); the circumstances in which the law grants the faculty to confirm to special ministers (c. 883); the concession of the faculty to confirm to special ministers by competent authority (c. 884); the pastoral responsibilities of all ministers of confirmation (c. 885); and territorial limitations on all ministers' power to confirm (886–888). While the canons expand the circumstances in which presbyters can exercise the faculty to confirm, the primacy of the bishop as the ordinary minister of the sacrament is reaffirmed explicitly or implicitly in every canon except the last, which deals with the right of bishops and presbyters to confirm in exempt places.

---

[284] Barrett, 702.

[285] Ibid.

[286] See *CIC* 782, §2.

[287] SCSacr, decr *Spiritus Sancti munera,* September 14, 1946, *AAS* 38 (1946) 352–353.

[288] For a listing of these additional concessions to confirm, see Woestman, *Sacraments,* 82.

[289] Paul VI, *mp Pastorale munus,* November 30, 1963, *AAS* 56 (1964) 8.

[290] *RConf* 7, *DOL* 2516.

[291] The canon avoids the term "extraordinary" used in the 1917 code (*CIC* 792, §2) for ministers of confirmation.

Ordinary and Special Ministers

Canon 882 — The ordinary minister of confirmation is a bishop; a presbyter provided with this faculty in virtue of universal law or the special grant of the competent authority also confers this sacrament validly.

The canon singles out the bishop as the "ordinary minister" of confirmation. Vatican II's reference to the bishop as the "primary"[292] or "original" minister of the sacrament was a more historically accurate term than "ordinary minister." "Original minister" respected the tradition of the Eastern churches where the bishop could hardly be called the "ordinary" minister, since presbyters were and are the ordinary ministers of confirmation. The term "original minister" also reflected the tradition of the Latin rite where the bishop was indeed the original minister of the sacrament. "Original minister" is also a more theological term than "ordinary minister." It suggests, perhaps, that the power which the Eastern rite bishops exercised originally is a power rooted in orders, so that Eastern rite presbyters also enjoy this same power to confirm.

In the early stages of the revision of the code,[293] "original minister" was changed to "ordinary minister," on the ground that this code applied only to the Latin rite[294] in which the bishop was not only the original minister but the ordinary minister as well. "Ordinary minister" was also selected to emphasize that the power and the faculty to confirm are rooted in the episcopal order, so that presbyters confirm not by reason of their order, but only by reason of the power granted to them as a faculty, either by law or by concession from competent authority.[295] By using the term "ordinary" rather than "original," the canon skirts

the question of the theological basis for granting the faculty to confirm to presbyters.

A presbyter acquires the faculty to confirm either from the law[296] or from a concession by competent authority.[297] In the revised code, the authority competent to concede to presbyters the faculty to confirm is not the Holy See alone as it was in canon 782, §2 of the 1917 code. However, this change in discipline had already been introduced prior to the promulgation of the 1983 code.[298]

Special Ministers by Law

Canon 883 — The following possess the faculty of administering confirmation by the law itself:

1° within the boundaries of their jurisdiction, those who are equivalent in law to a diocesan bishop;

2° as regards the person in question, the presbyter who by virtue of office or mandate of the diocesan bishop baptizes one who is no longer an infant or admits one already baptized into the full communion of the Catholic Church;

3° as regards those who are in danger of death, the pastor or indeed any presbyter.

This canon and the following one are the cardinal canons of chapter 2, for they specify those presbyters who have the faculty to confirm either from the law (c. 883) or from the concession of competent authority (c. 884). Canon 883 recognizes three circumstances in which the common law of the Church grants presbyters the faculty to confirm.

---

[292] *LG* 26. See *RConf* 7, *DOL* 2516. The bishop was called the "original minister" in the proposed *Lex Ecclesiae Fundamentalis*.

[293] See *Comm* 3 (1971) 204.

[294] Canon 1.

[295] *Comm* 3 (1971) 204.

[296] *RConf* 7, *DOL* 2516; c. 883.

[297] Canon 884. The treatment of the minister of chrismation in the Eastern code is greatly simplified, since all presbyters have by law the faculty to administer this sacrament to infants and adults alike, either in the context of the celebration of baptism or apart from it, and regardless of the rite *sui iuris* to which the one to be chrismated belongs. They need no special faculty by concession as do presbyters in the West. See *CCEO* 694, 696, §1.

[298] See, for example, *Pastorale munus* 8 by which bishops are the "competent authority" to grant faculties for confirmation to presbyters.

First, the law grants those who are equivalent in law to a diocesan bishop the faculty to confirm within the territory assigned to them. Those equivalent in law to a diocesan bishop are not themselves bishops, but presbyters who preside over particular churches that have not yet been raised to the status of a diocese. The canon repeats the norm already contained in the revised *Rite of Confirmation.*[299] Those who are equivalent in law to a diocesan bishop are identified in canons 381, §2 and 368: they are the prelates who preside over territorial prelatures, territorial abbeys, apostolic vicariates, apostolic prefectures, and apostolic administrations erected on a stable basis. Although canon 368 does not mention diocesan administrators (formerly called "vicars capitular") as equivalent in law to a diocesan bishop, they are included among those granted the faculty to confirm by the law in liturgical law, for they are explicitly mentioned in the *Rite of Confirmation.*[300]

Both the *Rite* and the code are careful to specify that those equivalent in law to a bishop have the faculty to confirm only "within the limits of their territory." Outside their territory, they have no faculty and, therefore, confer confirmation there invalidly. This restriction on the valid exercise of the faculty to confirm by these presbyters is mentioned again in canon 887.

Second, the law grants the faculty to confirm to presbyters who, in virtue of their office or the mandate of the diocesan bishop, have a particular relationship with the one to be confirmed. The canon again draws heavily from the revised *Rite of Confirmation:*

> The law gives the faculty to confirm to the following besides the bishop: . . . priests who, in virtue of an office they lawfully hold, baptize an adult or a child old enough for catechesis or receive a validly baptized adult into the full communion of the Church.[301]

This extension to presbyters of the faculty by law to confirm is a direct result of the restoration of the unity of the sacraments of initiation called for by Vatican Council II. Since the normative rite for adult initiation calls for candidates to be confirmed immediately following their baptisms and in the same liturgical celebration, presbyters who baptize adults need the faculty to confirm. The law also calls for adults who have already been baptized in a non-Catholic church or ecclesial community and who now seek full communion with the Catholic Church to be confirmed as part of the celebration of their reception into the Church. Thus, canon 883 incorporates into the code the grant to presbyters of the faculty to confirm previously made by liturgical law in the revised *Rite of Confirmation* and in the *Rite of Christian Initiation of Adults.*[302]

The canon, however, slightly expands the scope of the faculty presbyters enjoy by law. In the *Rite of Confirmation,* the law grants presbyters the faculty to confirm adults whom they baptize or receive into full communion in virtue of their office; the canon adds that the law grants the faculty to confirm to presbyters who baptize adults or receive them into full communion in virtue of a "mandate of the diocesan bishop." This expansion of the faculty covers those cases when a priest has no ecclesiastical office, but has the pastoral care of souls as would be the case for certain chaplains whose duties do not normally include baptizing adults. Canon 833, 2° grants the faculty to confirm to presbyters who, in virtue of their office or mandate, already possess the faculty to baptize adults and to receive them into full communion. Essentially, the law extends their faculty to baptize to include the faculty to confirm as well. A presbyter's office or mandate to baptize or receive adults into full communion may be territorially limited. If so, canon 887 confines his valid exercise of his faculty to confirm to the limits of this territory.

Since parish priests have the faculty to confirm by law, the diocesan bishop cannot revoke it or restrict its exercise. The diocesan bishop may, how-

---

[299] *RConf* 7, *DOL* 2516.
[300] Ibid.
[301] Ibid.

[302] *RCIA* 46, *DOL* 2373.

ever, reserve to himself the baptisms of adults fourteen years of age or older (c. 863). If he does so, the bishop must also confirm them.[303]

The canon lists several conditions which must met for parish priests to exercise validly the faculty to confirm adults they baptize or receive into full communion. First, the confirmation must follow immediately after the baptismal washing or the reception of an already baptized person into full communion by a profession of faith, and not at a later time or in a different liturgical celebration. Second, this faculty from the law to confirm can be exercised only on behalf of adults. Presbyters cannot confirm children under seven years of age when they baptize them or when they receive them into the Church, except in danger-of-death situations.

Thus, the canon mentions only two cases when a presbyter can confirm in virtue of office or mandate in ordinary circumstances: when baptizing an adult and when receiving an adult into full communion.[304] However, there are two other cases in which a priest with the faculty or mandate to baptize or receive into full communion may also lawfully confirm. These two additional circumstances arise from two authentic interpretations of the decrees of Vatican Council II. Both of these authentic interpretations concern the readmission to full communion of persons who had previously been baptized in the Catholic Church.

The first interpretation dealt with the case of readmission to the Church of Catholics who were never confirmed and who apostatized from the faith. A presbyter may validly confirm these baptized Catholics upon their readmission into full communion.[305] The second interpretation concerned the case of readmission to the Catholic Church of a person who was baptized in the Catholic Church as an infant but "who without fault has been instructed in a non-Catholic religion or adhered to a non-Catholic religion."[306] If this instruction in or adherence to a non-Catholic religion was not the fault of the person, then a presbyter may validly and lawfully confirm that person upon his or her readmission to full practice of the faith.

Thus, the law foresees four situations in which a presbyter may lawfully confirm in virtue of office or mandate: when he baptizes an adult; when he receives a previously baptized non-Catholic into full communion; when he readmits into full communion a previously baptized Catholic who apostatized from the faith; and when he readmits into full communion a previously baptized Catholic who through no personal fault was instructed in or adhered to a non-Catholic religion.

Neither the law nor authentic interpretations of the law have made provision for presbyters to confirm in other frequently occurring situations. Thus, a presbyter cannot validly confirm: baptized Catholics who were instructed in or adhered to a non-Catholic religion by their own fault; baptized Catholics who were not raised as Catholic but who never belonged to any other church; and baptized Catholics who have never left the Church but were never confirmed. The law's failure to provide presbyters with the faculty to confirm in these situations does create pastoral problems when people in these situations enter a parish RCIA program as part of their return to the full practice of the faith. Although the parish priest has no faculty from the

---

[303] *RConf* 11, *DOL* 2520; c. 866.

[304] *CCEO* 696, §2 gives Latin rite presbyters the right to confer chrismation on the faithful of the Eastern churches, to the extent of their faculties as Latin rite presbyters. Thus, while an Eastern rite presbyter validly administers the sacrament to any of the faithful of the Latin rite, Latin rite presbyters validly administer the sacrament only to those members of Eastern churches for which they have the faculty to confirm the faithful of the Latin rite. Note, however, that *CCEO* 696, §3 requires for *liceity* that Eastern presbyters confer chrismation on the faithful of other churches *sui iuris* "with regard for the agreements entered between the Churches *sui iuris* in this matter."

[305] Pontifical Commission for the Interpretation of the Decrees of Vatican Council II, reply, April 25, 1975, *AAS* 67 (1975) 348, *DOL* 2352.

[306] Pontifical Commission for the Interpretation of the Decrees of Vatican Council II, reply, December 21, 1979, *AAS* 72 (1980) 105.

law to confirm these people, he could seek from the diocesan bishop the concession of the faculty to confirm them (c. 884).

In virtue of canon 144 the Church supplies faculties to confirm which are absent in cases of common error. For an application to the present canon, see the commentary on canon 144.

In danger-of-death situations, any presbyter has the faculty by law to confirm. The canon is drawn from the *Rite of Confirmation:*

> The law gives the faculty to confirm to the following besides the bishop:...in danger of death, provided a bishop is not easily available or is lawfully impeded: pastors, and parochial vicars; in their absence their associate pastors; priests who are in charge of special parishes lawfully established; administrators, substitute and assistant priests; in the absence of all of the preceding, any priest who is not disqualified by censure or canonical penalty.[307]

The canon is less restrictive than the *Rite* in this situation in three respects. First, unlike the *Rite,* the canon makes no reference to the absence of a bishop as a condition for the licit exercise of the faculty to confirm in danger-of-death situations. Second, the canon expresses no preference for the presbyter who should confirm if more than one of them is present in a danger-of-death situation as the *Rite* does. Only the pastor is singled out for special mention. Third, the canon makes no reference at all to a censure or canonical penalty which, according to the *Rite,* would disqualify a presbyter from confirming. In short, the canon greatly simplifies the exercise of the faculty given by the law to presbyters to confirm in danger-of-death situations.

Faculty by Concession

Canon 884 — §1. The diocesan bishop is to administer confirmation personally or is to take

[307]*RConf* 7, *DOL* 2516.

care that another bishop administers it. If necessity requires it, he can grant the faculty to one or more specific presbyters, who are to administer this sacrament.

§2. For a grave cause the bishop and even the presbyter endowed with the faculty of confirming in virtue of the law or the special grant of the competent authority can in single cases also associate presbyters with themselves to administer the sacrament.

The previous canon stipulated those situations in which a presbyter has the faculty to confirm by the law itself. The present canon provides the means by which a presbyter may obtain the faculty by concession of competent authority for situations in which he does not have the faculty by law. In the 1917 code and in church law prior to Vatican Council II, the sole authority competent to concede to presbyters the faculty to confirm was the Holy See. The council called for the extension of this authority to the diocesan bishop. The present canon reflects this development. The canon treats two ways in which the faculty to confirm can be conceded: the concession of the faculty by the diocesan bishop to permit one or more designated presbyters to confirm in his absence, and the concession of the faculty by the bishop or delegated minister to associate other ministers with him in a concelebration of confirmation.

By recalling the particular obligation of the diocesan bishop to administer the sacrament personally, the canon reaffirms that the bishop is the ordinary minister of confirmation. If it is at all possible, the diocesan bishop should administer the sacrament throughout the diocese entrusted to him. If he is unable to do so, another bishop is the preferred alternate minister, since he too is an ordinary minister of the sacrament. The *Rite of Confirmation* explains this preference for a bishop as the minister of confirmation:

> The primary minister of confirmation is the bishop. Normally a bishop administers the sacrament so that there will be a clearer ref-

erence to the first pouring forth of the Holy Spirit on Pentecost: after the apostles were filled with the Holy Spirit, they themselves gave the Spirit to the faithful through the laying on of hands. Thus the reception of the Spirit through the ministry of the bishop shows the close bond that joins the confirmed to the Church and the mandate received from Christ to bear witness to him before all.[308]

The designation of a presbyter as minister of confirmation is clearly less desirable than employing another bishop, as is indicated by the canon's qualification of this option with the clause "if necessity requires." No such qualification is attached to the selection of a bishop other than the diocesan bishop. The canon does not specify what constitutes a case of necessity. Situations such as the absence of the bishop from his diocese, his illness, distance, and the large number of parishes in a diocese would be sufficient to constitute a situation of necessity. The canon specifies that one or more "specific" presbyters can be conceded the faculty in cases of necessity. This limitation on the bishop's concession of the faculty to presbyters is meant to safeguard the primacy of the bishop as ordinary minister of confirmation. Thus, a diocesan bishop is not to grant the faculty to confirm to all or most of the priests in his diocese. The canon imposes no additional limitations on the bishop's discretion to choose the presbyter or presbyters to whom he concedes the faculty to confirm. Thus, any priest may be so delegated.

Canon 884, §2 foresees the situation in which the number of those to be confirmed is so large that the minister of the sacrament needs to be assisted by one or more co-ministers of the sacrament. The concelebration of the sacrament would prevent an unduly protracted celebration of confirmation. Since confirmation is generally celebrated in the context of the Eucharist, the use of co-ministers of the sacrament would also prevent the conferral of confirmation from overshadowing the celebration of the Eucharist.[309]

The text of paragraph two is inspired by the *Rite of Confirmation:*

On the basis of true need and a special reason, as sometimes is present because of the large number of those to be confirmed, the minister of confirmation mentioned in n. 7 [the bishop] or the extraordinary minister designated by special indult of the Apostolic See or by law may associate other priests with himself in the administration of this sacrament.

It is required that these priests either have a particular function or office in the diocese, being, namely, vicars general, episcopal vicars or delegates, district or regional vicars, or those who by mandate of the Ordinary are counted as equal to these *ex officio;* or be the pastors of the places where confirmation is conferred, pastors of the places where the candidates belong, or priests who have had a special part in the catechetical preparation of the candidates.[310]

The most obvious difference between the canon and the *Rite* is the simplification of the criteria for selecting presbyters to join the principal minister in the celebration of the sacrament. The rite shows a marked preference for a priest who holds some diocesan office, probably to reflect the connection between the designated priest and the bishop who is the ordinary minister. In the absence of a diocesan official, the pastor of the place of confirmation, or of the candidates, or a priest who played a principal part in the catechesis of the candidates is to be designated by the principal minister in that order. On the other hand, the canon expresses no order of preference for the presbyters who are to join the principal minister in celebrating the sacrament.

---

[308] Ibid.

[309] See McManus, in *CLSA Com,* 637.
[310] *RConf* 8, *DOL* 2517.

The canon treats this concelebration of confirmation as an exceptional event, since it is permitted only "for a grave cause." The *Rite* gives an example of what constitutes such a grave cause: "the large numbers of those to be confirmed." That concelebration is exceptional is also evident in the canon's stipulation that concelebration is permitted only "in single cases."

Both the canon and the rite state that the bishop (the canon is more specific in qualifying him as the "diocesan bishop") and the presbyter who has the faculty to confirm either by law or by concession can concede to other priests the faculty to confirm. Although the diocesan bishop can designate a priest to confirm in his absence, the designated priest can associate other priests with him to confirm only in a ceremony at which he personally exercises his faculty to confirm. He cannot "subdelegate" the faculty to another priest to confirm in his absence.

The rite describes how these associated priests function in the celebration of confirmation. They extend hands over the candidates along with the principal celebrant, but do not join in the prayer which accompanies this "laying on of hands."[311] They confer the anointing in the same way as the principal minister.[312]

Obligations of Ministers

Canon 885 — §1. The diocesan bishop is obliged to take care that the sacrament of confirmation is conferred on subjects who properly and reasonably seek it.

§2. A presbyter who possesses this faculty must use it for the sake of those in whose favor the faculty was granted.

Since bishops have the power and some presbyters the faculty to confirm, they have the obligation to use the power or faculty on behalf of those for whom it was given. As the ordinary minister of confirmation, the bishop has the ultimate responsibility to see that confirmation is conferred on his subjects who properly and reasonably request it. Since the sacrament of confirmation is necessary for full initiation into the Church, baptized members of the faithful are entitled to this sacrament,[313] provided that they are properly prepared and request it freely.

The priest who has the faculty to confirm, whether by law or by special concession, has the obligation to use that faculty on behalf of those for whom it was granted. Thus, a presbyter is bound to confirm adults he baptizes or receives into full communion with the Catholic Church on the occasion of the baptism or rite of admission. No presbyter should neglect to confirm a person in danger of death.

Rights of and Restrictions on the Ordinary Minister

Canon 886 — §1. A bishop in his diocese legitimately administers the sacrament of confirmation even to faithful who are not his subjects, unless their own ordinary expressly prohibits it.

§2. To administer confirmation licitly in another diocese, a bishop needs at least the reasonably presumed permission of the diocesan bishop unless it concerns his own subjects.

The remaining canons of this chapter deal with the rights of and restrictions on ministers of the sacrament of confirmation.[314] Canon 886 treats of the rights of bishop ministers; canon 887 of the rights of presbyter ministers. Canon 888 addresses the particular situation when confirmation is celebrated in exempt places. The context of all three of these canons is the effect of the territory or place in which confirmation is conferred on the lawfulness and validity of the celebration.

---

[311] *RConf* 9, *DOL* 2518.
[312] *RConf* 45.

[313] See c. 213.
[314] The Eastern code presents a simplified version of the restrictions on the minister of chrismation in c. 696, §3. These restrictions are only for liceity.

Canon 886 deals with the situation in which a bishop is the minister of confirmation. Within the confines of his own diocese, the bishop has the right to confirm his own subjects. He confirms validly and licitly the subject of another ordinary, unless that ordinary has expressly prohibited him from doing so. Outside his own diocese, a bishop confirms licitly with at least the implied permission of the local diocesan bishop. Even without this permission and even if expressly prohibited, the bishop confirms his own subjects validly and licitly in another ordinary's territory. Since the canon does not speak of a "diocesan bishop" but simply of a "bishop" without qualification, auxiliary bishops and retired bishops enjoy the same rights as does the diocesan bishop in the exercise of their ministry to confirm.

Rights of and Restrictions on Presbyter Ministers

Canon 887 — A presbyter who possesses the faculty of administering confirmation also confers this sacrament licitly on externs in the territory assigned to him unless their proper ordinary prohibits it; he cannot confer it validly on anyone in another territory, without prejudice to the prescript of can. 883, n. 3.

Canon 887 has more juridical significance than the preceding canon because it determines not only when a presbyter exercises the faculty to confirm lawfully, but also when he does so validly. Thus, the canon can be seen as an implicit reaffirmation of the primacy of the bishop as ordinary minister of confirmation, since he always confirms validly. The liceity and validity of confirmation by presbyters depends on the territory for which the faculty to confirm was granted.

Territorial restrictions on presbyters' faculty to confirm were already stipulated in canon 883, 1° which grants the faculty to confirm to presbyters who are equivalent in law to a diocesan bishop but only within the limits of their territory. The "territory" of those equivalent in law to a diocesan bishop

is the entire territory of the particular churches under their direction. Outside that territory, they have no faculty, and, therefore, confirmations administered by them are invalid. Canon 887 imposes a similar territorial restriction on the faculty of other presbyters to confirm. However, the territory of these other presbyters may be more restricted than that of those equivalent in law to diocesan bishops. Since the mandate to baptize or receive into full communion, which forms the basis for the faculty by law to confirm, may not have been given for the entire territory of the particular church, "the territory assigned to him" may be restricted to a particular region or parish. The diocesan bishop's designation of a presbyter to confirm in his absence may be restricted to a particular parish or to a single celebration of confirmation in a determined area which becomes by the deputation "the territory assigned to him."

Within the confines of his own territory, a presbyter who has the faculty to confirm, either by law or by special mandate, always confirms validly and licitly those who live in his territory. Within the scope of his faculty, a presbyter may also validly and licitly confirm externs (those not domiciled in the territory assigned to him) who happen to be in his territory, as long as their own ordinary has not prohibited this. Should the presbyter confirm externs despite their own ordinary's express prohibition, the confirmation would be valid but illicit. Thus, a presbyter's confirmation of an extern despite the prohibition of the extern's proper ordinary has the same juridic effect as a bishop's.

While a bishop confirms validly but illicitly outside his own territory unless he has the at least presumed permission of the diocesan bishop of that place, a presbyter has no faculty to confirm outside his own territory. Therefore, a confirmation outside the presbyter's assigned territory is invalid, whether the one confirmed is the presbyter's own subject or not. However, the faculty of a presbyter to confirm is not territorially restricted when confirmation is administered in danger-of-death situations.

There are also other instances when a presbyter may confirm outside the territory where his pastoral ministry is normally exercised. For example, if a pastor who has the faculty to baptize an adult invites a presbyter from another diocese to baptize the adult in his parish, the extern priest must also confirm the neophyte (c. 866). Since the extern priest has the faculty to baptize the adult from the pastor, the law itself grants him the faculty to confirm as well. Similarly, a diocesan bishop may designate a priest from another diocese to minister confirmation in his absence. A priest designated by a diocesan bishop to confirm may also associate with him in the concelebration of confirmation a priest from another diocese. In all of these situations, the confirmations are both valid and licit. However, these examples are not really exceptions to the rule that presbyters validly confirm only in their own territory, but rather cases in which "the territory" is expanded. An extern priest can confirm a person he baptizes because, although the priest is incardinated elsewhere, he is confirming within the "territory assigned to him" by his mandate from the pastor to baptize. When a diocesan bishop designates a priest from another diocese to confirm during his absence, the bishop makes his own diocese the presbyter's proper territory for purposes of confirmation. In the same way, when a priest who has the faculty to confirm associates an extern priest with himself for confirmation, this priest is within the territory assigned to him for purposes of this particular confirmation.

Rights of Ministers in Exempt Places

Canon 888 — Within the territory in which they are able to confer confirmation, ministers can administer it even in exempt places.

The final canon of this chapter on the minister of confirmation speaks of the rights of the minister in "exempt places." "Exempt places" are those religious houses or territories within the geographical boundaries of a particular church or dio-

cese which are exempt from the jurisdiction of the diocesan bishop or person equivalent to him in law. Normally, this term is used to designate houses of clerical religious institutes of pontifical right. However, their exemption does not restrict the right and obligation of the bishop to regulate the liturgical life of the diocese.[315] Exempt places are subject to the authority of the diocesan bishop in what pertains to the public exercise of divine worship (c. 678, §1). Canon 888 is an application of this principle. It allows any lawful minister, whether he is a bishop or a presbyter, to celebrate confirmation in places otherwise exempt from his jurisdiction.

CHAPTER III
THOSE TO BE CONFIRMED
[cc. 889–891]

With canon 889, the code begins its consideration of those to be confirmed. This is a short chapter (three canons) by comparison with the parallel chapter on baptism (eight canons).[316] In the normative rite for the celebration of sacraments of initiation for adults, the celebration of confirmation takes place in the same ceremony as the celebration of baptism. Thus, there is no need to repeat the norms governing the confirmation of adults immediately following baptism. Canon 889 determines the basic requirements for confirmation. Canon 890 treats the obligation of the faithful to receive the sacrament and the obligation of parents and pastors to see that the faithful are properly prepared for it. Canon 891 treats the proper age for confirmation.

---

[315] See c. 838, §4.

[316] The Eastern code devotes only one canon to this matter. *CCEO* 693 simply states that those who are baptized are to be chrismated. Since the faithful of the Eastern churches are confirmed as infants, there is no need for the distinction between adults and children or for any stipulation of the appropriate age, as there is in the Latin code.

Capacity for Confirmation

Canon 889 — §1. Every baptized person not yet confirmed and only such a person is capable of receiving confirmation.

§2. To receive confirmation licitly outside the danger of death requires that a person who has the use of reason be suitably instructed, properly disposed, and able to renew the baptismal promises.

The first paragraph of canon 889 is distilled from two previous canons: canon 842, §1 which states that no other sacrament may be received prior to baptism and canon 845 which lists confirmation as one of those sacraments which imposes a character and so cannot be repeated.

The second paragraph is a justification for the practice in the Latin church of deferring confirmation until the candidate has reached the age of discretion: the kind of preparation necessary for the reception of confirmation is beyond the intellectual capacity of infants.

The canon mentions three elements of such preparation: the person is to be suitably instructed; the person is to be properly disposed; and the person is to be able to renew the baptismal promises. The absence of even a mention of the catechumenate as a possible means by which this preparation can be provided is another indication that the canons on confirmation presume that this sacrament will be celebrated in a distinct ceremony apart from baptism.

Paragraph two of the canon foresees circumstances when these requirements for confirmation are not binding. The text is drawn from the *Rite of Confirmation*, but the canon expands into two exceptions what is presented in the rite as a single exception. The *Rite* states:

> If one who has the use of reason is confirmed in danger of death, there should, as far as possible, be some spiritual preparation beforehand, suited to the individual situation.[317]

The *Rite* mentions only one situation when preparation for confirmation is not required: the case when a person who has the use of reason is in danger of death. The canon expands this one exception into two: the case when any person is in danger of death, and the case when a person does not have the use of reason, even when there is no danger of death.

The *Rite of Christian Initiation of Children of Catechetical Age* presents a more extensive overview of the sort of preparation for confirmation the law expects.

> The initiation of children requires both a conversion, which is personal and somewhat developed according to their age, and the assistance of the education needed at this age. From then on their initiation is to be adapted both to the spiritual progress of the candidates, that is, their growth in faith, and to the catechetical instruction they receive. Accordingly, as with adults, their initiation is to be extended over several years, if need be, before they receive the sacraments. It is also divided into different stages and periods and is marked by liturgical rites.[318]

> The children's progress in the formation they receive depends as much on the help and example of their companions as on their parents. This should be taken into account.

> Generally the children to be initiated belong to a group of their companions who are already baptized and are preparing for confirmation and Eucharist. Therefore, their initiation is based on this catechetical group and shares in its progress.

> It is to be hoped that the children will also receive as much help and example as possible from their parents, who must assent to their initiation and to their leading a Christian life from this time forward. The period of initiation will also provide a good

---

[317] *RConf* 12, *DOL* 2521.

[318] *RCIA* 307, *DOL* 2459.

opportunity for the family to have contact with priests and catechists.[319]

Obligation of Confirmation

Canon 890 — The faithful are obliged to receive this sacrament at the proper time. Parents and pastors of souls, especially pastors of parishes, are to take care that the faithful are properly instructed to receive the sacrament and come to it at the appropriate time.

The canon treats the obligation to receive confirmation, an obligation which binds the Christian faithful in general and parents and pastors in particular. The Christian faithful are to receive this sacrament at the proper time. What constitutes the "proper time" will be determined in the next canon. This preceptive norm is very different from the parallel canon in the 1917 code[320] which stressed that the sacrament was not necessary for salvation, but that the faithful who have the opportunity to receive it should not neglect to do so.

Like the 1917 code, the present canon stresses the obligation of pastors to see that candidates for confirmation are properly prepared to receive it. However, it extends this obligation to parents as well. By specifically mentioning parents, the canon reveals the underlying presumption of almost all the canons on confirmation that the sacrament is conferred at a separate celebration distinct from baptism when those to be confirmed are children still under the care of their parents, rather than in the normative celebration together with baptism in the case of adults.

The rite gives an extensive treatment of the role of the parents and pastors and recognizes the role of the entire Christian community in this preparation, about which the code is silent.

One of the highest responsibilities of the people of God is to prepare the baptized for confirmation. Pastors have the special responsibility to see that all the baptized reach the completion of Christian initiation and therefore that they are carefully prepared for confirmation.

Adult catechumens who are to be confirmed immediately after baptism have the help of the Christian community and, in particular, the formation that is given to them during the catechumenate. Catechists, sponsors, and members of the local Church participate in the catechumenate by means of catechesis and community celebration of the rites of initiation. For those who were baptized in infancy and are confirmed only as adults, the plan for the catechumenate is used with appropriate adaptation.

The initiation of children into the sacramental life is ordinarily the responsibility and concern of Christian parents. They are to form and gradually increase a spirit of faith in the children and, at times with the help of religious education classes, prepare them for the fruitful reception of the sacraments of confirmation and the Eucharist. The role of the parents is also expressed by their active participation in the celebration of the sacraments.[321]

Age for Confirmation

Canon 891 — The sacrament of confirmation is to be conferred on the faithful at about the age of discretion unless the conference of bishops has determined another age, or there is danger of death, or in the judgment of the minister a grave cause suggests otherwise.

Prior to the revision of the rites of Christian initiation, particularly the *Rite of Christian Initiation of Adults,* confirmation was sometimes referred to, somewhat sarcastically, as a sacrament in search of a theology. The commentary on canon 879 noted the different emphases, some

---

[319] *RCIA* 308, *DOL* 2460.
[320] *CIC* 787.

[321] *RConf* 3, *DOL* 2512.

complementary, some competing, but all justifiable, that are present in current theological treatments of confirmation. Of those different theological emphases, those that appear most in competition are the one that emphasizes confirmation as the completion of baptism, and the one that emphasizes confirmation as the sacrament of mature faith and adult commitment. These two recurring emphases partly explain why the age for celebrating confirmation has varied so much throughout the history of the Church, and varies still, particularly in the differing practices of the several autonomous ritual churches that comprise the Catholic Church.

In the earliest days of the Church, it was the bishop who conferred the sacraments of baptism and confirmation. As the Church grew, it became necessary for presbyters to confer baptism, and in the Eastern churches confirmation as well. The Latin church deferred confirmation until a later age, not for any compelling theological reason, but simply because it took several years for the bishop to visit all his local communities to confer the sacrament. The gradual development of a theology of confirmation as a sacrament of adult or mature faith was an attempt to justify theologically the historical and "accidental" separation of confirmation from baptism, and to give more meaning to a sacrament that was normally celebrated apart and seen as distinct from baptism.

With the promulgation of Pius X's *Quam singulari* at the beginning of this century, the age for the reception of first communion (and, with it, the age for the reception of first penance) became the age of discretion. The practical problems involved in catechizing young people for the reception of three sacraments at the age of discretion led to the deferral of the reception of confirmation until a still later age. Thus, the traditional ordering of the sacraments which had remained constant throughout the history of the Church was altered. The normal order in which these sacraments have been received during most of this century became: baptism, penance, Eucharist, and finally confirmation. Thus, throughout the long develop-

ment of the sacrament of confirmation, it has been conferred at every possible age.

The 1917 code determined not a normative age, but a "preferred" age for the reception of confirmation: it "should preferably be postponed in the Latin Church until the seventh year of age."[322] At the time, pastoral practice generally deferred the reception of confirmation well beyond the age of seven. Canon 5 of the 1917 code allowed bishops to retain the practice of confirming at a later age or even an earlier age than seven, if this was a centennial or immemorial custom in their region.[323] However, a 1952 authoritative interpretation prohibited postponing confirmation beyond the age of ten.[324]

Prior to Vatican Council II, there had been only limited official recognition by Rome of the actual pastoral situations in local churches where confirmation was postponed well beyond the age of seven and often well beyond the age of ten. However, after the promulgation of the revised *Rite of Confirmation* in 1971, wider concessions were made in order to recognize divergent practices. Episcopal conferences were charged to determine an age for confirmation more suitable for their local cultures and customs.[325]

> With regard to children, in the Latin Church the administration of confirmation is generally delayed until about the seventh year. For pastoral reasons, however, especially to implant deeply in the lives of the faithful complete obedience to Christ the Lord and a firm witnessing to him, the conferences of bishops may set an age that seems more suitable. This means that the sacrament is given, after the formation proper to it, when the recipients are more mature.[326]

---

[322] *CIC* 788.
[323] See McManus, in *CLSA Com,* 639–640.
[324] CodCom, March 26, 1952, *AAS* 44 (1952) 496; *CLD* 3, 314.
[325] McManus, in *CLSA Com,* 640.
[326] *RConf* 11, *DOL* 2520.

Since the age for confirmation established in the 1917 code was not normative but only "preferred," and since the *Rite of Confirmation* allowed episcopal conferences to determine an age for confirmation in light of local conditions, the 1980 schema of the revised code proposed suppressing the age of seven as the preferred age for confirmation and leaving the determination of the age at which to confirm to local custom or to a decree of the conference of bishops.[327]

However, canon 891 is considerably different from the norm proposed in the 1980 schema. Although it speaks of the "age of discretion," the revised code retains the age of seven not just as the "preferred" age, but as the normative age for confirmation. Nevertheless, the canon continues to allow episcopal conferences to determine another age. This is an important development, since it allows for an exception to the normative age to become a general policy within the territory of an episcopal conference.

The age at which confirmation is conferred varies widely in the dioceses of the United States. As a result of this divergent practice, the National Conference of Catholic Bishops debated for ten years before determining the age for confirmation. In 1993, the conference determined not a specific age but a range of ages for the conferral of confirmation: from seven to eighteen. This determination was approved by the Holy See for a five-year period beginning on July 1, 1994. However, the National Conference of Catholic Bishops will soon have to decide whether to determine another age or range of ages for confirmation or to reaffirm the present rather elastic norm. The Canadian Conference of Catholic Bishops took another approach to determining the age for confirmation. They decreed "that the sacrament of confirmation in the Latin rite shall be conferred at the age determined in the approved catechetical programmes."[328]

Canon 891 differs from its source, the *Rite of Confirmation,* in another respect. The rite states that episcopal conferences could determine an age other than seven "when the recipients are more mature."[329] The canon is less restrictive. It allows the episcopal conference to determine "another age," and does not require that it be a more mature age than seven. Thus, a bishops' conference could establish an age younger than seven for the reception of confirmation.

Exceptions can be made to both the normative age of discretion and the age determined by the conference of bishops when there is danger of death or when, in the judgment of the minister, some other grave cause is present.

CHAPTER IV
SPONSORS
[cc. 892–893]

The two canons which comprise chapter 4 give only a summary treatment of the role of sponsors for confirmation and are dependent on the parallel canons on sponsors at baptism.

The CLSA translation of the code renders the Latin *patrinus* or *matrina* ("godfather" or "godmother") as "sponsor." The term "sponsor" has a more technical sense in the *Rite of Christian Initiation of Adults,* where the sponsor is one who presents a candidate for the catechumenate, and may, but need not, be chosen as the godparent prior to the celebration of the rite of election.

Role of Sponsor

Canon 892 — Insofar as possible, there is to be a sponsor for the person to be confirmed; the sponsor is to take care that the confirmed person behaves as a true witness of Christ and faithfully fulfills the obligations inherent in this sacrament.

The sponsor is the person charged with seeing that the one confirmed lives as a true witness to

---

[327] 1980 Schema, c. 845.
[328] See Woestman, *Sacraments,* 92.

[329] *RConf* 11, *DOL* 2520.

Christ and fulfills faithfully the obligations connected with the sacrament.

A sponsor is required at confirmation only "insofar as possible." Canon 793 of the 1917 code[330] had noted the presence of a sponsor at confirmation as "a very ancient custom of the Church."[331] Thus, the present canon agrees with the 1917 code that a sponsor is not necessary for the celebration of the sacrament, but that it is a preferred custom.

The *Rite of Confirmation* expands somewhat on the role of the sponsor during the celebration of the sacrament and makes a forceful argument for the presence of a sponsor:

> As a rule there should be a sponsor for each of those to be confirmed. These sponsors bring the candidate to receive the sacrament, present them to the minister for the anointing, and will later help them to fulfill their baptismal promises faithfully under the influence of the Holy Spirit whom they have received.[332]

Requirements for Sponsors

Canon 893 — §1. To perform the function of sponsor, a person must fulfill the conditions mentioned in can. 874.

§2. It is desirable to choose as sponsor the one who undertook the same function in baptism.

The requirements or prerequisites for a person to serve as a sponsor at confirmation are the same as those for sponsors at baptism (c. 874).[333] In the normative celebration of confirmation of adults, the sponsors for baptism and those for confirma-

tion are the same, since both sacraments are conferred in the same liturgical celebration. As a result, it is understandable that the requirements for baptismal and confirmation sponsors should be the same.

This connection between baptismal and confirmation sponsors is made even more explicit in the second paragraph of canon 893 which states that it is desirable that those who earlier exercised the office of sponsor at baptism should also exercise this office when the previously baptized person is confirmed. The *Rite of Confirmation* provides an explicit rationale for this preference for the sponsor at baptism continuing as the sponsor at confirmation:

> In view of contemporary pastoral circumstances, it is desirable that the godparent at baptism, if available, also be the sponsor at confirmation; *CIC* 796, 1° is therefore amended. This change expresses more clearly the link between baptism and confirmation and also makes the function and responsibility of the sponsor more effective.
>
> Nonetheless the option of choosing a special sponsor for confirmation is not excluded. Even the parents themselves may present their children for confirmation. It is for the local ordinary to determine diocesan practice in the light of local conditions and circumstances.[334]

Both the code and the *Rite* are in agreement that it is not necessary for godparents at baptism to continue as sponsors at confirmation. There appears to be a substantial difference between the code and the *Rite,* however, with regard to the possibility of parents serving as sponsors at the confirmation of their children. It is clear in the above text cited from the rite that parents can function as sponsors for the confirmation of their own child. The *Rite of Confirmation* 5 is devoted exclusively to sponsors. After mentioning that sponsors "bring

---

[330] *CIC* 793.

[331] See McManus, in *CLSA Com,* 641.

[332] *RConf* 5, *DOL* 2514.

[333] The Eastern code makes no mention of sponsors in the canons on chrismation, since this sacrament is always conferred with baptism and the sponsors for chrismation are always the same as those for baptism.

[334] *RConf* 5, *DOL* 2514.

the candidates to receive the sacrament" and "present them to the minister for the anointing," the *Rite* states a preference for the baptismal sponsors continuing as confirmation sponsors. It then makes provision for "special" sponsors, i.e., those who were not also the sponsors at baptism. The rite adds immediately that "even parents may present their children for confirmation." From the context there can be no question that the rite allows for parents to be sponsors. It uses the same terminology ("presenting" for anointing or confirmation) for sponsors in the first part of the paragraph as it does for parents in the latter part of the paragraph.

The code, however, bars parents from serving as the children's confirmation sponsors. Canon 893, §1 refers back to the requirements for baptismal sponsors in canon 874, since the requirements for confirmation sponsors are identical to those for baptismal sponsors. However, canon 874, §1, 5° stipulates that neither the mother nor the father of a child to be baptized can be the sponsor for that child. Thus, there is a contradiction between the code which states that parents cannot be their children's confirmation sponsors and the *Rite* which states expressly that they can serve as sponsors.

To hold that the *Rite of Confirmation* allows parents to be the confirmation sponsors for their children is not a misinterpretation of the law, as some have claimed.[335] In the last redaction of the 1980 schema the contradiction between the draft code and *Rite* was brought to the attention of the Commission for the Revision of the Code in a report submitted by four consultors. These consultors argued that the canon treating the require-

ments for sponsors had to be amended to allow parents to be confirmation sponsors for their children and so to harmonize the draft code with the *Rite of Confirmation*.[336] However, the Commission rejected this proposal. The Commission claimed that parents' presentation of their children for confirmation was distinct from the sponsors' presentation of candidates for confirmation and that, if parents did present their children and no other sponsor was present, then it must be said that sponsors were lacking.[337]

This argumentation is not very convincing. The *Rite* stipulates that "sponsors bring the candidates to receive the sacrament" and "present them to the minister for the anointing." Nevertheless, the Code Revision Commission claimed that what parents do when they present their children for the anointing is somehow essentially different from what sponsors do when they present children for the sacrament. Speaking about the role of parents, the *Rite* singled out the parents as an example of the "special sponsor," that is, a sponsor who was not the sponsor at baptism.

In 1984 the Congregation for Divine Worship and the Discipline of the Sacraments released a clarification to an inquiry concerning the contradiction between the code and the rite on this very point, but the clarification does little more than repeat the response of the Commission for the Revision of the Code the previous year:

> From what has been said, it is clear that parents and the godparents exercise different functions in the sacrament of confirmation. For this reason parents may present their children according to the indicated rubric, even though they cannot be admitted to the function of godparent as this function would not add anything to their duty as parents.[338]

---

[335] For example, see Woestman, *Sacraments,* 94: "The second sentence of the last paragraph [of the *Rite of Confirmation,* 5] caused a problem of interpretation for some. They read the sentence to mean that the parents could be the sponsors of the one confirmed. It is to be noted that the text says nothing about the parents being sponsors, but says that they can present (*praesentent*) their children for confirmation."

[336] *Comm* 15 (1983) 188–189.
[337] *Comm* 15 (1983) 189.
[338] CDWDS, clarification, *N* 20 (1984) 86; *CLD* 11, 202–203.

The Commission for the Revision of the Code responses to proposals from consultors for revisions of drafts of the revised code are not authoritative interpretations of the code that was eventually promulgated. Nor is the "clarification" offered by the congregation, which was issued as a *documentorum explanatio,* an authoritative interpretation. Texts of this kind are guides for interpretation, but they are not official, and therefore not authentic, interpretations.[339] (Authentic interpretations are always published in the *Acta Apostolicae Sedis;* this "clarification" was not.)

The contradiction between the code and the *Rite* has given rise to a doubt of law (*dubium iuris*) regarding the current law that governs the possibility of parents serving as sponsors at their children's confirmations. Thus, one is free to interpret the rite as allowing parents to act as sponsors of their children until an authoritative interpretation resolves the conflict.

CHAPTER V
THE PROOF AND REGISTRATION OF THE CONFERRAL OF CONFIRMATION
[cc. 894–896]

The three final canons on confirmation deal with the methods of proving the sacrament's conferral, the information to be recorded in the register, and those responsible for recording this information.[340] The canons are clear and self-explanatory.

Proof of Confirmation

Canon 894 — To prove the conferral of confirmation the prescripts of can. 876 are to be observed.

Proof that confirmation was conferred is to be established in the same ways that the conferral of baptism is to be proven (c. 876). The juridic consequences of confirmation for a person's status and rights in the Church are not nearly as critical as are those of other sacraments, especially baptism, sacred orders, and matrimony. Consequently, cases in which people need to secure records proving their reception of confirmation are less frequent. Proof of confirmation is required for reception of orders[341] and may be requested prior to the celebration of marriage.[342] It may also be necessary to establish that a person was confirmed for him or her to serve as a sponsor for baptism or confirmation, since full initiation into the Church is a requirement for assuming these offices.[343] Since establishing proof of confirmation is only rarely an urgent matter, the issue is given a more summary treatment here than in the parallel canons on proof of baptism (cc. 875–876).

Registration and Notification

Canon 895 — The names of those confirmed with mention made of the minister, the parents and sponsors, and the place and date of the conferral of confirmation are to be recorded in the confirmation register of the diocesan curia or, where the conference of bishops or the diocesan bishop has prescribed it, in a register kept in the parish archive. The pastor must inform the pastor of the place of baptism about the conferral of confirmation so that a notation is made in the baptismal register according to the norm of can. 535, §2.

After indicating the names and other information to be recorded, canon 895 presents two options for the place in which the record is to be kept. Curiously, first preference is given to a diocesan register to be kept in the central office of the diocese. No such diocesan record is foreseen

---

[339] See *N* 1 (1965) 136; see also Woestman, *Sacraments,* 94–95.

[340] Since in the Eastern churches chrismation is usually celebrated with baptism, there is no treatment in the Eastern code of the registration and proof of chrismation. Only in the case where chrismation was celebrated apart from baptism is the minister of chrismation to notify the pastor of the place where the person was baptized (*CCEO* 695, §2.)

[341] Canon 1050, 3°.

[342] Canon 1065, §1.

[343] Canon 874, §1, 3°.

in the parallel canons on baptism. The purpose of such a diocesan register for confirmation is an implicit affirmation of the primacy of the bishop as ordinary minister of the sacrament. Since the bishop is usually the most common minister of the sacrament, a diocesan register may facilitate securing a confirmation record when it is needed.

The second option, a parochial register, is also allowed by the canon. This, however, is seen as a secondary preference, since the selection of this possibility appears to require the approval of the conference of bishops.

Regardless of which option is adopted, the pastor of the place where the confirmation took place is required to send notification of the confirmation to the pastor of the place where the confirmed person was baptized. The canon refers to canon 535, §2 which describes the kind of information that is to be added to the baptismal register, most notably those sacraments received and other events which determine the canonical status of the person after baptism.

Notification of the Pastor
of the Place of Confirmation

Canon 896 — If the pastor of the place was not present, the minister either personally or through another is to inform him as soon as possible of the conferral of confirmation.

The canon is the parallel to canon 878 which deals with notifying the pastor of the parish in which a baptism was celebrated but at which he was not the minister or not present. This notification is called for to ensure that the proof of baptism is recorded. The present canon applies this same principle to confirmation.[344] It has special relevance for the situation in which a person was confirmed in danger of death. If the pastor himself did not confirm the person, then the minister who did so is to notify the pastor so that the conferral of confirmation may be recorded.

[344] See the parallel canon in *CCEO* 695, §2.

BIBLIOGRAPHY

(The following bibliographical material provides further information regarding the sacraments discussed in the titles of Book IV on baptism and confirmation.)

Books

Abbo, J., and J. Hannan. *The Sacred Canons.* 2nd rev. ed. 2 vols. St. Louis: B. Herder Book Co., 1960.

Austin, G. *The Rite of Confirmation: Anointing with the Spirit.* Studies in the Reformed Rites of the Catholic Church, Vol. III. New York: Pueblo, 1985.

Bouscaren, T., and A. Ellis. *Canon Law: A Text and Commentary.* 2nd ed. Milwaukee: Bruce Publishing Co., 1955.

Chiappetta, L. *Dizionario del Nuovo Codice di Diritto Canonico.* Naples: Dehoniane, 1986.

———. *Prontuario di Diritto Canonico e Concordatario.* Rome: Dehoniane, 1994.

Cogan, P., ed. *CLSA Advisory Opinions: 1984–1993.* Washington, D.C.: CLSA, 1995.

Echeverria, L., et al., eds. *Code de Droit Canonique.* Trans. A. Soria-Vasco, H. LaPlane, and M. Chueca. Paris: Cerf, 1989.

Huels, J. *The Pastoral Companion.* Chicago: Franciscan Herald, 1986.

Kavanagh, A. *Confirmation: Origins and Reform.* New York: Pueblo, 1988.

NCCB. "National Statutes for the Catechumenate." *Rite of Christian Initiation of Adults* (Appendix III). Chicago: Liturgy Training Pub., 1988.

Paralieu, R. *Guide Pratique du Code de Droit Canonique.* Bourges: Tardy, 1985.

Pfnausch, E., ed. *Code, Community, Ministry.* 2nd rev. ed. Washington, D.C.: CLSA, 1992.

Reedy, W., ed. *Becoming a Catholic Christian.* New York: Sadlier, 1981.

Regatillo, E. *Ius Sacramentarium.* 3rd ed. Santander: Sal Terrae, 1960.

Woestman, W. *Sacraments: Initiation, Penance, Anointing of the Sick.* 2nd ed. Ottawa: St. Paul University, 1996.

Woywod, S., and C. Smith. *A Practical Commentary on the Code of Canon Law.* Rev. ed. New York: Joseph F. Wagner, Inc., 1957.

Articles

Barrett, R. "Confirmation: A Discipline Revisited." *J* 52 (1992) 697–714.

Covino, P. "The Postconciliar Infant Baptism Debate in the American Church." *W* 56 (1982) 240–260.

Daly, B. "Canonical Requirements of Parents in Cases of Infant Baptism according to the 1983 Code." *Stud Can* 20 (1986) 409–438.

Green, T. "The Church's Sanctifying Office: Reflections on Selected Canons in the Revised Code." *J* 44 (1984) 357–411.

Levada, W. "Reflections on the Age of Confirmation." *TS* 57 (1996) 302–312.

Rehrauer. A. "Welcome In! Canonical Issues and the RCIA." *CLSA Proceedings* 52 (1990) 161–169.

TITLE III
THE MOST HOLY EUCHARIST
[cc. 897–958]

The third and final sacrament of full Christian initiation is the Eucharist, the subject of the sixty-two canons of this title. The canons are arranged in three chapters: "The Eucharistic Celebration," "The Reservation and Veneration of the Most Holy Eucharist," and "The Offering Given for the Celebration of Mass." This division better integrates the various aspects of eucharistic discipline than did the former code which dealt with reservation and worship of the Eucharist not in the section on the sacraments but in that on divine worship, which included such topics as sacred furnishings and vows and oaths. The new arrangement bespeaks the essential unity of the Eucharist celebrated, received, and reserved. Some members of the *coetus* (committee) of the Pontifical Commission for the Revision of the Code of Canon Law which prepared this title of the code believed that the section on Mass offerings should be treated in Book V on church property, but it was decided to leave it in this title given its special relation to the celebration of the Eucharist.[1]

The principal sources for title III are the 1917 code, Vatican II's constitution on the sacred liturgy, *Sacrosanctum Concilium,* the 1967 instruction *Eucharisticum mysterium* on the worship of the Eucharist,[2] the 1973 *Rite of Holy Communion and Worship of the Eucharist outside Mass,* and the 1975 revised edition of the *General Instruction of the Roman Missal.* The canons also draw on numerous other postconciliar documents mentioned in the footnotes of the commentary.

[1] ComCICRec, *Schema Documenti Pontificii quo Disciplina Canonica de Sacramentis Recognoscitur* (Rome: Typis Polyglottis Vaticanis, 1975) 8.
[2] SCRit, May 25, 1967, *AAS* 59 (1967) 539–573, *DOL* 179; hereafter cited as *Eucharisticum mysterium.*

The Eastern code is considerably different from the Latin code in its treatment of the Divine Eucharist. While the Latin code covers the subject in sixty-two canons in three chapters, the Eastern code has only twenty canons in one chapter (*CCEO* 698–717). The Eastern code better recognizes the active role of deacons and laity in the celebration (*CCEO* 698, §§2–3) than does the Latin code, and it relegates many matters of detail to the particular laws of the various churches *sui iuris.* The reception of first communion by infants at their baptism and chrismation is permitted in accord with particular law (c. 710). In addition to offerings for the celebration of the Divine Liturgy, a priest is permitted to accept offerings for the Liturgy of the Presanctified and for commemorations in the Divine Liturgy in accord with established custom (c. 715).

The most noteworthy developments in the Latin law on the Eucharist since 1983 have occurred by means of authentic interpretations of the Pontifical Commission for the Authentic Interpretation of the Canons of the Code of Canon Law and its successor, the Pontifical Council for the Interpretation of Legislative Texts. These developments are treated in the commentary at canons 906, 910, 917, and 951. Other significant developments came about in a 1995 Congregation for the Doctrine of the Faith letter on the matter of the Eucharist, treated at canon 924, and in a 1991 Congregation for the Clergy decree, treated at canon 948.

FOUNDATIONAL CANONS

Canon 897 — The most august sacrament is the Most Holy Eucharist in which Christ the Lord himself is contained, offered, and received and by which the Church continually lives and grows. The eucharistic sacrifice, the memorial of the death and resurrection of the Lord, in which the sacrifice of the cross is perpetuated through the ages is the summit and source of all worship and

Christian life, which signifies and effects the unity of the people of God and brings about the building up of the body of Christ. Indeed, the other sacraments and all the ecclesiastical works of the apostolate are closely connected with the Most Holy Eucharist and ordered to it.

Canon 898 — The Christian faithful are to hold the Most Holy Eucharist in highest honor, taking an active part in the celebration of the most august sacrifice, receiving this sacrament most devoutly and frequently, and worshiping it with the highest adoration. In explaining the doctrine about this sacrament, pastors of souls are to teach the faithful diligently about this obligation.

Canon 899 — §1. The eucharistic celebration is the action of Christ himself and the Church. In it, Christ the Lord, through the ministry of the priest, offers himself, substantially present under the species of bread and wine, to God the Father and gives himself as spiritual food to the faithful united with his offering.

§2. In the eucharistic gathering the people of God are called together with the bishop or, under his authority, a presbyter presiding and acting in the person of Christ. All the faithful who are present, whether clerics or laity, unite together by participating in their own way according to the diversity of orders and liturgical functions.

§3. The eucharistic celebration is to be organized in such a way that all those participating receive from it the many fruits for which Christ the Lord instituted the eucharistic sacrifice.

Canons 897 and 898 introduce the entire title on the Eucharist, including the chapters on eucharistic reservation and worship and on Mass offerings. Canon 899 is an additional introductory canon for the first chapter on the eucharistic celebration, but it is best treated in connection with these two foundational canons. Canons 897 and 899 establish the doctrinal foundations for the disciplinary canons which follow, i.e., they are doctrinal in the broad sense, in that they include statements of dogma as well as authoritative teachings

which lack a strictly dogmatic character. The canons manifest an effort to harmonize past doctrine, such as the real presence and the sacrificial nature of the Mass, with Vatican II emphases such as the Eucharist as meal as well as its celebrational and memorial character. The ecclesial dimensions of the Eucharist which were highlighted at the council are also evident: the Eucharist as source and sign of the unity of the body of Christ; as source and summit of the Church's life and worship, its nourishment and growth; and as action of the whole people of God participating in the sanctifying function of the Church and reflecting its hierarchical structure through diverse and distinct liturgical roles and ministries.

Canon 898 is an exhortation on the general obligations of the faithful regarding the Eucharist and on the duty of pastoral ministers (*animarum pastores*) to elucidate eucharistic doctrine. This duty, which binds all ecclesiastical officeholders who exercise pastoral care, is also stated in canon 843, §2 for the sacraments in general. More specific directives on the obligation of pastors of parishes (*parochi*) to provide catechetical and experiential formation in the Eucharist are found in canons 528, §2; 777, 2°; and 914. Canon 898 also introduces three principal aspects of the Eucharist which are treated in the code: the Eucharistic action or celebration, holy communion, and the veneration of the Eucharist.

The history of these three canons is rather complex. A major part of canon 897 was derived from canon 66, §1 of the proposed *Lex Ecclesiae Fundamentalis;* the original version of canon 898 was canon 72 of the 1975 schema introducing the proposed section on the subject of the Holy Eucharist; the core of canon 899, §§1–2 was canon 61 of the same schema. Major revisions in the formulation and positioning of the canons were made by the *coetus* on the sacraments in response to critiques received during the consultation process, and final changes were made before the 1981 plenary session of the Pontifical Commission for the Revision of the Code of Canon Law.[3]

---

[3] *Comm* 13 (1981) 233–238, 408–410; *Rel* 209–210.

The immediate and proximate sources of the canons are chiefly certain texts of Vatican II, but the canons also draw on preconciliar sources such as the Council of Trent and the 1917 code, as well as postconciliar sources such as the *General Instruction of the Roman Missal*.[4]

CHAPTER I
THE EUCHARISTIC CELEBRATION
[cc. 899–933]

This chapter of thirty-three canons—more than half of all the canons on the Eucharist—is divided into four articles: "The Minister of the Most Holy Eucharist," "Participation in the Most Holy Eucharist," "The Rites and Ceremonies of the Eucharistic Celebration," and "The Time and Place of the Celebration of the Eucharist." The former code treated the Eucharist in two chapters, one on the eucharistic sacrifice and one on the sacrament. The more integral approach of the revised code better manifests the continuity and unity of the sacrificial and sacramental dimensions of the eucharistic action. The doctrinal canon (c. 899) which introduces the chapter on the eucharistic celebration was discussed above in the commentary on the foundational canons.

ARTICLE 1: THE MINISTER
OF THE MOST HOLY EUCHARIST
[cc. 900–911]

The twelve canons of this article deal with a wide variety of issues relative to the ministers of the Eucharist, who include the celebrant and concelebrants at Mass, and the ordinary and special ministers of communion and Viaticum. The canons establish the discipline for the following matters: valid and licit celebration (c. 900), Mass intentions (c.

901), concelebration (c. 902), the celebret (c. 903), the frequency of celebration (c. 904), binations and trinations (c. 905), the necessity of the presence of some faithful (c. 906), functions restricted to the priest (c. 907), the prohibition of interdenominational concelebration (c. 908), the personal prayer of the priest (c. 909), eucharistic ministers (c. 910), and ministers of Viaticum (c. 911).

Valid and Licit Celebration

Canon 900 — §1. The minister who is able to confect the sacrament of the Eucharist in the person of Christ is a validly ordained priest alone.

§2. A priest not impeded by canon law celebrates the Eucharist licitly; the provisions of the following canons are to be observed.

The 1917 code (*CIC* 802) spoke of the priest's having the "power to offer the sacrifice of the Mass," whereas this canon speaks of validly confecting the sacrament of the Eucharist. Despite the change in terminology, the meaning remains the same: only a validly ordained priest may preside at or concelebrate the Eucharist and validly consecrate the bread and wine.[5] Lay persons who attempt the liturgical action of the Eucharist automatically incur the penalty of interdict and deacons the penalty of suspension (c. 1378, §2, 1°).

The second paragraph of the canon, which is new in the revised code, deals with the licit celebration of the Eucharist. While any priest may validly consecrate the sacrament, some priests may not do so licitly, such as those who have been deprived of the exercise of their order by an irregularity or impediment,[6] or by a penalty,[7] or who have lost the clerical state.[8] Other requirements for the licit celebration of the Eucharist are specified in the canons which follow.

---

[4] See, e.g., *SC* 14, 26, 28, 41, 47, 48; *LG* 11; *PO* 2, 5, 6; Trent, sess. XIII, cap. 1, c. 1; sess. XXII, cap. 1, cc. 1–2; *CIC* 801; Intro. to *GIRM* 1–15; *GIRM* 1–5, 7, 48, 58–62, 74, 326.

[5] See SCDF, letter *Sacerdotium ministeriale,* August 6, 1983, *AAS* 75 (1983) 1:1001–1009; *CLD* 10, 151–158.
[6] Canon 1044. See W. H. Woestman, "Restricting the Right to Celebrate the Eucharist," *Stud Can* 29 (1995) 155–178.
[7] Canons 1331, §1, 2°; 1332; 1333, §1, 1°; 1338, §2.
[8] Canons 290, 292, 1336, §1, 5°.

Mass Intentions

Canon 901 — A priest is free to apply the Mass for anyone, living or dead.

A Mass may be applied for anyone,[9] living or deceased, baptized or non-baptized, sinner or saint. A non-Catholic may not be mentioned in the eucharistic prayer, however, since "ancient Christian liturgical and ecclesiological tradition permits the specific mention in the Eucharistic Anaphora only of the names of persons who are in full communion with the Church celebrating the Eucharist."[10]

The canon is considerably different from its correlate in the 1917 code (*CIC* 809) which said that Mass may be applied for the dead in purgatory or for the living with the exception of public Masses for the excommunicated. Private Masses could be applied for tolerated excommunicates (*excommunicati tolerati*), which included baptized non-Catholics, but for the excommunicates who must be avoided (*excommunicati vitandi*), a private Mass could be applied only for their conversion (*CIC* 2262, §2, 2°). A "private Mass" excluded any publicizing of the name of the person for whom the Mass was being applied. A 1976 Sacred Congregation for the Doctrine of the Faith decree derogated from the 1917 code to permit public Masses to be applied for deceased non-Catholic Christians when their families, friends, or subjects expressly request it and the ordinary judges that scandal is absent.[11] These conditions no longer bind since the revised code does not mention them.

This canon was dropped from the second draft of the schema on the sacraments in 1978 because it was considered more theological than juridical, but it was reinstated in 1981.[12]

<hr />

[9] See the introductory commentary to cc. 945–958 for an explanation of what it means to apply a Mass.

[10] *Ecum Dir* 121.

[11] *Accidit in diversis regionibus,* June 11, 1976, *AAS* 68 (1976) 621; *CLD* 8, 864; *DOL* 163.

[12] *Comm* 13 (1981) 244; *Rel* 209.

Concelebration

Canon 902 — Unless the welfare of the Christian faithful requires or suggests otherwise, priests can concelebrate the Eucharist. They are completely free to celebrate the Eucharist individually, however, but not while a concelebration is taking place in the same church or oratory.

Various forms of concelebration have existed in the Western and Eastern churches since at least the third century. Even before the liturgical reforms decreed by Vatican II, the *Roman Pontifical* had prescribed concelebration at Masses for the ordination of priests and the consecration of bishops. *Sacrosanctum Concilium* derogated from canon 803 of the 1917 code to permit much wider opportunity for concelebration.[13] It also directed that a new rite for concelebration be prepared, and this was accomplished by 1965.[14] The liturgical laws governing concelebration are found principally in the *General Instruction of the Roman Missal* 153–208.[15] Concelebration is required at the ordinations of bishops and presbyters and at the Chrism Mass. The liturgical law recommends concelebration, unless the needs of the faithful require otherwise, at: (a) the evening Mass of Holy Thursday; (b) the Mass for councils, meetings of bishops, or synods; (c) the Mass for the blessing of an abbot; (d) the conventual Mass and the principal Mass in churches and oratories; (e) the Mass for any kind of gathering of priests, either secular or religious. The diocesan bishop, in accord with the law, has the right to regulate concelebration in his diocese, also in the churches and oratories of

<hr />

[13] *SC* 57.

[14] *SC* 58; *Ritus servandus in concelebratione Missae et Ritus Communionis sub utraque specie* (Rome: Typis Polyglottis Vaticanis, 1965); P. Jounel, *The Rite of Concelebration of Mass and of Communion under Both Species* (New York: Desclée, 1967). Hereafter cited as either *Rite of Concelebration* or *Rite of Communion under Both Kinds.*

[15] See also NCCB, Guidelines for the Concelebration of the Eucharist, rev. ed., September 23, 1987, *BCLN* 23 (1987) 83–87.

clerical religious institutes and clerical societies of apostolic life when the eucharistic celebration is open to the faithful.[16]

The first part of the canon is based substantially on a statement from *Eucharisticum mysterium* 47. Concelebration is preferred over multiple private Masses because it manifests the Church gathered "in the unity of sacrifice and priesthood and the single offering of thanks around the one altar with the ministers and holy people."[17] However, priests should not insist on concelebration at the expense of the welfare of the faithful, such as when more than one Mass is required to meet pastoral needs.

The second part of the canon is based on *Sacrosanctum Concilium* 57, §2, n. 2 which says that each priest should have the opportunity (*facultas*) to celebrate an individual Mass. The canon reaffirms this by saying that priests are completely free to celebrate the Eucharist individually. This does not apply to Holy Thursday, however, when liturgical law prohibits all Masses without a congregation. Furthermore, priests are forbidden from celebrating an individual Mass at the time when there is a concelebration occurring in the same place, and they are also subject to the law of canon 906 on celebrating with at least some faithful present.

Concelebration among priests of different Catholic churches *sui iuris* can be done with permission of the diocesan/eparchial bishop for a just cause, especially that of fostering charity, and for the sake of manifesting unity between the churches.[18] The liturgical rite of the principal celebrant is to be observed, and he is to wear the appropriate vestments and insignia of his own church *sui iuris* (*CCEO* 701). Ordinarily the concelebrants wear the vestments of their own church,

but for a just cause and having removed any wonderment on the part of the faithful, they may wear the liturgical vestments of another church *sui iuris* (*CCEO* 707, §2).

The Celebret

Canon 903 — A priest is to be permitted to celebrate even if the rector of the church does not know him, provided that either he presents a letter of introduction from his ordinary or superior, issued at least within the year, or it can be judged prudently that he is not impeded from celebrating.

The law on the celebret from the 1917 code (*CIC* 804) is retained here but is greatly simplified. A celebret is a letter of introduction from a priest's ordinary or superior which attests to the priest's ordination and good standing, and certifies that there is nothing to prevent him from celebrating Mass. Secular priests obtain the celebret from their local ordinary, and priests who are religious or members of clerical societies of apostolic life may obtain it from their local ordinary, major superior, or local superior. To be valid it must be dated within a year of its presentation to the rector of the church where the priest wishes to celebrate. In this canon the term "rector" includes anyone who has the care of a church or an oratory, such as a pastor or religious superior, and not only the rector mentioned in canon 556. In many places the celebret is not requested of visiting priests, and the canon states that it is not necessary when the rector prudently judges that a priest is not impeded from celebrating.[19] The need for a celebret is even less if a priest merely wishes to celebrate Mass privately, in accord with canon 906.

Frequency of Celebration

Canon 904 — Remembering always that in the mystery of the eucharistic sacrifice the work of redemption is exercised continually, priests are to celebrate frequently; indeed, daily celebration is

---

[16] See cc. 678, §1; 1214; 1223.

[17] SCRit, decr *Ecclesiae semper,* March 7, 1965, *AAS* 57 (1965) 410, *DOL* 1792. See also *GIRM* 59; and CDW, decl *In celebratione Missae,* August 7, 1972, *AAS* 60 (1972) 561–562, *DOL* 208.

[18] One opinion holds that the bishop's permission is necessary only in the case of a publicly announced celebration. See *Pospishil Com,* 299.

[19] See commentary above on c. 900, §2.

recommended earnestly since, even if the faithful cannot be present, it is the act of Christ and the Church in which priests fulfill their principal function.

The daily celebration of the Eucharist by each priest was not an ancient practice in the Church, nor was it required by universal law even when it became common. The 1917 code obliged priests to celebrate several times a year, which the commentators interpreted as only three or four times a year. The former law also directed bishops and religious superiors to see that their priests celebrated Mass at least on Sundays and holy days of obligation (*CIC* 805).

Canon 904, unlike the directives in the 1917 code, does not speak of a binding obligation to celebrate but instead uses a milder form of preceptive language: "priests *are to* celebrate frequently," not *must* celebrate. Moreover, daily celebration by priests is earnestly recommended or, in the words of canon 276, §2, 2°, they are "earnestly invited" to offer the Eucharist daily. While there is no law binding priests to celebrate Mass daily, it is highly commended for the reasons adduced in the canon.

The wording of canon 904 is very similar to that of *Eucharisticum mysterium* 44, which in turn draws on *Presbyterorum ordinis,* the conciliar decree on the ministry and life of priests, and Paul VI's encyclical *Mysterium fidei,* on the doctrine and worship of the Holy Eucharist.[20] The statement that "priests fulfill their principal function" by celebrating the Eucharist originates in *Presbyterorum ordinis* 13 and must be interpreted in that context where the council was speaking expressly of priests' *sanctifying* function only. The same article also develops the priests' functions of ruling (in the broad sense of pastoral care) and teaching.

The 1994 *Directory on the Ministry and Life of Priests* 49 speaks of the importance of daily Eucharist for priestly spirituality. It says that the

Mass should be for the priest "the central moment of his day and of his daily ministry, fruit of a sincere desire and an occasion for a deep and effective encounter with Christ."[21]

Bination and Trination

Canon 905 — §1. A priest is not permitted to celebrate the Eucharist more than once a day except in cases where the law permits him to celebrate or concelebrate more than once on the same day.

§2. If there is a shortage of priests, the local ordinary can allow priests to celebrate twice a day for a just cause, or if pastoral necessity requires it, even three times on Sundays and holy days of obligation.

While priests may celebrate daily, they are forbidden from celebrating or concelebrating more than once each day except when the law permits it. The purpose of canon 905, §1 is to prevent the abuse of priests' celebrating multiple Masses for inadequate reasons or from improper motives. Similar prohibitions have been a part of church law since the eleventh century.[22] The law also serves to ensure that the manner of celebrating by priests does not become too hurried or routine due to the pressures of multiple Masses.

The principal occasions when the law permits a priest to celebrate or concelebrate more than once a day are: (1) on Holy Thursday at the Chrism Mass and at the evening Mass of the Lord's Supper; (2) at the Easter Vigil and the second Mass of Easter; (3) at the three Masses of Christmas, provided that the Masses are at their proper times according to the liturgical books; and (4) at concelebrations with the bishop or his delegate at a synod or pastoral visitation, or on the occasion of a meeting of priests, or gatherings of

---

[20] *PO* 13; ency *Mysterium fidei,* September 3, 1965, *AAS* 57 (1965) 762, *DOL* 176. See also *PO* 2, 5; *LG* 28; *AG* 39.

[21] CFC, *Directory on the Ministry and Life of Priests* (London: Catholic Truth Society, 1994) 51–52. See also John Paul II, letter *Dominicae cenae* 2, February 24, 1980, *AAS* 72 (1980) 113–149; *CLD* 9, 531–532.

[22] C. 53, D. I, *de cons.;* c. 3, 12, X, *de celebratione missarum,* III, 41; *CIC* 806.

religious—and another Mass celebrated for the benefit of the people.[23]

The 1917 code (*CIC* 806, §1) permitted trination on All Souls' Day, a practice that had existed in the universal Church only since 1915.[24] The revised code has abolished this practice because the former code is explicitly abrogated (c. 6, §1, 1°). Nevertheless, some canonists continue to maintain that this trination has not been abrogated.[25]

In 1963 Paul VI granted to diocesan bishops the faculty to permit priests to celebrate twice on weekdays for a just cause and when there is a shortage of priests, and even three times on Sundays and holy days of obligation when there is true pastoral need.[26] Canon 905, §2 extends this faculty to all local ordinaries.[27] The law permits bination and trination only for priests who preside at the Eucharist but not for concelebration except in the cases mentioned above. Local ordinaries may permit a priest to binate when there is a just cause, such as to provide for the needs of the faithful, and only when there is an insufficient number of priests available. For permission to trinate on Sundays and holy days, there must be a case of genuine pastoral need as, for example, when a priest has the care of more than one church or when the church is unable to accommodate all the faithful who wish to attend. The mere convenience of the faithful would not be an adequate reason to trinate unless a sufficient number of them could not otherwise attend Mass.

The Apostolic See discourages the multiplication of Masses when a church is large enough to accommodate the faithful at a smaller number of Masses. According to *Eucharisticum mysterium* 26, the pastoral effort is weakened by multiple Masses because the participation of the people in a scattered congregation is diminished and the effectiveness of overworked priests is reduced. The same document adds that small religious communities and other groups should take part in the parish Mass on Sundays and feast days rather than at separate celebrations. Multiple Masses attended by a few and small group Masses on the Lord's Day tend to detract from the value of the Eucharist as a sign and source of ecclesial unity.

The vigil Mass on the evening before a Sunday, in respect to this canon, counts as a Mass celebrated on Saturday, not Sunday; likewise a vigil Mass on the evening before a holy day of obliga-

---

[23] *GIRM* 158. See also SCSacr, rescript, March 10, 1970; *CLD* 7, 38–39, which permits priests who celebrate a Mass for the faithful on Holy Thursday to concelebrate at the evening Mass.

[24] Benedict XV, apconst *Incruentum,* August 10, 1915, *AAS* 7 (1915) 401.

[25] Most canonists who have commented on this canon assume or claim that the All Souls' trination is still permissible, and they cite the 1915 apostolic constitution of Benedict XV as their source. W. Woestman, e.g., says that the constitution is liturgical law and lies outside the domain of the code in keeping with c. 2. See "Three Masses on All Souls' Day," *J* 47 (1987) 521–530. However, the principal provision of the 1915 constitution, that Mass may be celebrated by each priest three times on All Souls' Day, was taken up by the 1917 code and is therefore subject to the provision of c. 22 of that code, as well as c. 20 of the 1983 code, that a later law abrogates a former one if it entirely reorders it. Even if the 1915 apostolic constitution may be called liturgical law, it is still subject to the same rules of interpretation and revocation as are other ecclesiastical laws. Since permission for the All Souls' trination is no longer included in the code or the *current* liturgical law, it has been formally abrogated. If this was unintentional, as some infer, then the legislator must correct this in a subsequent edition of the *GIRM*. It cannot be corrected by liturgical ordos, even if published by the Apostolic See; the compiler of the ordo is not the legislator.

If a revised *GIRM* does not explicitly provide for priests to trinate on All Souls, it should be clear that this faculty has indeed been abrogated. If there is no change in the Missal and three Mass texts continue to be provided for November 2, this would mean, as it now does, that a priest has a choice of Mass texts for that day, not that he may celebrate all three Masses in virtue of the law itself.

[26] *PM* I, 2.

[27] Chiappetta maintains that this faculty probably pertains also to ordinaries of religious institutes and societies of apostolic life of pontifical right relative to their subjects. However, his interpretation is contrary to the proper meaning of the words of this canon. See *Chiappetta Com,* 3218.

tion counts for that day, not the holy day. If pastoral need requires that a priest regularly celebrate more than two Masses on weekdays, including Saturdays, or more than three times on Sundays and holy days, the diocesan bishop may dispense in individual cases. However, the bishop may not give general permission without an indult from the Congregation for Divine Worship and the Discipline of the Sacraments.

Presence of Faithful Necessary

Canon 906 — Except for a just and reasonable cause, a priest is not to celebrate the eucharistic sacrifice without the participation of at least some member of the faithful.

The prohibition against celebrating the Eucharist without the presence of some member of the faithful has been a part of church law at least since the pontificate of Alexander III in the twelfth century, and it was reaffirmed in the 1917 code in terms of the requirement of a server for every Mass.[28] Vatican II insisted:

> When rites, according to their specific nature, make provision for communal celebration involving the presence and active participation of the faithful, it is to be stressed that this way of celebrating them is to be preferred, as far as possible, to a celebration that is individual and, so to speak, private. This applies with special force to the celebration of Mass.[29]

Lest this conciliar teaching be misunderstood, in 1965 Pope Paul VI reaffirmed the traditional practice of priests' celebrating Mass with only a server present:

> Although it is eminently in accord with the very nature of the celebration of Mass that large groups of the faithful participate ac-

tively, nevertheless, there is to be no disparagement but full approval of a Mass that, in conformity with the prescriptions and lawful traditions of the Church, a priest for a sufficient reason offers in private, that is, with no one present except the server.[30]

The Sacred Congregation for the Discipline of the Sacraments in 1949 stated that according to the approved authors there are only four cases in which Mass may be celebrated without a server: when it is necessary to give Viaticum to a sick person; to enable the people to satisfy the precept of hearing Mass; in time of pestilence, when a priest would otherwise be obliged to abstain from celebrating for a notable time; and when the server leaves during the course of the Mass.[31] Pius XII would not grant an indult for Mass to be said without a server unless some member of the faithful were present to assist.[32] The server in the former law was required not primarily for the material assistance of the priest but because the Eucharist is essentially an action of the whole Church, priest and people. In the words of Thomas Aquinas, the server "represents the whole Catholic people, and in that capacity answers the priest in the plural."[33] These principles are equally applicable to the present law, although the server's place may now be taken by any member of the faithful.

Canon 906 alters the previous discipline in two ways. First, the server is no longer necessary, but there must be the *participation* of at least some member of the faithful, i.e., of at least one other Christian who can make the responses in place of the congregation. For individual celebration the *Roman Missal* provides a "Rite of Mass without a Congregation," and the server's responses in it may be made by any member of the faithful. Sec-

---

[28] C. 6, X, *de filiis presbyt. ord. vel non,* I, 17; *CIC* 813, §1.
[29] *SC* 27, *DOL* 27.

[30] *Mysterium fidei* 32, September 3, 1965, *AAS* 57 (1965) 761–762, *DOL* 1176.
[31] Instr *Quam plurimum,* October 1, 1949, *AAS* 41 (1949) 507; *CLD* 3, 318.
[32] Instr *Quam plurimum,* October 1, 1949, *AAS* 41 (1949) 508.
[33] *STh* III, q. 83, art. 5, ad 12.

ond, the requirement that there be serious necessity for a priest to celebrate alone is changed to "a just and reasonable cause." Such a cause would be demonstrated whenever a member of the faithful is unavailable and when the priest is unable to participate in a communal celebration, e.g., as a result of illness, infirmity, or travel. A just and reasonable cause would not be the mere convenience of the priest or his preference for celebrating alone. Canon 902, while granting priests the freedom of celebrating individually instead of concelebrating, does not excuse the priest from the law requiring the presence of at least some member of the faithful.

Female Altar Servers

The former law corresponding to canon 906 is canon 813 of the 1917 code. This canon had barred females from serving Mass. Since certain liturgical documents before 1983 had also contained the ban on female servers, there was some doubt as to whether the ban was still in effect in keeping with the principle of canon 2, or whether it had been abrogated in keeping with canon 6, §1. There was also a question as to whether the code implicitly permitted female servers as one of the "other functions" mentioned in canon 230, §2. In 1992 the Pontifical Council for the Interpretation of Legislative Texts gave an authentic interpretation of canon 230, §2 which acknowledged that women or girls could be altar servers at Mass.[34] This was a merely declarative interpretation, since the prohibitions of canon 813 of the 1917 code against females serving Mass and approaching the altar during Mass were not included in canon 906 of the 1983 code.[35]

Functions Restricted to the Priest

Canon 907 — In the eucharistic celebration deacons and lay persons are not permitted to offer prayers, especially the eucharistic prayer, or to perform actions which are proper to the celebrating priest.

In the tradition of Jewish ritual meals and of the Last Supper, certain functions in the Eucharist have always been reserved to a presider, who as leader of the community prays and acts in its name. The Second Vatican Council established the general principle that those who have a liturgical ministry should perform only and all those functions which pertain to them according to the nature of the rite and the liturgical norms.[36] The hierarchical structure of the liturgy flows from the hierarchical ordering of the people of God who "all take part in this liturgical service, not indeed all in the same way, but all in their proper way."[37] The more the faithful clearly understand their proper role in the liturgical assembly and in the eucharistic action, "the more conscious and fruitful will be the active participation that belongs to a community."[38]

The eucharistic prayer is the preeminent prayer of the priest.[39] In this central prayer of praise and thanksgiving the priest unites the community with himself as he addresses the Father through the Son in the name of all, and "the entire congregation joins itself to Christ in acknowledging the great things God has done and in offering the sacrifice."[40] The priest's voice alone must be heard "as the assembly gathered to celebrate the liturgy maintains a reverent silence."[41] When non-priests join in the eucharistic prayer or when concelebrants are more than barely audible, the sign of the celebrant as leader of worship and president

---

[34] *AAS* 86 (1994) 541; *BCLN* 30 (1994) 13. See also BCL, "Suggested Guidelines Regarding Altar Servers," *BCLN* 30 (1994) 165–166.

[35] See J. Huels, "Female Altar Servers: The Legal Issues," *W* 57 (1983) 513–525; *Disputed Questions in the Liturgy Today* (Chicago: Liturgy Training Publications, 1988) 27–38.

[36] *SC* 28.

[37] *LG* 11.

[38] *Eucharisticum mysterium* 11; see also n. 12, *DOL* 1240–1241.

[39] *GIRM* 10.

[40] *Eucharisticum mysterium* 54, *DOL* 1444.

[41] SCDW, littcirc *Eucharisticae participationem* 8, April 27, 1973, *AAS* 65 (1973) 343, *DOL* 1982.

of the community is diminished and the role of silence, fostered by *Sacrosanctum Concilium,* is neglected.[42] Moreover, the common recitation of the eucharistic prayer destroys its dialogical character whereby the priest proclaims and the people listen attentively and respond. Among the most important responses of the people is the "Amen" when they affirm the whole prayer at its end. To accentuate its importance, the "Amen" should be embellished with song and never overwhelmed by reciting the doxology in common.[43]

Besides the eucharistic prayer, the other prayers and actions in the Eucharist proper to the celebrating priest are specified in the *Roman Missal.* Although canon 907 is new, it is related to canon 818 of the 1917 code which stated that the priest celebrant must observe accurately and devoutly the rubrics of the liturgical books and beware of adding other ceremonies or prayers on his own. The canon is closely related to the basic principle expressed in canons 835, §4 and 899, §2 that the faithful have their proper part to play in the sanctifying office and actively participate in liturgical celebrations, especially the Eucharist, in their own way.

Interdenominational Concelebration Prohibited

Canon 908 — Catholic priests are forbidden to concelebrate the Eucharist with priests or ministers of Churches or ecclesial communities which do not have full communion with the Catholic Church.

The 1993 *Directory for the Application of Principles and Norms on Ecumenism* gives a rationale for this law: eucharistic concelebration is a visible

manifestation of full communion in the faith, worship, and community life of the Catholic Church, expressed by ministers of that Church.[44] According to this principle, there can be no concelebration with ministers of other Christian churches and ecclesial communities until full communion exists with them. A Catholic priest who concelebrates at a non-Catholic Eucharist is subject to a just penalty (c. 1365).

Although there was no comparable canon in the 1917 code, the content of this canon is not new. Two decrees of Vatican II and several postconciliar documents issued by the Secretariat for Promoting Christian Unity considered the question of sacramental sharing in general and of common participation in the Eucharist in particular.[45] A 1970 declaration of the secretariat specifically mentions the issue of "a communal Eucharist celebrated together by ministers belonging to still separated churches and ecclesial communities."[46] A 1972 instruction of this same secretariat affirmed the basic principle that "of its very nature, the celebration of the Eucharist signifies the fullness of profession of faith and the fullness of ecclesial communion."[47]

Personal Prayer of Priest

Canon 909 — A priest is not to neglect to prepare himself properly through prayer for the celebration of the eucharistic sacrifice and to offer thanks to God at its completion.

The appendix to the *Roman Missal* provides several optional prayers of preparation for and

---

[42] *GIRM* 170; BCL, *Study Text 5: Eucharistic Concelebration* (Washington, D.C.: USCC, 1978) 25, n. 6; *SC* 30. See also F. R. McManus, *Liturgical Participation: An Ongoing Assessment,* American Essays in Liturgy 10 (Washington, D.C.: Pastoral Press, 1988) 11–14.

[43] *GIRM* 191; *IDon* 4; BCL, *Music in Catholic Worship* (Washington, D.C.: USCC, 1972) 53–54; *BCLN* 16 (1980) 230.

[44] *Ecum Dir* 104 e.

[45] *OE* 27–29; *UR* 8, 14, 22; *ED* 42–44, 55, 59; SPCU, decl *Dans ces derniers temps,* January 7, 1970, *AAS* 62 (1970), 184–188, *DOL* 150; SPCU, instr *In quibus rerum circumstantiis,* June 1, 1972, *AAS* 64 (1972) 518–525; SPCU, interpretation *Dopo la pubblicazione,* October 17, 1973, *AAS* 65 (1973) 616– 619; SPCU, *Ecumenical Collaboration at the Regional, National and Local Levels* IIIa, private, February 22, 1975, *CLD* 8, 879–880.

[46] *Dans ces derniers temps* 1, *DOL* 1024.

[47] *In quibus rerum circumstantiis* IV, 1.

thanksgiving after Mass. The priest may use these prayers or choose other ways to observe this canon. Canon 909 is substantially the same as canon 810 of the 1917 code.

Eucharistic Ministers

Canon 910 — §1. The ordinary minister of holy communion is a bishop, presbyter, or deacon.

§2. The extraordinary minister of holy communion is an acolyte or another member of the Christian faithful designated according to the norm of can. 230, §3.

Canon 845 of the 1917 code stated that the priest alone is the ordinary minister of communion, and the deacon is the extraordinary minister who could exercise this ministry only with permission of the local ordinary or the pastor, and for a grave reason. The current canon 910 states the church discipline that has been in effect since 1967 when the permanent diaconate was restored and deacons were made ordinary ministers of the Eucharist.[48]

The second paragraph of the canon treats the extraordinary, or special, minister of the Eucharist. *Minister extraordinarius,* which refers to a minister other than the ordinary minister, is translated as "special minister" by the International Commission on English in the Liturgy; this avoids the connotation of the English word "extraordinary" meaning "unusual."[49] According to canon 230, §3, acolytes and other special ministers of the Eucharist may distribute communion when the needs of the Church require it and when (ordinary) ministers are lacking. This may be either during the celebration of Mass or outside Mass, and they may administer either the bread or the cup.

In 1987 the Pontifical Commission for the Authentic Interpretation of the Canons of the Code of Canon Law made an authentic interpretation of this canon which stated that the special minister

may not exercise his or her function "when ordinary ministers, who are not in any way impeded, are present in the church, though not taking part in the Eucharistic celebration."[50] This interpretation reinforces the fact that special ministers have an auxiliary function and are to be used only if there are insufficient ordinary ministers present who are not impeded. An ordinary minister may be impeded if he is not vested, has not been notified that he is to assist in this ministry, or cannot easily approach the sanctuary.[51]

Diocesan bishops also have the faculty to permit individual priests to appoint a qualified person to distribute communion for a single occasion when there is a genuine need.[52] This faculty provides for the exceptional cases when the number of available ordinary ministers and regularly deputed special ministers is insufficient to meet pastoral needs. Those who would make use of the provision are required to obtain advance permission from their diocesan bishop, who may also give general permission. In cases of pressing need, tacit permission may be presumed unless the contrary is evident.

The special minister is to be deputed in accord with canon 230, §3. In keeping with the norm of canon 231, §1, it is desirable to provide a suitable program of formation or instruction for the candidates who are to be commissioned as special min-

---

[48] *SDO* 3.

[49] See *Rite of Commissioning Special Ministers of Holy Communion, BB* chap. 63.

[50] Reply, February 20, 1987, *AAS* 80 (1988) 1373; *BCLN* 24 (1988) 104; *Pamplona ComEng,* 1293.

[51] See *CLSGBI Com,* 500.

[52] SCSacr, instr *Immensae caritatis* 2, 6, January 29, 1973, *AAS* 65 (1973) 264–271, *DOL* 2076, 2080. The Vatican English translation of the 1997 "Instruction on Certain Questions Regarding the Collaboration of the Non-Ordained Faithful in the Sacred Ministry of Priests," art. 8, §1, *Origins* 27 (November 27, 1997) 406, leaves out the word "also" (*etiam*). It should read: "A non-ordained member of the faithful in cases of true necessity may be deputed by the diocesan bishop...to act as an extraordinary minister to distribute Holy Communion *also* outside of liturgical celebrations." The mistake in the Vatican translation makes it appear that the appointment applies only to distributing communion outside the liturgy. See CC et al., instr, *Ecclesiae de ministerio,* August 15, 1997, *AAS* 89 (1997) 871.

isters.[53] A diocesan bishop is free to mandate special ministers as he sees fit provided that the individual candidates' names are approved by the diocesan bishop himself; he may also delegate this faculty.

Legal History

In 1927 and 1930 extraordinary faculties were granted to ordinaries in Mexico and Russia permitting "pious lay men" to bring holy communion to the sick and to prisoners.[54] A wider use of special ministers of communion was permitted in 1969 by the routine granting of indults from the Holy See.[55] During the next few years numerous indults were granted to individual bishops and even to entire bishops' conferences, including the National Conference of Catholic Bishops.[56] When the minor orders were abolished by Paul VI in 1972, the new lay ministry of acolyte was created, among whose duties is that of distributing the Eucharist whenever ordinary ministers are not available or the number of communicants is great.[57]

The 1973 instruction of the Sacred Congregation for the Discipline of the Sacraments, *Immensae caritatis,* provided for the creation of special ministers without the necessity of the competent authorities applying for particular indults.[58] With the appearance of the instruction, local ordinaries had the faculty to appoint qualified persons of either sex to serve as special ministers for a given occasion, for a stated period of time, or even permanently, if needed. *Immensae caritatis* noted three circumstances, each of which would warrant the exercise of this ministry: (1) the absence of a priest, deacon, or acolyte; (2) the inconvenience to these same persons or their inability to distribute communion due to their involvement in some other pastoral ministry or because of ill health or advanced age; and (3) the presence of so many people who wish to receive communion that the celebration of Mass or the distribution of communion outside Mass would take an excessively long time.

Ministers of Viaticum

Canon 911 — §1. The pastor, parochial vicars, chaplains, and, with regard to all those dwelling in the house, the superior of a community in clerical religious institutes and societies of apostolic life have the duty and right of bringing the Most Holy Eucharist as Viaticum to the sick.

§2. In the case of necessity or with at least the presumed permission of the pastor, chaplain, or superior, who must be notified afterwards, any priest or other minister of holy communion must do this.

The minister of Viaticum in the 1917 code was principally the pastor; other priests could administer it only in cases of necessity or with at least the presumed permission of the pastor or ordinary.[59] The chief change in the law governing the minister of Viaticum occurred in the 1972 revision of the rites of anointing and Viaticum, which added as ordinary ministers both parochial vicars and priests who care for the sick in hospitals.[60] This canon includes not only those who care for the sick in hospitals, but all chaplains as ordinary ministers of Viaticum. General norms governing

---

[53] Some worthwhile instructional aids are W. J. Belford, *Special Ministers of the Eucharist* (New York: Pueblo, 1979); and BCL, *Study Text I: Holy Communion, Commentary on the Instruction Immensae Caritatis* (Washington, D.C.: USCC, 1973).

[54] D. Sheehan, *The Minister of Holy Communion, CanLawStud* 298 (1950) 108–117.

[55] SCSacr, instr *Fidei custos,* April 30, 1966, not published, *DOL* 259. This instruction required that the person for this ministry be chosen in this order of preference: subdeacons, clerics in minor orders, those who have received tonsure, men religious, women religious, male catechists (unless, in the prudent judgment of the pastor, a male catechist is preferable to a woman religious), laymen, laywomen. See n. 3, *DOL* 2046. This hierarchy no longer applies.

[56] *CLD* 7, 648–652.

[57] *MQ* VI.

[58] *DOL* 264; see also *HCWE* 17.

[59] *CIC* 850; see also *CIC* 397, 3°; 464, §2; 1368.

[60] *RAnointing* 29.

chaplains are found in canons 564–572; canon 566, §1 specifically mentions the administration of Viaticum as one of the chaplain's chief duties. The right of the pastor to administer Viaticum is also implicit in canon 530, 3° where it is listed as one of the functions specially committed to the pastor.

The ordinary ministers of Viaticum for religious remain nearly the same as in the 1917 code (*CIC* 514). For clerical religious institutes and clerical societies of apostolic life, the ordinary minister of Viaticum is the superior of the house. He has the right and duty to administer the sacrament to all who live in the house, including boarders who are not members of the institute. The ordinary minister for houses of lay religious is the pastor, parochial vicar, or chaplain of the house. The ordinary minister of Viaticum for a diocesan seminary is the seminary rector or his delegate in accord with canon 262.

The administration of Viaticum by the ordinary minister is both a right and a duty. By making it a duty incumbent on priests who have positions of pastoral care, the legislator assures that the faithful have access to the full benefits of spiritual comfort provided by the Church, including penance and anointing. The administration of Viaticum is also a right, which means that the ordinary minister may reserve this ministry to himself in all cases or in individual instances, unless he is impeded.

Ministers of Viaticum other than the ordinary ministers may be used either in case of need or if the minister has at least the presumed permission of the ordinary minister. A case of need is demonstrated when someone is in danger of death and the ordinary minister is unavailable. One can always presume the permission of the ordinary minister in cases of danger of imminent death because the right of the faithful to receive the last sacrament supersedes the right of the ordinary minister to give it. Since the administration of Viaticum is a canonical duty of the ordinary minister, he should be notified when this duty is fulfilled by another. A deacon follows the rite of Viaticum outside Mass prescribed for priests in the *Rite of Anointing* 101–114.[61] Lay ministers follow the *Rite of Holy Communion and Worship of the Eucharist outside Mass*.[62]

ARTICLE 2: PARTICIPATION IN THE MOST HOLY EUCHARIST [cc. 912–923]

The twelve canons of this article treat various aspects of participation in the Eucharist, all of which are related to the reception of holy communion. The norms regulate the following: the recipient of communion (c. 912), reception of communion by children (c. 913), duties of parents and pastors (c. 914), the prohibition of the Eucharist to public sinners (c. 915), obligation to confess serious sins (c. 916), communion twice a day (c. 917), communion outside Mass (c. 918), the eucharistic fast (c. 919), the eucharistic precept (c. 920), the recipient of Viaticum (cc. 921–922), and the Eucharist in other churches *sui iuris* (c. 923).

Recipient of Communion

Canon 912 — Any baptized person not prohibited by law can and must be admitted to holy communion.

Eligible baptized persons may and *must* be admitted to the Eucharist because they have a right to the sacrament in accord with canon 213. According to canon 842, §1, which is considered divine law, the recipient of communion must be baptized. For good reason the Church can prohibit baptized persons from receiving the sacrament or limit their reception of it. The law greatly restricts access to the Eucharist by baptized non-Catholics (c. 844, §§ 3–4). Further restrictions are specified in the canons which follow.

---

[61] The version approved for the United States is *Pastoral Care of the Sick: Rites of Anointing and Viaticum* 197–211.

[62] *RAnointing* 29, 112. See also commentary on cc. 910 and 921–922.

Reception of Communion by Children

Canon 913 — §1. The administration of the Most Holy Eucharist to children requires that they have sufficient knowledge and careful preparation so that they understand the mystery of Christ according to their capacity and are able to receive the body of Christ with faith and devotion.

§2. The Most Holy Eucharist, however, can be administered to children in danger of death if they can distinguish the body of Christ from ordinary food and receive communion reverently.

Since 1910 it has been the practice of the Latin church to give communion to children from the age of seven.[63] The ancient custom of giving communion to infants had largely ceased in the West by the twelfth century, but it is still maintained in Eastern churches. The Council of Trent decreed that it is not necessary to give the Eucharist to children before they have reached the age of discretion, but it did not condemn the practice.[64]

The intent of canon 913 is to ensure that children who receive the Eucharist have adequate catechetical and spiritual preparation.[65] Paragraph one states in broad terms the minimal requirements for admitting children to the Eucharist in ordinary circumstances. It does not specify what constitutes sufficient knowledge or how much faith and devotion is expected of the child but rather allows the persons mentioned in canon 914 to make such determinations while advising that the preparation be according to the child's capacity. The careful preparation required is something more than the intellectual preparation indicated by the words "sufficient knowledge." It includes formative experiences in faith such as are promoted by active participation in the Eucharist even before the children receive the first holy communion. The liturgy itself has formative value,[66] especially when it is adapted to the children's level as suggested by the principles contained in the *Directory on Children's Masses*. The use of the approved eucharistic prayers and lectionary for children can also encourage greater participation in and a fuller understanding of the "mystery of Christ" referred to in the canon.[67]

Children who are in danger of death may receive communion even if they do not have the sufficient knowledge and careful preparation specified in paragraph one. However, paragraph two requires that they be able to distinguish the body of Christ from ordinary food and to receive it reverently. The latter requirement is a change from the 1917 code (*CIC* 854, §2), which stated that the child must be able "reverently to adore" the host.

Duties of Pastors and Parents

Canon 914 — It is primarily the duty of parents and those who take the place of parents, as well as the duty of pastors, to take care that children who have reached the use of reason are prepared properly and, after they have made sacramental confession, are refreshed with this divine food as soon as possible. It is for the pastor to exercise vigilance so that children who have not attained the use of reason or whom he judges are not sufficiently disposed do not approach holy communion.

Canon 914 gives greater responsibility to parents and guardians in the preparation of children for the Eucharist than did the 1917 code (*CIC* 854, §5) which saw this principally as the pastor's

---

[63] SCSacr, decr *Quam singulari,* August 8, 1910, *AAS* 2 (1910) 577–583.

[64] Sess. XXI, *Decr. de comm.,* c. 4.

[65] See *Eucharisticum mysterium* 14, *DOL* 1243; SCDW, *Directory for Masses with Children, Pueros baptizatos* 12, November 1, 1973, *AAS* 66 (1974) 30–46, *DOL* 276.

[66] *SC* 33.

[67] CDW, decr *Postquam de precibus,* Eucharistic Prayers for Masses with Children, November 1, 1974, *N* 11 (1975) 4–6, *DOL* 249; NCCB, *Lectionary for Masses with Children,* December 28, 1992, Liturgy Documentary Series 12: *Masses with Children* (Washington, D.C.: USCC, 1996) 27–47.

duty.[68] Once children have attained the use of reason at about the age of seven,[69] and are judged sufficiently prepared and disposed, parents (or guardians) and pastors are responsible for seeing that these children receive communion as early as possible so that they not be deprived of a sacrament to which they have a right in law. The pastor has an additional obligation to see that children who do not have the use of reason or who are not sufficiently disposed do not receive the Eucharist. The canon gives broad discretionary latitude to the pastor for determining whether the child meets these requirements. However, in view of the right of the baptized to receive the sacraments, a doubt about the use of reason or sufficient disposition should be resolved in favor of the child's receiving communion.

Persons with Developmental Disabilities

The issue of the use of reason is especially problematic in the case of persons who are mentally retarded or who have other developmental disabilities, or who have Alzheimer's or other diseases that affect mental functioning. Traditionally the use of reason has been viewed in terms of the possession of abstract, cognitive skills, but the law does not exclude a broader definition which places primacy on symbolic and intuitive ways of knowing. For example, persons with developmental disabilities may not be able to conceptualize and articulate the difference between the body of Christ and ordinary food, but they can often appreciate the sacredness of the eucharistic food in the context of the reverence shown the sacrament by their families and the Christian community. The policy of the U.S. episcopal conference recognizes this:

It is important to note, however, that the criterion for reception of holy communion is the same for persons with developmental and mental disabilities as for all persons, namely that the person be able to distinguish the body of Christ from ordinary food, even if this recognition is evidenced through manner, gesture or reverential silence rather than verbally. Pastors are encouraged to consult with parents, those who take the place of parents, diocesan personnel involved with disability issues, psychologists, religious educators and other experts in making their judgment [about whether such persons may be admitted to communion].[70]

Since the baptized have a fundamental right to the Eucharist, any doubts about the sufficiency of the use of reason should be resolved in favor of the person.[71]

Penance before First Communion

In the years following Vatican II there was widespread experimentation with the practice of delaying first penance until after first communion, but the Apostolic See repeatedly ordered that these experiments be halted.[72] Since the context of

---

[68] On the role of parents in forming children for the Eucharist, see the *Directory for Masses with Children* 10, *DOL* 2143. It is the function of the pastor not so much to attend personally to the catechesis as to see that it is given, both before and after first communion. See c. 777, nn. 1–3. See also cc. 528; 843, §2; and 898.

[69] See c. 97, §2; *GCD* Addendum, n. 1.

[70] NCCB, "Guidelines for Celebration of the Sacraments with Persons with Disabilities" 20, June 15, 1995, *Origins* 25 (1995) 107–110. See also the pastoral statement of the Roman Catholic Bishops of England and Wales, *All People Together* 15–19 (London: CSP Studios, 1981).

[71] On the right of persons with developmental disabilities to the Eucharist, see J. Huels, "Canonical Rights to the Sacraments," in *Developmental Disabilities and Sacramental Access: New Paradigms for Sacramental Encounters*, ed. E. Foley (Collegeville: Liturgical Press, 1994) 94–115; and D. Wilson, "The Church, the Eucharist, and the Mentally Handicapped," *CR* 60 (1975) 69–84.

[72] SCSacr and SCC, decl *Sanctus Pontifex,* May 24, 1973, *AAS* 65 (1973) 410, *DOL* 379, *CLD* 8, 563; SCSDW, letter, April 30, 1976, *DOL* 380, *CLD* 8, 603; SCSDW and SCC, letter *In quibusdam Ecclesiae partibus, DOL* 381; SCSDW and SCC, reply, May 20, 1977, *AAS* 69 (1977) 427, *DOL* 382, *CLD* 8, 607. In contrast, the *General Catechetical Directory* of 1971 had previously manifested an

this canon is the preparation of children for first communion, the requirement of penance before first communion should be seen as a means to assist the child's preparation to receive communion fruitfully. Children should be prepared for and should be encouraged to approach the sacrament of penance as part of their preparation for first communion. However, penance before communion is a doctrinal requirement only if a person is in a state of serious sin, and exceptions are permitted even in that case (c. 916). Therefore, if the parents, who have the primary responsibility for the child's catechesis,[73] should determine that their child is not yet ready for first penance but is ready for first communion, the child should not be denied the right to the sacrament.[74]

Prohibition of Eucharist to Public Sinners

Canon 915 — Those who have been excommunicated or interdicted after the imposition or declaration of the penalty and others obstinately persevering in manifest grave sin are not to be admitted to holy communion.

The canon is directed to individual ministers of the Eucharist who are to refuse the sacrament in the cases mentioned in the canon. A principal effect of the penalties of excommunication and interdict is the prohibition against receiving the sacraments (cc. 1331, §1, 2°; 1332). If the censure was imposed or declared, it is a public fact of the external forum and the minister is bound to refuse the Eucharist or other sacrament whether or not the community actually knows of the penalty.

Eucharistic ministers are also to refuse holy communion when they are certain: (1) that a person has committed a sin that is objectively grave, (2) that the sinner is obstinately persevering in this sinful state, and (3) that this sin is manifest. A manifest sin is one which is publicly known by a large part of the parish or other community; if the sin is not publicly known, refusing communion would be a violation of a person's right to a good reputation (c. 220). The sin in question is one which is repeated habitually, e.g., by a gangster, a drug dealer, an abortionist. This canon would not, as a rule, apply to a single grave sin, even if manifest, since obstinacy must be evident.

Obstinate perseverance is indicated when the pastor or other church authority has expressly warned the offending party to cease committing the sin, but this warning is not heeded. If there is no advance warning before communion is denied, there is no way to be certain of obstinacy. The warning should include the express threat that communion will be refused to the manifest grave sinner in order to permit the sinner to avoid the shame of a public refusal of communion. The warning should be given to the sinner in the external forum, either orally or in writing, but it cannot be given if knowledge of the sin is gained from the internal forum (cc. 983–984). The confessor may admonish an obstinate penitent to refrain from communion, but the confessor may not himself refuse it unless he had knowledge of the sin from the external forum before it was confessed.

There is another serious difficulty in applying this canon in the case of persons who obstinately persevere in manifest grave sin. The state of one's conscience is a matter of the internal forum, yet this canon addresses ministers in the external forum. It is possible that a person may have repented of the sin and now may be in the state of grace, but this might not be evident in the external forum, e.g., in the case of the internal forum solution to an irregular marriage.[75] Since there is always some risk of injustice when this canon is ap-

---

openness to continued experimentation, provided the Holy See was kept informed; see *GCD* 5.

[73] Canons 226, 793, 797, 798, 835, §4. See F. G. Morrisey, "The Rights of Parents in the Education of the Children," *Stud Can* 23 (1989) 429–444; P. E. Baillargeon, "The Rights and Duties of Parents in the Sanctification of Their Children," *CLSAP* 54 (1992) 55–71.

[74] For more on this issue see J. Provost, "The Reception of First Penance," *J* 47 (1987) 294–340; J. Huels, *Disputed Questions in the Liturgy Today* (Chicago: Liturgy Training Publications, 1988) 67–74.

[75] See *FC* 84 e.

plied apart from the evident cases of public excommunication or interdict, it is necessary that there be some urgent need that pertains to the common good, in particular, the need to preclude grave scandal on the part of the community that would arise from the public sinner's reception of communion.

The fact of actual scandal is, moreover, culturally relative. What causes scandal in one part of the world may not cause scandal elsewhere. In North America the faithful often are more scandalized by the Church's denial of sacraments and sacramentals than by the sin that occasions it, because it seems to them contrary to the mercy and forgiveness commanded by Christ. Thus, this canon should be applied to cases of obstinate perseverance in manifest grave sin only when the common good of the Church is truly being harmed due to grave scandal. It is not the minister's own scandal that must be precluded, but the scandal that exists or would likely arise within the community.

The prohibition of the Eucharist by a minister in one community does not require that the person also be barred elsewhere where the sin may be known only to a few. This canon is directed to individual ministers of communion who must interpret it in the situation of their own community. Thus, it may not be applied by the diocesan bishop or other competent authority in order to prevent a person from receiving communion from all ministers. This may be done only through a penal process, since the deprivation of the sacraments is a penalty. Penalties may be imposed only after due process of law has been observed (c. 221, §3).[76]

Obligation to Confess Serious Sins

Canon 916 — A person who is conscious of grave sin is not to celebrate Mass or receive the body of the Lord without previous sacramental confession unless there is a grave reason and there is no opportunity to confess; in this case the person is to remember the obligation to make an act of perfect contrition which includes the resolution of confessing as soon as possible.

This canon, a composite of canons 807 and 856 of the 1917 code, is based on Tridentine doctrine. Citing the scriptures (1 Cor 11:28–29), Trent confirmed the Church's teaching that one who is conscious of grave sins may not receive the Eucharist.[77] *Eucharisticum mysterium* 35 affirmed this discipline, adding that confessions should not be heard during the celebration of Mass. Canon 916 adds nothing new to past discipline in requiring those who are conscious, i.e., *certain,* of having committed a grave sin to return to the state of grace by sacramental confession or an act of perfect contrition when sacramental confession is not possible. Perfect contrition (contrition of charity) arises from a love by which God is loved above all else; such contrition remits venial sins and also obtains forgiveness of mortal sins if it includes the intention to confess as soon as possible.[78]

A grave reason for celebrating Mass before confessing is the need to celebrate Mass for the faithful. Grave reasons for going to communion without confessing include danger of death and serious embarrassment if communion is not taken. Lack of opportunity to confess includes absence of a confessor, inability to approach the confessor at a scheduled time for the sacrament, and the availability only of a confessor who is known personally and who cannot be approached without embarrassment.

Communion Twice a Day

Canon 917 — A person who has already received the Most Holy Eucharist can receive it a second time on the same day only within the eucharistic celebration in which the person participates, without prejudice to the prescript of can. 921, §2.

---

[76] See F.G. Morrisey, "Denial of Access to the Sacraments," *CLSAP* 52 (1990) 170–186.

[77] Sess. XIII, *de euch.,* cap. 7, c. 11.
[78] *CCC* 1452.

In 1984 the Pontifical Commission for the Authentic Interpretation of the Canons of the Code of Canon Law issued an authentic interpretation on this canon to clarify that the word *iterum* as used here means "a second time," not "again and again" as often as one participates in the Eucharist.[79] Only as Viaticum, or in the case of the priest who has permission to trinate, may anyone receive communion a third time in one day. The purpose of this law is twofold: on the one hand, to promote active participation in the Eucharist including the full sacramental sharing in the Lord's body and blood; on the other hand, to prevent the abuse of receiving multiple communions out of superstition, ignorance, or misguided devotion.

The 1917 code (*CIC* 857) forbade the reception of communion more than once a day except in danger of death or to prevent impending irreverence. The law was mitigated repeatedly after Vatican II to allow more frequent opportunities to receive twice on the same day.[80] This canon greatly simplifies the postconciliar legislation by permitting the reception of communion twice in a day for any reason, provided the second reception is in the context of participation in the eucharistic celebration.

Communion outside Mass

Canon 918 — It is highly recommended that the faithful receive holy communion during the eucharistic celebration itself. It is to be administered outside the Mass, however, to those who request it for a just cause, with the liturgical rites being observed.

The 1917 code was rather liberal in its provision for communion outside Mass. In addition to communion for the sick and dying, any priest could give communion outside Mass in a church at the hours during which Mass could be celebrated and even at other times for a reasonable cause; it could also be given immediately before or after a private (low) Mass.[81]

Since the pontificate of Pope Pius XII, the Church's attitude toward communion outside Mass has become more restrictive.[82] Vatican II decreed that communion received during the eucharistic celebration is "the more complete form of participation in the Mass."[83] The 1967 instruction *Eucharisticum mysterium* said that it is highly recommended (*valde commendatur*) that the faithful receive communion during Mass. It also stated that it is necessary to accustom the faithful to receive communion during the Eucharist, and that there must be a just cause for distributing communion outside Mass.[84] The canon reflects this change in attitude, and it even more strongly (*maxime commendatur*) recommends that the faithful receive communion during the eucharistic celebration. Because the mind of the Church is that communion be given primarily during Mass, the requirement of a just cause for communion outside Mass should be strictly observed. Some examples of a just cause include the inability to participate in the eucharistic celebration due to illness or old age or the absence of a priest who can preside at Eucharist. Liturgical law requires pastors to see to it that the sick and aged be given every opportunity to receive the Eucharist frequently, especially during the Easter season.[85]

The liturgical rites to be observed in distributing communion outside Mass are contained in the *Roman Ritual* under the title, "Holy Communion and Worship of the Eucharist outside Mass." The

---

[79] August 7, 1984, *AAS* 76 (1984) 746; *Pamplona ComEng*, 1293–1295.

[80] *IO* 60; *Rite of Concelebration* 15; SCRit, instr *Tres abhinc annos* 14, May 4, 1967, *AAS* 59 (1967) 442–448, *DOL* 460; *Eucharisticum mysterium* 28, *DOL* 1257; *Immensae caritatis,* pt. 2, *DOL* 2082–2084.

[81] *CIC* 846; 867, §4.

[82] Ency *Mediator Dei,* November 20, 1947, *AAS* 39 (1947) 565.

[83] *SC* 55.

[84] *Eucharisticum mysterium* 31, 33a, *DOL* 1260, 1262. See also *HCWE* 13.

[85] *RAnointing* 46. *Pastoral Care of the Sick: Rites of Anointing and Viaticum* provides rites of communion outside Mass for the sick in ordinary circumstances. See also commentary on cc. 921–922.

ritual prescribes an introductory rite and a celebration of the word preceding the distribution of communion. Options are provided for a shorter reading of the word when the entire service of the word is pastorally unsuitable, such as when there are only one or two communicants. The eucharistic prayer may never be said in communion services outside Mass.[86] Special directives for communion services held on Sundays are given in the 1988 *Directory for Sunday Celebrations in the Absence of a Presbyter*.[87]

Communion may be given outside Mass on any day and at any hour, with several exceptions. On Holy Thursday and Good Friday the sacrament may be administered only during the Eucharist or the celebration of the Lord's passion, respectively; communion may be given to the sick at any time on these days. On Holy Saturday only Viaticum may be administered. In this way the ancient tradition of the single Eucharist of a community is maintained at least on the principal days of the church year.

Eucharistic Fast

Canon 919 — §1. A person who is to receive the Most Holy Eucharist is to abstain for at least one hour before holy communion from any food and drink, except for only water and medicine.

§2. A priest who celebrates the Most Holy Eucharist two or three times on the same day can take something before the second or third celebration even if there is less than one hour between them.

§3. The elderly, the infirm, and those who care for them can receive the Most Holy Eucharist even if they have eaten something within the preceding hour.

The custom of fasting before the Eucharist arose after the third century and was mandated by early councils. The Church considers fasting a means of spiritual preparation for the Eucharist and a way of showing reverence for the sacrament.

Paragraph one of the canon reflects the discipline of the Church that has been in force since 1964. The traditional total fast from midnight, prescribed in the 1917 code (*CIC* 808, 858), was reduced to a three-hour fast in 1957[88] and to a one-hour fast in 1964.[89] Already in 1953 Pius XII had granted permission to take water and medicine at any time before reception of communion.[90] The medicine may be in solid or liquid form, and it need not be prescribed by a physician.

Paul VI allowed residential bishops to permit priests who binate or trinate to take nourishment in liquid form before the celebration of the next Mass.[91] Paragraph two of this canon extends this to all priests even without the bishop's permission, and it also allows the taking of solid foods. Priests therefore need observe the eucharistic fast only for their first Mass of the day. The word "celebrates" in §2 should be understood also as including priests who concelebrate.

Paragraph three represents a change from the previous law which required a fast of about a quarter of an hour for the sick in hospitals or at home, for those who are confined to their homes because of old age, or for those who live in nursing homes. Those who care for the sick and aged and their families were bound to a fast of about fifteen minutes if they could not observe the one-hour fast without inconvenience.[92] The sick were able to take non-alcoholic drink at any time before communion.[93] According to paragraph three of the canon, those who are advanced in age or who suffer from any infirmity and those who care for the sick and aged are not bound by any fast. The terms "elderly" and "infirm" are subject to

---

[86] SCDW, instr *Liturgicae instaurationes* 6e, September 5, 1970, *AAS* 62 (1970) 692–704, *DOL* 524.

[87] For references and commentary, see c. 1248.

[88] Pius XII, *mp Sacram communionem*, March 19, 1957, *AAS* 49 (1957) 177; *CLD* 4, 286.

[89] Paul VI, decr, November 21, 1964, *AAS* 57 (1964) 186; *CLD* 6, 566; *DOL* 272.

[90] Apconst *Christus Dominus,* January 6, 1953, *AAS* 45 (1953) 15; *CLD* 4, 269.

[91] *PM* I, 3.

[92] *Immensae caritatis*, pt. 3, *DOL* 2085–2086.

[93] *Sacram communionem* 4.

broad interpretation. Certainly anyone too old or too infirm to go to church need not fast. Those who care for the sick or aged are exempted from the fast only when they are actually caring for the sick or aged at the time they receive communion, such as when communion is given in a home or an institution. This category of persons may also be broadly understood to include those who contribute in non-material ways to the care of the sick, such as visitors and family members who provide moral and emotional support.

By specifying that the fast is to be *at least* one hour, the legislator appears to be encouraging the faithful to fast for a longer period, if they desire. The one-hour fast is computed from the time of the completion of the consumption of food or drink until the reception of communion, not the onset of Mass. Prior to the 1983 code, dispensations from the eucharistic fast were reserved to the Apostolic See;[94] now the diocesan bishop may dispense.

Eucharistic Precept

Canon 920 — §1. After being initiated into the Most Holy Eucharist, each of the faithful is obliged to receive holy communion at least once a year.

§2. This precept must be fulfilled during the Easter season unless it is fulfilled for a just cause at another time during the year.

As a result of widespread neglect of the sacrament in the Middle Ages, various church councils from the sixth century onward enacted disciplinary laws obliging the faithful to receive the Eucharist, especially on the principal feasts. Lateran IV in 1215 established a general law for the Latin church requiring the reception of communion at least once a year at Easter by those who had attained the age of discretion, unless for some reasonable cause one's priest advised against it for a time.[95] This law, confirmed by Trent,[96] is basically the same as that incorporated into the 1917 code

(*CIC* 859, §1). The 1983 code retains the annual precept but with some changes.

One change is greater latitude in the time permitted for the fulfillment of the eucharistic precept. The *coetus* which prepared the original draft of this canon understood Easter time as the period from Palm (Passion) Sunday to Pentecost Sunday.[97] The dioceses of the United States have an indult which allows the Easter duty to be satisfied from the First Sunday of Lent to Trinity Sunday.[98] The satisfaction of the eucharistic precept outside this period requires a just cause, such as illness, but it must be satisfied within the space of one year. The year is reckoned from the previous communion.

Another change from the former law is the elimination of the exception which allowed the *sacerdos proprius,* understood as one's pastor or confessor, to permit an individual to postpone satisfaction of the eucharistic precept for a reasonable cause. The annual precept is now absolute, barring excusing causes such as physical or moral impossibility.

Under the former law, all who had attained the use of reason were bound by the eucharistic precept. The revised law specifies that all the faithful who have been initiated into the Eucharist (i.e., those who have made their first communion) are bound. Unlike the 1917 code (*CIC* 859, §3), the 1983 code does not require that the pastor of one's parish be notified when the eucharistic precept is fulfilled outside one's own parish.

Also dropped from the present law are canons 860 and 861 of the first code. The former canon specified the duty of those who have the care of children to see that they fulfill the paschal precept, while the latter stated that a sacrilegious communion did not satisfy the precept.

Viaticum

Canon 921 — §1. The Christian faithful who are in danger of death from any cause are to be nourished by holy communion in the form of Viaticum.

---

[94] *EM* IX, 20.
[95] Cap. 21.
[96] Sess. XIII, *de euch.,* c. 9.

[97] *Comm* 13 (1981) 417–418.
[98] Second Plenary Council of Baltimore, n. 257.

§2. Even if they have been nourished by holy communion on the same day, however, those in danger of death are strongly urged to receive communion again.

§3. While the danger of death lasts, it is recommended that holy communion be administered often, but on separate days.

Canon 922 — Holy Viaticum for the sick is not to be delayed too long; those who have the care of souls are to be zealous and vigilant that the sick are nourished by Viaticum while fully conscious.

Viaticum is the last sacrament of Christian life, holy communion given to those at or near the time of death. Vatican II called for the revision of the rite of Viaticum and for a new continuous rite of penance, anointing, and Viaticum.[99] This was implemented with the 1972 *Rite of Anointing of the Sick* and the 1973 *Rite of Holy Communion and Worship of the Eucharist outside Mass.* The liturgical law urges that Viaticum be given during Mass when possible and that it be given under both species of bread and wine. If the Eucharist is not celebrated, the Precious Blood is brought to the dying person in a sealed vessel and then poured into a chalice for administration.[100] The dying who are unable to receive under the form of bread may receive under the form of wine alone (c. 925).

The 1917 code (*CIC* 864) considered the reception of Viaticum by the faithful in danger of death as a "precept" to which they were bound by law. The revised code uses a milder form of command to express this duty, but the strict legal obligation still exists in the liturgical law which states that "all the baptized who can receive communion are bound by obligation to receive viaticum" in danger of death.[101] Baptized non-Catholics may, but are not obliged to, receive Vi-

aticum from a Catholic minister.[102] Children in danger of death who are able to distinguish the body of Christ from ordinary food and receive it reverently may, but are not obliged to, receive Viaticum (c. 913, §2).

The code does not define "danger of death" but, given the Church's desire that Viaticum be the final sacrament of passage from death to eternal life, a strict interpretation is in order. Viaticum should be received only by those who are in some real danger of dying, whether from intrinsic causes such as a grave illness or extrinsic sources such as the execution of a criminal. In doubt about the degree of danger, Viaticum may be given.

Viaticum should be administered as soon as possible after the faithful are in danger of death, even if they have already received communion once or twice that day. Terminally or seriously ill persons, although not in immediate danger of death, should not postpone its reception too long lest they lose consciousness or die. Canon 921, §3 recommends that "holy communion" be given each day while the danger lasts, whereas canon 864, §3 of the 1917 code said it was fitting to give "holy Viaticum" in these same circumstances. Thus, Viaticum is to be administered only once to a dying person.

Eucharist in Other Churches Sui Iuris

Canon 923 — The Christian faithful can participate in the eucharistic sacrifice and receive holy communion in any Catholic rite, without prejudice to the prescript of can. 844.

The reference to "any Catholic rite" means any Catholic church *sui iuris*. This canon is substantially the same as canon 866 of the 1917 code. The chief difference was that according to the 1917 code communion could be received "for reasons of piety" in another Catholic rite, but the law urged that the paschal precept be satisfied and Vi-

---

[99] *SC* 74.

[100] *RAnointing* 26, 95–96; NCCB, *Pastoral Care of the Sick: Rites of Anointing and Viaticum* (1983) 26, 181.

[101] *RAnointing* 27; *Pastoral Care of the Sick* 237; author's trans.

[102] See c. 844, §§ 3–4. The liturgical law binding all baptized Christians to receive Viaticum must be considered as derogated in view of cc. 11 and 2.

aticum received in one's own rite. Now there are no qualifications concerning the participation in and reception of the Eucharist in other Catholic churches *sui iuris*. However, the faithful may not receive the Eucharist of a church or ecclesial community which is not in full communion with the Catholic Church except for the case mentioned in canon 844, §2.

ARTICLE 3: THE RITES AND CEREMONIES OF THE EUCHARISTIC CELEBRATION [cc. 924–930]

The seven canons of this article treat the following: the matter of the Eucharist (c. 924), communion under one or both kinds (c. 925), the requirement of unleavened bread (c. 926), serious abuses (c. 927), the language of the Eucharist (c. 928), vestments (c. 929), and aged and infirm celebrants (c. 930).

Matter of the Eucharist

Canon 924 — §1. The most holy eucharistic sacrifice must be offered with bread and with wine in which a little water must be mixed.

§2. The bread must be only wheat and recently made so that there is no danger of spoiling.

§3. The wine must be natural from the fruit of the vine and not spoiled.

In keeping with the Last Supper narratives, the Church has always regarded bread and wine as the only matter essential for the eucharistic meal and sacrifice. A small quantity of water (*modica aqua*) is to be added to the wine by the deacon or priest at the preparation of the gifts. Cyprian of Carthage saw in this ritual mixing of water and wine a sign of the unity between Christ and his people, a tradition also reflected at the Council of Trent.[103]

---

[103] *Epistula 63 ad Caecilianum* 13, *PL* 4:395–396; Trent, sess. XXII, *Decr. de Missa*. Trent also mentioned that it was symbolic of the blood and water that came from Christ's side while on the cross.

In a 1929 instruction, the Sacred Congregation for the Discipline of the Sacraments taught that bread made of any substance other than wheat is invalid matter, as is bread to which has been added such a great quantity of another substance that it can no longer be considered wheat bread in the common estimation. The requirements that the bread be recently made and not corrupt are for liceity; however, if the bread is so corrupt that it is no longer considered bread in the common estimation, it is invalid matter.[104] The *General Instruction of the Roman Missal* 284 stipulates that the bread for the Eucharist should have the appearance of real food and be made in such a way that the priest is able to break it into parts and distribute them to at least some of the faithful. Subsequent instructions from the Apostolic See have attempted to clarify the meaning of this law by indicating that the "appearance" of bread applies to its color, taste, and thickness rather than to its shape.[105]

Persons who suffer from celiac disease may be given permission from the ordinary to receive communion in the form of bread which is low in gluten content. In fact, so called "gluten-free" wafers have been found by scientists to contain trace amounts of gliadin and would therefore be valid matter.[106] Bread without any gluten is invalid matter.[107]

Wine not made from grapes is invalid matter for the Eucharist, as is wine to which water has been added in greater or equal quantity.[108] The *General Instruction of the Roman Missal* 284 says the wine should be natural and pure, i.e., not mixed with any foreign substance. Wine may be

---

[104] *Dominus Salvator noster* I, March 26, 1929, *AAS* 21 (1929) 632, *CLD* 1, 353; *Missale Romanum* of Pius V, *De defectibus* III.

[105] SCDW, instr *Liturgicae instaurationes* 5, September 5, 1970, *AAS* 62 (1970) 692–704, *DOL* 523; *IDon* 8.

[106] W. H. Woestman, *Sacraments: Initiation, Penance, Anointing of the Sick* (Ottawa: Saint Paul University, 1996) 161.

[107] CDF, letter, June 19, 1995, *Origins* 25 (1995) 191–192; *BCLN* 31 (1995) 217–218.

[108] *Dominus Salvator noster* I.

corrupt in several ways: that which has totally turned to vinegar is invalid matter; that which has partially become vinegar, or contains unapproved additives or foreign matter, or which loses most of its alcohol, is used illicitly. Over the course of time, the Apostolic See has established specific regulations governing the wine-making process, alcoholic content, and use of additives.[109]

Alcoholic Priests

When concelebrating, priests recovering from alcoholism who are unable to consume wine may receive communion by intinction or they may receive under the species of the bread alone; this is a general faculty for which no specific permission is needed. The local ordinary may permit those who celebrate alone to receive by intinction, leaving it to an assistant to consume the consecrated wine.[110]

Canonists and theologians have commonly held that must (*mustum*), or the unfermented juice of ripe grapes, is valid matter for the Eucharist but is gravely illicit except in necessity.[111] With the permission of their ordinary after presentation of a medical certificate, priests recovering from alcoholism or other conditions which prevent the ingestion of even the smallest quantity of alcohol may consecrate grape juice instead of wine for themselves. A separate cup of wine is to be consecrated for others present whenever communion is given under both kinds. As for deacons and lay persons, permission to receive consecrated grape juice can be given only by the Apostolic See in very rare instances, as when individuals are medically unable to consume either wine or bread.[112]

Communion under One or Both Kinds

Canon 925 — Holy communion is to be given under the form of bread alone, or under both species according to the norm of the liturgical laws, or even under the form of wine alone in a case of necessity.

In contrast to the 1917 code (*CIC* 852) which prescribed that communion be given only in the form of bread, this canon reflects the restored practice of communion under both kinds and the revised liturgical law permitting communion under the form of wine alone in cases of need. Communion under the species of the bread is given on the tongue or, where permitted by the conference of bishops, in the hand.[113]

Communion under Both Kinds

Throughout the history of the Church, communion under both kinds was always the ideal in keeping with the Lord's Supper, but the Church also permitted communion under one kind for "just causes and reasons."[114] For the first twelve centuries, communion under both kinds was the general practice of the Church. Communion under one kind was given in special cases, such as to the sick, and it could even be given under the form of wine alone when the communicant was unable to consume bread. By at least the thirteenth century, the custom of administering only the eucharistic bread had become dominant in the West, and the Council of Constance in 1415 decreed that this custom should be considered as law.[115] With few exceptions, the distribution of communion under the form of bread alone remained the practice of the Latin church until the liturgical renewal following Vatican II. In *Sacrosanctum Concilium* 55 b, the council took the first step toward a return to the Church's earlier practice of giving commu-

---

[109] E. Regatillo, *Ius sacramentarium*, 3rd ed. (Santander: Sal Terrae, 1960) 110–112. Hereafter cited as Regatillo.

[110] SCDF, letter, September 12, 1983, *CLD* 11, 208–209.

[111] The chief authorities for this view are Pope Julius I, C. 7, D. II, *de cons.,* and Thomas Aquinas, *STh* III, q. 74, art. V ad 3.

[112] CDF, letter, May 18, 1995, *N* 31 (1995) 608–610; *BCLN* 31 (1995) 218, n. II E.

[113] *HCWE* 21.

[114] Trent, sess. XXI. See J. Huels, "Trent and the Chalice: Forerunner of Vatican II?" *W* 56 (1982) 386–400.

[115] Sess. XIII.

nion under both kinds to all communicants. The 1965 *Rite of Communion under Both Kinds* permitted the practice in specified cases with the consent of the bishop, and this and later developments were included in the 1970 *Roman Missal*.

Communion under both kinds is permitted in accord with the liturgical laws which chiefly appear in the *General Instruction of the Roman Missal* 240–252. Communion under both kinds is said more fully to express the sign of the eucharistic meal; of the new and eternal covenant ratified by the blood of the Lord; and of the relationship between the eucharistic banquet and the eschatological banquet.[116] The clear implication is that communion under both kinds is the ideal, or normative, practice.

The *General Instruction of the Roman Missal* 242 enumerates the cases for which ordinaries may permit communion under both kinds, adding that episcopal conferences may establish guidelines for the ordinaries to concede the faculty on other occasions as well. The ordinaries are to determine the extent of the practice within their respective jurisdictions, namely, local ordinaries for their territories and pontifical right major superiors of clerical religious institutes and societies of apostolic life for their subjects. In the United States the NCCB has extended the list of cases to all Masses, including those on Sundays and holy days, with the exception of several situations involving unprepared or excessively large congregations, as at a Mass in a stadium, when communion from the cup could not be given in an orderly and reverent manner.[117]

Wine Alone

In the late 1950s and early 1960s, the Holy Office granted indults for the reception of commu-

nion under the form of wine alone on behalf of persons who were medically unable to consume the bread; permission was even granted to take the Precious Blood through a stomach tube.[118] *Eucharisticum mysterium* 41 derogated from canon 852 of the 1917 code by allowing communion to be given under the form of wine alone to those who are unable to receive communion under the form of bread in case of need and in the judgment of the bishop. The instruction directed the priest to celebrate the Eucharist in the house of the sick person or to bring the Blood of the Lord to the sick person in a sealed vessel. Since 1972 the judgment of the bishop is not required.[119]

The canon requires that there be a case of need for administering communion under the form of wine alone. This is demonstrated whenever a person is physically or psychologically unable—whether permanently or temporarily—to consume the eucharistic bread.

Unleavened Bread

Canon 926 — According to the ancient tradition of the Latin Church, the priest is to use unleavened bread in the eucharistic celebration whenever he offers it.

The requirement of unleavened bread is for liceity.[120] In the early centuries, both Eastern and Western churches used leavened bread for the Eucharist, but in the eighth and ninth centuries the use of unleavened bread became the general custom in the West. In keeping with the limited scope of the code, the canon properly addresses only the practice of the Latin church, unlike the 1917 code (*CIC* 816) which alluded to the Eastern usage.

---

[116] *GIRM* 240.

[117] *This Holy and Living Sacrifice: Directory for the Celebration and Reception of Communion under Both Kinds* 22 (Washington, D.C.: USCC, 1985); text also in *The Liturgy Documents: A Parish Resource,* 3rd ed. (Chicago: Liturgy Training Publications, 1991) 249–268.

[118] *CLD* 5, 434; 6, 562–565.

[119] *RAnointing* 95.

[120] Council of Florence, *Decree for the Greeks, Ench* 1303; Pius X, apconst *Tradita ab antiquis* II, September 14, 1912, *AAS* 4 (1912) 614–616.

Serious Abuses

Canon 927 — It is absolutely forbidden, even in extreme urgent necessity, to consecrate one matter without the other or even both outside the eucharistic celebration.

Theological opinion has not been in agreement on whether the consecration of only one of the elements suffices for the validity of the Mass.[121] Neither the 1917 code (*CIC* 817) nor the revised code resolves the issue of validity, but instead both use the authority of the Church to forbid absolutely the consecration of only one element in or outside of Mass, or the consecration of even both elements apart from the eucharistic celebration. The phrase "it is absolutely forbidden" (*nefas est*) most strongly conveys the Church's desire to maintain the integrity of the eucharistic celebration and the two signs of bread and wine. Excluded are even cases of extreme necessity, such as lack of time to celebrate an entire Eucharist in the case of a person in danger of death or lack of bread or wine due to war or persecution.

Language of Eucharist

Canon 928 — The eucharistic celebration is to be carried out in the Latin language or in another language provided that the liturgical texts have been legitimately approved.

Latin is the official common language of the Latin church *sui iuris,* the language in which all the official liturgical books are first published. However, the use of the vernacular usually allows for greater participation in the liturgy and a fuller appreciation of it. Although the vernacular is generally pastorally preferable, the Eucharist may be celebrated in Latin provided the revised texts are employed,[122] and in special cases it may even be genuinely advantageous to do so.[123] Local ordinaries are encouraged by the Apostolic See to provide Masses in Latin in at least some churches, especially in areas where groups of people speak different languages.[124] The use of music with Latin texts, particularly Gregorian chant, is often suitable even in Masses in the vernacular.[125] The so-called "Tridentine rite" Mass according to the 1962 edition of the *Missale Romanum* may be used only with the permission of the diocesan bishop or the Pontifical Commission *Ecclesia Dei.*[126]

It is also possible to celebrate the Eucharist using approved texts of two or more vernacular languages that are spoken by significant numbers of people in the assembly.[127] Vernacular texts are legitimately approved according to the norm of canon 838, §§ 2–3. Sign language may be used in Masses at which deaf persons are present.[128]

Vestments

Canon 929 — In celebrating and administering the Eucharist, priests and deacons are to wear the sacred vestments prescribed by the rubrics.

The rubrics governing Mass vestments are chiefly found in the *General Instruction of the Roman Missal* 297–310. The principal changes

---

[121] Regatillo, 178–179.

[122] See CDW, "Declaration on Eucharistic Prayers and Liturgical Experimentation," March 21, 1988, *BCLN* 24 (1988) 110–111.

[123] SCRit, instr *Musicam sacram* 48, March 5, 1967, *AAS* 59 (1967) 314, *DOL* 4169; John Paul II, letter *Dominicae cenae* 10, February 24, 1980, *N* 16 (1980) 143, *Origins* 9 (1980) 661.

[124] SCDW, notification, June 14, 1971, *AAS* 63 (1971) 714, *DOL* 216.

[125] *SC* 54; *Musicam sacram* 51, *DOL* 4172.

[126] John Paul II, *mp Ecclesia Dei,* March 27, 1988, *AAS* 80 (1988) 1495–1498, *Origins* 18 (1988) 149; Pontifical Commission *Ecclesia Dei,* letter, *Origins* 21 (1991) 144–145.

[127] Instituto de Liturgia Hispana and the Federation of Diocesan Liturgical Commissions, "Guidelines for Multilingual Masses," *BCLN* 22 (1986) 25–28. See also M. R. Francis, *Liturgy in a Multicultural Community* (Collegeville: Liturgical Press, 1991).

[128] Consilium for the Implementation of the Constitution on the Sacred Liturgy, reply, December 10, 1965, *DOL* 274.

from past liturgical law are the elimination of the maniple and the optional use of amice and cincture when the design of the alb does not functionally require them. A cassock or habit need not be worn under the alb.

Conferences of bishops may determine adaptations regarding the material and form of vestments.[129] The NCCB allows both natural and artificial fabrics for sacred vesture provided that they are suitable for liturgical use, subject to the further judgment of the local ordinary in doubtful cases.[130] The Apostolic See has approved the use of the chasuble-alb at concelebrations, Masses for special groups, celebrations outside a sacred place, and similar occasions in several countries, including the United States and Canada. The stole is worn over the chasuble-alb and should be the color appropriate to the Mass being celebrated.[131]

When communion is given in a church or oratory, the appropriate vesture for the ordinary ministers of communion is alb and stole, or a surplice and stole over a cassock or habit. Special ministers should wear whatever is customary in the region or whatever has been approved by the ordinary. For communion outside a church, the vesture of the ministers should be appropriate and in accord with local circumstances.[132]

Aged and Infirm Celebrants

Canon 930 — §1. If an infirm or elderly priest is unable to stand, he can celebrate the eucharistic sacrifice while seated, but not before the people except with the permission of the local ordinary; the liturgical laws are to be observed.

§2. A blind or otherwise infirm priest licitly celebrates the eucharistic sacrifice by using any approved text of the Mass with the assistance, if needed, of another priest, deacon, or even a properly instructed lay person.

---

[129] SC 128; GIRM 304, 308.
[130] "Appendix to the GIRM for the Dioceses of the U.S.A.," 305.
[131] CLD 8, 528; Woestman, Sacraments, 176–177.
[132] HCWE 20.

Paragraph one provides for priests who by reason of age or illness are unable to stand while presiding at Eucharist. The incapacitating illness may be of any nature or origin, either temporary or permanent. The intent of paragraph two is to provide for celebrants who are blind or who have disorders which would make it difficult to follow diverse Mass texts, such as a priest who is disoriented as a result of illness or old age. The prior law required the permission of the priest's bishop or general superior before making use of provisions similar to those which this canon grants outright to the priests in question.[133]

ARTICLE 4: THE TIME AND PLACE OF THE CELEBRATION OF THE EUCHARIST [cc. 931–933]

The three canons of this article treat the proper times for the Eucharist (c. 931), the place of celebration (c. 932), and Mass in another Christian church (c. 933).

Proper Times for the Eucharist

Canon 931 — The celebration and distribution of the Eucharist can be done at any day and hour except those which the liturgical norms exclude.

The discipline on the proper time for the celebration of the Eucharist and the distribution of communion is much simpler in canon 931 than it was in the former code (cc. 820, 821, 867). The Eucharist may be celebrated and communion may be distributed at any hour with several exceptions. The anticipated Mass of Sunday and holy days of obligation may be celebrated only in the evening (c. 1248, §1), i.e., not earlier than 4:00 P.M. on Saturday or the day before the holy day.[134]

The other exceptions for the time of celebration and the distribution of the Eucharist are for

---

[133] PM I, 5, 6, 10; Secretary of State, rescript Cum admotae I, 2, 3, 5, November 6, 1964, AAS 59 (1967) 374–375; CLD 6, 147; DOL 940, 941, 943.
[134] See commentary on c. 1248.

the days of the Easter triduum. On Holy Thursday the Mass of the Lord's Supper is celebrated in the evening at a convenient hour. In cases of true necessity the local ordinary may permit an earlier Mass but only for those who find it impossible to participate in the evening Mass. Where pastoral reasons require it, the local ordinary may also permit a second evening Mass. Holy communion may be given to the faithful only during Mass, but it may be taken to the sick at any time of the day. According to the Church's ancient tradition, the sacraments are not celebrated on Good Friday or Holy Saturday. Holy communion may be given to the faithful only at the celebration of the Lord's passion on Good Friday, but it can be brought at any time to the sick. On Holy Saturday communion may be given only as Viaticum. The liturgy of the Easter Vigil takes place at night and should not begin before dark on Saturday and should end before sunrise on Sunday.[135]

Canon 931 represents little change from the previous discipline since canons 821 and 867 of the 1917 code had already been derogated from or mitigated by Pius XII in 1953 and 1957, and later by Paul VI.[136]

Place of Celebration

Canon 932 — §1. The eucharistic celebration is to be carried out in a sacred place unless in a particular case necessity requires otherwise; in such a case the celebration must be done in a decent place.

§2. The eucharistic sacrifice must be carried out on a dedicated or blessed altar; outside a sacred place a suitable table can be used, always with a cloth and a corporal.

The eucharistic celebration should take place in a church, oratory, or other sacred place that has been appointed for divine worship by dedication or blessing in accord with canons 1205–1209.

The altar may be fixed or movable and should be dedicated or blessed in accord with canon 1237. In particular cases of need, the Eucharist may be celebrated in some other place suitable for celebrating the liturgy with the active participation of the people.[137] Particular cases are not only single occasions but also situations in which an individual priest must regularly celebrate outside a sacred place by reason of necessity. Cases of need include sickness, old age, distance from a church, and, in general, whenever there is some pastoral advantage to celebrating outside a sacred place, such as at occasional Masses for children and other particular groups.[138] Canon 932 of the 1917 code had required the permission of the ordinary to celebrate the Eucharist outside a sacred place. The present law leaves this to the judgment of the individual priest.

The altar used for the Eucharist in sacred places is to be dedicated or blessed.[139] At Masses outside a sacred place any suitable table may be used instead of an altar.[140]

Mass in Another Christian Church

Canon 933 — For a just cause and with the express permission of the local ordinary, a priest is permitted to celebrate the Eucharist in the place of worship of some Church or ecclesial community which does not have full communion with the Catholic Church so long as there is no scandal.

The local ordinary is the final judge of whether there may be scandal but, in many areas, especially where non-Catholic Christians are numerous, the possibility of scandal is remote. A just cause is required for this permission, i.e., any good reason,

---

[135] See the rubrics of the *Roman Missal* for the triduum.
[136] *Christus Dominus* VI, *CLD* 4, 269; *Sacram communionem* 1, *CLD* 4, 286; *PM* I, 4; *Cum admotae* I, 1, *DOL* 939.
[137] *GIRM* 253.
[138] *Directory for Children's Masses* 25, *DOL* 2158; SCDW, instr *Actio pastoralis* 3, May 15, 1969, *AAS* 61 (1969) 806–811, *DOL* 2124; *Directory* 85, *DOL* 2655. Masses for special groups outside a sacred place are "abnormal" and should be done rarely. See A. Kavanaugh, *Elements of Rite* (New York: Pueblo, 1982) 13–14, 67–68.
[139] See commentary on c. 1237.
[140] *GIRM* 260.

not just a case of necessity. Since the phrase, "some Church or ecclesial community which does not have full communion with the Catholic Church," refers only to separated Christian churches, canon 933 does not apply to non-Christian churches. Hence, there is no strict obligation to obtain the local ordinary's permission to celebrate in such places, especially in interdenominational chapels at hospitals, universities, military bases, and other places of worship where the possibility of scandal is slight. The diocesan bishop may also permit non-Catholic Christians to use a Catholic church or other building if they lack a place of their own.[141]

Canon 933 alters the previous discipline in the following ways: (1) the prohibition against celebrating Mass in the churches of heretics or schismatics is abrogated;[142] (2) permission of the diocesan bishop is no longer required to celebrate the Eucharist at sea and on rivers;[143] (3) the specific prohibition against celebrating Mass in a bedroom has been removed.[144]

CHAPTER II
THE RESERVATION AND VENERATION OF THE MOST HOLY EUCHARIST
[cc. 934–944]

The custom of reserving the Eucharist originated in the early church primarily to provide for the administration of Viaticum. Other purposes for reservation included providing communion to those absent from the assembly, particularly the sick, and for the Liturgy of the Presanctified during Lent. The place of reservation varied according to period, locale, and circumstances; it included private houses, the dwellings of eremitical religious, and the sacristy or a similar place in a church. It was also the custom of many centuries for priests and monks to carry the Eucharist with them on journeys. By the end of the ninth century, regulations in some areas directed that the Eucharist be reserved within the church itself in proximity to the altar; this had become the rule in many places by the twelfth century. The practice of burning a continuous light, or sanctuary lamp, near the reserved Eucharist began toward the end of the twelfth century and became widespread by the sixteenth. The use of a tabernacle on the altar did not become a general practice in the Western church until the post-Tridentine period.[145]

The Council of Trent upheld the legitimacy of reserving the Eucharist for administration to the sick, and it also defended the adoration of the eucharistic species in general and the practice of eucharistic processions in particular.[146] Certain customs regarding the veneration of the Eucharist outside Mass had arisen during the late Middle Ages. Eucharistic processions—particularly on the feast of Corpus Christi—and visits to the Blessed Sacrament were derived from practices originating in the eleventh century. The first reliable evidence for exposition and benediction comes from the fourteenth century. It was only in the seventeenth and subsequent centuries that benediction became prevalent.[147]

In accordance with *Eucharisticum mysterium* 49–67, the revised *Roman Ritual* provides several forms of worship of the Eucharist outside Mass: (1) exposition of the Blessed Sacrament for a lengthy period or a brief period of adoration by religious communities; (2) a rite of eucharistic exposition and benediction; (3) eucharistic processions; it also has a section on eucharistic congresses. The canons of this chapter are based chiefly on the norms of this and of other parts of the section of the *Roman Ritual* entitled, "Holy Communion and Worship of the Eucharist outside Mass"; the *General Instruction of the Roman Missal* is also a key source.

---

[141] *Ecum Dir* 137.

[142] *CIC* 823, §1.

[143] *PM* I, 8.

[144] *CIC* 822, §4; *PM* I, 7; *Cum admotae* I, 4, *DOL* 942; *Actio pastoralis* 4, *DOL* 2125.

[145] See A. King, *Eucharistic Reservation in the Western Church* (New York: Sheed and Ward, 1965).

[146] Sess. XIII, cap. 6, c. 7; cap. 5, c. 6.

[147] See N. Mitchell, *Cult and Controversy: The Worship of the Eucharist outside Mass* (New York: Pueblo, 1982).

Several principles specifically on eucharistic devotions from *Eucharisticum mysterium* provide the doctrinal foundation for the liturgical law and the canons of this chapter of the code. The chief principles are:

(1) The celebration of the eucharistic sacrifice is the origin and consummation of eucharistic worship outside it.

(2) The Eucharist is no less an object of adoration because it was instituted by Christ to be eaten.

. (3) The primary and original purpose for reserving the Eucharist is the administration of Viaticum; the secondary reasons are the giving of communion and the adoration of the sacrament.

(4) The eucharistic presence of Christ is the real presence par excellence, but Christ is also present in the assembly of the faithful, in the word proclaimed, and in the person of the minister.

(5) Prayer before Christ the Lord sacramentally present, no less than the reception of the sacrament, should move the faithful to lead lives of witness and service in human society.[148]

The seven canons of this chapter treat obligatory and optional reservation of the blessed sacrament (c. 934), personal retention of the Eucharist (c. 935), religious and pious houses (c. 936), accessibility to churches (c. 937), the tabernacle (c. 938), the quantity and renewal of hosts and the vessels for reservation (c. 939), the sanctuary lamp (c. 940), exposition of the blessed sacrament (c. 941), lengthy exposition (c. 942), ministers of exposition and benediction (c. 943), and eucharistic processions (c. 944).

---

[148]*Eucharisticum mysterium* 3e, 3f, 49, 55, 13, *DOL* 1232e, f, 1278, 1284, 1242; *HCWE* 2, 3, 5, 6, 81.

Obligatory and Optional Reservation

Canon 934 — §1. The Most Holy Eucharist:
   1° must be reserved in the cathedral church or its equivalent, in every parish church, and in a church or oratory connected to the house of a religious institute or society of apostolic life;
   2° can be reserved in the chapel of the bishop and, with the permission of the local ordinary, in other churches, oratories, and chapels.
   §2. In sacred places where the Most Holy Eucharist is reserved, there must always be someone responsible for it and, insofar as possible, a priest is to celebrate Mass there at least twice a month.

This canon specifies those sacred places in which the Eucharist must be reserved and those in which it may be reserved, and it establishes the conditions for eucharistic reservation. The first condition is that there be someone who has charge of the place where the Eucharist is reserved. This person need not have any ecclesiastical office or be a cleric, since the chief purpose of this law is to prevent the desecration of the blessed sacrament. The second condition is that a priest celebrate Mass in that place at least twice a month, insofar as possible. This ensures the frequent renewal of the consecrated hosts in accord with canon 939 and, more important, it reinforces the primacy of the eucharistic action and its intimate connection to the sacrament reserved. Although the phrase "insofar as possible" admits of exceptions, there still should be provision for the regular celebration of Mass even if it cannot always be done twice a month. Canon 1265, §1 of the former code required that Mass be celebrated at least once a week as a condition for reservation.

When the two conditions of paragraph two are met, the law mandates eucharistic reservation in the sacred places specified in paragraph one, section one, all of them places where there are active communities of the faithful and where there could be need for communion for the sick and dying.[149] The Eucharist may optionally be reserved, with permission of the local ordinary, in the sacred places mentioned in paragraph one, section two, also observing the conditions of paragraph two. The Eucharist may not be reserved outside a sacred place, i.e., outside a church, oratory, or private chapel that has been lawfully established by decree of the competent ordinary.[150] This applies also to small communities in informal houses of religious institutes and other pious houses which lack a proper oratory for eucharistic celebration but which have a small room for prayer and meditation. Such a space, unconnected to a sacred place, is unsuitable for eucharistic reservation because the reserved sacrament is severed from its ecclesial and liturgical context.

Personal Retention of the Eucharist

Canon 935 — No one is permitted to keep the Eucharist on one's person or to carry it around, unless pastoral necessity urges it and the prescripts of the diocesan bishop are observed.

The retention of the Eucharist by private persons was common in the early church, especially in times of persecution, but by the fifth or sixth centuries the practice had died out and was forbidden in places. In contrast to canon 1265, §3 of the 1917 code, which absolutely prohibited the personal retention of the Eucharist and the carrying of it on a trip, this canon allows some flexibility. Normally the blessed sacrament may not be kept in one's private possession, either on one's person or in a fixed place, except when in transit to bring communion to someone. However, there may be times when it is necessary for a priest, deacon, or other eucharistic minister to keep the sacrament in the home or other place outside the church, e.g., when the minister lives at a great distance from the church and needs access to the Eucharist for visits to the sick

and Viaticum for the dying. In such cases of urgent pastoral need, the diocesan bishop may grant permission to reserve the Eucharist temporarily or as long as the urgent need remains. The bishop may also issue prescripts regulating the renewal of hosts, the tabernacle, and similar matters.

Religious and Pious Houses

Canon 936 — In the house of a religious institute or some other pious house, the Most Holy Eucharist is to be reserved only in the church or principal oratory attached to the house. For a just cause, however, the ordinary can also permit it to be reserved in another oratory of the same house.

The purpose of this canon is to prevent the duplication of places for eucharistic reservation in the same house. There should be only one focus for Christ's eucharistic presence in each religious house, seminary, etc.; duplicate reservation distorts the symbolic potential of Christ's eucharistic presence and diminishes its power. Duplicate reservation also suggests that the reserved Eucharist is a commodity that can be multiplied by the community for its own convenience, rather than the divine gratuitous gift that it is.

The Eucharist should be reserved only in the principal church or oratory attached to the house, namely, the church or oratory at which the Eucharist is celebrated, or in a special blessed sacrament chapel. If the members of the house worship in an oratory separate from the church or oratory attended by the faithful, the Eucharist may be reserved in each. If there is more than one distinct community under the same roof, there may be reservation in the oratory of each community.[151] In all other cases permission of the ordinary and a just cause are required for reserving the Eucharist in a second oratory of the same house. An example of such a cause would be a separate oratory in the infirmary for sick and aged religious.

---

[149] See also cc. 608, 1214, 1223, and 389.
[150] See the commentary on cc. 1214–1229.

[151] CodCom, interpretation, June 3, 1918, *AAS* 10 (1918) 346; *CLD* 1, 53.

Accessibility to Churches

Canon 937 — Unless there is a grave reason to the contrary, the church in which the Most Holy Eucharist is reserved is to be open to the faithful for at least some hours every day so that they can pray before the Most Blessed Sacrament.

This canon refers only to churches in the strict sense of canon 1214, not to oratories and other sacred places. In contrast to canon 1266 of the 1917 code, this canon, for a grave reason, allows exceptions to the rule that churches which reserve the Eucharist should be open to the faithful for at least some hours each day.[152] In some areas it is necessary to lock the church in order to prevent vandalism and burglary. This is a sufficiently grave reason to lock the church when it is not possible to arrange for parishioners or others to watch the church during the hours when it is open. "Some hours" means more than one hour.

The Tabernacle

Canon 938 — §1. The Most Holy Eucharist is to be reserved habitually in only one tabernacle of a church or oratory.

§2. The tabernacle in which the Most Holy Eucharist is reserved is to be situated in some part of the church or oratory which is distinguished, conspicuous, beautifully decorated, and suitable for prayer.

§3. The tabernacle in which the Most Holy Eucharist is reserved habitually is to be immovable, made of solid and opaque material, and locked in such a way that the danger of profanation is avoided as much as possible.

§4. For a grave cause, it is permitted to reserve the Most Holy Eucharist in some other fitting and more secure place, especially at night.

§5. The person responsible for the church or oratory is to take care that the key of the tabernacle in which the Most Holy Eucharist is reserved is safeguarded most diligently.

The canon regulates the place, construction, and custody of the tabernacle, somewhat simplifying canons 1268–1269 of the 1917 code. The norms largely repeat some of the liturgical laws on this matter found in the *General Instruction of the Roman Missal* 276–277 and the *Rite of Holy Communion and Worship of the Eucharist outside Mass* 6, 9, and 10.

The Eucharist may be reserved in only one place in the church or oratory of each parish, religious house, or other sacred place approved for reservation.[153] If a blessed sacrament chapel is connected to the church, the Eucharist may be reserved only there and not also in the body of the church. Nor may it be reserved in another building of the parish, unless it be another sacred place at some distance from the main church.

Paragraph two must be read in conjunction with the liturgical laws which strongly recommend a separate blessed sacrament chapel as the most fitting place for eucharistic reservation.[154] If it is not possible to have a separate chapel for reservation, the Eucharist may be reserved in the sacred place where Mass is celebrated. Traditional options for placement of the tabernacle include inside a wall niche, on a pillar, or in a eucharistic tower.[155] In 1983 the Holy See eliminated from the *Roman Ritual* any mention of an altar as a possible place for eucharistic reservation.[156] Since 1977 it has been a requirement that new churches that are built have only one altar,[157] and the blessed sacrament is not to be reserved on the altar of celebration in newer churches.[158] Older

---

[152] See also *Eucharisticum mysterium* 51, *DOL* 1280.

[153] See the commentary at c. 936 for reasons for this law.
[154] *GIRM* 276, *HCWE* 9.
[155] BCL, *Environment and Art in Catholic Worship* (Washington, D.C.: USCC, 1978) 80.
[156] See *Emendations in the Liturgical Books Following upon the New Code of Canon Law* (Washington, D.C.: USCC, 1984) 10.
[157] *RDCA* IV, 7.
[158] Cf. *CB* 49.

churches may retain the custom of reserving the Eucharist on a side altar or the old main altar, especially if this is necessary to preserve the architectural and artistic integrity of the old altar and its tabernacle.[159]

Paragraph three treats the design of the tabernacle. Wood, marble, and metal are traditionally acceptable materials for the construction of tabernacles, but the canon says that any solid and opaque material can be used. Like this canon, liturgical law leaves much leeway for determining the shape, size, and ornamentation of the tabernacle. Paragraphs four and five treat the custody of the tabernacle. A grave cause for removing the Eucharist from the tabernacle to a safer place, especially at night, would be a serious danger of desecration.

Quantity and Renewal of Hosts

Canon 939 — Consecrated hosts in a quantity sufficient for the needs of the faithful are to be kept in a pyx or small vessel; they are to be renewed frequently and the older hosts consumed properly.

This canon, a simplification of canons 1270 and 1272 of the 1917 code, treats the quantity and renewal of the reserved Eucharist and the vessels for it. The number of consecrated hosts which are to be reserved is dependent on the needs of the sick and other faithful who will be receiving communion outside Mass.[160] In order for the sign of communion to be expressed more clearly as a sharing in the sacrifice actually being celebrated, communion should not be given during Mass from the reserved elements but from the bread and wine consecrated at the Mass.[161] Therefore the quantity of reserved hosts should be kept to the minimum necessary for communion outside

Mass, and this will also facilitate the requirement of frequent renewal.

The person in charge should see that the hosts do not spoil or become too hard and easily broken.[162] The frequency of renewal of the consecrated hosts depends on climatic and other conditions. As a rule, the hosts should be renewed at least twice a month insofar as possible (cf. c. 934, §2).

The hosts should be reserved in a ciborium or other suitable vessel such as a pyx. The vessel may be made from any materials that are prized in a region, including ebony or other hard woods, as long as they are suited to sacred use.[163] The consecrated wine should not be reserved except for communion of the sick. It should be kept in a properly covered chalice and placed in the tabernacle after Mass until it is needed. When it is brought to the sick or dying, it must be carried in a closed vessel to eliminate all danger of spilling.[164]

The Sanctuary Lamp

Canon 940 — A special lamp which indicates and honors the presence of Christ is to shine continuously before a tabernacle in which the Most Holy Eucharist is reserved.

The canon speaks only of a "special lamp" without specifying a wax candle or a lamp fueled by olive oil as did canon 1271 of the 1917 code. Nevertheless, liturgical law prefers an oil lamp or a lamp with a wax candle.[165] The oil may be of any kind, although the law has traditionally favored vegetable oil, especially olive oil. Under the former law the candle was to be made at least in part from beeswax, olive oil, or another kind of vegetable oil.[166] Ordinaries were able to permit substi-

---

[159] See J. Huels, *More Disputed Questions in the Liturgy* (Chicago: Liturgy Training Publications, 1996) 153–159.
[160] *HCWE* 7.
[161] *SC* 55, *GIRM* 56 h.

[162] *GIRM* 285.
[163] *GIRM* 292.
[164] *HCWE* 55; *RAnointing* 95; *IDon* 14.
[165] *HCWE* 11.
[166] SCRit, decr, December 13, 1957, *AAS* 50 (1960) 50; *CLD* 5, 613.

tutions for oil lamps and wax candles when these were unavailable or could not be obtained without grave inconvenience or expense. In such a case any oil, especially a vegetable oil, could be substituted; as a last resort, even an electric light could be used.[167] Such substitutions may now freely be made by the persons in charge of sacred places, in keeping with particular laws and customs.

Liturgical law states that the presence of the Eucharist in the tabernacle is to be shown also by a veil or in another suitable way determined by the competent authority.[168] In many places the custom has developed not to cover tabernacles, especially when they are artistically notable.

Exposition

Canon 941 — §1. In churches or oratories where it is permitted to reserve the Most Holy Eucharist, there can be expositions with the pyx or the monstrance; the norms prescribed in the liturgical books are to be observed.

§2. Exposition of the Most Blessed Sacrament is not to be held in the same area of the church or oratory during the celebration of Mass.

The liturgical laws governing exposition of the Eucharist are found chiefly in the *Rite of Holy Communion and Worship of the Eucharist outside Mass* 82–100. The ritual contains a rite of simple exposition and a rite of exposition and benediction. Several principles from the introduction to the rite are noteworthy for understanding this canon:

(1) Exposition stimulates the faithful to spiritual union with Christ which culminates in sacramental communion.

(2) The arrangements for exposition must carefully avoid anything which might obscure the principal desire of Christ in instituting the Eucharist, namely, to be received as food, healing, and consolation.

(3) The celebration of the eucharistic mystery includes in a more perfect manner the spiritual communion to which exposition is intended to stimulate the faithful.[169]

The ritual distinguishes three kinds of exposition: that for a lengthy period, that for a brief period, and that for adoration by religious communities. Brief periods of exposition must always include time for readings of the word of God, hymns, prayers, and a period of silent prayer. Exposition merely for the purpose of giving the benediction is forbidden. There may never be exposition, whether lengthy or brief, in the same part of the church or oratory where Mass is being celebrated. Exposition should be interrupted during Mass, unless the Mass is celebrated in a chapel apart from the exposition and at least some of the faithful remain in adoration.[170]

Lengthy Exposition

Canon 942 — It is recommended that in these churches and oratories an annual solemn exposition of the Most Blessed Sacrament be held for an appropriate period of time, even if not continuous, so that the local community more profoundly meditates on and adores the eucharistic mystery. Such an exposition is to be held, however, only if a suitable gathering of the faithful is foreseen and the established norms are observed.

Canon 1275 of the former code had required an exposition of forty hours, but the 1983 code speaks only of an annual solemn exposition for an "appropriate period of time," which the liturgical law refers to as an "extended period of time." Liturgical planners are free to determine the length of this period in keeping with local custom. Exposition should not be held unless the partici-

[167] SCRit, decr *Urbis et orbis,* August 18, 1949, *AAS* 41 (1949) 476; *CLD* 3, 518.
[168] *HCWE* 11.

[169] *HCWE* 82–83.
[170] *HCWE* 83, 89.

pation of a reasonable number of the faithful is assured.[171] Exposition need not be continuous during the extended period, especially when it goes beyond one day, and the Eucharist may be replaced in the tabernacle at times which have been prearranged and duly announced. This may not be done more than twice in the day, e.g., at midday and at night.[172]

Parishes and other communities wishing to have perpetual adoration may do so, provided it is before the tabernacle and not the sacrament exposed. Permission of the local ordinary is needed for perpetual adoration before the blessed sacrament exposed. He may give permission to a pious association of the laity which has perpetual exposition as part of its constitution, but perpetual exposition may not take place in a parish church unless there is a separate blessed sacrament chapel and the sacrament is placed inside the tabernacle during Mass.[173]

Ministers

Canon 943 — The minister of exposition of the Most Blessed Sacrament and of eucharistic benediction is a priest or deacon; in special circumstances, the minister of exposition and reposition alone without benediction is the acolyte, extraordinary minister of holy communion, or someone else designated by the local ordinary; the prescripts of the diocesan bishop are to be observed.

The canon restates the liturgical law on the ministers of exposition and benediction.[174] The ordinary minister of exposition is a priest or deacon who may also bless the people with the sacrament at the end of the period of adoration. In the absence of a priest or deacon, an acolyte, special

minister of communion, or another person deputed by the local ordinary may publicly expose the Eucharist for adoration and later repose it. These ministers may open the tabernacle, put the host in the monstrance, and place it or the vessel containing the Eucharist on the altar or place of exposition. At the end of the adoration they may replace the Eucharist in the tabernacle, but they may not give the blessing.

Canon 1274, §2 of the former code limited the minister of exposition and reposition to the priest or deacon, and only the priest could give the benediction. This law was derogated from in 1967 to permit deacons to give the blessing and in 1972 to allow acolytes to expose and repose the Eucharist.[175]

Eucharistic Processions

Canon 944 — §1. When it can be done in the judgment of the diocesan bishop, a procession through the public streets is to be held as a public witness of veneration toward the Most Holy Eucharist, especially on the solemnity of the Body and Blood of Christ.

§2. It is for the diocesan bishop to establish regulations which provide for the participation in and the dignity of processions.

There is little evidence for eucharistic processions before Pope Urban IV established the feast of Corpus Christi in 1264, but in the fourteenth century such processions became widespread. The Council of Trent approved this custom in response to Protestants who denied the legitimacy of various forms of eucharistic cult outside Mass.

The liturgical laws governing eucharistic processions are quite broad and allow great latitude for local customs provided that they are in accord with the directives of the diocesan bishop.[176] The intent of the canon is to encourage public processions of the Eucharist provided the bishop approves the practice. The bishop is to decide whether processions are advisable in today's conditions, whether

---

[171] *HCWE* 86. A helpful collection of documents, in English translation, that treat solemn exposition is found in *Liturgy Documentary Series 11: Solemn Exposition of the Holy Eucharist* (Washington, D.C.: USCC, 1996).
[172] *HCWE* 88.
[173] CDWDS, reply, *BCLN* 31 (1995) 213–214.
[174] *HCWE* 91.

[175] *SDO* V, 22, §3; *MQ* VI.
[176] *HCWE* 101.

they can be carried out with decorum and reverence, and whether they can truly be a sign of common faith and adoration.[177] These conditions are more likely to be met in a predominantly Roman Catholic culture where such processions remain solidly rooted in popular piety today.

The 1917 code had an entire title of six canons (*CIC* 1290–1295) devoted to the subject of eucharistic processions. The reduction to one canon in the present code is reflective of the actual decline in the popularity of public eucharistic processions in the contemporary life of the Church.

CHAPTER III
THE OFFERING GIVEN
FOR THE CELEBRATION OF MASS
[cc. 945–958]

Historical Background

The custom of accepting Mass offerings arose in the Western church as a result of several key developments. In the early Church the faithful brought gifts to the Sunday assembly, especially the bread and wine for the Eucharist, and the excess was given to the Church's ministers and distributed to the poor. By the seventh or eighth century, gifts of money were frequently substituted and their purpose became chiefly the support of the clergy. Other contributing factors included the growth of votive Masses, which were offered for the intentions and desires (*vota*) of a group or an individual, and of private Masses, which were celebrated with only a server present out of a priest's personal devotion.

By the Carolingian period all of these developments had taken hold and contributed to the custom of the priest's accepting a single donation, or "stipend," for each Mass in return for remembering a special intention. This practice became widespread in the eleventh and twelfth centuries and remained popular thereafter. One of the reasons for its popularity was that it was one of the few ways

that the faithful had to take a more active role in the liturgy.[178] From the Middle Ages until the liturgical reforms of the twentieth century, the liturgy was largely a clerical affair and the laity were silent spectators; most did not understand the Latin language, and the reception of communion was rare. Thus, to give an offering for the priest to remember one's intention at Mass became a way of participating more closely in the action of the priest.

Theological Considerations

Scholastic theologians of the Middle Ages attempted to provide a rationale for Mass offerings by devising a theory of the "threefold fruits of the Mass," of which the priest applies the "special fruit" for the intention of the donor, but this theory was never officially adopted as such by the Church. The Council of Constance in 1415 and Pope Pius VI in 1794 upheld the Mass stipend practice against adversaries who opposed it on theological grounds and who charged that it was simoniacal.[179]

The Council of Trent's teaching on the sacrificial nature of the Mass, which was enunciated in part to defend the system of Mass offerings and intentions, stressed that the Mass is an unbloody representation and commemoration of Christ's sacrifice on the cross. Through the Eucharist, Christians in all ages are able to participate sacramentally in Christ's unique sacrifice on the cross and the once-and-for-all redemption he won by that sacrifice. The sacrifice of the Mass is not a new sacrifice offered each time by the Church, but a memorial (*anamnesis*) of Christ's sacrifice on the cross. The fruits of the Mass, therefore, represent a sharing in the merits gained for humanity by Christ's redemptive death on the cross.

The pertinent dogmatic teaching of Trent is that Mass may be "offered for the living and the dead, for sins, punishments, satisfactions, and

---

[177] Ibid.

[178] See M. F. Mannion, "Stipends and Eucharistic Praxis," *W* 57 (1983) 194–214.

[179] Constance, sess. VIII, errors of J. Wycliff, nn. 19 and 25; Pius VI, const *Auctorem fidei*, August 28, 1794, nn. 30 and 54, *Ench* 2630, 2654.

other necessities."[180] Thus, the fruits of the Mass bring about in some way the remission of sins of both the living and the dead. In the theological introduction to its canons on the Mass, Trent taught:

> The fruits of that bloody sacrifice [of the cross], it is well understood, are received most abundantly through this unbloody one, so far is the latter from derogating in any way from the former. Wherefore, it is rightly offered not only for the sins, punishments, satisfactions and other necessities of the faithful who are living, but also for those departed in Christ but not yet fully purified.[181]

Canon 901 and several of the canons of this chapter speak of the "application of the Mass" for a specific intention. The Church does not have any firm doctrine on what it precisely means to "apply the Mass." In fact, the Council of Trent, which debated this issue extensively in three sessions, eliminated from its definitive text any specific mention of the words "apply" or "application" of the fruits of the Mass by the priest. Nor did the council adopt any particular theory about the way that the fruits of the Mass were received, whether this was *ex opere operato* or by way of intercession. This allowed room for the different opinions expressed by the council fathers as well as for further theological clarification and development. Trent was content to conclude, in the words of David Power, that "the Mass celebrated by a duly ordained priest, under whatever circumstances, is beneficial for those for whom it is offered, and that through this offering some grace of remission of sin flows."[182] That there is spiritual benefit for the Mass offering intention is the Church's belief; all that this entails, and how it is

accomplished, are matters that remain in the realm of theological opinion.

The Mass offering system's greatest value for today is most likely as a vehicle for the remembrance of the dead. It may be seen as a way for the living to honor the memory of their beloved dead, to pray for them, and to stay in communion with them in a special way at the eucharistic celebration.

Discipline

Canons 945–958 principally reflect the discipline enacted by various popes over three centuries, including the 1974 apostolic letter of Paul VI, *Firma in traditione*.[183] Perhaps the most important change in the revised code's treatment of Mass offerings occurs in the title of this section which in the 1917 code was "Mass Alms or Stipends." No longer does the law refer to the donation for the application of Mass as a "stipend" (*stipendium*), but rather as an "offering" (*stips*) given by one of the faithful. The word "stipend" suggests a mercantile exchange of goods for services or the remuneration of a *do ut facias* contract. The word "offering," however, clearly signifies that it is given freely by the faithful primarily out of their concern for the Church and their desire to support its material needs. Mass offerings can be understood as gifts to the Church or its ministers on behalf of some intention, much as a donation or bequest is made to any charitable institution *in the name of* some person, living or deceased.

The fourteen canons of this chapter treat the following matters: offerings and intentions (c. 945), the donor (c. 946), exclusion of trafficking or trading (c. 947), separate and collective intentions (c. 948), lost offerings (c. 949), the procedure for an unspecified number of Masses (c. 950), the limit of one offering per day to be retained by each priest (c. 951), the amount of the offering (c. 952), the limit on the number of offer-

---

[180] Sess. XXII, c. 3, *de ss. Missae sacrificio,* September 17, 1562.

[181] Sess. XXII, *Decr. de Missa,* cap. 2.

[182] D. Power, *The Sacrifice We Offer: The Tridentine Dogma and Its Reinterpretation* (Edinburgh: T & T Clark, 1987) 128; see also idem, *The Eucharistic Mystery: Revitalizing the Tradition* (New York: Crossroad, 1992) 250–263.

[183] Innocent XII, const *Nuper,* December 2, 1697; Pius X, decr *Ut debita,* May 11, 1904; *CIC* 824–844; Paul VI mp *Firma in traditione,* June 13, 1974, *AAS* 66 (1974) 308–311, *DOL* 287, *CLD* 8, 530.

ings that may be accepted (c. 953), excess Mass offerings (c. 954), the transferal and satisfaction of Mass obligations (c. 955), unsatisfied Mass obligations (c. 956), the exercise of vigilance (c. 957), and the Mass record (c. 958).

Offerings and Intentions

Canon 945 — §1. In accord with the approved practice of the Church, any priest celebrating or concelebrating is permitted to receive an offering to apply the Mass for a specific intention.

§2. It is recommended earnestly to priests that they celebrate Mass for the intention of the Christian faithful, especially the needy, even if they have not received an offering.

The canon says that the priest "is permitted" to receive Mass offerings. Thus a legal right is granted which cannot be denied or restricted without the consent of the priest. In some dioceses all Mass offerings are given to the parish or diocese and in return the priests receive a salary equal to or higher than their income had they kept the offerings. This is legitimate provided it is voluntary, i.e., provided that each priest is free to retain the Mass offerings rather than the additional salary.

In the recommendation of paragraph two the legislator has in mind the spiritual benefit that may come to the persons or concerns for whose intentions the Masses are celebrated, but it neglects the other benefits of the Mass offering system. Canon 946 and *Firma in traditione,* as will be seen, assert that Mass offerings also benefit the *donors* themselves by their sharing in the Church's support of its ministers and through an increased participation in Christ's self-offering. However, these worthy benefits cannot be achieved if there is no donation. It would seem that poor people would profit more if they gave some donation, even if very small.

The Donor

Canon 946 — The Christian faithful who give an offering to apply the Mass for their intention con-

tribute to the good of the Church and by that offering share its concern to support its ministers and works.**

The donor who gives the offering also participates in the eucharistic celebration because the donation concretizes the donor's own prayer on behalf of his or her intention. Moreover, the donor's financial contribution to the good of the Church, even though small, is a means of sharing in the Church's concern for the support of its ministers and works. This canon, new to the 1983 code, is taken from Paul VI's *Firma in traditione.* This document states that the donors of Mass offerings "associate themselves more closely with Christ's act of offering himself as victim and in so doing experience its effects more fully."[184] This does not occur automatically upon the giving of the offering, but depends upon the extent of the donor's own faith, devotion, and actual participation in the Eucharist.

Trafficking or Trading Excluded

Canon 947 — Any appearance of trafficking or trading is to be excluded entirely from the offering for Masses.

This canon, identical to canon 827 of the 1917 code, sums up numerous disciplinary measures enacted over the centuries, including a reform decree of the Council of Trent.[185] Since the acceptance of Mass offerings has frequently led to accusations of simony, the Church wishes to regulate the practice strictly to avoid all appearances of commercialism. According to canon 1385, those who illegitimately profit from Mass offerings are to be punished with a censure or another just penalty. Canon 947 and the following canons of this chapter are intended to preclude profiteering and other abuses connected with Mass offerings.

---

[184] *DOL* 2234.

[185] Sess. XXII, *de observandis et evitandis in celebratione missae.*

Separate and Collective Intentions

Canon 948 — Separate Masses are to be applied for the intentions of those for whom a single offering, although small, has been given and accepted.

This canon is worded somewhat differently than canon 828 of the 1917 code, but the meaning is the same: the celebrant and concelebrants each may accept only one offering for one Mass, even if a smaller amount than customary is accepted. Although the donor's intention can include more than one person, only one offering can be taken.

In 1991 the Congregation for the Clergy derogated from this canon to permit priests to accept several offerings for a "collective intention" at a single Mass. The following regulations must be observed if this practice is followed:

(1) the donors must be informed of and consent to the combining of their offerings before the Mass for the collective intention is celebrated;

(2) the place and time for the Mass must be announced;

(3) the practice may not be observed more than twice a week;

(4) the celebrant may keep for himself no more than the usual amount of a single Mass offering and must send any excess to his ordinary in keeping with canon 951, §1.[186]

Lost Offerings

Canon 949 — A person obliged to celebrate and apply Mass for the intention of those who gave an offering is bound by the obligation even if the offerings received have been lost through no fault of his own.

[186] Decr *Mos iugiter,* February 22, 1991, *AAS* 83 (1991) 436–446; *BCLN* 27 (1991) 13–16.

This rule was also found in canon 829 of the former code. Once an offering has been accepted, the priest is obliged to apply the Mass for the intention of the donor, and that obligation ceases only when the Mass has been celebrated. If a large number of Mass offerings has been lost or stolen, the provisions of canons 1308–1309 could be applied.

Unspecified Number of Masses

Canon 950 — If a sum of money is offered for the application of Masses without an indication of the number of Masses to be celebrated, the number is to be computed on the basis of the offering established in the place where the donor resides, unless the intention of the donor must be presumed legitimately to have been different.

Canon 1300 states the general principle that the intentions of the donor are to be observed, but this canon deals with a case when it is not possible to learn the intention of the donor as, for example, when a sum of money is left in a will for Masses to be celebrated without specification of the number of Masses. The general rule is that the number of Masses be based on the amount of a Mass offering established for the place where the donor resides.

One Offering per Day

Canon 951 — §1. A priest who celebrates several Masses on the same day can apply each to the intention for which the offering was given, but subject to the rule that, except on Christmas, he is to keep the offering for only one Mass and transfer the others to the purposes prescribed by the ordinary, while allowing for some recompense by reason of an extrinsic title.

§2. A priest who concelebrates a second Mass on the same day cannot accept an offering for it under any title.

A priest is free to accept an offering for each Mass at which he presides, but he may keep only one offering for himself each day. The other offerings go to his ordinary, namely, the local ordinary for the diocesan clergy and the major superior for members of clerical religious institutes and societies of apostolic life. All pastors and parochial vicars, not just diocesan priests, are bound to send the offering for additional Masses celebrated each day to the local ordinary.[187] This rule applies only to parish Masses for which offerings have been received through the parish. Thus, a religious priest who is pastor or parochial vicar and who binates with an offering received from the sacristan of his own religious institute should send that offering to his own ordinary, not to the local ordinary, since the intention of the donor was to benefit the institute, not the diocese. Moreover, a visiting priest in the parish is entitled to all offerings for the Masses he celebrates, including binations and trinations, which he then sends to his own ordinary, not the local ordinary, unless they are the same.

While the priest may not retain more than one offering each day, except on Christmas, he may be compensated for celebrating additional Masses by virtue of some extrinsic title. For example, the priest may be paid for his services in celebrating the Mass even though he may not keep personally the offerings from any extra Masses celebrated in one day. Unlike the 1917 code (*CIC* 824, §2), the present law permits pastors and others who are obliged to celebrate the *Missa pro populo* on Sundays and holy days to take an offering for another Mass which they celebrate that day.

A priest may not take another offering, even one on behalf of his ordinary, when he concelebrates on the same day that he celebrates or concelebrates another Mass.[188] The reason for this rule is to avoid the appearance that concelebration, an optional practice, might be done merely for the sake of taking an offering. The rule applies to a second Mass, i.e., any additional Mass (*altera Missa*), whether it comes first or second in sequence. For example, if a priest concelebrates a Mass in the morning and presides in the evening, he may take an offering only for the Mass in the evening (unless he had already concelebrated the morning Mass before he learned that it would be necessary to celebrate Mass again in the evening). If a priest *presides* at a concelebrated Mass and must also preside at one or more additional Masses, he may receive offerings for each Mass, though retaining only one for himself and giving the others to the cause prescribed by his ordinary.

Amount of Offering

Canon 952 — §1. It is for the provincial council or a meeting of the bishops of the province to define by decree for the entire province the offering to be given for the celebration and application of Mass, and a priest is not permitted to seek a larger sum. Nevertheless, he is permitted to accept for the application of a Mass a voluntary offering which is larger or even smaller than the one defined.

§2. Where there is no such decree, the custom in force in the diocese is to be observed.

§3. Members of all religious institutes must also observe the same decree or local custom mentioned in §§1 and 2.

This canon makes two significant changes in canons 831–832 of the former law. The competent authority for determining the amount of Mass offerings is no longer the local ordinary but the provincial council or the meeting of bishops of a province, a change which ensures uniformity of practice among neighboring dioceses of a province. A second change from the former law is the absence of any provision allowing the local ordinary to prevent priests from accepting an offering that is lower than the defined or customary amount. While a priest may not demand a larger amount than that defined or customary in the province, he may accept an offering in any amount that is freely given.

---

[187] CodCom, interpretation, Feb. 20, 1987, *AAS* 79 (1987) 1132; *Pamplona ComEng*, 1295.

[188] This rule was first established by the SCDW in 1972 and was affirmed by Paul VI in 1974. See *In celebratione Missae* 3b, *DOL* 1816; and *Firma in traditione* IIIa, *DOL* 2238.

The competence of the meeting of bishops of a province to issue a decree is an exception to the usual norm that the bishops at such meetings, as a group, lack the power of governance. This is an example of a special grant of legislative power by the supreme legislator to the bishops of a province, on a par with the exception mentioned in canon 434. The decision of the majority of the bishops would be binding on all (c. 119, 2°).

If there is no such decree, each priest may accept an offering in any amount according to the custom, i.e., the majority practice of the diocese. Moreover, the bishop has the power to enact his own law on this matter if the bishops of the province have not done so.

It does not seem that paragraph three is really necessary, since diocesan bishops and provincial councils have such authority without this law,[189] which authority also extends to priests belonging to societies of apostolic life and to personal prelatures.

Limitation on Offerings Accepted

Canon 953 — No one is permitted to accept more offerings for Masses to be applied by himself than he can satisfy within a year.

This rule is to prevent the possibility of an individual priest amassing many obligations, which might go unsatisfied in the event of his incapacity or death. The rule applies only to Mass obligations to be satisfied by oneself, not to the acceptance of offerings to be transferred to others.

Excess Mass Offerings

Canon 954 — If in certain churches or oratories more Masses are asked to be celebrated than can be celebrated there, it is permitted for them to be celebrated elsewhere unless the donors have expressly indicated a contrary intention.

[189] See cc. 391; 392; 445; 835, §1; 838, §4; 678, §1; 738, §2.

The canon allows excess Mass offerings to be transferred from one place to another unless the donor has expressly indicated otherwise. When the one who accepts the offering agrees to have the Mass celebrated in that place, the Mass obligation cannot be satisfied elsewhere without the donor's permission or without the permission of the competent authority according to canon 1309. If a Mass offering has been accepted on the condition that it be celebrated in that place, this fact should be noted in writing along with the intention.

Transferal and Satisfaction of Mass Obligations

Canon 955 — §1. A person who intends to entrust to others the celebration of Masses to be applied is to entrust their celebration as soon as possible to priests acceptable to him, provided that he is certain that they are above suspicion. He must transfer the entire offering received unless it is certain that the excess over the sum fixed in the diocese was given for him personally. He is also obliged to see to the celebration of the Masses until he learns that the obligation has been accepted and the offering received.

§2. The time within which Masses must be celebrated begins on the day the priest who is to celebrate them received them unless it is otherwise evident.

§3. Those who entrust to others Masses to be celebrated are to record in a book without delay both the Masses which they received and those which they transferred to others, as well as their offerings.

§4. Every priest must note accurately the Masses which he accepted to celebrate and those which he has satisfied.

The rules of this canon are mostly self-evident, but a few words and phrases call for some explanation. In paragraph one, the words "as soon as possible" refer to the action of the person who entrusts the Mass obligations, i.e., the one who sends the offerings. In the case of a priest who has already accepted sufficient Mass obligations for a year's time (c. 953), he must send to one or more other priests the excess offerings as soon as possible. Or, in the case of transferring Mass obligations elsewhere (c. 954), this is to be done as soon as possible after it is determined that there are too many Masses to be celebrated in a given place.

A priest who is above suspicion is anyone about whom there is no doubt that he will satisfy the Mass obligations received. This is to be presumed of all priests in good standing unless the contrary is evident. One may also presume that the Mass obligations have been accepted by the other priest if he has received and keeps the offerings. The time within which the Masses are to be celebrated is one year from the day on which the offerings were received (cf. c. 953), unless it is evident that one or more Masses are to be celebrated sooner.

Unsatisfied Obligations

Canon 956 — Each and every administrator of pious causes or those obliged in any way to see to the celebration of Masses, whether clerics or laity, are to hand over to their ordinaries according to the method defined by the latter the Mass obligations which have not been satisfied within a year.

This canon applies to anyone entrusted with seeing that Mass obligations are satisfied. The year is to be reckoned as 365 days from the acceptance of the Mass offering, unless the donor specified that the Masses in question had to be celebrated within the calendar year (c. 202, §1).

Vigilance

Canon 957 — The duty and right of exercising vigilance that Mass obligations are fulfilled belong to the local ordinary in churches of secular clergy and to the superiors in churches of religious institutes or societies of apostolic life.

The canon speaks of *churches,* and this should be understood in the technical sense of canon 1214. A church of the secular clergy means, for purposes of this canon, a church served by secular clergy; a church of a religious institute or society of apostolic life means, for purposes of this canon, not only churches owned by them, but also churches owned by a parish or diocese and served by clergy of religious institutes and societies of apostolic life. Although the bishop has jurisdiction over all churches, to which the faithful have the right to come, the Mass offerings received in them belong to the clergy themselves, not to the churches. Oversight of the finances of clergy of religious institutes and societies of apostolic life is the competence of the internal superiors of the institute or society and is part of the just autonomy that institutes and societies enjoy.[190] In *parish churches* served by members of religious institutes and societies of apostolic life, it would be advisable to keep a separate account or list of all binations and trinations of the pastor and parochial vicars, in respect to the offerings for the Masses that come by way of the parish or diocese, since this income would be subject to the local ordinary's jurisdiction (as above in the commentary under c. 951).

As for the *oratories* of clerical religious institutes and clerical societies of apostolic life, the major superiors have exclusive jurisdiction over the Mass accounts there. For oratories of lay religious institutes and lay societies of apostolic life, the local ordinary has jurisdiction.

Mass Record

Canon 958 — §1. The pastor and the rector of a church or other pious place which regularly receives offerings for Masses are to have a special book in which they note accurately the number of Masses to be celebrated, the intention, the offering given, and their celebration.

§2. The ordinary is obliged to examine these books each year either personally or through others.

---

[190] See cc. 586, 732, 628, 734, 397, §2.

In place of a book, it is becoming customary in some places to use a computer program for keeping the Mass offering account. The Mass offering records are to be examined each year by the ordinary, either personally or by others delegated by him, either at the time of the canonical visitation or at some other time.[191]

[191] See cc. 396, 397, 628, 734, 1301. See the commentary on the previous canon for the proper ordinary.

BIBLIOGRAPHY

Books

Bugnini, A. *The Reform of the Liturgy: 1948–1975.* Collegeville: Liturgical Press, 1990.

Huels, J. M. *Disputed Questions in the Liturgy Today.* Chicago: Liturgy Training Publications, 1988. [The chapters related to the Eucharist treat: female altar servers, concelebration, Mass intentions, reducing the number of Masses, mixed marriages, and the Eucharist.]

———. *The Interpretation of the Law on Communion under Both Kinds.* CanLawStud 505. Washington, D.C.: Catholic University of America, 1982.

———. *More Disputed Questions in the Liturgy.* Chicago: Liturgy Training Publications, 1996. [The chapters related to the Eucharist treat: unauthorized liturgical adaptations, preparation for the sacraments, daily Mass, sacramental sharing with other Christians, reception of sacraments by divorced and remarried persons, lay preaching at liturgy.]

———. *One Table, Many Laws: Essays on Catholic Eucharistic Practice.* Collegeville: Liturgical Press, 1986. [Essays on the interpretation of liturgical law, communion under both kinds, the matter of the Eucharist, reception of communion by the mentally handicapped, the internal forum solution, eucharistic sharing, Mass offerings.]

The Liturgy Documents: A Parish Resource. 3rd ed. Chicago: Liturgy Training Publications, 1991. [Contains twelve key documents on the Eucharist, each with an introduction by a different scholar.]

McManus, F., ed. *Thirty Years of Liturgical Renewal: Statements of the Bishops' Committee on the Liturgy.* Washington, D.C.: NCCB, 1987, with introduction and commentaries. [Many of the statements are related to the Eucharist.]

McSherry, P. J. *Wine as Sacramental Matter and the Use of Mustum.* Washington, D.C.: National Clergy Council on Alcoholism, 1986.

Pearson, J. T. *The Reservation and Veneration of the Blessed Sacrament.* Ottawa: St. Paul University, 1986.

Rau, S. *Die Feiern der Gemeinden und das Recht der Kirche.* Altenberge: Telos, 1990. [A doctoral dissertation on liturgical law; chapter 5 treats the 1983 code.]

Seasoltz, R. K. *New Liturgy, New Laws.* Collegeville: Liturgical Press, 1980. [Pages 84–111 and 131–141, in particular, are devoted to the Eucharist.]

Woestman, W. H. *Sacraments: Initiation, Penance, Anointing of the Sick.* Ottawa: Saint Paul University, 1996. [Pages 97–216 are on the Eucharist.]

Articles

Fuenmajor, A. "Sobre el destino de los estipendios de misas binadas o trinadas." *IC* 28 (1988) 201–211.

Green, T. J. "Sacramental Law Revisited—Reflections on Selected Aspects of Book IV of the Revised Code: *De Ecclesiae munere sanctificandi.*" *Stud Can* 17 (1983) 277–330.

Hendriks, J. "Ad sacram communionem ne admittantur... Adnotationes in Can. 915." *P* 79 (1990) 163–176.

Huels, J. M. "Canonical Rights to the Sacraments." In *Developmental Disabilities and Sacramental Access: New Paradigms for Sacramental Encounters,* ed. E. Foley, 94–115. Collegeville: Liturgical Press, 1994.

———. "Communion under Both Kinds on Sundays—Is It Legal?" *J* 42 (1982) 70–106.

———. "Liturgy, Inclusive Language, and Canon Law." In *Living No Longer for Ourselves: Liturgy and Justice in the Nineties,* ed. K. Hughes and M. R. Francis, 138–152. Collegeville: Liturgical Press, 1991.

———. "Preparation for the Sacraments: Faith, Rights, Law." *Stud Can* 28 (1994) 33–58.

———. "Select Questions of Eucharistic Discipline." *CLSAP* 47 (1985) 48–65.

———. "Stipends in the New Code of Canon Law." In *Living Bread, Saving Cup,* ed. R. K. Seasoltz, 347–356. Collegeville: Liturgical Press, 1987.

Manzanares, J. "De stipendio pro missis ad intentionem 'collectivam' celebratis iuxta decretum *Mos iugiter.*" *P* 80 (1991) 579–608.

Miralless, A. "Il pane e il vino per l'Eucaristia: sulla recente lettera della Congregazione per la Dottrina della Fede." *N* 31 (1995) 616–626.

Morrisey, F. G. "Denial of Access to the Sacraments." *CLSAP* 52 (1990) 170–186.

Mosso, D. "L'Eucaristia nel nuovo Codice." *Rivista Liturgica* 71 (1984) 268–282.

Provost, J. H. "NCCB Guidelines for Receiving Communion." *W* 61 (1987) 223–230.

Rincón Pérez, T. "El Decreto de la Congregación para el Clero sobre acumulación de estipendias." *IC* 31 (1991) 627–656.

———. "La facultad para comulgar dos veces al día a tenor del c. 917." *IC* 24 (1984) 769–781.

Schmitz, H. "Taufe, Firmung, Eucharistie: Die Sakramente der Initiation und ihre Rechtsfolgen in der Sicht des CIC von 1983." *AkK* 152 (1983) 369–407.

Urtasun, C. "Perceptio Corporis et Sanguinis Domini. Quoties. Quomodo." *P* 74 (1985) 534–574.

Zielinski, P. "Pious Wills and Mass Stipends in Relation to Canons 1299–1310." *Stud Can* 19 (1985) 115–154.

TITLE IV
THE SACRAMENT OF PENANCE
[cc. 959–997]

The thirty-nine canons of this title form four chapters, the first three of which deal with the sacrament of penance or reconciliation, the fourth with indulgences. After an introductory canon, the title treats: (1) celebration of the sacrament (cc. 960–964); (2) the minister (cc. 965–986); and (3) the penitent (cc. 987–991), along with (4) indulgences (cc. 992–997). A disproportionate number of canons affect the priest (bishop or presbyter) who acts as an ordained minister of the Church in the sacrament, partly because of the detailed norms that govern the canonical faculty or capacity to minister. The additional six basic norms on indulgences, related to but carefully distinguished from sacramental reconciliation, will also be commented upon together with the special law on this institute, a law which is outside the code.

The canons of this title have force, like the rest of the code, for the Latin church only. The parallel Eastern discipline is governed by canons 718–736 of the Code of Canons of the Eastern (Catholic) Churches; the canons make up chapter 4 of title XVI. The canons on penance in the Eastern collection are not further subdivided into articles or sections.

The Eastern code is sometimes almost literally dependent on the Latin code, for example, with regard to general sacramental absolution or the broadening of the faculty to absolve. The Eastern code also includes a discipline suppressed in the Latin church's canons, namely, the reservation of absolution from certain sins (see *CCEO* 727–729). Of course the Eastern code includes nothing on indulgences, an institute foreign to the Eastern tradition.

Vatican II mandated a reform of the Roman rite for celebrating all liturgical services, including the sacrament of penance: "The rites and formularies for the sacrament of penance are to be revised so that they more clearly express both the nature and effect of the sacrament."[1] In this text of *Sacrosanctum Concilium* the reference to "nature" is to the social and ecclesial nature of sacramental reconciliation, a dimension that needed to be restored or recovered. This is obviously a primary, indeed necessary, aspect of all seven sacraments but one that is less apparent in the ordinary circumstances of individual or auricular confession of sins and their absolution.[2]

The conciliar constitution, treating penance also in a broader sense and in relation to the church year, introduces and stresses the same neglected ecclesial dimension: "The baptismal and penitential aspects of Lent are to be given greater prominence in both the liturgy and liturgical catechesis."[3] Hence:

a. More use is to be made of the baptismal features proper to the Lenten liturgy; some of those from an earlier era are to be restored as may seem advisable.

b. The same is to apply to the penitential elements. As regards catechesis, it is important to impress on the minds of the faithful not only the social consequences of sin but also the essence of the virtue of penance, namely, detestation of sin as an offense against God; the role of the Church is not to be neglected and the people are to be exhorted to pray for sinners.

[1] *SC* 72.
[2] *AcSynVat* 1, 2:567. See pp. 558–559 on the restoration of the laying on of the hand or hands, "even without physical contact," as "a sign of reconciliation and of restored communion with the Church" (Cyprian).
[3] *SC* 109.

During Lent penance should be not only inward and individual, but also outward and social.[4]

The liturgical reform carried out this mandate, specifically in the 1973 *Rite of Penance* of the *Roman Ritual*. This includes not only the three rites and texts for the sacrament itself, described below, but also an appendix of models for communal penitential celebrations, including those that are seasonal in orientation.[5] These services are the occasion of conversion and reconciliation. In themselves they are kept distinct from the sacrament itself, but the possible combination of such freely developed penitential services with celebration of the sacrament is also contemplated:

Sometimes these services will include the sacrament of penance. In such cases after the readings and homily the rite for reconciling several penitents with individual confession and absolution is to be used (*Rite of Penance* nn. 54–59) or, in those special cases for which the law provides, the rite for general confession and absolution (*Rite of Penance* nn. 60–63).[6]

The canons of this title of the code do not directly address the enhanced ecclesial dimension of the liturgical reform of penance except in passing. Nor is the nature of the sacrament of penance as public cult offered to God formally treated; this is left to the general affirmation about the seven sacraments in canon 840.[7] The discipline of the 1917 code is generally retained, especially the traditional norms of conduct af-

fecting the ministers of the sacrament, bishops and presbyters, and the avoidance of misconduct and abuse. The major developments may be summarized in this way:

(1) The few norms for celebration (cc. 960–964) include new canons on general sacramental absolution when individual, auricular confession of sins has not preceded the absolution or reconciliation. Under this heading, too, the norms on the lawful place of celebration have been included and certain restrictions lifted. Nevertheless, most of the strictly liturgical law on the celebration of the sacrament remains outside the code, in accord with canon 2.

(2) Proposals that those ordained to the presbyterate should by the very fact of ordination be empowered to minister the sacrament were rejected in the process of recodification.[8] Instead, the requisite faculty over and above holy orders was retained, but one radical extension or enlargement was introduced in canon 967, §§2–3. This was done in accord with the basic pastoral purposes of the recodification. Thus, although the norms on faculties remain largely intact, most presbyters with a regular or habitual faculty to minister may exercise it everywhere unless canonically prohibited (see below).

(3) The chapter of the 1917 code on the reservation of sins (*CIC* 893–900) was abrogated, at the recommendation of the Apostolic Penitentiary.[9] Thus the whole canonical institute was abolished whereby the minister of the sacrament could be limited or restricted in his canonical and sacramental power of absolution with regard to certain reserved cases of sins. The institute of reservation of sins, which had been rigorously limited by the 1917 code to "very grave and atrocious" cases and hemmed

---

[4] *SC* 109–110; see cc. 1249–1253 on days of penance, although neither the social and ecclesial nor the liturgical elements of penance are stressed in those canons.

[5] *RPenance,* Appendix II, "Samples of Penitential Services," nn. 1–73. Another appendix gives a "Form of Examination of Conscience."

[6] *RPenance* 4, *DOL* 3109.

[7] *Rel* 224–225.

[8] *Comm* 10 (1978) 56.

[9] *Rel* 230–231.

in by restraints against excessive or abusive reservations,[10] was pastorally obsolescent or obsolete. Such a "reservation of sins," however, is found in the Code of Canons of the Eastern Churches (cc. 727–730), as already noted.

Liturgical Reform

Because the canons are principally concerned with the extrinsic discipline affecting the celebration, minister, and penitent, it is necessary to refer to the *Rite of Penance* for a broader treatment of the canonical discipline of sacramental celebration. The 1973 reform of the ritual of the sacrament has three distinct rites for the celebration of sacramental reconciliation, all of them enhanced with prayers, biblical readings, and other elements as part of the general reform of the liturgical books of the Roman liturgy, all in fulfillment of *Sacrosanctum Concilium* 23–25 and 35, 1.

1. Rite for Reconciliation of Individual Penitents

The first rite, although historically and traditionally derivative, is treated as "ordinary," primary, and basic because it has been the common usage of the Western church in medieval and modern times. As the rite for individual or auricular confessions of sins followed by individual absolution, it is the celebration with which the canons are almost exclusively concerned.

2. Rite for Reconciliation of Several Penitents with Individual Confession and [Individual] Absolution

In its present form—as a communal celebration which constitutes a framework for individual confession and individual absolution—the "second" rite is an innovation. Aside from the individual absolution of sins which it includes, however, it follows the more venerable tradition of the general or communal reconciliation of penitents by the bishop on Holy Thursday; the understanding was that any individual confession of sins to presbyters had

taken place earlier and traditionally prior to the Lenten observance, the period when "satisfaction" for at least public sins might be made. This older rite of reconciliation—expulsion of penitents on Ash Wednesday and their reconciliation on Holy Thursday—had been retained in the modern *Roman Pontifical* (1596) but had long been obsolete; the liturgical revision follows this tradition except that it requires individual confession and absolution in the course of the second rite.[11]

The canons of the code do not refer to this new second rite of the *Roman Ritual*, although it was this rite which Paul VI anticipated might become common:

> It [the second rite] combines the two values of being a community act and a personal act. It is a preferable form of reconciliation for our people when it is possible but it usually presupposes the presence of many ministers of the sacrament and this is not always easy. Still, we hope that especially for homogeneous groups—children, youth, workers, the sick, pilgrims, etc.—it may become the normal way of celebration, since it involves a more complete preparation and a more structured service.[12]

3. Rite for Reconciliation of Several Penitents with General Confession and Absolution

This third rite is also new. Prior to the publication of the *Rite of Penance* in 1973, general or communal absolution without previous individual confession of sins had to be celebrated according to the ritual for individual penance, with the liturgical texts simply changed to the plural. The present rite, however, is fully developed and

---

[10] *CIC* 897; see also *CIC* 895, 898, 900.

[11] In the *Roman Pontifical,* part three, "De expulsione publice poenitentium ab ecclesia, in feria quarta cinerum"; "De reconciliatione poenitentium, quae fit in feria quinta Coenae Domini." An early redaction of the second rite in the liturgical reform of the *RPenance* followed the older tradition of communal absolution.

[12] Address, April 3, 1974, *N* 10 (1974) 225–227, *DOL* 3112. The text did not appear in *AAS*.

elaborated: opening song, greeting of the assembly, and prayer; a full celebration of the liturgy of the word, followed by examination of conscience; general confession and general absolution; proclamation of praise and conclusion. The ritual and new canons 961–963 determine the limited conditions under which the third rite for reconciliation may be used.

As a whole, the *Rite of Penance* is characterized by greater openness to adaptation and accommodation than several other sections of the *Roman Ritual*. This results from a recognition that (1) the public and ecclesial nature of penance is fundamentally the same as that of the other sacraments, but (2) the sacrament has nonetheless been celebrated ordinarily in quasi-private circumstances in which only two members of the Christian community are present, namely, the penitent and the minister.

With regard to ritual adaptation to circumstances, no matter which of the three rites is followed, it is for priests and especially pastors

in celebrating reconciliation with individuals or with a community to adapt the rite to the concrete circumstances of the penitents. They must preserve the essential structure and the entire form of absolution, but if necessary they may omit some parts of the rite for pastoral reasons or enlarge upon them, may select texts of readings or prayers, and may choose a place more suitable for the celebration according to the regulations of the conference of bishops, so that the entire celebration may be enriching and effective.[13]

Unlike the law on several other sacraments, there is no canon that directly addresses the required form of words for the sacrament of penance, as approved in the liturgical books. With certain variants for communal absolution, for the Latin church this formulary is:

God the Father of mercies, / through the death and resurrection of his Son / has reconciled the world to himself / and sent the Holy Spirit among us / for the forgiveness of sins; / through the ministry of the Church / may God give you pardon and peace, / and I absolve you from your sins / in the name of the Father, and of the Son, / and of the Holy Spirit. / R. Amen.[14]

This is the integral text which may not be altered and is referred to as the "entire form of absolution" in the text on adaptation quoted above; the essential words begin "I absolve you . . ." and suffice in emergency circumstances, such as the imminent danger of death.

Although a restoration of the more traditional and venerable deprecative form of reconciliation was not included in the *Rite of Penance*,[15] the above formulary was newly introduced for the following reasons:

The form of absolution indicates that the reconciliation of the penitent comes from the mercy of the Father; it shows the connection between the reconciliation of the sinner and the paschal mystery of Christ; it stresses the role of the Holy Spirit in the forgiveness of sins; finally, it underlines the ecclesial aspect of the sacrament, because reconciliation with God is asked for and given through the ministry of the Church.[16]

The introduction (*praenotanda*) to the *Rite of Penance* gives a summary but important treatment of the mystery of reconciliation in the history of salvation, the reconciliation of penitents in the Church's life, and the several offices and ministries of reconciliation, including the role of the Christian community as a whole:

---

[13] *RPenance* 40, *DOL* 3105.

[14] *RPenance* 46; 19; 21; *DOL* 3084, 3086.
[15] See A. Bugnini, ed., *The Reform of the Liturgy* (1948–1975) (Collegeville: Liturgical Press, 1990) 667–670.
[16] *RPenance* 19, *DOL* 3084.

The whole Church, as a priestly people, acts in different ways in the work of reconciliation that has been entrusted to it by the Lord. Not only does the Church call sinners to repentance by preaching the word of God, but it also intercedes for them and helps penitents with a maternal care and solicitude to acknowledge and confess their sins and to obtain the mercy of God, who alone can forgive sins. Further, the Church becomes the instrument of the conversion and absolution of the penitent through the ministry entrusted by Christ to the apostles and their successors.[17]

Remission of Canonical Censures

The title on penance is concerned with the sacramental remission of sins. This is kept distinct from the remission of the canonical sanctions with which Book VI of the code is concerned—both the medicinal penalties or censures defined in canons 1331–1335 and the expiatory penalties of canons 1336–1338. Nevertheless, the remission or cessation of censures (excommunication, interdict, and the suspension of ordained ministers) may take place in connection with and on the occasion of sacramental reconciliation. The minister of the sacrament, if he is empowered by the law to remit censures (in particular by c. 1357), must on this occasion observe the norms of Book IV, title IV, the present series of canons on the sacrament itself.

While the act of remitting canonical censures differs clearly from the sacramental absolution of sins and is defined rather as the remission of an ecclesiastical penal sanction, the *Roman Ritual* makes special provision:

The form of [sacramental] absolution is not to be changed when a priest, in keeping with the provision of law, absolves a properly disposed penitent from a censure *latae sententiae*. It is enough that he intend also to absolve from censures. Before absolving

[17] *RPenance* 8, *DOL* 3073. See Mt 18:18; Jn 20:23.

from sins, however, the confessor may [separately and distinctly] absolve from the censure, using the formula which is given below for absolution from censure outside the sacrament of penance.

When a priest, in accordance with the law, absolves a penitent from a censure outside the sacrament of penance, he uses the following formula: By the power granted to me, / I absolve you / from the bond of excommunication (*or* suspension *or* interdict). / In the name of the Father, and of the Son, + / and of the Holy Spirit. The penitent answers: Amen.[18]

Thus two possibilities are envisioned for the celebration of the sacrament of penance for one who is also under canonical censure: (1) The minister, if the law permits him to do so, first remits the canonical censure in a distinct act—using the extra-sacramental formula already quoted—before the absolution from sin. (2) Alternatively, the minister of the sacrament, again if the law permits him to do so, remits the censure in the very act of absolving from sin, with or even without the specific formula.

Nature of the Sacrament

Canon 959 — In the sacrament of penance the faithful who confess their sins to a legitimate minister, are sorry for them, and intend to reform themselves obtain from God through the absolution imparted by the same minister forgiveness for the sins they have committed after baptism

[18] *RPenance*, Appendix I, 1–2. The text of the first paragraph, as it appeared in the *RPenance*, has been altered slightly (omitting "Until other provision is made and as may be necessary, the present regulations which make recourse to the competent authority obligatory are to be observed") in the light of the recodification. See CDW, decr *Promulgato Codice Iuris Canonici*, September 12, 1983, *N* 20 (1983) 540–555 [cited as *Variationes*]; in English, *Emendations in the Liturgical Books Following upon the New Code of Canon Law* (Washington, D.C.: ICEL, 1984) 20.

and, at the same time, are reconciled with the Church which they have wounded by sinning.

The text of canon 959 expands considerably canon 870 of the 1917 code. It deliberately removes the description of absolution as "judicial" (but see c. 978, §1) and adds a specific mention of the several acts of the penitent: confession of sins, sorrow for the sins confessed, proposal or resolution to reform—the latter corresponding to the nature of penance as conversion or change. (For the act or acts of satisfaction, see c. 981.) Moreover, the text mentions, as the older law did not, that the forgiveness is from God (alone) and adds the concept of reconciliation with the church community, as intended by the conciliar fathers of Vatican II.[19]

This succinct doctrinal canon may and should be supplemented by the introduction to the *Rite of Penance* already mentioned. Later canons such as 987 also enlarge upon the disposition of the penitent who comes to celebrate the sacrament.

Subsequent to the code and in the aftermath of the 1983 ordinary assembly of the synod of bishops, John Paul II issued an important apostolic exhortation, with reflections upon "reconciliation and penance in the mission of the Church."[20] The document, however, did not alter the canonical discipline of the sacrament in such matters as general sacramental absolution, a matter much controverted at the 1983 synod, nor did it concentrate greatly upon the ecclesial dimension of the sacrament.

CHAPTER I
THE CELEBRATION OF THE SACRAMENT
[cc. 960–964]

This brief chapter of five canons treats in succession: (1) individual and integral confession of sins and absolution (c. 960); (2) general absolution without previous individual confession (cc. 961–

963); and (3) the place for the celebration of the sacrament with individual confession (c. 964). Nothing is said directly about the liturgical celebration itself, aside from the penitent's confession of sins and the discipline affecting absolution or reconciliation; the norms for celebration are left to the *Rite of Penance* in the *Roman Ritual*. Nor is there reference to the second rite of reconciliation, namely, communal celebration of the sacrament with individual confession and individual absolution, or to communal penitential celebrations without sacramental reconciliation—both of which are significant elements in the reformed Roman liturgy of penance.

Canons 961–963 have been introduced in the light of the greater possibility of general sacramental absolution, to which the *Roman Ritual* devotes a full and lengthy rite described already: song and opening prayer, celebration of the word of God with homily, general confession and absolution, concluding thanksgiving, song or hymn, and blessing —but only "for cases foreseen in the law."[21]

Individual Reconciliation

Canon 960 — Individual and integral confession and absolution constitute the only ordinary means by which a member of the faithful conscious of grave sin is reconciled with God and the Church. Only physical or moral impossibility excuses from confession of this type; in such a case reconciliation can be obtained by other means.

The first clause of canon 960, in dealing with individual reconciliation of penitents, does so in contrast to the three canons that follow. The mention of integral confession of sins made by the penitent to the minister of the sacrament is based upon the teaching of the Council of Trent. Reflecting the developed Scholastic doctrine of the sacrament, the council anathematized those who held

that in the sacrament of penance for the remission of sins it is not necessary by divine

---

[19] *SC* 72; see the beginning of the commentary on this sacrament.

[20] *Reconciliatio et Paenitentia,* December 2, 1984, *AAS* 77 (1985) 185–275.

[21] *RPenance* 60–63.

law to confess each and every mortal sin, which one recalls upon due and diligent prior reflection, even occult sins and those which are against the two final precepts of the decalogue, and the circumstances which change the species of the sin.[22]

Although there has been some dispute concerning the expression *iure divino* in this text, since the traditions of penitential discipline were so diverse in earlier centuries, the present canon does not depart from the expectation of the integrity and specificity of the confession of sins. The matter is taken up directly in canon 988, §1.

The statement of the canon has been rephrased somewhat from canon 901 of the 1917 code. The latter explained the meaning of integral confession as requiring mention of all sins of which the penitent is conscious and of the circumstances which make a specific change in the sin. This has been understood, again in accord with Tridentine teaching, not in reference to aggravating circumstances but only to circumstances which make the sin a violation of a specifically different precept or virtue.[23]

These elements of the canon anticipate what is determined in greater detail in chapter 3 about the penitent, especially canons 987–989. What is distinctive in the present canon is the limited acknowledgment that this primary manner of celebrating the sacrament (the "first rite for reconciliation"), with full and individual confession of sins prior to absolution or reconciliation, is the only ordinary means or mode by which a believer conscious of a grave sin committed after baptism is reconciled to God and the Christian community. This provides an opening to canons 961–963 on the exceptional, out-of-the-ordinary, mode of reconciliation.

In addition, the language of the first part of the canon reflects contemporary theology and the teaching of Vatican II, which have recovered the tradition that sacramental penance involves ecclesial reconciliation. This was of course more evident in antiquity and the early medieval period, for example, when one acknowledged his or her grave (and public) sins at the beginning of Lent and was reconciled publicly on Holy Thursday in the common assembly (as described above).

The second part of canon 960 introduces the common teaching of moral theology which recognizes excuses from individual and integral confession because of physical or moral impossibility, a matter that was not mentioned in this context by the 1917 code. These kinds of impossibility may embrace a variety of physical and moral (even psychological) incapacities on the part of the penitent, the latter's relationship to the only available ministers, circumstances of time or place, etc. The alternative means of sacramental reconciliation which are referred to include a less than complete individual confession of sins followed by individual absolution and, in addition, the exceptional mode regulated by the three canons which follow. Reconciliation with God and the Church may of course also be accomplished by means of sacraments other than penance, above all through the eucharistic celebration, as well as by nonsacramental penance and contrition.

The succinct statement of this canon is enlarged upon in the introduction to the *Rite of Penance* where, after a doctrinal exposition of the mystery of reconciliation, there is a section on "Reconciliation of Penitents in the Church's Life."[24] This part of the *Roman Ritual* deals successively with the Church itself as both holy and always in need of purification; penance in the Church's life and liturgy; reconciliation with God and with the Church; the traditional "parts" of the sacrament: contrition, confession, the act of penance or expiation, and the actual absolution or reconciliation; and the need for and benefit of sacramental penance as the celebration of the Church's faith, thanksgiving, and sacrifice.

Although the code fails to advert to the "second rite for reconciliation" spelled out at length in the

---

[22] Sess. XIV, *de poenitentia,* c. 9.

[23] J. Abbo and J. Hannan, *The Sacred Canons,* 2 vols. (St. Louis: B. Herder, 1960) 2:28–29.

[24] *RPenance* 3–7, *DOL* 3068–3072.

Rite of Penance, that rite falls under canon 960 as an ordinary means of celebrating the sacrament, inasmuch as the individual and integral confession of sins and also individual absolution fall within it, that is, as the canon defines "ordinary."

Canon 720, §1 of the Code of Canons of the Eastern Churches is derived verbatim from Latin church canon 960. Similarly, in cases of general reconciliation (below), canon 720, §2 is substantially the same as Latin canon 961, §2; canon 720, §3 is derived from Latin canon 961, §2; and canon 721 from Latin canon 962. Latin canon 963, however, has no parallel in the Eastern code.

General Reconciliation

Canon 961 — §1. Absolution cannot be imparted in a general manner to many penitents at once without previous individual confession unless:

1° danger of death is imminent and there is insufficient time for the priest or priests to hear the confessions of the individual penitents;

2° there is grave necessity, that is, when in view of the number of penitents, there are not enough confessors available to hear the confessions of individuals properly within a suitable period of time in such a way that the penitents are forced to be deprived for a long while of sacramental grace or holy communion through no fault of their own. Sufficient necessity is not considered to exist when confessors cannot be present due only to the large number of penitents such as can occur on some great feast or pilgrimage.

§2. It belongs to the diocesan bishop to judge whether the conditions required according to the norm of §1, n. 2 are present. He can determine the cases of such necessity, attentive to the criteria agreed upon with the other members of the conference of bishops.

The immediate antecedent of the three new canons, 961–963, on general sacramental absolution without previous individual confession of sins is the 1973 *Rite of Penance.* This third rite, as given in the *Roman Ritual,* appears there to be an ordinary and usual mode of communal reconciliation. The introduction to the *Rite of Penance,* however, is based on the *Normae pastorales* issued in the preceding year by the Congregation for the Doctrine of the Faith; this document[25] had severely restricted the "ordinary" celebration of the third rite. The norm of the *Roman Ritual,* prior to the promulgation of the code, was revised in the light of the 1972 pastoral norms and reads:

Special, occasional circumstances may render it lawful and even necessary to give general absolution to a number of penitents without their previous individual confession.

In addition to the danger of death, general absolution for many of the faithful who have confessed generically, but have been rightly disposed for penance, is lawful if there is a serious need. This means a case in which, given the number of penitents, not enough confessors are available to hear the individual confessions properly within a reasonable time, with the result that, through no fault of their own, the faithful would be forced to be for a long time [*diu*] without the grace of the sacrament [of penance] or without communion. Such a situation may occur in mission lands particularly, but in other places as well and in groups of people to whom the serious need mentioned clearly applies.

When confessors can be made available, however, the procedure is not lawful solely on the basis of a large number of penitents, for example, at some great festival or pilgrimage.

It belongs exclusively to the local Ordinary, after consultation with other members of the conference of bishops, to make the judgment on whether the conditions stated

---

[25] CDF, *Normae pastorales circa absolutionem generali modo impertiendam,* June 16, 1972, *AAS* 64 (1972) 510–514, *DOL* 3038–3051.

already are verified and therefore to decide when it is lawful to give general absolution.

If, apart from the instances established by the local Ordinary, any other serious need arises for general absolution, a priest is bound first, whenever possible, to have recourse to the local Ordinary in order to give the general absolution. If this is not possible, he is to inform the same Ordinary as soon as possible of the need in question and of the fact of the absolution.[26]

The terms of this pre-codal law reflect in part the existing discipline of 1973, i.e., before the issuance of the *Rite of Penance*. During World War II, the Apostolic Penitentiary had issued an instruction on the subject, indicating that (1) general sacramental absolution is permissible for serious and urgent cause even in circumstances other than the danger of death; (2) local ordinaries are competent to permit this absolution; and (3) the (individual) rite for the sacrament of penance in the existing *Roman Ritual* should be followed but with the liturgical texts in the plural—since the ritual did not then contain a special rite for these circumstances.[27]

As already mentioned, the revised *Rite of Penance* does provide such a rite, relying upon the canonical discipline in force but including the substance of the 1972 pastoral norms of the Congregation for the Doctrine of the Faith as part of the prenotes. (It also has a very brief rite for general absolution in emergency circumstances, such as the imminent danger of death, i.e., when none of the three rites can be used in its entirety.)

When the norms of the *Roman Ritual* quoted above are compared with canon 961, several changes are evident: (1) greater specificity con-

cerning the danger of death as one of the reasons permitting the use of the third rite; (2) suppression (but not denial) of the ritual's positive observation concerning instances in mission lands and elsewhere where the serious need "clearly applies"; (3) restriction of the permission to diocesan bishops rather than local ordinaries; (4) requirement that the bishop's decision be made in the light of "criteria agreed upon" with the other members of the conference of bishops, if such criteria have been enacted (and not merely after consultation with the other bishops); and (5) omission of a possible judgment by a minister of the sacrament that general absolution may be given when recourse to the diocesan bishop is impossible.[28]

With regard to this last matter, the possible decision of the minister himself, the ordinary principles of moral theology about impossibility of recourse in situations of necessity may be applied.[29] The canonical obligation to report to the diocesan bishop after the fact no longer exists; it has been removed from the ritual along with specific mention of impossibility of recourse.

The other changes listed above, especially (3) and (4), are further restrictions placed by the canon upon the celebration of general reconciliation. This has been recognized in variants introduced into the *Rite of Penance,* so that its norms conform literally with the present canon.[30] The Apostolic See has repeatedly expressed concern lest the norms limiting general sacramental absolution be exceeded to the (further) diminution of auricular confession.[31]

The language of the canon, even with these further inhibitions, continues to permit the cele-

[26] *RPenance* 31–32, *DOL* 3096–3097.

[27] Apostolic Penitentiary, instr March 25, 1944, *AAS* 36 (1944) 155–156. The development of the third rite of penance, although introduced in the light of recommendations by the conciliar fathers of Vatican II, was closely tied to the discipline of this document. See Bugnini, 651–655.

[28] The dispositions of cc. 961–963 replace, to the extent necessary, the corresponding norms of the introduction to *RPenance* 31–34 (and also the *Normae pastorales* of 1972, from which cc. 961–963 likewise differ, as noted in the text). See CDW, *Emendations* 17–20 (note 18, above).

[29] *Rel* 228.

[30] See note 18, above.

[31] CDF, letter January 14, 1977, *BCLN,* November 13, 1977, 57–58, *DOL* 3127–3132. Paul VI, address April 3, 1974, *N* 10 (1974) 225–227, *DOL* 3110–3113.

bration of the third rite if the conditions are fulfilled. As Paul VI explicitly asserted, the enlarged possibility of general sacramental absolution was introduced "with our special approval and by our mandate."[32] With particular reference to the language of canon 961, the availability of confessors is a relative matter: it depends on the size of the congregation of penitents, the period of time needed for the proper celebration of the sacrament of penance (i.e., in accord with the third rite found in the revised ritual), the remoteness of the community and its size, which might deny freedom of choice of confessors or desired anonymity to penitents, etc.

The extended deprivation of sacramental grace mentioned in the canon as justifying general absolution refers to the grace of the sacrament of penance;[33] this deprivation may create a spiritual hardship for those not conscious of grave sin as well as for those who are conscious of grave sin and who would therefore be deprived not only of sacramental penance but also of sacramental communion. Finally, the lengthy period of time has to be understood relatively, as in other instances, in terms of a rather limited time, even a day's deprivation of the sacrament of penance.[34] In the United States, an interpretation of the meaning of "a long while" [diu] as "one month" was made by the National Conference of Catholic Bishops in 1988, but no decree was issued to this effect.[35]

The canon balances carefully the exceptional character of the rite of general absolution with pastoral criteria, to be judged by the diocesan bishop in harmony with any criteria that may have been approved by the conference of bishops.

The judgment of the bishop or the criteria of the conference may justify or require the celebration even though the serious need cannot be characterized as creating an emergency situation.

It is of course true that, even in the circumstances in which the law does not permit the celebration of general reconciliation without prior individual confession of sins, those conscious of grave sin may indeed receive divine pardon in view of the degree and kind of their contrition ("perfect contrition") apart from the sacrament itself.[36] Such persons are nonetheless deprived of the grace of the sacrament of penance[37] and share less perfectly in the dimension of ecclesial reconciliation. The same is true of those who are conscious of only lesser or venial sins, which may indeed be remitted in ways other than the sacrament; in the circumstances such persons are likewise deprived of sacramental reconciliation.

In the Code of Canons of the Eastern Churches, Latin code canons 960 and 961 are combined—in substantially the same language, with allowance for different hierarchical names—into canon 720 (960 in §1 of CCEO 720, 961 in §2). This Eastern dependence on the (new) discipline of the Latin church on general sacramental absolution is continued in the next canon: canon 721 of the Eastern code is derived from Latin canon 962—but with the single significant omission of any reference to validity in canon 721, §1.

Canon 962 — §1. For a member of the Christian faithful validly to receive sacramental absolution given to many at one time, it is required not only that the person is properly disposed but also at the same time intends to confess within a suitable

---

[32] Paul VI, address April 20, 1978, AAS 70 (1978) 328–332, DOL 3138–3139.

[33] "gratia sacramentali aut sacra communione diu carere cogantur."

[34] See E. F. Regatillo and M. Zalba, *Theologiae Moralis Summa,* III (Madrid: BAC, 1954) 917 (cited as Regatillo-Zalba).

[35] Approved, general meeting, June 1988; CDWDS indicated that the interpretation was not a decree and needed no *recognitio:* "Complementary Norms" (Washington, D.C.: NCCB, 1991) 12. See also *CLD* 11, 238–244.

[36] International Theological Commission, report "Penance and Reconciliation," 1983, C, II, 4, *Origins* 13 (1984) 513–524.

[37] The various redactions of this text (*Normae pastorales, RPenance,* and the schemata of the code) differ, but they always refer to the *gratia sacramentalis* of penance and distinguish it from (the deprivation of) holy communion, a deprivation which affects only those conscious of the continuing guilt of grave sin. See also the commentary on c. 988, §2, below.

period of time each grave sin which at the present time cannot be so confessed.

§2. Insofar as it can be done even on the occasion of the reception of general absolution, the Christian faithful are to be instructed about the requirements of the norm of §1. An exhortation that each person take care to make an act of contrition is to precede general absolution even in the case of danger of death, if there is time.

Canon 962, §1 makes a twofold demand: (1) suitable disposition and (2) intent to confess (later) the serious sins that cannot be confessed at the time of general sacramental absolution.

The disposition to which paragraph one refers includes the inner conversion which "embraces sorrow for sin and the intent to lead a new life... expressed through confession made to the Church, due expiation, and amendment of life. God grants pardon through the Church, which works by the ministry of priests."[38] The *Rite of Penance,* even prior to the 1983 recodification, had specified these dispositions in relation to general sacramental absolution, namely, that those present "repent individually of their sins, have the intention of refraining from them, are resolved to rectify scandal or injuries they may have caused..."[39] The purpose of paragraph one of the canon is to repeat, under pain of invalidity of the absolution (which the *Roman Ritual* had not mentioned), a resolution or disposition special to the exceptional circumstances of general sacramental reconciliation. This disposition includes the intent to confess individually in due time the grave sins which could not be confessed individually on the occasion of general absolution.

The due time to which paragraph one refers for individual confession is further specified in the next canon ("as soon as possible") and, more generally, by the traditional precept of at least annual confession of grave sins, as found in canon 989.

Next, the norm of paragraph two of canon 962 may be seen as a specification of canon 988, §1, which speaks of the fundamental obligation to confess grave sins committed after baptism that have not yet been confessed in individual or auricular confession. In this way the usual ecclesiastical or canonical discipline is maintained. The mention of "even in the case of danger of death, if there is time" is applicable to the short rite of absolution[40] rather than to the complete and lengthy third rite of reconciliation of several penitents with general confession and absolution.

Canon 962, §2 is derived immediately from a similar injunction in the *Rite of Penance* and the specific norm that, after the homily of the third rite, there be a brief instruction or *monitio* concerning the requisite and special dispositions of penitents. The act of contrition, which is called simply a "general confession," follows this pattern in the full rite of general absolution:

> The deacon, another minister, or the priest then [after the homily and instruction] calls upon the penitents to show their intention by some sign (for example, by bowing their heads, kneeling, or giving some other sign determined by the conference of bishops). They should also say together a form of general confession (for example, the prayer *I confess to almighty God*), which may be followed by a litany or a penitential song. Then the Lord's Prayer is sung or said by all...
>
> Then the priest pronounces the invocation that expresses prayer for the grace of the Holy Spirit to pardon sin, the proclamation of victory over sin through Christ's death and resurrection, and the sacramental absolution given to the penitents.[41]

For the United States, the National Conference of Catholic Bishops decreed in 1974 that the sign of penance before general sacramental absolution should be determined and announced by the min-

---

[38] *RPenance* 6, *DOL* 3071; on the Church's ministry, see the revised formula of the sacrament, at the beginning of the commentary on this title.
[39] *RPenance* 33, *DOL* 3098.

[40] *RPenance* 64–65.
[41] *RPenance* 35, *DOL* 3100.

ister, namely, an "appropriate external sign of penance to be shown, e.g., kneeling, bowing of the head, bowing deeply, standing (if the penitents have been kneeling), a gesture such as the sign of the cross, etc."[42]

Canon 963 — Without prejudice to the obligation mentioned in can. 989, a person whose grave sins are remitted by general absolution is to approach individual confession as soon as possible, given the opportunity, before receiving another general absolution, unless a just cause intervenes.

This canon contains a precept distinct from that of canon 989, in which the annual confession of grave sins is prescribed as a minimum. In other words, the present norm may oblige even before the lapse of a year's time, i.e., as soon as possible after the celebration of general sacramental reconciliation. Since the divine and ecclesial sacramental reconciliation has already taken place, the norm must be considered an ecclesiastical law specifying when the intention to confess individually (c. 962) should be fulfilled.

Nonetheless, the language of the canon recognizes, as did the *Rite of Penance* and the *Normae pastorales* which preceded it, that there may be a just cause which may excuse from individual confession "as soon as possible." This just cause may be the same as the one which justified the general sacramental absolution in the first place, such as the remoteness of the area and the lack of ministers of the sacrament, so long as that condition or cause continues. There is of course no obligation to confess sins which are not grave, as canon 988, §1 makes clear, however much the confession of venial sins may be recommended (c. 988, §2).

The Eastern code departs from the Latin discipline on general sacramental absolution by omitting anything comparable to the above canon 963.

Place of Celebration

Canon 964 — §1. The proper place to hear sacramental confessions is a church or oratory.

§2. The conference of bishops is to establish norms regarding the confessional; it is to take care, however, that there are always confessionals with a fixed grate between the penitent and the confessor in an open place so that the faithful who wish to can use them freely.

§3. Confessions are not to be heard outside a confessional without a just cause.

The final form of this canon is the result of several variant redactions during the recodification process. In particular, canons 909–910 of the former code had singled out the confessions of women for special restrictions, indicating that the confessional for their celebration of the sacrament should be in an open and conspicuous place, while permitting the sacrament to be celebrated for male penitents even in private homes. In some places, moreover, it was customary and acceptable for the confessions of men to take place regularly in rooms, sacristies, and other areas without the use of a special confessional. It was (and is) always understood, finally, that in many circumstances such as sickness the sacrament is properly celebrated in any appropriate or available place.

In the revised *Roman Ritual* the prescriptions of the 1917 code were referred to as continuing in force,[43] but it was left to the conferences of bishops to make further (and different) determinations "about the place proper for the ordinary celebration of the sacrament of penance" and to priests and especially pastors to "choose a place more suitable for the celebration according to the regulations of the conference of bishops, so that the entire celebration may be enriching and effective."[44] In the light of this, with the development of chapels or rooms of reconciliation as alternatives to the modern style of confessional (or in combination with such a confessional), the con-

---

[42] *BCLN 1965–1975* (December 1974) 450; see R. Keifer and F. R. McManus, *The Rite of Penance: Commentaries; I, Understanding the Document* (Washington, D.C.: Liturgical Conference, 1975) 128–129.

[43] *RPenance* 12, *DOL* 3077.
[44] *RPenance* 38b, *DOL* 3103; 40, *DOL* 3105.

ference of bishops in 1974 decreed for the United States that it is

> considered desirable that small chapels or rooms of reconciliation be provided in which penitents might choose to confess their sins through an informal face-to-face exchange with the priest, with the opportunity for appropriate spiritual counsel. It would also be regarded as desirable that such chapels or rooms be designed to afford the option of the penitent's kneeling at the fixed confessional grille in the usual way, but in every case the freedom of the penitent is to be respected.[45]

A further elaboration was later given by the United States Bishops' Committee on the Liturgy, which recommended:

> A room or rooms for the reconciliation of individual penitents may be located near the baptismal area (when it is at the entrance) or in another convenient place. Furnishings and decoration should be simple and austere, offering the penitent a choice between face-to-face encounter or the anonymity provided by a screen, with nothing superfluous in evidence beyond a simple cross, table and bible. The purpose of this room is primarily for the celebration of the reconciliation liturgy; it is not a lounge, counseling room, etc. The word "chapel" more appropriately describes this space.[46]

Early drafts of the recodification left the matter generally to the conference of bishops, with the requirement that there be available a confessional with a fixed screen or grille. Later in the process a norm was introduced or reintroduced to require that the confessions of women take place in a confessional with a fixed screen "except by rea-

son of infirmity or other necessity."[47] In the final promulgated text, the present form of paragraph three appears without any reference to or restriction upon the confessions of women.

The reasoning behind paragraph one of this canon is that the sacrament, even though celebrated regularly in a rather individualized and private rite, is an ecclesial celebration for which the place of the communal liturgical assembly, namely, a church or oratory, is appropriate.

The provision of the confessional or confessional seat is retained in paragraphs two and three. The common form of booth, with a place for the penitent (either open to public view or enclosed but separate from the seat of the minister), is not prescribed, unless by particular law. Confessionals in one or other of these styles, e.g., with or without a door or doors, with or without curtains or drapes, were introduced after the Council of Trent and spread widely in the Latin church.[48] The canon, however, prescribes only that the seat of the confessor be in an open place and that there be a screen or grille between the penitent and the confessor; no norm is given concerning the style or form of the fixed dividing barrier.

The purpose of this norm is of course to afford the penitent anonymity if he or she desires and to make certain that there is no suspicion of impropriety in the confessor-penitent relationship. The chapel or room of reconciliation in which a "confessional" area with a fixed screen is incorporated fully satisfies the norm. If the chapel or room does not itself incorporate an area with a fixed screen, the latter must be available elsewhere.

In accord with paragraph three, the use of the usual confessional remains prescribed, but the confession may take place elsewhere for a just cause, namely, a lesser reason than the "necessity" earlier intended by the codifiers. The value

---

[45] *BCLN 1965–1975* (December 1974) 450.

[46] *Environment and Art in Catholic Worship* (Washington, D.C.: USCC: 1978), n. 81.

[47] *Comm* 10 (1978) 68–69.

[48] On the introduction of such confessionals, and the several styles, see J. B. O'Connell, *Church Building and Furnishing: The Church's Way* (Notre Dame: University of Notre Dame Press, 1955) 72–73.

of opportunities for informal face-to-face exchange and for spiritual counsel cited by the National Conference of Catholic Bishops (above) is a just cause for that body's encouragement of and preference for the chapels or rooms in which the penitent remains free to choose face-to-face confession or the anonymity provided by the confessional screen. As is obvious, the "just cause" also includes the very many circumstances outside churches and oratories, whether homes or hospitals or entirely secular places, where the hearing of confessions is reasonably requested.

A different and much simpler discipline concerning the place of celebration of penance is followed in the Eastern churches. Canon 736 of the Eastern code states that the proper place is a church, but, with due regard for particular law on the matter in case of infirmity or other just cause, the celebration may take place outside a church (§2).

CHAPTER II
THE MINISTER OF THE SACRAMENT OF PENANCE
[cc. 965–986]

The first half of this chapter deals directly with the priest as minister of this sacrament and with his faculty to minister. After an introductory canon, the acquisition of the faculty (cc. 966–969) is treated, along with special qualifications in those who may have the faculty and the terms of the faculty itself (cc. 970–973), and finally the cessation of the faculty (cc. 974–975).

The other eleven canons of the chapter deal with several matters closely related to the exercise of the sacramental ministry of reconciliation by priests: (1) special cases of absolution (cc. 976–977); (2) the manner of receiving the confession of sins, granting absolution, and imposing an act of penance or satisfaction (c. 978–981); (3) the false denunciation of confessors (c. 982); (4) confidentiality, including above all the sacramental seal (cc. 983–985); and (5) the duty or respon-

sibility to exercise the ministry of reconciliation (c. 986).

There is relatively little on the canonical faculty to minister in the revised *Roman Ritual*, except for a brief pastoral exhortation to priests[49] and a basic statement in which the priest's ministry is placed in an ecclesial context:

The whole Church, as a priestly people, acts in different ways in the work of reconciliation that has been entrusted to it by the Lord...

The Church exercises the ministry of the sacrament of penance through bishops and presbyters. By preaching God's word [newly introduced as a formal element of the actual rite of sacramental reconciliation] they call the faithful to conversion; in the name of Christ and by the power of the Holy Spirit they declare and grant the forgiveness of sins.

In the exercise of this ministry presbyters act in communion with the bishop and share in his power and office as the one who regulates the penitential discipline.

The competent minister of the sacrament of penance is a presbyter who has the faculty to absolve in accordance with canon law.[50]

Thus the role of the minister is asserted to include both declaring and granting the forgiveness of sins. This is in accord with the teaching of the Council of Trent, which repudiated any assertion that ecclesial reconciliation was merely a matter of declaring God's forgiveness or was void of judgmental (as well as other) dimensions.[51] The relationship of the presbyter to the bishop, who is the moderator of the liturgy and of the penitential

---

[49] *RPenance* 10, *DOL* 3075.

[50] *RPenance* 8–9, *DOL* 3073–3074. On the bishop of the particular church as *moderator* of penitential discipline, see *LG* 26.

[51] Sess. XIV, *de poenitentia*, c. 9.

discipline in the local church, is expressed in two ways: fundamentally as communion within the presbyterate headed by the bishop and canonically as possession of the faculty to reconcile or absolve sinners. There is concern in the new redaction of canons, however, not to speak of the sacramental exercise of the faculty as jurisdiction, as was done in the past, even though the actual concession of the faculty by law or otherwise is an exercise of the executive power of governance.

The faculty to minister this sacrament to penitents is generally referred to in the canons as the faculty to "hear" confessions, although such terminology refers to only part of the rite. The terminology always has to be understood as referring to the authorization to minister the sacrament, to absolve from sins as well as to receive ("hear") the confession of sins.

A similar usage is found in the canonical reference to the minister as "confessor," which is regularly retained in the canons. It corresponds also to the popular and even traditional practice of referring to the sacrament as "confession" rather than penance or reconciliation, although the revised ritual is careful to retain "penance" and to introduce "reconciliation."[52] The popular and canonical emphasis upon the confessional dimension of the sacrament has been explained as reflecting a modern concentration upon this aspect, which was less prominent in ancient and medieval times:

> The form of the acts of the penitent was also subject [in the historical development of the sacrament] to a noteworthy change. It often happened that one of these was emphasized so much that the others were relegated to the background. Public penance in the primitive Church stood under the sign of public satisfaction which lasted for a set period of time; private penance in the Middle Ages and in the modern period, on the other

hand, underlined the importance of contrition; in our own time, the accent is more on confession.[53]

The accent on confession is indeed greater in the canons of this chapter and the next. The ritual's emphasis, on the other hand, is on divine and ecclesial reconciliation as well as on contrition, confession, and satisfaction.

The present chapter 2 introduces a more generous recognition of confessional faculties than in the past, as already mentioned at the beginning of the commentary on the sacrament of penance. More important, it suppresses jurisdictional language in relation to the exercise of confessional faculties.

A certain analogy with the sacrament of confirmation is possible: over and above sacramental ordination and participation in the ordained presbyterate, some faculty or capacity or concession is needed by the minister in both cases. The analogy with confirmation is supported by canon 144, §2, which applies the institute of supplied executive power of governance or jurisdiction equally to both sacraments or, more precisely, to the concession which permits the valid exercise of the ministerial office in these instances. The pastoral purpose of that canon is clear enough: to give assurance to ministers and penitents who might otherwise succumb to scrupulosity in regard to validity of the respective sacrament.

In the case of confirmation, the addition to the power of holy orders has been variously explained; in the case of penance, the addition to the power of holy orders has been explicitly described in the past as an augmentation of jurisdiction or the power of governance.[54] The recodification, however, carefully avoids jurisdictional language in this connection. At the same time, it is clear that the church authority which is the ultimate source of the faculty to absolve or reconcile

---

[52] The preference of the revisers of the ritual of Paul VI is evident in the use of the term "reconciling" in the name of each of the three rites of the sacrament.

[53] International Theological Commission, report, 1983, B, IV, 6, 5, *Origins* 13 (1984) 520.

[54] E.g., Regatillo-Zalba, 280; see *CIC* 872–881; these canons regularly speak of jurisdiction.

is a person, ordinarily the bishop, who himself exercises a power of governance or jurisdiction in the act of conferring the faculty.

The minister of reconciliation in these canons is the priest (bishop or presbyter) who may absolve from sins in the celebration of the sacrament of penance. Insofar as the remission of canonical sanctions is concerned, see canons 1354–1363 and, with specific reference to confessors and the remission of certain censures, canon 1357. In itself distinct from the remission of sins, this discipline has been explained briefly above, at the beginning of the commentary on the present title on the sacrament of penance.

Sacerdotal Ministry of Reconciliation

Canon 965 — A priest alone is the minister of the sacrament of penance.

Canon 966 — §1. The valid absolution of sins requires that the minister have, in addition to the power of orders, the faculty of exercising it for the faithful to whom he imparts absolution.

§2. A priest can be given this faculty either by the law itself or by a grant made by the competent authority according to the norm of can. 969.

In the first of the canons of this chapter, the Latin *sacerdos* is used to refer to both bishops and presbyters. The text follows the Council of Trent, which condemned the teaching of those who held that

> priests are not the only ministers of absolution but it was said to each and every Christian: "Whatever you declare bound on earth shall be held bound in heaven, and whatever you declare loosed on earth shall be held loosed in heaven" and "For those whose sins you forgive, they are forgiven; for those whose sins you retain, they are retained."[55]

As already suggested, the faculty or capacity to absolve or remit sins through the celebration of sacramental reconciliation is understood as rooted in holy orders—and thus is a power for which episcopal or presbyteral ordination is necessary—but it is also understood as requiring a distinct, additional concession which permits the valid exercise of the ministry on behalf of God and the Church. This is the sense of canon 966.

Vatican II refrained from using the medieval distinction between the power of orders and the power of jurisdiction (now alternatively and preferably called the power of governance or governing).[56] Nonetheless, the distinction between the power of orders and the capacity to exercise that power is retained in relation to sacramental absolution, while avoiding any reference to jurisdiction exercised in the act of reconciling or absolving. The concept, for example, of ordinary or delegated confessional jurisdiction has been suppressed.

In principle, the determination of the faculty to absolve is based on the relationship of the minister to the penitents, namely, the particular members of the faithful who seek reconciliation. Thus, in succeeding canons the faculty is related either to the office of ministry which the priest has in respect to the penitents or to the governing power which the grantor of the faculty has in respect to the penitents.

Next, in paragraph two of canon 966 the distinction between ordinary and delegated jurisdiction, the categories employed by canon 872 of the 1917 code, has been replaced by a distinction between a faculty from the law and a faculty from a concession or grant.

In cases of error or doubt concerning the possession of the faculty of canon 966, the Church supplies the faculty, in accord with canon 144, §2, as explained above. See the commentary on canon 144, §1, which speaks of instances of "factual or legal common error and in positive and probable doubt of law or of fact." In effect, canon

---

[55] Sess. XIV, *de poenitentia*, c. 10. The biblical texts are Mt 18:18 and Jn 20:23.

[56] See *LG* 18–29 (chap. 3); the jurisdictional terminology is used only once (*LG* 23) in treating the hierarchical constitution of the Church.

144, §2 employs the institute of supplied jurisdiction (now called and limited to supplied executive power of governance) to the faculty of the minister of the sacrament of penance, although it is not considered a jurisdictional faculty as such.

Faculty from the Law

Canon 967 — §1. In addition to the Roman Pontiff, cardinals have the faculty of hearing the confessions of the Christian faithful everywhere in the world by the law itself. Bishops likewise have this faculty and use it licitly everywhere unless the diocesan bishop has denied it in a particular case.

§2. Those who possess the faculty of hearing confessions habitually whether by virtue of office or by virtue of the grant of an ordinary of the place of incardination or of the place in which they have a domicile can exercise that faculty everywhere unless the local ordinary has denied it in a particular case, without prejudice to the prescripts of can. 974, §§2 and 3.

§3. Those who are provided with the faculty of hearing confessions by reason of office or grant of a competent superior according to the norm of cann. 968, §2 and 969, §2 possess the same faculty everywhere by the law itself as regards members and others living day and night in the house of the institute or society; they also use the faculty licitly unless some major superior has denied it in a particular case as regards his own subjects.

Here as elsewhere, the faculty to "hear" confessions is understood as the faculty to exercise the power of orders to "absolve" penitents from their sins. This usage is without prejudice to the natural meaning of hearing a confession of sinful actions, which may be done by anyone. Here and in succeeding canons it is simply a canonical usage referring to the sacerdotal ministry of presiding over all the elements of the sacrament of penance.

A certain distinction is made in paragraph one. The Bishop of Rome himself, who is also the head of the college of bishops, and the cardinals, as the principal ministers of the Roman diocese, absolve both validly and licitly everywhere and without restriction. Bishops other than the Roman Pontiff, whether diocesan bishops or not, are also members of the same college of bishops, and they likewise absolve validly everywhere. It is illicit, however, for them to absolve if the diocesan bishop (explicitly) prohibits the use of the universal faculty in a particular case.

A substantial reform of the discipline of confessional faculties is found in paragraph two of canon 967. The text anticipates what is determined in detail in succeeding canons and makes a broad, general determination in favor of those presbyters whose faculty is derived from their office or granted by the local ordinary—of the place of their incardination or, if they are incardinated elsewhere or are religious or others who lack diocesan incardination, from the ordinary of their place of domicile. An additional condition is that the faculty thus held or granted is habitual or regular, that is, not conceded for a particular occasion or for particular circumstances or for the benefit of a particular group alone. Once they possess the faculty in the stated circumstances, such presbyters may validly and licitly absolve the Christian faithful everywhere unless in a particular case the local ordinary refuses to permit this; they have this extended or universal faculty from the law, i.e., from canon 967, §2.

A local ordinary may not, in contravention of the common law, refuse to permit all priests from other dioceses or priests in general to exercise the faculty, as conceded here, but for cause (not specified in the canon) he may deny it to an individual presbyter or on an individual occasion. The presumption always favors the right of the minister, who possesses the faculty according to the terms described here, to exercise it everywhere.

The pastoral and practical advantages of this broadening of the discipline are evident, and the concession is related to recent, limited developments: for the convenience of penitents and ministers alike, some bishops had already agreed to concede confessional faculties to all the priests of the same province or region who had the faculty within their own particular church. An underlying reason for such concessions, including the one made in the canon, is a more authentic recognition of the communion of local or particular churches—over and above the evident pastoral convenience.

Nothing is said expressly in paragraph two concerning the validity of sacramental absolution by a presbyter who has been denied the right to exercise his faculty by a local ordinary. According to the principle set down in canon 10, an express determination of the law is needed to render an act invalid, and thus the priest in these circumstances would at first appear to act validly but illicitly.

Nevertheless, canon 974, §§2–3, to which reference is made, equates this denial or refusal by the local ordinary with the revocation of the faculty in that ordinary's territory. It is stated in canon 974, §2 that the presbyter whose faculty is revoked by a local ordinary (other than the ordinary of his place of incardination or domicile) loses the faculty but only in the territory of the revoking ordinary. As paragraph two of canon 967 indicates, its terms must be understood in conjunction with the later canon, both as to loss of the faculty (c. 974, §2) and the notification of the presbyter's own ordinary or superior (c. 974, §3). Moreover, a comparison with paragraph three of the present canon, to be discussed next, supports the position that the presbyter who is denied the faculty by a particular local ordinary absolves invalidly in the latter's territory.

The third and final paragraph of canon 967 extends a somewhat similar concession, by operation of the law, to confessors who are superiors or who have received the faculty from a competent superior of a religious institute or society of apostolic life, if it is a clerical institute of pontifical right or status. In this case, however, the faculty is limited to the absolution of penitents who are members of the institute or society or who live regularly ("day and night") in some house of the institute or society. As in paragraph two, the faculty may be exercised everywhere in respect to the penitents who are mentioned; it is exercised illicitly but validly if in a particular case the competent major superior denies the right to absolve.

A comparison of paragraphs two and three reveals that the cases are indeed analogous, but, according to the fundamental principle affecting confessional faculties, the concession within institutes and societies is restricted to the benefit of those penitents who are subject in some way—as members or as those living in religious or similar communities—to the authorities of the individual institute or society. More notably, in paragraph three it is clear that the absolution given in contravention to the will of a major superior is valid if illicit, whereas in paragraph two this more generous expression is not present.

Faculty from Office

Canon 968 — §1. In virtue of office, a local ordinary, canon penitentiary, a pastor, and those who take the place of a pastor possess the faculty of hearing confessions, each within his jurisdiction.

§2. In virtue of their office, superiors of religious institutes or societies of apostolic life that are clerical and of pontifical right, who have executive power of governance according to the norm of their constitutions, possess the faculty of hearing the confessions of their subjects and of others living day and night in the house, without prejudice to the prescript of can. 630, §4.

The preceding canon indicates at least in general terms those whose faculty to absolve comes from the law. Canon 968 determines those who have the faculty, again from the law, in virtue of an office which they hold.

The enumeration in paragraph one includes the local ordinaries named in canon 134, §§1–2 (over and above bishops, already covered by c. 967, §1) for the particular church, as the latter is defined in canon 368; the canon penitentiary of canon 508, again for the particular church; and the pastor and those who take the place of a pastor, as determined in the canons of Book II, title III, chapter 6 (cc. 515–552), for the parish or quasi-parish. Since the officeholders so enumerated have the faculty to absolve from the law and on a habitual basis, they possess it elsewhere and indeed everywhere in accord with canon 967, §2.

In canon 968, §2, a similar determination is made in favor of superiors of clerical religious institutes and societies of apostolic life of pontifical right, but it is limited to the celebration of the sacrament for their members and for those who live regularly in their religious houses, that is, day and night. Again, canon 967, §3 provides that the superiors in question have the same faculty throughout the institute or society. Superiors are reminded, however, that canon 630, §4 prohibits them from hearing confessions of the members subject to their authority "unless the members request it on their own initiative."

Faculty from Concession

Canon 969 — §1. The local ordinary alone is competent to confer upon any presbyters whatsoever the faculty to hear the confessions of any of the faithful. Presbyters who are members of religious institutes, however, are not to use the faculty without at least the presumed permission of their superior.

§2. The superior of a religious institute or society of apostolic life mentioned in can. 968, §2 is competent to confer upon any presbyters whatsoever the faculty to hear the confessions of their subjects and of others living day and night in the house.

The two paragraphs of canon 969 rest on the principle or rule already stated: the concession of the faculty to absolve (namely, to those presbyters who do not have it in virtue of their office or by the operation of the law itself) depends upon a power residing in the grantor over those for whom the presbyter ministers the sacrament. Thus, although the faculty to absolve is no longer considered a governing or jurisdictional power, its concession to another demands (executive) power of governance[57]—ordinary or delegated—in the grantor, and this power is in respect to the penitents rather than to the minister.

In paragraph one of canon 969, the usual situation in the particular church is envisioned in which the diocesan bishop (or one equated in law to a diocesan bishop)[58] or other local ordinary grants the faculty. The terms or conditions under which this is to be done are determined in subsequent canons (especially cc. 970–973), and paragraph one requires only that, while they may possess the faculty by concession of the respective local ordinary, presbyters who are members of religious institutes should not use it without the permission of their own superior. This permission they may presume unless the contrary is established.

Although the language of canon 874, §1 of the 1917 code, to which this canon corresponds, has been simplified, there is no restriction placed on the extent of the faculty: it is applicable for the benefit of all members of the faithful who fall within the authority of the grantor of the faculty. The required "special jurisdiction to hear, validly and licitly, the confessions of any women religious and novices whatsoever" of canon 876 of the 1917 code has simply been suppressed. Moreover, as already noted, once a presbyter receives the faculty from the local ordinary of his place of incardination or domicile on a habitual or regular basis, he possesses the faculty everywhere, in accord with canon 967, §2 and with the restriction mentioned there.

In paragraph two the same principle is applied to determine who, in addition to the local ordinary, may grant the faculty to presbyters in the case of penitents who are (1) members of a religious institute or of a society of apostolic life of pontifical right or (2) not members of the particular institute or society, but who live in the house of the institute or society. The rationale for the norm is convenience, illustrated by a reference in the 1917 code to those who dwell regularly in the

[57] See cc. 135–144.
[58] Canon 381, §2 collated with c. 368.

religious house "by reason of service, education, hospitality, or illness" (c. 514, §1).

The period of one's stay in the house of an institute or society need not be protracted—a single day suffices—in order to render operative the terms of the canon by which the superior may grant the faculty or, in the usual situation, by which the presbyter who has received such a faculty from his superior may exercise it to minister to an individual.[59]

The common law does not limit the concession of this faculty to major superiors, as defined in canon 620, but the constitutions may do so, since by cross reference paragraph two incorporates the full terms of canon 968, §2: "superiors of religious institutes or societies of apostolic life that are clerical and of pontifical right, who have executive power of governance according to the norm of their constitutions." As in the parallel case of paragraph two of the present canon, once a presbyter—whether a member of the institute or society or not—receives the faculty, he possesses it throughout the institute or society, in accord with canon 967, §3 and with the restriction mentioned there.

Qualifications of Ministers

Canon 970 — The faculty to hear confessions is not to be granted except to presbyters who are found to be suitable through an examination or whose suitability is otherwise evident.

The form of examination, written or oral, is not prescribed, nor is its precise content (moral and sacramental theology, with some attention to the presbyter's pastoral capabilities). In addition to the requisite knowledge, the minister must of course satisfy the other expectations of the law, such as the discretion and prudence mentioned in canon 979, the integrity of character which confidentiality demands (cc. 983–984), etc., along with a willingness to observe the canons and the liturgical law on the sacrament.

[59] Abbo-Hannan, *Sacred Canons* 1:524.

On the other hand, in countries like the United States where it is usual that all priests be conceded the faculty upon ordination without restriction as to the persons to be absolved or as to the occasions for the celebration of the sacrament, the evidence of qualifications for presbyteral ordination may serve the same purpose as the examination referred to here. See canons 1050–1052, especially canon 1051 concerning the testimonial to and inquiry into an ordinand's doctrine, piety, morals, suitability, and state of physical and psychological health. In other circumstances, it is for the local ordinary to determine the form of examination and the persons to conduct the examination (the former office of synodal examiners having been suppressed in the recodification); in the case of externs or religious he may be satisfied, for example, with the evidence of qualifications or other recommendation submitted by the respective ecclesiastical superiors.

Concession to Externs

Canon 971 — The local ordinary is not to grant the faculty of hearing confessions habitually to a presbyter, even one having a domicile or quasi-domicile in his jurisdiction, unless he has first heard the ordinary of the same presbyter insofar as possible.

The canon has in mind the common situation in which the local ordinary confers the (habitual) faculty upon diocesan presbyters incardinated elsewhere or upon presbyters who are members of religious institutes and societies of apostolic life. It does not demand that the priest have a domicile or quasi-domicile within the territory of the local ordinary—although it is only in the case of the concession to presbyters who do have a domicile in the grantor's territory that the terms of canon 967, §2 become operative. In the present canon, consultation with the presbyter's own ordinary is required, if possible, before the concession of the faculty. Even if the presbyter's own ordinary advises against the grant, the local ordinary may concede the faculty, provided the other canons, and especially canon 970, are observed; in the case of a religious, however, although the local ordinary may grant the faculty, the presbyter should not use it "without at least the presumed permission" of his superior, in accord with canon 969, §1.

The norm of canon 874, §2 of the 1917 code has been suppressed: on the one hand, it obliged local ordinaries not to give the faculty to religious who had not been formally presented by their own superior; on the other hand, it required local ordinaries not to deny the faculty, without grave cause, to religious thus presented.

Period of Concession

Canon 972 — The competent authority mentioned in can. 969 can grant the faculty to hear confessions for either an indefinite or a definite period of time.

The distinction here between an indefinite and a definite period of time is somewhat different from the concept of a habitual or regular concession of the faculty in the following canon and in canon 967, §2. The grant of the faculty for an extended period of time, but still limited ("definite"), may be considered a habitual faculty, as of course is any concession for an indefinite or unlimited period.

A limitation of time may be in relation to a specified period, for example, for a year or for a specified number of months; such a limitation may be more likely in the case of presbyters who are not incardinated in the diocese of the grantor or in the case of religious who serve during a protracted but not indefinite period in the diocese. The limitation of time may also be in such terms as "for as long as you remain in the diocese." If no such limitation is expressed, the concession is presumed to be for an indefinite period, and this is usual in the case of members of the local diocesan presbyterate, whose incardination is permanent or indefinite.

It is clear, moreover, that such simple cessation of the faculty because of the terms of its concession renders subsequent absolutions invalid, unless the presbyter has the faculty under another title.

Concession in Writing

Canon 973 — The faculty to hear confessions habitually is to be granted in writing.

This canon represents a somewhat stricter norm than the corresponding canon 879, §1 of the former code, which demanded only an express concession of the faculty whether in writing or orally ("for the valid hearing of confessions"). The revision makes a written grant obligatory if the faculty is to be habitual in character, but the requirement of a written concession is not necessary for the validity of the faculty. The canon is of course not retroactive in the case of those who have received the faculty by oral concession prior to the effective date of the code.

Canon 879, §2 of the 1917 code, which prohibited any charging of a fee or payment for the faculty, has been suppressed, but such a charge would be considered simoniacal.

Revocation and Cessation

Canon 974 — §1. The local ordinary and the competent superior are not to revoke the faculty to hear confessions habitually except for a grave cause.

§2. When the faculty to hear confessions has been revoked by the local ordinary who granted it as mentioned in can. 967, §2, a presbyter loses the faculty everywhere. If some other local ordinary has revoked the faculty, the presbyter loses it only in the territory of the one who revokes it.

§3. Any local ordinary who has revoked the faculty of some presbyter to hear confessions is to inform the proper ordinary of incardination of the presbyter or, if he is a member of a religious institute, his competent superior.

§4. If the proper major superior of a presbyter has revoked the faculty to hear confessions, the presbyter loses the faulty to hear the confessions of members of the institute everywhere. If some other competent superior has revoked the faculty, however, the presbyter loses it only with regard to the subjects in the jurisdiction of that superior.

Canon 975 — Besides by revocation, the faculty mentioned in can. 967, §2 ceases by loss of office, excardination, or loss of domicile.

The direct concern of canon 974, the first of these two canons, is the possible revocation of the faculty for cause. Although not specified here, the faculty also ceases, as is evident, either upon loss of office, if in accord with canon 968 the minister possesses the faculty by reason of his office, or upon completion of the period, if in accord with canons 969–973 he possesses it by concession and the concession has been made for a definite period of time.

With regard to revocation for cause, canon 974, §1 omits any mention of "suspension" of the faculty and so removes any possible dispute about validity or invalidity of the exercise of a suspended faculty. In effect, any kind of suspension must now be equated with revocation; a subsequent concession of the faculty, after the reasons for revocation have ceased, is treated as a new grant and is necessary for the validity of absolution.

The grave cause for revocation includes such matters as the transgression of the norms of the subsequent canons on the proper conduct of the minister, if the transgression is serious, or the loss of the qualifications mentioned in canon 970.

Both paragraphs two and four of canon 974, the meaning of which is evident, are new norms made necessary by the introduction of the concession of the faculty by law in canon 967, paragraphs two and three respectively, namely, the universal exercise of a habitual or regular faculty. On the other hand, paragraph three of canon 974 simply imposes upon local ordinaries an obligation of notification should they, for serious cause, revoke the fac-

ulty of an extern or of a member of a religious institute. The prescriptions of canon 880, §§2–3 of the 1917 code, concerning revocation or similar action in the case of a pastor, of the canon penitentiary, or of all the confessors of a religious house have been omitted as unnecessary or otherwise covered; a proposed paragraph five of canon 974, on loss of the faculty because of deprivation of office and the like, was not introduced.[60]

Finally, canon 975 again treats the specific case of canon 967, §2, in which ministers "can exercise that faculty everywhere unless the local ordinary has denied it in a particular case." If the ministers who enjoy this faculty habitually in virtue of office or by grant of the ordinary of the place of incardination or the place where they have a domicile lose that office, incardination, or domicile respectively, they also lose the faculty in other places—i.e., by revocation, loss of office, excardination, or loss of domicile. (The rather analogous case of canon 967, §3 is not mentioned in canon 975 because, in the situation in question, the loss of the faculty comes about by revocation, a matter specifically covered in canon 974, §4.)

Absolution in Danger of Death

Canon 976 — Even though a priest lacks the faculty to hear confessions, he absolves validly and licitly any penitents whatsoever in danger of death from any censures and sins, even if an approved priest is present.

As noted at the beginning of the commentary on this chapter, the second half of the norms, beginning with canon 976, deals with the exercise of the ministry by the priest (bishop or presbyter) who has the requisite faculty and with certain special cases and abuses.

Canon 976 is derived from canon 882 of the 1917 code, from which it does not differ substantially. The absolution from the ecclesiastical sanction of censure in the internal forum of the sacra-

[60] *Comm* 10 (1978) 63.

ment of penance has been mentioned at the beginning of the commentary on this title: it is distinct from the absolution of sins and in ordinary situations requires that the minister have a special faculty to remit a censure or censures.

The present canon, however, is all embracing: it attributes to every ordained priest the capacity to remit censures as well as to absolve from sins if a penitent is in danger of death. As understood in other contexts,[61] the danger of death does not mean that the person need be at the point of death or *in extremis*. As is clear, the final clause of canon 976 assures to the penitent in danger of death complete freedom in the choice of the available ministers of the sacrament. Finally, the revised canon has suppressed the norm that the absolution of an accomplice in these circumstances would be valid but illicit (*CIC* 884)[62] or that the penitent upon recovery would in certain circumstances be obliged to have further recourse (*CIC* 2252).

For the case of the penitent in danger of death seeking reconciliation from a minister who is not a Catholic, see canon 844, §2.

Absolution of an Accomplice

Canon 977 — The absolution of an accomplice in a sin against the sixth commandment of the Decalogue is invalid except in danger of death.

As noted under the preceding canon, the norm of canon 977 no longer declares illicit the absolution of an accomplice who is in danger of death.[63] In all other cases it is both illicit and invalid for a priest to absolve an accomplice, female or male, from a sin against the sixth commandment in which he and the penitent have been accomplices. There is no further restriction under pain of invalidity of absolution if the minister absolves an ac-

---

[61] See c. 1004, §1.

[62] Benedict XIV, apconst *Sacramentum poenitentiae,* June 1, 1741, Document III among the documents appended to the 1917 code.

[63] Ibid.

complice from other sins—whatever may be the impropriety. The matter is treated in detail by moral and pastoral theologians.

In addition to the prohibition in this canon, see canon 1378, §1 for the sanction for such a transgression, namely, automatic (*latae sententiae*) excommunication reserved to the Apostolic See.

Ministry of the Confessor

Canon 978 — §1. In hearing confessions the priest is to remember that he is equally a judge and a physician and has been established by God as a minister of divine justice and mercy, so that he has regard for the divine honor and the salvation of souls.

§2. In administering the sacrament, the confessor as a minister of the Church is to adhere faithfully to the doctrine of the magisterium and the norms issued by competent authority.

Canon 979 — In posing questions, the priest is to proceed with prudence and discretion, attentive to the condition and age of the penitent, and is to refrain from asking the name of an accomplice.

Canon 980 — If the confessor has no doubt about the disposition of the penitent, and the penitent seeks absolution, absolution is to be neither refused nor deferred.

The three canons quoted above form a unit to describe and direct the exercise of the ministry of reconciliation by priests.

Canon 978, §1 gives equal weight to the minister's role as judge and as healer. The *Roman Ritual* enlarges upon the conduct of the minister, placing the judgmental role in a somewhat secondary position:

In order that he may fulfill his ministry properly and faithfully, understand the disorders of souls and apply the appropriate remedies to them, and act as a wise judge, the confessor must acquire the needed knowledge and prudence by constant study under the guidance of the Church's magisterium and especially by praying fervently to God. For the discernment of spirits is indeed a deep knowledge of God's working in the human heart, a gift of the Spirit, and an effect of charity. . . .

By receiving repentant sinners and leading them to the light of the truth, the confessor fulfills a paternal function: he reveals the heart of the Father and reflects the image of Christ the Good Shepherd. He should keep in mind that he has been entrusted with the ministry of Christ, who accomplished the saving work of human redemption by mercy and by his power is present in the sacraments.[64]

The second paragraph of canon 978 is new and reflects the text of the ritual. The magisterium referred to is presumed to be the official or episcopal magisterium, as exercised by the pope and the other bishops, singly or together, in ordinary or more solemn mode. Attention has to be given to the gradations in the weight of such teaching; see canons 749–750, 752–754. What was once understood to be the magisterium of theologians is not mentioned as such in the canons, although common adherence of the Christian faithful under leadership of the sacred magisterium is affirmed as an element in holding to the one deposit of faith (c. 750).

In some ways the concern for orthodox doctrine, especially as regards moral teaching, in the context of sacramental confession and ministerial counsel differs from the concern for orthodoxy in preaching, catechesis, or other teaching. On the occasion of the sacrament of penance, and specifically on the occasion of auricular confession, there is a special importance in avoiding any disturbance of the penitent's conscience by the aberrant opinions of the minister, whether these are rigid or lax. The mention of the norms issued by

authority refers to the juridical norms emanating, for example, from the diocesan bishop or the conference of bishops or found in the common law.

Canon 979 which follows is a simpler version of canon 888, §2 of the 1917 code: the priest "is to avoid entirely any inquiry concerning the name of the [penitent's] accomplice, pressing anyone with prying or useless questions, above all those concerned with the sixth commandment, and especially imprudent questions addressed to young persons about matters of which they are ignorant." Though now stated more briefly, the intent of the norm and exhortation in canon 979 remains the same as before.

Although inquiry in the course of sacramental confession about the identity of an accomplice was not uncommon in some places during the eighteenth century, it could easily lead to violation of confidentiality, as demanded in canons 983–984, and was therefore condemned as a serious abuse on the part of confessors.[65]

Finally, canon 980 affirms the presumption that the penitent has confessed his or her sins in good faith and has the requisite disposition. This does not restrict the judgmental authority of the minister in the case of the penitent who refuses to express sorrow or resolution of amendment of life. Even in these circumstances, however, the minister should make every effort to move and assist the penitent toward the proper disposition, namely, a true conversion of life.

A 1997 curial document may supplement canons 978–980 for confessors in cases involving aspects of married life and the sacrament of reconciliation.[66]

---

[64] *RPenance* 10 a and c, *DOL* 3075; on the presence of Christ, see *SC* 7.

[65] Among the sources of *CIC* 888, §2: Benedict XIV, ency *Suprema,* July 7, 1745; apconst *Ubi primam,* June 2, 1746; *Ad eradicandum,* September 28, 1746; *Apostolici ministerii,* December 9, 1749; *CICFontes* 360, 370, 373, 405, respectively. These documents and *Sacramentum poenitentiae* (appended to *CIC*) indicate the extreme seriousness of violations or potential violations of the discipline of this sacrament, and specifically of the sacramental seal.

[66] PCF, "Vade Mecum for Confessors Concerning Some Aspects of the Morality of Conjugal Life," March 1, 1997, *Origins* 26 (1997) 617, 619–625.

Penances or Acts of Satisfaction

Canon 981 — The confessor is to impose salutary and suitable penances in accord with the quality and number of sins, taking into account the condition of the penitent. The penitent is obliged to fulfill these personally.

The act or acts of the penitent called satisfaction or, commonly, the "penance" had to take place, in the ancient tradition and specifically in the case of grave and public offenses, during the period between the act of confession and the later reconciliation and absolution. In the development of the sacrament the act came to be postponed until after the sacramental absolution; instead the imposition of the act of satisfaction and its acceptance (i.e., the stated or implied will to fulfill the penance) suffice before sacramental reconciliation. The doctrine is expressed in the *Rite of Penance* of the *Roman Ritual* in this language:

> True conversion is completed by expiation for the sins committed, by amendment of life, and also by rectifying injuries done. The kind and extent of the expiation must be suited to the personal condition of penitents so that they may restore the order they have upset and through the corresponding remedy be cured of the sickness from which they have suffered. Therefore, it is necessary that the act of penance really be a remedy for sin and a help to renewal of life. Thus penitents, "forgetting the things that are behind" (Phil 3:13), again become part of the mystery of salvation and press on to the things that are to come.[67]

Aside from the kind of restitution or reparation for the evil that has been directly done by the sin-

ful act of the penitent, the choice of the act or satisfaction is left to the discretion of the minister (who may, according to circumstances, leave the further choice of a specific and appropriate act to the penitent). It may be a charitable or other virtuous action, prayer, or fasting, but its correspondence to the extent and character of the sins confessed and the particular capacity of the individual penitent must be judged by the confessor.

The present canon follows canon 887 of the former law with slight changes of language. In the 1917 code there was explicit mention of the penitent's "willing acceptance" of the penance or act of satisfaction directed by the confessor. Although this has been suppressed, the refusal of the penitent to perform the proposed penance would, in the case of the confession of grave sins, be reason for the minister not to absolve. In both the former and the revised law the mention of "suitable penances" and the "condition of the penitent" suggests that the confessor not excessively burden the penitent whose resolution seems weak or who is otherwise limited and, of course, the penitent who is sick or dying.

This whole matter is further explained in the *Rite of Penance:*

> A penitent who has been the cause of harm or scandal to others is to be led by the priest to resolve to make due restitution.
>
> Next, the priest imposes an act of penance or expiation on the penitent; this should serve not only as atonement for past sins but also as an aid to new life and an antidote for weakness. As far as possible, therefore, the penance should correspond to the seriousness and nature of the sins. This act of penance may suitably take the form of prayer, self-denial, and especially service to neighbor and works of mercy. These will underline the fact that sin and its forgiveness have a social aspect.[68]

---

[67] *RPenance* 8c, *DOL* 3071. See Trent, sess. XIV, *de poenitentia,* cap. 8; Paul VI, apconst *Indulgentiarum doctrina,* January 1, 1967, nn. 2–3, *AAS* 59 (1967) 5–24, *DOL* 3156–3157.

[68] *RPenance* 18, *DOL* 3083.

False Denunciation of Confessors

Canon 982 — Whoever confesses to have denounced falsely an innocent confessor to ecclesiastical authority concerning the crime of solicitation to sin against the sixth commandment of the Decalogue is not to be absolved unless the person has first formally retracted the false denunciation and is prepared to repair damages if there are any.

Both the crime of solicitation, as here defined, and the false denunciation with which canon 982 is concerned are the subject of canonical sanctions as well. The priest who is guilty of the crime of solicitation "in the act, on the occasion, or under the pretext of confession" is to be punished according to canon 1387 (suspension, prohibitions, and deprivations in accord with the seriousness of the offense and, in more serious cases, dismissal from the clerical state). The penitent, female or male, who falsely accuses a confessor of this crime before ecclesiastical authority is punished, in accord with canon 1390, §1, with a *latae sententiae* interdict and, if a cleric, by suspension as well. (With regard to the different question of the validity of absolution of an accomplice, see c. 977.)

Canon 982 itself deals only with the absolution from sin of a penitent who confesses having committed false denunciation. The condition for absolution is twofold: (1) In this instance the law requires that the act of satisfaction—here formal retraction of the denunciation before an ecclesiastical authority—must have taken place before the confessor may absolve. (2) It is not necessary that other elements of damage to the falsely denounced confessor be repaired before absolution, but the penitent must declare himself or herself prepared to make such reparation.

Formerly the absolution from false denunciation was the only instance of an absolution from sin reserved by the common law to the Apostolic See, and canon 894 of the 1917 code on this matter appeared in the now suppressed chapter on the

reservation of sins. The reservation has ceased in virtue of the present canon and has been replaced by the stated conditions for absolution.

A related canon of the 1917 code, on the obligation of reporting an actual case of solicitation to the local ordinary or to the Apostolic See, has been suppressed, and the relevant constitution of Benedict XIV, *Sacramentum poenitentiae,*[69] is no longer a part of the common law. These changes, however, do not alter the gravity or nature of the sin of solicitation or of false denunciation, as treated by moral theologians in the light of the teaching of Benedict XIV.

Confidentiality of Confession

Canon 983 — §1. The sacramental seal is inviolable; therefore it is absolutely forbidden for a confessor to betray in any way a penitent in words or in any manner and for any reason.
§2. The interpreter, if there is one, and all others who in any way have knowledge of sins from confession are also obliged to observe secrecy.

Canon 984 — §1. A confessor is prohibited completely from using knowledge acquired from confession to the detriment of the penitent even when any danger of revelation is excluded.
§2. A person who has been placed in authority cannot use in any manner for external governance the knowledge about sins which he has received in confession at any time.

The two canons, 983 and 984, deal with distinct aspects of the confidentiality which the minister—and others who may obtain similar knowledge from the celebration of this sacrament—must maintain with regard to matters learned from the individual confession of sins by penitents. Canon 983 is concerned with any kind of betrayal of a penitent, whose confession of sins is said to be under or protected by an inviolable sacramental seal, and this even if he or she has not been ab-

[69] June 1, 1741. See note 62, above, and *CIC* 904.

solved. It is any betrayal of a person who has simply confessed in the context of the sacrament.

Canon 984 is next concerned with other use of knowledge obtained in the course of the individual celebration of the sacrament, even when there is no disclosure of a person's sins, that is, without any betrayal of sacramental confidentiality.

The two canons, it should be noted, do not touch upon extra-sacramental confidentiality, to which the ordained minister is bound as is any recipient of confidences, but bound even more so when the relationship of the minister to the individual is analogous to that of a professional counselor or other professional person.

First, canon 983, §1 gives a definition of the seal of the sacrament. In order to stress the gravity of the violation of the norm, without entering into the question of the gravity of the moral guilt (which is left to moral theologians), the canon uses the strong word *nefas* (criminal, abominable). Neither the canon nor earlier interpretations admit exceptions to the norm; this is the intent of the emphasis: "in any way...in words or in any manner and for any reason." No distinction is made among the matters confessed, whether the sinful action itself or attendant circumstances, or the acts of satisfaction or penances imposed, etc. The secrecy to be maintained concerning the penitent and his or her confession of sins is properly described as total.

In another context, that of ecclesiastical sanctions, without lessening the obligatory force of canon 983, §1, a distinction is made between direct and indirect violations of sacramental confidentiality. A direct violation, namely, one in which the penitent's identity becomes known or may readily become known (e.g., from the circumstances described or by implication) is punished by the *latae sententiae* excommunication of the minister, with remission of the canonical penalty reserved to the Apostolic See, in accord with canon 1388, §1. The same canon states that an indirect violation of the seal, namely, when there is only some slighter possibility or danger that the penitent may be betrayed, "is to be pun-

ished according to the gravity of the delict." Canon 983, §1 proscribes both direct and indirect violations of sacramental confidentiality.

The sacramental seal is also referred to briefly but forcefully in the ritual: "Conscious that he has come to know the secret of another's conscience only because he is God's minister, the confessor is bound by the obligation of preserving the seal of confession absolutely unbroken."[70]

The obligation of the canon is not affected by a contrary disposition of civil law in jurisdictions where communications to an ordained minister, whether sacramental or extra-sacramental, are not considered privileged at law.[71]

Since canon 990 permits (but does not oblige) penitents to confess their sins through interpreters, the latter are mentioned explicitly in paragraph two of canon 983, although the inviolability of the sacramental secrecy extends equally to all who, deliberately or indeliberately, accidentally or in any other way, come to a knowledge of sins from confession. Canon 889, §2 of the 1917 code has been somewhat rephrased so that the obligation of confidentiality which persons other than the minister have is no longer called the sacramental seal.

In this case, that of a person other than the minister himself, the canonical sanction differs from that incurred by the minister, as described above. Other persons who betray a penitent "are to be punished with a just penalty, not excluding excommunication," in accord with canon 1388, §2.

In canon 984, the second of the two related canons, other use of knowledge gained from a penitent's confession of sins may be permitted— or, according to a more prudent judgment, tolerated—only if there is no danger of revelation (i.e., of the matters disclosed in the confession and the identity of the penitent) and if no harm will come to the penitent from the confessor's use of infor-

---

[70] *RPenance* 10d, *DOL* 3075.
[71] See *Origins* 26 (1997) 537, 539–545, for a ruling of the 9th U. S. Circuit Court of Appeals, dated January 27, 1997, in which the confidentiality of sacramental confession is upheld at civil law.

cc. 983-986

mation. Any other use of such knowledge, even if it does not constitute a direct or indirect violation of the sacramental seal of canon 983, §1, is entirely prohibited by canon 984, §1.

The sense of paragraph one of canon 984 is that the confessor may come to the knowledge of various types of incidental information in the course of a confession or confessions. Such information may not be disclosed or even used in any way that may be detrimental to the penitent; an instance might be the use of such information in a way advantageous to the confessor, always excluding any hurt or disadvantage to the penitent.

An older instruction of the Holy Office counseled against even references in the course of preaching to matters learned in confession: even though all danger of disclosure or injury might be absent, the broad confidence of penitents in the inviolability of the sacramental secrecy might be lessened.[72] As an example, a preacher might legitimately employ information learned from confession for illustrative purposes, provided there is no possibility that the transgression might be linked to a given individual penitent; even in this case, however, if the preacher does indicate that the source of the information is a confession, he might weaken the confidence of his hearers in the inviolability of the sacramental seal.

In paragraph two of canon 984 the prohibition against the use of knowledge about sins, as distinct from any other knowledge, is directed toward ecclesiastical authorities of all kinds, lest they employ such knowledge, quite apart from any disclosure of sins, in external governance. As is evident from a reading of the text, the norm is applicable whether the action of the superior is to the advantage or disadvantage of the penitent.

Restriction of Confessors

Canon 985 — The director of novices and his associate and the rector of a seminary or other institute of education are not to hear the sacramen-

[72] June 9, 1915, *ME* 29 (1917) 199–201.

tal confessions of their students residing in the same house unless the students freely request it in particular cases.

The purpose of the prohibition contained in the present canon is clear: to assure the freedom of choice of a confessor by penitents, in accord with canon 991, in the case of special relationships which might be intimidating to a penitent or might create a needless burden for a penitent. Canon 985 does relax somewhat the norm of canon 891 of the former law, which it otherwise follows: the 1917 code permitted the persons named in the canon to hear confessions only if requested "spontaneously, in particular cases, and for a grave and urgent cause." The third of these conditions has been suppressed.

Canon 240, §2 deals with a related matter in the formation of ordained ministers, namely, that the opinion of spiritual directors and confessors may never be sought when it is a question of admission to orders or dismissal from seminaries. In addition, canon 630, §4 simply prohibits religious superiors from hearing the confessions of those subject to their authority unless requested upon the penitent's own initiative.

Responsibility for the Ministry of Reconciliation

Canon 986 — §1. All to whom the care of souls has been entrusted in virtue of some function are obliged to make provision so that the confessions of the faithful entrusted to them are heard when they reasonably seek to be heard and that they have the opportunity to approach individual confession on days and at times established for their convenience.

§2. In urgent necessity, any confessor is obliged to hear the confessions of the Christian faithful, and in danger of death, any priest is so obliged.

The canon corresponds to canon 892 of the 1917 code, except that a moral distinction of obligations, out of justice (*CIC* 892, §1) or out of charity (*CIC* 892, §2), has been omitted; the distinction is not necessarily a matter for canonical determination. The norms of canon 986 are of course an application of ministerial obligations determined in canon 843, §1 to the sacramental ministry of penance. In addition, paragraph one reflects a recent pastoral concern that more generous opportunities for auricular confession be available. Thus there is new language in the text: "and that they [the Christian faithful] have the opportunity to approach individual confession on days and at times established for their convenience." The obligation of paragraph one rests with those who have the care of souls, and it is an obligation to make provision for the sacrament even though they may not in every case celebrate the sacrament personally with penitents.

A similar but briefer statement appears in the *Rite of Penance:* "The confessor should always show himself to be ready and willing to hear the confessions of the faithful whenever they reasonably request this."[73] More directly, the pastoral norms on penance (1972) had stated: "To enable the faithful to fulfill without difficulty the obligation of individual confession, steps are to be taken to ensure that there are confessors available in places of worship on days and at times assigned for the convenience of the faithful."[74]

Although the practice of establishing fixed times for the celebration of individual reconciliation is required by paragraph one, this practice does not completely satisfy the obligation of those mentioned in that paragraph: it is also an obligation to hear the confessions of any of the faithful who reasonably seek this at times other than those scheduled. It has to be presumed that such requests are reasonable.

In addition, the otherwise appropriate practice of scheduling appointments for individual confessions does not excuse from the requirement of the

designated "days and…times established for their [the faithful's] convenience," for example, before Sundays and feasts and on penitential occasions (below). The scheduled times should not be during the eucharistic celebration, and the following norms of the liturgical law are pertinent:

> The reconciliation of penitents may be celebrated in all liturgical seasons and on any day. But it is right that the faithful be informed of the day and hours at which the priest is available for this ministry. They should be encouraged to approach the sacrament of penance at times when Mass is not being celebrated ["so that the administration of the sacrament may be unhurried and that people will not be impeded from active participation in the Mass"] and preferably at the scheduled times.

> Lent is the season most appropriate for celebrating the sacrament of penance. Already on Ash Wednesday the people of God hear the solemn invitation, "Turn away from sin and be faithful to the Gospel." It is therefore fitting to have several penitential services during Lent, so that all the faithful may have an opportunity to be reconciled with God and their neighbor and so be able to celebrate the paschal mystery in the Easter triduum with renewed hearts.[75]

The tradition of celebrating the sacrament of reconciliation in the week before Easter, in particular on Holy Thursday before the beginning of the Easter triduum, should also be taken into account.

In paragraph two of this canon a distinction is made between a confessor and any other priest. The confessor referred to is a bishop or, if he has the necessary faculty, a presbyter. Thus the terms of the canon are that any confessor is obliged to hear confessions in cases of urgent necessity.

---

[73] *RPenance* 10b, *DOL* 3075.

[74] N. IX, *DOL* 3047. See also n. XII: Priests "are to extol its ['devotional' confession's] great benefits for the Christian life and to make it clear that they are always ready to hear such confessions whenever the faithful request," *DOL* 3050.

[75] *RPenance* 13, *DOL* 3078; the words quoted in brackets are the explanation given in SCRit, instr *Eucharisticum mysterium,* May 25, 1967, *AAS* 59 (1967) 539–573, n. 35, *DOL* 1264.

"Any priest" includes those who lack the faculty to absolve and describes the obligation in danger of death, in conformity with canon 976.

CHAPTER III
THE PENITENT
[cc. 987–991]

Only five canons treat the member of the faithful who confesses his or her sins and seeks absolution: a single canon on the penitent's disposition (c. 987) is followed by two canons on the obligation to confess (cc. 988–989), a canon on the possibility or option of confessing with the intervention of an interpreter (c. 990), and a final canon on the penitent's freedom of choice in the selection of a minister (c. 991).

On the matter of "ecumenical" sharing of sacraments, and specifically the sacrament of penance, with Christians of other churches and ecclesial communities, see canon 844, §§1–4.

The canons correspond rather closely to the chapter of the 1917 code (*CIC* 901–907) entitled "The Subject of the Sacrament of Penance," with some omissions: (1) canon 902, which defined "sufficient but not necessary matter" for the sacrament, namely, mortal sins already confessed and venial sins—the definition remains accurate but is not needed canonically; (2) canon 904, as already noted in the commentary on canon 982, so that the canonical obligation to denounce a confessor guilty of the crime of solicitation in confession is now suppressed; and (3) canon 907, which stated that one could not satisfy the precept of confessing sins by a sacrilegious or voluntarily null confession.

The norms of this chapter—aside from oblique references to general confession and absolution—are for individual confessions of sins. For norms affecting the penitent in the case of general absolution without prior specific confession of sins, see canons 961–963. The exposition of the *Roman Ritual,* over and above what is said about the penitential ministry of the whole Church (quoted at the beginning of the commentary on

this title of the code), may serve as introduction to the canons:

> The parts that penitents themselves have in the celebration of the sacrament are of the greatest importance.
>
> When with the proper dispositions they approach this saving remedy instituted by Christ and confess their sins, their own acts become part of the sacrament itself, which is completed when the words of absolution are spoken by the minister in the name of Christ.
>
> In this way the faithful, even as they experience and proclaim the mercy of God in their own life, are celebrating with the priest the liturgy of the Church's self-renewal.[76]

In this connection, the reform of the rite of individual confession, as decreed by Vatican II in *Sacrosanctum Concilium* 72, embraces liturgical elements not found in the 1614 *Roman Ritual.* These directly affect the penitent and make the celebration a prayerful act of public worship as well as a healing source of grace for the penitent:

> (1) A less formal welcome to the penitent has been introduced so that the priest may greet penitent Christians "with fraternal charity and, if need be, address them with friendly words." The sign of the cross is followed by some form of exhortation by the priest to the penitent to have confidence in God. Then "penitents who are unknown to the priest are advised to inform him of their state of life [for example, if they are married persons, ordained ministers, or religious], the time of their last confession, their difficulties in leading the Christian life, and anything that may help the confessor in the exercise of his ministry."[77]
>
> (2) A brief reading of the word of God by the priest or the penitent is an optional part of

[76] *RPenance* 11, *DOL* 3076.
[77] *RPenance* 16, *DOL* 3081.

the rite at this point: "For through the word of God Christians receive light to recognize their sins and are called to conversion and to confidence in God's mercy."[78]

(3) After the confession of sins and acceptance of penance, a distinct prayer for forgiveness, in the penitent's own words or in some set form of prayer, is singled out in the revised rite as a distinct ritual element: "Next, through a prayer for God's pardon the penitent expresses contrition and the resolution to begin a new life. It is advantageous for this prayer to be based on the words of Scripture."[79] For this reason, examples or models of such a prayer are given in the *Rite of Penance*.[80]

(4) After the prayer of sorrow and for forgiveness and after the form of absolution (explained above at the beginning of this commentary on the sacrament), accompanied by the ritual laying on of the minister's hands (or at least right hand), the celebration concludes with a proclamation of praise by the minister and the penitent ("Give thanks to the Lord, for he is good." R. "His mercy endures for ever.") and a liturgical dismissal. Finally, "the penitent continues the conversion thus begun and expresses it by a life renewed according to the Gospel and more and more steeped in the love of God, for 'love covers a multitude of sins' (1 Pt 4:8)."[81]

Because the sacrament of penance, as a liturgical celebration even in the case of individual confession, involves priest and penitent in a dialogue, the canons on the penitent have to be understood in the context of the preceding chapter on the minister. In that chapter, for example, the minister's imposition of an act of penance or satisfaction, in accord with canon 981, must be understood as coupled with the penitent's acceptance of this act and resolution to carry it out.

Disposition of the Penitent

Canon 987 — To receive the salvific remedy of the sacrament of penance, a member of the Christian faithful must be disposed in such a way that, rejecting sins committed and having a purpose of amendment, the person is turned back to God.

As is evident, the canon, which was newly redacted for the recodification, can give only a succinct statement of the requisite conditions of disposition that the penitent must have, just as *Sacrosanctum Concilium* 11 can speak only in general about the disposition of all who celebrate the liturgy. Under the consideration of the parts of the sacrament prior to the act of absolution and reconciliation, the ritual enlarges upon the requisite elements—both of spiritual disposition and of submission to the Church's ministry:

> The most important act of the penitent is contrition, which is "heartfelt sorrow and aversion for the sin committed along with the intention of sinning no more."[82] "We can only approach the Kingdom of Christ by *metanoia*. This is a profound change of the whole person by which we begin to consider, judge, and arrange our life according to the holiness and love of God, made manifest in his Son in the last days and given to us in abundance" (see Heb 1:2; Col 1:19 and passim; Eph 1:23 and passim).[83] The genuineness of penance depends on this heartfelt contrition. For conversion should affect a person from within toward a progressively deeper enlightenment and an ever-closer likeness to Christ.

The sacrament of penance includes the confession of sins, which comes from true

---

[78] *RPenance* 17, *DOL* 3082.
[79] *RPenance* 19, *DOL* 3084.
[80] *RPenance* 45, 85–92.
[81] *RPenance* 20, *DOL* 3085.

[82] See Trent, sess. XIV, *de poenitentia,* cap. 4.
[83] Paul VI, apconst *Paenitemini,* February 17, 1966, *AAS* 58 (1966) 179, *DOL* 3017–3030.

knowledge of self before God and from contrition for those sins. However, the inner examination of heart and the outward accusation must be made in the light of God's mercy. Confession requires on the penitent's part the will to open the heart to the minister of God and on the minister's part a spiritual judgment by which, acting in the person of Christ, he pronounces his decision of forgiveness or retention of sins in accord with the power of the keys.

True conversion is completed by expiation for the sins committed, by amendment of life, and also by rectifying injuries done. The kind and extent of this expiation must be suited to the personal condition of the penitents so that they may restore the order that they have upset and through the corresponding remedy be cured of the sickness from which they suffered [see c. 981]. Therefore, it is necessary that the act of penance really be a remedy for sin and a help to renewal of life. Thus penitents, "forgetting the things that are behind" (Phil 3:13), again become part of the mystery of salvation and press on to the things that are to come.[84]

Finally, the ritual attempts to balance the more evident effects of the sacrament upon the penitent as an individual and the ecclesial significance referred to in canons 959–960:

Just as the wounds of sin are varied and multiple in the life of individuals and the community, so too the healing that penance provides is varied. Those who by grave sin have withdrawn from communion with God in love are called back in the sacrament of penance to the life they have lost. And those who, experiencing their weakness daily, fall into venial sins draw strength from a repeated celebration of penance to reach the full freedom of the children of God....

[84] RPenance 6, DOL 3071.

In order that this sacrament of healing may truly achieve its purpose among the faithful, it must take root in their entire life and move them to more fervent service of God and neighbor.

The celebration of this sacrament is thus always an act in which the Church proclaims its faith, gives thanks to God for the freedom with which Christ has made us free (see Gal 4:31), and offers its life as a spiritual sacrifice in praise of God's glory, as it hastens to meet the Lord Jesus.[85]

Obligation of the Penitent to Confess

Canon 988 — §1. A member of the Christian faithful is obliged to confess in kind and number all grave sins committed after baptism and not yet remitted directly through the keys of the Church nor acknowledged in individual confession, of which the person has knowledge after diligent examination of conscience.

§2. It is recommended to the Christian faithful that they also confess venial sins.

Canon 989 — After having reached the age of discretion, each member of the faithful is obliged to confess faithfully his or her grave sins at least once a year.

The first of these two canons is derived from canons 901–902 of the 1917 code, but with considerable reworking of the texts and, as already noted, without an explicit definition of "sufficient but not necessary matter" for the sacrament.[86]

In paragraph one of canon 988 the phrase "in kind and number" has been added to the earlier text, in order to make explicit the obligation of the penitent to inform the minister of the nature and number of grave sins being confessed so that he may make his judgment with sufficient knowledge. The phrase in question replaces the norm of canon 901 of the 1917 code, which required the

[85] RPenance 7, DOL 3072.
[86] See Comm 10 (1978) 70–71.

penitent to "explain in confession the circumstances which may change the species of sin." The penitent is not directly obliged to indicate the circumstances of the sins in themselves, provided that he or she expresses clearly the nature and kind of sin that is confessed.

The reference to sins "not yet remitted directly through the keys of the Church," i.e., through the power and ministry of the Church, indicates the precise nature of the confessional obligation. Divine forgiveness for the sin may already have taken place; the contrition of the penitent may have been such that he or she has indeed been pardoned by God. Nevertheless, the obligation remains to submit oneself to the power and ministry of the Church in the sacrament of reconciliation. Moreover, although grave sins forgotten and thus omitted at the time of confession are indirectly remitted, the canon indicates that these too must be confessed when remembered and thus be submitted for "direct remission."

No judgment is made in the canon (or elsewhere in the law) whether such grave sins may be few or many; the distinction is at another level, namely, that grave sins committed after baptism must at some point be confessed. See the commentary on canon 960 for the law's recognition that there may be a physical or moral impossibility which excuses from the obligation expressed here in paragraph one of canon 988.

Finally, the phrase "nor acknowledged in individual confession" has been added to the original language to emphasize, in accord with canons 962, §1 and 963, that, despite the generic confession of sins before general sacramental absolution, the obligation of individually confessing grave sins remains—although they have already been remitted in the sacrament of penance in the rite of general absolution.[87]

The norm of canon 988, §1 is expressed in the ritual in less juridic terms but to the same effect: "To obtain the saving remedy of the sacrament of penance, according to the plan of our merciful God, the faithful must confess to a priest each and

every grave sin that they remember after a diligent examination of conscience."[88]

According to canon 916, those conscious of grave sin not yet confessed are not to celebrate Mass or receive Holy Communion "without previous sacramental confession unless there is a grave reason and there is no opportunity to confess; in this case the person is to remember the obligation to make an act of perfect contrition which includes the resolution of confessing as soon as possible."

It is not for canon law to determine what sins, including transgressions of the ecclesiastical law itself, are grave and what sins are non-grave or venial.[89] A contemporary statement of the International Theological Commission is to the point:

Already in the parenesis and the practice of the early Christian communities distinctions were made:

a. sins which exclude from the Kingdom of God, such as leading an immoral life, idolatry, adultery, pederasty, avarice, and so on (cf. 1 Cor 6:9f.), and which also lead to exclusion from the community (cf. 1 Cor 5:1–13);

b. the so-called daily sins (*peccata quotidiana*).

The fundamental difference between grave and non-grave sins is taught by the entire tradition of the Church, even if important differences in terminology [e.g., grave, mortal, lethal, etc.] and in the appraisal of individual sins occur.[90]

A careful distinction is drawn between the two paragraphs of canon 988. Any canonical obliga-

---

[87] Ibid.

[88] *RPenance* 7a, *DOL* 3072; see Trent, sess. XIV, *de poenitentia*, cc. 7–8.

[89] See *Rel*, 234.

[90] Report, 1983, C, III, 2, *Origins* 13 (1984) 523; see also, on the canonical avoidance of distinctions between "grave" and "mortal" sins, *Comm* 10 (1978) 70.

tion to confess is limited to grave sins, in accord with paragraph one. But in paragraph two there is a recommendation that venial sins (and, as is understood, grave sins that have already been directly remitted) be confessed, either in so-called confessions of devotion or in connection with the confession of a grave sin.

The *Rite of Penance* enlarges upon this recommendation:

> The frequent and careful celebration of this sacrament is also very useful as a remedy for venial sins. This is not a mere ritual repetition or psychological exercise, but a serious striving to perfect the grace of baptism so that, as we bear in our body the death of Jesus Christ, his life may be seen in us ever more clearly [see 2 Cor 4:10]. In confession of this kind, penitents who accuse themselves of venial faults should try to be more closely conformed to Christ and to follow the voice of the Spirit more attentively.[91]

It is in accord with this understanding of the sacrament, as remedy for sins both grave and lesser, that penitents are encouraged to repeat at least generically the confession of past venial (or even grave) sins and to follow on occasion the practice of a general confession, in the sense of a confession of the sins of one's life or of an extended period of one's life.

The forgiveness of venial sins may of course be sought and obtained in many non-sacramental ways, aside from the Eucharist or penance, through both individual and communal acts, none of which is excluded by the exhortation of canon 988, §2. This recommendation of paragraph two, however, is based upon an understanding of the altogether distinct nature of sacramental reconciliation with God and the Church, a special appreciation of the doctrine of sacramental grace, and the teaching of Vatican II. In another context, while praising extra-liturgical communal and individual acts of devotions, the council asserted that the

liturgy (above all, the Eucharist and the other sacraments) "by its very nature far surpasses any of them."[92] Similarly, without denigrating any of the other means or occasions of divine forgiveness, canon 988, §2 urges the celebration of the sacrament of penance even in the case of the confession of venial sins only.

For related norms concerning ordained ministers, see canon 276, §2, 5°; concerning students for the ordained ministry, see canon 246, §4; concerning religious, see canon 664; concerning members of secular institutes, see canon 719, §3. Also related to canon 988 is the reference in canon 914 to sacramental confession preceding the first communion of children who have reached the use of reason. If the child is conscious of grave sin, he or she is bound by canon 988, §1 (and c. 916); otherwise, in the absence of any consciousness of grave sin, canon 914 may be understood in the light of canon 988, §2, namely, as a recommendation but without any canonical obligation to confess.

The second of the above canons, canon 989, specifies the time when the obligation of canon 988, §1 is to be fulfilled, but without suggesting that it is desirable to postpone the confession of a grave sin for a period of an entire year. The canon is rephrased from canon 906 of the 1917 code, itself based upon the norm introduced by the Fourth Lateran Council in 1215.[93] The former norm was somewhat more specific, defining the age of discretion in terms of attaining the use of reason; in effect, the possible obligation begins when one becomes capable of committing grave sin. The present law states, in canon 97, §2, that "with the completion of the seventh year... [one] is presumed to have the use of reason." Once that presumption is fulfilled and the age of discretion is attained, if one then should commit a grave sin, the canon requires that he or she confess at least within a year. The

---

[91] *RPenance* 7b, *DOL* 3072.

[92] *SC* 13.

[93] Const. 21: "Each member of the faithful, of both sexes, after he or she has reached the years of discretion, is to confess individually [*solus*] all his or her sins at least once a year."

failure of the earlier law to make clear that this obligation of annual confession is applicable only in the case of grave sins has now been corrected in the text of canon 989.[94]

The canon is entirely distinct from the precept of Easter communion in canon 920 (now somewhat mitigated as to time or liturgical season of fulfillment), which obliges once a person has completed his or her Christian initiation through receiving the Holy Eucharist.

Confession through an Interpreter

Canon 990 — No one is prohibited from confessing through an interpreter as long as abuses and scandals are avoided and without prejudice to the prescript of can. 983, §2.

The canon permits, but does not require, that a penitent make use of the service of an interpreter if the minister, for example, does not know or know well the penitent's language. The choice remains that of the penitent. If the penitent is unwilling to use the services of an interpreter, the integral confession of sins may be morally impossible, in accord with canon 960. The cross reference to canon 983, §2 is concerned with the obligation of secrecy incurred by an interpreter.

Freedom to Choose a Confessor

Canon 991 — Every member of the Christian faithful is free to confess sins to a legitimately approved confessor of his or her choice, even to one of another rite.

The final canon of the chapter articulates and assures a right of the Christian believer to a free choice of a confessor or, put negatively, not to be obliged to confess to a confessor designated by an ecclesiastical superior and not to be coerced in any way in the choice of a minister of individual

confession. See canon 240, §1 for an application of this norm in seminaries, canon 630 for an application in religious communities.

Since in this matter there is no disciplinary distinction of rites, one bound by the Code of Canon Law for the Latin church may celebrate the sacrament of penance with a minister of any of the Eastern (Catholic) churches. It was proposed that the canon should speak only of a legitimately approved confessor of another Catholic rite.[95] Such a qualification of the text was unnecessary and was therefore omitted; the question of confession to and absolution from a minister of another church or ecclesial community is adequately covered by canon 844, §2.

CHAPTER IV
INDULGENCES
[cc. 992–997]

The six canons of this chapter are a major simplification of the former discipline on indulgences. This simplification, however, was mostly achieved by eliminating from the code norms which in some instances are still in force (below). The revised canonical discipline about indulgences—found principally in the apostolic constitution *Indulgentiarum doctrina* of 1967[96] and the norms of the *Enchiridion indulgentiarum* of 1968[97]—is still in effect for the Latin church. (The Eastern churches do not have a corresponding institute in their tradition, even though those churches in full communion with the Roman See may have adopted, under Latin influence, a parallel discipline. The Code of Canons of the Eastern Churches does not have any canons corresponding to chapter 4 of title IV on indulgences.)

The few canons on the subject remaining in the revised code are simply basic norms: (1) defini-

---

[94] See *RPenance* 34, *DOL* 3099, where the mention of annual confession is also referred explicitly to "all those grave sins not hitherto confessed one by one."

[95] *Rel* 234.

[96] Paul VI, apconst, January 1, 1967, *AAS* 59 (1967) 5–24, *DOL* 3155–3187.

[97] Apostolic Penitentiary, June 29, 1968 (Typis Polyglottis Vaticanis, 1968), *DOL* 3193–3228.

tions of indulgences (cc. 992–993); (2) applicability of indulgences (c. 994); (3) right to grant indulgences (c. 995); (4) capacity to gain indulgences (c. 996); and (5) canonical prescriptions outside the code (c. 997).

The chapter on indulgences appears within the title on the sacrament of penance because of their historical development in the medieval period as a parallel to the remission of canonical penances and with some relationship to sacramental reconciliation. Because of both controversy and serious abuse, however, indulgences are now carefully and absolutely distinguished from sacramental reconciliation itself and from the forgiveness of sins. While the act of piety or prayer to which an indulgence is attached may indeed be an act of reconciliation with God and the Church, in the refined doctrine elaborated in late medieval and modern times an indulgence is understood as a remission of temporal or purgatorial punishment still due *after* the forgiveness of sins. For this reason the definitions of indulgences speak of remission of punishment for sins already forgiven insofar as culpability or guilt is concerned; the indulgence itself is never a remission or absolution of sin.

A short time before the conclusion of Vatican II in 1965, the conciliar fathers heard reports from the conferences of bishops on a document about indulgences that had been drawn up by the Apostolic Penitentiary.[98] This draft was not intended for conciliar debate or action but only as a means of general consultation in preparation for a papal document on the subject. The reactions of the bishops to the proposed simplification of the canonical discipline were mixed, and the apostolic constitution of Paul VI which appeared at the beginning of 1967 included a doctrinal and historical exposition preceding its twenty norms in order to introduce changes "that are suited to the times and take into account the wishes of the conferences of bishops."[99] The norms, which otherwise left intact canons 911–936 of the 1917 code, were summarized by Paul VI as

concerned mainly with three points: to fix a new measure for partial indulgences [in place of the medieval measure in years, days, and so-called quarantines]; to lessen the number of plenary indulgences; to reduce and organize into a simpler and worthier form the matters related to indulgences attached to objects and places ("real" and "local" indulgences).[100]

A rationale for limiting the number of plenary indulgences was given by the pope: "The usual receives scant attention; the plentiful is not highly valued. Also many of the faithful need time sufficient for a right preparation to gain a plenary indulgence." Similarly, the suppression of the very terms, "real" and "local" indulgences, was explained as making it clear "that the Christian's acts are the subject of indulgences, not things and places; these are merely the occasions for gaining indulgences."[101] "An [indulgenced] act sometimes has a connection with a particular object or place."[102]

These steps to elevate the doctrine and practice of gaining indulgences to a spiritual and religiously virtuous plane, while eliminating the apparently mechanistic or quantitative elements, were carried forward in the 1968 publication of a radically reduced collection or enchiridion of indulgences (formerly called a *raccolta*) by the Apostolic Penitentiary.[103] This collection of indulgenced acts and prayers was preceded by thirty-six norms, embracing both the papal norms of the year before and a revision of the remainder of canons 911–936 of the 1917 code. The norms of the 1968 enchiridion remain in force, as will be mentioned again in the commentary on canon 997.

Of specific historical interest are the suppression of the so-called *toties quoties* plenary indulgences,[104] understood as available with unlimited

[98] *AcSynVat* 4, 6:131–197, 292–307, 315–335.
[99] *ID* 12, *DOL* 3166.

[100] Ibid.
[101] Ibid.
[102] *ID*, norm 12, *DOL* 3179; *EI* 7, *DOL* 3199.
[103] See note 97, above.
[104] *ID*, norm 19, *DOL* 3185; *EI* 30, *DOL* 3222.

frequency, and the suppression of the "privileged" altar, to which plenary indulgences for the dead were attached on the occasion of eucharistic celebrations. Instead, "like a devoted mother, the Church in its special concern for the faithful departed establishes that in every sacrifice of the Mass suffrages are most lavishly offered on behalf of the dead; any privilege in this matter is suppressed."[105]

Within the Roman Curia, the tribunal of the Apostolic Penitentiary is competent concerning the concession and use of indulgences (except in matters of doctrine in which the Congregation of the Doctrine of the Faith has oversight), in accord with *Pastor bonus*.[106] Thus from time to time the Penitentiary may make new concessions of indulgences related to certain prayers or actions. In addition, it may issue general concessions, for example, to permit the gaining of certain plenary indulgences by persons who are unable to be present for papal blessings given by bishops, "provided they follow the rites with pious mental intention while they are being transmitted live by television or radio" with the usual conditions (below).[107]

Definitions of Indulgences

Canon 992 — An indulgence is the remission before God of temporal punishment for sins whose guilt is already forgiven, which a properly disposed member of the Christian faithful gains under certain and defined conditions by the assistance of the Church which as minister of redemption dispenses and applies authoritatively the treasury of the satisfactions of Christ and the saints.

Canon 993 — An indulgence is partial or plenary insofar as it partially or totally frees from the temporal punishment due to sins.

The first of these two canons gives a definition from Paul VI's 1967 constitution on indulgences. It follows canon 911 of the 1917 code: "All shall hold in high esteem indulgences or remission before God of the temporal punishment due to sins whose guilt has already been removed. This remission is granted by the ecclesiastical authority from the treasury of the Church, for the living by way of absolution [of penalty or punishment], for the dead by way of suffrage." In canon 993, the text is more carefully nuanced to summarize the doctrinal exposition in the apostolic constitution, which offers the following statement of the Church's purpose in this institute:

An indulgence has certain features in common with other methods and means of taking away the remnants of sin, but at the same time is clearly distinct from the others.

This means that in the case of an indulgence the Church, using its power as minister of Christ the Lord's redemption, not only offers prayers, but authoritatively dispenses to the faithful rightly disposed the treasury of expiatory works of Christ and the saints for the remission of temporal punishment.

The purpose intended by ecclesiastical authority in granting indulgences is not only to help the faithful to pay the penalties due to sin, but also to cause them to perform works of devotion, repentance, and charity —especially works that contribute to the growth of faith and the good of the community.[108]

Although not expressed in the canon, the underlying doctrine on indulgences, often articulated in the past almost exclusively in terms of the authoritative intervention of church authority, is equally or more significantly the doctrine of the communion of saints:

---

[105]*ID,* norm 20, *DOL* 3186; *EI* 21, *DOL* 3213.
[106]*PB* 120.
[107]Decree, December 14, 1985, *OssRomEng,* December 23–30, 1985; *CLD* 11, 246–247.

[108]*ID* 8, *DOL* 3162.

The life of each of God's children is in Christ and through Christ conjoined with the life of all other Christians....

This is the basis of the "treasury of the Church." The treasury of the Church is not to be likened to a centuries-old accumulation of wealth. It means rather the limitless and inexhaustible value that the expiation and merits offered by Christ have in the eyes of God for the liberation of all humanity from sin and for the creation of communion with the Father.... Added to this treasure is also the vast, incalculable, ever increasing value in God's eyes of the prayers and good works of the Blessed Virgin Mary and the saints....

The union between those who are still pilgrims and their brothers and sisters who have died in the peace of Christ is therefore not broken, but rather strengthened by a communion in spiritual blessings.[109]

The second of the two canons, canon 993, is also derived from the papal document of 1967.[110] It radically changes the measure of indulgences, formerly related to the period of days or years of canonical penances (or, until recent years, the "quarantines" or Lenten periods) or indeed to a specified period of punishment in purgatory. On the contrary, the partial character of most indulgences is now defined indefinitely, i.e., simply as less than the full or plenary indulgence or remission of temporal punishment. A further authoritative elaboration of this concept is as follows: "Any of the faithful who, being at least inwardly contrite, perform a work carrying with it a partial indulgence, receive through the Church the remission of temporal punishment equivalent to what their own act already receives."[111] In this language there is an effort to maintain the me-

dieval and traditional doctrine of remission of punishment but to relate it directly to the goodness of the act or work for which the indulgence is conceded.

The requisite conditions are stated more forcefully in the current law with regard to the plenary indulgence, which except in the case of persons on the verge of death may be gained only once on any single day. These conditions attempt to avoid any mere multiplication of acts or, as it were, frequent and repeated "total" remissions of temporal punishment:

The requirements for gaining a plenary indulgence are the performance of the indulgenced work and the fulfillment of three conditions: sacramental confession; eucharistic communion; prayer for the pope's intentions. A further requirement is the exclusion of all attachment to sin, even venial sin.

Unless this unqualified disposition and the three conditions are present, the indulgence will be only partial....

Several plenary indulgences [on different days] may be gained on the basis of a single sacramental confession; only one may be gained, however, on the basis of a single communion and prayer for the pope's intention.

The condition requiring prayer for the pope's intentions is completely satisfied by reciting once the Our Father and Hail Mary for his intentions; nevertheless all of the faithful have the option of reciting any other prayer suited to their own devotion and their reverence for the pope.[112]

---

[109] *ID* 5, *DOL* 3159.
[110] *ID,* norm 2, *DOL* 3168; *EI* 2, *DOL* 3194.
[111] *ID,* norm 5, *DOL* 3171; *EI* 6, *DOL* 3198.

[112] *ID,* norms 7, 9, 10, *DOL* 3173, 3175, 3176; *EI* 26, 28, 29, *DOL* 3218, 3220, 3221.

Applicability of Indulgences

Canon 994 — Any member of the faithful can gain partial or plenary indulgences for oneself or apply them to the dead by way of suffrage.

The text of the canon needs no interpretation. The concept of applying indulgences for the dead was explained by Paul VI: "The faithful who apply indulgences as suffrages for the dead are practicing charity in a superior way and with their thoughts on the things of heaven are dealing more virtuously with the things of earth."[113]

The traditional reference to indulgences for the dead as granted only by way of suffrage, prayer, or petition indicates that the Church asserts no power of authoritative declaration concerning the extent of purgatorial punishment remitted for those who have already died.

An evident corollary of this canon is that "no one gaining an indulgence may apply it to other living people."[114]

Right to Grant Indulgences

Canon 995 — §1. In addition to the supreme authority of the Church, only those to whom this power is acknowledged in the law or granted by the Roman Pontiff can bestow indulgences.

§2. No authority below the Roman Pontiff can entrust the power of granting indulgences to others unless the Apostolic See has given this expressly to the person.

Since the 1967 norms of Paul VI on indulgences did not suppress all the canons of the 1917 code on the subject, it was only in the following year that canons 911–924 of the former code were revised.

Thus the general reference in paragraph one of canon 995 can be explained by listing those permitted by the 1968 law to grant indulgences:

Diocesan bishops and their equivalents in law possess from the outset of their pastoral office the right to:

§1. grant partial indulgences to persons or in the places subject to their jurisdiction;

§2. bestow the papal blessing with a plenary indulgence, using the prescribed formulary, three times a year on solemn feasts that they will designate, even if they only assist at the solemn Mass.

Metropolitans may grant partial indulgences in their suffragan dioceses just as in their own.

Patriarchs [of the Eastern Catholic churches] may grant partial indulgences in every place, even those exempt, of their patriarchate, in churches of their own rite outside the boundaries of their patriarchate, and everywhere in the world in favor of their own people. Archbishops major [of the Eastern Catholic churches] have the same power.

Cardinals possess the power to grant partial indulgences in every place or institution and in favor of those persons subject to their jurisdiction or protection. They may do so elsewhere, but only regarding indulgences to be gained by the people present on each occasion.[115]

None of the persons listed above may communicate or delegate the power to grant indulgences to others, as decreed in paragraph two of canon 995. The mention of Eastern patriarchs or other hierarchs in the norms of the *Enchiridion indulgentiarum,* moreover, must be understood only in the case of Eastern Catholic churches which have assimilated the Western institute of indulgences.

---

[113] *ID* 8, *DOL* 3162.
[114] *EI* 3, *DOL* 3195.

[115] *EI* 11–14, *DOL* 3203–3206.

Capacity to Gain Indulgences

Canon 996 — §1. To be capable of gaining indulgences, a person must be baptized, not excommunicated, and in the state of grace at least at the end of the prescribed works.

§2. To gain indulgences, however, a capable subject must have at least the general intention of acquiring them and must fulfill the enjoined works in the established time and the proper method, according to the tenor of the grant.

This canon states the fundamental requisites in the person who is desirous of gaining a plenary or partial indulgence. According to paragraph one, catechumens may not gain indulgences.[116]

In addition, it has been usual to recommend to the faithful that they have a general intention of gaining all indulgences available to them in order to satisfy one of the requirements of paragraph two of this canon.

These conditions are in addition to the dispositions mentioned above in the commentary on canon 993.

Special Laws on Indulgences

Canon 997 — As regards the granting and use of indulgences, the other prescripts contained in the special laws of the Church must also be observed.

Earlier redactions of this canon referred to the 1968 *Enchiridion indulgentiarum* by name, but this reference was too particularized.[117] There is a certain parallel between this canon and canon 2, since it incorporates by reference extra-codal norms on indulgences as canon 2 affirms the canonical force of all the extra-codal laws on liturgical celebration. See canons 335, 344, and 346, where there is also reference to special law outside the code.

As already noted, the principal current, universal law on indulgences was established by Paul VI's 1967 constitution *Indulgentiarum doctrina*. With the exception of some interim provisions, however, the twenty norms of Paul VI were included among the thirty-six norms of the 1968 enchiridion. With regard to the latter, it should be pointed out that, aside from the reform of the canonical discipline of indulgences, the collection itself was radically changed. This was done principally by a large-scale reduction in the number of indulgenced works and prayers. There are now some seventy such indulgences, a few of which are attached to good works in broad terms, for example, to acts of charity for those in need; the majority of the listed indulgences are attached to traditional and devotional prayers. (As mentioned before, from time to time the Apostolic Penitentiary may add to the number of indulgenced acts or prayers.)

The following are the principal norms of the 1968 enchiridion, those not mentioned already and not touched directly by the canons. They remain in effect in virtue of canon 997:

15. §1. No book, booklet, or pamphlet listing indulgences granted is to be published without the permission of the local Ordinary or local [Eastern] Hierarch.

§2. The publication, in no matter what language, of an authentic collection of prayers and devotional works to which the Apostolic See has attached indulgences requires the express permission of the same Apostolic See ...[118]

32. An indulgence annexed to any prayer may be gained no matter what the language of recitation, provided the accuracy of the translation is supported by a declaration either of the Apostolic Penitentiary or of one of the Ordinaries or Hierarchs in the region

---

[116] See c. 1170 on blessings for catechumens (and persons who are not Catholics).

[117] For a contrary opinion, see *Rel,* 235.

[118] *DOL* 3207.

where the language of the translation is in general use.[119]

From the second of these norms, n. 32, it is clear that devotional prayers, even if they carry indulgences, are carefully distinguished from liturgical prayers and other liturgical texts in the vernacular, for which the approbation is conceded solely by the respective conference of bishops for the churches of its territory, in accord with canon 838, §§2–3; such decrees of the conferences must be reviewed or confirmed by the Apostolic See. Nevertheless any diocesan bishop or other (local) ordinary of a region where the language of the prayer text is one of those in general use may declare that a vernacular translation of an indulgenced prayer, originally in Latin or some other language, is accurate.

As far as English versions of indulgenced prayers are concerned, there are often several texts in legitimate use, texts which have been approved or accepted at different periods. Some are variants of traditional or archaic forms; others are in modernized form or in new and contemporary translation. No uniformity of such devotional prayers is required, although on occasion liturgical texts will have indulgences attached for devotional use; in such cases the texts will already have a single official version for a given territory, with the canonical approbation and confirmation referred to above.

A new translation of the devotional prayers to which indulgences are now attached has been provided for members of the conferences of bishops in countries where English is spoken. Prepared by the International Commission on English in the Liturgy, these alternatives to the (various) translations already in use are available for inclusion in devotional books, along with other contemporary translations.[120] The publication of all such texts for the use of the church community is governed by canon 826, §3, which requires the permission of a local ordinary for the publication of "books of prayers for the public or private use of the faithful." Such books (or booklets, pamphlets, leaflets, etc.; see c. 824, §2) ordinarily contain both indulgenced texts and other devotional material.

The other, related norm of the enchiridion quoted above (n. 15) is distinct from but in harmony with what has been said. In norm 15, §1, books (or other publications) listing indulgences are required to have the permission of the local ordinary, just as is required by canon 826, §3 for all prayer books, whether for public or private use. In paragraph two of the same norm 15, however, any authentic collection of (all the) prayers and devotions to which the Apostolic See has attached indulgences requires express permission of that See, namely, a permission given by the Apostolic Penitentiary.[121] In effect, this refers to any integral and official version, in any language, of the *Enchiridion indulgentiarum* itself; it does not refer to the publication of the indulgenced prayers in other kinds of collections, listing of the indulgences or indulgenced prayers, publication of prayers or indulgences from sources other than the Apostolic See, etc., for all of which local ordinaries remain competent.

[119] *DOL* 3224.

[120] *A Book of Prayers* (Washington, D.C.: ICEL, 1982).
[121] *EI* 9, *DOL* 3201.

BIBLIOGRAPHY

Bibliographical material on canons 959–997 can be found after the commentary on canon 1007.

TITLE V
THE SACRAMENT OF THE ANOINTING
OF THE SICK
[cc. 998–1007]

After an introductory canon, the other nine canons of this title treat in separate chapters the celebration of the sacrament of the anointing of the sick (cc. 999–1002), the minister of anointing (c. 1003), and those to be anointed (cc. 1004–1007).

Without entering into complex historical, liturgical, and theological questions concerning this sacrament, the conciliar fathers of Vatican II proposed in 1963 to reform and strengthen its discipline as well as its ritual celebration:

"Extreme unction," which may also and more properly be called "anointing of the sick," is not a sacrament for those only who are at the point of death. Hence, as soon as any one of the faithful begins to be in danger of death from sickness or old age, the fitting time for that person to receive this sacrament has certainly already arrived.

In addition to the separate rites of the sick and for viaticum, a continuous rite shall be drawn up, structured so that the sick person is anointed after confessing and before receiving viaticum.

The number of anointings is to be adapted to the circumstances; the prayers that belong to the rite of anointing are to be so revised that they correspond to the varying conditions of the sick who receive the sacrament.[1]

Several distinct pastoral and doctrinal questions were addressed in this decision of the council:

(1) The nature of the sacrament—a healing anointing of those seriously ill—had been compromised by the almost universal pastoral practice which treated it principally as the sacrament for the dying, or even exclusively for those whose death was imminent and almost certain. This in turn had diluted or distorted the significance of eucharistic Viaticum as the sacrament of the dying; the name of extreme, final, or last anointing and the inclusion of anointing among "last rites" had contributed to this confusion. On the Eucharist as Viaticum, see canons 921–922.

(2) The medieval practice and doctrine of anointing clearly distinguished sacramental anointing from other anointings of the sick and also distinguished anointings of the sick by ordained ministers from anointings by lay persons, practices that were common in the earlier period. The close association of anointing with (final) penance helped in turn to create a requirement that the gravity or perilous situation of the sick person had to be certain or proved. Modern ecclesiastical documents which spoke to the contrary and permitted or encouraged a broader use of the sacrament, while recognizing the more common usage, were not widely accepted in church practice.[2]

Prior to Vatican II, a certain recovery of much older traditions had been initiated, especially when particular rituals returned to the sequence of anointing before Viaticum.[3] (This is the "con-

---

[1] *SC* 73–75. For a commentary on these articles, see F. R. McManus, "The Sacrament of Anointing: Some Ecumenical Considerations," in *Miscellanea Liturgica in onore di S. E. il Cardinale Giacomo Lercaro,* II (Rome: Desclée, 1967) 809–840.

[2] This was true of papal letters which sought to encourage the celebration of the sacrament without any scruple over the perilous state of the sick person: Benedict XV, aplett *Sodalitatem,* May 31, 1921, *AAS* 13 (1921) 345; Pius XI, aplett *Explorata res,* February 2, 1923, *AAS* 15 (1923) 105.

[3] E.g., *Collectio Rituum ad Instar Appendicis Ritualis Romani pro Omnibus Germaniae Dioecesibus* (Ratisbon:

tinuous rite" mentioned in *Sacrosanctum Concilium* 74, quoted above. It was added to the revised *Roman Ritual* in fulfillment of the conciliar mandate.) Such rituals accepted the fact that in many circumstances the person to be anointed might in fact be close to death or even at the point of death, but they moved in the direction of celebrating anointing much earlier, that is, as soon as the seriousness of the illness becomes evident.

(3) Although not directly touched in the conciliar constitution or in the canons, an underlying question is the relation of the sacrament, as understood in medieval and modern times, to the anointing described in the letter of James: "Is there anyone sick among you? Let him send for the presbyters of the Church and let them pray over him, anointing him with oil in the name of the Lord. The prayer of faith will save the sick man and the Lord will raise him up. If he has committed any sins, they will be forgiven him."[4] Before the medieval period this text was very broadly understood in reference to various anointings, for example, by Pope Innocent I (401–417): "There is no doubt that these words [of the letter of James] are to be understood of the faithful who are sick, and who can be anointed with the holy oil of chrism, which has been prepared by the bishop, and which not only priests but all Christians may use for anointing, when their own needs or those of their family demand."[5]

The healing effect of this anointing is mentioned first in the biblical text, without primary reference to the conditional effect of the forgiveness of sins. Nevertheless, the integral healing (physical and spiritual) and raising up by the Lord and in-

deed the relationship to sickness (physical healing) were relegated both in pastoral practice and in theory to a secondary place: emphasis was placed almost entirely upon spiritual healing of sin and sinfulness and upon final "anointing for glory." This was in contradiction to the (ancient) prayers for anointing retained in the 1614 *Roman Ritual;* their lack of suitability, on the occasion when the person is not anointed until all human hope of survival is gone, is one of the reasons for the reform decreed in the conciliar text quoted above.

(4) *Sacrosanctum Concilium* does no more than recover a simpler and older tradition. By declaring that it is "certainly" and "already" time for the sacrament when the person "begins" to be in danger, it deliberately leaves open the question whether a wider extension can legitimately develop. In this, the language does not propose or insinuate any trivialization of the sacrament or its indiscriminate celebration in cases of lesser or slight illness. In the period after Vatican II papal and curial documents, to be mentioned under canon 1004, §1, entertained and supported a further development in full harmony with the conciliar decision.

The Roman rite for the sacrament of the anointing of the sick (simply called "the oil of the sick" in some Eastern churches) is given, in revised form, in the *Rite of Anointing and Pastoral Care of the Sick.* This section of the *Roman Ritual* not only deals with anointing and other elements of sacramental and pastoral ministry to the members of the Christian community who are sick but also includes rites for the sacrament for the dying, namely, the Eucharist as Viaticum. The introduction (*praenotanda*) has an important treatment of sickness in relation to the paschal mystery of the death and resurrection of the Lord Jesus.[6]

For countries where English is spoken, the several conferences of bishops have approved, and the Apostolic See has confirmed, the liturgical book, *Pastoral Care of the Sick: Rites of Anoint-*

Pustet, 1950) 50–64; *Collectio Rituum ad Instar Appendicis Ritualis Romani pro Dioecesibus Statuum Foederatorum Americae Septentrionalis* (Milwaukee: Bruce, 1954) 64–82.

[4] Jas 5:14–15.

[5] Ep. 25, 8, *PL* 20:559; trans. P. Palmer, *Sacraments and Forgiveness, Sources of Christian Theology,* II (Westminster: Newman, 1959) 283.

[6] *RAnointing* (1972) 1–7, *DOL* 3321–3327.

ing and Viaticum.[7] The title reflects both the breadth of the Latin edition, concerned with the total ministry of the Church to its sick members, and the distinct significance of the two sacraments: (1) anointing for the sick who are not literally "dying" (but also for the sick who are close to death and could not be anointed earlier, at a more fitting time) and (2) Viaticum for the dying. A rearranged format, along with additional pastoral notes and newly composed prayers, also supports more clearly the necessary distinctions made in the conciliar reform of the sacramental celebration of anointing of the sick.

In the Eastern churches, the actual rite of anointing differs considerably from that of the Roman and other rites of the Latin church, in particular in the tradition of anointing of an individual Christian by several priests. The canonical discipline of the sacrament is much the same and may be found, in succinct form, in six canons of the Code of Canons of the Eastern Churches (*CCEO* 737–742).

Nature of Anointing of the Sick

Canon 998 — The anointing of the sick, by which the Church commends the faithful who are dangerously ill to the suffering and glorified Lord in order that he relieve and save them, is conferred by anointing them with oil and pronouncing the words prescribed in the liturgical books.

This text replaces the former name of the sacrament (extreme or final unction or anointing), adds a brief doctrinal exposition of the nature of the sacrament, and eliminates the specific mention of olive oil. The development is based upon the conciliar constitution already quoted; the doctrinal language of the canon was also used in the Dogmatic Constitution on the Church (1964):

By the sacred anointing of the sick and the prayer of priests the entire Church commends the sick to the suffering and glorified Lord, asks that he lighten their suffering and save them (see Jas 5:14–15); the Church exhorts them, moreover, to contribute to the welfare of the whole people of God by associating themselves freely with Christ's passion and death (see Rom 8:17; Col 1:24; 2 Tm 2:11–12; 1 Pt 4:13).[8]

This conciliar text was quoted by Paul VI in the apostolic constitution on the revised rite of the sacrament of anointing, in which the required use of blessed olive oil was modified:

Since olive oil, which has been prescribed until now for the valid celebration of the sacrament, is unobtainable or difficult to obtain in some parts of the world, we have decreed, at the request of a number of bishops, that from now on, according to circumstances, another kind of oil can also be used, provided it is derived from plants and is thus similar to olive oil.[9]

Parallel to the norms about the essential formula for other sacraments, canon 998 speaks of the words prescribed in the liturgical books. In this case the same apostolic constitution of Paul VI altered, for the Latin church, the medieval form then found in the *Roman Ritual* ("May the Lord forgive you by this holy anointing and his most loving mercy whatever sins you have committed by the use of your sight..."): "We have thought fit to modify the sacramental form in such a way that, by reflecting the words of James, it may better express the effects of the sacrament."[10]

The revised form—the first clause of which is said by the minister while anointing the forehead

---

[7] This English language ritual is arranged to include not only the section of the *Roman Ritual* cited in the preceding note but also excerpts from other rites, as appropriate.

[8] *LG* 11.
[9] *Sacram unctionem infirmorum,* November 30, 1972, *AAS* 65 (1973) 5–9, *DOL* 3317. See *ROils* 3, *DOL* 3863.
[10] *Sacram unctionem infirmorum, DOL* 3318; also *RAnointing* 25, *DOL* 3345.

of the sick person, the second while anointing the hands—is: "Through this holy anointing / may the Lord in his love and mercy help you / with the grace of the Holy Spirit. / R. Amen. May the Lord who frees you from sin / save you and raise you up. / R. Amen."[11] The form explicitly invites the two responses, "Amen." This is the integral formula referred to in canon 1000, §1 and replaces the formulas for the anointing of each of the senses. While giving a certain priority to spiritual healing (in the reference to grace and in the clause "who frees you from sin"), the formula is completed by the petition that the Lord may "save you and raise you up."

Parallel to but different from canon 998 is the introductory canon in the Eastern law on anointing (*CCEO* 737). The defining description of the sacrament (§1) expresses more expansively the effects of anointing: forgiveness of sins and strengthening "by hope of eternal reward." The faithful are then said to be disposed "to correct their lives and are helped to overcome their infirmity or patiently to suffer it" [*ad infirmitatem superandam patienterve sufferandam adiuvantur*]. This concluding phrase appears to be better nuanced than the Latin law, indicating more clearly the potential of physical healing or recovery in addition to the spiritual effects.

The same canon, in its second paragraph, requires that the rite of anointing by several priests, already mentioned above, be preserved so far as possible in the churches *sui iuris* where it is the custom.

CHAPTER I
THE CELEBRATION
OF THE SACRAMENT
[cc. 999–1002]

This first chapter includes the determination of the minister of the blessing of oil for the sick (c.

999), a general canon on the rite of anointing (c. 1000), and norms affecting both the responsibility to see to the celebration of the sacrament (c. 1001) and the case in which several or many sick persons are to be anointed together (c. 1002).

Blessing of Oil

Canon 999 — In addition to a bishop, the following can bless the oil to be used in the anointing of the sick:
    1° those equivalent to a diocesan bishop by law;
    2° any presbyter in a case of necessity, but only in the actual celebration of the sacrament.

The canon speaks in terms of what is considered the usual situation: the use of oil blessed by the diocesan bishop at the annual Chrism Mass, celebrated ordinarily on Holy Thursday, in accord with the rite of the *Roman Pontifical*.[12]

Although there is a special significance to the use of oils blessed by the bishop who presides over the local church and is its principal moderator of liturgical celebration and discipline,[13] this canon does not exclude the possibility that another bishop may be deputed to bless the oils. The *Roman Ritual* adds that the minister of anointing "should make sure that the oil remains fit for use and should replenish it from time to time, either yearly when the bishop blesses the oil on Holy Thursday or more frequently if necessary."[14]

As indicated in canon 368 together with canon 381, §2, the law equates with the diocesan bishop those persons who preside over portions of the flock (particular churches) that are not formally constituted as dioceses: territorial prelatures and abbacies, vicariates and prefectures apostolic, and apostolic administrations established in a sta-

---

[11] Ibid.; also *Pastoral Care* 94 (n. 124).

[12] *ROils* 9–10, *DOL* 3869–3870.
[13] Canon 835, §1.
[14] *RAnointing* 22, *DOL* 3342.

ble manner. Like diocesan bishops, they bless the oil for the sick, ordinarily in the Chrism Mass, and require no additional concession or faculty to do this.

The second category of ministers of the blessing of oil is treated differently, namely, for cases when oil blessed by the bishop is not available.[15] Blessing of the oil by the minister of the sacrament during the actual celebration is considered not uncommon by the ritual, which provides alternatives: either the blessing by the minister of anointing or a prayer of thanksgiving over the oil if it has already been blessed by the bishop.[16] This practice of blessing by the minister himself is followed in some other, non-Roman rites; it has a certain parallel in the blessing of the baptismal water in the course of the celebration of that sacrament[17] and as in that case allows for a fuller liturgical catechesis about the oil.[18]

Canon 999 permits the minister to bless the oil for the sick only "in a case of necessity" but does not determine the nature or degree of this necessity, given the fact that the minister may already judge the practice to be liturgically and spiritually suitable. The ritual explains that, in this case, the minister "may bring the unblessed oil with him, or the family of the sick person may prepare the oil in a suitable vessel. If any of the oil is left after the celebration of the sacrament, it should be absorbed in cotton or cotton wool and burned."[19] The canon does lessen the degree of necessity stressed in the ritual, which speaks of "true necessity,"[20] but still looks upon the blessing of the oil by the minister as exceptional.

In this connection, the reference to the actual celebration of the sacrament has been added to the canon for clarity. It is only a bishop or a presbyter whose office is equated with that of a diocesan bishop who blesses the oil of the sick during the Chrism Mass, i.e., apart from the celebration of the sacrament of anointing.

The Eastern churches have a different and simpler discipline about the minister who may bless the oil of the sick. It does not require any kind of necessity for the minister of the sacrament to carry out this blessing. Canon 741 of the Eastern code says only that he blesses the oil "unless the particular law of the Church *sui iuris* determines otherwise."

See canon 847 for norms concerning the holy oils in general, norms which are not repeated here. Older authors discussed related questions: the possibility of using other blessed oils for anointing the sick and the validity or invalidity of the sacrament if unblessed oil were used, as well as the addition of unblessed oil in smaller quantities (as a kind of blessing by contact). These questions no longer arise, since some kind of plant oil should be readily available for the minister himself to bless during the sacramental celebration, whenever needed.

Manner of Anointing

Canon 1000 — §1. The anointings with the words, order, and manner prescribed in the liturgical books are to be performed carefully. In a case of necessity, however, a single anointing on the forehead or even on some other part of the body is sufficient, while the entire formula is said.

§2. The minister is to perform the anointings with his own hand, unless a grave reason warrants the use of an instrument.

Although the entire rite for the anointing of the sick—including introductory rites and brief liturgy of the word, laying on of hands, and concluding prayers—is of significance, the canon concentrates on the anointing with oil and the required sacramental form. On the latter, see the commentary above on canon 998.

The *Roman Ritual* of 1614 had prescribed the anointing of eyes, ears, nose, hands, feet, and

---

[15] *RAnointing* 21, *DOL* 3341.
[16] *RAnointing* 75–75bis; *Pastoral Care* 92–93 (n. 123).
[17] See *RBaptC* 54–55, 223–224.
[18] *RCIA* 215; *RBaptC* 54–55.
[19] *RAnointing* 22, *DOL* 3342.
[20] *RAnointing* 21, *DOL* 3341; *ROils* 8, *DOL* 3868.

(until prohibited by *CIC* 947, §2) loins. The 1925 edition of that ritual, revised somewhat in its prenotes in the light of the 1917 code, also permitted the anointing of the feet to be omitted for a reasonable cause (in accord with *CIC* 947, §3). The same edition added or restored a ritual laying on of hands[21] because of the repeated examples of this healing gesture in the New Testament.[22] Vatican II decreed that, in the course of the revision of all the Roman liturgical rites, "the number of the anointings is to be adapted to the circumstances."[23] Thus, in the revised ritual of Paul VI the anointings were simplified, as described in the canon, and the accompanying formula altered for the Latin church (above).

The conferences of bishops remain free, in the preparation of particular rituals for their territories, to make further adaptations of the anointings: "Depending on the culture and traditions of different peoples, the number of anointings may be increased and the places to be anointed may be changed."[24]

Although paragraph one of this canon retains a reference to the order or sequence of anointings, it is now ordinarily a matter of anointing forehead and hands only. In effect the present canon allows the anointing of the hands to be omitted in case of necessity, e.g., if the person is in imminent danger of death (when Viaticum should be given immediately after the single anointing), if there is some physical obstacle to the anointing of the hands, if there is a large number of persons to be anointed and time is short, etc. Similarly, paragraph one recognizes the situation in which even the single anointing of the forehead is not possible, e.g., if in case of accident the head is not accessible, and indicates that another part of the body be anointed "because of the particular condition of the sick person."[25] It says nothing, however, about the style of anointing, e.g., the use of sufficient oil so that the sacramental sign may be perceived as an authentic gesture of healing, as contemporary authors urge.[26]

The serious reason which, according to paragraph two of the canon, may permit the minister to use an instrument to avoid direct physical contact with the body of the sick person may be the danger of infection or even extreme repugnance in some cases. Ordinarily, however, whatever the sick person's condition, the minister will be able to take the same safeguards against infection as do nurses and doctors in their ministry to the sick.[27]

Responsibility to the Sick

Canon 1001 — Pastors of souls and those close to the sick are to take care that the sick are consoled by this sacrament at the appropriate time.

The thrust of this canon is to establish the responsibility for celebrating the sacrament of the anointing of the sick at an opportune time. This time is related to the question, treated in canons 1004–1006, of those who may and should be anointed. Vatican II explicitly defined the appropriate, proper, and ideal time: "*As soon as* any one of the faithful *begins* to be in danger of death from sickness or old age, the fitting time for that person to receive this sacrament *has certainly already arrived*."[28] Thus, in order to broaden the interpretation of the sacramental discipline of anointing,[29] the conciliar fathers determined that—leaving open the possibility of an even earlier time—it is certainly opportune at the very beginning of serious illness.

The responsibility at this point in the Christian's illness rests with those who have the pas-

---

[21] Title VI, c. 2, n. 11.

[22] See Mk 6:5; 16:18; Lk 13:11–13; Acts 9:12, 17; 28:8; *Rituale Romanum* (1925), title VI, c. 2, n. 7.

[23] *SC* 75.

[24] *RAnointing* 24, *DOL* 3344.

[25] *RAnointing* 23, *DOL* 3343.

[26] See L. Bouyer, *Rite and Man* (Notre Dame: University of Notre Dame Press, 1963) 212.

[27] See J. Abbo and J. Hannan, *The Sacred Canons,* 2 vols. (St. Louis: B. Herder, 1960) 2:69.

[28] *SC* 73. Emphasis added.

[29] *AcSynVat* II, 2:568–569, 5:653–654.

toral office and those who are close to the sick person by family relationship, friendship, or the ministry of healing (such as nurses and doctors). The canon does not mention, since it is sufficiently obvious, that the sick person himself or herself should ask for the sacrament if those who have the responsibility of caring and healing are negligent.[30]

Anointing of Several Persons

Canon 1002 — The communal celebration of the anointing of the sick for many of the sick at once, who have been suitably prepared and are properly disposed, can be performed according to the prescripts of the diocesan bishop.

This canon, which did not appear in early drafts of the recodification, does not refer to the communal celebration of the sacrament for a single person (or of a very few persons). It is always desirable that at least some small community of the Christian people assemble and participate;[31] this dimension of communal celebration is always stressed in the revised ritual.[32]

The canon is instead concerned with cases in which there are several or many persons to be anointed together in a single rite, and it is based on the new *Roman Ritual:* "The local Ordinary has the responsibility of supervising celebrations at which sick persons from various parishes or hospitals may come together to receive the sacrament."[33] (The text of the canon employs "diocesan bishop" rather than "local Ordinary," a change which indicates the role of the bishop as president and moderator of the liturgy in the particular church.)[34]

Directions are provided in the ritual itself for the "Celebration of Anointing in a Large Congregation," suited to occasions such as large gatherings whether of a diocese, city, parish, or society for the sick or smaller groups in hospitals, nursing homes, and the like.[35] The first contemporary exemplar of large-scale celebrations of the sacrament was a gathering at Lourdes in 1969, at which a trial use of the rite was allowed.[36]

A pastoral note is added in English-language editions of the ritual: "In particular, the practice of indiscriminately anointing large numbers of persons on these occasions simply because they are ill or have reached an advanced age is to be avoided. Only those whose health is seriously impaired by sickness or old age are proper subjects for the sacrament."[37] For more on this issue, see the commentary on canon 1004.

CHAPTER II
THE MINISTER OF THE ANOINTING OF THE SICK
[c. 1003]

Canon 1003 — §1. Every priest and a priest alone validly administers the anointing of the sick.

§2. All priests to whom the care of souls has been entrusted have the duty and right of administering the anointing of the sick for the faithful entrusted to their pastoral office. For a reasonable cause, any other priest can administer this sacrament with at least the presumed consent of the priest mentioned above.

§3. Any priest is permitted to carry blessed oil with him so that he is able to administer the sacrament of the anointing of the sick in a case of necessity.

The first two paragraphs of this canon distinguish between validity and licitness: the ministration of the anointing of the sick may be done validly by any priest (bishop or presbyter) and only by a priest. At the same time, out of respect

[30] *RAnointing* 13, *DOL* 3333.
[31] In accord with *SC* 26–27 and c. 837.
[32] *RAnointing* 35–36, *DOL* 3355–3356.
[33] *RAnointing* 17, *DOL* 3337.
[34] Canon 835, §1.

[35] *RAnointing* 83–85.
[36] *N* 6 (1970) 13–33; *CLD* 7, 687.
[37] *Pastoral Care* 78.

for those exercising the pastoral office in a particular place or community, the law declares that not every priest acts lawfully in the celebration of the sacrament. Those who have the pastoral office called the "care of souls," moreover, have not only the right but also the duty to celebrate the sacrament with the sick entrusted to their care.

In the last stages of the revision, an unsuccessful effort was made to remove the words *valide* (much debated in the process of revision) and *omnis et solus* from the text of paragraph one, which follows canon 938, §1 of the 1917 code closely. The omission was proposed on the grounds that the statement cannot be supported historically, at least for the first eight centuries; the new *Roman Ritual* does not refer to validity in this connection; and the Council of Trent simply used the expression "proper minister" in regard to the priest.[38] The redacting commission preferred to retain the 1917 text. The Latin text has *sacerdos,* to include both bishops and presbyters.

This canon precludes, at least for the present time and discipline, the celebration of the sacrament by deacons, although this concession is widely desired in the United States, Germany, and other countries. The restriction is partly because of a desire to retain the relationship of the sacrament to the anointing mentioned in the letter of James, which speaks of presbyters or elders, who are understood to be those in positions of authority in the local Christian community.[39] The anathema of Trent, concerned with those who held that lay persons could administer anointing, did not speak directly to the question of validity, nor did it have any direct bearing upon the possibility of anointing by deacons.[40] The extent to which the question may remain open to future development depends upon the complex relation

of sacramental anointing to other kinds of anointing, whether by lay persons or by the ordained, referred to in the commentary at the beginning of this title of canons.

In paragraph two the obligation of those who have the pastoral office (pastors, parochial vicars, chaplains, etc.) to administer the sacrament is coupled with a right. This right excludes other priests, if they do not have a reasonable cause, from intervening in this sacramental ministry to the sick of a given parish or community. It is generally not difficult to presume the permission of those who have the pastoral responsibility, but this presumption should not result in a needless repetition of the sacrament, in accord with the limitation prescribed in canon 1004, §2.

The ritual enlarges upon the ministry of the priest in relation to anointing of the sick. The ministers

> have the pastoral responsibility both of preparing and helping the sick and others who are present, with the assistance of religious and laity, and of celebrating the sacrament.
>
> The local Ordinary [now, the diocesan bishop] has the responsibility of supervising celebrations at which sick persons from various parishes or hospitals may come together to receive the sacrament.
>
> Other priests also confer the sacrament of anointing with the consent of the minister mentioned [bishops, pastors, vicars, priests responsible for the sick or aged in hospitals, and superiors of clerical religious institutes]. Presuming such consent in a case of necessity, a priest need only inform the parish priest (pastor) or hospital chaplain later.
>
> When two or more priests are present for the anointing, one of them may say the prayers and carry out the anointings, saying the sacramental form. The others may take the remaining parts, such as the introducto-

---

[38] *Rel,* 237; Trent, sess. XIV, *de extr. unctione,* c. 3.

[39] *Jerome Biblical Commentary* (Englewood Cliffs: Prentice-Hall, 1968) 377; K. Condon, "The Sacrament of Healing," in T. Worden, ed., *Sacraments in Scripture* (Springfield, Ill.: Templegate, 1966) 176–179.

[40] Trent, sess. XIV, *de extr. unctione,* c. 4.

ry rites, readings, invocations, etc. Each priest may lay hands on the sick person.[41]

Given the reduction in the number of anointings, it is not feasible to follow the Eastern usage, in which several priests participate in the several anointings of a single person; as noted above and in the commentary on canon 1002, if there are several or many sick persons, a number of priests may perform the anointings. The ritual, moreover, treats at length the offices and ministries to the sick of non-ordained Christians.[42]

The keeping of the oil of the sick in a suitable and worthy manner is required by canon 847, §2. In particular, the prohibition of keeping of the oils in the parochial residence, mentioned in the former law, is effectively replaced by the concession of paragraph three of canon 1003. This change had been anticipated along the same lines in a decree of 1965, which gave local ordinaries power to allow priests "the permission to carry the oil of the sick with them, especially when using the various means of transportation to travel."[43] As is evident from canon 999, this 1965 concession and that of canon 1003, §3 are now less significant since any priest may bless any (plant) oil in case of necessity when he is to minister the sacrament of anointing of the sick.

CHAPTER III
THOSE ON WHOM THE ANOINTING
OF THE SICK IS TO BE CONFERRED
[cc. 1004–1007]

The four canons of this final chapter on anointing give, first, the basic norm for the celebration and even repetition of the sacrament (c. 1004),

then special cases of doubtful capacity to receive the sacraments (cc. 1005–1006) and of persons who persist in public circumstances of sinful life (c. 1007).

In particular, the chapter, while providing adequate clarity for canonical purposes, represents a development and broadening with regard to those who may and should be strengthened spiritually, physically, and psychologically by anointing, both the changes directly sought by Vatican II and the further changes found in postconciliar papal and curial documents. As commented upon at the beginning of the title on anointing of the sick, this reflects the contemporary sense of the Church to enlarge the occasions when the sacrament may and should be celebrated.

The anointing of the sick is one of the three sacraments governed by canon 844 so far as interconfessional sharing is concerned; see paragraphs two to four of that canon.

Those to Be Anointed

Canon 1004 — §1. The anointing of the sick can be administered to a member of the faithful who, having reached the use of reason, begins to be in danger due to sickness or old age.

§2. This sacrament can be repeated if the sick person, having recovered, again becomes gravely ill or if the condition becomes more grave during the same illness.

From one viewpoint, paragraph one of canon 1004 simply determines which Christian believers are eligible to receive the anointing of the sick. The reference to "member of the faithful" must not be understood to exclude those persons of other churches and ecclesial communities covered by canon 844, §§3–4.

From another viewpoint, by the phrase, "begins to be in danger," paragraph one specifies what is called in canon 1001 the appropriate time to celebrate this sacrament, namely, at the beginning of serious illness or of old age. The reference to the Christian's having reached the use of rea-

---

[41] *RAnointing* 17–19, *DOL* 3337–3339.
[42] *RAnointing* 32–37, *DOL* 3352–3357.
[43] SCRit, decr *Pientissima Mater Ecclesia,* March 4, 1965, *AAS* 57 (1965) 409, *DOL* 3314; see also SCC, general directory *Peregrinans in terra,* April 30, 1969, *AAS* 61 (1969) 3605, *DOL* 2616.

son is a concern because of the aspect of anointing as consummating or completing Christian penance,[44] namely, in the divine forgiveness of (personal) sin; on this question, however, see the commentary on canon 1005, below.

The nature of the illness is not addressed in the canon, only its seriousness. This leaves open to further development the question of serious psychological illness. Although the sacrament has ordinarily been associated with physical impairment, the gravity and even peril or danger of some psychological disorders are undeniable, and thus English-language rituals, without attempting to give a final resolution to this issue, have the following pastoral note: "Some types of mental illness are now classified as serious. Those who are judged to have a serious mental illness and who would be strengthened by the sacrament may be anointed."[45]

During the process of drafting paragraph one of this canon, it was planned to add, in slightly adapted form, but explicitly, the following norms from the revised ritual:

A sick person may be anointed before surgery whenever a serious illness is the reason for the surgery.

Elderly people may be anointed if they have become notably weakened even though no serious illness is present.

Sick children may be anointed if they have sufficient use of reason to be strengthened [confortari] by this sacrament.[46]

It was determined, however, that these paragraphs should be deleted from the draft of the canon because the matter was already regulated adequately by the revised ritual, i.e., by the litur-gical law. In the final stages of consideration by the codifying commission, attempts to add these references and to add the mention of danger "of death" to paragraph one of this canon were not successful.

Thus it becomes important to refer to the introduction to the section of the *Roman Ritual* on the sacrament. This took as its starting point the conciliar intent to improve pastoral practice and, without replacing those traditions of anointing that were judged sound, to expand the potential occasions for its celebration in the Christian community.[47]

Both in the ritual and in the apostolic constitution introducing it, the degree of gravity or seriousness of the illness is left somewhat open, without explicit mention of the relationship of this seriousness to death, which may be a rather remote danger. This was done not to minimize the seriousness of the condition which calls for the celebration of the sacrament but to remove all hesitation about when it will be proper and fruitful to celebrate the sacrament. It also serves to correct what are now considered abuses[48] or aberrations in the tradition: to reserve the sacrament for cases of persons *in extremis*, to postpone the celebration until there is a high likelihood or near certainty of death, to insist upon medical confirmation of the possibility or even proximity of death, or to consider the anointing in itself or primarily the sacrament of the dying.

The Council of Trent, reflecting the problematical traditions and the pastoral practice of the period, recognized in effect two possibilities, giving primacy to anointing as the sacrament of the sick but attributing to it a secondary "name" of sacrament of the departing[49] because of the fre-

---

[44] *RAnointing* 6, *DOL* 3327 (following the Tridentine teaching on anointing, in the places cited above in notes 38 and 40).

[45] *Pastoral Care* 27 (n. 53).

[46] *RAnointing* 10–12, *DOL* 3330–3332.

[47] *AcSynVat* II, 5:654, where the conciliar commission speaks of, and seeks, an *interpretatio latior.*

[48] In submitting the matter to the conciliar fathers for their vote, the commission on the liturgy was explicit: "We intend to suppress the abuse of administering this sacrament only to those *in articulo mortis* or extreme danger to life" (*AcSynVat* II, 2:568).

[49] Sess. XIV, *de extr. unctione,* c. 3.

quent (and, in later centuries, usual and almost exclusive) occasions when the sacrament was given to the dying. The recovery of an older and sounder tradition, and indeed an enlargement of that tradition, is demanded by the other postconciliar expositions of the matter, in particular that of the *Roman Ritual:*

> The Letter of James states that the sick are to be anointed in order to raise them up and save them. Great care should be taken to see that those of the faithful whose health is seriously impaired by sickness or old age receive this sacrament.
>
> A prudent or reasonably sure judgment, without scruple, is sufficient for deciding on the seriousness of the illness; if necessary a doctor may be consulted.[50]

Commenting upon this development on the occasion of a communal anointing of a large number of sick persons, Paul VI explained:

> Here as in the other sacraments the Church's main concern is, of course, the soul, pardon for sin, and the increase of God's grace. But also, to the extent that it is up to the Church, its desire and intent is to obtain relief and, if possible, even healing for the sick. . . . The revision's intent was to make the overall purpose of the rite clearer and to lead to a wider availability of the sacrament and to extend it—within reasonable limits—*even beyond cases of mortal illness.*[51]

The careful balance between the wrongful restriction of the sacrament and its celebration for those not seriously ill is reflected also in an explanatory note attached, in English-language rituals, to the text of the *praenotanda* which refers to health as "seriously impaired by sickness or old age":

The word *periculose* has been carefully studied and rendered as "seriously," rather than as "gravely," "dangerously," or "perilously." Such a rendering will serve to avoid restrictions upon the celebration of the sacrament. On the one hand, the sacrament may and should be given to anyone whose health is seriously impaired; on the other hand, it may not be given indiscriminately or to any person whose health is not seriously impaired.[52]

The same introduction of the *Roman Ritual* enlarges pastorally upon what is in paragraph one of canon 1004 (and also in c. 1001):

> In public and private catechesis, the faithful should be educated to ask for the sacrament of anointing and, as soon as the right time comes, to receive it with full faith and devotion. They should not follow the wrongful practice of delaying the reception of the sacrament. All who care for the sick should be taught the meaning and purpose of the sacrament.[53]

The Latin code's reference to "danger due to sickness or old age" is expressed somewhat differently in the corresponding Eastern code canons 738 ("The Christian faithful freely receive the anointing of the sick when they are gravely ill") and 740 (the presumption that those who lack consciousness or the use of reason "want this sacrament to be administered to them in danger of death and even at another time according to the judgment of the priest"). This language appears to have the effect of opening even more broadly than the Latin law the right of the gravely ill Christian to receive this sacrament.

Less commentary is required by paragraph two. It is the canonical tradition of the teaching on the repetition of the sacrament (in the same ill-

---

[50] *RAnointing* 8, *DOL* 3328.
[51] Homily, October 5, 1975, *N* 11 (1975) 257–258, *DOL* 3365. Emphasis added.

[52] *Pastoral Care* 13 (n. 8).
[53] *RAnointing* 13, *DOL* 3333.

ness) by the Council of Trent.[54] In the preparation of the constitution on the liturgy, the intent was to remove this restriction; after the conciliar debate, any mention of repetition of anointing was omitted from the constitution because of uncertain historical and theological precedents.[55]

The text of paragraph two also represents developments since Vatican II, in particular the teaching of Paul VI: "The sacrament may be repeated if the sick person recovers after being anointed and then again falls ill or if during the same illness the person's condition becomes more serious."[56]

Even before the broadening statement quoted, it had been understood that repetition of the sacrament "through the mere lapse of a long time without recovery"[57] was permissible, since a lengthy period might itself create the presumption of a newly critical or more seriously impaired condition. This presumption in favor of celebrating the sacrament is analogous to those situations mentioned in canon 1005, that is, the sacrament may be administered in case of doubt of a new seriousness of condition. It does not mean, however, that the sacrament should be administered on some regular basis, such as weekly or monthly, to the ill person, without any reference to the progress of the illness.

Special Cases

Canon 1005 — This sacrament is to be administered in a case of doubt whether the sick person has attained the use of reason, is dangerously ill, or is dead.

This canon differs from canon 941 of the 1917 code principally by the omission of any reference to *conditional* ministration in these instances of doubt. To avoid scruple on the part of the minister

—and thus again to correct pastoral abuses which had denied the sacrament to some of the faithful who were seriously ill—any condition attached to the formula of anointing ("If you have attained the use of reason..." or "If you are living...," etc.) is simply suppressed. In addition, the second of the three doubtful situations has been rephrased from the somewhat narrower text of the earlier code (doubt "whether he or she is truly in danger of death"). The canon, it should be noted, goes beyond the ritual and retains the language of obligation (*ministretur*) in all the cases of doubt which are mentioned.

(1) With regard to the first case of doubt (whether the age of reason has been attained), the canon is applicable to infants and young children incapable of sin and also to those who because of mental or other incapacity have never attained the use of reason. The norm of the ritual may be somewhat clearer: "Sick children may be anointed [in accord with the canon: *are to be anointed*] if they have sufficient use of reason to be strengthened [*confortari*] by this sacrament."[58] Canon 1005 in effect adds that the sacrament is to be administered even if it remains doubtful whether the child (or the retarded person) has sufficient reasoning power to be (spiritually, physically, and/or psychologically) strengthened by anointing. Although the limited requirement of the use of reason is related to the forgiving nature and effect of the sacrament, there is no demand that the child should have committed any sin or be repentant for any sin. Finally, there is no application of this canon (or of c. 1004, §1) to those who have had the use of reason and then have become mentally incompetent; no doubt whatever exists in such cases, and such persons are to be anointed, much the same as the persons referred to in canon 1006.

(2) With regard to the second case of doubt (whether there is dangerous illness), canon 1005 simply extends the norm of canon 1004, §1 to all cases in which the seriousness of impaired health is doubtful.

---

[54] Sess. XIV, *de extr. unctione*, c. 3.

[55] *AcSynVat* II, 2:569 ("lest the Council enter into disputed questions").

[56] *Sacram unctionem infirmorum, DOL* 3318; *RAnointing* 9, *DOL* 3329.

[57] Abbo-Hannan 2:63.

[58] *RAnointing* 12, *DOL* 3332.

(3) With regard to the third case of doubt (whether the person is alive or dead), it is certain that the sacrament of the anointing of the sick—which is also the sacrament of the dying in the case of those who were unable to be anointed or in fact were not anointed at an earlier and proper time in the illness—may not be given to a dead person. This would be improper; none of the seven sacraments may be given to a person who is dead. The norm of the *Roman Ritual* is explicit on this point: "When a priest has been called to attend those who are already dead, he should not administer the sacrament of anointing. Instead he should pray for them, asking that God forgive their sins and graciously receive them into the kingdom."[59] For this reason, English-language rituals add a number of appropriate prayers, psalms, and biblical readings so that the minister may follow the direction just quoted if indeed the person is dead.[60] Some of these texts are taken from the *Order of Christian Funerals,* as is suggested by the *Roman Ritual* itself.[61]

The canon, however, rephrases the liturgical law ("But if the priest is doubtful whether the sick person is dead, he may give the sacrament conditionally"—but without mention of the condition) and reinstates the language of obligation. In other words, if there is genuine doubt whether death has occurred, the person should be anointed. The judgment is one that it should be possible for the minister himself to make; alternatively, he should ordinarily be able to rely upon medical judgment.[62]

Canon 1006 — This sacrament is to be conferred on the sick who at least implicitly requested it when they were in control of their faculties.

Since often the nature of a serious illness is such that the person is unable consciously to ask for the sacrament, the canon is substantially the same as the current liturgical and pastoral norm:

"The sacrament of anointing may be conferred [in accord with the canon: *is to be conferred*] upon sick people who, although they have lost consciousness or the use of reason would, as Christian believers, probably have asked for it were they in control of their faculties."[63]

In effect, a presumption is established that the Christian believer is desirous of receiving the sacrament of anointing of the sick—unless there is contrary evidence such as that described in canon 1007, which follows. In the past the desire of the believer to receive the sacrament has been called an implicit habitual intention, sufficient even if it is merely internal.

Canon 1007 — The anointing of the sick is not to be conferred upon those who persevere obstinately in manifest grave sin.

The canon is derived from canon 942 of the 1917 code: "The sacrament is not to be conferred upon those who, impenitent, contumaciously persist in manifest serious sin; if this is doubtful, it should be conferred conditionally." A comparison of the language of the former and revised canons indicates substantial agreement. As in other cases in which doubt exists, the presumption favors the celebration of the sacrament but—again, as in other doubtful cases such as those mentioned in canon 1005—the revised law suppresses the reference to conditional anointing. This change may be attributed to a development that sees no need for the minister of the sacrament to advert to a potential invalidity of the sacrament because of lack of intention on the part of the one to be anointed; quite the contrary, this intention may be presumed in every case.

In any event, the prohibited case is that of a public sinner whose obstinate perseverance in a sinful life is known.[64] The contemporary judgment of the Christian community will almost always appreciate and accept the likelihood of repentance.

---

[59] *RAnointing* 15, *DOL* 3335.
[60] *Pastoral Care* 189–198 (nn. 223–231).
[61] *RAnointing* 151.
[62] *RAnointing* 8, *DOL* 3328.

[63] *RAnointing* 14, *DOL* 3334.
[64] For similar cases, see cc. 915; 1184, §1, 3°.

BIBLIOGRAPHY

(The following bibliographical material provides further information regarding the sacraments discussed in the titles of Book IV on penance and the anointing of the sick.)

Crichton, J. *The Ministry of Reconciliation.* London: Geoffrey Chapman, 1974.

Empereur, J. *Prophetic Anointing.* Wilmington, Del.: Glazier, 1982.

Green, T. "The Revision of Sacramental Law: Perspectives on the Sacraments Other Than Marriage." *Stud Can* 11 (1977) 261–327.

Gusmer, C. *And You Visited Me: Sacramental Ministry to the Sick and the Dying.* Revised ed. New York: Pueblo, 1989.

Häring, B. *Shalom: Peace: The Sacrament of Reconciliation.* New York: Farrar, Straus, 1967.

ICEL. *Pastoral Care of the Sick: Rites of Anointing and Viaticum.* Collegeville: Liturgical Press, 1983.

———. *The Rites of the Catholic Church.* 2 vols. New York: Pueblo, 1976–1980.

Keifer, R., and McManus, F. *The Rite of Penance: Commentaries.* I, *Understanding the Document.* Washington: Liturgical Conference, 1975.

Örsy, L. *The Evolving Church and the Sacrament of Penance.* Denville, N.J.: Dimension Books, 1978.

Osborne, K. *Reconciliation and Justification: The Sacrament and Its Theology.* New York: Paulist, 1990.

Palmer, P. ed. *Sources of Christian Theology.* II, *Sacraments and Forgiveness.* Westminster, Md.: Newman 1955.

Schillebeeckx, E., ed. *Sacramental Reconciliation* (*Con* 61). New York: Herder and Herder, 1971.

TITLE VI
ORDERS
[cc. 1008–1054]

Canons 1008–1054 primarily concern the specific juridic and sacramental act of ordination to sacred ministry and the preparation which precedes it. The canons focus most particularly on ordination to the diaconate (whether transitional or permanent) and to the ministerial priesthood.[1] The sources of these canons fall primarily into three groups: (1) documents of the Second Vatican Council, most notably *Lumen gentium, Presbyterorum ordinis, and Optatam totius;* (2) the 1917 Code of Canon Law; and (3) writings by various popes and Vatican dicasteries.[2]

Canons 1008–1054 remind us of the remarkably early and enduring foundation of the Church's juridic understanding of ordained ministry, as well as the elasticity of that understanding as it has developed through the ages. For instance, the articulation of the matter and form of presbyteral ordination has developed, as has the understanding of the episcopacy, as a distinct degree of orders requiring its own ordination; minor orders, once an innovation, are nearly beyond living memory, while the permanent diaconate is now a commonplace in many particular churches.

Many, if not most, of canons 1008–1054 are properly open to interpretation in light of local circumstances. All of these canons are derived from a fundamental mystery of grace beyond the Church's

control: God calls certain persons in specific time-and-place-dependent settings to come forth for ordained service to the Catholic Christian faithful. Grounded in mystery, subject to historical vicissitudes, and composed of ancient and constant elements, these canons call us less to an immersion in a canonical science marked by precision than to an appreciation of the Church's evolving attentiveness to the Spirit's movement regarding sacred ministry. Canons 1008–1054 invite us to appreciate ordained ministry as central to the sacramental efficacy of God's graces present in and through the Church. The canons also remind us of our adherence to the faith as it is revealed and lived in a hierarchically constituted Church.

Nature of Sacrament of Orders

Canon 1008 — By divine institution, the sacrament of orders establishes some among the Christian faithful as sacred ministers through an indelible character which marks them. They are consecrated and designated, each according to his grade, to nourish the people of God, fulfilling in the person of Christ the Head the functions of teaching, sanctifying, and governing.

Sacred ministry was intended by Jesus Christ, and the Church has traditionally recognized ordination to ministry as being one of the seven sacraments instituted by Christ for the good of his Church. Within this sacrament are three orders: the episcopate, the presbyterate, and the diaconate (c. 1009, §1). Ordination is one of the three sacraments which bestow an indelible character on the recipient (c. 845, §1). This character of orders is received but once, regardless of how many of the three orders one receives in his lifetime. Once validly received, an ordination cannot be invalidated (c. 290). A valid ordination is performed by a bishop who intends to ordain the candidate according to the mind of the Church; the candidate

---

[1] Regarding the title *De ordine* (instead of, for instance, *De ordinatione*), see *Comm* 10 (1978) 179.

[2] For different and accessible sources and histories of specific themes relative to canons 1008–1054, see the following: E. Gilbert, in *CLSA Com,* 713–736; J. González del Valle, in *Pamplona ComEng,* 632–659; and D. Kelly, in *CLSGBI Com,* 548–571. For a treatment of parallel issues in the Eastern code, see V. Pospishil, *Pospishil Com,* especially regarding *CCEO* 743–775.

is a validly baptized adult male who intends to be ordained for sacred ministry, as understood by the Church. The ordination follows a proper ritual, the execution of which includes the imposition of hands and the prayer of consecration.

Canon 1008 refers to "sacred ministers," a phrase canonically synonymous with "clerics." The Code of Canons of the Eastern Churches makes this equality of terms explicit (*CCEO* 323, §1). Even one who is laicized or dismissed from the clerical state (e.g., c. 290, 2°–3°) is still properly considered a sacred minister in certain situations (e.g., c. 976).

Sacred ministers are "consecrated and designated" according to a specific grade. Hierarchically constituted by Christ, the Church recognizes the equality of all human persons (c. 208) but regards certain functions as reliant upon specific sacramental powers and teaching authority. Just as the rights, obligations, and functions within the Church will differ according to one's canonical status, so deacons, priests, and bishops are differentiated by their sacramental ordination, most notably by the manner in which they fulfill for the faithful "in the person of Christ the Head the functions of teaching, sanctifying, and governing."

The functions and demands associated with various states of life differ. However, as noted above, this does not negate a true equality among all the Christian faithful of whatever state of life (c. 208). In an often cited passage from *Sedes sapientiae,* Pius XII taught that because God is the principal author of all states of life, and of all natural and supernatural gifts, a true vocation to any state of life can be considered divine.[3] Marriage, for instance, is a vocation. Building on themes introduced in *Gaudium et spes* 47–52 and *Apostolicam actuositatem* 9–11, canon 226, §1 reminds us that married persons enjoy a vocation in which they participate in a unique way in the formation of the people of God. However, there are real differences within the body of the Church,

according to each person's condition, state of life, or office (c. 208). Sacred ministers have unique responsibilities placed upon them. John Paul II unites theory and practice when he writes:

> What the Apostle Paul says of all Christians, that they must attain "to mature manhood, to the measure of the stature of the fullness of Christ" (Eph 4:13), can be applied specifically to priests, who are called to the perfection of charity and therefore to holiness, even more so because their pastoral ministry itself demands that they be living models for all the faithful.[4]

Canon 1008 suggests as much: sacred ministers, by divine institution through the sacrament of ordination, are consecrated and deputed so that, fulfilling in the person of Christ the Head the offices of teaching, sanctifying, and ruling, they feed the people of God. Much of what follows in the ensuing canons will concern expectations for those to be ordained to sacred ministry.

Three Grades of Orders

Canon 1009 — §1. The orders are the episcopate, the presbyterate, and the diaconate.

§2. They are conferred by the imposition of hands and the consecratory prayer which the liturgical books prescribe for the individual grades.

Canon 1009 specifies the diaconal, sacerdotal, and episcopal grades of orders. While the canonical distinctions among them are clarified throughout the code, the sacramental distinctions (especially between the orders of the presbyterate and the episcopate) are open to discussion among sacramental theologians. The distinction between the diaconate and the other two orders, however, is quite clear: the presbyterate and the episcopate

---

[3] Pius XII, apconst *Sedes sapientiae,* May 31, 1956, *AAS* 48 (1956) 357.

[4] John Paul II, apexhort *PDV* 156. English translation published by Libreria Editrice Vaticana, Vatican City, 1992.

are grades in the ministerial priesthood, to which the diaconate does not belong.

The conferral of each order requires its own ordination rite. In recent centuries, the Church had recognized seven grades of orders. However, Paul VI amended this sevenfold understanding in 1972,[5] suppressing the minor orders of porter, lector, exorcist, and acolyte and instituting the ministries of lector and acolyte; tonsure no longer admitted one to the clerical state.

Conferral of sacred ordination consists in the laying on of hands and the prayer of consecration. Canon 744 of the Eastern code corresponds with this.

CHAPTER I
THE CELEBRATION AND MINISTER OF ORDINATION
[cc. 1010–1023]

Time of Ordination

Canon 1010 — Ordination is to be celebrated within the solemnities of the Mass on a Sunday or holy day of obligation. For pastoral reasons it can take place also on other days, even weekdays.

Ordination is conferred licitly only within the celebration of a Mass. The preferred day for such a ceremony is Sunday or a holy day of obligation, for several reasons. First, the presumption is that a Sunday or holy day worship carries with it an inherent solemnity befitting the occasion of a diaconal, sacerdotal, or episcopal ordination. Second, a priest or deacon will regularly exercise his sacred ministry, among other times, within the context of eucharistic liturgies on a Sunday or holy day of obligation. Third, practically speaking, on a Sunday a full congregation would likely participate in the ordination ritual, which is desirable (c. 1011, §2).

[5] Mp *Ministeria quaedam,* August 15, 1972, *AAS* 64 (1972) 529–534.

Canon 1010, however, is somewhat flexible regarding the preferred day, if pastoral reasons warrant the selection of another day, even a weekday. Such pastoral reasons might well be liturgical in nature, since the ordination itself might overshadow the community's Sunday or holy day liturgy. A primary pastoral reason for selecting a day other than a Sunday or other holy day might well be the convenience of those who would wish to attend, and for whom weekday travel might be an inhibiting factor.

Setting for Ordination

Canon 1011 — §1. Ordination generally is to be celebrated in the cathedral church; for pastoral reasons, however, it can be celebrated in another church or oratory.

§2. Clerics and other members of the Christian faithful must be invited to the ordination so that as large an assembly as possible is present at the celebration.

While canon 1010 governs the timing of an ordination, canon 1011, §1 regulates the proper place for such a ceremony. As with canon 1010, the rule is to be interpreted broadly so as to permit appropriate exceptions. Because of its centrality in the life of the community, a cathedral is an appropriate location, especially for those ordained for the service of a diocese. Further, the cathedral is an especially apt location for the ordination of diocesan priests, who will enjoy a strong priestly and, ideally, personal relationship with their bishop. However, an ordinand's home parish church, or a church where he has served, might be just as appropriate, as long as there is sufficient room for all congregants wishing to attend. Religious might find a church under their care to be an appropriate setting.

Canon 1011, §2 reinforces the obvious: because of the importance of an ordination in the corporate life of the faithful, laity and clergy alike are to show their support of the ordinand(s) by attending the service in as large a number as possible. Obviously, the selection of day, time, and place should take this into account.

Minister of Ordination

Canon 1012 — The minister of sacred ordination is a consecrated bishop.

The minister of sacred ordination is a consecrated bishop; this corresponds to Eastern code canons 743 and 744. Canon 1012 affirms the current and universal practice of the Church.

For purposes of this canon (1012) and canons 1013 and 1014, episcopal consecration is synonymous with episcopal ordination. The consecrating bishop himself must be validly ordained. A bishop who is himself illicitly but validly ordained in turn illicitly but validly ordains candidates to the diaconate and presbyterate. Even one who has removed himself from the episcopal college united with Rome ordains validly, though certainly illicitly.

Tradition has never held that more than one validly ordained bishop is absolutely necessary for episcopal ordination. However, the practice prior to the Council of Nicea (325) and continuing into the present affirms that at least three bishops ordain a bishop (one principal consecrator with two designated co-consecrators). Symbolically, the collegiality of the episcopate is apparent; practically, the Church is undoubtedly assured of the validity of the ordination, as three bishops participate in an ordination which requires only one of them for validity.

Pontifical Mandate for Episcopal Ordination

Canon 1013 — No bishop is permitted to consecrate anyone a bishop unless it is first evident that there is a pontifical mandate.

Canon 1013 safeguards hierarchical communion. The ordinary minister of valid and licit episcopal ordination is a consecrated bishop who is certain that a pontifical mandate has been issued in favor of the bishop-designate. A bishop illicitly

but validly ordained himself illicitly but validly ordains to the episcopate. If a pontifical mandate is lacking for the one to be ordained, both the ordaining minister and the minister ordained incur a *latae sententiae* excommunication reserved to the Apostolic See (c. 1382). Obviously, if the ordaining bishop himself is under a canonical penalty due to circumstances regarding his own episcopal ordination, the imputability of his participation in another episcopal ordination, especially one lacking a pontifical mandate, is seriously aggravated. The autonomy of the Holy See in designating bishops is notably threatened in some nations by forces external to the Church. At least regarding internal order, canons 1013 and 1382 seek to assure that there will be no threat to the security of pontifical (ecclesiastical) independence in these matters. One notable example in recent history is the episcopal ordination, without pontifical mandate, by the late Archbishop Marcel Lefebvre.[6]

Co-consecrators of a Bishop

Canon 1014 — Unless the Apostolic See has granted a dispensation, the principal bishop consecrator in an episcopal consecration is to be joined by at least two consecrating bishops; it is especially appropriate, however, that all the bishops present consecrate the elect together with the bishops mentioned.

Co-consecrating bishops who assist the principal ordaining bishop are not essential for the validity of the episcopal ordination, but they are necessary for its liceity. However, unlike an episcopal ordination lacking a pontifical mandate, no penalty is expressly incurred if such bishops are absent. In particular situations, it may not be possible for three bishops to be present, in which case a dispensation from this requirement is to be requested from the Holy See. The traditional practice of assisting or co-consecrating bishops emphasizes the symbolic unity and the practical col-

[6] O. Bucci, "Lo scisma di Lefebvre documentazione," *Apol* 61 (1988) 529–555.

legiality of the episcopate. Eastern code canon 746 refers simply to ordination by three bishops, rather than a consecrating bishop and two co-consecrators.

Dimissorial Letters

Canon 1015 — §1. Each person is to be ordained to the presbyterate or the diaconate by his proper bishop or with legitimate dimissorial letters from him.

§2. If not impeded by a just cause, the proper bishop is to ordain his own subjects personally; without an apostolic indult, however, he cannot ordain licitly a subject of an Eastern rite.

§3. The person who can give dimissorial letters to receive orders can himself also confer the same orders personally if he possesses the episcopal character.

A candidate for the diaconate or priesthood should be ordained by his own proper bishop, or by another bishop in possession of an appropriate dimissorial letter (c. 1015, §1). It is a matter of interpretation as to whether the ordering of options in this canon reflects a priority, although at least in the case of secular clergy their proper bishop is to be preferred; this is confirmed in the first sentence of the next canon.

The diocesan bishop should be the ordaining prelate who welcomes secular deacons and priests who will be serving the particular church. An auxiliary bishop of that same diocese can make the same point less credibly. For religious clergy, the diocesan bishop of the place of the ordination might still be preferred, since his presence enables him to thank the institute for its pastoral assistance, and in turn permits the institute to manifest publicly its pastoral commitment to the particular church and its bishop. On the other hand, a religious institute might invite one of its own members to be the ordaining minister, should it have a bishop in its ranks. An ordaining religious bishop highlights in his person the availability of religious clergy for pastoral cooperation with and in particular churches.

In the case of diocesan clergy, a dimissorial letter is issued by one's proper diocesan bishop (cc. 1016 and 1018), who presents the candidate for ordination and, indeed, grants permission for that order to be conferred by another competent bishop. In this way, there is no confusion about the diocese of incardination; and there is assurance that the ordination is licit as well as valid. In the case of religious clergy, a dimissorial letter is issued by the competent major superior (c. 1019), presenting the candidate for orders and requesting ordination for him by a duly authorized bishop.

A dimissorial letter is issued only by one's proper bishop, in the case of secular clergy, or one's competent major superior, in the case of religious clergy. For an ordination to occur licitly, if it is not being performed by the bishop of one's diocese of incardination, canon 1015, §1 requires the presentation of a dimissorial letter from the candidate's proper ordinary.

Ordained according to Rite, or Church Sui Iuris

Canon 1015, §2 states that a Latin rite bishop is to ordain his own subjects; one infers from this canon that Eastern rite subjects are to be ordained by their proper ordinaries. The reference here, of course, is to candidates for the diaconate (whether transitional or permanent) or the priesthood. The Latin rite bishop is obliged to care for Eastern rite Catholics in his diocese (c. 383, §2). However, his obligation to care for Eastern Catholics does not encompass a right to ordain ministers to serve them, though indeed such an ordination would be valid. Questions arise rarely with orders (but more commonly with certain marriage situations) in which one's actual rite is uncertain, or one's perceived or preferred rite is in conflict with one's actual rite (cc. 111–112). That is, a man may have been baptized in one church *sui iuris* but reared and educated in another; he may not even know the facts regarding his infant baptism, which surface when documentation is sought during his training. In such cases, one's actual rite should be brought into conformity with one's perceived or preferred rite, according to the norm of law.

In cases in which the competent authorities and the man himself agree on the necessity or even advisability of the ordination of an Eastern rite subject by a Latin rite bishop, an indult from the Holy See is necessary for the licit celebration of the sacrament. If the competent authorities (e.g., a Latin rite bishop and an eparchial bishop) do not agree on who should ordain the man, the aspirant maintains the right to pursue the matter of an indult nonetheless. His decision to do so may be linked with his own discernment regarding an eventual petition for a change of rite, depending on the response to the indult request.

An Apparent Tautology

Canon 1015, §3 states that the person who can give dimissorial letters for a diaconal or presbyteral candidate may also be competent by law to perform the ordination itself. The canon is somewhat tautological; indeed, a bishop who can grant dimissorial letters is likely the preferred minister of ordination. According to c. 1015, §1 and §2, at least in the case of secular clergy, the proper diocesan bishop should be the minister of ordination for presbyters and deacons in his diocese. If that bishop is not the ordaining minister, he would also be the source of dimissorial letters granting the ordaining authority to another bishop. Hence, according to this canon, one who can issue such a letter could have performed the ordination. An auxiliary bishop may not issue dimissorial letters in normal circumstances, and so he may not ordain licitly unless he receives such a letter from the ordinary who has jurisdiction over the candidate or candidates (cc. 1018–1019).

Proper Bishop for Ordination

Canon 1016 — As regards the diaconal ordination of those who intend to be enrolled in the secular clergy, the proper bishop is the bishop of the diocese in which the candidate has a domicile or the bishop of the diocese to which the candidate is determined to devote himself. As regards the presbyteral ordination of secular clerics, it is the bishop of the diocese in which the candidate was incardinated through the diaconate.

According to canon 1016, the proper bishop for a diaconal candidate is the bishop in whose diocese that candidate has established domicile (c. 102), or the bishop of the diocese in which that candidate will minister. The applicability of one or the other is the fruit of discernment between the candidate and the bishops in question. However, the decision to admit the willing candidate to the diaconate belongs ultimately and solely to the bishop of the diocese in which the man will be incardinated (cc. 265–272). Once a secular transitional deacon is incardinated into a diocese, that same bishop (or his successor) will be his proper bishop for all matters relating to his presbyteral preparation and ordination. Whether a permanent or transitional deacon, the incardinated secular cleric enjoys all clerical rights proper to his state, and is bound by all its obligations as enunciated in universal (cc. 273–289) and particular law.

Territoriality and Conferral of Orders

Canon 1017 — A bishop cannot confer orders outside his own jurisdiction without the permission of the diocesan bishop.

Permission must be granted by the local diocesan bishop before another bishop may confer orders in the former's jurisdiction. This is distinct from the matter of dimissorial letters. Dimissorials concern the permission to ordain a man as granted by the competent authority to which he will be accountable ministerially. Canon 1017, in contrast, concerns the one who has episcopal authority not over the ordinand, but over the place where the ordination is to occur. Canon 1017 should be read as a concrete example of the territoriality of jurisdiction (see principle eight for the revision of the code).

A dimissorial letter permits a secular candidate to be ordained by someone other than his own proper bishop, or enables ordination by a duly authorized bishop in the case of a religious candidate. The ordaining minister may well be the bishop of another diocese; if the ceremony takes place within that bishop's jurisdiction, then the dimissorial letter suffices, and of course would not be necessary if the candidate is the bishop's subject.

However, if that bishop is to ordain licitly someone in a ceremony outside the jurisdiction of his particular church or outside of his own personal jurisdiction, he must receive the express permission of the bishop of the diocese in which the ceremony will take place. This permission is required for the licit ordination of any candidate, whether a subject of the ordaining bishop or not, if the ceremony takes place outside his jurisdiction. Likewise, any titular bishop, auxiliary bishop, or religious bishop who is not the local episcopal authority must receive the latter's explicit permission to ordain licitly anyone in that bishop's territory.

Dimissorial Letters for Seculars

Canon 1018 — §1. The following can give dimissorial letters for secular clergy:
  1° the proper bishop mentioned in can. 1016;
  2° an apostolic administrator and, with the consent of the college of consultors, a diocesan administrator; with the consent of the council mentioned in can. 495, §2, an apostolic pro-vicar and an apostolic pro-prefect.
§2. A diocesan administrator, apostolic pro-vicar, and apostolic pro-prefect are not to grant dimissorial letters to those who have been denied admission to orders by the diocesan bishop, the apostolic vicar, or the apostolic prefect.

For diocesan clergy, dimissorial letters usually are issued by the proper bishop (c. 1016). Clearly, the proper bishop of the ordinand's diocese of incardination has legal authority to issue dimissorials. Canon 1018 states expressly that an apostolic administrator with proper jurisdiction also has the authority to issue dimissorials, once proper consultation has been undertaken. In the case of a vacant see or a particular church other than a diocese, the diocesan administrator, apostolic pro-vicar, or apostolic pro-prefect is to seek the consent of the relevant council prior to the issuance of the dimissorial.

Canon 1018, §1, 2° presents an important restriction: a diocesan administrator must have the consent of his college of consultors to issue such dimissorials. It is true that canon 428, §1 restricts the administrator from any diocesan innovation or alteration, or any exercise of authority prejudicial to the subsequent diocesan bishop. However, the ordination of those in the normal course of formation would hardly constitute such an innovation and thus is permissible.

Canon 495, §2 is referenced in canon 1018 as it applies to apostolic pro-vicars and apostolic pro-prefects. While express mention is not made of them, apostolic vicars and apostolic prefects also presumably enjoy jurisdiction to issue dimissorials, in light of canon 368, which likens the vicariate and prefecture to a diocese. Their jurisdiction is analogous to that enjoyed by a diocesan bishop over his particular church (c. 381, §2).

Those temporarily presiding over a community implicitly referred to in canon 1018 may not countermand a prior decision of the one who last held that office permanently. Canon 1018, §2 attempts to preclude a potential abuse here: if a diocesan bishop, apostolic vicar, or apostolic prefect has earlier denied a man admission to orders, that denial must stand until a successor takes stable possession of the office. This is true despite the contrary opinion of the college of consultors or missionary council, or despite an earlier decision which may have been unfair.

Dimissorial Letters for Religious

Canon 1019 — §1. The major superior of a clerical religious institute of pontifical right or of a clerical society of apostolic life of pontifical right

is competent to grant dimissorial letters for the diaconate and the presbyterate to their subjects who are enrolled perpetually or definitively in the institute or society according to their constitutions.

§2. The law for secular clerics governs the ordination of all other candidates of any institute or society; any other indult granted to superiors is revoked.

While the previous canon governs those who may grant dimissorial letters for secular clergy, canon 1019 addresses those ordination candidates who are members of certain religious institutes or apostolic societies. Specifically, a major superior of a pontifical clerical religious institute may issue dimissorials for those perpetually vowed to that institute; the same is true for a major superior of a pontifical clerical society of apostolic life as regards those definitively ascribed to that society. This applies to candidates for the diaconate and the presbyterate. Dimissorials presume the completion of the preparatory formation of the candidate and the fulfillment of all binding legal norms, including incorporation into the institute. Those not yet perpetually incorporated into the institute must seek early profession, by indult if necessary, or possess an indult from the Holy See permitting the ordination prior to perpetual incorporation. Major superiors of diocesan institutes may not issue dimissorials.

Canon 1019, §2 enunciates two further points. First, if the candidate is not a definitively incorporated member of a pontifical society or institute, then the pertinent norms on dimissorials are those governing candidates for the diocesan clergy (c. 1018). Hence, for instance, candidates to be ordained for service in religious institutes, or in societies of apostolic life which are not clerical and of pontifical right receive dimissorials from the proper bishop. Second, if a non-clerical or non-pontifical right institute or society had enjoyed an indult permitting the superior to issue dimissorials, it was revoked on November 27, 1983, when the current code took effect.

Necessary Testimonials and Other Documents

Canon 1020 — Dimissorial letters are not to be granted unless all the testimonials and documents required by law according to the norm of cann. 1050 and 1051 have been obtained beforehand.

A testimonial letter primarily certifies a candidate's fitness for orders. Minimally, this certification regards the man's academic preparation, his reception of diaconate (if he is to be ordained a priest), and his sacramental history (c. 1050, 1°–3°); also included is an affirmation that he has received the ministries of lector and acolyte, and that he has freely and knowingly requested, in writing, the reception of orders (c. 1050, 3°). Well-informed parties are to attest that the candidate is morally fit and generally apt for orders (c. 1051). For a married man to be ordained to the permanent diaconate, the testimonial letter prepared on his behalf is to include the affirmation that his spouse consents to his ordination (c. 1050, 3°). Such information differs technically from a dimissorial letter, which specifically concerns only the bishop who may ordain a given candidate.[7]

Canon 1020 indicates a certain priority in the issuance of documentation regarding an ordinand. The materials associated with testimonials (regarding, for example, a man's sacramental history and fitness for orders) are to be assembled and known to be complete before the issuance of any dimissorial. The logic of such a provision is obvious: attestations of a man's aptness for orders must be finalized before the practical details of his ordination (e.g., designation of the ordaining prelate) are resolved.

While the ordaining prelate, in possession of a proper dimissorial if necessary, must be morally certain of a candidate's fitness,[8] he need not himself review all pertinent testimonials for those not

---

[7] See commentary on c. 1015, §1.

[8] See cc. 1025, §1 and §2; 1052, §1 and §3.

his subjects,[9] and such a review would normally not take place. Careful assessment of testimonial materials is the obligation of the candidate's proper ordinary. After a review of the documentation which finds a candidate suitable for orders, the dimissorial is issued (if necessary); and the ordination may proceed without the ordaining prelate's revisiting the matter of testimonials.

Eligibility to Receive Dimissorials

Canon 1021 — Dimissorial letters can be sent to any bishop in communion with the Apostolic See except to a bishop of a rite different from the rite of the candidate unless there is an apostolic indult.

With a correctly issued dimissorial in hand, any bishop in union with Rome may ordain a man presented him, provided that the bishop belongs to the same ritual church as the candidate he is to ordain. If the two are not of the same *sui iuris* church, an apostolic indult is required before the ordination may proceed. Without an apostolic indult (c. 1015, §2), a Latin rite bishop may not licitly ordain an Eastern rite candidate. Eastern code canon 747 affirms that a candidate to the diaconate or presbyterate should be ordained by his own eparchial bishop, or by another bishop who is in possession of authentic, legitimate dimissorial letters.

Authenticity of Dimissorials

Canon 1022 — After the ordaining bishop has received legitimate dimissorial letters, he is not to proceed to the ordination unless it is clearly evident that the letters are authentic.

The lengthy and comprehensive process of preparing one for orders should not be marred by dishonesty on the part of anyone associated with the process. A dimissorial letter represents the culminating moment in the process of finding a man fit for ordination. While even its issuance does not guarantee his ordination (as no one ever has a right to ordination), a dimissorial letter serves as a final clearance for his reception of orders. Since the dimissorial alone suffices as permission for an ordaining prelate to proceed,[10] its authenticity must be beyond question. Given the written correspondence and oral conversation which can easily take place today between an ordaining prelate and a candidate's proper ordinary, the falsification of such a document is now highly unlikely. Nonetheless, canon 1022 underscores the care which the Church demands in all matters concerning such a momentous act as diaconal or presbyteral ordination.

Conditions Regarding Issuance of Dimissorials

Canon 1023 — Dimissorial letters can be limited or revoked by the one who granted them or by his successor, but once granted they do not lapse when the authority of the one who granted them ceases.

The issuance of a dimissorial is a singular administrative act subject to norms governing executive power and administrative decrees (cc. 35–58). Canon 1023 specifies that the proper author of the dimissorial may condition its legal efficacy. For instance, the ordination in question might be subject to restrictions of time (after or prior to a given date) or place. Furthermore, a dimissorial is necessarily always ordinand-specific.

Canon 1023 also clearly states that the one who can grant a dimissorial can also revoke it according to the norm of law. This is also true for the legitimate successor of the dimissorial's author. Finally, the dimissorial itself is not dependent on the continued authority of its author. When he leaves office, the permission for ordination which the dimissorial grants does not cease.

---

[9] See c. 1052, §2.

[10] See commentary on c. 1020.

CHAPTER II
THOSE TO BE ORDAINED
[cc. 1024–1052]

Requisites for Validity of Ordination

Canon 1024 — A baptized male alone receives sacred ordination validly.

Canon 1024 is unambiguous: a baptized male alone receives sacred ordination validly. This is the authentic teaching of the Catholic Church. Eastern code canon 754 corresponds with this canon, with the exception of the Latin term *recipit,* which reads *suscipere potest* in the Eastern code.

Canon 842, §1 underlies canon 1024: baptism is a prerequisite for valid admission to, or reception of, all other sacraments. Besides the restriction that only baptized persons are ordained validly, canon 1024 states that such persons must be male.[11] The baptized male must be ordained by a consecrated bishop (c. 1012) according to the consecratory prayer and imposition of hands prescribed by the Church (c. 1009, §2).

Intentionality

In the actual ordination the ordaining bishop must intend to do what the Church intends him to do as minister of the sacrament. For his part, the ordinand must voluntarily, actively, and positively intend to receive the sacrament; he must have at least the habitual intention (or an actual intention not revoked) of receiving the Church's sacrament through ordination.[12] Pope John Paul II has spoken of this intention as "a conscious and free choice to do in his ministerial activities what the Church intends to do."[13] In this case, the positive intention manifested throughout formation by the candidate suffices, unless of course by some act of the will during the ordination the candidate renounces that intention. It can be argued that the subsequent voluntary celebration of liturgical acts proper to the diaconate or priesthood reflects the integrity of the cleric's intention to have received orders. In his ministerial activity, however halting at first, he effectively accepts the graces made available to him at his ordination; he publicly presents himself as the minister he intended to become, and which the Church intended him to become.

Requirements for Liceity of Ordination

Canon 1025 — §1. To confer the presbyteral or diaconal orders licitly, it is required that the candidate, having completed the period of probation according to the norm of law, is endowed in the judgment of his own bishop or of the competent

---

[11] One contemporary magisterial document is of central relevance: John Paul II, aplett *Ordinatio sacerdotalis,* May 22, 1994, *AAS* 86 (1994) 545–548, *Origins* 24 (June 9, 1994) 49, 51–52. A subsequent CDF statement sought to clarify the authoritative nature of the teaching: CDF *dubium,* October 28, 1995, *AAS* 87 (1995) 1114, *Origins* 25 (November 30, 1995) 401, 403. For a significant document prior to *Ordinatio sacerdotalis* which addresses the pertinent issues in greater detail, see CDF decl *Inter insigniores,* October 15, 1976, *AAS* 69 (1976) 98–116, *Origins* 6 (February 3, 1977) 517, 519–524. For a succinct treatment of this issue, see Kelly, in *CLSGBI Com,* 554–555. For a consideration of the weight to be given these magisterial teachings, see B. Ferme, "The Response (28 October 1995) of the Congregation for the Doctrine of the Faith to the *Dubium* concerning the Apostolic Letter, *Ordinatio Sacerdotalis* (22 May 1994): Authority and Significance," *P* 85 (1996) 689–727; and F. Morrisey, "The Weight to Be Given to Recent Vatican Documents Regarding the Ordination of Women," in *Proceedings of the Annual Conference of the Canon Law Society of Great Britain and Ireland* (1997) 55–66. See also CTSA, "Study, Prayer Urged Regarding Women's Ordination 'Responsum,'" *Origins* 27 (June 19, 1997) 75–79; and NCCB Doctrine Committee Staff, "Response to CTSA Report on Women and Ordination," *Origins* 27 (October 2, 1997) 265, 267–271.

[12] "In adulto requiritur quoque *intentio,* seu voluntas saltem *habitualis,* i.e., quae actualis fuit et non est revocata, suscipiendi ordines." J. Creusen and A. Vermeersch, *Epitome Iuris Canonici, Tomus II: Liber III Codicis Iuris Canonici* (Malines, Belgium: H. Dessain, 1924) 140.

[13] *PDV* 51.

major superior with the necessary qualities, is prevented by no irregularity and no impediment, and has fulfilled the prerequisites according to the norm of cann. 1033–1039. Moreover, the documents mentioned in can. 1050 are to be obtained and the investigation mentioned in can. 1051 is to be completed.

§2. Furthermore, it is required that he is considered in the judgment of the same legitimate superior as useful for the ministry of the Church.

§3. The bishop ordaining his own subject who is destined to the service of another diocese must be sure that the one to be ordained is going to be attached to this other diocese.

Canon 1025 succinctly introduces the key themes of canons 1026 through 1039. Those to be ordained should be fit for ministry. One would not be called to ministry by God or, presumably, the community were it not for his potential to become an effective sacred minister.

Those to be ordained licitly must be free of canonical impediments and irregularities. A thorough investigation, which is the culmination of the ordinand's clerical formation, should affirm this freedom. Aspirants to sacred orders, even prior to being canonically designated as candidates, should be desirous of living a holy life and availing themselves of the Church's sacramental graces. They should be exceptionally well catechized and well informed regarding the order which they are about to receive. Personal holiness, sacramental practice, catechesis, and proper education regarding the clerical state are themes recurring often in the canons treating the formation of clerics (cc. 232–264), with particular attention given to those preparing for presbyteral ordination.

A formal admission to candidacy, which affirms the probable ministerial fitness of the candidate, welcomes those aspiring to diaconal and presbyteral orders (c. 1034, §1). To avoid confusion, the term "aspiring" is used for those not yet admitted to candidacy. The completion of a course of academic study of several years' duration serves to form future presbyters according to

the mind of the Church.[14] All candidates must be assessed in terms of concerns not always easy to discern, such as correct intention (cc. 241, §1; 1029), and in areas easily assessed, such as completion of a pre-ordination retreat (cc. 246, §5; 1039).

Suitability of the Candidate and His Probable Usefulness in Ministry

The Church exercises its declared right to prepare its diaconal and presbyteral candidates as it sees fit for the service of the faithful (c. 232). Prior to any diaconal or presbyteral candidate's advancement to or within sacred orders, the bishop must be certain that the candidate's fitness (c. 1025, §1) has been proven by means of positive arguments (c. 1052, §1).

Canon 1025, §2 specifically reminds the ordaining prelate, the ordinand's ordinary, and (if applicable) the religious ordinary that the candidate must be considered useful for the Church's ministry. If he is useful for the particular church or institute into which he is to be incardinated, a candidate is useful to the universal Church (c. 368). From this concern flows a moral obligation which binds the relevant ordinary and his successors. It is presumed that the minister useful enough to be ordained will continue to be useful, and therefore fit for assignment, until the contrary is established. This expression of the notion of ministerial utility is not found in the Eastern code.

Given all that can be known about a candidate and the current and likely future needs of the faithful whom he will serve, canon 1025, §2 requires the ordinary to judge that the candidate will be able to fulfill his ministerial obligations. While no one can predict the future absolutely, the candidate's pastoral and apostolic efficacy must be assured in light of the needs of the particular church or institute for which he is to be ordained.

---

[14] See, for example, cc. 235, §1; 248–252; 256; and 1032, §1 and §2.

The Benefit of the Doubt

Canon 1025, §2 raises a couple of practical questions: what is a given candidate capable of doing as a sacred minister, and can he productively serve as such according to the mind of the Church? For cases in which probable, or at least potential, fitness and long-term utility are not clear, an aspirant should be dismissed from formation early if there is moral certitude that he is not a risk worth taking. Further, if a man's potential for future utility in the service of the faithful is in doubt, a strong moral argument can be made that the faithful deserve the benefit of the doubt more than does the aspirant, especially since he enjoys no right to ordination. Canon 1025, §2 discourages a minimalist approach in approving a man for orders.

Ordinaries must be cautious indeed not to encourage persons whose ministerial fitness and utility are in doubt. One might hope that a man will develop positively, but if such growth is not likely, it is unjust to all parties concerned to encourage him. If he later must be dismissed from formation because of problems which were known earlier and not considered remediable, then he has been treated unjustly if he has not been advised to pursue another vocation. If after ordination it becomes clear in practice that a man is ministerially inept, as earlier suspected, then he has been unjustly encouraged by superiors to believe that he might be something he cannot be. In such situations, the faithful have had thrust upon them a sacred minister who might well be a burden—and even a source of damage or scandal—in their common and individual spiritual lives.

Suitability for an Assignment

Despite being based on certain objective factors, the assessment of ministerial suitability is an unavoidably subjective process. Also, certain circumstances (e.g., cases of contemplatives) will call for unique applications of canon 1025, §2. Still, there must be positive arguments which convince the man's legitimate superior that the aspi-

rant, as an ordained minister, will be useful for the Church. Advancement to ordination is tantamount to an affirmative response to this question. Once a deacon or priest, after thorough investigation, has been deemed fit and useful for ministry, he must be considered as such on an ongoing basis until there is manifest, positive evidence to the contrary. While no person has a right to ordination, canon 1025, §2 indicates that a man can expect to exercise orders already received, since by the fact of his ordination he has been positively deemed fit and useful for sacred ministry.[15]

Usefulness in Light of Clergy Shortage

A consideration of canon 1025, §2 should not be concluded without a mention of the clergy shortage. An ordinary might well determine that a shortage of ordained clergy, especially priests, limits or even precludes access by the faithful to the sacraments (c. 213). Properly disposed members of the faithful have a right to reception of the sacraments. Hence, it could be argued simplistically that in such a situation, any cleric who can supply needed sacramental assistance is deemed useful. Certainly, sacramental graces in general are efficacious regardless of the fitness or overall pastoral usefulness of the minister. However, as is obvious from even a cursory reading of canons 1025–1054, the Church has a serious concern to assure the ministerial quality of a candidate beyond his minimal ability to fulfill basic sacramental tasks. A dire need for clergy in particular circumstances must be weighed against the Church's care that its ministers meet fairly exacting standards for comprehensive pastoral activity.

Usefulness in Light of Clergy Abundance

Conversely, where there is a sufficiency or even abundance of ministerial candidates, the obligation for careful assessment is all the stronger. Benedict

---

[15] This prior assessment of a man's ministerial fitness is relevant to the application of c. 1044, especially §2, 2° on an irregularity for the exercise of orders.

XIV cautioned in 1740 that "in fact progress is better made by having fewer ministers, but superior, fit, and useful, than many ministers, who might be worthless in the building up of the body of Christ, which is the Church."[16] Writing to the archbishops and bishops of Italy in 1906, Pope Pius X forcefully lamented the ordination of many simply for the sake of numbers. Particularly in places where there exists an abundance of willing candidates, bishops were and are to choose their ordinands carefully.

> We know there to be cities and dioceses where, far from being able to lament a scarcity of clergy, the number of priests is far superior to the need of the faithful. Indeed, what reason [is there], venerable brethren, to render so frequently the imposition of hands? If the scarcity of clergy cannot be reason enough to hurry into an affair of so great a gravity, [then] there, where the clergy exceeds the needs, there is nothing which excuses from the more discerning precautions and the total rigor in the selection of those who are to be admitted to the sacerdotal honor.[17]

Canon 1025, §3 addresses certain cases in which a diocesan clerical candidate's proposed place of incardination differs from his diocese of

domicile. A man may be ordained a deacon (at which time he becomes an incardinated cleric) by his proper bishop for service outside the diocese of his domicile. The bishop must be certain that appropriate arrangements have been made for that service.

ARTICLE 1: REQUIREMENTS IN THOSE TO BE ORDAINED [CC. 1026–1032]

Freedom of Candidates for Orders

Canon 1026 — A person must possess due freedom in order to be ordained. It is absolutely forbidden to force anyone in any way or for any reason to receive orders or to deter one who is canonically suitable from receiving them.

Canon 1026 directly and unequivocally addresses the candidate's moral freedom in approaching orders (c. 219). First, he must enjoy requisite freedom. Presumed, of course, is the unhindered use of reason: the candidate must be *able* to understand and must *in fact* understand that ordination is but one of several states of life available to him. He further must understand the rights and obligations of this particular state which he is now freely choosing. Not only must his intention be real and firm; it also must be free of any coercion which would lead one toward or away from ordination. This should be the case throughout formation: according to the age and personal development of each proposed candidate, care ought to be taken that he always advance with right intention and free exercise of his own will.[18]

Freedom to Request Ordination

Under no circumstances may one who is fit and prepared for ordination be turned away from his desired path. However, this does not refer to a

---

[16] "Melius enim profecto est pauciores habere Ministros, sed probos, sed idoneos, atque utiles, quam plures, qui in aedificationem Corporis Christi, quod est Ecclesia, nequicquam sint valituri." Benedict XIV, ency *Ubi primum*, September 13, 1740, in *Benedicti XIV Pont. Opt. Max. Opera Omnia*, vol. 15 (Prato, 1845) 4.

[17] "Sappiamo esservi città e diocesi, ove, lungi dal potersi lamentare scarsità nel clero, il numero dei sacerdoti è di gran lunga superiore alla necessità dei fedeli. Deh! qual motivo, o Venerabili Fratelli, di rendere così frequente la imposizione delle mani? Se la scarsità del clero non può essere ragione bastevole a precipitare in negozio di tanta gravità; là dove il clero sovrabbonda al bisogno, nulla è che scusi dalle più sottili cautele e da somma severità nella scelta di coloro, che debbano assumersi all'onore sacerdotale." Pius X, ency *Pieni l'animo*, July 28, 1906, *ASS* 39 (1906) 323.

[18] *OT* 6.

denial of orders by legitimate authority, which may always preclude the ordination of doubtfully fit candidates in view of the good of the Church. Rather, the reference is here to a man's own withdrawal from consideration for ordination due to some external influence (e.g., friends, family, paramour, colleagues, or even a superior); such influence is absolutely forbidden.

Freedom Not to Be Ordained

Conversely, one who is apparently fit and prepared for the reception of orders but who wishes to remove himself from consideration for ordination is morally free to do so. No outside agent (e.g., friends, family, colleagues, confessor, spiritual director, or even superior) may lead a candidate to advance to ordination when he desires otherwise. The candidate's moral freedom to choose ordination is a firm requirement for that ordination. It should be noted that sometimes the sources of external influences (e.g., parents) do not intend to be coercive, or they may be unaware that their son perceives in them a desire that he be ordained.

Lack of Moral Freedom, and Alleged Invalidity

Because intentionality is so difficult to assess, the possible invalidity of orders due to defective intention is difficult to prove, yet such a case could be tried according to canons 1708–1712. The presumption of validity (c. 124, §2) would be basic to any investigation into alleged invalidity, as would the fact that orders once validly received never become invalid (c. 290).

One apparently validly ordained might believe that, due to his lack of freedom, he consciously intended other than what the Church intended. Perhaps some irresistible force prompted his ordination (c. 125, §1). If, consequently, he believes in conscience that his orders are invalid, he may justly request that this alleged nullity be formally examined (cc. 1708–1712) so that he might demonstrate the truth of his claim. However, he does not have a right to an affirmative response to

his petition. On the other hand, if over time he has lived his priesthood effectively and with a degree of contentment, and he is not troubled in conscience as he recalls his state of mind at the time of ordination, he simply should accept the apparent validity of his ordination.

A Perceived Deficiency of Freedom, and Release from Obligations of the Clerical State

Lacking a conscience-driven conviction about the invalidity of his ordination, or aware that supportive data to prove nullity might be lacking, a man could humbly request from the Holy See a dispensation from the obligations of the clerical state, including celibacy. The ordination is valid, but the man only later appreciates the moral freedom that was wanting at the time of his ordination. In such a situation, a man may find that he cannot live up to the demands of sacred ministry and cannot fulfill the obligations of the clerical state (including celibacy). He can petition the Holy See to be freed from those obligations through the process commonly known as laicization.[19] The petitioner asks that this grace be granted by the Holy See for pastoral reasons relevant to his unique circumstances; however, he has no right to such a favor.

Formation of Candidates for Orders

Canon 1027 — Those aspiring to the diaconate and presbyterate are to be formed by careful preparation, according to the norm of law.

Candidates for the transitional diaconate, the permanent diaconate, and the priesthood are to be formed by careful preparation. The Church's principal expectations of such candidates are presented particularly in this article (cc. 1026–1032), in the following one (cc. 1033–1039), and in the canons concerning the formation of clerics (cc. 232–264). Canon 1027 also implicitly encompasses particular law promulgated by the proper episcopal con-

---

[19] See cc. 290, 3°; 291; 292; and 1078, §2, 1°.

ference, most notably programs for priestly or dia-conal formation.[20] Also, formational goals are to be particularized even at the level of the local seminary itself (c. 243).

Instruction on Obligations of Orders

Canon 1028 — The diocesan bishop or the competent superior is to take care that before candidates are promoted to any order, they are instructed properly about those things which belong to the order and its obligations.

In formally petitioning for admission to sacred orders, a candidate presumably acts freely and knowingly. Canon 1028 clarifies certain concerns about the knowledge such candidates should have regarding clerical and ministerial obligations. Not only are candidates to be "formed by careful preparation, according to the norm of law" (c. 1027), but they are also to be particularly versed in the order itself and its obligations. The responsibility for assuring this awareness on the part of the candidate belongs to his proper ordinary.

Those involved in a candidate's formation should be particularly concerned about assessing his knowledge of the order to which he aspires. Attention to both universal law (cc. 232–264) and particular law (local or national programs of priestly formation), as well as practical, supervised pre-ordination pastoral experience should offer the aspirant correct information regarding these obligations. However, negligence or ignorance in this area, which may lead to a cleric's subsequent disregard of his obligations, does not in itself invalidate his ordination.

A candidate validly receives orders even if he is thoroughly confused about the essential obligations of the clerical life. This confusion may significantly impair his exercise of ministry. The ordinand is only partially to blame for such a situation, as a man's proper ordinary is ultimately responsible for the formation of candidates under

---

[20] Such programs are specifically referenced in cc. 242, 249, 250, 260, and 261.

his care. However, pronounced ignorance of the order received or its attendant obligations would certainly figure prominently in an argument for the ordinand's ultimate release from clerical obligations, should the presentation of a laicization petition later appear warranted.

Requisites for Orders

Canon 1029 — Only those are to be promoted to orders who, in the prudent judgment of their own bishop or of the competent major superior, all things considered, have integral faith, are moved by the right intention, have the requisite knowledge, possess a good reputation, and are endowed with integral morals and proven virtues and the other physical and psychic qualities in keeping with the order to be received.

Attentive to the unique pastoral circumstances confronting him, the proper ordinary must decide on the promotion to orders of each candidate presented. Along with those assisting him in the formation of clerics, the ordinary must be convinced of the aptitude of each candidate regarding integral faith, right intention, requisite knowledge, good reputation, integral morals, proven virtues, and other relevant physical and psychological qualities. Canon 1029 reiterates points raised in canon 241, §1 regarding the suitability of those admitted to the seminary. It is not always easy to evaluate whether or not a given man fulfills these criteria.

Denial of Presbyteral Ordination

Canon 1030 — Only for a canonical cause, even if occult, can the proper bishop or competent major superior forbid admission to the presbyterate to deacons subject to him who are destined to the presbyterate, without prejudice to recourse according to the norm of law.

No one has a right to presbyteral ordination, a sacrament to be conferred contingent upon the positive judgment of the competent authority. Canon 1052, §3 declares that, all matters of examination and documentation notwithstanding and even if the transitional deacon appears fully prepared to be ordained a priest, an ordaining bishop who has a sound reason to doubt the deacon's fitness may not promote him. A question arises about the meaning of the phrase "all these notwithstanding." Minimally, it refers to the immediately preceding canons which concern the requisite documentation attesting to the candidate's proven fitness (cc. 1050; 1051; 1052, §1 and §2). Canon 1051, 1° details relevant virtues in the candidate, recalling canon 1029. Weighty data not previously known may come to light, whether in the public forum or not, such that ordination to the priesthood would not be prudent. Lest the possibility of a refusal of priestly ordination mentioned in canon 1052, §3 be abused, canon 1030 offers protection to the transitional deacon, stating that any reason to deny him advancement to the priesthood must be canonically defensible.

"Only for a Canonical Cause"

Canon 1030 states that a transitional deacon awaiting presbyteral ordination can be prevented from such by legitimate authority only for a canonical reason. What this means precisely is unclear and hence it may give rise to abusive interpretation. The canonical reason might not be known publicly (i.e., may be hidden or "occult"), complicating the matter further.

Although such a prohibition is not technically a penalty, the transitional deacon might not see it that way, especially if he is not given a fair explanation as to the problem that has arisen since his diaconal ordination. Further, though he does not have a canonical right to presbyteral ordination, the deacon might argue that he has a moral right, given the encouragement, even in writing, that was offered him throughout his formation. After all, he was previously found fit for ordination when he was ordained a deacon. Though canon 1030 articulates the canonical expectation that a transitional deacon will be advanced, the man does not enjoy a right to presbyteral ordination;

hence canon 18 regarding strict interpretation of the law when rights are at stake apparently does not apply.

Unless very serious reasons justify the contrary, a transitional deacon should be advanced to the presbyterate; this is a serious canonical expectation. It seems that an ordinary's choice not to fulfill this legal expectation "only for a canonical cause" would have to be considered an administrative act. Hence, canons 50 and 51 would apply: proof about the deacon's unsuitability for presbyteral ordination would have to be gathered, and reasons for the decision would have to be issued in writing. However, those parties having knowledge of the problem—which necessarily must be serious—are obligated to protect the deacon's good name (c. 220). This may be difficult to do while gathering data, pursuing a consultation, and issuing a summary decree. In order to protect confidentiality, even less would the ordinary give his reasons to any members of the public at large, however interested they might be, and however much he might wish to defend his decision before them.

Compared with the 1917 code (*CIC* 970), canon 1030 represents a noteworthy shift in favor of the transitional deacon and away from arbitrary appraisals by legitimate authority. The canon states that a transitional deacon may seek canonical recourse should he determine that he has been unjustly denied promotion to the presbyterate (cc. 1732–1739). Ultimate recourse can be made to the Holy See.

Age, Marital Status, Interstices, and Sufficient Maturity

Canon 1031 — §1. The presbyterate is not to be conferred except on those who have completed the twenty-fifth year of age and possess sufficient maturity; an interval of at least six months is to be observed between the diaconate and the presbyterate. Those destined to the presbyterate are to be admitted to the order of deacon only after completing the twenty-third year of age.

§2. A candidate for the permanent diaconate who is not married is not to be admitted to the diaconate until after completing at least the twenty-fifth year of age; one who is married, not until after completing at least the thirty-fifth year of age and with the consent of his wife.

§3. The conference of bishops is free to establish norms which require an older age for the presbyterate and the permanent diaconate.

§4. A dispensation of more than a year from the age required according to the norm of §§1 and 2 is reserved to the Apostolic See.

Canon 1031 contains certain minimum requirements for licit ordination regarding: age, maturity, and prior diaconal ordination for presbyteral candidates; and age, marital status, and spousal consent for married candidates to the permanent diaconate.

The requirement that presbyteral candidates must "possess sufficient maturity" does not derive directly from any canonical source. Canon 1031, §1 refers to legitimate authority's evaluation of the presbyteral candidate's maturity prior to ordination.[21] Presbyteral ordination requires positive proof of maturity manifested before the fact even though it may not always be clear what "sufficient maturity" means here. In contrast, the minimum ages set forth in the canon, and the interstices between the diaconate and the priesthood, are not ambiguous.

The Latin church sets twenty-three as the minimum age for diaconal ordination for transitional deacons, while for the Eastern churches that minimum is twenty-three for all deacons. In the Latin church permanent deacons may not be ordained until they have completed twenty-five years of age if they are unmarried or thirty-five years if they

are married. In the latter instance the consent of the diaconal candidate's spouse is required.[22] The Latin church sets the minimum age for presbyteral ordination at twenty-five, while for the Eastern churches one need be only twenty-four (*CCEO* 759, §1). Canon 1031, §3 also stipulates that an episcopal conference may determine a later, but not earlier, age of ordination for candidates to the priesthood and the permanent diaconate; however, the conference may not adjust the minimum age for the transitional diaconate. Particular law in the *sui iuris* Eastern churches may alter the minimum age for both the priesthood and the transitional diaconate (*CCEO* 759, §1).

The minimum age of ordination may be lowered for up to one year by the diocesan bishop, in individual cases; beyond that, a dispensation from the Holy See is required (c. 1031, §4). In light of canon 87, §1, the diocesan bishop may shorten the interstices, i.e., the required period of at least six months between diaconal and presbyteral ordination.

Canons 200–203 offer guidelines for computing when the minimum age for ordination has been reached. The first available licit ordination date would be the day after the birthday of the year mentioned in canon 1031, §1 and §2; for example, an unmarried permanent deacon is first available for licit ordination on the day following his twenty-fifth birthday.

Academic and Pastoral Prerequisites for Ordination

Canon 1032 — §1. Those aspiring to the presbyterate can be promoted to the diaconate only after they have completed the fifth year of the curriculum of philosophical and theological studies.

§2. After a deacon has completed the curriculum of studies and before he is promoted to the presbyterate, he is to take part in pastoral care, ex-

---

[21] Admittedly, "in all too many cases psychological defects, sometimes of a pathological kind, reveal themselves only after ordination to the priesthood." CCE, instr "A Guide to Priestly Formation," in *Norms for Priestly Formation,* vol. 1 (Washington, D.C.: USCC, 1993) 176.

[22] As regards the required consent of the spouse of a married candidate for the permanent diaconate, see commentary on c. 1050, 3°.

ercising the diaconal order, for a suitable time defined by the bishop or competent major superior.

§3. A person aspiring to the permanent diaconate is not to be promoted to this order unless he has completed the time of formation.

Canon 1032 specifies the basic academic and pastoral requirements for ordination. Candidates for sacerdotal ministry may be promoted to the transitional diaconate only after having completed the fifth year of the curriculum of philosophical and theological studies (§1). Canon 235, §1 stipulates that at least four years of the training leading to priestly ordination are to take place in the setting of a major seminary.

Canon 1032, §1 should be read in conjunction with canons 232–264 regarding ministerial formation, especially canons 233, §2; 245; 248–252; and 256–258. The national and local implementation of the program of studies belongs to the proper episcopal conference (c. 242) and the proper bishop (c. 243).

Training in Directly Pastoral Work

Canon 1032, §2 distinguishes formal study from training in pastoral ministry. The transitional deacon exercises his order for a designated period of time. The implementation of this canon varies widely, depending on the norms of national programs of priestly formation and the adaptations unique to particular local preparation programs.

Canon 1032, §2 does not mandate that the transitional deacon be supervised by experienced parochial personnel, although such supervision would understandably be beneficial for all parties concerned. Canon 232 does not limit the training of clergy to seminary faculties and proper ordinaries; rather, all the faithful participate in this training. As the exercise of diaconal ministry falls within the period of time set aside to form the future presbyter, so care for his pastoral development belongs, at least in part, to the faithful he serves and, all the more so, to the leaders within the designated pastoral setting. While the transitional deacon is to be treated respectfully as a trained cleric, careful supervision of him during his pastoral internship is desirable.

Training for Permanent Deacons

Canon 1032, §3 addresses training for those destined to the permanent diaconate. Local training for aspirants to the permanent diaconate varies as widely as the manner in which their ministry will be exercised. In dioceses in which successive bishops have permitted and encouraged the training, ordination, and ministry of permanent deacons, preparation programs are organized accordingly. Canon 236 regulates the regional or local adaptation of universal norms governing formation requirements concerning residency and duration.

ARTICLE 2: THE PREREQUISITES FOR ORDINATION [cc. 1033–1039]

Confirmation

Canon 1033 — A person is promoted licitly to orders only if he has received the sacrament of confirmation.

Reception of the sacrament of confirmation normally precedes acceptance into a clerical formation program, whether religious or secular. In the case of a religious program, proof of a man's confirmation precedes admission into the institute (c. 645, §1). In the case of a secular program, proof of confirmation precedes admission to the major seminary (c. 241, §2).

If one is born a Catholic, confirmation is received at the age customary according to approved local norms, unless there is some extraordinary circumstance (c. 891). If one is baptized into another church or ecclesial community and later received into the Catholic Church, confirmation would likely accompany his reception into the Church (c. 883, 2°). One baptized a Catholic as an adult generally is asked to wait for a period of time prior to admission to a seminary or a religious institute, thereby assuring a more than sufficient passage of time between confirmation and ordination.[23]

Canon 1033 mentions no time period which ought to elapse between confirmation and ordination. Confirmation could even proximately precede ordination, with proper permission; the validity of the ordination is not threatened even if the candidate is not confirmed.

Canon 1033 corresponds to Eastern code canon 758, §1, 1°, which calls for aspirants in the Eastern churches to have received chrismation with holy myron prior to ordination.

Formal Admission to Candidacy

Canon 1034 — §1. A person aspiring to the diaconate or presbyterate is not to be ordained unless he has first been enrolled among the candidates through the liturgical rite of admission by the authority mentioned in cann. 1016 and 1019; his petition is previously to have been written in his own hand, signed, and accepted in writing by the same authority.

§2. A person who has been received into a clerical institute through vows is not bound to obtain this admission.

The term "candidacy" is commonly used to include all those accepted into formal preparation for an eventual but not distant conferral of orders. More precisely, however, it refers to those who have been enrolled as candidates through the appropriate liturgical rite by the competent authority (cc. 1016 and 1019). The aspirant's petition is to be written in his own hand with his signature affixed; the competent authority is to indicate acceptance of the petition in writing. The petition states the aspirant's desire to be ordained to the diaconate or the presbyterate. Members of clerical institutes who have taken vows are not bound by

[23] See commentary on c. 1042, 3°.

this admission process. Renewable promises, however, do not exempt one from such a requirement.

Canon 1034 does not indicate when the candidacy enrollment should take place. While the simple liturgical rite itself should be duly solemn, perhaps the more significant moment for the candidate should be his prior, prayerful realization of the import of his petition. While distinct from the reception of orders, of course, the aspirant's signature and designation as a candidate for ordination should represent his sober, free acknowledgment of his present and future willingness to accept a calling which will bring him both joys and burdens.

Conferral and Exercise of Ministries

Canon 1035 — §1. Before anyone is promoted to the permanent or transitional diaconate, he is required to have received the ministries of lector and acolyte and to have exercised them for a suitable period of time.

§2. There is to be an interval of at least six months between the conferral of the ministry of acolyte and the diaconate.

Before his licit promotion to sacred orders, the candidate must have received the ministries of lector and acolyte. The code does not generally legislate regarding liturgical rites or functions (c. 2). However, some functions of assisting at the altar and proclaiming sacred scripture properly belong to the non-ordained; candidates for ordained ministry benefit from having earlier fulfilled these non-clerical liturgical roles. By exercising them for a suitable length of time, ideally one becomes more comfortable with such public roles. This experience helps the future presider in recognizing the importance of well-trained lectors and acolytes. These ministries can be exercised in or out of the seminary setting. While canon 1035 lists no specific interstices regarding the ministry of lector, at least six months must transpire between the conferral of the ministry of acolyte and one's diaconal ordination.

*Declaration of Freedom
and Petition for Ordination*

Canon 1036 — In order to be promoted to the order of diaconate or of presbyterate, the candidate is to present to his bishop or competent major superior a declaration written in his own hand and signed in which he attests that he will receive the sacred order of his own accord and freely and will devote himself perpetually to the ecclesiastical ministry and at the same time asks to be admitted to the order to be received.

Candidates for the diaconate or the priesthood must freely request reception of that order. The moral freedom enjoyed by the petitioning candidate must be beyond doubt.[24] Besides requesting conferral of the order, the candidate promises to commit himself forever to exercise the relevant ecclesiastical ministry according to the mind of the Church; he will act not for himself but for the good of the faithful, in the person of Christ (c. 1008).

The candidate for sacred ministry has presumably established himself during his formation as one apt to fulfill various teaching,[25] sanctifying,[26] and ruling[27] functions. The fit[28] and knowing[29] candidate understands the object of his intention, and has been judged worthy to be admitted to the order in question. Legitimate authority[30] receives this free petition as a reflection of the ordinand's intention to receive the sacrament. In accepting the freely given, aptly informed petition of a candidate for diaconal or sacerdotal ordination, the Church presumes that the ordinand will further develop his Christian commitment in his future exercise of the sacred ministry to which the Church admits him.[31]

---

[24] See cc. 1025, §1; 1026; 1034, §1; and 1050, 3°.
[25] See, for example, cc. 757; 760; 762; 764–765; 767; and 833, 6°.
[26] See, for example, cc. 835, §2 and §3; 843; 844; and 846.
[27] See, for example, cc. 129, §1 and 274.
[28] See cc. 1025 and 1029.
[29] See cc. 1027–1028.
[30] See cc. 265–266, 1016, and 1019.
[31] See c. 276.

*Assumption of the Obligation
of Clerical Celibacy*

Canon 1037 — An unmarried candidate for the permanent diaconate and a candidate for the presbyterate are not to be admitted to the order of diaconate unless they have assumed the obligation of celibacy in the prescribed rite publicly before God and the Church or have made perpetual vows in a religious institute.

Notwithstanding the controversy which attends it in some cultures, and the sanctioned exceptions which highlight the rule, the Church's teaching on clerical celibacy in the Latin rite is clear.

One who is married and aspires to the permanent diaconate must accept the fact that, if he is later rendered otherwise free to marry, he may not ordinarily contract marriage again. While this is the norm, the Congregation for Divine Worship and the Discipline of the Sacraments entertains requests from widowed deacons wishing to be exempted. Factors which may prompt the congregation to permit remarriage would be: the care of minor children; the care of elderly or infirm parents; or the serious needs of the particular church for which the deacon is exceptionally useful.

Canon 1037 presupposes that celibacy is to be observed by unmarried candidates for the priesthood or the transitional diaconate.[32] The celibacy obligation binds all Latin rite clergy, secular or regular, who are not married permanent deacons.

For religious, canon 1037 assumes one's prior vow to remain a chaste celibate.[33] The religiously vowed candidate for ordination should be mindful, however, that his publicly professed commitment to chastity is distinct from the clerical promise of celibacy, in that canonical release from the former does not necessarily entail canonical release from the latter (cc. 701; 291).

For secular clerics, the obligation of perpetual celibacy is expressed in the ordination rite itself. Admission to the transitional diaconate or the

---

[32] See also c. 277.
[33] See also cc. 599 and 1088.

presbyterate entails the unmarried ordinand's promise of celibacy. The Holy See alone admits of exceptions to this rule, e.g., in cases of non-Catholic Christian married ministers who convert to Catholicism and request admission to sacred orders.

Canon 1037 does not explicitly consider the case of one who cohabits with someone as if he were married to that person, when in fact he is not. Such a man must be able to promise celibacy and live it, which means he would begin by realizing the objective sinfulness of such a living arrangement. He would have to cease this behavior prior to any serious consideration of his advancement to the permanent diaconate or any sacred order.

Denial of Exercise of Diaconal Ministry

Canon 1038 — A deacon who refuses to be promoted to the presbyterate cannot be prohibited from the exercise of the order received unless he is prevented by a canonical impediment or another grave cause to be evaluated in the judgment of the diocesan bishop or competent major superior.

While no one has a right to ordination, the law protects a cleric's right to the exercise of orders already received. A validly ordained transitional deacon who opts not to advance to the presbyterate obviously never stops being a deacon. As one freely requests advancement to sacred orders, canon 1038 presumes that such a deacon may freely request that he remain a deacon who can exercise his sacred ministry. As an incardinated cleric whose fitness and usefulness have otherwise been established with moral certitude (cc. 1025, §1; 1052), the deacon rightfully may expect an assignment, unless his proper ordinary is morally certain about the former's lack of fitness for the exercise of diaconal ministry (c. 1044).

"Another Grave Cause"

Canon 1038 remains vague as to what "another grave cause" for prohibiting the exercise of dia-

conal ministry might be. The entirety of the canon suggests that the cause is ordinand-dependent, i.e., it is tied personally to the man and his ministerial fitness, personal will, or practical ability to function usefully as a deacon. The cause ought not depend wholly on external circumstances, and certainly not on an ordinary's whims.

One is not ordained to the diaconate only because one is going to be later ordained to the priesthood. While presumably one ordained to the transitional diaconate will likely proceed to priestly ordination, the transitional diaconate is nonetheless a distinct state and not simply a step to the priesthood.

Canon 1038 implies that the deacon's eventual sacerdotal ordination is probable but not necessary, and in some situations a transitional deacon in fact may remain such indefinitely. Since neither the ordinary nor the ordinand, at the time of the latter's ordination, intended that the latter should enter the permanent diaconate, the question of whether or not a diocese has a permanent diaconate program is not a relevant issue. If, in fact, a diocese lacks a permanent diaconate program, this reality alone does not constitute the "grave cause" to deny the deacon the exercise of the distinct ministry for which he has been deemed fit and useful. On the other hand, if the transitional deacon freely desires release from all his clerical obligations, he should pursue laicization (cc. 290–292).

Pre-ordination Retreat

Canon 1039 — All candidates for any order are to make a spiritual retreat for at least five days in a place and manner determined by the ordinary. Before the bishop proceeds to ordination, he must be certain that the candidates properly made this retreat.

An ordinand must approach ordination freely and knowledgeably. Furthermore, he should enter the clerical state with a humble spirit, appreciative of how he will need to rely upon the Lord's constant care for him. The ordinand's cooperation with the graces afforded him will necessitate his own hard work and the support of the community of believers. Accordingly, the law appropriately requires a period of intense prayer just prior to ordination.

The candidate's retreat is subject to regulation by his legitimate superior, especially as regards place and time. The ordaining prelate is to ascertain that this requirement has been fulfilled. The canon does not specify how soon the retreat should be made before the ordination. By referring to "all candidates for any order," the law encompasses those to be ordained deacons, priests, or bishops.

Though the canon does not explicitly refer to continuous time (c. 201, §1), the days noted in canon 1039 should be understood to be consecutive, as the canon refers to one retreat of five days. The canon delineates both a right and an obligation on the part of the ordinand, as well as an obligation on the part of the ordinaries involved. That is, an ordinand has a right to his ordination retreat. Hence, the norm governing useful time (c. 201, §2) is pertinent in reckoning an individual's ability to make the retreat. Individual days are computed in accord with canons 202, §1 (what constitutes a day); 203, §1 (when the first day of the retreat has been completed); and 203, §2 (the total number of days of the retreat).

While canon 1039 explicitly refers to a retreat of at least five days, Eastern code canon 772 makes no time stipulation, requiring only that the candidate make a retreat in the manner determined by particular law. There is also no reference to an ordaining prelate's obligation to be certain that the retreat has been made.

ARTICLE 3: IRREGULARITIES AND OTHER IMPEDIMENTS [cc. 1040–1049]

Simple and Perpetual Impediments to Ordination

Canon 1040 — Those affected by any impediment, whether perpetual, which is called an ir-

regularity, or simple, are prevented from receiving orders. The only impediments incurred, however, are those contained in the following canons.

Canons 1040 through 1049 govern impediments and irregularities for the reception and exercise of sacred orders. The broader category delimited is that of impediments, some of which are known as irregularities. While irregularities are perpetual impediments, all other impediments are simple impediments. A simple impediment to the reception of orders can cease when the impediment's cause ceases.

An impediment must be established with moral certitude, since it restricts a person's right to present himself for ordination or to exercise orders already received. The matter is also serious because it may result in the faithful's having one less priest, deacon, or bishop available for sacramental ministry.

The fact of an impediment, whether public or hidden, does not invalidate an ordination, but renders it illicit by the law itself. Whether an impediment exists is one question; if a delict gives rise to the impediment, a separate but related question will concern whether a canonical penalty is warranted. Such delicts may be punished by a *latae sententiae* or a *ferendae sententiae* penalty.

Canon 1040 indicates that only those impediments listed in canons 1040–1049 bar a candidate from the licit reception or exercise of orders. However, the practical applicability of these canons will vary. For instance, while it can generally be known objectively whether someone is bound by the impediment of an existing marital bond (c. 1042, 1°), it might be more difficult to determine if a person is impeded due to amentia or insanity (c. 1041, 1°) or heresy (c. 1041, 2°).

Irregularities for Reception of Orders

Canon 1041 — The following are irregular for receiving orders:
    1° **a person who labors under some form of amentia or other psychic illness due to which, after experts have been consulted,**

he is judged unqualified to fulfill the ministry properly;

2° a person who has committed the delict of apostasy, heresy, or schism;

3° a person who has attempted marriage, even only civilly, while either impeded personally from entering marriage by a matrimonial bond, sacred orders, or a public perpetual vow of chastity, or with a woman bound by a valid marriage or restricted by the same type of vow;

4° a person who has committed voluntary homicide or procured a completed abortion and all those who positively cooperated in either;

5° a person who has mutilated himself or another gravely and maliciously or who has attempted suicide;

6° a person who has placed an act of orders reserved to those in the order of episcopate or presbyterate while either lacking that order or prohibited from its exercise by some declared or imposed canonical penalty.

Persons falling into any of six categories may not receive orders licitly because they are bound by perpetual impediments, or irregularities. Since all parties properly disposed and capable according to law enjoy the right at least to be considered for orders, canon 18 implicitly applies to all six categories. The provisions of canon 1041 are to be applied strictly, and only in those situations in which they seem genuinely relevant. Eastern code canon 762 corresponds almost entirely to canons 1041 and 1042, excepting canon 1042, 1°. However, the Eastern code makes no distinction between simple and perpetual impediments.

"Amentia or Other Psychic Illness"

Persons who suffer from "amentia or other psychic illness" are not to advance to orders (c. 1041, 1°). The specifically impeding quality of the amentia or other psychic illness is seen in its effect: the candidate's condition is such that he will not be able to fulfill the ministerial duties flowing from ordination.[34]

Canon 1041, 1° does *not* state explicitly that the psychically impaired person is judged to be utterly *incapable* of fulfilling the demands of sacred ministry. Hence, he need not lack the use of reason or labor under an irremediable psychosis. The criterion is simply stated: the psychic disorder renders the person unqualified to fulfill ministry properly. For instance, a paranoid schizophrenic whose delusions cannot be regulated quite likely would be bound by this impediment; one who suffers inordinately from a fear of high places likely would not. The canon does not state whether the psychic problem need inhibit the person merely in liturgical ministry (e.g., presiding at Mass or hearing confessions), or rather in a broader pastoral sense as well (e.g., preaching, teaching, visiting, or parish administration).

The Perpetual Problem

An irregularity is a perpetual impediment; however, many psychic illnesses are in fact temporary. For instance, marked depression could seriously detract from an aspirant's overall qualifications for ministry. However, that depression may be situationally contingent, and professional therapy may help the person to function moderately well, or better. Even if such a temporary depression significantly and overtly limited a person for several months or longer, it might not be perpetual. Also, proper clinical diagnosis and an appropriate medical regimen may render one able to function quite well in ministerial settings.

Consultation with Experts

Though he enjoys a certain latitude in determining the applicability of canon 1041, 1° in a given candidate's case, the presenting ordinary or the ordaining bishop may not be arbitrary. The investigation must be thorough and complete and include an examination by experts. While the law recognizes that the ordinary's judgment is ultimately a subjective one, the decision must be

---

[34] See also commentary on c. 1044, §2, 2°.

based on solid objective data which lead him to moral certitude regarding the presence or absence of the impeding amentia or other psychic illness. The problem must be recognizable and determined by experts, and must directly affect the person's ability to exercise his office fittingly.

Canon 1041, 1° presumably refers to psychological experts; however, this is not explicitly stated. Hence, such experts need not be exclusively those credentialed in psychology or psychiatry. Persons may be consulted who are considered expert in some other pertinent field (e.g., civil or criminal law; education; clerical formation), depending on a candidate's specific situation and always with great deference to his right to privacy and the protection of his good name (c. 220).

Apostasy, Heresy, or Schism

A person who has committed the delict of apostasy, heresy, or schism (c. 751) is irregular for the reception of orders (c. 1041, 2°). The present canon implies that one has notoriously distanced himself from Catholicism.[35]

Contumacy and imputability are presumed: heresy requires an obstinate denial of a true teaching of the Church, apostasy a total repudiation of the Christian faith, and schism a genuine refusal to remain in faithful Catholic communion. Hence, a future seminarian's past single act, promptly repented, likely would not suffice for the declaration of this irregularity. If the requirements of canon 1321 on imputability are met, if canons 1323, 1324, and 1330 on factors exempting one from imputability or mitigating it do not apply, and if the man engages persistently in acts of heresy, apostasy, or schism, he incurs the *latae sententiae* excommunication set forth in canon 1364, §1. An open question remains just how public and notorious the acts of heresy, apostasy, or schism must be in order for a person to be recognized as irregular for the reception of orders. Canon 1330 states that the offense must be made evident by some public declaration or manifestation.

[35] See commentary on c. 751.

The delict is technically necessary if the irregularity of canon 1041, 2° is to be incurred. The remission of the penalty associated with the delict must be dealt with separately from the dispensation of the irregularity associated with it; the remission and the dispensation constitute two acts. Further, even if the revelation of certain facts should exempt the man from imputability, or at least mitigate it, he might still be unsuitable morally, if not irregular canonically, for advancement to orders.

Finally, simply falling away from the practice of the faith does not constitute an irregularity, though formal and seriously imputable admission into a non-Catholic or non-Christian denomination would. A public liturgical act or written declaration whereby a party separates himself from the Catholic faith might well entail a canonical delict and hence the irregularity understood by canon 1041, 2°. A formal declaration of the prior *latae sententiae* penalty would offer clarity in such a situation, though it would not technically be necessary to incur certain effects of the penalty (c. 1364, §1, 1°). In cases in which it is uncertain as to whether a delict has occurred (and an irregularity incurred), a doubtful irregularity does not bind.

Attempted Marriage

Also barred from the licit reception of orders is one who is or was involved in a canonically prohibited marriage (c. 1041, 3°). The attempted marriage could have been invalid because the man or his civil spouse already was bound by a prior valid matrimonial bond at the time of the attempted marriage, or because he or his civil spouse was impeded by a public perpetual vow of chastity (c. 1088), or because he himself had attempted marriage while a cleric (c. 1087). The current canon refers to the fact of the invalid attempt at marriage, which gives rise to scandal; hence, the irregularity occurs even if the marriage is ended by death or civil divorce, as irregularities are by their nature perpetual.

The Church here is particularly concerned about the scandal prompted by the failure of certain Christians to live chastely, according to their state of life. This obligation must be lived faithfully, whether one is in orders or not. Canon 1041, 3° clearly refers to those whose marriages cannot objectively be recognized by the Catholic Church as valid; therein rests the violation against chastity. A further concern is the impropriety of ordaining someone not faithful to a prior commitment, be it in virtue of orders, perpetual religious profession, or marriage.

Canon 1041, 3° does not pertain to parties freed—or declared free—by the Church to marry validly. For instance, a former member of a religious institute of pontifical right who earlier was committed by a perpetual vow to remain celibate and chaste can be released from that vow and enabled to marry according to church law (c. 1078, §2, 1°). Likewise, a marriage presumed to be valid can later be declared as having been ecclesiastically invalid. Such parties, if otherwise legally able and capable of marrying, enter marriage validly.

The focus of the canon is on the scandalous situation of those who have attempted a marriage which is viewed as invalid, regardless of whether or not the bond endures. A Catholic who wishes to marry and live a chaste marital life must do so according to the pertinent ecclesiastical norms. Hence, if an aspirant to the permanent diaconate is already in a valid marriage, he must not subsequently have divorced and attempted marriage with another. Or, if one has taken a perpetual vow of chastity, he must not subsequently have abandoned that vow and attempted marriage without the proper dispensation issued by legitimate authority.

Furthermore, for a man to be regular for orders, he cannot have attempted marriage with a woman bound by a presumably valid prior marriage bond, or by a prior perpetual, non-dispensed vow of chastity. A secular transitional deacon is bound not to marry, by virtue of his ordination; his attempt at marriage prior to his sacerdotal ordination would render him irregular for it. A religious deacon in perpetual vows is bound doubly, both by his public vow to remain a chaste celibate and by his commitment to celibacy reinforced by his ordination to the transitional diaconate. One already ordained who attempts marriage cannot be advanced licitly to another order, loses any ecclesiastical office he holds (c. 194, §1, 3°), and is subject to a *latae sententiae* suspension (c. 1394, §1).

Homicide and Abortion

One who has voluntarily committed a homicide or positively participated in a completed abortion is irregular for the reception of orders (c. 1041, 4°). The canon does not refer to participation in an incomplete abortion. A man is irregular if his complicity in planning such a death resulted directly in the completion of the act, even if he were not present for its completion. The heinous act must have been completed and one must be seriously culpable in the planning or execution of it. The participation must have been necessary to the execution of the act in some way; that is, without that participation, the act would not have taken place. The irregularity does not apply if one's participation is not voluntary and deliberate, or if one's participation is a sin of omission rather than commission, or if one's participation is ultimately negligible in the commission of the act.

One's participation in the death need not necessarily result in the imposition of a canonical penalty, whether *latae sententiae* (automatic) or *ferendae sententiae* (declared or imposed), since canon 1041, 4° does not refer to an offense or delict, technically speaking, or to the imposition of penalties. That is, the irregularity applies to one who has been instrumental in the death of a person or fetus, as long as that participation was voluntary, active, and effective. The question of a possible delict and related penalties (cc. 1329; 1397–1398) must be taken up separately.

Canon 1041, 4° must be carefully considered by church authorities who assess its applicability in a given case. In many situations the irregularity will not have been incurred, e.g., a soldier's participation in a recognizably just war, or a medical professional's participation in a procedure resulting in the unintended yet tragic death of a fetus.

Unresolved Questions

Some situations pose problems regarding the proper interpretation of canon 1041, 4°. What of a person who commits vehicular homicide while knowingly driving recklessly through a clearly marked school zone at recess? What of a son who agonizes with and supports his terminally ill mother in her request for a doctor-assisted or self-directed method of ending her life? What of a pharmacist who regularly sold abortifacients prior to his entrance into the seminary? On the one hand, a doubtful irregularity would not bind; on the other hand, the facts of a specific situation may not admit of much doubt. A just interpretation of the canon would require prudently considering how voluntary, active, and effective a person's participation was.

Yet a further question concerns the time at which a possibly irregularity-generating incident occurred. For instance, what if one's voluntary, active, and effective participation in a homicide or a procured abortion took place prior to one's baptism or reception into Catholicism? It appears that the irregularity of canon 1041, 4° would be doubtful, and therefore not binding. The non-Catholic person would not have been subject at that time to the peculiarly Catholic ecclesiastical norms governing irregularities which would apply to him only after he became a Catholic (see c. 11). Another relevant datum to be considered is Eastern code canon 762, §2, which states that impediments do not result from those actions corresponding to canons 1041, 2°–6° unless they were serious, external sins and were perpetrated *after* baptism.

While granting that the irregularity apparently is not incurred in the situation just described, a look at the counter-argument is in order. Canon 1041, 4° does not set any limits as to when an act occurs, i.e., before or after baptism or reception into the Catholic Church. Further, prohibitions against procured abortion and willful homicide certainly transcend ecclesiastical law and pertain to natural law, rooted in divine law. Also, Eastern code canon 762, §2 implies that the impediment is incurred by one baptized but not yet received into Catholicism, which suggests an applicability to non-Catholic Christians; this apparently would diminish the relevance of canon 11. However, to repeat, non-Catholics engaging in the activity outlined in canon 1041, 4° apparently would not incur the irregularity, as a doubtful irregularity does not bind; further, the canons on irregularities and simple impediments are to be interpreted strictly (c. 18), as a man has a right at least to have himself considered for orders.

Mutilation and Attempted Suicide

Grave and malicious mutilation of oneself or another also makes one irregular for the reception of orders, as does attempted suicide (c. 1041, 5°). Standards of gravity and maliciousness—and mutilation—may be culturally relative. For example, tattoos or ornamental artifices voluntarily appended to one's body may be considered beautiful, or at least acceptable, in one culture, yet maliciously mutilating in another. As another example, attitudes toward female or male circumcision are not only not universally consistent but indeed are the subject of heated transcultural controversy.

The contemporary application of canon 1041, 5° gives rise to some difficult questions, two of which are mentioned here by way of example: vasectomy, and doubtfully genuine suicide attempts.

Canonists disagree on whether or not a man's prior vasectomy renders him irregular for orders. In one view, a vasectomy is a gravely sinful act in which a man intends to render himself permanently sterile by means of an invasive and physically unnatural procedure, in direct violation of natural law.[36] An argument from a different perspective notes that while the vasectomy certainly constitutes an objectively grave moral evil, the procedure itself is simple and not truly mutilating in any physical sense. As a procedure which is usually a very pri-

---

[36] For a succinct presentation of this opinion, see J. Jukes, "Irregularity for the Reception of Orders: CIC 1041. n. 5," *CLS-GBIN* 108 (1996) 85–87.

vate matter, the threat of public scandal is limited. Since it is doubtful that such a procedure is truly physically mutilating, this argument holds that the irregularity would not be incurred.

In addition to self-mutilation, the current canon addresses attempted suicide. Any genuine, serious effort to end one's life incurs the irregularity. However, some attempts are so feeble as to be nothing more than attention-getting devices or desperate cries for help. Would the irregularity be incurred by an impulsive, desperate, perhaps misunderstood young person who ingests a moderate overdose of nonprescription medication? Yes, it would seem so, as the canon makes no distinction about the seriousness of the effort, or the age or state of mind of the person. However, if there is considerable doubt about whether or not an action qualifies as a genuine attempt to end one's life, the irregularity is not incurred. A doubtful irregularity does not bind. In any case, church authorities should not ignore any activity which highlights a candidate's prior or current self-destructive tendencies.

Simulation or Abuse of Sacramental Administration

Persons who are not priests or bishops and who have simulated an act proper to either order are themselves irregular for the reception of orders (c. 1041, 6°). The act of a lay person could involve the simulation of a sacrament such as penance or the Eucharist. The act of a cleric could involve the simulation of a sacrament not proper to that order (e.g., a deacon granting absolution) or the placement of an act not proper in a given instance (e.g., a priest attempting to confirm though he knowingly lacks the necessary faculty). Canon 1041, 6° may be relevant even if a canonical penalty has not been incurred (cc. 1378–1379 and 1384).

Further, a cleric is irregular for advancement to a higher order (a deacon to the presbyterate, a priest to the episcopacy) who exercises his order while prohibited by a canonical penalty which bars the exercise of that order, except in certain emergency pastoral situations such as caring for the faithful in danger of death.[37]

Canon 1041, 6° is clear that the penalty must be declared or imposed. Hence, the irregularity is not incurred if a *latae sententiae* penalty has not been declared. Properly disposed members of the faithful certainly have a right to the sacraments, but the offending deacon or priest has a corresponding obligation to seek the remission of the penalty so as to be fully restored to the communion of the Church.

Simple Impediments to Reception of Orders

Canon 1042 — The following are simply impeded from receiving orders:

    1° a man who has a wife, unless he is legitimately destined to the permanent diaconate;

    2° a person who exercises an office or administration forbidden to clerics according to the norm of cann. 285 and 286 for which he must render an account, until he becomes free by having relinquished the office or administration and rendered the account;

    3° a neophyte unless he has been proven sufficiently in the judgment of the ordinary.

Marriage

A currently married man is impeded from orders (c. 1042, 1°). This includes even one who is legitimately separated from his spouse (cc. 1151–1155). The impediment ceases with the death of a spouse, or when the marriage is dissolved or declared null by competent church authorities.

Since marriages attempted invalidly do not result in a canonically recognized husband-wife relationship, canon 1042, 1° refers to those bonds that are truly binding or apparently binding. The

---

[37] See cc. 976; 1335; 1338, §3; and 1352, §1.

canon refers to persons in presumably valid marital relationships, which distinguishes them from those affected by canon 1041, 3°. Excepted from the impediment in canon 1042, 1° would be a married man destined for the permanent diaconate. While one in an apparently valid marital bond is validly but illicitly ordained to the presbyterate or episcopate (unless permission from the Holy See assures liceity), the reverse is not true. One validly ordained and not laicized attempts marriage invalidly (c. 1087), and is subject at least to an automatic suspension (c. 1394, §1).

Marriages Declared Ecclesiastically Invalid by a Tribunal

Some commentators raise the possibility of the applicability of canon 1041, 1° to an aspirant whose marriage has been declared ecclesiastically invalid by legitimate authority, during which formal process his psychological incapacity to posit marital consent may have been determined. Such an incapacity could ground both a decision in favor of marital nullity, and an irregularity regarding the licit reception of orders due to amentia or other psychic illness, precluding the proper exercise of ministry. Though matrimony and orders are two very different sacraments, information regarding a person's fundamental psychological health as he attempted marriage *may* be relevant in assessing his fitness for ordained ministry.[38]

However, the protection of confidentiality (c. 220) is a serious concern. First, the acts of a tribunal proceeding contain confidential data relative to the lives of other persons (e.g., former spouse, children, witnesses) who have a right to privacy. Second, data surfacing during such a proceeding is usually understood to be restricted to it; parties offering testimony or expert assessments do so in the belief that their accounts will go no further than the annulment investigation. One could argue that the candidate could authorize a judge to release data pertinent to him alone. Such a gesture may be appropriate in light of a man's moral obligation to inform legitimate authority of any factors which touch upon his fitness for the valid and licit reception of orders. However, sifting through case acts and concentrating on data pertinent to only one party is a difficult task for a judge. Another possibility is that the applicant could ask proper judicial authorities to release to seminary admissions personnel a copy of the judicial sentence (and only the sentence), or at least those portions which concern the applicant.[39]

The diocesan bishop is the highest local judicial authority in his diocese (c. 1419, §1); hence, if the "formal process" declaration of nullity were granted in his own diocese, he would have access to the attendant tribunal case acts as well as to the file attendant to the man's seminary application. It would be entirely proper for him to consider the former in weighing the latter. A more complex question arises regarding the sharing of such data between different dioceses. For example, a declaration of nullity is granted in one diocese and a man applies for seminary admission elsewhere. One could argue that, since the acts of a formal annulment investigation belong to a judicial process in the external forum, they can be used—discreetly and by legitimate authority only—for the good of the ecclesial community at large. As noted earlier, this would presume the aspirant's free authorization, and the release of data pertinent to him alone. However, one still must confront the general principle that the use of information surfacing in a marriage nullity case should be restricted to that case. Ultimately, the discussion regarding the use of marriage tribunal documentation in weighing admissibility to sacred ministry is more properly a moral and ethical one, and less a canonical one. Universal law does not explicitly treat this topic.

---

[38] See P. Smith, "Lack of Due Discretion and Suitability for Ordination," *Stud Can* 21 (1987) 125–140.

[39] For a discussion of some of these issues, see F. Morrisey, "La formation des séminaristes et le respect de la personne," *Stud Can* 22 (1988) 5–25, esp. 18–19.

Offices and Administration Forbidden to Clerics

One who exercises an office or administration forbidden to clerics, either personally or through another (cc. 285–286), is simply impeded from the reception of orders (c. 1042, 2°). While it may be fairly easy to establish whether a man is married and thereby simply impeded from receiving orders (c. 1042, 1°), the applicability of canon 1042, 2° is less clearly determined. For instance, a man interested in the diocesan presbyterate at a later age (e.g., late thirties or older) may have held financially lucrative positions; while he may relinquish his office when he enters into seminary formation, the question of his administration of assets still remains. Canon 285, §2 is sufficiently broad so as to be subject to varying interpretations, relative to a given cultural and social context.

A question arises in relation to candidates for the priesthood who, of necessity or due to reasonable parental request, are nominated as executors of parental estates or are granted durable powers of attorney for their parents (c. 285, §4). While the proper ordinary's permission suffices for the assumption of such duties, canon 1042, 2° bears consideration. Once incurred, if the simple impediment of canon 1042, 2° does not cease with the cessation of the circumstance which gives rise to it, a dispensation is in order.

Neophytes

A neophyte in the faith is simply impeded from the reception of orders, unless his ordinary determines him to be sufficiently grounded in his new identity as a Catholic Christian (c. 1042, 3°). Given the minimum age requirements (c. 1031, §1), one would have to be at least in his twenties to be simultaneously a neophyte and a candidate for ordained ministry.

The notion of a neophyte, in this context, is a liturgical and catechetical construction, and not a defined legal category; in other words, canonically one is either a baptized Catholic or not. The law does not determine precisely how long one has to have been a baptized Catholic to be no longer considered a neophyte, though the period of three years is common in practice. Formal entrance into formation programs usually presupposes that one is no longer a neophyte; however, the canon does not refer to whether the neophyte may begin training for orders, but rather to whether he may be licitly ordained.

Notification of Known Impediments

Canon 1043 — If the Christian faithful are aware of impediments to sacred orders, they are obliged to reveal them to the ordinary or pastor before the ordination.

Ideally, the Christian faithful recognize their moral obligation to assist in ensuring that only fit candidates are ordained. Knowledge of existing irregularities and/or simple impediments is to be shared with the competent authority. Such an obligation unfortunately is vulnerable to a certain moral relativism in its fulfillment (or not). A person with such knowledge may not feel it to be his or her place to bring the impediment to light, lest he or she be perceived as judging another. Or one might think that surely such an impediment must have surfaced for review during the candidate's training. Or, perhaps most likely, a person might have no idea that such a fact indeed creates a problem; or the person might think that the Church should not be concerned about it in any case. Because of the ecclesial importance of ordained ministers, the community bears a moral responsibility to encourage the ordination of only fit candidates or, at the very least, candidates who are not bound by impediments. This is a very serious moral obligation on the part of the faithful.

Irregularities, Simple Impediments, and the Exercise of Orders Already Received

Canon 1044 — §1. The following are irregular for the exercise of orders received:

1° a person who has received orders illegitimately while affected by an irregularity to receive them;

2° a person who has committed a delict mentioned in can. 1041, n. 2, if the delict is public;

3° a person who has committed a delict mentioned in can. 1041, nn. 3, 4, 5, 6.

§2. The following are impeded from the exercise of orders:

1° a person who has received orders illegitimately while prevented by an impediment from receiving them;

2° a person who is affected by amentia or some other psychic illness mentioned in can. 1041, n. 1 until the ordinary, after consulting an expert, permits the exercise of the order.

The law distinguishes between those who are barred from the licit reception of orders and those who are barred from their licit exercise. The distinction is an important one.

The presence of a non-dispensed irregularity or simple impediment at the time of ordination may provoke subsequent hand wringing; however, whether or how it should have affected the man's earlier advancement to orders is merely academic. After the fact, the pertinent question becomes whether the man licitly exercises the order received. Canon 1044 addresses irregularities present at the time of ordination (c. 1044, §1, 1°; §2, 1°) as well as those arising after ordination.

The Effect of a Prior Irregularity

Canon 1044, §1, 1° presents an overarching principle: if an irregularity existed which made illegitimate the prior, presumably valid reception of orders, then the cleric may not legitimately exercise that order. The only apparent exception foreseen is indicated in canon 1044, §1, 2°. Public delicts of apostasy, heresy, or schism make one irregular for the exercise of orders. However, perhaps one's prior apostasy, heresy, or schism (c. 751) was an occult or not widely known delict (*CIC* 2197, 1° and 4°), yet it rendered him irregular for the reception of orders; that same act need not nec-

essarily make him irregular for their exercise, unless it becomes public.

As with canon 1044, §1, 2°, canon 1044, §1, 3° is not time-specific. That is, perhaps the delict occurred in such circumstances that it rendered illicit the candidate's reception of orders. Or perhaps the delict occurred *after* the ordination. Though the canon is formulated in the past tense, it does not state precisely *when* in the past the delict was committed. While canon 1044, §1, 2° implicitly suggests the two distinct categories of public and occult delicts, canon 1044, §1, 3° refers to both public and occult delicts mentioned in canon 1041, 3°, 4°, 5°, and 6°, since no distinction is made, as in canon 1044, §1, 2°.

Canon 1044, §2, 1° parallels canon 1044, §1, 1°: if a simple impediment existed which made illicit the prior, valid reception of orders, then the cleric may not legitimately exercise that order. There is one qualification made, however, concerning those who suffer from "amentia or some other psychic illness." Canon 1041, 1° states that those experiencing such a psychological debility are irregular for the licit reception of orders. However, canon 1044, §2, 2° does not state that the impediment need have existed as an irregularity at time of ordination.

Irregularity or Simple Impediment?

As discussed earlier,[40] questions arise as to *how* the perpetual character of "amentia or other psychic illness" should be understood, though the *fact* that its perpetuity is inherent in canon 1044, §1, 1° is not debatable. According to canon 1044, §1, 1°, such a person is irregular (perpetually) for the exercise of that order,[41] though canon 1044, §2, 2° treats this same subject under the simple heading of one who is "impeded" from the exercise of orders. Canons 1044, §1, 1° and 1044, §2, 2° are apparently inconsistent: is one irregular or simply impeded?

---

[40] See commentary on c. 1041, 1°.

[41] There are certain exceptions to this prohibition; see, for instance, c. 976.

Canon 1044, §2, 2° indicates that the ordinary, after having consulted at least one expert, can dispense from the simple impediment to the exercise of orders. Herein rests the confusion. If the irregularity arising from "amentia or other psychic illness" (c. 1041, 1°) is understood to be perpetual, as irregularities by their nature are (c. 1040), it necessarily must be dispensed from for both the reception and the exercise of orders. However, if it is understood as a simple impediment (c. 1044, §2, 2°), then a dispensation might not be necessary for the exercise of orders, and indeed might not even be necessary for the reception of orders if the debilitating cause ceased prior to ordination.

Like canon 1044, §1, the norm of canon 1044, §2, 2° is not time-specific. Hence, the "amentia or some other psychic illness"—whether creating an irregularity or a simple impediment—might not have been present even latently at the time of ordination, but may have manifested itself only after ordination, in the judgment of the ordinary and experts consulted by him. A man in such a situation can be declared impeded from the exercise of orders. Since canons treating of irregularities are careful to call them such, and given its placement in the midst of a discussion of simple impediments, one infers that the impediment of canon 1044, §2, 2° is to be understood as a simple impediment. Hence, it may cease with therapeutic treatment or perhaps merely with the passage of time. The competent ordinary is to confirm the continuing existence of the impediment and its consequential prohibition of a man's exercise of orders.

Further Issues Arising from Canon 1044, §2, 2°

A fair application of canon 1044, §2, 2° requires an appreciation of the qualitative and quantitative difference in standard from that of canon 1041, 1°. The latter explicitly refers to a man as being *inhabilis* (not necessarily incapable, but certainly "unqualified to fulfill the ministry properly"). In contrast, canon 1044, §2, 2° does not state that the man need have been rendered *inhabilis,* but merely that he suffer from the debilitation described in canon 1041, 1°. This would seem to give notable latitude to an ordinary in declaring a subject to be impeded from the exercise of his diaconal or presbyteral order because the ordinary judges him to suffer from "amentia or some other psychic illness." However, one might reasonably argue that the *inhabilis* qualifier of canon 1041, 1° is presumably implied in canon 1044, §2, 2°, and that the former norm is relevant to the interpretation of the latter. Hence, it seems that the man also needs to be declared *inhabilis* for the exercise of orders already received, though canon 1044, §2, 2° does not explicitly require this declaration.

The declaration that the impediment is incurred and that the cleric may not exercise orders, or that the cleric may in fact exercise his ministry in spite of the impediment, is an administrative act (c. 35), an individual decree (c. 48). If a man is declared prohibited from exercising his order, competent authority may permit exceptions by means of another administrative act (c. 59), e.g., so that a restricted priest might celebrate the funeral of one of his parents. Furthermore, any such prohibition would not preclude a priest from hearing confessions in a danger-of-death situation (c. 976).

Besides the declaration that one is impeded from the exercise of orders, the canons on removal from an ecclesiastical office may also be relevant in this situation. Removal from an office currently held (cc. 192–195) would require a just or grave reason depending on the situation. Such reasons must be weighed in light of comments of those whose rights might be injured (c. 50), reasons which in turn must be communicated to the cleric in writing, in at least a summary fashion (cc. 51 and 193, §4). The removed cleric's possible recourse follows canons 1732–1739.

Unresolved Questions
Arising from Canon 1044, §2, 2°

There exists the real potential for abusive application of canon 1044, §2, 2° by an ordinary against a man he wishes removed from active ministry. First, the canon could be interpreted broadly. Second, perceptions (including the ordinary's) of the complexities of the situation are always tinged by subjectivity. Third, the psychological sciences are not exact sciences, and evaluations made in light of them are not always precise. Fourth, the canon is vague regarding the proper methods of consultation necessary for the ordinary to achieve the moral certitude warranting the declaration of this impediment concerning the exercise of orders.

As noted earlier, fundamental questions remain about the relationship of canon 1044, §2, 2° with canons 1044, §1, 1° and 1041, 1°; about whether canon 1044, §2, 2° actually refers to an irregularity or a simple impediment; and about the timing and duration of the psychic impairment. Other uncertainties persist. How exactly is the psychological infirmity of canons 1041, 1° and 1044, §2, 2° to be determined? How are the Latin terms *rite* and *inhabilis* in canon 1041, 1° to be understood, and how do they relate to canon 1044, §2, 2°? What precisely is meant by the term *ministerium,* and what process is proper to the judgment of psychic impairment (*iudicatur*—c.1041, 1°)? How strictly is canon 1044, §2, 2° to be interpreted and applied, and in whose favor (the cleric's, the ordinary's, or the faithful's)? Who precisely is an "expert"? What financial, insurance, or pension benefits are appropriate for a priest who has been declared incapable of exercising orders, at least temporarily, in accord with canon 1044, §2, 2°? Is the prohibition of the exercise of orders total, or is it comparable to a suspension,[42] which might admit of some sacramental priestly activity on an ongoing basis? May the prohibition be imposed on public ministry only, while permitting certain private ministerial acts (e.g., a private celebration of Mass, in so far as a eucharistic celebration can ever be understood to be private)? Various commentators have vigorously discussed certain of these questions.[43]

Ignorance of Impediments

Canon 1045 — Ignorance of the irregularities and impediments does not exempt from them.

The aspirant to any of the sacred orders is morally bound to know what his condition is relative to the order which he desires to receive; if he is irregular for, or simply impeded from, the reception of or the exercise of that order, he is morally bound to know that, too. Ignorance of pertinent irregularities and simple impediments does not exempt him from them.

Practically speaking, the ignorance need not be culpable (i.e., negligent unawareness regarding what one should have known); or the error may be either of fact or of law. Hence, one might possibly incur an impediment or an irregularity but not be sinful in that regard. Canon 1045 implies that irregularities and simple impediments are rooted in some objective reality of the person's situation, apart from what he may understand about them.

While one who reads canons 1041, 1042, and 1044 carefully and sees his situation referred to can no longer be said to be ignorant, one should not dismiss canon 1045 as occurring only rarely. By way of example, a man might conceivably suffer from a significant psychic illness apparent to everyone but himself; or, while aware of it on some level, he may deny it even to himself. Unwilling as he may be to admit his illness, he is no less impeded from both the legitimate reception of orders (c. 1041, 1°) and their legitimate exercise (cc. 1044, §1, 1° and 1044, §2, 2°).

Or possibly a person could consciously commit a public act of heresy with what might be for him the best of intentions, genuinely if erroneously believing the law does not apply in his case

---

[42] See c. 1333.

[43] For a helpful treatment of some of these questions, see, for instance, W. Woestman, "Too Good to Be True: An Interpretation of Canons 1041, 1° and 1044, §2, 2°," *ME* 120 (1995) 619–629, and the rejoinder of J. Beal, "Too

Good to Be True? A Response," *ME* 121 (1996) 431–463; also, P. Lagges, "The Use of Canon 1044, §2, 2° in the Removal of Parish Priests," *Stud Can* 30 (1996) 31–69, and G. Read, "Administrative Approaches to Cases of 'Problem Clergy,'" *CLS-GBIN* 105 (1996) 16–22.

because he is serving what he has personally determined to be some higher good. Another individual might believe that he deliberately ought to join an ostensibly charitable organization, consciously accepting that it also fosters activity that would be characteristic of an apostolate. While in his specific case all the elements might not be present for the commission of a delict, such a person may be truly ignorant of the *potential* for an irregularity in light of canons 1041, 2° and 1044, §1, 2°, especially if no one educates him as to their possible applicability. Such ignorance is ultimately irrelevant to the impediment's application in a given case. This is consistent with canon 15, §1, which indicates that ignorance or error does not prevent the effect of certain laws.[44] Such ignorance of the law is normally not presumed (c. 15, §2).

With due regard for the fact that the Eastern code makes no distinction between irregularities and simple impediments, Eastern code canon 765 parallels canon 1045. The same is true of Eastern code canon 766 and canon 1046, to which we now turn.

Multiplication of Impediments

Canon 1046 — Irregularities and impediments are multiplied if they arise from different causes. They are not multiplied, however, if they arise from the repetition of the same cause unless it is a question of the irregularity for voluntary homicide or for having procured a completed abortion.

Irregularities and simple impediments may arise from a psychological, physical, or moral condition (e.g., cc. 1041, 1°; 1042, 1° or 3°). They may also arise from an action (e.g., cc. 1041, 2° or 3°; 1042, 2°). If there are multiple conditions or multiple actions, the irregularity or simple imped-

iment is considered to be only one if the cause be the same, with certain exceptions.

If, for example, a person in his spiritual journey has been received into several non-Catholic religious denominations consecutively (c. 1041, 2°), he would be considered irregular for the reception of orders only once, and need be dispensed but once. Likewise, if a person has twice attempted marriage and both invalid marriages end in civil divorce, he would be irregular for the reception of orders (c. 1041, 3°) in a manner which would require but one dispensation.

However, there would be "different causes" for the irregularity if a priest who has attempted civil marriage (c. 1044, §1, 3° deriving from c. 1041, 3°) and incurred the resultant suspension (c. 1394, §1) nonetheless carries out distinctly priestly duties (c. 1044, §1, 3°, deriving from c. 1041, 6°). Such a priest would be irregular for the exercise of orders already received for two different reasons, i.e., his attempted marriage and his unauthorized sacramental actions. It is less clear whether one who has attempted suicide (c. 1041, 5°) as a result of his having suffered from a psychological infirmity (c. 1041, 1°) should be considered irregular for the reception of orders as a result of a single cause (his suicide attempt being directly attributable to his psychic imbalance) or different causes (the suicide attempt differentiated from his mental problem). In cases of doubt, the dispensation request should simply spell out the person's situation in its entirety; whether there are distinct causes would probably be only an academic question in most cases.

There are two exceptions to the non-multiplication norm of canon 1046: repeated direct, voluntary, active, and effective participation in the procurement of abortions and repeated direct, voluntary, active, and effective participation in homicides. A dispensation is to be sought for each involvement in procuring an abortion; it is likewise to be sought for each involvement in a willful homicide. Each distinct act produces a distinct irregularity. The number of related and relevant actions becomes crucial, then, in presenting a dispensation petition, due to the gravity of the matter.

---

[44] An important distinction here is that c. 15, §1 expressly refers to invalidating and incapacitating laws, which are not the focus of cc. 1040–1049 on irregularities and simple impediments.

Dispensation from Irregularities and Simple Impediments

Canon 1047 — §1. Dispensation from all irregularities is reserved to the Apostolic See alone if the fact on which they are based has been brought to the judicial forum.

§2. Dispensation from the following irregularities and impediments to receive orders is also reserved to the Apostolic See:

1° irregularities from the public delicts mentioned in can. 1041, nn. 2 and 3;

2° the irregularity from the delict mentioned in can. 1041, n. 4, whether public or occult;

3° the impediment mentioned in can. 1042, n. 1.

§3. Dispensation in public cases from the irregularities from exercising an order received mentioned in can. 1041, n. 3, and even in occult cases from the irregularities mentioned in can. 1041, n. 4 is also reserved to the Apostolic See.

§4. An ordinary is able to dispense from irregularities and impediments not reserved to the Holy See.

Canon 1047 represents a practical application of the principle of subsidiarity: an ordinary generally is competent to grant dispensations from irregularities and simple impediments, without recourse to the Apostolic See. However, there are exceptions to this principle. The dispensation permitting licit reception of orders is reserved to the Holy See in certain situations in which a case has achieved public notoriety, e.g., its introduction into the judicial forum. Further, the Apostolic See alone is competent to grant such a dispensation if a case concerns: apostasy, heresy, or schism; valid marriage binding one desiring ordination (unless to the permanent diaconate); marriage attempted by one not free to do so; or abortion or willful homicide. A dispensation for the exercise of orders is reserved to the Apostolic See for cases involving attempted marriage, or abortion, or willful homicide. The ordinary can dispense from all other irregularities and

simple impediments. We now consider briefly the cases reserved to the Apostolic See.

If the cause of the irregularity or simple impediment has been brought to the judicial forum, the dispensation from the impediment belongs to the Holy See alone. The primary concern here is the public notoriety, even if not widespread, occasioned by the matter's treatment in a court. The traditional opinion holds that the judicial forum can be either ecclesiastical or civil, though this issue needs to be clarified further.

Canon 1047, §1 refers to any matter resulting in an irregularity or simple impediment which has been brought to an external judicial forum for consideration. Because of the threat of subsequent scandal, given the involvement of a cleric or a prospective cleric, the Apostolic See alone may dispense from the impediment. If the matter is occult and treated in the internal forum, it is addressed by the Apostolic Penitentiary; if it concerns heresy, apostasy, or schism, the Congregation for the Doctrine of the Faith should be consulted; and if the irregularity is public or in the external forum, the Congregation for Divine Worship and the Discipline of the Sacraments is competent for non-religious lay persons and secular clerics, while the Congregation for Institutes of Consecrated Life and Societies of Apostolic Life is competent for members of such institutes or societies.

For those who are to receive orders licitly, canon 1047, §2 lists explicitly all irregularities or simple impediments (beyond those brought to the judicial forum) whose dispensation is reserved to the Holy See. Such irregularities or impediments are those resulting from: public delicts of apostasy, heresy, or schism (c. 1041, 2°); a publicly attempted yet ecclesiastically invalid marriage (c. 1041, 3°); any direct participation in a willful homicide or a procured abortion (c. 1041, 4°); and, except for those seeking admission to the order of permanent deacon, a valid and ongoing marriage (c. 1042, 1°).

For those who are to exercise their orders licitly, canon 1047, §3 lists explicitly all impediments (beyond those brought to the judicial forum) whose dispensation is reserved to the Holy See. Again, a publicly attempted yet ecclesiastically invalid marriage requires particular attention (c. 1041, 3°). This would include, for instance, a priest who has left the active ministry, has publicly attempted marriage which ended in civil divorce, and has expressed his desire to return to active ministry. Likewise, one who has at any time directly participated in a willful homicide or a procured abortion, be it public or occult, must request a dispensation from the Holy See alone for the licit exercise of his office (c. 1041, 4°).

All other irregularities or simple impediments are not reserved to the Holy See and can be dispensed by the ordinary. It is worth noting that canon 1047 does not nominate a particular ordinary; that is, the canon does not state that a man subject to a diocesan bishop must approach his bishop and only that bishop, or that a religious must approach his major superior. Given all the canons governing dimissorial letters, testimonials of fitness, and—perhaps most important—the centrality of one's proper ordinary in one's approval for ordination, it stands to reason that the ordinary who should take up the matter of the irregularity is one's proper ordinary.

Finally, as has been noted, both irregularities and simple impediments may arise from a single action or condition, though certain acts may result in an irregularity or simple impediment while not giving rise to a penalty. The dispensation of an irregularity or simple impediment does not necessarily entail the lifting of a related penalty, which must be remitted according to law.

Exceptional Exercise of Orders in spite of Prohibition

Canon 1048 — In more urgent occult cases, if the ordinary or, when it concerns the irregularities mentioned in can. 1041, nn. 3 and 4, the Penitentiary cannot be approached and if there is imminent danger of grave harm or infamy, a person impeded by an irregularity from exercising an order can exercise it, but without prejudice to the obligation which remains of making recourse as soon as possible to the ordinary or the Penitentiary, omitting the name and through a confessor.

Recalling canons 1041, 3° and 4°, canon 1048 presents an exceptional situation in which a priest or deacon irregular for the reception of his order may exercise it, as long as the cause of that irregularity is not a public matter. If, for some credible reason, the Holy See cannot be approached for a dispensation through the Apostolic Penitentiary, such a cleric may exercise his office if there be serious threat to himself or others were he not to do so. Damage to his good name, and thereby to the Church, would be one such danger. The specific irregularities cited in canon 1048 are those related to a marriage attempted by one not free to do so (c. 1041, 3°) and direct participation in an abortion or willful homicide (c. 1041, 4°). A cleric who has incurred these irregularities may seek a temporary resolution in the internal sacramental (i.e., confessional) forum. However, the Apostolic Penitentiary is still to be approached for a final resolution of the matter as soon as reasonably possible. That the matter is addressed in this forum indicates the genuine care of the Church for the protection of the man's good name and his spiritual welfare, as well as the avoidance of scandal. Again, this applies only in matters involving urgency; only in matters occult; and only in matters relative to canon 1041, 3° and 4°.

A question arises as to why canon 1048 (which pertains to the exercise of orders) refers back to canon 1041, 3° and 4°, which deals with those irregular for the *reception* of orders. The answer is twofold. First, the only place in which those two irregularity-inducing causes are enunciated in detail is canon 1041, 3° and 4°. Subsequent references to them are by canon number only. Second, a reference here instead to canon 1044, §1, 3°, which concerns the exercise of orders, would be confusing, because it covers more than the subjects of canon 1041, 3° and 4°. The former canon also includes mutilation, attempted suicide, and acts of orders not permitted a given person in a specific time, place, or circumstance.

Dispensation Procedure

Canon 1049 — §1. Petitions to obtain a dispensation from irregularities or impediments must indicate all the irregularities and impediments. Nevertheless, a general dispensation is valid even for those omitted in good faith, except for the irregularities mentioned in can. 1041, n. 4, and for others brought to the judicial forum, but not for those omitted in bad faith.

§2. If it is a question of the irregularity from voluntary homicide or a procured abortion, the number of the delicts also must be mentioned for the validity of the dispensation.

§3. A general dispensation from irregularities and impediments to receive orders is valid for all the orders.

Canon 1049, §1 notes that the relevant irregularity and/or simple impediment must be stated explicitly in any request for a dispensation. In a particularly complex case involving, for instance, irregularities or simple impediments of different types having different causes, a general dispensation may be requested and granted, and would be effective even for an impediment not named explicitly, but omitted in good faith. There are two exceptions to the rule stated in the canon. First, if an irregularity or simple impediment is knowingly omitted or otherwise left out as a result of bad faith, it is not considered dispensed. Second, irregularities arising from participation in a willful homicide or a procured abortion are excluded from any general dispensation.

Canon 1049, §2 reinforces canon 1046: in cases of willful homicide and procured abortion, the irregularity is multiplied, and so its dispensation must cover all cases. Hence, the number of discrete delicts must be stated. Finally, canon 1049, §3 declares that an irregularity or simple impediment need be removed but once; a general dispensation for the reception of orders is valid for all orders.

ARTICLE 4: THE REQUIRED DOCUMENTS AND INVESTIGATION
[cc. 1050–1052]

Documents Required for Ordination

Canon 1050 — For a person to be promoted to sacred orders, the following documents are required:

1° **a testimonial that studies have been properly completed according to the norm of can. 1032;**

2° **for those to be ordained to the presbyterate, a testimonial that the diaconate was received;**

3° **for candidates to the diaconate, a testimonial that baptism, confirmation and the ministries mentioned in can. 1035 were received; likewise, a testimonial that the declaration mentioned in can. 1036 was made, and if the one to be ordained to the permanent diaconate is a married candidate, testimonials that the marriage was celebrated and the wife consents.**

Canon 1050 lists documents which must be amassed prior to the conferral of sacred orders. Some of the material listed here in canon 1050 has been treated elsewhere,[45] especially in referencing the distinction between dimissorials and testimonials.[46] Still, two remarks are in order here.

The Parties Responsible for Documentation

Canon 1050 permits a certain latitude as regards who precisely collects the pre-ordination documents or who finally is responsible for reviewing them to see that they are in order. Since the next two canons indicate that a candidate's major superior or diocesan bishop of incardination is central throughout the formation process, this same ordinary is understandably responsible for

[45] See commentary on cc. 1032, 1035, and 1036.
[46] See commentary on cc. 1015, §1 and 1020.

executing this documentary task, or having it executed by others properly delegated. The care of the pertinent files is often delegated to seminary rectors or formation directors. The documentation should clearly present any exemptions, dispensations, or other particular material unique to the ordinand. A mere statement of the issue and its resolution suffices, included in a manner befitting the candidate's right to privacy and the preservation of his good name.

The ordaining prelate, if different from the candidate's proper ordinary, is responsible for at least nominally checking to see that the matters of prior diaconal ordination (if pertinent), academic preparation, sacramental history, and matrimonial status have been investigated. In fact, the inquiry is made as part of the ordination ritual itself, as the bishop asks whether or not those to be ordained have been found worthy.

Respect for a Candidate's Marriage

The last phrase of canon 1050, 3° implies the obvious: the law permits a permanent deacon to be in a valid marriage, provided that the marriage precedes the diaconal ordination. Canon 1050, 3° also states a not so obvious point: the deacon's wife must consent to her spouse's ordination. If the husband's marriage is likely to suffer because of his wife's lack of support for his diaconal ministry, then the ordination should not proceed. This protects and upholds the sacred, intimate, and exclusive bond enjoyed by the spouses. The Church should never threaten in any way the communion of life and love between a wife and her husband, equal partners who must support each other's commitments (cc. 1055–1057).

A wife's agreement to her husband's diaconal ordination does not imply that she intends to participate actively in his ministry, although she may wish to do so; the consent rather suggests simply that she will support him in his exercise of sacred ministry. Most fundamentally, the wife's consent assures all parties that she foresees no threat to her marriage. This question of spousal agreement generally is addressed early and often in forma-

tion programs for those aspiring to the permanent diaconate. Canon 1050, 3° affirms that documentation of this agreement is essential for the licit ordination of the man as a permanent deacon.

Final Pre-ordination Inquiries

Canon 1051 — The following prescripts regarding the investigation about the qualities required in the one to be ordained are to be observed:

1° **there is to be a testimonial of the rector of the seminary or house of formation about the qualities required to receive the order, that is, about the sound doctrine of the candidate, his genuine piety, good morals, and aptitude to exercise the ministry, as well as, after a properly executed inquiry, about his state of physical and psychic health;**

2° **in order to conduct the investigation properly, the diocesan bishop or major superior can employ other means which seem useful to him according to the circumstances of time and place, such as testimonial letters, public announcements, or other sources of information.**

Much of the material presented in canon 1051 has been treated elsewhere.[47] A few further reflections are in order.

First, the law here apportions to seminary rectors and formation directors a share in the difficult assessment of the areas mentioned in canon 1051, 1°. Prior references to candidates' human, moral, spiritual, psychological, and intellectual qualities (e.g., cc. 241, §1; 1029) have indicated that the final assessment is left to the proper ordinary. Although these prior references may presume that he has delegated such an assessment, canon 1051, 1° is the first to make explicit the duty of seminary rectors and formation directors.

Second, care must be taken to respect the provisions of canon 220. For instance, data regarding a

---

[47] See, for instance, commentary on cc. 1015; 1025; 1029; 1030; 1031, §1; and 1041, 1°.

candidate's psychological and physical health must be guarded carefully. The information is confidential, whether it may justify his dismissal from formation or affirm his suitability. The materials relevant to the testimonials of canon 1051, 1° are part of a man's official approval process for reception of a given order. Testimonials composed in accord with canon 1051, 1° are usually succinct; however, there should be nothing perfunctory about the prior testing and investigation which culminate in the issuance of these testimonials.

Third, according to canon 1051, 2°, the proper diocesan bishop or competent major superior is charged with the investigation set forth in canon 1051, 1°. Obviously, this frees from particular responsibility the ordaining prelate who, if not ordaining his own subjects, need only be assured that this documentation is in order (see c. 1052, §2). Further, canon 1051, 2° grants the aforementioned ordinaries broad discretion in gathering information about a candidate: they can employ other means which seem useful to them according to the circumstances of time and place, pursuing "other sources of information."[48]

Persons who have known and observed a candidate's apostolic and personal development during formation often offer data which is particularly pertinent. Given the weightiness of the decision to be made regarding ordination (or not) and the significant responsibility of the candidate's proper ordinary, that authority is permitted, indeed encouraged, to utilize appropriate means to attain sufficient data so that moral certitude be reached about a candidate's fitness for orders. To this end, with due regard for the bounds of privacy, justice, and good taste, the inquiry may be as creative as the ordinary will allow.

One Document, Dual Purpose

The documentary requirements of canons 1050 and 1051 may be integrated into one statement,

---

[48] It is not entirely clear what is intended by the phrase "other sources of information."

beginning with the affirmation that after proper consultation, the candidate is qualified to receive orders in accord with these two canons. Explicit mention is to be made of his successful completion of studies and formation in general (c. 1032), and his reception of baptism (c. 1024), confirmation (c. 1033), and certain ministries (c. 1035). His declaration of freedom in seeking orders should be noted (c. 1036). A copy of the candidate's *curriculum vitae* is presented. As best as can be established outside the necessarily restricted non-sacramental internal forum, a candidate's good character is to be attested to, as are his fitness and usefulness for sacred ministry. Pertinent dispensations should be noted briefly. Moral certitude of the candidate's physical and psychic health is referenced, as is the candidate's suitability in accord with the general requirements of canons 1026–1039.

Responsibilities of Ordaining Bishop

Canon 1052 — §1. For a bishop conferring ordination by his own right to proceed to the ordination, he must be sure that the documents mentioned in can. 1050 are at hand and that, after the investigation has been conducted according to the norm of law, positive arguments have proven the suitability of the candidate.

§2. For a bishop to proceed to the ordination of someone who is not his subject, it is sufficient that the dimissorial letters mention that the same documents are at hand, that the investigation has been performed according to the norm of the law, and that the suitability of the candidate has been established. Moreover, if the candidate is a member of a religious institute or a society of apostolic life, the same letters must also attest that he has been received definitively into the institute or society and is a subject of the superior who gives the letters.

§3. If, all these notwithstanding, the bishop doubts for specific reasons whether a candidate is suitable to receive orders, he is not to promote him.

To ordain one who is his subject, a bishop must be certain that the testimonials mentioned in canon 1050 have in fact been collected and are in order. This serves as a final check that the candidate lacks nothing regarding: the fulfillment of academic requirements; the prior conferral of diaconal ordination (for sacerdotal candidates only); the reception of Christian baptism, Catholic confirmation, and the ministries of lector and acolyte; and the declaration of personal moral freedom in advancing to orders. For married candidates to the permanent diaconate only, there must be documentation of the candidate's current valid marriage, along with proof of his wife's consent to his ordination.

For bishops ordaining subjects not their own, the dimissorial letter not only grants permission to confer the orders but also explicitly states that the necessary documentation is in order. While the dimissorial letter is not in itself a testimonial, it presents the candidate as one who has been examined and found suitable, at least because he has fulfilled all the requirements of canon 1052, §1, deriving from canon 1050.

Members of religious institutes or societies of apostolic life must be received definitively into the institute or society prior to conferral of orders, and this fact must be affirmed formally in the dimissorial. Definitive incorporation implies perpetual vows or an equivalent assimilating action as understood in the approved proper law of the institute or society. Canon 1052, §2 also requires an explicit statement that the granter of the dimissorial in fact is the candidate's major superior.

The Final Judgment

Two portions of canon 1052 are especially noteworthy: the closing phrase of canon 1052, §1 (that positive arguments must prove the suitability of the candidate) and the entirety of canon 1052, §3 (regarding the possible refusal of ordination by the ordaining bishop). This latter obligation carries with it the emphatic reminder that the final decision on ordination belongs to the legitimate authority of the Church. No one has a right to ordination.

The final judgment about a man's ordination belongs first to the ordinand's proper ordinary; however, when ordaining a subject not his own, a bishop enjoys the right and has the obligation to act on any reasonable doubt regarding that candidate's fitness. Canon 1052, §3 does not qualify such a doubt. Given how much a man is tested throughout his formation, any last minute doubt must be significant in order for the ordaining bishop to withhold orders from this previously approved candidate. Further, this presumption is all the stronger for sacerdotal candidates who already are deacons, as they have once been found worthy and useful ministerially,[49] and free to exercise their diaconal ministry.[50] It is noteworthy that Eastern code canon 770 indicates that this doubt arises from the ordaining bishop's conscience, which is not stated explicitly in the Latin code.

CHAPTER III
THE NOTATION AND TESTIMONIAL
OF ORDINATION CONFERRED
[cc. 1053–1054]

Canon 1053 — §1. After an ordination has taken place, the names of those ordained and of the ordaining minister and the place and date of the ordination are to be noted in a special register to be kept carefully in the curia of the place of ordination; all the documents of individual ordinations are to be preserved carefully.

§2. The ordaining bishop is to give to each of the ordained an authentic testimonial of the reception of ordination; if a bishop other than their own promoted them with dimissorial letters, they are to show the testimonial to their own ordinary for notation of the ordination in a special register to be kept in the archive.

[49] See cc. 1025–1026, 1029, and 1031, and accompanying commentary.
[50] See cc. 1030 and 1038, and accompanying commentary.

Canon 1053, §1 states that all fundamental data pertinent to an ordination is to be recorded in the appropriate registry of the diocese of ordination, to be located at the diocesan chancery. This data includes the names of the ordained parties, the name of the ordaining prelate, and the place and date of ordination. The canon also calls for the careful and accurate preservation of all documents related to an ordination, though it does not refer expressly to these being kept in the same place. Formation files—which document a candidate's progress in preparation for orders—are often kept, securely, at the major seminary where he trained (for seculars) or in the provincial archives (for religious). The canon refers more particularly to those items directly tied to the ceremony itself, e.g., testimonials; dimissorials; and certification of completion of ceremony.

Canon 1053, §2 states that the ordaining minister is to see that each ordinand has an authentic certification that an order has been conferred. It is a fundamental principle of church order that each person has a right to know and have verification of his or her status in the Church (c. 487, §2). Fulfillment of this obligation by the ordaining minister protects the ordinand's right to assure others of his valid ordination. Experience has shown that there can be confusion about who has proof of what; the canon clarifies that the ordinand himself is to be sure that his superiors receive proper documentation about orders conferred, even if he himself must pursue the communication of such documentation.

As regards secular clergy properly ordained by an ordinary not their own (i.e., with legitimate dimissorial letters), the ordinary of incardination is to be presented with a certificate of orders conferred, so that the records are complete in the ordinand's own diocese. The proper ordinary of a religious deacon or priest should be presented with a similar certification.

Canon 1054 — The local ordinary if it concerns seculars, or the competent major superior if it concerns his own subjects, is to send notice of each ordination celebrated to the pastor of the place of baptism, who is to record it in his baptismal register according to the norm of can. 535, §2.

Canon 1054 reminds all principal parties to an ordination of the centrality of the baptismal registry in the sacramental life of a person. A notation of orders conferred must be made in the ordinand's baptismal registry, since one's sacramental history is recorded there (c. 535, §2). The obligation to provide such information does not belong to the ordinand or even necessarily to the staff of the ordaining minister, but rather to the ordinand's proper ordinary of incardination (e.g., local ordinary in the case of diocesan clergy; major superior in the case of religious clergy). Any subsequent development involving the cleric's status such as laicization or advancement to another order (e.g., from the diaconate to the priesthood) should also be noted carefully in the baptismal registry.

BIBLIOGRAPHY

Sources

CDF. Littcirc *Per litteras ad universos. AAS* 72 (1980) 1132–1135.

Paul VI. Aplett *Summi Dei Verbum. AAS* 55 (1963) 979–995.

———. Ency *Sacerdotalis caelibatus. AAS* 59 (1967) 657–697.

Pius XI. Ency *Ad Catholici Sacerdotii. AAS* 28 (1936) 5–53.

Reference Works, Studies, and Articles

Alesandro, J. *Canonical Delicts Involving Sexual Misconduct and Dismissal from the Clerical State.* Washington, D.C.: USCC, 1995.

Christensen, J. *Character Requisites for Reception of Holy Orders. CanLawStud* 424. Washington, D.C.: Catholic University of America, 1964.

Cox, C. "Processes Involving Irregularities and Impediments to the Exercise of Orders." In *Clergy Procedural Handbook,* ed. R. Calvo and N. Klinger, 178–205. Washington, D.C.: CLSA, 1992.

Del Prete, F. *The Juridical Elements of a Priestly Vocation: A Canonical Analysis of the Legislation of the Church from the Seventeenth Century to the Present.* Doctoral dissertation, Faculty of Canon Law, Pontifical University of St. Thomas Aquinas. Rome: Graziani, 1992.

De Maere, L. *La maturité psychique des candidats au sacerdoce selon le Code de droit canonique de 1983.* Doctoral dissertation, Faculty of Canon Law, Pontifical University of St. Thomas Aquinas. Rome: Graziani, 1990.

Gannon, J. *The Interstices Required for the Promotion to Orders. CanLawStud* 196. Washington, D.C.: Catholic University of America, 1944.

Hendriks, J. "On the Sacramentality of the Episcopal Consecration." *Stud Can* 28 (1994) 231–239.

Lendakadavil, A. *Candidates for the Priesthood: A Study of Their Suitability according to the New Code of Canon Law.* Shillong, India: Vendrame Institute Pub., 1989.

Magee, P. *Dispensation from the Obligations of Priestly Celibacy: An Interpretation of the Cases of Those Who Should Not Have Received Priestly Ordination according to "Per Litteras" §5a.* Doctoral dissertation, Faculty of Canon Law, Pontifical Gregorian University. Rome: Pioda, 1988.

McIntyre, J. "In Persona *Christi Capitis:* A Commentary on Canon 1008." *Stud Can* 30 (1996) 371–401.

McKay, G. "The Reconciliation of Schismatically Ordained Married Clergy." *P* 84 (1995) 355–368.

Pelliccia, G. *La preparazione ed ammissione dei chierici ai santi Ordini nella Roma del Secolo XVI: Studio storico con fonti inedite.* Rome: Pia Società San Paolo, 1946.

Poitras, S. "La figure du prêtre dans l'enseignement pontifical (1903–1985)." Excerpt of doctoral dissertation, Institute of Spirituality, Pontifical Gregorian University, Rome, 1988.

Quinn, J. *Documents Required for the Reception of Orders: A Historical Synopsis and Commentary. CanLawStud* 266. Washington, D.C.: Catholic University of America, 1948.

Smith, P. "Lack of Due Discretion and Suitability for Ordination." *Stud Can* 21 (1987) 125–140.

Szentmártoni, M. "Celibato per il Regno dei cieli e maturità della persona." *P* 83 (1994) 247–271.

Vogelpohl, H. *The Simple Impediments to Holy Orders: An Historical Synopsis and Commentary. CanLawStud* 224. Washington, D.C.: Catholic University of America, 1945.

Woestman, W. "Restricting the Right to Celebrate the Eucharist." *Stud Can* 29 (1995) 155–178.

TITLE VII[1]
MARRIAGE
[cc. 1055–1165]

Historical Overview

Since marriage has always been the state of life, indeed the vocation, of the vast majority of the Christian faithful, it has been a central theme of the Church's teaching and the canonical discipline rooted in that teaching in every era. From the beginning the Church's approach to marriage has been anchored in a few New Testament texts: Jesus' own stinging condemnation of divorce as a distortion of the Creator's original intention for marriage and a concession to human hardness of heart (Mt 19:3–12; Mk 10:2–12; Mt 5:31–32; Lk 16:18); Paul's response to questions from feuding members of the church in Corinth about marriage, divorce, and virginity (1 Cor 7); and the reflection by the author of the epistle to the Ephesians on the analogy between the relationship of husband and wife and that between Christ and the Church (Eph 5:22–33).

Theological reflection on these key texts fostered—and continues to foster—the gradual development of a distinctively Christian understanding of marriage. An appreciation of the evolution of this theology of marriage and the canonical discipline based on it is essential for understanding the treatment of marriage in the revised Code of Canon Law. This historical introduction will sketch the beginnings of a Christian theology of marriage, the consolidation of this reflection in the medieval synthesis, the response of the Church

to challenges to its doctrine on marriage from the sixteenth century reformers and secular authorities, and the renewal of Catholic thinking about marriage at Vatican II whose teaching has left its unmistakable imprint on the revised code.[2]

The Early Church

The early Christians did not radically alter the customs according to which marriage was constituted and lived out. Instead, they entered and lived out their marriages according to the traditional practices of their culture, first Jewish and later Greco-Roman, but they did so "in the Lord" (1 Cor 7:39).

However, from an early date, perhaps as early as New Testament times, traditional understandings of marriage were challenged by a somewhat amorphous movement now known as Gnosticism, which attacked the body ecclesiastic like a virus. Its struggle with Gnosticism enabled the Church to begin to articulate its own vision of marriage.

In its manifold, syncretistic forms, Gnosticism espoused an ethical, metaphysical, and theological dualism according to which the material world, including the human body, was seen as the creation of an evil demiurge who had imprisoned fallen, spiritual souls in physical bodies. Salvation came through special, esoteric knowledge (*gnosis*) that enabled these fallen souls to escape their material imprisonment and rise to spiritual contem-

---

[1] See T. Doyle, in *CLSA Com,* 737–746; K. Lüdicke, in *Münster Com,* Überblick vor 1055/1–1062/1; J. Hervada, in *Pamplona ComEng,* 659–732; D. Kelly, in *CLSGBI Com,* 571–578.

[2] For more complete accounts of the development of the Christian understanding of marriage, see E. Schillebeeckx, *Marriage: Secular Reality and Saving Mystery,* 2 vols. (London: Sheed and Ward, 1965); G. LeBras, "Le Mariage," *Dictionnaire de Théologie Catholique (DTC)* 9–2: col. 2123–2317; C. Brooke, *The Medieval Idea of Marriage* (Oxford: Clarendon, 1989); J. Brundage, *Law, Sex and Christian Society in Medieval Europe* (Chicago: University of Chicago, 1987); T. Mackin, *What Is Marriage?* (New York: Paulist, 1982).

plation of the true God.[3] Gnosticism rejected procreation as evil, since it resulted in the imprisonment of still more souls in corporeality. Gnostics of a rigorist bent urged their adherents to avoid both procreation and marriage and to practice perfect continence; those of a more antinomian bent adopted a radically realized eschatology according to which sharers in the special revelation already enjoyed the resurrected life and were immune from all moral laws. For the latter groups, sexual experience of all kinds was permissible (and, at times, obligatory), as long as procreation was avoided.[4]

Orthodox Christian teachers like Clement of Alexandria responded to the Gnostic challenge by marshaling resources from the New Testament, the Old Testament, Philo's Platonic reading of the Old Testament, and Stoic philosophy.[5] In response to Gnostic rigorists, they affirmed that marriage and procreation were good because they were created and enjoined by God (Gen 1:28), but not as good as virginity for the sake of the coming kingdom of God. In response to Gnostic antinomians, they insisted with the Stoics that sexuality, though fraught with moral dangers, was good as long as it was confined to marriage and exercised only for the procreation of offspring. These responses to Gnosticism soon became the orthodox Christian position on the nature and ends of marriage.[6]

In both Jewish and Greco-Roman cultures, the law recognized marriage as a "social fact" with certain juridic consequences, but marrying was almost exclusively a family matter, which took place without the necessary involvement of either religious or civil authority. Although liturgical rites for the celebration of marriage gradually emerged, their observance was not necessary for the ecclesial recognition of the validity of marriage until after the Council of Trent in the sixteenth century.[7]

The cultures in which Christianity was born and raised did, however, challenge its understanding of marriage. Jesus had pointedly rejected divorce, but both Judaic and Greco-Roman laws made provision for relatively easy divorce, at least by the husband. Throughout the patristic era, every major Christian teacher excoriated divorce as a grave violation of divine law and contrasted the permanence of marriages among Christians with the instability of the unions of their non-Christian neighbors.[8] Nevertheless, there is little evidence that, even after Christianity became the established religion of the Roman Empire, church leaders sought to bring relatively liberal Roman divorce law into conformity with the gospel (or that they could have done so had they been so inclined).[9]

Augustine provided the most coherent and influential synthesis of the emerging Christian understanding of marriage. He defended the essential goodness of marriage against the attacks of the Manicheans, a syncretistic sect which espoused a radical ontological dualism and held that marriage and procreation were to be shunned as intrinsically evil, a sect to which Augustine himself had once been an adherent. Augustine identified a threefold goodness in marriage: the good of fidelity (*bonum fidei*), the good of children (*bonum prolis*), and the good of the sacrament or permanence (*bonum sacramenti*). He explained:

> This good is threefold: fidelity, offspring, sacrament. Fidelity means that one avoids all sexual activity apart from one's marriage. Offspring means that the child is accepted in love, is nurtured in affection, is brought up in religion. The sacrament means

[3] P. Brown, *The Body and Society* (New York: Columbia University, 1988) 103–121; and J. Noonan, *Contraception* (New York: Mentor-Omega, 1967) 78–97.

[4] Noonan, 80–81.

[5] Brown, 122–139, and Noonan, 97–107.

[6] Noonan, 107–111, and Brown, 133.

[7] K. Stevenson, *To Join Together: The Rite of Marriage* (New York: Pueblo, 1987) 16–55.

[8] H. Crouzel, *L'Église primitive face au divorce du premier au cinquième siècle* (Paris: Beauchesne, 1970).

[9] P. Reynolds, *Marriage in the Western Church* (Leiden: E. J. Brill, 1994) 151–153.

that the marriage is not severed nor the spouse abandoned.... This is a kind of rule set for marriage, by which nature's fruitfulness is honored and vicious sexual vagrancy is restrained.[10]

For Augustine, it was chiefly "the sacrament" that distinguished the marriages of Christians from those of other people. Because of its essential goodness, marriage was a sacred reality and he analogized its permanence to the permanent character arising from baptism.[11] "The sacrament" was primarily the property of perpetuity or indissolubility and not "sacramentality" in its later medieval and modern sense of a sacred rite that causes grace. So strong was this "sacrament" that, even after the irretrievable breakdown of a marriage through divorce, a "conjugal something" (*quiddam coniugale*) remained and prevented a new marriage.[12] Augustine's teaching on the perdurance of the sacrament even after divorce sowed the seed from which later generations reaped an understanding of marriage as one of the seven sacraments, one of whose effects was an indissoluble bond (*vinculum*).

Although Augustine defended the goodness of marriage, he clearly saw it as less good than virginity. Fallen humans were infected with the spiritually deadly virus of concupiscence. Concupiscence was evident in every form of human activity, but it was nowhere more evident than in the sexual instinct, which stubbornly refused to be mastered by reason and will. Hence, even within marriage, sexual relations could rarely be had without the commission of at least venial sin.[13] This dark view of sexual relations in marriage was also part of Augustine's legacy to subsequent generations.

---

[10] Augustine, *De Genesi ad litteram,* ix, 7, 12, *Corpus Scriptorum Ecclesiasticorum Latinorum (CSEL)* 28: 275–276.

[11] Reynolds, 293–297.

[12] Augustine, *De nuptiis et concupiscentia,* I, 11, *CSEL* 42:223. See also idem, *De bono coniugali,* 6–7, *CSEL* 41:196–197; and *De adulterinis coniugiis,* II, 4, *CSEL* 41:386.

[13] Idem, *De bono coniugali,* 6–7, *CSEL* 41:194–195.

The Middle Ages

With the fall of the Roman Empire in the West and the settlement by largely Germanic peoples in its former territory, the Church confronted marriage customs that were markedly different from those of the Roman Empire. For these people, marriage did not come about when the parties exchanged consent, but as the end of a process involving several steps, each of which was necessary to constitute marriage: a man's (or his father's) petition to a woman's father for her hand (*petitio*), betrothal by public agreement of the parties' families (*desponsatio*), provision of a dowry to the woman's family (*dotatio*), the handing over of the woman to the man (*traditio*), and the physical consummation of the union by sexual intercourse (*consummatio*). Until all of these steps had been completed, the marriage was incomplete.[14]

Since decisions about the legitimacy of children and inheritance often hinged on whether a marriage existed, it was important to be clear about what constituted marriage. As the Church gradually acquired jurisdiction over marriage, it was forced to adjudicate matrimonial disputes. Two schools of thought emerged: the School of Paris, represented especially by Peter Lombard, held that marriage was constituted solely by the spouses' consent in words concerning the present (as opposed to words concerning the future, which gave rise only to betrothal); while the School of Bologna, represented especially by Gratian, held that consent initiated a marriage but a marriage was not fully constituted (and, therefore, could be dissolved) until it had been physically consummated. This scholarly dispute with its enormous practical implications was ultimately resolved by a series of decisions by Alexander III and his successors in the twelfth century.[15] These popes held that consent by the parties alone made a marriage[16] but that, prior to consummation, it could be dissolved for sufficiently grave cause

---

[14] Reynolds, 75–88.

[15] See C. Brooke, 264–270.

[16] X, 4.4.3.

(e.g., entry by one of the parties into religious life)[17] and that consent in words concerning the future followed by consummation transformed betrothal into marriage without the interposition of consent in words concerning the present.[18] The consequence of these papal decisions was to transfer power to constitute marriage from families to the parties themselves and, thereby, to open the door to the social scourge of clandestine marriages, unions entered into without any public form.

Since it was now clear that marriage was constituted by consent and gave rise to certain rights and obligations, the path was open to understand marriage according to the model of a contract, another kind of agreement entered into by consent and giving rise to rights and obligations. While the contractual model for understanding marriage soon triumphed in the West,[19] it was not accepted with the same enthusiasm by the Eastern churches. Marriage was analogized to a contract in later secular Roman law and in the *Nomocanon in Fourteen Titles,* a collection of conciliar canons and secular laws governing ecclesiastical affairs compiled around 629. Nevertheless, the Eastern churches have preferred to view marriage as a "sacrament" or "mystery of the Church."[20]

It was also in the Middle Ages that reflection on Ephesians 5 and Augustine's teaching on the "good of the sacrament" led the Church to an explicit consciousness of marriage's sacramentality among the baptized. The first inclusion of marriage among the seven sacraments of the New Law by the Church's magisterium occurred at the Council of Verona in 1184, perhaps in response to the resurgence of the rejection of marriage and procreation among the Cathars, a heretical sect with Manichaean tendencies.[21] Although theologians had spoken of marriage as a "sacrament" prior to Verona, there was no clear consensus that

the sacrament of matrimony was on the same level as baptism and Eucharist or that marriage was a cause of grace.[22] However, at Verona, the magisterium was running ahead of theology. In subsequent years, scholars struggled to elaborate a cogent theology of the sacramentality of marriage. While there was a consensus among theologians that marriage was the sacrament of the faithful and indissoluble union of Christ with his Church, there was considerable disagreement among them about how a natural institution had been elevated by Christ to sacramental dignity, what were the matter and form of the sacrament, whether the sacrament was a cause of grace, and, if so, what species of grace it caused.[23]

The Council of Trent and the Post-Tridentine Era

The sixteenth-century reformers challenged the Catholic Church's teaching and discipline on marriage. They rejected the sacramentality of marriage, the Church's jurisdiction over marriage, and its prohibition of remarriage after divorce in cases of adultery. They also sharply criticized the Church's failure to impose a mandatory public form for the celebration of marriage to eradicate clandestine marriages.[24]

The Council of Trent responded to this challenge by defining matrimony "as truly and properly one of the seven sacraments of the evangelical law, instituted by Christ the Lord"[25] and by reaffirming the Church's authority to establish impediments to marriage, to dispense from them, and, generally, to regulate marriage.[26] The council also condemned the reformers who had claimed the "church had erred when it taught and teaches" that the bond of marriage could not be dissolved because of the adultery of one of the partners.[27] The council, nevertheless, studiously

---

[17] X, 4.1.16.

[18] X, 4.1.15–16.

[19] LeBras, "Le Mariage," *DTC* 9:2182–2186.

[20] J. Meyendorf, *Marriage: An Orthodox Perspective* (Crestwood, N.Y.: St. Vladimir Seminary, 1975) 19–23.

[21] X, 5.7.9. See Schillebeeckx, 2:165–170.

[22] LeBras, "Le Mariage," *DTC* 9:2196–2201.

[23] LeBras, "Le Mariage," *DTC* 9:2196–2224.

[24] Brundage, 552–561.

[25] Council of Trent, sess. XXIV, *de doctrina,* c. 1.

[26] Council of Trent, sess. XXIV, *de doctrina,* cc. 2–12.

[27] Council of Trent, sess. XXIV, *de doctrina,* c. 7.

avoided condemning Eastern Christians whose discipline allowed for remarriage after divorce because of adultery.[28] Finally, the council decreed that henceforth, for the validity of their marriages, couples were required to express their consent before their proper pastors and two witnesses.[29] However, the council decided to make its decree effective only in parishes in which it had been promulgated. As a result, the decree lacked effect in many areas of the world where it could not be promulgated or its promulgation was judged inopportune, until the Sacred Congregation for the Council extended the obligation of observing the canonical form of marriage to Catholics throughout the world.[30]

As the Age of Enlightenment dawned, secular authorities sought to reclaim jurisdiction over marriage from the Church. To do so, they exploited the purported distinction between the marriage contract and the marital sacrament. The Church could have exclusive jurisdiction over marriage insofar as it was a sacrament, they argued, but, insofar as marriage was a contract, the State had jurisdiction over marriage, like other contracts. The Church's response to this secular challenge to its jurisdiction over marriage was to affirm with increasing vehemence the inseparability and, at times, the identity of the marriage contract and the marital sacrament among the baptized. In 1852, Pius IX affirmed: "It is a doctrine of the Church that the sacrament is not an adventitious quality superimposed on the contract; it pertains to the essence of marriage itself."[31] This teaching was reaffirmed in 1880 by Leo XIII: "Thus there can be no true and legitimate contract which is not thereby a sacrament."[32] This teaching was in-

corporated into canon 1012, §2 of the 1917 code which held that, since the matrimonial contract among the baptized had been raised by Christ to sacramental dignity, a valid matrimonial contract could not exist among the baptized "without its being by that fact a sacrament."

The 1917 code also consolidated a number of other aspects of the Church's theology and discipline on marriage that had been slowly developing during the post-Tridentine era. Throughout this era, there had been a pronounced tendency toward juridicizing moral theology in general and the theology of marriage in particular.[33] This tendency was clearly evident in the 1917 code's hierarchical ordering of the ends of marriage and its narrowing the object of matrimonial consent. Canon 1013, §1 of the 1917 code asserted: "The primary end of marriage is the procreation and education of children; the secondary, mutual assistance and the remedy of concupiscence." So secondary and subordinate were mutual assistance and the remedy of concupiscence to the primary end of marriage that the secondary end could be explicitly excluded from consent without invalidating the marriage, since it was not a *sine qua non* for the achievement of the primary end.[34] Canon 1081, §2 defined the object of matrimonial consent as "the perpetual and exclusive right to the body for acts which are per se apt to generate offspring." While the 1917 code's articulation of the ends of marriage and the object of consent had the advantage of juridic clarity, it was far removed from the lived experience of most married members of the faithful and smacked of arid legalism.

Consequently, not long after the promulgation of the 1917 code, some theologians, while acknowledging the essential ordering of marriage to the procreation and education of offspring, argued that more emphasis should be given to the so-called secondary end of marriage and its personal dimensions. These "personalists"

[28] P. Fransen, "Divorce on the Ground of Adultery—the Council of Trent (1563)," *Concilium* 7 (1970) 95–96.

[29] Council of Trent, sess. XXIV, *de ref.,* c. 1.

[30] SCConc, decr *Ne temere,* August 2, 1907, *ASS* 40 (1907) 525–530.

[31] Pius IX, letter, September 19, 1852, *CICFontes* 2: n. 515.

[32] Leo XIII, ency *Arcanum divinae sapientiae,* February 10, 1880, *ASS* 12 (1879–1880) 394.

[33] J. Mahoney, *The Making of Moral Theology* (Oxford: Clarendon, 1989) 224–258.

[34] C. Wynen, January 22, 1944, *AAS* 36 (1944) 189; *SRRDec* 36 (1944) 66–67.

felt that the true Catholic teaching would be more clearly presented if less emphasis were placed on what [had] hitherto been commonly called the primary end of marriage, and more emphasis on the personal elements of conjugal love and the conjugal community of life.[35]

The "personalist" project received an icy reception from the Holy See. In 1944, the Holy Office responded negatively to the question "whether the opinion of certain modern writers can be admitted, who...teach that the secondary ends are not essentially subordinate to the primary end, but are equally principal and independent?"[36] In 1951, Pius XII affirmed that the essential subordination of the secondary ends of marriage to the primary end is a principle which

the very internal structure of the natural order reveals, which the heritage of the Christian tradition embodies, which the Supreme Pontiffs have repeatedly taught, and which finally is crystallized into legal form by the Code of Canon Law.[37]

Vatican II

The Second Vatican Council devoted paragraphs 48 to 52 of its Pastoral Constitution on the Church in the Modern World to marriage. Although the council sought only to highlight "some major features of the church's teaching,"[38] its teaching marked a watershed in the Church's understanding of marriage. Avoiding the familiar term "contract," the council consistently spoke of marriage as a "covenant." Although the explicit reason given for this preference for "covenant" was that it was a

term more congenial to the tradition of the Eastern churches,[39] the term was also more in harmony with the personalist approach to marriage that suffuses *Gaudium et spes.*

This personalist approach was evident in the council's description of marriage as "an intimate sharing (*communitas*) of married life and love"[40] and in its repeated emphasis on the importance of conjugal love. The council did not present this conjugal love as a purely spiritual reality. Instead, it taught:

This love is uniquely expressed and perfected through the marital act. The actions within marriage by which the couple are united intimately and chastely are noble and worthy ones. Expressed in a manner which is truly human, these actions signify and promote that mutual self-giving by which spouses enrich each other with a joyful and thankful will.[41]

Ignoring the 1917 code's articulation of the object of consent as the perpetual and exclusive right to the body, the council defined consent as "that human act whereby spouses mutually bestow and accept each other."[42] Despite its teaching on the importance of conjugal love, the council reiterated traditional teaching that the "sacred bond" of marriage is indissoluble and that its continued existence is not dependent on the continued love of the spouses[43] and deplored the "plague of divorce."[44]

The council also reiterated the traditional teaching that "by their nature, the institution of matrimony itself and conjugal love are ordained for the procreation and education of children, and find in them their ultimate crown."[45] It recog-

---

[35] J. Ford, "Marriage: Its Meaning and Purpose," *TS* 3 (1942) 333.

[36] SCOf, decr, April 1, 1944, *AAS* 36 (1944) 103; *CLD* 3, 401–402.

[37] Pius XII, alloc, October 29, 1951, *AAS* 43 (1951) 849; *CLD* 3, 403.

[38] *GS* 47.

[39] Vatican II, *AcSynVat,* IV/4:536.

[40] *GS* 48.

[41] *GS* 49.

[42] *GS* 48.

[43] Ibid.

[44] *GS* 47.

[45] *GS* 48.

nized, however, that marriage is endowed by God "with various benefits and purposes"[46] and that its focus on the procreative end of marriage should not be understood as "making the other purposes of matrimony of less account."[47] In this, the council passed over in silence the strict hierarchical ordering of ends enunciated in the 1917 code and insisted on by the preconciliar magisterium.

The revised code has attempted to translate this conciliar teaching into canonical language as well as to integrate it with the rest of the canonical tradition. Toward that end, the code has devoted 111 canons to marriage, more than to any other sacrament. After several foundational canons, the material is divided into ten chapters: pastoral care and what must precede the celebration of marriage (cc. 1063–1072), diriment impediments in general (cc. 1073–1082), diriment impediments specifically (cc. 1083–1094), matrimonial consent (cc. 1095–1107), the form of the celebration of marriage (1108–1123), mixed marriages (cc. 1124–1129), marriages celebrated secretly (cc. 1130–1133), the effects of marriage (cc. 1134–1140), the separation of spouses (cc. 1141–1155), and the convalidation of marriage (cc. 1156–1165).

FOUNDATIONAL CANONS[48]
[cc. 1055–1062]

The Nature of Marriage

Canon 1055 — §1. The matrimonial covenant, by which a man and a woman establish between themselves a partnership of the whole of life and which is ordered by its nature to the good of the spouses and the procreation and education of off-

---

spring, has been raised by Christ the Lord to the dignity of a sacrament between the baptized.[49]

Unlike the 1917 code, which offered no definition of marriage, the present code begins its treatment of marriage with a description or "working definition" of marriage. This description, derived largely from *Gaudium et spes* 48, is essentially a theological statement, but one that has been cast in juridic language. Although the main clause of this paragraph of the canon affirms the traditional doctrine that Christ raised the marriages of the baptized to sacramental dignity, the subordinate clause of the sentence describes the natural or human reality of marriage. It is precisely this natural, human institution that Christ has raised to sacramental dignity for the baptized. Thus, the canon's description of marriage purports to be an authoritative interpretation of natural law and to provide the standard according to which all marriages are to be measured, whether the spouses are baptized or not.

In their discussions of marriage, canonists have traditionally distinguished *matrimonium in fieri* ("marriage in the act of being constituted") from *matrimonium in facto esse* ("marriage in the act of being lived out"). Although this distinction is not mentioned in either the 1917 or the 1983 code, it has an enduring significance for properly interpreting the meaning of the term "matrimony" in both codes. In brief, *matrimonium in fieri* is the act of consent that directly and immediately gives rise to *matrimonium in facto esse*. If *matrimonium in fieri* is fundamentally flawed, no *matrimonium in facto esse* results. But the converse is not true. *Matrimonium in facto esse*, once constituted by the legitimate consent of the parties, continues in existence even if seas of troubles cause the shipwreck of the existential relationship of the spouses.

In a sort of shorthand, commentators on the 1917 code customarily spoke of *matrimonium in*

---

[46] Ibid.

[47] *GS* 50.

[48] See Doyle, in *CLSA Com,* 740–746; Lüdicke, in *Münster Com,* Überblick vor 1055–1062; Hervada, in *Pamplona ComEng,* 659–662; Kelly, in *CLSGBI Com,* 571–578.

[49] See *CCEO* 776, §1. The Eastern code describes only the natural reality of marriage in this section and addresses the sacramentality of marriage in a separate section (*CCEO* 776, §2).

fieri as "the contract" and of *matrimonium in facto esse* as "the bond" (*vinculum*) and devoted little attention to the latter, except insofar as it precluded a subsequent marriage. However, following the lead of Vatican II, canon 1055, §1 identifies *matrimonium in fieri* as "the matrimonial covenant" and *matrimonium in facto esse* as the "partnership of the whole of life . . . ordered by its nature to the good of the spouses and the procreation and education of offspring" which results from the conjugal covenanting. A partnership of the whole of life ordered to both the good of the spouses and the procreation and education of children is a much richer understanding of *matrimonium in facto esse* than "the legitimate, perpetual and exclusive union of a man and a woman, arising from their mutual consent, ordered to the procreation and education of offspring"[50] of the 1917 code. In addition, greater maturity and interpersonal integration are required to establish a partnership of the whole of life than to give and accept the right to the body for acts suitable for the procreation of children.

Marriage as Covenant and Contract

In describing marriage, the revised code follows Vatican II in designating marriage as a "covenant," rather than as a "contract." It is not, however, as consistent as *Gaudium et spes* in its use of covenant language. In fact, the revised code refers to marriage as a "covenant" in only three canons;[51] but it uses contractual language in reference to marriage at least forty-three times.[52] This

contractual emphasis in the revised code is, in part, the result of the long canonical tradition that, at least since the Middle Ages, has understood marriage according to the model of a Roman law consensual contract. This was a contract from which obligations arose not from the exchange of a verbal formula or from the handing over of the object of the contract, but from the agreement of the wills of the consenting contractants.[53]

The code's juxtaposition of covenantal and contractual language and the predominance of the latter also reflect the fact that its drafters saw "covenant" and "contract" as interchangeable terms. In response to an objection from a code commission member to the use of both "covenant" and "contract" in what would become canon 1055, the Secretariat responded: "The terms 'contract' and 'covenant' are used in one and the same sense, indeed deliberately, so that it may be more clearly evident that the matrimonial covenant concerning which *Gaudium et spes* speaks can be constituted for the baptized in no other way than through a contract, even if it is *sui generis*."[54]

One may view the tendency of the code commission and of the revised code to equate "contract" and "covenant" as a matter of little consequence. Thus, Örsy suggests: "This new relationship between contract and covenant is best understood if the movement from contract to covenant is considered as a move to a higher viewpoint. Nothing is lost, everything is enriched; contract is contained in the covenant but does not exhaust it."[55] When one considers the decisive role played by the contractual model in articulating the Church's understanding of marriage since the Middle Ages, however, it is difficult to be sanguine about the predominance of contractual language about marriage in the revised code. At the very least, this

[50] F. Cappello, *De Matrimonio* (Rome: Marietti, 1961) n. 3; P. Gasparri, *De Matrimonio* (Vatican City: Typis Polyglottis Vaticanis, 1932) n. 8; F. X. Wernz and P. Vidal, *Ius Canonicum* (Rome: Gregorian University, 1946) 5: n. 21.
[51] See cc. 1055, §1; 1057, §2; and 1063, 4°.
[52] See cc. 1055, §2; 1058; 1068; 1073; 1085, §2; 1086, §3; 1089; 1094; 1095; 1096, §1; 1097, §2; 1098; 1101, §2; 1102, §1; 1104, §1 (bis); 1105, §1, 1° and §4 (bis); 1106; 1108, §1 and §2; 1114; 1115; 1117; 1120; 1121, §2 (bis) and §3; 1122, §§1–2; 1125, §3; 1125, 3°; 1127, §1; 1143, §1; 1144, §1; 1146; 1147; 1148, §2; 1149; 1160; 1684, §1; and 1706.

[53] A. Gauthier, *Roman Law and Its Contribution to the Development of Canon Law* (Ottawa: St. Paul University, 1996) 64–67.
[54] *Comm* 15 (1983) 222.
[55] L. Örsy, *Marriage in Canon Law* (Wilmington, Del.: Michael Glazier, 1986) 50.

predominance could possibly eviscerate the conciliar teaching on marriage as a covenant by providing a license to use the Roman law of contracts, understood as the natural law, as the interpretive key for the revised code.

"Covenant" has at least three advantages over "contract" as the prime analogue for articulating an understanding of marriage.

(1) A first advantage of the covenant analogy is that a covenant is a sacred reality, while a contract is essentially secular in nature. Although "covenant" was also used for ordinary pacts between peoples, it was the term chosen by the Old Testament authors to designate the faithful and loving relationship between Yahweh and his chosen people Israel. Especially in the prophetic books, this covenant was analogized to a marriage between Yahweh and his people, a marriage to which Yahweh was unfailingly faithful but to which his people were chronically unfaithful. This covenantal analogy was carried forward in the New Testament, especially in Ephesians 5 where the love of husband and wife is called a "great foreshadowing" that "refers to Christ and the Church."

Marriage was first assimilated to a contract not in classical Roman law but in the works of the commentators on Roman law as early as the twelfth century revival of the study of Roman law at Bologna. Once introduced by secular legal scholars, the contractual model for marriage spread "by a sort of contagion" first among canonists and then among theologians after the triumph of the theory that marriage was established by consent alone.[56] Although it was recognized that marriage was a unique contract, the use of the contractual model encouraged theologians and canonists to employ the tools of the Roman law of contracts to analyze marriage. While this sort of analysis fostered juridical clarity and was useful for adjudicating concrete marriage cases, it also opened the door for a legalistic approach to marriage and inhibited the development of a genuinely theological understanding of marriage.

[56] LeBras, "Le Mariage," *DTC* 9:2183.

(2) The covenantal model of marriage, while recognizing that marriage gives rise to mutual rights and obligations, places primary emphasis on the mutual personal commitment of the spouses. Thus, it is an apt vehicle for expressing the personalist dimension of marriage stressed by *Gaudium et spes* and the postconciliar magisterium. The contractual model, on the other hand, emphasizes the rights and obligations that are mutually given and accepted to constitute marriage and, when these rights and obligations are overemphasized, the personal dimension of marriage can be altogether or at least largely lost from view.

(3) As a result of its emphasis on rights and obligations, the contractual model has encouraged a narrow focus on *matrimonium in fieri,* the moment when marriage and its attendant rights and obligations come into being. This primary focus has historically led to a relative neglect of *matrimonium in facto esse,* the spouses' living out of their marital commitment amid the vicissitudes of daily life. One consequence of this neglect is that the Church has invested considerable resources in developing and implementing effective marriage preparation programs, but has invested considerably fewer resources and has had considerably less success in developing programs to assist couples in living out their marriages.[57] The covenantal model with its emphasis on the personal aspects of marriage can foster more balanced attention to both dimensions of marriage and more effective pastoral support to the married.

A Partnership of the Whole of Life

By describing marriage as a partnership or *consortium* of the whole of life, the revised code retrieves the classic Roman law definition of the

[57] M. Lawler, "Doing Marriage Preparation Right," *America* (December 30, 1995) 12; J. Provost, "Marriage Preparation in the New Code: Canon 1063 and the *Novus Habitus Mentis*," in *Ius Sequitur Vitam,* ed. J. Provost and K. Walf (Louvain: Leuven University, 1991) 190.

jurist Modestinus.[58] Although the term *consortium* defies precise translation, it connotes a close association or community of persons who share a common lot. Less intimate than a communion (*communio*), a *consortium* is more than a partnership (*societas*) for business purposes.[59] The qualification of this *consortium* as one "of the whole of life" underscores that the spouses' destinies are inextricably intertwined "in good times and in bad, in sickness and in health."[60]

Canon 1008 of the 1980 schema had spoken of marriage not as a *consortium* but as a communion, a more intimate union of minds and hearts. However, the code commission replaced the term "communion" with *consortium* in the 1982 schema. The reason given for this change was that the term *consortium* was less ambiguous than *communio* and better rooted in the juridical tradition.[61] Nevertheless, "communion" was the term preferred by John Paul II in his 1982 apostolic exhortation *Familiaris consortio*.[62]

The Ends of Marriage

To say that marriage is, by its nature, ordered to the good of the spouses and the procreation and education of offspring means that, as a natural institution, marriage has certain ends or finalities that are embedded in the nature of the institution itself (*fines operis*) and are independent of the will or intention of the spouses (*fines operantis*). Since the achievement of the ends of marriage is somewhat beyond the power of the spouses, the failure to attain them does not in itself affect the validity of a marriage. For example, even though marriage is ordered to the procreation and education of offspring, childless marriages are presumed to be valid. However, if one or both parties exclude this essential

end of marriage from their consent (i.e., refuse to give and accept the right to these ends) by a positive act of the will, they contract invalidly.[63]

Unlike the 1917 code, the revised code does not propose a hierarchical ordering of the ends of marriage. Neither the good of the spouses nor the procreation and education of offspring is designated as the primary end of marriage. Instead, both are equally essential to and inseparable in marriage. As John Paul II notes:

> Conjugal love, while leading the spouses to the reciprocal "knowledge" which makes them "one flesh," does not end with the couple, because it makes them capable of the greatest possible gift, the gift by which they become cooperators with God for giving life to a new human person. Thus the couple, while giving themselves to one another, give not just themselves but also the reality of children.[64]

Since the nascent Church's struggle with Gnosticism, it has taught that the procreation and education of offspring is an essential end of marriage. While primary emphasis has traditionally been given to the procreation of offspring, their nurture and education are equally important. Parents have both the obligation and the right to see to "the physical, social, cultural, moral, and religious education of their offspring" (c. 1136). This education is to take place in "a family atmosphere so animated with love and reverence for God and others that a well-rounded personal and social development will be fostered among the children."[65] For this reason, Christian parents' efforts to provide for the formation of their children is "truly a 'ministry' of the church at the service of building up her members."[66]

The 1917 code did not speak of the good of the spouses as an end of marriage. It spoke rather of

---

[58] D. 23.2.1: "Marriage is the union of a man and a woman, and a lifelong fellowship (*consortium omnis vitae*), a sharing of sacred and human law."

[59] Örsy, 51.

[60] *Rite of Marriage*, 45.

[61] *Comm* 15 (1983) 222.

[62] See *FC* 18–21.

[63] See the commentary on cc. 1095 and 1101.

[64] *FC* 14.

[65] *GE* 3; *FC* 36.

[66] *FC* 38. See also c. 835, §4.

"mutual assistance and the remedy of concupiscence" as the secondary end of marriage.[67] The Second Vatican Council employed the phrase "the good of the spouses," but it used the phrase to explain why the bond of marriage "does not depend on human decision" but is, of its nature, perpetual.[68] In speaking of conjugal love, however, *Gaudium et spes* taught:

> Fully human as it is, in being willed by one person for another, such love embraces the good of the entire person [*totius personae bonum*] and is therefore capable of endowing human expressions with a particular dignity and of ennobling them as special features and manifestations of married friendship.[69]

This love embracing the good of the whole person of the spouses prompts their "persevering endeavor to bring each other to the state of perfection."[70]

While canonists agree that the "good of the spouses" is an end of marriage, the relative novelty of the phrase has led them to disagree about how this good fits into the systematic structure of marriage. Some note that, while the Augustinian "goods" identify inherent properties of marriage that make *it* good, the good of the spouses is an end of marriage or an orientation toward the personal good of the spouses themselves. For them, the good of the spouses includes, but is richer than, the mutual assistance and remedy of concupiscence mentioned in the 1917 code. It "consists in the growth and maturing of the spouses as persons, through the aids, comforts and consolations, but also the demands and hardships, of conjugal life, when lived according to God's plan."[71] As such, the

good of the spouses gives rise to a right that marriage be lived out in accord with the three traditional *bona,* but not to a right whose content is independent of them. Thus, the good of the spouses is reduced to the good that accrues to the parties when the goods of children, fidelity, and sacrament are lived out faithfully in good times and in bad.

Other canonists have objected that such reductionism is contrary to the intent of the code commission and the mainstream of Rotal jurisprudence before and since the promulgation of the revised code. They propose instead that the good of the spouses is a fourth *bonum* distinct from but complementary to the three traditional "goods" of marriage first articulated by Augustine. For them, the good of the spouses consists in conjugal love and gives rise to the right to a loving relationship.[72]

Those who would reduce the content of the good of the spouses to the commitment to the three traditional "goods" object that conjugal love "cannot be the *bonum coniugum,* because love is not an end of marriage but an ingredient necessary for marriage to succeed, and a successful marriage is a sign of the achievement of the 'good of the spouses.'"[73] It is certainly true that a successful marriage is hardly imaginable without the presence of genuine love. Nevertheless, the fact that conjugal love is an essential ingredient of a successful marriage does not imply that it cannot also be an end of marriage, something to which marriage is ordered by its very nature. Indeed, the necessity of conjugal love for the success of a marriage suggests that, unless the spouses at least intended from the beginning of their union to give

---

[67] *CIC* 1013, §1.

[68] *GS* 48.

[69] *GS* 49.

[70] Pius XI, ency *Casti connubii,* December 30, 1930, *AAS* 22 (1930) 548. See also Pius XII, alloc, October 29, 1951, *AAS* 43 (1951) 848–849.

[71] D. Kimengich, *The Bonum Coniugum: A Canonical Appraisal* (Rome: Pontificium Athenaeum Sanctae Crucis,

1997) 113; C. Burke, "The 'Bonum Coniugum' and the 'Bonum Prolis': Ends or Properties of Marriage?" *J* 49 (1989) 704–713.

[72] L. Wrenn, "Refining the Essence of Marriage," *J* 46 (1986) 532–555; L. De Luca, "L'esclusione del *bonum coniugum,*" in *La simulazione del consenso matrimoniale canonico,* ed. P. Bonnet (Vatican City: Libreria Editrice Vaticana, 1990) 132–134; S. Villeggiante, "Il *bonum coniugum* e l'oggetto del consenso matrimoniale in diritto canonico," *ME* 120 (1995) 295.

[73] Kimengich, 46.

and accept the right to a loving relationship, their union was fundamentally flawed.

Even though the good of children has long been considered an end of marriage, a couple's failure to produce offspring has not been considered a basis for the nullity of their union, unless one or both of them were incapable of completing a sexual act that was at least potentially open to the conception of new life[74] or excluded the other spouse's right to such acts by a positive act of the will.[75] The spouses' post-matrimonial incurrence of impotence or withdrawal of openness to the procreation and education of children in no way affects the validity of consent already elicited. In a similar way, spouses may fail, in fact, to persevere in their love for one another or may become incapable of sustaining a loving relationship with each other. However, if one or both of them were, at the time of the marriage, incapable of appreciating and sustaining a loving relationship even minimally or did not intend to commit themselves to such a relationship, the marriage was invalid. The critical problem for jurisprudence is to establish with some clarity what type and degree of love is necessary for the validity of marriage.[76]

Since the promulgation of the 1983 code, canonical jurisprudence has quietly but steadily gone about the task of elucidating the meaning of the phrase "the good of the spouses" by adjudicating concrete cases in which a spouse's incapacity for marriage has been alleged.[77] Although mainstream jurisprudence has been reluctant to identify the good of the spouses with the right to a loving relationship, it has been more favorable to the position

that the good of the spouses, is an end of marriage whose content is distinct from the three traditional goods than to one that would reduce the good of the spouses to a function of the traditional goods. In its insistence that the interpersonal dimension is essential to a valid marriage, jurisprudence has left the door ajar for further precision of the nature of the good of the spouses.

Negatively, the good of the spouses is not to be identified with the spouses' subjective happiness, sense of fulfillment, or achievement of personal aspirations.[78] Nor is the lack of personal harmony between the spouses as a result of their "differences in character, nature, perspective on life, individual sensitivity, grade of particular love,"[79] or other accidental aspects of married life to be equated with incapacity for or exclusion of the good of the spouses. However, the good of the spouses is something more than a "communion of hearth, table and cohabitation."[80]

More positively, the good of the spouses is "the sum of all the goods which flow from the interpersonal relationship of the spouses,"[81] which, "at least as to their substance, bring about and promote the spiritual, intellectual, physical, moral, and social good of the spouses."[82] If this good of the spouses is to be realized, the spouses themselves must enjoy the minimum psychosexual integration "without which...the very communion of conjugal life would become impossible."[83] This psychosexual integration presupposes that the spouses possess at least the minimum affective maturity for marriage.[84] They must also have the capacity for and the willingness to engage in gen-

[74] See the commentary on c. 1084.
[75] See the commentary on c. 1101.
[76] See the commentary on c. 1057, §2.
[77] See E. Pfnausch, "The Good of the Spouses in Rotal Jurisprudence: New Horizons?" *J* 56 (1996) 527–558; and L. De Luca, 125–138. As of this writing, no cases have been decided by the Rota on the ground of the exclusion of the "good of the spouses." Nevertheless, the consensus of canonists is that both the incapacity for the good of the spouses and its exclusion by a positive act of the will result in the nullity of marriage.

[78] *Coram* Pompedda, April 11, 1988, *SRRDec* 80 (1988) 201.
[79] *Coram* Colagiovanni, February 2, 1988, *SRRDec* 80 (1988) 47–48.
[80] *Coram* Bruno, July 19, 1991, *SRRDec* 83 (1991) 465.
[81] Ibid., 466.
[82] *Coram* Bruno, December 17, 1987, *SRRDec* 79 (1987) 765.
[83] *Coram* Stankiewicz, May 28, 1991, *SRRDec* 83 (1991) 347–348.
[84] *Coram* Bruno, December 16, 1988, *SRRDec* 80 (1988) 748.

uine interpersonal communication,[85] to establish a mutually satisfactory sexual relationship,[86] and to establish at least a minimally "tolerable" personal relationship.[87]

The Sacrament of Matrimony

The Council of Trent capped a long development by defining as a dogma of the faith the proposition that marriage is "truly and properly one of the seven sacraments of the evangelical law, instituted by Christ the Lord."[88] It is precisely the natural institution of marriage, the partnership of the whole of life brought about by the spouses' consent, that Christ raised to sacramental dignity. Although marriage as a natural institution had existed since the beginning of time, Jesus Christ "merited for us by his passion the grace that would perfect natural love, strengthen the unbreakable unity and sanctify the spouses."[89] Four hundred years later, the Second Vatican Council returned to the Council of Trent's teaching on the very human love of the spouses, expressed in their consent and lived out in their daily lives, as the sign of the sacrament of matrimony: "Genuine married love is taken up into the divine love and is directed and endowed by the redeeming power of Christ and the saving action of the Church, so that married couples may be successfully led to God and be helped and strengthened in their noble task as father and mother."[90]

In short, in the marriages of Christians, the spouses' love for one another becomes the vehicle through which the faithful and irrevocable love of God in Jesus Christ becomes visible and tangible.

The love and faithfulness existing between Christ and his Church is therefore not simply an image or example of marriage, nor is the self-giving of man and wife an image and likeness of Christ's giving of himself to the Church. The love that exists between man and wife is rather a sign that makes the reality present, in other words, an epiphany of the love and faithfulness of God that was given once and for all time in Jesus Christ and is made present in the Church.[91]

By their efforts to love one another faithfully and perpetually, husband and wife slowly and sometimes painfully struggle to rise above the narcissistic alienation from self, others, and God, which is the condition of sin-wounded humanity. In this way, they participate in the Church's own mission of being "a sort of sacrament or sign of intimate union with God, and of the unity of all mankind . . . [and] an instrument for the achievement of such union and unity."[92] As a result, the family can be called "the domestic church,"[93] the tiniest but most essential cell of the Body of Christ which is the Church.

As a result of its emphasis on the consent of the spouses as the efficient cause of marriage, the Latin church has come to see the spouses themselves as the ministers of the sacrament of matrimony. The sacred minister present for the exchange of consent functions primarily as an official witness who asks for and receives the spouses' consent in the name of the Church (c. 1108, §2). In the Eastern churches, both Catholic and non-Catholic, however, it is the assisting priest who is the minister of the sacrament. While the spouses' consent is essential, it is not sufficient. From an Eastern perspective, it is hard to imagine how a marriage could be considered a sacrament without the priestly blessing. Thus, it is somewhat anomalous that the Eastern code makes provision for mar-

---

[85] Ibid., 746–749.

[86] *Coram* Colagiovanni, February 2, 1988, *SRRDec* 80 (1988) 49; *coram* Stankiewicz, April 20, 1989, *SRRDec* 81 (1989) 289; *coram* Bruno, July 19, 1991, *SRRDec* 83(1991) 472.

[87] *Coram* Stankiewicz, April 20, 1989, *SRRDec* 81 (1989) 280–293.

[88] Council of Trent, sess. XXIV, *de doctrina*, c. 1.

[89] Ibid., *doctrina de sacramento matrimonii*.

[90] *GS* 48.

[91] W. Kasper, *Theology of Christian Marriage* (New York: Seabury, 1980) 30.

[92] *LG* 1.

[93] *LG* 11.

riage according to the extraordinary form without the presence of a priest (*CCEO* 832, §1)[94] and for dispensations from the obligation of observing the form of marriage (*CCEO* 835). This seems to be an instance of the "Latinization" of the Eastern discipline.

The Sacramental Character of All Marriages of the Baptized

§2. For this reason, a valid matrimonial contract cannot exist between the baptized without it being by that fact a sacrament.[95]

The affirmation that marriage among baptized Christians has been raised by Christ to the dignity of a sacrament does not necessarily entail that, in the marriages of the baptized, the marital contract and the marital sacrament are so inseparably joined that the one cannot exist without the other. In fact, many fathers of the Council of Trent could support the imposition of a mandatory form for entering marriage because they believed that the marital contract and the sacrament were not only distinct but separable. Although they denied that the Church had any authority to alter the essence of the sacrament (i.e., the consent of the parties) as it had been instituted by Christ, they held that the Church did have the competence to regulate marriage insofar as it was a human contract. The principle that the marital contract and the marital sacrament were separable received support in diverse ways from reputable theologians from Duns Scotus to Alphonsus Liguori.[96]

The position that the inseparability of marital contract and marital sacrament is grounded in the will of Christ was most clearly articulated by Robert Bellarmine. He pointed out that neither revelation nor the magisterium specifies the mat-

ter, form, and minister of the sacrament of marriage. This silence has two possible explanations: either the matter, form, and minister of the sacrament are identical with those of the contract or marriage is not a sacrament. Since it is a dogma of the faith that marriage is a sacrament, Bellarmine concluded, the contract and the sacrament must be identical.[97] Bellarmine's argument was adopted (and adapted) by Suarez and Sanchez.[98]

The position that the contract and the sacrament were inseparable eventually gained the support of the Church's magisterium for reasons that were as much political as theological. During the eighteenth and nineteenth centuries, royalists and secularists exploited the alleged distinction between the marital contract and the sacrament to contest the Church's exclusive jurisdiction over marriage. The Church reacted to this attempt to usurp its jurisdiction over marriage by asserting ever more vehemently the inseparability of contract and sacrament in the marriages of the baptized. This conflict during the eighteenth and nineteenth centuries is the backdrop for the assertion of canon 1055, §2 that "a valid matrimonial contract cannot exist between the baptized without it being by that fact a sacrament."

The participants in the debate of the eighteenth and nineteenth centuries shared a common, albeit implicit, assumption—that the baptized who married possessed at least a scintilla of living faith. However, the discussion of the separability of the marital contract and the marital sacrament has re-emerged in recent years because of a less political and more theological concern, the phenomenon of baptized unbelievers. If, as the *Rite of Marriage* insists, "the sacrament of matrimony presupposes and demands faith,"[99] it has been asked, are those who, although baptized, lack even a semblance of faith capable of giving and receiving the sacrament of matrimony?[100]

---

[94] See the commentary on c. 1116.

[95] Cf. *CCEO* 776, §2.

[96] C. Caffarra, "Marriage as a Reality in the Order of Creation and Marriage as a Sacrament," in *Contemporary Perspectives on Christian Marriage,* ed. R. Malone and J. Connery (Chicago: Loyola University, 1984) 119–132.

[97] Ibid., 127.

[98] Ibid., 127–130.

[99] *Rite of Marriage,* 7.

[100] For a discussion of this issue, see W. Cuenin, "The Marriage of Baptized Non-believers: Questions of Faith,

The International Theological Commission has answered this question in the negative. While insisting that the question of the spouses' intention with regard to marriage should not be confused with that of their personal faith, the commission acknowledged that the two issues "must not be totally separated either."[101] The commission concluded:

In the last analysis the real intention is born from and feeds from living faith. Where there is no trace of faith (in the sense of "belief"—being disposed to believe), and no desire for grace and salvation is found, then a real doubt arises as to whether there is the above-mentioned and truly sacramental intention and whether the contracted marriage is validly contracted or not.[102]

The recognition that a total absence of faith can vitiate the spouses' sacramental intention and render their marital consent invalid has led some to ask a further question: how much faith is necessary for a genuinely sacramental intention? The

response of the magisterium to this question has been cautious. John Paul II asserts:

As for wishing to lay down further criteria for admission to the ecclesial celebration of marriage, criteria that would concern the level of faith of those to be married, this would above all involve grave risks. In the first place, the risk of making unfounded and discriminatory judgments; second, the risk of causing doubts about the validity of marriages already celebrated, with grave harm to Christian communities and new and unjustified anxieties to the consciences of married couples; one would also fall into the danger of calling into question the sacramental nature of many marriages of brethren separated from full communion with the Catholic Church, thus contradicting ecclesial tradition.[103]

Despite these prudential cautions, John Paul II acknowledges that, when even the best efforts of pastoral ministers to awaken a semblance of living faith in a couple preparing for marriage fail, "the pastor of souls cannot admit them to the celebration of marriage."[104]

While the reflections of the International Theological Commission and Pope John Paul II contain much pastoral wisdom, they fail to resolve a troubling problem resulting from the Church's teaching, enshrined in canon 1055, §2, that the marital contract and the marital sacrament are inseparable in the marriages of the baptized. If the total absence of faith in one or both parties to a marriage prevents them from entering a sacramental marriage, it also prevents them from entering a valid marriage. This unintended consequence of the insistence on the inseparability of marital contract and marital sacrament for the baptized means that "baptized non-believers" forfeit their natural right to marry as a result of their lack of faith. Since they lack faith, baptized

---

Sacrament and Law," *CLSAP* 40 (1978) 38–48; R. Cunningham, "Marriage and the Nescient Catholic: Questions of Faith and Sacrament," *Stud Can* 15 (1981) 263–284; L. Örsy, "Faith, Marriage, Contract, and Christian Marriage: Disputed Questions," *TS* 43 (1982) 379–398; Denis Baudot, *L'inséparabilité entre le contrat et le sacrement de mariage: La discussion après le Concile Vatican II,* Analecta Gregoriana 245 (Rome: Editrice Pontificia Università Gregoriana, 1987); M. Pompedda, "Faith and the Sacrament of Marriage—Lack of Faith and Matrimonial Consent—Juridical Aspects," in *Marriage Studies IV,* ed. J. Alesandro (Washington, D.C.: CLSA, 1990) 33–65; D. Faltin, "The Exclusion of the Sacramentality of Marriage with Particular Reference to the Marriage of Baptized Nonbelievers," in *Marriage Studies IV,* 66–104; M. Himes, "The Intrinsic Sacramentality of Marriage: The Theological Ground for the Inseparability of Validity and Sacramentality in Marriage," *J* 50 (1990) 198–220; M. Lawler, "Faith, Contract and Sacrament in Christian Marriage: A Theological Approach," *TS* 52 (1991) 712–731.

[101] International Theological Commission, "Propositions on the Doctrine of Christian Marriage," 2.3, *Origins* 8 (1978–1979) 237.

[102] Ibid.

[103] *FC* 68.

[104] Ibid.

unbelievers cannot enter a sacramental marriage; but, since they are baptized, they cannot have a valid marriage that is not a sacrament. As the International Theological Commission notes somewhat obliquely, "This gives rise to new problems for which a satisfactory answer has yet to be found."[105]

The Essential Properties of Marriage

Canon 1056 — The essential properties of marriage are unity and indissolubility, which in Christian marriage obtain a special firmness by reason of the sacrament.[106]

Unlike the ends of marriage, the essential properties of marriage (c. 1056) are not goals external to marriage but qualities inherent in the institution of marriage itself. These properties inhere in any genuine marriage independently of the will or intention of the partners. Unity and indissolubility are considered by the Church to be properties of marriage in virtue of the natural law. Thus, they are properties of all marriages and not just those of Christians. However, in the marriages of the baptized, these properties "obtain a special firmness by reason of the sacrament."

To say that *unity* is a property of marriage means that marriage is an exclusive relationship between one man and one woman. In marriage, a man and a woman mutually give and accept each other. To include anyone else within this privileged sphere of marital intimacy violates the unity proper to marriage. Thus, traditionally canonists have scored polygamy, whether simultaneous or serial, as violative of the unity of marriage. However, postconciliar reflection on marriage as a consortium of the whole of life has led to the recognition that violations of the unity of marriage need not involve extramarital sexual relationships. For example, a man may marry to have a wife for sexual relations, children, and companionship, but continue an unhealthily "close emotional relationship to his mother after marriage with even daily visits, frequent telephone conversations, dependence in decision making, sharing intimate aspects of marital life, often unknown to his wife."[107] In such a case, the man may be judged to have violated the unity of marriage.

To say that marriage is *indissoluble* means that it is a perpetual relationship which not only *should not* be terminated but *cannot* be terminated, even if the couple's existential relationship is irretrievably broken. Canonical tradition distinguishes between the intrinsic and extrinsic indissolubility of marriage.[108] All marriages, whether the spouses are baptized or not, are intrinsically indissoluble. That is, once the marriage is validly entered, it cannot be dissolved by the subsequent withdrawal of consent of the parties. A marriage is extrinsically indissoluble when it cannot be dissolved either by the intervention of external authorities or by the realization of certain conditions. While the Church does not recognize the power of civil authorities to dissolve marriages, it does claim the authority, under certain conditions, to dissolve non-sacramental marriages involving at least one unbaptized person and sacramental marriages that have not been consummated.[109] Thus, current church law considers only sacramental marriages that have been consummated to be extrinsically indissoluble by any cause except death.[110]

Matrimonial Consent

Canon 1057 — §1. The consent of the parties, legitimately manifested between persons qualified by law, makes marriage; no human power is able to supply this consent.[111]

---

[105] International Theological Commission, 2.3, 237.
[106] Cf. *CCEO* 776, §3.

[107] E. Pfnausch, "Simulated Consent: A New Way of Looking at an Old Way of Thinking—Part II," *J* 55 (1995) 727.
[108] Cappello, n. 45; Gasparri, nn. 1122–1127; Wernz-Vidal, 5: n. 27.
[109] See the commentary on cc. 1142–1150.
[110] See the commentary on c. 1141.
[111] Cf. *CCEO* 817.

The linchpin of the canon law governing marriage is the principle, derived from Roman law and reinforced by the decretals of twelfth century popes, that "consent not cohabitation makes a marriage."[112] So firmly is this principle rooted in canonical tradition that it has been cited by distinguished canonists as a matter of divine law.[113] Consent is not only an indispensable element of marriage but the efficient cause that brings marriage into being. As a result, no human power can supply for the absence of consent by one or both parties. Moreover, since consent is the essence of marriage, a marriage invalid because of an impediment or lack of form can be convalidated without renewal of consent by a radical sanation as long as the naturally sufficient consent originally given has continued.[114]

Even if it is naturally sufficient to bring about marriage, consent fails to achieve its juridic effect of bringing about an actual marriage unless it is exchanged between persons who are "qualified by law." The law has established a number of impediments to marriage which disqualify persons either from any marriage (e.g., the impediment arising from sacred orders) or from particular marriages (e.g., the impediment of consanguinity).[115] In addition, to be qualified for marriage, persons must possess at least the minimal psychological capacity to establish and nurture an intimate partnership of life, sufficient knowledge of the nature of this partnership, and the intention to undertake it. If these psychological, intellectual, or volitional requirements are lacking, a person's consent is deficient and fails to give rise to a marriage.[116]

For matrimonial consent to achieve its intended juridic effect, it must be legitimately manifested. Although consent itself is an internal act imperceptible to the senses, the social significance of the institution of marriage requires that it be given some public expression. For Latin Catholics, legitimate manifestation of consent normally entails the observance of the canonical form[117] or, in the case of Eastern Catholics, of the prescribed sacred rite.[118] Although consent alone is naturally sufficient to constitute marriage, unbaptized persons are bound to the observance of any civilly prescribed form for entering marriage.[119]

The Latin code is silent about the form for entering marriage that binds baptized non-Catholics when they marry one another. However, canon 781, 2° of the Eastern code stipulates that, when the Catholic Church judges marriage cases involving two baptized non-Catholics, it

> recognizes any form prescribed or admitted by the law to which the parties were subject at the time of the celebration of the marriage, provided that the consent be expressed in a public form and, when at least one of the parties is a baptized member of an Eastern non-Catholic Church, the marriage be celebrated with a sacred rite.

If this prescription of the Eastern code is supplementary law for the Latin church (c. 19),[120] baptized non-Catholics are always bound to manifest their consent according to some public form. Moreover, they are obliged to observe the form of marriage prescribed by the law of their church or ecclesial community, if it has one, or that to which their church or ecclesial community defers.[121] Thus, Eastern non-Catholics are bound to marry according to their church's sacred rite which includes the priestly blessing and Protestants, whose churches generally defer to the authority of the State in matrimonial matters, are bound by the form prescribed by civil law.

---

[112] D. 35.1.15.

[113] Cappello, n. 573; Gasparri, n. 775; Wernz-Vidal, 5: n. 451.

[114] See the commentary on cc. 1161–1165.

[115] See the commentary on cc. 1073, 1083–1094.

[116] See the commentary on cc. 1095–1107.

[117] See the commentary on cc. 1108–1123.

[118] See *CCEO* 828–842.

[119] Cappello, n. 78; Gasparri, nn. 240–246; Wernz-Vidal, 5: nn. 67–73.

[120] See J. Abbass, "Canonical Interpretation by Recourse to 'Parallel Passages': A Comparative Study of the Latin and Eastern Code," *J* 51 (1991) 296–298.

[121] *CCEO* 780, §2, 1°–2°.

Canon law, with its almost exclusive focus on the moment of the spouses' personal consent when marriage is constituted, is not easily harmonized with the marriage customs of cultures which envisage marriage as coming about in progressive stages and recognize a significant role for parents and other family members in "consent" to marriage. On the one hand, the Church's insistence on the principle that "consent makes a marriage" is often perceived as a manifestation of a cultural imperialism that denigrates traditional customs. On other hand, uncritical accommodation to traditional customs can lead to uncertainty about the status of couples who are on the continuum leading toward marriage and compromise the freedom of the spouses themselves. It seems unlikely that a genuine inculturation of the Church's law on marriage in traditional cultures can be achieved without some willingness on the part of the Church to soften its position on the exclusive role of the personal consent of the parties in effecting marriage.

§2. Matrimonial consent is an act of the will by which a man and a woman mutually give and accept each other through an irrevocable covenant in order to establish marriage.

The definition of matrimonial consent as "an act of the will" reflects the code's reliance on the rational psychology originated by Aristotle, Christianized by the Scholastic theologians, especially Thomas Aquinas, in the Middle Ages, and enshrined as the privileged vehicle for communicating Catholic doctrine at least since the neo-Scholastic revival of the nineteenth century. According to this traditional system, the human soul consists of two rational faculties or "proximate or immediate principles of mental operations":[122] the intellect, whose purpose is to discern the truth, and the will, whose purpose is to pursue the good.

Since the will is essentially a blind faculty which can choose only what is proposed to it by

the intellect, the two faculties are reciprocally related and play complementary roles in every genuinely human act, such as the act of matrimonial consent. Nevertheless, Scholastic philosophy and the ecclesiastical jurisprudence based on it has not always adverted sufficiently to this essential complementarity, but has sometimes succumbed to "an exaggerated objectification of the faculties."[123] When the intellect and will are objectified and dichotomized, jurisprudence loses sight of the essential unity of the human person, and its findings are not easily harmonized with those of contemporary empirical psychology. While one cannot understand the code's presentation of matrimonial consent without a rudimentary grasp of Scholastic rational psychology, an adequate understanding of consent also requires an appreciation of modern behavioral sciences. "Matrimonial consent is in fact much more than a mere act of the will. Everything in a human psyche contributes to it in varying degrees."[124]

Matrimonial consent is an act of the will exchanged between "a man and a woman." The phrase "a man and a woman" replaces the phrase "both parties" of canon 1081, §2 of the 1917 code. The change was prompted by a desire to underscore the personal dimension of consent. Consent is no longer exchanged by impersonal contractants but between a concrete man and a concrete woman for the purpose of establishing an irrevocable covenant. This phrasing is also closer to classical Roman law definitions of marriage by Modestinus[125] and Ulpian,[126] both of which speak of "a man and a woman." There is no evidence that this phrasing was meant to respond to the contemporary phenomenon of "same sex marriages." Nevertheless, the new wording does suggest that an exchange of consent between persons of the same sex is not truly "marital," and does not, therefore, give rise even to the semblance of marriage.

---

[122] J. Donceel, *Philosophical Psychology* (New York: Sheed and Ward, 1961) 99.

[123] Ibid., 318.
[124] Örsy, *Marriage in Canon Law,* 63.
[125] D. 23.2.1.
[126] Inst. 1.9.1.

Canon 1081, §2 of the 1917 code specified the formal object of matrimonial consent (i.e., what the parties mutually gave and accepted) as "the perpetual and exclusive right to the body ordered to acts per se apt for the generation of offspring," a formulation that was susceptible to, and often received, a primarily biological interpretation. Vatican II attempted to transcend this narrowly biological understanding of the object of matrimonial consent by describing it as "that human act whereby spouses mutually bestow and accept each other (*sese mutuo tradunt atque accipiunt*)."[127] This conciliar formulation has been incorporated into the revised code.

Both the conciliar articulation of the object of matrimonial consent and its canonical formulation have been criticized as overly pastoral and insufficiently juridical in nature.[128] It is certainly true that the spouses' mutual giving and accepting of each other "cannot mean a total surrender of all human faculties annihilating the spouses' sense of autonomy fundamental to human dignity."[129] Nevertheless, the oblative self-donation of the spouses in matrimonial consent, which was stressed in *Gaudium et spes* and has continued to be underscored by the papal magisterium,[130] cannot be reduced to the right to the body for acts per se apt for the generation of children. Indeed, this right to the body is "a real symbol of the giving of the whole person."[131] For the spouses to give themselves and accept one another in the act of matrimonial consent, they must have the capacity for and the intention to establish a genuine interpersonal relationship, characterized by fidelity and steadfastness "in good times and in bad" and ordered to "the good of the spouses and the procreation and education of offspring" (c. 1055, §1). Thus, the spouses must have the minimal capacity for and willingness to give themselves to one another not only physically but also emotionally and spiritually and to accept the other as a unique and equal partner.

In giving and accepting each other, the spouses themselves are what the Scholastics called the *material* object of matrimonial consent. They give and accept one another, however, not in an unqualified way, but "in order to establish marriage." The somewhat tautological phrase "to establish marriage" expresses the *formal* object of matrimonial consent. The phrase encompasses the whole complex of specifically marital rights and obligations that arise from the conjugal partnership of the whole of life. Although efforts have been made to identify these rights and obligations, no exhaustive listing yet exists. It will be the ongoing task of jurisprudence to undertake the painstaking task of articulating these rights and obligations.

The emphasis on conjugal love in *Gaudium et spes, Humanae vitae,* and *Familiaris consortio* has prompted the question whether love is an essential dimension of matrimonial consent. Since the question first was posed in the postconciliar period, the magisterium and ecclesiastical jurisprudence have consistently rejected the notion that romantic or erotic love is essential for valid matrimonial consent.[132] Such love is not a juridic element of marriage, but it is important as "a kind of force of the psychological order" without which "the spouses lack the strong inducement for carrying out with mutual sincerity all the tasks and duties of the conjugal community."[133] Indeed, at least in Western cultures where a genuine marriage can scarcely be conceived without the presence of romantic love, the absence of such love at

---

[127] *GS* 48.

[128] See U. Navarrete, "Structura iuridica matrimonii secundum Concilium Vaticanum II," *P* 57 (1968) 137–142; and C. Scicluna, *The Essential Definition of Marriage according to the 1917 and 1983 Codes of Canon Law* (Lanham, Md.: University Press of America, 1995) 292–295.

[129] Scicluna, 167.

[130] See Paul VI, ency *Humanae vitae,* July 27, 1968, §8, *AAS* 60 (1968) 485–487; and *FC* 11.

[131] *FC* 80.

[132] See Paul VI, alloc, February 9, 1976, *AAS* 68 (1976) 206–207; *CLD* 8, 794. See also ApSig, decision, November 29, 1975, *Apol* 49 (1976) 31–48; *CLD* 8, 768–790.

[133] Paul VI, alloc, February 9, 1976, *AAS* 68 (1976) 207; *CLD* 8, 794.

the time of consent may give rise to a strong presumption that one or both parties did not intend a
permanent union.[134]

In its most basic sense, however, "love" is not a
mere subjective disposition, infatuation, or erotic
inclination, but an act of the will. In fact, as Saint
Thomas noted, "this is to love someone: to wish
him or her good."[135] Matrimonial consent must
will the good of the other spouse in this fundamental sense and must, therefore, be an act of
love. Indeed, "unless this act of the will, which is
essentially self-donative—and, hence, an act of
love—is elicited, marriage is not entered into."[136]
In this sense, love is essential to the formation of
marriage. Thus, in the infamous hypothetical case
proposed by Jemolo,[137] the marriage of a man who
married with the intention to be open to children, to
be faithful, and to enter a perpetual union but also
with the intention, as part of a family vendetta, to
make his wife's life absolutely miserable, would be
invalid, because he "substituted hate" for loving
mutual self-donation in his consent.[138]

Despite frequent assertions that "conjugal love
is not included in the province of law,"[139] there
does seem to be an emerging consensus that conjugal love does have juridic relevance, at least insofar as it is an essential dimension of the dynamic
of mutual giving and accepting that is matrimonial
consent.[140] Nevertheless, those who recognize the
juridic relevance of conjugal love tend so to emphasize its oblative character that it seems reduced
to mere impersonal benevolence or goodwill
which Saint Thomas called the "beginning of friendship."[141] Such a one-sided emphasis on the oblative or "giving" dimension of conjugal love over-
looks another essential dimension suggested in the
revised code's emphasis that in matrimonial consent the spouses "mutually give *and accept* each
other."

Wrenn proposes that the love necessary for
matrimonial consent is "an affective tendency toward another person which is dialogical in nature
and involves union with the other."[142] According
to Aquinas, love is a function of the appetitive
faculty[143] and one of the soul's passions,[144] but a
passion that remains under the command of the
will[145] and tends inexorably toward union of affection.[146] Love involves an ongoing "give and
take." As Wrenn explains:

> These two poles were called by Aquinas
> *amor concupiscentiae* and *amor benevolen-
> tiae,* which Karl Rahner translates as love
> of desire and love of generosity. Love of
> desire, as the term implies, involves desir-
> ing the other as a source of legitimate self-
> fulfillment, whereas love of generosity in-
> volves wanting the best for one's beloved
> for one's beloved's own sake. In all healthy
> human love, however, both poles coexist
> and are more or less constantly active.[147]

Jurisprudence has, however, been slow to recognize a right to a loving relationship as an essential
element of a valid marriage, perhaps because a
thing as many splendored as love does not fit
neatly into the inherited contractual model.

---

[134] *Coram* Palazzini, June 2, 1971, *SRRDec* 63 (1971) 473–
474.

[135] Thomas Aquinas, *STh,* I-II, q. 77, a. 4.

[136] ApSig, decision, November 29, 1975, *Apol* 49 (1976)
42; *CLD* 8, 782.

[137] A. C. Jemolo, *Il matrimonio nel diritto canonico* (Milan:
Casa Editrice Dr. Francesco Vallardi, 1941) 76.

[138] ApSig, decision, November 29, 1975, *Apol* 49 (1976)
43; *CLD* 8, 783.

[139] Paul VI, alloc, February 9, 1976, *AAS* 68 (1976)
206–207; *CLD* 8, 794.

[140] In addition to the aforementioned 1976 allocution of
Paul VI and the 1975 decree of the Apostolic Signatura,
see Navarrete, 208; Z. Grocholewski, "De 'communione
vitae' in novo schemate 'De matrimonio' et de momento
iuridico amoris coniugalis," *P* 68 (1979) 469.

[141] Thomas Aquinas, *STh,* II-II, q. 27, art. 2, *sed contra.*

[142] L. Wrenn, "Refining the Essence of Marriage," *J* 46
(1986) 543.

[143] Thomas Aquinas, *STh,* I-II, q. 26, art. 1.

[144] Ibid., q. 26, art. 2.

[145] See, e.g., ibid., q. 26, art. 1–2.

[146] Ibid., q. 28, art. 1.

[147] Wrenn, "Refining the Essence of Marriage," 544–545.

The Right to Marry

Canon 1058 — All persons who are not prohibited by law can contract marriage.[148]

Every person enjoys the natural right to marry. This fundamental right is rooted in the social nature of the human person and is recognized by Catholic social teaching.[149] Therefore, the right to marry and to marry freely must be respected by both civil and ecclesiastical authority. Marriage is not, however, a merely private matter that concerns only the spouses themselves. It is also a societal institution whose health and vitality have a significant impact on the common good. Consequently, civil and ecclesiastical authorities have the right to regulate the exercise of the right to marry in the interest of the common good.[150]

A traditional way of regulating the exercise of the right to marry is the establishment of impediments that preclude certain marriages which experience has shown are inimical to the stability of marriage itself or to basic community values.[151] Since impediments impinge on the natural right to marry, they may be legitimately established only when the dangers posed by these marriages genuinely threaten the common good. The Church has attempted to prevent the hasty and unconsidered introduction of impediments by reserving to the supreme authority of the Church the competence to declare what are divine law impediments and to enact ecclesiastical law impediments (c. 1075). The Church also makes provision for dispensations from ecclesiastical law impediments when adequate precautions have been taken to prevent the dangers threatened by certain marriages (cc. 1078–1080).

---

[148] Cf. *CCEO* 778.
[149] See John XXIII, ency *Pacem in terris,* 1963, §15; and *GS* §26.
[150] Canon 223, §2.
[151] See the commentary on cc. 1073 and 1075.

The Church's Authority over Marriage

Canon 1059 — Even if only one party is Catholic, the marriage of Catholics is governed not only by divine law but also by canon law, without prejudice to the competence of civil authority concerning the merely civil effects of the same marriage.[152]

All marriages, whether they involve a Catholic spouse or not, are governed by what the Church teaches to be the divine law. Thus, baptized non-Catholics and unbaptized persons, even when they marry among themselves, are bound by the canonical norms defining the nature and ends of marriage (c. 1055, §1), its essential properties (c. 1056), and the necessity and nature of matrimonial consent (c. 1057), since these norms are considered to derive from natural law. For the same reason, non-Catholics also enjoy the natural right to marry (c. 1058) and, once they have legitimately entered marriage, their unions are presumed to be valid (c. 1060). They are also bound by other norms of the code (e.g., certain impediments) that are considered to be founded in divine law.

Throughout history, the Church has accepted the human laws of various nations, especially those of imperial Rome, and has enacted its own laws to regulate the marriages of its members. Canon 1016 of the 1917 code bound all baptized persons, whether they were Catholic or not, to the observance of these merely ecclesiastical marriage laws, unless the law expressly exempted them.[153] By contrast, canon 11 of the revised code

---

[152] The originally promulgated version of the revised code and the original CLSA translation had read, "even if only one party is baptized [*etsi una tantum pars sit baptizata*]." This error was subsequently corrected by the Holy See. *Acta Ioannis Pauli PPII,* "Codex Iuris Canonici," *AAS* 75 (1983) 324. This emended version of the canon is also found in *CCEO* 780, §1.
[153] This canon practically applied *CIC* 12, which subjected all the baptized to merely ecclesiastical laws, unless they were expressly exempted. The 1917 code did exempt baptized non-Catholics from the impediment of

exempts baptized non-Catholics from the observance of merely ecclesiastical laws, including those governing marriage, when they marry other non-Catholics. However, canon 1059 stipulates an exception to this exemption of non-Catholics from the observance of ecclesiastical laws. Non-Catholics, whether baptized or not, are bound by ecclesiastical marriage laws when they marry Catholics.

The revised code has introduced the category of persons who were once baptized in or received into full communion with the Catholic Church, but who subsequently left it by a formal act.[154] Although such persons may consider themselves non-Catholics and even be popularly considered to be no longer Catholics, their leaving the Church by a formal act does not exempt them from the observance of ecclesiastical laws, unless the law expressly provides the contrary. The law exempts those who have left the Catholic Church by a formal act from only three ecclesiastical laws. They are not bound by the regulations for mixed marriage (1124), the impediment of disparity of worship (c. 1086, §1), and the obligation of observing the canonical form of marriage (c. 1117).

Since the Church considers the marital sacrament and the marital contract to be inseparable, it does not recognize the State's competence to regulate marriage itself when it involves a Catholic. Nevertheless, the Church does normally encourage the faithful to observe the prescriptions of civil law regarding marriage when they are reasonable and designed to promote the common good. Thus, it usually insists that Catholics comply with civil laws governing such issues as matrimonial impediments, obtaining a marriage license, and the form to be observed when celebrating marriage. The Church, however, reserves the right to ignore such laws if they are contrary to divine law or unreasonably restrict the freedom of Catholics to marry.[155]

The Church defers to the authority of the State over the "merely civil effects" of the marriages of Catholics. These merely civil effects are those that do not necessarily flow from the essence of marriage, such as conjugal rights and obligations, the unity and indissolubility of the bond, the legitimacy of children, and the mutual rights and responsibilities of parents and children. The merely civil effects of marriage, which fall within the proper competence of the State, include such things as inheritance rights, tax status, and other civil rights, obligations, and privileges based on marital status.

The marriages of the unbaptized are governed by laws enacted by civil authority, provided that these are not contrary to divine law and do not unreasonably abridge the right to marry.[156] Thus, the unbaptized are bound by the impediments and form for entering marriage required by civil law. The 1983 code frees baptized non-Catholics from the obligations of observing merely ecclesiastical marriage laws when they marry among themselves, but it makes no explicit provision for the regulation of these marriages by any other law, except, of course, divine law.

The provisions of divine law concerning marriage are relatively few, however. The health and stability of the institution of marriage are so important to the public good of society that it seems anomalous that the marriages of baptized non-Catholics should be subject to no additional positive legislation whatsoever. It seems equally anomalous that the sacramental marriages of baptized non-Catholics should be directly and immediately subject to the regulatory authority of the secular State. The only alternative is that the marriages of baptized non-Catholics be subject to the laws of the churches or ecclesial communities to which these Christians belong. This, at least, is the solu-

disparity of worship (*CIC* 1070, §1) and from the obligation of observing the canonical form of marriage (*CIC* 1099, §2).

[154] For a discussion of leaving the Catholic Church "by a formal act," see the commentary on c. 1117.

[155] See the commentary on cc. 1130–1133. See also Cappello, n. 69.

[156] See Cappello, nn. 75–81; Wernz-Vidal, 5: n. 67.

tion of the Eastern code.[157] Baptized non-Catholics are bound by the marriage laws of their church or ecclesial community, if it has its own law, or by the law to which their church defers, if it lacks a proper law. Thus, baptized non-Catholics are subject indirectly and mediately to civil marriage law if their church or ecclesial community lacks a proper law but defers to the State for marriage regulations.[158]

The Favor of the Law

Canon 1060 — Marriage possesses the favor of law; therefore, in a case of doubt, the validity of a marriage must be upheld until the contrary is proven.[159]

Once it has been properly celebrated, a marriage is presumed to be valid unless the contrary is proven. When doubts are raised about its validity, this presumption requires that the validity of the marriage be upheld by refusing to allow the celebration of a new marriage until the invalidity or dissolution of the previous union has been demonstrated legitimately and certainly according

to the norm of law (c. 1085, §2). This legal presumption is a "favor" accorded to marriage by the Church's law.

Although the law presumes the validity of marriage once it is properly celebrated, the fact that it was celebrated is not presumed, but must be proven. According to traditional commentators, however, the favor of the law also extends to a marriage whose celebration cannot be demonstrated with certainty but which is "in possession." A marriage is considered "in possession" when the parties in good faith consider themselves to be married and are commonly considered to be married by others in the community.[160] Both when a marriage has been properly celebrated and when it is in peaceful possession, the presumption of its validity is a simple one, which cedes to contrary proof.

This presumption of validity is a particular application of the general principle of law that "a juridic act placed correctly with respect to its external elements is presumed valid" (c. 124, §2). The presumption is considered necessary from the viewpoint of the community to protect the stability of marriage against all the more or less well-founded reasons that can be used to call the validity of any marriage into question. It is also considered necessary from the viewpoint of couples to prevent possible doubts of overscrupulous spouses about the validity of their marriages from discouraging them from dedicating themselves to salvaging difficult marriages and carrying out their marital obligations.

In its earliest formulation by Innocent III,[161] the presumption of validity was meant to favor an existing marriage's claim to legitimacy when doubts about its validity surfaced because of a possible impediment. The validity of the existing marriage was to be upheld until its nullity had been certainly proved. At the present time, however, the effect of the favor of the law has been reversed. The presumption now favors the marriage that has, existentially at least, ceased over an existing subse-

---

[157] *CCEO* 780, §2, 1°–2°.

[158] A similar argument was advanced by commentators on the 1917 code to establish that the non-baptized, who were not subject to ecclesiastical laws of the Catholic Church, were bound by civil law. See Cappello, n. 76; Wernz-Vidal, 5: n. 70. Although these commentators were loath to recognize any authority other than the Catholic Church and the State as competent to regulate marriage, in the more ecumenical climate of the postconciliar era with its recognition of the existence of many elements of the Church of Christ outside the boundaries of the Catholic Church (*UR* 3), it is no longer unthinkable that non-Catholic churches and ecclesial communities might legitimately regulate the marriage of their members. In fact, the Catholic recognition that the diriment impediment of mixed religion enacted by the Council of Trullo had been abrogated implicitly (ApSig, decision, July 1, 1972, *CLD* 8, 3–29) acknowledged the existence of some legislative authority over marriage in the Orthodox churches. See the commentary on cc. 1124–1129.

[159] Cf. *CCEO* 779.

[160] Cappello, n. 51; Wernz-Vidal, 5: n. 44; Gasparri, n. 18.

[161] X, 2.20.47.

quent marriage in peaceful possession.[162] In addition, the presumption is at odds with the general principle that doubtful laws, contracts, and moral obligations do not oblige.[163]

Most commentators on the 1917 code held that the presumption favoring the validity of marriage was rooted in divine law.[164] During the code revision process, suggestions that this traditional presumption be modified at least implicitly questioned its divine law character. Justifying its refusal to modify the norm, the code commission asserted: "Although it is not of divine law itself, it is founded on the fundamental properties of marriage."[165] Since the presumption articulated in canon 1060 is applicable not only to the marriages of Catholics but also to those of non-Catholics, whether baptized or not, and since it is generally considered to bind in both the internal and the external fora, it is clearly something more than a merely ecclesiastical law or a procedural norm binding tribunal personnel.

While most commentators concentrate on the presumption of validity of a properly celebrated marriage as the "favor" accorded marriage by the law, there are various other ways in which the law favors marriage. The children of marriages enjoying the presumption of validity are considered legitimate, even if the marriage is subsequently proven to be invalid (c. 1137). The favor of the law toward marriage can also be seen in procedural law: a marriage whose validity is challenged is represented by its own attorney, the defender of the bond (c. 1432); marriage nullity cases are normally reserved to panels of at least three judges (c. 1425, §1, 1°); and affirmative decisions in marriage nullity cases must at least be reviewed and confirmed by a second and independent tribunal before the parties are free to remarry (c. 1684).

Some Definitions

Canon 1061 — §1. A valid marriage between the baptized is called *ratum tantum* if it has not been consummated; it is called *ratum et consummatum* if the spouses have performed between themselves in a human fashion a conjugal act which is suitable in itself for the procreation of offspring, to which marriage is ordered by its nature and by which the spouses become one flesh.

§2. After a marriage has been celebrated, if the spouses have lived together consummation is presumed until the contrary is proven.

§3. An invalid marriage is called putative if at least one party celebrated it in good faith, until both parties become certain of its nullity.[166]

A valid marriage between two baptized persons which has not yet been consummated is said to be "ratified" (*matrimonium ratum*). Ratified marriages are always sacramental and enjoy the essential properties of unity and indissolubility. Nevertheless, for a just cause, the obligations of a merely ratified marriage can be dispensed from, or it can be dissolved at the request of one of the spouses.[167]

A marriage between baptized persons is said to be ratified and consummated (*matrimonium ratum et consummatum*) if, after it has been validly entered into by consent, the spouses engage in a completed act of sexual intercourse in a human manner. A ratified and consummated marriage cannot be dissolved by any human power or for any cause (c. 1141). The sequence of ratification and consummation is critical. No matter how frequently a couple has had sexual relations prior to marriage, during an invalid marriage, or before it has become sacramental through the baptism of both spouses, this sexual activity does not constitute the consummation of a ratified marriage, because one cannot consummate or "complete" what does not yet exist.[168]

---

[162] R. Thrasher, "Canon 1014 and the External Forum and Internal Forum Solutions: An Update," in *Marriage Studies I*, ed. T. Doyle (Toledo, Ohio: CLSA, 1980) 146.

[163] See, e.g., cc. 14; 1084, §2; 1086, §3. But, on the contrary, see c. 1091, §4.

[164] Cappello, n. 54; Wernz-Vidal, 5: n. 44.

[165] *Comm* 3 (1971) 169–170.

[166] The Eastern code has no comparable canon.

[167] See the commentary on c. 1142 and cc. 1697–1706.

[168] Gasparri, n. 1093.

The 1917 code defined the act by which marriage is consummated as "a conjugal act to which the matrimonial contract is by its nature ordered and by which the spouses become one flesh."[169] Commentators agreed that the minimum necessary for consummation was that the man's penis penetrate the woman's vagina at least partially and deposit semen there. Consummation was not effected, however, by *coitus interruptus* in which the man penetrated the woman's vagina but withdrew before ejaculation or by intercourse using a condom.[170] In both cases, consummation did not occur because of the failure to ejaculate semen in the vagina. Even though illicit, other methods of birth control which did not prevent the ejaculation of semen in the vagina did not prevent consummation. The marriage law *coetus* explicitly restated the traditional view that natural sexual intercourse constituted consummation and that contraception did not prevent consummation as long as the physical integrity of the act was maintained.[171] Unlike the 1917 code, the revised code does explicitly require that, for consummation to occur, the act of sexual intercourse be performed "in a human fashion," i.e., it must be a natural and voluntary act.[172]

Also unlike the 1917 code, the revised code has defined the conjugal act by which marriage is consummated as one "which is suitable in itself for the procreation of offspring." This expression has a long canonical history. Canon 1081, §2 of the 1917 code used it to specify the perpetual and exclusive right to the body that was considered the object of matrimonial consent, and it meant non-contraceptive sexual relations, even if conception did not result from the act of intercourse.[173] In the 1983 code, however, the expression "suitable in itself for the procreation of offspring" no longer qualifies the conjugal acts by which the right to the body is exercised but the conjugal act by which a marriage is consummated. The choice of these words in this context (c. 17) and in accord with canonical tradition (c. 6, §2) seems to require the interpretation that a conjugal act (or even numerous conjugal acts) performed while practicing some form of artificial birth control does not result in the consummation of a marriage. Thus, despite the protestation of the code commission to the contrary, the revised code seems to have introduced a radical revision of the traditional understanding of the consummation of marriage. Since this revision seems to have been unintended and has not been followed in the practice of the Holy See, canon 1061, §1 should be emended so that the mind of the legislator is expressed clearly in language consonant with the canonical tradition.

Once a couple has begun to cohabit, their marriage is presumed to have been consummated (c. 1061, §2). Couples who have cohabited after their marriage and who subsequently claim that their marriages were never consummated bear the burden of proving non-consummation. This presumption of the law is, however, a simple one that yields to contrary proof. Not stated in the code is a corollary to this presumption. If a couple has not cohabited after marriage, consummation is not presumed but must be proven.

A marriage is said to be "putative" when it is in fact invalid but was entered into in good faith by at least one of the partners (c. 1061, §3). In other words, he or she was unaware of the existence of an undispensed impediment or of a defect of consent, which de facto rendered the marriage invalid. A party may also be in good faith if he or she was aware of the condition giving rise to an impediment (e.g., a prior marriage) or a defect of consent (e.g., a firm intention never to have children) but was unaware of its invalidating effect. Since ignorance of or error about the law is not presumed (c. 15, §2), however, the party who claims to have been in good faith must prove that he or she was unaware of the invalidating effect

---

[169] *CIC* 1015, §1.

[170] Cappello, n. 383; Wernz-Vidal, 5:20–21.

[171] *Comm* 6 (1976) 180. See M. Pompedda, "La nozione di matrimonio 'rato e consumato' secondo il can. 1061, §1 del C.I.C. e alcune questioni processuali di prova in merito," in *Studi di diritto matrimoniale canonico* (Milan: Giuffrè, 1993) 367–371.

[172] See the commentary on c. 1142.

[173] Cappello, n. 574.

of an impediment or defect of consent. Given the widespread ignorance of canon law among people today, most non-Catholics and even most lay Catholics should not have a great difficulty proving their good faith.

For a marriage to be considered putative, it must have been celebrated according to the required form and, therefore, have the appearance of a marriage. Thus, when a Catholic enters marriage without observing the canonical form and without being dispensed from its observance, the attempted marriage is not considered putative but simply invalid. If, however, the canonical form was observed but was substantially defective (e.g., the official minister was not properly delegated), the marriage would be considered putative.

The most significant effect of a putative marriage is that any children born of it are considered legitimate, even if it is subsequently declared invalid (c. 1137). A putative marriage also enjoys the favor of the law. It remains putative until both spouses become certain of its nullity. Thus, the spouses' doubts, even grave doubts, about the validity of their marriage are not sufficient to deprive it of its status as putative. The spouses on their own may become certain of the invalidity of their marriage because of an impediment. However, most couples become certain that their marriage was invalid because of a defect of consent only through the decision of a church tribunal.

Canon 1015, §3 of the 1917 code called a validly celebrated marriage between unbaptized persons a "legitimate marriage" (*matrimonium legitimum*). Although the revised code has not retained this category, the term continues to be used in ecclesiastical practice to designate valid marriages between two unbaptized persons and between a baptized person and an unbaptized person.

Engagement

Canon 1062 — §1. A promise of marriage, whether unilateral or bilateral, which is called an engagement, is governed by the particular law established by the conference of bishops, after it has considered any existing customs and civil laws.

§2. A promise to marry does not give rise to an action to seek the celebration of marriage; an action to repair damages, however, does arise if warranted.[174]

For much of human history, engagement or betrothal was a necessary prelude to marriage at least for the upper classes of society and an institution fraught with social and juridical consequences. Thus, engagement has historically been regulated by laws setting requirements for its validity and liceity, the form in which the promise of marriage is to be made, the dowry, the effects of an engagement, and the requirements for its valid and lawful termination.[175] In most Western societies, however, engagements have lost most of their social and legal significance. An engagement is now a more or less formal but unenforceable promise to marry at some future date. As a result of the decline in significance of engagement in many places, the revised code has not attempted to regulate it in universal law.

The task of regulating engagements is left to particular law to be enacted by episcopal conferences for their own territories. To date, episcopal conferences in the English-speaking world have not regulated engagements. Possible subjects for particular legislation might be a liturgical rite for engagement, the form in which the promises are to be made, witnesses to the promises, and the role, if any, of parents in entering an engagement. Particularly in societies where engagement remains an important social institution, particular law governing engagements should take into account local customs and pertinent civil laws.

Although an engagement is expected to be a serious and morally binding promise to marry, it does not give rise to a legally enforceable right. Thus, a broken engagement does not give the disappointed fiancé an action or a right to sue in ec-

---

[174] Cf. *CCEO* 782.

[175] Although *CIC* 1017 was the only canon on engagements in the 1917 code, Cappello devoted 59 pages of commentary to this canon. See Cappello, nn. 82–143, and Gasparri, nn. 50–125.

clesiastical court to compel the other party to go ahead with the celebration of the marriage. To authorize an ecclesiastical tribunal to compel unwilling persons to honor promises to marry that they have now retracted would compromise the freedom that is essential for true marital consent (cc. 219 and 1103). Nevertheless, a disappointed fiancé does have the right to approach an ecclesiastical tribunal to recoup material damages suffered as a result of a broken engagement. For example, a woman whose family made a non-refundable deposit for a wedding reception and forfeited this deposit when her fiancé abruptly broke their engagement could bring an action in an ecclesiastical tribunal to recover financial losses. Nevertheless, the absence of particular law governing engagements could make the successful prosecution of such a suit difficult.

BIBLIOGRAPHY

Bibliographical material for canons 1055–1062 can be found after the commentary on canon 1165.

CHAPTER I
PASTORAL CARE AND THOSE THINGS WHICH MUST PRECEDE THE CELEBRATION OF MARRIAGE[1]
[cc. 1063–1072][2]

The concerns in this chapter are broader than the parallel section of the 1917 code (*CIC* 1019–1034). The old code emphasized ensuring the freedom of the parties to marry, with some concern for their proper instruction concerning marriage (*CIC* 1033). The present code emphasizes more strongly the proper preparation of the parties for a valid and fruitful celebration of the sacrament.

Canons 1063–1065 speak of marriage preparation. Although the canons speak of the preparation required for sacramental and non-sacramental unions, the importance of the sacrament in the life of both parties and of the community is highlighted. These canons also remind us that concern for marriage involves much more than concern for the valid exchange of the consent of the parties. Preparation for forming children to become responsible Christian adults who understand and appreciate the sacrament in their lives is essential, as is the providing of support to those who are already married. The wedding is only the beginning of a long life together, a life that will include times of hardship. The Christian community has a duty to support married people in their vocation and to help them live out their married lives.

The canons emphasize the importance of marriage preparation and highlight a potential weakness. It is difficult to legislate adequate preparation for the sacraments and adequate care for those who are married. These canons and the 1996 document of the Pontifical Council for the Family on marriage preparation[3] depend for their implementation on the good will and concern of the Christian community. It is a pastoral challenge to ensure that these canons are well implemented in each diocese and parish, for the good of those receiving the sacrament of marriage, and for the good of the entire Christian community.

Canons 1066–1070 are concerned with ensuring that the canonical requirements for a valid and lawful celebration of marriage are met through the pre-nuptial inquiry. Canon 1071 addresses a number of difficult situations where the permission of the local ordinary is required for a lawful celebration of marriage to take place. Canon 1072 speaks of the concern that pastors should have for the marriages of young people who are below the age customary for marriage in the region.

Catechesis and Preparation for Marriage[4]

Canon 1063 — Pastors of souls are obliged to take care that their ecclesiastical community offers the Christian faithful the assistance by which the matrimonial state is preserved in a Christian spirit and advances in perfection. This assistance must be offered especially by:

    1° preaching, catechesis adapted to minors, youth, and adults, and even the use of instruments of social communication, by which the Christian faithful are instructed about the meaning of Christian marriage and about the function of Christian spouses and parents;

    2° personal preparation to enter marriage, which disposes the spouses to the holiness and duties of their new state;

    3° a fruitful liturgical celebration of marriage which is to show that the spouses

---

[1] See T. Doyle, in *CLSA Com,* 746–757; J. Fornés, in *Pamplona ComEng,* 663–667; D. Kelly, in *CLSGBI Com,* 578–588.

[2] Cf. *CCEO* 783–789.

[3] PCF, "Preparation for the Sacrament of Marriage," May 13, 1996, *Origins* 26 (1996–1997) 97, 99–109.

[4] Cf. *CCEO* 783, §1 and §3.

signify and share in the mystery of the unity and fruitful love between Christ and the Church;

4° **help offered to those who are married, so that faithfully preserving and protecting the conjugal covenant, they daily come to lead holier and fuller lives in their family.**

In speaking of the Church in the modern world, Vatican II addressed "some more urgent problems deeply affecting the human race," the first of which was "Marriage and the Family in the Modern World."[5] The council recognized that, while esteem for Christian marriage was growing among some people, in modern culture the dignity of Christian marriage was often "overshadowed by polygamy, the plague of divorce, so-called free love, and similar blemishes."[6]

Canon 1063 emphasizes the importance of marriage preparation. On May 13, 1996 the Pontifical Council for the Family published "Preparation for the Sacrament of Marriage,"[7] a document which addresses the three stages of preparation for marriage that are considered in the canon. The document sees preparation for marriage as "a broad and thorough process of education for married life which must be considered in the totality of its values."[8] It reflects the canon by stating: "Christian marriage preparation can be described as a journey of faith which does not end with the celebration of marriage but continues throughout family life."[9]

The canon begins by speaking generally about how the Christian community, specifically through its pastors, can preserve the marital state in a Christian spirit and perfect it further. This will be accomplished both through marriage preparation

and the pastoral care of married couples. "Pastors of souls" (those bishops and priests who are entrusted with the pastoral care of a community) have the primary function of ensuring that Christian marriage is valued and lived in the community. All others in the community are encouraged to participate in this important task. Such participation could be furthered by enlisting the help of married couples, as well as others whose work or expertise would be useful to the couples preparing for marriage (e.g., lawyers, doctors, psychologists, etc.).[10] The canon does not explain in detail how pastors of souls and the community are to help married couples. Depending on local needs and resources, different programs exist in different places and include, for example, marriage preparation courses, pre-Cana programs, engaged encounter, marriage encounter, pastoral marriage counseling, etc. The programs chosen should respond to the pastoral needs of the community.

Because marriage between baptized Christians is a sacrament, the prospective spouses should be prepared to receive the sacrament as fruitfully as possible. Such preparation should be accomplished through the various means highlighted in the canon, especially preaching and catechesis, which seek to strengthen and nourish the faith of the parties.

Marriage is not only a private commitment between two individuals. As a sacrament, it is a commitment before God and the church community, and it involves the good of the community. Hence, marriage should be highly esteemed and cared for by the community. The document issued by the Pontifical Council for the Family calls for the entire diocese to be involved in marriage preparation and recommends creating a "diocesan commission for marriage preparation, including a

---

[5] *GS* 46–47.

[6] *GS* 47b.

[7] This document consists of guidelines from the Pontifical Council for the Family, which is an administrative body. In other words, the text is not a legislative document. It cannot derogate from universal law. Rather, it seeks to explain the law and give suggestions for practice.

[8] "Preparation for the Sacrament of Marriage," 101, n. 10.

[9] Ibid., 102, n. 16.

[10] Number 12 of the introduction to the new ritual of marriage speaks of the whole community as being responsible for marriage preparation. Number 26 also notes that the ministry of marriage preparation, while a concern of the whole Church, is of particular concern for the lay members of the faithful.

group for the pastoral care of the family."[11] The document emphasizes that marriage preparation relates not merely to the pre-marriage period but also to the couple's ongoing commitment to live out the marriage in the fullest way possible. The canon too sees marriage preparation as something that takes a lifetime.

Remote, Proximate, and Immediate Preparation

We speak of marriage preparation that is remote, proximate, and immediate. Remote preparation takes place in infancy, childhood, and adolescence, in the family, in school, and in formation groups. The purpose of this remote preparation is to "attain the goal whereby every member of the faithful called to marriage will understand completely that, in the light of God's love, human love takes on a central role in Christian ethics."[12] Through preaching, catechesis, and social communication, children, young people, and adults can learn more about the meaning of marriage and what being a Christian spouse entails (1°). Effective marriage preparation must begin in childhood. Children and young people who learn what the obligations of marriage are, and who learn to appreciate the importance of the sacrament, will be better able to apply those teachings to their own lives when they marry.

The canon emphasizes the importance of proximate preparation for those who are about to marry (2°). The document issued by the Pontifical Council for the Family foresees proximate preparation as a time during which the couple will have the opportunity to deepen their faith as well as to "identify any difficulties they may have in living an authentic Christian life."[13] Normally, proximate preparation takes place in marriage preparation courses offered by pastoral workers who have a solid formation. The preparation should include:

instruction regarding the natural requirements of the interpersonal relationship between a man and a woman in God's plan for marriage and the family: awareness regarding freedom of consent as the foundation of their union, the unity and indissolubility of marriage, the correct concept of responsible parenthood, the human aspects of conjugal sexuality, the conjugal act with its requirements and ends, and the proper education of children.[14]

By the end of this period of proximate preparation, the engaged couple should have a good idea of what marriage entails and how they will take their place in the Christian community, as well as how to "preserve and cultivate marriage love later...and how to overcome the inevitable conjugal 'crises.'"[15]

Immediate preparation is the final stage before the wedding takes place (3°). As the couple prepares to celebrate the marriage, they should review all they have learned and receive spiritual and liturgical preparation.[16] Immediate preparation is all the more necessary in those cases where couples have not participated in a marriage preparation course.

What of those couples who refuse to take part in marriage preparation programs? "Is preparation for the sacrament of marriage a *sine qua non?* Or is it only a pastoral option?"[17] Huels notes that canon 1077, §1 could be used to delay a marriage temporarily until the couple are considered ready. However, it is very difficult to deny the celebration of a marriage only because of a couple's failure to participate in a specific marriage preparation program. One distinction that should be made is between concrete marriage preparation programs and preparation for marriage. What is important is that the couple be prepared for mar-

---

[11] "Preparation for the Sacrament of Marriage," 102–103, n. 20.

[12] Ibid., 103, n. 25.

[13] Ibid., 104, n. 32.

[14] Ibid., 104, n. 35.

[15] Ibid., 106, n. 46.

[16] Ibid., 106, n. 50.

[17] J. Huels, "Preparation for the Sacraments: Faith, Rights, Law," *Stud Can* 28 (1994) 56–57.

riage. How that preparation takes place might not be the same for every couple. Whether a couple is prepared for marriage must be assessed individually and objectively. If the couple is not prepared, then canon 1077, §1 could be invoked and the marriage temporarily delayed. However, the basic human right to marry (c. 1058) must also be taken into account in making such a decision and in evaluating such programs

Continued Pastoral Care after Marriage

The canon does not forget those who are already married: they too need to have continued pastoral care in order to sustain them in this vocation and to help them live it in an ever more fruitful manner (4°). This is especially important during the first five years of married life as the couple are adjusting to their new responsibilities as married people and possibly as parents. Continued pastoral care could take the form of "post-marriage courses to be carried out in parishes or deaneries."[18]

The Vocation to the Married or to the Celibate Life

We should speak of the married vocation and the vocation to the priestly or religious life in the same context.[19] It is important that young people understand the different vocations, and it is essential that married life be given its proper due. It is not a vocation that is secondary vis-à-vis the priestly or religious life, but the road to holiness that most of the baptized will follow.

Obligation of the Local Ordinary to Provide Marriage Preparation

Canon 1064 — It is for the local ordinary to take care that such assistance is organized fittingly, after he has also heard men and women proven by experience and expertise if it seems opportune.

[18] "Preparation for the Sacrament of Marriage," 108, n. 73; see also *FC* 66.
[19] *FC* 66; see also *CCC* 1620.

It is the local ordinary (cf. c. 134) who should ensure that appropriate forms of pre- and post-matrimonial help spoken of in the previous canon are provided. The canon is practical in stating that the ordinary should consult, if it is opportune, with men and women whose experience in these matters can help him provide the best help possible. This means that the ordinary should do more than provide generic pre-marriage courses. He should ensure that assistance appropriate to the situation of the people living in the diocese is provided. He can learn what is appropriate through the people whom he consults. Such courses or assistance should be updated regularly to keep in touch with any changing issues that should be addressed.

Reception of Confirmation, Penance, and the Eucharist

Canon 1065 — §1. Catholics who have not yet received the sacrament of confirmation are to receive it before they are admitted to marriage if it can be done without grave inconvenience.
§2. To receive the sacrament of marriage fruitfully, spouses are urged especially to approach the sacraments of penance and of the Most Holy Eucharist.

This canon is concerned with the spouses' spiritual preparation for marriage. The canon presumes that the parties are baptized, or that at least the Catholic party is. However, it also refers to the other sacraments of initiation—confirmation and Eucharist—and mentions penance. The reception of these three sacraments should facilitate a fruitful reception of marriage. Although reception of these sacraments is not necessary for the validity of the marriage, they are important for the faith of the parties and the fruitfulness of marriage, whether that marriage is sacramental or not. For this reason the faithful are "urged especially" to receive the sacraments of Eucharist and penance.

Confirmation should be received from a bishop, unless a priest has been deputed to do so according to canon 884, §1. The present canon stresses that confirmation should be conferred only if it can be done "without grave inconvenience." The person should not be rushed into reception of the sacrament. Adequate preparation should take place so that the importance of confirmation in the person's life is realized (c. 889, §2).

The question of the fruitfulness of the sacrament of marriage is an especially delicate one. The canons presume that the parties who approach the Church have at least a basic faith and a willingness to do as the Church intends when they receive the sacrament. Preparation for the fruitful reception of the sacrament advocated in paragraph two of this canon is the ideal situation, one in which both parties are persons of faith who are approaching the sacrament with the best of intentions. However, the opposite situation can occur, where the parties are not especially interested in a fruitful reception of the sacrament, or even in the sacrament at all.[20]

Certitude of Valid and Licit Celebration[21]

Canon 1066 — Before a marriage is celebrated, it must be evident that nothing stands in the way of its valid and licit celebration.

This general canon leads into the more particular requirements of the following canons (cc. 1067–1070) which establish ways to ensure the valid and lawful celebration of a marriage. The pastoral minister preparing the couple for marriage must be certain that nothing impedes a valid and lawful celebration. For a marriage to be valid, the parties must be canonically free to marry one another. In other words, an impediment to marriage must not exist (cc. 1083–1094), the parties must marry freely and give true matrimonial consent (cc. 1095–1107), and the marriage must be celebrated with the proper canonical form (c. 1108). For a marriage to be celebrated lawfully, the prescriptions of canons 1067–1072 as well as canon 1102, §3 should be followed.

[20] In the commentary on c. 1055 see the discussion of the related question of faith and sacrament.
[21] Cf. *CCEO* 785, §1.

The Investigation of Freedom to Marry[22]

Canon 1067 — The conference of bishops is to establish norms about the examination of spouses and about the marriage banns or other opportune means to accomplish the investigations necessary before marriage. After these norms have been diligently observed, the pastor can proceed to assist at the marriage.

Since marriage preparation is a matter in which it is desirable to have some uniformity in each region, the code empowers each conference of bishops to lay down the norms which establish the freedom of the parties to marry and all other prerequisites for marriage. However, the conference may still leave a certain amount of discretion to the diocesan bishop. Once the pertinent norms have been observed, then the pastor may proceed to assist at the marriage.

The canon states explicitly that there is to be some kind of examination of the spouses. Usually they are examined separately. The purpose of this examination is to ascertain, not merely the absence of impediments, but also the freedom of the parties to marry, their capacity to marry, their understanding of the obligations and rights of marriage, and their capacity to undertake those obligations and exercise those rights.

The canon does not state that a recent baptismal certificate must be produced. However, episcopal conference norms may so prescribe. A recent baptismal certificate is a useful tool for ascertaining the freedom of the parties to marry, since it may contain other pertinent information regarding a person's canonical status. Canon 535, §2 prescribes that a baptismal register, in addition to noting the fact of baptism, is to contain notations of the reception of confirmation, as well as any details regarding the aforementioned canonical status (marriage, adoption, reception of sacred orders, perpetual religious profession, change of *sui iuris* church, declaration of nullity or dissolution of a previous marriage, dispensation from the obligation of celibacy, etc.).

[22] Cf. *CCEO* 784.

Publication of Banns

The present canon allows for the possible publication of banns[23] if the local situation warrants it. Episcopal conferences and diocesan bishops should assess local situations to determine whether the publication of banns would be an effective way of proving that the parties to a proposed union are free to marry. In modern society, especially in cities, publishing banns would not be an effective means of determining people's freedom to marry, since people move around so much and are not necessarily well known in the area where they are living, not even in their parishes. In other circumstances (e.g., rural areas), however, banns could be an effective method of establishing freedom to marry.

Process to Be Followed in Establishing the Freedom of Catholic Parties Who Have Attempted Marriage without Following the Canonical Form

On August 7, 1984, the Pontifical Council for the Interpretation of Legislative Texts published a response to the following question:

Whether, in order to prove the state of freedom of those who, although bound to the canonical form, attempted marriage before a civil official or a non-Catholic minister, is the documentary process mentioned in c. 1686 necessarily required, or does the pre-nuptial investigation dealt in cc. 1066–1067 suffice?

The council replied that the process outlined in canons 1066–1067 would suffice to prove the freedom to marry of someone who was bound to the canonical form of marriage yet who contracted a marriage without observing this form.[24] Nevertheless, many diocesan bishops have reserved the determination of freedom to marry in these cases to the chancery or to the tribunal.

Procedure in Danger of Death[25]

Canon 1068 — In danger of death and if other proofs cannot be obtained, the affirmation of the contracting parties, even sworn if the case warrants it, that they are baptized and are prevented by no impediment is sufficient unless there are indications to the contrary.

This canon provides an alternate method for examining the parties in cases where one or both of the parties is in danger of death. If both parties affirm that they are baptized and that they are not impeded by any impediments to marriage, they may marry. The danger of death may come from illness (intrinsic danger) or war, natural disaster, etc. (extrinsic danger). The danger is presumably grave enough that there is not enough time to proceed with the usual investigations.

The canon requires that the statement of the parties regarding their baptismal status be made under oath only "if the case warrants it," in other words, only "where there is real doubt about the truthfulness of the parties."[26]

The Obligation of the Faithful to Reveal Impediments[27]

Canon 1069 — All the faithful are obliged to reveal any impediments they know about to the pastor or local ordinary before the celebration of the marriage.

---

[23] CIC 1022 required the pastor publicly to announce those who were to be married. This was known as publishing the banns of marriage, which occurred on three successive Sundays and other holy days of obligation (CIC 1024).

[24] PCILT, response, August 7, 1984, in *Pamplona ComEng,* 1295. See L. Wrenn, *Authentic Interpretations on the 1983 Code* (Washington, D.C.: CLSA, 1993) 13–14.

[25] Cf. *CCEO* 785, §2.

[26] Kelly, in *CLSGBI Com,* 582.

[27] Cf. *CCEO* 786.

This obligation is similar to that of canon 1027 of the 1917 code: anyone who knew anything that would invalidate the proposed union was to inform the pastor or the local ordinary. This obligation envisioned not only the good of the couple, but also the good of the community, since marriage affects the entire community.

Generally, anyone who is aware of any impediments to marriage, or anything that would invalidate the consent of one of the parties (an incapacity, an intention excluding one of the goods of marriage, etc.) is obliged to reveal this information to the pastor or the local ordinary before the marriage. Then, it is up to the pastor or the local ordinary to act on the information after having considered the nature and gravity of what he has learned, who informed him of it, how that person acquired the information, and whether it can be corroborated. The pastor or the local ordinary may need to speak with the parties or their parents to understand the situation more clearly.

However, not everyone who learns of an impediment affecting one of the parties is obliged to reveal it. Those who learn of it in sacramental confession can speak to the penitent about it only in the context of the confessional unless the penitent brings it up again in the extra-sacramental forum. Those who learn of such information in other confidential relationships (doctor-patient, lawyer-client, etc.) may not be free to reveal what they know. However, it is not universally held that these latter people are excused from the obligation of this canon. While upholding the confidential relationship is important, the good of the person who is perhaps unknowingly entering an invalid marriage must also be protected.[28]

---

[28] Those who learn information in a professional confidential context are excused from testifying about the information in a subsequent formal process, while those who learn information in the context of a sacramental confession are incapable of doing so. See cc. 1548, §2, 1° and 1550, §2, 2°.

Notification of the Parties' Completed Examination[29]

Canon 1070 — If someone other than the pastor who is to assist at marriage has conducted the investigations, the person is to notify the pastor about the results as soon as possible through an authentic document.

Because prospective spouses often live in different parishes, and because they may live in a parish different from the one in which they will be married, it is necessary to inform the pastor of the parish where the marriage is to take place of any preparations occurring outside his parish. In this way, he will be assured that the appropriate preparation and investigations have been accomplished. Since the pastor is responsible for fostering the spiritual welfare of his parish, he is responsible for ensuring proper preparation for marriages that take place in his parish. Even if he does not personally prepare the couple for marriage, he must be informed that all the prerequisites for a valid and lawful celebration have been fulfilled.

The canon states that the pastor should be informed by an "authentic document," which is a document that has been dated, signed by the person who conducted the investigation, and sealed with the parish seal (c. 535, §3).

Marriage Situations Requiring the Local Ordinary's Permission[30]

Canon 1071 — §1. Except in a case of necessity, a person is not to assist without the permission of the local ordinary at:
  1° a marriage of transients;
  2° a marriage which cannot be recognized or celebrated according to the norm of civil law;
  3° a marriage of a person who is bound by natural obligations toward another party or children arising from a previous union;

---

[29] Cf. *CCEO* 787.
[30] Cf. *CCEO* 789.

4° a marriage of a person who has notoriously rejected the Catholic faith;

5° a marriage of a person who is under a censure;

6° a marriage of a minor child when the parents are unaware or reasonably opposed;

7° a marriage to be entered into through a proxy as mentioned in can. 1105.

§2. The local ordinary is not to grant permission to assist at the marriage of a person who has notoriously rejected the Catholic faith unless the norms mentioned in can. 1125 have been observed with necessary adaptation.

This canon lists a number of situations in which the person who officially assists at the marriage (the priest, deacon, or lay person delegated in virtue of c. 1112) on behalf of the Church needs the local ordinary's permission to do so. These delicate situations require special pastoral care when the couple is being prepared for marriage. If the prescriptions of this canon are not followed, the validity of the marriage is not affected. However, the appropriate permission from the local ordinary is necessary for the lawfulness of the marriage. The prescriptions of this canon should be followed even when only one party fits into one of the categories mentioned in the canon. In all these instances, referral to the local ordinary is obligatory except in case of necessity, that is, in instances of danger of death and

any situation in which an undue delay could involve a serious pastoral risk. It will be for the person who is to assist at the marriage to make a prudent judgement in this regard, bearing in mind that the purpose of the rule is to protect both the sacrament and the ultimate well-being of the partners.[31]

The cases that the canon highlights as requiring special care are the following:

[31] Kelly, in *CLSBGI Com,* 584.

*1° – A Marriage of Transients or Wanderers (*Vagi*)*

These are people who have no domicile or quasi-domicile (cc. 100–101). The fact of their having no fixed address can make it difficult to establish their freedom to marry. In addressing these cases, it is important to determine the reason why the person has no domicile or quasi-domicile. For example, some people have no fixed address because of their lifestyle; they are transients, travelers, migrants. However, other transient people live this way because of mental or physical illness. The local ordinary would need to take extra care in such cases to ensure that the person is capable of entering marriage.

2° – A Marriage Prohibited by Civil Law

Civil law impediments (for example, minimum age required for marriage, degree of consanguinity permitted, etc.) or laws regarding remarriage may be different from canon law impediments. If a marriage cannot be recognized in civil law, special care needs to be taken so that church practice is not unnecessarily in conflict with civil law. However, there may be circumstances in which, for good reason, the local ordinary can allow a marriage to be celebrated despite the prohibition of civil law.

3° – A Marriage of a Person Bound by Previous Marital and Parental Obligations

If a marriage involves a person who has been married before but who is free to marry in the eyes of the Church (because of a dissolution or declaration of nullity, the death of a former spouse, a civil union that was not recognized by the Church, or a common law union followed by a separation), that person may be bound by natural obligations toward children from the previous union. Such obligations cannot be ignored (see cc. 1136, 1154). In the same way, obligations to a former spouse may still bind. In such cases, the children or the previous spouse may need financial or other assistance that would put a strain on the second union, or the community could be scandalized if the new union were to take place and the children or spouse of the previous union were not being provided for.[32] The Church could not condone the abandonment of a person's obligations to dependents. The local ordinary must assess the situation to ensure that all who need support and care are being provided for. If in his view the person is neglecting his or her obligations to a former spouse or children, the ordinary could even forbid the proposed marriage, at least for a time (c. 1077, §1).

4° – A Marriage of Someone Who Has Notoriously Rejected the Catholic Faith

The difficulty here is evaluating when someone has notoriously rejected the Catholic faith. To reject the faith means more than simply no longer practicing the Catholic faith. Rejecting the faith can mean professing to believe something contrary to the Catholic faith or joining a sect or a group that does not profess the Catholic faith.[33] One can reject the faith without embracing another religion.

Proving *notorious* rejection is a serious matter. It must be demonstrated that the person has consciously rejected the Catholic faith and that the rejection is publicly known. This understanding of the term "notorious" is taken from canon 2197 of the 1917 code which spoke of notorious delicts. A crime is notorious if "it is publicly known and was committed under such circumstances that no maneuver can conceal nor any legal defense ex-

cuse it."[34] A person who notoriously rejects the Catholic faith is different from someone who simply no longer practices the faith or who has stopped believing what the Church teaches without absolutely rejecting that teaching publicly.

In evaluating a notorious rejection of the faith, one can be guided by the words of Pope John Paul II in *Familiaris consortio:*

> When in spite of all efforts engaged couples show that they reject explicitly and formally what the Church intends to do when the marriage of baptized persons is celebrated, the pastor of souls cannot admit them to the celebration of marriage.[35]

For most of the situations listed in paragraph one of this canon, the resolution of the pastoral issues is left entirely to the discretion of the local ordinary. Paragraph two of the canon, however, somewhat qualifies that discretion with regard to those who have notoriously rejected the Catholic faith. Because this is such a serious situation for the faith of the person as well as for the faith of his or her prospective spouse and children, the ordinary is not to permit the marriage to take place unless the promises required of the partners in mixed marriages are made (c. 1125) with appropriate adaptations. This is necessary to ensure that both parties realize the religious obligations they have undertaken and what it will mean to live them out in their marriage.

5° – A Marriage of a Person under Censure

Canon 209 speaks of the obligation of the faithful to remain in communion with the Church. Implicit in this number of canon 1071 is the person's responsibility to try to restore the communion that has been broken.

A person under certain censures (excommunication or interdict) is forbidden to receive any of

---

[32] What are these obligations? Canon 1689 speaks of "moral and even civil obligations." In addition to financial or material assistance, such obligations could also include such things as the education of the children and the emotional and spiritual support of the children or the other spouse.

[33] Kelly, in *CLSGBI Com,* 586, notes that this notorious rejection of the Catholic faith "is not to be confused with that of a 'defection from the Catholic Church by a formal act' (see Cann. 1086, §1, 1117, 1124...)." In his opinion, this canon is addressing something less strong than that. It is addressing those persons who have not defected, but who, at the same time, cannot be considered Catholics in good standing.

[34] T. L. Bouscaren and A. C. Ellis, *Canon Law: A Text and Commentary,* 3rd rev. ed. (Milwaukee: Bruce, 1957) 838.

[35] *FC* 68g.

the sacraments (cc. 1331, §1, 2°; 1332). The purpose of the present provision is to balance the effects of the censure (exclusion from the sacraments) with a person's natural right to marry. Thus it is important for the local ordinary to be involved in order to help rectify the situation and to facilitate reconciliation with the Church on the part of the person under censure.

6° – A Marriage of a Minor

Because parents play such an important role in the education and upbringing of their children, they can help in the discernment of their children's choice of a state in life, without forcing their children into such a choice (c. 219) especially as regards a marriage partner (*GS* 52). It is natural that parents normally be part of the decision to marry. This is especially true if the children are still young adults, or for some reason not prepared to make a responsible choice of a marriage partner. Although the code also upholds the right of such minors to marry, the parents should usually be informed of what is happening, and should agree to the proposed marriage.

This number of the canon speaks only of marriages of minors whose parents are unaware of the proposed marriage, or whose parents are opposed to it. A minor is a person who has not completed his or her eighteenth year (c. 97, §1). Not all marriages of minors must be referred to the ordinary, but only those cases in which the parents of the person (or persons) to be married are unaware that the marriage is to take place, or have reasonable objections to it. Here the law presumes that the parents know the young people well enough to help them decide if they have the necessary maturity to enter marriage. However, if the young people have serious reasons why their parents should not be notified, or why the marriage should take place even though their parents oppose it, the local ordinary can permit the marriage, after assessing the reasons presented.

7° – A Marriage to Be Entered by Proxy

In a marriage entered by proxy one of the parties (or both) is not present and is represented by

another person (c. 1105). Such marriages raise certain pastoral questions, e.g., how well do the parties know one another and how genuine and free is their consent? Furthermore, if such marriages are prohibited in a particular place, certain civil law issues might arise. Thus, such marriages should be referred to the local ordinary.

Eastern Code

Canon 789, 5° of the Eastern code adds another situation in which the permission of the local ordinary is to be obtained before proceeding with the wedding:

> the marriage of one who is forbidden by an ecclesiastical sentence to enter into a new marriage unless the person fulfills certain conditions.

This is the potentially delicate situation in which a judgment has been given in a marriage nullity case and a prohibition (*vetitum*) to remarry has been imposed (*CCEO* 1370, §1). Such a prohibition might be imposed on a person when a marriage is declared invalid because one party was incapable of consenting, or did not understand what he or she was consenting to, or had a different view of marriage from the one the Church teaches. The prohibition would state that this person cannot marry again in the Catholic Church unless it is clear that through adequate preparation he or she understands the commitment that is being undertaken. Such cases are more difficult if the prohibition states that the person was incapable of understanding or committing himself or herself to the obligations of marriage. Sometimes, however, it can be shown that the person has grown and is now able to understand and embrace what marriage entails.

It is interesting that this provision is not included in canon 1071 of the Latin code. However, in practice, the permission of the local ordinary is required to lift any such prohibition and permit the marriage to take place. Thus, although the provision is not explicit in this chapter of the Latin code, the necessity of official consultation to ensure that adequate preparation for marriage has taken place should be the same in practice under both codes.

Marriages of the Young

Canon 1072 — Pastors of souls are to take care to dissuade youth from the celebration of marriage before the age at which a person usually enters marriage according to the accepted practices of the region.

A man cannot validly marry before he is sixteen, and a woman before she is fourteen (c. 1083, §1). However, episcopal conferences may establish an older minimum age for the lawful celebration of marriage than that prescribed by the code (c. 1083, §2). This last norm provides for the fact that there are different customs in different parts of the world. In some cultures, children mature early and are expected to take a responsible place in society at an earlier age than in other cultures. Nevertheless, even the minimum age prescribed by the episcopal conference may be younger than is the norm according to the culture of the country. Recently it has become clear that marriages of the very young often fail because they do not possess sufficient maturity to cope with the stresses and obligations of marriage. Thus, the canon exhorts pastors of souls to take care that the youth to whom they minister do not marry before they are ready. This is not an absolute prohibition, but a pastoral guideline based on experience.

BIBLIOGRAPHY

Bibliographical material for canons 1063–1072 can be found after the commentary on canon 1165.

CHAPTER II
DIRIMENT IMPEDIMENTS IN GENERAL[1]
[cc. 1073–1082][2]

The code devotes ten canons to general principles about impediments to marriage and their dispensation. These canons treat: general notions about impediments (cc. 1073–1076), the prohibition of a particular marriage (c. 1077), dispensations from impediments in various circumstances (cc. 1078–1080), and the recording of dispensations (cc. 1081–1082).

BASIC PRINCIPLES

The Nature and Effect of an Impediment

Canon 1073 — A diriment impediment renders a person unqualified to contract marriage validly.

An impediment is a circumstance that bars a person from marrying. An impediment is called *impedient* if it results only in the unlawfulness of the marriage;[3] it is called *diriment* (from the Latin *dirimere,* to put an end to or terminate) if it results in the invalidity of an attempted marriage. Laws establishing diriment impediments to marriage (cc. 1083–1094) are disqualifying laws (c. 10) in that they render a person ineligible either for any marriage or for a particular marriage. Diriment impediments invalidate attempted marriages even

[1] See T. Doyle, in *CLSA Com,* 757–764; K. Lüdicke, in *Münster Com,* 1073/1–1082/1; J. Fornés, in *Pamplona ComEng,* 667–674; and D. Kelly, in *CLSGBI Com,* 588–598.

[2] This material is treated also in *CCEO* 790–799. Because of its close similarity to the Latin code, the Eastern code will be discussed explicitly only where it is substantially different.

[3] Although the 1983 code contains no impedient impediments, canon 1083, §2 authorizes episcopal conferences to establish an impedient impediment of lack of age.

when the parties bound by them are ignorant of or in error about them and their effects (c. 15, §1).

Although it is difficult to render the nuances of Latin in English, it is important to distinguish an incapacity (*incapacitas*) for marriage from the disqualification (*inhabilitas*) for marriage that results from an impediment. Those incapable of marriage suffer from a serious deficiency, often psychological in nature, that prevents them from giving true marital consent;[4] those bound by an impediment are generally capable of marriage but are legally disqualified from it.

Impediments restrict the exercise of the natural right to marry, which has long been understood in the Church's positive law and its social teaching as a fundamental human right.[5] Nevertheless, both civil and ecclesiastical law have long restricted the freedom to marry in the interest of the common good by establishing impediments. These restrictions are justified by appeal to the experience that certain marital relationships are injurious to both civil and ecclesiastical society and to the institution of marriage and often harm the parties themselves and their children.

Historical Overview

Impediments to marriage emerged rather early in the history of church law. The early Church observed, absorbed, and adopted impediments from Roman law and, to a lesser extent, the Old Testament. Early councils, both local and ecumenical, established new impediments and modified or abrogated existing ones. The current discipline of the Eastern churches on impediments was essentially in place by the time of the Council of Trullo in 691. Although its legislation was not received by the churches of the West, they observed some

[4] See the commentary on c. 1095.
[5] See the commentary on c. 1058.

elements of it as custom (e.g., the impediment of disparity of worship). In addition, conciliar activity throughout the Middle Ages down to Trent continued to add, modify, and occasionally abrogate matrimonial impediments.

The existence of impediments induced by custom and their modification through conciliar activity led to considerable confusion in the post-Tridentine period. Among canonists estimates of the number of diriment impediments ranged from fourteen to nineteen and of impedient impediments from two to eleven.[6] The confusion was dispelled by the 1917 code which established an exhaustive list of impediments and abolished all others. This approach of limiting impediments to those explicitly mentioned in the positive law has been continued in the 1983 code, which has also eliminated impedient impediments.

Classifications of Impediments

Besides the distinction between impedient and diriment impediments, canonical tradition has used various other distinctions to classify impediments. The most important of these is the distinction between those impediments considered to be founded in divine law, whether natural or positive, and those established by positive ecclesiastical law alone. Most commentators speak of the impediments of impotence, prior bond, and consanguinity, at least in all degrees of the direct line and up to and including the second degree of the collateral line, as deriving from divine law. Some include in this category the impediment of age if one or both parties have not yet reached the age of discretion and the impediment of disparity of worship to the extent that there is grave danger of the Catholic party apostatizing. The rest of the impediments are considered matters of merely ecclesiastical law.

The implications of this distinction are two-fold. First, to the extent that impediments derive from divine law, they bind all persons, whether they are baptized or not, whether they marry Catholics or not; ecclesiastical law impediments bind only Catholics and non-Catholics who marry them. Second, ecclesiastical law impediments are, in principle, subject to dispensation; impediments said to be of divine law are not.

Canonists also distinguish impediments as absolute or relative and as perpetual or temporary. Absolute impediments bar a person from any marriage (e.g., prior bond); relative impediments preclude only specific marriages (e.g., consanguinity). An impediment is perpetual if it does not cease with the passage of time (e.g., sacred orders); otherwise it is temporary (e.g., age).

Public and Occult Impediments

Canon 1074 — An impediment which can be proven in the external forum is considered to be public; otherwise it is occult.

An impediment is considered public not because its existence is well known in the community but because it is susceptible to proof in an ecclesiastical process, either judicial or administrative. Otherwise, the impediment is considered occult. The public character of an impediment depends on the availability of one or more of the types of evidence admissible in ecclesiastical processes that can provide full proof of the existence of the impediment when evaluated in accord with the norm of law. Some impediments (e.g., age, prior bond, sacred orders) arise from a public event whose occurrence can often be established by a public document which is fully probative of the existence of the resulting impediment (c. 1541). Although these impediments are sometimes referred to as "of their nature public," the reality may be quite different. One has only to think of the clandestine ordinations conducted in the former Czechoslovakia during the Soviet era and the consequent difficulty of proving the existence of the impediment of sacred orders to realize that the public or occult character of an impediment depends less on its nature than on attendant circumstances.

---

[6] F. Wernz and P. Vidal, *Ius Canonicum* (Rome: Apud Aedes Universitatis Gregorianae, 1946) 5: n. 148.

Whether an impediment is public or occult does not alter its disqualifying effect. The public or occult character of an impediment does, however, determine who is the authority competent to dispense from it, what is required to convalidate a marriage invalid because of the impediment, and whether the invalidating effect of the impediment can be declared in the external forum to permit the parties to enter new marriages in the Church.

The Authority to Establish Impediments

Canon 1075 — §1. It is only for the supreme authority of the Church to declare authentically when divine law prohibits or nullifies marriage.

§2. Only the supreme authority has the right to establish other impediments for the baptized.

Only "the supreme authority of the Church" may declare authoritatively when divine law establishes impediments to marriage and establish additional impediments. This same authority has sole competence to interpret the meaning and define the scope of impediments of both divine and ecclesiastical law. As Vatican II taught (*LG* 22), this "supreme authority" is the Roman Pontiff as head of the college of bishops and the college of bishops acting together with its head. In this context, the reference to "the supreme authority of the Church" recognizes the significant role played by ecumenical councils in shaping canonical discipline on matrimonial impediments. The term "supreme authority of the Church" is not simply interchangeable with the terms "the Apostolic See" or "the Holy See." In law, the latter terms denote the Roman Pontiff and the institutions of the Roman Curia through which he carries out his ministry for the universal Church (c. 361). These curial agencies have no authority to establish and interpret impediments except to the extent that the Roman Pontiff has delegated this authority to them.

Since impediments gravely restrict the exercise of the natural right to marry, they should be established only when the common good clearly requires it and should be construed as narrowly as is consistent with protection of the common good (c. 18). Moreover, the fact that their invalidating effect may disrupt the social order suggests that they should be uniform throughout the Church. By restricting the authority to establish and interpret impediments to the supreme authority of the Church, the law seeks to ensure that there is uniformity and consistency in ecclesiastical discipline and that impediments are established only after due deliberation.[7]

Custom and Impediments

Canon 1076 — A custom which introduces a new impediment or is contrary to existing impediments is reprobated.

The Church has long recognized custom as a source of law and as the best interpreter of laws.[8] Throughout history, impediments have been introduced by custom. For example, the impediment of disparity of worship was binding in the Latin church by virtue of universal custom long before it was incorporated into statutory law in the 1917 code. Similarly, custom has been influential in shaping the interpretation and application of the law on impediments. For example, in the early Middle Ages, custom largely influenced the shift from the Roman to the Germanic method of computing degrees of consanguinity and affinity[9] and the extension of the scope of these impediments far beyond the degrees prohibited in Roman law.

Following the lead of the 1917 code (*CIC* 1041), the present code bars the introduction of new impediments through custom. It also bars customary interpretations of existing impediments that are contrary to a strict construction of the

---

[7] Out of deference to the autonomy of the Eastern churches, *CCEO* 792 allows for the establishment of other diriment impediments in the particular law of Eastern churches *sui iuris* after consultation with the Apostolic See and with the eparchial bishops of other interested churches *sui iuris*.

[8] See the commentary on cc. 23–28.

[9] See the commentary on c. 108.

canons themselves. By reprobating such customs, the law not only abrogates any such pre-1983 code customs but also declares them unreasonable and, therefore, incapable of obtaining binding force as customs in the future (c. 24, §2).

Prohibition of Particular Marriages

Canon 1077 — §1. In a special case, the local ordinary can prohibit marriage for his own subjects residing anywhere and for all actually present in his own territory but only for a time, for a grave cause, and for as long as the cause continues.

§2. Only the supreme authority of the Church can add a nullifying clause to a prohibition.

Nature and Source of a Prohibition

Impediments are general laws that disqualify or prohibit specified categories of people from marriage. While only the supreme authority of the Church can establish impediments, local ordinaries can, for a grave cause, prohibit the celebration of a marriage in a particular case. This authority, which is an exercise of the executive power of governance in the form of a personal precept (c. 49), derives from the obligation of ecclesiastical authorities to promote the common good of the particular and the universal Church and to prevent abuses of ecclesiastical discipline, especially in the celebration of the sacraments (c. 392).[10] The local ordinary can prohibit the marriage of a person who has a domicile (c. 102, §1) or quasi-domicile (c. 102, §2) in his territory even if the marriage is to be celebrated elsewhere. He can also prohibit the marriage in his territory of a person who is actually present there although he or she resides elsewhere.

The prohibition of a particular marriage by ecclesiastical authority emerged as a canonical insti-

tute distinct from matrimonial impediments in the twelfth century.[11] The prohibition seems to have been used especially to bar a couple from marriage while the status of one party's previous marriage was under investigation by an ecclesiastical court and to prevent the celebration of a marriage when the existence of some other impediment seemed probable. These prohibitions were issued by popes, bishops, and, at times, pastors. Failure to obey a personal prohibition did not of itself invalidate the marriage although, if proven to exist, the impediment that prompted the prohibition might do so. Observance of a personal prohibition was enforced by the threat of penal sanctions.

The current law states that only the local ordinary may prohibit a marriage. However, this authority can be delegated to others.[12] The local ordinary may issue a personal prohibition only for a particular case. Thus, he cannot prohibit all marriages of a particular class, e.g., all marriages in which the parties are cohabiting before marriage or all marriages involving teenagers. Such a blanket prohibition would be equivalent to a new impediment.

A personal prohibition differs from a minister's refusal to witness a marriage because of doubts as to whether its celebration will be valid and licit (c. 1066). In the case of such a refusal, the couple may seek another minister who will be more sympathetic to their situation; however, when a personal prohibition has been imposed, it binds other ministers as well. When a local ordinary prohibits

---

[10] See S. Gherro, "Il divieto al matrimonio stabilito dall'ordinario ex can. 1077," in *Gli impedimenti al matrimonio canonico* (Vatican City: Libreria Editrice Vaticana, 1989) 41–52.

[11] See J. Waterhouse, *The Power of the Local Ordinary to Impose a Matrimonial Ban, CanLawStud* 317 (Washington, D.C.: Catholic University of America, 1952) 9–56.

[12] Canon 1684, §1 empowers tribunal judges to impose prohibitions on parties to marriage cases when the evidence brought forward during the process suggests the continuing existence of problems that led to the nullity of a prior union (e.g., psychological disorders, deeply rooted errors about the substance of marriage) and that threaten to vitiate a subsequent union. Although an administrative act, the prohibition by a judge is distinct from the prohibition by a local ordinary because the basis of the former is the evidence collected during the judicial process and its aim is solely to avert another invalid marriage. See Gherro, 42–43.

a marriage of people who reside in his territory, the prohibition binds them (and indirectly potential official witnesses to their marriage) even when they are outside his territory. However, when a local ordinary prohibits the marriage of a couple who do not have a stable residence in his territory, the prohibition does not bind them when they depart from his territory.

Conditions for Imposing a Prohibition

The legitimacy of a personal prohibition depends on the existence of a grave cause. The proposed marriage must threaten serious harm to the parties themselves, to the good of the community, or to the dignity of the sacrament. Historically, the prohibition has most frequently been used to avert marriages that would probably be null because of an impediment or a defect of consent. However, the probable invalidity of a proposed marriage is not the only ground for a personal prohibition. Failure to allay the concerns that prompted the law to require the local ordinary's permission in the seven cases mentioned in canon 1071, §1, especially the reasonable objections of parents to the marriage of their minor children, could justify a prohibition. The threat of scandal posed by the proposed marriage could also justify a personal prohibition. Commentators on the 1917 code suggested that the existence of a communicable disease, especially a sexually transmitted disease, about which the other party was unaware was a reason to prohibit a particular marriage until either the other party was informed or the disease had been cured or at least rendered non-communicable.[13] This opinion is still valid. However, withholding such information today would probably nullify the marriage on the basis of fraud (c. 1098).

Cessation of a Prohibition

Although the existence of a grave cause is sufficient reason to issue a personal prohibition of marriage, this prohibition can only be temporary

[13] Waterhouse, 110–114.

and must be revoked when the motivating cause ceases. Personal prohibitions of marriage are not meant as punishments but as protections of the personal good of the spouses and the public good of the community. Once imposed, a prohibition of a marriage can be revoked by the local ordinary who issued it, another competent local ordinary, or the delegate of either of them.[14]

Issuing a Prohibition

Whatever the grave reason prompting the prohibition of a marriage in a particular case, such a prohibition restricts the exercise of the fundamental right to marry. Therefore, a careful effort to establish the relevant facts and to weigh the harm that might result from allowing the celebration of the marriage against the hardships that may result from deferring it should always precede the imposition of a personal prohibition (c. 50). When concern about the maturity of young people or the impact of a premarital pregnancy on their freedom are issues, mental health professionals should be consulted. As a precept, a prohibition should be issued in writing with at least a summary of the reasons prompting it (c. 51) and be communicated to the affected persons (cc. 54–56). If a prohibition is imposed, the affected persons should be assisted in overcoming the problems that prompted it.

Effect of a Prohibition

A prohibition of the celebration of a marriage by a local ordinary affects only the lawfulness and not the validity of a marriage celebrated in violation of the prohibition. Only prohibitions imposed by the supreme authority of the Church invalidate the subsequent attempt at marriage.[15] The provi-

[14] For the conditions for the validity of the revocation of a personal prohibition, see the commentary on c. 58, §1.
[15] CCEO 794, §2 provides that the patriarch can add an invalidating clause to the prohibition of a local hierarch who exercises his authority within the territorial boundaries of the patriarchal church.

sion of canon 1077, §2 resolves a controversy about the juridic effect of prohibitions attached to sentences of the Roman Rota. Although it is a tribunal of the Apostolic See, the Roman Rota does not enjoy the supreme power of the Church. Thus, its prohibitions affect only the lawfulness and not the validity of marriages celebrated in contravention of them.

DISPENSATION FROM IMPEDIMENTS

Although impediments are established to prevent grave harm to the common good, to the institution of marriage, and to the spouses and their children, there are often circumstances in which there are adequate protections against the feared harm that prompted the establishment of an impediment or in which the damage resulting from the refusal to permit a marriage may outweigh the harm from allowing it. Thus, church law makes provision for dispensations or relaxations of the law in particular cases to permit the valid and licit celebration of otherwise proscribed marriages when there is a proportionate cause for doing so. The current law contains specific norms governing the granting of dispensations from impediments in ordinary circumstances, in situations of danger of death, and in situations where the impediment is discovered only after all preparations have been made for the wedding.

Dispensations in Ordinary Circumstances

Canon 1078 — §1. The local ordinary can dispense his own subjects residing anywhere and all actually present in his own territory from all impediments of ecclesiastical law except those whose dispensation is reserved to the Apostolic See.

§2. Impediments whose dispensation is reserved to the Apostolic See are:

1° the impediment arising from sacred orders or from a public perpetual vow of chastity in a religious institute of pontifical right;

2° the impediment of crime mentioned in can. 1090.

§3. A dispensation is never given from the impediment of consanguinity in the direct line or in the second degree of the collateral line.

Before Vatican II, only the Holy See had ordinary power to dispense from matrimonial impediments in ordinary circumstances, but local ordinaries were often authorized to dispense from certain impediments through delegations contained in quinquennial faculties. *Christus Dominus* §8b and postconciliar legislation[16] recognized the authority of diocesan bishops to dispense from universal disciplinary laws unless their dispensation had been reserved to a higher authority. Canon 1078 reflects these conciliar and postconciliar developments by situating the authority to dispense from most matrimonial impediments of ecclesiastical law at the level of the particular church. Unlike the more general canon 87, however, canon 1078 extends this dispensing power over matrimonial impediments to all local ordinaries, a category broader than that of diocesan bishops (see c. 134). This dispensing power is ordinary, i.e., it is joined to the office of local ordinary (c. 131, §1). It can, therefore, be delegated either generally for all cases or specifically for a particular case (c. 137, §1).

A local ordinary can exercise this dispensing authority on behalf of those who have a domicile or quasi-domicile in his territory even if he or they are in fact temporarily absent from it. A local ordinary can also exercise his dispensing power on behalf of travelers who are actually present in his territory but who habitually reside elsewhere (c. 136).

The dispensing power of local ordinaries in ordinary circumstances extends only to ecclesiastical law impediments. Thus, a local ordinary can never dispense from the impediments of prior bond, impotence, or consanguinity in any degree of the direct line and up to the second degree inclusive of the collateral line.[17] Also beyond the

---

[16] *EM* 11–16, *CLD* 6, 399.

[17] Canon 1078, §3 states: "A dispensation is never given from the impediment of consanguinity in the direct line

scope of the dispensing power of local ordinaries in ordinary circumstances are the impediments arising from sacred orders, a perpetual vow of chastity in a religious institute of pontifical right, and crime as defined in canon 1090. In ordinary circumstances, dispensations from these three impediments are reserved to the Apostolic See.[18] If these impediments are public, dispensations should be sought from the Congregation for Divine Worship and the Discipline of the Sacraments for the impediments of sacred orders and crime and from the Congregation for Institutes of Consecrated Life and Societies of Apostolic Life for the impediment of perpetual vow of chastity in a religious institute of pontifical right.[19] If the impediments are occult, the dispensation is to be sought from the Apostolic Penitentiary.

In light of the circumstances of the case and the gravity of the dangers the impediment is intended to avert, a cause that is just and reasonable is required for the validity of a dispensation from an impediment by a local ordinary.[20] Although commentators on the 1917 code had suggested various causes that could be sufficient to dispense from impediments, Paul VI held that "the spiritual good of the faithful is a legitimate cause for a dispensation."[21] The phrase "spiritual good of the faithful" should not, however, be used as a shibboleth that excuses from a careful examination of the merits of individual cases.

---

or in the second degree of the collateral line." This oblique wording reflects the doubts expressed by some as to whether consanguinity in the second degree of the collateral line is a divine law impediment. In fact, on at least one occasion, Pope Paul VI, asserting that it was a matter of ecclesiastical law, granted a dispensation to permit the convalidation of the marriage of a blood half brother and sister. See *CLD* 9, 627–628.

[18] *CCEO* 795, §2 allows the patriarch of an Eastern church *sui iuris* to dispense from the impediments arising from conjugicide and from a perpetual vow of chastity.

[19] See the commentary on c. 1088.

[20] See the commentary on c. 90.

[21] *EM* viii, *CLD* 6, 397.

Dispensations in Situations of Danger of Death

Canon 1079 — §1. In urgent danger of death, the local ordinary can dispense his own subjects residing anywhere and all actually present in his territory both from the form to be observed in the celebration of marriage and from each and every impediment of ecclesiastical law, whether public or occult, except the impediment arising from the sacred order of presbyterate.

§2. In the same circumstances mentioned in §1, but only for cases in which the local ordinary cannot be reached, the pastor, the properly delegated sacred minister, and the priest or deacon who assists at marriage according to the norm of can. 1116, §2 possess the same power of dispensing.

§3. In danger of death a confessor possesses the power of dispensing from occult impediments for the internal forum, whether within or outside the act of sacramental confession.

§4. In the case mentioned in §2, the local ordinary is not considered accessible if he can be reached only through telegraph or telephone.

In situations of danger of death, the law expands both the scope of the authority of local officials to dispense from matrimonial impediments and the range of authorities empowered to do so. A person is considered to be "in urgent danger of death" (*urgente mortis periculo*) not only when death is imminent (*in articulo mortis*) but also when a life-threatening condition is present or very near and the person's survival or death is equally probable. The life-threatening condition can come from within (e.g., illness) or from without (e.g., capital punishment, major surgery, impending combat). It is not necessary that both parties be in danger of death or that the one in danger of death be the cause of the impediment.

In situations of danger of death, the local ordinary can dispense from all ecclesiastical law impediments *except* the impediment arising from the order of presbyterate. Thus, the scope of the local ordinary's dispensing power is expanded in these situations to include the impediments arising from the diaconate, a perpetual vow of chastity in a religious institute of pontifical right, and crime. He is also empowered to dispense from the observance of the canonical form of marriage, even if both parties are Catholic. However, even in these dire situations, the local ordinary cannot dispense from the impediments considered to be based in divine law. While a just cause for a dispensation is required even in danger-of-death situations, it seems that it would always be for the spiritual good of the parties to dispense when death threatens.

When the local ordinary cannot be reached in a danger-of-death-situation, the law extends the power to dispense to pastors, presbyters, and deacons who are properly delegated to assist at the marriage in question, and presbyters or deacons who lack the faculty to witness the marriage but who are present for its celebration according to the extraordinary form (c. 1116, §2). In these circumstances, pastors and sacred ministers who are either delegated to witness a marriage or present for an extraordinary form celebration enjoy the same competence as local ordinaries to dispense from ecclesiastical law impediments and from observance of the canonical form. Notably absent from this list of persons who may dispense in danger-of-death situations is the lay person delegated to assist at marriages (c. 1112).

Canon 1079, §4 incorporates into the code a 1922 authentic interpretation by the then code commission clarifying when the local ordinary is to be considered inaccessible in danger-of-death situations.[22] The local ordinary is considered inaccessible if he can be reached only by telephone or telegraph. A fortiori, he is inaccessible if he can be reached by facsimile transmission or electronic mail. Positively stated, the local ordinary is considered accessible if a petition for a dispensation can be brought to him in person or by ordinary mail. Thus, the accessibility of the local ordinary is dependent on the efficiency of local mail and transportation services. Commentators on the

1917 code noted that it was not necessary to use the time needed to deliver a petition by air mail as the criterion for determining the accessibility of the local ordinary. By analogy, it is not necessary to send the petition by express mail or next day service by a commercial carrier.

Even if the local ordinary is accessible in danger-of-death situations, confessors may dispense from occult impediments for the internal forum. In situations of danger of death, every validly ordained presbyter is to be considered a legitimate confessor (c. 976). Unlike canon 1044 of the 1917 code, canon 1079, §3 does not make the dispensing power of confessors in danger-of-death situations coextensive with that of local ordinaries or restrict the confessor's use of this faculty to danger-of-death situations when the local ordinary is inaccessible. In danger-of-death situations, the confessor can dispense only from occult impediments but the law places no explicit restriction on the occult impediments from which he can dispense. A confessor cannot dispense from the so-called divine law impediments in danger-of-death situations. However, the designation of his competence as "occult impediments" with no further qualification does not seem to exclude his dispensing from the impediment arising from the order of presbyterate if this impediment were truly occult.

The confessor's dispensing power in danger-of-death situations is explicitly limited to occult impediments. However, it is disputed whether the phrase "occult impediments" in this canon is to be understood as occult impediments in the strict sense of those that cannot be proved in the external forum (c. 1074) or in the more popular sense of those which are *de facto* unknown when it can be prudently foreseen that they will not be divulged in the future. The discussions of the code revision committee suggest that it was the latter sense that was intended.[23] However, since dispensing power is to be strictly interpreted (c. 92), canon 1079, §3 should be understood as limiting

---

[22] CodCom, November 12, 1922, *AAS* 14 (1922) 662; *CLD* 1, 502.

[23] *Comm* 9 (1977) 348–350.

the dispensing power of confessors to "occult impediments" in the strict sense. Moreover, the confessor's dispensing power does not extend to the canonical form of marriage.

The 1917 code had restricted the dispensing power of confessors to the internal sacramental forum, i.e., to the act of sacramental confession. At the suggestion of the Apostolic Penitentiary,[24] the current legislation extends that competence in danger-of-death situations to the internal non-sacramental forum as well.

Dispensations When Everything Is Prepared for the Wedding

Canon 1080 — §1. Whenever an impediment is discovered after everything has already been prepared for the wedding, and the marriage cannot be delayed without probable danger of grave harm until a dispensation is obtained from the competent authority, the local ordinary and, provided that the case is occult, all those mentioned in can. 1079, §§2–3 when the conditions prescribed therein have been observed possess the power of dispensing from all impediments except those mentioned in can. 1078, §2, n. 1.

§2. This power is valid even to convalidate a marriage if there is the same danger in delay and there is insufficient time to make recourse to the Apostolic See or to the local ordinary concerning impediments from which he is able to dispense.

The law makes provision for dispensation from impediments in other situations which are less dire than danger of death but, nonetheless, extraordinary, namely, when an impediment is discovered only after everything has been prepared for the wedding. An impediment is "discovered" not when it becomes known to the public or to the parties themselves but when it comes to the attention of the local ordinary or the pastor responsible for preparing the couple for marriage.[25] Thus, if the parties either inadvertently or intentionally fail

to reveal the existence of an impediment until shortly before the wedding, it is not considered to have been discovered until it is actually divulged. On the other hand, the conditions for the exercise of the dispensing power regulated by canon 1080 are not meant to include cases when the pastor is aware of the existence of the impediment but neglects to seek a dispensation from the competent authority until the wedding is imminent.

There is a lack of unanimity among commentators on when everything is to be considered prepared for the wedding. It is clear that the dispensing power of canon 1080 must be strictly interpreted (c. 92). However, to subject it to such a strict interpretation that the dispensing power is rendered unusable would thwart the purpose of the law. To insist that each and every preparation for the marriage be made before a hitherto undisclosed impediment could be dispensed would, in practice, limit the use of this dispensing power to rare cases when the impediment is discovered in the sacristy minutes before the wedding is to begin. On the other hand, to allow this dispensing power to be exercised when an impediment is discovered after a wedding date has been set or after the required canonical examination of the spouses (c. 1067)[26] has taken place would ignore the clear meaning of the words of the canon and implicitly encourage lackadaisical marriage preparation.

Canon 1080 clearly intends to provide for dispensations from impediments in cases of grave and urgent necessity other than situations of danger of death when the authority ordinarily competent to grant the dispensations cannot be reached. The canon establishes two criteria for the exercise of dispensing power: (1) everything has already been prepared for the wedding and (2) the marriage cannot be delayed until a dispensation can be obtained from the competent authority without "probable danger of grave harm." These two criteria are not independent of but complementary to one another. The more preparations that have been made for the wedding and the shorter the

[24] Ibid., 350.
[25] CodCom, March 1, 1921, *CLD* 1, 502.
[26] Fornés, in *Pamplona ComEng,* 673–674.

time until its celebration, the more probable the danger of harm and the more grave this harm resulting from a delay of the wedding will become. The harm is not simply financial, but especially spiritual in nature. Nevertheless, the exercise of dispensing power in these extraordinary circumstances still requires a sufficient cause for granting the dispensation, a cause which is independent of the urgency of the situation.

In these urgent situations, the dispensing power of the local ordinary is extended slightly to encompass the impediment of crime. However, the praxis of the Holy See suggests that there is rarely if ever sufficient cause to dispense from this impediment if it is public. The local ordinary still cannot dispense from divine law impediments or from the reserved impediments arising from any sacred order and a perpetual vow of chastity in a religious institute of pontifical right. Nor can he dispense from the observance of the canonical form in the urgent situations foreseen by canon 1080.

When the local ordinary is inaccessible (in the sense described in canon 1079, §4) in situations where everything is prepared for the wedding before the impediment is discovered, pastors, sacred ministers who are properly delegated for the marriage or are participating in an extraordinary form celebration, and confessors (but *not* lay ministers delegated in accord with canon 1112) have the same dispensing power as local ordinaries. However, their dispensing power extends only to "occult cases." This category is broader than that of occult impediments and includes not only impediments that cannot be proved in the external forum but also those that are public in nature but are *de facto* occult.[27] Since pastors and the others mentioned in canon 1080 are authorized to dispense only for occult cases in *omnia parata* situations, the dispensation is usually granted in the internal forum.

Dispensing power for situations when an impediment is detected only after all preparations for the wedding have been made is applicable as well to convalidations of invalidly attempted mar-

riages.[28] However, convalidations often involve much less extensive and expensive social preparations than weddings and allow for much more flexible scheduling. Thus, in the case of a convalidation it may be difficult to demonstrate the urgency required to resort to the dispensing power of canon 1080.

Recording Dispensations

Canon 1081 — The pastor or the priest or deacon mentioned in can. 1079, §2 is to notify the local ordinary immediately about a dispensation granted for the external forum; it is also to be noted in the marriage register.

Dispensations from matrimonial impediments in the external forum are public records with juridic effects. Therefore, they should be committed to writing even if they are granted orally (c. 37) and should be recorded in the curia where they were granted or, in the case of a dispensation granted by the Holy See, the curia from which the dispensation was requested, as well as in the matrimonial register of the place where the marriage was celebrated (c. 1121). The rescript granting the dispensation is usually retained in the prenuptial file in the parish where the marriage was celebrated or, in the case of a dispensation from the observance of the canonical form for a mixed marriage, in the parish of the Catholic party from which the petition for a dispensation came. When a dispensation is granted for the external forum by someone other than the local ordinary in a danger-of-death situation, that person must report the fact to the local ordinary and to the pastor so that it can be properly recorded.

Canon 1082 — Unless a rescript of the Penitentiary provides otherwise, a dispensation from an occult impediment granted in the non-sacramental internal forum is to be noted in a book which must be kept in the secret archive of the curia; no other dispensation for the external forum is nec-

---

[27] CodCom, December 28, 1927, III, *CLD* 1, 503.

[28] See the commentary on cc. 1156–1160.

essary if afterwards the occult impediment becomes public.

A dispensation granted for the internal non-sacramental forum is also to be recorded, but in a manner that preserves the couple's privacy and the occult character of the impediment or case. The ordinary way of recording these dispensations is to enter them in a special book to be maintained in the secret archives of the diocesan curia.[29] When a dispensation has been granted in the internal non-sacramental forum, the one who granted it will have to approach the diocesan bishop, who alone has a key to the secret archive (c. 490, §1), in order to record the dispensation. Pastors and the others mentioned in canon 1079, §2 as well as confessors who dispense from occult impediments in danger-of-death situations or from impediments in occult cases in other urgent situations will also have to approach the diocesan bishop to fulfill their obligation to see that the dispensations are properly recorded.

If those who grant these dispensations were required to reveal the names of the parties and the nature of the impediment to the diocesan bishop in order to have the dispensation recorded, the confidentiality of the internal forum would be breached. Thus, they should inform the bishop only of their need for access to the secret archives to record dispensations, and they should be permitted to record them personally. The special book for this purpose should be arranged so that those recording dispensations cannot see previous entries. These dispensations are not to be recorded in parish marriage registers.

When the Apostolic Penitentiary grants dispensations in the internal non-sacramental forum, it sometimes attaches provisions to its rescripts mandating an alternate method for recording these dispensations. Such dispensations are always recorded in the secret archive of the Apostolic Penitentiary itself. However, whether the dispensation is to be recorded in the particular church and what form it is to take must be determined from the rescript in the particular case.[30] Rescripts from the Penitentiary sometimes prohibit revelation of the dispensation to the diocesan bishop, presumably because he previously had refused to grant it or his knowledge of the circumstances attendant to the dispensation would prejudice his ability to conduct the external forum governance of the diocese (c. 984).

When a dispensation has been granted in the internal non-sacramental forum because an impediment or case is occult, no additional dispensation is required for the external forum if the impediment subsequently becomes public. Dispensations granted by confessors for the internal sacramental forum are not to be recorded anywhere, nor can the confessor attest to its granting should the existence of the impediment later become public. To record the dispensation or attest to its granting would violate the sacramental seal (c. 983). Thus, when an impediment legitimately dispensed by a confessor in the internal sacramental forum becomes public, a new dispensation and a convalidation of the marriage may be necessary for the external forum.

CHAPTER III
DIRIMENT IMPEDIMENTS SPECIFICALLY[31]
[cc. 1083–1094][32]

Lack of Age

Canon 1083 — §1. A man before he has completed his sixteenth year of age and a woman before she has completed her fourteenth year of age cannot enter into a valid marriage.

---

[29] See the commentary on cc. 489–490.

[30] For an example of a case where the dispensation was to be recorded in the secret archive of the parish from which the petition arose, see *CLD* 1, 503.

[31] See Doyle, in *CLSA Com,* 764–774; Fornés, in *Pamplona ComEng,* 674–684; Kelly, in *CLSGBI Com,* 598–610; Lüdicke, in *Münster Com,* 1083/1–1094/2; J. Banares and J. Mantecón, in *Com Ex,* 1160–1210.

[32] *CCEO* 800–812.

§2. The conference of bishops is free to establish a higher age for the licit celebration of marriage.

Matrimonial consent is an act of the will which establishes between the spouses a partnership of the whole of life, which, of its nature, is exclusive and perpetual (cc. 1055, §1 and 1057, §2). To give valid consent, a person must possess sufficient intellectual and emotional maturity to appreciate and assume the responsibility for lifelong obligations and the physical maturity to consummate the marriage by sexual relations. Even ancient societies recognized that a person's chronological age is an important indicator of the attainment of both intellectual-emotional and physical maturity. Thus, to avert the often detrimental effects of youthful marriages on the spouses, their children, and the common good, societies, including the Church, have long stipulated a minimum age for entering marriage.

In Roman law the minimum age for marriage was fourteen for men and twelve for women. These were the ages by which most young people had reached biological puberty. Fourteen was also the age at which boys were freed from guardianship and acquired the full rights of citizenship.[33] Thus, the law presumed that by these ages young people had achieved both the physical and the intellectual-emotional maturity necessary for marriage. Although some jurists held that this law was merely a presumption that ceded to contrary proof, Justinian established fourteen and twelve as the statutory ages for the marriage of men and women, regardless of when biological puberty actually occurred.[34] Since the emperor was more actively involved in the life of the Church in the East than in the West, Eastern canon law incorporated many imperial constitutions.[35] In this way, legal puberty rather than actual puberty became the minimum age for marriage in the Eastern churches.

In the West, however, the Church received the Roman law on the minimum age for marriage as a rebuttable presumption rather than as a strict legal norm. Preoccupation with the parties' capacity for sexual intercourse soon overshadowed concern for their capacity for personal responsibility. Marriages were not recognized as valid until the man had completed his fourteenth year and the woman her twelfth, unless the couple demonstrated that they had actually reached puberty by engaging in sexual relations. In these cases, "wickedness had supplied for [lack of] age."[36] Actual puberty rather than legal puberty remained the norm in the West until the 1917 code.

The 1917 code raised the minimum age for marriage to sixteen for men and fourteen for women and invalidated marriages entered into before these minimum ages regardless of the level of physical and psychological maturity the partners had attained.[37] The 1983 code retains these minimum ages for valid marriage. Thus, a marriage is invalid if it is entered into by a man who has not yet completed his sixteenth year or by a woman who has not yet completed her fourteenth year.[38]

Although the natural law invalidates marriages of those who lack sufficient psychological maturity for matrimonial consent (c. 1095), the impediment of lack of age is a matter of ecclesiastical law. The local ordinary can dispense from the impediment for a sufficiently grave cause, but prudence suggests that such dispensations should rarely be granted.[39] The impediment invalidates

---

[33] S. Treggiari, *Roman Marriage* (Oxford: Clarendon, 1991) 39–43. See also F. Ameriso, *El fundamento del impedimento de edad* (Rome: Athenaeum Romanum Sanctae Crucis, 1995) 19–32.

[34] Cod. 5.60.3. See W. Onclin, "L'âge requis pour le mariage dans la doctrine canonique médiéval," *Proceedings of the Second International Congress of Medieval Canon Law,* in *Monumenta Iuris Canonici,* Series E: Subsidia 1 (Vatican City: Sacra Congegatio de Seminariis et Studiorum Institutibus, 1965) 237; and Ameriso, 25–32.

[35] See C. van de Wiel, *History of Canon Law* (Louvain: Peeters, 1991) 30–32, 41–45.

[36] X, 4.2.9.

[37] *CIC* 1067.

[38] See c. 203, §2 on the computation of time.

[39] Gasparri noted that "the necessary discretion of mind, even if it is had before this age, is weak, and the use of marriage usually greatly harms the health both of parents

marriages involving at least one Catholic party, whether the party who lacks the required age is Catholic or not. Unbaptized persons are bound by minimum age requirements established by civil authority. Eastern non-Catholics are bound by the impediment of lack of age in their own law (*CCEO* 780, §2, 1°). Eastern code canon 780, §2, 2° suggests that other non-Catholics are bound by the minimum age requirement of the law of their own church or ecclesial community, if there is one, or by that of civil law, if their church or ecclesial community defers to it.

During the code revision process, it was suggested that the minimum age for marriage be raised to spare young people the tragedy of divorce, which, experience shows, is often the fate of youthful marriages, and to bring ecclesiastical law into conformity with the civil law of many places.[40] These suggestions were rejected, however, because it was thought a code for the universal Church should not legislate in light of conditions prevailing only in some regions and because marriage is a natural right whose exercise should not be unduly restricted.[41] As a concession, however, the code authorizes episcopal conferences to establish for their territories a higher minimum age for marriage than the one specified in the code. However, this higher age would not affect a marriage's validity but only its liceity.

To set such a higher age for marriage is to establish an impedient impediment, that is, one that renders marriage illicit but not invalid. Since this provision is an exception to the law that only the supreme authority of the Church can establish impediments (c. 1075, §2), it must be strictly interpreted (c. 18). Thus, no ecclesiastical authority below the level of the episcopal conference may establish an age for marriage higher than the one set by the code. However, if there is sufficient evidence of immaturity, local ordinaries can prohibit the celebration of particular marriages until the young people give evidence of the required maturity.[42]

Impotence

Canon 1084 — §1. Antecedent and perpetual impotence to have intercourse, whether on the part of the man or the woman, whether absolute or relative, nullifies marriage by its very nature.

§2. If the impediment of impotence is doubtful, whether by a doubt about the law or a doubt about a fact, a marriage must not be impeded nor, while the doubt remains, declared null.

§3. Sterility neither prohibits nor nullifies marriage, without prejudice to the prescript of can. 1098.

The Nature of Impotence

Impotence is the incapacity of a spouse to perform a complete conjugal act. To be potent, a man must have a penis, be capable of maintaining an erection long enough to penetrate the vagina at least partially, and to ejaculate there; a woman must have a vagina and be capable of receiving the erect penis. While plastic surgery may be able to create an artificial vagina where one is lacking or to open or widen one that is severely occluded, these procedures are dangerous and painful and are, therefore, considered to be extraordinary medical means, to which resort need not be made.

By defining the impotence that gives rise to an impediment as "impotence to have intercourse [*impotentia coeundi*]," the 1983 code has settled several controverted jurisprudential issues. A woman is not considered impotent but sterile if she lacks post-vaginal reproductive organs, either because of a defect of nature or because of surgical intervention, or if her vagina does not open into

---

and children." P. Gasparri, *De Matrimonio* (Vatican City: Typis Polyglottis, 1932) n. 493.

[40] See *Comm* 9 (1977) 360.

[41] Ibid. See also U. Navarrete, "Gli impedimenti relativi alla dignità dell'uomo: aetas, raptus, crimen," in *Gli impedimenti al matrimonio canonico,* Studi giuridici 19 (Vatican City: Libreria Editrice Vaticana, 1989) 73–77.

[42] See the commentary on c. 1077.

the uterus.[43] The definition of impotence also implicitly incorporates a 1977 CDF ruling on the nature of male impotence. Following Sixtus VI's 1587 constitution *Cum frequenter,*[44] many distinguished canonists held that a man was impotent if he could not ejaculate semen articulated in his testicles, whether the incapacity was the result of a natural defect, an accident, or surgery.[45] In a 1977 decree, the CDF ruled that impotence results only from incapacity for complete conjugal intercourse and not from the composition of the ejaculate.[46]

Canonists distinguish between organic and functional impotence. Organic impotence results from the absence, malformation, or underdevelopment of the genital organs, which renders the completion of intercourse impossible. Functional impotence results from a nervous or psychological condition that prevents the person from completing the act of sexual intercourse despite his or her possession of intact genital organs. Either type of impotence can be absolute or relative. Absolute impotence prevents marital relations with any partner; relative impotence renders one incapable of marital relations only with some partners.

Antecedence and Perpetuity

To invalidate marriage, impotence must be both antecedent to the exchange of consent and perpetual. If a person's inability to complete a conjugal act emerges during the first attempt at marital relations and continues thereafter, the antecedence of the impotence can often be presumed. The existence and antecedence of organic impotence can often be proved by the testimony of medical experts who have examined the affected person. Organic impotence is considered perpetual when it cannot be cured by licit and ordinary means. Licit means are forms of treatment that do not violate Christian sexual morality. What constitutes ordinary or extraordinary treatment depends on the state of medical science and the practical availability of treatments to affected persons.

Rotal judges have been reluctant to find that functional impotence is either antecedent or perpetual, especially when it does not have a psychosomatic substratum.[47] Since it is often difficult to identify the precise cause of functional impotence, judges cannot easily rule out the possibility that the post-marital conditions (including such things as "performance anxiety" at the time of attempts at consummation) contributed to this impotence. It can also be difficult to reach certainty about the perpetuity of functional impotence when its cause or causes are purely psychological in nature.

The different standards of certainty used respectively by medical experts and judges have fostered misunderstandings in impotence cases before tribunals. *Scientific* certainty (what Pius XII called "absolute certainty"[48]) is the standard used by medical experts when they offer their prognoses in impotence cases. Thus, they tend to couch their opinions in language that suggests they harbor prudent doubts about the perpetuity of impotence ("It is very likely," "I am inclined to believe"). This cautious language can lead a judge unfamiliar with the standard of certainty being used by experts to conclude erroneously that they cannot reach *moral* certainty (the exclusion of a well-founded doubt but not the absolute possibility of the contrary[49]) about the perpetuity of impotence in a particular case.[50] Only such moral certainty is required in church tribunals.

[43] *Comm* 6 (1974) 196–197. See G. Candelier, "Impuissance: Empêchement et signe d'une incapacité," *RDC* 44 (1994) 101–108. For a debate regarding whether the absence of post-vaginal organs constitutes impotence, see F. Cappello, *De Matrimonio* (Rome: Marietti, 1961) nn. 354–358.

[44] *CICFontes* 1:298–299.

[45] Cappello, *De Matrimonio,* nn. 343 and 377; Gasparri, n. 506; Wernz-Vidal, 5: nn. 224 and 232.

[46] CDF, decree, May 13, 1977, *AAS* 69 (1977) 426; *CLD* 8, 676–677.

[47] See Candelier, 108–124.

[48] Pius XII, alloc, October 1, 1942, *AAS* 34 (1942) 339.

[49] Ibid., 360.

[50] *Coram* Serrano, October 22, 1971, *SRRDec* 63 (1980) 770. See Candelier, 112–117.

Doubts about Impotence

Since the impediment of impotence is intimately connected to the essential purposes of marriage, it is generally considered to derive from divine natural law. It is not, therefore, subject to dispensation. Nevertheless, doubts can easily arise about the existence of impotence and about its antecedence or perpetuity. These doubts can be about the law (e.g., whether the 1977 CDF decree on "true semen" has retroactive effect) or about the facts of a concrete case (e.g., whether the impotence of a particular paraplegic is perpetual). Since the impediment of impotence restricts the free exercise of the natural right to marry, marriage is to be impeded only if the existence of the impediment is certain. Thus, if a doubt about impotence arises but cannot be resolved prior to a marriage, the person is to be permitted to marry.

As long as prudent doubt about the existence of impotence or its antecedence or perpetuity persists, the marriage may not be declared null. This is simply a practical application of the principle that, once properly celebrated, a marriage is presumed to be valid until the contrary is proven (c. 1060). In many doubtful cases, however, it is possible to refer the matter to the Congregation for Divine Worship and the Discipline of the Sacraments with a petition for the dissolution of the unconsummated marriage.

Sterility

While impotence, the incapacity to complete a conjugal act, invalidates marriage, sterility, the incapacity to generate offspring, does not. In matrimonial consent, the spouses exchange the perpetual and exclusive right to conjugal acts per se apt for the generation of children, but not the right to have children. Although marriage is of its nature ordered to the procreation and education of children (c. 1055, §1), the Church has long held that those incapable of procreation still have the right to marry. Thus, *Gaudium et spes* 50 insisted:

Marriage to be sure is not instituted solely for procreation.... Therefore, marriage persists as a whole manner and communion of life, and maintains its value and indissolubility, even when offspring are lacking—despite, rather often, the very intense desire of the couple.

Although sterility itself does not invalidate marriage, it may be a circumstance that suggests an invalidating defect of consent. Sterility is a quality that can seriously disrupt the partnership of conjugal life. Hence, a marriage may be invalid because of deceit, if, to induce the other party to marry, one party deliberately fails to disclose his or her sterility (c. 1098). Voluntary sterilization (tubal ligation or vasectomy) shortly before or after marriage may be an index of an intention against the good of children (c. 1101, §2).

Prior Marriage Bond

Canon 1085 — §1. A person bound by the bond of a prior marriage, even if it was not consummated, invalidly attempts marriage.

§2. Even if the prior marriage is invalid or dissolved for any reason, it is not on that account permitted to contract another before the nullity or dissolution of the prior marriage is established legitimately and certainly.

Valid matrimonial consent gives rise to a perpetual and exclusive bond (*vinculum*) between the spouses, whether they are baptized or not (c. 1134). At least since the time of Augustine, this bond has been understood to be not merely moral but ontological in nature.[51] That is, the continued existence of the marriage bond even after the existential breakdown of the marital relationship renders a new marriage during the lifetime of one's spouse not only immoral but impossible.

This long tradition was reaffirmed in personalist language by the Second Vatican Council:

---

[51] See the commentary before c. 1141.

[Marriage] is rooted in the conjugal cove-nant of irrevocable personal consent.... For the good of the spouses and their offspring as well as of society, the existence of this sa-cred bond no longer depends on human de-cisions alone.... As a mutual gift of two per-sons, this intimate union, as well as the good of the children, imposes total fidelity on the spouses and argues for an unbreakable one-ness between them.[52]

The impediment of prior bond is generally un-derstood to have its source in divine law, both positive and natural. As a result, the impediment invalidates all subsequent marriages, not merely those of Catholics. The divine law origin of the impediment of prior bond also entails that it is not dispensed even in danger-of-death situations. However, the impediment ceases with the death of one of the spouses. In some cases, moreover, the bond can be dissolved. Unconsummated sacra-mental marriages can be dissolved (the canons speak of "dispensation") by the Roman Pontiff for a just cause at the request of one of the spouses (c. 1142). Marriages entered into by two unbaptized persons can be dissolved in virtue of the Pauline privilege after the baptism of one of them and the departure of the still unbaptized spouse (c. 1143). Non-sacramental marriages can be dissolved by the Roman Pontiff in favor of the faith of a Catholic party.[53] Only the bond arising from sacra-mental, consummated marriages is not subject to dissolution.

The impediment of prior bond arises only from a valid marriage, whether it is consummated or not. Its existence is presumed once the marriage has been lawfully celebrated (c. 1060). A declara-tion of nullity is an assertion that a particular union gave rise to no bond. Thus, when a mar-riage is declared null, a new marriage entered after the civil divorce but before the formal decla-ration of nullity may be valid.

To avoid confusion and uncertainty about the validity of second and subsequent marriages, canon 1085, §2 prohibits the celebration of a new marriage until the nullity or dissolution of all the party's previous marriages is legitimately proven. Some see this prohibition as an ecclesiastical law impediment of prior bond, which complements the divine law impediment.[54] Whether or not it should be classified as an impediment, the prohi-bition does not invalidate marriages entered into in violation of it (c. 10) and does not bind non-Catholics when they marry among themselves (c. 11). If a Catholic re-marries according to the canonical form after a divorce but before a decla-ration of nullity is granted, the marriage is illicit but valid and need not be convalidated after the previous marriage is declared null. The validity of second and subsequent marriages of two non-Catholics depends on whether their previous marriage was, in fact, valid. However, their first marriages are presumed to be valid until the con-trary is proven (c. 1060). Since an ecclesiastical dissolution terminates a valid bond, marriages entered before dissolutions are granted are in-valid.

Those who maintain that canon 1085, §2 estab-lishes a distinct impediment of ecclesiastical law have also advanced a novel approach to dealing in a tribunal setting with a petitioner who had multi-ple marriages. They propose that the tribunal de-clare the petitioner's second and subsequent mar-riages invalid on the ground of the impediment of prior bond and then declare the nullity of the first union, the presumed source of the impediment, on the ground of some defect of consent. This ap-proach, while convenient, has been "directly con-demned" by the Apostolic Signatura as having

---

[52] GS 48.
[53] See the commentary after c. 1149.

[54] F. Morrisey, "The Impediment of *Ligamen* and Multiple Marriages," *J* 40 (1980) 406–418; and B. Griffin, "The Samaritan Woman and the Matrimonial Tribunal," in *Marriage Studies II,* ed. T. Doyle (Washington: CLSA, 1982) 99–110. For a critique of this position, see J. John-son, "*Ligamen* and Multiple Marriages: Too Good to Be True?" *J* 42 (1982) 222–228.

"no trace in law or approved doctrine."[55] A tribunal must deal with each of a petitioner's marriages as a separate case and on its own merits.

Disparity of Worship

Canon 1086 — §1. A marriage between two persons, one of whom has been baptized in the Catholic Church or received into it and has not defected from it by a formal act and the other of whom is not baptized, is invalid.

§2. A person is not to be dispensed from this impediment unless the conditions mentioned in cann. 1125 and 1126 have been fulfilled.

§3. If at the time the marriage was contracted one party was commonly held to have been baptized or the baptism was doubtful, the validity of the marriage must be presumed according to the norm of can. 1060 until it is proven with certainty that one party was baptized but the other was not.

The Church has long recognized that marriages between Catholics and non-Catholics pose particular dangers to the Catholic's continued practice of the faith and to the Catholic baptism and formation of children. The Church's concern is especially grave when a Catholic proposes to marry a non-Christian. As an expression of this concern, ecclesiastical law has established the impediment of disparity of worship, which invalidates marriages between Catholics and unbaptized persons.

Although marriages between Christians and pagans were prohibited by several early councils, disparity of worship was established as an invalidating impediment for the Eastern churches at the Council of Trullo in 692.[56] Although the canons of Trullo were not received by the Church in the West, the impediment spread throughout the West between the seventh and the eleventh centuries and ultimately obtained the force of a universal custom. It was finally incorporated into church legislation in canon 1070 of the 1917 code.

As an ecclesiastical law impediment, disparity of worship binds only Catholics and those who marry them. Exempt from the impediment are baptized non-Catholics and those who have left the Catholic Church by a formal act.[57] However, Eastern non-Catholics (i.e., Orthodox) remain bound by the impediment of their own church's law which invalidates marriages between the baptized and the unbaptized (CCEO 781, 1°).

A dispensation can be granted to permit a Catholic to marry an unbaptized person if there is sufficient assurance that the proposed marriage will not pose a threat to the Catholic's ability to continue the practice of his or her faith and to hand on the Catholic faith to their children. This assurance is given the Catholic party in the form of promises (cautiones). He or she must declare a readiness to remove all dangers of lapsing from the Catholic faith and promise to do all within his or her power to ensure the Catholic baptism and formation of all children. The unbaptized party is not required to make a promise, but must be made aware of what the Catholic party has promised.[58] If this declaration and promise are not made, a dispensation from the impediment of disparity of worship is invalid.

When, at the time a marriage was celebrated, one of the parties was generally reputed to be baptized or doubts had arisen about his or her baptism or its validity, the validity of the marriage is to be upheld until it has been proven that one party was baptized and the other was not. However, if the doubts about the baptism of one party or its validity surfaced prior to the marriage, the impediment of disparity of worship can be dispensed conditionally (ad cautelam) if the doubt cannot be resolved.[59]

Sacred Orders

Canon 1087 — Those in sacred orders invalidly attempt marriage.

---

[55] ApSig, "Procedure to Deal With Serial (i.e., Multiple and Successive) Marriages," *RRAO 1987,* 60.

[56] Council of Trullo, c. 72.

[57] See the commentary on c. 1117 for a discussion of the notion of leaving the Catholic Church by a formal act.

[58] See the commentary on cc. 1125–1126.

[59] See the commentary on c. 869, §§1–2.

From its origin, the Church has cherished the charisms of virginity and celibacy as witnesses to the Kingdom of God. Consequently, the celibate state was seen as particularly appropriate, even if not strictly required, for ordained ministers. As celibates, the ordained

> more easily hold fast to [Christ] with undivided heart. They more freely devote themselves to Him and through Him to the service of God and men. They more readily minister to His kingdom and to the work of heavenly generation, and thus become more apt to exercise paternity in Christ, and do so to a great extent. (*PO* 16)

It was only gradually, however, that the Latin church came to require celibacy of most candidates for ordained ministry (c. 1042, 1°) and to establish sacred orders as an impediment to marriage.

As the qualification in the pastoral epistles that various ministers "be married only once" suggests,[60] the early Church routinely ordained married men. Nevertheless, once ordained, these ministers were prohibited from marrying if they were unmarried at the time of their ordinations or from remarrying if their wives died. Ordained ministers who married in violation of this prohibition were subject to the penalty of deposition but their marriages were not declared invalid.[61] The Eastern churches have continued the tradition of ordaining married men but of subjecting those who attempt marriage after ordination to the penalty of deposition (*CCEO* 1453, §2). Moreover, the impediment of sacred orders now invalidates these attempted marriages (*CCEO* 804).

In the West, from the early fourth century there were periodic movements to require continence of all ordained ministers, even those who were married, and to prohibit the ordained from marrying. The prohibition of marriage by ordained ministers

was enforced by threatening penal sanctions such as deposition rather than by invalidating their marriages. However, the Second Lateran Council in 1139 established the sacred orders of bishop, presbyter, deacon, and subdeacon as a diriment impediment to marriage. The rationale given for this impediment was that ordination entailed a tacit solemn vow of chastity.[62]

The impediment of sacred orders arises from the valid reception of the orders of bishop, presbyter, and deacon. In addition, the one ordained must have received the order freely and with sufficient knowledge of his obligation not to marry (or, in the case of one who is already married at the time of his ordination, not to remarry).[63] Ignorance of this obligation cannot be presumed (c. 15, §2). The requirements that all candidates for ordination attest in writing that they are receiving sacred orders "of [their] own accord and freely" (c. 1036) and that unmarried candidates publicly assume the obligation of celibacy or perpetual vows (c. 1037) are designed to ensure that candidates possess the requisite freedom and knowledge.

In ordinary circumstances, dispensations from the impediment of sacred orders are reserved to the Apostolic See. In danger-of-death situations, the local ordinary and, when he is not available, pastors and the others mentioned in canon 1079, §2 can dispense from the impediment arising from the order of deacon. The Apostolic See does not grant dispensations to those ordained to the episcopate. Dispensations from the impediment arising from the order of presbyter are normally granted only by the pope as part of the process of returning to the lay state (cc. 290, 3°; 291). Until recently dispensations from the impediment arising from the order of deacon were also rarely granted except as part of the process of return to the lay state. However, in a 1997 circular letter, the Congregation for Divine Worship and the Discipline of the Sacraments expressed a willingness to dispense widowed permanent deacons from the impediment of sacred orders if their ministry is of

---

[60] See 1 Tim 3:2 (bishops); 1 Tim 3:12 (deacons); Titus 1:6 (presbyters).

[61] *Apostolic Constitutions* 6, c. 17; Council of Neo-Caesarea, c. 1; Council of Trullo, cc. 3 and 6.

[62] Lateran II, c. 6; VI 3.15.

[63] Cappello, *De Matrimonio,* n. 437.

"great and proven usefulness" to their dioceses or they need assistance from wives to care for minor children or aging parents (including the aging parents of their deceased wives).[64]

A person in sacred orders who attempts marriage not only does so invalidly, but is subject to penal sanctions. He *ipso facto* loses any ecclesiastical office he may hold (c. 194, §1, 3°) and incurs a *latae sententiae* suspension. If he continues to give scandal after a warning, he can be subjected to progressively graver deprivations, including eventually dismissal from the clerical state (c. 1394, §1).

Perpetual Vow of Chastity

Canon 1088 — Those bound by a public perpetual vow of chastity in a religious institute invalidly attempt marriage.

Throughout the history of the Church, men and women have sought to live together in community according to the evangelical counsels of poverty, chastity, and obedience. These communities eventually received recognition by the Church as what are now called institutes of consecrated life. The Church cherishes the celibate chastity promised and lived in these institutes.

> For it liberates the human heart in a unique way and causes it to burn with love for God and all mankind. It is therefore an outstanding token of heavenly riches, and also a most suitable way for religious to spend themselves readily in God's service and in works of the apostolate (*PC* 12).

Because of the incompatibility between marriage and the life of chaste celibacy in community promised in religious profession, the Church has

made a public and perpetual vow of chastity in a religious institute an impediment to marriage.

A vow is "a deliberate and free promise made to God about a possible and better good [which] must be fulfilled by reason of the virtue of religion" (c. 1191, §1). A vow is public "if a legitimate superior accepts it in the name of the Church" (c. 1192, §1). A vow is perpetual if a person intends to be bound by it for the rest of his or her life; otherwise it is temporary. To give rise to an impediment, a public and perpetual vow of chastity must be made in a religious institute, i.e., "a society in which members, according to proper law, pronounce public vows, either perpetual or temporary which are to be renewed, however, when the period of time has elapsed, and lead a life of brothers or sisters in common" (c. 607, §2). Thus, the "sacred bonds" taken by members of secular institutes (c. 712) and some societies of apostolic life (c. 731, §2) do not give rise to an impediment to marriage.

Although the obligation to fulfill a vow derives from the virtue of religion, the impediment is a matter of ecclesiastical law. In ordinary circumstances, dispensations from the impediment are reserved to the Apostolic See for members of pontifical right institutes and to the local ordinary for members of diocesan right institutes. In danger-of-death situations, local ordinaries can also dispense members of pontifical right institutes, and when the local ordinary is unavailable, pastors and the others mentioned in canon 1079, §2 can dispense members of all religious institutes.

Although dispensations from the impediment alone are possible in theory, they are rarely granted in practice since marriage and the demands of religious life in community are radically incompatible. Hence, the usual practice is to dispense a religious who desires to marry from the obligation of observing all the vows as part of an indult of departure from the institute (cc. 691–693). When this indult is accepted by the member, both the obligation of the vows and the impediment based on them cease.

Religious who attempt marriage are ipso facto dismissed from their institutes (c. 694, §1, 2°). A

---

[64] CDWDS, "Circular Letter to Diocesan Ordinaries and to Superiors General of Institutes of Consecrated Life and Societies of Apostolic Life," June 6, 1997, Prot. N. 263/97, 8; *Origins* 27 (1997) 171.

religious who is not a cleric also incurs a *latae sententiae* interdict (c. 1394, §2).

Abduction

Canon 1089 — No marriage can exist between a man and a woman who has been abducted or at least detained with a view of contracting marriage with her unless the woman chooses marriage of her own accord after she has been separated from the captor and established in a safe and free place.

A corollary of the Church's acceptance of the principle that the personal consent of the parties alone constitutes marriage (c. 1057, §1) is that this consent must be free (c. 219). The freedom of this consent is inevitably called into question when one of the parties (usually the woman) has been violently abducted. To avoid uncertainty and protracted litigation about the freedom of consent in these cases, the Church has established the impediment of abduction. This impediment creates an unrebuttable presumption (*praesumptio iuris et de iure*) that, as long as she remains in the control of her abductor, the abducted woman lacks the freedom to consent to marriage with him.

For the impediment to arise, a woman must be abducted or kidnapped against her will or at least forcibly retained in a place to which the abductor has access.[65] The abductee could even be detained in her own home if the abductor has free access to it. The violence involved in the abduction or detention can be either physical (e.g., use of force) or moral (e.g., threats to harm the woman's family members or her reputation). Thus, the impediment does not arise when a woman more or less voluntarily cooperates in her being spirited away as in cases of elopement or seduction. The vio-

lence involved in the abduction or detention can be inflicted either by the abductor himself or by others acting as his agents.

The existence of the impediment also requires that the abduction or forcible detention be for the sake of marriage with the abductee. The impediment does not arise, therefore, in cases where the abduction was motivated by factors unrelated to marriage (e.g., ransom). However, an abduction or detention may begin for purposes other than marriage but later continue for the sake of marriage. In this case, the impediment arises only from the time when the abductor's intention changed.

The impediment ceases when the abducted woman is separated from her abductor and placed in a safe place, i.e., one where she is free from the abductor's power over her. Only when she is released from the abductor's control is the woman considered sufficiently free to decide whether she wishes to marry her onetime abductor. Since abduction is an ecclesiastical law impediment, it can be dispensed by the local ordinary while the woman is still in the abductor's power. The strong presumption of the woman's lack of freedom in these circumstances would, however, counsel against granting a dispensation.

Crime

Canon 1090 — §1. Anyone who with a view to entering marriage with a certain person has brought about the death of that person's spouse or of one's own spouse invalidly attempts this marriage.

§2. Those who have brought about the death of a spouse by mutual physical or moral cooperation also invalidly attempt a marriage together.

The "crime" that gives rise to an impediment to marriage is conjugicide, although historically the primary focus of this impediment was adultery.[66] The principle underlying this impediment is

---

[65] While the Latin code establishes an impediment only for the abduction of a woman by a man, c. 806 in the Eastern code makes this impediment applicable also to situations where a woman has abducted a man.

[66] See Navarrete, "Gli impedimenti relativi alla dignità dell'uomo," 88–94; and Wernz-Vidal, *Ius Canonicum,* 5: n. 322.

that no one should receive a benefit as a direct result of his or her crime.

The impediment arises when, for the sake of marriage with a definite person, one murders his or her own spouse or the spouse of that other person. Since an impediment that restricts the free exercise of the right to marry must be interpreted strictly (c. 18), the impediment arises only when the marriage bond which ceases with the murder is a valid one. Otherwise, the crime involved would not be conjugicide but homicide.

It is not required that the other person participate in or even be aware of the murderer's actions and intent. It is required, however, that one's actions actually bring about the death of a spouse and that the murder be carried out for the purpose of marrying a certain person. Thus, the impediment does not arise from the accidental killing of one's own or another person's spouse. Nor is it sufficient that one murder one's own spouse for the purpose of becoming free to re-marry in general; the murder must open the way to a marriage with a definite person.

The impediment of crime also arises when two people conspire to bring about the death of the spouse of one of them. The impediment arises whether or not the murder was prompted by the conspirators' desire to marry, whether their cooperation in the murder was physical or moral, and whether the murder was carried out by the parties personally or through their agents.

The impediment of crime is of its nature relative but perpetual. In ordinary circumstances, a dispensation from the impediment is reserved to the Apostolic See, which does not usually grant the dispensation when the facts on which it is based are public.[67] In danger-of-death situations, the impediment can be dispensed by the local ordinary and, when he is not accessible, by pastors and the others mentioned in canon 1079, §2. In situations when the impediment is detected only after everything is prepared for the wedding, the local ordinary and, as long as it is an occult case

and the local ordinary is inaccessible, pastors and the others mentioned in canon 1079, §§2–3 can dispense from the impediment. In the latter situation, however, it seems unlikely that there would be a sufficiently grave cause to dispense validly from the impediment.[68]

Consanguinity

Canon 1091 — §1. In the direct line of consanguinity marriage is invalid between all ancestors and descendants, both legitimate and natural.

§2. In the collateral line marriage is invalid up to and including the fourth degree.

§3. The impediment of consanguinity is not multiplied.

§4. A marriage is never permitted if doubt exists whether the partners are related by consanguinity in any degree of the direct line or in the second degree of the collateral line.

Consanguinity is the blood relationship between persons who descend, either legitimately or illegitimately, from a common ancestor. All societies, both ancient and modern, have attempted to prevent marriage between close blood relatives. This aversion to consanguineous marriages has its roots in the near universal incest taboo and the experience of the deleterious effects on family harmony and stability of tolerating sexual relations between close relatives. In more modern times, the opposition to these marriages has been buttressed by scientific data about their negative genetic consequences for children.

The canonical impediment of consanguinity was influenced by Mosaic law[69] and Roman law[70] prohibitions of marriages between those related by blood or marriage. Between the sixth and the tenth centuries, however, the Church shifted the method of computing degrees of consanguinity from the Roman practice of counting the persons descending from a common ancestor to the Ger-

---

[67] T. Bouscaren and A. Ellis, *Canon Law* (Milwaukee: Bruce, 1946) 487.

[68] See the commentary on c. 90.
[69] Lev 18:6–18.
[70] Treggiari, *Roman Marriage,* 37–39.

manic practice of counting the generations after the common ancestor. At the same time, the scope of the impediment was expanded so that it invalidated marriage up to and including the seventh generation of the collateral line. While this expansion of the impediment (and a similar expansion of the impediment of affinity) strongly encouraged exogamy, it also caused an explosion of annulment cases. The Fourth Lateran Council reduced the scope of the impediment to the fourth generation in the collateral line.[71] The impediment was further reduced to the third generation in the collateral line by canon 1076, §2 of the 1917 code.

The 1983 code has returned to the Roman law method of computing degrees of consanguinity by counting persons descending from a common ancestor.[72] Consanguinity invalidates marriage in all degrees of the direct line (father-daughter-granddaughter) and up to the fourth degree of the collateral line inclusive (first cousins). The impediment of consanguinity no longer invalidates marriages of second cousins (sixth degree of the collateral line in the current method of computation, third degree in the old).[73]

Commentators agree that consanguinity in any degree of the direct line is a divine law impediment and that consanguinity in the third and fourth degrees of the collateral line is an ecclesiastical law impediment. There is, however, some disagreement as to whether consanguinity in the second degree collateral line (brother-sister) is a divine law or ecclesiastical law impediment.[74] To avoid having to resolve this issue, the code says simply that "a dispensation is never given from

the impediment of consanguinity in the direct line or in the second degree of the collateral line" (c. 1078, §3). The local ordinary can dispense from the impediment in the third (uncle-niece) and fourth degrees (first cousins) of the collateral line. Nevertheless, civil laws may well prohibit marriages within these degrees of consanguinity.

The 1917 code foresaw the possibility that the impediment of consanguinity could be multiplied in the collateral line when a couple shared more than one common ancestor (CIC 1076, §2). The multiplication of the impediment necessitated multiple dispensations. However, the current law has eliminated the multiplication of the impediment.

When the existence of an impediment is doubtful, the general principle is that the parties should not be impeded from marrying.[75] However, canon 1091, §4 establishes an exception to this principle for the impediment of consanguinity. Marriage is never permitted if there is any doubt as to whether the parties are related by consanguinity in any degree of the direct line or the second degree of the collateral line.

Affinity

Canon 1092 — Affinity in the direct line in any degree invalidates a marriage.

While the impediment of consanguinity arises from a blood relationship, the impediment of affinity is based on a marital relationship. Affinity arises from a *valid* marriage, whether it is consummated or not, between the man and the blood relatives of the woman and between the woman and the blood relatives of the man (c. 109, §1). It does not arise, however, between the blood relatives of the man and those of the woman. Like consanguinity, affinity is computed in lines and degrees. A person is related by affinity to his or her spouse's blood relatives in the same line and degree as his or her spouse is related to them by consanguinity (c. 109, §2). Thus, a man is related to his wife's mother in the first degree of the di-

---

[71] Lateran IV, c. 50. See J. Brundage, *Law, Sex and Christian Society in Medieval Europe* (Chicago: University of Chicago, 1987) 191–193, 355–356.

[72] See the commentary on c. 108.

[73] CIC 1076, §2.

[74] In one reported case, Paul VI declared that consanguinity in the second degree of the collateral line was an ecclesiastical law impediment and dispensed from it to permit the convalidation of a marriage of a blood half-brother and half-sister who had been raised apart. Paul VI, rescript, January 21, 1977, *CLD* 9, 627–628.

[75] See cc. 1084, §2 and 1086, §3.

rect line and a woman is related to her husband's brother in the second degree of the collateral line.

The impediment of affinity invalidates marriage in all degrees of the direct line. The 1917 code made affinity in the collateral line a diriment impediment up to the fourth degree (second degree according to the Germanic method of counting) inclusive.[76] Thus, if a woman's husband died, she was barred from marrying his brother or first cousin. The 1983 Latin code abrogated affinity as an impediment in the collateral line. Nevertheless, affinity in the second degree of the collateral line (e.g., a woman and her deceased husband's brother) remains an impediment in the law of the Eastern churches (CCEO 809, §1). Hence, attention must be paid to the possible impediment of affinity in the collateral line in inter-ritual marriages.

Since affinity is an ecclesiastical law impediment, it no longer affects the marriages of two non-Catholics, whether baptized or not. It does, however, invalidate a marriage involving a Catholic who has left the Church by a formal act. The local ordinary and, when he is inaccessible in urgent situations, those mentioned in canons 1079–1080 can dispense from the impediment of affinity.

Public Propriety

Canon 1093 — The impediment of public propriety arises from an invalid marriage after the establishment of common life or from notorious or public concubinage. It nullifies marriage in the first degree of the direct line between the man and the blood relatives of the woman, and vice versa.

Although neither an invalid marriage nor public concubinage gives rise to the impediments of affinity or, except with regard to the offspring of the union, of consanguinity, the Church has judged that there is something unseemly about the marriage of one of the parties to such irregular unions with close relatives of the other. This sense of the

[76] CIC 1077, §1.

inappropriateness of such marriages is the basis for the impediment of public propriety.

The impediment arises from an invalid marriage after a common life has been established and, therefore, there is a presumption that the union has been consummated (c. 1061, §2). It also arises from notorious and public concubinage. Concubinage is the more or less stable cohabitation of a man and a woman. It is considered public if it is known in the community and notorious if it is publicly known and carried out in such circumstances that it cannot be concealed or excused.[77] Thus, the impediment arises from the fact that a couple "lives together" without marriage, but not from the mere fact that they engaged in premarital sexual relations.

Strictly speaking, a union entered into without the observance of the required canonical form is not an invalid marriage since it lacks even the semblance of marriage. Nor can such a union be reduced to mere concubinage because "there is at least a certain commitment to a properly defined and probably stable state of life."[78]

In 1929, the code commission held that the impediment of public propriety arises as a result of such unions after cohabitation has begun.[79] The issue has been further clarified by canon 810, §1, 3° of the Eastern code, which stipulates that the impediment of public propriety arises "from the establishment of common life of those who, although bound to a required form for the celebration of marriage, attempted it before a civil official or non-Catholic minister."

The impediment of public propriety invalidates marriage between the man and the blood relatives of the woman and the woman and the blood relatives of the man, but only in the first degree of the direct line. That is, the impediment invalidates a marriage between the man and the woman's mother or daughter from another union and between the woman and the man's father or son from another union. Public propriety is an impediment of eccle-

[77] CIC 2197, 3°.
[78] FC 82c.
[79] CodCom, response, March 12, 1929, CLD 1, 516–517.

siastical law and can be dispensed by the local ordinary in ordinary circumstances and by those mentioned in canons 1079–1080 in the exceptional circumstances foreseen in those canons.

Those who validly marry after a period of notorious concubinage or who convalidate an invalid union become, by that fact, bound by the impediment of affinity. However, they remain bound by the impediment of public propriety as well. Thus, if one of the spouses seeks to marry a blood relation of the other in the first degree of the direct line after his or her spouse's death or the ecclesiastical dissolution of their marriage, dispensations from both the impediment of affinity and the impediment of public propriety are necessary for the validity of the new marriage.[80]

Adoption

Canon 1094 — Those who are related in the direct line or in the second degree of the collateral line by a legal relationship arising from adoption cannot contract marriage together validly.

Although adopted children are not related either by blood or marriage to their adoptive parents and siblings, the possibility of marriage between adopted children and the immediate members of their adoptive families raises the same concerns about family harmony and stability that led to the establishment of the impediments of consanguinity and affinity. Hence, these concerns have long prompted civil and ecclesiastical authorities to restrict the possibility of marriage between those adopted and their adoptive family members.

Roman law barred marriages between those adopted and the ones who adopted them, their spouses, and their other children. This impediment arising from the legal relationship of adoption was taken into canon law by Gratian.[81] The 1917 code abandoned the impediment of adoptive

relationship derived from Roman law and deferred completely to the civil law governing the region where the marriage was to be contracted. If the prevailing civil law had no such impediment, there was no canonical impediment; if the civil law impediment merely prohibited marriage, the canonical impediment was also only impedient (*CIC* 1059); but, if the civil law impediment invalidated marriage, it was invalid in canon law as well (*CIC* 1080).

The 1983 Latin code and the 1990 Eastern code establish an ecclesiastical law impediment arising from an adoptive relationship, an impediment which is independent of the existence or not of a civil law impediment. The impediment invalidates marriage between the adopted person and those related to him or her by adoption in all degrees of the direct line and up to the second degree of the collateral line. That is, adopted persons cannot validly marry their adoptive parents and grandparents or their adoptive siblings.

Although the existence of an ecclesiastical law impediment arising from an adoptive relationship no longer depends on the existence of a comparable civil law impediment, establishing what constitutes legal adoption remains within the competence of civil law. The impediment of adoptive relationship does not arise unless there is first an adoption recognized by civil law. Consequently, a person incurs no impediment if he or she grows up in a family with a stepparent and children from that stepparent's previous marriage but who is not legally adopted by the stepparent.

The impediment arising from an adoptive relationship is one of ecclesiastical law. The local ordinary can dispense from it as can those mentioned in canons 1079–1080 in the circumstances foreseen in those canons. Before a dispensation is granted, however, one should ascertain whether there is also a civil law impediment based on adoption.

Spiritual Relationship

Canon 1079 of the 1917 code continued a long tradition by establishing as a diriment impediment

---

[80] J. Gallagher, *The Matrimonial Impediment of Public Propriety, CanLawStud* 304 (Washington, D.C.: Catholic University of America, 1952) 140–141.
[81] C. 30 q. 3 c. 5.

the spiritual relationship arising from baptism. This impediment invalidated marriages between the person baptized and both the minister of baptism and the godparents.[82] This impediment was abrogated by the 1983 Latin code. However, the Eastern code has retained the impediment. It arises between the godparents and both the person baptized and his or her parents (*CCEO* 811, §1). If baptism is conferred conditionally, the impediment does not arise unless the godparents at the conditional baptism are the same as those at the doubtfully valid baptism (*CCEO* 811, §2). This impediment may be an issue not only in marriages between two Eastern Catholics but also in inter-ritual marriages.

CHAPTER IV
MATRIMONIAL CONSENT[83]
[cc. 1095–1107][84]

Since consent alone brings marriage into existence, substantial defects in consent render the

---

[82] *CIC* 768.

[83] See Doyle, in *CLSA Com,* 774–792; Lüdicke, in *Münster Com*, Überblick vor 1095/1–1107/1; F. Aznar Gil, in *Pamplona ComEng,* 684–700; Kelly, in *CLSGBI Com,* 610–622.

[84] Cf. *CCEO* 817–827. Although the Eastern code's treatment of matrimonial consent is generally parallel to that of the 1983 Latin code, there are some noteworthy differences between the two codes. *CCEO* 817 introduces this section by defining matrimonial consent. This definition is substantially the same as the one the Latin code places among the foundational canons in c. 1057, §2. *CCEO* 826 on conditioned consent is located after the treatment of the invalidating effect of force and fear, while the Latin code deals with these two defects of consent in the opposite order. The Latin code allows for marriage to be entered validly with a condition concerning the past or the present, but the Eastern code declares invalid marriages contracted with any type of condition. The Eastern code has no regulations governing marriages by proxy like the regulations in c. 1105 of the Latin code, but the former does allow particular law to make provision for such marriages (*CCEO* 837, §2). The Eastern code also has no provision for marriage through an interpreter like c. 1106 of the Latin code. Finally, the

marriage invalid. Although titled "Matrimonial Consent," the present chapter is devoted primarily to an enumeration of invalidating defects of consent, the "dark" or "shadow" side of matrimonial consent.

The definitive triumph in the twelfth century of the Roman law principle that consent makes a marriage coincided both with the movement first among canonists and then among theologians to treat marriage as a consensual contract and with the flowering of Scholasticism. As a result, the Roman law of contracts was the primary source for deriving and analyzing invalidating defects of matrimonial consent. These defects, which were generally considered to be rooted in natural law, were, in turn, interpreted by canonists and theologians in light of Scholastic rational psychology which distinguished intellect and will as the faculties of the soul.

Since consent is an act of the will, all defects of consent ultimately invalidate marriage because of their impact on the will. Nevertheless, valid consent requires the harmonious interaction of all of a person's mental faculties—the cognitive, the critical or deliberative, and the volitional. Thus, to use the Scholastic framework, consent is defective: (1) when a lack or disturbance of the use of reason disables the will; (2) when, as a result of the absence of even the most rudimentary knowledge of the nature of marriage or an error about the identity or a critical quality of one's partner or about the essential nature of marriage, a substantially defective object is proposed by the intellect to the will; and (3) when the will itself either lacks freedom because of external coercion or intends something other than marriage as it is defined by the Church. In fact, however, it is two concrete human persons in all their complexity, who "mutually give and accept each other...to establish marriage" (c. 1057, §2). Consequently, consent cannot be adequately understood merely as a disembodied juridic act. An adequate understanding of consent must also

---

Eastern code transfers the requirement that the spouses be present when they exchange consent to the article on the form for celebrating marriage (*CCEO* 837, §1).

include an appreciation of its personal and inter-personal dimensions and its concreteness. Thus, one can never overlook the influence of culture, society, family, and personal experience on individual couples' consent.

The present chapter begins with an exposition of consensual incapacity because of difficulties of a psychological nature (c. 1095). The chapter then treats the impact on the validity of consent of various defects of the intellect: ignorance (c. 1096), error concerning the person or a critical quality of one's spouse (c. 1097), error about a quality of one's spouse imposed by error (c. 1098), and error about the essential nature of marriage (c. 1099). Interjected at this point is the presumption that knowing or believing that a marriage will be invalid does not necessarily preclude a person from consenting validly (c. 1100). Three canons then treat defects of the will itself: positive intentions excluding marriage itself or one of its essential elements or properties (c. 1101), conditional consent (c. 1102), and consent extracted by force and fear (c. 1103). There follow three canons on the manner in which consent is to be expressed: the requirement that the parties be present together, either personally or through their proxy, for the exchange of consent (c. 1104), the requirements for the celebration of marriage by proxy (c. 1105), and the possibility of celebrating marriage through an interpreter (c. 1106). A final canon asserts the presumption that, when a marriage is entered invalidly, the consent given perdures until the contrary is proven (c. 1107).

Consensual Incapacity

Canon 1095 — The following are incapable of contracting marriage:

1° those who lack the sufficient use of reason;

2° those who suffer from a grave defect of discretion of judgment concerning the essential matrimonial rights and duties mutually to be handed over and accepted;

3° those who are not able to assume the essential obligations of marriage for causes of a psychic nature.

To consent to marriage, a person must: (1) possess sufficient use of reason to posit a responsible human act; (2) be able to evaluate the nature of marriage itself and the concrete marriage to be entered and so to choose it freely; and (3) be capable of assuming and carrying out the essential obligations of marriage. All of these capacities can be substantially undermined by disturbances, both transient and permanent, that are psychic or psycho-somatic in nature.[85]

Lack of Sufficient Use of Reason

Canonists have long recognized that serious mental disorders or disturbances can incapacitate a person for the performance of responsible human acts in general and for marital consent in particular. Gratian cited a Roman law fragment from Justinian's *Digest* as authority for the proposition that "neither a madman nor a madwoman can contract marriage,"[86] and Innocent III authorized the separation of a woman from a habitually insane man on the ground that "because of the alienation of the madness, consent could not occur."[87] Nevertheless, insanity (amentia) did not figure prominently in matrimonial jurisprudence until relatively recently.

The marginal role played by the ground of amentia in traditional jurisprudence was due, in part, to widespread ignorance about mental illness both in the Church and in society at large. Consequently, the claim was often raised that an otherwise habitually insane person had consented to marriage during a "lucid interval" and that the consent was, therefore, valid. Moreover, following Sanchez, the test for capacity for consent was generally the degree of the use of reason required for someone to commit a mortal sin, a level that

---

[85] *Coram* Ragni, Nov. 26, 1985, *SRRDec* 77 (1985) 554. See A. Mendonça, "Consensual Incapacity for Marriage," *J* 54 (1994) 482–486.

[86] C. 32 q. 7 c. 26. Gratian's source goes on to add, "But if it has been contracted let them not be separated." The reason for not separating the spouses was presumably because the insanity surfaced only after consent had occurred. See Gasparri, n. 785.

[87] X, 4.1.24.

was normally achieved around a person's seventh year. Later jurists argued that, although children may have sufficient use of reason to perform a human act after the age of discretion, they usually lack sufficient knowledge of the nature of marriage to consent to it until they reach the age of puberty (twelve for women, fourteen for men).[88] In both cases, setting the bar at such minimal levels was thought necessary to prevent simple folk from being judged incapable of marriage and thus depriving them of access to the only legitimate remedy for concupiscence.[89]

During the twentieth century, an enhanced understanding of mental illness has prompted jurisprudence to reject both the "mortal sin" and the "puberty" tests for assessing the level of mental functioning necessary for eliciting valid matrimonial consent. Although the law continues to presume that young people have achieved the use of reason by the age of seven (c. 97, §2) and thus may be able to commit mortal sins whose consequences concern the present, they may not necessarily be able to consent to marriage whose consequences affect the future. The law also presumes that those who have reached the age of puberty have sufficient use of reason to know the substance of marriage (c. 1096, §2), but consent requires more than due knowledge. Thus, jurisprudence has come to insist that a person must possess the use of reason proportionate to the act of matrimonial consent itself which entails obligations that are both serious and perpetual.[90]

Consequently, canon 1095, 1° declares incapable of contracting marriage not only those who lack the use of reason altogether but also those who lack "sufficient use of reason." When a disruption of the "psychological process involved in forming the human act...seriously impeded the rational function of the mind" and deprived a person "of any meaningful deliberation concerning personal capacity for marital commitment and the choice of the object of consent,"[91] he or she may be judged to lack sufficient use of reason. To deprive a person of sufficient use of reason to contract marriage, a mental impairment must be relatively severe and pervasive in its effect. The cause can be a habitual disorder such as a psychosis or severe mental retardation or a transient disturbance such as drug or alcohol intoxication or a serious psychic trauma.[92]

In judging cases on the ground of lack of sufficient use of reason, careful attention must be paid to the mental competence of the person at the time consent was elicited. Although jurisprudence has largely abandoned its former preoccupation with so-called "lucid intervals," some habitual mental disorders are susceptible to treatment by medications that restore a person's "sufficient use of reason." For example, persons suffering from bi-polar disorder (manic-depressive syndrome) may have experienced periods when they lacked sufficient use of reason for marriage, but, thanks to medication, may possess sufficient use of reason at the time of consent, even though they may lose the use of reason again later in the marriage when they cease taking their medication. In a similar way, a person may habitually possess the use of reason and have formed an intention to enter a particular marriage in the future, but, if the person was completely drunk at the time of the wedding, he or she may have lacked sufficient use of reason for marriage. At the time of the actual consent, the parties must be capable of manifesting their consent by a human act.[93]

When a person's lack of sufficient use of reason appears to be caused by a serious and habitual mental disorder, proof of this ground usually re-

---

[88] J. Keating, *The Bearing of Mental Impairment on the Validity of Marriage* (Rome: Gregorian University, 1973) 124–136.

[89] J. Noonan, *The Power to Dissolve* (Cambridge: Belknap, 1972) 123–158.

[90] Keating, 123–170.

[91] Mendonça, "Consensual Incapacity for Marriage," 490.

[92] Ibid.; L. Wrenn, *The Invalid Marriage* (Washington, D.C.: CLSA, 1998) 22.

[93] See *coram* Heard, December 4, 1943, *SRRDec* 35 (1943) 885–903; *coram* Grazioli, July 1, 1933, *SRRDec* 25 (1933) 403–419; and *coram* Jullien, July 30, 1932, *SRRDec* 24 (1932) 364–382.

quires the services of psychological experts. However, in cases involving serious but transient disturbances such as intoxication, psychological experts may shed little light on the critical issues, and the judge may have to rely on the declarations of the parties and the testimony of witnesses.

Lack of Due Discretion

A person may possess sufficient use of reason to have a rudimentary and abstract understanding of marriage and its obligations and to intend marriage so understood but still be incapable of consent, if he or she lacks the ability to deliberate critically about this choice in the concrete. For example, a teen-aged girl captivated by the story of Romeo and Juliet may have adequate abstract knowledge of marriage and intend a marriage with her first boyfriend like the one portrayed in Shakespeare's play, but still be unable to consent validly to the marriage because of her immature assessment of her own and her boyfriend's readiness for marriage. Canon law calls this incapacity for critical deliberation lack of maturity or discretion of judgment.

The Church requires the human maturity proportionate to the state of life in question for all life-choices, since they entail lifelong obligations.[94] The minimum age for marriage is sixteen for men and fourteen for women (c. 1083, §1), two years higher than the ages for puberty. At these ages, men and women respectively presumably possess the minimal maturity or discretion of judgment to consent to marriage. Following Aquinas, canon law has traditionally set a lower minimum age for marriage than for professing vows in a religious institute or for embracing celibacy as an ordained minister because marriage is something to-

ward which people are inclined by nature and, therefore, marriage consent requires less maturity or discretion than does entry into the other states.[95] The presumption that men and women possess minimally sufficient discretion for marriage at the ages of sixteen and fourteen respectively is a simple one that cedes to contrary proof. Such contrary proof may not be difficult to acquire in Western cultures where adolescence with its attendant dependence and immaturity is typically extended well into a person's twenties.

The maturity or discretion of judgment that is required for capacity for matrimonial consent must be proportionate to the serious and perpetual obligations of marriage. Mature or due discretion requires that consent be informed, prudent, and free.[96] Consent is informed if the person has "sufficient cognitive (intellectual) knowledge of self and of the other, and of the essential rights and duties, constitutive of the permanent and exclusive 'consortium totius vitae.'"[97] While such cognitive knowledge is necessary for a person to consent to marriage, it is not in itself sufficient. The person must also be capable of critically evaluating this knowledge in view of a decision about a concrete pending marriage.

In an often cited 1957 decision, Felici explained: "To be able to perform a responsible act, which can be characterized as morally imputable, it certainly does not suffice to be capable of exercising the cognitive function, but one must exercise the critical faculty, which alone renders one capable of forming judgments and moving the will."[98] This critical faculty, a function of the practical intellect, is the capacity to evaluate knowledge of one's self, one's prospective partner, and the complex of rights and obligations constitutive of the partnership of the whole of life by comparing, integrating, and deducing new judgments. In

---

[94] For example, superiors of religious institutes are to admit only those who have "sufficient qualities of maturity to embrace the proper life of the institute" (c. 642); candidates must be at least seventeen for valid entrance into the novitiate (c. 643, §1, 1°), eighteen for valid temporary profession (c. 656, 1°), and twenty-one for valid perpetual profession (c. 658, 1°).

[95] Thomas Aquinas, *STh,* III, suppl., q. 58, a. 5, ad 1–2.
[96] M. Pompedda, "Maturità psichica e matrimonio nei canoni 1095, 1096," *Apol* 57 (1984) 134 and idem, "L'incapacità consensuale," *IC* 31 (1991) 107–138.
[97] Mendonça, "Consensual Incapacity for Marriage," 495.
[98] *Coram* Felici, December 3, 1957, *SRRDec* 49 (1957) 788.

short, the critical faculty is the capacity to make a prudent judgment about *this* marriage with *this* person at *this* time.

To be a genuinely human act, matrimonial consent must be free from both external coercion and internal compulsion. While human actions are never entirely free from instinctual and unconscious influences, valid consent requires freedom "from immature, obsessive and overpowering ideas, fantasies, instinctual excitations, fear, and so forth in the process of choosing the object of consent."[99] In other words, a person must be able to evaluate his or her motives for marriage and to exercise mastery over impulses and anxieties.[100]

The notion of due discretion that has emerged in jurisprudence is well summarized in a 1979 decision by Pinto:

Discretion of judgment that is proportionate to marriage demands the capacity firstly of understanding the essential obligations of marriage, at least in substance, and secondly of freely choosing to assume those obligations. As regards the capacity of *understanding,* a speculative or abstract understanding is not enough; one must also have a practical understanding, which presupposes experience in living, about the particular marriage to be celebrated, with this person, in these circumstances, with some understanding of the particular difficulties both present and future insofar as they can be seen and with a sense of the responsibility and seriousness of the obligations that are being undertaken. As regards the capacity of *freely* choosing marriage, it is required that the decision to enter marriage be based on reasonable motives after sufficient deliberation and not on pathological motives, and it is also required that the will be able to order the decision into execution.[101]

The maturity or discretion of judgment required for matrimonial consent can be subverted by a variety of habitual mental disorders. Psychoses can deprive a person of the capacity for critical deliberation; neuroses can compromise a person's internal freedom. Personality disorders are "enduring patterns of perceiving, relating to, and thinking about the environment and oneself in a wide range of social and personal contexts" which "are inflexible and maladaptive and cause significant functional impairment."[102] These disorders are sometimes treated in jurisprudence as disorders that impair critical deliberation and sometimes as disorders that restrict internal freedom.[103] Since consent requires the harmonious interaction of the intellect and the will, "it cannot be determined a priori when the judge should examine someone's intellective capacity alone, and when he or she should investigate the volitive capacity."[104] In practice, whether to concentrate on the impact of a personality disorder on a person's critical faculty or internal freedom is dictated by the facts of the particular case.

Despite the firm assertion of John Paul II that "the hypothesis of a real incapacity is to be considered only when an anomaly of a serious nature is present,"[105] Rotal jurisprudence has continued to issue affirmative decisions in cases where lack of due discretion is alleged, not only when the basis for the defect is a serious habitual mental disorder, but also when the defect is rooted in a serious but transitory disturbance of the mind.[106] Thus, traumatic events or stress-related experiences can induce psychological disturbances that temporarily deprive a person of the due discretion for marriage.

[99] Mendonça, "Consensual Incapacity for Marriage," 496.
[100] Pompedda, "Maturità psichica e matrimonio," 134.
[101] *Coram* Pinto, December 18, 1979, *SRRDec* 71 (1979) 587–588. Emphasis in the original.

[102] American Psychiatric Association, *Diagnostic and Statistical Manual of Mental Disorders,* 4th ed. (Washington, D.C.: American Psychiatric Association, 1994) 630.
[103] See A. Mendonça, "The Effect of Personality Disorders on Matrimonial Consent," *SC* 21 (1987) 67–123.
[104] C. Lefebvre, "De defectu discretionis iudicii in rotali jurisprudentia," *P* 69 (1980) 562.
[105] John Paul II, alloc, February 25, 1987, *AAS* 79 (1987) 1457.
[106] Mendonça, "Consensual Incapacity for Marriage," 500–504.

A not uncommon example of a traumatic event that can disturb a person's psychological equilibrium is the discovery of a premarital pregnancy.[107] A person can also be temporarily deprived of due discretion by desperation arising from the need to flee an intolerable situation (e.g., an abusive home situation) or by extreme dependence on one's parents arising from an infantile relationship.[108]

Due discretion can also be undermined by mentalities and attitudes that pervade the socio-cultural milieu in which a person is immersed. For example, where family honor is a prominent cultural value, a person who has committed an act that, if disclosed, would bring disgrace on the family may feel compelled, even without external coercion, to marry in order to prevent damage to the family name.[109] Moreover, inveterate attitudes contrary to the Christian understanding of marriage can also result in a fundamentally flawed decision-making process. Thus, in a case involving a young man who married while steeped in the "hippy" life-style, the Rotal turnus concluded: "This sentence presents the clearest example of deliberation which was simply not there, perhaps not because of some psychopathy, but because of a life-style which precludes any serious consideration of the value of things."[110]

In cases where lack of due discretion is suspected, judges must reconstruct the marital decision-making process, as investigators reconstruct the scenes of traffic accidents, to attempt to identify critical faults or omissions in the reasoning process that may have rendered it fatally flawed. Often, this reconstruction involves a two-step process. First, one identifies an underlying disorder or disturbance that has impaired a person's psychic functioning. Then one weighs the seriousness of the impact of this impairment on the faculties involved in the decision-making process against the seriousness of marital rights and obligations. Psychological experts can provide invaluable assistance to judges in identifying the nature, seriousness, and impact of psychic disorders and disturbances and in reconstructing the dynamics of the process that led to the choice of marriage.[111]

Inability to Assume the Essential Obligations of Marriage

Jurisprudence has long recognized that physical impotence, i.e., the incapacity to complete the marital act in a human manner, invalidates marriage, when the impotence is both antecedent to marriage and perpetual. During the last half century, tribunals encountered cases involving people who seemed to have an adequate grasp of the nature of marriage, intact discretionary capacity, and proper intentions toward marriage, but who were affected by disorders that prevented them from fulfilling its obligations. Many of these cases involved sexual disorders (usually satyriasis and nymphomania) that compelled people to engage in promiscuous behavior despite their intention to remain faithful to their spouses. Jurisprudence began to treat such cases as cases of "psychic" or "moral" impotence, by analogy to physical impotence.[112]

Following the teaching of Vatican II, jurisprudence gradually began to recognize that the essential rights and obligations of marriage extend well beyond the perpetual and exclusive right to the body for acts in themselves apt for the procreation of offspring, which was formerly articulated as the formal object of marital consent (*CIC* 1081, §2) and considered its only truly essential obligation in the jurisprudence based on the 1917 code.[113] As the range of marital obligations considered essential expanded, jurisprudence quietly abandoned the analogy to physical impotence and

---

[107] *Coram* Ragni, July 11, 1986, *SRRDec* 78 (1986) 444–457.

[108] *Coram* Giannecchini, June 17, 1986, *SRRDec* 78 (1986) 382.

[109] *Coram* Faltin, November 11, 1988, *SRRDec* 80 (1988) 626.

[110] *Coram* Davino, March 20, 1985, *SRRDec* 77 (1985) 187.

[111] Mendonça, "Consensual Incapacity for Marriage," 497–499.

[112] See Keating, 176–200.

[113] See *coram* Wynen, January 22, 1944, *SRRDec* 36 (1944) 55–79 and *AAS* 36 (1944) 179–200.

began to speak of the inability to assume or fulfill the essential obligations of marriage as an autonomous ground for the invalidity of marriage because of consensual incapacity.

The incapacity for consent of persons unable, at the time of consent, to fulfill an essential marital obligation follows from the general principle rooted in natural law that "no one can be obliged to the impossible."[114] The defect lies not in the elements of consent itself but in its object. What is at issue is not the person's capacity for critical deliberation, but his or her inability to put into effect one or more of the rights and obligations given and accepted in consent. Canon 1095, 3° roots the incapacity for consent not in the inability to "fulfill" the essential obligations of marriage but rather in the inability to "assume" them. The word "assume" makes clear that the psychic defect that gives rise to the incapacity must be present at the moment of consent and not something that emerges during common life. Moreover, the source of the inability to "fulfill" the essential obligations of marriage may be extrinsic to consent, e.g., when the inability arises from a person's physical impotence or his incarceration. However, the source of the inability to "assume" them is always intrinsic, i.e., it "pertains to the content of the very act of consent as its object."[115]

To be incapable of consent, a person must be prevented from assuming an *essential* obligation of marriage. While postconciliar jurisprudence has continued to require that the spouses enjoy the capacity to give and accept the perpetual and exclusive right to the body for acts appropriate for the procreation of offspring, it has tended to cast this essential obligation in more personalist terms. Thus, Stankiewicz speaks of the essential "obligation to the gift of conjugal love, ordered to procreate and educate the child, to be shared with the partner in a human way perpetually and exclusively."[116] How-

ever, this jurisprudence has also devoted particular attention to the capacity of the spouses to establish and sustain the partnership of the whole of life that is perpetual and exclusive and ordered both to the good of the spouses and to the procreation and education of offspring.[117] Initiating and sustaining such a partnership presupposes the capacity for a genuinely interpersonal relationship. "Two persons should, before anything else, be able and willing to be friends, to love, to respect, to trust, to relate to and communicate with each other, or in Wrenn's words, be capable of 'self-revelation,' 'understanding' and 'loving.'"[118]

To invalidate marriage, the incapacity to assume the essential obligations of marriage must be rooted in "causes of a psychic nature." In his 1987 allocution to the Rota, John Paul II explained that the cause of this incapacity must be "a serious form of anomaly which, however it may be defined, must substantially impair the contractant's capacity to intend and/or will."[119] In his 1988 allocution, the Holy Father was more specific. He insisted that "only very serious forms of psychopathology reach the point of impairing substantially the freedom of the person."[120] Although some have interpreted the Holy Father's remarks as requiring the existence of an identifiable mental illness for declaring a marriage invalid because of a party's incapacity to assume the essential obligations of marriage,[121] most commentators have not accepted this interpretation. Instead, they recognize that any disorder or disturbance of the human mind, if it is sufficiently severe, can prevent a person from assuming the essential obligations of marriage, whether the disorder or disturbance is a recognized mental illness or

---

[114]*RI* 6. See also A. Stankiewicz, "De accommodatione regulae 'impossibilium nulla obligatio est' ad incapacitatem adimplendi matrimonii obligationes," *P* 68 (1979) 643–672.

[115]Mendonça, "Consensual Incapacity for Marriage," 507.

[116]*Coram* Stankiewicz, December 16, 1982, *EIC* 39 (1983) 258–259.

[117]M. Pompedda, "Determining What Are Essential Obligations," in *Incapacity for Marriage: Jurisprudence and Interpretation,* ed. R. Sable (Rome: Gregorian University, 1987) 190–193.

[118]Mendonça, "Consensual Incapacity for Marriage," 515. See also L. Wrenn, *The Invalid Marriage,* 45–46.

[119]John Paul II, alloc, February 5, 1987, *AAS* 79 (1987) 1457.

[120]John Paul II, alloc, January 25, 1998, *AAS* 80 (1988) 1182.

[121]*Coram* Burke, July 22, 1991, *Forum* 4 (1993) 110–111.

not. For them, "anomaly should not be confused with psychiatric illness. 'In reality, every true dysfunction of the psychic or psychological process constitutes a real psychopathology; but this does not mean that here one is faced with a person who suffers from a psychic illness.'"[122]

The mental disorder or disturbance that incapacitates a person from assuming the essential obligations of marriage must be antecedent to marriage, i.e., present at the time of consent. Psychological problems that surface only during the marriage cannot invalidate consent already given. Nevertheless, a disorder or disturbance that only became apparent during the marriage may actually have been present at the time of consent, but was overlooked or not recognized for what it was. To invalidate marriage, it is not sufficient that the disorder or disturbance render the assumption and fulfillment of essential marital obligations *difficult;* it is necessary that it render the fulfillment of these obligations *impossible.* As John Paul II has made clear, "For the canonist the principle must remain clear that only *incapacity* and not *difficulty* in manifesting consent and in realizing a true community of life and love invalidate marriage."[123]

Since the ground of incapacity to assume essential marital obligations emerged by analogy to the impediment of impotence, some canonists have maintained that, in order to invalidate marriage, the incapacity must be perpetual or incurable by ordinary means, like the incapacity involved in impotence.[124] This position has not, however, been embraced by the mainstream of Rotal jurisprudence,[125] which has treated the incapacity to assume essential marital obligations as a ground of nullity distinct from impotence. Adherents of this position argue that, although the essential obligations of marriage bind perpetually, an incapacitating disorder need not be perpetual or incurable. It is enough that the person be incapable of assuming essential obligations of marriage at the time of consent.[126]

Since a marriage can be declared invalid only if a party is truly incapable of assuming essential marital obligations and not merely because the party experienced difficulty in fulfilling them, the underlying disorder or disturbance must be severe. Identifying the nature of the disorder and assessing its severity usually require the services of a psychological expert.[127] "Practically all recent rotal sentences speak of the necessity of using experts in cases of 'consensual incapacity.'"[128]

Ignorance

Canon 1096 — §1. For matrimonial consent to exist, the contracting parties must be at least not ignorant that marriage is a permanent partnership between a man and a woman ordered to the procreation of offspring by means of some sexual cooperation.

§2. This ignorance is not presumed after puberty.

Ignorance is the absence of knowledge. One cannot consent to marriage without at least a minimal knowledge of what one is intending and willing. Canon 1096 deals not with the critical knowledge discussed in canon 1095, 2°, but with the required abstract or speculative knowledge for marriage. However, ignorance invalidates a juridic act, including matrimonial consent, only if it

---

[122]*Coram* Colagiovanni, March 20, 1991, *ME* 117 (1992) 33. See also Pompedda, "Determining What Are Essential Obligations," 197, and Mendonça, "Consensual Incapacity for Marriage," 526–529.

[123]John Paul II, alloc, February 5, 1987, *AAS* 79 (1987) 1457. Emphasis in the original.

[124]J. Pinto Gomez, "L'immaturità affettiva nella giurisprudenza rotale," in *L'immaturità psico-affettiva nella giurisprudenza della Rota Romana,* ed. P. Bonnet and C. Gullo (Vatican City: Libreria Editrice Vaticana, 1990) 50–51.

[125]*Coram* Bruno, July 19, 1991, *ME* 117 (1992) 171.

[126]M. Pompedda, "Annotazioni circa la 'incapacitas adsumendi onera coniugalia,'" in *Studi di diritto matrimoniale canonico* (Milan: Giuffré, 1993) 97–100. See Mendonça, "Consensual Incapacity for Marriage," 531–534.

[127]See the commentary on cc. 1574–1581.

[128]Mendonça, "Consensual Incapacity for Marriage," 541.

involves an element of the object of the act which constitutes its *substance* (c. 126). The substance of an act does not encompass all its elements or even all of its essential elements, but only those which must be explicitly intended for the act to exist.[129] For example, perpetuity or indissolubility is a property that belongs to the essence of marriage (c. 1056), but, for a valid marriage, it is sufficient that a person know only that marriage is permanent, i.e., that it is a stable relationship.

According to canon 1096, the substance of marriage is "a permanent partnership between a man and a woman ordered to the procreation of offspring by means of some sexual cooperation." Although the 1917 code had required only that parties know that marriage is a *societas,* a term that was often used for a business partnership, the revised code requires knowledge that it is a *consortium,* a partnership that involves mutual cooperation, support, and companionship. They must also know that this partnership is permanent (i.e., a stable relationship of some duration), but not necessarily that it is perpetual (i.e., that it is indissoluble).[130] Finally, the partners must know at least that marriage is heterosexual in nature (but not that it is exclusive). The parties cannot be ignorant that marriage is ordered to the procreation of children or that this procreation comes about by sexual cooperation between a man and a woman. It is not necessary that the parties have extensive knowledge of human sexuality, but they must know at least that procreation comes about through the bodily interaction of specific organs of the man and the woman.[131] Thus, a marriage would be invalid because of ignorance if a person thought that marriage entailed no exchange of the right to the body or that this right was substantially

different from what it is (e.g., that it consisted in a right to warm hugs.)[132]

Invalidating ignorance is most likely to be found in those who are developmentally disabled, who are quite young and naive, or who experienced a very sheltered upbringing. Ignorance is not presumed after puberty. It is, however, presumed prior to puberty. Although the revised code sets the age for valid marriage at sixteen for men and fourteen for women, the age of puberty remains twelve for women and fourteen for men, as it was in Roman law and in pre- and post-1917 code canon law.[133]

Error about the Person

Canon 1097 — §1. Error concerning the person renders a marriage invalid.

§2. Error concerning a quality of the person does not render a marriage invalid even if it is the cause for the contract, unless this quality is directly and principally intended.

Error of Person

While ignorance involves a lack of knowledge, error is a positive judgment that is objectively false. Like ignorance, error does not invalidate a juridic act unless it concerns an element "which constitutes its substance or which amounts to a condition *sine qua non*" (c. 126). Since the parties to a marriage are themselves the material object of consent and, therefore, an element of the substance of the act, error about the identity of the physical person one marries invalidates consent. Thus, had the Code of Canon Law been in effect at the time, Jacob's marriage to Leah would have been invalid because of his error about the person of his spouse.[134] In Western societies where young people usually enjoy a relatively long and unregulated courtship before they marry, cases involving error of person are rare. Nonetheless, such cases

---

[129] F. Urrutia, *Les normes générales* (Paris: Tardy, 1994) 296; and G. Michiels, *Principia generalia de personis in Ecclesia* (Tournai: Desclée, 1955) 653.

[130] But see *coram* Di Felice, December 14, 1977, *SRRDec* 69 (1987) 505–508, where a marriage was declared null because of the woman's ignorance that marriage is indissoluble.

[131] See *coram* Masala, March 30, 1977, *SRRDec* 69 (1987) 157–171.

[132] Wrenn, *The Invalid Marriage,* 94.

[133] *CIC* 88, §2.

[134] Gn 29:15–30.

may occur in societies where families play the primary role in arranging marriages or where personal contacts between young people are strictly restricted before their marriage. Error of person may also occur when people use "mail-order-bride" services.

Error of Quality of the Person

While cases involving error about the physical identity of one's spouse may be rare, not so rare are cases in which people claim to have been in error about qualities of their spouses that were so important that their absence made their spouses fundamentally different persons from the ones they thought they were marrying. A quality is an enduring characteristic of person that significantly defines who that person is. Qualities include such things as one's physical and mental health, marital status, religious adherence, educational attainment, occupation, legal status, and socio-economic status. In themselves, errors about such qualities in a prospective spouse do not affect the validity of marital consent, but sometimes a particular quality may be so important to a person that he or she implicitly makes its presence (or, in some cases, its absence) a condition attached to consent.

Jurisprudence has, until recently, been reluctant to recognize the invalidating effect of an error about a quality of the person. Saint Thomas held:

> If, however, the error about a person's rank or position amounts to an error about the person [*redundat in errorem personae*], it is an impediment to matrimony. Hence, if the woman consent directly to this particular person, her error about his rank does not void the marriage; but if she intend directly to consent to marry the king's son [or, a king's son (*filium regis*)], whoever he may be, then, if another man than the [or a] king's son be brought to her, there is error about the person, and the marriage will be void.[135]

[135] Thomas Aquinas, *STh*, suppl., q. 51, a. 2, ad 5.

Unfortunately, the absence of definite and indefinite articles in Latin has left Aquinas's meaning ambiguous. If he meant that consent was invalid if the woman directly intended to marry *the* son of the king, then the invalidating error concerned a quality that individuated or distinguished Prince Charles from Prince Andrew and amounted to an error of person. If, however, Aquinas meant that the woman directly intended to marry *a* king's son, the error redounding to an error of person concerned the quality of "princeship" and would invalidate marriage with anyone not of princely rank. Sanchez interpreted Aquinas in the first sense and limited the category of invalidating errors strictly to qualities that definitively distinguished one individual from another;[136] Alphonsus Liguori interpreted Aquinas more broadly and extended the category of invalidating error to qualities that, although common to many people, were directly and principally intended by the one giving consent.[137] Canon 1083, §2, 1° of the 1917 code declared that consent was invalid if it was elicited under the influence of an error of quality that amounted to an error of person. However, Sanchez's narrow interpretation of *error redundans* prevailed in jurisprudence until 1970, when a Rotal decision by Canals rejected this jurisprudence as not faithful to Saint Thomas and based on social conditions that no longer exist and espoused the position of Liguori.[138] Canals's view quickly became the predominant position in Rotal jurisprudence.[139]

This development in jurisprudence is reflected in canon 1097, §2, which avoids the traditional phrase an "error of quality which amounts to (*redundet in*) an error of person." Instead, error about a quality of a person invalidates consent only if that quality was directly and principally intended.

[136] T. Sanchez, *De matrimonio,* lib. 7, 18, 38.
[137] A. Liguori, *Theologia Moralis,* 5, 6, 31.
[138] *Coram* Canals, April 21, 1970, *SRRDec* 62 (1980) 370–375; *CLD* 8, 796–801.
[139] See *coram* Funghini, February 24, 1988, *SRRDec* 80 (1988) 144; and *coram* Jarawan, February 6, 1991, *SRRDec* 83 (1991) 77.

"In marriage a quality is *directly* intended when the quality rather than the person is intended in and of itself; it is *principally* intended when the quality is more important than the person."[140] Thus, when a woman marries a man whom she erroneously believes to be a physician, her error does not invalidate her consent unless the quality of "being a physician" was so important to her that she intended the quality more than the person of her spouse and, if the quality was not present, she did not want the marriage.

The mere fact that an error about a quality of a person caused the contract is not, in itself, sufficient to invalidate consent. In other words, it is not enough to show that a person decided to marry another precisely because he erroneously believed that she possessed a particular quality and that he would not have married her had he known that she did not possess that quality. One must be able to show in addition that he directly and principally intended the quality. However, proof that an error about a quality caused the marriage contract may generate a strong presumption that the quality was indeed directly and principally intended.

To invalidate marriage, one must directly and principally intend by a positive act of the will a quality erroneously believed to be present in one's spouse. Thus, this intention must be something more than a presumed intention (i.e., one that can be surmised from facts known about the person), an interpretive intention (i.e., one that the person would have had if she had stopped to think about the matter), a generic intention (i.e., a disposition or general preference), or a habitual intention (i.e., a more or less firm and long-standing inclination which remains merely an intellectual preference). On the other hand, the intention need not be actual (i.e, formulated at the time of the actual consent) or explicit (i.e., articulated in precise and definite terms). It is sufficient that the intention be virtual (i.e., formulated prior to the marriage cere-

mony but never retracted) and implicit (i.e., expressed only indirectly or obliquely).[141]

In his celebrated 1970 decision, Canals suggested a third way in which error about a quality of a person could invalidate consent. "The third interpretation considers the case of a moral, social or juridical quality which is so intimately connected with the physical person that the person would be altogether different if that quality did not exist.... The reason for this invalidity would not arise from any implicit condition, but due to an error of quality amounting to an error concerning the person understood in a more complete and integral way."[142]

For example, this approach would allow a marriage to be declared invalid because of a person's error about a quality of her spouse that is of such great objective importance (e.g., not being a member of the Mafia) that the absence of the quality rendered him an essentially different person from the one she thought she was marrying, whether the quality was directly and principally intended or not. However, this "third way" has been rather pointedly rejected by Rotal jurisprudence because this "more complete and integral way" of understanding the person has been judged at odds with the traditional Scholastic understanding of "person."[143] In addition, it is feared that, by eliminating the requirement that a quality be directly and principally intended, this third way would open the door to a spate of claims of nullity when spouses turned out to be less than the men and women of the others' dreams.

Fraud or Imposed Error

Canon 1098 — A person contracts invalidly who enters into a marriage deceived by malice, perpetrated to obtain consent, concerning some quality of the other partner which by its very nature can gravely disturb the partnership of conjugal life.

---

[140] Wrenn, *The Invalid Marriage,* 97. Emphasis in the original. See *coram* Stankiewicz, October 24, 1991, *SR-RDec* 83 (1991) 676.

[141] Wrenn, *The Invalid Marriage,* 101.

[142] *Coram* Canals, April 21, 1970, *SRRDec* 62 (1970) 371.

[143] See U. Navarrete, "Error in persona (c. 1097, §1)," *P* 87 (1998) 351–401.

As a rule, juridic acts performed under the influence of deceit are valid unless the law provides otherwise (c. 125, §2), as it does here with regard to marriages entered under the influence of error induced by deceit. Thus, although mere error about a quality of a person does not per se invalidate marriage unless it is directly and principally intended, such an error can invalidate marriage if it results from fraud or deceit.

The personalist understanding of marriage flowing from the teaching of Vatican II prompted the incorporation of deceit as a ground of nullity into the revised code. Consent consists in the spouses' mutually giving and accepting of one another. When one spouse has been deprived of knowledge of an important quality of the other by deceit, what is given and accepted in consent is incomplete or truncated. Thus, the material object of consent is defective. Moreover, such deceit is inimical to the honesty and self-revelation that is necessary to establish and sustain the partnership of the whole of life. To bind a person perpetually in marriage to a person who has deceived him or her about a significant personal quality is now deemed so unjust that the deceit leads to the invalidity of the marriage.

It is somewhat misleading, however, to speak of the ground of nullity treated in canon 1098 as that of fraud or deceit. It is not the deceiver who marries invalidly, but the one deceived. It is not the fraud or deceit itself that causes invalidity, but the error about a quality of the person of the spouse that results from it. Thus, it is more accurate to call this ground of nullity "imposed error" (*error dolosus*).

Several essential elements must be proved for a marriage to be declared null on this ground.

(1) *Deceit must be employed to secure the other party's consent to marriage.* The deceiver must know or, at least, suspect that the other party would not consent to marriage if he or she were aware of the existence (or absence) of a particular quality. Although deceit is always morally wrong, the motivation for it need not be malicious. One may sincerely think that what his future spouse "doesn't know won't hurt her," that the presence or absence of the quality on which the deceit bears will never come to light, that his spouse's discovery of the presence or absence of the quality after the marriage would cause only a temporary ripple in conjugal life, or that the quality is of no objective importance. Nor is it necessary that the deceit be perpetrated by one of the parties to the marriage. For example, family members may intentionally conceal from a prospective spouse their son's history of mental illness or the family's history of genetic abnormalities for fear that she will break the engagement. What is critical is that the deceit be aimed at securing consent to marriage.

(2) *The deceit must bear on a quality of the person "which by its very nature can gravely disturb the partnership of conjugal life."* A quality of a person is an inherent or distinguishing characteristic or trait of a person. Isolated actions in the past are not normally considered to be qualities. Thus, the fact that a man once smoked marijuana is not one of his qualities, but the fact that he was once incarcerated for drug possession and, therefore, has a criminal record or that he is a recovering drug addict is one of his qualities.

To disturb the partnership of conjugal life by its very nature, the quality that is the object of deception must be grave. The quality is considered objectively grave if most people would consider it so important to the happy outcome of a marriage that they would consider its concealment a serious injustice to the other party. However, a quality that is considered of little importance by most people may be subjectively grave for some individuals. For example, most people would not consider the quality of being a social drinker to be of its nature disruptive of conjugal life, but, for the child of alcoholic parents, it may be serious. The use of the phrase "by its very nature" (*suapte natura*) suggests that the quality that is the object of deceit must have some objective gravity to give rise to the invalidity of consent. Among the qualities that Rotal sentences have mentioned as of their nature possibly disruptive of conjugal life are: deceit about one's chronological age, having contracted AIDS, feigned affection for one's future spouse's children of a previous marriage, homosexuality, mental illness, marital status, membership in a subversive group, pregnancy, sterility, moral rectitude, and virginity.[144] These qualities do appear to be objectively grave. Nevertheless, some Rotal decisions have found for invalidity on the basis of imposed error about qualities that do not seem especially objectively grave. These decisions seem to emphasize more the injustice of the deceit itself than the objective gravity of the quality that was the object of deceit.[145]

(3) *The quality must be present (or absent) at the time of consent.* The quality that is the object of the deceit cannot be one that is expected or hoped for in the future. Thus, a woman who married a man who had led her to believe that he intended to enter law school, even though he had no such intention, cannot claim that her marriage was invalid because of the deceit. On the other hand, a woman who was led to believe that the man she was about to marry already was a lawyer or had been accepted at a law school may have a basis for claiming that her marriage was invalid as a consequence of this deceit.

(4) *The deceived person must be unaware that the quality that is the object of the deceit is (or is not) present in the other person.* The essential requirement for this ground of nullity is that a person is actually led into error about a quality of the other party as a result of deceit. Thus, if, despite a fiancé's efforts to deceive her, a woman independently becomes aware or strongly suspects that he lacks an important quality, the validity of the marriage cannot be challenged on this ground because the deceit has failed to induce error about the quality. A crucial indicator of whether deceit has led to error is the response of the allegedly deceived person on discovering the presence (or absence) of the quality that had been the object of the deceit. If she promptly moves to terminate the conjugal relationship, the deceit presumably had been effective and she had been unaware of the quality.

Since the promulgation of the 1983 code, jurists have debated whether the source of the invalidity of marriage because of error resulting from deceit is the natural law or positive ecclesiastical law.[146] The answer to this question is not merely of theoretical interest. If this ground of nullity is based in natural law, then canon 1098 has retroactive application and can also be used to resolve marriage cases involving two non-Catholics. If, however, it is based in positive ecclesiastical law, it cannot be applied to marriages entered prior to November 27, 1983 and is inapplicable to cases involving two non-Catholics, who are normally no longer bound by merely ecclesiastical law (c. 11).

In 1986, the then Commission for the Interpretation of the Code of Canon Law responded privately to the request from the Archbishop of Freiburg for a clarification of the possible retroactivity of canon 1098. While noting that a definitive judgment on the natural or positive law character of the canon was a matter of doctrine and, therefore, beyond its competence, the commission stated that it was

---

[144] J. Johnson, "Fraud and Deceit in the Rota: The First Ten Years," *J* 56 (1996) 577.

[145] See *coram* Pompedda, February 6, 1992, *IE* 6 (1994) 573–591, where the man and his family had led the woman to believe that he was thirty years old when, in fact, he was thirty-eight. See Johnson, "Fraud and Deceit," 569–577.

[146] See U. Navarrete, "Canon 1098 de errore doloso estne iuris naturalis an iuris positivi ecclesiastici?" *P* 76 (1987) 161–181; Johnson, "Fraud and Deceit," 559–569; idem, "On the Retroactive Force of Canon 1098," *Stud Can* 23 (1989) 61–83; and *coram* Stankiewicz, January 27, 1994, *Forum* 8 (1997) 382–390.

inclined to regard the wording of Canon 1098 as of merely positive law and consequently as *nonretroactive*. Given, however, the great variety of cases which the canon could embrace, one could not rule out a priori the possibility that some of those cases could involve nullity deriving from the natural law, in which case it would be legitimate to render an affirmative decision.[147]

Thus, canon 1098 is primarily a norm of positive ecclesiastical law and, as such, is not applicable to marriages celebrated before the revised code took effect or to marriages of two non-Catholics. Nevertheless, there may be cases in which the error induced by deceit so bears on "qualities of the partner which are necessary for the exercise of the essential rights and obligations of marriage" that, when a quality is assessed in the light of the demands of marriage, the error is substantial and, therefore, invalidates marriage in virtue of the natural law, even though the quality had not been directly and principally intended by the deceived party.[148] In other words, deceit induces substantial error when its object is a quality that is so objectively important that its presence (or absence) renders the deceiver an essentially different person than he or she pretended to be.

Error of Law or Determining Error

Canon 1099 — Error concerning the unity or indissolubility or sacramental dignity of marriage does not vitiate matrimonial consent provided that it does not determine the will.

In 1767, Benedict XIV articulated the presumption that, when people marry, their general intention to marry as Christ willed prevails over any personal or private errors they may harbor about the nature of marriage.[149] This presumption dominated jurisprudence until recent decades and was reflected in canon 1084 of the 1917 code which stipulated that "simple error concerning the unity or indissolubility or sacramental dignity of marriage, even if it gives cause to the contract, does not vitiate matrimonial consent."

For many years, this presumption that the general will to marry according to the will of Christ prevailed over private errors about the nature of marriage corresponded with everyday experience. Although people might know that civil divorce was available as a solution to an unhappy marriage, they generally did not apply this knowledge to their own practical judgment when they decided to marry. Despite their theoretical knowledge about the availability of divorce, they wanted the marriage they entered into with this person at this time to be "forever." However, the validity of the presumption has been steadily eroded in recent years as a result of the secularization of society and the proliferation of divorce. Consequently, Pompedda opines:

> In our judgment it is not a legitimate conclusion from canon 1084 [*CIC* 1917] to say there exists a presumption in favor of marriage for those people who, perhaps largely because of their religious beliefs or secular education, are laboring under a misunderstanding of the essential properties of marriage. This is particularly true since such a presumption is arrived at only by gratuitously conjecturing to a second presumption, namely, that it never occurs to such people, when they enter marriage, to apply their intellectual error to their intention.[150]

During the code revision process, the changing social situation led to a reassessment of the impact of error about the nature of marriage on mar-

---

[147] CodCom, private response, December 12, 1986, *AkK* 155 (1986) 482; Wrenn, *The Invalid Marriage,* 109.

[148] *Coram* Stankiewicz, January 27, 1994, *Forum* 8 (1997) 389–390. See also Navarrete, "Canon 1098 de errore doloso," 179–181.

[149] Benedict XIV, *De synodo dioecesana* 1, 13, c. 22, nn. 3 and 8.

[150] *Coram* Pompedda, January 23, 1971, *SRRDec* 63 (1971) 54.

ital consent. Canon 1099 reiterates the traditional position that error about the unity, indissolubility, or sacramental dignity of marriage does not invalidate consent but adds, "provided that it [the error] does not determine the will." The implication is clear: if an error about the unity, indissolubility, or sacramental dignity of marriage does determine the will, consent is invalid.

The recognition of the relevance of such errors for the validity of consent is not an innovation of the revised code. Rotal jurisprudence had already recognized that firmly held errors about the nature of marriage can so infect people's minds that they cannot will any other kind of marriage than the erroneous version they know. Thus, as early as 1954, Felici held:

> If error is so rooted in the mind of the contractant that it constitutes, as it were, a new nature, it is more difficult to admit the dissension about which we have spoken [the dissension between the positive act of the will and the erroneous opinion]. For generally man acts as he deeply believes on account of the dynamic nature of ideas and images, whereby the more vivid and profound they are and the deeper they lie within the personality, then to that extent they possess more influence and they more forcefully induce to action.[151]

By the 1970s, jurisprudence had universally recognized that deeply rooted or stubborn error (*error pervicax*) can cause the invalidity of marriage.[152] If it is sufficiently intense, the error itself can invalidate marriage. Even less intense error can, however, bring about invalidity when some circumstance, albeit slight, prompts the person to translate his or her erroneous idea of marriage into the act of the will by which he or she consents to a concrete marriage and thereby to simulate consent.[153]

Jurists agree that, to affect the validity of marriage, error about the nature of marriage must "acquire such intensity as to condition the act of the will."[154] There is less unanimity, however, about *how* error brings about marital invalidity. Some hold that the error that determines the will referred to in canon 1099 is equivalent to the "condition *sine qua non*" mentioned in canon 126. Thus, the error brings about marital nullity by attaching to the will an implicit condition *sine qua non* contrary to the substance of marriage. In other words, the person says, "If I cannot have a marriage as I understand it, I do not want the marriage at all."[155] Others agree that such determining error is not an autonomous ground of nullity. However, they argue, error influences the will by prompting an implicit positive act of the will excluding an essential property or the sacramental dignity of marriage. Thus, determining error is a species of implicit simulation.[156] Still others hold that error of law is an autonomous ground of nullity. Since the will is a "blind" faculty that can intend only what is presented to it by the intellect, stubborn error determines the will and brings about marital invalidity by presenting the will with a fundamentally deficient object.[157]

---

151 *Coram* Felici, July 13, 1954, *SRRDec* 46 (1954) 616.

152 I. Parisella, "De pervicaci seu radicato errore circa matrimonii indissolubilitatem: Iurisprudentia Rotalis recentior," in *Ius Populi Dei* (Rome: Gregorian University, 1972) 3: 513–540.

153 D. Fellhauer, "The Exclusion of Indissolubility: Old Principles and New Jurisprudence," *Stud Can* 9 (1975) 128–130. See also the commentary on c. 1101.

154 John Paul II, alloc, January 30, 1993, *AAS* 85 (1993) 1259.

155 U. Navarrete, "De sensu clausulae 'dummodo non determinet voluntatem' can. 1099," *P* 81 (1992) 469–520; and J. Kowal, "L'errore circa le proprietà essenziali o la dignità sacramentale del matrimonio (c. 1099)," *P* 87 (1998) 287–327.

156 Z. Grocholewski, "L'errore circa l'unità, indissolubilità e la sacramentalità del matrimonio," in *Error determinans voluntatem (can. 1099),* Studi giuridici 35 (Vatican City: Libreria Editrice Vaticana, 1995) 7–22; and V. De Paolis, "L'errore che determina la volontà," *ME* 120 (1995) 69–98.

157 A. Stankiewicz, "L'errore di diritto nel consenso matrimoniale e la sua autonomia giuridica," *P* 83 (1994)

No matter how error determines the will, it results in marital invalidity only if it bears on the unity, indissolubility, or sacramental dignity of marriage. Unity requires that marriage be an exclusive relationship between one man and one woman and that it exclude polygamy. Since polygamy is barred by the secular law of most Western countries and is held in disrepute by societal mores, error about the unity of marriage is likely to be relatively rare in these countries. Such error may occur more frequently, however, among peoples shaped by non-Western cultures in which polygamy continues to be practiced and socially accepted.

Error about marital indissolubility is likely to be encountered with some frequency in societies like those of the West where civil divorce is readily available and fairly common. A "divorce mentality" is a fertile breeding ground for erroneous conceptions of marriage according to which marriage is a purely personal relationship that is dissoluble at the will of the parties when it no longer meets their needs and expectations. In this climate, people easily come to believe that civil divorce dissolves all obligations of the spouses to one another and leaves them free to enter new marriages. One cannot, however, leap from a person's favorable attitude toward divorce to the conclusion that his or her marriage was invalid because of determining error. One must always assess the intensity of the error and demonstrate how it determined the person's will to enter a concrete marriage.

The Church teaches that every valid marriage between the baptized is by that fact a sacrament (c. 1055, §2). This teaching is rejected by the vast majority of Protestant churches and their members. It has also been rejected by many of those who, although baptized in the Catholic Church as infants, have drifted from the practice of the faith

635–668; K. Lüdicke, "Der Willensbestimmende Irrtum über das Wesen der Ehe nach c. 1099 CIC als eigenständiger Ehenichtigkeitsgrund," *OAKR* 40 (1991) 54; D. Campbell, "Canon 1099: The Emergence of a New Juridic Figure," *Quaderni Studio Rotale* 5 (1990) 35–72.

or have even abandoned the Christian faith altogether. These people are, therefore, in error about the sacramental dignity of marriage. However, their error does not in itself invalidate marriage unless it is so deeply rooted and intense that it determines the will.

Knowledge or Opinion about Nullity

Canon 1100 — The knowledge or opinion of the nullity of a marriage does not necessarily exclude matrimonial consent.

The fact that one or both parties know (or, at least, consider it probable) that the marriage they are about to enter is invalid does not, in itself, preclude their eliciting naturally sufficient consent. A person who is aware of the existence of a diriment impediment or of the fact that failure to observe the canonical form of marriage will invalidate the marriage can still offer consent that is naturally sufficient to establish marriage. If the person is mistaken about the existence of an impediment or about the obligation to observe canonical form, the marriage cannot be presumed to be invalid merely because he or she believed it was invalid.

Somewhat more problematic is the situation of people who enter marriage knowing or believing that the marriage will be invalid because of defects in their own or their spouse's consent. If the consent is, in fact, defective, the marriage is invalid, not because of the prior knowledge or suspicion about its nullity, but because of the defective consent itself. However, people's judgment about the invalidity of their own or their spouses' consent may be erroneous. For example, some may wrongly believe that their intention to practice artificial birth control constitutes an invalidating intention against the good of offspring or that their spouses had absolutely excluded this good from consent. In such cases, the erring parties cannot be presumed to have consented invalidly. On the other hand, those who enter marriage precisely because they know or believe that the marriage is invalid and that they will subsequently be able to regain their freedom have feigned or simulated marital consent. In this case, the belief, even the erroneous belief, that the marriage will be invalid has become the cause of consent.

Simulation of Consent

Canon 1101 — §1. The internal consent of the mind is presumed to conform to the words and signs used in celebrating the marriage.

§2. If, however, either or both of the parties by a positive act of the will exclude marriage itself, some essential element of marriage, or some essential property of marriage, the party contracts invalidly.

As an act of the will, matrimonial consent is internal to the mind and invisible to sensory perception. The existence of consent must, therefore, be deduced from its external manifestations in perceptible words, signs, and behavior. For evaluating the existence and adequacy of consent, the law gives priority to the words or signs used in the celebration of marriage. The law presumes that the internal consent of the will corresponds with the words or signs employed to give it external expression during the marriage ceremony. Thus, when a couple exchange consent according to the formula of the *Rite of Marriage,* they are presumed to have consented internally to marriage as it is understood by the Church. On the other hand, if they wrote their own wedding vows and promised to love and honor each other "as long as our love endures," they are presumed to have entered a union from which the property of indissolubility has been excluded. This presumption of law is a simple one that cedes to contrary proof.

Although canon 1101 does not use the term "simulation" to denote the exclusion of the substance of marriage by a positive act of the will,[158] the term has a long history in jurisprudence. Simulation occurs when a person desires to enter marriage or, at least, to go through a marriage ceremony to enjoy certain benefits of marriage, but intends marriage in such a truncated form that the object of consent is substantially defective. Thus, there are two conflicting acts of the will, one directed toward marriage or a semblance of marriage and the other rejecting marriage as understood by the Church. If the act of the will rejecting marriage prevails over the one seeking it, the marriage is invalid.

Invalidating simulation requires a positive act of the will which excludes either marriage itself or one of its essential elements or properties. This positive act of the will "can be absolute or hypothetical, explicit or implicit, actual or virtual; an habitual will, or mere inclination, or an interpretive opinion or will, which remain in the intellect and do not move into the will, do not invalidate marriage."[159]

On the one hand, the positive act of the will must be more than a habitual or interpretive will. A *habitual* will is a more or less enduring tendency toward a particular intention. Although it does not in itself invalidate marriage because it remains in the intellect, a habitual intention is always a near occasion of simulation. For example, a person who has a general disposition favorable to divorce as a solution to an unhappy marriage may be easily prompted by pre-matrimonial tensions and conflicts to intend a marriage lacking the property of perpetuity. An *interpretive* will is what a person would have intended had he or she been aware of a particular circumstance at the time of consent. For example, a person may accurately claim that had she known that her spouse was HIV positive, she would not have intended to have children with him. However, since this intention was never actually elicited but is an after-the-fact judgment, it does not affect the validity of consent.

On the other hand, an act of the will need not be actual, absolute, or explicit to invalidate marriage; it is sufficient that the act be virtual, hypothetical, or implicit. An act of the will is actual if

---

[158] See, however, c. 1379 which calls for a just penalty for those who "simulate" a sacrament.

[159] *Coram* Bruno, February 1, 1991, *SRRDec* 83 (1991) 67–68.

it is, in fact, elicited at the time of the wedding; it is virtual if it is formulated prior to the external exchange of consent, even a long time prior to it, and never retracted. An act of the will is absolute if it excludes marriage itself or one of its essential elements or properties without qualification; it is hypothetical when it excludes marriage or one of its essential elements or properties only if certain conditions are met. Thus, a man who reserves the right to regain his freedom by seeking a divorce whenever it suits his fancy excludes indissolubility absolutely, but a woman who resolves to seek a divorce if her fiancé continues to abuse her physically after the marriage excludes indissolubility hypothetically.

The positive act of the will simulating marriage can also be either explicit or implicit. An explicit act of the will excludes marriage or one of its essential elements or properties directly. For example, a person who goes through a marriage ceremony with no intention of sharing a life with his spouse but solely to regularize his immigration status simulates explicitly. A positive act of the will may also be implicit or contained in another act. Often this implicit act of the will involves intending a form of marriage that is radically incompatible with the Christian understanding. For example, a person who has thoroughly appropriated the "hippy" ideology of free love and rejects the notion that permanent commitments are possible may simulate implicitly.[160]

To invalidate marriage, this positive act of the will must exclude from consent either marriage itself (*total simulation*) or one of its essential elements or properties (*partial simulation*). In total simulation, a person does not want marriage at all, but goes through a marriage either as a sham or solely as a means to achieve some end totally extrinsic to marriage. In partial simulation, a person may want a "marriage," but a marriage on one's own terms and devoid of an essential ele-

ment or property of marriage. Since simulation involves a positive act of the will, simulators must be aware, at least in an inchoate way, of what they are intending, but they need not be aware of the invalidating effect of their intentions.

Total simulation can occur in various ways. A person can simulate totally:

(1) by not intending to contract marriage at all, i.e., by reducing the ceremony to an empty show;
(2) by undergoing the ceremony solely to obtain an end absolutely extrinsic to marriage itself;
(3) by excluding from the object of his/her consent the very core of marriage, i.e., the exchange of the perpetual and exclusive right over the body;
(4) by excluding sacramentality from the marriage;[161]
(5) by substituting for the Christian idea of marriage some other notion which is genuinely antithetical to marriage.[162]

The essential properties of marriage are unity and indissolubility (c. 1056). Unity requires that marriage be an exclusive relationship between one man and one woman. Thus, a person who reserves the right to have more than one spouse simulates unity. However, recent jurisprudence has expanded the notion of unity to include the right to fidelity.

There are many ways by which the right of fidelity can be removed: a) through direct ex-

[160] See R. Jenkins, *Recent Rotal Jurisprudence on Simulation* contra Bonum Sacramenti *by an Implicit Act of the Will,* CanLawStud 551 (Washington, D.C.: Catholic University of America, 1999).

[161] Not all canonists, or even all Rotal judges, agree that exclusion of the sacramental dignity of marriage necessarily leads to total simulation. See A. Mendonça, "Exclusion of the Sacramentality of Marriage: Recent Trends in Rotal Jurisprudence," *Stud Can* 31 (1997) 5–48. See also the discussion below about exclusion of the sacramental dignity of marriage from consent.

[162] J. Johnson, "Total Simulation in Recent Rotal Jurisprudence," *Stud Can* 24 (1990) 423. This recapitulates the principles articulated in *coram* Ragni, July 19, 1983, *SRRDec* 75 (1983) 471.

clusion of the right itself; b) through the attachment to consent of a condition contrary to the obligation of fidelity; c) through concession of the right to the conjugal act to a third person; d) through an intention, even an implicit one, of excluding the obligation by manifesting a firm plan of having sexual relations with others, even those of his or her own sex; e) because of a stubborn conviction about the impossibility for frail human nature to observe the good of fidelity; f) through the limitation of the right or obligation to a definite or indefinite period of time; g) through an intention to commit adultery which prevails over the intention of giving and accepting the obligation of fidelity.[163]

Although the fact that fidelity is violated during the marriage does not dissolve the marriage, entering marriage while refusing one's spouse the right to a faithful relationship excludes the good of fidelity. Traditional jurisprudence has, however, distinguished the intention to exclude the right to a faithful relationship from the intention to concede one's spouse the right but to abuse it. The former invalidates consent, but the latter does not. Thus, a person can enter marriage intending to recognize his or her spouse's right to a faithful relationship, but foreseeing that he or she will be unfaithful should the opportunity present itself. In practice, distinguishing an intention to exclude the right itself from an intention to abuse or not to honor the right can be difficult. Often, the key to discerning the intention of the suspected simulator is his or her pattern of behavior. If a person was promiscuous or maintained a liaison with a third party before and during the marriage, he or she presumably excluded the right to fidelity; but, if the person was guilty only of a few discrete indiscretions, he or she presumably conceded the right to a faithful relationship but abused that right.

With the perhaps overly subtle distinction between the intention to deny the right and the inten-

tion to abuse the right, jurisprudence has left a certain amount of room for hedging on the *bonum fidei*. However, there is no such room for hedging on the *bonum sacramenti* or indissolubility. One either intends a perpetual union or one does not. The increased availability of civil divorce and the increased willingness of people, including Catholics, to avail themselves of this option have led jurisprudence to reconsider the various ways in which people can exclude indissolubility from their marital consent.

A person who knows the Church's teaching on marriage but consciously rejects it as "old fashioned" or "too demanding" and marries "with the understanding that he has the option, albeit hypothetical, of dissolving the bond and recovering his former status of full freedom" to enter another marriage explicitly excludes indissolubility from consent.[164] Moreover, people, whether aware of the Church's teaching on marriage or not, may be convinced that marriage is such a personal reality that its terms are defined by the spouses themselves. Such persons may formulate their own doctrine of marriage which, explicitly or implicitly, excludes indissolubility.[165] More common is the situation where people exclude indissolubility hypothetically, i.e., by retaining the right to seek a divorce if some circumstance is realized. For example, a person who grew up in a home where her father physically abused her mother may reserve the right to seek a divorce should her husband abuse her. To exclude the good of permanence, people need not be aware of the Church's teaching on the indissolubility of marriage or of the invalidating effect of their intention or desire or even anticipate the marriage will fail. What is essential is that they reserve the right to terminate the relationship either at will or if a particular circumstance occurs.

The revised code has introduced the expression "some essential element" of marriage as a possible object of simulation. The relative novelty of the expression has resulted in a lack of consensus

---

[163] *Coram* Bruno, June 15, 1990, *SRRDec* 82 (1990) 515–516.

[164] *Coram* Pompedda, July 1, 1969, *SRRDec* 61 (1969) 691.
[165] Ibid.

about which elements of marriage are so essential that their exclusion by a positive act of the will causes marital invalidity. There is, however, agreement that among marriage's essential elements are at least its ordination to the procreation and education of offspring, its ordination to the good of the spouses, and, for some commentators at least, its sacramental dignity.

Whether a particular marriage gives rise to children is, in some measure, beyond the control of the spouses. The failure to have children, whether because of the sterility of the parties or because of their conscious intention, does not in itself invalidate consent, but exclusion of the right to potentially procreative conjugal acts by a positive act of the will is invalidating. Exclusion of marriage's ordination to the procreation and education of offspring occurs when a spouse reserves to himself or herself the right to determine whether, when, and under what circumstances conjugal relations will be open to the procreation of children. Thus, the good of offspring is excluded when:

1. The right to acts per se apt for the generation of children is excluded absolutely;
2. The right to such acts is limited, even for a time;
3. The exclusion of the right, even for a time, is made a condition for marriage;
4. The exclusion of the right is implicit in the exclusion of children from the marriage;
5. The right to conjugal acts is limited to contraceptive acts only, or to conjugal acts only during the "safe time."[166]

As it has done with the *bonum fidei,* jurisprudence has distinguished the exclusion of the right to the *bonum prolis* from its non-exercise or abuse. In an age in which contraceptives are readily available, it can be difficult to determine whether a couple's decision to practice birth control constitutes an exclusion of the right to potentially procreative conjugal acts which invalidates marriage

or a decision not to exercise this right or even to abuse it, which may be morally illegitimate but does not affect marital validity. The persistent refusal by one of the spouses to honor the other's insistence that conjugal relations be open to procreation can often lead to the presumption that the right itself was excluded. Even in cases where openness to children was not a source of contention during the period of common life, an exclusion of the right may be implicit "in the consistent use of contraceptives so that acts per se apt for the generation of children never occur in the time of conjugal life, and there is no responsible objective cause for this."[167]

Marriage is ordered not only to the procreation of offspring but also to their education. Under the 1917 code, jurisprudence recognized that, for a person to marry validly, it was not sufficient for spouses to be open to the procreation of offspring. In addition, they could not validly enter marriage with an intention of bringing about the death of a fetus once conceived (e.g., by securing an abortion) or of exposing the child once born directly or indirectly (e.g., by neglect) to the danger of death.[168] However, the 1917 code did not include the exclusion of the education of children among the essential elements of marriage whose exclusion resulted in the invalidity of marriage.[169]

The 1983 code does not rule out the positive exclusion of the education of children as a basis for marital nullity. In fact, the revised code extends the obligation of parents beyond ensuring their children's physical survival and safety to include their "social, cultural, moral, and religious education" (c. 1136). This obligation has both moral and juridic dimensions, but the implications of the juridic dimension for marital consent have not yet been plumbed. Jurisprudence still needs to determine "'what is the essential minimum' of education, in which the right-duty to the transmission of human life is joined to the right-duty of its

---

[166] J. Provost, "Simulated Consent: A New Way of Looking at an Old Way of Thinking—Part I," *J* 55 (1995) 719.

[167] Ibid.
[168] See K. Schmidt, "*Educatio prolis* and the Validity of Marriage," *J* 55 (1995) 261–263.
[169] *CIC* 1086, §2.

protection, reception, and growth, as a human person, in the conjugal community."[170]

The good of the spouses to which marriage is ordered by its very nature is also an essential element of marriage. Therefore, to exclude this good from one's consent by a positive act of the will invalidates marriage. The lack of consensus about the content of the good of the spouses[171] makes it difficult to offer concrete examples of the sort of intentions *contra bonum coniugum* that would render marriage invalid.[172] Moreover, as of this writing, there are no reported decisions of the Rota that deal directly with an alleged exclusion of the good of the spouses.[173] This somewhat confused situation suggests the need for caution in admitting cases to marriage tribunals on the ground of this type of exclusion. Nevertheless, the Rota is unlikely to decide a case on such a ground unless the case reaches it on appeal from a lower court. Thus, the need for caution when dealing with this ground is not a warrant for avoiding it altogether.

Simulation of the good of the spouses may occur if a person, perhaps for motives quite extraneous to marriage, excludes from consent "'the right to the intimate partnership of persons,' which is an essential part of the formal substantial element of marital consent."[174] Such a situation may be the hypothetical case formulated by Jemolo in which a man marries a woman solely to make her life miserable to avenge the injuries her family had inflicted on his. Such extreme cases may, however,

be rather rare and may be difficult to distinguish from cases of total simulation.[175]

According to the Church's teaching, when two baptized persons marry validly, their marriage is by that fact a sacrament (c. 1055, §2). When one baptized person marries another while excluding the sacramental dignity of marriage from his consent, the marriage is invalid. This much is traditional jurisprudence. Recently, however, canonists have discussed how cases in which the exclusion of marriage's sacramental dignity is alleged should be dealt with in tribunals. The traditional position is that exclusion of sacramental dignity is a species of total simulation. The marriage contract and the marital sacrament are so intimately intertwined that to exclude one is to exclude the other.[176] More recently, canonists have argued that, at least from a psychological perspective, a person can genuinely desire a marriage, but one bereft of the quality of sacramentality. Thus, simulation of sacramental dignity is a species of partial simulation in which an essential element or property of marriage is excluded from consent.[177]

The mere fact that a baptized person adheres to a non-Catholic church whose doctrine rejects the sacramentality of marriage is not sufficient to prove that he or she excluded sacramental dignity from consent. The person's religious beliefs would be presumed to be at most a general or habitual intention and not the positive act of the will required for simulation. Nevertheless, during the course of preparation for a Catholic wedding, the Church's teaching on the sacramentality of marriage may be brought to the non-Catholic's attention so pointedly that he is prompted to translate this habitual will

---

[170] A. Stankiewicz, "L'esclusione della procreazione ed educazione della prole," in *La simulazione del consenso matrimoniale canonico,* ed. P. Bonnet (Vatican City: Libreria Editrice Vaticana, 1990) 169. For suggestions as to where jurisprudence may be moving in this area, see Schmidt, 243–280.

[171] See the commentary on c. 1055.

[172] See L. DeLuca, "L'esclusione del 'bonum coniugum,'" in *La simulazione del consenso matrimoniale canonico,* 125–137; and *Il "bonum coniugum" nel matrimonio canonico* (Vatican City: Libreria Editrice Vaticana, 1996).

[173] Some first instance decisions on the ground of exclusion of the good of the spouses have been issued, however. See *Il Diritto Ecclesiastico* 104 (1993) 21–76.

[174] E. Pfnausch, "The Good of the Spouses in Rotal Jurisprudence: New Horizons," *J* 56 (1996) 555.

[175] Ibid.

[176] Gasparri, n. 827. More recently, see C. Burke, "The Sacramentality of Marriage: Canonical Reflections," *ME* 119 (1994) 556.

[177] Z. Grocholewski, "Crisis doctrinae et iurisprudentiae rotalis circa exclusionem dignitatis sacramentalis in contractu matrimoniali," *P* 67 (1978) 283–295; and D. Faltin, "The Exclusion of the Sacramentality of Marriage with Particular Reference to the Marriage of Baptized Non-Believers," in *Marriage Studies IV,* ed. J. Alesandro (Washington, D.C.: CLSA, 1990) 66–104.

into a positive act of the will excluding sacramental dignity from consent to this marriage.[178]

Conditional Consent

Since the canonical tradition has treated marriage as a contract, marriage can, like other contracts, be entered into conditionally. A condition is a circumstance attached to consent by a positive act of the will in such a way that the validity of the marriage is made dependent on the verification of the circumstance. In other words, people condition their marital consent when "a particular circumstance is so important to them that they rate it higher than marriage itself and that, if they cannot have the circumstance or quality, they do not want the marriage either."[179] Conditions can concern the future (e.g., I marry you on condition that you are drafted in the first round of the NBA draft next year), the present (e.g., I marry you on condition that you are a virgin), or the past (e.g., I marry you on condition that you have never been married before).

Since in conditional consent some circumstance is so important to the person that the marriage is subordinated to it, it is important to distinguish true conditions from other circumstances that do not enter into marital consent itself. A condition is not the same as the cause of the contract or the motive for marrying a particular person (e.g., I marry you because you are rich). Nor is a condition equivalent to a mode or "the addition of a certain obligation to a contract already completed"[180] (e.g., I marry you,

but, after our marriage, you must return to active practice of the Catholic faith). A condition is also distinct from a demonstration or a quality that is more or less taken for granted in one's future spouse (e.g., I marry you who are Irish).[181] Finally, a condition is not the same as a "prerequisite" (sometimes called a "postulate" or a "presupposition") or a quality that prompts the initial decision to marry and significantly affects the decision to enter an engagement but does not, in theory, influence the subsequent decision to marry.[182]

Causes of the contract, modes, demonstrations, and prerequisites are not equivalent to conditions because they do not directly enter into the actual marital contracting itself, but are side issues. Nevertheless, these neat canonical distinctions should not obscure the fact that none of these quasi-conditions is any more than a hair's breadth from a true condition. Thus, in practice, tribunals need to be attentive not only to the way in which parties articulate their intentions with regard to marriage, but also to what they really meant. In the end, the concrete facts of the particular case are more important than canonical distinctions.

To invalidate marriage, a condition attached to consent can be either explicit or implicit. A person positing a condition need not be aware that such a condition has the potential for invalidating consent.

> People are generally unaware of such legalities and in no way realize that entering marriage conditionally results in invalidity. . . . And consequently Rotal jurisprudence, especially as it has evolved in recent years, holds that a true condition can coexist with ignorance of its invalidating effect as long as it is clear that the person would not have consented to marry unless the quality had been present.[183]

Often a person's doubt about a quality or circumstance prompts him or her to attach a condi-

---

[178] See A. Mendonça, "Exclusion of the Sacramentality of Marriage: Recent Trends in Rotal Jurisprudence," *Stud Can* 31 (1997) 5–48. Some Rotal judges have also treated exclusion of sacramental dignity as a species of determining error (c. 1099). See A. Stankiewicz, "Errore circa le proprietà e la dignità sacramentale del matrimonio," *ME* 109 (1984) 470–486; and M. Pompedda, "Faith and the Sacramentality of Marriage—Lack of Faith and Matrimonial Consent: Juridical Aspects," in *Marriage Studies IV,* 33–65.

[179] *Coram* Pinto, June 26, 1971, *SRRDec* 63 (1971) 560.

[180] R. Colantonio, "La condicio de futuro," in *Il consenso matrimoniale condizionato: Dottrina e giurisprudenza recente* (Vatican City: Libreria Editrice Vaticana, 1993) 40.

[181] Ibid., 37.

[182] Ibid. See also Wrenn, *The Invalid Marriage,* 158–159.

[183] *Coram* Pinto, June 26, 1971, *SRRDec* 63 (1971) 560.

tion to consent. While the existence of such a doubt can be extremely helpful in proving that a condition was appended to consent and Rotal jurisprudence has often insisted on it as a necessary element of proof, a particular quality can be so important to a person that his or her obsession with it prompts the attachment of a condition even without a doubt.[184]

For a person to make consent to marriage conditional on the verification of some circumstance, that circumstance should have some objective importance, and its presence or absence should have the potential to have a significant impact on a couple's future life. Often, the values of the culture in which a person is immersed may help to identify circumstances important enough to be the object of a condition. For example, in some cultures a woman's virginity at the time of marriage is more highly prized than in others. Nevertheless, it is ultimately the individual's subjective assessment of the importance of a particular circumstance that determines whether it became the object of a condition.

Future Conditions

Canon 1102 — §1. A marriage subject to a condition about the future cannot be contracted validly.

The 1917 code declared that future conditions that were not contrary to the substance of marriage but were necessary (e.g., if the sun rises tomorrow), impossible (e.g., if you grow wings and fly), or indecent (e.g., if you will submit to unnatural sexual acts) were presumed not to have been attached to consent. Future conditions contrary to the substance of marriage were treated as the equivalent of simulation and invalidated marriage. However, licit future conditions suspended the validity of marriage until the condition was realized or not.[185] To suspend the validity of marriage, it was sufficient that the future licit condition con-

cern a circumstance that would occur within a few years of the wedding and be reasonably specific (e.g., I marry you on condition that you earn your law degree within three years).[186]

The 1983 code has thoroughly revised the law governing future conditions attached to consent. Since November 27, 1983, all marriages entered into with a condition concerning the future are invalid. The recognition that consent whose validity was made dependent on some future contingency is incompatible with consent as the self-giving of the spouses to establish a partnership of the whole of life prompted this change in the law. Moreover, allowing a future condition to suspend the validity of marriage is "a 'corrupting yeast,' that is, a device that undermines the principle of the indissolubility of the matrimonial bond and introduces into marriage a state of uncertainty that is absolutely alien to and therefore incompatible with it."[187]

Nevertheless, the revised law invalidating marriages entered into with future conditions is considered to be a matter of positive law.[188] Therefore, this law does not have retroactive effect and cannot be used to judge cases involving marriages entered prior to November 27, 1983. These cases must be judged in accord with the law and jurisprudence that developed under the 1917 code. If canon 1102, §1 is a matter of positive ecclesiastical law, it is also not applicable to the marriages of two non-Catholics (c. 11).

Past and Present Conditions

§2. A marriage entered into subject to a condition about the past or the present is valid or not insofar as that which is subject to the condition exists or not.

§3. The condition mentioned in §2, however, cannot be placed licitly without the written permission of the local ordinary.

---

[184] *Coram* Stankiewicz, January 30, 1992, in *Il consenso matrimoniale condizionato,* 150–151.

[185] *CIC* 1092, 1°–3°.

[186] Wrenn, *The Invalid Marriage,* 157.

[187] Colantonio, 46.

[188] *Comm* 3 (1971) 77. See L. Notaro, "Retroattività-irretroattività del. can. 1102, par. 1," in *Il consenso matrimoniale condizionato,* 61–71.

If marriage is entered into with a condition concerning the past or the present, the validity of the marriage depends on the existence of the circumstance that is the object of the condition at the time of consent. Only a true condition that was attached to consent and never revoked influences the validity of marriage. Proof of such a condition usually requires that the person had harbored doubts about the existence of the circumstance or quality or at least was subjectively obsessed with it so that the doubts or obsession prompted him or her to subordinate the marriage to the existence of the circumstance or quality. If the person who is said to have consented conditionally took steps to terminate the marriage as soon as the presence or absence of the circumstance or quality that was the object of the condition was verified, he or she presumably consented conditionally.[189]

It is not sufficient, however, that the person took the quality for granted but would have formulated a condition had there been any evident reason for doubting the quality's presence or even that most people would have formulated such a condition had they had reason to think about the circumstance. Such conditions are interpretive, not actual. Thus, when, prior to their marriage, a woman had no reason to think that her fiancé was a "cross-dresser" and she left him immediately after discovering, while on the honeymoon, that he was, the marriage would probably not be invalid because of her conditional consent. It may, however, be invalid because of the error imposed on her by his deceit (c. 1098).

To attach a past or present condition to consent lawfully, a person must have the written permission of the local ordinary. Although this stipulation was not found in the 1917 code, it was recognized as normative by most canonists.[190] If a local ordinary is aware that a couple is planning to marry conditionally, there may be compelling pastoral reasons not only to refuse the permission but to prohibit the marriage until the condition

has been verified or revoked (c. 1077, §1). However, the refusal of permission or the failure to seek it affects only the lawfulness of the marriage and not its validity. The marriage will be valid or not depending on whether the condition is met.

The Eastern code differs from the Latin discipline on past and present conditions attached to consent. Consent to marriage with a condition of any kind attached is invalid.[191] Thus, an Eastern Catholic who attaches a past or present condition to consent marries invalidly even if the condition is verified. For example, an Eastern Catholic man who marries a woman on condition that he is the father of the child she is carrying does so invalidly even if he is the father of her child.

Force and Fear

Canon 1103 — A marriage is invalid if entered into because of force or grave fear from without, even if unintentionally inflicted, so that a person is compelled to choose marriage in order to be free from it.

Freedom in choosing one's state of life and, if that choice is for marriage, in choosing one's spouse is a basic human right recognized by the Church's teaching office.[192] External coercion that seriously compromises a person's marital freedom violates this right and is, therefore, unjust. Moreover, external coercion contradicts the very nature of marriage as an intimate partnership of life and love.[193] Thus, canon law invalidates marriages entered into as a result of grave fear even though consent, the efficient cause of marriage, is given, albeit under duress.[194]

The ultimate reason why fear has an invalidating effect . . . is that marriage by its very

---

[189] *Coram* Stankiewicz, January 20, 1992, in *Il consenso matrimoniale condizionato*, 152.

[190] See Wernz-Vidal, 5: n. 515.

[191] *CCEO* 826.

[192] *GS* 26.

[193] *GS* 48.

[194] This is the reason that juridic acts in general are invalid only if the extrinsic force is irresistible (c. 125, §1) but are valid but rescindable if the force is merely grave and unjust (c. 125, §2). Thus, c. 1103 is an exception to the general norm governing the validity of juridic acts.

divine institution is a community of life and love between the spouses. Where there is not love but aversion, a fundamental element of this communion of life and love is lacking.[195]

Force (*vis*) is physical or moral coercion brought to bear on another person; fear (*metus*) is the result of this force on the one on whom it is inflicted. If the force exerted is irresistible (as may be the case when a "shotgun wedding" includes a real, loaded shotgun), the resulting marriage is invalid. Outside such cases of irresistible force, fear must be grave, extrinsic, and causative to invalidate a marriage.

Common Fear

Fear may be absolutely or relatively grave. Fear is absolutely grave when it results from a cause that would intimidate a mature and well-balanced person sufficiently to compel that person to enter an unwanted marriage. Examples of causes of absolutely grave fear are threats of death, imprisonment, or disinheritance. Immature, vulnerable, or insecure people may be browbeaten into marriage by threats of lesser gravity. Relatively grave fear may be induced by threats of defamation, withdrawal of college tuition assistance, loss of a job, or eviction from a home. Although relatively grave fear may be somewhat subjective, it must have some objective weight, and there must be a prudent reason to believe that threats would be carried out if the person refused to marry. Otherwise, the force prodding a person toward marriage would be intrinsic or self-imposed.[196]

Invalidating force and fear must come from a source outside the affected person. The fear cannot result from scrupulosity, a sense of moral or social obligation, or some other internal psychological process. Moreover, since coercing a person to marry is unjust and only a human act can be just or unjust, the source of the fear must be a human agent and not some impersonal cause. Thus, a man who marries his pregnant girlfriend out of fear that he will be killed in an impending military operation and will be punished by God for failing "to do the right thing" or the pregnant young woman who marries out of fear that she would otherwise be unable to support herself and her child do not marry invalidly because of the influence of grave fear inflicted *ab extrinseco*. In such cases, however, the fear, if sufficiently grave, may temporarily impede a person's ability to exercise due discretion (c. 1095, 2°).

Grave fear from without must also cause marriage in order to invalidate it. "Marriage, in other words, must be the effect, of which the cause (the principal and determining cause) is fear, so that if the fear (the cause) were not present, marriage (the effect) would not take place."[197] Under the pressure of moral coercion, the person must have no other realistic option except marriage to escape the evil threatened. If a person has realistic courses of action available besides marriage, even if they are no more attractive than marriage, he or she presumably marries "with fear" but not "because of fear." Thus, a young Arab woman who is pregnant out of wedlock may have no option but to marry to avoid being killed to preserve her family's "honor," but a twenty-something career woman in North America also pregnant out of wedlock may have several options for dealing with her predicament.

To invalidate marriage, the force that gives rise to grave fear need not be exerted directly to bring about a marriage. It is sufficient that the force be present and that it bring about the marriage indirectly.[198] For example, when the father of a woman, who is a junior at Harvard, discovers that his daughter has been living with her boyfriend and insists that she transfer to a small liberal arts college near their home and live at home while completing her degree, the father does not

---

[195] U. Navarrete, "Oportetne ut supprimantur verba 'ab extrinseco et iniuste incussum' in can. 1087, circa metum irritantem matrimonium?" in *Ius Populi Dei* (Rome: Gregorian University, 1972) 3:591.

[196] Wrenn, *The Invalid Marriage,* 163.

[197] Ibid., 164.

[198] *Comm* 16 (1983) 234.

directly intend to force his daughter to marry. In fact, his primary intention may be to break up her relationship with her boyfriend. However, the unintended consequence of his intervention may be to prompt her decision to marry the man, even though she knows she does not love him, because she can see no other way to maintain the benefits of a Harvard education. The one exerting the force that leads to grave fear need not be aware of the consequences of his actions. What is critical is that, even unintentionally, the person's actions result in grave fear.

The 1917 code had stipulated that grave fear invalidated marriage only if it were "unjustly inflicted."[199] In the revised code, the phrase "unjustly inflicted" no longer qualifies the fear that invalidates marriage. This deletion is a recognition that, no matter how justified one's anger or disappointment at a person may be, there is no justification for compelling him or her to choose marriage unwillingly.

The grave fear that invalidates marriage is one by which "a person is compelled to choose *marriage* in order to be free from it" (c. 1103). It is not necessary that the person be compelled to choose a marriage with a particular person; it is sufficient that he or she be compelled by the fear to enter an unwanted marriage, even if he or she is free in the choice of a partner. For example, a person whose parents stipulate that he must marry by the age of twenty-five or forfeit a substantial inheritance may have no choice except to marry to avoid a grave financial loss, but still be free in the choice of the person he marries.

The acid test for determining whether grave fear caused a marriage is evidence of aversion or repugnance on the part of the one who claims to have experienced such fear. A person compelled to marry by grave fear may exhibit aversion toward the unwanted partner. However, a person may genuinely like his or her partner as a friend but exhibit repugnance not toward this person, but toward marriage with him or her. "The ordinary signs or symptoms of aversion are crying and complaining before the marriage, sadness and denial of affection. The absence of such signs after the marriage proves nothing since it is then presumed that one is making the best of a bad situation."[200] While it is virtually impossible to prove a case of force and fear without some evidence of aversion, aversion itself gives rise only to a presumption of grave fear. The presence of fear itself must be proven.

Reverential Fear

A person in a relationship of dependence or subordination to another is particularly susceptible to moral coercion to enter marriage, even when the duress inflicted might not be considered objectively grave if the victim of the coercion were not dependent on or subordinate to the coercer. On the one hand, the subject person in such a relationship has an instinctive respect for and desire to please the superior; on the other hand, the subject is fearful of offending the superior and incurring his or her indignation. In a situation in which the subject can avoid offending or can assuage the indignation of the superior only by marrying, the resulting fear can compel him or her to choose an unpalatable marriage. Although such "reverential fear" can easily arise in any relationship of dependence or subordination, it most commonly occurs in the relationship of parents with their children. The kind of fear that can arise in the parent-child relationship highlights the fact that the specific object of reverential fear is not a particular evil threatened by the parent but the parental indignation itself. Thus, a young woman, pregnant out of wedlock and threatened by disinheritance by her father if she does not marry her lover may know that her father will not carry out his threat to disinherit her. However, knowing also that he will never forgive her if she does not marry, she may marry out of reverential fear because of the credible threat of ongoing parental indignation.

Nevertheless, to invalidate marriage, the fear of parental indignation must have some objective

---

[199] *CIC* 1087, §1.

[200] Wrenn, *The Invalid Marriage,* 165.

gravity. In other words, the person must have some probable basis for believing that his or her refusal to marry will result in harsh and enduring parental indignation. Indignation is not to be confused with efforts of parents to advise their children, to warn them, or even to try to persuade them to marry or to marry a particular person. While these moderate efforts at persuasion may prompt a child to marry freely but reluctantly, they are not usually sufficient to induce invalidating reverential fear. Such fear is more likely to be evoked by "severities, cruelties, absolute and imperious commands, threats, curses, a grim and gloomy mien, angry badgering, ceaseless and uncivil complaining, constant and annoying requests"[201] that leave the child with no option but marriage to escape this importuning.

Applicability of Force and Fear to Marriages of Non-Catholics

Since canon 1103 is an exception to the general principle that merely grave fear does not invalidate a juridic act (c. 125, §2), it could be argued that the canon is a matter of merely ecclesiastical law and, therefore, no longer applicable to the marriages of non-Catholics (c. 11). However, on April 23, 1987, the then Pontifical Commission for the Interpretation of the Code of Canon Law responded affirmatively to the question "whether the defective consent of canon 1103 can be applied to the marriages of non-Catholics."[202] Since non-Catholics are no longer bound by merely ecclesiastical laws (c. 11), this authentic interpretation seems to affirm that grave force and fear invalidate marriage by the natural law.[203]

Presence of the Spouses at the Exchange of Consent

Canon 1104 — §1. To contract a marriage validly the contracting parties must be present together, either in person or by proxy.

§2. Those being married are to express matrimonial consent in words or, if they cannot speak, through equivalent signs.

Before the 1917 code, it was legitimate to contract marriage by letter.[204] This practice was abrogated by canon 1088, §1 of the 1917 code, which has been repeated virtually verbatim in the present canon. Since matrimonial consent is an act of the will by which the spouses mutually give and accept one another (c. 1057, §2), the presence of the spouses for the exchange of consent either personally or through their duly appointed proxies is required for the validity of the marriage. The revised code has added the word "together" (*una*) to canon 1088, §1 of the 1917 code to emphasize that the spouses must be present simultaneously for the exchange of consent. Thus, a marriage would be invalid if one spouse appeared before the official witness to give his consent while the other spouse appeared to give consent at another time or before a different official minister or in a different place.

In June of 1949, the Holy Office declared that the presence of both spouses for the exchange of consent was required for validity not only for marriages involving at least one Catholic but also for those involving all baptized Christians, whether Catholic or not.[205] A month later, the Holy Office issued a private reply declaring that a marriage could be declared invalid if the parties were not present together for the exchange of consent, if at least one of them was certainly baptized.[206] These responses were little more than applications to marriage of canon 12 of the 1917 code which

---

[201] Ibid., 166.

[202] CodCom, response, April 23, 1987, *AAS* 79 (1987) 1132.

[203] See L. Wrenn, "Urban Navarrete, S.J., and the Response of the Code Commission on Force and Fear," *J* 51 (1991) 119–137; and U. Navarrete, "Responsa Pontificiae Commissionis Codici Iuris Canonici authentice interpretando," *P* 73 (1988) 497–510.

[204] F. Cappello, *Summa Iuris Canonici* (Rome: Gregorian University, 1962) 382.

[205] SCOf, decl, June 30,1949, *AAS* 41 (1949) 427.

[206] SCOf, response, July 15, 1949, *CLD* 3, 446–447.

bound all baptized persons, whether Catholic or not, to observe merely ecclesiastical laws unless they were expressly exempted and of canon 1016 of the same code which subjected the marriages of the baptized to the requirements of ecclesiastical law. However, baptized non-Catholics are no longer bound by merely ecclesiastical laws (c. 11). Thus, the apparent basis for the congregation's declaration has been undermined. The simultaneous presence of two baptized non-Catholics is now required for the validity of their consent only if it is required by the law of their church or ecclesial community or the law to which it defers.[207] The marriages of the unbaptized are governed by civil law.[208]

If the spouses can speak, they are to express their consent in words. If not, they can express their consent in equivalent signs. In either case, the expression of consent must clearly and unequivocally communicate to those present the spouses' intent to enter marriage. For the marriages of Catholics, including mixed marriages celebrated according to the canonical form, marital consent should be exchanged through one of the formulae prescribed in the approved liturgical books. While episcopal conferences can propose formulae for the exchange of consent that differ from those in the Roman Ritual,[209] spouses and official witnesses are not free to alter the approved formulae or to compose their own. Such adaptations do not necessarily invalidate consent, but they do render it illicit.[210] Adaptations of the formulae for the exchange of consent and original compositions need to be scrutinized carefully to ensure that their content is consistent with the Church's teaching on marriage. If these formulae exclude an essential element or property of marriage, the marriage must be presumed to be invalid (c. 1101, §1).

[207] See *CCEO* 780–781.
[208] See the commentary on c. 1057, §1.
[209] *Rite of Marriage,* 17.
[210] J. Huels, *The Pastoral Companion* (Quincy, Ill.: Franciscan Press, 1995) 248.

Proxy Marriages

Canon 1105 — §1. To enter into a marriage validly by proxy it is required that:
 1° there is a special mandate to contract with a specific person;
 2° the proxy is designated by the one mandating and fulfills this function personally.
 §2. To be valid the mandate must be signed by the one mandating and by the pastor or ordinary of the place where the mandate is given, or by a priest delegated by either of them, or at least by two witnesses, or it must be made by means of a document which is authentic according to the norm of civil law.
 §3. If the one mandating cannot write, this is to be noted in the mandate itself and another witness is to be added who also signs the document; otherwise, the mandate is invalid.
 §4. If the one mandating revokes the mandate or develops amentia before the proxy contracts in his or her name, the marriage is invalid even if the proxy or the other contracting party does not know this.

Since the canonical tradition has treated marriage as a contract, it has logically made provision for marriage to be entered into by proxy like other contracts. A proxy is an agent who is authorized to perform juridic acts on behalf of a principal. The juridic acts performed by the proxy entail the same obligations for the principal as if he or she had performed them personally. Thus, a marriage entered into by a lawful proxy binds the principal to a perpetual and exclusive relationship with the other party.

Since a proxy marriage entails serious obligations for the principal, a proxy must have a special mandate that expressly authorizes him or her to contract marriage on behalf of the principal. Only the principal can grant such a mandate and the authorization cannot be delegated by the designated proxy. For its validity, the mandate must be signed by the principal and by the pastor or the local ordinary of the place where it was issued or by a priest delegated by either of them. Other legitimate options are for the mandate to be signed by the principal and two witnesses and for it to be prepared in a form recognized by civil law. If the principal cannot write, that fact is to be mentioned in the mandate, and an additional witness is to sign it. If all these requirements are not fulfilled, both the mandate and the marriage contracted pursuant to it are invalid.

Proxy marriages usually occur when the parties cannot be physically present to exchange consent but there is some compelling reason for marrying without delay. This might occur, for example, when a man is on military duty overseas and there is an urgent need to contract marriage to legitimate a child or to make his spouse eligible for dependent's benefits. Before a marriage can be entered into by proxy, all of the usual canonical and civil requirements for the valid and lawful celebration of marriage must be observed. In addition, the permission of the local ordinary is required for the lawfulness of a proxy marriage (c. 1071, §1, 7°). Although canon law permits proxy marriages, most civil jurisdictions in the United States do not.[211]

Proxies can be of the same or the opposite sex as the principal. Although proxies must intend to carry out the mandates of their principals, their own intentions with regard to marriage are irrelevant. Although the principal need not be aware when or where the proxy contracts marriage on his or her behalf, the principal must intend a perpetual and exclusive marriage ordered to the good of the spouses and the procreation and education of offspring when he or she mandates the proxy and not retract this intention before the mandate is executed. However, if the principal revokes the mandate or becomes insane before the proxy contracts marriage on his or her behalf, the marriage is invalid even if the proxy and the other party are unaware of these developments.

The law presumes that proxy marriages will be contracted in accord with the canonical form

of marriage before an authorized minister and two witnesses. The *Rite of Marriage* does not explicitly prohibit the use of the nuptial Mass and blessing for proxy marriages as had the preconciliar Roman Missal.[212] Nevertheless, the full liturgical celebration of marriage is quite inappropriate for proxy marriages. The Eastern code does not provide norms regulating proxy marriages. Eastern law has never been as enamored of the contractual model for marriage as has the Latin tradition. However, the Eastern code does mention the possibility for the particular law of a church *sui iuris* to allow such marriages.[213]

Marriage Consent through an Interpreter

Canon 1106 — A marriage can be contracted through an interpreter; the pastor is not to assist at it, however, unless he is certain of the trustworthiness of the interpreter.

Marriage consent can be expressed through an interpreter if the official witness or the other witnesses do not understand the language of the parties. The spouses express their consent in their own language, and the interpreter then translates their expressions of consent for the benefit of the others present. The pastor of the place where the marriage is to be celebrated is not to assist at such a marriage or delegate someone else to do so unless he has first satisfied himself that the interpreter is reliable.

The services of an interpreter may also be needed because the parties themselves do not share a common language. For example, military personnel on duty overseas have often married natives, even though neither spouse can speak more than a few words in the other's language. While the use of an interpreter for the celebration of marriage would be appropriate, such cases do raise difficult pastoral questions. Without a common language, the spouses' ability to communicate with one another will be severely impaired and the prospect for a happy outcome of the marriage dubious.

---

[211] Proxy marriages are permitted in Florida, Kansas, Oklahoma, Idaho, Iowa, Montana, Nebraska, Nevada, and New Mexico. They are permitted in Texas only if the couple is separated by military service. No other jurisdictions recognize proxy marriages. See Doyle, in *CLSA Com,* 791.

[212] *Missale Romanum,* xxvi, nn. 379–381.
[213] *CCEO* 837, §2.

*Presumed Continuance of Consent
to Invalid Marriages*

Canon 1107 — Even if a marriage was entered into invalidly by reason of an impediment or a defect of form, the consent given is presumed to persist until its revocation is established.

Impediments disqualify persons from marriage, but they do not deprive them of the capacity to elicit true matrimonial consent. Similarly, persons bound by canonical form can elicit naturally sufficient consent, but the consent lacks juridic efficacy if this form is not observed. Consequently, the law presumes that, when a person consents to a marriage that is invalid because of an impediment or a defect of form, the consent continues until its revocation has been proven.

This presumption is of particular relevance when there is a question of granting a radical sanation of a marriage invalid because of an impediment or defect of form (cc. 1161–1165). The continuation of naturally sufficient consent is an essential precondition for the granting of a radical sanation (c. 1162). The presumption that such consent continues allows the granting of a radical sanation without proof that consent has continued. It is rather the revocation of consent that must be proved.

CHAPTER V
THE FORM OF THE CELEBRATION
OF MARRIAGE[214]
[cc. 1108–1123][215]

The form of marriage is the complex of external formalities and ceremonies required by law for its proper celebration. The *canonical* form consists in those solemnities required for the Church to recognize the union as a valid marriage. The *litur-*

gical form consists in those rites required to ensure that the celebration adequately expresses "the mystery of the unity and fruitful love between Christ and the Church" in which the spouses share (c. 1063, 3°). The form of marriage has evolved in different ways in the churches of the East and West. The Latin church has primarily emphasized the role of the consent of the spouses in bringing marriage into existence and so has considered them the ministers of the sacrament of matrimony. The Eastern churches, while acknowledging the necessity of the spouses' personal consent, have primarily emphasized the role of the priest's crowning and blessing of the couple in effecting the sacrament and so see him as its minister.[216]

Historical Synopsis

The early Church had no distinctively Christian ritual for the celebration of marriage. Instead, it accepted the forms of marrying customary among the various peoples who had accepted the gospel. In time, Christian elements were grafted on to these customary forms, and a role for the ecclesial community in the celebration of marriage was recognized. It became increasingly common for the local bishop or presbyter to be present at the weddings of members of his flock and to bless them. Eventually liturgical rites emerged that incorporated elements of family-centered wedding customs into the context of the celebration of the Eucharist. The faithful were encouraged to observe these liturgical rites to solemnize their marriages, but observance of these rituals was not a condition for ecclesial recognition of the validity of marriage until rather late.[217]

Although Roman law regulated the social consequences of marriage in considerable detail, it

---

[214] See Doyle, in *CLSA Com,* 792–800; Lüdicke, in *Münster Com,* Einführung vor 1108/1–1123/1; R. Navarro Valls, in *Pamplona ComEng,* 701–710; and Kelly, in *CLSGBI Com,* 622–632.

[215] See *CCEO* 828–842.

[216] See F. McManus, "Marriage in the Canons of the Eastern Catholic Churches," *J* 54 (1994) 56–80; and U. Navarrete, "De ministro sacramenti matrimonii in Ecclesia latina et in Ecclesiis Orientalibus: Tentamen explicationis concordantis," *P* 84 (1995) 711–733.

[217] See K. Stevenson, *To Join Together: The Rite of Marriage* (New York: Pueblo, 1987) 16–104.

showed little interest in the formalities by which marriage was constituted. Consent with *affectio maritalis* between the spouses was necessary and sufficient to constitute a marriage, but the form in which this consent was exchanged was a matter of indifference.[218] The Latin church's reception of the principle that consent alone constitutes marriage impeded the emergence of a mandatory ecclesiastical form for entering marriage. A mandatory form emerged earlier in the Eastern churches in response to the heightened significance attributed to the crowning and blessing of the spouses by the priest. For the churches of the Byzantine tradition, Emperor Leo VI (886–912) made observance of the liturgical form obligatory for all free persons. The obligation of observing this form was extended to slaves by Emperor Alexis Comnenos (1088–1118).[219]

In the West, the Roman law consensual model of marriage coexisted rather uneasily with Germanic marriage customs that highlighted the public nature of marriage by emphasizing the importance of the role of parents and of consummation in constituting a marriage. Ultimately, the consensual model triumphed through the decretals of Alexander III and his successors during the twelfth century. However, this triumph opened the door to a flood of clandestine marriages, i.e., marriages contracted without any public form and not susceptible to proof, and their socially disruptive consequences. Conciliar legislation attempted to compel compliance with the public liturgical form by threatening penal sanctions for its nonobservance.[220] However, this legislation did not declare clandestine unions invalid because it was believed that consent had been established by Christ as the essential form of the sacrament of matrimony and, therefore, it was beyond the Church's power to add to or detract from that form.

Stung by the Protestant reformers' castigation of the Catholic Church's failure to extirpate clandestine marriages, the Council of Trent in its decree *Tametsi* declared disqualified for marriage those who failed to solemnize their unions "in the presence of the parish priest or another priest with the permission of the parish priest or ordinary, and two or three witnesses."[221] The rationale for this decree was that, although the Church lacked authority to alter the substance of the sacrament of matrimony, it did possess the authority to establish impediments to marriage insofar as it was a contract. Thus, Trent made failure to marry before the proper pastor or his delegate and two witnesses a disqualifying impediment to marriage.

The Tridentine decree succeeded only partially in stamping out clandestine marriages. Since it was binding only in areas where it had been promulgated, it was without effect in most Protestant areas of Europe and in the colonies of Protestant powers. For example, in what is now the United States, *Tametsi* was never promulgated except in a few isolated pockets of originally French and Spanish colonies. In addition, the decree created new problems. Where it had been promulgated, it bound all the baptized, whether they were Catholic or not. Nor did it make clear whether the pastor of the man or the woman was competent to witness marriages or to delegate another priest to do so. Moreover, by requiring only the priest's physical presence at the marriage and not his active and voluntary participation, *Tametsi* recognized the validity of marriages at which the pastor's presence was coerced.

To overcome these problems, the Congregation for the Council eventually promulgated the decree *Ne temere* in 1909. This new decree extended the obligation of observing the canonical form of marriage to the whole Latin church, but it bound only those who had been baptized in or received into the Catholic Church and those who sought to marry them. *Ne temere* specifically required that the priest participate in the ceremony actively by asking for and receiving the consent of the parties and that his participation be voluntary. The decree also authorized pastors and ordinaries to witness

---

[218] Treggiari, *Roman Marriage*, 170.

[219] J. Meyendorf, *Marriage: An Orthodox Perspective* (Crestwood, N.Y.: St. Vladimir Seminary, 1975) 30–31.

[220] Lateran IV (1215), c. 51.

[221] Council of Trent, sess. XXIV, *de ref. matrim.*, cap. 1.

marriages validly within their respective territories whether the spouses resided there or not.

The discipline of *Ne temere* was substantially incorporated into the 1917 code. However, this code exempted from the obligation of observing the canonical form those born of non-Catholic parents who were baptized into the Catholic Church as infants but who had not been raised as Catholics.[222] The difficulty of determining whether people baptized in the Catholic Church as infants had been raised as Catholics prompted Pius XII to abrogate this exemption effective January 1, 1949.[223]

The Function of the Form of Marriage

Although a mandatory form for celebrating marriage was introduced in the Latin church to attempt to address the late medieval problem of clandestine marriages, its function is not limited to ensuring the public character of marriage. Nor has modern civil legislation preventing clandestine marriages rendered the canonical form redundant. At a pastoral level, the requirement of canonical form provides a privileged opportunity for the Church's ministers to help couples to assess their suitability and readiness for marriage and to provide them with appropriate catechesis and immediate preparation for marriage and its liturgical celebration (c. 1063). At a more theological level, the mandatory form ensures that celebration of marriage will embody at least the minimal ecclesial and liturgical dimensions consistent with the celebration of a sacrament of the Church. The fact that the Eastern churches have also evolved a mandatory form for celebrating marriage, albeit by a very different path, suggests that the historical circumstances that led the Latin church to impose a mandatory form for marriage and a typically Western preoccupation with juridic formalities have obscured the necessary relationship between

the manner in which marriage is celebrated in the Church and its sacramental nature.

The 1983 code devotes sixteen canons to the form of marriage. These canons deal with: the elements of canonical form (c. 1108), the requisites for valid assistance at marriage (cc. 1109–1112), the requisites for licit assistance at marriage (cc. 1113–1115), the extraordinary canonical form (c. 1116), those bound by the canonical form of marriage (c. 1117), the place where marriage is to be celebrated (c. 1118), the liturgical form of marriage (cc. 1119–1120), and the recording of marriages (cc. 1121–1123).

THE ELEMENTS OF CANONICAL FORM

Canon 1108 — §1. Only those marriages are valid which are contracted before the local ordinary, pastor, or a priest or deacon delegated by either of them, who assist, and before two witnesses according to the rules expressed in the following canons and without prejudice to the exceptions mentioned in cann. 144, 1112, §1, 1116, and 1127, §§1–2.

An Authorized Witness

When a Catholic enters marriage, the Church ordinarily recognizes the union as valid only if the canonical form of marriage is observed in its celebration. In other words, one must exchange marital consent in the presence of an authorized minister of the Church and at least two additional witnesses. Subsequent canons regulate in detail who is considered an authorized minister of marriage in the Church.

Two Additional Witnesses

The presence of at least two additional witnesses is as essential for the valid celebration of a marriage as the presence of an authorized minister. Unlike sponsors at baptism (c. 872) and confirmation (c. 892), these witnesses at marriage assume no responsibility to attest to the faith of those entering marriage or to assist them in living

---

[222] *CIC* 1099, §2.

[223] Pius XII, *mp Abrogatur alterum comma paragraphi secundae canonis 1099,* August 1, 1948, *AAS* 40 (1948) 305; *CLD* 3, 463–464.

out its obligations. Their sole function is to witness to the fact that the marriage was legitimately celebrated. Thus, the code stipulates no detailed qualifications for those fulfilling this role. To function as witnesses to the celebration of the marriage, they should possess the use of reason and be capable of understanding the events they are witnessing. Although no minimum age is specified for these witnesses, those who have not completed their fourteenth year may not serve as witnesses in canonical processes (c. 1550, §1). Thus, preference should be given to witnesses fourteen or older. Clearly excluded from the function of witness are those who are insane, intoxicated, or severely developmentally disabled.

Commentators on the 1917 code also excluded the deaf from serving as witnesses at marriages. This position reflected a long and unfortunate history of assimilating the deaf to those habitually lacking the use of reason. Current research demonstrates that this assimilation was erroneous. While they may not be able to hear the words by which the spouses exchange consent, they may be able to witness the exchange of consent in other ways, e.g., by lip reading, signing, or other gestures.

Exceptional Cases

Canon 1108, §1 concludes by referring to four canons which contain exceptions to the required observance of the canonical form for the validity of a marriage. The Church supplies the power to assist at marriages in cases of common error (c. 144). In certain circumstances, lay people can be delegated to witness marriages in the name of the Church (c. 1112, §1). Marriage may be validly celebrated by the use of an extraordinary form in some urgent cases (c. 1116). When Catholics marry non- Catholics, they can be dispensed from the obligation of observing the canonical form (c. 1127, §2).

Eastern Discipline

Canon 828, §1 of the Eastern code also makes the validity of marriage contingent on the observance of a form. However, it prefers to speak of the observance of a "sacred rite." In all of the Eastern Catholic churches, the sacred rite for celebrating marriage includes the spouses' exchange of consent, but the central focus is on the blessing imparted by the authorized priest. As a result, only a priest (presbyter or bishop) can be the authorized minister of marriage. Thus, Eastern law makes no provision for the celebration of marriage in the presence of a deacon or lay person.

§2. The person who assists at a marriage is understood to be only that person who is present, asks for the manifestation of the consent of the contracting parties, and receives it in the name of the Church.

The Role of the Authorized Witness

The authorized witness of a marriage must be not only physically present but also an active and willing participant in the event. This active participation involves asking the spouses to manifest their consent and receiving that consent in the name of the Church. In the liturgical rite, the authorized witness, after asking three questions to ascertain the spouses' freedom and marital intent, invites them "to declare [their] consent before God and the Church." After they have exchanged consent, the authorized witness accepts this consent in the name of the Church by saying: "You have declared your consent before God and the Church. Let no man separate what God has joined."[224]

The authorized witness must ask for and receive the consent of both parties, even if one of them is not a Catholic. When other priests or deacons or, in the case of mixed marriages, non-Catholic ministers are present, the responsibility for asking for and receiving the consent of the spouses is not to be divided. Unless the authorized witness alone asks for and receives the spouses' consent, the marriage is invalid.[225] Other ministers

---

[224] *Rite of Marriage*, 25–26.
[225] CDF, private reply, November 28, 1975, *CLD* 8, 820–821.

present merely observe the exchange of consent, but they can be given other appropriate liturgical roles in the celebration.

REQUISITES FOR VALID ASSISTANCE AT MARRIAGE

Authorization by Office

Canon 1109 — Unless the local ordinary and pastor have been excommunicated, interdicted, or suspended from office or declared such through a sentence or decree, by virtue of their office and within the confines of their territory they assist validly at the marriages not only of their subjects but also of those who are not their subjects provided that one of them is of the Latin rite.

Offices Delimited by Territory

By virtue of their offices, local ordinaries (c. 134) and pastors are authorized to witness marriages. This authorization extends also to parochial administrators (c. 540, §1), pastors of quasi-parishes or missions (c. 516, §1), and members of the team of priests to whom the pastoral care of a parish has been entrusted *in solidum* (c. 543, §1), who are considered equivalent to pastors. However, the rector of a non-parochial church (c. 558) or a chaplain (c. 566, §1) is not so authorized, unless in the latter case particular or special law provides otherwise. In fact, the special law governing military ordinariates extends to the office of military chaplain the authorization to witness marriages of those persons entrusted to his care.[226]

The authorization of local ordinaries and pastors to witness marriages is territorially based. By virtue of office, they may validly assist at marriages only within the territory assigned to them.[227]

Local ordinaries within the boundaries of their dioceses or vicariates and pastors within the boundaries of their parishes validly assist at marriages not only of their subjects but also of others who are physically present in their territory. However, by virtue of office local ordinaries and pastors may not assist at the marriages of their subjects when they are absent from their territory. In these cases, local ordinaries and pastors must be delegated by the local ordinary or pastor of the place where the marriage is to be celebrated.

Since the authority to assist at marriages is connected to their offices, local ordinaries and pastors enjoy this authority from the moment they legitimately assume their offices. They lose this authority when they lose office in any of the ways specified in canon 184, §1. Thus, local ordinaries and pastors who have submitted their resignations or whose terms have expired retain the power to witness marriages in their territories until they are notified in writing that they have ceased from office (cc. 189, §3 and 186).

Local ordinaries and pastors lose their power to assist at marriages without necessarily losing office when the penalty of excommunication, interdict, or suspension from office is imposed or declared by a judicial sentence or administrative decree.[228] However, they do not forfeit their authority to witness marriages as a result of incurring one of these censures *latae sententiae*. Only after one of these censures has been declared pursuant to a judicial or administrative process does a local ordinary or pastor lose the authority to assist at marriages.

The authority of local ordinaries and pastors to assist at marriages is limited not only territorially but personally. They can validly assist at marriages in their territory only if at least one of the parties "is of the Latin rite."[229] Thus, when both parties are Eastern Catholics and, in mixed marriage situations, when the Catholic party belongs

---

[226] John Paul II, apconst *Spirituali militum curae,* vii, April 21, 1986, *AAS* 78 (1986) 484.

[227] By way of exception, *CCEO* 829, §3 recognizes the patriarch's authority to bless marriages anywhere in the world, as long as at least one of the spouses belongs to his church *sui iuris.*

[228] See the commentary on canons 1314 and 1331–1335.

[229] On the determination of "rite" or ascription to a ritual church *sui iuris,* see the commentary on cc. 111–112 and *CCEO* 29–38.

to an Eastern church, the Latin local ordinary or pastor must seek delegation from the competent Eastern hierarch or pastor in order to assist validly at the marriage (*CCEO* 830, §1).[230] Since ascription to a ritual church *sui iuris* is neither lost nor altered by even longtime practice of the Catholic faith in another church *sui iuris* (c. 112, §2), particular care should be taken to determine the ritual status of spouses during the pre-nuptial investigation, especially if their names or ethnic backgrounds suggest affiliation with an Eastern church.

Latin local ordinaries and pastors can validly assist at marriages by virtue of office when the Catholic party or parties belong to an Eastern Catholic church which does not have an organized hierarchy in their country. However, most of the larger Eastern Catholic churches do have hierarchical organs in North America.

Canon 1110 — By virtue of office, a personal ordinary and a personal pastor assist validly only at marriages where at least one of the parties is a subject within the confines of their jurisdiction.

Offices Delimited by Persons

Besides local ordinaries and pastors, whose jurisdiction is defined by territorial boundaries, there are also ordinaries and pastors whose authority is limited to a defined group or class of persons. The most familiar personal ordinaries and pastors are those who have been entrusted with the pastoral care of particular language or ethnic communities. However, the pastoral needs of other groups may suggest the advisability of establishing personal ordinaries and pastors (e.g., university communities or military personnel). When they are established at the level of the particular church, personal jurisdictions always have a secondary territorial delimitation. Thus, the authority of a personal pastor for a Polish community is limited to the territory of the

diocese for which the personal parish was erected and may be further limited to a defined section of that diocese. However, personal jurisdictions established by the Apostolic See often lack a territorial delimitation. Thus, military ordinariates have responsibility for military personnel and some others when they are on active duty anywhere in the world.[231]

Personal ordinaries and pastors validly assist at marriages only if one of the spouses belongs to the special group entrusted to their care. Moreover, they can delegate other presbyters or deacons to assist only at marriages involving at least one party over whom they have personal jurisdiction.

Authorization by Delegation

Canon 1111 — §1. As long as they hold office validly, the local ordinary and the pastor can delegate to priests and deacons the faculty, even a general one, of assisting at marriages within the limits of their territory.

§2. To be valid, the delegation of the faculty to assist at marriages must be given to specific persons expressly. If it concerns special delegation, it must be given for a specific marriage; if it concerns general delegation, it must be given in writing.

Delegation of Sacred Ministers

Both local and personal ordinaries and pastors can delegate other priests or deacons to witness

---

[230] *CCEO* 829, §1 limits the authority of an Eastern local hierarch and a territorial pastor to bless marriages to situations in which at least one of the spouses is "enrolled in his Church *sui iuris*."

[231] *Spirituali militum curae*, iv, 1°, *AAS* 78 (1986) 483. The "others" over whom military ordinariates have jurisdiction must be derived from the statutes of the particular ordinariate. The Statutes of the Military Archdiocese U.S.A., xv lists as subjects of the ordinariate: (1) all who serve in the military service; (2) those on active duty in the Coast Guard, National Guard, Air National Guard, and Civil Air Patrol; (3) the families of these military personnel; (4) those who attend military and related academies or reside in military or Veterans Administration hospitals; (5) those who dwell on military installations or homes reserved for military personnel; and (6) those employed overseas by the United States government, including diplomatic personnel, and their families.

marriages in the territory assigned to them, i.e., they can delegate others to assist only at those marriages at which they could validly assist themselves. Delegation is general when it is granted for all marriages within the delegator's territory; it is special if it is given only for a specific marriage. The 1917 code had permitted general delegation to assist at marriages only to parochial vicars for the parish to which they were assigned.[232] This restriction has been abrogated by the revised code. Thus, both local ordinaries and pastors can now grant such general delegations more broadly.[233]

The norms governing the power to assist at marriages are more exacting than the general norms governing delegation of executive power.[234] The power to assist at marriages must be made *expressly* to a specific person. An express delegation can be explicit ("I delegate you") or implicit ("Here are the keys to open the church for the wedding") but never tacit or presumed. The express grant must be made to a specific individual. Thus, a local ordinary or pastor cannot validly delegate a priest or deacon to be named later by a religious superior (e.g., "I delegate whatever priest you designate to provide weekend coverage of my parish while I am on vacation").[235] Special delegation must be expressly granted to a specific priest or deacon for a specified marriage.

General delegations can be validly granted only in writing. Special delegations can be granted orally. However, since the validity of the marriage hinges on whether the priest or deacon was properly delegated, some written record of the special delegation should be retained.

Those who have been granted general delegation to witness marriages in a particular territory may subdelegate that authority but only for an in-dividual case; however, those who have been granted special delegation cannot subdelegate the authority unless expressly authorized by the delegator (c. 137, §3). Subdelegated power cannot be further subdelegated, unless this power was expressly granted by the delegator (c. 137, §4).

Canon 1112 — §1. Where there is a lack of priests and deacons, the diocesan bishop can delegate lay persons to assist at marriages, with the previous favorable vote of the conference of bishops and after he has obtained the permission of the Holy See.

§2. A suitable lay person is to be selected, who is capable of giving instruction to those preparing to be married and able to perform the matrimonial liturgy properly.

Delegation of Lay People

Although the authority to witness marriages in the name of the Church is normally reserved to priests and deacons, in the Latin church it is not a function that *per se* requires the power of orders. The current law makes provision for lay men and women to be delegated to assist at marriages when priests and deacons are lacking. The absence of priests and deacons may be physical (e.g., remote communities without a resident pastor) or moral (e.g., ordained ministers who do not speak the language or understand the marriage customs of a particular group). The current law incorporates with some modifications the discipline on delegating lay people to witness marriages of the Congregation for the Sacraments instruction *Sacramentalem indolem* of May 15, 1974.[236]

Before the diocesan bishop can delegate lay people to assist at marriages, a favorable vote of the episcopal conference is required. The episcopal conference can express itself in favor of allowing an individual diocesan bishop, a group of them, or even all the diocesan bishops who are members of the conference to open this role to lay

---

[232] *CIC* 1096, §1.

[233] Besides limiting delegations to bless marriages to priests, *CCEO* 830, §2 restricts the authority to grant general delegations to bless marriages to local hierarchs. However, in virtue of *CCEO* 302, §2, pastors can grant a general faculty, but only to their own parochial vicars.

[234] See the commentary on cc. 137–138.

[235] CodCom, May 20, 1923, *CLD* 1, 540–541.

[236] *CLD* 8, 815–818. See also SCSacr, private reply, January 20, 1983, *CLD* 10, 178–181.

people.[237] After this favorable vote, interested bishops must individually seek the permission of the Holy See. Once this permission is received, the diocesan bishop and those equivalent in law, but not vicars general and episcopal vicars, may validly delegate lay people to witness marriages in the name of the Church. This delegation can be either general or special. The current law has not retained the requirement of *Sacramentalem indolem* that lay witnesses of marriages be delegated by the diocesan bishop personally. Thus, the diocesan bishop could presumably delegate another official to subdelegate lay people for particular cases.

Care should be exercised in selecting lay people to assist at marriages. They should possess both the personal qualities that make them suitable for this task and the ability to provide appropriate pre-marital instruction to couples and to perform the liturgical rites fittingly. At the wedding itself, the lay delegate presides at a liturgy of the word during which he or she may preach and asks for and receives the spouses' consent.[238] Since authorized lay people can administer sacramentals (c. 1168), the lay delegate can bless the wedding rings. However, the lay delegate may not dispense from certain impediments in the urgent cases mentioned in canons 1079–1080, nor is he or she authorized to impart the nuptial blessing.

---

[237] Since the *votum* of the episcopal conference is not a general decree but merely an expression of a favorable opinion, it does not seem to require the review (*recognitio*) of the Apostolic See. Nevertheless, on September 16, 1983, the Canadian episcopal conference approved a decree allowing the use of lay people to witness marriages in all the dioceses of Canada. This decree was confirmed by the Holy See on April 4, 1984. See *CLD* 11, 267. Kelly, in *CLSGBI Com*, 626, says: "Strangely, however, in some countries the Conference has approved the delegation of lay people in principle but in such terms that each Bishop must apply directly to the Holy See for permission before actually delegating anyone." In fact, there is nothing "strange" about this approach; the two-step process is precisely what a fair reading of the canon requires.

[238] The 1991 edition of the *Ordo Celebrandi Matrimonium* contains a Rite for the Celebration of Marriage before a Lay Person.

Although delegation of a lay person to witness a marriage in the name of the Church ensures that the marriage will be recognized as canonically valid, it does not assure that the State will recognize the union as valid. Before delegating a lay person, the diocesan bishop should see that the lay person has been certified or licensed to witness marriages by the State as well.

REQUIREMENTS FOR LICIT ASSISTANCE AT MARRIAGES

Responsibility of the Delegator

Canon 1113 — Before special delegation is granted, all those things which the law has established to prove free status are to be fulfilled.

Before he grants special delegation to witness a marriage, a local ordinary or pastor must ascertain that the required pre-nuptial investigation (c. 1066) has been conducted to establish that the parties are entering marriage freely, are not bound by any impediment, and are willing and able to assume the obligations of Christian marriage. Failure to fulfill this obligation does not render the delegation invalid, but it does constitute a serious dereliction of pastoral responsibility.

Responsibilities of All Authorized Witnesses

Canon 1114 — The person assisting at marriage acts illicitly unless the person has made certain of the free status of the contracting parties according to the norm of law and, if possible, of the permission of the pastor whenever the person assists in virtue of general delegation.

Whether they are authorized to assist at marriages by virtue of office or by virtue of delegation, priests, deacons, and lay people may not witness a marriage unless they are satisfied that the pre-marital investigation has been completed. Even if the official witness has not conducted this investigation personally, he or she has a pastoral obligation to ensure that care has been taken to establish that nothing stands in the way of a valid and licit celebration before witnessing a marriage.

When an official witness is acting by virtue of general delegation, he or she still must seek the permission of the pastor of the place where the marriage is to be celebrated. Although the current law no longer reserves this function to pastors,[239] assistance at marriages remains one of the functions "especially entrusted" to them (c. 530, 4°). Since the pastor is "the proper pastor (*pastor*) of the parish entrusted to him" (c. 519), he should at least be made aware of significant events affecting the ecclesial status of those entrusted to his care, even if he does not have the exclusive prerogative of celebrating these events himself. The requirement that, if possible, the one acting by virtue of general delegation receive the pastor's permission before witnessing a particular marriage attempts to ensure that the latter is aware of the pending marriage and may voice any concerns or cautions. However, failure to seek this permission does not affect the validity of the marriage, and the qualification of the obligation to seek it by the phrase "if possible" suggests that, in many cases, failure to seek this permission does not render the marriage illicit. Nevertheless, willful neglect of this requirement would amount to a violation of pastoral courtesy.

The Authorized Witness and the Pastor

Canon 1115 — Marriages are to be celebrated in a parish where either of the contracting parties has a domicile, quasi-domicile, or month-long residence or, if it concerns transients, in the parish where they actually reside. With the permission of the proper ordinary or proper pastor, marriages can be celebrated elsewhere.

The normal place for the celebration of marriage is the place where at least one of the parties

[239] *CIC* 462, 4°.

if both are Catholic or, in the case of mixed marriages, the Catholic party has a domicile, quasi-domicile, or month-long residence. The marriages of those who have no domicile or quasi-domicile are normally celebrated where they actually reside. The permission of the ordinary or pastor of one of the spouses is required to licitly celebrate the marriage elsewhere.[240]

The revised Latin code has dropped the preference of the 1917 code for celebrating marriage in the parish of the bride.[241] However, the Eastern code stipulates that marriages are to be celebrated before the pastor of the groom "unless either particular law determines otherwise or a just cause excuses."[242] This norm is somewhat less stringent than the previous Eastern discipline that required that mixed rite marriages be celebrated before the pastor of the groom and that dispensations be sought to permit deviations from this norm.[243] The less restrictive norms of both the Latin and the Eastern codes governing the place of inter-ritual marriages gives the spouses greater freedom to choose either of their churches *sui iuris* as the site

[240] *CCEO* 831, §1, 3° adds that a local hierarch or pastor lawfully blesses a marriage in "a place exclusively of another Church *sui iuris,* unless the hierarch who exercises power in that place expressly refuses." This canon reverses the Commission for the Codification of the Oriental Canon Law's 1952 authentic interpretation of *Crebrae allatae,* c. 86, §1, 2°. According to this extensive interpretation, ministers of one church *sui iuris* could validly exercise their jurisdiction in a place dedicated exclusively for an other church *sui iuris* only with the express *permission* of the official responsible for that place. See Pius XII, *mp Crebrae allatae,* February 22, 1949, c. 86, §1, 2°, *AAS* 41 (1949) 106; and Commission for the Codification of the Oriental Canon Law, reply, July 8, 1952, *AAS* 44 (1952) 552; *CLD* 3, 32. It is not clear whether, by analogy, a Latin local ordinary or pastor can now bless a marriage in a place exclusively of an Eastern church *sui iuris* unless the Eastern hierarch expressly refuses.

[241] See *CIC* 1097, §2.

[242] *CCEO* 831, §2.

[243] Pius XII, *mp Crebrae allatae,* c. 88, §3. See CDF, private reply, February 1, 1967, *CLD* 6, 411–412; and CEC, private reply, February 7, 1969, *CLD* 7, 8–9.

for the celebration of their marriage.[244] Nevertheless, in inter-ritual marriages where the man is an Eastern Catholic, the permission of his pastor should be obtained before celebrating the marriage in the woman's Latin church.

THE EXTRAORDINARY CANONICAL FORM

Latin Discipline

Canon 1116 — §1. If a person competent to assist according to the norm of law cannot be present or approached without grave inconvenience, those who intend to enter into a true marriage can contract it validly and licitly before witnesses only:
1° in danger of death;
2° outside the danger of death provided that it is prudently foreseen that the situation will continue for a month.
§2. In either case, if some other priest or deacon who can be present is available, he must be called and be present at the celebration of the marriage together with the witnesses, without prejudice to the validity of the marriage before witnesses only.

The Church's requirement that the canonical form be observed as a condition for the validity of marriage could unduly abridge the exercise of the natural right to marry when authorized witnesses are lacking or rarely available. The provision for the delegation of lay people to witness marriages when priests and deacons are lacking is an attempt to avoid conflicts between that natural right and the demands of ecclesiastical law. The same purpose is served by the extraordinary form of marriage (c. 1116). The availability of this extraordinary form in certain urgent circumstances attempts to honor the natural right to marry while preserving the public character of marriage.

[244] V. Pospishil, *Eastern Catholic Marriage Law* (Brooklyn: St. Maron Publications, 1991) 383.

Unavailability of an Authorized Minister

Resort to the extraordinary form is legitimate only when those authorized to witness marriages in the name of the Church are unavailable because access to them is impossible "without grave inconvenience." It must be gravely inconvenient both for the parties who seek marriage to go to an authorized witness and for a witness to come to them. The impossibility may result from physical circumstances (e.g., distance, inadequate means of transportation or communication) or moral factors (e.g., persecution, war, unjust civil laws). The "impossibility" that makes resort to the extraordinary form legitimate can be relative. For example, traveling twenty-five miles may be only a minor inconvenience for persons with access to good roads and an automobile but a grave inconvenience for people who must make the journey on foot.

Circumstances Warranting Use of the Extraordinary Form

Canon 1116 foresees two situations in which the inaccessibility of authorized witnesses justifies resort to the extraordinary form: danger of death and situations when it can be prudently judged that an authorized witness will be unavailable for a month. Death need not be imminent or certain. It is sufficient that the death of one of the parties from internal or external causes is at least probable.

It is sufficient that the parties prudently foresee that an authorized witness will be unavailable for at least a month. If events prove them to have been mistaken, their marriage entered into according to the extraordinary form is still valid. However, the conditions for use of the extraordinary form are not met if the long-term unavailability of an authorized witness results from a prohibition of the marriage by a local ordinary, a diocesan policy that requires couples to meet with a priest or deacon several months prior to the wedding to begin marriage preparation, or the fact that the available witness does not meet the couple's personal criteria for orthodoxy.

Celebrations Pursuant to the Extraordinary Form

If these criteria for use of the extraordinary form are met, the couple validly contracts marriage by exchanging consent before two witnesses. However, the urgent circumstances justifying the use of this form bring no automatic dispensation from any impediments. The couple must intend marriage as understood by the Church, but they need not grasp all of the implications of the extraordinary form. If a priest or deacon who has no authorization to assist at marriages is available, he should be asked to participate in the extraordinary form celebration. However, failure to call him does not affect the validity of marriage before witnesses alone. However, this priest or deacon may dispense from certain impediments in the urgent situations foreseen by canons 1079–1080.

Eastern Discipline

Although a valid celebration of marriage without the priestly blessing is hard to reconcile with the Eastern theology of marriage, canon 832 of the Eastern code provides for an extraordinary form for the celebration of marriage that is substantially the same as that prescribed in canon 1116 of the Latin code. However, if a non-Catholic priest is available, he is to be present to bless the marriage, "without prejudice to the validity of a marriage in the presence of the witnesses alone" (*CCEO* 832, §2). In addition, the spouses who marry according to the extraordinary form are admonished to seek the priestly blessing of their marriage as soon as possible (*CCEO* 832, §3).

THOSE BOUND BY THE CANONICAL FORM OF MARRIAGE

Canon 1117 — The form established above must be observed if at least one of the parties contract-ing marriage was baptized in the Catholic Church or received into it and has not defected from it by a formal act, without prejudice to the prescripts of can. 1127, §2.

General Principle

All who have been baptized in the Catholic Church or received into full communion with it must observe the ordinary or the extraordinary canonical form when they marry, whether they marry another Catholic or not. The failure of a Catholic to observe this form results in the nullity of his or her marriage. The fact that a person was not raised in the Catholic Church after baptism or has lapsed from the active practice of the faith does not exempt him or her from the obligation of observing the canonical form.

Those Who Have Left the Catholic Church by a Formal Act

However, the present law does exempt from the observance of this form those who have "defected from [the Catholic Church] by a formal act."[245] The concept of "defection from the Catholic Church by a formal act" is an innovation of the 1983 code, and its exact meaning has yet to be determined.[246] It is distinguished from the "notorious defection from the communion of the Church" that disqualifies a person from voting in a canonical election (c. 171, §1, 4°) by its note of formality. Throughout the 1983 code, the terms

---

[245] Those who have defected by a formal act are also not bound by the impediment of disparity of worship (c. 1086, §1) and the prohibition on entering a mixed marriage (c. 1124), but are exempt from no other merely ecclesiastical laws.

[246] See V. De Paolis, "Alcune annotazioni circa la formula 'actu formali ab Ecclesia catholica deficere,'" *P* 84 (1995) 570–608; J. Doyle, "The Formal Act of Leaving the Catholic Church," *CLSAP* 52 (1990) 152–160; A. Stenson, "The Concept and Implications of the Formal Act of Defection of Canon 1117," *Stud Can* 21 (1987) 175–194.

formale (formal) and *formaliter* (formally) consistently denote a juridic act which is both public and intended to effect a change in the ecclesial status of some person or group.[247] Thus, the formal act of defection from the Catholic Church is a juridic act which can be proven in the external forum and whose intended effect is to separate oneself from the Church.

In addition to freedom and deliberation, the validity of a juridic act requires that the person who posits it be qualified to do so (c. 124). The Council for the Interpretation of Legal Texts has ruled that the formal act of defecting from the Catholic Church must "be a strictly personal act and thus the subject who poses it must be naturally and juridically capable."[248] Consequently, since minors lack the full exercise of their rights (c. 98, §2), they are incapable of positing a formal act of defection for themselves, and their parents are incapable of making this act for them. Children who were baptized in the Catholic Church but whose parents subsequently enrolled them in a non-Catholic church may ratify this parental decision when they come of age, but, to do so by a formal act, they would have to be aware of their Catholic baptism (c. 126).[249]

The following may be considered to have defected from the Catholic Church by a formal act: those who have made a public declaration of their abandonment of the Catholic faith, either in writing or orally before two witnesses, and those who have formally enrolled by some external sign in another Christian church or another religion.[250]

Lengthy participation in the worship of another church or religion without formal enrollment and a long-standing lapse in Catholic practice lack the formality required for defection by a formal act.

Since intent is integral to the formality of the act of defection, care should be taken to examine each case before deciding that the conditions for defection by a formal act have been met. For example, in countries where the only way to escape the "church tax" is to renounce membership in the Church before a civil official, the intent of this renunciation may be to relieve oneself of a burdensome tax and not to defect from the Church.[251] Even enrollment in another church may not qualify as defection by a formal act if it were done solely to appease a fiancé or future in-laws but without the intention of abandoning the Catholic Church.[252]

Non-Catholics

Those who have never been baptized in the Catholic Church or received into it are not bound by the canonical form when they marry among themselves. However, they may be bound by some other public form for entering marriage. The unbaptized are bound by any form required by the State for the civil recognition of marriage. The law of the Eastern non-Catholic churches requires a sacred rite which includes the priestly blessing of the couple as a condition for ecclesial recognition of the marriage. Canon 781, 2° of the Eastern code recognizes this law as the standard to be used by

---

[247] The term *formale* is used to qualify the decree by which a private association acquires private juridic personality (c. 322, §1), an institute of consecrated life of diocesan right is erected (c. 579), and an institute of consecrated life is erected or approved as one of pontifical right (c. 589). Canon 982 requires that, before sacramental absolution is imparted to a person who has falsely denounced a confessor for solicitation, he or she must retract the denunciation *formaliter.*

[248] PCILT, reply, January 4, 1994, in *De processibus matrimonialibus* 3 (1996) 319.

[249] Ibid.

[250] See Kelly, in *CLSGBI Com,* 603.

[251] E. Corecco, "Dimettersi dalla Chiesa per ragioni fiscali," *Apol* 55 (1982) 470.

[252] At this writing, the PCILT is conducting a survey of the experience of dioceses in applying concretely the notion of defection by formal act and of the usefulness of this canonical innovation. Canon 1099, §2 of the 1917 code exempted "those born of non-Catholics" from the obligation of observing canonical form. The vagueness of this phrase and difficulties in its practical application led Pius XII to delete it from the code in 1948. Vagueness and difficulty in practical application may doom to a similar fate the exemption of those who leave the Catholic Church by a formal act.

the Catholic Church when it assesses the validity of a marriage involving an Eastern non-Catholic.[253]

Canon 781, 2° of the Eastern code also stipulates that "with regard to the form of the celebration, the Church recognizes any form prescribed or admitted by the law to which the parties were subject at the time of the celebration of the marriage." Churches and ecclesial communities stemming from the Protestant Reformation of the sixteenth century generally do not have their own law governing marriage (the Anglican communion is a notable exception). They have instead deferred to civil authority to regulate marriage. Thus, the Eastern code seems to say that the validity of marriages of baptized Protestants depends on their observance of the formalities required by civil law (see also *CCEO* 780, §2). The Latin code, on the other hand, is silent about the possible competence of civil authority to prescribe a form for marriages between baptized non-Catholics, which are, by definition, sacramental (c. 1055, §2). The Council for the Interpretation of Legal Texts could assist practitioners by clarifying whether on this issue the Eastern code is to be considered supplementary law for the Latin church.

THE PLACE WHERE MARRIAGE IS TO BE CELEBRATED

Canon 1118 — §1. A marriage between Catholics or between a Catholic party and a non-Catholic baptized party is to be celebrated in a parish church. It can be celebrated in another church or oratory with the permission of the local ordinary or pastor.

§2. The local ordinary can permit a marriage to be celebrated in another suitable place.

§3. A marriage between a Catholic party and a non-baptized party can be celebrated in a church or in another suitable place.

Parish Church

A parish church is the ordinary place for the celebration of a marriage involving two Catholics or a Catholic and a baptized non-Catholic. Since the marriages of two baptized persons are sacraments, they are not merely private or familial celebrations but ecclesial events. The spouses declare their consent "before God and the Church" and live out that commitment in and with the support of the local ecclesial community. It is, therefore, fitting that this celebration should take place in the parish church. It is here that the local community is "gathered together by the preaching of the Gospel of Christ, and the mystery of the Lord's supper is celebrated, 'so that the whole fellowship is joined together by the flesh and blood of the Lord's body.'"[254]

Another Church or Oratory

The local ordinary or pastor can permit a marriage between Catholics or between a Catholic and a baptized non-Catholic to be celebrated in another church or oratory. In this canon, the term "church" denotes a building dedicated to Catholic worship to which the faithful have the right of free access (c. 1214). An oratory is a place designated for Catholic worship for the benefit of some community to which the access of the faithful is regulated by the competent authority of that community (c. 1223). Unlike the 1917 code,[255] the current law does not prohibit the celebration of marriages in the oratories (often popularly, but imprecisely, called "chapels") of seminaries and religious houses. However, the consent of the rector of the church or the superior responsible for the oratory is required in addition to the permission of the local ordinary or pastor.

---

[253] *CCEO* 833 authorizes local hierarchs to grant to priests of any Catholic church the faculty to bless the marriages of Eastern non-Catholics when these members of the faithful cannot approach a priest of their own church and spontaneously seek the blessing. A priest so delegated should, if possible, inform the competent authority of the non-Catholic church before he blesses the marriages.

[254] *LG* 26.
[255] *CIC* 1109, §2.

Another Suitable Place

A local ordinary, but not a pastor, can permit a marriage between two Catholics or between a Catholic and a baptized non-Catholic to be celebrated in some suitable place other than a Catholic church or oratory. Suitable places might include the non-Catholic church or place of worship of one of the parties to a mixed marriage, a non-denominational chapel attached to a college, university, or other institution, or even a private home.[256] When judging the suitability of a place for the celebration of a marriage, care should be taken to ensure that the nature of the place is consistent with a religious celebration. Particular law or policy might establish criteria for determining the suitability of places for the celebration of marriage or determine which places in the diocese are suitable and under which conditions.

When a Catholic marries an unbaptized person, a (Catholic) church, whether parochial or not, remains the preferred place for the celebration. However, these marriages can also be celebrated in some other suitable place. The canon does not require the permission of the local ordinary for the selection of another suitable place, nor does it specify the one competent to select the place.[257] Therefore, the selection is presumably left to the discretion of the assisting minister. Although marriages between Catholics and unbaptized persons are not considered sacraments, they are significant religious events. A suitable place for the celebration should enhance rather than distract from the religious dimension of the marriage. Therefore, the assisting minister should consult local guidelines on suitable places for marriages and use common sense.

Canon 1118 presumes that, no matter where a marriage is celebrated, the canonical form will

normally be observed. When marriages are celebrated outside a parish church, those who assist at those marriages in the name of the Church need to be particularly attentive to the requirements of this form. Delegation must be received from the pastor or local ordinary of the place where the marriage is to be celebrated if that place is outside the territorial boundaries of one who assists by virtue of office even if the parties are his subjects. The marriage is to be recorded in the parish where it was actually celebrated rather than in the parish where the spouses have a domicile (c. 1121, §1).

The Liturgical Form of Marriage

Canon 1119 — Outside the case of necessity, the rites prescribed in the liturgical books approved by the Church or received by legitimate customs are to be observed in the celebration of a marriage.

Although the essential form of marriage is the exchange of consent by the spouses, the Church has long surrounded this element with liturgical rites that elucidate the place of marriage in the mystery of salvation. This liturgical form is to be observed in the celebration of all marriages, except in cases of grave necessity. The liturgical norms and rubrics to be used in the celebration of marriage are found in the official liturgical book, *The Rite of Marriage*. The current ritual offers a rich variety of options for readings, prayers, and blessings to allow the liturgical celebration to be adapted to the circumstances of individual couples.

Marriages between two Catholics are normally celebrated in the context of a nuptial Mass. However, for a just cause, these marriages may be celebrated according to the "Rite for Celebrating Marriage outside Mass" which includes a liturgy of the word and the nuptial blessing as well as the required exchange of consent.

The 1917 code prohibited the celebration of marriages between Catholics and non-Catholics in a Catholic church. The local ordinary could dispense from this prohibition to avoid serious diffi-

---

[256] The 1983 code abrogates the former prohibition on marriages in private buildings except in extraordinary circumstances of *CIC* 1109, §2.

[257] *CCEO* 838, §1 reserves to the local hierarch alone the authority to permit a marriage involving a Catholic anywhere other than in a Catholic sacred place.

culties, but a sacred rite was rarely permitted for the celebration of these marriages.[258] Paul VI abrogated this prohibition in 1970.[259] The current ritual reflects this postconciliar change in discipline.[260] Marriages between Catholics and baptized non-Catholics are normally celebrated according to the "Rite for Celebrating Marriage outside Mass." However, the local ordinary can permit these marriages to be celebrated within the context of the Eucharist.[261] Marriages between Catholics and unbaptized persons are always to be celebrated outside the Mass and according to the special rite provided for these situations, which allows the option of using only one scriptural reading from the Old Testament.[262]

When marriage takes place during the celebration of the Eucharist, the readings and prayers for the wedding Mass are normally employed. However, if the marriage takes place on a Sunday or solemnity, the readings and prayers of the day are to be used, except on Sundays during the Christmas season and ordinary time when the wedding Mass may be used at celebrations that are not regular parish Masses. When the Mass texts of the day must be used, one of the readings from the wedding Mass can be substituted, except during the Triduum and on Christmas, Epiphany, Ascension, Pentecost, Corpus Christi, and other holy days of obligation.[263]

All of the rites for the celebration of marriage contain a nuptial blessing. The current discipline has eliminated previous restrictions on when and to whom this blessing may be imparted. Thus, the nuptial blessing can be granted to those entering second marriages or entering mixed marriages, when marriage is celebrated outside a Mass, and during any liturgical season.

Canon 1120 — The conference of bishops can produce its own rite of marriage, to be reviewed by the Holy See, in keeping with the usages of places and peoples which are adapted to the Christian spirit; nevertheless, the law remains in effect that the person who assists at the marriage is present, asks for the manifestation of consent of the contracting parties, and receives it.

The liturgical role of episcopal conferences is not limited to preparing and publishing vernacular versions of the typical editions of the marriage ritual (c. 838, §3). They may also prepare their own marriage rituals, which incorporate and adapt the customs and usages of their cultures in a Christian spirit. Perhaps no human institution is more intimately intertwined with culture than marriage. This authorization for inculturation of the rite of marriage is derived from *Sacrosanctum Concilium* 77. It embodies the Church's desire to preserve and foster those elements of a people's cultural heritage that are "not indissolubly bound up with superstition and error."[264]

While episcopal conferences may adapt the words by which the spouses exchange consent, their inculturated rituals must retain the exchange of consent in the presence of the assisting minister. Like all liturgical books, these particular rituals for marriage may not be used until they have received the *recognitio* of the Holy See (c. 838, §3).

THE RECORDING OF MARRIAGES

Registration of Marriages

Canon 1121 — §1. After a marriage has been celebrated, the pastor of the place of the celebration or the person who takes his place, even if neither assisted at the marriage, is to note as soon as possible in the marriage register the names of the spouses, the person who assisted, and the witnesses, and the place and date of the celebration

---

[258] *CIC* 1109, §3 and 1102, §2.

[259] Paul VI, *mp Matrimonia mixta,* March 31, 1970, 11, *CLD* 7, 716–717.

[260] See *Ecum Dir* 159–160.

[261] *Rite of Marriage,* 8.

[262] Ibid., 56.

[263] Ibid., 11.

[264] *SC* 37.

of the marriage according to the method prescribed by the conference of bishops or the diocesan bishop.

§2. Whenever a marriage is contracted according to the norm of can. 1116, a priest or deacon, if he was present at the celebration, or otherwise the witnesses *in solidum* with the contracting
parties are bound to inform as soon as possible
the pastor or local ordinary about the marriage
entered into.

§3. For a marriage contracted with a dispensation from canonical form, the local ordinary who
granted the dispensation is to take care that the
dispensation and celebration are inscribed in the
marriage registers of both the curia and the
proper parish of the Catholic party whose pastor
conducted the investigation about the free status.
The Catholic spouse is bound to notify as soon as
possible the same ordinary and pastor about the
marriage celebrated and also to indicate the place
of the celebration and the public form observed.

Since marriage is a public event that affects the
spouses' status in the Church and in society, it is
important that there be a public record by which
the fact of the celebration can be proved. Each
parish is to have a marriage register (c. 535, §1).
The responsibility for ensuring that every marriage celebrated within the boundaries of the
parish is registered rests ultimately with the pastor
(or the one who takes his place), even if he did
not assist at the marriage.

The entry in the marriage register is to include
the names of the spouses, the names of the person
who assisted at the marriage and of the two other
witnesses, and the place and date of the celebration. The conference of bishops or the diocesan
bishop can provide additional directives on what is
to be entered in the register and the manner in
which it is to be done. Since the marriage register
records public events that affect the status of persons, the spouses and other interested parties have
a right to an authentic copy of the data pertaining
to them that is recorded in the marriage register (c.
487, §2). An authentic copy of the entry in the

marriage register is a public ecclesiastical document that is fully probative of the fact that the
marriage was properly celebrated (cc. 1540, §1;
1541).

When the extraordinary form of marriage has
been legitimately employed (c. 1116), the obligation to report the marriage to the local ordinary or
pastor of the place where the celebration took
place rests with the priest or deacon who was in
fact present but not authorized to assist. If no such
priest or deacon was present, the spouses together
with the witnesses are to report the matter to the
pastor or local ordinary. In either case, the event
is to be reported as soon as possible.

If a marriage is celebrated after a dispensation
from canonical form has been granted,[265] the local
ordinary who granted the dispensation is responsible to see that both the dispensation and the subsequent marriage are properly recorded. In these
cases, the relevant information is to be entered
into marriage registers in the diocesan curia from
which the dispensation was granted and in the
parish of the Catholic party whose pastor conducted the pre-nuptial investigation.

When a Catholic seeks to marry a non-Catholic,
whether baptized or not, the one competent to dispense from the canonical form is the local ordinary of the place where the Catholic has a domicile or quasi-domicile.[266] The proper pastor of a
Catholic is normally the pastor of the place of his
or her domicile or quasi-domicile (c. 107). However, in many cases, the proper pastor is not the
one who conducts the pre-nuptial investigation
and submits the petition for a dispensation from
canonical form. The NCCB norms attempt to
avoid this ambiguity in the law by stipulating that
the marriage is to be registered in "the marriage

---

[265] See the commentary on c. 1127, §2.

[266] Although c. 1121, §3 seems to envision only dispensations from canonical form for mixed marriages, the
same norms for recording the dispensation and the marriage entered pursuant to it seem to apply to cases when
the form was dispensed in danger-of-death situations (c.
1079) and the unusual cases when the Holy See has dispensed from the form for the marriage of two Catholics.

records of the parish from which the application for the dispensation was made."[267]

The Catholic on whose behalf a dispensation from canonical form was granted has an obligation to report to the local ordinary who granted it and his or her proper pastor when, where, and by what public form the marriage was contracted. This information is usually contained in the petition for a dispensation from the obligation of canonical form. However, the Catholic spouse has an obligation to confirm the fact that the marriage was in fact celebrated in the manner previously specified.

Canon 1122 — §1. The contracted marriage is to be noted also in the baptismal registers in which the baptism of the spouses has been recorded.

§2. If a spouse did not contract marriage in the parish in which the person was baptized, the pastor of the place of the celebration is to send notice of the marriage which has been entered into as soon as possible to the pastor of the place of the conferral of baptism.

The fact that a marriage has been celebrated is also to be recorded in the baptismal register of the place where the Catholic party or parties were baptized. If the marriage is celebrated in the same place where the baptism occurred, the pastor of the place of marriage is responsible for seeing that the required information is entered into both parish registers. The pastor of the place where the marriage took place also has the responsibility to notify the pastor of the place of baptism and to assure that the marriage is properly recorded there if one or both spouses was baptized elsewhere.

Canon 1123 — Whenever a marriage is either convalidated in the external forum, declared null, or legitimately dissolved other than by death, the pastor of the place of the celebration of the marriage must be informed so that a notation is

properly made in the marriage and baptismal registers.

Parish marriage and baptismal registers should also contain notations of external forum convalidations of marriages,[268] dissolutions of marriage for causes other than death,[269] and declarations of nullity. When a marriage null because of the failure to observe the canonical form is convalidated, it is to be recorded in the place where the convalidation occurred. The convalidation of a marriage invalid for other causes is recorded both in the parish where the original ceremony took place and the parish where the convalidation occurred. Convalidations in the internal non-sacramental forum are recorded only in the secret archive of the diocesan chancery. Tribunals and chanceries that prepare marriage cases leading to the declaration of nullity or dissolution usually notify the parishes of baptism and marriage directly when the decision can be executed (cc. 1685 and 1706). The notation should indicate that the marriage was decreed null or dissolved, the date, and the protocol number of the document.

CHAPTER VI[270]
MIXED MARRIAGES
[cc. 1124–1129][271]

In the strict canonical sense, a "mixed marriage" is one entered into by a Catholic with a person who is a baptized member of a Christian church or ecclesial community that lacks full communion with the Catholic Church. In a broad sense, a mixed marriage is any union between a Catholic and a non-Catholic, whether baptized or not. While this

---

[267]NCCB, particular norms, November 16, 1970, §12, *CLD* 7, 738.

[268] See the commentary on cc. 1161–1165.
[269] See the commentary on cc. 1142–1150.
[270] See Doyle, in *CLSA Com,* 800–806; Lüdicke, in *Münster Com,* Einführung vor 1124/1–1129/1; Navarro Valls, in *Pamplona ComEng,* 710–715; Kelly, in *CLSGBI Com,* 633–638.
[271] See *CCEO* 813–816, 834–835, 839.

broad sense is frequently used in popular discourse, the strict sense will be used here because the canonical issues and implications of marriages between Catholics and other baptized Christians are quite different from those raised by marriages between Catholics and the unbaptized.

Historical Synopsis

Since the patristic era, the Church has exhibited pastoral concern about the marriages of Catholics with those who do not share the faith of the Church. The basis for this concern is the fear, grounded in experience, that mixed marriages provide the occasion for Catholics to lapse from the practice of the faith or even to fall into heresy or schism (c. 751) and for the loss to the Church of the children born of the marriage. More recently, the Church has highlighted the potential for the religious differences endemic to mixed marriages to undermine the community of married life. As Paul VI observed, "There are very many difficulties inherent to a mixed marriage as such since a kind of division is introduced into a living cell of the Church as the Christian family is deservedly called."[272]

Early councils prohibited marriages between Christians and heretics and schismatics, at least when they involved clerics or their children.[273] The most draconian legislation on mixed marriages was that of the Council of Trullo in 691 which decreed:

It is not allowed that an Orthodox man be joined with an heretical woman, nor, indeed that an Orthodox woman be united with an heretical man. But if anything of this kind appears to have been done by any at all, the marriage is considered invalid and the nefarious union dissolved.[274]

Although the canons of Trullo were not received by the churches of the West, its diriment impediment of mixed religion remained the law of the Eastern churches for many centuries.[275] In the West, although local councils and popes continued to prohibit the marriages of the faithful with heretics and schismatics, marriages in contravention of this prohibition were generally not considered invalid. Prior to Trent, there is scant evidence of dispensations from what had become the impedient impediment of mixed religion, which prohibited but did not invalidate mixed marriages.

With the Protestant Reformation, European Catholics often found themselves living in close proximity with large numbers of people whom the Church considered to be heretics. Catholics in the new missionary territories were even more isolated from other Catholics. As a result, intermarriage with non-Catholics became an increasingly acute pastoral problem. The Council of Trent did not address this situation directly. However, its decree *Tametsi,* where it was promulgated, had the effect of enforcing the traditional prohibition on marriage with heretics since the proper (Catholic) pastor would refuse to be present at these weddings. Normally, mixed marriages were permitted only after the non-Catholic party abjured heresy.

The refusal of Catholic pastors to assist at mixed marriages as well as the scarcity of Catholic pastors in many areas where the Tridentine decree had been promulgated caused a proliferation of marriages invalid for failure to observe the canoni-

---

[275] As late as 1969, the Rota declared invalid the marriage of an Orthodox communicant with a Protestant on the basis of the Trullan impediment. The changed ecumenical climate of the postconciliar era prompted a rethinking of the continuing force of the Trullan impediment. It was eventually held that this impediment had been abrogated either by immemorial custom or by legislation of the various Orthodox churches. See the Rotal decision *coram* Canals, October 21, 1970, *CLD* 7, 10–14; and ApSig, decision, July 1, 1972, *CLD* 8, 3–29. See also J. Myers, *The Trullan Controversy, CanLawStud* 491 (Washington, D.C.: Catholic University of America, 1977).

---

[272] Paul VI, *mp Matrimonia mixta,* March 31, 1970, *CLD* 7, 712.

[273] Elvira (306), c. 16; Laodicaea (between 343 and 381), cc. 10 and 31; Hippo (393), c. 12; Chalcedon (451), c. 14.

[274] Council of Trullo, c. 72.

cal form. To address this pastoral problem, Benedict XIV exempted non-Catholics in the Netherlands from the observance of the Tridentine form when they married among themselves or with Catholics.[276] This Benedictine privilege was eventually extended to other regions. In addition, some, including Alphonsus Liguori, held that, in German-speaking areas, the prohibition of mixed marriages had been displaced by contrary custom.[277]

For the sake of the public good, the pope occasionally granted dispensations to allow Catholic monarchs and members of the nobility to marry non-Catholics. Dispensations were granted only after the successful negotiation of treaty-like compacts in which the freedom of the Catholic to worship and raise any children in the Catholic faith was guaranteed. The form of these compacts, which gradually became the style of the Roman Curia, provided the model for the *cautiones* or "promises" that became the essential condition for the granting of dispensations for mixed marriages, when the Church began granting these dispensations for ordinary people in the late eighteenth and early nineteenth century. Although the authority to dispense for mixed marriages belonged to the pope, the faculty was increasingly delegated to diocesan bishops and their equivalents from the early nineteenth century on.[278] In the 1917 code, the impedient impediment of mixed religion prohibited but did not invalidate marriages between Catholics and baptized non-Catholics. A dispensation from this impediment could be granted only if the non-Catholic promised to remove all dangers of the Catholic spouse's lapsing from the Catholic Church and both parties promised unconditionally to have all children baptized and educated as Catholics.[279]

The new ecumenical climate ushered in by Vatican II prompted a reconsideration of the Church's discipline on mixed marriages. The recognition of the existence of elements of the Church of Christ outside the Catholic Church and of various degrees of communion between the Catholic Church and other Christian churches and ecclesial communities[280] made it impossible to continue to treat baptized non-Catholics simply as heretics and schismatics. Moreover, the conciliar teaching on religious freedom seemed incompatible with the practice of requiring non-Catholic parties to mixed marriages to make promises that might violate their consciences.[281]

In 1966, the CDF issued new norms governing mixed marriages, which called for the non-Catholic party to be invited to promise not to interfere with the Catholic spouse's fulfillment of the obligation to practice the Catholic faith and to ensure the Catholic baptism and upbringing of children. If the non-Catholic declined to make this promise, the case was to be referred to the congregation.[282] In 1970, after the issue of mixed marriages had been studied and discussed by the 1967 Synod of Bishops, Paul VI promulgated the *motu proprio Matrimonia mixta* which completely revised the discipline governing mixed marriages.

This revised discipline has been incorporated into the revised code.[283] The six canons devoted to mixed marriages treat: the prohibition of mixed marriages (c. 1124), the conditions for granting permissions for mixed marriages (c. 1125), the role of episcopal conferences in regulating mixed marriages (c. 1126), the form for celebrating mixed marriages (c. 1127), the pastoral care of spouses in mixed marriages (c. 1128), and the extension of the discipline governing mixed marriages to marriages involving the impediment of disparity of cult (c. 1129).

[276] Benedict XIV, bull *Matrimonia,* November 4, 1741, in *Bull. Ben. XIV,* 1:178.

[277] Cappello, *De Matrimonio,* n. 659.

[278] For a more detailed treatment of these post-Tridentine developments, see F. Schenk, *The Matrimonial Impediments of Mixed Religion and Disparity of Cult, CanLawStud* 51 (Washington, D.C.: Catholic University of America, 1929) 45–69.

[279] *CIC* 1061, §1, 2°.

[280] *LG* 15; *UR* 3.

[281] See *DH,* especially 2–5.

[282] CDF, instr *Matrimonii sacramentum,* March 18, 1966, I, 3, *CLD* 6, 594–595.

[283] See *Ecum Dir* 143–160.

Prohibition of Mixed Marriages

Canon 1124 — Without express permission of the competent authority, a marriage is prohibited between two baptized persons of whom one is baptized in the Catholic Church or received into it after baptism and has not defected from it by a formal act and the other of whom is enrolled in a Church or ecclesial community not in full communion with the Catholic Church.

The revised code repeats the traditional prohibition of marriages between Catholics and baptized members of non-Catholic Christian churches and ecclesial communities. In fact, the language of the code ("is prohibited") seems somewhat stronger than that used by Paul VI in *Matrimonia mixta* ("may not be contracted").[284] Nevertheless, the revised code situates the discipline on mixed marriages in a wholly new context that profoundly but subtly changes its meaning.

From Dispensation to Permission

The 1917 code, which was still in effect when *Matrimonia mixta* was promulgated, based its prohibition of mixed marriages on the impedient impediment of mixed religion (see *CIC* 1060–1064). To enter a mixed marriage lawfully, a Catholic had first to be dispensed from this impediment. The law views dispensations negatively. Since church law aims to protect important communal values, dispensations should be granted rarely and in circumstances where the values the law upholds are not threatened and there are objectively grave reasons for departing from the usual discipline in an individual case. In brief, the legislator wants the faithful to avoid certain activities, but is willing, sometimes reluctantly, to make exceptions. However, during the twentieth century dispensations from the impediment of mixed religion were increasingly granted as a matter of course.

[284] *Matrimonia mixta, CLD* 7, 712, 715.

The revised code no longer categorizes mixed religion as an impediment and requires not a dispensation but a permission (*licentia*) before a mixed marriage is contracted. Unlike dispensations, permissions are not viewed negatively by the law. Elsewhere in the code, permissions are required for activities that the legislator views favorably but that entail certain inherent risks. The requirement of prior permission is an attempt to ensure that these risks are removed or at least minimized before the faithful engage in the activity in question.[285] By abrogating mixed religion as an impediment and requiring only permission for Catholics to enter into mixed marriages, the revised code has taken a decidedly more positive view of mixed marriages than did the previous code and the tradition underlying it.

Concerns Surrounding Mixed Marriages

This more positive assessment of mixed marriages has not blinded the Church to the particular problems to which these marriages can give rise. As Paul VI pointed out, mixed marriages pose "an obstacle to the full spiritual communion of the parties."[286] Despite their sharing a common faith in Christ, the scriptures, and other elements of the Christian heritage, spouses in mixed marriages bring with them the tragically divided state of the Church of Christ. The different ways in which their respective churches understand and live out the common Christian heritage can be a source of tensions and misunderstandings within their marriage. Nor can the danger of the Catholic party's lapse from the Catholic Church be discounted. Mixed marriage is the single most significant factor in the decision of a Catholic to join another

[285] See, for example, c. 933, which requires the permission of the local ordinary to celebrate Mass in a sacred edifice of a non-Catholic church or ecclesial community, and c. 934, §1, 2°, which requires permission of the local ordinary to reserve the Eucharist in non-parochial churches and oratories and chapels not connected to a religious house.

[286] *Matrimonia mixta, CLD* 7, 715.

Christian church and an important factor in lapse from religious practice altogether.[287]

As a result of these pastoral concerns, Catholics must seek the permission of the competent authority before entering into a mixed marriage. Those who have left the Catholic Church by a formal act[288] are not bound by this obligation, unless they wish to marry a Catholic (see c. 1071, §2). The authority competent to grant this permission is the local ordinary of the place where the Catholic party has a domicile or quasi-domicile or of the place where he or she is actually staying (c. 136). Failure to seek this permission does not of itself invalidate a mixed marriage, but it does render it illicit.

Conditions for Granting Permission for a Mixed Marriage

Canon 1125 — The local ordinary can grant a permission of this kind if there is a just and reasonable cause. He is not to grant it unless the following conditions have been fulfilled:

1° **the Catholic party is to declare that he or she is prepared to remove dangers of defecting from the faith and is to make a sincere promise to do all in his or her power so that all offspring are baptized and brought up in the Catholic Church;**

2° **the other party is to be informed at an appropriate time about the promises which the Catholic party is to make, in such a way that it is certain that he or she is truly aware of the promise and obligation of the Catholic party;**

3° **both parties are to be instructed about the purposes and essential properties of marriage which neither of the contracting parties is to exclude.**

A "just and reasonable cause" must exist for a local ordinary to grant permission for a mixed

marriage. By saying that the local ordinary can grant such a permission (*concedere potest*), the canon leaves some room for discretion in assessing the sufficiency of the reasons for permitting a mixed marriage. However, since the Church ordinarily grants this permission "provided that a just reason is had"[289] and the spiritual good of the faithful is a legitimate cause,[290] it would be an abuse of pastoral discretion to refuse the permission if it would truly serve the spiritual good of the parties and they are otherwise prepared for marriage. Thus, assessing the sufficiency of the cause for this permission can be reduced in practice to determining whether there are adequate safeguards for the faith of the Catholic party and the children. Without these safeguards, the permission would hardly serve the spiritual good of the faithful.

The local ordinary is not to permit a mixed marriage unless three conditions are met: the declaration and promise of the Catholic party, the notification of the non-Catholic party, and catechesis for both parties.

1. Declaration and Promise of the Catholic Party

Following the path blazed by Paul VI, the revised code requires no promises by the non-Catholic party but places on the Catholic party the burden for ensuring continuance of his or her own Catholic practice and seeing to the Catholic formation of children. The Catholic must first declare his or her readiness to remove dangers of lapsing from the Catholic faith. He or she should be willing to recognize the potential problems arising from differences of religion that have already surfaced during the courtship or are reasonably foreseeable. An anti-Catholic attitude on the part of the non-Catholic or his or her family, lack of respect for the Catholic's religious convictions or practice, and differences of attitude about the frequency of religious practice or church support are issues that should be discussed and resolved

---

[287] A. Greeley, *The Catholic Myth* (New York: Scribners, 1990) 111.

[288] See the commentary on c. 1117.

[289] *Matrimonia mixta,* 3, *CLD* 7, 715.

[290] *EM*, viii, *CLD* 6, 397.

prior to the marriage in a manner consonant with the parties' consciences. If the non-Catholic is absolutely indifferent to matters religious, the Catholic should be aware of how difficult it will be to maintain religious observance and see to the religious formation of children without the support of his or her spouse.

The Catholic party must also promise "to do all in his or her power so that all offspring are baptized and brought up in the Catholic Church." Marriage is ordered to the procreation and education of children (c. 1055, §1). "Since they have given life to their children, parents have a most grave obligation and possess the right to educate them" (c. 226, §2). This right and obligation of parents extends to the physical, social, cultural, moral, and religious upbringing of their children (c. 1136). Catholic parents have a particular duty to see that their children are baptized soon after birth (c. 867, §1), that they are prepared for the sacraments of confirmation and Holy Eucharist and approach these sacraments at the appropriate time (cc. 890 and 914), and that they receive appropriate catechesis at home (c. 774, §2) and have access to the available opportunities for further Catholic formation outside the home (c. 793, §1). As a condition for permission for a mixed marriage, the Catholic must promise to make a sincere effort to fulfill these obligations.

The promise extends to all children who will be born of the marriage. Thus, it is not permissible to agree in advance to raise any male children in one church and the female children in the other or to baptize or raise the children in both churches (or neither) and allow them to choose for themselves when they are of age.[291] In its strict sense, the promise refers only to children to be born

after the proposed marriage. It does not extend to children already born out of wedlock or in an invalid union that is to be convalidated or in a previous marriage of either of the parties.[292] However, Catholics should be reminded of their moral obligation to see to the religious formation of these children.

The revised code has omitted the 1917 code's requirement that, before permission for a mixed marriage was granted, the competent authority have moral certainty that the promises would be fulfilled.[293] Instead, the Catholic must promise to "do all in his or her power" to see to the Catholic baptism and rearing of the children, not to guarantee that these efforts will be successful. In fact, he or she may foresee that his or her efforts will probably be ineffective because of the strongly held convictions of his or her non-Catholic fiancé. The canonical and pastoral problems are whether a Catholic can, in good faith, promise to do all that he or she can to see to the Catholic baptism and formation of children while realizing the likely futility of these efforts and whether his or her promise in these circumstances is sufficient basis for granting permission for the mixed marriage.

The phrase "to do all in his or her power" is derived from *Matrimonia mixta*. Various episcopal conference norms[294] implementing this *motu proprio* have specified the manner in which the Catholic's promise is to be made, but they have shed little light on the meaning of the phrase. More helpful are CDF responses in cases referred to it pursuant to the instruction *Matrimonii sacramentum* when one or both parties refused to make the required promises.[295] These replies indicate that the phrase "to do all in his or her power" is to be understood literally. Permission for a mixed marriage can be granted even when it is foreseen

---

[291] Canon 1366 threatens penal sanctions for Catholic parents who allow their children to be baptized or raised in a non-Catholic religion. However, *Ecum Dir* 151 notes: "If, notwithstanding the Catholic's best efforts, the children are not baptized and brought up in the Catholic Church, the Catholic parent does not fall subject to the censure of Canon Law. At the same time, his/her obligation to share the Catholic faith with the children does not cease."

[292] SCOf, reply, January 16, 1942, *CLD* 2, 286.

[293] *CIC* 1061, §1, 3°.

[294] See *CLD* 7, 714–741.

[295] See CDF, replies of May 17, 1966; June 18, 1966; July 9, 1966; December 10, 1966; December 12, 1966; February 27, 1967; *CLD* 6, 597–604.

that the Catholic's efforts to pass on the Catholic faith will probably be fruitless because of the resistance of the non-Catholic spouse. In these circumstances, the Catholic party can fulfill his or her obligation, at least in part,

> by playing an active part in contributing to the Christian atmosphere of the home; doing all that is possible by word and example to enable the other members of the family to appreciate the specific values of the Catholic tradition; taking whatever steps are necessary to be informed about his/her own faith so as to be able to explain and discuss it with them; praying with the family for the grace of Christian unity as the Lord wills it.[296]

Doing all that one can does not include so insisting on the Catholic formation of children that the stability of the marriage is threatened. What is necessary is a sincere promise by the Catholic to do all in his or her power to assure the Catholic formation of children. The sincerity of that promise is to be presumed, unless there is evidence to the contrary.

2. Informing the Non-Catholic

The declaration and promise by the Catholic spouse are necessary but not sufficient for the granting of permission for a mixed marriage. The non-Catholic party must also be informed of the declaration and promise the Catholic has made, in such a way that he or she understands that the Catholic has undertaken a genuine obligation.

Although the non-Catholic is not required to make a promise comparable to that of the Catholic and the dictates of the former's conscience are to be respected, the obligations of the Catholic party should be addressed early enough in the marriage preparation process to allow a thorough airing of the concerns and possible objections of both parties. The parish priest or pastoral minister responsible for marriage preparation should attempt to draw the couple into a candid discussion of the religious issues in their marriage, possible sources of tension, and strategies for dealing with conflicts. The pastoral minister should assist the couple to reach an understanding on these issues, and especially the religious nurture of children, that is consonant both with the Catholic's obligations and with their respective consciences. Sound pastoral care does not defer resolution of potentially divisive religious issues to some indefinite time after the marriage.

3. Catechesis for Marriage

Both parties to a mixed marriage are to be catechized about the nature, properties, and ends of marriage. This catechesis should be positive in tone and should highlight those areas where the couples' respective traditions share a common vision of marriage and married life. However, it should not overlook areas where their religious traditions espouse divergent positions. This catechesis should establish a context for ascertaining that neither party excludes an essential end or property of marriage from his or her consent.[297]

Competence of the Episcopal Conference

Canon 1126 — It is for the conference of bishops to establish the method in which these declarations and promises, which are always required, must be made and to define the manner in which they are to be established in the external forum and the non-Catholic party informed about them.

Like *Matrimonia mixta,* the revised code leaves to episcopal conferences the task of issuing specific norms adapted to the conditions of their territory about how the Catholic's declaration and promise is to be made, how this declaration and promise are to be proven in the external forum, and how the non-Catholic is to be informed. Like all conference decrees, these mixed marriage norms have force only after they have received the *recognitio* of the Holy See and been properly promulgated.

---

[296]*Ecum Dir* 151.

[297]*Ecum Dir* 148–149.

Since permission for a mixed marriage always requires the declaration and promise by the Catholic and the notification of the non-Catholic, there should always be some written documentation to prove that these requirements have been met. The Catholic should normally make the declaration and promise in writing, but he or she may make them orally. In either case, they should be made in the presence of a priest or deacon who certifies with his own signature that they were made. The notification of the non-Catholic party should also be attested to in writing by the responsible priest or deacon. While printed formulas to which the required signatures are affixed may be employed, the priest or deacon should indicate in some way that the declaration and promise were made sincerely.

Since the norms of the code governing mixed marriages are substantially the same as those of *Matrimonia mixta,* many episcopal conferences, including that of the United States, simply reiterated the norms they issued in response to *Matrimonia mixta* after the revised code was promulgated.[298]

Canonical and Liturgical Form

Canon 1127 — §1. The prescripts of can. 1108 are to be observed for the form to be used in a mixed marriage. Nevertheless, if a Catholic party contracts marriage with a non-Catholic party of an Eastern rite, the canonical form of the celebration must be observed for liceity only; for validity, however, the presence of a sacred minister is required and the other requirements of law are to be observed.

Mixed Marriage in a Catholic Church

When a Catholic receives permission to enter into a mixed marriage, he or she remains bound to observe the canonical form when celebrating the marriage. The exchange of consent is to take

place in the context of the liturgical rite specified in *The Rite of Marriage.* Mixed marriages are normally not to be celebrated during the Eucharist,[299] especially because of the awkwardness, confusion, and misunderstandings that can arise from the Catholic Church's discipline on *communicatio in sacris* (c. 844, §§3–5), which would bar most non-Catholic spouses and their families from the reception of the Eucharist.[300] However, the local ordinary can permit the celebration of mixed marriages during Mass either in individual cases or in general at the discretion of the pastor.

A non-Catholic priest or minister may be present and actively participate in a Catholic liturgical celebration of marriage. He or she may be invited to give "additional prayers, blessings, or words of greeting or exhortation. If the marriage is not part of the eucharistic celebration, the minister may also be invited to read a lesson and/or to preach."[301] However, only the Catholic minister may validly ask for and receive the consent of the parties in the name of the Church.

Marriages of Catholics and Eastern Non-Catholics

The canonical form of marriage must be observed for liceity, but *not* for validity when a Catholic marries an Eastern non-Catholic.[302] However, to be recognized as valid, the marriage must be celebrated in the presence of a non-Catholic Eastern priest who conducts the sacred rite according to the norm of the law of his church and imparts the customary blessing to the couple. Although the Catholic Church is willing to recognize the Eastern sacred rite as a suitable substitute for

---

[298] NCCB-*CompNm,* 16 and 35–49.

[299] *Rite of Marriage,* 8.
[300] *Ecum Dir* 159.
[301] NCCB-*CompNm,* 43. See also *Ecum Dir* 158.
[302] This exception was introduced for marriages between Eastern Catholics and Eastern non-Catholics by the conciliar decree *OE* 18. It was extended to include marriages of Latin Catholics with Eastern non-Catholics by the decree *Crescens matrimoniorum* of the CEC on February 22, 1967. *CLD* 6, 605–606.

the usual canonical form, the Church would not recognize the validity of the marriage if one of the parties were bound by a diriment impediment such as prior bond. Although non-observance of the canonical form does not affect the validity of the marriage in these cases, its lawfulness requires that a Catholic who plans to marry in an Orthodox ceremony first seek permission for a mixed marriage and a dispensation from the obligation of observing canonical form from his or her own local ordinary.

Dispensation from Canonical Form

§2. If grave difficulties hinder the observance of canonical form, the local ordinary of the Catholic party has the right of dispensing from the form in individual cases, after having consulted the ordinary of the place in which the marriage is celebrated and with some public form of celebration for validity. It is for the conference of bishops to establish norms by which the aforementioned dispensation is to be granted in a uniform manner.

Latin Discipline

Prior to 1970, the competence to dispense Catholics from the observance of canonical form was reserved to the Apostolic See, except in cases of danger of death. *Matrimonia mixta* authorized local ordinaries to dispense from the observance of this form for mixed marriages when grave difficulties stand in the way of its observance. This reformed discipline has been incorporated into the revised code.

Dispensations from canonical form for mixed marriages can be granted by the local ordinary of the Catholic party, i.e., the local ordinary of the place where the Catholic has a domicile or quasi-domicile.[303] If the marriage is to be celebrated in an-

other diocese, the Catholic's local ordinary is not to grant the dispensation without first consulting the ordinary of the place of celebration. Although this consultation does not affect the validity of the dispensation and the local ordinary of the place of celebration exercises no veto power, the consultation aims to prevent confusion or wonderment when a Catholic marries in a non-Catholic ceremony with perhaps a Catholic minister present.

In its norms implementing *Matrimonia mixta,* the NCCB had authorized both the local ordinary of the Catholic party and the local ordinary of the place of celebration to dispense from canonical form.[304] With the promulgation of the revised code, the authorization for this dispensation to be granted by the local ordinary of the place of celebration has been abrogated.[305]

For a dispensation to be granted, grave obstacles must stand in the way of the observance of canonical form. While it is impossible to provide an exhaustive listing of all possible obstacles to the observance of form, the following have been suggested as legitimate pastoral reasons:

> to achieve family harmony or to avoid family alienation, to obtain parental agreement to the marriage, to recognize the significant claims of relationship or special friendship with a non-Catholic minister, to permit the marriage in a church that has particular importance to the non-Catholic.[306]

In many areas, the long-standing custom of celebrating marriages in the church of the bride may also be a sufficient reason.

Even though a dispensation from *canonical* form has been granted, the law requires the observance of some public form as a condition for the

---

[303] Catholics serving in the armed forces are subject to the concurrent jurisdiction of the military ordinary and the local ordinary of the place where they have a domicile or

quasi-domicile. Thus, either ordinary may dispense from the obligation of canonical form for mixed marriages.

[304] NCCB, "Statement of the National Conference of Catholic Bishops on the Implementation of the Apostolic Letter on Mixed Marriages," 10, *CLD* 7, 737.

[305] NCCB-*CompNm,* 17.

[306] NCCB-*CompNm,* 42. See *Ecum Dir* 154.

validity of the marriage. A public form is one that allows the fact of the marriage to be proved in the external forum. Dispensations from canonical form are usually granted to permit the celebration of the marriage in the church or place of worship of the non-Catholic party, but, especially in cases of marriages between Catholics and non-Christians, these dispensations can be granted to permit civil ceremonies. While the form required by the civil jurisdiction for the recognition of marriage would usually meet the criteria for a public form, "common law" marriages would not do so even where they are recognized by civil law.

Episcopal conferences are to issue norms to regulate the granting and registration of dispensations from canonical form. These norms can establish conditions which must be observed for the valid celebration of a mixed marriage pursuant to a dispensation. The local ordinary who grants the dispensation can also attach conditions that must be observed in the celebration of the marriage under pain of nullity. Thus, the local ordinary can require for validity that the marriage be celebrated on the date, in the place, and before the official mentioned in the petition for the dispensation.[307]

If a Catholic priest or deacon is present at a religious celebration of a mixed marriage after a dispensation from the canonical form, he may participate in the celebration at the invitation of the competent non-Catholic authority. He may offer words of greeting, prayers, or blessings or read scriptural lessons, but only at the invitation of the representative of the host church.[308]

Outside of situations of danger of death (c. 1079), the competence to dispense from the observance of canonical form for the marriage of two Catholics remains reserved to the Apostolic See.[309] There seems to be an openness on the part of the Holy See to grant these dispensations on behalf of recent converts to the Catholic Church when insistence on observance of canonical form would alienate them from their families and perhaps weaken their own commitment to the Church.[310]

Eastern Discipline

For Eastern Catholics, the blessing of the couple by the priest is an integral part of the celebration of marriage and, in ordinary circumstances, necessary for its validity. Thus, the authority to dispense Eastern Catholics from the obligation of observing canonical form or the sacred rite is "reserved to the Apostolic See or the patriarch, who will not grant it except for a most grave reason" (*CCEO* 835). In North America, dispensations from canonical form for the celebration of mixed marriages involving Latin Catholics have become relatively common. Especially where Eastern Catholics practice their faith in Latin churches, often due to a shortage of priests of their own church *sui iuris,* the expectation has arisen that dispensations from the canonical form will be granted to allow them to celebrate their marriages in the church of their non-Catholic fiancées. Out of sensitivity to the pastoral needs that arise because of this situation, the Congregation for the Eastern Churches has granted the apostolic pronuncio the faculty to dispense from canonical form for mixed marriages involving an Eastern Catholic.[311] Nevertheless, a most grave reason is still necessary for this dispensation to be granted.

Prohibition of Duplicate Ceremonies

§3. It is forbidden to have another religious celebration of the same marriage to give or renew matrimonial consent before or after the canonical celebration according to the norm of §1. Likewise, there is not to be a religious celebration in which the Catholic who is assisting and a non-Catholic minister together, using their own rites, ask for the consent of the parties.

---

[307] Com. Vat. II Interp., reply, April 9, 1979, *CLD* 9, 659.
[308] *Ecum Dir* 157.
[309] CodCom, reply, July 5, 1985, *AAS* 77 (1985) 771.

[310] SCSacr, reply, June 6, 1973, *CLD* 8, 818–820.
[311] Apostolic Pro-Nuncio, letter No. 5895/7, November 12, 1991 in *RRAO 1992,* 48–50.

When a mixed marriage is celebrated according to canonical form, another religious ceremony in which consent is exchanged or renewed is strictly forbidden either before or after the Catholic ceremony. Similarly, when a dispensation from canonical form is granted, a Catholic ceremony before or after the public celebration is prohibited. Duplicate ceremonies of this kind at least implicitly call into question the validity of the original celebration of the marriage. Also forbidden are religious services in which Catholic and non-Catholic ministers "co-officiate" and ask for and receive the consent of the spouses according to their respective liturgical books. However, the Holy See has been willing to permit two religious ceremonies for the marriage of a Catholic and an Orthodox communicant as long as consent was exchanged before a Catholic minister and the Orthodox priest confers the nuptial blessing with no new exchange of consent.[312]

This canon expressly prohibits only reduplication of religious ceremonies. Thus, it does not bar Catholics from observing the civil form prior to the religious ceremony in those places where the civil form is required for recognition of the marriage by the State.

Pastoral Care for Mixed Marriages

Canon 1128 — Local ordinaries and other pastors of souls are to take care that the Catholic spouse and the children born of a mixed marriage do not lack the spiritual help to fulfill their obligations and are to help spouses foster the unity of conjugal and family life.

Despite the Church's willingness to allow the faithful to enter into mixed marriages, it also recognizes the particular problems that couples in such marriages often encounter. Thus, the law reminds local ordinaries and pastors of their pastoral responsibility to assist these couples to transcend the tensions occasioned by their religious differences and to come to experience the mystery of unity that exists between Christ and the Church despite its divisions. Pastors should be particularly attentive to supporting and assisting the Catholic spouse to remain faithful to the commitments he or she made in the declaration and promises.

The responsibility of pastors toward couples in mixed marriages is a particular application of the general obligation of the Christian community to assist married couples to "lead holier and fuller lives in their family" (c. 1063, 4°). However, the special needs and problems of couples in mixed marriages may outstrip the resources of the Catholic community and its pastors. Thus, adequate pastoral care of mixed marriages will often require ecumenical cooperation.[313]

Application to Disparity-of-Cult Marriages

Canon 1129 — The prescripts of cann. 1127 and 1128 must be applied also to marriages which the impediment of disparity of cult mentioned in can. 1086, §1 impedes.

When a Catholic seeks to marry an unbaptized person, he or she must first secure a dispensation from the diriment impediment of disparity of cult. This dispensation can be granted only after the *cautiones* required by canon 1125 and further specified by episcopal conference norms have been made (c. 1086, §2). Since in marriages between Catholics and unbaptized persons the spouses do not share a common Christian faith, their religious differences and the tensions arising from them are likely to be more acute. Thus, particular attention must be given to safeguarding the

---

[312] SCOf, reply of October 26, 1964 and SCDF reply of June 16, 1966, *CLD* 6, 22–23.

[313] *Ecum Dir* 147 suggests: "In fulfilling this responsibility, where the situation warrants it, positive steps should be taken, if possible, to establish contacts with the minister of the other Church or ecclesial Community, even if this may not always prove easy. In general, mutual consultation between Christian pastors for supporting such marriages and upholding their values can be a fruitful field of ecumenical collaboration."

faith of the Catholic and ensuring the handing on of the faith to children.

The norms governing the canonical and liturgical celebration of mixed marriages are to be applied to marriages involving the impediment of disparity of cult as well. If the canonical form is observed, the marriage can be celebrated in a Catholic church but always outside the Mass.[314] Dispensations from the obligation of observing canonical form can be granted under the same conditions as for mixed marriages.

CHAPTER VII[315]
MARRIAGE CELEBRATED SECRETLY
[cc. 1130–1133][316]

The Tridentine decree *Tametsi* aimed at eradicating clandestine marriages and their attendant social problems by requiring that henceforth only those marriages celebrated in the presence of the proper local ordinary or pastor and two witnesses would be considered valid. Where it was promulgated, *Tametsi* largely succeeded in its desired effect, but it gave rise to several new and unforeseen problems. One of these problems was the dilemma of couples who sincerely desired to marry and who often sought marriage to salve their consciences, but who feared there would be seriously negative repercussions if their marrying were to be publicly known. The oft cited example was the couple who had lived in concubinage for a long time and were universally thought to be married. On the one hand, if the couple remained as they were, they would still be "living in sin" and their children would remain canonically (and often civilly) illegitimate. On the other hand, if they married according to the canonical form, the publication of the

banns and the public celebration of their marriage would highlight their irregular situation and so destroy their reputations in the community.[317]

In his encyclical *Satis vobis* of November 17, 1741, Benedict XIV enacted legislation for dealing with these awkward situations in a way that struck a delicate balance between the complete privacy characteristic of clandestine unions with its harm to the public good and the full publicity required by the Tridentine form with its possible harm to the private good.[318] The legislation of Benedict XIV created the new canonical institute of "marriage of conscience" (*matrimonium conscientiae*), which was incorporated largely unchanged into canons 1104–1107 of the 1917 code. This legislation is repeated with some minor emendations in the 1983 code under the more descriptive rubric of "Marriage Celebrated Secretly."

Justification for Secret Celebration of Marriage

Canon 1130 — For a grave and urgent cause, the local ordinary can permit a marriage to be celebrated secretly.

To understand the discipline governing the secret celebration of marriage, it is necessary to be clear about what these marriages are not. They are not clandestine marriages. Clandestine marriages are entered into with no public form and no public record of their celebration. They are, therefore, not subject to proof in the external forum. However, marriages secretly celebrated are entered into with the observance of canonical form, and a written record of them is kept. Therefore, their celebration can be proved, if this proof becomes necessary later.

Nor is a marriage celebrated secretly the sort of morganatic marriage once employed by Euro-

---

[314] *Rite of Marriage,* 8.

[315] See Doyle, in *CLSA Com,* 806–807; Lüdicke, in *Münster Com,* Einführung vor 1130/1–1133/1; Navarro Valls, in *Pamplona ComEng,* 715–716; and Kelly, in *CLSGBI Com,* 638–639.

[316] See *CCEO* 840.

[317] For a more thorough discussion of these problems and the attempt to address them, see V. Coburn, *Marriages of Conscience, CanLawStud* 191 (Washington, D. C.: Catholic University of America, 1944).

[318] Benedict XIV, ency *Satis vobis,* November 17, 1741, *CICFontes,* n. 319.

pean nobility. A morganatic marriage is a marriage "of a man, of noble or illustrious birth, with a woman of inferior status, upon condition that neither the wife nor her children shall partake of the titles, arms, or dignity of the husband or succeed to his inheritance."[319] A marriage celebrated secretly entails equal obligations and rights of both spouses in all that pertains to the community of life (c. 1135).

A marriage celebrated secretly is not one celebrated in the internal forum. The Apostolic Penitentiary has occasionally granted radical sanations of marriages in the internal forum when it was impossible to prove the invalidity of the previous marriage of one of the spouses in the external forum.[320] In itself, an internal forum sanation does not allow the spouses to act in the external forum (e.g., receiving holy communion publicly), except to the extent that their situation is occult. Should their situation be made public, they are barred from acting in the external forum, if the sanation was granted in the internal sacramental forum or if there is no proof of the granting of the sanation in the internal non-sacramental forum.[321] However, the secret celebration of marriage takes place in the external forum in the presence of an authorized priest or deacon and two witnesses. If the fact of their marriage becomes public or their situation a source of scandal, the fact that it was celebrated secretly is also made public.

The local ordinary may permit the secret celebration of marriage. The 1917 code stipulated that the vicar general needed a special mandate to permit a secret celebration.[322] This stipulation has been omitted in the revised code. Nevertheless, the potential repercussions of a secret celebration of marriage, especially the possible conflicts between canon and civil law, suggest that a vicar general or episcopal vicar should not grant this permission without at least consulting with the diocesan bishop.

A grave and urgent cause is required to permit the secret celebration of marriage. The 1917 code had required a "most grave and most urgent" cause (*gravissima et urgentissima causa*).[323] This change in wording does not mean that permission for the secret celebration of marriage can be granted more lightly under the new legislation. The phrase "a most grave and most urgent cause," which appeared only once in the 1917 code, meant that the cause for maintaining secrecy was more than ordinarily grave *and* the celebration of marriage was a pressing necessity.[324]

The mere desire of the couple to keep their marriage secret is not sufficient to grant this permission. Commentators on the 1917 code suggested reasons that could justify permission for a secret celebration of marriage:

1. the couple had been living in concubinage and were generally believed to be already married;
2. the spouses were of radically unequal social status and their marriage would result in permanent alienation from family or disinheritance;
3. a widow would lose custody of her children or her inheritance or both as a result of remarriage;
4. a widow would lose the job on which she depended to support herself and her children;
5. the couple are barred from marriage by an unjust civil law (e.g., anti-miscegenation statutes).[325]

Even in these situations, the couple would have to have a compelling reason for marrying at this time rather than waiting until the situation changed.

---

[319] *Black's Law Dictionary,* s.v. "Marriage. Morganatic marriage."

[320] See ApPen, private reply, May 22, 1950, *CLD* 5, 712–713.

[321] See commentary on c. 1082.

[322] *CIC* 1104.

[323] Ibid.

[324] Coburn, 74.

[325] Ibid., 76–83; Cappello, *De Matrimonio,* n. 723; Wernz-Vidal, 5: n. 567.

At present, the most common reason why couples seek to celebrate marriage secretly is that, as a result of a public marriage, one of them (usually the woman) will lose government entitlements (e.g., Social Security survivors benefits, "welfare") on which she depends for sustenance.[326] The local ordinary may be sympathetic to the plight of couples who may suffer financial hardship as a result of a public marriage, but he should consider the possible consequences of permitting a secret celebration. This permission may render the local ordinary liable to a civil suit or criminal prosecution for conspiracy to defraud the government.

Laws providing for the cut-off of entitlements after marriage are not *per se* unjust. They are based on the presumption that the new spouse will provide for the dependent one. Nevertheless, these laws can work disproportionate hardship on couples whose income is marginal. Before permitting a secret celebration of marriage in such a case, the local ordinary should determine whether loss of entitlements would leave the couple indigent or only render their lifestyle somewhat less comfortable.

Implications of Secret Celebration

Canon 1131 — Permission to celebrate a marriage secretly entails the following:
1° **the investigations which must be conducted before the marriage are done secretly;**
2° **the local ordinary, the one assisting, the witnesses, and the spouses observe secrecy about the marriage celebrated.**

Permission for the secret celebration of a marriage does not exempt the assisting local ordinary or parish priest from the obligation of establishing the parties' freedom to marry through a pre-nuptial investigation. However, this investigation must be conducted secretly. After the marriage, the record of the pre-nuptial investigation is not to be retained in the archives of the parish where the marriage is celebrated. Instead, the pre-nuptial file should be destroyed after the marriage is properly recorded.[327]

Permission for the secret celebration of marriage also obliges the local ordinary, the assisting minister, the two other witnesses, and the spouses themselves to maintain secrecy about the event. All participating in a secret celebration must be informed of the seriousness of this obligation.

Cessation of the Obligation of Secrecy

Canon 1132 — The obligation of observing the secrecy mentioned in can. 1131, n. 2 ceases on the part of the local ordinary if grave scandal or grave harm to the holiness of marriage is imminent due to the observance of the secret; this is to be made known to the parties before the celebration of the marriage.

The obligation of maintaining secrecy binds the assisting minister (if he is distinct from the local ordinary) and the witnesses absolutely, but it binds the local ordinary only conditionally. The spouses themselves are always free by mutual agreement to make the fact of the marriage public. If maintaining secrecy about the celebration of a marriage threatens to provoke serious scandal or damage to the sanctity of marriage, the local ordinary is released from this obligation. The conditions that will release the local ordinary from his obligation of secrecy must be explained to the parties prior to the marriage.

To release the local ordinary from the obligation of secrecy, the harm to the sanctity of marriage must be grave; its existence or continuation must be facilitated by the secrecy; and it must be present or imminent.[328] Such harm to the sanctity of marriage could arise from one spouse's attempted public marriage with a third party. Scandal could also easily arise if the couple is widely known to be co-

---

[326] The same situation can arise when re-marriage will result in the loss of private benefits such as alimony, child support payments, or income from a deceased spouse's estate.

[327] Coburn, 127.
[328] Ibid., 114.

habiting and the Church's silence creates the impression that it approves of this activity.

Registration of Secret Celebrations

Canon 1133 — A marriage celebrated secretly is to be noted only in a special register to be kept in the secret archive of the curia.

Marriages celebrated secretly are not to be recorded in the parish where they took place. Nor are entries to be made in the baptismal registers of the places where the parties were christened. The marriage is to be recorded only in a special book maintained in the secret archives of the diocesan curia. Once this entry is made, all documentation related to the marriage should be destroyed.

BIBLIOGRAPHY

Bibliographical information for canons 1073–1133 can be found after the commentary on canon 1165.

CHAPTER VIII
THE EFFECTS OF MARRIAGE[1]
[cc. 1134–1140][2]

This chapter describes the effects of marriage, namely, the "bond that arises from the valid exchange of promises and the equal rights and duties that flow from the spouses' new status, especially concerning the education of children."[3] The canons describe the effects of the bond of marriage in the lives of the spouses (c. 1134), the equality of the spouses (c. 1135), and the obligations and rights of parents (c. 1136). The final canons in the chapter speak of the canonical understanding of the legitimacy of children (cc. 1137–1140).

The Marriage Bond

Canon 1134 — From a valid marriage there arises between the spouses a bond which by its nature is perpetual and exclusive. Moreover, a special sacrament strengthens and, as it were, consecrates the spouses in a Christian marriage for the duties and dignity of their state.

While the first sentence of this canon speaks of all marriages, natural and sacramental, the second sentence speaks only of sacramental marriages, i.e., those between two baptized persons. The canon speaks of the "bond" that arises from a valid marriage. By this bond, the partners become husband and wife in the relationship that is marriage. The bond is such that

in each partner a set of new obligations arises. The spouses, by committing themselves mutually to each other, give a new orientation to their own life. . . . A clearer and simpler way of conveying the same meaning would be to say that the spouses are bound to each other.[4]

This bond is "by its nature . . . perpetual and exclusive," which recalls the properties of marriage described in canon 1056. The properties in both natural and sacramental marriages are unity and indissolubility, but those properties are made firmer in a sacramental union.

The canon continues with its distinction between natural and sacramental unions: both are intrinsically good, but in a Christian marriage the spouses are strengthened to fulfill the duties of their state by the sacrament. Marriage, like the other sacraments, confers grace on those who receive the sacrament in a fruitful manner.[5]

The Mutual Obligations of the Spouses

Canon 1135 — Each spouse has an equal duty and right to those things which belong to the partnership of conjugal life.

The rights and obligations are equal for each spouse in marriage. These rights and obligations include family duties as well as the rights and obligations inherent in the interpersonal relationship of the spouses and their relations with their children. All these aspects are important, and neither party is ever a "lesser" partner in a marriage. "In spite of social and cultural inequalities which may be imposed from without, Christian marriage

---

[1] See T. Doyle, in *CLSA Com,* 807–811; R. Navarro Valls, in *Pamplona ComEng,* 716–718; D. Kelly, in *CLSGBI Com,* 639–642.

[2] For the most part there is no equivalent to this section in the Eastern code. Only *CCEO* 777 in the introductory canons on marriage corresponds to c. 1135.

[3] L. Örsy, *Marriage in Canon Law* (Wilmington, Del.: Michael Glazier, 1986) 201.

[4] Ibid., 203.

[5] See commentary on c. 1065 for a discussion of the fruitful reception of the sacrament.

imposes equal obligations of the spouses toward one another."[6]

It is impossible to make a complete listing of the rights and obligations that the spouses have toward one another and to the marriage. As examples of such rights and obligations that have been determined by jurisprudence, Doyle lists "the right to heterosexual acts,... mutual respect and support, cohabitation, and an interpersonal relationship."[7] Canon 1095, 3° speaks of the *essential* rights and obligations of marriage. The basic expression of the essential rights and obligations is found in canons 1055 and 1056, which speak of the elements and properties of marriage: the good of the spouses, the procreation and education of children, and the properties of unity and indissolubility.[8] All rights and obligations can be traced back to these essentials and to the understanding that marriage is an interpersonal relationship, a partnership of the whole of life which involves the participation and contribution of both spouses.

Duties of Parents toward Children

Canon 1136 — Parents have the most grave duty and the primary right to take care as best they can for the physical, social, cultural, moral, and religious education of their offspring.

> Canon 1136 underscores the fact that the procreative purpose of marriage is not simply fulfilled in the act of procreation, but is completed in the education of offspring.[9]

Parents have the right and duty to provide for the education of their children. This education is to be physical, social, cultural, moral, and religious. The objective of such education is that the children not only become responsible Christians, but also responsible and contributing members of society. Thus, the parents are responsible for providing food, clothing, medical care, and appropriate living conditions for their children, as well as fostering their psychological and spiritual development. This care of the children begins at the moment of their conception. Children will live in society, and they should be prepared to do so. Their moral development is essential so that they can make informed moral choices as they get older. Religious education beginning with baptism (c. 867) is also in the first place the responsibility of the parents (cf. c. 226, §2). Religious education should bring the children to an adult, mature practice and understanding of their faith.[10]

Legitimacy of Children

Canon 1137 — The children conceived or born of a valid or putative marriage are legitimate.

Both civil and canon law speak of the legitimacy of children. This was especially important when being legitimate or illegitimate had consequences in the law. Although the 1983 code retains the norm on legitimacy, in fact, this norm has little or no practical consequence in the law today.

The canon speaks only of the legitimacy of children of valid or putative marriages. This means that children conceived or born of marriages that are known to be null would be considered illegitimate. This situation of illegitimacy is true if the nullity is due to the presence of a known diriment impediment, or if it is due to a lack of canonical form.[11] In the case of a declaration of nullity of marriage, the children conceived or born of that union while it was considered putative (c. 1061, §3) are considered to be legitimate. In the case of the dissolution of a marriage (cc. 1142–1150), the children conceived or born

---

[6] Doyle, in *CLSA Com,* 809.

[7] Ibid.

[8] For more on these essential rights and obligations, see commentary on cc. 1095 and 1055–1056.

[9] M. Foster, "The Promotion of the Canonical Rights of Children," *CLSAP* 59 (1997) 176.

[10] See also cc. 793; 796, §2; 890.

[11] A marriage is putative if it was celebrated in good faith by at least one of the parties (c. 1061, §3).

of that union prior to the dissolution also remain legitimate.

If an invalid marriage becomes valid through a sanation (*sanatio in radice*) (cc. 1161–1165), the sanation legitimizes the children conceived or born of that marriage (c. 1161, §2). In the case of a simple validation of a marriage (cc. 1156–1160), the children are legitimated from the time of the validation.

Presumptions Concerning Legitimacy

Canon 1138 — §1. The father is he whom a lawful marriage indicates unless clear evidence proves the contrary.

§2. Children born at least 180 days after the day when the marriage was celebrated or within 300 days from the day of the dissolution of conjugal life are presumed to be legitimate.

Normally, if a married woman gives birth to a child, her lawful husband is presumed to be the father (§1). That presumption may be proven incorrect, however, by clear arguments to the contrary, such as, for example, the fact that the couple have lived apart for more than ten months (300 days) before the baby's birth, etc.

Paragraph two speaks of approximate periods of gestation, from about six months to about ten months. With due regard for modern technology and the fact that children are being born and survive at ever earlier ages, this paragraph offers a reasonable definition of the limits of the rebuttable legal presumption for establishing the legitimacy of a child.

Legitimation of Children

Canon 1139 — Illegitimate children are legitimated by the subsequent valid or putative marriage of their parents or by a rescript of the Holy See.

There are two ways of legitimating illegitimate children (both those who are born to parents who are not married and those who are born to parents in an invalid union): through the marriage of their parents after their birth, or through a rescript of the Holy See in a case where the requirements of the previous two canons have not been fulfilled.[12] An example of the latter would be a case in which the parties could not marry because they were not free to do so (e.g., prior valid marriage of one party), yet they had children together. Then, by the time they were free to marry, one of the parties had died. In such a case, a rescript of legitimation could be requested.

Effects of Legitimation

Canon 1140 — As regards canonical effects, legitimated children are equal in all things to legitimate ones unless the law has expressly provided otherwise.

In the present code there are no effects caused by illegitimacy, unlike in the 1917 code where being illegitimate had certain negative implications, especially for those wishing to be priests, cardinals, abbots, and bishops (*CIC* 1363, §1; 232, §2, 1°; 320, §2; 331, §1, 1°). However, there may be some restrictions on persons who are illegitimate in particular law, proper law, or concordats. If there are no effects of illegitimacy in the code, why did the redactors choose to keep canons 1137–1140 in the code? Because, as they noted,

> even though all the effects of illegitimacy have been removed from the universal law, the canons more appropriately remain since they can have application in particular law and, for another reason, they can highlight the sanctity of marriage in this way.[13]

---

[12] It should be noted, however, that such a rescript would not validate the invalid marriage of the parents.

[13] *Comm* 15 (1983) 240, as translated by J. Abbass, "Marriage in the Codes of Canon Law," *Apol* 68 (1995) 527.

CHAPTER IX[1]
THE SEPARATION OF SPOUSES
[cc. 1141–1155][2]

Once legitimately exchanged, marital consent gives rise to a relationship that is, in principle, perpetual and beyond the power of the spouses themselves to revoke or alter. This relationship transcends the existential relationship of the spouses and can perdure even after the definitive breakdown of the latter. Traditional canonical terminology designates this relationship as "the bond" (*vinculum*). The conjugal bond entails the equal right and obligation of the spouses to "those things which belong to the partnership of conjugal life" (c. 1135). Among these things is the right to enjoy and the obligation to preserve conjugal cohabitation or the sharing of a common bed, table, and dwelling.

Despite the principle that the conjugal bond and its attendant rights and obligations are perpetual, church law recognizes that circumstances can and do arise which render the maintenance of conjugal life impossible or, at least, intolerable. In some circumstances, the bond itself can be dissolved or dispensed.[3] These circumstances are regulated by canons 1141–1150. In other circumstances, the law allows the spouses to cease their common life and relieves them of many of their spousal obligations but without the freedom to enter a new marriage. Separations of this kind are regulated by canons 1151–1155.

ARTICLE 1: DISSOLUTION OF THE BOND
[cc. 1141–1150]

Historical Synopsis

Patristic Era

Fidelity to the teaching of Jesus as it is handed down in the synoptic tradition[4] prompted the early Church to reject the rather permissive attitude toward divorce enshrined in Roman law[5] and to treat remarriage after a divorce as a grave sin. With the notable exception of the anonymous author known as Ambrosiaster,[6] all patristic authors taught the immorality of remarriage after a divorce even when the divorce was occasioned by the other spouse's adultery.[7] While the teaching of the Fathers is clear and consistent, it is less clear that ecclesial practice was equally consistent.

---

[1] See T. Doyle, in *CLSA Com,* 811–822; K. Lüdicke, in *Münster Com,* Einführung vor 1141/1–1155/1; J. Hervada, in *Pamplona ComEng,* 719–726; and D. Kelly, in *CLSGBI Com,* 642–653.

[2] *CCEO* 853–866.

[3] Although most canonists speak of the "dissolution" of the bond of marriage in certain circumstances, the law itself regularly uses the term "dispensation" rather than "dissolution" to refer to the situation in which spouses are allowed to enter a new marriage after a sacramental marriage that was not consummated. See cc. 1697; 1698; 1699, §1; 1704; and 1706. The same preference for "dispensation" over "dissolution" was found in the 1917 code's canons 1119, 1962, 1963, and 1973 and the rubric of chapter 3 of title XX of Book IV, *De processibus.* This usage suggests that "dispensation from the obligations of a marriage" may be a more accurate description than "dissolution of the bond" of what happens when a person is permitted to enter a new marriage after a valid but failed marriage.

[4] Mk 10:9, 11–12; Mt 5:32, 19:9; Lk 16:18; as well as 1 Cor 7:10–11. See R. Collins, *Divorce in the New Testament* (Collegeville: Liturgical, 1992).

[5] See S. Treggiari, *Roman Marriage* (Oxford: Clarendon, 1993) 435–482.

[6] Ambrosiaster, *Ad Corinthios prima* 7:11, *Corpus Scriptorum Ecclesiasticorum Latinorum (CSEL)* 81, 2:75.

[7] See H. Crouzel, *L'Église primitive face au divorce* (Paris: Beauchesne, 1971); and A. Bevilacqua, "The History of the Indissolubility of Marriage," *CTSAP* 22 (1972) 253–308.

At least by the time of Cyprian in the mid-third century, adultery was ranked among the deadly sins to be submitted to the Church's penitential discipline. Since the gospels equate remarriage after divorce with adultery, the question of the ecclesial status of Christians who had divorced and remarried in accord with Roman law could not be avoided. The extant sources do not clearly indicate how the Church dealt with divorced Christians during the first four centuries, and it may be that practice differed from church to church. However, scattered ecclesiastical texts and new divorce legislation of the Christian emperors suggest that, in many places at least, the practice was to excommunicate or bar from the eucharistic table those who remarried after a divorce and to subject them to a period of penance which could last several years. At the end of this period, they were reconciled to the Church but not necessarily required to separate.[8]

This somewhat lenient practice of concession and toleration continued in the East. However, it was displaced in the West during the fourth and early fifth centuries by a more rigorist practice which was crystallized in the writings of Jerome and especially Augustine. Augustine's meditation on the New Testament led him to the conclusion that, if remarriage after divorce constituted adultery, then some residue of marriage (*quiddam coniugale*) must survive the *de facto* and *de iure* disintegration of the social fact of marriage.[9] This "marital something" was "the bond" (*vinculum*) whose perdurance even after divorce precluded the establishment of another marriage. In this way, Augustine quietly moved the prohibition of

divorce beyond the realm of morality into the realm of ontology: remarriage after a divorce was not only forbidden but impossible as long as the original spouse was alive.[10]

Middle Ages

The Augustinian position, which triumphed in the West, enabled the Church to judge not only whether a marriage was morally legitimate but also whether it was valid. No matter what their status in secular law, only marriages in conformity with divine law could be considered valid. Although it took the Church centuries to elaborate the implications of Augustine's heritage,[11] the principle was established that the bond of marriage between Christians could be sundered only by death and was, therefore, indissoluble.

The emergence of this doctrine of indissolubility required that the Church clearly identify those unions that it would recognize as marriages. The patristic Church absorbed the Roman law principle that the consent of the parties with marital affection (*affectio maritalis*) established marriage. "Marital affection" was a rather slippery standard[12] that did not always make clear which unions were legitimate marriages and which mere concubinages. However, Roman law and societal conventions provided a framework for distinguishing concretely between a marriage which was binding until death and a concubinage which was, in principle, dissoluble.[13]

Determining who was truly married was complicated by the influx of Germanic peoples and the collapse of the Roman Empire in the West.

---

[8] G. Cereti, "The Reconciliation of Remarried Divorcees according to Canon 8 of the Council of Nicea," in *Ius Sequitur Vitam*, ed. J. Provost and K. Walf (Louvain: Leuven University, 1991) 193–207. For a fuller presentation of this position, see G. Cereti, *Divorzio, nuove nozze et penitenza nella Chiesa primitiva* (Bologna: Dehoniane, 1977). See also J. Noonan, "Novel 22," in *The Bond of Marriage*, ed. W. Bassett (Notre Dame: University of Notre Dame, 1968) 41–96.

[9] *De nupt. et conc.* 1,11, *CSEL* 42, 223.

[10] P. L. Reynolds, *Marriage in the Western Church* (Leiden: E. J. Brill, 1994) 149–152, 280–311.

[11] See C. Lefebvre, "L'évolution de l'action de nullité," *RDC* 26 (1976) 25; and J. Gaudemet, "Le lien matrimonial," *RDC* 21 (1971) 81–105.

[12] J. Noonan, "Marital Affection in the Canonists," *Studia Gratiana* 12 (1975) 479–509.

[13] See Reynolds, 159–169; and J. Brundage, *Law, Sex and Christian Society in Medieval Europe* (Chicago: University of Chicago, 1987) 98–103.

The laws and customs of many of these peoples attributed considerably greater significance than had Roman law to physical consummation and the role of families in the establishment of marriage. The resulting cultural clash crystallized in the dispute between the school of Bologna (Gratian) and the school of Paris (Peter Lombard).

The school of Bologna taught that marriage was initiated (*coniugium initiatum*) by the consent at the time of the betrothal but that it was not completed until it had been ratified by an act of sexual intercourse (*coniugium consummatum* or *ratum*).[14] As a result, a consummated marriage was indissoluble, but one initiated by consent could be dissolved prior to consummation because it still lacked firmness. The school of Paris distinguished clearly between engagement or betrothal (*verba de futuro*) and marriage consent itself (*verba de praesenti*). The latter was necessary and sufficient to establish an indissoluble marriage whether or not it was subsequently consummated by sexual intercourse.

The dispute between the schools, which reflected the deeper conflict of cultures, was resolved by Pope Alexander III (1159–1181) and his successors. In a series of decretals, these popes held that consent alone was sufficient to establish a true and valid sacramental marriage that was indissoluble in principle. However, prior to consummation, this marriage could be dissolved or dispensed by solemn religious profession on the part of one of the spouses or, for a proportionate cause, by the intervention of ecclesiastical authority. Thus, only after consummation was a marriage indissoluble in fact.

Pauline Privilege

The teaching on indissolubility was further qualified by the medieval development and juridicization of the Pauline privilege. While patristic authors conceded that Jews and pagans married legitimately, they showed little interest in the status of the unions of unbelievers who divorced and remarried. However, the prevailing view, again enunciated clearly by Augustine, was that Christian spouses of unbelievers, whether they were Christians at the time of the marriage or subsequent converts, could separate from their unbelieving spouses but could not remarry.[15] However, by the early Middle Ages most authors followed the position of Ambrosiaster who understood Paul's concession in 1 Corinthians 7:12–15 as allowing the newly converted spouse to remarry if the unbelieving spouse departed.[16] This position was enshrined in church law in the decretals of Innocent III.[17]

Three constitutions by sixteenth century popes extended the provisions of the Pauline privilege to polygamous situations encountered by missionaries in the Americas.[18] Although the limited concessions contained in the constitutions were originally given only as special faculties for missionaries in particular regions, canon 1125 of the 1917 code extended them to all countries where the same conditions existed. Following the promulgation of the 1917 code, Pius XI and his successors moved beyond the traditional framework of the Pauline privilege to dissolve in favor of the faith marriages involving at least one unbaptized person after a conversion to the Catholic Church and eventually without a conversion in favor of the faith of a new Catholic spouse.[19]

---

[14] C. 27, q. 2; Dictum post C. 29, q.1.

[15] Augustine, *De sermone Domini in monte, Corpus Christianorum Series Latina* 35: 1.16.48.

[16] Ambrosiaster, *Ad Corinthios prima* 7:13, *PL* 17:219.

[17] See c. 7, X, *de divortiis,* iv, 19 and c. 8, X, *de divortiis,* iv, 19. For a history of the development of this institute, see J. Noonan, *Power to Dissolve* (Cambridge: Belknap, 1972) 341–347; and D. Gregory, *The Pauline Privilege, CanLawStud* 68 (Washington, D.C.: Catholic University of America, 1931) 12–36.

[18] Paul III's constitution *Altitudo* of June 1, 1537, Pius V's constitution *Romani Pontificis* of August 2, 1571, and Gregory XIII's constitution *Populis* of January 25, 1585 were first published as appendices to the 1917 code.

[19] See Noonan, *The Power to Dissolve,* 366–392.

The Notion of Indissolubility

The gradual expansion of the classes of marriages that are susceptible to dissolution or dispensation has necessitated a somewhat nuanced approach to indissolubility. Traditional authors distinguish between intrinsic and extrinsic indissolubility. All marriages, whether they involve baptized persons or not, are intrinsically indissoluble in that they cannot be dissolved by the will of the parties. However, not all marriages are extrinsically indissoluble, since they can sometimes be dissolved either by the intervention of competent ecclesiastical authority or by the realization of conditions specified in law.[20]

A. THE PRINCIPLE

Canon 1141 — A marriage that is *ratum et consummatum* can be dissolved by no human power and by no cause, except death.

A *ratum* or ratified marriage is a valid marriage between two baptized persons, whether Catholic or not (c. 1061, §1). The Eastern code, which generally eschews the technical Latin vocabulary for types of marriages, speaks simply of the "sacramental bond of marriage" (*CCEO* 853). Marriages of this kind are intrinsically indissoluble. However, these marriages are also extrinsically indissoluble if they have been consummated by an act of sexual intercourse (c. 1061, §1). The extrinsic indissolubility of ratified and consummated marriages means that they "can be dissolved by no human power and by no cause, except death."

The slow evolution of the Church's practice of dissolving, or acknowledging the dissolution, of various types of marriages has left the category of *ratum et consummatum* marriages as the only one that is both intrinsically and extrinsically indissoluble. The power to dissolve marriages that

are ratified but not consummated and non-sacramental marriages "in favor of the faith" has been explained as one by which "God dissolves [the bond] and thus allows a party to pass licitly to a new marriage" through the vicarious action of the Roman Pontiff.[21] If this explanation is correct, the power in virtue of which the Roman Pontiff dissolves marriages is not a merely human power.[22] Consequently, there have been periodic suggestions that the Roman Pontiff's vicarious power could, in certain circumstances, extend to ratified and consummated marriages, but that the Church has never found it opportune to exercise this power.[23] This opinion has never gained a wide following. However, the fact that it resurfaces periodically indicates that the theological basis for the Roman Pontiff's power to dissolve some marriages has not yet been adequately articulated.

The assertion that a ratified and consummated marriage can be dissolved "by no human power and by no cause, except death [*praeterquam morte*]" suggests that death does dissolve the matrimonial bond. The death of one spouse certainly frees the surviving spouse to enter a new marriage. Although many patristic authors viewed remarriage after the death of a spouse as a sign of weakness and lack of self-control, the early Church did permit widows and widowers at least one remarriage by way of concession. Nonetheless, they were often subjected to a period of penance.[24]

---

[20] F. Cappello, *De Matrimonio* (Rome: Marietti, 1961) n. 45.

[21] Pius XII, "Address to the Rota," October 3, 1941, *AAS* 33 (1941) 426; *CLD* 2, 458. See also Paul VI, *EM* V, *CLD* 6, 397: "...but not the divine laws, natural or positive, from which the Supreme Pontiff alone, using his vicarious power, can dispense...."

[22] See Cappello, n. 762.

[23] See W. O'Connor, "The Indissolubility of a Ratified, Consummated Marriage," *Ephemerides Theologicae Lovanienses* 13 (1936) 692–722; and J. Gerhartz, "L'indissolubilité du mariage et sa dissolution par l'Église dans la problématique actuelle," *RDC* 21 (1971) 198–234.

[24] See, for example, Council of Laodicea, c. 1, Mansi 2: 563–564; Basil of Caesarea, *Epistola* 188, 4, *PG* 32: 673–674. For a survey of patristic views on the remarriage of widows and widowers see, L. Godefroy, "Mariage dans les Pères: Les secondes noces," *Dictionnaire de Théologie Catholique* 9–2: 2096–2101.

The view that death actually dissolves the matrimonial bond finds support in Jesus' rejoinder to the Sadducees: "When people rise from the dead, they neither marry nor are given in marriage but live like the angels in heaven."[25] However, the Orthodox tradition has long maintained that "marriage is not dissolved by the death of one of the partners, but creates between them—if they so wish and if 'it is given to them' (Matthew 19: 11)—an eternal bond."[26] Because remarriage falls short of the ideal, the Orthodox liturgy for the second marriages of those whose spouses have died (as well as those who have divorced) has a profoundly penitential character.[27] This perspective in which "human decision and action acquire an eternal dimension"[28] resonates better with the experience of couples who hope that "as they come together to [the Lord's] table on earth, so they may one day have the joy of sharing [his] feast in heaven"[29] than does the position that implicitly holds that death is stronger than love.

B. THE EXCEPTIONS

1) Dissolution of a Ratified but Non-consummated Marriage

Canon 1142 — For a just cause, the Roman Pontiff can dissolve a non-consummated marriage between baptized persons or between a baptized party and a non-baptized party at the request of both parties or of one of them, even if the other party is unwilling.

A valid marriage between two baptized persons or between a baptized and an unbaptized person can be dissolved if it has not been consummated by an act of sexual intercourse performed

in a human manner.[30] The dissolution is effected only by the personal intervention of the Roman Pontiff. Canon 1119 of the 1917 code had retained the traditional provision that solemn religious profession dissolved a ratified but unconsummated marriage by the law itself. This provision has been deleted from the 1983 code in part because of the absence of a procedure for verifying the fact of non-consummation.

Conditions for Dissolution

A ratified but unconsummated marriage can be dissolved at the request of both spouses or at the request of one of them even if the other objects. In either case, there must be a just cause for the dissolution. The following are generally considered just causes: discord in the marriage without hope of reconciliation; civil remarriage by one of the parties after a divorce; civil divorce with danger of incontinence to the innocent party; probable impotence with danger of incontinence; an incurable disease contracted after the marriage; and partial proof of defect of consent.[31] When a just cause is absent, the dissolution is invalid.[32] The Roman Pontiff does not dissolve unconsummated sacramental marriages without a petition from at least one spouse.[33]

The Notion of Consummation

A sacramental marriage is considered to have been consummated when

---

[25] Mt 22:30; Mk 12:25; Lk 20:34–35.

[26] J. Meyendorf, *Marriage: An Orthodox Perspective* (Crestwood, N.Y.: St. Vladimir Seminary, 1975) 42–43.

[27] Ibid., 33–34.

[28] Ibid., 26.

[29] *Rite of Marriage*, 33.

[30] In the present discipline, the marriages of the unbaptized, whether consummated or not, can be dissolved by the Roman Pontiff in favor of the faith.

[31] B. Marchetta, *Scioglimento del matrimonio canonico per inconsummazione* (Padua: Antonio Milani, 1981) 17–18; and W. Woestman, *Special Marriage Cases* (Ottawa: St. Paul University, 1992) 21–22.

[32] Cappello, n. 762.

[33] The procedure to be observed in preparing a case for dissolution is discussed in cc. 1697–1706 and SCSacr, littcirc "De processu super matrimonio rato et non consummato," December 20, 1986, *ME* 112 (1987) 423–429. An English translation of the circular letter appears in Woestman, *Special Marriage Cases,* 119–126.

the spouses have performed between themselves in a human fashion a conjugal act which is suitable in itself for the procreation of offspring, to which marriage is ordered by its nature and by which the spouses become one flesh. (c. 1061, §1)

The marriage can be consummated only after it has become ratified by the legitimate manifestation of consent by the spouses. Thus, if a couple engaged in sexual relations prior to marriage, their subsequent exchange of consent does not of itself give rise to a consummated marriage. According to traditional canonical doctrine, the conjugal act that consummates a marriage requires that the man's penis penetrate the woman's vagina at least partially and deposit semen in the vagina. Often, the failure to consummate the marriage is the result of impotence on the part of one spouse. However, it can also result from the conscious intent of the parties. Thus, a marriage is not consummated by *coitus interruptus,* by intercourse with the use of a condom or vaginal sheath, or by artificial insemination.[34]

Consummation "in a Human Manner"

The conjugal act which consummates a marriage must be performed in a human fashion (*humano modo*). The precise determination of what constitutes sexual relations in a human fashion will have to developed gradually in the jurisprudence of the Congregation for the Sacraments.[35] However, it is already clear that, in order to effect the consummation of a marriage, the conjugal act must be a human and voluntary act. That is,

for a marriage to be consummated it is necessary that there be a human act on the part of both spouses; it is sufficient for it to be virtually voluntary, provided that it was not

extorted through violence. No weight is given to other psychological elements which render the act easier or more loving.[36]

Thus, true consummation does not result from sexual acts performed as a result of physical or moral violence that deprives a spouse of his or her freedom. Nor is a marriage consummated by a sexual act performed on a person who is asleep or unconscious because of the influence of drugs or alcohol. However, the use of drugs, alcohol, or aphrodisiacs does not impede consummation if the person under their influence had previously consented to the sexual act.[37]

Suggestions of a Broader Notion of Consummation

The significance of the conjugal act by which a sacramental marriage is consummated was suggested in the conciliar pastoral constitution *Gaudium et spes*:

Married love is uniquely expressed and perfected by the exercise of the acts proper to marriage. Hence the acts in marriage by which the intimate and chaste union of the spouses takes place are noble and honorable; the truly human performance of these acts fosters the self-giving they signify and enriches the spouses in joy and gratitude.[38]

Despite the antiquity of the tradition that a marriage is consummated and thereby rendered extrinsically indissoluble by the initial act of sexual intercourse by the spouses, some have argued that the personalist theology of marriage introduced by Vatican II requires a broadening of the definition of consummation.

They suggest that a more adequate definition of consummation would include not only the

---

[34] Woestman, *Special Marriage Cases,* 19.
[35] See P. Jugis, *A Canonical Analysis of the Meaning of* Humano Modo *in Canon 1061, §1, CanLawStud* 541 (Washington, D.C.: Catholic University of America, 1993).

[36] SCSac, circular letter, December 20, 1986. English translation in Woestman, *Special Marriage Cases,* 119–126.
[37] SCOf, response, February 2, 1949, *CLD* 3, 473–474.
[38] *GS* 49.

spouses' physical union but also their existential and spiritual union.[39] Nevertheless, proposals of this kind had no discernible impact on the drafting of the current law. However, the possibility of a more existential understanding of consummation cannot be precluded. The International Theological Commission has conceded that it cannot "be excluded that the Church can further define the concepts of sacramentality and consummation by explaining them even better, so that she can present the whole doctrine on indissolubility in a deeper and more precise way."[40] Commenting on this thesis, Philippe Delhaye, then secretary of the commission, observed:

> As we learn more about the way in which the conjugal bond comes to be constituted, the consummation theory of medieval canonists may well turn out to be too inadequate to be tenable any longer. According to this theory, marriage is consummated by one act of sexual intercourse, no more, no less. However, no one has yet elaborated another acceptable theory.[41]

2) Dissolution by the Pauline Privilege

Canon 1143 — §1. A marriage entered into by two non-baptized persons is dissolved by means of the pauline privilege in favor of the faith of the party who has received baptism by the very fact that a new marriage is contracted by the same party, provided that the non-baptized party departs.

While addressing a series of pastoral problems raised by the Church in Corinth, Paul dealt with the situation of believers married to unbelievers. Lacking a solution from what "the Lord has said," Paul offered his own recommendation:

> If any brother has a wife who is an unbeliever and she is willing to go on living with him, he should not divorce her; and if any woman has a husband who is an unbeliever, and he is willing to go on living with her, she should not divorce her husband.... If the unbeliever separates, however, let him separate. The brother or sister is not bound in such cases. God has called you to peace.[42]

By the twelfth century, this pastoral solution emerged in a highly juridicized form as the Pauline privilege, which authorized a newly baptized Christian to enter a new marriage after a divorce from his or her unbaptized first spouse under certain conditions.

Conditions for the Application of the Pauline Privilege

The essential conditions for the application of the Pauline privilege are:

(a) a marriage entered into by two unbaptized persons;
(b) the subsequent baptism of one and only one of the spouses; and
(c) the "departure" of the still unbaptized spouse.

If all three of these conditions are met, the newly baptized spouse may enter a new marriage. The original marriage bond is dissolved not by the intervention of ecclesiastical authority as in the case of a ratified but unconsummated marriage, but by

---

[39] J. Bernhard, "Réinterpretation existentielle et dans la foi de la legislation canonique concernant l'indissolubilité du mariage chrétien," *RDC* 21 (1971) 243–277; and idem, "Perspectives renouvellées de la 'consommation existentielle et dans la foi' du mariage chrétien," *RDC* 24 (1974) 334–349. For a sympathetic but critical treatment of this approach, see O. Fumagalli Carulli, "Innovazioni conciliari e matrimonio canonico," *Il Diritto Ecclesiastico* 89 (1978) 331–425.

[40] International Theological Commission, "Propositions on the Doctrine of Christian Marriage," 4.4., in *Origins* 8 (1978–1979) 238.

[41] P. Delhaye, "Propositions on the Doctrine of Christian Marriage: Introduction and Commentary," in *Contemporary Perspectives on Christian Marriage,* ed. R. Malone and J. Connery (Chicago: Loyola University, 1984) 30.

[42] 1 Cor 7:12–13, 15 (NAB).

the second marriage. The only role of ecclesiastical authority in the operation of the Pauline privilege is to verify that the conditions for its application have been met.

The sequence in which the baptism of the one spouse and the departure of the other occur is not of critical importance. Thus, whether the departure of the unbaptized party occurs before or after the baptism of the other spouse, the newly baptized party may use the privilege. Nor must the unbaptized spouse's departure be prompted by the other's actual or intended baptism. Baptism in the Catholic Church is not necessary for the Pauline privilege to be applicable; valid baptism in any Christian church or ecclesial community is sufficient.[43]

Departure of the Unbaptized Spouse

§2. The non-baptized party is considered to depart if he or she does not wish to cohabit with the baptized party or to cohabit peacefully without affront to the Creator unless the baptized party, after baptism was received, has given the other a just cause for departing.

The unbaptized spouse is considered to have departed when he or she either refuses to continue conjugal cohabitation with the baptized party or is willing to continue cohabitation but not "peacefully without affront to the Creator [*sine contumelia Creatoris*]." "Departure" does not necessarily mean that the unbaptized spouse takes the initiative to effect a physical separation. The unbaptized spouse is also considered to have departed if he or she made the common life so physically or morally intolerable that the baptized party initiated a separation. When the baptized spouse (or the spouse to be baptized) has initiated a separation for any of the grounds mentioned in canons 1152–1153,[44] the unbaptized spouse is deemed to have refused to cohabit peacefully (*pacifice*) and, therefore, to have "departed."

The expression "affront to the Creator," which has been in ecclesiastical usage at least since Ambrosiaster in the fourth century, refers to a situation in which the unbaptized spouse's manner of living threatens the neophyte spouse's ability to live out the obligations of the Christian life. When the unbaptized spouse interferes with the neophyte's practice of the Christian faith, refuses to allow the Christian education of their children, or insists on engaging in immoral sexual activity, he or she is considered to have refused to cohabit "without affront to the Creator." Thus, in such cases, the unbaptized spouse is deemed to have departed.

The nature of the unbaptized spouse's motives for departing does not affect the availability of the Pauline privilege to the other spouse, unless his or her behavior after baptism has given the unbaptized spouse just cause for departing. Thus, a spouse who after his or her baptism commits adultery or unjustly deserts the unbaptized spouse cannot use the Pauline privilege. However, if the behavior that led to the failure of the marriage occurred before the spouse was baptized, this fault does not impede his or her use of the Pauline privilege "since it has been blotted out by the bath of regeneration."[45]

The Interpellations

Canon 1144 — §1. For the baptized party to contract a new marriage validly, the non-baptized party must always be interrogated whether:
    1° he or she also wishes to receive baptism;
    2° he or she at least wishes to cohabit peacefully with the baptized party without affront to the Creator.

Although the fact that a marriage occurred when both parties were still unbaptized and the fact that one of them subsequently received baptism can often be established without great difficulty, it is not always clear whether the unbaptized spouse "departed" as defined in canon 1143,

---

[43] CDF, reply, August 30, 1976, *CLD* 8, 837–840.
[44] See the commentary on cc. 1152–1153.

[45] Cappello, n. 770.

§2. Consequently, before the newly baptized spouse celebrates a new marriage in virtue of the Pauline privilege, the still unbaptized spouse must be interrogated to establish the fact of his or her departure. This interrogation, designated in canonical terminology as "the interpellations," attempts to determine whether the unbaptized spouse has departed or not. Toward this end, he or she is to be asked: (a) whether he or she also wishes to receive baptism and (b) whether he or she wishes at least to cohabit peacefully with the other party without affront to the Creator.

Possible Responses to the Interpellations

The unbaptized spouse's responses to these two questions determine whether ecclesiastical authority will permit the other spouse to use the Pauline privilege to enter a new marriage. The unbaptized spouse's responses to the interpellations can take several forms.[46]

(a) If the unbaptized spouse responds negatively to both questions, he or she is considered to have departed and the now baptized spouse may enter a new marriage as long as his or her own post-baptismal conduct has not given the unbaptized spouse cause to depart.

(b) If the unbaptized spouse responds affirmatively to both questions, the baptized spouse may not enter a new marriage. Even if it was the fault of the unbaptized spouse that resulted in the couple's separation, the baptized spouse should be urged to reconcile with him or her since the unbaptized spouse's baptism will remit the sin. At most, the baptized spouse can be allowed to remain separated but without the possibility of remarriage. However, if the unbaptized spouse sincerely responds affirmatively to the interpellations but it is de facto impossible to restore conjugal cohabitation because of distance, confinement, or some other circumstance, he or she is considered to have departed, and the other spouse may enter a new marriage after baptism.[47]

(c) If the unbaptized responds that he or she wishes to be baptized but not to cohabit peacefully with the baptized spouse, careful consideration must be given to his or her refusal to resume cohabitation. If the refusal is for reasons, legitimate or illegitimate, unrelated to any culpable conduct on the part of the baptized spouse, the latter may enter a new marriage. If the unbaptized spouse's refusal results from the other spouse's illegitimate post-baptismal conduct, the latter is not permitted to enter a new marriage. However, if the convert's pre-baptismal conduct prompts the unbaptized spouse's refusal to renew cohabitation, the convert may enter a new marriage if pastoral efforts to effect a reconciliation of the spouses prove fruitless. In these cases, care should be taken to ensure that the convert enters a new marriage before the other spouse is baptized.[48] Otherwise, the baptism of the other spouse will make the marriage ratified but not consummated and, therefore, one to which the Pauline privilege is not applicable.

---

[46] Woestman, *Special Marriage Cases,* 43, and Kelly, in *CLSGBI Com,* 645, hold that only if the unbaptized spouse gives negative responses to both questions can the other spouse be permitted to enter a new marriage. This position fails to take into account the complexity of the issue and the long-standing CDF practice in dealing with Pauline privilege cases.

[47] E. Woeber, *The Interpellations, CanLawStud* 172 (Washington, D.C.: Catholic University of America, 1942) 85–87.

[48] Ibid., 89. Some authors have suggested that a desire to be baptized is inconsistent with a refusal to reconcile and live at peace with an estranged spouse. They suggest that such a mixed response to the interpellations may indicate insincerity on the part of the unbaptized spouse. If a lack of sincerity can be established, the unbaptized spouse's affirmative response is to be interpreted as actually negative and the convert permitted a new marriage. See D. Gregory, *The Pauline Privilege, CanLawStud* 68 (Washington, D.C.: Catholic University of America, 1931) 75; and A. Abate, *The Dissolution of the Matrimonial Bond* (Rome: Desclée, 1962) 75.

d) If the unbaptized spouse does not wish to be baptized but sincerely desires to resume or continue peaceful cohabitation with the convert, the latter may not enter a new marriage. Authors as distinguished as Sanchez have argued that, since cohabitation with an unbeliever always constitutes a proximate danger of lapsing from the faith for a convert, the refusal of the unbaptized spouse to receive baptism is sufficient cause for the other spouse to separate and enter a new marriage.[49] This position has not, however, become the basis for ecclesial praxis.[50] Nevertheless, the baptized spouse who continues or renews a common life with an unbaptized spouse who has promised to cohabit peacefully does not forfeit the right to separate from the latter and enter a new marriage should the unbaptized spouse subsequently break this promise.

Timing of the Interpellations

§2. This interrogation must be done after baptism. For a grave cause, however, the local ordinary can permit the interrogation to be done before baptism or can even dispense from the interrogation either before or after baptism provided that it is evident at least by a summary and extrajudicial process that it cannot be done or would be useless.

Since the purpose of the interpellations is to establish the fact of the unbaptized spouse's departure, they are normally to take place only after the baptism of the other spouse. Only then is he or she eligible to use the Pauline privilege. Nevertheless, the local ordinary can permit the interpellations to be made before the catechumen's baptism if there is a serious reason for doing so. For example, the catechumen may have already entered a civil marriage with a Catholic and it is desirable to convalidate this union as soon as possible after his or her

baptism. The unbaptized spouse is usually questioned early in the process to establish the fact of his or her non-baptism. Making the interpellations at the same time as this preliminary inquiry can prevent the unbaptized spouse from feeling badgered by the Catholic Church because of repeated interrogations and avert the danger that he or she will be unavailable or uncooperative later after the other spouse's baptism.

Dispensation from the Interpellations

The local ordinary can now dispense from the interpellations if conducting them would be impossible or useless. This dispensing power, which the 1917 code had reserved to the Apostolic See,[51] can be delegated without restriction (c. 137).[52] The dispensation can be from the obligation of asking either or both of the questions that constitute the interpellations. Before dispensing from the interpellations, the local ordinary or his delegate must conduct a brief and informal investigation to verify the impossibility or uselessness of making the interpellations. Making the interpellations is useless if it is clear from other sources that the unbaptized spouse's responses to one or both questions will be negative. The interpellations can also be dispensed when making them would harm the newly baptized spouse or the children of the marriage.[53]

Manner of Making the Interpellations

Canon 1145 — §1. The interrogation is regularly to be done on the authority of the local ordinary of the converted party. This ordinary must grant

---

[49] T. Sanchez, *De Matrimonio,* lib. vii, disp. lxxiv, n. 9.
[50] Woeber, 91–93.

[51] *CIC* 1121, §2.
[52] In 1963, the *mp Pastorale munus* I, 23, granted diocesan bishops the faculty to dispense from the interpellations. However, this faculty could be delegated only to coadjutor and auxiliary bishops and vicars general. See *CLD* 6, 371. Diocesan bishops in the United States were subsequently authorized to delegate this faculty to their chancellors, but not to their vice chancellors. See *CLD* 6, 385 and 380.
[53] SCOf, reply, July 2, 1965, *CLD* 6, 387.

the other spouse a period of time to respond if the spouse seeks it, after having been advised, however, that his or her silence will be considered a negative response if the period passes without effect.

§2. Even an interrogation made privately by the converted party is valid and indeed licit if the form prescribed above cannot be observed.

§3. In either case, the fact that the interrogation was done and its outcome must be established legitimately in the external forum.

The interpellations are normally to be made by the authority of the local ordinary of the spouse who has been or is about to be baptized. If the unbaptized spouse requests a reasonable period of time to consider his or her answers to the interpellations, it is to be granted. However, the unbaptized spouse is to be notified that, if the period elapses without any answer to the interpellations, his or her response will be presumed to be negative.

The local ordinary can conduct this interrogation personally or through a delegate. The interpellations can even be made privately by the converted party himself or herself. Interpellations made privately are always valid; this method is also lawful if they cannot be made in the usual public way. In either case, however, there should be a written record of the fact that the interpellations took place and of their result so that there is proof for the external forum.

Right to Remarry

Canon 1146 — The baptized party has the right to contract a new marriage with a Catholic party:

   1° if the other party responded negatively to the interrogation or if the interrogation had been omitted legitimately;

   2° if the non-baptized party, already interrogated or not, at first persevered in peaceful cohabitation without affront to the Creator but then departed without a just cause, without prejudice to the prescripts of cann. 1144 and 1145.

Although ecclesiastical usage has long referred to a dissolution of this kind as a "privilege," the law asserts the right (*ius*) of the baptized party to enter a new marriage with a Catholic if the unbaptized party responds negatively to the interpellations or the interpellations are legitimately omitted. The baptized spouse does not forfeit this right to a new marriage by continuing cohabitation with the unbaptized spouse. No matter how long the cohabitation continues, the baptized spouse retains the right to a new marriage if the unbaptized spouse later departs without just cause as long as the latter has not been baptized in the meantime. Before the baptized spouse exercises this right, however, the interpellations must be conducted.

Since the new marriage of the baptized party dissolves the bond of the original marriage, this new marriage leaves the unbaptized party free to remarry. Thus, the unbaptized party may enter a new marriage or convalidate a civil union with a Catholic after a dispensation from the impediment of disparity of worship has been granted. A new marriage by the unbaptized spouse with a non-Catholic, whether baptized or not, is to be presumed valid if it was entered into after the baptized spouse's new marriage. However, if it was entered into prior to the baptized spouse's remarriage, it is invalid because of the impediment of prior bond.

Possibility of a Mixed Marriage

Canon 1147 — For a grave cause, however, the local ordinary can allow a baptized party who uses the pauline privilege to contract marriage with a non-Catholic party, whether baptized or not baptized; the prescripts of the canons about mixed marriages are also to be observed.

Since in the Pauline privilege the bond of the original marriage is dissolved in favor of the faith of the newly baptized person, the convert does not have a strict right to enter a new marriage with a non-Catholic. To the extent that it threatens the convert's continued practice of the Catholic faith, a marriage to a non-Catholic cannot be said to be in favor of the faith of the Catholic. However, for a serious reason and after adequate safeguards for the faith of the newly baptized, the local ordinary can permit him or her to enter a new marriage with a non-Catholic, baptized or not. Canons 1124–1129 governing mixed marriages are to be observed in these cases.

3) Dissolution in Virtue of Three Sixteenth Century Papal Constitutions

Historical Synopsis

During the age of exploration, Catholic missionaries in Asia, South and Central America, and the Caribbean frequently encountered natives who were favorably disposed toward the Christian faith but who were impeded from receiving baptism because they were living in polygamy. The Church could not tolerate polygamy among Christians, but the traditional discipline governing the Pauline privilege did not seem to apply to these cases. In addition, because of the slave trade, missionaries encountered men and women who were potential converts but who had been forcibly separated from their wives and husbands. Since the whereabouts of these first spouses were usually unknown, it was impossible to conduct the interpellations. Moreover, it was impossible to know whether these first spouses might have been baptized after the forced separation.

Three sixteenth century popes issued constitutions to address these hardship situations in missionary territories. In 1537, Paul III's constitution *Altitudo* allowed a convert with several wives, either simultaneously or serially, who could not remember which of them was the first, to contract marriage with any one of them without the necessity of the interpellations and to dismiss the others. However, if the convert could recall which of his wives was the first, he was bound to remain with her, unless the usual conditions for the Pauline privilege applied. Pius V's constitution *Romani Pontificis* of 1571 allowed a convert with several wives to remain with the one who was

baptized with him and dismiss the others. In 1585, the constitution *Populis* of Gregory XIII authorized certain missionaries to permit new marriages of African converts who had been separated from their then unbaptized spouses because of the slave trade. These new marriages dissolved the original ones even if the interpellations were omitted as impossible and the other spouses had subsequently received baptism.

These constitutions, which were never promulgated, were originally given as special faculties to certain missionaries and as privileges for the peoples of certain regions. Knowledge of these constitutions and their provisions was not widespread. Even one as knowledgeable and well connected as Benedict XIV seems to have had only secondhand knowledge of them.[54] Perhaps as a result of the limited awareness of these constitutions, little was done to assess the significance of their innovations. Nor is there evidence of much reflection on the manner in which or the authority by which the other bonds were dissolved. However, it can be argued that the sixteenth century popes merely adapted the Pauline privilege to make it applicable to situations the Apostle could not have foreseen and, in the case of *Populis*, provide for an *ipso iure* dissolution of a ratified but non-consummated marriage.

Canon 1125 of the 1917 code extended these constitutions to the universal Church, and excerpts from them were published as appendices of that code. The gist of these constitutions has been distilled in canons 1148–1149 of the 1983 code.

Situations of Polygamy

Canon 1148 — §1. When he receives baptism in the Catholic Church, a non-baptized man who has several non-baptized wives at the same time can retain one of them after the others have been dismissed, if it is hard for him to remain with the first one. The same is valid for a non-baptized woman who has several non-baptized husbands at the same time.

[54] Benedict XIV, *De synodo dioecesana* l. xiii, c. 21, n. 2–7.

§2. In the cases mentioned in §1, marriage must be contracted in legitimate form after baptism has been received, and the prescripts about mixed marriages, if necessary, and other matters required by the law are to be observed.

§3. Keeping in mind the moral, social, and economic conditions of places and of persons, the local ordinary is to take care that the needs of the first wife and the others dismissed are sufficiently provided for according to the norms of justice, Christian charity, and natural equity.

Canon 1148, §1 is based on the provisions of the constitutions *Altitudo* and *Romani Pontificis*. It allows a newly baptized man who had several unbaptized wives simultaneously while he was himself unbaptized to retain one of them and dismiss all the others if it would be difficult for him to remain with the one he married first. These provisions are also applicable to women who had several unbaptized husbands simultaneously prior to their baptisms. It is no longer necessary that the convert not be able to remember which of the spouses was his or her first or that the spouse retained be the one who is willing to be baptized with him or her.

The New Marriage

After baptism, the convert wishing to use this privilege must contract marriage with his or her chosen spouse according to a legitimate form. Since this privilege extends only to those who have received baptism in the Catholic Church, the legitimate form is usually the canonical form. However, if the chosen spouse opts not to be baptized or to be baptized in a non-Catholic church, a dispensation from the canonical form could be granted to permit this marriage to be contracted according to some other legitimate form (c. 1127, §2).

Concern for Dismissed Wives

The use of this privilege by the convert can result in severe hardship for the first wife and any other wives who are dismissed. In some places dismissed wives are reduced to supporting themselves through prostitution. Thus, the local ordinary is to see that appropriate provision is made for their support, presumably by their former husband. Criteria for the adequacy of this support are to be derived from the moral, cultural, and economic conditions of the area. This support is not merely a matter of charity. It is also due as a matter of justice and natural equity.

The canon's failure to advert to the obligation of support for dismissed husbands probably results from the fact that polygyny is much more common than polyandry and that dismissed wives are exposed to much greater hardships than are dismissed husbands. Less understandable is the canon's failure to mention explicitly the convert's obligations toward the children born of these dismissed wives.

Separation Due to Captivity or Persecution

Canon 1149 — A non-baptized person who, after having received baptism in the Catholic Church, cannot restore cohabitation with a non-baptized spouse by reason of captivity or persecution can contract another marriage even if the other party has received baptism in the meantime, without prejudice to the prescript of can. 1141.

This canon incorporates into the code the basic provisions of the constitution *Populis*. A non-baptized person who married another unbaptized person from whom he or she is now separated as a result of captivity or persecution can enter a new marriage after baptism in the Catholic Church if he or she cannot restore cohabitation with the first spouse. The interpellations may be omitted as superfluous in the circumstances envisaged by the canon. The new marriage is permitted even if the original spouse has received baptism since the separation as long as the marriage was not consummated after both spouses were baptized. The dissolution of the first marriage seems to take place by the law and without the personal intervention of the Roman Pontiff.

4) Dissolution of a Non-sacramental Marriage "In Favor of the Faith"

Historical Synopsis

Shortly after the promulgation of the 1917 code, cases began to be reported in which the Roman Pontiff had dissolved marriages involving only one unbaptized spouse in favor of the faith either of the unbaptized spouse who now wished to be baptized in the Catholic Church or of a baptized non-Catholic spouse who wished to become a Catholic. These dissolutions could not be explained by the traditional principles governing the application of the Pauline privilege or even by the extensions of this privilege by the sixteenth-century constitutions. Thus, these dissolutions were soon recognized as exercises of a heretofore unknown papal prerogative to dissolve non-sacramental marriages. The scope of this power to dissolve expanded steadily, albeit sometimes in fits and starts, until it extended to the power of the pope to dissolve a marriage of two unbaptized persons without the baptism of either of them in favor of the faith of a Catholic third party who wished to marry (or convalidate a civil marriage with) one of them.[55]

Essential Conditions

The dissolution of non-sacramental marriages in favor of the faith is now governed by the CDF instruction *Ut notum est* of December 6, 1973 and the procedural norms attached to it.[56] There are three essential conditions for the dissolution of a marriage in favor of the faith:

(a) at least one of the parties to the marriage must have been unbaptized at the time of the marriage and throughout the duration of the common life;

(b) if only one party was unbaptized at the time of the marriage and he or she subsequently received baptism, no sexual relations occurred after his or her baptism;[57] and

(c) if the dissolution is requested to permit the marriage of a Catholic with an unbaptized person or a baptized non-Catholic, the non-Catholic must yield to the Catholic full freedom to practice and to raise all children in the Catholic faith by means of written *cautiones*.[58]

Unlike dissolution by the Pauline privilege, dissolution in favor of the faith does not require that an unbaptized spouse be baptized or that a baptized non-Catholic spouse seek full communion with the Catholic Church. If the other conditions are met, the marriage can be dissolved in favor of the faith of a Catholic who wishes to marry one of the parties to the marriage to be dissolved.

Other Conditions

The dissolution is not granted if the one seeking it was responsible for the failure of the marriage or if the person he or she desires to marry was instrumental in the break-up of the marriage. This lack of culpability for the failure of the marriage is to be established by questioning the former spouse, if possible, and the future spouse. If

---

[55] For a treatment of this twentieth century development, see Noonan, *The Power to Dissolve*, 366–392.

[56] CDF, instruction and procedural norms, December 6, 1973, *CLD* 8, 1177–1184. Although this instruction has been communicated to diocesan bishops, it has never been published in the *AAS*. During the process of revising the Latin code, various schemata incorporated the essence of the norms of this instruction. However, these norms were deleted prior to the promulgation of the 1983 code. In a private response of September 8, 1983, the CDF stated through the then apostolic delegate to the United States that the 1973 norms remained in effect

even after the promulgation of the revised code. However, dissolution in favor of the faith is cryptically mentioned in *CCEO* 1384, with a reference to special norms of the Apostolic See.

[57] In the case of a marriage entered into by two unbaptized persons, there must have been no sexual relations after both of them had received baptism.

[58] CDF, *Ut notum est* I, *CLD* 8, 1177.

all the other conditions have been met, a marriage between a Catholic and an unbaptized person entered into after a dispensation from the impediment of disparity of worship can be dissolved in favor of the faith.[59]

Although there have been a few reports of favor-of-the-faith dissolutions without the immediate prospect of a new marriage by the petitioner, the present CDF practice is not to recommend the granting of the dissolution until the petitioner intends marriage with a person who is free to marry.[60] The dissolution can be granted to permit a new marriage between a Catholic and a baptized non-Catholic or even an unbaptized person. In the latter case, the dispensation from the impediment of disparity of worship is granted by the congregation.[61] However, if the petitioner is a Catholic whose first marriage was entered after a dispensation from the impediment of disparity of worship, the dissolution will be granted only in view of a new marriage to a validly baptized person.[62]

Procedure

Unlike Pauline privilege cases which can be dealt with locally, petitions for dissolution in favor of the faith are instructed by the petitioner's local ordinary and forwarded to the CDF which has exclusive competence over matters touching on the privilege of the faith.[63] The congregation reviews the dossier accompanying the petition and, if all the conditions have been met, recommends a dissolution to the Roman Pontiff. The pope then dissolves the non-sacramental marriage in favor of the faith in virtue of the personal, non-delegable vicarious power which he possesses from Christ. Since the dissolution of a marriage in favor of the faith is a privilege and not a right, the congregation does not customarily recommend dissolution of marriages entered into or

convalidated after the dissolution of a previous non-sacramental marriage.[64]

The Favor of the Law and the Privilege of the Faith

Canon 1150 — In a doubtful matter the privilege of faith possesses the favor of the law.

Meaning and Scope of "Privilege of the Faith"

The phrase "privilege of the faith" is a rather recent coinage, which seems to have first appeared in canon 1127 of the 1917 code as a conflation of the more traditional phrase "favor of the faith" (*favor fidei*) and "Pauline privilege."[65] This conflation was suggested by the juxtaposition of these two phrases in canon 1120.[66] At the time of the promulgation of the 1917 code, the "privilege of the faith" that was granted the favor of the law in cases of doubt could have meant only the Pauline privilege and its extensions by the sixteenth century constitutions, the only forms of dissolution in favor of the faith then known.

The creeping twentieth century expansion of papal power over non-sacramental marriages also enlarged the scope of the privilege of the faith. Changes in the designation of the competence of the Holy Office (later, CDF) in the area illustrate this expansion. In 1917, the Holy Office was assigned exclusive authority over matters concerning "the Pauline, as they call it, privilege."[67] When Paul VI reorganized the Roman Curia in 1967, this exclusive competence was designated as pertaining to "all that concerns the privilege of the faith,"[68] a phrase that now clearly included dissolutions of

---

[59] CDF, *Ut notum est* II, §§3–4 and V, *CLD* 8, 1178–1179.
[60] CDF, reply formula, 1977, *CLD* 8, 1186.
[61] CDF, reply, September 16, 1974, *CLD* 8, 1185.
[62] CDF, *Ut notum est* V, *CLD* 8, 1179.
[63] *PB* 53.

[64] CDF, *Ut notum est* VI, *CLD* 8, 1179.
[65] U. Navarrete, "Commentarium decreti Signaturae Apostolicae de recta applicatione canonum 1150 et 1608, §4," *P* 85 (1996) 368–370. See also idem, "'Favor fidei' e 'salus animarum,'" *Ius* 27 (1980) 83.
[66] *CIC* 1120, §1: "A legitimate marriage between non-baptized persons, even though consummated, is dissolved in favor of the faith by the Pauline privilege."
[67] *CIC* 247, §3.
[68] *RE* 34. This same designation is retained in *PB* 53.

non-sacramental marriages in favor of the faith by the Roman Pontiff.

The "privilege of the faith" is not, however, simply identical with the "favor of the faith." The latter has an application beyond cases of the dissolution of non-sacramental marriages; the former does not.[69] However, the principle that the privilege of the faith enjoys the favor of the law in doubtful matters is limited to cases of the dissolution of non-sacramental marriages. This is clear from its context of this principle in the code. Canon 1150 appears immediately after the canons governing dissolution of marriages entered into by two unbaptized persons in virtue of the Pauline privilege and the sixteenth century constitutions. This context appears to limit the applicability of the principle asserted in canon 1150 to these canons.[70]

Possible Doubts

Various doubts can arise about the possibility of dissolving a marriage by the Pauline privilege and its sixteenth century extensions. There can be doubt about: whether the conversion of one of the spouses is sincere, whether the unbaptized spouse's response to the interpellations is sincere, whether the unbaptized spouse departed, whether the baptized spouse gave the other spouse just cause to separate, whether the interpellations were lawfully made, or whether there was just cause for dispensing from the interpellations. In all of these cases, the doubt is to be resolved in favor of the freedom of the newly baptized party to enter a new marriage (c. 1150).

Doubt can also arise about whether one or both spouses were baptized at the time of the marriage or whether the baptism received by one of the spouses after the marriage was valid. Since the unbaptized status of both parties at the time of the marriage is an essential condition for the valid use of the Pauline privilege and its extensions, cases where there is a doubt about the baptismal status of one or both parties must be referred to the CDF.[71] If doubts about the validity of the baptism of the converted spouse cannot be resolved, he or she can use the privilege after being baptized conditionally.[72]

Doubt about the Validity of the Marriage

There can also be a doubt about the validity of the marriage whose dissolution is sought. If all the conditions for the Pauline privilege or its extensions are met, there is little reason to invoke the principles of canon 1150. If a new marriage can dissolve an unquestionably valid marriage, it can surely dissolve one of doubtful validity. Moreover, papal dissolutions of non-sacramental marriages, which involve the privilege of the faith in its broad sense, "are more readily granted if on some other ground there is serious doubt about the validity of the marriage itself."[73]

Some authors interpreted canon 1014 of the 1917 code and canon 1608, §4 of the 1983 code as granting the favor of the law to the privilege of the faith and not to the marriage in cases where its validity is doubtful.[74] These authors have pro-

---

[69] Navarrete, "Commentarium," 370.

[70] This argument from context is corroborated by the history of the revision of the Latin code. All schemata placed draft norms on the papal dissolution of non-sacramental marriages after what is now canon 1150. *CCEO* 862, which deals with the dissolution of ratified but non-consummated marriages, is located immediately after the canon asserting the favor of the law enjoyed by the privilege of the faith, as if to preclude any possible confusion about the applicability of this favor to sacramental marriages.

[71] SCOf, decree, June 10, 1937, *AAS* 29 (1937) 305–306; *CLD* 2, 343.

[72] See c. 869.

[73] CDF, *Ut notum est* III, *CLD* 8, 1178.

[74] *CIC* 1014: "Marriage enjoys the favor of the law; wherefore when a doubt exists the validity of a marriage is be upheld until the contrary is proven, with due regard for the prescription of canon 1127." The "*salvo praescripto can. 1127*" clause has been deleted from the otherwise identical c. 1060 of the 1983 code. Nevertheless, some have found a similar provision in c. 1608, §4 which requires a judge who cannot reach moral certainty to find

posed that canon 1150 can be used by tribunal judges to resolve marriage nullity cases. For example, Wrenn suggested that, when an insoluble doubt remained about the validity of a marriage, the judge was bound to render a negative decision with regard to its nullity. However, if

> one of the parties is doubtfully baptized, then, since a doubtful privilege of the faith is one of those cases which "enjoys the favor of the law" (c. 1150), the judge must (or so it appears to this author) give a *constat pro ipsa,* i.e., the person's freedom to marry must be recognized.[75]

The Apostolic Signatura, after consultation with the CDF, has declared that this position is utterly lacking in foundation in law and that practice based upon it "must be stopped immediately."[76]

While canon 1150 is indeed a "doubt-solving canon," its function is limited to resolving doubts about the applicability of the Pauline privilege and its now traditional extensions. As a traditional principle, it may guide the CDF's dealing with cases of dissolution of non-sacramental marriages in favor of the faith, but this type of case falls outside the parameters of the law of the codes. In any case, canon 1150 is not intended as a tool for resolving doubts about the validity of marriage in ecclesiastical tribunals.

---

for the defendant "unless there is a question of a case which enjoys the favor of the law."

[75] L. Wrenn, in *CLSA Com,* 995. A more adventuresome approach was proposed by R. Carney, "A New Application of Canon 1127," *CLSAP* 39 (1977) 49–52. Carney proposed that the "favor of the faith" could be invoked to declare a party to a doubtfully valid marriage free to marry whenever a declaration of this kind would benefit the faith of either the petitioner or a third party. This position, which is wholly without any basis in canonical tradition, was severely criticized in L. Örsy, "An Evaluation of 'New Applications of Canon 1127,'" *J* 38 (1978) 163–170.

[76] Apostolic Signatura, "Canon 1608: An Unusual Manner of Handling Nullity Cases," *RRAO 1996,* 39–45. See Navarrete, "Commentarium," 360–385.

ARTICLE 2: SEPARATION WITH THE BOND REMAINING
[cc. 1151–1155]

The Principle: Common Life

Canon 1151 — Spouses have the duty and right to preserve conjugal living unless a legitimate cause excuses them.

Echoing *Gaudium et spes* 48, canon 1055 describes marriage as "a partnership of the whole of life . . . which is ordered by its nature to the good of the spouses and the procreation and education of offspring." The achievement of the twofold ends of marriage normally requires that the spouses share a common life (*convictus coniugalis*). Long experience has shown that lengthy interruptions of a common life have a deleterious effect on the spouses themselves, their ability to sustain their marital obligations, and the well-being of children. Therefore, the spouses have a duty to one another and to their children to maintain a common life and a mutual right to expect one another to maintain this common life, unless a legitimate cause excuses. Although the code frames this duty and right in the language of positive law, it is rooted in the nature of marriage as a partnership of the whole of life.

While recognizing that marriage is the most intimate and personal of relationships, the Church refuses to treat marriage as a purely private matter between the spouses alone. It is also an institution which has a societal impact. A separation represents at least the temporary failure of a marriage and has a particularly profound effect on the well-being of any children born of the marriage.[77] Thus, spouses may not take the initiative to terminate their common life unless there is a legitimate cause. Canons 1692–1696 outline the process by which ecclesiastical authority determines the existence of a legitimate cause and, if one is proven,

---

[77] See J. Wallerstein and S. Blakeslee, *Second Chances* (New York: Ticknor and Fields, 1989).

permits a separation of the spouses. Permission for such a separation does not, however, free the parties to enter new marriages. In practice, however, the substantive and procedural canons governing separation are largely ignored both by separating couples and by ecclesiastical authority in the English-speaking world.

GROUNDS FOR SEPARATION

Adultery as a Ground for Separation

Canon 1152 — §1. Although it is earnestly recommended that a spouse, moved by Christian charity and concerned for the good of the family, not refuse forgiveness to an adulterous partner and not disrupt conjugal life, nevertheless, if the spouse did not condone the fault of the other expressly or tacitly, the spouse has the right to sever conjugal living unless the spouse consented to the adultery, gave cause for it, or also committed adultery.

§2. Tacit condonation exists if the innocent spouse has had marital relations voluntarily with the other spouse after having become certain of the adultery. It is presumed, moreover, if the spouse observed conjugal living for six months and did not make recourse to the ecclesiastical or civil authority.

§3. If the innocent spouse has severed conjugal living voluntarily, the spouse is to introduce a cause for separation within six months to the competent ecclesiastical authority which, after having investigated all the circumstances, is to consider carefully whether the innocent spouse can be moved to forgive the fault and not to prolong the separation permanently.

Canon law has long recognized adultery as a legitimate ground for the innocent spouse to effect a separation. Although the innocent spouse is strongly encouraged to forgive an adulterous spouse out of a Christian spirit of forgiveness and reconciliation and for the good of the family and to maintain common life, separation is asserted as a right of the innocent spouse. Only actual adultery, i.e., a completed act of sexual intercourse with a third party,

gives rise to the innocent spouse's right to separate.[78] Inappropriate expressions of affection, intense but platonic relationships, and even "affairs" in cyberspace with a third party may be considered breaches of the obligation of marital fidelity. However, these indiscretions do not constitute the "adultery" that gives the wronged spouse a right to a separation.

The innocent spouse cannot claim a right to a separation from an adulterous spouse if he or she has consented to or given cause for the other's adultery or if he or she is also guilty of adultery. The innocent spouse also forfeits the right to a separation if, after becoming aware of the other spouse's adultery, he or she has "condoned" or, more accurately, pardoned it.[79] The pardon of an adulterous spouse can be express or tacit. It is tacit if the innocent spouse freely continues common life with the guilty spouse after becoming aware of the adultery. Tacit pardon is presumed if the innocent spouse continues conjugal cohabitation for six months after becoming aware of the adultery and fails to seek permission for a separation from ecclesiastical or civil authority. However, this presumption cedes to contrary proof.

If an innocent spouse unilaterally initiates a separation after learning of the other spouse's adultery, he or she is to initiate an action for a formal separation before the competent ecclesiastical authority within six months. Before granting the requested separation, the diocesan bishop or ec-

[78] Although in its strict sense adultery was understood to involve sexual relations by a married person with a person of the opposite sex, commentators on the 1917 code equated homosexual relations and bestiality with adultery as causes for legitimate separation. See F. Wernz and P. Vidal, *Ius Canonicum* (Rome: Apud Aedes Universitatis Gregorianae, 1946) 5: n. 639; and A. Vermeersch and J. Creusen, *Epitome Iuris Canonici* (Mechelen: H. Dessain, 1927) 2:270. But for a contrary view, see Cappello, n. 826.

[79] The decision to translate *condono* and its derivatives as "condone" in English versions of the code is unfortunate and misleading. In contemporary English, "condone" denotes "pardon" or "overlook," but it also connotes vague approval or at least indifference. These connotations do not attach to the Latin root word.

clesiastical judge is to attempt to persuade the innocent spouse to forgive the adulterous spouse and resume their common life.

Other Grounds for Separation

Canon 1153 — §1. If either of the spouses causes grave mental or physical danger to the other spouse or to the offspring or otherwise renders common life too difficult, that spouse gives the other a legitimate cause for leaving, either by decree of the local ordinary or even on his or her own authority if there is danger in delay.

§2. In all cases, when the cause for the separation ceases, conjugal living must be restored unless ecclesiastical authority has established otherwise.

The canonical discipline governing marital separation is based on the "fault" of one of the spouses, even though a psychological disorder may diminish or, at times, extinguish the spouse's moral culpability. This fault-based system for separation provided the model for the fault-based legislation for divorce that prevailed in most Western countries until recently.[80] Although this fault-based approach has been largely abandoned by secular divorce legislation, canon law has resisted the trend toward allowing "no fault" separation.

Canon 1131, §1 of the 1917 code listed various causes besides adultery that could justify marital separation. The revised code instead speaks generally of actions or inactions by one spouse that pose a physical or spiritual danger to the other spouse or the children or that "render common life too difficult." The language of canon 1153, §1 is flexible enough to include a large variety of behaviors on the part of one spouse as justifications for requests for separation. Nevertheless, it does not include a spouse's pervasive dissatisfaction with the quality of the marital relationship, difficulties for which neither spouse bears objective

responsibility, or problems caused by the one seeking the separation. Although the causes of marital breakdown are rarely black and white, the granting of permission to separate by ecclesiastical authority presupposes that one spouse was relatively innocent and the other relatively guilty.

The innocent spouse is normally to seek from the local ordinary the prior permission to separate.[81] The intervention of church authority prior to the separation provides an opportunity for pastoral action to attempt to effect a reconciliation of the spouses (c. 1695). However, the innocent spouse may initiate a separation without prior approval if a delay would expose him or her or the children to danger.

Canon law recognizes only adultery as a legitimate ground for a permanent separation. Permission to separate for other causes normally lapses when the cause ceases to exist. However, the causes of separations are often deep-rooted problems of long standing that do not suddenly vanish. Moreover, these causes often have resulted in such a complete unraveling of the spouses' relationship that it is practically impossible for them to resume a common life. Thus, ecclesiastical authority can allow a separation to continue even after the original cause for it has ceased.

POST-SEPARATION ISSUES

Care for Children after a Separation

Canon 1154 — After the separation of the spouses has taken place, the adequate support and education of the children must always be suitably provided.

A couple's children often suffer the most serious consequences of marital separation. In most cases, they experience a notable decline in their economic standard of living after their parents' separation. In addition, they often experience

---

[80] M. A. Glendon, *The Transformation of Family Law* (Chicago: University of Chicago Press, 1989) 28.

[81] Canon 1692 stipulates that permission to separate can be granted by the decree of the diocesan bishop or the sentence of an ecclesiastical judge.

emotional problems which can be severe and sometimes persist into their adulthood. Although the details of child custody, visitation, and child support are the province of the civil courts, the Church must also be solicitous of the needs of these children.[82] A separation is an occasion for the Church to bring its pastoral resources to bear to assist the children themselves, to provide the spouses with the resources for dealing with them, and to remind the spouses of their ongoing legal and moral obligations to the children.

Reconciliation and the Right to Separate

Canon 1155 — The innocent spouse laudably can readmit the other spouse to conjugal life; in this case the innocent spouse renounces the right to separate.

Even though an innocent spouse has been granted permission to separate, he or she is encouraged to reconcile with the other spouse if that is possible. By resuming a common life, the innocent spouse forfeits the right to separate because of cause given by the other spouse in the past. However, the innocent spouse can initiate a new request for permission to separate if the other spouse once again gives just provocation.

In most cases, a marital separation, whether formalized by ecclesiastical authority or not, is a prelude to civil divorce. In some jurisdictions, a civil divorce is the only vehicle available to spouses for securing their legal and financial status and for clarifying mutual rights and obligations regarding the children. Although the Church does not consider a civil divorce to have any effect on the bond of marriage, it imposes no sanctions or disabilities on members of the faithful who receive a civil divorce. However, since the bond of marriage remains intact despite the cessation of common life, remarriage after a civil di-

vorce puts spouses in an irregular situation that bars them from the reception of the sacraments.[83]

CHAPTER X
THE CONVALIDATION OF MARRIAGE[84]
[cc. 1156–1165][85]

The spouses' legitimately manifested matrimonial consent brings a marriage into existence. Sometimes, however, the consent elicited by the parties fails to achieve its end. Consent that is fundamentally flawed by a defect recognized in ecclesiastical jurisprudence does not give rise to a valid marriage. Moreover, consent that is in itself naturally sufficient is juridically inefficacious if one or both parties are bound by a diriment impediment or if the parties fail to observe the form required by law in manifesting their consent. In these cases, the parties' consent may result in a meaningful and enriching human relationship, but it does not result in a valid marriage.

Convalidation is the canonical procedure for making valid a marriage that was invalid from its origin because of a defect of consent, a diriment impediment, or a defect of the required form. The law contains two methods for convalidating an invalid marriage: simple convalidation and radical

---

[82] See M. Foster, *The Promotion of the Canonical Rights of Children in Situations of Divorce and Remarriage,* CanLawStud 545 (Washington, D.C.: Catholic University of America, 1994).

[83] John Paul II, *FC* 84; and CDF, letter "Concerning the Reception of Holy Communion by Divorced-and-Remarried Members of the Faithful," September 14, 1994, *Origins* 24 (1994–1995) 337, 339–341. The latter was a response to a more open approach to the admission of the divorced and remarried to the sacraments by Bishops Karl Lehmann, Oscar Saier, and Walter Kasper. See Three German Bishops, "Pastoral Ministry: The Divorced and Remarried," *Origins* 23 (1993–1994) 670–676. For a review of recent literature on the ecclesial status of divorced-remarried Catholics, see J. Provost, "Intolerable Marriage Situations Revisited," *J* 40 (1980) 141–196; and idem, "Intolerable Marriage Situations: A Second Decade," *J* 50 (1990) 573–612.

[84] See Doyle, in *CLSA Com,* 822–829; Lüdicke, in *Münster Com,* Einführung vor 1156/1–1160/1; Hervada, in *Pamplona ComEng,* 727–732; Kelly, in *CLSGBI Com,* 653–659.

[85] *CCEO* 843–852.

sanation. The former requires a renewal of consent by the parties; the latter is an intervention of church authority that gives naturally sufficient and still perduring consent retroactive validity. Neither method can be applied unless any impediment has been dispensed or has ceased and any defect of consent has been overcome. The effect of simple convalidation is to render a marriage valid from the moment consent is renewed; the effect of radical sanation is to render a marriage valid from the moment the original, naturally sufficient consent was exchanged.

Both simple convalidation and radical sanation are matters of merely ecclesiastical law. Consequently, they directly bind only Catholics (c. 11); but they indirectly bind non-Catholics, whether baptized or not, when they seek to enter into a marriage or to convalidate an invalid union with a Catholic (c. 1059).[86] The code contains no explicit

[86] Since the promulgation of the 1983 code, some have suggested that canon 11 exempts non-Catholics from the ecclesiastical law governing convalidation even if they are seeking to convalidate a marriage with a Catholic or, at least, that, since the apparent conflict between canons 11 and 1059 has given rise to a doubt of law, non-Catholics are not bound by these norms as long as this doubt continues (c. 14). See Doyle, in *CLSA Com*, 824, 826; L. Örsy, *Marriage in Canon Law* (Wilmington, Del.: Michael Glazier, 1986) 64–65; L. Pivonka, "Ecumenical or Mixed Marriage in the New Code of Canon Law," *J* 43 (1983) 122; Woestman, *Special Marriage Cases,* 90–91; and P. Cogan, "The Non-Catholic and Convalidation," *CLSAP* 56 (1994) 84–86.

Although the exemption of non-Catholics from the canonical norms governing convalidation of their marriages to Catholics would resolve a pressing pastoral problem (see J. Johnson, "The 'Simple' Convalidation as a Pastoral Problem," *Stud Can* 15 [1981] 461–479), the arguments against the existence of such an exemption in the current law seem compelling.

(1) Despite the general principle of canon 11 that merely ecclesiastical laws do not bind non-Catholics, the code does contain norms governing non-Catholics when they seek certain benefits from the Catholic Church. For example, canon 844, §§3–5 stipulates the conditions under which baptized non-Catholics may receive the sacraments of Eucharist, penance, and anointing of the sick from Catholic ministers. Non-Catholics who exer-

provision for the convalidation of invalid marriages of two non-Catholics. Marriages between two non-Catholics, whether baptized or not, are convalidated by the natural law by the continuation of the naturally sufficient consent of both parties after the obstacle to validity has been re-

cise their right to bring a case to an ecclesiastical tribunal (c. 1476) become subject to all ecclesiastical procedural laws. Similarly, canon 1059 subjects to merely ecclesiastical marriage law a non-Catholic who seeks to marry (or convalidate a marriage with) a Catholic.

(2) Almost without exception, commentators on the 1917 code held that canon 1016, which is parallel to canon 1059 of the 1983 code, bound non-baptized persons, who were otherwise exempt from merely ecclesiastical laws, to ecclesiastical law governing marriage when they sought to marry Catholics. Similarly, canon 1059 obviously intends to subject non-Catholics, whether baptized or not, to ecclesiastical discipline when they marry Catholics.

(3) If canon 1059 does not bind non-Catholics to merely ecclesiastical laws when they seek to marry Catholics, the clause "even if only one party is Catholic" is redundant and the canon tautological.

(4) Those who claim that non-Catholics are not bound by merely ecclesiastical norms when they seek the convalidation of their marriages to Catholics are rather selective in their application of canon 11. If non-Catholics are exempt from the laws governing convalidation, they should also be exempt from the merely ecclesiastical laws governing marriage preparations, impediments, canonical form, and the like when they seek marriage with a Catholic. However, no responsible canonist has proposed so broad an exemption.

(5) Since the matrimonial covenant is indivisible, the Church's claim of authority to regulate the marriages of Catholics extends to the non-Catholic party to a mixed marriage. This extension applies the traditional principle that "marriage cannot be divided" (*matrimonium non potest claudicare*). Similarly, a mixed marriage is invalid if the Catholic minister asks for and receives the consent of the Catholic party but a non-Catholic minister asks for and receives the consent of the non-Catholic party (*Ecum Dir* 156); and non-Catholic parties to mixed marriages are considered bound by impediments of merely ecclesiastical law. In short, while exempt from merely ecclesiastical law in most cases, non-Catholics are bound by ecclesiastical marriage laws, including those governing convalidation, when they marry Catholics.

moved.[87] However, the convalidations of invalid unions involving two non-baptized persons are also governed by the norms, if any, of civil law.[88]

ARTICLE 1: SIMPLE CONVALIDATION
[cc. 1156–1160]

Historical Synopsis

Although the Church has long attempted to address the problem of marriages invalid because of an impediment that has subsequently ceased or been dispensed, a coherent discipline governing the validation of these marriages has emerged only relatively recently. During the first Christian millennium, local councils, beginning with one held at Agde in 506, allowed some couples who had entered into marriage within the forbidden degrees of consanguinity and affinity to continue to cohabit as husband and wife. Some see these conciliar canons as early examples of the exercise of the power to dispense from matrimonial impediments and subsequently to convalidate marriages without requiring a renewal of consent.[89] However, these sources are too scattered and obscure to permit a definitive conclusion that they represent the earliest antecedents of the institute of simple convalidation.

From the late tenth century on, it became increasingly common for dispensations from matrimonial impediments to be granted for individual cases. Some of these dispensations were granted to permit the recognition of marriages contracted invalidly because of an impediment. Although renewal of consent was not generally required for the marriage to be recognized as valid, continued cohabitation and voluntarily engaging in marital intercourse after the dispensation were considered an implicit confirmation of consent. The first known requirement of explicit renewal of consent for the validation of a marriage is found in a rescript from the Holy See in 1281. However, until the Council of Trent this requirement appears only sporadically in Holy See rescripts granting dispensations.[90]

To reduce the number of invalid marriages, the Council of Trent considerably pared back the degrees in which the impediments of spiritual relationship, public propriety, and affinity arising from fornication invalidated marriage.[91] Trent also sought to reduce the number of dispensations granted to permit or to validate marriages contracted within the forbidden degrees. Only those who entered marriage in probable ignorance of the existence of an impediment were to be granted retroactive dispensations.[92] However, Trent said nothing about a renewal of consent after the granting of a dispensation as a condition for the validity of the marriage in these cases. Despite Trent's intention to reduce the number of invalid marriages, its decree *Tametsi* which imposed a mandatory form of marriage[93] and the confusion resulting from the rather haphazard way of promulgating it introduced a new cause for the proliferation of invalid marriages.

In the post-Tridentine era, the council's hard line on granting dispensations from diriment impediments soon softened because of the Church's concern to prevent leakage to Protestant churches. However, the clause "after consent has been given anew" (*de novo praestito consensu*) was routinely appended to Holy See rescripts granting dispensations to allow the validation of marriages already contracted invalidly. The requirement of renewal of consent for the validation of marriages became such a fixed part of Roman curial practice that some authors opined that it was a matter of divine law.[94] In places where the decree *Tametsi* had

---

[87] L. Bogdan, "Simple Convalidation of Marriage in the 1983 Code of Canon Law," *J* 46 (1986) 527–530.

[88] J. Brennan, *The Simple Convalidation of Marriage, CanLawStud* 102 (Washington, D.C.: Catholic University of America, 1937) 114–120.

[89] Ibid., 10–14.

[90] Ibid., 14–20.

[91] Council of Trent, sess. XXIV, *de ref. matrimonii,* cap. 2–4.

[92] Ibid., cap. 5.

[93] Ibid., cap. 1.

[94] Brennan, 37–38.

been promulgated, consent was to be renewed according to the Tridentine form, unless the marriage had originally been celebrated according to this form and an occult impediment was later detected. Although renewal of consent for convalidation was insisted on in practice throughout the post-Tridentine period, it was incorporated into church law only with the 1917 code.[95] The discipline of the 1917 code on simple convalidation is substantially incorporated into the revised code.

Marriages Invalid because of Diriment Impediments

Canon 1156 — §1. To convalidate a marriage which is invalid because of a diriment impediment, it is required that the impediment ceases or is dispensed and that at least the party conscious of the impediment renews consent.

§2. Ecclesiastical law requires this renewal for the validity of the convalidation even if each party gave consent at the beginning and did not revoke it afterwards.

The essential precondition for the simple convalidation of a marriage invalid because of a diriment impediment is that the impediment either be dispensed by competent authority or cease. After the impediment has been dispensed or has ceased, at least the party who is aware of its existence must renew consent. The restriction of the obligation to renew consent to the party aware of the impediment was introduced in the 1917 code to sidestep a prickly pastoral issue. Pre-code law required that both parties be aware of the invalidity of a marriage because of an impediment and renew consent. Thus, when only one party was aware of an occult impediment, he or she had to inform the other of the invalidity of their marriage. Since affinity arising from fornication was a diriment impediment at that time, informing one's spouse of the invalidity of the marriage so that it could be convalidated could create an embarrassing and potentially volatile situation.

95 Ibid., 22–29.

The renewal of consent for convalidation is explicitly presented as a requirement of merely ecclesiastical law. It is necessary even if the original consent of both parties was naturally sufficient and has never been revoked. The result of the failure of the party or parties aware of the impediment to renew consent according to the norm of law is the invalidity of the convalidation and, consequently, the continued invalidity of the marriage.

While non-Catholics aware of an invalidating impediment must renew their consent when they convalidate marriages with Catholics, renewal of consent is not necessary for the convalidation of the marriages of two non-Catholics.[96] These marriages are convalidated by the continuation of naturally sufficient consent after the cessation of a divine law impediment. Thus, when the marriage of two non-Catholics is invalid because of the impediment of prior bond, the marriage is convalidated by their continued consent to the invalid marriage after the death of one party's first spouse.

Necessity of Renewal of Consent

Canon 1157 — The renewal of consent must be a new act of the will concerning a marriage which the renewing party knows or thinks was null from the beginning.

For the convalidation of a marriage invalid because of an impediment, it is not sufficient for the party aware of the impediment to confirm his or her original consent after the impediment has ceased or been dispensed. Renewal of consent requires a new act of the will, one both materially and formally distinct from the original consent. Such a new act of the will is probably psychologically impossible unless the person is aware that the marriage is or may be invalid. Thus, the law requires that to renew consent a person must know

96 Although those who were baptized in or received into full communion with the Catholic Church but who subsequently left it by a formal act are exempted from observing some ecclesiastical marriage laws, they remain bound by the laws governing convalidation.

or at least think that the marriage was null from the beginning. Certitude of the invalidity of the marriage is not necessary; awareness that it may be invalid or that the Church considers it to be invalid is sufficient. If the party or parties aware of the impediment do not at least think the marriage is invalid or if they fail to elicit a new act of consent, the convalidation is itself invalid.

Cases Where an Impediment Can Be Proven

Canon 1158 — §1. If the impediment is public, both parties must renew the consent in canonical form, without prejudice to the prescript of can. 1127, §2.

It is an impediment's susceptibility to proof in the external forum (c. 1074) and not the extent to which it is actually known that renders it public. Marriages invalid because of a public impediment are convalidated by the renewal of consent of both parties according to the canonical form.

The requirements for renewal of consent can pose pastoral problems for the convalidation of mixed marriages invalid because of an impediment when the non-Catholic party is aware of the facts that give rise to an impediment but refuses to recognize their juridic effect. For example, a non-Catholic may acknowledge that he was married prior to his present marriage to a Catholic but sincerely believe that his present marriage is valid, since the civil divorce dissolved that prior bond. Unable to acknowledge the invalidity of the current marriage, he may not be able to renew consent by a new act of the will. These situations need to be approached with great pastoral sensitivity.

The original published version of canon 1158, §1 contained an erroneous cross-reference to canon 1127, §3. This erratum has since been corrected with a cross-reference to canon 1127, §2,[97] which deals with the authority of local ordinaries to grant dispensations from the obligation of observing the canonical form of marriage for mixed marriages.

Although one might imagine cases of invalid mixed marriages for which the local ordinary might dispense to allow a convalidation according to "some public form" other than the canonical form,[98] cases when the civil authority or a non-Catholic church or ecclesial community recognizes the invalidity of a marriage and the need for its convalidation are relatively rare. Thus, Lüdicke suggests that the correct cross-reference should be to canon 1127, §1 according to which the convalidation of a marriage between a Catholic and an Eastern non-Catholic before the Eastern non-Catholic priest would be valid but illicit.[99]

Impediments That Cannot Be Proved

§2. If the impediment cannot be proven, it is sufficient that the party conscious of the impediment renews the consent privately and in secret, provided that the other perseveres in the consent offered; if the impediment is known to both parties, both are to renew the consent.

An impediment whose existence cannot be proven in the external forum is considered occult (c. 1074). If only one party is aware of the existence of the impediment, private and secret renewal of consent by that party alone is sufficient to convalidate the marriage, on condition that the other party has not withdrawn his or her consent. If both parties are aware of the unprovable impediment, then both must renew consent privately and secretly. No particular form needs to be observed for the private and secret renewal of consent in these cases. However, the party or parties renewing consent must be aware of the possible invalidity of the marriage and give a new act of consent. Private renewal of consent is insufficient, however, to convalidate marriages invalid because of impediments that are susceptible to proof but are not known in the region.

---

[97] Appendix, *AAS* 75 (1983) pars II, 324.

[98] Woestman, *Special Marriage Cases,* 85, n. 30.
[99] Lüdicke, in *Münster Com* 2: 1158/1–2, n. 4.

Marriages Invalid
because of Defects of Consent

Canon 1159 — §1. A marriage which is invalid because of a defect of consent is convalidated if the party who did not consent now consents, provided that the consent given by the other party perseveres.

Since the consent of the parties gives rise to marriage and no human power can supply for the absence of this consent (c. 1057, §1), a marriage is invalid if the consent of one or both parties was substantially defective, even though the parties were bound by no impediment and observed the required form in the celebration of the marriage. Canons 1095–1105 catalogue the defects of consent that can invalidate marriage.[100] Simple convalidation of a marriage invalid because of a defect of consent presents a very different problem than does the convalidation of a marriage invalid because of a diriment impediment. In the latter case, presumably valid and perduring consent (c. 1107) was juridically inefficacious; in the former case, the consent itself was lacking. Thus, the critical issue is not the "renewal" of consent, but the supplying of consent that has been hitherto lacking.

Requirement of Consent

The convalidation of a marriage invalid because of a defect of consent requires that the party who had initially failed to consent altogether or whose original consent was fundamentally defective now give a true consent to the marriage. This consent must be a new act of the will that is distinct from the original and fundamentally flawed act that invalidated the marriage. This new or, more accurately, true act of consent can convalidate the marriage only if the original consent of the other spouse has continued without revocation. Since it is the mutual consent of the parties

that constitutes marriage (c. 1057, §2), it is only when the true consent of the party whose original consent was defective is joined to the continuing consent of the other party that their consent is at least morally mutual.

Canon 1159, §1 does not repeat the stipulation of canon 1157 that the one proffering consent to a marriage invalid because of his or her defective consent know or at least think that the marriage is invalid. On the one hand, a person ignorant of the defect of consent and the consequent invalidity of the marriage has little motivation to give genuine consent. Although ignorance or error about the law or about a fact concerning oneself is not presumed (c. 15, §2), the jurisprudence on defects of consent is so complex that most non-specialists are ignorant of the juridic effect of their defective consent. Evidence of marital affection and satisfaction can be understood as a continuation and confirmation of consent to the invalid marriage. On the other hand, the experience of a satisfying union might prompt a person to substitute true consent for his or her originally defective consent. For example, a person who entered marriage invalidly because of a positive intention against the good of offspring may change his or her mind later and consent to a marriage ordered to their procreation and education.[101]

Manner of Giving Consent

§2. If the defect of consent cannot be proven, it is sufficient that the party who did not consent gives consent privately and in secret.
§3. If the defect of consent can be proven, the consent must be given in canonical form.

If the defect of consent cannot be proven in the external forum, the marriage is convalidated when the party responsible for the defect gives consent privately and secretly, provided the naturally sufficient consent of the other party perdures. This consent can be an internal act of the will with no

---

[100] See the commentary on cc. 1095–1105.

[101] Cappello, n. 846.

additional external manifestation. However, if the defect of consent can be proven in the external forum, the marriage is convalidated by the external manifestation of the consent of the parties according to the canonical form.

Defects of Consent That Cannot Be Proven

The norms of the 1917 code governing the manner in which a marriage invalid because of a defect of consent was to be convalidated distinguished between cases in which the defect was merely internal and those in which it had been externally manifested, in either a public or an occult manner.[102] The revised code has abandoned this distinction between merely internal and externally manifested defects of consent in favor of a distinction between defects of consent that can be proven and those that cannot. However, changes in the canonical discipline governing the evaluation of proofs may have rendered this distinction unworkable in practice. Since the declaration or confession of a party or the testimony of one witness can provide full proof if fully corroborated by circumstantial evidence,[103] most, if not all, defects of consent are susceptible to proof, at least in principle.[104]

Despite the potential for proving most defects of consent, tribunal practitioners are aware that, in practice, proving these defects can be an arduous task. The primary purpose of requiring consent according to the canonical form when a defect of consent can be proven is to ensure public proof that a marriage known to be invalid from its origin has now been convalidated. Thus, a rule of thumb for determining whether a marriage invalid because of a defect of consent must be convalidated according to the canonical form might be whether knowledge of the defect of consent is sufficiently widespread that it would raise doubts about the validity of the marriage in the minds of members of the community if they were aware of the invalidating effects of such a defect.

In cases of marriages invalid because of an unprovable defect of consent, the law does not insist on the "renewal" of consent by the party whose original consent was naturally sufficient. Even if this party is aware of the defect of consent, all that is required for convalidation to be effective is that his or her original consent not be revoked. However, when the defect of consent can be proven, the party whose original consent was naturally sufficient must participate in the convalidation of the marriage according to the canonical form. However, canon 1159, §3 rather pointedly avoids saying that the party whose consent has perdured must "renew" that consent as canon 1158, §1 does. Therefore, this party's expression of his or her continuing consent is sufficient to convalidate the marriage.

The requirement that marriages invalid because of a defect of consent be convalidated according to the canonical form is clearly a matter of merely ecclesiastical law. Consequently, it does not bind non-Catholics when they convalidate marriages with other non-Catholics. All that is necessary is that the party whose consent was originally defective purge the defect and give true internal consent privately and secretly. This consent can be expressed explicitly in the form of a conscious intention or implicitly in a pattern of behavior expressive of marital intent.[105] Consequently, tribunal practitioners need to exercise caution when evaluating marriages of two non-Catholics which endured many years despite a somewhat rocky beginning. Especially when the proposed ground is the lack of due discretion, one or both parties may well have purged the defect and implicitly consented to marriage once the early turmoil subsided.

---

[102] CIC 1136, §§2–3.

[103] See the commentary on cc. 1536–1537 and 1572–1573.

[104] M. Pompedda, "La questione dell'ammissione ai sacramenti dei divorziati civilmente risposati," in *Studi di diritto matrimoniale canonico* (Milan: Giuffrè, 1993) 503–506.

[105] Brennan, 81.

Marriages Invalid
because of Defect of Canonical Form

Canon 1160 — A marriage which is null because of defect of form must be contracted anew in canonical form in order to become valid, without prejudice to the prescript of can. 1127, §2.

The phrase "defect of form" has two senses in canon law. In a narrow sense it refers to the absence of some essential element (e.g., the faculty to witness the marriage on the part of the Church's official witness) from the celebration of a marriage according to the canonical form. In a broad sense, it refers to the complete failure to observe the canonical form (e.g., when one bound by the form marries before a civil official). Traditional canonists held that a marriage invalid because of a defect of form in the narrow sense had the appearance or semblance of marriage (*species seu figura formae matrimonii*), but a marriage invalid because of a defect of form in the broad sense did not. When a Catholic contracted marriage before a civil official or a non-Catholic minister, the union was considered the equivalent of mere concubinage. Thus, these unions were not subject to convalidation in the proper sense; they could be rendered valid only if the parties contracted marriage anew as if for the first time.

Since the distinction between the narrow and broad senses of "defect of form" is still operative in the revised code,[106] some authors have continued to view unions contracted by Catholics without the observance of canonical form as mere concubinage.[107] However, John Paul II has insisted that civil marriages by Catholics cannot simply be identified with mere concubinage:

> Their situation cannot of course be likened to that of people simply living together

without any bond at all, because in the present case there is at least a certain commitment to a properly defined and probably stable form of life.... By seeking public recognition of their bond on the part of the State, such couples show that they are ready to accept not only its advantages but also its obligations.[108]

Moreover, the Church's long-standing practice of granting radical sanations of civil marriages involving Catholics suggests that these unions are something more than mere concubinage. They have enough of an appearance of marriage to be considered invalid marriages subject to simple convalidation.

Contracting a Marriage Anew

Whether a marriage is invalid because of a defect of form in the narrow or the broad sense, the requirements for simple convalidation are the same: the parties must contract marriage anew (*denuo*) according to the canonical form. Commentators on canon 1137 of the 1917 code agreed that to contract marriage anew the parties had to recognize the possible invalidity of their marriage and elicit a new act of consent.[109] This position was adopted in Rotal jurisprudence.[110] Canon 1160 of the present code repeats canon 1137 of the previous code almost verbatim.[111] Hence, it should apparently be interpreted "in accord with canonical tradition" (c. 6, §2).

[108] *FC* 82.

[109] See L. Bender, *Forma iuridica celebrationis matrimonii* (Rome: Desclée, 1960) 218.

[110] See *coram* Wynen, June 1, 1940, *SRRDec* 32 (1940) 432; and *coram* Rogers, January 21, 1969, *SRRDec* 61 (1969) 63–67.

[111] Canon 1160 speaks of "canonical form" rather than "legitimate form" as a recognition of the fact that this norm no longer binds baptized non-Catholics when they marry other non-Catholics. Its cross-reference to canon 1127, §2 is new but does not in any way alter the sense of the canon.

[106] See PCILT, reply, June 26, 1984, *AAS* 76 (1984) 747; *CLD* 11, 351.

[107] Lüdicke, in *Münster Com,* 1160/1, n. 2; Hervada, in *Pamplona ComEng,* 729.

Since the promulgation of the revised code, some have argued that, in virtue of canon 11, non-Catholics are no longer bound to renew consent to convalidate their marriages with Catholics. This argument, which ignores the clear sense of canon 1059, is seriously flawed and is insufficient to give rise to a doubt of law.[112] Others argue that it is illegitimate to apply the requirements of 1157 for the renewal of consent in cases of the convalidation of marriages invalid due to a diriment impediment to cases of convalidation of marriages invalid due to a defect of form.[113] They are correct that the context of canon 1157 is the norms governing the convalidations of marriages invalid because of impediments and that, at least in the present law, defect of form is not classified as an impediment. Nevertheless, it is incorrect to conclude that the requirements of canon 1157 for the renewal of consent are irrelevant for the convalidation of marriages vitiated by a defect of form. These requirements are implicit in canon 1160.

Canon 1160 requires for the convalidation of a marriage invalid because of a defect of form that the marriage be contracted anew (*denuo*) according to the canonical form. In five of the other six uses of *denuo* in the revised code, the term refers to a juridic act that is both materially and formally distinct from a previous one.[114] An act of consent that is both materially and formally distinct from the original consent can only be a new act of the will. It is highly unlikely, if not psychologically impossible, that a person will elicit such a new act of the will unless he or she is aware that the marriage may be invalid. Since the promulgation of the revised code, the Rota has reaffirmed the requirement that a person convalidating a marriage invalid due to defect of form recognize the possible invalidity of the marriage and proffer a new consent.[115]

Pastoral Problems Arising from the Law

The requirements for renewal of consent in cases of marriages invalid because of a defect of form create a difficult pastoral challenge. Since neither ignorance nor error prevents invalidating laws from having their effect (c. 15, §1), many non-Catholics in invalid marriages with Catholics and non-practicing or ill-informed Catholics do not in fact, and perhaps cannot, effect the simple convalidation of their marriages. The problem Johnson described in 1982 remains a problem today:

> The pastor who softens the language of the law, who tries to suggest that the parties are simply receiving the Church's blessing on their union, is only complicating the situation.... The sensitive priest might shrink from confronting the couple with the harshness of the law's view of their situation. The more delicate his exposition of the matter, however, the less likely he is to bring the parties to the subjective state out of which a new act of consent can arise. Bluntness appears to be what the law demands, and the pastoral consequences of such bluntness can be unfortunate.[116]

---

[112] See note 86 above. The fact that several reputable canonists advance an erroneous interpretation of the law is not, in itself, sufficient to give rise to a doubt of law.

[113] J. O'Rourke, "Considerations on the Convalidation of Marriage," *J* 43 (1983) 390.

[114] See cc. 293 (on a person who has lost the clerical state being ascribed *denuo* as a cleric); 921, §2 (on a person who has already received holy communion receiving it *denuo* on the same day as Viaticum); 1004, §2 (on repetition of the anointing of the sick after a person who has recovered falls into a serious sickness *denuo*); 1505, §3 (on submitting *denuo* an amended petition after the original was rejected because of technical defects); 1570 (on calling witnesses who have already testified for examination *denuo*); and 1705, §3 (on submitting *denuo* a petition for a dissolution of a ratified but not consummated marriage after the original petition was rejected by the Holy See). Although *denuo* does not refer to a juridic act in c. 1004, §2, it does refer to a new personal

health crisis distinct from the one that prompted the original anointing.

[115] *Coram* Funghini, June 30, 1988, *SRRDec* 80 (1988) 440–444.

[116] Johnson, "The 'Simple' Convalidation," 478–479.

The norms governing renewal of consent in these cases are merely ecclesiastical law—and rather recent ecclesiastical law at that. If the pastoral consequences of this law are unacceptable, perhaps the time has come to change it.

ARTICLE 2: RADICAL SANATION
[cc. 1161–1165]

Historical Synopsis

The origins of the institute of radical sanation are shrouded in the mists of history.[117] It arose out of a desire to legitimate children born of marriages invalid because of impediments, who suffered serious civil and ecclesiastical disabilities because of their status. In the Middle Ages, it was generally conceded that the Church could legitimate children insofar as spiritual effects were concerned, but to legitimate them insofar as temporal effects were concerned seemed a usurpation of the power of civil authorities. What was needed was an approach to legitimation that avoided a direct confrontation between Church and State.

Joannes Andrea (d. 1348) is generally credited, if not with the invention of radical sanation, at least with its first systematic articulation.[118] At the time, all sides conceded that the Church had exclusive jurisdiction over the sacrament of marriage. Since the Church could cause marriages to be invalid by establishing diriment impediments and could dispense from these impediments, Joannes Andrea reasoned that the Church could dispense from an impediment that had already invalidated a marriage in a way that allowed the dispensation to undo the consequences the impediment had previously wrought. Thus, by healing or validating the marriage directly at its root, the Church could indirectly legitimate the offspring of the marriage. There was

precedent for this approach since the Church had often retroactively abrogated or dispensed from other ecclesiastical laws.

Because of its origin and purpose, this institute was first called "the fullest legitimation" (*legitimatio plenissima*). Later it became known as a "dispensation in the root" (*dispensatio in radice*) and ultimately a "healing in the root" (*sanatio in radice*). At first, the institute was used to validate marriages in particular cases, usually to permit the succession to the throne of the illegitimate offspring of invalidly married monarchs. In time, however, it was used to give a general validation of numerous marriages invalidly contracted during turbulent times. Thus, in 1554, Julius III delegated the legate Reginald Pole to sanate marriages invalidly contracted during the reign of Henry VIII in England, and in 1801 and again in 1809 Pius VII granted general sanations of invalid marriages contracted during the turmoil following the French Revolution.[119]

Since the institute of radical sanation rests on the Church's power to establish, abrogate, and dispense from ecclesiastical law, it was originally used to validate marriages invalid because of an impediment of ecclesiastical law and later a defect of canonical form. However, in 1890, the Holy See began granting radical sanations of marriages invalid because of the divine law impediment of prior bond, when the impediment had ceased. The practice was curtailed in 1904 when the Holy Office declared that the Church lacks the power to grant radical sanations of marriages invalid because of a divine law impediment.[120] However, Cardinal Gasparri convinced Pius X to incorporate into the 1917 code a formulation that somewhat weakened the Holy Office's declaration. Canon 1139, §2 of the 1917 code declared not that the Church *cannot* sanate marriages invalid because of an impediment of divine law but that it *does not* do so.[121] However, practice soon outstripped theory. The Holy See's

---

[117] See R. Harrigan, *The Radical Sanation of Invalid Marriages,* CanLawStud 116 (Washington, D.C.: Catholic University of America, 1938) 19–42.

[118] Ioannes Andrea, *glos. ord.* to Clem. 3.17.cap.unic. ad v. *Pro infectis.*

[119] Harrigan, 28–34.

[120] *CICFontes,* n. 1270.

[121] Harrigan, 36–38.

practice of sanating marriages invalid because of the impediment of prior bond despite the explicit norm of canon 1139, §2 of the 1917 code was first formalized in law in Paul VI's 1966 *motu proprio De episcoporum muneribus.*[122]

The authority to grant a radical sanation was originally articulated as a power proper to the Roman Pontiff. In the course of time, this power was exercised on his behalf by various offices of the Roman Curia. By the nineteenth century, this power had been widely delegated for individual cases to diocesan bishops in the form of quinquennial faculties. In the 1963 *motu proprio Pastorale munus,* Paul VI listed the power to sanate marriages in certain cases among the faculties that belong by right to the diocesan bishop.[123] Three years later, he recognized the power to sanate marriages in individual cases as belonging by right to the office of the diocesan bishop and reserved to the Holy See the sanation of marriages only in cases where the marriage is invalid because of an impediment whose dispensation is reserved to the Holy See or is of divine law and where the conditions for the celebration of a mixed marriage have not been met.

The Nature of Radical Sanation

Canon 1161 — §1. The radical sanation of an invalid marriage is its convalidation without the renewal of consent, which is granted by competent authority and entails the dispensation from an impediment, if there is one, and from canonical form, if it was not observed, and the retroactivity of canonical effects.

§2. Convalidation occurs at the moment of the granting of the favor. Retroactivity, however, is understood to extend to the moment of the celebration of the marriage unless other provision is expressly made.

§3. A radical sanation is not to be granted unless it is probable that the parties wish to persevere in conjugal life.

A radical sanation is a fiction of law by which competent ecclesiastical authority renders retroactively valid a marriage which was invalid from its origin without the renewal of consent by either party. An essential precondition for a radical sanation is that both parties gave naturally sufficient but juridically inefficacious consent to marriage in the past and that this consent continues into the present. In addition, the obstacle to the juridic efficacy of the parties' consent must be removed either by its dispensation or by its cessation. Since by definition a radical sanation entails a dispensation from any impediment of ecclesiastical law that may have caused the invalidity of the marriage and from the parties' obligation to renew consent, the rescript granting the sanation need not explicitly mention these dispensations. However, the one granting the sanation must have the authority to dispense from the impediment at issue.

Effect of Radical Sanation

The effect of a radical sanation is to render a marriage valid not only from the moment the sanation is granted but from the moment naturally sufficient consent was initially given. Unless the law asserts an express provision to the contrary, the radical sanation makes the validity of a marriage retroactive to its beginning. Canon 1162, §2 expressly limits the retroactive effect of the sanation of a marriage invalid because of a defect of consent on the part of one or both parties to the moment when true consent was given by both parties. Commentators on the 1917 code generally held that, since the Church cannot dispense from the impediment of prior bond, it could grant a radical sanation of a marriage invalid because of this impediment only to the time when the impediment ceased.[124] The revised code makes no such express provision limiting the scope of a radical sanation of a marriage invalid because of a divine law impediment that has now ceased.

[122] *EM* 18.
[123] *PM* 21–22.

[124] Harrigan, 96–99.

Since a radical sanation can be granted validly only if the naturally sufficient consent of both parties has perdured, an effort must be made to ascertain that the original consent has not been revoked before a sanation is granted. Chronic marital instability or long-standing marital problems may be signs that the original consent has been revoked by one or both parties. Thus, canon 1161, §3 cautions that a radical sanation is not to be granted unless it seems probable that the couple intends to persevere in conjugal life. Well-meaning pastoral ministers ignore this caution when they seek a radical sanation to allow a return to the sacraments by an invalidly married Catholic whose partner has refused to convalidate the union by renewal of consent. Despite its "pastoral" intent, this approach may make the last state of the person worse than the first.

RADICAL SANATION IN VARIOUS CIRCUMSTANCES

1. Sanation and Defective Consent

Canon 1162 — §1. A marriage cannot be radically sanated if consent is lacking in either or both of the parties, whether the consent was lacking from the beginning or, though present in the beginning, was revoked afterwards.

§2. If this consent was indeed lacking from the beginning but was given afterwards, the sanation can be granted from the moment the consent was given.

Since no human power can supply consent that was withheld or fundamentally flawed, a marriage invalid because of a defect of consent cannot be the subject of a radical sanation as long as that defect continues. Nor can a radical sanation be granted if the party whose original consent was defective gives true consent only after the other party has withdrawn his or her consent. A radical sanation of a marriage invalid because of a defect of consent is possible after the party whose consent was defective gives consent as long as the

consent of the other party endures. However, the sanation is retroactive only to the moment when the true consent was given.

Since a simple convalidation of a marriage invalid because of a defect of consent that cannot be proven in the external forum requires only that the party responsible for the defect of consent give true consent privately and secretly (c. 1159, §2), a radical sanation will rarely if ever be employed for the validation of these marriages. In these cases, the intervention of ecclesiastical authority would be superfluous. However, a radical sanation might be employed to validate a marriage invalid because of a defect of consent that can be proved in the external forum but now is healed, when one party refuses to consent according to the canonical form.

2. Sanation and Impediments or Defect of Form

Canon 1163 — §1. A marriage which is invalid because of an impediment or a defect of legitimate form can be sanated provided that the consent of each party perseveres.

§2. A marriage which is invalid because of an impediment of natural law or of divine positive law can be sanated only after the impediment has ceased.

One effect of a radical sanation is an implicit dispensation from ecclesiastical law impediments that prevented consent from having juridic effect. However, the dispensation from some of these impediments and, therefore, the radical sanation of marriages invalid because of them are reserved to the Apostolic See. The implied dispensation is effective from the time of the original consent.

A radical sanation does not dispense from impediments considered to be based in divine law, whether natural or positive. These impediments are: prior bond, antecedent and perpetual impotence, and consanguinity in the direct line and up to and including the second degree of the collateral line (i.e., brother-sister). For the granting of a radical sanation of a marriage invalid because of one of these impediments, the impediment must first cease. The impediment of prior bond ceases with the death of the first spouse or the dissolution of the bond by competent authority.[125] The impediment of impotence may cease in some cases after surgery or some other form of medical treatment that moral theologians would consider extraordinary means. Of its nature, the impediment of consanguinity does not cease.

A marriage that is invalid solely because of lack of form in either the narrow or the broad sense can be the subject of a radical sanation. Indeed, radical sanation may be the only practical method of validating a marriage invalid because of a defect of form when one of the parties will not or cannot contract marriage anew according to the canonical form. Nevertheless, care should be taken to ensure that the party's refusal to renew consent does not indicate the revocation of his or her original consent.

3. Sanation without the Awareness of the Parties

Canon 1164 — A sanation can be granted validly even if either or both of the parties do not know of it; nevertheless, it is not to be granted except for a grave cause.

A radical sanation is often granted at the request of one or both parties to an invalid marriage to regularize their union in the eyes of the Church and to allow them to return to the reception of the sacraments. If only one party requests the sanation, the other party does not have to be informed or even aware of the granting of the sanation. What is critical is that the naturally sufficient consent of both parties continues at the time the radical sanation is granted.

The parties do not have to be present at the granting of the sanation nor is its effect dependent on their acceptance of it. In fact, a radical sanation can be granted without the knowledge of either party. Since a radical sanation is a favor, it does not necessarily presuppose a request on the part of the parties. It can be granted ex officio by competent

---

[125] See the commentary on cc. 1141–1150.

ecclesiastical authority. Often, a radical sanation is granted to correct invalidating defects for which the parties are not responsible and about which they are totally ignorant. For example, a parish minister may discover after the wedding that he neglected to seek a dispensation from an impediment or from the observance of canonical form, that he lacked the faculty to witness the marriage, or that only one other witness was present at the celebration. A radical sanation heals these defects without disturbing the consciences of the parties.

The longer the time between the celebration of the marriage and the discovery of an invalidating defect, the riskier the granting of radical sanations ex officio becomes. With the passage of time, the difficulties and trials of married life can prompt one or both parties whose original consent was naturally sufficient to revoke it. If consent has been withdrawn by even one party, the radical sanation is without effect.

Competence to Grant Sanations

Canon 1165 — §1. The Apostolic See can grant a radical sanation.

§2. The diocesan bishop can grant a radical sanation in individual cases even if there are several reasons for nullity in the same marriage, after the conditions mentioned in can. 1125 for the sanation of a mixed marriage have been fulfilled. He cannot grant one, however, if there is an impediment whose dispensation is reserved to the Apostolic See according to the norm of can. 1078, §2, or if it concerns an impediment of natural law or divine positive law which has now ceased.

The institute of radical sanation was given its first coherent juridic articulation during the height of medieval papal absolutism. As a result, the power to grant a radical sanation was traditionally reserved to the Roman Pontiff or to the curial offices that exercised the power in his name. However, especially during the nineteenth and early twentieth centuries, the power was delegated to papal legates, missionaries, and diocesan bishops in the form of habitual faculties.

Sanations of Multiple Marriages

In the current law, only the Apostolic See can grant a general sanation of a number of marriages simultaneously. This power has usually been exercised only to restore ecclesial order and peace after an extended period of social and ecclesial turmoil resulting in numerous invalid marriages, e.g., during the Catholic restoration under Mary Tudor in sixteenth century England and in the aftermath of the Revolution in early nineteenth century France. The Apostolic See also retains the authority, in some cases the exclusive authority, to grant radical sanations in individual cases. However, even the Apostolic See can grant radical sanations only on condition that the naturally sufficient consent of both parties continues in existence.

Sanations by Authority of the Diocesan Bishop

The power to grant radical sanations in individual cases, but only in individual cases, is now understood to be inherent in the office of the diocesan bishop. The power is reserved to diocesan bishops and those equivalent to them in law[126] and is not granted by the law to local ordinaries such as vicars as is much of the authority to dispense in matrimonial matters (e.g., cc. 1078, §1; 1127, §2). Nevertheless, the granting of a radical sanation is an exercise of executive power which can be freely delegated by the diocesan bishop.

The granting of radical sanations is governed by the general norms governing the exercise of executive power. While it can be exercised whether the diocesan bishop or his delegate is present in the diocese or not, it can be exercised validly only on behalf of "subjects," i.e., those who have a domicile or quasi-domicile in the diocese, and travelers who are actually present in the diocese at the time the sanation is granted (c. 136). Thus, if a couple returns to a diocese in which they no longer reside to celebrate their marriage but the official witness fails to obtain the necessary faculty to witness the marriage, the bishop of the diocese where the marriage was celebrated cannot grant a radical sanation of this marriage invalid because of a defect of form, unless perchance the couple happens to be still de facto present there.

The competent diocesan bishop can grant a radical sanation of an invalid marriage between a Catholic and a non-Catholic, whether baptized or not, only if the conditions for a mixed marriage (c. 1125) have been met. If these conditions have not been met, the case must be referred to the CDF.

Sanations Reserved to the Apostolic See

The authority of a diocesan bishop to grant radical sanations in individual cases is also restricted to the limits of his dispensing power over matrimonial impediments. Marriages invalid because of impediments whose dispensation is reserved to the Apostolic See can be sanated only by the same Apostolic See. The impediments whose dispensation is reserved to the Apostolic See are those arising from sacred orders, from a public and perpetual vow of chastity in a pontifical religious institute, and from the conjugicide defined in canon 1090 (c. 1078, §2). The Congregation for Divine Worship and the Discipline of the Sacraments can dispense from the impediments of sacred orders and crime; the Congregation for Institutes of Consecrated Life and Societies of Apostolic Life from the impediment of a perpetual vow.[127] Petitions for radical sanations of marriages invalid because of these impediments should be directed to these congregations or, in occult or non-public cases, to the Apostolic Penitentiary.

---

[126] See cc. 381, §2 and 368 and the commentary on these canons for an explanation of those considered equivalent in law to the diocesan bishop.

[127] In practice, the impediment arising from a perpetual vow of chastity in a pontifical religious institute is not dispensed directly. Rather, the petitioner is granted a dispensation from his or her vows as part of an indult of departure from the institute. With the dispensation from vows, the impediment ceases. See cc. 691–692.

Also reserved to the Apostolic See is the radical sanation of marriages invalid because of a divine law impediment which has now ceased. Marriages invalid because of the impediment of prior bond are the most common, if not the only, cases involving divine law impediments for which radical sanations are sought. If one party to the invalid marriage is a Catholic, the invalidity is usually compounded by lack of form. However, the fact that the marriage is also invalid because of lack of form does not empower the diocesan bishop to grant a radical sanation. The request for a sanation should be directed instead to the Congregation for Divine Worship and the Discipline of the Sacraments with proof of the cessation of the impediment (certificate of death of the first spouse, other proof of death, or an authentic document verifying an ecclesiastical dissolution of the marriage), an explanation of the serious reasons why a simple convalidation is not possible, and the *votum* of the diocesan bishop regarding the merits of the petition.

A declaration of nullity of a first marriage acknowledges that there never was a true impediment of prior bond. If one party to a marriage that has been declared null has subsequently entered a civil marriage and a party to this second marriage was bound to observe the canonical form, the only real cause for the invalidity of this second marriage is the lack of form. Therefore, it can be radically sanated by the diocesan bishop if one of the parties refuses to contract the marriage anew according to canonical form.[128]

---

[128] If a party to a marriage that has been declared null is a non-Catholic who has entered a second marriage with another non-Catholic but who now is seeking baptism in or reception into full communion with the Catholic Church, neither a simple convalidation nor a radical sanation is necessary to achieve ecclesial recognition of the second marriage, as long as the new spouse was free to marry. The declaration of nullity recognizes that the person was not bound by the impediment of prior bond when he or she entered the second marriage. All things being equal, the second marriage is presumed valid.

(The material listed below serves as a comprehensive bibliography for title VII of Book IV—canons 1055–1165.)

MARRIAGE IN GENERAL

Books

Brooke, C. *The Medieval Idea of Marriage.* Oxford: Clarendon, 1989.

Brundage, J. *Law, Sex, and Christian Society in Medieval Europe.* Chicago: University of Chicago, 1987.

Cappello, F. *Tractatus Canonico-Moralis de Sacramentis.* Vol. 5: *De Matrimonio.* Rome: Marietti, 1961.

Gasparri, P. *Tractatus Canonicus de Matrimonio.* Vatican City: Typis Polyglottis Vaticanis, 1932.

Gramunt, I., J. Hervada, and L. Wauck. *Canons and Commentaries on Marriage.* Collegeville: Liturgical Press, 1987.

Kasper, W. *Theology of Christian Marriage.* New York: Seabury, 1980.

McAreavey, J. *The Canon Law of Marriage and the Family.* Dublin: Four Courts, 1997.

Mackin, T. *Divorce and Remarriage.* New York: Paulist, 1984.

———. *The Marital Sacrament.* New York: Paulist, 1989.

———. *What Is Marriage?* New York: Paulist, 1982.

Il matrimonio sacramento nell' ordinamento canonico vigente. Studi giuridici 31. Vatican City: Libreria Editrice Vaticana, 1993.

Mendonça, A. *Rotal Anthology: An Annotated Index of Rotal Decisions from 1971 to 1988.* Washington, D.C.: CLSA, 1992.

La nuova legislazione matrimoniale canonica. Studi giuridici 10. Vatican City: Libreria Editrice Vaticana, 1986.

Örsy, L. *Marriage in Canon Law: Texts and Comments, Reflections and Questions.* Wilmington, Del.: Michael Glazier, 1986.

Reynolds, P. *Marriage in the Western Church.* Leiden: E. J. Brill, 1994.

Schillebeeckx, E. *Marriage: Secular Reality and Saving Mystery.* 2 vols. London: Sheed and Ward, 1965.

Wrenn, L. *The Invalid Marriage.* Washington, D.C.: CLSA, 1998.

———, trans. *Law Sections.* Washington, D.C.: CLSA, 1994.

Articles

Burke, C. "The Sacramentality of Marriage: Canonical Reflections." *ME* 119 (1994) 545–565.

Caffara, C. "Marriage as a Reality in the Order of Creation and Marriage as a Sacrament." In *Contemporary Perspectives on Christian Marriage,* ed. R. Malone and J. Connery, 119–132. Chicago: Loyola University, 1984.

Decanay, A. N. "Matrimonium ratum: significatio termini." *P* 79 (1990) 69–89.

Errazuriz, C. "La rilevanza canonica della sacramentalità del matrimonio e della sua dimensione familiare." *Ius Ecclesiae* 7 (1996) 561–572.

Finn, R. C. "Faith and the Sacrament of Marriage: General Conclusions from a Historical Study." In *Marriage Studies III,* ed. T. Doyle, 95–111. Washington, D.C.: CLSA, 1985.

Gherro, S. "Sulla sacramentalità del matrimonio (*in fieri* e *in facto*)." *Ius Ecclesiae* 7 (1995) 573–578.

Hendriks, J. "Battesimo, fede e sacramentalità del matrimonio (c. 1055 §2)." *Ius Ecclesiae* 8 (1996) 663–676.

Himes, M. J. "The Intrinsic Sacramentality of Marriage: The Theological Ground for the Inseparability of Validity and Sacramentality." *J* 50 (1990) 198–220.

International Theological Commission. "Propositions on the Doctrine of Christian Marriage. *Origins* 8 (1978–1979) 235–239.

Lawler, M. G. "Faith, Contract, and Sacrament in Christian Marriage: A Theological Approach." *TS* 52 (1991) 712–731.

McAreavey, J. "Faith and the Validity of Marriage." *Irish Theological Quarterly* 59 (1993) 177–187.

McManus, F. R. "The Ministers of the Sacrament of Marriage in the Western Tradition." *Stud Can* 20 (1986) 85–104.

O'Callaghan, D. "Faith and the Sacrament of Marriage." *Irish Theological Quarterly* 52 (1986) 161–179.

Pompedda, M. "Faith and the Sacrament of Marriage: Lack of Faith and Matrimonial Consent: Juridical Aspects." In *Marriage Studies IV,* ed. J. Alesandro, 33–65. Washington, D.C.: CLSA, 1990.

———. "Mancanza di fede e consenso matrimoniale." In *Studi di diritto matrimoniale canonico,* 399–448.

Reynolds, L. "Marriage, Sacramental and Indissoluble: Sources of the Catholic Doctrine." *Downside Review* 109 (1991) 105–150.

PRELIMINARY NORMS

Books

Il *"bonum coniugum" nel matrimonio canonico.* Studi giuridici 40. Vatican City: Libreria Editrice Vaticana, 1996.

Navarrete, U. *Structura Iuridica Matrimonii Secundum Concilium Vaticanum II.* Rome: Gregorian University, 1968.

Scicluna, C. *The Essential Definition of Marriage according to the 1917 and 1983 Codes of Canon Law.* Lanham, Md.: University Press of America, 1995.

Articles

Burke, C. "The 'Bonum Coniugum' and the 'Bonum Prolis': Ends or Properties of Marriage?" *J* 49 (1989) 704–713.

Carreras, J. "Il 'bonum coniugum' oggetto del consenso matrimoniale." *Ius Ecclesiae* 6 (1994) 117–158.

Fagiolo, V. "Le proprietà essenziali del matrimonio." *ME* 119 (1993) 145–178.

Pfnausch, E. "The Good of the Spouses in Rotal Jurisprudence: New Horizons?" *J* 56 (1996) 527–558.

Wrenn, L. "Refining the Essence of Marriage." *J* 46 (1986) 532–551.

CHAPTER I:
Pastoral Care and Those Things Which Must Precede the Celebration of Marriage

Articles

Lawler, M. "Doing Marriage Preparation Right." *America,* December 30, 1995, 12–15.

Provost, J. "Marriage Preparation in the New Code: Canon 1063 and the *Novus Habitus Mentis.*" In *Ius Sequitur Vitam,* ed. J. Provost and K. Walf, 173–192. Louvain: Leuven University, 1991.

CHAPTER II:
Diriment Impediments in General

Books

Gli impedimenti al matrimonio canonico. Studi giuridici 19. Vatican City: Libreria Editrice Vaticana, 1989.

Waterhouse, J. *The Power of the Local Ordinary to Impose a Matrimonial Ban.* CanLawStud 317. Washington, D.C.: Catholic University of America, 1952.

CHAPTER III:
Diriment Impediments Specifically

Books

Ameriso, F. *El fundamento del impedimento de edad.* Rome: Athenaeum Sanctae Crucis, 1995.

Articles

Candelier, G. "Impuissance: Empêchement et signe d'une incapacité." *RDC* 44 (1994) 93–145.

Johnson, J. "*Ligamen* and Multiple Marriages." *J* 42 (1982) 222–228.

CHAPTER IV:
Matrimonial Consent

C. 1095

Books

Keating, J. *The Bearing of Mental Impairment on the Validity of Marriage.* Rome: Gregorian University, 1973.

L'immaturità psico-affettiva nella giurisprudenza della Rota Romana. Studi giuridici 23. Vatican City: Libreria Editrice Vaticana, 1990.

Pompedda, M. *Studi di diritto matrimoniale canonico.* Milan: Giuffré, 1993.

Sable, R. M., ed. *Incapacity for Marriage: Jurisprudence and Interpretation.* Acts of the III Gregorian Colloquium. Rome: Pontificia Università Gregoriana, 1987.

Articles

Aznar Gil, F. R. "Incapacidad de asumir (c. 1095.3) y jurisprudencia de la Rota Romana." *REDC* 53 (1996) 15–65.

Bauhoff, R., and A. Mendonça. "Psychic Impotence." *Stud Can* 24 (1990) 205–240, 293–333.

Burke, C. "Some Reflections on Canon 1095." *ME* 117 (1992) 133–150.

Burke, R. "Canon 1095: Canonical Doctrine and Jurisprudence, Part I: Canon 1095.1 and 2." *CLSAP* 48 (1986) 94–107.

———. "Lack of Discretion of Judgement: Canonical Doctrine and Legislation." *J* 45 (1985) 171–209.

Egan, E. "The Nullity of Marriage for Reason of Insanity or Lack of Due Discretion of Judgment." *EIC* 39 (1983) 9–53.

Errazuriz, C. J. "Riflessioni sulla capacità consensuale nel matrimonio canonico." *Ius Ecclesiae* 6 (1994) 449–464.

Fellhauer, D. "Canon 1095: Canonical Doctrine and Jurisprudence, Part II: Canon 1095.3." *CLSAP* 48 (1986) 107–117.

Ferme, B. "The Shifting Boundaries on Incapacity for Marriage." *Forum* 3 (1992) 25–43.

Gramunt, I., and L. Wauck. "Capacity and Incapacity to Contract Marriage." *Stud Can* 22 (1988) 147–168.

———. "Lack of Due Discretion—Incapacity or Error?" *IC* 32 (1992) 533–558.

McGrath, A. "On the Gravity of Causes of a Psychological Nature in the Proof of Incapacity to Assume the Essential Obligations of Marriage." *Stud Can* 22 (1988) 67–75.

Mendonça, A. "Consensual Incapacity for Marriage." *J* 54 (1992) 477–569.

———. "The Effect of Paranoid Personality Disorder on Matrimonial Consent." *Stud Can* 18 (1984) 253–289.

———. "The Effects of Multiple Sclerosis on Matrimonial Consent." *Stud Can* 21 (1987) 429–450.

———. "The Incapacity to Contract Marriage: Canon 1095." *Stud Can* 19 (1985) 259–325.

———. "Narcissistic Personality Disorder: Possible Effects on Matrimonial Consent." *Stud Can* 27 (1993) 97–143.

———. "Recent Jurisprudence on the Effects of Mood Disorders and Neuroses on Matrimonial Consent." In *Unico Ecclesiae servitio,* ed. M. Thériault and J. Thorn, 148–179. Ottawa: St. Paul University, 1991.

———. "Recent Rotal Jurisprudence on the Effects of Sexual Disorders on Matrimonial Consent." *Stud Can* 26 (1992) 209–233.

———. "Recent Trends in Rotal Jurisprudence." *Stud Can* 28 (1994) 167–230.

———, and N. Sangal. "The Effects of Anorexia and Bulimia Nervosa on Marital Consent." *ME* 121 (1996) 539–610.

Pavanello, P. "Il requisito della perpetuità nell'incapacità di assumere le obbligazioni essenziali del matrimonio (c. 1095.3)." *P* 83 (1994) 119–144.

Pompedda, M. "De incapacitate assumendi obligationes matrimonii essentiales." *P* 75 (1986) 129–152.

———. "Lecture du canon 1095 du Code de 1983." *AC* 35 (1992) 259–284.

Provost, J. H. "Canon 1095: Past, Present, Future." *J* 54 (1994) 81–112.

Sabbattani, A. "L'évolution de la jurisprudence dans les causes de nullité de mariage pour incapacité psychique." *Stud Can* 1 (1967) 143–161.

Sangal, N. "The Effects of Incest on Matrimonial Consent." *Stud Can* 30 (1996) 5–30.

Sanson, R. "Narcissistic Personality Disorder: Possible Effects on the Validity of Marital Consent." *ME* 113 (1988) 541–581; 114 (1989) 405–424.

C. 1096

Parisella, I. "Ignoranza 'in re matrimoniali.'" *EIC* 43–44 (1987–1988) 17–32.

Sherba, J. "Canon 1096: Ignorance as a Ground for Nullity." *CLSAP* 59 (1997) 282–299.

C. 1097

Carmignani Caridi, S. "The *Error Personae vel Qualitatis Personae* in Rotal Jurisprudence." *Forum* 3 (1992) 67–96.

Hennessey, P. "Canon 1097: A Requiem for *Error Redundans?*" *J* 49 (1989) 146–181.

Hilbert, M. "Error in qualitate personae (c. 1097, §2)." *P* 87 (1998) 403–442.

Navarrete, U. "Error circa personam et error circa qualitates communes seu non identificantes personam (c. 1097)." *P* 82 (1993) 639–667.

———. "Error in persona (c. 1097, §1)." *P* 87 (1998) 351–401.

C. 1098

Bonnet, H. "Quelques pistes nouvelles pour le dol en matière de mariage." *AC* 35 (1992) 147–179.

Canale, G. "Primi contributi della giurisprudenza rotale alla configurazione del dolo come vizio del consenso matrimoniale." *Il Diritto Ecclesiastico* 104 (1993) 343–360.

Cuneo, J. J. "Deceit/Error of Person as a *Caput nullitatis.*" *CLSAP* 45 (1983) 154–166.

Gressier, G. "La nullité du mariage conclu sous l'effet du dol qualifié du canon 1098 est de droit naturel." *Stud Can* 30 (1996) 343–370.

Gullo, C. "Riflessioni sulla retroattività del can. 1098." *Ius Ecclesiae* 4 (1992) 225–234.

Johnson, J. "Fraud and Deceit in the Roman Rota: The First Ten Years." *J* 56 (1996) 557–585.

———. "On the Retroactive Force of Canon 1098." *Stud Can* 23 (1989) 61–83.

Navarrete, U. "Canon 1098 de errore doloso estne iuris naturalis an iuris positivi ecclesiastici?" *P* 76 (1987) 161–181.

Vann, K. "*Dolus:* Canon 1098 of the Revised Code of Canon Law." *J* 47 (1987) 371–393.

C. 1099

Boccafola, K. "Error Concerning Sacramental Dignity: Limits of the Object and Proof." *Forum* 7 (1996) 305–325.

Campbell, D. M. "Canon 1099: The Emergence of a New Juridic Figure." *Quaderni Studio Rotale* 5 (1990) 35–72.

Grocholewski, Z. "De errore circa matrimonii unitatem, indissolubilitatem et sacramentalem dignitatem." *P* 84 (1995) 395–418.

Kowal, J. "L'erore circa la proprietà essenziale o la dignità sacramentale del matrimonio (c. 1099)." *P* 87 (1998) 287–327.

Navarrete, U. "De sensu clausulae 'Dummodo non determinet voluntatem' can. 1099." *P* 81 (1992) 469–493.

Provost, J. "Error as a Ground in Marriage Nullity Cases." *CLSAP* 57 (1995) 306–324.

Stankiewicz, A. "De errore voluntatem determinante (can. 1099) iuxta rotalem iurisprudentiam." *P* 78 (1990) 441–494.

———. "L'errore di diritto nel consenso matrimoniale e la sua autonomia giuridica." *P* 83 (1994) 635–668.

C. 1101

Books

La simulazione del consenso matrimoniale canonico. Studi giuridici 22. Vatican City: Libreria Editrice Vaticana, 1990.

Jenkins, R. *Recent Rotal Jurisprudence on Simulation* contra Bonum Sacramenti *by an Implicit Act of the Will.* CanLawStud 551. Washington, D.C.: Catholic University of America, 1999.

Articles

Dewhirst, J. A. "*Consortium vitae, bonum coniugum,* and their Relation to Simulation." *J* 55 (1995) 794–812.

Faltin, D. "The Exclusion of the Sacramentality of Marriage with Particular Reference to the Marriage of Baptized Non-believers." In *Marriage Studies IV,* ed. J. Alesandro, 66–104. Washington, D.C.: CLSA, 1990.

Grocholewski, Z. "L'esclusione della dignità sacramentale del matrimonio come capo autonomo di nullità matrimoniale." *ME* 121 (1996) 223–239.

Johnson, J. "Total Simulation in Recent Rotal Jurisprudence." *Stud Can* 24 (1990) 383–425.

Kitchen, P. "Matrimonial Intention and Simulation." *Stud Can* 28 (1994) 347–406.

Mendonça, A. "Exclusion of the Sacramentality of Marriage: Recent Trends in Rotal Jurisprudence." *Stud Can* 31 (1997) 5–48.

Pfnausch, E. "The Good of the Spouses in Rotal Jurisprudence: New Horizons?" *J* 56 (1996) 527–556.

Provost, J., and E. Pfnausch. "Simulated Consent: A New Way of Looking at an Old Way of Thinking." *J* 55 (1995) 698–744.

Robitaille, L. "Proofs in Defect of the Will Cases." *CLSAP* 57 (1995) 337–354.

———. "Simulation, Error Determining the Will, or Lack of Due Discretion? A Case Study." *Stud Can* 29 (1995) 397–432.

Sanson, R. "Implicit Simulation: Grounds for Annulment?" *J* 48 (1988) 747–770.

Schmidt, K. "*Educatio prolis* and the Validity of Marriage." *J* 55 (1995) 243–280.

———. "The 'Raising of Children' as an Essential Element of Marriage." *CLSAP* 59 (1997) 223–266.

Stankiewicz, A. "De iurisprudentia Rotali recentiore circa simulationem totalem et partialem." *ME* 122 (1997) 189–234.

———. "L'esclusione della procreazione ed educazione della prole." *Apol* 63 (1990) 625–654.

Villeggiante, S. "L'esclusione del 'bonum sacramenti.'" *ME* 115 (1990) 351–386.

C. 1102

Books

Il consenso matrimoniale condizionato. Studi giuridici 30. Vatican City: Libreria Editrice Vaticana, 1993.

Articles

Lagges, P. "Conditioned Consent to Marriage." *CLSAP* 58 (1996) 236–260.

Leuzzi, A. "La condizione del consenso matrimoniale canonico." *Apol* 66 (1993) 371–437.

McGrath, J. B. "The Effects of Pre-nuptial Agreements on the Validity of Marriage." *J* 53 (1993) 385–395.

Robitaille, L. "Conditioned Consent: Natural Law and Human Positive Law." *Stud Can* 26 (1992) 75–110.

C. 1103

Lagges, P. "Force or Fear." *CLSAP* 58 (1996) 261–282.

Smilanic, D. A. "Reverential Fear." *CLSAP* 58 (1996) 283–291.

Wrenn, L. "Urban Navarrete, S.J., and the Response of the Code Commission on Force and Fear." *J* 51 (1991) 119–137.

CHAPTER IX:
The Separation of Spouses

Books

Abate, A. *The Dissolution of the Matrimonial Bond.* Rome: Desclée, 1962.

Cereti, G. *Divorzio, nuove nozze et penitenza nella Chiesa primitiva.* Bologna: Dehoniane, 1977.

Gregory, D. *The Pauline Privilege. CanLawStud* 68. Washington, D.C.: Catholic University of America, 1931.

Jugis, P. *A Canonical Analysis of the Meaning of* Humano Modo *in Canon 1061, §1. CanLawStud* 541. Washington, D.C.: Catholic University of America, 1993.

Marchetta, B. *Scioglimento del matrimonio canonico per inconsummazione.* Padua: Antonio Milani, 1981.

Noonan, J. *The Power to Dissolve.* Cambridge, Mass.: Belknap, 1972.

I procedimenti speciali nel diritto canonico. Studi giuridici 27. Vatican City: Libreria Editrice Vaticana, 1992.

Woeber, E. *The Interpellations. CanLawStud* 172. Washington, D.C.: Catholic University of America, 1942.

Woestman, W. *Special Marriage Cases.* 3rd ed. Ottawa: St. Paul University, 1994.

Articles

Cereti, V. "The Reconciliation of Remarried Divorcees according to Canon 8 of the Council of Nicea." In *Ius sequitur vitam,* ed. J. Provost and K. Walf, 193–207. Louvain: Leuven University, 1991.

Gerhartz, J. "L'indissolubilité du mariage et sa dissolution par l'Église dans la problématique actuelle." *RDC* 21 (1971) 198–234.

O'Connor, W. "The Indissolubility of a Ratified, Consummated Marriage." *Ephemerides Theologicae Lovanienses* 13 (1936) 692–722.

CHAPTER X:
The Convalidation of Marriage

Books

Brennan, J. *The Simple Convalidation of Marriage. CanLawStud* 102. Washington, D.C.: Catholic University of America, 1937.

Harrigan, R. *The Radical Sanation of Invalid Marriages. CanLawStud* 116. Washington, D.C.: Catholic University of America, 1938.

Articles

Bogdan, L. A. "Simple Convalidation of Marriage in the 1983 Code of Canon Law." *J* 48 (1986) 511–531.

Johnson, J. "The 'Simple' Convalidation as a Pastoral Problem." *StudCan* 15 (1981) 461–479.

Matthews, K. "Validations or Convalidations: That Is the Question." In *Unico Ecclesiae servitio,* ed. M. Thériault and J. Thorn, 133–147. Ottawa: St. Paul University, 1991.

O'Rourke, J. J. "Considerations on the Convalidation of Marriage." *J* 43 (1983) 387–391.

MARRIAGE IN GENERAL: EASTERN CODE

Books

Il matrimonio nel Codice dei canoni delle Chiese orientali, Studi giuridici 32. Vatican City: Libreria Editrice Vaticana, 1994.

Pospishil, V. *Eastern Catholic Marriage Law according to the Code of Canons of the Eastern Churches.* Brooklyn: St. Maron Publications, 1990.

Prader, J. *Il matrimonio in Oriente e Occidente.* Kanonika 1. Rome: Pontificium Institutum Orientalium Studiorum, 1992.

Articles

Abbass, J. "Marriage in the Codes of Canon Law." *Apol* 68 (1995) 521–565.

Gallagher, C. "Marriage in the Revised Canon Law for the Eastern Catholic Churches." *Stud Can* 24 (1990) 69–90.

Gallaro, G. "The Mystery of Crowning: An Interecclesial Perspective." *CLSAP* 51 (1989) 185–200.

McManus, F. "Marriage in the Canons of the Eastern Catholic Churches." *J* 54 (1994) 56–80.

Prader, J. "Differenze fra il diritto matrimoniale del Codice latino e quello del Codice orientale che influiscono sulla validità del matrimonio." *Ius Ecclesiae* 5 (1993) 469–494.

Vadakumcherry, J. "Marriage Laws in the *Code of Canon Law* and the *Code of Canons of the Eastern Churches.*" *Stud Can* 26 (1992) 437–460.

John M. Huels, O.S.M.

Part II
OTHER ACTS
OF DIVINE WORSHIP
[cc. 1166–1204]

The other acts of divine worship in part two of Book IV are those other than sacraments, treated in five titles dealing with: (1) sacramentals in general; (2) the liturgy of the hours; (3) funerals; (4) the cult of saints, sacred images, and relics; (5) vows and oaths. The principal sources for these sections are the 1917 Code of Canon Law, *Sacrosanctum Concilium* (Vatican II's constitution on the liturgy), and the liturgical rites that had been revised before 1983, namely, the 1970 *Liturgy of the Hours*[1] and the 1969 *Rite of Funerals*.[2] The source of some of the canons on dedications and blessings is the 1977 *Rite of Dedication of a Church and an Altar.*

Since the promulgation of the 1983 code, two revised titles of the *Roman Ritual* and a revised liturgical book which are pertinent to matters treated in this section have been published. The first of these is *De benedictionibus* of 1984 which was significantly adapted by the International Commission on English in the Liturgy (ICEL) and the National Conference of Catholic Bishops (NCCB) and was published under the name *Book of Blessings*.[3] The liturgical book is the revised

Caeremoniale episcoporum of 1984; the English version, the *Ceremonial of Bishops,* appeared in 1989. The other section of the *Ritual* revised after the code is *De exorcismis et supplicationibus quibusdam* of 1999, which contains the Rite of Major Exorcism. Other documents containing provisions related to this section are the 1993 *Directory for the Application of Principles and Norms on Ecumenism* of the Pontifical Council for the Promotion of Christian Unity and the revised and adapted *Order of Christian Funerals* that went into effect in 1989 for the dioceses of the United States.[4]

The Eastern code differs significantly from the Latin code in its treatment of these matters. It has only one canon on sacramentals (*CCEO* 867). Funerals are treated along with cemeteries (*CCEO* 874–879) in a section on sacred places. Like the Latin code, the Eastern code has distinct sections on the veneration of the saints, sacred images and relics (*CCEO* 884–888), and vows and oaths (*CCEO* 889–895). The liturgy of the hours is not treated.[5]

---

[1] *DOL* 424.

[2] *DOL* 416.

[3] The English translation of *De benedictionibus* was published in 1987 by ICEL; newly composed blessings were published by the USCC in 1988. The completed *Book of Blessings* went into effect for the dioceses of the U.S. on December 3, 1989.

[4] The commentary that follows does not give the legal history of the canons since that is readily available in other English-speaking commentaries. See, e.g., *CLSA Com* for the corresponding canons.

[5] Further references to the Eastern code will be made only when there is a noteworthy difference from the Latin code.

TITLE I
SACRAMENTALS
[cc. 1166–1172]

The seven canons of this title treat the definition of sacramentals (c. 1166), authority over sacramentals (c. 1167), minister of sacramentals (c. 1168), minister of consecrations, dedications, blessings (c. 1169), recipients of blessings (c. 1170), sacred objects (c. 1171), and exorcism (c. 1172).

Definition of Sacramentals

Canon 1166 — Sacramentals are sacred signs by which effects, especially spiritual effects, are signified in some imitation of the sacraments and are obtained through the intercession of the Church.

Sacramentals are similar to sacraments but differ from them in both their origin and nature. The seven sacraments were instituted by Christ and cannot be substantially changed or abolished. The sacramentals are instituted by the Church; new ones can be created and old ones suppressed. Like sacraments, sacramentals are sacred signs[6] which signify and bring about spiritual effects. Unlike sacraments, which produce their effects *ex opere operato*—through the action itself—the spiritual effects of sacramentals are obtained through the intercession of the Church.

Sacramentals may be either things or actions. Sacramentals that are things are those which remain after the liturgical action has taken place, e.g., holy water, blessed palms or ashes, or blessed candles. Sacramentals usually involve a brief liturgy of the word, and they always include a prayer; often the prayer is accompanied by a distinctive gesture, such as the laying on of hands, the sign of the cross, or the sprinkling of holy water

which recalls baptism.[7] Since sacramentals involve liturgical actions, the Second Vatican Council directed that sacramentals be revised according to the basic principle of the liturgical reform that the faithful might participate in them intelligently, actively, and easily.[8] The council treated the sacraments and sacramentals together in chapter 3 of *Sacrosanctum Concilium*. Through the sacramentals, the council taught, persons are disposed to receive the chief effect of the sacraments and various occasions in life are rendered holy.[9]

> Thus, for well-disposed members of the faithful, the liturgy of the sacraments and sacramentals sanctifies almost every event of their lives with the divine grace which flows from the paschal mystery of the passion, death and resurrection of Christ. From this source all sacraments and sacramentals draw their power. There is scarcely any proper use of material things which cannot thus be directed toward the sanctification of people and the praise of God.[10]

Some examples of sacramentals are rites of blessing, dedications of churches and altars, the consecration of virgins and chrism, exorcism, religious profession, institution of lectors and acolytes, crowning of images of the Blessed Virgin Mary, the use of blessed objects like scapulars, holy water, etc. Sacramentals bring the reality of the sacred to numerous situations in the lives of Christians, situations beyond those directly touched by the sacraments. For example, the sacrament of the anointing of the sick is intended only for persons who are seriously ill, but other sick persons, not eligible for the sacrament, can find spiritual comfort in a sacramental such as a blessing.

[6] *SC* 60.

[7] *CCC* 1668.
[8] *SC* 79.
[9] *SC* 60; see also *CCEO* 867, §1 and *CCC* 1670.
[10] *SC* 61.

Authority over Sacramentals

Canon 1167 — §1. The Apostolic See alone can establish new sacramentals, authentically interpret those already received, or abolish or change any of them.

§2. In confecting or administering sacramentals, the rites and formulas approved by the authority of the Church are to be observed carefully.

The Apostolic See makes the final determination on the establishment, authentic interpretation, and abolition of sacramentals and changes to them. However, this does not mean that the Apostolic See has total and exclusive authority. The authority of the conferences of bishops and the diocesan bishops over the liturgy, stated at Vatican II[11] and reiterated in canon law (cc. 838, 835), applies as much to the sacramentals as to other liturgical celebrations. The principal rites of the sacramentals, like other liturgical rites, specifically mention the adaptations that can be made by conferences of bishops.[12] Vatican II, in keeping with traditional practice, allowed for particular rituals of the sacraments and sacramentals to be revised and developed, and it expressly allowed for the possibility of new sacramentals to be added to these rituals as the need for them becomes apparent.[13] The NCCB created forty-two new blessings when it issued in 1989 the *Book of Blessings*. Therefore, the words of the canon which state that only the Apostolic See can establish new sacramentals must be interpreted to refer to entirely new classes of sacramentals, not to new sacramentals within the same category. The NCCB is the true legislative authority which created the new blessings, even though the blessings could not be promulgated until after their confirmation, or review (*recognitio*), by the Apostolic See.[14]

The second paragraph of canon 1167 is a specification with reference to sacramentals of a well-known general rule stated at Vatican II[15] and repeated elsewhere in the code in reference to the sacraments (c. 846, §1). It is restated somewhat differently here although its basic meaning is the same, that the sacramentals are to be celebrated according to the rites and formulas prescribed in the liturgical books. "Rite" refers to the entirety of the rite of a sacramental, whereas "formula" means the key words of the rite, akin to the form of the sacraments. Unauthorized alterations of a sacramental would result in its invalidity if it is so altered that it could no longer be judged as substantially the rite approved by the Church. However, such invalidity is not comparable to the invalidity of the sacraments, since sacramentals achieve their effects through the prayer of the Church, not through the ritual action itself as do sacraments. A sacramental would also be juridically invalid, i.e., not recognized as the official rite of the Church, if it were celebrated by an unauthorized minister.[16]

Minister of Sacramentals

Canon 1168 — The minister of sacramentals is a cleric who has been provided with the requisite power. According to the norm of the liturgical books and to the judgment of the local ordinary lay persons who possess the appropriate qualities can also administer some sacramentals.

The canon refers to the public celebration of the sacramentals, not to their private use, since some of them can be used by anyone. Clerics (bishops, presbyters, and deacons) are the ordinary ministers of sacramentals in accord with the norm of law. As indicated in the liturgical laws, lay persons may celebrate certain sacramentals, with the authorization of the local ordinary in those cases for which express authorization is required. The most common sacramentals that may be celebrated

[11] *SC* 22.
[12] See, e.g., *DB/BB* 39.
[13] *SC* 63, 79. See also CDWDS, *Instruction on the Roman Liturgy and Inculturation* 55, 59 (Rome: 1994) 25–27.
[14] Canons 455, 838, §3.

[15] *SC* 22, §3.
[16] See, e.g., c. 1169, §1.

by lay persons are certain blessings, as discussed in the commentary on the following canon. The rule of canon 230, §3 is applicable to the public celebration of sacramentals by lay persons. Theirs is an extraordinary ministry which may be exercised in the absence of a cleric, or when they are assisting a cleric in the administration of sacramentals to many persons, such as in the distribution of blessed ashes on Ash Wednesday.

Ministers of Consecrations, Dedications, Blessings

Canon 1169 — §1. Those marked with the episcopal character and presbyters permitted by law or legitimate grant can perform consecrations and dedications validly.

§2. Any presbyter can impart blessings except those reserved to the Roman Pontiff or bishops.

§3. A deacon can impart only those blessings expressly permitted by law.

Consecrations and dedications are like blessings, but they are sacramentals of greater importance. The term "consecration" is used in various ways in canon law and the liturgy, but here it refers to consecrations which are sacramentals, namely, the consecration of virgins and the consecration of the sacred chrism.[17] The consecration of the chrism belongs exclusively to a bishop; the minister for the consecration of virgins is the bishop who is the local ordinary.[18] While persons and things are consecrated, places —namely churches and altars—are dedicated.[19] Sacred places that are dedicated must be solely and permanently destined for assembling the people of God and carrying out sacred functions.[20]

Bishops are ordinary ministers of consecrations and dedications; presbyters may be ministers of a dedication when permitted by law or by special concession as seen, for example, in canon 1206.

Ministers of Blessings

The *Cathechism of the Catholic Church,* n. 1669, gives a general principle on the minister of blessings: the more a blessing concerns ecclesial and sacramental life, the more its administration is reserved to the clergy. *Presbyters* may celebrate all blessings except those reserved to the Roman Pontiff or to bishops. Vatican II desired that reserved blessings be very few and in favor of bishops and ordinaries.[21] Moreover, the diocesan bishop may reserve certain blessings to himself, particularly those celebrated with special solemnity or at celebrations that involve the entire diocesan community with a large attendance of the faithful. Presbyters preside especially at those blessings that involve the community they are appointed to serve. However, if a bishop is present as presider, the blessing is given by the bishop.[22]

Deacons may give blessings at rites at which they preside, including the liturgy of the hours, baptism, marriage, holy communion and Viaticum outside Mass, eucharistic benediction, and nonsacramental penitential services. Deacons may also give twenty-one of the blessings in *De benedictionibus* and additional ones in the *Book of Blessings.* Whenever a priest is present, it is more fitting that the office of presiding at a blessing be assigned to him.[23] This rule would not apply if the priest is morally absent, such as when his presence is anonymous or unforeseen.

In *De benedictionibus,* the ritual of blessings for the universal Latin church, there are thirteen blessings which *lay persons* may celebrate, including two which have multiple uses for things,

---

[17] SCDW, *Rite of Consecration to a Life of Virginity,* May 31, 1970, *DOL* 3253; *Rites* 2:237. SCDW, *Rite of the Blessing of Oils; Rite of Consecrating the Chrism,* December 3, 1970, *DOL* 3861; *Rites* 2:327.

[18] *Rite of Blessing of Oils; Rite of Consecrating the Chrism* 6; *Rite of Consecration to a Life of Virginity* 6.

[19] See *RDCA.*

[20] *RDCA* II, 2. The ordinary may grant permission for other uses in accord with c. 1210.

[21] *SC* 79. The papal blessing with a plenary indulgence is an example of a blessing reserved to the diocesan bishop or his juridical equivalent. See *CB* 1122.

[22] *DB/BB* 18 a.

[23] *DB/BB* 18 c.

places, animals, harvests, before and after meals, favors received, and various other circumstances. The *Book of Blessings* for use in the United States has additional blessings which lay persons may celebrate. Whenever a priest or deacon is present, lay persons may not preside at official blessings, unless the cleric is morally unavailable as above.

According to the liturgical law,[24] formally instituted acolytes and readers are to be preferred as the ministers of blessings over other lay ministers. Other lay persons may be ministers of blessings primarily because they share in the common priesthood of the faithful in virtue of their baptism and confirmation. Their specific authorization as ministers of blessings comes from either of two sources: (1) from the law itself in virtue of their office, e.g., parents on behalf of their children; or (2) by appointment of the local ordinary for some special liturgical ministry or in fulfillment of a particular charge in the Church, e.g., lay religious or catechists. These latter who have a special charge are to be appointed ministers of blessings only after the local ordinary has determined that they have the proper pastoral formation and prudence in the apostolate.[25]

Recipients of Blessings

Canon 1170 — Blessings, which are to be imparted first of all to Catholics, can also be given to catechumens and even to non-Catholics unless there is a prohibition of the Church to the contrary.

Blessings are liturgical celebrations consisting of two parts: (1) the proclamation of the word of God and the praise of God's goodness and (2) the petition for God's help. In addition, there are usually rites for the beginning and conclusion that are proper to each celebration.[26] In the canonical tradition two kinds of blessings are distinguished.[27]

Constitutive blessings are similar in their effects to consecrations and dedications because the place or thing so blessed becomes a sacred place or thing set aside for divine worship (e.g., blessing of an oratory, blessing of a chalice and paten). The blessing of an abbot or abbess is also constitutive because the official rite of blessing actually constitutes the monk or nun the abbot or abbess of the monastery. An *invocative* blessing has no such constitutive effect; the persons so blessed retain their status, and the places or things so blessed retain their secular character.

Blessings are given, in the first place, to Catholics; they have the right to be enriched by the spiritual goods of the Church (c. 213), among which are liturgies of blessing. Catechumens, since they are already connected to the Church in a special way and are to be introduced to the sacred rites (c. 206), may also be given all appropriate blessings—not just the blessings of the *Rite of Christian Initiation of Adults* (*RCIA*) intended specifically for them. Blessings may be given to non-Catholic Christians who request them, according to the nature and object of the blessing.[28] Indeed all persons, even non-Christian believers, may receive blessings provided they have the proper dispositions.[29]

Sacred Objects

Canon 1171 — Sacred objects, which are designated for divine worship by dedication or blessing, are to be treated reverently and are not to be employed for profane or inappropriate use even if they are owned by private persons.

The current liturgical books speak of "dedication" only in reference to places—to churches and altars. "Blessings" are given to all objects which are destined for divine worship; the only exception is the chrism which is consecrated. The liturgical books have blessings for the following objects related to divine worship: a foundation stone of a

[24] *DB* 18 d.
[25] *BB* 18d; see also c. 231, §1.
[26] *DB/BB* 20.
[27] *CIC* 1148, §2.
[28] *Ecum Dir* 121.
[29] *DB/BB* 15.

new church; a chalice and paten; other articles for the liturgical celebration such as the ciborium or pyx, the monstrance, vestments, linens, hymnals, and service books; a baptistery or a new baptismal font; a repository for holy oils; an episcopal or a presidential chair, a lectern, a tabernacle, a confessional; church doors; a cross for public veneration; images for public veneration; bells; an organ; holy water; stations of the cross.[30]

The diocesan bishop has the right of visitation of places where blessed objects are kept, except the houses of pontifical religious institutes and societies of apostolic life.[31] Sacred objects may not be used for secular purposes unless they have lost their blessing.[32] A person who profanes a sacred thing is to be punished by a just penalty (c. 1376).

Exorcism

Canon 1172 — §1. No one can perform exorcisms legitimately upon the possessed unless he has obtained special and express permission from the local ordinary.

§2. The local ordinary is to give this permission only to a presbyter who has piety, knowledge, prudence, and integrity of life.

An exorcism is a sacramental by which "the Church asks publicly and authoritatively in the name of Jesus Christ that a person or object be protected against the power of the Evil One and withdrawn from his dominion."[33] The canon pertains to solemn exorcisms observing the Rite of Exorcism of the *Roman Ritual*,[34] not to the simple exorcisms that are part of the *Rite of Christian Initiation of Adults* or the baptism of infants.

One of the *praenotanda* to the 1998 Rite of Exorcism (n. 13) has completely reordered this canon. There are significant differences between the new law and the canon.

(1) An exorcist is to be a priest (*sacerdos*), not a presbyter (*presbyterus*) as in the canon, which means bishops as well as presbyters may be appointed exorcist.

(2) The priest must have specific preparation for this office.

(3) "For the most part" (*plerumque*), the local ordinary who appoints the exorcist should be the diocesan bishop, which implies that the vicar general and episcopal vicar should not do it without a special mandate, except in a case of need when the bishop cannot be reached.

(4) The exorcist, whether appointed to the stable office of exorcist or *ad actum*, is to fulfill this ministry under the direction of the diocesan bishop.

Other aspects of the canon are repeated in the liturgical law: special and express permission is needed to function as exorcist, and the priest must be endowed with piety, knowledge, prudence, and integrity of life.[35] Permission of the diocesan bishop/local ordinary is required for each case, unless a priest has been appointed to the office of exorcist in a diocese where this office has been established at the request of the conference of bishops and with the approval of the Apostolic See.[36]

Belief in the devil is consistent with the scriptures and church tradition. However, the Holy See urges prudence and caution whenever there is a claim of demonic possession.

---

[30] *RDCA* I, VII; *DB*, pt. 3; *BB*, ch. 31–42.

[31] Canons 397, 683, 738.

[32] Canon 1269. Presumably the loss of blessing occurs for sacred objects in the same way as for sacred places. See c. 1212 on sacred places and c. 19 on laws enacted for similar matters.

[33] *CCC* 1673.

[34] *De exorcismis et supplicationibus quibusdam* (Rome: Typis Vaticanis, 1999). The rite was promulgated by a decree of the CDWDS, November 22, 1998.

[35] Thus, this is a derogation by complete reordering, not an abrogation. See c. 20.

[36] *MQ, DOL* 2923; *CLD* 7, 692. On certain abuses regarding exorcisms see CDF, letter, September 29, 1985, *AAS* 77 (1985) 1169–1170; *CLD* 11, 276–277.

When a possible demonic intervention is suggested, the Church always imposes a critical assessment of the facts, as in the case of miracles. Reserve and prudence are in fact demanded. It is easy to fall victim to imagination and to allow oneself to be led astray by inaccurate accounts distorted in their transmission and incorrectly interpreted.[37]

The Rite of Exorcism, nn. 14–16, takes a most cautious approach to this phenomenon and requires the exorcist to have moral certainty of demonic possession before proceeding to celebrate the rite.

Title II
The Liturgy of the Hours
[cc. 1173–1175]

It is fitting that the code include a section, although brief, on the liturgy of the hours, also known as the divine office. This form of liturgical prayer has been consistently celebrated by the Church since ancient times, and together with the Eucharist it remains today the principal form of daily prayer throughout the Church. The various hours center on the singing or reciting of scriptural psalms and canticles which are so arranged "that the whole course of the day and night is made holy by the praises of God."[38] The Second Vatican Council desired that the liturgy of the hours be reformed so that clergy and religious could pray it with greater understanding and devotion, and so that the laity too could more readily make this prayer their own. Among the principal goals of the reform of the hours was that, whenever possible, the hours be celebrated communally, at the proper times of day and, in parishes, together with the laity.

The three canons of this title treat the following: a theological description of the liturgy of the hours (c. 1173), those who celebrate the liturgy of the hours (c. 1174), and the time of celebration (c. 1175).

Theological Description

Canon 1173 — Fulfilling the priestly function of Christ, the Church celebrates the liturgy of the hours. In the liturgy of the hours, the Church, hearing God speaking to his people and recalling the mystery of salvation, praises him without ceasing by song and prayer and intercedes for the salvation of the whole world.

This is a concise theological description of the liturgy of the hours. A fuller theological exposition of the liturgy of the hours is found in *Sacrosanctum Concilium* 83–86 and in the *General Instruction on the Liturgy of the Hours* 1–19.

Celebrants

Canon 1174 — §1. Clerics are obliged to carry out the liturgy of the hours according to the norm of can. 276, §2, n. 3; members of institutes of consecrated life and societies of apostolic life, however, are bound according to the norm of their constitutions.
§2. Other members of the Christian faithful, according to circumstances, are also earnestly invited to participate in the liturgy of the hours as an action of the Church.

The liturgy of the hours is the prayer of the whole Church, and all the faithful are deputed to celebrate this liturgy. Priests and transitional deacons are obliged to pray the liturgy of the hours daily; permanent deacons are to recite the parts of the hours prescribed by the conference of bishops.[39]

---

[37] SCDF, Christian Faith and Demonology, June 26, 1975, *La documentation catholique* 72 (1975) 708–718; *The Pope Speaks* 20 (1975) 209–233.
[38] *SC* 84.

[39] Canon 276, §2, 3°. See NCCB, *Permanent Deacons in the United States: Guidelines on Their Formation and Ministry* 97, 3rd ed. (Washington, D.C.: USCC, 1985).

The Church deputes the clergy to celebrate the hours to ensure that at least some of its members are regularly carrying out the duty of the whole community.[40] In fulfilling this obligation clerics are to be aware of the "hierarchy" of the hours, with morning and evening prayer of greatest importance.[41] The celebration of the hours in common is preferred.[42] Even clergy who are not obliged to communal celebration, if they live together or when they gather for a meeting, should celebrate at least morning and evening prayer in common.[43] Dispensations or commutations of the clerical obligation can be given by the cleric's ordinary, including a clerical major superior.[44]

Lay members of religious institutes are "to celebrate worthily the liturgy of the hours" in accord with the norm of their constitutions (c. 663, §3). Seminarians "are to be formed in the celebration of the liturgy of the hours."[45] Other lay members of the faithful are "earnestly invited" to participate in the liturgy of the hours, as stated in this canon. Clergy and other pastoral ministers are obliged by the liturgical law to see that the people are invited and instructed to celebrate the principal hours, especially on Sundays and holy days.[46] Whenever possible, groups of the faithful should celebrate the liturgy of the hours communally in church, especially in parish churches.[47] Those who cannot participate in the communal celebration are to be encouraged to pray morning and evening prayer in private.[48] Also recommended is the praying of the hours at special gatherings of the lay faithful and in families.[49]

Time of Celebration

Canon 1175 — In carrying out the liturgy of the hours, the true time for each hour is to be observed insofar as possible.

Vatican II decreed the restoration of the proper sequence of the hours so that they may genuinely correspond to the correct time of the day at which they are to be prayed.[50] Morning prayer is celebrated upon rising or at some convenient hour of the morning. Evening prayer is celebrated anytime in the evening, which may be understood as after 4:00 in the afternoon.[51] Mid-morning prayer is celebrated at 9:00, or anytime after morning prayer and before midday prayer. Midday prayer is celebrated at noon or before or after the midday meal. Mid-afternoon prayer is celebrated at 3:00 or anytime in the afternoon until late afternoon. The office of the readings is celebrated anytime during the day or even during the night hours of the previous day after evening prayer. Night prayer is the last prayer of the day, said before retiring, even if after midnight.[52]

TITLE III
ECCLESIASTICAL FUNERALS
[cc. 1176–1185]

The principal source for the canons of this title is the 1969 *Ordo exsequiarum*. The particular law in the United States on funerals is found chiefly in the 1989 *Order of Christian Funerals* which has an original general introduction and original introductions to the various sections of the order, and which contains a number of adaptations made in accord with *Ordo exsequiarum* 21. Also pertinent are the "Christian Burial Guidelines" which

---

[40] *General Instruction on the Liturgy of the Hours* 28. Hereafter cited as *GILH*.
[41] *GILH* 29, 77.
[42] *GILH* 33.
[43] *SC* 99, *GILH* 25.
[44] *SC* 97.
[45] Canon 246, §2. See NCCB, *Program of Priestly Formation* 153, 215, 273, 277, 313, 481, 4th ed. (Washington, D.C.: USCC, 1993).
[46] *SC* 100, *GILH* 23.
[47] *GILH* 21.
[48] *GILH* 40.
[49] *GILH* 27.

[50] *SC* 88, 94.
[51] Cf. Pius XII, apconst *Christus Dominus* VI, January 6, 1953, *AAS* 45 (1953) 14–24; *CLD* 4, 275–276.
[52] *GILH* 59, 84.

serve as a basis for particular law in the dioceses of the U.S.A. and Canada.[53]

Basic Values and Rules

Canon 1176 — §1. Deceased members of the Christian faithful must be given ecclesiastical funerals according to the norm of law.

§2. Ecclesiastical funerals, by which the Church seeks spiritual support for the deceased, honors their bodies, and at the same time brings the solace of hope to the living, must be celebrated according to the norm of the liturgical laws.

§3. The Church earnestly recommends that the pious custom of burying the bodies of the deceased be observed; nevertheless, the Church does not prohibit cremation unless it was chosen for reasons contrary to Christian doctrine.

The values expressed in this canon are the importance of ecclesiastical funeral rites, their proper celebration, and the preferred custom of burying the dead. The first paragraph is preceptive: the faithful *must be given* funeral rites according to the norm of law. This implies an obligation on the part of pastors, that they see that church funeral rites are celebrated for their deceased parishioners (cf. c. 530, 5°), as well as an obligation on the next of kin to see that church funeral rites are accorded a deceased Catholic. Moreover, it implies a right to have one's funeral in one's parish, in accord with the norm of law.[54]

The first part of paragraph two succinctly expresses the purposes of church funeral rites. The second is really only a reminder that there are liturgical laws that must be observed in celebrating funeral rites, laws which are primarily found in the *Ordo exsequiarum* and the translations and adaptations of same approved by the conferences of bishops.

The first statement of paragraph three is a recommendation: the Church prefers that the bodies of the

deceased faithful be buried, because it manifests Christian faith in the resurrection and the dignity of the body; but burial is not required. The second statement expresses the right of the faithful to choose cremation, with one exception. Cremation is not tolerated by the Church if it is chosen for reasons which are contrary to Christian teaching (cf. c. 1184, 2°). The 1917 code had forbidden cremation (*CIC* 1203; 1240, §1, 5°), but this was derogated in 1963 by an instruction of the Holy Office which stated that the Church "never opposed nor now opposes cremation under certain circumstances, that is, whenever it is certain that it is done through innocent motives and for grave reasons, especially of a public order."[55] No longer is it necessary to have positive reasons for choosing cremation. Anyone may choose cremation unless it is done for reasons contrary to Christian teaching.

When cremation is chosen, it is preferable to celebrate the funeral Mass in the presence of the body before it is cremated. Nevertheless, the dioceses of the United States and Canada have an indult permitting the celebration of the funeral Mass in the presence of the cremated remains of the body.[56] However, there is good reason to conclude that an indult for this practice is not strictly necessary; it is likely that it is within the competence of the diocesan bishop to permit this practice since it is not expressly excluded by law.[57]

CHAPTER I
THE CELEBRATION OF FUNERALS
[cc. 1177–1182]

This chapter consists of six canons treating: the place of funerals (c. 1177), funerals of dioce-

---

[53] National Catholic Cemetery Conference, January 28, 1975, *CLD* 9, 688–702. Hereafter cited as NCCC Guidelines.

[54] See especially cc. 1177 and 1184.

[55] *Piam et constantem*, May 8, 1963, *AAS* 56 (1964) 822; *CLD* 6, 666–667; *DOL* 3366.

[56] *Order of Christian Funerals* (Ottawa: Canadian Conference of Catholic Bishops, 1990) appendix 4, 432; for the U.S. see CDWDS, letter, March 21, 1997, *BCLN* 33 (1997) 13–15.

[57] See cc. 835, §1; 838, §4; 135, §2. This issue is addressed by M. J. Henchal in "Cremation: Canonical Issues," *J* 55 (1995) 281–298.

san bishops (c. 1178), funerals of religious and members of societies of apostolic life (c. 1179), place of burial (c. 1180), monetary offerings for funerals (c. 1181), and parish death registers (c. 1182).

Place of Funerals

Canon 1177 — §1. A funeral for any deceased member of the faithful must generally be celebrated in his or her parish church.

§2. Any member of the faithful or those competent to take care of the funeral of a deceased member of the faithful are permitted to choose another church for the funeral rite with the consent of the person who governs it and after notification of the proper pastor of the deceased.

§3. If a death occurred outside the person's own parish, and the body was not transferred to it nor another church legitimately chosen for the funeral rite, the funeral is to be celebrated in the church of the parish where the death occurred unless particular law has designated another church.

Catholics have a right to funeral rites in their parish. The rites in question are all the funeral stages (*stationes*) that are observed in a region (e.g., vigil service, funeral Mass, committal).[58] The canon says that generally funerals for the faithful departed must be celebrated in their own parish, which obliges the pastor to see that they are given a funeral. Membership in a parish is determined by domicile or quasi-domicile in the parish territory, not by registration or participation in the parish (c. 102). An exception is membership in a personal parish which is based on rite, language, nationality, or some other determining factor (c. 518). Transients (*vagi,* c. 100) have a right to a church funeral in the parish of the territory where they were living at the time of death.

While the faithful have a right to a funeral in their own parish, they or the persons in charge also have the freedom to request that their funeral be in another church. This requires the consent of the

rector of the church, namely, the priest in charge of the church. If the rector permits the funeral in his church, he or the person making the funeral arrangements must inform the proper pastor of the deceased, even if the deceased was unknown to the pastor, and the name of the deceased is to be recorded in the parish death register unless particular law provides otherwise. (Cf. cc. 535, §1; 1182.)

Since the code mentions only a "church" and not an "oratory," funerals may not be held in the oratories of religious communities or other oratories or private chapels without a dispensation from the diocesan bishop, unless legitimate custom, an acquired right, or a privilege is in force.[59] Although Catholics may not have their funerals celebrated in oratories, non-Catholic Christians may do so in certain oratories. The 1993 *Directory for the Application of Principles and Norms on Ecumenism* says that Catholic hospitals, homes for the aged, and similar institutions should afford priests and ministers of other denominations every opportunity to provide spiritual and sacramental ministrations, under dignified and reverent conditions, including the use of the chapel.[60] The diocesan bishop's permission is necessary for other cases involving use of Catholic churches and oratories by non-Catholic Christians for funerals or other purposes.[61]

The third paragraph gives a rule for a special case when a person dies away from the parish and the body is not returned. In such a case the parish of the territory in which the person died is required to celebrate the funeral rites, unless particular law has designated another church.

Funerals of Diocesan Bishops

Canon 1178 — The funeral of a diocesan bishop is to be celebrated in his own cathedral church unless he has chosen another church.

---

[58] *Ordo exsequiarum* 4, *OCF* 50.

[59] See cc. 1214, 1223. See also c. 1179 on the funerals of religious and members of societies of apostolic life in their own oratories.

[60] *Ecum Dir* 142.

[61] *Ecum Dir* 137.

This canon is applicable to diocesan bishops who were either active or retired at the time of their death. The *Ceremonial of Bishops* gives regulations to be observed upon the death and for the funeral of the diocesan bishop.[62] These norms presume that the diocesan bishop's funeral rites will be in the cathedral, and they must in fact be celebrated there unless the bishop himself left other instructions.

Funerals of Religious

Canon 1179 — The funerals of religious or members of a society of apostolic life are generally to be celebrated in their own church or oratory by the superior if the institute or society is clerical; otherwise by the chaplain.

This canon gives a general rule but is open to other possibilities. The funeral arrangements of religious and members of societies of apostolic life are handled by the competent superior. The superior, keeping in mind the wishes of the deceased, determines in which church or oratory of the community the funeral will take place. If the superior wishes to have the funeral in another church, the rules of canon 1177 are to be observed.

Place of Burial

Canon 1180 — §1. If a parish has its own cemetery, the deceased members of the faithful must be buried in it unless the deceased or those competent to take care of the burial of the deceased have chosen another cemetery legitimately.

§2. Everyone, however, is permitted to choose the cemetery of burial unless prohibited by law.

If the parish has a cemetery, the faithful who are resident in the parish territory or who are members of a personal parish have a right to be buried in it. This does not mean that parishioners may have cemetery plots free of charge but that, all things being equal, they are to be given priority

over non-parishioners in the parish cemetery. No one is obliged to be buried in the parish cemetery, or even in a Catholic cemetery, but may choose another cemetery, mausoleum, or a place where cremated remains are kept. In a non-Catholic cemetery the individual grave is to be blessed at the time of committal (c. 1240).

All the faithful, or those responsible for their burial, may choose any place for burial unless prohibited by law. This refers to a prohibition of particular law since the universal law has no such prohibitions. The right to choose a cemetery does not carry with it an obligation on the part of the Catholic cemetery owner to accede to the request, except in the case of a parish cemetery whereby, all things being equal, the pastor is obliged to give a parishioner preference over a non-parishioner.

Offerings for Funerals

Canon 1181 — Regarding offerings on the occasion of funeral rites, the prescripts of can. 1264 are to be observed, with the caution, however, that there is to be no favoritism toward persons in funerals and that the poor are not deprived of fitting funerals.

The mention of canon 1264 refers to number 2 of that canon which states that it is the competence of the bishops of the province to determine the amount of the offerings to be given on the occasion of the administration of the sacraments and sacramentals, unless another law prescribes something else. The caution against depriving the poor of a funeral is akin to that of canon 848 in reference to offerings for the administration of sacraments. Precaution is also to be taken against any favoritism toward persons.[63] For example, it would not be lawful to celebrate a funeral Mass only for contributing parishioners while limiting others to a liturgy of the word celebrated by a deacon or lay person. Deacons may celebrate the funeral liturgy without a Mass, or lay persons may celebrate funeral rites in accord with the law

---

[62] *CB* 1157–1165.

[63] Cf. *SC* 32.

in situations of pastoral need,[64] but not in consideration of persons.

Death Register

Canon 1182 — When the burial has been completed, a record is to be made in the register of deaths according to the norm of particular law.

Every parish is to have a register to record the deaths of parishioners (c. 535, §1). In regard to the case of a person whose funeral is celebrated in another parish, it is advisable to record the death both in that parish and in the person's own parish, unless this matter is regulated otherwise in particular law.

CHAPTER II
THOSE TO WHOM ECCLESIASTICAL FUNERALS MUST BE GRANTED OR DENIED
[cc. 1183–1185]

The three canons of this chapter treat: non-Catholics who may be granted a church funeral (c. 1183), Catholics who must be deprived of a church funeral (c. 1184), and the denial of any kind of funeral Mass to those who must be deprived of a church funeral (c. 1185).

Non-Catholics Granted a Church Funeral

Canon 1183 — §1. When it concerns funerals, catechumens must be counted among the Christian faithful.

§2. The local ordinary can permit children whom the parents intended to baptize but who died before baptism to be given ecclesiastical funerals.

§3. In the prudent judgment of the local ordinary, ecclesiastical funerals can be granted to baptized persons who are enrolled in a non-Catholic Church or ecclesial community unless their intention is evidently to the contrary and provided that their own minister is not available.

The Church grants certain prerogatives to catechumens which are proper to Christians (c. 206). The right to a church funeral is one of these prerogatives.[65] The catechumenate begins with the rite of acceptance into the order of catechumens.[66] A catechumen is entitled to the full funeral rites of Catholics in accord with local laws and customs, such as the vigil service, funeral Mass, and committal service. The particular law in force in the United States on this matter offers pastoral guidance that could be helpful elsewhere as well.

[For the funerals of catechumens], the funeral liturgy, including the funeral Mass, should be celebrated as usual, only omitting language referring directly to the sacrament. ... In view of the sensibilities of the immediate family of the deceased catechumen, however, the funeral Mass may be omitted at the discretion of the pastor.[67]

Children of a Catholic parent (or guardian) who die before baptism may be given church funeral rites if at least one parent or guardian had intended to have them baptized. Although they are unbaptized, the Church entrusts these children to the mercy of God who desires that all people should be saved.[68] The Eastern code permits ecclesiastical funerals not only for unbaptized children whose parents intended to have them baptized, but also for unbaptized persons "who in some way were considered to be close to the Church" (*CCEO* 876, §2).

The local ordinary may permit Catholic funerals for non-Catholics under the following conditions:

(1) the deceased must have been validly baptized;

---

[64] *Ordo exsequiarum* 19, *OCF* 14.

[65] For a discussion of the prerogatives and obligations of catechumens, see J. Huels, *The Catechumenate and the Law: A Pastoral and Canonical Commentary for the Church in the United States* (Chicago: Liturgy Training Publications, 1994) 5–13.

[66] *RCIA* 14, U.S. version, 41; c. 788, §1; NSC 2.

[67] NSC 9.

[68] *CCC* 1261.

(2) the non-Catholic minister must be unavailable;

(3) there is no indication that the person would not have wanted a Catholic funeral.

In case of doubt about the validity of baptism, the funeral may be permitted. The minister may be either physically or morally unavailable. An example of physical unavailability is when there is no church of that denomination in the area. Examples of moral unavailability are: when the deceased had not practiced his or her faith whereas the next of kin is a practicing Catholic; or if the non-Catholic had been intending to become a Catholic.[69] If a funeral Mass is celebrated, the name of the deceased non-Catholic may not be mentioned in the eucharistic prayer.[70]

Catholics Deprived of a Church Funeral

Canon 1184 — §1. Unless they gave some signs of repentance before death, the following must be deprived of ecclesiastical funerals:
   1° notorious apostates, heretics, and schismatics;
   2° those who chose the cremation of their bodies for reasons contrary to Christian faith;
   3° other manifest sinners who cannot be granted ecclesiastical funerals without public scandal of the faithful.
   §2. If any doubt occurs, the local ordinary is to be consulted, and his judgment must be followed.

These three cases of deprivation of ecclesiastical funeral rites apply only to persons who were baptized Catholic or who were received into the Catholic Church. Funerals may not be denied to someone who gave a sign of repentance before

death. The sign of repentance should in some way indicate that the person wanted to be reconciled to God and the Church, such as summoning a priest at the time of death, making an act of perfect contrition, or stating a desire to die in the state of grace. It is not sufficient that the person merely make an act that indicates belief in God, since even heretics, schismatics, and many apostates believe in God. If the deceased had manifested a sign of repentance, this should be made known if it would preclude scandal.[71]

Apostasy, heresy, and schism are defined in canon 751. Since number one of canon 1184 does not distinguish between notoriety in law and notoriety in fact, the word "notorious" should be understood in the ordinary sense of the word, namely, publicly known. Those who are publicly known in the parish to be apostates, heretics, or schismatics are to be denied a church funeral. If they had formally joined another Christian or non-Christian faith, it should be presumed they would want to have their funeral celebrated in that faith unless contrary indications are present. Those who ceased practicing their Catholic faith without formally abandoning it do not fall in this category and may not be denied Catholic funeral rites.

A case of a Catholic choosing cremation for reasons contrary to the faith is so rare that the provision of number two is hardly necessary. Such would occur if the person were, for example, choosing cremation as a way to manifest unbelief in the doctrine of the resurrection of the dead.

Cases in number three require the presence of two conditions: (1) that a person be a manifest sinner, i.e., be publicly known to be living in a state of grave sin; and (2) that a church funeral would cause public scandal. Cases when both of these conditions are verified are rare but they do occur, e.g., when the murder of a celebrated criminal is accompanied by great publicity. Also included would be those under an imposed or declared penalty of excommunication or interdict if they could not be granted a funeral without public scan-

---

[69] The permission required of the local ordinary could appropriately be delegated to pastors and parochial vicars in the diocesan list of faculties. See also *Ecum Dir* 120.
[70] *Ecum Dir* 121.

[71] Cf. SCDF, decr *Patres Sacrae Congregationis*, September 20, 1973, *AAS* 65 (1973) 500; *DOL* 418.

dal. Not included are persons in irregular marriages[72] or persons who committed suicide.[73] Since deprivation of a church funeral not infrequently causes as much if not more scandal than granting it, it would be prudent to refer any such case to the local ordinary, even if not doubtful.

The Eastern code differs from the Latin code in some respects.

(1) In the case of those choosing cremation, instead of focusing on motives contrary to the faith, it says that a church funeral is not to be denied "provided it does not obscure the preference of the Church for the burial of bodies and that scandal is avoided" (*CCEO* 876, §3).

(2) Instead of the distinctions made in canon 1184, §1, 1° and 3°, the Eastern code simply states that "sinners" who gave no sign of repentance are to be deprived of a church funeral if there would be public scandal (*CCEO* 877).

Denial of Any Kind of Funeral Mass

Canon 1185 — Any funeral Mass must also be denied a person who is excluded from ecclesiastical funerals.

While canon 1184 speaks of the deprivation of the official funeral rites of the Church, which includes the funeral Mass, canon 1185 adds that "any funeral Mass" is excluded. Thus, it is not lawful to have a public Mass for someone who is to be deprived of a church funeral, even if the body is not present and the special rites connected with the funeral Mass are not observed. Although a Mass celebrated later, such as on the anniversary of death, is not excluded, this should be done only without publicity so as to preclude scandal or wonderment.

TITLE IV
THE VENERATION OF THE SAINTS, SACRED IMAGES, AND RELICS
[cc. 1186–1190]

Since the canons of this title treat the cult of the saints, they only indirectly apply to Book IV, part two which is on acts of divine cult, the worship of God. However, since the veneration of the saints is expressed most notably through the sanctoral cycle at the Eucharist and the liturgy of the hours, which are acts of divine worship, it is not inappropriate to locate this title here. The five canons of this title treat: the veneration of Mary and the other saints (c. 1186), public veneration (c. 1187), sacred images in churches (c. 1188), restoration of precious images (c. 1189), and alienation of relics and images (c. 1190). The Eastern canon law governing these matters is substantially the same as the Latin law (*CCEO* 884–888).

Veneration of Mary and the Saints

Canon 1186 — To foster the sanctification of the people of God, the Church commends to the special and filial reverence of the Christian faithful the Blessed Mary ever Virgin, Mother of God, whom Christ established as the mother of all people, and promotes the true and authentic veneration of the other saints whose example instructs the Christian faithful and whose intercession sustains them.

The Church venerates the Blessed Virgin Mary and the other saints first of all through the celebrations of the sanctoral cycle at the liturgy of the hours and the Eucharist. In addition to the many feasts in honor of Mary during the liturgical year, there is a special sacramentary and lectionary, the

---

[72] See SCDF, letter *Complures Conferentiae Episcopales,* May 29, 1973, *DOL* 417; *CLD* 8, 862–863. See also the commentary at this canon in *Salamanca Com,* 573–574.

[73] See NCCC Guidelines, *CLD* 9, 694. The ritual for the U.S.A. provides special prayers for persons who committed suicide. See *OCF* 398, prayers 44 and 45. The 1917 code, *CIC* 1240, §1, nn. 3–4, had prohibited from ecclesiastical funerals persons who committed suicide and those who were killed in a duel.

Collection of Masses of the Blessed Virgin Mary.[74] Mary and the other saints are also venerated by means of art and music, popular devotions, and sacramentals such as the 1981 *Order of Crowning an Image of the Blessed Virgin Mary* of the *Roman Pontifical.*[75] Veneration of the Mother of God is especially recommended to seminarians, clergy, and religious (cc. 246, §3; 276, §2, 5°; 663, §4). Exercises of popular piety are subject to the supervision of local ordinaries in accord with canon 839, §2.

Public Veneration

Canon 1187 — It is permitted to reverence through public veneration only those servants of God whom the authority of the Church has recorded in the list of the saints or the blessed.

The public veneration (*cultus*) mentioned here is the official liturgical worship of the Church approved by competent ecclesiastical authority and offered in the name of the Church by lawfully deputed persons (cf. c. 834, §2). Only saints of more universal significance are included for public veneration in the general calendar of the Church, whereas particular calendars include the blessed as well as saints of significance to particular churches and religious institutes. Ecclesiastical authority has designated the saints and blessed either by recognizing an immemorial cult or by the formal process of canonization and beatification. The 1917 code contained a lengthy section of procedures for beatification and canonization (*CIC* 1999–2141). This matter is now regulated outside the code by special pontifical law (c. 1403, §1).[76]

Sacred Images in Churches

Canon 1188 — The practice of displaying sacred images in churches for the reverence of the faithful is to remain in effect. Nevertheless, they are to be exhibited in moderate number and in suitable order so that the Christian people are not confused nor occasion given for inappropriate devotion.

This canon, which restates *Sacrosanctum Concilium* 125, deals with the display of statues and paintings in churches as well as images on stained glass, mosaics, tapestries, banners, and other artistic images in churches. The liturgical law adds that there is to be only one image of any one saint and that the devotion of the entire community is the criterion for displaying images and adorning and arranging a church.[77] The canon speaks only of churches, not of sacred places in general, but the principle expressed is equally applicable to oratories and private chapels which are used for divine worship.

The liturgical law also demands that the highest artistic standards be met in selecting works of art for churches.[78] Moreover, Vatican II exhorted bishops to "carefully remove from the house of God and from other places of worship those works of artists that are repugnant to faith and morals and to Christian devotion and that offend true religious sense either by their grotesqueness or by the deficiency, mediocrity, or sham in their artistic quality."[79] However, the Holy See has also condemned as gravely harmful to ecclesiastical heritage the removal from churches of true works of art under the pretext of liturgical renewal.[80] Since not all pastors are capable of making judgments about what constitutes good art, it is necessary that

---

[74] (Collegeville: Liturgical Press, 1992); Sacramentary and Lectionary published separately.

[75] *Rites* 2:453.

[76] John Paul II, apconst *Divinus perfectionis Magister,* January 25, 1983, *AAS* 75 (1983) 349–355; *CLD* 10, 266–273; Sacred Congregation for Causes of the Saints, Norms to Be Observed by Bishops When Making Investigations in Causes of Saints, February 7, 1983, *AAS* 75 (1983) 396–404; *CLD* 10, 273–282.

[77] *GIRM* 278. Special blessings are to be celebrated on the occasion of placing in a church an image for public veneration by the faithful. See *DB* ch. 29, *BB* ch. 36.

[78] *GIRM* 254.

[79] *SC* 124, *DOL* 124.

[80] SCC, littcirc, *Opera artis,* April 11, 1971, *AAS* 63 (1971) 315–317; *DOL* 4327.

any significant alterations in church decor "never proceed without the approval of the commissions on sacred art, on liturgy and, when applicable, on music, or without prior consultation with experts. The civil laws of the various countries protecting valuable works of art are also to be taken into account."[81]

Restoration of Precious Images

Canon 1189 — If they are in need of repair, precious images, that is, those distinguished by age, art, or veneration, which are exhibited in churches or oratories for the reverence of the faithful are never to be restored without the written permission of the ordinary; he is to consult experts before he grants permission.

A precious image is one that has a special historical, artistic, cultural, or monetary value. Before undertaking the restoration of a precious image of any kind, the written permission of the ordinary is necessary to ensure that the restoration will be done by persons who are truly expert. The ordinary is the major superior in the case of churches and oratories owned by clerical religious institutes and clerical societies of apostolic life, or the local ordinary in the case of all other churches and oratories. The experts that the ordinary is to consult include the commissions mentioned in the commentary on the previous canon. The ordinary does not personally have to consult the experts, provided he is given a report of the consultations that have been undertaken and the recommendations that have been made by the experts.[82]

Alienation of Relics and Images

Canon 1190 — §1. It is absolutely forbidden to sell sacred relics.
§2. Relics of great significance and other relics honored with great reverence by the people can-

not be alienated validly in any manner or transferred permanently without the permission of the Apostolic See.

§3. The prescript of §2 is valid also for images which are honored in some church with great reverence by the people.

The canon treats two kinds of relics. Paragraph one refers to all authentic relics of the saints and the blessed. Paragraph two treats only relics which are significant (*insignes*) or relics which are honored with great veneration by the people. A significant relic was defined in the previous code as a part of a saint's body (arm, forearm, heart, tongue, leg) or the part of a martyr's body that had suffered the wound that caused death, provided the part was entire and not too small (*CIC* 1281, §2).

The prohibition against selling any sacred relic is expressed in the code's strongest language, *nefas est,* meaning "it is absolutely forbidden." Relics may be given away by their owners, except for the second category of relics, which may not be given away without permission of the Apostolic See.[83] A just penalty is to be inflicted on anyone who alienates such relics or who alienates any images that are displayed in churches and honored with great veneration by the faithful (c. 1377). The penal sanction applies to the relics in the second category wherever they are displayed. In reference to images, it applies only to those images found in churches as defined by canon 1214, not in oratories, private chapels, or elsewhere, since penal law must be interpreted strictly (c. 18). Rules governing alienation are found in cc. 1291–1296.

---

[81] Ibid., n. 4; *DOL* 4331. See also *SC* 126.
[82] For further rules governing precious goods, see cc. 1220, §2; 1270; 1283, 2°–3°; 1292, §2.

[83] In 1994 the Apostolic Sacristy published new norms regulating relics. According to the norms, very small pieces of the bones or flesh of saints and martyrs will be distributed "only for public veneration in a church, oratory or chapel. No relic from the Apostolic Sacristy will be given to individual faithful for private veneration." See *Norme per la concessione delle reliquie del Sacrario Apostolico,* February 15, 1994, *N* 30 (1994) 349–350; *BCLN* 32 (1996) 6.

TITLE V
A VOW AND AN OATH
[cc. 1191–1204]

Vows and oaths are not acts of worship (*cultus*) in the sense of liturgical celebrations, but they are acts of religion that have a sacred character and impose obligations of religion.[84] Thus they are treated in Book IV of the code which deals with the sanctifying function of the Church. Vows and oaths are, moreover, juridic acts which have juridic effects and which are governed by both general laws[85] and the specific canons that follow. Although canon law does not bind non-Catholics as a general rule (c. 11), the laws on vows and oaths apply to non-Catholics if the law in question is based on the divine law or if the merely ecclesiastical law includes non-Catholics, e.g., the taking of an oath by a non-Catholic in an ecclesiastical process. The canons on vows in the Eastern code (*CCEO* 889–894) are similar to those in the Latin code, but there is only one canon in the Eastern code on oaths (*CCEO* 895). This canon recognizes the canonical efficacy only of oaths made before the Church in cases established by canon law.

CHAPTER I
A VOW
[cc. 1191–1198]

The following canons refer to private vows and, as applicable, also to public vows. Members of religious institutes profess public vows, which are also governed by the laws of Book II, part three, especially canons 607, 654–658, and 688–701, as well as the constitutions and other laws proper to each institute. The canons of this chapter treat: the definition of a vow, the capability of vowing, and the nullity of a vow (c. 1191); the different kinds of vows (c. 1192); the obligation of a vow (c. 1193); the cessation of a vow (c. 1194); the suspension of a vow (c. 1195); dispensation (c. 1196); commutation (c. 1197); and suspension of private vows by religious profession (c. 1198).

Definition, Capability, Nullity

Canon 1191 — §1. A vow, that is, a deliberate and free promise made to God about a possible and better good, must be fulfilled by reason of the virtue of religion.

§2. Unless they are prohibited by law, all who possess suitable use of reason are capable of making a vow.

§3. A vow made out of grave and unjust fear or malice is null by the law itself.

A vow is a promise made to God, the fulfillment of which is a serious religious obligation. A promise implies more than a wish or a desire but rather is a firm decision to fulfill what is vowed. A vow must be made with sufficient deliberation, knowingly, and with due discernment. The object of the vow must be something good; otherwise it is not a vow and has no effect. It must be something that the one vowing is capable of fulfilling, and it must be something better, i.e., better than not doing it, or better than its opposite. The good that is vowed may be relatively better depending on the person and circumstances. For example, whether a vow to perpetual virginity is a better good than matrimony would depend on whether the person has a true vocation to a life of celibacy.

Not only must the one vowing have the use of reason, but it must be a sufficient use of reason appropriate to the object of the vow. For example, the minimal use of reason normally required of children for reception of first communion (c. 914) would not be sufficient for the profession of vows in a religious institute (cf. c. 656, 1°).

The vow must be freely made, i.e., without grave and unjust fear, or as a result of malice. A vow made under such circumstances would be invalid. Fear is grave when, in order to escape some serious harm that is perceived, a person sees no

---

[84] Thomas Aquinas, *STh* II-IIae, q. 88, a. 5 et q. 89, a. 4.
[85] Among these laws see especially cc. 124–126, 11, 96–100.

alternative other than to take the vow. Fear is unjust if it is inspired by a threat that is not deserved; it is just if it is inspired by a threat that is deserved. For example, a secular cleric living in concubinage is told by the bishop to take a vow in his presence never to repeat that sin or, if the cleric does not take the vow, he will be given an onerous penance. The cleric takes the vow motivated by grave fear of the penance, but the vow is valid insofar as the penance is deserved and is just.

Malice (*dolus*) in the context of this canon is the deliberate act of lying or of concealing the truth in order to get another person to make a vow which he or she would not do if the truth were known, or in order for oneself to get permission to make a vow, which would not be permitted if the truth were known. For example, a novice conceals from her superiors some external forum fact that, if known, would result in her not being admitted to profession of vows. Such malice invalidates the profession of vows (cf. c. 656, 4°).

Also invalid is a vow made out of ignorance or error concerning an element which constitutes the substance of the vow or which amounts to a condition *sine qua non* (c. 126). Ignorance is lack of knowledge; error is mistaken judgment. Ignorance or error invalidates a vow if the person vowing lacked knowledge of, or erred in judgment about, something that is of the substance of the vow. For example, a woman who, believing her husband to have survived a war, vows in gratitude to go to Mass every day, and only later discovers that he in fact was killed in the final hours of battle, is not bound by the vow.

A condition *sine qua non* is one which is so important that the vow would not have been taken if it had been known that the condition was not verified or could not be fulfilled. For example, a religious brother, who is unaware of or mistakes the juridical effects of a solemn vow of poverty and believes he can keep his property, takes solemn vows in a religious institute on the condition, whether explicit or implicit, that he retain

ownership of his goods (cf. c. 668, §§4–5).[86]

Distinctions

Canon 1192 — §1. A vow is *public* if a legitimate superior accepts it in the name of the Church; otherwise, it is *private*.

§2. A vow is *solemn* if the Church has recognized it as such; otherwise, it is *simple*.

§3. A vow is *personal* if the person making the vow promises an action; *real* if the person making the vow promises some thing; *mixed* if it shares the nature of a personal and a real vow.

This distinction between a public and private vow is not exact because members of some secular institutes and some associations of the faithful take vows which are accepted by a legitimate superior, yet these are considered private vows or, in the case of secular institutes, "semi-public vows."[87] A more accurate distinction, modeled on the difference between solemn and simple vows, is simply this: a public vow is one which is recognized as such by the Church; otherwise it is private. An essential element of religious life is the profession of vows which are recognized as public (cc. 607, §2; 654). Members of secular institutes assume vows or some other sacred bond as determined by the constitutions (c. 712). Societies of apostolic life, by definition, do not take "religious" vows, but in some of them the members assume the evangelical counsels by some bond (vow, oath, promise) as defined in the constitutions (c. 731).

This is the only place in the revised code where solemn and simple vows are mentioned. The older religious orders (monastics, canons regulars, mendicants, Jesuits) have perpetual solemn vows, and the more recent apostolic congregations have perpetual simple vows. The chief juridical difference between the two is that religious who profess a solemn vow of poverty renounce ownership of all their temporal goods (c. 668, §§ 4–5), whereas re-

---

[86] If this situation existed and the brother wanted to leave religious life due to his error, he should seek an indult of departure in the usual way (c. 691) rather than attempt to prove that his profession was invalid.

[87] See J. Zammit, *Il voto e la promessa* (Rome: Pontifical Lateran University, 1995) 201.

ligious who profess a simple vow of poverty have a right to retain ownership of their patrimony but must give up its use and any revenue (c. 668, §1). A temporary vow, which expires after a stated period of time, is always a simple vow.

A personal vow binds the person to perform some act, e.g., to make a pilgrimage or to fast. A real vow binds the person to give a thing, e.g., a donation of property to a religious institute. A mixed vow consists of both personal and real elements, e.g., to make a pilgrimage to a shrine and to contribute funds for a new chapel there.

Obligation

Canon 1193 — By its nature a vow obliges only the person who makes it.

This is a change from the previous law (*CIC* 1310, §1), which said that the obligation of a real vow, or the real part of a mixed vow, passes on to the heirs of the one who died without having fulfilled the vow. There might be a moral or legal obligation on the part of heirs to fulfill the vow of a deceased person, but there is no obligation arising from that person's vow itself.

Cessation

Canon 1194 — A vow ceases by the lapse of the time designated to fulfill the obligation, by a substantial change of the matter promised, by the absence of a condition on which the vow depends, by the absence of the purpose of the vow, by dispensation, or by commutation.

A vow ceases to bind when the obligation of the vow is fulfilled. There are six other ways by which a vow ceases to bind:

(1) when the time appointed for the fulfillment of the obligation has passed, e.g., one vows to make a pilgrimage to Rome during the Holy Year and it is not possible to fulfill the vow during that year;

(2) when there has been a substantial change in the matter promised, i.e., the thing promised becomes impossible or wrongful whether in itself or due to circumstances, e.g., one vows to attend Mass each year at a certain church and the church is closed, or one vows to give a large donation to the parish building fund and it becomes necessary to use the money to pay for emergency medical care;

(3) when a condition on which the vow depends no longer exists, e.g., one vows to give a donation to the Church if one's mother is cured of cancer and she is not;

(4) when the purpose for which a vow was made no longer exists, e.g., one vows to fast every day because of obesity, and the excess weight is lost;

(5) by dispensation (c. 1196); and

(6) by commutation (c. 1197).

Suspension

Canon 1195 — The person who has power over the matter of the vow can suspend the obligation of the vow for as long a time as the fulfillment of the vow brings disadvantage to that person.

Suspension is a temporary cessation of the fulfillment of a vow; the obligation of the vow resumes when the reason for the suspension ceases. A person who has power over the matter of a vow is a person whose own rights are affected by the vow of another. If this person's rights are adversely affected by the fulfillment of the vow, he or she may suspend the vow in question, even against the will of the one who made the vow.

Dispensation

Canon 1196 — In addition to the Roman Pontiff, the following can dispense from private vows for a just cause provided that a dispensation does not injure a right acquired by others:

1° the local ordinary and the pastor with regard to all their subjects and even travelers;

2° the superior of a religious institute or society of apostolic life if it is clerical and of pontifical right with regard to members, novices, and persons who live day and night in a house of the institute or society;

3° those to whom the Apostolic See or the local ordinary has delegated the power of dispensing.

Dispensation from a vow is its complete cancellation for a just reason by an authority competent in law. Just reasons include the public good, a serious difficulty in fulfilling the vow, excessive scrupulosity. In doubt or error about the adequacy of the reason, the dispensation may be lawfully given.

The acquired right (cf. c. 4) which may be injured must be understood in a strict sense, i.e., only a right which has been lawfully acquired, not something which is merely promised. For example, some years ago a man had vowed to endow a chair at a Catholic university and had established a foundation for this purpose upon which the funding of the chair has since depended, but recently his personal fortune suffered losses and now he wants to dissolve the foundation which he controls; he may not be dispensed from his vow without the agreement of the university since its acquired right to these funds would be harmed.

Commentators on the 1917 code said that only the Holy See was able to dispense from a vow if those who would be harmed by the dispensation refused to consent to it.[88] Since Vatican II it must be presumed that the diocesan bishop also has this power.[89] Although canons 85–93 are not applicable here since they deal only with dispensation from laws, not vows, these canons may be helpful as a parallel passage (cf. c. 17).

Transients (vagi) are not expressly mentioned here, but they are included in number one because they are subjects of the local ordinary and the pastor in the place where they are staying (cf. c. 102, §2). The local ordinary or pastor may give the dispensation to his subjects whether they are in or outside the territory at the time of the dispensation, and whether he himself is in or outside his own territory when he dispenses.

Those who stay day and night in a house of a religious institute or society of apostolic life include students and other residents, lay staff, and even guests who stay overnight.

Commutation

Canon 1197 — The person who makes a private vow can commute the work promised by the vow into a better or equal good; however, one who has the power of dispensing according to the norm of can. 1196 can commute it into a lesser good.

The commutation of a vow is the substitution of the act or work (opus) promised by the vow to some other act. If the act to be substituted is as good or better than the original act that was vowed, the person who made the vow can commute it. If the act to be substituted is a lesser good than the original act that was vowed, the commutation is validly granted only by a competent superior as in the previous canon. The authorities competent to dispense are also competent to commute the vow to a greater or equal good—not just to a lesser good—if this is desired by the person seeking the commutation.[90]

Suspension by Religious Profession

Canon 1198 — Vows made before religious profession are suspended while the person who made the vow remains in the religious institute.

Any private vow is suspended by the law itself at the first profession of a religious (c. 655), and it continues to be suspended as long as the reli-

---

[88] See, e.g., S. Woywod, *A Practical Commentary on the Code of Canon Law,* rev. by C. Smith (New York: Joseph F. Wagner, 1946) n. 1333.

[89] *LG* 27; *CD* 8, 11; c. 381, §1.

[90] This may happen if the person is ignorant of or reluctant to use his or her own power to commute.

gious remains in the institute, i.e., until definitive departure at which time the vow begins to bind again.[91] A religious may continue to observe the non-binding vow if he or she wishes, but only with the permission of the competent superior if the act in question is incompatible with religious obligations or arouses public notice, e.g., if the religious must miss a common act of the community in order to perform the deed privately vowed. This canon does not apply to members of societies of apostolic life who should seek a dispensation from a private vow if this is warranted.

CHAPTER II
AN OATH
[cc. 1199–1204]

The six canons of this chapter treat: the definition of an oath and the prohibition of a proxy (c. 1199); the obligation and nullity of oaths (c. 1200); the nature of a promissory oath (c. 1201); the cessation of the obligation of an oath (c. 1202); suspension, dispensation, and commutation of oaths (c. 1203); and the strict interpretation of oaths (c. 1204).

Definition, Proxy

Canon 1199 — §1. An oath, that is, the invocation of the divine name in witness to the truth, cannot be taken unless in truth, in judgment, and in justice.

§2. An oath which the canons require or permit cannot be taken validly through a proxy.

By swearing an oath, one takes God as a witness to the truth or sincerity of what one says or promises. While the essence of a vow is a *promise* made to God, an oath is an *invocation* of the divine name. No precise wording for an oath is prescribed; any suitable formula may be used provided God is invoked.

Oaths are classified as *assertory* or *promissory.* An assertory oath is one by which God is invoked to bear witness to the truth of an affirmation or to the denial of some fact. A promissory oath is one by which God is invoked to attest to the sincerity of intention of the oath-taker with regard to a future act or omission of an act which he or she is now promising. The promissory oath always concerns the future.[92] An example of a promissory oath is the oath of fidelity on assuming an office to be exercised in the name of the Church.[93] In a judicial proceeding, an oath taken before testifying is a promissory oath by which the person promises to tell the truth; an oath taken after the testimony is an assertory oath by which the person asserts that he or she has told the truth (cf. c. 1532).

The words "in truth, in judgment, and in justice" come from Jeremiah 4:2. The elements of truth, judgment, and justice pertain to both assertory and promissory oaths. Regarding *truth,* in an assertory oath a person swears to assert the truth as he or she knows it; in a promissory oath the person must have a true and sincere intention to fulfill the promise made. A false assertion or promise made under oath before an ecclesiastical authority constitutes the crime of perjury which is to be punished by a just penalty (c. 1368). *Judgment* requires careful discernment or judgment of the reason for taking an oath; only some cause of real necessity or importance justifies the taking of an oath. *Justice* demands, in the case of an assertory oath, that the affirmation or negation which the person wishes to corroborate be lawful; in the case of a promissory oath, justice requires that the person be able to assume morally and lawfully the obligation of fulfilling the promise (cf. c. 1201, §2).

The second paragraph prohibits a person from using another to swear an oath on his or her behalf. Although in the strict sense this requirement pertains only to oaths demanded or admitted in the canons, i.e., in the code, it may be taken as a gen-

---

[91] Applicable to definitive departure are cc. 684, §5; 688; 689; 692; 694–700; but not 686 on exclaustration.

[92] E. J. Moriarty, *Oaths in Ecclesiastical Courts, CanLawStud* 110 (1937) 3.

[93] See commentary at c. 833; cf. also cc. 380, 1454, 1283, 1°.

eral rule applicable also to oaths required or admitted by ecclesiastical laws outside the code. It does not apply, however, to oaths that are not required or admitted by the law. An oath submitted on one's own initiative could be taken by a proxy.

Obligation, Nullity

Canon 1200 — §1. A person who freely swears to do something is bound by a special obligation of religion to fulfill what he or she affirmed by oath.

§2. An oath extorted by malice, force, or grave fear is null by the law itself.

The first paragraph applies only to promissory oaths. A religious obligation is incurred by a promise made under oath, unlike a simple promise which does not invoke the divine name. The second paragraph applies to all oaths. Malice, force, or grave fear can invalidate an oath; also, an oath is invalid if it was sworn in ignorance or error concerning an element which constitutes its substance or which amounts to a condition *sine qua non*.[94] In contrast with canon 1191, §3 which expressly mentions that fear or malice must be unjust, this canon implicitly suggests the element of injustice through the use of the word "extorted."[95]

Nature of Promissory Oath

Canon 1201 — §1. A promissory oath follows the nature and conditions of the act to which it is attached.

§2. If an oath is added to an act which directly tends toward the harm of others or toward the disadvantage of the public good or of eternal salvation, then the act is not reinforced by the oath.

The first paragraph states the principle that an oath does not change the nature of the promise or any conditions that might be attached to it. The oath reinforces the promise by making it a religious obligation, but the promise itself is in no

---

[94] See c. 126 and commentary on c. 1191, §3.
[95] *Comm* 12 (1980) 378.

way altered. For example, a wealthy woman swears to donate a large sum of money to the diocese if the bishop builds a certain shrine, but the bishop wants the money for another purpose. The woman is not bound to give him the money, even though she swore an oath, because the promise was conditioned.

The second paragraph says, in effect, that an oath is invalid if the act that is promised directly tends to be harmful to others or disadvantageous to the public good or eternal salvation. An act that would have deleterious effects would be contrary to the virtue of religion, specifically the virtue of justice which is a defining element of an oath (c. 1199, §1). An oath sworn to fulfill such an act would have no effect.

Cessation of Obligation

Canon 1202 — The obligation arising from a promissory oath ceases:

1° if it is remitted by the person for whose benefit the oath was made;

2° if the matter sworn to is substantially changed or if, after the circumstances have changed, it becomes either evil or entirely indifferent or, finally, impedes a greater good;

3° if the purpose or a condition under which the oath may have been taken ceases;

4° by dispensation or commutation, according to the norm of can. 1203.

A promissory oath ceases to bind when the promised act has been fulfilled. The obligation ceases before its fulfillment in the nine ways mentioned in the canon:

(1) if the beneficiary remits the thing sworn, e.g., the bishop refuses to accept a donation a person has sworn to give for a specific purpose;

(2) if what is sworn is substantially changed, e.g., a man swears to donate his house to a religious community but the house is destroyed by fire;

(3) if due to changed circumstances what is sworn becomes evil, e.g., a man swears to marry a certain woman but then discovers she does not want children;

(4) if due to changed circumstances what is sworn becomes entirely indifferent, e.g., a woman swears to give the parish a certain statue sought by the pastor, but a new pastor does not care whether she gives it or not;

(5) if due to changed circumstances what is sworn would impede a greater good, e.g., a man swears to make a pilgrimage at a certain time, but it becomes necessary to care for his ailing mother;

(6) if the purpose for which the oath was taken no longer exists, e.g., a woman swears to leave a bequest to her parish, but the parish is closed before she dies;

(7) if a condition under which an oath was taken no longer exists, e.g., a man swears to assist an impoverished neighbor (the fact of his poverty being an implied condition), but then the neighbor gets a good job;

(8) by dispensation; or

(9) by commutation.

Suspension, Dispensation, Commutation

Canon 1203 — Those who can suspend, dispense, or commute a vow have the same power in the same manner over a promissory oath; but if the dispensation from the oath tends to the disadvantage of others who refuse to remit the obligation of the oath, only the Apostolic See can dispense the oath.

Canons 1195–1197 on the suspension, dispensation, and commutation of vows are also applicable to promissory oaths. There is one significant difference: this canon expressly restricts to the Apostolic See a dispensation from an oath when the dispensation may disadvantage others who have refused to remit its obligation. Under these circumstances, a dispensation from an oath by an authority inferior to the Apostolic See would be invalid.

While canon 1198 allows for the automatic suspension of private vows made by a person before his or her religious profession, there is no such provision with regard to promissory oaths. If a promissory oath conflicts in any way with the religious life, it should be suspended, dispensed, or commuted in accord with canons 1195–1197.

Strict Interpretation

Canon 1204 — An oath must be interpreted strictly according to the law and according to the intention of the person taking the oath or, if that person acts out of malice, according to the intention of the person to whom the oath is made.

Oaths are to be interpreted according to the strict wording of what is sworn. In the case of some oaths, the law itself is the principal basis for understanding the meaning of the oath. For example, many church officials must swear to assume certain obligations when they take the oath of fidelity on assuming an office to be exercised in the name of the Church.[96] These obligations must be interpreted according to the strict meaning of the words of the oath and only in reference to the requirements of the law to which they refer.

If there is doubt about the meaning of an oath, the intention of the person taking the oath should be considered. For example, a woman swears an oath before her pastor to give the parish a gold chalice. The woman's intention in swearing the oath determines the meaning of "gold chalice," whether it be solid gold or gold plated. However, if the oath is sworn deceitfully, the intention of the person to whom the oath was made prevails. For example, a pawn shop dealer swears an oath

---

[96] See commentary on c. 833.

that the chalice he is selling the pastor is gold, and the pastor thinks he is getting a solid gold chalice because the price is too high for a gold-plated chalice. The pastor buys the chalice, discovers it is only gold plated, and wants his money back. In interpreting the meaning of "gold chalice," the pastor's intention to buy a solid gold chalice prevails over the intention of the dealer to sell a gold-plated chalice because the pastor was deceived by the ambiguous wording of the oath.

BIBLIOGRAPHY

Anandarayar, A. "Cremation and Ecclesiastical Legislation." *Indian Theological Studies* 30 (1993) 131–144.

D'Ostilio, F. "Il culto dei santi beati venerabili servi di Dio: Ciò che è dovuto permesso vietato auspicabile." *ME* 117 (1992) 63–90.

Henchal, M. J. "Cremation: Canonical Issues." *J* 55 (1995) 281–298.

Huels, J. M. "The Liturgy of the Hours in Parishes." In *More Disputed Questions in the Liturgy,* 85–96. Chicago: Liturgy Training Publications, 1996.

———. *The Pastoral Companion: A Canon Law Handbook for Catholic Ministry,* chapter 13. 2nd rev. ed. Quincy, Ill.: Franciscan, 1995.

McIntyre, J. P. "An Apology for the 'Lesser Sacraments.'" *J* 51 (1991) 390–414.

Seasoltz, R. K. *New Liturgy, New Laws,* chapters 9–10. Collegeville: Liturgical Press, 1980.

Spirito, P. "Il giuramento nel diritto canonico." *Apol* 61 (1988) 807–815.

Sucheski, Z. "La cremazione nella legislazione della chiesa." *Apol* 66 (1993) 653–728.

Zammit, J. *Il voto e la promessa.* Rome: Pontifical Lateran University, 1995.

John M. Huels, O.S.M.

Part III
SACRED PLACES AND TIMES
[cc. 1205–1253]

Part three is divided into two titles, one on sacred places and the other on sacred times. The principal sources for this section are the 1917 Code of Canon Law, *Sacrosanctum Concilium* (Vatican II's constitution on the liturgy), the 1977 *Rite of Dedication of a Church and an Altar* of the *Roman Pontifical*, the 1975 *General Instruction of the Roman Missal*, the 1969 *General Roman Calendar*,[1] and the 1966 apostolic constitution of Pope Paul VI, *Poenitemini*,[2] which was a major revision of the Church's penitential discipline.

Since the promulgation of the 1983 code, a revised title of the *Roman Ritual* and a revised liturgical book which are pertinent to matters treated in this section have been published. The first of these is *De benedictionibus* of 1984 which was significantly adapted by the International Commission on English in the Liturgy (ICEL) and the National Conference of Catholic Bishops (NCCB) and was published under the name *Book of Blessings*.[3] The revised liturgical book is the *Caeremoniale episcoporum* of 1984; the English version, the *Ceremonial of Bishops*, appeared in 1989. Another important document that touches on some of the matters treated here, and which has actually changed the previous discipline,[4] is the 1993 *Directory for the Application of the Principles and Norms on Ecumenism*. Other ecclesiastical documents containing provisions related to this section are mentioned in the footnotes.

In reference to sacred places, the Eastern code treats only churches and cemeteries (*CCEO* 868–874); funerals are treated in the same section with cemeteries (cc. 874–879). Feast days and days of penance are treated together (*CCEO* 880–883).[5]

---

[1] Paul VI, *mp Mysterii paschalis,* February 14, 1969, *AAS* 61 (1969) 222–226; *DOL* 442.

[2] February 17, 1966, *AAS* 58 (1966) 177–198; *The Pope Speaks* 11 (1966) 363–371; excerpts in *DOL* 358.

[3] The English translation of *De benedictionibus* was published in 1987 by ICEL; newly composed blessings were published by the USCC in 1988. The completed *Book of Blessings* (Collegeville: Liturgical Press, 1989) went into effect for the dioceses of the U.S. on December 3, 1989.

[4] See the commentary on c. 1248.

[5] Further references to the Eastern code are made only when there is a notable difference from the Latin law.

TITLE I
SACRED PLACES
[cc. 1205–1243]

Title I has an introductory section on sacred places in general (cc. 1205–1213) followed by five chapters on churches (cc. 1214–1222), oratories and private chapels (cc. 1223–1229), shrines (cc. 1230–1234), altars (cc. 1235–1239), and cemeteries (cc. 1240–1243). The introductory section has nine canons that treat: the definition of sacred places (c. 1205), the minister of dedications (c. 1206), the minister of blessings (c. 1207), certificate of blessing or dedication (c. 1208), proof of dedication or blessing (c. 1209), sacred and profane uses of sacred places (c. 1210), the desecration of sacred places (c. 1211), the loss of dedication or blessing (c. 1212), and the right of ecclesiastical authority vis-à-vis sacred places.

Definition

Canon 1205 — Sacred places are those which are designated for divine worship or for the burial of the faithful by a dedication or a blessing which the liturgical books prescribe for this purpose.

A sacred place is a place that: (1) has been lawfully designated for divine worship or the burial of the faithful by the competent ordinary, and (2) has been dedicated or blessed according to the proper liturgical rite. Churches, oratories, private chapels, shrines, and altars are dedicated or blessed according to the *Rite of Dedication of a Church and an Altar.*[6] Cemeteries are blessed according to the *Rite of Blessing a Cemetery.*[7] Only those places which

are destined for divine worship or the burial of the faithful should be dedicated or blessed according to these rites.[8] For example, a church hall that is to be used for Sunday Mass and for other purposes during the week should not be dedicated or blessed as a sacred place, but should be given an appropriate blessing from the *Book of Blessings,* which blessing would not make it a sacred place.[9]

Minister of Dedications

Canon 1206 — The dedication of any place belongs to the diocesan bishop and to those equivalent to him by law; they can entrust the function of carrying out a dedication in their territory to any bishop or, in exceptional cases, to a presbyter.

Only churches and altars are dedicated; other sacred places are blessed. A dedication is a sacramental that makes a church or an altar a sacred place.[10] Once dedicated, the church or altar is excluded from profane uses. The ordinary minister of dedication is the diocesan bishop,[11] but if he is unable to preside, he is to entrust it to another bishop, preferably to one who assists him in the pastoral care of the community for which the church has been built or, in altogether special circumstances, to a presbyter to whom he must give a special mandate.[12] The mandate may be given orally or in writing.

Minister of Blessings

Canon 1207 — Sacred places are blessed by the ordinary; the blessing of churches, however, is reserved to the diocesan bishop. Either of them,

---

[6] This is the general title of what are actually several separate rites, individually titled and numbered. There are rites for the laying of the foundation stone or commencement of work on the building of a church, dedication of a church, dedication of a church already in use for sacred celebrations, dedication of an altar, blessing of a church, blessing of an altar, blessing of a chalice and paten.

[7] *DB* ch. 35, *BB* ch. 43.

[8] See c. 1210 for an exception to the rule that sacred places must be used solely for religious purposes.

[9] See *BB* ch. 16, "Order for the Blessing of a Parish Hall or Catechetical Center."

[10] See the commentary on cc. 1169 and 1217.

[11] This includes the canonical equivalents of the diocesan bishop. See cc. 381, §2 and 427, §1.

[12] *RDCA* II, 6; IV, 12.

moreover, can delegate another priest for this purpose.

The general rule is that the blessing of a sacred place is celebrated by the ordinary who is competent in accord with canon 134, §1. The blessing of churches, in the strict sense of canon 1214, is reserved to the diocesan bishop, as is the dedication of altars.[13] Delegation for the blessing of a sacred place would usually be a special delegation for a specific case, but general delegation is not excluded.

Certificate of Blessing or Dedication

Canon 1208 — When the dedication or blessing of a church or the blessing of a cemetery has been completed, a document is to be drawn up, one copy of which is to be kept in the diocesan curia and another in the archive of the church.

The canon is concerned only with churches and cemeteries, not other sacred places. Nevertheless, it would be helpful to observe this canon also for other places to have written proof of their blessing, especially in later years when witnesses are no longer living. The liturgical law gives rules for recording the dedication of a church and altar, which in part may also serve as a suppletory norm (c. 19) for the blessing of other sacred places:

> The record of the dedication of the church should be drawn up in duplicate, signed by the bishop, the rector of the church, and representatives of the local community; one copy is to be kept in the diocesan archives, the other in the archives of the church.... In this record mention should be made of the day, month, and year of the church's dedication, the name of the bishop who celebrated the rite, also the titular of the church and, where applicable, the names of the martyrs

or saints whose relics have been deposited beneath the altar.[14]

Proof of Dedication or Blessing

Canon 1209 — The dedication or blessing of any place is sufficiently proven by one witness who is above suspicion, provided that no harm is done to anyone.

Anyone who has the use of reason can act as a witness. A witness above suspicion is a person of good reputation who would have no reason to lie. An oath (c. 1199) can be administered to give additional juridical value to the witness's testimony. The testimony of a single witness does not suffice if that testimony could harm anyone's interests. The interests in question would principally be either those of the owner of the place or of the persons who use the place.[15]

Sacred and Profane Uses

Canon 1210 — Only those things which serve the exercise or promotion of worship, piety, or religion are permitted in a sacred place; anything not consonant with the holiness of the place is forbidden. In an individual case, however, the ordinary can permit other uses which are not contrary to the holiness of the place.

---

[13] The commentary at c. 1217 explains when a church should be dedicated and when it should be blessed.

[14] RDCA II, 25.

[15] For example, a pontifical lay religious institute wants to demolish an old shrine, dear to some faithful, that requires costly repairs, and sell the property it stands on. Provided the value of the shrine and property does not exceed the limit for an alienation, the religious could have it demolished on their own authority if it were not blessed. If it had been blessed, the diocesan bishop could block demolition by refusing to decree the loss of blessing (c. 1212), and the institute would be faced with taking recourse to the Holy See or submitting to the will of the bishop. In this case the shrine's blessing could not be proved merely on the basis of one witness, since the witness's testimony would harm the interests of the religious institute.

The ordinary's permission is not needed to use a sacred place for a purpose that serves the exercise or promotion of worship, piety, or religion, e.g., a concert of sacred music,[16] a sacred drama, a retreat conference. The pastor, superior, or other person in charge of the sacred place could permit this. The ordinary's permission is necessary for each case to use a sacred place for a secular purpose, e.g., a concert of classical music which is secular in inspiration, graduation exercises, a talk on a secular topic in the interest of the public good. No permission may be given to use a sacred place for anything that offends against the holiness of the place, e.g., a concert of loud rock music, a political rally, merchandising.

Desecration

Canon 1211 — Sacred places are violated by gravely injurious actions done in them with scandal to the faithful, actions which, in the judgment of the local ordinary, are so grave and contrary to the holiness of the place that it is not permitted to carry on worship in them until the damage is repaired by a penitential rite according to the norm of the liturgical books.

The *Ceremonial of Bishops* has a chapter devoted to "Public Prayer after the Desecration of the Church," but a footnote explains that the rite of public prayer to be observed, described as a penitential rite of reparation, is to be used for the desecration of any sacred place.[17] The canon speaks of "violation" rather than "desecration" but, since the Ceremonial was published after the code, it is clear that the term "desecration" is not obsolete.

The *Ceremonial of Bishops* speaks of the harmful, scandalous actions that desecrate a sacred place as crimes: "The crimes in question are those that do grave dishonor to sacred mysteries, especially to the eucharistic species, and are committed to show contempt for the Church, or are crimes that are serious offenses against the dignity of the person and of society."[18] Since the profanation of a sacred thing, movable or immovable, is itself a crime (c. 1376), it is not necessary that any additional canonical delict be committed, but the action must be objectively serious, cause serious harm and scandal to the faithful, and be contrary to the holiness of the place. The local ordinary judges whether these conditions exist. If so, the penitential rite of reparation is to be celebrated. In the case of a church that has been dedicated, the diocesan bishop is the proper minister,[19] but delegation of another bishop or presbyter is not excluded. For places that have been blessed, the rite may be fittingly celebrated by the bishop, other ordinary, the priest in charge of the place, or another priest who has their permission, whether express or at least presumed.

The reparation rite is to be celebrated as soon as possible, either as part of Mass or a liturgy of the word. Until that time, no sacrament or other rite may be celebrated in the place. Instead there should be preaching and devotional exercises to prepare the people for the penitential rite of reparation, and they should be encouraged to celebrate the sacrament of penance for their own inner con-

---

[16] See CDW, letter to the presidents of episcopal conferences and the presidents of national liturgical commissions, November 5, 1987, *N* 24 (1988) 3–10. In n. 10 of this letter it says that the ordinary's permission is necessary for a concert in the church, but it fails to distinguish between concerts of sacred or religious music and concerts of secular music. In keeping with c. 1210, the ordinary's permission is needed only for concerts of secular music, since a concert of sacred or religious music falls within the meaning of serving the promotion of piety or religion. See J. Huels, "Canonical Comments on Concerts in Churches," *W* 62 (1988) 165–172; and idem, *Disputed Questions in the Liturgy Today* (Chicago: Liturgy Training Publications, 1988) 111–120.

[17] *CB* VI, ch. 20.
[18] *CB* 1070. *CIC* 1172 listed the crimes that brought about the desecration of a church, provided they were certain, notorious, and committed within the church itself: (1) homicide; (2) a sinful and serious shedding of blood; (3) godless and disgraceful uses to which the church has been converted; (4) burial of an infidel or of a person excommunicated by condemnatory or declaratory sentence.
[19] *CB* 1072.

version.[20] The sacrament of penance would have to be celebrated in some other church or oratory (c. 964, §1) since no sacrament may be celebrated in the sacred place before the rite of reparation.

Loss of Dedication or Blessing

Canon 1212 — Sacred places lose their dedication or blessing if they have been destroyed in large part, or have been turned over permanently to profane use by decree of the competent ordinary or in fact.

If a sacred place cannot be used before major repairs due to destruction by war, arson, vandalism, natural disasters, etc., it loses its dedication or blessing. The mere deterioration of a church that has been in steady use and requires temporary repairs during which the place cannot be used would not result in the loss of dedication or blessing. However, in the case of a major restoration of a sacred place which includes a new altar, there should be a new dedication or blessing. If the same altar is used and there has been no major destruction, there may not be a new dedication of the church after restoration because the dedication of the altar is a central part of the rite of dedication. A church that has been elevated in status, such as a church being ranked as a parish church, may have a new dedication provided a new altar is to be dedicated.[21]

If a sacred place is to be given over permanently for profane uses, the competent ordinary should first issue a decree in writing, directed to the person responsible for the sacred place, stating that the place in question is no longer a sacred place and has by the decree lost its dedication or blessing. The issuance of the decree is subject to the rules for individual administrative acts and individual decrees (cc. 35–47, 48–58), and recourse may be taken against it if a person, physical or juridic, is aggrieved by it. Although a sacred place also loses its dedication or blessing when in fact it

has been permanently given over for secular purposes, this is not a legal option for omitting a decree but simply a provision of law in case a decree is not issued. A decree should be issued because it recognizes the authority of the ordinary who had the competence to establish the sacred place, it leaves no uncertainty about the status of the place, and it allows the possibility of recourse.

Right of Church Authority

Canon 1213 — The ecclesiastical authority freely exercises its powers and functions in sacred places.

This is a statement of the right of competent church authorities to conduct their own legitimate affairs in any sacred place without interference from the state or other entity or person. This assertion may have practical effects. In some places the secular courts may defer to canon law when it is not contrary to the civil law. In other places where canon law is not recognized, and even in places where the rights of the Church are violated by the State, it is all the more important that the Church's rights be stated unambiguously in law so that there is a secure basis for protesting offenses against the free exercise of the Catholic faith in sacred places and for seeking redress.[22]

CHAPTER I
CHURCHES
[cc. 1214–1222]

The nine canons of this chapter treat: the definition of a church (c. 1214), the necessity of the bishop's consent to establish a church (c. 1215), the liturgical norms and expert advice to be followed (c. 1216), the dedication of a new church (c. 1217), the title of a church (c. 1218), the right to divine worship in a church (c. 1219), care for

---

[20] CB 1071.
[21] RDCA III, 1.

[22] The right of a fugitive to seek asylum in a church, recognized in the former law (CIC 1179), was suppressed in the revised code.

churches (c. 1220), free entry to churches for divine worship (c. 1221), and the relegation of churches to profane uses (c. 1222).

Definition

Canon 1214 — By the term church is understood a sacred building designated for divine worship to which the faithful have the right of entry for the exercise, especially the public exercise, of divine worship.

The principal juridical element defining a church—as distinct from an oratory (c. 1223) or a private chapel (c. 1226)—is the right of the faithful to go there. The most common examples of churches are cathedrals and parish churches. Because churches have a public character, they are subject to the authority and oversight of the diocesan bishop.[23]

Consent of Bishop

Canon 1215 — §1. No church is to be built without the express written consent of the diocesan bishop.
§2. The diocesan bishop is not to give consent unless, after having heard the presbyteral council and the rectors of the neighboring churches, he judges that the new church can serve the good of souls and that the means necessary for building the church and for divine worship will not be lacking.
§3. Although religious institutes have received from the diocesan bishop consent to establish a new house in the diocese or the city, they must also obtain his permission before building a church in a certain and determined place.

The rules of this canon apply for both the building of a new church and the canonical establishment of a church in a place where an oratory or chapel already exists. Consultation with the presbyteral council and the rectors of the neighboring churches is a requirement for the validity

[23] See cc. 397; 557; 683, §1; 738, §2.

of the act (cc. 124, 127). The term "rector" as used here refers to the pastor, religious superior, chaplain, or anyone in charge of the neighboring churches, not just the rectors of canon 556. The neighboring churches are only those churches in the sense of canon 1214, not oratories, shrines, or private chapels. The bishop must listen to the advice of the presbyteral council and the neighboring rectors and afterward decide whether the new church will serve the pastoral good and whether it has adequate financial prospects.

If the bishop approves the establishment of a formal religious house in accord with canons 608–611, the religious institute, if it is clerical, has a right to *have* a church (c. 611, 3°). Thus, the bishop can give the institute a church already established. The institute does not have a right to *build* a new church, though it does have the right to build a new oratory. To build a church requires the additional consent of the bishop as prescribed by this canon, which includes the bishop's approval of the exact site for it.

Liturgical Norms and Expert Advice

Canon 1216 — In the building and repair of churches, the principles and norms of the liturgy and of sacred art are to be observed, after the advice of experts has been taken into account.

Principles and norms on church art and architecture are chiefly found in Vatican II's constitution on the liturgy, *Sacrosanctum Concilium,* and the liturgical books.[24] These principles and norms require that churches be designed in keeping with their proper liturgical function and that they be worthy of the rites to be celebrated there.

[24] *SC* 122–128, *GIRM* 253–280, *RDCA* II, 3. Also helpful is the BCL statement, *Environment and Art in Catholic Worship* (Washington, D.C.: USCC, 1978). Although this statement of itself has no binding force, it is based on principles and norms of the liturgy and of sacred art which themselves are binding. The statement was prepared by experts under the authority of the bishops' committee and is a reliable and authoritative resource for matters of church art and architecture.

Churches and other places of worship should be suited to celebrating the liturgy and to ensuring the active participation of the faithful. Further, the places and requisites for worship should be truly worthy and beautiful, signs and symbols of heavenly realities.[25]

The very nature of a church demands that it be suited to sacred celebrations, dignified, evincing a noble beauty, not mere costly display, and it should stand as a sign and symbol of heavenly realities. The general plan of the sacred edifice should be such that in some way it conveys the image of the gathered assembly. It should also allow the participants to take the place most appropriate to them and assist all to carry out their individual functions properly.[26]

Among those whose advice must be sought in the construction, restoration, or remodeling of churches are the diocesan commissions on liturgy and art.[27] Other experts to be consulted should include a reputable architect and, when possible, a liturgical consultant.[28]

Dedication of a New Church

Canon 1217 — §1. After construction has been completed properly, a new church is to be dedicated or at least blessed as soon as possible; the laws of the sacred liturgy are to be observed.

§2. Churches, especially cathedrals and parish churches, are to be dedicated by the solemn rite.

The ideal expressed in the canon is that a new church should be dedicated or at least blessed as

soon as it is completed and before it is used for divine worship. The reason for this is primarily to bring out fully the symbolism and meaning of the rite of dedication.[29] Moreover, without the dedication or blessing it is not a sacred place and Mass may not be celebrated there except in a particular case of need (c. 932, §1). It is preferable to dedicate rather than bless churches; cathedral and parish churches must be dedicated.[30] However, a church must be blessed rather than dedicated if there is no altar to be dedicated, or if the place is only temporarily set aside for divine worship, e.g., a building destined to become a parish hall after the church is built.[31] The solemn rites of dedication and blessing are those in the *Rite of Dedication of a Church and an Altar.*[32]

When a church is dedicated, such appointments as the baptismal font, cross, images and statues, organ, bells, and stations of the cross are to be considered as blessed, duly erected, and installed.[33] This rule also applies to the *blessing* of a church.

The Eastern code uses the term "consecration" of a church rather than "dedication." The consecration of churches is reserved to the eparchial bishop, who can grant the faculty of consecrating only to another bishop (*CCEO* 871).

Title of Church

Canon 1218 — Each church is to have its own title which cannot be changed after the church has been dedicated.

The title that is given may be the Blessed Trinity, a mystery in the life of Christ, or a title already accepted in the liturgy, the Blessed Virgin Mary under a title already accepted in the liturgy, the Holy Spirit, one of the angels, or an approved

---

[25] *GIRM* 253, *DOL* 1643.

[26] *RDCA* II, 3; *DOL* 4371.

[27] *GIRM* 256, *SC* 126.

[28] The Federation of Diocesan Liturgical Commissions in Washington, D.C. publishes a national directory of consultants. Some helpful publications are M. B. Mauck, *Places for Worship: A Guide to Building and Renovating* (Collegeville: Liturgical Press, 1995); and idem, *Shaping a House for the Church* (Chicago: Liturgy Training Publications, 1990).

[29] *RDCA* III, 1.

[30] *GIRM* 255.

[31] *RDCA* III, 1; V, 1.

[32] Cf. also *CB* VI, 864–971. For further discussion on the dedication or blessing of a church, see the commentary on cc. 1169 and 1205–1209.

[33] *CB* 864.

saint. The title may not be that of a blessed without an indult of the Apostolic See. There may be only one title, except in the case of saints listed together in the Roman Calendar.[34] The titular feast of the church is celebrated annually with the rank of a solemnity. The feast of the Assumption is the feast day for all churches named after the Blessed Virgin Mary without a particular mystery or title or with a title that lacks its own liturgical day.[35]

Additional norms governing the titles of churches were issued in 1999. Chief among these are:

(1) Once a blessed is approved by the Holy See for insertion in a diocesan liturgical calendar, it is not necessary to have a further indult to name a church after that blessed in that diocese.

(2) Once a church is dedicated, the title may not be changed except for grave reasons and with an indult of the Apostolic See.

(3) If the church has not been dedicated but only blessed, the diocesan bishop may change the title for a grave reason after carefully considering all the circumstances.

(4) If several parishes are suppressed and a new one is established using one of the churches, its title must be retained, but it may be changed if it is a new building. The churches of the suppressed parishes are also to retain their own titles if they are considered to be "co-parishes."

(5) If several parishes are each suppressed and united into one new parish, it is permitted, for pastoral reasons, to give it a new name different from the previous title of the parish church.[36]

Right to Divine Worship

Canon 1219 — In a church that has legitimately been dedicated or blessed, all acts of divine worship can be performed, without prejudice to parochial rights.

This is a statement of the right to celebrate liturgical actions in a church once it has been dedicated or blessed. Certain liturgical celebrations are ordinarily reserved to parish churches and cathedrals, notably infant baptism, confirmation, adult initiation, the reception of a baptized person into full communion with the Catholic Church, marriages, and funerals.[37] The right to liturgical celebrations in a church is lost when the dedication or blessing is lost in accord with canons 1212 and 1222.

Care for Churches

Canon 1220 — §1. All those responsible are to take care that in churches such cleanliness and beauty are preserved as befit a house of God and that whatever is inappropriate to the holiness of the place is excluded.
§2. Ordinary care for preservation and fitting means of security are to be used to protect sacred and precious goods.

This is an exhortation directed to those responsible for the upkeep of churches. It expresses common sense values which may hardly seem necessary in a code of law. However, the canon would serve a useful purpose if an abuse needed to be corrected.

Free Entry for the Liturgy

Canon 1221 — Entry to a church is to be free and gratuitous during the time of sacred celebrations.

---

[34] *RDCA* II, 4. See V. Lanzani, "*Pastor Bonus* art. 69: I patroni," *N* 25 (1989) 226–233.

[35] SCSDW, *Decreta authentica* 2529.

[36] CDWDS, notification *Omnis ecclesia titulum,* February 10, 1999, *N* 35 (1999) 158–159. See also idem, notifica-

tion *Ad spirituale fidelium bonum,* November 29, 1998, *N* 34 (1998) 664; English translation in *RR* (1999) 20–21.

[37] See cc. 530; 857, §2; 1118, §1; 1177, §1. See also cc. 558, 559, and 560.

This rule, which follows from the right of the faithful to go to a church (c. 1214), applies to all liturgical celebrations. It does not apply at times when no liturgical celebrations are occurring,[38] including special events, such as concerts, held in a church.[39] In some churches of great historic or artistic value a small fee is charged to tourists. Where that is the case, provision should be made for the free entry, at least for some period each day, of those who wish to pray before the blessed sacrament (cf. c. 937).

Relegation to Profane Use

Canon 1222 — §1. If a church cannot be used in any way for divine worship and there is no possibility of repairing it, the diocesan bishop can relegate it to profane but not sordid use.

§2. Where other grave causes suggest that a church no longer be used for divine worship, the diocesan bishop, after having heard the presbyteral council, can relegate it to profane but not sordid use, with the consent of those who legitimately claim rights for themselves in the church and provided that the good of souls suffers no detriment thereby.

The decision to relegate a church to profane use pertains solely to the diocesan bishop, even if the church is owned by a juridic person other than the diocese or parish. Since the diocesan bishop grants permission for the establishment of a church, he is the competent authority to issue the decree that removes its dedication or blessing and relegates it to secular use (c. 1212).

Paragraph one treats a case when it is impossible to repair a badly damaged church. The impos-

sibility of restoring the church does not mean only an architectural impossibility but would also include an impossibility due to insufficient funds available from the parish, religious institute, or other juridic person that owns the church.

The second paragraph covers other situations of grave need when the church still is able to be used for divine worship or when it is possible to restore it to such use. Before relegating such a church to profane use, the diocesan bishop must observe all the requirements of the law.

(1) He must determine if there is a grave reason for doing so, e.g., inadequate finances to maintain the church properly, or a small number of parishioners together with a shortage of priests.

(2) He must consult the presbyteral council (c. 127, §1).

(3) He must have the consent of those who could legitimately claim rights for themselves in the church, which consent is necessary for the validity of his act (c. 127, §2, 1°).

(4) He must determine that the good of souls would not be harmed.

(5) He must determine that the proposed use of the place will not be sordid, which judgment should be made in keeping with cultural variables and local circumstances.

Those who could lawfully claim rights for themselves in the church would in every case be the juridic person or persons who own the church property. For example, a parish owns the church building and a religious institute owns the land on which it was built. The bishop would have to obtain the consent of both the pastor (cc. 515, §3; 532) and the competent authority of the religious institute (c. 638), but not the pastor if the parish has already been suppressed (cc. 515, §2; 123). A physical person might also be able to claim rights, e.g., a major donor to the church whose donation

---

[38] A suggestion to make admission to churches free at all times was deliberately rejected in the code revision process. See *Comm* 12 (1980) 388.

[39] Nevertheless, the CDWDS suggested to ordinaries, as one of the rules they might require for granting permission for a concert in a church, that admission be free of charge. See letter, n. 10 c, English version, *N* 24 (1988) 3–10. This is only a suggestion and is not binding unless the ordinary makes it binding on his own authority.

was accepted on the condition that the church would continue in use as a sacred place for a certain period (cf. c. 1284, §1, 3°).

Those who contributed unconditional donations to the building, restoration, or upkeep of the church would not have any claim to the church and the bishop need not consult them or obtain their consent (cf. cc. 1255–1257, 1267), but appropriate consultations of such persons likely would be pastorally beneficial. Although offerings given by the faithful for building or maintaining a church may be used only for that purpose (c. 1267, §3), this principle of law is not a basis for the donors' claiming a right of consent to the relegation of the church to a profane use. Nor is it a basis for claiming a return of the donation that was initially used for the purpose of building or maintaining the church when at a later time that church is lawfully designated by the bishop for a profane purpose. The Church, in the sense of canon 1258, owns the church building; the donors do not. The competent authorities of the Church, in accord with the law, have sole authority to make determinations about the use of a church.

CHAPTER II
ORATORIES AND PRIVATE CHAPELS
[cc. 1223–1229]

The seven canons of this chapter treat: the definition of an oratory (c. 1223), establishment and conversion to profane use (c. 1224), the right to liturgical celebrations (c. 1225), the definition of a private chapel (c. 1226), the right of bishops to have a private chapel (c. 1227), permission for Mass or other sacred celebrations in a chapel (c. 1228), and the blessing of oratories and private chapels (c. 1229).

Definition of an Oratory

Canon 1223 — By the term oratory is understood a place for divine worship designated by permission of the ordinary for the benefit of some community or group of the faithful who gather in it and to which other members of the faithful can also come with the consent of the competent superior.

An oratory, frequently called a "chapel" in ordinary discourse, is different from a church principally in virtue of who has a right to make use of it. All the faithful have the right to go to a church, but only that community or group of people for whom an oratory was established has the right to make use of it. An oratory may be established for any specified community or group of the faithful: a religious community, people in a nursing home, students and staff in a school, etc. Unless the matter is regulated by particular law, the competent superior who may permit others to have access is the person in charge of the institution or other place of which the oratory is a part, such as the superior of a religious house, the administrator of a nursing home, the rector of a seminary, the principal of a school, etc. The competent ordinary whose permission is needed to establish an oratory is defined in canon 134, §1. The permission is to be given in writing (c. 37).

In every house of a religious institute there must be an oratory or a church in which the Eucharist is celebrated and reserved (c. 608). This applies only to religious houses that have been erected with all the formalities of the law (c. 609), not to informal communities of religious. Moreover, the permission of the ordinary for the establishment of the oratory must be obtained even if he has already granted permission to establish a religious house or informal community.[40]

Houses of societies of apostolic life have a right to have an oratory in which the Eucharist is celebrated and reserved but, unlike houses of religious institutes, they are not required to do so (c. 733, §2). For all houses of religious institutes and societies of apostolic life, the rule of canon 934, §2 must also be observed on the custody of the blessed sacrament and the necessity of having a

---

[40] The reason for this separate permission is seen in c. 1224: the ordinary must first inspect the place before he can decree its canonical erection as an oratory.

priest celebrate Mass in the oratory on a regular basis, at least twice a month insofar as possible.

Any oratory other than that of a house of a religious institute or society of apostolic life requires the permission of the local ordinary for the reservation of the Eucharist. This permission is separate from the permission necessary to establish the oratory. Before granting this permission the local ordinary should make certain that provision has been made for the regular celebration of Mass there in accord with canon 934, §2.

Establishment and Conversion to Profane Use

Canon 1224 — §1. The ordinary is not to grant the permission required to establish an oratory unless he has first visited the place destined for the oratory personally or through another and has found it properly prepared.

§2. After permission has been given, however, an oratory cannot be converted to profane use without the authority of the same ordinary.

The canon restricts the ordinary's power: he may not grant permission to establish an oratory unless he or a delegate has visited the place and has found the space and its appointments suitable for its intended uses, especially for the liturgical services that are to be celebrated there. In making this judgment the ordinary should be guided by pertinent principles and norms of liturgy and of sacred art (cf. c. 1216). Once this permission is granted, the oratory may not be used for domestic purposes, but it does not become a sacred place until it has been blessed.[41]

The ordinary who may establish an oratory is the one who is competent to decree that it may be converted to profane uses. Whether or not the oratory was blessed, the ordinary should decree in writing the fact of the oratory's conversion to a secular purpose so that there be legal clarity about the status of the place.[42]

Right to Liturgical Celebrations

Canon 1225 — All sacred celebrations can be performed in legitimately established oratories except those which the law or a prescript of the local ordinary excludes or the liturgical norms prohibit.

This is a statement of a right to have any liturgical celebration in an oratory unless a particular celebration is excluded by law (*ius*), whether universal or particular, including general administrative norms and legal customs, or by a prescript of the local ordinary. The canon must also be read in conjunction with canon 932, §1 which requires that the Eucharist ordinarily be celebrated in a sacred place. For the oratory to be a sacred place, it must be blessed (c. 1205).

Infant baptism, adult initiation, and marriage are generally celebrated in parish churches, but the universal law also makes provision for them to be celebrated in other churches and oratories (cc. 530, 857, 1118). Funerals may be celebrated only in churches (c. 1177); a dispensation from the diocesan bishop would be necessary to celebrate a Catholic funeral in an oratory unless a legitimate custom, acquired right, or privilege is in force.

Small lay religious communities and other similar communities are encouraged to participate in Mass on Sundays at the parish church.[43] The celebration of the principal liturgies of the Easter triduum by all small communities in oratories and churches is discouraged by the Holy See:

> It is fitting that small religious communities, both clerical and lay, and other lay groups should participate in the celebration of the Easter Triduum in neighboring principal churches. Similarly where the number of participants and ministers is so small that the celebrations of the Easter Triduum cannot be carried out with the requisite solem-

---

[41] Cf. cc. 1205, 1229; *Comm* 12 (1980) 339.
[42] See commentary on c. 1212.

[43] SC Rites, instr *Eucharisticum mysterium* 26, May 25, 1967, *AAS* 59 (1967) 539–573; *DOL* 1255.

nity, such groups of the faithful should assemble in a larger church.[44]

A prescript in the context of this canon refers to a singular administrative decree or precept issued by the local ordinary.[45] The local ordinary could prohibit one or more specific liturgical celebrations in an oratory. He should not prohibit the eucharistic celebration in an oratory since it is the central act of divine worship of all communities and groups in the Church and is a chief purpose for having an oratory. Rather, if the competent ordinary has a most serious reason for wanting Mass prohibited in a certain oratory, he should remove by decree the status of the place as an oratory (cc. 1224, §1; 1212).

The bishop may not prohibit the celebration of Sunday Mass in oratories, which the faithful attend with the consent of the competent superior, in order to compel them to attend a parish church. It is clear from canon 1248, §1 that the Sunday Eucharist is not a parochial right.

Definition of a Private Chapel

Canon 1226 — By the term private chapel is understood a place for divine worship designated by permission of the local ordinary for the benefit of one or more physical persons.

Unlike an oratory, which is established for a specific community or group of the faithful, a chapel is established only for one or several persons, e.g., a bishop or a noble family. Except for the case mentioned in the following canon, only the local ordinary may permit the establishment of a private chapel; personal ordinaries may not. By definition, a private chapel is established for the purpose of divine worship, specifically for those liturgical acts that ordinarily are not to be celebrated outside a sacred place. A chapel without the reservation of the blessed sacrament, one that is to be used only for private meditation, the liturgy of the hours, or popular devotions, is not the private chapel of this canon and therefore its erection does not require authorization from the local ordinary.

Privilege of Bishops

Canon 1227 — Bishops can establish a private chapel for themselves which possesses the same rights as an oratory.

The rights of a bishop's chapel are the right to celebrate Mass there, to reserve the blessed sacrament (c. 934, §1, 2°), and to celebrate all other liturgical actions that may be celebrated in an oratory. The right applies to all bishops—diocesan bishops, titular bishops, retired bishops.

Sacred Celebrations

Canon 1228 — Without prejudice to the prescript of can. 1227, the permission of the local ordinary is required for Mass or other sacred celebrations to take place in any private chapel.

The sacred celebrations intended in this canon must be understood as only those liturgical actions which as a rule are to be celebrated in a church or oratory. The local ordinary's permission would not be required to celebrate in a private chapel the liturgy of the hours or most sacramentals. The local ordinary's permission would also not be needed for the celebration of a non-sacramental marriage there.[46]

---

[44] CDW, littcirc *Paschalis sollemnitatis* 43, January 16, 1988, *N* 24 (1988) 81–107; *Origins* 17 (1988) 679–687. The *Roman Missal,* in the rubrics for the evening Mass of the Lord's Supper on Holy Thursday, says that only one Mass of the Lord's Supper may be celebrated in churches and oratories without the permission of the local ordinary.

[45] See cc. 35–58. A restriction on the right to celebrate a specific liturgical act or acts in oratories must be given by the local ordinary observing the formalities of the law. Otherwise the right to that liturgical celebration is not lost.

[46] See c. 1118, §3. The officiating priest or deacon would, of course, need the faculty to assist at the marriage.

The permission to hold sacred celebrations habitually in a private chapel is preferably given in writing as proof of its being granted, especially in later years when there is a new local ordinary. The permission should specify exactly which liturgical celebrations are permitted. Before permission is granted, the local ordinary or his delegate should inspect the place and see if it is suitable for the liturgical celebrations requested (cf. c. 1224, §1). Separate authorization is required to reserve the blessed sacrament in a private chapel (c. 934, §1, 2°). This permission should not be granted unless there is a priest who can celebrate Mass there at least twice a month, as far as possible (c. 934, §2). This rule maintains the intimate connection between the Eucharist celebrated and reserved.[47] Moreover, the local ordinary should require that the chapel be blessed as a condition for granting permission to celebrate the Eucharist there (cc. 932, §1; 1205).

Blessing of Oratory/Private Chapel

Canon 1229 — It is fitting for oratories and private chapels to be blessed according to the rite prescribed in the liturgical books. They must, however, be reserved for divine worship alone and free from all domestic uses.

Oratories and private chapels are blessed, not dedicated. The blessing prescribed for oratories and private chapels is found in chapter 5 of the 1977 *Rite of Dedication of a Church and an Altar* of the *Roman Pontifical*. The minister of blessing is the competent ordinary or his delegate (c. 1207). When an oratory or chapel is blessed, such things in it as the cross, images, organ, and stations of the cross are considered blessed and installed by the one rite of blessing and therefore should not be blessed separately.[48]

An oratory or private chapel that has not been blessed with the official rite of blessing is not a sacred place and is not subject to the limitations

on its uses mentioned in canon 1210. Nevertheless the law requires that all oratories and private chapels, even if not blessed, be reserved only for divine worship and be free from all domestic use. This would not exclude occasional non-religious use, provided the use does not cause offense or wonderment to the group or community or persons for whom the oratory or chapel has been established. Although this is not expressly stated in the law, it is evident from the fact that the ordinary may grant permission to use even dedicated churches for a non-religious purpose in individual instances provided it is not contrary to the holiness of the place (c. 1210).[49]

It is appropriate, but not required, that an oratory or a chapel be blessed. Even if an oratory or a chapel has been in use for a long time, it may still be blessed and should be blessed if it is regularly used for the celebration of the Eucharist.[50] If a multi-purpose room is to be used for both cultic and non-cultic activities, it may be blessed by an appropriate blessing from the *Roman Ritual*,[51] but not with the rite from the Pontifical.

CHAPTER III
SHRINES
[cc. 1230–1234]

The five canons of this chapter treat: the definition of a shrine (c. 1230), national and international shrines (c. 1231), shrine statutes (c. 1232), privileges of shrines (c. 1233), and religious services and votive offerings of art and piety at shrines (c. 1234).

---

[47] *HCWE* 1–6.
[48] *CB* 954.
[49] The one who is permitted to do the more is also permitted to do the less. See *RI* 53.
[50] See cc. 932, §1 and 1205. In contrast, a church must be dedicated or at least blessed and this should be done, if possible, when the church is first opened for use (*RDCA* III, 1). The law does not say the same about an oratory or private chapel, so either may be used, even for a long time, before it is blessed; but if Mass is to be celebrated there on a regular basis, it should be blessed as soon as possible.
[51] Cf. *BB* ch. 16; c. 932, §1.

Definition

Canon 1230 — By the term shrine is understood a church or other sacred place to which numerous members of the faithful make pilgrimage for a special reason of piety, with the approval of the local ordinary.

The notion of a shrine contains two essential elements: (1) it is a sacred place and (2) the local ordinary has approved it for the purpose of pilgrimage by the faithful. A sacred place is one which: (1) has been designated for divine worship or the burial of the faithful, and (2) has been dedicated or blessed with the prescribed liturgical rite (c. 1205). It is necessary that the sacred place and the devotion that is fostered be approved by the local ordinary so that the faithful may go there on pilgrimage if they wish. It is not juridically necessary that a shrine arise out of the people's devotion or even that they actually frequent it; a shrine could be approved with the hope or expectation that this would occur after the shrine is built.

This section on shrines is new to the 1983 code and is not retroactive. In the case of new shrines established since the 1983 code, the local ordinary's approval must be expressed.[52] Prior to the 1983 code, religious institutes or other juridical persons could establish shrines without the express approval of the local ordinary. It is fitting that this approval now be required in the law since divine worship and popular piety are areas subject to regulation by and the vigilance of the diocesan bishop or other local ordinary.[53]

Shrines that have the title of "minor basilica" are also subject to a 1989 Congregation for Divine Worship and the Discipline of the Sacra-

ments decree.[54] This decree lays down the conditions for obtaining the title of minor basilica, the liturgical and pastoral offices and works that are to be provided at basilicas, and special concessions granted to basilicas.

National and International Shrines

Canon 1231 — For a shrine to be called a national shrine, the conference of bishops must give its approval; for it to be called an international shrine, the approval of the Holy See is required.

Shrines that had already been called national or international before the 1983 code went into effect may continue using that title even without the approbation of the competent authority. In the case of competing claims to the title of national or international shrine, the ecclesiastical authorities mentioned in this canon may decide the issue in keeping with the law as well as customs, privileges, acquired rights, the patrimony of institutes of consecrated life (c. 578), and other pertinent facts. In a case of recourse the Congregation for the Clergy has competence.[55]

Statutes

Canon 1232 — §1. The local ordinary is competent to approve the statutes of a diocesan shrine; the conference of bishops for the statutes of a national shrine; the Holy See alone for the statutes of an international shrine.

§2. The statutes are to determine especially the purpose, the authority of the rector, and the ownership and administration of goods.

The law does not require that every shrine have its own statutes, but simply points out who is competent to approve such statutes when they are drawn up. However, the competent authority could

---

[52] Before the 1983 code, the official definition of a shrine, a definition approved by Pope Pius XII in 1955, made no mention of the local ordinary's permission being necessary for a shrine's erection. See *DDC* 7:870. Local ecclesiastical authority did, however, have competence over pious pilgrimages. See SCConc, decree, February 11, 1936, *AAS* 28 (1936) 167; *CLD* 2, 573–575.

[53] See cc. 392; 397; 678, §1; 838, §4; 839, §2.

[54] Decree *Domus ecclesiae,* November 9, 1989, *N* 26 (1990) 13–17; *BCLN* 26 (1990) 217–219. See J. Evenou, "*Pastor bonus* art. 69: basiliche minori," *N* 25 (1989) 234–236.

[55] *PB* 97, 1°.

require such statutes before granting the approval required by the preceding canon. There is an implied preference in this canon that each shrine have its own statutes in order to regulate with clarity the matters mentioned in paragraph two of the canon.

Privileges

Canon 1233 — Certain privileges can be granted to shrines whenever local circumstances, the large number of pilgrims, and especially the good of the faithful seem to suggest it.

Privileges may be granted by a legislator, namely, the diocesan bishop, a particular council, the pope, an ecumenical council, or by an executive authority who has delegation (cf. c. 76). Privileges for a shrine might include the absolution of censures, special indulgences, the celebration of specified parochial functions, etc.

Shrine Services, Votive Offerings

Canon 1234 — §1. At shrines the means of salvation are to be supplied more abundantly to the faithful by the diligent proclamation of the word of God, the suitable promotion of liturgical life especially through the celebration of the Eucharist and of penance, and the cultivation of approved forms of popular piety.

§2. Votive offerings of popular art and piety are to be kept on display in the shrines or nearby places and guarded securely.

This is an exhortation which is preceptive in its general orientations, but the details are left to the shrine director and staff under the vigilance of the diocesan bishop.

CHAPTER IV
ALTARS
[cc. 1235–1239]

This chapter of five canons treats: fixed or movable altars (c. 1235), the altar's construction

(c. 1236), the dedication or blessing of an altar and the relics under it (c. 1237), the loss of dedication or blessing (c. 1238), and the reservation of the altar's use to divine worship, also excluding burial beneath it (c. 1239).

Fixed or Movable

Canon 1235 — §1. An altar, or a table upon which the eucharistic sacrifice is celebrated, is called *fixed* if it is so constructed that it adheres to the floor and thus cannot be moved; it is called *movable* if it can be removed.

§2. It is desirable to have a fixed altar in every church, but a fixed or a movable altar in other places designated for sacred celebrations.

In oratories and private chapels the altar may be fixed or movable. It is preferable, though not required, that the altar in a church be fixed. An altar is not an object but a sacred *place,* a place that symbolizes Christ.[56] This symbolism is more clearly manifest if the altar is permanently positioned in one place. In new churches there should be only one altar in the church "so that in the one assembly of the people of God the one altar may signify our one Savior Jesus Christ and the one eucharist of the Church."[57] A second altar is permitted in a separate blessed sacrament chapel at which weekday Mass may be celebrated; additional altars are prohibited.[58] Since the altar is a symbol of Christ, the duplication of altars distorts this symbolism. Moreover, in churches constructed since 1977, statues and pictures of saints may not be placed above the altar.[59]

The altar should be freestanding to allow the ministers to walk around it easily and to allow Mass to be celebrated facing the people. It should be posi-

---

[56] See *RDCA* IV, 7.

[57] *RDCA* IV, 7.

[58] *RDCA* IV, 7. Churches, oratories, and private chapels erected before the *Rite of Dedication of a Church and an Altar* went into effect in 1977 are not affected by the law stipulating that there be only one altar.

[59] *RDCA* IV, 10.

tioned to be the focal point on which the attention of the whole congregation centers naturally.[60]

Construction

Canon 1236 — §1. According to the traditional practice of the Church, the table of a fixed altar is to be of stone, and indeed of a single natural stone. Nevertheless, another worthy and solid material can also be used in the judgment of the conference of bishops. The supports or base, however, can be made of any material.

§2. A movable altar can be constructed of any solid material suitable for liturgical use.

The law favors a fixed altar's construction from stone, preferably from a single, natural stone. The use of stone conveys a sense of solidity and permanence and is thus appropriate for symbolizing Christ's presence in a sacred place. Other worthy and solid materials may be used if permitted by the conference of bishops. The material used for the construction of a movable altar is not said to be subject to regulation by the conference of bishops, but it should be "becoming, solid material suited to liturgical use, according to the traditions and customs of different regions."[61] The appropriate material to be used in the construction of a movable altar can be determined by local authorities who are competent to make decisions about church design and furnishings.

Dedication or Blessing, Relics

Canon 1237 — §1. Fixed altars must be dedicated, and movable altars must be dedicated or blessed, according to the rites prescribed in the liturgical books.

§2. The ancient tradition of placing relics of martyrs or other saints under a fixed altar is to be preserved, according to the norms given in the liturgical books.

The rites of dedication and blessing of altars are found in the *Rite of Dedication of a Church and an Altar,* chapters 4 and 6. The minister of dedication is the diocesan bishop. If he cannot be present in person, he may delegate another bishop, especially an episcopal vicar or auxiliary who has the pastoral care of that community. In special circumstances the diocesan bishop may give a special mandate to another priest to dedicate an altar.[62] The dedication of an altar is a more elaborate rite than a blessing and includes the anointing of the altar with sacred chrism.

An option in the *Rite of Dedication of an Altar* is the bishop's placing of relics in an aperture beneath the table of a fixed altar of a church.[63] The following are the principal liturgical laws governing relics vis-à-vis altars:[64]

(1) A reliquary must not be placed on the altar or set into the table of the altar, but placed beneath the table of the altar, as the design of the altar permits.

(2) The relics should be of a size sufficient for them to be recognizable as parts of human bodies; very small relics may not be used.

(3) The relics must be authentic; relics of doubtful authenticity may not be used.[65]

(4) When any relics are exposed for veneration, they should not be placed on the table of the altar.

(5) Only fixed altars may have relics placed beneath them.

Loss of Dedication or Blessing

Canon 1238 — §1. An altar loses its dedication or blessing according to the norm of can. 1212.

---

[60] *GIRM* 262.
[61] *GIRM* 264, *DOL* 1654.

[62] *RDCA* IV, 12.
[63] *RDCA* IV, 47.
[64] *RDCA* IV, 10–11.
[65] The CCS is competent to authenticate relics. See *PB* 74.

§2. Altars, whether fixed or movable, do not lose their dedication or blessing if the church or other sacred place is relegated to profane uses.

An altar loses its dedication or blessing if it suffers major destruction or if it has been given over permanently to profane use in fact or by a decree of the competent ordinary. If a church, oratory, or private chapel loses its dedication or blessing, the altar in it may be transferred for use in another sacred place and is not dedicated or blessed again unless the competent ordinary previously secularized the altar by decree. In the event of an altar's desecration, its dedication or blessing is not lost but the provisions of canon 1211 are applicable.

Reserved for Divine Worship

Canon 1239 — §1. An altar, whether fixed or movable, must be reserved for divine worship alone, to the absolute exclusion of any profane use.

§2. A body is not to be buried beneath an altar; otherwise, it is not permitted to celebrate Mass on the altar.

Proper reverence for the altar means that the only objects that may be placed on it are those which are necessary for the liturgical celebration. The document, *Environment and Art in Catholic Worship,* is instructive on this point:

> The altar, the holy table, should be the most noble, the most beautifully designed and constructed table the community can provide.... It is holy and sacred to this assembly's action and sharing, so it is never used as a table of convenience or as a resting place for papers, notes, cruets, or anything else.[66]

The body of a saint may be placed beneath a fixed altar since it is a relic. If any other corpse is buried under an altar, Mass may not be celebrated on it. According to canon 1202 of the 1917 code, Mass could be celebrated in a church in which a corpse had been buried as long as the place of burial was at least a meter away from the altar; the present law makes no provision for this situation.

CHAPTER V
CEMETERIES
[cc. 1240–1243]

The four canons of this chapter treat: the establishment and blessing of cemeteries (c. 1240), optional cemeteries (c. 1241), burial in churches (c. 1242), and particular laws on cemeteries (c. 1243).

Establishment and Blessing

Canon 1240 — §1. Where possible, the Church is to have its own cemeteries or at least areas in civil cemeteries that are designated for the deceased members of the faithful and properly blessed.

§2. If this cannot be achieved, however, then individual graves are to be properly blessed.

Catholic cemeteries, as well as parts of cemeteries that are reserved for the burial of the Catholic faithful, should be blessed according to the appropriate rite in the *Book of Blessings.*[67] The blessing makes it a sacred place subject to the canons on sacred places in general (cc. 1205–1213). In a blessed cemetery (or in that part of a non-Catholic cemetery that has been blessed for Catholics), a cross is to be erected as a sign of hope in the resurrection. The rite of blessing is preferably celebrated by a bishop, but he may entrust it to a priest, particularly one involved in the pastoral care of the faithful who have established the cemetery. Sunday is the preferred day for the blessing, but it may be done on any day except Ash Wednesday and the days of Holy Week. If a new cemetery is to be used jointly by various Christian denominations, there

[66] BCL (Washington, D.C.: USCC, 1978) n. 71.

[67] *BB* ch. 43, *DB* ch. 34.

should be an ecumenical celebration to mark its opening.[68] A document is to be drawn up in duplicate recording the blessing of the cemetery with one copy for the diocesan curia and the other for the cemetery archives.[69]

If a Catholic is to be buried in a cemetery that has not been blessed, the individual grave is blessed at the time of the burial in accord with the *Rite of Funerals*.[70] Non-Catholic Christians, if they do not have their own cemetery, may be buried in a Catholic cemetery with the permission of the diocesan bishop, which permission may be given on a general basis or reserved for individual cases.[71]

The wording of this canon, unlike that of the following one, is preceptive. The Church *is to have* its own cemeteries where possible. This obligation is binding on the diocese itself, unless there is sufficient space in parish or other Catholic cemeteries for the burial of all the faithful. Reasons for the impossibility of having Catholic cemeteries include lack of available land, insufficient funds, and serious difficulties posed by civil law or civil authorities.

Optional Cemeteries

Canon 1241 — §1. Parishes and religious institutes can have their own cemetery.

§2. Other juridic persons or families can also have a special cemetery or tomb, to be blessed according to the judgment of the local ordinary.

Parishes, religious institutes, other juridic persons, and even Catholic families may have their own cemeteries. The cemeteries of parishes and religious institutes should be blessed. The cemeteries of other juridic persons and of private families may be blessed with the permission of the local ordinary. This canon does not refer to diocesan cemeteries, which are considered in the previous canon.

---

[68] *BB* 1418–1421, *DB* 1115–1118.
[69] *CB* 1056.
[70] *OEx* 53, *OCF* 218.
[71] *Ecum Dir* 137.

Burial in Churches

Canon 1242 — Bodies are not to be buried in churches unless it is a question of burying in their own church the Roman Pontiff, cardinals, or diocesan bishops, including retired ones.

The wording of this canon would indicate that the diocesan bishop may not be buried in any church except his own cathedral. However, the liturgical law of the 1984 *Ceremonial of Bishops,* number 1164, extended this privilege of burial in a church: "The body of a deceased bishop is buried in a church, and as a rule in the cathedral church of his diocese. A retired bishop is buried in the cathedral church of his last see, unless he has made other arrangements." Excluded from burial in churches are auxiliary and other titular bishops and all other persons except the pope, cardinals, and diocesan bishops.

Several commentators, basing their view on rulings of the Holy See on the old law, state that the general prohibition on burial in churches applies also to oratories and private chapels.[72] However, this interpretation extends the meaning of "churches" beyond its canonical sense (c. 1214). Such a change in meaning would require an authentic interpretation (c. 16, §1).

Particular Laws

Canon 1243 — Particular law is to establish appropriate norms about the discipline to be observed in cemeteries, especially with regard to protecting and fostering their sacred character.

The universal law here upholds the value of protecting and fostering the sacred character of cemeteries. However, it specifies that this goal is to be accomplished by means of particular law— at the level of the nation or other region, the province, and/or the diocese. The canon speaks of *ius particulare* rather than *lex*. This includes true

---

[72] See, e.g., *Pamplona ComEng,* 767–768; *CLSGBI Com,* 698; *CLSA Com,* 852; *Chiappetta Com,* 350.

laws enacted by legislative authority, but it also includes executory decrees, guidelines, instructions, and other kinds of executory norms. All of these are acceptable means to fulfill the requirement of this canon.[73]

TITLE II
SACRED TIMES
[cc. 1244–1253]

The two chapters of this title are divided according to the two kinds of sacred times: feast days and days of penance. "Feast days" in this context refer only to Sundays and holy days of obligation, not to celebrations that have the rank of "feast" in universal or particular liturgical calendars. Further principles and rules on the subject matter of this section are found in *Sacrosanctum Concilium,* chapter 5,[74] and the *General Norms for the Liturgical Year and the Calendar.*[75] Two introductory canons establish the competent authorities over feast days and days of penance (c. 1244) and the authorities who may grant dispensations from and commutations of the obligations of feast days and days of penance (c. 1245).

The Eastern code treats feast days and days of penance together in one section (*CCEO* 880–883). The holy days common to all the Eastern churches *sui iuris* are Sundays, Christmas, Epiphany, the Ascension, the Dormition of Mary, and Saints Peter and Paul (*CCEO* 880, §3). Eastern Catholics are obliged either to participate in the Divine Liturgy (Eucharist) on these days or, if the prescripts or the legitimate custom of their own church *sui iuris* requires it, in the celebration of the divine praises (*CCEO* 881, §1). The faithful who are outside the territorial boundaries of their

own church *sui iuris* may observe the feast days and days of penance in force where they are staying; families in which parents are of different churches *sui iuris* may observe the norms of either church in regard to feast days and days of penance (*CCEO* 883).

Competent Authorities

Canon 1244 — §1. It is only for the supreme ecclesiastical authority to establish, transfer, and suppress feast days and days of penance common to the universal Church, without prejudice to the prescript of can. 1246, §2.

§2. Diocesan bishops can decree special feast days or days of penance for their dioceses or places, but only in individual instances.

The first paragraph refers only to feasts and days of penance in the universal Latin church. The feast days in question are the days of obligation specified in canon 1246, §1; the days of penance are those specified in canon 1250. The supreme authority is the pope alone or the college of bishops acting together with the pope (cc. 331, 336). The transference of a feast refers to a change of its day of celebration.

Since feast days and days of penance in the code imply a legal obligation to observe them in a certain way (cc. 1247, 1251), the special feast day or day of penance established by the diocesan bishop may be understood as one with *a legally binding obligation* to participate in Mass on the feast day or to do a specified penitential act or acts on the day of penance. The bishop can establish such a day in an individual instance (*per modum tantum actus*), but not on an ongoing basis. To be legally binding, the obligation should be stated in a general decree establishing the special feast or day of penance, which decree must be promulgated (cc. 29; 8, §2). A decree is not necessary if the bishop does not intend to impose a legal obligation but only to encourage or invite the people to observe a special feast day or day of penance. The word translated "to decree" (*indicere*) in paragraph two has other meanings, non-

---

[73] See the January 28, 1975 Christian Burial Guidelines of the National Catholic Cemetery Conference, *CLD* 9, 688–702. These guidelines are used as a basis for particular law in the dioceses of the U.S.A. and Canada.

[74] *SC* 102–111.

[75] *DOL* 440.

preceptive in nature, including "to proclaim," "to declare," "to announce."

The nature of feast days approved for universal and particular calendars suggests that the special feast day of obligation decreed by the bishop should be a celebration of some mystery or title of God, Jesus, or the Blessed Virgin Mary, or the feast day of a saint or blessed. The day chosen may not conflict with liturgical days of greater precedence.[76]

The bishop may wish to decree a special day of penance for particular reasons—even of a social or civil character—that commend the urgency of prayer, reparation, or reconciliation. The day chosen should not be a day or time of rejoicing, such as a Sunday, a solemnity, or the octave of Easter.

Dispensation and Commutation

Canon 1245 — Without prejudice to the right of diocesan bishops mentioned in can. 87, for a just cause and according to the prescripts of the diocesan bishop, a pastor can grant in individual cases a dispensation from the obligation of observing a feast day or a day of penance or can grant a commutation of the obligation into other pious works. A superior of a religious institute or society of apostolic life, if they are clerical and of pontifical right, can also do this in regard to his own subjects and others living in the house day and night.

Dispensation from or commutation of the obligation to observe a feast day or day of penance (in universal law) refers to the obligations of canons 1247 or 1251. Diocesan bishops have general competence to dispense from universal disciplinary laws (c. 87, §1), but pastors, other priests, and deacons may dispense from universal or particular laws only when this power is specifically given to them (c. 89), as in this canon for the benefit of pas-

tors and clerical superiors. The canons on the use of executive power of governance and on dispensations are applicable to the dispensation of this canon (cc. 136–144, 85–93). A just reason for dispensing is required for the validity of the dispensation (c. 90).

"Individual cases" refers not only to a single instance, but also to an individual situation that is ongoing, e.g., a person who must be at work each week during the times of Sunday Mass. In an ongoing case, it is advisable to commute rather than dispense. For example, the pastor could commute the obligation to attend Mass on Sunday to another day each week. An individual case also refers to a situation affecting several or many persons, e.g., those attending a banquet on a day of abstinence. Those staying day and night in the house of a religious institute or society of apostolic life include not only students, maintenance personnel, etc., who stay on a regular basis, but even guests who stay only one night.

The bishop may issue prescripts (norms, guidelines, instructions, policies, etc.) governing dispensations and commutations from the obligations of feast days and days of penance, e.g., by establishing general cases that would constitute a just reason for dispensing in order to give guidance to pastors and superiors in judging the sufficiency of reasons.

CHAPTER I
FEAST DAYS
[cc. 1246–1248]

The three canons of this chapter treat: Sundays and holy days (c. 1246), holy day obligations (c. 1247), and feast day observance.

Sundays and Holy Days

Canon 1246 — §1. Sunday, on which by apostolic tradition the paschal mystery is celebrated, must be observed in the universal Church as the primordial holy day of obligation. The following days must also be observed: the Nativity of our

---

[76] "Table of Liturgical Days according to Their Order of Precedence," index of *General Norms for the Liturgical Year and the Calendar, DOL* 3825.

Lord Jesus Christ, the Epiphany, the Ascension, the Body and Blood of Christ, Holy Mary the Mother of God, her Immaculate Conception, her Assumption, Saint Joseph, Saint Peter and Saint Paul the Apostles, and All Saints.

§2. With the prior approval of the Apostolic See, however, the conference of bishops can suppress some of the holy days of obligation or transfer them to a Sunday.

The paschal mystery is the life, passion, death, resurrection, and ascension of Jesus Christ—the central theological realities of every liturgical celebration which are most especially experienced by the Christian community on Sunday, the day of the resurrection. The canon reflects the renewed importance placed on Sunday by the Second Vatican Council:

> The Lord's Day is the first holyday of all and should be proposed to the devotion of the faithful and taught to them in such a way that it may become in fact a day of joy and of freedom from work. Other celebrations, unless they be truly of greatest importance, shall not have precedence over the Sunday, the foundation and core of the whole liturgical year.[77]

Solemnities, feasts of the Lord, and All Souls take precedence over Sundays in ordinary time, but not over the Sundays of Advent, Lent, and Easter.[78]

The ten holy days of obligation in the universal Latin church are on the same dates as those of the 1917 code (*CIC* 1247). In the order in which they appear in canon 1246 of this code they are: December 25, January 6, the sixth Thursday after Easter, the Thursday after Trinity Sunday, January 1, December 8, August 15, March 19, June 29, and November 1. The only changes are in the feasts themselves. Instead of the Solemnity of Mary Mother of God, the feast of the Circumcision was celebrated on January 1; the Body and Blood of Christ was formerly called the Most Holy Body of Christ.

Due to the demands of work and life it is difficult for people to observe all ten solemnities as days of obligation. Moreover, not all of these feasts have equal importance in the many cultures of the world's Catholics. Thus it is appropriate that the law grants to conferences of bishops the authority to suppress the obligation of some of them or transfer them to a Sunday, which decisions become effective after confirmation by the Congregation for Bishops. The practice of the Holy See is that there must be at least two holy days in every country—Christmas and a solemnity of Mary. For those feasts not retained as holy days of obligation, the episcopal conference has two options: either to transfer the feast to a Sunday or to retain the feast on its proper day but to abolish the obligation to participate in the Eucharist and abstain from servile work.

In the United States, Epiphany and the Body and Blood of Christ are transferred to Sundays; Saint Joseph and Saints Peter and Paul are celebrated on their proper days, but the obligations are suppressed. Whenever January 1, August 15, or November 1 fall on a Saturday or a Monday, the obligation to attend Mass is suppressed.[79] The decision whether to transfer the Solemnity of the Ascension to the Seventh Sunday of Easter is left to each ecclesiastical province.[80]

---

[77] *SC* 106, *DOL* 106. See also John Paul II, aplett *Dies Domini,* May 31, 1998, *AAS* 90 (1998) 713–766; *Origins* 28 (1998) 133–151.

[78] In 1990, Norm 5 of the *General Norms for the Liturgical Year and the Calendar* was changed as follows: When December 8 occurs on a Sunday, the Immaculate Conception is transferred to December 9. When March 19 or 25 occurs on a Sunday, St. Joseph's or the Annunciation are transferred to the next day respectively, unless either occurs on Passion Sunday or Easter, in which case they will be celebrated on the Monday following the second Sunday of Easter. See CDWDS, decr, April 22, 1990, *N* 26 (1990) 160–161; *BCLN* 26 (1990) 225–226.

[79] *BCLN* 28 (1992) 95–96. The decisions of other English-speaking conferences of bishops are given in *Pamplona ComEng,* indexed on p. 1307.

[80] *BCLN* 34 (1999) 82.

Holy Day Obligations

Canon 1247 — On Sundays and other holy days of obligation, the faithful are obliged to participate in the Mass. Moreover, they are to abstain from those works and affairs which hinder the worship to be rendered to God, the joy proper to the Lord's day, or the suitable relaxation of mind and body.

The obligations are twofold: participation in the Mass and abstention from unnecessary and burdensome work or business. Participation at Mass minimally means physical presence and consciousness. Although the precept to attend Mass may be fulfilled the evening before the feast day, the precept of rest obliges only on the day itself.[81] Both precepts are binding on the faithful according to the ordinary rules for the subject of ecclesiastical laws (c. 11).

Those whose livelihood requires them to work on holy days and/or Sundays are morally excused from the observance of the rest, but not necessarily from participation in the Mass. Those who have a just reason for missing Mass on Sundays or holy days on a regular basis should seek a dispensation, or preferably a commutation, in accord with canon 1245. Those who find it impossible, or impossible without serious inconvenience, to attend Mass in individual instances are morally excused from the observance of the obligation and need not seek a dispensation.

Feast Day Observance

Canon 1248 — §1. A person who assists at a Mass celebrated anywhere in a Catholic rite either on the feast day itself or in the evening of the preceding day satisfies the obligation of participating in the Mass.

§2. If participation in the eucharistic celebration becomes impossible because of the absence of a sacred minister or for another grave cause, it is strongly recommended that the faithful take part in a liturgy of the word if such a liturgy is celebrated in a parish church or other sacred place according to the prescripts of the diocesan bishop or that they devote themselves to prayer for a suitable time alone, as a family, or, as the occasion permits, in groups of families.

The obligation to participate in the Mass may be satisfied at any time during the twenty-four hours of the feast day itself, or on the evening before it. "Evening" should be understood as anytime from 4:00 P.M. onward.[82] The legislator uses the word "evening" (*vesper*), not "afternoon" (*post meridiem*); in keeping with the proper meaning of the word (cf. c. 17), an afternoon Mass before 4:00 is not an evening Mass and does not satisfy the obligation. The precept may be satisfied at *any* Catholic Mass, i.e., not only when the texts are those of the Sunday or holy day. For example, attendance at a wedding Mass after 4:00 on a Saturday fulfills the Sunday obligation. The Mass must be celebrated in a Catholic rite, i.e., in the liturgical rite of any Catholic church *sui iuris,* but not in a church which is not in full communion with the Catholic Church, although using a Catholic liturgical rite. The former *Ecumenical Directory* of 1967 granted a privilege permitting Catholics to fulfill their Sunday and holy day obligation at the divine liturgy of a separated Eastern church.[83] This privilege was suppressed in the 1993 *Directory for the Application of the Principles and Norms on Ecumenism.*[84]

The second paragraph is a recommendation, not a binding obligation, directed toward Catholics who are not able to participate in the Sunday Eucharist due to the absence of a priest or another

---

[81] *Comm* 12 (1980) 359.

[82] See Pius XII, apconst *Christus Dominus* VI, January 6, 1953, *AAS* 45 (1953) 14–24; *CLD* 4, 275–276. See also J. Huels and T. Willis, "What Time for Anticipated Masses?" *Emmanuel* 96 (1990) 34–41.

[83] *ED* 47.

[84] See *Ecum Dir* 115. One could argue that the privilege had already been revoked in 1983 by this canon since it made no exception for the separated Eastern churches.

grave cause. The recommendations given are not alternative ways for fulfilling one's Sunday obligation; rather, the obligation morally ceases to bind when it is impossible to fulfill it. In 1988 the Congregation for Divine Worship issued the *Directory for Sunday Celebrations in the Absence of a Presbyter.*[85] The Directory recommends a liturgy of the word, morning or evening prayer, or occasionally the celebration of a sacrament or sacramental, each of which should include the Sunday readings. The service is to be led by a deacon, acolyte, lector, or other lay minister for the benefit of the faithful who are unable to go to a neighboring church for Mass. The Directory specifies that there may be only one celebration of this nature in a church on a Sunday, and it may not be done if Mass is celebrated that day or the evening before. Masses that are televised are not to be recommended as an alternative for persons who are able to gather for a Sunday celebration; they are intended for the sick, home-bound, prisoners, etc., who are unable to go to church.[86]

CHAPTER II
DAYS OF PENANCE
[cc. 1249–1253]

In addition to feast days, Christian time is made sacred by days of penance. Pope Paul VI's 1966 apostolic constitution, *Poenitemini,* provides the historical, doctrinal, and disciplinary back-

ground for the following canons on penitential days and times.[87] The five canons of this chapter treat: individual and common observance of penance (c. 1249), penitential days and times (c. 1250), abstinence and fast (c. 1251), those bound to fast and abstinence (c. 1252), and the competence of the conferences of bishops over the observance of fast and abstinence (c. 1253).

Individual and Common Observance

Canon 1249 — The divine law binds all the Christian faithful to do penance each in his or her own way. In order for all to be united among themselves by some common observance of penance, however, penitential days are prescribed on which the Christian faithful devote themselves in a special way to prayer, perform works of piety and charity, and deny themselves by fulfilling their own obligations more faithfully and especially by observing fast and abstinence, according to the norm of the following canons.

Penitence is a part of the Christian life binding all the faithful in virtue of the divine law.[88] Although the faithful are free to choose their own forms of penitence, particular penitential days and times, specified in canon 1250, are established by ecclesiastical law in order to promote a *common* observance of penance. The canon mentions several ways that days of penance are observed. The first three (prayer, works of piety and charity, and self-denial by fulfilling one's obligations more faithfully) are left to the individual faithful to observe in their own way or to the regulations of the conference of bishops.[89] The final ways (fast and abstinence) are specific penitential acts binding the faithful in accord with canons 1251 and 1252. The adverb "especially" (*prae-*

---

[85] June 2, 1988, *N* 24 (1988) 366–378; *Origins* 18 (1988) 301–307. For the dioceses of the U.S., see *Sunday Celebrations in the Absence of a Priest: Leader's Edition* (New York: Catholic Book Publishing Company, 1994) and *Gathered in Steadfast Faith: Statement of the Bishops' Committee on the Liturgy on Sunday Worship in the Absence of a Priest* (Washington, D.C.: USCC, 1991). For commentaries see M. Henchal, *Sunday Celebrations in the Absence of a Priest* (Washington, D.C.: Federation of Diocesan Liturgical Commissions, 1992); and J. Huels, "Sunday Liturgies without a Priest," *W* 64 (1990) 451–460.

[86] See NCCB, "Guidelines for Televising the Liturgy," *BCLN* 33 (1997) 1–5. See also *SC* 20.

[87] February 17, 1966, *AAS* 58 (1966) 177–198; *The Pope Speaks* 11 (1966) 363–371; excerpts in *DOL* 358.

[88] *Poenitemini* I, *DOL* 3021; cf. Mt 3:2, 4:2–4; Mk 1: 12–15; Lk 4:1–2.

[89] See *Comm* 12 (1980) 364.

sertim) recalls the words of Paul VI that "fast and abstinence have a privileged place" among the forms of penance.[90]

Penitential Days and Times

Canon 1250 — The penitential days and times in the universal Church are every Friday of the whole year and the season of Lent.

Friday is a day of penance in memory of the passion and death of Christ. Penitential practices during the season of Lent dispose the faithful to celebrate the paschal mystery.[91] The Second Vatican Council said that Lenten penance should not only be internal and individual but also external and social, that it should be suitable to the present time, to different regions and circumstances, and that the conferences of bishops should make recommendations in this regard.[92]

Abstinence and Fast

Canon 1251 — Abstinence from eating meat or some other food according to the prescripts of the conference of bishops is to be observed on every Friday of the year unless a Friday occurs on a day listed as a solemnity. Abstinence and fasting, however, are to be observed on Ash Wednesday and Good Friday.

The law of abstinence prohibits the eating of meat, but eggs, milk products, and sauces made from animal fats may be eaten, as may fish and all cold-blooded animals (e.g., frogs, clams, turtles). The law of the fast means that only one full meal may be taken during the day; two light meals are permitted in accord with local custom as to the amount and kind of food. The consumption of solid food between meals is prohibited, but liquids may be taken at any time.[93] *Sacrosanctum Concilium* also recommends fasting on Holy Saturday.[94] The conference of bishops may substitute for abstinence from meat abstinence from some other food. This adaptation is more meaningful in countries where the people rarely eat meat.[95]

Those Bound to Abstain/Fast

Canon 1252 — The law of abstinence binds those who have completed their fourteenth year of age. The law of fasting, however, binds all those who have attained their majority until the beginning of their sixtieth year. Nevertheless, pastors of souls and parents are to take care that minors not bound by the law of fast and abstinence are also educated in a genuine sense of penance.

The completion of the fourteenth year occurs at midnight at the end of one's fourteenth birthday. The age of majority begins at midnight at the end of one's eighteenth birthday. The beginning of the sixtieth year occurs at midnight at the end of one's fifty-ninth birthday.[96] Unlike the fast, there is no upper age at which the law of abstinence ceases to bind. It should be noted that these norms are unrelated to the law of the eucharistic fast of canon 919 which gives no age limits but does except the elderly and the infirm.

Competence of Episcopal Conference

Canon 1253 — The conference of bishops can determine more precisely the observance of fast and abstinence as well as substitute other forms of penance, especially works of charity and exercises of piety, in whole or in part, for abstinence and fast.

---

[90] *Poenitemini* III, *DOL* 3020. See also *Comm* 12 (1980) 366.

[91] *General Norms for the Liturgical Year and the Calendar* 27, *DOL* 3793.

[92] *SC* 109.

[93] Cf. *Paenitemini* III, §§1–2; *DOL* 3023.

[94] *SC* 109.

[95] See *Comm* 12 (1980) 364 for a record of the discussion by the *coetus* on sacred times and places/divine worship.

[96] See cc. 97, §1; 203.

Fasting and abstinence must be observed everywhere on Ash Wednesday and Good Friday, but for other Fridays and the season of Lent the conferences of bishops have broad competence to establish both obligatory and recommended penitential practices. In the United States, fasting on all weekdays of Lent is strongly recommended; on all Fridays of the year the NCCB recommends abstinence from meat, prayer, penance (especially by eating less food), and almsgiving for the sake of world peace. Abstinence from meat is obligatory on all the Fridays of Lent.[97]

[97] NCCB, pastoral statement, November 18, 1966, *CLD* 6, 679–684. NCCB, *The Challenge of Peace: God's Promise and Our Response* 298, May 3, 1983. For the policies of other English-speaking conferences see *Pamplona ComEng*, 1307.

BIBLIOGRAPHY

Agnelo, G. "Santuari, pellegrinaggi e liturgia." *N* 28 (1992) 247–260.

Foster, M. S. "The Violation of a Church (Canon 1211)." *J* 49 (1989) 693–703.

Fox, J. "Notes on the Canonical Status of Shrines." *N* 28 (1992) 261–269.

Fuentes, J. A. "Regulación canónica de las celebraciones dominicales en ausencia de presbítero." *IC* 24 (1984) 559–574.

Henchal, M. "Sunday Celebrations in the Absence of a Priest." *J* 49 (1989) 607–631.

———. *Sunday Celebrations in the Absence of a Priest*. Washington, D.C.: Federation of Diocesan Liturgical Commissions, 1992.

Huels, J. M. "Concerts in Churches." In *Disputed Questions in the Liturgy Today,* 111–120. Chicago: Liturgy Training Publications, 1988.

———. "Preparing and Celebrating the Paschal Feasts." *W* 63 (1989) 71–79.

———. "Sunday Liturgies without a Priest." *W* 64 (1990) 451–460.

———. "The Sunday Mass Obligation." In *More Disputed Questions in the Liturgy,* 61–72. Chicago: Liturgy Training Publications, 1996.

———, and T. Willis. "What Time for Anticipated Masses?" *Emmanuel* 96 (1990) 34–41.

Longhitano, A. "Il sacro nel Codice di Diritto Canonico." *Ius Ecclesiae* 6 (1994) 709–730.

Manzanares, J. "De celebrationibus dominicalibus absente presbytero iuxta Directorium *Christi Ecclesia.*" *P* 78 (1989) 477–501.

Martín, J. L. "El directorio para las celebraciones dominicales en ausencia de presbítero." *REDC* 66 (1989) 615–639.

Mathieu, M.-T. "Réflexion sur le jeune." *Vie Consacrée* 58 (1986) 113–122.

Poveda, A. B. "Precepto Dominical y la nueva cultura del ocio." *Apol* 59 (1986) 513–531.

BOOK V
THE TEMPORAL GOODS OF THE CHURCH
[cc. 1254–1310]

A fundamentalist reading of some passages in the New Testament can lead to the conclusion that ownership of material goods is antithetical to the gospel and, hence, is forbidden to the Church. Passages susceptible to such an interpretation include those which recount the command of Jesus to his apostles to "take no gold, nor silver, nor copper in your belts, no bag for your journey, nor two tunics, nor sandals, nor a staff" (Mt 10:9–10), the challenge of Jesus to the rich member of the ruling class to "sell all that you have and distribute the money to the poor, and you will have treasure in heaven and come, follow me" (Lk 18:22), and the warning of Jesus to the assembled multitude that "none of you can be my disciple unless you give up all your possessions" (Lk 14:33).

Fundamentalist interpretation takes such passages out of context and isolates them from other relevant passages, such as those which speak of Jesus and his apostles having a common fund out of which they met their own needs and those of the poor (Jn 12:6; 13:29), or which recount the practice in early Christian communities of possessing material goods in common and from their sale providing for the needy members of the community (Acts 2:44–45; 4:34–35), or the early practice of taking up collections to aid the poor of other communities (Rom 15:25–28).

In the light of a reading of sacred scripture in its entirety, the magisterium has consistently made a distinction between the laudable observance of evangelical poverty in pursuit of spiritual perfection, on the one hand, and the practice of ordinary virtue necessary for salvation, on the other. With equal consistency the magisterium has affirmed the Church's right to own material goods necessary for the fulfillment of its spiritual mission, and denied the existence of theological obstacles to its doing so.

The Second Vatican Council, while reaffirming the excellence of evangelical poverty, individual and corporate (*PC* 13; *PO* 17), reiterated in a number of passages the need of the Church for material resources in order to carry out its mission (*LG* 8; *GS* 76; *PC* 13; *DH* 4), and specified in still other passages the particular aspects of the mission for which material goods are essential, namely, the proper ordering of divine worship (*PO* 17; *SC* 128), the fitting support of the clergy (*PO* 17, 20, 21; *CD* 21, 31) and others who devote themselves to the service of the Church (*AA* 22; *AG* 17), and the exercise of charity toward those in need (*PO* 17; *GS* 88; *GE* 8; *IM* 3). In addition to reaffirming these traditional teachings, the council, as an aspect of the ecclesiology of *communio,* emphasized the need for dioceses and other ecclesial communities to contribute from their material resources to assist one another to fulfill their common mission (*LG* 13, 23; *CD* 6; *AA* 10; *PO* 21; *AG* 19, 29, 38), and recommended that the laity, called to active participation in the life and activity of the Church, contribute their knowledge, experience, and special skills to make more efficient the administration of the material resources of the Church (*AA* 10; *AG* 41; *PO* 17, 21).

In the context of such conciliar teachings, Book V sets forth the guiding principles and disciplinary norms to govern the acquisition, use, administration, and disposition of what the title of Book V calls the "temporal goods of the Church." By "temporal goods" is meant all non-spiritual assets, tangible or intangible, that are instrumental in fulfilling the mission of the Church: land, buildings, furnishings, liturgical vessels and vestments, works of art, vehicles, securities, cash, and other categories of real or personal property. The phrase "of the Church" is less easily defined, partly because of the diverse meanings of the word "church" throughout the code, ranging from the community of the baptized (c. 204) to a sacred building (c. 1214). Book V itself, in one of its early canons, accords a specialized meaning to "church" in the area of temporal goods (see c. 1258), but that specialized meaning is said to apply only if the context or nature of a particular matter does not dictate otherwise. Different meanings are in fact dictated by context or subject matter in a number of canons in Book V. The word "church," then, in the title of Book V must have a signification broad enough to include its several meanings throughout the book.

Difficulty in interpreting the title of Book V is due also to use of the apparently possessive "of" in referring to the temporal goods "*of* the Church." The implication is that Book V is dealing with temporal goods belonging to a single owner known as "the Church." In fact, however, the goods which form the subject matter of Book V belong to many owners: the Apostolic See, individual dioceses, institutes of consecrated life, societies of apostolic life, parishes, other public juridic persons, private juridic persons, and natural persons individually and in association. The universal Church, although said to have the capacity to own temporal goods (c. 1255), does not in fact own any such goods.

What is common to all the temporal goods which form the subject matter of Book V, then, is not ownership, since the goods belong to many different owners, nor is it a relationship to a univocal understanding of "church" which in fact has multiple meanings within Book V. Rather, it is a common orientation to the work of the Church, that is, to the worship of God, to proclaiming the good news of the gospel, and to facilitating the flourishing of God's kingdom of justice and charity. This is spiritual work, but work which on this earth necessarily involves the use of temporal goods which are said to be "of the Church," not because of who owns them but because of the supernatural mission they serve.

In regard to temporal goods, that mission needs the support and assistance of carefully drafted and faithfully observed laws of the Church designed to guard against improper acquisition, excessive accumulation, and imprudent administration, and to ensure the protection, faithful use, and wise disposition of the things of this world which have been placed in the service of a kingdom that is not of this world. That is the rationale for the inclusion of Book V in the Code of Canon Law, and that should be the motivation for careful study and faithful observance of its provisions.

The canons of Book V are divided into five sections:

- Introductory Canons (cc. 1254–1258)
- The Acquisition of Goods (title I: cc. 1259–1272)
- The Administration of Goods (title II: cc. 1273–1289)
- Contracts and Especially Alienation (title III: cc. 1290–1298)
- Pious Wills in General and Pious Foundations (title IV: cc. 1299–1310)

Five preliminary canons set forth fundamental principles underlying the disciplinary norms of Book V and define technical terminology important to proper interpretation of those norms. The principles include the right of the Church to own material possessions, the purposes for which the Church does so, the independence of the Church from civil authority in the exercise of the Church's property rights, the essential elements of ownership, and the competence of the Church to confer upon juridic persons of the Church's own creation the capacity to own temporal goods. Terminological precision is given to the term "ecclesiastical goods" (*bona ecclesiastica*) and the word "church" when used in relation to temporal goods, as in the expression "church property."

Independence from Civil Authority

Canon 1254 — §1. To pursue its proper purposes, the Catholic Church by innate right is able to acquire, retain, administer, and alienate temporal goods independently from civil power.

Book V opens with a declaration of the Church's independence from civil authority in regard to temporal goods. More is claimed than simply the independent *origin* of the Church's property rights; the Church also claims independence from civil authority in the *exercise* of its rights to acquire, possess, administer, and dispose of temporal goods.[1]

The claim is rooted in centuries of conflicts between the Catholic Church and civil governments which, at various times and in various ways, have sought to deprive the Church of its material possessions. Restrictions on acquisitions, excessive taxation, forced alienations, and the outright seizure of church lands and revenues have, since the early Middle Ages, evoked strong reactions from bishops, local and ecumenical councils, and popes. The severity of the deprivations left little room for moderation in papal and conciliar pronouncements condemning the confiscations and insisting upon freedom of the Church from the jurisdiction of civil authorities in regard to temporalities.[2] The insistence found succinct expression in canon 1495, §1 of the 1917 code, and is reiterated, in substantially the same wording, in canon 1254, §1 of the present code.

While historically the result of Church-State conflicts, the Church's claim to independence, when interpreted in an absolute sense as it often has been, has itself spawned among some church leaders attitudes of defiance of civil authority, ranging from ignoring the provisions of civil law to open hostility toward civil government, both of which have given rise to added Church-State conflicts which have often resulted in harm to the Church.

The teaching of the Second Vatican Council affords needed moderation to the Church's claim by nuancing the understanding of the independence sought by the Church. According to the council, the degree of independence needed by the Church will be achieved wherever the principle of religious freedom set forth in *Dignitatis humanae* is put into practice.

> [W]here the principle of religious freedom is not only proclaimed in words or simply

[1] The earlier CLSA translation, in affirming that the Church "has" an innate right independently of civil power, gave rise to an ambiguity as to whether the claim is simply one of independent *origin* of the Church's rights or of their *exercise* as well. The new translation better comports with the Latin text which contains no such ambiguity.

[2] Brief summaries of many of the Church-State struggles over temporal possessions and of related statements of the magisterium may be found in J. Goodwine, *The Right of the Church to Acquire Temporal Goods*, CanLawStud 131 (Washington, D.C.: Catholic University of America, 1941) 50–98; U. Wiggins, *Property Laws of the State of Ohio Affecting the Church*, CanLawStud 367 (Washington, D.C.: Catholic University of America, 1956) 3–39.

incorporated in law but also given sincere and practical application, there the Church succeeds in achieving a stable situation of right as well as of fact and the *independence* which is necessary for the fulfillment of her divine mission. *This independence* is precisely what the authorities of the Church claim in society.[3]

The principle of religious freedom set forth in *Dignitatis humanae,* however, acknowledges the right and duty of civil authority to regulate the exercise of religious freedom in the interests of public order.[4] The independence of the Church spoken of in *Dignitatis humanae,* then, is an independence compatible with reasonable regulation by civil authority in the interests of public order.[5] It is solely the degree of independence necessary for the fulfillment of the Church's mission; it is not an absolute independence, but simply freedom from unreasonable regulation or restriction.

Such a nuanced understanding of the Church's independence from civil authority should guide the interpretation of canon 1254, §1, for the code is to be interpreted in the light of the image of the Church proposed by the council. *Dignitatis humanae* itself, in speaking of the right of religious bodies to acquire and use suitable funds and properties, prefaces its assertion with the words "provided the just requirements of public order are observed."[6] And several canons in Book V belie a claim to absolute independence by exhorting compliance with the provisions of civil law,[7] and even, at times, by "canonizing" such provisions.[8]

In view of the conciliar teaching, it would perhaps have been preferable to omit altogether in canon 1254 the claim to independence from civil authority, limiting the canon to a simple affirma-

tion of the Church's innate rights of ownership, as was proposed during the revision process[9] and as has been done in the parallel canon in the more recently promulgated Code of Canons of the Eastern Churches.[10] Notwithstanding the continued presence of the claim in canon 1254, §1, administrators of church property need to be aware of both the theoretical and practical propriety of recognizing in civil authority a limited but significant regulatory role in the ownership of temporal goods by the Church.

Use of the adjective "innate" in canon 1254, §1 affirms that the right to own temporal goods without unreasonable interference from civil authority is indigenous to the Church, both as a society of human beings and as a divinely instituted body whose mission requires the use of temporal goods. It is not a right which has been conferred upon the Church by any civil government or legal system. The term "Catholic Church" in this canon should be understood, in accord with canon 1, as referring only to the Latin church; as noted above, the parallel canon in the Eastern code omits any claim to independence from civil authority.

Canon 1254, §1 lists four essential elements of ownership of temporal goods: acquisition, retention, administration, and alienation. Acquisition, administration, and alienation are governed, respectively, by titles I, II, and III of Book V; retention is governed by individual canons in each of these titles. The 1917 code listed only the first three elements of ownership; the fourth, alienation, was regarded as an act of extraordinary administration. The drafters of the revised code, however, considered alienation a juridic act that is essentially different from administration,[11] to be governed by different norms. This distinction appears not to have been universally assimilated as

---

[3] *DH* 13 (emphasis added).
[4] *DH* 7.
[5] The council understood the essential elements of public order to be justice, peace, and public morality. *DH* 7.
[6] *DH* 4.
[7] See cc. 1284, §2, 2°, 3°; 1286, 1°; 1299, §2.
[8] See cc. 1268, 1290.

[9] The original draft omitted the claim of independence from civil authority as polemical and needlessly reminiscent of past Church-State conflicts. The 1980 draft restored the claim in deference to those who feared that the omission might give rise to unforeseen doctrinal interpretations. *Comm* 5 (1973) 94; 12 (1980) 396.
[10] *CCEO* 1007.
[11] *Comm* 12 (1980) 396.

yet, leading to considerable confusion and not a few canonical errors.[12]

Purposes of Church Ownership

§2. The proper purposes are principally: to order divine worship, to care for the decent support of the clergy and other ministers, and to exercise works of the sacred apostolate and of charity, especially toward the needy.

Since the time of Gratian,[13] the purposes given in this paragraph as justifications for the Church's ownership of material goods had been traditional. The 1917 code, however, after listing divine worship and support of clerical and other ministers, substituted the vague "other proper purposes" for the traditionally specific reference to charity.[14] The Second Vatican Council restored the traditional formulation,[15] and canon 1254, §2 repeats the conciliar language virtually verbatim.

The restoration is significant. Omission of specific mention of charity as one of the principal purposes for the acquisition of material goods was instrumental in the development among some church administrators of an excessive possessiveness. The revised code seeks to reverse that unfortunate trend, in service to the conciliar teaching that "the spirit of poverty and of charity are the glory and authentication of the Church of Christ."[16]

Authors have differed as to whether or not the listing of the purposes in canon 1254, §2 is taxative. Insertion of the word "principally" indicates, for some, the existence of other purposes,[17] while others suggest that the insertion was made solely because the paragraph speaks generally of the purposes of the Church, not just of the ownership

of temporal goods by the Church, and that the purposes of church ownership are, in fact, taxatively stated.[18] In any event, in light of the conciliar definition of the apostolate as all activity of the Church directed to bringing the world to Christ,[19] it would be difficult to conceive of any ecclesial purpose not included in "works of the sacred apostolate."

The question has been raised as to whether or not the purposes are listed in order of priority.[20] A negative answer would seem dictated by the different ordering of the same purposes in canon 222, §1 and in the parallel canon in the Code of Canons of the Eastern Churches.[21] While circumstances may dictate that one or another purpose be given priority at a given time, church administrators need to be vigilant that none of the purposes becomes so dominant as to preclude fulfillment of the others. In particular, it should not be forgotten that one of the principal purposes for the acquisition of material possessions by the Church is to use them for, or give them to, the poor and needy.

Capacity for Ownership

Canon 1255 — The universal Church and the Apostolic See, the particular churches, as well as any other juridic person, public or private, are subjects capable of acquiring, retaining, administering, and alienating temporal goods according to the norm of law.

This canon is an immediate exercise of the independence asserted in the preceding canon; it affirms the capacity for ownership of temporal goods not only in the universal Church and Apostolic See, but also in particular churches and other

---

[12] See commentary on cc. 1277, 1291, 1295.

[13] See *Decretum,* C. 12 q. 1 c. 23 (Friedberg I, 684–685).

[14] *CIC* 1496.

[15] *PO* 17.

[16] *GS* 88. See also cc. 640, 1285.

[17] V. De Paolis, *De Bonis Ecclesiae Temporalibus: Adnotationes in Codicem: Liber V* (Rome: Gregorian University, 1986) 29; F. Morrisey, "Acquiring Temporal Goods for the Church's Mission," *J* 56 (1996) 591.

[18] A. Maida and N. Cafardi, *Church Property, Church Finances, and Church-Related Corporations: A Canon Law Handbook* (St. Louis: Catholic Health Association, 1984) 10.

[19] *AA* 2.

[20] G. Roche, "The Poor and Temporal Goods in Book V of the Code," *J* 55 (1995) 316.

[21] *CCEO* 1007.

juridic persons of the Church's own creation. No intervention of civil authority is necessary; ecclesiastical authority is considered fully competent to confer capacity for ownership upon ecclesiastical entities and other church-related institutions.

Like the claim to independence itself, however, the conferral of proprietary capacity is minimally enforceable in contemporary society in the absence of a concordat or similar agreement between ecclesiastical and civil authorities. No such agreement exists in many nations, including the United States. Consequently, it is necessary in such nations to seek civil-law recognition, with accompanying civil-law capacity for the ownership of temporal goods, through incorporation or some other civil-law structuring of ecclesiastical entities such as dioceses and parishes and of other church-related institutions. Notwithstanding the Church's claim to independence, church authorities are exhorted to safeguard the ownership of ecclesiastical goods through civilly valid methods (c. 1284, §2, 2°). Once civil-law status has been acquired, the entity then has two sovereigns, canonical and civil, and is subject to the provisions of two legal systems. Church administrators are obliged by the law of the Church to comply with the provisions of both canon and civil law (c. 1284, §2, 3°).

The reference to particular churches includes dioceses, apostolic vicariates and prefectures, stably erected apostolic administrations, territorial prelatures and abbacies, and personal prelatures (cc. 368–373). The reference to juridic persons is to artificial persons, distinct from natural persons, created by competent ecclesiastical authority either by law or by decree, for an apostolic purpose, with the capacity for continuous existence and with rights and obligations conferred by canon law, to which they are wholly accountable (see cc. 113–123). In addition to particular churches, juridic persons include parishes, religious institutes and their provinces and houses, societies of apostolic life, secular institutes, seminaries, episcopal conferences, and, if so erected by decree of competent authority, church-related colleges, universities, hospitals, and other health-care and charitable institutions. Juridic persons whose personality is conferred upon them by law (e.g., dioceses, parishes, religious institutes) are *public* juridic persons, and act "in the name of the Church"; *private* juridic persons receive their personality only by decree of competent authority, and act only in their own name (see c. 116). Where not conferred by law, public juridic personality, like private juridic personality, may be conferred by decree. Thus, for example, a university or hospital could be either a public or private juridic person depending upon the decree which conferred the personality (see commentary on c. 116).

The term "Apostolic See" in this canon is used in the broad sense to include the various dicasteries of the Roman Curia (see c. 361). The term "universal Church" refers, anomalously, only to the Latin church (see c. 1).

Canon 1255 is not a taxative listing of all subjects capable of owning temporal goods in service to the mission of the Church. Individuals, and associations of natural persons as co-owners, are also recognized as capable of such ownership (see, e.g., cc. 310, 1269). A considerable amount of property used in the life and work of the Church is owned by individuals, from crucifixes and bibles in private homes and vestments and chalices used by priests in liturgical celebrations, to automobiles and countless other privately owned temporal goods used by individual members of the faithful in a myriad of charitable works. The purpose of canon 1255 is simply to affirm proprietary capacity in nonnatural ecclesial entities;[22] the capacity of natural persons, individually or in association, is presumed.

Ownership

Canon 1256 — Under the supreme authority of the Roman Pontiff, ownership of goods belongs to that juridic person which has acquired them legitimately.

---

[22] The law allows the possibility of a religious institute excluding or restricting, by the terms of its constitution, the capacity to own temporal goods, but not its juridic personality (c. 634, §1).

Whereas the preceding canon affirms the capacity of juridic persons to own temporal goods, this canon asserts the simple truth that actual ownership resides in the juridic person which has legitimately acquired the goods. Thus, property legitimately acquired by a parish—which, by law, is a juridic person (c. 515, §3)—is owned by the parish, not by the diocese, which is a distinct juridic person (c. 373). Property legitimately acquired by a religious province belongs to the province, not to the religious institute; province and institute are distinct juridic persons (c. 634, §1).

Notwithstanding its simplicity and seemingly obvious truth, canon 1256 gives rise to a number of Church-State conflicts as well as internal ecclesial disputes between diocesan bishops and pastors or other administrators of church property. The problems arise when the civil-law structure of a diocese does not mirror, or is otherwise incompatible with, the canonical structure, resulting in divergent views of the ownership of church-related property and of the appropriate persons to administer and alienate such property. A prime illustration exists in those dioceses in the United States where the diocese is civilly structured as a corporation sole. In such a diocese all, or nearly all, church-related assets are civilly owned by a single corporation whose sole member is the diocesan bishop. While such a structure is considered desirable by some because of the high degree of centralized control it affords, and because of its capacity to offer ample collateral as security for large construction and other loans, the corporation sole is viewed by others as highly undesirable from the viewpoint of liability, exposing as it does all parochial and other church-related assets within a diocese to satisfy creditors' claims against any individual parish or institution, and because centralized ownership and control of all church property within a diocese is contrary to the law of the Church.

Early in the twentieth century, the Holy See expressed to American bishops its disapproval of the corporation sole as a method of holding title to church property:

Among the methods which are now in use in the United States for holding and administering church property, the one known as *Parish Corporation* is preferable to the others, but with the conditions and safeguards which are now in use in the State of New York. The Bishops therefore should immediately take steps to introduce this method for the handling of property in their dioceses, if the civil law allows it. If the civil law does not allow it, they should exert their influence with the civil authorities that it may be made legal as soon as possible. Only in those places where the civil law does not recognize *Parish Corporations,* and until such recognition is obtained, the method commonly called *Corporation sole* is allowed, but with the understanding that in the administration of ecclesiastical property the Bishop is to act with the advice, and in more important matters with the consent, of those who have an interest in the premises and of the diocesan consultors, this being a conscientious obligation for the Bishop in person.[23]

Although economic conditions have changed since that reply was issued, the law of the Church regarding ownership of each juridic person's property has not. In fact, liability considerations in contemporary American society, and the enhanced emphasis on subsidiarity in the 1983 code, argue strongly for the continued inappropriateness of the corporation-sole method of holding civil title to church-related property.[24] Where such a method remains in use, diocesan bishops and their finance officers and councils should make every effort to see that the laws of the Church governing the acquisition, retention, administration, and alienation of temporal goods are faithfully fulfilled.

[23] SCConc, July 29, 1911, *CLD* 2 (1956) 444–445.

[24] A contrary opinion, arguing the merits of the corporation sole, is presented in R. Kealy, "Methods of Diocesan Incorporation," *CLSAP* (1986) 163–177.

The term "legitimately" in canon 1256 refers to valid acquisition of ownership, not to licit acquisition. As long as the essentials of valid acquisition have been fulfilled, ownership accrues to the juridic person. Failure to fulfill a requirement for liceity (e.g., obtaining permission of the ordinary for a public juridic person to accept a gift with conditions attached—see c. 1267, §2) would render an acquisition of property illicit, but not illegitimate for purposes of canon 1256.

Reference to the authority of the Roman Pontiff is simply a reference to the teaching and governing authority of the Pontiff in regard to the ownership and use of property dedicated to one or another of the Church's purposes. It is not a suggestion of ownership by the Roman Pontiff.[25] Like canon 1255, however, canon 1256 is not taxative. Its purpose is to affirm ownership in juridic persons which have legitimately acquired temporal goods; ownership in natural persons, individually or in association, is presumed.

Canonical writing in English-speaking countries often points to the more complex, sophisticated understanding of ownership in the common-law system compared with what is thought to be a more simplistic notion conveyed by the Roman-law term *dominium* which is translated as "ownership" in canon 1256 and elsewhere in the code. Whereas common law acknowledges many forms of split or divided ownership (e.g., legal v. equitable ownership, various estates in land, and several forms of concurrent ownership), Roman-law *dominium* is said to have been undivided and absolute, much like common law's fee-simple ownership. The implication seems to be that use of the word *dominium* in the code limits the scope of the canons in which the word is used to instances of full, undivided ownership, and does not allow the application of such canons to contemporary forms of partial or divided ownership. Such a view is untenable for a number of reasons, principally because later Roman law used *dominium* interchangeably with *proprietas* (as

does the code, which uses *dominium* in c. 1256 and *proprietas* in c. 1284, §2, 2°) which, less technical and broader in scope than classical *dominium*, embraced not only full ownership but several inferior modes of limited or partial ownership as well.[26] Moreover, virtually all ownership, partial or full, is acquired by juridic persons in the Church either by gift or contract, with the result that either the intention of the donor, which the code demands must be fulfilled (c. 1300), or the local civil law of contracts, which the code canonizes (c. 1290), determines the extent of ownership conveyed. *Dominium* in the code, then, is not confined to its meaning in classical Roman law, but refers to all forms of ownership, divided or undivided, recognized in contemporary society.

Ecclesiastical Goods

Canon 1257 — §1. All temporal goods which belong to the universal Church, the Apostolic See, or other public juridic persons in the Church are ecclesiastical goods and are governed by the following canons and their own statutes.

§2. The temporal goods of a private juridic person are governed by its own statutes but not by these canons unless other provision is expressly made.

This is a terminological canon giving a technical meaning to the expression "ecclesiastical goods" (*bona ecclesiastica*) as the temporal goods of a *public* juridic person, and subjecting such goods to all of the disciplinary norms of Book V in addition to the provisions of the statutes which govern the particular public juridic person to which the goods belong. The temporal goods of *private*

---

[25] *Comm* 12 (1980) 398.

[26] J.-P. Schouppe, *Elementi di Diritto Patrimoniale Canonico* (Milan: Giuffrè, 1997) 20, n. 28; F. Schulz, *Classical Roman Law* (Oxford: Oxford University, 1961) 338–344; W. Buckland, *A Text-Book of Roman Law from Augustus to Justinian* (Cambridge: Cambridge University, 1966) 186–194.

juridic persons are not ecclesiastical goods and, though governed by the statutes of the private juridic person to which they belong, are not governed by the norms of Book V except where expressly provided otherwise. Canons providing otherwise include such canons as 1263; 1265, §1; 1267, §1; and 1269.

Distinguishing the property of private juridic persons from that of public juridic persons, with the latter subject to a greater number of disciplinary norms, is consistent with the greater autonomy which characterizes a private juridic person (see commentary on c. 116), and may often be an influential factor in the choice of canonical status for a church-related charitable institution, particularly in the health-care field where fulfillment of the detailed norms which govern the administration and alienation of ecclesiastical goods may be unduly burdensome and, at times, obstructive of efficient fiscal management.

Meaning of "Church"

Canon 1258 — In the following canons, the term Church signifies not only the universal Church or the Apostolic See but also any public juridic person in the Church unless it is otherwise apparent from the context or the nature of the matter.

This is another terminological canon, according a restrictive and somewhat anomalous signification to the word "church" as used in the remaining canons of Book V. Unless otherwise apparent from the context or nature of the matter, the term "church" throughout the remainder of Book V signifies not only the universal Church but also the Apostolic See and any *public* juridic person within the ecclesial community. It does not include private juridic persons, despite their orientation to works of the apostolate (see c. 114, §§1, 2), nor private associations of the faithful, despite their similar orientation (see cc. 298, 299).

The curious terminology derives from a post-Tridentine inclination to identify the Church with the hierarchy, an inclination found in the 1917

code[27] but scarcely reconcilable with the people-of-God ecclesiology of the Second Vatican Council. According to canon 1258, "church" property is not simply any property dedicated to or used in the work of the Church, but only that which belongs to juridic persons which are closely governed by ecclesiastical authority (the characteristic that differentiates a public from a private juridic person[28]). Failure to advert to this technical meaning of "church" when used in regard to temporal goods in Book V can lead to considerable confusion and to not a few canonical errors.

TITLE I
THE ACQUISITION OF GOODS
[cc. 1259–1272]

This title begins with general principles regarding acquisition of material possessions needed for the Church's mission (cc. 1259–1261). Succeeding canons contain regulatory norms for unsolicited (c. 1267) and specific types of solicited contributions, namely, fund-raising in general (c. 1262), taxation (c. 1263), prescribed fees and offerings (c. 1264), begging for alms (c. 1265), and collections taken up in church (c. 1266). There follow three canons regarding prescription as a means of acquiring temporal goods (cc. 1268–1270), one canon concerning acquisition of goods for the support of the Holy See (c. 1271), and a final canon regarding the regulation and gradual suppression of benefices (c. 1272). A comprehensive knowledge of the provisions of the code governing the acquisition of goods requires knowledge also of canons 121–123, which provide for acquisition on the occasions of the consolidation (c. 121), division (c. 122), or extinction (c. 123) of public juridic persons in the Church.

---

[27] See, e.g., *CIC* 684–686 where establishment of associations of the faithful by hierarchical authority was called establishment "by the Church" (*ab Ecclesia*).

[28] See commentary on c. 116.

Right of Public Juridic Persons to Acquire

Canon 1259 — The Church can acquire temporal goods by every just means of natural or positive law permitted to others.

The right to acquire material possessions, affirmed generally in canon 1254, §1, is here specifically affirmed as belonging, pursuant to the norm of canon 1258, to each public juridic person within the Church. Further, the canon asserts the right to acquire by every just means of natural or positive law.

While the laudable intent of the canon is to claim for the Church's public juridic persons equality with similarly situated secular entities in the use of just means for the acquisition of goods, the references to natural and positive law are problematical. It may be doubted that the natural law contains much of anything regarding specific modes of acquisition (other than to prohibit theft and fraud), or can appropriately be said to apply to nonnatural entities such as juridic persons. Positive law, in keeping with canonical tradition, refers here to civil as well as canon law;[29] but civil laws frequently contain regulatory provisions that treat churches and church-related institutions differently from others as regards inheritances, accumulation of assets, and some forms of fund-raising. These differences in treatment need not be due to invidious discrimination but may be, and often are, motivated by considerations of sound public policy (e.g., maintaining, in the light of liberal tax exemptions for religious and charitable organizations, an adequate and fair tax base for the citizenry). Accordingly, canon 1259 would seem best understood as claiming for public juridic persons in the Church freedom from unjust restriction in the acquisition of temporal goods, a claim less problematically stated

in the Code of Canons of the Eastern Churches, which omits all reference to natural or positive law.[30]

Support from the Faithful

Canon 1260 — The Church has an innate right to require from the Christian faithful those things which are necessary for the purposes proper to it.

This canon asserts a right of the Church to demand from the Christian faithful what is necessary for fulfillment of ecclesial purposes. The text and context make clear that here "church" cannot be understood in the technical sense of public juridic person (see c. 1258), for the right is said to be "innate." Nothing is innate to a juridic person; as an artificial construct of a legal system, a juridic person cannot be said to have "innate" rights. Nor can "church" in this canon refer generally to the Christian faithful, since the canon asserts a right of the Church to make demands of the Christian faithful, clearly envisioning the Christian faithful as other than the Church, as the terms are used in this canon.

The word "church" appears to be used in canon 1260 to denote ecclesiastical authority, as the word frequently was used in the 1917 code (see commentary on c. 1258), despite the ecclesiological incongruity of such usage today. What appears to be asserted in canon 1260 is the right of ecclesiastical authority to require from the Christian faithful necessary financial support for ecclesial purposes. Confirmation of such an interpretation would seem to exist in the parallel canon in the Code of Canons of the Eastern Churches:

> The competent authority has the right to require from the Christian faithful whatever is necessary to attain the ends proper to the Church.[31]

[29] F. Cappello, *Summa Iuris Canonici,* 5th ed. (Rome: Gregorian University, 1951) 2:550; A. Vermeersch and J. Creusen, *Epitome Iuris Canonici,* 6th ed. (Rome: H. Dessain, 1940) 2:570.

[30] *CCEO* 1010.
[31] *CCEO* 1011.

In light of the obligation of the Christian faithful, stated in canon 222, §1, to assist with the needs of the Church, and the obligation of diocesan bishops, stated in canon 1261, §2, to urge fulfillment of the faithful's obligation, the affirmation of canon 1260 may seem to be superfluous. The focus of canons 222 and 1261, however, is on the internal raising of funds within the Church; the focus of canon 1260 appears to be on the right to raise funds vis-à-vis any attempts by civil authority to deny or restrict such a right, a focus that was explicit in the parallel canon in the 1917 code.[32] The import of canon 1260 is to affirm in members of the hierarchy an innate right (indigenous to their divinely instituted office) to require necessary support from the faithful vis-à-vis any attempts, especially by civil authority, to deny, interfere with, or unreasonably restrict such a right.

Canon 1261 — §1. The Christian faithful are free to give temporal goods for the benefit of the Church.

§2. The diocesan bishop is bound to admonish the faithful of the obligation mentioned in can. 222, §1 and in an appropriate manner to urge its observance.

Having stated as general principles the right of public juridic persons to acquire temporal goods by all just means (c. 1259) and the right of ecclesiastical authority to demand needed support from the faithful (c. 1260), canon 1261 sets forth two additional correlative principles: the right of the faithful freely to contribute, and the responsibility of diocesan bishops to urge the faithful to fulfill their obligation to meet the temporal needs of the Church.

Affirmation of the right freely to contribute appears to be directed at those, within or outside the Church, who would seek to deny or discourage such an exercise of religious liberty. Detailing the bishop's duty to admonish the faithful and urge fulfillment of their obligation of material support is a specification of the general responsibility of

diocesan bishops to urge participation and assistance of the faithful in the various works of the apostolate (c. 394, §2), and to promote the discipline of the Church by urging the observance of all ecclesiastical laws (c. 392, §1). Fulfillment of the faithful's obligation is to be urged by the bishop "in an appropriate manner." Appropriateness of manner would include full, honest disclosure of needs and available resources, a preference for persuasion rather than coercion, and the offering of truly Christian motivation.

Fund-Raising in General

Canon 1262 — The faithful are to give support to the Church by responding to appeals and according to the norms issued by the conference of bishops.

The preceding three canons set forth general principles regarding the acquisition of material possessions; canon 1262 is the first of several canons dealing with specific modes of acquisition. Primacy[33] is given to the solicitation of funds through appeals to which the faithful freely respond by contributing in the manner and amount of their own choice.[34]

Since such appeals can take many different forms and give rise to widely differing problems in different cultures, the canon wisely invokes the principle of subsidiarity in calling upon episcopal conferences to issue appropriate regulatory norms. In accord with canon 1258, the term "Church" in this canon refers to public juridic persons.

---

[32] CIC 1496.

[33] During the revision process, what is now c. 1262 had earlier followed what is now c. 1263 on taxation. The positions of the two canons were reversed precisely to avoid the impression that taxation, rather than free-will responses to fund-raising appeals, is the preferred mode of acquisition. *Rel* 282.

[34] The earlier CLSA translation, which rendered *subventiones rogatas* as "collections," led to a truncated understanding of this canon as having to do with offerings taken up in churches. Collections in churches are the subject matter of c. 1266.

In 1977, the National Conference of Catholic Bishops (NCCB) issued guidelines for fund-raising by dioceses, diocesan agencies, and religious institutes in the United States.[35] The guidelines were developed in conjunction with the Leadership Conference of Women Religious and the Conference of Major Superiors of Men. Preceding the 1983 code by six years, the guidelines appear to have anticipated the intent of canon 1262 for regional norms to govern fund-raising in general by public juridic persons.

Under four topics dealing with motivation, official authorization, accountability, and technique, the NCCB guidelines offer practical wisdom in a laudably theological context. Emphasis is placed on the need to offer prospective donors theologically sound Christian motivation for financially participating in apostolic works. This is a needed antidote to secular motivations which often seem to infect contemporary religious fund-raising, such as the satisfaction of self-interest through lotteries, bingos, raffles, tax deductions, and guilt-assuaging expressions of gratitude for receipt through the mail of unsought and unwanted religious trinkets.

The guidelines draw attention to the inappropriateness among Christians of efforts to fund undefined future needs or total financial security as contrary to the gospel mandate to live by faith and trust in God, and warn against the incongruity of excessive fund-raising costs, especially when based on a percentage of the contributions which have been given for apostolic purposes. Protection of the Church's integrity is given as the rationale for requiring antecedent authorization and ongoing supervision by appropriate ecclesiastical authority of the scope and method of each fund-raising endeavor.

Noting that religious fund-raising gives rise to a sacred relationship of trust, the NCCB guidelines offer a challenging view of the extent of a fund-raiser's accountability:

Fund-raising reports should be prepared in scope and design to meet the particular concerns of those to whom reports are due: namely, the governing body and membership of the fund-raising organization itself, religious authorities who approved and must monitor the fund-raising effort, donors to the particular organization and the giving public at large, and those who are beneficiaries of the funds given.[36]

It is regrettable that in seeking to fulfill its responsibility under canon 1262 to issue norms for fund-raising in general, the NCCB did not reaffirm the insights contained in its 1977 guidelines. The 1984 implementation of canon 1262 by the NCCB reads simply:

> The National Conference of Catholic Bishops authorizes diocesan bishops to establish norms for Church support by the faithful for their own dioceses.[37]

Notwithstanding the fact that the NCCB did not reissue as norms under canon 1262 the guidelines of 1977, there is nothing to prevent diocesan bishops from looking to those guidelines for inspiration in drafting norms for their own dioceses.

Canon 1262 and the NCCB guidelines are both confined to fund-raising by and for public juridic persons. This leaves fund-raising by private juridic persons and by church-related institutions which do not have juridic personality without regulatory norms or even guiding principles. Some solicitation of funds on behalf of such institutions may qualify as begging for alms, and so be regulated by the provisions of canon 1265, or as collections taken up in churches, and so be subject to canon 1266. For the rest, it would seem regrettable that in a matter such as this a lacuna exists in the law, one remedy for which would be an analogical application of the norms issued pursuant to canon 1262 (see c. 19).

---

[35] NCCB, *Principles and Guidelines for Fund Raising in the United States by Arch/Dioceses, Arch/Diocesan Agencies and Religious Institutes* (Washington, D.C.: USCC, 1977); *CLD* 8 (1978) 415–421.

[36] *CLD* 8 (1978) 418.
[37] NCCB-*CompNm* 20.

Taxation

Canon 1263 — After the diocesan bishop has heard the finance council and the presbyteral council, he has the right to impose a moderate tax for the needs of the diocese upon public juridic persons subject to his governance; this tax is to be proportionate to their income. He is permitted only to impose an extraordinary and moderate exaction upon other physical and juridic persons in case of grave necessity and under the same conditions, without prejudice to particular laws and customs which attribute greater rights to him.

Having accorded primacy to free-will offerings given in response to fund-raising appeals, the code turns next to the matter of ecclesiastical taxation. Canon 1263 is the result of much debate and several revisions during the drafting process in an effort to meet the desires both of those who felt the need to expand the power of diocesan bishops beyond the severely restricted power to tax which had been granted to them in the 1917 code,[38] and those who opposed giving the bishop too much power to burden by diocesan taxes the finances of parishes and others doing the work of the Church in the diocese. The debated issues resolved by the final text of canon 1263 included: who can impose a tax (any local ordinary or only the diocesan bishop), who can be taxed, what can be taxed, to what extent, for what reasons, and only after what, if any, consultation.[39]

The canon has two parts. The first confers on the diocesan bishop the right, after consultation, to impose, for the needs of the diocese, a moderate tax proportionate to income upon public juridic persons subject to his governance. Unlike the second part, the first part makes no mention of grave necessity nor does it designate the tax as "extraordinary." This makes clear that the tax referred to in the first part could be a regularly recurring means of raising funds to meet regularly recurring diocesan needs, and, in that sense, may be considered to be an "ordinary" tax in contradistinction to the extraordinary tax referred to in the second part of the canon. Reluctance to use the word "ordinary" in the canon's first part appears to have been in deference to the decision to give primacy to voluntary responses to fund-raising appeals as the preferred mode of acquisition (see footnote 33); explicit reference to an "ordinary" tax could be misunderstood as an indication that taxation is to be an expected or preferred mode of acquiring needed funds.

The required consultation is to involve two bodies, the diocesan finance council and the entire presbyteral council, not just the college of consultors as is often the case (see, e.g., cc. 1277, 1292). Consultation should include such matters as the genuineness and relative importance of the diocesan need for which the tax is to be imposed, the appropriate meaning in the particular circumstances of "moderate" (a relative term but clearly indicative of limits), and the criteria for determining what qualifies as taxable income. Nothing would appear to preclude the tax from being a graduated income tax, but, in such a case, consultation should also include the various levels and percentages to be used.

If a tax is to be annual, or otherwise regularly recurring, a single consultation at the time of original imposition would appear insufficient to fulfill the intent of the consultation requirement. Consultation should be repeated prior to each renewal of the tax. While the bishop is not obliged to follow the advice he receives from either of the consultative bodies, failure to consult them would invalidate a tax, relieving those upon whom it had been imposed of the obligation to pay it (see c. 127, §1).[40]

---

[38] See *CIC* 1504–1506; D. Frugé, "Taxes in the Proposed Law," *CLSAP* (1982) 274–278.

[39] The legislative history of c. 1263 is amply traced in R. Kealy, *Diocesan Financial Support: Its History and Canonical Status* (Rome: Gregorian University, 1986) 312–330; see also Frugé, 279–287.

[40] The Eastern code, while requiring consultation of only the finance council, stipulates that the eparchial bishop receive the *consent* of the council before imposing a tax. *CCEO* 1012, §1.

Canon 1263 requires consultation of only two ecclesial bodies. When it comes to taxation, however, maximum representation of those who are to bear the burden of taxation is part of the ethos of some cultures. A diocesan bishop in the United States, for example, would be well advised to consult also the diocesan pastoral council, if one exists, the superiors of religious institutes of diocesan right, if such institutes are to be taxed, and representatives of other categories of public juridic persons to be subject to the proposed tax.

The Pontifical Council for the Interpretation of Legislative Texts was asked if, in the first part of the canon, the words "public juridic persons subject to his authority" include external schools of religious institutes of pontifical right; the council replied in the negative.[41] Few, if any, schools of such religious institutes have been established as public juridic persons in their own right; most, therefore, would not be subject to such a tax imposed directly on the schools simply because they are not public juridic persons. Nor could the pontifical religious institute to which such a school belongs be taxed under the first part of canon 1263, because such an institute is not generally subject to the governance of the diocesan bishop and specifically enjoys autonomy regarding the internal management of its schools (c. 806, §1). Similarly, schools which, though established as public juridic persons in their own right, continue to be sponsored and governed by religious institutes of pontifical right, would not, according to the authentic interpretation, be subject to the authority of the diocesan bishop for purposes of a tax imposed in accord with the first part of canon 1263.[42]

The second part of canon 1263 empowers the diocesan bishop to impose an extraordinary tax upon other persons, physical and juridic, in cases of grave necessity and "under the same conditions." It is clear that this extraordinary tax cannot be regularly recurring and cannot be for regularly recurring diocesan needs. It is also clear that in order to be under the same conditions, it must be moderate, proportionate to income, and imposed only after consultation with the diocesan finance council and presbyteral council. Finally, it is clear that it can be imposed on natural (physical) persons, either individually or gathered in associations, and on private juridic persons; all of these qualify as "other physical and juridic persons."

What is considerably less clear is whether or not an extraordinary tax can be imposed on a public juridic person not otherwise subject to the diocesan bishop (e.g., a religious institute of pontifical right). Is the phrase "subject to his governance" in the first part of canon 1263 a "condition" which must also be fulfilled in an extraordinary tax imposed under the second part, or is "subject to his governance" simply part of the description of the persons taxable under the first part of the canon, leaving all other persons, including public juridic persons not subject to the diocesan bishop, taxable in the event of an extraordinary tax?

Arguments can be offered in support of either interpretation[43] and commentators, often without giving their reasons, have reached opposite con-

---

[41] *AAS* 81 (1989) 991.

[42] See L. Wrenn, *Authentic Interpretations on the 1983 Code* (Washington, D.C.: CLSA, 1993) 57–58.

[43] Arguments in favor of limiting extraordinary taxes to persons subject to the governance of the diocesan bishop could point to the fact that imposition of a tax, even extraordinary in nature, on persons not otherwise subject to the legislator is highly unusual. Moreover, during the revision process, the Secretariat at one point intimated that the taxing power of a diocesan bishop would be confined to persons subject to his governance (*Rel* 282). Contrary arguments could point to the fact that the Latin text of c. 1263 uses, in the first part, the word *tributum*, which connotes the classical notion of tribute being paid by subjects, but, in the second part, the canon uses the word *exactionem*, a broader term suggesting a legislative intention to reach beyond those who, strictly speaking, are subjects. Also, canon 264, providing for the support of a diocesan seminary, authorizes the imposition of a tax on juridic persons which have an establishment in the diocese, even if they are not otherwise subject to the diocesan bishop, thereby affording a precedent within the code for a more extensive interpretation of the second part of c. 1263.

clusions.[44] This leads to the practical conclusion that, until such time as an authentic interpretation is given, an attempt by a diocesan bishop to impose an extraordinary tax under canon 1263 on a public juridic person (or any person) not otherwise subject to his governance would be doubtfully valid and, hence, not binding (c. 14).

Although canon 1263 empowers diocesan bishops to impose taxes, it does not oblige them to do so. A diocesan bishop who chooses not to use the coercive instrument of taxation in order to meet the needs of the diocese, but who prefers to rely on free-will offerings in response to fund-raising appeals, is free to do so. Any attempt to assign a mandatory quota to parishes or other entities, however, would transform a fund-raising appeal into a tax, requiring the fulfillment of all the conditions of canon 1263.

Unlike the 1917 code[45] and the Code of Canons of the Eastern Churches,[46] the 1983 code contains no provision prohibiting the imposition of a tax on Mass stipends. Early in the revision process, there was made known the intention to transfer the prohibition on such a tax to a more appropriate place in the code[47] (most likely to the section of canons governing Mass stipends). Accordingly, although the notion that no tax could be imposed on Mass stipends continued to be agreed upon by those drafting canon 1263,[48] no such prohibition was included in the revised canons on temporal goods. Apparently through inadvertence, the prohibition was not inserted into any other part of the code. This leaves Mass stipends technically taxable under the 1983 code, though in light of the

expressed intention simply to relocate, not eliminate, the prohibition, and in light of the Eastern code's retention of the prohibition, a diocesan bishop may well choose to exempt Mass stipends from any tax he may impose.

The final clause in canon 1263 suggests that particular laws and customs could attribute more extensive taxing power to a diocesan bishop. A particular law of such a sort obviously could not originate at the diocesan level; it would have to be supradiocesan in origin, which would require review by the Apostolic See (cc. 446, 455). To acquire the force of law, a custom must be introduced by a community of the faithful with the intention of introducing a law (cc. 23, 25), an unlikely occurrence in the area of taxation. The clause, which was added after submission of the proposed code to the Pope, may have been inserted to accommodate the situation of the Church in some European nations where taxes for the support of churches are collected by civil authorities.[49]

Prescribed Fees and Offerings

Canon 1264 — Unless the law has provided otherwise, it is for a meeting of the bishops of a province:

　1°　to fix the fees for acts of executive power granting a favor or for the execution of rescripts of the Apostolic See, to be approved by the Apostolic See itself;

　2°　to set a limit on the offerings on the occasion of the administration of sacraments and sacramentals.

In keeping with tradition, canon 1264, 1° makes provision for seeking financial assistance on the occasion of the granting of a favor by executive authority in the Church. Such would include dispensations, privileges, and other juridic concessions granted by rescript in response to a request (see c. 59). The concession may originate

---

[44] Canon 1263 is interpreted as limiting extraordinary taxes to persons subject to the governance of the bishop in F. Aznar Gil, *La Administracion de los Bienes Temporales de la Iglesia,* 2nd ed. (Salamanca: University of Salamanca, 1993) 166; and M. López Alarcón, in *Pamplona ComEng,* 781. The contrary opinion is expressed in J.-C. Périsset, *Les Biens Temporels de l'Église* (Paris: Tardy, 1996) 87; and J. Myers, in *CLSA Com,* 865.

[45] *CIC* 1506.

[46] *CCEO* 1012, §1.

[47] *Comm* 5 (1973) 95.

[48] *Comm* 12 (1980) 402.

[49] See V. De Paolis, *I Beni Temporali della Chiesa* (Bologna: Dehoniane, 1995) 111–112; K. Walf, "The Church Tax as a Means of Subsistence," *Con* 117 (1979) 20–27.

at the diocesan level or may consist of executing a rescript issued by the Holy See or extending a rescript previously issued by the Holy See (see c. 72). The purpose of assessing fees on such occasions is to provide a specific source of support for the administrative expenses of chanceries and other offices engaged in executive governance.

The canon directs that the amount to be sought on such occasions is to be determined by the bishops of the province. The determination need not be made in a formal provincial council, nor are auxiliary bishops excluded from a decision-making role. The syntax of the Latin text makes clear that approval of the Apostolic See must be obtained for all such fees, not just those for execution of rescripts of the Apostolic See itself.

The determination of fees for marriage dispensations, which received separate treatment under the 1917 code[50] but which receives no mention in the present code, is now subject to the prescriptions of c. 1264, 1°. Fees for expenses incurred by tribunals in their exercise of judicial governance, however, are regulated in an entirely different manner (see c. 1649).

Also, in keeping with long-standing tradition but arguably at variance with contemporary ecclesial thought, canon 1264, 2° makes provision for seeking financial assistance on the occasion of the administration of sacraments and sacramentals. The 1971 Synod of Bishops had stated:

> It seems greatly to be desired that the Christian people be gradually instructed in such a way that priests' incomes may be separated from the acts of their ministry, especially sacramental ones.[51]

The fact that in many regions of the world there as yet appears to be no other means of supporting priests and other clergy precluded the abolition of what had become known as "stole fees," but it

was agreed that the term "fees" (*taxas*) should be replaced by the term "offerings" (*oblationes*) when referring to financial support given on the occasion of the administration of sacraments and sacramentals.[52] It was also agreed that the verb *praefinire* ("to fix"), used to describe the determination of fees for rescripts in c. 1264, 1°, should be replaced by the verb *definire* ("to set a limit on") when referring in canon 1264, 2° to offerings on the occasion of administering sacraments and sacramentals.[53] The import of number two is that provincial bishops are to set a limit above which it is not permissible to request an offering, though voluntary offerings in excess of the limit may be accepted.[54]

Determination of fees and offerings at the provincial level was retained notwithstanding the new structure of the episcopal conference because of varying economic conditions within many episcopal conferences. A suggestion that determination be made by each ordinary was rejected on the ground that fees and defined offerings should be uniform, at least within a province, as had been the discipline under the 1917 code.[55]

Offerings on the occasion of funerals, which received separate treatment under the 1917 code,[56] are explicitly said to be governed by canon 1264, taking care that the needy are not, because of their poverty, deprived of appropriate funeral rites (c. 1181). A similar provision for the needy is made

---

[50] *CIC* 1056.

[51] 1971 Synod of Bishops, *The Ministerial Priesthood* (Washington, D.C.: USCC, 1972) 29; *Comm* 5 (1973) 95.

[52] *Comm* 12 (1980) 403.

[53] Ibid.

[54] The recommendation of the 1971 synod is reflected in cc. 531 and 551 which provide that offerings given on occasions of pastoral ministry are to be put into the parochial account unless, in regard to voluntary offerings (those in excess of the defined amount for the province), the contrary intention of the donor is clear.

[55] *CIC* 1507; *Rel* 283. Canon 952 of the present code also commits to the bishops of a province the determination of what offering may be sought on the occasion of the celebration and application of a Mass for a particular intention. A different method of determining the amount of fees and stipends is prescribed for the Eastern churches. *CCEO* 1013.

[56] *CIC* 1234.

in regard to offerings on the occasion of reception of the sacraments (c. 848).

In its opening words, canon 1264 allows for the possibility that different provisions might exist in other laws (as was the case, noted above, in regard to marriage dispensations and funerals in the 1917 code). No such other law exists in the 1983 code, but a future universal law (e.g., in regard to the execution of some papal rescripts) or particular law of an episcopal conference could contain provisions different from those of canon 1264. Such a law would take precedence. It would appear to be invalid as a violation of canon 1264, however, for an individual diocesan bishop or for a province of bishops to attempt to enact contrary legislation.

Begging for Alms

Canon 1265 — §1. Without prejudice to the right of religious mendicants, any private person, whether physical or juridic, is forbidden to beg for alms for any pious or ecclesiastical institute or purpose without the written permission of that person's own ordinary and of the local ordinary.

§2. The conference of bishops can establish norms for begging for alms which all must observe, including those who by their foundation are called and are mendicants.

The phenomenon of face-to-face begging for alms existed long before the advent of Christianity[57] and continues in modern society. The problems to which it gives rise are of concern to civil society and, when the object of the begging is alleged to be religious, to ecclesial society as well.

Among the ills the law of the Church seeks to minimize in this area are misrepresentation, fraud, exploitation of generosity, indecorous sales-pitches, and interference with the effectiveness of fund-

raising by dioceses, parishes, religious institutes, and other public juridic persons. To guard against these and other ills associated with begging, canon 1265 requires all private persons, natural or juridic, intending to beg for alms for any religious purpose, to obtain written permissions from their own ordinary (diocesan or religious) and the ordinary of place where the begging is to take place. That the permissions be in writing is essential to verification of the authorization should it be challenged.

Although the canon makes no distinction between oral and written forms of begging, the majority of commentators on the parallel canon in the 1917 code concluded that only oral, person-to-person begging (as in door-to-door solicitation) was within the intended scope of the law.[58] It has generally been thought that written appeals entail far less imposition and coercion and can far more easily be dismissed, and hence do not lead to the kind of abuses the law is seeking to guard against; also, as a practical matter, it is virtually impossible to obtain written permission from the ordinary of every place into which a written appeal may go.

The begging that is restricted is that which is intended to reach, not just a few friends or acquaintances, but many persons approached individually or in groups of two or three. Solicitation of funds from large groups or from the faithful or public at large is subject to the norms for fund-raising in general (see c. 1262) or for collections to be taken up in churches (see c. 1266). So, too, solicitation of funds not by private persons but by official representatives of public juridic persons (such as diocesan bishops and pastors) is subject to the norms for fund-raising in general and for collections in churches.

The opening words of canon 1265, §1, stating that the provisions which are to follow are with-

---

[57] The expression *stipem cogere,* a technical expression derived from Roman law, signifies face-to-face begging. Cappello, 2:553. The earlier CLSA translation, mistaking the expression for fund-raising in general, gave c. 1265 an excessively broad scope.

[58] Vermeersch-Creusen, 2:573; G. Vromant, *De Bonis Ecclesiae Temporalibus,* 3rd ed. (Paris: Desclée de Brouwer, 1953) 89–90; T. Bouscaren, A. Ellis, and F. Korth, *Canon Law: A Text and Commentary,* 4th rev. ed. (Milwaukee: Bruce, 1966) 813.

out prejudice to the right of religious mendicants, do not imply that religious mendicants can beg for alms whenever and wherever they wish without the required permissions; the words are intended simply to remind relevant ordinaries that begging for alms is indigenous to the life of a true mendicant and that, therefore, caution must be exercised when considering denying or restricting permission to mendicants, in order to assure that their right to beg is adequately being honored.[59] Since begging for alms is essential to the life of true mendicants, the consent of a diocesan bishop to erect a religious house of a mendicant institute within the diocese brings with it permission to beg for alms in that diocese;[60] in order for members of the house to beg in another diocese, however, permission of the relevant local ordinary is required.

Canon 1265, §2 authorizes episcopal conferences to supplement the provisions of paragraph one by additional norms which, like the provisions of paragraph one, must be observed by all, including true mendicants. The National Conference of Catholic Bishops in the United States has not, to date, issued any such norms.

Collections

Canon 1266 — In all churches and oratories which are, in fact, habitually open to the Christian faithful, including those which belong to religious institutes, the local ordinary can order the taking up of a special collection for specific parochial, diocesan, national, or universal projects; this collection must be diligently sent afterwards to the diocesan curia.

In the absence of a controlling norm in the 1917 code, commentators were generally of the opinion that, without an apostolic indult, a local ordinary could not order exempt religious to take up a collection in their churches unless they were also parish churches.[61] Canon 1266 expands the power of local ordinaries in this regard.[62]

Local ordinaries can order the taking up of special collections in all churches and oratories, even those belonging to religious institutes, if the churches or oratories are, as a matter of fact, open to the faithful at large on a regular basis. Churches and oratories differ in that all the faithful have a right of access to a church for divine worship, but no such right in regard to an oratory which, by definition, exists for the benefit of a particular community (compare cc. 1214 and 1223). Canon 1266 rests the right to order a collection on the *de facto,* rather than *de iure,* use of an oratory.

The collection must be for a specific, not indeterminate, undertaking, but it need not be diocesan; it can be parochial (e.g., aid to a poor or struggling parish) or national or international. Nor does the undertaking or project which is the object of a mandated collection have to rise to the level of a need or necessity, as in the case of a tax (see c. 1263), suggesting that the motivating causes for collections can be less urgent than those for taxes. The legislative history of canon 1266, however, indicates that mandated collections are envisioned as extraordinary means of raising funds and, hence, ought not to be employed immoderately.[63]

Among the several differences between ordering a collection, which can be done by any local ordinary, and imposing a tax, which can be done only by the diocesan bishop, the most significant is the absence of required consultation when mandating the taking up of a collection. This is no doubt due to the difference in nature between a noncoercive collection, in which no preset amount is designated as due, and a tax, which, of its nature, is coercive. It is arguable, however, that a multiplicity of mandated collections taken up during liturgical celebrations can cumulatively lead to a high level of frustration and disaffection among the faithful

---

[59] See *ES* I, 27.
[60] See c. 611, 1°.

[61] See, e.g., Vermeersch-Creusen, 2:574; Cappello, 2:553.
[62] The canon has its source in *ES* I, 37.
[63] *Comm* 12 (1980) 405.

that could perhaps be avoided by antecedent consultation with appropriately representative bodies. The placing of a mandatory quota upon a collection (e.g., requiring a parish to return a designated amount) transforms a collection into a tax, subjecting it to the consultative and other requirements of canon 1263.

The final clause in canon 1266 requires that the proceeds of a mandated collection be sent diligently (*sedulo*) to the diocesan curia. The import of the adverb is twofold: that the proceeds be sent without delay and in their entirety. Unless contributors have been so informed in advance, no part of the proceeds may be withheld at the parish or any other level; not to turn over the entirety of the collection immediately is to violate the intentions of the donors and, as such withholding becomes known, seriously to compromise the perceived integrity of fund-raising in the Church.

Unsolicited Offerings

Canon 1267 — §1. Unless the contrary is established, offerings given to superiors or administrators of any ecclesiastical juridic person, even a private one, are presumed given to the juridic person itself.

§2. The offerings mentioned in §1 cannot be refused except for a just cause and, in matters of greater importance if it concerns a public juridic person, with the permission of the ordinary; the permission of the same ordinary is required to accept offerings burdened by a modal obligation or condition, without prejudice to the prescript of can. 1295.

§3. Offerings given by the faithful for a certain purpose can be applied only for that same purpose.

While in its opening words the first paragraph of this canon acknowledges the possibility of gifts to superiors or administrators being intended for their personal use, the paragraph reaffirms the traditional presumption that offerings made to such persons are intended for the juridic entity they represent and administer.[64] A contrary intention must be morally certain (*constet*). During the revision process it was suggested that this presumption be altered to accord with what seems to be contemporary practice to the contrary. The suggestion was rejected, and the presumption was explicitly made applicable to private as well as public juridic persons.[65]

The second paragraph contains three provisions. The first, applicable to the administrators of both public and private juridic persons, requires a just cause for the refusal of donations, a requirement entirely consistent with the fiduciary nature of an administrator's responsibilities. Depending upon the property being offered, there can be many just causes for refusal to accept (e.g., funds unethically acquired, property needing massive repairs).

The remaining provisions in canon 1267, §2 apply only to public juridic persons. If it is a matter of greater importance, an administrator of a public juridic person who wishes to decline an offering must have, in addition to a just cause, the permission of the proper ordinary. Definition of "greater importance" in this regard, purposefully left vague in the canon, should be determined in the statutes of the public juridic person (see commentary on c. 117).

The final provision in canon 1267, §2 concerns acceptance by public juridic persons of donations and requires permission of the proper ordinary for acceptance of a gift to which has been attached a modal obligation or condition, as well as fulfillment of the provisions of canon 1295, when relevant. A modal obligation, according to Roman law whence the term is derived, is an obligation undertaken at the time of accepting a gift which is enforceable against the donee but the breach of which does not result in reversion of the gift to the donor. A conditional gift, on the other hand, conditions transfer of ownership upon fulfillment of the condition; breach results in a reversion of ownership to the donor. Canon 1295 applies all

[64] *CIC* 1536, §1.
[65] *Comm* 12 (1980) 405.

the norms which govern restricted alienation of the property of public juridic persons (cc. 1291–1294) not only to alienation but also to transactions which entail risk of harm to the patrimonial condition of the juridic person. It can happen that the burden of a particular condition or modal obligation is such that acceptance of the gift to which it is attached entails risk of serious harm to the financial condition of the donee; in such situations, not only must the provisions of canon 1267, §2 be fulfilled, but also those of canons 1291–1294.

The third paragraph of canon 1267 restates a fundamental canonical principle, expressed in several other canons,[66] that the intentions of donors must be carefully and diligently fulfilled. The presence of such a principle in many civil-law systems owes its origin to centuries-old canonical jurisprudence.

Prescription Applied to Temporal Goods

Canon 1268 — The Church recognizes prescription as a means of acquiring temporal goods and freeing oneself from them, according to the norm of cann. 197–199.

Prescription, in both canon and civil law, is a means of acquiring or losing a right, or of freeing oneself from an obligation, by the passage of time under conditions prescribed by law (see c. 197). Canon 1268 affirms the application of prescription to temporal goods, where it is a means of acquiring or losing the ownership of property or of discharging debts. Though included under the title "The Acquisition of Goods," prescription is of importance in the practical life of the Church not so much as a means of acquisition but as a means of losing church property. Administrators on diocesan, parochial, religious, and other levels need to be alert to the dangers of losing property, through inadvertence, by prescription.

The rationale behind allowing transfer of ownership by prescription includes the concern to prevent issues of ownership from remaining uncertain or confused for long periods of time, the desire to encourage cultivation and care of property without fear of one day losing it to a long-dormant claim of ownership by another, and the demand of justice that legal action to vindicate a claim of ownership be brought within a time-frame when witnesses and relevant documentary evidence may reasonably be expected to be available.

The law of the Church "canonizes" the relevant civil law of prescription by according it the same effects at canon law except where the code provides otherwise (c. 197). Exceptions regarding the quality and duration of good faith (c. 198) and the ineligibility of certain matters for prescription (c. 199) are found in the fundamental canons governing prescription in Book I of the code.[67] Additional exceptions to the application of the civil law of prescription to temporal goods are provided in canons 1269 and 1270.

In the United States, there is considerable diversity in the laws of the fifty states concerning what is generally called "adverse possession" when referring to realty, and "prescription" when referring to personalty. Notwithstanding the diversity in detailed provisions, it is commonly required that possession of the property at issue be sufficiently open or public to arrest the attention of the true owner to the fact that the property is being appropriated by another. Also common is the requirement that the possession be pursuant to a claim that is adverse or hostile to the interests of the true owner; prescription does not operate, for example, in favor of a tenant, guardian, partner, agent, or trustee. It is universally required that the adverse possession be continuous, that is, uninterrupted throughout the statutory period of time.

Civil-law statutes of limitation, though technically not effective of transfers of ownership, have

---

[66] See, e.g., cc. 121; 122; 123; 1284, §2, 3°; 1300; 1303, §2; 1304, §1; 1307, §1; 1310, §2.

[67] Among matters declared in c. 199 not to be subject to prescription are the certain boundaries of ecclesiastical territories and Mass stipends and obligations.

the same practical effect by precluding the bringing of legal action to vindicate one's ownership after expiration of the designated period of time. The code uses the term "prescription" in its broadest sense to include the prohibition of legal actions after expiration of designated time periods (see cc. 1362, 1363, 1492, 1512, 4°), and hence, with exceptions provided in the code, canonizes civil-law statutes of limitation (see commentary on c. 197).

Canon 1269 — If sacred objects are privately owned, private persons can acquire them through prescription, but it is not permitted to employ them for profane uses unless they have lost their dedication or blessing; if they belong to a public ecclesiastical juridic person, however, only another public ecclesiastical juridic person can acquire them.

Sacred objects are those which are destined for divine worship by dedication or blessing (c. 1171). Examples would include relics, chalices, vestments, altar linens, and some religious images. Ownership of sacred objects often vests in dioceses, parishes, religious institutes, and other public juridic persons, but it may also vest in natural or private juridic persons. Canon 1269 limits to public juridic persons the acquisition by prescription of sacred objects owned by other public juridic persons. Sacred objects owned by private persons, natural or juridic, may be acquired through prescription by other private persons or by public juridic persons. A privately owned chalice, for example, left by its owner in a parish church when the owner goes to a foreign mission, could, through prescription, become the property of the parish. A chalice owned by a parish, however, could not, according to canon law, become the property of an individual priest by prescription. Canon 1269, in addition to placing a limitation on the canonization of the civil law of prescription, also prohibits any profane use of a sacred object (e.g., use of a blessed chalice or vestment as a prop in a theatrical production) unless the object

has lost its dedication or blessing (usually by decree of a competent ordinary; see, for analogy, c. 1212).

Canon 1270 — If they belong to the Apostolic See, immovable property, precious movable objects, and personal or real rights and actions are prescribed by a period of a hundred years; if they belong to another public ecclesiastical juridic person, they are prescribed by a period of thirty years.

From the viewpoint of Church-State conflicts, the most troublesome of the canonical exceptions to the civil law of prescription concern the length of the prescription period. According to canon 1270, immovable property and precious movable objects as well as other real or personal property rights and claims belonging to the Apostolic See are subject to a one-hundred-year prescription period; those of other public juridic persons are subject to a thirty-year period.[68] Civil-law periods of time are generally briefer. In the United States, for example, prescription periods would rarely exceed twenty years for realty (the equivalent of immovable property) or six years for personalty (the equivalent of movable objects).

The code offers no explicit definition of precious movable objects. It does, however, define precious images as those distinguished by age, art, or veneration (c. 1189), and, in the context of alienation, speaks of goods precious for artistic or historical reasons (c. 1292, §2). The 1917 code had defined as precious those temporal goods which were of notable artistic, historical, or mate-

---

[68] The Eastern code, in addition to stipulating one-hundred-year and thirty-year prescription periods, adds a fifty-year period for property belonging to a church *sui iuris* or to an eparchy. *CCEO* 1019. By apostolic privileges granted long ago, the property of some religious institutes (e.g., Benedictines, Cistercians) is protected by lengthy prescription periods, such as sixty or one hundred years. Such privileges remain in effect (c. 4). See D. Tirapu, in *Com Ex* IV/1, 97; F. Morrisey, in *CLSGBI Com,* 717, n. 3.

rial value,[69] a definition incorporated into the Code of Canons of the Eastern Churches.[70] Canonical principles of interpretation[71] dictate, therefore, that in canon 1270 the expression "precious movable objects" be understood to refer to objects of notable value due to their material composition (e.g., gold, platinum, diamonds) or because of their status as antiques, artistic or historical treasures, or objects of veneration.

A real right or claim is one whose object is a *res,* a particular piece of property, movable or immovable (e.g., a right to possess or use a building or remove minerals from the land of another); a personal right has as its object not property but a person against whom one has a claim for damages (e.g., for a breach of contract) or for the cessation or initiation of some activity. In common-law nations, such as the United States, actions to vindicate or enforce a real or personal right or claim are subject to statutes of limitation which vary in length depending upon the particular right at issue and the particular state in which the action is brought.

During the revision process it was suggested that no canonical exceptions be made to the relevant civil-law periods of time. The suggestion was rejected on the ground that it would lead to too much diversity.[72] The wisdom of that decision would seem questionable, not only because acceptance of diversity would appear to have been implied in the decision to canonize civil law in the first place, but also because disparity between the law of the Church and civil law leads inevitably to Church-State conflicts which, while always undesirable, are particularly regrettable in an area like prescription where no theological value is at stake. Moreover, the reluctance to allow diversity in the time periods required for the acquisition by prescription of real or personal property belonging to public juridic persons seems inconsistent with the allowance of such diversity in regard to the acquisition of property belonging to private juridic persons, and the adoption, as a general rule, of diverse civil-law periods for the initiation of actions in ecclesiastical tribunals (see c. 1492, §1).

Support of the Apostolic See

Canon 1271 — By reason of the bond of unity and charity and according to the resources of their dioceses, bishops are to assist in procuring those means which the Apostolic See needs, according to the conditions of the times, so that it is able to offer service properly to the universal Church.

While this canon is new, the notion of financial contributions to support the work of the Apostolic See is not, and has, for a long time, found practical expression in the annual Peter's Pence collection throughout the world. Canon 1271 was drafted in order to insert into the code a canonical obligation to mirror the moral obligation which dioceses have to contribute the means necessary for the Apostolic See to fulfill its functions in service to the universal Church.[73]

The obligations, moral and canonical, flow from the communion and catholicity of the particular churches that together constitute the Catholic Church.[74] The Apostolic See is the principal earthly instrumentality of the unity and mutuality of concern through which the good of all the churches is fostered and furthered. Financial support of the various offices of the Apostolic See, therefore, is a common responsibility of all dioceses; long recognized as a moral obligation, it is now also a canonical obligation.

Although the canon speaks only of bishops, without the modifier "diocesan," and although the bonds of unity and charity of which the canon speaks bind all members of the episcopacy, the obligation of the canon would seem to fall only on diocesan bishops, and not also on auxiliary

---

[69] *CIC* 1497, §2.
[70] *CCEO* 1019.
[71] See cc. 6, §2; 17; 19.
[72] *Comm* 12 (1980) 407.

[73] *Comm* 12 (1980) 411.
[74] See *LG* 13, 23; *CD* 6; *AG* 38; *Directory* 46–49, 138.

bishops. In speaking of bishops, the canon refers to the resources of "their" dioceses (*suae dioecesis*); use of the possessive pronoun implies reference only to bishops to whom the governance of a diocese has been entrusted in their own name, that is, diocesan bishops.

The legislative history of canon 1271 suggests that, in the mind of the drafters, the ordering of a special collection to be taken up in all churches (see c. 1266) would be the means used by diocesan bishops to obtain financial support for the Apostolic See.[75] There is nothing in the law, however, that would confine diocesan bishops to the use of collections as the only appropriate means through which to fulfill the obligation of canon 1271. It would seem that even the imposition of a tax would be permissible for, while taxation must be for diocesan needs (c. 1263), enabling the Apostolic See to fulfill its responsibility of service to all dioceses is truly a need of each diocese flowing from the ecclesiology of communion and catholicity.

Since November 1992, it has been the practice of diocesan bishops in the United States to seek to fulfill canon 1271 by including an annual contribution to the Holy See, separate from the Peter's Pence collection, in the annual budget of each diocese. The amount of this voluntary contribution, which is sent directly to the Apostolic Nunciature, is expected by the National Conference of Catholic Bishops to equal the annual assessment paid by each diocese to the NCCB to defray its expenses. Methods of raising funds to meet annual budgets vary from diocese to diocese.

Reform of Benefices

Canon 1272 — In regions where benefices properly so called still exist, it is for the conference of bishops, through appropriate norms agreed to and approved by the Apostolic See, to direct the governance of such benefices in such a way that the income and even, insofar as possible, the en-

dowment itself of the benefices are gradually transferred to the institute mentioned in can. 1274, §1.

A benefice in the strict sense is an endowed ecclesiastical office. In many countries, though not in the United States, bishoprics, pastorates, and other offices have long been established as benefices. The theoretical advantage of a benefice has been thought to be the freeing of the officeholder for ministry without having to be concerned with obtaining personal financial support. Practically, however, the system has led to financial inequities which in turn have frequently spawned the subordination of ministry to ecclesiastical ambition and avarice. To counter the undesirable effects, the Second Vatican Council sought the reform, even suppression, of the benefice system:

> The chief emphasis should be given to the office which sacred ministers fulfill. Hence the so-called benefice system should be abandoned or at least it should be reformed in such a way that the beneficiary aspect, that is, the right to revenues accruing to an endowed office, will be treated as secondary, and the main consideration in law will be accorded to the ecclesiastical office itself.[76]

Canon 1272 reflects a compromise between those who wanted total suppression of benefices and those who, because of particular circumstances including civil-law implications in certain regions, wanted a more nuanced approach supervised by episcopal conferences through norms approved by the Apostolic See.[77] The canon is of minimal relevance to the Church in some countries, including the United States, because of the absence of benefices in the strict sense.

---

[75] *Comm* 12 (1980) 411–412.

[76] *PO* 20.
[77] *Comm* 12 (1980) 412.

TITLE II
THE ADMINISTRATION OF GOODS
[cc. 1273–1289]

The organization of this title is essentially hierarchical, beginning with the affirmation of the Roman Pontiff as supreme administrator of all ecclesiastical goods (c. 1273), followed by norms dealing with administration by diocesan bishops and other ordinaries (cc. 1274–1278), and concluding with norms dealing with administration by persons other than ordinaries (cc. 1279–1289). Topics include remuneration of clergy and others who serve the Church, duties of administrators, acts of ordinary and extraordinary administration, required consultation by diocesan bishops and other administrators, social justice, responsibility for acts of administrators which are contrary to law, and required reporting by administrators.

Roman Pontiff as Supreme Administrator

Canon 1273 — By virtue of his primacy of governance, the Roman Pontiff is the supreme administrator and steward of all ecclesiastical goods.

Ownership of ecclesiastical goods is vested in public juridic persons in the Church (cc. 1256, 1257, §1). Administration, an essential element of ownership (see commentary on c. 1254, §1), must be undertaken on behalf of public juridic persons by natural persons designated for some public juridic persons by law and for others by the documents of foundation, statutes, or legitimate custom or, where these make no designation, by appointment by the ordinary to whom the public juridic person is subject (c. 1279). Acts of administration include maintenance, repair, and renovation of property, borrowing money, investment of revenues, entering into contracts, and all other actions necessary to preserve, make fruitful, or put to proper use temporal goods once acquired.

Canon 1273 affirms that, pursuant to his primacy of governance over the whole Church, the Roman Pontiff is supreme administrator and

steward of all ecclesiastical goods. This acknowledges in the Roman Pontiff the right, rarely exercised, to supersede the designated administrator and place, directly or indirectly, any act of administration, ordinary or extraordinary, on behalf of any public juridic person in the Church.[78] Originally drafted to apply to all temporal goods in the Church,[79] canon 1273 was narrowed to ecclesiastical goods on the curious ground that the notion of ecclesiastical goods is used in preceding canons and so should be the focus of this one.[80] As a consequence, the Roman Pontiff is not said to be the supreme administrator or steward of goods belonging to private juridic persons. While this may be consistent with the greater degree of autonomy that characterizes private juridic persons as compared with public juridic persons (see commentary on c. 116), it is difficult to reconcile with the Roman Pontiff's "supreme, full, immediate, and universal ordinary power in the Church, which he is always able to exercise freely" (c. 331), or with the provision in canon 1256 that ownership belongs to juridic persons "under the supreme authority of the Roman Pontiff."[81]

In affirming that it is pursuant to his primacy of governance that the Roman Pontiff is supreme administrator of ecclesiastical goods, canon 1273 makes clear that acts of administration of temporal goods are acts of governance.[82] Since it is the

---

[78] De Paolis, *De Bonis Ecclesiae Temporalibus,* 81; Z. Combalía, in *Com Ex* IV/1, 109; López Alarcón, in *Pamplona ComEng,* 787.

[79] *Comm* 12 (1980) 412.

[80] *Comm* 12 (1980) 413.

[81] Some authors are of the opinion that, notwithstanding the wording of c. 1273, the Roman Pontiff is supreme administrator of the goods of private as well as public juridic persons. See, e.g., Combalía, in *Com Ex* IV/1, 109.

[82] Treatises on the theory of governance in the Church have traditionally divided governance into legislative, judicial, and executive, and subdivided executive governance into coactive, gubernative, and administrative functions, with the last of these identified with the administration of temporal goods. See, e.g., A. Ottaviani, *Institutiones Iuris Publici Ecclesiastici* (Vatican City: Vatican Press, 1958) 1:94–95, 325–346.

position of the code that lay persons as well as clerics may serve as administrators of ecclesiastical goods,[83] it would seem undeniable that lay persons can and do perform acts of governance. Whether or not, in doing so, lay persons exercise "power of governance" (jurisdiction) may be considered debatable,[84] but canon 1273 would seem clearly relevant to the debate.

Diocesan, Interdiocesan, and Supradiocesan Funds

Canon 1274 — §1. Each diocese is to have a special institute which is to collect goods or offerings for the purpose of providing, according to the norm of can. 281, for the support of clerics who offer service for the benefit of the diocese, unless provision is made for them in another way.

§2. Where social provision for the benefit of clergy has not yet been suitably arranged, the conference of bishops is to take care that there is an institute which provides sufficiently for the social security of clerics.

§3. Insofar as necessary, each diocese is to establish a common fund through which bishops are able to satisfy obligations towards other persons who serve the Church and meet the various needs of the diocese and through which the richer dioceses can also assist the poorer ones.

§4. According to different local circumstances, the purposes mentioned in §§2 and 3 can be obtained more suitably through a federation of diocesan institutes, through a cooperative endeavor, or even through an appropriate association established for various dioceses or for the entire territory of the conference of bishops.

§5. If possible, these institutes are to be established in such a way that they also have recognition in civil law.

Canon 1275 — An aggregate of goods which come from different dioceses is administered according to the norms appropriately agreed upon by the bishops concerned.

Several conciliar concerns led to the formulation of canon 1274.[85] Not least among them was replacement of the benefice system with more equitable remuneration for clergy who serve the diocese (see c. 1272). The first paragraph of canon 1274 mandates the establishment of a diocesan fund for the support, according to the norms of c. 281,[86] of clergy who devote themselves to ministry, unless other provision for their support has been made. In several nations, including the United States, the support of clergy who serve in a diocese is provided by the parishes and other institutions in which they serve. Canon 1274, §1 makes clear, however, that the obligation is a diocesan obligation. To the extent, therefore, that such support is, in fact, equitable in the light of diverse conditions of time and place, canon 1274, §1 imposes no obligation on a diocese; where such support is not equitable, however, the need of a diocese to supplement remuneration coming from parishes or other institutions would argue for the implementation of canon 1274, §1 by establishment of a diocesan fund to meet such a need. Whether or not the beneficiaries of such a fund are to be limited to clergy incardinated in the diocese, or should also include religious and externs serving within a diocese, is a matter for determination in the statutes of the fund.[87]

---

[83] See cc. 1282, 1287.

[84] For opposite views see F. Urrutia, "Delegation of the Executive Power of Governance," *Stud Can* 19 (1985) 343; and D-M. Jaeger, "The Relationship of Holy Orders and the Power of Governance according to the Revised Code of Canon Law or: Are the Laity Capable of the Power of Governance?" *CLS-GBIN* 62 (1984) 27. See also the commentary on c. 129.

[85] See *PO* 21.

[86] Among other noteworthy provisions, the norms of c. 281 make a distinction between married deacons who devote themselves completely to ministry and those who continue to receive remuneration from a civil profession which they continue to exercise.

[87] See *Comm* 12 (1980) 409.

The second paragraph of canon 1274 obliges the episcopal conference to see that a fund is established to provide adequate social security for clergy, where no such system exists. The canonical understanding of social assistance includes provision for suitable support during disability, illness, and old age (c. 281, §2).[88] The Social Security, Medicare, and Medicaid programs presently in effect in the United States may be thought to obviate the need for action in this regard by the National Conference of Catholic Bishops. Such programs, however, rarely suffice to provide adequate sustenance and medical care, making private pension plans and additional medical insurance virtually necessary. These may be, and in the United States usually are, part of the diocesan support of clergy, the subject matter of paragraph one of canon 1274. Paragraph two, however, while not obliging the episcopal conference to establish a fund for the various aspects of social security, does oblige the conference to see that such funds are established at appropriate levels. This would seem to place upon the episcopal conference an antecedent responsibility to learn if adequate provision for disability, illness, and old age among the clergy is being made through diocesan, regional, or other funds.

The third paragraph of canon 1274 reminds diocesan bishops of additional financial obligations flowing from their office as taught by the Second Vatican Council, namely, to provide for adequate remuneration to nonordained religious and laity who serve the Church, to meet the many educational, charitable, and other needs of the diocese for which temporal goods are needed, and to aid poorer dioceses. Remuneration for laity who serve the diocese should include disability, health, and retirement benefits (c. 231, §2). The mandate to establish a diocesan fund in order to fulfill these obligations is contingent upon such a fund or institute being necessary because of the absence of other available means of doing so.

Monies to fulfill these various obligations can come from free-will offerings of the faithful, responses to fund-raising appeals, taxes, prescribed fees, collections, and canonically approved alienations of diocesan property. Explicit reference to canon 1274, §1 is made in canon 1272 regarding what is to happen to the income and endowment of gradually suppressed benefices, and in canon 1303, §2 regarding the disposition of the principal of some non-autonomous foundations upon their termination.

The fourth paragraph of canon 1274 recognizes one of the salient features of contemporary economics, namely, the benefit of pooling or combining funds so as to produce higher yields on investments and greater rates of growth. Accordingly, paragraph four suggests and authorizes interdiocesan and supradiocesan approaches to the funds mentioned in paragraphs two and three. No similar suggestion is made in regard to the core support of clergy who serve the diocese (§1), perhaps in deference to the doctrinal position that priests form one presbyterate with their bishop and are not to be thought of as constituting a national or other supradiocesan presbyterate.[89] Canon 1275 directs that interdiocesan and supradiocesan funds are to be administered according to norms agreed upon by the diocesan bishops involved.

Notwithstanding the Church's claim of independence from civil authority in regard to temporal goods (see c. 1254), the fifth paragraph of canon 1274 urges the establishment of diocesan, supradiocesan, and interdiocesan funds in such a way as to ensure their protection under civil law. Liability concerns will often argue for separate civil-law incorporation of various diocesan funds; canonical separateness, by establishing funds as autonomous foundations (see cc. 115, §3; 1303, §1, 1°) and hence as ecclesiastical juridic persons distinct from the diocese, will often also be advisable in order to match civil-law separateness and thereby lessen liability of the diocese in ecclesiastical tribunals, and perhaps also in civil courts as well (see the discussion of the canonical status of

---

[88] Prior to its mention of support for priests burdened by infirmity and ill health, the conciliar source for c. 1274 makes explicit reference to appropriate programs of preventive medicine and health benefits. *PO* 21.

[89] See *PO* 7, 8; *CD* 28.

church-related institutions following the commentary on cc. 113–123).

Supervisory Role of Ordinaries

Canon 1276 — §1. It is for the ordinary to exercise careful vigilance over the administration of all the goods which belong to public juridic persons subject to him, without prejudice to legitimate titles which attribute more significant rights to him.

§2. With due regard for rights, legitimate customs, and circumstances, ordinaries are to take care of the ordering of the entire matter of the administration of ecclesiastical goods by issuing special instructions within the limits of universal and particular law.

In marked contrast to canon 1273, which declares the Roman Pontiff to be supreme administrator of all ecclesiastical goods, canon 1276 does not declare the diocesan bishop or other ordinary to be the preeminent administrator of all ecclesiastical goods within the diocese or other jurisdiction. Rather, canon 1276 attributes to all ordinaries a supervisory role in regard to the administration of goods belonging to public juridic persons subject to them.

The administrator of ecclesiastical goods is ordinarily the person who directly governs the public juridic person to whom the goods belong (c. 1279, §1).[90] Thus, for example, a pastor is the administrator of the temporal goods belonging to a parish (c. 532). A diocesan bishop is the administrator of goods belonging to the public juridic person known as the diocese, but he is not the administrator of parochial and all other ecclesiastical goods situated within the diocese. In regard to the administration of such goods his role is supervisory. He has a responsibility to urge the observance of all laws of the Church by those whose responsibility it is to administer ecclesiastical goods, and to ensure that abuses do not creep into such administration. In this regard, canon 1276 is a specification of the general norms found in canon 392.

Supervision of administration by an ordinary extends, according to canon 1276, §1, only to public juridic persons. This is in keeping with the greater autonomy of private juridic persons. Canon 1276, §1, however, allows for lawful titles which give an ordinary greater rights. Such titles could include the statutes of a private juridic person which accord supervisory rights to the ordinary, or statutes of a public or private juridic person (e.g., a healthcare, educational, or other charitable institution or foundation) designating the ordinary as administrator of its temporal goods.

The elements that constitute the supervisory role of an ordinary include the responsibility to issue appropriate regulatory instructions for the administration of ecclesiastical goods, with due regard for rights, lawful customs, and relevant circumstances (c. 1276, §2). Instructions must always be within the law; they cannot derogate from the law (e.g., by attempting to take away from pastors their right and duty to administer the goods of their parishes). Any instruction which cannot be reconciled with the law lacks all force (c. 34, §2).

Other elements of an ordinary's supervisory role are found in subsequent canons and include:

- appointment of administrators for public juridic persons whose governing documents fail to make provision for them (c. 1279, §2);
- reception, personally or through a delegate, of the required oath of an administrator regarding faithful performance of duty (c. 1283, 1°);
- determination of the limits of ordinary administration where the relevant statutes fail to do so (c. 1281, §2);[91]
- authorization of acts of extraordinary administration (c. 1281, §1);
- consent to long-term investments (c. 1284, §2, 6°);

---

[90] Particular law, statutes, or lawful custom can provide otherwise (c. 1279, §1), and, in the rare instance where no designation exists, the ordinary is to appoint a suitable person as administrator (c. 1279, §2).

[91] The wording of c. 1281, §2 commits such a determination to diocesan bishops, not to all ordinaries.

- intervention in cases of negligence by an administrator (c. 1279, §1);
- reception of annual reports and transmittal of them to the financial council (c. 1287, §1);[92]
- granting or denying permission to initiate or contest a legal proceeding in civil court (c. 1288);
- granting or denying permission to accept a non-autonomous foundation (c. 1304, §1);
- approval of provisions for the safe-keeping and investment of the endowment of a non-autonomous foundation (c. 1305);
- approval of the renunciation of the trial of an issue involving temporal goods (c. 1524, §2).

Ordinary and Extraordinary Administration by Diocesan Bishop

Canon 1277 — The diocesan bishop must hear the finance council and college of consultors to place acts of administration which are more important in light of the economic condition of the diocese. In addition to the cases specially expressed in universal law or the charter of a foundation, however, he needs the consent of the finance council and of the college of consultors to place acts of extraordinary administration. It is for the conference of bishops to define which acts are to be considered of extraordinary administration.

As the one who directly governs the public juridic person known as the diocese, the diocesan bishop is the administrator of temporal goods owned by the diocese (c. 1279, §1). The bishop's role in regard to diocesan property, then, is far greater than his supervisory role in regard to the administration of other ecclesiastical goods within the diocese. Yet, the law of the Church does not allow a diocesan bishop in his administration of diocesan financial matters always to act alone. Consultation with others, and at times even ob-

taining their consent, is required of him in important matters.

The rationale for this is twofold: first, to guard against the dangers of grave harm to the financial condition of a diocese from decisions hastily made in the absence of accurate and adequate information from truly knowledgeable and skilled experts; second, to free the diocesan bishop from the felt need to spend inordinate amounts of time attending to financial matters to the neglect of his many responsibilities in the teaching and sanctifying offices of the Church and in the nonfinancial areas of the governing office.

Canon 1277 has two parts, the first dealing with a diocesan bishop's acts of *ordinary* administration of greater importance, for which consultation of both the diocesan finance council and the college of consultors is required (for validity, according to the norm of c. 127, §1).[93] In general, acts of ordinary administration are those which occur regularly or whose financial consequences are moderate. Despite requests during the revision process for precise determination of what is meant by acts of ordinary administration *of greater importance,* the canon, in deference to economic diversity among the dioceses of the world, offers no specification of the term other than to indicate that its meaning is relative to the financial condition of each diocese.[94] Accordingly, the proper place in which to find a precise determination is in the statutes of each diocese. Well-drafted statutes (ideally the result of widespread consultation themselves) should indicate what kinds of ordinary transactions, and above what monetary limits, are considered to be of greater importance within the diocese. The law of the Church expects such a determination to be made; without it, the first part of canon 1277

---

[92] The wording of c. 1287, §1 requires that an annual report be made to a local ordinary, not to all ordinaries.

[93] Although the canon does not use the word "ordinary," it is clear from the use of the word "extraordinary" in the second part of the canon, which requires consent of the two consultative bodies, that the first part, which requires only that the two bodies be heard, concerns the more important acts of ordinary administration.

[94] See *Comm* 12 (1980) 414.

cannot be implemented. Such a determination, whether made in diocesan statutes or elsewhere, serves to remind the diocesan bishop, the finance council, and the college of consultors of the need for consultation, an exercise of shared responsibility without which the administration of diocesan property and finance may be qualitatively flawed.

The second half of canon 1277 deals with a diocesan bishop's acts of *extraordinary* administration, for which consent of both the finance council and the college of consultors is required (for validity, according to c. 127, §1). In general, acts of extraordinary administration are those which occur irregularly or whose financial consequences are considerable. The canon places upon the episcopal conference the responsibility to determine which acts of a diocesan bishop are to be regarded as acts of extraordinary administration, and additionally requires the consent of the finance council and college of consultors whenever another provision of universal law or the charter of a foundation requires it.

In implementing the directive of canon 1277 to define which of a diocesan bishop's acts of administration are to be considered extraordinary administration, the National Conference of Catholic Bishops in the United States seems not to have adverted to the fact that the 1983 code, unlike the 1917 code, regards extraordinary administration as a category of financial transaction distinct from alienation and other transactions governed by the norms for alienation.[95] The NCCB implementation of canon 1277, promulgated in June 1986, reads as follows:

> In accord with the norms of canon 1277, the National Conference of Catholic Bishops determines that the following are to be considered acts of extraordinary administration

and therefore subject to the limits of canons that regulate such acts.

1. To alienate (in the strict sense, convey or transfer ownership) goods of the stable patrimony when the value exceeds the minimum limit (c. 1292, §1).

2. To alienate goods donated to the Church through a vow, or to alienate goods that are especially valuable due to their artistic or historical value regardless of the appraised value (c. 1292, §2).

3. To incur indebtedness (without corresponding increase in the assets of the diocese) that exceeds the minimum limit (c. 1295).

4. To encumber stable patrimony the value of which exceeds the minimum limit (c. 1295).

5. To lease church property when the annual lease income exceeds the minimum limit (c. 1297).

6. To lease church property when the value of the leased property exceeds the minimum and the lease is for more than nine (9) years (c. 1297).[96]

The first four acts of extraordinary administration defined by the NCCB are transactions already subject to the more exacting requirements of the canons governing alienation. The remaining two acts of extraordinary administration defined by the NCCB concern leasing which, in the 1983 code, is viewed as distinct both from extraordinary administration and alienation and is made subject to a distinct set of norms (see commentary on canon 1297).

Implementation of canon 1277 in other nations appears to evidence a better understanding of the

[95] See *Comm* 12 (1980) 396; De Paolis, *I Beni Temporali,* 149–150; 179, n. 1; 183–184; López Alarcón, in *Pamplona ComEng,* 792; F. Morrisey, "Ordinary and Extraordinary Administration: Canon 1277," *J* 48 (1988) 722–723.

[96] NCCB-*CompNm* 21.

nature of acts of extraordinary administration and the differences between them and acts of alienation or leasing. Some conferences classify as extraordinary administration certain types of transaction, such as the acceptance of onerous gifts or bequests, acquisition of real estate, creation or suppression of institutions, alteration of buildings, relocation of artistic or historical works, or erection of a cemetery. Others base the classification on the amount of money involved (but below the minimum set for application of the norms governing alienation). Still others require a combination of type of transaction and amount of money involved for classification as an act of extraordinary administration.[97] Perhaps opportunity will be afforded to the episcopal conference in the United States to reconsider and revise its complementary norms for canon 1277.

Role of Finance Officer

Canon 1278 — In addition to the functions mentioned in can. 494, §§3 and 4, the diocesan bishop can entrust to the finance officer the functions mentioned in cann. 1276, §1 and 1279, §2.

Each diocese is required by law to have a finance officer whose duty is to administer, under the authority of the bishop, the temporal goods belonging to the public juridic person known as the diocese (c. 494). The finance officer is not the administrator of such property, but acts as canonical agent for the diocesan bishop who remains the administrator.

Canon 1278 authorizes the diocesan bishop also to entrust to the finance officer fulfillment of the bishop's supervisory responsibilities in regard to the administration of other ecclesiastical goods within

the diocese (see commentary on c. 1276), and specifically the appointment and re-appointment of suitable administrators of the temporal goods of public juridic persons subject to the bishop for which no such administrators have otherwise been provided (see c. 1279, §2).

The need for canon 1278 may be questioned by those who regard the diocesan bishop's supervisory role in regard to the administration of temporal goods by others to be within the exercise of the bishop's ordinary (attached to his office by law) executive power of governance.[98] As such, the supervisory responsibilities may be delegated in whole or in part without the need for any additional authorization (c. 137, §1). Delegation to a finance officer who is a member of the laity, however, might by some be considered questionable in the absence of an express provision such as canon 1278.

Administrators Other Than Ordinaries

Canon 1279 — §1. The administration of ecclesiastical goods pertains to the one who immediately governs the person to which the goods belong unless particular law, statutes, or legitimate custom determine otherwise and without prejudice to the right of the ordinary to intervene in case of negligence by an administrator.

§2. In the administration of the goods of a public juridic person which does not have its own administrators by law, the charter of the foundation, or its own statutes, the ordinary to whom it is subject is to appoint suitable persons for three years; the same persons can be reappointed by the ordinary.

This is the first in a series of canons that govern administration of temporal goods by persons other than ordinaries. The first paragraph sets forth the general principle that administration of ecclesiastical goods is the responsibility of the person who immediately governs the public juridic person that owns the goods. Canon 532, which designates the

[97] "Canon 1277. Particular Legislation: Definition of Acts of Extraordinary Administration," *CLD* 11, 303–308; "Complementary Norms to the Code Promulgated by English-Language Conferences of Bishops," in *Pamplona ComEng* 1312, 1331, 1353, 1389, 1407; J. Martín de Agar, *Legislazione delle Conferenze Episcopali Complementare al C.I.C.* (Milan: Giuffrè, 1990) passim.

[98] See footnote 82 above.

pastor as the person responsible for the administration of the goods of the parish, is a specification of this general principle. Exceptions to the principle can be made by particular law, statutes of a public juridic person, or lawful custom; no particular law or statute, however, can derogate from universal laws such as canon 532 which contain no express provision for particular law to the contrary (c. 6, §1, 2°), and no custom contrary to current law can become lawful until it has been observed for thirty years by a community intending thereby to introduce a law (cc. 25, 26).

The second paragraph provides that in instances where no law (legislated or customary) or provision in a governing document (charter or statutes) designates an administrator, the ordinary (diocesan or religious) to whom the public juridic person is subject is to appoint a suitable person for a term of three years, and may reappoint the person for additional terms. The 1917 code had restricted appointment of administrators by ordinaries to suitable men and had discouraged reappointment.[99] The 1983 code reflects a deliberate change to allow the appointment of women and to allow reappointment.[100]

A concluding clause in the first paragraph of canon 1279 acknowledges the right of the relevant ordinary to intervene in case of negligence by an administrator. The right of intervention in the event of negligence is an essential element of supervision (see commentary on c. 1276). Negligence, however, is not the same as prudential disagreement, and ordinaries should exercise caution in seeking to override the judgments of those to whom the law or other governing documents, in service to the values of subsidiarity and shared responsibility, have entrusted the responsibilities of administration. Conversely, administrators must respect not only the legitimate supervisory role of ordinaries but also the competence of ecclesiastical authority to regulate the exercise of rights, including the rights of administrators, in the interest of the common good (see c. 223, §2).

The incompatibility with canon law of the corporation-sole approach to the ownership of church property in the United States (see commentary on c. 1256) is nowhere more evident than in the provisions of canon 1279. The right and responsibility of a diocesan bishop to appoint administrators of public juridic persons where they are lacking, and to intervene in cases of negligence by an administrator, make clear that according to the law of the Church the diocesan bishop himself is not the administrator of all ecclesiastical property within the diocese. Decision-making concerning temporal goods, within the parameters of canon law and legitimate instructions issued by the diocesan bishop, and the implementation of such decisions once made are responsibilities of the pastor in the case of a parish and of others who immediately govern other public juridic persons within a diocese.

Finance Council or Advisors

Canon 1280 — Each juridic person is to have its own finance council or at least two counselors who, according to the norm of the statutes, are to assist the administrator in fulfilling his or her function.

As is true of diocesan bishops in their administration of temporal goods belonging to the diocese (see c. 1277), so too in regard to other administrators the law of the Church does not favor financial administration by a single individual acting alone. This is particularly true when the administrator, such as a pastor, is called upon to fulfill many other responsibilities.

The need for financial, civil-law, and canonical expertise is critical in a complex modern world. Accordingly, canon 1280 requires administrators to be assisted by finance councils or at least two counselors,[101] and mandates the inclusion of norms to govern the role of such councils or advisors (e.g., when they must be consulted or when

---

[99] *CIC* 1521, §1.
[100] *Comm* 12 (1980) 416.

[101] A parish is required to have a financial council, not simply the less formal counselors (c. 537).

their consent must be obtained) in the statutes of the juridic person. The composition and functions of the diocesan finance council (see cc. 492–493, 1277, 1292) can serve as models for similar provisions in the statutes of other public juridic persons.

The first words of canon 1280 give rise to an ambiguity found also in some subsequent canons in this title: is the canon binding on private as well as public juridic persons? The norms given in canon 1257 provide that the canons of Book V apply only to public juridic persons unless express provision is made to the contrary. Express provisions can be explicit or implicit. Canon 1280 contains no explicit reference to private juridic persons, but it is unclear if use of the phrase "each juridic person" is intended to imply inclusion of private juridic persons.

An affirmative response is suggested by the fact that the immediately preceding canon explicitly refers to ecclesiastical goods in paragraph one and to public juridic persons in paragraph two; use of the expression "each juridic person" in canon 1280 may reasonably be read, therefore, as indicating the legislator's intention to extend the scope of canon 1280 to all juridic persons, private as well as public. On the other hand, canons 1279, 1280, and 1281 may reasonably be read as a cluster of canons all referring to the same administrators, namely, the administrators of ecclesiastical goods explicitly referred to in canon 1279. Such a reading finds support in the legislative history of canon 1280 which was originally proposed as an addition to canon 1279.[102] Further support derives from the fact that canon 1267, §1, which uses the expression "any ecclesiastical juridic person," immediately adds the phrase "even a private one" to signal the intention to include private juridic persons; no such specification has been included in canon 1280. Doubt regarding the applicability of canon 1280 to private juridic persons would seem resolvable through the application of canon 14, leading to the conclusion that, pending authentic interpreta-

[102]*Comm* 12 (1980) 415–416.

tion to the contrary, the provisions of canon 1280 are not binding on private juridic persons.[103]

It is, nonetheless, certainly advisable that private juridic persons, no less than public ones, be so structured as to make available to their administrators the assistance of expert financial advice, and it may fairly be presumed that most, if not all, private juridic persons are so structured. The practical importance of resolving the ambiguity in canon 1280 may, therefore, be minimal. The same ambiguity arises, however, in other canons where the practical consequences for private juridic persons can be considerable. It has seemed appropriate, therefore, to introduce the issue here where it first arises, and to continue the discussion when commenting upon subsequent canons.

Acts of Extraordinary Administration

Canon 1281 — §1. Without prejudice to the prescripts of the statutes, administrators invalidly place acts which exceed the limits and manner of ordinary administration unless they have first obtained a written faculty from the ordinary.

§2. The statutes are to define the acts which exceed the limit and manner of ordinary administration; if the statutes are silent in this regard, however, the diocesan bishop is competent to determine such acts for the persons subject to him, after having heard the finance council.

§3. Unless and to the extent that it is to its own advantage, a juridic person is not bound to an-

[103] That the applicability of c. 1280 to private juridic persons is doubtful seems amply confirmed by the divergent opinions of authors. De Paolis, in his earlier work, acknowledged the doubt without attempting to resolve it (*De Bonis Ecclesiae Temporalibus,* 90), but in his later work, relying solely on the words "each juridic person," takes the position that the canon is applicable to private juridic persons (*I Beni Temporali,* 163). See also L. de Echeverria, in *Salamanca Com,* 608; Morrisey, in *CLSGBI Com,* 725. Others hold that, despite the generality of its opening words, c. 1280 applies only to public juridic persons. See, e.g., Périsset, 165; V. Rovera, "I Beni Temporali della Chiesa," in *La Normativa del Nuovo Codice,* ed. E. Cappellini, 2nd ed. (Brescia: Querinian, 1985) 284.

swer for acts invalidly placed by its administrators. A juridic person itself, however, will answer for acts illegitimately but validly placed by its administrators, without prejudice to its right of action or recourse against the administrators who have damaged it.

There is nothing, explicit or implicit, in the wording of any of the paragraphs of canon 1281 to suggest that the canon applies to private juridic persons. Accordingly, canon 1257, §2 requires the conclusion that the canon applies only to public juridic persons.

Echoing the invalidating restrictions placed upon diocesan bishops when performing acts of extraordinary administration (see cc. 1277, 127, §1), the first paragraph of canon 1281 imposes an invalidating restriction upon acts of extraordinary administration by other administrators of temporal goods. For validity, a faculty is required from the ordinary (diocesan or religious) to whom the public juridic person whose goods are being administered is subject. In accord with principles of good governance, the law requires the faculty to be in writing; canonical tradition, however, regards an oral grant of faculties to be valid, viewing the additional requirement that the grant be in writing as designed only to facilitate proof and, therefore, as affecting only liceity.[104]

The requirement of a written faculty from a relevant ordinary is in addition to whatever requirements, for validity or liceity, are contained in the statutes of the public juridic person regarding acts of extraordinary administration. That is the import of the opening phrase in the first paragraph of canon 1281. Such statutory requirements could include, for example, hearing or obtaining the consent of the public juridic person's finance council or advisors (see c. 1280).

Use of the term "faculty" (imprecisely translated as "authority" in the earlier CLSA translation) in canon 1281 is not without relevance to the continuing debate over lay exercise of the power

of governance. Unlike permission, a faculty is in the genus of power;[105] where required, as in canon 1281, its absence affects validity.[106] Since lay persons as well as clerics may serve as administrators of ecclesiastical goods (see cc. 1282, 1287), canon 1281 affords an instance where the law of the Church allows a faculty to be given to a lay person, something not acknowledged in the canons which govern preaching or assisting at marriage.[107]

The second paragraph of canon 1281 remits to the statutes of individual public juridic persons the determination of what kinds of financial transactions (e.g., purchasing, borrowing, renovating), and above what monetary limits, are to be regarded as acts of extraordinary administration. Only where the statutes fail to do so is the determination to be made by the diocesan bishop for public juridic persons subject to him. It seems unnecessary, and often ecclesiologically and economically inappropriate, for all parishes (or other public juridic persons) in the same diocese to have identical designations of acts of extraordinary administration; what is an extraordinary financial transaction, in kind or amount, for an inner-city parish may be quite routine, and hence ordinary, in an affluent suburban parish. Recognition of financial diversity is but one facet of truly catholic unity-in-diversity, even as such unity leads, or should lead, to effective concern on the part of rich ecclesial units for poorer ones.

The third paragraph of canon 1281 expresses three propositions the content of which seems self-evident: a public juridic person is not liable for acts invalidly placed by its administrators, but is liable for validly placed acts even if they are illicit, and in all cases has the right to hold liable any administrator who by invalid or illicit action has injured the public juridic person. An administrator's individual liability for causing financial damage is a specification of the general norm of canon 128.

---

[104] Cappello, 2:577; Vromant, 194; Vermeersch-Creusen, 2:591–592; De Paolis, *I Beni Temporali,* 177.

[105] See, e.g., c. 132.

[106] The sole exception is in regard to preaching (see c. 764) where the notions of validity and invalidity are inapposite.

[107] Compare c. 764 with c. 766, and c. 1111 with c. 1112.

Even though a public juridic person is not canonically liable for an action that is canonically invalid (e.g., because of an administrator's failure to obtain the requisite faculty before placing an act of extraordinary administration), the action may have been civilly valid, resulting in consequent conflict and harm to the public juridic person. Civil lawyers representing public juridic persons in the Church would be well advised to see to it that canon 1281 is incorporated-by-reference in by-laws and other civilly governing documents so that the invalidity of canonically unauthorized actions by administrators will be honored at civil law as well as canonically.

If a canonically invalid financial transaction in fact proves advantageous, the public juridic person is free to ignore the invalidity and allow the transaction to stand. Administrators who place such actions should be reminded, however, that despite the ensuing advantage to the public juridic person, the law of the Church has been broken and the administrator's fidelity to the duties of office may thereby have been diminished.

Notwithstanding the technical inapplicability of canon 1281 to private juridic persons, the seemingly self-evident propositions of paragraph three would appear relevant to private as well as to public juridic persons.

Duties of Administrators

Canon 1282 — All clerics or lay persons who take part in the administration of ecclesiastical goods by a legitimate title are bound to fulfill their functions in the name of the Church according to the norm of law.

Canon 1283 — Before administrators begin their function:
  1° they must take an oath before the ordinary or his delegate that they will administer well and faithfully;
  2° they are to prepare and sign an accurate and clear inventory of immovable property, movable objects, whether precious or of some cultural value, or other goods,

with their description and appraisal; any inventory already done is to be reviewed;
  3° one copy of this inventory is to be preserved in the archive of the administration and another in the archive of the curia; any change which the patrimony happens to undergo is to be noted in each copy.

Canon 1284 — §1. All administrators are bound to fulfill their function with the diligence of a good householder.
  §2. Consequently they must:
  1° exercise vigilance so that the goods entrusted to their care are in no way lost or damaged, taking out insurance policies for this purpose insofar as necessary;
  2° take care that the ownership of ecclesiastical goods is protected by civilly valid methods;
  3° observe the prescripts of both canon and civil law or those imposed by a founder, a donor, or legitimate authority, and especially be on guard so that no damage comes to the Church from the non-observance of civil laws;
  4° collect the return of goods and the income accurately and on time, protect what is collected, and use them according to the intention of the founder or legitimate norms;
  5° pay at the stated time the interest due on a loan or mortgage and take care that the capital debt itself is repaid in a timely manner;
  6° with the consent of the ordinary, invest the money which is left over after expenses and can be usefully set aside for the purposes of the juridic person;
  7° keep well organized books of receipts and expenditures;
  8° draw up a report of the administration at the end of each year;
  9° organize correctly and protect in a suitable and proper archive the documents and records on which the property rights of the Church or the institute are based,

and deposit authentic copies of them in the archive of the curia when it can be done conveniently.

§3. It is strongly recommended that administrators prepare budgets of incomes and expenditures each year; it is left to particular law, however, to require them and to determine more precisely the ways in which they are to be presented.

The paramount duty of all administrators, clerical or lay, of temporal goods belonging to public juridic persons is that they fulfill their responsibilities in the name of and in accord with the law of the Church. It is the essence of a public juridic person that all of its activity is undertaken in the name of the Church, that is, pursuant to a mission received from competent ecclesiastical authority and closely governed by that authority (see commentary on c. 116). It is in that sense that lay administrators of ecclesiastical goods, no less than clerics, act "in the name of the Church."

In view of the meaning of acting in the name of the Church, it was perhaps unnecessary to insert into canon 1282 the admonition to act in accord with the norm of law; such a mode of action is clearly included in the notion of acting in the name of the Church. The claim has occasionally, and erroneously, been made that altering the membership of a board of directors or trustees of a public juridic person, or of an institution (e.g., a hospital or university) canonically belonging to a public juridic person, so as to result in a board the majority of whose members are lay persons, has the effect of removing the entity and its property from the ambit of canon law, as if lay persons were not members of the Church or not competent to fulfill its laws. Canon 1282 makes it clear that lay persons, no less than clerics, act in the name of the Church and are bound by all applicable laws of the Church in their administration of temporal goods canonically belonging to public juridic persons.

Canon 1283 prescribes two preliminary obligations to be fulfilled by administrators before undertaking the duties of their office: the taking of an oath to serve well and faithfully, and the preparation of an up-to-date inventory and appraisal of all temporal goods to be administered. In the absence of a thorough, authenticated, and up-to-date inventory, serious conflicts can arise between individual administrators (such as pastors) and their successors over which assets belong personally to the administrator and which to the juridic person. It is the purpose of canon 1283 to prevent such conflicts by requiring up-to-date copies to be kept in the archives both of the juridic person and of the relevant curia.

There is nothing, explicit or implicit, in the wording of canon 1283 to suggest that its provisions are applicable to private juridic persons. Therefore, in accord with the norms of canon 1257, the obligations of canon 1283 are binding only on administrators of public juridic persons.[108] This seems entirely appropriate. Taking an oath before an ordinary and filing an inventory in the curial archive would be inconsistent with the relative autonomy of a private juridic person. Moreover, the administrators to whom canon 1283 refers seem clearly to be the same as those referred to in canon 1282, which is explicitly directed to administrators of ecclesiastical goods.

Canon 1284 begins with the words "All administrators," raising yet again the issue first raised in canon 1280 as to whether the canon is intended to

---

[108] The parallel canon in the 1917 code (*CIC* 1522) explicitly applied to administrators of ecclesiastical goods "referred to in the preceding canon," namely, those appointed by the local ordinary to serve as administrators of ecclesiastical goods where no administrator had otherwise been provided (*CIC* 1521). The principal focus of *CIC* 1521, §2 was on lay men appointed to serve as administrators. Early in the revision process, it was decided to omit the phrase "referred to in the preceding canon" so that what was to become c. 1283 would apply to "administrators in general." *Comm* 5 (1973) 98. It is unclear whether "administrators in general" was intended only to mean clerical as well as lay, or those serving pursuant to law or statute as well as those appointed by a local ordinary, or was intended also to include administrators of private as well as public juridic persons. The promulgated text contains nothing to suggest its application to private juridic persons, and therefore, in accord with c. 1257, it is here interpreted to apply only to public juridic persons.

apply only to administrators of public juridic persons or to all administrators of juridic persons, private as well as public. No explicit mention is made of private juridic persons (as, e.g., in cc. 1265, §1 and 1267, §1); the doubt concerns whether they are implicitly included in the reference to "all" administrators. The parallel canon in the 1917 code made explicit reference to administrators *of ecclesiastical goods;*[109] this phrase has been omitted in the 1983 code. It is not clear if the omission was made in order to extend the canon to cover private juridic persons, or simply because the words were seen as superfluous in view of an intention that canon 1284 should be considered part of a cluster of canons beginning with canon 1282, or even 1279, both of which make explicit the application only to public juridic persons.

Nearly all of the provisions of canon 1284 are nothing more than commonly recognized principles of sound administration, and, on that basis, would be as applicable to private as to public juridic persons. But paragraph two, number six, requiring the consent of the ordinary for the investment of surplus funds, seems too close an involvement with hierarchical authority for a private juridic person (whose distinguishing feature, when compared with a public juridic person, is greater autonomy), especially since the effect of investment is to stabilize funds, making them part of stable patrimony the alienation of which is subject to regulatory norms only in the case of public juridic persons (see commentary on c. 1291). Also, in requiring the consent of the ordinary, paragraph two, number six makes clear that the words "all administrators," with which canon 1284 begins, cannot literally mean "all," since it clearly does not include administrators who are ordinaries. Moreover, paragraph two, number two makes explicit reference to ecclesiastical goods, and paragraph two, number three uses the word "church" in the specialized meaning given in canon 1258, which restricts it to public juridic persons. While it is arguable that only these two subparagraphs, because

of their explicit references, are limited to administrators of public juridic persons, leaving all the other subparagraphs to apply to administrators of private juridic persons as well, there seems to be no sufficient reason for supposing the legislator thought the duties of paragraph two, numbers two and three important only for public juridic persons, while thinking the other duties important for private juridic persons as well. It seems more reasonable to conclude that the references to ecclesiastical goods in paragraph two, numbers two and three are indicative of the intended scope of the entire canon. As with canon 1280, doubt regarding the technical applicability of the provisions of canon 1284 to private juridic persons would seem resolvable, pending authentic interpretation, by the application of canon 14, leading to the conclusion that the provisions of canon 1284 are not, at the present time, canonically binding on private juridic persons.[110]

As noted above, the provisions of canon 1284 are, for the most part, basic dictates of sound financial administration. Most are self-explanatory; only a few warrant a word or two of comment. Notwithstanding the Church's claim of independence from civil authority in regard to temporal goods (c. 1254), administrators of ecclesiastical goods are enjoined to employ civilly valid methods of ownership (§2, 2°) and to observe all relevant civil laws so that no harm ensues to a public juridic person from nonobservance of such laws (§2, 3°). This confirms the need for a nuanced understanding of the independence claimed by the Church in regard to temporal goods (see commentary on c. 1254). Administrators are also enjoined to observe the intentions of founders and donors (§2, 3°, 4°), a concern of paramount importance repeatedly emphasized throughout the code.[111]

---

[109] *CIC* 1523.

[110] In the Latin text of the Eastern code, all the canons in the chapter dealing with administration (*CCEO* 1022–1033) make explicit reference to ecclesiastical goods. This is of minimal relevance in interpreting the 1983 code, however, since in the Eastern code there is no division of juridic persons into public and private.

[111] See footnote 66 above.

Whereas an earlier draft of paragraph two, number five had called for the payment of the principal (translated as "capital debt") due on a loan or mortgage as soon as possible,[112] the promulgated canon wisely substitutes "in a timely manner," thereby recognizing the economic prudence of retaining a debt at advantageous interest rates rather than, in order to pay the debt, sacrificing capital which may be invested at a higher rate of return. Investment of surplus funds remaining after payment of expenses requires consent of the relevant ordinary, diocesan or religious (§2, 6°). This requirement, like the others in canon 1284, is for liceity, there being nothing to indicate the contrary (see c. 10); but the statutes, or in their absence the diocesan bishop, could declare investment over a certain amount to be an act of extraordinary administration (c. 1281, §2), in which case failure to obtain a faculty from the ordinary would canonically invalidate the investment (c. 1281, §1). By investment is here meant a long-term investment sufficient to make the funds part of stable patrimony (see commentary on c. 1291), not deposits in savings accounts or short-term certificates of deposit.

Annual budgets, recommended but left to particular law to require and regulate (§3), are in fact required by the code in the case of one administrator, namely, the diocesan bishop; an annual budget of diocesan income and expenditures is to be prepared by the diocesan finance council according to the directions of the diocesan bishop (c. 493). All budgeting in the Church should be done, not just with a view to increasing income, meeting expenditures, and providing for unforeseen circumstances, but also in the light of the demands of social justice (see c. 1286) and in the light of one of the principal purposes of raising funds in the Church, namely, to be able to perform the works of charity toward the needy (see c. 1254, §2).[113]

---

[112] *Comm* 5 (1973) 98.
[113] Roche, 326–328.

Charitable Donations by Administrators

Canon 1285 — Within the limits of ordinary administration only, administrators are permitted to make donations for purposes of piety or Christian charity from movable goods which do not belong to the stable patrimony.

This is an instance where the force of the Latin is lost in English translation. The Latin *fas est administratoribus,* translated "administrators are permitted," is stronger than mere permission; *fas* connotes a religiously based right or responsibility. It can be translated "it is lawful," but with the connotation of lawful by divine command as distinguished from lawfulness by human command or right (*ius est*).

Canon 1285 recalls one of the principal purposes for the acquisition of material goods by the Church, namely, to give them away in acts of charity to the poor (see commentary on 1254, §2). The canon in effect places upon administrators the responsibility to fulfill this purpose by acts of piety and charity.[114]

The canon does limit charitable gifts by administrators to movable goods which are not part of stable patrimony and which are within the limits of ordinary administration. Movable goods are best understood as all temporal goods, tangible or intangible (e.g., securities), which are not immovable; the latter are land, buildings, and fixtures attached to the land (e.g., trees, shrubs, fences, large statues, sheds). The notion of stable patrimony is explained in the commentary on canon 1291. The limits of ordinary administration are to be defined in the statutes or, if the statutes are silent in this regard, by the diocesan bishop, after consulting

---

[114] The parallel canon in the 1917 code (*CIC* 1535), located among the canons restricting alienation, was negative in tone, prohibiting gifts other than small amounts according to local custom unless there was an intervening just cause, and providing that successors could reclaim unjustified donations. The parallel canon in the Eastern code is similarly negative in tone, though it does not provide for reclamation of unjustified donations (*CCEO* 1029).

his finance council, for public juridic persons subject to him (c. 1281, §2).

Nothing is expressed in canon 1285 to suggest that its provisions apply to private juridic persons, and hence, in accord with canon 1257, §2, they do not. A similar canon applies to religious institutes (c. 640).

Social Justice

Canon 1286 — Administrators of goods:
   1° in the employment of workers are to observe meticulously also the civil laws concerning labor and social policy, according to the principles handed on by the Church;
   2° are to pay a just and decent wage to employees so that they are able to provide fittingly for their own needs and those of their dependents.

This is one of several canons in the code intended to give practical effect in the life of the Church to the social teaching of the magisterium as developed in preconciliar, conciliar, and postconciliar documents (see also cc. 222, §2; 287, §1; 528, §1; 747, §2; and 768, §2).[115] Canon 1286,

1° in effect calls upon church administrators to follow meticulously the teachings of the Church as well as the provisions of civil law regarding labor and social policy. It is regrettable that this meaning of the canon is somewhat obscured both by an awkward word order in the Latin text and by the English translation.

The translation accurately reflects the word order in the Latin text which refers first to civil law and then to church principles, a curious alignment of priorities for a Church that, in the opening canon of Book V, declares its independence from civil authority. The word order can give the erroneous impression that the principal articulation of the demands of social justice is to be found in the provisions of civil law rather than in the teachings of the Church. The sad truth is that in most if not all nations, including the United States, many people live and work in social and economic conditions far below the level demanded by the dignity of the human person as taught by the Church, and they do so despite the existence of civil laws ostensibly designed to further social justice. Meticulous conformity to civil laws that fall short of serving the fullness of social justice is hardly the measure of institutional behavior sought by the law of the Church. That is why in canon 1286, 1° observance of civil law is joined to fulfillment of the principles of social justice taught by the Church.[116]

---

[115] Leading magisterial documents include Leo XIII, ency *Rerum Novarum, ASS* 23 (1890–1891) 641; Pius X, *mp Fin Dalla Prima, ASS* 36 (1903–1904) 339; Pius XI, ency *Quadragesimo Anno, AAS* 23 (1931) 177, ency *Divini Redemptoris, AAS* 29 (1937) 65; Pius XII, ency *Sertum Laetitiae, AAS* 31 (1939) 635, *1941 Pentecost Message, AAS* 33 (1941) 195, *1942 Christmas Message, AAS* 35 (1943) 9, alloc *To Italian Workers, AAS* 35 (1943) 171, alloc *Questa Grande Vostra Adunata, AAS* 37 (1945) 284; John XXIII, ency *Mater et Magistra, AAS* 53 (1961) 401, ency *Pacem in Terris, AAS* 55 (1963) 257; Vatican II, *Gaudium et spes,* nn. 63–72, *AAS* 58 (1966) 1084–1094; Paul VI, ency *Populorum Progressio, AAS* 59 (1967) 257, aplett *Octogesima Adveniens, AAS* 63 (1971) 401; John Paul II, ency *Redemptor Hominis, AAS* 71 (1979) 257, ency *Laborem Exercens, AAS* 73 (1981) 577, ency *Sollicitudo Rei Socialis, AAS* 80 (1988) 513, ency *Centesimus Annus, AAS* 83 (1991) 793; Synod of Bishops, *De Iustitia in Mundo, AAS* 63 (1971) 923; NCCB, *Economic Justice for All: Pastoral Letter on Catholic Social Teaching and the U.S. Economy* (Washington, D.C.: USCC, 1986).

[116] The corresponding canon in the 1917 code made no reference to civil law, but was markedly more specific than the present canon in detailing what at the time were the Church's embryonic concerns for the welfare of employees (*CIC* 1524). The published legislative history of c. 1286, 1° is silent as to the reason for inserting the admonition to observe civil law. The explanation has been offered that, since 1917, secular legislation has developed sufficiently to make it possible for the law of the Church to refer to such legislation rather than offer a specific enumeration of canonical standards of social justice. CLSA, "Canonical Standards in Labor-Management Relations: A Report," *J* 47 (1987) 553, n. 20. The continuing inadequacy of the scope of social justice in civil legislation, however, makes it incumbent upon church employers to supplement their meticulous observance of civil law with equally meticulous observance of the more exacting demands of church teaching.

The uniquely valuable contribution of canon 1286, 1° is to remind church administrators that there are in the Church two sources of authentic guidance for appropriate behavior, the law and the magisterium. Neither is to be neglected. Administrators are called to look beyond the law, not only civil but canonical as well, to the teaching of the Church and conform their actions to its dictates and not just to those embodied in law.[117]

Unfortunately, this message may be clouded not only by the word order which can be misinterpreted as putting emphasis on meticulous observance of civil law, but also because of a translation that renders the Latin *iuxta* in its secondary meaning of "according to" rather than in its primary meanings of "alongside" or "immediately after" (from which is derived the English word "juxtapose"). The result is a translation which enjoins church administrators to observe civil laws "according to the principles handed on by the Church" instead of "alongside (or together with) the principles handed on by the Church." To speak of meticulous observance of civil law "according to the principles handed on by the Church" reduces church teaching to the role of placing occasional limitations upon the obligations of civil law,[118] as in the commonplace restriction that no one is bound to observe a civil law that is contrary to divine law, rather than recognizing in church teaching additional positive demands which transcend the content of civil law and which, on that account, must be followed by church employers as an affirmative duty.[119]

During the revision process efforts were made to expand the reference in canon 1286, 2° to a just and decent wage so that it would go beyond simply meeting *necessitates* (benignly translated as "needs"). It was recommended that reference be made to wages sufficient to enable employees and their families to enjoy not just the bare necessities of life, but the benefits of social and cultural life as well, and recommendations were made to add to the canon still other aspects of the betterment of the condition of workers.[120] Expansion beyond "necessities" was rejected, however, on the ground that the economic condition of many church entities could not sustain such an approach.[121] The approach, however, is part of the teaching of the Church;[122] even if not expressed in law, it cannot justifiably be ignored in practice by church administrators.

A particular cause of tension in some nations is the effort of church employees to exercise their human right to form labor unions or otherwise organize in order collectively to protect their interests. The teaching of the Church affirming such a right is clear, nowhere more so than in the conciliar document *Gaudium et spes:*

> Among the basic rights of the human person must be counted the right of freely founding labor unions. These unions should be truly able to represent the workers and to contribute to the proper arrangement of economic life. Another such right is that of tak-

---

[117] Brief but useful studies of the code's treatment of social justice in the context of the teachings of the Church may be found in T. Grant, "Social Justice in the 1983 Code of Canon Law: An Examination of Selected Canons," *J* 49 (1989) 112–145; D. Hermann, "The Code of Canon Law Provisions on Labor Relations," *J* 44 (1984) 153–193.

[118] The phrase is so interpreted in Grant, 134; Myers, in *CLSA Com,* 877.

[119] Other English translations of c. 1286, 1° also render *iuxta* as "according to." See *CLSA Com, CLSGBI Com, Pamplona ComEng.* The Eastern code replaces *iuxta*

with *secundum,* the primary meaning of which is "after, behind, in the second place," which effectively accords appropriate priority to Church teachings by enjoining administrators to observe civil law after, or secondarily to, the principles handed down by the Church; the English translation, however, renders *secundum* as "according to" (*CCEO* 1030, 1°).

[120] *Comm* 12 (1980) 420.

[121] *Rel* 287. Though efforts to go beyond a wage sufficient to meet "necessities" failed in the drafting of c. 1286, explicit mention of pension, health, and social security benefits is included in c. 231, §2. See also the commentary on c. 1274.

[122] See, e.g., *GS* 67.

ing part freely in the activity of these unions without risk of reprisal.[123]

Resistance to the exercise of these rights cannot be justified on the ground that relevant civil law does not extend its jurisdiction to include employer-employee relationships in church-related enterprises. Church administrators should be motivated by the teaching of the Church to transcend the confines of civil law.[124]

Accountability

Canon 1287 — §1. Both clerical and lay administrators of any ecclesiastical goods whatever which have not been legitimately exempted from the power of governance of the diocesan bishop are bound by their office to present an annual report to the local ordinary who is to present it for examination by the finance council; any contrary custom is reprobated.

§2. According to norms to be determined by particular law, administrators are to render an account to the faithful concerning the goods offered by the faithful to the Church.

The focus of this canon is on administrators' accountability to ecclesiastical authority and to other members of the faithful. The canon explicitly refers to ecclesiastical goods and to both clerical and lay administrators of ecclesiastical goods which have not been exempted from the power of governance of the diocesan bishop. The juxtaposition of the references to lay administrators and to goods subject to the power of governance of the diocesan bishop has unavoidable implications for the meaning of lay cooperation in the exercise of the power of governance (see c. 129; see also

commentary on c. 1273). While religious institutes of pontifical right are subject to the diocesan bishop in works of the apostolate (c. 678, §1), the bishop's power of governance does not extend to temporal goods owned by a religious institute; no report need be made to the local ordinary by such religious in regard to the administration of the institute's assets.[125]

Receiving an annual report is one of the elements of an ordinary's supervision of the administration of goods belonging to public juridic persons subject to him (see commentary on c. 1276). Transmission of the report to the finance council serves the values of having the details of financial administration examined by those whose expertise qualifies them to discern and call to the local ordinary's attention both commendable and troublesome aspects, and of freeing the local ordinary from having to take time from other duties to make such an examination himself. The reprobation of contrary customs has the canonical effect of rendering such customs unreasonable and, hence, incapable of obtaining the force of law (c. 24, §2).

The second paragraph of canon 1287 remits to norms of particular law the rendering of an account to the faithful concerning offerings made by the faithful to a public juridic person (the specialized meaning given by c. 1258 to the word "church" as used in Book V). It is not just the manner of reporting, but the very rendering of a report at all that is left up to particular law.[126] Accordingly, paragraph two does not speak of an annual report as does paragraph one.

During the revision process, unsuccessful efforts were made to expand the scope of this report

---

[123] GS 68. See also John XXIII, *Mater et Magistra, AAS* 53 (1961) 425–426; John Paul II, *Laborem Exercens,* n. 20, *AAS* 73 (1981) 629–632; NCCB, *Economic Justice for All,* n. 353.

[124] See Hermann, 190–193; CLSA, "Canonical Standards," 557–563.

[125] A 1972 reply from SCRIS declared religious associations of pontifical right, and their provincial and individual houses, not subject to the reporting requirements of the 1917 code's less precisely worded parallel canon (*CIC* 1525). *CLD* 9 (1983) 911. Reference in c. 1287 to goods which are not "exempted from the power of governance of the diocesan bishop" is apparently designed to incorporate into the revised code the content of that reply.

[126] *Rel* 287.

to include an account not just of offerings from the faithful but of all the financial holdings of the public juridic person, including returns on investments, sales of property, and other sources of income. Such a broad scope, while considered praiseworthy in certain circumstances, was judged to be unwise in circumstances where the faithful may not be sufficiently educated in the propriety of the Church's possession of material goods.[127] A far less cynical view characterizes the broader accountability provisions in the fund-raising guidelines issued several years ago by the National Conference of Catholic Bishops in the United States (see commentary on c. 1262).

Lawsuits in Civil Courts

Canon 1288 — Administrators are neither to initiate nor to contest litigation in a civil forum in the name of a public juridic person unless they have obtained the written permission of their own ordinary.

Civil litigation involving church-related entities raises both problems and opportunities, not just for the entities involved but also for the particular church or institute of consecrated life of which the church-related litigant is a part, and, at times, for the Church itself at a national or international level. Litigation involving church-related entities is nearly always accompanied by publicity; the resolution of issues in one case often has implications for other situations not yet litigated; and in a common-law nation, such as the United States, the precedent-setting nature of court decisions can have long-range effects that transcend the interests of present litigants. These among other considerations underlie the wisdom of requiring permission of one's ordinary (diocesan or religious) before initiating or contesting litigation in civil court. The canon is explicitly applicable only to administrators of public juridic persons, consistent with the greater autonomy of

private juridic persons, but, for the reasons just given, administrators of private juridic persons would evidence appropriate ecclesial sensitivity if they consulted their ordinaries before reaching a decision on a course of action involving civil litigation.

An earlier draft of canon 1288 had also required public juridic persons to obtain permission from the ordinary of the place where the litigation was to occur.[128] Such a provision seemed wise, especially from the point of view of the local publicity likely to be generated by the litigation, but the provision was dropped from the final text with no reason given in the published legislative history.[129]

Civil litigation does not give rise only to problems; it also affords the Church opportunities. Apart from the possibilities of vindicating rights and putting an end to discrimination and various forms of injustice, litigation affords the Church in common-law nations such as the United States the opportunity actively to participate in the making of the law of the land. Common law is primarily judicial in nature; the courts, not the legislatures, are the ultimate architects of the law. In the United States, enactments of legislatures are subject to the courts not only for definitive interpretation and application but also for ultimate determination of validity and constitutionality. To be true to its heritage of active participation in the forging of Church-State relationships, and in the development of value-oriented law, the Church in the United States belongs in the courts where the law is ultimately determined. The route to appellate courts is through trial courts, and ordinaries whose permission is sought in accord with canon 1288 would be well advised to consider the long-range benefits, and not just the short-term disadvantages, of involvement in civil litigation.

[127]*Comm* 12 (1980) 421.

[128]*Comm* 5 (1973) 99; 12 (1980) 421.

[129]*Comm* 12 (1980) 421. The parallel canon in the 1917 code had required permission of the local ordinary or, in an urgent case, from the dean (*CIC* 1526).

Abandonment of Duty by Administrators

Canon 1289 — Even if not bound to administration by the title of an ecclesiastical office, administrators cannot relinquish their function on their own initiative; if the Church is harmed from an arbitrary withdrawal, moreover, they are bound to restitution.

Although for many public juridic persons (e.g., dioceses and parishes) administrators of temporal goods are designated by law and, for many others, by statute, lawful custom, or appointment by an ordinary (see c. 1279), there are instances where the functions of an administrator are fulfilled by persons not so designated who, either voluntarily or in response to a request from some office-holder, undertake such functions. The care of real estate, the maintenance of buildings, the keeping of accounts, managing investment portfolios, supervising the work of employees, and a host of other activities are often performed by such "unofficial" administrators who render invaluable service to church entities. Based on long experience, the Church seeks in canon 1289 to remind all administrators, including unofficial ones, that once they have undertaken to fulfill administrative responsibilities, they have an obligation not to abandon them suddenly without affording appropriate authorities ample opportunity to arrange for others to assume the responsibilities. Sudden interruption in the stewardship of temporal goods can result in grave harm, for which the canon holds responsible the administrator, even an unofficial one, upon whom reliance had justifiably been placed and whose arbitrary withdrawal occasioned the harm. The requirement of restitution in such a case is a specific application of the general norm of canon 128. In accord with canon 1258, use of the word "church" in this canon has the canonical effect of restricting its application to public juridic persons. The moral principle underlying the canon, however, would apply as well to private juridic persons.

TITLE III
CONTRACTS AND ESPECIALLY ALIENATION
[cc. 1290–1298]

Contracts play a large and important role in the financial life of the Church. This title begins with an extensive though not unlimited canonization of civil law in regard to contracts (c. 1290). Canonical limitations on the canonization of civil law occur chiefly in regard to contracts involving transfer of ownership, known canonically as alienation (cc. 1291–1294). Such limitations also occur in regard to transactions which pose risk of harm to the overall financial condition of a public juridic person (c. 1295), and in regard to leasing (c. 1297). Directives are given for handling situations where a canonically invalid alienation is civilly valid (c. 1296), and regarding the sale or lease of ecclesiastical goods to administrators or family members of administrators of such goods (c. 1298).

Limited Canonization of Civil Law

Canon 1290 — The general and particular provisions which the civil law in a territory has established for contracts and their disposition are to be observed with the same effects in canon law insofar as the matters are subject to the power of governance of the Church unless the provisions are contrary to divine law or canon law provides otherwise, and without prejudice to the prescript of can. 1547.

Stewardship of temporal goods often involves entering into and fulfilling the terms of contracts of various kinds. Some, like those for the routine payment of salaries, purchase of supplies, or maintenance of real estate, usually fall within the sphere of ordinary administration; others, not routine and involving larger sums of money, are often designated as acts of extraordinary administration (see cc. 1277, 1281); still others fall into the categories of alienation or related transactions (see cc. 1291, 1295).

Rather than enact its own norms regarding capacity to contract, mutuality of obligations, requisite formalities, and other aspects of contractual transactions, the Church elects to adopt (canonize) the provisions of civil law applicable in the territory, except where such provisions are contrary to divine law or canon law provides otherwise. Contracts involving church-related entities or institutions rarely contain provisions explicitly contrary to divine law but could do so implicitly, especially in areas such as health care and education where, in nations such as the United States, governmental regulatory provisions are required to be incorporated by reference into many contracts. Some regulatory provisions are designed to protect constitutionally protected but, according to the teaching of the Church, morally objectionable civil rights in such areas as medical procedures or services, or are designed to implement public policies which, according to church teaching, are violative of social justice or other moral requirements.[130] Contractual provisions which are explicitly or implicitly contrary to divine law are, of course, not canonized and are not enforceable in ecclesiastical tribunals.

Other exceptions to the canonization of secular contract law derive from express provisions of canon law, notably those which govern acts of extraordinary administration (see cc. 1277, 1281), alienation (cc. 1291–1294) and related transactions (c. 1295), and leasing (c. 1297). For the most part, the canons do not so much contradict provisions of civil law as they add requirements (e.g., consultation, consent, permission) to those of civil law; it is principally in that sense that they constitute exceptions to the canonization of the provisions of civil law.

In at least one regard, however, a canonical provision does contradict the civil law of many nations, and that is the directive in canon 1547, referred to in canon 1290, that in ecclesiastical tri-

bunals proof by the testimony of witnesses, under the supervision of the judge, is always admissible. Civil laws, including those in the United States, often require documentary proof of the existence and terms of some kinds of contracts (e.g., the purchase and sale of real estate). Under the 1917 code, the question arose and remained a subject of controversy as to whether or not the canonization of the civil law of contracts included the procedural requirement of written proof where such a requirement existed in civil law. The 1983 code resolves the controversy by the explicit reference in canon 1290 to canon 1547 which allows proof by means of witnesses in all cases.[131]

The canonization of secular contract law in canon 1290 would seem to place upon professional canonists a responsibility to become reasonably familiar with the basics of the secular legal system under which they live, and in particular its approach to the law of contracts, in order more effectively to cooperate with civil attorneys representing dioceses, parishes, and church-related institutions. Conversely, it would seem to be in the best interests of such entities for their civil attorneys to become familiar with the canonical exceptions to the canonization of the civil law of contracts that are set forth in the following canons.

Restricted Alienation

Canon 1291 — The permission of the authority competent according to the norm of law is required for the valid alienation of goods which constitute by legitimate designation the stable patrimony of a public juridic person and whose value exceeds the sum defined by law.

The Latin verb *alienare* means "to make something another's." Alienation of temporal goods is the transfer of ownership. Ownership may be total (as in fee simple ownership of real estate) or partial (as in a life estate or a remainder interest in real estate); alienation is a transfer of either total

---

[130] See W. Bassett, "A Note on the Law of Contracts and the Canonical Integrity of Public Benefit Religious Organizations," *CLSAP* 59 (1997) 63–67.

[131] See *Comm* 12 (1980) 427–428.

or partial ownership. It is effected nearly always by sale, gift, or exchange.[132]

As a juridic act, alienation differs radically from administration. Acts of administration, either ordinary or extraordinary, have as their purpose the preservation, proper use, improvement, or enhanced productivity of temporal goods; acts of alienation have as their purpose the termination of ownership. While many commentators on the 1917 code classified alienation as an act of extraordinary administration, they did so because of the particular wording of that code;[133] alienation in the 1983 code, which in this regard is worded more precisely, has been deliberately and appropriately categorized differently (see commentary on cc. 1254, §1; 1277)[134] and is governed by norms that differ from the norms that govern acts of extraordinary administration.

Since alienation is the transfer of ownership, there is no alienation if no transfer of ownership takes place. Mortgaging property is not an act of alienation. A mortgage gives rise to rights in regard to property, and creates the potential of a future loss of ownership in the event of default in payments on the loan for which the mortgage serves as collateral, but there is no immediate transfer of ownership and, hence, no alienation. The same is true of assuming a mortgage when

purchasing property which already has a mortgage on it. Granting a right of way or an easement to come across or otherwise use one's land, since it does not involve a transfer of ownership, is not an act of alienation.[135] Nor is leasing, or granting an option to purchase one's property, or borrowing or loaning sums of money with or without collateral, or refusing a gift.

None of these transactions entails a transfer of ownership by the initiator of the action. Many of these transactions, however, may constitute acts of extraordinary administration and thereby be subject to the norms governing such acts (see cc. 638, §1; 1277; 1281); and, under certain circumstances, many may fall into the category of transactions which endanger the patrimonial condition of a public juridic person and, on that account, be subject, according to canon 1295, to the norms governing alienation, even though the actions themselves are not acts of alienation. Since canon 1295 transactions are required to conform to the laws governing alienation, some authors refer to such transactions as alienation "in the broad sense" and to transfers of ownership as alienation "in the strict sense." While a basis for such a distinction existed in the 1917 code,[136] no basis for such a distinction exists in the 1983 code and, consequently, continuing to speak of alienation "in the broad sense" can lead to confusion and to canonical errors (see commentary on c. 1295). Clarity and canonical accuracy are best served by

---

[132] Alienation may also result from the decision in an arbitration proceeding or the settlement in a conciliation proceeding (see c. 1715).

[133] Whereas the 1983 code speaks of four essential elements of ownership, namely, acquisition, retention, administration, and alienation (see cc. 1254, §1; 1255), the 1917 code spoke of only three, namely, acquisition, retention, and administration (see *CIC* 1495). Accordingly, without a category of its own, alienation was considered to be an act of extraordinary administration. See, e.g., Vromant, 162, 210; Bouscaren-Ellis-Korth, 835. Even among the commentators on the 1917 code, however, the view was expressed that alienation and administration are two distinct juridic acts. See Cappello, 2:573.

[134] De Paolis, *De Bonis Ecclesiae,* 98; idem, *I Beni Temporali,* 149–150; 179, n. 1; 183–184; López Alarcón, in *Pamplona ComEng,* 792. See *Comm* 12 (1980) 396.

[135] If the easement also includes the right to remove minerals, timber, or other natural resources from the land, then, of course, the easement would entail alienation of such resources.

[136] Canon 1533 of the 1917 code, the antecedent of canon 1295 of the present code, provided that the norms governing acts of alienation must be followed not only in an alienation properly so called (*proprie dicta*) but also in any transaction which could worsen the condition of the moral person. The latter transactions became known among commentators as alienation *improprie dicta* or alienation in the broad sense. The modifier *proprie dicta* has been deleted in the 1983 code, thereby removing the textual basis for the confusing distinction between alienation in the strict sense and alienation in the broad sense.

confining use of the term "alienation" to transfers of ownership.

Confusion has also been caused by authors who suggest that a transfer of ownership from one public juridic person in the Church to another public juridic person is not alienation because the property remains "church property"; it is still the property of a public juridic person, albeit a different one, such authors say, and so the amount of church property in the world has not lessened. The purpose of the Church's laws restricting alienation, however, is not to maintain a reservoir of property dedicated to the work of the Church, as if that were the meaning of "church property" (see c. 1258), but rather to protect the economic viability and stability of each public juridic person by guarding against imprudent loss of temporal goods by any individual public juridic person in the Church.

A minority view under the 1917 code held that a transfer of property from one province of a religious institute to another province of the same institute should not be considered alienation because members of the same religious family are supposed to help each other and, hence, such a transfer should not be subject to the laws governing restricted alienation.[137] This view was contrary not only to the views of the vast majority of canonists but also to the practice of the Roman Curia.[138] The view still finds occasional expression today, however, and at times is expanded to include transfers from parishes to the diocese, especially in areas where civil-law ownership of church property has been vested in one corporation sole.[139] The view appears to confuse having a

[137] E. Regatillo, *Institutiones Iuris Canonici,* 6th ed. (Santander: Sal Terrae, 1961) 2:230.

[138] This was acknowledged by Regatillo himself (ibid.). See also Cappello, 2:583; Vermeersch-Creusen, 2: 594–595; S. Sipos, *Enchiridion Iuris Canonici,* 7th ed. (Rome: Herder, 1960) 697.

[139] See F. Morrisey, "The Conveyance of Ecclesiastical Goods," *CLSAP* 38 (1976) 129; idem, "The Alienation of Temporal Goods in Contemporary Practice," *Stud Can* 29 (1995) 307. For a brief description of the corporation sole, see commentary on c. 1256.

just cause, which is required for every act of alienation (c. 1293, §1, 1°), with not being in the category of restricted alienation at all, as if only unjustified transfers of ownership were subject to the laws governing alienation. Such a view misunderstands the meaning of alienation and the purpose of the Church's laws governing it (see commentary on c. 1293, §1).

In addressing issues of alienation, it is important to keep in mind the true stance of the Church in regard to it. Contrary to the beliefs of some church administrators who go to great lengths to avoid having a transaction regarded as alienation as if it were a prohibited evil, the code does not view alienation as always undesirable. At times it is highly desirable, even encouraged. One of the principal purposes for the acquisition of material possessions by the Church is to use them for or give them to the poor and needy (c. 1254, §2). Accordingly, alienation for purposes of charity is recommended (see cc. 640, 1285). Though not prohibited, and though often encouraged, alienation is nevertheless restricted at times. As canon 1291 directs, it is restricted when the property to be alienated is part of the lawfully designated stable patrimony of a public juridic person and of a value in excess of a legitimately established minimum.

Stable patrimony is all property, real or personal, movable or immovable, tangible or intangible, that, either of its nature or by explicit designation, is destined to remain in the possession of its owner for a long or indefinite period of time to afford financial security for the future. It is the opposite of free or liquid capital which is intended to be used to meet operating expenses or otherwise disposed of within a reasonably short period of time (within one or, at most, two years).

There are four general categories of stable patrimony: (1) real estate (land, buildings); (2) non-fungible personalty (tangible movable property that is not consumed in its use, such as automobiles, furniture, books); (3) long-term (over two years) investments in securities (stocks, bonds, treasury notes); (4) restricted funds, that is, funds, even if comprised of cash or short-term securities, that have been set aside for a specific purpose, such as pension funds or certain building or educational funds. As a general rule, these four categories of assets are intended to afford reliable security for the future, enabling a juridic person to continue to serve the purposes for which it was created.[140] They are said to be immobilized, stabilized, frozen; they are what is meant by "stable patrimony." Cash and its equivalents (e.g., checking and regular savings accounts, short-term certificates of deposit, securities to be held only for a short term), on the other hand, are considered to be liquid or free capital; it is intended that they be consumed in their use within a relatively short period of time (e.g., to meet operating expenses) and, hence, they are not stable patrimony.

Alienation is restricted, according to canon 1291, when the ecclesiastical goods to be alienated are part of the legitimately designated stable patrimony. "Legitimate designation" can be explicit or implicit. It is implicit when the property is of such a nature that ordinarily it is acquired with the intention of retaining it for a long or indefinite period of time; in such cases, the act of acquisition implicitly designates the property as part of the stable patrimony.[141] Classic examples of property implicitly designated as stable patrimony are parcels of land, buildings, books, and fine furniture. Rarely are such assets acquired by public juridic persons in the Church without an intention to retain ownership of them indefinitely. On occasion, however, such an asset, a parcel of land for example, could be acquired not to be held for future use or to be developed over a long period of time, but with a view toward a quick resale; in such a circumstance, the asset could be explicitly designated as not part of stable patrimony. Absent such an explicit designation, the parcel of land would implicitly be allocated to stable patrimony by virtue of the kind of asset it is.

When assets are acquired which of their nature are not usually retained indefinitely (e.g., cash,

some categories of stocks or bonds), they become part of stable patrimony only by explicit designation by the administrator of the acquiring public juridic person as happens, for example, when such assets are allocated to pension funds or other restricted funds or portfolios.[142] Without such explicit designation, such assets would not be part of stable patrimony and, hence, not subject to the norms governing restricted alienation. Sound administration dictates that assets belonging to stable patrimony should be clearly identified in the up-to-date inventory required by canon 1283, 2°, 3°.[143]

Alienation, then, is restricted when the property to be alienated is the property of a public juridic person which, by legitimate designation either explicit or implicit, is stable patrimony, and the value of which exceeds a determined amount. In addition to delineating these prerequisites for restricted alienation, canon 1291 sets forth the first of the restrictions, namely, the invalidating requirement of permission of competent authority. Alienation is one of two instances in the code where permission, which ordinarily is required only for liceity, is said to be required for validity.[144] The reference to competent authority is in need of further specification, as is the determined amount above which permission is required for validity; both items receive further specification in the following canon.

Canon 1292 — §1. Without prejudice to the prescript of can. 638, §3, when the value of the goods whose alienation is proposed falls within the min-

---

[140] See Rovera, 277; Schouppe, 131; Aznar Gil, 408; J. Mantecón, in *Com Ex* IV/1, 154; Périsset, 199–200; De Paolis, *I Beni Temporali,* 185–188.

[141] See Schouppe, 132; De Paolis, *I Beni Temporali,* 187.

[142] Explicit designation to stable patrimony may be pursuant to the intention of founders or donors, or may be dictated by provisions in the statutes of a juridic person. Schouppe, 132; Mantecón, in *Com Ex* IV/1, 154; De Paolis, *I Beni Temporali,* 187.

[143] Périsset, 199, 200.

[144] Canons requiring permission for the validity of alienation (and other transactions subject to the norms governing alienation) include, in addition to c. 1291, cc. 638, §3; 1190, §2; 1292, §2. The other instance where permission is said to be required for validity concerns the acceptance of a non-autonomous pious foundation (c. 1304, §1).

imum and maximum amounts to be defined by the conference of bishops for its own region, the competent authority is determined by the statutes of juridic persons if they are not subject to the diocesan bishop; otherwise, the competent authority is the diocesan bishop with the consent of the finance council, the college of consultors, and those concerned. The diocesan bishop himself also needs their consent to alienate the goods of the diocese.

§2. The permission of the Holy See is also required for the valid alienation of goods whose value exceeds the maximum amount, goods given to the Church by vow, or goods precious for artistic or historical reasons.

§3. If the asset to be alienated is divisible, the parts already alienated must be mentioned when seeking permission for the alienation; otherwise the permission is invalid.

§4. Those who by advice or consent must take part in alienating goods are not to offer advice or consent unless they have first been thoroughly informed both of the economic state of the juridic person whose goods are proposed for alienation and of previous alienations.

The first concern of canon 1292 is to afford some specification to the preceding canon's reference to a "sum defined by law." It does so by calling for a two-tiered sum, a minimum and a maximum, to be established according to the principle of subsidiarity by each episcopal conference and legitimately promulgated after having been reviewed by the Apostolic See (see c. 455, §2). For all religious institutes the maximum amount is to be determined by the Holy See (c. 638, §3); the minimum amount, however, since religious institutes are bound by the norms of Book V except where expressly provided otherwise (c. 635, §1), is that set by the episcopal conference for its region, there being no provision to the contrary for religious.[145]

[145] De Paolis argues that canon 683, §3 leaves the determination of the minimum amount to the proper law of each religious institute (*I Beni Temporali,* 190). While

The amounts promulgated for various nations may be found among their published complementary norms.[146] In the United States the current maximum amount, promulgated after review by the Holy See, is three million dollars.[147] Technically, no minimum amount has been promulgated after review by the Holy See but, as a matter of practice, the National Conference of Catholic Bishops regards $500,000 as the currently operative minimum amount.[148] In establishing the minimum amount,

his argumentation is interesting, it is difficult to reconcile his position with the wording of c. 638, §3 which, unlike c. 638, §1, makes no mention of proper law. Moreover, allowing proper law to determine the minimum would result in religious institutes within the same region having minimums that differ not only from each other but from other public juridic persons in the region, a result the Holy See appears not to favor in regard to the maximum since it is the practice of the Holy See to set the same maximum for religious as has been set by the episcopal conference for others. Also, allowing proper law to determine the minimum, rather than holding religious to the minimum set for each region by the episcopal conference, would result in international religious institutes being bound by one uniform minimum despite wide economic discrepancies between different regions of the world.

[146] See "Canon 1292. Particular Legislation: The Determination of Minimum and Maximum Amounts for Alienation," *CLD* 11, 308–314; "Complementary Norms to the Code Promulgated by English-Language Conferences of Bishops," in *Pamplona ComEng,* 1312, 1332, 1341, 1353, 1363, 1390, 1407, 1415; J. Martín de Agar, *Legislazione delle Conferenze Episcopali Complementare al C.I.C.,* passim.

[147] NCCB, *Decree of Promulgation,* May 24, 1993. This decree was issued subsequent to the April 1991 publication of the volume of complementary norms by the NCCB. A brief history of earlier NCCB action in regard to canon 1292 may be found in the published volume, NCCB-*CompNm* 22–24. A fuller history may be found in *RR* (1982) 30–34 and *RR* (1986) 41–42.

[148] NCCB-*CompNm* 23. In 1985, the NCCB requested from the Holy See *recognitio* of a five-million-dollar maximum and a minimum of $500,000. The Holy See rejected the five-million-dollar maximum, insisting upon a maximum of one million dollars. In its reply the Holy See made no mention of the $500,000 minimum which had been requested in relation to the five-million-dollar maximum but simply stated that the minimum

it is important for episcopal conferences to keep in mind that the minimum they set is not just for alienations of diocesan property by diocesan bishops, but also for alienations by parishes, religious institutes, and all other public juridic persons within the territory of the episcopal conference. Below the minimum, the Church's norms restricting alienation of stable patrimony by public juridic persons, such as parishes, do not apply. One may wonder if the episcopal conference in the United States had this in mind when approving a minimum as high as $500,000.[149]

Under certain circumstances, when several assets owned by the same public juridic person are alienated, their individual values coalesce for the purpose of reaching the minimum or maximum lev-

els. Three circumstances give rise to such coalescence: intention, time, and purpose. When the *intention* at the time of alienating the first asset is to alienate several assets (e.g., separate lots of land, paintings), though at different times, the total value of all the assets to be alienated must be used to determine at the time of the first alienation whether the minimum or maximum levels will be reached.[150] So, too, when two or more assets are alienated within a short period of *time* (one month or less), apart from any initial intention to do so, the separate alienations are considered to be morally one; as soon as the cumulative value of the separate assets reaches the minimum or maximum level, the required authorizations must be obtained for the canonical validity of the remaining alienations, even though, standing alone, the value of each remaining individual alienation would be below the minimum.[151] When various items are alienated for the same *purpose* (e.g., to finance the construction of a new building), their value coalesces regardless of how much time has elapsed between alienations and notwithstanding the absence of any initial expectation of having to alienate multiple assets. Thus, after some holdings have been alienated in order to finance construction, if additional costs arise making a further alienation necessary, the entire outlay, united by purpose, coalesces and the required authorizations must be obtained for the additional alienation even though, standing alone, it is below the minimum.[152]

The second concern of canon 1292 is to afford specification to the preceding canon's reference to "the authority competent according to the norm of law." It does so, first, by acknowledging the provisions of canon 638, §3 which include designation of the authorities competent to grant permission for alienation in religious institutes. Canon 1292, §1 then distinguishes public juridic persons subject to the diocesan bishop (e.g., parishes, cer-

may be established in accord with c. 1292, §1. See NCCB-*CompNm* 22–23; RR (1986) 42; *Pamplona ComEng,* 1419, n.18. This would require a vote of the NCCB, with subsequent submission of the agreed upon minimum to the Holy See for *recognitio.* No further action in regard to a minimum has been taken by the NCCB, even when requesting (and receiving) the new maximum of three million dollars in 1993.

[149] By particular law in many dioceses of the United States, pastors are forbidden, without the permission of the diocesan bishop, to alienate parochial property valued in excess of an amount far below the minimum of $500,000. Rarely, however, do such particular laws contain language expressly invalidating alienations contrary to the law; without such language, prohibited alienations, although illict, are canonically valid (see c. 10). In a few dioceses, alienations in excess of an amount far below the minimum of $500,000 have been designated as acts of extraordinary administration with the result that such alienations, without a faculty from the ordinary, are thereby rendered invalid (see c. 1281, §1). In such cases, however, as in all cases of prohibited alienations below the minimum established by the episcopal conference, the consultations (of finance council, college of consultors, and interested parties) required by c. 1292, §1 for restricted alienations above the minimum, since not required below the minimum, are often omitted. While some diocesan bishops may view as desirable the absence of an obligation to consult, the underlying concerns in the law of the Church for expert advice, shared responsibility, and the rights of interested parties may be thwarted when an episcopal conference sets an excessively high minimum.

[150] See *CLD* 2, 447–448; Vromant, 260; Bouscaren-Ellis-Korth, 844.

[151] See *CLD* 1, 731; López Alarcón, in *Pamplona ComEng,* 803.

[152] See Bouscaren-Ellis-Korth, 844–845.

tain diocesan foundations) from those not so subject (e.g., supradiocesan entities such as regional seminaries or national universities). For the latter, canon 1292, §1 remits to their statutes the designation of authorities competent to authorize alienations above the minimum level. For public juridic persons subject to the diocesan bishop, canon 1292, §1 designates as the authority competent to authorize alienations above the minimum level the diocesan bishop with the consent of the diocesan finance council, the college of consultors, and "those concerned" (e.g., founders, donors, beneficiaries, and others whose rights might be affected by the proposed alienation). The same threefold consent is required for valid alienations by the diocesan bishop of stable patrimony of the diocese above the minimum level.

For alienations above the maximum level (as determined by the episcopal conference in accord with c. 1292, §1 or by the Holy See in accord with c. 638, §3) by any public juridic person, whether subject to the diocesan bishop or not, the permission of the Holy See is required in addition to the permissions already required for alienations above the minimum level.[153] Permission of the Holy See is also required, regardless of monetary value, for the canonically valid alienation of goods considered precious for artistic or historical reasons or given to a public juridic person (the specialized meaning accorded the word "church" in c. 1258) in fulfillment of a vow. Canonical tradition has long regarded goods given pursuant to a vow as

somehow sharing in the sacredness of a vow as a religious act, and for that reason as being directly subject to the authority of the Holy See. A similar concern for the sacred underlies the reservation to the Holy See of permission to alienate significant relics or other relics or images which are the objects of great veneration (see c. 1190).

In addition to the invalidating law requiring permission of competent authority, there is an additional requirement for the validity of an act of restricted alienation when the property to be alienated is divisible, that is, of such a nature that portions of it can be alienated separately (e.g., a library, a collection of paintings, a tract of land capable of being divided into separate lots). Canon 1292, §3 requires disclosure of previously alienated parts of divisible property; in the absence of such disclosure, permission to alienate a subsequent portion is invalid. The invalidating clause in paragraph three is a specification of the general norm found in canon 63, §1. The concern of the legislator is to prevent the bit-by-bit dissipation of valuable assets without the knowledge and approval of proper ecclesiastical authority.

Canon 1292, §4 sets forth the sensible directive that all whose advice (where statutes call for it) or consent is required are not to offer their advice or consent unless they have been thoroughly informed both of the overall financial condition of the public juridic person involved and of previous alienations of the juridic person's stable patrimony. The law seeks informed, not *pro forma*, advice and consent, and therefore calls for accurate and thorough information to be given, among others, to finance councils, colleges of consultors, interested parties, diocesan bishops, and the Holy See. While the directive of paragraph four refers explicitly only to consultation on the occasion of proposed alienation, the principle of informed consultation and consent is a principle of sound governance applicable, by analogy, to all situations of consultation (see also c. 127, §3).[154]

---

[153] When the Holy See is involved, the competent congregations are CICLSAL for institutes of consecrated life and societies of apostolic life, and CFC for all others (*PB* 108, 98). The congregations are particularly interested in knowing if all required consultations have taken place, if all necessary informed consents have been obtained, and if all other procedural requirements both for validity and liceity have been fulfilled. The interest of the congregations in the merits of a proposed alienation focuses chiefly on just cause, the adequacy of compensation, the continuing Catholic identity of an institution whose assets are being alienated, and the potential effect upon the financial security and pastoral mission of the alienating public juridic person.

[154] T. Green, "Shepherding the Patrimony of the Poor: Diocesan and Parish Structures of Financial Administration," *J* 56 (1997) 712.

Canon 1293 — §1. The alienation of goods whose value exceeds the defined minimum amount also requires the following:

1° a just cause, such as urgent necessity, evident advantage, piety, charity, or some other grave pastoral reason;

2° a written appraisal by experts of the asset to be alienated.

§2. Other precautions prescribed by legitimate authority are also to be observed to avoid harm to the Church.

Canon 1294 — §1. An asset ordinarily must not be alienated for a price less than that indicated in the appraisal.

§2. The money received from the alienation is either to be invested carefully for the advantage of the Church or to be expended prudently according to the purposes of the alienation.

In addition to the requirements for the validity of an act of restricted alienation, the code also prescribes requirements for the liceity of such an act. Canons 1293 and 1294 together contain five such requirements: just cause, appraisal by experts, alienation ordinarily not below appraisal, restricted use of proceeds, and observance of additional precautions prescribed by legitimate authority. Failure to comply leaves the transaction valid[155] but contrary to the law of the Church and, hence, subjects those responsible for the noncompliance to possible reprisals, including having to make restitution to the public juridic person for any resulting harm.[156]

The first of these requirements is the presence of a just cause. Essentially this means that the gain to the public juridic person must outweigh the loss of the portion of stable patrimony to be alienated. Ordinarily the gain is to be assessed in financial terms, but not always. Canon 1293, §1,

1° includes as examples of just causes such nonfinancial considerations as piety, charity, and serious pastoral concerns. Illustrative of the latter would be the desire on the part of the sponsor of a Catholic hospital to maintain a Catholic presence in institutional health care in a given locality by entering into a form of partnering or networking with a secular institution that involves alienation of assets canonically owned by the sponsor; monetary return to the sponsor in such a situation may be minimal but intangible justification may be found not only in securing the effective continuation of Catholic presence but also in the corporate witness given by the sponsor to charity and poverty (see c. 640).

Confusion has resulted from the expressed view that whenever prudence dictates that ownership of a particular piece of property should be relinquished (as, for example, where it is heavily taxed because it is not presently being used for religious, educational, or charitable purposes, or where expenses of maintaining the property far outweigh the revenues it produces), the laws restricting alienation do not apply and, hence, there is no need to obtain the requisite permissions or fulfill any of the other requirements for restricted alienation.[157] Such a view seems to assume that the presence of a justifying reason removes a transfer of ownership from the category of restricted alienation. As canon 1293, §1, 1° makes clear, however, a just cause is always necessary for an act of restricted alienation; it is one of the first items consultative bodies and ecclesiastical authorities should look for in a proposed alienation. It is never a justification for omitting consultation and ignoring the need to obtain authorization. Alienation is not the unjustified transfer of ownership; it must always be justified, since otherwise the requisite authorization cannot licitly be given.

Canon 1293, §1, 2° prescribes the second of the requirements for licit alienation, namely, writ-

---

[155] Nothing in cc. 1293 or 1294 either explicitly or implicitly suggests that any of their provisions affect validity; consequently, they do not (see c. 10).

[156] See cc.128; 1281, §3; and, by analogy, cc.1289 and 1296.

[157] See Morrisey, "The Conveyance of Ecclesiastical Goods," 130; idem, "The Alienation of Temporal Goods in Contemporary Practice," 308.

ten appraisal by experts of the value of the asset to be alienated. Use of the plural makes clear that appraisals should be obtained from at least two experts. The concern of the legislator is that judgments of administrators, consultative bodies, interested parties, and ecclesiastical authorities be informed judgments based on data and advice of the highest quality (see commentary on c. 1292, §4). Even when there is to be no monetary return, as in cases of alienation motivated by charity or other intangible concerns as noted above, expert appraisals must still be obtained to form part of the basis upon which to judge the appropriateness of the proposed alienation. Caution should be exercised in utilizing governmental valuations of property made for the purpose of assessing real estate or personal property taxes, since such valuations are often out of date or otherwise not in accord with present market value.

The requirement to obtain appraisals gives rise to the correlative requirement that assets ordinarily not be alienated for less than the lowest appraised amount. Obviously, whenever charity or some other pastoral motivation provides the justification for an alienation, attaining the appraised value will not be a consideration. So, too, ecclesial values such as precluding unethical future use of alienated property may dictate the sale of property to a purchaser whose ethical commitments are in accord with those of the Church even though the price being offered is less than the appraised value which could be obtained from a less ethically committed purchaser. Such considerations are illustrative of those which led to the insertion of the word "ordinarily" into canon 1294, §1.[158]

The fourth requirement for licit acts of restricted alienation concerns the disposition of the proceeds realized from the alienation. Canon 1294, §2 requires that, to the extent the proceeds are not expended for the purpose of the alienation (as, for example, if the alienation yields more than needed for payment of a debt for which the alienation had been authorized), the money received is to be rein-

vested into some form of stable patrimony of the public juridic person (the specialized meaning of the word "church" according to c. 1258). The law restricts alienation in order to protect the stable patrimony of a public juridic person; accordingly, canon 1294, §2 requires that all proceeds not expended for the authorized purpose of the alienation be returned by legitimate designation to stable patrimony.

The final requirement for the liceity of an act of restricted alienation acknowledges the possibility that particular circumstances of time or place may suggest that additional precautions be prescribed by legitimate authority; canon 1293, §2 requires that all such precautions be observed. Requiring that a proposed sale of real estate receive a certain measure of publicity in order to attract suitable offers,[159] or requiring collateral to secure the payment of future installments,[160] or the insertion of invalidating clauses into civil documents to assure comparable civil invalidity in the event of canonical invalidity[161] are illustrative of such additional precautions.

Other Restricted Transactions

Canon 1295 — The requirements of cann. 1291–1294, to which the statutes of juridic persons must also conform, must be observed not only in alienation but also in any transaction which can worsen the patrimonial condition of a juridic person.

The first concern of this canon, expressed in the subordinate clause, is to mandate conformity between the statutes of public juridic persons and the provisions of canons 1291–1294. This means that the statutes must either include the provisions of canons 1291–1294 or incorporate them by reference. Seemingly a strange requirement, since public juridic persons are bound by canons 1291–1294 whether or not their statutes make reference

---

[158] See *Comm* 5 (1973) 100; 12 (1980) 426.

[159] Aznar Gil, 411.
[160] Mantecón, in *Com Ex* IV/1, 162.
[161] Ibid., 163.

to them, the expressed purpose of the requirement is to ensure that failure to fulfill any of the invalidating requirements will render an attempted alienation not only canonically invalid but civilly invalid as well.[162] The laudable intent is to preclude situations where a canonically invalid transfer of ownership is civilly valid, thereby creating serious problems for the public juridic person whose property has been wrongfully alienated (see c. 1296).[163] Notwithstanding the laudable intent, attainment of the desired goal presupposes that the statutes of the Church's public juridic persons are civilly recognized, a premise not verified in many nations including the United States. In such nations, it is necessary to have canons 1291–1294 incorporated by reference in the relevant civil documents (in the United States, these would chiefly be the by-laws of corporations or particular forms of trust agreements). The effect of such incorporation by reference is to put all persons dealing with the entity or institution on notice that the canonical requirements, as well as the civil, must be met in order to have a civilly binding transaction. It is incumbent upon ecclesiastical authorities responsible for approving the statutes of public juridic persons (see commentary on c. 117) to see to it that the statutes do conform to canons 1291–1294,[164] and, where necessary to achieve the purpose of such conformity, that the appropriate civil documents conform also.

Although the view has been expressed that canon 1295 applies to private as well as public juridic persons,[165] such a view seems untenable. Canon 1257, §2 is clear that private juridic persons are not bound by the canons of Book V unless expressly so provided. There is nothing in the wording of canon 1295 that either explicitly or implicitly expresses an intention to include private juridic persons within its scope. Moreover, canon 1291 makes clear that the norms governing

alienation found in canons 1291–1294 apply only to the stable patrimony of public juridic persons, and it is the chief purpose of canon 1295 to apply canons 1291–1294 to transactions other than alienation. That would seem to make clear that canon 1295 is similarly limited to public juridic persons. It is also noteworthy that the modifier "public," absent in canon 1295, is also absent in canons 1292–1294, though there can be no doubt that those canons, forming a cluster with canon 1291, apply only to public juridic persons. Canon 1295, explicitly referring to canons 1291–1294, seems clearly to be part of the same cluster. To hold otherwise is effectively to undermine the distinction, so pivotal throughout Book V, between the temporal goods of public juridic persons and those of private juridic persons.[166]

The second and principal concern of canon 1295 is to place restrictions upon another category of financial transactions, distinct from acts of alienation, which are of considerable importance in the life of the Church. Canon 1295 embraces a variety of contracts and other financial transactions whose common characteristic is the risk they pose to the overall economic well-being of a public juridic person. From the canonical point of view, economic well-being is rooted in stable patrimony, namely, in all property destined to remain in the possession of its owner for a long or indefinite period of time and, hence, property on which the financial future of a public juridic person depends (see commentary on c. 1291). That is the meaning of the "patrimonial condition" referred to in canon 1295.

Mortgaging a parcel of real estate or pledging valuable items of personal property as collateral to secure the repayment of a loan are often given as examples of canon 1295 transactions, as are granting easements, licenses, liens, or options to purchase, contracting to pay annuities, making unsecured loans, acting as guarantor or surety, transferring operational control of one's assets while retaining ownership, and incurring debts even if unsecured by collateral. Such a listing can

[162] *Comm* 12 (1980) 426.

[163] Périsset, 215–216; De Paolis, *De Bonis Ecclesiae,* 107; idem, *I Beni Temporali,* 197.

[164] Périsset, 216.

[165] Aznar Gil, 427–429.

[166] Mantecón, in *Com Ex* IV/1, 167.

be misleading, however, since each of the examples may or may not be a canon 1295 transaction depending upon the potential impact upon the overall patrimonial condition of the public juridic person. The application of canon 1295 is necessarily relative, depending upon both the degree of risk involved and the economic condition of the public juridic person. A debt that so burdens the stable patrimony of an inner-city parish as to threaten the future financial security of the parish may pose little or no risk to the future security of an affluent suburban parish. In the case of the inner-city parish, contracting such a debt would be a canon 1295 transaction, whereas in the case of the affluent parish it would not. What is placed at risk must be viewed in light of the total value of the patrimony in general.[167] That is the clear import of canon 1295.

To take another example of the inherent relativity of canon 1295, a mortgage in the contemporary world of finance, so far from always risking harm to economic stability, often enhances rather than endangers an organization's financial condition. Instead of paying construction or other costs with available surplus funds, it frequently is more advantageous to "use someone else's money" by borrowing what is needed to cover costs, placing a mortgage on a building under construction or on a parcel of real estate as collateral for the loan, and investing one's available surplus in securities whose long-term growth will far surpass the total interest payments due on the loan and often will even surpass the value of the mortgaged property itself.

Hence, mortgages and other means of financing that at the time commentaries were written on the 1917 code were uniformly viewed negatively as risk-laden ventures that imperiled one's financial future are today viewed as among the fundamentals of sound, productive fiscal management. While it remains true that, under certain circumstances, placing a mortgage upon a parcel of valuable real estate might pose a risk to the general

economic condition of a diocese, parish, religious institute, or other public juridic person, and therefore fall into the category of transactions governed by canon 1295, it is also true that in the contemporary world of finance such a transaction in other circumstances may pose little or no risk at all. It is surprising that many commentators on the 1983 code simply adopt *carte blanche* the pre-code list of transactions that were considered perilous under the 1917 code and assume, in apparent disregard of the evolutionary nature of modern finance and the inherent relativity of a norm of law that seeks to protect "patrimonial condition," that such transactions today always threaten the economic future of all public juridic persons. To suppose that transactions considered perilous in the early-twentieth-century world of finance remain so in all circumstances today seems as canonically unsophisticated as it is financially naive.

It is also surprising that a number of contemporary commentators cite *Pastorale munus* as an authoritative source for viewing individual acts of mortgaging, pledging, leasing, or contracting debts as acts that always risk harm to one's patrimonial condition and, hence, pursuant to canon 1295, are always subject to the norms governing acts of alienation.[168] It is true that, in 1963, Paul VI listed such transactions along with alienation when granting to residential bishops the faculty to grant permission up to a sum to be determined by a national or regional conference of bishops and approved by the Holy See.[169] It does not follow, however, that Paul VI considered such individual transactions in each and every case to risk harm to the overall financial condition and for that reason

---

[167] López Alarcón, in *Pamplona ComEng,* 805.

[168] See, e.g., López Alarcón, in *Pamplona ComEng,* 804–805; Mantecón, in *Com Ex* IV/1, 166; De Paolis, *De Bonis Ecclesiae,* 107; F. Salerno, in *Urbaniana Com,* 737.

[169] *PM* I: "Faculties which belong by right to a residential Bishop...32. To grant permission, for a legitimate reason, to alienate, pledge, mortgage, rent out, or perpetually lease ecclesiastical property and to authorize ecclesiastical moral persons to contract debts to the sum of money determined by the National or Regional Conference of Bishops and approved by the Holy See."

to be subject to the norms governing alienation in accord with canon 1533 of the 1917 code (the forerunner of c. 1295 of the present code). Unlike the 1983 code, the 1917 code, in addition to its canon 1533, contained separate restrictive provisions for individual acts of mortgaging (*CIC* 1538), pledging (*CIC* 1538), leasing (*CIC* 1541, 1542), and contracting debts (*CIC* 1538); each of these provisions required permission, depending upon the value of the property involved, of the same ecclesiastical authorities whose permission was required for acts of alienation. *Pastorale munus* equated such acts to acts of alienation for the purpose of obtaining prior permissions, not because such acts were always subject to the general provision of canon 1533 of the 1917 code, but because they were in each case subject to the specific restrictions of other canons which required the same or similar permissions. The deletion in the 1983 code of the separate provisions governing mortgages, pledges, and debts, and the total change of discipline regarding leasing (see c. 1297 and accompanying commentary), results in an entirely different juridic status for such transactions. They, like many of the transactions traditionally viewed as always constituting a risk to one's economic condition, would, under the 1983 code, likely be classified as acts of extraordinary administration because they are not routine and not financially insignificant, and therefore would be subject to the regulatory norms for acts of extraordinary administration (see cc. 1277, 1281); but such acts do not rise to the level of a canon 1295 transaction unless they realistically threaten to weaken the general patrimonial condition of the public juridic person.

In the framework of the 1983 code, canon 1295 transactions are the more important acts of extraordinary administration, analogous to the more important acts of ordinary administration referred to and specially regulated in canon 1277. Just as the latter cannot be determined in the abstract but only in light of the financial condition of each diocese (see c. 1277), so too a transaction cannot be determined to be one of the more important acts of extraordinary administration, and hence a canon

1295 transaction, except in the light of its likely impact on the overall financial condition of the relevant public juridic person. Nor is it sufficient that there be a purely theoretical possibility of harm; based on an examination of the proposed transaction in the concrete, it must appear to constitute a realistic danger of worsening the economic well-being of the public juridic person.[170] To suppose that canon 1295 restricts every nonroutine financial transaction, subjecting them all to the cumbersome requirements of canons 1291–1294 without regard to the economic contexts in which they are placed, would mean that all acts of extraordinary administration are *ipso facto* also canon 1295 transactions, an interpretation which would render superfluous the norms enacted for acts of extraordinary administration and would blur the distinctions between such acts, canon 1295 transactions, and alienation.

While canon 1295 transactions are subject to the same norms that govern alienation, the wording of the canon makes clear that canon 1295 transactions are not acts of alienation. This is also evident from canon 1267, §2 which acknowledges the possibility that in some circumstances canon 1295 applies to the acceptance of offerings burdened by a condition or modal obligation; in such circumstances, canon 1295 applies to an act of *acquisition* of temporal goods, a matter far different from an act of alienation. Clarity and canonical precision are not well served by referring to canon 1295 transactions, as a number of authors do, as "alienation in the broad sense."[171]

Alienation is the transfer of ownership (see commentary on c. 1291). An act of alienation reduces, through sale or gift, the quantity of stable patrimony owned by a public juridic person or, where one asset is exchanged for another which by legitimate designation is to be part of stable patrimony, alters the identity of stable patrimony owned by a public juridic person. A canon 1295

---

[170] Schouppe, 136.

[171] Brief summaries of the views of several authors, followed by his own view, may be found in De Paolis, *I Beni Temporali*, 212–221.

transaction, on the other hand, leaves unchanged the quantity and identity of stable patrimony owned by a public juridic person, but nonetheless entails a risk to its future financial stability. Whereas the focus of the law restricting alienation is primarily on a specific asset proposed for sale or donation or exchange, the focus of the law restricting canon 1295 transactions is not primarily on the specific asset which is the subject of the transaction but on the "condition" of the public juridic person and, hence, on the potential of the transaction to weaken the future financial security of the public juridic person *as a whole,* which it is the purpose of stable patrimony to protect. An act of alienation is easy to recognize, since it involves a transfer of ownership; a canon 1295 transaction is less readily identified because it could be any of a great variety of actions (not involving a transfer of ownership) and in each case its categorization is contingent upon the degree of risk it poses to the overall patrimonial condition of the public juridic person involved. Assistance could be given to administrators in fulfilling their responsibility to identify canon 1295 transactions by carefully drawn and regularly updated statutes which, in the light of the patrimonial condition of each public juridic person, offer concrete criteria for determining when a proposed financial transaction should be judged to threaten the overall financial stability and future well-being of the juridic person. Such criteria cannot be offered in universal law or even in particular law; the complexities of contemporary finance preclude it. The inherent relativity of canon 1295, which defies antecedent juridical precision and certainty, well serves the flexibility and diversity needed in the administration of church property by church administrators in the modern world of finance.

In the 1983 code, the administration of church property falls into one of five categories: acts of ordinary administration, acts of ordinary administration of greater importance (see c. 1277), acts of extraordinary administration (see cc. 1277, 1281), acts of alienation (see cc. 1291–1294), and acts of extraordinary administration of greater importance because of the risk of harm they pose to a

public juridic person's overall economic condition (c. 1295 transactions). Each category has its own defining characteristics and is governed by its own canonical norms. Those who have been entrusted with the stewardship of church property need to be aware of the different categories, their defining characteristics, and the norms which govern them. Such awareness is an essential prerequisite for faithful fulfillment of the responsibilities of stewardship.

Civilly Valid but Canonically Invalid Alienations

Canon 1296 — Whenever ecclesiastical goods have been alienated without the required canonical formalities but the alienation is valid civilly, it is for the competent authority, after having considered everything thoroughly, to decide whether and what type of action, namely, personal or real, is to be instituted by whom and against whom in order to vindicate the rights of the Church.

This canon addresses situations where a civilly valid transfer of ownership is canonically invalid because of the failure to obtain the necessary permissions of ecclesiastical authorities or the necessary consents of those entitled to have been consulted, or because of the failure to disclose previously alienated parts of divisible assets. These are the invalidating requirements for an act of restricted alienation; they are what is meant by the expression "required canonical formalities [*solemnitates*]."[172] Canon 1296 speaks only of alienation; its wording does not include canon 1295 transactions, which the wording of canon 1295 makes clear are not alienation (see commentary on c. 1295). The possibilities of corrective action of which canon 1296

---

[172] The preceding canon speaks more comprehensively of the "requirements" (*requisita*) of cc. 1291–1294, thereby including not only the invalidating formalities (*solemnitates*) but also the prescriptions for liceity. Less precise in this regard, the 1917 code used the term *solemnitates* in both c. 1533, the antecedent of c. 1295 of the 1983 code, and in c. 1534, the antecedent of c. 1296 of the 1983 code.

speaks, however, could by analogy be applied to many canon 1295 transactions as well.

In situations of civil validity but canonical invalidity, canon 1296 calls for a decision to be made as to whether any action should be taken and, if so, whether it should be a real[173] or personal action, and by whom and against whom it should be brought, to vindicate the canonical rights of the public juridic person (the specialized meaning of "church" according to c. 1258) whose property has been civilly alienated. The law wisely refrains from mandating corrective action in all cases. Attempts to recover property the ownership of which has been validly transferred according to civil law are likely to succeed only in instances where the transferee of the property acknowledges the authority of canon law, and even in such cases, as in many others, such attempts can give rise to considerable ill will toward the Church. Moreover, at times canonically invalid alienations may in fact prove economically advantageous, suggesting that no steps should be taken to try to undo them; in certain circumstances, it may be more prudent to take no action and allow the canonical situation to heal by the passage of time through prescription (see commentary on cc. 1268–1270).[174]

While the view has been expressed that the competent authority referred to in canon 1296 is the authority whose permission was required for the alienation,[175] it would seem more appropriate for decisions about corrective action to be made by the immediate canonical superior of the person responsible for the canonically invalid alienation,

since otherwise the decision-making process in regard to corrective action could involve several authorities, consultative bodies, and interested parties. Whether or not to institute administrative or judicial proceedings to recover the invalidly alienated property, or to seek damages from those who wrongfully transferred civil ownership, would seem best left to the judgment of local authorities in a position to evaluate all relevant circumstances rather than involving the complex authority structure appropriate for initially authorizing an act of restricted alienation. This interpretation would seem to be confirmed by the parallel canon in the more recently promulgated Code of Canons of the Eastern Churches:

> Whenever ecclesiastical goods are alienated contrary to the prescriptions of canon law, but the alienation is civilly valid, the authority superior to the one who carried out the alienation decides, after a thorough review of the situation, whether and what type of action is to be taken to vindicate the rights of the Church as well as by whom and against whom this action is to be taken.[176]

Leasing

Canon 1297 — Attentive to local circumstances, it is for the conference of bishops to establish norms for the leasing of Church goods, especially regarding the permission to be obtained from competent ecclesiastical authority.

Nowhere in Book V, and perhaps nowhere in the code, is the principle of subsidiarity more fully applied than it is in regard to the leasing of church property. Virtually the entire matter is remitted by canon 1297 to norms enacted by episcopal conferences. A lease, of course, is a contract, and is therefore governed by the civil law of contracts unless a particular provision of civil law is contrary to divine or canon law (see commentary on c. 1290). Except for canon 1298, which

---

[173] A real action is one which has as its object a *res,* a particular piece of property as, for example, an action to recover possession of property invalidly alienated. A personal action has as its object a person against whom one has a claim for damages as, for example, an action to recover damages from an administrator who wrongfully alienated an asset of a public juridic person.

[174] Canonically invalid alienations cannot usually be sanated by ecclesiatical authority, since sanation cannot supply the missing consents of consultative bodies or individuals, often among the causes of canonical invalidity.

[175] Myers, in *CLSA Com,* 882.

[176] *CCEO* 1040.

prohibits leasing of ecclesiastical goods to their own administrators or members of their families, there are no laws in the code specifically applicable to leasing other than canon 1297, which does not itself constitute an exception to the canonization of civil law but simply calls for regulations to be enacted by episcopal conferences to supplement the regulations contained in civil law.

Leasing is not alienation because there is no transfer of ownership (see commentary on c. 1291). Were it not for canon 1297, some long-term leasing might qualify as a canon 1295 transaction because of the risk of harm to the overall financial condition of a public juridic person (e.g., by removing for lengthy periods of time the use of substantial portions of stable patrimony, by subjecting stable patrimony to the perils of cumulative wear and tear by long-term lessees, or by risking economic loss due to inflation in real estate values while bound to the terms of an ill-advised long-term lease). The effect of canon 1297, however, is to remove leasing from the ambit of canon 1295 by subjecting leasing to a separate discipline to be found in regulatory norms enacted by the episcopal conference in the light of local circumstances. That the entire matter of leasing is remitted to the episcopal conference is clear from the canon's explicit mention of conference norms regarding permission to be obtained from ecclesiastical authority. It is left to each episcopal conference to designate authorities competent to grant permission for different kinds or monetary levels of leasing. It is also left to episcopal conferences to determine if permission is to be required for validity or simply for liceity.[177]

Leasing also received separate treatment in the 1917 code where it was governed by a lengthy, complex canon[178] which commentators generally concluded had the effect of removing leasing from the category of what they called "alienation in the broad sense" (see commentary on cc. 1291, 1295).[179] Continuing the tradition of separate treatment for leasing, the 1983 code simplifies the matter by recognizing the inadvisability of attempting to legislate universally for leasing which is so heavily influenced by local circumstances, economics, and civil law.[180] Despite the separate treatment accorded leasing in both codes, and the view of leading commentators on the 1917 code that, precisely because of the separate treatment, leasing was not to be included among transactions which risk harm to the patrimonial condition so as to make applicable the norms governing alienation, several commentators on the 1983 code inexplicably include leasing among what they understand to be canon 1295 transactions, thereby subjecting at least some leasing to the norms of canons 1291–1294 governing alienation.

The episcopal conference in the United States, perhaps not realizing the extent of its responsibility to enact norms for the leasing of property belonging to public juridic persons throughout the territory of the conference, attempted to fulfill its responsibility under canon 1297 by issuing norms solely for the leasing of diocesan property by a diocesan bishop. Action taken by the National Conference of Catholic Bishops to implement canon 1297 reads simply:

See canon 1277: Acts of Extraordinary Administration for reference to leasing of church property by the diocesan bishop.[181]

---

[177] Permission is ordinarily required only for liceity. In two instances, however, the code requires permission for validity: acts of restricted alienation (and other transactions subject to the norms governing alienation) and acceptance of a non-autonomous pious foundation. See note 144 above.

[178] *CIC* 1541. This canon contained detailed prescriptions regarding renting to the highest bidder, safeguarding the boundaries of rented property, care of the property, payment of rent, guarantees of the fulfillment of all terms, and various levels of requisite permissions depending upon the value of the property, amount of the rent, and length of the term.

[179] See, e.g., Cappello, 2:582; Vermeersch-Creusen, 2:594.

[180] See *Comm* 5 (1973) 101; 9 (1977) 272; De Paolis, *I Beni Temporali,* 195; Aznar Gil, 433; Mantecón, in *Com Ex* IV/1, 170–171.

[181] NCCB-*CompNm* 25.

The reference is to the NCCB implementation of canon 1277 which requires episcopal conferences to determine what are to be regarded as acts of extraordinary administration by a diocesan bishop. The final two of such acts, as determined by the NCCB, concern the leasing of church property by the diocesan bishop (see commentary on c. 1277). The net effect of the NCCB action is to leave much of the Church in the United States without canonical norms governing the leasing of ecclesiastical goods.[182] Except for canon 1298, which prohibits leasing to administrators and their families, and canon 1547, which would allow in an ecclesiastical tribunal proof by witnesses alone of any lease regardless of civil-law requirements to the contrary,[183] the matter of leasing church property in the United States at the present time is, for most public juridic persons in the Church, governed solely by civil law. This includes leasing by religious institutes, provinces, and houses, all of which are governed by the canons of Book V except where express provision to the contrary has been made (c. 635, §1); there is no separate provision for leasing by religious institutes. In the absence of canonical norms enacted by the NCCB,[184] provisions regarding leasing could, of course, be included in the proper law of a religious institute or in the statutes of any other juridic person.[185]

---

[182] For norms issued by other episcopal conferences, see "Particular Legislation: Norms for Leasing Church Property," *CLD* 11, 315–317; "Complementary Norms to the Code Promulgated by English-Language Conferences of Bishops," in *Pamplona ComEng*, 1312, 1332–1333, 1353, 1408, 1415; J. Martín de Agar, *Legislazione delle Conferenze Episcopali Complementare al C.I.C.*, passim.

[183] See commentary on c. 1290.

[184] The view has been expressed that continued absence of substantial implementation of c. 1297 in the United States gives rise to the impression that such legislation is not important, an impression that may be difficult to overcome if left uncorrected for long. See F. Morrisey, "Leasing of Goods," in *CLSA Advisory Opinions 1984–1993*, ed. P. Cogan (Washington, D.C.: CLSA, 1995) 421.

[185] The Code of Canons of the Eastern Churches contains no canon dealing with the leasing of ecclesiastical goods.

Avoiding Conflict of Interest

Canon 1298 — Unless an asset is of little value, ecclesiastical goods are not to be sold or leased to the administrators of these goods or to their relatives up to the fourth degree of consanguinity or affinity without the special written permission of competent authority.

The wisdom of this canon is self-evident.[186] It is simply a specification of the general obligation of all ecclesial administrators, not just those of public juridic persons, always to act in the best interests of the entity they have been appointed to serve, unmoved by selfish considerations, careful to avoid even the appearance of conflict of interest, and ever conscious that in financial matters the Church can lose a great deal more than money. Without the unyielding integrity of its administrators, the Church can lose credibility, and a witness without credibility is worthless.

TITLE IV
PIOUS WILLS IN GENERAL
AND PIOUS FOUNDATIONS
[cc. 1299–1310]

The canons of this title make unmistakably clear, in principle and in disciplinary regulations, the Church's commitment to the faithful observance of the declared intentions of those who contribute temporal goods in service to the mission of the Church. After affirming the natural right of all persons so to contribute, and echoing the Church's claim of independence from civil law in such matters (c. 1299), the canons in this title require exact fulfillment of even the subsidiary intentions of donors (c. 1300), the exercise of vigilant supervision by ordinaries (c. 1301) especially in regard to trusts (c. 1302) and founda-

---

[186] For the determination of the degrees of consanguinity and affinity, see the commentary on cc. 108 and 109.

tions (cc. 1303–1305), the taking of careful precautions to prevent long-term continuing obligations from being forgotten (cc. 1306–1307), and the fulfillment of stringent conditions as a prerequisite to any alteration by ecclesiastical authority of the designated intentions of donors (cc. 1308–1310). Interwoven through the canons of this title are the notions of pious cause, pious will, pious trust, and two categories of pious foundation, notions which, though unexpressed in the earlier titles of Book V, permeate those titles and are essential to a thorough understanding of the canonical norms they contain.

Pious Causes

Canon 1299 — §1. A person who by natural law and canon law is able freely to dispose of his or her goods can bestow goods for pious causes either through an act *inter vivos* or through an act *mortis causa*.

§2. In dispositions *mortis causa* for the good of the Church, the formalities of civil law are to be observed if possible; if they have been omitted, the heirs must be admonished regarding the obligation, to which they are bound, of fulfilling the intention of the testator.

Although the term "pious cause," found in canon 1299, §1, is used sparingly in the code,[187] the concept pervades not only this title but all of Book V. By "pious cause," is meant any endeavor undertaken for a supernatural motive.[188] Some such endeavors are recognizable by the very nature of the endeavor, such as acts of worship, preaching the gospel, or the pursuit of Christian perfection. Others are recognizable as works of a juridic person in the Church, for all such works

must be oriented to piety, charity, or the apostolate (see c. 114, §2). Still others are less easily identified because, while at times certain works may be undertaken for a supernatural motive, at other times they may not, as is true of many humanitarian works which may or may not be motivated by love of God or supernatural love of neighbor. Purely philanthropic motivation is insufficient to constitute a pious cause.[189]

Canon 1299 proclaims the freedom of all persons who are naturally and canonically capable of disposing of their own assets to donate goods for pious causes. Since a pious cause is a work or endeavor, it is inappropriate to speak of goods being donated *to* a pious cause; ownership resides in persons, natural or juridic, not in works or endeavors. The revised CLSA translation, unlike the earlier CLSA translation, avoids the expression "*to* pious causes" and consistently uses the precise formulation "*for* pious causes."

Pious causes are undertaken by natural as well as juridic persons, and by private as well as public juridic persons. Donations for pious causes, therefore, may or may not become ecclesiastical goods (*bona ecclesiastica*), depending upon whether or not the goods have been bestowed on a public juridic person (see c. 1257, §1). So, too, notwithstanding their inevitable relationship to the mission of the Church, goods donated for pious causes may or may not constitute *church property* depending upon whether or not they have been bestowed on a public juridic person (see commentary on c. 1258). Accordingly, many of the canons in this title, unlike the canons in the preceding title governing alienation, are not restricted to *bona ecclesiastica* but apply also to temporal goods belonging to private juridic persons and to natural persons, individually or jointly.[190]

---

187 The term occurs in cc. 325, §2; 956; 1299, §1; 1300; 1302, §§1, 3; 1310, §1; the cognate term "pious works" occurs in c. 1245.

188 De Paolis, *I Beni Temporali,* 224; idem, *De Bonis Ecclesiae,* 109–110. See also Vromant, 137; Bouscaren-Ellis-Korth, 821; J. Abbo and J. Hannan, *The Sacred Canons* (St. Louis: B. Herder, 1960) 2:720, n. 45.

189 De Paolis, *I Beni Temporali,* 225, n.5; Vromant, 137; Bouscaren-Ellis-Korth, 821.

190 Since a non-autonomous foundation, defined in c. 1303, §1, 2°, involves only goods belonging to a public juridic person, canons referring only to non-autonomous foundations are limited in scope to *bona ecclesiastica.* Such canons include 1303, §2; 1304; 1305; 1306; and 1307.

Bestowal of goods for pious causes is said to be through an act *inter vivos* when the transfer of ownership takes effect during the life of the donor; bestowal is said to be through an act *mortis causa* when the transfer of ownership is effective only upon death. *Inter vivos* bestowal of goods is commonly referred to simply as a gift; *mortis causa* bestowal can be either of two kinds: a *last will and testament* or a *gift in contemplation of death*. The latter shares some of the characteristics of an *inter vivos* gift and some of the characteristics of a last will and testament.

Though not often thought of as such, an *inter vivos* gift is a contract,[191] requiring natural and canonical contractual capacity in the donor, delivery (actual or constructive) of the goods,[192] acceptance by the donee, and fulfillment of civil-law requirements (that are not contrary to divine or canon law) in accord with the canonization of the civil law of contracts (see c. 1290).[193] Each of these elements is essential; the absence of any one precludes the effective making of a gift. Natural contractual capacity requires the use of reason, sufficient maturity (commensurate with the nature

of the gift), and physical and psychological freedom. Canonical capacity includes the canonized requirements of civil law as well as specific canonical exceptions to the capacity to dispose of one's goods, such as those applicable to members of religious institutes (see c. 668).

As noted above, acceptance by the donee is an essential element of a gift *inter vivos*. Not every gift should be accepted. Potential burdens of maintenance and repair, incompatibility with the mission or ecclesial nature of a particular donee, and burdensome conditions or modal obligations attached to some gifts are among the considerations that often argue against acceptance of a gift.[194] While a just cause is required for a gift to a juridic person to be refused (see c. 1267, §2), many such causes exist. Once accepted, however, an *inter vivos* gift effectively transfers ownership immediately and the transfer is irrevocable.

A last will and testament differs from an *inter vivos* gift in several respects. Unlike the making of a gift *inter vivos,* the making of a last will and testament entails no delivery of goods and requires no acceptance by the beneficiaries in order to be effective;[195] also unlike an *inter vivos* gift, a last will and testament is not effective to transfer ownership until death and, consequently, remains revocable, in whole or in part, until such time. These differences flow from the fact that, both canonically and civilly, a last will and testament, unlike an *inter vivos* gift, is not a contract.[196] This

[191] De Paolis, *I Beni Temporali,* 196–197; Périsset, 231; Aznar Gil, 202; Schouppe, 85–87. See also Vromant, 138; Cappello, 2:567; Bouscaren-Ellis-Korth, 821.

[192] Delivery is said to be constructive when the nature of the property being transferred is such that an actual "handing over" of the property is impracticable or impossible and it is necessary to substitute some recognized symbol of delivery, such as a deed to real estate or documentary title to a motor vehicle.

The essentiality of delivery derives from the concerns to make vivid to the donor the loss of ownership that is taking place, to make unambiguous to witnesses the meaning of the transaction, and, by transferring possession to the donee, to give the donee *prima facie* evidence of the gift having been made.

[193] De Paolis, *I Beni Temporali,* 196–197; Périsset, 231. See also Vromant, 138; Cappello, 2:569.

Since by definition an *inter vivos* gift is gratuitous, it is sometimes said to be a unilateral contract because of the absence of a *quid pro quo*. Use of such terminology, however, should not be allowed to obscure the mutuality of obligations on the part of both donor and donee to respect the transfer of ownership effected by a gift *inter vivos*.

[194] A public juridic person requires the permission of its ordinary to accept a gift to which has been attached a condition or modal obligation (c. 1267, §2) and may, in some circumstances, need additional consents and permissions as well (see c. 1295). For an explanation of modal obligation, see commentary on c. 1267, §2.

[195] A beneficiary may, of course, decline a bequest, thereby causing the object of the bequest to become part of the residuary estate of the decedent; but, absent a refusal, canonical ownership (or, according to some, the right to ownership) passes to the beneficiary immediately upon the death of the testator without the need for acceptance.

[196] See J. Hannan, *The Canon Law of Wills, CanLawStud* 86 (Washington, D.C.: Catholic University of America, 1934) 53; Aznar Gil, 203.

accounts for the inapplicability to last wills and testaments of the canonization of the civil law of contracts found in canon 1290; accordingly, although in order to minimize Church-State conflicts canon 1299, §2 urges the observance of the formalities required by civil law for a valid last will and testament, such observance is not necessary to give rise to the canonical obligation to fulfill the intention of the testator.

The difficulty with canon 1299, §2 is its apparent assumption that the formalities of civil law are unrelated to ascertaining the true intention of the testator; yet that is their very purpose. Testamentary formalities such as the simultaneous presence of a designated number of witnesses at the signing of a last will and testament, signing by the testator on each page and by the witnesses on the final page, explicit statement by the testator that the document being witnessed is a last will and testament, careful and precise dating of the document, explicit revocation of all previous wills and codicils, and other formalities are precisely designed both to make vivid to the testator what is transpiring and to afford ample proof of the true intention of the testator. In the absence of some or all civilly required formalities, it is incumbent upon ecclesiastical authorities to obtain adequate alternative proof of true intention before attempting to impose or enforce the obligation of canon 1299, §2.

Bestowal of temporal goods for pious causes may also be accomplished by a *gift in contemplation of death* (*donatio mortis causa*) which, as noted above, shares some of the characteristics of an *inter vivos* gift and some of the characteristics of a last will and testament. Of Roman origin,[197] the gift in contemplation of death transfers personal property in expectation of imminent death, with the understanding that if the donor survives the danger of death or revokes the gift, the property must be returned. If not revoked, ownership transfers at death. Like a gift *inter vivos*, a gift in con-

templation of death is a contract and requires delivery of the goods and acceptance by the donee, but like a last will and testament it does not transfer ownership until death.[198] Not recognized in the civil law of some nations,[199] the gift in contemplation of death continues to be recognized in the United States[200] but would seem rarely to be used today as a means of donating temporal goods for pious causes.[201]

The expression "for the good of the Church" in canon 1299, §2 does not refer solely to public juridic persons according to the specialized meaning given to the word "church" in canon 1258, but refers more generally to all pious causes, whether undertaken by natural persons or by public or private juridic persons.[202] This is apparent both from the context and the nature of the matter, and was the opinion of the majority of canonists in interpreting the same wording in the parallel canon of the 1917 code (*CIC* 1513, §2).[203]

The parallel canon in the Code of Canons of the Eastern Churches[204] replaces the words "in dispositions *mortis causa*" with the words "in last wills" (*in ultimis voluntatibus*), the language used

---

[197] R. Brown and W. Raushenbush, *The Law of Personal Property*, 3rd ed. (Chicago, Ill.: Callaghan, 1975) 130–132.

[198] See Aznar Gil, 203; Cappello, 2:567; Hannan, 42–47; Bouscaren-Ellis-Korth, 822.

[199] See Vromant, 145, n. 5; Cappello, 2:567. Non-recognition in the civil laws of several nations may account for the absence of any reference to gifts in contemplation of death in some commentaries on the 1983 code.

[200] J. Kennel, "Gifts," in *American Jurisprudence*, 2nd ed. (n.p.: West Group, 1999) 38:707–711; Brown and Raushenbush, 130–145.

[201] Since a gift in contemplation of death is a contract subject to the provisions of c. 1299, §2, which applies not just to last wills and testaments but to all dispositions *mortis causa*, the gift in contemplation of death is an exception to the canonization of the civil law of contracts, as provided in c. 1290, since c. 1299, §2 merely urges rather than requires observance of the formalities of civil law.

[202] De Paolis, *De Bonis Ecclesiae*, 112; idem, *I Beni Temporali*, 228–229; Myers, in *CLSA Com*, 884.

[203] See, e.g., Vromant, 145; Regatillo, 2:215; Cappello, 2:569; Vermeersch-Creusen, 2:583, n.2; Hannan, 286–287.

[204] *CCEO* 1043, §2.

in the 1917 code (*CIC* 1513, §2). This should not be understood, however, as a narrowing of the scope of the canon to last wills and testaments, since in canonical tradition the expression "last wills" includes all acts by which one disposes of all or part of one's goods as of one's death, including a gift in contemplation of death (*donatio mortis causa*).[205]

Pious Wills

Canon 1300 — The legitimately accepted wills of the faithful who give or leave their resources for pious causes, whether through an act *inter vivos* or through an act *mortis causa,* are to be fulfilled most diligently even regarding the manner of administration and distribution of goods, without prejudice to the prescript of can. 1301, §3.

The wording of this canon makes it clear that the term "will" in canonical parlance has a much broader scope than it has in the civil law of many nations, including the United States, where the term usually refers to the written instrument declaring one's intentions regarding the disposition to be made of one's estate upon death, and is often used as shorthand for the fuller expression "last will and testament." Canonically, the term "pious will" includes all dispositions of temporal goods (tangible or intangible), whether made *inter vivos* or *mortis causa,* for pious causes. Pious wills, therefore, include gifts, gifts in contemplation of death (see commentary on c. 1299), and last wills and testaments. Nor is the notion of a pious will restricted to bestowal of temporal goods upon a public juridic person resulting in *bona ecclesiastica* (see c. 1257, §1), but is all-inclusive of dispositions made for pious causes however undertaken.

Faithful fulfillment of pious wills is a cardinal principle of canon law, given expression not only in canon 1300 but frequently throughout the

code.[206] Fidelity to the intentions of donors is rooted in the right of all natural persons to dispose of their temporal goods as they wish. To accept a gift or testamentary bequest and not to honor the expressed intentions of the donor in regard to its use or disposition is, therefore, a violation of justice. Canon 1300 makes it clear that diligent fulfillment of a pious will extends not just to its general purpose but also to detailed directives as to how the temporal goods which comprise the matter of the pious will are to be applied to the general purpose or distributed in accord with it.[207] Unwillingness to comply with such directives should lead to refusal of the gift or bequest unless, in the case of an *inter vivos* gift or a gift in contemplation of death, efforts can successfully be made to induce the donor to change the directives. Only in the rarest of circumstances does the law of the Church allow ecclesiastical authority to alter the terms of a pious will once accepted (see cc. 1308–1310).[208]

In recognition of the fact that a gift or bequest for a pious cause may at times be justifiably refused, canon 1300, unlike the parallel canon in the 1917 code,[209] adds the modification "legitimately accepted" to its reference to wills of the faithful which give rise to the obligation of faithful fulfillment. In this connection, it should be re-

---

[205] See De Paolis, *I Beni Temporali,* 224; Aznar Gil, 203; Vermeersch-Creusen, 2:581–582; Regatillo, 2:214–215; Vromant, 138; Hannan, 51, 65.

[206] See cc. 121; 122; 123; 326, §2; 531; 616, §1; 706, 3°; 954; 1267, §3; 1284, §2, 3°, 4°; 1299, §2; 1303, §2; 1304, §1; 1307, §1; 1310, §2.

[207] For a brief historical summary of the roots of this canon in Roman, decretal, and post-Tridentine canon law, see J. Lahey, *Faithful Fulfillment of the Pious Will: A Fundamental Principle of Church Law as Found in the 1983 Code of Canon Law, CanLawStud* 521 (Washington, D.C.: Catholic University of America, 1987) 8–39; W. Doheny, *Church Property: Modes of Acquisition, CanLawStud* 41 (Washington, D.C.: Catholic University of America, 1927) 96–98.

[208] In this regard, the law of the Church is generally stricter than what is known in some civil laws, including those in the United States, as the *cy pres* doctrine which allows a more liberal substitution of alternative charitable dispositions where fulfillment of the original intent has become unduly burdensome or impractical.

[209] *CIC* 1514.

called that licit acceptance of some gifts requires permission of ecclesiastical authority (see c. 1267, §2); acceptance of such gifts without permission renders the acceptance illegitimate, thereby requiring the return of the gift or bequest and negating the obligation to fulfill the pious will.

The final clause in canon 1300 calls attention to an apparent exception, found in canon 1301, §3, to the firm canonical commitment to faithful fulfillment of the detailed directives of legitimately accepted pious wills. The exception is more apparent than real, however, as is explained in the commentary on the following canon.

Canon 1301 — §1. The ordinary is the executor of all pious wills whether *mortis causa* or *inter vivos*.

§2. By this right, the ordinary can and must exercise vigilance, even through visitation, so that pious wills are fulfilled, and other executors are bound to render him an account after they have performed their function.

§3. Stipulations contrary to this right of an ordinary attached to last wills and testaments are to be considered non-existent.

A reading of paragraph two of this canon is essential to a correct understanding of paragraph one, for it is paragraph two that makes it clear that the ordinary referred to in paragraph one as the executor of all pious wills is not the executor in the sense in which that term is generally used in the civil laws of many nations, including the United States. The ordinary does not have the primary responsibility to implement the terms of every pious will.[210] Primary responsibility belongs to the "other executors" referred to in paragraph two; it is they who have been designated by the donors or testators to fulfill the pious will.

In accord with canonical tradition, the term "executor" is applied to the ordinary in the sense of one who, as part of executive governance, has the right and duty to see that the laws of the

Church are faithfully observed and, in regard to temporal goods, that no abuses enter into the management or distribution of resources which have been placed in the service of one or more of the goals proper to the Church (see cc. 392, 1276, 325).[211] The role of the ordinary is independent of the will of the benefactors; it derives not from their will but from the hierarchical structure of the Church.[212] As paragraph two makes clear, it is a role of vigilant supervision.

In the exercise of vigilance, ordinaries (diocesan or nondiocesan) have the right and responsibility to learn when and how pious wills within their jurisdiction are being fulfilled. Paragraph two mentions visitation and reporting as principal means of acquiring such information. Diocesan bishops can exercise their right to obtain relevant information either personally or indirectly through the diocesan finance officer (see c. 1278) or through a delegate; religious or other nondiocesan ordinaries can monitor the fulfillment of pious wills through finance officers or delegates. Only in the event of neglect by a designated executor, or if no executor had been named, would the ordinary have responsibility to implement, personally or through a delegate, the terms of a pious will.[213]

According to paragraph three, stipulations in a last will[214] that are contrary to the supervisory

---

[210] See *Comm* 12 (1980) 429.

[211] De Paolis, *I Beni Temporali,* 230; Périsset, 234–235; Cappello, 2:570.

[212] Salerno, in *Urbaniana Com,* 740; Périsset, 235; Cappello, 2:570.

[213] See *Comm* 12 (1980) 429; Aznar-Gil, 221–222; Regatillo, 2:217.

[214] The Latin text of paragraph three, which refers to last wills (*in ultimis voluntatibus*) and hence includes gifts in contemplation of death as well as last wills and testaments (see note 205 above and accompanying text), is broader in scope than the English translation which limits the provision to last wills and testaments.

Differentiating last wills from gifts *inter vivos* is apparently based on the fact that, in instances of last wills, opportunity rarely (in the case of gifts in contemplation of death) and not at all (in the case of last wills and testaments) exists for altering the pious will to eliminate the unacceptable provision denying the supervisory right of the ordinary.

right of an ordinary are to be ignored. This provision can be thought of as an exception to the principle of faithful fulfillment, even as to the manner of administration, of the will of donors but it is also possible, and perhaps preferable, to interpret the principle of faithful fulfillment as applicable only to matters subject to the free choice and control of a donor or testator. Altering the hierarchically allocated responsibilities of ecclesiastical authority is not so subject. Moreover, the supervisory role of ordinaries is designed to assure the diligent fulfillment of donative intentions; to give effect to stipulations which would negate this supervision would be counterproductive to the faithful fulfillment of donative intent. It is for these reasons that the final clause in canon 1300 was said in the commentary above to point to an exception to the principle of faithful fulfillment of pious wills that is more apparent than real.

Pious Trusts

Canon 1302 — §1. A person who has accepted goods in trust for pious causes either through an act *inter vivos* or by a last will and testament must inform the ordinary of the trust and indicate to him all its movable and immovable goods with the obligations attached to them. If the donor has expressly and entirely prohibited this, however, the person is not to accept the trust.

§2. The ordinary must demand that goods held in trust are safeguarded and also exercise vigilance for the execution of the pious will according to the norm of can. 1301.

§3. When goods held in trust have been entrusted to a member of a religious institute or society of apostolic life and if the goods have also been designated for some place or diocese or for the assistance of their inhabitants or pious causes, the ordinary mentioned in §§1 and 2 is the local ordinary; otherwise, it is the major superior in a clerical institute of pontifical right and in clerical societies of apostolic life of pontifical right or the proper ordinary of the member in other religious institutes.

To the notions of pious cause and pious will this canon adds the notion of a pious trust. The three notions are interrelated. A pious trust is a pious will which requires ongoing administration; temporal goods are conveyed to a person (natural or juridic), called a trustee, to be managed over a period of time, with the income or principal or both being used to benefit one or more pious causes. A pious trust differs from other restricted gifts precisely in the need for ongoing investment, management of funds, and periodic distribution of principal or income. A gift which is immediately to be applied to a specific purpose without the need of ongoing administration is not a trust. Hence, not every executor of a pious will is a trustee.

Nor is the notion of trustee in canon 1302 to be confused with the meaning of the term in such expressions as "board of trustees" frequently used in the United States to designate the board of directors or governing body of a civilly incorporated university or hospital. Though the members of such a board have fiduciary responsibilities according to the governing documents (canonical and civil) of the institution, they do not in any sense own the temporal goods of the institution; civil ownership resides in the corporation, and canonical ownership resides in the canonical juridic person being served by the members of the board. A change in the composition of such a board is not a change in ownership.[215] The trustee of a pious trust, on the other hand, has received ownership of the temporal goods which form the *corpus* of the trust;[216] the ownership is qualified, of course, by the requirements of use and distribution imposed by the terms of the trust.

A pious trust can be created by an act *inter vivos* or by a last will and testament. It cannot be

---

[215] See the discussion of the canonical status of church-related institutions following the commentary on cc. 113–123.

[216] Hannan, 1–2, 69–70, 468. Anglo-American law recognizes in such situations a form of split ownership; the trustee is said to be the legal owner while the intended beneficiaries of the trust are said to be the equitable or beneficial owners.

created by a gift in contemplation of death, which transfers revocable possession but not ownership (until death); creation of a trust requires a transfer of ownership. Accordingly, unlike canon 1301, §3, the Latin of canon 1302 does not use the broader term "last wills" which would include gifts in contemplation of death, but refers instead to trusts created by last will and testament (*ex testamento*).[217]

Since a pious trust is a pious will, fulfillment of the terms of the trust is subject, according to canon 1302, §2, to the supervision of the ordinary in accord with the provisions of canon 1301. This places upon trustees the obligation to inform the ordinary of the existence of the trust, the movable and immovable temporal goods which constitute the *corpus* of the trust, and the terms of the trust (c. 1302, §1), so that the ordinary can fulfill his obligation to exercise vigilance over the fulfillment of the trust. If a donor or testator prohibits this expressly and entirely (that is, so firmly as to make the prohibition a *sine qua non* of the gift[218]), the trust is not to be accepted (c. 1302, §1). While this provision is sensible and practical in the case of a trust to be established by an act *inter vivos* where, prior to acceptance, the donor may be persuaded to revise the terms of the trust so as to eliminate the ecclesially unacceptable prohibition, the provision has far less to commend it in the case of a trust established by last will and testament. As noted above, a last will and testament does not require acceptance to be effective (see commentary on c. 1299). Refusal to implement a trust established by last will and testament, therefore, amounts to repudiation of a pious will after the ownership (or, according to some, the right to ownership) of temporal goods has already been transferred, simply because the testator has included a directive attempting to impede the supervisory rights of the ordinary which derive from the hierarchical structure of the Church and are

not dependent upon the free will of the testator (see commentary on c. 1301). Since those supervisory rights are precisely intended to secure the faithful fulfillment of the testator's donative intent, it would seem disingenuous to refuse fulfillment of that intent entirely simply because the testator sought ineffectively to negate a law of the Church designed to protect his or her intent. Since canon 1302, §2 makes specific mention of canon 1301, it would seem canonically more sound to confine the last clause of canon 1302, §1 to trusts established *inter vivos*[219] and, in instances of trusts established by last will and testament, to apply canon 1301, §3 to consider nonexistent the ecclesially unacceptable provision and sustain the supervisory rights of the ordinary.

If a member of a religious institute or society of apostolic life is chosen to be the trustee of a pious trust, the issue can arise as to which ordinary, the proper ordinary of the trustee or the ordinary of place where the trust is to be fulfilled, has the right and duty of supervising the fulfillment of the trust. Canon 1302, §3 resolves the issue in favor of the local ordinary whenever the temporal goods which form the *corpus* of the trust are to be used for the benefit of a diocese or other place or for its inhabitants or pious causes, and in favor of the proper ordinary of the trustee in other cases (as, for example, where the goods are to be used for the benefit of the religious institute or society of apostolic life). While that distinction will often suffice to resolve a doubt or controversy, it is likely that situations will arise where it will not be clear whether the purpose of a trust is primarily to benefit an apostolic work (such as education or health care) within a particular diocese or primarily to benefit the members of the institute or society who are engaged in the work. In such situations, determination of which ordinary will fulfill the responsibility of supervision would seem best made collaboratively by the ordinaries involved.

---

[217] The same precision in the use of terminology was found in the 1917 code (compare *CIC* 1516, §1 with *CIC* 1513, §2 and 1515, §3).

[218] Vromant, 152.

[219] In this connection, it is noteworthy that the final clause of c. 1302, §1 speaks only of a donor (*donator*) and not also of a testator (the term used in both Latin and English in c. 1299, §2).

Pious Foundations

Canon 1303 — §1. In law, the term pious foundations includes:

    1° *autonomous pious foundations,* **that is, aggregates of things (*universitates rerum*) destined for the purposes mentioned in can. 114, §2 and erected as a juridic person by competent ecclesiastical authority;**

    2° *non-autonomous pious foundations,* **that is, temporal goods given in some way to a public juridic person with the obligation for a long time, to be determined by particular law, of celebrating Masses and performing other specified ecclesiastical functions or of otherwise pursuing the purposes mentioned in can. 114, §2, from the annual revenues.**

§2. If the goods of a non-autonomous pious foundation have been entrusted to a juridic person subject to a diocesan bishop, they must be remanded to the institute mentioned in can. 1274, §1 when the time is completed unless some other intention of the founder had been expressly manifested; otherwise, they accrue to the juridic person itself.

The law of the Church provides for two markedly different kinds of pious foundation. An *autonomous* foundation is a juridic person which has as its substratum temporal goods which have been set aside for one or more pious causes. It can be either a public or private juridic person. The term "autonomous foundation," therefore, is synonymous with *universitas rerum* when the latter is used to designate one of the two principal categories of juridic person, namely, those which have as their substratum goods rather than people (see c. 115, §3). Since a juridic person is an artificial person, a singular subject of rights and obligations, and not a collectivity or aggregate (see commentary on cc. 113, 115), it is unfortunate that the CLSA translation of canon 1303, §1, 1° renders *universitates rerum* as "aggregates of things." Autonomous pious foundations are not aggregates; they are individual juridic persons

whose substratum, or basis in reality, is an aggregate of goods.[220]

Creation of an autonomous pious foundation requires the establishment of a fund or other substratum of goods, the approval of statutes, and the conferral of either public or private personality by decree of competent ecclesiastical authority (see commentary on cc. 114, 116, 117).[221] The management of an autonomous foundation is governed by its statutes and the laws of the Church governing juridic persons (see cc. 117–123). Like all juridic persons, the autonomous pious foundation is of its nature perpetual but can, under certain circumstances, be terminated (c. 120). The distribution of its assets upon consolidation, division, or extinction is governed by canons 121–123.

A *non-autonomous* foundation is not a juridic person. It is a long-term pious trust, with a public juridic person as trustee, according to the terms of which the annual income (but not the principal) is to be used for a pious cause. The code leaves to particular law the determination of how long such a trust must be intended to last in order to qualify as a non-autonomous foundation, and for how long a time it may last.[222]

---

[220] The code occasionally uses the term *universitas rerum* to refer to an aggregate or accumulation of temporal goods *prior* to the creation of a juridic person (see, e.g., cc. 114, §3; 117); in these instances, translation of *universitas rerum* as "aggregate of things" is appropriate (see commentary on cc. 115, 117).

[221] Although the code provides for conferral of juridic personality by law (c. 114, §1), no law of the Church confers juridic personality on any *universitas rerum.*

[222] The present code speaks only of long-term, not perpetual, obligations in recognition of contemporary economic conditions which do not lend themselves to guaranteeing the perpetual availability of sufficient income to fulfill obligations *in perpetuum. Comm* 12 (1980) 431. It was apparently not the intention of the revisers of the code, however, to prohibit perpetual obligations, but simply to acknowledge modern economic reality by not supposing such obligations to be undertaken frequently enough to warrant mention in universal law, and by leaving to particular law the enactment of whatever relevant regulations may be thought advisable. See *Comm* 9 (1977) 273.

Prior to prescribing norms for the creation and governance of non-autonomous foundations (cc. 1304–1307), the code, in canon 1303, §2, addresses the issue of what is to happen to the principal of such a foundation upon expiration of its term. Unless expressly provided otherwise in the terms of the foundation, the principal of a non-autonomous foundation entrusted to a public juridic person subject to the diocesan bishop is to be distributed to the diocesan institute prescribed in canon 1274, §1 for the support of clergy serving the diocese. The existence of such an institute, however, is contingent upon the absence of other ways to support the clergy; in many nations, including the United States, clergy are supported from other sources, making unnecessary the establishment of a canon 1274, §1 institute and thereby exposing a lacuna in the law governing the distribution of the principal of a non-autonomous foundation.

Even more problematic is the fact that the category of public juridic persons subject to the diocesan bishop includes a number of juridic persons, such as institutes of women religious of diocesan right or lay societies of apostolic life of diocesan right, whose members, not being clerics, would, under this provision, derive no benefit from distribution of the principal of a foundation which the juridic person had administered for a long period of time. Such an outcome would undoubtedly be contrary to the intention of many founders, which makes it imperative that in the documentation establishing a non-autonomous foundation there be a clear expression of the founder's intent regarding the distribution of the principal upon the expiration of the term of the foundation.

Acceptance of Non-autonomous Foundations

Canon 1304 — §1. For a juridic person to be able to accept a foundation validly, the written permission of the ordinary is required. He is not to grant this permission before he has legitimately determined that the juridic person can satisfy both the new obligation to be undertaken and

those already undertaken; most especially he is to be on guard so that the revenues completely respond to the attached obligations, according to the practice of each place or region.

§2. Particular law is to define additional conditions for the establishment and acceptance of foundations.

Although the wording of this canon speaks of "juridic person" and "foundation" without, in either case, a modifier, the content of the canon makes clear that it is speaking only of *public* juridic persons and only of *non-autonomous* foundations, for the canon concerns the acceptance of a foundation by a juridic person. Only a non-autonomous foundation is accepted by a juridic person; an autonomous foundation is a juridic person in its own right (c. 1303, §1, 1°). And, by definition, a non-autonomous foundation is accepted only by a public juridic person (1303, §1, 2°).

For the valid acceptance of a non-autonomous foundation, canon 1304 requires the written *permission* of the proper ordinary. This is one of the few canons in the code where permission (*licentia*) is said to be required for validity.[223] Generally throughout the code, as in canonical tradition, permission is required only for liceity, not validity. Where validity is at stake, the code usually requires a faculty (*facultas*) or power (*potestas*).

That the permission be written, however, would seem to be required for proof, not validity, and hence only for liceity, as is generally true in canonical tradition.[224] The fact that the non-autonomous foundation itself can be established orally (see c. 1306, §1) reinforces the conclusion that the permission may also be given orally. This in no way diminishes the importance of committing the permission to writing as soon as possible, however, since proof that permission was in fact

---

[223] All other instances have to do with alienation and other transactions subject to the norms governing alienation (see cc. 638, §3; 1190, §2; 1291; 1292, §2).

[224] See commentary on c. 1281, §1 and authors cited in note 104.

given will be necessary to sustain the validity of the acceptance of the foundation if it should be challenged.

Since a non-autonomous pious foundation is a form of pious trust (see c. 1303, §1, 2°), the ordinary referred to in canon 1304 is to be determined according to canon 1302, §3. Prior to giving permission, the proper ordinary must determine if the public juridic person is able, both in terms of available personnel and available resources, to fulfill the obligations of the non-autonomous foundation for the proposed length of time for which it is to exist. It is canonically and ethically reprehensible to accept, or approve the acceptance of, a non-autonomous foundation knowing in advance that it will be necessary to seek from competent ecclesiastical authority the reduction or commutation of the obligations of the foundation because of the impossibility of their being fulfilled.

Requiring a public juridic person to obtain authorization from the ordinary to accept a non-autonomous foundation echoes the general norm requiring public juridic persons to obtain permission when accepting any gift to which is attached a condition or modal obligation (c. 1267, §2)[225] and, since the authorization required by canon 1304 is for validity, in effect makes the acceptance of a non-autonomous foundation an act of extraordinary administration (see c. 1281, §1).

Evidencing an awareness of the multiplicity of factors and diversity of conditions that can affect the wisdom of accepting and the manner of establishing non-autonomous foundations, canon 1304, §2, in accord with the principle of subsidiarity, remits to particular law (which, in this instance, includes the proper law of religious institutes and societies of apostolic life) the enactment of additional requirements for the acceptance and establishment of non-autonomous foundations.[226]

Administration of Non-autonomous Foundations

Canon 1305 — Money and movable goods assigned to an endowment are to be deposited immediately in a safe place approved by the ordinary so that the money or value of the movable goods is protected; as soon as possible, these are to be invested cautiously and usefully for the benefit of the foundation, with express and specific mention made of the obligation; this investment is to be made according to the prudent judgment of the ordinary, after he has heard those concerned and his own finance council.

The distinctions between autonomous and non-autonomous foundations and between public and private juridic persons were not found in the 1917 code. The only foundation known to the 1917 code was the equivalent of a non-autonomous foundation in the present code, namely, temporal goods entrusted to a juridic person (called "moral person" in the 1917 code) with the obligation to use the income perpetually or for a long time for a designated pious cause or causes (*CIC* 1544, §1). Such foundations were regulated by canons 1545–1550 of the former code, the content of which was virtually identical to the content of canons 1305–1307 of the present code. This fact alone strongly suggests the limited application of these canons in the present code to non-autonomous foundations; autonomous foundations, as juridic persons in their own right, are governed by canons 116–123 and by their own statutes in such details as form the subject matter of canons 1305–1307. Moreover, the context and content of each of these can-

---

[225] Aznar Gil, 236; Salerno, in *Urbaniana Com,* 743.

[226] Some authors are of the opinion that c. 1304, §2 applies also to autonomous foundations. See L. Chiappetta, *Il Codice di Diritto Canonico: Commento Giuridico-Pastorale,* 2nd ed. (Rome: Dehoniane, 1996) 2:574;

J. M. Vázquez García-Peñuela, in *Com Ex* IV/1, 206. While particular law can indirectly affect the constitution of autonomous foundations by requiring the inclusion of certain provisions in the statutes, which must be approved by competent authority (c. 117), the context of c. 1304 (the *acceptance* of a foundation) would seem to confine the application of all its provisions to non-autonomous foundations. See De Paolis, *I Beni Temporali,* 234, n. 21; Schouppe, 104.

ons lends its own weight to the conclusion that they are intended to apply only to non-autonomous foundations.

The context of canon 1305 is the safeguarding and eventual investment of the endowment of foundations accepted according to canon 1304. The need for the ordinary's approval of the "safe place" in which to deposit the endowment pending its investment, and the need for additional approval of the investment itself, reinforce the conclusion that canon 1305 is speaking only of non-autonomous foundations. Such close supervision would be inconsistent with the autonomy of a private juridic person, which an autonomous foundation often is.

Sound administration of a non-autonomous foundation entails safeguarding the movable goods, including money, which form the principal (or part of the principal[227]) of the foundation prior to their being invested and, as soon as economically advisable,[228] carefully and prudently investing these goods so as to realize the income needed to fulfill the obligations of the foundation. By investment is here meant a long-term investment sufficient to make the goods part of the stable patrimony (see commentary on c. 1291) of the public juridic person to which the foundation belongs. Deposits in savings accounts in banks or in short-term certificates of deposit, while appropriate vehicles for safeguarding the principal of the foundation pending investment, are not themselves considered canonically to constitute an *investment* (see commentary on canon 1284, §2, 6°).

In accord with the general norm for administrators of public juridic persons, the investment is to be made with the approval of the ordinary (see c. 1284, §2, 6°).[229] Since a non-autonomous pious foundation is a form of pious trust (see c. 1303, §1, 2°), the ordinary referred to here is to be determined according to canon 1302, §3. Canon 1305 adds the requirement that, in judging the prudence of investments, the ordinary must consult interested parties (e.g., living donors, members of the families of deceased donors, beneficiaries of the foundation, and others who have an interest in seeing that appropriate investments will be made to assure the fulfillment of the purposes of the foundation) and the ordinary's own financial council. In the case of a local ordinary, the relevant council is the diocesan finance council; in the case of a religious ordinary (major superior of a clerical religious institute of pontifical right[230]) or ordinary of a society of apostolic life (major superior of a clerical society of apostolic life of pontifical right[231]) the relevant council is that which has been established pursuant to the directive of canon 1280 (which allows at least two advisors in lieu of a formal financial council) to which religious institutes and societies of apostolic life are subject (cc. 635, §1; 741, §1). In judging the prudence of investments, ordinaries must also keep in mind the obligation to honor, when fulfilling any pious will, the intentions of donors regarding even the manner of administration (c. 1300), which might include the inclusion or exclusion of certain kinds of investments.

Canon 1306 — §1. Foundations, even if made orally, are to be put in writing.

§2. One copy of the charter is to be preserved safely in the archive of the curia and another copy in the archive of the juridic person to which the foundation belongs.

---

[227] Nothing in either the nature of things or in the code precludes assigning immovable goods such as land or buildings to the endowment of a non-autonomous foundation.

[228] The immediate sale of goods, especially income-producing goods, in order to invest the proceeds may not be economically advisable given the nature of the goods or current market conditions. See López Alarcón, in *Pamplona ComEng,* 811–812.

[229] See commentary on c. 1284 for the reasons which support interpreting c. 1284 as applicable only to public juridic persons despite its apparently broad reference to "all" administrators.

[230] See c. 134, §1.

[231] Ibid.

Since an autonomous foundation, which is it-self a juridic person (c. 1303, §1, 1°), comes into being only by decree of competent authority, there being no autonomous foundation established *a iure* (see c. 114, §1), and since a decree of its na-ture is to be in writing (see cc. 51, 55), only non-autonomous foundations can be established orally as, for example, by the acceptance of an *inter vivos* gift with the stipulation that it be invested and the income alone be used over a long period of time for a designated pious cause or causes. Canon 1306, then, like the two canons that imme-diately precede it and the canon that immediately follows it, is speaking of non-autonomous founda-tions. After acknowledging the possibility that some such foundations can be established orally, canon 1306, §1 sets forth the sensible requirement that such foundations be put in writing. By defini-tion a non-autonomous foundation is long-term; its obligations (e.g., the offering of Masses, conduct-ing of pilgrimages, works of charity) are to be ful-filled over a long period of time (c. 1303, §1, 2°). To assure fulfillment, it is imperative that those obligations be detailed in writing so that succes-sive administrators of the public juridic person to which the foundation belongs will be aware of them.

The same concern underlies the provisions of canon 1306, §2 requiring two copies of the char-ter of the foundation, one to be kept in the archive of the curia of the ordinary who has the responsi-bility of supervising the non-autonomous founda-tion, the other to be kept in the archive of the ju-ridic person to which the foundation belongs.

Canon 1307 — §1. A list of the obligations incum-bent upon pious foundations is to be composed and displayed in an accessible place so that the obligations to be fulfilled are not forgotten; the prescripts of cann. 1300–1302 and 1287 are to be observed.

§2. In addition to the book mentioned in can. 958, §1, another book is to be maintained and kept by the pastor or rector in which the individ-ual obligations, their fulfillment, and the offer-ings are noted.

Canon 1307 continues the sequence of direc-tives begun in canon 1304 to assure the faithful fulfillment of the obligations of non-autonomous foundations. A list of all obligations (e.g., number and dates of Masses to be celebrated, liturgical functions to be conducted, meals to be served to the poor) is to be prepared and displayed in a readily accessible place so that those in a position to fulfill the obligations will be reminded to do so. For Masses and other liturgical functions, the proper place for displaying such a list would seem to be a sacristy; for other obligations, the office of the administrator or financial officer of the public juridic person to which the non-autonomous foun-dation belongs would seem appropriate.

Reference to canons 1300–1302 is intended to remind relevant administrators that non-autonomous pious foundations also share the na-ture of pious wills (cc. 1300, 1301) and pious trusts (c. 1302) and, as such, are also governed by the disciplinary regulations found in those canons. Moreover, in view of the fact that the temporal goods which comprise the principal of a non-autonomous foundation are ecclesiastical goods, since they have been entrusted to a public juridic person (see cc. 1303, §1, 2°; 1257, §1), the report-ing requirements of canon 1287 are also applicable; clerical and lay administrators of non-autonomous foundations are reminded of their responsibili-ties to report to local ordinaries and to the faith-ful in accord with the norms set forth in canon 1287.

Concluding the sequence of directives designed to assure faithful fulfillment of the obligations of non-autonomous foundations is the requirement in canon 1307, §2 that a special book be kept, dis-tinct from the book required by canon 958, §1 for the recording of the acceptance and fulfillment of individual Mass stipends, in which all the obliga-tions of non-autonomous foundations (including Mass obligations) be recorded, along with their fulfillment and the offerings taken from the in-come of the foundation for their fulfillment. The careful maintaining of such a written record of ful-fillment of obligations is itself an efficacious in-strument of faithful fulfillment. The specific mention of pastors and rectors suggests that this provision is limited to non-autonomous foundations entrusted to parochial or other churches, or to seminaries, for the celebration of Masses or other liturgical functions. The wording of the provision makes clear that canon 1307 is not intended to apply to autonomous foundations, private or public, although the keeping of a similarly mandated written record, as well as the readily accessible display of obligations mandated in paragraph one, could appropriately be required in the statutes of such foundations.

ALTERATION OF PIOUS WILLS
[cc. 1308–1310]

No amount of care in the articulation of a pious will of any kind, *inter vivos* or *mortis causa,* can eliminate all possibility of the need for some future modification in the terms of the will, especially if the will establishes a trust or foundation which is to last for a long time. Economic and other changes (such as revisions in the Church's liturgical practices) make the need for such modifications inevitable. The Church's commitment to faithful fulfillment of all pious wills, however, gives rise to strict norms governing any alterations. These norms are found in canons 1308–1310.

The first two of these canons pertain exclusively to the reduction of Mass obligations. The strictness of the Church's stance in this regard is foreshadowed by the exclusion of Mass stipends and obligations from prescription (c. 199, 5°) and in the several disciplinary norms governing the acceptance, timely fulfillment, transfer, and accurate recording of Mass stipends (cc. 947–958).

Canon 1308 — §1. A reduction of the obligations of Masses, to be made only for a just and necessary cause, is reserved to the Apostolic See, without prejudice to the following prescripts.

§2. If it is expressly provided for in the charters of the foundations, the ordinary is able to reduce the Mass obligations because of diminished revenues.

§3. With regard to Masses independently founded in legacies or in any other way, the diocesan bishop has the power, because of diminished revenues and for as long as the cause exists, to reduce the obligations to the level of offering legitimately established in the diocese, provided that there is no one obliged to increase the offering who can effectively be made to do so.

§4. The diocesan bishop also has the power to reduce the obligations or legacies of Masses binding an ecclesiastical institute if the revenue has become insufficient to pursue appropriately the proper purpose of the institute.

§5. The supreme moderator of a clerical religious institute of pontifical right possesses the same powers mentioned in §§3 and 4.

Canon 1309 — The authorities mentioned in can. 1308 also have the power to transfer, for an appropriate cause, the obligations of Masses to days, churches, or altars different from those determined in the foundations.

Canon 1308, §1 sets forth the general norm that reduction of Mass obligations is reserved to the Apostolic See,[232] the only exceptions being those found in the remaining provisions of canon 1308 and in canon 1309. Evidencing the seriousness with which the law views any such alteration is the requirement of a just and necessary cause in all cases, even when the reduction is made by the Apostolic See. Mere convenience is never a sufficient cause.[233]

---

[232] Four dicasteries of the Holy See are competent to deal with issues concerning Mass obligations, pious wills in general, and pious foundations in particular: CFC for the Latin church in general (*PB* 97, 2°), CICLSAL for such matters involving institutes of consecrated life or societies of apostolic life or individual members thereof (*PB* 108, §1), ApPen for internal forum issues (*PB* 118), and CEC for the Eastern churches (*PB* 56, 58, §1).

[233] The expression "just and necessary cause" occurs only in cc. 1308 and 1310, both having to do with the alteration of pious wills. The expression would appear to require a greater justification than the more frequently occurring expressions "just cause," "just and reasonable cause," and

Paragraph two affords the first of three mitigations of the reservation to the Holy See of the power to reduce Mass obligations. This first mitigation is limited, however, to Mass obligations attached to foundations (autonomous or non-autonomous, there being nothing to suggest restriction to one or the other category) and to reductions made necessary by diminished revenues (often due to economic inflation) which are no longer sufficient to provide stipends for the originally designated number of Masses. In such circumstances, the proper ordinary may reduce the number of Mass obligations if, but only if, express authorization to do so has been given in the governing document (charter) of the foundation.

Paragraph three affords a second mitigation, though more limited than the first. As in paragraph two, the mitigation in paragraph three affects only foundation Masses, whether the foundation be autonomous or non-autonomous,[234] and

the reduction is restricted to the sole circumstance of diminished revenue. In paragraph three, however, reduction is further limited to the level of offering established in accord with canon 952, solely for as long as the income is diminished, and only if there is no one with an obligation to increase the offering who can be persuaded to do so in order to sustain the originally designated number of obligations.[235] Even in such circumstances, further restriction limits the power to reduce Mass obligations to diocesan bishops and to supreme moderators of clerical religious institutes of pontifical right (§5), rather than extending the power to all ordinaries as in paragraph two.

Paragraph four affords a third and final mitigation, authorizing a diocesan bishop (and, pursuant to §5, the supreme moderator of a clerical religious institute of pontifical right) to reduce Mass obligations binding an ecclesiastical institute (e.g., hospital, school, university) if the revenue has become insufficient to continue to sustain the work of the institute. Unlike the provisions in paragraphs two and three, this provision (taken from *PM* 12) does not refer to foundations, autonomous or non-autonomous, established for the sole purpose of providing for the celebration of Masses, but to situations where gifts or testamentary bequests have been made primarily to support the work of various institutions, with accompanying modal obligations (see commentary on c. 1267) to arrange for the celebration of a designated number of Masses for a specified intention (often for the living or deceased members of the donor's family).

---

even "grave cause." See Périsset, 258–259; Aznar Gil, 270; Myers, in *CLSA Com,* 888. Curiously, the Eastern code omits all reference to cause when referring to reduction of Divine Liturgy obligations by the Apostolic See (*CCEO* 1052, §1), but retains "just and necessary cause" when referring to the alteration of pious wills by a hierarch to whom such power has been expressly committed by the donor (*CCEO* 1054, §1).

[234] Paragraph three of c. 1308 is limited to Mass obligations "independently" founded in testamentary bequests (legacies) or in any other way, such as in *inter vivos* establishment of a foundation. The modifier "independently" translates *quae sint per se stantia,* a phrase taken from *PM* 11. The phrase has been variously translated as "perpetual" (*CLD* 6, 372), "autonomous" (*Urbaniana Com; Pamplona ComEng*), "solely for the purpose of Masses" (original British, Canadian, Australian translation), and "which are separately endowed" (*CLSGBI Com*). Prior to the promulgation of the 1983 code, the phrase was interpreted by some as referring only to Mass foundations established as distinct juridic persons (see Bouscaren-Ellis-Korth, 827), which would correspond only to the autonomous foundation under the 1983 code. Though the issue has not been addressed by many commentators on the 1983 code, the prevailing interpretation seems to be that the phrase refers to all foundation Masses, whether the foundation is autonomous or non-

autonomous. See Aznar Gil, 275; Morrisey, in *CLSGBI Com,* 745. In both kinds of foundations, the goods set aside for the celebration of Masses are "independent" of all other goods and obligations.

[235] Rarely would a person have such an obligation; it would have to be imposed (e.g., on a member of the family) by the founder of the foundation or, in the rarest of circumstances, by ecclesiastical authority as a form of mandatory restitution for an injustice done either to the founder or to those for whom the foundation Masses are to be offered.

The 1977 draft of what was to become canon 1308 contained a provision limiting the diocesan bishop's delegation of the powers given in paragraphs three and four to coadjutors, auxiliary bishops, vicars general, and episcopal vicars, which had been the situation under *Pastorale munus* from which paragraphs three and four were derived. The provision was deleted on the ground that there is no sufficient reason to limit the bishop's power to delegate in this matter.[236] The parallel canon in the Code of Canons of the Eastern Churches, however, does limit the eparchial bishop's power to delegate these powers to certain officials, and prohibits all subdelegation.[237]

It was suggested during the revision process that diocesan bishops be given general power to reduce the obligations of nonfoundation Masses (known under the 1917 code as *manual* Masses[238]), but it was thought preferable to refer such reductions to the Holy See in order to avoid abuses.[239]

As noted above, paragraph five extends to supreme moderators, but not to other major superiors, of clerical religious institutes of pontifical right the same powers accorded to diocesan bishops in paragraphs three and four. The decision not to extend the powers to the supreme moderators or other major superiors in clerical societies of apostolic life of pontifical right was deliberate,[240] even though they, like many major superiors in clerical religious institutes of pontifical right who are also excluded from these powers, may be ordinaries (see c. 134, §1). This may be seen as further evidence of the strictness of the law's approach to the reduction of Mass obligations.[241]

Distinct from the reduction in the number of Masses to be celebrated, which is the concern of canon 1308, is the alteration of what the law considers to be ancillary or secondary intentions regarding the celebration of Masses, namely, specifications of particular churches in which, or days or altars on which, Masses are to be offered. It is to these ancillary intentions that canon 1309 is directed, but only to such intentions as have been attached to foundation Masses. For an appropriate cause (which is less stringent, as befits an ancillary obligation, than the just and necessary cause required for reducing the number of Masses) the authorities mentioned in canon 1308 can transfer to other days or places the obligations of Masses. Reference to the authorities mentioned in canon 1308 is somewhat problematic. While paragraph one of that canon refers to the Apostolic See and paragraph two refers to ordinaries, paragraphs three, four, and five more narrowly refer only to the diocesan bishop and to supreme moderators of clerical religious institutes of pontifical right. Had the legislator intended to restrict the powers of canon 1309 to only some of the authorities mentioned in canon 1308, however, limited reference to one or another paragraph of canon 1308 would have been appropriate. In the absence of such a limited reference, canon 1309 should be interpreted as referring to any or all of the authorities mentioned in canon 1308, namely, to the Apostolic See and to all ordinaries.[242]

Canon 1310 — §1. The ordinary, only for a just and necessary cause, can reduce, moderate, or

---

[236] *Comm* 12 (1980) 433–434.

[237] *CCEO* 1052, §6.

[238] See *CIC* 826. Technically, it was the stipend that was called *manual,* but the practice soon developed of referring to *manual* Masses as distinct from *foundation* Masses, due perhaps to the wording of *CIC* 826, §3.

[239] *Comm* 12 (1980) 434.

[240] *Rel* 290; *Comm* 16 (1984) 37. A critique of this decision may be found in Périsset, 261–262, 268.

[241] The Eastern code, while stricter than the Latin code in regard to the delegatability of the power to reduce Mass

obligations, is broader in its inclusion of superiors general of some societies of common life (*CCEO* 1052, §5).

[242] De Paolis expresses the same conclusion (*I Beni Temporali,* 237) but Aznar Gil, without explanation, restricts competent authorities to the Apostolic See, diocesan bishops, superiors general of clerical religious institutes of pontifical right, and superiors general of clerical societies of apostolic life of pontifical right, despite the fact that the latter have no authority under c. 1308 except under paragraph two which includes all ordinaries, not just those he lists (Aznar Gil, 276).

commute the wills of the faithful for pious causes if the founder has expressly entrusted this power to him.

§2. If through no fault of the administrators the fulfillment of the imposed obligations has become impossible because of diminished revenues or some other cause, the ordinary can equitably lessen these obligations, after having heard those concerned and his own finance council and with the intention of the founder preserved as much as possible; this does not hold for the reduction of Masses, which is governed by the prescripts of can. 1308.

§3. In other cases, recourse is to be made to the Apostolic See.

This canon concerns the alteration of pious wills other than those for the celebration of Masses. Paragraph one speaks of three different forms of alteration: reduction, moderation, and commutation. By reduction is meant lessening the number of obligations; by moderation is meant changing a secondary or ancillary aspect of an obligation, such as those spoken of in canon 1309; by commutation is meant the substitution of a different pious cause for the one provided for in the pious will (e.g., aiding the foreign missions in lieu of educating seminarians in one's own nation).[243]

Canon 1310, §1 authorizes an ordinary to reduce, moderate, or commute a pious will only for a just and necessary cause and only if the founder (in this case, the maker of any pious will, not just those which establish foundations[244]) has expressly

entrusted such power to the ordinary. Paragraph two empowers an ordinary to alter the obligations (by reduction, moderation, or commutation), even in the absence of express authorization by the founder if, through no fault of the administrators, fulfillment of the designated obligations has become impossible. Such alteration, which should be made by decree,[245] is to preserve as much as possible of the founder's intention, is to be equitable, and is to take place only after the ordinary has consulted those concerned (e.g., the founder, family members of a deceased founder, intended beneficiaries) and his own finance council. Failure of the ordinary to consult would canonically invalidate the alteration of the pious will (see c. 127).

The depth of the Church's commitment to faithful fulfillment of pious wills, *inter vivos* or *mortis causa,* and the strong reluctance to allow modifications in those wills are amply evidenced by the reservation to the Apostolic See in paragraph three of canon 1310 of all alterations other than those sought in the rarely occurring circumstances delineated in paragraphs one and two.

---

[243] Vázquez García-Peñuela, in *Com Ex* IV/1, 218–219; Aznar Gil, 269; Bouscaren-Ellis-Korth, 826–827.

[244] Use of the term "founder" (*fundator*) in paragraph one of this canon has lead some to conclude that the canon applies only to pious foundations. See, for example, P. Zielinski, "Pious Wills and Mass Stipends in Relation to

Canons 1299–1310," *Stud Can* 19 (1985) 150–151. But, unless the text or context of a canon otherwise confines it to foundations, as is true, for example, of c. 1303, §2, there is no reason to limit the meaning of the word *fundator* in a canon to the founder of a pious foundation. The word is used with several other connotations in the code, such as founders of institutes of consecrated life (cc. 576; 578; 588, §§2, 3) or of other public juridic persons which are *universitates personarum* (cc. 121; 122; 123; 1284, §2, 3°, 4°). There is no compelling reason to interpret *fundator* in c. 1310 as referring only to the founder of a foundation, and ample reason, beginning with the wording of paragraph one itself, to understand c. 1310 as referring to all wills of the faithful for pious causes. See Aznar Gil, 268–272.

[245] Vázquez García-Peñuela, in *Com Ex* IV/1, 219.

BIBLIOGRAPHY

Treatises

Aznar Gil, F. *La Administracion de los Bienes Temporales de la Iglesia.* 2nd rev. ed. Salamanca: Universidad de Salamanca, 1993.

De Paolis, V. *De Bonis Ecclesiae Temporalibus: Adnotationes in Codicem, Liber V.* Rome: Gregorian University, 1986.

―――. *I Beni Temporali della Chiesa.* Bologna: Dehoniane, 1995.

Kealy, R. *Diocesan Financial Support: Its History and Canonical Status.* Rome: Gregorian University, 1986.

Périsset, J.-C. *Les Biens Temporels de l'Église.* Paris: Tardy, 1996.

Schouppe, J.-P. *Elementi di Diritto Patrimoniale Canonico.* Milan: Giuffrè, 1997.

Articles

Abbass, J. "The Temporal Goods of the Church: A Comparative Study of the Eastern and Latin Codes of Canon Law." *P* 83 (1994) 669–714.

Bassett, W. "A Note on the Law of Contracts and the Canonical Integrity of Public Benefit Religious Organizations." *CLSAP* 59 (1997) 61–86.

De Paolis, V. "Negozio Giuridico, 'quo condicio patrimonialis personae iuridicae peior fieri possit' (cf. c. 1295)." *P* 83 (1994) 493–528.

Farrelly, A. "The Diocesan Finance Council: Functions and Duties according to the *Code of Canon Law*." *Stud Can* 23 (1989) 149–166.

Frugé, D. "Diocesan Taxation of Parishes in the United States, Sign of *Communio* or Source of Tension?" *CLSAP* 60 (1998) 68–81.

Grant, T. "Social Justice in the 1983 Code of Canon Law: An Examination of Selected Canons." *J* 49 (1989) 112–145.

Green, T. "Shepherding the Patrimony of the Poor: Diocesan and Parish Structures of Financial Administration." *J* 56 (1996) 706–734.

Hermann, D. "The Code of Canon Law Provisions on Labor Relations." *J* 44 (1984) 153–193.

Hollenbach, D. "Corporate Investments, Ethics, and Evangelical Poverty: A Challenge to American Religious Orders." *TS* 34 (1973) 265–274.

Kealy, R. "Methods of Diocesan Incorporation." *CLSAP* 48 (1986) 163–177.

Kennedy, R. "McGrath, Maida, Michiels: Introduction to a Study of the Canonical and Civil-Law Status of Church-Related Institutions in the United States." *J* 50 (1990) 351–401.

―――. "The Declaration on Religious Liberty Thirty Years Later: Challenges to the Church-State Relationship in the United States." *J* 55 (1995) 479–503.

Morrisey, F. "Ordinary and Extraordinary Administration: Canon 1277." *J* 48 (1988) 709–726.

―――. "The Alienation of Temporal Goods in Contemporary Practice." *Stud Can* 29 (1995) 293–316.

―――. "Acquiring Temporal Goods for the Church's Mission." *J* 56 (1996) 586–603.

Roche, G. "The Poor and Temporal Goods in Book V of the Code." *J* 55 (1995) 299–348.

Documents

CLSA. *Canonical Standards in Labor-Management Relations: A Report. J* 47 (1987) 545–575.

NCCB. *Principles and Guidelines for Fund Raising in the United States by Arch/dioceses, Arch/diocesan Agencies and Religious Institutes.* Washington, D.C.: USCC, 1977. *CLD* 8, 415–421.

BOOK VI
SANCTIONS IN THE CHURCH
[cc. 1311–1399]

INTRODUCTION

Thomas J. Green

During the post-1983 code period, the tragedy of clerical sexual abuse of minors among other things has highlighted the significance of a well-ordered and pastorally responsible ecclesiastical penal system. First of all the following introductory observations consider the phenomena of delicts, or offenses, against the Church's faith or order and its response in the form of penalties. The commentary will then briefly consider the 1917 code and its postconciliar revision to contextualize the subsequent reflections on Book VI.

While the Church is a graced community empowered by the Spirit, its members are sinners reflecting the limitations of the human condition.[1] Occasionally their attitudes are contrary to the faith (e.g., heresy) or their behavior contradicts the Christian way of life (e.g., clerical sexual abuse of minors). This disturbs the community of faith and brings such persons into conflict especially with those in authority whose responsibility is to foster the integrity of the community's faith, communion, and service.

Hence there needs to be a framework to restore ecclesial peace and order and reintegrate the offending party within the community. This challenge to resolve conflicts arising from breaches of public order is common to Church and State; hence there are certain similarities between ecclesiastical and civil penal law. However, the Church's salvific purpose gives its penal order a unique character which must constantly be remembered.

Delicts against the Community

The Church's penal order does not refer primarily to the individual's relationship with the Lord in conscience. This is largely inaccessible to church authority and hence beyond its competence. Rather, what is principally envisioned is a public act or omission adversely affecting the community. However, ecclesiastical penal law also deals with certain occult, or non-public, delicts known only to a few individuals, e.g., solicitation in confession. This is because such acts may significantly harm the community and hence are deemed matters of penal discipline.

Not every sin is an ecclesiastical delict warranting a penalty, yet every delict is a seriously sinful act or omission reflecting significant, if not full, freedom and knowledge. Certain factors notably impairing such freedom (e.g., fear) and knowledge (e.g., ignorance) may diminish or completely preclude imputability, or responsibility, for one's apparently criminal behavior.

Furthermore, not every canonical violation is a delict warranting a penalty. In fact, the violation of relatively few laws in the 1983 code constitutes a delict. Historically there have been different understandings of what patterns of thought or behavior so impair the Church's spiritual integrity as to require an ecclesiastical penalty, i.e., the deprivation of some spiritual or temporal good within the Church's control. The determination of such delicts has reflected at least an implicit hierarchy of values. Both such delicts and their corresponding penalties are historically conditioned.[2] Throughout the ages there has been a continuing effort to clarify the boundaries of ecclesial communion and specify those breaches of ecclesial values which the community cannot tolerate.

A significant historical factor affecting ecclesiastical penal discipline has been a change in Church-State relations. Until relatively recently, the Church occasionally had recourse to the secular arm to enforce its own discipline, and at times church authorities implemented distinctly civil

---

[1] The author is grateful to Rev. Ladislas Örsy, S.J., whose unpublished reflections entitled "Breach of Law and Punishment" were helpful in preparing these observations. See also A. Marzoa, in *Com Ex,* 222–245.

[2] For a brief overview of the evolution of ecclesiastical delicts and penalties, see G. Michiels, *De Delictis et Poenis* (Paris: Desclée, 1961) 1: 30–40.

discipline. Such close Church-State relations are largely a thing of the past today. There is now a clearer sense of the proper autonomy of ecclesiastical and civil penal orders.

This has facilitated the structuring of the Church's penal discipline according to primarily theological-pastoral considerations. Yet that discipline still reflects significant vestiges of a so-called perfect society ecclesiology. Such a view considered the Church from an unduly institutional perspective as a society comparable to the State but independent from it, with both the Church and State possessing all the institutional means necessary to achieve their respective purposes. Such an approach, however valid, does not do justice to the rich conciliar view of the Church as a *sui generis* hierarchical community of believers with its implications for penal law.[3]

The Reaction of the Community

If the peace of the community disturbed by the delict is to be responsibly restored, church authorities, rather than private individuals, should deal with those seriously violating community faith or order. The community can ill afford to be indifferent to such violations. Otherwise its identity as a sign of the union of God and human persons would be seriously jeopardized. While some types of diversity (e.g., theological, canonical, ascetical, liturgical) clearly enrich the Church, it cannot tolerate certain divergent patterns of thought and activity if it is to be faithful to its teaching, sanctifying, and serving mission. Clarifying the difference between the two types of diversity is a continuing task for believers.

The Church's penal activity will reflect its redemptive, healing character if it primarily affirms ecclesial unity through faith and charity rather than condemning individuals expressing heterodox positions or behaving in an ecclesially detrimental fashion. Church authorities should deal pa-

tiently and charitably with those violating community ideals even while being appropriately firm.

Actually, official penal action is not taken primarily at the initiative of church authorities. Rather, such action responds to the action of an individual breaking entirely with the Church or seriously disturbing his or her communion with it. The community must take notice of those whose conduct significantly impairs its mission. While most Latin Catholics[4] are theoretically subject to the code's penal discipline, in practice it generally affects only clerics and other significant leadership figures.

The official response to canonical violations has assumed different historical forms. The key ecclesiastical penalties have been censures, or so-called medicinal penalties (e.g., excommunication) and expiatory penalties (e.g., dismissal from the clerical state). The Church's penal order has various purposes: repairing scandal, restoring justice, and reforming the offender (c. 1341). One distinction among such penalties is their principal orientation. Censures strongly emphasize reconciling the offender with the community. Their operative force depends on the individual's dispositions vis-à-vis the community; hence, once the offender sincerely repents the canonical violation, the penalty must be remitted. This is not true for expiatory penalties, which more notably emphasize restoring community order, repairing scandal, and deterring would-be violators of ecclesiastical discipline. Such penalties (e.g., deprivation of office) may be operative even after the offender has fully repented.

The complex issue of penalties can hardly be explored adequately here.[5] Throughout history questions have been raised about the effectiveness of

---

[3] For a review of contemporary discussions regarding a proper theological rationale for penal law and related issues, see T. Green, "The Future of Penal Law in the Church," *J* 35 (1975) 215–235.

[4] This commentary nearly exclusively focuses on the 1983 Latin code; however, occasional references will be made to the 1990 Eastern code. See T. Green, "Penal Law in the *Code of Canon Law* and in the *Code of Canons of the Eastern Churches:* Some Comparative Reflections," *Stud Can* 28 (1994) 407–451.

[5] For helpful discussions of such issues see the introduction to the Münster commentary; A. Borras, *Les Sanctions dans l'Eglise* (Paris: Tardy, 1990) 197–220; T. Green, in *CLSA Com*, 893–894.

various penalties and about the ecclesiastical penal system itself. At times a non-penal pastoral approach may lead an offender to a fuller life in Christ more effectively than penalties. Fullness of life in Christ is the ultimate rationale for penal as well as non-penal disciplinary measures in the Church.

Book V of the 1917 Code[6]

Despite some noteworthy differences, Book VI of the 1983 code (cc. 1311–1399) has much in common with Book V of the 1917 code (*CIC* 2195–2414). Hence some comments about that latter text are in order.

Book V of the 1917 Code was the first serious effort to systematize universal penal discipline. It was a complex of norms on establishing, applying, and remitting penalties. It articulated general principles on delicts (*CIC* 2195–2213) and penalties (*CIC* 2214–2240) and considered specific penalties such as censures and so-called vindictive penalties (*CIC* 2241–2313). A concluding section specified penalties for individual delicts organized according to certain fundamental ecclesial values (*CIC* 2314–2414).

While a few individual penalties were changed, the basic presuppositions of Book V were generally unchallenged during the preconciliar period.[7] The Church's penal system was reexamined seriously only during the postconciliar revision of the 1917 code.

Contemporary Penal Law Revision

Code Commission Penal Law Committee

After Vatican II a special *coetus* or committee of the Latin code commission was established to revise Book V of the 1917 code. This committee met nine times from November 1966 until January 1970 when a tentative schema, or draft, of canons was approved. A particularly significant event during the drafting process was the 1967 synod of bishops, which approved certain principles to guide contemporary Latin canonical reform.

Principle nine reaffirmed the continuing need for penal law since a certain coercive power is necessary in every society. Nevertheless, the number of penalties was to be reduced; and penal discipline was to be confined to the so-called external forum (public arena of church life). *Ferendae sententiae,* or imposed, penalties requiring official ecclesiastical intervention were to be the rule. *Latae sententiae* penalties, which are incurred because of a seriously imputable legal violation without such intervention, were to be limited to the most notable ecclesiastical delicts.

In December 1973 a somewhat shortened version of the aforementioned schema was sent for evaluation to the bishops of the world and other consultative organs.[8] Book VI of the 1983 code largely reflects the subsequent reworking of that schema by the aforementioned committee in light of that evaluation.[9]

The Basic Structure and Sources of Book VI

Book VI is divided into two parts, one on delicts and penalties in general (cc. 1311–1363) and the other on penalties for specific delicts (cc. 1364–1398). A concluding canon 1399 indicates the extraordinary conditions under which a penalty may be imposed even without an existing penal law.

The first part of Book VI contains six titles. Four deal with the establishment of penalties: the punishment of delicts in general (cc. 1311–1312),

---

[6] Since the 1983 code is the primary focus of this commentary, 1917 code references will be less numerous than in the original CLSA commentary. See Green, in *CLSA Com,* 894–896.

[7] For post-1917 code preconciliar changes in penal law, see various editions of *CLD* under headings of *CIC* 2195–2414. Also J. O'Connor, "Trends in Canon Law: The Question of Penalties," *Stud Can* 3 (1969) 209–237.

[8] For critical reflections on this schema, see Green, "Future of Penal Law," 248–274.

[9] For an overview of penal law committee activities, see J. Fox, "A General Synthesis of the Work of the Pontifical Commission for the Revision of the Code of Canon Law," *J* 48 (1988) 829–832.

penal law and penal precepts (cc. 1313–1320), those subject to penal sanctions, or imputability (cc. 1321–1330), and penalties and other punishments (cc. 1331–1340). One title governing the application of penalties (cc. 1341–1353) must be read in connection with norms on penal processes in Book VII (cc. 1717–1731). Finally, a single title considers the cessation of penalties (cc. 1354–1363).

The second part of Book VI also contains six principal titles, highlighting various types of delicts warranting similar treatment throughout the Church. These canons penalize delicts against religion and church unity (cc. 1364–1369), delicts against church authorities (cc. 1370–1377), delicts in exercising ecclesiastical functions (cc. 1378–1389), delicts involving falsehood (cc. 1390–1391), delicts involving violations of clerical and religious obligations (cc. 1392–1396), and delicts against human life, integrity, and freedom (cc. 1397–1398).

The 1983 code depends significantly on the canons of the 1917 code, occasionally modified in light of subsequent legal developments. Conciliar sources rarely seem to influence Book VI directly. However, certain conciliar themes indirectly shape it, e.g., an increased respect for human dignity and freedom and an emphasis on expanded legal-pastoral discretion for bishops and other ordinaries.[10]

Noteworthy Aspects of the 1983 Code

Certain universal norms are necessary for a proper application of penal law throughout the Latin church. However, the principle of subsidiarity calls for increased legislative competency for infra-universal church authorities such as diocesan bishops. This should facilitate the adaptation of penal discipline to differing pastoral circumstances. Hence, universal penal laws are notably

---

[10] T. Green, "Penal Law: A Review of Selected Themes," *J* 50 (1990) 221–256; E. McDonough, "A *Novus Habitus Mentis* for Sanctions in the Church," *J* 48 (1988) 727–746.

reduced in number. Only those fundamental principles necessary for a basic framework of penal discipline are maintained in part one (cc. 1311–1363). Only those delicts so ecclesially detrimental as to require relatively uniform treatment everywhere are presumably included in part two (cc. 1364–1398). However, lest increased infra-universal penal discretion be arbitrary and pastorally counterproductive, the code encourages penal law uniformity in neighboring particular churches of a given region (c. 1316).

A renewed recognition of human dignity and freedom and of the salvific character of church law underlies the code's forceful emphasis on penalties only as a last resort when all other legal-pastoral measures have failed to deal with problematic behavior (c. 1341). The judicial or administrative discretion of ecclesiastical authorities in confronting various pastoral problems is notably enhanced. Appeal or recourse to a higher authority against a penal sentence or decree always suspends its effects until higher authority upholds the sentence or decree (c. 1353).

Penal discipline is simplified in several respects. The code notably reduces the number of penalties and simplifies the formerly complex system of reserving the remission of numerous penalties to the Holy See. Likewise, bishops may more easily remit penalties and thereby minister more effectively to their fellow believers (cc. 1354–1356).

Penal discipline is largely an external forum reality within the exclusive competence of bishops, other ordinaries, and judges. Confessors may remit only certain *latae sententiae* penalties if there has been no formal declaration that they have been incurred (c. 1357).

The 1983 code prefers judicial rather than administrative procedure in imposing penalties to protect better the rights of all concerned (c. 1342). Yet, the competent penal authority may generally impose penalties administratively for a just cause (c. 1720). However, the code explicitly requires judicial process for perpetual, or irrevocable, penalties such as deprivation of office (c. 1336, §1, 2°).

Finally, concerns about ensuring the personal involvement of church authorities in dealing with potential offenders account for the emphasis on *ferendae sententiae* penalties (c. 1314). These penalties can be imposed only after a formal procedure, unlike *latae sententiae* penalties, which an imputable offender incurs by the very commission of the delict. Presumably, these latter penalties are

incurred only for the most serious delicts (c. 1318), and the legislator occasionally minimizes their practical effects, e.g., lack of operative force given mitigating circumstances (c. 1324, §3).[11]

[11] For lists of penalties and corresponding delicts in the 1983 code, see *CLSA Com*, 932–940.

CANONS AND COMMENTARY

Part I
DELICTS AND PENALTIES IN GENERAL
[cc. 1311–1363][12]

TITLE I
THE PUNISHMENT OF DELICTS IN GENERAL
[cc. 1311–1312][13]

Church Penal Rights[14]

Canon 1311 — The Church has the innate and proper right to coerce offending members of the Christian faithful with penal sanctions.

Despite requests for a statement of the theological-canonical foundations of the Church's penal authority, the code simply affirms the Church's

innate and proper right to penalize lawbreakers. Generally the code commission avoided dealing with foundational theological-canonical issues.

The Church presumably possesses an "innate" penal right, i.e., one based on its nature and not derivative from any human power such as the State.[15] This right is also "proper," i.e., exercised in its own name rather than for another higher authority (e.g., the State). This formulation reflects an overly institutional, perfect society ecclesiology, which highlights the Church's distinctive governmental competencies. Conciliar themes such as the Church as a divine-human mystery and a communion of believers seem not to have influenced this formulation.[16]

Unlike the 1917 code, the present code does not define terms such as ecclesiastical "delict" that prompt the exercise of such coercive power.[17] However, canon 1321 on penal imputability (to be

[12] For observations on this material in the *CCEO*, see Green, "Comparative Reflections," 429–435.

[13] Besides the Münster commentary, see Borras, 200–207; Green, in *CLSA Com*, 897–898; J. Martin, in *CLSGBI Com*, 749–750; Marzoa, in *Com Ex*, 246–257; W. Rees, *Die Strafgewalt der Kirche* (Berlin: Duncker & Humblot, 1993) 365–372.

[14] See *CCEO* 1401, highlighting the pastoral, reconciling spirit that should characterize penal law.

[15] For comparable formulations of ecclesiastical rights vis-à-vis the State, see cc. 232 (ministerial formation), 800, §1 and 807 (establishment of schools and universities), and 1254, §1 (disposition of temporal goods).

[16] For a more detailed exploration of these issues, see the Münster commentary on c. 1311.

[17] *CIC* 2195. Recourse to the former code and the canonical tradition occasionally helps to clarify the meaning of similar terms in the 1983 code (cf. c. 6, §2). However, the present code must always be interpreted primarily in light of Vatican II.

considered later) states that no one may be punished unless a sanctionable external violation of a law or precept[18] is gravely imputable because of malice or negligence.

In principle the "Christian faithful" liable to sanctions are baptized Latin Catholics with the sufficient use of reason (c. 11). However, canon 1323, 1° exempts those under sixteen from any ecclesiastical penalties.

While canon 1311 affirms the Church's penal competency, several canons call for penal restraint. For example, canon 1317 cautions legislators to establish penalties only if they are truly necessary to provide more suitably for ecclesiastical discipline. Canon 1318 advises against multiplying *latae sententiae* penalties, especially excommunications. Furthermore, canon 1341 warns ordinaries not to initiate penal processes unless there is no other way of repairing scandal, restoring justice, and reforming the alleged offender.

Types of Sanctions

Canon 1312 — §1. The following are penal sanctions in the Church:

    1° medicinal penalties or censures, which are listed in cann. 1331–1333;

    2° expiatory penalties mentioned in can. 1336.

§2. The law can establish other expiatory penalties which deprive a member of the Christian faithful of some spiritual or temporal good and which are consistent with the supernatural purpose of the Church.

§3. Penal remedies and penances are also used; the former especially to prevent delicts, the latter to substitute for or to increase a penalty.

The code here briefly deals with various sanctions geared to addressing problematic ecclesial behavior. The generic term "sanctions" encompasses both penalties in the strict sense and quasi-penal measures such as penal remedies and penances.

Paragraph one neither defines nor indicates the purpose of the various types of penalties but simply mentions them and refers to title IV on their effects. The primary, but not exclusive, purpose of medicinal penalties, or censures (e.g., excommunication), is breaking contumacy, or contempt of church authority, and reintegrating the offender within the community (cc. 1331–1335). In contrast, expiatory penalties such as deprivation of office primarily envision restoring justice and repairing the ecclesial damage done by the offender (cc. 1336–1338). Unlike the remission of a censure, their remission does not depend primarily on the offender's change of heart but rather on church authority's determination that such ecclesial damage has been repaired. Censures emphasize reforming the offender, whereas expiatory penalties more notably highlight protecting the Church's fundamental socio-juridical goods.[19]

While censures are exhaustively listed in canons 1331–1335, there may be expiatory penalties besides those enumerated in canon 1336 (§2). Such penalties are deprivations of a spiritual or temporal good, which are consistent with the Church's supernatural purpose. The Church's integrity is to be protected against breaches of its faith and order, but the human dignity and freedom of conscience even of offenders are to be respected.

Despite explicitly referring only to expiatory penalties, this description actually applies to all penalties. However, not every deprivation of an ecclesial good is a penalty, e.g., removal of a pastor (cc. 1740–1747). Rather, only those deprivations prompted by an ecclesiastical delict are technically penalties.

Penal remedies or external forum penances (cc. 1339–1340) may be employed in a somewhat ancillary fashion vis-à-vis penalties (§3). Since penalties are last resort provisions, such quasi-penal measures may help to preclude ecclesiastical delicts or address problematic, yet non-delictual

---

[18] Subsequently when the commentary refers to "penal law," the "penal precept" is also understood unless it is otherwise indicated.

[19] For more detailed reflections on various sanctions, see the Münster commentary on c. 1312.

disciplinary situations. Furthermore, after a delict has been proven, such measures may replace a penalty in cases of mitigated imputability (c. 1348) or increase the force of a *latae sententiae* penalty given aggravating circumstances (c. 1326, §2).

TITLE II
PENAL LAW AND PENAL PRECEPT
[cc. 1313–1320][20]

Change of Law Situation[21]

Canon 1313 — §1. If a law is changed after a delict has been committed, the law more favorable to the accused is to be applied.

§2. If a later law abolishes a law or at least the penalty, the penalty immediately ceases.

A benign interpretation of penal law is pastorally necessary (*CIC* 2219, §1; *CCEO* 1404, §1). If the meaning of a text is doubtful, the interpretation favoring the alleged offender is preferable.[22] Furthermore, since penal law is always burdensome, it is always to be strictly interpreted (c. 18; *CCEO* 1500). Hence one should restrict rather than enlarge a canon's potential applicability.

The present canon exemplifies the aforementioned benign approach. If the law changes after a delict is committed but before the penalty is imposed, the law more favorable to the alleged offender at the time of the penal process is applicable (§1). This may mean a less severe penalty (a "just penalty" rather than an excommunication) or possibly a *ferendae sententiae* penalty requiring a

process rather than a *latae sententiae* penalty incurred by the commission of the delict.[23]

This moderate approach is even more evident when the law or at least the penalty attached to its violation is repealed after a delict is committed and a *latae sententiae* penalty incurred or a *ferendae sententiae* penalty imposed. In this case the offender is no longer subject to the penalty even without a formal declaration of such although other pastoral measures may be warranted (§2; c. 1348).

This situation was verified when the present code took effect on November 27, 1983. Numerous 1917 code penalties lost their force (c. 6, §1, 3°), e.g., excommunication for fully imputable Masonic membership (*CIC* 2335).[24]

Ferendae Sententiae *Orientation of Law*

Canon 1314 — Generally, a penalty is *ferendae sententiae*, so that it does not bind the guilty party until after it has been imposed; if the law or precept expressly establishes it, however, a penalty is *latae sententiae*, so that it is incurred ipso facto when the delict is committed.

A significant postconciliar discussion has concerned the continuing viability of *latae sententiae* penalties, i.e., those incurred by committing a delict without any formal procedure.[25] This canon embodies a principal code commission concern: an emphasis on *ferendae sententiae* penalties as normative. A service-oriented exercise of authority requires that church authorities normally address the concrete circumstances of every alleged delict. Hence, before the exercise of rights is curtailed by a penalty, there must normally be a formal judicial or administrative process, usually after a preliminary inquiry (cc. 1717–1719).

---

[20] Besides the Münster commentary, see Borras, 50–62; Green, in *CLSA Com,* 898–901; Martin, in *CLSGBI Com,* 750–753; Rees, 371–377; J. Sanchis, in *Com Ex,* 258–281.

[21] Cf. *CCEO* 1412, §2–§3.

[22] This benign approach also prohibits recourse to the usual rules on supplying for a lack of penal legislation. In other words, if a specific legal norm is lacking when a church authority deals with a penal situation, he may not create such a norm in light of the provisions of c. 19.

[23] An exception to this benign approach are special norms governing prescription of penal actions for sexual abuse of minors in the United States. See commentary on cc. 1362 and 1395.

[24] See c. 1374.

[25] Green, "Future of Penal Law," 224–228; V. De Paolis, "De legitimate et opportunitate poenarum latae sententiae in iure poenali canonico," *P* 63 (1974) 37–67.

By way of exception, *latae sententiae* penalties may be established in situations of grave scandal or when the public good cannot be adequately served by *ferendae sententiae* penalties (c. 1318). Presumably certain occult, or non-public, delicts, such as absolution of an accomplice (c. 1378, §1), might not be punished without *latae sententiae* penalties.

For the sake of legal precision, such uniquely Latin church penalties appealing to the offender's conscience must be expressly stated in the law threatening them. Furthermore, the code occasionally limits their impact on the person who must observe them. Actually, such an observance seems to presuppose a certain depth of spiritual motivation in the offender which may not always be verified.[26]

No explicit reference is made here to the declaration or official clarification that such penalties have been incurred. However, this is necessary to enforce their full effects.[27]

Competence to Establish Penal Law[28]

Canon 1315 — §1. A person who has legislative power can also issue penal laws; within the limits of his competence by reason of territory or of persons, moreover, he can by his own laws also strengthen with an appropriate penalty a divine law or an ecclesiastical law issued by a higher authority.

§2. The law itself can determine a penalty, or its determination can be left to the prudent appraisal of a judge.

§3. Particular law also can add other penalties to those established by universal law for some delict; however, this is not to be done except for very grave necessity. If universal law threatens an indeterminate or facultative penalty, particular law can also establish a determinate or obligatory one in its place.

The remaining canons in this title seem to refer primarily to infra-universal church authorities, particularly legislators. Such authorities enjoy expanded legislative and administrative penal discretion to be exercised with restraint according to the following canons.

Only those with legislative authority can establish their own penal laws or penalize violations of divine or higher level ecclesiastical laws lacking a distinctive sanction (c. 1315, §1). Such authority is exercised by individuals such as diocesan bishops (c. 391) and by corporate bodies, such as conferences of bishops, under certain conditions (c. 455). To preclude abuses, such authority is to be exercised only within the territorial or personal limits of the particular legislator's competence. Furthermore, neighboring diocesan bishops are normally to consult with one another before establishing penal laws (c. 1316). They are also to observe the principle of legislative restraint (cc. 1317–1318).

At times a *ferendae sententiae* penalty is determined in the law establishing it, e.g., c. 1395, §1. At other times, however, an indeterminate *ferendae sententiae* penalty must be determined by the competent penal authority after a formal process, e.g., c. 1365. However, *latae sententiae* penalties are always determinate (c. 1315, §2).

The preceding examples involve obligatory, or preceptive, *ferendae sententiae* penalties, which is generally the case in the code. However, occasionally it leaves the disposition of the matter up to the judge or ordinary (facultative, or discretionary, penalties), e.g., c. 1390, §3. The aforementioned obligatory-facultative distinction concerns the penal discretion exercised by the competent penal authority.[29] Such a distinction, however, is not relevant to *latae sententiae* penalties, which are incurred by an imputable offender upon committing the delict.

---

[26] See, for example, cc. 1318; 1324, §3; 1329, §2; 1335; 1338, §3. See also the Münster commentary on c. 1314.

[27] See, for example, c. 1331, §1–§2 on the different effects of a non-declared and declared excommunication.

[28] Cf. *CCEO* 1405, §1–§2.

[29] On such penal discretion, see especially cc. 1343–1346; 1349. Far from being a dereliction of duty, such discretion of the judge or ordinary is permissible and at times pastorally desirable even if penalties are theoretically obligatory (c. 1344).

The aforementioned principle of legislative restraint is also operative here (§3). Barring an extremely grave necessity, infra-universal legislators are not to add to those penalties specified in the code, since multiplying penalties may be pastorally detrimental. However, if the code does not specify a penalty for a delict or indicates that it is facultative, infra-universal legislators may impose a determinate penalty or require some type of penalty. This would probably be prompted by a particularly problematic legal-pastoral situation, e.g., serious human rights violations.

Desirable Penal Law Uniformity[30]

Canon 1316 — Insofar as possible, diocesan bishops are to take care that if penal laws must be issued, they are uniform in the same city or region.

The conciliar enhancing of episcopal pastoral governance authority implies that bishops should have a certain penal legislative discretion given their responsibility to see to the observance of the code in their dioceses (c. 392). The penal law committee rejected a proposal to limit infra-universal penal law initiatives to episcopal conferences, since this would unduly restrict the pastoral governance role of diocesan bishops.

However, while some penal law diversity might be justified, such expanded episcopal discretion might be a mixed blessing. Notable discrepancies among neighboring dioceses in punishing delicts might be ecclesially counterproductive and weaken the effectiveness of the penal system. Hence, neighboring bishops should strive for a uniform legislative approach to possible delicts. Hopefully this will check arbitrary episcopal discretion violating Christian dignity and freedom.[31]

Cautious Establishment of Penal Law

Canon 1317 — Penalties are to be established only insofar as they are truly necessary to provide more suitably for ecclesiastical discipline. Particular law, however, cannot establish a penalty of dismissal from the clerical state.

The next two canons wisely advise infra-universal legislators to establish new penal laws cautiously, especially those threatening *latae sententiae* penalties or censures such as excommunications. Since penalties are last resort measures (c. 1341), they should be limited to instances in which they are absolutely necessary from a disciplinary standpoint. The sharp reduction in penalties for specific delicts in the code might prompt lower level legislators to multiply particular penal laws.

To protect clerics against possibly arbitrary episcopal discretion, particular law may not determine additional grounds for dismissal from the clerical state (c. 1336, §1, 5°).[32] Such a last resort penalty is warranted only in those extremely serious cases of clerical intransigence expressly stated in the code.[33] The serious effects of dismissal for the cleric (c. 292) and the need to facilitate the exercise of his right of defense require special care in determining violations warranting dismissal and normally a collegiate tribunal of at least three judges in imposing it (c. 1425, §1, 2a). Somewhat surprisingly, however, during 1998 John Paul II, at the request of their bishops, administratively dismissed certain clerics for sexual abuse of minors. As problematic as such behavior

---

[30] Cf. *CCEO* 1405, §3.

[31] Such episcopal penal consultation seemed lacking in February 1996 when Bishop Fabian Bruskewitz of Lincoln, Nebraska forbade membership in twelve organizations under penalty of interdict (initially) and excommunication (subsequently). See *Origins* 25/42 (April 11,

1996) 725; G. Read, "Lincoln, Nebraska Excommunications," *CLS-GBIN* no. 107 (September 1996) 18–24.

[32] See also c. 1350 on support for even penalized clerics.

[33] See cc. 1364, §2 (heresy, apostasy, or schism); 1367 (violation of sacred species); 1370, §1 (physical attack on the pope); 1387 (confessional solicitation); 1394, §1 (attempted marriage); 1395 (various sexual offenses). Martin also includes violations of c. 1397 as a basis for dismissal (752, n. 2). However, a strict interpretation of law seems to preclude this, since c. 1397 speaks explicitly of the privations and prohibitions mentioned in c. 1336 (§1, 2°–3°) but not precisely of dismissal (§1, 5°).

may be, questions could possibly be raised about how well such an expeditious process honored the aforementioned right of defense which the pope has strongly and repeatedly emphasized, especially in marriage cases.

Caution Regarding Latae Sententiae *Penalties*

Canon 1318 — A legislator is not to threaten *latae sententiae* **penalties except possibly for certain singularly malicious delicts which either can result in graver scandal or cannot be punished effectively by** *ferendae sententiae* **penalties; he is not, however, to establish censures, especially excommunication, except with the greatest moderation and only for graver delicts.**

This canon's cautious approach to *latae sententiae* penalties in general and censures (especially excommunication) in particular continues the prior canon's emphasis on penal legislative restraint.[34] The present canon embodies the law's preference for *ferendae sententiae* penalties (c. 1314). The canon also reflects a penal hierarchy of values since *latae sententiae* penalties are among the most serious in the law. Such caution is probably related to the absence of a direct encounter between church authority and the offender before the penalty is incurred although it can later be formally declared judicially or administratively. Furthermore, the serious liturgical and governmental prohibitions resulting from excommunication (c. 1331) probably account for the legislator's special caution in that regard.

The seriousness of the penalty should be proportionate to the gravity of the delict. Hence, *latae sententiae* penalties are warranted only for extraordinary, singularly malicious delicts not arising from mere negligence. Such penalties are justified only if there is serious scandal[35] or the

delict cannot be addressed adequately through a *ferendae sententiae* penalty.

Issuing of Penal Precepts

Canon 1319 — §1. Insofar as a person can impose precepts in the external forum in virtue of the power of governance, the person can also threaten determinate penalties by precept, except perpetual expiatory penalties.

§2. A penal precept is not to be issued unless the matter has been considered thoroughly and those things established in cann. 1317–1318 about particular laws have been observed.

This canon on penal precepts reflects this title's cautious approach to the establishment of penalties. Here the code refers to a more particularized situation than is envisioned by the law's more generalized focus. An administrative authority (c. 134) (e.g., a vicar general) may order an individual or a group to do or cease doing something under threat of a penalty for non-compliance (cc. 35; 49). For example, a bishop might threaten a priest with suspension for continuing partisan political activities (c. 287, §2). Generally speaking, a precept differs from a law by focusing somewhat more on the private rather than the common good and by being personal rather than territorial in character. Much more so than a law, a precept takes cognizance of the particular circumstances of the potential offender.

Administrative authorities should impose penal precepts cautiously and only after careful deliberation. The code explicitly refers to canons 1317–1318 on moderation in establishing any penalties and special care in threatening *latae sententiae* penalties, es-

---

[34] The 1983 code contains seventeen *latae sententiae* penalties. See *CLSA Com,* 937. Of nine possible excommunications, seven are *latae sententiae.* See *CLSA Com,* 932.

[35] Book VI speaks of "scandal" eleven times without defining it. See cc. 1318; 1328, §2; 1339, §2; 1341; 1344, §2;

1347, §2; 1352, §2; 1357, §2; 1364, §2; 1394, §1; and 1395, §1. In this regard see *CCC* 2284–2287. Such scandal probably refers to delicts significantly dishonoring the Church and its teachings and creating in the faithful an attitude conducive to delictual behavior. Such scandal is particularly grave if church authorities cause it or especially vulnerable persons are adversely influenced by them (c. 1326).

pecially censures such as excommunication. This is because of their significant consequences for the exercise of Christian rights. The rules on individual administrative decrees[36] and administrative recourse (cc. 1732–1739) are relevant here.

The code forbids precepts threatening indeterminate penalties because these depend too much on the will of the superior and hence may unduly jeopardize the rights of an alleged offender. Even more notably, the code prohibits precepts threatening perpetual expiatory penalties because of their irrevocable implications, e.g., deprivation of an office (c. 1336, §1, 2°).

Penalties for Religious

Canon 1320 — The local ordinary can coerce religious with penalties in all those matters in which they are subject to him.

The bishop is the primary moderator of the exercise of the apostolate in his diocese (c. 394). This has particular relevance to apostolic religious. With due regard for their legitimate autonomy (c. 586), such religious are subject to him regarding pastoral care, the exercise of divine worship, and other works of the apostolate.[37]

Accordingly, the bishop may visit various institutions of religious in the diocese although the scope of his visit is somewhat more restricted in dealing with pontifical institutes than with their diocesan counterparts (c. 397). During such a visitation or possibly in other circumstances, questions may arise about the compliance of religious with church discipline in the aforementioned apostolic areas.

The present canon must be situated in that larger context of the integration of religious into diocesan life. The canon explicitly accords the "local ordinary" (c. 134, §2: e.g., an episcopal vicar for reli-

gious) coercive power over religious in his diocese in those matters in which they are subject to him, especially the aforementioned apostolic concerns.

It is not entirely clear why the code needed to express this principle of coercive authority here. Perhaps it is because of the principle of exemption of institutes of consecrated life from the governance of the local ordinary (c. 591).[38] In any event, the principle of penal restraint suggests that every effort be made to minimize the need for recourse to penalties in bishop-religious relationships. Hopefully regular pastoral consultation between bishops and religious superiors may facilitate the achievement of this goal.[39]

TITLE III
THE SUBJECT LIABLE TO PENAL SANCTIONS
[cc. 1321–1330][40]

This significant title should be read in connection with canons 1341–1353 on applying penalties, for the current title articulates basic principles aiding penal authorities in determining whether a delict has been committed and what might be an appropriate penalty.[41]

After specifying the basis of penal imputability (c. 1321), the legislator indicates various factors affecting it (cc. 1322–1327). Subsequently, the canons consider an attempted delict (c. 1328), delictual collaboration (c. 1329), and delicts involving declaring one's mind or intent (c. 1330).

---

[36] Canons 48–58. See especially c. 50 on necessary consultation before issuing an administrative decree such as a precept. Furthermore, c. 51 requires a written decree giving the reasons for the precept at least in summary fashion.

[37] See especially the commentary on cc. 673–683.

[38] Borras, 61.

[39] Although it is not technically a penal canon, see c. 679 empowering the bishop, for a very serious reason, to prohibit a member of a religious institute from living in his diocese. However, if the religious superior fails to comply with the bishop's request, the latter cannot act on his own but must refer the matter to CICLSAL.

[40] Besides the Münster commentary, see also Borras, 13–44; Green, in *CLSA Com,* 901–906; Martin, in *CLSGBI Com,* 753–761; Marzoa, in *Com Ex,* 282–351; Rees, 377–385.

[41] For less detailed Eastern code provisions, see *CCEO* 1413–1418.

While these canons focus on individual offenders, a key penal law concern is protecting the integrity of the Church's faith and order and somewhat distancing the community from behavior patterns violating such integrity.[42]

Notion of Imputability[43]

Canon 1321 — §1. No one is punished unless the external violation of a law or precept, committed by the person, is gravely imputable by reason of malice or negligence.

§2. A penalty established by a law or precept binds the person who has deliberately violated the law or precept; however, a person who violated a law or precept by omitting necessary diligence is not punished unless the law or precept provides otherwise.

§3. When an external violation has occurred, imputability is presumed unless it is otherwise apparent.

It is a basic Christian right not to be punished except according to law (c. 221, §3). The exercise of one's rights cannot be curtailed by a penalty unless it is proven that a delict has been committed (§1). One may neither be penalized nor subjected to other disciplinary action merely because a delict has been alleged. Normally penalties are imposed through a judicial or administrative process (*ferendae sententiae*); however, *latae sententiae* penalties are incurred by the very commission of a delict.

A key penal consideration is the meaning of an ecclesiastical "delict," which is not defined here.[44] However, this initial canon can facilitate a working understanding of the concept. There are objective, subjective, and legal dimensions to any delict. First of all, there must be an external or perceivable violation of a law provable in the external forum (objective dimension). However, the violation need not be public, or known to many people; certain legal violations may be occult, or known only to a few people. Furthermore, the mere breaking of the law does not necessarily mean that a delict has been committed. There must also be grave juridical imputability, rooted primarily in a free and deliberate intent to violate the law or secondarily in culpable negligence (subjective dimension). Finally, prescinding from serious moral culpability, which must always be verified, not every legal violation constitutes a delict. The violation must normally be expressly sanctioned in universal or particular law (legal dimension).[45]

This title deals largely with the second element of a delict, i.e., grave imputability. Given its importance, the code provides detailed guidelines to assist judges and ordinaries in making prudent penal judgments after weighing the relevant factors. The code articulates various factors influencing imputability, some within an individual's control (e.g., culpable drunkenness) and others beyond such control (e.g., grave fear).

The significant notions here are *dolus* and *culpa.* Normally *dolus,* or a deliberate intent to violate the law, is necessary for penal imputability (criminal intent). *Culpa,* or culpable negligence in observing the law, normally does not give rise to such imputability (§2).[46] A certain penal proportionality is operative: one should normally not be punished except for a free and knowing violation of the law.

How does one assess penal imputability in particular cases, since various complex factors may influence a given legal violation? If there is an external violation of the law, imputability is presumed (§3). This seems to involve *dolus,* or crim-

---

[42] For a more detailed discussion of penal imputability, see the Münster commentary's introduction to this title; also Marzoa, in *Com Ex,* 282–289.

[43] For detailed reflections on this canon see Marzoa, in *Com Ex,* 282–303.

[44] *CIC* 2195, §1.

[45] See especially cc. 1364–1398, most of the sanctionable violations in the code.

[46] The only canon in Book VI explicitly penalizing negligent behavior is c. 1389, §2, requiring a just penalty if one harms another through the culpably negligent exercise of ecclesiastical power, ministry, or function. Yet see also c. 1326, §1, 3°, indicating as a factor aggravating imputability a type of negligence hardly distinguishable from criminal intent. *Culpa* also may mean culpable ignorance of the law (*CCEO* 1414, §1).

inal intent; yet since *culpa*, or negligence, at times grounds imputability, this factor must also be considered. Presumably one violating the law acts in a human fashion with a certain freedom and knowledge. However, since penal law is to be interpreted benignly, the judge or ordinary should not too easily attribute criminal intent to the alleged offender. By contrast, the former code simply presumed criminal intent (*dolus*) if the law were broken (*CIC* 2200, §2).[47]

In short the present code requires the alleged offender to demonstrate that grave imputability is not verified in the case in question. However, the current burden of proof is less stringent than in the former code, which required that the presumption of criminal intent be overturned with moral certitude, i.e., beyond a reasonable doubt. The present code states simply that the presumption of imputability is verified unless the contrary is otherwise evident. Hence any evidence posing reasonable questions about such imputability suffices to overturn the presumption.

The retention of such a presumption of imputability still seems questionable, although it is less objectionable than the prior presumption of criminal intent. This legal change reflects the present code's somewhat more pastoral thrust, since it enhances the penal rights of alleged offenders and better protects their reputations by placing a more stringent burden of proof on the ordinary or promoter of justice (c. 1430).

However, the traditional Anglo-American presumption of innocence until one is proven guilty seems still more appropriate, since it better protects the reputation of alleged offenders by placing an even more stringent burden of proof on the institution. Church law should vindicate freedom, justice, and equity even more forcefully than civil law does. Accordingly, the code should presume purity of intent until the guilt of alleged offenders is formally demonstrated.[48]

Insanity and Imputability

Canon 1322 — Those who habitually lack the use of reason are considered to be incapable of a delict, even if they violated a law or precept while seemingly sane.

To assist the competent penal authorities, the next seven canons address various aspects of individual imputability in committing a delict. Separate canons indicate the various factors eliminating, diminishing, or increasing imputability or those factors not to be taken into account in assessing it. Limitations of space permit only brief comments on these factors.[49]

Imputability essentially presupposes a free, deliberate human act. Hence, whatever factors significantly impair one's ability to function freely and deliberately thereby affect imputability, or one's being held accountable for certain actions or omissions.

Such factors are similar to certain grounds for marital nullity (cc. 1095–1107)[50] since certain factors mentioned here which impair one's decisional integrity can affect one's ability to express free and deliberate marital consent.

Canon 1322 deals with the most radical situation, i.e., the insane person or one habitually deprived of the use of reason. The canon does not state a refutable legal presumption. Rather, the person habitually deprived of the use of reason is viewed as incapable of a delict despite appearing normal when breaking the law. Such an individual is not in possession of his or her faculties and

---

[47] For a comparable Eastern code presumption, see *CCEO* 1414, §2.

[48] See Green, "Penal Law: A Review of Selected Themes," 243–244; M. Hughes, "The Presumption of Imputability

in Canon 1321, §3," *Stud Can* 21 (1987) 33–35; E. Mc-Donough, "A Gloss on Canon 1321," *Stud Can* 21 (1987) 383–384.

[49] See also the commentaries on the 1983 code indicated earlier. Commentators on the 1917 code are also helpful given significant continuity between the two codes. For example, see T. L. Bouscaren, A. Ellis, and F. Korth, *Canon Law*, 4th ed. (Milwaukee: Bruce, 1962) 866–869; A. Vermeersch and I. Creusen, *Epitome Iuris Canonici*, 7th ed. (Malines-Rome: H. Dessain, 1956) 227–233.

[50] See also cc. 125 and 126 on various factors affecting the validity of a juridic act, e.g., force, fear, ignorance, or error.

hence cannot function freely and deliberately. Such a one is comparable to an infant and hence absolved of responsibility before the community, however serious the legal violation (c. 99).[51]

Factors Exempting from a Penalty[52]

Canon 1323 — The following are not subject to a penalty when they have violated a law or precept:

  1° a person who has not yet completed the sixteenth year of age;

  2° a person who without negligence was ignorant that he or she violated a law or precept; inadvertence and error are equivalent to ignorance;

  3° a person who acted due to physical force or a chance occurrence which the person could not foresee or, if foreseen, avoid;

  4° a person who acted coerced by grave fear, even if only relatively grave, or due to necessity or grave inconvenience unless the act is intrinsically evil or tends to the harm of souls;

  5° a person who acted with due moderation against an unjust aggressor for the sake of legitimate self-defense or defense of another;

  6° a person who lacked the use of reason, without prejudice to the prescripts of cann. 1324, §1, n. 2 and 1325;

  7° a person who without negligence thought that one of the circumstances mentioned in nn. 4 or 5 was present.

In contrast to the preceding canon involving the radically impaired individual, the legislator here deals with various violators of a law who are normally in possession of their faculties. However, they are not penalized because of certain factors significantly diminishing their knowledge or freedom. Hence, there is generally no real penal im-

putability since there is neither criminal intent nor culpable negligence.

The canon lists different factors prompting the legislator to exempt one breaking the law from a penalty. Such factors will be briefly considered in terms of the aforementioned limitations of human awareness and freedom, which are less serious in some cases than others, e.g., age (1°). However, it may be difficult at times to differentiate sharply such imputability-exempting considerations in a given case.

Those under sixteen years of age are entirely exempt from penal imputability (1°).[53] This provision somewhat reflects the civil law tendency to treat juvenile offenders more leniently than other lawbreakers given the former's presumed lack of full maturity.

The impairment of one's understanding is a factor underlying several other numbers of the canon. First of all, inculpable ignorance of a law exempts one from penal imputability since it impairs the deliberateness of one's functioning (2°).[54] Such lack of knowledge about a law, penalty, or fact concerning oneself is not presumed (c. 15, §2) but must be proven if one claims such an exemption from penal imputability. Equally relevant factors exempting from imputability are error, or a false judgment about a given matter,[55] and inadvertence, or a lack of attentiveness to a given matter.

The legislator also exempts from penalties the individual erroneously yet inculpably believing that his or her behavior was attributable to the freedom-impairing circumstances of grave fear, serious inconvenience, necessity, or legitimate self-defense (7°). Likewise, such error is not presumed but must be demonstrated to exempt one from imputability.

The impairment of personal freedom is a key factor elsewhere in the canon. For example, one

---

[51] See c. 1095, 1° on the marital incapacity of those lacking the sufficient use of reason.

[52] For helpful reflections see Marzoa, in *Com Ex,* 306–314.

[53] By contrast, the Eastern code speaks of fourteen years of age (*CCEO* 1413, §1).

[54] On ignorance invalidating marital consent, see c. 1096.

[55] On the effect of ignorance or error on the validity of juridic acts, see c. 126; on error invalidating marital consent, see c. 1097.

is exempt from all imputability if the law is violated in the circumstances of a purely unforeseeable accident. This exemption also applies if the legal violation could have been foreseen but not prevented or if one's actions result from irresistible external physical force (3°).[56]

A comparable pressure situation is one in which a person violates the law out of necessity. This means that one breaks the law to preclude the threat of some personal or social evil arising from its observance. Furthermore, while it may be burdensome to observe any law, serious inconvenience in observing positive ecclesiastical law possibly exempts one from a penalty. This is because such a law does not bind in circumstances in which there is no reasonable alternative to its violation. Likewise subject to coercion is one who acts out of grave fear, even if only relative, i.e., sufficient to intimidate the accused even if not necessarily all persons (4°).[57]

However, if the legal violations mentioned in the prior paragraph are intrinsically evil acts[58] or will cause significant pastoral damage, an offender is not exempt from all imputability. This is because certain significant ecclesial values to be fostered[59] are at stake, and their violation needs to be addressed by church authorities.

One violating a law in legitimate defense of self or another against an actual threat is likewise exempt from a penalty if the person used only that amount of force necessary to repel the unjust aggressor (5°). A certain moderation must be verified if the legal violation is not to reflect criminal intent.

Finally, the prior canon indicated that the person habitually lacking the use of reason was incapable of a delict. A somewhat comparable situation involves a person who temporarily but involuntarily lacks the use of reason and hence cannot place a human act, e.g., involuntary drunkenness, subjection to drugs or uncontrollable passion (6°). If this is the case when the law is violated, such a person is exempt from any penalty.

Factors Diminishing Imputability[60]

Canon 1324 — §1. The perpetrator of a violation is not exempt from a penalty, but the penalty established by law or precept must be tempered or a penance employed in its place if the delict was committed:

1° **by a person who had only the imperfect use of reason;**

2° **by a person who lacked the use of reason because of drunkenness or another similar culpable disturbance of mind;**

3° **from grave heat of passion which did not precede and hinder all deliberation of mind and consent of will and provided that the passion itself had not been stimulated or fostered voluntarily;**

4° **by a minor who has completed the age of sixteen years;**

5° **by a person who was coerced by grave fear, even if only relatively grave, or due to necessity or grave inconvenience if the delict is intrinsically evil or tends to the harm of souls;**

6° **by a person who acted without due moderation against an unjust aggressor for the sake of legitimate self-defense or defense of another;**

7° **against someone who gravely and unjustly provokes the person;**

8° **by a person who thought in culpable error that one of the circumstances mentioned in can. 1323, nn. 4 or 5 was present;**

---

[56] On the impact of force and grave fear on the validity of juridic acts, see c. 125, §1; on the invalidating effect of such factors on marital consent, see c. 1103.

[57] For a practical example, see the commentary on c. 1382.

[58] Certain acts are said to be seriously wrong in themselves prescinding from circumstances or the human agent's intention. See *CCC*, 1755–1756. For various positions in the contemporary Catholic discussion of this issue, see C. Curran and R. McCormick, eds., *Readings in Moral Theology, No. 1: Moral Norms and Catholic Tradition* (New York: Paulist, 1979).

[59] The headings of the first six titles of part two of Book VI (cc. 1364–1398) indicate some pertinent ecclesial values.

[60] For helpful reflections see Marzoa, in *Com Ex*, 316–324.

9° **by a person who without negligence did not know that a penalty was attached to a law or precept;**

10° **by a person who acted without full imputability provided that the imputability was grave.**

§2. A judge can act in the same manner if another circumstance is present which diminishes the gravity of a delict.

§3. In the circumstances mentioned in §1, the accused is not bound by a *latae sententiae* penalty.

Various factors do not exempt one breaking the law from a penalty but diminish imputability (§1). Hence, the judge or ordinary in a *ferendae sententiae* penalty situation must temper the penalty specified in law or substitute a lesser measure such as a penance (c. 1340). Since this canon largely restates the preceding factors, a briefer treatment of the pertinent issues should suffice.

Instead of the integrity of the alleged offender's decisional process being significantly, if not totally, impaired (c. 1323), here it is only partially impaired. Hence, the person functions somewhat freely and deliberately and accordingly is somewhat accountable for the legal violation. The graver the delict and the imputability, the graver the penalty; and the less serious the delict and the imputability, the less serious the penalty (principle of penal proportionality).

Such limited imputability is verified in the following cases in paragraph one: those without the full use of their faculties, e.g., those who are senile (1°); those culpably lacking the use of reason due to voluntary, yet not premeditated, drunkenness or another mental disturbance possibly caused by voluntarily using mind-altering drugs (2°); those driven by culpable, yet not premeditated, passion which does not totally deprive them of the use of their faculties (3°); the minor between sixteen and eighteen years of age (4°);[61] the person acting out of grave fear or other freedom-impairing factors if the legal

violation is intrinsically evil or seriously pastorally detrimental (5°); the person using excessive force in self-defense or in defending another against an unjust attack (6°); the person breaking the law in resisting a serious and unjustified provocation by another (7°); the person erroneously but culpably thinking that the excusing causes of grave fear or legitimate self-defense are verified in a given situation (8°), the person aware of a law but inculpably unaware that its violation carries a sanction (9°).

Finally, besides the aforementioned specific factors mitigating imputability, the code states generically and logically that if one breaking the law were not fully imputable but at least gravely imputable, a diminished penalty is warranted (10°; *CIC* 2218, §2). The competent penal authority needs to assess not simply the offender's personal situation but also the ecclesial damage done by the delict.

Once again the code provides ample latitude for judicial or administrative discretion in dealing with legal violations. The present canon should be read in connection with canon 1345 empowering penal authorities to abstain from imposing any penalty in certain situations of mitigated imputability if the offender's spiritual well-being can be better served otherwise. The present canon also reflects the difficulty of comprehensively listing the factors that diminish imputability. Hence, it empowers, but does not require, the penal authority to consider other imputability-mitigating circumstances relevant to a particular case (§2).

Finally, if any of the imputability-mitigating factors mentioned in paragraph one are verified, a *latae sententiae* penalty is not incurred, e.g., the excommunication possibly warranted for a procured abortion (§3; c. 1398). This is another example of legislative caution regarding such penalties and an effort to preclude needless anxiety regarding the incurring of the penalty. This provision would probably be operative primarily during a process to declare, or formally confirm, the existence of such a penalty. The competent penal authority should weigh carefully the penal significance of those factors.

---

[61] Realistically speaking, few, if any, ecclesiastical penalties seem relevant to minors.

Factors Not Mitigating Imputability

Canon 1325 — Crass, supine, or affected ignorance can never be considered in applying the prescripts of cann. 1323 and 1324; likewise drunkenness or other disturbances of mind cannot be considered if they are sought deliberately in order to commit or excuse a delict, nor can passion which is voluntarily stimulated or fostered.

This canon precludes certain offenders from deliberately taking advantage of some of the previously mentioned imputability-exempting or mitigating factors to excuse themselves from penal imputability. First of all, it is not mitigated by crass, supine, or affected ignorance. Crass ignorance means gross ignorance about what a reasonable person should know. Supine ignorance means a careless indifference to knowing what other persons regard as necessary knowledge. Affected ignorance is deliberately cultivated to excuse a legal violation.

Furthermore, imputability is not mitigated by drunkenness or another mental disorder, such as a drug-induced stupor, deliberately sought to violate a law or excuse such a violation. This is also true for voluntarily stimulated or fostered passion. In such situations of premeditated behavior, the offender consciously and voluntarily precipitates certain factors subsequently impairing personal deliberation and freedom.

While acts influenced by such factors are not entirely deliberate or free, they reflect a certain bad faith and criminal intent. Hence, the offender is to be dealt with as if these ordinarily mitigating factors were not operative.

Factors Aggravating Imputability [62]

Canon 1326 — §1. A judge can punish the following more gravely than the law or precept has established:

    1° a person who after a condemnation or after the declaration of a penalty contin-

[62] Cf. *CCEO* 1416.

ues so to offend that from the circumstances the obstinate ill will of the person can prudently be inferred;

    2° a person who has been established in some dignity or who has abused a position of authority or office in order to commit the delict;

    3° an accused person who, when a penalty has been established against a delict based on negligence, foresaw the event and nonetheless omitted precautions to avoid it, which any diligent person would have employed.

§2. If the penalty established in the cases mentioned in §1 is *latae sententiae*, another penalty or a penance can be added.

Besides the lengthy list of factors exempting one from a penalty or diminishing imputability, the code specifies a few factors aggravating imputability. In such cases, because of the seriousness of the delict, the offender might warrant a more severe penalty than that stated in the law. However, while canon 1324 requires the penal authority to temper the penalty given mitigated imputability, here the possible increasing of the penalty is left entirely to the discretion of that authority.

For example, after a *ferendae sententiae* penalty is imposed or a *latae sententiae* penalty declared, an offender may commit the same delict again so that continuing bad faith can reasonably be presumed (§1, 1°). Traditionally such bad faith has been viewed as a significant penal factor, especially in the case of censures, whose primary purpose is to break such bad faith and foster ecclesial reconciliation. In such cases of legal recidivism, the original penalty has not had the intended deterrent effect, and the legislator hopes that more severe penalties will facilitate the offender's conversion.

Penal imputability is also aggravated if one with an established ecclesiastical rank violates the law (§1, 2°). The precise meaning of the term *dignitas* here is not entirely clear. However, it probably refers to certain clerics who have received special honors.[63] Their dishonoring their significant ecclesial status seems to underlie this provision.

Yet not only such clerics may be punished more severely than other believers. The abuse of one's authority or office to break the law also aggravates imputability.[64] This applies to both clerics and laity in official ecclesiastical positions (§ 1, 2°). Such persons violate their institutional trust and significantly fail to exercise authority in a spirit of ecclesial service, e.g., the episcopal ordinations carried out by Archbishop Lefebvre in the early 1980s without a pontifical mandate (cc. 1382; 1013).

As noted earlier, imputability generally presupposes criminal intent, not negligence in observing the law. In fact, only one delict in Book VI arises from negligence, i.e., damage caused another by negligently positing or omitting an act of ecclesiastical power, ministry, or function (c. 1389, §2). Here or whenever particular law penalizes negligence, the imputability of the offender may be aggravated at times. This would be true if an offender foresaw the detrimental consequences of such negligence yet took no reasonable precautions to preclude them (§1, 3°). The presumably obstinate defiance of the law probably grounds the heightened imputability. There is only a very fine line between such negligence and genuine criminal intent.

The legislator's intention to deal severely with such heightened imputability is also evident in paragraph two, which permits an additional *ferendae sententiae* penalty or penance (c. 1340) in a *latae sententiae* penalty situation. Presumably this

would occur when the latter penalty is formally declared. It is a rare exception to the code's general tendency to mitigate the force of such penalties.

Particular Law on Imputability

Canon 1327 — Particular law can establish other exempting, mitigating, or aggravating circumstances besides the cases in cann. 1323–1326, either by general norm or for individual delicts. Likewise, circumstances can be established in a precept which exempt from, mitigate, or increase a penalty established by the precept.

The enhancing of particular penal law options (c. 1315) explains this provision for particular law discretion in determining other factors affecting imputability (cc. 1323–1326) either as a general rule or regarding specific delicts. Such discretion may not be exercised often, but it enables diocesan bishops and other infra-universal penal legislators to adapt the code in dealing with distinctive local problems, e.g., clerical or lay financial malfeasance. Such penal discretion is also pertinent to precepts, which should be viewed in relationship to the laws they are intended to enforce (c. 1319).

Attempted Delict[65]

Canon 1328 — §1. A person who has done or omitted something in order to commit a delict and yet, contrary to his or her intent, did not commit the delict is not bound by the penalty established for a completed delict unless the law or precept provides otherwise.

§2. If the acts or omissions are by their nature conducive to the execution of the delict, however, their perpetrator can be subjected to a penance or penal remedy unless the perpetrator voluntarily ceased from carrying out the delict which had been initiated. If scandal or some other grave damage or danger resulted, however, the perpetrator, even if he or she voluntarily desisted, can

---

[63] For example, on the episcopal *dignitas,* see cc. 339, §2 and 481, §2; on the cardinalatial *dignitas,* see cc. 351, §3 and 833, §2. The 1917 code, unlike the 1983 code, used this term to designate certain significant figures in chapters of canons. See *CIC* 391–422 *passim.* One might also note that occasionally in cc. 1364–1398 clerics are subject to additional penalties besides those envisioned for the laity, e.g., a suspension as well as an interdict for the cleric falsely accusing a confessor of confessional solicitation (c. 1390, §1).

[64] This provision seems unnecessary given c. 1389, §1 on punishment of abuse of ecclesiastical power or function unless the code otherwise penalizes such an abuse.

[65] Cf. *CCEO* 1418.

be punished with a just penalty, although one lesser than that established for a completed delict.

This canon deals with a somewhat complex issue, i.e., the implications for penal imputability of situations in which a delict is not actually committed, or completed, after being initiated.[66] Paragraph one envisions a situation in which a person does or omits something to commit a delict. However, the individual's delictual purpose is not achieved because of circumstances beyond his or her control or intent. Normally the penalty specified in law is not warranted if the delict has not been completed because of the lack of ecclesial damage (cf. c. 1321, §1). However, a law could penalize even an attempt at breaking the law, e.g., the attempted marriage of certain clerics and religious (c. 1394).

Nevertheless, merely because the penalty specified for the completed delict is not incurred does not prevent church authorities from employing certain legal-pastoral measures to deal with the situation. Paragraph two envisions a situation in which the aforementioned action or omission is naturally conducive to the commission of the delict. A quasi-penal measure such as a penal remedy or a penance (cc. 1339–1340) might still be imposed to highlight the ecclesial seriousness of the issue. However, if the person involved has a change of heart after initiating the delict, no such measure is normally warranted because of the lack of contempt of church authority. By way of exception, if even the attempted delict causes great ecclesial scandal or damage, an indeterminate just penalty may be imposed on such an individual. Yet it is to be less than that determined for the completed delict since penalties normally presuppose completed delicts (penal proportionality). There is ample room here for penal discretion in assessing the relevant ecclesial values (c. 1349).

Collaboration in Delict[67]

Canon 1329 — §1. If *ferendae sententiae* penalties are established for the principal perpetrator, those who conspire together to commit a delict and are not expressly named in a law or precept are subject to the same penalties or to others of the same or lesser gravity.

§2. Accomplices who are not named in a law or precept incur a *latae sententiae* penalty attached to a delict if without their assistance the delict would not have been committed, and the penalty is of such a nature that it can affect them; otherwise, they can be punished by *ferendae sententiae* penalties.

Thus far the discussion of imputability has focused largely on individual offenders. Yet at times a law may be broken by several people acting together, e.g., procuring an abortion (c. 1398).[68] This canon presupposes a distinction between so-called necessary and secondary collaborators despite the absence of such terminology.

Necessary collaborators are those without whose cooperation the delict could not have been committed, e.g., persons living in concubinage with a cleric (c. 1395, §1). Such collaborators are normally punished as severely as the principal offender given their significant delictual involvement. The involvement of secondary collaborators, on the other hand, is not essential to the commission of the delict, e.g., the co-consecrating bishop during an illicit episcopal consecration (c. 1382). Given their lesser delictual involvement, such secondary collaborators are correspondingly punished less severely than the principal offender.

The canon deals with the frequent situation in which such collaborators are not expressly named in the penal law that has been violated. Paragraph

---

[66] For a more detailed discussion of this canon, see Borras, 34–38; Marzoa, in *Com Ex,* 334–341.

[67] Cf. *CCEO* 1417.

[68] For a thoughtful examination of such collaboration, see J. Coriden, "Canon 1398: Canonical Penalty for Abortion as Applicable to Administrators of Clinics and Hospitals," in *RRAO 1986,* 80–85.

one on *ferendae sententiae* penalties states that such collaborators are subject to the same penalties as the principal offender or to other similar or lesser penalties. Understandably, the penalties for necessary collaborators will be the same or at least similar to those for the principal offender. However, the penalties for secondary collaborators will be less serious. In all such instances the penal authority must assess the relevance of the aforementioned circumstances affecting imputability. This is also true for the following paragraph.

Paragraph two on *latae sententiae* penalties somewhat more explicitly differentiates between necessary collaborators (accomplices strictly speaking) and secondary collaborators. Necessary collaborators are liable to the same penalty as the principal offender if it can affect them. However, at times this is impossible; for example, a layperson collaborating with a cleric in a delict cannot be suspended. However, such a layperson (e.g., the partner of the cleric attempting marriage—c. 1394, §1) could be liable to a comparable *ferendae sententiae* penalty, e.g., interdict. In a *latae sententiae* context so-called secondary collaborators could also be liable to less severe *ferendae sententiae* penalties given the principle of penal proportionality.[69] Here is another area characterized by ample penal discretion options.

Declaration of Mind or Intent

Canon 1330 — A delict which consists in a declaration or in another manifestation of will, doctrine, or knowledge must not be considered completed if no one perceives the declaration or manifestation.

The final canon in this title is similar to canon 1328 on the attempted delict. The present canon

clarifies what is meant by a completed delict whenever a person expresses his or her mind or intent verbally or in writing presumably in a fashion contrary to ecclesial values. The necessary "externalization factor" characterizing any delict (c. 1321, §1) is important here.

For example, whatever may be one's moral culpability, it is not a delict technically simply to hold heretical views. Someone must perceive the expression of such views if it is to be penally imputable. The implications of such a perception ideally should be clarified during the penal process. For example, such a perception might refer to the reaction of a class listening to a lecturer espousing allegedly heretical views (c. 1364). Another example of such a perception might be that of a church authority figure who initiates a preliminary penal investigation based on what turns out to be a false denunciation of a priest for confessional solicitation or some other delict (c. 1390, §1–§2).[70]

TITLE IV
PENALTIES AND OTHER PUNISHMENTS[71]
[cc. 1331–1340]

The present title does not describe the various penalties in detail; rather, it simply clarifies their principal effects for those breaking the law. Separate chapters consider censures and expiatory penalties (penalties) and penal remedies and penances (other punishments). This is a distinctly Latin code phenomenon. The Eastern code contains numerous similar provisions but does not explicitate the aforementioned distinction.[72]

---

[69] Martin seems incorrect in asserting that this part of the canon deals solely with necessary collaborators (761). So-called secondary collaborators are also "accomplices" but are understandably treated less severely than necessary collaborators because of the former's lesser delictual involvement. Here again the code mitigates the force of *latae sententiae* penalties.

[70] The following other delicts might exemplify the aforementioned declaration or manifestation: perjury (c. 1368), blasphemy (c. 1369), or teaching a condemned but not heretical doctrine (c. 1371, 1°).

[71] Besides the Münster commentary, see Borras, 45–50; 62–100; Green, in *CLSA Com*, 906–911; Martin, in *CLSGBI Com*, 762–770; Rees, 385–398; various authors in *Com Ex*, 352–388.

[72] Cf. *CCEO* 1426–1435.

CHAPTER I
CENSURES
[cc. 1331–1335]

The first chapter of the title deals with various censures, i.e., medicinal penalties depriving obstinate offenders of access to various ecclesiastical goods, such as the sacraments or church offices, until they are restored to full ecclesial communion. Such a restoration is a basic Christian obligation (c. 209).

Unlike expiatory penalties, censures focus more sharply on the offender's reform and reintegration within the community. *Ferendae sententiae* censures require a formal warning by a competent penal authority, usually an ordinary, before being imposed validly (c. 1347, §1). However, for *latae sententiae* censures the warning is presumably given by the law itself.

Censures are always indefinite in duration, since they must be remitted when the offender ceases being contumacious and is willing to be reintegrated within the communion (cc. 1358, §1; 1347, §2; cf. c. 980). Such censures include excommunication, interdict, and suspension; the first two can be incurred by any believer, while the last one is reserved to clerics. Unlike the subsequent illustrative listing of expiatory penalties, this listing of censures is comprehensive. The following reflections highlight key features of such censures.

Effects of Excommunication[73]

Canon 1331 — §1. An excommunicated person is forbidden:
  1° to have any ministerial participation in celebrating the sacrifice of the Eucharist or any other ceremonies of worship whatsoever;
  2° to celebrate the sacraments or sacramentals and to receive the sacraments;

  3° to exercise any ecclesiastical offices, ministries, or functions whatsoever or to place acts of governance.
  §2. If the excommunication has been imposed or declared, the offender:
  1° who wishes to act against the prescript of §1, n. 1 must be prevented from doing so, or the liturgical action must be stopped unless a grave cause precludes this;
  2° invalidly places acts of governance which are illicit according to the norm of §1, n. 3;
  3° is forbidden to benefit from privileges previously granted;
  4° cannot acquire validly a dignity, office, or other function in the Church;
  5° does not appropriate the benefits of a dignity, office, any function, or pension, which the offender has in the Church.

The present code does not define excommunication (*CIC* 2257, §1), which prohibits the exercise of certain subjective spiritual rights rooted primarily in one's irrevocable baptismal incorporation in the Church (c. 96). However, the excommunicated person remains a member of the Church and subject to its legislation unless the delict prompting the penalty entails a formal leaving of the Church, e.g., schism (cc. 751; 1364). Even such persons remain subject to most church laws but need not observe the canonical form for marriage (c. 1117) or obtain a permission or dispensation to marry a non-Catholic (cc. 1124; 1086, §1–§2).

Interestingly enough, the degree to which an excommunicated person is separated from the Catholic communion varies greatly depending on the nature of the delict. For example, one is excommunicated for heresy, schism, or apostasy (c. 1364, §1), which significantly alienate a person from the Church. However, a confessor is also excommunicated for directly violating the seal of confession (c. 1388, §1). Such a breach of the priest-penitent relationship, however morally culpable, hardly constitutes the same ecclesial alienation as the prior delicts.

---

[73] Cf. *CCEO* 1434. For a detailed discussion of the effects of excommunication, see Borras, 69–77; J. Bernal, in *Com Ex,* 354–360. For a list of Latin code excommunications, see *CLSA Com,* 932.

Nevertheless, in all instances of excommunication, like interdict (c. 1332), all of its effects are operative. This is not true for suspension (c. 1333), whose potential effects can be adapted by the competent penal authority to fit different legal-pastoral situations.

Canon 1331 distinguishes between a non-declared *latae sententiae* excommunication and a declared *latae sententiae* or a *ferendae sententiae* excommunication. The formal church intervention in the latter two instances entails more extensive legal restrictions for the excommunicated person than were operative before such intervention.[74] For example, the confessor may not remit a declared *latae sententiae* excommunication in certain situations of pastoral urgency outside of danger of death (c. 1357).

Some effects of excommunication are liturgical in character, e.g., prohibition of active ministerial participation[75] in the Eucharist and other acts of public worship (§1, 1°) and prohibition of celebrating the sacraments or sacramentals or receiving the sacraments (§1, 2°).[76] These prohibitions do not simply reflect the will of the legislator but rather flow from the nature of the ecclesial alienation underlying the delict warranting excommunication.

Such prohibitions affect the liceity but not the validity of such acts. Furthermore, the penalty does not prevent such persons from attending the Eucharist or other liturgical services, much less prohibit private prayers or devotions. Such participation may actually prompt conversion of heart and lead to full reintegration into ecclesial communion.

The second set of restrictions affects the excommunicated person's participation in church governance. Such a one is not deprived of any ecclesiastical offices, ministries, or functions (c. 1336, §1, 2°), but may neither licitly exercise them nor posit acts of legislative, executive, or judicial power, ordinary or delegated (§1, 3°). However, in the case of a *ferendae sententiae* or declared *latae sententiae* excommunication, such acts of governance are invalid and not simply illicit (§2, 2°).

The third set of restrictions concerns the eligibility of the excommunicated individual to receive certain ecclesiastical benefits. Declaration of a *latae sententiae* penalty or imposition of a *ferendae sententiae* penalty prohibits one from: (a) enjoying privileges (c. 76, §1) already acquired (§2, 3°); (b) validly acquiring any ecclesiastical dignity, office, or function (§2, 4°); and (c) receiving the income from any ecclesiastical dignity, office, function, or pension (§2, 5°). In the case of clerics, however, this last provision must be interpreted in light of canon 1350, §1 on the basic right to support of even the excommunicated cleric.[77] Furthermore, the civil law implications of possible deprivations of income must be considered in preparing contracts for church employees.

The most significant revision process issue regarding excommunication was whether it should continue to preclude access to all the sacraments. The original schema would have permitted the excommunicated (or interdicted) individual to receive penance and anointing for peace of conscience even prior to formal external forum remission of the penalty.

Sharp criticism of this innovation undoubtedly influenced a special May 1977 code commission meeting to vote to maintain the traditional prohi-

---

[74] Comparable restrictions are also operative for interdicts and suspensions.

[75] This refers to either formally installed lay ministries (c. 230, §1) or ordained ministry (cc. 1008–1009).

[76] Theoretically, after the excommunication is declared or imposed, the excommunicated individual challenging this prohibition is to be ejected from the sacred place and the liturgical action discontinued barring a grave reason for continuing it. This seems true for most liturgical celebrations, hence this part of the canon seems unrealistic (§2, 1°). On not admitting to Holy Communion those whose excommunication has been declared or imposed, see c. 915.

[77] For examples of other canonical restrictions on those who are excommunicated, see c. 171, §1, 3° on voting in canonical elections, c. 316 on membership in public associations of the faithful, and c. 1109 on officially assisting at a marriage.

bition on such persons' receiving any sacraments. The original schema presumably failed to take adequate cognizance of the ecclesial implications of sacramental reconciliation and of the interrelationship between excommunication and the sacrament of penance. It seemed somewhat incongruous to the commission that one could be absolved from sins yet still be subject to a censure indicating an irregular ecclesial status.[78]

Effects of Interdict[79]

Canon 1332 — The prohibitions mentioned in can. 1331, §1, nn. 1 and 2 bind an interdicted person. If the interdict has been imposed or declared, however, the prescript of can. 1331, §2, n. 1 must be observed.

The current notion of interdict simplifies the 1917 code, which envisioned personal or local interdicts, depending on whether the penalty affected individuals or a group of believers directly or rather indirectly because they lived in a certain territory (*CIC* 2268). In the latter instance even individuals not technically guilty of a delict might have been deprived of certain ecclesial goods such as access to some liturgical ministries.

Despite criticism of this penalty, the code reaffirms the personal interdict while not retaining local interdicts, reflecting a pastoral concern that penalties not be imposed indiscriminately on the guilty and innocent alike.

The interdict entails the same liturgical restrictions as excommunication. However, the interdict does not affect any governmental functions or personal prerogatives, such as privileges, eligibility for various offices, or the reception of income.[80]

Effects of Suspension[81]

Canon 1333 — §1. Suspension, which can affect only clerics, prohibits:
  1° either all or some acts of the power of orders;
  2° either all or some acts of the power of governance;
  3° the exercise of either all or some of the rights or functions attached to an office.
  §2. A law or precept can establish that a suspended person cannot place acts of governance validly after a condemnatory or declaratory sentence.
  §3. A prohibition never affects:
  1° the offices or the power of governance which are not under the power of the superior who establishes the penalty;
  2° the right of residence which the offender may have by reason of office;
  3° the right to administer goods which may pertain to the office of the person suspended if the penalty is *latae sententiae*.
  §4. A suspension prohibiting a person from receiving benefits, a stipend, pensions, or any other such thing entails the obligation of making restitution for whatever has been received illegitimately, even if in good faith.

Unlike excommunication and interdict, which all believers may incur, only clerics may incur a suspension, which totally or partially restricts their liturgical and governmental functioning. However, unlike the expiatory privation of office (c. 1336, §1, 2°), the suspended cleric does not lose his office. Suspensions also differ from the preceding censures since their effects are separa-

---

[78] See T. Green, "Penal Law Revisited: The Revision of the Penal Law Schema," *Stud Can* 15 (1981) 155–156.

[79] Cf. *CCEO* 1431. The Eastern code actually speaks not of "interdict" but of "minor excommunication." For a helpful discussion of interdicts in the Latin code, see Borras, 80–84. For a list of such interdicts, see *CLSA Com,* 932.

[80] For some effects of interdict indicated elsewhere in the code, see cc. 874, §1, 4° and 893, §1 prohibiting the in-

terdicted person from being a baptism or confirmation sponsor, 1071, 1, 5° requiring the local ordinary's permission for an interdicted person to marry, and 1109 prohibiting a local ordinary or pastor from validly assisting at the marriages of their subjects after the interdict has been declared or imposed.

[81] Cf. *CCEO* 1432. For some helpful reflections on suspension, see Borras, 84–87; Bernal in *Com Ex,* 364–369. For a list of Latin code suspensions, see *CLSA Com,* 933.

ble and more or less comprehensive depending on the penal authority's assessment of the seriousness of the offense. Like any censure, such restrictions seek to motivate the cleric to be reintegrated into ecclesial communion and restored to full ministerial functioning.

Unlike the prior two canons, which clarify precisely the inseparable effects of excommunication and interdict, the first two paragraphs of this canon are rather open-ended in specifying the effects of suspension. Its precise scope is clarified in the next canon, permitting significant discretion for the competent penal authority.

Paragraph one of this initial canon on suspension differentiates between total or partial (a) prohibitions of the exercise of the power of orders, e.g., celebration of Eucharist, (b) restrictions on the power of governance, e.g., deciding a marriage case, and (c) limitations of the exercise of various rights or responsibilities related to an office, e.g., rights and duties of pastors (cc. 528–538).

Unlike the Eastern code (*CCEO* 1432, §3), paragraph two provides for the possible invalidity of governmental acts of the suspended cleric, which are otherwise only illicit without formal church intervention. However, the pertinent law (e.g., c. 1109) must indicate that such an invalidating effect follows the judicial sentence or administrative decree. The law seeks to protect the faithful's access even to such suspended clerics for various governmental acts.

The code's intent to circumscribe the effects of suspension is clear in its limiting the power of ecclesiastical superiors to penalize clerics (§3). This protection of clerics is somewhat comparable to canon 1317 limiting causes of dismissal to those delicts mentioned in the code.

Particular law suspensions, unlike those specified in the code, affect only those offices or aspects of the power of governance under the authority of the penalizing superior. Hence, if a cleric's office were conferred by an authority other than his own bishop, he could still exercise it even if he were suspended in his own diocese due to particular law (§3, 1°).

Another protection of the suspended cleric is the humanitarian provision that he still enjoys the right of residence connected with his office, e.g., the suspended pastor living in his rectory (§3, 2°; c. 533). If the suspension were *latae sententiae,* he would also have the right to administer the goods pertaining to his office, e.g., parish property (§3, 3°; cc. 532; 1281–1288). The code intends to protect the parish financial patrimony and assure its continuing administration. In a *ferendae sententiae* situation, the competent penal authority presumably would address this significant administrative issue, e.g., by appointing a temporary parish financial administrator.

If the suspended cleric profits illegitimately from the income related to his office, he is to make restitution to the Church in justice even if he acted in good faith (§4). However, even the suspended cleric has a right to decent support (cc. 281; 1350, §1).

Scope of Suspension

Canon 1334 — §1. Within the limits established by the preceding canon, either the law or precept itself or the sentence or decree which imposes the penalty defines the extent of a suspension.

§2. A law, but not a precept, can establish a *latae sententiae* suspension without additional determination or limitation; such a penalty has all the effects listed in can. 1333, §1.

Since the effects of suspension vary notably, its exact scope must be determined in the law establishing it or the sentence or decree imposing it (§1).[82] Presumably the suspension is generalized in focus unless it is explicitly limited to certain acts of orders or governance or the exercise of certain rights or office-related functions (c. 1333, §1, 3°).

However, the legislator cautions against the indiscriminate use of a general *latae sententiae* sus-

---

[82] The former suspension *ex informata conscientia* (from an informed conscience) not requiring a process has been abolished (*CIC* 2186–2194). Every *ferendae sententiae* suspension must be imposed pursuant to a formal process.

pension (§2). Only the law (universal or particular) but not a precept may establish such with the corresponding liturgical, governmental, and office restrictions (c. 1333, §1). This is another example of administrative restraint regarding penal precepts (c. 1319, §2).

Suspension of Prohibition[83]

Canon 1335 — If a censure prohibits the celebration of sacraments or sacramentals or the placing of an act of governance, the prohibition is suspended whenever it is necessary to care for the faithful in danger of death. If a *latae sententiae* censure has not been declared, the prohibition is also suspended whenever a member of the faithful requests a sacrament or sacramental or an act of governance; a person is permitted to request this for any just cause.

The code recognizes a need to provide for the spiritual welfare of the faithful, particularly but not exclusively in certain extreme pastoral situations (c. 1752). Hence, this exceptional measure temporarily suspends the liturgical-governmental prohibitions affecting any censured cleric even if another cleric is available. Quite secondarily there is a concern to protect the penalized cleric's reputation (c. 220) if his irregular status is unknown to the faithful. Once again the degree of authoritative penal intervention notably qualifies the types of situations in which the censured cleric may respond to the sacramental or governmental requests of the faithful.

In danger of death the censured cleric's activity is not restricted, whatever the nature of the censure. However, outside of this extreme pastoral situation, the same ministerial options are generally[84] available only to the cleric whose *latae sententiae* censure has not been formally declared by

church authority. In such situations the faithful may generally seek such ministry for any just cause, e.g., deepening one's spiritual life.

In contrast, the cleric subject to a declared *latae sententiae* or a *ferendae sententiae* censure may not minister to the faithful outside of danger of death, whether they legitimately seek a sacrament, sacramental, or act of governance. If he attempts to do so, acts of the power of orders are valid but illicit. Furthermore, governmental acts are valid or not depending on whether the declaratory or condemnatory sentence invalidates such acts.

This canon exemplifies the less stringent canonical effects of the non-declared *latae sententiae* penalty. Similar pastoral provisions also govern the observance of expiatory penalties (c. 1338, §3; cf. also c. 1352 on observing penalties). In such situations the penalty is not remitted; its observance is temporarily suspended because of prevailing community pastoral interests.

CHAPTER II
EXPIATORY PENALTIES
[cc. 1336–1338]

Despite criticism that expiatory penalties seem overly punitive and inadequately pastoral, the Latin code maintains them,[85] specifying some general principles regarding them and especially

---

[83] Cf. *CCEO* 1435.

[84] The term "generally" is used because of a May 19, 1997 PCILT declaration that clerics attempting marriage and thereby incurring a *latae sententiae* suspension (c. 1394, §1) may normally not licitly minister to the faithful ac-

cording to this canon even if their suspension is undeclared. Although certain married clerics may legitimately function in the Latin church, the attempted marriage of clerics not so authorized allegedly entails an objective ministerial unfitness. Hence the faithful may not legitimately seek the ministry of such clerics. No other cleric whose censure is undeclared is subject to such restrictions. However, even such "married clerics" may minister to the faithful in danger of death (e.g., c. 976). See PCILT, "Declaration on Married Priests and Sacramental Ministry," *Origins* 27/4 (June 12, 1997) 64.

[85] The Eastern code stresses the medicinal character of penalties and does not explicitly distinguish between censures and expiatory penalties. However, it provides in practice for "expiatory" penalties (*CCEO* 1429–1430).

their effects. These penalties certainly envision the offender's spiritual well-being. However, more forcefully than censures, "expiatory" penalties emphasize remedying the societal damage done by the delict and deterring others from similar behavior. Besides this difference in orientation, expiatory penalties do not require a warning before being imposed. They may be imposed perpetually, or forever (e.g., clerical dismissal), indefinitely, or for a definite period of time (e.g., c. 1383 prohibiting a bishop from conferring a sacred order for a year). The rules on their cessation, which differ somewhat from the rules on the cessation of censures, will be addressed later.

Various Expiatory Penalties

Canon 1336 — §1. In addition to other penalties which the law may have established, the following are expiatory penalties which can affect an offender either perpetually, for a prescribed time, or for an indeterminate time:

    1° a prohibition or an order concerning residence in a certain place or territory;

    2° privation of a power, office, function, right, privilege, faculty, favor, title, or insignia, even merely honorary;

    3° a prohibition against exercising those things listed under n. 2, or a prohibition against exercising them in a certain place or outside a certain place; these prohibitions are never under pain of nullity;

    4° a penal transfer to another office;

    5° dismissal from the clerical state.

    §2. Only those expiatory penalties listed in §1, n. 3 can be *latae sententiae*.

As in the case of censures, the code does not define expiatory penalties but simply lists some of them, yet not in an exhaustive fashion. Hence, additional ones may be established in universal or particular law.[86]

Some penalties affect only religious according to their constitutions (residence restrictions in §1, 1°) or clerics (e.g., residence restrictions in §1, 1° or dismissal in §1, 5°). Others, however rarely, may possibly affect the laity, especially those holding ecclesiastical office, who are not subject to suspension (e.g., privations in §1, 2° or prohibitions in §1, 3°).

Several penalties are irrevocable in character, e.g., various privations of the power of governance (not orders), office, function, etc. (§1, 2°) and penal transfer to another office (§1, 4°),[87] all of which require a formal judicial process (c. 1342, §2).

The most serious perpetual expiatory penalty is dismissal from the clerical state, whose comprehensive effects are specified in canons 291–293, e.g., loss of all clerical rights (§1, 5°).[88] Dismissal can be imposed only for the delicts specifically mentioned in the code.[89] It is a last resort provision after other measures to deal with an intransigent cleric have failed. Furthermore, to protect his rights adequately, it can normally be imposed only after a formal judicial process involving a collegiate tribunal of three judges.

The other expiatory penalties do not have such an irrevocable character, e.g., the restrictions on residence in §1, 1° and various prohibitions of the exercise of the power of governance, office, or function in §1, 3°. Such temporary expiatory penalties never affect the valid exercise of such competencies. The list is not exhaustive to permit legislators to determine other expiatory penalties corresponding to differing pastoral situations.

---

[86] For a detailed discussion of expiatory penalties in the code, see Borras, 89–95; G. Di Mattia, in *Com Ex,* 372–383.

[87] On the general provisions for a non-penal transfer of an officeholder, see cc. 190–191. On the transfer of an unwilling pastor, which primarily envisions enhancing the spiritual welfare of the faithful rather than punishing him, see cc. 1748–1752. In expediting a penal transfer, however, the judge should consult with the pertinent ordinary regarding the penalized individual's eligibility to assume the new office.

[88] Cf. *CCEO* 1433, §2 (deposition). Unlike the Latin code, the Eastern code also envisions demoting a cleric to a lower grade (*CCEO* 1433, §1).

[89] See commentary on c. 1317, n. 33.

The code's tendency to restrict the scope of *latae sententiae* penalties is also evident here, since only the prohibitions of §1, 3° may be used as *latae sententiae* penalties (§2). For example, one could be prohibited from exercising a certain office but not deprived of it, e.g., diocesan finance officer (c. 494). Furthermore, such prohibitions never invalidate acts performed contrary to such restrictions. A concern to protect the ministerial rights of the faithful underlies this provision. Apparently, if the delict were serious enough, ecclesiastical authority should judicially deprive the offender of a certain power, office, function, etc. (§1, 2°).

Territorial Restrictions [90]

Canon 1337 — §1. A prohibition against residing in a certain place or territory can affect both clerics and religious; however, the order to reside in a certain place or territory can affect secular clerics and, within the limits of the constitutions, religious.

§2. To impose an order to reside in a certain place or territory requires the consent of the ordinary of that place unless it is a question of a house designated for clerics doing penance or being rehabilitated even from outside the diocese.

The next two canons specify the practical implications of certain penalties in canon 1336. Canon 1337 regarding a prohibited or prescribed residence (c. 1336, §1, 1°) affects only clerics and religious,[91] not lay persons who are not religious. Paragraph one differentiates between a prohibition against living in a certain place, which affects clerics and religious, and a prescription to live in a certain place, which affects secular clerics and religious in accord with their constitutions. This restrictive provision should be viewed in terms of the residence obligation of secular clerics (c. 283)

and religious (c. 665). Furthermore, while this measure is similar to possible non-penal restrictions on the accused during the penal process (c. 1722: so-called "administrative leave"),[92] here it is a penalty presupposing the commission of a delict.

If the penalizing authority is not the proper ordinary of the one penalized, the former should consult the latter before imposing such a restriction on residence to ascertain its practical implications for the diocese or religious institute. Furthermore, the local ordinary of the place of confinement normally must consent, presumably because of the potentially disruptive behavior of the penalized cleric or religious. However, such consent is not required if a house is specifically established to rehabilitate clerics (c. 1337, §2).

What explains such possible restrictions on freedom of movement, which may be difficult to enforce in practice? Certain delicts may cause particularly serious damage to a community, e.g., sexual abuse of minors in a parish or school. This may require the offender's having no further contact with such a community both for its protection and his rehabilitation. Furthermore, at times medical reasons may require an offender to reside in a certain place for a specified time, e.g., a recognized treatment center for sex offenders or substance abusers.

Such restrictions of personal mobility are justified only for very serious reasons, e.g., reparation of scandal and reform of the offender. This is especially true if they are imposed for a long time. Furthermore, a cleric can be prevented from living in his diocese of incardination only as long as the continuance of the penalty is clearly warranted.[93]

---

[90] Cf. *CCEO* 1429.

[91] Strictly speaking (c. 18), this provision affects only members of religious institutes, not members of secular institutes or societies of apostolic life.

[92] For a somewhat comparable non-penal administrative disciplinary measure, see c. 679.

[93] For various reasons a formerly penalized diocesan cleric may not be able to be assigned even if he is dedicated to ministry. However, he is at least entitled to decent support (c. 281) and is to be enabled to fulfill his obligation to reside in his diocese of incardination (c. 283). See J. Provost, "Effects of Incardination," in *Clergy Procedural*

Limitations on Prohibitions[94]

Canon 1338 — §1. The privations and prohibitions listed in can. 1336, §1, nn. 2 and 3, never affect powers, offices, functions, rights, privileges, faculties, favors, titles, or insignia which are not subject to the power of the superior who establishes the penalty.

§2. Privation of the power of orders is not possible but only a prohibition against exercising it or some of its acts; likewise, privation of academic degrees is not possible.

§3. The norm given in can. 1335 for censures must be observed for the prohibitions listed in can. 1336, §1, n. 3.

The code limits the force of certain penalties. Only those powers of governance and offices subject to the authority of the penalizing superior are affected by the penalty (§1; c. 1333, §3, 1°).

Once the power of orders has been conferred, it cannot be taken away; only its exercise may be limited. For example, a priest may be forbidden to celebrate the Eucharist licitly in a particular parish. There is also a certain irrevocability about the granting of an academic degree. Nevertheless, the exercise of an office presupposing such a degree may be restricted. Furthermore, attempting to deprive a penalized person of such a degree would raise civil law problems (§2).

Finally paragraph three embodies a certain penal hierarchy of values. In principle the penalty should normally be observed. However, certain pressing pastoral considerations may suggest otherwise, e.g., primarily the spiritual welfare of the faithful (c. 1752) but secondarily the penalized cleric's reputation (c. 220). Accordingly, the code suspends the expiatory sacramental and governmental prohibitions on him in various situations of pastoral need. This is especially true if a *latae sententiae* expiatory penalty has not been declared (cf.

Handbook, ed. R. Calvo and N. Klinger (Washington, D.C.: CLSA, 1992) 38–49.
[94] Cf. *CCEO* 1430.

c. 1335). However, the penalty still must be remitted subsequently.

CHAPTER III
PENAL REMEDIES AND PENANCES[95]
[cc. 1339–1340]

We can briefly consider these quasi-penal measures designed to protect the community against illegal behavior. They may preclude possible delicts[96] (penal remedies), replace a penalty in a case of diminished imputability,[97] or increase a penalty[98] in a case of aggravated imputability (penances) (c. 1312, §3). Furthermore, an additional corrective measure may occasionally be required even after a penalty has been remitted.[99]

Penal Remedies

Canon 1339 — §1. An ordinary, personally or through another, can warn a person who is in the proximate occasion of committing a delict or upon whom, after investigation, grave suspicion of having committed a delict has fallen.

§2. He can also rebuke a person whose behavior causes scandal or a grave disturbance of order, in a manner accommodated to the special conditions of the person and the deed.

---

[95] For a helpful discussion of these canonical institutes, see Borras, 95–100; Sanchis, in *Com Ex,* 384–388.

[96] See c. 1328 on an attempted delict and c. 1348 regarding an accused person who has been acquitted of an accusation or upon whom no penalty has been imposed. The protection of the public good may still warrant such penal remedies.

[97] See cc. 1324, §1 on diminished imputability, 1328 on an attempted delict, 1343 on facultative penalties, and 1344, §2 on preceptive penalties. In such instances a penance rather than a penalty may be warranted.

[98] See c. 1326, §2 on situations of aggravated imputability involving *latae sententiae* penalties.

[99] For instance, c. 1357, §2 requires the confessor remitting a non-declared *latae sententiae* excommunication or interdict to impose a penance. Canon 1358 enables the authority figure remitting any censure to impose such a penance.

§3. The warning or rebuke must always be established at least by some document which is to be kept in the secret archive of the curia.

The revised code speaks only of warnings and rebukes as penal remedies. This formal canonical warning may be appropriate if one is in the proximate occasion of committing a delict or if a preliminary investigation (c. 1717) raises grave suspicion about its already being committed (§1). Such an investigation seems necessary to protect the reputation of the one warned and preclude frivolous penal processes. For example, legitimate questions may be raised about whether certain relationships of a cleric may jeopardize his observance of continence (c. 277).

The somewhat more severe measure called a rebuke[100] may be required if an individual causes scandal or gravely disturbs church order (§2). This is true although a penal process may be impossible due to significant imputability-mitigating circumstances or evidentiary problems in proving a delict. While no explicit reference is made to an investigation as in the prior paragraph, this seems presupposed for the same reasons. Such a rebuke is to be tailored to the specifics of a given situation, e.g., the individual's ecclesial status and the ecclesial damage.

The need to prove that such legal-pastoral steps have been taken explains the requirement that they be recorded in writing (§3). Such warnings or rebukes must follow the normal rules on administrative decrees, e.g., canons 35–58. Such a record is to be retained in the secret curial archive (c. 489, §1).[101] Later such information may be needed in a penal process, e.g., to prove aggravated imputability (c. 1719).

The imposition of such measures is a rather delicate issue. Hence the alleged delict is to be carefully investigated, and the rights of the alleged offender are to be duly protected, especially the right to reputation (cc. 220; 1717, §2). This is

true even given the equally legitimate right of the community to protect itself against serious violations of its integrity and mission and damage to its most vulnerable members, such as minors.

Penances

Canon 1340 — §1. A penance, which can be imposed in the external forum, is the performance of some work of religion, piety, or charity.

§2. A public penance is never to be imposed for an occult transgression.

§3. According to his own prudent judgment, an ordinary can add penances to the penal remedy of warning or rebuke.

This canon speaks generically of a work of religion, piety, or charity without listing such works (*CIC* 2313) or indicating their purpose (§1). Such external forum penances may help to preclude the need for a penalty or complete the steps necessary for its remission. There should be a proportion between the penance and the transgression; therefore, no public penance may be imposed for an occult transgression out of respect for the reputation of the offender (§2).[102] Where appropriate, penances, such as prayers, fasting, almsgiving, a retreat, or community service,[103] may be added to the above-mentioned penal remedies (§3). These provisions are administrative acts, hence they follow the normal rules on such acts. They should enable church authorities to deal sensitively with problematic disciplinary situations and thereby preclude penal processes except as a last resort.

---

[102] While the present code does not define the terms "public" or "occult," see *CIC* 2196. A public delict was commonly known or committed in such circumstances that it would likely become known. Otherwise it was occult.

[103] Unlike the Latin code, the Eastern code views penalties more as a positive imposition of a good work than as the privation of some good, while providing for the latter. Hence the Eastern code envisions as possible penalties certain prayers, a pious pilgrimage, a special fast, alms, or spiritual retreats (*CCEO* 1426, §1).

---

[100] Cf. *CCEO* 1427.
[101] Ibid.

TITLE V
THE APPLICATION OF PENALTIES [104]
[cc. 1341–1353]

This significant title expresses some fundamental principles regarding a judicious pastoral approach in imposing *ferendae sententiae* penalties.[105] The judge or ordinary may not simply determine that a law has been broken before penalizing someone; rather, he must weigh carefully the relevant factors that put the violation in perspective, e.g., the factors affecting imputability (cc. 1322–1327). This is because only a seriously imputable violation of a law to which a sanction is attached is penalizable as a delict (c. 1321, §1–§2).

At times an examination of such factors may indicate that a delict has not been committed, and hence a penalty may not be imposed. At other times a delict may have been committed, but mitigating circumstances suggest that no penalty be imposed, that it be deferred, or that a penal remedy (c. 1339) or a lesser penalty than that specified in law be imposed. However, at certain times the damage done to the Church's integrity and mission may require a heavier penalty than that specified in law. In short, both judges and ordinaries have ample discretion in realizing the Church's penal goals and delineating the boundaries of tolerable behavior and possible transgressions.

Most canons in this title govern the conducting of the penal process,[106] especially the judicial or administrative discretion to be exercised at the end of the process. However, the last canon (c. 1353) governs the appeal of a penal sentence or recourse against a penal decree. Furthermore, several canons deal with the post-process observance of the penalty by the offender (cc. 1350–1352).

---

[104] Besides the Münster commentary, see Borras, 101–124; V. De Paolis, in *Com Ex,* 389–429; Green, in *CLSA Com,* 911–915; Martin, in *CLSGBI Com,* 770–777; Rees, 398–407.

[105] Some of these principles are also relevant in declaring *latae sententiae* penalties.

[106] This title constantly needs to be interpreted in relationship to cc. 1717–1731 on the penal process.

Penalties as a Last Resort

Canon 1341 — An ordinary is to take care to initiate a judicial or administrative process to impose or declare penalties only after he has ascertained that fraternal correction or rebuke or other means of pastoral solicitude cannot sufficiently repair the scandal, restore justice, reform the offender.

This very significant canon should be read together with the next one to understand the appropriate procedure to be used in imposing *ferendae sententiae* penalties or declaring *latae sententiae* penalties. The present canon reflects a principal pastoral concern underlying penal law interpretation. Penalties are never ends in themselves but should be employed only as a last resort after all other pastoral measures have failed to deal with a problematic situation. Church authorities should normally not impose penalties too quickly but rather use all available non-penal legal-pastoral options before imposing penalties. Among such options are penal remedies (c. 1339) and penances (c. 1340), traditional moral measures such as retreats or fraternal correction, or possibly treatment at a specialized rehabilitation center. While procedural considerations are important in such matters, a concern for the spiritual good of all persons, alleged victims and offenders, should be a key pastoral priority (c. 1752).

Canon 1341 is the only provision in Book VI expressing the key purposes of penal discipline: the repairing of scandal, the restoring of justice, and the reform of the offender.[107] The first two interrelated purposes, which emphasize the protection of certain institutional values, especially characterize expiatory penalties while the last one on the offender's conversion especially characterizes censures. However, unduly sharp distinctions between such purposes and penalties should be avoided.

---

[107] Within the context of consecrated life see c. 695, §1 on the mandatory dismissal of a religious. See also *CCEO* 1401 and *CIC* 2214, §2.

Another noteworthy point in canons 1341–1342 is the emphasis on the discretion of the ordinary or superior (usually the diocesan bishop). He may determine not only whether there will be a penal procedure, usually after a preliminary investigation (c. 1717), but also whether to follow a judicial or administrative procedure (c. 1718). This latter type of discretion is qualified, however, by the code's preference for judicial procedure to protect better the right of defense (cc. 1342, §1; 221, §3).

If the ordinary decides on a penal process, his administrative decree (c. 1718) should indicate at least briefly what non-penal measures were employed and why they failed to achieve the aforementioned penal purposes, or it should note why non-penal measures were judged insufficient and not used.

Penal Procedure To Be Used[108]

Canon 1342 — §1. Whenever just causes preclude a judicial process, a penalty can be imposed or declared by extrajudicial decree; penal remedies and penances, however, can be applied by decree in any case whatsoever.

§2. Perpetual penalties cannot be imposed or declared by decree, nor can penalties be so applied when the law or precept establishing them prohibits their application by decree.

§3. What a law or precept states about the imposition or declaration of a penalty by a judge in a trial must be applied to a superior who imposes or declares a penalty by extrajudicial decree unless it is otherwise evident or unless it concerns prescripts which pertain only to procedural matters.

A basic canonical question confronting an ordinary who has decided that a penal process is appropriate is whether to follow a judicial or administrative process (c. 1718). The present canon answers that question.

There is ample room for the ordinary's discretion. Yet the legislator implicitly prefers judicial

[108] Cf. *CCEO* 1402.

procedure since just (*iustae*) causes are necessary to use administrative procedure.[109]

The canon does not indicate the reasons for not using judicial procedure, which unfortunately do not have to be especially compelling.[110] For example, at times the tribunal staff may be unduly burdened with marriage cases and hence ill-equipped to conduct a formal penal procedure. It might be necessary to proceed expeditiously in certain scandalous situations, e.g., serious financial malfeasance by a church administrator. Yet, such a situation might precisely require a somewhat more formal process if an overemphasis on expediting the case might undercut the proper vindication of the substantive and procedural rights of all concerned.

According to canon 1341 the ordinary decides whether such reasons for an administrative procedure exist even if that is not explicitly stated here (see c. 1718, §1, 3°). In such a serious matter, consultation at least with the judicial vicar, other legal experts, or some other significant diocesan official is appropriate even if not strictly required (c. 1718, §3).

Penal remedies (c. 1339) or penances (c. 1340) may always be applied by decree, or administratively. Since they do not have especially weighty consequences, judicial formalities are not required (c. 1342, §1).

On the contrary, certain serious penalties such as those of a perpetual, or irrevocable, character (e.g., privation of office—c. 1336, §1, 2°) can be imposed only through formal judicial procedure. There is a proportion between the seriousness of the penalty and the seriousness of the procedure imposing it. When the consequences of a penalty are so weighty, the accused should enjoy maximal

[109] Wisely, the Eastern code more strongly emphasizes the need for judicial penal procedure while admitting administrative procedure for weighty (*graves*) reasons if proofs of the delict are certain. Besides the perpetual penalties mentioned in canon 1342, §2, that code also requires judicial penal procedure to impose a major excommunication and a suspension for more than one year (*CCEO* 1402, §1–§2).

[110] For the discussion of this issue by the penal law committee, see *Comm* 9 (1977) 161–162.

legal protection, e.g., services of an advocate, access to all relevant documentation for self-defense purposes, possible appeal of an adverse decision to a higher court. Furthermore, the law establishing a penalty, universal or particular, may require its being imposed judicially (c. 1342, §2).

Paragraph three indicates the equivalence of a judge (judicial procedure) and a superior or ordinary (administrative procedure)[111] relative to the subsequent canons on applying penalties. Such equivalence is particularly relevant to the broad discretion enjoyed by the one presiding over the penal procedure. When the canons refer to the judge, they also apply to the ordinary unless judicial procedure is clearly envisioned, e.g., the detailed provisions on examining witnesses (cc. 1558–1571).

Facultative Penalties

Canon 1343 — If the law or precept gives the judge the power to apply or not apply a penalty, the judge can also temper the penalty or impose a penance in its place, according to his own conscience and prudence.

Numerous canons in this title stress the prudent discretion of the judge in applying *ferendae sententiae* penalties. Such discretion is to be exercised after it is judged that a delict has been committed, even given certain mitigating circumstances. The penal authority must then decide how to deal with the guilty party. Presumably such discretion is an appropriate way of realizing the law's pastoral purposes and dealing sensitively with the specifics of each case.[112] While fostering the offender's

conversion, the judge must also consider legitimate community concerns, especially those persons whose rights have been violated by the delict.

Canon 1343 states that if a *ferendae sententiae* penalty is facultative, or discretionary[113] (e.g., c. 1391), the judge may either not impose a penalty at all, lighten the specified penalty, or substitute a penance (c. 1340).[114] Generally speaking, when a canon mentions only such a facultative penalty, the delict is viewed as less significant than other delicts. However, at times when a preceptive penalty is specified for a given delict, the code also mentions possible additional facultative penalties, even dismissal from the clerical state (e.g., c. 1395, §2). This happens when delicts are particularly serious or clerics continue to scandalize the community.

Preceptive Penalties[115]

Canon 1344 — Even if the law uses preceptive words, the judge can, according to his own conscience and prudence:

1° **defer the imposition of the penalty to a more opportune time if it is foreseen that greater evils will result from an overly hasty punishment of the offender;**

2° **abstain from imposing a penalty, impose a lighter penalty, or employ a penance if the offender has reformed and repaired the scandal or if the offender has been or, it is foreseen, will be punished sufficiently by civil authority;**

3° **suspend the obligation of observing an expiatory penalty if it is the first offense**

---

[111] Despite this canon's use of the term "superior," the canons and this commentary normally refer to the "ordinary" (c. 134) to describe the significant administrative figure before, during, and after the penal procedure. Subsequent procedural references to the "judge" alone also generally envision the "ordinary."

[112] Such authoritative discretion is not operative in marriage nullity cases in which the judge must decide solely whether the nullity of the marriage has been proven or not.

[113] See the list of such penalties in *CLSA Com,* 940.

[114] In this instance and in the circumstances addressed in the next two canons, the accused can still appeal or take recourse against the judge's action (cc. 1727, §1; 1353). Although the judge may treat the accused rather benignly, a declaration of innocence (c. 1726) by the higher authority would more effectively vindicate such a party's reputation.

[115] Cf. *CCEO* 1409, §1, 1°–2° and 4°.

**of an offender who has lived a praisewor-
thy life and if the need to repair scandal
is not pressing, but in such a way that if
the offender commits an offense again
within the time determined by the judge,
the person is to pay the penalty due for
each delict unless in the interim the time
for the prescription of a penal action has
elapsed for the first delict.**

Normally, rather serious delicts, such as teaching a condemned doctrine, call for a preceptive,
or obligatory, *ferendae sententiae* penalty (c.
1371, 1°).[116] In those instances the judge must
generally impose some penalty if a delict has
been committed although the present canon permits responsible penal discretion even there.

For example, the imposition of the penalty
may be deferred if prompt penal action would
cause more pastoral problems than prudently delaying such. For example, the faithful in a parish
might be notably "scandalized" as well as deprived of access to sacramental ministry if their
pastor were penalized and there were a shortage
of clergy (1°). However, the penalty is only temporarily waived, not technically remitted.

Another option is somewhat comparable to the
preceding canon. Perhaps occasionally no penalty
need be imposed; possibly the prescribed penalty
may be tempered (e.g., a suspension from preaching in a given church instead of a total suspension
from preaching); or perhaps a penance (c. 1340)
may be imposed (2°). Here the judge must weigh
carefully the twin values of reforming the offender and repairing scandal to the community. This
option seems to presuppose that the offender has
reformed and the scandal caused by the delict has
been repaired after the penal process has been
initiated.

The possible civil law implications of an ecclesiastical delict must also be considered at times.[117]
The offender may have been punished civilly to repair the societal damage caused by the delict. If so,
an ecclesiastical penalty may be inappropriate even
given the different penal objectives of Church and
State. The legislator attempts to prevent the penal
system from being overly punitive and overwhelm-
ing the offender rather than fostering ecclesial reconciliation; yet legitimate community concerns
also must be addressed (2°; cf. also c. 1346).

Finally, canon 1344 deals with the effects of
expiatory penalties (c. 1336) on first offenders
who have otherwise led a praiseworthy life (3°).
The judge may suspend the obligation of observing such a penalty provided no serious scandal
still needs to be repaired.[118] An equitable concern
for the offender's spiritual well-being presumably
outweighs the institutional interest in repairing societal damage, normally the primary focus of such
penalties.

However, this arrangement is provisional since
the offender may be penalized if another delict is
committed during a probationary period specified
by the judge. In fact the offender may be penalized for both delicts unless the statute of limitations (prescription) has run out for enforcing the
punishment of the first delict (c. 1363). After the
probationary period has elapsed without a new
delict and the aforementioned penal action has
been prescribed, the expiatory penalty whose observance has been suspended definitively ceases.

This canon embodies the pastoral purposes of
the Church's penal order. Penalties, even preceptive
in character, are not simply to be applied mechani-
cally. Rather equity demands that church authority
consider their rationale and use them if necessary to
foster the good of both the community and the individual offender (principle of penal proportionality).

---

[116] For a listing of such preceptive penalties, see *CLSA
Com,* 938–939. While the current title focuses on *ferendae sententiae* penalties, the most serious delicts are actually punished by *latae sententiae* penalties listed in
CLSA Com, 937.

[117] For ecclesiastical delicts with possible civil law ramifications, see cc. 1370; 1395; 1397; 1398.

[118] On suspending the observance of censures and expiatory penalties in critical pastoral situations, see cc. 1335,
1338, §3 and 1352.

Waiving of Penalty

Canon 1345 — Whenever the offender had only the imperfect use of reason or committed the delict from fear, necessity, the heat of passion, or mental disturbance from drunkenness or something similar, the judge can also abstain from imposing any penalty if he thinks that reform of the person can be better accomplished in another way.

This somewhat open-ended and pastorally inspired canon envisions judicial or administrative discretion in dealing with offenders whose imputability is notably diminished. Without mentioning canon 1324, the present canon notes certain factors in that canon mitigating penal imputability.[119] However, the present canon views the issue from the judge's standpoint rather than from that of the offender. Furthermore, the present canon goes beyond that earlier formulation, which required tempering a penalty or imposing a penance in such circumstances. Here the judge may abstain from imposing any penalty if the offender can be rehabilitated better otherwise. At times fraternal correction, rebuke, or other means of pastoral care might reflect the Church's reconciling nature better than properly punitive measures. This canon, unlike the preceding one, focuses explicitly only on the reform-of-the-offender dimension of the penal system.

Multiple Delicts[120]

Canon 1346 — Whenever the offender has committed several delicts, it is left to the prudent decision of the judge to moderate the penalties within equitable limits if the sum of the *ferendae sententiae* penalties appears excessive.

Technically if several delicts have been committed, several penalties may be warranted, especially if such penalties are different, e.g., suspension and certain expiatory penalties. For example, a soliciting confessor (c. 1387) may also engage in prohibited sexual activity (c. 1395). Both the offender's spiritual welfare and the good of the community may justify such a cumulation of penalties. However, even here the penal authority may exercise a certain discretion.

It may be pastorally counterproductive to burden the penalized individual, however guilty, with various *ferendae sententiae* penalties although they may be canonically justified. In other words, a benign interpretation of penal law (*CCEO* 1404, §1) might militate against "penal overkill" and suggest an equitable imposition of penalties reflecting a responsible pastoral approach to this issue. However, a concern for the integrity of the community suggests caution in exercising such discretion. No such discretion, however, is operative for *latae sententiae* penalties, which bind the imputable offender upon commission of the delict.

Conditions for a Censure[121]

Canon 1347 — §1. A censure cannot be imposed validly unless the offender has been warned at least once beforehand to withdraw from contumacy and has been given a suitable time for repentance.
§2. An offender who has truly repented of the delict and has also made suitable reparation for damages and scandal or at least has seriously promised to do so must be considered to have withdrawn from contumacy.

This canon on imposing censures should be read in conjunction with canons 1331–1335 on specific censures. It illustrates a key feature of such penalties: the offender is to be formally warned to withdraw from contumacy, or contempt

---

[119] The present canon explicitly mentions only certain factors in c. 1324, §1 mitigating imputability, i.e., an imperfect use of reason (1°), fear or necessity (5°), passion (3°), or drunkenness or another similar mental disturbance (2°).
[120] Cf. *CCEO* 1409, §1, 3°.

[121] While the Eastern code technically does not differentiate between censures and expiatory penalties, see *CCEO* 1407, §1–§2.

of church authority, within a certain period of time (§1).[122] The mere fact that a law has been broken does not necessarily mean that the offender is contumacious. Only if this is true can such a penalty be validly inflicted since its primary rationale is breaking such contumacy and reintegrating the offender within the community.[123] In contrast, no such warning normally must be given to impose expiatory penalties.[124]

The criteria for determining when such contumacy has ceased are genuine repentance for the delict and an effort, or at least a serious promise, to repair the damage or scandal it causes, e.g., making a public retraction for damaging another's reputation (c. 1390, §2). The focus is not simply on the offender's personal conversion of heart; rather any societal damage is to be remedied as much as possible.

The pre-process determination whether contumacy has ceased is made by the ordinary competent to initiate the penal process (cc. 1341; 1718). The judge conducting the penal process also must consider this factor before imposing or declaring the censure. Subsequently such a determination rests with the authority competent to remit the penalty (cc. 1354–1358).

Quasi-Penal Options

Canon 1348 — When an accused is acquitted of an accusation or when no penalty is imposed, the ordinary can provide for the welfare of the person and for the public good through appropriate warnings and other means of pastoral solicitude or even through penal remedies if the matter warrants it.

---

[122] Such a formal warning, normally by the ordinary or his delegate, applies only to *ferendae sententiae* censures. In *latae sententiae* censures the warning is presumably contained in the law threatening the penalty.

[123] This warning is similar to, yet technically different from, the penal remedy mentioned in c. 1339, §1. The warning to cease contumacy is likewise to be confirmed by a document to be kept in the secret archive (c. 1339, §3).

[124] By way of exception, a warning may sometimes be required for an expiatory penalty, e.g., c. 1395, §1.

The issue of administrative discretion surfaces again here. This canon focuses not on the one conducting the penal process but on the ordinary alone exercising his oversight role relative to the welfare of the community.

The penal process may end with the judgment that the charges against the accused are unfounded, hence he or she is declared innocent (c. 1726). In such instances this canon is inapplicable. At other times, however, the accused may be acquitted because the alleged delict could not be proven, e.g., lack of criminal intent or the presence of significant imputability-mitigating factors (c. 1324). Furthermore, occasionally the accused may be guilty; however, no penalty is imposed because penal discretion is exercised (cc. 1343–1346). Perhaps the offender has reformed and the societal damage has been repaired, or the goals of the penal system can be better achieved in a non-penal fashion.

In such circumstances institutional or personal pastoral considerations may still require the ordinary's warning the individual, imposing a penal remedy (c. 1339), or providing some other pastoral measure such as appropriate counseling. Why is this so? The fact that no penalty is imposed does not necessarily mean that all is in order ecclesially or personally. The public order may have been seriously disturbed by the accused even if there has technically been no delict. Furthermore, the accused person who has not been totally exonerated may benefit spiritually from such pastoral measures.

However, this somewhat extraordinary administrative measure presupposes hearing the person in question whose rights may be jeopardized (c. 50). Furthermore, administrative recourse to higher authority is available under the usual conditions (cc. 1732–1739).

Judicious Application of Penalties[125]

Canon 1349 — If a penalty is indeterminate and the law does not provide otherwise, the judge is not to impose graver penalties, especially censures,

---

[125] Cf. *CCEO* 1409, §2.

unless the seriousness of the case clearly demands it; he cannot, however, impose perpetual penalties.

This title constantly stresses judicial or administrative discretion in dealing with individual penal situations. However, this canon introduces a prudent restriction on such discretion. It is comparable to the principle of legislative penal restraint affirmed in canons 1317–1318.

At times the law (not a precept) specifies a possible penalty in indeterminate terms, e.g., a "just penalty." Then the judge is normally to refrain from imposing particularly serious penalties such as censures, probably because they frequently preclude access to the sacraments. Generally the legislator does not view a legal violation quite as seriously as other delicts if the corresponding penalty is formulated in indeterminate terms.[126]

At times, however, a censure may be appropriate even in such indeterminate penalty circumstances, e.g., c. 1388, §2. Furthermore, the seriousness of the delict may require heavier penalties; for example, imputability-aggravating circumstances may be operative in situations of persistent disobedience to one's ecclesiastical superiors (cc. 1326; 1371, 2°).

With due regard for such provisions, however, perpetual penalties, such as privation of office or dismissal from the clerical state, may never be imposed in an indeterminate penalty situation. Given their irrevocable implications, the code must specify them explicitly as an appropriate punishment of very serious delicts.

Support of Penalized Cleric[127]

Canon 1350 — §1. Unless it concerns dismissal from the clerical state, when penalties are im-

posed on a cleric, provision must always be made so that he does not lack those things necessary for his decent support.

§2. In the best manner possible, however, the ordinary is to take care to provide for a person dismissed from the clerical state who is truly in need because of the penalty.

There is an institutional responsibility to support the penalized yet non-dismissed cleric (§1). While the original schema referred only to clerics subject to expiatory penalties and not to those under censure, the code makes no such distinction. Although the cleric has seriously violated the law, his basic right to appropriate support is to be honored by the institution (c. 281).[128]

Obviously the ecclesial status of the penalized cleric differs from that of his peers in good standing who discharge their ministerial obligations and deserve an appropriate remuneration. However, the ordinary must respect the penalized cleric's right to support, whose specific implications must be assessed in light of the penalty to which he is subject.[129] Diocesan or possibly provincial personnel norms might appropriately address this issue and its implications for lay persons in full-time church service (c. 231, §2).

Only dismissal from the clerical state technically extinguishes such a right in strict justice (c. 292). However, even the dismissed cleric is not totally beyond his ordinary's pastoral care and charity. While charity is the motivating factor here, the ordinary is juridically obliged (*providere curet*) to provide as best he can for the dismissed cleric who is truly needy because of the penalty (§2). Even after being dismissed, the cleric maintains a certain relationship to the institution in which he has been incardinated (c. 266). The code

---

[126] Because of their vague formulation, one may wonder how effectively such penalties foster the goals of the penal system. Such penalties seem to be conducive to an arbitrary exercise of authority, yet they do permit the penal authority to take cognizance of differing degrees of imputability. De facto numerous penalties are indeterminate in character. See *CLSA Com,* 935–936.

[127] Cf. *CCEO* 1410.

[128] See c. 384 on the bishop's obligation to be solicitous for his priests, including providing for their decent support and social assistance. See also c. 195.

[129] For examples of clerical penalties with possible financial implications, see cc. 1331, §2, 5°; 1333, §4; and 1336, §1, 2°. Such ecclesiastical penalties, however, must take cognizance of legitimate civil law claims of such individuals, e.g., regarding pensions.

here also seems to recognize his service to the aforementioned institution.[130]

Territorial Scope of Penalty[131]

Canon 1351 — Unless other provision is expressly made, a penalty binds the offender everywhere, even when the authority of the one who established or imposed the penalty has lapsed.

This canon notes the universally binding force of a penalty even if the ecclesiastical authority establishing (legislator) or imposing it (judge or ordinary) no longer holds office (cc. 184–196). A concern to ensure the proper enforcement of the law and protect the public good underlies this provision. The penalty is related primarily to nonterritorial factors, i.e., the ecclesial damage and/or problematic dispositions of the offender. Hence, his or her mobility should not affect the impact of the penalty.

Although this broad territorial scope of the penalty is the general rule, the penal law might provide otherwise. For example, the penalty might cease at the death of the ordinary who imposed it. Or a cleric might be prohibited from functioning only in a certain place where his continued ministry might be pastorally detrimental (c. 1336, §1, 2°). Furthermore, certain expiatory penalties specifically affect one's residence, e.g., canon 1336, §1, 1° on prohibited or prescribed residence. Finally, at times the observance of various penalties is temporarily suspended (cc. 1335; 1338, §3; 1344, 3°; 1352).

Observance of Penalty Suspended

Canon 1352 — §1. If a penalty prohibits the reception of the sacraments or sacramentals, the prohibition is suspended as long as the offender is in danger of death.

§2. The obligation to observe an undeclared *latae sententiae* penalty which is not notorious in the place where the offender is present, is suspended totally or partially whenever the offender cannot observe it without danger of grave scandal or infamy.

The code here also deals with the practical impact of a penalty on the guilty party. It addresses two particularly urgent situations in which observing a penalty might be pastorally harmful, i.e., danger of death or danger of infamy or scandal.[132] Once this pastoral contingency has passed, the penalty must be observed.

Under certain conditions the personal spiritual needs of the individual offender prevail over considerations of good ecclesial order. Certain penalties such as excommunication (c. 1331, §1, 2°) and interdict (c. 1332) normally forbid the reception of the sacraments. However, this prohibition is suspended in danger of death (§1).[133] The present canon should be read in connection with canon 976, another emergency provision empowering any priest[134] to absolve the faithful in danger of death from any sins or censures. However, unless the censure were unreserved and undeclared, the recovering offender must make recourse to a competent penal authority (c. 1357, §3).

The code also addresses significant problems arising in a less critical pastoral situation than danger of death (§2). If certain penalties were observed, the individual offender might suffer personal infamy or serious loss of reputation (c. 220), or the community might be gravely scandalized. Either condition suffices to justify suspending the observance of the penalty.

---

[130] See c. 702, §2 for an analogous provision regarding those who legitimately leave or are dismissed from a religious institute. See also *CCEO* 1410 explicitating the cleric's vested right to insurance and social security as well as health insurance for himself and his family if he is married.

[131] Cf. *CCEO* 1412, §4.

[132] See also cc. 1335 and 1338, §3 enabling penalized church ministers to serve the faithful in various pastoral contingencies.

[133] Cf. *CCEO* 1435, §1.

[134] Even priests without confessional faculties or subject to an ecclesiastical penalty or laicized may absolve the penitent in such circumstances.

For example, a priest might commit an occult[135] delict, or one known only to a few persons, e.g., absolution of an accomplice (cc. 977; 1378, §1). Observing the excommunication would prevent his performing certain spiritual functions for a particular community, such as a parish. Although this canon was originally formulated fairly broadly, the present text limits such non-observance of penalties to undeclared *latae sententiae* penalties even if reserved. This is another example of the legislator's mitigating their impact. However, if a *latae sententiae* penalty has been declared or a *ferendae sententiae* penalty imposed, the competent penal authority would presumably consider the offender's existential situation. This would preclude the need for recourse to this extraordinary measure of non-observance (not remission) of the penalty.

Suspensive Effect of Appeal or Recourse against Penalty[136]

Canon 1353 — An appeal or recourse from judicial sentences or from decrees, which impose or declare a penalty, has a suspensive effect.

In the 1917 code, unlike the rules on vindictive (now expiatory) penalties (*CIC* 2287), appeals against sentences imposing censures or recourses against decrees imposing them were without suspensive effect. Hence, the declared or imposed censure had to be observed immediately although an appeal or recourse was pending (*CIC* 2243).

Now, however, such a suspensive effect is operative for both censures and expiatory penalties. This change reflects a benign interpretation of penal law (*CCEO* 1404, 1). It embodies the legislator's concern to foster the pastoral purposes of penal law and respect the dignity and basic rights of the offender, e.g., reputation (c. 220).

Another such right is challenging an adverse penal sentence (cc. 1628–1640; 1727, §1) or decree (cc. 1732–1739). The defendant's exercise of basic Christian rights should normally not be restricted until the original sentence is confirmed by the ordinary appellate court or by the Rota, a concurrent appellate court (c. 1444, §1, 1°). Likewise the defendant's ecclesial status should normally not be jeopardized until the original administrative decree is confirmed by the penal authority's hierarchic superior, usually a Roman congregation, e.g., the Congregation for the Clergy in most cases involving clerics.

In short, the pre-penalty status quo is maintained during the appeal or recourse. However, certain non-penal disciplinary measures possibly taken against the defendant during the process remain in effect if still warranted, e.g., prohibition from exercising a certain office such as the pastorate (c. 1722). This restriction, however, is not technically a privation of office (c. 1336, §1, 2°), which is an expiatory penalty requiring a judicial process.

TITLE VI
THE CESSATION OF PENALTIES[137]
[cc. 1354–1363]

Thus far the code has discussed the meaning of delicts and penalties (titles I–IV) and the practical

---

[135] Such a suspension of the observance of an undeclared *latae sententiae* penalty is operative only if the penalty is not "notorious" in the place where the offender is actually present. Unfortunately the 1983 code does not define the term "notorious." The 1917 code spoke not of penalties but of certain delicts as being "notorious in fact" if they had been committed in circumstances in which there were no mitigating factors (*CIC* 2197, 3°). In short, a notorious penalty likely means a situation of reasonably broad public awareness of the gravity of a delict despite no formal penal process. See also the commentary on c. 1335 regarding "married priests."

[136] See *CCEO* 1319 regarding a judicial appeal and *CCEO* 1487, §2 regarding administrative recourse in penal processes.

[137] Besides the Münster commentary, see Borras, 124–150; idem, in *Com Ex*, 430–460; Green, in *CLSA Com*, 915–919; Martin, in *CLSGBI Com*, 777–784; Rees, 407–414.

application of the latter (title V). This final title of part one of Book VI indicates the various ways in which penalties cease once they have been incurred (*latae sententiae*) or imposed (*ferendae sententiae*).

The generic term "cessation" in the title encompasses the different ways in which an offender is released from a penalty, e.g., death, expiation of expiatory penalty, remission of penalty. However, de facto this chapter exclusively considers the "remission" of penalties by a church authority figure usually in the external forum (cc. 1355–1356), but sometimes in the internal sacramental forum of confession (c. 1357).

The code normally uses only the generic term "remission" for all types of penalties.[138] However, the remission of censures and expiatory penalties differs somewhat. Censures, which are always indefinite in duration, are to be remitted when the guilty party is properly disposed (c. 1358, §1). This is somewhat comparable to the penitential context: the absolution of the disposed penitent is neither to be refused nor deferred (c. 980). In other words, the discretion of the competent authority is somewhat restricted since such a remission is a matter of justice. Finally, censures may sometimes be remitted in the internal forum.

Expiatory penalties, on the other hand, may be imposed for a certain period of time and cease once it elapses, e.g., loss of salary for three months (expiation of penalty). If they are imposed for an indefinite period, they cease only at the discretion of the competent authority, who technically grants a favor and is not bound to remit the penalty merely because the offender is contrite, for institutional concerns may still preclude such a remission, e.g., long-term damage experienced by victims of notable financial malfeasance. Furthermore, certain perpetual expiatory penalties such as deprivation of office and dismissal from the clerical state are not remitted (c. 1336, §1, 2° and 5°). Finally, there are generally no internal forum remissions of such penalties.

Power of Remitting Penalties[139]

Canon 1354 — §1. In addition to the persons listed in cann. 1355–1356, all who can dispense from a law which includes a penalty or who can exempt from a precept which threatens a penalty can also remit that penalty.

§2. Moreover, a law or precept which establishes a penalty can also give the power of remission to others.

§3. If the Apostolic See has reserved the remission of a penalty to itself or to others, the reservation must be interpreted strictly.

Title II on the penal law/precept deals largely with the exercise of legislative power (penal law: cc. 1313–1318) and relatively minimally with executive power (penal precept: c. 1319). The previous title V on applying penalties deals with either executive or judicial power (cc. 1341–1353).

However, title VI deals solely with executive power since the remission of a penalty is viewed implicitly as an act of executive power, somewhat like a dispensation from a law (§1; c. 85). The competent authority figure "dispenses" or releases the guilty party from the obligation of observing the penalty for due cause, somewhat comparable to releasing one from the obligation of observing the law. Such executive authority figures are spelled out more precisely in the subsequent canons 1355–1356.[140] The present canon should probably also have explicitly referred to canon 1357 enabling confessors to remit certain censures under specific conditions; however, the external forum focus of the code here is quite clear.

A penal law or precept may permit broader remission options than those specified in paragraph one (§2). However, a broad delegation of such power has not been common in the past given the seriousness of penal discipline. In such instances the general rules on delegated power are opera-

[138] By way of exception certain canons refer to "absolution" of censures as in the 1917 code. See cc. 508, §1; 566, §2; and 976.

[139] Cf. *CCEO* 1419.

[140] While it is not stated explicitly here, obviously those competent to establish penal laws may also dispense from them and remit penalties flowing from their violation.

tive, e.g., canon 137.[141] The penal authority of those who are simply judges, e.g., judicial vicar, and not ordinaries (c. 134) is rather limited. Those possessing only judicial authority may only apply an established penal law in a given case. This is an example of a generally strict judicial-executive power differentiation for authority figures other than the pope and the diocesan bishop.

A noteworthy change from the prior code is the significant reduction of the number of penalties whose remission was reserved to the Holy See.[142] Lower level authorities such as ordinaries could not remit them presumably because of the particular seriousness of the delict, the exigencies of ecclesiastical discipline, and the need to foster more effectively the spiritual welfare of offenders (*CIC* 2246, §1). Such reservations made the former penal discipline overly complex and burdensome, especially for confessors, who were more frequently involved in such remissions than currently.

The Holy See theoretically may reserve the remission of certain penalties to itself[143] or to another authority. However, only five *latae sententiae* excommunications are actually reserved: canon 1367 (violation of sacred species); canon 1370, §1 (physical attack on pope); canon 1378, §1 (absolution of accomplice); canon 1382 (unauthorized episcopal consecration); and canon 1388, §1 (direct violation of confessional seal by confessor). Hence generally any ordinary and exceptionally any confessor may remit penalties under specific conditions.

This simplification of the law enhances the options for remission of penalties for properly disposed offenders. Furthermore, such reservations must be strictly interpreted since they limit the free exercise of remitting power by ordinaries (c. 18).

---

[141] Occasionally a diocesan bishop will delegate the priests of the diocese the faculty to remit certain penalties, e.g., the excommunication resulting from an abortion (c. 1398).

[142] In the external forum this means the appropriate Roman congregation, depending on the nature of the issue (see *PB* 48–116); in the internal forum this means the ApPen (see *PB* 117–120).

[143] Cf. *CCEO* 1423.

Remitting Penalties Established by Law

Canon 1355 — §1. Provided that the penalty has not been reserved to the Apostolic See, the following can remit an imposed or declared penalty established by law:

   1° the ordinary who initiated the trial to impose or declare a penalty or who personally or through another imposed or declared it by decree;

   2° the ordinary of the place where the offender is present, after the ordinary mentioned under n. 1 has been consulted unless this is impossible because of extraordinary circumstances.

§2. If the penalty has not been reserved to the Apostolic See, an ordinary can remit a *latae sententiae* penalty established by law but not yet declared for his subjects and those who are present in his territory or who committed the offense there; any bishop can also do this in the act of sacramental confession.

Canons 1355 and 1356 reflect the enhanced postconciliar legal-pastoral authority of bishops although the code speaks more broadly of "ordinaries" (c. 134). The two canons exemplify the generally external forum focus of penal discipline. Canon 1355 deals with unreserved penalties established by law, while canon 1356 treats of unreserved penalties established by precept. No distinction is made between censures and expiatory penalties; however, the *ferendae sententiae–latae sententiae* distinction is relevant.

The code provides broad penalty-remitting options, both for the ordinary of the place where the offender is actually present and for the ordinary who initiated the judicial penal process or declared or imposed the penalty administratively (the penalizing ordinary). The options for the former ordinary take special cognizance of increased societal mobility. However, canon 1355 also refers generically to penalties reserved to the Holy See, and here the aforementioned ordinaries may not remit the penalty.

Paragraph one[144] deals with declared *latae sententiae* and *ferendae sententiae* penalties. The penalty-remitting options are somewhat more restricted here than in paragraph two on non-declared *latae sententiae* penalties, probably because of the formal ecclesiastical intervention in the prior instance. Both the penalizing ordinary and the offender's local ordinary may remit such penalties. Yet, barring extraordinary circumstances, the latter is normally to contact the former before remitting the penalty. Presumably the penalizing ordinary can clarify the possibly complex legal-pastoral circumstances surrounding the imposition or declaration of the penalty and any continuing detrimental ecclesial impact of the delict. A pastorally responsible remission of a penalty normally presupposes access to such information; however, the penalizing ordinary does not have to approve the remission of the penalty.

Paragraph two of the canon concerns the undeclared, unreserved *latae sententiae* penalty. Remitting options are broader here than in paragraph one, presumably since no authority figure has been directly involved in the case, prescinding from the legislator's establishing the penalty. Hence no reference is made to consultation with the penalizing ordinary. The focus is on the local ordinary's power vis-à-vis his subjects, those actually in his territory even if they are not his subjects, and those who committed a delict in his territory (c. 136).

Furthermore, besides the aforementioned external forum option, any bishop, diocesan or titular (c. 376), may remit such undeclared *latae sententiae* penalties, yet only in sacramental confession and for the internal forum. The rationale for introducing this exceptional internal forum dimension in the otherwise external forum remission process is not entirely clear; however, it parallels the comparable role of confessors (c. 1357). It is another example of the pastoral thrust of penal law and its limiting the impact of *latae sententiae* penalties.

[144] Cf. *CCEO* 1420, §1.

Remitting Penalties Established by Precept

Canon 1356 — §1. The following can remit a *ferendae sententiae* or *latae sententiae* penalty established by a precept not issued by the Apostolic See:

1° the ordinary of the place where the offender is present;

2° if the penalty has been imposed or declared, the ordinary who initiated the trial to impose or declare the penalty or who personally or through another imposed or declared it by decree.

§2. The author of the precept must be consulted before remission is made unless this is impossible because of extraordinary circumstances.

Contrary to the more generalized situation of a penal law (c. 1355), this canon deals with the more individualized penal precept issued by an executive authority other than the Holy See. The remitting options are more limited than in the preceding canon. No reference is made to internal forum remissions, and the canon does not differentiate between declared and undeclared *latae sententiae* penalties.

Either the offender's local ordinary or the penalizing ordinary can remit the penalty (§1).[145] However, the need to consider the circumstances surrounding the issuing of the penal precept underlies the requirement that its author be consulted before the penalty is remitted unless this is impossible for some extraordinary reason (§2). Such a burden of consultation makes sense for the offender's local ordinary but not so much for the penalizing ordinary, who should be familiar with the case. In any event, the author of the precept does not have to approve the remission of the penalty.

Power of Confessors[146]

Canon 1357 — §1. Without prejudice to the prescripts of cann. 508 and 976, a confessor can

[145] Cf. *CCEO* 1420, §2.

[146] For a thoughtful discussion of this issue, see Borras, 136–145.

remit in the internal sacramental forum an unde-clared *latae sententiae* censure of excommunica-tion or interdict if it is burdensome for the peni-tent to remain in the state of grave sin during the time necessary for the competent superior to make provision.

§2. In granting the remission, the confessor is to impose on the penitent, under the penalty of reincidence, the obligation of making recourse within a month to the competent superior or to a priest endowed with the faculty and the obliga-tion of obeying his mandates; in the meantime he is to impose a suitable penance and, insofar as it is demanded, reparation of any scandal and damage; however, recourse can also be made through the confessor, without mention of the name.

§3. After they have recovered, those for whom an imposed or declared censure or one reserved to the Apostolic See has been remitted according to the norm of can. 976 are also obliged to make recourse.

The present canon reflects the 1977 code com-mission decision generally not to permit excom-municated or interdicted persons to receive penance and anointing before remission of the censure. However, for pressing pastoral reasons limited provisions should be made for the remis-sion of certain censures in the internal sacramen-tal forum.

The confessor may remit undeclared *latae sen-tentiae* excommunications or interdicts even if they are reserved to the Apostolic See. Accord-ingly he may not remit undeclared *latae senten-tiae* suspensions, *ferendae sententiae* censures, or expiatory penalties. In practice, however, there may be significant options for confessors since numerous *latae sententiae* excommunications and interdicts may never be declared, especially those affecting the laity, e.g., the excommunication for a procured abortion (c. 1398).

When is such an option available? It must be hard for a penitent to remain in serious sin until a competent superior remits the penalty (§1). Actu-

ally, if a penitent finds it burdensome to remain in mortal sin for only one day, this canon is relevant. The "competent superior" refers to those autho-rized to remit penalties in canons 1355–1356, an-other authorized priest, or the appropriate Holy See dicastery.

Canon 1357 also mentions the canon peniten-tiary, who ex officio may remit in confession any unreserved and undeclared *latae sententiae* cen-sures (c. 508, §1).[147] This official functions only in dioceses with chapters of canons (cc. 503–510). Yet technically a comparable internal forum offi-cial must be appointed even by bishops without such chapters (c. 508, §2). The present canon also alludes to the broad powers of remitting sins and censures enjoyed by any priest in a danger-of-death situation even if he is laicized or otherwise unauthorized to hear confessions (c. 976).

The confessor's special penalty-remitting pow-ers are not unqualified. Hence, he must impose on the penitent the burden of making recourse within a month to the competent penal superior or to an authorized priest and observing such an authori-ty's mandates or instructions (§2).[148] Should such recourse not be made, the censure technically re-curs (reincidence), presumably because of the penitent's obstinate refusal to follow the confes-sor's directions.

Does the censure also recur if the penitent makes such recourse yet does not observe the aforemen-tioned mandates? The phrase "under the penalty of reincidence" directly qualifies the recourse obliga-tion but not the obligation to obey such mandates. The censure probably is incurred again since the penitent's disobedience seemingly reflects contempt of church authority. However, the structure of the canon might suggest that non-compliance with such

---

[147] Certain chaplains may also absolve penitents from un-declared, unreserved *latae sententiae* censures wherever they minister (e.g., in hospitals and prisons and on sea journeys) with due regard for c. 976 in a danger-of-death situation in such settings (c. 566, §2).

[148] Such a recourse obligation is operative neither in the case of the canon penitentiary (c. 508, §1) nor the chap-lain (c. 566, §2).

mandates does not entail reincidence of the censure. Furthermore, a strict interpretation requires that such reincidence be proven conclusively. Just as serious imputability is necessary if one is to be penalized initially, similar imputability seems necessary for the reincidence of the censure.

Besides informing the penitent of the recourse obligation, the confessor must also impose a suitable penance (c. 1340) and require the repairing of any damage or scandal, if necessary, as an integral part of remitting the censure.[149] The offender's willingness to accept such a penance and make a reasonable effort to repair any damage caused by the delict is a significant sign of the cessation of contumacy necessary to remit a censure (c. 1347, §2; 1358, §1).

Realistically many penitents may find the required recourse difficult given their unfamiliarity with the law. In such instances the confessor may fulfill this duty without mentioning any names to protect the penitent's reputation.

A comparable but different recourse obligation binds those for whom censures are remitted in danger of death (§3; c. 976). Only those subject to unreserved, undeclared *latae sententiae* censures are exempt from such a recourse obligation after recovering from the crisis. The pastoral urgency of this situation warrants broader faculties for any priest than is envisioned for confessors in the present canon. However, the principally external forum thrust of penal discipline is still exemplified by the post-recovery recourse obligation, which may also be fulfilled by the confessor.

Remission of Censure[150]

Canon 1358 — §1. Remission of a censure cannot be granted unless the offender has withdrawn from contumacy according to the norm of can. 1347, §2; it cannot be denied, however, to a person who withdraws from contumacy.

---

[149] See c. 981 on a penance to be imposed by a confessor in a regular penitential context.
[150] Cf. *CCEO* 1424.

§2. The person who remits a censure can make provision according to the norm of can. 1348 or can even impose a penance.

The cessation of contumacy is indispensable for the remission of a censure. If such a disposition is verified (c. 1347, §2), the offender has a certain claim to its remission (§1). Such a cessation of contumacy, however, involves both the offender's conversion of heart and serious efforts at remedying any ecclesial damage or scandal. Should such a remission be denied, the offender could take appropriate hierarchic recourse (cc. 1732–1739). This provision notably differentiates censures from expiatory penalties, whose remission is not exclusively related to the cessation of contumacy. Restoring justice and repairing scandal are even more relevant considerations in that context.

The remission of the censure, however, does not necessarily preclude the competent authority from employing certain non-penal legal-pastoral measures (e.g., warning) or imposing a penance (c. 1340). According to canon 1348 the offender may be subject to such measures at the ordinary's discretion (§2). Some detrimental ecclesial effects of the delict may need to be addressed even after the cessation of contumacy, e.g., notable parish divisions occasioned by illegitimate protests against episcopal restructuring of parishes (c. 1373). However, no new penalties may be imposed unless a new penal process indicates that a new delict has been committed.

Remission of Multiple Penalties[151]

Canon 1359 — If several penalties bind a person, a remission is valid only for the penalties expressed in it; a general remission, however, takes away all penalties except those which the offender in bad faith omitted in the petition.

An offender committing several delicts may be liable to multiple penalties although a sense of eq-

---

[151] Cf. *CCEO* 1425.

uity might suggest moderation in their application lest the offender be unduly burdened (c. 1346). One must examine the rescript (c. 59) of remission to see which penalties are remitted since, unlike the sacramental remission of sins, which is total, the remission of penalties may be partial. Such a rescript may be specific or general in character. If it is specific, it is valid only for the penalties expressly mentioned. On the contrary, if it is general, it covers all penalties except those concealed in bad faith when the offender sought such a remission.[152]

This canon emphasizes the offender's good faith in acknowledging honestly whatever penalties have been incurred. Such good faith indicates a spirit of conversion, a primary concern in remitting censures (c. 1358) but also pertinent to remitting expiatory penalties.

Coerced Remission of Penalty

Canon 1360 — The remission of a penalty extorted by grave fear is invalid.

This provision invalidating a coerced remission of a penalty illustrates the general principle that legal acts posited through grave fear unjustly induced or through deceit are valid unless the law provides otherwise (c. 125, §2). Here the law provides otherwise regarding grave fear because of the serious ecclesial threat posed by the possible intimidation of church authorities to remit penalties.[153] In such a situation one may question the genuineness of the cessation of contumacy. The canon's legal history and interpretation and the use of the term *extorta* qualifying the fear seem to indicate that the fear must be unjust in itself or in the manner of its application.

---

[152] On the relevance of concealing the truth or lying in seeking rescripts, see c. 63.

[153] Interestingly the Eastern code states that, besides grave fear, force or fraud also invalidates the remission of a penalty (*CCEO* 1421). Although the Latin code does not explicitly state it here, irresistible extrinsic force prompting grave fear also invalidates a remission of a penalty (c. 125, §1).

Format of Remission[154]

Canon 1361 — §1. A remission can also be given conditionally or to a person who is absent.

§2. A remission in the external forum is to be given in writing unless a grave cause suggests otherwise.

§3. Care is to be taken that the petition of remission or the remission itself is not divulged except insofar as it is either useful to protect the reputation of the offender or necessary to repair scandal.

In principle the remission of a penalty is an external forum act of executive power not per se sacramental (cc. 1354–1356). Hence it can technically be expedited without the offender's being present, however desirable that may be (§1). However, the various exceptional internal forum remissions of certain censures[155] obviously presuppose the presence of the penitent.

The remission of a penalty, like other acts of executive governance in the external forum, can be expedited absolutely or conditionally. The condition (e.g., making appropriate restitution) may concern the past, present, or future. However, that conditional factor is also operative in certain internal forum remissions requiring recourse to a competent superior under penalty of reincidence of the censure (c. 1357, §2–§3).

Barring a serious reason for not doing so, an external forum remission is normally to be put in writing like any other administrative act (cc. 37 and 51) so that it can be proved easily (§ 2). However, such a written instrument is not necessary for validity.

The remission should be publicized only if necessary to protect the offender's reputation (c. 220) or to repair damage to the community. The remission of the penalty should be no more public than the delict and the corresponding penalty. The concern about protecting the offender's reputation might be especially valid for one occupying a po-

---

[154] Cf. *CCEO* 1422.

[155] See cc. 508, §1; 566, §2; 976; 1355, §2; and 1357.

sition of public ecclesial trust, e.g., vicar, pastor, school principal, etc. (§3). However, one must proceed very carefully here.

Prescription of Criminal Action [156]

Canon 1362 — §1. Prescription extinguishes a criminal action after three years unless it concerns:
    1° delicts reserved to the Congregation for the Doctrine of the Faith;
    2° an action arising from the delicts mentioned in cann. 1394, 1395, 1397, and 1398, which have a prescription of five years;
    3° delicts which are not punished in the common law if particular law has established another period for prescription.
    §2. Prescription runs from the day on which the delict was committed or, if the delict is continuous or habitual, from the day on which it ceased.

Somewhat surprisingly the next two canons on prescription (c. 197) of criminal and penal actions are not placed in Book VII on procedural law. They may have been placed here because such canons presumably are best situated in the section of the law dealing with the matter subject to prescription. While this may be true, it would have been systematically more appropriate to situate at least the present canon in connection with canon 1718 on the factors an ordinary considers in determining whether to initiate a penal process.[157]

Prescription in Book VI means a statute of limitations or a prohibition of pursuing a criminal

action to impose or declare a penalty or a penal action to enforce a penalty after a certain period of time. A concern for the public good requires that criminal actions be pursued expeditiously. The evidence may become stale if too long a time lags between the commission of an alleged delict and its formal prosecution. Furthermore, the legal security of the accused is unduly jeopardized if church authorities do not pursue potential criminal actions with reasonable expeditiousness.

Generally speaking, criminal actions are subject to prescription three years after the commission of the delict or the cessation of a so-called continuing or habitual delict, e.g., membership in a forbidden society plotting against the Church (c. 1374).

However, a different period of time is pertinent for the prosecution of certain delicts. For example, one needs to consult CDF rules for delicts of faith or morals referred to it (PB 52). A five-year period of prescription is envisioned for certain serious moral delicts of clerics or religious (cc. 1394–1395) and certain serious violations of persons, i.e., abduction, mutilation, homicide, and abortion (cc. 1397–1398).

Furthermore, particular law might prescribe a longer or shorter period of prescription for certain delicts it punishes.[158] The specification of a longer period of time to pursue a criminal action indicates that certain delicts are viewed as more destructive of ecclesial values than others.

Prescription of Penal Action [159]

Canon 1363 — §1. Prescription extinguishes an action to execute a penalty if the offender is not notified of the executive decree of the judge mentioned in can. 1651 within the time limits mentioned in can. 1362; these limits are to be computed from the day on which the condemnatory sentence became a _res iudicata_.

---

[156] Cf. _CCEO_ 1152. Unlike the Latin code, which deals explicitly only with prescription, the Eastern code also refers to the extinction of the penal action by the death of the accused or by an authoritative pardon (§1). Rather than referring specifically to the CDF, the Eastern code refers generically to delicts reserved to the Apostolic See (§2).

[157] This is true although technically c. 1363 on the prescription of an action to execute a penalty presupposes that the penalty has already been imposed after a process. The prescription of such an action is one way in which a penalty ceases.

[158] See commentary on c. 1395, §2 for special particular law provisions in clerical sexual abuse of minors cases in the United States.

[159] Cf. _CCEO_ 1153.

§2. Having observed what is required, the same is valid if the penalty was imposed by extrajudicial decree.

This final canon deals with a complex canonical point warranting only a brief consideration given its lack of relevance in practice. One may distinguish between initiating 1) a criminal action leading to a decree or sentence penalizing an offender (c. 1362) and 2) a penal action to enforce the penalty determined in the criminal action (c. 1363).

Although an offender might be condemned for committing a delict, the judge may defer enforcing the penalty if certain pastoral goals can better be achieved otherwise. Furthermore, the observance of an expiatory penalty for a first offender might be suspended for the same reasons (c. 1344, 1° and 3°). When the penalty is deferred or its observance is suspended, the institute of prescription is also operative from the time the penal sentence is technically a definitively adjudged matter (*res iudicata*, c. 1641, §1). The same holds true for an administrative penal decree with due regard for the fact that the code does not explicitly envision such a decree's becoming technically a definitively adjudged matter (§2).

In other words, if three (or possibly five) years elapse after a penal sentence becomes a definitively adjudged matter and no judge has ordered the enforcement of the penalty (c. 1651), then no one can press the issue further. Such a provision is to ensure the legal security of the offender, who otherwise would be indefinitely liable to the penalty in question.

The present canon refers explicitly only to *ferendae sententiae* penalties since it mentions the condemnatory sentence. Technically there is no executory decree for *latae sententiae* penalties, which take effect upon commission of the delict, barring mitigating circumstances (c. 1324, §3). However, additional legal effects follow the formal declaration of such penalties (e.g., c. 1331, §2). Hence an executory decree seems warranted in such cases, and the ordinary rules on prescription also seem applicable there.

Part II
PENALTIES FOR INDIVIDUAL DELICTS
[cc. 1364–1399][160]

This second part of Book VI lists various delicts deemed serious enough to require similar treatment throughout the Church if its penal purposes are to be achieved, i.e., repairing scandal, restoring justice, and reforming the offender (c. 1341).[161] Instead of 101 canons on specific delicts (*CIC* 2314–2414), the present code contains only 35 canons organized under six titles as well as a concluding general norm penalizing legal violations not specifically sanctioned in the code.[162] Such titles reflect various values to be promoted in fostering the Church's mission. These values will be clarified when we examine individual delicts.

This part of the commentary will be briefer than part one, which seems somewhat more significant since it clarifies basic penal principles. We will briefly introduce the seven titles, comment on the relevant canons, and refer to pertinent canons elsewhere in the revised code or in its 1917 predecessor.[163]

This part of the code can be properly appreciated only by regularly referring to the commen-

---

[160] See the helpful reflections of Marzoa, in *Com Ex*, 461–467.

[161] Furthermore, infra-universal legislators such as bishops and episcopal conferences can penalize specific delicts other than those indicated here under certain conditions (e.g., cc. 1315–1318).

[162] The Eastern code contains slightly fewer delicts (*CCEO* 1436–1467). It neither systematically lists them under certain titles nor penalizes otherwise unsanctioned legal violations. The text will be referred to solely for comparison purposes. See Green, "Comparative Reflections," 435–441.

[163] The 1917 code will be considered in detail only if necessary to explain the current law or clarify significant differences from it.

tary on the substantive law contained elsewhere in the code. However, some brief reflections on that substantive law are necessary in explaining the penal canons addressing serious violations of that law.[164]

The commentary will briefly clarify the nature of the delict, indicate possible offenders, and note the pertinent penalties. As frequently noted, penal law must be interpreted strictly; hence, in doubt, the strictest possible understanding of a delict is to be followed (c. 18). Furthermore, the factors affecting imputability (cc. 1321–1330) and options for exercising penal discretion (cc. 1343–1346; 1349)[165] are constantly to be considered.

Individual delicts should be defined precisely so that the faithful are clear about the legislator's expectations regarding the observance of the law. This is important to protect the right of believers not to be deprived of their freedom except according to law (c. 221, §3). Generally the canons in this part of the code precisely define sanctionable behavior. However, occasionally this is not true, which makes legal interpretation somewhat difficult.[166]

TITLE I
DELICTS AGAINST RELIGION AND THE UNITY OF THE CHURCH
[cc. 1364–1369][167]

Apostasy, Heresy, and Schism[168]

Canon 1364 — §1. Without prejudice to the prescript of can. 194, §1, n. 2, an apostate from the faith, a heretic, or a schismatic incurs a *latae sententiae* excommunication; in addition, a cleric can be punished with the penalties mentioned in can. 1336, §1, nn. 1, 2, and 3.

§2. If contumacy of long duration or the gravity of scandal demands it, other penalties can be added, including dismissal from the clerical state.

Canon 751, not the present canon, defines heresy, apostasy, and schism, three different yet at times interrelated delicts. Heresy is an obstinate post-baptismal denial of or doubt concerning some truth which must be believed with divine and catholic faith. Apostasy means a total repudiation of the Catholic faith. Schism is the refusal of submission to the Supreme Pontiff or of communion with those subject to him (c. 209).

These very serious violations of ecclesial faith and communion warrant a *latae sententiae* excommunication.[169] The present formulation of the canon surfaced late in the revision process,[170] during most of which a *ferendae sententiae* excommunication had been envisioned. Although a *latae*

---

[164] Not all penalties for specific delicts are found in Book VI. For example, see cc. 1457 and 1489 on penalties for tribunal personnel, advocates, and procurators. Furthermore, penalties are specified for certain violations of papal election norms. See John Paul II, apconst *Universi dominici gregis,* February 22, 1996, nn. 55; 58; 78, *Origins* 25/37 (March 7, 1996) 626; 628.

[165] For example, the penal authority need not necessarily impose even obligatory *ferendae sententiae* penalties (c. 1344). Furthermore, if penalties are indeterminate, only relatively light penalties are generally in order; and perpetual penalties are prohibited (c. 1349). These observations will not be repeated throughout the commentary, which simply refers to these canons as appropriate.

[166] See, for example, cc. 1384 on illegitimately performing a priestly function or another sacred ministry and 1389 on abusing power and negligently harming another through an official ecclesiastical act.

[167] Besides the Münster commentary, see Borras, 159–172; Green, in *CLSA Com,* 920–921; Martin, in *CLSGBI Com,* 785–789; Rees, 426–439; various authors in *Com Ex,* 461–494.

[168] See *CCEO* 1436, 1 (heretic and apostate) and 1437 (schismatic).

[169] The penalty does not bind non-Catholics, whatever their doctrinal positions, since they are generally not bound by church law (c. 11). See numbers 19–20 of the May 14, 1967 SPCU ecumenical directory.

[170] For thoughtful reflections on this process, see Marzoa, in *Com Ex,* 470–474.

sententiae excommunication is presumably incurred for such delicts, church authorities must be sensitive to the complex theological-pastoral issues raised by these delicts.

At times it is difficult to determine precisely when an individual or group is canonically guilty of apostasy, heresy, or schism. This is especially true given increased theological pluralism, expanded contacts with other Christians and members of other religious traditions, and confessional boundaries not as sharply defined as formerly. Furthermore, penal measures may be inappropriate in dealing responsibly with persons so distancing themselves from the Church. It might be better simply to declare formally an incompatibility between their faith and that of the Church.

In any event, juridical certainty about such delicts presupposes a careful inquiry into the pertinent facts, especially the obstinate, external (c. 1330) rejection of a doctrine of faith (c. 750, §1) or ecclesial communion (c. 209). This is certainly warranted before any formal declaration of the penalty, only after which are all the effects of the excommunication verified (c. 1331, §2).[171]

On balance, the penalty should have remained *ferendae sententiae* in character as initially proposed, for the determination of doctrinal orthodoxy is a delicate enterprise, which has been publicized occasionally during the past decade due to formal investigations of various theologians, e.g., Boff, Curran, Drewermann. Yet, interestingly enough,

such theologians were not declared heretics although administrative measures were taken against them, e.g., withdrawal of mandate/ canonical mission to teach theology.

The most notable recent declaration of heresy involved the Sri Lankan theologian Tissa Balasuriya. This controversial CDF action in January 1997 raised various questions about the appropriate procedure in such doctrinal matters, the significance of the profession of faith, and the ecumenical appropriateness of such penal measures.[172] The relevant doctrinal issues can be dealt with constructively and various ecclesial values preserved only through workable procedures for regular informal, and perhaps formal, dialogue between the magisterium and various scholars.[173]

Occasionally special penalties bind clerics committing particularly serious delicts. Here additional expiatory prohibitions or privations (c. 1336, §1, 1°–3°) may be imposed on them besides the aforementioned excommunication (§1). Despite the basic equality of believers (c. 208), clerics have special institutional responsibilities; hence, their legal violations are especially serious delicts.

Furthermore, long-standing contumacy, or contempt for the law, or serious scandal undercutting the faith of believers may justify additional penal-

---

[171] See Doctrinal Congregation, "Regulations for Doctrinal Examination," June 29, 1997, *Origins* 27/13 (September 11, 1997) 221–224. These CDF regulations on reviewing possibly erroneous theological writings were specifically approved by the pope, which is necessary for a congregation to issue legislation. Article 28 provides for the congregation's declaration of a *latae sententiae* excommunication for heresy, apostasy, or schism after reviewing writings said to be "clearly and certainly erroneous," whose dissemination could gravely harm the faithful. Somewhat surprisingly, recourse against such a declaration is prohibited, contrary to the usual rule to protect the right of defense (c. 1353). Presumably the involvement of the pope, congregation officials and advisors, the author, and the author's ordinary precludes the need for such recourse. See Regulations, 23–24.

[172] For some pertinent documentation on the case see *Origins* 26/32 (January 30, 1997) 528–536. See also L. Örsy, "A Profession of Faith and an Excommunication in Ecumenical Perspective," *America* (February 22, 1997) 6–8; G. Read, "The Excommunication of Fr. Balasuriya, O.M.I.," *CLS-GBIN* no. 109 (March 1997) 24–29. Father Balasuriya was subsequently reconciled with the Church on January 15, 1998. See "Father Tissa Balasuriya's Reconciliation with the Church," *Origins* 27/32 (January 29, 1998) 529; 531–32.

[173] This complex issue can hardly be dealt with adequately here. See L. O'Donovan, ed., *Cooperation between Theologians and the Ecclesiastical Magisterium* (Washington, D.C.: CLSA, 1982). Subsequent discussions involving CLSA, CTSA, and NCCB representatives ultimately led to an official document on theologian-magisterium relationships. See NCCB, *Doctrinal Responsibilities Approaches to Promoting Cooperation and Resolving Misunderstandings between Bishops and Theologians* (Washington, D.C.: USCC, 1989).

ties for clerics including the last resort measure of dismissal from the clerical state (c. 1364, §2). The seriousness of the penalty is proportionate to the obstinacy of the offender and the seriousness of the ecclesial damage. The dismissal reflects the radical incompatibility between one's public ministerial commitment (c. 1008) and the notable and obstinate distancing of self from the Catholic communion.

Excommunication in principle does not entail the loss of ecclesiastical office but rather a prohibition of its exercise, sometimes with invalidating effects (c. 1331). However, any ecclesiastical office is lost as an administrative consequence of abandoning the Catholic communion (c. 194, §1, 2°).[174] Understandably the exercise of such an office presupposes a continuing commitment to the Catholic communion.

Prohibited Participation in Sacred Rites[175]

Canon 1365 — A person guilty of prohibited participation in sacred rites (*communicatio in sacris*) is to be punished with a just penalty.

The postconciliar period has witnessed the development of notably closer relationships between Catholics and members of other religious traditions, especially those in other Christian churches or ecclesial communities. Catholic ecumenical involvement, liturgical and otherwise, is subject to the direction of the college of bishops, the Holy See, individual bishops, and the episcopal conference (c. 755).

Given diverse ecumenical situations throughout the Church, the code understandably articulates only generic norms while leaving ample room for more specific lower level determinations. The cur-

rent canon was apparently deemed necessary to cope with serious ecumenical abuses, e.g., risk of indifferentism through indiscriminate sacramental sharing (*communicatio in sacris*). Yet, other than prohibited concelebration (c. 908), it is not entirely clear to what this penal text applies, for the significant canon 844 states general principles on permissible sacramental sharing but contains no explicit prohibitions.

Hence the vagueness of this canon poses problems for its responsible implementation. Like the preceding canon, it should be interpreted strictly lest legitimate options for sharing spiritual activities and resources be unduly jeopardized and the vitality of the ecumenical movement impaired.[176] The canon envisions an obligatory yet indeterminate *ferendae sententiae* penalty for clerics or laity violating the law (cc. 1344; 1349). Hence, the delict is viewed as notably less serious than apostasy, heresy, or schism.

Non-Catholic Baptism or Education of Children[177]

Canon 1366 — Parents or those who take the place of parents who hand over their children to be baptized or educated in a non-Catholic religion are to be punished with a censure or other just penalty.

Catholic parents, natural or adoptive, or their surrogates (e.g., foster parents) are primarily responsible for the religious initiation and formation of their children.[178] This canon penalizes a serious breach of those responsibilities by the free and deliberate handing over of children to be baptized and/or educated in a non-Catholic religious tradition.[179] Mere negligence in fulfilling those

---

[174] A member of a religious institute or society of apostolic life notoriously defecting from the Catholic faith is *ipso facto* dismissed from the institute (c. 694, 1°) or society (c. 746). For other implications of the delicts in c. 1364, see cc. 316 (public associations of the faithful), 1041, 2° and 1044, §1, 2° (irregularities for orders); 1071, 4° (permission for marriage); 1184, §1, 3° (ecclesiastical burial).

[175] Cf. *CCEO* 1440.

[176] See *Ecum Dir,* nn. 102–142, especially nn. 122–136 on sacramental sharing.

[177] Cf. *CCEO* 1439. For a thoughtful discussion of c. 1366, see J. Escriva Ivars, in *Com Ex,* 482–487.

[178] On the right and responsibility of parents to see to the baptism and education of their children, see cc. 867; 226, §2; 774, §2; 1136.

[179] This provision intends no disrespect for the spiritual values of other religious traditions. Rather, the code highlights the richness of the Catholic tradition and the par-

baptismal and educational responsibilities, however problematic morally, is not a delict. Furthermore, the preceptive (c. 1344), *ferendae sententiae* censure or other just penalty (c. 1349) envisioned here does not apply to parents or their surrogates who legitimately send their children to non-Catholic schools for various reasons (e.g., unavailability of a Catholic school) but share their Catholic faith with them.

Such a penal situation, however unlikely, would probably be relevant only in mixed marriages. One must also consider possible pressures on Catholic spouses including those making the requisite declarations and promises prior to a mixed marriage (c. 1125, 1°). A concern to foster marital and family harmony may lead the Catholic spouse to permit the baptism and/or education of the children in another church or ecclesial community. However, even in such difficult circumstances, the Catholic is still obliged to share the faith with the children.[180]

The discretion of the penal authority in assessing the situation is important here. The positive initiative, serious imputability, and bad faith of the Catholic parent(s) in handing over the children for non-Catholic baptism and/or education are key penal considerations. Yet intensive evangelization or catechetical efforts would likely foster ecclesial values more effectively than penalties.[181]

Violation of Sacred Species[182]

Canon 1367 — A person who throws away the consecrated species or takes or retains them for a sacrilegious purpose incurs a *latae sententiae* excommunication reserved to the Apostolic See; moreover, a cleric can be punished with another penalty, not excluding dismissal from the clerical state.

ents' sacramentally based obligation to share it with their children. Cavalier disregard for one's Catholic heritage is viewed as especially problematic.

[180] For a nuanced discussion of this issue, see *Ecum Dir,* n. 151.

[181] On the responsibility of pastors to support ecumenical marriages, see c. 1128.

[182] Cf. *CCEO* 1442.

This canon reflects the importance of reverence for the Eucharist, the summit and source of Christian worship and life (cc. 897–898). The present canon is the most serious of a series of canons penalizing deliberate and free violations of sacred realities, i.e., persons and objects.[183]

The canon envisions three possible delictual situations: disrespectfully throwing away the sacred species (usually consecrated hosts) or scattering them in an inappropriate place, intentionally taking them from the tabernacle for sacrilegious purposes (e.g., satanic ritual), or keeping them for such obscene purposes although they were obtained legitimately (e.g., at a Eucharist).[184]

The *latae sententiae* excommunication envisioned for any Catholic violating the law and the reservation of its remission to the Holy See[185] indicate the seriousness of the violation. Furthermore, clerics are especially obliged to foster eucharistic piety (cc. 246, §1; 276, §2, 2°; 898). Hence, they may be liable to additional discretionary *ferendae sententiae* penalties including dismissal from the clerical state for a very serious violation.

Perjury[186]

Canon 1368 — A person who commits perjury while asserting or promising something before ecclesiastical authority is to be punished with a just penalty.

This canon attempts to ensure the authenticity of ecclesial commitments and protect the integrity

[183] See also c. 1370 on physically attacking certain persons, c. 1376 on profaning sacred things, and c. 1380 on simoniacally celebrating or receiving the sacraments.

[184] Since the essence of the delict is disrespect for the Lord, it is not a delict if one inadvertently drops the consecrated host, keeps the Blessed Sacrament in his or her possession out of misguided devotion (c. 935), or fails to care properly for the tabernacle (c. 938).

[185] See also c. 1370, §1 on the delict of physically attacking the pope, whose remission is also reserved to the Holy See.

[186] Cf. *CCEO* 1444.

of church processes. Perjury means deliberately violating the serious obligation before God to tell the truth under oath (c. 1199, §1).[187] The breaking of such an oath violates the virtue of religion, which accounts for the placement of this canon here and not in title IV on crimes of falsehood (cc. 1390–1391).

The canon envisions two situations of Catholics knowingly and freely violating an oath, i.e., supporting an assertion or confirming a promise. For example, one may falsely take an oath confirming the truth of one's assertions in a formal case (c. 1532). Or a person may falsely promise to discharge faithfully a diocesan curial office (c. 471, 1°).[188]

The delict presupposes that the false assertion or promise is made knowingly and freely to a church authority figure functioning officially. Such perjury in a private context or in a civil law setting is not a delict, whatever its moral or civil law implications. Furthermore, there is no delict if one errs about the status of the person before whom one is swearing, if one fails to recognize the religious character of the oath, or if an inculpably ignorant person erroneously believes he or she is telling the truth.

The canon provides for a preceptive, indeterminate, *ferendae sententiae* penalty to be assessed according to the seriousness of the situation (cc. 1344; 1349).

Abuse of Church/Religion[189]

Canon 1369 — A person who in a public show or speech, in published writing, or in other uses of the instruments of social communication utters blasphemy, gravely injures good morals, expresses insults, or excites hatred or contempt against religion or the Church is to be punished with a just penalty.

Late in the revision process, the penal law committee thought that the code should address certain contemporary evils, particularly those directly and adversely affecting the Church's social order at a time of serious attacks on traditional moral values. This generically formulated, rather sweeping canon embodies such a concern.

The canon generically envisions four possible violations of church integrity or moral values. Blasphemy means deliberately speaking irreverently or contemptuously of God; at issue is the degrading character of a presentation and the potentially scandalous impact upon a group's religious sensibilities, e.g., incitement to evil. Also envisioned is an intentional attack on good morals, e.g., promotion of pornography. Third, the legislator prohibits direct attacks on religion or the Church even if no particular individual is insulted; and finally he penalizes behavior prompting hatred or contempt of religion or the Church.[190]

There is a distinctly public, external character about the aforementioned delicts (c. 1330). They involve the improper use of the media (e.g., radio, TV, or film)[191] or other public activity, e.g., a public gathering or a written publication. The context is such that the religious sensibilities of a significant number of persons may be grievously offended.

The code also provides here for a preceptive, indeterminate, *ferendae sententiae* penalty (cc. 1344; 1349). However laudable the legislator's intent, the practical relevance of this canon seems questionable because of its sweeping, imprecise character. Furthermore, one may wonder whether those normally guilty of such outrageous behavior would be significantly affected by such a penalty.

---

[187] For example, on the obligation to tell the truth in a formal case, see cc. 1531 (principals) and 1548, §1 (witnesses).

[188] Among other situations in which perjury may be possible in taking an oath, see cc. 380 (new bishop vis-à-vis Holy See); 1283, 1° (new administrator of church property); 1454 and 1455, §3 (tribunal personnel).

[189] Cf. *CCEO* 1448, §1.

[190] See also c. 1373 penalizing one publicly inciting animosities or hatred among the subjects of the Apostolic See or an ordinary because of an act of ecclesiastical power or ministry.

[191] On the importance of a human and Christian use of the media, see cc. 822–823.

TITLE II
DELICTS AGAINST ECCLESIASTICAL AUTHORITIES AND THE FREEDOM OF THE CHURCH
[cc. 1370–1377][192]

Physical Attacks on Religious Figures [193]

Canon 1370 — §1. A person who uses physical force against the Roman Pontiff incurs a *latae sententiae* excommunication reserved to the Apostolic See; if he is a cleric, another penalty, not excluding dismissal from the clerical state, can be added according to the gravity of the delict.

§2. A person who does this against a bishop incurs a *latae sententiae* interdict and, if he is a cleric, also a *latae sententiae* suspension.

§3. A person who uses physical force against a cleric or religious out of contempt for the faith, the Church, ecclesiastical power, or the ministry is to be punished with a just penalty.

The penal law committee rejected criticisms of the need for this canon given civil law provisions, its questionable effectiveness in deterring potential offenders, and its penalizing physical attacks only on clerics and religious, prescinding from other believers. There is a descending scale of penalties proportionate to the official ecclesial status of the victim of violence, of which the attacker must be aware.

The Church's public good is presumably harmed more or less seriously depending on the institutional dignity of the victim of physical (not verbal—c. 1369) violence. Clerics (c. 1008) represent the Church in a special way in exercising their public ministry, and religious represent a special gift for its mission given their public commitment (c. 573, §1).

Accordingly one of the few reserved *latae sententiae* excommunications punishes those intentionally doing physical violence to the *pope* for whatever reason given his preeminent ecclesial status (§1; cc. 331; 333, §1). He may be physically assaulted (e.g., shooting) or deprived of his freedom (e.g., abduction). If the attacker is a cleric, additional expiatory penalties may be warranted, including dismissal from the clerical state, depending on the seriousness of the delict.[194] Such penalties may be imposed even prescinding from the cessation of contumacy, which warrants the lifting of the excommunication.

Somewhat less serious penalties are envisioned for those physically attacking a *bishop* for whatever reason given his significant ecclesial status (§ 2; c. 375). Any attacker is subject to a *latae sententiae* interdict, and a cleric is also liable to a *latae sententiae* suspension.

A still less serious preceptive, indeterminate, *ferendae sententiae* penalty binds those deliberately attacking another *cleric* or *religious* physically (§3; cc. 1344; 1349).[195] Interestingly enough here, such an attack must be prompted by contempt for the faith, the Church, ecclesiastical power, or ministry. An attack motivated by other reasons (e.g., strong personal dislike), however morally problematic, is not technically a delict.

---

[194] Clerics are subject to additional penalties due to their special obligation of reverence for and obedience to the pope and their own ordinary (c. 273). In the Eastern code attacks on bishops warrant a preceptive "appropriate penalty" possibly including deposition, i.e., dismissal. However, attacks on patriarchs, metropolitans, and the pope warrant a major excommunication, reserved to the pope in the last instance (*CCEO* 1445, §1).

[195] The term "cleric" refers to bishops, priests, and deacons (cc. 207, §1; 1008–1009). The term "religious" means members of religious institutes (c. 607). Hence, nonclerical members of secular institutes or societies of apostolic life are technically not envisioned by the canon, which must be strictly interpreted (c. 18). The Eastern code, however, also penalizes physical attacks on members of a society of common life in the manner of religious as well as on lay persons exercising an ecclesiastical function (*CCEO* 1445, §2).

[192] Besides the Münster commentary, see Borras, 172–178; Green, in *CLSA Com,* 922–924; Martin, in *CLSGBI Com,* 789–793; Rees, 439–451; various authors in *Com Ex,* 495–525.

[193] Cf. *CCEO* 1445.

Doctrinal Violations

Canon 1371 — The following are to be punished with a just penalty:

1° in addition to the case mentioned in can. 1364, §1, a person who teaches a doctrine condemned by the Roman Pontiff or an ecumenical council or who obstinately rejects the doctrine mentioned in can. 750, §2 or in can. 752 and who does not retract after having been admonished by the Apostolic See or an ordinary;

Like canon 1364 on apostasy, heresy, and schism, this text requires careful interpretation given its broad formulation.[196] What is envisioned is the offender's persistent, deliberate refusal to comply with an authoritative warning to change an erroneous way of teaching or thinking. Such a warning is to be established by some document to be kept in the secret curial archive (c. 1339, §3).

The scope of the canon was expanded during the papal consultation prior to promulgation of the code. All prior drafts of the canon, including that approved by the October 1981 commission *Plenarium,* would have penalized only the teaching of a doctrine clearly condemned by the pope or an ecumenical council even if the doctrine were not technically heretical. However, the Latin code, unlike its Eastern counterpart (*CCEO* 1436, §2), refers also to the pertinacious rejection of a doctrine which calls not for an assent of faith (c. 750) but rather for religious submission (*obsequium*) of mind and will (c. 752). This latter response is appropriate because the doctrine in question is not proclaimed definitively as requiring an assent of faith.

The scope of this canon was further explicitated in a May 18, 1998 apostolic letter of John Paul II entitled *Ad tuendam fidem.*[197] The letter added a second paragraph to canon 750 of the Latin code

and canon 598 of its Eastern counterpart. The new paragraph calls for a firm acceptance and holding of whatever is proposed definitively by the magisterium regarding doctrine concerning faith and morals. According to the present canon, whoever obstinately rejects such a doctrine and does not retract after an official warning is also to be punished with a just penalty (cf. *CCEO* 1436, §2).[198]

The delict presupposes an exercise of authoritative magisterial teaching, not simply a private expression of a theological opinion by a bishop. The delict is viewed as considerably less serious than apostasy, heresy, or schism since it warrants only a preceptive, indeterminate, *ferendae sententiae* penalty (cc. 1344; 1349) instead of a *latae sententiae* excommunication (c. 1364, §1).[199]

The penalty for the doctrinal violations envisioned here should correspond to the seriousness of the ecclesial damage done by the offender's doctrinal obstinacy. The warning mentioned would be issued by the Apostolic See, i.e., CDF (*PB* 51–52) or an ordinary (c. 134). While the penalty for knowingly teaching a condemned doctrine probably affects only Catholic teachers, any Catholic may theoretically be penalized for deliberately rejecting such authoritative doctrine.

Actually, penal measures here may be decidedly counterproductive both in the Church and in the larger society. Regular magisterium-scholar-pastor dialogue rather than penal measures will more likely protect and foster the integrity of ecclesial faith and ensure appropriate freedom of in-

---

[196] See the commentary on cc. 749–754 regarding the complex doctrinal issues underlying this canon.

[197] See John Paul II, aplett *Ad tuendam fidem, Origins* 28/8 (July 16, 1998) 113; 115-116.

[198] For a more detailed discussion of the pertinent doctrinal issues, see the commentary on cc. 750 and 833.

[199] Fortunately the proposed penalty here is *ferendae sententiae* in character, unlike the *latae sententiae* provision in c. 1364. Hence, c. 1371, 1° envisions a judicial or administrative procedure hopefully facilitating a careful examination of the pertinent doctrinal issues. See CDF Regulations, art. 29, *Origins* 27/13 (September 11, 1997) 222–223. Unlike the less serious indeterminate penalty here, the 1917 code required the removal of faculties to preach and hear confessions, removal from any teaching office, and other penalties deemed necessary to repair scandal (*CIC* 2317).

quiry and expression for those engaged in the sacred disciplines (c. 218).[200]

Disobedience of Legitimate Church Authority

2° a person who otherwise does not obey a legitimate precept or prohibition of the Apostolic See, an ordinary, or a superior and who persists in disobedience after a warning.

Canon 1371 likewise envisions an obligatory, indeterminate, *ferendae sententiae* penalty in the case of free and deliberate disobedience of ecclesiastical superiors functioning according to law (cc. 1344; 1349).[201] Such law includes the constitutions of religious institutes, secular institutes, and societies of consecrated life.[202] This number of canon 1371 is somewhat vaguely formulated and could possibly lead to certain abuses. The code here envisions a serious breach of ecclesiastical discipline involving an obstinate failure to comply with a legitimate prescription (e.g., taking an assignment) or prohibition of church authority (e.g., cessation of political activity) even after a formal warning.

---

[200] For some thoughtful theological reflections on c. 1371, 1°, see J. Boyle, *Church Teaching Authority: Historical and Theological Studies* (Notre Dame, Ind.: University of Notre Dame, 1995) 117–118. Boyle is concerned about the canon's insufficiently nuanced approach to violations of c. 752, which embraces a wide range of papal or episcopal teaching and implies the commitment of teaching authority in varying degrees (*LG* 25). Canon 1371, 1° does not seem to take sufficient cognizance of sophisticated theological distinctions (e.g., the tradition of theological notes) and seems to impede legitimate dissent from the teaching of the ordinary magisterium. See also A. Naud, *Un Aggiornamento et Son Eclipse* (n.p.: Fides, 1996) 141–142.

[201] On the basic Christian obligation to obey one's sacred pastors as teachers of the faith and rulers of the Church, see c. 212, §1. On the special clerical obligation of reverence for and obedience to the Supreme Pontiff and one's own ordinary, see c. 273.

[202] On the counsel of obedience of "religious," see c. 601. The Eastern code requires only an appropriate penalty for disobedience of one's hierarch (*CCEO* 1446).

Recourse against Pope

Canon 1372 — A person who makes recourse against an act of the Roman Pontiff to an ecumenical council or the college of bishops is to be punished with a censure.

This somewhat perplexing canon, without an Eastern code counterpart, emerged late in the revision process. It apparently reflects the serious intra-ecclesial conflict of the conciliarist period of the fifteenth century. In contrast, despite certain tensions, there has been very fruitful, contemporary papal-episcopal collaboration, especially during Vatican II and subsequent episcopal synods.

The canon's basic rationale is the denial of papal primacy (cc. 331 and 333, §1). Such recourse would create the impression of an ecclesial authority higher than the pope. Deliberate recourse against him to either the ecumenical council (cc. 337–341) or the college of bishops (c. 336) would represent an illegitimate effort to separate him from an integral and preeminent relationship with his brother bishops. Such an effort is technically impossible given our theological-canonical understanding of papal-episcopal relationships.

Canon 1372 generically refers to "making recourse against an act of the Roman Pontiff," not a curial act unless it were specifically approved by the pope. Since the term "recourse" (*recurrit*) must be strictly interpreted (c. 18), the canon seems to envision an act of *administrative* papal governance as distinct from judicial[203] or legislative governance.[204]

The code speaks generically of a preceptive (c. 1344), *ferendae sententiae* censure rather than a reserved *latae sententiae* excommunication as in

---

[203] On the impossibility of an appeal or recourse against a papal sentence or decree, see c. 333, §3. For other pertinent canons in the judicial arena, see cc. 1404; 1405, §2; and 1629, 1°.

[204] See Marzoa, in *Com Ex,* 504–508, who adopts an unduly broad view of the delict as also encompassing appeals against papal sentences.

the 1917 code (*CIC* 2332). An excommunication or interdict might be imposed for clerics or laity or a suspension for clerics depending on the seriousness of the issue. This is the only canon providing solely for an unspecified censure.

Opposition to Church Authority [205]

Canon 1373 — A person who publicly incites among subjects animosities or hatred against the Apostolic See or an ordinary because of some act of power or ecclesiastical ministry or provokes subjects to disobey them is to be punished by an interdict or other just penalties.

The next three canons deal with illegitimate opposition to church authority, which might significantly jeopardize the Church's threefold mission.

One can appreciate the legitimate concern to protect the unimpeded exercise of church authority, which is essential to the common good. However, this canon's concern to repress destructive hostility to church institutions must be interpreted judiciously. Otherwise a responsible expression of opinion regarding their effectiveness might be arbitrarily curtailed. Yet this is indispensable if the Church is adequately to fulfill its mission amid changing pastoral circumstances (c. 212, §2–3).[206]

The canon differentiates between two delictual situations, which might involve any Catholic[207] inciting those subject to authority to insubordination or disobedience. First of all one may deliberately stir up hostility to the Apostolic See or an ordinary (c. 134) because of some act of power or ecclesiastical ministry, e.g., the closing of a parish (c. 515, §2). The second situation does not neces-

sarily involve a specific act of governance but rather entails provoking disobedience to the aforementioned authorities. In both instances the canon requires a certain success of the conspiratorial efforts. Thus hostility to church authority must be generated in the first case, and actual disobedience must occur in the second instance.

The conspiratorial mindset differentiates the present delict from the simple disobedience of canon 1371, 2°. The former may have more detrimental ecclesial consequences than the latter because of the fostering of a general climate of public insubordination. Hence, the provision for a preceptive, *ferendae sententiae* interdict or other just penalties (cc. 1344; 1349).

Membership in Forbidden Societies [208]

Canon 1374 — A person who joins an association which plots against the Church is to be punished with a just penalty; however, a person who promotes or directs an association of this kind is to be punished with an interdict.

This canon was added during the revision of the original schema at the request of the CDF. The code notably simplifies its 1917 predecessor, which explicitly condemned the Masons and also mentioned plotting against civil powers (*CIC* 2335). Furthermore, the 1983 code is formulated rather generically, neither providing special penalties for clerics or religious nor requiring their denunciation to the then Holy Office (*CIC* 2336).

However, the 1983 code, unlike its Eastern counterpart, differentiates between simple membership (just penalty) and the deliberate promoting of or holding office in a society plotting against the Church (interdict). Since the latter activities are presumably more ecclesially detrimental, they require a somewhat more severe penalty. Both penalties are preceptive (c. 1344), indeterminate (c. 1349), and *ferendae sententiae* in character unlike the former *latae sententiae* excommunication simply reserved to the Holy See. The delict pre-

---

[205] Cf. *CCEO* 1447, §1.

[206] Ongoing critique of the law is integral to church reform. See J. Provost, "Canon Law: True or False Reform in the Church," *J* 38 (1978) 257–267; J. Coriden, "Law in Service to the People of God," *J* 41 (1981) 1–20.

[207] For the view that the offender is an authority figure such as a pastor inciting his subjects to insubordination or disobedience of higher authority, see Borras, 175–176, and Martin, 791.

[208] Cf. *CCEO* 1448, §2.

supposes that the offender is duly aware of the society's hostile attitude toward the Church.

These developments reflect changing historical circumstances and diverse ecclesial conditions, especially but not exclusively regarding the anti-ecclesial nature of the Masons. If they or other groups actively plot against the Church, this canon is possibly relevant.

In this connection one might note an official development at the time of promulgation of the code. During the revision process various bishops, especially from Germany, sought an explicit condemnation of the Masons because of their anti-ecclesial stance. However, both the commission secretariat and the October 1981 *Plenarium* rejected this proposal since the problem was not perceived to be a universal one warranting a general provision.

Somewhat surprisingly, just before the code took effect, a CDF declaration, which did not technically have the force of law, indicated that Catholic Masons are involved in serious sin and are barred from the Eucharist.[209] This judgment was based on the alleged irreconcilability of Masonic principles and Catholic doctrine. The declaration also precluded contrary episcopal judgments mitigating the force of the CDF declaration. This posture seems somewhat contrary to earlier CDF pronouncements apparently open to recognizing the differences in various Masonic associations while opposing formal episcopal conference pronouncements on the general nature of such associations.

The complex implications of this issue have prompted different canonical opinions.[210] However, in dealing with practical questions that may arise, one must interpret the pertinent penal law strictly (e.g., cc. 1364 and 1374) with due regard for the factors affecting imputability (cc. 18; 1323–1327). Such prudence is also necessary in practically judging the serious sinfulness of Masonic affiliation, especially by one in good faith. The traditional principles of moral theology are pertinent here.

Furthermore, every effort should be made to clarify the precise nature of Masonic associations throughout the world to assist local church authorities in prudently assessing membership in such groups. Only such authorities seem able to clarify precisely whether a given society actively plots against the Church.

Violations of Church Freedom [211]

Canon 1375 — Those who impede the freedom of ministry, of election, or of ecclesiastical power or the legitimate use of sacred goods or other ecclesiastical goods or who greatly intimidate an elector, one elected, or one who exercises ecclesiastical power or ministry can be punished with a just penalty.

This generically formulated canon also attempts to ensure the free exercise of various significant ecclesial functions. While this goal is laudable, the canon seems somewhat difficult to interpret because of its sweeping and generic character. The implementation of the law might be facilitated if the sanctionable legal violations were more precisely delineated.[212] Furthermore, those most likely to hinder the Church's mission may not even be Catholics subject to this legislation, e.g., governmental or military figures persecuting the Church in areas of notable Church-State conflict.

There are two general types of delicts here. First of all, one may deliberately and successfully obstruct the exercise of ecclesiastical ministry, authority,[213] or office, the holding of ecclesiastical elections (c. 170), and finally the legitimate use of sacred goods (c. 1171) or other ecclesiastical goods (c. 1257, §1).[214] Furthermore, one may deliberately and seriously intimidate those involved

---

209 *Origins* 13/27 (November 15, 1983) 450.

210 See R. Jenkins, "The Evolution of the Church's Prohibition against Catholic Membership in Freemasonry," *J* 56/2 (1996) 735–755. Also Marzoa, in *Com Ex,* 512–517.

211 Cf. *CCEO* 1447, §2.

212 For example, various penalties are specified for violations in connection with the papal election. See supra, n. 164.

213 For example, see c. 1401 affirming the Church's proper and exclusive right to judge certain cases.

214 See c. 1254, §1 on the Church's claim to legitimate freedom in disposing of its temporal goods.

in ecclesiastical elections (c. 172, 1°) or exercising ecclesiastical power or ministry.

Since the code envisions only a discretionary, indeterminate, *ferendae sententiae* penalty, these possible delicts are probably not viewed as especially urgent concerns (cc. 1343; 1349).

Profanation of Sacred Things[215]

Canon 1376 — A person who profanes a movable or immovable sacred object is to be punished with a just penalty.

This canon should be read in relationship to other violations of sacred realities: canons 1367 on desecrating the sacred species, 1370 on attacking certain clerics and religious, and 1380 on simoniacally celebrating or receiving the sacraments. A concern for reverence for sacred objects (c. 1171) underlies this provision. Sacred things are those destined for divine worship through their dedication or consecration, be they immovable, e.g., church, or movable, e.g., chalice. They are to be treated reverently and are not to be used for profane or inappropriate use even if owned by private persons.[216]

The seriousness of the preceptive, indeterminate, *ferendae sententiae* penalty obviously should correspond to the gravity of the delict (cc. 1344; 1349). At issue is deliberately putting such objects to profane, common, or sordid use for a time contrary to their cultic orientation. The sacred character of the object, the offender's sacrilegious intent, and possible scandal of the faithful are to be considered in assessing imputability.

Unlawful Alienation of Church Property[217]

Canon 1377 — A person who alienates ecclesiastical goods without the prescribed permission is to be punished with a just penalty.

---

[215] Cf. *CCEO* 1441.
[216] However, the delict is not verified if church authorities have authorized the profane (non-sacral) but not sordid use of such objects, e.g., cc. 1210; 1212.
[217] Cf. *CCEO* 1449.

A concern for fiscal accountability in administering church resources gives rise to possible penalties for those deliberately violating the norms on alienating ecclesiastical goods (c. 1257, §1) by not obtaining the requisite permission of the competent authority.[218] What is envisioned is transferring the ownership of goods constituting the stable patrimony of a public juridic person (c. 116, §1).

The current law leaves the determination of the seriousness of the delict up to the competent penal authority. Theoretically any Catholic can be liable to the preceptive, indeterminate, *ferendae sententiae* penalty envisioned here (cc. 1344; 1349). However, practically speaking, the offender would probably be an authority figure administering the goods of a public juridic person and deliberately disregarding the norms on the aforementioned permission.[219] Nevertheless, inculpable ignorance of such norms, while not presumed (c. 15, §2), exempts one from penal imputability.

TITLE III
USURPATION OF ECCLESIASTICAL FUNCTIONS AND DELICTS IN THEIR EXERCISE
[cc. 1378–1389][220]

While this title mentions both usurping ecclesiastical functions and delicts in their exercise, only one canon deals with such usurpation (c. 1381). Most canons penalize serious violations of

---

[218] On the alienation of church property, see cc. 1291–1296 esp. c. 1292 on such permission. On the property of religious, see c. 638, §3–§4.
[219] Such action by church administrators seems to be a breach of their fiduciary responsibilities (c. 1284) and may constitute an abuse of office warranting its privation (c. 1389, §1). For a possible, but probably unlikely, non-penal ecclesiastical action against one invalidly alienating ecclesiastical goods, see c. 1296.
[220] Besides the Münster commentary, see Borras, 178–189; Green, in *CLSA Com,* 924–927; Martin, in *CLSGBI Com,* 794–800; Rees, 452–467; various authors in *Com Ex,* 526–563.

public ecclesial trust especially regarding sacramental ministry.

Delicts involving the sacrament of penance are especially prominent, e.g., cc. 1378 on absolving an accomplice and simulating the sacrament, 1387 on solicitation in confession, and 1388 on the seal (secret) of confession.[221]

Absolution of Accomplice [222]

Canon 1378 — §1. A priest who acts against the prescript of can. 977 incurs a *latae sententiae* excommunication reserved to the Apostolic See.

Canon 1378 penalizes particularly serious eucharistic and penitential abuses violating the sacramental rights of believers (c. 213). The most serious delict meriting a reserved excommunication involves an authorized priest knowingly attempting to absolve his accomplice of either sex in an external sexual sin[223] (§ 1). Such an absolution is invalid except in danger of death, in which case it is valid even if another priest is available. The pastoral urgency of the situation is the prevailing legal consideration here.

To incur the penalty, the priest need not know the invalidity of such an absolution; it suffices that he knows he may not absolve his accomplice from their joint sexual sin. If the priest hears the confession but does not attempt to absolve his accomplice from the sexual sin or does not recognize the penitent as his accomplice, there is no delict. Sins other than the sexual sin in question do not fall under the invalidating and penal provisions.

The reason for these measures is the impropriety of the confessor's absolving one in whose sin

he has shared whenever it occurred. This sinful complicity violates the integrity of the priest-penitent relationship, the fostering of which is a key value underlying the canons on penance. Furthermore, the faithful should be protected from being deceived when they seek the Church's sacramental ministry. The seriousness of the delict is clear because it is one of only five excommunications reserved to the Holy See. One may wonder, however, why only sexual sins are envisioned, since sinful complicity in other areas may be more ecclesially detrimental, e.g., collusion in unjust treatment of church workers.

Simulation of Eucharist/Penance [224]

§2. The following incur a *latae sententiae* penalty of interdict or, if a cleric, a *latae sententiae* penalty of suspension:
    1° a person who attempts the liturgical action of the eucharistic sacrifice though not promoted to the sacerdotal order;
    2° apart from the case mentioned in §1, a person who, though unable to give sacramental absolution validly, attempts to impart it or who hears sacramental confession.
§3. In the cases mentioned in §2, other penalties, not excluding excommunication, can be added according to the gravity of the delict.

Canon 1378, §2 mentions two violations of the rules on properly differentiating sacramental functions. Number one penalizes those who are not priests who violate canon 900, §1 on the valid celebrant of the Eucharist. Such persons would have to recite the eucharistic prayer deliberately including the words of institution so that others would conclude erroneously that the Eucharist was being celebrated.[225]

---

[221] For various penalties outside Book VI prompted by a lack of professional accountability in ecclesiastical processes, see cc. 1457; 1470, §2; 1488–1489.

[222] Cf. *CCEO* 1457.

[223] On the difficulty of interpreting the phrase "sin against the sixth commandment of the Decalogue" used throughout the code, see the commentary on c. 1395, §2. For helpful reflections on c. 1378, see De Paolis, in *Com Ex*, 526–534.

[224] Cf. *CCEO* 1443.

[225] This sanction might apply to those involved in "feminist liturgies." See also c. 907 prohibiting deacons and laity from saying prayers and performing actions proper to the priest celebrant.

Number two penalizes those violating canons 965–975 on confessional faculties who deliberately attempt to impart sacramental absolution or simply pretend to hear confessions without such an attempt. In other words, the offender intentionally fosters the erroneous impression that penitents may be absolved of their sins.

This may rarely be a real issue, especially given the broad confessional faculties for priests (c. 967, §2). Furthermore, two other canons providing for valid absolution in certain pastoral contingencies are pertinent here, i.e., canon 144, §2 on common error or positive and probable doubt about such faculties and canon 976 on absolution in danger of death. In neither instance are the penalties specified here incurred.

Canon 1378 differentiates between clerics and lay people regarding the censure for such violations. Deacons in numbers one and two and priests without appropriate faculties in number two are subject to a *latae sententiae* suspension. Lay people incur a *latae sententiae* interdict.[226] Yet, to foster the aforementioned values, the offender may also be subject to other just penalties, including an excommunication, depending on the seriousness of the violation. This is the only discretionary excommunication in the code.

Other Sacramental Simulations [227]

Canon 1379 — In addition to the cases mentioned in can. 1378, a person who simulates the administration of a sacrament is to be punished with a just penalty.

A similar concern for liturgical integrity and the sacramental rights of believers underlies this generic canon penalizing a deliberately simulated or inauthentic celebration of sacraments other than penance and the Eucharist. For example, a lay health care minister attempts to anoint the sick (c. 1003, §1).[228]

The preceptive, indeterminate, *ferendae sententiae* penalty provision indicates that the legislator views such violations as less serious than the preceding eucharistic and penitential violations given the ecclesial centrality of such sacraments (cc. 1344; 1349).

Simony and Sacraments [229]

Canon 1380 — A person who celebrates or receives a sacrament through simony is to be punished with an interdict or suspension.

Unlike its predecessor (*CIC* 727), the code does not define sacramental simony.[230] It means an explicit or implicit and externally manifest agreement whereby one party deliberately agrees to confer a sacrament on another in exchange for some temporal good, e.g., money or property. The delict essentially is the deliberate intent to equalize the spiritual and the temporal, i.e., to deal commercially in sacred things. However, this is not verified regarding the legally regulated offerings of the faithful for the celebration of the Eucharist or other sacraments (cc. 945–958; 1264).

Concerns about precluding irreverence toward the Church's salvific mysteries underlie these penalties for those involved in the simoniacal celebration or reception of the sacrament.[231] How-

---

[226] See cc. 1041, 6° and 1044, §1, 3° declaring irregular for receiving or exercising orders one placing an act of episcopal or presbyteral orders while lacking the order.

[227] Cf. *CCEO* 1443.

[228] On simulating marital consent, see c. 1101. This means positively excluding marriage itself or one of its essential elements or properties (c. 1056).

[229] Cf. *CCEO* 1461. Unlike the Latin code, the Eastern code also penalizes the simoniacal provision of ecclesiastical office (*CCEO* 1462). On the invalidating effect of such a provision except for the papacy, see c. 149, §3; *CCEO* 946; *Universi dominici gregis,* 78.

[230] On different aspects of simony, see J. Abbo and J. Hannan, *The Sacred Canons* (St. Louis: B. Herder, 1952) 1: 723–733.

[231] See also the comparable c. 1385 on trafficking in Mass offerings.

ever, an arrangement for a third party to celebrate or receive a sacrament is not technically a delict.

The legislator envisions a preceptive (c. 1344), *ferendae sententiae* interdict or suspension for simoniacal celebration or reception of the sacraments. The former penalty may affect clerics and laity while the latter envisions only clerics.[232]

Usurpation of Ecclesiastical Office[233]

Canon 1381 — §1. Whoever usurps an ecclesiastical office is to be punished with a just penalty.

§2. Illegitimate retention of a function after its privation or cessation is equivalent to usurpation.

The realization of the Church's mission presupposes an orderly provision and exercise of various offices. Such order is seriously jeopardized by violations of the rules on their provision.[234] This is especially true for illegitimate attempts to assume an office on one's own initiative without the intervention of the competent authority even if such a claim is not recognized (§1). A preceptive, indeterminate, *ferendae sententiae* penalty is warranted in such cases (cc. 1344; 1349).

The orderly transfer of authority crucial to ecclesial life is also impeded by individuals who deliberately and illegally retain a function (*munus*) after being deprived of it (§2)[235] or losing it, e.g., expiration of term, removal, or transfer.[236] A preceptive, indeterminate, *ferendae sententiae* penalty is also envisioned for a former officeholder usurping a vacant office in such a fashion, e.g., a removed pastor refusing to leave the rectory and fa-

cilitate a smooth transition to his successor (cc. 1747, §1; 1344; 1349).

Unauthorized Episcopal Consecration[237]

Canon 1382 — A bishop who consecrates someone a bishop without a pontifical mandate and the person who receives the consecration from him incur a *latae sententiae* excommunication reserved to the Apostolic See.

This delict concerning a major violation of hierarchical communion was added during the revision of the original schema. Perhaps the increasingly intense Holy See–Archbishop Lefebvre conflict in the late 1970s and early 1980s especially influenced this development.[238] The present canon reflects the pope's central leadership role within the college of bishops, the notable ecclesial significance of the episcopal office, and the importance of close papal-episcopal relationships for orderly church government.[239] The seriousness of this violation is evident in its being one of only five *latae sententiae* excommunications reserved to the Holy See.

---

[232] The Eastern code views simony more seriously than its Latin counterpart. For the former distinguishes between simony regarding holy orders warranting deposition (dismissal) of the clerics involved, and the other sacraments requiring an appropriate penalty, possibly a major excommunication (*CCEO* 1461).

[233] Cf. *CCEO* 1462.

[234] Canons 146–183.

[235] Canons 196; 1336, §1, 2°; 1342, §2; 1389, §1; 1396.

[236] See cc. 184–196 on the loss of church office and cc. 1740–1752 on the removal and transfer of pastors.

[237] Cf. *CCEO* 1459, §1. The Eastern code differs from its Latin counterpart in two respects. The former speaks of a "mandate of the competent authority" rather than a "pontifical mandate" given varied Eastern episcopal selection procedures. Furthermore, the former does not reserve the major excommunication to the Holy See.

[238] However, on April 9, 1951 a Holy Office decree specified a *latae sententiae* excommunication for illegitimate episcopal consecrations in China after the Communist takeover had seriously impeded communications with the Holy See. See *CLD* 3, 649. For a thoughtful examination of such consecrations and the possible exemption from a penalty of those involved due to extreme governmental pressure, see G. King, "The Catholic Church in China: A Canonical Evaluation," *J* 49 (1989) 69–94.

[239] On the pope's central leadership role within the episcopal college, see cc. 330–331; 336. For the pontifical mandate required prior to an episcopal consecration, see cc. 1013 and 377, §1. Also relevant are the new bishop's obligatory profession of faith and oath of fidelity to the Apostolic See (c. 380).

If the consecration is valid, both the principal consecrating bishop and the consecrated bishop engaging knowingly and freely in the episcopal consecration liturgy without the pontifical mandate are subject to the *latae sententiae* excommunication. Co-consecrating bishops technically do not commit the delict of consecrating without a mandate since their complicity is not necessary theologically or canonically for the validity of the consecration (cc. 18; 1329, §2). However, if they participate knowingly and freely, they may be subject to a *latae sententiae* excommunication for schism (c. 751).[240]

This and the following canon are the only two canons explicitly penalizing bishops although theoretically they could commit most of the delicts specified in Book VI.[241]

Illicit Presbyteral or Diaconal Ordination [242]

Canon 1383 — A bishop who, contrary to the prescript of can. 1015, ordains without legitimate dimissorial letters someone who is not his subject is prohibited for a year from conferring the order. The person who has received the ordination, however, is ipso facto suspended from the order received.

This is the other canon explicitly penalizing a bishop. Without explanation it appeared first in the 1980 schema. The canon attempts to protect the right of the faithful to competent ministry by ensuring appropriate accountability in admitting candidates to the diaconate and the priesthood. An ordaining bishop other than a candidate's proper ordinary (cc. 1016; 1019) presumably does not know the candidate as well as the latter. Accordingly, dimissorial letters testifying to the candidate's suitability for ordination (cc. 1050–1051) are to be forwarded by the proper ordinary to the ordaining bishop.

If the latter knowingly ordains the candidate without such dimissorials (c. 1015), he may not confer the order[243] for a year. This is the only *latae sententiae* expiatory penalty in Book VI. Only such penalties, unlike censures, can be incurred for a specified time (c. 1336, §1). While the penalty automatically ceases after the year has elapsed, if the bishop seeks its remission sooner, the pope or his delegate must intervene (c. 1405, §1, 3°).

The candidate knowingly receiving diaconate or priesthood without proper dimissorials is subject to a *latae sententiae* suspension from exercising the order in question until he ceases being contumacious.

Other Instances of Illegitimate Sacred Ministry

Canon 1384 — In addition to the cases mentioned in cann. 1378–1383, a person who illegitimately performs a priestly function or another sacred ministry can be punished with a just penalty.

Despite criticism during the revision process of the sweeping, rather unfocused character of this canon[244] and canon 1389 on abuse of office, they are restated unchanged in the code.

---

[240] The *latae sententiae* excommunication of Archbishop Lefebvre for consecrating without a pontifical mandate and the similar penalty for schism of his co-consecrator were formally declared by the CFB on July 1, 1988. See *Origins* 18 (1988) 151. On the establishment of the papal commission *Ecclesia Dei* to reconcile members and associates of the Lefebvre-inspired Priestly Fraternity of St. Pius X, see John Paul II, aplett *Ecclesia Dei adflicta,* July 7, 1988, *Origins* 18 (1988) 149–152. For pertinent documents on the Lefebvre affair, see O. Bucci, "Lo scisma di Lefebvre," *Apol* 61 (1988) 529– 555.

[241] J. Huels, "The Correction and Punishment of a Diocesan Bishop," *J* 49 (1989) 507–542. Only the pope or his delegate may judge bishops in penal matters (c. 1405, §1, 3°).

[242] Cf. *CCEO* 1459, §2.

[243] A strict interpretation (c. 18) of the singular Latin term *ordinem* means that the bishop is prohibited from conferring only the order in question and not all orders as Martin affirms (797).

[244] This canon raises questions about the relevance of the basic Christian right not to be penalized except according to law (c. 221, §3). How can one defend oneself when the legislator so minimally articulates the profile of the delict? The judge or ordinary conducting the penal process assumes an unduly significant determinative role here.

Two significant values must be considered in interpreting both canons. First of all, the faithful have a right to expect ministerial accountability from clerics[245] occupying positions of public trust. Second, such ministers deserve a clear description of their responsibilities lest they be uncertain about the Church's expectations of them. They also have a right not to be subject to arbitrary penal discretion, which may significantly restrict their exercise of office and impair their reputation. Accordingly, precise norms on ministerial accountability should be articulated as far as possible, reflecting both the code's expectations and possibly more detailed particular law provisions given local pastoral circumstances.[246]

The canon specifies a discretionary, indeterminate, *ferendae sententiae* penalty for illegitimately exercising the sacred ministry in areas other than those specified in canons 1378–1383. Hence, such violations are hardly viewed as seriously as the delicts addressed in those canons. Serious penalties such as censures are generally to be avoided, and perpetual penalties such as deprivation of office are prohibited (c. 1349). Furthermore, the penalty may also be tempered or replaced by a penance (cc. 1343; 1340).

Trafficking in Mass Offerings

Canon 1385 — A person who illegitimately makes a profit from a Mass offering is to be punished with a censure or another just penalty.

A need to foster reverence for the Eucharist and preclude the commercializing of sacred realities[247] accounts for this generically formulated canon penalizing trafficking in Mass offerings. Such "trafficking" means profiting unlawfully

from the money or goods received for the celebration of Mass. With due regard for the legitimacy of such offerings (c. 945), this canon seems to penalize deliberate violations of the following canons among others: canon 947 prohibiting any appearance of trafficking in or trading Mass offerings and canon 948 requiring that as many Masses be celebrated as offerings are accepted, thereby prohibiting the illegitimate accumulation of such offerings.[248] The present canon also seems to apply to canon 955, §1. The latter requires that in transferring Mass offerings the entire sum received is to be forwarded unless any excess over the offering determined by law or custom is clearly intended to benefit the recipient of the original offerings.

The preceptive, *ferendae sententiae* censure or other just penalty for various violations is to be proportionate to their seriousness, e.g., risk of "scandalizing" the faithful and damage to the institutional Church (cc. 1344; 1349). Presumably priests are normally envisioned as possible violators of the pertinent canons. However, lay administrators of pious causes might seriously violate their ecclesial trust regarding the disposition of such offerings (c. 956).

Bribery of Church Official[249]

Canon 1386 — A person who gives or promises something so that someone who exercises a function in the Church will do or omit something illegitimately is to be punished with a just penalty; likewise, the one who accepts such gifts or promises.

An understandable concern for integrity in exercising ecclesiastical office underlies this canon, which penalizes deliberate attempts to influence ecclesiastical officials to act illegally by doing or omitting something. Such deliberate efforts to subvert the faithful discharging of ecclesiastical

---

[245] The references to a "priestly function" or another "sacred ministry" seem to restrict the canon's applicability to clerics (c. 207, §1) although numerous lay persons fulfill various ecclesiastical functions and ministries.

[246] Green, "Penal Law Revisited," 197–198.

[247] Such concerns underlie the provisions on Mass offerings in cc. 945–958.

[248] See CFC, decr *Mos iugiter,* February 22, 1991, *AAS* 83 (1991) 443–446. English translation in *Origins* 20 (1991) 705–706.

[249] Cf. *CCEO* 1463.

responsibilities might occasion a betrayal of public ecclesial trust.

The delict requires a definite link between the gift (e.g., cash) or promise of a future gift (e.g., stock options) and a desired future illegal course of action or inaction. However, payment of an officeholder after such illegal activity does not constitute a delict, however morally questionable. The just penalty must be imposed even if the attempted bribery fails and the officeholder does not break the law, e.g., by violating appropriate chancery secrecy (c. 471, 2°).[250]

Canon 1386 provides for a preceptive (c. 1344), indeterminate (c. 1349), *ferendae sententiae* penalty for the one bribing a church official (active bribery) as well as the official accepting the bribe, whether or not it leads to illegal behavior (passive bribery). Obviously any believer could be guilty of active bribery, while only an officeholder can be guilty of passive bribery. Furthermore, the bribed officeholder may commit another delict if the illegal activity itself constitutes a delict, e.g., various tribunal violations in c. 1457, §1.

Solicitation in Confession[251]

Canon 1387 — A priest who in the act, on the occasion, or under the pretext of confession solicits a penitent to sin against the sixth commandment of the Decalogue is to be punished, according to the gravity of the delict, by suspension, prohibitions, and privations; in graver cases he is to be dismissed from the clerical state.

Concerns about the integrity of the priest-penitent relationship underlie this canon on solicitation, the following one on the confessional seal,

and canon 1378 punishing absolution of an accomplice and other penitential violations.

There are some noteworthy differences between the present canon and the 1917 code, which obliged the solicited penitent to denounce the offending priest (*CIC* 904) and penalized both the soliciting priest and the penitent knowingly failing to denounce him (*CIC* 2368).

First of all, the current law on penance neither obliges the solicited penitent to denounce the soliciting priest nor requires another confessor to advise the one solicited of such an obligation.

Second, unlike the 1917 code, the present canon describes the circumstances of solicitation even if not its precise meaning. It is a deliberate invitation by the priest to commit a serious sin against the sixth commandment.[252] The delict could happen during the sacramental celebration, immediately before or after it, or in a setting in which the penitent could reasonably expect the hearing of his or her confession.

The delict is essentially the solicitation itself, and the penitent need not necessarily welcome the priest's abusive sexual overture. Furthermore, the delict might also be verified if the solicited sexual activity involves the penitent and a third party, not necessarily the priest and the penitent.

Third, like the canons on penance, the present canon does not refer to the penitent knowingly failing to denounce an offending priest. The code penalizes only the soliciting priest according to the seriousness of the delict. While the *ferendae sententiae* penalty is obligatory (c. 1344), the penal authority may impose a suspension (censure), prohibitions (c. 1336, §1, 3°), and/or privations (c. 1336, §1, 2°) (expiatory penalties). The potential gravity of the situation is clear, since in more serious cases the priest is to be dismissed from the clerical state.[253]

Penal authorities should proceed very cautiously here, particularly because of the vulnerable situation

---

[250] See also several canons on tribunal discipline addressing similar concerns, cc. 1488, §1 and 1489 on possible penalties for advocates and procurators for similar offenses. A related non-penal canon 1456 prohibits judges and other tribunal officials from accepting gifts on the occasion of a trial.

[251] Cf. *CCEO* 1458.

[252] However questionable, the law envisions only sexual sins. See c. 1378, §1.

[253] This is the only canon on clerical dismissal that speaks in obligatory terms (*dimittatur*).

of the priest,[254] who is bound by the seal of confession and hence is somewhat impaired in defending his integrity. Should a priest be denounced, pertinent Holy See instructions are to be followed.[255]

In this general connection, canon 982 binds one making a false denunciation of solicitation in confession to retract it formally and repair any damage done before being absolved. Furthermore, canon 1390, §1 subjects the false denunciator to the *latae sententiae* penalties of interdict and possibly suspension if he is a cleric. Both canons primarily envision protecting the innocent priest, whose reputation (c. 220) and ministerial effectiveness could be seriously jeopardized.

Violation of Confessional Seal [256]

Canon 1388 — §1. A confessor who directly violates the sacramental seal incurs a *latae sententiae* excommunication reserved to the Apostolic See; one who does so only indirectly is to be punished according to the gravity of the delict.

§2. An interpreter and the others mentioned in can. 983, §2 who violate the secret are to be punished with a just penalty, not excluding excommunication.

Traditionally one of the most severely penalized delicts has been the violation of the confessional seal because of the serious breach of the priest-penitent relationship. The sacramental seal is the strict and inviolable obligation of keeping secret whatever has been related to the confessor to obtain absolution, the revelation of which would render the sacrament odious and onerous.

If the penitent and the sin are easily known from the confessor's deliberate revealing of such information, there is a *direct* violation of the seal, punishable by a *latae sententiae* excommunication. However, there is no delict if the confessor honestly believes such information is available from extra-confessional sources. Direct betrayal of the penitent's trust (c. 983, §1)[257] is very serious, since it is one of only five excommunications reserved to the Holy See (CDF in external forum; SP in internal forum).[258]

However, if there is only a danger that the penitent's identity and the sin will be revealed, there is an *indirect* violation of the seal, to be punished according to the seriousness of the confessor's indiscretion (§1; c. 1344).

While the canon primarily concerns the confessor, given his key ministerial role, occasionally others, such as interpreters or bystanders (cc. 983, §2; 990), may know the contents of a confession. If they deliberately violate its secrecy (not technically the seal), they are subject to a preceptive, indeterminate, *ferendae sententiae* penalty (§2; cc. 1344; 1349). Although the code here does not distinguish between direct and indirect violations, the penalty should correspond to the seriousness of the violation. In particularly serious cases (e.g., a direct violation) an unreserved excommunication may be warranted.

Some post-1983 code developments pertinent to the seal seem noteworthy. In 1988 the CDF with specific papal authorization decreed a *latae sententiae* excommunication for anyone deliberately

---

[254] A priest does not have to be an authorized confessor to commit this delict.

[255] For further information on the 1917 code, see Abbo-Hannan, 2:30–33. According to *PB* 52, the CDF is exclusively competent in penal matters regarding the sacrament of penance which are brought to its attention. The investigation of solicitation still seems regulated by an unpublished 1962 Holy Office instruction, which is to be preserved in the diocesan secret archives.

[256] Cf. *CCEO* 1456.

[257] If the penitent is not betrayed and permits the confessor to reveal certain confessional information, there is no delict. On this delicate issue calling for extreme caution, see D. Brewer, "The Right of a Penitent to Release the Confessor from the Seal: Considerations in Canon Law and in American Law," *J* 54 (1994) 424–476. However, the confessor may not testify about confessional knowledge in a church process although the penitent requests such testimony (c. 1550, §2, 2°).

[258] On possible questions regarding a direct violation suggested by an October 24, 1983 letter *Pro memoria* of SP, see *CLD* 11, 51.

using technical instruments to record and/or publish in the mass media anything said in sacramental confession by the confessor or the penitent, real or feigned. The law, which took effect on September 13, 1988, seems to have been prompted by the outrageous public abuse of the priest-penitent relationship for commercial purposes.[259]

Recently a controversy erupted in Oregon when the district attorney of Lane County authorized the taping of a prisoner's confession in the county jail without his or his confessor's knowledge. This act was declared illegal on January 27, 1997 by the 9th U.S. Circuit Court of Appeals.[260]

Finally, certain Church-State tensions in the United States have been occasioned by conflicts between the canons on the confessional seal and civil reporting statutes binding civil and ecclesiastical authority figures in alleged sex abuse cases especially involving minors.[261]

Abuse of Authority/Negligence [262]

Canon 1389 — §1. A person who abuses an ecclesiastical power or function is to be punished according to the gravity of the act or omission, not ex- cluding privation of office, unless a law or precept has already established the penalty for this abuse.

§2. A person who through culpable negligence illegitimately places or omits an act of ecclesiastical power, ministry, or function with harm to another is to be punished with a just penalty.

A fundamental conciliar theme restated in *Sacrae disciplinae leges* is that church authority must be exercised in a spirit of ecclesial service. This explains the present canon penalizing both abuse of power or function (§1) and culpable official negligence damaging others (§2). The latter provision was added during the revision of the original schema.

While such abuse is not defined, presumably it means deliberately exercising the power of orders or jurisdiction or some other ecclesiastical function in a fashion contrary to its basic ecclesial purpose. For example, a pastor might employ parish funds for his own personal use rather than responsibly stewarding the parish financial patrimony (cc. 532; 1284).

Such a concern to preclude abuse by the Church's public servants is laudable. However, the earlier comments on canon 1384 are relevant here. Canon 1389, §1 is formulated in such a sweeping, generic fashion that it seems difficult to implement practically. The legislator seems to leave the articulation of the delict exclusively to the penalizing judge or ordinary, which notably expands their competence beyond applying existing law. Furthermore, because the canon is so vaguely articulated, it raises concerns about the ability of the defendant to exercise the right of defense. This paragraph presumably provides the basis for a criminal action against church authorities whenever the code does not explicitly penalize a given abuse of office.

---

[259] CDF, decr *Urbis et orbis, AAS* 80 (1988) 1367. See also c. 1369 on media attacks against the Church and religion.

[260] See, for example, "A Prisoner's Secretly Taped Sacramental Confession," *Origins* 26/3 (June 6, 1996) 33; 35–36; "Recording of Prisoner's Sacramental Confession Violated Rights," *Origins* 26/33 (February 6, 1997) 537; 539–545.

[261] See M. Fitzgerald, *The Sacramental Seal of Confession in Relation to Selected Child Abuse Statutes in the Civil Law of the United States* (Rome: Gregorian University, 1991); D. Ioppolo, "Civil Law and Confidentiality: Implications for the Church," in idem et al., *Confidentiality in the United States: A Legal-Canonical Study* (Washington, D.C.: CLSA, 1988) 3–48; idem, "Appendix: Statutes and Court Decisions of the Fifty States," in *Confidentiality,* 49–92; R. Stake, "Grounding the Priest-Penitent Privilege in American Law," in *Confidentiality,* 145–162.

[262] Cf. *CCEO* 1464. In the context of abuse of office another Eastern penal canon must be mentioned; it is the only one explicitly said to bind Latin Catholics. Canon 1465 requires an appropriate penalty for one exercising an office, ministry, or function who presumes to induce a be-

liever to change affiliation to another *sui iuris* or autonomous church, Latin or Eastern. At times the law permits such a transfer of affiliation (*CCEO* 29–38; cc. 111–112). However, *CCEO* 1465 prohibits proselytism or deliberately manipulating a person to abandon his or her religious heritage. See *Pospishil Com,* 118.

An equally generic and sweeping canon 1389, §2 penalizes culpable negligence in illegitimately placing or omitting an act of ecclesiastical power or function which damages others. This is the only canon in part two of Book VI where negligence (*culpa*), not malice (*dolus*), grounds penal imputability (c. 1321, §2). For example, an ordinary may neglect to conduct a preliminary investigation of an alleged delict (c. 1717). This may damage its possible victims and perhaps the Church itself, especially but not exclusively if the Church is found civilly liable because of such negligence.

The legislator's interest in precluding the culpably negligent exercise of office is clearly legitimate. However, this paragraph also raises some of the aforementioned questions about the legislator–judge/ordinary relationship and the right of defense.

Both paragraphs of the canon need to be interpreted strictly. Furthermore, the penalizing authority needs to proceed especially carefully, clearly articulating the due cause(s) for the criminal action. Ample provision must also be made for exercising the right of defense. The necessary cautions indicated in connection with canon 1399 are equally relevant here.

Only those exercising ecclesiastical power or some function are possible offenders here. The legislator envisions a gradated scale of preceptive, indeterminate, *ferendae sententiae* penalties for abuse of office (§1) depending on the seriousness of the delict (cc. 1344; 1349). In especially grave situations one may even be deprived of office (c. 196); only this canon and canon 1396 on serious violations of residence explicitly mention such a penalty.

In cases of culpable negligence (§2) involving the illegitimate exercise of office, the legislator also provides for a preceptive, indeterminate, *ferendae sententiae* penalty (cc. 1344; 1349). Obviously the extent and nature of the damage to another are the prime criteria for determining an appropriate penalty.

A possible separate contentious action for damages (cc. 1729–1731) may be warranted, whatever the extent of penal imputability, for any-

one illegitimately damaging someone by a juridic act or any other act placed with malice or negligence must repair such damage (c. 128).

TITLE IV
THE CRIME OF FALSEHOOD
[cc. 1390–1391][263]

Violations of Reputation[264]

Canon 1390 — §1. A person who falsely denounces before an ecclesiastical superior a confessor for the delict mentioned in can. 1387 incurs a *latae sententiae* interdict and, if he is a cleric, also a suspension.

The first canon in this brief title considers delicts involving violations of personal reputation. This issue was placed very forcefully before the American Catholic consciousness in the mid-1990s when a young man falsely accused the late Cardinal Joseph Bernardin of sexual abuse. The second canon addresses violations of the integrity necessary in public ecclesial life, especially but not exclusively during ecclesiastical procedures.[265]

The first two paragraphs of canon 1390 deal with three violations of a person's reputation (c. 220), not all of which are viewed equally seriously.

The most serious delict here is the deliberate false accusation of a confessor of solicitation in

[263] Besides the Münster commentary, see Borras, 189–190; A. Calabrese, in *Com Ex*, 564–572; Green, in *CLSA Com*, 928; Martin, in *CLSGBI Com*, 801–802; Rees, 467–470.

[264] The Eastern code differs somewhat from its Latin counterpart in dealing with violations of reputation. The former treats of the issue in two canons rather than one canon. One canon addresses a calumnious injuring of another or seriously impairing another's reputation (*CCEO* 1452). The other punishes false accusations of an ecclesiastical delict, especially if the accused is a confessor, cleric, religious, or lay person holding a church office (*CCEO* 1454). A separate sacramental canon requires a formal retraction prior to absolving one falsely accusing a confessor of solicitation in confession (*CCEO* 731).

[265] See also c. 1368 on perjury.

confession (§1; see c. 1387). Given the serious violation of the priest-penitent relationship, the solicitation should be denounced to the competent ecclesiastical authority although no canon explicitly requires such a denunciation. This authority figure is likely the accused confessor's ordinary, who must investigate probable allegations of delicts (c. 1717, §1). Yet it might be the ordinary of the place of the alleged delict. Furthermore, the judicial vicar, the promoter of justice, or another official might be authorized to address such complaints.

With due regard for the obligation to denounce a soliciting confessor, a deliberately false accusation can seriously harm the reputation and future ministry of an innocent confessor, who is especially impaired in defending himself due to the obligation of the confessional seal. Hence, the competent authority must be very cautious in accepting such denunciations. Furthermore the legislator specifies a *latae sententiae* interdict for anyone so harming the confessor. If the false accuser is a fellow cleric, he is also liable to a *latae sententiae* suspension.

The legislator's concern for restoring the innocent confessor's reputation is clear from canon 982, which prohibits absolving one confessing the sin of false denunciation before the penitent formally retracts it and is prepared to repair any possible damages (cf. c. 1390, §3).

§2. A person who offers an ecclesiastical superior any other calumnious denunciation of a delict or who otherwise injures the good reputation of another can be punished with a just penalty, not excluding a censure.

§3. A calumniator can also be forced to make suitable reparation.

Canon 1390 deals with other deliberate violations of the right to a good reputation (§2; c. 220). Such violations, however problematic, do not have such grievous institutional implications as the false accusation of a confessor. Accordingly, a discretionary, *ferendae sententiae,* just penalty or possibly a censure may be imposed depending on the seriousness of the damage caused by the delict (cc.

1343; 1349). Two possible profiles of a delict are indicated: 1) a calumnious, or false, denunciation to a competent ecclesiastical superior of a delict other than confessional solicitation and 2) a deliberate, even if non-calumnious, injuring of another's reputation without any reference to a delict.[266]

At times the offender may be required to make restitution for harming the victim (§3). This would likely occur in connection with the remission of the penalty as a sign of good faith. The nature of the restitution, monetary or otherwise, will depend on the nature of the damages suffered by the victim.

In this general context one should also note a possible contentious action for damages, which can be pursued independently of or along with a criminal action (cc. 1729–1731).

Falsification of Documents [267]

Canon 1391 — The following can be punished with a just penalty according to the gravity of the delict:

1° a person who produces a false public ecclesiastical document, who changes, destroys, or conceals an authentic one, or who uses a false or altered one;

2° a person who uses another false or altered document in an ecclesiastical matter;

3° a person who asserts a falsehood in a public ecclesiastical document.

Documents of various types, both public and private (c. 1540), are of particular ecclesial significance, e.g., clarifying the status of physical or juridic persons. Such documents are admissible as proof in any trial, contentious or penal, in accord with the canons (cc. 1539–1546).

---

[266] For a Vancouver case involving an action for damages based on an alleged violation of reputation, see P. Lopez-Gallo, "Case of Rights and Defamation," *J* 49 (1989) 286–302.

[267] Cf. *CCEO* 1455. Unlike the Latin code, this Eastern text is not subdivided into three numbers; furthermore, it envisions a preceptive, not a discretionary, penalty for various delicts involving falsifying documents.

This canon attempts to preclude injustice and protect the integrity of the Church's public life and procedures. It envisions possible penalties for various delicts involving deliberately tampering with public ecclesiastical documents (1°),[268] intentionally using other altered documents[269] in various ecclesiastical procedures (2°), as well as knowingly stating a falsehood in a public ecclesiastical document (3°).[270]

While the delicts in numbers two and three seem fairly clear, some clarifications may be helpful regarding the various forms of tampering with public ecclesiastical documents in number one. Such a document may be fabricated to convey the impression that it is authoritative, e.g., a letter of appointment. The content of an authentic document may be changed so that it distorts the author's intent, e.g., a report of preliminary penal investigation. A document may be destroyed, thereby making it unavailable to prospective readers. Furthermore, a document might be concealed temporarily or permanently so that it is inaccessible in a given process, e.g., a psychological report on marital capacity. Finally, a false or altered public ecclesiastical document might be used to support one's position in a given process.

While any penally liable Catholic may commit the delicts mentioned in numbers one and two, presumably only an officeholder may assert a falsehood in a public ecclesiastical document (3°). The delicts here seem less serious than other legal violations, since only a discretionary, indeterminate, *ferendae sententiae* penalty is provided (cc. 1343; 1349). This is to be assessed in light of the seriousness of the injustice and the violation of the integrity of the ecclesiastical institution. A church officeholder might be punished more severely than other believers due to the breach of institutional trust. The penalty may be imposed even if the offender does not achieve the purpose(s) of such varied deceptions, e.g., obtaining of an annulment.

TITLE V
DELICTS AGAINST SPECIAL OBLIGATIONS
[cc. 1392–1396][271]

Except for a generic text on violations of obligations imposed by penalties (c. 1393), the following delicts concern violations of clerical or religious obligations related to their significant ecclesial role (cc. 1392; 1394–1396).[272] Since penalties are envisioned for violations of the following obligations, they are presumably viewed as somewhat more serious than other obligations. However, delicts elsewhere in Book VI involve violations of other obligations.[273]

Prohibited Business Activities [274]

Canon 1392 — Clerics or religious who exercise a trade or business contrary to the prescripts of the canons are to be punished according to the gravity of the delict.

This canon penalizes violations of canons 286 and 672 prohibiting unauthorized clerics and religious from intentionally conducting business (*negotiatio*) or trade (*mercatura*). Given the difficulty of clarifying precisely what constitutes such pro-

---

[268] See, for example, c. 428, §2 prohibiting the diocesan administrator or others from removing or destroying any curial documents or from changing anything in them, whether personally or through another.

[269] This could be a public civil document (c. 1540, §2), e.g., a forged marriage certificate, or a private document (c. 1540, §3), e.g., a premarital letter indicating a prospective spouse's views on children, fidelity, or permanence.

[270] See c. 1368 on perjury.

[271] Besides the Münster commentary, see Borras, 191–194; Di Mattia, in *Com Ex,* 573–584; Green, in *CLSA Com,* 929–930; Martin, in *CLSGBI Com,* 802–807; Rees, 471–479.

[272] On clerical obligations and rights, see cc. 273–289; on the obligations and rights of religious institutes and their members, see cc. 662–672; for societies of apostolic life, see c. 739.

[273] For example, for various sexual offenses of priests, see cc. 1378, §1 and 1387.

[274] Cf. *CCEO* 1466.

hibited commercial activities, the penal canon is formulated somewhat generically, comparable to the aforementioned substantive canons.[275]

The code seeks to foster an appropriate simplicity of life for clerics (c. 282, §1) and poverty of life for religious (c. 600) while assuring their serious ministerial commitment. This might be notably compromised by a significant investment of time and energy in commercial pursuits. However, since such pursuits may be necessary at times, canon 286 empowers the competent ecclesiastical authority to permit them.

Canon 1392 provides for an obligatory, indeterminate, *ferendae sententiae* penalty depending on the seriousness of the delict, i.e., the deliberate failure to seek appropriate authorization for business or trade (cc. 1344; 1349). Presumably the code envisions an habitual involvement in such prohibited commercial ventures.

The canon envisions as possible offenders clerics or "religious." However, permanent deacons are subject neither to the prohibition of canon 286 nor the penalty specified here unless particular law (e.g., diocesan norms) provides otherwise (c. 288). Furthermore, the penalty binds only clerics and non-clerical members of religious institutes (see c. 18), not non-clerical members of secular institutes or societies of apostolic life.[276]

Violation of Penal Obligations [277]

Canon 1393 — A person who violates obligations imposed by a penalty can be punished with a just penalty.

This generic new provision pertinent to any penalty seems somewhat out of place in this title on violations of specifically clerical and religious obligations. It might fit better in title II on delicts against ecclesiastical authorities.

The canon attempts to foster the effectiveness of the penal system by indicating that one who deliberately disregards the obligations imposed by a penalty (cc. 1331–1333; 1336) may be liable to another just penalty for such contempt of church authority. Examples of disregarding obligations include continuing to discharge the functions of an office whose exercise has been prohibited or receiving sacraments from which one has been barred.

The present canon is similar to canon 1326, §1, 1°, which indicates as an imputability-aggravating factor the recidivism of one who commits a delict even after being penalized. The basic obligation of anyone subject to a penalty is to restore ecclesial communion (c. 209) by complying with the legitimate precepts of the penal authority. However, the opposite kind of behavior is penalized here. In a certain sense it indicates the Church's relative helplessness regarding an intransigent offender given its lack of coercive resources. The effectiveness of the Church's penal system significantly depends on the willingness of such offenders to observe its provisions.

Since the situations and attitudes of various offenders may vary notably, the present canon envisions a discretionary, indeterminate, *ferendae sententiae* penalty, to be assessed in light of the seriousness of the offender's obstinacy (cc. 1343; 1349).

Violation of Celibacy [278]

Canon 1394 — §1. Without prejudice to the prescript of can. 194, §1, n. 3, a cleric who attempts marriage, even if only civilly, incurs a *latae sententiae* suspension. If he does not repent after being warned and continues to give scandal, he can be punished gradually by privations or even by dismissal from the clerical state.

§2. A perpetually professed religious who is not a cleric and who attempts marriage, even if only civilly, incurs a *latae sententiae* interdict, without prejudice to the prescript of can. 694.

---

[275] See the commentary on c. 286 for examples of prohibited business or trade.

[276] However, members of such societies are subject to an appropriate penalty in *CCEO* 1466.

[277] Cf. *CCEO* 1467.

[278] Cf. *CCEO* 1453, §2–§3.

One of the most serious obligations of most clerics (cc. 277, §1; 1037)[279] and all religious (c. 599) is observing perfect and perpetual continence (non-use of the sexual faculty) as well as celibacy, which prevents them from marrying. Canons 1087–1088 invalidate the attempted marriages[280] of clerics as well as members of religious institutes in perpetual (not temporary) vows. Married deacons may not remarry validly after the death of their spouses and continue their official ministry without a Holy See dispensation from canon 1087.[281]

If a cleric illegally attempts marriage, he incurs a *latae sententiae* suspension restricting his exercise of various ministerial functions (c. 1333).[282] One may wonder how realistic is the possibility of his giving up this new relationship, especially if children are involved. However, if after a formal warning the cleric contumaciously and scandalously persists in that relationship, he is liable to increasingly severe *ferendae sententiae* privations (c. 1336, §1, 2) including dismissal from the clerical state (§1).[283] This is one of the few delicts for which such a penalty is warranted.[284] Furthermore, by the law itself the cleric loses any ecclesiastical offices he may hold (c. 194, §1, 3°), yet the enforcement of this provision requires an authoritative declaration.

The non-clerical religious illegally attempting marriage incurs a *latae sententiae* interdict and, like the religious cleric, is also *ipso facto* dismissed from the religious institute given the radical incompatibility between the attempted marriage and one's religious commitment.[285] This dismissal is to be formally declared by the major superior with the council after gathering pertinent proofs of the attempted marriage (c. 694, §1, 2°–§2).

While canon 1394 does not explicitly refer to the partner of the above-mentioned cleric or religious, canon 1329, §2 on knowing and free complicity in a delict punished by a *latae sententiae* penalty is relevant here. Such a partner is a necessary accomplice, without whose cooperation there would be no delict. The partner of the cleric would be subject to a discretionary, *ferendae sententiae* penalty to be determined by the competent penal authority since she cannot incur a suspension. However, the partner of the non-clerical religious is subject to the same *latae sententiae* interdict. In assessing possible penalties, the penal authority needs to take cognizance of the norms on imputability (cc. 1323–1327), e.g., ignorance, grave fear, etc.

One might note briefly another administrative non-penal consequence of such a delict. A layman committing such a delict is irregular for receiving orders while a cleric is irregular for receiving further orders, e.g., a deacon vis-à-vis the priesthood (c. 1041, 3°). Such a cleric is also irregular for exercising the orders he has received (c. 1044, §1, 3°).

Various Violations of Clerical Continence [286]

Canon 1395 — §1. A cleric who lives in concubinage, other than the case mentioned in can. 1394, and a cleric who persists with scandal in another external sin against the sixth commandment of the Decalogue is to be punished by a suspension.

---

[279] An exception to the general rule of celibacy for Latin clerics is the married deacon (c. 1042, 1°).

[280] The code speaks technically about "attempting" marriage. This means that the cleric or religious may be mature enough to exchange naturally sufficient marriage consent, i.e., prescinding from church regulations. However, that consent is legally ineffective or not recognized by the Church because of the aforementioned marriage impediments.

[281] See June 6, 1997 circular letter of CDWDS in *Origins* 27/11 (August 28, 1997) 169; 171.

[282] See commentary on c. 1352.

[283] Interestingly enough, this is one of two instances where the Eastern code requires the deposition of a cleric (*CCEO* 1453, §2). The other is *CCEO* 1461 on the simoniacal conferral or reception of orders.

[284] The delict is viewed as so serious that the statute of limitations (prescription) for pursuing a criminal action is five years instead of the usual three years (c. 1362, §1, 2°).

[285] A strict interpretation of penal law means that the *latae sententiae* interdict here (c. 1394, §2) does not apply to non-clerical members of secular institutes or societies of apostolic life. However, they are *ipso facto* dismissed from the institute or society (cc. 729; 746).

[286] Cf. *CCEO* 1453, §1 and §3.

If he persists in the delict after a warning, other penalties can gradually be added, including dismissal from the clerical state.

§2. A cleric who in another way has committed an offense against the sixth commandment of the Decalogue, if the delict was committed by force or threats or publicly or with a minor below the age of sixteen years, is to be punished with just penalties, not excluding dismissal from the clerical state if the case so warrants.

A similar concern for an authentic observance of clerical[287] continence for the sake of the Kingdom prompts this canon penalizing other violations of that obligation[288] besides attempted marriage. Paragraph one treats of concubinage, an ongoing non-marital sexual relationship between a cleric and a woman, married or single. It also encompasses other scandalous, habitual, clerical sexual offenses with persons of either sex not entailing the exclusivity of concubinage.

A preceptive (c. 1344), *ferendae sententiae* suspension is envisioned initially, with subsequent increasingly severe penalties depending on the cleric's obstinate refusal to heed official warnings to change his scandalous behavior. The issue is quite serious since dismissal from the clerical state is possible in cases of notable intransigence. Further-

more, the statute of limitations (prescription) for pursuing a criminal action here and in most situations mentioned in the next paragraph is five years instead of the usual three years (c. 1362, §1, 2°).

While the canon does not explicitly refer to the cleric's accomplice in the ongoing sexual relationship, canon 1329, §1 on complicity in a delict punished by a *ferendae sententiae* penalty seems relevant. Such an accomplice is to be punished with a penalty comparable to suspension (e.g., interdict) or a less serious one depending on the level of imputability.

Paragraph two addresses certain occasional, non-habitual clerical sexual delicts,[289] which are especially serious if they are perpetrated publicly (i.e., in a public place), or with force, or with threats, or with a person of either sex under sixteen years of age.[290] These four criteria must be carefully considered in determining whether a delict has been committed. If any one of them is verified in an instance of external, seriously imputable, clerical sexual behavior, there may be a delict. In fact occasionally more than one of these criteria may be exemplified, e.g., the use of force or manipulation in sexual abuse of minors.

The issue of possibly diminished imputability is a critical one here, especially but not exclusively in cases of pedophilia. This means the experiencing of and acting upon recurrent, intense sexual urges and/or fantasies involving a prepubescent child for at least six months.[291] Church authorities

---

[287] Unlike c. 1394, §2, which also dealt with non-clerical religious, the present canon deals solely with clerics, secular and "religious" of all types.

[288] Besides concubinage, the present canon speaks generically of an external sin "against the sixth commandment of the Decalogue." See also cc. 977 and 1378, §1 (absolution of an accomplice) and c. 1387 (solicitation in confession). Regrettably, the exact meaning of this phrase is not entirely clear. It may mean technically adultery or sexual delicts involving clerics and married women. However, it is also used as a circumlocution for other types of sexual misconduct, heterosexual or homosexual, e.g., rape, fornication, or incest. For a thoughtful examination of this complex issue, including the contemporary problems of sexual harassment, exploitation, and abuse, see J. Provost, "Offenses against the Sixth Commandment: Toward a Canonical Analysis of Canon 1395," *J* 55 (1995) 632–663.

[289] Interestingly enough, the Eastern code penalizes only ongoing sexual delicts (c. 1395, §1), not the occasional sexual delict (c. 1395, §2).

[290] The age of "minors" here has been temporarily raised to eighteen years of age in the United States due to a special Holy See modification of the code for five years beginning April 25, 1994. On November 30, 1998 John Paul II extended this provision for ten years until April 25, 2009.

[291] For further discussion of the psychological implications of pedophilia, ephebophilia, and other sexual disorders involving clerics see P. Cimbolic, "The Identification and Treatment of Sexual Disorders and the Priesthood," *J* 52 (1992) 598–614.

should exercise great care in developing policies in this delicate area, and consultation with psychological and other experts is imperative before disciplinary or penal measures are taken.[292]

Such authorities must be sensitive to the diverse situations of clerics accused of sexual misconduct, which require different legal-pastoral approaches. For example, the cleric accused of recent repeated sexual abuse of children or minors seems notably different from the one accused of one or possibly several sexual offenses many years ago who has sought treatment and subsequently exercised the ministry laudably. Furthermore, the cleric engaging in consensual sexual activity with another adult, however morally objectionable, is different from the one forcefully engaging in non-consensual sexual activity with a minor or another vulnerable person such as a counselee. Complicity in the delict is to be assessed in terms of the free, deliberate sexual involvement of an individual with the guilty cleric (c. 1329, §1).

At times the most beneficial approach may be pastoral and therapeutic in character rather than penal, especially if the cleric's imputability is notably diminished. Concerns about his dignity, well-being, and future ministerial options[293] are key legal-pastoral considerations. However, one must also seriously consider the significant damage possibly done to the ecclesial community and certain individuals within it, especially the most vulnerable. Furthermore, there may be legitimate community outrage regarding the serious betrayal of trust involved in clerical sex abuse of minors.

This may heighten the imputability of the offending cleric (c. 1326, §1, 2°).[294]

Somewhat surprisingly, the code does not seem to view such delicts as seriously as other violations of clerical continence since, initially at least, the canon envisions only obligatory, indeterminate, *ferendae sententiae* penalties (c. 1344; 1349) rather than the suspension indicated in canons 1394, §1 and 1395, §1.[295] Furthermore, possible civil penalties such as incarceration may possibly preclude the need for canonical penalties if the various purposes of the penal system have been otherwise achieved (c. 1344, 2°). Nevertheless, if such penal and other remedial measures do not repair the ecclesial damage, the seriously imputable cleric may be dismissed from the clerical state, another illustration of the seriousness of this delict.[296]

---

[292] A helpful resource in this area are two volumes entitled *Restoring Trust,* prepared in 1994–1995 by the NCCB Ad Hoc Committee on Sexual Abuse. They review various diocesan sexual abuse policies, report on various treatment/evaluation centers, and provide useful articles on various aspects of the clergy sex abuse issue. See also *From Pain to Hope,* Report from the CCCB Ad Hoc Committee on Child Sexual Abuse (Ottawa: Publications Service CCCB, 1992).

[293] In assessing the possible reintegration of such a cleric in ministry, see, for example, F. Morrisey, "The Pastoral and Juridical Dimensions of Dismissal from the Clerical State and of Other Penalties for Acts of Sexual Misconduct," *CLSAP* (1991) 221–239, esp. 237–239.

[294] See *Canonical Delicts Involving Sexual Misconduct and Dismissal from the Clerical State* (Canonical Delicts) (Washington, D.C.: USCC, 1995). Pages 46–47 contain a helpful bibliography on clerical sexual abuse. See also *J* 52/2 (1992) containing articles by canonists Beal (642–683) and Provost (615–641) and psychologist Cimbolic (598–614) mentioned earlier.

[295] One must remember that the code was drafted and promulgated in the 1970s and early 1980s, somewhat prior to the notable emergence of the scandal of clerical sex abuse of minors in the United States and elsewhere. At that time church authorities and canonists were much less aware than today of the broad and complex implications of this tragic development.

[296] Another example of the seriousness with which this delict is viewed in the United States is a change in the statute of limitations (prescription) for initiating a criminal action based on alleged sexual abuse of minors. The aforementioned special April 1994 Holy See norms (cf. supra, n. 290) modified c. 1362, §1, 2°, which normally provides for a five-year period after the commission of such a delict. For alleged delicts committed with minors *under 18* years of age *between April 25, 1994 and April 24, 1999,* such a criminal action may be initiated until the minor celebrates his/her 28th birthday or one year has elapsed from the denunciation of the delict expedited prior to that 28th birthday. For alleged delicts committed with minors *under 16* years of age (former rule) *before April 25, 1994,* such a criminal action may be initiated until the minor in question celebrates his/her 23rd birthday. See *Canonical Delicts,* 38–39. On

Finally, the delicts in canon 1395 are normally the basis for a mandatory dismissal of a religious cleric from his institute or society after an appropriate procedure (cc. 695; 729; 746). This is a separate issue from dismissal from the clerical state. However, somewhat surprisingly, the delicts mentioned in paragraph two may not necessarily require such a dismissal from the institute or society. The superior may decide that such action is not completely necessary since the correction of the member, the restitution of justice, and the reparation of scandal can be achieved otherwise.

Violation of Residence Obligation

Canon 1396 — A person who gravely violates the obligation of residence which binds by reason of ecclesiastical office is to be punished by a just penalty, not excluding, after a warning, even privation from office.

This provision penalizes those gravely violating the residence obligation attached to certain pastoral offices, e.g., bishop,[297] pastor,[298] or parochial vicar.[299] This traditional obligation seeks to ensure the availability of clerics to the communities which they are called to serve. The obligation is especially serious given the conciliar emphasis on authority as service, a value reaffirmed in *Sacrae disciplinae leges*. Furthermore, the code highlights certain basic spiritual rights of the faithful, such as being nurtured in word and sacrament (c. 213) and educated in the faith (c. 217).

The present canon initially envisions a preceptive (c. 1344), indeterminate, *ferendae sententiae* penalty for such illegitimate absence from ministry, which does not seem especially serious. However, if, even after a warning, the cleric obstinately and habitually is absent from the community

he is called to serve, he may be deprived of his office.[300] Key concerns would be the frequency, duration, and pastorally detrimental implications of such absence. Normally such indeterminate penalty delicts do not permit perpetual penalties (c. 1349). However, this exception to the rule is one of only two delicts entailing possible privation of office (see c. 1389, §1). Given its notable impact on the offender's life and ministry, such a privation of office presupposes a judicial penal process (c. 1342, §2).

TITLE VI
DELICTS AGAINST HUMAN LIFE AND FREEDOM
[cc. 1397–1398][301]

The two canons here deal with ecclesiastical delicts with civil law implications although unfortunately there is more statutory diversity in various countries regarding abortion (c. 1398) than regarding the other violations of human life, integrity, and freedom (c. 1397).

Physical Violations of Human Life, Integrity, and Freedom [302]

Canon 1397 — A person who commits a homicide or who kidnaps, detains, mutilates, or gravely

November 30, 1998 John Paul II extended the aforementioned norms for ten years until April 25, 2009.

[297] Canons 395 (diocesan bishops) and 410 (coadjutor and auxiliary bishops).

[298] Canons 533 (individual pastors) and 543, §2, 1° (team ministry).

[299] Canon 550.

[300] The diocesan bishop would penalize pastors and parochial vicars. The metropolitan would report a problem involving a suffragan to the Holy See, which is to take appropriate action; if the metropolitan is at fault, the senior suffragan would inform the Holy See (c. 395, §4). Nothing is said explicitly about a seriously delinquent coadjutor or auxiliary bishop; presumably the diocesan bishop would report the matter to the Holy See for appropriate action, for only the pope or his delegate can judge bishops in penal cases (c. 1405, §1, 3°).

[301] Besides the Münster commentary, see also Borras, 194–196; Green, in *CLSA Com,* 930; Martin, in *CLSGBI Com,* 807–810; F. Pérez-Madrid, in *Com Ex,* 585–594; Rees, 479–485.

[302] See *CCEO* 1450, §1 (homicide) and 1451 (other violations of personal freedom and integrity). Also *CCC,* nn.

wounds a person by force or fraud is to be punished with the privations and prohibitions mentioned in can. 1336 according to the gravity of the delict. Homicide against the persons mentioned in can. 1370, however, is to be punished by the penalties established there.

With due regard for the civil ramifications of such violations of persons, the code also views them as significant ecclesiastical concerns. Nevertheless, realistically speaking, the competent civil authorities, rather than church officials, will likely deal with such criminal behavior initially, given its destructive societal impact. Accordingly, ecclesiastical and civil authorities should cooperate as much as possible given their presumed mutual interest in fostering the good of society.

There are several different profiles of a delict. The code presupposes freedom and deliberation on the part of the assailant or victimizer, whatever his or her intent, unless it is a case of legitimate self-defense or defense of another (see cc. 1323, §1, 5° and 1324, §1, 6°). The most serious delict involves the willful taking of life (homicide). However, the canon also penalizes serious violations of human freedom, e.g., kidnapping or forcible or fraudulent detention of an individual. The legislator also envisions certain notable violations of bodily integrity, e.g., forcible or fraudulent mutilation or serious wounding of a person.

The legislator views these delicts and abortion (c. 1398) as quite serious, since the statute of limitations (prescription) for initiating a criminal action is five years rather than the usual three years from the commission of the delict (c. 1362, §1, 2°).

The code generically requires *ferendae sententiae* privations (c. 1336, §1, 2°) and prohibitions (c. 1336, §1, 1°–3°) according to the gravity of the delict (c. 1344). They are much less severe than the corresponding civil penalties. This is one of very few canons generically requiring such expiatory penalties. Because of their irrevocable char-

acter, the "privations" are more serious than the "prohibitions" and must be imposed judicially.

The aforementioned delicts, however serious, technically do not warrant either a penal transfer of office (c. 1336, §1, 4°) or dismissal from the clerical state (c. 1336, §1, 5°). Nevertheless, in penalizing the killing of the pope, a bishop, cleric, or religious, the competent authority must apply canon 1370, including the possible dismissal of a cleric for an attack on the pope. The significant ecclesial status of such figures underlies this special provision.

Since ecclesiastical authorities may normally not be involved in initially penalizing such delicts, canon 1344, 2° may be relevant. In short, a distinctly canonical penalty may not be necessary, or a lighter penalty than that envisioned by the code or a penance (c. 1340) may be appropriate. This is true if the offender has reformed, repaired any scandal, and been sufficiently punished civilly. Obviously the exercise of such penal discretion presupposes a careful assessment of the seriousness of the delict and its detrimental ecclesial impact.

Finally, several implications of the aforementioned delicts are noteworthy. First of all, religious, members of secular institutes, and members of societies of apostolic life are to be dismissed from the institute or society after an appropriate process (cc. 695; 729; 746). Secondly, laymen or clerics who have committed voluntary homicide or mutilated another gravely and maliciously are irregular either for receiving orders (c. 1041, 4°–5°)[303] or for exercising orders already received (c. 1044, §1, 3°).

Abortion [304]

Canon 1398 — A person who procures a completed abortion incurs a *latae sententiae* excommunication.

---

[303] While the fact on which this irregularity is based may be a delict, one may incur the irregularity even without technically committing a delict.

[304] Cf. *CCEO* 1450, §2.

2268 (homicide) and 2297 (other violations of personal freedom and integrity).

The present code restates the main thrust of the 1917 code (*CIC* 2350). However, explicit reference is made neither to the mother undergoing the abortion nor to the obligatory deposition (dismissal) of a cleric who might be involved.

The penal law committee refused to define abortion here since presumably the Church's teaching[305] was well known. Traditionally abortion has been defined as the ejection of a live, immature or non-viable fetus from the mother's womb. A related but technically distinct moral evil was feticide, i.e., the killing of the fetus within the womb. Since penal law must be strictly interpreted, most canonists have judged that abortion, but not technically feticide, however horrendous, was the delict envisioned by both codes.

Tragically, however, most abortions today occur by procedures involving killing the fetus in the womb, e.g., suction, dilation and curettage, or the use of a prostaglandin drug often in connection with the RU 486 pill. Hence, not surprisingly, a May 23, 1988 authentic Code Commission interpretation broadened the canonical understanding of abortion to maximize the protection of the fetus. Abortion means not simply the deliberate ejection of an immature fetus but also any intentional killing of the fetus through whatever means at any time after conception. This broadened view of abortion is an extensive interpretation of the code, which is not retroactive but operative only after the interpretation.[306]

According to canon 1398, a person who knowingly and freely procures a completed[307] abortion incurs a *latae sententiae* excommunication. A proposed *ferendae sententiae* penalty was rejected as possibly undercutting the canon's effectiveness, especially if the abortion were occult, or non-public. Canon 1329, §2 on complicity in a delict punished by a *latae sententiae* penalty is especially relevant, since numerous persons may be involved in procuring the abortion, e.g., parents of the aborted fetus, their families, doctor, nurses, etc. Those whose assistance is indispensable for the abortion presumably incur the excommunication since they are necessary accomplices. Others involved before or after the abortion may be subject to otherwise unspecified *ferendae sententiae* penalties. In assessing such penalties, the penal authority must consider various factors affecting imputability, e.g., age, ignorance, fear, etc. (cc. 1323–1327).[308]

This is probably the most common situation in which a confessor might remit a penalty, since this *latae sententiae* excommunication would rarely be formally declared (c. 1357). While counseling the penitent about the moral evil of abortion, the confessor should also consider possible mitigating circumstances precluding the incurring of the penalty (cf. canons 1323–1324).

Finally, certain other canonical implications of involvement in an abortion are noteworthy. Members of religious institutes, secular institutes, or societies of apostolic life must be dismissed for committing such a delict (cc. 695; 729; 746). Furthermore, anyone who has procured a completed abortion or positively cooperated in it is irregular for receiving orders even if there is technically no delict (c. 1041, 4°). In similar circumstances, if there has technically been a delict, such a one is irregular for exercising orders already received (c. 1044, §1, 3°).

---

[305] See, for example, *CCC*, nn. 2270–2275; also John Paul II, ency *Evangelium vitae*, March 25, 1995, *Origins* 24 (1995) 689–727, esp. nn. 58–62.

[306] *AAS* 80 (1988) 1818. For a translation and brief commentary on the interpretation, see L. Wrenn, *Authentic Interpretations on the 1983 Code* (Washington, D.C.: CLSA, 1983) 48–49.

[307] An attempted or failed abortion, however morally culpable, is not technically a delict. Yet see c. 1328.

[308] For a thoughtful examination of delictual cooperation here, see J. Coriden, "The Canonical Penalty for Abortion as Applicable to Administrators of Clinics and Hospitals," *J* 46 (1986) 652–658. A properly strict interpretation means that the canon applies primarily to those directly participating in the abortion, not those removed from such participation. Hence, however morally questionable the behavior, this particular canon applies neither to such administrators nor to political officials facilitating abortions by advocating abortion rights and voting to fund abortions.

TITLE VII
GENERAL NORM
[c. 1399][309]

Canon 1399 — In addition to the cases established here or in other laws, the external violation of a divine or canonical law can be punished by a just penalty only when the special gravity of the violation demands punishment and there is an urgent need to prevent or repair scandals.

Book VI closes with a general norm providing for a penalty in certain extraordinary circumstances even if no canon explicitly penalizes the particular violation of a divine or canonical law. This general norm might be situated more logically in title III following canon 1321 on penal imputability. This general norm, not found in the Eastern code, raises the issue of the ecclesial relevance of the so-called principle of legality (*nulla poena sine lege*—"no penalty without a law"). In canon law the axiom *nulla poena sine culpa* ("no penalty without culpability") is actually more pertinent.

The original schema (c. 73) contained such a penalty like the 1917 code (*CIC* 2222, 1). Some favored such a canon because it is impossible to list comprehensively all delicts notably impairing the Church's integrity and mission. Others, however, questioned its practical effectiveness and feared arbitrary action by church authorities which might violate basic Christian rights, e.g., the right not to be penalized except according to law (cf. c. 221, §3). They also felt that problematic disciplinary situations entailing no legal sanction could be responsibly addressed by issuing pertinent penal precepts.

A significant factor influencing the current canon was the approval of the underlying principle by the May 1977 Code Commission *Plenarium*. Apparently legitimate concerns about protecting the integrity of the Church's mission and precluding spiritual damage to persons prevailed over reasonable concerns for legal security and the rights of believers.[310]

Great caution should be employed in applying this canon, which provides for a discretionary (c. 1343), indeterminate, *ferendae sententiae* penalty for any believer in exceptional situations where the code does not penalize a legal violation. There is a special burden of proof on the penalizing authority here, since the canon speaks of the "special gravity of the violation" and the "urgent need to prevent or repair scandals." Both criteria must be verified to impose the penalty, which should normally be less severe than for delicts specified in the law, for the alleged offender, however imputable, could neither have anticipated the penalty nor adequately defended himself or herself. In fact, inculpable ignorance of the law (not presumed) normally exempts one from penal imputability (c. 1323, 2°), and ignorance of the penalty mitigates it (c. 1324, 9°).

The penalty is expiatory rather than a censure, since no warning is necessary for its imposition and its primary focus is not reforming the offender but restoring the violated ecclesial order. Accordingly, censures such as excommunication or suspension cannot be imposed. Furthermore, canon 1349 restricting penal discretion in applying indeterminate penalties is relevant. Hence, perpetual expiatory penalties such as privation of office and dismissal from the clerical state cannot be imposed.

[309] Besides the Münster commentary, see Borras, 23–25; Green, in *CLSA Com*, 930–931; idem, "Penal Law: A Review of Selected Themes," 244–246; Martin, in *CLSGBI Com*, 810; Rees, 75–76, 485–486; Sanchis, in *Com Ex*, 595–598.

[310] On the tensions between conciliar ecclesiology and a so-called "perfect society" ecclesiology underlying this canon, see especially pp. 5–6 of the Münster commentary.

BIBLIOGRAPHY

Commentaries on the 1917 Code

Abbo, J., and J. Hannan. *The Sacred Canons.* Vol. 2: 779–871. St. Louis: B. Herder, 1952.

Bouscaren, T. L., A. Ellis, and F. Korth. *Canon Law.* 4th ed., 863–975. Milwaukee: Bruce, 1962.

Michiels, G. *De Delictis et Poenis.* 3 vols., 2nd ed. Paris: Desclée, 1961.

Vermeersch, A., and I. Creusen. *Epitome Iuris Canonici.* 7th ed., 219–400. Malines-Rome: H. Dessain, 1956.

Code Commission Reports on the Revision of Penal Law[311]

Commentaries on the Original 1973 Schema and Its Revision[312]

Green, T. "The Future of Penal Law in the Church." *J* 35 (1975) 212–275 (for postconciliar penal law reform literature, see 274–275).

---

[311] Green, in *CLSA Com,* 941.
[312] Ibid.

Green, T. "Penal Law Revisited: The Revision of the Penal Law Schema." *Stud Can* 15 (1981) 135–198.

Commentaries on Book VI of the 1983 Code

Arias, J. In *Pamplona ComEng,* 817–867.

Borras, A. *Les Sanctions dans l'Eglise.* Paris: Tardy, 1990.

Green, T. In *CLSA Com,* 891–941.

Ludicke, K. In *Münster Com.*

Martin, J. In *CLSGBI Com,* 749–810.

Rees, W. *Die Strafgewalt der Kirche.* Berlin: Duncker & Humblot, 1993.

Various authors in *Com Ex,* 222–598.

Commentaries on Penal Law in the Eastern Code

T. Green. "Penal Law in the *Code of Canon Law* and in the *Code of Canons of the Eastern Churches:* Some Comparative Reflections." *Stud Can* 28 (1994) 407–451.

BOOK VII
PROCESSES
[cc. 1400–1752]

Lawrence G. Wrenn

Ecclesial Judgments before Constantine

The Church, it may be said, is one, holy, catholic, apostolic, and adjudicative. Courts and trials have been part of our community life from the very beginning.

According to Matthew, the Evangelist, it was Jesus himself who drafted the first procedural canon of the Church's law.

> If your brother should commit some wrong against you, go and point out his fault, but keep it between the two of you. If he listens to you, you have won your brother over. If he does not listen, summon another, so that every case may stand on the word of two or three witnesses. If he ignores them, refer it to the church. If he ignores even the church, then treat him as you would a Gentile or a tax collector. I assure you, whatever you declare bound on earth shall be held bound in heaven, and whatever you declare loosed on earth shall be held loosed in heaven.[1]

St. Paul obviously approved of the notion of having every case "stand on the word of two or three witnesses," because he twice reiterated that advice, once in his second letter to the Corinthians[2] and again in his first letter to Timothy.[3]

Paul regretted that there should ever be litigations among the followers of Jesus, but he nevertheless accepted them as necessary and inevitable in a sinful Church. In his first letter to the Corinthians, Paul urged that the incestuous man among them be driven from the community:

> What business is it of mine to judge outsiders? Is it not those inside the community you must judge? God will judge the others, "Expel the wicked man from your midst."[4]

In the next (sixth) chapter of that letter, Paul, amplifying on the notion of Christians judging insiders, suggests, in effect, that the Church establish a kind of court system of its own in order to settle its problems internally:

> How can anyone with a case against another dare bring it for judgment to the wicked and not to God's holy people? Do you not know that the believers will judge the world? If the judgment of the world is to be yours, are you to be thought unworthy of judging in minor matters? Do you not know that we are to judge angels? Surely, then, we are up to deciding everyday affairs. If you have such matters to decide, do you accept as judges those who have no standing in the church? I say this in an attempt to shame you. Can it be that there is no one among you wise enough to settle a case between one member of the church and another? Must brother drag brother into court, and before unbelievers at that?[5]

By the year 197, when Tertullian wrote his *Apology* in an effort to convince the provincial governors of the Roman Empire that Christians were good, decent people, undeserving of the persecutions directed against them, he cited as one example of the uprightness of Christians their laudable court system. In the beautiful thirty-ninth chapter of the *Apology,* Tertullian reminded the Roman rulers that

> family possessions, which generally destroy brotherhood among you, create fraternal

---

[1] Mt 18:15–18.
[2] 2 Cor 13:1.
[3] 1 Tm 5:19.

[4] 1 Cor 5:12–13.
[5] 1 Cor 6:1–6.

bonds among us. One in mind and soul, we do not hesitate to share our earthly goods with one another. All things are common among us but our wives.... But it is mainly the deeds of a love so noble that lead many to put a brand upon us. "See," they say, "how they love one another."... We are a body knit together by a common religious profession, by unity of discipline, and by the bond of a common hope.... We assemble to read our sacred writing.... In the same place also exhortations are made, rebukes and sacred censures are administered. *For with a great gravity is the work of judging carried on among us, as befits those who feel assured that they are in the sight of God; and you have the most notable example of judgment to come when anyone has sinned so grievously as to require his severance from us in prayer, in the congregation and in all sacred intercourse. The tried men of our elders preside over us, obtaining that honor not by purchase, but by established character.*[6]

It is clear from this text that the Matthaean exhortation about bringing one's brother before the community for judgment was still in practice, and, indeed, of some import at the time of Tertullian. The *Didascalia,* however, probably written within a few decades of the *Apology,* spells out even more clearly what immense importance was attached to the role of judging in the early Church. Page after page of the *Didascalia* is devoted to the Church's court system, with detailed instructions on such matters as how the bishop-judge ought to handle the case of a falsely accused person, how the judge ought not to accept bribes, how both sides should be given a hearing, how the judge ought not to be a respecter of persons, and even how the judicatures of Christians

ought to be held on the second day of the week, so that the matter might be settled before the next Sabbath.[7]

The "earliest Church historian," Eusebius, who was the bishop of Caesarea early in the fourth century, tells us that in the year 268, the then bishop of Antioch had to be deposed because of his heretical beliefs and certain misdemeanors. Among the specific complaints against the bishop were several that referred to his role as judge. It was alleged, and eventually proved, according to Eusebius that

he extorts from the brethren, depriving the injured of their rights and promising to assist them for reward, yet deceiving them, and plundering those who in their trouble are ready to give that they may obtain reconciliation with their oppressors... and ... that he practices chicanery in ecclesiastical assemblies, contrives to glorify himself, and deceive with appearances, and astonish the minds of the simple, preparing for himself a Tribunal and lofty throne, not like a disciple of Christ, and possessing a "secretum," like the rulers of the world, and so calling it, and strike his thigh with his hand and stamping on the Tribunal with his feet; or in that he rebukes and insults those who do not applaud, and shake their handkerchiefs as in theaters, and shout and leap about like the men and women that are stationed around him.[8]

It seems, therefore, that ecclesiastical courts, both good and bad, grew up along with the Church itself as part of the family. They were used and abused, admired and detested; but, above all, they were a fixture.

---

[6] *The Ante Nicene Fathers* (New York: Scribner's, 1926) III:46–47. Order of sentences slightly altered; italics the author's.

[7] *Constitutions of the Holy Apostles*, Book II, Sections III–VI, *The Ante Nicene Fathers,* VII:398–421.

[8] *The Church History of Eusebius*, VII, 30. *The Nicene and Post Nicene Fathers,* Second Series (New York: Christian Literature Co., 1890) I:314.

*Ecclesial Judgments from Constantine
to the Decretals of Pope Gregory IX*

Once Constantine, the Roman emperor, became a Christian and, in particular, once he granted to bishops the same authority as civil judges in cases brought before them by the mutual consent of the parties,[9] it was inevitable that the procedural law of the Roman civil courts would influence and change the procedures of the church courts. And so it did.

Perhaps the clearest single illustration of that influence of Roman law on church law is found in Gregory the Great's letter to John the Defender, the letter listed as number 45 in Book XIII of his collected letters.[10] Gregory was born in Rome sometime around 540 to a distinguished patrician family. Before his ordination, Gregory was himself a judge in the civil system, prefect of the city of Rome, and president of the Roman Senate. When, therefore, he became pope in 590, he was a true expert in law and government. At a point in his pontificate, news came to Gregory of a couple of particularly delicate matters in Spain that had already come to the attention of the local church courts. Gregory sent John the Defender to Spain and, in Letter 45, Gregory instructed John, who had in effect been designated as Gregory's judicial vicar for these particular cases, how to proceed. The pope told John that he wanted him to review and evaluate the procedures, testimony, and merits of the first instance hearing; and time and time again, Gregory quoted chapter and verse for John from Justinian's *Code* and *Novels*. Gregory was saying, in other words, that the rules and directives of Roman civil law (the *Code* and *Novels,* along with two other works called the *Institutes* and *Digest,* which were a systematic collection of several centuries of imperial legislation ordered by and published under Emperor Justinian shortly before Gregory was born) could and should be utilized in church courts.

The influence of Roman law on ecclesiastical court procedures still endures. The following chapter headings, for example, which are immediately familiar to anyone conversant with the Codes of Canon Law, are in fact lifted verbatim from the *Corpus Iuris Civilis* (as Justinian's four collections came to be known): *De ordine iudiciorum, De foro competenti, De litis contestatione, De dilationibus, De procuratoribus, De actionibus et exceptionibus, De praescriptionibus, De re iudicata, De effectu sententiarum,* and *De restitutionibus in integrum.*[11]

The Decretals *of Pope Gregory IX*

Although a complete history of procedural law in the Church is far beyond the scope of these few introductory remarks, still there is one essential link between the early Church and the contemporary Church which is altogether too important to go unmentioned: the *Decretals* of Pope Gregory IX. In the year 1234, Gregory IX collected several centuries' worth of ecclesiastical laws and arranged them (following the order utilized by Bernard of Pavia in his *Collectio Prima* of some forty years earlier) into five books: *Iudex, Iudicium, Clerus, Connubia,* and *Crimen.*

Book II of the *Decretals* (*Iudicium*) was divided into the following thirty titles:

> *De iudiciis*
> *De foro competenti*
> *De libelli oblatione*
> *De mutuis petitionibus*
> *De litis contestatione*
> *Ut lite non contestata non procedatur ad testium receptionem vel ad sententiam definitivam*
> *De iuramento calumniae*
> *De dilationibus*
> *De feriis*
> *De ordine cognitionum*

---

[9] *Codex Theodosianus*, I 27, 1: Mommson-Meyers (Berlin, 1905) 62.
[10] *PL* 77, 1294–1300.

[11] *Institutiones* IV 6, 13; *Digesta* IV 1, XLII 1, XLIV 1, 2; *Codex* II 13, III 8, 9, 11, 13.

De plus petitionibus
De causa possessionis et proprietatis
De restitutione spoliatorum
De dolo et contumacia
*De eo, qui mittitur in possessionem causa rei
    servandae*
Ut lite pendente nihil innovetur
De sequestratione possessionum et fructuum
De confessis
De probationibus
De testibus et attestationibus
De testibus cogendis vel non
De fide instrumentorum
De praesumptionibus
De iureiurando
De exceptionibus
De praescriptionibus
De sententia et re iudicata
*De appellationibus, recusationibus, et relatio-
    nibus*
De clericis peregrinantibus
De confirmatione utili vel inutili[12]

The titles, chapters, and articles of the 1983 code as they appear in this commentary are in English, but a perusal of them in the Latin version of the code dramatically illustrates the continuity of procedural law in the Church over the centuries. Many of them are exact repetitions of the titles found in the *Decretals* of the year 1234, some of which, in turn, were found in Justinian's collection of the year 534.

Some General Observations

1. The procedural law of the 1983 code consists of 353 canons (cc.1400–1752) and is divided into five parts: I "Trials in General" (cc. 1400–1500); II "The Contentious Trial" (cc. 1501–1670); III "Certain Special Processes" (cc. 1671–1716); IV "The Penal Process" (cc. 1717–1731); and V "The Method of Proceeding in Administrative Recourse and in the Removal and Transfer of Pastors" (cc. 1732–1752).

[12] *CorpusIC* II, 239–448.

2. Marriage cases (which constitute practically the entire work load of our tribunals) have their own special norms and are treated under part three, "Certain Special Processes," title I, "Marriage Processes" (cc. 1671–1707). Besides those special norms, however, the canons that regulate contentious cases also apply to marriage cases (cc. 1425, §1, 1° and 1691). In his 1996 allocution to the Roman Rota, however, Pope John Paul II noted certain difficulties that result from the fact that the procedure used for marriage cases "is set in the broader framework of contentious procedures" and called, therefore, for "corrective measures by the legislator or for specific norms" that would apply to marriage cases.[13] These norms are presently being drafted.

3. The matter of "Methods of Avoiding Trials" (part three, title III, cc. 1713–1716) seems rather oddly placed in both the 1917 and the 1983 codes, though interestingly, it was assigned the same relative position in the third-century *Didascalia*'s own rather lengthy treatment of ecclesiastical judicatories.[14]

The Eastern code, however, positioned its chapter on "Methods of Avoiding a Trial" (*CCEO* 1164–1184) immediately before its section on "The Contentious Trial" (*CCEO* 1185–1356), which seems a more logical placement.

Chronology of the Revision of the 1917 Code

The early years of this revision were marked by four significant dates:

- January 15, 1959 — when Pope John XXIII issued the initial call for a revision of the 1917 code;
- March 28, 1963 — when the Pontifical Commission for the Revision of the Code was established;

[13] *Origins* 25 (February 29, 1996) 615–616.
[14] See the commentary on cc. 1713–1716 but one should also see the commentary on c. 1446.

- November 12, 1963 — when it was decided to postpone the work of revision until the end of the Second Vatican Council;
- November 20, 1965 — when Pope Paul VI inaugurated the work of the commission.

Following Pope Paul's inauguration, the consultors comprising the various study groups began their meetings. The *De processibus* group had its first meeting in May 1966 and for the next several years met, for a week or so at a time, two or three times a year.[15]

Finally, after ten years of work, the commission issued on November 3, 1976, the *Schema Canonum de Modo Procedendi pro Tutela Iurium seu de Processibus,* which was distributed to the various bishops of the world and other consultative organs. It was accompanied by a request that they return to the commission any observations they might have on the schema by September 1977. Using these observations, the consultors then met:

- in April and May of 1978 — to revise the present canons 1400–1490;[16]
- in October, November, and December of 1978 — to revise canons 1491–1649;[17]
- in March and May of 1979 — to revise canons 1650–1752.[18]

The final draft was then incorporated into the 1980 draft of the revised code and from there, with some few more revisions, into the final text.

Some Basic Definitions

A *process* (*processus*) is a complex of acts or solemnities, prescribed by law and to be observed

by public authority, for solving questions or settling business.

A *procedure* (*procedura*) is simply a way of proceeding (*modus procedendi*); it can be either judicial or extra-judicial.

A *trial* (*iudicium*) is a hearing, discussion, and settlement by a judge of a legal controversy which arises between a plaintiff and a respondent.

An *ecclesiastical trial* is a discussion and settlement by an ecclesiastical tribunal of a controversy in a matter in which the Church enjoys competence.

Basic Elements of a Trial

There are five basic elements to a trial: the material object, the formal object, the active subject, the passive subject, and the form. These five elements comprise the subject matter of part one of this book on procedural law. The elements are discussed according to the following order:

Canon 1400 — *the material object,* i.e., the matters that can, in general, be addressed by a court.

Canon 1401 — *the active subject,* i.e., the judge or tribunal before whom the case is tried. Canon 1401 states the general principle that the Catholic Church does indeed have the proper and exclusive right to hear certain cases. Canons 1404–1475 (titles I–III) treat this matter in greater detail.

Canon 1402 — *the form,* i.e., the procedures or solemnities that are followed in the adjudication of certain matters. This canon states the general rule.

Canon 1476 — *the passive subject,* i.e., the petitioner or respondent whose case is being heard. This matter, along with the procurators and advocates for the parties, is treated in canons 1476–1490 (title IV).

Canon 1491 — *the formal object,* i.e., the precise claim or counterclaim made by the parties in a particular hearing. This matter is treated in canons 1491–1500 (title V).

[15] These meetings are described in *Comm* 6 (1974) 37–43, 216–219.
[16] These meetings are described in *Comm* 10 (1978) 209–272.
[17] These meetings are described in *Comm* 11 (1979) 67–162.
[18] These meetings are described in *Comm* 11 (1979) 243–296.

The Eastern Canons

One of the guiding principles in revising the procedural law for the Eastern churches was that all Catholics, as far as possible, should observe the same procedural norms. In general, therefore, the Latin canons and the Eastern canons regarding trials are uniform. As a table of corresponding canons easily shows, there are some Latin canons

without an Eastern counterpart and vice versa, but these are relatively rare. There are also certain norms that are common to both codes and that differ somewhat.[19] When deemed significant, the specific differences between the two codes will be discussed in their proper place.

[19] J. Abbass, "Trials in General: A Comparative Study of the Eastern and Latin Codes," *J* 55 (1995) 834–874.

CANONS AND COMMENTARY

Book VII on "Processes" is divided into five parts: "Trials in General" (I), "The Contentious Trial" (II), "Certain Special Processes" (III), "The Penal Process" (IV), and "The Method of Proceeding in Administrative Recourse and in the Removal and Transfer of Pastors" (V).

Part I
TRIALS IN GENERAL
[cc. 1400–1500]

After four introductory canons, part one is divided into five titles: "The Competent Forum" (I), "Different Grades and Kinds of Tribunals" (II), "The Discipline to be Observed in Tribunals" (III), "The Parties in a Case" (IV), and "Actions and Exceptions" (V).

INTRODUCTORY CANONS
[cc. 1400–1403]

The Material Object of a Trial

Canon 1400 — §1. The object of a trial is:
1° the pursuit or vindication of the rights of physical or juridic persons, or the declaration of juridic facts;

2° the imposition or declaration of a penalty for delicts.
§2. Nevertheless, controversies arising from an act of administrative power can be brought only before the superior or an administrative tribunal.

Paragraph one of this canon states what, in general, the object of a trial *is;* paragraph two speaks of a situation which is *not* the object of a trial.

When the object is to prosecute or vindicate the rights of persons or to declare juridic facts, as in §1, 1°, the trial is called *contentious;* when the object is to impose or declare a penalty, as in §1, 2°, the trial is called *penal* (see c. 1425, §1).

Not all vindication of rights, however, is the object of a judicial trial. Paragraph two notes that controversies that arise from an act of administrative power are handled administratively, or, as the canon says, "can be brought only before the superior or an administrative tribunal." If, for example, a person is aggrieved by a decision or decree of a bishop, recourse is had not to an ordinary tribunal but to the appropriate Roman congregation. In turn, recourse against the decision of that congregation is made to the Signatura acting as an administrative, not an ordinary tribunal.

Paragraph two, it should be noted, applies only to those controversies that arise from "an act of administrative power." It does not therefore suggest that any controversy involving an administrator, i.e., one who has administrative or executive power, is handled administratively. A penal or contentious case involving the person of the bishop, for example, is heard either by the Holy Father or the Rota (c. 1405, §1, 3° and §3, 1°). And when the rights or temporal goods of a juridic person represented by a bishop are at issue, the case is heard by the court of appeal (c. 1419, §2). It is, in other words, only those controversies that stem from an actual administrative act that are heard before the hierarchic superior rather than an ordinary tribunal.

Prior to 1967 there was no administrative tribunal in the Church. On August 15 of that year, however, as part of the apostolic constitution *Regimini Ecclesiae universae,* a second section was established within the Signatura to serve as an administrative tribunal empowered to decide on "contentions which have arisen from the exercise of administrative ecclesiastical power."[20]

For a time, indeed, it was envisioned that there would be not only a supreme administrative tribunal in the Church but local administrative tribunals as well. In the 1980 draft of this code, part five of this Book VII was not entitled "The Method of Proceeding in Administrative Recourse and in the Removal and Transfer of Pastors" as it is now, but simply "The Administrative Procedure," and that part five in the 1980 draft

contained twenty canons (cc. 1689–1692, 1697–1698, and 1702–1715) which explained in considerable detail how administrative courts—which were envisioned as optional—could be constituted at the episcopal conference level and how they would function.

In preparation for the October 1981 meeting of the commission, three members of the commission recommended that these administrative courts be made obligatory rather than facultative for each conference. The Secretariat responded:

> Although it is devoutly to be wished that administrative tribunals be regularly established in the Conference of Bishops, for the safeguarding of subjective rights and for the better ordering of administrative justice, it does not seem opportune to impose such a burden by universal law. Just to establish ordinary tribunals has been replete with difficulties since oftentimes qualified, experienced personnel are lacking; this would be all the more true in setting up administrative courts since the work of such courts is extremely sensitive and important and demands a profound grasp of the law and of justice. Besides, such courts constitute a major innovation in church law and it therefore seems appropriate to move somewhat gradually and voluntarily in a way that is tailored to local resources. Nor should we forget, finally, that hierarchic recourse is always available with the possibility of approaching the Signatura for a final decision. Nevertheless, let the matter be referred to the Plenary Commission.[21]

In October 1981 the matter was referred to the Plenary Commission, and the vote was fifty-three to six in favor of retaining administrative courts as optional rather than mandatory.

Nevertheless, when the code finally appeared in 1983, all twenty canons dealing with local ad-

---

[20] See paragraph 106 of that constitution in *CLD* 6, 351. For a discussion of the nature of an administrative tribunal, i.e., whether it is judicial, extra-judicial, or quasi-judicial, see I. Gordon, "De iustitia administrativa ecclesiastica tum transacto tempore, tum hodierno," *P* 61 (1972) 251–378; idem, "De objecto primario competentiae 'Sectionis Alterius' Supremi Tribunalis Signaturae Apostolicae," *P* 58 (1979) 505–542. See also *Comm* 10 (1978) 217–218. For other helpful observations on administrative tribunals, see K. Matthews, "The Development and Future of the Administrative Tribunal," *Stud Can* 18 (1984) 1–233; and M. Moodie, "Defense of Rights: Developing New Procedural Norms," *J* 47 (1987) 423–448. Regarding the matter of sections within the Signatura, see the commentary on c. 1445.

[21] *Comm* 16 (1984) 85–86.

ministrative courts had been deleted, and we are now left with the so-called "second section" of the Signatura as the sole administrative tribunal in the Church.

Because this "section" of the Signatura is the only administrative tribunal in the Church and because canon 1400, §2 indicates that a person aggrieved by an act of administrative power could have recourse to "the superior *or an administrative tribunal,*" there was, upon promulgation, some initial confusion about the meaning of the canon. Some canonists wondered whether an option was really being offered. They wondered, for example, where an administrative act of a bishop was at issue, whether recourse either to the appropriate congregation or to the Signatura was really being allowed. It soon became apparent, however, especially after 1988 when article 123 of *Pastor bonus*[22] made it perfectly clear, that recourse was first to the congregation and only after that to the Signatura.

Accordingly, the parallel canon in the Eastern code (*CCEO* 1055, §2), not promulgated until 1990, simply omits all mention of an administrative tribunal, making it entirely clear that the initial recourse is only to the hierarchic superior.

The Active Subject of a Trial

Canon 1401 — By proper and exclusive right the Church adjudicates:
  1° cases which regard spiritual matters or those connected to spiritual matters;
  2° the violation of ecclesiastical laws and all those matters in which there is a question of sin, in what pertains to the determination of culpability and the imposition of ecclesiastical penalties.

Canon 1401 makes it clear that it is the Church itself, in its various judicial roles, that has

the right to adjudicate certain issues. These issues are (a) spiritual matters, e.g., the validity of a sacrament, (b) matters connected with the spiritual, e.g., the right of a pastor to serve in a particular parish, (c) the violation of a law, and (d) cases in which there is the *ratio peccati,* that is to say, actions which disturb the social order of the Church.

The phrase *ratio peccati* has a long and interesting history.[23] It was first used by Pope Innocent III in 1204 in the famous decretal *Novit.* In that decretal Innocent intervened in a dispute between King Philip of France and King John of England, assuring them that, although he had no intention of diminishing or disturbing a king's power, he was nevertheless intervening in the dispute because it had been alleged that a sin had been committed and judgment regarding sin belonged to the Church. The phrase *ratio peccati* appeared in canon 1553 of the 1917 code in the same context as it does here, and indeed also appeared in the 1909 draft of the procedural law for that code as canon 3, §1.[24] In all cases in the past, as well as in the present canon, the phrase "a question of sin" refers not to theological sin (which is treated in the internal forum) but rather to an ecclesially disruptive action where judgment in the external forum is appropriate.

The Eastern code has elected to omit the present norm altogether because, although the substance of it "is very dear to every Catholic, it is nevertheless based on an undoubtedly true, but very complex, theology (e.g., what is the *ratio peccati?*)." "Nevertheless," as Abbass says, "the theological rule on which it is based is undoubtedly applicable in the whole Church."[25]

American civil law generally recognizes this right of the Church to judge church matters, at

---

[22] See *Code of Canon Law, Latin-English Edition: New English Translation* (Washington, D.C.: CLSA, 1999) 721.

[23] L. Wrenn, "The Scope of the Church's Judicial Competence," *J* 45 (1985) 639–652.
[24] J. Llobell, E. DeLeon, J. Navarrete, *Il Libro "De Processibus" nella Codificazione del 1917* (Milan: Giuffrè, 1999) 754.
[25] Abbass, 842.

least to the extent that it does not impinge on any civil right. *American Jurisprudence,* for example, the standard and authoritative encyclopedia on American civil law, notes the following:

> If civil rights, as contradistinguished from ecclesiastical questions, are passed upon by a church tribunal, the secular courts will usually decide the merits of the case for themselves. But, according to the rule broadly stated by some courts, when a civil right depends upon some matter pertaining to ecclesiastical affairs, the civil tribunal tries the right and nothing more, taking the ecclesiastical decisions out of which the civil right has arisen as it finds them, and accepting such decisions as matters adjudicated by another legally constituted tribunal. Thus the decisions of the church tribunals as to questions of discipline, faith or ecclesiastical rules, customs or law affecting the members of the church must be accepted by legal tribunals as final and binding upon them in their application to a case before them.[26]

The Applicability of the Canons

Canon 1402 — The following canons govern all tribunals of the Church, without prejudice to the norms of the tribunals of the Apostolic See.

Canon 1403 — §1. Special pontifical law governs the causes of canonization of the servants of God.

§2. The prescripts of this Code, however, apply to these causes whenever the special pontifical law refers to the universal law, or norms are involved which also affect these causes by the very nature of the matter.

As noted in the introduction, the procedures or solemnities that are observed in a trial constitute one of the five basic elements of a trial, namely the *form.*

These two canons note that although, in general, all tribunals of the Church are regulated by the canons that follow, nevertheless the tribunals of the Holy See (c. 1402) and the Congregation for the Causes of Saints (c. 1403) are often ruled by their own special norms.

The tribunals of the Apostolic See are the Apostolic Penitentiary, the Apostolic Signatura, the Roman Rota,[27] and, perhaps, the Congregation for the Doctrine of the Faith when it deals with more serious offenses.[28] The Apostolic Penitentiary deals only with the internal forum. The norms followed by the Signatura were issued in 1968;[29] the most recent revision of the norms for the Rota appeared in 1994;[30] the norms followed by the Congregation for the Doctrine of the Faith when it investigates more serious offenses are unavailable. The congregation, however, issued norms for privilege-of-the-faith cases in 1973,[31] for dispensations from clerical celibacy in 1980,[32] and for doctrinal examinations in 1997.[33]

Regarding the procedure in causes of canonization, Pope John Paul II issued the apostolic constitution *Divinus perfectionis Magister* on January 25, 1983 (the same day on which the code was promulgated), revising the mode of procedure in the drawing up of causes of canonization and giving new regulations for the Congregation for the Causes of Saints.[34] The following month further norms were issued to be followed by bishops when investigating causes of saints.[35]

[26] *American Jurisprudence,* 2nd ed. (Rochester, N.Y.: Lawyers Cooperative Publishing Company, 1973) 66: 784. As regards marriage cases, see cc. 1671–1672.

[27] *PB* 117–120.
[28] *PB* 52.
[29] *CLD* 7, 246–272.
[30] *AAS* 86 (1994) 508–540.
[31] *CLD* 8, 1177–1184.
[32] *CLD* 9, 92–101.
[33] *Origins* 27/13 (September 11, 1997) 221–224.
[34] *CLD* 10, 266–273.
[35] *CLD* 10, 273–281. See also *J* 43 (1983) 366–375.

TITLE I
THE COMPETENT FORUM
[cc. 1404–1416]

Title I on the competent forum treats three main topics: the extraordinary forum, sometimes called the singular forum (cc. 1404–1406); the ordinary forum, sometimes called the common or concurrent forum (cc. 1407–1415); and the disputed forum (c. 1416).

The Extraordinary Forum

a. Judicial Immunity of the Pontiff

Canon 1404 — The First See is judged by no one.

Canon 1404 is not a statement about the personal impeccability or inerrancy of the Holy Father. Should, indeed, the pope fall into heresy, it is understood that he would lose his office. To fall from Peter's faith is to fall from his chair.[36] The question, however, of who or what body (probably a general council) would determine whether, in fact, the pope had fallen into heresy is unclear historically and is obviously not settled by this canon.

While not a statement about impeccability or inerrancy, canon 1404 is a statement about the judicial immunity of the First See. It says that the Holy Father cannot be tried by a secular or religious court and, perhaps particularly, given the history of the question, by a general council. The Constitution on the Church of Christ of the First Vatican Council, for example, said,

> We also teach and declare that he [the Roman Pontiff] is the supreme judge of all

the faithful to whose judgment appeal can be made in all matters which come under ecclesiastical examination. But the verdict of the Apostolic See may be rejected by no one, since there is no higher authority, and no one may pass judgment on its judgment. Hence they stray from the right path of truth who affirm that it is permissible to appeal to a General Council against the judgments of the Roman Pontiffs, as if the General Council were a higher authority than the Roman Pontiff.[37]

b. Right of Pontiff to Judge

Canon 1405 — §1. It is solely the right of the Roman Pontiff himself to judge in the cases mentioned in can. 1401:
1° **those who hold the highest civil office of a state;**
2° **cardinals;**
3° **legates of the Apostolic See and, in penal cases, bishops;**
4° **other cases which he has called to his own judgment.**
§2. A judge cannot review an act or instrument confirmed specifically (*in forma specifica*) by the Roman Pontiff without his prior mandate.
§3. Judgment of the following is reserved to the Roman Rota:
1° **bishops in contentious matters, without prejudice to the prescript of can. 1419, §2;**
2° **an abbot primate or abbot superior of a monastic congregation and a supreme moderator of religious institutes of pontifical right;**
3° **dioceses or other physical or juridic ecclesiastical persons which do not have a superior below the Roman Pontiff.**

As regards canon 1405, §1, 1°, the purpose of reserving such cases to the Holy See is not to provide a privilege to the governmental head but

---

[36] See T. Izbicki, "Infallibility and the Erring Pope," in *Law, Church and Society*, ed. K. Pennington and R. Somerville (Philadelphia: University of Pennsylvania, 1977) 97–111; M. Schmaus, "Pope," in *Readings, Cases, Materials in Canon Law*, ed. J. Hite, G. Sesto, and D. Ward (Collegeville: Liturgical Press, 1980) 109–123; S. Ozment, *The Age of Reform 1240–1550* (New Haven: Yale University, 1980) 160–164.

[37] *Ench* 1830.

rather to remove the possibility of a local judge being pressured to give a favorable decision.

As regards canon 1405, §2, the sense is that once an act has been confirmed *in forma specifica*[38] by the pope, it can no longer be adjudicated by an inferior judge without a specific mandate. In effect, therefore, it becomes a fifth type of case (added to the four in §1) that is reserved to the pope himself.

As regards canon 1405 §3, article 129 of *Pastor bonus* adds to the three types of cases listed a fourth, namely cases which the Holy Father commits to the Roman Rota for adjudication. The article further notes that all four types of cases are heard at the Rota not only in first instance but in other instances as well.[39] One should also see canon 1444, §2.

c. Incompetence of Lower Courts

Canon 1406 — §1. If the prescript of can. 1404 is violated, the acts and decisions are considered as not to have been placed.

§2. In the cases mentioned in can. 1405, the incompetence of other judges is absolute.

Canon 1406 brings up the matter of jurisdictional incompetence in terms of the extraordinary forum.

Incompetence can be either relative or absolute. (1) Relative incompetence stems from a territorial defect (c. 1407, §§1–2), while absolute incompetence stems from the fact that a case is already legitimately pending before another tribunal (c. 1512, 2°) or from the grade of the tribunal, the dignity of the parties, or the quality of the issue;[40] (2)

relative incompetence results in the judge acting illicitly, while absolute incompetence results in his or her acting invalidly;[41] (3) relative incompetence need not be declared by the judge after the *contestatio litis* or joinder of issue, while absolute incompetence should be declared at any stage;[42] (4) relative incompetence may be challenged as an exception only before the *contestatio litis,* while absolute incompetence may be challenged at any time;[43] (5) relative incompetence can be prorogated or extended while absolute incompetence generally cannot;[44] and (6) relative incompetence does not result in the nullity of the sentence, whereas absolute incompetence results in a sentence that is incurably null.[45]

The Ordinary Forum

Canon 1407 — §1. No one can be brought to trial in first instance except before an ecclesiastical judge who is competent by reason of one of the titles determined in cann. 1408–1414.

§2. The incompetence of a judge supported by none of these titles is called relative.

§3. The petitioner follows the forum of the respondent. If the respondent has more than one forum, the choice of forum is granted to the petitioner.

After the general principles stated in this canon, this title then goes on to list the eight sources or titles of competence recognized in law. For the special titles of competence in marriage cases, one should see canon 1673. It is to be noted that canon 1673, 3° on the forum of the petitioner

---

[38] For observations on the phrase *in forma specifica,* see F. Urrutia, "Quandonam Habeatur Approbatio 'In Forma Specifica,'" *P* 80 (1991) 3–17.

[39] *Comm* 20 (1988) 46.

[40] S. Goyeneche, *De processibus,* Part I (Messina: Scuola Tipografica Antoniana "Cristo Re," 1958) 40. See also footnote 94 of this commentary, and A. Stankiewicz, "De nullitate sententiae iudicialis propter absolutam iudicis incompetentiam," *P* 81 (1992) 537.

[41] E. Regatillo, *Institutiones iuris canonici,* vol. II (Santander: Sal Terrae, 1956) par. 350.

[42] Canon 1461; *Comm* 10 (1978) 257.

[43] Canon 1459, §§1, 2.

[44] Canon 1405 (where other tribunals are absolutely incompetent) admits of no exceptions, whereas cc. 1411 and 1414 (where other tribunals are relatively incompetent) admit of an extension either by the parties or by the law itself.

[45] Canon 1620, 1°.

somewhat modifies the ancient principle mentioned in canon 1407, §3 that "the petitioner follows the forum of the respondent."

(1) The Tribunal of Domicile or Quasi-Domicile

Canon 1408 — Anyone can be brought to trial before the tribunal of domicile or quasi-domicile.

For the acquisition and loss of domicile and quasi-domicile, one should see canons 102–106. This present canon clearly refers to the domicile or quasi-domicile of the respondent. In a case accepted on this basis, should the respondent relocate after the citation, the hearing is completed in the court in which it was initiated (c. 1512, 2°).

(2) The Tribunal of the Transient and of the Unlocatable

Canon 1409 — §1. A transient has a forum in the place of his or her actual residence.
§2. A person whose domicile, quasi-domicile, and place of residence are unknown can be brought to trial in the forum of the petitioner provided that no other legitimate forum is available.

It bears noting that, in the case of an unlocatable person, the forum of the petitioner acquires competence only if no other legitimate forum is available. To illustrate: a woman petitioner approaches her own United States diocese, e.g., New York, requesting a declaration of invalidity. The marriage took place in San Juan, Puerto Rico. The husband is certainly somewhere in Puerto Rico but is unlocatable. Since San Juan is a legitimate forum, New York does not enjoy competence by reason of canon 1409, §2, though it might by reason of canon 1673, 4° on the forum of proofs.

(3) The Tribunal of the Disputed Object

Canon 1410 — By reason of the location of an object, a party can be brought to trial before the tri- bunal of the place where the object in dispute is located whenever the action is directed against the object or concerns damages.

When ownership of some object is at issue and the plaintiff brings an action either to obtain or to recover that object (*actio in rem aut de spolio*), that action by the plaintiff may be lodged at the tribunal where the object is located. If, however, the plaintiff is accusing the respondent of stealing the object or of some other delict, then it is not the tribunal of the disputed object that is competent but the tribunal where the offense was perpetrated (c. 1412). In both cases, of course, another tribunal, e.g., the tribunal where the respondent is domiciled, might also be competent.

(4) The Tribunal of Contract, Quasi-Contract, and Election

Canon 1411 — §1. By reason of a contract, a party can be brought to trial before the tribunal of the place where the contract was entered into or must be fulfilled unless the parties agree to choose some other tribunal.
§2. If the case concerns obligations which originate from another title, a party can be brought to trial before the tribunal of the place where the obligation either originated or must be fulfilled.

Paragraph one of this canon closes with the words, "unless the parties agree to choose some other tribunal." This tribunal chosen by the parties is known as the tribunal of election.[46]
Paragraph two of this canon notes that in what might be called quasi-contracts, i.e., other agreements and business arrangements, the tribunals where the agreement was made and where it is to be implemented are competent. In such cases, however, the tribunal of election is not available to the parties.

[46] *Comm* 10 (1978) 225.

(5) The Tribunal of the Delict

Canon 1412 — In penal cases the accused, even if absent, can be brought to trial before the tribunal of the place where the delict was committed.

For an example of when the diocese where the delict was committed would enjoy jurisdiction, one should see the commentary on canon 1414. The rationale for this being a source of competence is that it is often the place where the delict was committed that, first of all, facilitates the investigation of the facts and, second, most stands in need of having the wounds resulting from the delict healed by a fair trial.

(6) The Tribunal of Administration or Bequest

Canon 1413 — A party can be brought to trial:
   1° in cases which concern administration, before the tribunal of the place where the administration was conducted;
   2° in cases which regard inheritances or pious legacies, before the tribunal of the last domicile, quasi-domicile, or place of residence, according to the norm of cann. 1408–1409, of the one whose inheritance or pious legacy is at issue unless it concerns the mere execution of the legacy, which must be examined according to the ordinary norms of competence.

(7) The Tribunal of Connection

Canon 1414 — By reason of connection, interconnected cases must be adjudicated by one and the same tribunal in the same process unless a prescript of law prevents this.

One example of a tribunal enjoying competence by reason of connection would involve the hearing of penal cases concerning two similar delicts committed by the same person, one committed within the diocese undertaking the hearing of the case in accord with canon 1412 but the other delict committed outside the diocese, with

the diocese in question having no source of jurisdiction other than canon 1414.

Another example would be the counterclaim mentioned in canon 1495 and discussed in the commentary on that canon.

(8) The Tribunal of Prevention

Canon 1415 — By reason of prevention, if two or more tribunals are equally competent, the right of adjudicating the case belongs to the one which legitimately cited the respondent first.

Although the wording of this canon (*ratione praeventionis,* paralleling *ratione rei sitae* of c. 1410, *ratione contractus* of c. 1411, etc.) suggests that prevention is, like the others, a genuine source of competence, some prefer to view it rather as a mechanism by which one tribunal obtains definitive competence over others that initially enjoyed a legitimate title to hear the case.

For a similar use of the notion of prevention, one should see the commentary on canon 1482.

The Disputed Forum

Canon 1416 — The appellate tribunal resolves conflicts of competence between tribunals subject to it; if the tribunals are not subject to the same appellate tribunal, the Apostolic Signatura resolves conflicts of competence.

Conflicts of competence can arise either when two or more tribunals claim to have competence over a case (prevention not having solved the conflict) or when two or more tribunals claim to lack competence. It is always to be hoped that the conflict can be settled locally, through a more thorough investigation. Appeal to a higher court should be a matter of last resort.[47]

The corresponding canon in the Eastern code deals with this matter in its own way. Unlike the Latin canon, which directs that the conflict be set-

---

[47] *Comm* 16 (1984) 54.

tled by the ordinary appellate tribunal when the conflicting tribunals are subject to the same appellate tribunal, and by the Signatura when they are not, the Eastern canon (*CCEO* 1083) directs that the matter be settled by the appellate tribunal of the judge who was first petitioned. No mention is made of the Signatura. The Eastern canon does, however, note that if one of the tribunals happens to be the appellate court of the other, then the matter is settled by the tribunal of third instance of the judge who was first petitioned. Even in this case, however, the intervention of the Holy See is usually not involved.

TITLE II
DIFFERENT GRADES AND KINDS OF TRIBUNALS
[cc. 1417–1445]

INTRODUCTORY OBSERVATIONS AND CANONS
[cc. 1417–1418]

1. Outline of Title

After two introductory canons, title II consists of three chapters: "The Tribunal of First Instance" (I), "The Tribunal of Second Instance" (II), and "The Tribunals of the Apostolic See" (III).

2. Grades and Kinds (Species) of Tribunals

The grade of a tribunal is the place it holds in the judicial hierarchy. There are four grades of church tribunals: the first is the diocesan, the second is the metropolitan, the third is the regional, and the fourth is the tribunals of the Holy See.[48] It should be noted that the grade of tribunal does not always coincide with the grade of hearing or instance (*gradus iudicii*). A tribunal of the fourth

grade, for example, may hear a case in the first instance (c. 1417).

3. Subordination of Tribunals

Tribunals follow the rules of subordination of canon 1438 when competence is not disputed, and the rules of canon 1416 when competence is disputed.

4. Petitioning a Roman Tribunal

Canon 1417 — §1. By reason of the primacy of the Roman Pontiff, any member of the faithful is free to bring or introduce his or her own contentious or penal case to the Holy See for adjudication in any grade of a trial and at any stage of the litigation.

§2. Recourse brought to the Apostolic See, however, does not suspend the exercise of jurisdiction by a judge who has already begun to adjudicate a case except in the case of an appeal. For this reason, the judge can prosecute a trial even to the definitive sentence unless the Apostolic See has informed the judge that it has called the case to itself.

One should see canon 1442 for a discussion of this issue.

5. Cooperation Between Tribunals

Canon 1418 — Any tribunal has the right to call upon the assistance of another tribunal to instruct a case or to communicate acts.

When one tribunal requests another to receive the testimony of someone residing within the territory of that second tribunal, this request is made by a rogatorial letter,[49] and it is called a rogatorial commission.[50]

---

48 S. Sipos, *Enchiridion Iuris Canonici* (Rome: B. Herder, 1954) 713.

49 M. Lega and V. Bartocetti, *Commentarius in iudicia ecclesiastica*, 3 vols. (Rome: Anonima Libraria Cattolica Italiana, 1938) I:103.

50 M. Reinhardt, *The Rogatory Commission*, CanLawStud 288 (Washington, D.C.: Catholic University of America, 1949).

For an alternative procedure, one should see canon 1469, §2. As regards the precise place for receiving testimony, one should see canon 1558.

CHAPTER I
THE TRIBUNAL OF FIRST INSTANCE
[cc. 1419–1437]

Chapter 1 consists of three articles: "The Judge" (1), "Auditors and Relators" (2), and "The Promoter of Justice, the Defender of the Bond, and the Notary" (3).

ARTICLE 1: THE JUDGE
[cc. 1419–1427]

Article 1 treats of the judge under five different categories: the diocesan judge, the regional judge, the single judge with assistance, plural judges acting as a college, and the judge of religious.

1. The Diocesan Judge

a. The Diocesan Bishop

Canon 1419 — §1. In each diocese and for all cases not expressly excepted by law, the judge of first instance is the diocesan bishop, who can exercise judicial power personally or through others according to the following canons.

§2. If a case concerns the rights or temporal goods of a juridic person represented by the bishop, the appellate tribunal judges in first instance.

Canon 375 notes that a bishop, by the fact of his episcopal consecration, receives the functions of sanctifying, teaching, and ruling. Canon 381, §1 notes that a diocesan bishop, in the diocese committed to him, possesses all the ordinary, proper, and immediate power which is required for the exercise of his pastoral office; and canon 391, §1 observes that a diocesan bishop is to rule the particular church committed to him with legislative, executive, and judicial power.

In terms of the topic under discussion, namely the diocesan judge, canon 1419 sums up the principles enunciated in these canons by stating that, apart from those cases expressly excepted by law, the judge of first instance is the diocesan bishop.

The principal cases that are, in fact, expressly excepted by law are found in canons 1400, §2; 1404; 1405; 1427, §§1 and 2; and paragraph two of this canon, which deals with an action that concerns the rights or the temporal goods of a juridic person represented by the bishop. The matter of representing a juridic person is discussed in canon 118. As canon 393 indicates, "The diocesan bishop represents his diocese in all its juridic affairs." Clearly, then, if a case involved diocesan property, it would not be the diocesan bishop but the appellate tribunal of that diocese that would hear the case in first instance.

b. The Judicial Vicar and His Adjutant

Canon 1420 — §1. Each diocesan bishop is bound to appoint a judicial vicar, or officialis, with ordinary power to judge, distinct from the vicar general unless the small size of the diocese or the small number of cases suggests otherwise.

§2. The judicial vicar constitutes one tribunal with the bishop but cannot judge cases which the bishop reserves to himself.

§3. The judicial vicar can be given assistants who are called adjutant judicial vicars, or vice-officiales.

§4. Both the judicial vicar and adjutant judicial vicars must be priests, of unimpaired reputation, doctors or at least licensed in canon law, and not less than thirty years of age.

§5. When the see is vacant, they do not cease from their function and cannot be removed by the diocesan administrator; when the new bishop arrives, however, they need confirmation.

The judicial vicar or officialis is a priest chosen by the bishop to judge cases with ordinary power.

Although his jurisdiction is ordinary, not delegated, and vicarious, not proper (c. 131), the judicial vicar is distinct from the episcopal vicars discussed in canons 476–481. This is clear from the following: (1) canons 463, §1, 2° and 833, 5° both speak of the episcopal vicars *and* the judicial vicar, clearly indicating that the judicial vicar is not included among the episcopal vicars; (2) canon 472 says that those who exercise judicial power follow different norms from those who exercise administrative power; (3) canon 479 says that episcopal vicars have executive (rather than judicial) power to place administrative (rather than judicial) acts, and (4) canon 481, §1 says that episcopal vicars lose their power when the see is vacant (see also c. 418, §2, 1°) whereas the judicial vicar does not (c. 1420, §5).

The judicial vicar, therefore, though he enjoys ordinary power, is not included when the law speaks about the "ordinary" (c. 134). Neither is he included in the episcopal council (c. 473, §4).

Like the episcopal vicar, however (c. 477, §1), the judicial vicar should be appointed for a definite but unspecified time; and the bishop is not to remove him from office prior to the vicar's term having expired unless the bishop has a legitimate and serious cause (c. 1422).

Paragraph two of this canon notes that "the judicial vicar constitutes one tribunal with the bishop." This implies that an appeal against a decision of the tribunal cannot be lodged with the bishop, and that the bishop is not free to change or modify a decision given by his judicial vicar.

It is to be noted, finally, that, in accord with canon 135, §3, judicial power cannot be delegated by the vicar or any other judge, except to carry out acts which are preparatory to a decree or decision.

c. The Judges

Canon 1421 — §1. In a diocese, the bishop is to appoint diocesan judges, who are to be clerics.

§2. The conference of bishops can also permit the appointment of lay persons as judges; when it is necessary, one of them can be selected to form a college.

§3. Judges are to be of unimpaired reputation and doctors or at least licensed in canon law.

Canon 1422 — The judicial vicar, adjutant judicial vicars, and other judges are appointed for a definite time, without prejudice to the prescript of can. 1420, §5 and cannot be removed except for a legitimate and grave cause.

(1) The 1917 code (*CIC* 1574) did not permit lay persons to serve as judges. This was at least partly based on the common assumption that jurisdiction could be exercised only by those in holy orders.

After the Second Vatican Council, however, interest spread in permitting lay persons as well as clerics to function as judges.[51] In 1971, *Causas matrimoniales* permitted the lay man but not the lay woman to serve as a judge (V, 1); and this regulation was incorporated into the 1976 and 1980 drafts of procedural law. Finally, this 1983 code, in accord with the October 1981 vote of the members of the commission to eliminate the discriminatory restriction, allowed that a qualified lay person of either sex may be appointed a judge.

For a discussion of the exercise of jurisdiction by lay persons, one should see the commentary on canons 129; 228, §1; and 274, §1.[52]

(2) Canon 1574 of the 1917 code noted that diocesan judges exercised *delegated* power. The present canon has deleted that observation and, in accord with the definitions found in canon 131 §1, a diocesan judge would now seem to be exercising *ordinary* power.[53]

(3) The law's interest in having key court personnel equipped with academic degrees is partic-

---

[51] See, for example, P. Frattin, "Lay Judges in Ecclesiastical Tribunals," *J* 28 (1968) 177–184.

[52] See also J. Provost, "The Participation of the Laity in the Governance of the Church," *Stud Can* 17 (1983) 417–448; and J. Beal, "The Exercise of the Power of Governance by Lay People: The State of the Question," *J* 55 (1995) 1–92.

[53] For more on this question, see G. Graham, *Synodal and Pro-Synodal Judges* (Washington, D.C.: Catholic University of America, 1967) 74–83; and A. Diacetis, *The Judgment of Formal Matrimonial Cases: Historical Reflections, Contemporary Developments, and Future Possibilities* (Washington, D.C.: Catholic University of America, 1977) 129–132.

ularly apparent in canons 1420, §4; 1421, §3; and 1435. In dioceses where there are not a sufficient number of degreed people to staff the tribunal adequately, the Signatura is willing to grant dispensations from this requirement to non-degreed but otherwise qualified people until such time as the diocese is able to arrange for a full complement of degreed personnel.

(4) Canon 1421, §2 speaks of the conference of bishops as the authority that can permit lay persons to be appointed judges. Since conferences of bishops are not part of the hierarchical ordering of the Eastern Catholic churches, the parallel canon in the Eastern code (*CCEO* 1087, §2) utilizes a somewhat different system for the granting of the permission.

2. The Regional Judge

Canon 1423 — §1. With the approval of the Apostolic See, several diocesan bishops can agree to establish a single tribunal of first instance for their dioceses in place of the diocesan tribunals mentioned in cann. 1419–1421. In this case, the group of bishops or a bishop they designate has all the powers which a diocesan bishop has over his own tribunal.

§2. The tribunals mentioned in §1 can be established either for any cases whatsoever or only for certain types of cases.

The 1917 code did not specifically mention regional tribunals. They were, however, adverted to in *Regimini Ecclesiae universae* of 1967;[54] the Signatura issued special norms to govern them in 1970;[55] and canon 1445, §3, 3° directs that the Signatura "promote and approve the erection" of these tribunals.[56]

Once erected, regional tribunals, of course, remain under the vigilance of the Signatura. Indeed, several regional tribunals that had been erected in the United States during the early 1980s were later suppressed because the Signatura found

some of their structures and practices unacceptable. The Signatura's principal objection in respect to these regional tribunals was that the defenders and judges on those tribunals were also serving as defenders and judges on first instance tribunals which were hierarchically subordinate to the regional tribunal. Although, in a given case, the judges and defender in second instance were always different from those who had served in first instance, the Signatura nevertheless found the system unacceptable.

3. The Single Judge with Assistance

Canon 1424 — In any trial, a single judge can employ two assessors who consult with him; they are to be clerics or lay persons of upright life.

This canon notes that a single judge may utilize the services of one or at the most two assessors who serve as consultors or advisors. It should be noted that the single judge as well as the collegiate tribunal may also, in accord with canon 1428, designate an auditor to carry out the instruction of the case.

For occasions when a case alleging the invalidity of a marriage may be heard by a single judge, one should see canon 1425, §4.

4. Plural Judges Acting as a College

Canon 1425 — §1. With every contrary custom reprobated, the following cases are reserved to a collegiate tribunal of three judges:

　　1° contentious cases: a) concerning the bond of sacred ordination; b) concerning the bond of marriage, without prejudice to the prescripts of cann. 1686 and 1688;

　　2° penal cases: a) concerning delicts which can entail the penalty of dismissal from the clerical state; b) concerning the imposition or declaration of an excommunication.

§2. The bishop can entrust more difficult cases or those of greater importance to the judgment of three or five judges.

---

[54] *CLD* 6, 351.
[55] *CLD* 7, 920–926.
[56] This directive was repeated in *PB* 124, 4°.

§3. Unless the bishop establishes otherwise in individual cases, the judicial vicar is to assign the judges in order by turn to adjudicate individual cases.

§4. If it happens that a collegiate tribunal cannot be established in the first instance of a trial, the conference of bishops can permit the bishop, for as long as the impossibility continues, to entrust cases to a single clerical judge who is to employ an assessor and auditor where possible.

§5. The judicial vicar is not to substitute judges once they have been assigned except for a most grave cause expressed in a decree.

Canon 1426 — §1. A collegiate tribunal must proceed collegially and render its sentences by majority vote.

§2. The judicial vicar or an adjutant judicial vicar must preside over a collegiate tribunal insofar as possible.

Canon 1425, §1 reserves to a collegiate tribunal of three judges several categories of cases, including those cases in which the invalidity of a marriage is alleged, which, as is well known, constitute more than 95 percent of all cases heard by ecclesiastical tribunals. Canon 1425, §4 outlines the circumstances under which such cases can be heard by a single clerical judge rather than by a collegiate tribunal.

This institute has an interesting history. For centuries prior to Pope Benedict XIV these cases were heard by a single judge. In 1741 that pope reformed the Church's procedural law for the hearing of marriage cases with his constitution *Dei miseratione,* but even though several procedural practices were changed by that constitution, such cases were still expected to be heard by a single judge.[57] In 1840 a new instruction on marriage procedures, *Cum moneat,* was issued, but still the rule of the single judge was maintained.[58] Four years later *Causae matrimoniales* was issued

specifically for tribunals of the United States, and this instruction likewise directed that marriage cases be heard by a single judge.[59]

Canon 1576, §1 of the 1917 code, however, broke with this centuries-long tradition and required marriage cases to be heard by a college of three judges, "with every contrary custom reprobated and every contrary privilege revoked." For the next five decades or so, few cases were heard in the United States; but finally, in 1970, the *American Procedural Norms* were approved for use in the United States. Norm 3 allowed that, under certain conditions, the NCCB, in accordance with faculties to be sought from the Holy See, could permit tribunals to have these cases adjudicated by a single clerical judge rather than by a collegiate tribunal.[60] The following year, Pope Paul VI issued for the universal Church the *motu proprio, Causas matrimoniales,* Norm V §2 of which contained a regulation similar to that of Norm 3 of the *American Procedural Norms.*[61] Canon 1425, §§1 and 4 are clearly derived from this *motu proprio.*

Canon 1425, §4 notes that it is the conference of bishops which can permit the bishop to entrust cases to a single clerical judge. As noted in the commentary on canon 1421, §2, conferences of bishops do not exist in the Eastern churches. Accordingly, the parallel Eastern canon (*CCEO* 1084, §3) arranges for the permission to be granted by a different authority.

Canon 1425, §5 notes that once a judge is assigned to a case he or she is to remain on the case without being replaced by a substitute unless there is "a most grave cause," which cause, the canon notes, is to be expressed in the decree of substitution. It would seem, however, that the inclusion of the cause (e.g., other duties, serious illness) in the decree is required for liceity but not for validity.[62]

[57] *CICFontes* I, n. 318, §4, p. 699.
[58] *CICFontes* VI, n. 4069, p. 346.
[59] *CICFontes* VII, n. 4901, 6, p. 480.
[60] *CLD* 7, 952.
[61] *Comm* 10 (1978) 234.
[62] Ibid.

Canon 1426, §1 notes that a collegiate tribunal should proceed collegially. For more on this matter, one should see canon 1609.

Finally, it should be noted that if a sentence was rendered by an illegitimate number of judges contrary to the prescription of canon 1425, §1, the sentence is vitiated by remediable nullity (c. 1622, 1°).

5. The Judge of Religious

Canon 1427 — §1. If there is a controversy between religious or houses of the same clerical religious institute of pontifical right, the judge of first instance is the provincial superior unless the constitutions provide otherwise; if it is an autonomous monastery, the local abbot judges in first instance.

§2. Without prejudice to a different prescript of the constitutions, if a contentious matter arises between two provinces, the supreme moderator will judge in first instance either personally or through a delegate; if the controversy is between two monasteries, the abbot superior of the monastic congregation will judge in first instance.

§3. Finally, if the controversy arises between physical or juridic religious persons of different religious institutes or of the same clerical institute of diocesan right or of the same lay institute, or between a religious and a secular cleric or lay person or a non-religious juridic person, the diocesan tribunal judges in first instance.

The three paragraphs of this canon speak of the three categories of judges who sit in first instance on various types of cases involving a religious person, physical or juridic. Paragraph one outlines the cases heard by the provincial superior or local abbot. Paragraph two refers to those cases heard by the supreme moderator of a religious institute or the abbot superior of a monastic congregation. Paragraph three speaks of those cases heard by a diocesan tribunal.

ARTICLE 2: AUDITORS AND RELATORS
[cc. 1428–1429]

1. The Auditor

Canon 1428 — §1. The judge or the president of a collegiate tribunal can designate an auditor, selected either from the judges of the tribunal or from persons the bishop approves for this function, to instruct the case.

§2. The bishop can approve for the function of auditor clerics or lay persons outstanding for their good character, prudence, and doctrine.

§3. It is for the auditor, according to the mandate of the judge, only to collect the proofs and hand those collected over to the judge. Unless the mandate of the judge prevents it, however, the auditor can in the meantime decide what proofs are to be collected and in what manner if a question may arise about this while the auditor exercises his or her function.

(a) The question of whether or not it is wise to involve auditors (or judge instructors, as they have been called)[63] in the judicial process, has long been hotly disputed. Cardinal Roberti, one of the more prestigious of the commentators on the procedural law of the 1917 code, was of the opinion that judge instructors did more harm than good, since their involvement necessarily resulted in the principal judge losing that immediate contact with the parties and witnesses that is so important in deciding a case.[64] The same argument

---

[63] CIC 1614, §1 juxtaposed the auditor with the "principal judge" as though to imply that the auditor was the "subsidiary judge." CIC 1580 referred to the auditor as "instructor of the acts," and several commentators used the term "judge instructor." The term "auditor" goes back to the early days of the Rota when the pope judged the case but employed others to audit (in an auditorium) the witnesses and collect and prepare the evidence. As a matter of fact, the men who even now serve as judges on the Rota are still referred to as auditors.

[64] F. Roberti, De processibus, 2 vols. (Rome: Libreria Pontificii Instituti Utriusque Iuris, 1941) I:295.

was made in an attempt to suppress the office of auditor in the 1983 code at the April 8, 1978 meeting of the consultors of the commission.[65]

The office has, however, been retained in the 1983 code, and it has indeed been found immensely useful in some tribunals for many years now. Some American tribunals employ a great many instructors who are responsible for collecting and presenting all the evidence to the defender of the bond and the judge, thus enabling the tribunal to be of assistance to far more people than would ever be possible if the judge had to do all the auditing personally. Roberti's point is, of course, a valid one, but it must be weighed against the demands being made on tribunals today to serve such large numbers of petitioners.

(b) In its treatment of the auditor, the 1917 code (*CIC* 1580–1583) completely neglected any mention of the qualities to be found in the auditor, except to say that if possible he should be selected from among the synodal judges. This may have been a lacuna but, more likely, it is just another indication that the 1917 code viewed the auditor as a true, if subsidiary, judge and assumed, therefore, that he should possess the same qualities as the judge. The post-1917 code commentators, furthermore, were in general agreement that since the auditor exercised judicial power, it would be necessary for him to be a cleric.[66] The present canon 1428, §2, however, explicitly permits the lay person (*Causas matrimoniales* permitted the lay *man*) to serve as auditor.[67]

(c) For the distinction between an auditor and a "designated receiver," one should see canon 1528.

2. The Relator or Ponens

Canon 1429 — The president of a collegiate tribunal must designate one of the judges of the col-

lege as the *ponens* or *relator* who is to report about the case at the meeting of the judges and put the sentence into writing. For a just cause the president can substitute another in place of the original *relator*.

For more regarding the duties of the *ponens,* one should see canons 1609, §3; 1610, §2; and 1677, §§1, 2, and 4.

An example of a just cause for which the president might replace the original *ponens* with one of the other judges on the panel might occur when, at the voting session (c. 1609), the original *ponens* is in strong disagreement with the other two judges and is outvoted.

The relator or *ponens* has also been called the referee.[68]

ARTICLE 3: THE PROMOTER OF JUSTICE, THE DEFENDER OF THE BOND, AND THE NOTARY [cc. 1430–1437]

THE PROMOTER AND DEFENDER [cc. 1430–1436]

1. Need to Be Appointed

Canon 1430 — A promoter of justice is to be appointed in a diocese for contentious cases which can endanger the public good and for penal cases; the promoter of justice is bound by office to provide for the public good.

Canon 1431 — §1. In contentious cases, it is for the diocesan bishop to judge whether or not the public good can be endangered unless the intervention of the promoter of justice is prescribed by law or is clearly necessary from the nature of the matter.

---

[65] *Comm* 10 (1978) 232.

[66] Dugan, quoting D'Angelo, disagreed. H. Dugan, *The Judiciary Department of the Diocesan Curia* (Washington, D.C.: Catholic University of America, 1925) 52.

[67] See also the commentary on c. 1421.

[68] C. Augustine, *A Commentary on the New Code of Canon Law*, vol. VII, *Ecclesiastical Trials* (St. Louis: B. Herder, 1923) 40; W. Doheny, *Canonical Procedure in Matrimonial Cases*, 2 vols. (Milwaukee: Bruce, 1944) I:81.

§2. If the promoter of justice has intervened in a previous instance, such intervention is presumed necessary in a further instance.

Canon 1432 — A defender of the bond is to be appointed in a diocese for cases concerning the nullity of sacred ordination or the nullity or dissolution of a marriage; the defender of the bond is bound by office to propose and explain everything which reasonably can be brought forth against nullity or dissolution.

The promoter of justice is involved in all penal cases and in those contentious cases in which the public welfare is involved. The public welfare is involved (1) when the bishop decides it is (as, for example, when a quarrel between two priests over the possession of an office is judged to have become sufficiently public as to have caused considerable scandal), or (2) when the law says it is (as, for example, when c. 1691 indicates that the public good is involved in all marriage nullity cases and when c. 1696 declares that any separation case involves the commonweal), or (3) when the matter is obviously public (as, for example, when it is a highly publicized matter involving well-known people).

A particular promoter may be appointed, as canon 1436, §2 notes, either permanently or on an ad hoc basis, but canon 1430 indicates that there should be a promoter in every diocese.

The office of defender postdates that of the promoter,[69] and some authors regard the defender as a species of promoter. This linkage between the defender and the promoter dates back to the days just prior to *Dei miseratione* when some authors were urging that, just as the promoter was active in other cases as a protector of law and of justice, so he should also be active in matrimonial cases as a protector of the bond of marriage against the possible fraud and/or collusion of the parties. *Dei miseratione* then incorporated the idea, but, as it were, gave the promoter a new name, namely that of defender.[70]

The role of the defender, as canon 1432 points out, is to propose and clarify everything which can be reasonably adduced against nullity or dissolution. In those cases where, in the judgment of the defender, nothing can be reasonably adduced against nullity, the defender may not speak in favor of nullity but may entrust the decision to the wisdom and justice of the tribunal.[71]

Like the promoter, a particular defender may be appointed either permanently or on an ad hoc basis (c. 1436, §2), but canon 1432 indicates that there should be a defender in every diocese.

Although the public good is, to some extent, present in every case that alleges the invalidity of a marriage, the intervention of the promoter is considered necessary only when the promoter impugns the marriage or when it is judged that the intervention of the promoter is deemed important for safeguarding the procedures. Otherwise, the intervention of the defender of the bond is regarded as sufficient. Perhaps this reflects Coronata's opinion that the defender is, as it were, a species of promoter.

2. Need to Be Cited

Canon 1433 — If the promoter of justice or defender of the bond was not cited in cases which require their presence, the acts are invalid unless they actually took part even if not cited or, after they have inspected the acts, at least were able to fulfill their function before the sentence.

---

[69] The promoter served as a prosecutor during the Inquisition, whereas the office of defender was not instituted until 1741 by Benedict XIV in the constitution *Dei miseratione*.

[70] M. Coronata, *Institutiones iuris canonici*, vol. III, *De processibus* (Rome: Marietti, 1956) 45 and J. Glynn, *The Promoter of Justice, His Rights and Duties* (Washington, D.C.: Catholic University of America, 1936) 39.

[71] For a neat description of the role of the defender, see *RRAO 1992*, 125–127, and *CLSA Advisory Opinions 1984–1993*, ed. P. Cogan (Washington, D.C.: CLSA, 1995) 452–454.

3. Rights

Canon 1434 — Unless other provision is expressly made:
1° **whenever the law requires the judge to hear either both or one of the parties, the promoter of justice and the defender of the bond must also be heard if they take part in the trial;**
2° **whenever the request of a party is required in order for the judge to be able to decide something, the request of the promoter of justice or defender of the bond who takes part in the trial has the same force.**

Although this canon indicates that the rights of the promoter and defender are somewhat akin to those of the parties, there is, of course, a difference since the parties are protecting a private interest whereas the promoter and defender are providing for the public good.

4. Nomination and Qualities

Canon 1435 — It is for the bishop to appoint the promoter of justice and defender of the bond; they are to be clerics or lay persons, of unimpaired reputation, doctors or licensed in canon law, and proven in prudence and zeal for justice.

5. Separateness and Removal

Canon 1436 — §1. The same person can hold the office of promoter of justice and defender of the bond but not in the same case.
§2. The promoter and the defender can be appointed for all cases or for individual cases; however, the bishop can remove them for a just cause.

THE NOTARY
[c. 1437]

Canon 1437 — §1. A notary is to take part in any process, so much so that the acts are null if the notary has not signed them.

§2. Acts which notaries prepare warrant public trust.

For more on the notary, one should see canons 483–485.

CHAPTER II
THE TRIBUNAL OF SECOND INSTANCE
[cc. 1438–1441]

Chapter 2 comprises four canons. The first two treat of the sources of competence of various second instance tribunals, the third speaks of the incompetence of an illegitimate second instance tribunal, i.e. one not endowed with one of the titles of competence mentioned in the two former canons; and the fourth summarizes the way in which second instance tribunals are constituted.

Competent Second Instance Tribunals

1. For the Diocesan Tribunal

Canon 1438 — Without prejudice to the prescript of can. 1444, §1, n. 1:
1° **from the tribunal of a suffragan bishop, appeal is made to the metropolitan tribunal, without prejudice to the prescript of can. 1439;**

Canon 1438 begins with the words "Without prejudice to the prescript of can. 1444, §1, n. 1." The sense, then, is that ordinarily an appeal from the tribunal of a suffragan bishop goes to the tribunal of the metropolitan bishop, but a party always has a right to appeal the sentence of a diocesan tribunal (or, for that matter, the first instance decision of a metropolitan or religious tribunal) *directly* to the Roman Rota.

Canon 1438, 1° also notes that the prescription of canon 1439 is to be observed. If, in other words, the tribunal of a diocese is a first instance *regional* tribunal, the rules of canon 1439 apply.

2. For the Metropolitan Tribunal

2° in cases tried in first instance before the metropolitan, appeal is made to the tribunal which the metropolitan has designated in a stable manner with the approval of the Apostolic See;

Once a tribunal has been designated as the appellate tribunal for a metropolitan tribunal, it is understood that the designation is a stable one and not merely a temporary arrangement.

3. For a Religious Tribunal

3° for cases tried before a provincial superior, the tribunal of second instance is under the authority of the supreme moderator; for cases tried before the local abbot, the tribunal of second instance is under the authority of the abbot superior of the monastic congregation.

4. For a Regional Tribunal

Canon 1439 — §1. If a single tribunal of first instance has been established for several dioceses according to the norm of can. 1423, the conference of bishops must establish a tribunal of second instance with the approval of the Apostolic See unless the dioceses are all suffragans of the same archdiocese.

§2. With the approval of the Apostolic See, a conference of bishops can establish one or more tribunals of second instance in addition to the cases mentioned in §1.

§3. Over the tribunals of second instance mentioned in §§1–2, the conference of bishops or the bishop it designates has all the powers which a diocesan bishop has over his own tribunal.

Canon 1438 notes that from the tribunal of a suffragan bishop appeal is made to the metropolitan tribunal. In some instances, all or some of the suffragan dioceses, instead of maintaining their own individual tribunals, will, in accord with canon 1423, form one regional tribunal. Ordinarily the decisions of that regional tribunal will be appealed for a second instance hearing to the metropolitan tribunal, but canon 1439, §2 notes that an alternative arrangement can be established. In some countries, for example, there is a single national appellate tribunal which serves as the second instance tribunal for all cases, whether those cases were heard in first instance by a diocesan, metropolitan, or even regional tribunal. This is one of several possible options envisioned in canon 1439, §2.

Canon 1439, §1 mentions another situation which is not optional but obligatory. When a first instance regional tribunal is established which comprises several dioceses, all of which are *not* suffragans of the same archdiocese (for example, when the regional tribunal comprises all of the suffragans of the metropolitan tribunal plus the metropolitan itself, i.e., all the tribunals of a single province), then a tribunal of second instance for that regional tribunal must be constituted by the conference of bishops with the approval of the Apostolic See, i.e., the Apostolic Signatura.

Finally, it should be noted that since the Eastern churches have a somewhat different hierarchical ordering than the Latin church, the parallel Eastern canons (*CCEO* 1064–1069) deal with this matter in a manner that is appropriate to their own structures.

Incompetent Second Instance Tribunal

Canon 1440 — If competence by reason of grade according to the norm of cann. 1438 and 1439 is not observed, the incompetence of the judge is absolute.

Regarding the implications of absolute incompetence, one should see the commentary on canon 1406.

The Constitution of Second Instance Tribunals

Canon 1441 — The tribunal of second instance must be established in the same way as the tribunal of first instance. Nevertheless, if a single

judge rendered a sentence in the first instance of the trial according to can. 1425, §4, the tribunal of second instance is to proceed collegially.

This canon deals with the way in which a tribunal of second instance is *constituted*. As in first instance, in other words, there should be a judicial vicar, judges, auditors, relators, a promoter of justice, a defender of the bond, and a notary. For the way in which an appellate tribunal *functions* one should see canon 1640.

The canon does not say that *every* trial settled by a single judge in first instance must be heard by a college in second, but only those trials which were settled by a single judge in virtue of canon 1425, §4. If, therefore, the case is a minor one (as when the tribunal is settling a dispute between two persons) and not consequently reserved to a college, it may be heard by a single judge in both instances.

CHAPTER III
THE TRIBUNALS OF THE APOSTOLIC SEE
[cc. 1442–1445]

Chapter 3 comprises four canons. The first canon speaks of the supreme judge; the next two canons treat of the Roman Rota, and the fourth concerns the Apostolic Signatura.

The Supreme Judge

Canon 1442 — The Roman Pontiff is the supreme judge for the entire Catholic world; he renders judicial decisions personally, through the ordinary tribunals of the Apostolic See, or through judges he has delegated.

Since, as canon 331 notes, the Roman Pontiff enjoys supreme, full, immediate, and universal power in the Church, and since, according to canon 135, §1, the power of governance in the Church is legislative, executive, *and judicial,* it follows, as canon 1442 says, that "the Roman Pontiff is the supreme judge for the entire Catholic world."

One should also see canon 1417, §1 on the broad right of the faithful to introduce cases for adjudication at the Holy See.

The Roman Rota

According to canons 1443 and 1444 the Roman Rota may act either as an ordinary appellate tribunal or as a delegated tribunal.

1. As Ordinary Appellate Tribunal

Canon 1443 — The Roman Rota is the ordinary tribunal established by the Roman Pontiff to receive appeals.

Canon 1444 — §1. The Roman Rota judges:
  1° in second instance, cases which have been adjudicated by the ordinary tribunals of first instance and brought before the Holy See through legitimate appeal;
  2° in third or further instance, cases which the Roman Rota or any other tribunals have already adjudicated unless the matter is a *res iudicata*.

Although an appeal from a first instance decision is usually lodged with the domestic tribunal of appeal in accord with canon 1438, appellants are also free, in accord with canon 1444, §1, 1° to appeal directly to the Roman Rota for the second instance hearing. In accordance with canon 1444, §1, 2°, a case generally goes to the Roman Rota for the third instance when the two lower tribunals are not in agreement. There are, however, exceptions to this general rule. Both Spain[72] and Hungary[73] have had stable third instance tribunals for many years, and during World War II both Austria and the United States were also allowed a third instance hearing within their own countries.[74] In more recent years some conferences of bishops

---

[72] *AAS* 39 (1947) 155–163.
[73] A. Szentirmai, "The Primate of Hungary," *J* 21 (1961) 36 and 44.
[74] *CLD* 2, 459–460.

have periodically shown an interest in obtaining an indult to establish a third instance court in their own countries, but Rome has generally taken a dim view of such efforts—partly perhaps because of a concern that a proliferation of third instance courts might give rise to national inbreeding and so result in a loss of jurisprudential catholicity, and partly because of a concern that the individual conferences would not be able to staff these courts with the kind of Solomonic judges that would be necessary at that level.[75]

The Rota (the name means "wheel") probably takes its name either from the fact that the judges originally sat in a circle or because there was a circle on the chamber floor at Avignon where the title is first known to have been used (ca. 1350), or because the cases under consideration were moved from judge to judge on a book stand which was on wheels. At any rate, the Rota has not only retained the name but still uses the wheel as its logo.

The Roman Rota dates back to the twelfth century, though in those days the auditors, who were the pope's chaplains, were only auditors (c. 1428) and not judges as they are today.

In 1870, when the Papal States were incorporated into the Kingdom of Italy, the Rota lost most of its jurisdiction and thereafter the auditors acted as judges only in causes of beatification and canonization. In 1908, however, Pope Pius X reconstituted the Rota as the ordinary judicial forum of the Holy See, and this marks, as it were, the beginning of the Rota's modern history.[76]

In accord with canon 1402 the Rota follows its own norms.[77]

2. As Delegated Tribunal

§2. This tribunal also judges in first instance the cases mentioned in can. 1405, §3 and others

which the Roman Pontiff, either *motu proprio* or at the request of the parties, has called to his own tribunal and entrusted to the Roman Rota; unless the rescript entrusting the function provides otherwise, the Rota also judges these cases in second and further instance.

Some authors have pointed out that the Rota is here functioning with delegated power.[78] The reference in the canon to "the rescript entrusting the function" suggests that the point may be well made.

The Apostolic Signatura

The three paragraphs of canon 1445 outline the three areas in which the Apostolic Signatura functions:

1. In Judicial Matters

Canon 1445 — §1. The supreme tribunal of the Apostolic Signatura adjudicates:
1° **complaints of nullity, petitions for *restitutio in integrum* and other recourses against rotal sentences;**
2° **recourses in cases concerning the status of persons which the Roman Rota refused to admit to a new examination;**
3° **exceptions of suspicion and other cases against the auditors of the Roman Rota for acts done in the exercise of their function;**
4° **conflicts of competence mentioned in can. 1416.**

2. In Contentious Administrative Matters

§2. This tribunal deals with conflicts which have arisen from an act of ecclesiastical administrative power and are brought before it legitimately, with other administrative controversies

---

[75] Regatillo, 253–259. See also E. Egan, "Appeal in Marriage Nullity Cases," *CLSAP* (1981) 135–138.

[76] J. Noonan, *Power to Dissolve* (Cambridge, Mass.: Belknap, 1972) 183.

[77] *AAS* 86 (1994) 508–540.

[78] Lega-Bartocetti, I:182–183, and Coronata, 56, nn. 5 and 6.

which the Roman Pontiff or the dicasteries of the Roman Curia bring before it, and with a conflict of competence among these dicasteries.

3. In Noncontentious Administrative Matters

§3. Furthermore it is for this supreme tribunal:

   1° to watch over the correct administration of justice and discipline advocates or procurators if necessary;

   2° to extend the competence of tribunals;

   3° to promote and approve the erection of the tribunals mentioned in cann. 1423 and 1439.

According to both *Regimini Ecclesiae universae* and the Special Norms of Government of the Signatura, judicial matters (§1) and noncontentious administrative matters were handled by the so-called "first section" of the Signatura,[79] while contentious administrative matters (§2) were heard by the "second section."[80] Since, however, neither *Pastor bonus*[81](which supplanted *Regimini Ecclesiae universae*) nor the 1983 code speaks of different sections of the Signatura, some authors have concluded that the Signatura is a single tribunal with different functions.[82]

The Apostolic Signatura had its origins in the referendaries or reporters who worked in civil chanceries in the beginning of the Middle Ages. In the Church the referendaries studied and sorted out the various requests received by the popes. By the fifteenth century they came to be called "Referendaries of the Signature" because they pre-

sented for the signature of the pope drafts of rescripts, and during that same century Pope Eugene IV established the "Signatura" as a separate department. Initially it was composed of two sections: the *Signatura Gratiae* and the *Signatura Justitiae,* but by the nineteenth century the former had lost its importance and was suppressed while the latter became the prototype of the present Apostolic Signatura. Over the centuries the Signatura of Justice developed and was reorganized several times. Finally in 1908 it was restored by Pope Pius X and declared to be the supreme tribunal of the Apostolic See.[83]

TITLE III
THE DISCIPLINE TO BE OBSERVED IN TRIBUNALS
[cc. 1446–1475]

Title III is divided into five chapters: "The Duty of Judges and Ministers of the Tribunal" (I); "The Order of Adjudication" (II); "Time Limits and Delays" (III); "The Place of the Trial" (IV); and "Persons to Be Admitted to the Court and the Manner of Preparing and Keeping the Acts" (V).

CHAPTER I
THE DUTY OF JUDGES AND MINISTERS OF THE TRIBUNAL
[cc. 1446–1457]

This chapter contains twelve canons and may be viewed as consisting of two basic sections. The first section, comprising canons 1446–1456, concerns the duties or obligations of the judge and other tribunal ministers; the second section, consisting only of canon 1457, concerns the

---

[79] *RE* 105 in *CLD* 6, 351, and Special Norms, 17, §2 in *CLD* 7, 250–251.

[80] *RE* 106 in *CLD* 6, 351, and Special Norms, 96 in *CLD* 7, 263.

[81] *PB* 122–124.

[82] B. Gangoiti, "Sfera materiale e ottica del processo amministrativo ecclesiastico," *Studia Lateranensia* 1 (1989) 352. But see F. Ramos, *I Tribunali Ecclesiastici, Costituzione, Organizzazione, Norme Processuali* (Rome: Millennium Romae, 1998) 178–182.

[83] *NCE* 13, 209–210.

penalties for failing to carry out the substantial duties of office.

Duties

1. The Duty of Urging an Out-of-Court Settlement

Canon 1446 — §1. All the Christian faithful, and especially bishops, are to strive diligently to avoid litigation among the people of God as much as possible, without prejudice to justice, and to resolve litigation peacefully as soon as possible.

§2. Whenever the judge perceives some hope of a favorable outcome at the start of litigation or even at any other time, the judge is not to neglect to encourage and assist the parties to collaborate in seeking an equitable solution to the controversy and to indicate to them suitable means to this end, even by using reputable persons for mediation.

§3. If the litigation concerns the private good of the parties, the judge is to discern whether the controversy can be concluded advantageously by an agreement or the judgment of arbitrators according to the norm of cann. 1713–1716.

This is a generic statement about encouraging a peaceful solution to the problem. It is repeated in more specific form in canons 1341 (penalties as a last resort); 1659, §1 (regarding the oral contentious process); 1676 (on receiving a petition in a marriage case); 1695 (on receiving a petition for separation of spouses); 1713–1716 (regarding contentious matters); 1733 (when one considers himself or herself aggrieved by a decree); and 1742 and 1748 (regarding the removal or transfer of a pastor).

2. The Duty to Avoid Serving in Another Instance on the Same Case

Canon 1447 — A person who has taken part in a case as a judge, promoter of justice, defender of the bond, procurator, advocate, witness, or expert cannot later in another instance validly decide the same case as judge or perform the function of assessor.

The use of the word "validly" in the canon should be noted. If, therefore, a person were to contravene this canon, the sentence in the later instance would be irremediably null (c. 1620, 1°).

3. The Duty to Withdraw When Required

Canon 1448 — §1. A judge is not to undertake the adjudication of a case in which the judge is involved by reason of consanguinity or affinity in any degree of the direct line and up to the fourth degree of the collateral line or by reason of trusteeship, guardianship, close acquaintance, great animosity, the making of a profit, or the avoidance of a loss.

§2. In these circumstances the promoter of justice, the defender of the bond, the assessor, and the auditor must abstain from their office.

Canon 1449 — §1. If in the cases mentioned in can. 1448 the judge does not withdraw, a party can lodge an objection against the judge.

§2. The judicial vicar deals with the objection; if the objection is lodged against him, the bishop who presides over the tribunal deals with it.

§3. If the bishop is the judge and the objection is lodged against him, he is to abstain from judging.

§4. If the objection is lodged against the promoter of justice, the defender of the bond, or other officials of the tribunal, the president in a collegiate tribunal or the single judge deals with this exception.

Canon 1450 — If the objection is accepted, the persons must be changed but not the grade of the trial.

Canon 1451 — §1. The question of an objection must be decided as promptly as possible (expeditissime) after the parties have been heard as well as the promoter of justice or defender of the bond, if they take part in the trial and are not the ones against whom the objection has been lodged.

§2. Acts placed by a judge before an objection is lodged are valid; nevertheless, those acts placed

after the objection has been lodged must be rescinded if a party requests it within ten days from the acceptance of the objection.

This grouping of canons deals with two species of possible conflict of interest. Canon 1448 discusses voluntary withdrawal from a case by a major tribunal official when that official has a personal interest in the case, while the following three canons treat of the case in which a party lodges an objection (known as a "recusal") against an official when the official, despite a personal interest in the case, declines to withdraw voluntarily.

Canon 1448 lists the reasons on account of which an official should withdraw. These basically are consanguinity/affinity, guardianship/curatorship, friendship/animosity, and profit/loss. Doheny noted that some authors regarded that list (which is identical in the two codes) as exhaustive while others considered it demonstrative.[84] Doheny himself took a middle ground, saying that, in terms of strict obligation to withdraw, the list is exhaustive, but in terms of an optional withdrawal, the list is only demonstrative. The Pamplona commentary observes that the list is also merely demonstrative in terms of canon 1449 where the party is lodging an exception to an official who, despite personal interest, has declined to withdraw.[85]

Canon 1451, §1 notes that the issue of an objection is to be handled as promptly as possible (*expeditissime*), which means, according to canon 1629, 5°, that there is no appeal against the decision. There are, in the code, five other examples of decisions that do not admit of appeal because the issues are to be handled *expeditissime:* recourse against the rejection of a libellus (c. 1505, §4); recourse against the joinder of issues (c. 1513, §3); the insistence by a party that a proof rejected by the judge be admitted (c. 1527, §2); a decision in an incidental case (c. 1589, §1); and a question regarding the right of appeal (c. 1631).

[84] Doheny, I:90.

[85] L. Del Amo and R. Rodriguez Ocaña, in *Pamplona ComEng*, 904.

4. The Duty to Proceed Properly in All Cases

Canon 1452 — §1. In a matter which concerns private persons alone, a judge can proceed only at the request of a party. Once a case has been legitimately introduced, however, the judge can and must proceed even *ex officio* in penal cases and other cases which regard the public good of the Church or the salvation of souls.

§2. Furthermore, the judge can supply for the negligence of the parties in furnishing proofs or in lodging exceptions whenever the judge considers it necessary in order to avoid a gravely unjust judgment, without prejudice to the prescripts of can. 1600.

This canon distinguishes between two categories of cases: a) those which concern private individuals only and b) penal cases, cases involving the public good, and cases involving the salvation of souls. In the former, judges may proceed only at the request of a party, whereas in the latter, they may proceed on their own initiative. In both categories of cases, however, a judge may, in accord with paragraph two, supply for the neglect of the parties when appropriate. Canon 1530 serves as an example of this sort of judicial activity.

For more on cases involving the public good, one should see the commentary on canon 1430. To say that a judge may proceed *ex officio* in cases involving the public good does not, of course, mean that the judge himself may initiate such a case but only that, once the case has been legitimately introduced, the judge may, in the interest of justice and of obtaining a fuller truth, actively participate in the progress of the investigation.

5. The Duty to Conclude Cases Expeditiously

Canon 1453 — Without prejudice to justice, judges and tribunals are to take care that all cases are completed as soon as possible and that in a tribunal of first instance they are not prolonged beyond a year and in a tribunal of second instance beyond six months.

The Church has a centuries-old interest in avoiding all unnecessary delays in ecclesiastical trials, an interest reiterated by many popes and councils.[86]

6. The Duty to Take an Oath

Canon 1454 — All who constitute a tribunal or assist it must take an oath to carry out their function correctly and faithfully.

This oath customarily includes not only the obligation to fulfill one's function properly and faithfully but also to maintain secrecy (c. 1455) and not to accept any gifts in one's tribunal ministry (c. 1456). The oath is generally made while touching a book of the gospels or, in the case of a priest, while touching his heart.[87]

In accord with the policy of the Pontifical Commission for the Revision of the Code of Eastern Canon Law to limit the taking of oaths to an absolute minimum in the Eastern code,[88] canon 1112 of that code requires tribunal personnel to make a promise rather than to take an oath.

7. The Duty to Maintain Secrecy

Canon 1455 — §1. Judges and tribunal personnel are always bound to observe secrecy of office in a penal trial, as well as in a contentious trial if the revelation of some procedural act could bring disadvantage to the parties.

§2. They are also always bound to observe secrecy concerning the discussion among the judges in a collegiate tribunal before the sentence is passed and concerning the various votes and opinions expressed there, without prejudice to the prescript of can. 1609, §4.

§3. Whenever the nature of the case or the proofs is such that disclosure of the acts or proofs will endanger the reputation of others, provide opportunity for discord, or give rise to scandal or some other disadvantage, the judge can bind the witnesses, the experts, the parties, and their advocates or procurators by oath to observe secrecy.

Paragraph one speaks of the distinction between secrecy in a penal trial and secrecy in a contentious trial. Paragraph two speaks of the secrecy the judges are to maintain regarding their deliberative session described in canon 1609. Paragraph three speaks of the right of the judge to oblige to secrecy even those who are not formally part of the tribunal.

In general this canon is to be understood in the context of canon 1598 which permits the parties and their advocates to inspect the acts prior to the conclusion and discussion of the case. The sense of the present canon is that the officers of the court may not discuss the case with any *third* party, i.e., any party not having legitimate access to the acts.[89]

8. The Duty Not to Accept Gifts

Canon 1456 — The judge and all officials of the tribunal are prohibited from accepting any gifts on the occasion of their acting in a trial.

Penalties for Abuse of Office

Canon 1457 — §1. The competent authority can punish with fitting penalties, not excluding privation from office, judges who refuse to render a judgment when they are certainly and manifestly competent, who declare themselves competent with no supporting prescript of law and adjudicate and decide cases, who violate the law of secrecy, or who inflict some other damage on the litigants out of malice or grave negligence.

§2. The ministers and personnel of a tribunal are subject to these same sanctions if they fail in

---

[86] F. D'Ostilio, "Le sollecitudini della Chiesa in favore della giusta rapidità dei processi," *ME* 112 (1987) 347–377; idem, "La durata media delle cause matrimoniali," *ME* 114 (1989) 185–236.

[87] *CIC* 1622, §1, and *Provida Mater Ecclesia* 96, §1.

[88] *Nu* 18 (1984) 57 (c. 97 of the original 1981 schema on general norms and temporal goods).

[89] See also c. 1470, §1.

their office as described above; the judge can also punish all of them.

CHAPTER II
THE ORDER OF ADJUDICATION
[cc. 1458–1464]

Chapter 2 comprises seven canons. The first canon deals with the order in which different cases are to be heard; the other six canons discuss the order in which subordinate issues are to be heard.

Different Cases

Canon 1458 — Cases are to be adjudicated in the order in which they were presented and inscribed in the register unless one of them requires speedier treatment than the others; this fact must be established through a special decree which gives the substantiating reasons.

Subordinate Issues

Upon receiving a petition, a court does not always move uninterruptedly toward the settlement of the principal issue. Occasionally it gets sidetracked in the settlement of subordinate issues. This section explains at what stage of the proceedings such subordinate issues should be handled. Other aspects of these subordinate issues are discussed elsewhere and at greater length under canons 1491–1500 (actions and exceptions) and under canons 1587–1597 (incidental cases). The present section concerns itself primarily with the question: at what stage of the proceedings should such matters be settled by the court?

The subordinate issues discussed in this chapter are five: dilatory exceptions (c. 1459), exceptions against the competence of the judge or the judge's own awareness of incompetence (cc. 1460–1461), peremptory exceptions (c. 1462), counterclaims (c. 1463), and questions about judicial expenses (c. 1464).

Dilatory Exceptions

Canon 1459 — §1. Defects which can render the sentence null can be introduced as exceptions at any stage or grade of the trial; the judge can likewise declare them *ex officio*.

§2. In addition to the cases mentioned in §1, dilatory exceptions, especially those which regard the persons and the manner of the trial, must be proposed before the joinder of the issue unless they emerged after the issue was already joined; they must be decided as soon as possible.

An *exception* is a claim or complaint (strictly speaking, a complaint made by the defendant) which either modifies the procedure in some way or quashes the action altogether. A *dilatory* exception is one which does not aim at extinguishing the action but only at modifying it in some way, e.g., asking that the joinder of issues be changed.

Dilatory exceptions can be either major or minor. A *major* dilatory exception points out some procedural defect that will result in the nullity of the sentence, e.g., that the sentence does not contain the reasons for the decision (c. 1622, 2°). A *minor* dilatory exception refers to procedural points or other matters that do not affect the validity of the sentence.

Canon 1459 points out that major dilatory exceptions can be introduced at any stage or grade of a trial,[90] whereas minor dilatory exceptions should generally be proposed prior to the joinder of issues.

Exceptions against the Competence of the Judge

Canon 1460 — §1. If an exception is proposed against the competence of the judge, that judge must deal with the matter.

§2. In the case of an exception of relative incompetence, if the judge finds for competence, the decision does not admit of appeal; a com-

---

[90] But see cc. 1621 and 1623 for the time periods during which one may lodge a complaint against irremediably and remediably null sentences.

plaint of nullity and *restitutio in integrum,* however, are not prohibited.

§3. If the judge finds for incompetence, however, the party who feels injured can appeal to the appellate tribunal within fifteen useful days.

Canon 1461 — A judge who becomes aware of being absolutely incompetent at any stage of the case must declare the incompetence.

Canon 1460, §1 states the general rule that the judge whose competence is in question is the judge who deals with the exception.

Canon 1460, §§2 and 3 deal with the *relative* incompetence of the judge and would therefore constitute a *minor* dilatory exception.[91] Generally, therefore, the judge would resolve the case by a decree rather than by an interlocutory sentence.[92]

According to the general rule (c. 1629, 4°) there is normally no room for appeal either from a judicial decree or from an interlocutory sentence which does not have the force of a definitive sentence. The issue of the relative incompetence of the judge, however, follows its own, rather unusual, rule, namely: if the judge finds *against* incompetence, then there is no appeal;[93] but if the judge finds *for* incompetence, then the decision does admit of appeal.

Canon 1461 deals not with relative but with *absolute* incompetence. It notes that judges who become aware of their absolute incompetence (either on their own or through an exception lodged against their competence) must declare that incompetence.

Exceptions against the absolute incompetence of the judge are considered major dilatory exceptions because when the incompetence is absolute[94]

it renders the sentence invalid and, indeed, effectively brings an end to the instance. Such exceptions, however, are not considered peremptory because they do not altogether extinguish the action since the action may then be brought to another tribunal that does enjoy competence.

Peremptory Exceptions

Canon 1462 — §1. Exceptions of *res iudicata,* of agreement, and other peremptory exceptions which are called *litis finitae* must be proposed and adjudicated before the joinder of the issue. A person who proposes them later must not be rejected but is liable for expenses unless the person proves that the presentation was not delayed maliciously.

§2. Other peremptory exceptions are to be proposed during the joinder of the issue and must be treated at the proper time according to the rules for incidental questions.

A peremptory exception is a complaint that quashes the action altogether. Peremptory exceptions can be either *closed case* exceptions (*litis finitae*) or exceptions *to the action.*

Closed case exceptions (c. 1462, §1) claim, in effect, that the case has already been settled either by another tribunal or perhaps by a negotiated settlement *(transactio)* or arbitration.[95] Such exceptions should ordinarily be lodged before the joinder of issues but may be lodged later as well in accord with canon 1462, §1.

Exceptions *to the action* (c. 1462, §2), on the other hand, do not claim that the case was otherwise settled but do claim that, for some reason, the matter should not be heard. For example: the plaintiff sues the defendant, stating that the defendant never paid him or her the agreed upon $50,000 for the purchase of a piece of property. The defendant then lodges a peremptory excep-

---

[91] Regatillo, par. 350.

[92] Canon 1589, §1.

[93] The other two standard "remedies" against a sentence, however, namely, the complaint of nullity (cc. 1619–1627) and reinstatement (cc. 1645–1648), are permitted.

[94] See cc. 1406, §2 (where judges other than the Roman Pontiff are absolutely incompetent in cases reserved to

him); 1417, §2 (where the Apostolic See has called a case to itself); and 1440 (where competence by reason of grade has not been observed).

[95] See cc. 1446, §3 and 1713–1715.

tion, claiming that the so-called bill of sale is a forgery and that it was always the respondent and never the petitioner who owned the property. Such exceptions are treated according to the rules on incidental cases as found in canons 1587–1597.

Counterclaims

Canon 1463 — §1. Counterclaims cannot be proposed validly except within thirty days from the joinder of the issue.

§2. They are to be adjudicated, however, along with the original action, that is, in the same grade with it unless it is necessary to adjudicate them separately or the judge considers it more opportune to do so.

The counterclaim is known in Latin as *actio reconventionalis,* or *reconventio,* i.e., a reconvening of the petitioner by the respondent. It is also referred to as a second convening, or reciprocal petition. It may be defined as a petition made by the respondent in order to offset the original petition. One party in a marriage, for example, sues for a separation; the other party then sues for a declaration of invalidity.

For the difference between an exception and a counterclaim or counteraction, one should see the commentary on canons 1494–1495.

Questions about Judicial Expenses

Canon 1464 — Questions concerning the provision for judicial expenses or a grant of gratuitous legal assistance which had been requested from the very beginning and other such questions as a rule must be dealt with before the joinder of the issue.

CHAPTER III
TIME LIMITS AND DELAYS
[cc. 1465–1467]

Time limits are of three kinds: legal (when they are defined by the law), judicial (when they

are defined by the judge), and conventional (when they are defined by the parties).

All three kinds of time limits can be either peremptory or non-peremptory. Peremptory time limits are those which extinguish the right in question if the time limit is not met. Non-peremptory time limits, if unmet, do not extinguish the right.

As regards *legal* time limits, the rule of thumb is that those that refer to the parties are peremptory, whereas those that refer to the tribunal (or judge) are non-peremptory.[96] An example of the former is canon 1505, §4 which gives the petitioner ten days to appeal a rejection of a petition; after those ten days the right is considered extinguished. See also canons 1460, §3; 1623; 1630, §1; 1633; and 1646. An example of the latter is canon 1453 which says that a tribunal should complete a first instance hearing in a year and a second instance hearing in six months; if, however, the tribunal has not in fact completed the instances in the allotted time, no right is extinguished. For another example of the legal non-peremptory time limit, one might look at canon 1609, §5 where the judges, at their deliberative session, can postpone sentencing but not more than a week; again, if the meeting is deferred beyond that time limit, no right is extinguished.

For an exception to the second part of this rule of thumb regarding legal time limits (namely, that those limits that refer to the tribunal are non-peremptory), one should see canon 1506 where the right of the judge to accept or reject a petition is extinguished when the judge remains silent for ten days after the petitioner has legitimately insisted that the judge fulfill his duty.

Judicial and *conventional* time limits can also be either peremptory or non-peremptory. In this case, however, the rule of thumb is different. It is that all such time limits are non-peremptory unless they are expressly declared to be peremptory either by the law itself or by the judge.[97] An example of a non-peremptory judicial time limit is

---

[96] Coronata, 81.
[97] Coronata, 82.

the assignment by the judge of a date for the presentation of defense briefs (c. 1601). Examples of peremptory judicial time limits are the deadline for presenting the procurator's mandate as described in canon 1484, §2, and the deadline for presenting the items of discussion (*articuli argumentorum*) for the interrogation of witnesses as described in canon 1552, §2.

Legal Time Limits

Peremptory

Canon 1465 — §1. *Fatalia legis,* that is, the time limits established by law for extinguishing rights, cannot be extended nor validly shortened unless the parties request it.

For an exception to the principle that peremptory legal time limits cannot be extended (or prorogated), one should see canon 1633 which requires that an appeal be prosecuted within a month of its being filed, but then allows the judge *a quo* to extend that time limit.

Non-Peremptory

The canons do not explicitly say that non-peremptory (or simple) legal time limits (the ones that usually put limits on the judge or the tribunal) may or may not be extended, but presumably those limits follow the rules that pertain to judicial and conventional time limits.

Judicial and Conventional Time Limits

§2. Before the judicial or conventional time limits lapse, however, the judge can extend them for a just cause after the parties have been heard or if they request it; the judge, however, can never shorten those limits validly unless the parties agree.

§3. Nevertheless, the judge is to take care that such an extension does not overly prolong the litigation.

Canon 1466 — When the law in no way establishes time limits for completing procedural acts, the judge must define them after having taken into consideration the nature of each act.

Holidays

Canon 1467 — If the tribunal is closed on the day scheduled for a judicial act, the time limit is extended to the first day following which is not a holiday.

For details regarding the computation of time, one should see canon 203.

CHAPTER IV
THE PLACE OF THE TRIAL
[cc. 1468–1469]

Stable Location for the Tribunal

Canon 1468 — Insofar as possible, every tribunal is to be in an established location open during stated hours.

The Judge outside His Territory

Canon 1469 — §1. A judge expelled by force from his territory or impeded from the exercise of jurisdiction there can exercise jurisdiction and render a sentence outside that territory; the diocesan bishop, however, is to be informed of this.

§2. In addition to the case mentioned in §1, for a just cause and after having heard the parties, the judge can also go outside the territory to acquire proofs. This is to be done, however, with the permission of the diocesan bishop of the place where the judge goes and in the location designated by that bishop.

It has always been recognized, both in Roman[98] and in canon law, that as a general rule, a judge

[98] *Digesta* V, I, 59.

cannot exercise his jurisdiction outside of his own territory. This principle was stated explicitly in canon 201, §2 of the 1917 code. The corresponding canon in the 1983 code, canon 135, §3, simply says, however, that judicial power should be exercised "in the manner prescribed by law." This apparent softening of the principle of territoriality in the 1983 code does not, of course, negate the principle of territoriality but does seem to leave room for broader exceptions.

The exception mentioned in paragraph one of this canon, about the judge who has been expelled from his own territory, is a traditional one that was recognized both in medieval law and in the 1917 code.[99] The exception mentioned in paragraph two, however, is new to this code.[100] For an alternative procedure to this second paragraph, one should see canon 1418 which recognizes the right of every tribunal to call upon other tribunals for assistance.

CHAPTER V
PERSONS TO BE ADMITTED
TO THE COURT
AND THE MANNER OF PREPARING
AND KEEPING THE ACTS
[cc. 1470–1475]

This chapter, as its title indicates, refers to two general subjects: persons and acts; or, more specifically, the *persons* to be admitted to the courtroom and the manner of preparing and keeping the *acts*.

Persons to Be Admitted

Necessary Persons

Canon 1470 — §1. Unless particular law provides otherwise, while cases are being heard before the tribunal, only those persons are to be present in

[99] *Clem* II, 2, *CorpusIC* II, 1144, *CIC* 1637.
[100] See *CIC* 1770, §2, 3°.

court whom the law or the judge has established as necessary to expedite the process.

This paragraph, like canon 1455, refers to the publicity of the trial in terms of a third party, whereas canon 1598 discusses the publicity of the trial in terms of the two parties.

Clearly, an ecclesiastical trial is much more private regarding third parties than are most civil trials to which private citizens and the press, and sometimes even television cameras, have access.

The necessary people at the hearing of a witness are, besides the judges or auditor, the notary, the defender, and the promoter when they are involved in the case, and, in accord with canon 1559, ordinarily the procurators and advocates and sometimes the parties.

If the tribunal is collegiate, only the judges are present at the deliberation prior to sentencing (cc. 1455, §2 and 1609). At the session during which the sentence is signed, only the judge(s) and the notary are present (c. 1612, §4).

Respectful Persons

§2. With appropriate penalties, the judge can call to task all those present at a trial who are gravely lacking in the respect and obedience due the tribunal; furthermore, the judge can also suspend advocates and procurators from the exercise of their function in ecclesiastical tribunals.

Regarding the penalties mentioned in the canon, one should see canons 1331–1353 regarding penalties, other punishments, and their application.

Regarding advocates and procurators in particular, one should see canons 1487–1489.

Interpreters

Canon 1471 — If a person to be questioned speaks a language unknown to the judge or the parties, an interpreter designated by the judge and under oath is to be used. The statements, however, are to

be put into writing in the original language and a translation added. An interpreter is also to be used if a speech or hearing impaired person must be questioned unless the judge may prefer the person to answer the questions in writing.

The Acts

Drafting the Acts

Canon 1472 — §1. The judicial acts, both the acts of the case, that is, those regarding the merit of the question, and the acts of the process, that is, those pertaining to the procedure, must be put in writing.

§2. The individual pages of the acts are to be numbered and authenticated.

Canon 1473 — Whenever judicial acts require the signature of the parties or witnesses and the party or witness is unable or unwilling to sign, this is to be noted in the acts; the judge and the notary are also to attest that the act was read to the party or the witness verbatim and that the party or the witness was either not able or unwilling to sign.

Canon 1472 introduces the distinction between the acts of the case (*acta causae*) and the acts of the process, sometimes called the procedural acts (*acta processus*). The acts of the case are all those materials which pertain to the merits of the case, like the proofs and the sentence, whereas the acts of the process are those materials which pertain to the formalities of the case, like the constitution of the tribunal and the acceptance of the petition. All of the acts must be committed to writing since *quod non est in actis non est in mundo*[101] and because, at the conclusion of the instance, the judge must base his decision *ex actis et probatis,* that is to say, on the acts and what is proved therein (c. 1608, §2).

---

[101] Loosely translated, this reads, "Whatever is not included in the acts is considered non-existent."

Should the instance be terminated by peremption or renunciation (cc. 1522 and 1525), the acts of the process are extinguished but not the acts of the case.

Transmitting the Acts

Canon 1474 — §1. In the case of an appeal, a copy of the acts authenticated by the attestation of a notary is to be sent to the higher tribunal.

§2. If the acts were written in a language unknown to the higher tribunal, they are to be translated into one known to that tribunal, with due precautions taken that the translation is a faithful one.

This canon deals with *what* is to be transmitted to the appeal court, and is therefore appropriately included in the chapter. Later canons (cc. 1633–1635) will deal with such questions as when, how, and to whom the acts will be transmitted.

Conserving the Acts

Canon 1475 — §1. When the trial has been completed, documents which belong to private persons must be returned; a copy of them, however, is to be retained.

§2. Without a mandate of the judge, notaries and the chancellor are forbidden to furnish a copy of the judicial acts and documents acquired in the process.

Canon 469 indicates that the tribunal is part of the diocesan curia. Canon 1475, §2, however, since it establishes a special rule regarding the conservation of judicial acts that is different from the rules that apply to other diocesan documents (cc. 486–491), suggests that the tribunal should have its own special archive.

Although the code does not indicate for exactly how long judicial acts should be conserved, the Apostolic Signatura has permitted tribunals to destroy the original acts of marriage cases after ten years following the conclusion of the process, provided that the original sentences and decrees be preserved and the other judicial acts be stored on microfilm.[102]

TITLE IV
THE PARTIES IN A CASE
[cc. 1476–1490]

This title comprises two chapters, the first on the petitioner and the respondent, the second on procurators and advocates.

CHAPTER I
THE PETITIONER AND THE RESPONDENT
[cc. 1476–1480]

General Principles

Canon 1476 — Anyone, whether baptized or not, can bring action in a trial; however, a party legitimately summoned must respond.

As noted in the introduction, one of the five basic elements of a trial is the *passive subject,* namely the petitioner and respondent.

The Latin terms for petitioner and respondent are *actor* (the one who institutes the action by a petition—c. 1501) and *pars conventa* (the convened party). They are sometimes referred to, especially in penal cases, as the plaintiff and the defendant.

The basic principle of canon 1476 is twofold: a) anyone can act in a trial (*quilibet potest agere*) and b) the respondent must respond (*pars conventa respondere debet*). Neither part of the principle, however, is quite as simple as it might seem.

Canon 1478, for example, speaks of several groups of people, like minors and the fiscally incompetent, who have only limited capacity to serve as *petitioners;* and canon 1508, §3 notes that there are groups of people, like those who do not have the free exercise of personal rights, whose capacity to act as *respondents* is also limited.

The canon makes a point of saying that anyone, *whether baptized or not,* can act in a trial. In order to understand why the code makes an issue of the fact that one's baptismal status is irrelevant, one needs to know something about the history of this institute. It was understood under the 1917 code, particularly on the basis of canon 87, that a non-baptized person did not have the right to act as petitioner in a case. In 1970, however, Norm 8 of the *American Procedural Norms* permitted "any spouse without qualification" to petition for a declaration of marriage invalidity, and on January 8, 1973, the Pontifical Commission for the Interpretation of the Decrees of Vatican Council II declared that, even outside of the United States, unbaptized people needed no special permission to act as petitioners in marriage cases.[103] This right of the unbaptized is now extended to all types of cases.

A similar situation existed under the 1917 code for baptized non-Catholics. Because they were baptized, it was granted that they enjoyed "judicial capacity," but because they were not Catholic, they were considered to lack the "procedural capacity" to petition in a Catholic tribunal. This was specifically spelled out in article 35, §3 of *Provida Mater Ecclesia*[104] but it was reversed by the *American Procedural Norms* and the interpretation of January 8, 1973 as indicated above.[105] Prior to that, however, in those cases in which a non-Catholic did wish a Catholic tribunal to declare his or her marriage invalid (so that he or she would be free to remarry a Catholic), the procedure was for the non-Catholic to "denounce" the

---

[102]*RRAO 1985,* 17, and *RRAO 1990,* 22. See also *RRAO 1981,* 2–3, and c. 489, §2 on periodically purging the acts in criminal cases involving morals.

[103]*CLD* 8, 1092.

[104]Doheny, I:116. Canon 1505, §1 and §2, 2° also mentions procedural capacity.

[105]For the implications of this development in marriage invalidity procedures, see c. 1674, 1°.

marriage and then for the promoter of justice to petition for the declaration of invalidity.

Canon 1477 — Even if the petitioner or respondent has appointed a procurator or advocate, they themselves are nevertheless always bound to be present at the trial according to the prescript of the law or of the judge.

The parties, for example, may be required by the law or the judge to offer their declarations in person (c. 1530) or to meet in person with a witness in order to settle a discrepancy (c. 1560, §2). This is true even if they have appointed a procurator or advocate.

Minors and Those Lacking Use of Reason

Canon 1478 — §1. Minors and those who lack the use of reason can stand trial only through their parents, guardians, or curators, without prejudice to the prescript of §3.

§2. If the judge thinks that the rights of minors are in conflict with the rights of the parents, guardians, or curators or that the latter cannot adequately protect the rights of the former, then the minors are to stand trial through a guardian or curator appointed by the judge.

§3. Nevertheless, in spiritual cases and those connected with spiritual matters, if the minors have attained the use of reason, they can petition and respond without the consent of their parents or guardian. They can do so personally if they have completed their fourteenth year of age; otherwise, they do so through the curator appointed by the judge.

According to canon 97, §1, minors are those persons under the age of eighteen. According to canon 99 those who habitually lack the use of reason are equated with infants, i.e., those under the age of seven (c. 97, §2). Despite the broad, general principle stated in canon 1476, minors and those lacking the use of reason do not generally enjoy procedural capacity (*ius standi in iudicio*) except through parents, guardians, or curators.

The legislation incorporated into paragraph three dates back to Pope Boniface VIII (d. 1303) and is designed to protect minors whose parents or guardian has allowed their own selfish, perhaps monetary, interests to prevail over the spiritual welfare of the minor.[106]

Although the law often uses the terms "guardian" and "curator" interchangeably, some authors regard the guardian as one who looks after the interests of those who are minors, while a curator performs the same office for those who suffer from some mental debility. This more specific usage is also found in the code on occasion. See canon 98, §2 regarding the guardian and canon 1478, §4 for the curator.

The Fiscally Incompetent and Weak-Minded Persons

§4. Those deprived of the administration of goods and those of diminished mental capacity can stand trial personally only to answer for their own delicts or at the order of the judge; otherwise, they must petition and respond through their curators.

This paragraph notes that, except in the two cases mentioned, those of diminished mental capacity must act *and respond* through their curators. The question might arise here: does the phrase "those of diminished mental capacity" include all those who are listed in canon 1095, namely, those who lack the due reason, discretion, or competence for marriage? The answer seems clearly to be no. A respondent, for example, whose severe personality disorder deprived him or her of the capacity to enter a marital covenant is not necessarily deprived by that disorder of the capacity to enter a non-marital type of contract, or to conduct his or her own legal or judicial affairs. Few people who suffer from personality disorders are appropriately referred to as "those of diminished mental capacity," i.e., *ii qui minus firmae mentis sunt*. Therefore, not all

---

[106] Lega-Bartocetti, I:136.

those respondents in marriage cases whose marital incompetence is alleged need have guardians appointed for them, but only those who either lack the use of reason altogether or are weak minded.

Appointment of Guardian and Curator

Canon 1479 — Whenever a guardian or curator appointed by civil authority is present, the ecclesiastical judge can admit the guardian or curator after having heard, if possible, the diocesan bishop of the person to whom the guardian or curator was given; if the guardian or curator is not present or does not seem admissible, the judge will appoint a guardian or curator for the case.

The appointment of a guardian or curator should, of course, be made promptly, since at the very beginning of the case it is the guardian, not the respondent, who is cited in all those cases where a guardian or curator is required (c. 1508, §3). Also, in the appointing of a guardian or curator, the welfare of the minor or of the legally incompetent person should always be paramount in the mind of the judge.

Juridic Persons

Canon 1480 — §1. Juridic persons stand trial through their legitimate representatives.

§2. In a case of the lack of or negligence of the representative, however, the ordinary himself can stand trial personally or through another in the name of juridic persons subject to his authority.

Canon 118 notes that they alone represent a *public* juridic person who are acknowledged to have this competence either by universal or particular law or by its own statutes, and that they represent a *private* juridic person who have been given this competency by statute.

Among those recognized by universal law as representatives of public juridic persons are the bishop for his diocese (c. 393) and the pastor for his parish (c. 532).

CHAPTER II
PROCURATORS FOR LITIGATION
AND ADVOCATES
[cc. 1481–1490]

Definitions and Functions

A *procurator* or proxy is one who, by legitimate mandate, performs judicial business in the name of someone else. The procurator, in other words, is a representative of the party and is, in effect, the *alter ego* of the party.

An *advocate* is a person approved by ecclesiastical authority who safeguards the rights of a party in a canonical process by arguments regarding the law and the facts. Besides providing advice and technical assistance, preparing the evidence, etc., an advocate may be present at the examination of the parties, witnesses, and experts (c. 1561), may inspect the acts, even though not published, and review the documents produced by the parties (c. 1678, §1, 2°), and is, of course, expected to write a brief (c. 1601). In his famous 1944 allocution to the Rota, Pope Pius XII outlined the functions of the advocate and also noted that the advocate "must not withdraw himself from the sole and common final purpose: the discovery, the ascertainment, the legal affirmation of the truth of the objective fact."[107]

Optional and Required Appointments

Canon 1481 — §1. A party can freely appoint an advocate and procurator; except for the cases established in §§2 and 3, however, the party can also petition and respond personally unless the judge has decided that the services of a procurator or advocate are necessary.

§2. In a penal trial, the accused must always have an advocate either appointed personally or assigned by the judge.

§3. In a contentious trial which involves minors or in a trial which affects the public good, with the exception of marriage cases, the judge is

---

[107] *CLD* 3, 617.

to appoint *ex officio* a defender for a party who does not have one.

Paragraph one notes that in contentious trials that involve adults and only the private good, the appointment of an advocate or procurator is optional for the parties unless the judge has decided that the services of an advocate are necessary, in which case either the party appoints the advocate at the insistence of the judge or the judge appoints the advocate to assist the party.

Paragraphs two and three address the penal trial and the contentious trial involving minors or the public good (except for marriage cases) where an advocate or *defensor* is required. It is understood that, in a marriage case, the respondent *may* appoint an advocate but that, in a sense, that role is already being fulfilled by the defender of the bond, and that a personal advocate for the respondent is ordinarily unnecessary and tautological.[108]

Occasionally the person mandated to serve as advocate for the petitioner is also mandated to serve as procurator so that one and the same person would serve as procurator/advocate.[109] In a marriage case, however, a party generally performs personally, and not through a proxy, any judicial business that needs to be done.

Number

Canon 1482 — §1. A person can appoint only one procurator who cannot substitute another unless the procurator has been given the expressed faculty to do so.

§2. If a person appoints several procurators for a just cause, however, they are to be designated in such a way that prevention is operative among them.

§3. Nevertheless, several advocates can be appointed together.

A party may appoint only one procurator but may appoint several advocates. This rule follows from the nature of the two offices. Only one procurator is permitted because a procurator is the *alter ego* of the party and is uniquely identified with the party; several advocates are permitted and, in complex cases, even desired so that the party may profit from expert advice from different advocates, each of whom may specialize in a different aspect of the case.

The term "prevention" mentioned in paragraph two has the same basic meaning here that it had in canon 1415. In that canon the first judge (among those competent) to cite the respondent thereby acquired competence over the case *ratione praeventionis*. According to the present canon, the first procurator to undertake the judicial business becomes the active procurator—by prevention.

The notion of prevention is also expressed in canon law by the term *in solidum* (as opposed to *collegialiter,* where the function is performed by several people together as a group).[110]

Qualities

Canon 1483 — The procurator and advocate must have attained the age of majority and be of good reputation; moreover, the advocate must be a Catholic unless the diocesan bishop permits otherwise, a doctor in canon law or otherwise truly expert, and approved by the same bishop.

It is to be noted that unlike judges (c. 1421, §3), promoters of justice, and defenders of the bond (c. 1435), it is not absolutely necessary for an advocate to hold a doctorate or licentiate in canon law.

Ordinary Mandate

Canon 1484 — §1. Before the procurator and advocate undertake their function, they must present an authentic mandate to the tribunal.

§2. To prevent the extinction of a right, however, the judge can admit a procurator even if the

---

[108] *Comm* 10 (1978) 268 and 16 (1984) 61. See also c. 1723 in penal cases.
[109] *Comm* 10 (1978) 269.

[110] See c. 140.

mandate has not been presented, once a suitable guarantee has been furnished if the case warrants it; the act, however, lacks any force if the procurator does not correctly present the mandate within the peremptory time established by the judge.

Paragraph one speaks of the requirement that the procurator and advocate submit a mandate to the tribunal. In all marriage cases which receive an affirmative decision in the first instance tribunal, the acts of the case are forwarded to the appellate tribunal for further action (c. 1682). It bears noting that, unless the mandate signed at the beginning of the hearing specifically empowers the procurator or advocate to serve in both tribunals, the mandate is presumed to be valid only for the first instance tribunal.

Paragraph one also notes that the mandate must be authentic. It is unclear whether "authentic" in this context means that it must be signed by a notary (see cc. 483, §1 and 1437, §1) or simply that it must be a genuine, original document truly signed by the party (see cc. 1070 and 1544).

Paragraph two speaks of a circumstance where a procurator may validly place an act on behalf of a party even before presenting an authentic mandate, provided that the mandate is later presented prior to the deadline presented by the judge. According to canon 1465, §2 the judge can ordinarily extend the time limit; but canon 1484, §2 specifically mentions that the particular judicial time limit is peremptory, that is, that if unmet, the right is extinguished, so that if the mandate is not submitted prior to the deadline, any act placed by that procurator is considered invalid.

Also, according to canon 1620, 6°, should one act in the name of another without an authentic mandate, the sentence would be irremediably null.

Special Mandate

Canon 1485 — Without a special mandate, a procurator cannot validly renounce an action, an instance, or judicial acts nor come to an agreement, make a bargain, enter into arbitration, or in general do those things for which the law requires a special mandate.

This canon says, in effect, that the general mandate is a mandate only to act on behalf of a party in a trial that leads to a judicial decision. The general mandate, therefore, does not empower a procurator to terminate the trial either by renunciation or by reaching some sort of out-of-court settlement.

Removal by the Mandator

Canon 1486 — §1. For the removal of a procurator or advocate to take effect, they must be informed; if the issue has already been joined, the judge and the opposing party must also be informed about the removal.

§2. After the definitive sentence has been issued, the right and duty to appeal, if the mandating person does not refuse, remains with the procurator.

Although, as noted, the mandate of the *advocate* in first instance ordinarily expires at the time of the definitive judgment in first instance, the mandate of the *procurator* ordinarily extends through the lodging of an appeal.

Expulsion by the Judge

Canon 1487 — For a grave cause, the judge either *ex officio* or at the request of the party can remove the procurator and the advocate by decree.

For a serious or grave cause the judge may expel a procurator or advocate from the trial. Gross dereliction of duty, malfeasance, dishonesty, and disrespect for the tribunal (c. 1470, §2) would no doubt qualify as grave causes.

Sanctions for Reprehensible Actions

Canon 1488 — §1. Both the procurator and the advocate are forbidden to resolve the litigation by bribery or to make an agreement for an excessive profit or for a share in the object in dispute. If they do so, the agreement is null, and the judge can fine them. Moreover, the bishop who presides over the tribunal can suspend the advocate from office and even remove him or her from the list of advocates if it happens again.

§2. Advocates and procurators can be punished in the same way if in deceit of the law they withdraw cases from competent tribunals so that the cases will be decided more favorably by other tribunals.

Canon 1489 — Advocates and procurators who betray their office for gifts, promises, or any other reason are to be suspended from the exercise of legal assistance and punished with a fine or other suitable penalties.

Permanent Staff

Canon 1490 — As far as possible, legal representatives are to be appointed in a stable manner in each tribunal, who receive a stipend from the tribunal and are to exercise, especially in marriage cases, the function of advocate or procurator on behalf of parties who wish to select them.

This canon seems to encourage as an ideal the establishment in every diocese of a permanent staff of procurators and advocates to serve the needs of interested parties. Although the ideal is perhaps beyond the realistic grasp of some dioceses, the canon nevertheless embodies the pastoral interest of the Church in being of service to people seeking justice, and encourages each diocese to do whatever is possible in providing skilled personnel to assist them in judicial proceedings.

TITLE V
ACTIONS AND EXCEPTIONS
[cc. 1491–1500]

As noted in the introduction, the basic elements of a trial are the subject, the form, and the object. The subject is twofold: active (the tri-

bunal), and passive (the parties). The form is the procedures. The object, like the subject, is also twofold: material (rights, juridic facts, and penalties) and formal, namely the actions and exceptions which are the subject of this title V.

Title V comprises two chapters, the first on actions and exceptions in general, the second on actions and exceptions specifically.

CHAPTER I
ACTIONS AND EXCEPTIONS IN GENERAL
[cc. 1491–1495]

Preliminary Observations

An *action* is a request made by a petitioner (Latin: *actor)* for a judicial decision on some matter. An *exception* is a claim or complaint made by the respondent which either modifies the court procedure in some way (these are called dilatory exceptions) or quashes the suit altogether (these are called peremptory exceptions).

Exceptions and a certain type of action (the reconvening action or counterclaim) are also discussed in canons 1458–1464 in chapter 2 of title III ("The Order of Adjudication"). That treatment, however, confines itself to the question of the particular stage of the trial at which such matters should be introduced. The present treatment is more general.

Availability

Canon 1491 — Every right is protected not only by an action but also by an exception unless other provision is expressly made.

This is a simple statement to the effect that in general whenever a right is disputed, some adjudicative process must normally be available to the parties. St. Lawrence's Parish, for example, sells a piece of property to St. Robert's Parish. A bill of sale exists as proof of the transaction, but St. Lawrence's continues to occupy and use the property. St. Robert's is entitled to bring an *action* against St. Lawrence's in order to obtain possession of the property. But St. Lawrence's can then bring an *exception* against St. Robert's, claiming that the contract was, for a stated reason, null and void.

The canon notes that an action and an exception are always available to protect a right "unless other provision is expressly made." An example of "an express other provision" is found in canon 1062, §2 which indicates that a promise to marry does not give rise to an action to seek the celebration of marriage.

Extinction

Canon 1492 — §1. Every action is extinguished by prescription according to the norm of law or by some other legitimate means, with the exception of actions concerning the status of persons, which are never extinguished.

§2. Without prejudice to the prescript of can. 1462, an exception is always available and is perpetual by its very nature.

It is axiomatic that actions are temporary while exceptions are perpetual. This principle, which seems to the advantage of the respondent, is, in fact, meant to correct the respondent's previous disadvantage in that the petitioner comes to court freely, whereas the respondent is convened and is obliged to appear. If, therefore, a right of a respondent is imperiled by his or her having been summoned and sued, his or her right then to lodge an exception is in no way limited by time.

To this general principle, however, there are exceptions on both sides. Some *actions,* namely those regarding the status of persons (those, for example, which refer to the bond of marriage, the separation of spouses, religious profession, or the clerical state) are perpetual. And some *exceptions* can cease. In particular, canon 1459, §2 requires that dilatory exceptions be proposed before the joinder of issues. If, however, the party fails to do that, the exception ceases to be available because

the party is considered, in effect, to have renounced the exception.[111]

Concerning the prescription that extinguishes actions, one should see canons 197–199, 1268–1270, and 1362.[112]

Multiple Actions

Canon 1493 — A petitioner can bring a person to trial with several actions at once, either concerning the same or different matters, so long as the actions do not conflict among themselves and do not exceed the competence of the tribunal approached.

An example of multiple actions would be a person petitioning both for a separation from his or her spouse and for the custody of the children.

Counteractions

Canon 1494 — §1. The respondent can file a counterclaim against the petitioner before the same judge in the same trial either because of the connection of the case with the principal action or to remove or diminish the claim of the petitioner.

§2. A counterclaim to a counterclaim is not allowed.

Canon 1495 — The counterclaim must be presented to the judge before whom the first action was filed even if the judge was delegated for only one case or is otherwise relatively incompetent.

---

[111] Lega-Bartocetti, I:258; Goyeneche, 183. See also P. Coyle, *Judicial Exceptions, CanLawStud* 193 (Washington, D.C.: Catholic University, 1944) 8, 24–25. It is also to be noted that c. 1492, §2 includes the phrase "without prejudice to the prescript of can. 1462."

[112] Regarding the prescription (or statute of limitations) that pertains to a cleric's sexual abuse of a minor, one should see the commentary on c. 1362 and J. Alesandro, "Dismissal from the Clerical State in Cases of Sexual Misconduct: Recent Derogations," *CLSAP* 56 (1994) 28–67.

The commentaries on canons 1459 and 1463 discussed exceptions and counteractions in terms of their order of adjudication. The basic difference between the two is this: an *exception* always remains tied to the original action and is never separate from it, whereas a *counteraction*, in effect, begins a new case and is, as it were, independent of the original action.

Canon 1494, §1 notes that there are basically two types of counteractions. The first type is directly connected to, but still independent of, the original action, as in the case of the two parties to a marriage, the first of whom sues for a separation whereupon the second countersues for a declaration of invalidity. The second type of counteraction aims at removing or diminishing the petition, as when the original petition sues a person for a sum of money whereupon that person countersues the original petitioner for a piece of property.

Where, in other words, a *counteraction* is instituted, there are, in effect, two different cases with the petitioner in the first case being the respondent in the second and vice versa.[113] But where an *exception* is lodged, there remains only the one case, with the respondent remaining the respondent. It is true that, according to the old axiom "in lodging an exception the respondent becomes the petitioner";[114] but this is to be understood only in the sense that, in accord with canon 1526, §1, it is then incumbent upon the one lodging the exception to prove that the exception has merit. In fact, however, when a respondent lodges an exception, he or she remains the respondent in the one and only principal case under consideration.[115]

Canon 1495 notes that even though the judge is acting in virtue of delegated power and the terms of delegation empowered him to judge only the one issue, nevertheless his jurisdiction is, by this canon, extended to include the counterclaim. Equity in fact dictates that the counterclaim, like any connected case, not only *may* be but indeed *should* be proposed before the original judge. Canon 1414 reads *cognoscendae sunt,* and this canon *proponenda est.*[116]

CHAPTER II
SPECIFIC ACTIONS AND EXCEPTIONS
[cc. 1496–1500]

This chapter deals with sequestration, injunctions, and possessory actions. In North America, such matters are, in fact, almost always brought before civil courts rather than ecclesiastical tribunals, but the principles of justice inherent in these institutes (which date back to medieval and even Roman law) are of both historical and practical interest.

Object Sequestration

Canon 1496 — §1. A person, who through at least probable arguments has shown a right over something held by another and the threat of damage unless the thing is placed in safekeeping, has the right to obtain its sequestration from the judge.

Injunctions

§2. In similar circumstances, a person can obtain an order to restrain another from the exercise of a right.

Object sequestration is the temporary entrusting of a disputed object to a third party.[117] An in-

---

[113] Canon 1463, §2, however, directs that the two cases, depending on the circumstances, may be heard together or separately.

[114] *Reus excipiendo fit actor.*

[115] Some exceptions are handled as incidental cases. See cc. 1462, §2 and 1587–1591.

[116] See also c. 1588 on the proposal of an incidental case.

[117] Although c. 1496, §1 speaks only of a "thing" (*super aliqua re* and *res ipsa*) as the object of sequestration, it sometimes happens that a person can also be sequestered. In a child custody case, for example, the child can sometimes be placed in the care of a neutral party until the suit is settled.

junction is the temporary prohibition of exercising a disputed right because of probable infringement on the prevailing right of someone else.

It is to be noted that, in object sequestration, a person can obtain the right to have an object sequestered even when the person's right to the object is demonstrated only through probable arguments (*probabilibus saltem argumentis*).

Security Sequestration

Canon 1497 — §1. Sequestration of a thing is also allowed as security for a loan provided that the right of the creditor is sufficiently evident.

§2. Sequestration can also be extended to the goods of the debtor which are discovered in the possession of others under any title and to the loans of the debtor.

Security sequestration is the temporary entrusting to a third party of assets owned by a debtor as security for the creditor.

In security sequestration, in order for the creditor to obtain the right to have assets sequestered or attached, it is not enough for the creditor to demonstrate that the other party probably owes the creditor something; rather, the creditor must set forth arguments that convince the judge with a degree of certitude (*satis constet*) that the creditor truly enjoys the right to a security sequestration.

It is clear from the rubric of chapter 2 that sequestrations and injunctions may be entered either as actions or as exceptions

Sequestration and Injunctions as Extraordinary Procedures

Canon 1498 — Sequestration of a thing and restraint upon the exercise of a right can in no way be decreed if the harm which is feared can be repaired in another way and suitable security for its repair is offered.

When there are means, other than sequestration or injunction, of repairing the harm or damage, and when the respondent guarantees that the damage will indeed be repaired, then the judge is not allowed to issue a writ or decree of sequestration or of injunction.

Protection of the Respondent

Canon 1499 — A judge who grants the sequestration of a thing or a restraint upon the exercise of a right can first impose an obligation upon the person to compensate for damages if that person's right is not proven.

In some instances a judge will impose a surety bond on the petitioner to compensate the respondent for any damage suffered in the event that the petitioner's alleged right is not proven.

Possessory Actions

Canon 1500 — The prescripts of the civil law of the place where the object whose possession is in question is located are to be observed regarding the nature and force of a possessory action.

A possessory action is a defense submitted to a judge for the obtaining, retaining, or recovery of the possession of some object or right.

As already noted, all of the matters included in this chapter (sequestrations, injunctions, and possessory actions) are, in North America, heard virtually exclusively by civil courts rather than ecclesiastical tribunals. In regard to possessory actions in particular, however, this canon decrees for the universal Church that, should such an action be submitted to a tribunal, the prescriptions of the civil law of the place where the disputed object is located should be observed.[118]

[118] See c. 1410.

BIBLIOGRAPHY

Books

Augustine, C. *A Commentary on the New Code of Canon Law*. Vol. VII, *Ecclesiastical Trials*. St. Louis: B. Herder, 1923.

Bartocetti, V. *De causis matrimonialibus*. Rome, 1950.

Bassett, W., and P. Huizing, eds. *Judgment in the Church*. New York: Seabury, 1977.

Coronata, M. *Institutiones iuris canonici*. Vol. III, *De processibus*. Rome: Marietti, 1956.

Della Rocca, F. *Canonical Procedure*. Milwaukee: Bruce, 1961.

Diacetis, A. *The Judgment of Formal Matrimonial Cases: Historical Reflections, Contemporary Developments, and Future Possibilities*. Washington, D.C. : Catholic University of America, 1977.

Doheny, W. *Canonical Procedure in Matrimonial Cases*, Vol. I. 2 vols. Milwaukee: Bruce, 1944.

Gordon, I., and Z. Grocholewski, eds. *Documenta recentiora circa rem matrimonialem et processualem*, Vol. I. 2 vols. Rome: Pontificia Universitas Gregoriana, 1977.

Goyeneche, S. *De processibus*. Part I. Messina: Scuola Tipografica Antoniana "Cristo Re," 1958.

Graham, G. *Synodal and Pro-Synodal Judges*. Washington, D.C.: Catholic University of America, 1967.

Grocholewski, Z., ed. *Documenta recentiora circa rem matrimonialem et processualem*, Vol. II. 2 vols. Rome: Pontificia Universitas Gregoriana, 1980.

Lega, M., *Praelectiones de iudiciis ecclesiasticis*. 4 vols. Rome: Typis Vaticanis, 1905.

Lega, M., and V. Bartocetti. *Commentarius in iudicia ecclesiastica*, Vol. I. 3 vols. Rome: Anonima Libraria Cattolica Italiana, 1938.

Noonan, J. *Power to Dissolve*. Cambridge, Mass.: Belknap, 1972.

Ramos, F. *I Tribunali Ecclesiastici, Costituzione, Organizzazione, Norme Processuali*. Rome: Millennium Romae, 1998.

Regatillo, E. *Institutiones iuris canonici*, Vol. II. 2 vols. Santander: Sal Terrae, 1956.

Roberti, F. *De processibus*, Vol. I. 2 vols. Rome: Libreria Pontificii Instituti Utriusque Iuris, 1941.

Sheehy, G., R. Brown, D. Kelly, and A. McGrath, eds. *Canon Law, Letter and Spirit*. Collegeville: Michael Glazier, 1995.

Sipos, S. *Enchiridion Iuris Canonici*. Rome: B. Herder, 1954.

Smith, S. *The Marriage Process in the United States*. New York: Benziger Brothers, 1893.

—————. *Elements of Ecclesiastical Law*. Vol. II, *Ecclesiastical Trials*. New York: Benziger Brothers, 1887.

Wernz, F. *Ius Decretalium*. 6 vols. Rome: Typis Vaticanis, 1898.

Wernz, F., and P. Vidal. *Ius Canonicum*. Vol. VI, *De processibus*. Rome: Universitas Gregoriana, 1949.

Woywod, S., and C. Smith. *A Practical Commentary on the Code of Canon Law*, Vol. II. 2 vols. London: B. Herder, 1948.

Articles

Abbass, J. "Trials in General: A Comparative Study of the Eastern and Latin Codes." *J* 55 (1995) 834–874.

Beal, J. "Have Code Will Travel: Advocacy in the Church of the 1990s." *J* 53 (1993) 263–283.

———. "The Exercise of the Power of Governance by Lay People: The State of the Question." *J* 55 (1995) 1–92.

Burke, R. "The Distinction of Personnel in Hierarchically-Related Tribunals." *Stud Can* 28 (1994) 85–98.

Coriden, J. "Alternative Dispute Resolution in the Church." *CLSAP* (1986) 61–82.

Frattin, P. "Lay Judges in Ecclesiastical Tribunals." *J* 28 (1968) 177–184.

Gil de la Heras, F. "Organización Judicial de la Iglesia en el Nuevo Código." *IC* 24 (1984) 123–197.

Grocholewski, Z. "Theological Aspects of the Judicial Activity of the Church." *J* 86 (1986) 552–567.

Hayward, P. "Changes in Ecclesiastical Administrative Justice Brought About by the New Competence of the 'Sectio Altera' of the Apostolic Signatura to Award Damages." *Ius Ecclesiae* 5 (1993) 643–673.

Hesch, J. "The Right of the Accused Person to an Advocate in a Penal Trial." *J* 52 (1992) 723–734.

Matthews, K. "The Development and Future of the Administrative Tribunal." *Stud Can* 18 (1984) 1–233.

Moodie, M. "Defense of Rights: Developing New Procedural Norms." *J* 47 (1987) 423–448.

Morrisey, F. "Some Thoughts on Advocacy in Non-matrimonial Cases." *J* 53 (1993) 301–318.

Provost, J. "The Participation of the Laity in the Governance of the Church." *Stud Can* 17 (1983) 417–448.

Part II
THE CONTENTIOUS TRIAL
[cc. 1501–1670]

Part one of Book VII on procedures, canons 1400–1500, is concerned with the nature and structure of tribunals, the officers of the court, the parties and their representatives, and some basic rules governing all types of trials. Part two, canons 1501–1670, governs the actual unfolding of a trial. Commentators sometimes refer to this as the *dynamic* part of procedural law.

Contentious trials may be distinguished as "ordinary" (cc. 1501–1655) or "oral" (cc. 1656–1670). Weightier matters are reserved to the ordinary contentious process. The oral contentious process is a streamlined process that, as its name indicates, resolves issues by means of an oral hearing.[1]

There are also special procedures which somewhat modify ordinary or oral contentious trials. These include norms for marriage nullity cases (cc. 1671–1691), norms governing the separation of spouses (cc. 1692–1696), procedures for investigating the nullity of sacred orders (cc. 1708–1712), and norms for the imposition or declaration of ecclesiastical penalties (cc. 1717–1731).

The norms for ordinary contentious trials must be understood in light of an especially significant purpose of all ecclesiastical trials, namely, vindicating rights and declaring juridic facts (c. 1400, §1, 1°). Thus, the ultimate goal is discovering the truth in order to do justice. As the designation "contentious" indicates, this goal is sought through a contention, a legal dispute over some specified question or questions. The judicial con-

tention is the means through which the Church seeks truth and justice.[2]

Contentious trials unfold in stages. While commentators vary in the manner in which they distinguish the stages, the principal phases of the ordinary contentious trial can be identified as follows:

1. an introductory phase (cc. 1501–1512),
2. the clarification and specification of the dispute (cc. 1513–1516),
3. the trial proper, principally focused on the gathering of proofs, often referred to as the "instruction" of the case (cc. 1517–1597),
4. the publication of acts and discussion of the case (cc. 1598–1606),
5. the decision (cc. 1607–1618),
6. challenges to the decision (cc. 1619–1648), and
7. the execution of the decision (cc. 1650–1655).

Implementing procedural law effectively requires an appreciation of the interrelationship of these differing stages, the contribution each makes to the whole process, and the overall flow of the trial.[3]

The norms for contentious trials in the Code of Canons for the Eastern Churches are very similar, in many cases identical, to those of the Latin code. This reflects a deliberate decision of the Eastern Code Commission to keep procedural law

---

[1] See the commentary on cc. 1656–1670 for further information on the nature of this process and when it can be employed.

[2] E. Egan, "Appeal in Marriage Nullity Cases: Two Centuries of Experiment and Reform," *CLSAP* 43 (1981) 132–135.

[3] For a more detailed outline sketching the various steps in the development of a trial, see M. Wijlens, *The Ordinary Contentious Trial: A Schematic Overview* (privately published, 1992). This text is available through the CLSA, Catholic University, Caldwell Hall 431, Washington, DC 20064.

substantially the same throughout the Church.[4] Because of that basic similarity, in this portion of the commentary reference will be made to parallel passages in the Eastern code only when there is a significant or otherwise instructive difference between the two codes.[5]

At present, the most common use of the contentious trial is to adjudicate marriage nullity cases. In this commentary, therefore, special attention will be given to the application of the basic procedural law to trials of marriage nullity.

[4] *Nu* 3 (1976) 23 (canons "De processibus," n. 2).
[5] For a discussion of such differences, see J. Abbass, "Con-

tentious Trials: A Comparative Study of the Eastern and Latin Codes," *J* 56 (1996) 875–904.

CANONS AND COMMENTARY

SECTION I
THE ORDINARY CONTENTIOUS TRIAL
[cc. 1501–1655]

TITLE I
THE INTRODUCTION OF THE CASE[6]
[cc. 1501–1512]

CHAPTER I
THE INTRODUCTORY *LIBELLUS*
OF LITIGATION
[cc. 1501–1506]

Requirement of a Petition

Canon 1501 — A judge cannot adjudicate a case unless the party concerned or the promoter of justice has presented a petition according to the norm of the canons.

[6] L. Wrenn, in *CLSA Com*, 970–973; M. Coyle, in *CLSGBI Com*, 862–868; C. de Diego-Lora, in *Pamplona ComEng*, 934–942; M. J. Arroba Conde, in *Valencia Com*, 660–666; R. Rodríguez-Ocaña, in *Com Ex*, IV/2, 1162–1216; S. Panizo Orallo, in *Com Ex* IV/2, 1217–1231.

An ecclesiastical judge may act only in response to a legitimately prepared petition presented by a person with a recognized interest in the matter. Without such a petition, a trial has no basis and any action taken is vulnerable to a plaint of irremediable nullity (c. 1620, 4°). Once a trial is initiated, however, even if it concerns only the private good of the parties, the judge has the right and even the duty to proceed in order to serve the goal of doing justice (c. 1452).[7]

FORM AND CONTENTS OF A PETITION
[cc. 1502–1504]

Canon 1502 — A person who wishes to bring another to trial must present to a competent judge a *libellus* which sets forth the object of the controversy and requests the services of the judge.

Canon 1503 — §1. The judge can accept an oral petition whenever the petitioner is impeded from presenting a *libellus* or the case is easily investigated and of lesser importance.
§2. In either case, however, the judge is to order the notary to put the act into writing; the

[7] M. F. Pompedda, "Decision-Sentence in Marriage Trials," *QuadStR* 5 (1990) 80.

written record must be read to and approved by the petitioner and has all the legal effects of a *libellus* written by the petitioner.

By definition, a *libellus* is a written petition presented by the one wishing to initiate a trial. It must request the assistance of a tribunal that has a claim to legal competence or jurisdiction (cc. 1404–1416, 1673), and must specify what is being sought from the judge.

While the norm is the presentation of a written petition, canon 1503 empowers a judge to accept an oral petition when a petitioner is impeded, for instance, by illiteracy, or when the matter is of lesser importance. When an oral petition is presented, a tribunal notary must commit the substance of that petition to writing and that written petition must be approved by the petitioner. This gives the document full legal force as a *libellus*.

Canon 1504 — The *libellus*, which introduces litigation, must:

1° **express the judge before whom the case is introduced, what is being sought and by whom it is being sought;**

2° **indicate the right upon which the petitioner bases the case and, at least generally, the facts and proofs which will prove the allegations;**

3° **be signed by the petitioner or the petitioner's procurator, indicating the day, month, and year, and the address where the petitioner or procurator lives or where they say they reside for the purpose of receiving the acts;**

4° **indicate the domicile or quasi-domicile of the respondent.**

The essential elements of a *libellus* are defined in this important canon. These elements enable a tribunal to clarify whether there is a genuine claim and whether the tribunal has jurisdiction to adjudicate that claim. In the absence of one or more of these elements, the petition is liable to rejection. Every *libellus* must:

1. be directed to a specific tribunal (to assist in clarifying jurisdiction);

2. indicate the goal sought by the petitioner (e.g., vindication of good reputation; declaration of the nullity of a marriage);

3. identify the petitioner (to determine whether he or she has standing to introduce the suit);

4. refer in general terms to the right upon which the action is sought (to establish that a matter appropriate to a judicial process is at issue);

5. identify the facts and proofs which the petitioner intends to use to establish the right (to establish that a means of argumentation exists);

6. be signed and dated and include the address of the petitioner and/or procurator;[8]

7. identify the respondent and, if possible, the respondent's domicile or quasi-domicile (to determine jurisdiction and facilitate citation).

RESPONSE TO THE LIBELLUS
[cc. 1505–1506]

Canon 1505 — §1. When a single judge or the president of a collegiate tribunal has seen that the matter is within his competence and the petitioner does not lack legitimate personal standing in the trial, he must accept or reject the *libellus* as soon as possible by decree.

§2. A *libellus* can be rejected only:

1° **if the judge or tribunal is incompetent;**

2° **if without doubt it is evident that the petitioner lacks legitimate personal standing in the trial;**

3° **if the prescripts of can. 1504, nn. 1–3 have not been observed;**

4° **if it is certainly clear from the *libellus* itself that the petition lacks any basis and that there is no possibility that any such basis will appear through a process.**

---

[8] For a description of the role of the procurator, and the distinction between a procurator and an advocate, see the commentary on cc. 1481–1490.

The *libellus* must be either accepted or rejected by the court in a formal decree. As is true of any decree (cc. 51 and 1617), it is to be in writing and must include a summary of the reasons for the decision.[9]

A petition can be rejected only for reasons specified in this canon; otherwise it must be admitted for a hearing.

In deciding to accept or reject a *libellus,* the single judge or president of a college of judges first considers two questions: (1) whether there is a basis for the tribunal to assume jurisdiction immediately or at least to seek authorization to assume it, and (2) whether the petitioner has legal standing to initiate the suit. If the answer to either of these threshold questions is negative, the petition must be rejected (c. 1505, §2, 1°–2°).

Next, the formalities of the *libellus* are examined to assure that all requirements are met. Then the judge assesses whether a *fumus boni iuris,* a sign that there is at least some basis for the claim, is present. Finally, the judge assesses whether there is at least some hope of bringing forward proof for the claim. If the formalities required for a *libellus* have not been observed or if there is no basis or potential proof of the claim, the judge rejects the *libellus.*

§3. If the *libellus* has been rejected because of defects which can be corrected, the petitioner can resubmit a new, correctly prepared *libellus* to the same judge.

§4. A party is always free within ten available days to make recourse with substantiating reasons against the rejection of a *libellus* either to the appellate tribunal or to the college if the *libellus* was rejected by the presiding judge; the question of the rejection is to be decided as promptly as possible (*expeditissime*).

---

[9] A decree accepting a *libellus* could be viewed as "merely procedural" (c. 1617) and need simply state that the *libellus* contains the elements specified in c. 1504 without any further discussion of reasons. A decree rejecting the *libellus,* however, should provide the reasons for the rejection so that a petitioner will have some idea on how the *libellus* might be amended.

In face of a rejection of a *libellus,* a petitioner can remedy the defects and re-present the petition (c. 1505, §3). While a canonical advocate is not specifically mentioned by this canon, equity suggests that the tribunal make the services of an advocate available to a petitioner to assist in this attempt.

Within ten days "available time" (*tempus utile*),[10] the petitioner also has the right to "make recourse against" the decision rejecting a *libellus.*[11] This recourse means more than simply objecting to the decision; it entails a "reasoned" argument that the rejection was inappropriate.

If the initial rejection was issued by a sole judge, then recourse is taken to the court of appeals. If the petition was rejected by the president of a college of judges, the appeal normally is directed to the full panel.[12]

The appellate court or the college of judges is charged to decide the recourse "as promptly as possible" (*expeditissime*). In accord with canon 1629, 5°, there is no appeal beyond this decision.[13]

---

[10] *Tempus utile* is distinguished from continuous time, and refers to a period within which a party has the ability to act. See the commentary on cc. 200–203 for reflections on the computation of time in canon law.

[11] The Church's procedural law distinguishes between an "appeal" (a challenge directed against the merits of a formal judicial decision) and "recourse" (a challenge against administrative decisions or against certain procedural decisions in a judicial trial such as the rejection of a *libellus*).

[12] While the canon envisions this as the normal approach, nothing prevents a petitioner from immediately taking recourse against the rejection to the appellate tribunal rather than to the full college of judges.

[13] Realistically, since cases involving the status of persons are never a *res iudicata* (see cc. 1641–1644), a prospective petitioner would be free to "try again" by lodging a totally new petition at some future date. For example, several years after the rejection of a *libellus,* a petitioner might learn new information that would open up previously unsuspected avenues of investigation. In such a case (while not ignoring a prior rejection), an ecclesiastical judge rightly would examine the merits of the new petition.

Canon 1506 — If within a month from the presentation of the *libellus* the judge has not issued a decree which accepts or rejects the *libellus* according to the norm of can. 1505, the interested party can insist that the judge fulfill his function. If the judge takes no action within ten days from the request, then the *libellus* is to be considered as accepted.

Since ecclesiastical trials are vehicles for vindicating rights, the law provides a remedy when a judge fails to act in response to a legitimate petition. If neither a decision to accept or reject the *libellus* is made within one month after its submission, the petitioner can insist that the judge act on it. The petitioner would be wise to do this in writing, documenting the fact that the action was taken. If ten further days pass without a response, the *libellus* is accepted by virtue of the law itself.[14]

CHAPTER II
THE CITATION AND NOTIFICATION
OF JUDICIAL ACTS
[cc. 1507–1512]

Canon 1507 — §1. In the decree which accepts the *libellus* of the petitioner, the judge or the presiding judge must call the other parties to trial, that is, cite them to the joinder of the issue, establishing whether they must respond in writing or present themselves before the judge to come to agreement about the doubts. If from the written responses the judge perceives it necessary to convene the parties, the judge can establish that by a new decree.

§2. If the *libellus* is considered as accepted according to the norm of can. 1506, the decree of citation to the trial must be issued within twenty days from the request mentioned in that canon.

§3. If the litigating parties de facto present themselves before the judge to pursue the case, however, there is no need for a citation, but the notary is to note in the acts that the parties were present for the trial.

In the decree accepting the petition, the court also issues an official citation (or summons) to the respondent and to the other parties whose involvement in the case is required (e.g., a defender of the bond or promoter of justice).[15] The judicial citation informs these parties of the fact of the petition and its acceptance. The citation invites their participation in the first substantive action of the court—the "joinder of issues" at which the *dubium* (i.e., the "doubt," the terms of the controversy) is to be defined. Thus, sufficient information needs to be sought at this time to identify the essential question(s) and to narrow the focus of the subsequent investigation. At this stage of the trial, seeking a written response from the respondent and other participants is an option. The citation should specify whether the response to the citation is to be in writing or in person.

It may be that, having requested and reviewed written responses to the citation, the judge determines that the nature of those responses requires seeing the parties in person before it is possible to define the issue. In this case, the judge issues a new decree delaying the joinder and calling the parties to an initial hearing.

If a petition was accepted in the extraordinary manner provided in canon 1506, the court is required to issue this initial citation within twenty days of the party's insistence on action (hence, within ten days of the automatic acceptance of the petition).

Finally, the citation is a means to an end and not the end in itself. Thus, if the parties to the trial

---

[14] In a properly staffed and well-organized tribunal, the acceptance of a *libellus* by default should never occur. If, however, a petition is accepted in this extraordinary fashion, petitioners and their procurators may need to exercise special care to assure that the petition is handled appropriately.

[15] For a description of the role of these critically important officers of the court, see the commentary on cc. 1430–1436.

are actually present to prosecute the case, their rights are respected and a formal citation would be unnecessary. When this occurs, the notary is responsible to assure that the acts of the case reflect the presence of the parties.

Canon 1508 — §1. The decree of citation to the trial must be communicated immediately to the respondent and at the same time to others who must appear.

§2. The *libellus* which introduces litigation is to be attached to the citation unless for grave causes the judge determines that the *libellus* must not be made known to the party before that party makes a deposition in the trial.

A notification of the citation is to be communicated immediately to the respondent and other concerned parties. Normally, the *libellus* presented by the petitioner is to be attached to the citation. A judge may, however, delay the communication of the *libellus* in order first to seek initial testimony from a respondent. For example, the judge may see a need to obtain preliminary information from a respondent because his or her review of the petitioner's claims might give rise to anger or excessive defensiveness which could color subsequent testimony. Should the judge deem this necessary, however, the decree of citation should specify why the judge has chosen this course of action.

§3. If litigation is introduced against someone who does not have the free exercise of his or her rights or the free administration of the things in dispute, the citation must be communicated, as the case may be, to the guardian, curator, or special procurator, that is, the one who is bound to undertake the trial in the name of that person according to the norm of law.

When someone lacks the ability to stand trial personally, the norms governing the process of recognizing or appointing a guardian or other curator

to protect the person's rights are to be observed.[16] In such a situation, the citation is communicated to the guardian.

Canon 1509 — §1. The notification of citations, decrees, sentences, and other judicial acts must be made through the public postal services or by some other very secure method according to the norms established in particular law.

§2. The fact of notification and its method must be evident in the acts.

While this canon is located in the context of the initial citation, its norms apply to the notification of all judicial decrees, sentences, and other acts issued by the tribunal in the course of a trial.

Since the communication of a citation has very significant consequences, it is vital that those cited receive this notification.[17] To forestall any charge that a person's rights were violated, it is also critical that the acts of a case contain some indication that the citation was properly communicated. The canon expressly accepts delivery through postal services as an appropriate means of notification. Recognizing, however, that different circumstances render any one method inadequate for a worldwide Church, this canon provides for particular law to determine other secure means of notification.

Obviously, the participation of the parties establishes the fact of citation. When a party does not participate, it is especially critical that the acts reflect that the party was duly cited. In this circumstance, one "secure" practice is to use "return receipt" registered mail.

---

[16] See the commentary on cc. 1478–1480. Those norms identify persons unable to stand trial personally and govern the appointment of guardians and curators.

[17] Significantly, a properly cited party who neither appears nor provides a reasonable excuse for being unable to appear may be decreed absent (see c. 1592). As a consequence, those absent parties effectively waive a number of their rights in the trial. See the commentary on cc. 1592 and 1594.

Canon 1510 — A respondent who refuses to accept the document of citation or who prevents its delivery is considered to be legitimately cited.

This norm protects a petitioner from a respondent who might attempt to obstruct the trial by evading the citation. When there is evidence that a citation was evaded or refused, the tribunal is to consider the respondent duly notified and is to proceed with the trial.

Canon 1511 — If the citation was not communicated legitimately, the acts of the process are null, without prejudice to the prescript of can. 1507, §3.

Canon 1512 — When the citation has been communicated legitimately or the parties have appeared before the judge to pursue the case:
  1° the matter ceases to be *res integra;*
  2° the case becomes proper to the otherwise competent judge or tribunal before which the action was initiated;
  3° the jurisdiction of a delegated judge is fixed in such a way that it does not cease when the authority of the one delegating expires;
  4° prescription is interrupted unless other provision is made;
  5° the litigation begins to be pending; therefore, the principle *while litigation is pending, nothing is to be altered* immediately takes effect.

These norms specify the effects of the transmittal or failure to transmit a citation. If the citation is not properly communicated, the procedural acts of the process are null and void (unless the party *de facto* participated). Any resulting decision certainly would be vulnerable to a complaint of remediable nullity (c. 1622, 5°), and likely would be irremediably null as a violation of the right of defense (c. 1620, 7°).

What of the situation where a respondent's whereabouts cannot be determined? Does the inability to cite a respondent prevent the process from moving forward? No. Provided all reasonable efforts have been made to locate a respondent, a tribunal may hear a case when the respondent's whereabouts remain unknown.[18] Great care needs to be taken in these circumstances, first to assure that genuine efforts were made to locate the respondent and, second, to assure that the rights of the respondent are not ignored or violated if the process moves ahead. If the whereabouts of a respondent are discovered during the trial, that person must then be cited and invited to participate in the process. There is no need, however, to declare null the procedural acts posited up to that point.[19]

A properly communicated citation (or the fact of the participation of the one cited) brings with it a number of judicial effects.

  1. First, the matter in question ceases to be a *res integra*. In other words, the contested nature of the right or object involved is officially recognized and considered subject to judgment.

  2. Second, presuming that there is a sufficient legal basis, the jurisdiction of the tribunal is secured. Therefore, other potentially competent tribunals are "prevented" from acting (c. 1415). Furthermore, any changes of circumstances subsequent to this do not interfere with the tribunal's competence. Thus, for example, if a court has jurisdiction as the domicile of the

---

[18] That the law envisions this possibility is evident in c. 1409, §2, which makes provision for a petition to be accepted at the tribunal of the domicile of the petitioner when the domicile or quasi-domicile of a respondent is unknown and no other legitimate forum is available. See ApSig, decr *De foro competenti in causa nullitatis matrimonii,* April 6, 1973, *P* 62 (1973) 590–591. Translated in *CLD* 8, 1196–1197. See also J. Provost, "Competent Tribunal When Respondent's Address Is Unknown," *J* 44 (1984) 244–246.

[19] Of course, if a respondent shows that the petitioner was aware of his or her whereabouts and concealed that information, then that attempt to deny the right of defense would render the process invalid.

respondent when it issues the citation, a subsequent move of the respondent to another diocese would not deprive the tribunal of its competence to complete the case.

3. Similarly, the jurisdiction of a delegated judge (*iudice delegato*)[20] appointed to process the case is firmly established and will perdure even if the authority of the one who initially delegated the judge later expires.

4. The passage of time affecting possible prescription (cc. 197–199) is interrupted, unless the law provides otherwise.

5. The matter is considered "pending" or officially under adjudication.[21] This has the consequence of prohibiting the introduction of any innovation, any transfer of control, or any other action that might prejudice the rights of one or more of the parties to the trial.

---

[20] The term "delegated judge" is found in the Latin code only in this canon, although reference to delegating judges is also made in cc. 1427, §2 (a judge delegated by a supreme moderator of a religious institute of pontifical right); 1442 (a papal delegate); and 1495 (a judge delegated for one case only). Other sorts of delegated judges are found in canonical tradition. For example, c. 1607, 2° of the 1917 code speaks of a judge delegated by a local ordinary.

In the 1983 code, however, the idea of a delegated judge seems to be an exception to c. 135, §3 (*CCEO* 985, §3) which states that judicial power, except for the performance of some preliminary acts, cannot be delegated. Clearly, a "delegated judge" as used in c. 1512, 3° is not an auditor or merely someone delegated to handle some preparatory acts but a true judge. Does this refer only to the religious and papal delegates of cc. 1427 and 1442? J. Abbass thinks not. In "Contentious Trials," 888–889, nn. 56–57, he states that the prohibition against delegating judicial power extends only to individual judges and judicial colleges. According to Abbass, a bishop remains free to delegate a judge, and he notes that *CCEO* 1102, §2 foresees this possibility.

[21] Canon 1194, 5° of the Eastern code differs, stating that with the citation the "instance of the suit begins." For the significance of this difference, see Abbas, "Contentious Trials," 891–892.

TITLE II
THE JOINDER OF THE ISSUE[22]
[cc. 1513–1516]

The Notion and Purpose of the Joinder

Canon 1513 — §1. The joinder of the issue (*contestatio litis*) occurs when the terms of the controversy, derived from the petitions and responses of the parties, are defined through a decree of the judge.

§2. The petitions and responses of the parties, besides those in the *libellus* which introduces the litigation, can be expressed either in a response to the citation or in the oral declarations made before the judge; in more difficult cases, however, the judge must convene the parties to resolve the doubt or doubts which must be answered in the sentence.

The joinder of the issue is the definition of the terms of the controversy by a decree of the judge. Normally, the issue is phrased in the form of a question or questions to which an affirmative or negative response is given at the completion of the process (e.g., "Whether the marriage between the petitioner and the respondent has been proven invalid on the ground(s) of A and B?").

The purpose of the joinder of the issue is to focus the investigation of the tribunal on the specific question or questions to be decided. It establishes the "matter about which the entire controversy will revolve."[23] Thus, it is a critical moment in the process and shapes the subsequent instruction of the case.

The definition of the issue(s) is an act of the judge, specified in a judicial decree.[24] It reflects

---

[22] Wrenn, in *CLSA Com,* 973–974; Coyle, in *CLSGBI Com,* 869–870; L. Madero, in *Pamplona ComEng,* 943–945; Arroba Conde, in *Valencia Com,* 667–668; A. Stankiewicz, in *Com Ex* IV/2, 1232–1246.

[23] Pompedda, "Decision-Sentence," 82.

[24] Thus, while it initiates the process, the "entire controversy . . . is not totally expressed in a *'libellus,'*" and the court is not limited to the potential grounds brought forward in the *libellus* or in any counterclaims of the respondent. Pompedda, "Decision-Sentence," 82.

the court's evaluation of the pleadings and responses of the petitioner and the respondent (as well as the defender of the bond and promoter of justice when the nature of the case requires their participation).

The canon envisions two means whereby the issue may be joined. Most commonly, the judge reviews the written and oral statements of the parties to the case and defines the issue on the basis of that information. Alternatively, in more difficult cases, the judge may call the parties together and define the issue by means of a discussion. Ideally, both parties would agree on the formulation of the issue, although nothing prevents the judge from defining the question(s) at issue if the parties cannot agree.

Notification and Potential Challenge to the Definition of the Issue

§3. The decree of the judge must be communicated to the parties; unless they have already agreed to the terms, the parties can make recourse to the judge within ten days in order to change them; a decree of the judge, however, must resolve the question as promptly as possible (*expeditissime*).

Once the issue has been defined, the parties are to be informed of the decision of the judge and given ten days to request the amendment of the ground(s), or the addition of a different ground, or the deletion of one or more of the grounds. The judge's decision in the face of a challenge is to be made *expeditissime* and hence is not subject to appeal (c. 1629, 5°).

Clearly, the very structure of these norms indicates the high value placed on obtaining input from both the petitioner and respondent in specifying the question(s) at issue. What should be done, then, if a respondent does not reply to the citation? There are a number of options. The judge may choose to decree the respondent absent and determine the issue without any testimony from the respondent. In this case, the absent respondent has effectively waived his or her right to

participate in the formulation of the ground (see the commentary on c. 1592). If there is a founded hope that the respondent will eventually participate, the judge could delay for a time the definition of the issue while further efforts are made to secure the respondent's input. Given the expectations of canon 1453, however, such a delay must not infringe on the petitioner's right to a decision within a reasonable time.[25]

Changing the Definition of the Issue

Canon 1514 — Once established, the terms of the controversy cannot be changed validly except by a new decree, for a grave cause, at the request of a party, and after the other parties have been heard and their arguments considered.

Once the issue has been defined, it acquires a certain stability. A change in the terms of the controversy can *validly* be made only in accord with the provisions of this canon. Four things are required.

1. One party (including the defender of the bond or promoter of justice when they are involved) must request the amendment or addition of a ground. While enjoying a great deal of autonomy in managing the trial, a judge cannot change the ground without such a request.

2. There must be a "grave cause" for the change (e.g., assuring a just decision).

3. The other parties to the case must be consulted about the proposed change and their arguments carefully considered. An objection by one or more of the parties, however, does not prevent the judge from admitting the change.

---

[25] If it seems just to delay joining the issue in the hope that some additional time will secure the respondent's input, the judge may deem the avoidance of excessive delays as the "grave cause" required to gather at least some proofs before the joinder (c. 1529).

4. The judge must issue a decree specifying the change and summarizing the reasons for admitting the change (cc. 51 and 1617).

In the absence of any of these steps, an alteration of the ground is *invalid;* any subsequent decision is vulnerable to a complaint of remediable nullity under canon 1622, 5°.[26]

Effect of the Joinder on Possession of Property

Canon 1515 — After the issue has been joined, the possessor of the property of another ceases to be in good faith; therefore, if the possessor is sentenced to restore the property, the person must also return the profits made from the day of the joinder and repair any damages.

If the contention concerns a dispute over property, the joinder of the issue puts the possessor on notice that the ownership of the property is under adjudication. Officially, the possession is no longer "in good faith."[27]

Should the trial result in a decision mandating that the possessor hand over the property, all profit made from the point of the joinder must also be handed over, and restitution must be made for any damages suffered as the result of the possession.

Time Limits for Proposing Proofs

Canon 1516 — After the issue has been joined, the judge is to prescribe a suitable time for the parties to present and complete the proofs.

The joinder of the issue completes the preliminary stage of the trial and inaugurates the "instruction" of the case (i.e., the evidence-gathering phase). While the parties have the chief responsibility to bring forward appropriate proofs of their claims,[28] the judge has the authority to establish reasonable time limits suitable for the nature of the case. Those time limits may be extended in accord with the provisions of canon 1465, §2, provided there are no undue delays (c. 1465, §3).

For marriage cases, canon 1677, §4 further specifies that the judge is to arrange for the instruction of the case ten days after the notification of the decree of the joinder, unless objections were raised against that decree.

TITLE III
THE TRIAL OF THE LITIGATION[29]
[cc. 1517–1525]

The Life Span of a Trial

Canon 1517 — A trial begins with the citation; it ends not only by the pronouncement of a definitive sentence but also by other methods defined by law.[30]

The first part of this norm reiterates the provisions of canon 1512 indicating that the citation (summons) begins the trial.[31]

---

[26] The value of stability in the definition of the issue is also protected by c. 1639, §1, which prohibits the introduction of a new ground in the appeal process. Canon 1683, however, makes an exception for marriage nullity cases, permitting the introduction of a new ground on the appellate level which is adjudicated as if in first instance.

[27] Canon 198 provides that the possession must be in "good faith" throughout the "entire course of time required for prescription." In the circumstances of a trial, however, prescription was already interrupted by the communication of the citation (c. 1512, 4°).

[28] The judge, however, has a role in seeking out evidence to supply for the parties' negligence or inability to bring forward appropriate proof (see c. 1452, §2).

[29] Wrenn, in *CLSA Com,* 975–976; Coyle, in *CLSGBI Com,* 870–873; Madero, in *Pamplona ComEng,* 945–949; Arroba Conde, in *Valencia Com,* 668–671; J. Carreras, in *Com Ex* IV/2, 1247–1268.

[30] There is no counterpart to c. 1517 in the Eastern code. See Abbass, "Contentious Trials," 880–881.

[31] Wrenn, in *CLSA Com,* 975, explains that the 1917 code's distinction between the beginning of the litigation and the beginning of the instance has been eliminated by this norm of the 1983 code.

Once initiated, the normal means of bringing the trial to conclusion is through a judicial sentence. Other ways in which a trial can be interrupted or terminated are suspension (cc. 1518–1519 and 1681), peremption or abatement (cc. 1520–1523), renunciation (cc. 1524–1525), and reconciliation or arbitration (cc. 1713 and 1676).

Suspension of a Case and Its Effects

A trial may be interrupted due to factors relating to the parties (c. 1518) or their representatives (c. 1519). In marriage nullity cases, a case may also be suspended to investigate the possible non-consummation of the union (c. 1681).

During a suspension, the development of the trial proper ceases until the cause of the suspension is addressed. The trial may then resume, and the time during which the case was suspended is not computed relative to peremption.[32]

Suspension Due to a Change in the Status of a Party to the Trial

Canon 1518 — If the litigating party dies, changes status, or ceases from the office in virtue of which action is taken:

1° if the case has not yet been concluded, the trial is suspended until the heir of the deceased, the successor, or an interested party resumes the litigation;

2° if the case has been concluded, the judge must proceed to the additional acts, after having cited the procurator, if there is one, or otherwise the heir of the deceased or the successor.

When death or some other change of status affecting a party's capacity to act in the litigation occurs, two possibilities result depending on how far the process has advanced.

1. The process is suspended by the law itself as long as it has not reached the stage of formal conclusion of the probative phase of the process (c. 1599). The trial may be resumed only if a person with standing to do so pursues the matter.[33]

2. If the process has been formally concluded, the judge must proceed to a final decision, first citing the procurator, heir, or successor of the party whose status has changed. Canon 1675, §2 specifies that, if one of the parties dies, this norm applies in marriage nullity cases.

Lawrence Wrenn suggested that the phrase *causa conclusa* might be interpreted to refer to the issuance of the definitive decision rather than the "conclusion" spoken of in canon 1599.[34] Most commentators, however, do not agree with this interpretation.

Suspension Due to a Change in the Status of a Representative of a Party

Canon 1519 — §1. If the guardian, curator, or procurator who is necessary according to the norm of can. 1481, §§1 and 3 ceases from that function, the trial is suspended in the meantime.

§2. The judge, however, is to appoint another guardian or curator as soon as possible; the judge can appoint a procurator for the litigation if the party has neglected to do so within the brief time period established by the judge.

---

[32] Wrenn, in *CLSA Com*, 975.

[33] Carreras, in *Com Ex* IV/2, 1257–1258, and Madero, in *Pamplona ComEng*, 946, argue that this situation provides an exception to the norm of c. 1674 and allows a third party with an interest involved to continue the process of impugning a marriage. While the text of c. 1518 makes this argument reasonable, the interest must be compelling. The situation envisioned in c. 1675, §1, where the resolution of some other controversy depends on the question of the validity of the marriage, could provide an example of a legitimate interest in proceeding.

[34] Wrenn, in *CLSA Com*, 975.

A temporary suspension of the process takes place only in the narrow circumstance of a trial where a representative for the parties is *required* by canon 1481, §1 or §3 (e.g., contentious trials involving the public good or a minor).[35]

When this suspension occurs, if a *guardian or curator* is needed (see c. 1478–1479), the judge is to provide for a new one as quickly as possible.

If a *procurator* is needed, the judge is to give a brief period of time for the affected party to appoint a new representative. If such an appointment is not made within the allotted time, the judge is to appoint a procurator *ad litem* so that the litigation can be resumed.

Peremption (Abatement)

Canon 1520 — If the parties, without any impediment, propose no procedural act for six months, the trial is abated. Particular law can establish other terms of abatement.

Peremption or abatement occurs as a result of the failure of the parties to place any procedural act for a period of six months. If, however, some legitimate cause has impeded the parties from acting, abatement does not take effect. Particular law may establish a different period of time, longer or shorter, after which abatement takes effect. It should be noted that abatement does not take effect as a result of the mere passage of time, but rather from the failure of the petitioner and respondent to act within the specified time. Thus, delays resulting from a backlog in the tribunal or as a result of the negligence of the court itself do not bring about abatement.

[35] Canon 1481, §3 specifically excludes marriage nullity cases from those contentious trials involving the public good where a judge *is required* to appoint a legal representative when a party lacks one. In marriage nullity cases, however, judges retain the discretion to do so if they deem it necessary.

Canon 1521 — Abatement takes effect by the law itself against all persons, including minors or those equivalent to minors, and must be declared *ex officio,* without prejudice to the right of seeking indemnity against guardians, curators, administrators, or procurators, who have not proved that they were not negligent.

Canon 1522 — Abatement extinguishes the acts of the process but not the acts of the case; indeed these acts can also have force in another trial provided that the case involves the same persons and the same issue; regarding those not party to the case, however, the acts have no force other than that of documents.

Canon 1523 — Each litigant is to bear the expenses of the abated trial which that litigant has incurred.

Abatement takes effect automatically, by the force of the law itself, and affects all parties to the case. The judge, however, is to make the parties aware of the fact by declaring that abatement has taken effect.

Since abatement may stem from negligence (e.g., the failure of a procurator to act), canon 1521 recognizes the right of a party injured by abatement to bring an action against those at fault. Canon 1523 provides that the parties are liable for the court's expenses incurred prior to abatement.

Abatement extinguishes the judicial instance. In other words, all procedural acts taken up to that point lose their force. Abatement does not, however, vitiate the value of the substantive acts of the case. Therefore, any testimony secured prior to abatement remains in the file and can be employed in a new instance involving the same parties and same issues. Those substantive acts may also serve as documentary evidence in other ecclesiastical trials. An authentic interpretation of May 17, 1986 clarified the fact that, should one of the parties wish to initiate a new petition subsequent to the abatement of a prior instance, it is not necessary to lodge the petition before the original tribunal.[36] Any court with recognized jurisdiction at the time of the new petition may accept the *libellus* and may employ the substantive acts from the earlier process.[37]

Renunciation

Canon 1524 — §1. The petitioner can renounce the trial at any stage or grade of the trial; likewise both the petitioner and the respondent can renounce either all or only some of the acts of the process.

§2. To renounce a trial, guardians and administrators of juridic persons need the counsel or consent of those whose involvement is required to place acts which exceed the limits of ordinary administration.

§3. To be valid, a renunciation must be written and signed by the party or by a procurator of the party who has a special mandate to do so; it must be communicated to the other party, accepted or at least not challenged by that party, and accepted by the judge.

Since the petitioner initiated the process, only the petitioner may renounce the instance itself. Both parties, however, have the right to renounce any or all procedural acts. Should all the procedural acts be renounced and that renunciation admitted, the instance is effectively ended.

A renunciation can take place at any point in the trial. It can be lodged before a tribunal of first, second, or any further instance.

Renunciation is considered an extraordinary matter. Thus, before placing an act of renunciation, a guardian or administrator may need to seek counsel or consent from the appropriate person or bodies as required by law (cf. cc. 638, 1277). Nor is a procurator free to posit a renunciation unless given a special mandate to do so (c. 1485).

For the validity of a renunciation, the following must occur:

1. the renunciation must be expressed in writing and signed by the party (or procurator with a special mandate) placing it;
2. the renunciation must be communicated to the other party;
3. the other party must either accept the renunciation or at least raise no opposition to it;[38]
4. the renunciation must be admitted by the judge, who retains the discretion to refuse to accept a renunciation in order better to serve justice.

If any of these elements is lacking, the renunciation has no force and the trial continues.

Canon 1525 — A renunciation accepted by the judge has the same effects for the acts renounced as the abatement of the trial; it also obliges the renouncing party to pay the expenses for the acts renounced.

The judicial effects of a renunciation that has been admitted are identical to the effects of abatement (c. 1522), with the exception that the court expenses become the responsibility of the renouncing party.

---

[36] PCILT, *responsa ad proposita dubia,* May 17, 1986, *AAS* 78 (1986) 1324. Also see L. Wrenn, *Authentic Interpretations on the 1983 Code* (Washington, D.C.: CLSA, 1993) 29–30.

[37] In fact, the original tribunal may have lost any claim to jurisdiction. For instance, jurisdiction may originally have been based on the domicile of the respondent. But if at the time of the new petition the respondent is no longer domiciled in that diocese, the original court has lost that basis to adjudicate the case. Unless some other basis for jurisdiction is present, the original court would be prevented from reopening the case.

[38] There is a more stringent norm in penal trials where, for a valid renunciation, the accused *must accept* the renunciation (unless the accused was decreed absent from the trial). See the commentary on c. 1724, §2.

TITLE IV
PROOFS[39]
[cc. 1526–1586]

Introduction

The title on proofs constitutes the longest section of Book VII. The process of gathering and assessing evidence, commonly known as the "instruction" of the case, is under the direction of the judge. It is on the basis of the proofs assembled that the judge must reach moral certitude and pronounce a decision in the controversy (c. 1609, §2).

A proof is a demonstration, in whole or in part, of the truth of matters relevant to the question at issue. Proofs may be direct or indirect in nature. Certain forms of evidence may provide "full proof," although more commonly it is in the "aggregate of proofs and indications" that the truth is discovered.[40]

After a series of introductory canons referring to proofs in general, the six chapters of this title discuss distinct sources of proof recognized at canon law. Those sources yield various types of evidence of differing probative value.

The instruction of a case is not merely a matter of assembling information. Sifting, weighing, and evaluating the evidence is also crucial. These norms contain principles to assist the judge in that art.

Burden of Proof

Canon 1526 — §1. The burden of proof rests upon the person who makes the allegation.

In accord with ancient principles of law, the canon clearly asserts the responsibility of the one making a claim to bring forth evidence establishing that claim. Initially, that burden rests on the petitioner, although a respondent may assume the burden of proof in establishing any counterclaims made in response to the initial petition.

Once a trial is initiated, however, the judge also assumes a responsibility to seek and act in accord with the truth. Thus, while not removing the burden of proof from the parties, this canon must be interpreted in light of canon 1452, §2, which affirms the judge's right and duty to "supply for the negligence of the parties in furnishing proofs" in order to avoid a "gravely unjust judgment."

Matters Not Requiring Proof

§2. The following do not need proof:
1° matters presumed by the law itself;
2° facts alleged by one of the contending parties and admitted by the other unless the law or the judge nevertheless requires proof.

Some matters require no proof, such as when the law itself establishes a presumption. For example, canon 1060 establishes a presumption in favor of the validity of a marriage; canon 1061, §2 presumes the consummation of a marriage subsequent to the cohabitation of the parties; canon 1321, §3 establishes the presumption of imputability whenever an external violation of ecclesiastical law or precept has occurred. Such presumptions, however, can be overturned by sufficient evidence to the contrary.

Also exempted from the requirement of proof are facts alleged by one party and admitted by the other party (see c. 1536, §1). This holds *unless* the law or the judge requires additional proof. The law does provide otherwise in cases concerning the public good (c. 1536, §2), which include marriage nullity cases (c. 1691). In these cases, the declarations of the parties alone do not normally constitute full proof.[41]

---

[39] Wrenn, in *CLSA Com,* 976–988; R. Bourgon, in *CLSGBI Com,* 873–895; J. Calvo, in *Pamplona ComEng,* 949–983; Arroba Conde, in *Valencia Com,* 671–688; J. P. Schouppe et al., in *Com Ex* IV/2, 1269–1430.

[40] Pius XII, alloc, October 1, 1942, *AAS* 34 (1942) 338–343. Translation in *CLD* 3, 605–611.

[41] See the commentary on cc. 1536–1537 and 1679 for circumstances in which the declarations of the parties might constitute full proof.

Admissible Proofs

Canon 1527 — §1. Proofs of any kind which seem useful for adjudicating the case and are licit can be brought forward.

§2. If a party insists that a proof rejected by a judge be accepted, the judge is to decide the matter as promptly as possible (*expeditissime*).

This title identifies various types of proof that are licit (e.g., declarations of the parties, documents, etc.). The canon also leaves the door open for the admission of types of proof not foreseen by the code, such as videotapes and various forms of electronic transmissions.[42] Normally, a judge will be flexible and provide sufficient latitude for the parties to bring forward proofs. Ruling on the liceity and utility of any particular proof, however, is the responsibility of the judge. For example, a judge could refuse to admit a proof obtained by an immoral means. Similarly, a judge can refuse useless proofs or those brought forward as delaying tactics, such as the multiplication of witnesses (c. 1553).

If a judge rejects a proposed proof, the one proposing it can ask for a reconsideration of that rejection. The judge is then to rule *expeditissime,* meaning that no further appeal can be made against the decision (c. 1629, 5°).

Alternative Methods for Obtaining Testimony

Canon 1528 — If a party or a witness refuses to appear before the judge to testify, it is permissible to hear them through a lay person designated by the judge or to require of them a declaration either before a notary public or in any other legitimate manner.

Since discovering the truth is the primary goal of the instruction of a case, great latitude is afforded the judge or auditor in obtaining evidence from a less than fully cooperative party or witness. When people refuse to appear at the tribunal and testify in the usual manner, their testimony may be sought through third parties designated by the tribunal, by means of a written and notarized declaration, or in "any other legitimate manner." What might constitute another legitimate manner? The code does not specify, and certain questions have arisen over the manner in which tribunals sometimes seek testimony. The use of written questionnaires has been challenged by Zenon Grocholewski, who concludes that this "may not be accepted as an ordinary means of questioning the parties and/or the witnesses."[43] Grocholewski argues that testimony taken in this way does not satisfy the requirements governing the way the examination of the parties and witnesses is to be carried out, and results in evidence of very limited probative force. John Beal, on the other hand, questions whether such a restrictive reading of canon 1528 is justifiable, and argues that the practice can be justified especially in situations "where a party or a witness would, in the judgment of a tribunal, refuse or be reluctant to appear personally."[44]

The practice of seeking testimony by telephone is not authorized by the code,[45] but neither is it ruled out in the canons themselves. Seeking testimony by telephone, however, has been strongly criticized by Grocholewski and others.[46] Certainly,

---

[42] As more and more communication is handled electronically, these sources of proof will grow in importance. Much as with documents (see c. 1543), care will need to be taken to assure the authenticity of the proof brought forward. Assessing whether electronic communications have been altered may present a new area in which tribunals will need to employ the services of experts (see cc. 1574–1581).

[43] Z. Grocholewski, "Interrogation by Letter or Telephone," in *CLSA Advisory Opinions 1984–1993*, ed. P. Cogan (Washington, D.C.: CLSA, 1995) 460–465.

[44] J. Beal, "Making Connections: Procedural Law and Substantive Justice," *J* 54 (1994) 162.

[45] A proposal to authorize the use of the telephone was made but not accepted during the code revision process because of a fear of abuses (*Comm* 11 [1979] 114). Also see the commentary on c. 1558.

[46] Grocholewski, "Interrogation," 460–465. He does, however, leave the door partly open to alternative means of taking testimony by concluding that "an interrogation by letter or telephone could be justified only by the most exceptional circumstances" (464).

there are dangers connected with attempting to secure testimony by telephone. Yet the tribunal has a responsibility to seek the truth in order to make a just decision. When a party or witness is unwilling to provide evidence in any other fashion, that underlying responsibility can be in tension or conflict with a stance that would never admit testimony obtained by telephone. Certainly, Grocholewski is correct in concluding that obtaining testimony by telephone is not an "ordinary" manner of proceeding.[47] Creative approaches might well provide means to alleviate many of the concerns related to this method of taking testimony. For example, a witness could be asked to go to the offices of a local parish and present testimony by telephone from that location. The parish priest or other parish official could verify the identity of the party and serve as notary while the judge or auditor posed questions by telephone. Similarly, the use of videoconferencing technology could also provide an effective means of interrogating the parties and witnesses that would ease the burdens on them while preserving many of the values of an interview in the tribunal's offices.

Prohibition of Evidence Gathering before the Joinder of the Issues

Canon 1529 — Except for a grave cause, the judge is not to proceed to collect the proofs before the joinder of the issue.

Since the purpose of the joinder of issues is to focus the investigation on the central question(s) to be decided by the court, that investigation is most fruitfully conducted after the issue has been defined. The nature of the questions asked, the appropriate witnesses to contact, the other sorts of proofs to be admitted are all affected by the nature of the matter at issue. Additionally, to respect the rights of the respondent, the investigation should not proceed until he or she has at least had an opportunity to contest the claims of the petitioner, to secure the services of an advocate, and to nominate witnesses.

The canon, however, provides for an exception to this norm, which permits the gathering of at least some evidence before the joinder when there is a "grave cause" for doing so. In the drafting of this canon, a specific decision was made to use the term "grave" cause rather than simply a "just" cause,[48] thus emphasizing the exceptional nature of this possibility. No list of grave causes is provided. The canonical tradition, however, provides guidance. Canon 1730 of the 1917 code specifically provided for securing the testimony of a witness who was in danger of death or who would be otherwise unavailable at a later time. Certainly, these two circumstances continue to constitute grave causes.[49] In practice, it is the judge who must weigh the gravity of arguments for collecting any proof before the joinder of the issue. While collecting proof prior to the joinder must never become the usual practice, the principle that justice should not be unduly delayed may sometimes provide a cause that is sufficiently grave.[50]

---

[47] Grocholewski, "Interrogation," 461. Should a judge deem it necessary to seek testimony by telephone, great care needs to be taken to assure the identity and freedom of the one making the deposition in order to eliminate or significantly mitigate the dangers feared by the code commission.

[48] *Comm* 16 (1984) 64.

[49] S. Raica, *Canon 1529: A Historical and Canonical Study* (Rome: Pontificia Universitas Gregoriana, 1996) 97–100, discusses the meaning of "grave cause" as used in this canon and concludes that the criterion to be used in determining such gravity is whether failure to seek the evidence prior to the joinder "would imperil the attainment of the truth" (100). Raica persuasively argues that fidelity to this norm is vital not only to the credibility of the trial process (avoiding the impression that the "process has occurred before the process") but also to maintain the right of privacy of the parties (90–91, 103).

[50] For example, in a particular case a respondent may not reply by the originally scheduled time of the joinder of the issues. When there is a good prospect that the respondent will take part in the trial, the judge may choose to delay the determination of the issue so that the ground or grounds joined are not based solely on the claims of the petitioner. Mindful, however, of the requirements of c. 1453, the judge may also conclude that these circum-

In practice, in the face of a persuasive argument that a grave cause is present, the judge would be able to issue a decree authorizing evidence gathering prior to the joinder.[51]

CHAPTER I
THE DECLARATIONS OF THE PARTIES
[cc. 1530–1538]

An important innovation of the 1983 code was the decision to include in the title on proofs the norms governing the collection and assessment of the declarations of the parties. The prior code had placed the canons on the declarations of the parties (*CIC* 1742–1746) in a separate title, distinct from the title on proof. In interpreting and implementing that code, the instruction *Provida Mater Ecclesia* had specifically excluded the "judicial declarations" of the parties as sufficient to constitute proof in marriage nullity cases.[52] The change in attitude toward such declarations reflects developments in the praxis and jurisprudence of the Roman Rota as well as a less suspicious and more respectful stance toward the parties and their testimony.[53]

Judge's Right to Question the Parties

Canon 1530 — The judge can always question the parties to draw out the truth more effectively and indeed must do so at the request of a party or to prove a fact which the public interest requires to be placed beyond doubt.

The judge is entrusted with the responsibility of discovering and ruling in accord with the truth. In light of this responsibility, the judge (or auditor)

has a fundamental right to question the parties. Additionally, the judge must interrogate a party (1) when requested by one of the parties to the case (including the defender of the bond or promoter of justice) or (2) when the public good of the Church requires that some fact be established.

The Obligation to Testify Truthfully

Canon 1531 — §1. A party legitimately questioned must respond and must tell the whole truth.

A party to an ecclesiastical trial has an underlying obligation to testify truthfully. That obligation is nuanced in several ways. First, the questioning must be conducted in a legitimate fashion, by the judge or auditor and in accord with the norms for posing questions (see c. 1564). Further, the accused in a penal trial is not obligated to confess the crime and cannot be forced to testify under oath (c. 1728, §2).

If a party violates the obligation to tell the truth and commits perjury, he or she is possibly subject to an ecclesiastical penalty (c. 1368).

Evaluation of a Refusal to Answer

§2. If a party refuses to respond, it is for the judge to decide what can be inferred from that refusal concerning the proof of the facts.

When a party refuses to reply to a question, the significance of that refusal must be evaluated by the judge. Silence cannot automatically be interpreted as a tacit admission, and hence each situation must be carefully assessed.

Oath to Testify Truthfully

Canon 1532 — In cases where the public good is at stake, the judge is to administer an oath to the parties to tell the truth or at least to confirm the truth of what they have said unless a grave cause suggests otherwise; the same can be done in other cases according to the judge's own prudence.

---

stances provide a grave cause to gather at least some proofs before the joinder. See also the discussion at c. 1513, §3 above.

[51] Beal, "Making Connections," 154–159.

[52] SCSacr, instr *Provida Mater Ecclesia,* August 15, 1936, art. 117, *AAS* 28 (1936) 337. Translation in *CLD* 2, 500.

[53] P. Felici, "Juridical Formalities and Evaluations of Evidence in the Canonical Process," *J* 38 (1978) 153–157. Also see Pompedda, "Decision-Sentence," 90–91.

In cases which concern the public good (which according to c. 1691 always includes marriage nullity cases), the judge is to administer to the parties an oath to tell the truth or to confirm the truth of information previously provided. An oath is "the invocation of the divine name in witness to the truth" (c. 1199, §1). The fact that testimony was given under oath is a factor to be considered in the evaluation of evidence.

A judge may forego the oath for a grave cause, for example a conscientious objection to the taking of an oath. In cases that do not involve the public good, the administration of an oath is left to the judge's discretion.

In penal cases, the accused may not be compelled to take an oath (see c. 1728, §2), but he or she may wish to present testimony under oath.[54]

Preparation of Questions

Canon 1533 — The parties, the promoter of justice, and the defender of the bond can present the judge with items about which the party is to be questioned.

Canon 1534 — The provisions of cann. 1548, §2, n. 1, 1552, and 1558–1565 concerning witnesses are to be observed to the extent possible when questioning the parties.

While the judge or auditor directs the instruction of the case, the responsibility to seek the truth belongs to all participants in an ecclesiastical trial. In furtherance of that goal, the parties, their advocates, the defender of the bond, and the promoter of justice all have the right to ask the judge or auditor to interrogate the parties concerning various subjects or even to suggest specific questions to be posed. The judge or auditor then determines whether and in what manner to use these questions.[55]

The manner of conducting the interview is governed by the canons for the interrogation of witnesses adapted appropriately for the questioning of the parties.

Definition of a Judicial Confession

Canon 1535 — A judicial confession is the written or oral assertion of some fact against oneself before a competent judge by any party concerning the matter of the trial, whether made spontaneously or while being questioned by the judge.

With careful precision, this canon defines a judicial confession. Such a confession must involve a statement:

1. concerning factual matters (not speculation or statements of opinion);
2. made as part of the trial process, that is, to a judge or auditor, whether orally or in writing, whether spontaneously volunteered or admitted in response to questioning;
3. made by either the petitioner or respondent directly (a third party report of a statement allegedly made by one of the parties is not a judicial confession);
4. against the interests of the party in the trial (not every admission of fault or weakness is a confession, for such a statement may serve the interest of the party in the trial; similarly, a confession may consist of admissions of positive behaviors which are against the interests of the party);
5. and about a matter pertinent to the issue being investigated.

---

[54] Bourgon (in *CLSGBI Com,* 876) asserts that "in penal cases an oath may not be administered to the accused person." That conclusion goes beyond the norm of the canon. While it would never be appropriate subtly to pressure an accused to take an oath (which even a simple invitation might do), there is no reason to prevent the accused from volunteering to take the oath, an opinion held by J. Martin, in *CLSGBI Com,* 959.

[55] Canon 1561 leaves room for particular law to allow persons other than the judge or auditor to pose questions directly to witnesses. Since c. 1534 applies the norms for the interrogation of witnesses to the questioning of parties, similar particular law provisions could be enacted to allow direct questioning of parties by persons other than the judge or auditor.

Probative Force of Judicial Confessions

Canon 1536 — §1. The judicial confession of one party relieves the other parties from the burden of proof if it concerns some private matter and the public good is not at stake.

In matters where the public good is not at stake, a judicial confession relieves the other parties of the burden of proof (see c. 1526, §2, 2°). The judge must still evaluate the confession for its veracity and its relevance to the matter at issue. Thus, it may or may not provide full proof.

§2. In cases which regard the public good, however, a judicial confession and declarations of the parties which are not confessions can have a probative force which the judge must evaluate together with the other circumstances of the case; the force of full proof cannot be attributed to them, however, unless other elements are present which thoroughly corroborate them.

In cases involving the public good, both judicial confessions and other declarations made by the parties are attributed some, though normally not full, probative force.[56] The appropriate probative value must be determined by the judge in light of the evidence taken as a whole. In weighing these declarations, the judge is to consider "the other circumstances of the case" (*ceteris causae adiunctis*) and whether there are "other elements [*alia elementa*] ... which thoroughly corroborate" those declarations.[57] For marriage nullity cases, canon 1679 provides for the use of testimony regarding the credibility of the parties as

---

[56] Pompedda in "Decision-Sentence," 91, asks whether the depositions of the spouses are of themselves sufficient to induce moral certitude, and he responds that the answer "according to prevalent rotal jurisprudence is without a doubt in the affirmative."

[57] Pompedda, "Decision-Sentence," 91. For an analysis of the role of circumstances and corroborative elements in proof, see J. Beal, "The Substance of Things Hoped For: Proving Simulation of Matrimonial Consent," *J* 55 (1995) 751–753.

well as other "indications and supporting factors" (*indicia et adminicula*) in the evaluation of the declarations of the parties.

Extrajudicial Confessions

Canon 1537 — After considering all the circumstances, it is for the judge to decide how much value must be accorded an extrajudicial confession introduced into the trial.

An extrajudicial confession shares all of the characteristics of a judicial confession as described above, with the exception that the statement was made outside of the context of the trial. The statement is later brought to the attention of the court, often by a witness who heard the confession.

With due regard for the norm of canon 1538, the judge is to evaluate the weight of the confession in context of the evidence as a whole. For example, the judge would consider circumstances such as the confession's consistency with other statements and behaviors of the party, any ambiguity which the statement might contain, the quality of the memory of the person reporting the confession, etc. It should be noted, however, that there is no restriction against attributing full probative force to extrajudicial confessions.

The time at which an extrajudicial confession was made is significant in assessing its value. The judge would attribute greater weight to a confession uttered at a "non-suspect" time, i.e., before any thought of a trial arose, than to a statement made only after the contention was under way. While this canon refers only to confessions, the principles for evaluation are applicable to any extrajudicial declaration made by one of the parties.

Effect of Error, Force, or Fear

Canon 1538 — A confession or any other declaration of a party lacks any force if it is shown that it was made due to an error of fact or extorted by force or grave fear.

This norm protects the integrity of the tribunal's search for the truth. Any confession or declaration of the parties, judicial or extrajudicial, has no force at all if made through an error of fact, or if it was extorted through grave force or fear.[58]

CHAPTER II
PROOF THROUGH DOCUMENTS
[cc. 1539–1546]

Admissibility of Documents

Canon 1539 — In any kind of trial, proof by means of both public and private documents is allowed.

Proof by documents is admitted in all types of trials, whether involving the public or the private good, whether concerning marriage nullity, property issues, penal matters, or any other issue. The canon refers to "public" and "private" documents; the distinctions are clarified in the following canon.

Modern technological developments require an expanded understanding of this type of proof. The term *documenta* traditionally referred to various sorts of written materials. But other documentary evidence might include photographs, audio and video tape recordings, and information from other electronic media.[59]

---

[58] This norm makes "other provision" adapting the basic principles of law found in cc. 125 and 126 which govern the effect of force, fear, fraud, ignorance, or error on juridic acts. Precisely because the need to obtain the truth is so critical in an ecclesiastical trial, c. 1538 is more demanding than cc. 125–126, which at times recognize the validity of acts posited under the influence of such factors.

[59] Although the code commission chose not to adopt the broader term "instrument" rather than "document," this decision did not preclude the admission into evidence of these or other forms of documentary materials. See *Comm* 11 (1979) 105.

ARTICLE 1: THE NATURE AND TRUSTWORTHINESS OF DOCUMENTS
[cc. 1540–1543]

Kinds of Documents

Canon 1540 — §1. Public ecclesiastical documents are those which a public person has drawn up in the exercise of that person's function in the Church, after the solemnities prescribed by law have been observed.

§2. Public civil documents are those which the laws of each place consider to be such.

§3. Other documents are private.

The first paragraph of the canon specifies those elements which make an ecclesiastical document "public" in nature. The document must (1) be drawn up by a designated ecclesiastical official (2) in the exercise of his or her office or function (3) after having observed the proper formalities for preparing the document in question. Without these elements, the document is private. Examples of public ecclesiastical documents include rescripts of the Apostolic See and other ecclesiastical authorities, tribunal decrees, and certificates of baptism and the reception of other sacraments.

Paragraph two is an example of the canonization of civil law (c. 22), since canon law accepts the legal definition of documents provided by the civil authority of the place. Depending on such civil norms, examples of public civil documents could include birth, marriage, and death certificates, the rulings of civil courts, and police and other governmental records.

All documents that do not meet the standards of the first two paragraphs are considered private. Examples include letters, diaries, financial records, tape recordings, calendar entries, and a host of other materials.

Value of Public Documents

Canon 1541 — Unless contrary and evident arguments prove otherwise, public documents are to

be trusted concerning everything which they directly and principally affirm.[60]

Public documents, whether ecclesiastical or civil, carry probative weight. Such documents are presumed by canon law to be fully accurate about the facts which these documents "directly and principally affirm." Like any presumption of law, however, this can be overturned by clear proof to the contrary.

Public documents may contain a mixture of information, only some of which is directly and principally affirmed. For example, in marriage nullity cases, it is not unusual for a petitioner or respondent to submit a restraining order issued by a civil court as evidence of harassment or mistreatment by the other party. What is directly and principally affirmed in such a document is that the civil court legally restrained the party or parties named therein from a number of specified actions on the date and under the conditions indicated. The document establishes that the court was convinced that there was sufficient cause to restrict the rights of the person or persons restrained. But, unless it is accompanied by specific findings of fact, the document does not directly and principally affirm that every claim made by the one who petitioned the order is fully accurate. Thus, the document constitutes proof of the restraining order itself; it may be a source of proof of the existence of certain patterns of abuse, but the document does not provide full proof of such allegations. Further evidence would be required to corroborate information contained in but not directly affirmed by the document.

Value of Private Documents

Canon 1542 — A private document, whether acknowledged by a party or approved by the judge, has the same force of proof against the author or signatory and those deriving a case from them as an extrajudicial confession. It has the same force against those who are not parties to the case as declarations of the parties which are not confessions, according to the norm of can. 1536, §2.

The probative force of private documents varies. The wording of the canon is rather dense and requires close attention. *With regard to its author or signer,* a private document is to be assessed in the same way that extrajudicial confessions or declarations are assessed (c. 1537). *With regard to "outsiders,"* i.e., persons other than the author or signer, private documents have the same force as declarations of the parties which are not confessions (c. 1536, §2).

These documents can be extremely important forms of proof, since they may contain information not available from any other source. At the same time, the judge must cautiously weigh information in private documents. Not only is there a need to establish that private documents are authentic, but information contained in such documents may be erroneous or ambiguous and needs to be interpreted as much as possible within its original context.

Defects or Alterations in Documents

Canon 1543 — If the documents are shown to have been erased, emended, falsified, or otherwise defective, it is for the judge to decide what value, if any, must be afforded them.

Documents may deteriorate, be officially corrected or unofficially amended, forged, or otherwise tampered with. Thus, when any document gives indication of alteration or lack of authenticity, the court must be on guard. Wisely, however, this canon does not mandate automatic rejection of these documents. The judge is given the responsibility to evaluate the value and probative weight of the questionable document. In assessing such documents, the court may well secure the assistance of an expert in the field.

---

[60] The parallel canon in the Eastern code (*CCEO* 1222) differs, adding the clause "with due regard for other requirements for public civil documents in the civil law of the place." For the rationale and significance of this difference, see Abbass, "Contentious Trials," 893–894.

ARTICLE 2: THE PRESENTATION OF DOCUMENTS
[cc. 1544–1546]

Authentic Copies

Canon 1544 — Documents do not have probative force in a trial unless they are originals or authentic copies and deposited at the tribunal chancery so that the judge and the opposing party can examine them.

In assessing the probative value of documents, the judge must distinguish between the authenticity of the document itself (i.e., that it is an original or a fully exact copy of an original) and the trustworthiness of the information contained in the document (e.g., a letter submitted in evidence may not be subject to challenge as an authentic document, but the information contained in the letter may be erroneous or incomplete and, hence, subject to challenge). This canon reminds tribunals of the need to assure the authenticity of the documents themselves.

Probative force is not attributed to documents unless originals or authentic copies are deposited with the tribunal. This enables the judge and the "opposing party" to examine them,[61] either to contest their authenticity as documents or to challenge the accuracy of the information contained in them.

What constitutes an "authentic" copy? Ultimately, any copy that faithfully and completely reproduces an original has an *internal authenticity* in that the copy is genuine; it has not been altered. How can a tribunal, however, be sure that a purported original or copy has not been tampered with? One means to help assure the trustworthiness of documents is the use of formally authenticated copies, i.e., copies prepared by ecclesiasti-

cal or civil notaries or certified by such notaries as concordant with the originals. Of course, as the history of forged papers amply attests, this sign of *external authenticity* is not an absolute guarantee of their actual authenticity. Thus, the requirement that all documents be lodged at the tribunal allows documents to be examined and their authenticity challenged.

In normal practice, the parties often present photocopies or even fax copies of documents to tribunals. Since these do not have a notary's certification of their external authenticity, there is greater danger that they may have been illegitimately altered. Such copies of documents, nonetheless, may well be completely faithful to the original and trustworthy. Thus, internal authenticity cannot be totally denied to documents presented in these fashions.[62]

As a general rule, judges should insist on the presentation of original documents (with authentic copies made at the tribunal) or certified copies. Occasionally, however, there are grave reasons why an original document or certified copy is simply unavailable.[63] When an original or certified copy of a document is not available, but a photocopy or other abstract is, the judge cannot uncritically accept the document as authentic. The judge may, however, incorporate the copy into the acts and then evaluate its authenticity and genuineness in light of other evidence. Since external authenticity is simply a means to assure that the copy faithfully reproduces the information contained in the original, it would be pure formalism rigidly to refuse to consider the potential veracity of a non-authenticated copy when

---

[61] Certainly, the defender of the bond and promoter of justice, if involved in a case, also have the right to examine all documentary evidence. This is explicitly provided for in marriage cases by c. 1678, §1, 2°.

[62] For example, in recent times some congregations of the Roman Curia have used faxes to communicate official documents so that their execution can be expedited. The original documents are later sent by mail, but the expectation is that the ecclesiastical authority receiving the fax transmission will act on the basis of that electronically communicated copy.

[63] For instance, the destruction of records by fire, flood, war, or other disasters is not uncommon, especially among refugee peoples.

circumstances make it impossible to compare it to the original.

Mandate to Produce Documents

Canon 1545 — The judge can order a document common to both parties to be presented in the process.

When a document common to both parties is in the possession of only one of the parties, the judge has the authority to order that the document be presented and incorporated into the acts of the case. Should the possessor of the document refuse to provide that document without a legitimate reason for the refusal (see c. 1546), it is the judge's responsibility to evaluate the significance of that refusal in a manner similar to the evaluation of the refusal of a party to answer a question (see c. 1531, §2).

Exemptions from Obligation to Produce Documents

Canon 1546 — §1. Even if documents are common, no one is bound to present those which cannot be communicated without danger of harm according to the norm of can. 1548, §2, n. 2 or without danger of violating an obligation to observe secrecy.

§2. Nonetheless, if at least some small part of a document can be transcribed and presented in copy without the above-mentioned disadvantages, the judge can decree that it be produced.

The judge's authority to demand the presentation of a document is not unlimited. There is also a need to balance conflicting rights and responsibilities, and to protect the parties and other persons from damage that might result from the disclosure of confidential documents. Thus, two circumstances exempt from the obligation to present a document.

1. First, the obligation is mitigated when exhibiting a document would cause serious dangers either to the possessor of the document or to his or her spouse, relatives, or in-laws.[64] It should be noted that this exemption must involve a genuine danger. The mere existence of some fear (which may have little real foundation) or a preference not to make the information contained in the document known is insufficient to claim the exemption. Likewise, a fear that the disclosure of the information in the document will result in embarrassment or will damage one's position in the ecclesiastical trial does not dispense one from the obligation to communicate the document.[65]

2. Second, a document may be withheld when exhibiting it would violate an obligation of secrecy which the tribunal must respect. The Church recognizes both moral and legal obligations to maintain secrecy. See the commentary on canon 1548 for additional reflections on this obligation.

In balancing the conflicting needs for the court both to discover the full truth and to avoid other dangers, the solution may be a partial disclosure of a document or some portion thereof. Canon 1546, §2 provides for the presentation of a transcript of a document in place of the full document. The transcript might remove the names of parties who could be injured, or remove sections of the document with no relevance to the issue in the trial but which contain harmful information. It is for the judge to determine whether, and how, such a partial presentation might be made.

---

[64] The types of dangers recognized as dispensing one from the obligation to provide a document are the same as those which exempt a witness from the obligation of testifying. See the commentary on c. 1548, §2, 2°.

[65] Penal procedure contains an exception to this rule. Given the right of parties not to incriminate themselves (c. 1728, §2), an accused is not obliged to produce a purely private document which would be tantamount to his or her confessing to the delict.

CHAPTER III
WITNESSES AND TESTIMONIES
[cc. 1547–1573]

Often the single most important source of evidence is the testimony of witnesses.[66] There are various types of witnesses, and the nature and quality of their knowledge can vary tremendously. This chapter first identifies those who can and cannot serve as witnesses, and then discusses the introduction and exclusion of witnesses. It next specifies norms for the proper examination of witnesses, and concludes with provisions for the evaluation of their testimony. Precisely because witnesses are so vital in the search for truth, careful attention to these norms is critical in the tribunal's ministry of justice.

Proof through Witnesses Admissible in All Cases

Canon 1547 — Proof by means of witnesses is allowed under the direction of the judge in cases of any kind.

This initial canon asserts the principle that testimony from witnesses is admissible in any sort of ecclesiastical trial.[67] While the assertion of canon 1527 on the admissibility of proofs of any sort that are useful and licit might seem to render canon 1547 redundant, the *coetus* decided to retain it to avoid any confusion about the admissibility of witness testimony in trials when the civil law of the place might not permit proof by means

of witnesses in contractual disputes.[68] By mandating that proof by witnesses be admitted only under the judge's supervision, the canon carefully preserves the judge's role in directing the course of the trial. Thus, for example, the judge retains the right to allow a minor to testify (c. 1550, §1), to set time limits for identifying the information to be sought from a witness (c. 1552, §2), to curb an excess number of witnesses (c. 1553), to rule on a request to exclude a witness (c. 1555), and to examine a witness in secret (c. 1559).

The Obligation of the Witness to Tell the Truth

Canon 1548 — §1. When the judge questions witnesses legitimately, they must tell the truth.

The obligation to tell the truth in an ecclesiastical trial, whether under oath or not, is a grave one. Since discovering the truth and deciding in accord with it is the very goal of the trial, the integrity of the process depends on witnesses being fully honest.

The obligation to tell the truth is, however, subject to some limitations. In addition to those exempted from testifying in virtue of the second paragraph of this canon, a witness is obliged to respond only to the judge or auditor in the course of the process.[69] The witness has no obligation, however, to respond to questions posed by third parties outside the context of the trial. The obligation to respond also depends on the legitimacy of the questions posed by the judge or auditor. For

---

[66] For a brief description of the etymology of the terms "witness" and "testimony," see Wrenn, in *CLSA Com,* 981.

[67] In contrast to the position of Bourgon (in *CLSGBI Com,* 880, note 1) and Arroba Conde (in *Valencia Com,* 677), this author holds that proof by means of witnesses is not totally barred from a supplementary role in the documentary process for certain marriage nullity cases (cc. 1686–1688). In addition to the clear wording of c. 1547, this fact is verified in the canonical tradition. See the commentary on c. 1686 for the argument supporting this conclusion.

[68] See the commentary on c. 1290 dealing with contracts, and the discussion in *Comm* 11 (1979) 108. Thus, although the Church usually defers to civil law regarding contracts, the Church will admit testimony from witnesses in contractual matters even if the civil law does not recognize such testimony as admissible evidence. Of course, if the resulting judgment lacked civil recognition, the Church's ability to enforce a judgment might be thwarted.

[69] By extension, that obligation also holds if particular law permits a defender of the bond, advocate, or other official taking part in the interview to pose questions (see c. 1561).

example, questions not pertinent to the case (see c. 1564) are unlawful and, hence, the witness would have the right to refuse to answer.

Those Exempt from Testifying

§2. Without prejudice to the prescript of can. 1550, §2, n. 2, the following are exempted from the obligation to respond:
> **1° clerics regarding what has been made known to them by reason of sacred ministry; civil officials, physicians, midwives, advocates, notaries, and others bound by professional secrecy even by reason of having given advice, regarding those matters subject to this secrecy;**
> **2° those who fear that from their own testimony ill repute, dangerous hardships, or other grave evils will befall them, their spouses, or persons related to them by consanguinity or affinity.**

An exemption from testifying, either in whole or in part, is extended to two groups of persons:

1. Those who have an obligation of secrecy connected with their office or function.
2. Those who are likely to suffer harm as a consequence of their participation as witnesses.

These exemptions from testifying may or may not be claimed by a witness. For example, a witness who may suffer harm and would have a right to claim an exemption from testifying may, nonetheless, choose to testify despite the dangers present. Such an "exemption" differs from "exclusion" from testifying by the law itself (c. 1550).

The exemption extends first to clerics (c. 266, §1) concerning any information learned in the course of their ministry.[70] The exemption also ex-

tends to others who learn information in the course of their official duties and who consequently have an obligation of secrecy.[71] These exemptions, however, extend only to information learned by the witness in the course of his or her official duties.[72]

In addition to those bound by professional secrecy, an exemption from testifying is extended to prospective witnesses who might suffer dangerous consequences should they testify. To invoke this exemption there must be a genuine danger to the witness personally or to his or her spouse, relatives, or in-laws. The canon refers to three sorts of dangers: (1) "ill repute" (*infamiam*), the loss of good reputation (c. 220); (2) "dangerous hardships" (*periculosas vexationes*); and (3) "other grave evils" (*aliave mala gravia*).

If witnesses fear that their testimony will result in these consequences, a conflict of values results. The court needs to obtain the truth, but the witnesses need to protect themselves and their families. In these situations, it is the judge's responsibility to work with witnesses to assess the degree of danger to which their testimony might expose them. The judge may then determine whether there are ways to obtain their testimony while avoiding or minimizing these dangers.[73] Not every

---

[70] Information learned by a priest or interpreter in the sacrament of penance is completely inadmissible. See the commentary on c. 1550, §2, 2°.

[71] The canon lists a number of persons who are able to claim such professional secrecy. The list, however, is not taxative, since it concludes with the generic description of "others bound by professional secrecy." The identification of some of those persons so bound would be a matter on which canon law would defer to the civil law (c. 22).

[72] Thus, without duly executed consents for release of confidential information, therapists are exempt from testifying concerning clients. Such therapists, however, could not claim exemptions from testifying concerning persons whom they know, not in the context of the therapist-client relationship, but as friends, family members, neighbors, and the like.

[73] While in some circumstances it is appropriate to exempt the witness from testifying at all, other options can be considered. For instance, the court may agree to question a witness only about certain limited matters and to avoid areas which might create dangers but which have less relevance to the specific issue in the trial. The serious-

claim of exemption fits under the provisions of this canon. Some fears may have little or no foundation. Not every hardship or embarrassment that might be connected with testifying dispenses from the obligation to testify. The court, however, has no choice but to take the concerns of fearful witnesses very seriously since, in most of the world, ecclesiastical tribunals have neither genuine power to subpoena testimony nor means to protect witnesses from retribution.

ARTICLE 1: THOSE WHO CAN BE WITNESSES [cc. 1549–1550]

The Principle

Canon 1549 — All persons can be witnesses unless the law expressly excludes them in whole or in part.

As a basic principle, all persons, whatever their background, condition, or ecclesial status, can serve as witnesses unless the law expressly excludes them. The exclusions, specified in canon 1550, are narrow.[74] For example, there are no restrictions prohibiting a person who has incurred an ecclesiastical penalty (e.g., an excommunication) from serving as a witness.

In practice, however, not all persons are appropriate witnesses. Most important, a witness must have knowledge relevant to the dispute at issue. A knowledgeable witness must also be able and willing to provide testimony to the tribunal. Tribunals should provide guidance to the parties, especially when they do not have the assistance of qualified

advocates, concerning the qualities needed in a good witness.[75]

Those Unsuited as Witnesses

Canon 1550 — §1. Minors below the fourteenth year of age and those of limited mental capacity are not allowed to give testimony; they can, however, be heard by a decree of the judge which declares such a hearing expedient.

Normally, minors "below the fourteenth year of age" are not permitted to testify.[76] Nor are those of "limited mental capacity" (*mente debiles*) admitted as witnesses. Since there is no definition of the term "limited mental capacity," the assess-

---

[75] In marriage nullity cases, the parties sometimes wish to name their children as witnesses. When the children are minors under fourteen, normally their testimony is not to be admitted (see the commentary on c. 1550, §1). Furthermore, many tribunals have a policy of not seeking testimony from the children in marriage cases involving their parents, even if the children are adults. As a standard practice, such a policy is wise since, presumably, the children are not knowledgeable about the events of the courtship and the earliest years of their parents' marriage, the period of greatest relevance to the tribunal's investigation. The policy of not seeking testimony from children also recognizes that children often find it distasteful to testify about (and perhaps against) their parents and even risk alienating one or both of their parents if they do. Hence, they could claim an exemption under c. 1548, §2, 2°.

The law, however, does not "expressly exclude" children from service as witnesses in marriage nullity cases. Thus, a tribunal policy of this kind, while defensible as a standard procedure, needs to provide room for exceptions. Especially when no other witnesses can supply the relevant information, a tribunal cannot absolutely prohibit the parties from naming as witnesses children fourteen and older who are willing to testify. Children, for instance, while not having "first-hand knowledge" of critical events, may be able to report important information learned secondhand, at a non-suspect time. The assessment of such testimony, however, must be very judicious.

[76] Canon 97, §1 defines a minor as anyone under the age of eighteen. The restriction of c. 1550, §1, however, applies only to those minors under the age of fourteen. Minors fourteen and older may serve as witnesses.

---

ness of the danger may also suggest that a witness may be permitted to testify with the understanding that the testimony or some portion of it will be exempted from the publication of the acts, provided this exemption from publication does not deny the right of defense of the parties (c. 1598, §1).

[74] While not technically a matter of excluding witnesses, the right of judges to limit the number of witnesses (c. 1553) should also be noted.

ment of whether there is such a limiting factor is left to the judge.

The rationale for this provision is a presumption that the very young and the seriously mentally impaired are not capable of providing the sort of reliable testimony a tribunal needs. The judge, however, is free to set aside this prohibition by means of a decree which explains the reasons why the witness is to be heard.[77] In fact, in justice, it is incumbent upon the judge to do precisely this in those situations where the witness in question is the only one who has knowledge concerning a matter of importance. In these cases, however, the interrogation of the witness should be limited to the crucial issues, and the questions posed should be adapted to the capacity of the witness.

Those Disqualified from Testifying

§2. **The following are considered incapable:**

1° **the parties in the case or those who stand for the parties at the trial, the judge and the judge's assistants, the advocate, and others who assist or have assisted the parties in the same case;**

2° **priests regarding all matters which they have come to know from sacramental confession even if the penitent seeks their disclosure; moreover, matters heard by anyone and in any way on the occasion of confession cannot be accepted even as an indication of the truth.**

Some potential witnesses are disqualified by the law itself. Obviously, the parties to the trial itself are not witnesses, although their declarations are a form of proof to be considered (cc. 1530–1538). The procurators of the parties are similarly excluded, as are the judge, defender of the bond, advocates, notaries, and all involved in the case.

More significantly, out of respect for the sacramental seal (cc. 983, 1388), the law absolutely

forbids a priest or bishop from testifying about anything he has learned in the sacrament of penance. Even the penitent's explicit request that the confessor testify does not release him from the obligation to maintain the confessional seal.[78] Likewise, information revealed in confession cannot be released by an interpreter or by anyone else who may have overheard the contents of a confession (see cc. 983, §2 and 1388, §2).

ARTICLE 2: THE INTRODUCTION AND EXCLUSION OF WITNESSES [cc. 1551–1557]

Who Can Introduce or Renounce Witnesses

Canon 1551 — The party who has introduced a witness can renounce the examination of that witness; the opposing party, however, can request that the witness be examined nevertheless.

A party who had previously proposed a witness may choose to renounce the request that the person be interrogated.[79] Since foregoing the hearing of a witness is a renunciation of a procedural act,

---

[77] As with any decree that is not merely procedural, it must contain the reasons which motivated the decision (cc. 50, 51, 1617).

[78] This is an absolute prohibition, differing in kind from the exemption which can be claimed from providing information learned in other aspects of ecclesial ministry (c. 1548, §2, 1°). To protect the integrity of the penitential relationship, the inviolability of the seal of confession (cc. 983, §1 and 1388, §1) is never to be compromised. On the delicate question of a possible release of the confessor from the obligation of the seal, where one must proceed very cautiously, see D. Brewer, "The Right of a Penitent to Release the Confessor from the Seal: Considerations in Canon Law and American Law," *J* 54 (1994) 424–476.

[79] Parties may renounce the hearing of a witness for a variety of reasons. For example, if a previously named witness has subsequently suffered health problems, the person who proposed that witness may wish to spare him or her the burden of testifying, especially if there are other witnesses or sources of proof available. Less altruistically, a fear that the testimony of a witness would be damaging to the party's claims might be a motive for renunciation and a motive for the other party to oppose the renunciation.

the norms of canon 1524 must be followed. The renunciation must be made in writing and signed by the party (or by the party's procurator with the necessary special mandate). The renunciation must be communicated to the other party (and to the defender of the bond and promoter of justice if their involvement is required). The other party must accept or at least not oppose the renunciation, and the judge has discretion to admit the renunciation or not. If the other party opposes the renunciation, then the witness is to be interrogated. Judges may choose not to admit the renunciation should they determine that the interrogation is necessary to reach a just decision (c. 1452).

How Witnesses Are Introduced

Canon 1552 — §1. When proof through witnesses is requested, their names and domicile are to be communicated to the tribunal.

§2. The items of discussion about which questioning of the witnesses is sought are to be presented within the time period set by the judge; otherwise, the request is to be considered as abandoned.

If the tribunal is to arrange for the interrogation of witnesses, the person proposing them must provide their full names and addresses. The one naming witnesses is also to identify the sort of information each witness is able to provide. This enables the court to focus its interrogation on areas in which the witness has knowledge, and to avoid questions that would simply waste the time of the witness and the auditor. A party's failure to provide this information about proposed witnesses within the time limit established by the judge is to be interpreted as his or her abandonment of the request to obtain testimony from these witnesses.[80]

Curbing an Excessive Number of Witnesses

Canon 1553 — It is for the judge to curb an excessive number of witnesses.

The right and duty of judges to curb an excessive number of witnesses is an example of their discretion in directing the trial and their responsibility to see that cases are concluded in a reasonable time (c. 1453). If a party lodges recourse against the judge's decision not to interrogate certain witnesses, that recourse is to be decided by the judge *expeditissime* (c. 1527, §2), a decision that cannot be appealed (c. 1629, 5°).

Notification of Witnesses' Names to the Parties

Canon 1554 — Before the witnesses are examined, their names are to be communicated to the parties; if in the prudent judgment of the judge, however, that cannot be done without grave difficulty, it is to be done at least before the publication of the testimonies.

As a rule, the names of the witnesses nominated by one party are to be made known to the other prior to any attempt to obtain their testimony.[81] It should be noted that the canon requires only that the names of the witnesses be provided, not their addresses or telephone numbers.

This notification provides the opportunity for the petitioner and respondent to lodge an exception requesting that a witness be excluded (cc. 1555, 1491). The judge, however, may determine that because of serious difficulties, the identities of the witnesses are not to be made known before they are interrogated.[82] If so, the judge issues a de-

---

[80] The CLSA's previous translation of c. 1552, §2 stated that the "petition" was to be considered as abandoned. That translation was ambiguous. It is only the request to interrogate the witness which is considered as abandoned, not the *libellus* itself..

[81] This modifies the norms of the 1917 code as elucidated by the instruction *Provida Mater Ecclesia*. See Wrenn, in *CLSA Com,* 982, for a description of the prior practice.

[82] For example, a concern that a party might try to coach a witness or impede him or her from testifying would be a solid reason for the judge to delay the notification. The situations envisioned by c. 1455, §3 provide other exam-

cree, explaining the reasons for delaying this notification (c. 1617). The decree allows only a delay in the disclosure; the identities of the witnesses must still be made known to the parties after their testimony has been obtained at some point prior to the publication of the acts.

Exclusion of Witnesses

Canon 1555 — Without prejudice to the prescript of can. 1550, a party can request the exclusion of a witness if a just cause for the exclusion is shown before the questioning of the witness.

A party may request that a witness be excluded. The judge, however, has the final authority to determine whether or not to exclude a witness. The right to present proofs, among which proposing witnesses is often the most important (cc. 1527, 1547, 1549), is an integral element of the right of defense.[83] Therefore, a party's objection to the introduction of a witness must indicate a "just cause" for the exclusion. Just causes would include claims that a witness is unsuitable or legally incapable for any of the reasons mentioned in canon 1550. Just causes might also include the contention that the witness has no relevant knowledge, that he or she has been coached, that his or her testimony may be coerced (c. 1538), or that a proposed witness is prejudiced. On the other hand, the possibility that the testimony of a witness might reflect negatively on the party is not a just cause for exclusion.

Recourse against the decision of a judge to admit or to exclude testimony from a witness is to be made before that same judge and must be decided *expeditissime* (c. 1527, §2). Hence, the judge's resolution of the recourse is not subject to appeal (c. 1629, 5°).

Citation of Witnesses

Canon 1556 — The citation of a witness occurs through a decree of the judge legitimately communicated to the witness.

Canon 1557 — A witness who has been cited properly is to appear or to inform the judge of the reason for the absence.

The citation of witnesses is accomplished in a decree which is communicated to the witness in accord with the same norms as those for the citation of the parties (c. 1509).

The duly cited witness has an obligation to present testimony as requested. If he or she is unable to do so, there is an obligation to inform the judge of this fact. In theory, at least, the tribunal could penalize a Catholic witness who fails to comply with the citation (c. 1371, 2°). In practice, however, this is neither prudent nor possible. Since the tribunals of most countries have no power to compel an uncooperative witness to testify, the judge must employ the other legitimate methods permitted by canon 1528 to attempt to secure at least some testimony from a reluctant witness. Should a witness continue to refuse to testify, the judge is to evaluate the significance of this refusal (c. 1531, §2).

ARTICLE 3: THE EXAMINATION OF WITNESSES
[cc. 1558–1571]

Place of the Examination

Canon 1558 — §1. Witnesses must be examined at the tribunal unless the judge deems otherwise.

§2. Cardinals, patriarchs, bishops, and those who possess a similar favor by civil law are to be heard in the place they select.

§3. The judge is to decide where to hear those for whom it is impossible or difficult to come to the tribunal because of distance, sickness, or some impediment, without prejudice to the prescripts of cann. 1418 and 1469, §2.

---

ples of reasons for deferring the disclosure of the identity of witnesses.

[83] ApSig, decr, April 11, 1987, *P* 77 (1988) 341. *Coram Burke,* nullity of sentence, November 15, 1990, *Stud Can* 25 (1991) 510.

Paragraph one states the standard expectation that witnesses are to testify at the office of the tribunal. The judge, however, is given latitude to make other appropriate arrangements as circumstances warrant.

Paragraph two contains an exception, enumerating certain persons who enjoy the privilege of selecting the place where they are to be interrogated.

Paragraph three describes more fully the discretion of the judge to take testimony in places other than the tribunal office. When illness, distance, or some other impediment makes it impossible or very difficult for a witness to travel to the tribunal office, the judge may select an alternate location (e.g., the offices of a parish in the vicinity of the witness, a conference room in the rest home in which the witness resides). When a witness resides outside of the diocese in which the trial is being conducted, the judge may call upon the assistance of another tribunal to appoint an auditor and arrange for securing the testimony of a witness (c. 1418).

Another possibility is for the judge or auditor to travel outside of his or her own territory to obtain testimony directly from a witness. First, however, the judge or auditor must secure the permission of the diocesan bishop[84] of the place where the testimony is to be taken, and the testimony is to be obtained at the site designated by that bishop (c. 1469, §2).[85]

Manner of the Examination

Canon 1559 — The parties cannot be present at the examination of the witnesses unless the judge

has decided to admit them, especially when the matter concerns a private good. Their advocates or procurators, however, can be present unless the judge has decided that the examination must proceed in secret due to the circumstances of the matters and persons.

As a rule, the parties to the case are not permitted to be present for the examination of the witnesses, but their procurators or advocates may be present.

By way of exception, the judge can authorize or even require the presence of the parties, especially in cases involving the private as opposed to the public good. Conversely, the judge may determine that the examination of a particular witness should be carried out in secret without the presence of the parties' procurators and advocates. If either of these exceptions is warranted, the judge should issue a decree summarizing the reasons for the exception (c. 1617).[86]

When the canons speak of the "parties," that usually includes the defender of the bond and the promoter of justice (c. 1434, 1°), unless the clear wording or the context makes the contrary obvious. May a judge, then, determine that the defender and the promoter may not be present for the examination of a particular witness? No. Although the 1983 code creates much greater parity between the advocates and the defender of the bond, it does not create complete parity.[87] In cases involving marriage nullity or the nullity of sacred orders, the judge cannot exclude the defender or promoter because of the norms of canons 1678, §1, 1° and 1711. These give the defender, the advocates, and the promoter the right (*ius*) to be present for the examination of the parties and wit-

---

[84] Canon 1469, §2 uses the technical term *Episcopi dioecesani* and hence, in accord with c. 134, §3, the permission may not be given by a local ordinary or judicial vicar unless he has been specially mandated to do so.

[85] The controversial practice of securing testimony over the telephone is neither authorized by the code, nor is it reprobated (see Bourgon, in *CLSGBI Com,* 885, note 1). For further comment on this contested issue, see the commentary on c. 1528.

[86] In marriage nullity cases, c. 1678, §2 supersedes the general norm of c. 1559. Thus, judges do not have the discretion to permit the parties to be present for the examination of witnesses in these cases. Also see *Comm* 11 (1979) 114, 262–263.

[87] C. A. Cox, *Procedural Changes in Formal Marriage Nullity Cases from the 1917 to the 1983 Code* (Washington, D.C.: Catholic University of America, 1989) 48–54.

nesses. Laws which restrict the free exercise of a right must be strictly interpreted (c. 18). Therefore, unless a right is clearly restricted, it cannot be infringed. Canon 1559 permits a judge to restrict this right for procurators and advocates only; it does not give a corresponding authority to restrict the right of the defender or the promoter of justice. Certainly, a judge might request that the defender or promoter not be present, perhaps because of a concern that the presence of several people besides the judge would intimidate a timid witness. The defender and promoter, however, retain the right to be present.

Witnesses Examined Individually

Canon 1560 — §1. Each witness must be examined separately.

To preserve the court's ability to obtain evidence that has not been "contaminated" by one witness hearing the testimony of another, all witnesses are to be examined individually. It is for this same reason that judges commonly ask witnesses to promise not to divulge the content of their testimony to anyone until the completion of the trial, and may even bind witnesses to secrecy concerning their testimony (c. 1455, §3).

Possibility of Confrontation

§2. If witnesses disagree among themselves or with a party in a grave matter, the judge, after having removed discord and scandal insofar as possible, can have those who disagree meet together or confront one another.

When there is disagreement concerning serious issues among witnesses or between witnesses and one or both of the parties, the judge has the option of bringing the witnesses together for a confrontation or otherwise directing that the witnesses come to some agreement. This extraordinary step is rarely employed, and great care is to be taken to preclude disputes or scandal if such a confrontation is necessary.

Those Who May Question Witnesses

Canon 1561 — The judge, the judge's delegate, or an auditor examines the witness; the examiner must have the assistance of a notary. Consequently, if the parties, the promoter of justice, the defender of the bond, or the advocates present at the examination have any questions to be put to the witness, they are to propose them not to the witness but to the judge or the one who takes the place of the judge, who is to ask the questions, unless particular law provides otherwise.

The examination of a witness is conducted by the judge, a special delegate of the judge, or an auditor with the assistance of a notary who is charged to make a record of the session. If others are present and wish to pose questions, they are not to do so directly. Rather, they are to propose the questions to the judge or auditor, who determines whether the questions are appropriate. If so, the judge or auditor then poses the questions to the witness. The values behind this canon are (1) to assure that the judge or auditor conducts the interview in an orderly and reasonable fashion, and (2) to protect the witness from being "bombarded" with questions from multiple directions.

This is an area where provision is made for particular law to make other arrangements, permitting the defender of the bond, an advocate, an expert, or another person who is legitimately present to question a witness directly. If particular law makes such provisions, the judge should nonetheless retain overall direction of the questioning in order to minimize the burden on witnesses.

Obligation and Oath to Testify Truthfully

Canon 1562 — §1. The judge is to call to the attention of the witness the grave obligation to speak the whole truth and only the truth.
§2. The judge is to administer an oath to the witness according to can. 1532; a witness who refuses to take it, however, is to be heard without the oath.

At the beginning of every examination, the judge or auditor is to remind the witness of the grave obligation to tell the truth and only the truth. This obligation binds witnesses whether or not they take the customary oath.

Ordinarily, the witness is asked to take an oath to tell the truth (c. 1199). Should a witness choose not to take the oath (c. 1532), however, his or her testimony is still to be taken.

The Manner of Questioning

Canon 1563 — The judge is first of all to establish the identity of the witness, then ask what relationship the witness has with the parties, and, when addressing specific questions to the witness concerning the case, also inquire about the sources of his or her knowledge and the precise time when the witness learned what he or she asserts.

Crucial to the gathering and assessment of the evidence are a number of preliminary matters. Thus, the judge or auditor is first to establish the identity of the witness. Normally, this would be through the presentation of some form of photo identification. The judge is then to establish the relationship which the witness has with the parties to the case. This information assists the court in appreciating the scope of the person's knowledge.

After these preliminaries, the judge or auditor proceeds to substantive questions about the issue(s) in dispute. The judge or auditor is to probe not only what the witness knows, but also how he or she came to know it. Was the information learned by direct observation? Was it learned indirectly, perhaps confided to the witness by one or both of the parties? Was it learned through a document, perhaps one that no longer exists? The time at which a witness learned information is also critical to assessing the value of the testimony. The canonical tradition values information learned at a "non-suspect time" (i.e., a time prior to the presentation of the *libellus* or the inception of the dispute between the parties) much more highly than information learned at a later time.

The Nature of the Questions

Canon 1564 — The questions are to be brief, accommodated to the mental capacity of the person being questioned, not comprised of several points at the same time, not deceitful or deceptive or suggestive of a response, free from any kind of offense, and pertinent to the case being tried.

The nature of the questions posed to a witness is also crucial. The questions are to be: (1) brief, (2) crafted to correspond to the level of intelligence and sophistication of the witness, (3) simple and focused on one point rather than complicated, (4) never deceitful or tricky, (5) not leading or suggestive of the answer, (6) not offensive, and (7) relevant to the specific issues in the case. Questions that go beyond these limits are illegitimate, and the witness is not bound to respond (c. 1548, §1 obliges witnesses to respond when interrogated legitimately).

The questioning of a witness is an art not easily mastered. The subject matter which an ecclesiastical tribunal needs to probe is often sensitive. Frequently, witnesses are nervous and not very articulate; sometimes they are wary about sharing confidential information. Non-Catholics named as witnesses may be ill at ease, perhaps resentful, and not convinced that the Catholic Church has any right to be conducting the investigation. Thus, to question a witness effectively requires tact, patience, and sometimes gentle probing. In difficult interviews it is particularly tempting for a judge or auditor to "lead a witness." Thus, great care must be taken to assure that the questioning is legitimate and at the service of the truth.

Questions Normally Not Communicated in Advance

Canon 1565 — §1. Questions must not be communicated to the witnesses beforehand.

§2. Nonetheless, if the matters about which testimony must be given are so remote to memory that they cannot be affirmed with certainty un-

less previously recalled, the judge can advise the witness beforehand on some matters if the judge thinks this can be done without danger.

The questions to be posed to a witness or to the parties are not to be communicated to them in advance. This norm seeks to prevent the coaching of a witness or collusion among the parties or witnesses.

An exception to this norm permits the judge or auditor to advise witnesses of the nature of the questioning in advance when it cannot be reasonably expected that they would accurately recall the information without some time for prior reflection. The decision whether to do this rests solely with the judge or auditor, who is free to do so if there seems to be no danger that it would render suspect the resulting testimony.

Responses of Witnesses

Canon 1566 — Witnesses are to give testimony orally and are not to read written materials unless they are computations and accounts; in this case, they can consult the notes which they brought with them.

The norm is for witnesses to give their testimony orally and without the assistance of any written material, except when the testimony concerns accounts and calculations. This norm recognizes that a face-to-face interview is usually the best means for discovering the truth in all of its dimensions. The personal contact with a witness permits the judge or auditor to pose follow-up questions to important or ambiguous responses as well as to observe body language, gauge facial reactions and tone of voice, and hence make a better assessment of the knowledge and credibility of the witness.

Excursus: The Use of Affidavits

The canons, however, do provide alternative means for securing evidence when a personal interview is either impossible or excessively bur-

densome. For example, the initial response of a respondent may be in writing (c. 1507, §1). Also, the judge is empowered to obtain testimony through a lay person, through declarations made before public notaries, or "in any other legitimate manner" (c. 1528).

Among these other legitimate means is a form of documentary evidence, the submission of a sworn affidavit offering written responses to questions posed by the judge or auditor.[88] While formal testimony taken from witnesses is always to be preferred, a judge may admit sworn responses to written questionnaires as affidavits. Technically, the person submitting written information is not a "witness" and does not "testify." Rather, the person serves as an affiant and the evidence is evaluated in accord with the norms for assessing documentary evidence. Many tribunals employ this alternative method of gathering evidence. In relying too heavily or resorting too quickly to the use of written questionnaires, tribunals may unnecessarily sacrifice the security and other benefits that can come only from a personal interview. Thus, the practice of using questionnaires as an "ordinary" means of securing proof has been strongly and understandably criticized.[89] Yet, this means of proof has a long canonical tradition and cannot be ruled out *a priori*. For example, William J. Doheny, the foremost English-language commentator on the procedural law of the 1917 code, noted that documentary and written proof has long been considered a particularly cogent form of evidence at canon law, and he offered numerous citations from the *Corpus Iuris* to justify his claim.[90] Doheny discussed sworn affidavits as a

---

[88] This author disagrees with Bourgon (in *CLSGBI Com*, 888) that the use of written questionnaires is "[p]articularly prohibited." L. Wrenn, in *Procedures* (Washington, D.C.: CLSA, 1987) 44–46, 52–53, also agrees that written affidavits may be employed.

[89] Grocholewski, "Interrogation by Letter or Telephone," 460–465.

[90] W. J. Doheny, *Canonical Procedure in Matrimonial Cases*, vol. 1, *Formal Procedure*, 2nd ed. (Milwaukee: Bruce, 1948) 399, especially n. 22.

form of evidence, and cited a Rotal decision[91] which indicated that affidavits may be employed although they are not considered judicial depositions and cannot constitute full proof.[92] Another commentator on the 1917 code, Francis Wanenmacher, likewise spoke of sworn depositions and other written testimonies. While they are "not generally nor *per se* to be approved," he noted that it "would be too much to say that the judge cannot under any circumstances admit proof of that kind."[93] Wanenmacher cited the 1923 rules of procedure for proving non-consummation cases as one source for accepting the practice of admitting affidavits into evidence.[94] The revised rules of procedure for this process contain similar provisions.[95] Likewise, the current norms for the instruction of petitions for a papal dissolution of a marriage in favor of the faith make limited provision for affidavits or depositions given before a notary public or other trustworthy person. This is permitted for those who are not Catholic and who refuse to appear before a Catholic priest to give evidence.[96]

In this author's opinion, the problem is not the use of affidavits *per se,* but the almost total re-liance of many tribunals on written depositions to the exclusion of testimony taken in a formal manner. Without obtaining testimony from the parties and witnesses through judicial depositions, the trustworthiness of the evidence is less secure and its quality is apt to be much poorer. On the other hand, the judicious use of a combination of formal testimony supplemented with additional written affidavits provides a better-balanced and more secure foundation upon which the court may reach certitude.

The Record of the Testimony

Canon 1567 — §1. The notary is to write down the response immediately and must report the exact words of the testimony given, at least in what pertains to those points which touch directly upon the material of the trial.

§2. The use of a tape-recorder can be allowed, provided that the responses are afterwards transcribed and, if possible, signed by the deponents.

The responses of the party or witness to the judge's or auditor's questions are to be put into writing immediately by the notary present for the interview. The notary must record both the questions posed and the responses, which are to be in the words of the one giving testimony. The notary's report, however, need not be a transcription of everything said. The notary is charged to record the witness's exact words "at least in what pertains to those points which touch directly upon the material of the trial." Frequently, however, witnesses go off the point, make asides, or engage in significant repetition, none of which is directly relevant to the issue. Hence, the notary's record should focus on evidence germane to the tribunal's search for the truth of the matters at issue.

As an alternative to the notary's report, a tape recording may be made of the testimony. Subsequently, however, a transcript must be made of the tape. It is preferred, although not essential, that the transcript later be reviewed and signed by the one making the deposition.

[91] *Coram* Florczak, June 5, 1926, #7, *SRRDec* 18 (1926) 194–195.

[92] Doheny, *Canonical Procedure,* I:400–401, 406–407.

[93] F. Wanenmacher, *Canonical Evidence in Marriage Cases* (Philadelphia: Dolphin, 1935) 144 (at #234). Wanenmacher discussed a role for affidavits as public or private civil documents on pp. 210 (at #343), 211–212 (at #345), and 230 (at #373).

[94] SCSacr, *Decretum et regulae servandae in processibus super matrimonio rato et non consummato,* May 7, 1923, art. 75, *AAS* 15 (1923) 407. Translated in *CLD* 1, 784.

[95] CDWDS, *Litterae circulares "De processu super rato et non consummato,"* December 20, 1986, art. 9, *ME* 112 (1987) 425. Translated in W. H. Woestman, *Special Marriage Cases,* 3rd ed. (Ottawa: St. Paul University, 1994) 124.

[96] CDF, instr *Ut notum est,* December 6, 1973, art. 5, in *Leges Ecclesiae post Codicem iuris canonici editae,* ed. X. Ochoa, vol. 5 (Rome: Commentarium pro Religiosis, 1980) #4244, col. 6704. Translated in *CLD* 8, 1180–1181.

Other Elements in the Notary's Report

Canon 1568 — The notary is to make mention in the acts of whether the oath was taken, excused, or refused, of the presence of the parties and other persons, of the questions added *ex officio,* and in general of everything worth remembering which may have occurred while the witnesses were being examined.

In addition to making a record of the testimony, the notary is charged to note who was present for the interview, whether or not the oath was taken (and, if not, why), and to call attention to anything noteworthy which occurred during the interview. For example, such things as changes in the demeanor of the one testifying, his or her excessive nervousness, signs of evasiveness, and refusal to make eye contact may be relevant to the assessment of the credibility of the one testifying. Yet, unless these events or signs are mentioned in the record, the classical principle *quod non est in actis, non est in mundo* (what is not in the acts does not exist) precludes their use in making the decision.

Concluding the Interview

Canon 1569 — §1. At the end of the examination, what the notary has written down from the deposition must be read to the witness, or what has been recorded with the tape-recorder during the deposition must be played, giving the witness the opportunity to add, suppress, correct, or change it.
§2. Finally, the witness, the judge, and the notary must sign the acts.

At the conclusion of the interview, to assure that the testimony is accurate, the notary is to read the record back to the one testifying, who is free to excise elements of the statement, amend errors, or supplement the testimony. Similarly, if the interview has been recorded, the witness has the right to listen to the tape to request that correc-

tions, additions, or deletions be made. Of course, should the witness wish, he or she may waive this right, or choose to review only selected portions of the testimony. Once this review is completed, the witness, the judge, and the notary are to sign the acts.[97]

Rehearing a Witness

Canon 1570 — Although already examined, witnesses can be recalled for examination before the acts or testimonies are published, either at the request of a party or *ex officio,* if the judge decides it is necessary or useful, provided that there is no danger of collusion or corruption.

As the instruction of a case develops, new questions often emerge. Thus, provision is made for recalling witnesses for further examination. The judge can recall a witness at his or her own discretion or in response to the request of a party to the case. It is the judge, however, who determines whether such a new examination is either necessary or useful. The judge also is responsible to assure that the information obtained in the new examination is not tainted. This new examination of a witness must occur *prior to* the publication of the acts (see c. 1598). A reexamination of witnesses after the publication of the acts is governed by the provisions of canon 1600.

Expenses of a Witness

Canon 1571 — Both the expenses which the witnesses incurred and the income which they lost by giving testimony must be reimbursed to them according to the just assessment of the judge.

Witnesses may incur expenses in connection with their testimony. At times, these expenses are negligible, but at other times the expenses may be

---

[97] If a witness is unable or refuses to sign the record of his or her testimony, the notary and judge or auditor make note of this in accord with c. 1473.

substantial, including travel expenses or loss of income due to time taken away from employment in order to testify. Witnesses have a right to reimbursement for their legitimate expenses. The judge is to make a determination of the appropriate reimbursement due each witness. While not specifically mentioned in canon 1571, the reimbursement of witnesses is an area for regulation by particular law or tribunal policy (see c. 1649). When the sentence is issued (c. 1611, 4°) or the instance is concluded in another way (cc. 1523 and 1525), the judge is to issue appropriate decrees allocating the expenses incurred during the trial.

ARTICLE 4: THE TRUSTWORTHINESS OF TESTIMONIES
[cc. 1572–1573]

Obtaining the testimony of the parties and witnesses is only one step in the development of evidence. These testimonies must be sifted, pondered, and assessed so that appropriate conclusions may be drawn from them. The two canons of this title offer the judge basic principles for weighing the value of testimony. Jurisprudence, especially that of the Roman Rota, provides further assistance in this essential and delicate task.

General Criteria of Evaluation

Canon 1572 — In evaluating testimony, the judge, after having requested testimonial letters if necessary, is to consider the following:
  1° **what the condition or reputation of the person is;**
  2° **whether the testimony derives from personal knowledge, especially from what has been seen or heard personally, or whether from opinion, rumor, or hearsay;**
  3° **whether the witness is reliable and firmly consistent or inconsistent, uncertain, or vacillating;**
  4° **whether the witness has co-witnesses to the testimony or is supported or not by other elements of proof.**

It is the judge who is responsible for evaluating testimony. There are a number of touchstones which assist the judge in this task:

  1° The character and reputation of the person testifying must be taken into account.[98] Usually, greater weight is attributed to the testimony of a person well known for integrity than to that of a person whose reputation for honesty is tarnished. That does not mean, however, that the judge automatically accepts the former as fully credible and automatically rejects the testimony of the latter as suspect. Reputation is an aid in assessing evidence, not the sole determining factor. A person with a reputation for dishonesty may have been unjustly labeled; a person of great integrity may be in error; and a person who often stoops to dishonesty may, in fact, testify truthfully. The "condition" of a witness refers to a variety of qualities that can affect the quality of that person's testimony. This includes a witness's relationship to the parties, age and life experience, and religious, educational, and cultural background, among other factors. The term "condition" also refers to whether the person is testifying in virtue of some official capacity (see c. 1573).

  2° The source of a witness's knowledge is also crucial. When the witness reports what he or she has personally seen or heard, his or her testimony normally has greater weight than when a witness is reporting information learned second hand, or is simply offering an opinion rather than describing events. Canon law admits as proof, however, hear-

---

[98] Often an ecclesiastical judge has no personal knowledge of the character and integrity of a witness. Given the mention of testimonial letters in the introduction of c. 1572, clearly a judge may seek testimonial letters to assist in establishing the character and reputation of a witness. For marriage nullity cases, c. 1679 provides that credibility testimony regarding the parties to the case may be employed in assessing the value of their testimony.

say evidence and even the opinion of a witness. This is particularly important in marriage cases, where witnesses may rarely be in a position directly to observe events, but where a witness may well have learned information indirectly, or even served as a confidant of one or both of the spouses. A witness with this sort of knowledge is able to offer important and credible reports to the tribunal concerning matters relevant to the issue under adjudication. In weighing this type of testimony, however, the judge must take into account the indirect nature of the witness's knowledge.

3° The manner in which the witness presents testimony is also an important touchstone.[99] If the testimony of the witness is internally consistent, it is to be accorded greater weight than if the testimony is riddled with internal contradictions. If the witness speaks with great certitude about some issues, but with hesitation concerning others, that fact too needs to be taken into account when the judge evaluates the various parts of the deposition.

4° The testimony of each party and witness must be assessed in light of all the evidence before the tribunal. If the testimony of a number of witnesses, while exhibiting understandable differences in perspective and detail, is basically consistent and also in accord with other sources of evidence (such as that obtained from documents), its probative value is enhanced. If, however, there is significant contradiction or disagreement between the testimony of one party or witness and that of all the others, the court rightly would doubt the value of the former testimony. When the testimony of the parties to a case is in serious disagreement, it happens frequently that the testimony of the witnesses

named by each tends to mirror those disagreements. In these circumstances, the judge's responsibility to proceed *ex officio* (c. 1452) in order to try to resolve the contradictions becomes critical.[100]

Deposition of a Single Witness

Canon 1573 — The testimony of one witness cannot produce full proof unless it concerns a qualified witness making a deposition concerning matters done *ex officio*, or unless the circumstances of things and persons suggest otherwise.

Canon 1573 reiterates a principle that has long been part of the canonical tradition, namely, that the deposition of one witness normally does not provide full proof. Traditionally, the principle was phrased absolutely (*unus testis, nullus testis*) but it is not an absolute rule. While the norm that a single witness is generally insufficient remains, canon 1573 provides two exceptions.

First, the testimony of a witness acting in an official capacity may be accorded full probative weight. For example, the testimony of a priest concerning what he did or did not do in exercising his priestly office (e.g., in administering the sacrament of baptism) can be accorded full probative value.

Second, in a significant departure from canonical tradition, the law and jurisprudence now recognize occasions when the testimony of a single witness not acting in an official capacity may be afforded full probative value.[101] It is not possible to provide a list of circumstances in which the judge could lawfully accord full probative value to the testimony of a single witness. Ultimately, it

---

[99] Also see the comments above at c. 1568 on the behavior of a witness during the presentation of testimony.

[100] Pompedda, "Decision-Sentence," reflects on the dilemma of "uncertain proofs" and emphasizes that such doubt serves as "a further impetus to find the truth of the matter" (87). He refers to the need for judges to have a "sagacious intelligence" and, when faced with an impasse, to strive to resolve the *dubia* by seeking all reasonable means to discover the truth (93–95).

[101] Pompedda, "Decision-Sentence," 90–91.

is the judge who must determine whether the testimony of a single witness provides a sufficient basis for moral certitude. He or she does so in light of the criteria for evaluating testimony and of the unique circumstances of things or persons present in a particular case. Wrenn uses the example of a marriage lasting only a few weeks and entered for the obvious purpose of gaining legal entrance into the country as a circumstance where the testimony of a single witness could be afforded full probative value.[102] Other circumstances could include testimony provided by a particularly trustworthy witness whose credibility is beyond challenge.[103] Similarly, when a witness has offered particularly insightful testimony that is balanced and internally consistent, based on personal knowledge, and meshes with the circumstances of the case, the judge may responsibly attribute full probative value to such testimony. Full probative force cannot be attributed, however, to the testimony of a witness that is superficial, inconsistent, unbalanced, or flies in the face of contrary indications.

CHAPTER IV
EXPERTS[104]
[cc. 1574–1581]

Notion of an Expert

Lawrence Wrenn defines an expert (*peritus*) as "a specialist who is learned, experienced, and skilled in his or her science or profession and whose scientific report is required either to prove some fact or to diagnose the true nature of something."[105]

The analyses of those expert in a variety of disciplines are highly valued as a form of proof.[106] The canons of this chapter describe when evidence from experts is either necessary or useful, how experts are named and carry out their function, and how the evidence deriving from experts is to be assessed.

Experts may come from many different fields —psychology, anthropology, sociology, theology, finance, the authentication of documents, etc. In marriage nullity cases, it is common to employ experts in the fields of psychology and psychiatry. Too often, the value of calling on experts from other disciplines is overlooked. For example, experts in the doctrines of differing religious traditions may help a tribunal judge whether a person raised in that tradition simulated by excluding the good of marital permanence or was in such deeply rooted error that it determined the will. Experts in anthropology can help judges understand the cultural roots of marital practices of immigrant peoples. Experts in sociology can shed light on the factors that influence the consent of people due to their careers or socioeconomic condition.

The Necessity of Experts

Canon 1574 — The assistance of experts must be used whenever the prescript of a law or of the judge requires their examination and opinion based on the precepts of art or science in order to establish some fact or to discern the true nature of some matter.

While an ecclesiastical judge always retains the right and sometimes even has a duty to secure

---

[102]Wrenn, in *CLSA Com,* 985. Wrenn also notes that c. 876 establishes circumstances under which the testimony of a single witness is sufficient to prove the administration of baptism.

[103]Bourgon, in *CLSGBI Com,* 890.

[104]Wrenn, in *Procedures,* 54–58.

[105]Wrenn, in *CLSA Com,* 985–986.

[106]While maintaining the preeminent role of the judge and the independence of the canonical judgment, Rotal jurisprudence manifests a long tradition of respect for the conclusions of experts. For example, see decisions *coram* Felici, November 23, 1954, *SRRDec* 46 (1954) 836; *coram* Parisella, July 13, 1968, *SRRDec* 60 (1968) 564–565; *coram* Parisella, November 25, 1976, *SRRDec* 68 (1976) 462–463; and *coram* Masala, December 17, 1985, *SRRDec* 77 (1985) 604–605.

the services of experts as part of the court's search for the truth, at times the use of experts is required by the law itself. The text of the canon is carefully worded. Experts *must be used* whenever their examination and opinion, rooted in their field of expertise, is necessary:

1. to establish some fact, or
2. to discern the true nature of some matter.

Thus, if the facts are well established and their meaning is truly clear, there is no need for the use of an expert. If, however, there is need to establish facts or clarify certain ambiguities concerning their significance, experts are to be employed.[107] For example, canon 1680 specifies that one or more experts are to be used in marriage nullity cases involving impotence or defects of consent due to mental illness unless such intervention would be useless.[108]

Admission of Experts

Canon 1575 — After having heard the parties and their suggestions, it is for the judge to appoint the experts or, if the case warrants, to accept reports already drawn up by other experts.

Canon 1576 — Experts are excluded or can be objected to for the same reasons as a witness.

The judge is either to appoint experts after consulting with the parties (including the defender of the bond and the promoter of justice if they are involved) and considering the names they propose,

or to admit into evidence the reports that have already been drawn up by experts.[109] The code does not spell out the qualifications necessary in an expert. Clearly, lay persons may serve as experts (see c. 228, §2). There is nothing that would automatically disqualify a person who is not Catholic from service as an expert. The judge, therefore, must determine whether a proposed expert has the background, knowledge, experience, and wisdom to serve as an expert in a particular case.[110]

The question of the admission or exclusion of an expert is handled in the same fashion as the admission or exclusion of a witness (see c. 1555). For example, the reasons which would disqualify a judge from adjudicating a case (c. 1448, §1) would also be reasons for excluding a proposed expert.

While respecting the special competence of a particular expert, the judge must take care to discern whether the service of an individual proposed as an expert would be helpful to the discovery of the truth. For example, in Rotal allocutions of 1987 and 1988, Pope John Paul II warned against the use in marriage nullity cases of psychological experts who operate out of an anthropology at odds with the Christian understanding of human nature.[111]

---

[107] M. F. Pompedda, "Incapacity to Assume the Essential Obligations of Marriage," in *Incapacity for Marriage: Jurisprudence and Interpretation,* ed. R. Sable (Rome: Pontificia Universitas Gregoriana, 1987) 208–210. In asserting that the use of experts remains facultative, Pompedda emphasizes that this does not mean that the choice is purely arbitrary. Rather, as a general rule, a judge should not prescind from utilizing such expertise, although there are cases where this is simply not necessary.

[108] See the commentary on that canon for further discussion of the need for experts in marriage cases.

[109] T. G. Doran, "Some Thoughts on Experts," *QuadStR* 4 (1989) 62, notes that the 1983 code provides for greater judicial discretion in the selection of experts "than did the previous legislation."

[110] A. Mendonça in "The Role of Experts in 'Incapacity to Contract' Cases (Canon 1095)," *Stud Can* 25 (1991) 431–433, discusses the qualifications of experts that are found in Rotal jurisprudence. Specifically, there is great concern that the expert not only possess the appropriate technical skills but be formed by value systems in alignment with Catholic doctrine.

[111] John Paul II, alloc, February 5, 1987, *AAS* 79 (1987) 1453–1459; alloc, January 25, 1988, *AAS* 80 (1988) 1178–1185. Translated in W. H. Woestman, *Papal Allocutions to the Roman Rota 1939–1994* (Ottawa: St. Paul University, 1994) 191–203. For reflections on the consequences of differing anthropological perspectives on marriage cases, see G. Versaldi, "The Dialogue between Psychological Science and Canon Law," in R. Sable, ed., *Incapacity for Marriage,* 25–78.

The Task of Experts

Canon 1577 — §1. Attentive to what the litigants may bring forward, the judge is to determine in a decree the individual items upon which the services of the expert must focus.

§2. The acts of the case and other documents and aids which the expert can need to fulfill his or her function correctly and faithfully must be turned over to the expert.

§3. After having heard the expert, the judge is to determine the time within which the expert must complete the examination and produce the report.

The judge is responsible to delineate clearly the task of the expert. After having heard and considered the points which the parties wish the expert to consider, the judge through a decree frames the questions and issues for the expert's consideration and response. Within these parameters, however, the judge must respect the expert's competence and the methodology of his or her discipline.

The judge is to make available to the expert the materials which he or she needs to conduct a thorough analysis and offer a well-considered professional opinion.[112] The extent of the access to the acts which a judge gives to an expert will depend on the specific role the expert is asked to play. An expert in the authentication of documents might need to see only one part of the acts. A psychological expert in a marriage nullity case, on the other hand, should have access to the testimonies, documents, and other evidence collected in the course of the trial and, ideally, should also be able to examine the parties.[113]

An expert may conclude that further information is needed in order to reach a responsible conclusion. The expert, however, is not an auditor and, therefore, has no right to take additional testimony. Thus, an expert might well request that the judge provide for further examinations of the parties and witnesses. Of course, it is the responsibility of the judge to determine whether such additional instruction of the case is warranted. Normally, however, the judge should respect the request of the expert and strive to secure the data the expert needs, unless there is some persuasive reason to the contrary.

In the course of testing or examining a party, an expert may learn significant information not otherwise contained in the acts of the case. Since the expert shares the court's responsibility to serve the truth, that new information should be brought to the attention of the judge. The judge would then determine whether further questioning of the parties or witnesses or other additional instruction is required to corroborate the new information.[114]

Finally, after consulting the expert, the judge is to fix a realistic time period within which the expert is to complete his or her examination and submit a report. Once the time limit has been established, adjustments to it may be made in accord with canon 1465, §2.

The Expert's Report

Canon 1578 — §1. Each of the experts is to prepare a report separate from the others unless the judge decrees that one report signed by the experts individually be drawn up; if this is done, differences of opinion, if there are any, are to be noted carefully.

§2. Experts must indicate clearly by what documents or other suitable means they gained cer-

---

[112] For example, in a marriage nullity case DiFelice urged caution when an expert's report was based solely on the declaration of the petitioner. *Coram* DiFelice, May 6, 1970, *SRRDec* 62 (1970) 448.

[113] T. G. Doran, in "Some Thoughts on Experts," 64, indicates that the expert's service could involve a direct examination of the parties or an indirect examination through a study of the acts, but that "a *peritia* should involve both, if possible."

[114] See J. J. García Faílde, "El perito psicólogo y psiquiatra en las causas canónicas de nulidad matrimonial," in *Memorias* 20 (1996) 107, for the situation when an expert discovers new information. García Faílde notes that the expert must bring the new facts to light, but that the expert's report does not, of itself, provide proof of the new information.

tainty of the identity of the persons, things, or places, by what manner and method they proceeded in fulfilling the function entrusted to them, and above all on which arguments they based their conclusions.

§3. The judge can summon the expert to supply explanations which later seem necessary.

The norm is that each expert prepares an independent report. While written reports are preferable, an oral report is acceptable.[115] If the report is given orally, a notary should be present to prepare a record of the report for inclusion in the acts of the case.

If multiple experts are employed, however, the judge may ask them to collaborate in the preparation of a single report, which, if written, each signs. Should the experts disagree in their conclusions, those differences of opinion are to be noted and explained in the report.

In addition to their findings or conclusions, other important information must be incorporated in the reports of experts. Such information includes:

1. descriptions of the documentation employed in their investigation;
2. brief descriptions of the methodology employed in analyzing the data;
3. explanations of the reasons which form the foundation of the conclusions of the report.

After the expert has submitted a report to the court, the judge is free to propose additional questions to seek further explanation or clarification from the expert.[116]

Weighing the Reports of Experts

Canon 1579 — §1. The judge is to weigh carefully not only the conclusions of the experts, even if they are in agreement, but also the other circumstances of the case.

§2. When giving reasons for the decision, the judge must express what considerations prompted him or her to accept or reject the conclusions of the experts.

While fully respecting the competence of experts, the judge cannot abdicate the responsibility for making a judgment about the issues in a case. Canonical tradition considers the judge to be the *peritus peritorum,* the expert of the experts.[117] In assessing the value of the reports of experts, the judge must take into consideration all of the circumstances of the case. Even when several experts have agreed in their conclusions, judges cannot abandon their own responsibility to sift the evidence.[118] Ultimately, the judgment of the court is a canonical one.[119] While other sciences can and must contribute to that judgment, the conclusions of experts remain one element of the proof, but not the sole determinative one.[120]

Judges are not, however, to act arbitrarily in dealing with the reports of experts. Rather, they must express their reasons for either adopting or rejecting the conclusions of experts.[121] This may be done in a separate decree, or as part of the judicial sentence. It should be noted that the judges must give their reasons not only for rejecting the

---

[115] Doran, "Some Thoughts on Experts," 65. On November 23, 1978, while discussing what eventually became c. 1577, §3, the *coetus* on procedures considered and rejected a proposal to require that experts' reports be written. See *Comm* 11 (1979) 122–123.

[116] See B. de Lanversin, "L'importance du can. 1578, §3, dans les procès matrimoniaux ('judex peritus peritorum')," *QuadStR* 4 (1989) 49–58, for a discussion of the importance of this judicial authority in understanding and weighing the conclusions of experts.

[117] *Coram* Parisella, November 25, 1976, *SRRDec* 68 (1976) 463.

[118] See Mendonça, "The Role of Experts," 443.

[119] John Paul II, alloc, February 5, 1987, *AAS* 80 (1987) 1457–1458. Translated in Woestman, *Papal Allocutions,* 194–195.

[120] For further reflections on assessing the reports of experts, see Z. Grocholewski, "The Ecclesiastical Judge and the Findings of Psychiatric and Psychological Experts," *J* 47 (1987) 462–466; Mendonça, "The Role of Experts," 440–446; and García Faílde, "El perito psicólogo," 106–108.

[121] Doran, "Some Thoughts on Experts," 65.

conclusions of experts, but also for *accepting* them.

Expenses of the Expert

Canon 1580 — The judge must justly and equitably determine the expenses and fees to be paid to the experts, with due regard for particular law.

Particular law is to provide for the appropriate remuneration of experts (see c. 1649, §1, 2°). Within the framework of such local legislation, it is the responsibility of the judge to make determinations concerning honoraria for experts.

Private Experts

Canon 1581 — §1. The parties can designate private experts whom the judge must approve.

§2. If the judge allows them, the private experts can inspect the acts of the case insofar as necessary and attend the presentation of the expert testimony; moreover, they can always present their own report.

"Private experts" may be proposed by the parties in ecclesiastical trials. A private expert (selected by a party) needs to be distinguished from an "expert witness" (a witness who happens to have some expertise) and from those experts appointed by the court.[122] Judges retain the responsibility for admitting them or not.[123]

Once admitted, these private experts should be given access to data upon which to draw responsible conclusions. Therefore, "insofar as necessary"

(a determination made by the judges),[124] the private expert has the right to study the evidence already assembled by the tribunal, to be present at the examination conducted by the tribunal's own experts, and to present a report. R. Bourgon concludes that private experts "are not allowed to inspect the reports of the appointed experts or to be present when these are questioned about their reports."[125] This author disagrees, and is convinced that judges retain the underlying discretion to allow private experts to review the reports of court-appointed *periti* or to be present when they are questioned.[126] Clearly, judges need not do so. But, if the judges become convinced that it would aid the search for the truth to permit private experts one or both of these functions, that is not prohibited by canon 1581.

CHAPTER V
JUDICIAL EXAMINATION AND INSPECTION
[cc. 1582–1583]

Canon 1582 — If, in order to decide a case, the judge considers it opportune to visit some place or to inspect some thing, the judge, after having heard the parties, is to order it by a decree describing in summary fashion those things which must be exhibited during the visit or inspection.

---

[122] A. Mendonça in "The Role of Experts," 430–431, briefly discusses the differences between these three figures.

[123] The use of private experts in public cases is an innovation in the 1983 code. Given the common experience of "dueling experts" in secular legal actions, the judge has the responsibility to assure that the involvement of private experts does not create a dynamic at odds with the chief aim of canonical trials, i.e., seeking the truth. For reflections on this issue, see Wrenn, in *CLSA Com,* 987.

[124] T. G. Doran, in "Some Thoughts on Experts," 64, emphasizes that the experts are to be given access only to those acts necessary to fulfill their tasks. For example, if certain acts or portions of acts have no relevance to the questions proposed for the experts' consideration, the judge should not make those acts available to them.

[125] Bourgon, in *CLSGBI Com,* 893.

[126] The 1976 schema on procedural law contained no canon permitting private experts. In its meeting of November 24, 1978, the *coetus* drafted a new text that eventually became canon 1581. In a series of votes taken concerning this new canon, the members of the *coetus* decided not to include reviewing the reports and being present for the questioning in the list of things the private experts can normally do (see *Comm* 11 [1979] 124–125). But that vote concerned the simple question of whether to include those possibilities specifically in the text; it was not a vote to prohibit those practices.

Canon 1583 — When the visit or inspection has been completed, a report about it is to be drafted.

At times, the just resolution of a dispute requires that the judge personally visit some site or inspect some object relevant to the issues in the case. Judicial examination or access (*accessus*) refers to the judge's visit to a location outside of the courtroom (e.g., a church or, in penal cases, the scene of an alleged ecclesiastical crime). Judicial inspection (*recognitio*) refers to bringing objects into the court for examination by the judge for possible admission into evidence as exhibits (e.g., photographs of the scene of an alleged crime).

Such a visit or inspection would be ordered by the judge only after first having heard the parties on the question of whether this is relevant and useful. The judge's decree would then specify the things that are to be examined during the visitation or inspection.

Once the inspection has taken place, a document reporting the results of the visit or inspection must be drawn up and included in the acts.[127] This document should clearly express the specific findings of the judge which resulted from the examination (e.g., what was observed, what was learned). The document then becomes part of the evidence and is to be weighed in the context of all other evidence.

CHAPTER VI
PRESUMPTIONS
[cc. 1584–1586]

Presumptions are a critical, inescapable, yet often neglected source of proof in any trial. While presumptions constitute an "indirect" rather than a direct form of proof, when properly used they are an important tool for discovering the truth and establishing moral certitude. The misuse of presump-

---

[127] Because of the canonical principle *quod non est in actis, non est in mundo* (what is not in the acts does not exist), this document reporting the results of the visit or inspection must be included in the acts.

---

tions, on the other hand, can create serious problems by obscuring rather than revealing the truth.

Definition and Distinctions

Canon 1584 — A presumption is a probable conjecture about an uncertain matter; a presumption of law is one which the law itself establishes; a human presumption is one which a judge formulates.

The definition of a presumption contained in this canon is simple and precisely worded.[128] First, presumptions always involve "uncertain matters." Where there is full certitude, there is no need for a presumption. Second, a presumption, no matter how well conceived, remains a conjecture. Thus, of their nature, presumptions must always cede to contrary proof.[129] But presumptions are not just any sort of conjecture; they are not even "educated guesses." They are "probable" conjectures supported by well-established facts and solid reasoning. A clear understanding of the nature of presumptions is critical to their proper use in the judicial forum.

The law distinguishes two types of presumptions. First there are presumptions of law (*praesumptio iuris*). These "legal presumptions" are established by the law itself and have the force given to them by the law.[130] Examples of legal

---

[128] Although the definition of a presumption and distinctions among their types are applicable in Eastern law, there is no comparable canon in the Eastern code. See Abbass, "Contentious Trials," 881–882.

[129] As Bourgon points out in *CLSGBI Com*, 894, presumptions, whether legal or human, may be overturned directly (by demonstrating that the "fact" being presumed is false) or indirectly (by demonstrating the falsehood of the "factual basis" used in formulating the presumption).

[130] The 1983 code eliminates the distinction made in *CIC* 1825, §2 between a simple legal presumption, *praesumptio iuris simpliciter,* and an absolute legal presumption, *praesumptio iuris et de iure* (i.e., that which was established by the law and considered so firm that it could be challenged only indirectly by attacking the supposed factual basis of the presumption).

presumptions in canon law are the presumption in case of doubt that a previous law is not revoked by a later law (c. 21); the presumption, for purposes of recourse, that an administrator's silence constitutes a negative reply to a petition (c. 57, §2); the presumption that a minor possesses the use of reason at age seven (c. 97, §2); the presumption that a properly celebrated marriage is valid (c. 1060); the presumption of consummation if the spouses have lived together after the exchange of consent (c. 1061, §2); the presumption that the internal consent of the mind conforms with the words and signs used in the celebration of marriage (c. 1101, §1); the presumption that consent to marriage that was inefficacious due to an impediment or defect of form nonetheless persists until its withdrawal has been established (c. 1107); and presumptions regarding paternity and the legitimacy of children (c. 1138). There is also a process for establishing the presumed death of a spouse (c. 1707), which, once established, then carries the force of a legal presumption.

Second, there are "human presumptions" (*praesumptio hominis*) which, during a trial, are formulated by the judge under the conditions described in canon 1586.

Force of Legal Presumptions

Canon 1585 — A person who has a favorable presumption of law is freed from the burden of proof, which then falls to the other party.

Presumptions of law have significant judicial consequences. Those matters enjoying a presumption of law need not be proved (c. 1526, §2, 1°). In a trial, the position supported by a favorable legal presumption stands unless and until sufficient proof is brought forward to overturn that presumption. Thus, for example, in marriage nullity cases, the validity of the bond is presumed (c. 1060) and the petitioner has the burden of proving otherwise (c. 1526, §1).

The limits of legal presumptions, however, must be clearly understood. Some legal presumptions come into play only if the foundation for the pre-

sumption has been proven. For example, in a marriage case the presumption concerning the conformity between internal consent and external words and deeds (c. 1101, §1) comes into play only when there is certitude that an exchange of vows actually took place. Legal presumptions, while exempting a party from the burden of proving the matter presumed, are not of themselves unimpeachable. These presumptions always cede to the truth.

Human Presumptions

Canon 1586 — The judge is not to formulate presumptions which are not established by law unless they are directly based on a certain and determined fact connected with the matter in dispute.

A judge is *not* to formulate human presumptions unless two clearly specified conditions are met.[131] First, the presumption, which remains a conjecture, requires a solid factual foundation. Without such a foundation, the conjecture is not probable and thus not a valid presumption.[132] Second, the certain fact upon which a presumption is based must have a direct connection with the question at issue. Otherwise, no matter how solid the conjecture may be, it is irrelevant.

Well-formed human presumptions "have long been staples of the jurisprudence of the Rota."[133] In fact, as Doheny rightly noted, "whenever the question of consent is concerned, presumptions must be frequently invoked by the judges in arriv-

---

[131] *CCEO* 1265 is worded more positively: "To come to a just sentence, the judge can formulate presumptions which are not established by the law itself as long as they arise from a certain and determined fact which is directly connected with the subject matter of the controversy." This provision concerning human presumptions is also placed first in the discussion, prior to *CCEO* 1266 on legal presumptions.

[132] Thus, a presumption cannot be based on another presumption. See Wrenn, in *CLSA Com,* 988.

[133] Beal, "The Substance of Things Hoped For," 771. Also see Wanenmacher, *Canonical Evidence,* 243–244 (at #391).

ing at their decisions. A great deal of information is necessary to enable them to formulate these presumptions prudently and correctly."[134] In order to form human presumptions rightly, judges must have a clear understanding of their nature and role in the development of proof.

Presumptions involve both inductive and deductive reasoning. John Beal describes well the process through which a presumption is formed. The "inductive moment consists in distilling from the data of experience a general principle that describes the causal relationship that generally exists between two discrete facts." This "generalization from experience" becomes the "major premise of a syllogism" whose minor premise is that the "factual situation foreseen in the generalization was indeed met in the concrete case being adjudged." The conclusion is then deduced from the syllogism.[135]

In marriage nullity cases, sometimes human presumptions may support a conclusion of nullity, but at other times they may support the validity of the bond. For example, a judge rightly might presume that a common life enduring forty-five years supports the presumption of validity. This is a reasonable presumption, but one which may be overturned by contrary evidence.

Presumptions have probative value only for the concrete case in which they are formulated.[136] It is not legitimate to draw up presumptions and apply them automatically or uncritically to entire classes of marriages.[137] Thus, caution is needed in

suggesting examples of human presumptions— precisely because genuine presumptions always must be rooted in the facts of specific cases. Nonetheless, jurisprudence provides helpful examples that can guide judges in the task of formulating presumptions appropriately. For instance, presumptions regularly come into play in marriage cases tried on the ground *vis vel metus* (force or fear). Rotal jurisprudence has traditionally employed presumptions as a mode of proof when there is evidence of strong aversion toward a prospective spouse.[138] When reverential fear is involved, the facts uncovered through documents and the testimony of the parties and witnesses may establish that: (1) the one being pressured was a teenager, (2) he or she was still living at home and financially dependent, and (3) the parents not only demanded that their son or daughter marry but reinforced that demand with weighty threats. On the basis of these facts, a judge may presume that the ensuing fear was sufficiently grave to compel the child to enter marriage. On the other hand, if the son or daughter was twenty-nine years of age, independent financially and emotionally, and the pressure to marry was not backed up with threats, a judge may understandably presume that any fear of going against the wishes of the parents was not so grave as to rob the person of freedom.[139]

---

[134] Doheny, *Canonical Procedure,* I:424–425.

[135] Beal, "The Substance of Things Hoped For," 771–772. Pompedda in "Decision-Sentence," 88–90, and J. J. García Faílde, *Nuevo derecho procesal canónico: Estudio sistemático-analítico comparado,* 3rd rev. ed. (Salamanca: Publicaciones Universidad Pontificia, 1995) 195–198, also describe how judges formulate and apply presumptions.

[136] García Faílde, *Nuevo derecho procesal canónico,* 199.

[137] Wanenmacher, *Canonical Evidence,* 242. More recently, the Signatura prohibited the use of a generalized list of presumptions. See ApSig, decr, December 13, 1995, "Formulation of 'Presumptions of Fact,'" *RRAO 1996,* 34–39.

[138] L. Wrenn, in "Notes, but Mostly Footnotes," *J* 30 (1970) 210–211, cites presumptions related to aversion used by several Rotal auditors.

[139] Other examples of pertinent presumptions include: (1) presumptions for or against antecedence given to various types of impotence and to certain severe personality disorders (see L. Wrenn, *The Invalid Marriage* [Washington, D.C.: CLSA, 1998] 16–17, 73, 88); (2) presumptions concerning the perpetuity and tenacity of attitudes in cases involving simulation or deeply ingrained error (see Wrenn, "Notes, but Mostly Footnotes," 211–214); (3) presumptions related to the intention of persons who engage in sexual activity with other partners immediately prior to a wedding (see Beal, "The Substance of Things Hoped For," 771); and (4) presuming that a spouse committed adultery in light of a series of proven facts concerning his behavior (see García Faílde, *Nuevo derecho procesal canónico,* 199–200].

The probative force of human presumptions varies. Some may be little more than suspicions, and are termed "light." Other presumptions may be grave and carry significant weight. Finally, jurisprudence recognizes the possibility of a vehement presumption of great and possibly even full probative value.[140]

While presumptions must be based on certain and determined facts directly connected with the matter at issue, presumptions may be related to incidental questions as well as to the central issue of a trial. For example, in the context of a trial, a question may arise concerning the credibility of a certain witness. Presumptions rooted in a person's reputation for great integrity (or, to the contrary, a reputation for mendacity) may well help the judge reach conclusions about the reliability of this witness's testimony. The presumption says nothing about the specific issue at the heart of the trial, but is directly related to the matter of weighing the evidence given by the witness.

Presumptions also have an auxiliary role in guiding the instruction of a case. For example, a certain constellation of facts may lead a judge to presume that a person was in substantial and determining error concerning the indissolubility of marriage or that a person labored under a serious mental illness. In these circumstances, the judge would conduct additional instruction of the case either to verify or disprove these conclusions.

Because presumptions involve hard work and careful reasoning, there can be a tendency to avoid their use. Or, on the other hand, there can be a tendency either to create presumptions rashly or uncritically to accept presumptions made by others. Yet, in the process of conducting the trial and seeking the truth, judges cannot abdicate their responsibility to formulate and apply well-reasoned presumptions.[141]

TITLE V[142]
INCIDENTAL CASES[143]
[cc. 1587–1597]

The Notion and Proposal of Incidental Cases

Canon 1587 — An incidental case arises whenever, after the trial has begun through the citation, a question is proposed which nevertheless pertains to the case in such a way that it frequently must be resolved before the principal question, even if it was not expressly contained in the *libellus* which introduced the litigation.

Canon 1588 — An incidental case is proposed in writing or orally before the judge competent to decide the principal case, indicating the connection between this and the principal case.

Before resolving the central issue in a trial, judges may have to resolve one or more secondary questions. These are called "incidental cases." Incidental cases may have been expressly included in the initial *libellus,* or they may arise during the trial. In either situation, they must be resolved by the judges before they rule on the central issue.

---

[140] Pompedda, "Decision-Sentence," 90.

[141] M. F. Pompedda in "Decision-Sentence," 85–90, situates his discussion on presumptions in the context of the judge's responsibility to use indirect as well as direct proofs (87) in seeking moral certitude. J. J. García Faílde in *Nuevo derecho procesal canónico,* 199, notes

that presumptions formulated by the judge have a special importance in marriage nullity cases.

[142] *CCEO* 1267–1277 on incidental cases corresponds to the Latin cc. 1587–1597. Unlike the current Latin code but like its predecessor (*CIC* 1865–1867), the Eastern code has an additional three canons (*CCEO* 1278–1280) governing "attempts to a pending suit." An "attempt" is an incidental matter introducing innovations that are against the will of and prejudicial to the interests of one or both parties to a case. For a brief comment on the decision to retain these norms in the Eastern code, see Abbass, "Contentious Trials," 886–888.

[143] Wrenn, in *CLSA Com,* 989–991; M. Ryan, in *CLSGBI Com,* 895–899; Madero, in *Pamplona ComEng,* 983–989; J. L. Acebal, in *Salamanca Com,* 772–777; Arroba Conde, in *Valencia Com,* 688–692; P. A. Bonnet, in *Com Ex* IV/2, 1436–1469; L. Madero, in *Com Ex* IV/2, 1470–1476.

By definition, incidental cases take place only after a trial is initiated by a citation. Thus, the court's initial assessment of its claim to assume competence over some dispute is not strictly speaking an incidental case. Should a challenge to the basis of jurisdiction be raised during the trial, however, the matter is an incidental case that must be resolved (see c. 1460). Examples of incidental cases that might arise include the question of whether to appoint a guardian (cc. 1478–1479), to admit or exclude a witness (c. 1555), or to respond to an exception (c. 1462, §2).

Incidental cases may be raised in written or oral form, but the connection between the secondary question and the principal issue must be clearly delineated. Competence over the resolution of incidental questions belongs to the judge who is responsible for the principal case.

Admission or Rejection

Canon 1589 — §1. After having received the petition and heard the parties, the judge is to decide as promptly as possible (*expeditissime*) whether the proposed incidental question seems to have a foundation and a connection with the principal trial or rather must be rejected at the outset. If the judge admits the incidental question, the judge is to decide whether it is of such gravity that it must be resolved by an interlocutory sentence or by a decree.

§2. If the judge decides not to resolve the incidental question before the definitive sentence, however, the judge is to decree that the question will be considered when the principal case is decided.

Upon receiving the petition to decide an incidental case, the judge is to give the parties the opportunity to comment on the issue. As soon as possible (*expeditissime*)[144] the judge then makes the following determinations:

(1) whether the secondary issue has any foundation;

(2) whether the proposed case is truly related to the principal trial, or whether it is an entirely separate question.

If the proposed incidental case has no foundation or has no reasonable connection to the principal issue, the judge, by decree, is to reject it entirely. If the judge admits the question, the court has three options for resolving the incidental case:

(1) when the question is a grave one, it is to be resolved by an interlocutory sentence;

(2) in other circumstances, the incidental case may be resolved by a decree of the judge;

(3) by decree, the judge may decide to resolve the incidental question in the context of the definitive sentence deciding the central issue.

Procedures Used in Incidental Cases

Canon 1590 — §1. If the incidental question must be resolved by sentence, the norms for the oral contentious process are to be observed unless the judge decides otherwise due to the gravity of the matter.

§2. If the matter must be resolved by decree, however, the tribunal can entrust the matter to an auditor or the presiding judge.

If the incidental question is of such a nature that it needs to be resolved by an interlocutory sentence, the matter normally is addressed by employing the oral contentious process.[145] When the issue is very serious or complex in nature, however, the judge has the discretion to order, and the parties have the right to insist, that the incidental question be addressed by means of the ordinary contentious process.

If the incidental matter is to be decided by a decree, the decision may be entrusted to an audi-

---

[144] The decision of the judge in this matter admits of no appeal (c. 1629, 5°).

[145] See the commentary on cc. 1656–1670.

tor.[146] The decision may also be made by the presiding judge alone rather than by the college if the principal case has been entrusted to a panel of judges.

Revocation or Correction of Decision

Canon 1591 — Before the principal case is completed, the judge or the tribunal can revoke or reform the decree or interlocutory sentence for a just reason either at the request of a party or *ex officio* after the parties have been heard.

Prior to the completion of the principal case, the college of judges or individual judge may revoke or revise any interlocutory sentence or decree issued in an incidental case. To do so, there must be a just cause. For example, new evidence may have emerged that sheds a different light on the incidental question. Also, for the revocation or revision to be valid (see c. 127, §2, 2°), the parties must be informed about the proposed revision and given the opportunity to comment.

This provision for amendment allows the court to correct any possible errors that might come to light during the instruction of the case concerning the principal issue. The revocation or amendment of the decision in the incidental case may be made by the judge or judges either at their own initiative or at the request of one or more of the parties.

CHAPTER I
PARTIES WHO DO NOT APPEAR
[cc. 1592–1595]

Declaring a Respondent Absent

Canon 1592 — §1. If the cited respondent has neither appeared nor given a suitable excuse for being absent or has not responded according to

the norm of can. 1507, §1, the judge, having observed what is required, is to declare the respondent absent from the trial and decree that the case is to proceed to the definitive sentence and its execution.

§2. Before issuing the decree mentioned in §1, the judge must be certain that a legitimately executed citation has reached the respondent within the useful time, even by issuing a new citation if necessary.

The citation issued by a tribunal carries with it the obligation to respond in the way directed by the citation (tribunal appearance, written reply). When a respondent has not replied to the citation or provided a reasonable excuse for being unable to respond at the time or in the manner requested, the judge has the responsibility to declare that person absent from the trial.

In the 1917 code, this institute was known as a decree of contumacy. The current legislation, recognizing that many factors might induce a respondent to ignore a citation, has removed the judgmental language.

Before issuing a decree of absence, the judge must be certain that: (1) there was a legitimate citation, (2) there was no appearance by the cited party, (3) the cited party gave no reasonable excuse for failing to appear, and (4) the cited party also did not respond in accord with canon 1507, §1, which permits a written response. With regard to the first of these, normally there must be evidence that the citation reached the respondent. If the initial citation was delivered by "return receipt" mail, the signed receipt provides such certainty, although there are other ways in which the judge can have such certitude (e.g., the testimony of witnesses verifying that the respondent received the citation). In case of doubt concerning whether a citation reached the respondent, the canon itself suggests the possibility of issuing a second citation. It should be remembered that a respondent who refuses to accept or otherwise evades the notification of a citation is considered legitimately cited (c. 1510). The fact that a respondent cooperates only selectively in the

---

[146] When this is done, the auditor, who may be a lay man or woman (c. 1428), exercises true decision-making authority.

process, however, is not a reason for a declaration of absence.[147]

The absence of a respondent significantly limits the tribunal's ability to discover and rule in accord with the truth. This is especially critical in marriage nullity cases, where testimony from both parties to the partnership provides the possibility of greater insight into its dynamics. Thus, a judge might decide to delay a decree of absence if there is hope that a respondent might be persuaded to reply. Eventually, however, should the respondent not participate, then he or she is to be decreed absent. Like any decree that is not merely procedural, this must be in writing, with a summary of its reasons (cc. 51, 1617).

The consequences of the respondent's absence are most significant. In effect, by their absence respondents waive most of their rights in the trial. In the absence of a respondent, the *"case is to proceed to the definitive sentence and its execution"* with the judge observing that which is required (*servatis servandis*). What, however, are those essentials which a judge must observe? The code does not specify what rights a respondent waives and what elements of the process must still be observed. The rules for interpretation enshrined in canons 17 and 19 and the norms governing the Roman Rota, however, can clarify the issue.[148] Article 60, paragraph 3 of these norms provides that those who have been decreed absent are to be notified of the decree of the joinder of the issues and

of the definitive sentence.[149] Article 79, by its cross-reference to article 60, clarifies that an absent respondent has effectively waived the right to review the published acts of the case.[150]

Occasionally, respondents may state expressly that they wish no further contact from the tribunal whatsoever. In this case, precisely out of respect for their demands, even the minimal notifications made to absent respondents need not be made.[151]

It should be noted that article 60 of the Rotal norms distinguishes the situation of an absent respondent (art. 60, §3) from that of a respondent who leaves the judgment up to the justice of the court (art. 60, §2). In this latter situation, the Rota does not declare such respondents absent, and they are notified not only of the definition of the issue and the decision but also of any new petitions and all pronouncements of the judge.[152]

The decree of absence is an essential tool protecting a petitioner's right to a just decision. Thus, a respondent cannot derail the ecclesiastical process by refusing to participate. The absence of a respondent, however, might well close important avenues of proof which could support a petitioner's contention.

When the court has been unable to locate the whereabouts of a respondent, it is *not* appropriate to decree such a respondent absent.[153] The decree

---

[147] A potential exception to this observation emerged in a case *coram* Colagiovanni, decr, March 30, 1993, *ME* 119 (1994) 535–544. Two earlier Rotal panels had issued conflicting rulings on whether the first instance decision was null on the basis of the denial of the respondent's right of defense. Eventually, the Colagiovanni *turnus* ruled that, because the respondent threatened a civil lawsuit, the first instance tribunal was justified both in declaring her absent from the trial (542–543) and in appointing ex officio a procurator for the absent respondent (543).

[148] F. Daneels, "The Right of Defence," *Stud Can* 27 (1993) 86, also notes that in view of c. 19 and papal teaching, the norms for the Rota provide a guide for local tribunals.

[149] RomRot, *Normae,* April 18, 1994, art. 60, *AAS* 86 (1994) 526. For a brief commentary on article 60 of these norms, see J. L. Acebal Luján, "Normas del Tribunal de la Rota Romana: Texto y comentario," *REDC* 52 (1995) 276.

[150] RomRot, *Normae,* April 18, 1994, art. 79, *AAS* 86 (1994) 531. See also Wrenn, *Procedures,* 62.

[151] Daneels, "The Right of Defence," 86.

[152] Jean Trudeau traces the canonical history of this institute in "La remise à la justice du tribunal dans les causes de nullité de mariage," *Stud Can* 32 (1998) 129–143. He argues that, although current Rotal norms employ the formula, the lack of any provision for this in the 1983 code means there is no longer any basis for local tribunals to use it. This author, however, is not fully persuaded by Trudeau's conclusion.

[153] A. Stankiewicz, "De citationis necessitate et impugnatione," *QuadStR* 4 (1989) 81.

of absence presupposes that the respondent has been notified of the process and invited to participate through a prior citation. Rather than issuing a decree of absence, therefore, the court should issue a decree specifying the nature of the efforts made to locate a respondent, concluding that all reasonable efforts to discover the respondent's whereabouts have failed, and ordering the trial to proceed even though it is not possible to cite the respondent.[154]

Subsequent Participation of an Absent Respondent

Canon 1593 — §1. If the respondent appears at the trial later or responds before a decision in the case, the respondent can offer conclusions and proofs, without prejudice to the prescript of can. 1600; the judge, however, is to take care that the trial is not prolonged intentionally through longer and unnecessary delays.

When a respondent who has legitimately been decreed absent later chooses to participate, the earlier refusal to reply is not to be held against that person. Within certain limits designed to protect against excessive delays and dilatory tactics, the previously absent respondent may exercise all the usual rights of a party to the case. If the case has already been formally concluded (c. 1599), however, a previously absent respondent can bring forward new proofs only in accord with the provisions of canon 1600.

Absent Respondents and Challenges to the Sentence

§2. Even if the respondent did not appear or respond before a decision in the case, the respondent can use challenges against the sentence; if the respondent proves that there was a legitimate impediment for being detained and there was no personal fault in its not being made known be-

forehand, the respondent can use a complaint of nullity.

A previously absent respondent, having received notification of the decision, is free to challenge the sentence in accord with the norms of canons 1619–1640. If the respondent can show that he or she was legitimately impeded from participation through no personal fault, then a complaint of remediable nullity of the sentence (c. 1622, 6°) may be lodged. If there was no legitimate impediment, the respondent's absence cannot be used to challenge the sentence on the basis of any alleged denial of the right of defense (c. 1620, 7°). The respondent decreed absent had waived his or her rights and, hence, the court did not deny the right to defense.

Absence of a Petitioner

Canon 1594 — If the petitioner has not appeared on the day and at the hour prescribed for the joinder of the issue and has not offered a suitable excuse:
  1° the judge is to cite the petitioner again;
  2° if the petitioner does not comply with the new citation, the petitioner is presumed to have renounced the trial according to the norm of cann. 1524–1525;
  3° if the petitioner later wishes to intervene in the process, can. 1593 is to be observed.

The absence of a petitioner, while less common, may occur. When petitioners fail to respond to a citation, they are to be cited again. If there is no response to the new citation, the court presumes that the petitioner has renounced the instance, and the norms of canons 1524–1525 apply.[155] As in any renunciation, the instance is not necessarily closed. The respondent must be notified of the petitioner's absence and may well urge that the suit nonetheless

---

[154] See the commentary on cc. 1409, §2 and 1511.

[155] Canon 1594 is an exception to the rule (c. 1524, §3) that a renunciation is not valid unless made in writing and signed by the renouncing party.

go forward. The judge is then to rule whether the suit should continue to be processed despite the petitioner's absence.

If the petitioner's absence did not lead to the closure of the instance, that petitioner may later intervene in the process in accord with the same norms permitting the involvement of a previously absent respondent. On the other hand, if the petitioner's absence resulted in the effective renunciation of the process and a decree closing the instance, that decree extinguished the procedural acts of the process (cc. 1525, 1522). Thus, a subsequent change of mind by a previously absent petitioner would require that he or she submit a *libellus* seeking a new trial. The substantive acts from the earlier instance may be deemed relevant and incorporated into the new trial, but the trial itself is new and must proceed from the beginning.

Expenses Occasioned by Absence

Canon 1595 — §1. A petitioner or respondent who is absent from the trial and has not given proof of a just impediment is obliged both to pay the expenses of the litigation which have accrued because of the absence and to indemnify the other party if necessary.

§2. If both the petitioner and the respondent were absent from the trial, they are obliged *in solidum* to pay the expenses of the litigation.

In theory, the expenses incurred because of the absence (without just impediment) of a party are the responsibility of that party. In practice, it may be impossible for a tribunal to collect from an absent party. This responsibility for expenses is one factor that may be taken into consideration if a previously absent party seeks to intervene subsequently. Similarly, if a petitioner's absence is presumed to be a renunciation but a respondent wishes the trial to go forward, the judge may take into consideration the respondent's willingness or unwillingness to accept responsibility for court costs in deciding to continue the trial or decree the process closed.

CHAPTER II
THE INTERVENTION OF A THIRD PERSON IN A CASE[156]
[cc. 1596–1597]

The legislator envisions two possible scenarios. In one case, a third party takes the initiative and seeks to be involved in a trial. In the other, one of the original parties or the judge might conclude that a just resolution of the issues requires the involvement of one or more third parties.

An "Interested" Third Party

Canon 1596 — §1. A person who has an interest can be admitted to intervene in a case at any instance of the litigation, either as a party defending a right or in an accessory manner to help a litigant.

§2. To be admitted, the person must present a *libellus* to the judge before the conclusion of the case; in the *libellus* the person briefly is to demonstrate his or her right to intervene.

§3. A person who intervenes in a case must be admitted at that stage which the case has reached, with a brief and peremptory period of time assigned to the person to present proofs if the case has reached the probatory period.

Normally, third parties may seek to intervene at any grade or stage of a trial.[157] They may seek to intervene independently in order to protect their own rights which might be jeopardized, or in an accessory fashion on behalf of the position of one or the other of the parties.

---

[156] Canons 1276–1277 of the Eastern code are nearly identical with cc. 1596–1597 of the Latin code. The Eastern code, however, makes an additional provision for involvement by third parties, permitting them, under certain circumstances, to attack a definitive sentence prior to its execution (*CCEO* 1330–1333). There is no parallel provision in the Latin code. For further commentary, see Abbass, "Contentious Trials," 889–890.

[157] There is an exception in penal trials in which a third party may be admitted only in first instance (c. 1729, §2).

The decision whether to admit a third party or not belongs to the judge. The potential third party must first present a *libellus* requesting admission and establishing the right to intervene. Such a *libellus* must be handled in accord with the norms for incidental cases (cc. 1587–1591). The judge is to respond to that request *expeditissime* (c. 1589, §1); hence, there is no appeal from the decree admitting or rejecting the intervention of the third party (c. 1629, 5°).

If the intervention is admitted, the trial continues from the point it had already reached, and procedural acts already placed remain in full force.[158] This prevents third parties from unnecessarily delaying the prosecution of a trial. If the third party is admitted during the instruction phase of a case, the judge assigns a brief but realistic period of time for the third party to present proofs. This deadline is *peremptory,* meaning that, once it has passed, the right to produce proofs is extinguished. If the third party was admitted only after the conclusion of the case (c. 1599), that party may present proofs only in accord with the provisions of canon 1600.

A "Necessary" Third Party

Canon 1597 — After having heard the parties, the judge must summon to the trial a third person whose intervention seems necessary.

When during the prosecution of a suit it becomes apparent that the involvement of one or more third parties is essential for the court to do justice, the judge is to cite those parties to join the suit.[159] That citation, however, is to be issued only after the judge consults those already involved as parties to the suit. That consultation is required for the validity of the judge's act, although the judge is free to accept or reject the counsel received (c. 127, §2, 2°).

TITLE VI
THE PUBLICATION OF THE ACTS,
THE CONCLUSION OF THE CASE,
AND THE DISCUSSION OF THE CASE[160]
[cc. 1598–1606]

This title contains norms governing the transition between the instruction or evidence-gathering phase of the trial and the decision-making phase. Three critically important institutes are discussed in this title: (1) the publication of the acts; (2) the conclusion of the evidence-gathering phase and provisions for exceptional gathering of evidence; and (3) the discussion of the case.

The Publication of the Acts

Canon 1598 — §1. After the proofs have been collected, the judge by a decree must permit the parties and their advocates, under penalty of nullity, to inspect at the tribunal chancery the acts not yet known to them; furthermore, a copy of the acts can also be given to advocates who request one. In cases pertaining to the public good to avoid a most grave danger the judge can decree that a specific act must be shown to no one; the judge is to take care, however, that the right of defense always remains intact.

---

[158] For example, if the joinder of issues was already completed, the involvement of the third party neither requires nor permits a new joinder. Should a third party wish the addition, subtraction, or amendment of a ground, that could be done only in the exceptional circumstances provided by c. 1514.

[159] This is not a citation of a witness to provide testimony. A witness is not a third party. This is a citation of an additional party, someone whose rights are bound up with the issue before the tribunal.

[160] Wrenn, in *CLSA Com,* 991–994; Ryan, in *CLSGBI Com,* 899–904; Diego-Lora, in *Pamplona ComEng,* 989–994; Acebal, in *Salamanca Com,* 778–782; Arroba Conde, in *Valencia Com,* 693–696; Rodríguez-Ocaña, in *Com Ex* IV/2, 1477–1520.

The text of canon 1598, §1 reflects compromises resulting from many differing concerns and a great deal of debate during the code revision process.[161] Since the promulgation of the code, the provisions of this canon have continued to receive a great deal of attention in the canonical literature.[162] Papal teaching[163] and Roman jurisprudence since 1983 have emphasized the vital nature of the publication of the acts, but the jurisprudence, while in complete agreement about the fundamental importance of this institute, has not been completely uniform regarding every detail.[164]

The term "publication" may be misunderstood and even create needless fears in the minds of the parties and witnesses. In English, the term "publi-

cation" is commonly understood as publicizing something, making it available for public consumption. That, however, is not what is meant in this context. When tribunals communicate with the parties and witnesses, the use of terminology such as "making the acts available for review" may help avoid such misunderstanding.

To interpret and implement the canon properly, it is vital not only to understand the text itself but also to identify and respect the values which the law strives to foster. Two chief values motivate the requirement of the publication of the acts: (1) to provide for the parties' right of defense and (2) to "test" the evidence, thus assuring the tribunal that the truth has been discovered. More will be said about the right of defense below. With regard to the second value, upon reviewing the acts the parties, while perhaps challenging one or two minor points, may indicate that the evidence assembled reflects the truth. This assures the judges that they have a solid basis upon which to rule. On the other hand, the publication of the acts may lead one or both of the parties to challenge certain statements as inaccurate, incomplete, misleading, or totally false. In this respect, publication has some of the benefits of a cross-examination. By identifying disputed claims, the tribunal may then take whatever further steps are needed to clarify the truth.

The canon is precisely worded. Thus, it is essential to examine the text closely in order to know exactly what the law does and does not require.

The General Rule for Publication

1. The publication of the acts occurs only after the evidence has been gathered. For the parties themselves, access to the acts prior to this time is limited to the inspection of documents as provided by canon 1544. In marriage nullity cases, canon 1678, §1, 2° permits the defender of the bond and the advocates of the parties to inspect the acts prior to the publication. But the parties themselves are invited to inspect the acts only after the proofs have been assembled. Withholding publication until all the evi-

---

[161] For summaries of the discussion on publication of the acts during the drafting process, see *Comm* 11 (1979) 134–135 and *Comm* 16 (1984) 68. For a review of the history of the institute and concerns raised during the revision process, see Cox, *Procedural Changes,* 77–85, and Wrenn, in *CLSA Com,* 991–992.

[162] Among the many canonists who address the publication of the acts, see: C. Gullo, "La pubblicazione degli atti e la discussione della causa," in *Il processo matrimoniale canonico: Nuova edizione riveduta e ampliata, Studi Giuridici* XXIX, ed. P. A. Bonnet and C. Gullo (Vatican City: Libreria Editrice Vaticana, 1994) 677–693; F. Daneels, "The Right of Defence," especially 87–89; A. Farret, "Publication des actes et publication de la sentence dans les causes de nullité de mariage," *Stud Can* 25 (1991) 115–138; J. G. Johnson, "Publish and Be Damned: The Dilemma of Implementing the Canons on Publishing the Acts and the Sentence," *J* 49 (1989) 210–240; M. R. Moodie, "Fundamental Rights and Access to the Acts of a Case," *Stud Can* 28 (1994) 123–154; D. Nau, "Publish and Be Damned: One Practitioner's Experience," *J* 51 (1991) 442–450; D. A. Smilanic, "The Publication of the Acts: Canon 1598, §1," *CLSAP* 57 (1995) 377–386; Wrenn, *Procedures,* 59–62.

[163] John Paul II, alloc, January 26, 1989, *AAS* 81 (1989) 924. Translation in Woestman, *Papal Allocutions,* 206.

[164] For examples, see *RRAO 1990,* 41–42, 47–50, 56–58, 58–61; *coram* Pinto, decr, May 24, 1985, *ME* 113 (1988) 314–319; *coram* Funghini, decr, May 11, 1994, *ME* 119 (1994) 526–534; *coram* Colagiovanni, decr, March 30, 1993, *ME* 119 (1994) 535–544. D. A. Smilanic, in "The Publication of the Acts," 382, briefly discusses different views evident in Rotal jurisprudence.

dence is gathered serves an important value. By reducing the possibility that testimony will be given primarily in reaction against the statements of others, the judge or auditor may more easily obtain a balanced and less defensive account when interrogating the parties and the witnesses. Secondarily, conducting the publication of the acts only after all the evidence is gathered, rather than piecemeal as each new proof is admitted, streamlines the trial and eases the burden on the parties and court officials.

2. The canon places a responsibility on the judge who, by means of a decree, *must permit* the parties and their advocates to review the acts. Note that the canon uses the Latin *et*. It is not the parties or their advocates, but the parties *and* their advocates who must be given this permission. In cases of marriage nullity or the nullity of sacred orders, this permission must be extended to the defender of the bond (cc. 1434; 1678, §1, 2°; 1711).

3. Since canon 1598 does not specifically establish a time limit for reviewing the acts, the judge must define a reasonable peremptory deadline (*fatalia legis;* see c. 1466). The deadline cannot validly be shortened without the consent of the parties; after hearing the parties it may be extended for a just reason, even without their consent (c. 1465, §2). Given the peremptory nature of the time limit, the right to review the acts ceases once the allotted time has expired.[165] This decree of publication must be communicated to the parties and their advocates in accord with the norms of canon 1509 and the particular law of the tribunal.

4. The permission to review the acts must be extended *under penalty of nullity.* If the permission was not given or if the notification was not made, the resulting sentence would be open to a complaint of remediable nullity due

to an invalid judicial act (c. 1622, 5°). More critically, failure to publish the acts might well be a ground for irremediable nullity as a denial of the right of defense (c. 1620, 7°), as will be discussed shortly.

5. It is vital to note that the validity of the process does not depend on whether the acts were, in fact, reviewed by the parties. It depends on whether a genuine permission was extended to them. The parties may choose not to exercise their right to review the acts, either by so informing the judge or by failing to act within the peremptory time limit.

6. The permission entails reviewing the acts at the tribunal office and not elsewhere. This provides appropriate security for the sensitive information contained in the acts. Thus, normally a party has no right to review the acts at a place of his or her choosing. Parties living outside of the territory of the tribunal trying the case, however, must be allowed to review the acts at the tribunal of their domicile.[166]

7. The permission is to review the acts which are "not yet known to them." A "republication" of acts already known to the parties is unnecessary since for those acts the purposes of publication (protecting the right of defense and testing the truth) would already have been fulfilled.

8. The advocates of the parties, but not the parties themselves, may request a copy of the acts. The advocate is not permitted to give a

---

[165] *RI,* n. 25, *CorpusIC* II, 1122.

[166] A tribunal has a right and responsibility to call on another tribunal to assist in the communication of the acts (c. 1418). See *RRAO 1990,* 57. If a genuine impediment (e.g., severe illness, military service) precludes a party from coming to the tribunal trying the case, what may be done? The norm of c. 1558, §3, on hearing witnesses outside of the tribunal's offices, is helpful. The judge, by way of exception, could permit the inspection to take place in some other location with due regard for privacy and adequate supervision of the review process.

copy of the acts to his or her client.[167] This norm is designed to balance the parties' right of defense while also assuring the independence and confidentiality of the ecclesiastical process.

The Possibility of Exempting an Act from Publication

The expectation of the canon is that all of the acts not yet known to the parties will be made available for inspection. As a result of the debate over the publication of the acts, however, the canon permits certain exemptions from publication. As a law which restricts the free exercise of a right, the exemption must be interpreted narrowly (c. 18).[168] Pope John Paul emphasized that it would "be a distortion of the norm of law and also a grave error of interpretation if the exception were to become the general rule."[169] The exemption, like the canon as a whole, is carefully worded.

1. An exemption from publication may be considered only in cases involving the *public good*. Marriage nullity cases (c. 1691), cases concerning the separation of spouses (c. 1696), and penal cases (c. 1728, §1) all involve the public good.[170]

2. The only motive permitting the exemption from publication is the avoidance of *a most grave danger*. The Latin uses the superlative form of the adjective (*gravissima pericula*). Thus, inconvenience, embarrassment, the preference or request of a party or a witness not to have their testimony made known are not sufficient motives to exempt an act from publication. The canon neither defines what factors constitute *gravissima pericula,*

nor identifies who it is that might be endangered by publication.[171] This wisely respects the judge's discretion to assess the dangers present in a specific case and make an appropriate determination. To assist the judge in exercising this discretion, some commentators point to canon 1548, §2, 2°, which identifies reasons that exempt a witness from the obligation to testify. This parallel can help clarify whether there is sufficient danger to withhold publication of an act.[172]

3. To exempt an act from publication, the judge must issue a decree. While the decree of publication proper is purely procedural in nature and need not contain a summary of its reasons (c. 1617), the decree to exempt an act from publication is not merely procedural. Thus, either the decree of publication itself must identify the exempted act and specify the dangers justifying the exemption, or a separate decree of exemption from publication needs to be included in the acts.

4. Only a specific act (*aliquod actum*), not the acts as a whole, may be exempted from publication. This might involve all the testimony of one person, or one part of someone's testimony. The canon neither permits a judge to exempt all of the acts from publication, nor limits a judge to exempting one and only one act in a particular case.

5. The decree may stipulate that the act not be shown to anyone. The judge, however, may choose not to extend the exemption so widely. For example, the judge could exempt an act from publication to the parties while permitting their advocates to review the material. This

---

[167] Ryan, in *CLSGBI Com,* 900–901.

[168] Johnson, "Publish and Be Damned," 213, n. 10.

[169] John Paul II, alloc, January 26, 1989, *AAS* 81 (1989) 924. Translation in Woestman, *Papal Allocutions,* 206.

[170] Even if a case is not specifically identified by law as involving the public good, a diocesan bishop may so designate a specific contentious case (c. 1431, §1).

[171] Johnson, in "Publish and Be Damned," 214 and 222, n. 32, indicates that the danger may be to one of the parties, to witnesses, to tribunal personnel, or to the Church itself.

[172] Rodríguez-Ocaña, in *Com Ex* IV/2, 1485; Wrenn, *Procedures,* 61.

could be done on the condition that the advocates not communicate the contents of the act to the parties, and would seem to protect the right of defense better than not allowing anyone to see the act.[173] In marriage nullity cases, however, this provision must be interpreted in light of the right of the defender of the bond, the advocates of the parties, and the promoter of justice (if involved in the trial) to inspect the judicial acts even if not yet published.[174]

6. In all cases, the exemption of an act from publication must leave the right of defense intact or the exemption cannot be justified.

Publication and the Right of Defense in Marriage Cases

Controversy over the publication of the acts has not abated in the more than fifteen years since the promulgation of the code. That should not be surprising, since the norm strives to balance important competing rights and interests. Controversy over the canon has centered on its application in marriage nullity cases. The debate has contributed to deeper reflection on the nature of marriage nullity cases[175] and on the meaning of the right of defense (c. 221, §1) in such cases.[176] Lawrence Wrenn has argued that in marriage nullity cases "the right of defense and the right of the parties to know are separable rights" because "the issue is not the

good name of either party but the validity of the marriage bond." Hence, as Wrenn understands it, the right of defense belongs primarily to the defender of the bond.[177] Michael Moodie has strongly challenged this, arguing that the role of the defender of the bond does not remove the right of defense from the parties.[178] Rather, Moodie argues, marriage cases always concern a person's state of life, and there is a fundamental right to vindicate one's state of life and protect one's personal dignity. Hence any "infringement upon the right to know would appear to violate fundamental rights of the individual."[179] Alain Farret, based on certain trends in Rotal jurisprudence, argues for an understanding of canon 1598 that is carefully nuanced in light of canon 1691.[180] He concludes that in publishing the acts, the key issue is whether the parties have real knowledge of the facts of the case and the practical opportunity of offering a defense. This allows a judge greater latitude for exempting acts from publication.[181]

Clearly, the right of defense cannot be simplistically identified with the right to review the acts. Otherwise, the exception permitting the exemption of some acts from publication would be a denial of the right of defense. Other canonical processes involving the status of marriages, while administrative in nature and not identical to marriage nullity trials, reinforce this conclusion. For example, the administrative process for a dispensation from a non-consummated marriage requires the intervention of the defender (c. 1701, §1), the hearing of the parties, and the use of many of the norms for ordinary contentious trials and marriage nullity cases (c. 1702). Yet, in this process the acts are *not*

---

[173] See Ryan, in *CLSGBI Com,* 901. D. A. Smilanic, in "The Publication of the Acts," 383–384, notes that "the quality of the advocate's activity is a pivotal point" in Rotal jurisprudence concerning the publication of the acts and the right of defense.

[174] See the commentary on c. 1678, §1, 2°.

[175] Z. Grocholewski, in "Quisnam est pars conventa in causis nullitatis matrimonii?" *P* 79 (1990) 357–391, argues convincingly that the nullity petition is against the presumption of validity (c. 1060), not against the other spouse. Hence, church authority is the true respondent in marriage nullity cases and is represented by the defender of the bond.

[176] The drafting commission specifically indicated that the publication of the acts was "intimately connected" with the right of defense. See *Comm* 16 (1984) 68.

[177] Wrenn, *Procedures,* 61–62; see also 72–73.

[178] Moodie, "Fundamental Rights and Access to the Acts," 127–138.

[179] Ibid., 140–141.

[180] The canon indicates that the norms concerning trials in general and the ordinary contentious process are to be applied in marriage nullity cases unless the nature of the case demands otherwise. See the commentary on c. 1691.

[181] Farret, "Publication des actes et publication de la sentence," 137–138.

to be published (c. 1703, §1). Similarly, the acts are not to be published or inspected in the administrative process for a papal dissolution in favor of the faith, even though the instruction of such cases is quasi-judicial and involves the intervention of the defender of the bond.[182] At the same time, even if the bond as upheld by church authority is the chief respondent, not only the defender but also the petitioner and respondent have significant rights at stake. Thus, when the respondent has not been declared absent from the trial,[183] respect for the right of defense would require only limited use of the exemption provided in canon 1598, §1.

Some Practical Possibilities

When there is a genuine concern that the information contained in the acts might be misused (e.g., risk of damage to the reputation of others, possible scandal or family quarrels, potential civil court actions), judges may consider other possibilities to mitigate the potential dangers.

1. Judges could invoke their authority to oblige the parties to swear an oath to use the information only in the canonical trial and otherwise to observe secrecy regarding the material (c. 1455, §3). There is a *lacuna* in the law, however, since nowhere does the code spell out the consequence of a party's refusal to take such an oath. May judges deny access to the acts if a party refuses to swear or otherwise solemnly promise to maintain secrecy? The refusal to make such a promise of secrecy would manifest a lack of respect for the fundamental nature of this ecclesiastical process. Such a refusal would seem to constitute the *gravissima pericula* envisioned by the canon, and this author believes judges are well within their rights to withhold the publication of the acts under these extraordinary circumstances.[184]

2. Certainly, there is no need to reveal the addresses and telephone numbers of the parties and witnesses, information which has no bearing on the right of defense.

3. In addition to excusing witnesses from testifying in the first place, judges could exclude entirely from the acts the testimony of a particularly fearful witness when other sources of evidence make any information provided by that witness unnecessary. The evidence initially presented by that witness, therefore, could not be used in any fashion.

4. Judges might also exclude from the acts materials that might be inflammatory but which have no relevance to the specific ground.[185] This situation tends to arise when tribunals use generalized questions eliciting a wide variety of information rather than more precisely focused interrogatories. For example, if the ground of nullity involves simulation on the part of the petitioner, certain information about the respondent may be vitally important to help identify the petitioner's motive for simulating. Other information about the respondent, however, may have no evidentiary value, and the judges could entirely exclude such information as irrelevant to the issue.

Further Instruction of Case Subsequent to Publication

§2. To complete the proofs, the parties can propose additional proofs to the judge. When these proofs have been collected, it is again an occasion for the decree mentioned in §1 if the judge thinks it necessary.

---

[182] See the private reply published in *RRAO 1998,* 29–30.

[183] See the commentary on c. 1592.

[184] A March 30, 1993 decision *coram* Colagiovanni does not speak directly to this *lacuna,* but is instructive. The

decision upheld the validity of a sentence in which the respondent was not allowed access to the acts of a case because of her threat to initiate a civil lawsuit. See *ME* 119 (1994) 535–544.

[185] Smilanic, in "Publication of the Acts," 384, notes that what is subject to publication is "all the evidence on which a sentence rests."

Based on their review of the acts, the parties may wish to present additional proofs to rebut allegedly false claims, or to supplement, nuance, or provide a context for other elements of the evidence. The judge determines whether to admit or reject the proposed new proofs (e.g., see cc. 1527, 1533, and 1547). If additional proofs are admitted into the acts of the case, there may be a need for a new decree of publication, permitting the parties to inspect the new evidence. This is not strictly required, however, and the judge may determine that a new publication is unnecessary. Often, there may be little or nothing new or relevant in the "new" proofs, in which case further publication would extend the trial for no benefit. On the other hand, if the additional evidence contains something of significance that sheds new light on the issues in the case, respect for the right of defense would lead the judge to publish the newly acquired acts.

The Conclusion of the Case

Canon 1599 — §1. When everything pertaining to the production of proofs has been completed, the conclusion of the case is reached.

§2. This conclusion occurs whenever the parties declare that they have nothing else to add, the useful time prescribed by the judge to propose proofs has elapsed, or the judge declares that the case is instructed sufficiently.

§3. The judge is to issue a decree that the case has reached its conclusion, in whatever manner it has occurred.

The term "conclusion of the case" (*conclusionem in causa*) may be somewhat misleading to one not trained in procedural law. The trial is not completed or concluded; rather, the case remains pending, since the decision regarding the doubt (*dubium*) has not yet been rendered. The instance remains open, and vitally important stages of the trial, such as the discussion of the case and the crafting and publication of the judicial sentence, remain. What is concluded at this point, except under the extraordinary circumstances described in canon 1600, is the evidence-gathering phase of the trial.

The conclusion occurs in one of three ways: (1) the parties to the case declare that they have no further evidence to bring forward; (2) the time limits established by the judge for producing proof have expired; (3) the judges declare that sufficient proof has been assembled to establish the truth of the matter. The recognition of the fact that the instruction is concluded is to be accomplished in the form of a judicial decree.

Admission of New Proofs after the Conclusion

Canon 1600 — §1. After the conclusion of the case, the judge can still summon the same or other witnesses or arrange for other proofs which were not requested earlier, only:

1° in cases which concern the private good of the parties alone, if all the parties consent;

2° in other cases, after the parties have been heard and provided that there is a grave reason and any danger of fraud or subornation is eliminated;

3° in all cases whenever it is likely that the sentence will be unjust because of the reasons mentioned in can. 1645, §2, nn. 1–3 unless the new proof is allowed.

Once the decree concluding the case has been issued, new evidence of any sort may be admitted only under very limited circumstances.[186] This norm is designed to assure that dilatory tactics do not unduly delay the verdict while at the same time providing a protection against an unjust decision. New evidence may be admitted after the conclusion of the case only in three circumstances.

1. New evidence may be admitted when the case involves the private as opposed to the public good[187] *and* all the parties to the case agree to admit the new evidence.

---

[186] Similarly, new evidence is admitted on the appellate level in accord with the same limited circumstances (c. 1639, §2).

[187] See the commentary on c. 1431 for the means of distinguishing cases involving the public good from cases involving the private good.

2. New evidence may also be admitted in cases involving the public good even if one of the parties has objected to the proposal to admit new evidence. This may be done when a grave reason (*gravis ratio*) exists for admitting the new evidence

    a) provided that the judges first consult the parties about the matter and

    b) provided all danger of fraud or subornation has been removed.[188]

The judges assess whether the reason is grave and have the responsibility to determine whether or not the possibility of fraud or subornation has been removed.

3. In all types of cases, new evidence may be admitted whenever it is *probable*[189] that, unless the evidence is admitted, the ultimate decision will be unjust and hence subject to a petition for a *restitutio in integrum* for the reasons described in canon 1645, §2, 1°–3°. Thus, new evidence is to be admitted when:

    a) it is probable that the judgment would be rendered on the basis of false evidence (1°),

    b) a document has been discovered demanding a contrary decision (2°),

    c) the court has learned that its judgment would be based on the deceitful testimony (*dolus*) of one of the parties which is harmful to the interests of another party.[190]

Introduction of a New Document after the Conclusion

§2. The judge, moreover, can order or allow a document to be shown, which may have been unable to be shown earlier through no negligence of the interested person.

Beyond the three circumstances just described, judges may admit a document (see cc. 1544–1546) into the evidence when a party was legitimately impeded from presenting it earlier in the trial. On their own authority, the judges may also request a new document at this time.

Publication of New Proofs

§3. New proofs are to be published according to can. 1598, §1.

If and when any new evidence has been admitted into the acts, that new material is to be published in accord with canon 1598, §1. Given the strict rules for admitting evidence subsequent to the conclusion of the case, that new material almost inevitably involves new or very weighty information. Hence, publication is necessary to protect the right of defense.[191]

The Discussion Phase: Time Limit for Arguments and Observations

Canon 1601 — After the conclusion of the case, the judge is to determine a suitable period of time to present defense briefs or observations.

---

[188] The admission of new evidence is invalid if the parties are not consulted. But, while they must listen to the parties, the judges need not follow their advice or obtain their consent (c. 127, §2, 2°).

[189] The text requires the probability (though not absolute certainty) that injustice may result unless the new evidence is admitted. The mere possibility of an injustice is not sufficient, since the moral certitude required for the ultimate judgment need not exclude every possibility of the contrary (c. 1608, §1).

[190] The existence of fraudulent testimony may not necessarily require the admission of new evidence, since the tribunal may well determine that its decision would not be based on the deceitful claims. If that is the case, the trial may

move forward to a decision, although the judge should consider an appropriate penalty for the person who attempted to deceive the court (see cc. 1531, §1 and 1368).

[191] One should note that the reference is to the first and not the second paragraph of c. 1598. When evidence is brought forward subsequent to the initial publication but prior to the conclusion of the case, the judge has the discretion to determine that a new publication is not required (c. 1598, §2). The judge, however, does not have the same degree of flexibility regarding evidence admitted in accord with c. 1600.

The discussion phase of the trial begins after the conclusion of the case. The judge has the authority and duty to establish a reasonable period of time within which the parties, their advocates, the defender of the bond, and the promoter of justice may study the evidence and present their observations and arguments. That period of time is most appropriately specified in the decree of conclusion. The code does not suggest an appropriate length of time, leaving the determination to the judge. In establishing the appropriate time, the judge needs to balance two concerns: (1) avoiding needless delays so that the law's expectation of an expeditious trial (c. 1453) is respected, while (2) providing sufficient time for adequate study of the case. The judge may extend the time limit for just cause provided the trial as a whole is not unduly prolonged (c. 1465, §§2–3).

Norms Governing the Pleadings

Canon 1602 — §1. The defense briefs and the observations are to be written unless the judge, with the consent of the parties, considers a debate before a session of the tribunal to be sufficient.

§2. To print the defense briefs along with the principal documents requires the previous permission of the judge, without prejudice to the obligation of secrecy, if such exists.

§3. The regulations of the tribunal are to be observed regarding the length of the defense briefs, the number of copies, and other matters of this kind.

Normally, the observations and pleadings of the parties are to be presented in writing. Only with the parties' consent[192] may an oral discussion be substituted for written briefs. If an oral discussion is held, a notary is to be present (c. 1605).

Generally, written briefs are typed or prepared using a word processing program. If, however, there is any need or desire that the written briefs

[192] The consent of all the parties is required or the action is invalid (c. 127, §2, 1°).

be printed for publication, the judge must issue a specific order authorizing this. Such an authorization may be extended only if the obligation of secrecy is fully protected so that the rights and reputations of those involved in the trial are not impaired.

Particular law is to provide appropriate norms with regard to other matters concerning the briefs.

Opportunity for Rebuttal

Canon 1603 — §1. When the defense briefs and observations have been communicated to each party, either party is permitted to present responses within the brief time period established by the judge.

§2. The parties are given this right only once unless the judge decides that it must be granted a second time for a grave cause; then, however, the grant made to one party is considered as given to the other also.

Upon their completion, the pleadings and observations of the parties are made available for review in accord with the tribunal's norms (c. 1602, §3). The parties then have the right to present counterarguments within the time limit established by the judge.

There is a *right* to only one such rejoinder. For a serious reason, however, the judge may provide the parties the opportunity to present a second (not a third or subsequent) rejoinder. This opportunity cannot be granted to one party alone; if it is extended, all the parties must have the opportunity to present an additional counterargument.

Right of Last Response

§3. The promoter of justice and the defender of the bond have the right to reply a second time to the responses of the parties.

The promoter of justice and defender of the bond, when involved in a trial, have the right to a final response after the rejoinders presented by the parties. An exception to this rule is found in canon 1725; in penal trials the accused (or the advocate or procurator of the accused) has the right to speak last, not the promoter of justice.

Norms Governing Any Oral Discussion

Canon 1604 — §1. It is absolutely forbidden for information given to the judge by the parties, advocates, or even other persons to remain outside the acts of the case.

§2. If the discussion of the case has been done in writing, the judge can order a moderate oral debate to be held before a session of the tribunal in order to explain certain questions.

To preserve the integrity of the trial and to respect the canonical principle *quod non est in actis non est in mundo* (what is not in the acts does not exist), under no circumstances may information be given to the judge that is not incorporated into the acts of the case.

When written arguments have been prepared in accord with canon 1602, the judge may but need not call for an oral discussion to clarify various issues.

Record of an Oral Discussion

Canon 1605 — A notary is to be present at the oral debate mentioned in cann. 1602, §1 and 1604, §2 so that, if the judge orders it or a party requests it and the judge consents, the notary can immediately report in writing about what was discussed and concluded.

The presence of a notary at the oral discussions provided by canons 1602 and 1604 enables the judge to assure that significant points which emerge from the debate are incorporated into the acts of the case. Often, the oral discussion will contain nothing new, and the notary will not need to provide any record. On other occasions, however, the discussion may open up a new perspective or shed new light on the facts. When this happens, the judge should order the notary to record

the relevant points, or one of the other parties to the discussion may ask the judge to have the notary do so.

The Waiver of a Final Argument

Canon 1606 — If the parties have neglected to prepare a defense brief within the time available to them or have entrusted themselves to the knowledge and conscience of the judge, and if from the acts and proofs the judge considers the matter fully examined, the judge can pronounce the sentence immediately, after having requested the observations of the promoter of justice and the defender of the bond if they are involved in the trial.

The parties may forego their right to present a final argument, either by explicitly renouncing that right and leaving the matter to the conscience of the judge, or by allowing the time limit to present a defense to pass without any action. When this occurs, the judge may proceed immediately to a decision after first requesting the intervention of the defender of the bond and the promoter of justice whenever they are involved in the trial.

TITLE VII
THE PRONOUNCEMENTS OF THE JUDGE[193]
[cc. 1607–1618]

During a trial, judges are empowered to issue three types of decisions corresponding to the nature of the matters to be decided. Two of them, *definitive judgments* and *interlocutory judgments,* are defined in canon 1607. A judge may also decide certain matters by means of *judicial decrees,* which may be either merely procedural or sub-

---

[193] Wrenn, in *CLSA Com,* 994–997; Ryan, in *CLSGBI Com,* 904–910; Diego-Lora, in *Pamplona ComEng,* 994–1001; Acebal, in *Salamanca Com,* 782–788; Arroba Conde, in *Valencia Com,* 696–701; C. de Diego-Lora, in *Com Ex* IV/2, 1521–1612.

stantive in nature (c. 1617). Decrees are the usual means by which the judge governs the development of a trial.[194]

Definitive and Interlocutory Sentences

Canon 1607 — When a case has been handled in a judicial manner, if it is the principal case, the judge decides it through the definitive sentence; if an incidental case, through an interlocutory sentence, without prejudice to the prescript of can. 1589, §1.

This canon distinguishes the two types of sentences issued by ecclesiastical judges. A *definitive sentence* resolves the central issue or issues before the court.[195]

Decisions concerning related but incidental matters are rendered in one of three ways.[196] The decision may be issued in a separate *interlocutory sentence,* it may be incorporated into the definitive sentence, or, if the judge deems a full judicial sentence unnecessary, the question may be decided by means of a decree (c. 1589, §1).

Need for Moral Certitude

Canon 1608 — §1. For the pronouncement of any sentence, the judge must have moral certitude about the matter to be decided by the sentence.

To issue a judgment, the judge must reach moral certainty about the matter to be decided. This, however, is not moral certainty about any and all aspects of a case. Thus, a judge may have the required degree of certainty about the central question at issue while remaining uncertain about one or more related events or their significance.

Moral certitude is distinguished from absolute certitude on the one hand, and probability on the other. Pope Pius XII gave the classic description of moral certitude in an address to the Roman Rota of January 10, 1942.[197] To reach moral certitude, judges must be able to exclude the probability of error but are not held to the impossible and paralyzing standard of excluding all possibility of error.[198]

Reaching Moral Certitude

§2. The judge must derive this certitude from the acts and the proofs.

§3. The judge, however, must appraise the proofs according to the judge's own conscience, without prejudice to the prescripts of law concerning the efficacy of certain proofs.

Moral certitude *must be rooted in the evidence* contained in the acts of the case.[199] Thus, the judge's merely subjective conviction is not sufficient. The great challenge facing ecclesiastical judges is to sift through that evidence, understand it, and weigh its significance in order to reach certitude about the truth of the matter. Only then will the judgment be just.

The weighing of the evidence is both a science and an art. It is, as well, a great challenge. Judges are charged to assess the evidence and reach a decision *according to their own consciences.* That judgment of conscience is to be guided by the law and jurisprudence concerning the efficacy of vari-

---

[194] For example, the *libellus* is accepted or rejected and the parties cited by means of decrees (cc. 1505, §1; 1507); the terms of the controversy are specified by decree (c. 1513). Similarly, decrees are required for citing witnesses (c. 1556), declaring a party absent from trial (c. 1592), etc.

[195] For a discussion of the nature and importance of this judicial act, see Pompedda, "Decision-Sentence," 73–99, esp. 74–77.

[196] See the canons on incidental cases (cc. 1587–1591) for further reflections on interlocutory judgments.

[197] Pius XII, alloc, January 10, 1942, *AAS* 34 (1942) 338–342; translated in *CLD* 3, 606–611.

[198] This balanced understanding of moral certitude continues to guide the jurisprudence of ecclesiastical tribunals. See Pompedda, "Decision-Sentence," 85–93. Also see John Paul II, alloc, February 4, 1980, *AAS* 72 (1980) 172–178. Translated in Woestman, *Papal Allocutions,* 159–164.

[199] John Paul II, alloc, February 4, 1980, *AAS* 72 (1980) 175. Translated in Woestman, *Papal Allocutions,* 161– 162.

ous types of proofs.[200] But the freedom and responsibility of the judges to weigh the evidence in order to discover the truth is crucial. As Pompedda explains, in this process

> judicial formalism must not be its first guiding principle. More important is the free weighing of proofs.[201]

Judges are to form their consciences so that their judgments are in accord with the truth. This requires careful study of the evidence assembled and reflection on its significance in light of the Church's teaching and law. As in any process of conscience formation, however, this involves not only study and reflection but also a prayerful commitment to truth and justice.[202]

At times, the evidence can be so persuasive that judges can reach moral certitude without much difficulty. At other times, however, finding the truth is quite challenging and demands intense study and careful assessment. When certainty is elusive, a judge should not give up the search for truth easily; rather, when faced with doubts of law or of fact, those doubts should serve as "a further impetus to find the truth."[203] Pompedda describes vital qualities necessary for judges to fulfill their office faithfully:

> The judge must not only be endowed with a sufficient scientific preparation (canonical),

but he must be capable of practical judgment. He must also have some experience of both reality and of human nature. He must have a sagacious intelligence.[204]

Absence of Moral Certitude

§4. A judge who was not able to arrive at this certitude is to pronounce that the right of the petitioner is not established and is to dismiss the respondent as absolved, unless it concerns a case which has the favor of law, in which case the judge must pronounce for that.

When the judges are unable to reach moral certitude that the claim of the petitioner is established, the law requires that they rule in the negative. This rule holds unless the case involves a *favor of the law* in which case the judges "must pronounce for that" [i.e., for the favored position]. A favor of the law creates an exception to the burden of proof. The person whose position enjoys such a favor is free from the burden of proof (c. 1526, §2, 1°). Several classic favors of the law involve marriage cases. Canon 1060 establishes a presumption in favor of the validity of marriage.[205] Canon 1101, §1 establishes the presumption that the internal consent of the mind is in agreement with the words employed in a marriage ceremony. Another example is canon 1150: "In a doubtful matter the privilege of faith possesses the favor of the law."[206]

When significant doubts of fact remain that seem to preclude moral certitude, before issuing a definitive ruling, judges should take care that "reasonable and prudent efforts have been put

---

[200] Some of those guidelines are codified (e.g., c. 1541 on the weight of public documents, c. 1536 on the judicial confession of a party, c. 1679 on the proof required in marriage nullity cases). Canonical jurisprudence, especially that of the Roman Rota as well as papal allocutions to the Rota, also provide sources of accumulated wisdom to assist judges in assessing the evidence and reaching a decision. For example, these sources are extremely helpful in assessing the reports of experts (see the commentary on c. 1579).

[201] Pompedda, "Decision-Sentence," 85.

[202] Canon 1612, §1 illustrates this need for an attitude of discernment with its requirement that the introduction to the judicial sentence include an invocation of the Divine Name.

[203] Pompedda, "Decision-Sentence," 87.

[204] Ibid., 93.

[205] See the commentary on c. 1060. This presumption does not constitute an exception to the obligation that judges rule against a petition in the absence of moral certitude, but serves to reinforce that requirement.

[206] The proper interpretation and application of this privilege have been disputed. For details, see the commentary on c. 1150. Also see A. Mendonça, "The Correct Interpretation of Canons 1150 and 1608, §4," *Stud Can* 31 (1997) 475–512.

forth to provide necessary information to resolve those doubts."[207] Accordingly, judges have the duty to supply for the negligence of the parties in order to avoid injustice (c. 1452, §2).[208] If judges still do not have moral certitude, they are bound to rule in the negative.

Collegial Discussion of the Case

Canon 1609 — §1. In a collegiate tribunal the president of the college is to establish the date and time when the judges are to convene for deliberation; unless a special reason suggests otherwise, the meeting is to be held at the tribunal office.

§2. On the date assigned for the meeting, the individual judges are to submit their written conclusions on the merit of the case with the reasons in law and in fact which led them to their conclusions; these conclusions are to be added to the acts of the case and must be kept secret.

§3. After the invocation of the Divine Name, the individual judges are to present their conclusions in order of precedence, always beginning, however, with the *ponens* or *relator* of the case. A discussion then follows under the leadership of the tribunal president, especially to determine what must be established in the dispositive part of the sentence.

When the case has been entrusted to a college (panel) of judges,[209] this canon regulates the process by which they jointly discuss and decide the case.[210] The presiding judge is to schedule the day and time for the judges to discuss the case. While the meeting would normally be held at the tribunal office, the presiding judge may designate another place if there is a reason for doing so.

Prior to this meeting, each judge is to study the evidence and prepare his or her preliminary conclusions in writing. The judges must not merely state those conclusions, but include a summary of their reasons in both law and fact. These written opinions (*vota*) become part of the acts of the case, although normally they are kept secret.

The college of judges meets in a context of prayer, beginning with an invocation of the Divine Name. Next, the judges in order of precedence, beginning with the *ponens* or *relator* (c. 1429), make known their conclusions. The presiding judge then leads a discussion, focusing primarily on the *dispositive part* of the sentence.[211]

Right of Judges to Retract Initial Conclusions

§4. In the discussion each judge is permitted to withdraw from his or her original conclusion. The judge who is unwilling to assent to the decision of the others, however, can demand that his or her conclusions be transmitted to the higher tribunal if an appeal is made.

---

[207] Pompedda, "Decision-Sentence," 94.

[208] Pompedda's remarks about the responsibility of the judges in this regard merit a fuller quotation: "It is the obligation of the judge to attempt to resolve the *dubia* which arise in the course of the trial by seeking out that information which could provide answers to the significant issues which remain unresolved in the instruction. It must be remembered that the ecclesiastical judge is the ruler of the cause (*'dominus causae'*). It would be a negligence of the judge were he not to investigate obvious elements or potential proofs which could afford a basis for moral certitude in the case" ("Decision-Sentence," 94).

[209] The general norms governing collegial acts apply to the acts of a judicial college. See the commentaries on cc. 115, §2; 119, 2°; and 166.

[210] *CCEO* 1292, §§1–2 differs in some respects. A clause was added to §1 indicating that only the judges of the college may be present for the meeting. Clauses were also added to §2 specifying that (1) the judges are not to indicate their names on their written conclusions and (2) those conclusions are to be authenticated by all the judges; (3) further, a specific reference was made to §4 of the same canon. For additional details, see Abbass, "Contentious Trials," 894–896.

[211] The dispositive part of the sentence is the decision itself, the affirmative or negative response to the doubt (*dubium*). While the judges will necessarily discuss the reasoning to be articulated in the sentence, the primary purpose of this session of the judges is not to draft the argument but to reach their decision.

In light of the discussion, the judges are free to retract their initial conclusions. While the written *vota* reflecting their prior conclusions remain a part of the acts of the case, those initial opinions do not bind the judges.

A college often reaches a unanimous verdict. When unanimity is not forthcoming, however, the judges' vote and the court's decision are determined by the majority (see c. 1426, §1). When a split vote occurs, the judge or judges in the minority may demand that their dissenting opinion(s) be transmitted to the higher tribunal *"if an appeal is made."* [212] The judge or judges in the minority, however, have no right to lodge an appeal. Only the parties (including the defender of the bond and promoter of justice when they are involved) may lodge an appeal. [213]

Deferral of a Decision

§5. If the judges are unwilling or unable to arrive at a sentence during the first discussion, the decision can be deferred to a new meeting, but not for more than a week, unless the instruction

[212] This is a new provision that did not exist in the 1917 code. The Eastern code differs, requiring that the written conclusions of all of the judges, without names indicated, be transmitted to the appellate court (*CCEO* 1292, §4; note that the CLSA translation does not accurately capture the Latin). See Abbass, "Contentious Trials," 896–897.

[213] In marriage nullity cases, c. 1682, §1 mandates the ex officio transmission of a first affirmative decision for review by the appellate tribunal. Technically, this is not an appeal, although the parties or defender of the bond may lodge appeals which are transmitted along with the case. If no genuine appeal is lodged, do dissenting judges retain the right to demand that their conclusions be transmitted to the higher tribunal as part of the ex officio transmission of the acts? Strictly speaking, c. 1609, §4 indicates that this right exists only *"if an appeal is made."* In practice, it would be appropriate to forward the dissenting opinion if the judge involved so requests. This would reflect a respect for the judge(s) in the minority, be in keeping with canonical equity, and manifest to the appellate tribunal the care with which the judgment was reached. Morrisey offers a similar opinion in *RRAO 1994,* 146–147.

of the case must be completed according to the norm of can. 1600.

When, as a result of their discussions, the judges are unable or unwilling to make a final determination, they may defer their decision for a brief period, normally not to exceed a week. This provides time for additional study and reflection. The presiding judge is responsible for scheduling this second and final meeting at which the decision is made. At times, however, the discussion among the judges may lead to the conviction that a just decision is not possible without further instruction of the case. When this occurs, the instruction phase may be reopened (c. 1600) and sufficient time allotted to complete the gathering of additional evidence. Once the new instruction is completed, the new proofs are published, the case is concluded, and the decision-making phase is reinitiated.

The Sentence of a Sole Judge

Canon 1610 — §1. If there is only one judge, he will write the sentence himself.

When the case is entrusted to a sole judge, the provisions of canon 1609 are unnecessary and the judge proceeds to making his decision and drafting the sentence. Prior to finalizing his decision, however, the judge may wish to discuss the evidence with one or more assessors (see cc. 1424 and 1425, §4). Such a discussion brings to the sole judge many of the benefits associated with a college. The assessors may provide alternative points of view and additional insights to help clarify the judge's thinking.

Sentence of a Judicial College

§2. In a collegiate tribunal, it is for the *ponens* or *relator* to write the sentence, selecting the reasons from those the individual judges brought forth during the discussion, unless a majority of the judges have already determined the reasons to be presented. The sentence must then be submitted for the approval of the individual judges.

In a collegial tribunal, the task of drafting the sentence is entrusted to the *ponens* or *relator* (c. 1429). The judges may give explicit instructions to the *ponens* concerning the line of argumentation to be used. In the absence of such directives, the *ponens* is to compose the sentence using the reasons which emerged in the judges' discussion. Once drafted, the sentence must be circulated to the individual judges for approval. If one or more of the judges is dissatisfied with the sentence, he or she may request that the *ponens* redraft the text. At times, the members of the judicial college may choose to meet in order to agree upon the final text.

Time Limits for Issuing Sentences

§3. The sentence must be issued no more than a month from the day on which the case was decided unless in a collegiate tribunal the judges set a longer period for a grave reason.

Whether rendered by a sole judge or a college, the sentence should be drafted and issued within a month of the decision. This norm is intended to prevent any serious delays in the final stage of the instance. When the case was decided by a judicial college, however, for a grave cause the judges may establish a longer period for issuing the sentence. This reflects the understandable reality that the process of having three or five judges come to agreement on a text may occasionally involve delays.

Nature and Essential Elements of a Sentence

Canon 1611 — The sentence must:
  1° decide the controversy deliberated before the tribunal with an appropriate response given to the individual doubts;
  2° determine what obligations have arisen for the parties from the trial and how they must be fulfilled;
  3° set forth the reasons or motives in law and in fact on which the dispositive part of the sentence is based;
  4° determine the expenses of the litigation.

This canon defines the nature and essential elements of the judicial sentence. The following canon (1612) deals with the formalities of a sentence.

Most important, the sentence must "decide the controversy." The terms of the controversy were determined at the joinder of issues (c. 1513) or in any subsequent legitimate amendment of the issue (c. 1514). If multiple grounds are at issue, the sentence must respond to each of the questions. Failure to respond to the terms of the controversy may lead to the irremediable nullity of the sentence (c. 1620, 8°). The requirement that the sentence settle the controversy also provides an important principle for the crafting of a judicial sentence. The argument of the sentence must be focused on the specific doubt or doubts (*dubium* or *dubia*), and not wander into unnecessary discussions of related but irrelevant information learned during the trial. A sentence will be much more convincing to the extent that its author focuses precisely on a response to the specific controversy.

The sentence must also explicitly specify the obligations of the parties resulting from the sentence. Since the sentence is a juridic act, it must clarify for the parties the consequences of the decision. At times, the law itself requires that a sentence include certain requirements. For example, in marriage nullity cases the sentence must remind the parties of their moral and legal obligations toward children (c. 1689).[214] At other times, the decision itself will impose an obligation which must be clearly communicated to the parties.

Third, the sentence must set forth the reasons motivating the decision both *at law* and *in terms of the facts* of each case. In other words, it must contain a reasoned argument in which the evidence adduced in the instruction phase is analyzed in light of the law and jurisprudence to justify the tribunal's decision. It is not enough for the sentence simply to assert a conviction; it must demonstrate the reasoning which led the judges to

---

[214] M. S. Foster, "Divorce and Remarriage: What about the Children?" *Stud Can* 31 (1997) 165–171.

reach moral certitude. A judicial argument, then, is much more than a summary or recapitulation of the testimony and other evidence. The sentence must establish the canonical bridge linking the specific facts of the case with the relevant law in order to support the decision. A sentence lacking the motives for the decision is remediably null (c. 1622, 2°).

Finally, the sentence is to apportion in a just manner the parties' obligations regarding the expenses of the trial (e.g., costs such as those envisioned in cc. 1571 and 1580). Normally, the particular law or policies of each tribunal would establish a standard schedule of fees and who is responsible for them (c. 1649). This enables the parties to have reasonable expectations regarding costs at the beginning of the trial. Even if a policy is in place, the sentence must apply that policy by specifying costs and addressing questions such as any additional expenses that were incurred. It also must reduce costs or provide gratuitous assistance for those parties unable to pay court costs (c. 1649, §1, 3°).

There is no separate appeal from the determination of expenses and fees, although there is a fifteen day period during which a person may have recourse to the original judge seeking an adjustment of the charges (c. 1649, §2).

Formalities of a Sentence

Canon 1612 — §1. After the invocation of the Divine Name, the sentence must express in order the judge or the tribunal, the petitioner, the respondent, and the procurator, with their names and domiciles correctly designated, and the promoter of justice and defender of the bond if they took part in the trial.

§2. Next, it must briefly relate the facts together with the conclusions of the parties and the formula of the doubts.

§3. The dispositive part of the sentence follows the above, preceded by the reasons on which it is based.

§4. It is to conclude with the indication of the date and the place where it was rendered, with the signature of the judge or, if it is a collegiate tribunal, of all the judges, and the notary.

This canon specifies the external formalities, sometimes termed the solemnities, required in a sentence. The sentence contains the following principal parts: (1) an introduction, (2) a report of certain essential facts, (3) the argument leading to and justifying the decision, and (4) a conclusion.

The Introduction: First, the sentence must contain an invocation of the Divine Name (see the commentary on c. 1608). Then it must include the following data:

1. the name(s) of the judge(s);
2. the names of the petitioner, the respondent, and (if any were appointed) their procurators;
3. the domiciles of the parties in the case (see cc. 102–106);
4. the names of the promoter of justice and the defender of the bond if they took part in the trial.

While not specifically mentioned, the specific title of competence (tribunal jurisdiction) should also be indicated here.

The Facts: Next, the sentence must "briefly relate the facts" along with the conclusions of the parties and the formulation of the doubt (*dubium*). The description is to be brief and, hence, need not involve a lengthy and detailed narrative. The content of the "Facts Section" will vary depending on the nature of the case at issue. For example, in a marriage nullity case, the relevant facts would include information such as the date and place of the exchange of consent, the length of the common life, whether children were born of the union, and similar information. The report on the facts must also include the specific formulation of the doubt, so as to clarify the exact nature of the issue(s), and the stance of the parties with regard to the issues.[215]

---

[215] The petitioner, as the initiator of the suit, will normally favor an affirmative response to the doubt. The stance of a

The Argument and Decision: This is the heart of the sentence. It must discuss both the applicable law and relevant facts in light of the specific question(s) at issue (c. 1611, 3°). Thus, the argument normally begins with a discussion *in iure,* an exposition of the law and jurisprudence applicable to the issues in the case. Next, in light of those issues, the argument must apply the law to the specific facts of the case. This part of the sentence is the most challenging to compose. A judicial sentence must not simply recite the story or sequence of events (e.g., of a marriage), but carefully analyze those events in light of the Church's law and doctrine. This discussion specifies the reasoning which led to the conclusions. That analysis leads to the decision or *dispositive section* of the sentence. The tribunal's verdict is phrased as a response in the affirmative or in the negative to the doubt(s) (*dubium*) specified in the joinder of issues (see c. 1611, 1°).

The Conclusion: The sentence concludes by indicating the date and place where it was rendered. It must also include the signature(s) of the judge(s) who issued it (not merely the signature of the presiding judge or that of the *ponens*) and the signature of the notary. Failure to include these formalities results in the remediable nullity of the sentence (c. 1622, 3° and 4°).

Adaptation of Rules
for an Interlocutory Sentence

Canon 1613 — The rules proposed above for a definitive sentence are to be adapted for an interlocutory sentence.

respondent, however, may vary significantly. The "Facts Section" should briefly indicate how the respondent has reacted to the issue. He or she may be opposed to the petitioner's plea in whole or in part or may agree with it wholly or partially. He or she may fail to respond to the citation and be decreed absent (c. 1592), or his or her whereabouts may be unknown (c. 1409, §2). Finally, anything unusual about the respondent's standing at trial (e.g., he or she was a minor who stood trial through a parent or guardian, cc. 1478–1479) should also be indicated.

This canon clarifies that the norms concerning definitive sentences (cc. 1608–1612) also apply to interlocutory sentences. Thus, while an interlocutory sentence involves issues of lesser moment, it is a true judicial sentence and must settle the specific controversy, indicate its motives, and follow the basic formalities required for a definitive sentence.[216]

Based on his analysis of the context of this canon, Wrenn concluded that the legislator did not intend that the norms of the following canons (cc. 1614–1616) be applied to interlocutory sentences.[217] Diego-Lora does not explicitly cite Wrenn's conclusion, but likewise argues that canon 1613 refers only to the requirements of canons 1608–1612.[218] Hence, given the context of canon 1613, the specific requirements of canons 1614–1616 concerning the publication of a sentence evidently do not apply to interlocutory sentences. This conclusion is supported by the fact that no appeal is possible against an interlocutory sentence which does not have the force of a definitive judgment (c. 1629, 4°). Thus, the provisions of the interlocutory sentence are published as part of the publication of the definitive sentence, and can be challenged along with the definitive judgment.

Publication of a Sentence

Canon 1614 — The sentence is to be published as soon as possible, with an indication of the means by which it can be challenged. It has no force before publication even if the dispositive part was made known to the parties with the permission of the judge.[219]

---

[216] One should recall that incidental cases need not be decided in interlocutory sentences, but may be decided within the definitive sentence (c. 1589, §2) or by judicial decrees (cc. 1589, §1 and 1590, §2).

[217] Wrenn, in *CLSA Com,* 996.

[218] Diego-Lora, in *Com Ex* IV/2, 1580–1582.

[219] *CCEO* 1297 differs in some respects. For example, to avoid any ambiguity, the term *intimetur* (communicate) is used rather than the term *publicetur* here and in *CCEO* 1298. For comments on the reasons for this and

This very brief canon, along with canon 1615, protects a vital value, namely, that of making the parties fully aware of the decision and its motives. Only in this way will the parties be able either to appropriate the decision and make it their own or lodge a reasoned challenge to the decision. The canon contains three vitally important provisions.

First, the sentence must be published "as soon as possible" (*quam primum*). While the canon does not further specify the time, justice requires that there be no delays and that the sentence be published immediately upon its completion,[220] or at the least within a day or two. The sentence is to be published even to a party who was decreed absent from the trial (see commentary on cc. 1592–1593).

Second, the parties are also to be informed of the means by which the sentence may be challenged. That information can be included in the text of the definitive sentence itself or in the decree or other document communicated as part of the publication. Such challenges to the sentence include an appeal (cc. 1628–1640) lodged against the substance of the decision and a complaint of nullity against the sentence (cc. 1619–1627) lodged against alleged procedural irregularities or violations of rights.[221] The "indication of the means by which it can be challenged" does not require a complete explanation, but a brief notice of the types of challenges available and direction on how to initiate such challenges.[222]

Finally, the right to challenge a sentence requires that the parties know both the decision and the reasoning justifying it.[223] Therefore, the time period for lodging an appeal does not begin until the sentence is published (see c. 1634, §2). Until it is legitimately published, the sentence *has no force,* even if the dispositive part (the decision proper) was communicated to the parties. Thus, failure to publish the sentence, while not resulting in the invalidity of the sentence itself, renders it legally ineffective and prevents the trial process from being completed.[224]

Canon 1614 is silent about how to handle the publication of a sentence which contains a discussion of a particular act that was exempted from publication (c. 1598, §1). Wrenn and Ryan both agree that this evidence should still be considered secret at the time of the publication of the sentence and that a portion of the sentence likewise could be restricted from publication.[225] Daneels would also permit this possibility, but only under very exceptional circumstances.[226]

Obviously, it is impossible to publish a sentence to a party who was not able to be located. In these circumstances, provided that all reasonable efforts were made to locate the person, the tribunal can move to the execution of the sentence. This reflects the ancient principle that no one can be held to the impossible.[227] Should the whereabouts of the missing party later come to light, the sentence should be published to that person.[228]

---

other differences, see J. Abbass, "Contentious Trials," 897–899.

[220] Canon 1610, §3 requires that the sentence be drafted and issued within a month of the decision, except when, for grave cause, a college of judges establishes a longer period.

[221] *CCEO* 1297 does not require that the sentence indicate all of the methods by which it may be challenged, but only the ways in which it may be appealed.

[222] An invitation to contact the judge or an advocate for further information is advisable as part of this indication.

[223] John Paul II, alloc, January 26, 1989, *AAS* 81 (1989) 924–925. Translated in Woestman, *Papal Allocutions,* 206–207.

[224] Johnson, "Publish and Be Damned," 223.

[225] Wrenn, in *CLSA Com,* 997; idem, *Procedures,* 69; Ryan, in *CLSGBI Com,* 910.

[226] Daneels, "The Right of Defence," 90. He states: "Perhaps, though, a certain analogy can be accepted with c. 1598, §1, with a caution that the exception not become the rule and that the right of defence always remains intact."

[227] *RI,* n. 6, *CorpusIC* II, 1122.

[228] Depending on the type of case, the nature of the subject matter, and the reasons why the respondent was not located, the decision may or may not be subject to challenge. See the commentary on challenges against the sentence (title VIII, cc. 1619–1640) and on *res iudicata* and *restitutio in integrum* (title IX, cc. 1641–1648).

Methods of Publication

Canon 1615 — Publication or communication of the sentence can be done either by giving a copy of the sentence to the parties or their procurators or by sending them a copy according to the norm of can. 1509.[229]

A sentence may be published in one of two ways. The first method is to hand a copy to the parties or their procurators. Note that this provision is not fulfilled by giving a copy of the sentence to an advocate of the parties, unless that advocate was also appointed a procurator.[230] No special mandate is required for a procurator to accept the sentence (see cc. 1484–1485).

The second method is to send a copy of the sentence to the parties in the same way that citations are communicated (see the commentary on canon 1509).

The 1917 code provided three methods of publishing the sentence. The first was to cite the parties to appear at the tribunal for a solemn reading of the sentence. The second was to inform the parties that the sentence was available for their inspection at the tribunal. Neither of these methods was adopted for the current code.[231] The third was to mail a copy of the sentence to the parties,

which corresponds to the second method of the current legislation.

Although it received less attention during the revision process, many of the concerns associated with the publication of the acts have also been raised concerning the publication of the sentence.[232] While this is not necessarily a problem in other contentious trials, in marriage nullity cases the publication is particularly sensitive because of the nature of the sentence. There are two audiences to which a sentence of marriage nullity is directed. First and foremost, the sentence is a legal argument crafted for the court of appeal. In order to address the appellate judges effectively, the sentence necessarily must narrow its focus tightly, discuss jurisprudential issues, strongly assert its conclusions, and perhaps even more strongly respond to counterarguments raised by the defender of the bond or one of the parties. The second audience of the sentence, however, are the two persons whose broken union was the focus of the tribunal's investigation. While the parties need to understand the tribunal's reasoning, the blunt legal manner in which a judicial sentence is crafted is not necessarily the most effective, sensitive, or helpful means to communicate that reasoning to them. A legally well-argued sentence does not communicate the whole picture of the broken relationship. It uses language that may be hard for the parties to understand. Its narrowly focused analysis of the broken relationship from the point of view of the Church's law and jurisprudence may be experienced as cold, harsh, foreign, or insensitive by the parties who lived through those tragic circumstances and whose emotions may still be rubbed raw. Thus, in marriage nullity cases, merely impersonally mailing

---

[229] *CCEO* 1298, consistent with *CCEO* 1297, uses only the term *intimatio sententiae* rather than the term *publicatio seu intimatio* of the Latin code. This amendment reflected a decision consistently to use one term and avoid the potential ambiguities connected with the Latin code's use of differing terms in cc. 1614, 1615, 1621, 1623, 1630, and 1646, §2. For a fuller treatment of the intent of the drafters of the Eastern code, see Abbass, "Contentious Trials," 899–901.

[230] The possibility of publishing the sentence to an advocate was rejected during the code revision process. See *Comm* 16 (1984) 68–69.

[231] These options were suppressed in the first schema of the revision process, *Comm* 8 (1976) 190. On December 13, 1978, the *coetus* on procedural law considered reinstating the option of a solemn reading, but decided against it (*Comm* 11 [1979] 142–143).

[232] See the commentary on c. 1598, §1 for further discussion. In addition to the sources cited there, see also J. Bernhard, "A propos de la publication de la sentence dans les procédures en déclaration de nullité de mariage," in *Iustus Iudex: Festgabe für Paul Wesemann zum 75. Geburtstag von seinen Freunden und Schülern,* ed. K. Lüdicke, H. Mussinghoff, and H. Schwendenwein, (Essen: Ludgerus-Verlag, 1990) 387–399.

the sentence to the parties often is counterproductive and even hurtful. Certainly, in marriage nullity cases judges face a tremendous challenge in composing sentences that are both legally correct and persuasive and pastorally sensitive and constructive. For these reasons, despite the added time required, many judges prefer to invite the parties to come to the tribunal where the sentence can be communicated personally and discussed in a manner that helps the parties to understand the court's findings.

Correction of a Sentence

Canon 1616 — §1. If in the text of the sentence an error in calculations turns up, a material error occurs in transcribing the dispositive section or in relating the facts or the petitions of the parties, or the requirements of can. 1612, §4 are omitted, the tribunal which rendered the sentence must correct or complete it either at the request of a party or *ex officio*, but always after the parties have been heard and a decree appended to the bottom of the sentence.

§2. If any party objects, the incidental question is to be decided by a decree.

If any of the errors or inaccuracies described in the first paragraph of this canon are discovered in the published sentence, those must be corrected. This, however, may be accomplished without a full challenge against the sentence. The tribunal may make such corrections *ex officio* or in response to the request of one of the parties.

If a correction needs to be made, the parties must first be notified and given the opportunity to comment. The amendment is then made by appending a decree at the end of the sentence.

If a party objects to the proposed amendment, that objection is dealt with as an incidental question and decided by a decree (not an interlocutory sentence). The presiding judge alone (rather than the full *turnus*) or an auditor is able to deal with this incidental case (c. 1590, §2). There is no appeal of the decision in this sort of incidental matter unless that appeal is made as part of a wider challenge of the sentence (c. 1629, 4°).

Requirements for Judicial Decrees

Canon 1617 — Other pronouncements of the judge besides the sentence are decrees, which have no force if they are not merely procedural unless they express the reasons at least in a summary fashion or refer to reasons expressed in another act.

In discharging their responsibility to conduct the trial, judges make numerous pronouncements and decisions. The most important of these are sentences, either definitive or interlocutory; other decisions are issued in the form of decrees. This canon reflects the general norm that decrees contain at least a summary of the motivating reasons (c. 51). But canon 1617 goes further, specifying that a judicial decree has no force unless the reasons are included in the decree itself or in some other procedural act to which the decree refers.[233]

Canon 1617 also contains an important exception. When the decree of a judge is merely procedural (e.g., that the parties be cited, that the acts be published), then it need not incorporate the reasons. This is because the reasons for procedural decrees are enshrined in the law and the process itself and require no further explanation.

Decrees and Interlocutory Sentences with Definitive Force

Canon 1618 — An interlocutory sentence or a decree has the force of a definitive sentence if it pre-

---

[233] A new periodical of the Roman Rota, *Decreta,* now publishes selected decrees which can serve as models for judges in crafting their own decrees. Volume 1 of *Decreta,* for instance, contains decrees confirming affirmative sentences in marriage cases (c. 1682, §2), admitting or rejecting a *libellus* (c. 1505), adding a new ground in marriage nullity cases (c. 1683), and dealing with complaints of nullity of sentences (cc. 1620 and 1622).

vents a trial or puts an end to a trial or some grade of a trial with respect to at least some party in the case.

This canon[234] generically defines the circumstances in which an interlocutory sentence or a decree has the force of a definitive sentence. These include, for example, a decree deciding a peremptory exception (c. 1462), a decree rejecting a *libellus* (c. 1505), a decree declaring a petitioner absent from the trial (c. 1594), and an appellate court's decree of confirmation of an affirmative marriage nullity decision (c. 1682, §2). Clarifying these circumstances is important because, in a case in which a decree or interlocutory sentence has such a definitive effect, it is treated differently when it comes to the question of an appeal. Decrees or interlocutory sentences that do not have the force of a definitive sentence are not subject to a direct appeal; however, those with the force of a definitive sentence are subject to an appeal (c. 1629, 4°).[235]

the sentence, allows a party to challenge the decision on the basis of a denial of rights or any significant procedural irregularity. The second, the appeal, allows a party to challenge the decision on the basis of its substance in law or in fact.

The right to challenge a sentence, however, is not unlimited. To prevent dilatory tactics and harassment through unending litigation, canon law provides a measure of juridic stability for the decisions of ecclesiastical tribunals. Thus, to understand fully both the possibilities and limits connected with challenges against a sentence, title VIII needs to be situated within the context of title IX, on the *res iudicata* (the adjudged matter) which gives certain decisions a stability that is not subject to most challenges. There are also the extraordinary challenges of a sentence known as: (1) a new presentation of a case, which is available for cases involving the status of persons only (c. 1644), and (2) the *restitutio in integrum* (cc. 1645–1648).

TITLE VIII
CHALLENGE OF THE SENTENCE[236]
[cc. 1619–1640]

One or more of the parties to a trial may be aggrieved by the decision of the tribunal. In these circumstances, the law provides avenues to challenge the sentence. Ordinarily, two avenues are available. The first, a complaint of nullity against

CHAPTER I
COMPLAINT OF NULLITY
AGAINST THE SENTENCE
[cc. 1619–1627]

Sanation of Some Null Acts

Canon 1619 — Without prejudice to cann. 1622 and 1623, whenever a case involves the good of private persons, the sentence itself sanates the nullities of acts established by positive law which were not declared to the judge before the sentence even though they were known to the party proposing the complaint.

The important values of assuring that justice is not thwarted by insignificant errors or dilatory tactics and of preserving the security of judicial decisions motivate the provision for the sanation (healing) of some procedural irregularities by the sentence itself. This occurs when the following conditions are verified:

---

[234] It might have been more logically placed near the beginning of this title, after c. 1607.

[235] Canon 1505, §4 specifies the manner in which recourse can be made against the rejection of a *libellus*.

[236] Wrenn, in *CLSA Com,* 997–1002; Ryan, in *CLSGBI Com,* 911–919; Diego-Lora, in *Pamplona ComEng,* 1001–1013; Acebal, in *Salamanca Com,* 788–796; Arroba Conde, in *Valencia Com,* 701–708; Stankiewicz, in *Com Ex* IV/2, 1613–1642; P. Moneta, in *Com Ex* IV/2, 1643–1672.

1. the nullity results merely from positive ecclesiastical law and not from the natural law;[237]

2. the party making the complaint knew of the cause of the nullity during the trial but did not raise the question earlier;[238]

3. the matter involves the private rather than the public good;[239]

4. the complaint does not involve one of the causes of remediable nullity (c. 1622), which a party may challenge for three months after the notification of the publication of the sentence (c. 1623).

Causes of Irremediable Nullity

Canon 1620 — A sentence suffers from the defect of irremediable nullity if:

1° it was rendered by an absolutely incompetent judge;

2° it was rendered by a person who lacks the power of judging in the tribunal in which the case was decided;

3° a judge rendered a sentence coerced by force or grave fear;

4° the trial took place without the judicial petition mentioned in can. 1501 or was not instituted against some respondent;

5° it was rendered between parties, at least one of whom did not have standing in the trial;

6° someone acted in the name of another without a legitimate mandate;

7° the right of defense was denied to one or the other party;

8° it did not decide the controversy even partially.

There are eight headings of irremediable or incurable nullity listed here.[240] Each touches on important values that the trial process must preserve. Thus, a failure to foster and protect those values robs the sentence of any force and leaves it vulnerable to challenge. Irremediable nullity results from the following causes:

1. The sentence was rendered by a judge who was *absolutely incompetent.* Absolute incompetence results from the nature of the issue (e.g., questions reserved to the Rota), the standing of the person (e.g., cases involving heads of state), or the grade of the trial (e.g., a

---

[237] For example, in its essence the right of defense is rooted in the natural law; hence a direct violation of that right is not sanated (see the commentary on c. 1620, 7°). The relative incompetence of a judge or the omission of a required signature are matters of positive law and hence may be sanated if the other conditions are verified.

[238] Wrenn in *CLSA Com,* 998, explains that the purpose here is to "dissuade parties from delaying to denounce invalid acts until after the sentence, with a view to undermining the entire proceedings."

[239] See the commentary on cc. 223 and 1431 for a discussion of the public good. By definition, cases involving marriage nullity, the separation of spouses, and penalties always concern the public good (cc. 1691, 1696, 1728, §1). When cases involve the private good, the judge proceeds only at the request of the parties. However, when the public good is at issue (i.e., when concerns of significance to the wider community are at stake), once the trial has been initiated, the judge has the duty to seek the truth and do justice (c. 1452).

[240] Canon 1669, however, explicitly establishes the nullity of a sentence reached by the oral contentious process when that process is excluded by law. Is this a ninth example of irremediable nullity? L. Wrenn, in *CLSA Com,* 1007, concludes the nullity is remediable. M. Ryan and D. Kelly, in *CLSGBI Com,* 912 and 931, L. Madero, in *Pamplona ComEng,* 1029, and A. Stankiewicz and L. Madero in *Com Ex* IV/2, 1622 and 1791, however, all hold it is irremediable. This author agrees that the use of the oral contentious process in a case where it is prohibited by law is a ninth example of irremediable nullity. This conclusion is based on the fact that c. 1669 treats this as a very serious form of nullity, making no exception for the appellate court to accept the sentence as sanated due to the passage of time. Unlike the other bases of irremediable nullity, however, the court itself is charged to act ex officio in voiding the sentence and not to wait for one of the parties to lodge a complaint of nullity.

first instance tribunal rendering judgment in second or higher instances), and is defined in canons 1406, §2 and 1440. All other incompetence is relative in nature (c. 1407, §2) and does not result in irremediable nullity.

2. The sentence was rendered by a person who "lacks the power of judging in the tribunal in which the case was decided." In other words, the person must be duly appointed as a judge for that specific tribunal by the ecclesiastical authority responsible for the provision of that office (see cc. 1419–1421).[241]

3. The judge issued the sentence coerced by force or grave fear. This canon applies the general norm concerning force (c. 125, §1) to ecclesiastical trials. In the case of grave fear, however, there is a modification. Generally, acts placed out of grave fear are valid "unless the law provides otherwise" (c. 125, §2). For ecclesiastical trials, canon 1620, 3° provides otherwise, and a sentence coerced by grave fear is irremediably null.

4. An ecclesiastical trial must be initiated through a judicial petition or *libellus* (cc. 1501–1504) lodged by someone with a right to do so (e.g., cc. 1674, 1708, 1721). In the absence of any such petition, signed by the petitioner or his or her procurator (c. 1504, 3°), the process is not a genuine trial and has no force. Similarly, the petition must be lodged against some respondent. If there is no respondent, there is no trial.[242] One should note that this

cause of irremediable nullity does not apply to cases in which a respondent cannot be located or is decreed absent from trial. In these situations, there is a respondent, even if that person is not involved in the trial.

5. Canons 1478, 1480, and 1674 (for marriage cases) clarify who has standing in court. A minor (see c. 97, §1) normally stands trial through a parent or guardian, although in some circumstances he or she may stand trial personally (c. 1478, §3). The question of a petitioner's right to stand in court should be resolved at the time of the presentation of the *libellus,* and the petition rejected when the petitioner lacks standing (c. 1505, §2, 2°). If, nonetheless, a sentence is issued in a case where any of the parties did not have standing in court, that sentence is irremediably null.

6. A mandate is a legally binding authorization to act in the name of another party. A procurator must present a mandate before representing a party in court (c. 1484, §1).[243] The mandate may be provided by the party directly or, in certain circumstances, may be granted by the judge.[244] An ordinary mandate provides a limited authorization for the procurator to act in the name of a party; without a special mandate, however, certain actions cannot be undertaken (see c. 1485). If one person acts in the name of another without a legitimate mandate or acts beyond the scope of a mandate, the right of de-

---

[241] This is rooted in the ancient rule of law that what judges do outside the scope of their office has no legal force. *RI,* n. 26, *CorpusIC* II, 1122.

[242] A person may request an ecclesiastical authority to clarify some matter that does not involve a respondent (e.g., baptismal status, qualification for an ecclesiastical office). In these cases, the responses of the ecclesiastical authority may be juridic acts with canonical consequences, but they are administrative in nature and do not involve a trial.

[243] See the commentary on c. 1484, §2 for the narrowly defined circumstances when a procurator may act without a mandate.

[244] Canon 1481, §3 allows the judge ex officio to appoint a "defender" (*defensor*) in contentious trials involving minors or the public good, except for marriage cases. Similarly, the judge may appoint or admit a guardian or curator for minors or those with diminished mental capacity or deprived of the administration of goods (c. 1478). F. Morrisey discusses the possibility of a judge appointing a procurator in marriage nullity cases in *RRAO 1995,* 105–106.

fense of the party is impaired, and the judicial actions of the procurator are invalid. If not corrected during the course of the trial (e.g., by the party personally placing the act or extending the mandate of the procurator who then places the act), the sentence is irremediably null.[245]

7. The right of defense is a natural human right as well as an ecclesiastical right enjoyed by the Christian faithful (see c. 221, §1).[246] Its denial offends against human dignity, and results in the irremediable nullity of the sentence. The canon speaks of a *denial* of the right of defense. Thus, it is important to distinguish the following:

a) The failure of a party to exercise the right of defense is not in any way a denial of that right.[247] Thus, if a party communicates a waiver of his or her rights, or if the tribunal legitimately decrees a party absent from the trial (c. 1592), no complaint of nullity can later be upheld on the basis of canon 1620, 7°.

b) Actions which might in some way limit a person's right of defense without denying it do not lead to the nullity of the sentence. Thus, a judge has the right to curb an excessive number of witnesses (c. 1553) or exclude a specific witness for a just cause (c. 1555). Similarly, a judge may decide

to exclude an expert (c. 1576) or not admit an expert designated by a party (c. 1581). Even actions that may impair the right of defense to some degree do not necessarily amount to a denial of the right of defense.[248]

The jurisprudence of the Roman Rota and the Apostolic Signatura helps to clarify the content of the right of defense.[249] In brief, the right of defense can be said to include the rights (a) to be notified of the trial, (b) to know the issue, (c) to present proofs, (d) to know the proofs relevant to deciding the issue, (e) to present arguments, and (f) to respond in defense of one's position.[250]

8. The object of the trial is formulated at the joinder of the issues, phrased in the form of one or more questions or doubts (the *dubium* or *dubia,* c. 1513). That formulation of the issue

---

[245] It should be noted that null judicial acts normally lead only to remediable nullity (see c. 1622, 5°). Because the right of defense is intimately involved in the null acts of a person acting without a mandate, however, the more severe remedy of irremediable nullity applies.

[246] John Paul II, alloc, January 26, 1989, *AAS* 81 (1989) 922–927. Translated in Woestman, *Papal Allocutions,* 204–208.

[247] If, however, a person fails to exercise his or her rights due to the manifest negligence of the tribunal to provide reasonable information concerning those rights, then the failure might amount to a denial. The manifest negligence of a person's advocate could also contribute to a denial of the right of defense.

[248] G. Erlebach, "Le fattispecie di negazione del diritto di difesa causanti la nullità della sentenza secondo la giurisprudenza Rotale: criteri generali e parte statica," *ME* 114 (1989) 508–513.

[249] Two recent Rotal decisions available in English are *coram* Burke, November 15, 1990, *ME* 119 (1991) 406–409, translated in *Stud Can* 25 (1991) 510–512; *coram* Burke, May 22, 1997, *Stud Can* 32 (1998) 517–520. Also see *coram* Parisella, July 3, 1980, *SRRDec* 72 (1980) 462–464; *coram* Pompedda, July 23, 1986, *SRRDec* 78 (1986) 480–482; *coram* Pinto, decr *nullitatis sententiae,* May 24, 1985, *Decreta* 3 (1985) 140–144; ApSig, *coram* Sabattani, January 17, 1987, *ME* 113 (1988) 272–275. For a discussion of the jurisprudence and further reflections, see Daneels, "The Right of Defence," 77–95; G. Erlebach, *La nullità della sentenza giudiziale "ob ius defensionis denegatum" nella giurisprudenza rotale,* Studi Giuridici XXV (Vatican City: Libreria Editrice Vaticana, 1991); Moodie, "Fundamental Rights and Access to the Acts of a Case," 123–154; F. Morlot, "Le droit de défense, en particulier dans la publication des actes," *Stud Can* 30 (1996) 133–162.

[250] The right of defense also includes the rights to have access to the published sentence and to challenge that sentence. These rights, however, come into play only after a sentence is issued. They could give rise to a challenge on the basis of c. 1620, 7° only to a subsequent sentence or decree of confirmation, not to the original sentence itself.

may be changed, but only as provided by canon 1514. If the sentence does not settle the controversy as formulated in the *dubia,* at least in part, then the sentence is irremediably null. Clearly, if the sentence does not give an affirmative or negative response to the *dubium,* the sentence is null. This type of nullity would also seem to apply when a sentence is manifestly incoherent in its application of the law to the facts. A sentence may "resolve" the *dubium* only in the purely formal sense of issuing a conclusion. But when that conclusion bears little or no reasonable relationship to the proofs adduced or the arguments made, then just as surely it fails to settle the controversy even partially.

Proposing a Complaint of Irremediable Nullity

Canon 1621 — The complaint of nullity mentioned in can. 1620 can be proposed by way of exception in perpetuity and also by way of action before the judge who rendered the sentence within ten years from the date of the publication of the sentence.

A complaint of nullity on the basis of one or more of the causes of nullity indicated in canon 1620 must be initiated by someone with the right to propose such an action or exception[251] as identified by canon 1626, §1. No one else has the standing in court to challenge the sentence.

The right to lodge most actions is extinguished by the period of prescription provided by law (c. 1492, §1). Canon 1621 establishes a period of ten years from the date of publication of the sentence[252] to lodge the action of a complaint of irre-

---

[251] See the commentary on cc. 1491–1500 on the nature and norms for actions and exceptions.

[252] There is a difference in the wording of cc. 1621 and 1623 regarding the point at which the time limit begins. Canon 1621 indicates that the time begins "from the date of the publication of the sentence" while c. 1623 indicates that it begins "from the notice of the publication of the sentence." *CCEO* 1303, §2 and 1304, §2 eliminate this discrepancy, indicating that the time limit

mediable nullity. The action is to be lodged before the tribunal that issued the original judgment. An action bearing on the status of persons, however, is not extinguished (c. 1492, §1), an application of the underlying principle that cases involving the status of persons never become *res iudicata* (c. 1643). In a marriage case, therefore, the radical right to propose an action remains available. To prevent the frivolous or vindictive use of the Church's tribunals, however, the right to lodge an action is circumscribed after two concordant decisions in favor of nullity by the requirement that the interested party meet the burden of making a new presentation of the case.[253]

The right to lodge most exceptions, however, is perpetual in nature (c. 1492, §2). Thus, canon 1621 specifies that a complaint of irremediable nullity can be made in perpetuity by means of an exception. The exception is also to be lodged before the tribunal that issued the original judgment.

Causes of Remediable Nullity

Canon 1622 — A sentence suffers from the defect of remediable nullity only if:

    1° it was rendered by an illegitimate number of judges contrary to the prescript of can. 1425, §1;

    2° it does not contain the motives or reasons for the decision;

    3° it lacks the signatures prescribed by law;

    4° it does not indicate the year, month, day, and place in which it was rendered;

    5° it is based on a null judicial act whose nullity was not sanated according to the norm of can. 1619;

    6° it was rendered against a party legitimately absent according to can. 1593, §2.

runs from the communication (*ab intimatione*) of the sentence. The CLSA translation, however, is inaccurate in not reflecting this clarification. See Abbass, "Contentious Trials," 900–901.

[253] See the commentary on c. 1684.

In contrast to the causes of irremediable nullity listed in canon 1620, there are other less serious procedural irregularities known as remediable nullities, since they may be sanated by the action of the law itself.

1. Certain cases are to be entrusted to a college of judges rather than to a sole judge (c. 1425, §1). If a sentence was not issued by the legitimate number of judges, it is remediably null.

2. If, contrary to the requirements of canons 1611, 3° and 1612, §3, the sentence does not contain the reasons for the decision, it labors under remediable nullity.

3. The sentence is remediably null if, contrary to canon 1612, §4, it does not contain the signatures required by law.

4. Similarly, if it does not indicate the date and place where it was issued (contrary to c. 1612, §4), the sentence is remediably null.

5. If the sentence is founded on a judicial act that is null and void, and if the nullity of that act was not sanated (c. 1619), then the sentence may be challenged as remediably null. Examples of such acts would be the relative incompetence of a judge to try the matter (c. 1407, §2) or the mistaken admission of a document into the acts prior to the joinder of issues (c. 1529).

6. If the sentence was rendered against a party who was decreed absent from the trial but had a just reason that impeded compliance with the tribunal's citation (c. 1593, §2), that party may lodge a complaint of remediable nullity. It should be noted that this possibility is not available to the party who was not truly impeded but simply chose not to take part in the trial.

Time for Proposing a Complaint of Remediable Nullity

Canon 1623 — A complaint of nullity in the cases mentioned in can. 1622 can be proposed within three months from the notice of the publication of the sentence.

Complaints of remediable nullity can be lodged only within a period of three months after the publication of the sentence.[254] This is a peremptory time limit which cannot be extended and after which the right to propose a challenge ceases (see c. 1465, §1). Thus, the law itself sanates the causes of remediable nullity once the time limit has passed.

Competent Judge to Hear a Complaint of Nullity

Canon 1624 — The judge who rendered the sentence deals with the complaint of nullity. If the party fears that the judge who rendered the sentence challenged by the complaint of nullity is prejudiced and therefore considers the judge suspect, the party can demand that another judge be substituted according to the norm of can. 1450.

Unless it involves a sentence issued by the Roman Rota (c. 1445, §1, 1°), or unless it is lodged together with an appeal (c. 1625), the complaint of nullity is to be lodged before the judge who issued the sentence. If the party making the complaint fears that the judge will not address the complaint in an unbiased manner, he or she may demand that another judge hear the complaint. While canon 1624 refers only to canon 1450, it necessarily incorporates the norms of canons 1449 and 1451 that stipulate how to handle the incidental question of an objection against a judge. If the objection to the judge is upheld, a

---

[254]There are differences in the wording of cc. 1621 and 1623 and their counterparts in the Eastern code concerning the point at which time limits begin to run. See the commentary on c. 1621 for a brief discussion.

new judge is substituted to decide the complaint of nullity.

Linking a Complaint of Nullity with an Appeal

Canon 1625 — A complaint of nullity can be proposed together with an appeal within the time established for an appeal.

A complaint of nullity may be filed in its own right, in which case it follows the norms of canon 1624. It may also be lodged jointly with an appeal, in which case it will be handled by the appellate tribunal (see cc. 1438, 1439, 1444, and 1632). The time limit of fifteen canonical days provided to lodge an appeal (c. 1630, §1) is much shorter than the period of three months within which a complaint of remediable nullity may be lodged. If an appeal is initiated within the allotted time, nothing prevents the person appealing from adding a complaint of irremediable nullity at any point during the appeal, or of remediable nullity within the three-month time limit.[255] If the appellate court upholds the complaint of nullity, it does not rule on the substantive issues but remands the case to the previous instance.[256]

Who May Lodge a Complaint of Nullity?

Canon 1626 — §1. Not only the parties who consider themselves aggrieved can introduce a complaint of nullity but also the promoter of justice and the defender of the bond whenever they have the right to intervene.

This canon identifies those who have standing to lodge a complaint of nullity. The parties to the

case, if they consider themselves aggrieved, may do so. Likewise, if they have been involved in the case, the promoter of justice and defender of the bond have the right to lodge a complaint of nullity. This right to lodge a complaint of nullity also belongs to the promoter or defender of the bond of a tribunal of higher grade.[257]

Retraction/Amendment of Sentence by Judges

§2. The judge can retract or emend *ex officio* a null sentence, which that judge has rendered, within the time limit for acting established by can. 1623 unless an appeal together with a complaint of nullity has been introduced in the meantime or the nullity has been sanated through the expiration of the time limit mentioned in can. 1623.

Even if a complaint of nullity has not been proposed, when judges recognize a cause of nullity in their sentences, they may on their own authority retract or correct the invalid judgments. Technically, the judges here do not propose complaints but simply remedy the errors. The judges must do this, however, within the three-month time period provided in canon 1623. Judges are not free to act in this fashion if an appeal joined to a complaint of nullity has already been lodged (c. 1625). This reflects the canonical principle that a judge is absolutely incompetent to deal with a matter pending before a superior tribunal (c. 1440).

When remediable nullity is involved, the judges may be able to correct the flaw. For example, the signatures or data missing in accord with canon 1622, 3° or 4° may be completed. When the cause of nullity cannot be remedied so easily, judges may retract their sentences and take the steps necessary to resolve the problems. For example, a sentence may be redrafted to include the missing reasoning (c. 1622, 2°). If a party was legitimately absent (c. 1622, 6°), the judges may re-

---

[255] Also see the commentary on c. 1629, 2°.

[256] See ApSig, private reply, April 17, 1989, in *RRAO 1990*, 46, which stated: "A court of appeal cannot simultaneously declare the sentence of a lower tribunal null and also look into the merits of the case; the nullity of a sentence of the first grade having been declared, the case is to be remanded to the tribunal of first instance that it may again take up the merits of the case."

[257] A. Mendonça, "The Structural and Functional Aspects of an Appeal Tribunal in Marriage Nullity Cases," *Stud Can* 32 (1998) 479.

tract a sentence, reopen the instruction in accord with canon 1600, and then follow the normal procedure of publication, conclusion, argument, and decision.

Does this ability to correct or amend a sentence apply to cases of irremediable nullity? At first glance, canon 1626, §2 would seem to permit this, since it refers to any invalid judgment. Diego-Lora, however, contends that this provision "can only be justified in cases of remediable nullity" which, he argues, explains the application of the three-month time limit of canon 1623.[258] Stankiewicz, on the other hand, argues that the power is not limited only to cases of remediable nullity.[259] This author agrees with Stankiewicz. As ministers of justice, judges would be negligent if they became aware of and then simply ignored a cause of irremediable nullity in one of their sentences. Thus, within the three-month period, judges may retract a sentence vitiated by irremediable nullity. Because irremediable nullity is more serious, the judges will not be able simply to correct the sentence. Rather, some or all parts of the process would need to be repeated in a way that resolves the underlying cause of nullity.

Process to Address Complaints of Nullity

Canon 1627 — Cases concerning a complaint of nullity can be treated according to the norms for the oral contentious process.

When a complaint of nullity, remediable or irremediable, is lodged, the judge may employ the oral contentious process (cc. 1656–1670) to resolve the issue expeditiously. The ordinary contentious process, however, must be employed if one of the parties requests it (c. 1656, §1)

[258] Diego-Lora, in *Pamplona ComEng,* 1005–1006. Ryan, in *CLSGBI Com,* 914, and Arroba Conde, in *Valencia Com,* 704, while not specifically raising the question, assume that the provision applies only to causes of remediable nullity.

[259] Stankiewicz, in *Com Ex* IV/2, 1640.

CHAPTER II
APPEAL[260]
[cc. 1628–1640]

An appeal is a challenge to the substance of a decision rather than to any procedural irregularity or violation of rights. All that is needed is for one with the right to appeal to provide notice of the appeal. Thus, no specific line of argumentation is required of the appellant, although failure to bring forth persuasive arguments would certainly impede the possibility of a successful appeal.

Right of Appeal

Canon 1628 — A party who considers himself or herself aggrieved by any sentence as well as the promoter of justice and the defender of the bond in cases which require their presence have the right to appeal the sentence to a higher judge, without prejudice to the prescript of can. 1629.

The canon specifies who has the right to lodge an appeal, with due regard for certain sentences not admitting any appeal (c. 1629). The right belongs to a party to the case at issue who feels aggrieved by the decision, as well as to the promoter of justice and defender of the bond if they were involved in the case. No one else has the standing to initiate an appeal.

The appeal is made to the appropriate hierarchically superior tribunal as defined in law (see c. 1632).

Decisions Not Subject to Appeal

Canon 1629 — There is no appeal:
   1° from a sentence of the Supreme Pontiff himself or the Apostolic Signatura;
   2° from a sentence tainted by a defect of nullity, unless the appeal is joined with a com-

[260] For an excellent review of the appellate tribunal and appeal process, see Mendonça, "The Structural and Functional Aspects," 441–500.

plaint of nullity according to the norm of can. 1625;

3° from a sentence which has become a *res iudicata;*

4° from a decree of a judge or from an interlocutory sentence which does not have the force of a definitive sentence, unless it is joined with an appeal from a definitive sentence;

5° from a sentence or a decree in a case where the law requires the matter to be decided as promptly as possible (*expeditissime*).

Certain decisions are not subject to any appeal. As limitations of rights, these exemptions from appeal must be understood narrowly (see c. 18). The underlying reasons justifying exemption from appeal vary, and may be rooted in the nature of the authority who issued the ruling or based on the nature of the matter decided. At times, the prohibition is absolute, admitting no exceptions; in other circumstances a direct appeal is prohibited, but an appeal may be made in conjunction with some other challenge to the sentence.

Specifically, because of the supreme authority of the pope (c. 333, §1), rulings of the Supreme Pontiff or the Apostolic Signatura may not be appealed (1°). Due to its nature, a judgment that is an adjudged matter (*res iudicata,* cc. 1641–1644) may not be appealed (3°), nor may any judgment concerning an issue which the law requires to be decided *expeditissime* or "as promptly as possible" (5°). An interlocutory sentence that does not have the force of a definitive sentence may not be appealed except when the appeal is lodged jointly with an appeal of the definitive sentence (4°). Finally, an appeal cannot be lodged against a judgment which is null (2°). Since a null judgment is legally non-existent, it logically cannot be appealed, since there is "no-thing" against which to appeal. The nullity of such a judgment, however, may not necessarily be obvious or may not have yet been recognized at law. Thus, an appeal is permitted when joined with a complaint of nullity (c. 1625). If the complaint of nullity is

upheld, the sentence is decreed null and the appellate court does not address the substantive issues connected with the appeal.[261] If the complaint of nullity is rejected, the sentence has legal standing and the appeal is handled on its merits.

Introduction of an Appeal

Canon 1630 — §1. An appeal must be introduced before the judge who rendered the sentence within the peremptory period of fifteen useful days from the notice of the publication of the sentence.

§2. If an appeal is made orally, the notary is to put it in writing in the presence of the appellant.[262]

Although the appeal is directed toward the appropriate hierarchically superior court, it is to be lodged with the judge who issued the judgment. This serves the practical value of enabling that judge to transmit the entire acts of the case along with the appeal to the designated appellate tribunal.

The appeal is to be lodged within fifteen useful days (*tempus utile;* see cc. 201, §2 and 203) after the notification of the publication of the sentence. This is a peremptory time limit, which means that the right to appeal is lost if it is not lodged within that time frame (cc. 1465, §1 and 1467). In cases which involve the status of persons and hence are never *res iudicata* (c. 1643), the peremptory nature of the time limit is somewhat mitigated in that a new challenge to the *status quo* remains

---

[261] ApSig, private reply, April 17, 1989, *RRAO 1990,* 46–47.

[262] *CCEO* 1311 is similar although, reflecting a decision to employ consistent terminology, it refers to the communication of the sentence (*intimatione*) rather than to the notification of publication. See the commentary on cc. 1615 and 1621. *CCEO* 1312, concerning an appeal against a decision of a delegated judge, has no counterpart in the Latin code. The CLSA translation of *CCEO* 1312 is inaccurate; for a better translation and brief commentary, see Abbass, "Contentious Trials," 888–889.

theoretically possible through a new presentation of the case (c. 1644, §1). Some commentators, therefore, conclude that in cases involving the status of persons, the time limit is not peremptory.[263] This, however, contradicts the text of the canon. For this author, the failure to lodge the appeal within the peremptory time (unless one is legitimately impeded) constitutes a waiver of the right to appeal but not a waiver of the right subsequently to question the status of persons. If there are not two concordant judgments, an "appeal" which arrives after the time limit should be treated as a new presentation of the case, asking the higher level tribunal to proceed to a resolution of the question of status.[264] If there are two concordant decisions, then the request must be handled as a new presentation of the case.[265]

Of course, a person may be legitimately impeded from lodging an appeal within the time limit. For example, because of travel he or she may not have received the notice of the publication of the sentence. In such a case, the useful time begins to run from the time the party had the knowledge and opportunity to act.

Normally, an appeal is to be presented in writing. If it is made orally, however, a notary must immediately draw up the appeal in writing in the presence of the one making it. While the notary's signature alone is sufficient to verify the fact of the appeal (c. 1437, §2), the one appealing should be asked to sign the document of appeal prepared by the notary.

Incidental Question about Right of Appeal

Canon 1631 — If a question arises about the right to appeal, the appellate tribunal deals with it as promptly as possible (expeditissime) according to the norms of the oral contentious process.

If a question emerges concerning the right of a party to appeal, this is the first issue that must be addressed by the appellate court. For example, a question of the right to appeal arises when a party lodges an appeal after the deadline but claims that he or she was impeded from doing so within the deadline. This question is handled by the oral contentious process (cc. 1656–1670) unless a party insists on the ordinary contentious process (c. 1656, §1). The decision concerning the right of appeal is to be made expeditissime, which means that it is not itself subject to further appeal (c. 1629, 5°).

Appropriate Appellate Court

Canon 1632 — §1. If the appeal does not indicate the tribunal to which it is directed, it is presumed to be made to the tribunal mentioned in cann. 1438 and 1439.

§2. If the other party has appealed to another appellate tribunal, the tribunal of higher grade deals with the case, without prejudice to can. 1415.[266]

This canon establishes a presumption at law, namely, that if there is no indication of the tribunal to which the appeal is directed, it is to be considered as directed to the usual appellate court as determined by canons 1438–1439. As is the case with any presumption, however, it must cede to the truth. Thus, the one appealing may clarify his or her intention to appeal to another competent appellate court, such as the Roman Rota (c. 1444, §1, 1°). If this is done before the usual appellate court has cited the parties, then the case can be transmitted in accord with the clarification. But if the usual appellate court has already cited the parties, any other tribunal is prevented from hearing the appeal (c. 1415).

---

[263] For example, Moneta, in *Com Ex* IV/2, 1655–1656.

[264] Since there were not two concordant decisions, however, this new presentation would not require the presentation of new and weighty evidence or arguments. See ApSig, private reply, June 3, 1989, *RRAO 1989,* 56.

[265] For further discussion of this question, see Mendonça, "The Structural and Functional Aspects," 475–477.

[266] There is no counterpart in the Eastern code. See Abbass, "Contentious Trials," 883–884.

It may happen, however, that more than one party appeals. For example, both a defender of the bond and a respondent might appeal an affirmative decision in a marriage nullity case. If the appeals are directed to different appellate courts, the matter is to be heard at the tribunal of the higher grade. This normal procedure does not apply, however, if the tribunal of the lower grade has already cited the parties, for the tribunal of the higher grade would then be prevented from hearing the case in that instance (c. 1415).[267]

Time for Pursuing an Appeal

Canon 1633 — An appeal must be pursued before the appellate judge within a month from its introduction unless the judge from whom appeal is made has established a longer period for a party to pursue it.

The law distinguishes between lodging the appeal and pursuing the appeal. Once an appeal is lodged (c. 1630), through an action as simple as a letter or other notice indicating the decision to appeal, the one appealing has a time limit of one month (thirty consecutive days; see c. 202, §1) to pursue that appeal before the appellate judge. If the appeal is not pursued within that time, it is considered as abandoned (see below, c. 1635). There are two exceptions to this rule. First, the judge who issued the original decision may extend the time limit for the party to pursue the appeal. Second, the time limit may be suspended by the law itself in accord with the norm of canon 1634, §2 (see below).

Means of Pursuing an Appeal

Canon 1634 — §1. To pursue an appeal it is required and suffices that a party calls upon the services of a higher judge for an emendation of the challenged sentence, attaches a copy of this sentence, and indicates the reasons for the appeal.

§2. If a party cannot obtain a copy of the challenged sentence from the tribunal from which appeal is made within the useful time, the time limits do not run in the meantime; the impediment must be made known to the appellate judge who is to bind the judge from whom appeal is made by a precept to fulfill that judge's duty as soon as possible.

§3. Meanwhile the judge from whom appeal is made must transmit the acts to the appellate judge according to the norm of can. 1474.

The first paragraph defines what is involved in pursuing the appeal. The requirements are minimal in that it is required and *suffices* that the party appealing:

1. request the assistance of the appellate tribunal to change the judgment;
2. attach a copy of the sentence being challenged;
3 indicate the reasons for appealing against the sentence.

Paragraph two provides a protection of the right of the one appealing.[268] The canonical time limit of thirty days is intended to give the one lodging an appeal the opportunity to study the judgment and prepare appropriate arguments. If the one appealing is unable to obtain a copy of the

---

[267] Provided the person lodges the appeal legitimately (i.e., before the judge who issued the original decision), this conflict between courts of appeals will never occur. The judge would wait until the peremptory time limit has passed in order to give every party the right of appeal. If there is more than one appeal and they are directed to different courts, the judge applies the principle of this canon and sends the appeal to the tribunal of higher grade. If, however, a party incorrectly sends an appeal directly to an appellate court, without the original judge having any awareness of that action, then a tribunal of lower grade might already have the case and be acting upon it, thus bringing the law on prevention into play.

[268] There is no parallel to paragraph two in the Eastern code. See Abbass, "Contentious Trials," 884–885.

judgment, then he or she does not have that opportunity. In this case, the thirty-day time limit is automatically suspended and the party retains the right to pursue the appeal.[269] The one appealing is to inform the judge of the appellate tribunal of the difficulty. The appellate judge is then to issue a precept (see c. 49) obliging the original judge to provide the copy to the one appealing.

Paragraph three would probably be more appropriately incorporated into canon 1630. It simply states the requirement that, when the original tribunal is notified of the appeal, all the acts of the case are to be forwarded to the appellate court. This is to be done as soon as possible, certainly within the thirty-day period provided for a party to pursue the appeal.[270] A notary is to certify the authenticity of the transmitted acts (c. 1474). If the acts are in a language unknown to the higher tribunal, an accurate translation is also to be provided.

`Abandonment of Appeal

Canon 1635 — Once the deadline for appeal has passed without action either before the judge from whom the appeal is made or before the appellate judge, the appeal is considered abandoned.

The appeal is to be considered as abandoned if either of the time limits provided in canons 1630, §1 or 1633 passes without an action being taken. The language of the canon seems strange as applied to the original fifteen-day time limit for lodging an appeal. It might have been more precise to say that once that time limit passes, any attempt to lodge an appeal is to be considered as having no effect. In this situation, an appeal was not deserted; rather, it never existed. Nonetheless, the practical consequences are the same.

Abandonment of an appeal carries with it all of the canonical consequences connected with renunciation (see cc. 1524–1525). Depending on the nature of the case, the case may become a *res iudicata* (c. 1641, 2°) and the sentence is to be executed appropriately. In cases involving the status of persons, including cases of marriage nullity, the matter does not become *res iudicata*. The judgment, however, may be executed if there are two conforming decisions (cc. 1644, §1 and 1684).

Renunciation of Appeal

Canon 1636 — §1. The appellant can renounce the appeal with the effects mentioned in can. 1525.

§2. If the defender of the bond or the promoter of justice has introduced the appeal, the defender of the bond or the promoter of justice of the appellate tribunal can renounce it, unless the law provides otherwise.

Whoever pursues an appeal may voluntarily renounce it at any point in the instance. To do so validly, the renunciation should fulfill the requirements of canon 1524, §3.[271] The effects of renunciation of an appeal are described in canon 1525. Although canon 1636 does directly refer to it, another effect of the renunciation of an appeal is that, unless it involves the status of persons, the matter becomes a *res iudicata* (c. 1641, 3°).

If either the promoter of justice or defender of the bond lodged appeals, the comparable officers of the appellate tribunal have the right to renounce the appeal. This renunciation also must meet the requirements of canon 1524, §3.

---

[269] A sentence that has not been legitimately published has no force (see the commentary on c. 1614).

[270] A more specific and limited time is provided in marriage nullity cases where all the acts are to be forwarded to the appeal tribunal within twenty days of the publication of the sentence (c. 1682, §1).

[271] The renunciation must be (1) in writing, (2) signed by the party or a procurator with the special mandate to do so, (3) communicated to the other party who must accept or not oppose it, and (4) admitted by the judge.

Effect of Appeal on the Parties

Canon 1637 — §1. An appeal made by the petitioner also benefits the respondent and vice versa.

§2. If there are several respondents or petitioners and the sentence is challenged by only one or against only one of them, the challenge is considered to be made by all of them and against all of them whenever the matter sought is indivisible or a joint obligation.

Canon 1637 establishes certain parameters and presumptions governing the appeal process. Paragraph one deals with a case involving one petitioner and one respondent. If either party appeals, the other party is equally affected and has equal rights in the prosecution of the appeal.

Paragraph two deals with cases involving multiple petitioners or respondents. When the matter at issue is neither indivisible nor a joint obligation, one person may lodge an appeal affecting only some of the other parties. When the obligation is joint or the matter indivisible, however, the appeal necessarily affects all the parties. Therefore, the law automatically considers the appeal as being made by all against all (*ab omnibus et contra omnes*).

Specifying the Focus of an Appeal

§3. If one party introduces an appeal against one ground of the sentence, the other party can appeal incidentally against other grounds within the peremptory period of fifteen days from the day on which the original appeal was made known to the latter, even if the deadline for an appeal has passed.

§4. Unless it is otherwise evident, an appeal is presumed to be made against all the grounds of a sentence.

When an appeal is lodged by one party against only a part of the sentence (e.g., against only one of two or more grounds), the other party or parties are to be informed of the fact and extent of the appeal. They then have the right to lodge what is known as an "incidental appeal" against other grounds of the sentence. Even if the time limit established in canon 1630, §1 has already expired, the right to lodge an incidental appeal extends for fifteen consecutive days from the time the notification of the appeal was communicated.[272]

Paragraph four establishes the presumption of law that an appeal is considered to be made against the judgment in its entirety, including each and every ground, unless the appeal clearly indicates otherwise. If the appeal is narrowly targeted and if no incidental appeals are lodged against other parts of the judgment, then the uncontested parts of the judgment are not considered in the appeal.[273]

Suspensive Effect of Appeal

Canon 1638 — An appeal suspends the execution of the sentence.

The general principle for the ordinary contentious process is that the appeal suspends the execution of the judgment.[274] There are, however, exceptions to this rule. In some circumstances, the judge has the discretion to order a provisional execution of a judgment (c. 1650, §§2–3).

Other challenges to the sentence do not have such an automatic suspensive effect. A complaint of nullity against a sentence does not carry sus-

---

[272] Unlike c. 1630, §1, this norm does not provide for the time limit to be counted as canonical days (*tempus utile*). For the computation of time, see cc. 200–203.

[273] An exception would be a marriage nullity case in which the entire judgment must be transmitted ex officio to the appellate court (c. 1682, §1). In that case, the entire judgment must be considered at the appellate level, even if technically only a part of the judgment is being formally appealed.

[274] See cc. 1650–1655 for the norms governing the execution of a sentence.

pensive effect. A new presentation of the case after two concordant sentences does not have automatic suspensive effect (cc. 1644, §2; 1684, §2), although the judge may decide to decree a suspension of execution (c. 1650, §3).

A petition for *restitutio in integrum,* however, does suspend the execution of the sentence provided that execution is not already under way or unless the judge decrees otherwise (c. 1647).

Admission of New Grounds/Proofs

Canon 1639 — §1. Without prejudice to the prescript of can. 1683, a new cause for petitioning cannot be admitted at the appellate grade, not even by way of useful accumulation; consequently, the joinder of the issue can only address whether the prior sentence is to be confirmed or revised either totally or partially.

§2. New proofs, however, are admitted only according to the norm of can. 1600.

As a general rule, a new ground may not be admitted at the appellate level (whether second, third, or higher instance). The issue joined before the court of appeals, therefore, is controlled by the manner in which the issue was joined in the previous instance or instances. The question to be addressed is whether that previous judgment is to be upheld, modified, or overruled.

An exception to this rule is provided for in marriage nullity cases in which an appellate court may admit and judge a new ground of nullity as if in first instance.[275]

In second and higher instances, new proofs may be admitted, but only under the provisions of canon 1600.[276] Thus, while the appellate court is free to further instruct a case, normally the judg-

ment on appeal is made on the basis of the evidence previously obtained.

Appellate Procedure

Canon 1640 — The appellate grade must proceed in the same manner as first instance with appropriate adjustments; immediately after the issue has been joined according to the norm of can. 1513, §1 and can. 1639, §1 and unless the proofs possibly must be completed, the discussion of the case is to take place and the sentence rendered.

In general, the court of appeals follows the procedure provided for trials of first instance. The law envisions, however, that a trial on the appellate level be a simpler and less time-consuming process. Thus, the procedures governing first instance trials are to be modified to take into account the nature of the appellate process. What are the key differences?

First, if the matter would normally be reserved to a college of judges (c. 1425, §1) but was nonetheless rendered in first instance by a sole judge (c. 1425, §4), the court of second instance must be constituted as a college and proceed in a collegial manner (c. 1441).

Second, except in marriage nullity cases, the appellate court is limited to joining the issue on the question of whether to confirm, modify, or overturn the judgment of the previous tribunal (c. 1639, §1).

Finally, the law normally does not envision gathering additional proofs at the appellate level. In fact, new proofs may be gathered only under limited circumstances (cc. 1639, §2; 1600). Thus, on appeal, usually the trial moves immediately from the joinder of the issues (c. 1513) to a discussion of the case (cc. 1601–1606), and then to the decision, the drafting of the sentence, and its publication (cc. 1607–1615). If new proofs need to be gathered by the appellate tribunal, then the norms governing the collection of proofs and the publication of the acts apply.

---

[275] See the commentary on c. 1683.

[276] This second paragraph of c. 1639 might better have been attached to c. 1640, since it contains an exception to the general provision that the procedure on the appellate level is the same as that of first instance.

TITLE IX[277]
RES IUDICATA
AND *RESTITUTIO IN INTEGRUM*[278]
[cc. 1641–1648]

CHAPTER I
RES IUDICATA
[cc. 1641–1644]

Among other safeguards to protect against endless lawsuits, canon law provides the institute known as *res iudicata*.[279] This is sometimes referred to as the "closed judgment" or "adjudged matter." A *res iudicata* is a definitive judicial sentence resolved in such a way that it is no longer subject to a direct challenge by means of an appeal (see the commentary on c. 1642, §1).

While a matter that is *res iudicata* cannot be appealed, in cases of manifest injustice it may be directly challenged by a petition for *restitutio in integrum* (see cc. 1645–1648).

Situations Resulting in a Res Iudicata

Canon 1641 — Without prejudice to the prescript of can. 1643, a *res iudicata* occurs:
  1° if a second concordant sentence is rendered between the same parties over the same issue and on the same cause for petitioning;

---

[277] Article X of the Eastern code corresponds with title IX of the Latin code in providing norms for *res iudicata* and *restitutio in integrum*. The Eastern code, however, contains additional norms for challenges based on the opposition of third parties (*CCEO* 1330–1333). For a discussion of these norms, see Abbass, "Contentious Trials," 889–890.

[278] Wrenn, in *CLSA Com,* 1002–1005; Ryan, in *CLSGBI Com,* 919–923; Diego-Lora, in *Pamplona ComEng,* 1013–1019; Acebal, in *Salamanca Com,* 797–801; Arroba Conde, in *Valencia Com,* 709–713; Diego-Lora, in *Com Ex* IV/2, 1673–1721; J. de Salas Murillo, in *Com Ex* IV/2, 1722–1738.

[279] An excellent analysis of this institute is provided by J. G. Johnson, "*Res iudicata, restitutio in integrum,* and Marriage Cases," *Stud Can* 28 (1994) 323–327.

  2° if an appeal against the sentence has not been introduced within the useful time;
  3° if at the appellate grade, the trial has been abated or renounced;
  4° if a definitive sentence has been rendered from which there is no appeal according to the norm of can. 1629.

This canon defines the circumstances under which a judicial decision becomes *res iudicata*. This canon must be understood in the light of canon 1643 which stipulates that a case involving the status of persons never becomes *res iudicata*[280] even if one or more of the provisions of canon 1641 are verified.

First, a *res iudicata* occurs when two concordant sentences have been issued concerning the same parties, regarding the same basic issue being petitioned (*de eodem petito*), and based on the same juridic facts or basis of petitioning (*ex eadem causa petendi*). Of course, those conforming sentences must have been issued by different tribunals ruling in different instances.[281]

Second, a judgment becomes *res iudicata* subsequent to the issuance of a sentence that is not challenged by an appeal within the peremptory time limit provided (see cc. 1630, §1, 1633, 1634, §2, and 1635).

Third, a judgment that was appealed becomes *res iudicata* if the appeal is renounced (see cc. 1524–1525) or the trial abated at the appellate level (see cc. 1520–1523).

Finally, by definition, a definitive sentence is *res iudicata* if it concerns one of the matters against which no appeal is permitted (c. 1629).[282]

---

[280] For the types of cases that involve status of persons, see the commentary on c. 1643.

[281] For reflections on conformity of sentences in marriage nullity cases, see the commentary on c. 1684.

[282] See the commentary on c. 1629, 1°, 2°, and 5°. Numbers 3 and 4 of c. 1629 do not apply, with 3° being tautological and 4° involving a decree or sentence that is not definitive in nature, and hence not a matter that becomes *res iudicata*.

Effect of a Res Iudicata

Canon 1642 — §1. A *res iudicata* possesses the stability of law and cannot be challenged directly except according to the norm of can. 1645, §1.

When a sentence becomes a *res iudicata,* it acquires a high degree of canonical stability, becoming "immune to any future direct attack."[283] This canon provides that a *res iudicata* can be "challenged directly" only through the institute known as *restitutio in integrum* (c. 1645, §1).

If a "direct" challenge is prohibited except through *restitutio in integrum,* does the law envision any "indirect" challenge? Specifically, is a *res iudicata* subject to a complaint of nullity in accord with canons 1620 or 1622? Wrenn states that the judgment "is so firm and final that it no longer admits either of appeal or complaint (*querela*) but only of reinstatement."[284] This author, however, disagrees.[285] When a sentence is vitiated by a cause of irremediable nullity (c. 1620), those causes of nullity are not sanated and remain open to challenge by an action for ten years and by means of exception in perpetuity (c. 1621).[286] A matter that is *res iudicata* would not, however, be open to a complaint of remediable nullity (c. 1622) once the three-month time limit (c. 1623) has passed.

---

[283] Johnson, *"Res iudicata,"* 325.

[284] Wrenn, in *CLSA Com,* 1002. Ryan agrees with Wrenn on this point (*CLSGBI Com,* 920).

[285] Diego-Lora likewise holds that a *res iudicata* remains open to an indirect challenge by means of a complaint of nullity. See *Com Ex* IV/2, 1686, 1697–1698, and *Pamplona ComEng,* 1014. Arroba Conde, in *Valencia Com,* 709, agrees with this conclusion. These commentators note that a complaint of nullity is not a direct challenge to the adjudged matter itself, but rather a challenge to the validity of the process employed to issue the decision.

[286] *CCEO* 1323, §1 supports this conclusion by specifically providing for a challenge to a *res iudicata* through a complaint of nullity. Unlike the Latin code, the Eastern code also allows a challenge by third parties.

Rights Flowing from a Res Iudicata

§2. It establishes the rights between the parties and permits an action for execution and an exception of *res iudicata* which the judge can also declare *ex officio* in order to prevent a new introduction of the same case.

The existence of a *res iudicata* has important legal consequences establishing rights that can be vindicated either by means of an action or an exception (cc. 1491–1495).

As an action: Unless the judge has already executed the judgment ex officio, any of the parties can petition for the execution of that judgment in accord with canon 1650, §2.

As an exception: Should anyone attempt to introduce the same case anew before any tribunal, a party may lodge the exception that there is no right to present the new petition because the matter is *res iudicata.* Similarly, the judge before whom the new petition has been presented need not wait for another party to lodge an exception, but may ex officio reject the new petition on the basis of the existence of a *res iudicata.*

Status-of-Persons Cases

Canon 1643 — Cases concerning the status of persons, including cases concerning the separation of spouses, never become *res iudicata.*

A case involving the "status of persons" never becomes a *res iudicata,* even if it otherwise fulfills all of the requirements of canon 1641. Nonetheless, such cases may attain a significant degree of judicial security in accord with the provisions of canon 1644.

Since canon 1643 creates an exception to the law, it must be interpreted strictly (c. 18). Thus, this norm applies only to those types of cases clearly involving the status of the persons themselves; it does not apply to other issues that may significantly affect the person (e.g., the exercise of a right or the holding of a particular ecclesiastical office) but do not change that person's underlying status. Which cases, then, involve the status of persons? This canon itself, reflecting an authentic interpretation of the 1917 code,[287] specifies that cases involving the separation of spouses (cc. 1692–1696) concern the status of persons. Canon 1691 expressly specifies that all marriage nullity cases, whether handled in the ordinary contentious process or the documentary process, involve the status of persons. Cases declaring the nullity of sacred orders (cc. 1708–1712) certainly involve the status of persons, as do cases involving the validity of religious profession (cc. 656, 658). Some commentators argue that penal actions involve the status of persons.[288] Others hold the contrary[289] and many are silent on the matter. This author agrees that of their nature penal actions are not status-of-persons cases.[290] This position is consistent with canon 1731, which recognizes that a judgment in a penal trial may become a *res iudicata.* Furthermore, canon 1728, §1, unlike canon 1691 in marriage cases, applies the norms for cases pertaining to the public good to penal trials, but not the norms for cases involving the status of persons.

New Presentation of a Case

Canon 1644 — §1. If a second concordant sentence has been rendered in a case concerning the status of persons, recourse can be made at any time to the appellate tribunal if new and grave proofs or arguments are brought forward within the peremptory time limit of thirty days from the proposed challenge. Within a month from when the new proofs and arguments are brought forward, however, the appellate tribunal must estab-

lish by decree whether a new presentation of the case must be admitted or not.

Since cases involving the status of persons do not become *res iudicata,* they remain radically open to challenge. Nonetheless, it is in the interest neither of the spiritual welfare of the parties, nor of the community of the Church, for frivolous or vindictive lawsuits to continue interminably. Thus, after two concordant decisions, cases involving the status of persons attain an important measure of judicial security.[291]

Once there are two concordant decisions, the aggrieved party does not enjoy the right simply to appeal those two judgments.[292] The threshold is raised and, instead of appealing, a party may seek recourse only by means of a "new presentation of the case" (*nova causae propositio*). The petition for a new presentation of the case must be lodged before a tribunal with jurisdiction superior to the two courts that rendered the first two decisions.[293]

This extraordinary challenge requires that the aggrieved party be prepared to bring forward "new and grave proofs or arguments." This requirement is not met simply by presenting the names of additional witnesses or by merely asserting that the party believes the two conforming sentences are wrong. It must be shown that addi-

---

[287] CodCom, *responsa,* April 8, 1941, *AAS* 33 (1941) 173. Translation in *CLD* 2, 552.

[288] Arroba Conde, in *Valencia Com,* 710.

[289] Diego-Lora, in *Com Ex* IV/2, 1707.

[290] Of course, some penal actions, such as dismissal from religious life (cc. 694–704) or dismissal from the clerical state (c. 1336, §1, 5°), affect the status of persons. But these are not status-of-persons cases, i.e., cases where a person's status is the primary focus of the inquiry.

[291] See the commentary on c. 1684 for reflections on conformity of sentences in marriage nullity cases.

[292] One should recall that the requirements for lodging and pursuing an appeal (cc. 1630 and 1634) are relatively minimal in nature.

[293] In the Latin church, this almost always involves a petition to the Roman Rota as the ordinary court of third and further instance (c. 1444, §1, 2°). In Spain, however, the Spanish Rota is competent in third instance (see J. L. Acebal, in *Salamanca Com,* 708–709), and a new presentation of the case may be lodged there. For the Eastern Catholic churches, the patriarchal tribunal is competent in third and further instances (*CCEO* 1063, §§3–4). In those particular churches *sui iuris* not subject to a patriarchal tribunal, particular law may provide an alternative tribunal competent to accept cases in third instance (*CCEO* 1065).

tional witnesses or other modes of proof bring forward genuinely new information of significant value, evidence that has the potential to shed a truly different light on the judgment. Likewise, the proposed argumentation must reflect a truly new, weighty, and compelling reading of the applicable law and facts.[294]

The new and grave proofs or arguments must be presented within a peremptory time limit of thirty continuous days (see cc. 201–203) from the lodging of the challenge. Hence, if those new proofs or arguments are not brought forward within that peremptory time, the request for a new presentation of the case is to be rejected.

Once the challenge has been lodged and the new proofs and arguments presented, the appellate judges have one month (30 consecutive days; see c. 202, §1) to consider the request and issue a decree either admitting or rejecting the new presentation of the case. This decree must contain at least a summary of the reasons for the judges' decision (c. 1617). The canon as well as the norms for the Roman Rota are silent concerning what happens if the appellate tribunal fails to act within the one-month period provided. By analogy with canon 1506 on the presentation of an initial *libellus,* the interested party could certainly insist on a ruling. It would not be realistic, however, to expect a response within ten additional days, and there is no provision for an "automatic" admission of a petition for a new presentation of the case.

A decree rejecting a new presentation of a case is subject to appeal, since it is a decree which has a definitive effect (cc. 1618 and 1629, 4°).

Should a new presentation of the case be admitted and lead to a decision contrary to the earlier conforming decisions, any party to the case aggrieved by the new judgment is free to appeal against it in accord with the usual norms governing appeals (cc. 1628–1640).

Petition for New Presentation
Not Automatically Suspensive

§2. Recourse to a higher tribunal in order to obtain a new presentation of the case does not suspend the execution of the sentence unless either the law provides otherwise or the appellate tribunal orders its suspension according to the norm of can. 1650, §3.

Although not constituting a *res iudicata,* two conforming decisions in a case involving the status of persons have significant juridical effects and permit the execution of the judgment (cc. 1650–1655).[295]

In the event a new presentation of the case is proposed, that petition does not suspend the execution of the sentence. There are two exceptions to this rule:

1. The law may provide otherwise and mandate an automatic suspension of execution for certain types of judgments. In fact, the code contains no such alternative provision for judicial trials involving the status of persons.[296]

2. Upon receiving the petition for a new presentation of a case, the appeal tribunal may issue a decree suspending the execution of the judgment in accord with canon 1650, §3.

If the execution of the sentence was suspended and the petition for a new presentation of the case subsequently is rejected, the tribunal would then move to the execution of the judgment (c. 1650). If the execution was not suspended and the new

---

[294] *RRAO 1993,* 33. Also see *RRAO 1990,* 68–69.

[295] See the commentary on c. 1684 for the specific application of this general rule to two concordant judgments in marriage nullity cases.

[296] For cases not involving the status of persons, the law provides for the suspension of the execution of a decision when that decision is challenged in penal cases (c. 1353) and in the administrative processes for the removal or transfer of a pastor (cc. 1747, §3; 1752).

presentation of the case is rejected, the acts of execution retain full force. If the new presentation is admitted and eventually results in a decision contrary to the earlier conforming decisions, the new decision should incorporate a revocation or amendment of the decree of execution in conformity with the new judgment. If the original decree of execution, in accord with canon 1650, §3, provided for some guarantee in the event of a subsequent contrary judgment, the provisions for the guarantee would then be activated unless further appeals or challenges of the judgment have been lodged.

CHAPTER II
RESTITUTIO IN INTEGRUM
[cc. 1645–1648]

Lawrence Wrenn defines *restitutio in integrum* as a "legal remedy by which a person who has been seriously injured by a judicial sentence that was manifestly unjust can, for reasons of natural equity, be restored by a competent judge to the status quo *ante,* i.e., before the injurious sentence."[297] Sometimes translated as "reinstatement" or "total reinstatement," this institute was modified significantly in the code revision process.[298] While no longer technically referred to as an "extraordinary" remedy, in practice its application would be rare given the requirement that there be clear proof of injustice in the original decision.

Clear Proof of Injustice

Canon 1645 — §1. *Restitutio in integrum* is granted against a sentence which has become *res iudicata* provided that its injustice is clearly established.

Restitutio in integrum is a remedy to be used when a matter is *res iudicata* provided that there

---

[297] Wrenn, in *CLSA Com,* 1004.
[298] For a detailed summary of the history of this institute, see Salas Murillo, in *Com Ex* IV/2, 1723–1726.

is manifest proof of injustice. While a potentially invalid sentence may be challenged by a complaint of nullity (see the commentary on cc. 1619–1627), a *restitutio in integrum* is the only challenge available against a valid sentence that is *res iudicata.*[299]

Wrenn argues that, as a result of the changes made in the 1983 code, a petition for *restitutio* may be lodged against even "a first instance decision in a marriage case" despite the fact that these never become *res iudicata.*[300] Most commentators disagree with this conclusion.[301] John Johnson discusses Wrenn's opinion at length. He concludes that

> Wrenn's reasons, taken individually or cumulatively, are finally not convincing.... Nevertheless, I do not find my own analysis to be so overpowering as to deprive his conclusions of all force.[302]

Johnson then carefully examines Wrenn's argument in the light of hypothetical cases where use of the remedy might be considered, concluding that experimenting with the use of *restitutio* in marriage cases might be justifiable but only under extremely rare circumstances.[303] Further, Johnson argues, any attempt to use it would be "rather risky" because it would likely raise "messy" procedural wrangles, especially with courts of appeal, that might well complicate rather than promote the effort to redress an injustice.[304] This author shares Johnson's skepticism and is of the opinion that evidence of manifest injustice in

---

[299] As noted above, *CCEO* 1323, §1 provides for an additional challenge against a valid sentence by a third party.
[300] Wrenn, *Procedures,* 79. Also see idem, in *CLSA Com,* 1004.
[301] Ryan, in *CLSGBI Com,* 922; Diego-Lora, in *Pamplona ComEng,* 1016; Sallas Murillo, in *Com Ex* IV/2, 1727–1728.
[302] Johnson, *"Res iudicata,"* 340.
[303] Ibid., 340–345.
[304] Ibid., 345. Thus, while very skeptical of Wrenn's position, Johnson is not willing to close the door totally to the possibility of a *restitutio* in marriage cases.

cases involving the status of persons would better be addressed through a complaint of nullity of sentence or a new presentation of the case.

The Five Manifest Injustices

§2. Injustice, however, is not considered to be established clearly unless:
1° **the sentence is based on proofs which afterwards are discovered to be false in such a way that without those proofs the dispositive part of the sentence is not sustained;**
2° **documents have been revealed afterwards which undoubtedly prove new facts and demand a contrary decision;**
3° **the sentence was rendered due to the malice of one party resulting in harm to the other party;**
4° **a prescript of the law which is not merely procedural was clearly neglected;**
5° **the sentence is contrary to a previous decision which has become *res iudicata*.**

A *restitutio in integrum* may be granted only when it is evident (*constare*) that the original judgment was unjust. What is required to conclude that a sentence was manifestly unjust? Canon 1645, §2 stipulates that such injustice is established if any one of the following factors was present:

1° The original judgment must have been based on proofs that subsequently have been discovered to be false. Whatever the source of that false evidence, be it honest mistake or deliberate deceit, it must have been so important that without it the original decision would not have been rendered. In other words, due to the false evidence, the dispositive part of the sentence (i.e., the decision of the tribunal in response to the issue) no longer has a foundation. Thus, discovering that some of the evidence in a case was false is not sufficient to prove injustice provided

the rest of the evidence provides a solid basis for the tribunal's decision.

2° Documents are later discovered that undoubtedly establish new facts, facts which demand a contrary decision. Again, the mere presentation of newly discovered relevant documents is insufficient. The probative force of the new documents must be incontrovertible and must establish facts that prove the original decision was not in accord with truth and justice.[305]

3° The original judgment was rendered due to the deceit (*dolus*) of one of the parties that harmed the other party or parties.[306] Such fraudulent manipulation of the trial would also provide a basis for a complaint of nullity of the sentence on the ground of the denial of the right of defense (c. 1620, 7°). Unless instigated or encouraged by one of the parties, the deceit of a witness or other person involved in the trial does not give rise to an action for *restitutio* under this heading, but may do so in terms of false proofs (1°).

4° Injustice may be proven if there was evident neglect of a provision of law that was not merely procedural. In other words, procedural flaws in themselves are not to be considered evidence of injustice unless they caused substantive injustice.[307]

5° A *restitutio* is granted against a judgment that was contrary to a previous decision that

---

[305] See the commentary on the nature and trustworthiness of documentary evidence (cc. 1540–1543).

[306] See the commentary on canon 1098 for a discussion on the meaning of the term *dolus*.

[307] While the cases did not involve petitions for *restitutio,* Mendonça gives examples of two Rotal decisions in which procedural formalities were seriously flawed, yet where the Rota concluded that the spirit and substance of the law had been observed. See A. Mendonça, "The Application of the Principle of Equity in Marriage Nullity Cases," *J* 55 (1995) 670–679.

had become *res iudicata*. Of course, this provision does not apply if a previous *restitutio* had been granted against that *res iudicata,* or if that decision had been declared null as the result of a complaint of nullity.

The *nisi* clause in this text (the injustice "is not considered to be established clearly *unless*")[308] indicates that this list is taxative, i.e., that it contains the only causes of injustice which can be the foundation of *restitutio in integrum.* Canon 1460, §2, however, speaks of the possibility of a *restitutio in integrum* in the situation where an exception has been made against a judge on the basis of relative incompetence (c. 1407, §§1–2). If in response to the exception the judge decrees the tribunal to be competent, there is no appeal against this ruling. The canon, however, indicates that a complaint of nullity and *restitutio in integrum* are not prohibited against the sentence as a whole on the basis of the relative incompetence of the judge. Relative incompetence is not listed as one of the causes of injustice providing a basis for *restitutio* in canon 1645, §2. The only one of the five categories under which it might fall is 4°, neglect of a provision of law that is not merely procedural. Yet, the rules governing relative incompetence are strictly procedural laws. To provide the basis for a *restitutio,* an incorrectly issued decree of competence would need to be not merely procedurally erroneous, but also substantively unjust.

Issues to Be Adjudicated
before the Original Judge

Canon 1646 — §1. *Restitutio in integrum* for the reasons mentioned in can. 1645, §2, nn. 1–3 must be sought from the judge who rendered the sentence within three months computed from the day the person became aware of these same reasons.

This first paragraph governs petitions for *restitutio in integrum* based on numbers one through three of canon 1645, §2 only. Unless the injured party is a minor (see the commentary on c. 1646, §3 below), such a petition is to be presented within a period of three months. This time limit is computed from the day on which the party became aware of the injustice, not from the day of the publication of the sentence. Thus, many years might pass between the issuance of the judgment and the discovery of its injustice. Petitions for *restitutio* on the bases of paragraphs one to three must be lodged before the judge who delivered the original judgment.[309]

Issues to Be Adjudicated
before the Appellate Tribunal

§2. *Restitutio in integrum* for the reasons mentioned in can. 1645, §2, nn. 4 and 5 must be sought from the appellate tribunal within three months from the notice of the publication of the sentence; if in the case mentioned in can. 1645, §2, n. 5 notice of the previous decision occurs later, however, the time limit runs from this notice.

This second paragraph governs petitions for *restitutio in integrum* based on items four and five of canon 1645, §2 only. Unless the injured party is a minor (see the commentary on c. 1646, §3 below), such a petition is to be presented within a period of three months from the notification of the publication of the sentence. This norm presumes, therefore, that the parties to the case are aware of the existence of the factors described in items four and five. When, however, the injured party had not received notice of the prior judgment that had become *res iudicata,* the three-month time limit to petition for a *restitutio* begins with the notification of the existence of that previous judgment.

---

[308] Canon 39, while referring directly to conditions in administrative acts rather than laws, explains the significant legal effect of the Latin terms *si, nisi,* and *dummodo.*

[309] If so much time has passed that the original judge is no longer available, the petition is lodged before the original tribunal where the judgment was issued.

Special Protection for Minors

§3. The time limits mentioned above do not run as long as the injured person is a minor.

In canon law, a minor is a person under the age of eighteen (c. 97, §1). Historically, the institute of *restitutio in integrum* developed as an extraordinary remedy to protect the rights of minors involved in litigation.[310] While its use has been expanded, this paragraph provides special protection for minors. Whatever the foundation that would justify *restitutio,* the time limits for seeking that remedy do not apply as long as the injured party is a minor. The minor's right to petition for a *restitutio* perdures until the person celebrates his or her eighteenth birthday, when the time limits begin to run in accord with the previous two paragraphs.

Effects of a Petition for Restitutio

Canon 1647 — §1. The petition for *restitutio in integrum* suspends the execution of a sentence if execution has not yet begun.

§2. If from probable indications there is a suspicion that a petition has been made in order to delay the execution, however, the judge can decree execution of the sentence, though with suitable guarantees to the one seeking the *restitutio* that there will be indemnity if the *restitutio in integrum* is granted.

The law gives a petition for *restitutio in integrum* suspensive effect preventing the execution of the judgment.[311] There are two exceptions to this general rule. First, if the execution of the judgment has already been completed or even initiated, the petition for *restitutio* does not suspend that execution. Second, judges before whom petitions for *restitutio* are lodged retain the discretion

to order a provisional execution of the sentences. Judges may exercise this power only if they are convinced that the request for reinstatement is merely a delaying tactic designed to prevent the execution of the sentence. When exercising the power to order the judgment executed despite the petition for *restitutio,* however, the judges must provide guarantees indemnifying the party petitioning for a *restitutio.*

Effects of Grant/Denial
of a Petition for Restitutio

Canon 1648 — If *restitutio in integrum* is granted, the judge must pronounce on the merits of the case.

When a petition for a *restitutio in integrum* is denied, the original judgment retains its full force. If it has not yet been executed, the execution may begin immediately.

If the petition for a *restitutio in integrum* is granted, however, the original judgment is completely overturned, leaving the original controversy at the heart of the trial unresolved. The law could have provided that the matter then be returned to the original court for the process to resume.[312] Instead, this canon stipulates that the judge or judges who granted the *restitutio* must then proceed to rule on the merits of the case. The judge would conduct the renewed trial according to the process suitable for the issue at stake (e.g., ordinary contentious process, oral contentious process, documentary process).[313]

---

[310] Johnson, *"Res iudicata,"* 327.

[311] This differs from the provisions for a new presentation of the case (see the commentary on c. 1644, §2).

[312] This is the situation, for example, when a second instance tribunal declares the nullity of a first instance sentence. See commentary on c. 1625.

[313] A *restitutio in integrum* could be granted only against the second of two conforming decisions rather than against both. If so, the first judgment remains in force, and the new trial is conducted at the same grade (instance) as that of the judgment that was overturned.

Title X
Judicial Expenses and Gratuitous Legal Assistance[314]
[c. 1649]

Particular Law on Fees and Legal Aid

Canon 1649 — §1. The bishop who directs the tribunal is to establish norms concerning:

1° the requirement of the parties to pay or compensate judicial expenses;

2° the fees for the procurators, advocates, experts, and interpreters and the indemnity for the witnesses;

3° the grant of gratuitous legal assistance or reduction of the expenses;

4° the recovery of damages owed by a person who not only lost the trial but also entered into the litigation rashly;

5° the deposit of money or the provision furnished for the payment of expenses and recovery of damages.

Rather than attempt the impossible task of providing detailed norms for the universal Church, this canon provides that the bishop governing each tribunal is to enact particular law to govern tribunal fees and legal aid.[315] Among other things, those norms would need to implement the provisions of canons 1523 and 1525 concerning expenses when a trial is abated or renounced.[316]

---

[314] Wrenn, in *CLSA Com,* 1005; Ryan, in *CLSGBI Com,* 924; Diego-Lora, in *Pamplona ComEng,* 1019–1020; Acebal, in *Salamanca Com,* 801–802; Arroba Conde, in *Valencia Com,* 712–713; E. de León, in *Com Ex* IV/2, 1739–1744.

[315] *CCEO* 1335 is worded slightly differently, noting that the "statutes of the tribunal" are to provide norms for this purpose. This wording is more precise, since interdiocesan tribunals may not be subject to a specific bishop.

[316] Particular law should also make a determination concerning the payment of the fees associated with appeal of cases to the Roman Rota. According to the current policy for the United States, a stipend of between $750 and $850 is to be forwarded to the Rota with an appeal (*RRAO 1994,* 26). The Rota does not determine whether

Whatever the determination of particular law, the provisions should be made clear to the parties at the beginning of the trial (c. 1464). Thus, when the specific determination of the expenses is made in the sentence (see c. 1611, 4°), the assessment of fees will not be seen as arbitrary, but as the application of the previously communicated policy.

Among the five areas listed, it is vital that realistic provisions for free legal aid or reduction of expenses (3°) be enacted. Otherwise, the exercise of the rights enunciated in canon 221 may be impaired or thwarted. Canon 1334 of the Eastern code specifies the following:

> The poor, that is, those who are totally unable to pay the court costs, have the right to gratuitous legal assistance; those who can pay only part of the court costs, to a diminution of expenses.

While the Latin code, unfortunately, has no parallel explicit proclamation of this right, the right to legal assistance nonetheless exists, is recognized implicitly, and must be respected.

Recourse against Court Fees

§2. There is no separate appeal from the determination of expenses, fees, and recovery of damages, but the party can make recourse within fifteen days to the same judge who can adjust the assessment.

There is no distinct appeal to a tribunal of higher grade concerning the provisions of a sentence regarding the apportionment of expenses. Within fifteen days of the notification of the fees,[317] how-

---

only one or both of the parties are responsible for this stipend, permitting the local tribunal to implement the norm provided that policy would "in no way compromise the right of appeal of one of the partners to the Apostolic Tribunal" (*RRAO 1998,* 31–32).

[317] The translation used in *CLSGBI Com* and *Pamplona ComEng* incorrectly states that the time limit is ten days. The Latin is *quindecim dies,* fifteen days.

ever, a party who is aggrieved at the provisions for expenses may have recourse to the judge who issued the sentence. That judge is free to modify the amount.

If a party lodges an appeal against the judgment as a whole, may that appeal include a complaint about the determination regarding expenses contained in the sentence? Certainly nothing can prevent a party from raising that issue. The court of appeals, however, does not have jurisdiction over the internal administration of the tribunals it oversees. The appellate court cannot legitimately usurp the role of the bishop as moderator of his tribunal. Thus, in response to a complaint about provisions for expenses, the court of appeals would probably be able to act only if it found evidence that the original tribunal violated its own policies concerning expenses.

TITLE XI
THE EXECUTION OF THE SENTENCE[318]
[cc. 1650–1655]

Lawrence Wrenn defines the execution of a sentence as that "judicial act by which the vindicated party in the trial is actually provided what was awarded in the sentence."[319] The canons of this title establish when a sentence may be executed, who is responsible for the execution, and how a sentence is executed. They also provide norms governing the role of the executor.

Execution of a Sentence That Has Become
Res Iudicata

Canon 1650 — §1. A sentence that has become a *res iudicata* can be executed, without prejudice to the prescript of can. 1647.

A sentence that has become *res iudicata* can be executed. The judge may issue the decree of execution ex officio or may do so in response to the request of a party to the case.

If, however, a petition for *restitutio in integrum* has been filed, that petition has suspensive effect and the judge is not to *begin*[320] the execution of the sentence unless a specific decree has been issued permitting the execution despite the petition for *restitutio*.[321]

Execution of a Sentence That Is Not
Res Iudicata

§2. The judge who rendered the sentence and, if an appeal has been proposed, also the appellate judge can order *ex officio* or at the request of a party a provisional execution of a sentence which has not yet become *res iudicata*, after having set suitable guarantees, if the case warrants, for provisions or payments ordered for necessary support; they can also do so if some other just cause urges it.

If a judgment has been reached that is not *res iudicata*, that judgment may nonetheless be accorded a provisional execution. For example, a decision may have been reached in one instance only. Since there are not two concordant decisions, that sentence has not attained the status of *res iudicata*. Yet, if the law does not mandate a review of the matter at issue and if the parties are satisfied with the judgment and will not challenge it, the case is effectively settled and the judgment may be executed. Or, if the matter has been appealed and the appellate tribunal nonetheless deems that a provisional execution is warranted, it may issue a decree executing the sentence.

The judge who rendered the sentence is the one with authority to issue the decree executing

---

[318] Wrenn, in *CLSA Com,* 1005–1006; Ryan, in *CLSGBI Com,* 924–927; Diego-Lora, in *Pamplona ComEng,* 1020–1024; Acebal, in *Salamanca Com,* 802–804; Arroba Conde, in *Valencia Com,* 713–715; de León, in *Com Ex* IV/2, 1745–1757.

[319] Wrenn, in *CLSA Com,* 1005.

[320] If the process of executing the sentence has already begun, the judge is not obliged to halt the process. And if the execution of the sentence was already completed, the judge is not to rescind the execution.

[321] See the commentary on c. 1647, §2.

the judgment. If an appeal was filed, the appellate judge likewise has the authority to order the provisional execution of the sentence. When the case involves the provision of basic sustenance to a person, the decree of execution must provide sufficient guarantees of support during the period of provisional execution. In like manner, a judge may include similar guarantees protecting a party's needs or rights if some other just cause warrants.

Suspending the Execution or Requiring Safeguards

§3. If the sentence mentioned in §2 is challenged, the judge who must investigate the challenge can suspend the execution or subject it to a guarantee if the judge sees that the challenge is probably well founded and irreparable damage can arise from execution.

This paragraph concerns a case in which a judicial sentence

1. has not become *res iudicata* and
2. has been challenged either by appeal (cc. 1628–1640) or by a complaint of nullity of sentence (cc. 1619–1627)

and a decree of provisional execution of the judgment already has been issued.

Before being able to rule definitively, the judge responsible for considering the challenge may realize that the challenge is solidly founded and that irreparable harm may result from the execution of the sentence. In these circumstances, the judge has the authority either to suspend the execution of the sentence or to incorporate appropriate safeguards into that execution to prevent the potential damage.

The Executory Decree

Canon 1651 — Execution cannot occur prior to the executory decree of the judge which declares that the sentence must be executed. This decree is

to be included in the text of the sentence or issued separately according to the particular nature of the cases.

The execution of the judgment requires a judicial decree of execution. This decree should not only order the execution but also specify the means to be used in executing the judgment.

Depending on the nature of the case, the decree of execution may be issued as a separate document or incorporated into the text of the sentence itself. For example, in a marriage nullity case there can be no decree of execution for an affirmative sentence issued in first instance, since two concordant decisions are required to establish freedom to marry. The conforming sentence or decree of ratification of that sentence in second instance, on the other hand, should incorporate a decree of execution.

Rendering of Accounts as an Incidental Case

Canon 1652 — If the execution of a sentence requires a prior rendering of accounts, it is an incidental question which the same judge who rendered the sentence ordering the execution must decide.

This canon governs trials involving disputes over property. In some circumstances, such a judgment may be executed without an exact rendering of accounts. In other circumstances, the nature of the judgment may require a full accounting before it can be properly executed. In these situations, the judge who rendered the decision is to arrange for that accounting according to the norms for incidental cases (cc. 1587–1591). Since the law itself proposes this particular incidental case, the provision of canon 1588 requiring a petition from one of the parties is unnecessary.

The Execution Proper

Canon 1653 — §1. Unless particular law establishes otherwise, the bishop of the diocese in which the sentence was rendered in the first

grade must execute the sentence personally or through another.

The law distinguishes between the specifically judicial acts of rendering a sentence (cc. 1610–1613) and issuing a decree of execution (c. 1651), and the actual execution of those judicial acts, which is understood as an administrative act.[322]

Unless particular law provides otherwise, the diocesan bishop[323] of the tribunal where the first instance judgment was rendered is responsible for the execution of the sentence. The execution may be handled personally or through a delegate, who is to fulfill that responsibility in accord with the canons of this title.[324]

Particular law is given a strictly limited role in the Church's procedural law. The latitude provided for particular law to establish norms for executing sentences reflects the realization that, to be effective, such an execution must take into account the unique cultural, educational, and linguistic backgrounds of the persons involved. Whether designated by particular law or delegated by the diocesan bishop, in practice the judicial vicar is frequently entrusted with the responsibility of executing sentences. The bishop, however, may entrust that responsibility to any other qualified person, cleric or lay.[325]

---

[322] de León, in *Com Ex* IV/2, 1746, 1754; Diego-Lora, in *Pamplona ComEng,* 1022.

[323] Since the term "diocesan bishop" is employed, local ordinaries such as a vicar general or episcopal vicar do not have the authority to execute a sentence without a special mandate to do so (c. 134, §3).

[324] Since the execution of a judicial act is an administrative function, the norms of cc. 40–45 are also applicable and may help executors resolve doubts about the correct means of fulfilling their functions.

[325] Wrenn indicates that only by exception should the judge act as executor (*CLSA Com,* 1006). His understandable concern seems to be emphasizing the distinction between judicial and administrative authority. Nothing in the law, however, prevents the bishop from entrusting this responsibility to judges who, in this situation, would be exercising delegated administrative power rather than distinctly judicial authority.

Remedying a Failure to Execute a Sentence

§2. If he refuses or neglects to do this, the execution of the sentence, either at the request of an interested party or even *ex officio,* pertains to the authority to whom the appellate tribunal is subject according to the norm of can. 1439, §3.

Failure to execute a sentence, except under the circumstances provided in canon 1654, §2, creates a serious injustice, since it prevents the judgment from coming into full force. Thus, if the diocesan bishop fails to see to the execution of the sentence originally issued by his court, the responsibility devolves on the ecclesiastical authority who oversees the appellate tribunal to which that first instance tribunal is subject.[326] That authority might be the archbishop of the metropolitan tribunal (c. 1438, 1°), the diocesan bishop of a tribunal designated as the court of second instance by the Apostolic See (c. 1438, 2°), or the episcopal moderator or governing bishops of an interdiocesan or national second instance tribunal (c. 1439, §3).

This authority may intervene and execute the sentence ex officio or, more likely, at the request of one of the parties aggrieved by the fact that it has not been executed.

Execution of Sentences of Religious Tribunals

§3. Among religious the execution of the sentence pertains to the superior who rendered the sentence to be executed or the superior who delegated the judge.

When the trial was conducted before a religious tribunal, the authority responsible to execute the sentence is the major superior who personally judged the case or who delegated the judge who tried the case.[327] Should the one re-

---

[326] The canon is poorly drafted, since it evidently should have referred to both cc. 1438 and 1439. The Eastern code is clearer (*CCEO* 1340, §2).

[327] See the commentary on c. 1427 which specifies the proper judge for various types of disputes involving reli-

sponsible to execute the sentence fail to do so (similar to the problem envisioned in c. 1653, §2), recourse would be taken to the appropriate superior as specified in the constitutions of the particular institute or society.

Role of the Executor

Canon 1654 — §1. Unless the text of the sentence leaves it to the judgment of the executor, the executor must execute the sentence according to the obvious sense of the words.

§2. The executor is permitted to deal with exceptions concerning the manner and force of the execution but not concerning the merit of the case. If it is discovered from another source that the sentence is null or manifestly unjust according to the norm of cann. 1620, 1622, and 1645, the executor is to refrain from executing it and, after having informed the parties, is to refer the matter to the tribunal which rendered the sentence.

Unless something is expressly left to the executor's discretion in the sentence or decree of execution, the executor must execute the judgment "according to the obvious sense of the words." Should there be any doubt, the executor should seek clarification from the one who issued the judgment.

The executor is not merely a robot, however, and enjoys some latitude as provided in the law. If an exception is raised concerning the manner and force of the execution, the executor may deal with that on his or her own authority. The executor may not, however, deal with any exception concerning the merits of the case, a matter which is the exclusive province of the tribunal.

Finally, an executor is bound not to execute the judgment if he or she encounters convincing evidence either:

(1) that the judgment is null (cc. 1620, 1622), and hence able to be challenged by a complaint of nullity of sentence; or

gious, whether individuals, houses, provinces, or juridic persons.

(2) that the judgment is manifestly unjust for one of the reasons specified in canon 1645, §2, and hence open to a petition for *restitutio in integrum.*

In this situation, the executor is to inform the parties of his or her inability to execute the judgment and then immediately refer the matter and any new information discovered to the tribunal that rendered the decision.

Time for Fulfillment of Obligations

Canon 1655 — §1. In real actions, whenever the petitioner is awarded something, it must be handed over to the petitioner as soon as there is a *res iudicata.*

§2. In personal actions, when the guilty party is condemned to furnish a movable thing, to pay money, or to give or do something else, the judge in the text of the sentence or the executor according to his or her judgment and prudence is to establish a time limit to fulfill the obligation; this time limit, however, is not to be less than fifteen days nor more than six months.

Normally, upon execution of a sentence, its provisions take immediate effect. This canon contains norms for establishing reasonable time limits to fulfill the obligations required by certain types of judgments.

Paragraph one refers to trials where the central issue involved real actions, that is, disputes about the ownership of property whether movable or immovable. When the tribunal's judgment determined that the property belongs to the plaintiff, the execution of the sentence should provide for the immediate transfer of the disputed property. This reflects the fact that, since the communication of the citation, the matter in dispute had ceased to be a *res integra* (see the commentary on c. 1512). Thus, since the possessor had been on notice that the property was under dispute and subject to the court's judgment, he or she cannot claim a need for further time to transfer possession to the plaintiff.

Paragraph two governs trials where the central issue involved personal actions, that is, disputes over the rights and obligations of persons. When the tribunal's resolution of the dispute includes the requirement to hand over some object, pay monetary compensation, or perform some other action to make restitution to the injured party (e.g., a public retraction or apology), the executor may establish a time limit within which the obligation must be fulfilled. Depending on the nature of the obligation and the arrangements required to fulfill it, the executor is to establish an appropriate time limit ranging from fifteen days to six months.

BIBLIOGRAPHY

Bibliographical material for canons 1501–1655 can be found after the commentary on canon 1691.

SECTION II
THE ORAL CONTENTIOUS PROCESS
[cc. 1656–1670][1]

Origin of the Process

A frequent complaint about the procedural law governing contentious trials in the 1917 code was that it was encumbered with unnecessary and outdated procedural formalities that inevitably resulted in long, protracted trials. Thus, early in its deliberations, the *coetus* of the code revision committee responsible for procedural law formulated a proposal for a streamlined judicial process. This initiative was eventually promulgated as the oral contentious process.

Although the oral contentious process is one of the procedural innovations of the revised code, it has historical precedents. In part, the oral contentious process was inspired by the summary procedure introduced by Clement V (1305–1314) in his decretal *Saepe,* which became, in practice at least, the normal form of canonical procedure until the promulgation of the 1917 code.[2] In part, the new process was modeled on the "contentious trial before a single judge" in the procedural law promulgated in 1950 by Pius XII for the Eastern churches[3] and a similar process in the Code of Civil Procedure for the Vatican City State.[4] In addition to these canonical antecedents, the elaboration of the oral contentious process was also deeply influenced by trends in continental European legal scholarship that emphasize the values

---

[1] *CCEO* 1343–1356 treat this institute as "The Summary Contentious Process" in chapter 2 of title XXV: "The Contentious Trial."

[2] *In Clem.* V, 11, 2.

[3] Pius XII, *mp Sollicitudinem nostram,* June 6, 1950, cc. 453–467, *AAS* 42 (1950) 98–99.

[4] A. Stankiewicz, "Il processo contenzioso orale," *Apol* 64 (1992) 570.

of oral testimony and discussion, direct personal interchanges between the parties and the judge, public trials, and the expeditious resolution of cases.[5]

Cases for Which the Oral Process Can Be Used

Canon 1656 — §1. All cases not excluded by law can be treated in the oral contentious process mentioned in this section unless a party requests the ordinary contentious process.

§2. If the oral process is used outside of the cases permitted in law, the judicial acts are null.

Despite the apparent openness to the use of the oral contentious process in paragraph one, its use is expressly prohibited for marriage cases (c. 1690), penal cases (c. 1728, §1), and cases involving the validity of ordination (c. 1710). Its use is allowed for cases involving the separation of spouses (c. 1693, §1), complaints of nullity against a sentence even in marriage and penal cases (c. 1627), resolution of incidental cases by interlocutory sentences (c. 1590, §1), and questions about the right to appeal (c. 1631). Even when the law does not preclude the use of the oral process, either party or, in cases where their intervention is required, the defender of the bond or promoter of justice can petition that the ordinary process be employed, and the judge must honor this request. However, there are two exceptions to this rule: the judge rather than the parties has discretion to use the oral process or not for the resolution of incidental cases, and the use of the oral process to resolve disputes concerning the right of appeal is mandatory.

If the oral contentious process is used in cases not permitted by law, all subsequent judicial acts are null. This nullity results both when the oral

---

[5] L. Madero, "El proceso contencioso oral," *IC* 24 (1984) 219–265.

process is used for cases expressly excluded by law and when the judge ignores a party's request that the ordinary process be employed.

Single Judge

Canon 1657 — The oral contentious process takes place in the first grade before a single judge according to the norm of can. 1424.

A single judge is the norm for this process at first instance. However, the use of two assessors is recommended (c. 1424). Since the oral process is designed to allow direct contact between the judge and the parties and witnesses, no mention is made of the use of an auditor. When a case has been resolved by a single judge at first instance, the appellate court normally consists of a single judge as well (c. 1441). A collegiate tribunal is necessary at any grade of trial for the judicial resolution of incidental cases when the principal case has been entrusted to a college (c. 1590, §1) and for the resolution of complaints of nullity when the impugned sentence has been issued by a college (c. 1624). The Roman Rota always proceeds collegially regardless of the process used.[6]

The Petition

Canon 1658 — §1. In addition to the things enumerated in can. 1504, the *libellus* which introduces the litigation must:
    1° set forth briefly, completely, and clearly the facts on which the requests of the petitioner are based;
    2° indicate the proofs by which the petitioner intends to demonstrate the facts but which cannot be presented at once, in such a way that the judge can collect them immediately.
  §2. The documents on which the petition is based must be attached to the *libellus,* at least in an authentic copy.

[6] Stankiewicz, 583.

Since a trial according to the oral process is brief, the petition initiating this process must be more complete than that for the ordinary process. In addition to the items mentioned in canon 1504, the petition must contain a thorough narration of the facts on which the case is based, a complete listing of the proofs on which the petitioner intends to rely, and any relevant documents in the petitioner's possession. The indication that the judge is to proceed to collect proofs immediately (*statim*) suggests that he begins to collect proofs even before the hearing. These proofs are primarily documents, but they may include the testimony of witnesses who can be heard only by rogatory commission (see. c. 1418) or through a written affidavit.

Citation

Canon 1659 — §1. If the attempt at reconciliation according to the norm of can. 1446, §2 proved useless and the judge thinks that the *libellus* has some foundation, the judge is to order within three days by a decree appended to the bottom of the *libellus* that a copy of the petition be communicated to the respondent, giving to the latter the opportunity to send a written response to the tribunal chancery within fifteen days.
  §2. This notification has the effect of the judicial citation mentioned in can. 1512.

Once a petition has been received, a tribunal is constituted. The judge's first responsibility is to ascertain whether an out-of-court settlement is possible. If efforts at conciliation prove fruitless, the judge is to determine within three days whether the petition should be accepted. The accepted petition along with proposed proofs and attached documents is then communicated to the other party. Appended to the petition is a judicial decree offering the other party an opportunity to respond in writing to the issues raised in the petition within fifteen useful days. This response should be as thorough as the original petition and should include a listing of all proofs the party intends to propose and all relevant documents in the respondent's possession. In fact, the judge's decree may request that the respondent produce documents mentioned by, but unavailable to, the petitioner. The response should also include any exceptions the party intends to raise and, if the party wishes, a request that the dispute be resolved by the ordinary process. The judge's decree has the legal effect of a judicial citation.

Rejoinder by the Petitioner

Canon 1660 — If the exceptions of the respondent demand it, the judge is to establish a time limit for the petitioner to respond, in such a way that from the points brought forth by both of the parties the judge clarifies the object of the controversy.

The respondent's reply to the citation may raise questions about the legal issues to be resolved in the dispute or, in the case of exceptions and countersuits, issues that were not dealt with in the petition. The judge may allow the petitioner a peremptory time period within which to reply to the respondent's rejoinder.

Joinder of Issues

Canon 1661 — §1. When the time limits mentioned in cann. 1659 and 1660 have elapsed, the judge, after an examination of the acts, is to determine the formula of the doubt. Next, the judge is to cite all those who must take part to a hearing which must be held within thirty days; the formula of the doubt is to be attached to the citation of the parties.

§2. In the citation the parties are to be informed that they can present a brief written statement to the tribunal to verify their claims at least three days before the hearing.

When the limits for replies have elapsed, the judge joins the issues ex officio on the basis of the submissions of the parties. There is no provision for recourse by the parties to seek a revision of

the grounds (c. 1513, §3). Instead, in a decree summoning the parties to a hearing to be held within thirty days of the joining of the issues, the judge informs the parties of the grounds that have been set. If a party has not petitioned for the use of the ordinary contentious process by the time of the joinder of the issues, he or she is estopped from making such a petition subsequently.[7]

The judge also cites parties, witnesses, and experts to be present at the hearing. At the same time, the parties are to be informed that they may present a brief written statement of their positions. These written statements are to be submitted at least three days prior to the hearing. Although the code is silent on the issue, fairness seems to demand that these written statements be made available to the opposing parties before the hearing.

The Hearing

Canon 1662 — At the hearing the questions mentioned in cann. 1459–1464 are treated first.

Canon 1663 — §1. The proofs are collected at the hearing without prejudice to the prescript of can. 1418.

§2. A party and his or her advocate can be present at the examination of the other parties, the witnesses, and the experts.

The hearing is the centerpiece of the oral contentious process. The judge directs the hearing and the parties and their advocates have the right to be present for the whole session. After disposing of any exceptions or motions, the judge proceeds to collect the outstanding evidence. Since no opportunity is foreseen for re-examining witnesses once the hearing has concluded, the judge must strictly enforce the norm requiring that the party seeking to introduce a witness inform the judge in advance of the hearing of the issues about which the witness ought to be questioned (c. 1552, §2). The judge personally interrogates

---

[7] Madero, 272.

the parties, witnesses, and experts. The parties or their advocates can suggest additional questions to the judge and, at the discretion of the judge, the parties' advocates can be permitted to address questions directly to a party or witness (cc. 1561, 1670).

The Role of the Notary

Canon 1664 — The notary must put into writing the responses of the parties, the witnesses, and the experts and the petitions and exceptions of the advocates, but in a summary fashion and only in those matters pertaining to the substance of the dispute; the deponents must sign these acts.

A notary must be present at the hearing to record the responses of the parties and witnesses to the judge's questions and any exceptions or petitions made by the advocates. The code does not, however, foresee the creation of a verbatim transcript of the hearing. Only a summary of the testimony relevant to the points in dispute needs be taken down. To determine the matters that ought to be recorded, the notary must have legal as well as stenographic skills. The notary's summaries must be reviewed and signed by the deponents.

Limits on New Evidence

Canon 1665 — The judge can admit proofs which are not brought forth or sought in the petition or response only according to the norm of can. 1452. After even one witness has been heard, however, the judge can only decide about new proofs according to the norm of can. 1600.

Evidence that was not presented or asked for in either the petition or the rejoinder of the respondent cannot be admitted at the hearing unless the judge believes that the failure to admit this evidence will result in an unjust decision. Once even a single witness has testified at the hearing, the judge can allow the admission of proofs not previously requested only under the conditions that would allow for the collection of new evidence after the conclusion of the case in the ordinary process.[8]

These rather severe restrictions on the freedom of the judge to admit evidence not mentioned in the petition and response of the parties are necessitated by the short time frame of the oral contentious process. All of the outstanding evidence is collected in one or, at most, two sessions. To admit evidence about which one or both parties had no prior notice leaves little time in which to prepare a defense or to unearth contrary evidence.

Conclusion of the Case and Oral Discussion

Canon 1666 — If all the proofs were not able to be collected during the hearing, a second hearing is to be scheduled.

Canon 1667 — When the proofs have been collected, the oral discussion takes place at the same hearing.

Unlike the ordinary contentious process, the oral process requires no formal decree publishing the acts of the case. Since the parties either had access to evidence prior to the hearing or assisted at its collection during the hearing, publication of the acts is superfluous. There is also no decree formally concluding the probatory phase of the trial. When all the evidence has been collected, the advocates are invited to discuss the case orally, perhaps after a brief recess.

The oral discussion requires of advocates skills different from those needed for the preparation of written briefs. It also requires that the judge have the skill to maintain courtroom decorum and prevent the discussion from degenerating into a shouting match while at the same time listening attentively to the substantive arguments being raised by the advocates. The notary is to take down a summary of the arguments made by the advocates to assist the judge in his deliberation.

[8] See the commentary on c. 1600.

Pronouncement of the Judge

Canon 1668 — §1. Unless the discussion reveals that something must be supplied in the instruction of the case or something else turns up which prevents a proper pronouncement of the sentence, at the completion of the hearing the judge in private is to decide the case immediately; the dispositive part of the sentence is to be read at once before the parties who are present.

§2. The tribunal can defer the decision up to the fifth useful day because of the difficulty of the matter or for some other just cause.

§3. The complete text of the sentence with the reasons expressed is to be communicated to the parties as soon as possible, ordinarily in not more than fifteen days.

Unless it becomes clear that additional evidence is needed, the judge is to decide the case at the end of oral discussion. He retires to consider the evidence and deliberate in private. The dispositive section of the decision is then read to the parties. If the difficulty of the issues prevents the judge from reaching a decision within a brief time after the conclusion of the hearing, the reading of the decision can be deferred for up to five days. The complete written text of the decision with reasons in law and in fact is to be communicated to the parties promptly, normally within fifteen days of the announcement of its dispositive section. The communication of the full text of the sentence to the parties is comparable to the publication of the sentence. Thus, it should be effected by one of the methods mentioned in canon 1615 and the peremptory period for lodging an appeal runs from the date of this notification.

Appellate Tribunal

Canon 1669 — If the appellate tribunal discovers that the oral contentious process was used at a lower grade of a trial in cases excluded by law, it is to declare the nullity of the sentence and remit the case to the tribunal which rendered the sentence.

In the case of an appeal, the appellate court is to declare the nullity of the sentence ex officio if it detects that the oral contentious process was employed to resolve a case for which the law expressly bars its use.

The nullity in this case is irremediable. Just as canon 1400, §2 removes controversies arising from acts of administrative power from the scope of the judicial process altogether and renders judges absolutely incompetent, so the various canons that expressly prohibit the use of the oral contentious process for certain types of cases withdraw these matters from the scope of the oral contentious process. Thus, the nullity of the sentence in these cases is irremediable because of the absolute incompetence of the judge (c. 1620, 1°).[9] After declaring the nullity of the sentence, the appellate tribunal remands the case to the lower tribunal for a new trial according to the ordinary contentious process.

Canon 1656, §1 distinguishes between "cases not excluded by law" for treatment according to the oral contentious process and cases in which one of the parties has requested the use of the ordinary contentious process. The repetition of the phrase "cases excluded by law" in canon 1669 suggests that the unlawful use of the oral contentious process results in the irremediable nullity of a sentence only when the law itself expressly bars the use of the oral process for particular types of cases, not when the oral process was employed despite a request of a party for the ordinary process. Only in the former case is the appellate tribunal authorized to declare the nullity of the sentence of the lower court ex officio.

Nevertheless, since the judge is bound to honor the request of a party for the ordinary process, use of the oral contentious process is not "permitted in law" when a party has made such a request (c. 1656, §2). Thus, failure to honor a party's request for the use of the ordinary process results in the nullity of all subsequent judicial acts (c. 1656, §2). Consequently, in a case affecting the public good, the failure to honor a party's request for the use of

[9] Stankiewicz, 581.

the ordinary process results in the remediable nullity of the sentence because the decision is based on null and as yet unsanated judicial acts (c. 1622, 5°). A party or, if he or she has intervened, the defender of the bond or promoter of justice can propose a complaint of nullity to the original judge within three months of the notification of the sentence (c. 1623) or join the complaint to an appeal of the sentence. In cases affecting only the private good, null judicial acts are sanated by the sentence unless a party denounced them to the judge prior to the sentence (c. 1619).[10]

Derogation from Procedural Norms

Canon 1670 — In other matters pertaining to the manner of proceeding, the prescripts of the canons for the ordinary contentious trial are to be observed. In order to expedite matters without prejudice to justice, however, the tribunal, by a decree expressing the reasons for its decision, can derogate from procedural norms which have not been established for validity.

The canons dealing specifically with the oral contentious process are to be supplemented as needed by the norms for the ordinary process. However, the judge has discretion to derogate from procedural norms whose observance is not required for validity.[11] These derogations are to be in the form of written decrees that explain the reasons for the departure from ordinary procedure. This provision for derogations from procedural norms is itself an exception to the general principle that procedural laws are not subject to dispensation (c. 87, §1).

[10] Ibid., 580–581.

[11] In the order in which they come into play in a contentious trial, procedural norms whose observance is required for the validity of the process include: cc. 1507; 1433; 1478, §§2–4; 1437, §1; 1598; 1611; 1612, §§3–4; 1614; 1622, 2°–4°.

BIBLIOGRAPHY

Bibliographical material for canons 1656–1670 can be found after the commentary on canon 1691.

Part III
CERTAIN SPECIAL PROCESSES
[cc. 1671–1716]

Part three of Book VII provides supplementary norms governing processes where the unique nature of the cases requires adjustments to the basic procedures. Besides norms governing various marriage processes (cc. 1671–1707), this part also contains a

title governing cases for declaring the nullity of sacred orders (cc. 1708–1712) and a title on methods of avoiding trial (cc. 1713–1716). The norms of the Eastern code are largely identical except for the chapter on methods of avoiding a trial.[1]

[1] *CCEO* 1164–1184 develops methods of avoiding a trial with much greater precision and detail. The Eastern code treats these norms in the title on trials in general, just before the norms on the contentious trial.

CANONS AND COMMENTARY

TITLE I
MARRIAGE PROCESSES[2]
[cc. 1671–1707]

This title contains the norms governing marriage nullity cases (cc. 1671–1691), cases of the separation of spouses (cc. 1692–1696), the process for the dispensation of a *ratum et non consummatum* marriage (cc. 1697–1706), and the process to be employed in investigating the presumed death of a spouse (c. 1707).

CHAPTER I
CASES TO DECLARE THE NULLITY
OF MARRIAGE
[cc. 1671–1691]

Marriage nullity cases form the vast majority of ecclesiastical trials.[3] The procedures governing

these cases are a means employed by the Church to serve its mission. In particular, the procedural law governing marriage nullity processes was designed to foster and to protect critically important values such as fidelity to truth, the protection of the rights and the spiritual welfare of persons, the Church's witness to the sacredness of marriage, canonical equity, and the Church's common good.[4] Thus, to avoid legalism or a pure juridical formalism, these procedures must always be understood and implemented in light of those foundational values.

The code structures marriage nullity procedures as a species of trials in general (cc. 1400–1500) and of the ordinary contentious process (cc. 1501–1655). This is specified in canon 1691, which

[2] For a brief history of the development of matrimonial procedures, see L. Wrenn, in *CLSA Com,* 1009–1011. For reflections primarily from the viewpoint of changes made in the current legislation governing matrimonial processes, see J. Llobell, in *Com Ex* IV/2, 1812–1828.

[3] In 1996 there were 60,677 formal marriage nullity cases introduced and 61,806 were closed. Of those closed,

49,512 received decisions in favor of nullity, 2,690 received negative decisions, and the remainder were perempted or renounced. Secretaria Status, *Statistical Yearbook of the Church 1996* (Vatican City: Libreria Editrice Vaticana, 1998) 421 and 440.

[4] For a discussion of the purpose of marriage nullity processes and the values which the tribunal system strives to foster, see C. A. Cox, *Procedural Changes in Formal Marriage Nullity Cases from the 1917 to the 1983 Code, CanLawStud* 528 (Washington, D.C.: Catholic University of America, 1989) 299–345.

along with the other "general norms" for marriage nullity cases (cc. 1689–1690) might have been more appropriately placed in the first article at the beginning of this chapter rather than in the seventh and concluding article. All of the canons of this chapter, then, specify and adapt the overall trial procedure for marriage nullity cases.

During the code revision process, suggestions were made to revise more drastically the procedures for handling such cases. Some recommended completely abandoning a judicial approach in favor of some other model. Others recommended that a modified judicial approach be maintained, but that marriage cases not be treated using a "contentious" process. These recommendations for more thoroughly rethinking the process were not admitted.[5]

In his 1998 allocution to the Roman Rota, Pope John Paul II announced the creation of an interdicasterial commission "charged with drafting an instruction on the conduct of trials concerning marriage cases."[6] Presumably, this may be similar to the instruction *Provida Mater Ecclesia* issued subsequent to the promulgation of the 1917 code.[7] As of the spring of 1999, the interdicasterial commission has prepared an initial draft of such an instruction that is being circulated to episcopal conferences and other consultative groups for evalua-

tion. There is no indication, however, when the proposed instruction might be forthcoming. If and when one is issued, the instruction's provisions would guide the interpretation and implementation of the current law (c. 34).

ARTICLE 1: THE COMPETENT FORUM[8]
[cc. 1671–1673]

The Church's Fundamental Right to Judge

Canon 1671 — Marriage cases of the baptized belong to the ecclesiastical judge by proper right.

This proclamation of the Church's right to adjudicate marriage cases in which at least one of the spouses is baptized specifies the right to judge cases concerning spiritual matters or connected to spiritual matters claimed in canon 1401, 1°. In comparison to its counterpart in the 1917 code (*CIC* 1960), canon 1671 does not claim this as an "exclusive" right of the Church, although canon 1401 claims such exclusivity. In reality, ecclesiastical tribunals do not insist on exclusive jurisdiction and recognize certain rights of other churches and of civil society to rule on some aspects of marriage.[9]

Canon 1671 claims a right to treat marriage cases involving *all validly baptized persons,* not just those baptized in the Catholic Church or who have been received into full communion with it. This claim is rooted first in the Church's teaching on the nature of baptism, which incorporates a

---

[5] It is beyond the scope of this commentary to delve further into this topic. For an in-depth review of various recommendations, see C. A. Cox, *Procedural Changes,* 108–204. For a brief discussion of unadopted proposals for changes within the context of the current system, see idem, "The Procedural Law That Might Have Been: Some Proposed Changes That Were Not Adopted during the Code Revision Process," *J* 50 (1990) 613–642. Since the promulgation of the code, there has been little formal discussion of the question of alternatives, since canonists have rightly focused on implementing the current legislation. Yet, interest in alternative approaches remains. For example, see the brief comments *coram* Burke, May 22, 1997, *Stud Can* 32 (1998) 516–517, and F. G. Morrisey, "*Decimo anno* . . . On the Tenth Anniversary of the *Code of Canon Law,*" *Stud Can* 28 (1994) 120.

[6] John Paul II, alloc, January 17, 1998, *AAS* 90 (1998) 784. Translated in *Origins* 27 (February 27, 1998) 585.

[7] SCSacr, instr *Provida Mater Ecclesia,* August 15, 1936, *AAS* 28 (1936) 313–361. Translated in *CLD* 2, 471–530.

[8] Wrenn, in *CLSA Com,* 1011–1012; D. Kelly, in *CLSGBI Com,* 932–934; L. Madero, in *Pamplona ComEng,* 1030–1032; J. L. Acebal, in *Salamanca Com,* 809–811; J. Martínez Valls, in *Valencia Com,* 720–721; Llobell, in *Com Ex* IV/2, 1829–1848.

[9] For example, the Church respects the regulations of the Orthodox and other ancient Christian churches of the East regarding impediments and the requirement of the priestly blessing (sacred rite) to enter marriage (see *CCEO* 780, §2 and 781). Ecclesiastical tribunals also respect the determinations of civil authority concerning the civil effects of marriage even for baptized Catholics (see cc. 1059, 1672 and *CCEO* 780, §1; 1358).

person into the Church of Christ (see c. 96) even if that person is not in full communion with the Catholic Church.[10] Furthermore, the Church teaches that the valid marriage of two baptized persons is a sacrament (see c. 1055), and without doubt that sacramental dignity is a "spiritual matter" as understood in canon 1401, 1°.

Since canon 1671 asserts the Church's right to adjudicate concerning the nullity of marriages in which one or both of the spouses was baptized, what of marriages in which neither party was baptized? Does the Church have any claim to judge their status? Normally, the Church leaves judgments concerning the marriages of persons who are not baptized to civil authority, provided the civil authority respects the divine and natural law. The Church claims jurisdiction to deal with such cases not by proper right over the union itself, but indirectly. The Church has the right and duty to serve those who seek its ministry. Accordingly, the Church respects the right of non-baptized persons seeking to be baptized in the Church or non-baptized persons hoping to marry a Catholic to seek a ruling regarding their marital status (see cc. 1476 and 1674).[11]

Finally, although this canon is situated within the context of marriage nullity cases, the right claimed here also is understood to include the right to judge in *ratum et non consummatum* dissolution cases (cc. 1697–1706) and privilege-of-the-faith cases (cc. 1141–1150 and norms for papal dissolutions in favor of the faith[12]).

---

[10] Merely ecclesiastical laws normally bind only those baptized or received into the Catholic Church. Here we have, however, an express provision to the contrary (see c. 11).

[11] See the summary of a Signatura response to a non-Catholic respondent concerning the Church's right to judge the marriages of non-Catholics in *RRAO 1997*, 25–26. Also see J. L. Acebal Luján, "La declaración de nulidad del matrimonio de dos acatólicos: Texto y comentario," *REDC* 49 (1992) 691–697.

[12] CDF, instr *Ut notum est*, December 6, 1973, in *Leges Ecclesiae post Codicem iuris canonici editae*, ed. X. Ochoa, vol. 5 (Rome: Commentarium pro Religiosis, 1980) #4244, cols. 6702–6705. Translated in *CLD* 8, 1177–1184. See also the commentary on c. 1150.

Competence Regarding the Civil Effects of Marriage

Canon 1672 — Cases concerning the merely civil effects of marriage belong to the civil magistrate unless particular law establishes that an ecclesiastical judge can investigate and decide these cases if they are done in an incidental or accessory manner.

This canon recognizes the right and duty of civil authorities to regulate the merely civil effects of marriage dealing with issues such as custody, alimony and child support, inheritance and other property issues, the restoration of the legal use of a maiden name, etc.

When particular ecclesiastical law makes appropriate provision, a judge handling a petition for marriage nullity may also decide such issues *but only as incidental matters*. A tribunal is not to accept a suit in which the civil effects of marriage are the principal issue. This provision primarily relates to tribunals in regions where particular law established in concordats between the Holy See and various countries (see c. 3) gives ecclesiastical tribunals sufficient civil standing to decide such questions in a way that will be honored by the civil authorities.

Identifying the Competent Ecclesiastical Court

Canon 1673 — In cases concerning the nullity of marriage which are not reserved to the Apostolic See, the following are competent:

1° the tribunal of the place in which the marriage was celebrated;

2° the tribunal of the place in which the respondent has a domicile or quasi-domicile;

3° the tribunal of the place in which the petitioner has a domicile, provided that both parties live in the territory of the same conference of bishops and the judicial vicar of the domicile of the respondent gives consent after he has heard the respondent;

4° the tribunal of the place in which in fact most of the proofs must be collected, pro-

vided that consent is given by the judicial vicar of the domicile of the respondent, who is first to ask if the respondent has any exception to make.

The general norms governing the legal competence or jurisdiction for a tribunal to adjudicate a petition are found in canons 1404–1414. Canon 1673 contains special provisions that apply to marriage nullity cases only.[13]

Cases reserved to the pope are enumerated in canon 1405, §1. Of these, only two numbers might apply to persons in marriage nullity cases: (1) unions involving heads of state (c. 1405, §1, 1°) or (2) unions involving persons in which the pope has specially reserved judgment to himself (c. 1405, §1, 4°).

Of the four bases of competence in marriage nullity cases, the first two have no conditions attached to them. The other two can be employed only when certain conditions are fulfilled. There is, however, no hierarchy of claims requiring the choice of one tribunal over the others. Thus, a prospective petitioner has the right to approach a tribunal under any of the four titles of competence. Of course, all four titles of competence may possibly be located in the same place; in this situation, only one tribunal is available to a petitioner.

Additionally, in assessing whether a particular tribunal is competent, the ritual church *sui iuris* within which the parties are inscribed must also be taken into account. For example, even if the marriage was celebrated within its boundaries, the tribunal of a Latin diocese is not competent to treat the marriage case of two Eastern Catholics.[14]

Place of Contract (1°)

The tribunal of the place where the marriage was celebrated is competent to accept a petition in marriage nullity cases. If the union in question is the convalidation[15] of a previous exchange of consent without canonical form, the place of contract is the tribunal where the convalidation was celebrated (not the tribunal of the prior ceremony).

Canon 1673, 1° applies the provisions of canon 1411, §1 on the forum of contract to marriage nullity cases. Unlike canon 1411, §1, however, the present canon does not permit the parties mutually to agree on some other tribunal.

Domicile or Quasi-Domicile of the Respondent (2°)

In canon law, traditionally the respondent's forum is privileged since the initiation of a suit places a burden on the respondent. This privilege is expressed in the ancient maxim *actor sequitur forum partis conventae,* the petitioner follows the forum of the respondent.[16] Thus, the tribunal of the place where the respondent has a domicile or quasi-domicile has unconditioned competence to accept a marriage nullity petition.

The terms "domicile" and "quasi-domicile" are defined in canon 102.[17] A respondent may have a domicile and a separate quasi-domicile. When this is verified, a prospective petitioner would have the right to approach the tribunal of either place.

---

[13] For a discussion of the major changes in the norms governing competence in marriage nullity trials and the rationale for those changes, see Cox, *Procedural Changes,* 14–28.

[14] The complex possibilities for court competence may be confusing. For a very helpful analysis, see J. H. Provost, "Canon 1673: Competency of Tribunals of Latin and Eastern Churches," *RRAO 1997,* 91–97.

[15] For a discussion of simple convalidation, see the commentary on cc. 1156–1160.

[16] See the commentary on c. 1407, §3 for further reflections on the history and rationale of this maxim. The privilege given to the forum of the respondent, however, does not prevent the petitioner from approaching another competent tribunal.

[17] Canon 104 provides for a common domicile for spouses. In marriage nullity cases, however, the parties are separated. Since domicile is lost by departure without the intent of returning (c. 106), it must be presumed that the separated spouses no longer have a common domicile or quasi-domicile.

Domicile of the Petitioner (3°)

The tribunal of the place in which a petitioner has a domicile[18] may be competent. Before the tribunal of the petitioner's domicile can admit a *libellus,* however, certain conditions must be verified. The conditions are introduced by the Latin term *dummodo* ("provided that"). In the canonical tradition, this term indicates that the conditions affect the validity of the act.[19] Two conditions apply:

1. The respondent must live within the territory of the same episcopal conference.[20] The boundaries of episcopal conferences may coincide with the boundaries of a particular nation, or they may include several different countries. For the United States, the territories of Puerto Rico, Guam, and the Virgin Islands, while part of the nation, are not part of the National Conference of Catholic Bishops.

2. The judicial vicar of the respondent's domicile must consent to the tribunal of the petitioner's domicile as the place for the trial "after he has heard the respondent" (*ipsa audita*).

This second condition raises a number of questions requiring careful consideration. Since those considerations apply to the similar condition regulating the "forum of proofs," they will be discussed below.

The Forum of Proofs (4°)

The tribunal of the place where, in fact, most of the proofs are to be collected may be competent, provided the judicial vicar of the respondent consents after first having asked the respondent if she or he has any exceptions to make. The wording used in 4° to describe the consultation with the respondent differs slightly from that of 3° in that it refers specifically to inquiring if the respondent has any exceptions to raise.[21] In practice, the purpose of hearing the respondent is broader than simply seeking out objections; rather, it is to assure that respondents will be able to participate fully and vindicate their rights in the process.

The use of this title of competence—unlike use of the domicile of the petitioner—does not require that the respondent live within the territory of the same conference of bishops.

By proofs must be understood all the types of proof discussed in canons 1526–1586 and 1679. Several factors help in determining whether a tribunal legitimately may claim to be the forum where most of the proofs must be collected. First, the proofs must be found in the diocese of that tribunal, not in the region or nation.[22] Second, the quality or weight of proofs rather than their numerical majority is crucial.[23] Often one witness with extensive knowledge may be able to offer far more important testimony than another five less knowledgeable witnesses combined. Furthermore, it is not only the witnesses and other proofs identified by the petitioner that must be taken into account, but also those identified by the respondent or ex officio by the judge.[24]

---

[18] See the commentary on c. 102. Unlike the case of the respondent described above, in this case only the tribunal of the petitioner's domicile, not of his or her quasi-domicile, has a claim to jurisdiction.

[19] Canon 39, while not speaking of laws themselves, explicitly applies this understanding to administrative acts. See J. Ochoa, "I titoli de competenza," in *Il processo matrimoniale canonico, Studi Giuridici* XXIX, ed. P. A. Bonnet and C. Gullo (Vatican City: Libreria Editrice Vaticana, 1994) 104.

[20] The Eastern code has a slightly different provision. *CCEO* 1359, 3° specifies that the respondent must reside within the "same nation."

[21] *CCEO* 1359, 3° and 4° eliminates this discrepancy and uses the same phrase (*ea audita*) in both numbers.

[22] ApSig, decl, April 27, 1989, *AAS* 81 (1989) 893. Translated in *RRAO 1989,* 46. F. Daneels briefly comments on the Signatura's declaration in "The 'Forum of Most of the Proofs,'" *J* 50 (1990) 289–309, which also contains a translation of the declaration.

[23] ApSig, decl, April 27, 1989, *AAS* 81 (1989) 893. Translated in *RRAO 1989,* 46.

[24] Ibid. Also see Z. Grocholewski, "Current Questions Concerning the State and Activity of Tribunals with Par-

The Required Consent
of the Respondent's Judicial Vicar

The use of both the domicile of the petitioner and the forum of proofs requires the consent of the respondent's judicial vicar after he has consulted with the respondent. It is not correct to speak of the respondent's judicial vicar "granting competence." Rather, the vicar's consent fulfills a condition that allows a tribunal to declare itself competent in virtue of the law.

A number of important clarifications about this condition have been made in response to questions raised since the promulgation of the 1983 code. First, who is the judicial vicar involved when an interdiocesan tribunal handles marriage cases for the respondent's diocese? An authentic interpretation issued February 28, 1986 clarified that the judicial vicar concerned was that of the respondent's diocese of domicile, not the judicial vicar of the interdiocesan tribunal. If the diocese of the respondent's domicile has no judicial vicar, then the consent of the diocesan bishop is required.[25]

Second, the consent of the respondent's judicial vicar cannot be presumed after a time limit established by the tribunal seeking consent.[26] In the absence of a reply, the tribunal seeking consent may not proceed, but should again contact the respondent's judicial vicar to inquire about the delay.[27]

Third, the respondent's judicial vicar may seek additional information from the tribunal requesting consent in order to make the appropriate determination.[28] Similarly, a respondent may seek additional information in determining his or her stance with regard to the trial.[29]

Fourth, by what means may a judicial vicar "hear" the respondent? A general decree of the Apostolic Signatura dated May 6, 1993 declared that the practice of the petitioner's tribunal directly contacting and hearing the respondent "cannot be allowed." Rather, the respondent's own judicial vicar must contact the respondent.[30] The judicial vicar, however, may hear the respondent and express the consent through another, such as an adjutant judicial vicar or a delegate.[31]

Fifth, what does it mean for the judicial vicar to hear the respondent? For example, if the respondent makes no reply whatsoever, can the judicial vicar still give consent? Yes.[32] Provided there is certainty that the respondent received the invitation to comment, the judicial vicar has, in fact, heard the respondent.[33] In these circumstances, the purpose of this norm, assuring that respondents have the opportunity to voice their concerns, has been accomplished. Although the respondent's silence cannot be construed as agreement with the process,

ticular Reference to the United States of America," in *Incapacity for Marriage,* ed. R. Sable (Rome: Pontificia Universitas Gregoriana, 1987) 243.

[25] CodCom, *responsa,* February 28, 1986, *AAS* 78 (1986) 1323. For a translation and brief discussion of the interpretation, see L. Wrenn, *Authentic Interpretations on the 1983 Code* (Washington, D.C.: CLSA, 1993) 23.

[26] ApSig, decl, April 27, 1989, *AAS* 81 (1989) 892. Translated in *RRAO 1989,* 45. While the Signatura's declaration spoke directly of the forum of proofs, a private reply clarified the fact that the requirement also applied to the forum of the petitioner. See *RRAO 1989, 47–49.*

[27] If the respondent's judicial vicar still does not reply, the petitioner's tribunal could seek a prorogation of competence from the Apostolic Signatura (see the discussion at the next heading of the commentary on this canon entitled "Other Sources of Tribunal Competence").

[28] ApSig, decl, April 27, 1989, *AAS* 81 (1989) 893. Also see *RRAO 1996,* 46–47.

[29] Daneels, "The 'Forum of Most of the Proofs,'" 296, n. 8.

[30] ApSig, decr, May 6, 1993, *AAS* 85 (1993) 969–970. Translated in *RRAO 1995,* 16–20. For the nature and force of general decrees, see the commentary on cc. 29 and 30. Also see J. L. Acebal Luján, "El fuero competente matrimonial, c. 1673, 3°: Texto y comentario," *REDC* 51 (1994) 185–189.

[31] While judicial power may not be delegated (c. 135, §3), the granting of consent is not a judicial but rather an administrative function. See ApSig, private reply, October 21, 1991, *RRAO 1992,* 44–46.

[32] Martínez Valls, in *Valencia Com,* 721, reaches the same conclusion.

[33] This is the wording of c. 1673, 3° (*ipsa audita*). Similarly, by giving the respondent the opportunity to make an exception, the judicial vicar has certainly fulfilled the requirement of c. 1673, 4° (*qui prius ipsam interroget, num quid excipiendum habeat*).

silence nonetheless is a response. In this situation, the judicial vicar should assess the meaning of the silence in light of the respondent's right of defense and may give the consent requested.[34]

Sixth, if the respondent raises objections, must the judicial vicar automatically deny his consent? No. A proposal to require the respondent's consent was raised during the code revision process,[35] but not incorporated. The law requires the consent of the judicial vicar, not that of the respondent. In determining whether to extend or deny consent, the judicial vicar is to give "due consideration" to the reasons for the respondent's opposition, weighing "carefully" the circumstances of the case and especially "the difficulties the respondent will encounter in defending himself before the other tribunal."[36] When, then, might the vicar extend consent in the face of the respondent's objections? For example, in hearing the respondent, the vicar may conclude that the objections being raised are unfounded, possibly even vindictive or dilatory. In these situations, the judicial vicar may give consent despite the respondent's objections, provided he is certain that the respondent may reasonably exercise his or her right of defense before the tribunal hearing the case.[37]

Finally, may competence be assumed on the basis of either the petitioner's domicile or the forum of proofs if the respondent's whereabouts is unknown? Canon 1673 does not address this situation.[38] At first glance, it would seem not, since the condition of obtaining the consent of the respondent's judicial vicar cannot be fulfilled. Many commentators, however, argue that these two titles of competence may be employed in such circumstances.[39] They reach this conclusion by applying both traditional canonical principles (e.g., the "rule of law" that no one is bound to the impossible[40]) and previous Signatura rulings in similar cases.[41] On the other hand, Joaquín Llobell, based on his reading of a 1989 Signatura declaration,[42] has misgivings about using these two titles of competence when the respondent's whereabouts is unknown. In support of Llobell's position is the fact that the Signatura's practice has not been consistent.[43] This author, however, holds that in these circumstances a tribunal may assume jurisdiction under either canon 1673, 3° or 4° provided that truly serious efforts are made to locate the respondent. Should a judge decree competence in these circumstances, the defender

---

[34] Canon 1531, §2, concerning the declarations of the parties in a trial, requires the judge to evaluate insofar as possible what can be deduced from a party's refusal to reply. If the respondent's silence indicated that he or she would not take part in the trial at all, to deny consent may well create undue burdens for the petitioner without any corresponding benefit to the respondent.

[35] The possibility was suggested at the March 28, 1979 meeting of the *coetus* on procedural law, *Comm* 11 (1979) 258.

[36] ApSig, decl, April 27, 1989, *AAS* 81 (1989) 893–894. Translated in *RRAO 1989*, 46–47.

[37] Kelly, in *CLSGBI Com*, 933, suggests that in the face of a respondent's objections the judicial vicar "ought to withhold his consent, unless he judges the respondent's objection to be wholly unreasonable." Sometimes, however, respondents make it clear that they have no intention of presenting testimony or cooperating with the trial in any way. In these situations, even if a respondent has some reasonable objections, the judicial vicar would very responsibly grant consent given the respondent's professed intent to be absent from the trial.

[38] For cases other than marriage nullity, c. 1409, §2 provides for a trial in the forum of the plaintiff provided no other legitimate forum is available.

[39] Wrenn, in *CLSA Com*, 1011–1012; Kelly, in *CLSGBI Com*, 934; J. Ochoa, "I titoli di competenza," in P. A. Bonnet and C. Gullo, eds., *Il processo matrimoniale*, 168–170; J. H. Provost, "Canon 1673: Competent Tribunal When Respondent's Whereabouts Unknown," in *CLSA Advisory Opinions 1984–1993*, ed. P. Cogan (Washington, D.C., 1995) 474–476; J. Hesch, "Canon 1673: Competent Tribunal When Respondent's Whereabouts Remain Unknown," *RRAO 1994*, 147–152.

[40] *RI*, n. 6, *CorpusIC* II, 1122.

[41] I. Gordon and Z. Grocholewski, eds., *Documenta recentiora circa rem matrimonialem et processualem* (Rome: Pontificia Universitas Gregoriana, 1977) 217–218. Translated in *CLD* 11, 350–351. Also see Daneels, "The 'Forum of Most of the Proofs,'" 305, n. 15.

[42] Llobell, in *Com Ex* IV/2, 1844–1845.

[43] See *RRAO 1994*, 54–59, where the Signatura prorogued competence rather than determining that the tribunal could proceed on the basis of canon 1673, 3°.

of the bond has the right to lodge an exception of incompetence. Such an exception is to be raised prior to the joinder of issues, and the judge's ruling in the matter is not subject to appeal although it may be challenged by means of a complaint of nullity (cc. 1459, §2 and 1460, §§2–3).

Other Sources of Tribunal Competence

There are two circumstances in which a tribunal that has no claim of competence under canon 1673 nonetheless may be given competence, either by the law itself or by a grant of the Apostolic Signatura.

Prorogation of Competence: The Apostolic Signatura has the authority to prorogue competence, i.e., grant competence to a tribunal that otherwise has no jurisdiction.[44] For example, a prospective petitioner who is a refugee from a place where the Church is persecuted may wish to introduce a *libellus* but be thwarted because the respondent remains in his or her native land and no functioning tribunals exist in the dioceses of the place of contract or the respondent's domicile. Or only one tribunal may be competent according to canon 1673, yet one party to the case is related to the diocesan bishop or an official of that tribunal. For this tribunal to adjudicate a petition may create the perception of favoritism, leaving the Church open to accusations of injustice. In these and similar situations, the Signatura may be asked to extend competence to another tribunal so that a prospective petitioner may vindicate his or her rights as assured by canon 221.[45] The Signatura requires a just cause to prorogue competence. In particular, it assesses whether well-founded reasons prevent the petitioner from approaching another legitimate forum and whether the respondent's rights can be guaranteed by the tribunal seeking the grant of competence.[46]

Competence of an Appellate Court Acting "as if in First Instance": Canon 1683 allows an appellate court treating a marriage nullity case to admit and judge a new ground "as if in first instance." In these circumstances, the appellate tribunal need not have a basis for competence under canon 1673. This is an example of competence by means of connection (c. 1414).

ARTICLE 2: THE RIGHT TO CHALLENGE A MARRIAGE[47] [cc. 1674–1675]

Canon 1674 — The following are qualified to challenge a marriage:
  1° the spouses;
  2° the promoter of justice when nullity has already become public, if the convalidation of the marriage is not possible or expedient.

The right to challenge the validity of marriage is clearly defined and strictly limited. Either spouse, whether baptized or not (see c. 1476), possesses an almost unqualified right to do so.[48] The norms of the 1917 code (*CIC* 1971) and subsequent legislation that limited the rights of non-Catholic spouses or those who caused the nullity or who incurred an ecclesiastical penalty have been suppressed. This modification is an example of the code's concern to respect human dignity and facilitate the vindication of rights.[49]

The promoter of justice, as the one bound to safeguard the public good (see c. 1430), may also

---

[44] See canon 1445, §3, 2° and John Paul II, apconst *Pastor bonus,* June 28, 1988, art. 124, 3°, *AAS* 80 (1988) 892. Translated in *Pamplona ComEng,* 1239.

[45] For examples of the Signatura's practice in admitting or rejecting the prorogation of competence, see *RRAO 1988,* 21–24; *RRAO 1989,* 32–39; *RRAO 1990,* 35–41; *RRAO 1991,* 50–55; *RRAO 1994,* 50–54.

[46] Daneels, "The 'Forum of Most of the Proofs,'" 295–296.

[47] Wrenn, in *CLSA Com,* 1012; Kelly, in *CLSGBI Com,* 934–935; Madero, in *Pamplona ComEng,* 1032–1033; Acebal, in *Salamanca Com,* 811–812; Martínez Valls, in *Valencia Com,* 721–722; R. Rodríguez-Ocaña, in *Com Ex* IV/2, 1849–1881.

[48] The right to challenge a marriage is limited after the death of one or both of the spouses. See the commentary on c. 1675.

[49] This norm implements the rights expressed in cc. 221, §1 and 1476. For further reflections, see Cox, *Procedural Changes,* 54–61.

challenge the validity of marriage, but only under two narrow circumstances. First, the invalidity of the marriage must already have been made public. The Latin wording here, *iam divulgata est,* clearly indicates a matter that has, in fact, become public.[50] Second, either the union in question cannot be convalidated (e.g., the underlying impediment has not ceased and cannot be dispensed), or convalidating the union is not expedient (e.g., both parties have attempted new unions and have no interest in reconciliation).

No one else has the standing to impugn the validity of a marriage.

Petition for Marriage Nullity Subsequent to the Death of One or Both of the Spouses

Canon 1675 — §1. A marriage which was not accused while both spouses were living cannot be accused after the death of either one or both of the spouses unless the question of validity is prejudicial to the resolution of another controversy either in the canonical forum or in the civil forum.

After the death of one or both parties, the favor of the law (see c. 1060) which their marriage had always enjoyed is given a special firmness. Thus, if the validity of a union is not challenged while both parties are still living, it cannot be challenged after the death of one or both unless the question of the validity of the union is prejudicial to the resolution of some other ecclesiastical or civil legal controversy.[51]

---

[50] This *fact of publicity* must be distinguished from something which is factually occult even if inherently public at law (i.e., able to be proven in the external forum). See c. 1074. Also see Rodríguez-Ocaña, in *Com Ex* IV/2, 1861–1862, who describes the evolution of the text as verifying that it focuses on actual public knowledge.

[51] Martínez Valls notes that this provision raises serious problems, since the declaration of nullity would not be sought for spiritual ends. He advises judges to be extremely cautious and admit such an action only when a decision about nullity is truly essential to resolving the other trial (*Valencia Com,* 722).

The canon is forcefully articulated. While it says nothing concerning the exact nature of the other controversy, it sets a very high standard for a posthumous challenge of the validity of a marriage. Unless the question is directly linked to the decision in the other controversy in such a way that failure to address the question of nullity would impair the rights of another, the petition cannot be admitted.[52]

A traditional example involves a controversy over property or an inheritance that hinges on whether the parties were validly married. If the surviving spouse wishes to present a *libellus* in this situation, he or she may approach a competent tribunal. The judge would then need to assess whether the conditions of canon 1675, §1 are verified. If not, the judge is to reject the *libellus* on the ground that the surviving spouse "lacks legitimate personal standing" (c. 1505, §2, 2°).[53] If, on the other hand, a ruling on the validity of the marriage is necessary to resolve a trial involving third parties (e.g., children or heirs), the interested party would have to approach the promoter of justice and request that he or she impugn the marriage on the basis of canon 1674, 2°.

Death of a Spouse during a Case

§2. If a spouse dies while the case is pending, however, can. 1518 is to be observed.

If a spouse dies after a case has already been under way (i.e., after the legitimate communication of a citation according to c. 1512), canon 1518 is relevant. There are two possibilities.

First, the death occurs *before the decree concluding the case* (c. 1599, §3) has been issued. In this situation, the trial is suspended by the law itself (c. 1518, 1°). The action remains suspended unless the heir or successor of the deceased or some other interested party resumes the suit. For

---

[52] See Rodríguez-Ocaña, in *Com Ex* IV/2, 1871 and 1873–1874.

[53] Recourse against this rejection would be possible (see c. 1505, §4).

example, subsequent to the death of a petitioner, the respondent may have an interest in clarifying his or her conscience, and may ask that the suit move forward for that purpose. Otherwise, in marriage nullity trials, it would be most unusual for an heir to wish to continue the process. An heir might wish to resume the suit in circumstances similar to those envisioned in the prior paragraph of this canon, namely, that the question of nullity was prejudicial to the resolution of some other matter.

Second, the death occurs only *after the decree concluding the case* (c. 1599, §3) was issued. In this situation, the case is to move forward to a decision after the duly mandated procurator (cc. 1481–1485) or heir of the deceased has been summoned.

ARTICLE 3: THE DUTY OF THE JUDGES[54] [cc. 1676–1677]

Canons 1676–1677 supplement or adapt to marriage nullity cases the many duties of judges described throughout Book VII.

Judge as Minister of Reconciliation

Canon 1676 — Before accepting a case and whenever there is hope of a favorable outcome, a judge is to use pastoral means to induce the spouses if possible to convalidate the marriage and restore conjugal living.

Due to the sacredness of marriage and its ecclesial and civil import, the Church is concerned to restore the common life of a broken union whenever possible. This is not a requirement to save a union "at any cost," but a recognition that pastoral efforts may help bring healing to relationships, es-

pecially in circumstances where people have separated hastily. Thus, before accepting a *libellus* and *whenever there is hope of success,* the judge is to use pastoral means to assist the parties to resolve their differences, restore common life, and, if needed, convalidate their marriage.[55] This is an application of the general principles of canon 1446 about avoiding lawsuits and seeking mutual resolution to controversies. Normally, when a petition reaches a tribunal, there is little or no reasonable hope of reconciliation. When such a hope exists, however, the judge should use pastoral means such as referral to counselors and spiritual directors to assist the parties to explore the possibility of saving their marriage.

Sometimes one party desires reconciliation, but the other is totally closed to the possibility and may even have attempted marriage with another. In these circumstances, having ascertained the attitudes of the parties, the judge is not authorized to hold the *libellus* in abeyance, since there is no real hope for a successful reconciliation. The judge must admit or reject the petition in accord with canon 1505.

Citation of the Respondent

Canon 1677 — §1. When the *libellus* has been accepted, the presiding judge or the *ponens* is to proceed to the communication of the decree of citation according to the norm of can. 1508.

This paragraph simply refers the judge to canon 1508 governing the manner of communicating a citation to a respondent.

One should note carefully the situation envisioned by canon 1508, §3. When there is a question as to whether a respondent enjoys the free exercise of his or her rights, the judge must determine whether the citation should be communicated to the legal guardian already appointed by civil au-

---

[54] Wrenn, in *CLSA Com,* 1012–1013; Kelly, in *CLSGBI Com,* 935–937; Madero, in *Pamplona ComEng,* 1033–1034; Acebal, in *Salamanca Com,* 812–813; Martínez Valls, in *Valencia Com,* 722–723; A. Stankiewicz, in *Com Ex* IV/2, 1882–1888.

[55] Pope John Paul II, in his January 18, 1990 allocution to the Rota, stressed that this duty is not to be seen as a mere formality. *AAS* 82 (1990) 876. Translated in Woestman, *Papal Allocutions,* 212.

thority, or whether the judge needs to appoint a guardian *ad litem,* i.e., a guardian for the marriage nullity process (cc. 1478–1479). Strictly speaking, this is not an incidental question (c. 1587), since by definition such questions arise only after the trial has formally begun through the citation of the parties. Nonetheless, the judge must examine carefully the question as to whether a guardian must be involved in the trial. Canon 1590 on incidental questions provides a parallel place (cc. 17, 19) suggesting the sort of procedure that would be appropriate. Certainly, consultation with the defender of the bond and the civil legal guardian, if one is available, will be necessary, as well as seeking appropriate evidence concerning the respondent's state of mind and capacity to stand personally at the trial. Finally, whatever the decision concerning the necessity of recognizing or appointing a guardian, the information discovered in dealing with this preliminary question may well be relevant to the central issue of the nullity trial (e.g., if the issue is later joined on a ground enunciated in canon 1095). Thus, any evidence unearthed at this time forms a part of the acts and proofs upon which moral certitude must be reached (c. 1608, §2).

The Joinder of Issues

§2. When fifteen days have passed from the communication and unless either party has requested a session for the joinder of the issue, the presiding judge or the *ponens* is to establish the formula of the doubt or doubts within ten days by *ex officio* decree and is to notify the parties.

§3. The formula of the doubt not only is to ask whether the nullity of the marriage is established in the case but also must determine on what ground or grounds the validity of the marriage is to be challenged.

These paragraphs supplement the norms of canon 1513. The determination of the doubt remains the prerogative of the judge, who defines the question by means of a decree. This canon governing how that decree is issued is clearly designed to prevent undue delays at the outset of the trial.

First, the parties must be cited. Next, the judge allows fifteen days to pass, which provides an opportunity for the petitioner and respondent to present written comments or request a session for the joinder of the issues. If no such request is made, once the fifteen days have passed, the judge has ten more days within which to formulate the doubt (*dubium*) and notify the parties.

If one or both of the parties requests a session for the joinder of issues, the canon does not require the judge to convene a meeting. Normally, however, the judge would accede to the request and schedule a session to determine the issue as soon as reasonably possible. Judges may also convene the parties for a session to determine the issue, even if neither party has requested such a session (c. 1513, §2).

Finally, the formulation of the doubt must be specific rather than generic in nature. It must ask whether the nullity of the union has been proven on one or more specific grounds (e.g., "total simulation on the part of the petitioner" or "conditioned consent posited by the respondent"). Once joined, the issue may be amended or supplemented only in accord with canon 1514.

§4. Ten days after the communication of the decree, the presiding judge or the *ponens* is to arrange for the instruction of the case by a new decree if the parties have lodged no objection.

After having been notified of the formulation of the issue, the parties have ten days within which to lodge an objection. If no objection is lodged, the judge is to issue a decree ordering the instruction (i.e., evidence-gathering phase) of the case to begin.

If an objection to the formulation of the doubt is lodged, the judge is to deal with that objection in accord with canon 1513, §3. The judge's decision may not be appealed, since this matter is to be resolved as promptly as possible (*expeditissime*) (c. 1629, 5°).

ARTICLE 4: PROOFS[56]
[cc. 1678–1680]

Rights of the Defender, Advocates, and Promoter

Canon 1678 — §1. The defender of the bond, the legal representatives of the parties, and also the promoter of justice, if involved in the trial, have the following rights:

    1° to be present at the examination of the parties, the witnesses, and the experts, without prejudice to the prescript of can. 1559;

    2° to inspect the judicial acts, even those not yet published, and to review the documents presented by the parties.

    §2. The parties cannot be present at the examination mentioned in §1, n. 1.

This norm specifies two critical rights extended to certain important figures in the trial, and reflects the legislator's decision to provide for a substantial degree of parity between defenders of the bond and advocates.[57]

First, the defender, the advocates of the parties (not their procurators if a different person fills that role), and the promoter of justice have the right to be present at the examination of the parties, witnesses, and experts. This right, however, may be limited by the judge who may order that the examination of someone should be carried out in secret (c. 1559).[58] Being present, however, does not give these persons the right to pose questions to the party or witnesses. Canons 1533 and 1561 provide that the judge or auditor poses the questions. Unless particular law makes other provision, the defender, advocates, or promoter of justice may only propose questions to the judge or auditor, who determines whether the questions should be asked of the party or witness.

The defender, promoter of justice, and advocates also have the right to inspect the judicial acts,[59] even those not yet published, as well as to review any documents submitted as evidence (see the commentary on cc. 1544–1546).

There is an apparent conflict between the right of the defender, promoter, and advocates to review the acts and the judge's ability to decree that a given act be shown to no one (*nemini*). May an act that was exempted from publication in accord with canon 1598, §1 be withheld from the defender, the advocates, and the promoter of justice in a marriage nullity case? The canon uses the phrase *etsi nondum publicata* (even those *not yet* published) rather than *etsi non publicata* (even those not published). This implies that the acts would eventually be published, but that the defender, promoter, and advocates may have access to them prior to the decree of publication. This temporally oriented phrasing, coupled with the use of *nemini* in canon 1598, §1, seems to indicate that judges could claim an authority to withhold a given act even from the defender of the bond as well as from the advocates and promoter of justice. Yet, this conclusion is at odds with the canonical tradition which gave defenders access to all of the acts.[60] It would almost certainly motivate a defender to appeal any affirmative judgment that might be rendered. Furthermore, canon 1598, §1 permits judges to exempt an act from publication only to avoid most grave dangers. What danger, however, could be present

---

[56] Wrenn, in *CLSA Com,* 1013; Kelly, in *CLSGBI Com,* 937–938; L. del Amo and J. Calvo, in *Pamplona ComEng,* 1035–1037; Acebal, in *Salamanca Com,* 813–814; Martínez Valls, in *Valencia Com,* 723–724; J. Carreras, in *Com Ex* IV/2, 1889–1899.

[57] Cox, *Procedural Changes,* 48–54.

[58] This is another example of the judicial discretion so frequently highlighted in the code. See the commentary on c. 1559 for the extent and limits of the judge's authority in this regard.

[59] At their meeting of March 29, 1979, the procedural law *coetus* changed the text from *acta processus* to *acta iudicialia.* Presumably, this was to clarify that all judicial acts, substantive and procedural, were intended. *Comm* 11 (1979) 263.

[60] See *CIC* 1969 and SCSacr, instr *Provida Mater Ecclesia,* art. 71, §1, *AAS* 28 (1936) 329. Translation in *CLD* 2, 490.

in allowing the defender of the bond and the promoter of justice to review all of the acts?[61] Similarly, if advocates are indeed of good repute and truly expert in the law (c. 1483), then there should be no danger giving them full access to the acts. This is all the more true since they can be bound to secrecy (c. 1455, §3) and are subject to disciplinary measures for violations of such secrecy (c. 1470, §2). Thus, quite apart from the theoretical question of whether they have the authority to do so, in marriage nullity cases judges should not withhold any acts from the defender of the bond, the promoter of justice, and the advocates of the parties.[62]

Canon 1678 does not specify when the right to inspect the acts may be exercised, although it implies that this may be done prior to the publication. It is most appropriate, however, to provide the defender, the promoter, and the advocates reasonable access to all the acts of the case throughout the course of the trial. This enables each better to perform his or her duties. Certainly, this must be done at the time of the official publication.

The parties themselves are not to be admitted to the examination of the other party or of the witnesses. This ensures the "complete freedom" of the other party, the witnesses, and the experts in presenting their testimony.[63] For trials in general, canon 1559 permits the judge to make an exception and admit the parties to the examination of witnesses, especially when the trial involves the private rather than the public good. In marriage nullity cases, however, the judge has no authority to do so.[64]

Proof through Use of Credibility Witnesses

Canon 1679 — Unless there are full proofs from elsewhere, in order to evaluate the depositions of the parties according to the norm of can. 1536, the judge, if possible, is to use witnesses to the credibility of those parties in addition to other indications and supporting factors.

Often only the parties themselves are aware of an underlying reality that may have vitiated their matrimonial consent. Sometimes, especially in cases involving simulation, only one party has such an awareness. Thus, proving marriage nullity is often very difficult, especially in light of the general principle governing proof in cases involving the public good.[65] That general principle states that "the force of full proof cannot be attributed" to the confessions[66] or other declarations of the parties "unless other elements are present which thoroughly corroborate them" (c. 1536, §2).[67]

Canon 1679 is an important innovation with no direct parallel in the 1917 code.[68] It specifically empowers the judge to make use of testimony

---

[61] Rodríguez-Ocaña, in *Com Ex* IV/2, 1486, notes that there is no danger that would require prohibiting a defender from examining all of the acts.

[62] A distinction could be made between the defender and promoter on the one hand (who are officers of the court), and the advocates on the other (who are advisors of the parties). Yet, one concern in the revision of the law was to provide much greater parity between the defender and the advocates in marriage nullity cases (see Cox, *Procedural Changes,* 48–54). Unless there were a reason to believe that a particular advocate could not be trusted, it does not seem appropriate to treat advocates differently from the defender in this regard.

[63] Kelly, in *CLSGBI Com,* 937.

[64] See the *coetus* discussion of this restriction in *Comm* 11 (1979) 114 and 263.

[65] Marriage nullity cases always pertain to the public good (c. 1691).

[66] For a discussion of the nature of confessions, whether judicial or extrajudicial, see the commentary on cc. 1535–1537.

[67] This text itself reflects an important shift away from a formal attitude of suspicion toward the depositions of the parties. See the commentary on c. 1536. Also see Cox, *Procedural Changes,* 65–71, and P. Felici, "Formalitates iuridicae et aestimatio probationum in processu canonico," *Comm* 9 (1977) 175–184. Translation in *J* 38 (1978) 153–157.

[68] There is an indirect parallel in that credibility testimony was not only admitted but required in non-consummation cases. See SCSacr, *Regulae servandae in processibus super matrimonio rato et non consummato,* arts. 57–58 and 60–61, May 7, 1923, *AAS* 15 (1923) 404– 405. Translated in *CLD* 1, 780–781.

concerning the credibility of the parties as an element which may corroborate their declarations. In fact, if full proof from other sources is lacking, the judge must seek out credibility witnesses whenever possible. This source of corroboration is vitally important in the judge's mission to serve truth and justice. It enables tribunal decisions to fulfill one of the key principles guiding the revision of the code, that of precluding conflicts between the internal and external *fora*.[69] Conflicts between the *fora* occur when a marriage is truly invalid but sources of proof to establish the invalidity are severely limited. The use of credibility testimony can help bridge the gap so that mere procedural formalities do not prevent the Church from officially recognizing the underlying spiritual reality (internal forum) of the parties' marital status.

The Use of Experts

Canon 1680 — In cases of impotence or defect of consent because of mental illness, the judge is to use the services of one or more experts unless it is clear from the circumstances that it would be useless to do so; in other cases the prescript of can. 1574 is to be observed.

Canon 1574 requires the use of experts (*periti*) "in order to establish some fact or to discern the true nature of some matter." In any particular case, the judge may mandate that an expert's assessment is necessary. Canon 1574 also speaks of cases where the expert is required by "the prescript of a law."

Canon 1680 is an example of the latter. It requires the use of experts in marriage nullity cases involving the impediment of impotence (c. 1084) or defects of consent due to mental illness. There has been some discussion concerning the scope of the second of these requirements. What is meant by the phrase "defect of consent because of men-

tal illness" (*mentis morbum*)? After briefly reviewing the evolution of canonical doctrine concerning *amentia* and other mental disorders, Mendonça concludes that the phrase "mental illness" as used in canon 1680 at least implicitly covers all of the psychic causes involved in the three parts of canon 1095.[70]

Canon 1680, however, contains an important exception. Experts are to be used "unless it is clear from the circumstances that it would be useless to do so." Like any exception to the law, this must be interpreted strictly (c. 18). How, then, is a judge to decide whether involving an expert would "be useless"? The presumption is that the services of an expert are necessary in cases involving impotence or mental illness; this presumption should not be overturned lightly.[71] When, however, the evidence has (1) certainly established the facts relevant to the ground at issue and (2) clarified the nature and meaning of those facts in light of jurisprudential issues such as antecedence and severity, then the involvement of experts is superfluous.[72] Since discovering the truth and ruling in accord with it are the purposes of the trial, the judge has the authority to proceed to a decision without involving an expert when the truth is manifestly evident.

Apart from impotence or defects of consent due to mental illness, in marriage cases psychic causes

---

[69] ComCICRec, "Principia quae Codicis Iuris Canonici recognitionem dirigant," *Comm* 1 (1969) 79. Also see R. Cunningham, "The Principles Guiding the Revision of the Code of Canon Law," *J* 30 (1970) 448.

[70] A. Mendonça, "The Role of Experts," *Stud Can* 25 (1991) 420–424. A. McGrath agrees, in "At the Service of Truth: Psychological Sciences and Their Relation to the Canon Law of Nullity of Marriage," *Stud Can* 27 (1993) 381.

[71] L. Wrenn, in *Procedures* (Washington, D.C.: CLSA, 1987) 55, states: "When the defect of consent is caused by a mental disorder...then the law wants the court, as a general rule, to use the services of an expert." See the commentary on c. 1574 for further reflections on when it is necessary to use experts. M. Breitenbeck, in "The Use of Experts in Marriage Nullity Cases," *CLSAP* 51 (1989) 35, indicates that the judge's prerogative to waive the use of experts should not be used lightly, but the utilization of an expert should not be "treated as a *pro forma* canonical hoop through which judge, expert, and parties must jump in order to satisfy the requirements of law."

[72] McGrath, "At the Service of Truth," 395–398.

of various sorts may be relevant in grounds other than those listed in canon 1095. Also, judges may need to employ one or more experts from disciplines other than psychology in order to establish facts and clarify their meaning. For example, experts may help clarify whether the teachings of a particular religious tradition concerning the unity, indissolubility, or sacramental dignity of matrimony would likely create an error that would determine the will (c. 1099). Experts in handwriting or the authentication of documents may be employed to assess documentary evidence. When judges recognize their need for expert assistance, they are to proceed in accord with the provisions of canons 1575–1578.

Finally, the judge has the important duty of carefully assessing the value of expert reports, translating their findings into canonical conclusions.[73]

ARTICLE 5: THE SENTENCE AND THE APPEAL[74] [cc. 1681–1685]

Potential Transfer to a Non-consummation Case

Canon 1681 — Whenever, during the instruction of a case, a very probable doubt emerges that consummation of the marriage did not occur, after suspending the case of nullity with the consent of the parties, the tribunal can complete the instruction for a dispensation *super rato* and then transmit the acts to the Apostolic See together with a petition for a dispensation from either one or both of the spouses and the *votum* of the tribunal and the bishop.

During a marriage nullity trial, substantial evidence may arise that the union was never consummated. In these circumstances, the judicial nullity action may be suspended in favor of a petition for a dispensation from a ratified but non-consummated marriage.[75] This option is available only under the following conditions:

(1) evidence exists that the fact of non-consummation is strongly probable;
(2) one or both of the parties petitions for a dispensation from their non-consummated marriage;
(3) both parties consent to the significant procedural shift of suspending the marriage nullity trial in favor of the non-consummation process.

If these conditions are met, the tribunal which was handling the nullity case completes the instruction of the non-consummation case. This is an exception to the normal rule of canon 1699, §1, regarding competence for accepting a *libellus* and instructing a non-consummation case. The tribunal proceeds to instruct the case in accord with canons 1697–1706, forwarding the acts of the case to the Congregation for Divine Worship and the Discipline of the Sacraments.[76] The judge or panel of judges prepares its opinion (*votum*) and also arranges for the petitioner's diocesan bishop to submit his *votum*.

Finally, the decision to exercise the option of canon 1681 does not amount to a renunciation of the instance (cc. 1524–1525). The nullity trial is only suspended, not closed, and the norms regard-

---

[73] McGrath, in "At the Service of the Truth," reflects on some dangers inherent in the use of experts (384–389) and offers helpful guidelines for the evaluation of their reports (389–393). For further reflections on the judge's critical responsibility to assess the reports of *periti*, including a discussion of the pertinent allocutions of Pope John Paul II, see the commentary on c. 1579.

[74] Wrenn in *CLSA Com*, 1013–1015; Kelly in *CLSGBI Com*, 938–941; Madero in *Pamplona ComEng*, 1037–1040; Acebal, in *Salamanca Com*, 814–815; Martínez Valls in *Valencia Com*, 724–726; Diego-Lora in *Com Ex* IV/2, 1900–1945.

[75] CDWDS, littcirc *De processu super rato*, December 20, 1986, arts. 7 and 23b, *ME* 112 (1987) 425 and 427. Translated in Woestman, *Special Marriage Cases*, 122 and 125.

[76] John Paul II, apconst *Pastor bonus*, June 28, 1988, art. 67, *AAS* 80 (1988) 877. Translated in *Pamplona ComEng*, 1221.

ing abatement (cc. 1520–1523) would be applicable only after six months have passed. Thus, if the non-consummation cannot be proven or for any other reason the dispensation cannot be granted, the original trial may be resumed. The procedural acts already undertaken in that trial retain their force, and the tribunal need not retrace those steps.

Mandatory Review
of First Affirmative Decisions

Canon 1682 — §1. The sentence which first declared the nullity of the marriage is to be transmitted *ex officio* to the appellate tribunal within twenty days from the publication of the sentence, together with the appeals, if there are any, and the other acts of the trial.

Canon 1986 of the 1917 code required defenders of the bond to appeal affirmative decisions in marriage nullity cases when those were issued by a tribunal of first instance or where, at higher instances, the judgment was the first affirmative decision issued in response to the petition. During the code revision process, this requirement was challenged and the institute was radically revised.[77]

It is no longer accurate to speak of a "mandatory appeal" in marriage nullity cases. Rather, quite apart from any appeal that may be lodged by the parties or the defender, canon 1682, §1 provides for a "mandatory review" of all sentences which first declare the nullity of marriage.[78]

Within twenty days of the publication of the sentence, the tribunal which issued the judgment must transmit ex officio to the appellate court the sentence, any appeals or other comments of the parties,[79] and all the substantive and procedural acts of the case.

Confirmation of Prior Sentence or New Hearing

§2. If a sentence in favor of the nullity of a marriage was given in the first grade of a trial, the appellate tribunal is either to confirm the decision at once by decree or to admit the case to an ordinary examination in a new grade, after having weighed carefully the observations of the defender of the bond and those of the parties if there are any.

Whether a first affirmative sentence in a marriage nullity case is formally appealed or transmitted for an ex officio review, canon 1682, §2 specifies how such a sentence is to be handled. The appellate tribunal must first consider the observations of the parties, if any. It must also consider the animadversions of the appellate level's own defender of the bond. The tribunal then has two options.

(1) It may, without delay, confirm the original affirmative sentence by means of a decree.[80] Such a decree of confirmation must contain the signatures of all the judges.[81]

(2) Or, if the tribunal cannot confirm the sentence, it opens the case to an ordinary examination at the new grade of trial. It should be noted that the option of confirming a sentence by decree applies only to affirmative sentences; a negative decision that is appealed must be examined anew.[82]

---

[77] For a discussion of these challenges and the debate which led to the revisions, see Cox, *Procedural Changes,* 95–105.

[78] *Comm* 16 (1984) 75.

[79] It should be recalled that the parties have a peremptory time limit of fifteen canonical days within which to lodge an appeal (c. 1630, §1).

[80] Such a decree of confirmation is not merely procedural in nature. Hence, it must contain a summary of the reasons motivating the decision or refer to those motives expressed in another act (cc. 1617 and 51). For samples of recent decrees of confirmation issued by the Rota, see *coram* Turnaturi, decr, November 15, 1994, *SRRDec* 86 (1994) 544–556; *coram* Huber, decr, September 28, 1995, *SRRDec* 87 (1995) 525–533; *coram* Pinto, decr, October 6, 1995, *SRRDec* 87 (1995) 540–545.

[81] See *RRAO 1989.*

[82] See the opinions of J. Provost and L. Wrenn in P. Cogan, ed., *CLSA Advisory Opinions 1984–1993,* 479–481.

Normally, a sentence in favor of marriage nullity given "in the first grade of a trial" involves the decision of a first instance tribunal. But should an appellate court of the second or higher instance issue an affirmative decision on a new ground of nullity "as if in first instance" (see c. 1683 below), then the court of the next instance may issue a decree of confirmation acting at second instance on that one particular new ground.[83]

Possible Admission of a New Ground of Nullity

Canon 1683 — If a new ground of nullity of the marriage is alleged at the appellate grade, the tribunal can admit it and judge it as if in first instance.

In ecclesiastical trials, a new ground may be admitted in the course of a first instance trial in accord with canon 1514 on amending the original formulation of the doubt. Normally, however, a new ground cannot be introduced at a second or higher instance (c. 1639, §1). Canon 1683, reflecting the crucial spiritual impact of clarifying the marital status of persons, makes an exception for marriage nullity cases.

The new ground may be admitted and judged "as if in first instance." If this is done, the appellate court need not have one of the bases of competence provided in canon 1673.

No procedure for admitting a new ground is provided in canon 1683. The provisions governing a change in the terms of the controversy (c. 1514) provide guidance for the appropriate manner of handling the admission of a new ground at the appellate level. Should information pointing to a new ground emerge during an appellate trial, however, it is not necessary that a new ground be

admitted. A conforming sentence may well be forthcoming on the original ground, and neither party may see a need to pursue a moot question. Or one or both of the parties might prefer to submit a new petition on the new ground to a competent court of first instance.

Finally, if a new ground is admitted at the appellate level, while it is judged as if in first instance, it remains a ruling of the court of second or higher instance. This has important implications for identifying the correct tribunal to which the affirmative decision must be sent for mandatory review (c. 1682, §1). For example, if the case had come to a metropolitan tribunal in second instance, the affirmative decision on the new ground may not be transmitted to the normal court of appeal for the first instance trials of that metropolitan tribunal. Rather, the transmission must be made to the appropriate court of third instance, normally the Roman Rota (c. 1444, §1, 2°).[84] Likewise, in the case of interdiocesan courts of second instance, the normal court of appeal is the Roman Rota. If, however, the statutes of that interdiocesan court were to assign a different court of third instance, then the mandatory review would be conducted there.

Effect of Conforming Judgments

Canon 1684 — §1. After the sentence which first declared the nullity of the marriage has been confirmed at the appellate grade either by a decree or by a second sentence, the persons whose marriage has been declared null can contract a new marriage as soon as the decree or second sentence has been communicated to them unless a prohibition attached to the sentence or decree or established by the local ordinary has forbidden this.

The issuance of two conforming decisions in favor of marriage nullity brings about a very significant change in the juridical status of the parties.

Prior to the second conforming decision, the parties were still legally impeded from entering a

---

[83] See, for example, decrees of confirmation issued *coram* Bruno, June 17, 1994, *SRRDec* 86 (1994) 337–344; *coram* López-Illana, December 12, 1994, *SRRDec* 86 (1994) 619–649; and *coram* Sable, December 13, 1994, *SRRDec* 86 (1994) 650–658. These decrees were all issued relative to affirmative decisions made by second instance courts that admitted new grounds as if in first instance.

[84] *CLSA Advisory Opinions 1984–1993,* 478.

new marriage by their previous union.[85] Subsequent to a conforming sentence, however, the prior exchange of consent no longer prevents the parties from entering a new marriage. Given the fundamental human right to marry affirmed by canon 1058, the parties are free to marry as soon as the decree of nullity is communicated to them[86] unless a prohibition (*vetitum*) has been attached to the decree of nullity. In a few countries in which ecclesiastical declarations of nullity may have civil effects, however, additional formalities in registering the decree of nullity may be necessary before the parties are civilly free to marry.[87]

Excursus: The Meaning of Conformity of Judgments

The jurisprudence concerning substantial or equivalent conformity of sentences in marriage nullity cases is not fully consistent.[88] Canon 1641, 1° identifies three criteria for conforming judgments. The decisions must concern the same parties (*inter easdem partes*), must be about the same

basic issue at the heart of the petition (*de eodem petito*), and must be based on the same cause of petitioning (*ex eadem causa petendi*). In a marriage case, there is no difficulty verifying the first two of these criteria. The two decisions would involve the same two parties. The basic issue being addressed is whether their union is valid or not. But the question arises, "Is the basis for petitioning (*causa petendi*) the same as the grounds of nullity (*caput nullitatis*)?"[89] Provost identifies two schools of thought and examines numerous Rotal decisions on the issue of conformity of sentences.[90] One school holds that *formal conformity* of sentences is necessary. This school identifies the basis of petitioning with the specific ground of nullity and requires that the conforming affirmative decisions be based on the same ground. The other school holds that the basis of petitioning is not to be strictly identified with the specific ground. This school argues that there can be *equivalent or substantial conformity* when the decisions address the same juridic facts even if they do so under different formal headings. For the most part, this school focuses less on the "different juridical names" given in the formulation of the grounds than on the "substance of the controversy."[91] Thus, the different headings of nullity matter less than whether "each ground is based on the *same juridical facts* admitted and accepted in both instances."[92]

In practice, when two sentences have been issued concerning the same parties and same matter with the exact same formulation of the ground(s), then there is formal conformity. If, however, the formulation of the grounds differs and the court of higher instance did not specifi-

---

[85] The Signatura clarified that this requirement of conforming decisions, although of ecclesiastical law, nonetheless applies to declarations of nullity of the marriages of two persons neither of whom were Catholic. See ApSig, *responsio,* February 1, 1990, *AAS* 84 (1992) 549–550. This author has found no published English translation. For a Spanish translation and brief commentary, see J. L. Acebal Luján, "La declaración de nulidad del matrimonio de dos acatólicos: Texto y commentario," *REDC* 49 (1992) 691–697.

[86] Canon 1684, §1 seems to eliminate the need for a separate decree of execution of the judgment which is normally required to implement the legal consequences of a judgment (cc. 1650–1655). At the very least, canon 1684, §1 presumes that the decree of confirmation or second conforming sentence incorporates a decree of execution of the judgment (c. 1651).

[87] See Madero, in *Pamplona ComEng,* 1039.

[88] A. McGrath, "Conformity of Sentence in Marriage Nullity Cases," *Stud Can* 27 (1993) 11–15; A. Mendonça, "The Structural and Functional Aspects of an Appeal Tribunal in Marriage Nullity Cases," *Stud Can* 32 (1998) 496–499.

[89] J. Provost, "Jurisprudential and Procedural Approaches to Traditional and Modern Grounds and the Question of Conformity of Sentences," in *Proceedings of the Canon Law Society of Australia and New Zealand* (Sydney, Australia: CLSANZ, 1996) 94.

[90] Ibid, 94–106.

[91] J. Cuneo, "Towards Understanding the Conformity of Two Sentences of Nullity," *J* 46 (1986) 600–601.

[92] McGrath, "Conformity of Sentence," 20.

cally decree that its decision is to be considered as conforming, then presumably the sentences are not concordant.[93]

Excursus: The Vetitum

A *vetitum* (plural *vetita*) may be imposed either by a tribunal or by the competent local ordinary. Since such a prohibition is mentioned solely in canons 1684 and 1685, some have argued that a *vetitum* may be issued only by a tribunal of second or higher instance.[94] In this author's opinion, however, a *vetitum* may be imposed by a tribunal of first instance as well as of second or any further instance.[95]

Vetita are limited in nature and do not have an invalidating effect (see the commentary on c. 1077). They do, however, stand in the way of a licit union (c. 1066). Thus, should a person upon whom such a prohibition has been imposed wish to enter a new marriage, the pastor or other person responsible to prepare a couple for marriage has the duty to address the provisions of the *vetitum*.

Such prohibitions serve several purposes. Ideally, *vetita* serve the parties upon whom they are imposed by helping them address the underlying problems that contributed to the breakdown of their previous unions. Second, the existence of a *vetitum* may help protect those interested in marrying persons whose prior unions have been declared null. The counseling or other steps required to remove the prohibition provide important information to these prospective spouses, enabling them better to assess the wisdom of marrying. A *vetitum* also manifests the Church's commitment to uphold the sacredness of marriage precisely by prohibiting a new marriage until there is evidence that the parties are truly willing and able to assume and live out that commitment.[96]

Most commonly, *vetita* are imposed when there is evidence of psychological factors that would impair a person's ability to exercise due discretion or to assume the essential obligations of marriage (c. 1095). But *vetita* also have their place when the nullity of the prior union was rooted in other causes. For example, a prohibition may be called for in cases of error determining the will or simulation (cc. 1099, 1101) when the evidence has indicated that a person's philosophy of life or value system is significantly at odds with the Church's teaching on marriage.

This author believes that the subject of prohibitions attached to declarations of nullity deserved a fuller treatment in the code. A prohibition restricts the free exercise of the right to marry (c. 1058), and hence the law concerning prohibitions must be interpreted strictly (c. 18). The code provides no process either for issuing or rescinding a prohibition to marry. Presumably, when issued during a marriage nullity trial, the trial procedures themselves protect the rights of the person whose freedom to marry is being restricted. When an ordinary issues a prohibition outside of the context of a marriage nullity trial, the procedural requirements of canons 50 51 ought to be observed.

Likewise, the decision to remove or lift a *vetitum* should never be taken lightly. Once imposed, the *vetitum* does indeed stand in the way of the licit celebration of a new marriage (c. 1066). Tribunal officials, however, often express the concern that those preparing couples for marriage do not always take these prohibitions seriously enough, sometimes ignoring them entirely or treating them superficially. In part, this may reflect the fact that marriage preparation ministers do not have access to the acts of the case. Thus, they may not fully appreciate why the judge imposed the prohibition.

---

[93] In these circumstances, a party might raise an incidental question and ask the tribunal to rule on the question of whether the sentences are conforming.

[94] See the opinion of B. A. Cusack in *CLSA Advisory Opinions 1984–1993*, 481–483.

[95] Custom is the best interpreter of the law (c. 27), and first instance tribunals have customarily imposed prohibitions.

[96] See J. Lucas, "The Prohibition Imposed by a Tribunal: Law, Practice, Future Development," *J* 45 (1985) 598.

Finally, while it is not provided for by the code, some tribunals issue *monita* (warnings or pastoral cautions). A *monitum* is not a prohibition, but identifies areas of concern to assist the minister preparing a couple for marriage in providing the appropriate preparation required by canon 1063, 2°.[97]

Decree of Confirmation Constitutes a Conforming Judgment

§2. The prescripts of can. 1644 must be observed even if the sentence which declared the nullity of the marriage was confirmed not by a second sentence but by a decree.

This paragraph stipulates that a decree of confirmation (c. 1682, §2) constitutes a conforming decision at law. It has the same force as a full judicial sentence issued subsequent to an ordinary examination of the case. This eliminates any confusion and prevents any attempt to downgrade the force of a decree of confirmation. Since confirmation of a first affirmative sentence is a true conforming decision, it cannot be challenged by means of an ordinary appeal.

It is true that conforming decisions in a case involving the status of persons do not result in a *res iudicata* or adjudged matter (see commentary on cc. 1643 and 1641). Thus, a challenge to the two conforming decisions remains radically possible. Such a challenge, however, requires a new presentation of the case (c. 1644). A new presentation of the case, however, does not suspend the execution of the sentence of marriage nullity (c. 1644, §2) unless the appellate tribunal has suspended its execution. The only other possible challenge to two conforming decisions in favor of nullity would involve a complaint of nullity of the process (cc. 1619–1627).

Recording Decrees of Nullity in Sacramental Registers

Canon 1685 — As soon as the sentence is executed, the judicial vicar must notify the local ordinary of the place in which the marriage was celebrated. The local ordinary must take care that the declaration of the nullity of the marriage and any possible prohibitions are noted as soon as possible in the marriage and baptismal registers.

Once executed, an ecclesiastical judgment takes legal effect. Canon 1651 provides that the decree of execution may be issued separately or incorporated into the judgment itself.

As soon as the sentence is executed, canon 1685 obliges the judicial vicar to assure that notations of the declaration of nullity and any prohibition (*vetitum*) are made in the appropriate sacramental registers. The canon, however, does not identify whether this is the responsibility of the judicial vicar of first instance or of the judicial vicar of the appellate court that issued the second conforming decision. Kelly assumes that it is the judicial vicar of the appellate level.[98] Martínez Valls, to the contrary, indicates that this is the responsibility of the judicial vicar of the first instance tribunal in which the petition was initially judged.[99] Given the doubt, canon 17 suggests recourse to parallel places. A potential parallel is found in canon 1653, §1, which entrusts the execution of a judgment to the bishop of the diocese in which the first instance judgment was issued. This is the responsibility of the bishop of the first instance tribunal even if the definitive judgment was issued by an appellate tribunal. Thus, while executing a judgment and seeing that proper notices are entered into sacramental registers are not identical tasks, this author agrees with Martínez Valls that the responsibility belongs to the judicial vicar of the first instance tribunal where the trial was initiated.

[97] Besides the sources already cited, also see J. Hopka, "The *Vetitum* and *Monitum* in Matrimonial Nullity Proceedings," *Stud Can* 19 (1985) 357–399, and R. Guiry, "Canonical and Psychological Reflections on the *Vetitum* in Today's Tribunals," *J* 49 (1989) 191–209.

[98] Kelly, in *CLSGBI Com,* 941.
[99] Martínez Valls, in *Valencia Com,* 726.

The judicial vicar is to provide notice of the decree of nullity and any prohibitions to the local ordinary (c. 134, §2) of the place where the marriage was celebrated. That local ordinary is then responsible to ensure that the relevant notation is made in the marriage register of the parish of contract, as well as in the register(s) of the parish(es) of baptism, even if those parishes are located outside of his jurisdiction.[100] In practice, to assure that notations are properly made, tribunals often send notices directly to the churches of marriage and baptism.

ARTICLE 6: THE DOCUMENTARY PROCESS[101]
[cc. 1686–1688]

The name "documentary process" was adopted by the procedural law *coetus* during its discussion of the 1976 schema.[102] The term emphasizes that this procedure may be employed only when the nullity of the marriage is established principally by means of a document that is not subject to contradiction.

The process, while streamlined, remains judicial in nature. This is evident both in the text of canons 1686–1688 and in the fact that they are situated in the context of tribunal actions (see c. 17). Furthermore, the judicial nature of the process was specifically affirmed in an authentic interpretation of canon 1990 of the 1917 code.[103] While some changes were made in the norms governing the documentary process, the new code did not change its underlying judicial nature.

The documentary process is frequently employed. In 1996, for example, 15,768 documentary cases were introduced worldwide, and 15,790 were closed. Of the closed cases, 15,437 were decided in favor of nullity, 51 received a sentence contrary to nullity, and the others were closed by peremption or renunciation.[104] Thus, to serve the people's needs, it is critical that tribunal officials properly understand and implement the norms for documentary cases.

Application and Nature of the Documentary Process

Canon 1686 — After receiving a petition proposed according to the norm of can. 1677, the judicial vicar or a judge designated by him can declare the nullity of a marriage by sentence if a document subject to no contradiction or exception clearly establishes the existence of a diriment impediment or a defect of legitimate form, provided that it is equally certain that no dispensation was given, or establishes the lack of a valid mandate of a proxy. In these cases, the formalities of the ordinary process are omitted except for the citation of the parties and the intervention of the defender of the bond.

This lengthy canon contains many elements which require careful study.

Types of Cases Where the Documentary Process May Be Used

The documentary process may be employed *only* for cases when the nullity of marriage is due to:

---

[100] This specifies the requirement of c. 535, §2 that a notation be made in a person's baptismal record of all matters pertaining to his or her canonical status, including marriage.

[101] Wrenn, in *CLSA Com*, 1015; Kelly, in *CLSGBI Com*, 941–942; C. de Diego-Lora, in *Pamplona ComEng*, 1040–1042; Acebal, in *Salamanca Com*, 816–817; Martínez Valls, in *Valencia Com*, 726–727; Diego-Lora, in *Com Ex* IV/2, 1946–1962. For a thorough study of the origins and development of this process, see T. L. Dupre, *The Summary Process of Canons 1990–1992* (Washington, D.C.: Catholic University of America, 1967) 1–61.

[102] *Comm* 11 (1979) 269. The 1917 code (*CIC* 1990–1992) referred to these as exceptional cases. More commonly, the process was known as the "summary judicial process" or "summary trial."

[103] CodCom, *responsa*, December 6, 1943, *AAS* 36 (1944) 94. Translation in *CLD* 3, 645.

[104] Secretaria Status, *Statistical Yearbook of the Church 1996*, 431 and 449.

(1) the existence of a diriment impediment (cc. 1083–1094)[105] that has not been dispensed (cc. 1078–1082);

(2) a defect of legitimate form that was not dispensed (cc. 1104, 1108–1123, 1127); and

(3) a defect of a valid mandate of a proxy (cc. 1104–1105).

A *defect of legitimate form* must be distinguished from those cases where there was no semblance of canonical form at all (*lack of form* cases). When canonical form was totally lacking, the documentary process is not used, and the nullity of the union is decided administratively as part of the prenuptial investigation (cc. 1066–1067).[106]

Other Conditions for Use of the Documentary Process

Furthermore, the documentary process may be employed for the aforementioned three types of cases only if there is a document "subject to no contradiction or exception" that "clearly establishes" (*certo constet*) the existence of the impediment or defect. Thus, when unimpeachable documentary evidence is lacking, cases involving impediments or defects of form or mandate must be tried in the formal process.

Use of Other Forms of Evidence

While the central proof of nullity must be found in a document, there is a role for other forms of evidence in the documentary process, including the testimony of witnesses.[107] This is verified in the interpretation and implementation of canon 1990 of the 1917 code.[108] An authentic interpretation of the former code clarified that other legitimate sources could be used in these cases.[109] Thus, the declarations of the parties, testimonies of witnesses, and other legitimate forms of proof may serve an important adminicular function in helping the judge, especially in establishing that impediments were not dispensed and that the union was not convalidated or sanated. For example, in the case of a defect of form due to the officiating minister's lack of delegation, besides the documents establishing that such delegation was necessary and that the marriage records contain no entry regarding the granting of delegation, the brief testimony of a priest or deacon that he neglected to seek the required delegation, or from the pastor or local ordinary that he failed to extend it, would be admissible and of great value.[110]

---

[105] The 1917 code permitted the use of the documentary process for some, but not all impediments (*CIC* 1990). That restriction is not present in c. 1686, and the documentary process may be used for any of the impediments provided the other conditions are met.

While there is no longer the impediment of spiritual relationship in the Latin code, prior to November 27, 1983, Latin Catholics were bound by that impediment (*CIC* 1079, 768). If the impediment existed and was not dispensed, marriages attempted before that date can be declared null through the documentary process.

[106] CodCom, *responsa,* July 11, 1984, *AAS* 76 (1984) 747. Translated in *CLD* 11, 351. For a brief explanation, see Wrenn, *Authentic Interpretations,* 13–14.

[107] For a differing opinion, see R. Bourgon, in *CLSGBI Com,* 880, n. 1.

[108] When one compares *CIC* 1990 with c. 1686 of the current code, the changes made are significant, but they have not totally reordered the institute. Thus, in accord with standard principles of interpretation (see c. 20), the praxis related to the exceptional process of the 1917 code provides important guidance in interpreting and implementing the current norms.

[109] CodCom, *responsa,* June 16, 1931, *AAS* 23 (1931) 353–354. Translation in *CLD* 1, 811–812. Also see SCSacr, instr, *Provida Mater Ecclesia,* art. 226, *AAS* 28 (1936) 358. Translation in *CLD* 2, 526.

[110] See W. J. Doheny, *Canonical Procedure in Matrimonial Cases,* vol. II, *Informal Procedure* (Milwaukee: Bruce, 1948) 13–28 for a full discussion of the proof required in documentary cases.

The Judge in Documentary Cases

Canon 1425, §1, 1°b) reserves contentious cases involving the bond of marriage to a college of three judges, but then specifically exempts the documentary process in both first and second instance from this requirement. Thus, marriage cases involving the documentary process may always be decided by a sole judge.

In the previous code, the "ordinary" was the competent authority to judge documentary cases (*CIC* 1990). In contrast, canon 1686 provides that the judicial vicar or a judge designated by him handle these petitions. While the canon seems to prefer that the judicial vicar personally adjudicate these matters, nothing prevents his designating another judge to fulfill this task.

May, however, a lay judge be designated to adjudicate documentary cases? This is a disputed question, related directly to the continuing debate over the nature of the power of governance and the meaning of "lay cooperation" in governance.[111] Most commentators do not directly address the question of whether a lay judge may adjudicate documentary cases, although many seem to assume that this should not be done. Grocholewski states that a lay judge can fulfill his or her function "only as part of a college" and cannot perform any function as a sole judge.[112] Burke argues that a decision by a sole lay judge would be invalid, not merely illicit.[113] Both indicate that this is not merely a disciplinary norm, but reflects doctrinal concerns. While neither specifically refers to the documentary process, they would undoubtedly reject the prospect of a sole lay judge adjudicating documentary cases. Provost, however, while admitting it is a minority opinion, argues that a lay judge may validly and licitly adjudicate documentary cases.[114] Despite Provost's suggestion that further serious consideration be given to this possibility, most commentators have not addressed the question.[115] Certainly, since some commentators contend that a lay judge acting solely acts invalidly, the prudent course is to assign documentary cases only to cleric judges. Yet, this author believes that Provost's position merits much fuller discussion.

The Process Employed in Documentary Cases

The process begins when the tribunal accepts a petition in accord with canon 1677. Upon acceptance of the petition, the judge must cite the parties, including the defender of the bond, and notify them of the citation in accord with canon 1508. Thus, the documentary process preserves the initial stages of the ordinary judicial process. The clause noting that the parties must be cited and the defender of the bond must intervene may be redundant given the explicit requirement that canon 1677 be observed. But that redundancy emphasizes the essential fact that the right of defense must be respected in the documentary process. The judge, however, may omit the remaining formalities of the judicial process (*praetermissis sollemnitatibus ordinarii processus*).

---

[111] See this commentary at cc. 129, §2; 1421; and 1425 for further reflections.

[112] Z. Grocholewski, in *Com Ex* IV/1, 784. He adds, however, that within the college the lay person is without doubt a true judge and has the same judicial power as the other members (785), although a lay judge may not serve as the presiding judge (785–786). Also see *RRAO 1989*, 49–50.

[113] R. L. Burke, "Nullity of a Decision by a Single Lay Judge," *RRAO 1994*, 145–146.

[114] J. Provost, "Roles for Lay Judges," in *CLSA Advisory Opinions 1984–1993*, 444–446; idem, "Role of Lay Judges," *J* 45 (1985) 329–332.

[115] R. Pagé briefly refers to Provost's opinion, but he concludes that, as a matter of purely ecclesiastical law, lay judges can exercise their authority only within a judicial college. See R. Pagé, "Juges laïcs et exercice du pouvoir judiciaire," in *Unico Ecclesiae Servitio: Canonical Studies Presented to Germain Lesage,* ed. M. Thériault and J. Thorn (Ottawa: St. Paul University, 1991) 209. F. G. Morrisey, in *"Decimo anno,"* 120, does not speak of documentary cases. He argues, however, that "there no longer seems to be any objectively valid reason preventing a qualified lay person from acting as a sole judge in a case. The power of orders is not at stake here; instead we are simply dealing with a fact to be ascertained by the court."

The canon neither specifies what "formalities" may be omitted nor identifies how they are distinguished from the constitutive elements of the judicial process. Commentators on the 1917 code were not in agreement on this point. Among the formalities which may be omitted, Doheny included the use of a collegiate tribunal, the formal *litis contestatio,* the depositions of witnesses (unless needed), the publication of the acts, and the mandatory appeal.[116] He concluded that essential elements which must be preserved were: (1) the generic and special norms governing competency in marriage cases, (2) the right of the parties to accuse the marriage, (3) the actual petition for a trial of nullity, (4) the right of defense, and (5) a judicial sentence.[117] Thomas L. Dupre, after extensively surveying the literature and historical background of the process, developed a helpful set of principles. He argued that all formalities may be omitted except those which are required by: (1) divine law, (2) the demands of justice, (3) the positive law for this process, and (4) the requirements of the public order. Finally, Dupre concluded that in each concrete case the judge had the discretion to resolve doubts about whether a specific formality was necessary or not.[118] Applying these principles to the *ius vigens,* this author suggests that the following essential elements must be preserved: (1) a petition from one with the right to impugn the marriage, (2) the rules of judicial competence for marriage nullity cases, (3) the citation of the parties, (4) the oral or written intervention of the defender

of the bond, (5) the requirement of moral certitude to overturn the presumption of validity, (6) a written sentence, and (7) the right of defense of the parties including their right to appeal the judgment.

The Decision

Upon reaching moral certitude, the judge declares the nullity by means of a judicial sentence. The essential elements of any judicial sentence must be present, although not necessarily all the formalities. Thus, the sentence must settle the controversy, determine the obligations of the parties, set forth reasons in law and in fact for the decision, and apportion the expenses of the trial (cc. 1611, 1612, 1689).

If the judge cannot reach moral certitude in the summary process, some authors indicate that a negative decision should not be issued, but that the case should be transferred to the formal process.[119] This opinion is supported by the fact that canon 1688 seems to assume that any appeal will be against an affirmative decision. Yet, canon 1687, §2 speaks of an appeal by a party who feels aggrieved, which would imply that a petitioner might be aggrieved by a negative decision. Normally, when the judge cannot reach moral certitude of nullity in the documentary process, it is most appropriate to order the matter transferred to the ordinary contentious process. Yet, the canon does not specifically preclude a negative decision. For example, the results of the investigation may firmly establish that no impediment exists, or that it was definitely dispensed, or that the alleged defect of form did not exist. In these situations, a transfer of the case to the ordinary process would be pure formalism, since there would be no hope of an affirmative decision on the ground at issue. Rather than drag out the process uselessly, the judge should issue a negative sentence.[120] The

---

[116] Doheny, *Canonical Procedure: Informal Cases,* 145–146.

[117] Ibid. 146. Doheny noted that some canonists argued that at least some of the formalities connected with judicial competence could also be omitted, a position which he refused to endorse or condemn, but with which he was not in full agreement (148–151).

[118] T. Dupre, *The Summary Process,* 122. He also suggested that, in keeping with the spirit of the summary process, the benefit of the doubt should be given to the elimination of procedural formalities unless they were at least probably essential to the judicial process, the public order, or the right of defense (121).

[119] Kelly, in *CLSGBI Com,* 941–942; Martínez Valls, in *Valencia Com,* 726.

[120] W. J. Doheny, in *Canonical Procedure: Informal Cases,* 173–174, concludes that normally there is little need to

fact that the Secretariat of State and Signatura collect statistics about negative decisions in documentary cases reinforces this conclusion. If it is necessary to issue a negative decision in a documentary case, ideally the judge might suggest that the petitioner consult a canonical advocate to assess whether some other ground of nullity might be present that could become the basis of a new petition.

The Appeal

Canon 1687 — §1. If the defender of the bond prudently thinks that either the flaws mentioned in can. 1686 or the lack of a dispensation are not certain, the defender of the bond must appeal against the declaration of nullity to the judge of second instance; the acts must be sent to the appellate judge who must be advised in writing that a documentary process is involved.

§2. The party who considers himself or herself aggrieved retains the right of appeal.

The mandatory review of first affirmative decisions in marriage nullity cases (c. 1682, §1) is not applicable to cases decided by the summary process. Presumably, this respects the nature of the process and the weight of the documentary proof on which the decision must be based. Thus, if neither the defender of the bond nor one of the parties lodges an appeal against an affirmative judgment, the decision stands and may be executed.

If, however, the defender of the bond believes that the existence of the impediment or other defect or the lack of dispensation is not certainly established, he or she must appeal to the court of second instance. A party who is aggrieved by the decision also retains the right of appeal.

In the face of an appeal, the first instance tribunal is to send the acts of the case to the appel-

late tribunal with a written indication that the case was decided using the documentary process.

Second Instance Process in Documentary Cases

Canon 1688 — The judge of second instance, with the intervention of the defender of the bond and after having heard the parties, will decide in the same manner as that mentioned in can. 1686 whether the sentence must be confirmed or whether the case must rather proceed according to the ordinary method of law; in the latter event the judge remands the case to the tribunal of first instance.

Canon 1441 states that the tribunal of second instance is to be constituted in the same way as the tribunal of first instance. Thus, a sole judge adjudicates the documentary process in second instance.[121] The defender of the bond of second instance must intervene, and the judge is to hear the parties.

Then, in the same manner as the first instance documentary trial, the second instance judge decides between two options: (1) to ratify by decree the decision of first instance (which seems to presume the decision was in the affirmative), or (2) to order that the case be tried in the ordinary contentious process. In this latter situation, the case is not opened at the court of second instance, but returned to the tribunal of first instance. This has the effect of vacating the initial affirmative decision and requiring the petitioner to accept again the burden of proving nullity. Clearly, in the documentary process the court of second instance is not free to issue a negative sentence with regard to the substance of the case, but only to order that the matter be more closely examined.

---

issue negative decisions in the summary process. He adds, however, that when the evidence against nullity is incontrovertible, the proper way to dispose of the case is to issue a negative sentence.

[121] The second sentence of c. 1441 applies only to cases normally reserved to a college but decided by a sole judge in light of the exception provided by c. 1425, §4. Since documentary cases are handled by a single judge as a matter of course, second instance documentary cases are also adjudicated by a sole judge.

ARTICLE 7: GENERAL NORMS[122]
[cc. 1689–1691]

The general norms in this final article apply to all marriage nullity cases, and might have been better placed as the first rather than the seventh article of this chapter on "Cases to Declare the Nullity of Marriage."

Reminder of the Parties' Moral and Civil Obligations

Canon 1689 — In the sentence the parties are to be reminded of the moral and even civil obligations which may bind them both toward one another and toward their children to furnish support and education.

A judicial sentence must determine the obligations of the parties resulting from the judgment (c. 1611, 2°). In marriage nullity cases, whether rendered in the affirmative or the negative, the sentence is to remind the parties of their moral and legal obligations to each other and their children, if any.[123] Legal obligations to children pertain to the civil effects of marriage which are determined by the appropriate civil authority (c. 1672). Quite apart from a reminder of any legal obligations imposed on them, the judge is also to point out additional moral obligations, especially any connected with the parties' vocation as parents.

This requirement must be read in conjunction with canon 1071, §1, 3°, which mandates that, except in a case of necessity, no one is to assist at a marriage of a person who has obligations toward a former partner or children arising from a prior union without the permission of the local ordi-nary.[124] If during the course of the trial credible information emerged indicating that civil or moral obligations were not being fulfilled, it would be appropriate not only to remind the parties of their obligations, but also to prohibit a new marriage (c. 1684, §1) until it was evident that such obligations were being properly fulfilled.

Marriage Cases and the Oral Contentious Process

Canon 1690 — Cases for the declaration of the nullity of a marriage cannot be treated in an oral contentious process.

The oral contentious process (cc. 1656–1670) cannot be used to decide questions of marriage nullity. A proposal to use the oral contentious process for such cases was specifically rejected during the drafting of the code.[125] Marriage nullity cases, therefore, are handled using the ordinary contentious process (c. 1691) or, when the conditions are verified, the documentary process (cc. 1686–1688).

This prohibition, however, only forbids the use of the oral contentious process to decide the principal case. Canon 1590 permits use of the oral contentious process to decide incidental cases connected with marriage cases.

Process in Formal Marriage Nullity Cases

Canon 1691 — In other procedural matters, the canons on trials in general and on the ordinary contentious trial must be applied unless the nature of the matter precludes it; the special norms for cases concerning the status of persons and

---

[122] Wrenn, in *CLSA Com,* 1015–1016; Kelly, in *CLSGBI Com,* 942–943; Madero, in *Pamplona ComEng,* 1043; Acebal, in *Salamanca Com,* 817; Martínez Valls, in *Valencia Com,* 727; Carreras, in *Com Ex* IV/2, 1963–1966.

[123] See M. S. Foster, "Divorce and Remarriage: What about the Children?" *Stud Can* 31 (1997) 165–171.

[124] Such obligations exist whether the prior union was putative (c. 1061, §3) or not. Parental obligations to children exist even if the union lacked any semblance of marriage.

[125] *Comm* 11 (1979) 271. F. G. Morrisey, in *"Decimo anno,"* 120, has issued a new call for use of the oral contentious process in marriage nullity cases.

cases pertaining to the public good are to be observed.

Despite proposals to elaborate a completely separate process for marriage nullity cases,[126] the code treats them as a species of the ordinary contentious trial. Thus, besides the special provisions of canons 1671–1690, the norms for trials in general (cc. 1400–1500) and for the ordinary contentious process (cc. 1501–1655) are to be employed in adjudicating marriage nullity cases "unless the nature of the matter precludes it" (*nisi rei natura obstet*). Few commentators have yet to suggest examples of the sorts of matters that might preclude the use of the ordinary contentious process in marriage nullity cases.[127] Clearly, the

nisi clause does not provide the authority to dispense from procedural law (c. 87, §1). In using the term *obstet,* the canon refers only to those situations where it is truly impossible to implement one of the norms of the ordinary contentious process. Thus, it is an example of the rule of law that no one is bound to the impossible.[128]

Canon 1691 also specifies that marriage nullity cases by their nature involve the status of persons and the public good.[129] Thus, the special norms for these types of cases must be observed.[130]

---

[126] Cox, *Procedural Changes,* 146–152, 170–176.

[127] A. Farret, for example, has suggested that the norms for publication of the acts and of the sentence need to be implemented in light of the special nature of marriage cases. See "Publication des actes et publication de la sentence," *Stud Can* 25 (1991) 128–138. Presumably, the proposed instruction being prepared by the interdicasterial commission (see n. 5 above) will clarify in-

stances in which the special nature of marriage cases will modify the requirements of the ordinary contentious process.

[128] *RI,* n. 6, *CorpusIC* II, 1122.

[129] For a brief explanation of what is meant by cases involving the "status of persons," see the commentary on c. 1643. For reflections on cases involving the public good, see the commentary on cc. 1430–1431.

[130] Norms making special provisions for status-of-persons cases are cc. 1445, §1, 2°; 1492, §1; 1643; and 1644, §1. Norms for cases involving the public good, which are defined either by the law itself (cc. 1691, 1696) or by the diocesan bishop (c. 1431, §1) are found in cc. 1452, §1; 1532; 1536, §2; 1598, §1; 1696; and 1715, §1.

BIBLIOGRAPHY

(The material listed below serves as a comprehensive bibliography for canons 1501–1691.)

Books

Bonnet, P.A., and Gullo, C., eds. *Il processo matrimonioniale canonico, Nuova edizione riveduta e ampliata. Studi Giuridici* XXIX. Vatican City: Libreria Editrice Vaticana, 1994.

Cox, C. A. *Procedural Changes in Formal Marriage Nullity Cases from the 1917 to the 1983 Code. CanLawStud* 528. Washington, D.C.: Catholic University of America, 1989.

Doheny, W. J. *Canonical Procedure in Matrimonial Cases.* Vol. 1, *Formal Procedure.* 2nd ed. Milwaukee: Bruce, 1948.

———. *Canonical Procedure in Matrimonial Cases.* Vol. 2, *Informal Procedure.* Milwaukee: Bruce, 1948.

Dupre, T. L. *The Summary Process of Canons 1990–1992. CanLawStud* 451. Washington, D.C.: Catholic University of America, 1967.

Erlebach, G. *La nullità della sentenza giudiziale "ob ius defensionis denegatum" nella giurisprudenza rotale. Studi Giuridici* XXV. Vatican City: Libreria Editrice Vaticana, 1991.

García Faílde, J. J. *Nuevo derecho procesal canónico: Estudio sistemático-analítico comparado.* 3rd rev. and enlarged ed. Salamanca: Publicaciones Universidad Pontificia, 1995.

Gordon, I., and Grocholewski, Z., eds. *Documenta recentiora circa rem matrimonialem et processualem.* Vol. I. 2 vols. Rome: Pontificia Universitas Gregoriana, 1977.

Lüdicke, K., Mussinghoff, H., and Schwendenwein, H., eds. *Iustus Iudex: Festgabe für Paul Wesemann zum 75. Geburtstag von seinen Freunden und Schülern.* Essen: Ludgerus-Verlag, 1990.

Ochoa, X., ed. *Leges Ecclesiae post Codicem iuris canonici editae.* Vol. V. 7 vols. Rome: Commentarium pro Religiosis, 1980.

Raica, S. J. *Canon 1529: A Historical and Canonical Study.* Rome: Pontificia Universitas Gregoriana, 1996.

Sable, R. M., ed. *Incapacity for Marriage: Jurisprudence and Interpretation: Acts of the III Gregorian Colloquium.* Rome: Pontificia Universitas Gregoriana, 1987.

Secretaria Status. *Statistical Yearbook of the Church 1996.* Vatican City: Libreria Editrice Vaticana, 1998.

Thériault, M., and Thorn, J., eds. *Unico Ecclesiae Servitio: Canonical Studies Presented to Germain Lesage.* Ottawa: St. Paul University, 1991.

Wanenmacher, F. *Canonical Evidence in Marriage Nullity Cases.* Philadelphia: Dolphin, 1935.

Wijlens, M. *The Ordinary Contentious Trial: A Schematic Overview.* Privately published, 1992.

Woestman, W. H. *Papal Allocutions to the Roman Rota 1939–1994.* Ottawa: St. Paul University, 1994.

———. *Special Marriage Cases.* Ottawa, St. Paul University, 1992.

Wrenn, L. G. *Authentic Interpretations on the 1983 Code.* Washington, D.C.: CLSA, 1993.

———. *Procedures.* Washington, D.C.: CLSA, 1987.

Articles

Abbass, J. "Contentious Trials: A Comparative Study of the Eastern and Latin Codes." *J* 56 (1996) 875–904.

Acebal Luján, J. L.. "El fuero competente matrimonial, c. 1673, 3°: Texto y comentario." *REDC* 51 (1994) 185–189.

———. "La declaración de nulidad del matrimonio de dos acatólicos: Texto y comentario." *REDC* 49 (1992) 691–697.

———. "Normas del Tribunal de la Rota Romana: Texto y comentario." *REDC* 52 (1995) 231–279.

Beal, J. P. "Making Connections: Procedural Law and Substantive Justice." *J* 54 (1994) 113–182.

———. "The Substance of Things Hoped For: Proving Simulation of Matrimonial Consent." *J* 55 (1995) 745–793.

Breitenbeck, M. "The Use of Experts in Marriage Nullity Cases." *CLSAP* 51 (1989) 30–47.

Cox, C. A. "The Procedural Law That Might Have Been: Some Proposed Changes That Were Not Adopted during the Code Revision Process." *J* 50 (1990) 613–642.

Cuneo, J. J. "Towards Understanding the Conformity of Two Sentences of Nullity." *J* 46 (1986) 568–601.

Daneels, F. "The 'Forum of Most of the Proofs.'" *J* 50 (1990) 289–309.

———. "The Right of Defence." *Stud Can* 27 (1993) 77–95.

de Lanversin, B. "L'importance du can. 1578, §3, dans les procès matrimoniaux." *QuadStR* 4 (1989) 49–58.

Doran, T. G. "Some Thoughts on Experts." *QuadStR* 4 (1989) 59–74.

Erlebach, G. "La fattispecie di negazione del diritto di defesa causanti la nullità della sentenza secondo la giurisprudenza Rotale: Criteri generali e parte statica." *ME* 114 (1989) 495–556.

Egan, E. M. "Appeal in Marriage Nullity Cases: Two Centuries of Experiment and Reform." *CLSAP* 43 (1981) 132–144.

Farret, A. "Publication des actes et publication de la sentence dans les causes de nullité de mariage." *Stud Can* 25 (1991) 115–138.

Felici, P. "Formalitates iuridicae et aestimatio probationum in processu canonico." *Comm* 9 (1977) 175–184. Translation in *J* 38 (1978) 153–157.

Foster, M. S. "Divorce and Remarriage: What about the Children? Canons 1071, 1077, 1684, 1689." *Stud Can* 31 (1997) 147–191.

García Faílde, J. J. "El perito psicólogo y psiquiatra en las causas canónicas de nulidad matrimonial." *Memorias* 20 (1996) 95–110.

Grocholewski, Z. "The Ecclesiastical Judge and the Findings of Psychiatric and Psychological Experts." *J* 47 (1987) 449–470.

———. "Quisnam est pars conventa in causis nullitatis matrimonii?" *P* 79 (1990) 357–391.

Guiry, R. W. "Canonical and Psychological Reflections on the *Vetitum* in Today's Tribunals." *J* 49 (1989) 191–209.

Hopka, J. "The *Vetitum* and *Monitum* in Matrimonial Nullity Proceedings." *Stud Can* 19 (1985) 357–399.

Johnson, J. G. "Publish and Be Damned: The Dilemma of Implementing the Canons on Publishing the Acts and the Sentence." *J* 49 (1989) 210–240.

———. "*Res iudicata, restitutio in integrum,* and Marriage Cases." *Stud Can* 28 (1994) 323–345.

Lucas, J. P. "The Prohibition Imposed by a Tribunal: Law, Practice, Future Development." *J* 45 (1985) 588–617.

Madero, L. "El proceso contencioso oral en el Codex Iuris Canonici de 1983." *IC* 24 (1984) 197–291.

Martinez Cavero, M. "El proceso contencioso oral." *REDC* 45 (1988) 677–696.

McGrath, A. "At the Service of Truth: Psychological Sciences and Their Relation to the Canon Law of Nullity of Marriage." *Stud Can* 27 (1993) 379–400.

———. "Conformity of Sentence in Marriage Nullity Cases." *Stud Can* 27 (1993) 5–22.

Mendonça, A. "The Application of the Principle of Equity in Marriage Nullity Cases." *J* 55 (1995) 664–697.

———. "The Role of Experts in 'Incapacity to Contract' Cases (Canon 1095)." *Stud Can* 25 (1991) 417–450.

———. "The Structural and Functional Aspects of an Appeal Tribunal in Marriage Nullity Cases." *Stud Can* 32 (1998) 441–500.

Moodie, M. R. "Fundamental Rights and Access to the Acts of a Case." *Stud Can* 28 (1994) 123–154.

Morlot, F. "Le droit de défense, en particulier dans la publication des actes." *Stud Can* (1996) 133–162.

Nau, D. "Publish and Be Damned: One Practitioner's Experience." *J* 51 (1991) 442–450.

Pompedda, M. F. "Decision-Sentence in Marriage Trials: Of the Concept and Principles for Rendering an Ecclesiastical Sentence." *QuadStR* 5 (1990) 73–99.

Provost, J. H. "Competent Tribunal When Respondent's Address Unknown." *J* 44 (1984) 244–246.

———. "Jurisprudential and Procedural Approaches to Traditional and Modern Grounds and the Question of Conformity of Sentences." *Proceedings of the Canon Law Society of Australia and New Zealand.* Sydney, Australia: CLSANZ, 1996, 92–113.

Smilanic, D. A. "The Publication of the Acts: Canon 1598, §1." *CLSAP* 57 (1995) 377–386.

Stankiewicz, A. "De citationis necessitate et impugnatione." *QuadStR* 4 (1989) 75–87.

———. "Il processo contenzioso orale." *Apol* 54 (1992) 563–591.

Trudeau, J. "La remise à la justice du tribunal dans les causes de nullité de mariage." *Stud Can* 32 (1998) 129–143.

Wirth, P. "Das mündliche Streitverfahren." In *Iustus Iudex,* ed. K. Lüdicke, H. Mussinghoff, and H. Schwendenwin, 631–653. Essen: Ludgerus Verlag, 1990.

Wrenn, L. G. "Notes, but Mostly Footnotes, on Presumptions." *J* 30 (1970) 206–215.

CHAPTER II
CASES OF SEPARATION OF SPOUSES
[cc. 1692–1696]

The process to decide the personal separation of baptized spouses is elaborated in the following canons. This chapter is new to the present code. The 1917 code did not contain any norms to guide the competent ecclesiastical authority in deciding separation cases. The 1917 code alluded only to the fact that separation could be effected by the sentence of an ecclesiastical judge or by the pronouncement of the ordinary.[1] The 1983 code, by contrast, explains the process to be used by the proper ecclesiastical authority in arriving at the decision for separation.

The Eastern code also elaborates the process to decide the separation of spouses. This is laid out in five canons very similar to those of the Latin code.[2]

No legal developments have taken place concerning this process since the promulgation of the 1983 code.

Ecclesiastical Forum

Canon 1692 — §1. Unless other provision is legitimately made in particular places, a decree of the diocesan bishop or a judicial sentence can decide the personal separation of baptized spouses according to the norm of the following canons.

Spouses have the duty and the right to preserve conjugal living in virtue of their marriage covenant, unless a legitimate cause excuses them. The Church has a special pastoral solicitude for married couples, and considers the separation of spouses even for a temporary period a serious matter.[3]

The case for separation may be decided by an administrative process or a judicial process. For the administrative process, the diocesan bishop of the domicile or quasi-domicile of the spouses is competent to issue the decree of separation (c. 107). The vicar general or episcopal vicar may issue this decree only by special mandate of the diocesan bishop.[4] Recourse against the decree of the diocesan bishop is governed by canons 1732–1739.

The following canons elucidate the important points of the judicial process.

Civil Forum

§2. Where an ecclesiastical decision has no civil effects or if a civil sentence is not contrary to divine law, the bishop of the diocese of the residence of the spouses, after having weighed the special circumstances, can grant permission to approach the civil forum.

§3. If a case concerns only the merely civil effects of marriage, the judge, after having observed the prescript of §2, is to try to defer the case to the civil forum from the start.

Marriage cases of the baptized belong to the ecclesiastical judge by proper right.[5] The diocesan bishop may exercise his discretion to have cases of separation decided in the ecclesiastical forum or deferred to the civil forum. Cases which concern the civil effects of marriage are more appropriately decided in the civil forum,[6] especially in those places where the decisions of ecclesiastical authority are not recognized by the civil authority. The civil effects of marriage concern such matters as property division, spousal support, child support, child custody, and the like.

---

[1] *CIC* 1130; 1131, §2.
[2] *CCEO* 1378–1382.
[3] Canon 1151. See cc. 1152–1153 for the legitimate causes for separation.

[4] Canon 134, §3.
[5] Canon 1671.
[6] Canon 1672.

The diocesan bishop may also grant permission for the spouses to approach the civil forum in those places where the civil sentence of separation is not contrary to the divine law. The divine law, for example, on the indissolubility and unity of marriage and the obligations of parents toward their children may not be contradicted by any civil sentence of separation.

The Judicial Process

Canon 1693 — §1. Unless a party or the promoter of justice requests the ordinary contentious process, the oral contentious process is to be used.

If the judicial process is chosen, the law prescribes that the oral contentious process be used (cc. 1656–1670). The spouses or the promoter of justice may exercise their right to choose the ordinary contentious process instead, if they so desire (cc. 1501–1655).

§2. If the ordinary contentious process has been used and an appeal is proposed, the tribunal of second grade, observing what is required, is to proceed according to the norm of can. 1682, §2.

If an appeal is proposed, and the ordinary contentious process was used, the appellate tribunal is either to confirm the decision at once by decree or admit the case to an ordinary examination in a new grade. If an appeal is proposed, and the oral contentious process was used, the appellate tribunal is also to proceed in accord with the oral contentious process.[7] Even with two concordant sentences, a case concerning the separation of spouses never becomes *res iudicata*.[8]

Competence of the Tribunal

Canon 1694 — The prescripts of can. 1673 are to be observed in what pertains to the competence of the tribunal.

The competence of the tribunal is determined by canon 1673, whether the oral or the ordinary contentious process is used. The case is tried before a single judge, who may associate two assessors with himself in the case.[9]

Reconciliation of the Spouses

Canon 1695 — Before accepting the case and whenever there is hope of a favorable outcome, the judge is to use pastoral means to reconcile the spouses and persuade them to restore conjugal living.

The spouses have the duty and the right to preserve conjugal living,[10] and pastoral means are to be used to help them maintain common life. Separation is the last resort.

The Promoter of Justice

Canon 1696 — Cases concerning the separation of spouses also pertain to the public good; therefore the promoter of justice must always take part in them according to the norm of can. 1433.

The participation of the promoter of justice is required for the validity of the acts of the case, whether the administrative or the judicial process is used. The public good is at stake in these cases because separation seriously alters the life of the spouses, the children, the family, and society.

CHAPTER III
PROCESS FOR THE DISPENSATION OF A MARRIAGE *RATUM ET NON CONSUMMATUM* [cc. 1697–1706]

In this chapter the 1983 code systematically presents the norms for the dispensation of a marriage that has been ratified but not consummated. The presentation here is markedly different from

---

[7] Canons 1670, 1640.
[8] Canons 1643–1644.

[9] Canons 1424, 1657.
[10] Canon 1151.

that found in the 1917 code. In the old code, the norms for the administrative process for dispensation from a ratified and non-consummated marriage were mixed together with the norms for the judicial process for cases of nullity of marriage.[11] In the new code the two processes are treated separately.

The ten canons in this chapter have as their primary sources the 1917 code and two major instructions issued by the Sacred Congregation for the Discipline of the Sacraments on May 7, 1923[12] and March 7, 1972.[13] Since the promulgation of the 1983 code the congregation has issued new norms in the form of a circular letter on December 20, 1986, to assist bishops in the instruction of this process.[14]

The Eastern code contains one canon on the process for the dispensation from a ratified and non-consummated marriage. That canon simply directs that the special norms issued by the Apostolic See are to be followed in instructing these cases.[15]

The Right to Petition

Canon 1697 — Only the spouses, or one of them even if the other is unwilling, have the right to petition for the favor of a dispensation from a marriage *ratum et non consummatum*.

This is a fundamental principle, found in the 1917 code and repeated in the major instructions.[16]

---

[11] *CIC* Book IV, part one, title XX.
[12] SCSacr, decr *Catholica doctrina* and *Regulae servandae in processibus super matrimonio rato et non consummato,* May 7, 1923, *AAS* 15 (1923) 389–413. Translation in *CLD* 1, 764–792.
[13] SCSacr, instr *Dispensationis matrimonii,* March 7, 1972, *AAS* 64 (1972) 244–252. Translation in *CLD* 7, 988–997.
[14] CDWDS, littcirc *De processu super matrimonio rato et non consummato,* December 20, 1986, *ME* 112 (1987) 423–429. Translation in W. Woestman, *Special Marriage Cases* (Ottawa: St. Paul University, 1994) 121–128.
[15] *CCEO* 1384.
[16] *CIC* 1119, 1973; *Regulae servandae,* art. 5, §1; *Dispensationis matrimonii,* I, b.

The right to petition for the dispensation is limited to the spouses to the marriage. The spouses together may request the dispensation. If only one spouse requests the dispensation and the other party, namely, the respondent, is unwilling to participate after having been cited, then the respondent is declared absent in accord with canon 1592 and the case proceeds.

The Right to Decide

Canon 1698 — §1. Only the Apostolic See adjudicates the fact of the non-consummation of a marriage and the existence of a just cause to grant a dispensation.

The exclusive competence of the Apostolic See to adjudicate these cases is well established in the old code and in subsequent documents.[17] The Congregation for Divine Worship and the Discipline of the Sacraments recommends to the pope the granting of the favor of the dispensation, after it has determined both that the fact of the non-consummation is proved and that there exists a just cause to grant the dispensation. The absence of either of these elements renders the dispensation of no benefit to the one who receives it.[18]

The Right to Grant a Dispensation

§2. Only the Roman Pontiff, however, grants the dispensation.

Although the congregation has the responsibility of studying the case and recommending to the pope the granting of the favor of a dispensation, it remains the exclusive prerogative of the pope to grant the dispensation. This is an exercise of the supreme ministerial authority of the Roman Pontiff.

---

[17] *CIC* 249, §3; 1962; *Regulae servandae,* art. 1; *Dispensationis matrimonii,* I.
[18] *Regulae servandae,* art. 103; *Dispensationis matrimonii,* I, f.

The Petition

Canon 1699 — §1. The person competent to accept a *libellus* seeking a dispensation is the diocesan bishop of the domicile or quasi-domicile of the petitioner, who must arrange for the instruction of the process if the petition is well founded.

Under the 1917 code, in order to instruct a process regarding dispensation, the diocesan bishop had to request the faculty each time from the Apostolic See.[19] It was only with the 1972 instruction from the congregation that the diocesan bishop was granted the general faculty in his own territory to draw up the process.[20] The new code in the present canon incorporates this competence of the diocesan bishop.

The canon names the diocesan bishop of the place in which the petitioner has a domicile or quasi-domicile as the competent person to accept a petition. In addition, the 1986 circular letter from the congregation has extended competence also to the bishop of the place in which most of the proofs in fact must be collected, provided that he requests the prorogation of competence in each case from the congregation and that the bishop of the place where the petitioner has a domicile or quasi-domicile consents.[21]

If, during the examination of a petition for dispensation, a prudent doubt arises concerning the validity of the marriage itself, the bishop is to advise the spouses to choose the judicial path if one of the spouses wishes to proceed with a case for marriage nullity, or else to arrange for the process for dispensation to continue if the case has good foundation.[22]

Upon receiving the petition for dispensation, if there is a hope of reconciling the spouses, the bishop is to urge the spouses to resolve their differences and restore conjugal living.[23]

Difficult Cases

§2. If the proposed case has special difficulties of the juridical or moral order, however, the diocesan bishop is to consult the Apostolic See.

Some cases of non-consummation are especially difficult to prove. These require prior consultation with the congregation before the bishop can proceed with the instruction of the case. Consultation is required in cases where there was an uncompleted conjugal act, conception through the absorption of semen, resort to artificial insemination, the birth of a child, a defect in the human fashion of consummating the marriage, the danger of scandal or of financial loss connected with the granting of the favor, and other such difficulties.[24]

The new requirement in canon 1061, §1 that the consummation of marriage take place by a conjugal act performed in a human fashion has been taken into account in the process for the dispensation from a ratified and non-consummated marriage. In its plenary congregation in April 1986, the Congregation for Divine Worship and the Discipline of the Sacraments decided to use the following criteria in those cases where a defect of consummation in a human fashion is alleged:

> Following the conclusions of the Plenary Congregation mentioned above, which were approved by the Supreme Pontiff, this Congregation uses the following mode of solving the cases submitted to it, namely that for the consummation of marriage, there must be a human act on the part of each party, but it is sufficient that it be virtually voluntary, provided that it is not demanded violently. Other psychological elements, which would

---

[19] *CIC* 1963, §1.

[20] *Dispensationis matrimonii,* I.

[21] *De processu,* n. 1.

[22] Ibid., n. 3.

[23] Ibid., n. 4.

[24] Ibid., n. 2. For the thinking of the congregation regarding difficult cases, see G. Orlandi, *I "Casi Difficili" nel Processo Super Rato* (Padua: Cedam, 1984). See also B. Marchetta, *Scioglimento del Matrimonio Canonico per Inconsumazione* (Padua: Cedam, 1981) 22–161.

make the human act easier or more loving, are not taken into account.[25]

In approving these conclusions, the pope reserved to himself the right to establish more exact criteria in individual cases, to determine if there was sufficient voluntariness for the consummation, and to decide if it is suitable to grant the dispensation.[26] Because the dispensation is always a favor freely granted by the pope and not a right demanded by the parties, the pope enjoys broad discretion regarding these criteria.

Based on the conclusions of the congregation we can say that a spouse is incapable of performing the human act required for consummation if he or she is deprived of all awareness during the conjugal act. This can happen when the party is under the intoxicating influence of drugs or alcohol. Likewise, a spouse is incapable of performing the human act required for consummation if will and freedom are taken away. This happens when the party is the victim of physical violence and the consummation takes place against the person's will.

Recourse

§3. Recourse to the Apostolic See is available against a decree by which a bishop rejects a *libellus*.

If the bishop rejects the petition, recourse to the expertise of the congregation could help clarify the merits of the case in order to determine if the case should be accepted.

The Forum for Instruction

Canon 1700 — §1. Without prejudice to the prescript of can. 1681, the bishop is to entrust the in-

struction of these processes either in a stable manner or in individual cases to his tribunal, that of another diocese, or a suitable priest.

The diocesan bishop enjoys the ordinary competence to accept the petition and arrange for the instruction of the process. The bishop will want to make sure that the instruction is in capable hands. For that reason, he enjoys the discretion of utilizing his own tribunal, another tribunal, or a suitable priest to carry out this instruction.

§2. If a judicial petition to declare the nullity of the same marriage has been introduced, however, the instruction is to be entrusted to the same tribunal.

Competence to instruct the case for the dispensation is always given to the tribunal that is considering nullity, whether the instruction of the petition for a dispensation started before or after the nullity case was introduced.[27] Having the proceedings take place in one tribunal helps assure that a marriage case will not be instructed in two different processes at the same time and that a dispensation will not be granted for a marriage that has been declared null.[28]

The Defender of the Bond

Canon 1701 — §1. The defender of the bond must always intervene in these processes.

The task of the defender of the bond is to propose and explain everything which reasonably can be brought forth against the dissolution of the marriage.[29] The defender can introduce questions for the parties, witnesses, and experts to answer and can be present at their examination. When the instruction has been completed, the defender examines all the records of the case and presents obser-

---

[25] *De processu,* introduction. *RRAO 1987,* 63.
[26] R. Melli, "Breve Commentarium ad Litteras Circulares 'De Processu Super Matrimonio Rato et Non Consummato,'" *ME* 112 (1987) 431.

[27] *De processu,* n. 5.
[28] Melli, "Breve Commentarium," 432.
[29] Canon 1432.

vations on whether the fact of non-consummation has been proved and whether there is sufficient cause to grant a dispensation.[30]

The Legal Expert

§2. A legal representative is not admitted, but because of the difficulty of a case, a bishop can permit the petitioner or the respondent to have the assistance of a legal expert.

Because the process for dispensation is administrative and not contentious in nature, an advocate is not allowed to participate. To admit an advocate would confuse the administrative process with the judicial process. More appropriate to the administrative process is the participation of a legal expert. Recognizing the fact that non-consummation is at times difficult to prove, the code allows a legal expert to participate in difficult cases.

The bishop is the person competent to designate the legal expert, who may be chosen ex officio or at the request of one of the parties.[31] The duty of the legal expert is to help the parties introduce the case and assist the parties in gathering the proofs. In the event that the congregation responds that non-consummation has not been established from the materials presented, canon 1705, §3 allows the legal expert to inspect all the acts of the case at the tribunal, except for the *votum* of the bishop, to help the parties produce new proofs in order to resubmit their petition.[32]

Proofs

Canon 1702 — In the instruction each spouse is to be heard, and the canons on the collection of proofs in the ordinary contentious trial and in cases of the nullity of marriage are to be observed

insofar as possible, provided that they can be reconciled with the character of these processes.

The integrity of the process demands that each spouse be heard during the instruction of the case. Thus, the respondent must always be cited. The congregation will reject a case for dispensation that has been instructed without the knowledge of the respondent. If the respondent does not respond to the citation, he or she is declared absent in accord with canon 1592 and the case proceeds.[33]

The canons on the collection of proofs in the ordinary contentious trial (cc. 1526–1586) and in cases of the nullity of marriage (cc. 1678–1680) assist the instructor in presenting the moral argument and the physical argument for non-consummation. The moral argument relies on the testimony given by the parties, witnesses, and experts, on authentic documents, and on inferences from circumstances and presumptions. The physical argument relies on the physical examination of the man or the woman, and confirms the proof offered by the moral argument. The physical examination may be omitted if moral certitude of the non-consummation of the marriage can be reached by the moral argument alone.

Serious Contradictions among Proofs

Canon 1703 — §1. There is no publication of the acts. If the judge perceives that the proofs brought forward seriously hinder the request of the petitioner or the exception of the respondent, however, he is prudently to inform the interested party.

Unlike the practice in marriage nullity cases, where publication of the acts is required, the general rule in the process for a dispensation from a ratified and non-consummated marriage is that

---

[30] Canons 1533, 1561, 1678; *Regulae servandae,* arts. 28, 98.

[31] *Dispensationis matrimonii,* II, e.

[32] *De processu,* n. 6.

[33] B. Marchetta, "Il Processo 'Super Matrimonio Rato et Non Consummato' nel Nuovo Codice di Diritto Canonico," in *Dilexit Iustitiam,* ed. Z. Grocholewski and V. C. Orti (Vatican City: Libreria Editrice Vaticana, 1984) 410.

the acts are not published. The acts are secret because of the delicate nature of the testimony. However, in the interest of arriving at the truth of the fact of non-consummation and of the existence of a just cause for granting the dispensation, the judge is obliged to inform the parties if any of the proofs brought forward seriously contradict their testimony. The interested party may then request to see a particular document or testimony in order to present observations to correct any falsehoods or errors.

§2. The judge can show a document introduced or a testimony received to a party who requests it and set a time to present observations.

As the person entrusted by the bishop with the instruction of the case, the judge has the responsibility of deciding whether or not it is proper to show a particular document or testimony to a party who requests it.[34] It is also the responsibility of the judge to determine the time for the party to present his or her observations.

The Votum *of the Bishop*

Canon 1704 — §1. When the instruction has been completed, the instructor is to give all the acts along with a suitable report to the bishop, who is to prepare a *votum* on the veracity of the fact of the non-consummation, the just cause for the dispensation, and the suitability of the favor.

When the instructor has completed his task, he hands all the acts of the case over to the bishop. The bishop has the responsibility of writing a *votum* to accompany the case to the Apostolic See. The bishop may personally prepare this opinion, or he may accept and make his own an opinion which was written by the vicar general or the episcopal vicar, to whom he had generally delegated by special mandate the faculty to write such opinions.[35]

In the preparation of his *votum,* the bishop has access to all the acts of the case, as well as the "suitable report" from the instructor. Lest it unduly influence the opinion of the bishop, the report of the instructor does not enter into the merits of the case, but merely narrates a summary of the entire process in order to assist the bishop in writing his opinion.[36]

The bishop must identify in his *votum* a just cause for granting the dispensation. Some reasons recognized as just causes in the practice of the congregation are profound aversion of the spouses to each other, the fear of continuing dissension and strife between the spouses, scandal due to another civil marriage already contracted by one of the spouses, the danger of incontinence for one party due to a civil divorce obtained by the other party, the danger of incontinence for one party due to the probable impotence of the other party, a serious and incurable contagious disease contracted after the wedding, the existence of a defect of consent or of another impediment to the marriage, and the danger of perversion. These or some other proportionately serious reason concerning the special circumstances of the parties are grounds for a just cause to grant the dispensation.[37]

In addition to weighing the fact of non-consummation and the just cause for the dispensation, the bishop must also consider the suitability of the favor, the absence of scandal, the possible wonderment of the faithful or any kind of damage that could result from granting the favor, and any other consequences related to the good of souls and the restoration of peace to consciences. He must explicitly refer to these pastoral concerns in his *votum.*[38]

§2. If the instruction of the process has been entrusted to another tribunal according to the norm of can. 1700, the observations in favor of the

---

[34] *Regulae servandae,* art. 97, §2.

[35] *De processu,* n. 23a.

[36] Ibid., n. 21. Marchetta, "Il Processo 'Super Matrimonio Rato et Non Consummato,'" 427.

[37] Marchetta, *Scioglimento,* 17–18.

[38] *De processu,* n. 23c.

bond are to be made in the same forum; the *votum* mentioned in §1, however, pertains to the entrusting bishop, to whom the instructor is to hand over a suitable report together with the acts.

The entrusting bishop prepares the *votum,* since he can best attest to the effect the concession of the papal dispensation will have on the faithful of his own diocese. The entrusting bishop is able to verify the suitability of the favor and the absence of scandal.

Transmission of the Acts

Canon 1705 — §1. The bishop is to transmit to the Apostolic See all the acts together with his *votum* and the observations of the defender of the bond.

The responsibility for the case rests with the bishop who first accepted the petition. It is he who arranges for the instruction of the case, and it is he who finally has the responsibility of sending all the acts of the completed instruction along with his *votum* to Rome. The Congregation for Divine Worship and the Discipline of the Sacraments commences its study of the case to determine if the fact of non-consummation has been proved and if a just cause for granting the dispensation has been given.[39]

Supplemental Instruction

§2. If supplemental instruction is required in the judgment of the Apostolic See, this requirement will be communicated to the bishop with an indication of the points on which the instruction must be completed.

Supplemental instruction is required if the congregation judges that sufficient information is lacking to decide on the fact of non-consummation

or the existence of a just cause. The congregation assists the bishop by informing him of exactly which points of the instruction need to be clarified or completed. Before the case is returned to the congregation, the bishop is requested to prepare a new *votum* and the defender of the bond is asked to prepare new observations taking into account the supplemental instruction.

Second Presentation

§3. If the Apostolic See replies that non-consummation has not been established from the materials presented, then the legal expert mentioned in can. 1701, §2 can inspect the acts of the process, though not the *votum* of the bishop, at the tribunal to consider whether any grave reason can be brought forth in order to resubmit the petition.

If the congregation replies that non-consummation has not been established (*non constare*), the parties may resubmit the petition for another examination if they have significant new proofs to offer. They may request the aid of a legal expert to inspect the acts of the case and to assist them in gathering new testimonies and documents. Access to the *votum* of the bishop is denied to the legal expert because of the confidential nature of the bishop's opinion regarding the case.

If the congregation replies negatively to the petition, the parties may not resubmit the petition for another examination. The congregation rejects the petition with a negative when the acts of the case show the marriage is not in fact non-consummated or there is no just cause for the dispensation.[40]

Rescript, Notification, and Recording

Canon 1706 — The Apostolic See transmits the rescript of the dispensation to the bishop who will notify the parties about the rescript and also as soon as possible will order the pastor both of the place where the marriage was contracted and of

---

[39] For sample forms of the acts, see Woestman, *Special Marriage Cases,* 150–174.

[40] Marchetta, *Scioglimento,* 109, n. 5.

the place of baptism to note the granting of the dispensation in the marriage and baptismal registers.

The rescript of the dispensation is effective from the moment the pope grants the dispensation on the day of his audience with the prefect of the congregation.[41] The bishop fulfills his final responsibilities in the case by receiving the rescript, notifying the parties, and ordering the appropriate notations in the marriage and baptismal registers.

CHAPTER IV
PROCESS IN THE PRESUMED DEATH
OF A SPOUSE
[c. 1707]

In this chapter the code presents the outline of a process for use in attaining moral certitude of the death of a missing spouse when no authentic document can be found to prove the fact of death. The process for a declaration of presumed death is included in the title on special marriage processes because a declaration of this sort is usually sought by a surviving spouse who wishes to enter a new marriage.

The canon is new in the present code. There was no comparable treatment of this material in the 1917 code. The primary source for the canon is the 1868 instruction *Matrimonii vinculo* of the Holy Office, which contained norms for ecclesiastical superiors to use when instructing cases of presumed death of a spouse.[42] Since the promulgation of the 1983 code, no legal developments have taken place concerning this process.

The Eastern code contains one canon on this process, and it is substantially the same as the present canon except in two regards. In paragraph three of the Eastern canon, an eparchial bishop

exercising his power within the territorial boundaries of a patriarchal church is directed to consult the patriarch in uncertain and complex cases; other eparchial bishops are to consult the Apostolic See. The Eastern canon also adds a paragraph four, which states that the process in the presumed death of a spouse requires the intervention of the promoter of justice but not of the defender of the bond.[43]

Declaration of Presumed Death

Canon 1707 — §1. Whenever the death of a spouse cannot be proven by an authentic ecclesiastical or civil document, the other spouse is not considered free from the bond of marriage until after the diocesan bishop has issued a declaration of presumed death.

The partner who wishes to remarry after the death of a spouse is the object of the special pastoral solicitude of the Church. Freedom to marry is normally established by an authentic ecclesiastical or civil document certifying the death of the other spouse. If the party has no authentic document proving the death of the other spouse, the Church establishes the freedom of the party to marry by issuing a declaration of the presumed death of the other spouse. The effect of this declaration is that the party is permitted to enter a new marriage.[44]

A declaration of presumed death does not dissolve a marriage. Only death can dissolve a ratified and consummated marriage.[45] Therefore, if a spouse who was presumed to be dead is later found to be alive, the other party must separate from the second partner and return to the first spouse. In this case, the bond of the first marriage never in fact ceased to exist because the absent spouse was not dead, and the second marriage is invalid because of the impediment of prior bond.

---

[41] *Regulae servandae*, art. 103.

[42] SCOf, instr *Matrimonii vinculo*, May 13, 1868, *AAS* 2 (1910) 199–203. Translation in Woestman, *Special Marriage Cases*, 141–144; and in W. Doheny, *Canonical Procedure in Matrimonial Cases* (Milwaukee: Bruce, 1944) 2:593–596.

[43] *CCEO* 1383.

[44] For a sample decree of presumed death, see L. Wrenn, *Decisions*, 2nd rev. ed. (Washington, D.C.: CLSA, 1983) 197–198.

[45] Canon 1141.

Proofs and Moral Certainty

§2. The diocesan bishop is able to issue the declaration mentioned in §1 only if, after having carried out appropriate investigations, he attains moral certitude of the death of the spouse from the depositions of witnesses, from rumor, or from evidence. The absence of a spouse alone, even for a long time, is not sufficient.

The diocesan bishop, either personally or through his delegate, is to conduct the investigations necessary to arrive at moral certitude concerning the death of a spouse. The bishop may conduct these investigations by means of an administrative process or a judicial process, but the administrative process is the ordinary and more convenient way to proceed.[46]

The depositions of at least two witnesses who knew the deceased and who agree on the fact of death, the place of death, and the circumstances of death provide the best evidence for a declaration of presumed death. Lacking this evidence, the testimony of hearsay witnesses who learned of the death at a non-suspect time, the use of presumptions regarding the age, the condition of health, and the moral character of the person, as well as a study of the circumstances of the disappearance of the person, a respectable rumor of death, and inquiry through newspaper notices may all help provide the moral certitude the bishop needs to presume that the spouse is dead.[47] Long-time absence by itself, without the support of other evidence, is not a sufficient criterion in canon law for a presumption of death, even though this criterion often suffices in civil law.

Uncertain and Complicated Cases

§3. The bishop is to consult the Apostolic See in uncertain and complicated cases.

If, after carrying out the investigations, the bishop still cannot arrive at moral certitude of the death of the spouse, the bishop is to consult the Congregation for Divine Worship and the Discipline of the Sacraments.

TITLE II

CASES FOR DECLARING THE NULLITY OF SACRED ORDINATION
[cc. 1708–1712]

The primary sources for this title are the 1917 code and the instruction issued by the Sacred Congregation of the Sacraments on June 9, 1931.[48] The 1917 code and the 1931 instruction covered the nullity of sacred ordination and the nullity of obligations inherent in sacred orders together. The 1983 code, on the other hand, addresses the nullity of sacred ordination alone in this present title. Thus, the treatment of the material is more focused. Since the promulgation of the 1983 code, no legal developments have taken place concerning this process.

The Eastern code covers the material on the nullity of sacred ordination in three canons. Its presentation is very similar to the presentation in this title, except in two regards. The Eastern code omits the canon concerning the competence of the

---

[46] Doheny, *Canonical Procedure in Matrimonial Cases,* 2: 596–597; M. Said, "De Processu Praesumptae Mortis Coniugis," in *Dilexit Iustitiam,* ed. Z. Grocholewski and V. C. Orti (Vatican City: Libreria Editrice Vaticana, 1984) 450.

[47] For a fuller discussion of each of these elements of the investigation, see the Holy Office instruction *Matrimonii vinculo.* For a study of some particular cases decided by the Sacred Congregation of the Sacraments, see Doheny, *Canonical Procedure in Matrimonial Cases,* 2:609–614; *CLD* 1, 508–511, and *CLD* 5, 507–508; and *Stud Can* 32 (1998) 229–239.

[48] *CIC* 1993–1998; SCSacr, decr *Ut locorum Ordinarii* and *Regulae servandae in processibus super nullitate sacrae Ordinationis vel onerum sacris Ordinibus inhaerentium,* June 9, 1931, *AAS* 23 (1931) 457–492. Translation in *CLD* 1, 812–832.

defender of the bond. Also, the Eastern code explicitly states that the canons on the summary contentious process cannot be used.[49]

The Right to Petition

Canon 1708 — The cleric himself, the ordinary to whom the cleric is subject, or the ordinary in whose diocese the cleric was ordained has the right to challenge the validity of sacred ordination.

The validity of sacred ordination may be challenged for a variety of reasons. The ordination may be invalid because the cleric was not a baptized male, did not have the intention of receiving sacred orders, or lacked consent because of force or because of a mental defect.[50] Sacred ordination may be invalid because the ordaining bishop himself was not validly ordained, or did not have the intention to ordain.[51] Sacred ordination may also be invalid because the essentials of the sacred rite were not observed.[52]

The cleric himself has the right to challenge the validity of his ordination. This right to challenge is also given to the particular ordinaries named in the canon in order that the public good be safeguarded.

The Petition

Canon 1709 — §1. The *libellus* must be sent to the competent congregation which will decide whether the congregation of the Roman Curia itself or a tribunal designated by it must handle the case.

The petition for a declaration of nullity is addressed to the Holy Father, and is sent to the Congregation for Divine Worship and the Discipline of the Sacraments or, in the case of a cleric of an Eastern church *sui iuris,* to the Congregation for the Eastern Churches. If the case involves a substantial defect of the sacred rite, the petition is sent to the Congregation for the Doctrine of the Faith.[53]

The competent congregation decides whether the administrative process or the judicial process will be used. If the administrative process is used, the congregation will usually delegate an ordinary to draw up the instruction.[54]

§2. Once the *libellus* has been sent, the cleric is forbidden to exercise orders by the law itself.

The immediate effect of sending the petition is the prohibition of the exercise of orders.

The Judicial Process

Canon 1710 — If the congregation refers the case to a tribunal, the canons on trials in general and on the ordinary contentious trial are to be observed unless the nature of the matter precludes it and without prejudice to the prescripts of this title.

If the congregation chooses to have the case instructed by a judicial process, then the tribunal which is selected must use the canons on trials in general (cc. 1400–1500) and the canons on the ordinary contentious trial (cc. 1501–1655), as well as the canons of this title as the framework for the instruction.

The Defender of the Bond

Canon 1711 — In these cases the defender of the bond possesses the same rights and is bound by the same duties as the defender of the marriage bond.

The defender of the bond of sacred orders is bound by office to propose and explain everything which reasonably can be brought forth

---

[49] *CCEO* 1385–1387.
[50] Canons 1024, 1026; *Regulae,* arts. 17; 46, §2; 62, §2; 68.
[51] Canon 1012.
[52] Canon 1009, §2.

[53] *CIC* 1993, §1; V. Pospishil, *Eastern Catholic Church Law* (Brooklyn: St. Maron Publications, 1993) 630.
[54] *Regulae,* art. 7.

against the nullity of ordination.[55] The defender takes part in the process whether the case follows the administrative path or the judicial path.

Two Conforming Affirmative Sentences

Canon 1712 — After a second sentence has confirmed the nullity of sacred ordination, the cleric loses all rights proper to the clerical state and is freed from all obligations.

[55] Canon 1432.

By a double conforming affirmative sentence the cleric loses the clerical state, and with it all the rights and obligations proper to the clerical state.[56]

Since a case for nullity of ordination concerns the status of a person, the case never becomes *res iudicata*. Recourse can be made for a new presentation of the case if new and grave proofs or arguments are brought forward.[57]

[56] Canon 290, 1°.
[57] Canons 1643–1644.

BIBLIOGRAPHY

Cases of Separation of Spouses
(cc. 1692–1696)

Articles

Diego-Lora, C. de. "Las Causas de Separación de Cónyuges según el Nuevo Código." In *Dilexit Iustitiam,* ed. Z. Grocholewski and V. C. Orti, 389–403. Vatican City: Libreria Editrice Vaticana, 1984.

García Faílde, J. J. "Juicio de Separación Conyugal." In *Nuevo derecho procesal canónico.* Salamanca: Universidad Pontificia de Salamanca, 1984.

Process for the Dispensation of a Marriage
Ratum et Non Consummatum
(cc. 1697–1706)

Sources

CDWDS. Littcirc *De processu super matrimonio rato et non consummato,* December 20, 1986. *ME* 112 (1987) 423–429.

SCSacr. Decr *Catholica doctrina* and *Regulae servandae in processibus super matrimonio rato et non consummato,* May 7, 1923, *AAS* 15 (1923) 389–413.

SCSacr. Instr *Dispensationis matrimonii,* March 7, 1972, *AAS* 64 (1972) 244–252.

Reference Works

Jugis, P. *A Canonical Analysis of the Meaning of Humano Modo in Canon 1061, §1. CanLawStud* 541. Washington, D.C.: Catholic University of America, 1993.

Marchetta, B. *Scioglimento del Matrimonio Canonico per Inconsumazione.* Padua: Cedam, 1981.

Orlandi, G. *I "Casi Difficili" nel Processo Super Rato.* Padua: Cedam, 1984.

Woestman, W. *Special Marriage Cases.* Ottawa: St. Paul University, 1994.

Articles

Marchetta, B. "Il Processo 'Super Matrimonio Rato et Non Consummato' nel Nuovo Codice di Diritto Canonico." In *Dilexit Iustitiam,* ed. Z. Grocholewski and V. C. Orti, 405–430. Vatican City: Libreria Editrice Vaticana, 1984.

Melli, R. "Breve Commentarium ad Litteras Circulares 'De Processu Super Matrimonio Rato et Non Consummato.'" *ME* 112 (1987) 430–434.

Process in the Presumed Death of a Spouse
(c. 1707)

Sources

SCOf. Instr *Matrimonii vinculo,* May 13, 1868, *AAS* 2 (1910) 199–203.

Reference Works

Doheny, W. *Canonical Procedure in Matrimonial Cases.* Vol. 2. Milwaukee: Bruce, 1944.

Woestman, W. *Special Marriage Cases.* Ottawa: St. Paul University, 1994.

Wrenn, L. *Decisions.* 2nd rev. ed. Washington, D.C.: CLSA, 1983.

Articles

Said, M. "De Processu Praesumptae Mortis Coniugis." In *Dilexit Iustitiam,* ed. Z. Grocholewski and V. C. Orti, 431–455. Vatican City: Libreria Editrice Vaticana, 1984.

Cases for Declaring the Nullity
of Sacred Ordination
(cc. 1708–1712)

Sources

SCSacr. Decr *Ut locorum Ordinarii* and *Regulae servandae in processibus super nullitate sacrae Ordinationis vel onerum sacris Ordinibus inhaerentium,* June 9, 1931, *AAS* 23 (1931) 457–492.

Reference Works

Pospishil, V. *Eastern Catholic Church Law.* Brooklyn: St. Maron Publications, 1993.

Articles

Ferrara, V. "Le Conseguenze della Sentenza di Dichiarazione di Nullità della Sacra Ordinazione dei Chierici nel Canone 1712." *Apol* 68 (1995) 567–586.

Moroni, A. "Spunti sull'*Ordo Sacer* e le Relative Cause di Invalidità nella Nuova Codificazione Canonica." In *Dilexit Iustitiam,* ed. Z. Grocholewski and V. C. Orti, 457–472. Vatican City: Libreria Editrice Vaticana, 1984.

TITLE III
METHODS OF AVOIDING TRIALS
[cc. 1713–1716]

It is important to note the context for these canons on methods of avoiding a trial: they come at the end of the part on certain special processes, following the canons on trials in general, the ordinary contentious trial, and the oral contentious process, but before the canons on the penal process and administrative recourse. The title and placement suggest that these methods are intended for avoiding a contentious trial in the ordinary contentious judicial process, i.e., a trial before a judge in an ecclesiastical tribunal (cc. 1501–1696).

In practice, however, ordinary contentious trials are used today almost exclusively for marriage annulment cases and only very rarely for other types of controversies between Christians.[1] There are several reasons for this. One is that St. Paul's exhortation that Christians should not summon other members of the faith community into a civil court (1 Cor 6:1–6) was written in a historical context in which the judges and other personnel in the civil courts were comprised entirely of non-believers; furthermore, the legal system itself was based on non-Christian principles.[2] Today, however, many civil legal systems are themselves evolutionary products of ecclesiastical courts[3] and, at times, even use principles and terminology

derived from canon law.[4] Also, the personnel of civil courts often are now themselves believers, acting out of a Judeo-Christian belief system and seeking to imbue the secular order with their religious values.[5] It would be overly optimistic to suggest that such efforts have been successful in transforming civil legal institutions in accordance with the demands of faith. Nevertheless, the legal concerns of Christians and the institutions of civil courts today are not necessarily incompatible, except when the latter are oppressive or hostile to the faith. Thus, recourse to civil courts by Christians against a peer is not always seen today as an evil to be avoided, e.g., when two Christians are involved in an automobile accident and one sues the other in civil court for damages.[6] In fact, as long as civil laws are not contrary to divine law or unless canon law provides otherwise, canon law often defers to civil laws (c. 22), especially civil contract law (c. 1290), labor laws (cc. 231, §2 and

---

[1] See M. Moodie, "Defense of Rights: Developing New Procedural Norms," *J* 47 (1987) 446.

[2] See C. T. Craig and J. Short, "The First Epistle to the Corinthians: Introduction, Exposition and Exegesis," in *The Interpreter's Bible,* ed. G. Buttrick et al. (New York: Abingdon, 1953) 10:69–71.

[3] See M. Cappelletti, J. Merriman, and J. Perillo, *The Italian Legal System* (Stanford, Calif.: Stanford University, 1967) 9–52; and H. Berman, *Law and Revolution: The Formation of the Western Legal Tradition* (Cambridge: Harvard University, 1983) 85–226.

[4] This is true not only in the continental civil law systems, but in the "common law" systems of English-speaking nations as well: "Already in Edward I's day the phrase 'common law' is current. It is a phrase that has been borrowed from the canonists—who used 'jus commune' to denote the general law of the Catholic Church; it describes that part of the law that is unenacted, non-statutory, that is common to the whole land and to all Englishmen. It is contrasted with statute, with local custom, with royal prerogative." F. W. Maitland, "Equity," in E. Re, *Equity and Equitable Remedies: Cases and Materials* (Mineola, N.Y.: Foundation Press, University Casebook Series, 1975) 2. (First published as F. W. Maitland, *Equity* [London: Macmillan, 1909].)

[5] See W. Droel, *The Spirituality of Work: Lawyers* (Chicago: National Center for the Laity, 1989).

[6] See W. Bassett, "Christian Rights in Civil Litigation: Translating Religion into Justiciable Categories," *J* 46 (1986) 229; and A. Adams and W. Hanlon, "Jones v. Wolf: Church Autonomy and the Religion Clauses of the First Amendment," *University of Pennsylvania Law Review* 128 (1980) 1291. While civil suits between Christians need not always be shunned, this should not be construed, however, as encouraging unwarranted litigation.

1286), prescription (cc. 197–199 and 1268–1270), the laws of wills and inheritance (c. 1299, §2), and probably also tort law (compensation for negligent and intentional harms and injuries; see c. 128).[7] As ecclesiastical courts have relinquished jurisdiction in these areas to the civil courts, diocesan tribunals are generally neither prepared to hear such matters nor to enforce injunctions or execute judgments for damages.[8]

Accordingly, most Christians today are more likely to sue a fellow Christian in civil court to vindicate a right than to bring an action for a contentious trial in a diocesan tribunal. The exception would be in the limited number of cases where a person feels his or her rights *as a Christian* have been violated by a peer in the community; however, canon 1400, §2 precludes the use of the judicial process when the alleged violation of rights arose from an "act of administrative power." In this case the process of administrative recourse must be used (cc. 1732–1739).

Although controversies between Christians are rarely litigated these days in a contentious judicial trial, the following canons provide helpful norms for resolving disputes through less formal means such as conciliation and arbitration.

Alternative Dispute Resolution

Canon 1713 — In order to avoid judicial contentions an agreement or reconciliation is employed usefully, or the controversy can be committed to the judgment of one or more arbitrators.

Transactio, or settlement, is "an agreement by which a controversial matter is settled without a formal trial."[9] *Reconciliatio* here is not meant in the sacramental sense of reconciliation, but in the more generic sense of conciliation or mediation between disputing parties. An *arbitrator* is a neutral party by whose decision the disputing parties have agreed in advance to be bound. Throughout Book VII, the use of conciliators, mediators, or arbitrators is encouraged to avert the ordinary contentious trial (c. 1446), the oral contentious process (c. 1659), marriage nullity cases (c. 1676), cases involving the separation of spouses (c. 1695), and administrative recourse (c. 1733). These methods of resolving controversies while avoiding a formal trial are commonly known as alternative dispute resolution.[10]

Process to Be Followed

Canon 1714 — For an agreement, a compromise, and an arbitrated judgment, the norms selected by the parties or, if the parties have selected none, the law laid down by the conference of bishops, if there is such a law, or the civil law in force in the place where the agreement is entered into is to be observed.

Compromissum is "a mutual agreement to be bound by the decision of an arbitrator."[11] Canon 1714 allows the parties in a dispute to select the norms to guide the process of conciliation, mediation, or arbitration. In practice, the parties most likely will agree to follow a process established by the national episcopal conference, the local diocesan bishop, or some civil authority.[12]

---

[7] T. Molloy and J. Folmer, "The Canonization of Civil Law," *CLSAP* 46 (1983) 46.

[8] See J. Beal, "Protecting the Rights of Lay Catholics," *J* 47 (1987) 157–158; and J. Coriden, "A Challenge: Make the Rights Real," *J* 45 (1985) 21.

[9] L. Stelten, *Dictionary of Ecclesiastical Latin* (Peabody, Mass.: Hendrickson, 1995), s.v. "transactio."

[10] The notion of "alternative dispute resolution" is discussed more fully in the commentary on c. 1733.

[11] *Cassel's Latin Dictionary* (1977), s.v. "compromissum."

[12] For example, see NCCB, *On Due Process,* rev. ed. (Washington, D.C.: NCCB, 1972); Archdiocese of Chicago, *Office of Conciliation: Norms and Procedures* (Chicago: Archdiocese of Chicago, 1987); R. Fleming, *The Labor Arbitration Process* (Urbana, Ill.: University of Illinois, 1965); American Arbitration Association, *Labor Arbitration: Procedures and Techniques* (New York: American Arbitration Association, 1979); and American Arbitration Association, *Voluntary Labor Arbitration Rules* (New York: American Arbitration Association, 1979).

Matters Not Subject to Agreement or Arbitration

Canon 1715 — §1. An agreement or compromise cannot be made validly concerning matters which pertain to the public good and other matters about which the parties cannot make disposition freely.

§2. For temporal ecclesiastical goods, the formalities established by law for the alienation of ecclesiastical goods are to be observed whenever the matter demands it.

While many objects of dispute can be resolved by agreement of the parties or by decision of an arbitrator, canon 1715 removes certain subject matters from the scope of alternative dispute resolution, viz., matters pertaining to the public good, such as cases involving the nullity of marriage and the nullity of sacred orders. Thus, the parties to a marital dispute could obviously agree on their own or through conciliation to resolve their differences and resume conjugal life, but they could not on their own or through any form of alternative dispute resolution conclude that their marriage was invalid.

Just as obviously, two parties cannot on their own decide the rights or interests of some third party. Similarly, if parties to a property dispute mutually agree to resolve their differences by alienating temporal ecclesiastical goods from one party to another, the canonical formalities on alienation (cc. 1291–1298) must still be observed if the matter would otherwise require this.

Civil and Canonical Effects of Arbitration

Canon 1716 — §1. If the civil law does not recognize the force of an arbitrated sentence unless a judge confirms it, an arbitrated sentence in an ecclesiastical controversy, in order to have force in the canonical forum, needs the confirmation of an ecclesiastical judge of the place where it was rendered.

§2. If civil law permits the challenge of an arbitrated judgment before a civil judge, however, the same challenge can be proposed in the canonical forum before an ecclesiastical judge competent to judge the controversy in the first grade.

The assumption of canon 1716 is that the civil law norms for arbitration are being followed in a given case. The object of this canon, then, is for the effects of arbitration to mirror each other in both civil law and canon law. Thus, if civil law requires a judge to confirm an arbitrator's decision in order for it to be recognized as civilly binding and effective, then canon law will also require a local ecclesiastical judge to confirm the arbitrator's decision in order for it to be recognized as canonically binding and effective. Conversely, if civil law allows an arbitrator's decision to be challenged before a judge in a civil court, canon 1716, §2 allows it to be challenged before the competent ecclesiastical judge in the proper canonical forum.

BIBLIOGRAPHY

American Arbitration Association. *Labor Arbitration: Procedures and Techniques.* New York: American Arbitration Association, 1979.

———. *Voluntary Labor Arbitration Rules.* New York: American Arbitration Association, 1979.

Archdiocese of Chicago. *Office of Conciliation: Norms and Procedures.* Chicago: Archdiocese of Chicago, 1987.

Fleming, R. *The Labor Arbitration Process.* Urbana, Ill.: University of Illinois, 1965.

NCCB. *On Due Process.* Rev. ed. Washington, D.C.: NCCB, 1972.

Part IV
THE PENAL PROCESS
[cc. 1717–1731]

Tribunal practitioners normally work almost exclusively with marriage nullity procedures (cc. 1671–1691), since such cases constitute by far the main agenda of church tribunals. However, certain tragic ecclesial developments during the past decade and a half (e.g., clerical sex abuse cases) have highlighted the importance of the Church's penal processes. Such processes are geared toward clarifying the existence of a delict, assessing the imputability of the defendant, and declaring or imposing an appropriate penalty.

Hopefully such processes will be used only rarely, i.e., when it is necessary to deal with serious breaches of faith and order. The following observations clarify the main features of such penal processes to assist practitioners in their ministry. Such observations must be situated within the broad framework of the commentary on Book VII.

The canons on the penal process are found in both Books VI and VII of the code. Canons 1717–1731 of Book VII must be read especially in connection with the commentary on canons 1341–1353 of Book VI on applying penalties.

The fifteen canons on the penal process are divided into three chapters. The first chapter on the preliminary investigation (cc. 1717–1719) deals with the appointment of a preliminary investigator after an allegation of a delict (c. 1717), the ordinary's subsequent decision regarding the appropriateness of a penal process (c. 1718), and the custody of the acts of the investigation (c. 1719). The second chapter on the development of the penal process (cc. 1720–1728) briefly considers the administrative process (c. 1720) but highlights the preferred judicial process (cc. 1721–1728). This chapter notes certain procedural principles and clarifies certain rights of the defendant; however, most of the relevant canons are found in the general norms on trials in general and on the ordinary contentious trial (cc. 1400–1655). Finally, the third chapter (cc. 1729–1731) governs an action for damages by one adversely affected by an ecclesiastical delict.[1]

The following schema attempts to sketch briefly the interrelationship between the aforementioned books of the code:

- prior investigation regarding necessity and appropriateness of penal process: canons 1717, 1719.
- decision whether to initiate penal process: canons 1718, 1341–1342, 1362.
- details of administrative penal process: canon 1720.
- details of judicial penal process: canons 1721–1728.
- exercise of discretion by penal authority in issuing administrative penal decree or judicial penal sentence: canons 1343–1346, 1349.
- appeal or recourse against penal sentence or decree: canons 1353, 1727.
- situation of one subject to a penalty after a sentence or decree: canons 1350–1353.
- related issue of action for damages distinct from the criminal action to declare *latae sententiae* penalty or impose *ferendae sententiae* penalty: canons 1729–1731.

[1] For brief reflections on changes from the 1917 code, see T. Green, in *CLSA Com*, 1023.

CHAPTER I
THE PRELIMINARY INVESTIGATION
[cc. 1717–1719]

Initiation of the Investigation[2]

Canon 1717 — §1. Whenever an ordinary has knowledge, which at least seems true, of a delict, he is carefully to inquire personally or through another suitable person about the facts, circumstances, and imputability, unless such an inquiry seems entirely superfluous.

§2. Care must be taken so that the good name of anyone is not endangered from this investigation.

§3. The person who conducts the investigation has the same powers and obligations as an auditor in the process; the same person cannot act as a judge in the matter if a judicial process is initiated later.

The penal process is not to be undertaken lightly given its potentially detrimental legal-pastoral consequences for the accused, i.e., the curtailment of the exercise of one's rights (c. 96). Before the process can be initiated, there must be a strong probability that an ecclesiastical delict has been committed. It is unjust to penalize someone merely because of an allegation of a delict. This clearly violates the right to one's good reputation (c. 220) and the right not to be penalized except according to law (c. 221, §3). Hence the code generally calls for a preliminary investigation to clarify such a probability in a given case. However, few details are mentioned regarding the specifics of such an investigation, which is not technically part of the penal process but related to it.[3]

The formal responsibility for initiating such an investigation rests with ecclesiastical authority and not with private individuals (§1). While the canon speaks of the "ordinary" (c. 134, §1) and hence theoretically of vicars general and episcopal vicars, practically speaking it probably means bishops and major superiors of pontifical clerical religious institutes and societies of apostolic life. Such an investigation is related to their preeminent responsibility for fostering the well-being of the diocese or religious institute or society and ensuring compliance with church discipline (cc. 392, 618–619).

Despite the importance of protecting the well-being of the community, the code is particularly concerned about safeguarding the reputation of the person(s) accused of an ecclesiastical delict (§2; c. 220). The investigation must be carried out discreetly and sensitively to preclude damaging anyone's good name. This key value is to be fostered especially by the person(s) conducting the preliminary investigation. Realistically speaking, most bishops would probably not conduct such an inquiry any more than they would be significantly involved in marriage cases. Such an investigator, a cleric or a lay person,[4] is comparable to an auditor gathering evidence but not making the final

---

[2] Cf. *CCEO* 1468. For Eastern penal procedure, see T. Green, "Penal Law in the *Code of Canon Law* and in the *Code of Canons of the Eastern Churches:* Some Comparative Reflections," *Stud Can* 28 (1994) 442–444.

[3] For helpful reflections on the preliminary investigation, especially in clerical sex abuse cases, see *Canonical Delicts Involving Sexual Misconduct and Dismissal from*

the Clerical State (Washington, D.C.: USCC, 1995) 8–10. See also the commentary on c. 1395, §2. For samples of helpful forms pertinent to conducting such an investigation and initiating a subsequent penal process, see G. Ingels, "Processes Which Govern the Application of Penalties," in *Clergy Procedural Handbook*, ed. R. Calvo and N. Klinger (Washington, D.C.: CLSA, 1992) 230–237.

[4] The following observation seems pertinent to cases of alleged clerical sex abuse: "Although the investigator need not be a priest, a priest may be more effective in speaking with those concerned, especially the accused; on the other hand, persons specially trained in dealing with children and their parents may be more effective for those persons. Thus, in some cases a team approach may be advisable, provided there is coordination of information and an assessment by one knowledgeable about the canonical process," (*Canonical Delicts*, 9).

decision in a regular judicial process (c. 1428). In the interests of judicial objectivity, the preliminary investigator may not validly serve as a judge in a subsequent judicial process (§3).

The preliminary investigation is geared to ascertaining whether there are solid grounds for judging that an ecclesiastical delict (e.g., cc. 1364–1399) has been committed. The investigator should carefully inquire about the character and background of the accuser(s) and differentiate facts from rumor, suspicion, opinion, the personal propensities of the accused, or even his/her past behavior (c. 1572). This investigation resembles the preliminary investigation in a marriage nullity case, which seeks to determine if there is a sufficient basis to pursue such a case.

The preliminary inquiry should examine the relevant facts of the case, factors affecting the imputability of the accused (cc. 1322–1327), and possible canonical and civil damages. In other words, this investigation should clarify an initial profile of the alleged delict. While the code does not explicitly require a written report from the investigator, it is implicitly presupposed (c. 1719). The investigator presents his or her findings to the ordinary, who ultimately makes the decision about the penal process in light of the pertinent legal-pastoral facts.[5]

However, such an investigation may be superfluous if the facts regarding a legal violation are notorious. In such a case, the ordinary can immediately assess the factors influencing his decision regarding a possible penal process (c. 1718).

At this point, whether the investigation has been conducted or not, it is not necessary that the alleged delict be certain; it suffices that there be a strong probability that it has been committed. This is different from evidence about the ineffective ministry of an officeholder, which may warrant disciplinary action (e.g., removal) but not a penalty. The determination of the existence of a delict with moral certitude (i.e., beyond a reasonable doubt) is the task of the subsequent penal process.

[5] See the canons on the judge-expert relationship in the formal judicial process (cc. 1574–1581).

Decree of Ordinary
Regarding the Penal Process[6]

Canon 1718 — §1. When it seems that sufficient evidence has been collected, the ordinary is to decide:
    1° whether a process to inflict or declare a penalty can be initiated;
    2° whether, attentive to can. 1341, this is expedient;
    3° whether a judicial process must be used or, unless the law forbids it, whether the matter must proceed by way of extrajudicial decree.

§2. The ordinary is to revoke or change the decree mentioned in §1 whenever new evidence indicates to him that another decision is necessary.

§3. In issuing the decrees mentioned in §§1 and 2, the ordinary is to hear two judges or other experts of the law if he considers it prudent.

§4. Before he makes a decision according to the norm of §1 and in order to avoid useless trials, the ordinary is to examine carefully whether it is expedient for him or the investigator, with the consent of the parties, to resolve equitably the question of damages.

This canon deals with the situation after the aforementioned investigation has been completed or deemed superfluous. The most basic issue is this: do the facts warrant a penal process (§1, 1°)? Perhaps the original complaint prompting the investigation was frivolous or vindictive, or perhaps there are indications but no solid evidence of an ecclesiastical delict. In such instances a process might not be warranted; however, in the latter case quasi-penal measures such as a warning, a rebuke, or a penance might appropriately foster the spiritual good of the alleged offender and the ecclesial community (cc. 1339–1340).

The ordinary also must determine whether a criminal action may be impossible because the statute of limitations for initiating it has run out

[6] Cf. *CCEO* 1469, §1–§3.

(prescription).[7] If so, the ordinary may decide to employ the aforementioned quasi-penal measures.

In other instances, however, although a process may be warranted and there is evidence of an ecclesiastical delict, such a process may not be expedient (§1, 2°). The Church's well-being and that of the offender might be better served by legal-pastoral measures other than a penal process, for penalties are to be imposed only as a last resort when all other legal-pastoral measures (e.g., fraternal correction, rebuke, therapy) have failed to repair scandal, restore justice, and reform the offender (c. 1341).

If a penal process is justified, other considerations then come into play. The code clearly favors a judicial process (c. 1342, §1) because it better safeguards the common good of the Church and provides more effective legal protections for all concerned. However, for a just cause to be considered very carefully, the ordinary may use an administrative process unless the law specifically requires a judicial process (§1, 3°; c. 1342, §2), e.g., perpetual penalties such as privation of office or dismissal from the clerical state.[8]

The personal and ecclesial significance of this issue requires the ordinary to be open to new evidence possibly altering his initial decision regarding the process (§2).[9] He should consult two judges or other legal experts before making his decision although, unlike the administrative penal process (c. 1720, 2°), the law does not oblige him to do so (§3).[10] Such experts should help to clarify especially the canonical and possible civil law ramifications of the case and foster informed decision-making.

This decision regarding the penal process follows the general rules on administrative decrees (cc. 35–58). For example, canon 50 requires the ordinary to seek out the necessary information and proofs and, insofar as possible, to hear those whose rights could be injured by the decree, e.g., the accused. Canon 51 requires a written decree with at least a summary expression of the reasons for the decision. Whether a process is conducted or not, the ordinary needs to terminate the investigation through a reasoned decree assessing the pertinent data.

The Latin and Eastern codes differ somewhat regarding the involvement of the accused during this pre-process phase. The Latin code does not explicitly require such involvement, although the aforementioned canon 50 implicitly calls for such. However, the Eastern code explicitly requires the hierarch to hear both the accused and the promoter of justice before deciding about the process (*CCEO* 1469, §3). This Eastern provision provides better for the fundamental right of defense so strongly emphasized in marriage cases and equally, if not more, relevant to penal cases.

In this general context another point seems noteworthy. Canon 1728, §2 protects the accused against self-incrimination during the penal process. However, the code's concern to protect the accused's reputation (c. 220) is equally relevant during the pre-process phase of any such investigation. Otherwise he or she might be pressured into admitting imputability with detrimental ecclesiastical and civil consequences. While access to canonical counsel is explicitly required only after the process has been initiated (c. 1723), a serious respect for the right of defense requires such counsel even during the preliminary investigation.

Finally, to avoid needless processes (c. 1446), the ordinary may resolve a claim for damages equitably either personally or through the aforementioned investigator, who presumably knows the situation well. In other words, a penal process may be unnecessary if the only issue is repairing certain damages, e.g., pastor's violation of a parish employee's job security or compensation rights (c. 1389). However, such a solution may not be imposed on unwilling parties; in such cir-

---

[7] See commentary on canon 1362. "Initiating an action" means formally citing the accused, which technically initiates the process (c. 1517).

[8] See commentary on c. 1342.

[9] See also cc. 1724 on dropping a penal case and 1726 on declaring the innocence of the accused.

[10] A similar concern for informed decision-making is operative in removal- or transfer-of-pastor procedures (cc. 1742, §1; 1745, 2°; 1750).

cumstances a formal judicial process may be necessary to resolve the complaint for damages (cc. 1729–1731).

Custody of the Acts[11]

Canon 1719 — The acts of the investigation, the decrees of the ordinary which initiated and concluded the investigation, and everything which preceded the investigation are to be kept in the secret archive of the curia if they are not necessary for the penal process.

Frequently the acts of the investigation and decrees of the ordinary are necessary for the penal process and are subsequently incorporated into the acts of the case by judicial decree. However, such a process may not be warranted because of the innocence of the accused, the presence of evidentiary problems, or the inappropriateness of a penal process to deal with the problem. In such a situation the aforementioned documents must be placed in the diocesan secret archives (c. 489). This is because of the sensitive nature of such materials regarding the alleged delict and the possible imputability of the accused and their potentially damaging effect on his/her reputation (c. 220).

Although no process may be conducted, the maintenance of such acts in the archives ensures their availability if a new accusation subsequently prompts a penal process or if it is necessary to prove to the civil court that the Church handled an accusation responsibly.

CHAPTER II
THE DEVELOPMENT OF THE PROCESS
[cc. 1720–1728]

The Latin and Eastern codes differ somewhat in organizing the penal process. This chapter of the Latin code deals very briefly with the administrative process (c. 1720) and somewhat more extensively with the judicial process (cc. 1721–

1728). Title 28 of the Eastern code on imposing penalties (*CCEO* 1468–1487) contains two chapters, a lengthier one on the penal trial (*CCEO* 1468–1485) and a very brief one on imposing penalties by extrajudicial (administrative) decree (*CCEO* 1486–1487).

Canon 1728, §1 states that the rules on trials in general and on ordinary contentious trials are generally operative here, especially the norms governing cases affecting the public good.[12]

This chapter is concerned both with vindicating the procedural rights of the accused and protecting the well-being of the community during the process. Out of respect for human dignity and freedom, the present code requires a process to impose most penalties. It drops a former questionable provision enabling a superior to prohibit a cleric from exercising his ministry or remove him from office without a process (*CIC* 2222, §2).[13]

Administrative Penal Process[14]

Canon 1720 — If the ordinary thinks that the matter must proceed by way of extrajudicial decree:

1° he is to inform the accused of the accusation and the proofs, giving an opportunity for self-defense, unless the accused neglected to appear after being properly summoned;

2° he is to weigh carefully all the proofs and arguments with two assessors;

---

[11] Cf. *CCEO* 1470.

[12] This fundamental canon should begin this chapter rather than end it. As a general provision it resembles the norms on formal marriage nullity cases. The aforementioned rules on contentious trials are operative there with due regard for the canons on marriage nullity cases (cc. 1671–1691) and on cases affecting the public good (c. 1691).

[13] The superior had the right and duty to employ these measures even if the delict were only probable or the statute of limitations for a criminal action had run out. Another similarly questionable procedure, the suspension of a cleric *ex informata conscientia* (from an informed conscience) (*CIC* 2186–2194), has also been dropped.

[14] Cf. *CCEO* 1486.

3° if the delict is certainly established and a criminal action is not extinguished, he is to issue a decree according to the norm of cann. 1342–1350, setting forth the reasons in law and in fact at least briefly.

At the outset one should recall that canon 1342 favors a judicial process unless a just cause precludes such. Furthermore, perpetual penalties such as dismissal from the clerical state and privation of office cannot be imposed administratively.

The general norms on administrative decrees (cc. 35–58) are relevant here, but were deemed insufficient to regulate the specifics of the administrative penal process. Accordingly, this canon guarantees the accused's right of self-defense, requires official consultation before the ordinary's decision, and calls for a reasoned decision applying the law to the pertinent facts. Hopefully these measures will preclude arbitrary penal decisions.

The involvement of the accused here is required by the basic right to be informed of proposed actions which might prejudicially affect one's rights and the right of self-defense (1°). If the accused chooses not to exercise that right, however, the ordinary or his delegate may decide the case. While the code does not explicitly require access to counsel as in the judicial process (c. 1481, §2), such access seems indispensable for a knowledgeable exercise of the right of defense in light of the accusation and the various proofs of such introduced in the process (c. 221).

The code here explicitly refers to assessors (c. 1424). By their canonical and/or civil counsel, such clerics or lay persons can clarify the pertinent issues in the case although they do not decide it. Hopefully their input will facilitate an informed decision by the ordinary, who, however, is not bound by their advice (c. 127, §2, 2°).[15]

Finally, if there is moral certitude (c. 1608, §1) about the delict and the criminal action has not been prescribed (c. 1362), the ordinary is to issue an appropriate penal decree in light of certain canons on applying penalties (cc. 1342–1350).[16] If such moral certitude is not attained, the accused is to be dismissed as absolved. Any such decree should succinctly clarify the relevant substantive, penal, and procedural canons and the pertinent facts to which the law is to be applied.[17]

Recourse against a penal decree follows the ordinary rules on administrative recourse (cc. 1732–1739). First of all, the ordinary issuing the decree is to be asked to revoke it. Should he refuse, recourse then is to be taken to his hierarchical superior. If the bishop is the penalizing authority, such recourse must be taken to a Roman congregation depending on the nature of the issue.[18] In any event, such recourse has a suspensive effect (c. 1353). Hence the defendant need not observe the penalty unless the ordinary's action is sustained by his superior.

The other canons in this chapter concern the judicial penal process, yet some of the above considerations are also relevant to that process. Furthermore, certain judicial process norms are somewhat pertinent to the administrative process, e.g., rules of evidence (cc. 1526–1586).

Role of the Promoter of Justice[19]

Canon 1721 — §1. If the ordinary has decreed that a judicial penal process must be initiated, he is to hand over the acts of the investigation to the promoter of justice who is to present a *libellus* of accusation to the judge according to the norm of cann. 1502 and 1504.

§2. The promoter of justice appointed to the higher tribunal acts as the petitioner before that tribunal.

---

[15] See also cc. 1742, §1; 1745, 2°; 1750.

[16] See the pertinent commentary.

[17] In the absence of specific rules on formulating such a decree, see c. 1612 on drafting a judicial sentence.

[18] For the competency of the various Roman dicasteries, including congregations, see the commentary on c. 360, which discusses the June 1988 apostolic constitution of John Paul II *Pastor bonus* reorganizing the Roman Curia.

[19] Cf. *CCEO* 1472.

The promoter of justice (c. 1430) initiates the judicial process at the request of the ordinary, who is to forward the acts of the preliminary investigation. Such acts presumably constitute a prima facie case against the accused. The promoter is institutionally responsible for fostering the public good, whose protection occasionally requires a penal process. He or she generally enjoys the same rights and is bound by the same obligations as the petitioner in a marriage case (c. 1434). The promoter is basically to support the accusation, organize the pertinent proofs, argue the case for a penalty, and appeal the decision if appropriate.

The promoter initially prepares a *libellus*, or petition of accusation, according to law (§1; cc. 1502, 1504). Without such a petition there can be no process (c. 1501). The petition should briefly indicate the purpose of the promoter's activity, i.e., the declaration or imposition of a penalty, and succinctly present the evidence that a delict has been committed. The burden of proof is on the promoter to demonstrate this to the tribunal with moral certitude; otherwise the defendant is to be dismissed and a *non constat* decision rendered (c. 1608, §4).

At the appellate level, the second instance promoter functions in the same way as the promoter in first instance given the similarity of functions in both instances (§2).

Restrictions on the Accused[20]

Canon 1722 — To prevent scandals, to protect the freedom of witnesses, and to guard the course of justice, the ordinary, after having heard the promoter of justice and cited the accused, at any stage of the process can exclude the accused from the sacred ministry or from some office and ecclesiastical function, can impose or forbid residence in some place or territory, or even can prohibit public participation in the Most Holy Eucharist. Once the cause ceases, all these measures must be revoked; they also end by the law itself when the penal process ceases.

[20] Cf. *CCEO* 1473.

Most of the canonical concerns noted thus far have primarily related to the accused. This canon, however, focuses on protecting the community against the potentially disruptive activities of the former. It empowers the ordinary (not the judge) at any stage of the process, but not before it, to restrict the defendant's exercise of ecclesiastical office or public participation in the Eucharist.[21] Theoretically he or she may also be prevented from living in a certain place (e.g., rectory where priest has been living) or ordered to live in a given place, e.g., retreat house.

Such measures reflect a concern for the integrity of the process, e.g., protecting the freedom of witnesses and expediting the course of justice. In addition, the accused may cause potential scandal by giving others the occasion for spiritual ruin or leading them to sin. Such restrictive measures are not to be taken lightly, and the right of the accused not to be unduly burdened is to be carefully honored. This is evident from both the required consultation of the promoter of justice by the ordinary and the required citation of the accused. With the aid of counsel, he or she may be able to challenge successfully the alleged reasons for such measures. However, if the accused does not appear in court, the provisions envisioned here can still be implemented.[22]

Furthermore, such measures are to be rescinded when there is no longer a reason for them, and they automatically cease at the end of the process. It is illegitimate to impose them indefinitely on an accused without any real relationship to a process, for, practically speaking, this is tantamount to imposing a perpetual expiatory penalty without a process.

The imposition of such "administrative leave" requires an administrative decree governed by the

[21] For a thoughtful examination of this canon, see J. Beal, "Administrative Leave: Canon 1722 Revisited," *Stud Can* 27 (1993) 293–320, esp. 314–315. He argues persuasively that the measures envisioned here are operative only *after* a formal process has been initiated, not during the preliminary investigation. He also suggests certain legal-pastoral provisions which may help to protect the community during that investigation.

[22] See the commentary on cc. 1592–1595.

rules on such decrees (cc. 35–58). Unlike the 1917 code (*CIC* 1959), the present code permits administrative recourse against such a decree according to the usual rules (cc. 1732–1739). However, unlike recourse against a penalty declared or imposed administratively, which has a suspensive effect (c. 1353), recourse against such restrictions does not have a suspensive effect; the accused must observe the restrictions specified here during the recourse. However onerous, they are not technically penalties presupposing a delict, although they are imposed during a criminal trial.

The code does not technically admit such measures during the preliminary investigation. If they are employed then, it would have to be according to particular law with appropriate protections of the accused. The welfare of the community may indeed require limiting the exercise of some rights by the accused before the process begins. However, the sweeping restrictions of canon 1722 may be unjustified, since the concerns underlying it may be able to be addressed by other less onerous measures. For example, the ordinary may issue a penal precept prohibiting contact of the accused with witnesses, use the penal remedies of warning and rebuke (c. 1339), closely supervise the accused (*CCEO* 1428; *CIC* 2311), or restrict certain faculties. Such measures may sufficiently protect both the rights of the community and those of the accused.

Counsel for the Defendant[23]

Canon 1723 — §1. The judge who cites the accused must invite the accused to appoint an advocate according to the norm of can. 1481, §1 within the time limit set by the judge.

§2. If the accused does not make provision, the judge is to appoint an advocate before the joinder of the issue; this advocate will remain in this function as long as the accused does not appoint an advocate personally.

Fundamental fairness requires that the defendant enjoy the services of counsel in protecting

[23] Cf. *CCEO* 1474.

his or her interests especially given the risk of a serious penalty. If the defendant does not choose an advocate, the judge must appoint one before the joinder of the issue (cc. 1513–1516) so that the former's right to defense may be effectively exercised throughout the process (c. 1481, §1–§2). The court-appointed advocate functions as long as the defendant neglects to choose someone else.[24] Should such counsel not be provided, any sentence would probably be irremediably null due to a lack of the right of defense (c. 1620, 7°).

Renunciation of the Penal Trial[25]

Canon 1724 — §1. At any grade of the trial the promoter of justice can renounce the trial at the command of or with the consent of the ordinary whose deliberation initiated the process.

§2. For validity the accused must accept the renunciation unless the accused was declared absent from the trial.

This provision is a specific example of the general rules on renouncing a trial (cc. 1524–1525). The preeminent role of the ordinary who initiated the penal process (c. 1718) is evident here. Without his initiative or approval, the promoter of justice cannot renounce the trial at any stage. Perhaps the initial allegations prove to be unfounded, or there are insoluble conflicts among the witnesses or experts. In any event, it may become clear that the criminal action cannot be pursued successfully and hence should be terminated.

Nevertheless, the trial cannot be renounced validly without the defendant's consent. Once the

[24] In connection with the accused's right of defense, one might note that the accuser's name does not have to be revealed initially to the accused. If, however, a given accusation were used as a proof in the process, the accuser would technically be a witness, and his or her name would then be revealed to the accused (*Comm* 12 [1980] 194). While the code does not normally envision the confrontation of the parties and witnesses in a case, occasionally this is possible under the judge's direction to resolve testimonial conflicts (c. 1560, §2).

[25] Cf. *CCEO* 1475.

trial commences with the citation of the defendant (c. 1517), a procedural relationship is established between the promoter of justice (petitioner) and the defendant (respondent). That relationship cannot normally be fundamentally altered without the consent of both parties. To restore his or her reputation, which is somewhat impaired by the process, the defendant may insist on its completion and preferably a declaration of innocence (c. 1726). However, if the defendant has been formally declared absent from the trial because of a lack of cooperation with the court (cc. 1592–1595), the trial may be renounced even without his or her consent.

Last Word for the Defendant[26]

Canon 1725 — In the discussion of the case, whether done in written or oral form, the accused, either personally or through the advocate or procurator, always has the right to write or speak last.

The code's concern to highlight the exercise of the right of defense is evident in this provision for the defendant to have the last word before the case is resolved. This equitable provision is relevant to the so-called discussion phase of the trial (cc. 1601–1605) just before the decision is rendered. Such a right to the last word orally or in writing may be exercised personally by the defendant or more likely by his or her advocate given the latter's legal expertise. This right of the defendant modifies the normal right of the promoter to reply a second time to the responses of the parties during this stage of the trial (c. 1603, §3).

Absolution of the Defendant[27]

Canon 1726 — If at any grade and stage of the penal trial it is evidently established that the accused did not commit the delict, the judge must declare this in a sentence and absolve the accused

even if it is also established that criminal action has been extinguished.

The basic legal interest in protecting the reputation of the defendant (c. 220) explains this requirement that the judge declare the defendant's innocence as soon as it is clear from the acts and proofs in the case. This is true at any grade of the trial (e.g., first or second instance) or at any stage (e.g., the gathering of evidence or the discussion of the case). This is also true even if the statute of limitations for a criminal action has run out (c. 1362). It is not enough simply to terminate the trial, for without such a formal declaration of innocence there might still be a continuing cloud over the reputation of the defendant. Such a declaration differs from a negative (*non constat*) decision, which still could leave such a cloud since it may indicate simply that insufficient evidence of a delict has been introduced.

Appeal by Defendant/Promoter[28]

Canon 1727 — §1. The accused can propose an appeal even if the sentence dismissed the accused only because the penalty was facultative or because the judge used the power mentioned in cann. 1344 and 1345.

§2. The promoter of justice can appeal whenever the promoter judges that the repair of scandal or the restoration of justice has not been provided for sufficiently.

Generally speaking, the usual rules on the appeal (cc. 1628–1640) apply to penal trials. Unlike marriage nullity cases (c. 1682, §1) there is no mandatory review of any penal sentence, affirmative or negative. Hence all penal appeals are at the discretion of the parties involved. The present canon contains several points regarding such appeals.

The canon does not explicitly mention the obvious case of an appeal, i.e., when the defendant is found guilty of a delict and penalized accordingly without any exercise of judicial discretion.

---

[26] Cf. *CCEO* 1478.
[27] Cf. *CCEO* 1482.

[28] Cf. *CCEO* 1481.

On the contrary, paragraph one deals with various exercises of such discretion. First of all, the defendant may not be penalized because the penalty for the delict was discretionary (e.g., c. 1391) and the judge chose not to impose a penalty (c. 1343). Second, the delict may have been committed, but the judge chose to abstain from imposing an obligatory penalty, impose a lighter penalty, defer its imposition, or suspend its observance due to various imputability-mitigating factors (cc. 1344–1345, 1324). The defendant may appeal such decisions, however benign, to obtain a declaration of innocence by a higher court (c. 1726).

The promoter of justice may also appeal a decision that does not seem to serve the public good adequately, i.e., the reparation of scandal and/or restitution of justice (§2). This does not refer simply to a declaration of innocence. The guilt of the defendant may be established, but no penalty may be imposed or lesser measures such as penal remedies or penances (cc. 1339–1340) may be employed in accord with judicial discretion.

As in the administrative penal process, any appeal against a sentence declaring or imposing a penalty has a suspensive effect (c. 1353). Hence the full effects of a *latae sententiae* penalty need not be observed until the sentence declaring it has been confirmed by the appellate court.[29] Similarly, a *ferendae sententiae* penalty need not be observed prior to a similar confirmation.

Pertinent Canons/ Self-Incrimination Privilege[30]

Canon 1728 — §1. Without prejudice to the prescripts of the canons of this title and unless the nature of the matter precludes it, the canons on trials in general and on the ordinary contentious trial must be applied in a penal trial; the special norms for cases which pertain to the public good are also to be observed.

§2. The accused is not bound to confess the delict nor can an oath be administered to the accused.

The first paragraph has been commented on earlier.[31] Systematically speaking, paragraph one should have been placed immediately after canon 1720, since it affects the remaining canons in this chapter.

The right of protection against self-incrimination (c. 220) means that the accused should not be required to take an oath or confess the alleged delict during the process (§2). This somewhat qualifies canon 1531, §1 requiring parties legitimately questioned to tell the whole truth. While the accused may freely confess the delict, he or she should have access to counsel throughout the process and not be pressured into such a confession.

Such a protection against self-incrimination is also relevant to the administrative penal process and during the preliminary investigation when such a confession may also be highly prejudicial. With due regard for the presumption of imputability when the law has been violated (c. 1321, §3), it is basically the promoter's task to prove the commission of the delict with moral certitude (c. 1608).

CHAPTER III
ACTION TO REPAIR DAMAGES
[cc. 1729–1731]

Conditions for the Action for Damages[32]

Canon 1729 — §1. In the penal trial itself an injured party can bring a contentious action to repair damages incurred personally from the delict, according to the norm of can. 1596.

§2. The intervention of the injured party mentioned in §1 is not admitted later if it was not made in the first grade of the penal trial.

---

[29] See, for example, the different effects of a *latae sententiae* excommunication before and after it is declared (c. 1331, §1–§2).

[30] Cf. *CCEO* 1471.

[31] See introductory comments prior to chapter 2 on the development of the process.

[32] Cf. *CCEO* 1483.

§3. The appeal in a case for damages is made according to the norm of cann. 1628-1640 even if an appeal cannot be made in the penal trial; if both appeals are proposed, although by different parties, there is to be a single appellate trial, without prejudice to the prescript of can. 1730.

Hopefully the following brief reflections should sufficiently clarify the key implications of canons 1729–1731.[33] There is a possible separate action for damages suffered as a result of a given delict (e.g., abuse of office—c. 1389), prescinding from, even if related to, the aforementioned penal process.[34] In fact the first two canons here envision the linking of such a criminal action and the action for damages since they presuppose the intervention of the allegedly aggrieved party during the criminal action (c. 1596). Such an intervention seeking compensation for damages must take place during the first instance of that action; otherwise it is not admissible although it may occur after that action is completed (c. 1729, §1–§2).

Like an appeal from the penal sentence, the appeal in a case for damages follows the usual rules governing the ordinary contentious process (cc. 1628–1640). Furthermore, there can be an appeal in the case for damages although one is not filed against the penal sentence, since they are independent actions involving possibly distinct appellants (c. 1729, §3). To expedite matters both appeals are normally to be addressed in a single appellate trial except for the provision of the next canon.

Deferral of the Action for Damages[35]

Canon 1730 — §1. To avoid excessive delays in the penal trial the judge can defer the judgment for damages until he has rendered the definitive sentence in the penal trial.

---

[33] See J. Martin, in *CLSGBI Com*, 959–960, for some brief but helpful reflections on this issue.

[34] See c. 128 on the obligation to repair the damage done by a malicious or negligent act illegitimately damaging another.

[35] Cf. *CCEO* 1484.

§2. After rendering the sentence in the penal trial, the judge who does this must adjudicate for damages even if the penal trial still is pending because of a proposed challenge or the accused has been absolved for a cause which does not remove the obligation to repair damages.

While the action for damages and the criminal action are usually handled simultaneously, the contentious action for damages may be deferred to expedite the criminal action, whose completion may be more urgent for the welfare of the community (c. 1730, §1). The two trials, however, are separate entities, and a decision in the criminal action does not exempt the first instance court from dealing with the action for damages (c. 1730, §2). Hence this latter action is to be addressed promptly although the criminal action is still pending due to a proposed challenge, e.g., an appeal or perhaps a complaint of nullity (cc. 1619–1627). This is also true if the defendant has been acquitted for a reason that does not take away the obligation of repairing damages. For example, the judge may abstain from imposing a penalty because of certain mitigating circumstances if the offender's spiritual well-being may be better fostered otherwise (c. 1345). However, the damage done to the community or to certain individuals may still need to be repaired.

Effect of Penal Sentence on the Action for Damages[36]

Canon 1731 — Even if the sentence rendered in a penal trial has become a *res iudicata*, it in no way establishes the right of the injured party unless this party has intervened according to the norm of can. 1729.

Conceivably the action for damages might not be pursued along with the criminal action as is envisioned in the prior two canons. If the sentence in that action has become a *res iudicata* or an adjudged matter (c. 1641), that does not prejudice

---

[36] Cf. *CCEO* 1485.

the initiating of an independent action for damages. The penal sentence affects only the parties involved in that trial, i.e., the promoter and the defendant and no one else including a possibly aggrieved third party (c. 16, §3). Such an independent action for damages may be treated somewhat expeditiously using the oral contentious process (cc. 1656–1670) unless one party insists on the ordinary contentious process. In such actions the one seeking damages is the petitioner and the one accused of causing damage through the delict is the respondent.

BIBLIOGRAPHY

The bibliographical material at the end of Books VI and VII gives a fairly thorough list of significant penal and procedural references. However, the following additional penal procedural sources may be useful.

Beal, J. "To Be or Not To Be: That Is the Question. The Rights of the Accused in the Canonical Penal Process." *CLSAP* (1991) 77–97.

———. "Administrative Leave: Canon 1722 Revisited." *Stud Can* 27 (1993) 293–320.

Canonical Delicts Involving Sexual Misconduct and Dismissal from the Clerical State. Washington, D.C.: USCC, 1995.

Ingels, G. "Processes Which Govern the Application of Penalties." In *Clergy Procedural Handbook*, ed. R. Calvo and N. Klinger, 206–237. Washington, D.C.: CLSA, 1992.

Martin, J. In *CLSGBI Com*.

Various authors in *Com Ex* IV/2, 953–960.

Part V
THE METHOD OF PROCEEDING IN ADMINISTRATIVE RECOURSE AND IN THE REMOVAL OR TRANSFER OF PASTORS
[cc. 1732–1752]

One of the more noteworthy features of the 1983 Code of Canon Law is the inclusion of listings of the rights and obligations of Christians (e.g., cc. 208–231 and 273–289). The identification and articulation of rights are only the first steps toward ensuring that these rights are honored. Without adequate means of vindicating and defending rights, the effect of recognizing them would be nugatory.

The importance of effective procedures for protecting rights quickly became evident in the early history of the United States. Defending the broad powers given to courts of justice in the new Constitution of the United States, Alexander Hamilton wrote, "Without this all the reservation of particular rights or privileges would amount to nothing."[1] This realization was not, however, an original discovery of the American Federalists. It had already been recognized by the great medieval canonist Henry de Susa Cardinal Hostiensis, who observed: "It is of little use to have rights in society unless there is someone to administer justice."[2]

Effective and practical ways must also be provided to pursue claims of injustice in the Church today. Archbishop Zenon Grocholewski, Prefect of the Supreme Tribunal of the Apostolic Signatura, has pointed out: "The proclamation of the rights of the faithful in the Church would be in vain if there were not the possibility of an adequate defense of such rights."[3]

Even the most eloquent assertions of rights lack substance and life unless there are effective administrative procedures to vindicate rights when they have been violated. In fact, it is vitally important for steps to be taken to prevent violations of the rights of Christians in the first place. Even when adequate remedies are available, violations of rights themselves create injustices harmful to the Christian community, and remedies are often at best imperfect attempts at reparation and reconciliation. Steps to prevent rights violations from occurring include education of church personnel and administrators about rights in the Church. Personal attitudes and a spirituality mindful of charity and justice are also indispensable elements which help prevent violations of rights.[4] In addition, diocesan policies can provide for consultation and other checks against arbitrary decisions and other abuses of authority.[5]

Protective measures or "prior process" to prevent violations of rights before they occur include confining, structuring, and checking authority to help prevent both rigid juridicism and discretionary arbitrariness.[6] Among the elements of "prior process" are consultation, communication of relevant information, and written findings

---

[1] A. Hamilton, J. Madison, and J. Jay [Publius, pseud.], *The Federalist: A Commentary on the Constitution of the United States,* 78 (1788; reprint, New York: Modern Library, 1945) 505.

[2] Quoted in C. Gallagher, *Canon Law and the Christian Community: The Role of Law in the Church according to the Summa Aurea of Cardinal Hostiensis* (Rome: Typis Pontificiae Universitatis Gregorianae, 1978) 162.

[3] Z. Grocholewski, "Aspetti Teologici dell'Attività Giudiziaria della Chiesa," *ME* 110 (1985) 197.

[4] See J. Provost, "Promoting and Protecting the Rights of Christians: Some Implications for Church Structure," *J* 46 (1986) 314.

[5] See J. Beal, "Confining and Structuring Administrative Discretion," *J* 46 (1986) 70–106.

[6] See J. Beal, "Protecting the Rights of Lay Catholics," *J* 47 (1987) 132–133.

and reasons. Consultation provides a means, before a decision is made, for authority to hear the views of those who may be affected by that decision. Adequate and reliable information is needed as a basis for the authority's decision to ensure that it achieves its goal and to prevent it from having unforeseen and unintended consequences. Those affected by administrative decisions also need adequate and reliable information to bring their behavior into conformity with them and to defend themselves if they are accused of acting contrary to them. By rendering the underlying rationale for decisions more comprehensible, written findings of fact and reasons help those affected by these decisions to accept and comply with them. Findings and reasons are required to also provide demonstrable evidence that the decisions of those exercising authority are well grounded.

Unfortunately, in an imperfect world there are no measures which can wholly prevent wrongs from occurring. Accordingly, when harm does happen, canon 221, §1 states that the "Christian faithful can legitimately vindicate and defend the rights which they possess in the Church" before the competent ecclesiastical authority. Having provided this guarantee, the Church must then assure that its procedures for vindicating rights are effective. As then-Bishop Joseph L. Bernardin said when he was General Secretary of the United States Catholic Conference and the National Conference of Catholic Bishops:

> In this age when the question of human rights and freedoms looms so large in the thinking of people the world over, surely the Church should exert her leadership by ensuring those rights and freedoms among her own members. We should not be afraid, therefore, to examine closely our legal apparatus to see if it will stand the test of today's needs and aspirations. We must listen to those who insist that our procedures are not adequate. Then, on the basis of actual fact rather than emotion or an effort to

prove some preconceived idea, we must decide whether changes are needed and, if so, what kind. Only in this way will the Church's credibility in this area remain intact.[7]

Part five of Book VII, then, provides the *administrative* processes for the vindication and defense of rights, in contrast to parts one through four, which address *judicial* processes. In speaking of rights, however, it must be noted that legal philosophy,[8] judicial opinion,[9] and canonical tradition[10] commonly hold that rights "correlate" with duties. In fact, there are those who see these two terms as simply opposite sides of the same coin. For them, assertions of rights "are merely the shadows cast by (other people's) duties."[11]

Canonical tradition generally maintains the close correlation between rights and duties. Thus, Pope Paul VI said that "the basic rights of the baptized are not efficacious, nor can they be exercised, unless one recognizes *the duties connected*

---

[7] J. Bernardin, "Due Process in the Church," *Homiletic and Pastoral Review* 69 (1969) 756–757.

[8] See D. Lyons, "The Correlativity of Rights and Duties," in *Philosophy of Law,* ed. J. Feinberg and H. Gross (Belmont, Calif.: Wadsworth, 1986) 319; S. I. Benn and R. Peters, *Social Principles and the Democratic State* (London: Allen & Unwin, 1959) 89; R. Brandt, *Ethical Theory* (Englewood Cliffs, N.J.: Prentice-Hall, 1959) 441; and W. Hohfeld, "Rights and Jural Relations," in *Philosophy of Law,* ed. J. Feinberg and H. Gross (Belmont, Calif.: Wadsworth, 1986) 308–309.

[9] "A duty or legal obligation is that which one ought or ought not to do. 'Duty' and 'right' are correlative terms. When a right is invaded, a duty is violated." Lake Shore & M.S.R. Co. v. Kurtz, 10 Ind. App. 60, 37 N.E. 303–4 (1894).

[10] For example, after describing the "fundamental obligation" to maintain communion, Gianfranco Ghirlanda states, "All other duties and rights are established and held so that this fundamental obligation may be fulfilled properly and faithfully." G. Ghirlanda, "De obligationibus et iuribus Christifidelium in communione ecclesiali deque eorum adimpletione et exercitio," *P* 73 (1984) 373.

[11] H. Warrender, *The Political Philosophy of Hobbes* (Oxford: Clarendon, 1957) 19.

with them by baptism."[12] Pope John Paul II echoed these words when he spoke of the "hoped-for reciprocity between the rights and duties" of the Christian faithful."[13]

The view that rights are related to duties may be the reason why specific language about rights did not develop more fully until rather late, perhaps not beginning until the fourteenth century.[14] The Latin word for duty, *officium,* suggests that duty is related to one's office, i.e., an official role or position. Indeed, Webster defines a duty as "obligatory tasks, conduct, service, or functions that arise from one's position (as in life or in a group)."[15]

In light of this close connection between rights and the duties of office, the placement of the canons on the removal and transfer of pastors

after those on administrative recourse is appropriate. While administrative recourse may be used affirmatively to vindicate and defend rights in the Church, the removal or transfer of pastors is related to the performance of their official duties and obligations.[16] Since the "Christian faithful have the right to receive assistance from the sacred pastors out of the spiritual goods of the Church, especially the word of God and the sacraments" (c. 213), it follows that there should be some procedure to remove a pastor who is not fulfilling this duty or to transfer one whose ministry is badly needed elsewhere. The very last section of the Code of Canon Law addresses such situations.

---

[12] Paul VI, "The Function of Juridical Structures in the Life of the Church: Address to the Judges of the Sacred Roman Rota," February 4, 1977, *AAS* 69 (1977) 149, trans. *OssRomEng,* February 24, 1977, 5 (emphasis added).

[13] John Paul II, "The Function of the Sacred Rota Increases through Exemplary Quality of Work Accomplished: Address to the Tribunal of the Sacred Roman Rota," February 26, 1983, *AAS* 75 (1983) 556, trans. *OssRomEng,* March 21, 1983, 6.

[14] A. White, *Rights* (Oxford: Clarendon, 1984) 22, n. 1.

[15] *Webster's New Collegiate Dictionary,* s.v. "duty."

[16] The approach in canon law seems to treat the terms "duty" and "obligation" synonymously. Thus, while title I of Book II ("The People of God") is designated "The Obligations and Rights of All the Christian Faithful," c. 223, §1 says, "In exercising their rights, the Christian faithful . . . must take into account . . . their own duties [*officiorum*] toward others." Sometimes this indiscriminate exchange can be seen within the same canon. Canon 209, §1 states, "The Christian faithful . . . are always obliged [*obligatione*] to maintain communion with the Church," while §2 of the same canon says that the Christian faithful are to fulfill "with great diligence . . . the duties [*officia*] which they owe to the universal Church."

CANONS AND COMMENTARY

SECTION I
RECOURSE AGAINST ADMINISTRATIVE DECREES
[cc. 1732–1739]

Scope of Administrative Recourse

Canon 1732 — What is established in the canons of this section concerning decrees must be applied to all singular administrative acts which are given in the external forum outside a trial except-

ing those which have been issued by the Roman Pontiff or an ecumenical council.

In canon law, rights can be vindicated and defended[17] juridically by means of a judicial trial. Canon 1400, §1 provides: "The object of a trial is:

[17] The Latin word *vindicare* means: "To lay legal claim to a thing. . . . To lay claim as to one's own, to make a claim upon, to demand, claim, arrogate, assume, appropriate. . . . To restore. . . . To deliver, liberate, protect, defend. . . . To make compensation for. . . ." Similarly, while the common connotation of *defendere* is "to defend, guard,

1° the pursuit or vindication of the rights of physical or juridic persons, or the declaration of juridic facts; 2° the imposition or declaration of a penalty for delicts." However, the next paragraph of the same canon quickly adds a significant limitation to this norm: "Nevertheless, controversies arising from an act of administrative power can be brought only before the superior or an administrative tribunal." To understand this canon, particular attention must be paid to the term "act of administrative power." The phrase "the superior or an administrative tribunal" must also be kept in mind when interpreting the canons on administrative recourse, since it implies that such recourse may be made either before a hierarchic superior or an administrative tribunal.

Act of Administrative Power

In keeping with the code commission's stated methodology of not providing definitions,[18] the 1983 code does not define the term "act of administrative power." The meaning of the phrase "act of administrative power" is a crucial threshold question, however, because on it hinges the determination of the competent forum in which to adjudicate some alleged violations of rights. If the controversy arose from an act of administrative power, the parties are precluded from litigating the matter in a contentious trial before an ordinary tribunal. Instead, they must use a process of administrative recourse.[19]

Most canon law commentators identify the phrase "act of administrative power" with the impugnable administrative act or *provvedimento amministrativo* of continental administrative law.[20] Dino Cardinal Staffa, formerly Prefect of the Supreme Tribunal of the Apostolic Signatura, elaborates:

> An impugnable administrative act, therefore, according to the norm of the Apostolic Constitution [*Regimini Ecclesiae universae*] is a decision or administrative decree (which, if they are such, are called a "*provvedimento amministrativo*" by practitioners of civil administrative law), even if they do not assume the properties of a decree. The notion of an impugnable administrative act or decree [is defined as]...: an act of the will, legitimately manifested, of an administrative authority acting within the sphere of the law as such and directed to the good of the Church, thereby immediately changing the juridic condition of the subjects in a concrete case.[21]

This interpretation appears to be confirmed by the use of the term "administrative act" in canon 1732. The fact that this was the sole canon under the heading "Administrative Procedure in General (*De Procedura Administrativa in Genere*)" as late in the code revision process as the 1982 schema indicates that this canon was intended as a general principle guiding the entire section dealing with administrative recourse.[22] This canon clearly removes from the scope of the procedure for administrative recourse legislative and judicial acts in the external forum, such as a diocesan bishop's

---

protect, cover, preserve, support, maintain," later juridical Latin denotes a technical meaning: "to claim, vindicate, or prosecute at law." Accordingly, the nouns which correlate with these verbs signify concomitant meanings: *vindicatio* is "a laying claim to a thing, a civil action or lawsuit, a taking into protection, defense, vindication"; *defensio*, again in juridical language, is "the legal maintenance of a right." Thus, *vindicatio* and *defensio* should be understood as virtually synonymous. C. Lewis and C. Short, *A Latin Dictionary* (Oxford: Clarendon, 1984), s.v. "vindico," "defendo," "vindicatio," and "defensio."

[18] *Comm* 2 (1970) 101.

[19] Note the technical distinction in canon law between "recourse" and "appeal": an "appeal" is a challenge to a judicial sentence (see cc. 1628–1638 and 1682–1684); "recourse" is a challenge to an administrative decision (see cc. 1732 and 1737–1739).

[20] See M. Moodie, "The Administrator and the Law," *J* 46 (1986) 57; and Beal, "Protecting the Rights," 152.

[21] D. Staffa, "Praesupposita recursus ad Alteram Sectionem Signaturae Apostolicae," *P* 67 (1978) 524–525.

[22] See ComCICRec (Vatican City: Libreria Editrice Vaticana, 1982) c. 1736.

general decree enacting a particular diocesan law (c. 29) or an ordinary tribunal's sentence declaring a marriage null (c. 1628). Nor can administrative acts made by a judge during a trial be challenged through administrative recourse. Moreover, no recourse is available against the administrative acts of the Roman Pontiff himself or an ecumenical council. Outside of these exceptions, the scope of administrative recourse is intended to be broadly inclusive. It can be used to challenge decrees and "all singular [or particular or individual] administrative acts."

Some commentators interpret canon 1732 as restricting recourse to controversies involving particular or individual administrative acts.[23] However, the canon begins with a straightforward reference to "decrees" without further qualification and then goes on to say that these canonical provisions for administrative recourse also apply (*eadem applicanda sunt*) to "all singular administrative acts." Thus, the initial unqualified reference to "decrees" suggests that the procedure for administrative recourse can be used to impugn not only particular or "singular administrative acts" but general administrative decrees.[24]

Individual or singular administrative acts (*actus administrativi singulares*) are given detailed treatment in canons 35–93. These acts include individual decrees and precepts (cc. 48–58), rescripts (cc. 59–75), privileges (cc. 76–84), and dispensations (cc. 85–93). Other acts of administrative power which may be subject to administrative recourse are general administrative acts, including general executory decrees (cc. 31–33), instructions (c. 34), statutes (c. 94), and rules of order (*ordines*) (c. 95).[25] Although a rescript must be issued in writing

(c. 59, §1) and any administrative act dealing with the external forum should be set forth in writing (c. 37), not all administrative acts are necessarily contained in written documents. For example, an individual or singular decree is defined in canon 48 as "an administrative act issued by a competent executive authority in which a decision is given or a provision is made for a particular case according to the norms of law." Since a competent executive authority can make a "decision" constituting an administrative act without issuing a written document, the notion of an "individual decree" is not limited to situations where a written document is issued. Such "decisions" are in fact rendered rather routinely by those who exercise leadership in the Church.[26]

While an "act of administrative power" can be identified with an "administrative act," it must be distinguished from an "act of administration." "Acts of administration" are activities that can be described broadly as "administrative" but lack one or more essential characteristics of an administrative act (see c. 35) and thus do not involve the Church's power of governance as such. Some illustrations of "acts of administration" are:

1. acts of church officials performed in their capacity as private persons;

---

[23] E.g., Moodie, "The Administrator and the Law," 68; E. Labandeira, in *Pamplona ComEng*, 1069.

[24] See T. Green, in *CLSA Com*, 1031, and M. Thériault, in *CLSGBI Com*, 961.

[25] See F. D'Ostilio, "Il ricorso contro i decreti amministrativi," in *Urbaniana Com*, 992. Another interpretation would exclude the general executory decrees and instructions described in cc. 31–34 from the scope of administrative recourse, instead restricting the procedure to conflicts arising from the individual administrative acts

mentioned in cc. 35–93. See L. de Echeverría, in *Salamanca Com*, 835. See also Green, in *CLSA Comm*, 1031. However, the position that general executory decrees and instructions (cc. 31–34) should also be subject to administrative recourse is based on the fact that these general administrative acts can be issued by persons who "possess executive power" (cc. 31, §1 and 34, §1), in contrast to general decrees establishing laws, which can be issued only by persons who possess legislative power (cc. 29–30).

[26] See F. Urrutia, "Administrative Power in the Church according to the Code of Canon Law," *Stud Can* 20 (1986) 261; F. Urrutia, "La potestà amministrativa secondo il diritto canonico," and Lorenzo Spinelli, "L'atto amministrativo nell'ordinamento della Chiesa," in *De Iustitia Administrativa in Ecclesia /La Giustizia amministrativa nella Chiesa*, ed. Pio Fedele (Rome: Officium Libri Catholici/Catholic Book Agency, 1984) 73–100, 167–195.

2. acts of church-related organizations which are not part of the public governance structure of the church;

3. acts of church authorities in their official capacity that partake in the nature of a private transaction.[27]

The distinction between "acts of administration" and "acts of administrative power" is important because the jurisdiction of the Administrative Tribunal (Second Section) of the Apostolic Signatura does not extend to cases involving "acts of administration" (compare c. 1445, §2, which gives the Apostolic Signatura competence over disputes arising from acts of administrative power, with c. 1413, 1°, which gives ordinary tribunals competence over contentions arising from [acts of] administration).[28] Controversies arising from acts of administrative power must be resolved according to administrative recourse, that is, recourse to the hierarchic superior and, after exhausting hierarchic recourse, to the Second Section of the Apostolic Signatura; cases involving acts of administration properly belong to the competence of ordinary diocesan tribunals.[29]

For example, in a particular dispute, one priest alleged that another priest had damaged his good reputation. The Apostolic Signatura decided that the basis of the alleged defamation was a telegraphic message sent by the respondent "in his capacity as general delegate for pastoral care" for members of a certain ethnic group living as alien residents in a foreign nation. As a result, the Signatura held that the ordinary tribunal was "absolutely incompetent, according to c. 1400, §2, to hear such a controversy arising from an act of administrative power." The Signatura determined that the "instance of the judicial vicar of the [in-

terdiocesan] tribunal could not be considered unless the case is certain to deal with harm to [the plaintiff's] good reputation by acts placed by [the respondent] as a private person and not in his official capacity."[30]

The Apostolic Signatura also held that the process of administrative recourse and not the ordinary tribunal's contentious judicial process was required in cases involving a dispute between a teacher and a principal in a Catholic parochial school[31] and a conflict between a religious sister and the mother general of a religious institute of diocesan right.[32] In the latter case, the decisions of both the first and second instance courts were declared irremediably null (c. 1620, 1°, 4°, and 5°). The case did not concern a private controversy between two women religious (c. 1427, §3), but a dispute between a religious and her superior as a result of acts placed in the exercise of her office. Moreover, the Signatura specifically pointed out that canon 1400, §2 provides that administrative recourse (cc. 1732–1739), and not a judicial trial in the ordinary diocesan or metropolitan tribunal, is the proper procedure to vindicate and defend rights in these cases.

The determination in this case is especially significant because it illustrates how the phrase "act of administrative power" is being interpreted in the jurisprudence of the Apostolic Signatura. It is quite clear from this case that the decision of a religious superior in the exercise of her authority is considered an "act of administrative power." Thus, the proper, and indeed only, forum in which to vindicate and defend rights in such cases is the procedure for administrative recourse.

Theoretically, there are two possible options for administrative recourse: an administrative tri-

---

[27] Beal, "Protecting the Rights," 156.

[28] Ibid.

[29] Advisory Opinion on Acts of Administrative Power, October 18, 1990, ApSig, Prot. No. 21362/89 V.T.; published with permission given November 27, 1990, Prot. No. 22258/90 VAR.

[30] Judgment of September 28, 1990, ApSig, Prot. No. 21955/90 C.P.; published with permission given November 27, 1990, Prot. No. 22258/90 VAR.

[31] Judgment of October 12, 1987, ApSig, Prot. No. 18679/86 V.T.; published with permission given November 27, 1990, Prot. No. 22258/90 VAR.

[32] Judgment of February 9, 1988, ApSig, Prot. No. 19764/88 V.T.; published with permission given November 27, 1990, Prot. No. 22258/90 VAR.

bunal or hierarchic recourse. In practice, however, only hierarchic recourse exists at the local level in most dioceses.

Administrative Tribunals

An administrative tribunal is a judicial forum in which a panel of judges adjudicates claims that an administrative decision violated the law, either because the procedure followed was defective or because the grounds on which it was based were erroneous.[33] Unlike hierarchic recourse, an administrative tribunal may only confirm, rescind, or declare null the administrative act, but may not amend or otherwise change the act itself. This is because the amending of the original act would itself be an administrative or executive act, not a judicial one.[34]

Provisions for local administrative tribunals were contemplated for the revised Code of Canon Law. The 1980 schema proposed that local administrative tribunals should be optional,[35] while earlier schemata had provided that they should be mandatory.[36] At its final plenary session in October 1981, members of the code commission voted fifty-three to six to leave to conferences of bishops the decision as to whether administrative tribunals should be established for their territories, rather than to impose such tribunals as a mandatory institute for all ecclesiastical regions.[37] The main reasons cited for not imposing administrative tribunals as mandatory were related to "regional differences in need and especially the varying level of resources required to implement such a directive world-wide."[38] It was apparently during the papal consultative processes in 1982 that it was decided to omit the detailed provisions for local administrative tribunals entirely from the code.[39]

The various features and propounded merits of local administrative tribunals have received extensive treatment in canonical literature.[40] Since

---

[33] See T. Molloy, "Administrative Recourse in the Revised Code of Canon Law," *CLSAP* 44 (1982) 271.

[34] See J. Meszaros, "Procedures of Administrative Recourse," *J* 46 (1986) 133.

[35] ComCICRec, *Schema Codicis Iuris Canonici* (Vatican City: Libreria Editrice Vaticana, 1980), c. 1689, §1.

[36] ComCICRec, *Schema Canonum de Procedura Administrativa* (Vatican City: Typis Polyglottis Vaticanis, 1972), c. 19.

[37] See L. Wrenn, in *CLSA Com,* 950; see also J. Alesandro, "Response to Bishop Malone's Address," *CLSAP* 50 (1988) 33.

[38] Alesandro, "Response," 33. Cardinal Bernardin verified these reasons in a telephone conversation on October 4, 1990 and reconfirmed the basic rationale in a personal interview with this author in Rome, October 16, 1990. These observations are further substantiated by the cardinal's notes and other documents from the 1981 plenary session. See Joseph Cardinal Bernardin, Code Commission Papers, Archdiocese of Chicago's Joseph Cardinal Bernardin Archives and Records Center, Chicago.

[39] See Green, "Procedure in Administrative Recourse," in *CLSA Com,* 1030. Archbishop Zenon Grocholewski, one of the members of the small group of canonists who advised the pope during the papal consultative process, in an interview stated that after they completed their deliberations with the Holy Father (which lasted more than a year and consisted of fourteen sessions, each lasting three to four hours), their recommendations were reviewed by still another small group of consultors, this one consisting of cardinals. Grocholewski said it was at the very last stages that the canons on administrative tribunals were deleted and offered two reasons why these canons were removed: (1) concerns expressed by many episcopal conferences about the lack of trained personnel to staff the proposed administrative tribunals in light of the difficulties in providing prepared canonists even for the ordinary diocesan tribunals; and (2) obstacles presented by the theological principle that a bishop can be judged by no one except the Apostolic See; thus, local administrative tribunals would not be able to review a bishop's administrative decisions. Z. Grocholewski, interview with the author, Rome, December 4, 1990.

[40] See, for example, I. Gordon, "De tribunalibus administrativis," *P,* 602–652; Z. Grocholewski, "I tribunali regionali amministrativi della Chiesa," in *De Iustitia Administrativa in Ecclesia/La Giustizia amministrativa nella Chiesa,* ed. P. Fedele (Rome: Officium Libri Catholici/Catholic Book Agency, 1984) 135–165; C. Lefebvre, "De tribunalibus administrativis," *P* 67 (1978) 583–591; K. Matthews, "The Development and Future of the Administrative Tribunal," *Stud Can* 18 (1984) 3–233; F. McManus, "Administrative Procedure," *J* 32

similar provisions for local administrative tribunals were also proposed for and omitted from the 1917 Code of Canon Law,[41] the critical question is why a model which has received widespread acclamation in theory has been consistently ignored and not implemented in practice.

Some of the reasons offered in answer to this question are doctrinal in nature; others are more practical. In its report on the observations made by episcopal conferences[42] and the dicasteries of the Holy See regarding the proposed schema on administrative tribunals, the code revision commission noted the following difficulties:

> There are those who call into doubt the very compatibility of administrative tribunals with the nature of the Church, or at least doubt whether the authority of bishops can be limited in such a way that it be submitted to administrative tribunals, since they are neither Ecumenical Councils nor the Supreme Pontiff.... Doubts have been proposed about the opportuneness of administrative tribunals, especially because of fear that pastoral action be impeded by too many conflicts and disputes, but also be-

cause of the difficulty of establishing them [administrative tribunals] in many places, and because of the paternal and pastoral, rather than juridic, character which is customary for relationships between administrative authority and its subjects in very many regions.[43]

More pragmatic concerns were offered by the Secretariat of the code commission when it argued that local administrative tribunals should be optional rather than obligatory:

> Although it is very much to be desired that administrative tribunals be regularly established by Conferences of Bishops, for protecting subjective rights and for ordering administrative justice better, it does not seem opportune however to impose such a burden by universal law. For indeed, if establishing ordinary tribunals is already replete with difficulties due to the fact that personnel who understand the law well and who have doctorates or licentiates in canon law are lacking, this would be all the more true in setting up administrative tribunals, since the function assigned to such courts is difficult and important and undoubtedly requires an exceptional grasp of laws and of justice. Besides, such courts constitute a significant innovation in church law, and therefore it seems appropriate to move gradually and in some way voluntarily, according to local possibilities and resources. In addition, hierarchic recourse is always available with the possibility of approaching the Signatura for a final decision.[44]

In response to the suggestion of the code revision commission, some local dioceses are moving gradually and voluntarily to experiment with ad-

(1972) 417–418; idem, "The Second Vatican Council and the Canon Law," *J* 22 (1962) 280; M. Moodie, *The Constitution and Competence of Interdiocesan Administrative Tribunals according to the 1980 Schema of the Code of Canon Law* (JCD diss., Pontifical Gregorian University, Rome, 1984).

[41] See Matthews, "Administrative Tribunal," 187. The reason offered for this omission was that those drafting the 1917 code considered the argument for these proposals as not yet sufficiently mature. Seen as especially problematic were the division between judicial and administrative procedures for resolving matters and controversies, the very concept of administrative processes, and the difficulty of arranging recourses through successive instances. See Gordon, "De tribunalibus administrativis," 606–607.

[42] The observations of the episcopal conferences are especially noteworthy, since the 1967 Synod of Bishops had previously voted to recommend establishing administrative tribunals. ComCICRec, "Principia quae dirigant," *Comm* 1 (1969) 83.

[43] ComCICRec, "Acta Commissionis," *Comm* 5 (1973) 236.

[44] ComCICRec, "Acta Commissionis: Relatio," *Comm* 16 (1984) 85–86.

ministrative tribunals.[45] However, since hierarchic recourse is universally available, while administrative tribunals are not, it is incumbent upon responsible canonists and ecclesial administrators to examine and devise ways to structure hierarchic recourse in order to provide for the vindication and defense of the rights of the Christian faithful within current administrative lines of authority and accountability in the local church.

Hierarchic Recourse

Hierarchic recourse is "a request to the superior of the author of an administrative act to confirm, amend, or revoke the [subordinate's] decision."[46] Although the part of the code containing canons 1732–1739 is entitled "Recourse against Administrative Decrees," the deletion of norms on administrative tribunals from the final text of the 1983 code means that, in practice, these canons are actually dealing solely with hierarchic recourse.[47]

Alternative Dispute Resolution

Canon 1733 — §1. Whenever a person considers himself or herself aggrieved by a decree, it is particularly desirable that the person and the author of the decree avoid any contention and take care to seek an equitable solution by common counsel, possibly using the mediation and effort of wise persons to avoid or settle the controversy in a suitable way.

§2. The conference of bishops can determine that each diocese establish in a stable manner an office or council whose function is to seek and suggest equitable solutions according to the norms determined by the conference. If the conference has not ordered this, however, the bishop can establish a council or office of this kind.

§3. The office or council mentioned in §2 is especially to be of assistance when the revocation of a decree has been requested according to the norm of can. 1734 and the time limits for making recourse have not elapsed. If recourse has been proposed against a decree, however, the superior who deals with the recourse is to urge the person making recourse and the author of the decree to seek a solution of this kind whenever he sees hope of a favorable outcome.

After the general introductory canon (c. 1732), there is a preliminary canon with three paragraphs concerning resolution of controversies through some alternative form of dispute resolution. The first paragraph reiterates the Church's concern, expressed repeatedly in the code,[48] to promote the gospel value of reconciliation between aggrieved parties:

> If you bring your gift to the altar and there recall that your brother has anything against you, leave your gift at the altar, go first to be reconciled with your brother, and then come and offer your gift. Lose no time; settle with your opponent while on your way to court with him. (Mt 5:23–24)[49]

When two disputing parties are unable to work out their differences by themselves, scripture indicates that the matter is to be brought to other members of the Church for their assistance in resolving the controversy:

---

[45] As of October 1996, the Archdiocese of St. Paul and Minneapolis and the Archdiocese of Milwaukee have established administrative tribunals as part of the CLSA's "Experiment in Due Process." See *CLSAP* 58 (1996) 427.

[46] Meszaros, "Procedures of Administrative Recourse," 113.

[47] See Labandeira, "Del Recurso contra los Decretos Administrativos," in *Pamplona Com,*1037; and Green, "Procedure in Administrative Recourse," in *CLSA Com,* 1030, n. 8.

[48] See cc. 1446; 1659, §1; 1676; 1695; 1713–1716; 1742; and 1748.

[49] For a study of scriptural approaches to resolving conflicts and disputes, see L. Buzzard, J. Buzzard, and L. Eck, *Readiness for Reconciliation: A Biblical Guide* (Oak Park, Ill.: Christian Legal Society, Christian Conciliation Service, 1982).

If your brother should commit some wrong against you, go and point out his fault, but keep it between the two of you. If he listens to you, you have won your brother over. If he does not listen, summon another, so that every case may stand on the word of two or three witnesses. If he ignores them, refer it to the church. If he ignores even the church, then treat him as you would a Gentile or tax collector. (Mt 18:15–17)[50]

This solicitude for reconciliation can be given institutional form through the creation of offices of conciliation (mediation) and arbitration, as the second paragraph of the canon provides. In practice, episcopal conferences in some countries, such as the United States and Italy, have left the establishment of such offices to the discretion of individual diocesan bishops rather than making their establishment mandatory.[51] While these offices and procedures are sometimes given the generic label of "due process,"[52] the more commonly used and more technically accurate terms for the functions of these offices are conciliation and arbitration.[53] In conciliation, a neutral person mediates the dispute with the hope of helping the parties to reach a mutually satisfactory solution; in arbitration, the parties create a binding contract in which they voluntarily agree in advance to abide by the decision of the arbitrator.[54] Where they have been established, these diocesan offices have proven to be somewhat effective in resolving administrative conflicts.[55] However, they have not been established in all the dioceses of the United States.[56]

Legal theorists explain the notion of due process by analyzing its twofold aspect. Substantively, due process means that certain fundamental rights or freedoms, for example the right to life or to own property, cannot be denied or taken away without proper justification, good reason or just compensation. Procedurally, due process guarantees a person adequate safeguards when his rights are challenged or questioned in administrative or judicial procedures." A. Maida, "Rights in the Church," in *A Pastoral Guide to Canon Law,* ed. G. Dyer (Dublin: Gill and Macmillan, 1977) 40. (First published in *CS* 15 [1976] 255–67.)

[53] See CLSA, *Due Process in Dioceses in the U.S.: 1970–1985: Report on a Task Force Survey,* ed. J. Provost (Washington, D.C.: CLSA, 1987) 12–13.

[54] See Archdiocese of Chicago, *Office of Conciliation: Norms and Procedures* (Chicago: Archdiocese of Chicago, 1987) 3–6; R. Fleming, *The Labor Arbitration Process* (Urbana, Ill.: University of Illinois, 1965); American Arbitration Association, *Labor Arbitration: Procedures and Techniques* (New York: American Arbitration Association, 1979); and American Arbitration Association, *Voluntary Labor Arbitration Rules* (New York: American Arbitration Association, 1979).

[55] "Since 1970 over 900 cases have been submitted for 'due process' consideration [in the U.S.] and decisions have been reached in nearly 500 of these." CLSA, *Due Process in the U.S.: Survey,* 6. For a detailed evaluation of these processes, see pp. 36–39 of the survey.

[56] "Seventy-six dioceses [in the U.S.] reported experience with cases submitted for 'due process' consideration. This is slightly over 40% of the 185 dioceses in the United States, of Latin and Eastern Catholic rites, at the time of the survey....8% of the dioceses with some case experience account for over two-thirds of the cases submitted for which we have statistics....In terms of cases

---

[50] A practical alternative to the civil courts based on Christ's command in this scriptural passage to settle disputes among believers is suggested by L. Buzzard and L. Eck, *Tell It to the Church: Reconciling out of Court* (Elgin, Ill.: David C. Cook Publishing Co., 1982). It should also be noted that the desire to avoid litigation is not confined to ecclesiastical clashes; cf. American Judicature Society, "Alternative Dispute Resolution and the Courts," *Judicature* 69 (February-March 1986) 252–314; S. Goldberg, E. Green, and F. Sander, "Litigation, Arbitration or Mediation: A Dialogue," *American Bar Association Journal* (June 1989) 70–72; K. Ehrman, "Why Business Lawyers Should Use Mediation," *American Bar Association Journal* (June 1989) 73–74; C. Blair, "A Court System on Overload: The Need for Alternative Dispute Resolution," *Chicago Bar Association Record* (November 1989) 12–13; and R. Byrne, J. Woodward, and J. Lapinski, "Court-Annexed Mandatory Arbitration Practice and Procedure in Illinois," *Chicago Bar Association Record* (May 1990) 14–20.

[51] See NCCB, *On Due Process,* 3; and *Chiappetta Com,* 2:786, citing "Delibera n. 15, 23 dicembre 1983," Enchir. CEI, vol. 3, p. 916, n. 1603.

[52] "Due process is a term whose roots are in the Anglo-American legal tradition. It is a principle of justice rather than a rule of law which can be defined categorically.

The final paragraph of canon 1733 urges that parties be encouraged to seek reconciliation even after formal recourse has been initiated. This paragraph also emphasizes that conciliation and arbitration must be seen as alternatives to formal recourse. Conciliation and arbitration, as well as similar forms of "due process," do not themselves constitute hierarchic recourse, since hierarchic recourse involves an authoritative resolution of the dispute by the hierarchic superior. In contrast, the parties themselves reach a solution through conciliation; in arbitration, the arbitrator, a private person chosen by the parties, determines the outcome. Thus, dioceses which have offices of conciliation and arbitration should not consider these as instruments of administrative or hierarchic recourse, strictly speaking, but as types of alternative dispute resolution.[57]

Unfortunately, however, parties to a controversy are not always amenable to working out their differences through conciliation or arbitration. In addition, conciliation and arbitration are not appropriate procedures for resolving some types of disputes, such as controversies arising from a bishop's exercise of his teaching office. Nor can a person whose rights have been violated by an ecclesiastical administrative act be obliged to renounce the protection of administrative procedures in a public forum and to submit the matter instead to an arbitrator.[58] In such cases, the formal procedures of recourse are needed. These begin with the next canon.

Petition to Revoke or Modify the Decree

Canon 1734 — §1. Before proposing recourse a person must seek the revocation or emendation of the decree in writing from its author. When this petition is proposed, by that very fact suspension of the execution of the decree is also understood to be requested.

This provision is an innovation in the 1983 code. Previously, a petitioner could proceed directly to formal recourse; now, a written request must be submitted to give the author of the administrative act an opportunity to revoke or amend the decree.[59] While it may seem futile to approach the source of the alleged harm, it could happen that the author of the administrative act is not aware that anyone has been aggrieved and may be quite willing to amend or revoke the decision if this fact

which have gone through the entire process, the number of dioceses with substantial experience is even smaller. Five dioceses, or 3% of the 185 dioceses in the United States at the time of the study, account for 69% of the cases decided." CLSA, *Due Process in the U.S.: Survey,* 27–29.

[57] "Alternative dispute resolution (ADR) typically refers to the use of negotiation, mediation, and conciliation as alternatives to the traditional practice of adjudication." L. Putnam and J. Folger, "Communication, Conflict, and Dispute Resolution: The Study of Interaction and the Development of Conflict Theory," *Communication Research* 15 (August 1988) 349. "The two most widely used ADR systems are arbitration and mediation. These two ADR systems can be readily distinguished by understanding the role of the neutral in those processes. In arbitration, a neutral adjudicates and makes a final binding decision on the merits. In mediation, the neutral does not make a decision on the merits, but is a facilitator to assist the parties to reach an agreement. Unless the parties in mediation agree, there is no decision." A. Schwartz, "A Primer on Alternative Dispute Resolution," *Chicago Bar Association Record* (Sept. 1988) 19. Note that the terms "mediation" and "conciliation" are often used synonymously, but not always: "In mediation, the third party is essentially a facilitator. His role is to help the parties see each other's point of view and to emphasize points of agreement; but it is not for him to suggest or promote particular solutions to the conflict. In conciliation, too, the third party is a facilitator, but in addition he may promote agreement by suggesting a solution and pointing

out its advantages." P. Cane, *An Introduction to Administrative Law* (Oxford: Clarendon, 1986) 94. For further examination of the notion of "alternative dispute resolution," see L. Ray, "Emerging Options in Dispute Resolution," *American Bar Association Journal* (June 1989) 66–68; and American Bar Association Standing Committee on Dispute Resolution, *Alternative Dispute Resolution: A Handbook for Judges* (Chicago: ABA Publications, 1987).

[58] See Grocholewski, "I tribunali regionali amministrativi," 156; Labandeira, in *Pamplona ComEng,* 1070.

[59] See Echeverría, "Del recurso," in *Salamanca Com,* 837.

becomes known. Also, this preliminary step once again underscores the legislator's preference for amicable resolution of disputes.

The last clause of this paragraph contains a further provision of considerable importance. The person petitioning for the revocation or emendation of a decree is understood to be automatically requesting suspension of the execution of the decree while the authority deliberates on the matter. This is significant, since the explicit request for suspension of the execution of the decree may be inadvertently omitted from the petition itself.

Peremptory Period for Petition

§2. The petition must be made within the peremptory period of ten useful days from the legitimate notification of the decree.

A "peremptory period" is one within which a person must act or else be precluded from doing so.[60] The person seeking the revocation or emendation of the decree must do so within ten "useful" or "available" days after receiving legal notice of the decree. "Available/useful time" (*tempus utile*) is defined by canon 201, §2: "Useful time is understood as that which a person has to exercise or to pursue a right, so that it does not run for a person who is unaware or unable to act."[61]

Thus, if a person is unaware of the administrative act which gives rise to the alleged harm, the "available time" period does not begin until the person learns of the administrative act. Also, the time does not run when a person is unable to act, whether that be the person's own subjective inability, such as because of illness, or an objective inability, such as when the last day of the time period falls on a holiday when the diocesan offices are closed. Although traditional authors took a different approach, the current praxis of the Holy See is to view "useful time" as running continuously, even on holidays unless the last day on which the person may act is a legal holiday. In the latter case, the time is extended until the next business day, since useful time cannot expire on a holiday. Thus, a person who is notified of a decree on Monday, February 16, has until Thursday, February 26, to petition for reconsideration of the decree, even though the chancery is closed for the weekend on February 21 and 22. However, a person notified of a decree on Thursday, February 12, has until Monday, February 23, to petition for reconsideration, since the tenth day of the peremptory period falls on Sunday, February 22, when the office is closed.

A special *caveat* should be noted when seeking to invoke subjective inability to act within the peremptory period of useful time: if a party has appointed a procurator (c. 1481), the inability of both the party and the procurator to act must be shown. For example, even if a party is unable to act personally due to illness or absence while on vacation, the Signatura has held that the party's procurator is expected to act as the proxy for the party.

Furthermore, the type of notice required must be "legitimate notification," that is, any required formalities of the law must be followed. When an individual decree is issued, for example, the provisions of canons 50–57 must be observed. Specifically, those whose rights can be injured should be heard before the decree is issued (c. 50), and the decree itself must be communicated (cc. 54, §1 and 56) in a written document (cc. 51 and 54, §2) or orally before a notary or two witnesses if a very grave reason prevents the handing over of the written text of the decree itself (c. 55).

Waiver of Petition to Amend or Revoke

§3. The norms of §§1 and 2 are not valid:
1° for recourse proposed to a bishop against decrees issued by authorities subject to him;

---

[60] The "peremptory period" (*peremptorium terminum*) is also known in Latin as *fatalia legis* (see c. 1465, §1).

[61] *Tempus utile* is also translated by some commentators as "canonical time." See A. Mendonça, in *CLSGBI Com*, 112; Thériault, in *CLSGBI Com*, 962; E. Molano, in *Pamplona ComEng*, 182; and Labandeira, in *Pamplona ComEng*, 1071.

2° for recourse proposed against a decree which decides a hierarchical recourse unless the bishop gave the decision;

3° for recourse proposed according to the norm of cann. 57 and 1735.

The petition asking the author of the offensive act to revoke or amend it is not necessary if the author is directly subordinate to the diocesan bishop (e.g., the vicar general, an episcopal vicar, a dean [vicar forane], an official of the diocesan curia, a pastor, etc.).[62] In such cases, the recourse is to be proposed directly to the bishop or a delegate designated by him. However, in a dispute between a religious and his or her superior, the member must first approach the superior of the institute before proposing recourse to the diocesan bishop or the Congregation for Institutes of Consecrated Life and Societies of Apostolic Life, depending on whether the institute is one of diocesan or pontifical right.

Second, an injured party need not make this petition to amend or revoke a decree when he or she is making further recourse against a decree which itself has decided a case of hierarchic recourse at a lower level, unless the decree deciding hierarchic recourse was issued by a bishop. For example, if a member of a religious institute feels aggrieved by a decision of the diocesan bishop that resolved a recourse against a decision of her superior, she would still need to ask him to review his decision before approaching the Congregation for Institutes of Consecrated Life and Societies of Apostolic Life in Rome. However, if, after the bishop confirmed his decision, she took her case to the congregation in Rome where she received a negative decision, she can have recourse directly to the Apostolic Signatura without asking the congregation to revoke or amend its decree.[63]

Third, the canon indicates two cases when a request to modify or withdraw a decree would be superfluous, and therefore is not necessary.[64] One is when an authority's silence or failure to act is automatically presumed by law to be a negative decision. Canon 57 asserts a legal presumption of a negative response if no answer is given within three months from the receipt of the petition or recourse, unless another time period has been prescribed by law. Canon 1735 provides that the period for making recourse begins to run when the authority fails to respond to the petition for reconsideration within thirty days. In such a case, the authority's response to the petition for reconsideration is presumed to be negative.

Similarly, a new petition to revoke or modify a decision is not required when the authority issues a decree modifying the original decree in response to the first petition (c. 1735).

Time Period for Recourse

Canon 1735 — If within thirty days after receiving the petition mentioned in can. 1734 the author of the decree communicates a new decree by which he either emends the earlier one or decides that the petition must be rejected, the time limits for making recourse run from the notification of the new decree. If the author makes no decision within the thirty days, however, the time limits run from the thirtieth day.

After receiving the aggrieved party's petition to modify or revoke the original decree, the author of the decree has thirty days in which to respond. The thirty days are apparently computed as "continuous time" (c. 201, §1), since there is no reference here to "available/useful time."[65] After thirty days, silence or inaction on the part of the authority is presumed to be a negative response.[66]

---

[62] See D'Ostilio, "Il ricorso," in *Urbaniana Com,* 992; and *Chiappetta Com,* 2:787.

[63] See Green, "Administrative Recourse," in *CLSA Com,* 1032.

[64] See Green, "Administrative Recourse," in *CLSA Com,* 1032.

[65] See Echeverría, "Del recurso," in *Salamanca Com,* 837–838; Labandeira, in *Pamplona ComEng,* 1071; and Thériault, in *CLSGBI Com,* 963.

[66] Note that the thirty-day period prescribed by c. 1735 is a special "other time period" mentioned in c. 57, §1,

After the thirty days have passed or after the authority has responded to the petition, whichever comes first, the aggrieved party then has fifteen available days to pursue recourse to a higher authority (c. 1737). Of course, if the original author of the administrative act accedes to the petition to revoke the decision or modifies it in a way that is acceptable to the aggrieved party, the issue becomes moot.

Suspension of the Effects of the Decree

Canon 1736 — §1. In those matters in which hierarchical recourse suspends the execution of a decree, the petition mentioned in can. 1734 also has the same effect.

§2. In other cases, if the author of the decree has not decreed the suspension of execution within ten days after receiving the petition mentioned in can. 1734, an interim suspension can be sought from his hierarchical superior who can decree a suspension only for grave reasons and always cautiously so that the salvation of souls suffers no harm.

§3. If the execution of the decree has been suspended according to the norm of §2 and recourse is proposed afterwards, the person who must deal with the recourse according to the norm of can. 1737, §3 is to decide whether the suspension must be confirmed or revoked.

§4. If no recourse is proposed against the decree within the established time limit, the interim suspension of the execution given according to the norm of §§1 or 2 ceases by that very fact.

This canon deals with the suspensive effect of recourse. In some cases, recourse automatically suspends the force of a decree by the law itself, e.g., a decree dismissing a member of a religious institute (c. 700), of a secular institute (c. 729), or of a society of apostolic life (c. 746), and an extrajudicial decree which imposes or declares a canonical sanction or penalty (c. 1353).[67] In the case of removal or transfer of a pastor, recourse against the decree suspends the removal or transfer to the extent that a new pastor cannot be named while the recourse is pending; however, the removed or transferred pastor must abstain from exercising the office of pastor, vacate the rectory, and hand over anything pertinent needed by the parochial administrator to whom the parish has been entrusted in the interim (see cc. 1747 and 1752). The ordinary power connected to the office does not cease when recourse is made against dismissal from other ecclesiastical offices; however, the ordinary power of the office is suspended (c. 143).

In cases where the recourse does not have automatic suspensive effect, the authority who issued the decree may voluntarily suspend its execution. If the author of the decree refuses or fails to do so within ten days after having received the petition for reconsideration, the aggrieved party may request the suspension from the author's hierarchic superior, who can grant it only "for grave reasons and always cautiously." The canon is particularly solicitous that the primary concern should always be the "salvation of souls" (*salus animarum*). Even if the effect of the decree is suspended as requested, when hierarchic recourse commences, the hierarchic superior to whom the recourse is proposed must decide whether to continue or revoke the suspension of the decree's execution. On the other hand, if recourse is not proposed within the peremptory fifteen days, the suspension of the execution of the decree terminates automatically.

Procedures for Hierarchic Recourse

Canon 1737 — §1. A person who claims to have been aggrieved by a decree can make recourse for any just reason to the hierarchical superior of the one who issued the decree. The recourse can be proposed before the author of the decree who must transmit it immediately to the competent hierarchical superior.

---

which supersedes that canon's usual three months' wait for a response. See Labandeira, in *Pamplona ComEng*, 1071.

[67] See *Chiappetta Com*, 2:788.

§2. Recourse must be proposed within the peremptory time limit of fifteen useful days which in the cases mentioned in can. 1734, §3 run from the day on which the decree was communicated; in other cases, however, they run according to the norm of can. 1735.

§3. Nevertheless, even in cases in which recourse does not suspend the execution of the decree by the law itself and suspension has not been decreed according to the norm of can. 1736, §2, the superior can order the execution to be suspended for a grave cause, yet cautiously so that the salvation of souls suffers no harm.

A person who feels injured by an administrative act can make recourse directly to the hierarchic superior of the author of the act. However, the aggrieved party may also propose the recourse to the author of the decree, who must then immediately transmit it to the proper hierarchic superior.[68] This is helpful, since the petitioner may not know who is the competent hierarchic superior to whom recourse should be made. Once recourse is initiated, the executive power of the lower authority is not suspended; however, the lower authority should refrain from further involvement in the case pending the superior's review, unless "a grave and urgent cause" dictates otherwise. In this case the lower authority should immediately notify the superior (c. 139). The following basic principles of hierarchic recourse can be deduced from canon 1737:

(a) Administrative acts are subject to review by the competent hierarchic authority. Within an institute of consecrated life or a society of apostolic life, the competent authority should be outlined in the constitutions of the institute or society (cc. 625, 717, 734, and 738). While the internal ordering of particular churches is specified in canons 460–572, diocesan bishops may designate various levels of authority under them or delegate power for resolving hierarchic recourse to appropriate diocesan offices.[69] Pastors of parishes with large

staffs could also delineate lines of authority in the parish by indicating the immediate supervisor of each member of the staff. In this way, recourses do not always have to come to the immediate personal attention of the pastor or bishop. When recourse is made against a decree of a diocesan bishop, however, the hierarchic superior to whom recourse must be made is neither the metropolitan archbishop nor the national conference of bishops, but only the Holy See. Thus, recourse against decrees of diocesan bishops should be directed to the Roman congregation in whose competence the subject matter of the recourse falls.[70]

(b) Any person has the procedural capacity or standing to propose recourse simply as "a person who claims to have been aggrieved by a decree." There is no further specification of this injury or harm, such as monetary damage, usurpation or abuse of power, violation of law, etc.[71]

(c) The reason or motive for the recourse is stated in the widest possible terms: "for any just reason." Just reasons include the possible illegality of the act, its infringement of a subjective right, its erroneous or inadequate basis, anticipated damage or danger from it, or even simply because the administrative act was "inopportune."[72]

The second paragraph of canon 1737 indicates the peremptory time limit for proposing recourse: fifteen useful or available days. This time limit runs from the day on which the decree was published, if no petition to amend or revoke it was required; from the day of the response to the petition to amend or revoke it, if there was a response; or from the thirtieth day if there was no response to the petition to amend or revoke the decree (cc.

---

[68] See 1982 schema, cc. 1747–1749.

[69] Meszaros, "Administrative Recourse," 120–122.

[70] *Chiappetta Com,* 2:790. While metropolitan archbishops have certain powers of vigilance within the suffragan dioceses, these are basically of a supervisory nature whereby any abuses against the faith or ecclesiastical discipline are to be reported to the Roman Pontiff; however, the metropolitan archbishop himself does not have any authority to intervene directly in the governance of the suffragan dioceses (c. 436).

[71] Echeverría, "Del recurso," in *Salamanca Com,* 838–839.

[72] Labandeira, "Del recurso," in *Pamplona Com,* 1041; and *Chiappetta Com,* 2:790.

1734, §3 and 1735). Once this peremptory time has elapsed, the hierarchic superior is no longer required to hear the recourse, but is not barred from doing so if he or she considers it appropriate.[73]

The third paragraph allows the superior to suspend the effects of the decree if this has not happened automatically by the law itself or was not previously granted pursuant to 1736, §2. Again, the code expresses solicitude that the "salvation of souls" be considered when this determination is being made.

Right to Counsel

Canon 1738 — The person making recourse always has the right to use an advocate or procurator, but useless delays are to be avoided; indeed, a legal representative is to be appointed *ex officio* if the person making recourse lacks one and the superior thinks it necessary. Nevertheless, the superior always can order the person making recourse to be present in order to be questioned.

The right to counsel in administrative recourse is a significant innovation in the 1983 code.[74] The canon expressly extends this right to "the person making recourse" at all stages of the proceedings. Nevertheless, there are some glaring omissions in the general statement of this right. Nothing is said about the right to counsel of the author of the administrative act, but equity would argue that neither party should be given any preference or advantage over the other. Also, nothing is stated in canon 1738 about the type of counsel or the qualifications of advocates or procurators. Elsewhere in Book VII of the 1983 code, canons 1481–1490 provide norms for the appointment, qualifications, disciplining, resignation and removal of advocates and procurators in judicial processes. These canons may be applied analogously to regulate the use of counsel in administrative recourse (c. 19).[75]

Furthermore, nothing is mentioned about payment of the fees and costs of the proceedings. Presumably, the expenses incurred during recourse could be paid from the administrative budget of the juridic person represented by the official whose administrative act was challenged; however, using canon 1649 by analogy, the local ordinary could determine some equitable apportionment of costs and fees among the parties involved. In any case, the canon does provide that if the aggrieved party lacks an advocate, one could be appointed ex officio if "the superior thinks it necessary."

One additional point is a reminder to avoid "useless delays" in the appointment of counsel.

Discretionary Authority of Hierarchic Superior

Canon 1739 — The superior who deals with the recourse, as the case warrants, is permitted not only to confirm the decree or declare it invalid but also to rescind or revoke it or, if it seems more expedient to the superior, to emend, replace, or modify it.

Unlike a judge in an administrative tribunal who would be able only to confirm, rescind, or annul an administrative act,[76] the hierarchic superior "has the widest possible range in deciding the recourse, since such a one has greater administrative authority than the one whose decision is being challenged."[77] Thus, the hierarchic superior is able not only to confirm the decree, declare it null, rescind it or revoke it, but can also substitute his or her own judgment by amending, subrogating, or obrogating the decree.

Confirmation of the decree, of course, upholds the decision of the lower authority.

Declaration of invalidity or nullity means that the decree itself is invalid due to some violation of law or technical defect.

[73] Green, "Administrative Recourse," in *CLSA Com,* 1033.

[74] D'Ostilio, "Il ricorso," in *Urbaniana Com,* 998; and *Chiappetta Com,* 2:783–784 and 791.

[75] Echeverría, "Del recurso," in *Salamanca Com,* 839.

[76] Moodie, "The Administrator and the Law," 49; and Meszaros, "Procedures of Administrative Recourse," 133.

[77] Green, "Administrative Recourse," in *CLSA Com,* 1034.

Rescission and revocation do not address the validity of the decree, but simply withdraw or quash it and make it unenforceable.

Amendment of the decree leaves the original decree in force, but with modifications.

Subrogation replaces the original decree with a new one that adds to or substitutes for the existing one.[78]

Obrogation abolishes or abrogates the original decree by issuing a new one contrary to the former one.[79]

If the hierarchic superior does not act within three continuous months of receiving the recourse, the law presumes that his or her response to the recourse is negative (c. 57). Once the three months have passed without response or after the hierarchic superior has issued a decision in accord with canon 1739, the person making recourse then has fifteen available days to make further recourse to the next hierarchical level (c. 1737, §2). However, for recourse to the Apostolic Signatura from the decision of one of the curial congregations, the peremptory time period is thirty useful days (*PB* 123, §1 and 125). These time periods, which are computed in accord with canons 201–203, must be observed closely or the right to make recourse can be extinguished simply by passage of these statutory time limits and without a decision on the merits of the recourse.

For example, if a priest feels aggrieved by a decision of his bishop, he has ten available days from his receipt of legal notice of the decree to ask his bishop to revoke or modify it (c. 1734). After thirty continuous days without answer from the bishop, the priest has fifteen available days to make recourse to the competent dicastery of the Roman Curia, e.g., the Congregation for the Clergy (cc. 1735 and 1737, §2). If three continuous months go by without answer from the congregation, the dicastery's answer is presumed negative (c. 57),[80] and the priest has thirty available days to make further recourse to the Apostolic Signatura (*PB* 123, §1). Of course, when a decision on recourse is rendered before the expiration of these peremptory periods of administrative silence, the time periods for making further recourse begin to run from the legal notice of the decision.

Note also that if the administrative act caused damage to the aggrieved party, canon 128 allows for compensation for damages.[81] In addition, canon 1281, §3 holds administrators liable for damage to juridic persons resulting from their illegitimate acts in the administration of temporal goods; and canon 1389 even provides for possible penal sanctions against those who abuse or negligently exercise power when issuing decrees.[82]

---

[78] Stelten, *Dictionary of Ecclesiastical Latin,* s.v. "subrogatio."

[79] Stelten, *Dictionary of Ecclesiastical Latin,* s.v. "obrogatio."

[80] The norms of the Roman Curia's *Regolamento* allow the dicastery to extend the time for resolving a recourse beyond ninety days, but it must inform the parties and give reasons. *AAS* 84 (1992) art. 120, §2.

[81] Response of the CodCom, May 22, 1923, *AAS* 16 (1924) 251; cited in D'Ostilio, "Il ricorso," in *Urbaniana Com,* 999; Labandeira, "Del recurso," in *Pamplona Com,* 1042; *Pamplona ComEng* 1075; and *Chiappetta Com,* 2:791. See also *PB* 123, §2.

[82] J. Krukowski, "Responsibility for Damage Resulting from Illegal Administrative Acts in the Code of Canon Law of 1983," in *Le Nouveau Code de Droit Canonique/The New Code of Canon Law: Proceedings of the 5th International Congress of Canon Law,* organized by St. Paul University and held at the University of Ottawa, August 19–25, 1984, ed. M. Thériault and J. Thorn (Ottawa: St. Paul University, 1986) 231–242. See also J. Krukowski, *Administracja w Kosciele: zarys koscielnego prawa administracyjnego [Administration in the Church: An Outline of Ecclesiastical Administrative Law]* (Lublin, Poland: Redakcja Wydawnictwo KUL, 1985) 290ff; P. Ciprotti, "Il risarcimento del danno nel progetto di riforma del Codice di diritto canonico," *EIC* 37 (1981) 169–170; F. D'Ostilio, *La responsabilità per atto illecito della pubblica amministrazione nel diritto canonico* (Rome: Pontificia Università Lateranense, 1966) 26; I. Gordon, "La responsabilità dell'amministrazione pubblica ecclesiastica," *ME* 98 (1973) 391–393; and J. F. Noubel, "La responsabilité administrative devant la S. R. Rote," *RDC* 18 (1968) 243.

EVALUATION OF CANONICAL PROVISIONS FOR ADMINISTRATIVE RECOURSE

A few years before the promulgation of the 1983 code, Adam Maida offered the following assessment of the processes for administrative recourse in the 1917 code:

> Why [are the 1917 provisions] for administrative recourse in the Church insufficient for the protection of individual rights?
>
> A number of reasons could be given to explain the deficiency of administrative recourse, but the following three highlight the parameters of the problem. First, the very minimum requirements of procedural due process, as we know them in the Anglo-American law, are not always operative in the resolution of such disputes. The right to counsel, to notice, to face one's accuser, to cross-examination, etc., are not required by the Canon Law....
>
> Secondly, the present system does not provide for a neutral and independent resolution. Often the superior authority to whom one has recourse is responsible for the appointment of the authority being challenged. In addition, there is a reluctance to question the unfavorable decision of a superior authority....
>
> Thirdly, when a person is aggrieved by the exercise of administrative authority in the local Church, it is unreasonable, and often impossible, from a practical standpoint, to have recourse to the Holy See. Distance, language, expense and cultural differences often create a situation in which the difficulty in protecting rights results in their denial. A legal procedure and an administrative forum need to be accessible and available if they are to be an effective instrument for the protection of individual rights.[83]

How well did the revised code remedy these deficiencies? The canons on administrative recourse in the 1983 code (cc. 1732–1739) have three innovations that were not present in the 1917 code:

(1) the petition to the author of the administrative act to amend or revoke it before proceeding directly to formal recourse (c. 1734, §1);

(2) the office of conciliation which can be instituted in each diocese (c. 1733);

(3) the right to counsel during administrative recourse (c. 1738).[84]

In other respects, the provisions for administrative recourse in the 1983 code are basically the same as they were in the 1917 code. In short, they simply state the existence of hierarchic recourse, time limitations for the various stages of the process, provisions for suspension of the decree pending resolution of the dispute, and the options available to the hierarchic superior in deciding the matter. Nothing is stated in the code concerning "due process" or any type of procedure, for that matter, which must be followed in administrative recourse.[85] For example, little is stated outside of the general norms governing issuance of decrees (Book I) about procedural safeguards normally associated with the notion of due process: the right to notice, the right to be heard, the right to confront one's accusers, the right to cross-examination, the gathering of evidence, proofs, testimony, witnesses, refutation, a written decision, statement of reasons, or the right not to be judged by one's accuser.[86] The hierarchic superior seems to enjoy unlimited discretion in resolving the controversy. While discretion is an important and necessary tool of administration, unstructured discretion leaves the administrator

---

[83] Maida, "Rights in the Church," 41.

[84] *Chiappetta Com,* 2:783–84.

[85] Echeverría, "Del recurso," in *Salamanca Com,* 839.

[86] Maida, "Rights in the Church," 40.

and the institution vulnerable to charges of misuse or abuse of discretionary authority due to real or perceived injustices in the manner in which a decision is reached.[87]

As a result, a number of canonists hold that there is still a real *lacuna iuris* in the administrative law of the Church.[88] A *lacuna iuris* means that there is a gap in the law or part of the law is missing. While canons 1732–1739 outline the rudimentary elements of administrative recourse and the general norms of canons 50–51 may be said to complement them in some sense, there is a *lacuna* to the extent that these canons do not fully lay out the step-by-step procedures to be followed in the process of administrative recourse. This vacuum is compounded by the fact that there are no sources listed for canons 1732–1739 in the code commission's publication of the fonts for the canons in the 1983 Code of Canon Law.[89]

Lamberto de Echeverría, Professor of Canon Law at the Pontifical University of Salamanca (Spain), believes that the lack of norms for procedures in administrative recourse should be supplied by observing canon 19, which gives directions for filling the void when apposite provisions are missing from the code itself. One possible approach suggested by Echeverría is to fill the procedural lacuna with analogous provisions from Book VII of the code governing the processes in ordinary tribunals.[90] However, these canons deal with contentious trials in the judicial forum; as previously noted, administrative recourse is an entirely different species of procedure for resolving disputes which arise from acts of administrative power. It would seem to be more appropriate, then, to look for analogous provisions in the jurisprudential science known as administrative law

or administrative justice, even though canon 19 does not explicitly refer to civil law as a supplementary source of law. This does not mean that administrative recourse *must* operate according to civil law processes of administrative justice, but that it *could* be done in this way, since neither church doctrine nor church law nor church custom either prohibits or impedes an appropriate adaptation of civil law principles of administrative justice in the local church. Since canon law has already borrowed the concepts of conciliation and arbitration virtually intact from the Roman law institutes of *transactio* and *compromissum inter arbitros*,[91] there should be no objection to borrowing from other civil law concepts in the development of procedures for handling administrative recourse.

Accordingly, complementing the canonical provisions for administrative recourse by accommodating civil law models of administrative justice to an ecclesial understanding of the Church as the family of God constituted in hierarchic communion, it is feasible to synthesize five basic procedural rights for administrative recourse in the Church, as follows:

1. THE RIGHT TO AN IMPARTIAL
   DECISION-MAKER:
   Anyone who claims to have been injured by an act of administrative power shall enjoy the right to make recourse for any just reason to the hierarchic superior of the author of the act, proposing such recourse directly to the superior or transmitting it through the author of the act; the competent hierarchic superior can decide the matter personally or appoint an impartial person as a delegate or vicar authorized to review the action or decision according to the laws of the Church.

2. THE RIGHT TO ADEQUATE NOTICE:
   The affected persons in administrative recourse shall have the right to adequate no-

---

[87] Beal, "Administrative Discretion," 70–74.

[88] Ibid., 74; Matthews, "Administrative Tribunal," 175; Meszaros, "Administrative Recourse," 113; Provost, "Promoting and Protecting the Rights of Christians," 313–314; G. Raab, *Rechtsschutz gegenüber der Verwaltung* (Rome: Università Gregoriana Editrice, 1978) 259.

[89] *CIC An,* cc. 1732–1739.

[90] Echeverría, "Del recurso," in *Salamanca Com,* 839.

[91] Matthews, "Administrative Tribunal," 55–82.

tice of the impending matter, including notice of the date, time, and place of any hearing; notice of the nature of the issue; and sufficient time to prepare their case.

3. THE RIGHT TO BE HEARD:

In administrative recourse, the right to a meaningful opportunity to be heard shall be observed, including the right to information relevant to one's case, especially opposing evidence; the right of defense; the right to present one's case orally or in writing or both; and the right to call and examine witnesses, confront contrary testimony, and refute adverse allegations.

4. THE RIGHT TO ASSISTANCE
AND REPRESENTATION:

All persons shall have the right to the assistance and representation of counsel or an advocate in administrative recourse; an advocate ex officio is to be constituted if the person taking recourse lacks assistance or representation and the superior considers an advocate necessary.

5. THE RIGHT TO AN EQUITABLE DECISION
AND REMEDIES:

The competent authority who examines a case in administrative recourse shall comply with the right to an equitable decision based on available information, including a written statement of findings and reasons; provision of appropriate remedies; and an indication of the avenues for further recourse or review, if any.[92]

The right to petition the Church for redress of grievances and the right not to be deprived of due

---

[92] T. Paprocki, *Vindication and Defense of the Rights of the Christian Faithful through Administrative Recourse in the Local Church* (JCD diss., Pontificia Universitas Gregoriana, Rome, 1991; repr., Ann Arbor, Mich.: University Microfilms International, 1993) 510–512.

process of law are themselves *substantive rights*. The procedures that specify the processes for exercising these rights are known as *procedural rights*. The observance of these procedural rights in administrative recourse would make a significant impact in advancing the vindication and defense of the substantive rights of the Christian faithful in the Church.

SECTION II
THE PROCEDURE IN THE REMOVAL OR TRANSFER OF PASTORS
[cc. 1740–1752]

CHAPTER I
THE MANNER OF PROCEEDING
IN THE REMOVAL OF PASTORS
[cc. 1740–1747]

General Reason for Removal of Pastors

Canon 1740 — When the ministry of any pastor becomes harmful or at least ineffective for any cause, even through no grave personal negligence, the diocesan bishop can remove him from the parish.

Since the Christian faithful enjoy the right to receive assistance from the sacred pastors out of the spiritual goods of the Church, especially the word of God and the sacraments (c. 213), pastors have a correlative duty to provide such pastoral care (cc. 519–535, 757, and 843). Diocesan bishops have an obligation to foster vocations (c. 385), to ordain only needed and suitable candidates for the priesthood (cc. 1024–1032), and to appoint only qualified priests as pastors of parishes (c. 521). It follows logically that pastors who are not fulfilling their duty should be removed from office. Canon 1740 codifies that principle.

Because this responsibility belongs uniquely to the diocesan bishop and those equivalent in law (see cc. 368 and 381, §2), vicars general and episcopal vicars cannot remove a pastor without a special mandate (see cc. 134, §3 and 479, §§1–2). Moreover, canons 1740–1752 refer to the removal and transfer only of pastors, not of associate pastors (parochial vicars) or priests assigned to other types of pastoral ministry, e.g., hospital chaplains.[93] For priests serving in offices other than pastor of a parish, the general canonical provisions for transfer or removal from ecclesiastical office apply (cc. 190–195), with the pertinent procedural safeguards provided by the canons on general norms (cc. 50–51).

The grounds stated for removal are most broad and leave wide discretion to the diocesan bishop. The pastor's ministry need be only "harmful or at least ineffective for any cause." There need be no finding of fault or culpability on the part of the pastor. Since the diocesan bishop freely confers the office of pastor unless someone else has a right of presentation (c. 523), a pastor normally does not hold this ecclesiastical office as a matter of substantive right,[94] although the pastor may be said to enjoy the procedural rights specified in the removal and transfer processes described in canons 1740–1752. Consequently, the canons on removal are to be construed broadly (c. 18). However, if the "removal" is really the privation of office imposed as a penalty, the norms for the judicial penal process must be observed.

In practice, therefore, if recourse is made against a pastor's removal, the bishop's decision will generally not be overturned by the Holy See for substantive reasons because of the breadth of the general grounds for removal. It is far more likely that a bishop will be overruled by the Holy See if he has failed to follow the procedures specified in these canons. For this reason, careful attention must be paid to the procedural requirements which follow the next canon.

Examples of Reasons for Removal

Canon 1741 — The causes for which a pastor can be removed legitimately from his parish are especially the following:

    1° a manner of acting which brings grave detriment or disturbance to ecclesiastical communion;

    2° ineptitude or a permanent infirmity of mind or body which renders the pastor unable to fulfill his functions usefully;

    3° loss of a good reputation among upright and responsible parishioners or an aversion to the pastor which it appears will not cease in a brief time;

    4° grave neglect or violation of parochial duties which persists after a warning;

    5° poor administration of temporal affairs with grave damage to the Church whenever another remedy to this harm cannot be found.

In light of the broad general basis for removal of pastors articulated in canon 1740, the catalog of reasons for removal in canon 1741 is almost superfluous. In fact, canon 1742 indicates that a bishop is to begin the process of removal if an inquiry "has established the existence of one of the causes mentioned in can. 1740." No mention is made of canon 1741 as the basis for beginning such a process. So why does canon 1741 exist? The answer can be seen in the use of the word "especially" (*praesertim*) in the introductory clause of canon 1741: "The causes for which a pastor can be removed legitimately from his parish are *especially* the following..." (emphasis added). In other words, the list which follows is *illustrative,* not taxative or exhaustive.[95] This

---

[93] The term *parochus* is usually translated as "pastor" in the United States, while many other English-speaking countries use the term "parish priest."

[94] While pastors enjoy security of tenure and stability of office unless provision has been made for a term of office, that is, for a specified period of time (c. 522), the distinction between removable and irremovable pastors has been dropped. See *CD* 31, *CIC* 454.

[95] ComCICRec, "Schema canonum de modo procedendi pro tutela iurium seu de processibus," *Comm* 8 (1976) 199, n. 73.

means that a pastor can be removed if the bishop decides that the pastor's ministry has become harmful or ineffective for any reason, as provided by canon 1740, even if none of the specific reasons listed in canon 1741 is present. Nevertheless, the bishop's decision would certainly be strengthened if he could also point to one of the causes given in canon 1741.

Even this listing of specific reasons for determining pastoral suitability must be seen in light of its underlying rationale, which is the Second Vatican Council's paramount concern for the "proper care of souls," a concern cited as one of the fonts for canon 1741.[96] The reasons listed in this canon are examples of instances when the "proper care of souls" is impeded or at least threatened.

(1) The "grave detriment or disturbance" is specifically related to the conciliar notion of ecclesiastical communion.[97] If it is the pastor himself who disturbs this communion, then there is a serious obstacle to the efficacy of his pastoral ministry. Behaviors involving moral turpitude, e.g., sexual misconduct with minors, may be said to constitute manners of acting that cause grave harm or disturbance to ecclesiastical communion.

(2) "Ineptitude" (*imperitia*) is defined as "ignorance, lack of skill or knowledge; inexperience."[98] This ineptitude or incompetence may be either absolute or relative, that is, the pastor may not be suited for ministry in one particular parish, but may do very well elsewhere.[99] For example, a priest with no knowledge of Spanish may find that over the years demographic shifts have changed his parish membership so that it is now comprised almost exclusively of Spanish-speaking people. If he refuses or is unable to learn Spanish, the bishop may decide that the priest is no longer suited to be pastor of this particular parish. He may, however, be quite effective elsewhere in an English-speaking parish. In such a case, transfer would be more appropriate if another suitable pastorate is available. If not, the pastor may need to be removed pending the availability of a suitable pastorate.

Another basis for removal mentioned here is a "permanent infirmity of mind or body." This condition, however, must be such that it renders the pastor unable to fulfill his official duties properly or usefully. Thus, it is not enough that the pastor have some sort of permanent disability; the infirmity must be such that it interferes with his ability to work effectively. The canon makes no mention of consulting with medical experts about the state of a pastor's health. However, even though it is the diocesan bishop who ultimately must decide about the pastor's suitability to continue in office, analogous provisions of other canons suggest that it would be well for the bishop to obtain an expert's assessment to assist the bishop in making his determination.[100]

(3) "Loss of a good reputation" by and "aversion" to the pastor are not absolutes. It is not sufficient that the pastor has lost his good reputation in the eyes of some parishioners or even of parishioners in general. Rather, these are factors to be considered only to the extent that they take place among "upright and responsible parishioners." This is an important distinction because of the need to protect the prophetic witness which a pastor may be called upon to give from time to time. For example, it may not be popular to preach against racism, abortion, or capital punishment, and a pastor who does so may become the object of scorn among some parishioners. Presumably, though, "upright and responsible parishioners" would not object if the pastor were teaching the authentic doctrine of the Church. Also, it must be apparent that the difficulty will not cease in a brief time. This means that the bishop must carefully discern whether the problem is an enduring one or merely a passing tension in the parish.

(4) "Grave neglect or violation of parochial duties" must be an enduring problem about which

---

[96] See *CIC An,* 475, listing *CD* 31 and *ES* I, 20, §1.

[97] See *LG* 18–28.

[98] Stelten, *Dictionary of Ecclesiastical Latin,* s.v. "imperitia."

[99] See J. Parizek, "The Manner of Procedure in Removing Pastors," in *CLSA Com,* 1037–1038.

[100] See cc. 1041, 1°; 1044, §2, 2°; 1574–1581; and 1680.

the pastor has been admonished. This reason for removal goes to the heart of the Church's pastoral concern for the "proper care of souls."

(5) "Poor administration of temporal affairs" is also a relative cause; that is, it must result in "grave damage to the Church" and there must be no other available remedy for this problem. It may be that the pastor is wonderfully capable in preaching the gospel and providing for the spiritual care of his parishioners, but he is an inept administrator. If the difficulty could be addressed by hiring a parish business manager, the canon suggests that this would be preferable to removing the pastor.

One of the most vexing and unfortunate problems facing the Church in recent times is that of clerical sexual misconduct with minors. Even Pope John Paul II felt the need to address "this problem of how the sins of clerics have shocked the moral sensibilities of many and become an occasion of sin for others."[101] It is scandalous for any priest to engage in such misconduct, but the difficulty is compounded if the accused priest is the pastor of a parish. Adding to the complexity is the fact that accusations often have to do with things that took place many years in the past, due to the length of time it takes victims (sometimes after years of therapy) to summon the courage to confront the alleged perpetrator. By the time this happens, the peremptory period of prescription may have passed for bringing a canonical process for the imposition of a penalty.[102]

In such cases, the accusation may be very public and the bishop may be morally convinced of the credibility of the allegation. Even if the allegation is not yet public, the bishop may be rightfully concerned about the scandal which would arise if the apparent problem were not adequately addressed. If he is barred by prescription from imposing a canonical penalty, is there not anything he can do?

While canon 2147, §2, 3° of the 1917 code allowed that a pastor could lose his good reputation by recent detection of an earlier crime, the 1983 code eliminated this and the "probable occult commission of a crime" (*CIC* 2147, §2, 4°) as bases for removal. Thus, it has been observed that attempting to predicate removal on a probable occult crime is improper "since all reasons for removal must be manifestly provable."[103] However, canon 1741, 3° added the reason of "aversion to the pastor," which had not been in the 1917 code.

One might expect that there would be a strong aversion to a pastor whom parishioners reasonably suspect has been involved in sexual misconduct with minors. This is not always the case, however, since people may refuse to believe that someone apparently otherwise so good could do something so bad. Certainly the possibility of false allegations must be considered as well as the priest's right to his good reputation (c. 220). But persistent, even if unfounded, rumors, media reports, and lawsuits can cause aversion to a pastor and render his ministry ineffective. In such cases, the diocesan bishop and the falsely accused pastor would need to weigh very carefully the protection of the priest's good name and reputation with the pastoral needs of the parish.

Sometimes the people remain convinced of the priest's innocence despite extensive adverse information to the contrary. In any event, clerical sexual misconduct with minors could be said to be a "manner of acting which brings grave detriment or disturbance to ecclesiastical communion" (c. 1741, 1°) as well as "loss of a good reputation" (c. 1741, 3°), and therefore be a basis for a priest's removal as pastor. The Holy See has upheld a pastor's removal on these grounds, even when the diocesan bishop was barred by prescription from imposing a penalty. Given the overriding canonical and pastoral concern for the

---

[101] John Paul II, Letter to Bishops of the United States of America, June 11, 1993, in *Origins* 23 (July 1, 1993) 102.

[102] See cc. 1395, §2 and 1362, §1, 2°, with derogations granted by rescript from an audience of Pope John Paul II for a period of five years, effective April 25, 1994, and subsequently extended for ten or more years until April 25, 2009.

[103] ComCICRec, "Schema canonum de modo procedendi," 199, n. 73.

"proper care of souls" and the need to take into account the "common good of the Church" (c. 223, §1), a pastor's removal is certainly warranted and morally required in such circumstances if the diocesan bishop has determined that the safety of children and the prevention of scandal require it.

Procedure for Removal

Canon 1742 — §1. If the instruction which was carried out has established the existence of one of the causes mentioned in can. 1740, the bishop is to discuss the matter with two pastors selected from the group established for this purpose in a stable manner by the presbyteral council at the proposal of the bishop. If the bishop then judges that removal must take place, he paternally is to persuade the pastor to resign within fifteen days, after having explained, for validity, the cause and arguments for the removal.

§2. The prescript of can. 682, §2 is to be observed for pastors who are members of a religious institute or a society of apostolic life.

The procedure for removal presupposes an inquiry to verify that one of the grounds mentioned in canon 1740 is present. The fact that canon 1741 is not mentioned indicates that the reasons listed there only illustrate examples of when the pastor's ministry has become harmful or at least ineffective. The canon does not mention who does this instruction or inquiry, so presumably the diocesan bishop could do it himself. For the sake of greater objectivity and to demonstrate that he is not acting out of some personal animosity or because of a personality clash, it would make sense for the bishop to ask someone else, such as the vicar general, dean, vicar for priests, or chancellor, to make this inquiry. Although the removal of a pastor is an administrative process and not a penal one, canon 1717 provides a helpful analogy by directing the ordinary "to inquire personally or through another suitable person about the facts, circumstances, and imputability, unless such an inquiry seems entirely superfluous."

If the bishop is satisfied that there is a justified basis for proceeding after this inquiry, the next step calls for consultation with two specially selected pastors. The manner of selecting these two pastors requires careful attention. The bishop cannot proceed by simply picking out two pastors in the diocese. First, the bishop must propose a list of pastors to the presbyteral council. From this list, the presbyteral council (*not* the bishop) establishes a group of pastors as a sort of standing committee, which might be called the "Pastors' Review Panel." The bishop then can select two pastors from this panel of names. The canon does not specify how many pastors should be in this group, but since the bishop is to select two pastors from the group, presumably the list contains more than two names. Having a larger pool to choose from is helpful in ensuring that there are two impartial pastors who would not be disqualified by close friendship with the pastor being reviewed or by some other conflict of interest which could impair their objective judgment. In establishing this Pastors' Review Panel, the presbyteral council can approve all of the names or only some of the names proposed by the bishop, but the stipulation that it is the bishop who proposes names to the council implies that the council cannot add names which are not on the bishop's list.

Since the consultation with the two pastors is required, it must be carried out properly for validity (c. 127). The minutes of the meeting during which the presbyteral council establishes the group of pastors proposed by the bishop should indicate that the council was properly convoked (c. 166) and that an absolute majority of council members consented to the selection of the group of pastors (c. 127, §1). When the bishop selects the two pastors with whom he will discuss the matter of removal, he is consulting with them as individual persons and not as a collegial body. Thus, for validity, the bishop must hear their counsel, but does not need their consent to act; however, he should not act contrary to their opinion unless, in the bishop's judgment, he has an overriding reason (c. 127, §2, 2°). Moreover, the pastors are obliged to offer their opinion sincerely and, if the bishop so indicates, maintain confidentiality (c. 127, §3). If a pastor believes he cannot fulfill these obligations, he should recuse himself and suggest that the bishop choose someone else to advise him.

If the consultation with the two pastors convinces the bishop to proceed with the removal, canon law once again expresses its preference for avoiding contentious litigation (cf. cc. 1446, 1713, and 1733). The bishop cannot simply decree the pastor's removal, but he "paternally is to persuade the pastor to resign," giving the pastor fifteen days to think about it. The canon does not say fifteen *useful* days, so it would seem these are fifteen continuous days. After all, the pastor in question does not need access to the diocesan offices during normal business hours to consider the matter. Most likely, he will think about little else for at least the next fifteen days.

In trying to persuade the pastor to resign, the bishop must explain his reasons for the request. This explanation is required for the validity of the process. If the bishop simply asks for the pastor's resignation but does not say why, and if the pastor initially offers it out of a sense of obedience, the pastor can later challenge the resignation as invalid on the ground that he was not provided with the required explanation.

The second paragraph of canon 1742 cites canon 682, §2 as a reminder that either the diocesan bishop or the religious superior, without the consent of the other, can remove a pastor who is a member of a religious institute or a society of apostolic life. Diocesan bishops and religious superiors are to keep each other informed before acting. The courtesy of providing this notice is required for liceity, but not for validity.

Resignation of the Pastor

Canon 1743 — A pastor can submit a resignation not only purely and simply but also conditionally, provided that the bishop can accept it legitimately and actually does accept it.

The possibility of a conditional resignation afforded by this canon allows the pastor to make the effectiveness of his resignation contingent on some fact. For example, the bishop explains that his reason for asking for the resignation is the pastor's embezzlement of church funds. The pastor is contrite and offers to make full restitution. As a sign that he intends to make good on this promise, he offers his resignation if the funds are not fully repaid by a certain date. In order for such a conditional resignation to be effective, the condition must actually be realized. In the example, if the specified date comes and goes without full repayment, the resignation takes effect. On the other hand, if the pastor in fact makes full restitution by the date promised, his resignation is avoided.

It must be legitimate for the bishop to accept the resignation. In the above example, should the pastor promise to make repayment if he can obtain an illegal loan, it would not be legitimate for the bishop to accept such a condition.

A problem arises when a pastor agrees to resign on condition that he be appointed to another parish or office, since canon 153, §3 provides that the promise of any office, regardless of who makes the promise, has no juridical effect.

The bishop must also in fact accept the resignation. Moreover, the general norms on resignation from ecclesiastical office must be observed (cc. 187–189).

Pastor Does Not Answer
or Simply Refuses to Resign

Canon 1744 — §1. If the pastor has not responded within the prescribed days, the bishop is to repeat the invitation and extend the useful time to respond.

§2. If the bishop establishes that the pastor received the second invitation but did not respond even though not prevented by any impediment, or if the pastor refuses to resign without giving any reasons, the bishop is to issue a decree of removal.

The lawgiver's pastoral solicitude to avoid contentious litigation continues. Apparently the fifteen-day period provided by canon 1742 is not a *fatalia legis,* since the bishop is required to repeat the invitation for the resignation if the pastor has not responded within the allotted time. Moreover, the bishop is to give the pastor more time to think about it. No particular period is specified, except that the time is to be "useful."

Not only must the bishop issue a second invitation to resign, but the law also requires the bishop to ascertain that the pastor in fact received the second invitation. If the invitations to resign are *not* extended in person with a witness present, they should be sent in writing by certified mail in order to have documentary proof for any possible later recourse. Moreover, the bishop must establish that the lack of response was not due to some impediment and that, in fact, the pastor has simply refused to resign without giving any reasons.

Only after the above steps have been exhausted can the bishop proceed to issue a decree of removal.

Pastor States Reasons Opposing the Removal

Canon 1745 — If the pastor opposes the cause given and its reasons and alleges reasons which seem insufficient to the bishop, the bishop, in order to act validly, is:

    1° to invite the pastor to organize his objections in a written report after he has inspected the acts, and offer any proofs he has to the contrary;

    2° when any necessary instruction is completed, to consider the matter together with the same pastors mentioned in can. 1742, §1, unless others must be designated because those pastors are unavailable;

    3° finally, to establish whether the pastor must be removed or not and promptly to issue a decree on the matter.

The preceding canon allows the bishop to issue a decree of removal if the pastor does not respond or if he simply refuses to resign but gives no reasons, and if the time specified has elapsed. However, canon 1745 deals with the situation in which a pastor refuses to resign and alleges reasons which the bishop judges to be insufficient. In this case, the bishop must defer issuing the decree of removal until after the pastor has had an opportunity to offer a defense and the bishop has consulted once again with the two pastors.

If the pastor properly expresses his opposition and his reasons within the peremptory period,[104] then the bishop can either acquiesce and refrain from issuing the decree of removal or he must proceed, for the validity of the removal, as outlined by canon 1745. Accordingly, the bishop must give the pastor to be removed an opportunity to inspect any and all of the acts and invite him to put his objections to his removal in writing and offer any proofs contrary to those of the bishop. Canon 1745, 1° does not mention how much time the pastor has to submit his written rebuttal, but equity would demand, on the one hand, that he be given sufficient time to organize his challenges to the removal and prepare his report; on the other hand, both the bishop and the pastor should proceed expeditiously so as not to impair the pastoral care of souls.

After the pastor's written rebuttal is submitted, the bishop is again to consult with the same two pastors from the "Pastors' Review Panel" previously consulted in this process. If one or both of these pastors is unavailable for any reason, substitution is permitted from the group established for this purpose by the presbyteral council from the list proposed by the bishop.

After all of this is done, the bishop must decide whether or not to remove the pastor and promptly issue a decree announcing his decision. For validity, the bishop must sign this decree (c. 474). For liceity, the decree must also give at least a sum-

---

[104] The peremptory period is within fifteen days of the first invitation to resign (c. 1742, §1) or, if the pastor has remained silent, within the additional time extended by the bishop in his second invitation to resign (c. 1744, §1).

mary of the reasons for the decision (c. 51) and be co-signed by the chancellor or other ecclesiastical notary (c. 474); the chancellor is also to inform the moderator of the curia of this decision (c. 474).

Nothing is said directly in the canons about the type of certitude the bishop is to have in making his decision. Canon 1742, §1 uses *constiterit* in referring to the causes for removal. *Consto* in the code generally means moral certitude,[105] but the moral certitude required concerns the cause mentioned in canon 1740, that is, "when the ministry of any pastor becomes harmful or at least ineffective for any cause." The moral certitude in the removal of a pastor involves the bishop's prudential judgment about the effectiveness of a pastor's ministry, but not necessarily about whether the pastor is guilty of committing a canonical crime. In comparison, canon 1608 requires judges to have "moral certitude" for the pronouncement of any kind of sentence; however, the removal of a pastor is an act of executive authority and is not a judicial sentence. Since a decree of removal is an individual administrative act (cc. 35 and 48), the diocesan bishop enjoys considerable administrative discretion in exercising his executive power. Such discretion is not to be exercised arbitrarily, but must be based on moral certitude about the pastor's effectiveness in the pastoral care of souls.

In addition to the specific requirements of these canons on the removal of pastors, canon 50 requires that an authority, before issuing an individual decree, is to "seek out the necessary information and proofs and, insofar as possible, to hear those whose rights can be injured."

Provision Following Decree of Removal

Canon 1746 — After the pastor has been removed, the bishop is to make provision either for an assignment to some other office, if he is suitable for this, or for a pension as the case warrants and circumstances permit.

[105] See, for example, c. 1066.

The preference of the law is for the bishop to provide the removed pastor with another ecclesiastical office. For the provision of any such office, however, the person must be suitable, in keeping with the qualities required for that office (c. 149). If he is not suitable for another office, he is to be given a pension. This follows the principle of at least minimum support due to a cleric even if he is unassigned (cc. 195 and 1350).

Effects of Removal

Canon 1747 — §1. The removed pastor must refrain from exercising the function of pastor, vacate the rectory as soon as possible, and hand over everything belonging to the parish to the person to whom the bishop has entrusted the parish.

§2. If, however, the man is sick and cannot be transferred elsewhere from the rectory without inconvenience, the bishop is to leave him the use, even exclusive use, of the rectory while this necessity lasts.

§3. While recourse against a decree of removal is pending, the bishop cannot appoint a new pastor, but is to provide a parochial administrator in the meantime.

Normally, the removed pastor must cease all pastoral activity in the parish, move out of the rectory, and give everything pertinent to the person assigned by the bishop to care for the parish. The law is solicitous, however, of a pastor who may have been removed because of illness; in such a case, the removed pastor can stay in the rectory and even retain its exclusive use as long as necessary if he cannot be conveniently moved elsewhere.

If the pastor makes recourse against the decree of removal, the recourse has quasi-suspensive effect: the removed pastor retains only title to the office, but otherwise loses his right to exercise the office. Until the recourse is decided, the bishop cannot name a new pastor, but he can and should appoint a parochial administrator (cc. 539–540).

CHAPTER II
THE MANNER OF PROCEEDING IN THE TRANSFER OF PASTORS
[cc. 1748–1752]

Reason for Transfer of Pastors

Canon 1748 — If the good of souls or the necessity or advantage of the Church demands that a pastor be transferred from a parish which he is governing usefully to another parish or another office, the bishop is to propose the transfer to him in writing and persuade him to consent to it out of love of God and souls.

Even though canon law no longer speaks of removable and irremovable pastors, the process for the transfer of pastors has an underlying assumption that pastors enjoy stability in office, and therefore should be appointed for an indefinite period of time (cf. c. 522). Appointment of a pastor for a specified term of office is done only by way of exception when the bishops' conference has provided for this.[106] When the term of a pastor appointed for a specified period of time expires, it is not necessary to use the process for removal or transfer if the diocesan bishop wishes to appoint the priest to another parish or even some other office. The bishop need only notify the priest in writing that he no longer holds the office of pastor by reason of the expiration of his term (c. 186).

It is also not necessary to follow these canons on the transfer of pastors if the pastor is the one initiating the change. Many dioceses now use a process of "open-listing" of parishes in need of a pastor. If a pastor applies for consideration as a candidate to be pastor of another parish, it is obvious that he is not opposed to being transferred.

The text and context of the canons on the transfer of a pastor make it clear that this process is intended for use when it is the bishop who is initiating the transfer and the pastor is likely not to be amenable to the change. Canon 190, §2 makes this explicit: when the officeholder is unwilling to accept a transfer, there must be grave cause for the transfer and the procedure prescribed by law is to be observed. The corollary of this norm is that there need not be grave reason and the procedure need not be followed if the officeholder is open to the transfer.

Although in effect all pastors are now removable, there must be sufficient reason for a pastor's involuntary transfer: the good of souls or the necessity or advantage of the Church.[107] Even if the bishop is convinced that such cause exists, he cannot act unilaterally. Again, with solicitude for the pastor's well-being and concern to avoid contentiousness, the legislator requires the bishop to propose the transfer to the pastor in writing and persuade the pastor to agree to the move out of love for God and the good of souls. If the pastor accedes to the proposal, the bishop can then transfer him to another parish or even to some nonparochial office. If the pastor does not agree, then the process outlined in the following canons must continue.

Pastor's Opposition to Transfer

Canon 1749 — If the pastor does not intend to submit to the counsel and persuasions of the bishop, he is to explain the reasons in writing.

If the bishop is not able to persuade the pastor to cooperate, the pastor must put his opposition and the reasons for his opposition in writing. The canon does not specify how much time the pastor is to be given to do this, but, using the analogy of canon 1744, §1, the bishop should indicate the period of time which the pastor has available for his response. Since canon 1752 includes a reminder that canonical equity is to be observed in cases of

---

[106] Six-year (except where noted) renewable terms for pastors are allowed by decree of the episcopal conferences of Australia, Canada, the Gambia, Liberia, Sierra Leone, India (period left up to individual local ordinaries), Ireland, Nigeria ("for a specified period of time"), the Philippines, and the United States of America. See *Pamplona ComEng,* Appendix III.

[107] See *ES* I, 20, §2.

transfer, the bishop should not set an unreasonably short period of time for the pastor's response, nor should the pastor be allowed to delay the process through procrastination. If the pastor chooses simply not to respond, the traditional rules of law indicate that silence may be interpreted as consent.[108]

Second Invitation to Be Transferred

Canon 1750 — Notwithstanding the reasons alleged, if the bishop decides not to withdraw from his proposal, he is to consider the reasons which favor or oppose the transfer with two pastors selected according to the norm of can. 1742, §1. If he then decides to implement the transfer, however, he is to repeat the paternal exhortations to the pastor.

If the pastor objects to the transfer and puts his reasons in writing, and if the bishop still insists on the transfer, the bishop is to discuss the reasons for and against the transfer with two pastors chosen according to the same process established for the removal of pastors in canon 1742, §1. The bishop is then to repeat his efforts to persuade the pastor to cooperate.

Decree of Transfer

Canon 1751 — §1. When this has been done, if the pastor still refuses and the bishop thinks that the transfer must be made, he is to issue a decree of transfer, establishing that the parish will be vacant after the lapse of a set time.

§2. If this period of time has passed without action, he is to declare the parish vacant.

Canonical equity again requires a reasonable period of time for the bishop's second effort to persuade the pastor to accept the transfer. After this period has elapsed, if the pastor is still opposed but the bishop continues to insist on the transfer, the bishop can proceed with issuing a de-

---

[108] *Qui tacet consentire videtur. RI,* 43.

cree of transfer. This decree, issued with the usual formalities (see commentary on canon 1745), is to specify a period of time after which the parish will be declared vacant.

The second paragraph of canon 1751, referring to the period of time passing without action, suggests that the bishop is to wait for some response from the pastor. Since at this point there is nothing to prevent the bishop from proceeding if he has correctly followed the process for transfer, the pastor may wish to indicate his willingness to cooperate and avoid the stigma of being transferred involuntarily, unless perhaps he wants to make a statement that he is being moved from the parish against his will. While he might choose not to cooperate in anticipation of having recourse against the decree of transfer, canon 1748 would not suggest great optimism for a successful challenge since the grounds for transfer are so broadly stated. The implication of this second paragraph, however, is that there is to be a second, separate juridic act by the bishop after waiting for the specified period to pass. In this act, the bishop is to declare the parish vacant. Presumably, this is also true when the transferred pastor is given his new assignment. If the pastor is not given a new assignment, he could argue that he has not, in fact, been transferred, but removed. In that case, the more stringent process for removal of a pastor would have to be followed (cc. 1740–1747).

Two additional topics of some practical importance concerning the procedures for the transfer of pastors should be noted:

1. The Apostolic Signatura has expressed concern about the abuse of the transfer process to effect the removal of a pastor by a less cumbersome procedure. The "grave cause" (c. 190, §2) for the transfer of a pastor is "the good of souls or the necessity or advantage of the Church" (c. 1748). In contrast, the ground for removing a pastor is when his ministry "becomes harmful or at least ineffective for any cause" (c. 1740). These are two very distinct situations.

2. The Signatura has also taken the position that the simultaneous transfer of multiple pastors (a common practice in most English-speaking countries) is invalid unless each pastor to be transferred has first resigned his parish. This is due to the provision of canon 153, §1, which states that "the provision of an office which by law is not vacant is by that fact invalid and is not validated by subsequent vacancy." An exception is provided in c. 153, §2, which allows for provision of an office within six months before the expiration of a predetermined time; however, it does not take effect until the day the office becomes vacant. In the case of appointment of a pastor, this can be done only if the conference of bishops has permitted term limits for pastors (c. 522).[109]

The Supreme Law of the Church

Canon 1752 — In cases of transfer the prescripts of can. 1747 are to be applied, canonical equity is to be observed, and the salvation of souls, which must always be the supreme law in the Church, is to be kept before one's eyes.

Just as the Latin language often places the most significant word at the end of a sentence for emphasis, the Latin Code of Canon Law puts its most important norm in the very last canon: the salvation of souls is the highest law of the Church. Many areas of Roman culture have been assimilated into the life of the Church, and even this "supreme law" is adapted from Roman law. The fonts for canon 1752 indicate that the source of this maxim is St. Ivo of Chartres (approx. 1040–1115 A.D.), St. Raymond of Peñaforte (1185–1275 A.D.), and St. Thomas Aquinas (approx. 1225–1274 A.D.).[110] However, further historical investigation actually traces the roots of this maxim to the Twelve Tables of Roman Law (approx. 450 B.C.) to which Cicero

refers: "the salvation (safety/welfare) of the people shall be the supreme law."[111]

Although this supreme law, substituting "souls" for "the people," is cited along with canonical equity as guiding principles in cases of transfer, the text and context suggest that this reminder is meant to apply to all areas of canonical jurisprudence. Having said that, one must not read too much into it, since such a broadly stated maxim could be cited for conflicting sides of the same argument. For example, the bishop may be convinced that the good of souls requires the pastor's transfer, while the pastor may sincerely believe that the parish will collapse if he leaves. Each could argue his position based on his concern for the supreme law of the Church, namely, the salvation of the parishioners' souls.

One must therefore provide greater specificity regarding the content and implications of this maxim. The effort to do just that is only one reason why the Code of Canon Law contains one thousand seven hundred and fifty-two canons instead of just this one supreme law! Since the details of the law are often daunting to the casual observer, a maxim such as "The salvation of souls is the supreme law of the Church" helps make the law approachable. Lest the law lose its effectiveness, however, by becoming too easily invoked in any and every situation, it must be formed to fit specific circumstances, as William Shakespeare pointed out:

> We must not make a scarecrow of the law,
> Setting it up to fear the birds of prey,
> And let it keep one shape, till custom make it
> Their perch and not their terror.[112]

---

[109] See the discussion of this issue in *CLS-GBIN* 104 (1995) 22–32.

[110] *CIC An,* c. 1752.

[111] *Salus populi suprema lex esto.* Cicero, *De Legibus* 3.3.8 (Loeb Classical Library, 1977) 466–467. See also B. Nicholas, *An Introduction to Roman Law* (Oxford: Clarendon, 1962) 15; and H. Jolowicz and B. Nicholas, *Historical Introduction to the Study of Roman Law,* 3rd ed. (Cambridge: Cambridge University Press, 1972) 5, 13, and 191, n. 1.

[112] William Shakespeare, "Measure for Measure" (1604), Act II, sc. i, l, 1.

The following is a checklist of steps to be followed in the removal of a pastor in accord with the procedures outlined in canons 1740–1747:

_____ 1. As provided by canon 1742, §1, the diocesan bishop should propose a list of pastors to the presbyteral council (unless this has already been done). From this list, the presbyteral council establishes a group of pastors to serve as the "Pastors' Review Panel" from which the bishop can select two pastors with whom he will consult as required in the various steps of this process.

_____ 2. Although it is not required by canon law, the diocesan bishop might speak informally and pastorally with the priest whose pastorate is in question to discuss the situation. .

_____ 3. If the bishop believes it is warranted by the circumstances, he can begin the canonical process for removal of the pastor by:

    _____ a. appointing a priest (e.g., vicar general/chancellor/vicar for priests) in writing to conduct an inquiry to determine if a cause mentioned in canons 1740–1741 is present which would warrant the removal the pastor.

    _____ b. sending letters to two priest-consultors appointing them to serve in accord with canon 1742, §1.

    _____ c. (optional:) sending a letter to the pastor informing him that this process is being initiated.

_____ 4. The diocesan bishop should meet with the two pastor-consultors, as required by canon 1742, §1, to discuss the matter with them and receive their recommendations. They should be reminded of the obligation of confidentiality (c. 127, §3) and the right to privacy (c. 220) of the parties involved. A memo recording the minutes of this meeting should be drawn up, notarized by a priest-notary, and filed (c. 483, §2).

_____ 5. If the diocesan bishop decides that the removal must take place, "he paternally is to persuade the pastor to resign within fifteen days, after having explained, for validity, the cause and arguments for the removal" (c. 1742, §1). This should be done by means of a personal meeting between the bishop and the pastor, with a priest-notary present. If the pastor desires, he should be allowed to have a canonical advocate present also. A letter from the bishop to the pastor, notarized by a priest-notary, should summarize the conversation and request for the pastor's resignation, along with the reasons and arguments for removal.

_____ 6. *First Scenario – Resignation:* If the pastor is willing to resign, this should be done in writing and the bishop should send the pastor a letter accepting the resignation (cc. 189 and 1743). The letter of acceptance should be notarized by a priest-notary (cc. 474 and 483, §2). If the priest resigns, he is no longer pastor and the remaining steps can be disregarded.

_____ 7. *Second Scenario – No Response or Simple Refusal:* "If the pastor has not responded within the prescribed days [15 days], the bishop is to repeat the invitation [to resign] and extend the useful time to respond" (c. 1744, §1). This should be done by means of a letter to the pastor from the bishop. The letter should be notarized by a priest-notary and sent by certified mail, return receipt requested (cf. c. 1744, §2). An additional time period of at least another fifteen days would be a reasonable extension.

_____ 8. After the additional time period has expired and the return receipt of certified mail delivery has been received, if there is no response although the pastor is "not prevented by any impediment, or if the pastor refuses to resign without giving any reasons, the bishop is to issue a decree of removal" (c. 1744, §2). Again, this decree should be notarized by a priest-notary.

_____ 9. *Third Scenario – Opposition to Removal:* If the pastor expresses his opposition to the removal and its reasons, alleging reasons which appear insufficient to the bishop, canon 1745 requires the bishop, *for validity:*

_____ a. "to invite the pastor to organize his objections in a written report after he has inspected the acts, and offer any proofs he has to the contrary";

_____ b. "when any necessary instruction is completed, to consider the matter together with the same pastors mentioned in can. 1742, §1, unless others must be designated because those pastors are unavailable";

_____ c. "finally, to establish whether the pastor must be removed or not and promptly to issue a decree on the matter."

_____ 10. After the removal is completed, the bishop is either to give the priest another assignment, if he is suitable for this, or the priest should be provided a pension, as the case requires and circumstances permit (c. 1746).

_____ 11. If the removed pastor has recourse to the Holy See, he can no longer function as pastor and cannot live in the rectory (c. 1747, §1) unless he is too sick to be transferred elsewhere (c. 1747, §2), but a new pastor cannot be named while the recourse is pending; meanwhile the bishop is to provide a parochial administrator (c. 1747, §3).

The following is a checklist of steps to be followed in the transfer of a pastor in accord with the procedures outlined in canons 1748–1752:

_____ 1. As provided by canon 1742, §1, the diocesan bishop should propose a list of pastors to the presbyteral council (unless this has already been done). From this list, the presbyteral council establishes a group of pastors to serve as the "Pastors' Review Panel" from which the bishop can select two pastors with whom he will consult as required in the various steps of this process.

_____ 2. Although it is not required by canon law, the diocesan bishop might speak informally and pastorally with the priest whose transfer is being considered to discuss the situation.

_____ 3. If the bishop believes it is warranted by the circumstances, he can begin the canonical process for transfer of the pastor by proposing the transfer to him in writing and persuading him to consent to it "out of love of God and souls" (c. 1748).

_____ 4. "If the pastor does not intend to submit to the counsel and persuasions of the bishop, he is to explain the reasons in writing" (c. 1749).

_____ 5. Having reviewed the pastor's reasons for opposing the transfer, if the bishop still wishes to proceed, he should

      _____ a. send letters to two priest-consultors, appointing them to serve in accord with canon 1750;

      _____ b. meet with the two pastor-consultors, as required by canon 1750, to discuss the matter with them and receive their recommendations. They should be reminded of the obligation of confidentiality (c. 127, §3) and the right to privacy (c. 220) of the parties involved. A memo recording the minutes of this meeting should be drawn up, notarized by a priest-notary, and filed (c. 483, §2).

_____ 6. If the diocesan bishop decides to implement the transfer, "he is to repeat the paternal exhortations to the pastor" (c. 1750). This should be done by means of a personal meeting between the bishop and the pastor, with a priest-notary present. If the pastor desires, he should be allowed to have a canonical advocate present also. A letter from the bishop to the pastor, notarized by a priest-notary, should summarize the conversation and request for the pastor's consent to the transfer, along with the reasons and arguments for the transfer.

_____ 7. If the pastor is still unwilling to be transferred, the bishop "is to issue a decree of transfer, establishing that the parish will be vacant after the lapse of a set time" (c. 1751, §1). If there is no action after the time period has expired, the bishop is to declare the parish vacant (c. 1751, §2). This should be done in a written document (c. 190, §3) notarized by a priest-notary (cc. 474 and 483, §2).

BIBLIOGRAPHY

Recourse against Administrative Decrees (cc. 1732–1739)

Alesandro, J. "Response to Bishop Malone's Address." *CLSAP* 50 (1988) 33.

American Arbitration Association. *Labor Arbitration: Procedures and Techniques.* New York: American Arbitration Association, 1979.

———. *Voluntary Labor Arbitration Rules.* New York: American Arbitration Association, 1979.

American Bar Association Standing Committee on Dispute Resolution. *Alternative Dispute Resolution: A Handbook for Judges.* Chicago: ABA Publications, 1987.

American Judicature Society. "Alternative Dispute Resolution and the Courts." *Judicature* 69 (February-March 1986) 252–314.

Archdiocese of Chicago. *Office of Conciliation: Norms and Procedures.* Chicago: Archdiocese of Chicago, 1987.

Beal, J. "Confining and Structuring Administrative Discretion." *J* 46 (1986) 70–106.

———. "Protecting the Rights of Lay Catholics." *J* 47 (1987) 132–133.

Bernardin, J. "Due Process in the Church." *Homiletic and Pastoral Review* 69 (1969) 756–757.

Blair, C. "A Court System on Overload: The Need for Alternative Dispute Resolution." *Chicago Bar Association Record* (November 1989) 12–13.

Buzzard, L., J. Buzzard, and L. Eck. *Readiness for Reconciliation: A Biblical Guide.* Oak Park, Ill.: Christian Legal Society, Christian Conciliation Service, 1982.

Buzzard, L., and L. Eck. *Tell It to the Church: Reconciling out of Court.* Elgin, Ill.: David C. Cook Publishing Co., 1982.

Byrne, R., J. Woodward, and J. Lapinski. "Court-Annexed Mandatory Arbitration Practice and Procedure in Illinois." *Chicago Bar Association Record* (May 1990) 14–20.

Cane, P. *An Introduction to Administrative Law.* Oxford: Clarendon, 1986.

CLSA. *Due Process in Dioceses in the U.S.: 1970–1985: Report on a Task Force Survey.* Ed. J. Provost. Washington, D.C.: CLSA, 1987.

Ehrman, K. "Why Business Lawyers Should Use Mediation." *American Bar Association Journal* (June 1989) 73–74.

Fleming, R. *The Labor Arbitration Process.* Urbana, Ill.: University of Illinois Press, 1965.

Goldberg, S., E. Green, and F. Sander. "Litigation, Arbitration or Mediation: A Dialogue." *American Bar Association Journal* (June 1989) 70–72.

Ghirlanda, G. "De obligationibus et iuribus Christifidelium in communione ecclesiali deque eorum adimpletione et exercitio." *P* 73 (1984) 373.

Krukowski, J. "Responsibility for Damage Resulting from Illegal Administrative Acts in the Code of Canon Law of 1983." In *Le Nouveau Code de Droit Canonique/The New Code of Canon Law: Proceedings of the 5th International Congress of Canon Law,* ed. M. Thériault and J. Thorn, 231–242. Ottawa: St. Paul University, 1986.

Lefebvre, C. "De tribunalibus administrativis." *P* 67 (1978) 583–591.

Maida, A. "Rights in the Church." In *A Pastoral Guide to Canon Law,* ed. G. Dyer, 40–41. Dublin: Gill and Macmillan, 1977.

Malone, J. "The Canon Law Society and the Church in the United States." *CLSAP* 50 (1988) 24–32.

Matthews, K. "The Development and Future of the Administrative Tribunal." *Stud Can* 18 (1984) 3–233.

McManus, F. "Administrative Procedure." *J* 32 (1972) 417–418.

―――. "The Second Vatican Council and the Canon Law." *J* 22 (1962) 280.

Meszaros, J. "Procedures of Administrative Recourse." *J* 46 (1986) 133.

Molloy, T. "Administrative Recourse in the Revised Code of Canon Law." *CLSAP* 44 (1982) 271.

Moodie, M. "The Administrator and the Law." *J* 46 (1986) 57.

―――. *The Constitution and Competence of Interdiocesan Administrative Tribunals according to the 1980 Schema of the Code of Canon Law.* JCD diss., Rome: Pontifical Gregorian University, 1984.

NCCB. *On Due Process.* Rev. ed. Washington, D.C.: NCCB, 1972.

Paprocki, T. "Parish Closings and Administrative Recourse to the Apostolic See: Recent Experiences of the Archdiocese of Chicago." *J* 55 (1995) 875–896.

―――. *Vindication and Defense of the Rights of the Christian Faithful through Administrative Recourse in the Local Church.* JCD diss., Rome: Pontificia Universitas Gregoriana, 1991. Reprint, Ann Arbor, Mich.: University Microfilms International, 1993.

Provost, J. "Promoting and Protecting the Rights of Christians: Some Implications for Church Structure." *J* 46 (1986) 314.

Putnam, L., and Folger, J. "Communication, Conflict, and Dispute Resolution: The Study of Interaction and the Development of Conflict Theory." *Communication Research* 15 (August 1988) 349.

Ray, L. "Emerging Options in Dispute Resolution." *American Bar Association Journal* (June 1989) 66–68.

Schwartz, A. "A Primer on Alternative Dispute Resolution." *Chicago Bar Association Record* (September 1988) 19.

Staffa, D. "Praesupposita recursus ad Alteram Sectionem Signaturae Apostolicae." *P* 67 (1978) 524–525.

Urrutia, F. "Administrative Power in the Church according to the Code of Canon Law." *Stud Can* 20 (1986) 261.

The Procedure in the Removal or Transfer of Pastors (cc. 1740–1752)

Parizek, J. "Canonical Changes of Procedures in the Administrative Removal and Transfer of Pastors since Maxima Cura." JCL thesis, Catholic University of America, 1978.

PROFESSION OF FAITH _____

(Formula for making the Profession of Faith in those cases where it is required by law)

I, N., with firm faith believe and profess each and every thing that is contained in the symbol of faith, namely:

I believe in one God, the Father, the Almighty, maker of heaven and earth, of all that is seen and unseen. I believe in one Lord, Jesus Christ, the only Son of God, eternally begotten of the Father, God from God, Light from Light, true God from true God, begotten, not made, one in Being with the Father. Through him all things were made. For us men and for our salvation he came down from heaven: By the power of the Holy Spirit he was born of the Virgin Mary, and became man. For our sake he was crucified under Pontius Pilate; he suffered, died and was buried. On the third day he rose again in fulfillment of the Scriptures; he ascended into heaven and is seated at the right hand of the Father. He will come again in glory to judge the living and the dead, and his kingdom will have no end. I believe in the Holy Spirit, the Lord, the giver of life, who proceeds from the Father and the Son. With the Father and the Son he is worshiped and glorified. He has spoken through the Prophets. I believe in one, holy, catholic and apostolic Church. I acknowledge one baptism for the forgiveness of sins. I look for the resurrection of the dead, and the life of the world to come. Amen.

With firm faith I also believe everything contained in God's word, written or handed down in tradition and proposed by the Church, whether by way of solemn judgment or through the ordinary and universal magisterium, as divinely revealed and calling for faith.

I also firmly accept and hold each and every thing that is proposed definitively by the Church regarding teaching on faith and morals.

Moreover, I adhere with religious submission of will and intellect to the teachings which either the Roman Pontiff or the college of bishops enunciate when they exercise the authentic magisterium, even if they proclaim those teachings by an act that is not definitive.

Oath of Fidelity on Assuming an Office to Be Exercised in the Name of the Church _____

(Formula to be used by the faithful mentioned in canon 833, nn. 5–8)

I, N., in assuming the office of _____, promise that both in my words and in my conduct I shall always preserve communion with the Catholic Church.

I shall carry out with the greatest care and fidelity the duties incumbent on me toward both the universal Church and the particular church in which, according to the provisions of the law, I have been called to exercise my service.

In fulfilling the charge entrusted to me in the name of the Church, I shall hold fast to the deposit of faith in its entirety, I shall faithfully hand it on and explain it, and I shall avoid any teachings opposed to that faith.

I shall follow and foster the common discipline of the whole Church and I shall observe all ecclesiastical laws, especially those which are contained in the Code of Canon Law.

In Christian obedience I shall unite myself with what is declared by the bishops as authentic doctors and teachers of the faith or established by them as those responsible for the governance of the Church; I shall also faithfully assist the diocesan bishops, in order that the apostolic activity exercised in the name and by mandate of the Church may be carried out in the communion of the same Church.

So help me God, and God's holy Gospels, on which I place my hand.

(Changes in paragraphs four and five of the formulary, for use by those faithful indicated in canon 833, n. 8)

I shall foster the common discipline of the whole Church, and I shall insist on the observance of all ecclesiastical laws, especially those which are contained in the Code of Canon Law.

In Christian obedience I shall unite myself with what is declared by the bishops as authentic doctors and teachers of the faith or established by them as those responsible for the governance of the Church; I shall also cooperate fully with the diocesan bishops, in order that, without prejudice to the character and purpose of my own institute, the apostolic activity exercised in the name and by mandate of the Church may be carried out in the communion of the same Church.

So help me God, and God's holy Gospels, on which I place my hand.

CHARLES D. BALVO is a priest of the Archdiocese of New York. Since 1987 he has worked in the diplomatic service of the Holy See and is currently assigned to the Apostolic Nunciature in Jordan. He obtained his J.C.L. and J.C.D. degrees respectively from The Catholic University of America and the Gregorian University in Rome.

DIANE L. BARR holds a J.C.D. from Saint Paul University in Ottawa, Ontario, and a J.D. from the University of Idaho, College of Law. She is currently director of the Office of Canonical Affairs for the Diocese of Boise, Idaho.

JOHN P. BEAL is associate professor of canon law at The Catholic University of America. He earned his J.C.L. and J.C.D. from The Catholic University of America. Before coming to Catholic University, he served for eight years as the judicial vicar of the Diocese of Erie, Pennsylvania. He has published articles in various scholarly journals, presented papers at regional and national conventions of canon lawyers, and served as consultor to several committees of the NCCB.

JAMES A. CORIDEN is professor of church law and dean emeritus at the Washington Theological Union. He earned an S.T.L. and a J.C.D. at the Gregorian University and a J.D. at The Catholic University of America. He has taught canon law for more than thirty years and has published several articles on canonical issues. He wrote *An Introduction to Canon Law* (1990) and *The Parish in Catholic Tradition* (1996), and served as one of the editors and authors of *The Code of Canon Law: A Text and Commentary* (1985). He was born in Hammond, Indiana, in 1932, and is a presbyter of the Diocese of Gary.

CRAIG A. COX, a priest of the Archdiocese of Los Angeles, is judicial vicar and chair of the Archdiocesan Theological Commission. He earned a J.C.D. at The Catholic University of America and a D.Min. at St. Mary's Seminary and University in Baltimore. He assists in parish ministry, teaches canon law, and has

served actively in the Canon Law Society of America on a number of committees and as a consultor on the Board of Governors.

RICHARD G. CUNNINGHAM is a professor of canon law at St. John's Seminary, Brighton, Massachusetts and Pope John XXIII National Seminary, Weston, Massachusetts. He also serves on the faculty of the Summer Program for the Licentiate in Canon Law at The Catholic University of America. He earned his J.C.L. at The Catholic University of America and his J.C.D. at the Lateran University in Rome. Formerly assistant judicial vicar of the Metropolitan Tribunal of the Archdiocese of Boston, he has taught canon law for the past twenty-six years, published various articles and reviews, and lectured in many dioceses on the revised Code of Canon Law.

BARBARA ANNE CUSACK is chancellor for the Archdiocese of Milwaukee and serves as a judge in second instance for the Metropolitan Tribunal of Milwaukee and the Interdiocesan Tribunal of the Province of Illinois. She also teaches at St. Francis Seminary and serves on the faculty of the Summer Program for the Licentiate in Canon Law at The Catholic University of America. She received a J.C.D. degree from The Catholic University of America.

SHARON A. EUART, R.S.M. is associate general secretary of the National Conference of Catholic Bishops. She holds master's degrees in liberal arts and in administration and supervision from Johns Hopkins University in Baltimore and a J.C.D. from The Catholic University of America. She has taught canon law at The Catholic University of America and has published articles on pastoral planning, religious life, lay pastoral ministry, the role of women in the Church, episcopal conferences, and the canonical mandate for theologians in Catholic colleges and universities. She has served as a member of the board of governors of the Canon Law Society of America.

JOHN D. FARIS, a priest of the Maronite Eparchy of Saint Maron, is assistant secretary general of the

Catholic Near East Welfare Association. He received a J.C.O.D. degree from the Pontifical Oriental Institute in Rome. He has published books and articles on Eastern churches and canon law. He is a former president of the Canon Law Society of America.

ROBERT J. GEISINGER, S.J. is professor of canon law at the Pontifical Gregorian University in Rome. He received his J.C.D. at the Pontifical Gregorian University. He is a former associate chancellor of the Archdiocese of Chicago, where he also served the Metropolitan Tribunal at various times as advocate, defender of the bond, and presiding judge. He enjoys parish ministry.

THOMAS J. GREEN is professor of canon law at The Catholic University of America. He received his S.T.L. and J.C.D. degrees from the Gregorian University in Rome. He has published articles in various canonical journals and served the Canon Law Society of America in several capacities. He also served as one of the editors and authors of *The Code of Canon Law: A Text and Commentary* (1985).

BERTRAM F. GRIFFIN is adjutant judicial vicar of the Metropolitan Tribunal of Portland, Oregon and pastor of St. Michael Parish in Portland. He received his M.Div. from the Sulpician Seminary of the Northwest and his J.C.D. from the Lateran University in Rome. He has taught canon law as adjunct professor at The Catholic University of America, Washington, D.C. and Mt. Angel Seminary, Oregon. He is a recipient of the Role of Law Award and has served the Canon Law Society of America in several capacities including that of president.

KEVIN T. HART has served both as judge and defender of the bond in the Tribunal of the Archdiocese of Washington and is the pastor of St. Mary Church, Piscataway, Maryland. He received his J.C.D. degree from the Angelicum University in Rome. He served as a lecturer in the Summer Program for the Licentiate in Canon Law at The Catholic University of America from 1991 to 1998.

SHARON L. HOLLAND, I.H.M. is on the staff of the Congregation for Institutes of Consecrated Life and Societies of Apostolic Life in Rome and teaches canon law at the Pontifical Institute *Regina Mundi*. She re-

ceived a J.C.D. from the Gregorian University and has been a contributor to a number of CLSA publications.

JOHN M. HUELS, O.S.M. is professor of canon law at Saint Paul University in Ottawa, Ontario. He received an M.Div. and an M.A. in theology at the Catholic Theological Union in Chicago and a J.C.D. at The Catholic University of America. He has published seven books and numerous articles on canonical and liturgical topics. He is an active member of the Canon Law Society of America, the Canadian Canon Law Society, and the North American Academy of Liturgy.

JOHN G. JOHNSON is currently pastor of St. Peter Parish in Columbus, Ohio and adjutant judicial vicar for the Diocese of Columbus. John G. Johnson was ordained in 1974. He has pursued graduate studies in English literature at Loyola University in Chicago, Illinois and has degrees in theology from the Pontifical College Josephinum and in canon law from The Catholic University of America. He has served as judicial vicar, taught canon law at the Josephinum, and lectured and published on questions of jurisprudence and procedural law.

PETER J. JUGIS is judicial vicar of the Diocese of Charlotte, North Carolina. He received his J.C.L. degree from the Gregorian University and his J.C.D. degree from The Catholic University of America.

ROBERT J. KASLYN, S.J. is adjunct professor of canon law at Weston Jesuit School of Theology, Cambridge, Massachusetts and a judge in the Diocesan Tribunal, Diocese of Worcester, Massachusetts. He also teaches in the Summer Program for the Licentiate in Canon Law at The Catholic University of America. He earned his S.T.L. degree from Regis College, University of Toronto and his J.C.D. from Saint Paul University, Ottawa. His work focuses on the ecclesiology of *communio*.

ROBERT T. KENNEDY is associate professor of canon law at The Catholic University of America. He holds a J.D. degree from Harvard University and a J.U.D. degree from the Lateran University in Rome. A past president of the Canon Law Society of America, he has served as consultant to several committees of the National Conference of Catholic Bishops and as a member of the Papal Commission for the Development of Administrative Law in the Church.

JOHN E. LYNCH, C.S.P. is professor of the history of canon law and medieval history at The Catholic University of America. He earned an M.S.L. at the Pontifical Institute of Mediaeval Studies and a Ph.D. at the University of Toronto. At The Catholic University of America he has served as chair of both the Department of Canon Law (1974 to 1978) and the Department of History (1983 to 1986) and was vice provost for graduate studies from 1991 to 1998. For the Canon Law Society of America he has served as vice president and board member and on various committees. He received the society's Role of Law Award in 1984. He has published many articles and one book dealing with history and canon law.

ROSE M. McDERMOTT, S.S.J. is associate professor of canon law at The Catholic University of America. She received an M.A. degree from Providence College and a J.C.D. degree from The Catholic University of America. She is a member of the Canon Law Society of America and an assistant editor of *Roman Replies* and serves as consultor for institutes of consecrated life and their members.

JOHN P. McINTYRE, S.J. is a writer in residence at St. Mary's Hall, Boston College. After receiving his J.C.L. and his J.C.D. at The Catholic University of America, he taught canon law at Saint Paul University in Ottawa, Ontario. He has presented a seminar for the Canon Law Society of America and has published in *The Jurist, Studia Canonica,* and *Periodica.* Presently he serves as a judge for the Canadian Appeal Tribunal.

FREDERICK R. McMANUS is professor emeritus of canon law at The Catholic University of America and formerly served as dean of the School of Canon Law and as academic vice president of the university. He received his J.C.D. degree from The Catholic University of America and holds several honorary doctorates as well as the John Courtney Murray award from the Catholic Theological Society, the Berakah award from the North American Academy of Liturgy, and the Michael Mathis award from the University of Notre Dame. After serving in pastoral, canonical, and educational positions in the Archdiocese of Boston, he joined the faculty of The Catholic University of Amer-

ica in 1958, where he also served as editor of *The Jurist.* He has published widely and served in various liturgical, ecumenical, and canonical positions, including the secretariat of the NCCB Bishops' Committee on the Liturgy, the Liturgical Consilium, and the Code Commission.

MICHAEL R. MOODIE, S.J. received a J.C.D. from the Pontifical Gregorian University in 1984. He has served as judge in the Archdiocesan Tribunals of San Francisco and Los Angeles. From 1984 to 1995 Fr. Moodie taught at Loyola Law School. From 1995 to 1996 he worked in the procurator general's office of the Society of Jesus in Rome. For the past two years he has been on the faculty of St. Ignatius College Preparatory, San Francisco, California.

MICHAEL A. O'REILLY, O.M.I. is judge of the Dublin Regional Marriage Tribunal. He received his J.C.D. degree from the Gregorian University in Rome. He has been a professor in the canon law faculty of Saint Paul University, Ottawa, Ontario, and has served as procurator general at the Holy See for the Oblates. He has published articles in various canonical periodicals.

LADISLAS M. ÖRSY, S.J. is visiting professor of philosophy of law and canon law at Georgetown University Law Center, Washington, D.C. Formerly, he taught at the Gregorian University in Rome, Fordham University in New York, and The Catholic University of America in Washington, D.C. He has graduate degrees in theology (Louvain), canon law (Gregorian), and civil law (Oxford).

ROCH PAGÉ is full professor and dean of the faculty of canon law at Saint Paul University in Ottawa, Ontario. He received a J.C.L. degree from the Gregorian University, a J.C.D. from Saint Paul University, and a Ph.D. from the University of Ottawa. He has published a number of books and has written and collaborated in the writing of numerous articles in various canonical journals.

THOMAS J. PAPROCKI is chancellor of the Archdiocese of Chicago, where he was ordained in 1978. He received an S.T.L. from St. Mary of the Lake Seminary in Mundelein, Illinois. After ordination, he obtained a J.D. at DePaul University College of Law and was admitted to the Illinois Bar in 1981. Working as a parish priest in South Chicago, he co-founded the Chicago Legal Clinic to provide legal services for the poor. He earned a J.C.D. at the Pontifical Gregorian University in Rome in 1991. He has authored several articles in various publications and also teaches as a member of the adjunct faculty at Loyola University School of Law in Chicago.

JAMES H. PROVOST is professor of canon law at The Catholic University of America. He earned M.A. and S.T.B. degrees at the University of Louvain and a J.C.D. degree at the Lateran University in Rome. He is managing editor of *The Jurist* and has published articles in various canonical journals. He is a former president and executive coordinator of the Canon Law Society of America.

JOHN A. RENKEN is vicar general/moderator of the curia, judicial vicar, and a pastor in the Diocese of Springfield, Illinois. He received his J.C.D. and S.T.D. degrees from the University of Saint Thomas Aquinas in *Urbe* and an M.A. in civil law at the University of Illinois at Springfield. He has published articles in various canonical journals and lectures widely. He teaches in the Summer Program for the Licentiate in Canon Law at The Catholic University of America. He has served the Canon Law Society of America in various capacities, including as a member of its board of governors, chairperson of the Committee for the New Translation of the Code of Canon Law, and CLSA president, 1999-2000.

LYNDA A. ROBITAILLE works as a judge for the Vancouver Regional Tribunal. She is also an adjunct professor of canon law at Saint Paul University, Ottawa, Ontario. She received her J.C.L. and J.C.D. as well as a specialization in jurisprudence from the Gregorian University in Rome. She has published articles in canonical journals and served as president of the Canadian Canon Law Society from 1997 to 1999.

FRANCIS J. SCHNEIDER is chancellor of the Diocese of Rockville Centre. He earned a J.C.L. from the Gregorian University and a J.C.D. from The Catholic University of America. He is an adjunct professor at the Seminary of the Immaculate Conception, Hunting-

ton, New York, and has served in various parish positions. He was born in Rockville Centre, New York in 1956.

ROSEMARY SMITH, S.C., a Sister of Charity of Saint Elizabeth, currently lives and works in Houston, Texas, where she serves as director of women's advocacy for a religious congregation, adjunct professor of canon law at St. Mary's Seminary, and judge in the Diocesan Tribunal. She received her J.C.D. from The Catholic University of America in Washington, D.C. and her M.A. in English literature from Montclair State University in New Jersey. She has held leadership positions in her religious congregation and has published several articles on religious life.

KNUT WALF is professor of canon law at The Catholic University of Nijmegen in the Netherlands. He received a J.C.D. degree and obtained his "Habilitation" in canon law from the University of Munich. From 1972 until 1977 he was a lecturer at the University of Munich. He was visiting professor at the University of Fribourg in Swtizerland, the University of Saarbrücken in Germany, and The Catholic University of America in Washington, D.C. and is the author of numerous canonical publications.

MYRIAM WIJLENS was born in 1962 in Losser, the Netherlands. She earned an S.T.L. in Nijmegen in 1986, a J.C.D. in Ottawa in 1990, and a "Habilitation" in canon law in Münster in 1997. Dr. Wijlens has been teaching in the Department of Canon Law (Institut für Kanonisches Recht) of the Westfälische-Wilhelms-Universität in Münster since 1992. She has served as a visiting professor at the Pontifical Beda College in Rome and on the staff of the Diocesan Tribunal of Münster since 1991. She is a member of several commissions of the Episcopal Conference and of the Conference for Major Superiors in The Netherlands.

LAWRENCE G. WRENN served as the judicial vicar of the Archdiocese of Hartford from 1965 to 1983 and as the judicial vicar of the Court of Appeals of the Province of Hartford from 1983 to 1995. He is presently a judge on the Metropolitan Tribunal of Hartford. He received his J.C.D. from the Lateran University in Rome and has published several articles and books.

NOTE: **Boldface** numbers indicate canon numbers. Roman numbers indicate page numbers.